C000121462

PHILIP'S
WORLD REFERENCE
ATLAS

PICTURE ACKNOWLEDGEMENTS:

Page 9 (centre left) – NASA: Olympus Mons, *The Universe Revealed*, page 47 (top).
Page 10 – Science Photo Library/National Optical Astronomy Observationaries:
Sun's corona (blue) *The Universe Revealed*, page 21.
Page 12 – Royal Greenwich Observatory, Herstmonceaux: Sun maximum,
Joy of Knowledge Science and Technology (c 1976 pic), page 221.
Page 13 – NASA: UV shot of prominences J*oy of Knowledge Science and Technology*,
page 223 (c 1976).
Page 14 – NASA: Mercury from Mariner. *The Universe Revealed*, page 25.
Page 15 – NASA: Venus (Octopus Publishing Group Ltd).
Page 16 (centre) – NASA: *Joy of Knowledge Science and Technology*, page 192.
Page 16 (bottom) – NASA: *The Universe Revealed*, page 35.
Page 17 – NASA: *The Universe Revealed*, page 47 (bottom).
Page 18 – NASA: Jupiter and Io (Octopus Publishing Group Ltd).
Page 19 – NASA: Saturn (Octopus Publishing Group Ltd).
Page 20 – NASA/Science Photo Library: Uranus.
Page 21 (centre) – NASA: Triton, moon of Neptune. *The Universe Revealed*, page 74.
Page 21 (bottom) – Space Telescope Science Institute/NASA/Science Photo Library:
Hubble computer images of Pluto hemispheres.
Page 23 – NASA: comet Hale-Bopp. *The Universe Revealed*, page 78.
Page 24 – NASA: asteroid Ida. *The Universe Revealed*, page 80.

The Solar System and the Physical Earth compiled by Richard Widdows.

PHILIP'S WORLD REFERENCE ATLAS

Bounty Books

This 2000 edition published
by Chancellor Press, an imprint of Bounty Books,
a division of Octopus Publishing Group Ltd,
2-4 Heron Quays, London E14 4JP.

Reprinted 2002, 2003, 2004

Cartography by Philips

ISBN 0-75370-906-6

A CIP catalogue record for this book is available from the British Library

Produced by Toppan (HK) Ltd
Printed in Hong Kong

Contents

The Solar System

8–9 Solar System: Evolution
10–11 Solar System: Profile
12–13 The Sun
14 Mercury
15 Venus
16 Earth
17 Mars
18 Jupiter
19 Saturn
20 Uranus
21 Neptune and Pluto
22 The Moon
23 Comets
24–25 Asteroids and Meteoroids

The Physical Earth

26–27 Time and Motion
28–29 Anatomy of the Earth
30–31 The Restless Earth
32 Earthquakes
33 Volcanoes
34–35 Shaping the Landscape
36–37 Oceans: Seawater
38–39 Oceans: Currents
40 Oceans: Waves and Tides
41 Oceans: The Seafloor
42–43 The Atmosphere and Clouds
44–45 Winds and the Weather
46-47 World Climate
48–49 The World's Water
50–51 Underground Water
52–53 Vegetation and Soil
54–55 The Earth in Figures
56 Understanding Maps

The Map Section

1 Map Symbols
2–3 World: Political 1:80 000 000
4 Arctic Ocean 1:35 000 000
5 Antarctica 1:35 000 000
6 Europe: Physical 1:20 000 000
7 Europe: Political 1: 20 000 000
8–9 Scandinavia 1:5 000 000
10–11 England and Wales 1:2 000 000
12 Scotland 1:2 000 000
13 Ireland 1:2 000 000
14 The British Isles 1:5 000 000
15 Netherlands, Belgium and Luxembourg 1:2 500 000
16–17 Middle Europe 1:5 000 000

18 France 1:5 000 000
19 Spain and Portugal 1:5 000 000
20–21 Italy and the Balkan States 1:1:5 000 000
22 The Balearics, the Canaries and Madeira 1:1 000 000/1:2 000 000
23 Malta, Crete, Corfu, Rhodes and Cyprus 1:1 000 000/1:3 000 000
24–25 Eastern Europe and Turkey 1:10 000 000
26–27 Russia and Central Asia 1:20 000 000
28 Asia: Physical 1:50 000 000
29 Asia: Political 1:50 000 000
30–31 Japan 1:5 000 000
32–33 China and Korea 1:15 000 000
34–35 Northern China and Korea 1:6 000 000
36–37 Indonesia and the Philippines 1:12 500 000
38–39 Mainland South-east Asia 1:6 000 000
40–41 South Asia 1:10 000 000
42–43 The Indo-Gangetic Plain 1:6 000 000
44–45 The Middle East 1:7 000 000
46 Arabia and the Horn of Africa 1:15 000 000
47 The Near East 1:2 500 000
48 Africa: Physical 1:42 000 000
49 Africa: Political 1:42 000 000
50–51 Northern Africa 1:15 000 000
52–53 Central and Southern Africa 1:15 000 000
54–55 East Africa 1:8 000 000
56–57 Southern Africa 1:8 000 000; Madagascar 1:8 000 000
58 Australia and Oceania: Physical and Political 1:50 000 000
59 New Zealand 1:6 000 000
60–61 Western Australia 1:8 000 000
62–63 Eastern Australia 1:8 000 000
64–65 Pacific Ocean 1:54 000 000
66 North America: Physical 1:35 000 000
67 North America: Political 1:35 000 000
68–69 Canada 1:15 000 000; Alaska 1:30 000 000
70–71 Eastern Canada 1:7 000 000
72–73 Western Canada 1:7 000 000
74–75 United States 1:12 000 000; Hawaii 1:10 000 000
76–77 Eastern United States 1:6 000 000
78–79 North-eastern United States 1:2 500 000
80–81 Middle United States 1:6 000 000
82–83 Western United States 1:6 000 000
84–85 Central and Southern California and Western Washington 1:2 500 000
86–87 Mexico 1:8 000 000
88–89 Central America and the West Indies 1:8 000 000
90 South America: Physical 1:35 000 000
91 South America: Political 1:35 000 000
92–93 South America – North 1:16 000 000
94–95 Central South America 1:8 000 000
96 South America – South 1:16 000 000

INDEX

97–176

SOLAR SYSTEM: EVOLUTION

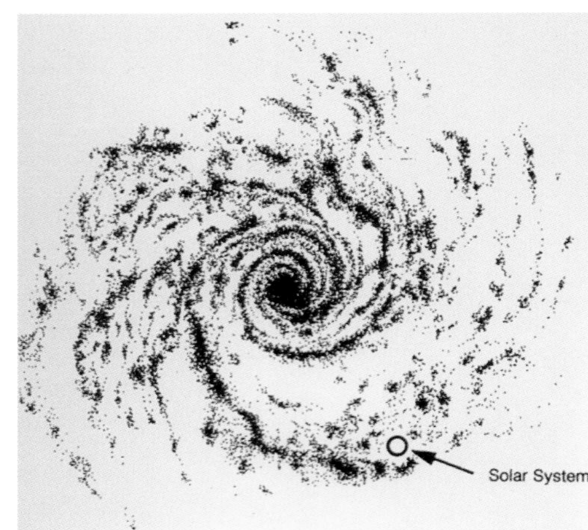

ABOVE Our Solar System is located in one of the home galaxy's spiral arms, a little under 28,000 light-years away from the galactic centre and orbiting around it in a period of about some 200 million years. There are at least 100 million other galaxies in the Universe.

ABOUT 15 BILLION years ago, time and space began with the most colossal explosion in cosmic history: the "Big Bang" that initiated the Universe. According to current theory, in the first millionth of a second of its existence it expanded from a dimensionless point of infinite mass and density into a fireball about 30 billion km (18.6 billion miles) across – and has been expanding at a phenomenal rate ever since.

It took almost a million years for the primal fireball to cool enough for atoms to form. They were mostly hydrogen, still the most abundant material in the Universe. But the new matter was not evenly distributed around the young Universe, and a few billion years later atoms in relatively dense regions began to cling together under the influence of gravity, forming distinct masses of gas separated by vast expanses of empty space.

At the beginning these first proto-galaxies were dark places – the Universe had cooled – but gravitational attraction continued its work, condensing matter into coherent lumps inside the galactic gas clouds. About three billion years later, some of these masses had contracted so much that internal pressure produced the high temperatures necessary to cause nuclear fusion: the first stars were born.

There were several generations of stars, each feeding on the wreckage of its extinct predecessors as well as the original galactic gas swirls. With each new generation, progressively larger atoms were forged in stellar furnaces and the galaxy's range of elements, once restricted to hydrogen, grew larger. About ten billion years after the Big Bang, a star formed on the outskirts of our galaxy with enough matter left over to create a retinue of planets. Some 4.6 billion years after that, a few planetary atoms had evolved into structures of complex molecules that lived, breathed and, eventually, pointed telescopes at the sky.

These early astronomers found that their Sun was just one of more than 100 billion stars in our home galaxy alone – the number of grains of rice it would take to fill a cathedral. Our galaxy, in turn, forms part of a local group of 25 or so similar structures, some much larger than ours. The most distant galaxy so far observed lies about 13.1 billion light-years away – and one light-year is some 9,461 million km (5,879 million miles).

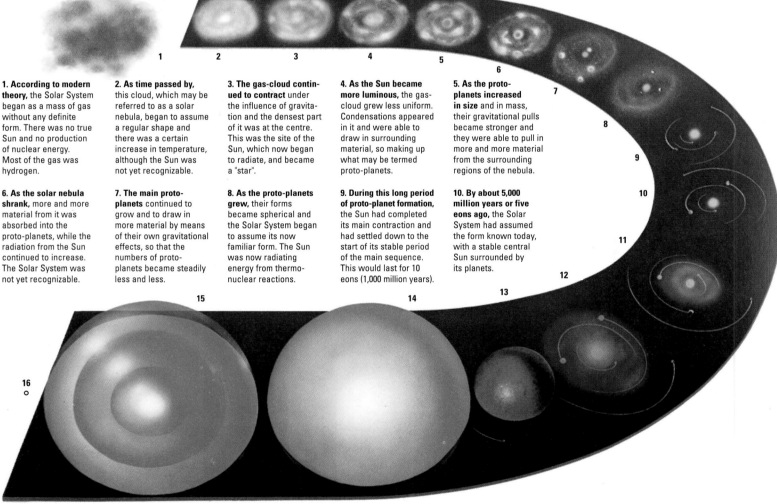

1. According to modern theory, the Solar System began as a mass of gas without any definite form. There was no true Sun and no production of nuclear energy. Most of the gas was hydrogen.

2. As time passed by, this cloud, which may be referred to as a solar nebula, began to assume a regular shape and there was a certain increase in temperature, although the Sun was not yet recognizable.

3. The gas-cloud continued to contract under the influence of gravitation and the densest part of it was at the centre. This was the site of the Sun, which now began to radiate, and became a "star".

4. As the Sun became more luminous, the gas-cloud grew less uniform. Condensations appeared in it and were able to draw in surrounding material, so making up what may be termed proto-planets.

5. As the proto-planets increased in size and in mass, their gravitational pulls became stronger and they were able to pull in more and more material from the surrounding regions of the nebula.

6. As the solar nebula shrank, more and more material from it was absorbed into the proto-planets, while the radiation from the Sun continued to increase. The Solar System was not yet recognizable.

7. The main proto-planets continued to grow and to draw in more material by means of their own gravitational effects, so that the numbers of proto-planets became steadily less and less.

8. As the proto-planets grew, their forms became spherical and the Solar System began to assume its now familiar form. The Sun was now radiating energy from thermo-nuclear reactions.

9. During this long period of proto-planet formation, the Sun had completed its main contraction and had settled down to the start of its stable period of the main sequence. This would last for 10 eons (1,000 million years).

10. By about 5,000 million years or five eons ago, the Solar System had assumed the form known today, with a stable central Sun surrounded by its planets.

11. In perhaps 5,000 million years from now the Sun will have exhausted its supply of available hydrogen and its structure will change. The core will shrink and the surface expand considerably, with a lower surface temperature.

12. The next stage of solar evolution will be expansion to the red giant stage, with luminosity increased by 100 times. The size of the globe will increase with the overall increase in energy output, and the inner planets will be destroyed.

13. With a further rise in core temperature, the Sun will begin to burn its helium, causing a rapid rise in temperature and increase in size. The Earth can hardly hope to survive this phase of evolution as the Sun expands to 50 times its size.

14. By now the Sun will be at its most unstable, with an intensely hot core and a rarefied atmosphere. The helium burning helium will give the so-called "helium flash". After a temporary contraction the Sun will be 400 times its present size.

15. Different kinds of reactions inside the Sun will lead to an even greater increase of core temperature. The system of planets will no longer exist in the form we know today, but the supply of nuclear energy will be almost exhausted.

16. When all the nuclear energy is used up, the Sun (as all stars eventually do) will collapse, very rapidly on the cosmic scale, into a small dense and very feeble white dwarf. It will continue to shine because it will still be contracting gravitationally.

Formation of the planets

The planets and larger satellites can be divided into two distinct classes. Mercury, Venus, Earth and Mars are all rocky "terrestrials", while Jupiter, Saturn, Uranus and Neptune are the large gaseous Jovian planets. Pluto can be classified, along with the large icy moons of the gas giants, as a third type. The terrestrial planets are closer to the Sun, have smaller masses and radii, and are more dense than the Jovian planets. These are big, low in density and have extensive satellite systems and rings.

The basic difference between the two families arose as a consequence of the temperature difference within the proto-solar cloud. This allowed icy material to condense well beyond the asteroid belt, producing cold proto-planets which effectively collected vast amounts of gas. The inner planets were too small and too hot to retain large amounts of original atmosphere in the face of the strong winds from the Sun.

Beyond the Solar System

Far beyond the gas giants, and outside the erratic orbit of Neptune, lie two regions of space that have intrigued astronomers since their discovery in the last half of the 20th century.

The Kuiper belt, named after one of the scientists who predicted its existence, is a disc of debris lying between about 35 and 100 astronomical units from the Sun; an astronomical unit (AU) is the average distance from the Earth to the Sun – 149,597,870km (92,958,350 miles). The first object was located there in 1992, so dim it was 10 million times fainter than the faintest stars seen by eye. It is now estimated that this belt may contain up to a billion comets, with a total mass just 1% of Earth.

Astronomers have now found over 60 Kuiper belt objects orbiting farther from the Sun than Neptune and Pluto, taking between 160 and 720 years to orbit the Sun. The smallest object seen is roughly 100km (60 miles) across, while the largest is 500 km (300 miles) in diameter, slightly smaller than Neptune's moon Triton. Indeed, Triton could be a body captured from the Kuiper belt, and Pluto and its moon Charon could be among its members.

Much further out in space is the Oort cloud, named in 1950 after the Dutch astronomer who identified it as a source of long-period comets. This is a rough sphere of rocky and icy debris left over from the solar nebula from which the Solar System formed. A vast size, it lies between 30,000 and 100,000AU from the Sun, a distance where gravity from passing stars could perurb it, sending comets in towards the Sun.

Future of the Solar System

We now know that dramatic consequences are in store for these terrestrial planets as a result of the dramatic changes that will happen to the Sun. Astronomers calculate that our star will be hot enough in 3 billion years to boil Earth's oceans away, leaving the planet a burned-out cinder, a dead and sterile place. Four billion years on, the Sun will balloon into a giant star, engulfing Mercury and becoming 2,000 times brighter than it is now. Its light will be intense enough to melt Earth's surface and turn the icy moons of the giant planets into globes of liquid.

Such events are in the almost inconceivably distant future, of course. For the present the Sun continues to provide us with an up-close laboratory of stellar astrophysics and evolution.

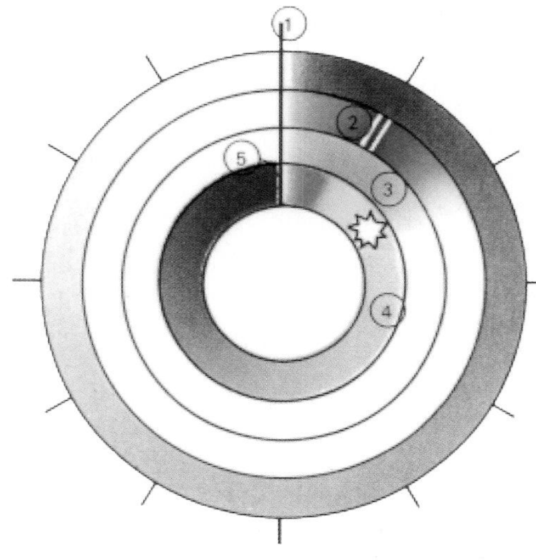

ABOVE The timescale of the Solar System can be represented on a 12-hour clock, tracing the lifespan of the Sun, the inner planets, Earth and the outer planets from the inner circle outwards. At the 12 o'clock position [1] the Solar System is created; after 4,000 million years, conditions on Earth are favourable for life [2]; as a red giant the Sun engulfs the inner planets [3] before collapsing as a white dwarf [4] and, possibly, end its long life as a brown dwarf [5].

BELOW The distance of the outermost planets – Jupiter, Saturn, Uranus, Neptune and Pluto – will save them from the Sun's helium burn, and each will continue its orbit. More precise predictions for their future are not possible.

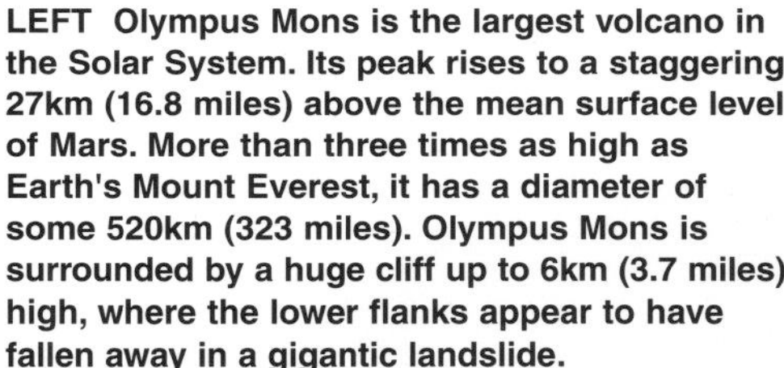

LEFT Olympus Mons is the largest volcano in the Solar System. Its peak rises to a staggering 27km (16.8 miles) above the mean surface level of Mars. More than three times as high as Earth's Mount Everest, it has a diameter of some 520km (323 miles). Olympus Mons is surrounded by a huge cliff up to 6km (3.7 miles) high, where the lower flanks appear to have fallen away in a gigantic landslide.

This collapse may have generated the peculiar blocky terrain of ridges separated by flat areas, the Olympus Mons aureole, that extends from the base of the cliff up to 1,000km (600 miles) from the volcano's summit. This contains a nested set of volcanic craters, the largest of them 80km (50 miles) across.

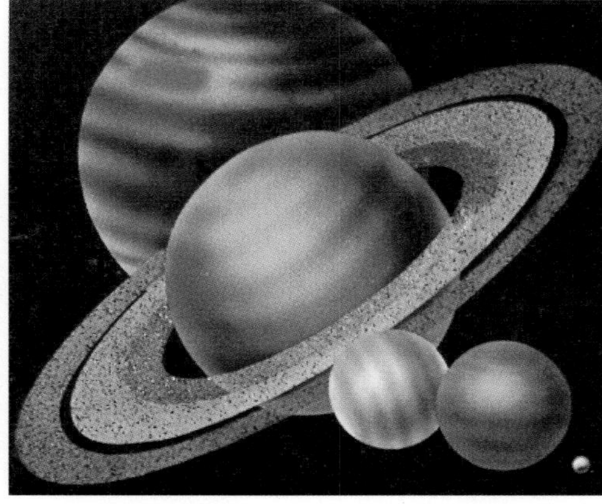

BELOW The lifespan of the Earth started from the material of the solar nebula [A] which at first had no regular form. When it reached its present size [B] the original hydrogen atmosphere had already been lost and replaced by a new one, caused by gases sent out from the interior. Life could begin and today the Earth is moving in a settled orbit round a stable star, so that it is habitable [C]. But this state of affairs will not persist indefinitely: long before the Sun enters the red giant stage, most scientists believe, the Earth will be overheated, the oceans will boil, and the atmosphere will be driven off [D]. Finally, the only planet known to have had life will be completely destroyed [E].

A

B

C

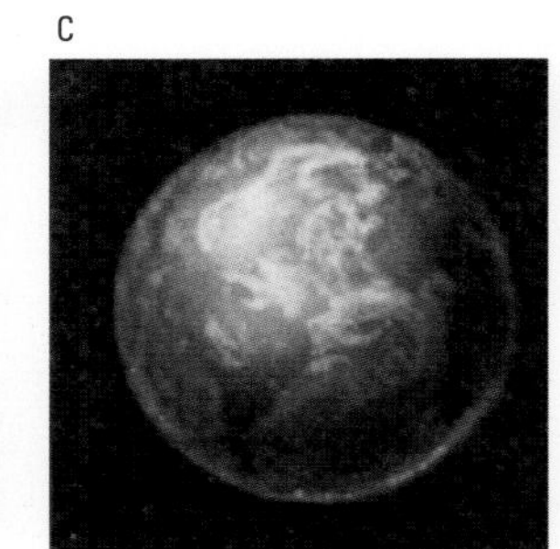

D

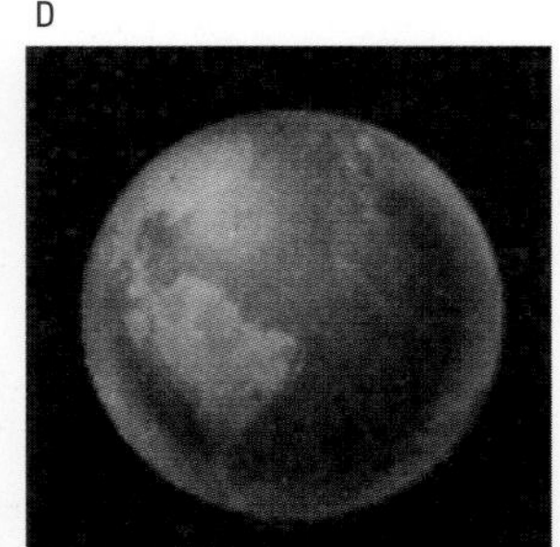

E

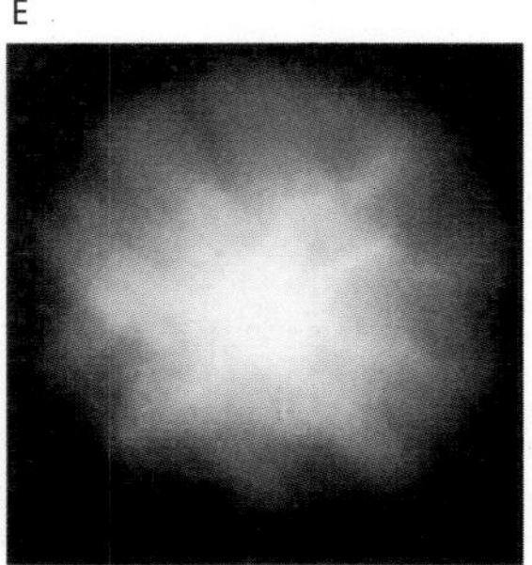

SOLAR SYSTEM: PROFILE

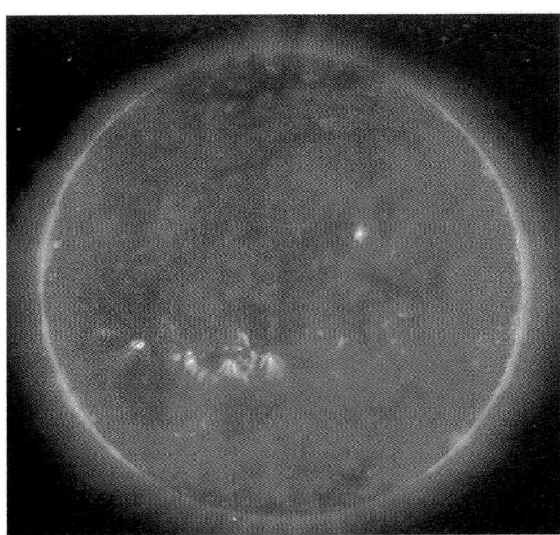

ABOVE The Sun's outer corona in ultraviolet light. The bright regions are areas of intense magnetism. This part of the corona is at a temperature of around 1,000,000°C. All the components of the Solar System are tethered by the immense gravitational pull of the Sun, the star whose thermonuclear furnaces provide them with virtually all their heat and light.

A TINY PART of one of the millions of galaxies (collections of stars) that make up the known Universe, the Solar System orbits at a mean distance of 29,700 light-years from the centre of our own galaxy, the "Milky Way". The present distance is 27,700 light-years, and it will reach the minimum distance of 27,600 in around 15 million years' time. It comprises one star, which we call the Sun, nine principal planets, and various bodies of lesser importance, including the satellites that attend some of the planets and a range of cosmic debris, notably asteroids, meteors and comets.

The system is entirely dependent on the Sun, which is by far the most massive body and the only one to be self-luminous: the remaining members of the Solar System shine by reflected sunlight and appear so brilliant in our skies that it is not always easy to remember that in universal terms they are nowhere near as large or important as they appear.

The inner planets

The planets are divided into two well-defined groups. First come the four relatively small planets of Mercury, Venus, Earth and Mars, with diameters ranging from 12,756km (7,926 miles) for Earth down to only 4,878km (3,031 miles) for Mercury. These planets have various factors in common. All, for example, have solid surfaces and are presumably made up of similar materials, although Earth and Mercury are more dense than Mars and Venus.

Although their orbits do not in general depart much from the circular, the paths of Mercury and Mars are considerably more eccentric than those of Earth and Venus. Mercury and Venus are known as the "inferior planets" because their orbits lie inside that of Earth; they show lunar-type phases from new to full and remain in the same region of the sky as the Sun. While Mercury and Venus are unattended by any satellites, Earth has one satellite (our familiar Moon) and Mars has two, Phobos and Deimos, both of which are very small and different in nature from the Moon.

Beyond Mars comes a wide gap, in which move thousands of small worlds known as the asteroids, or minor planets. Even Ceres, the largest, is only about 913km (567 miles) in diameter. This is much larger than was once thought, but still small by planetary standards. It is not therefore surprising that the asteroids remained hidden until relatively recent times, with Ceres discovered only in 1801. Just one of this new multitude, Vesta, is ever visible from Earth without the aid of a telescope.

The outer planets

Far beyond the main asteroid belt come the four giant planets of Jupiter, Saturn, Uranus and Neptune. These worlds are quite different from the terrestrial planets: they are fluid (that is, gas or liquid) rather than solid bodies with very dense atmospheres. Their masses are so great that they have been able to retain much of their original hydrogen; the escape velocity of Jupiter, for instance, is 60km (37 miles) per second as against

BELOW The planets of the Solar System shown to the same scale. On the right is a segment of the Sun [1]; from its surface rises a huge prominence [2]. Then come the inner planets: Mercury [3], Venus [4], Earth [5] with its Moon [6], and Mars [7]. Mars has two dwarf satellites Phobos [8] and Deimos [9], exaggerated here – if shown to the correct scale, they would be too small to be seen without a microscope. Then come the asteroids [10], of which even the largest is only about 913 (567 miles) in diameter. Beyond lie the giant planets: Jupiter [11], with its four largest satellites Io [12], Europa [13], Ganymede [14] and Callisto [15]; Saturn [16] with its retinue of satellites, of which the largest is Titan [17]; Uranus [18] with its many satellites; Neptune [19] with its large satellite Triton [20]; and finally misfit Pluto [21].

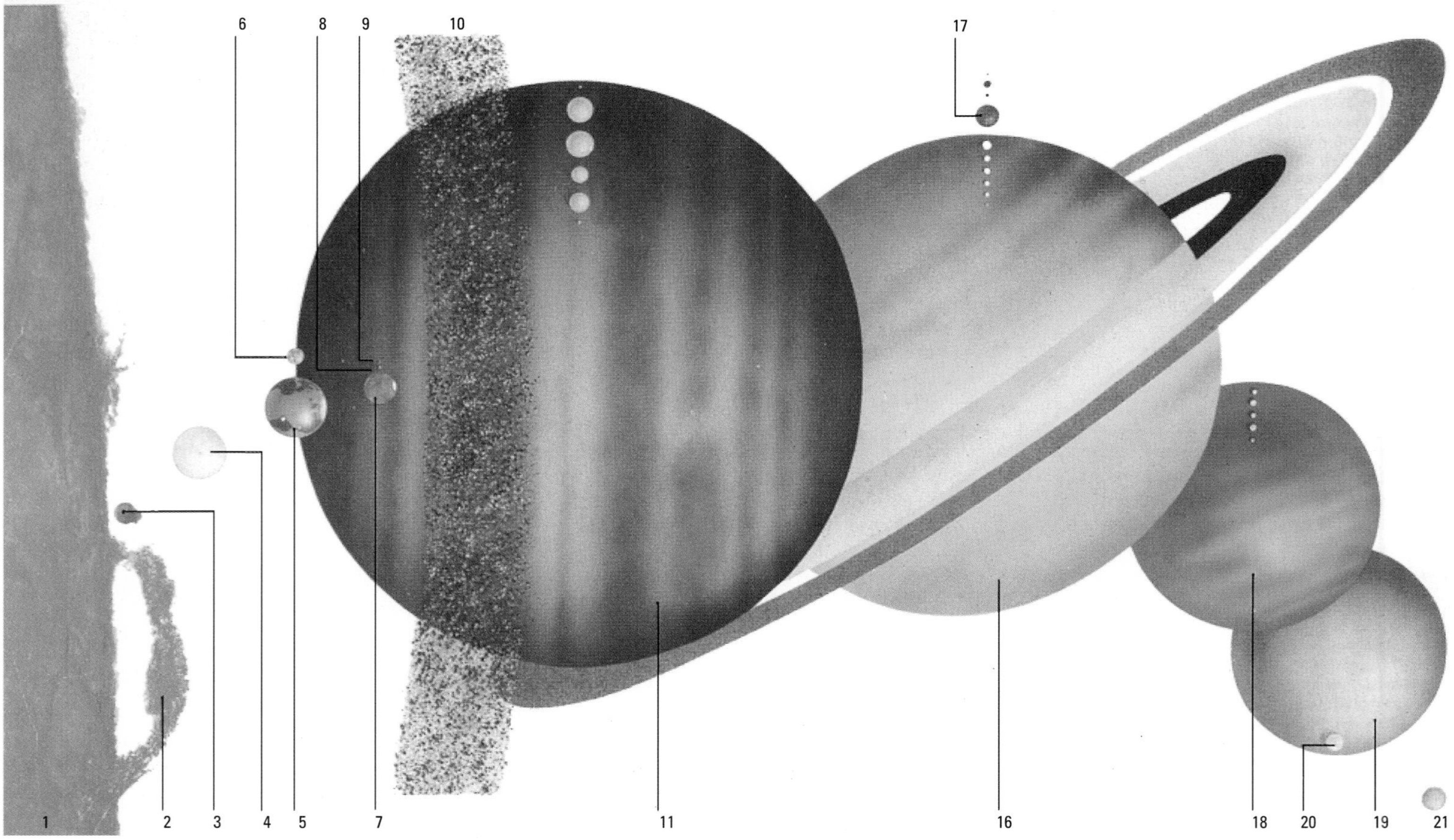

only 11.2km (7 miles) per second for Earth. Their mean distances from the Sun range from 778 million km (483 million miles) for Jupiter out to 4,497 million km (2,794 million miles) for Neptune. Conventional diagrams of the Solar System tend to be misleading as far as scale is concerned; it is tempting, for example, to assume that Saturn and Uranus are lying next to each other when in fact the distance of Uranus from the Earth's orbit is about twice that of Saturn.

The giant planets have various points in common, but differ markedly in detail. Their densities are comparatively low and the density of Saturn is actually less than that of water. Although Jupiter is seen solely by reflected sunlight, the planet does generate some heat of its own. However, even though the core temperature must be high, it is not nearly high enough for nuclear reactions to begin, so that Jupiter, though massive, cannot be compared to a star like the Sun.

Planetary discoveries

Five of the planets – Mercury, Venus, Mars, Jupiter and Saturn – have been known from ancient times, since all are prominent naked-eye objects. Uranus, just visible with the naked eye, was discovered fortuitously in 1781 by William Herschel and Neptune was added to the list of known planets in 1846 as a result of mathematical investigations carried out concerning movements of Uranus. All the giants are attended by satellites; Jupiter has 16 moons, Saturn 20, Uranus 15 and Neptune eight. Several of these are of planetary size, with diameters almost equal to Mercury's.

The outermost known planet is Pluto, discovered in 1930 by astronomers at the Lowell Observatory, Flagstaff, Arizona. It is far from another giant, being smaller than the Earth, and is usually ranked as a terrestrial-type planet, even though little is known about it.

Pluto's origin was long a mystery because of its size, rocky composition and highly unusual orbit. In recent years, however, it has become apparent that Pluto orbits within a "swarm" of tens of thousands of still smaller worlds orbiting well beyond the region of Neptune.

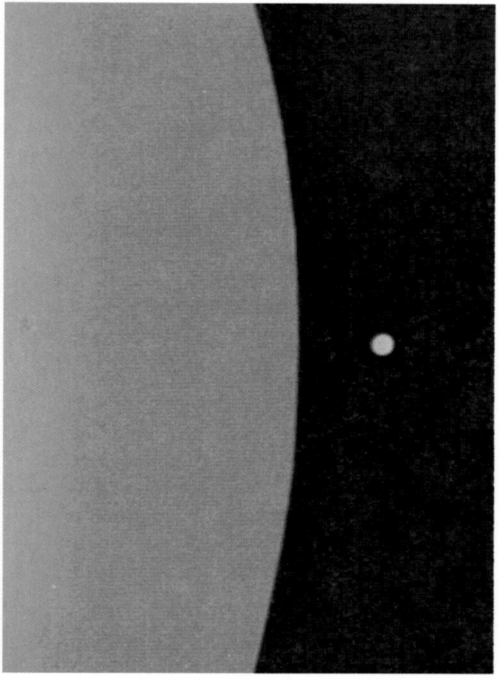

ABOVE Shown here in cross-section, the Sun has an equatorial diameter of 1,392,000km (865,000 miles), 109 times that of Earth. Despite the fact that its volume is more than a million times that of Earth, its mass is only 333,000 times greater because the density is lower: the mean specific gravity, on a scale where water = 1, is only 1.4.

LEFT While the Sun is the body on which the entire Solar System depends, and is more massive than all the planets combined, it is an ordinary main sequence star with a magnitude of +5 – small when compared with a giant star. The diagram shows the Sun alongside a segment of the red supergiant Betelgeuse, which marks Orion's right shoulder. Betelgeuse is of spectral class M2 – a very cool star – but has an absolute magnitude of –5.5. Its diameter is 300 to 400 times that of the Sun, and its globe is large enough to contain Earth's orbit. In 5 million years' time the Sun's life cycle will make it a modest red giant in its own right, and the solid inner planets of the Solar System will be destroyed by the heat and light that results from its phenomenal expansion.

RIGHT The ecosphere is the region around the Sun in which a planet can be at a suitable temperature for life as we conceive it to exist – assuming that the planet is of Earth "type". The inner yellow zone [1] is way too hot, and beyond the ecosphere [orange, 2], temperatures will become too low [3]. Earth [4] lies in the middle of the ecosphere, enjoying a near-perfect set of balanced conditions for life. Inhospitable Venus [5] orbits at the very inner limit and barren Mars [6] at the outer, but recent probes have proved that neither has the prerequisites for evolution. The best hope of finding life as we know it seems now to rest with a similar ecosphere – in one of the billions of other solar systems in the Universe.

THE SUN

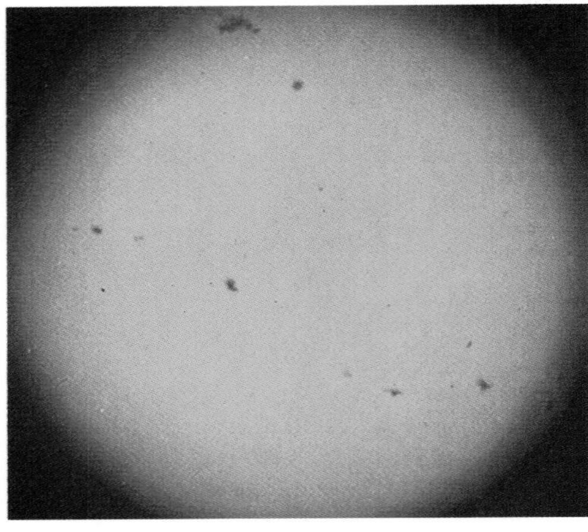

ABOVE The "solar maximum" of 1958, pictured here, was the most energetic phase of the solar cycle ever recorded, and sunspots are clearly visible. Occurring where there is a local strengthening of the Sun's magnetic field, sunspots are regions in the photosphere that are cooler than their surroundings and therefore appear darker. Varying in size from 1,000 to 50,000km (600 to 30,000 miles) and occasionally up to 200,000km (125,000 miles), they comprise a dark central region called the umbra, and a grey outer region, the penumbra. Their duration varies from a few hours to several weeks, or months for the biggest ones.

The number of spots visible depends on the stage of the solar cycle. This is fairly regular and lasts around 11 years and is part of a longer 22-year solar cycle, but at the intervening "spot minima" the disc may remain featureless for several days or even weeks. The exact cause of sunspots is not fully understood – and no theory has been able to explain their disappearance between 1645 and 1715.

Sunspots are seen to move across the face of the Sun as it rotates. Most appear in pairs, but often complex groups emerge. They can be seen if you project an image of the Sun onto a piece of white paper or card.

THE SUN is a star, one of 100,000 million stars in our galaxy. In the Universe as a whole it is insignificant – classed as a yellow dwarf star with a spectrum of type G – but in our planetary system it is the all-important controlling body.

Immensely larger than Earth, the Sun has a diameter of 1,392,000km (865,000 miles). Though big enough to contain more than a million bodies the volume of Earth, its mass is only 1.99 x 10^{30} kg – approximately 333,000 times that of Earth. The reason why it is not as massive as might be expected is that its density is lower than that of an Earth-type planet. The mean value for the specific gravity is 1.409 (that is, 1.409 times an equal volume of water), but the Sun is not homogenous and density, pressure and temperature all increase rapidly beneath the brilliant outer surface towards the centre. It consists of about 70% hydrogen (by weight) and some 28% helium, with the remainder mostly oxygen and carbon.

The Sun lies some 32,000 light-years from the centre of our galaxy and takes approximately 200 million years to complete one journey round the galactic nucleus. It has an axial rotation period of 25.4 days at its equator, but because the Sun does not rotate in the manner of a solid body, this period is considerably longer near the solar poles.

In ordinary light the Sun appears to have a clear edge. This is because only a 500-km (300-mile) layer of its atmosphere, the photosphere, is at the correct temperature to emit light at visible wavelengths – a very small layer in comparison to the star's vast diameter.

The Sun's magnetic field

Overall, the Sun's magnetic field is roughly the same strength as Earth's, but the mechanism is entirely different. The Sun is not a solid body but a plasma created by heat removing the electrons of hydrogen atoms to leave negatively charged electrons and, possibly, positively charged ions. Magnetic fields can be created by the motion of electrically charged particles, and the Sun's turbulence and rotation create localized fields.

As the Sun rotates, the magnetic field lines get "trapped" and move around with the rotation. As the top layers bubble with convection the field lines become twisted up, and this squashing together increases the strength of the magnetic field in those areas. These intense pockets cause many of the phenomena seen on the Sun, notably sunspots.

Prominences and flares

The part of the solar atmosphere lying immediately above the photosphere is called the chromosphere ("colour sphere") because it has a characteristically reddish appearance. This is also the region of the large and brilliant prominences. To observe the prominences, instruments based on the principle of the spectroscope are used. There are two main types of prominences: eruptive and quiescent. Eruptive prominences are in violent motion and have been observed extending to more than 50,000km (312,500 miles) above the Sun's surface; quiescent prominences are much more stable and may hang in the chromosphere for days before breaking up. Both are most common near the peak of the solar cycle of activity.

Prominences are often associated with major spot-groups. Active groups also produce "flares", which are not usually visible, although a few have been seen. The flares are short-lived and emit streams of particles as well as short-wave radiation. These emissions have marked effects on Earth, producing magnetic storms or disturbances of Earth's magnetic field that affect radio communications and compasses. They also produce the beautiful solar lights or aurorae.

The solar wind

Less dense areas of the corona, the outer layer of the Sun, called coronal holes by astronomers, appear where the Sun's magnetic field opens to interplanetary space rather than looping back down. These areas are believed to be the major source of the solar wind, where charged particles, mainly protons and electrons, stream out into the interplanetary medium.

It is this emission that has a strong effect on the tails of comets, forcing them to point away from the Sun. Even when it reaches Earth, the wind's velocity exceeds 950km (590 miles) per second.

BELOW The structure of the Sun cannot be drawn to an accurate scale, and attempts at full cross-sections are misleading. In the core, about 400,000km (250,000 miles) across, continual nuclear transformations create energy and the temperature is perhaps 15 million °C (27 million °F). Further out in the solar interior, the radiative zone [1] , about 300,000km (200,000 miles) wide, diffuses radiation randomly, and temperatures range from 15 million to 1 million °C. In the convective layer [2] heat travels outward for 200,000km (125,000 miles) on convection currents, cooling from a million to 6,000°C (11,000°F). The relatively rarefied photosphere [3], the fairly well-defined "sphere of light" from which energy is radiated into space and where temperatures average 5,500°C (10,000°F), is surprisingly narrow – only 500km (300 miles) wide; because it is the layer of the Sun that radiates in visible wavelengths, this is the part of the Sun that we see, including the sunspots [4].

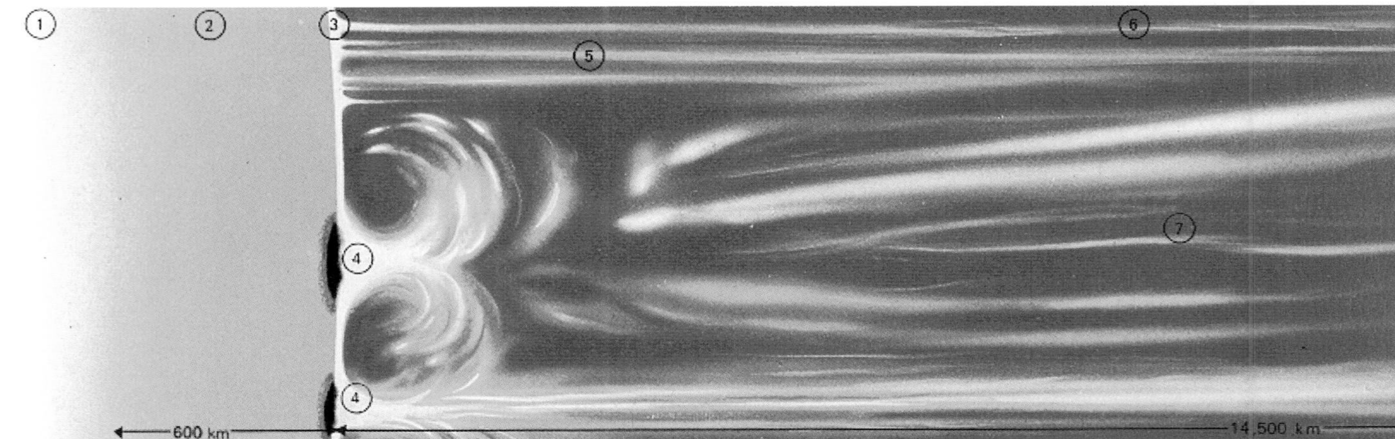

RIGHT Like all stars the Sun's energy is generated by nuclear reactions taking place under extreme conditions in the core. Here the Sun is continually converting four hydrogen atoms into one helium atom. The amount of energy produced in each individual reaction is tiny, but the Sun is converting 600,000 million kg (1,325,000 million lb) of hydrogen into helium every single second. The Sun's total power output, its luminosity, is 3.9 x 10^{26} watts (the equivalent of a million, million, million, million 100-watt light bulbs).

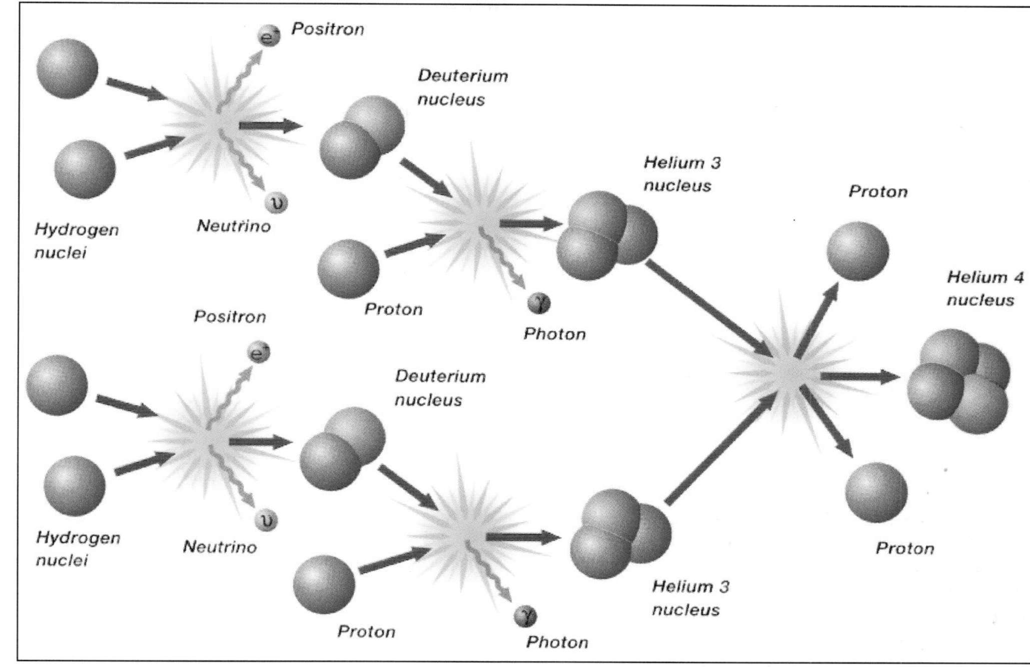

Powerhouse of a star

It is a mistake to think of the Sun burning in the same way that a fire burns. A star made up entirely of coal, and radiating as fiercely as the Sun does, would not last long on the cosmic scale, and astronomers believe that the Sun is at least 5,000 million years old.

The source of solar energy is to be found in nuclear transformations. Hydrogen is the main constituent and near the core, where the temperatures and pressures are so extreme that the second lightest element, helium, is formed from hydrogen nuclei by nuclear fusion. It takes four hydrogen nuclei to make one nucleus of helium; in the process a little mass is lost, being converted into a large amount of energy. The energy produced keeps the Sun radiating: the loss of mass amounts to four million tonnes per second. This may seem significant, but it is negligible compared with the total mass of the Sun – and there is enough hydrogen available to keep the Sun shining in its present form for at least another 5,000 million years.

Eventually the hydrogen will start to become exhausted and the Sun will change its structure drastically. According to current theory, it will pass through a red giant stage, when it will have a luminosity at least 100 times as great as it does today. Once all its nuclear fuel has been used up, it will start to collapse into a small dense star of the type known as a white dwarf. Earth will have long gone: it will not survive the heat of the Sun's red giant stage, and along with the other inner planets will be totally destroyed.

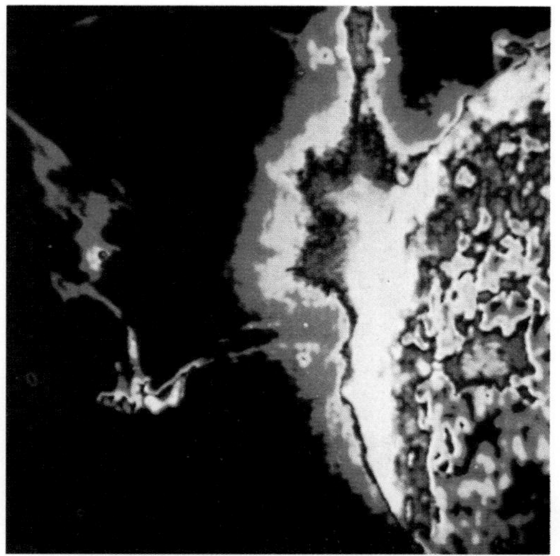

LEFT A solar prominence photographed by astronauts on board Skylab. In this extreme ultraviolet shot the colours are false: they represent the degree of radiation intensity from red, through yellow and blue, to purple and white, where the activity is most intense. This picture could only be taken with equipment carried above the layers of the Earth's atmosphere.

When viewed face-on against the bright photosphere, prominences are known as filaments. Narrow jets of gas called spicules can also be observed at the limb of the Sun. They move at around 20–30km (12–18 miles) a second from the lower chromosphere into the inner corona, and fall back or fade away after a few minutes. Flares, intense outpourings of energy, occur in complex sunspot groups, and can cause auroral activity and storms on Earth.

Above the photosphere lies the chromosphere [5], meaning "sphere of colour", and so-called because of its rosy tint when seen during a total solar eclipse. This is the region of flares and prominences [6], where the temperature rises from 6,000 to 50,000°C; temperature here is purely a measure of the speeds at which the atomic particles are moving and does not necessarily indicate extra "heat". In the chromosphere there are spicules [7], masses of high-temperature gases shooting up into the immensely rarefied corona [8], where temperatures can reach 1 million °C (1,800,000°F) – possibly due to the action of the Sun's magnetic field. Streamers [9] issue from the corona, which has no definite boundary and extends millions of kilometres out into space, eventually thinning to become the radiation we call the "solar wind". Together with the Sun's magnetic field, the solar wind dominates a vast indeterminate region of space called the heliosphere.

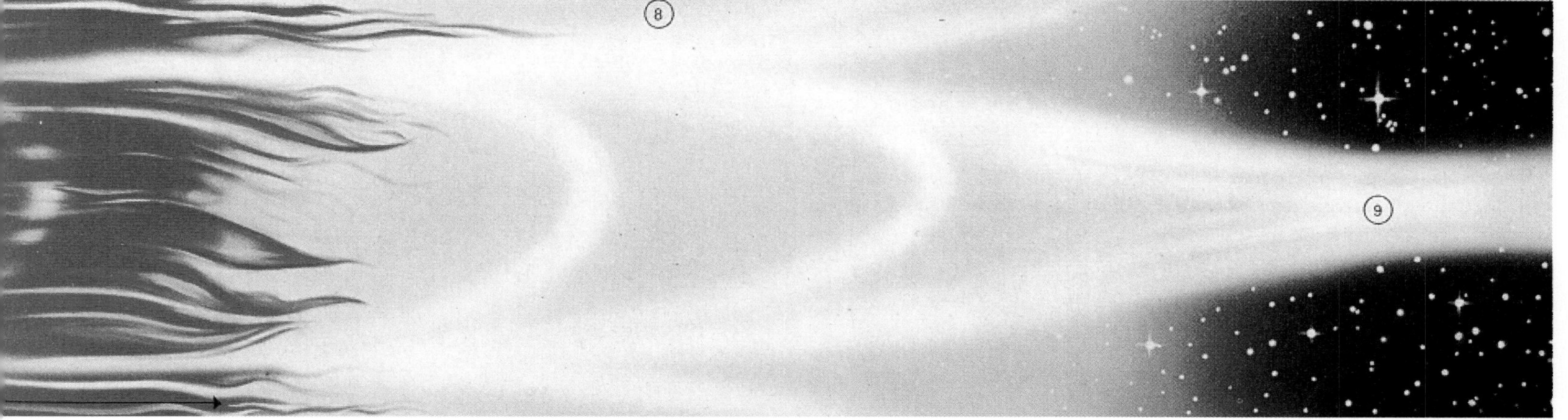

MERCURY

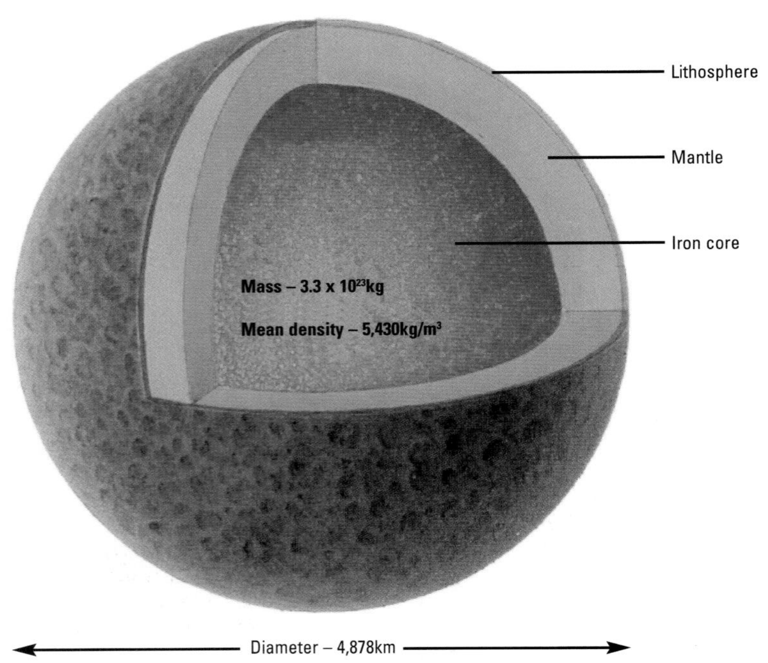

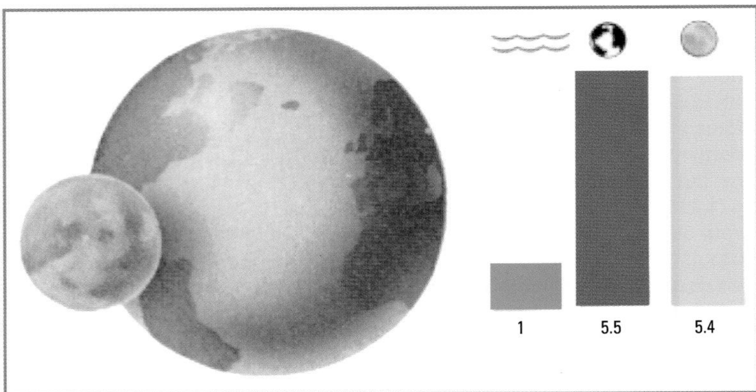

ABOVE **With a diameter of 4,878km (3,031miles), Mercury is dwarfed by Earth and is the Solar System's smallest planet after Pluto. However, its mean density (5.4 times that of water) is similar to Earth's. A small planet must contain a lot of iron to have so high a density, and astronomers believe that Mercury has twice as much, by proportion, as any other planet. Its iron core, thought to extend out to three-quarters of its entire radius, is surrounded by a mantle of rock and a thick hard crust. Mercury has a very tenuous and thin atmosphere, mostly hydrogen and helium, with a ground pressure only two-trillionths that of Earth.**

THE "FASTEST" planet, Mercury takes just 88 Earth days to orbit its massive close neighbour, the Sun – probably the reason the Romans named it after the fleet-footed messenger of the gods. It is the closest planet to the Sun and suffers the widest extremes of temperature: at noon, when the Sun is directly overhead, the temperature can soar to as high as 470°C (880°F), while during the long Mercurian night it can plunge to below –175°C (–283°F).

Mercury's orbit is elliptical: its aphelion (farthest point from the Sun) is 69,800,000km (43,400,000 miles), and its perihelion (closest point to the Sun) is 46,000,000km (28,600,000 miles).

The elusive planet

Although its existence has been known since the dawn of history, and it can appear to be brighter than the brightest star, Mercury is notoriously difficult to observe. This is because it is always too close to the Sun in the sky. The angle between Mercury and the Sun can never exceed 28°; this means that Mercury is lost in the Sun's glare because it sets no more than two hours after the Sun and rises no more than two hours before it. Once or twice a year, you may be able to see Mercury shining like a bright star close to the western horizon after sunset, or close to the eastern horizon before sunrise.

Mercury orbits the Sun in only 88 Earth days and undertakes the Earth at intervals of, on average, 115.88 days. On these occasions, Mercury lies between the Sun and Earth, but because of the tilt of its orbit (7°), usually passes above or below the Sun when viewed from Earth. Occasionally, when the alignment is right, Mercury passes directly in front of the Sun and can be seen as a small dot moving slowly across its face: such an event is called a transit. The alignments that allow transits of Mercury to take place occur only in the months of May or November, and the dates of early 21st-century transits are 7 May 2003, 8 November 2006, 9 May 2016, and 11 November 2019.

Until the 1960s, most astronomers believed that Mercury took exactly the same time to rotate on its axis as it took to orbit the Sun: one hemisphere would always face toward the Sun and constantly suffer its boiling heat, while the other was in constant darkness. However, radar measurements carried out since then have shown that this is not the case: Mercury rotates every 58.65 Earth days, precisely two-thirds of its orbital period or year.

Mercury's magnetic puzzle

The strength of the magnetic field at Mercury's surface is very low: only about 1% that of the Earth's. This is only just strong enough to deflect most of the incoming solar wind and to form a magnetosphere around the planet. Nevertheless, Mariner 10's discovery of the magnetic field came as a surprise to most astronomers. According to conventional theory, a planet can only sustain a magnetic field if it has an electrically conductive liquid interior and rotates rapidly on its axis.

Although Mercury has a large iron core, this should in theory have cooled and solidified by now because of the planet's small size. The presence of a magnetic field suggests that at least part of the deep interior must still be liquid – but even if this is the case, Mercury's slow rotation still makes the presence of a magnetic field puzzling.

RIGHT **A mosaic of Mercury created from images taken by Mariner 10, the first two-planet probe, on its outward journey in March 1974. The craft flew within 703km (437 miles) of the planet, and in three encounters during 1974–75 took more than 12,000 images covering over half its surface. Images returned by Mariner 10 revealed that most of Mercury's surface is heavily cratered from impacts by meteorites, asteroids and comets, with many over 200km (125 miles) wide. As on the Moon, some are surrounded by lighter-coloured ejecta – material splashed out by the impacts. The largest feature pictured by the probe was the Caloris Basin, measuring 1,300km (800 miles) across.**

VENUS

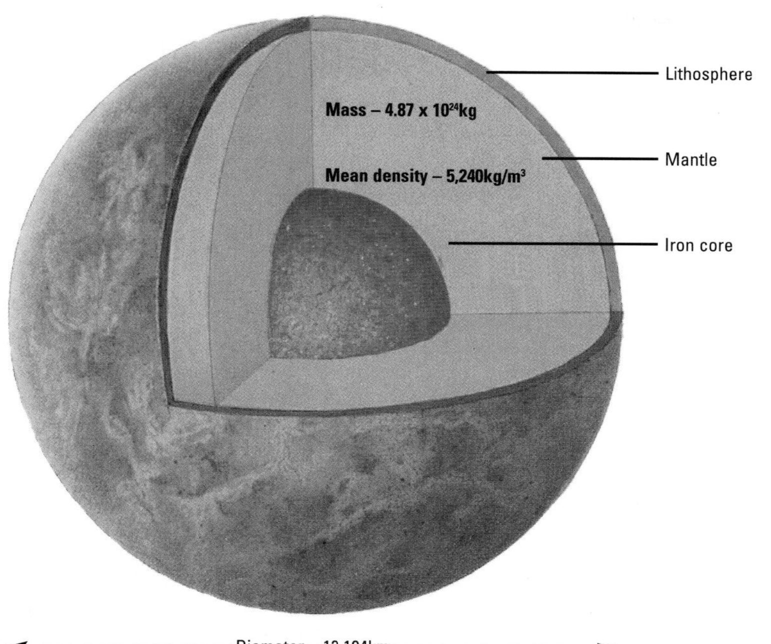

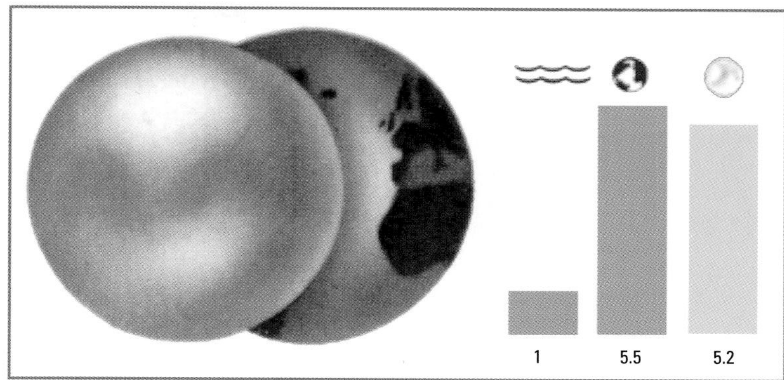

ABOVE The similarity in size, mass and density led to astronomers regarding Venus and Earth as "sister planets", formed at much the same time and part of space, but incredible heat and pressure make Venus an inhospitable body. Its internal structure, however, is probably much the same, with a nickel-iron core surrounded by a silicate mantle. The Mariner 2 probe of 1962 discovered it has a much weaker magnetic field than Earth, suggesting it may not have a liquid outer core. The lack of a strong magnetic field may also be a result of the planet's slow rotation of 243 days. Venus also rotates "backwards" (retrograde) as compared to other planets, but the reason remains a mystery.

TO THE NAKED EYE Venus is a splendid object and, as the evening and morning "star", is far brighter than any celestial object except the Sun and Moon – the reason it was named after the goddess of beauty. Telescopically, however, it has always been a disappointment, shrouded in cloud and, until very recently, mystery.

The orbit of Venus is nearer to circular than any planet, and the mean distance from the Sun – an average of 108,200,000km (67,200,000 miles) varies little. This revolution period is 224.7 Earth days, while the rotation takes 243 days.

Analysis of the sunlight reflected from the Venusian clouds revealed that the atmosphere was chiefly composed of carbon dioxide, and radio measurements suggested the surface was extremely hot. Space probe soundings of the atmosphere and surface later revealed a world completely devoid of all forms of water and confirmed searing surface temperatures that reached 480°C (895°F).

As if this were not enough, the dense atmosphere crushes down on the planet with a pressure 90 times that at the Earth's surface; a human being standing unprotected on the rock-strewn landscape of Venus would be simultaneously roasted, crushed and asphyxiated.

A dead planet

Liquid water is an essential ingredient for life as we know it, and without any water source it is extremely unlikely that any form of life ever existed on the planet. Venus's proximity to the Sun means that it probably started out with less water than the Earth – any water there would probably have existed as vapour rather than as liquid.

Even after the planets formed, the more intense solar radiation on Venus would have driven what little water remained from its atmosphere by breaking up the water molecules into their constituent parts of hydrogen and oxygen. Hydrogen is a very light gas and would have escaped off into space, while the oxygen would have been absorbed by the planet's surface. Even the rain of watery, icy comets that must have impacted Venus during its history was apparently insufficient to prevent the planet drying out.

The Venusian atmosphere

When the interiors of both Venus and Earth heated up from radioactivity, a great deal of volcanic activity occurred, causing vast amounts of carbon dioxide to be released. On Earth, the oceans dissolved some of this gas and carbonate rocks were formed, but on Venus there were no oceans and the carbon dioxide stayed in the atmosphere.

Findings in 1978 from the US Pioneer Venus 2 spacecraft, which parachuted through the atmosphere, established that Venus has sulphuric acid clouds concentrated in a layer at heights of 48–58km (30–36 miles) above the surface. Drops of the acid develop just like drops of water in our own clouds and when they are large enough, they fall as acid rain. However, this corrosive rain never reaches Venus' surface because the temperature difference, 13.3°C (56°F) at the top of the clouds and an oven-like 220°C (430°F) underneath them, causes them to evaporate at about 31km above the ground. Below this level, the Venera and Pioneer probes revealed that the atmosphere is remarkably clear, though the surface, subject to a fierce greenhouse effect, lies under a permanent overcast.

RIGHT This view of Venus was taken from 760,000km (450,000 miles) by Mariner 10's television cameras in 1974, en route to Mercury. Individual TV frames were computer-enhanced using invisible ultraviolet light: the blue appearance of the planet does not represent true colour, but is the result of darkroom processing of the images to enhance the UV markings on the clouds. It is this cloud cover that accounts for the brilliance of Venus. The picture is viewed with the predominant swirl at the South Pole. The clouds rotate 60 times faster than the planet's slow 243 days, taking only four days to go around Venus once, a rapid motion driven by the heating of the atmosphere by the nearby Sun.

EARTH

THE "THIRD rock from the Sun" is the heaviest of the stony planets and the most dense of all planets. The difference in size and mass between Earth and Venus is slight but Mars is much smaller

What makes Earth unique, however, is the fact that it has the perfect physical and chemical credentials for the evolution of life; slightly closer to the Sun, or slightly farther away, and life could not have developed. The "ecosphere", or the region in which solar radiation will produce tolerable conditions for terrestrial-type life, extends from just inside the orbit of Venus out to that of Mars. Until about 1960, it was thought that such life might exist throughout the region, but spaceprobes have shown both Venus and Mars to be incapable of creating and sustaining any form of life.

Approximately equal in density as well as size and mass, Venus absorbs about the same amount of solar energy as Earth because of the high reflecting power of its cloud. It was not until 1967, when the surface temperature of Venus was shown to register up to 480°C (895°F), that it was commonly accepted that advanced terrestrial life could develop only within a very limited zone.

Temperature depends not only on the distance of the planet from the Sun or the composition of its atmosphere; there is also the axial rotation period to be taken into account. Earth spins round once in approximately 24 hours, and the rotation period of Mars is only 37 minutes longer, but Mercury and Venus are very different – the periods are 58.7 days and 243 days respectively, leading to very peculiar "calendars". Were Earth a slow spinner, the climatic conditions would be both unfamiliar and hostile.

An atmosphere must not only enable living creatures to breathe, but also protect the planet from lethal short-wave radiations from space. There is no danger on the surface of Earth because the radiations are blocked out by layers in the upper atmosphere; had Earth been more massive, it might have been able to retain at least some of its original hydrogen (as the giants Jupiter and Saturn have done) and the resulting atmosphere might have been unsuitable for life.

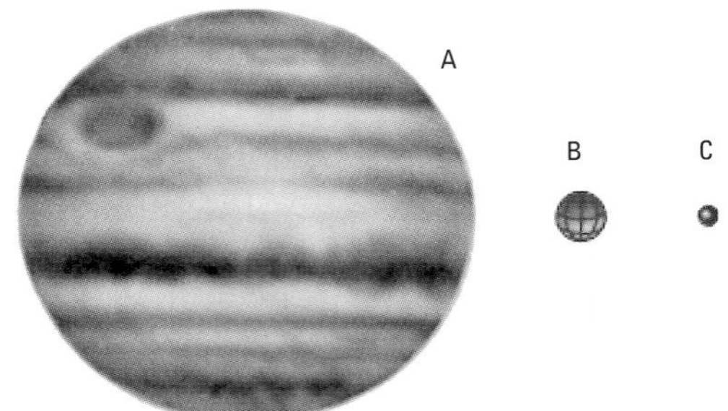

ABOVE The relative sizes of Jupiter [A], Earth [B] and Mercury [C]. Jupiter is the largest planet, Mercury the smallest (excluding the extraordinary misfit Pluto), and while Earth is intermediate in size, it is more nearly comparable with Mercury in the context of the Solar System. Earth is the largest of the so-called terrestrial planets – Mercury, Venus, Earth, Mars, Pluto – but far inferior in size even to the smallest of the four "gas giants", Neptune.

ABOVE Seen from space, Earth will show phases – just as the Moon does to us. These five photographs shown were taken from a satellite over a period of 12 hours.

RIGHT Earth as captured above the Moon's surface from an Apollo spacecraft. The contrast between the barren landscape of the Moon and the near-perfect balance of land, cloud and ocean on Earth is startling. Our planet is the only home of known life in the Solar System, though spheres in the same section of their ecospheres may well exist in the Universe.

Earth is unique in having a surface that is largely covered with water; thus although it is the largest of the four inner planets its land surface is much less than that of Venus and equal to that of Mars. There can be no oceans or even lakes on Mars, because of the low atmospheric pressure, and none on the Moon or Mercury, which are to all intents and purposes without atmosphere. On Venus the surface temperature is certainly too high for liquid water to exist, so that the old, intriguing picture of a "carboniferous" Venus, with luxuriant vegetation flourishing in a swampy and moist environment, has had to be given up.

Because Earth is so exceptional, it has been suggested that it was formed in a manner different from that of the other planets, but this is almost certainly not the case. The age of Earth, as measured by radioactive methods, is approximately 4,600 million years (4.6 eons) and studies of the lunar rocks show that the age of the Moon is the same; there is no reason to doubt that the Earth and all other members of the Solar System originated by the same process, and at about the same time, from the primeval solar nebula.

[For detailed profile of Earth, see pages 28–29; for Earth statistics, see page 54]

MARS

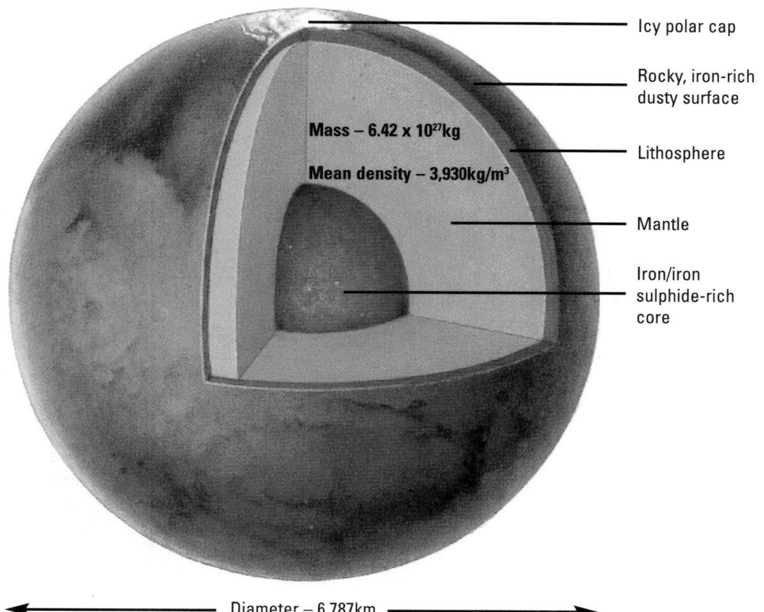

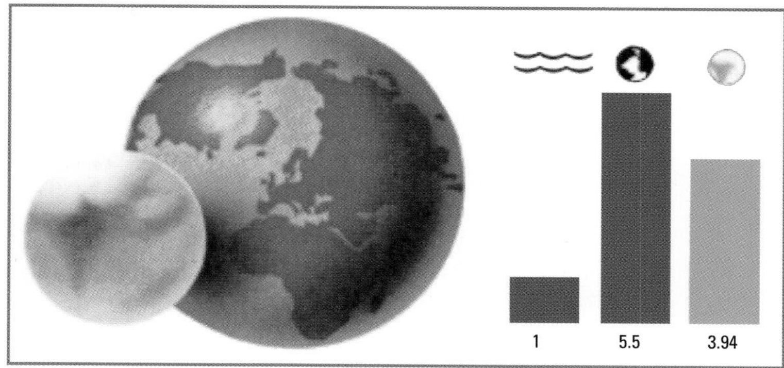

ABOVE The surface area of Mars is 28% that of Earth. Its diameter of 6,787km (4,217 miles) is a just over half that of Earth, and about twice that of the Moon. It has only a tenth of Earth's mass. Observations suggest that Mars contains an iron-rich core, about 1,700km (1,050 miles) in diameter. The low density of Mars compared to the other terrestrial planets hints that this core may also contain a significant amount of sulphur. Apparently, this core is not convecting enough to create as strong a magnetic field as Earth: indeed, it was not until 1997 that Mars Global Surveyor detected its weak and patchy magnetic field.

LIKE EARTH, Mars experiences seasons. Varying between 207 million km and 249 million km (129 and 158 million) miles from the Sun, its orbit is not circular and it is much closer to the Sun during the southern summer than in the northern summer, so that southern Martian summers are warmer than northern ones. But because the planet moves faster when it is closer to the Sun they are shorter and southern winters longer and colder than those in the north; one result is that the southern residual cap retains some frozen carbon dioxide (which melts at a lower temperature) as well as water.

In the late 1960s the Mariner 4, 6 and 7 spacecraft confirmed that the surface resides under only a thin atmosphere of carbon dioxide, with a pressure of only one hundredth of that at the Earth's surface at most, and in places even lower. They also revealed that Mars is cold, with mean annual temperatures ranging from –58°C (–72°F) at the equator to –123°C (–189°F) at the poles. At these temperatures and low pressures liquid water cannot currently exist on the Martian surface, although the Mariner and subsequent Viking pictures revealed evidence for the ancient action of flowing water.

RIGHT A mosaic image of the Schiaparelli hemisphere created from images taken by the Viking orbiter in 1980. Mars was once considered the likeliest of planets to share Earth's cargo of life, the seasonal expansion of dark patches strongly suggesting vegetation and the icecaps indicating the presence of water.

However, close inspection by spacecraft brought disappointment: some combination of chemical reactions, erosion and dark dust deposited by strong winds account for the "vegetation", and the "icecaps", though comprising a permanent layer of water ice, are covered from autumn to spring by a cover of carbon dioxide frost. Whatever oxygen the planet once possessed is now locked up in the iron-bearing rock that covers its cratered surface and gives it its characteristic red colour. The large crater near the centre is Schiaparelli, about 500km (370 miles) in diameter.

Mars is smaller and less "massive" than Earth or Venus, and so has a lower surface gravity and cannot hold on to a dense atmosphere. Mars' lower volume means that it could not generate and retain the same amount of internal heat as Venus or Earth, and does not maintain the same level of volcanic activity.

The core is surrounded by a molten rocky mantle denser and perhaps three times as rich in iron oxide as that of the Earth, overlain by a thin crust. The lack of plate tectonics and absence of current volcanic activity implies this mantle is also non-convecting – though one massive feature, the 4,500-km (2,800-mile) long Valles Marineris, may be a fracture in the crust caused by internal stresses.

Mars has two small moons, Phobos and Deimos, two potato-shape asteroids that were once captured by the planet's gravity.

JUPITER

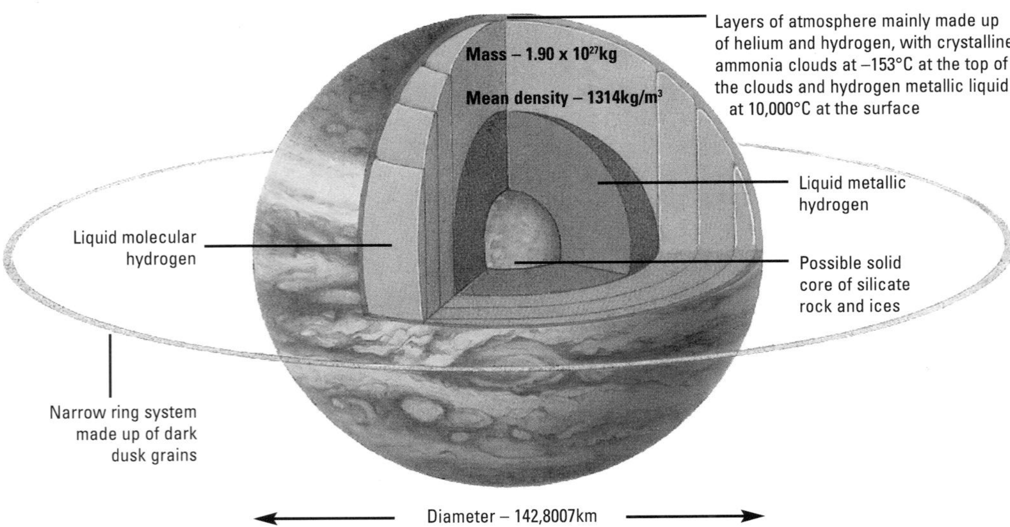

Jupiter's mean density is only 1.3 times that of water *(right)*, but the outer layers are tenuous and the core is far denser. The Earth's axis is tilted at an angle of 23½° from the perpendicular to the plane of orbit, but Jupiter's is only just over 3° *(below)*.

1 5.5 1.3

23.5° 3.1°

FAR BEYOND the main asteroid belt, at a mean distance of 778,300,000km (483,600,000 miles) from the Sun, lies Jupiter, the largest of the planets. This huge globe could swallow up 1,300 bodies the volume of Earth but its mass – despite being nearly three times as much as the other planets combined – is only 318 times that Earth because Jupiter is much less dense.

The planet is mostly gas, under intense pressure in its lower atmosphere above a core of fiercely compressed hydrogen and helium. The upper layers form strikingly coloured rotating belts, outward signs of the intense storms created by its rapid rotation of less than ten hours. This also means that the equator tends to bulge, and like Saturn the planet is clearly flattened at the poles: Jupiter's equatorial diameter is 143,000km (89,000 miles), whereas the polar diameter is less than 135,000km (84,000 miles).

When viewing the planet, you can only see the outermost part of its very deep atmosphere, which has several layers of cloud of different composition and colour. Jupiter rotates so fast that it spins the clouds into bands in which various spots, waves and other dynamic weather systems occur. The banded patterns in Jupiter's clouds arise because of the existence of convection cells in the atmosphere. The giant spots between, and sometimes within, the bands are giant eddies, or rotating masses of cloudy air, similar to enormous versions of our earthly hurricanes. Other weather systems, often of contrasting colour, appear embedded in the layers.

The Great Red Spot

While most of Jupiter's spots are short-lived, the Great Red Spot, by far the largest, is the notable exception. Under observation for over 300 years, it sometimes disappears but always returns, and has been prominent this time around since the mid-1960s. Occurring at a latitude of around 23° south, it is a huge, complex, cloudy vortex – variable in size but always far larger than the diameter of Earth – rotating in an anti-clockwise direction.

The "GRS" is believed to be a two-dimensional vortex which spirals outwards away from areas of high pressure, so although it appears like a hurricane it is a high- rather than low-pressure phenomenon. The reasons for its constant position and its characteristic colour, however, remain unclear.

Jupiter's rings

Recent investigations by spaceprobes have shown an orbiting ring system and discovered several previously unknown moons, and Jupiter has at least 16. The ring system is composed of three major components. The main ring is some 7,000km (4,350 miles) wide and has an average radius of about 126,000km (80,000 miles). At its inner edge this merges into the halo, a faint doughnut-shaped ring about 20,000km (12,400 miles) across, which extends over half the distance to the planet itself. Just outside the main ring is a faint gossamer ring made of fine material, extending out past the orbit of the innermost satellite Amalthea. These rings are not only more tenuous than Saturn's but are also darker, probably comprising dust rather than ice.

The magnetic field

Jupiter has a strong magnetic field, caused by the planet still cooling from its time of formation and constantly collapsing in on itself under its own gravitational pull. This gives off heat, producing dynamic convection movements in the fluid metallic interior. Coupled with the spin of Jupiter's rapid rotation, it produces an extensive magnetic field about 20,000 times stronger than that of the Earth – one which constantly alters size and shape in response to changes in the solar wind.

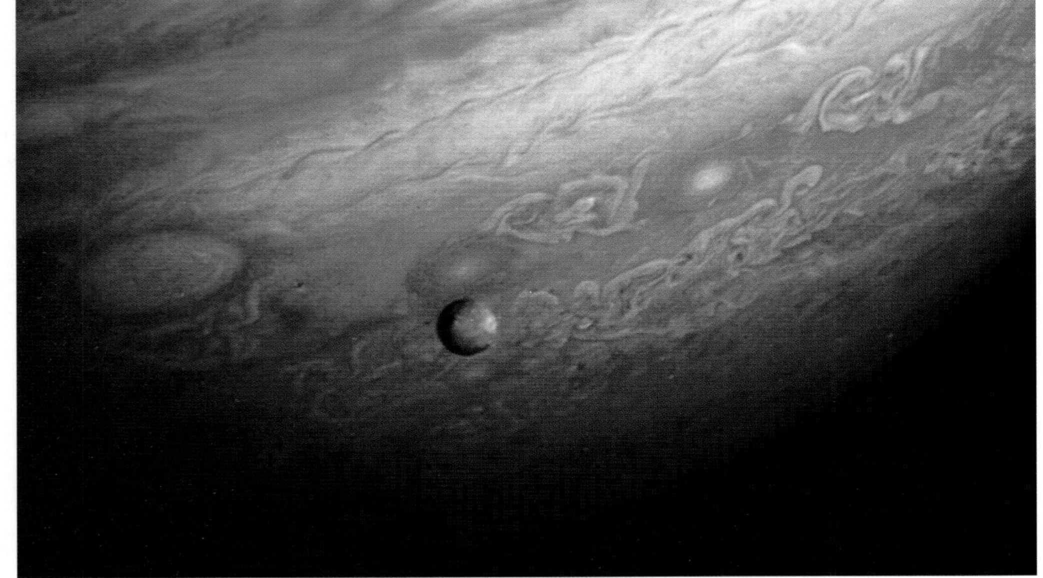

LEFT Voyager 1 took this photo of Jupiter and the innermost of its four Galilean satellites, Io, in 1979, with Io about 420,600km (260,000 miles) above Jupiter's Great Red Spot. The picture was taken about 20 million km (12,400,000 miles) from the planet. Slightly larger than our Moon, Io is the densest large object in the outer Solar System and most volcanically active, spewing material up to 300km (200 miles) into the air; in 1996, when Galileo detected an iron core and magnetic field, it found the moon's surface features had changed radically since the satellite was imaged by Voyager just 17 years before.

Jupiter's main moons are group-named after Galileo because it was his identification of their orbiting the planet that eventually led him to support Copernicus's revolutionary views that Earth revolved round the Sun. They are Europa, Callisto and Ganymede, the largest satellite in the Solar System and bigger than Mercury and Pluto, orbiting Jupiter at a distance of just over 1 million km (620,000 miles).

SATURN

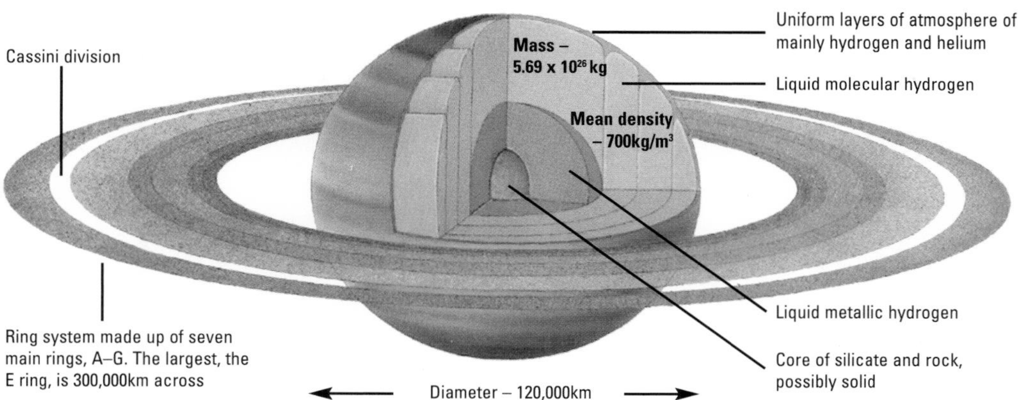

OUTERMOST OF the planets known to ancient man and named after the Roman god of agriculture, Saturn lies at a mean distance of 1,427 million km (88 million miles) from the Sun and has a revolution period of 29.46 years. The second largest planet in the Solar System, its polar diameter of 120,000km (75,000 miles) is considerably less than its equatorial diameter.

Astronomers believe the temperatures in the core of Saturn exceed 11,700°C (21,000°F), and the atmosphere must be deeply convective since this is the only plausible way to transport the interior heat to levels where it can be radiated to space. Like its neighbours Jupiter and Uranus, Saturn radiates more energy into space than it receives from the Sun. The atmosphere of Saturn broadly resembles that of Jupiter: it has 80–90% hydrogen, 10–20% helium and less than 1% traces of other gases, including methane and ammonia detected by Earth-based and Voyager spectroscopy. Because the cloud layers are cooler than those of Jupiter, they tend to be thicker and more uniform in shape, forming deeper in the atmosphere. Saturn's distinctive hazy yellow hue, plus the deeper orange-yellow of Titan, largest of its 18 moons, are thought to be caused by deep haze layers of condensed hydrocarbons.

Saturn's magnetosphere is smaller than that of Jupiter, though it still extends well beyond the orbits of the outer moons, while the field is about 30 times weaker than that of its huge neighbour.

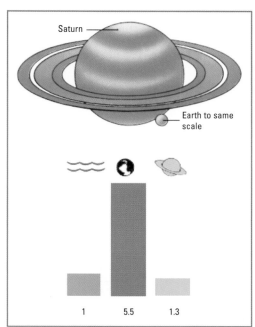

Saturn
Earth to same scale
1 5.5 1.3

ABOVE Though not as large as Jupiter, Saturn's globe is of impressive size – its volume is 1,000 times that of Earth. The mean density of Saturn is only 0.7 that of water, far less than any other planet, and it would float if it were dropped into an ocean. The low density is due to the preponderance of hydrogen.

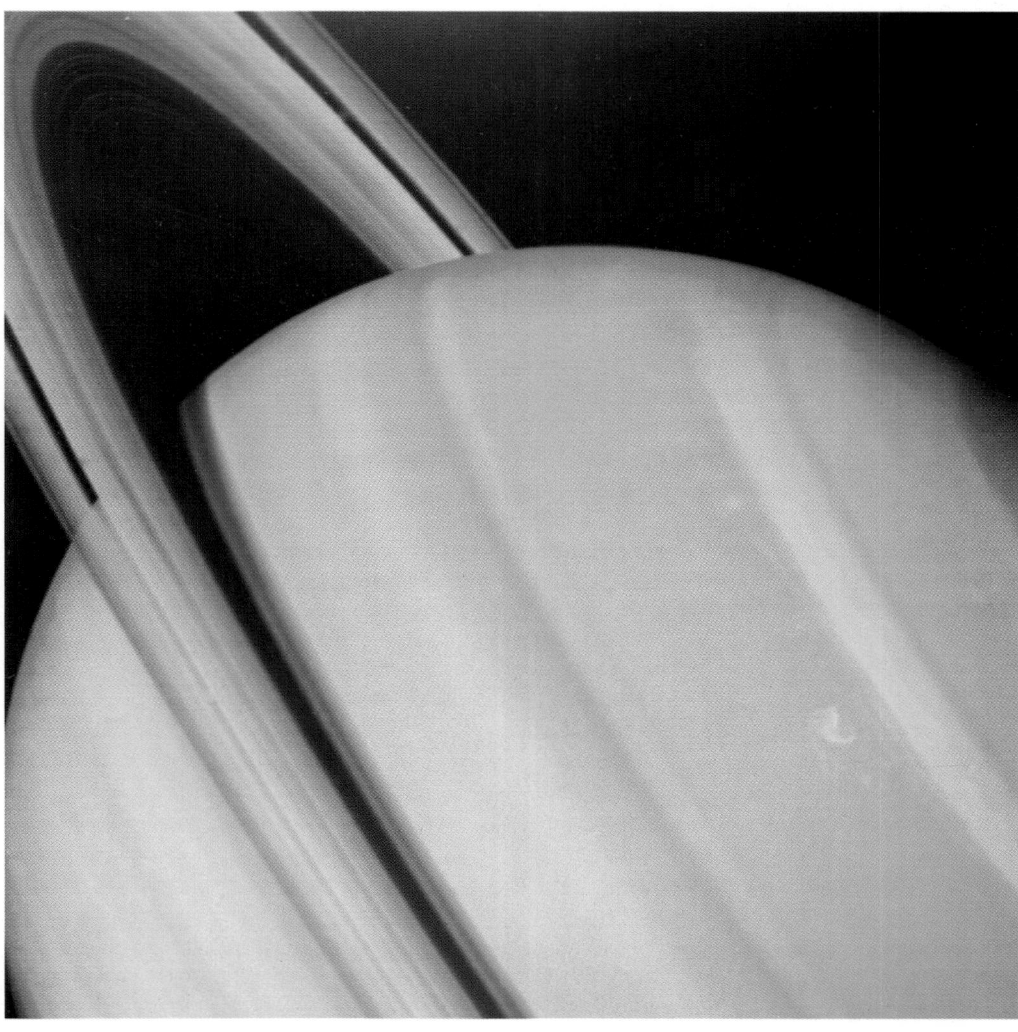

RIGHT Voyager 2 returned this view of Saturn in 1981, when the spacecraft was approaching the large, gaseous planet at about 1 million km (620,000 miles) a day.

The so-called "ribbon-like" feature in the white cloud band marks a high-speed jet at about 47° north; there, the westerly wind speeds are about 530km/h (330mph). Although less pronounced than on Jupiter, the bands, storms, ovals and eddies are all evident here, too, caused by the same combination of rapid rotation (just under 10 hours and 14 minutes) and convective atmosphere.

Saturn's stunning ring system – hundreds or even thousands of narrow ringlets – are grouped, giving the impression of broad bands, each of which has been designated a letter. Brighter than those of other outer planets and no more than 1.5km thick, they comprise millions of small objects ranging in size from tiny stones to rocks several metres long, and are composed at least in part of water ice, possibly plus rocky particles with icy coatings.

The bright A and B rings and the fainter C ring are visible from Earth through a telescope. The space between the A and B rings is called the Cassini division, while the much narrower Encke division splits the A ring. The complex structure is due to the gravitational effects of the satellites, which orbit close to and within the rings.

Saturn has 18 named satellites, six of them icy (resembling the three outer moons of Jupiter) and the others small and rocky. The unique atmosphere of Titan, second largest moon in the Solar System after Ganymede, make it the odd one out. About every 15 years we see Saturn's rings edge-on because of the orbital geometry between Saturn and Earth.

URANUS

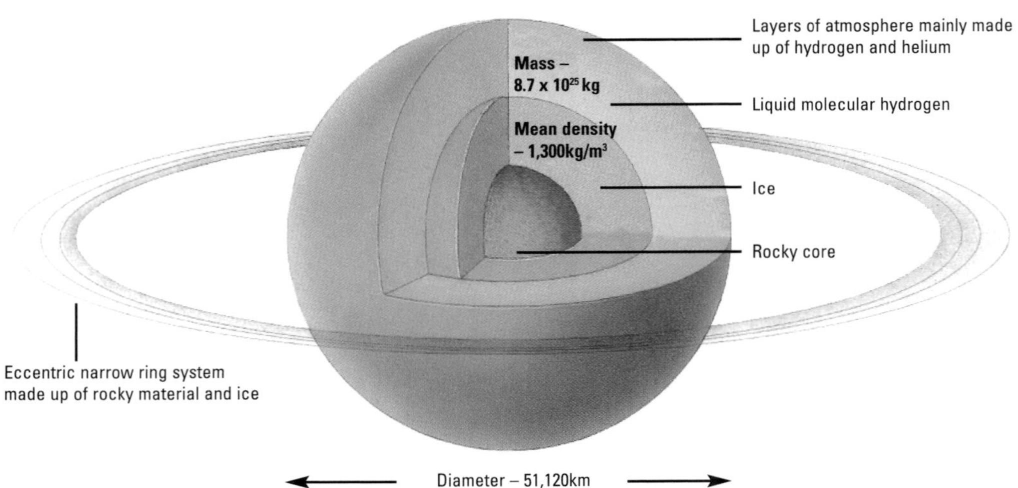

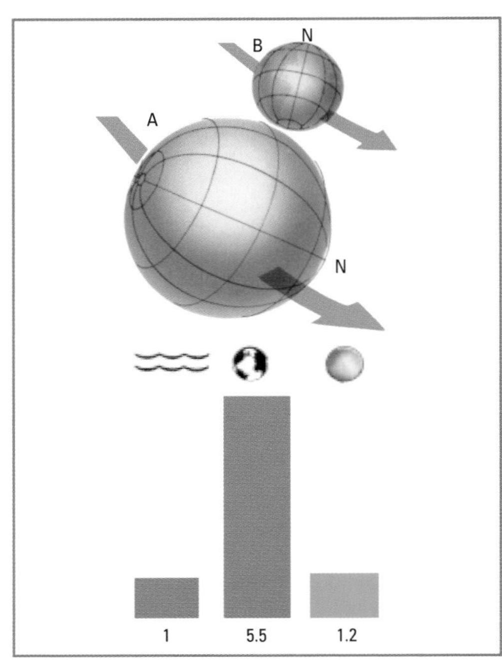

RIGHT The tilt of Uranus's axis [A] compared to Earth [B] is 98°, unique in the Solar System. Its density is 1.2 times that of water, more than Jupiter and Saturn but far less than Earth.

DISCOVERED BY William Herschel in 1781, Uranus appears as a smooth, aqua-coloured sphere with very subtle hints of bands, but this calm facade gives no hint of a history fraught with spectacular catastrophe: at some stage a mighty collision wrenched the young planet off its axis. As a result the planet is tipped over on its side so that its rotation axis lies almost in the plane of the planet's orbit, giving rise to the most striking seasonal changes. Another collision may have been responsible for the fantastic geology of its moon Miranda.

Uranus has a mean distance from the Sun of 2,869,600,000km (1,783 million miles) and a revolution period of just over 84 years. Its basic composition is the same as the other giant planets and similar to that of the Sun – predominantly hydrogen (about 80%) with some helium (15%), the remainder of the atmosphere being methane, hydrocarbons (molecular mixtures of carbon, nitrogen, hydrogen and oxygen) and other trace elements.

Uranus' colour is caused by the small amount of methane – probably less than 3% – that preferentially absorbs red light, meaning the reflected sunlight we see is greenish-blue.

Temperatures at the outer layers of the atmosphere are very cold, about –200°C (330°F), but pressures and temperatures rise with depth and the hydrogen and helium transform from gas to a liquid state. At still greater depth, a transition occurs to a thick, viscous, partly solidified layer of highly compressed liquid water, which may have traces of ammonia and methane. Deep within the centre of Uranus, at extremely high pressure, a core of rocky material is thought to exist, with a mass almost five times that of Earth.

BELOW A composite image of Uranus, the striking but featureless blue planet, and five of its 15 moons, made from photographs taken by Voyager 2 in 1986. The moons (clockwise from top left) are Umbriel, Oberon, Titania, Miranda and Ariel. While an unexplained jumble of huge geological features dominates Miranda, tectonic activity has given Ariel the youngest surface of the moons. Voyager 2's discovery of 10 moons tripled Uranus's known total, while in 1997 two unnamed satellites, probably captured asteroids, were found by the Palomar Observatory. In 1977, astronomers discovered that Uranus has a ring system: there are nine well-defined rings, plus a fainter one and a wider fuzzy ring.

NEPTUNE

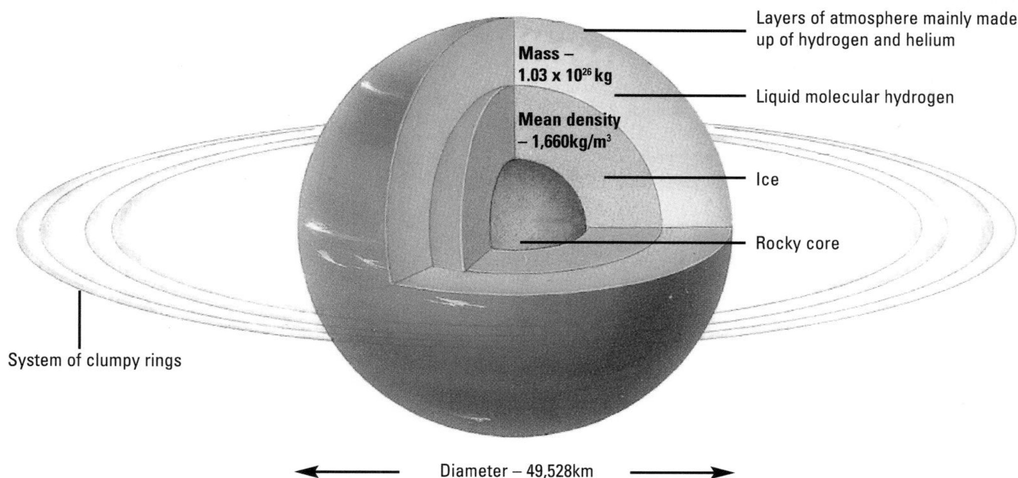

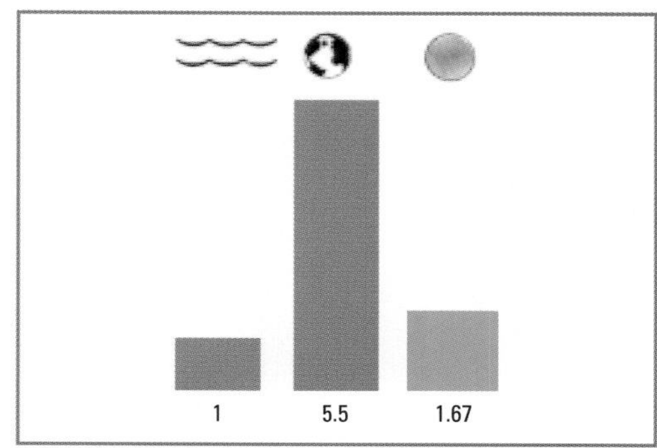

ABOVE Densest of the four main outer planets, Neptune's mass is 17.1 times that of Earth. Its almost circular orbit is always more than 4 billion km (2.5 billion miles) from Earth. Its rotation period is just over 16 hours.

A NEAR TWIN to Uranus in size, Neptune has a similar atmospheric make-up and internal structure, though its magnetic field is 60% weaker. A gas giant surrounded by clumpy rings and eight moons, it takes 164.8 years to orbit the Sun.

Unlike Uranus, which has no detectable internal heat source, Neptune has the strongest internal heat source of all the giant planets. It radiates almost three times more heat than equilibrium conditions would predict, as opposed to Jupiter and Saturn, which radiate about twice as much energy as expected.

Clouds and storms are the main features of Neptune's dynamic atmosphere. Dominating all is the Great Dark Spot, a hurricane-like storm in the southern hemisphere about half the size of Earth. Like all Neptune's weather conditions, it is constantly and rapidly changing. Neptune's winds are among the fastest in the Solar System, dwarfed only by Saturn's high-speed equatorial jet.

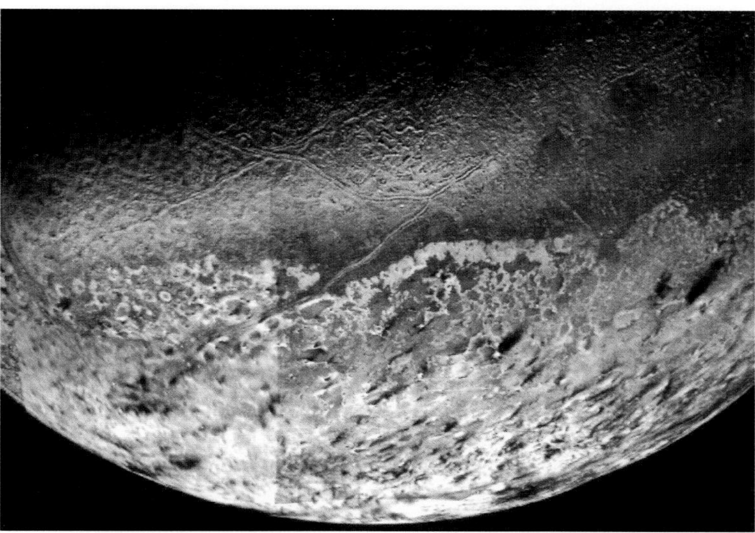

LEFT The southern hemisphere of Triton, largest of Neptune's eight moons, pictured from Voyager 2 in 1989. The large, lighter-coloured area is the polar icecap, probably nitrogen. Because of its retrograde and highly inclined orbit, it is thought Triton was captured by the gravitational pull of Neptune. Tiny Nereid was also known before 1989, when Voyager discovered six more satellites.

PLUTO

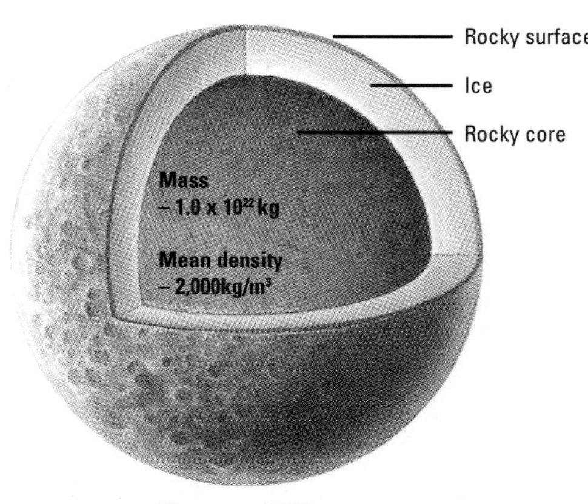

ABOVE Pluto has an average density about twice that of water ice, implying its interior is composed of rock; about 30% of its volume is thought to be water ice. Like Earth, Pluto's atmosphere is primarily nitrogen gas, but the changing surface pressure never exceeds about 10 millibars – around one hundred thousandth of the pressure on Earth at sea level.

FARTHEST PLANET from the Sun, Pluto's tiny size (smaller than Mercury) and rocky composition (like the terrestrial planets of the inner system) make it a real misfit among the gas giants of the outer system. In both size and surface constituents it is similar to Triton, a moon of Neptune, and many astronomers believe it is a former satellite of Neptune somehow separated from its parent.

Pluto has a long, elliptical and tilted orbit that takes over 248 Earth years to complete, of which about 20 years are inside the orbit of Neptune, the last occasion being from 1979 to 1999. Discovered only in 1930, its size and distance from Earth make it difficult to study, despite its high reflectivity: in our sky it is less than one 36,000th of a degree across – the equivalent of a walnut at a range of 50km (30 miles). It is thought that the surface of Pluto is largely nitrogen ice, with methane and carbon monoxide ices as impurities. At nearly half its size, the mysterious Charon (discovered in 1978) is the Solar System's largest moon in relation to its parent planet. Pluto did not form in isolation: it is simply the largest relic in space past Neptune left over from the formation of the Solar System.

RIGHT Hubble Space Telescope (HST) images from 1994 showing two hemispheres of Pluto. The two main images have been computer processed to show rotation and bring out the differences in brightness on the surface; the original "raw" images are at the top left of each panel. Twelve bright regions have been identified, including a large north polar cap.

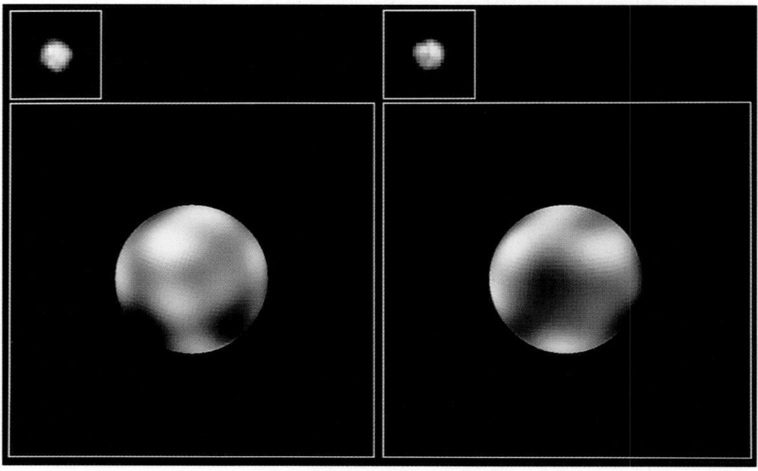

The Moon

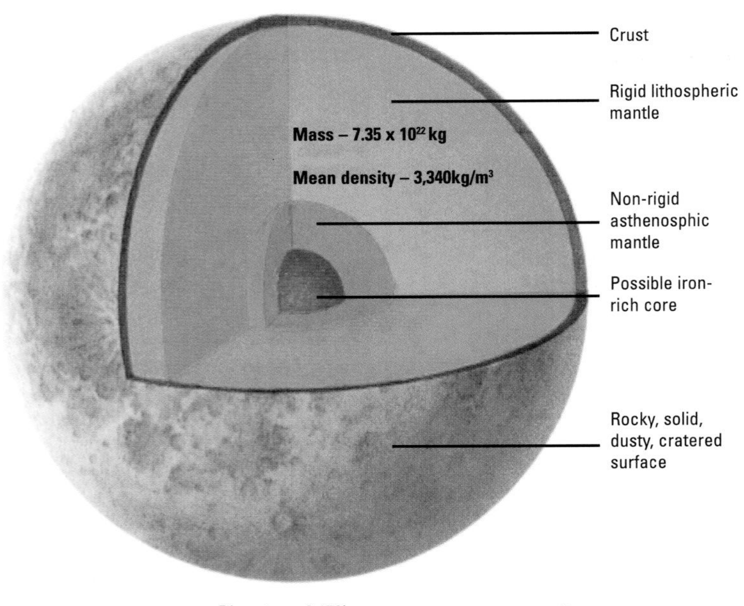

The average diameter of the Moon is 3,475km (2,159 miles), 0.27 times Earth. It has a mass of about 1/81 that of Earth, its surface gravity is one-sixth of Earth, and its density is 3.344 times that of water. It orbits the Earth at a mean distance of 384,199 km (238,731 miles) at an average speed of 3,683km/h (2,289mph) in relation to the Earth. It orbits its parent in 27.3 days.

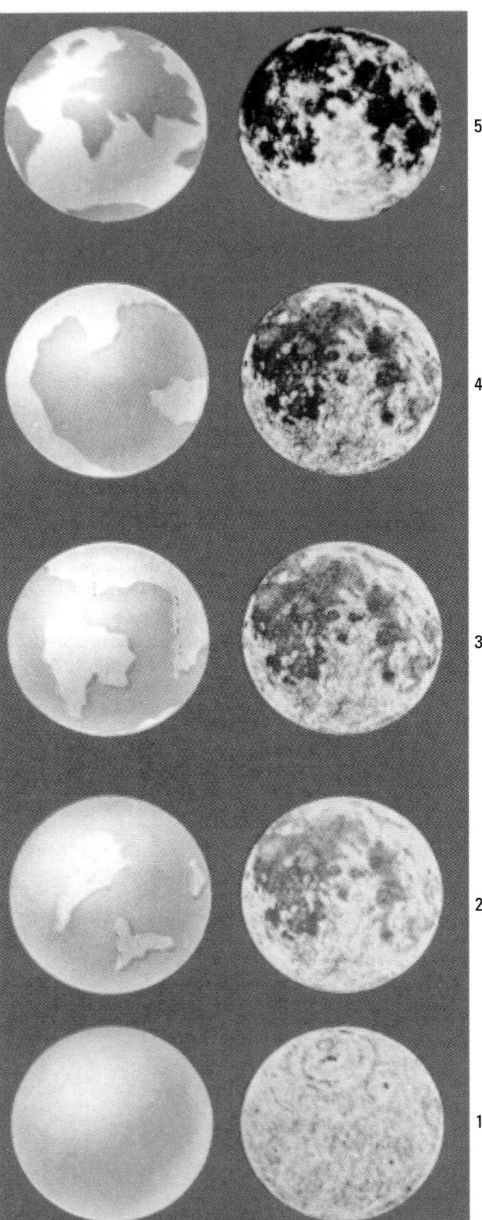

LEFT The lunar "seas" were formed, either by internal accretion or by impact, at an early stage development of Moon and Earth surfaces around 4,000 million years ago [1]. The general aspect of the Moon then must have been similar to that of today, although the basins were not filled. The surface of both the Earth and the Moon then remained the same for a considerable period. Some 2,000 million years ago the basins on the Moon were filled in; 1,000 million years later [4] lunar activity was almost over, while Earth has since seen fabulous change.

BECAUSE THE Moon is about 400 times smaller than the Sun, but about 400 times closer to Earth, humans have always seen them as roughly the same size. While the Moon is tiny in cosmic terms, however, its diameter is more than a quarter that of Earth, considerably more than Pluto and well over 70% that of Mercury. Despite its bright appearance it is a dark body, illuminated only by light reflected from the Sun.

Analysis of lunar samples suggests that the Moon was formed from the remnant of a Mars-sized body that collided with the juvenile planet Earth in a giant impact some 4,500 billion years ago. Any iron-rich core this body may have had appears to have been absorbed into the Earth's core, while the Moon grew out of the mostly rocky debris thrown into space by the crash. The lack of a large, fluid core explains the almost total lack of a magnetic field, which registers only one ten millionth of the strength of Earth's.

The Moon's characteristic dark patches – the face of the "Man in the Moon" – are low-lying regions once flooded by outpourings of basaltic lava, which scientists have dated as between 3 and 4 billion years ago. Known as the lunar seas (Latin *maria,* singular *mare*), they have appeared never to have contained any water, nor indeed any liquid.

Only about 59% of the Moon's surface is directly visible from Earth. Reflected light takes 1.25 seconds to reach us – compared to 8 minutes 27.3 seconds for light from the Sun. With the Sun overhead the temperature on the lunar equator can reach 117.2°C (243°F), and at night it can sink to –162.7°C (–261°C). An astronaut has only a sixth of his normal weight on the Moon, though his mass is unaltered. There is no local surface colour and the lunar sky is black, even when the Sun is above the horizon. There is no air or water – and there has never been any form of life.

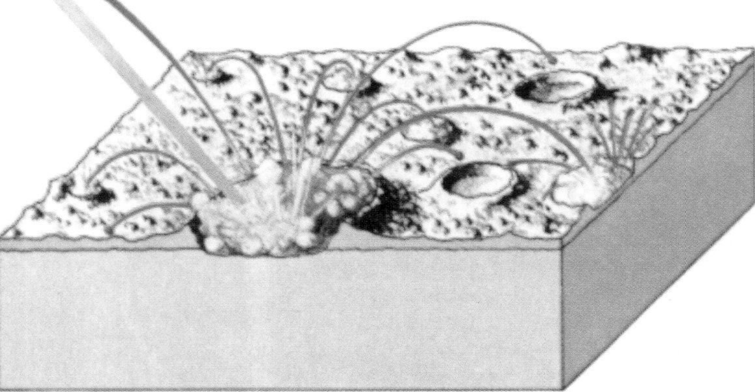

BELOW After the dark patches of the lunar seas, huge craters are the most noticeable features on the Moon. Once presumed volcanic in origin, it is now accepted they were caused by the impact of asteroids and comets travelling at tens of kilometres a second. Around 30 times the size of the foreign bodies that created them, the craters are always roughly circular unless, rarely, the angle of impact was extremely oblique. The Moon's lack of any atmosphere means that its surface remains unprotected from any form of impactors – an atmospheric layer, as on Earth, helps to burn up any encroaching objects – and this, combined with the fact that it has no geological processes, means that no crater is ever worn away or changed . . . except by the arrival of another foreign body.

Comets

A GREAT COMET, with a brilliant head and a tail stretching way across the sky, is a spectacular object – and it is easy to understand they caused such terror in ancient times. Comets have always been regarded as unlucky and fear of them is still not dead in some primitive societies.

Yet a comet is not nearly as important as it may look: it is made up of small rock and ice particles and tenuous gas. On several occasions Earth passed through a comet's tail without suffering the slightest damage. Since Edmund Halley first calculated the paths of several comets in 1695 – including Halley's, whose period is 76 years and which last appeared in 1986 – astronomers have found over 600 such bodies orbiting the Sun.

Analysis of a comet

At the heart of every comet is the nucleus, a solid mass of ice that also contains small solid particles of rock called "dust". Most nuclei are between 1 and 10km (0.6 and 6 miles) across, though they can reach 100km (60 miles). The dark thin crust of icy dust that covers them reflects only 4% of sunlight, making them difficult to detect when distant from the Sun. Over 80% of the ice is simple water ice – the nucleus of Halley's comet contains more than 300,000 tonnes of it – and another 10% or more is frozen carbon dioxide and carbon monoxide. The coma and tails appear only when the comet approaches the Sun, which can be from any angle; as the comet recedes the tail disappears.

Because a comet nucleus shrinks every time it passes the Sun – Halley's by perhaps about a metre (3ft) on each orbit – no comet can have been in its present orbit since the birth of the Solar System. It is now believed that while some comets come from the Kuiper belt beyond Pluto, far more spend most of their time in the Oort cloud much farther out in space. Collisions occur, too: in 1994 at least 21 fragments of Shoemaker-Levy 9 exploded in Jupiter's upper atrmosphere, and Jupuiter may well have swept up many comets from farther out in the Solar System in the past.

RIGHT There are three main classes of comet. The faint short-period comets [A] often have their aphelia (furthest points from the Sun) at approximately the distance of Jupiter's orbit [1], and their periods amount to a few years. Long-period comets [B] have aphelia near or beyond Neptune's orbit [2], though Halley's is the only conspicuous member of the class. Comets with very long periods [C] have such great orbital eccentricities that the paths are almost parabolic. Apart from Halley's, all the really brilliant comets are of this type. Half the known comets orbit almost entirely within the paths of Jupiter and Saturn, taking 20 or so years; the quickest, Encke, takes just 3.3 years. At the other extreme there are comets with huge orbits: Hyakutake, last seen in 1996, will not be near the Sun again for another 14,000 years.

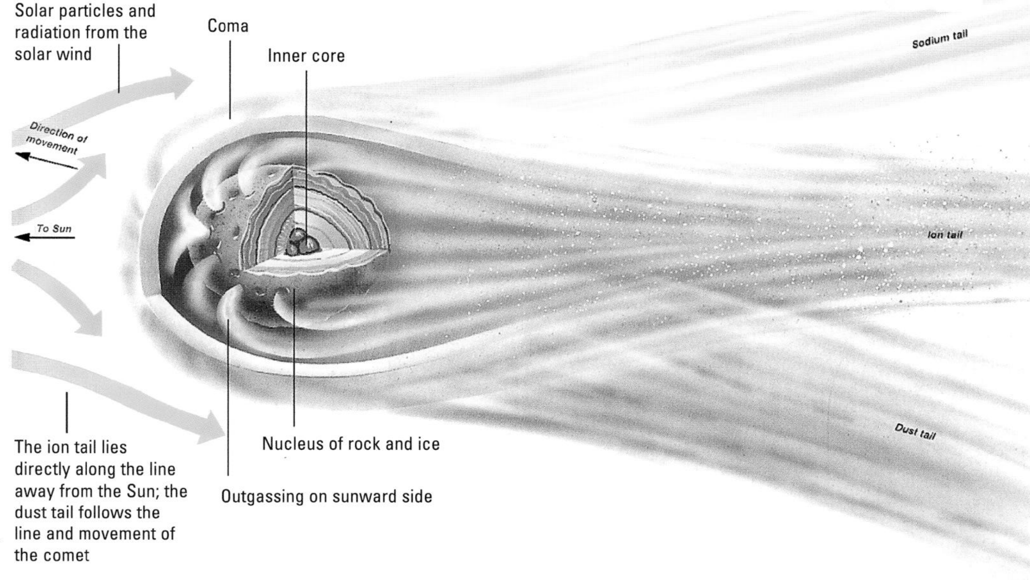

LEFT Hale-Bopp had its perihelion (closest approach to the Sun) in 1997, and it was easily seen with the naked eye from much of Earth for several days. Spectroscopy revealed 38 types of gas present in the comet's coma.

BELOW Following its visit in 1910, Halley's comet last returned to perihelion in 1986. Although not as bright as the great "non-periodical" comets, the increase and decline of the tail is clearly shown. As it approached perihelion the tail developed enormously; after the closest approach to the Sun the tail contracted, so that when the comet was last seen the tail had disappeared altogether. The seventh picture shows the tail shortly before perihelion.

ABOVE A comet has an irregular nucleus of rock and ice. As it nears the Sun, the ice vaporizes and combines with dust to produce the coma or head, hiding the nucleus from our view. The gas or ion tail, often blue and comprising charged electrons (ions) caught up in the solar wind, streams away from the direction of the Sun for up to 100 million km (60 million miles); the dust tail, often white in reflected sunlight, comprises tiny grains of rock and can stretch for up to 10 million km (6 million miles) behind the comet. When observing comet Hale-Bopp in 1997 astronomers also discovered a new type, the sodium tail, which accelerates a straight neutral gas tail up to 10 million km (6 million miles) behind the comet.

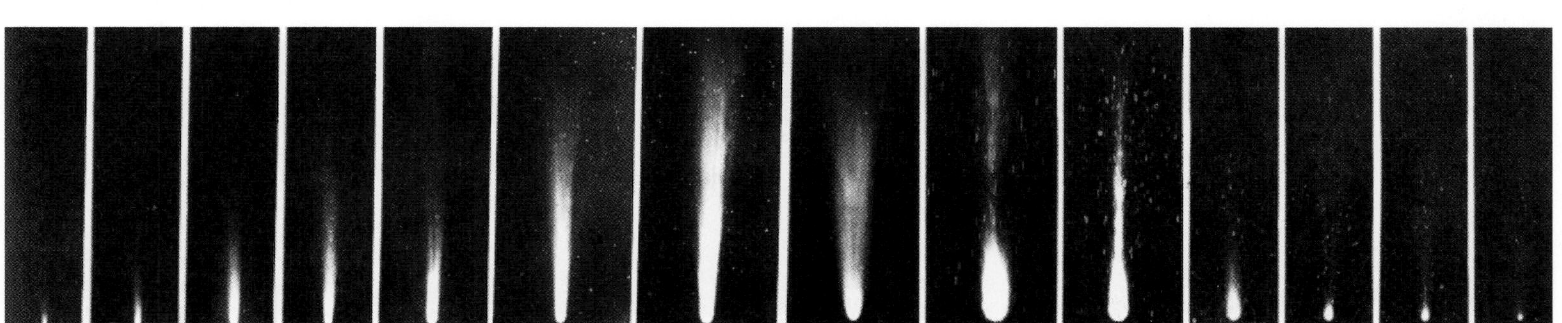

Asteroids and Meteoroids

Since the beginning of the 19th century, astronomers have catalogued more than 8,000 asteroids orbiting our Sun, and at least 10,000 more have been observed. It is estimated that there are at least a million of these rocky bodies with diameters of over 1km (0.6 miles), their numbers making nonsense of their previous description the "minor planets". Along with comets and meteoroids, they are better described as "space debris", though 95% are found in the main asteroid belt between Mars and Jupiter. Some tiny examples find their way to Earth as meteorites, but our knowledge of their formation and composition remains limited.

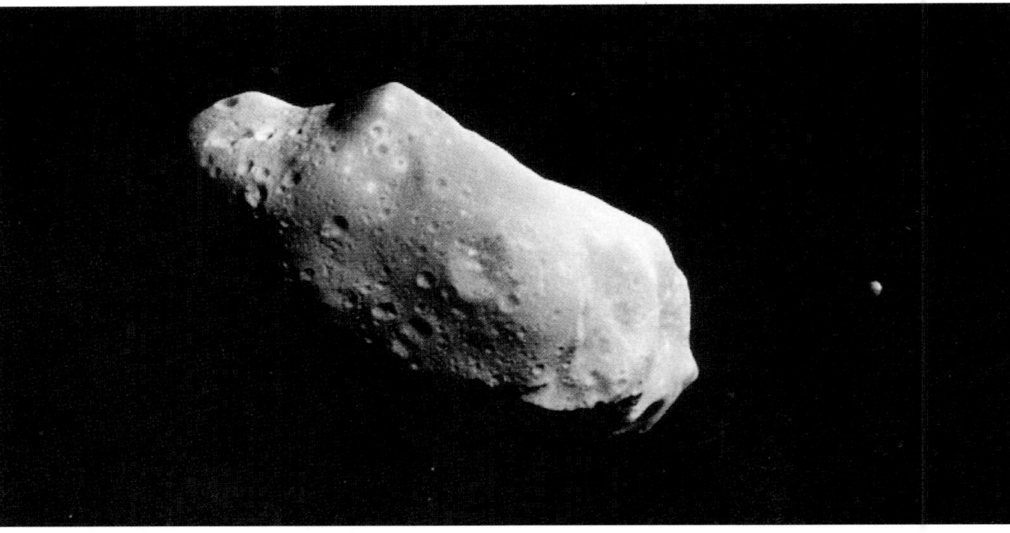

ABOVE The asteroid Ida as photographed by the Galileo spacecraft on its way to Jupiter in 1993. Galileo discovered a small moon, seen here on the right, orbiting at about 100km (60 miles); named Dactyl by surprised scientists, this irregularly shaped satellite measures only 1.7 cu. km (0.4 cu. miles). Galileo also passed the asteroids Gaspra and Mathilde, like Ida heavily cratered by small asteroids and meteorites: one crater on Mathilde was estimated at about 10km (6 miles) deep, huge in relation to the body's size.

Asteroid orbits

The main belt asteroids are not smoothly distributed in cloud between Mars and Jupiter. There are gaps in the main belt where very few asteroids exist. These were discovered by an American astronomer, Daniel Kirkwood, and are known as the Kirkwood gaps and mark places where the orbital period would be a simple fraction of Jupiter's. For example, an asteroid orbiting the Sun at a distance of 375 million km (233 million miles) would complete exactly three orbits while Jupiter orbited the Sun once. It would feel a gravitational tug from Jupiter, away from the Sun, every orbit, and quickly be moved out of that position.

However, in some places more asteroids are seen than expected: one such place is Jupiter's orbit. A swarm of a few hundred asteroids is found 60° ahead of and behind Jupiter in the same orbit. Known as the Trojans, they orbit the Sun at the same rate as Jupiter, but hardly ever come close enough to the planet for their orbits to be disturbed.

Swarms can also be found within the main belt of asteroids. These are known as asteroid families, and are formed when two larger asteroids collide. Astronomers then see the resulting fragments as many smaller asteroids sharing similar orbits around the Sun.

Formation and composition of asteroids

For some time it was thought that the asteroids were the debris of a collision that destroyed a "missing" planet, but it now seems unlikely that a large planet ever formed between Mars and Jupiter – mainly because of the latter's gravitational field. Most of the mass present in that region during the early days of the Solar System was probably rotating in elliptical orbits and ended up colliding with the planets, their satellites or even the Sun.

No asteroid has ever been shown to have an atmosphere, so the light we see must be sunlight reflected from the surface. An asteroid's composition depends on its distance from the Sun. In the inner main belt nearest Mars, they are made of silicate rocks (minerals containing silicon and oxygen) similar to those found on Earth. These are called "S-type" asteroids. In the middle of the belt are mostly "C-type": these appear to have rocks containing carbon, similar to some types of meteorites landing on Earth.

The outer belt has asteroids that are so dark they only reflect 5% of the sunlight that reaches them, and are very red. Our best assumption about these "D-type" asteroids is that there is a large amount of ices such as water ice and frozen carbon monoxide

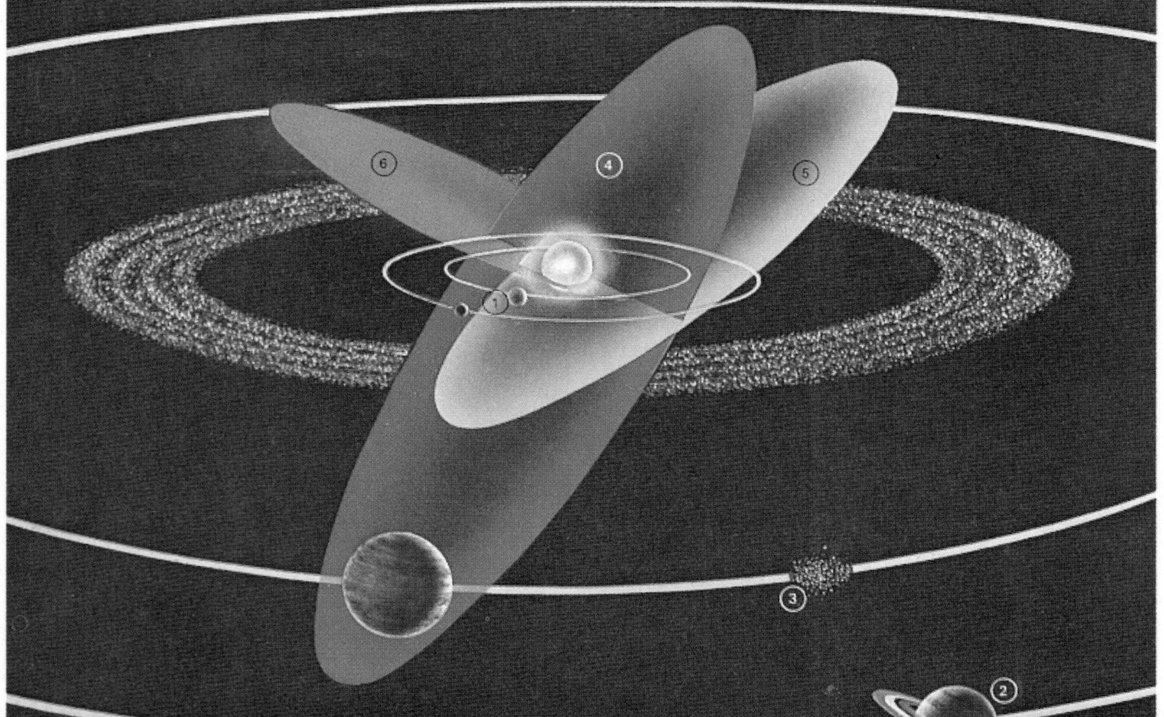

LEFT The orbits of the planets from Earth [1] out to Saturn [2], together with some notable asteroids (the illustration is not to scale). While most asteroids move in the region between the orbits of Mars and Jupiter, the so-called Trojan asteroids [3] move in the same orbit as Jupiter. They keep their distance, however, and collisions are unlikely to occur: one group moves 60° ahead of the planet and the other group 60° behind, though they move round for some distance to either side of their mean positions.

Hidalgo [4] has a path which is highly inclined and so eccentric – much like a comet – that its aphelion (farthest point from the Sun) is not far from the orbit of Saturn. Amor [5] and Apollo [6] belong to the so-called "Earth-grazing" asteroid group. All the Earth-grazers are very small: Amor has a diameter of 8km (5 miles) and Apollo only about 2km (1.25 miles). Both satellites of Mars, Phobos and Deimos, are asteroids captured by the gravitational pull of the planet.

mixed in with the rock, and that charged particles from the solar wind hitting them have created chemical reactions to form the dark red colour.

This change in asteroid make-up is logical if they were formed at the beginning of the Solar System, as this change in composition fits in with theories about how the planets formed. In addition, since their formation, asteroids nearer the Sun have been heated more than those farther out; this means that, over time, more ice melted and escaped. Farther away, lower temperatures mean that less of the ice has melted.

Asteroids undergo some of the most violent temperature changes in the Solar System. One asteroid, Icarus, actually approaches closer to the the Sun than the baked planet Mercury. At its perihelion (closest point), only 28 million km (17 million miles), its surface can reach more than 900°C (500°F); just 200 Earth days later it has reached its aphelion (farthest point), 295 million km (183 million miles) from the warmth of the Sun in the cool space beyond Mars.

RIGHT **The sizes of the first four asteroids to be discovered, Ceres [C], Vesta [D], Pallas [E] and Juno [F], together with the irregularly-shaped Eros [B], are compared here with the Moon [A]. Being so small, the diameters are difficult to measure: earlier assessments of Ceres gave 685km (426 miles), but new methods show that it is much larger at 913km (567 miles). Still the largest known asteroid, Ceres is two-fifths the size of Pluto. It was the first asteroid to be identified, by the Italian astronomer Guiseppe Piazzi in 1801.**

While Ceres and some other large asteroids are spherical, most are elongated and lumpy. All are pitted with craters – one on Mathilde is 10km (6 miles) deep. The average rotation period of an asteroid is eight hours, but while Florentina takes only three hours to spin once, Mathilde takes 17 days. They almost certainly originate from the time of the formation of the Solar System and are not remnants of a large planet that disintegrated, as was once thought. The largest asteroid is less than 1% of the mass of the Moon, and the known asteroids combined are less than 10% of Earth's mass. The first encounter by a space probe was made by the Galileo mission in 1989.

Asteroids and Earth

In 1937 Hermes, a mere 1km (0.6 miles) in diameter, passed just 780,000km (485,000 miles) from Earth, less than twice the distance of the Moon. What would happen if such an object hit Earth? Besides the tremendous heat, enough rock and dust would be deposited in the atmosphere to change the climate all over the Earth, while if it landed near water, huge tsunamis would devastate cities on the edge of the ocean all over the globe. Indeed, it is now widely thought that the impact of an asteroid or comet 65 million years ago, producing a crater 180km (112 miles) wide in the Yucatan Peninsula of Mexico assisted in the extinction of the dinosaurs. Luckily for us, it's estimated that such devastating impacts are likely to happen only once every 100 million years or so.

Meteors

Commonly known as shooting stars, meteors are flashes of light caused by particles of rock entering the Earth's atmosphere at altitudes of around 100km (60 miles), most of them only the size of a grain of sand. As they travel at between 10 and 30km (6 to 18 miles) per second, friction with the air molecules rapidly heats them to thousands of degrees, and they vaporize in a flash of heat. Larger and therefore brighter meteors are known as fireballs, and can be anything from the size of a small pebble up to a large boulder. Before the rocks enter our atmosphere, they are following their own orbit about the Sun.

A "meteor shower" occurs when Earth passes through one of the meteor streams, belts of dust particles sharing their orbits with comets but too heavy to be swept out of the Solar System. For example, the Leonid shower shares the orbit of comet Temple-Tuttle. The best showers occur on 12 August and 13 December each year. They are called the Perseid meteor shower and the Geminid meteor shower because their radiant points appear to be in the constellations of Perseus and Gemini.

Meteorites

While meteoroids usually burn up in the atmosphere, some are big enough to make it through the atmosphere without being completely vaporized and reach the ground; they are then called meteorites. Scientists estimate that about 300,000 meteorites reach the surface of the Earth every year, though many fall in the oceans or remote forests, deserts and mountains. Even those that fall near towns and cities can remain undiscovered, since many look like ordinary rocks to the untrained eye. Some meteorites are tiny particles, while others weigh up to 200 tonnes. Meteoroids weighing more than about 100 tonnes that don't break up are not decelerated as much as lighter bodies, and produce impressive impact craters.

When chemically analysed, there are many different types of meteorite. The most common finds are called chondrites, and appear to be the same type of iron- and silicon-bearing rock that S-type asteroids are made from. Much rarer are the carbonaceous chondrites, which have large amounts of carbon and appear to have come from the middle of the asteroid belt. Finally, about 10% of meteorites are the heavier stony-iron and iron-nickel type.

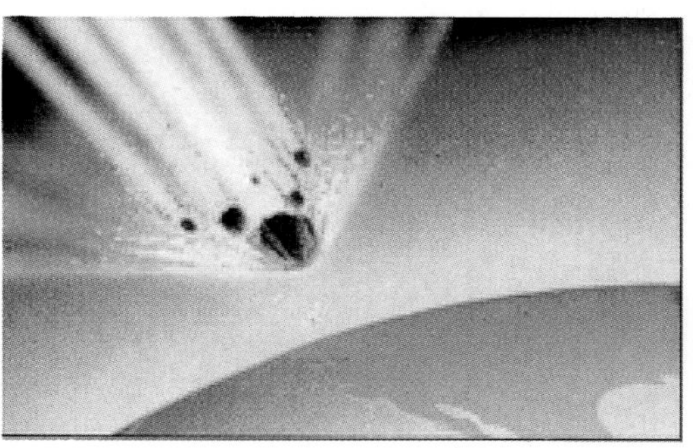

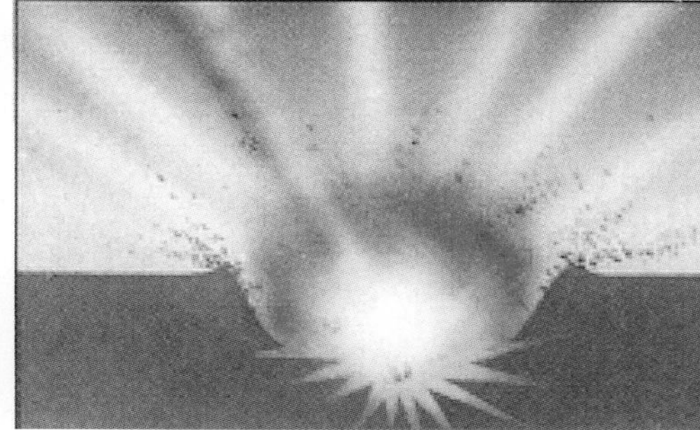

RIGHT **Research suggests that craters such as the Barringer in Arizona, 1.6km (1 mile) wide and 180m (600ft) deep, was formed by nickel-iron meteorites up to about 50,000 years ago. Burning up as they plunged through the atmosphere, they shattered the Earth's outer layer of rock on impact (*top right*). Because of their high speed they burrowed into the ground, causing friction, heat, compression and shockwaves, culminating in a violent explosion that left the huge crater. More than 130 craters have so far been identified, though many more were created before being subsequently destroyed by geological activity and erosion.**

Time and Motion

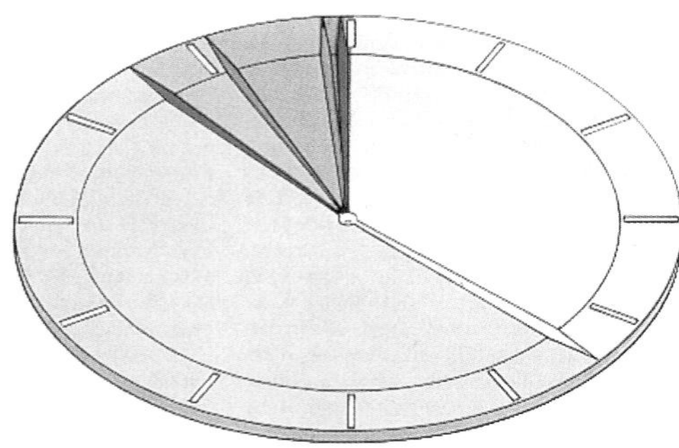

ABOVE **A "clock" of the Earth's history, with 12 hours representing the 4,600 million years the world has been in existence. The first 2 hours and 52 minutes are still obscure, but the earliest rocks are then formed – though the planet remains a lifeless desert until 04.20, when bacterial organisms first appear.**

Eons of time drag by until just after 10.30, when there is an explosion of invertebrate life in the oceans. Dinosaurs wander the land by 11.36, only to die out and replaced by birds and mammals 25 minutes later. Hominids arrive about 30 seconds before noon – and the last tenth of a second covers human civilization.

The oldest rocks of the great Precambrian shields of North America, Africa and Australia convey dates of up to about 3,500 million years ago. Only the past 570 million years show an abundance of plant and animal life. The most widely found fossil remains from any period are called index fossils and are used to correlate various rock formations of the same age.

THE BASIC unit of time measurement is the day, one rotation of the Earth on its axis. The subdivision of the day into hours, minutes and seconds is simply for our convenience. The present Western calendar is based on the "solar year", the 365.24 days the Earth takes to orbit the Sun.

Calendars based on the movements of the Sun and Moon, however, have been used since ancient times. The average length of the year, fixed by the Julian Calendar introduced by Julius Caesar, was about 11 minutes too long, and the cumulative error was eventually rectified in 1582 by the Gregorian Calendar. Pope Gregory XIII decreed that the day following 4 October that year was in fact 15 October, and that century years do not count as leap years unless they are divisible by 400. Britain did not adopt the reformed calendar until 1752 – by which stage it was lagging 11 days behind the continent; the Gregorian Calendar was imposed on all its possessions, including the American colonies, with all dates preceding 2 September marked O.S., for Old Style.

The seasons are generated by a combination of the Earth's revolution around the Sun and the tilt of its axis of $23\frac{1}{2}°$. The solstices (from the Greek *sol*, sun, and *stitium*, standing) are the two times in the year when the Sun is overhead at one of the Tropics of Cancer and Capricorn, $23\frac{1}{2}°$ North and South, furthest from the Equator. The equinoxes (from the Greek *aequus*, equal, and *nox*, night) are the two times in the year when day and night are of equal length due to the Sun being overhead at the Equator. The longest and shortest days in each hemisphere fall on or around the solstices, and are opposites in each hemisphere.

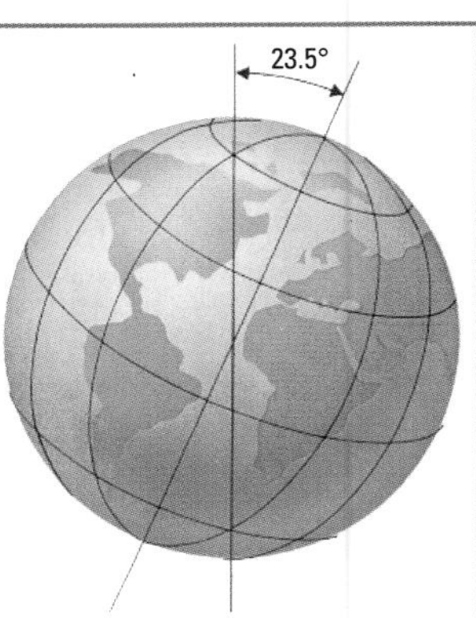

The Earth's axis is inclined at 23.5° to the perpendicular to the orbital plane. This angle accounts for the complex seasonal variations in climate, notably in mid-latitudes. The varying distance of the Earth from the Sun has only a minor effect.

Definitions of Time

Year: The time taken by the Earth to revolve around the Sun, or 365.24 days.
Month: The approximate time taken by the Moon to revolve around the Earth. The 12 months of the year in fact vary from 28 days (29 in a Leap Year – once every 4 years to offset the difference between the calendar and the solar year) to 31 days.
Week: An artificial period of 7 days. Unlike days, months and years – but like minutes and seconds – it is not based on astronomical time.
Day: The time taken by the Earth to complete one rotation (spin) on its axis.
Hour: A day comprises 24 hours, divided into hours a.m. (*ante meridiem*, before noon) and p.m. (*post meridiem*, after noon) – though timetables use the 24-hour system from midnight.

Northern Spring Equinox
Southern Autumn Equinox
21 March
Northern Summer Solstice
21 June
SUN
21 December
Northern Winter Solstice
Southern Winter Solstice
21 September
Southern Summer Solstice
Southern Spring Equinox
Northern Spring Equinox

LEFT **Seasons occur because the Earth's axis is tilted at a constant angle of $23\frac{1}{2}°$ as it spins. When the Northern Hemisphere is tilted to a maximum extent towards the Sun, on 21 June, the Sun is overhead at noon at the Tropic of Cancer ($23\frac{1}{2}°$ North): this is midsummer, or the summer solstice, in this hemisphere.**

On 22 or 23 September the Sun is overhead at the Equator, and day and night are of equal length throughout the world: this is the autumn or fall equinox in the Northern Hemisphere. On 21 or 22 December, the Sun is overhead at the Tropic of Capricorn ($23\frac{1}{2}°$ South), the winter solstice in the Northern Hemisphere. The overhead Sun then tracks north, until on 21 March it is overhead at the Equator: this is the spring equinox in the Northern Hemisphere.

In the Southern Hemisphere the seasons are the reverse of those in the Northern Hemisphere: autumn corresponds to spring and winter to summer.

21 June
21 December
N
N. Pole: 24 hours daylight
N. Pole: 24 hours darkness
$10\frac{1}{2}$ hours daylight
12 hours daylight
0°
SUN'S RAYS
$13\frac{1}{2}$ hours daylight
$13\frac{1}{2}$ hours daylight
0°
12 hours daylight
$10\frac{1}{2}$ hours daylight
S. Pole: 24 hours darkness
S. Pole: 24 hours daylight
S

LEFT **The Sun appears to "rise" in the east, reach its highest point at noon, and then "set" in the west, to be followed by night. In reality it is not the Sun that is moving but the Earth, rotating ("spinning" on its axis) from west to east. At the summer solstice in the Northern Hemisphere (21 June), the area inside the Arctic Circle has total daylight and the area inside the Antarctic Circle has total darkness. The opposite occurs at the winter solstice on 21 or 22 December. At the Equator, the length of day and night are almost equal all year round, with seasonal variations in between.**

RIGHT The Moon rotates more slowly than the Earth, making one complete turn on its axis in just over 27 days. Since this corresponds to its period of revolution around the Earth, the Moon always presents the same hemisphere or face to us, and we never see its "dark side".

The interval between one full Moon and the next (and thus also between two new Moons) is about 29½ days – a lunar month. The apparent changes in the shape of the Moon are caused by its changing position in relation to the Earth; like the planets, the Moon produces no light of its own and shines only by reflecting the rays of the Sun.

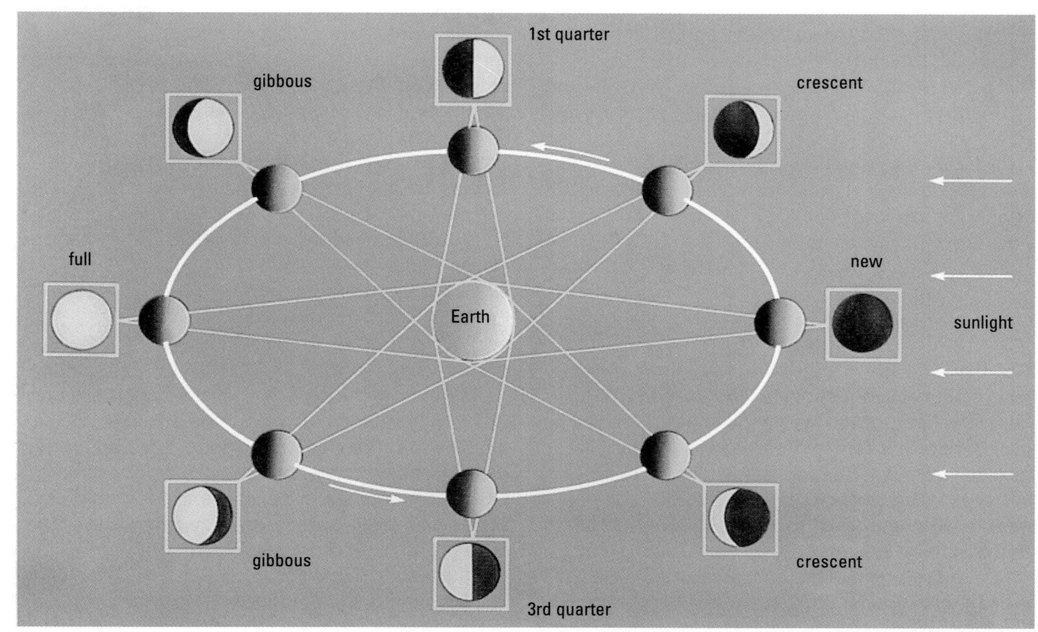

BELOW The Earth rotates through 360° in 24 hours, and therefore moves 15° every hour. The world is divided into 24 standard time zones, each centred on lines of longitude at 15° intervals, 7½° on either side of its central meridian.

The prime or Greenwich meridian, based on the Royal Observatory in London, lies at the centre of the first zone. All places to the west of Greenwich are one hour behind for every 15° of longitude; places to the east are ahead by one hour for every 15°.

When it is 12 noon at the Greenwich meridian, at 180° east it is midnight of the same day – while at 180° west the day is only just beginning. To overcome this problem the International Dateline was established, approximately following the 180° meridian. If you travelled from Japan (140° east) to Samoa (170° west) you would pass from the night into the morning of the same day.

While some countries cope with several time zones (Russia experiences no fewer than 11), others "bend" the meridians to incorporate their territory in certain zones, and China, despite crossing five, follows just one. Others, including Iran and India, employ differences of half an hour.

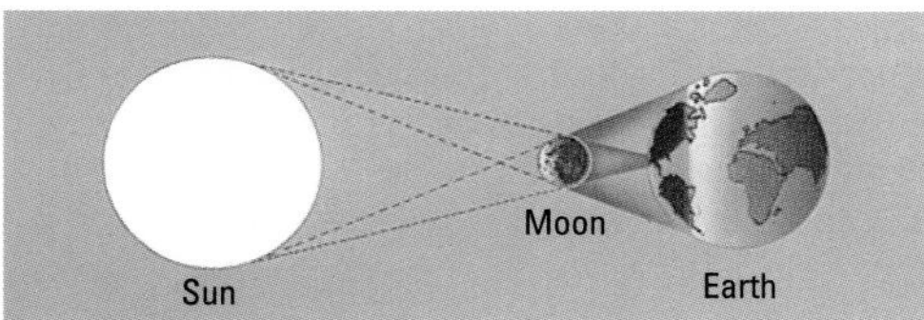

LEFT A solar eclipse occurs when the Moon passes between the Sun and the Earth. It will cause a partial eclipse of the Sun if the Earth passes through the Moon's outer shadow, or a total eclipse if the inner cone shadow crosses the Earth's surface. A total eclipse was visible in much of the Northern Hemisphere in 1999.

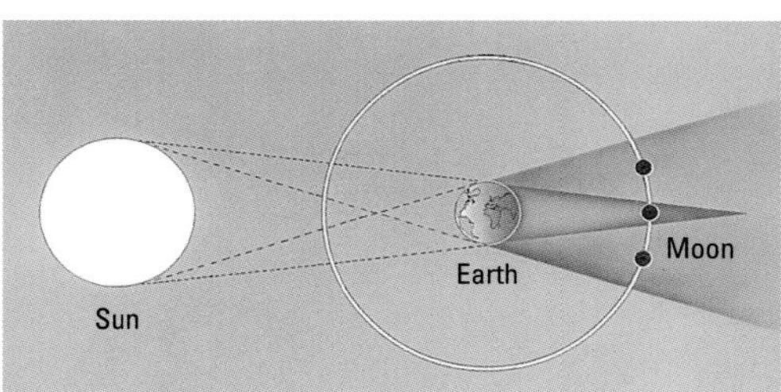

LEFT In a lunar eclipse the Earth's shadow crosses the Moon and, as with the solar version, provides either a partial or total eclipse. Eclipses do not occur every month because of the 5° difference between the plane of the Moon's orbit and the plane in which the Earth moves. In the 1990s, for example, only 14 eclipses were possible – seven partial and seven total – and each was visible only from certain and variable parts of the world.

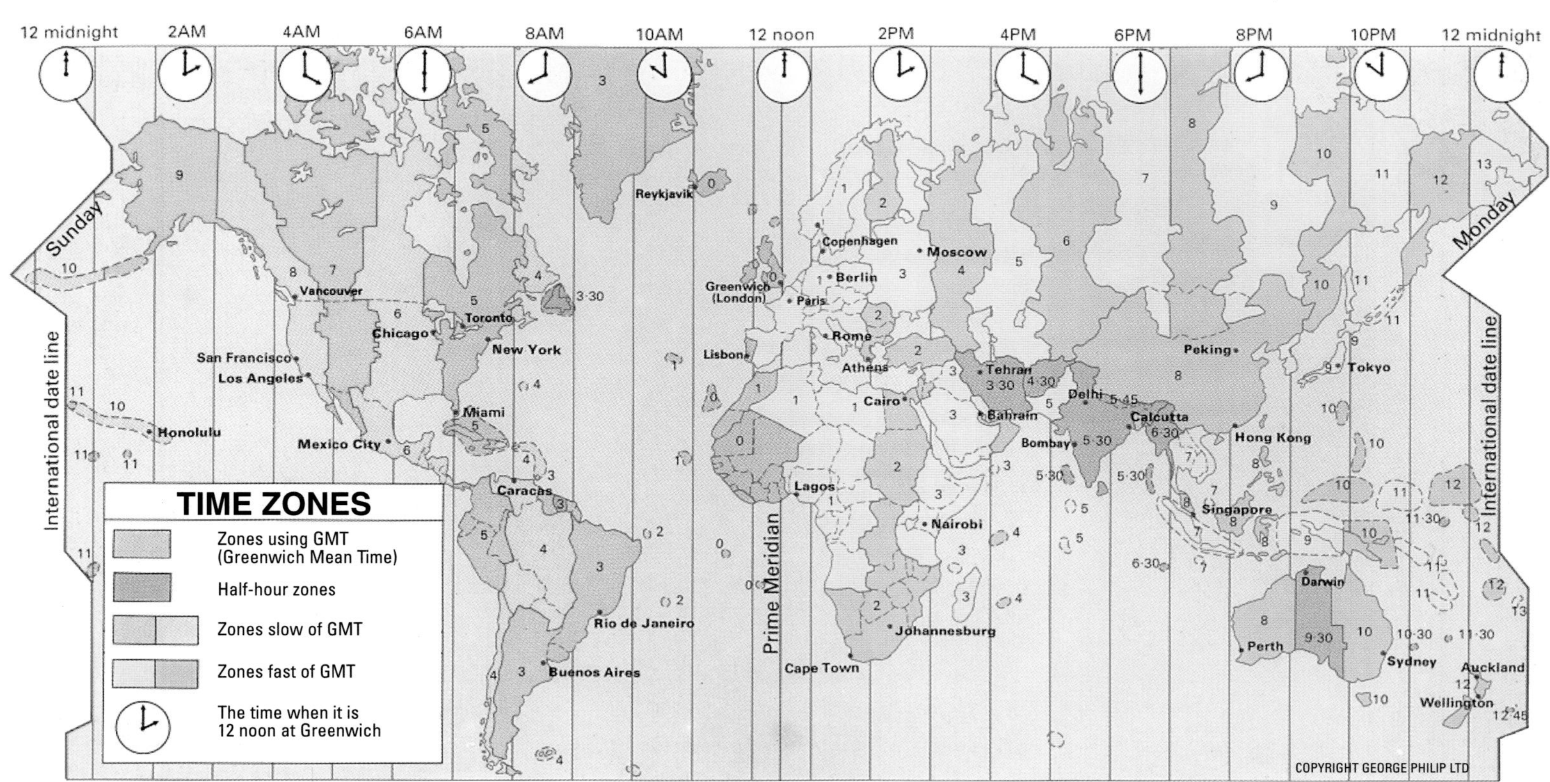

ANATOMY OF THE EARTH

THE EARTH is made up of several concentric shells, like the bulb of an onion. Each shell has its own particular chemical composition and physical properties. These layers are grouped into three main regions: the outermost is called the crust, which surrounds the mantle, and the innermost is the core. The solid, low-density crust on which we live is no thicker in relation to the Earth than an eggshell, taking up only 1.5% of the planet's volume. While the chemical distinction between crust and mantle is important, as far as physical processes go they behave as a single unit termed the lithosphere. It is a common fallacy that if you could drill through the Earth's crust you would find a molten mass: even well below the brittle outer shell that forms part of the lithosphere, the convecting part of the the mantle is still essentially solid, and pockets of liquid rock (magma) are relatively rare.

While the chemical composition of the crust and upper mantle is well known, little is absolutely certain about the layers beneath.

BELOW The Earth's crust varies in thickness from 40km (25 miles) under the continents to 5km (3 miles) under the seafloor. With the top of the mantle it forms the rigid lithosphere [1], which overlies a "plastic" layer, the asthenosphere [2], on which it may move. The upper mantle [3] goes down to about 700km (430 miles), where it overlies the lower mantle [4].

From the surface the temperature inside the Earth increases by 30°C for every kilometre (85°F for every mile), so that the asthenosphere is close to melting point. At 50km (30 miles), in the upper mantle, it reaches 800°C (1,480°F). After around 100km (60 miles) the rate of increase slows dramatically, and scientists now estimate the temperature to be 2,500°C (4,600°F) at the boundary of the lower mantle and core [5] – a depth of 2,900km (1,800 miles).

The mantle is separated from the outer core [6], which seismic observations suggest is in a liquid state. The density jumps from 5.5g/cm for the lower mantle to 10g/cm for the outer core, where it increases downwards to 12 or 13g/cm. The liquid outer core gives way to a solid inner core [7] at around 5,150km (3,200 miles] from the surface. Although the core is only around 16% of the Earth by volume, it represents 32% of its mass; it is thought to consist mostly of iron and some nickel, a hypothesis that fits the data and is inspired by iron-nickel meteorites which are probably the remnants of another planet. The temperature at the centre of the Earth (8) is estimated at least 3,000°C (5,400°F), and could be as high as 5,000°C (9,000°F).

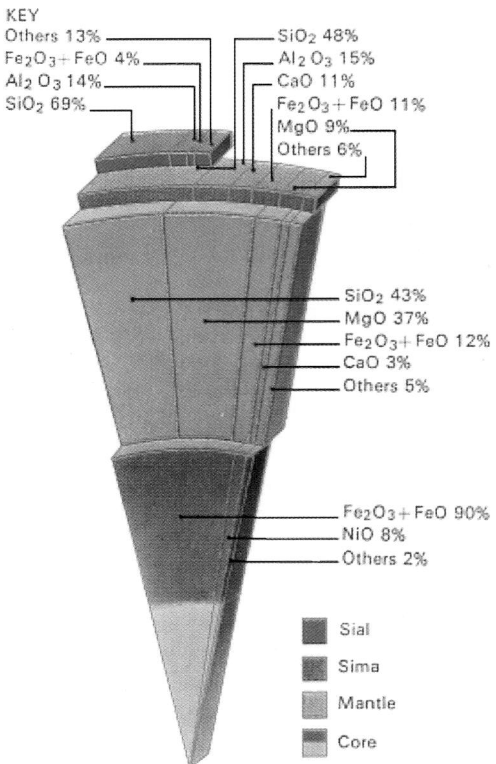

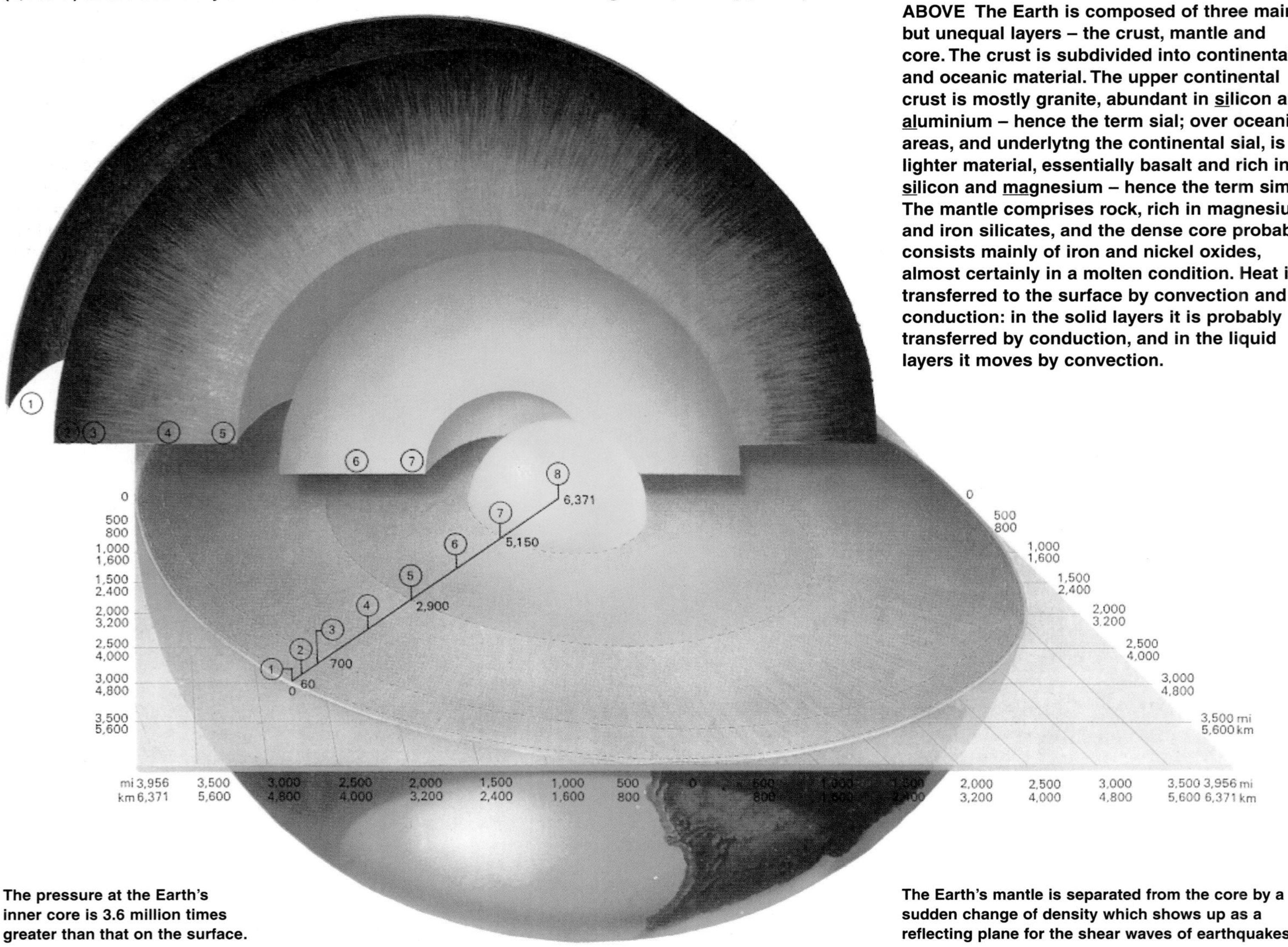

ABOVE The Earth is composed of three main but unequal layers – the crust, mantle and core. The crust is subdivided into continental and oceanic material. The upper continental crust is mostly granite, abundant in <u>si</u>licon and <u>al</u>uminium – hence the term sial; over oceanic areas, and underlytng the continental sial, is a lighter material, essentially basalt and rich in <u>si</u>licon and <u>ma</u>gnesium – hence the term sima. The mantle comprises rock, rich in magnesium and iron silicates, and the dense core probably consists mainly of iron and nickel oxides, almost certainly in a molten condition. Heat is transferred to the surface by convection and conduction: in the solid layers it is probably transferred by conduction, and in the liquid layers it moves by convection.

The pressure at the Earth's inner core is 3.6 million times greater than that on the surface.

The Earth's mantle is separated from the core by a sudden change of density which shows up as a reflecting plane for the shear waves of earthquakes.

The Magnetic Earth

As the Earth spins on its axis, the fluid layer of the outer core allows the mantle and solid crust to rotate relatively faster than the inner core. As a result, electrons in the core move relative to those in the mantle and crust. It is this electron movement that constitutes a natural dynamo and produces a magnetic field similar to that produced by an electric coil.

The Earth's magnetic axis is inclined to its geographical axis by about 11°, and the magnetic poles don't coincide with the geographic north and south poles. The Earth's magnetic axis is continually changing its angle in relation to the geographic axis, but over a long time – some tens of thousands of years – an average relative position is established.

A compass needle points to a position some distance away from the geographical north and south poles. The difference (the declination), varies from one geographical location to the next, with small-scale variations in the Earth's magnetism. The magnetosphere is the volume of space in which the Earth's magnetic field predominates.

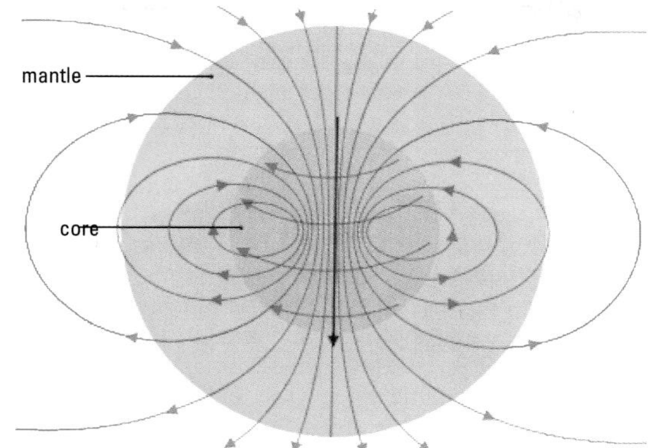

ABOVE The magnetic field originating inside the Earth makes up about 90% of the field observed at ground level: the remainder is due to currents of charged particles coming from the Sun and to the magnetism of rocks in the crust. The difference in rotation speed between the liquid outer core and the mantle creates a dynamo effect.

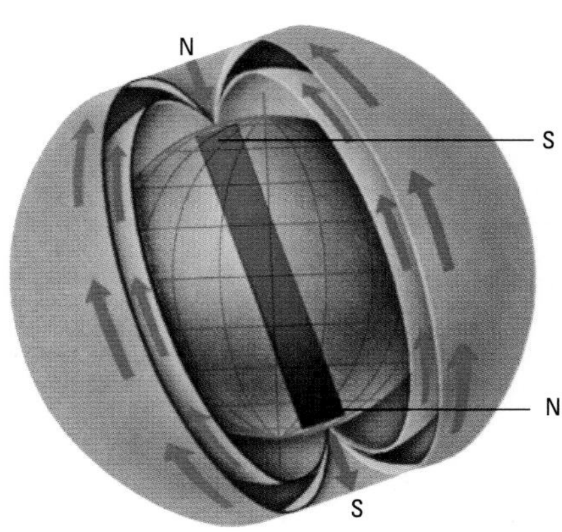

ABOVE The Earth's magnetic field is like that of a giant natural bar magnet placed inside the Earth, with its magnetic axis inclined at a small angle to the geographical axis. The poles of a compass needle are attracted by the magnetic poles of the Earth so that one end points to the north magnetic pole and the other to the south magnetic pole.

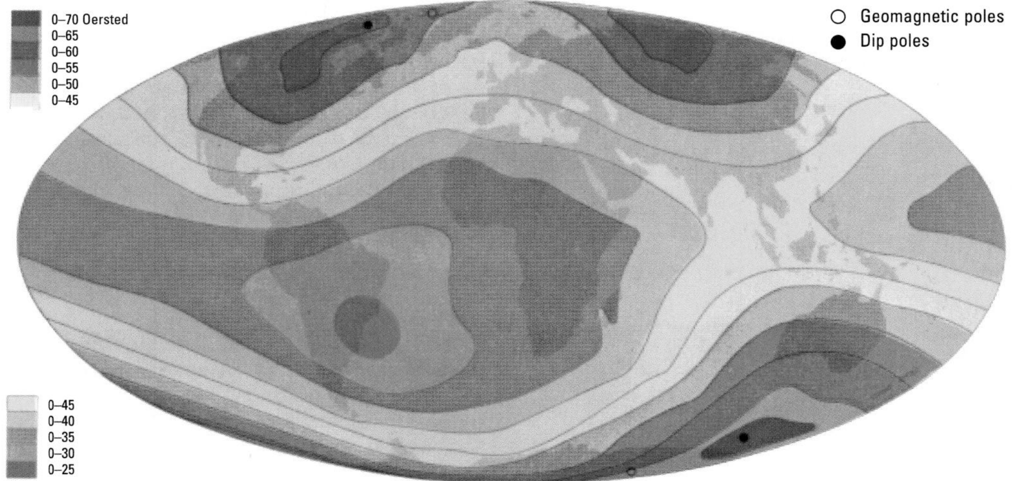

LEFT The intensity of the Earth's magnetic field is strongest at the poles and weakest in the equatorial regions. If the field were purely that of a bar magnet in the centre of the Earth and parallel to the spin axis, the lines of equal intensity would follow the lines of latitude and the magnetic poles would coincide with the geographic poles. In reality, however, the "bar magnet" field is inclined at about 11° to the spin axis and so are its geomagnetic poles.

Neither is the real field purely that of a bar magnet. The "dip poles", where the field direction is vertical (downwards at the north pole and upwards at the south dip pole), are themselves offset in respect to the geomagnetic poles – each by a different amount so that the south dip pole is not exactly opposite the north dip pole. Oersted is a traditional unit of magnetic field strength.

BELOW Until recent times taking account of the difference between the magnetic and geographic poles was crucial in navigation. The needle of a ship's magnetic compass, for example, swings to a position where its ends point to north and south along a line of force of the Earth's magnetic field. In navigation today, the magnetic compass is often replaced by the motor-driven gyrocompass, which indicates true north.

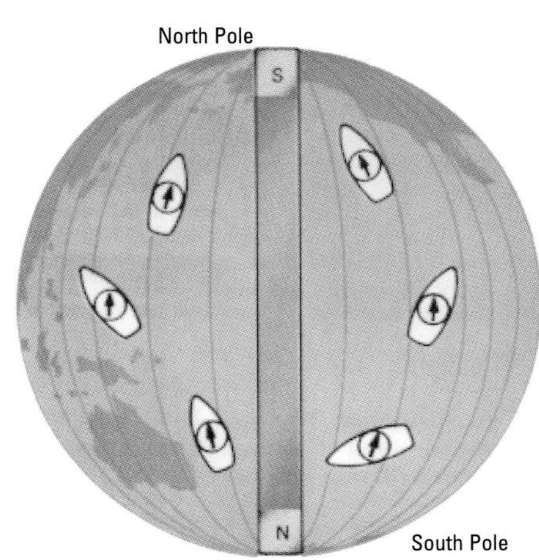

RIGHT The magnetosphere is the region in which the Earth's magnetic field can be detected. It would be symmetrical were it not for the "solar wind", electrically-charged particles from the Sun [A], which distort it to a teardrop shape. The particles meet the Earth's magnetic field at the shock front [1]. Behind this is a region of turbulence and inside the turbulent region is the magnetopause [2], the boundary of the magnetic field. The Van Allen belts [3] are two zones of high radiation in the magnetopause. The inner belt consists of high-energy particles produced by cosmic rays, the outer comprises solar electrons.

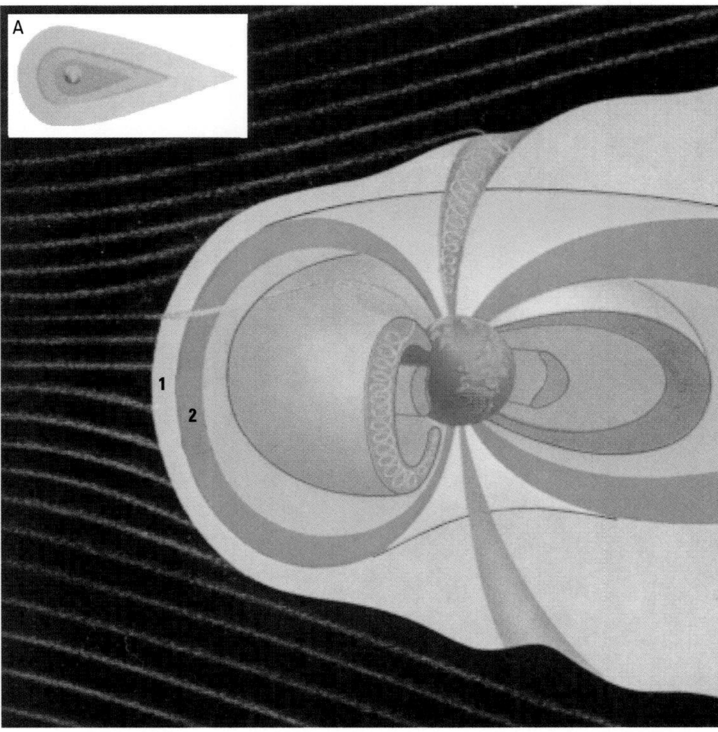

THE RESTLESS EARTH

THE THEORY of plate tectonics was advanced in the late 1960s and has had a revolutionary effect on the earth sciences. It is a unifying, all-embracing theory, offering a plausible and logical explanation for many of the Earth's varied structural phenomena, ranging from continental drift to earthquakes and mountain building.

The crust of the Earth, which together with the upper mantle forms the lithosphere, consists of rigid slabs called plates that are slowly but constantly moving their position in relation to each other. The plates are bounded by oceanic ridges, trenches and transform faults. Oceanic ridges are formed where two plates are moving apart, leaving a gap which is continuously filled by magma (molten rock) rising from the asthenosphere, on which the plates "float". As the magma cools, new crust is created on the ridges and becomes part of the oceanic plates.

This is the phenomenon known as seafloor spreading. Spreading rates, though slow, are not negligible: the North Atlantic is opening up by 4cm (1.6 in) a year, and the fastest rate is found at the East Pacific Rise, which creates 10cm (4 in) of new crust every year – 1,000km (620 miles) in the relatively short geological time of 10 million years.

Trenches as well as mountain ranges are formed where two plates converge. One of the plates slides steeply under the other and enters the mantle: the world's deepest trench, the Mariana, was formed when the Pacific plate was forced under the far smaller Philippine plate. Since the volume of the Earth does not change, the amount of crust created at the ridges is balanced by that destroyed at the trenches in an endless cycle of movement.

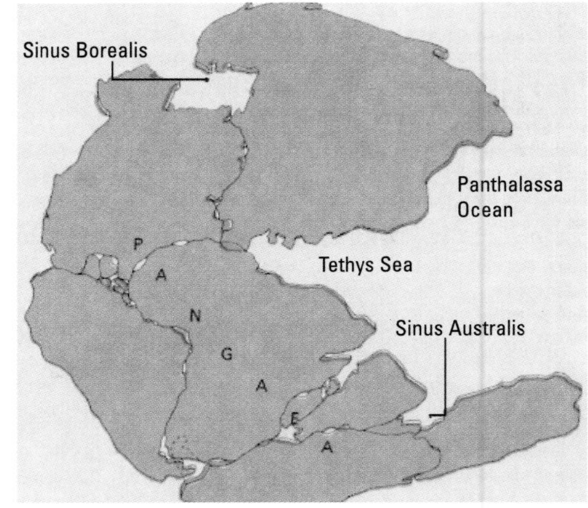

ABOVE First put forward by the German meteorologist Alfred Wegener in 1912, the theory of continental drift suggests the continents once formed a single land mass, Pangaea. The initial break-up created a northern mass, Laurasia, and a southern one, Gondwanaland, named after a province in India.

135 million years ago

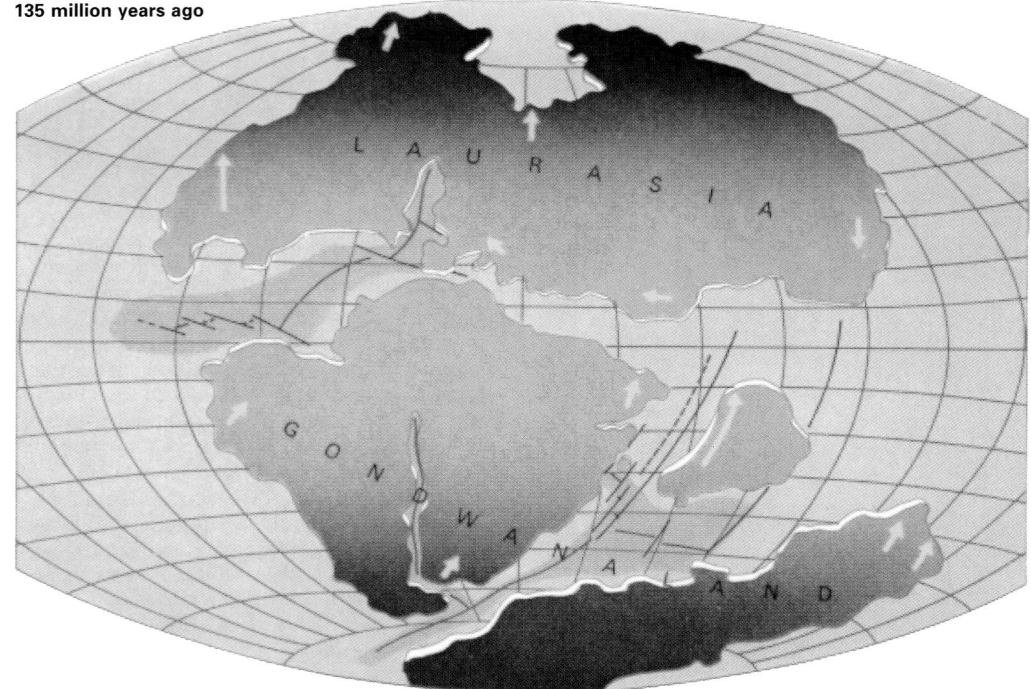

LEFT A map of Pangaea cannot be accurately constructed. The most suitable fit of the land masses is obtained by matching points midway down the continental slope, at about 200m (650ft). The easiest areas to fit together are the continents of Africa and South America, and while the linking of the northern lands is possible with a certain degree of accuracy, much remains to be learned of the complex fit of India, Antarctica and Australia with Africa and South America. The break-up of Pangaea began about 200 million years ago, and by the end of the Jurassic period, about 135 million years ago, the North Atlantic and Indian Oceans had become firmly established. The Tethys Sea was being diminished by the Asian land mass rotating in an anti-clockwise direction, and South America had begun to move away from Africa to form the South Atlantic.

65 million years ago

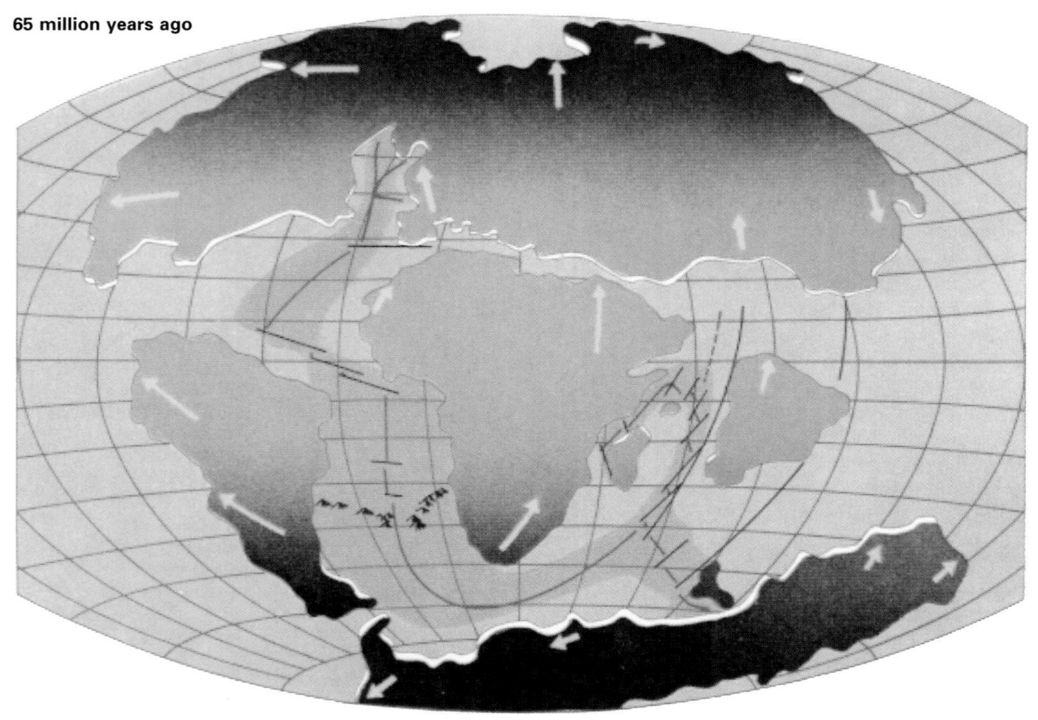

LEFT By the end of the Cretaceous period, about 65 million years ago, the South Atlantic had grown, Madagascar had parted from Africa and India had continued northwards. Antarctica was moving away from the central land mass, though still linked with Australia. The North Atlantic rift forked at the north, starting to form the island of Greenland.

Geological evidence that the continents were once linked is provided by distinctive rock formations that can be assembled into continuous belts when South America and Africa are juxtaposed; by the processes of mountain building, notably India grinding into Asia and crumpling up sediments to form the Himalayas; and by the dovetailed distribution of many plants and animals.

Perhaps the most important impetus to the theory of continental drift came from the twin theories of plate tectonics and seafloor spreading, which developed rapidly from the 1960s. One of the weakest points in Wegener's argument centred on the tremendous forces needed to drive the continents apart. The new plate theories, which have been substantially proven, provide an explanation of the source of the necessary power. Even so, much has still to be learned about the original continent.

RIGHT The debate about continental drift was followed by a more radical idea: plate tectonics. The basic theory proposes that the Earth's crust comprises a series of rigid plates that "float" on a softer layer of the mantle, and are moved about by continental convection currents within the Earth's interior. These plates slowly converge and diverge along margins marked by seismic (earthquake) activity.

Converging plates form either trenches (where the oceanic plate sinks below the lighter continental rock), or mountain ranges. The theory not only supports the notion of continental drift: it also explains the paradox that while there have always been oceans, none of the present seabeds contain sediments more than 150 million years old.

The six major mobile plates (the American, Eurasian, African, Indo-Australian, Pacific and Antarctic) contain smaller plates such as the Arabian and West Indian plates which "absorb" the geometrical discrepancies between major plates by creating or destroying compensating amounts of crustal material.

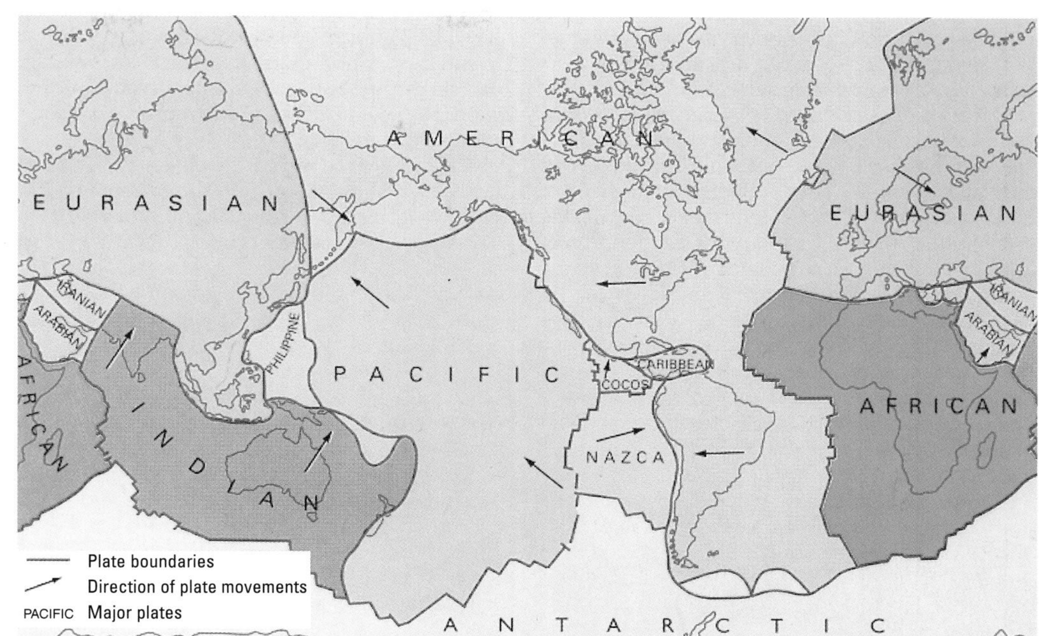

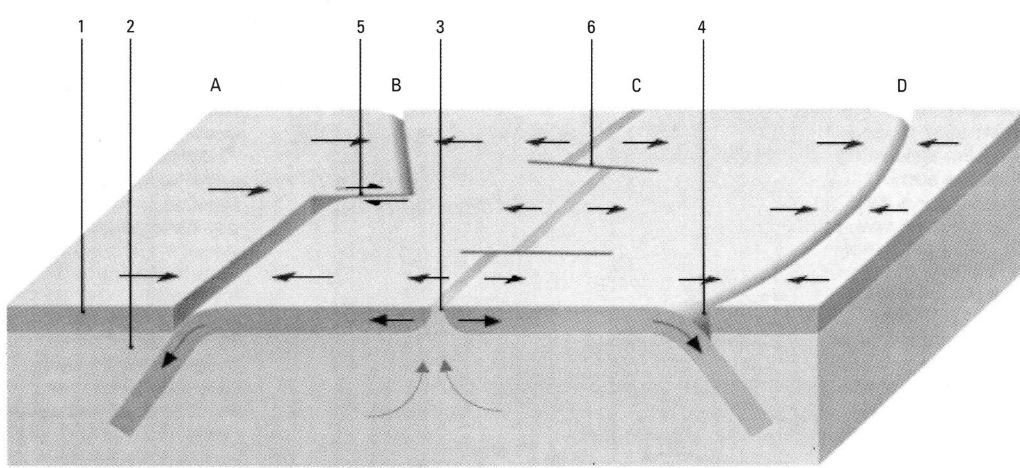

ABOVE The plate tectonics theory sees the Earth's lithosphere [1] as a series of rigid but mobile slabs called plates [A,B,C,D]. The lithosphere floats on a "plastic" layer called the asthenosphere [2]. There are three types of boundaries. At the mid-oceanic ridges [3], upwelling of mantle material occurs and new seafloor is formed. A trench [4] is formed where one plate of oceanic crust slides beneath the other, which may be oceanic or continental. The third type of boundary is where two plates slide past one another, creating a transform fault [5,6]. These link two segments of the same ridge [6], two ocean trenches [5] or a ridge to a trench. Plates move from ridges and travel like conveyor belts towards the trenches.

BELOW Collision zones are where two plates, each carrying a continental mass, meet. When one of the plates is forced beneath the other, the buoyant continental material is pushed upwards in a series of high overthrusts and folds, producing great mountain ranges. The Himalayas, formed when the northward-moving Indian plate crunched up against the Eurasian plate, were the result of such forces – as were other leading fold mountains such as the Alps in Europe (African/Eurasian plates), the Andes in South America (Nazca/American) and the western Rockies (Pacific/American).

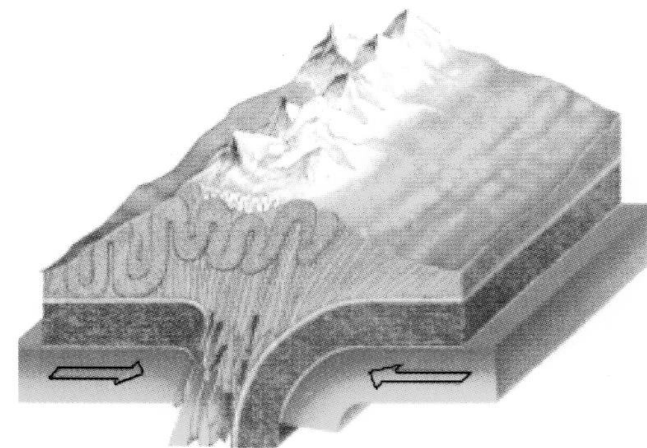

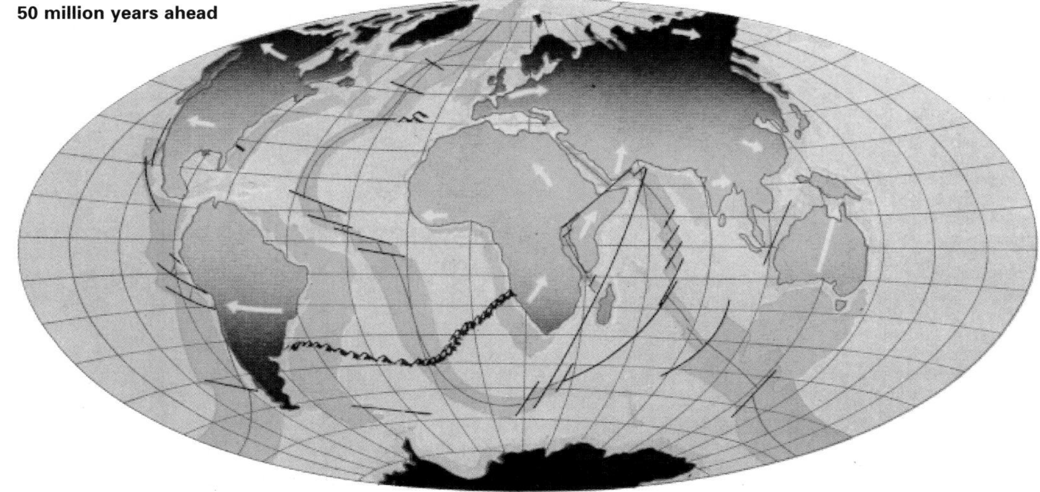

LEFT The continents are still drifting, and there is no reason to expect them to stop. This is how the world may look 50 million years from now if drift is maintained as predicted. The most striking changes in this "new world" are the joining of the Atlantic and Pacific Oceans; the splitting away from the USA of Baja California and the area west of the San Andreas fault line; the northward drift of Africa; the breaking away of that part of the African continent east of the present-day Great Rift Valley; and Australia's continued journey north towards Asia. The majority of the great continent of Antarctica, however, remains in its present southerly position. Plant fossils found in Antarctica's coal seams – remnants of its tropical past hundreds of millions of years ago – are among many examples of evidence supporting the tectonic theory of continent drift.

EARTHQUAKES

AN EARTHQUAKE is the sudden release of energy in the form of vibrations and tremors caused by compressed or stretched rock snapping along a fault in the Earth's surface. Rising lava under a volcano can also produce small tremors. It has been estimated that about a million earthquakes occur each year, but most of these are so minor that they pass unnoticed. While really violent earthquakes occur about once every two weeks, fortunately most of these take place under the oceans, and only rarely do they produce tsunamis.

Slippage along a fault is initially prevented by friction along the fault plane. This causes energy, which generates movement, to be stored up as elastic strain, similar to the effect created when a bow is drawn. Eventually the strain reaches a critical point, the friction is overcome and the rocks snap past each other, releasing the stored-up energy in the form of earthquakes by vibrating back and forth. Earthquakes can also occur when rock folds that can no longer support the elastic strain break to form a fault.

Shockwaves

Seismic or shockwaves spread outwards in all directions from the focus of an earthquake, much as sound waves do when a gun is fired. There are two main types of seismic wave: compressional and shear. Compressional waves cause the rock particles through which they pass to shake back and forth in the direction of the wave, and can be transmitted through both solids and liquids; they are therefore able to travel through the Earth's core. Shear waves make the particles vibrate at right-angles to the direction of their passage, and can travel only through solids; at the boundary of lower mantle and liquid outer core, they are reflected back to the Earth's surface. Neither type of seismic wave physically moves the particles – it merely travels through them.

Compressional waves, which travel 1.7 times faster than shear waves, are the first ones to be distinguished at an earthquake recording station. Consequently seismologists refer to them as primary (P) waves and to the shear waves as secondary (S) waves. A third wave type is recognized by seismologists – the long (L) wave which travels slowly along the Earth's surface, vertically or horizontally. It is L waves that produce the most violent shocks.

Measuring earthquakes

The magnitude of earthquakes is usually rated according to either the Richter or the Modified Mercalli scales, both formulated in the 1930s. Developed by the US geologist Charles Richter, the Richter scale measures the total energy released by a quake with mathematical precision, each upward step representing a tenfold increase in shockwave power. A magnitude of 2 is hardly felt, while a magnitude of 7 is the lower limit of an earthquake that has a devastating effect over a large area. Theoretically there is no upper limit, but the largest measured have been rated at between 8.8 and 8.9. The 12-point Mercalli scale, named after the Italian seismologist Guiseppe Mercalli, is based on damage done and thus varies in different places. It ranges from I (noticed only by seismographs) to XII (total destruction); intermediate points include VII (collapse of substandard buildings) and IX (conspicuous cracks in the ground).

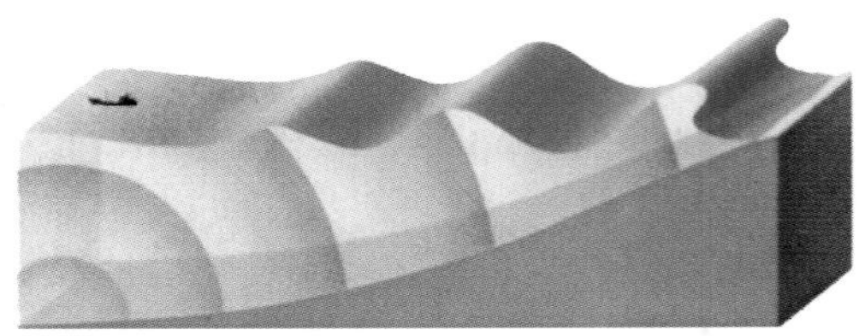

ABOVE The long wave length of tsunamis gives them tremendous speed. An earthquake in the Aleutian Trench in the far northern Pacific in 1946 triggered off a tsunami that devastated Honolulu; it took 4 hours 34 minutes to reach Hawaii, a distance of 3,220km (2,000 miles) – a speed of about 700km/h (440mph).

Tsunamis

Tsunami is the Japanese word for a seismic sea wave; they are often called tidal waves, though they have no connection with tides. Tsunamis are caused mainly by seismic disburbances below the seafloor (oceanic earthquakes), but also by submarine landslides and volcanic eruptions. Other tidal waves can be due to the surge of water when the barometric pressure is exceptionally low, such as in a hurricane. At sea, the height of the wave is seldom more than 60–90cm (2–3ft), but the wave length may be as long as 200km (120 miles), generating speeds of up to 750km/h (450mph).

Although the height of the crest is low out to sea, tsunamis have immense energy, which, as they lose speed in more shallow water, is converted into an increase in height. The waves, on reaching the shore, may be 40m (125ft) or more high. The most destructive tsunamis occur in the northern Pacific.

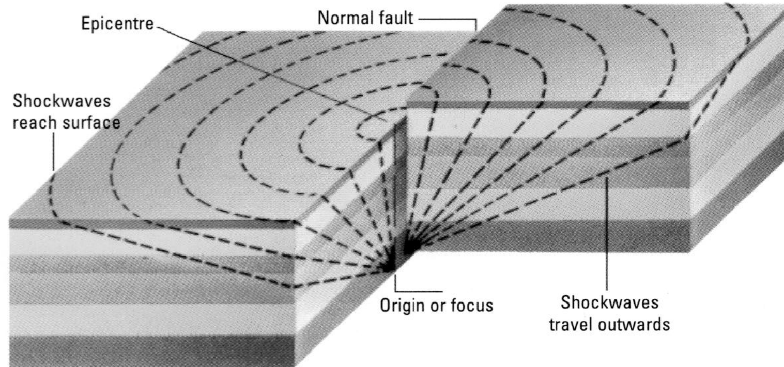

LEFT An earthquake takes place when two parts of the Earth's surface move suddenly in relation to each other along a crack called a fault. The point from which this movement originates is called the focus, usually located at depths between 8 and 30km (5 to 18 miles), and the point on the surface directly above this is called the epicentre. Shockwaves move outwards from the focus in a curved pattern; while speed varies with the density of rock, intensity decreases the farther the waves travel.

BELOW Earthquakes occur in geologically sensitive areas of the world such as mid-oceanic ridges and mountain-building regions, and can be classified according to the depth of their focus. Deep focus quakes occur at depths of between 300 and 650km (185-400 miles), intermediate focus quakes from 55 to 240km (35-150 miles), and shallow focus quakes from the surface down to a depth of 55km (35 miles).

EARTHQUAKE ZONES

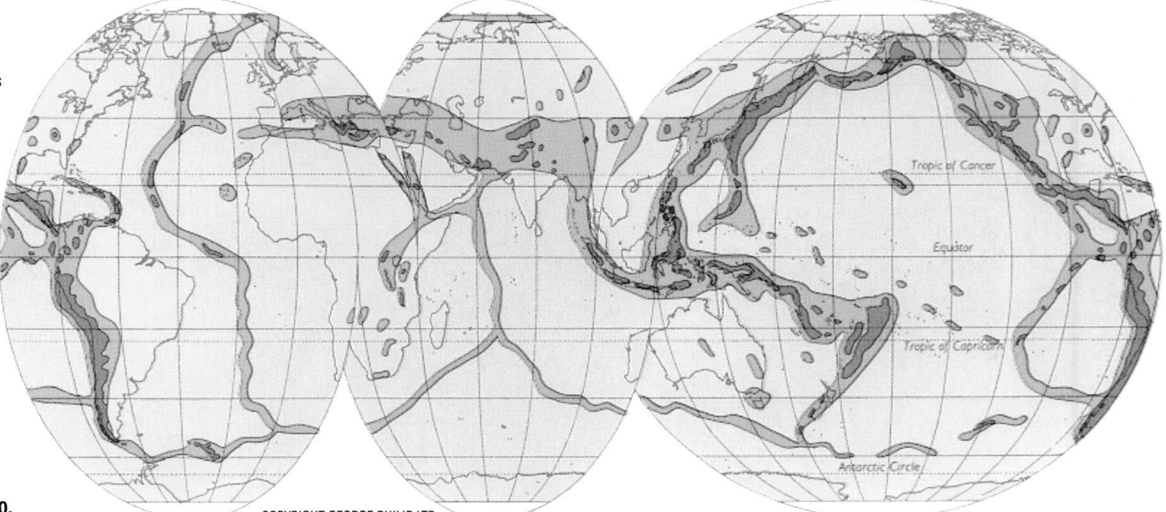

The highest magnitude recorded on the Richter scale is 8.9, for a quake that killed 2,990 people in Japan on 2 March 1933. The most devastating earthquake ever affected three provinces of central China on 2 February 1556, when it is believed that about 830,000 people perished. The highest toll in modern times was at Tangshan, eastern China, on 28 July 1976: the original figure of over 655,000 deaths has since been twice revised by the Chinese government to stand at 242,000.

VOLCANOES

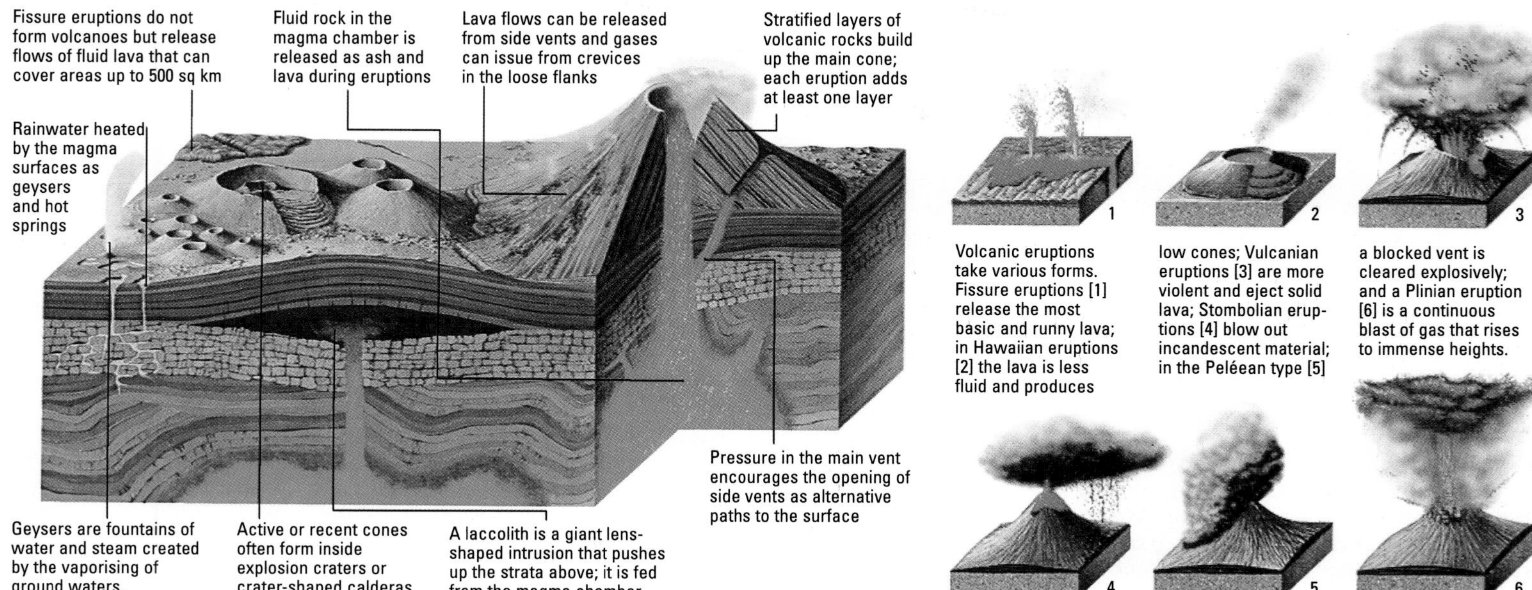
Fissure eruptions do not form volcanoes but release flows of fluid lava that can cover areas up to 500 sq km
Fluid rock in the magma chamber is released as ash and lava during eruptions
Lava flows can be released from side vents and gases can issue from crevices in the loose flanks
Stratified layers of volcanic rocks build up the main cone; each eruption adds at least one layer
Rainwater heated by the magma surfaces as geysers and hot springs
Pressure in the main vent encourages the opening of side vents as alternative paths to the surface
Geysers are fountains of water and steam created by the vaporising of ground waters.
Active or recent cones often form inside explosion craters or crater-shaped calderas
A laccolith is a giant lens-shaped intrusion that pushes up the strata above; it is fed from the magma chamber
1
2
3
4
5
6

Volcanic eruptions take various forms. Fissure eruptions [1] release the most basic and runny lava; in Hawaiian eruptions [2] the lava is less fluid and produces low cones; Vulcanian eruptions [3] are more violent and eject solid lava; Stombolian eruptions [4] blow out incandescent material; in the Peléean type [5] a blocked vent is cleared explosively; and a Plinian eruption [6] is a continuous blast of gas that rises to immense heights.

THE WORLD'S most spectacular natural displays of energy, volcanoes are responsible for forming large parts of the Earth's crust. Volcanoes occur when hot liquefied rock beneath the crust is pushed up by pressure to the surface as molten lava. They are found in places where the crust is weak – the mid-ocean ridges and their continental continuations, and along the collision edges of crustal plates. Some volcanoes erupt in an explosive way, throwing out rocks and ash, while others are effusive and lava flows out of the vent. Some, such as Mount Fuji in Japan, are both.

An accumulation of lava and cinders creates cones of various sizes and shapes. As a result of many eruptions over centuries Mount Etna in Sicily has a circumference of more than 120km (75 miles). Craters at rest are often filled by a lake – and the mudflow caused by an eruption can be as destructive as a lava flow and, because of its speed, even more lethal.

Despite the increasingly sophisticated technology available to geologists to monitor volcanoes, like earthquakes they remain both dramatic and unpredictable. For example, in 1991 Mount Pinatubo, located 100km (60 miles) north of the Philippines capital Manila, suddenly burst into life without any warning after lying dormant for over six centuries.

Most of the world's active volcanoes are located in a belt round the Pacific Ocean, on the edge of the Pacific crustal plate, called the "Ring of Fire" – a circle of fear that threatens over 400 million people. However, the soils formed by the weathering of volcanic rocks are usually exceptionally fertile, and despite the dangers large numbers of people have always lived in the shadows of volcanoes.

Climatologists believe that volcanic ash, if ejected high into the atmosphere, can influence temperature and weather conditions generally over a massive area and for several years afterwards. It has been estimated that the 1991 eruption of Mount Pinatubo in the Philippines threw up more than 20 million tonnes of dust and ash over 30km (18 miles) into the atmosphere, and it is widely believed that this accelerated the depletion of the ozone layer over large parts of the globe.

There are far more volcanoes on the seafloor than on the land, however. These "seamounts" exist because the oceanic crust is newer and thinner than continental crust and easily pierced by the underlying magma. The Pacific Ocean alone is thought to have more than 10,000 underwater volcanoes over 3,000m (9,850ft) high.

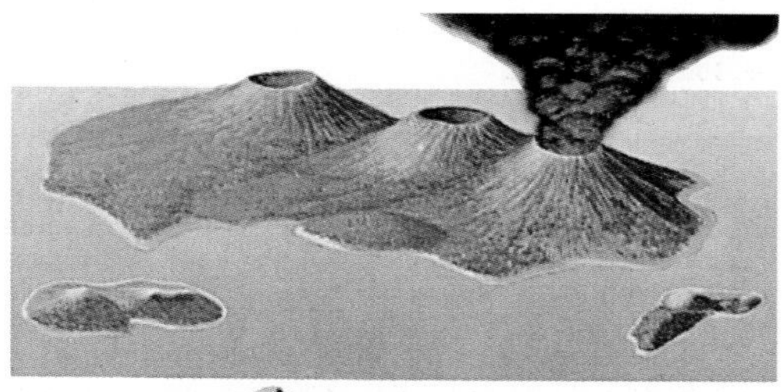

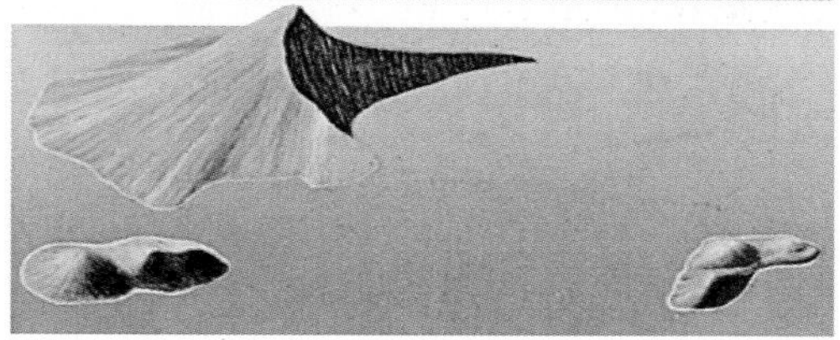

ABOVE Situated in the Sunda Strait of Indonesia, Krakatau was a small volcanic island inactive for over 200 years when, in August 1883, two-thirds of it was destroyed by a violent erruption. It was so powerful that the resulting tidal wave killed 36,000 people. Indonesia has the greatest concentration of volcanoes with 90, 12 of which are active.

VOLCANIC ZONES

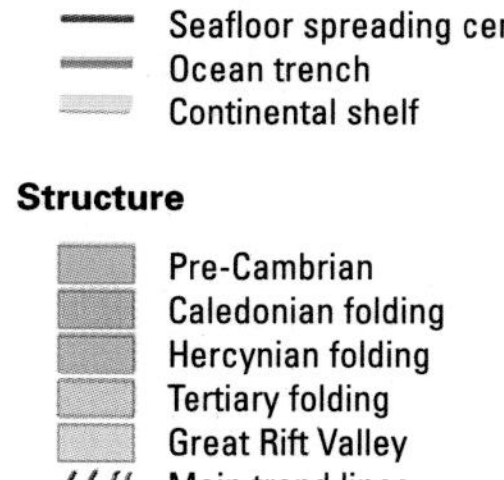
Volcanoes
Seafloor spreading centre
Ocean trench
Continental shelf
Structure
Pre-Cambrian
Caledonian folding
Hercynian folding
Tertiary folding
Great Rift Valley
Main trend lines

Of the 850 volcanoes to produce recorded eruptions, nearly three-quarters lie in the "Ring of Fire" that surrounds the Pacific Ocean on the edge of the Pacific plate.

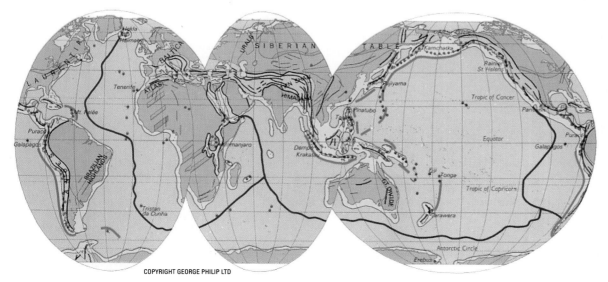

Shaping the Landscape

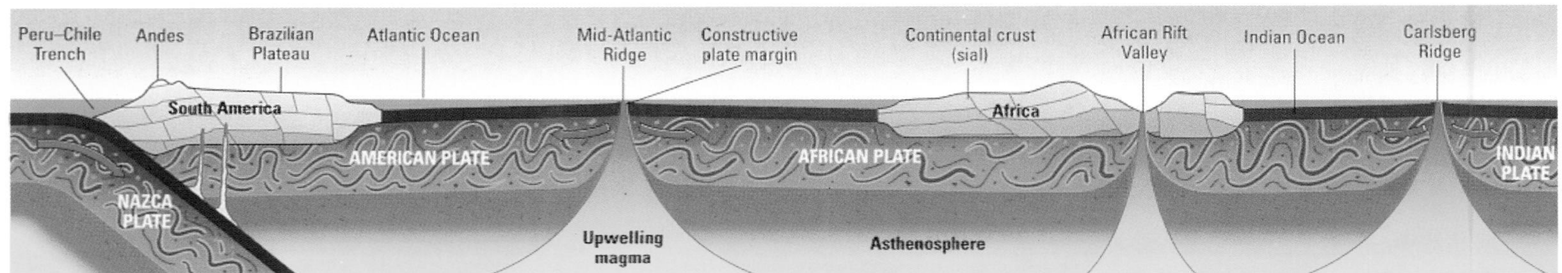

ABOVE A view of seafloor spreading along the Equator from the west coast of South America to the centre of the Indian Ocean. On the left, the Nazca plate has been subducted beneath the American plate to push up the Andes.

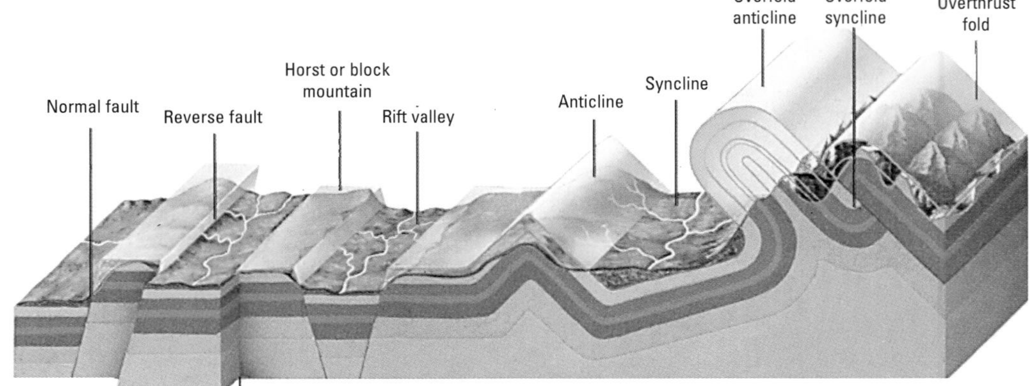

RIGHT A normal fault results when vertical movement causes the surface to break apart, while compression leads to a reverse fault. Horizontal movement causes shearing, known as a tear or strike-slip fault. When the rock breaks in two places, the central block may be pushed up in a "horst", or sink in a rift valley. Folds occur when rock strata are squeezed and compressed. Layers bending up form an anticline, those bending down form a syncline.

THE VAST ridges that divide the Earth beneath the world's oceans mark the boundaries between tectonic plates that are gradually moving in opposite directions. As the plates shift apart, molten magma rises from the mantle to seal the rift and the seafloor spreads towards the land masses. The rate of spreading has been calculated at about 40mm (1.6in) a year in the North Atlantic Ocean.

Near the ocean shore, underwater volcanoes mark the lines where the continental rise begins. As the plates meet, much of the denser oceanic crust dips beneath the continental plate at the "subduction zone" and falls back to the magma.

Mountains are formed when pressures on the Earth's crust caused by continental drift become so intense that the surface buckles or cracks. This happens where oceanic crust is subducted by continental crust, or where two tectonic plates collide: the Rockies, Andes, Alps, Urals and Himalayas all resulted from such impacts. These are known as fold mountains because they were formed by the compression of the sedimentary rocks, forcing the surface to bend and fold like a crumpled rug.

The other main mountain-building process occurs when the crust is being stretched or compressed so violently that the rock strata breaks to create faults, allowing rock to be forced upwards in large blocks; or when the pressure of magma inside the crust forces the surface to bulge into a dome, or erupts to form a volcano. Large and more complex mountain ranges may well reveal a combination of these features.

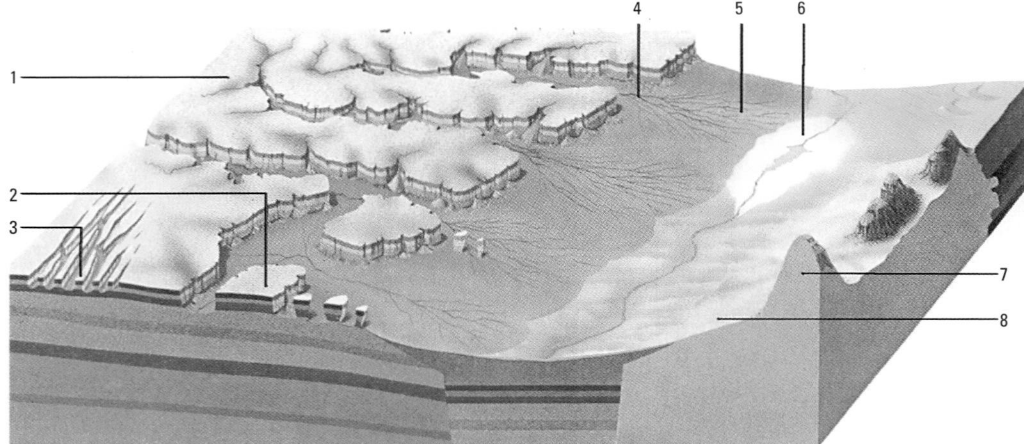

ABOVE The topography of a desert is characterized by the relative absence of the chemical weathering associated with water, and most erosion takes place mechanically through wind abrasion and the effect of heat – and cold.

Mesas [1] are large flat-topped areas with steep sides, while the butte [2] is a flat isolated hill, also with steep sides. Elongated in the direction of the prevailing wind, yardangs [3] comprise tabular masses of resistant rock resting on undercut pillars of softer material. Alluvial fans [5] are pebble-mounds deposited in desert deltas by flash floods, usually at the end of a wadi [4]. A saltpan [6] is a temporary lake of brackish water, also formed by flash floods. An inselberg [7] is an isolated hill rising from the plain, and a pediment [8] is a gently inclining rock surface.

Agents of Erosion

Destruction of the landscape, however, begins as soon as it is formed. Wind, ice, water and sea, the main agents of erosion, maintain a constant assault that even the hardest rocks cannot withstand. Mountain peaks may dwindle by only a few millimetres a year, but if they are not uplifted by further movements of the Earth's crust they will eventually disappear. Over millions of years, even great mountain ranges can be reduced to a low, rugged landscape.

Water is the most powerful destroyer: it has been estimated that 100 billion tonnes of rock are washed into the oceans each year. Three Asian rivers alone account for a fifth of this total – the Hwang Ho in China, and the Ganges and the Brahmaputra in Bangladesh.

When water freezes, its volume increases by about 9%, and no rock is strong enough to resist this pressure. Where water has penetrated fissures or seeped into softer rock, a freeze followed by a thaw may result in rockfalls or earthslides, creating major destruction in minutes.

Over much longer periods, acidity in rain water breaks down the chemical composition of porous rocks such as limestone, eating away the rock to form deep caves and tunnels. Chemical decomposition also occurs in river beds and glacier valleys, hastening the process of mechanical erosion.

Like the sea, rivers and glaciers generate much of their effect through abrasion, pounding or tearing the land with the debris they carry. Yet as well as destroying existing landforms they also create new ones, many of them spectacular. Prominent examples include the Grand Canyon, the vast deltas of the Mississippi and the Nile, the rock arches and stacks off the south coast of Australia, and the deep fjords cut by glaciers in British Columbia, Norway and New Zealand.

While landscapes evolve from a "young" mountainous stage, through a "mature" hilly stage to an "old age" of lowland plain, this long-term cycle of erosion is subject to interruption by a number of crucial factors, including the pronounced effects of plate tectonics and climate change.

Shaping forces: ice

Many of the world's most dramatic landscapes have been carved by icesheets and glaciers. During the Ice Ages of the Pleistocene epoch (over 10,000 years ago) up to a third of the land surface was glaciated; even today a tenth is still covered in ice – the vast majority locked up in the huge icesheets of Antarctica and Greenland.

Valley glaciers are found in mountainous regions throughout the world, except Australia. In the relatively short geological time scale of the recent Ice Ages, glaciers accomplished far more carving of the topography than rivers and wind.

They are formed from compressed snow, called névé, accumulating in a valley head or cirque. Slowly the glacier moves downhill, moving at rates of between a few millimetres and several metres a day, scraping away debris from the mountains and valleys through which it passes. The debris, or moraine, adds to the abrasive power of the ice. The sediments are transported by the ice to the edge of the glacier, where they are deposited or carried away by meltwater streams.

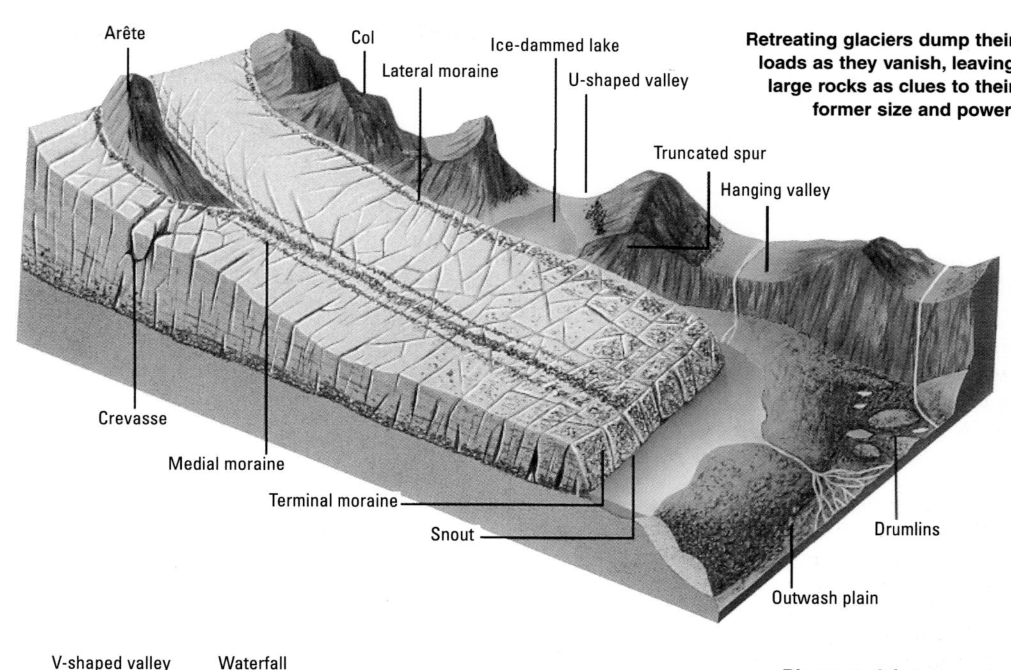

Retreating glaciers dump their loads as they vanish, leaving large rocks as clues to their former size and power.

Shaping forces: rivers

From their origins as small upland rills and streams channelling rainfall, or as springs releasing water that has seeped into the ground, all rivers are incessantly at work cutting and shaping the landscape on their way to the sea.

In highland regions flow may be rapid and turbulent, pounding rocks to cut deep gorges and V-shaped valleys through softer rocks, or tumbling as waterfalls over harder ones.

As they reach more gentle slopes, rivers release some of the pebbles and heavier sediments they have carried downstream, flow more slowly and broaden out. Levées or ridges are raised along their banks by the deposition of mud and sand during floods. In lowland plains the river drifts into meanders, depositing layers of sediment, especially on the inside of bends where the flow is weakest. As the river reaches the sea it deposits its remaining load, and estuaries are formed where the tidal currents are strong enough to remove them; if not, the debris creates a delta.

Shaping forces: the sea

Under the constant assault from tides and currents, wind and waves, coastlines change faster than most landscape features, both by erosion and by the building up of sand and pebbles carried by the sea. In severe storms, giant waves pound the shoreline with rocks and boulders; but even in much quieter conditions, the sea steadily erodes cliffs and headlands, creating new features in the form of sand dunes, spits and salt marshes. Beaches, where sand and shingle have been deposited, form a buffer zone between the erosive power of the waves and the coast. Because it is composed of loose materials, a beach can rapidly adapt its shape to changes in wave energy.

Where the coastline is formed from soft rocks such as sandstones, debris may fall evenly and be carried away by currents from shelving beaches. In areas with harder rock, the waves may cut steep cliffs and wave-cut platforms; eroded debris is deposited as a terrace. Bays and smaller coves are formed when sections of soft rock are carved away between headlands of harder rock. These are then battered by waves from both sides, until the headlands are eventually reduced to rock arches, which as stacks are later separated from the mainland.

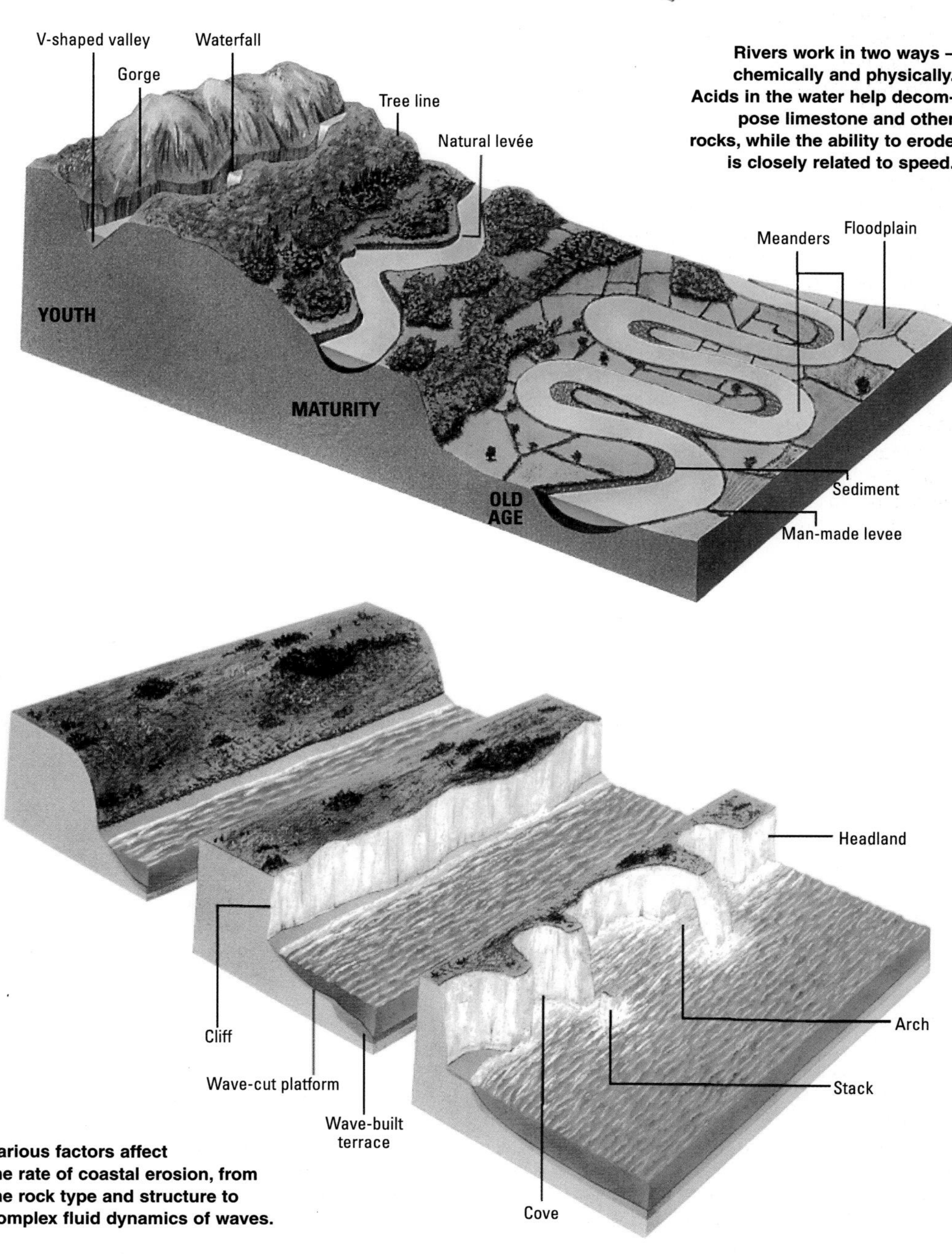

Rivers work in two ways – chemically and physically. Acids in the water help decompose limestone and other rocks, while the ability to erode is closely related to speed.

Various factors affect the rate of coastal erosion, from the rock type and structure to complex fluid dynamics of waves.

OCEANS: SEAWATER

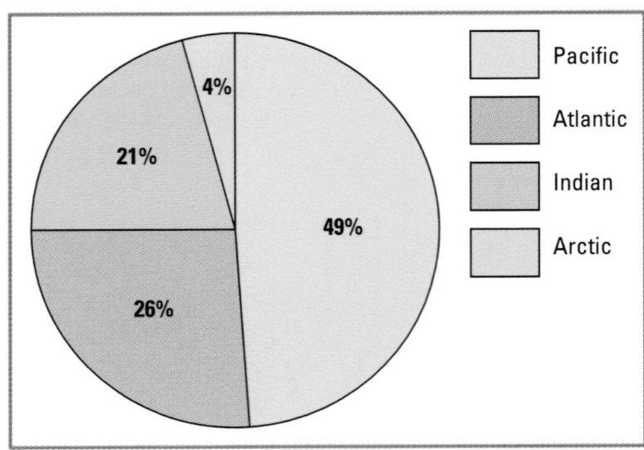

ABOVE In the strictest geographical sense the Earth has only three oceans – Atlantic, Indian and Pacific. The legendary "Seven Seas" would require these to be divided at the Equator and the addition of the smaller Arctic Ocean. Geographers do not recognize the Antarctic Ocean (much less the "Southern Ocean") as a separate entity.

The Earth is a watery planet: almost 71% of its surface is covered by its oceans and seas. This great liquid cloak gives our planet its characteristic and beautiful blue appearance from space, and is one of the two obvious differences between the Earth and its two near-neighbours, Venus and Mars. The other difference is the presence of life – and the two are closely linked.

ABOVE When sunlight strikes the surface of the ocean between 3% and 30% of it is immediately reflected. The amount reflected depends on the angle at which the light strikes – the smaller the angle the greater the reflection – which varies with latitude and the seasons.

Penetration of sunlight is selectively reduced according to wavelength. Radiation at the red or long-wave end of the visible spectrum is absorbed near the surface of the water, while the shorter blue wavelengths are scattered, giving the sea its characteristic blue colour.

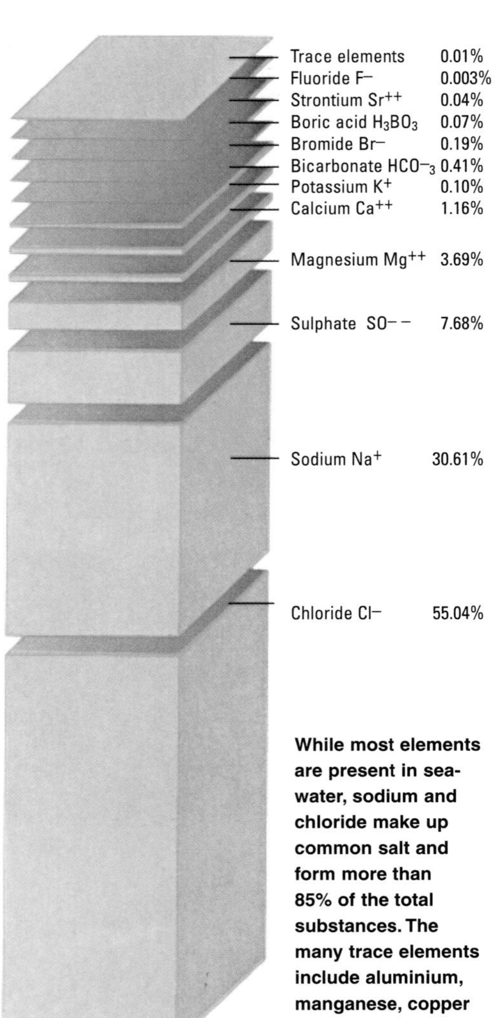

While most elements are present in seawater, sodium and chloride make up common salt and form more than 85% of the total substances. The many trace elements include aluminium, manganese, copper and gold.

EARTH IS something of a misnomer for our planet; "Ocean" would be a more suitable name, since the oceans and seas cover 70.8% of its total surface area. The oceans are not separate areas of water but form one continuous oceanic mass, and (as with some continental divisions) the boundaries between them are arbitrary lines drawn for convenience. The vast areas of interconnected oceans contain 97.2% of the world's total water supply.

The study of oceans, including their biology, chemistry, geology and physics, has now become a matter of urgency, because the future of humans on Earth may well depend on our knowledge of the ocean's potential resources not only of minerals and power but also of food.

Composition of seawater

The most obvious resource of the oceans is the water itself. But seawater is salty, containing sodium chloride (common salt), which makes it unsuitable for drinking or farming. One kilogramme (2.2lb) of seawater contains about 35g (1.2oz) of dissolved materials, of which chloride and sodium together make up nearly 30g (1oz) or about 85%.

Seawater is a highly complex substance in which 73 of the 93 natural chemical elements are present in measurable or detectable amounts. Apart from chloride and sodium it contains appreciable amounts of sulphate, magnesium, potassium and calcium, which together add up to over 13% of the total. The remainder, less than 1%, is made up of bicarbonate, bromide, boric acid, strontium, fluoride, silicon and various trace elements. Because the volume of the oceans is so great, there are substantial amounts of some trace elements: seawater contains more gold, for example, than there is on land, even though it's in a very low concentration of four-millionths of one part per million.

Also present in seawater are dissolved gases from the atmosphere, including nitrogen, oxygen and carbon dioxide. Of these, oxygen is vital to marine organisms. The amount of oxygen in seawater varies according to temperature. Cold water can contain more oxygen than warm water, but cold water in the ocean depths, which has been out of contact with the atmosphere for a long period, usually contains a much smaller amount of oxygen than surface water.

Other chemicals in seawater that are important to marine life include calcium, silicon and phosphates, all of which are used by marine creatures to form shells and skeletons. For building cells and tissue, marine organisms extract phosphates, certain nitrogen compounds, iron and silicon. The chief constituents of seawater – chloride, sodium, magnesium and sulphur – are hardly used by marine organisms.

Density, light and sound

The density of seawater is an important factor in causing ocean currents and is related to the interaction of salinity and temperature. The temperature of surface water varies between –2°C and 29°C (28°F and 85°F); ice will begin to form if the temperature drops below –2°C (28°F).

The properties of light passing through seawater determine the colour of the oceans. Radiation at the red or long-wave end of the spectrum is absorbed near the surface of the water, while the shorter blue wavelengths are scattered, giving the sea its characteristic colour.

The depth to which light can penetrate is important to marine life. In clear water light may reach to 110m (360ft), whereas in muddy coastal waters it may penetrate to only 15m (50ft). Below about 1,000m (3,300ft) there is virtually no light at all.

The most active zone in the oceans is the sunlit upper layer, falling to about 200m (650ft) at the edge of the continental shelf, where the water is moved around by windblown currents. This is the

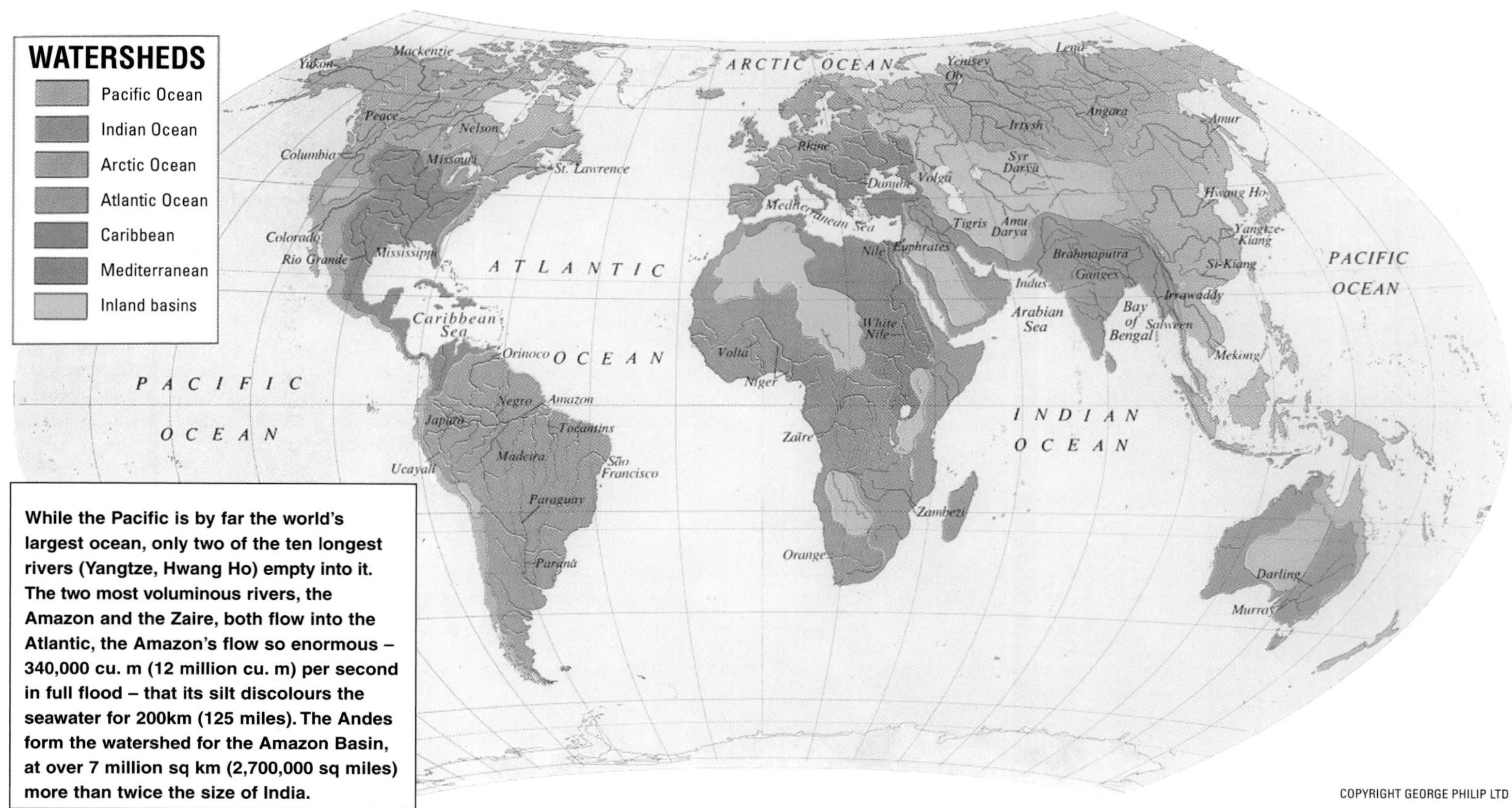

While the Pacific is by far the world's largest ocean, only two of the ten longest rivers (Yangtze, Hwang Ho) empty into it. The two most voluminous rivers, the Amazon and the Zaire, both flow into the Atlantic, the Amazon's flow so enormous – 340,000 cu. m (12 million cu. m) per second in full flood – that its silt discolours the seawater for 200km (125 miles). The Andes form the watershed for the Amazon Basin, at over 7 million sq km (2,700,000 sq miles) more than twice the size of India.

home of most sealife and acts as a membrane through which the ocean breathes, absorbing great quantities of carbon dioxide and partly exchanging it for oxygen.

As the depth increases light fades and temperatures fall until just before around 950m (3,000ft), when there is a marked temperature change at the thermocline, the boundary between the warm surface zones and the cold deep zones.

Water is a good conductor of sound, which travels at about 1,507m (4,954ft) per second through seawater, compared with 331m (1,087ft) per second through air. Echo-sounding is based on the measurement of the time taken for sound to travel from a ship to the seafloor and back again. However, temperature and pressure both affect the speed of sound, causing the speed to vary by about 100m (330ft) per second.

The salinity of the oceans

The volume of dissolved salts in seawater is called the salinity. The average salinity of seawater ranges between 33 and 37 parts of dissolved material per 1,000 parts of water. Oceanographers express these figures as 33 parts per thousand (33‰) to 37‰.

The salinity of ocean water varies with local conditions. Large rivers or melting ice reduce salinity, for example, whereas it is increased in areas with little rainfall and high evaporation.

To produce fresh water from seawater the dissolved salts must be separated out. This desalination can be carried out by electrical, chemical and change of phase processes. Change of phase processes involve changing the water into steam and distilling it, or changing it into ice, a process that also expels the salt. Eskimos have used sea ice as a source of fresh water for centuries, while primitive coastal tribes still take salt from the sea by damming water in pools and letting it evaporate in the Sun.

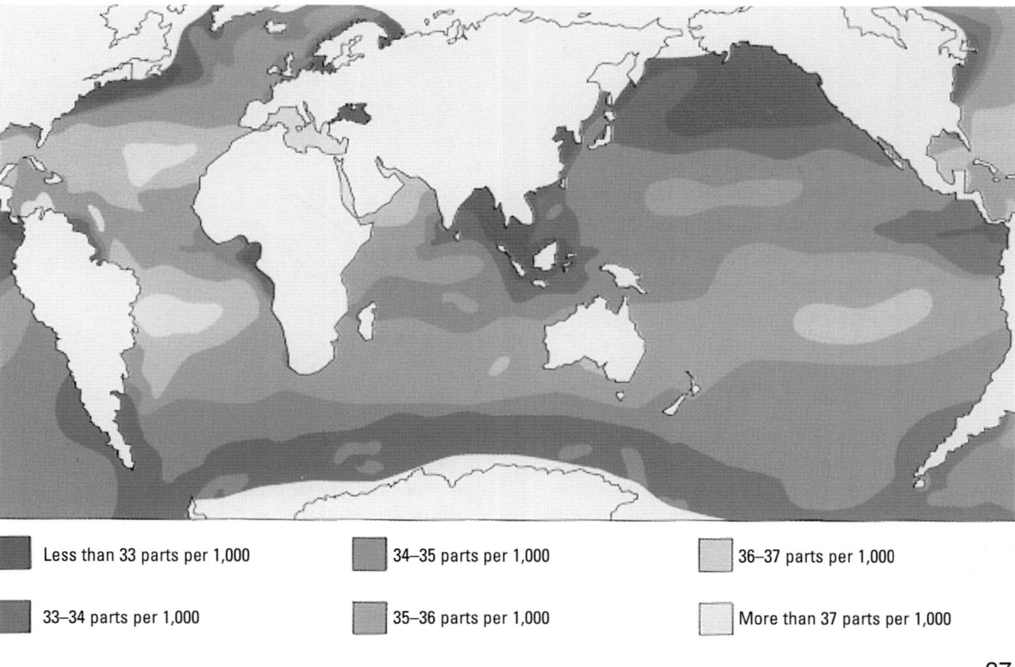

RIGHT The average salinity of seawater ranges between 33 and 37 parts of dissolved material per 1,000 parts of water. While the most saline water is generally found in semi-enclosed seas in temperate and tropical areas such as the Gulf of Mexico, Mediterranean and the Red Sea (where high rates of evaporation can produce a figure of 41 parts per thousand), the Baltic Sea, which receives large quantities of freshwater from rivers and melting snow, has a remarkably low salinity of 7.2‰.

In the oceans themselves, the least saline waters occur in areas of high freshwater discharge such as the edge of the Antarctic icecap and the mouths of large rivers. The most pronounced regional example of this is Southeast Asia, where a string of massive rivers – including the Ganges, Brahmaputra, Irrawaddy, Salween, Mekong, Si Kiang, Yangtze and Hwang Ho – flow into the coastal area from the Bay of Bengal to the Yellow Sea.

If the salt in the oceans were precipitated, it would cover the Earth's land areas with a layer more than 150m (500ft) thick.

THE OCEANS: CURRENTS

NO PART of the ocean is completely still – although, in the ocean depths, the movement of water is often extremely slow. Exploration of the deeper parts of the oceans has revealed the existence of marine life. If the water were not in motion, the oxygen on which all lifeforms depend would soon be used up and not replaced. No life would therefore be possible.

Prevailing winds sweep surface water along to form drift currents. These surface currents do not conform precisely with the direction of the prevailing wind because of the Coriolis effect caused by the rotation of the Earth. This effect, which increases away from the Equator, makes currents in the Northern Hemisphere veer to the right of the wind direction and currents in the Southern Hemisphere veer to the left. The result is a general clockwise circulation of water in the Northern Hemisphere and an anticlockwise circulation in the Southern.

Other factors affecting currents are the configuration of the ocean bed and the shapes of land masses. For example, in the Atlantic Ocean the North Equatorial Current flows towards the West Indies. Most of this current is channelled into the Gulf of Mexico where it veers northeastwards, bursting into the Atlantic between Florida and Cuba as the Gulf Stream.

OCEAN CURRENTS

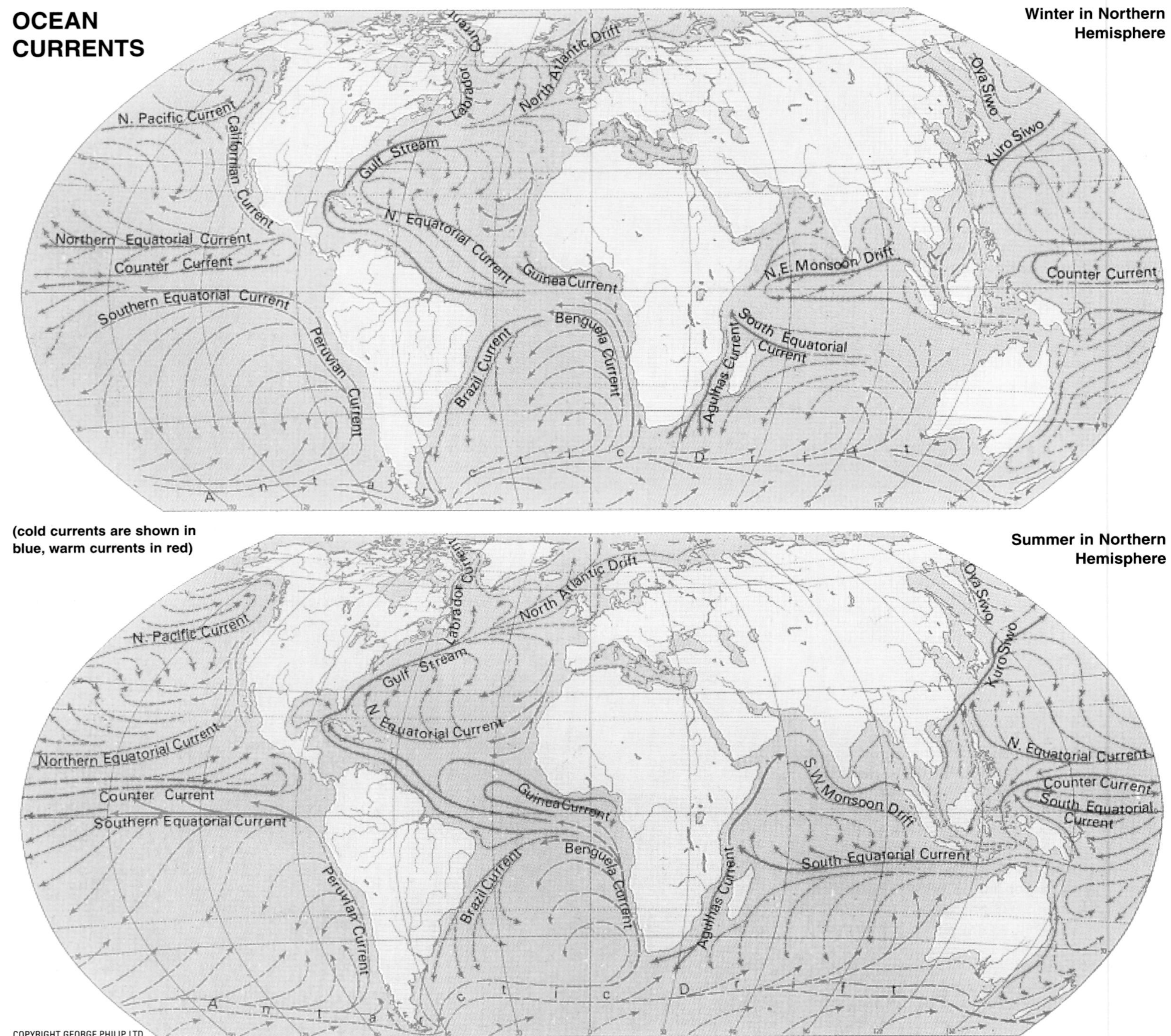

ABOVE The world's surface currents circulate in a clockwise direction in the Northern Hemisphere and in an anticlockwise direction in the Southern Hemisphere. These circulatory systems are called gyres. There are two large clockwise gyres in the Northern Hemisphere (North Atlantic and North Pacific) and three anticlockwise gyres in the Southern (South Atlantic, South Pacific and Indian Ocean).

Beneath the surface are undercurrents whose direction may be opposite to those at the surface. Under the Gulf Stream off the eastern USA lies a large, cold current flowing south from the Arctic. The Gulf Stream finally splits: while the North Atlantic Drift branches past eastern Greenland and western Europe, part of the current returns southwards to complete the gyre. Surface cold currents in the Northern Hemisphere generally flow southwards. In the Southern Hemisphere, cold water circulates around Antarctica, while offshoots flow northwards. The warm currents are very strong in tropical and subtropical regions, and include the various Equatorial currents.

The causes of currents that are not powered by winds are related to the density of ocean water, which varies according to temperature and salinity. Heating at the Equator causes the water to become less dense, while cooling round the poles has the opposite effect. Salinity is affected by the inflow of fresh water from rivers, melting ice and rainfall, and by evaporation. A high rate of evaporation increases the salinity and therefore the density.

Effects of ocean currents

One of the most important effects of ocean currents is that they mix ocean water and so affect directly the fertility of the sea. Mixing is especially important when subsurface water is mixed with surface water. The upwelling of subsurface water may be caused by strong coastal winds that push the surface water outwards, allowing subsurface water to rise up. Such upwelling occurs off the coasts of Peru, California and Mauritania, where subsurface water rich in nutrients (notably phosphorus and silicon) rises to the surface, stimulating the growth of plankton which provides food for great shoals of fish, such as Peruvian anchovies.

Water has a high heat capacity and can retain heat two and a half times as readily as land. The heat of the Sun absorbed by water around the Equator is transported north and south by currents. Part of the North Atlantic Drift flows past Norway, warming offshore winds and giving northwest Europe a winter temperature that is 11°C (20°F) above the average for those latitudes. The northward-flowing Peru and Benguela currents have a reverse effect, bringing cooler weather to the western coasts of South America and southern Africa.

In such ways, currents have a profound effect on climate. Currents from polar regions can also create hazards for shipping: the Labrador and East Greenland currents carry icebergs and pack ice into shipping lanes, and fog often occurs where cold and warm currents meet, most persistently off the coast of Newfoundland.

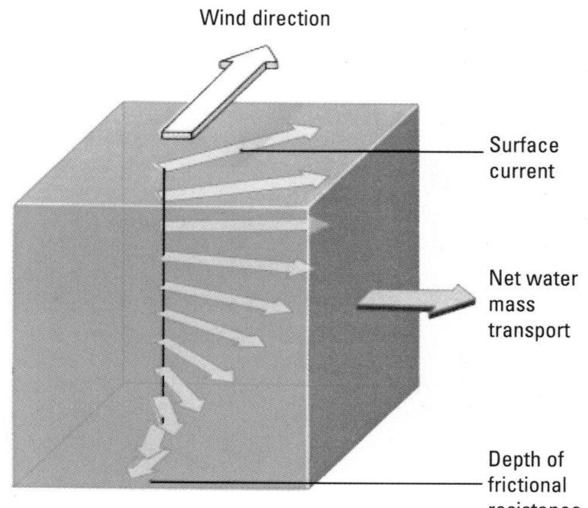

RIGHT Surface currents are caused largely by prevailing winds. The Coriolis effect caused by the rotation of the Earth results in the deflection of currents to the right of the wind direction in the Northern Hemisphere. In the same manner, the surface motion drags the subsurface layer at an angle to it, and so on.

Each layer moves at a slower speed than the one above it and at a greater angle from the wind. The spiral created has the overall effect of moving the water mass above the depth of frictional resistance at an angle of about 90° from the wind direction, while surface currents move at around 45°. The same effect reverses the direction of draining water from a bath in the Northern and Southern hemispheres.

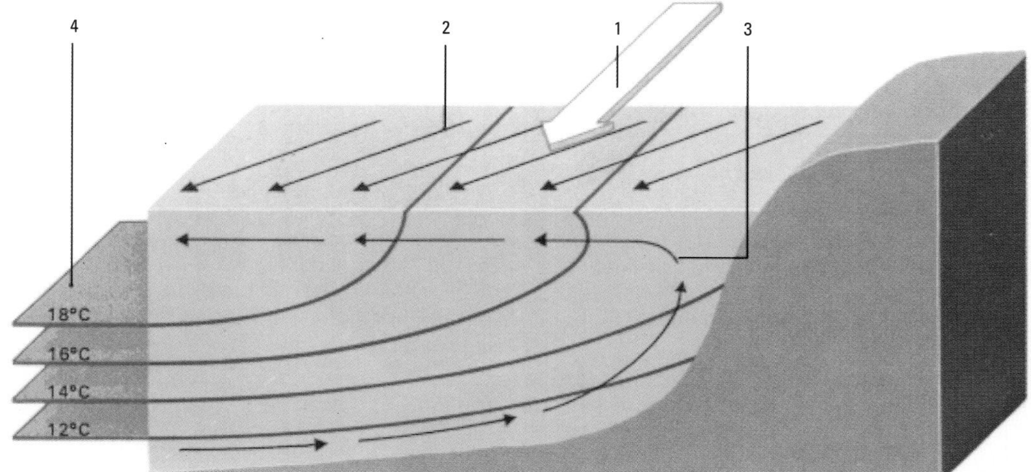

ABOVE Upwelling occurs when a longshore wind [1] pushes surface water away from a coast at an angle [2], allowing deeper water to rise [3]. The deeper water is not only colder [4] but usually rich in nutrients, and areas where upwelling occurs are often exceptional fishing grounds. A good example are the waters off the west coast of South America, the most productive in the world before the upwelling was suppressed by successive years of El Niño.

El Niño

El Niño is the most dramatic and influential of current reversals, producing devastating effects. Its 1997–98 visit was the most damaging yet, triggering (among other things) floods and landslides in northwest South America, storms in California, drought in southern Africa, monsoon failure in India and widespread rainforest fires in Southeast Asia. Estimates put the cost of the property damage alone as high as US$33 billion.

As the previous worst case in 1982–83 showed, the commercial cost is colossal and far-reaching. This includes declining fish stocks in the eastern Pacific (the anchovy catch dropped by over 90%), frost-wrecked orange groves in Florida, crop losses in Africa and brush fires in Australia.

While El Niño is unpredictable in both power and frequency – it used to appear every 2 to 7 years – the phenomenon now occurs more often, including five consecutive seasons from 1990 to 1994. It usually lasts about three months but can be far longer. The name was originally given by Peruvian fishermen to the warm but weak current that flowed south for a few weeks each year around Christmas – hence the name, which means "Christ child". Now the term is applied to a complex if irregular series of remarkable natural happenings.

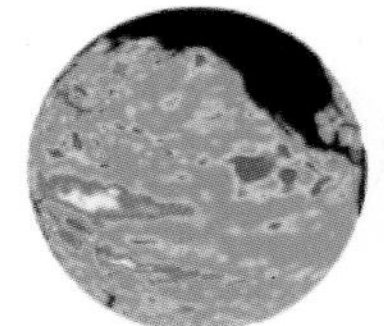

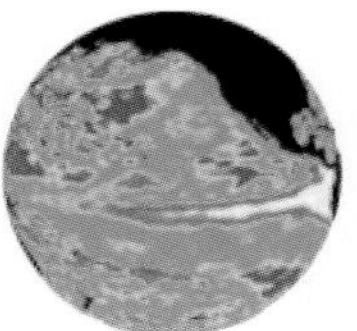

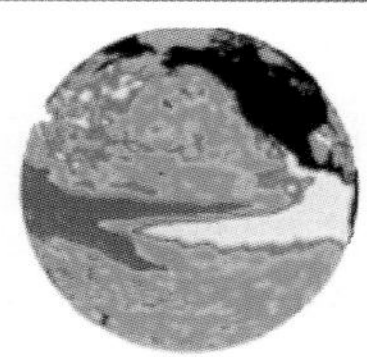

The El Niño sequence begins in the western Pacific. The mass of warm water (white in centre), 8°C higher than in the east and generally kept in check by the prevailing westerly trade winds, breaks free of its moorings as these winds subside and moves in an equatorial swell towards South America. There it raises both sea temperatures and sea levels, suppressing the normal upwelling of the cold and nutrient-rich Peruvian current. Meanwhile, the western Pacific waters cool (purple) as the warm water is displaced.

The movement of such vast amounts of warm water results in chaotic changes to wind patterns, in turn creating freak weather conditions well outside the Pacific tropics. The passage of El Niño's warm water is also tracked by rainfall, leading to droughts in Southeast Asia and Australia and excessive levels of precipitation in South America.

This sequence traces El Niño's passage from March 1997 *(above left)* to October 1998 *(below right)*, when normal oceanic conditions were finally resumed – until the next time. In 1983, 1987 and 1995 El Niño was followed by the cool current La Niña ("the little girl").

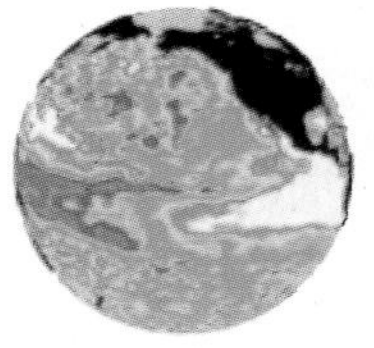
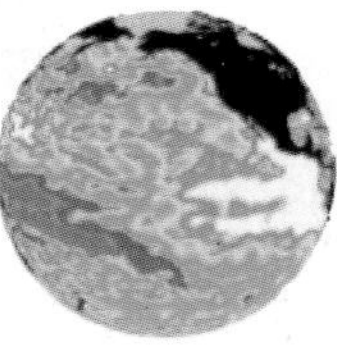

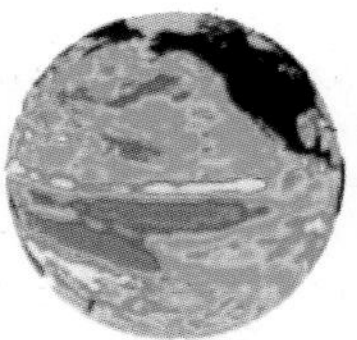

Oceans: Waves and Tides

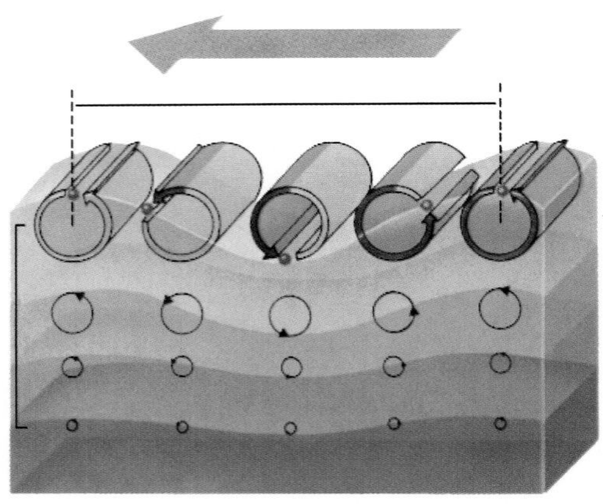

ABOVE Most waves are generated by the wind. As a wave travels in deep water, however, the water particles don't move up and down but rotate in circular orbits. As depth increases, the rotations of the water particles diminish rapidly – the reason why submarines escape the effects of severe storms at sea.

Because they affect coastal areas, waves and tides are the most familiar features of oceans and seas for most of us, but sometimes the energies of waves, tides and high winds combine with devastating effect. In January 1953 a high spring tide, storm waves and winds of 185km/h (115mph) combined to raise the level of the North Sea by 3m (10ft) higher than usual. This "surge" caused extensive flooding in eastern England, but in the Netherlands over 4% of the country was inundated: 1,800 people died and about 30,000 houses were destroyed or damaged by the seawater.

The motion of waves

While some wave motion occurs at great depth along the boundary of two opposing currents, most waves are caused by the wind blowing over an open stretch of water. This area where the wind blows is known as the "fetch". Waves there are confused and irregular and are referred to as a "sea". As they propagate beyond the fetch they combine into more orderly waves to form a "swell", which travels for long distances beyond the fetch. Waves are movements of oscillation – that is, the shape of the wave moves across the water, but the water particles rotate in a circular orbit with hardly any lateral movement. As a result, if there is no wind or current, a corked bottle bobs up and down in the waves, but is more or less stationary.

At sea, waves seldom exceed 12m (40ft) in height, although one 34m (115ft) high was accurately measured in the Pacific Ocean in 1933. Such a wave requires a long fetch measuring thousands of kilometres and high-speed winds.

Waves that break along a seashore may have been generated by storms in mid-ocean or by local winds. As a wave approaches shallow water, which is defined as a depth of half a wave length, it "feels" the bottom, gradually slowing down, and the crests tend to crowd together. When the water in front of a wave is insufficient to fill the wave form, the rotating orbit – and hence the wave – breaks. There are two main kinds of breakers: spilling breakers occur on gently sloping beaches, when the crests spill over to form a mass of surf, while plunging breakers occur on steeper slopes.

BELOW Waves have dimensions of both length and height. The wave length [14] is the distance between one crest [5] and another – in this case a peaking wave [4] – and between two crests is a trough [11]. The wave height [6] is the distance between the crest and the trough. If wave action ceased, the water would settle at the "still water level" [8]. Wave action extends to the wave base [7], where rotation becomes negligible. Wave distortion is caused by frictional drag on the seabed: if waves pass over a sandbar [10], a spilling breaker [9] may form. Sometimes, waves in shallow water move the whole body of the water forward in translation waves [2] towards the shore [1].

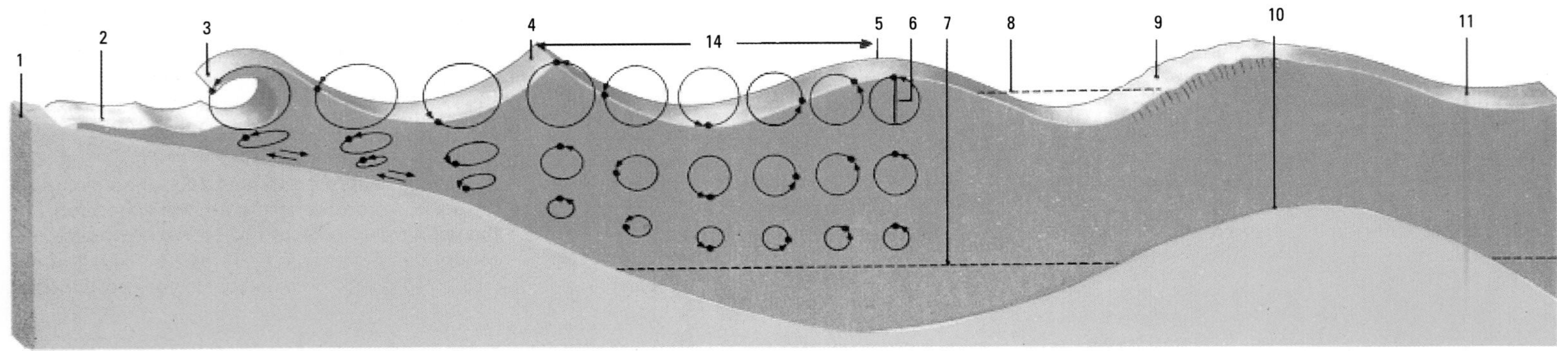

RIGHT Tides are the alternate rises and falls of the sea's surface level, caused by the gravitational pull of the Moon and the Sun. Although the Moon is much smaller than the Sun, it is much closer to Earth and its effect on the oceans is more than twice that of the Sun. The configurations of coasts and seafloors can accentuate these forces, while barometric pressure and wind effects can also superimpose an added "surge" element.

In the open sea the tidal range is small and in enclosed basins, such as the Mediterranean, it is little more than 30cm (12in). However, in shallow seas it may be more than 6m (20ft) and in tidal estuaries 12–15m (40–50ft). The highest tidal range recorded is about 16m (53ft) in the Bay of Fundy, which divides the peninsula of Nova Scotia from the Canadian mainland of New Brunswick.

In some 60 estuaries, such as Hangchow Bay in China and the Severn in England, tidal bores occur. These are bodies of water with a wall-like front that surge up rivers, formed because the estuaries act as funnels, leading to a rise in the height of the water. At spring tides the Hangchow bore attains heights of 7.5m (25ft) and speeds of 27km/h (17mph).

SPRING TIDE

Tidal bulge

Tidal bulge

Earth

Moon

Sun

When the Moon and Sun are roughly in the same direction (around the time of the new Moon), they each pull the oceans on the near side of the Earth towards them. They also pull the Earth towards them, away from the oceans on the far side of the Earth. The effect is to produce two bulges on opposite sides of the Earth. These will not rotate with the Earth but will stay with the forces that produced them, causing two high tides and two low tides a day.

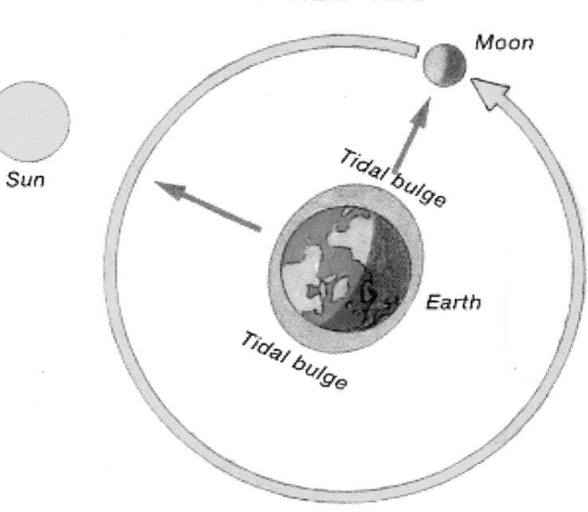

The effect is the same if the Moon and Sun are aligned on opposite sides of the Earth (at the time of full Moon). Thus the tides are greatest at the time of new Moon and full Moon (spring tides). Tides are less pronounced when the Sun, Moon and Earth are not aligned, and are least strong when the three are at right-angles to each other (near the Moon's first and third quarters). In this situation solar and lunar forces compete: the lunar tide wins, but the difference between high and low tides is much less (neap tides).

OCEANS: THE SEAFLOOR

THE DEEP ocean floor was once thought to be flat, but maps compiled from readings made by sonar equipment show that it's no more uniform than the surface of the continents. Here are not just the deepest trench – the Challenger Deep of the Pacific's Mariana Trench plunges 11,022m (36,161ft) – but also the Earth's longest mountain chains and its tallest peaks.

The vast underwater world starts in the shallows of the seaside. Surrounding the land masses is the shallow continental shelf, composed of rocks that less dense than the underlying oceanic crust. The shelf drops gently to around 200m (650ft), where the seafloor suddenly falls away at an angle of 3° to 6° via the continental slope. Submarine canyons such as the 1.5km (5,000ft) gorge off Monterey, California are found on the continental slopes. They can be caused either by river erosion before the land was submerged by the sea, or by turbidity currents – underwater avalanches that carry mud, pebbles and sand far out to sea, scouring gorges out of both slope rock and sediment.

The third stage, the continental rise, made up of sediments washed down from the shelves, is more gradual, with gradients varying from 1 in 100 to 1 in 700. At an average depth of 5,000m (9,000ft) there begins the aptly named abyssal plain, massive submarine depths where sunlight fails to penetrate and only creatures specially adapted to deal with the darkness and the pressure can survive.

Underwater highlands

While the abyss contains large plains it is broken by hills, volcanic seamounts and mid-ocean ridges. Here new rock is being continually formed as magma rises through the Earth's crust, pushing the tectonic plates on each side apart towards the continents in the process called seafloor spreading.

Taken from base to top, many of the seamounts which rise from these plains rival and even surpass the biggest of continental mountains in height. Mauna Kea, Hawaii's highest peak, reaches 10,203m (33,475ft), some 1,355m (4,380ft) more than Mount Everest, though only 4,205m (13,795ft) is above sea level. Nearby is Mauna Loa, the world's biggest active volcano, over 84% of which is hidden from view.

Life in the ocean depths

Manned submersibles have now established that life exists even in the deepest trenches, where the pressure reaches 1,000 "atmospheres" – the equivalent of the force of a tonne bearing down on every sq cm (6.5 tons per sq in).

Further exploration in the pitch-black environment of the oceanic ridges has revealed extraordinary forms of marine life around the scalding hot vents: creatures include giant tubeworms, blind shrimps, and bacteria, some of which are genetically different from any other known lifeforms.

In 1996 an analysis of one micro-organism revealed that at least half its 1,700 or so genes were hitherto unknown. Based on chemicals, not sunlight, this alien environment may well resemble the places where life on Earth first began.

ABOVE Continental shelves are the regions immediately off the land masses, and there are several different types. Off Europe and North America the shelf has a gentle relief, often with sandy ridges and barriers [A]. In high latitudes, floating ice wears the shelf smooth [B], and in clear tropical seas a smooth shelf may be rimmed with a coral barrier such as the Great Barrier Reef off eastern Australia, leaving an inner lagoon area "dammed" by the reef [C].

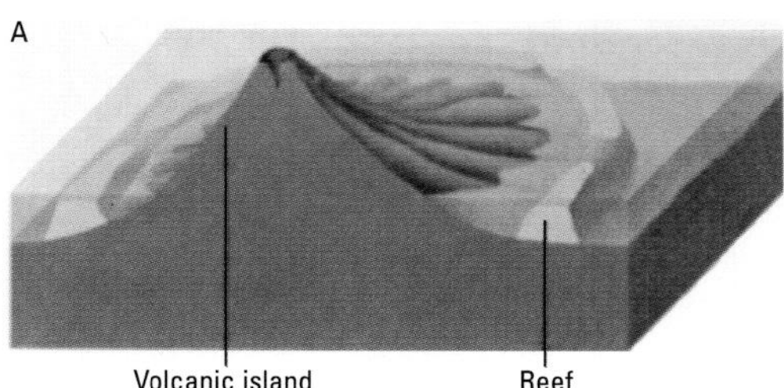

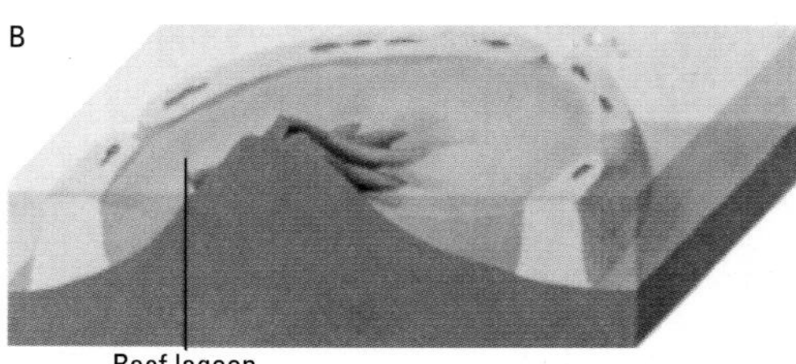

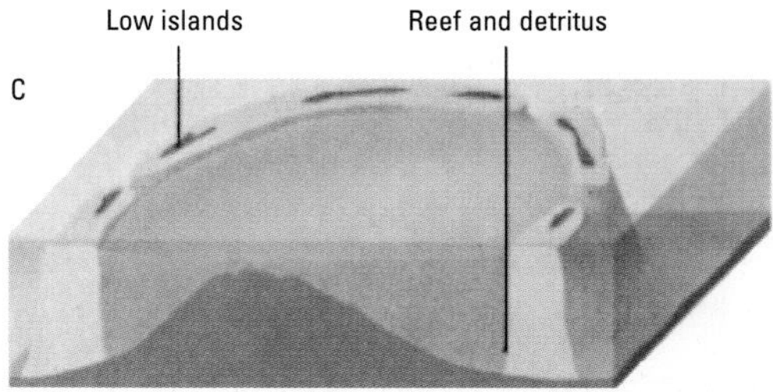

ABOVE The most intriguing of coral features, an atoll is a ring or horseshoe-shaped group of coral islands. Organisms with skeletons of calcium carbonate, corals grow in warm, fairly shallow water to depths of about 90m (300ft), but the depth of coral in many atolls is much greater than this.

The prevailing theory is that the coral began to form as a reef in the shallows of a volcanic island [A]. While the sea level began to rise and the island slowly sank [B], the coral growth kept pace with these gradual changes, leaving an atoll of hard limestone around its remnant [C]. In this way, coral can reach depths of up to 1,600m (5,250ft).

The world's largest atoll is Kwajalein in the Marshall Islands, in the central Pacific. Its slender 283-km (176-mile) coral reef encloses a lagoon of 2,850 sq km (1,100 sq miles).

RIGHT The seafloor consists of different zones, the most shallow being the continental shelf that lies between the coast and the 200m (650ft) depth contour. The shelf area occupies 7.5% of the seafloor and corresponds to the submerged portion of the continental crust. Beyond, the downward slope increases abruptly to form the continental slope (8.5%), an area that may be dissected by submarine canyons. The continental slope meets the abyssal basins at a more gentle incline (the continental rise). The basins lie at depths of 4,000m (13,200 ft) and feature mountain ranges and hills.

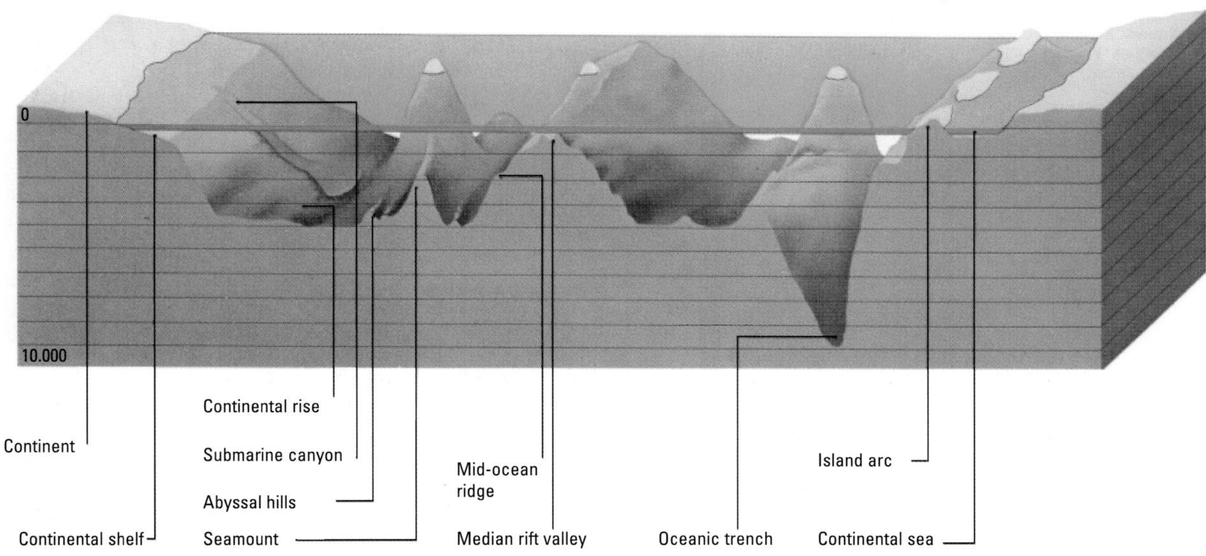

The Atmosphere and Clouds

The origin of the atmosphere was closely associated with the origin of the Earth. When the Earth was still a molten ball, it was probably surrounded by a large atmosphere of cosmic gases, including hydrogen, that were gradually lost into space. As the Earth began to develop a solid crust over a molten core, gases such as carbon dioxide, nitrogen and water vapour were slowly released to form an atmosphere with a composition not unlike the present emissions from volcanoes. Further cooling probably led to massive precipitation of water vapour – so that today it occupies less than 4% by volume of the atmosphere. At a much later stage, the oxygen content of the atmosphere was created by green plants releasing oxygen.

Extending from the Earth's surface far into space, the atmosphere is a meteor shield, a radiation deflector, a thermal blanket and a source of chemical energy for the Earth's diverse lifeforms. Five-sixths of its total mass is located in the first 15 km (9 miles), the troposphere, which is no thicker in relative terms than the skin of an onion. Almost all the phenomena we call the weather occur in this narrow layer.

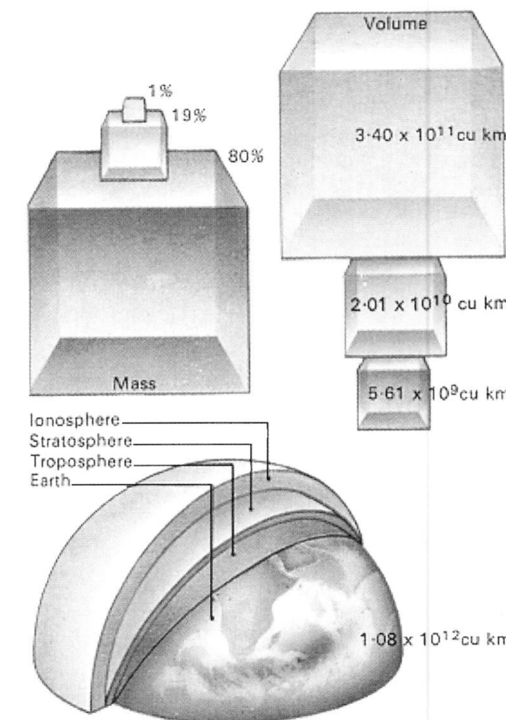

RIGHT Because air is easily compressed, the atmosphere becomes "squashed" by gravity. Thus the bulk of the atmosphere lies in the troposphere, occupying a volume of about 6 billion cu. km (1,560 million cu. miles). As air density decreases with altitude, the very much smaller amounts of air present in the stratosphere (19%) and the ionosphere and above (1%) occupy an increasingly greater volume.

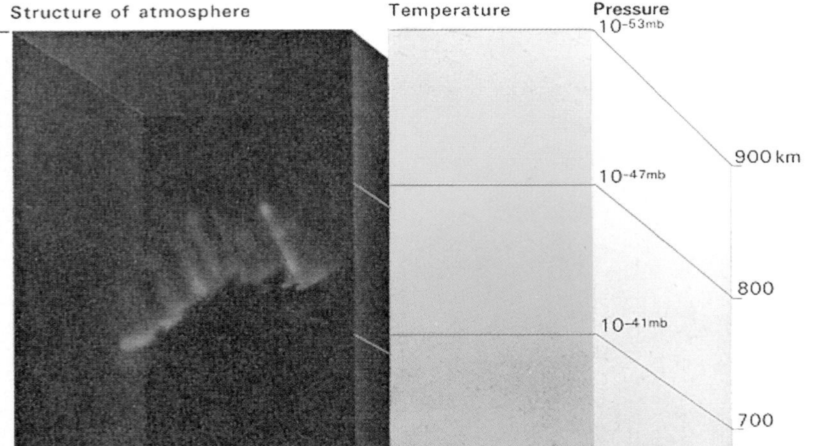

LEFT The discovery by British scientists of the hole in the ozone layer over Antarctica in 1985 triggered a growing interest in the structure of the atmosphere.

LAYERS OF THE ATMOSPHERE

1. EXOSHERE

The atmosphere's upper layer has no clear outer boundary, merging imperceptibly with interplanetary space. Its lower boundary, at an altitude of around 400km (250 miles), is almost equally vague. The exosphere is mainly composed of hydrogen and helium in changing proportions: helium vanishes with increasing altitude, and above 2,400km (1,500 miles) it is almost entirely hydrogen.

2. IONOSPHERE

Gas molecules in the ionosphere, mainly helium, oxygen and nitrogen, are ionized – electrically charged – by the Sun's radiation. Within the ionosphere's range of 50 to 400km (30 to 250 miles) they group themselves into four layers, known conventionally as D, E, F1 and F2, all of which can reflect radio waves of differing frequencies. The high energy of ionospheric gas gives it a notional temperature of more than 2000°C (3,600°F), although its density is negligible. The auroras – *aurora borealis* and its southern counterpart, *aurora australis* – occur in the ionosphere when charged particles from the Sun interact with the Earth's magnetic fields, at their strongest near the poles.

3. STRATOSPHERE

Separated at its upper and lower limits by the distinct thresholds of the stratopause and the tropopause, the stratosphere is a remarkably stable layer between about 15km and 50km (9 and 30 miles). Its temperature rises from –55°C (–67°F) at its lower extent to approximately 0°C (32°F) near the stratopause, where a thin layer of ozone – increasingly depleted with the acceleration in pollution by CFCs since the 1970s – absorbs ultraviolet radiation believed to cause skin cancer, cataracts and damage to the immune system in humans. Stratospheric air contains enough ozone to make it poisonous, although it is far too rarified to breathe. Overall, the stratopshere comprises 80% nitrogen, 18% oxygen, 1% argon and 1% ozone. "Mother-of-pearl" or nacreous cloud occurs at about 25km (15 miles).

4. TROPOSPHERE

The narrowest of all the atmospheric layers, the troposphere extends up to 15km (9 miles) at the Equator but only 8km (5 miles) at the poles. Since this thin region contains about 85% of the atmosphere's total mass and almost all of its water vapour, it is also the realm of the Earth's weather. Temperatures fall steadily with increasing height by about 1°C for every 100 metres (1.5°F for every 300 feet) above sea level. The main constituents are nitrogen (78%), oxygen (21%) and argon (1%).

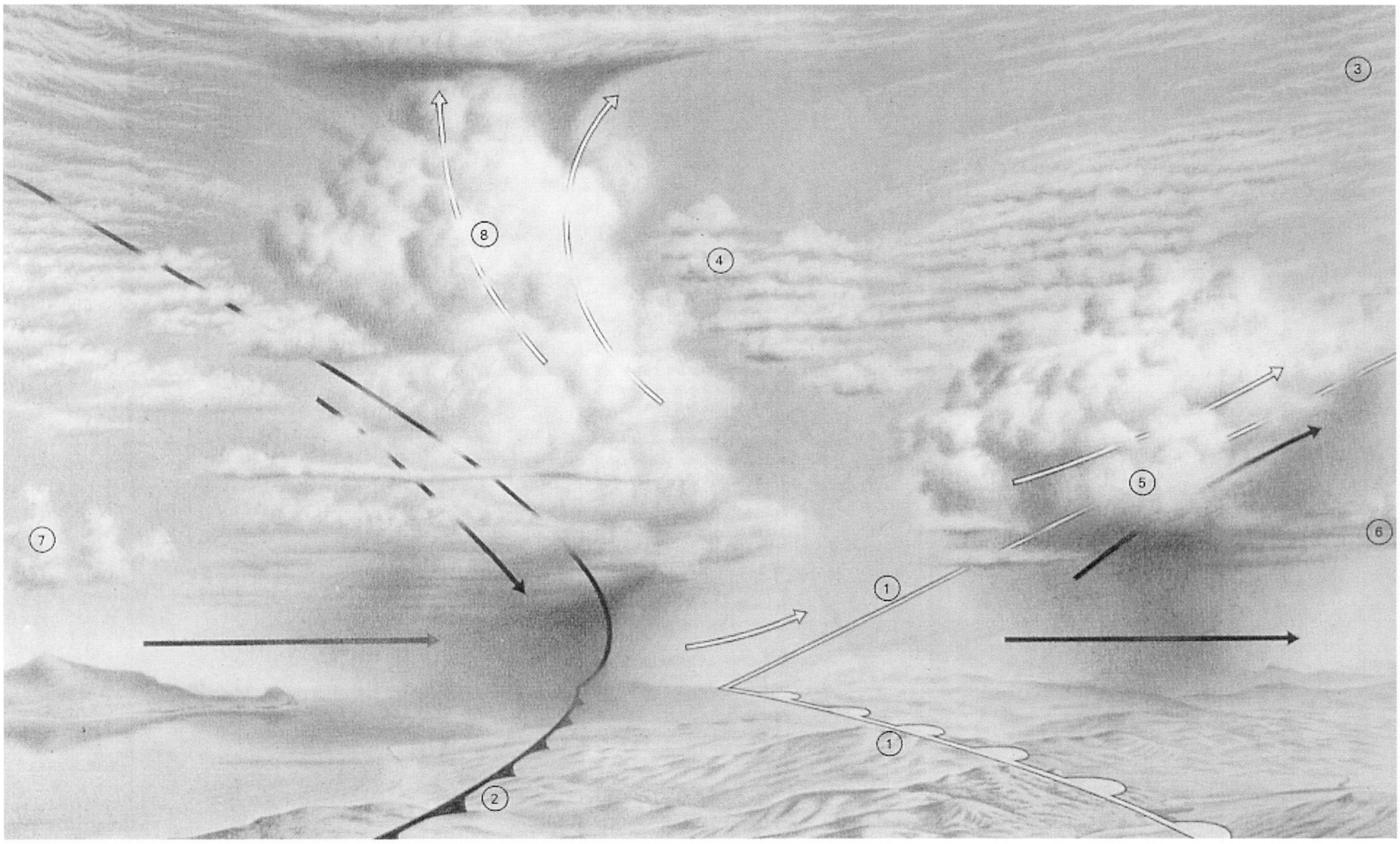

ABOVE The different cloud types are best illustrated within the context of the familiar mid-latitude frontal depression. Here a schematic, generalized Northern Hemisphere depression is viewed from the south as it moves eastwards, with both warm [1] and cold [2] fronts clearly visible. Over the warm front the air rises massively and slowly over the great depth of the atmosphere. This results in a fairly complete suite of layer-type clouds ranging from ice-crystal cirrus [3] and fluffy altocumulus [4] to grey-based nimbostratus [5].

The precipitation area often associated with such cloud types, and especially with nimbostratus, usually lies ahead of the surface warm front and roughly parallel to it [6]. Turbulence may cause some clouds to rise and produce heavy convective rainfall, as well as the generally lighter and more widespread classical warm front rainfall. Stratus often occupies the warm sector, but a marked change occurs at the cold front. Here the wind veers (blowing in a more clockwise direction) and cumulus clouds [7], brilliant white in sunlight, are often found in the cold air behind the front.

At the front itself the atmosphere is often unstable and cumulus clouds grow into dramatic cumulonimbus formations [8]. The canopy of cirrus clouds – of all types – may extend over the whole depression and is often juxtaposed with the anvil shape of the nimbus. These cloud changes are accompanied by changes in pressure, wind temperature and humidity as the fronts pass.

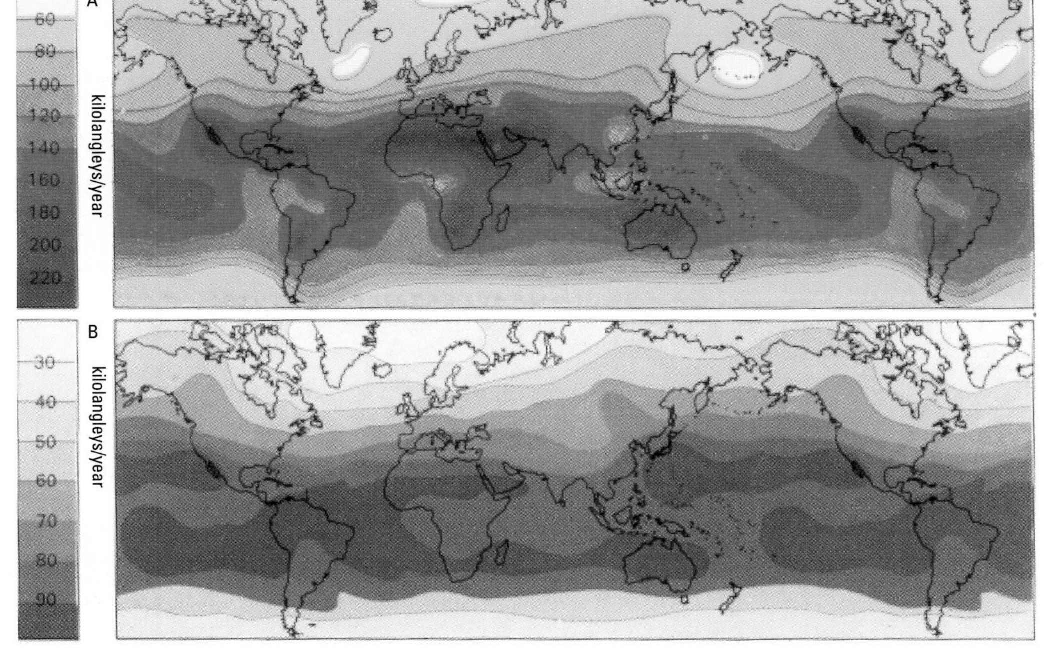

LEFT Temperatures in the atmosphere and on Earth result mainly from a balance of radiation inputs and outputs. Average annual solar radiation reaching the Earth, measured in kilolangleys – one calorie absorbed per sq cm (0.15 sq in) is highest in hot desert areas [A].

Comparison with the average annual long-wave radiation back from the Earth's surface [B] shows an overall surplus radiation for nearly all latitudes, but this is absorbed in the atmosphere and then lost in space, ensuring an overall balance. The extreme imbalance of incoming radiation between equatorial and polar latitudes is somewhat equalized through heat transfers by atmosphere and oceans. This balancing transfer between surplus and deficit radiation is greatest in mid-latitudes, where most cyclones and anticyclones occur.

WINDS AND THE WEATHER

WIND IS the movement of air, and large-scale air movements, both horizontal and vertical, are crucial in shaping weather and climate. The chief forces affecting horizontal air movements are pressure gradients and the Coriolis effect.

Pressure gradients are caused by the unequal heating of the atmosphere by the Sun. Warm equatorial air is lighter and therefore has a lower pressure than cold, dense, polar air. The strength of air movement from areas of high to low pressure – known as the pressure gradient – is proportional to the difference in pressure.

Along the Equator is a region called the doldrums, where the Sun's heat warms the rising air. This air eventually spreads out and flows north and south away from the Equator. It finally sinks at about 30°N and 30°S, creating subtropical high-pressure belts (the horse latitudes), from which trade winds flow back towards the Equator and westerlies flow towards the mid-latitudes.

The Coriolis effect is the deflection of winds caused by the Earth's rotation, to the right in the Northern Hemisphere and to the left in the Southern. As a result, winds don't flow directly from the point of highest pressure to the lowest; those approaching a low-pressure system are deflected round it rather than flowing directly into it. This creates air systems, with high or low pressure, in which winds circulate round the centre. Horizontal air movements are important around cyclonic (low-pressure) and anticyclonic (high-pressure) systems. Horizontal and vertical movements combine to create a pattern of prevailing global winds.

Weather and depressions

To most of us "weather" means rain and sunshine, heat and cold, clouds and wind. Humidity and visibility might be added to the list. If not precise in terminology, this layman's catalogue comprises the six main elements which also comprise weather for meteorologists: in their language they are precipitation, air temperature, cloud cover, wind velocity, humidity and barometric pressure.

Depressions occur when warm air flows into waves in a polar front while cold air flows in behind it, creating rotating air systems that bring changeable weather. Along the warm front (the boundary on the ground between the warm and cold air), the warm air flows upwards over the cold air, producing a sequence of clouds that help forecasters predict a depression's advance.

Along the cold front the advancing cold air forces warm air to rise steeply, and towering cumulonimbus clouds form in the rising air. When the cold front overtakes the warm front, the warm air is pushed up to form an occluded front. Cloud and rain persist along occlusions until temperatures equalize, the air mixes, and the depression dies out.

BELOW The world's zones of high and low pressure are both areas of comparative calm, but between them lie the belts of prevailing winds. West of Africa, wind patterns are remarkably constant between summer and winter, but in much of the east variations are caused by monsoons (reversals of wind flows) stemming in part from the unequal heating of land masses and the sea.

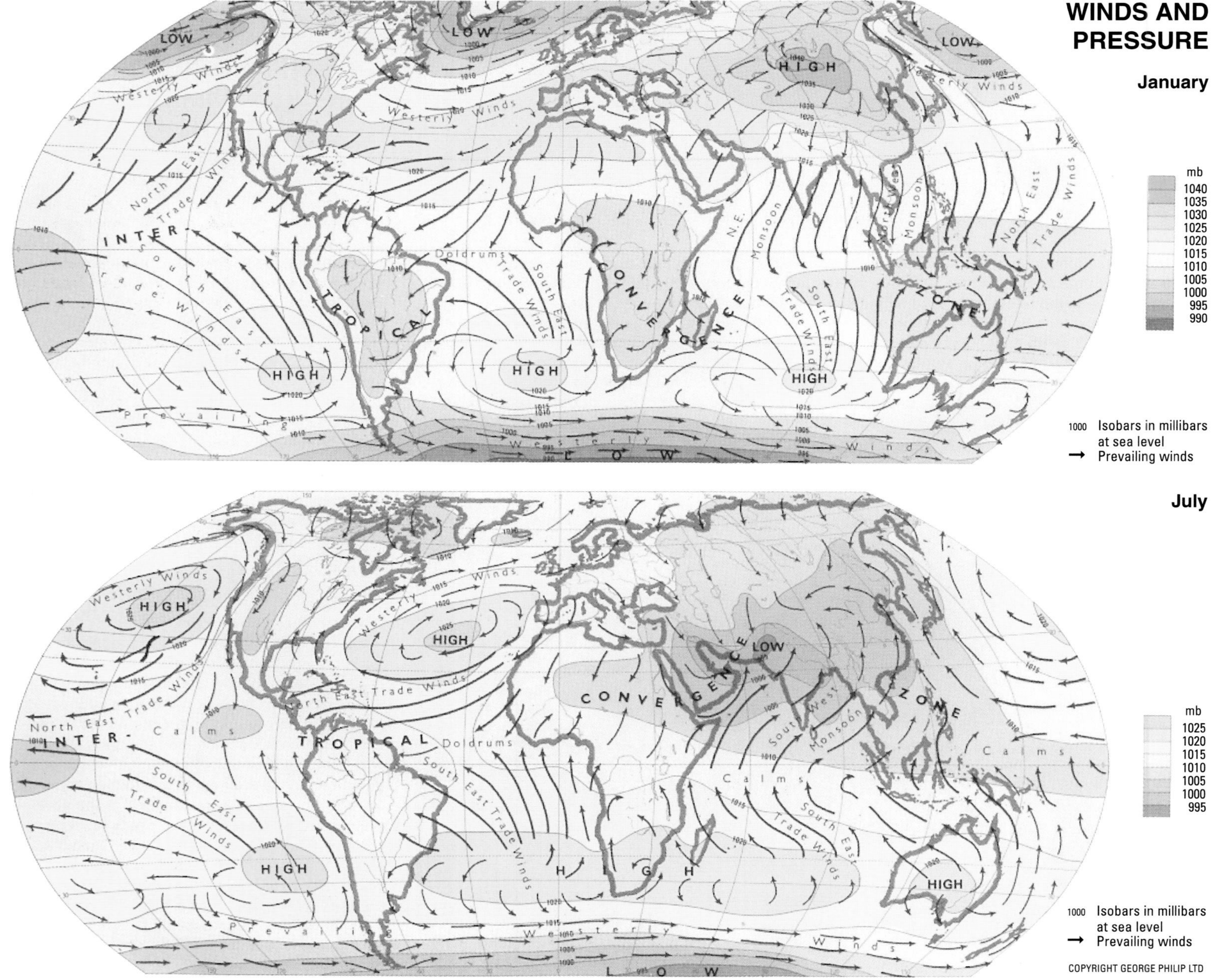

Warm air
Cool air
Cold air
Warm front
Cold front
H = High pressure
L = Low pressure

ABOVE The Earth's atmosphere acts as a giant heat engine. The temperature differences between the poles and the Equator provide the thermal energy to drive atmospheric circulation, both horizontal and vertical. In general, warm air at the Equator rises and moves towards the poles at high levels and cold polar air moves towards the Equator at low levels to replace it. Air also flows north and south from the high-pressure belts called the horse latitudes, and these airflows meet up with cold, dense air flowing from the poles along the polar front.

The basic global pattern of prevailing winds is complicated by the rotation of the Earth (which causes the Coriolis effect), by cells of high-pressure and low-pressure systems (depressions) and by the distribution and configuration of land and sea.

Climate Records

Highest barometric pressure: Agata, Siberia [at altitude of 262m (862ft)] 1,083.8 millibars, 31 December 1968.

Lowest barometric pressure: Typhoon Tip, 480km (300 miles) west of Guam, Pacific Ocean, 870 millibars, 12 October 1979.

Highest recorded wind speed: Mt Washington, New Hampshire, USA, 371km/h (231 mph), 12 April 1934; this is three times as strong as hurricane force on the Beaufort scale.

Worst recorded storm: Bangladesh (then East Pakistan) cyclone, 13 November 1970 – over 300,000 dead or missing; the 1991 cyclone in Bangladesh killed an estimated 138,000 people.

Worst recorded tornado: Missouri/Illinois/Indiana, USA, 18 March 1925 – 792 deaths; the tornado was only 275m (900ft) across.

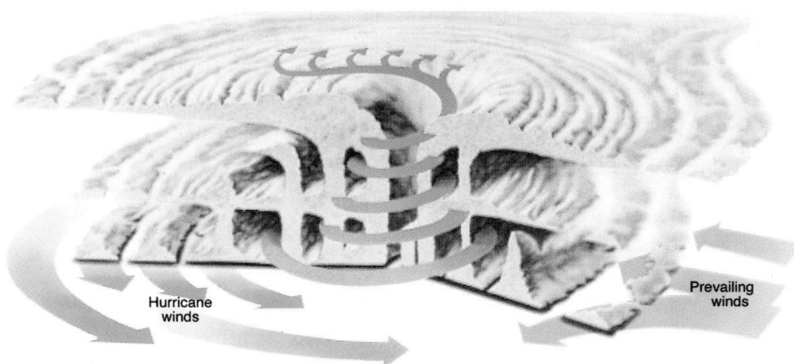

ABOVE Hurricanes consist of a huge swirl of clouds rotating round a calm centre – the "eye" – where warm air is sucked down. Hurricanes may be 400km (250 miles) in diameter and they extend through the troposphere, which is about 15-20km (9-12 miles) thick. Clouds, mainly cumulonimbus, are arranged in bands round the eye, the tallest forming the wall of the eye. Cirrus clouds usually cap the hurricane.

JANUARY

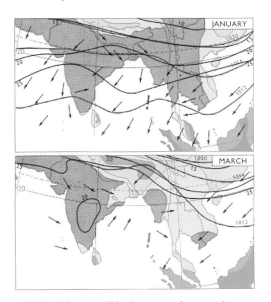

MARCH

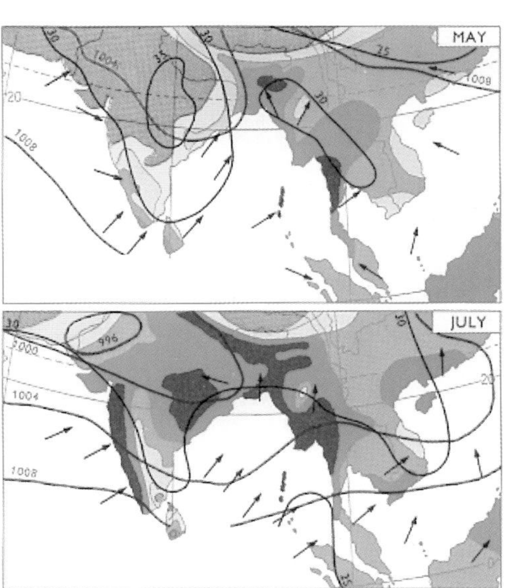

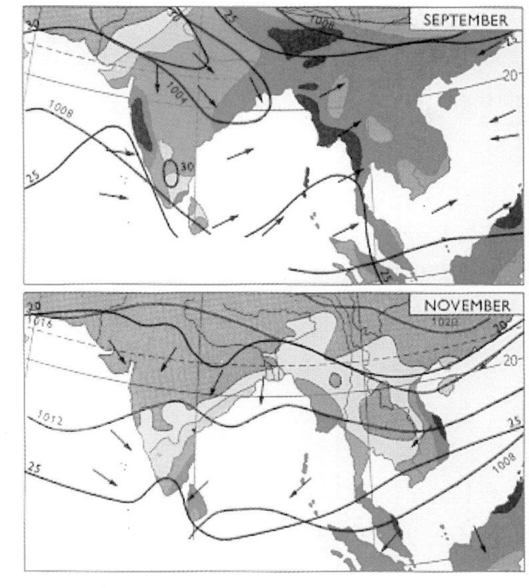

ABOVE "Monsoon" is the term given to the seasonal reversal of wind direction, most noticeably in South and Southeast Asia, where it results in very heavy rains. In January a weak anticyclone in northern India gives the clear skies brought by northeasterly winds; in March temperatures increase and the anticyclone subsides, sea breezes bringing rain to coastal areas; by May the north is hot and a low pressure area begins to form, while the south is cooler with some rain; in July the low-pressure system over India caused by high temperatures brings the Southwest Monsoon from the high-pressure area in the south Indian Ocean; in September the Southwest Monsoon – with its strong winds, cloud cover, rain and cool temperatures – begins to retreat from the northwest; by the end of the cycle in November the subcontinent is cool and dry, though still wet in the southeast.

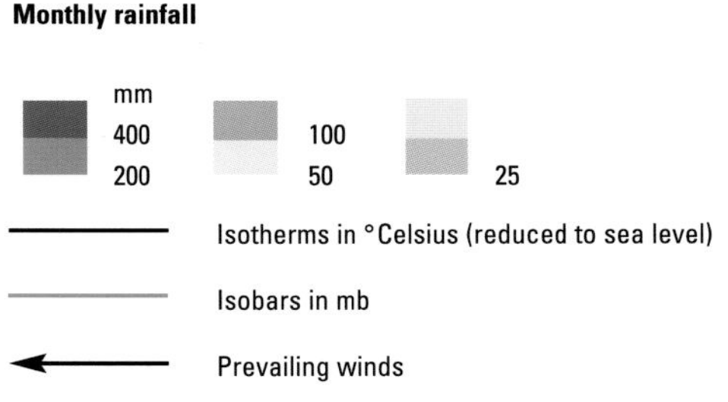

WORLD CLIMATE

CLIMATE IS weather in the longer term, the seasonal pattern of hot and cold, wet and dry, averaged over time. Its passage is marked by a ceaseless churning of the atmosphere and the oceans, further agitated by the Earth's rotation and the motion it imparts to moving air and water.

There are many classifications of world climate, but most are based on a system developed in the early 19th century by the Russian meteorologist Vladimir Köppen. Basing his divisions on two main features, temperature and precipitation, and using a code of letters, he identified five main climatic types: tropical (A), dry (B), warm temperate (C), cool temperate (D) and cold (E). Each of these main regions was then further subdivided. (A highland mountain category was added later to account for the variety of climatic zones found in mountainous areas due to changes caused by altitude.)

Although latitude is a major factor in determining climate, other factors add to the complexity. These include the influence of ocean currents, different rates of heating and cooling of land and ocean, distance from the sea, and the effect of mountains on winds. New York, Naples and the Gobi Desert all share the same latitude, for example, but their climates are very different.

Climates are not stable indefinitely. Our planet regularly passes through cool periods – Ice Ages probably caused by the recurring long-term oscillations in the Earth's orbital path from almost circular to elliptical every 95,000 years, variations in the Earth's tilt from 21½° to 24½° every 42,000 years, and perhaps even fluctuations in the Sun's energy output. In the present era, the Earth is closest to the Sun in the middle of winter in the Northern Hemisphere and furthest away in summer; 12,000 years ago, at the height of the last Ice Age, northern winter fell with the Sun at its most distant.

Studies of these cycles suggest that we are now

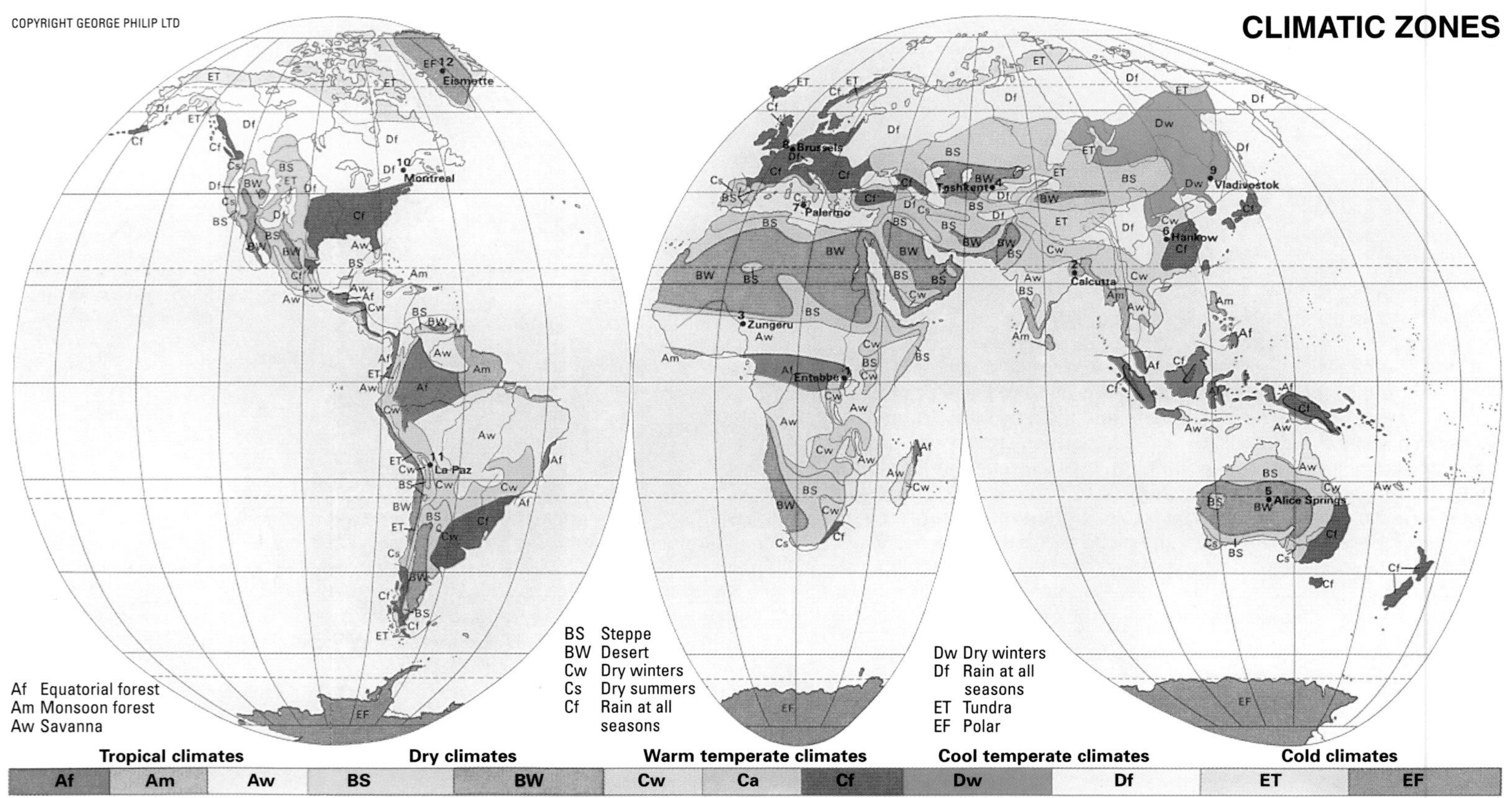

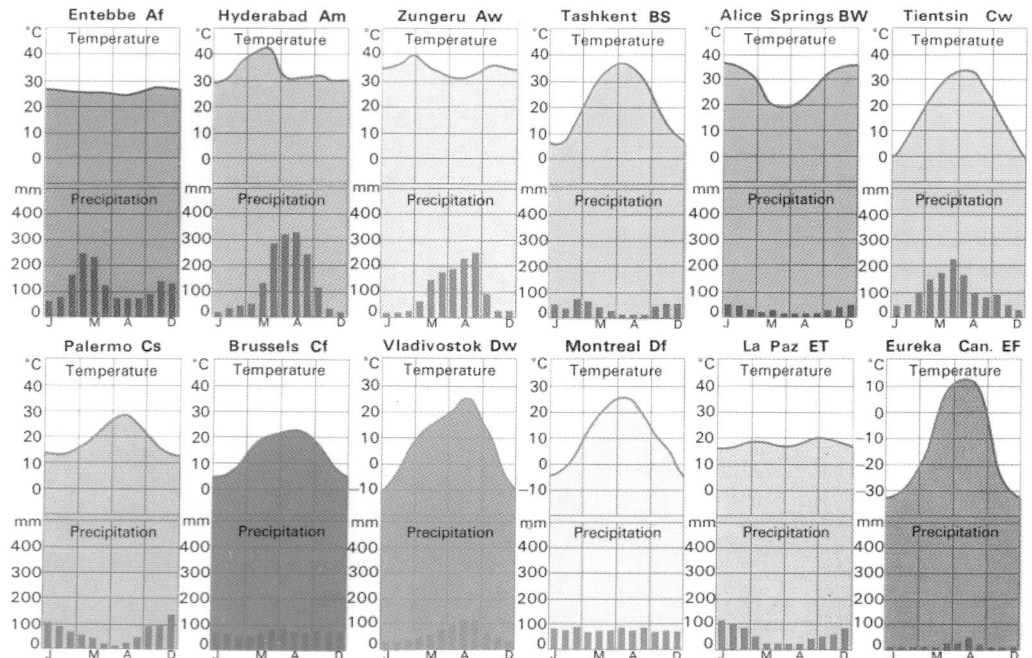

CLIMATE TERMS

Cyclone: Violent storm called a hurricane in N. America and a typhoon in the Far East.
Depression: Area of low pressure.
Frost: Dew when the air temperature falls below freezing point.
Hail: Frozen rain.
Humidity: Amount of moisture in the air.
Isobar: Line on a map connecting places of equal atmospheric pressure.
Isotherm: Line on a map connecting places of equal temperatutre.
Precipitation: Measurable amounts of rain, snow, sleet or hail.
Rain: Precipitation of liquid particles with diameter larger than 0.5mm (0.02 in); under this size is classified as drizzle.
Sleet: Partially melted snow.
Snow: Crystals formed when water vapour condenses below freezing point.
Tornado: Severe funnel-shaped storm that twists as hot air spins vertically; called a waterspout at sea.

in an interglacial period, but with a new glacial period on the way. For the forseeable future, however, the planet is likely to continue heating up because of global warming, caused largely by the burning of fossil fuels and deforestation. Figures show that average temperatures rose 1.7°C (0.9°F) in the 20th century, with most of that increase coming after about 1970, and despite attempts to stabilize the situation it's likely that the trend will continue. Such changes would not redraw Köppen's divisions, but they would make a significant difference to many local climates, with a dramatic effect on everything from agriculture to architecture.

Climate Records

TEMPERATURE

Highest recorded shade temperature: Al Aziziyah, Libya, 58°C (136.4°F), 13 Sep. 1922.

Highest mean annual temperature: Dallol, Ethiopia, 34.4°C (94°F), 1960-66.

Longest heatwave: Marble Bar, Western Australia, 162 days over 37.8°C (100°F), 23 October 1923 to 7 April 1924.

Lowest recorded temperature: Vostock Station, Eastern Antarctica, 21 July 1985, –89.2°C (–128.6°F)

(Lowest recorded temperature (outside poles): Verkhoyansk, Siberia, –68°C (–90°F), 6 February 1933.

Lowest mean annual temperature: Plateau Station, Antarctica, –56.6°C (–72.0°F).

PRECIPITATION

Longest drought: Calama, N. Chile – no recorded rainfall in 400 years to 1971.

Wettest place (12 months): Cherrapunji, Meghalaya, NE. India, 26,470mm (1,040 in), August 1860 to August 1861; Cherrapunji also holds the record for the most rainfall in a month: 2,930mm (115 in), July 1861.

Wettest place (average): Tututendo, Colombia, mean annual rainfall of 11,770mm (463.4 in).

Wettest place (24 hours): Cilaos, Réunion, Indian Ocean, 1,870mm (73.6 in), 15-16 March 1952.

Heaviest hailstones: Gopalganj, Bangladesh, up to 1.02kg (2.25lb), 14 April 1986 (92 people were killed).

Heaviest snowfall (continuous): Bessans, Savoie, France, 1,730mm (68 in) in 19 hours, 5-6 April 1969.

Heaviest snowfalls (season/year): Paradise Ranger Station, Mt Rainier, Washington, USA, 31,102mm (1,224.5 in), 19 February 1971 to 18 February 1972.

Conversions

°C = (°F -32) x 5/9; °F = (°C x 9/5) + 32; 0°C = 32°F

1 mm = 0.0394 in (100 mm = 3.94 in); 1 in = 25.4 mm

TEMPERATURE

Average temperature in January

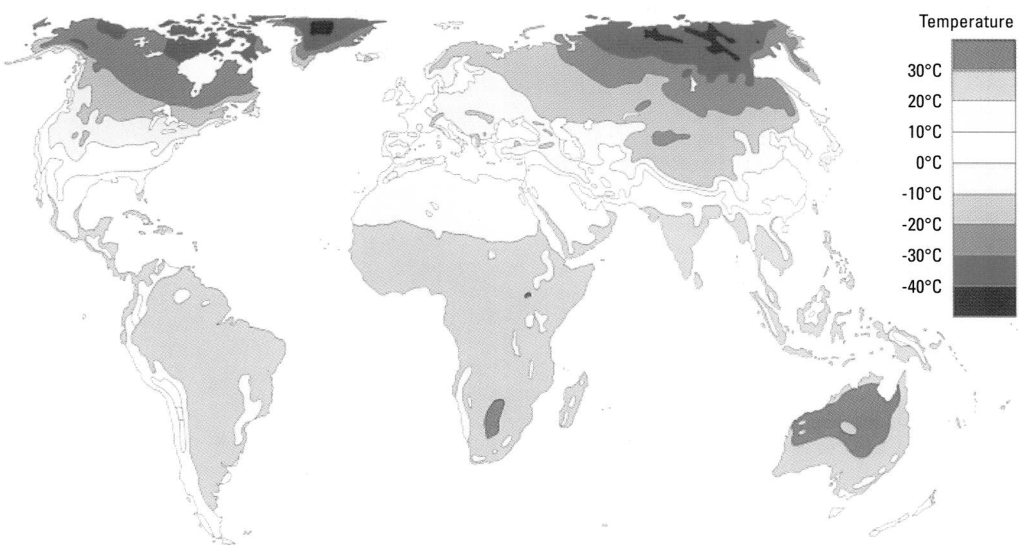

Average temperature in July

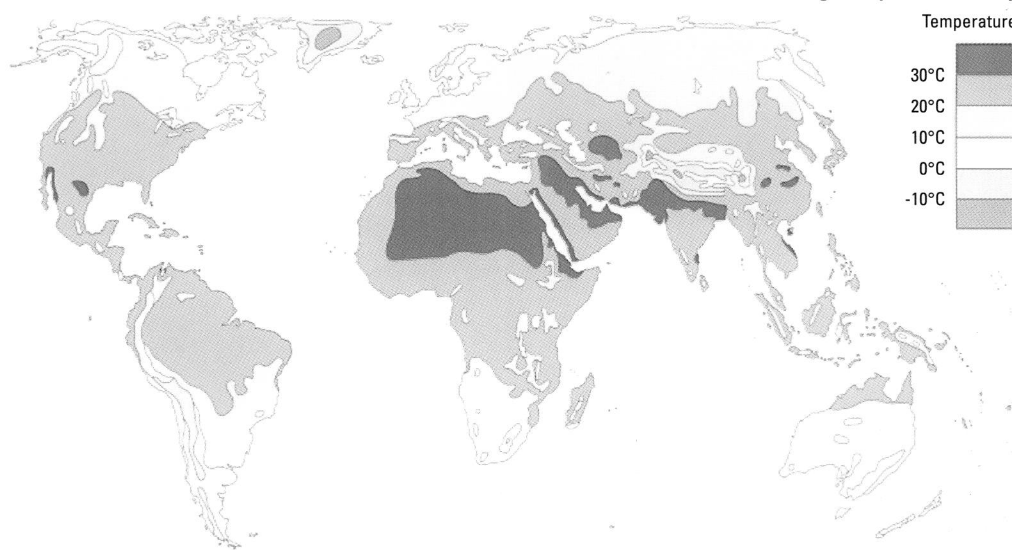

RAINFALL

Average annual precipitation

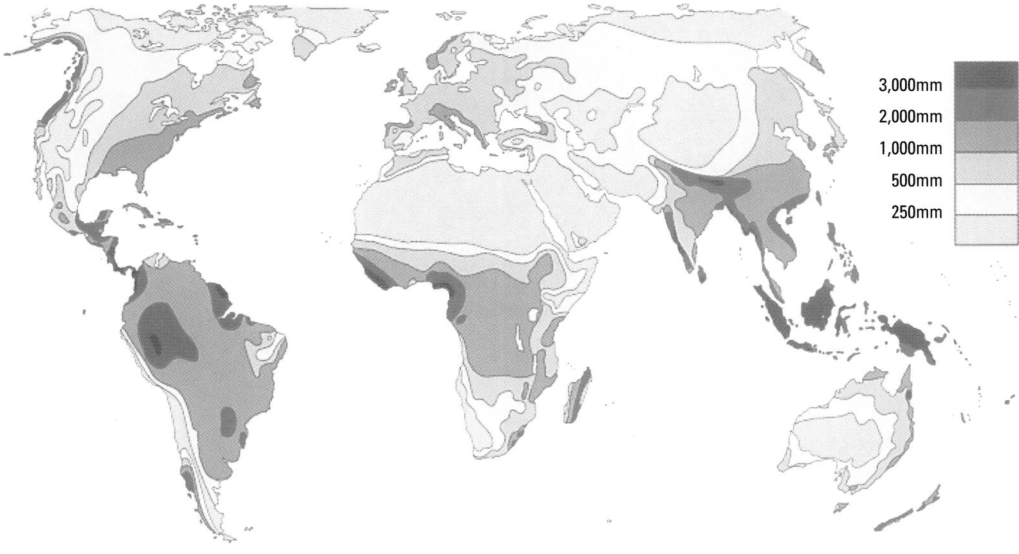

THE WORLD'S WATER

FRESH WATER is essential to all life on Earth, from the humblest bacterium to the most advanced technological society. Yet freshwater resources form a minute fraction of our 1.36 billion cu. km (326 million cu. miles) of water: most human needs must be met from the 2,000 cu. km (480 cu. miles) circulating in rivers.

Agriculture accounts for huge quantities: without large-scale irrigation, most of the world's people would starve. Since fresh water is just as essential for most industrial processes, the combination of growing population and advancing industry has put supplies under increasing strain.

Fortunately water is seldom used up: the planet's water cycle circulates it efficiently, at least on a global scale. More locally, however, human activity can cause severe shortages: water for industry and agriculture is being withdrawn from many river basins and underground aquifers faster than natural recirculation can replace it – a process exacerbated by global warming.

The demand for water has led to tensions between an increasing number of nations as supplies are diverted or hoarded. Both Iraq and Syria, for example, have protested at Turkey's dam-building programme, which they claim drastically reduces the flow of Tigris and Euphrates water to their land.

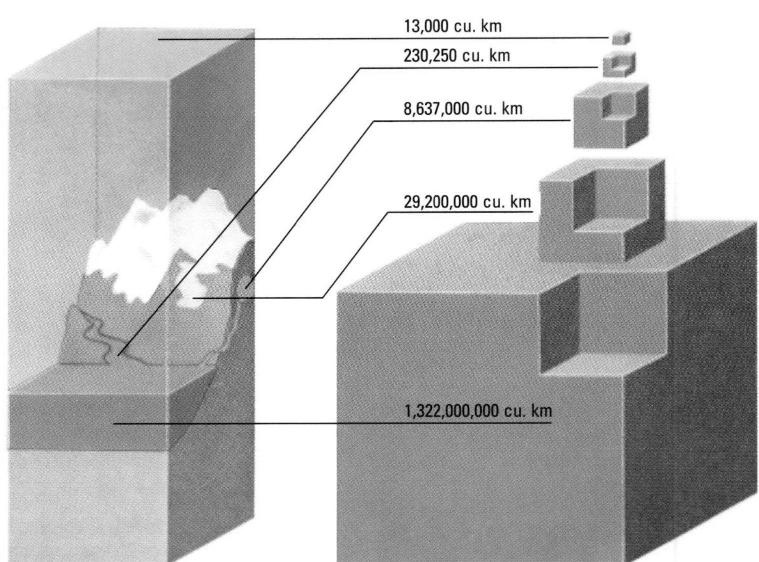

RIGHT Over 97% of the world's water is accounted for by the oceans. Of the total water on land more than 75% is frozen in icesheets and glaciers. Most of the rest, about 22%, is water collected below the Earth's surface (ground water). Relatively small quantities are in lakes and rivers (0.017% of the total), while water vapour represents only 0.001%. Without this, however, there would be no life on land.

The water cycle

Oceanic water is salty and unsuitable for drinking or farming. In some desert regions, where fresh sources are in short supply, seawater is desalinated to make fresh water, but most of the world is constantly supplied with fresh water by the natural process of the water or hydrological cycle, which relies on the action of two factors: gravity and the Sun's heat.

Over the oceans, which cover almost 71% of the Earth's surface, the Sun's heat causes evaporation, and water vapour rises on air currents and winds. Some of this vapour condenses and returns directly to the oceans as rain, but because of the circulation of the atmosphere, air bearing large amounts is carried over land, where it falls as rain or snow.

Much of this precipitation is quickly re-evaporated by the Sun. Some soaks into the soil, where it is absorbed by plants and partly returned to the air through transpiration; some flows over the land surface as run-off, which flows into streams and rivers; and some rain and melted snow seeps through the soil into the rocks beneath to form ground water.

In polar and high mountainous regions most precipitation is in the form of snow. There it is compacted into ice, forming icesheets and glaciers. The force of gravity causes these bodies of ice to move downwards and outwards, and they may eventually return to the oceans where chunks of ice break off at the coastline to form icebergs. Thus all the water that does not return directly to the atmosphere gradually returns to the sea to complete the water cycle. This continual movement of water and ice plays a major part in the erosion of land areas.

Of the total water on land, more than 75% is frozen in icesheets and glaciers, and two-thirds of all the Earth's fresh water is held in Antarctica. Twice the size of Australia, this frozen continent contains ice to depths of 3,500m (11,500ft) and land is covered in ice to an average depth of more than 2,000m (6,500ft). However, Antarctica receives very little precipitation, not even in the form of snow. It is, effectively, a polar desert.

Most of the rest of the water on land (about 22%) is collected below the Earth's surface and is called ground water; comparatively small but crucially important quantities are in lakes, rivers and in the soil. Water that is held in the soil and that nourishes plant growth is called capillary water: it is retained in the upper few metres by molecular attraction between the water and soil particles.

BELOW The water or hydrological cycle is the process whereby water, in its various forms, circulates from the oceans to land areas and back again. Fresh water is present on the Earth as water vapour in the atmosphere, as ice, and as liquid water.

The elements of the cycle are precipitation as rain [3], surface run-off [4], evaporation of rain in falling [5], ground water flow to rivers and streams [6], ground water flow to the oceans [7], transpiration from plants [8], evaporation from lakes and ponds [9], evaporation from the soil [10], evaporation from rivers and streams [11], evaporation from the oceans [13], flow of rivers and streams to the oceans [12], ground water flow from the oceans to arid land [16], intense evaporation from arid land [17], movement of moist air from and to the oceans [14,15], precipitation as snow [2], and ice-flow into the seas and oceans [1].

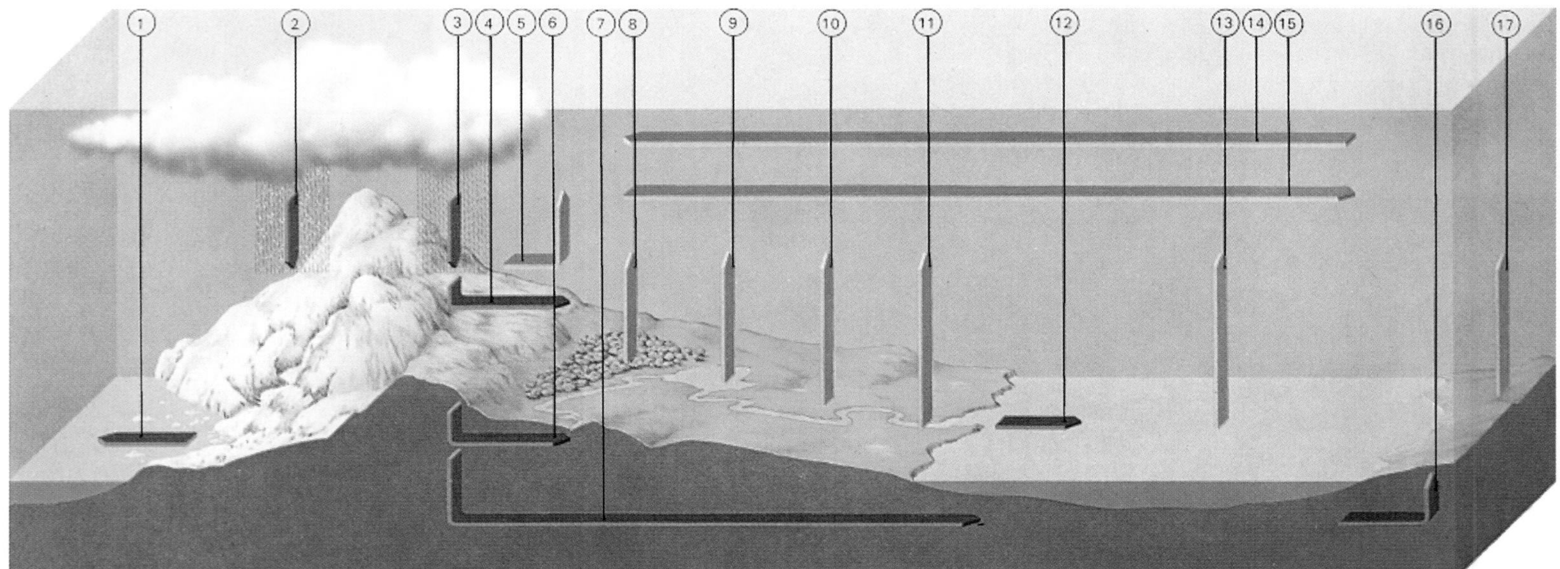

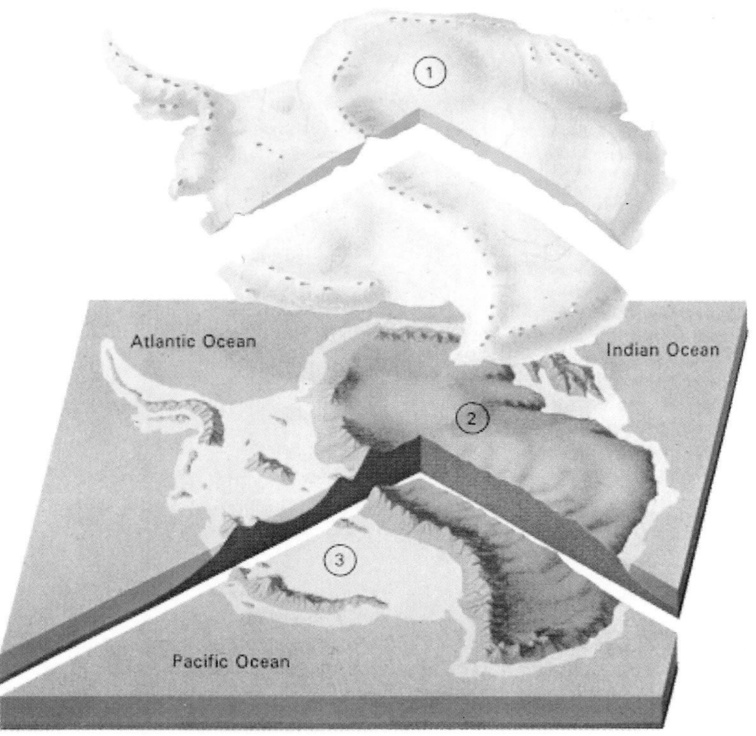

ABOVE While 75% of the world's fresh water is frozen, continental ice-sheets are now found only in Antarctica and Greenland. In Antarctica the ice [1] covers the land [2] but also permanently frozen sea [3]. Beneath the ice the terrain is rugged and variable in height, but because of the weight of the ice, about 40% of the land is depressed below sea level.

BELOW Almost all our water supply is 3 billion years old, and all of it cycles endlessly through the hydrosphere, though at very different rates. Water vapour circulates over days, even hours, and deep ocean water over millennia, while icecap water remains solid for millions of years.

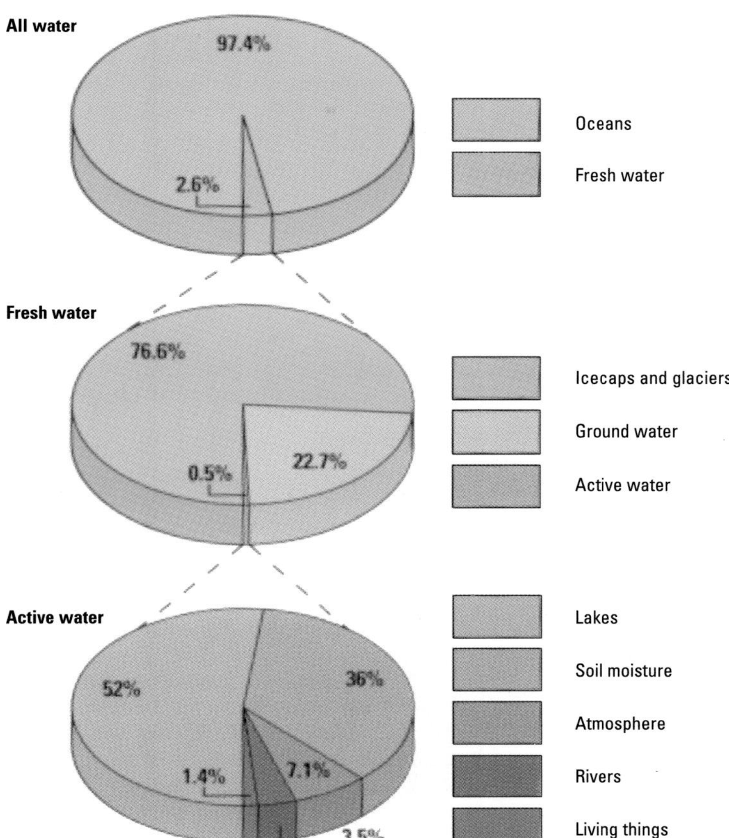

BELOW Ice in the form of icesheets and glaciers now covers 10% of the world's land area, but during the last glacial period, between about 110,000 and 10,000 years ago, icesheets covered up to 30% of the land. At periods of maximum glaciation, sea levels were 180m (600ft) lower than at the present time because of the large amount of water frozen in the ice. Many of today's islands were joined to adjacent continental masses: the British Isles, for example, would have been part of Europe.

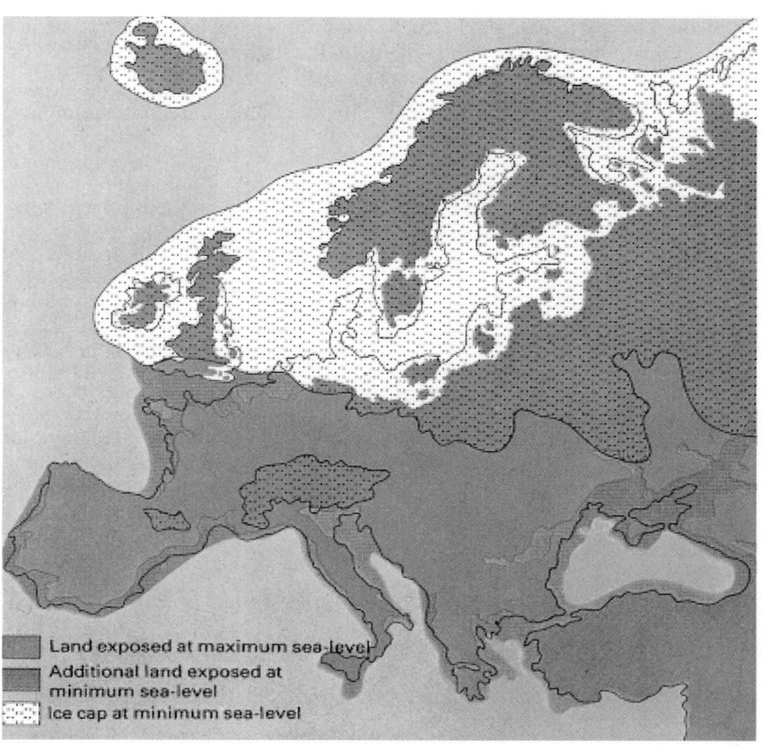

BELOW Rivers are the most visible part of the water cycle. The drainage pattern of a river and its tributaries is related primarily to the type of rocks on which it formed or flows. On rocks of equal or similar resistance (A), a dendritic pattern develops; in areas of alternating hard and soft rock (B), the water follows the softer rock to form a trellis pattern; and a radial pattern (C), forms on and around and rock domes and volcanoes.

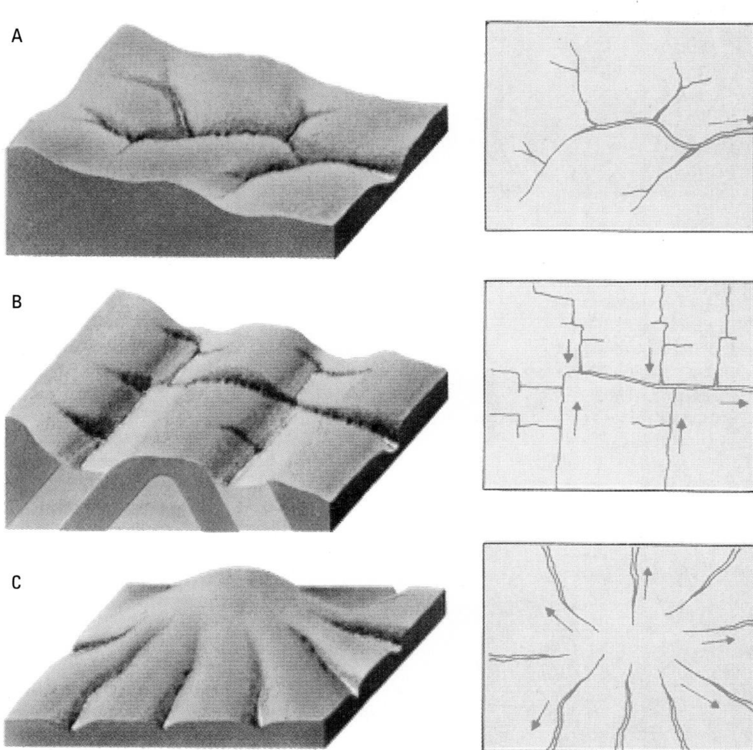

UNDERGROUND WATER

BELOW Gushes or seepages of water, springs are found where the water table or an aquifer appears at the surface, or where the aquifer is blocked by an impermeable rock such as a volcanic dyke. Spring water is usually fresh and clean because it passes through porous rocks.

Springs can occur where a fault brings an aquifer into contact with an impermeable layer [A]; where water pressure creates artesian springs at points of weakness [B]; where water seeps through jointed limestone until it emerges above an impermeable layer [C]; or where permeable strata overlay impermeable rock. An impermeable barrier may lead to the formation of a spring line [E].

A

B

C

D

E

GROUND WATER enters permeable rocks through what is called the zone of intermittent saturation, a layer that may retain water after continued rain but which soon dries up. Beneath this lies a rock zone where the pores or crevices are filled with water. Called the zone of saturation, this usually begins within 30m (100ft) of the surface, extending downwards until it reaches impermeable rock, through which it cannot percolate, lying below the water-holding layer (aquifer). The top of the saturated zone is the water table which, despite its name, is not level. It is often arched under hills, while beneath the softer rocks of plains it generally lies closer to the surface. The water table also varies in level during the year, depending on the amount of rainfall. In some places the water table intersects the surface, forming features such as oases in desert hollows, lakes, swamps and springs. Some springs

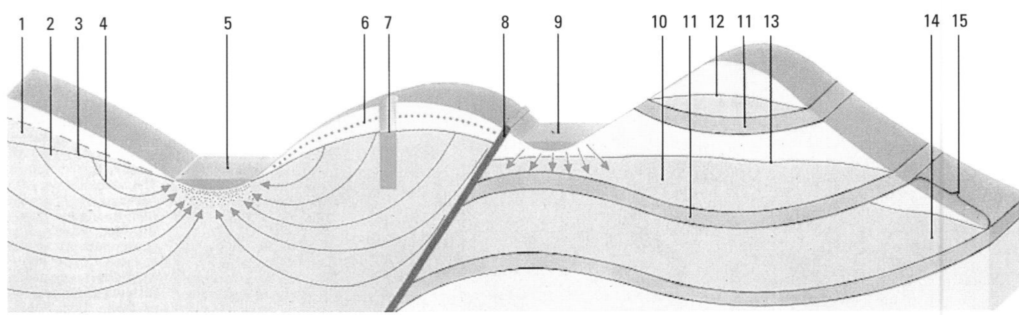

ABOVE Ground water seeps through the zone of intermittent saturation [1] until it reaches an impermeable layer, above which it forms the zone of saturation or aquifer [2,10]. The upper surface of the aquifer forms the water table [3,13], above which is the capillary fringe [6]. Because the capillary fringe is not saturated, wells [7] must be sunk to the water table.

Impermeable dikes [8] block the flow of ground water. In uniform material the water follows paths [4] that curve down and up again towards the nearest stream. If an aquifer is part of a series of strata including several impermeable layers [11], a "perched" water table [12] may result; if it lies between two impermeable strata it is said to be "confined" [14].

The recharge area [15] of the water table is where water enters the confined aquifer. A stream below the water table is called a gaining stream [5], while a stream flowing above it is known as a losing stream [9] because it loses water by seepage.

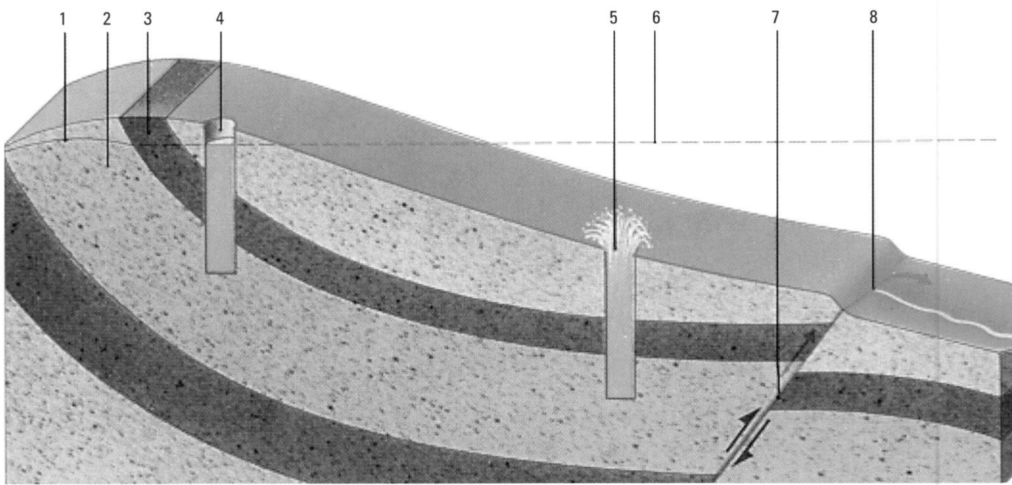

ABOVE The lowest level of the water table, reached at the driest time of the year, is called the permanent water table, and wells must be drilled to this depth if they are to guarantee a supply of water throughout the seasons.

Artesian springs and wells are found where ground water is under pressure, and in artesian wells water is forced to the surface by hydrostatic pressure. The water table [1] in the confined aquifer [2] lies near the top of the dipping layers. A well [4] drilled through the top impervious layer [3] is not an artesian well because the head of hydrostatic pressure [6] is not sufficient to force water to the surface; in such wells the water must be pumped or drawn to the surface.

The top of an artesian well [5] lies below the level of the head of hydrostatic pressure and so water gushes to the surface. Artesian springs [8] may occur along joints or faults [7] where the head of hydrostatic pressure is sufficient to force the water up along the fault.

Areas with artesian wells are called artesian basins. Artesian water is obtained from porous sandstone aquifers that underlie the Great Basin of Australia, which are supplied with water from rain that falls on the Eastern Highlands of Queensland and New South Wales. In the London and Paris artesian basins the water has been so heavily tapped in recent centuries that the water level has dropped below the level of the well-heads.

contain so much mineral substance in solution that their water is used for medicinal purposes and spa towns have grown up around them.

While sandstone is a highly porous rock through which water percolates easily, limestone is a permeable but non-porous rock. Ground water can seep through its maze of joints, fissures and caves, with apertures enlarged by the chemical action of rainwater containing dissolved carbon dioxide.

BELOW Limestone surfaces are often eroded into blocks called clints [1]. Surface streams flow into dissolved sink-holes [2] that lead to a deep chimney [3]; pot-holes [7] are dry chimneys. Gours [4] are ridges formed as carbonate is precipitated from turbulent water. Streams flow at the lowest level of the galleries [17], and abandoned galleries [13] are common. A siphon [12] occurs where the roof is below water level. Streams reappear at resurgences [20], and abandoned resurgences [19] may provide entrances to caves.

Stalactites [5] include macaroni stalactites [6], curtain stalactites or drapes [11] and "eccentric" stalactites [16], formed by water being blown sideways; stalagmites [14] sometimes have a fir-cone shape [15] caused by splashing, or resemble stacked plates [8]. Stalactites and stalagmites may also merge to form columns [10]. Signs of ancient humans [18] have been found in many caves, and they still harbour a variety of animal life adapted to the environment, including colourless shrimps and sightless newts – often called blind fish – which live in the dark pools [9].

Rain coming off the Atlantic Ocean and Mediterreanean Sea and falling on the Atlas Mountains of Morocco and Algeria then drains into porous rocks underlying the northern parts of the Sahara Desert. The water seeps through these rocks which, wherever they come to the surface, give rise to fertile oases.

BELOW As rain falls, it dissolves carbon dioxide from the atmosphere and becomes a weak carbonic acid that attacks carbonate rock (limestone and dolomite) by transforming it into the soluble bicarbonate. Carbonate rocks are criss-crossed by vertical cracks and horizontal breaks along bedding planes [A]. Some geologists believe the caves were formed when the rock was saturated by water; others reckon they formed gradually by solution [B] into a major cave network [C]. Limestone caves contain many features formed from calcium carbonate.

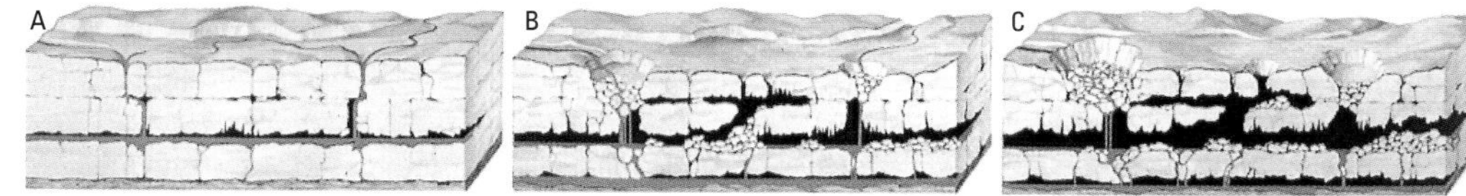

VEGETATION AND SOIL

THE DISTRIBUTION of natural resources over the Earth's surface is far from even. The whereabouts of mineral deposits depends on random events in a remote geological past, while patches of fertile soil depend on more recent events such as the flow of rivers or the movement of ice.

For agriculture, the activity that has been basic to the survival of humanity and our huge increase in population, about a fifth of the Earth's surface is barred by ice or perennially frozen soil; a fifth is arid or desert; and another fifth is composed of highlands too cold, rugged or barren for the cultivation of crops. Between 5% and 10% of the remainder has no soil, either because it has been scraped by ice or because it is permanently wet or flooded. This leaves only 30% to 35% of the land surface where food production is even possible.

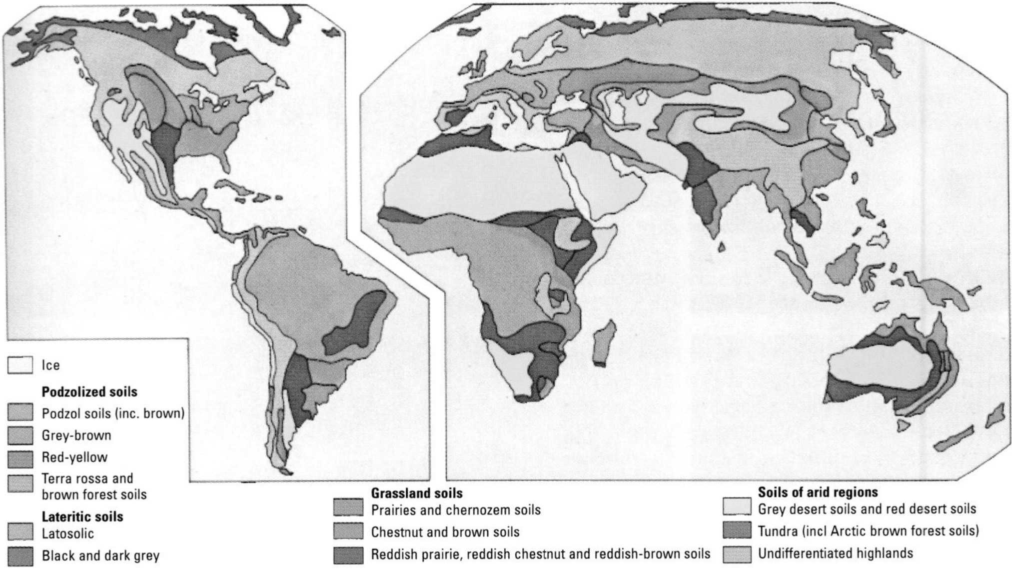

The importance of soil

The whole structure of life on Earth, with its enormous diversity of plant and animal types, is dependent on a mantle of soil which is rich in moisture and nutrients.

Soil is a result of all the processes of physical and chemical weathering on the barren, underlying rock mass of the Earth that it covers, and varies in depth from a few centimetres to several metres. The depth of soil is measured either by the distance to which plants send down their roots, or by the depth of soil directly influencing their systems. In some places only a very thin layer is necessary to support life.

Soil remains an unconsolidated mass of inorganic particles until it acquires a minimum organic content and plants take root and deposit their "litter". As the organic matter accumulates, fine humus builds up in the upper soil horizons, enriching them chemically and providing an environment for a wide variety of lifeforms. In the course of time plants, fungi, bacteria, worms, insects and burrowing animals such as rodents and moles reproduce in the soil and thrive in the complex ecosystem of a mature soil.

Formation of soil is the result of the complex interaction of five major elements – the parent rock (the source of the vast bulk of soil material), land topography, time, climate and decay. However, by far the most single important factor in the development of soil is climate, with water essential to all chemical and biological change. As it percolates through, water both leaches the surface layers and deposits material in the subsoil.

BELOW The map illustrates the natural "climax" vegetation of a region, as dictated by its climate and topography. In the vast majority of cases, however, human agricultural activity has drastically altered the pattern of vegetation. Western Europe, for example, lost most of its broadleaf forest many centuries ago, and in many areas irrigation has gradually turned natural semi-desert into productive land.

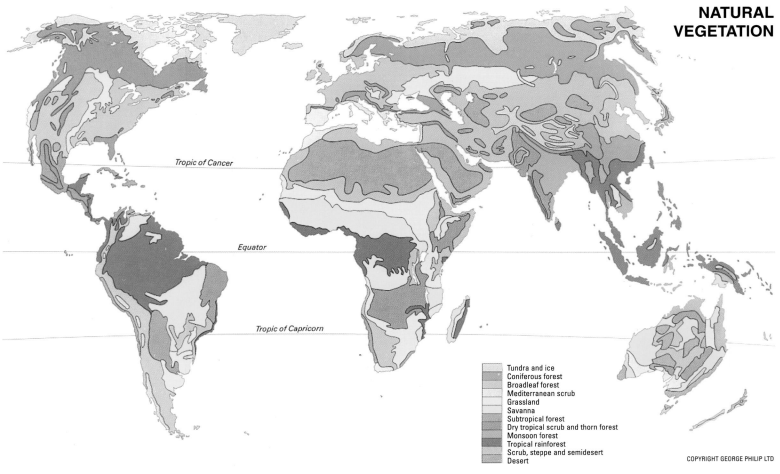

NATURAL VEGETATION

Tropic of Cancer

Equator

Tropic of Capricorn

Tundra and ice
Coniferous forest
Broadleaf forest
Mediterranean scrub
Grassland
Savanna
Subtropical forest
Dry tropical scrub and thorn forest
Monsoon forest
Tropical rainforest
Scrub, steppe and semidesert
Desert

RIGHT Some legume crops, such as clover, can obtain nitrogen from the air by the process known as fixation, but most plants need additional inorganic nitrogen and this element is the one most widely used in fertilizers.

Nitrogen undergoes a natural cycle. Together with its compounds it is involved in five basic processes: fixation of nitrogen from the air by micro-organisms and by lightning; use by plants of nitrates in the soil to make proteins; ammonium compound production in decaying plant and animal matter; nitrification of these to nitrites and then to nitrates; and denitrification of ammonium compounds back to nitrogen gas.

Nitrogen is removed from the soil whenever we consume food, but is replaced by the artificial addition of nitrogenous fertilizers to the soil by farmers. In its many forms nitrogen accounts for almost half of the world consumption of fertilizers: phosphoros makes up another 30% and potassium, the remaining primary nutrient, accounts for most of the balance.

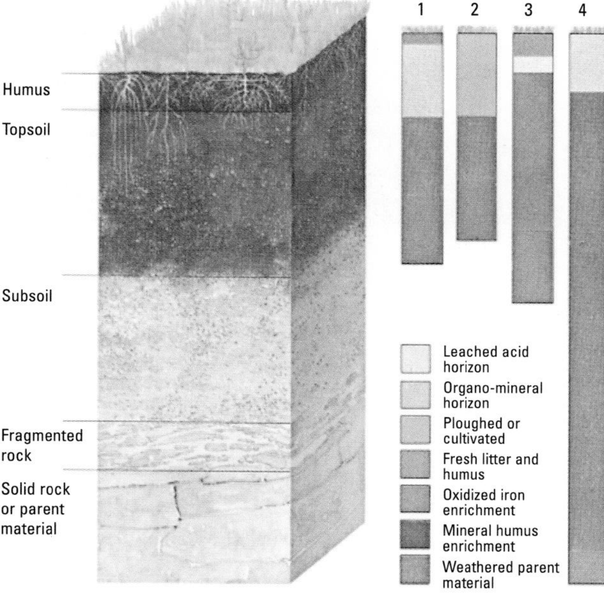

RIGHT Soil is identified by composition and colour. The tundra soil [1] has a dark, peaty surface. Light-coloured desert soil [2] is coarse and poor in organic matter. Chestnut-brown soil [3] and chernozem [4] – Russian for "black earth" – are humus-rich grassland soils typical of the central Asian steppes and prairies of North America. The reddish, leached latosol [5] of tropical savannas has a very thin but rich humus layer. Podzolic soils are typical of northern climates where rainfall is heavy but evaporation is slow: they include the organically rich brown forest podzol [6], the grey-brown podzol [8], and the grey-stony podzol [9] that supports mixed growths of conifers and hardwoods. All are relatively acid. The red-yellow podzol [9] is quite highly leached.

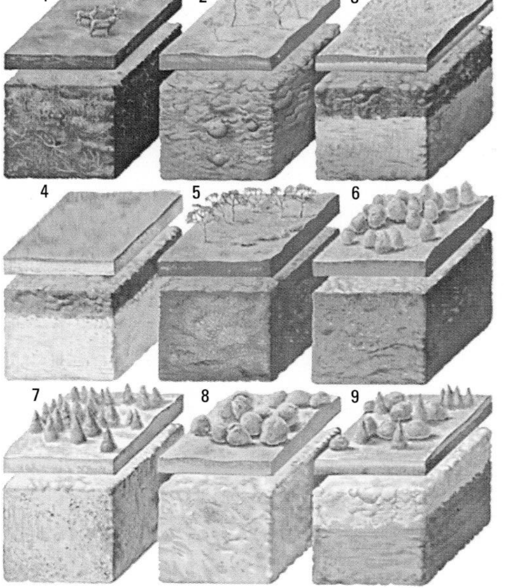

ABOVE Profile 1 is of acid brown earth found in temperate climates – this one on sandy rock – and 2 is a cultivated brown earth of the same region. Grey leached podzol [3] is typical of wet, cool climates such as the taiga in Russia – while oxisol [4], a thick red soil containing iron compounds, is found in humid, tropical lands with high chemical and biological activity.

BELOW The soil is a complex ecosystem. A cubic metre of fertile soil teems with more than 1,000 million individual forms of life, from microscopic organisms through insects and earthworms to large animals such as burrowing rodents. In the steppes, for example, these include marmots, susliks, hamsters and mole rats. All play an important part in helping to aerate the soil and to accelerate the processes of decay and humus formation.

The role of soil bacteria is perhaps the most crucial: they not only "fix" nitrogen from the air in a form that plants can use, but also promote the essential processes of decay. As they decay, plants provide the fine organic humus litter vital to healthy soil life.

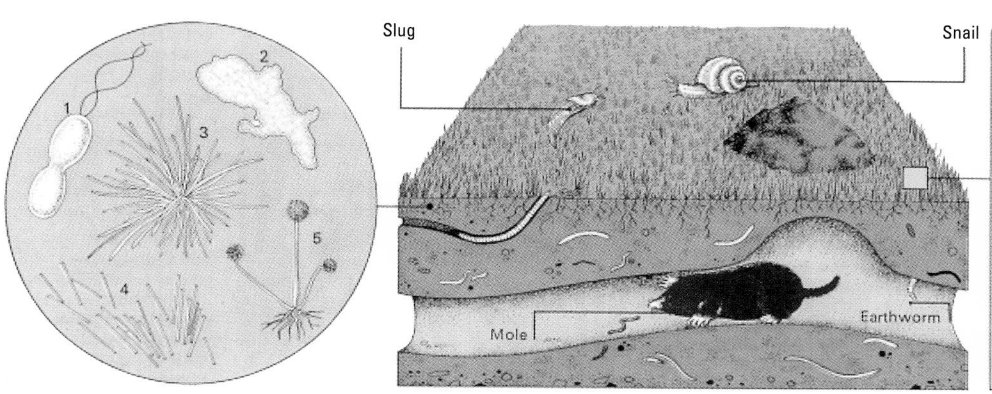

1. Bacterium
2. Protozoan
3. Alga
4. Virus
5. Fungus
6. Eelworm
7. Earwig
8. Woodlouse
9. Mite
10. Centipede
11. Millipede
12. Spider
13. Ant
14. Springtail
15. Cricket
16. Cockchafer lava

THE EARTH IN FIGURES

PLANET EARTH

Mean distance from the Sun	149,500,000km (92,860,000 miles)
Average speed around the Sun	108,000km/h (66,600mph)
Age	approx. 4,500,000,000 years
Mass	5,975 million million million tonnes
Density	5,515 times that of water
Volume	1,083,207,000,000cu. km (260,000,000,000 cu. miles)
Area	509,450,000sq km (196,672,000sq miles)
Land surface	149,450,000sq km (57,688,000sq mi) – 29.3% of total
Water surface area	360,000,000sq km (138,984,000sq mi) – 70.7% of total
Equatorial circumference	40,075km (24,902 miles)
Polar circumference	40,008km (24,860 miles)
Equatorial diameter	12,756km (7,926 miles)
Polar diameter	12,714km (7,900 miles)

INSIDE THE EARTH

	Density (g/cm)	Temperature		State	Thickness	
Sial	2.8	< 500°C	(930°F)	Solid	0-30km	(0-18miles)
Sima	2.9	< 650°C	(1,200°F)	Solid	20-80km	(12-50miles)
Upper mantle	4.3	< 800°C	(1,480°F)	Molten	*c.* 700km	(435miles)
Lower mantle	5.5	< 2,500°C	(4,600°F)	Solid	*c.* 1,700km	(1,050miles)
Outer core	10.0	< 3,000°C	(5,400°F)	Molten	*c.* 2,100km	(1,305miles)
Inner core	13.5	< 5,000°C	(9,000°F)	Solid	*c.* 1,370km	(850miles)

SELECTED EARTH RECORDS

Greatest tides	Bay of Fundy, Nova Scotia, Canada, 16.3m (53.5ft)
Deepest gorge	Colca River, Peru, 3,205m (10,515ft)
Longest gorge	Grand Canyon, Arizona, USA, 350km (217 miles)
Deepest lake	Lake Baikal, Siberia, Russia, 1,620m (5,315ft)
Highest navigable lake	Lake Titicaca, Peru/Bolivia, 3,812m (12,506ft)
Deepest cave	Réseau Jean Bernard, Haute-Savoie, France, 1,602m (5,256ft)
Longest cave system	Mammoth Cave, Kentucky, USA, 560km (348 miles)
Deepest valley	Kali Gandaki, Nepal, 5,883m (19,300ft)
Longest glacier	Lambert-Fisher Ice Passage, Antarctica, 515km (320 miles)
Deepest depression	Dead Sea, Israel/Jordan, 395m (1,296ft)

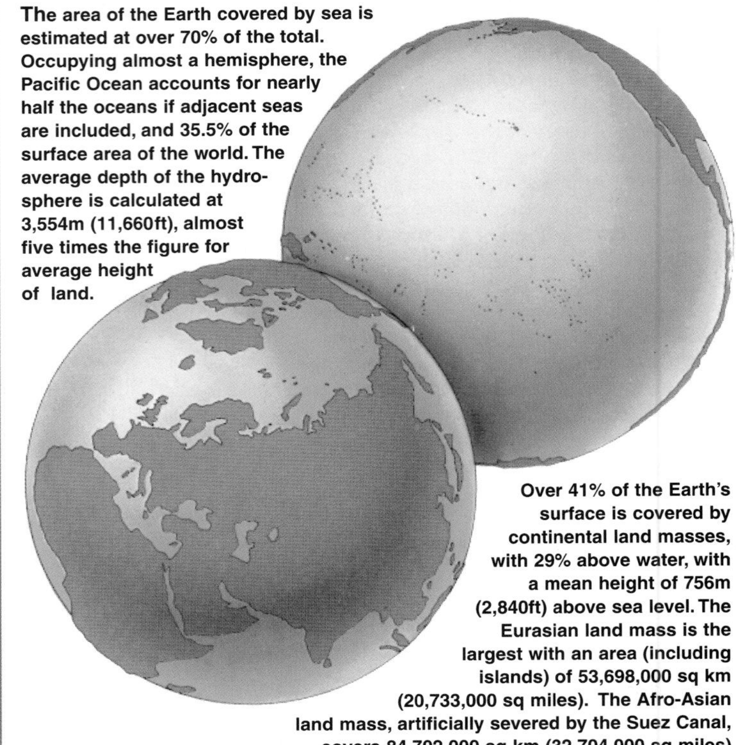

The area of the Earth covered by sea is estimated at over 70% of the total. Occupying almost a hemisphere, the Pacific Ocean accounts for nearly half the oceans if adjacent seas are included, and 35.5% of the surface area of the world. The average depth of the hydrosphere is calculated at 3,554m (11,660ft), almost five times the figure for average height of land.

Over 41% of the Earth's surface is covered by continental land masses, with 29% above water, with a mean height of 756m (2,840ft) above sea level. The Eurasian land mass is the largest with an area (including islands) of 53,698,000 sq km (20,733,000 sq miles). The Afro-Asian land mass, artificially severed by the Suez Canal, covers 84,702,000 sq km (32,704,000 sq miles) – or 57.2% of the Earth's land mass.

LARGEST ISLANDS

	sq km	sq miles
Europe		
Great Britain [8]	229,880	88,700
Iceland	103,000	39,800
Ireland	84,400	32,600
Novaya Zemlya (N)	48,200	18,600
Sicily	25,500	9,800
Corsica	8,700	3,400
Asia		
Borneo [3]	744,360	287,400
Sumatra [6]	473,600	182,860
Honshu [7]	230,500	88,980
Celebes	189,000	73,000
Java	126,700	48,900
Luzon	104,700	40,400
Mindanao	95,000	36,700
Hokkaido	78,400	30,300
Sakhalin	76,400	29,500
Sri Lanka	65,600	25,300
Africa		
Madagascar [4]	587,040	226,660
Socotra	3,600	1,400
Réunion	2,500	965
North America		
Greenland [1]*	2,175,600	839,800
Baffin Island [5]	508,000	196,100
Victoria Island [9]	212,200	81,900
Ellesmere Island [10]	212,000	81,800
Cuba	110,860	42,800
Newfoundland	96,000	37,100
Hispaniola	76,200	29,400
Jamaica	11,400	4,400
Puerto Rico	8,900	3,400
South America		
Tierra del Fuego	47,000	18,100
Falkland Island (E)	6,800	2,600
Oceania		
New Guinea [2]	821,030	317,000
New Zealand (S)	150,500	58,100
New Zealand (N)	114,700	44,300
Tasmania	67,800	26,200
Hawaii	10,450	4,000

** Geographers consider Australia to be a continental land mass*

LARGEST INLAND LAKES AND SEAS

	Location	sq km	sq mi
Europe			
Lake Ladoga	Russia	17,700	6,800
Lake Onega	Russia	9,700	3,700
Saimaa system	Finland	8,000	3,100
Vänern	Sweden	6,500	2,100
Asia			
Caspian Sea [1]	W. Central Asia	371,800	143,550
Aral Sea* [6]	Kazakhstan/ Uzbekistan	33,640	13,000
Lake Baikal [9]	Russia	30,500	11,780
Tonlé Sap	Cambodia	20,000	7,700
Lake Balkhash	Kazakhstan	18,500	7,100
Africa			
Lake Victoria [3]	East Africa	68,000	26,000
Lake Tanganyika [7]	Central Africa	33,000	13,000
Lake Malawi [10]	East Africa	29,600	11,430
Lake Chad*	Central Africa	25,000	9,700
Lake Turkana	Ethiopia/Kenya	8,500	3,300
Lake Volta†	Ghana	8,480	3,250
North America			
Lake Superior [2]	Canada/USA	82,350	31,800
Lake Huron [4]	Canada/USA	59,600	23,010
Lake Michigan [5]	USA	58,000	22,400
Great Bear Lake [8]	Canada	31,800	12,280
Great Slave Lake	Canada	28,500	11,000
Lake Erie	Canada/USA	25,700	9,900
Lake Winnipeg	Canada	24,400	9,400
Lake Ontario	Canada/USA	19,500	7,500
Lake Nicaragua	Nicaragua	8,200	3,200
South America			
Lake Titicaca‡	Bolivia/Peru	8,300	3,200
Lake Poopó	Peru	2,800	1,100
Australia			
Lake Eyre§	Australia	8,900	3,400
Lake Torrens§	Australia	5,800	2,200
Lake Gairdner§	Australia	4,800	1,900

** Shrinking in area due to environmental factors; until the 1980s it was the world's 4th largest*
† Artificial lake created by Akosombo Dam (1966)
‡ Lake Maracaibo, in Venezuela, is far larger at 13,260 sq km (5,120 sq miles), but is linked to the Caribbean by a narrow channel and therefore not an "inland" lake
§ Salt lakes that vary in size with rainfall

BEAUFORT WIND SCALE

Named after the 19th-century British naval officer who devised it, the Beaufort Scale assesses wind speed according to its effects. Originally designed in 1806 as an aid for sailors, it has since been adapted for use on land and was internationally recognised in 1874.

Scale	Wind speed km/h	Wind speed mph	Name
0	0-1	0-1	Calm
1	1-5	1-3	Light air
2	6-11	4-7	Light breeze
3	12-19	8-12	Gentle breeze
4	20-28	13-18	Moderate
5	29-38	19-24	Fresh
6	39-49	25-31	Strong
7	50-61	32-38	Near gale
8	62.74	39-46	Gale
9	75-88	47-54	Strong gale
10	89-102	55-63	Storm
11	103-117	64-72	Violent storm
12	118+	73+	Hurricane

WINDCHILL FACTORS

A combination of cold and wind makes the human body feel cooler than the actual air temperature. The charts below give approximate equivalents for combinations of wind speed and temperature. In sub-zero temperatures even moderate winds will significantly reduce effective temperatures: if human skin was exposed to winds of 48km/h (30mph) in a temperature of –34°C (–30°F) it would freeze solid in 30 seconds.

Temp. °C	Wind speed (km/h) 16	32	48	64*	Temp. °F	Wind speed (mph) 10	20	30	40*
15	11	9	8	6	30	16	4	–2	–5
10	6	3	2	–1	20	3	–10	–18	–21
5	1	4	–5	–8	10	–9	–24	–33	–37
0	–8	–14	–17	–19	0	–2	–39	–49	–53
–5	–14	–21	–25	–27	–10	–34	–53	–6	–69
–10	–20	–28	–33	–35	–20	–46	–67	–79	–84
–15	–26	–36	–40	–43	–30	–58	–81	–93	–100
–20	–32	–42	–48	–51	–40	–71	–95	–109	–115

** Wind speeds of more than about 64km/h (40mph) have only a marginal cooling effect*

THE CONTINENTS

Continent	Area sq km	Area sq miles	%	Highest point above sea level	metres	feet	Lowest point below sea level	metres	feet
Asia	44,500,000	17,179,000	29.8	Mt Everest (China/Nepal)	8,848	29,029	Dead Sea, Israel/Jordan	–396	–1,302
Africa	30,302,000	11,697,000	20.3	Mt Kilimanjaro, Tanzania	5,895	19,340	Lake Assal, Djibouti	–153	–502
North America	24,454,000	9,442,000	16.2	Mt McKinley, Alaska	6,194	20,321	Death Valley, California, USA	–86	–282
South America	17,793,000	6,868,000	11.9	Mt Aconcagua, Argentina	6,960	22,834	Peninsular Valdés, Argentina	–40	–131
Antarctica	14,100,000	5,443,000	9.4	Vinson Massif	4,897	16,066	*		
Europe	9,957,000	3,843,000	6.7	Mt Elbrus, Russia	5,633	18,481	Caspian Sea, W. Central Asia	–28	–92
Oceania	8,945,000	3,454,000	5.7	Puncak Jaya (Ngga Pulu), Indonesia	5,029	16,499	Lake Eyre (N), South Australia	–15	–50

**The Bentley trench (–2,540m/–8,333ft) is englacial and therefore not a surface point*

THE OCEANS

Ocean	Area sq km	Area sq miles	%	Average depth metres	Average depth feet	Greatest known depth	metres	feet
Pacific	179,679,000	69,356,000	49.9	4,300	14,100	Mariana Trench	11,022	36,161
Atlantic	92,373,000	35,657,000	25.7	3,700	12,100	Puerto Rico Deep*	9,200	30,138
Indian	73,917,000	28,532,000	20.5	3,900	12,800	Java Trench	7,450	24,442
Arctic	14,090,000	5,439,000	3.9	1,330	4,300	Molloy Deep	5,608	18,399

**7th deepest trench in the world; 8 of the deepest 10, including 1-6, are in the Pacific Ocean*

HIGHEST MOUNTAINS

	Location	metres	feet
Europe			
Elbrus*	Russia	5,642	18,510
Mont Blanc† ‡	France/Italy	4,807	15,771
Monte Rosa‡	Italy/Switzerland	4,634	15,203
Also			
Matterhorn (Cervino)‡	Italy/Switzerland	4,478	14,691
Jungfrau	Switzerland	4,158	13,642
Grossglockner	Austria	3,797	12,457
Mulhacen	Spain	3,478	11,411
Etna	Italy (Sicily)	3,340	10,958
Zugspitze	Germany	2,962	9,718
Olympus	Greece	2,917	9,570
Galdhopiggen	Norway	2,468	8,100
Ben Nevis	UK (Scotland)	1,343	4,406
Asia§			
Everest	China/Nepal	8,848	29,029
K2 (Godwin Austen)	China/Kashmir	8,611	28,251
Kanchenjunga‡	India/Nepal	8,598	28,208
Lhotse‡	China/Nepal	8,516	27,939
Makalu‡	China/Nepal	8,481	27,824
Cho Oyu	China/Nepal	8,201	26,906
Dhaulagiri‡	Nepal	8,172	26,811
Manaslu (Kutang)‡	Nepal	8,156	26,758
Nanga Parbat	Kashmir	8,126	26,660
Annapurna‡	Nepal	8,078	26,502
Also			
Pik Kommunizma	Tajikistan	7,495	24,590
Ararat	Turkey	5,165	16,945
Gunong Kinabalu	Malaysia (Borneo)	4.101	13,455
Fuji-san (Fujiyama)	Japan	3,776	12,388
Africa			
Kilimanjaro	Tanzania	5,895	19,340
Mt Kenya	Kenya	5,199	17,057
Ruwenzori	Uganda/Zaire	5,109	16,762
North America			
Mt McKinley (Denali)‡	USA (Alaska)	6,194	20,321
Mt Logan	Canada	5,959	19,551
Citlaltépetl (Orizaba)	Mexico	5,700	18,701
Mt St Elias	USA/Canada	5,489	18,008
Popocatépetl	Mexico	5,452	17,887
Also			
Mt Whitney	USA	4,418	14,495
Tajumulco	Guatemala	4,220	13,845
Chirripo Grande	Costa Rica	3,837	12,589
Pico Duarte	Dominican Rep.	3,175	10,417
South America			
Aconcagua#	Argentina	6,960	22,834
Ojos del Salado	Argentina/Chile	6,863	22,516
Pissis	Argentina	6,779	22,241
Mercedario	Argentina/Chile	6,770	22,211
Huascarán‡	Peru	6,768	22,204
Oceania			
Puncak Jaya	Indonesia (W Irian)	5,029	16,499
Puncak Trikora	Indonesia (W Irian)	4,750	15,584
Puncak Mandala	Indonesia (W Irian)	4,702	15,427
Mt Wilhelm	Papua New Guinea	4,508	14,790
Also			
Mauna Kea	USA (Hawaii)	4 205	13 796
Mauna Loa	USA (Hawaii)	4,170	13,681
Mt Cook (Aorangi)	New Zealand	3,753	12,313
Mt Kosciusko	Australia	2,237	7,339
Antarctica			
Vinson Massif	—	4,897	16,066
Mt Tyree	—	4,965	16,289

** The Caucasus Mountains include 14 other peaks higher than Mont Blanc, the highest point in non-Russian Europe*
† The highest point is in France; the highest point wholly in Italian territory is 4,760m (15,616ft)
‡ Many mountains, especially in Asia, have two or more significant peaks; only the highest ones are listed here
§ The ranges of Central Asia have more than 100 peaks over 7,315m (24,000ft); thus the first 10 listed here constitute the world's 10 highest mountains # Highest mountain outside Asia

HIGHEST WATERFALLS

Name	Total height m	Total height ft	Location	River	Highest fall m	Highest fall ft
Angel	979	3,212	Venezuela	Carrao	807	2,648
Tugela	947	3,110	Natal, South Africa	Tugela	410	1,350
Utigård	800	2,625	Nesdale, Norway	Jostedal Glacier	600	1,970
Mongefoseen	774	2,540	Mongebekk, Norway	Monge	—	—
Yosemite	739	2,425	California, USA	Yosemite Creek	739	2,425
Østre Mardøla Foss	656	2,154	Eikisdal, Norway	Mardals	296	974
Tyssestrengane	646	2,120	Hardanger, Norway	Tysso	289	948
Cuquenán	610	2,000	Venezuela	Arabopó	—	—
Sutherland	580	1,904	Otago, New Zealand	Arthur	248	815
Takkakaw	502	1,650	British Columbia, Canada	Daly Glacier	365	1,200
Ribbon	491	1,612	California, USA	Ribbon Fall Stream	491	1,612

The greatest falls by volume are the Boyoma (formerly Stanley) Falls on the Zaïre (formerly Congo), with a mean annual flow of 17,000 cu m/sec (600,000 cu ft/sec). The Niagara Falls come 4th and the Victoria Falls 9th in terms of volume, though both are relatively modest in height.

LONGEST RIVERS

	Outflow	km	miles
Europe			
Volga	Caspian Sea	3,700	2,300
Danube	Black Sea	2,850	1,770
Ural*	Caspian Sea	2,535	1,575
Asia			
Yangtze [3]	Pacific Ocean	6,380	3,960
Yenisey-Angara [5]	Arctic Ocean	5,550	3,445
Hwang Ho [6]	Pacific Ocean	5,464	3,395
Ob-Irtysh [7]	Arctic Ocean	5,410	3,360
Mekong [9]	Pacific Ocean	4,500	2,795
Amur [10]	Pacific Ocean	4,400	2,730
Africa			
Nile [1]	Mediterranean	6,620	4,140
Zaire (Congo) [8]	Atlantic Ocean	4,670	2,900
Niger	Atlantic Ocean	4,180	2,595
Zambezi	Indian Ocean	3,540	2,200
North America			
Mississippi-Missouri[4]	Gulf of Mexico	6,020	3,740
Mackenzie	Arctic Ocean	4,240	2,630
Mississippi	Gulf of Mexico	3,780	2,350
Missouri	Mississippi	3,780	2,350
Yukon	Pacific Ocean	3,185	1,980
Rio Grande	Gulf of Mexico	3,030	1,880
Arkansas	Mississippi	2,840	1,450
Colorado	Pacific Ocean	2,330	1,445
South America			
Amazon [2]	Atlantic Ocean	6,450	4,010
Paraná-Plate	Atlantic Ocean	4,500	2,800
Purus	Amazon	3,350	2,080
Madeira	Amazon	3,200	1,990
Sao Francisco	Atlantic Ocean	2,900	1,800
Australia			
Murray-Darling	Southern Ocean	3,750	2,830
Darling	Murray	3,070	1,905
Murray	Southern Ocean	2,575	1,600
Murrumbidgee	Murray	1,690	1,050

** Flows through Europe and Asia*

NOTABLE EARTHQUAKES*

Year	Location	Magnitude†	Deaths
1906	San Francisco, USA	8.3	503
1908	Messina, Italy	7.5	83,000
1920	Gansu (Kansu), China	8.6	180,000
1923	Yokohama, Japan	8.3	143,000
1927	Nan Xian, China	8.3	200,000
1932	Gansu (Kansu), China	7.6	70,000
1933	Sanriku, Japan	8.9 ‡	2,990
1935	Quetta, India §	7.5	60,000
1939	Chillan, Chile	8.3	28,000
1963	Skopje, Yugoslavia #	6.0	1,000
1964	Anchorage, Alaska	8.4	131
1970	N. Peru	7.7	86,794
1976	Guatemala	7.5	22,778
1976	Tangshan, China	8.2	242,000
1985	Mexico City, Mexico	8.1	4,200
1988	NW. Armenia	6.8	55,000
1990	N. Iran	7.7	36,000
1993	Maharastra, India	6.4	30,000
1995	Kobe, Japan	7.2	5,000
1995	Sakhalin Island, Russia	7.5	2,000
1997	NE Iran	7.1	2,400
1998	Takhar, Afghanistan	6.1	4,200
1999	NW Turkey	8.2	22,000
1999	Taiwan	7.6	4,600

** Since 1900 † On the Richter scale ‡ Highest ever recorded § Now Pakistan # Now Macedonia*

UNDERSTANDING MAPS

Mapmaking

While small areas can be mapped by plane (flat) surveying, larger areas must be done by geodesy, which takes into account the Earth's curvature. A variety of instruments and techniques is used to determine the position, height and extent of features – data essential to the cartographic process. Instruments such as graduated metal rods, chains, tapes and portable radar or radio transmitters are used for measuring distances, and the theodolite is used for angles. With measured distances and angles, further distances and angles as well as heights are calculated by triangulation.

Latitude and longitude

Accurate positioning of points on the Earth's surface is made possible by reference to latitude and longitude. Parallels of latitude are drawn west-east around the globe and numbered by degrees north and south of the Equator (0° of latitude). Meridians of longitude are drawn north-south and numbered by degrees east and west and the prime meridian (0° of longitude) which passes through the Royal Observatory at Greenwich in southeast London. Latitude and longitude are indicated by blue lines on the maps, and are straight or slightly curved according to the projection used.

Representing relief

Height and gradient can be represented on a map in many ways. Hachuring, in which fine lines follow the direction of the greatest slope, can give an excellent impression of the landscape but the lines may obscure other information. Hill shading, the representation of a landscape illuminated from one direction, is used alone or with colours. Contours can also be separated by colour and intermediate heights given as spot heights. These techniques are now often used in conjunction with sophisticated computerized technology, including digitalization.

ABOVE Any point on the Earth's surface can be located in terms of longitude and latitude – in degrees, minutes and seconds east or west of the prime meridian for longitude, and north or south of the Equator for latitude. The latitude of X (the angle between X, the centre of the Earth and the plane of the Equator [1]) equals 20°, while its longitude (the angle between between the plane of the prime meridian [2] and that passing through X and the North and South Poles [3]) equals 40°.

RIGHT Reference to lines of longitude and latitude is the easiest and most common way of determining the relative positions of places on different maps, and for plotting compass directions.

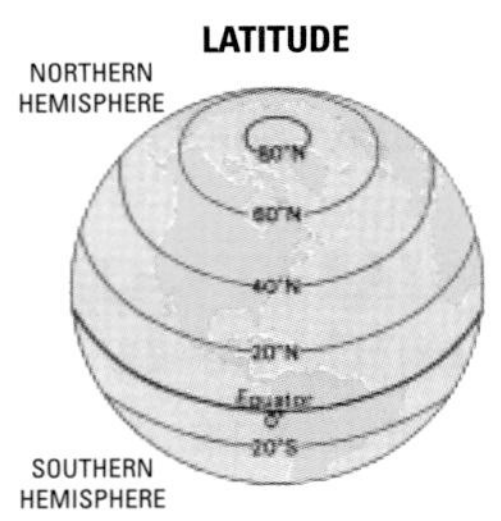

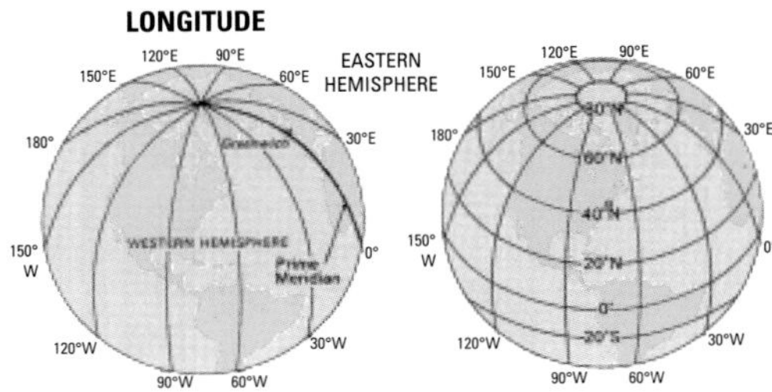

Projections

A map projection is the systematic depiction on a plane surface of the imaginary lines of latitude or longitude from a globe of the Earth. This network of lines is called the graticule and forms the framework on which an accurate depiction of the world is made. The basis of any map, the graticule, is constructed sometimes by graphical means but often by using mathematical formulas to give the intersections plotted as x and y co-ordinates.

The choice of projection is governed by the properties the cartographer wishes the map to possess, the map scale and also the extent of the area to be mapped. Since the globe is three-dimensional, it is not possible to depict its surface on a two-dimensional plane without distortion. Preservation of one of the basic properties involved – area, distance or shape – can only be secured at the expense of the others, and the choice of projection is often a compromise solution.

Map projections are constructions designed to maintain certain selected relationships of the Earth's surface. Most of the projections used for large-scale atlases, selected primarily to minimize distortion of size and distance, fall into one of three categories – conic [A], cylindrical [B] or azimuthal [C]. Each involves plotting the forms of the Earth's surface on a grid of lines of latitude and longitude, which may be shown as parallels, curved lines or radiating spokes *(see below)*.

Conical projections use the projection of the graticule from the globe onto a cone which is tangential to a line of latitude (termed the standard parallel). This line is always an arc and scale is always true along it. Because of its method of construction it is used mainly for maps depicting the temperate latitudes around the standard parallel – that is, where there is least distortion.

Cylindrical projections are constructed by the projection of the graticule from the globe onto a cylinder tangential to the globe, and permit the whole of the Earth's surface to be depicted on one map. Though they can depict all the land masses, there is colossal exaggeration of area and shape towards the poles at the expense of equatorial regions: Greenland, for example, grows to almost the size of Africa. However, the best known example, named after the pioneering 16th-century cartographer Gerardus Mercator, has been invaluable to navigators because any straight line drawn on it is a line of constant bearing.

Azimuthal projections, sometimes called zenithal, are constructed by the projection of part of the graticule from the globe onto a plane tangential to any single point on it. This plane may be tangential to the equator (equatorial case), the poles (polar case) or any other point (oblique case). Any straight line drawn from the point where the plane touches the globe is the shortest distance from that point and is known as a great circle.

A

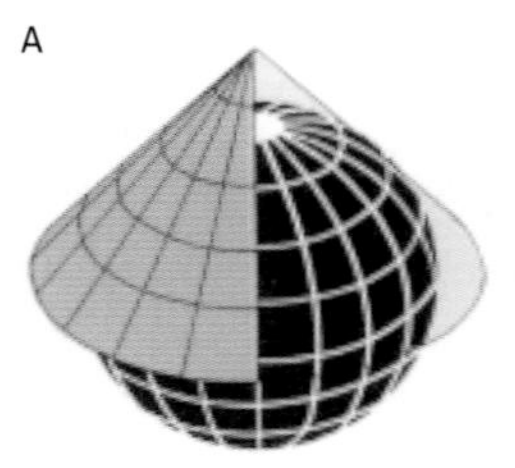

B

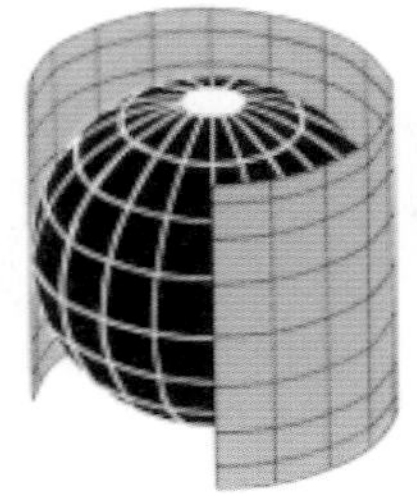

C

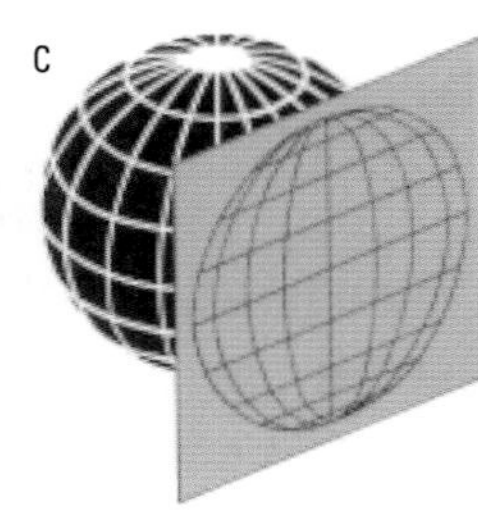

LEFT Most of the projections used for large-scale atlases, selected primarily to minimize distortion of size and distance, fall into one of three principal categories – conic [A], cylindrical [B] or azimuthal [C].

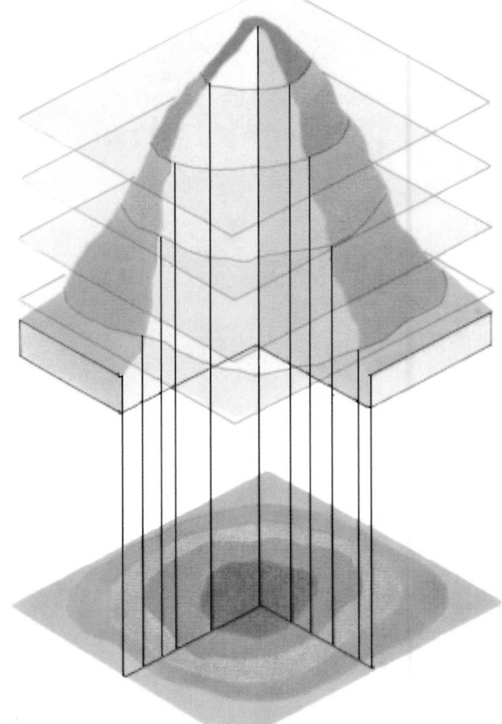

ABOVE Recording a three-dimensional shape on a flat surface can be achieved by contour scaling. Here the cross-sections of a hill at heights of 50, 100, and 150 metres (or feet) are projected onto a map of the hill. The topography of the hill can be visualized fairly well from such a map when graduated colour is employed – the closer the gradations the steeper the slope – though the crudeness of the contour intervals loses some finer detail.

WORLD MAPS

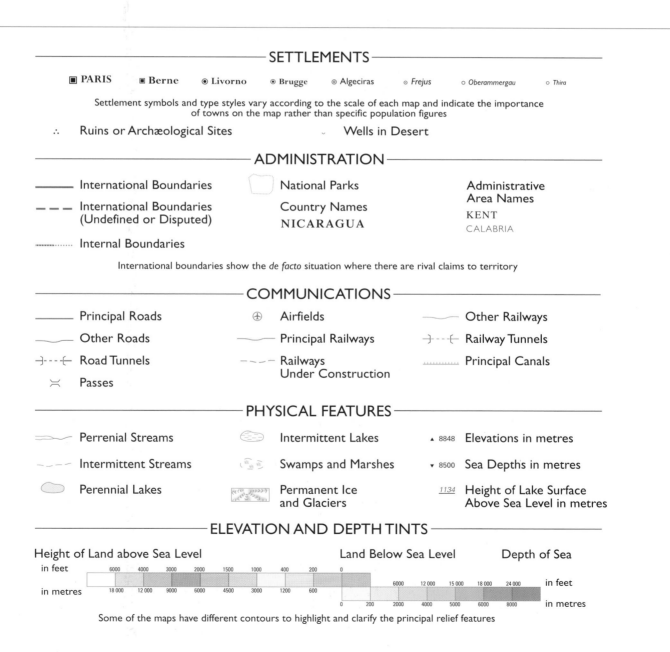

SETTLEMENTS

PARIS · Berne · Livorno · Brugge · Algeciras · *Frejus* · *Oberammergau* · *Thira*

Settlement symbols and type styles vary according to the scale of each map and indicate the importance of towns on the map rather than specific population figures

Ruins or Archæological Sites

Wells in Desert

ADMINISTRATION

International Boundaries

International Boundaries (Undefined or Disputed)

Internal Boundaries

National Parks

Country Names
NICARAGUA

Administrative Area Names
KENT
CALABRIA

International boundaries show the *de facto* situation where there are rival claims to territory

COMMUNICATIONS

Principal Roads

Other Roads

Road Tunnels

Passes

Airfields

Principal Railways

Railways Under Construction

Other Railways

Railway Tunnels

Principal Canals

PHYSICAL FEATURES

Perrenial Streams

Intermittent Streams

Perennial Lakes

Intermittent Lakes

Swamps and Marshes

Permanent Ice and Glaciers

▲ 8848 Elevations in metres

▼ 8500 Sea Depths in metres

1134 Height of Lake Surface Above Sea Level in metres

ELEVATION AND DEPTH TINTS

Height of Land above Sea Level

in feet	6000	4000	3000	2000	1500	1000	400	200	0
in metres	18 000	12 000	9000	6000	4500	3000	1200	600	

Land Below Sea Level

Depth of Sea

in feet		6000	12 000	15 000	18 000	24 000
in metres	0	200	2000	4000	5000	6000	8000

Some of the maps have different contours to highlight and clarify the principal relief features

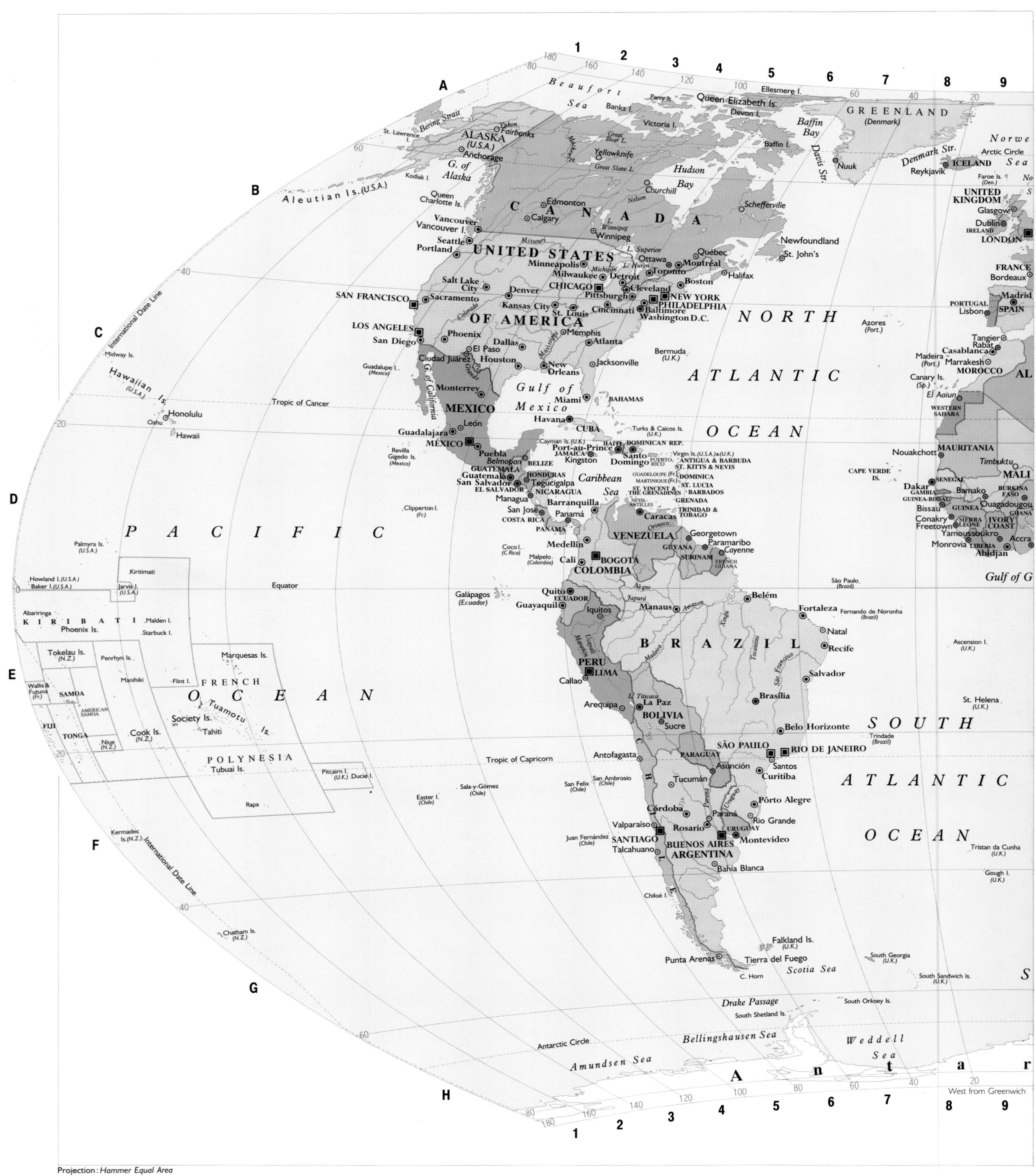

Projection: *Hammer Equal Area*

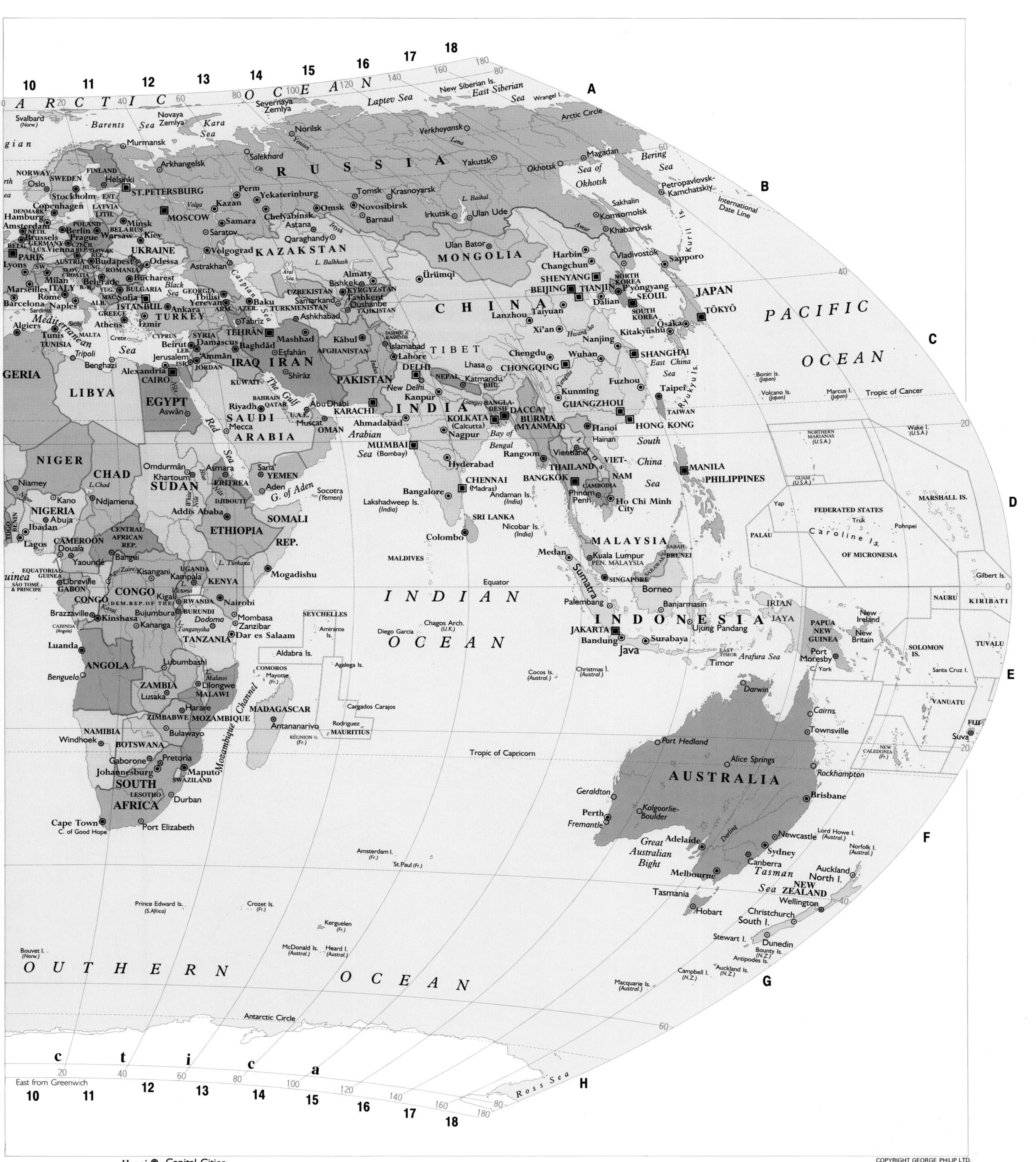

Hanoi ● Capital Cities

ARCTIC OCEAN 1:35 000 000

100 0 200 400 600 800 1000 1200 1400 km

100 0 200 400 600 800 1000 miles

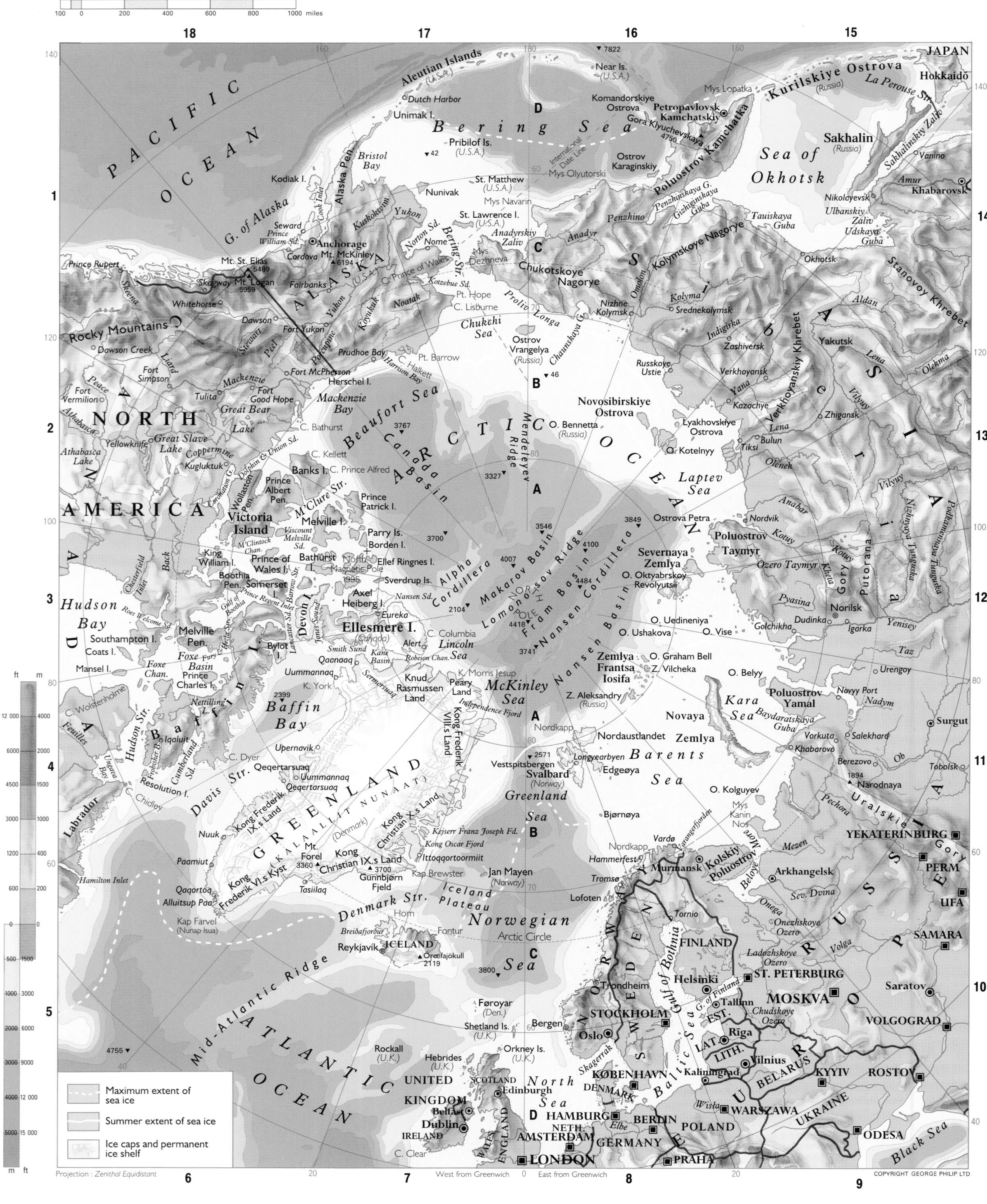

Maximum extent of sea ice

Summer extent of sea ice

Ice caps and permanent ice shelf

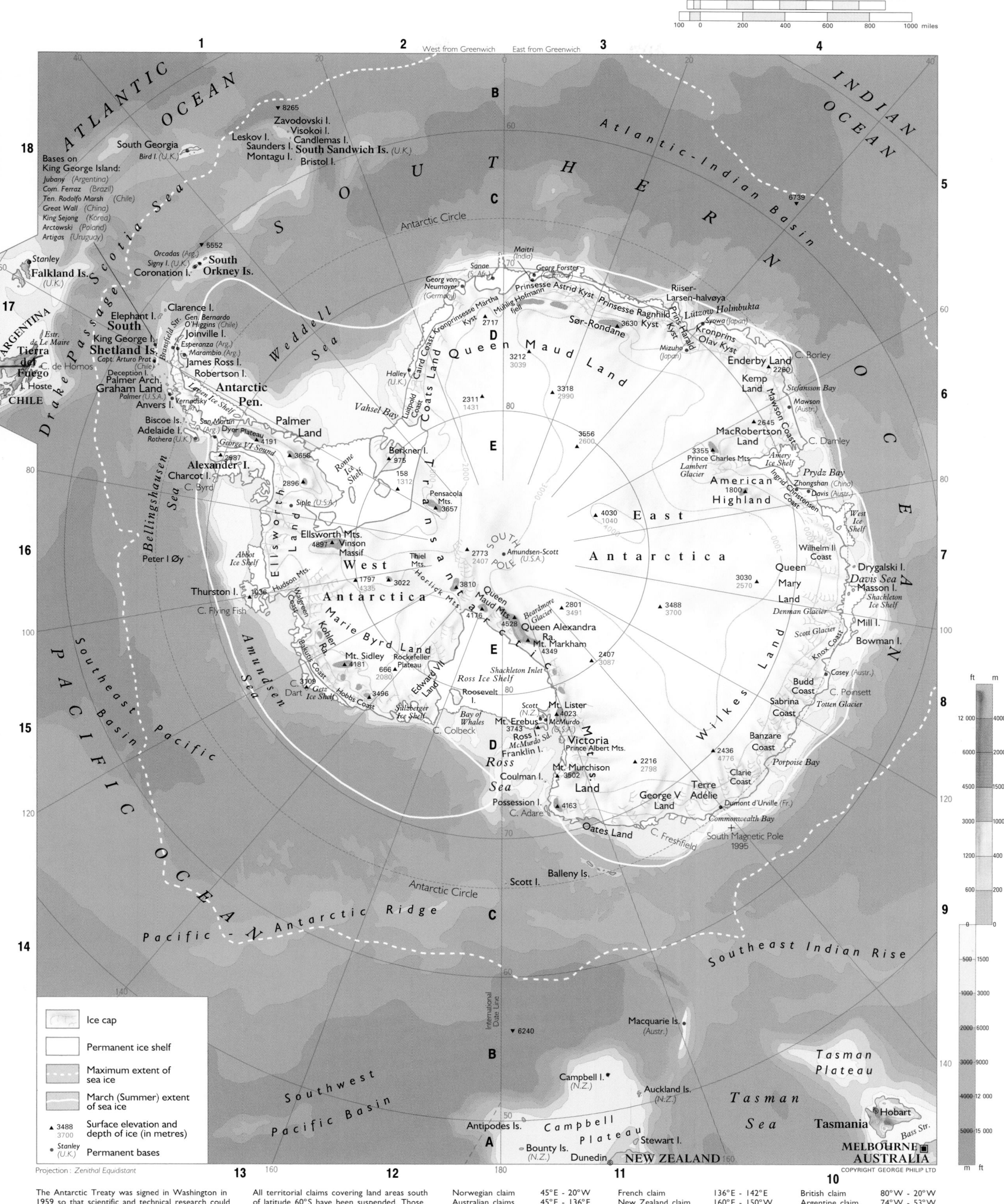

Projection: Zenithal Equidistant

COPYRIGHT GEORGE PHILIP LTD

The Antarctic Treaty was signed in Washington in 1959 so that scientific and technical research could continue unhampered by international politics.

All territorial claims covering land areas south of latitude 60°S have been suspended. Those claims were:

Norwegian claim	45°E - 20°W
Australian claims	45°E - 136°E
	142°E - 160°E
French claim	136°E - 142°E
New Zealand claim	160°E - 150°W
Chilean claim	90°W - 53°W
British claim	80°W - 20°W
Argentine claim	74°W - 53°W

EUROPE : Physical 1:20 000 000

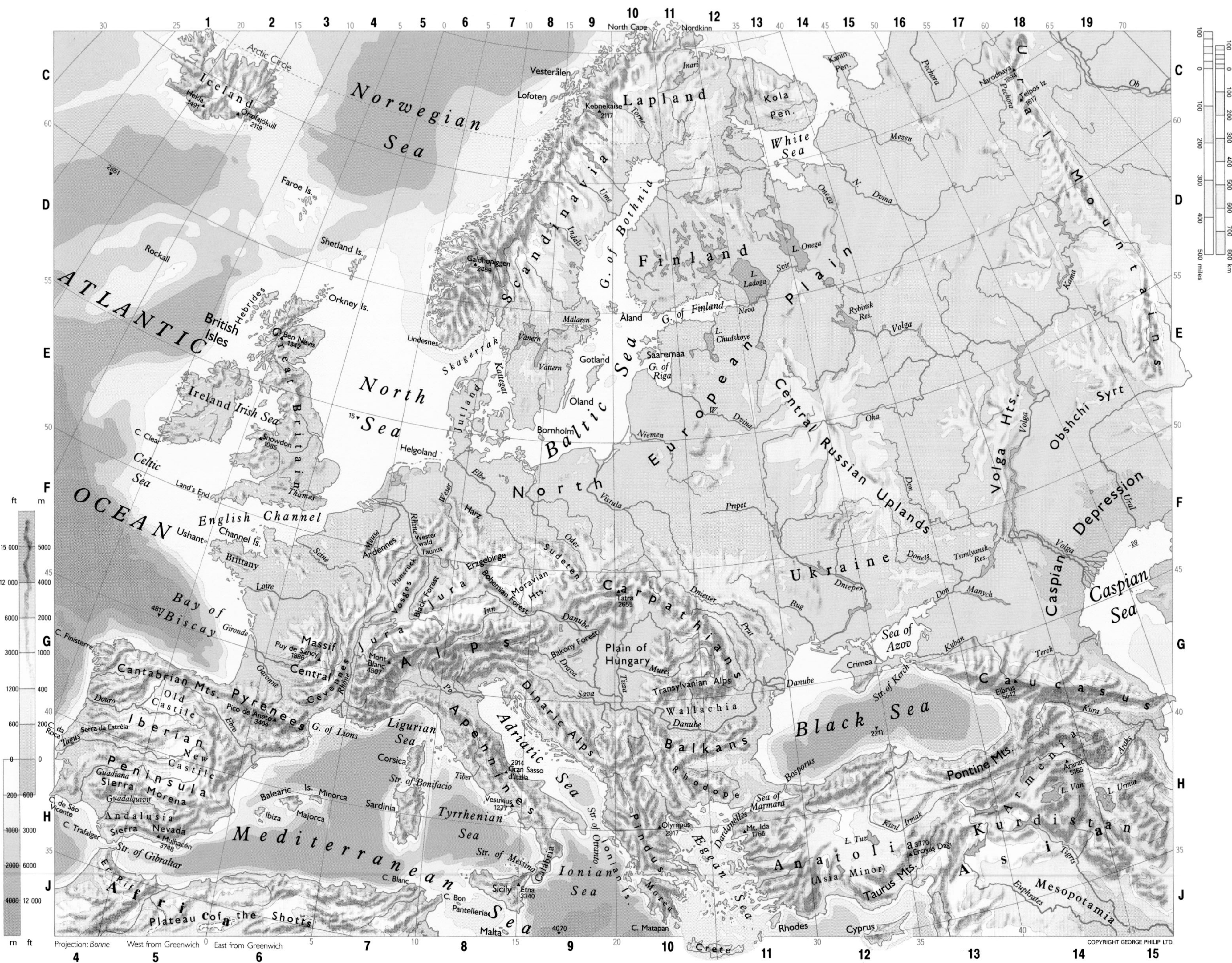

100 0 100 200 300 400 500 600 700 800 km
100 0 100 200 300 400 500 miles
ICELAND
Reykjavík
Arctic Circle
Norwegian Sea
Faroe Is. (Den.)
Shetland Is.
Orkney Is.
Hebrides
ATLANTIC OCEAN
UNITED KINGDOM
SCOTLAND
ENGLAND
WALES
N. IRELAND
IRELAND
Dublin
LONDON
North Sea
English Channel
Bay of Biscay
NORWAY
Oslo
SWEDEN
Stockholm
FINLAND
Helsinki
G. of Bothnia
Baltic Sea
White Sea
DENMARK
Copenhagen
ESTONIA
Tallinn
LATVIA
Riga
LITHUANIA
Vilnius
BELARUS
Minsk
RUSSIA
MOSCOW
ST. PETERSBURG
KAZAKSTAN
Caspian Sea
UKRAINE
Kiev
MOLDOVA
Kishinev
POLAND
Warsaw
GERMANY
Berlin
NETHERLANDS
Amsterdam
BELGIUM
Brussels
LUX.
FRANCE
PARIS
SWITZERLAND
LIECH.
AUSTRIA
Vienna
CZECH REP.
Prague
SLOVAK REP.
Bratislava
HUNGARY
Budapest
SLOVENIA
Ljubljana
CROATIA
Zagreb
BOSNIA-HERZ.
Sarajevo
YUGOSLAVIA
SERBIA
MONTENEGRO
Belgrade
MACEDONIA
Skopje
ALBANIA
Tirana
GREECE
Athens
ROMANIA
Bucharest
BULGARIA
Sofia
Black Sea
TURKEY
Ankara
İSTANBUL
GEORGIA
Tbilisi
ARMENIA
Yerevan
AZERBAIJAN
Baku
IRAN
IRAQ
SYRIA
CYPRUS
Nicosia
ITALY
Rome
SAN MARINO
MONACO
MALTA
Valletta
Adriatic Sea
Tyrrhenian Sea
Ionian Sea
Ægean Sea
Mediterranean Sea
Corsica
Sardinia
Sicily
Crete
Balearic Is.
SPAIN
Madrid
PORTUGAL
Lisbon
ANDORRA
MOROCCO
ALGERIA
TUNISIA
Africa
■ LONDON Capital Cities
Projection: Bonne
West from Greenwich 0 East from Greenwich
CARTOGRAPHY BY PHILIPS.

SCANDINAVIA 1:5 000 000

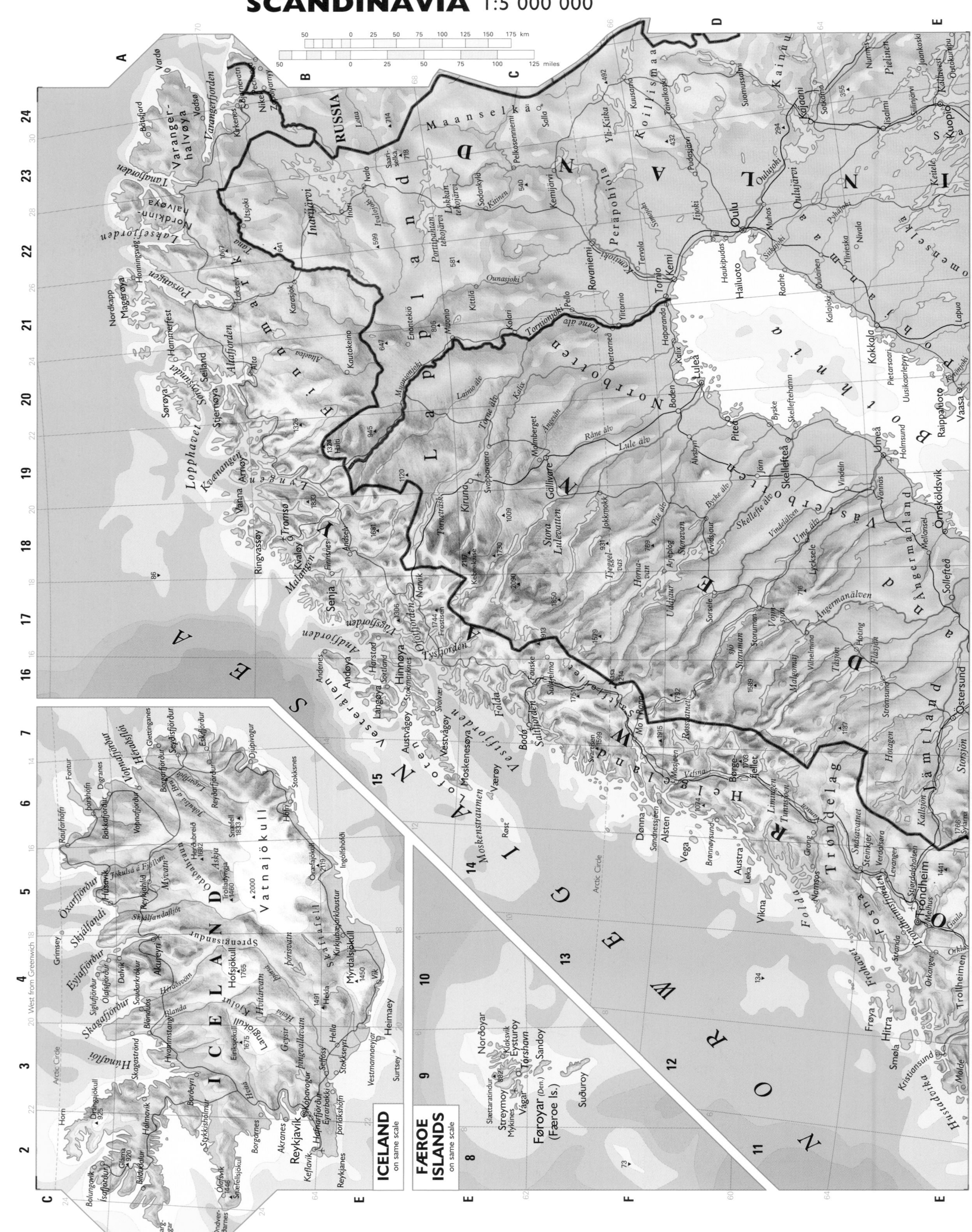

Projection: Conical with two standard parallels

East from Greenwich

12 13 14 15 16 17 18 19 20 21

m	ft
2000	6000
1500	4500
1000	3000
500	1500
200	600
0	0
50	150
100	300
200	600
500	1500
1000	3000
2000	6000

ENGLAND AND WALES 1:2 000 000

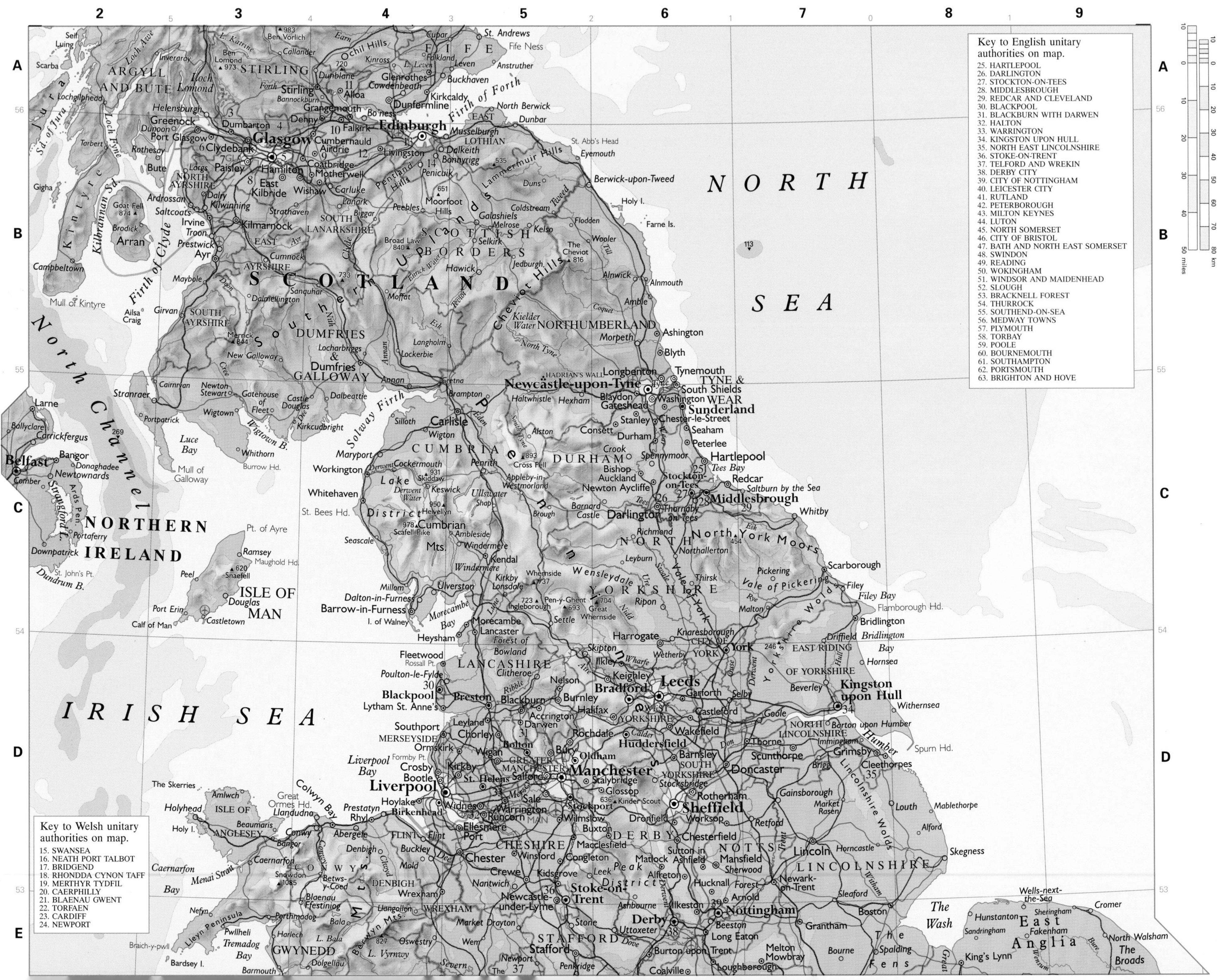

WALES
ENGLAND
FRANCE
ENGLISH CHANNEL
Bristol Channel
Cardigan Bay
Strait of Dover
Thames Estuary
Baie de la Seine
Baie de la Somme
Lyme Bay
CHANNEL ISLANDS (U.K.)
Guernsey
Jersey
Alderney
ISLE OF WIGHT
LONDON
BIRMINGHAM
Bristol
Cardiff
Southampton
Portsmouth
Plymouth
Brighton
Bournemouth
Le Havre
Rouen
Caen
Cherbourg
HAUTE-NORMANDIE
SEINE-MARITIME
CALVADOS
MANCHE
CORNWALL
DEVON
DORSET
SOMERSET
WILTSHIRE
OXFORD
BUCKS
HERTS
ESSEX
KENT
SURREY
SUFFOLK
NORFOLK
CAMBRIDGE
NORTHAMPTON
WARWICK
WORCESTER
HEREFORD
GLOUCS
POWYS
CEREDIGION
PEMBROKESHIRE
CARMARTHENSHIRE
Isles of Scilly
On same scale
Projection : Lambert's Conformal Conic
West from Greenwich
East from Greenwich
COPYRIGHT GEORGE PHILIP LTD.
ft
m
1
2
4
5
6
7
8
9
E
F
G
H
11

SCOTLAND 1:2 000 000

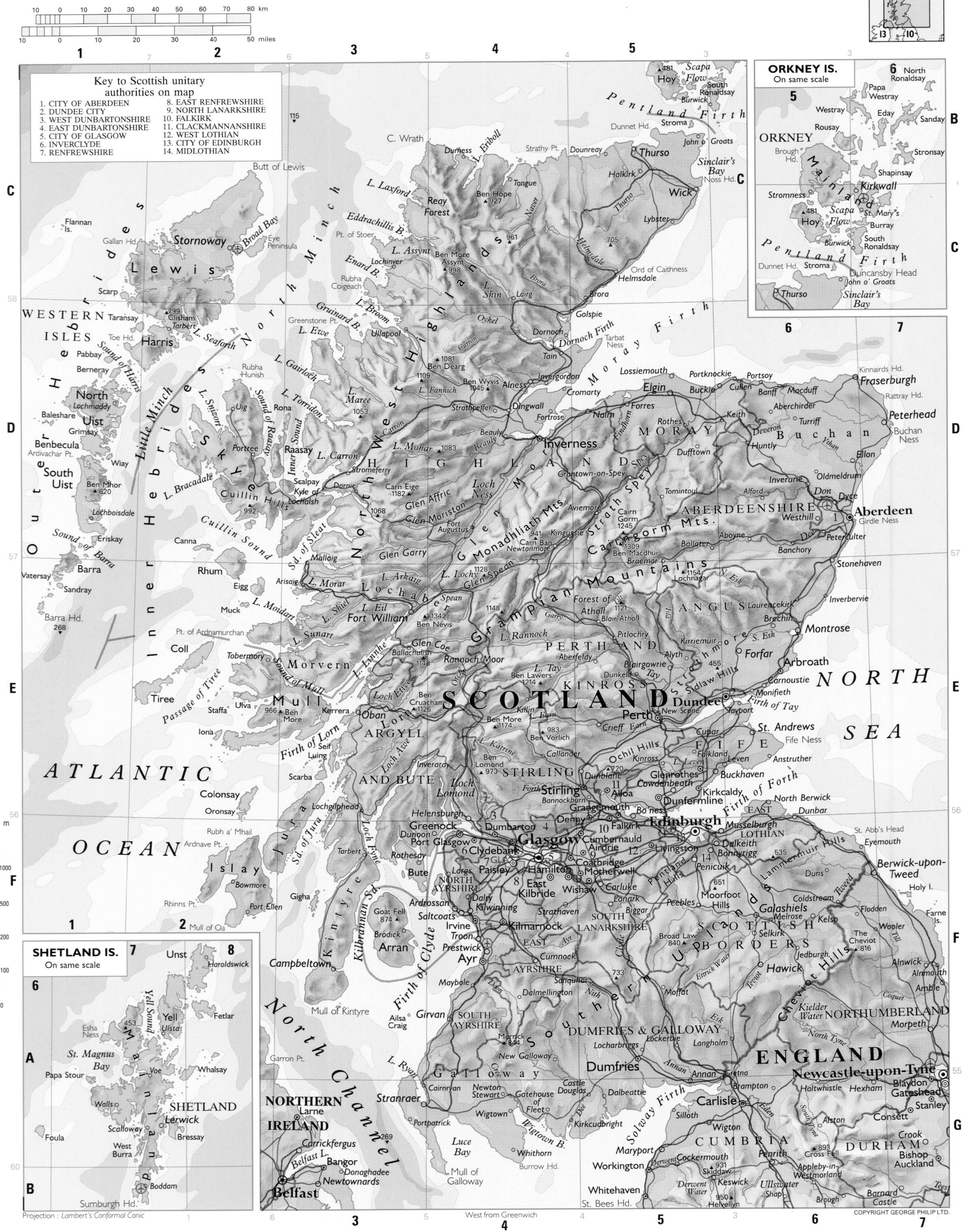

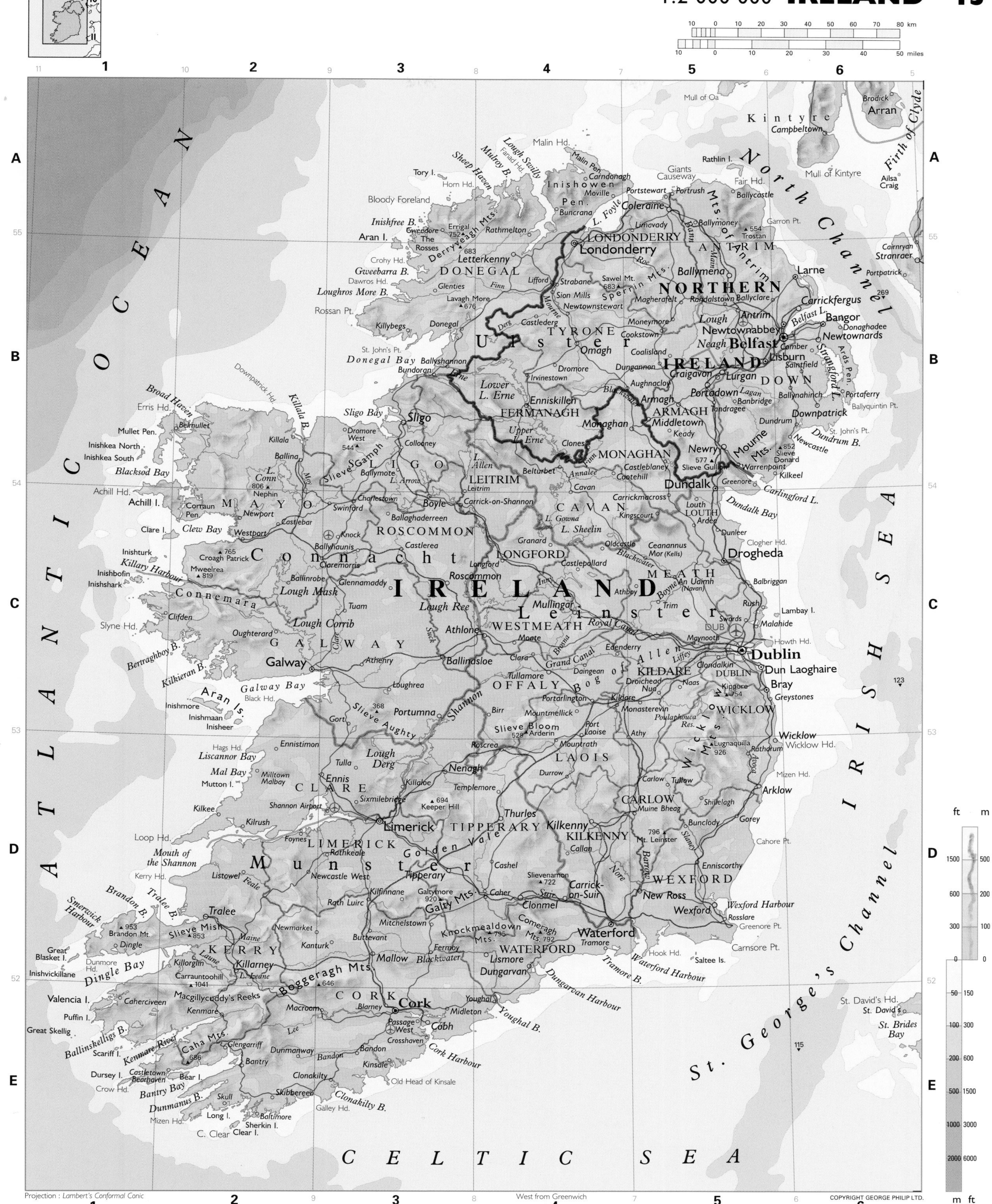
ATLANTIC OCEAN
CELTIC SEA
IRISH SEA
North Channel
St. George's Channel
IRELAND
NORTHERN IRELAND
Ulster
Connacht
Leinster
Munster
Dublin
Belfast
Cork
Limerick
Galway
Waterford
Londonderry
Projection : Lambert's Conformal Conic
West from Greenwich
COPYRIGHT GEORGE PHILIP LTD.

ATLANTIC OCEAN
NORTH SEA
IRISH SEA
CELTIC SEA
English Channel
UNITED KINGDOM
SCOTLAND
ENGLAND
WALES
IRELAND
NORTHERN IRELAND
NORWAY
NETHERLANDS
BELGIUM
FRANCE
Shetland Is.
Yell
Unst
Fetlar
Mainland
Lerwick
Foula
Fair Isle
Orkney Is.
Westray
Sanday
Stronsay
Kirkwall
Hoy
South Ronaldsay
Pentland Firth
Thurso
Wick
C. Wrath
Outer Hebrides
Lewis
Stornoway
Harris
St. Kilda
North Uist
Benbecula
South Uist
Barra
North Minch
Ullapool
North West Highlands
Lairg
Helmsdale
Golspie
Tain
Invergordon
Dingwall
Moray Firth
Buckie
Banff
Fraserburgh
Peterhead
Nairn
Elgin
Huntly
Inverurie
Aberdeen
Stonehaven
Portree
Skye
Inverness
L. Ness
Spey
Don
Dee
Ballater
Aviemore
Grampian Mts.
Mallaig
Rhum
Eigg
Ben Nevis
Fort William
Inner Hebrides
Coll
Tiree
Tobermory
Mull
Oban
Forfar
Montrose
Arbroath
Tay
Dundee
Perth
St. Andrews
L. Lomond
Stirling
Glenrothes
Kirkcaldy
Dunfermline
Dunbar
Colonsay
Jura
Islay
Greenock
Clyde
Glasgow
Edinburgh
Paisley
East Kilbride
Hamilton
Berwick-upon-Tweed
Irvine
Arran
Kilmarnock
Southern Uplands
Galashiels
Campbeltown
Ayr
Jedburgh
Hawick
Cheviot Hills
Alnwick
Firth of Clyde
North Channel
Girvan
Dumfries
Newcastle-upon-Tyne
South Shields
Sunderland
Malin Hd.
Buncrana
Coleraine
Aran I.
Letterkenny
Londonderry
Ballymena
Larne
Lifford
Antrim
Bangor
Lough Neagh
Belfast
Donegal
Omagh
Lisburn
Lurgan
Bundoran
Lower L. Erne
Portadown
Armagh
Enniskillen
Newry
Clones
Sligo
Ballina
L. Conn
Castleblaney
Dundalk
Achill I.
Castlebar
Leitrim
Cavan
Westport
Roscommon
Longford
Ceanannus Mor
Drogheda
Boyne
Lough Mask
Lough Corrib
Lough Ree
Athlone
Mullingar
Connemara
Galway B.
Galway
Ballinasloe
Tullamore
Dublin
Dun Laoghaire
Liffey
Bray
Aran Is.
Birr
Port Laoise
Athy
Wicklow Mts.
Ennis
Lough Derg
Shannon
Kilrush
Limerick
Nenagh
Thurles
Carlow
Kilkenny
Arklow
Listowel
Tipperary
Tralee
Clonmel
Carrick-on-Suir
Wexford
Rosslare
Dingle
Carrauntoohill
Killarney
Mallow
Blackwater
Waterford
Dungarvan
Valencia I.
Macgillycuddy's Reeks
Cork
Cobh
Youghal
Bantry
Bandon
Kinsale
C. Clear
Stranraer
Kirkcudbright
Mull of Galloway
Workington
Whitehaven
Annan
Carlisle
Cumbrian Mts.
Hexham
Gateshead
Durham
Hartlepool
Redcar
Pennines
Darlington
Middlesbrough
Stockton-on-Tees
Scarborough
Douglas
I. of Man
Barrow-in-Furness
Lancaster
Harrogate
York
Bridlington
Beverley
Kingston upon Hull
Blackpool
Burnley
Keighley
Leeds
Bradford
Preston
Blackburn
Halifax
Huddersfield
Scunthorpe
Humber
Bolton
Barnsley
Doncaster
Grimsby
Liverpool
Manchester
Oldham
Rotherham
Sheffield
Louth
Holyhead
Anglesey
Warrington
Stockport
Chesterfield
Lincoln
Skegness
Bangor
Colwyn Bay
Chester
Crewe
Mansfield
Boston
The Wash
Cromer
Snowdon
Wrexham
Stoke on Trent
Derby
Nottingham
Trent
Grantham
King's Lynn
Norwich
Pwllheli
Stafford
Great Yarmouth
Lowestoft
Shrewsbury
Telford
Leicester
Cambrian Mts.
Cardigan Bay
Aberystwyth
Welshpool
Wolverhampton
BIRMINGHAM
Nuneaton
Coventry
Corby
Peterborough
Thetford
Redditch
Rugby
Ely
Bury St. Edmunds
Worcester
Royal Leamington Spa
Northampton
Bedford
Cambridge
Ipswich
Hereford
Milton Keynes
Felixstowe
Fishguard
Stevenage
Harwich
Brecon
Cheltenham
Cotswold Hills
Hemel Hempstead
Luton
Harlow
Colchester
Carmarthen
Gloucester
Oxford
Chelmsford
Haverfordwest
Milford Haven
Pembroke
Merthyr Tydfil
Neath
Cwmbran
High Wycombe
Watford
Basildon
St. George's Channel
Llanelli
Swansea
Port Talbot
Rhondda
Newport
Cardiff
Bristol
Swindon
Slough
LONDON
Thames
Southend-on-Sea
Barry
Bath
Newbury
Reading
Chatham
Margate
Bristol Channel
Weston-super-Mare
Basingstoke
Reigate
Canterbury
Maidstone
Dover
Barnstaple
Exmoor
Salisbury
Guildford
Ashford
Folkestone
Taunton
Yeovil
Southampton
Winchester
Fareham
Crawley
Hastings
Str. of Dover
Bude
Exeter
Bournemouth
Poole
Havant
Portsmouth
Brighton
Worthing
Eastbourne
Dartmoor
Exmouth
Torbay
Newport
Weymouth
Isle of Wight
Newquay
Truro
St. Austell
Plymouth
Falmouth
Land's End
Penzance
Isles of Scilly
Askøy
Bergen
Osøyro
Stord
Bømlo
Leirvik
Haugesund
Kopervik
Åkrahamn
Boknafjorden
Stavanger
Sandnes
Bryne
Nærbø
Texel
Den Helder
Alkmaar
Haarlem
's-Gravenhage (Den Haag)
Hoek van Holland
ROTTERDAM
Dordrecht
Vlissingen
Zeebrugge
Antwerpen
Oostende
Brugge
Gent
Mechelen
Dunkerque
Calais
Flandre
BRUSSEL (Bruxelles)
Tourcoing
C. Gris-Nez
Boulogne-sur-Mer
St-Omer
Lille
Tournai
Béthune
Villeneuve-d'Ascq
Bruay-la-Buissière
Lens
Valenciennes
Le Touquet-Paris-Plage
Cambrai
Abbeville
Somme
Picardie
St-Quentin
Le Tréport
Dieppe
Amiens
Fécamp
Pays de Caux
Rouen
Seine
Elbeuf
Bolbec
Le Havre
Lisieux
Caen
Bayeux
Trouville-sur-Mer
Pte. de Barfleur
Cherbourg
Valognes
Cotentin
C. de la Hague
Alderney
Guernsey
St. Peter Port
Sark
Channel Is. (U.K.)
St. Helier
Jersey
1224
316
789
1182
1311
1342
1214
973
840
816
893
978
636
1085
926
953
1041
886
618
99
238
16
36
33
ft m
3000 1000
1500 500
600 200
0 0
50 150
100 300
200 600
500 1500
1000 3000
2000 6000
m ft
Projection: Conical with two standard parallels
East from Greenwich
West from Greenwich
COPYRIGHT GEORGE PHILIP LTD.

Underlined towns give their name to the administrative area in which they stand.

NORTH SEA
BALTIC SEA
UNITED KINGDOM
DENMARK
NETHERLANDS
BELGIUM
LUXEMBOURG
GERMANY
FRANCE
SWITZERLAND
LIECHTENSTEIN
AUSTRIA
CZECH R
SLOVENIA
ITALY
MONACO
SAN MARINO
ADRIATIC SEA
Golfo di Génova
Golfo di Venézia
AMSTERDAM
's-Gravenhage (Den Haag)
ROTTERDAM
BRUSSEL (Bruxelles)
PARIS
BERLIN
HAMBURG
MÜNCHEN (Munich)
PRAHA (Prague)
MILANO
TORINO (Turin)
LYON
MARSEILLE
Frankfurt
Köln (Cologne)
Zürich
Genève
Wien
Ljubljana
Zagreb
Nordfriesische Inseln
Ostfriesische Inseln
Deutsche Bucht
Kieler Bucht
Mecklenburger Bucht
Fehmarn Bælt
Niedersachsen
Nordrhein-Westfalen
Sachsen-Anhalt
Brandenburg
Mecklenburg
Hessen
Rheinland-Pfalz
Thüringer Wald
Erzgebirge
Bayern
Baden-Württemberg
Schwarzwald
Schwäbische Alb
Böhmerwald
Tirol
Tauern
Steiermark
Kärnten
Karawanken
Alsace
Lorraine
Champagne
Bourgogne
Franche-Comté
Jura
Massif Central
Provence
Alpes Maritimes
Dauphiné
Rhône
Piemonte
Lombardia
Liguria
Dolomiti
Île-de-France
Picardie
Ardennes
Harz
Projection: Conical with two standard parallels

LITHUANIA
BELARUS
POLAND
UKRAINE
SLOVAK REP.
HUNGARY
ROMANIA
MOLDOVA
YUGOSLAVIA
BOSNIA-HERZEGOVINA
BULGARIA
Carpathians
Transilvania
Walachia
Dobruja
Podilska Vysochyna
Pripet Marshes
Pojezierze Mazurskie
Pomorskie
Basarabia
Vojvodina
Carpaţii Meridionali
Vychodné Beskydy
Západné Beskydy
Nízke Tatry
Tatry
Slovenské Rudohorie
Malé Karpaty
Biele Karpaty
Bakony
Zatoka Gdańska
Zalew Wiślany
WARSZAWA (Warsaw)
MINSK
KYYIV (Kiev)
BUDAPEST
BUCUREŞTI (Bucharest)
BEOGRAD (Belgrade)
Chişinău
WIEN (Vienna)
Bratislava
Kaliningrad (Russia)
Vilnius
Gdańsk
Gdynia
Elbląg
Olsztyn
Białystok
Hrodna
Bydgoszcz
Toruń
Poznań
Łódź
Wrocław
Kraków
Katowice
Lublin
Radom
Kielce
Częstochowa
Rzeszów
Lviv (Lvov)
Lutsk
Rivne
Ternopil
Zhytomyr
Vinnytsya
Khmelnytskyy
Ivano-Frankivsk
Chernivtsi
Uzhhorod
Košice
Prešov
Miskolc
Debrecen
Nyíregyháza
Szeged
Pécs
Cluj-Napoca
Timişoara
Oradea
Arad
Braşov
Sibiu
Iaşi
Constanţa
Galaţi
Brăila
Ploieşti
Craiova
Brest
Pinsk
Homyel
Mahilyow
Babruysk
Baranavichy
Ostrava
Brno
Sarajevo
Novi Sad
Varna
Ruse
Dnister
Dunărea (Danube)
Dunaj
Duna
Dunav
Wisła (Vistula)
Tisza
Pripyat
Prut
Siret
Mureş
Sava
Drava
East from Greenwich

FRANCE 1:5 000 000

50 0 25 50 75 100 125 150 175 km

50 0 25 50 75 100 125 miles

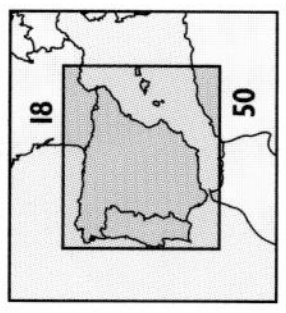

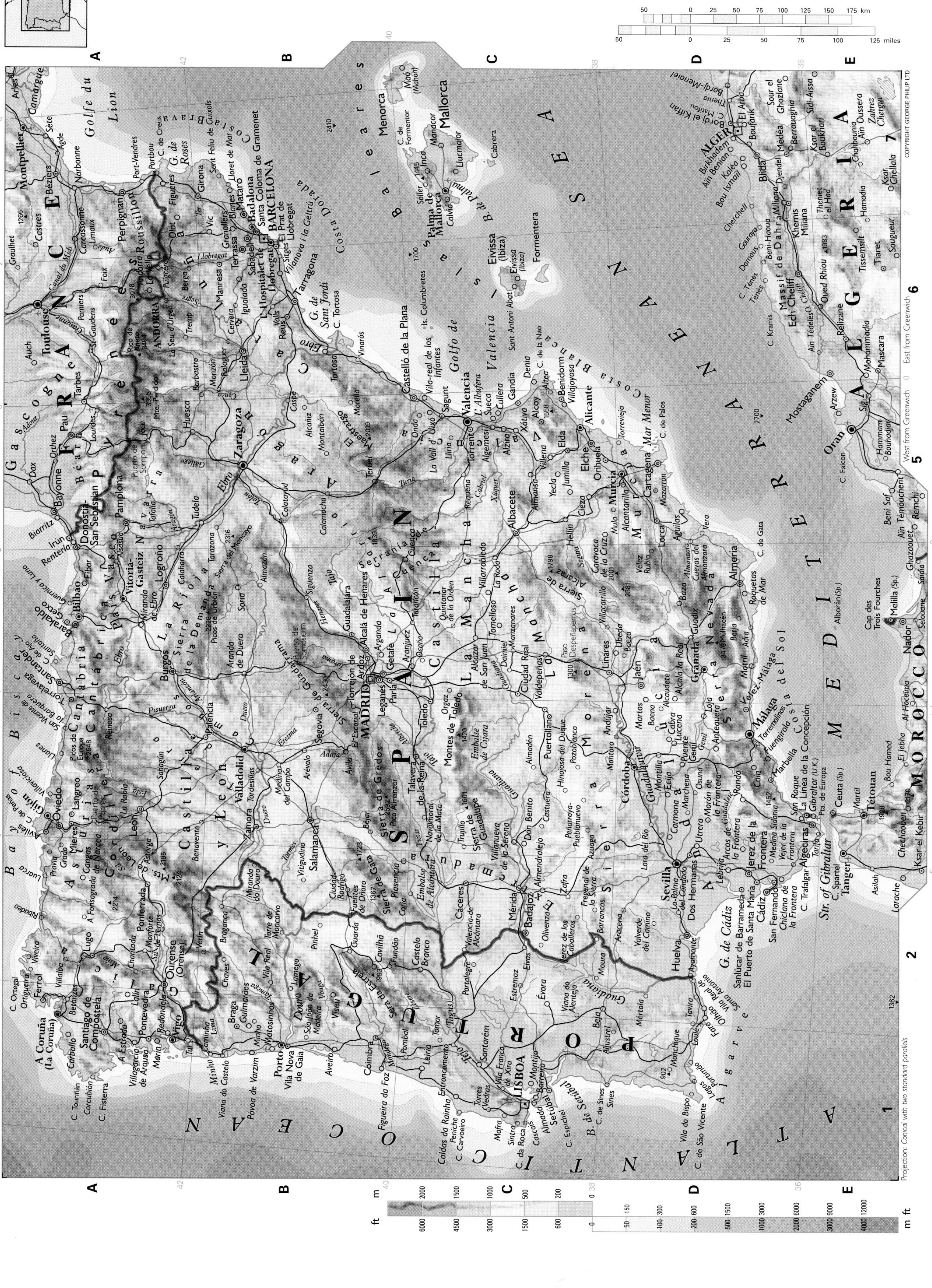

50 0 25 50 75 100 125 150 175 km

50 0 25 50 75 100 125 miles

Projection: Conical with two standard parallels

West from Greenwich 0 East from Greenwich

m 2000 1500 1000 500 200 0

ft 6000 4500 3000 1500 600 0

m 50 100 200 500 1000 2000 3000 4000

ft 150 300 600 1500 3000 6000 9000 12000

ITALY AND THE BALKAN STATES 1:5 000 000

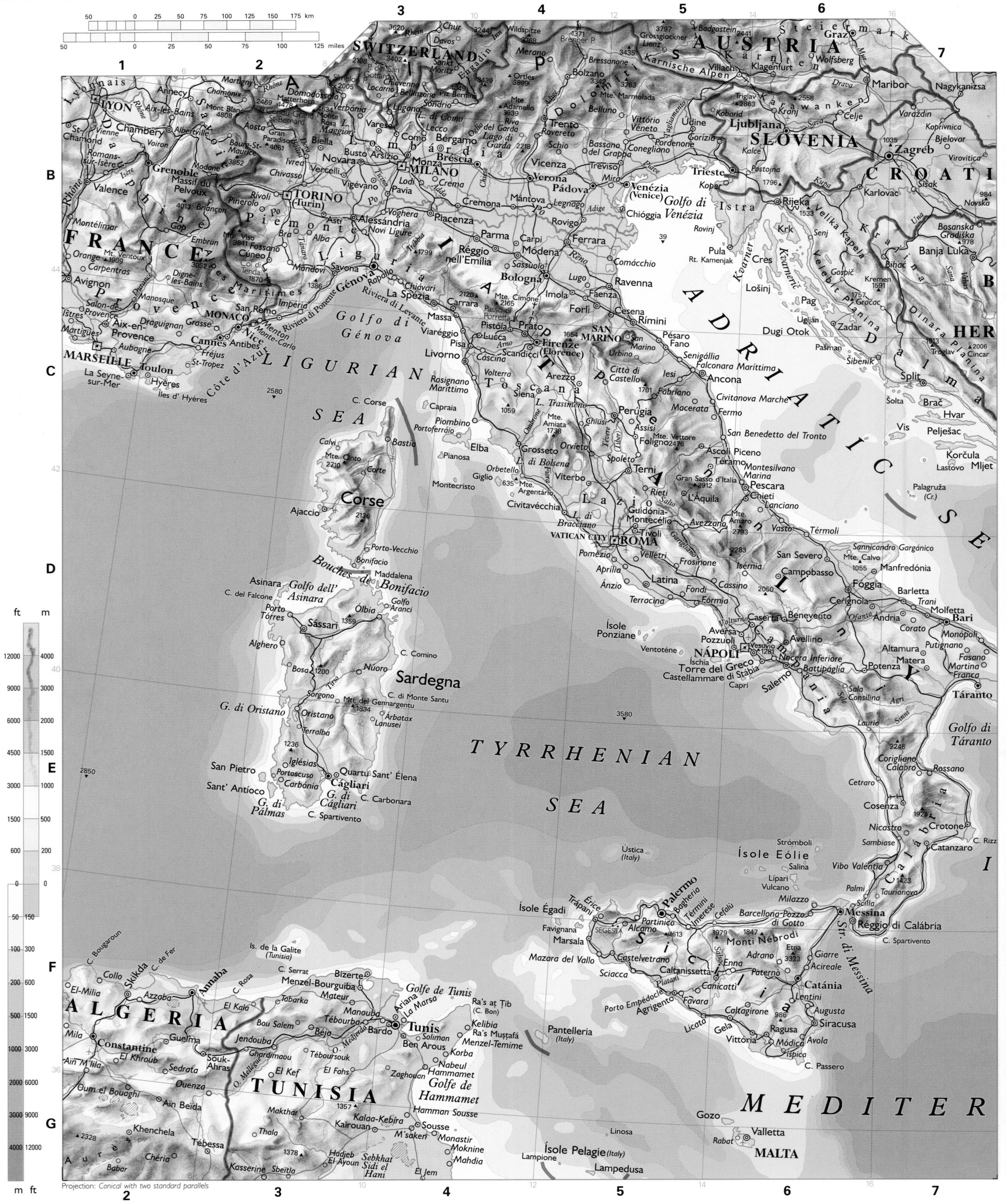

50 0 25 50 75 100 125 150 175 km

50 0 25 50 75 100 125 miles

Projection: *Conical with two standard parallels*

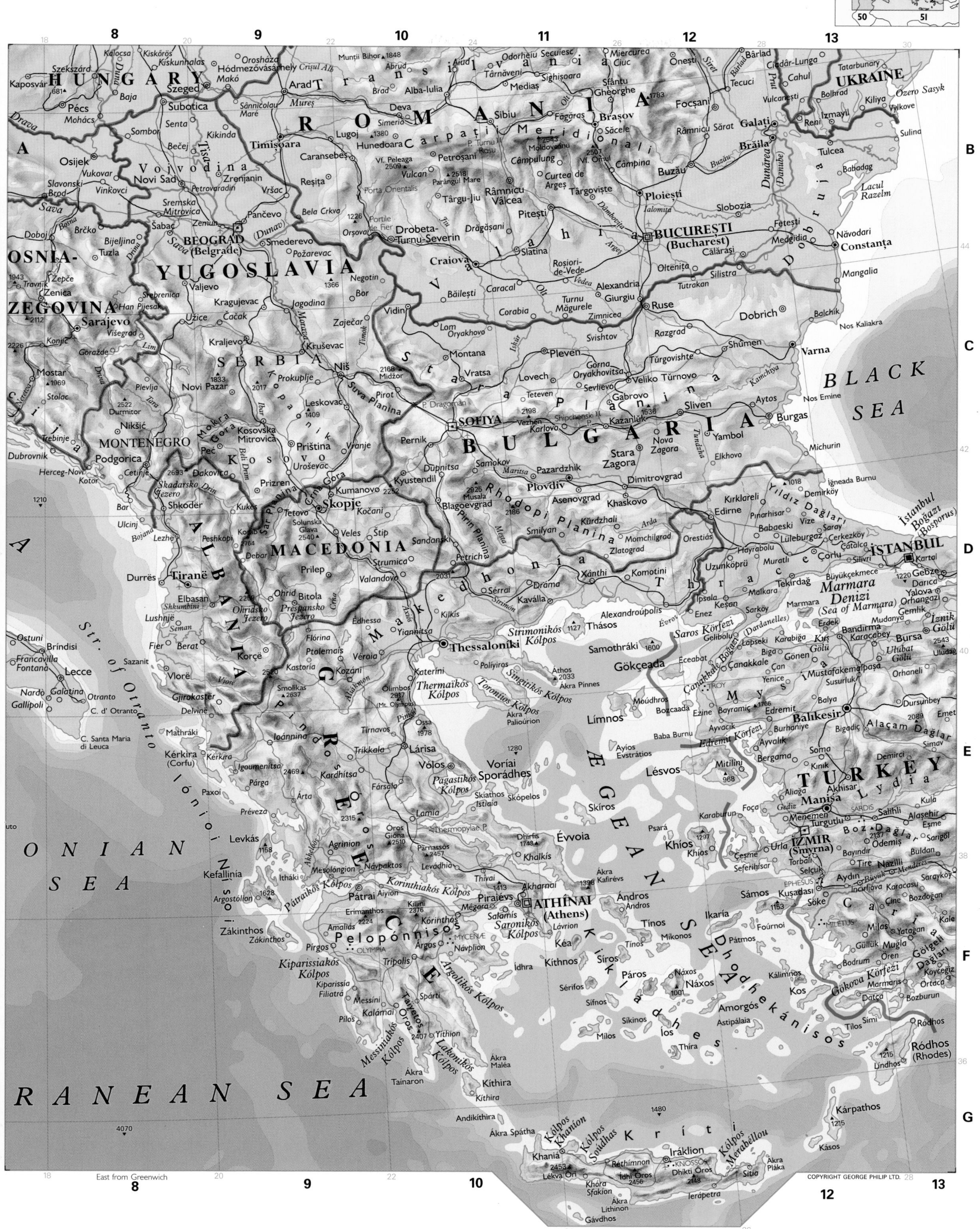
HUNGARY
ROMANIA
YUGOSLAVIA
SERBIA
MONTENEGRO
ALBANIA
MACEDONIA
BULGARIA
GREECE
TURKEY
UKRAINE
BLACK SEA
AEGEAN SEA
IONIAN SEA
MEDITERRANEAN SEA
BUCUREŞTI (Bucharest)
BEOGRAD (Belgrade)
SOFIYA
ATHÍNAI (Athens)
ISTANBUL
Marmara Denizi (Sea of Marmara)
Thessaloníki
Kríti
Pelopónnisos
Kikládhes
Dhodhekánisos
East from Greenwich
COPYRIGHT GEORGE PHILIP LTD.

THE BALEARICS, THE CANARIES AND MADEIRA

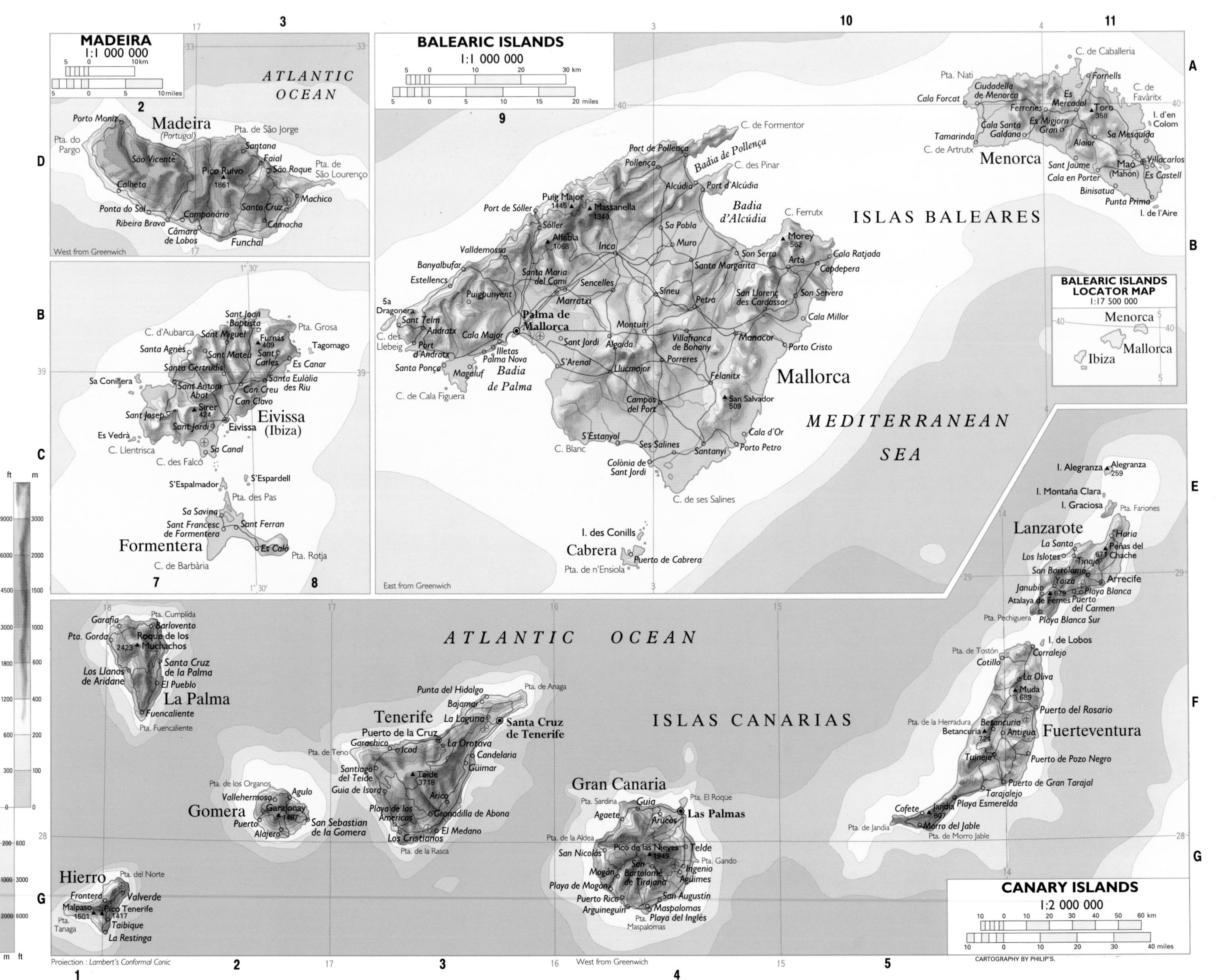

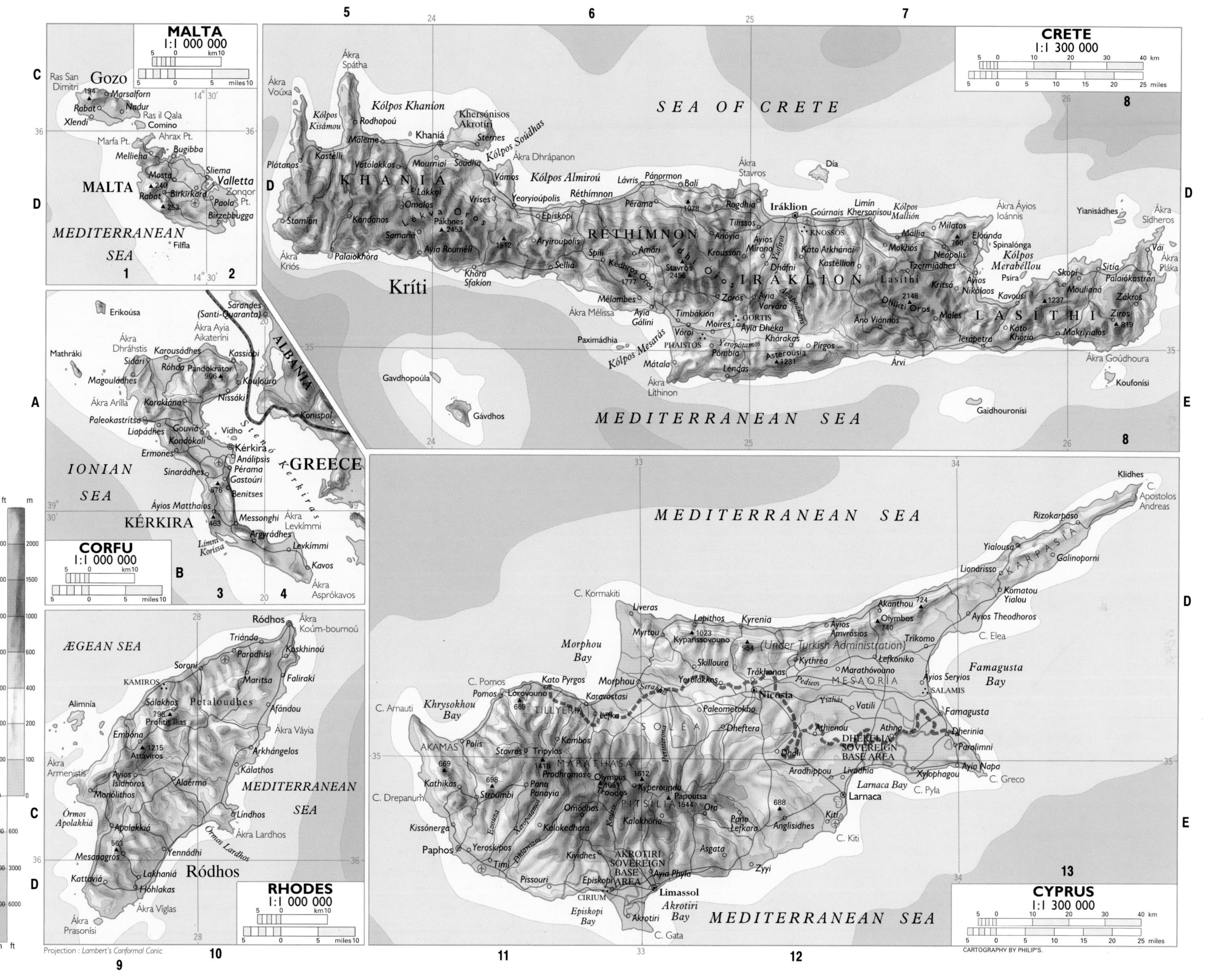
MALTA
1:1 000 000
Gozo
MALTA
Valletta
MEDITERRANEAN SEA
CRETE
1:1 300 000
SEA OF CRETE
Kríti
Khaniá
Iráklion
Réthimnon
MEDITERRANEAN SEA
CORFU
1:1 000 000
IONIAN SEA
KÉRKIRA
Kérkira
ALBANIA
GREECE
RHODES
1:1 000 000
ÆGEAN SEA
MEDITERRANEAN SEA
Ródhos
CYPRUS
1:1 300 000
MEDITERRANEAN SEA
Morphou Bay
Khrysokhou Bay
Famagusta Bay
Larnaca Bay
Akrotiri Bay
Episkopi Bay
Nicosia
Famagusta
Larnaca
Limassol
Paphos
(Under Turkish Administration)
DHEKELIA SOVEREIGN BASE AREA
AKROTIRI SOVEREIGN BASE AREA
CARTOGRAPHY BY PHILIP'S.
Projection : Lambert's Conformal Conic

EASTERN EUROPE AND TURKEY 1:10 000 000

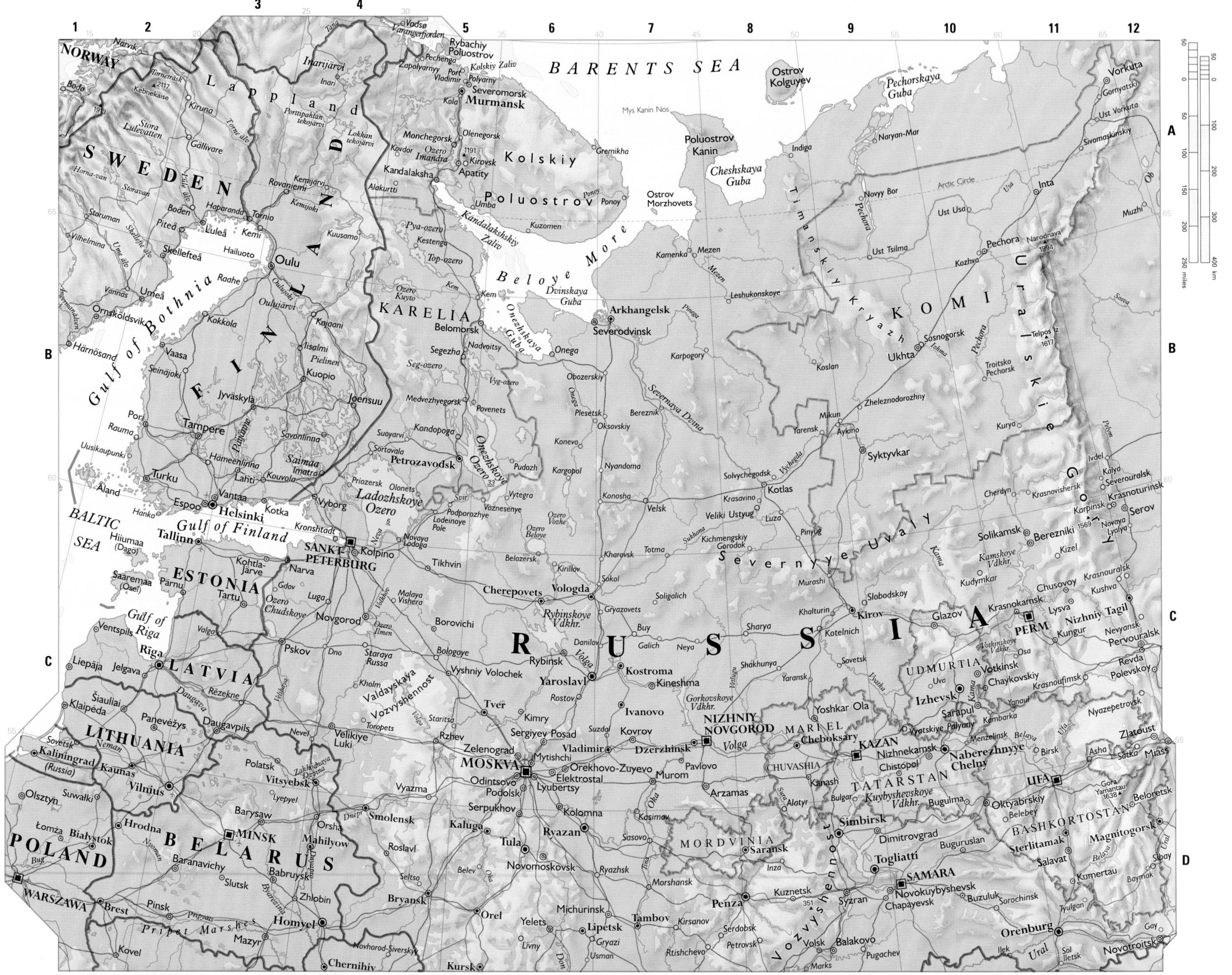

BLACK SEA
CASPIAN SEA
MEDITERRANEAN SEA
Sea of Azov
UKRAINE
KAZAKSTAN
ROMANIA
MOLDOVA
BULGARIA
TURKEY
GEORGIA
ARMENIA
AZERBAIJAN
TURKMENISTAN
IRAN
IRAQ
SYRIA
LEBANON
CYPRUS
CRIMEA
KALMYKIA
DAGESTAN
CHECHENIA
Kirgiziya Steppe
Caspian Depression
Carpathians
Caucasus Mountains
Kuzey Anadolu Dağları
Anadolu
Toros Dağları
Kurdistan
Reshteh-ye Kūhhā-ye Alborz
Bādiyat ash Shām
Dasht-e Kavīr
Garabogazköl Aylagy
KYYIV
KHARKIV
DNIPROPETROVSK
DONETSK
ODESA
ROSTOV
VOLGOGRAD
BUCUREŞTI
İSTANBUL
ANKARA
BURSA
IZMIR (Smyrna)
KONYA
ADANA
TBILISI
YEREVAN
BAKI
TABRĪZ
TEHRĀN
HALAB
DIMASHQ
BAYRŪT
Astrakhan
Saratov
Voronezh
Krasnodar
Sevastopol
Simferopol
Trabzon
Samsun
Erzurum
Kayseri
Sivas
Malatya
Diyarbakır
Al Mawşil
Arbīl
Kirkūk
Grozny
Makhachkala
Derbent
Aqtaū
Atyraū
Oral
Aqtöbe
Türkmenbashi
Rasht
Qom
Hamadān
Bākhtarān
Nicosia
Limassol
Projection: Conical with two standard parallels
East from Greenwich
COPYRIGHT GEORGE PHILIP LTD.
ft
m
12 000
9000
6000
4500
3000
1500
600
0
200
500
1000
2000
4000
3000
2000
1500
1000
500
200
0
600
1500
3000
6000

RUSSIA AND CENTRAL ASIA 1:20 000 000

ASIA : Physical 1:50 000 000

500 0 250 500 750 1000 1250 1500 1750 km

500 0 250 500 750 1000 1250 miles

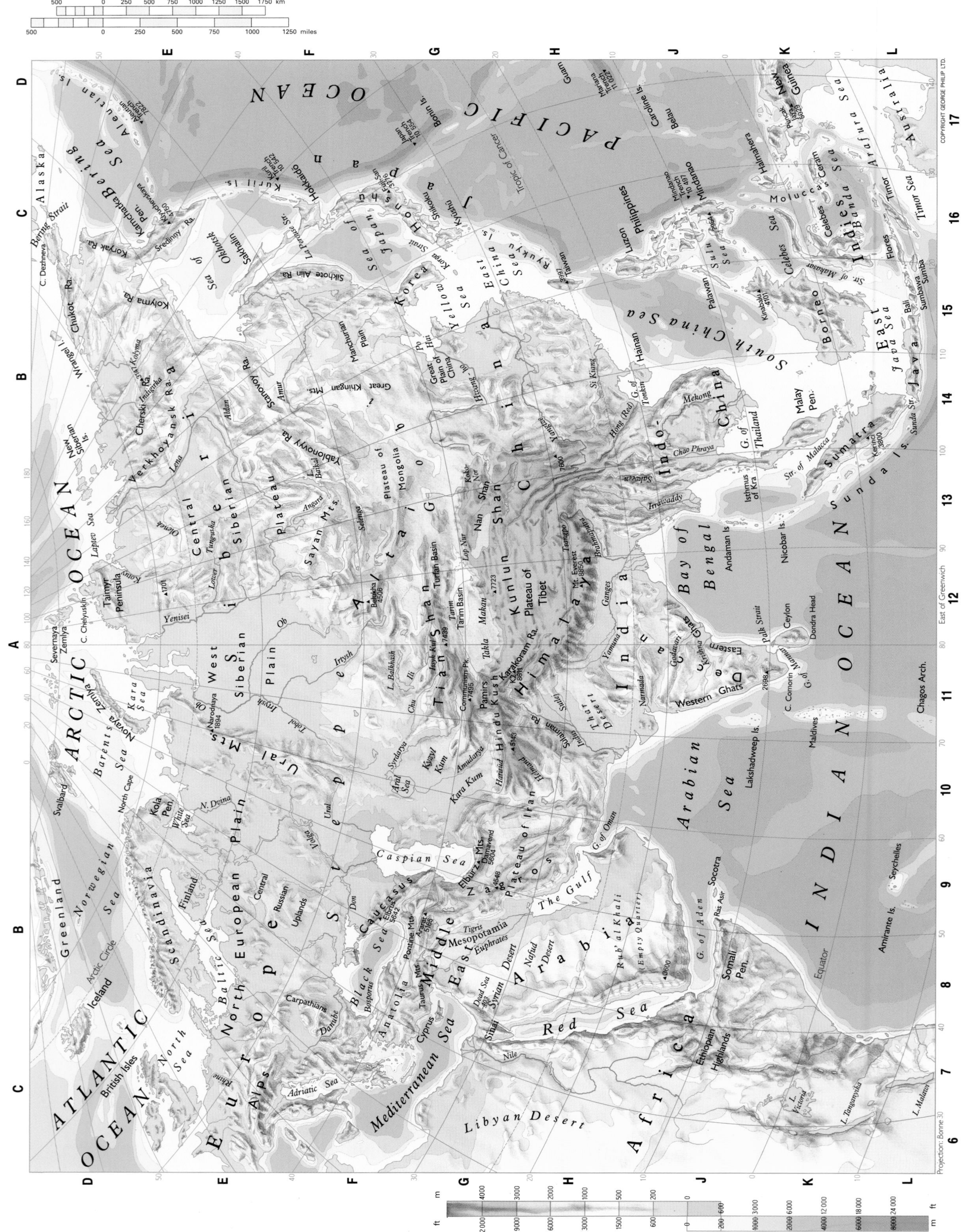

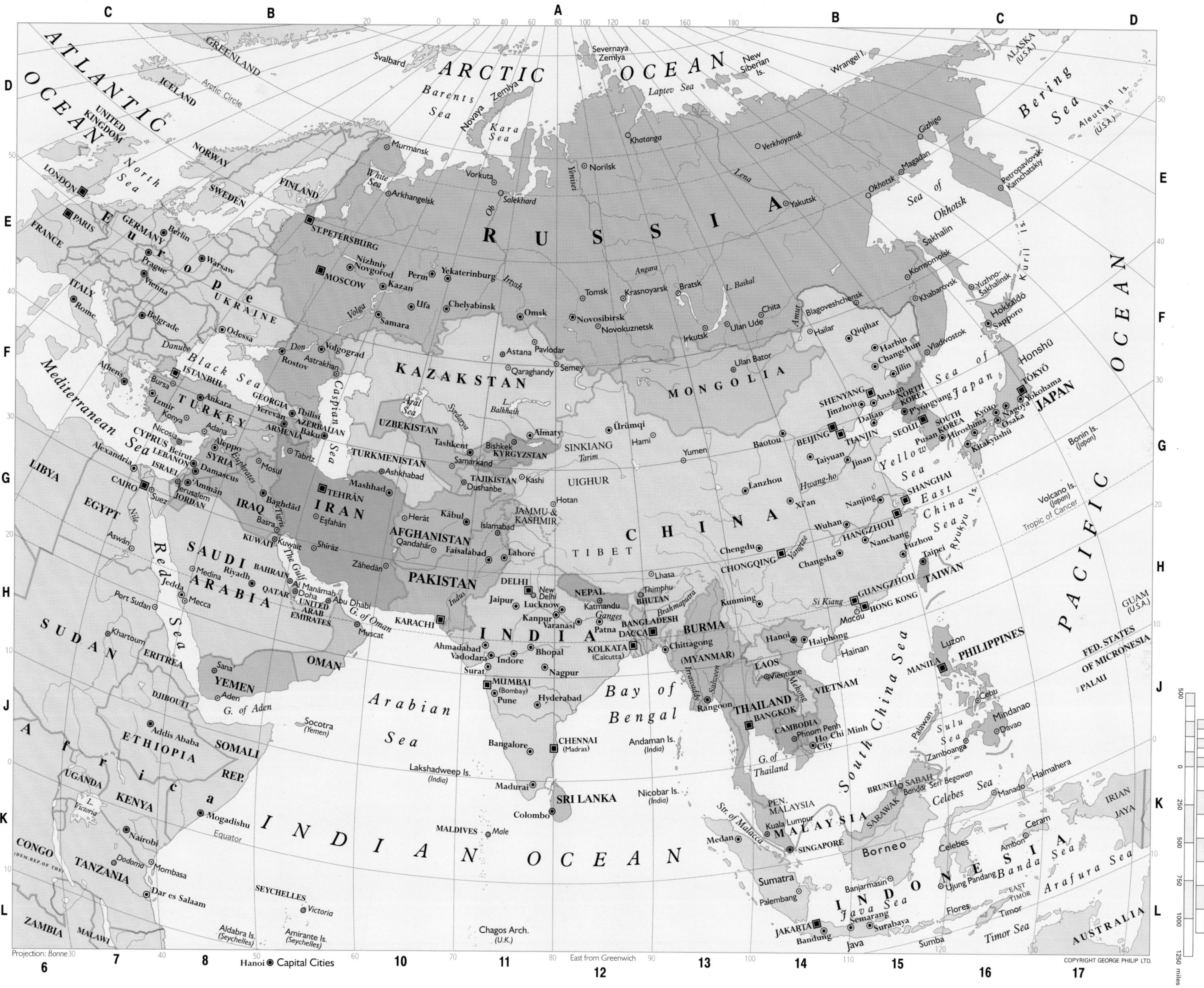
500 0 250 500 750 1000 1250 1500 1750 km
500 0 250 500 750 1000 1250 miles
ARCTIC OCEAN
PACIFIC OCEAN
INDIAN OCEAN
ATLANTIC OCEAN
Barents Sea
Kara Sea
Laptev Sea
Bering Sea
Sea of Okhotsk
Sea of Japan
Yellow Sea
East China Sea
South China Sea
Bay of Bengal
Arabian Sea
Caspian Sea
Black Sea
Mediterranean Sea
Red Sea
North Sea
The Gulf
G. of Oman
G. of Aden
G. of Thailand
Str. of Malacca
Java Sea
Banda Sea
Arafura Sea
Timor Sea
Celebes Sea
Sulu Sea
RUSSIA
KAZAKSTAN
MONGOLIA
CHINA
TIBET
SINKIANG UIGHUR
JAPAN
TOKYO
NORTH KOREA
SOUTH KOREA
SEOUL
BEIJING
SHANGHAI
TAIWAN
HONG KONG
PHILIPPINES
MANILA
VIETNAM
LAOS
CAMBODIA
THAILAND
BANGKOK
BURMA (MYANMAR)
MALAYSIA
SINGAPORE
INDONESIA
JAKARTA
BRUNEI
INDIA
DELHI
KOLKATA (Calcutta)
MUMBAI (Bombay)
CHENNAI (Madras)
SRI LANKA
BANGLADESH
DACCA
NEPAL
BHUTAN
PAKISTAN
KARACHI
AFGHANISTAN
IRAN
TEHRĀN
IRAQ
SAUDI ARABIA
YEMEN
OMAN
UNITED ARAB EMIRATES
QATAR
KUWAIT
SYRIA
JORDAN
ISRAEL
LEBANON
CYPRUS
TURKEY
GEORGIA
ARMENIA
AZERBAIJAN
TURKMENISTAN
UZBEKISTAN
TAJIKISTAN
KYRGYZSTAN
MOSCOW
ST. PETERSBURG
UKRAINE
EGYPT
CAIRO
SUDAN
ETHIOPIA
SOMALI REP.
KENYA
TANZANIA
AUSTRALIA
Tropic of Cancer
Arctic Circle
Equator
Hanoi ● Capital Cities
Projection: Bonne
East from Greenwich
COPYRIGHT GEORGE PHILIP LTD.

JAPAN 1:5 000 000

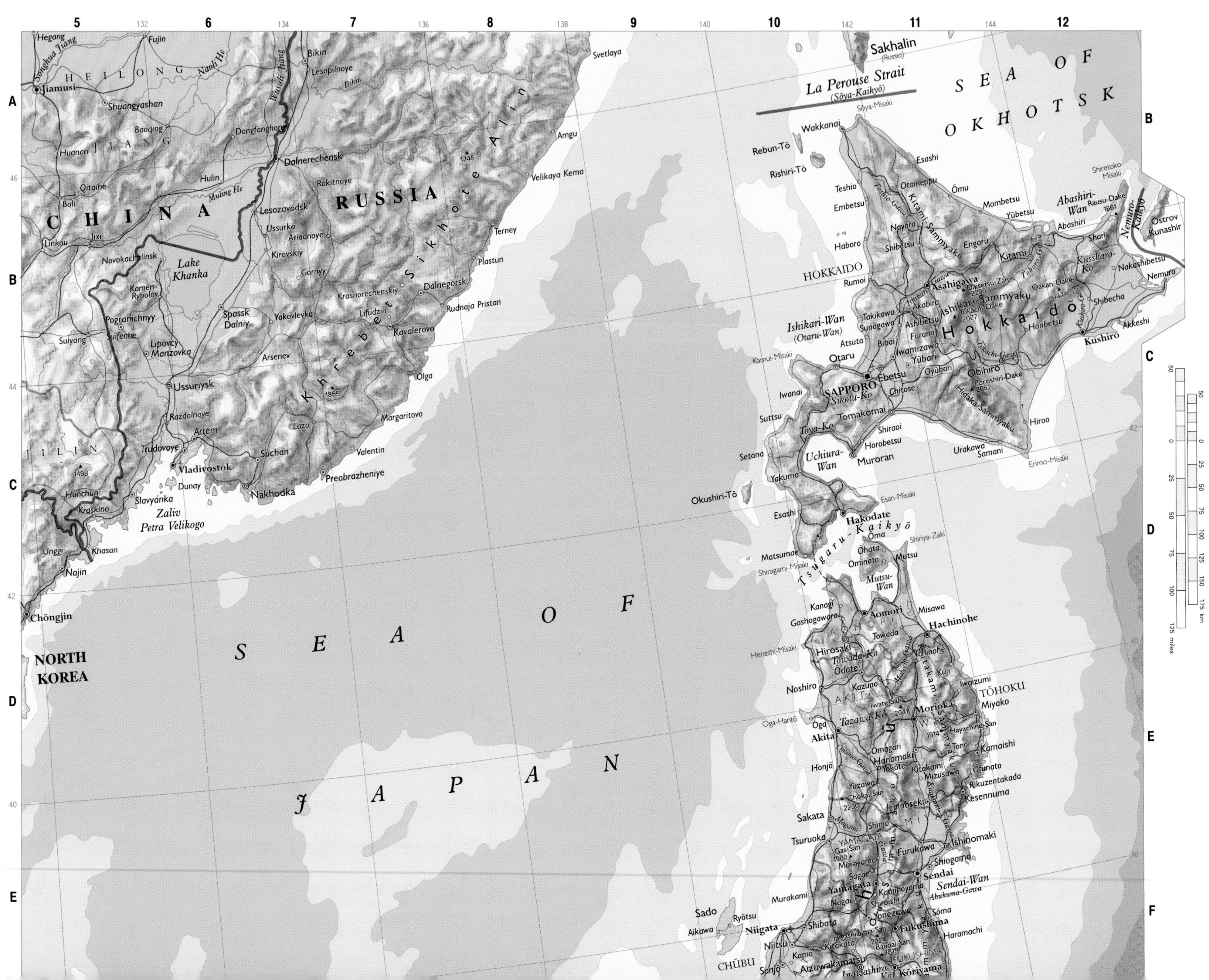

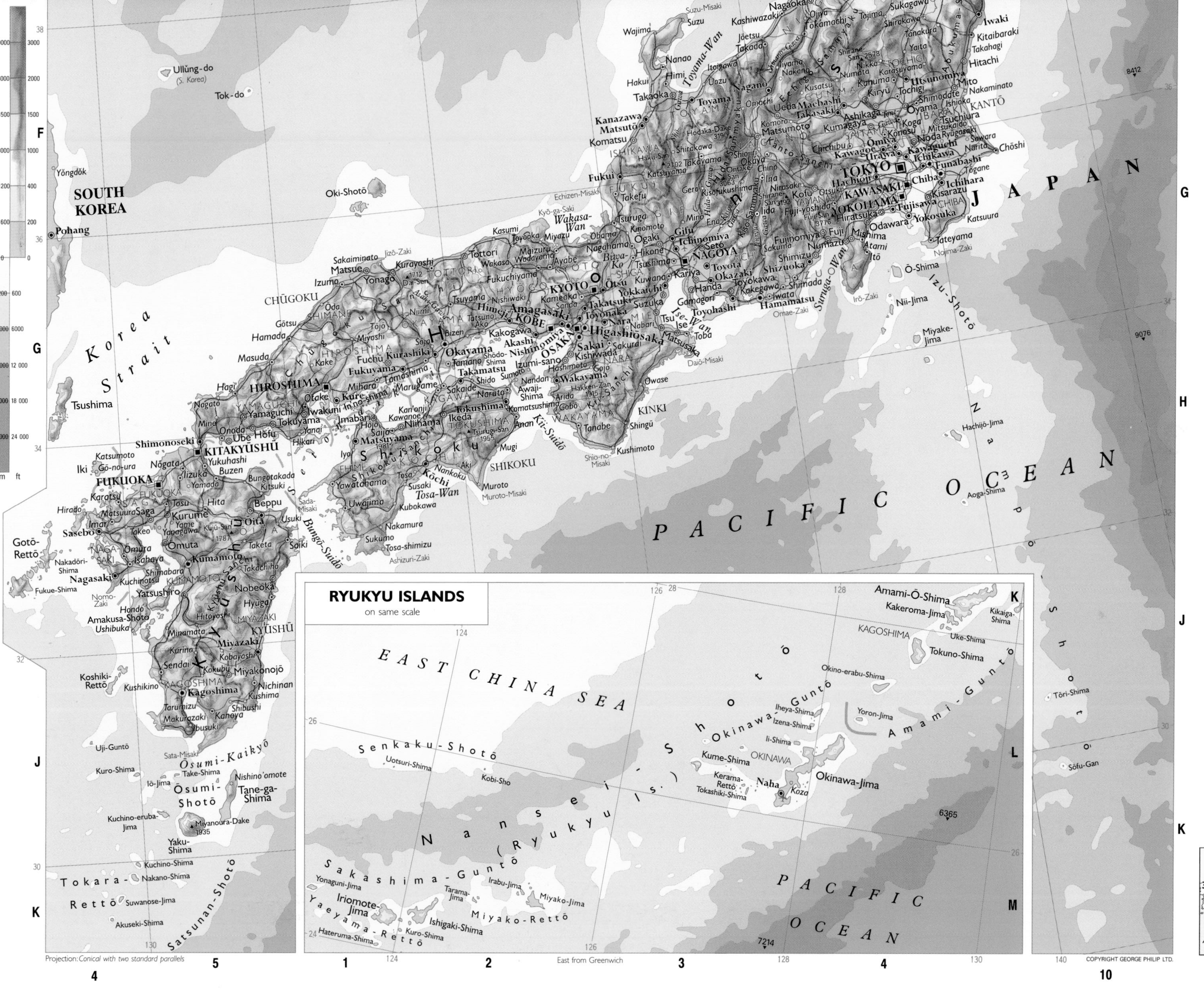
JAPAN
PACIFIC OCEAN
SOUTH KOREA
Korea Strait
Tsushima
Oki-Shotō
Ullŭng-do
(S. Korea)
Tok-do
Pohang
Yŏngdŏk
TOKYO
KAWASAKI
YOKOHAMA
NAGOYA
KYOTO
OSAKA
KOBE
HIROSHIMA
FUKUOKA
KITAKYŪSHŪ
Shikoku
SHIKOKU
KYŪSHŪ
CHŪGOKU
KINKI
KANTŌ
Izu-Shotō
Ōsumi-Shotō
Ōsumi-Kaikyō
Tokara-Rettō
Satsunan-Shotō
Gotō-Rettō
RYUKYU ISLANDS
on same scale
EAST CHINA SEA
PACIFIC OCEAN
Nansei-Shotō (Ryukyu Is.)
Senkaku-Shotō
Sakashima-Guntō
Okinawa-Guntō
Amami-Guntō
Okinawa-Jima
Amami-Ō-Shima
Naha
Koza
Miyako-Rettō
Yaeyama-Rettō
Projection: Conical with two standard parallels
East from Greenwich
COPYRIGHT GEORGE PHILIP LTD.

CHINA AND KOREA 1:15 000 000

100 0 100 200 300 400 500 600 km

100 0 100 200 300 400 miles

3 4 5

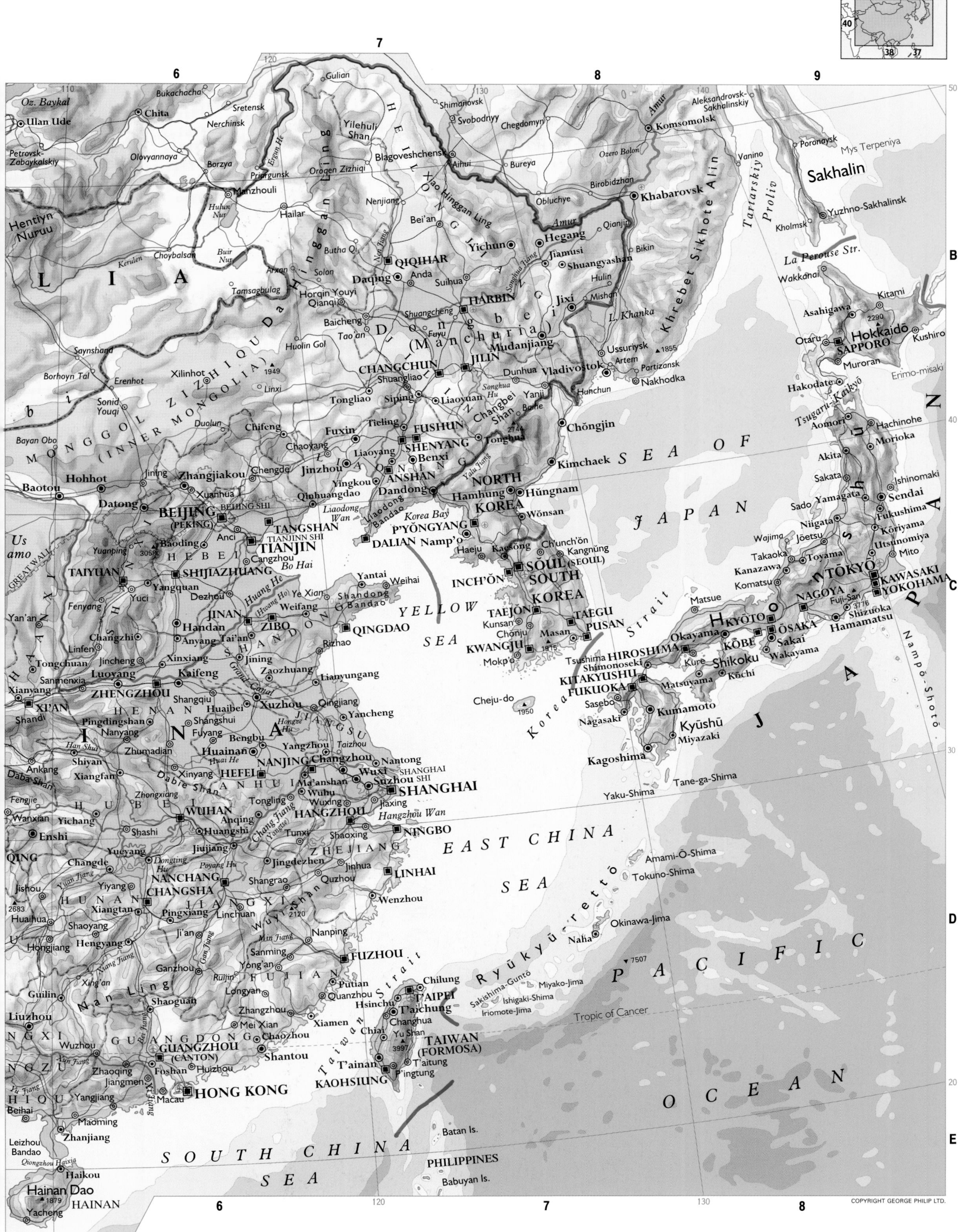
SEA OF JAPAN
YELLOW SEA
EAST CHINA SEA
PACIFIC OCEAN
SOUTH CHINA SEA
NORTH KOREA
SOUTH KOREA
JAPAN
TAIWAN (FORMOSA)
PHILIPPINES
HAINAN
Sakhalin
Hokkaidō
Honshū
Shikoku
Kyūshū
Hainan Dao
BEIJING (PEKING)
TIANJIN
SHANGHAI
HONG KONG
GUANGZHOU (CANTON)
P'YŎNGYANG
SŎUL (SEOUL)
TŌKYŌ
ŌSAKA
KYŌTO
NAGOYA
YOKOHAMA
KAWASAKI
SAPPORO
HARBIN
SHENYANG
CHANGCHUN
Vladivostok
Khabarovsk
Blagoveshchensk
Korea Strait
Taiwan Strait
La Perouse Str.
Tartarskiy Proliv
Ryūkyū-rettō
Tropic of Cancer
Nampō-Shotō
COPYRIGHT GEORGE PHILIP LTD.

NORTHERN CHINA AND KOREA 1:6 000 000

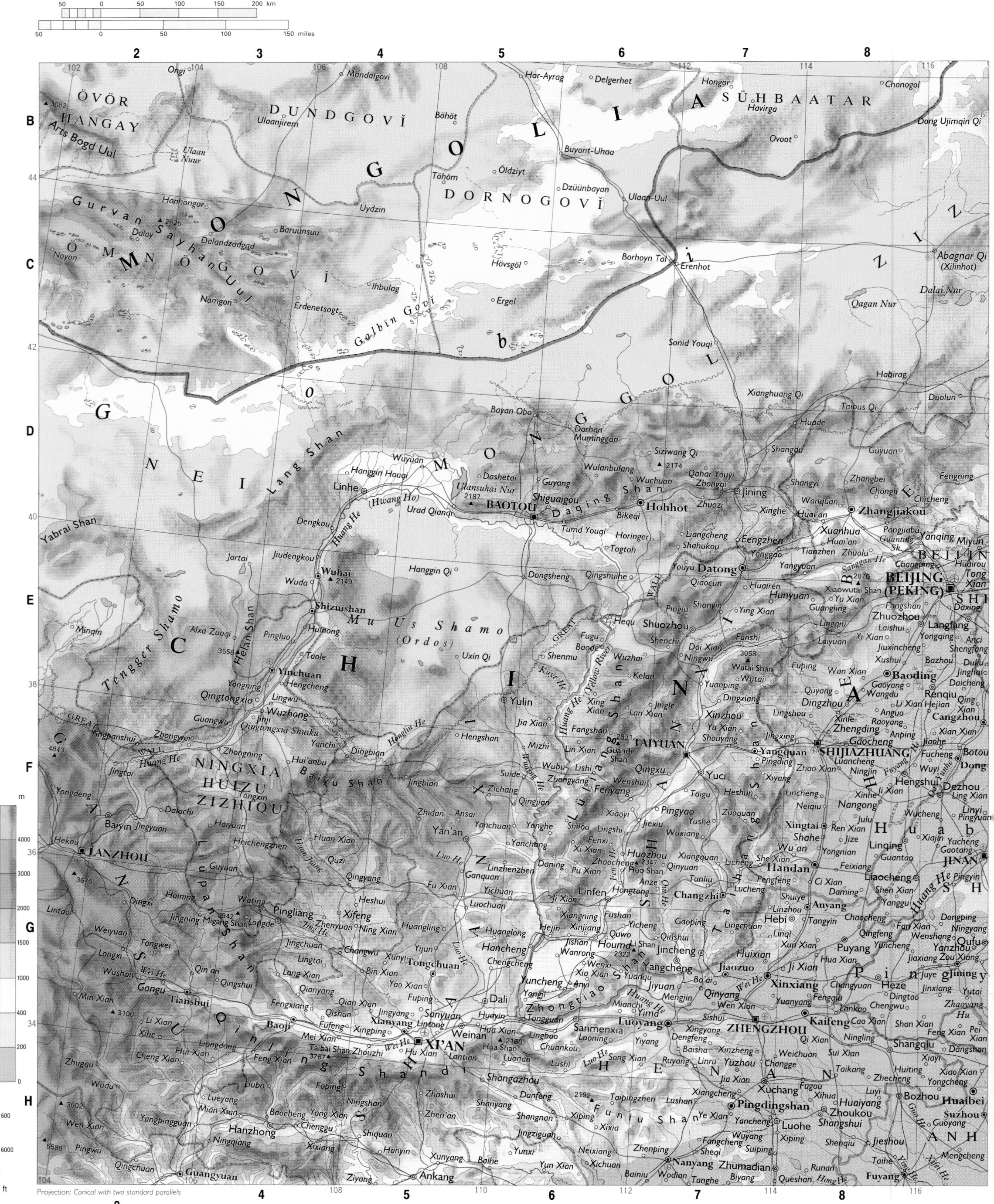

Projection: Conical with two standard parallels

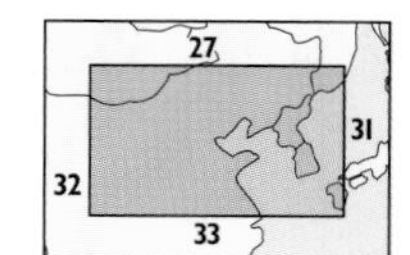

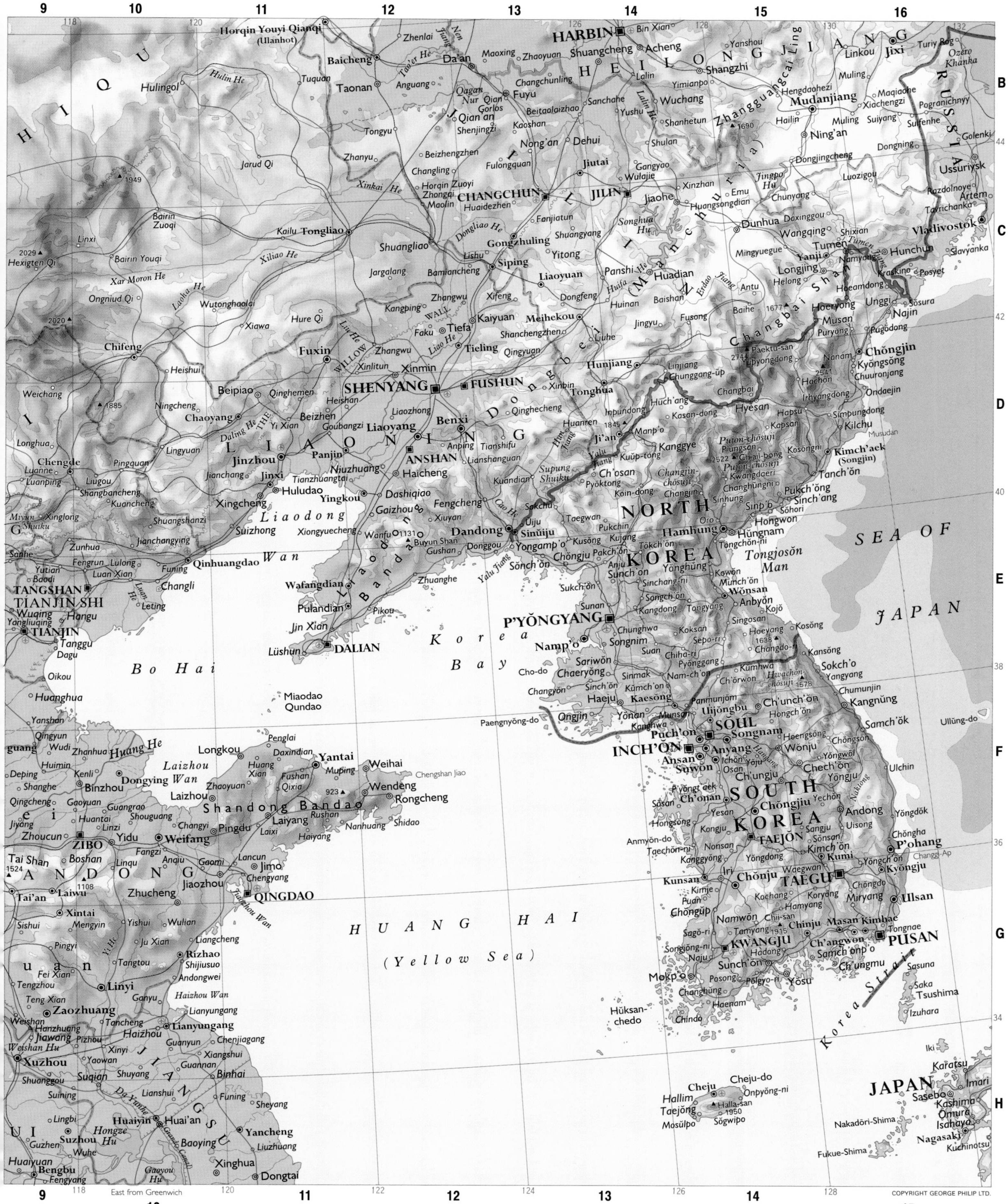

9 10 11 12 13 14 15 16

HEILONGJIANG
RUSSIA
HARBIN
Horqin Youyi Qianqi (Ulanhot)
Baicheng
Zhenlai
Da'an
Taonan
Hulingol
Tuquan
Anguang
Qagan Nur
Qian Gorlos
Shenjingzi
Fuyu
Maoxing
Zhaoyuan
Shuangcheng
Acheng
Bin Xian
Yanshou
Shangzhi
Linkou
Jixi
Turiy Rog
Ozero Khanka
Mudanjiang
Hailin
Ning'an
Muling
Suiyang
Suifenhe
Pogranichnyy
Dongning
Ussuriysk
Artem
Vladivostok
Slavyanka
Posyet
Kraskino
Zhangguangcai Ling
Yimianpo
Wuchang
Shanhetun
Shulan
Jiutai
Dehui
Nong'an
Kaoshan
Changchunling
Sanchahe
Yushu
Lalin
Beitaolaizhao
Tongyu
Zhanyu
Beizhengzhen
Changling
Horqin Zuoyi Zhongqi
Maolin
Fulongquan
CHANGCHUN
Huaidezhen
JILIN
Jiaohe
Xinzhan
Emu
Huangsongdian
Jingpo Hu
Chunyang
Dunhua
Daxinggou
Wangqing
Tumen
Shixian
Hunchun
Yanji
Longjing
Helong
Namyang
Hoeamdong
Unggi
Najin
Sŏsura
Hoeryong
Musan
Puryong
Pugodong
Chŏngjin
Kyŏngsŏng
Chuuronjang
Nanam
Hochon
Irhyangdong
Ondaejin
Sinpungdong
Kilchu
Hapsu
Kapsan
Kimch'aek (Songjin)
Tanch'ŏn
Pukch'ŏng
Sinch'ang
Sinp'o
Sŏhori
Hongwon
Hŭngnam
Hamhung
Tongjosŏn Man
SEA OF JAPAN
Jarud Qi
Bairin Zuoqi
Bairin Youqi
Linxi
Hexigten Qi
Xar Moron He
Xiliao He
Xinkai He
Kailu
Tongliao
Shuangliao
Jargalang
Bamiancheng
Lishu
Siping
Gongzhuling
Fanjiatun
Shuangyang
Yitong
Liaoyuan
Dongfeng
Panshi
Huadian
Songhua Hu
Huinan
Baishan
Antu
Baihe
Changbai Shan
Paektu-san
Ch'ŏngjin
Ongniud Qi
Wutonghaolai
Xiawa
Hure Qi
Kangping
Zhangwu
Faku
Tiefa
Kaiyuan
Xifeng
Meihekou
Shanchengzhen
Liuhe
Jingyu
Fusong
Chifeng
Fuxin
Xinlitun
Xinmin
Tieling
Qingyuan
Hunjiang
Linjiang
Chunggang-ŭp
Changbai
Hyesan
Heishui
Weichang
Ningcheng
Beipiao
Qinghemen
SHENYANG
FUSHUN
Xinbin
Tonghua
Heishan
Liaozhong
Qinghecheng
Huanren
Manp'o
Kanggye
Chaoyang
Yi Xian
Beizhen
Goubangzi
Liaoyang
Benxi
Ji'an
Longhua
Lingyuan
Chengde
Pingquan
Jinzhou
Panjin
ANSHAN
Anping
Tianshifu
Lianshanguan
Kuandian
Supung Shuiku
Ch'osan
Pyŏktong
Kanggye
LIAONING
Luanping
Liugou
Shangbancheng
Kuancheng
Jianchang
Jinxi
Huludao
Xingcheng
Tianzhuangtai
Niuzhuang
Haicheng
Yingkou
Dashiqiao
Gaizhou
Fengcheng
Xiuyan
Dandong
Sinŭiju
Uiju
Yongamp'o
Taegwan
Kusŏng
Pukchin
Kujang
Chŏngju
Pakch'ŏn
Anju
Sunch'ŏn
NORTH KOREA
Yŏnghŭng
Kowŏn
Munch'ŏn
Wŏnsan
Anbyŏn
Kojŏ
Miyun Shuiku
Xinglong
Shuangshanzi
Suizhong
Xiongyuecheng
Wafu
Liaodong Wan
Jianchangying
Zunhua
Fengrun
Luan Xian
Funing
Qinhuangdao
Changli
Leting
Yutian
Baodi
TANGSHAN
TIANJIN SHI
Wuqing
Hangu
Yangliuqing
TIANJIN
Tanggu
Dagu
Wafangdian
Pulandian
Pikou
Zhuanghe
Jin Xian
Lüshun
DALIAN
Liaodong Bandao
Buyun Shan
Gushan
Donggou
Sŏnch'ŏn
Yalu Jiang
Sukch'ŏn
Sunan
P'YŎNGYANG
Nampo
Songnim
Chunghwa
Koksan
Sepo-ri
Singosan
Hoeyang
Kosŏng
Changdo-ri
Kansŏng
Sokch'o
Yangyang
Bo Hai
Korea Bay
Oikou
Huanghua
Miaodao Qundao
Cho-do
Chaeryŏng
Sariwŏn
Sinmak
Suan
Chiha-ri
P'yŏnggang
Kumhwa
Ch'ŏrwŏn
Hwach'ŏn
Changyon
Sinch'ŏn
Haeju
Kaesŏng
Kŭmch'ŏn
Ongjin
Yŏnan
Paengnyŏng-do
P'anmunjŏm
Ŭijŏngbu
Ch'unch'ŏn
Hongch'ŏn
Chumunjin
Kangnŭng
Samch'ŏk
Ullŭng-do
SOUL
Songnam
INCH'ON
Puch'ŏn
Anyang
Ansan
Suwŏn
Osan
Ich'ŏn
Yoju
Wŏnju
Hoengsŏng
Chŏngsŏn
Yŏngwŏl
Chech'ŏn
Yŏngju
Ulchin
Yanshan
Qingyun
Wudi
Zhanhua
Huang He
Laizhou Wan
Longkou
Penglai
Daxindian
Yantai
Weihai
Huimin
Kenli
Deping
Shanghe
Dongying
Binzhou
Huang Xian
Fushan
Qixia
Muping
Wendeng
Rongcheng
Chengshan Jiao
Zhaoyuan
Laizhou
Shandong Bandao
Rushan
Shidao
Nanhuang
Haiyang
Laiyang
Laixi
Pingdu
Changyi
Weifang
Gaoyuan
Guangrao
Shouguang
Qingcheng
Huantai
Linzi
Jiyang
Zhoucun
ZIBO
Yidu
Tai Shan
Boshan
Fangzi
Anqiu
Gaomi
Linqu
Lancun
Jimo
Jiaozhou
Chengyang
QINGDAO
Jiaozhou Wan
Laiwu
Zhucheng
Tai'an
Xintai
Mengyin
Yishui
Wulian
Sishui
Ju Xian
Liangcheng
Rizhao
Shijiusuo
Andongwei
Pingyi
Tangtou
Fei Xian
Linyi
Tengzhou
Teng Xian
Ganyu
Haizhou Wan
Lianyungang
Zaozhuang
Tancheng
Tianyungang
Haizhou
Weishan
Hanzhuang
Jiawang
Pizhou
Weishan Hu
Xinyi
Guanyun
Chenjiagang
Xiangshui
Xuzhou
Yaowan
Guannan
Binhai
Shuanggou
Suqian
Shuyang
Lianshui
Funing
Sheyang
Suining
Da Yunhe
Lingbi
Huaiyin
Huai'an
Yancheng
Hongze Hu
Suzhou
Guzhen
Wuhe
Baoying
Liuzhuang
JIANGSU
Grand Canal
Huaiyuan
Bengbu
Fengyang
Gaoyou Hu
Xinghua
Dongtai
HUANG HAI (Yellow Sea)
P'yŏngt'aek
Sosan
Ch'ŏnan
Ch'ŏngju
SOUTH KOREA
Yech'ŏn
Andong
Yŏngdŏk
Hongsŏng
Yesan
Kongju
Sangju
Sŏnsan
Uisong
Chŏngha
Anmyŏn-do
Taech'ŏn-ni
TAEJŎN
Nonsan
Kimch'ŏn
Kumi
P'ohang
Yŏngch'ŏn
Kyŏngju
Changgi-Ap
Kanggyŏng
Yŏngdong
Iri
Kunsan
Chŏnju
Waegwan
TAEGU
Kimje
Chŏngdo
Miryang
Ulsan
Pu'an
Chŏngŭp
Kochang
Koryŏng
Hamyang
Namwŏn
Chii-san
Chinju
Masan
Kimhae
Tongnae
PUSAN
Sagŏ-ri
Tamyang
KWANGJU
Songjŏng-ni
Naju
Hadong
Ch'angwŏn
Samch'ŏnp'o
Ch'ungmu
Mokp'o
Sunch'ŏn
Posong
Polgyo-ri
Yŏsu
Changhŭng
Haenam
Chindo
Hŭksan-chedo
Korea Strait
Sasuna
Saka
Tsushima
Izuhara
Iki
Karatsu
Imari
Cheju
Cheju-do
Onpyŏng-ni
Hallim
Halla-san
Taejŏng
Mosŭlpo
Sŏgwipo
JAPAN
Sasebo
Kashima
Omura
Isahaya
Nakadōri-Shima
Nagasaki
Kuchinotsu
Fukue-Shima

9 10 11 12 13 14 15
East from Greenwich
118 120 122 124 126 128

INDONESIA AND THE PHILIPPINES 1:12 500 000

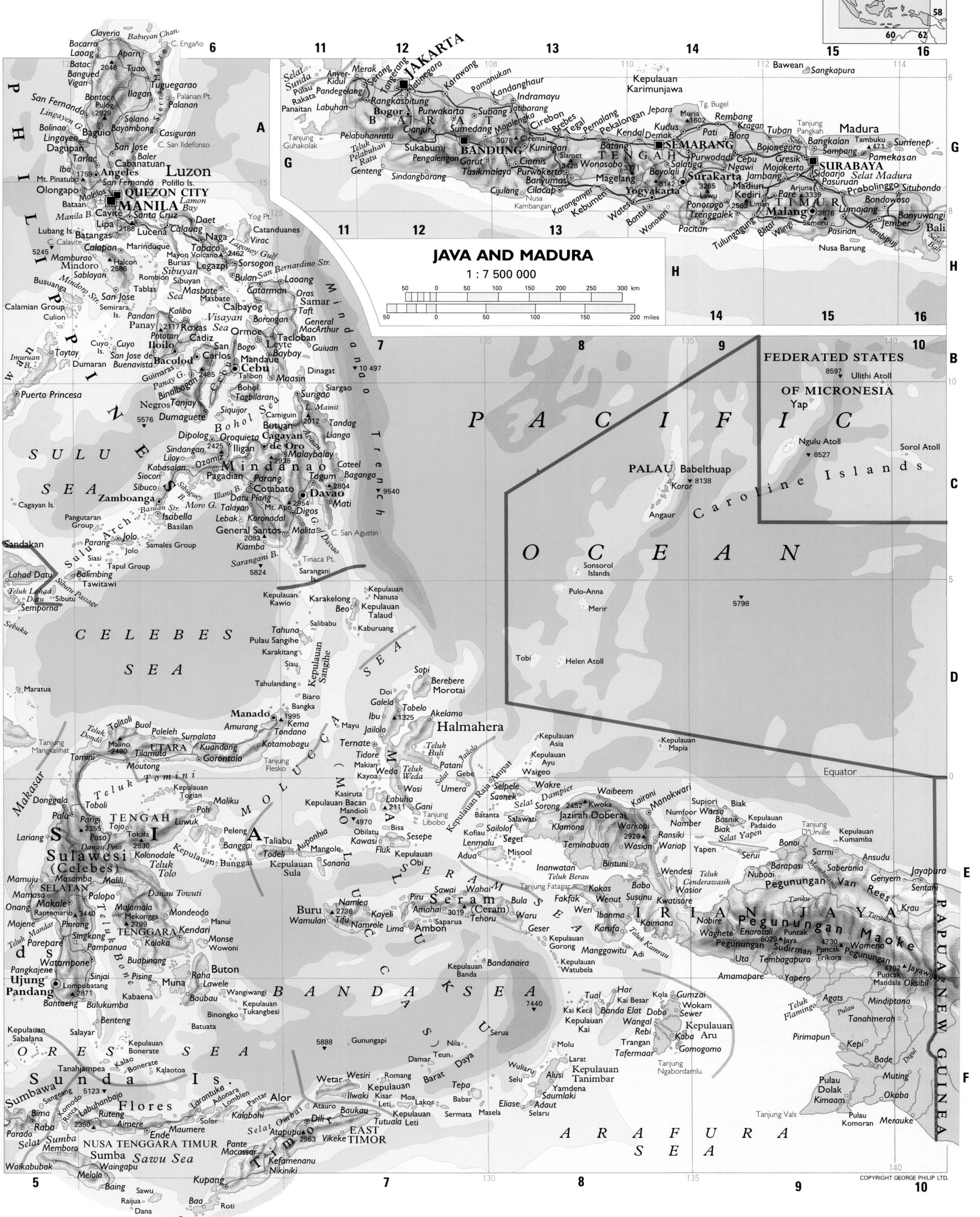
JAVA AND MADURA
1 : 7 500 000
50 0 50 100 150 200 250 300 km
50 0 50 100 150 200 miles
JAKARTA
BANDUNG
SEMARANG
SURABAYA
Bogor
Cirebon
Surakarta
Yogyakarta
Malang
Madura
Kepulauan Karimunjawa
Bawean
Selat Sunda
Selat Madura
Bali
Nusa Barung
PHILIPPINES
Luzon
QUEZON CITY
MANILA
Mindoro
Samar
Leyte
Cebu
Mindanao
Davao
Zamboanga
Mindanao Trench
SULU SEA
CELEBES SEA
Sulu Arch.
PACIFIC OCEAN
PALAU
Babelthuap
Koror
FEDERATED STATES OF MICRONESIA
Yap
Caroline Islands
Halmahera
MOLUCCA SEA
Manado
Sulawesi (Celebes)
Ujung Pandang
BANDA SEA
SERAM SEA
Seram (Ceram)
Ambon
Buru
IRIAN JAYA
Pegunungan Maoke
Jayapura
PAPUA NEW GUINEA
Kepulauan Aru
Kepulauan Tanimbar
ARAFURA SEA
FLORES SEA
Flores
Sumba
Sawu Sea
Timor
EAST TIMOR
NUSA TENGGARA TIMUR
Sunda Is.
Equator
COPYRIGHT GEORGE PHILIP LTD.

MAINLAND SOUTH-EAST ASIA 1:6 000 000

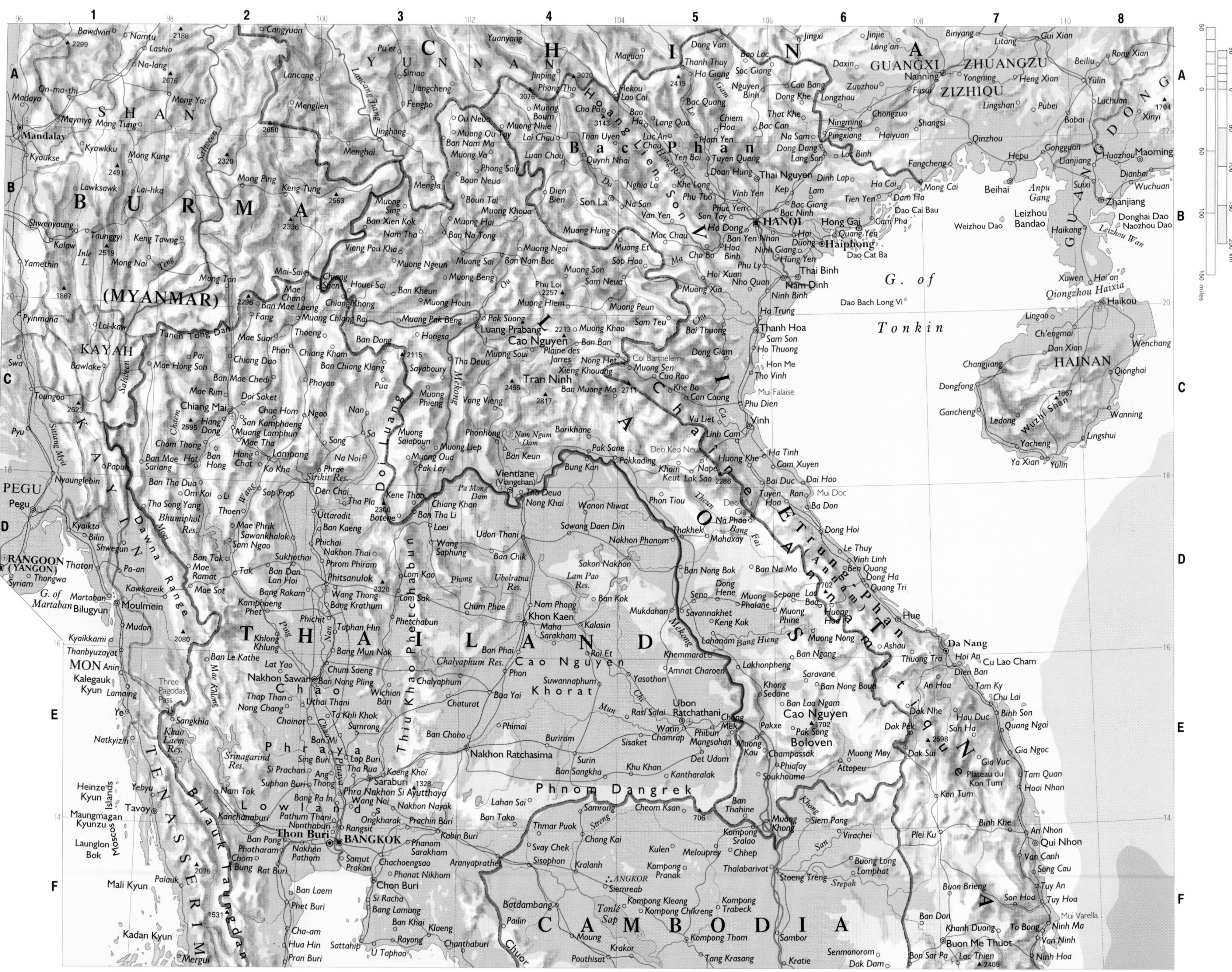

Gulf of Thailand
SOUTH CHINA SEA
MALAYSIA
PENINSULAR MALAYSIA
INDONESIA
Strait of Malacca
Myeik Kyunzu (Mergui Archipelago)
Phnom Penh
THANH PHO HO CHI MINH (SAIGON)
Kuala Lumpur
SINGAPORE
Straits of Singapore
George Town
Medan
Kuantan
Kuala Terengganu
Kota Baharu
Johor Baharu
Ipoh
Seremban
Melaka
Hat Yai
Songkhla
Nakhon Si Thammarat
Surat Thani
Phuket
Ko Samui
Ko Phangan
Kho Khot Kra
Cameron Highlands
Kepulauan Anambas (Indonesia)
Kepulauan Natuna Besar (Indonesia)
Kepulauan Natuna Selatan (Indonesia)
Borneo
Kuching
SARAWAK (Malaysia)
Con Son
Nha Trang
Da Lat
Phan Thiet
Can Tho
Bac Lieu
Ca Mau
Rach Gia
Long Xuyen
Dao Phu Quoc
Projection: Conical with two standard parallels
East from Greenwich
COPYRIGHT GEORGE PHILIP LTD.

Continuation Southwards on same scale
Projection: Conical with two standard parallels
ARABIAN SEA
AFGHANISTAN
PAKISTAN
INDIA
SRI LANKA
KARACHI
Hyderabad
Quetta
RAWALPINDI
Islamabad
LAHORE
FAISALABAD
Amritsar
DELHI
Jaipur
Ahmadabad
MUMBAI (BOMBAY)
Pune (Poona)
HYDERABAD
Bangalore
Chennai (Madras)
Colombo
Kabul
Herat
Qandahar
Gulf of Kachchh
Gulf of Khambhat
Gulf of Mannar
Palk Strait

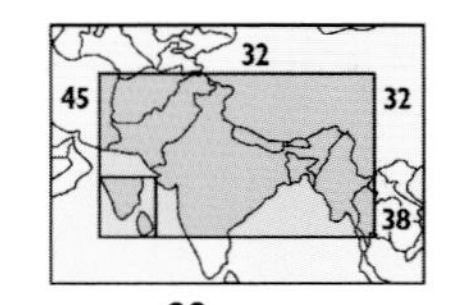

12 13 14 15 16 17 18 19 20 21 22

B C D E F G H J K L M

XINJIANG UYGUR ZIZHIQU
Kunlun Shan
Hoh Xil Shan
QINGHAI
Bayan Har Shan
CHINA
XIZANG ZIZHIQU (TIBET)
Tanggula (Dangla) Shan
Nganglong Kangri
Gangdisê Shan
Nyainqentanglha Shan
Lhasa
Nu Jiang (Salween)
Lancang Jiang (Mekong)
Jinsha Jiang
SICHUAN
YUNNAN
NEPAL
Katmandu
Mt. Everest 8850
Kanchenjunga 8598
SIKKIM
BHUTAN
Thimphu
ARUNACHAL PRADESH
ASSAM
MEGHALAYA
NAGALAND
MANIPUR
MIZORAM
TRIPURA
KACHIN
SAGAING
BIHAR
JHARKHAND
WEST BENGAL
CHHATTISGARH
ORISSA
Lucknow
Varanasi
Patna
Allahabad
Ranchi
Jamshedpur
Haora
KOLKATA (CALCUTTA)
Mouths of the Ganges
Sundarbans
BANGLADESH
DHAKA
Chittagong
Cox's Bazar
Brahmaputra
Ganga
Chindwin
Irrawaddy
Mandalay
SHAN
BURMA (MYANMAR)
ARAKAN
Sittwe (Akyab)
Arakan Coast
Ramree I.
Cheduba I.
MAGWE
KAYAH
KAYIN
PEGU
RANGOON (YANGON)
IRRAWADDY
MON
Moulmein
G. of Martaban
Mouths of the Irrawaddy
THAILAND
Chiang Mai
Tropic of Cancer
BAY OF BENGAL
INDIAN OCEAN
Preparis North Channel
Pariparit Kyun (Burma)
Preparis South Channel
Koko Kyunzu (Burma)
Moscos Is.
Northern Circars
Vishakhapatnam
Rajahmundry
Vijayawada
Machilipatnam
Kakinada

East from Greenwich 82 84 86 88 90 92 94 96

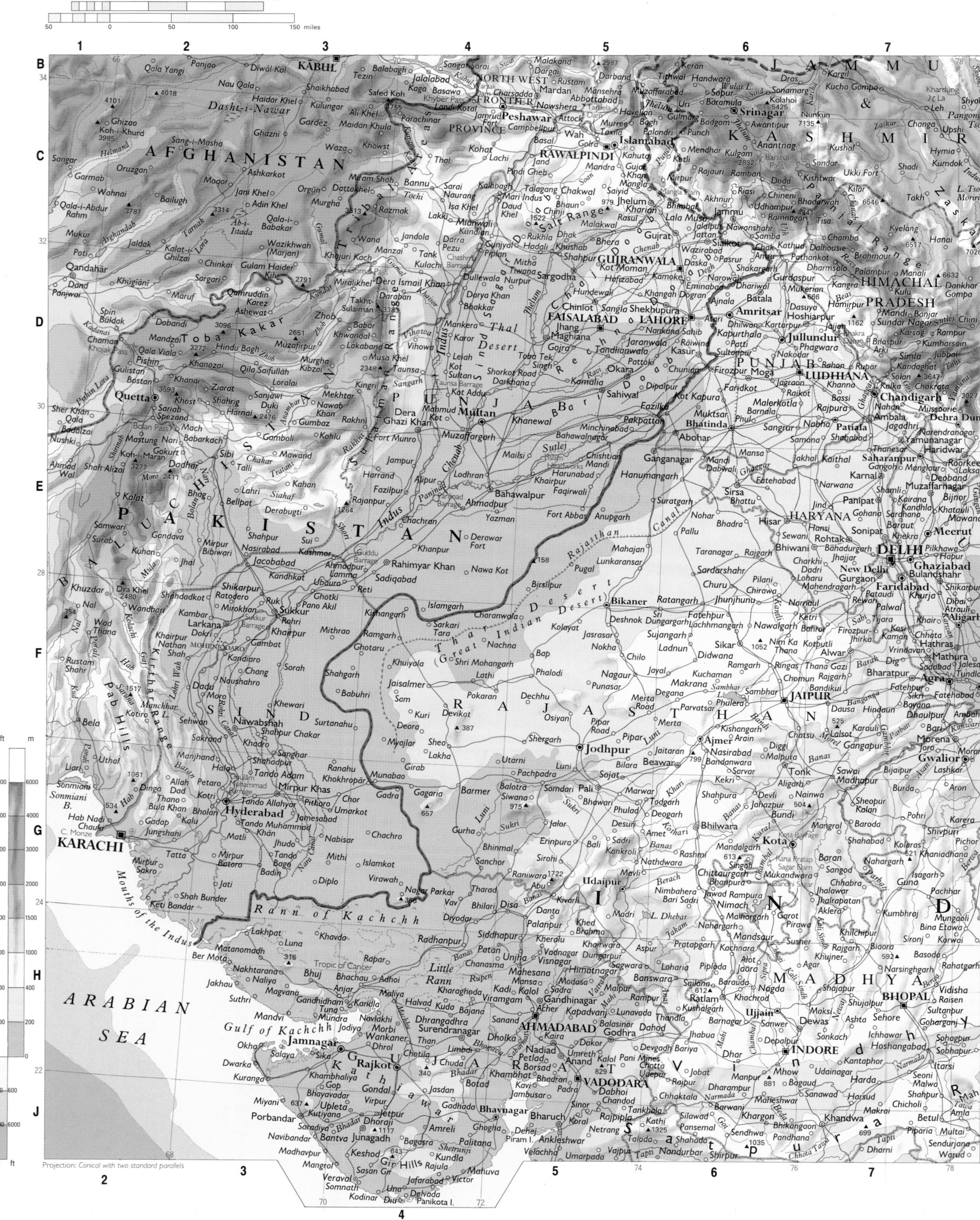
AFGHANISTAN
PAKISTAN
BALUCHISTAN
PUNJAB
SIND
RAJASTHAN
HARYANA
HIMACHAL PRADESH
JAMMU & KASHMIR
GUJARAT
MADHYA
NORTH WEST FRONTIER PROVINCE
Thar Desert (Great Indian Desert)
Thal Desert
Rann of Kachchh
Little Rann
Gulf of Kachchh
ARABIAN SEA
Mouths of the Indus
Kathiawar
Tropic of Cancer
Satpura
Vindhya
KABUL
Peshawar
Islamabad
RAWALPINDI
Srinagar
GUJRANWALA
FAISALABAD
LAHORE
Amritsar
Jullundur
LUDHIANA
Chandigarh
Quetta
Multan
Bahawalpur
Sukkur
Hyderabad
KARACHI
Bikaner
Jodhpur
Ajmer
JAIPUR
DELHI
New Delhi
Agra
Gwalior
Kota
Udaipur
AHMADABAD
VADODARA
Rajkot
Jamnagar
Bhavnagar
INDORE
BHOPAL
Hisar
Meerut
Ghaziabad
Faridabad
Aligarh
Projection: Conical with two standard parallels

32
40
41
40

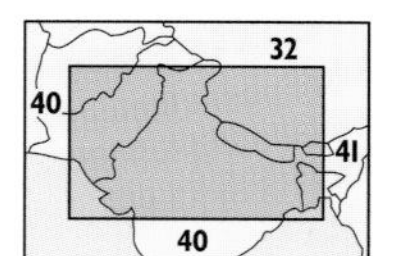

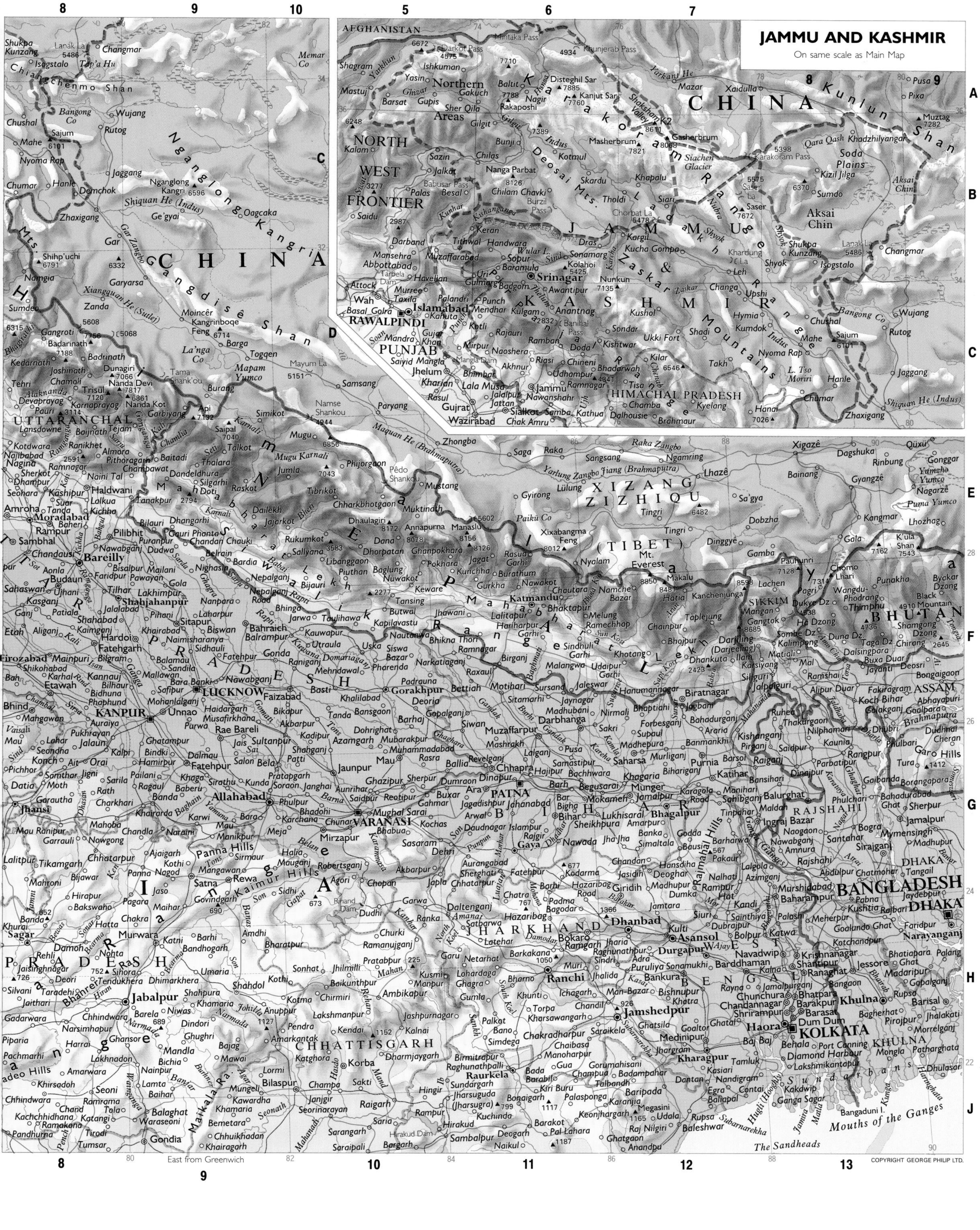

JAMMU AND KASHMIR
On same scale as Main Map
AFGHANISTAN
NORTH WEST FRONTIER
Northern Areas
Karakoram Range
CHINA
Kunlun Shan
Aksai Chin
Soda Plains
JAMMU & KASHMIR
Zaskar Mountains
Ladakh Range
Deosai Mts.
PUNJAB
HIMACHAL PRADESH
Islamabad
RAWALPINDI
Srinagar
Jammu
Leh
Kargil
Gilgit
K2
Siachen Glacier
Karakoram Pass
Nanga Parbat
Chiang Chenmo Shan
Nganglong Kangri
Gangdisê Shan
CHINA
UTTARANCHAL
XIZANG ZIZHIQU
(TIBET)
Mt. Everest
Mahabharat Lekh
Siwalik Range
NEPAL
Katmandu
SIKKIM
BHUTAN
Thimphu
ASSAM
BANGLADESH
DHAKA
UTTAR PRADESH
LUCKNOW
KANPUR
Allahabad
VARANASI
PATNA
BIHAR
JHARKHAND
WEST BENGAL
KOLKATA
MADHYA PRADESH
Jabalpur
CHHATTISGARH
Ranchi
Jamshedpur
Kaimur Hills
Rajmahal Hills
Garo Hills
Mouths of the Ganges
The Sandheads
Sundarbans
Yarlung Zangbo Jiang (Brahmaputra)
Ganga (Ganges)
East from Greenwich
COPYRIGHT GEORGE PHILIP LTD.

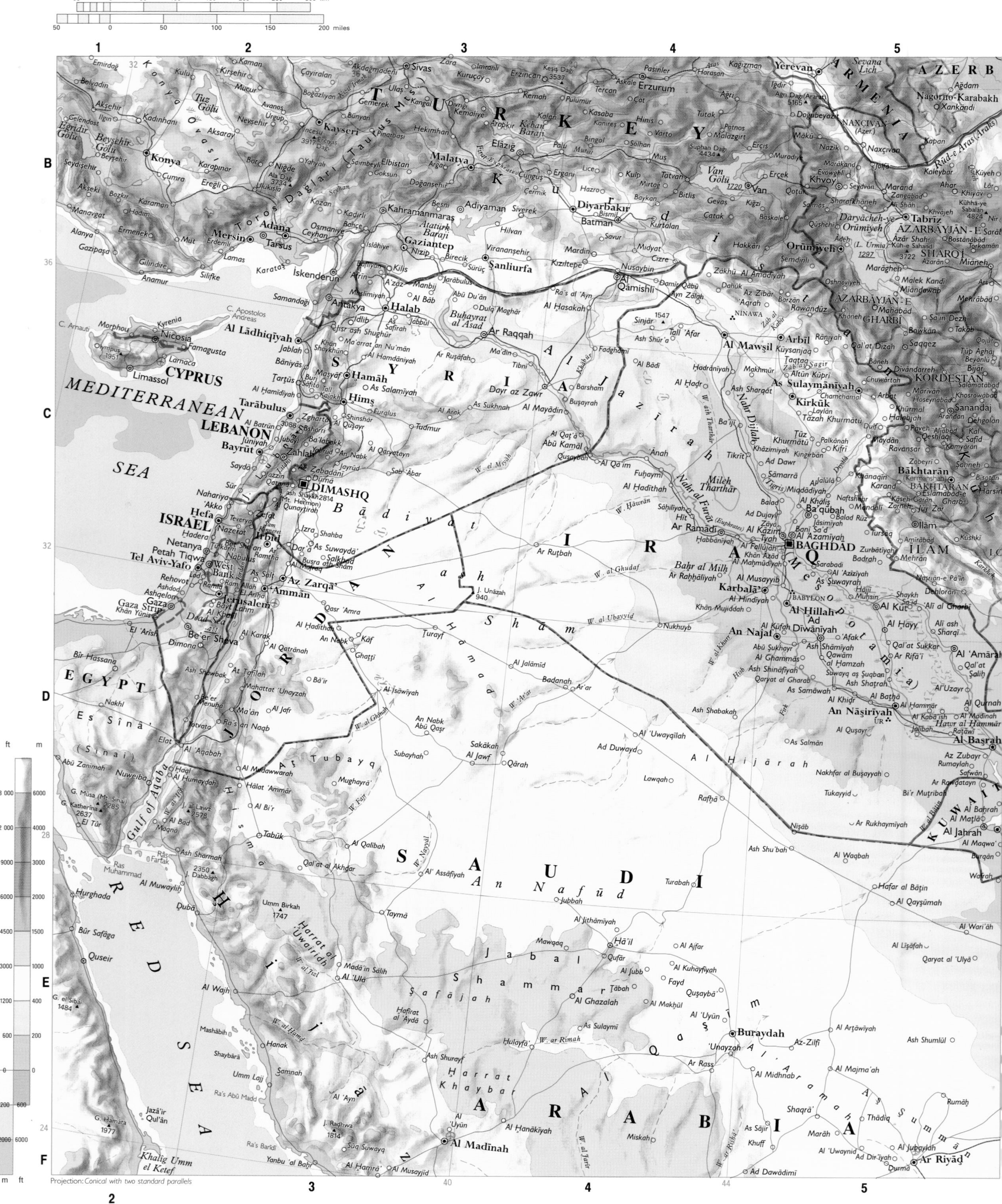

Projection: Conical with two standard parallels

25
25
40
51
46

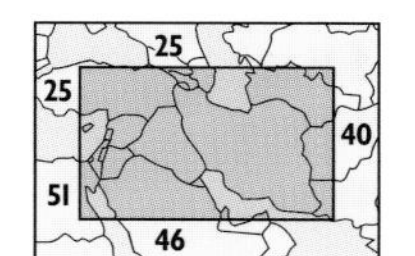

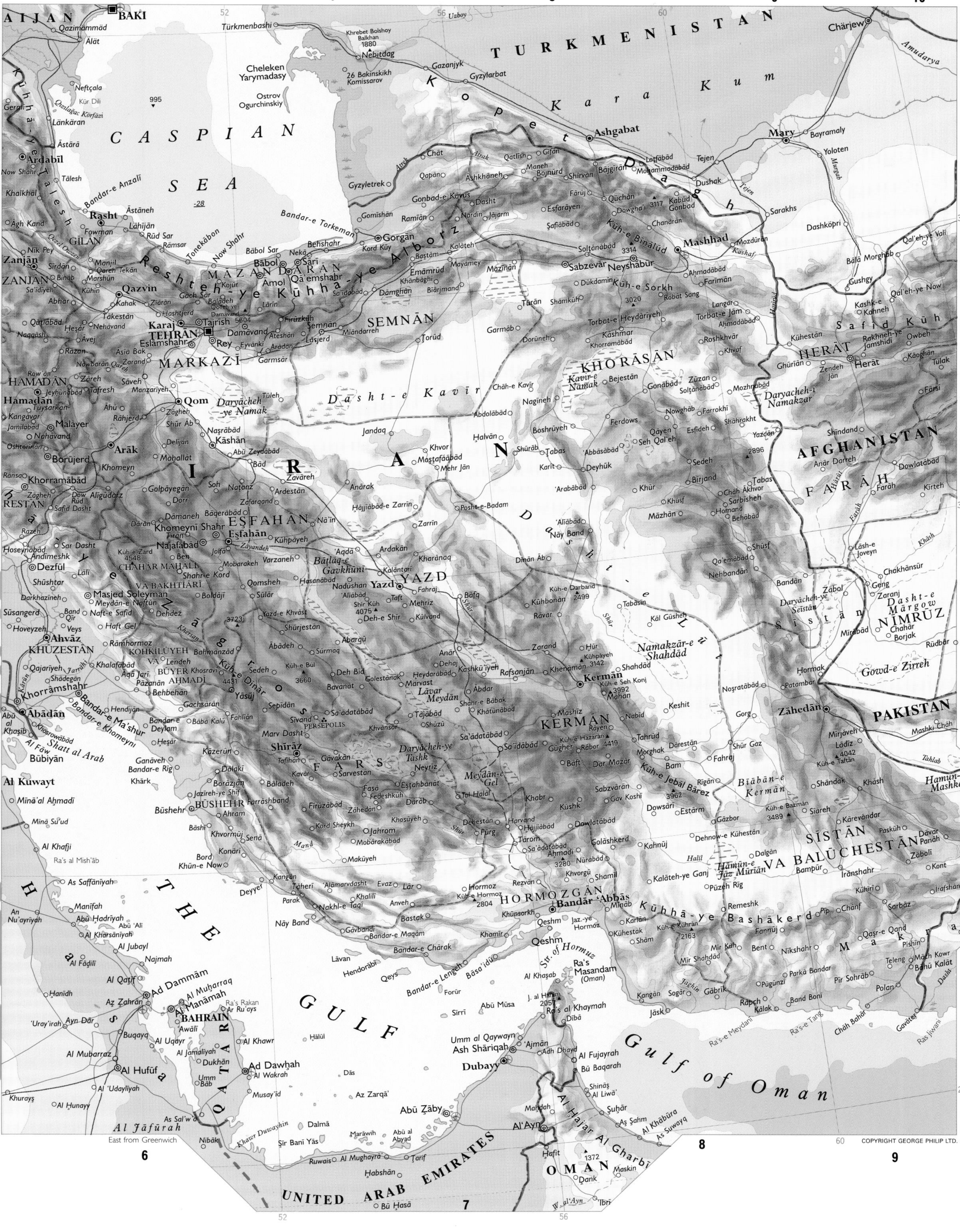

6
7
8
9
10
B
C
D
E
F
TURKMENISTAN
Kara Kum
Kopet Dagh
CASPIAN SEA
IRAN
AFGHANISTAN
PAKISTAN
OMAN
UNITED ARAB EMIRATES
QATAR
BAHRAIN
THE GULF
Gulf of Oman
Str. of Hormuz
Dasht-e Kavīr
Dasht-e Lūt
Reshteh-ye Kūhhā-ye Alborz
Kūhhā-ye Zāgros
Kūhhā-ye Bashākerd
Kūh-e Bīnālūd
Kūh-e Sorkh
Safīd Kūh
Dasht-e Mārgow
Gowd-e Zirreh
Hamun-i Mashkel
Makran
Al Hajar Al Gharbī
Al Jāfūrah
Daryācheh-ye Namak
Daryācheh-ye Tashk
Daryācheh-ye Sīstān
Daryacheh-i Namakzar
Namakzār-e Shahdād
Hāmūn-e Jaz Mūrīān
Bīābān-e Kermān
Kavīr-e Namak
Bātlāq-e Gavkhūnī
Lāvar Meydān
Meydān-e Gel
BAKI
Türkmenbashi
Cheleken Yarymadasy
Ostrov Ogurchinskiy
Nebitdag
Gazanjyk
Gyzylarbat
Ashgabat
Mary
Bayramaly
Yoloten
Tejen
Chärjew
Amudarya
Sarakhs
Gushgy
Herāt
Shīndand
Farāh
FARĀH
HERĀT
NĪMRŪZ
Zaranj
Zābol
Zāhedān
Mashhad
Neyshābūr
Sabzevār
Quchān
Bojnūrd
Gorgān
Sārī
Bābol
Āmol
Rasht
Ardabīl
Zanjān
Qazvin
Karaj
TEHRĀN
Rey
Qom
Kāshān
Arāk
Hamadān
Malāyer
Borūjerd
Khorramābād
Dezfūl
Ahvāz
Ābādān
Khorramshahr
Bandar-e Khomeynī
Eşfahān
Najafābād
Yazd
Shīrāz
PERSEPOLIS
Kermān
Rafsanjān
Sīrjān
Bandar 'Abbās
Jāsk
Chāh Bahār
Būshehr
Semnān
Dāmghān
Shāhrūd
Tabas
Bīrjand
Torbat-e Ḩeydarīyeh
Torbat-e Jām
Khorāsān
KHORĀSĀN
SEMNĀN
MARKAZĪ
MĀZANDARĀN
GĪLĀN
ZANJĀN
HAMADĀN
EŞFAHĀN
YAZD
KERMĀN
FĀRS
KHŪZESTĀN
BŪSHEHR
HORMOZGĀN
SĪSTĀN VA BALŪCHESTĀN
CHAHĀR MAḨALL VA BAKHTĪĀRĪ
KOHKĪLŪYEH VA BŪYER AḨMADĪ
Iranshahr
Bam
Dubayy
Ash Shāriqah
Abū Ẓaby
Al 'Ayn
Ad Dawḩah
Al Manāmah
Ad Dammām
Al Hufūf
Al Kuwayt
Ra's Masandam (Oman)
Qeshm
Hormoz
Lārak
Kīsh
Lāvān
Abū Mūsā
East from Greenwich
52
56
60
36
32
28
24

ARABIA AND THE HORN OF AFRICA 1:15 000 000

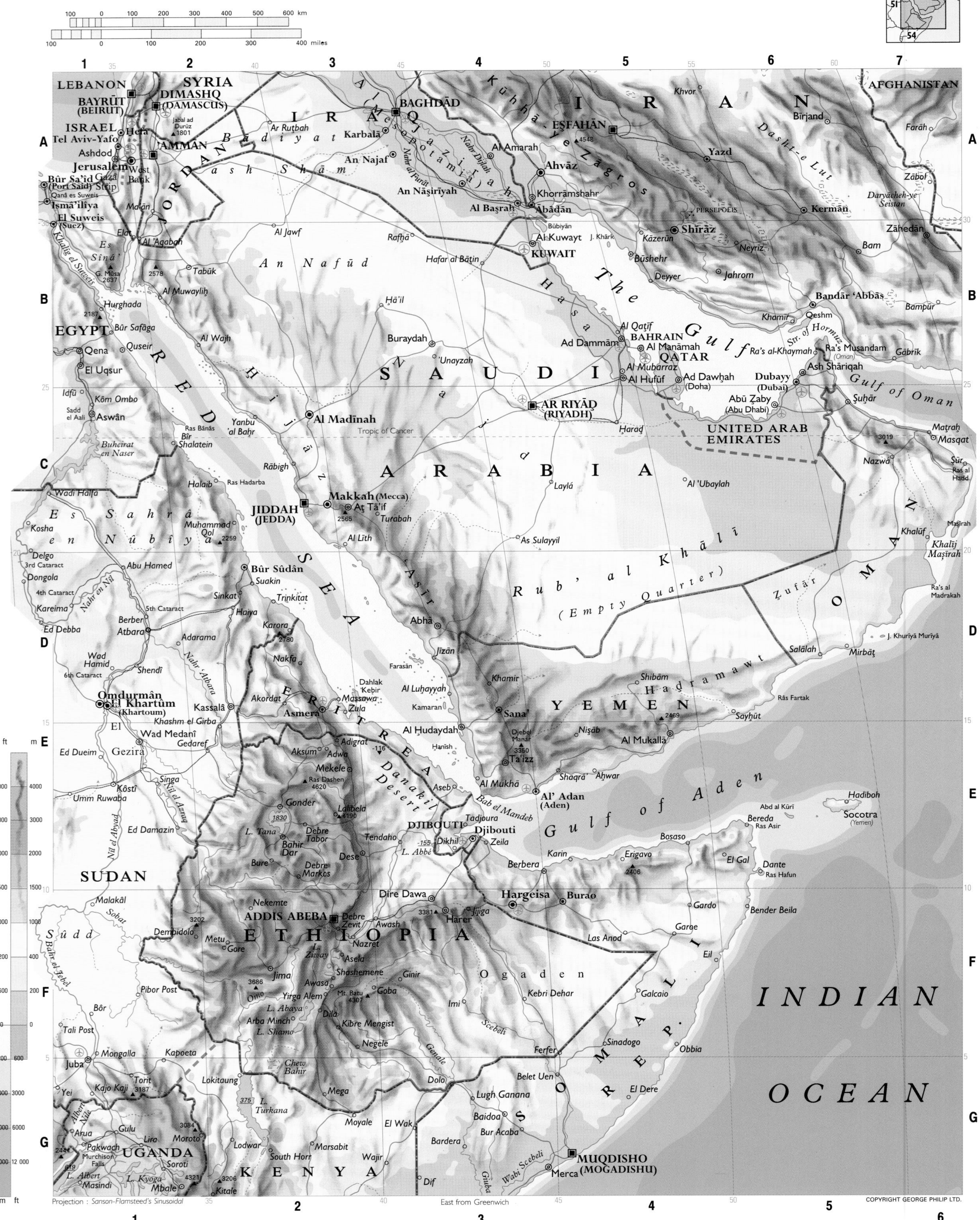

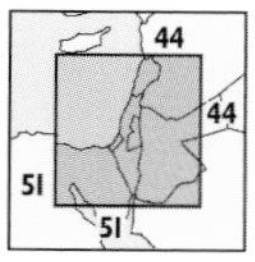

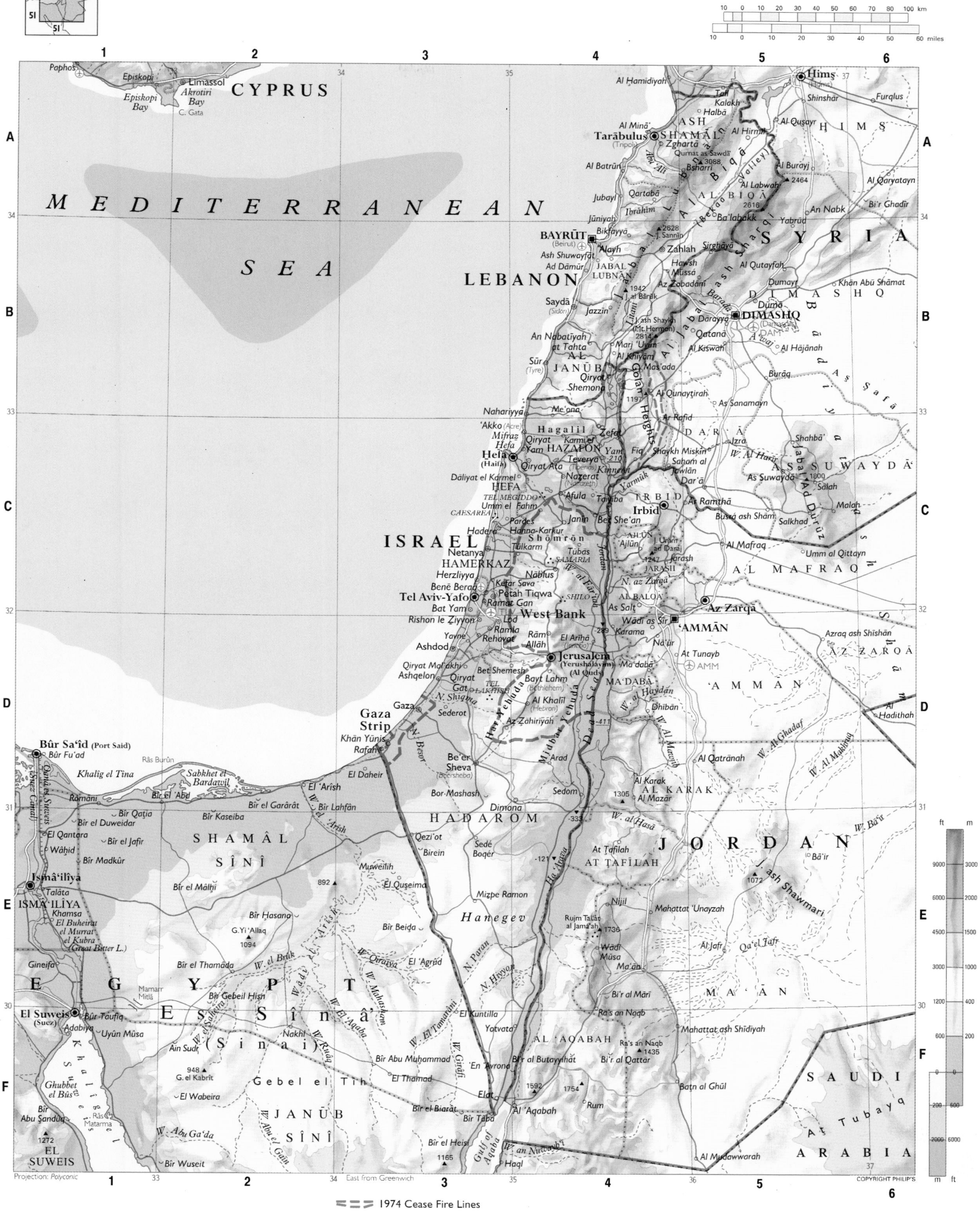

10 0 10 20 30 40 50 60 70 80 100 km

10 0 10 20 30 40 50 60 miles

CYPRUS
Paphos
Episkopi
Limassol
Akrotiri Bay
Episkopi Bay
C. Gata

MEDITERRANEAN SEA

LEBANON
Țarābulus (Tripoli)
Al Mīnā'
ASH SHAMĀL
Zghartā
Qurnat as Sawdā' 3088
Bsharri
Al Batrūn
Jubayl
Qartabā
Ibrāhīm
Jūniyah
Bikfayyā
BAYRŪT (Beirut)
Ash Shuwayfāt
Ad Dāmūr
JABAL LUBNĀN
'Alayh
J. Sannin 2628
Zahlah
Al Biqā' (Beqaa Valley)
AL BIQĀ'
Ba'labakk
Al Labwah
Al Hirmil
Tall Kalakh
Halbā
Jabal Lubnān
Jabal ash Sharqī
Saydā (Sidon)
Jazzīn
1942 al Bārūk
An Nabatīyah at Tahta
AL JANŪB
Şūr (Tyre)
Marj 'Uyūn
Al Khiyām

SYRIA
Al Ḥamīdiyah
Ḥimş (Homs)
Shinshār
Furqlus
Al Quşayr
ḤIMŞ
Al Burayj
2464
Al Qaryatayn
An Nabk
Bi'r Ghadīr
Yabrūd
2616
Sirghāyā
Al Quţayfah
Ḥawsh Mūssā
Az Zabadānī
Baradā
Dumayr
Khān Abū Shāmat
DIMASHQ
Dūmā
DIMASHQ (Damascus)
Dārayyā
J. ash Shaykh (Mt. Hermon) 2814
Qaţanā
Al Kiswah
Al Hājānah
Burāq
Al Quneyţirah
As Sanamayn
Ar Rafid
Golan Heights
DAR'Ā
Izra'
Shaykh Miskīn
Saḥam al Jawlān
Dar'ā
W. Al Harīr
Shahbā'
Jabal Ad Durūz
AS SUWAYDĀ'
As Suwaydā'
1800
Şalkhad
Salkhad
Malaḥ
Buşrá ash Shām
Ar Ramthā
Ḥarrat ash Shāmah
As Şafā
Bādiyat ash Shām

ISRAEL
Me'ona
Qiryat Shemona
Nahariyya
'Akko (Acre)
Hagalil
Karmi'el
Zefat
Mifraz Hefa
Qiryat Yam
HAZAFON
Yam Kinneret
Hefa (Haifa)
Qiryat Ata
Teverya (Tiberias)
Kinneret
Nazerat (Nazareth)
Dāliyat el Karmel
HEFA
TEL MEGIDDO
'Afula
Umm el Fahm
CAESAREA
Pardes Hanna-Karkur
Hadera
Netanya
HAMERKAZ
Herzliyya
Kefar Sava
Petah Tiqwa
Benē Beraq
Tel Aviv-Yafo
Ramat Gan
Bat Yam
Rishon le Ziyyon
Lod
Ramla
Rehovot
Yavne
Ashdod
Qiryat Mal'akhi
Ashqelon
Bet Shemesh
Qiryat Gat
TEL LAKHISH
N. Shiqma
Sederot
Be'er Sheva (Beersheba)
N. Besor
Bor-Mashash
Dimona
Arad
Sedom
HADAROM
Qezi'ot
Birein
Sedé Boqer
Mizpe Ramon
Hanegev
N. Paran
N. Hiyyon
'En Avrona
Elat
Yotvata
Ha 'Arava
Midbar Yehuda
Har Yehuda

West Bank
Jenin
Bet She'an
Shōmrōn
SAMARIA
Tūbās
Ţulkarm
Nāblus
SHILO
W. al Fār'ah
Rām Allāh
El Arīhā (Jericho)
Jerusalem (Yerushalayim) (Al Quds)
Bayt Lahm (Bethlehem)
Al Khalīl (Hebron)
Az Zāhirīyah
Dead Sea
-399
-411
Jordan
Yarmūk

Gaza Strip
Gaza
Khān Yūnis
Rafah

JORDAN
Irbid
IRBID
'AJLŪN
'Ajlūn
J. Umm ad Daraj 1247
Jarash
JARASH
Al Mafraq
AL MAFRAQ
Umm al Qiţţayn
N. az Zarqā
AL BALQĀ'
As Salţ
Az Zarqā
Wādī as Sīr
'AMMĀN
Karama
Nā'ūr
Mā'dabā
MA'DABA
At Tunayb
AMM
'AMMAN
Azraq ash Shīshān
AZ ZARQĀ'
W. al Haydān
Dhībān
W. Al Mawjib
Al Qaţrānah
W. Al Ghadaf
W. Al Mahmiyah
Al Hadīthah
Al Karak
AL KARAK
1305
Al Mazār
W. al Hasā
-333
-121
At Ţafīlah
AT TAFĪLAH
Bā'ir
W. Bā'ir
J. ash Shawmari
1072
Nijil
Maḥaţţat 'Unayzah
Rujm Tal'at al Jamā'ah 1736
Wādī Mūsā
Ma'ān
MA'ĀN
Al Jafr
Qā' el Jafr
Bi'r al Mārī
Ra's an Naqb
Maḥaţţat ash Shīdiyah
AL 'AQABAH
Ra's an Naqb 1435
Bi'r al Qaţţār
Bi'r al Butayyihāt
1592
1754
Rum
Baţn al Ghūl
Al 'Aqabah
Al Mudawwarah
Ḥaql
W. an Nuwaybi'
Gulf of Aqaba

SAUDI ARABIA
Aţ Ţubayq

EGYPT
Bûr Sa'îd (Port Said)
Bûr Fu'ad
Râs Burûn
Khalîg el Tîna
Sabkhet el Bardawîl
Romani
Bîr el 'Abd
Bîr el Garârât
El 'Arîsh
Bîr Lahfân
W. el 'Arîsh
El Daheir
Bîr Qaţia
Bîr el Duweidar
Bîr Kaseiba
El Qantara
Bîr el Jafir
Wâhid
Bîr Madkûr
SHAMÂL SÎNÎ
Ismâ'ilîya
ISMA'ILÎYA
Talâta
Bîr el Mâlhi
Muweilih
El Quseima
892
Bîr Hasana
G.Yi'Allaq 1094
Bîr Beida
Khamsa
El Buheirat el Murrat el Kubra (Great Bitter L.)
Qanâ el Suweis (Suez Canal)
Geneifa
Bîr el Thamâda
W. el Brûk
El 'Agrûd
W. Qiraiya
W. Mahashsh
Mamarr Mitlâ
Bîr Gebeil Hişn
El Suweis (Suez)
Bûr Taufiq
Adabiya
'Uyûn Mûsa
Sînâ' (Sinai)
W. el Sahera
W. El 'Aqaba
W. Rudâg
Nakhl
'Ain Sudr
W. El Tamarâni
El Kuntilla
W. Girâfi
Bîr Abu Muhammad
El Thamad
948 G. el Kabrît
Gebel el Tîh
El Wabeira
Khalîg el Suweis
Ghubbet el Bûs
Bîr Abu Sandûq
Râs Matarma
W. Abu Ga'da
W. Abu el Gain
JANÛB SÎNÎ
Bîr el Biarât
Bîr Tâba
Bîr el Heisi
1165
1272
EL SUWEIS
Bîr Wuseit

ft m
9000 3000
6000 2000
4500 1500
3000 1000
1200 400
600 200
0 0
200 600
2000 6000
m ft

Projection: Polyconic

East from Greenwich

COPYRIGHT PHILIP'S

1974 Cease Fire Lines

AFRICA : Physical 1:42 000 000

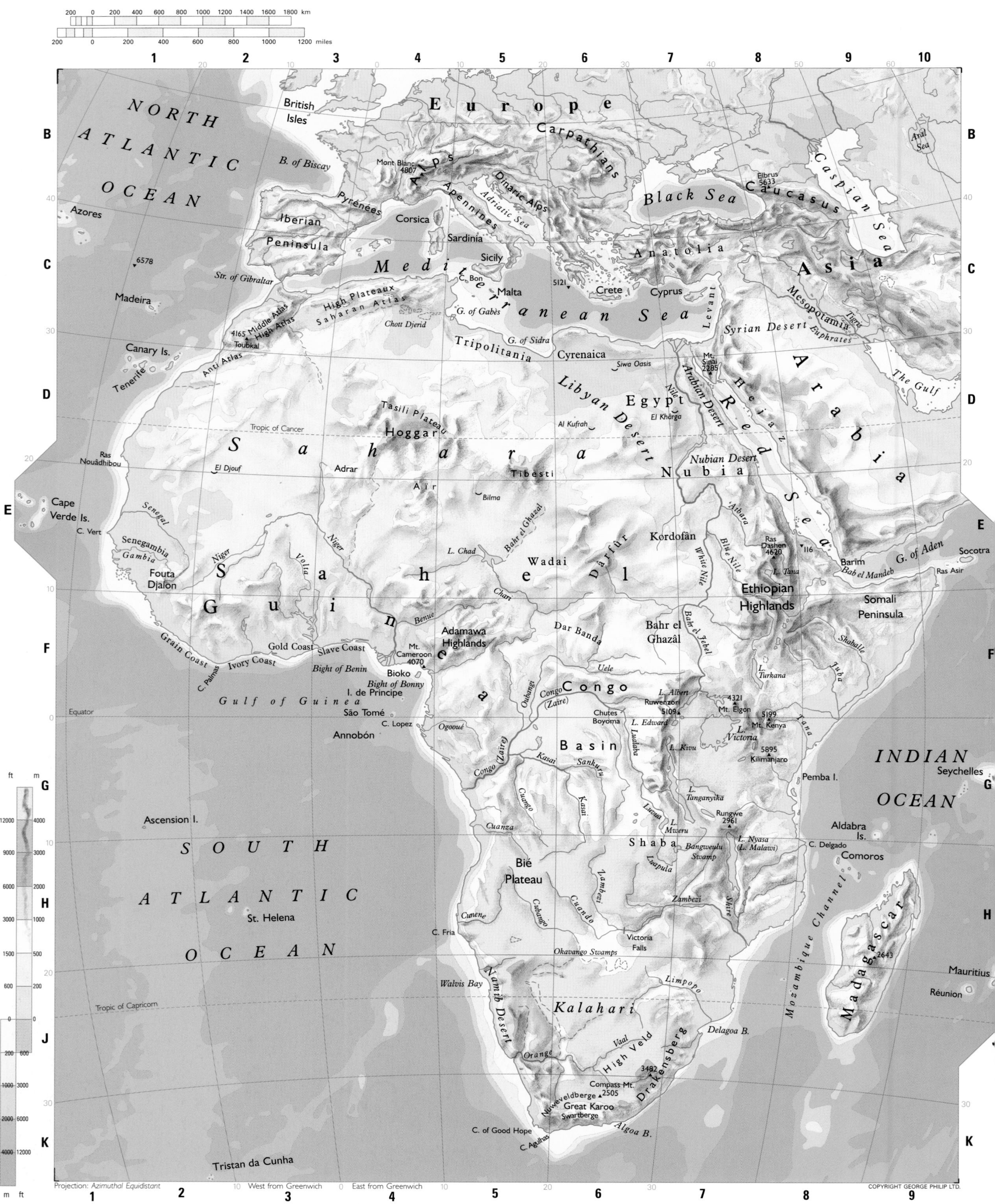

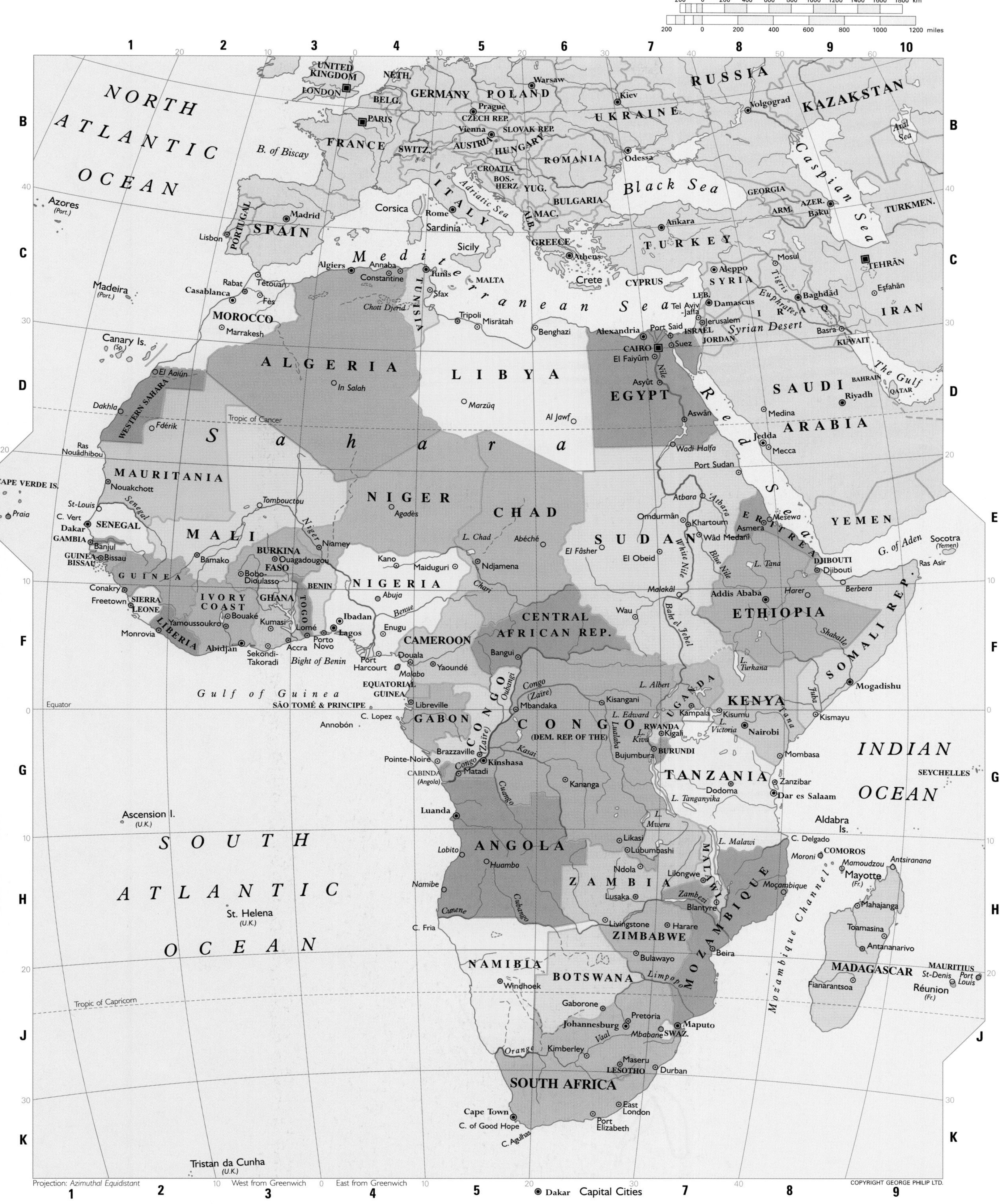
NORTH ATLANTIC OCEAN
SOUTH ATLANTIC OCEAN
INDIAN OCEAN
Mediterranean Sea
Black Sea
Caspian Sea
Red Sea
Sahara
ALGERIA
LIBYA
EGYPT
MOROCCO
WESTERN SAHARA
MAURITANIA
MALI
NIGER
CHAD
SUDAN
ETHIOPIA
ERITREA
DJIBOUTI
SOMALI REP.
KENYA
UGANDA
TANZANIA
SENEGAL
GAMBIA
GUINEA-BISSAU
GUINEA
SIERRA LEONE
LIBERIA
IVORY COAST
GHANA
TOGO
BENIN
BURKINA FASO
NIGERIA
CAMEROON
CENTRAL AFRICAN REP.
EQUATORIAL GUINEA
GABON
CONGO
CONGO (DEM. REP. OF THE)
RWANDA
BURUNDI
ANGOLA
ZAMBIA
MALAWI
MOZAMBIQUE
ZIMBABWE
NAMIBIA
BOTSWANA
SOUTH AFRICA
LESOTHO
SWAZ.
MADAGASCAR
COMOROS
SEYCHELLES
MAURITIUS
SAUDI ARABIA
YEMEN
IRAN
IRAQ
SYRIA
TURKEY
CYPRUS
LEB.
ISRAEL
JORDAN
KUWAIT
BAHRAIN
QATAR
SPAIN
PORTUGAL
FRANCE
ITALY
RUSSIA
UKRAINE
KAZAKSTAN
CAPE VERDE IS.
Tropic of Cancer
Tropic of Capricorn
Equator
Gulf of Guinea
Mozambique Channel
Projection: Azimuthal Equidistant
West from Greenwich
East from Greenwich
Dakar Capital Cities
COPYRIGHT GEORGE PHILIP LTD.

NORTHERN AFRICA

1:15 000 000

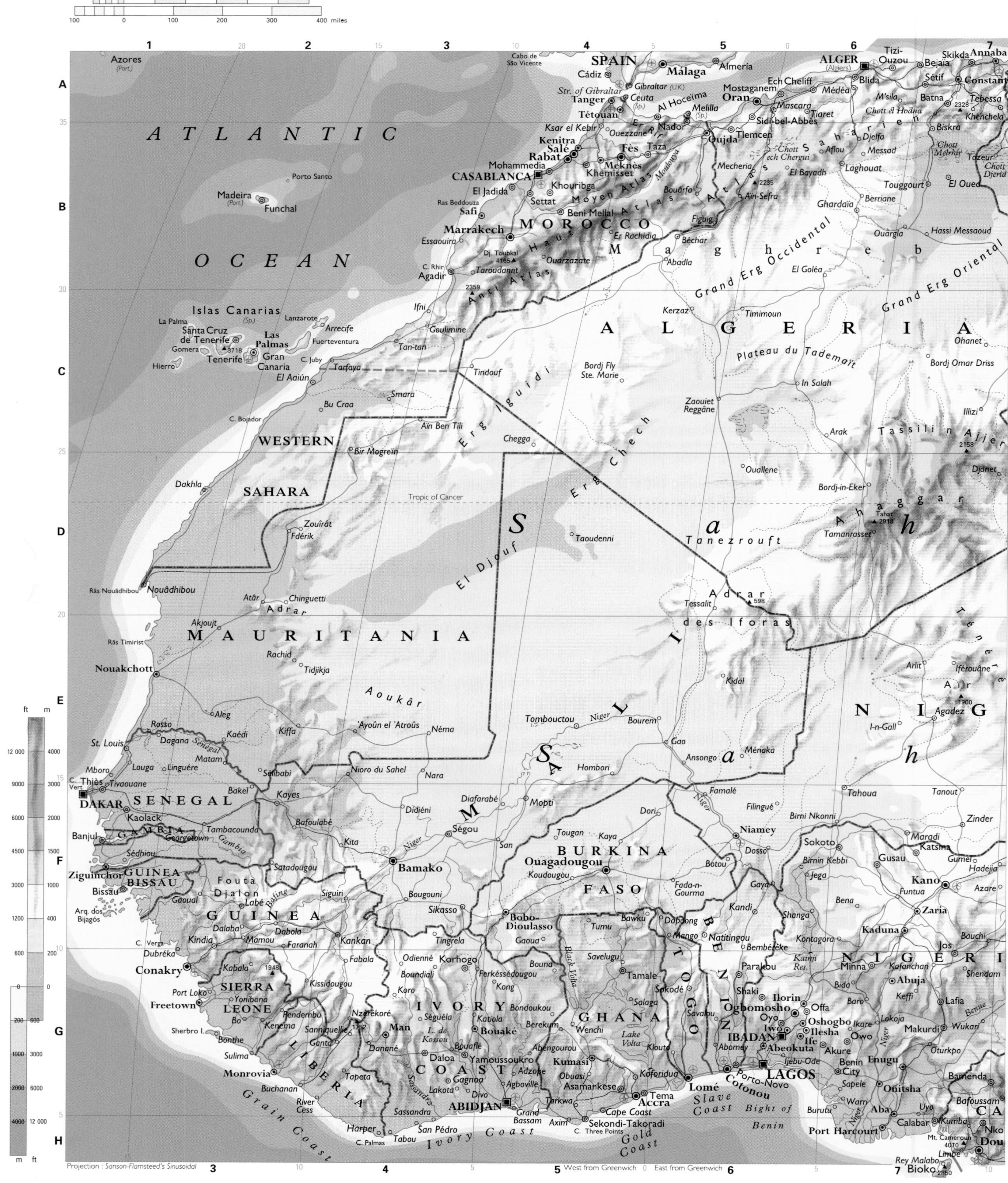

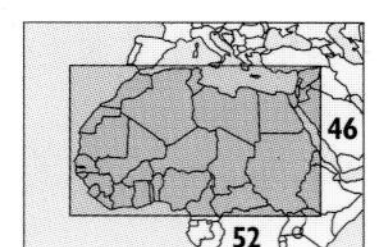

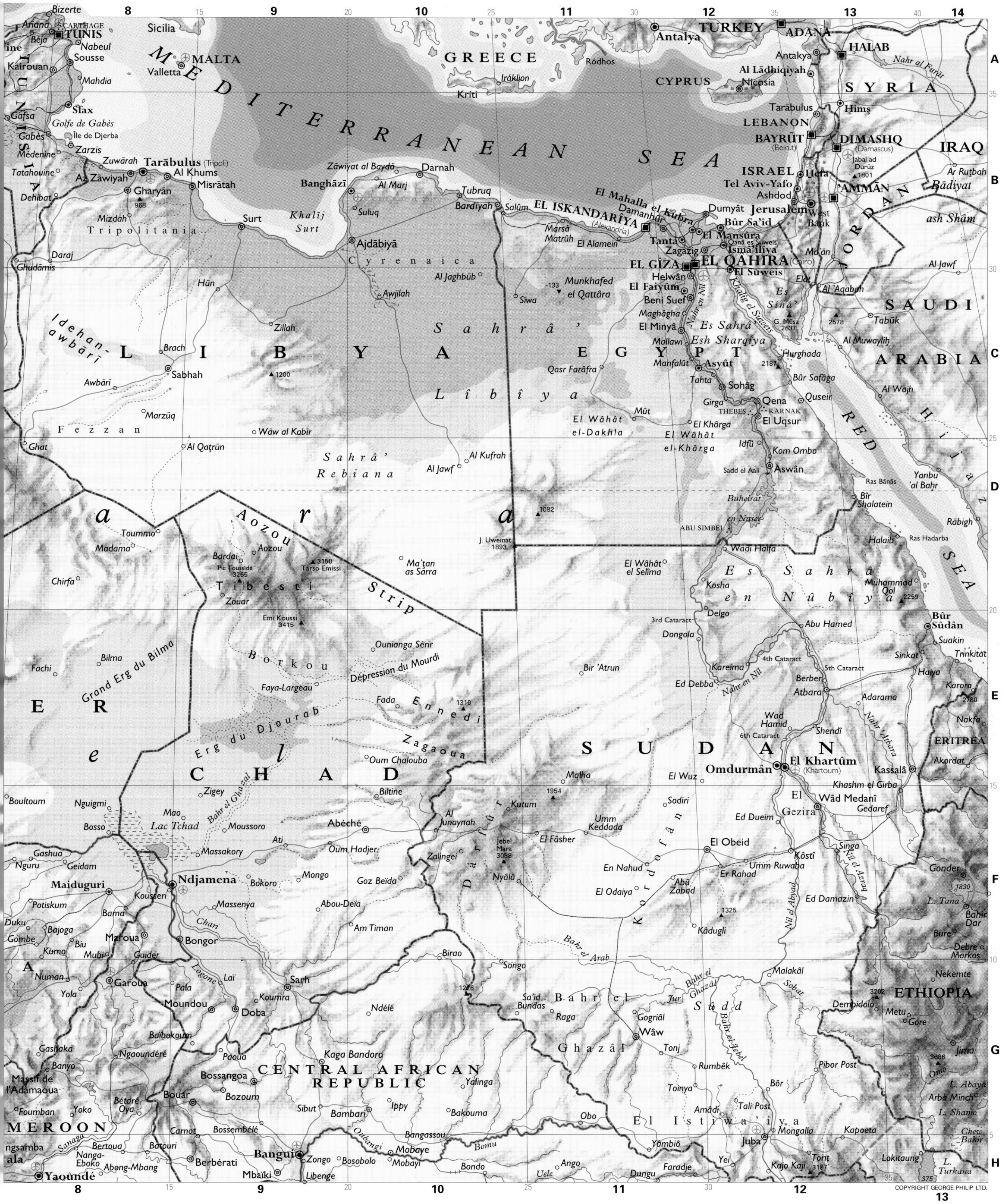

8 15 9 20 10 25 11 30 12 35 13 40 14

A B C D E F G H

MEDITERRANEAN SEA

Bizerte, Ariana, CARTHAGE, TUNIS, Béja, Nabeul, Sousse, Kairouan, Mahdia, Sfax, Gafsa, Golfe de Gabès, Île de Djerba, Gabès, Médenine, Zarzis, Tatahouine, Dehibat, TUNISIA

Sicilia, MALTA, Valletta

Zuwārah, Tarābulus (Tripoli), Az Zāwiyah, Al Khums, Gharyān 968, Misrātah, Mizdah, Tripolitania, Surt, Khalīj Surt, Daraj, Ghudāmis

Zāwiyat al Baydā, Darnah, Banghāzī, Al Marj, Suluq, Tubruq, Bardīyah, Ajdābiyā, Cyrenaica, Al Jaghbūb, Awjilah, Hūn, Zillah, Idehan Awbārī, Brach, Sabhah, LIBYA, 1200, Awbārī, Marzūq, Fezzan, Ghat, Al Qaṭrūn, Wāw al Kabīr, Sahrâ' Rebiana, Al Jawf, Al Kufrah, Sahrâ' Lîbîya

GREECE, Ródhos, Iráklion, Kríti, Antalya, TURKEY, ADANA, CYPRUS, Nicosia, Antakya, HALAB, Al Lādhiqiyah, Nahr al Furāt, SYRIA, Ḥimṣ, Tarābulus, LEBANON, BAYRŪT (Beirut), DIMASHQ (Damascus), Jabal ad Durūz 1801, IRAQ, ISRAEL, Haifa, Tel Aviv-Yafo, Ashdod, Jerusalem, West Bank, 'AMMĀN, JORDAN, Ar Ruṭbah, Bādiyat ash Shām, Ma'ān, Al Jawf

Salûm, EL ISKANDARÎYA (Alexandria), El Mahalla el Kubra, Damanhûr, Dumyât, Bûr Sa'îd, El Mansûra, Qanâ es Suweis, Ismâ'ilîya, Tanta, Zagazig, Marsâ Matrûh, El Alamein, EL GÎZA, EL QÂHIRA (Cairo), El Suweis, Helwân, El Faiyûm, Beni Suef, Maghâgha, El Minyâ, Mallawi, Manfalût, Asyût, Tahta, Sohâg, Girga, THEBES, KARNAK, Qena, El Uqsur, Munkhafed el Qattâra, -133, Siwa, Qasr Farâfra, EGYPT, Es Sahrâ Esh Sharqîya, Nahr en Nîl, Khalîg el Suweis, Es Sînâ', G. Mûsa 2637, Elat, Al 'Aqabah, 2578, Tabūk, SAUDI ARABIA, Al Muwayliḥ, 2187, Hurghada, Bûr Safâga, Quseir, Al Wajh, Hijaz, Mût, El Wâhât el-Dakhla, El Khârga, El Wâhât el-Khârga, Idfû, Kom Ombo, Sadd el Aali, Aswân, RED SEA, Ras Bânâs, Yanbu 'al Baḥr, Bîr Shalatein, Buheirat en Naser, ABU SIMBEL, Rābigh, 1082, J. Uweinat 1893

Toummo, Madama, Chirfa, Aozou, Aozou Strip, Bardaï, Pic Toussidé 3265, Tarso Emissi 3150, Tibesti, Zouar, Emi Koussi 3415, Ma'tan as Sarra, Sahara, Fachi, Bilma, Grand Erg du Bilma, ER, Borkou, Ounianga Sérir, Dépression du Mourdi, Faya-Largeau, Fada, Ennedi, 1310, Erg du Djourab, Zagaoua, Oum Chalouba, CHAD, Biltine, Zigey, Mao, Lac Tchad, Bahr el Ghazal, Moussoro, Abéché, Ati, Oum Hadjer, Massakory, Boultoum, Nguigmi, Bosso, Gashua, Nguru, Geidam, Maiduguri, Ndjamena, Kousseri, Bokoro, Mongo, Goz Beïda, Massenya, Abou-Deïa, Am Timan, Chari, Potiskum, Bama, Duku, Gombe, Bajoga, Biu, Marova, Kumo, Mubi, Guider, Bongor, Numan, Yola, Garoua, Logone, Laï, Pala, Moundou, Doba, Koumra, Sarh, Baïbokoum, Gashaka, Banyo, Ngaoundéré, Paoua, Massif de l'Adamaoua, Bossangoa, Bozoum, Bouar, Bétaré Oya, Yoko, Foumban, CAMEROON, Carnot, Bossembélé, Bertoua, Batouri, Nanga-Eboko, Abong-Mbang, Berbérati, Mbaïki, Yaoundé, Sanaga, Bangui, Zongo, Libenge, Bosobolo, Mobaye, Mobayi, Oubangi, Bangassou, Bomu, Bondo, Uele, Ango, Dungu, CENTRAL AFRICAN REPUBLIC, Kaga Bandoro, Ndélé, Yalinga, Ippy, Bambari, Sibut, Bakouma, Birao, 1226

Wâdi Halfa, El Wâhât el Selîma, Kosha, Es Sahrâ en Nûbîya, Muhammad Qol, 2259, Halaib, Ras Hadarba, Delgo, 3rd Cataract, Dongola, Abu Hamed, Bûr Sûdân, Suakin, Sinkat, Trinkitat, Haiya, Kareima, 4th Cataract, 5th Cataract, Bir 'Atrun, Ed Debba, Nahr en Nîl, Berber, Atbara, Adarama, Nahr Atbara, Karora, 2780, Nakfa, ERITREA, Wad Hamid, 6th Cataract, Shendî, Akordat, Kassalâ, SUDAN, Omdurmân, El Khartûm (Khartoum), El Wuz, Malha, 1954, Kutum, Dârfûr, Al Junaynah, El Fâsher, Umm Keddada, Sodiri, Kordofân, Ed Dueim, El Gezira, Wad Medanî, Gedaref, Khashm el Girba, Jebel Mara 3088, Zalingei, Nyâlâ, El Obeid, Kôstî, Umm Ruwaba, Singa, Nîl el Azraq, En Nahud, Er Rahad, Abû Zabad, El Odaiya, Nîl el Abyad, Ed Damazin, 1325, Kâdugli, Gonder, 1830, L. Tana, Bahir Dar, Bure, Debre Markos, Bahr el Arab, Songo, Sa'id Bundas, Bahr el Ghazal, Raga, Jur, Sudd, Gogriâl, Wâw, Tonj, Bahr el Jebel, Malakâl, Sobat, Nekemte, ETHIOPIA, 3202, Dembidolo, Metu, Gore, Jima, 3686, Omo, L. Abaya, Arba Minch, L. Shamo, Rumbêk, Pibor Post, Bôr, Toinya, Amadi, Tali Post, Obo, El Istiwâ'iya, Yambio, Juba, Mongalla, Kapoeta, Chew Bahir, Lokitaung, Yei, Faradje, Kajo Kaji, Torit, 3187, L. Turkana, 375

8 15 9 20 10 25 11 30 12 35 13

CENTRAL AND SOUTHERN AFRICA 1:15 000 000

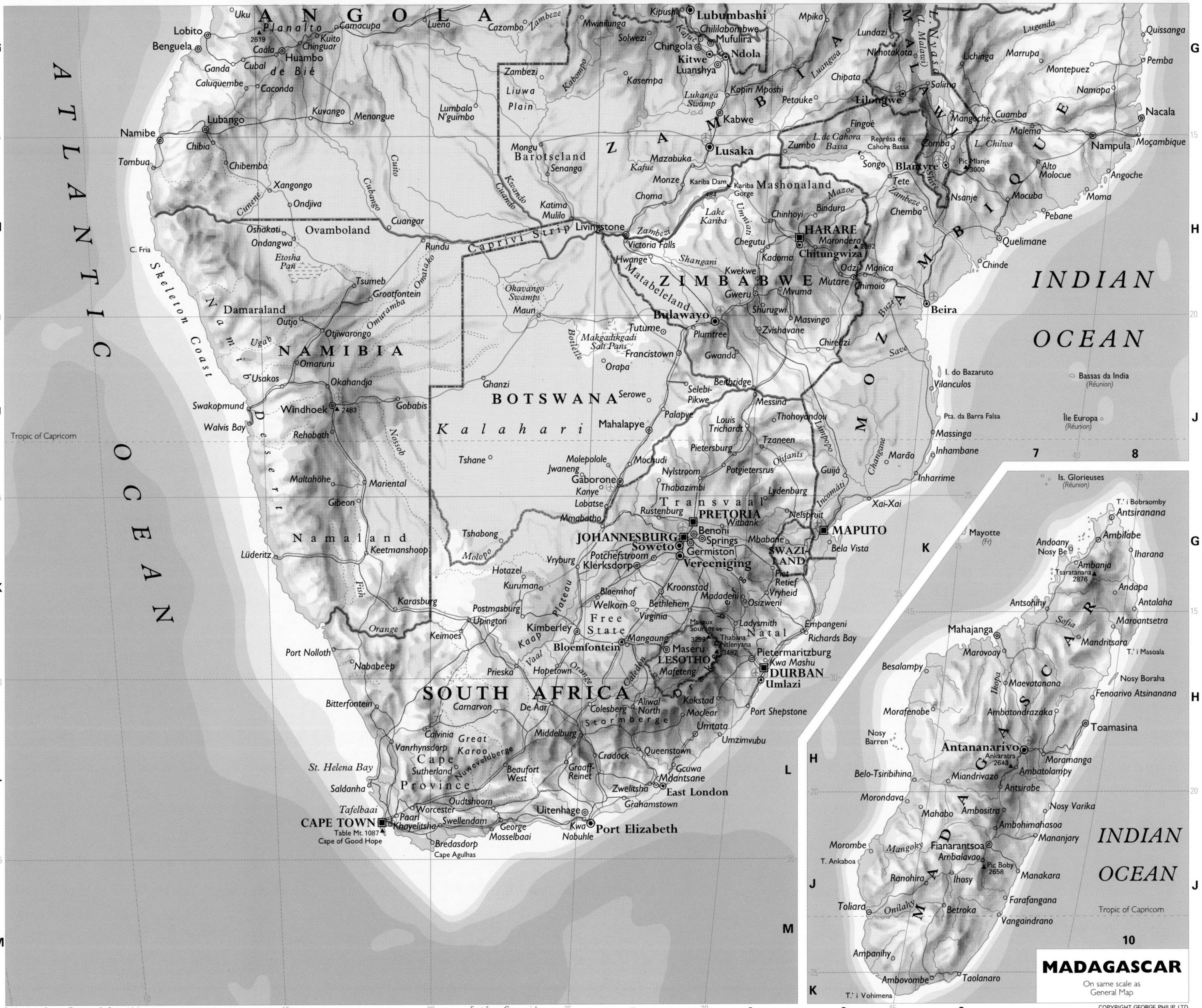

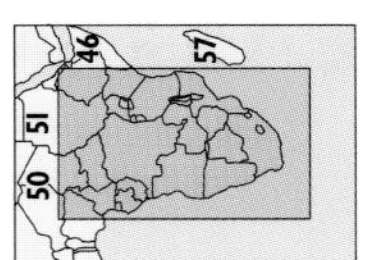

ANGOLA

ZAMBIA

MALAWI

MOZAMBIQUE

ZIMBABWE

NAMIBIA

BOTSWANA

SOUTH AFRICA

LESOTHO

SWAZILAND

INDIAN OCEAN

ATLANTIC OCEAN

Kalahari

Namib Desert

Skeleton Coast

Caprivi Strip

Transvaal

Orange Free State

Natal

Cape Province

Great Karoo

LUSAKA

HARARE

PRETORIA

JOHANNESBURG

MAPUTO

MASERU

CAPE TOWN

DURBAN

Windhoek

Gaborone

Bulawayo

Blantyre

Lilongwe

Beira

Port Elizabeth

East London

Bloemfontein

Kimberley

Livingstone

Victoria Falls

Lake Kariba

L. Nyasa (L. Malawi)

Tropic of Capricorn

East from Greenwich

Projection : Sanson-Flamsteed's Sinusoidal

MADAGASCAR

On same scale as General Map

Antananarivo

Toamasina

Mahajanga

Fianarantsoa

Toliara

Taolanaro

Antsiranana

INDIAN OCEAN

m	ft
4000	12 000
3000	9000
2000	6000
1500	4500
1000	3000
400	1200
200	600
0	0
200	600
1000	3000
2000	6000
4000	12 000

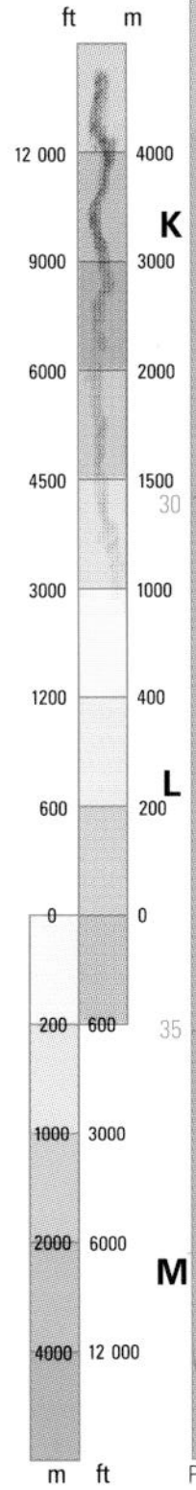

EAST AFRICA 1:8 000 000

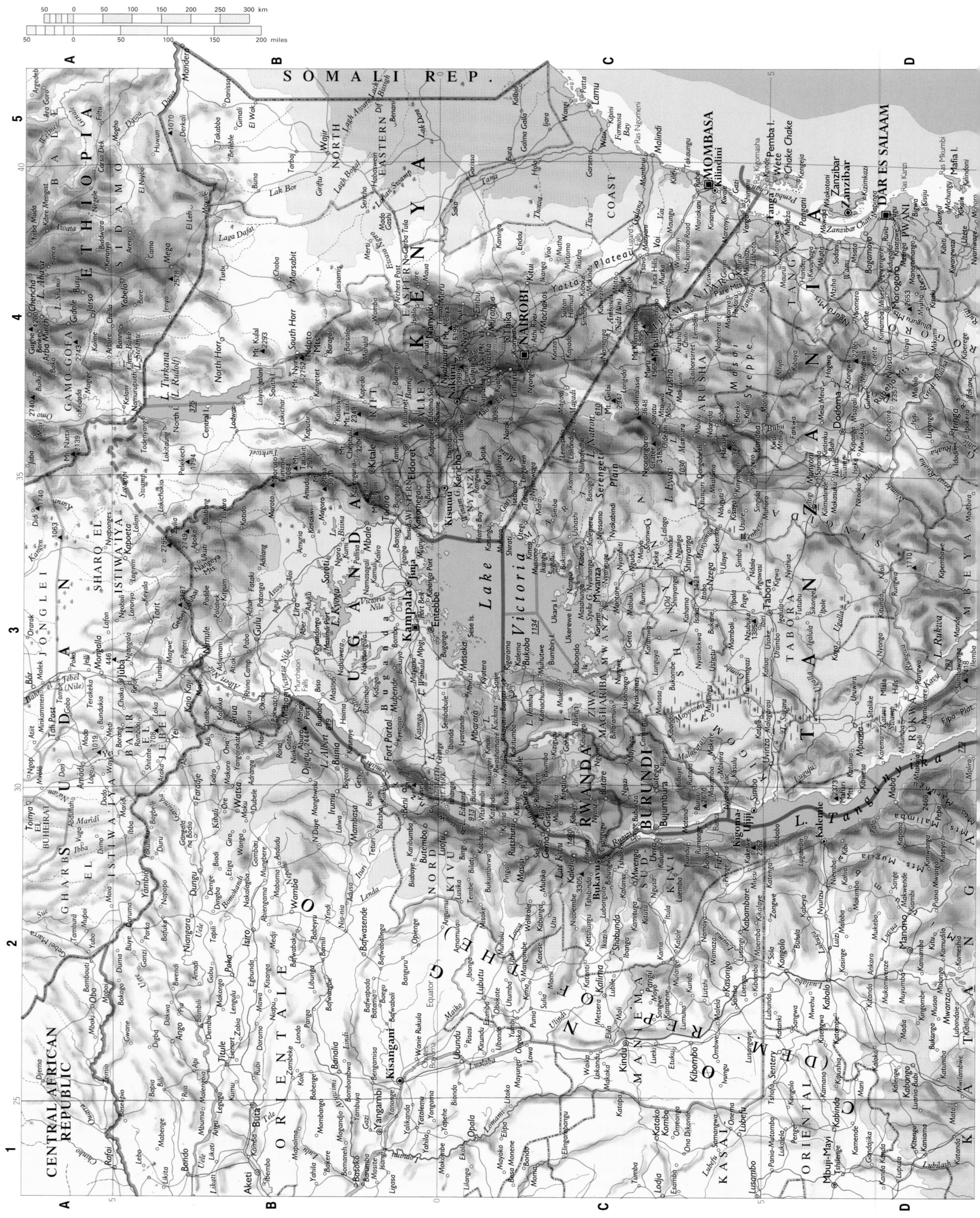

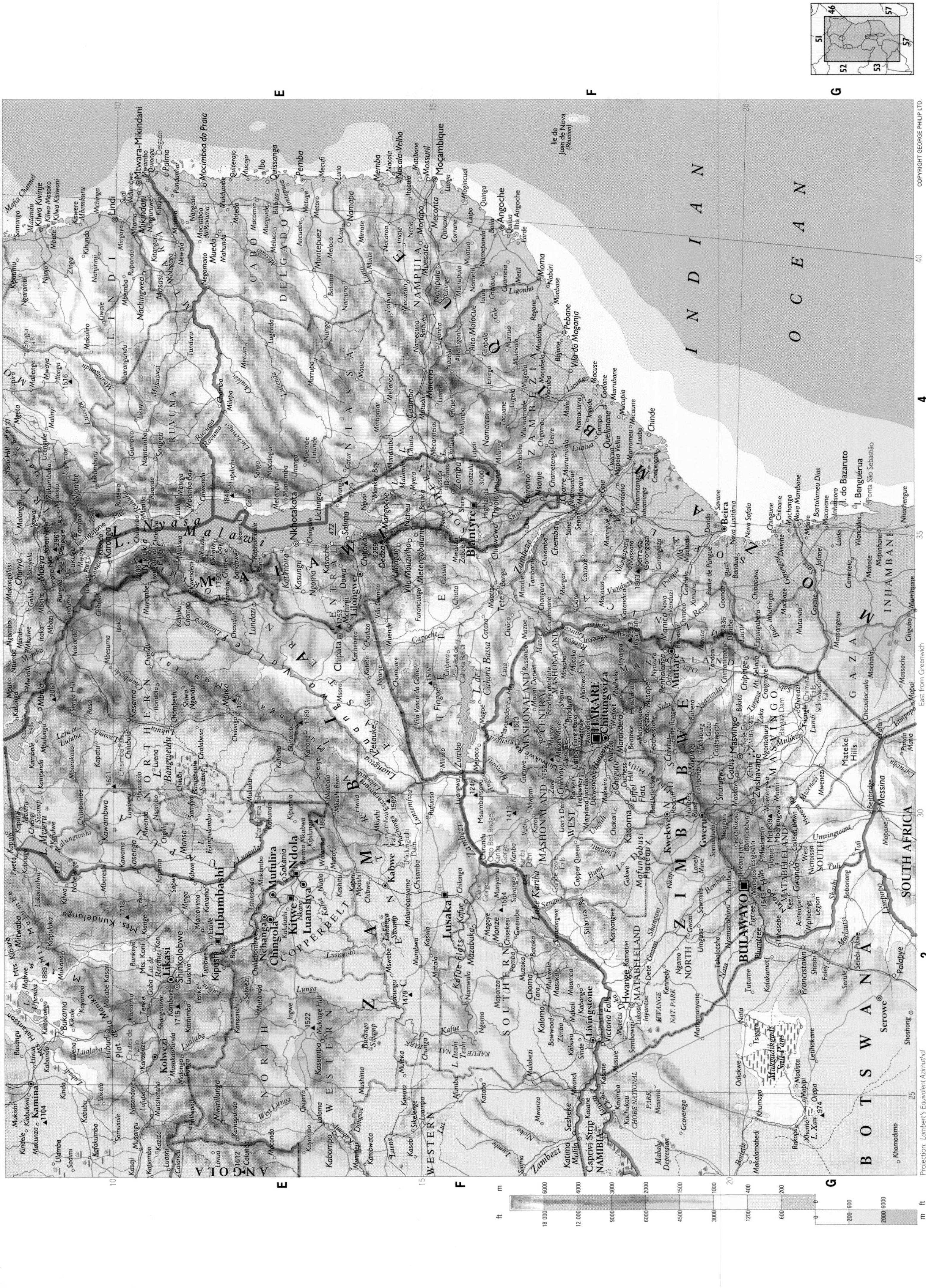

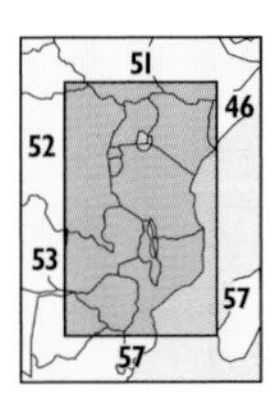

ZAMBIA

MALAWI

MOZAMBIQUE

ZIMBABWE

BOTSWANA

SOUTH AFRICA

NAMIBIA

ANGOLA

INDIAN OCEAN

L. Nyasa Malawi

Lake Kariba

L. de Cahora Bassa

HARARE

BULAWAYO

Lusaka

Lubumbashi

Blantyre

Lilongwe

Beira

Quelimane

Moçambique

Nampula

Lindi

Mtwara-Mikindani

Ile de Juan de Nova (Réunion)

E

F

G

1 2 3 4 5

Projection: Lambert's Equivalent Azimuthal

East from Greenwich

ft m

18 000 6000

12 000 4000

9000 3000

6000 2000

4500 1500

3000 1000

1200 400

600 200

0 0

200 600

2000 6000

m ft

SOUTHERN AFRICA 1:8 000 000

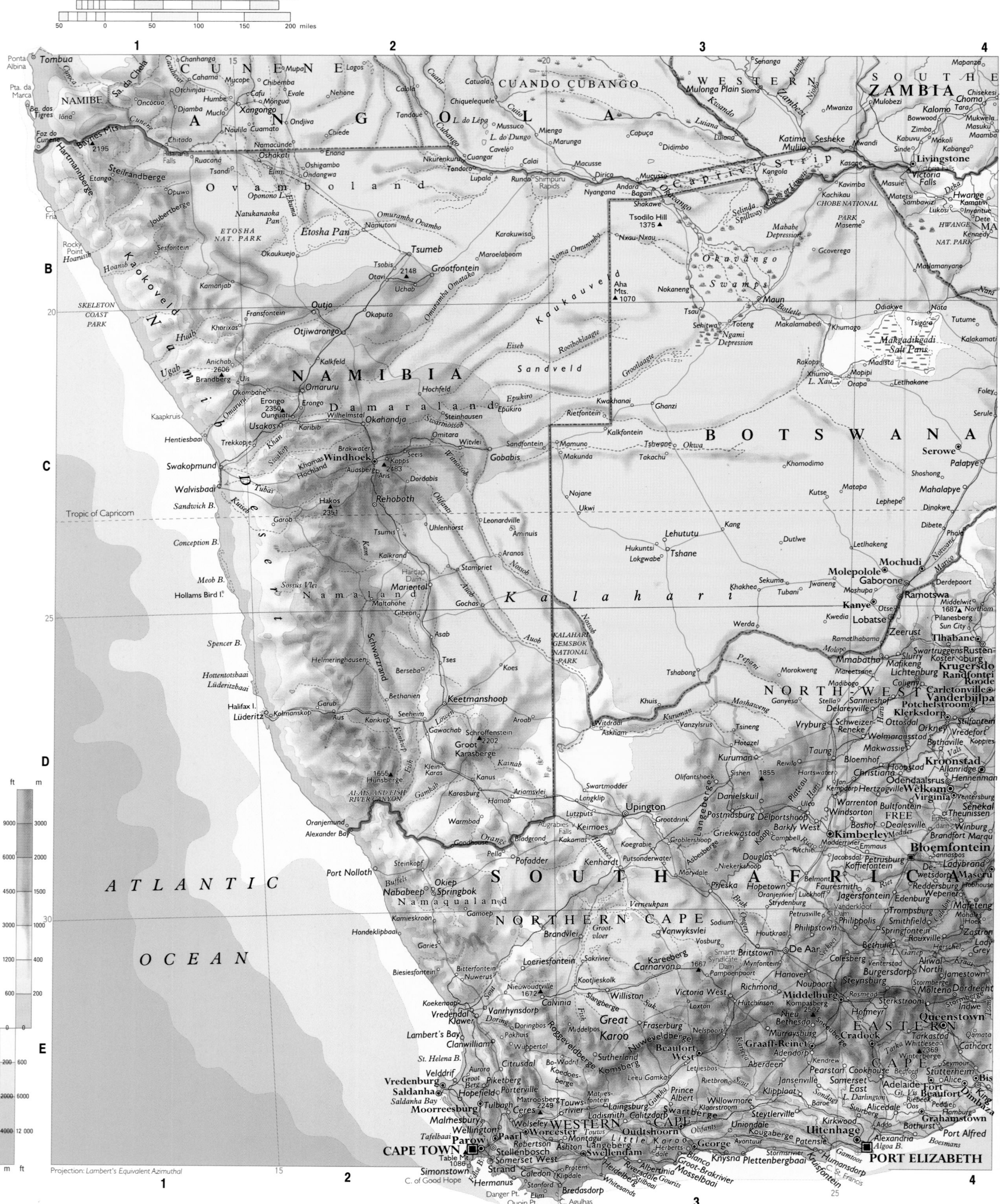

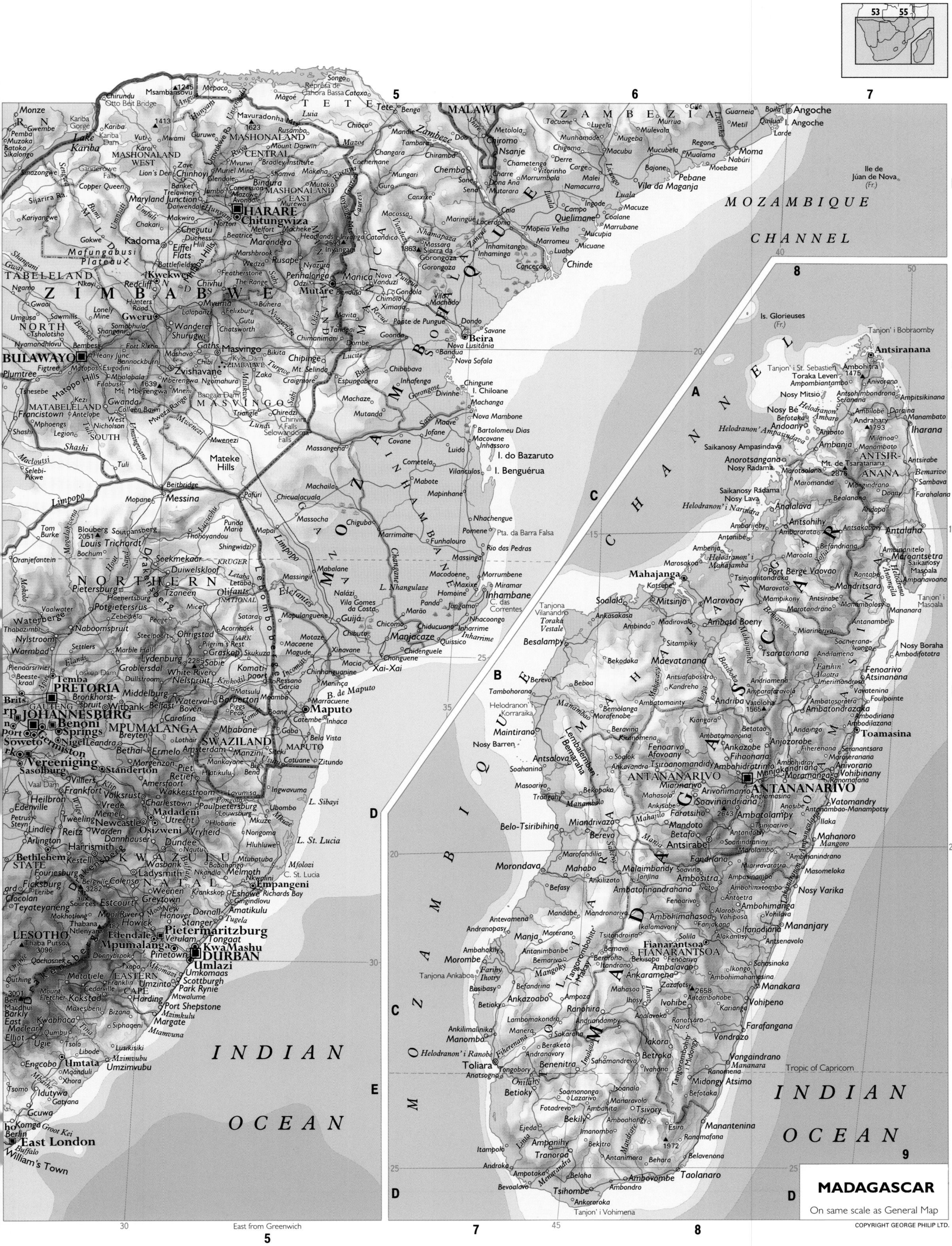

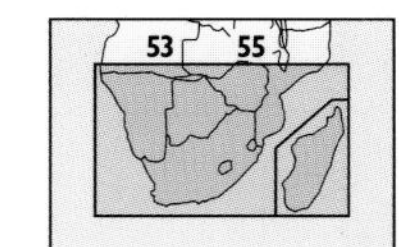

MOZAMBIQUE CHANNEL

INDIAN OCEAN

MADAGASCAR

On same scale as General Map

East from Greenwich

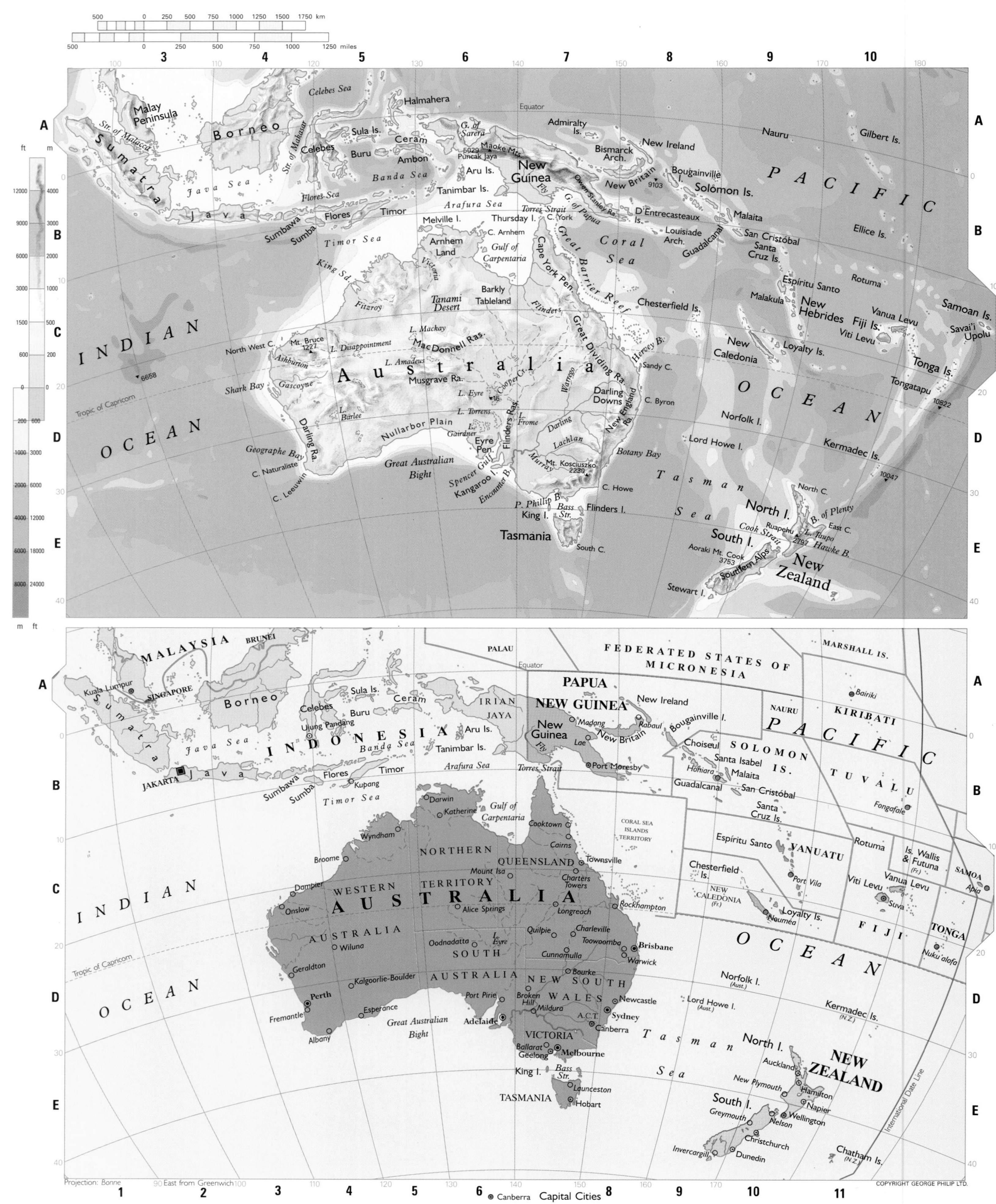

500 0 250 500 750 1000 1250 1500 1750 km
500 0 250 500 750 1000 1250 miles
ft m
12000 4000
9000 3000
6000 2000
3000 1000
1500 500
600 200
0
200 600
1000 3000
2000 6000
4000 12000
6000 18000
8000 24000
Malay Peninsula
Str. of Malacca
Sumatra
Borneo
Celebes Sea
Halmahera
Str. of Makasar
Celebes
Sula Is.
Ceram
Buru
Ambon
Java Sea
Java
Banda Sea
G. of Sarera
Maoke Mts.
5029 Puncak Jaya
Aru Is.
New Guinea
Fly
Tanimbar Is.
Flores Sea
Sumbawa
Sumba
Flores
Timor
Arafura Sea
Timor Sea
Equator
Admiralty Is.
Bismarck Arch.
New Ireland
New Britain
9103
Owen Stanley Ra.
Bougainville I.
Solomon Is.
Nauru
Gilbert Is.
PACIFIC
Torres Strait
C. York
G. of Papua
D'Entrecasteaux Is.
Louisiade Arch.
Guadalcanal
Malaita
San Cristóbal
Santa Cruz Is.
Ellice Is.
Melville I.
Thursday I.
C. Arnhem
Arnhem Land
Gulf of Carpentaria
Great Barrier Reef
Coral Sea
Cape York Pen.
King Sd.
Victoria
Fitzroy
Tanami Desert
Barkly Tableland
Flinders
Chesterfield Is.
Espíritu Santo
Rotuma
Malakula
New Hebrides
Fiji Is.
Vanua Levu
Viti Levu
Samoan Is.
Savai'i
Upolu
INDIAN
OCEAN
North West C.
Mt. Bruce 1227
L. Disappointment
L. Mackay
MacDonnell Ras.
Ashburton
L. Amadeus
Australia
Great Dividing Ra.
Hervey B.
New Caledonia
Loyalty Is.
Tonga Is.
Tongatapu
10822
Sandy C.
6658
Gascoyne
Musgrave Ra.
Shark Bay
Tropic of Capricorn
Warrego
Cooper Cr.
L. Eyre
-16
Darling Downs
C. Byron
L. Barlee
L. Torrens
L. Frome
Darling
New England Ra.
Norfolk I.
Nullarbor Plain
L. Gairdner
Flinders Ras.
Lachlan
Darling Ra.
Geographe Bay
C. Naturaliste
C. Leeuwin
Eyre Pen.
Great Australian Bight
Spencer Gulf
Kangaroo I.
Encounter B.
Murray
Mt. Kosciuszko 2230
Botany Bay
Lord Howe I.
Kermadec Is.
10047
C. Howe
Tasman Sea
P. Phillip B.
King I.
Bass Str.
Flinders I.
Tasmania
South C.
North C.
North I.
B. of Plenty
East C.
Ruapehu 2797
L. Taupo
Hawke B.
Cook Strait
South I.
Aoraki Mt. Cook 3753
Southern Alps
New Zealand
Stewart I.
MALAYSIA
BRUNEI
PALAU
FEDERATED STATES OF MICRONESIA
MARSHALL IS.
Kuala Lumpur
SINGAPORE
Sumatra
Borneo
Sula Is.
Ceram
Celebes
Buru
IRIAN JAYA
PAPUA NEW GUINEA
New Ireland
Madang
Rabaul
Bougainville I.
Bairiki
KIRIBATI
Ujung Pandang
INDONESIA
Aru Is.
New Guinea
Lae
New Britain
NAURU
PACIFIC
Java Sea
Banda Sea
Tanimbar Is.
Fly
Choiseul
SOLOMON IS.
Santa Isabel
Honiara
Malaita
TUVALU
JAKARTA
Java
Flores
Timor
Arafura Sea
Torres Strait
Port Moresby
Guadalcanal
San Cristóbal
Sumbawa
Sumba
Kupang
Timor Sea
Darwin
Katherine
Gulf of Carpentaria
Cooktown
CORAL SEA ISLANDS TERRITORY
Santa Cruz Is.
Fongafale
Wyndham
Cairns
Espíritu Santo
VANUATU
Rotuma
Is. Wallis & Futuna (Fr.)
SAMOA
NORTHERN TERRITORY
QUEENSLAND
Townsville
Broome
Mount Isa
Charters Towers
Chesterfield Is.
Port Vila
Viti Levu
Vanua Levu
Apia
INDIAN
Dampier
WESTERN AUSTRALIA
AUSTRALIA
NEW CALEDONIA (Fr.)
Suva
Onslow
Alice Springs
Longreach
Rockhampton
Loyalty Is.
Nouméa
FIJI
TONGA
Wiluna
Oodnadatta
L. Eyre
Quilpie
Charleville
Toowoomba
Brisbane
OCEAN
SOUTH AUSTRALIA
Cunnamulla
Warwick
Nuku'alofa
Geraldton
Tropic of Capricorn
Kalgoorlie-Boulder
Bourke
NEW SOUTH WALES
Norfolk I. (Aust.)
OCEAN
Perth
Port Pirie
Broken Hill
Newcastle
Lord Howe I. (Aust.)
Kermadec Is. (N.Z.)
Fremantle
Esperance
Mildura
Sydney
A.C.T.
Canberra
Adelaide
Great Australian Bight
VICTORIA
Tasman Sea
North I.
Albany
Ballarat
Geelong
Melbourne
Auckland
NEW ZEALAND
King I.
Bass Str.
New Plymouth
Hamilton
International Date Line
Launceston
Napier
TASMANIA
Hobart
South I.
Wellington
Greymouth
Nelson
Christchurch
Invercargill
Dunedin
Chatham Is. (N.Z.)
Projection: Bonne
East from Greenwich
Canberra Capital Cities
COPYRIGHT GEORGE PHILIP LTD.

50 0 50 100 150 200 km
50 0 50 100 150 miles

PACIFIC OCEAN

TASMAN SEA

North Island

South Island

C. Reinga
C. Maria van Diemen
North C.
Rangaunu B.
Doubtless B.
Mangonui
Whangaroa Harb.
Houhora Heads
Ahipara B.
Kaitaia
Tauroa Pt.
Northland
B. of Islands
Okaihau
C. Brett
Rawene
Opua
Kaikohe
Hokianga Harbour
Hikurangi
Whangarei
Whangarei Harb.
Donnelly's Crossing
Bream Hd.
Dargaville
Waipu
Bream B.
Little Barrier I.
Great Barrier I.
Warkworth
C. Rodney
C. Colville
Kaipara Harbour
Hauraki Gulf
Cuvier I.
Helensville
Takapuna
Devonport
Coromandel
AUCKLAND
Whitianga
Manukau
Papakura
Thames
Pukekohe
Waiuku
Waikato
Mercer
Waihi
Mayor I.
Paeroa
Tauranga Harb.
Huntly
Te Aroha
Morrinsville
Hamilton
Raglan
Tauranga
Te Puke
White I.
C. Runaway
Mount Maunganui
Bay of Plenty
Cambridge
Te Awamutu
Whakatane
Kawhia Harbour
Kawerau
Opotiki
East C.
Otorohanga
Putaruru
Rotorua
L. Rotorua
Te Teko
L. Tarawera
Te Araroa
Tokoroa
Murupara
Raukumara Ra.
Hikurangi 1753
Waipiro
Te Kuiti
Kinleith
Motu
Tolaga Bay
Mokau
Mokai
Wairakei
Ormond
North Taranaki Bight
Waitara
Ongarue
Taumarunui
L. Taupo
Taupo
Gisborne
Poverty Bay
New Plymouth
Inglewood
Turangi
Tarawera
Nuhaka
Waikokopu
Mt. Taranaki (Mt. Egmont) 2518
Whangamomona
Wairoa
Mahia Pen.
C. Egmont
Opunake
Stratford
Eltham
Ruapehu 2797
Ohakune
Raetihi
Kaimanawa Mts.
Hawke Bay
Bay View
Napier
Kapuni
Hawera
Waiouru
Taihape
South Taranaki Bight
Patea
Waverley
Mangaweka
Ruahine Ra.
Hastings
C. Kidnappers
Wanganui
Hunterville
Waipawa
Marton
Halcombe
Waipukurau
Bulls
Feilding
Palmerston North
Dannevirke
Foxton
Shannon
Woodville
Pahiatua
Levin
Otaki
Eketahuna
C. Turnagain
Paraparaumu
Kapiti I.
Tararua Ra.
Masterton
Carterton
Greytown
Martinborough
Featherston
Upper Hutt
Petone
Lower Hutt
Eastbourne
WELLINGTON
Cook Strait
Wairarapa
C. Farewell
Golden B.
Collingwood
Takaka
D'Urville I.
Tasman B.
Tasman Mts.
Pelorus Sd.
Motueka
Karamea
Karamea Bight
Nelson
Havelock
Tadmor
Richmond
Wakefield
Picton
Blenheim
Seddonville
Granity
Seddon
Ward
Westport
Lyell
Matiri Ra.
Murchison
Inangahua
L. Rotoroa
2885 Tapuaenuku
Mt. Travers 2338
Reefton
Spenser Mts.
Kaikoura Ra.
Blackball
Runanga
Greymouth
Stillwater
Lewis Pass
Hanmer Springs
Kaikoura
Kumara
L. Brunner
Jacksons
Hokitika
Ross
Waiau
Culverden
Hurunui
Arthur's Pass
Westland Bight
Abut Hd.
Waikari
Waipara
Amberley
Rangiora
Kaiapoi
Pegasus Bay
Oxford
New Brighton
Christchurch
Springfield
Whitecliffs
Coleridge
Riccarton
Lincoln
Lyttelton
Banks Pen.
Aoraki Mt. Cook 3753
Southern Alps
Methven
Staveley
Plains
Akaroa
Little River
L. Ellesmere
Southbridge
Rakaia
Ashburton
Mount Cook
Tekapo
Rangitata
Jackson B.
Okuru
Haast
Fairlie
L. Pukaki
Temuka
Timaru
Canterbury
Canterbury Bight
St. Andrews
Mt. Aspiring 3027
L. Wanaka
L. Hawea
L. Ohau
Waitaki
Milford Sd.
Sutherland Falls
Mt. Earnslaw 2818
Bligh Sound
George Sound
Milford Sound
Wanaka
Arrowtown
Dunstan Mts.
Kurow
Waimate
Queenstown
Cromwell
Tokarahi
Ngapara
Secretary I.
Doubtful Sd.
Wakatipu
Alexandra
Naseby
Kakanui Mts.
Oamaru
Maheno
Hampden
Te Anau
Kingston
Clyde
Otago
Dunback
Palmerston
Breaksea Sd.
L. Manapouri
Eyre Mts.
Garvie Mts.
Umbrella Mts.
Roxburgh
Waikouaiti
Resolution I.
Dusky Sd.
Manapouri
Mossburn
Lumsden
Port Chalmers
Otago Harbour
Saunders C.
Southland
Nightcaps
Edievale
Kelso
Lawrence
Tapanui
Mosgiel
Fairfield
Dunedin
L. Poteriteri
Ohai
Winton
Chalky Inlet
Preservation Inlet
Clifden
Tuatapere
Gore
Clinton
Milton
Balclutha
Te Waewae B.
Orepuki
Hedgehope
Mataura
Wyndham
Kaitangata
Nugget Pt.
Riverton
Invercargill
Owaka
Tahakopa
South Invercargill
Bluff
Tokanui
Foveaux Str.
Ruapuke I.
Halfmoon Bay
Stewart I.
Southwest C.
Port Pegasus

SAMOA ISLANDS
1:12 000 000

SAMOA
AMERICAN SAMOA
Savai'i
Apia
Upolu
Pago Pago
Tutuila
West from Greenwich

Futuna
Wallis & Futuna (Fr.)
Niuafo'ou (Tonga)
Thikombia
Labasa
Vanua Levu
FIJI
Yasawa Group
Taveuni
Koro
Vanua Balavu
Lautoka
Nandi
Viti Levu
1323
Levuka
Ovalau
Koro Sea
Gau
Lakeba
Lau Group
Suva
Moala
TONGA (Friendly Is.)
Kandavu
Vava'u
Vatoa
Tofua
East from Greenwich
Tongatapu
Nuku'alofa
West from Greenwich

FIJI AND TONGA ISLANDS
1:12 000 000

50 0 50 100 150 200 km
50 0 50 100 150 miles

ft m
9000 3000
6000 2000
3000 1000
1200 400
600 200
0 0
200 600
2000 6000
4000 12 000
6000 18 000
m ft

Projection : *Conical with two standard parallels*
East from Greenwich

WESTERN AUSTRALIA 1:8 000 000

WESTERN AUSTRALIA
SOUTH AUSTRALIA
INDIAN OCEAN
SOUTHERN OCEAN
Great Australian Bight
Great Victoria Desert
Nullarbor Plain
Hampton Tableland

PERTH
Fremantle
Kwinana
Rockingham
Mandurah
Bunbury
Busselton
Albany
Geraldton
Carnarvon
Kalgoorlie-Boulder
Esperance
Norseman
Northam
Merredin
Katanning
Collie
Narrogin
Meekatharra
Wiluna
Leonora
Laverton
Menzies
Coolgardie
Southern Cross
Kambalda
Eucla
Nullarbor
Cocklebiddy
Madura
Balladonia
Hopetoun
Ravensthorpe
Denham
Kalbarri
Northampton
Dongara
Moora
Pinjarra
Harvey
Australind
Manjimup
Augusta
Margaret River
Walpole
Denmark
Mount Barker

Ayers Rock 868
Mt. Olga 1069
Yulara
ULURU NAT. PARK
Petermann Ranges
Musgrave Ranges
Mt. Woodroffe 1440
Everard Ranges
Docker River
Warburton
Mt. Augustus 1105
Mt. Essendon 906
Mt. Eureka 499
Mt. Redcliffe 576
Tallering Peak 439
Wyemandoo 543
Mt. Singleton 677
Mt. Burges 554
Peak Eleanora 503
Mt. Ragged 585
Bluff Knoll
Stirling Ra. 1073
Pt. Lillian 466
Saunders Pt. 466
Mt. Aloysius 1058

L. Amadeus
L. Carnegie
L. Wells
L. Austin
L. Moore
L. Barlee
L. Ballard
L. Carey
L. Minigwal
L. Cowan
L. Dundas
L. Lefroy
L. Johnston
L. Magenta
L. Throssell
L. Yeo
L. Darlot
L. Way
L. Annean
L. Gregory
L. Nabberu
L. Gillen
L. Breaden
L. Burnside
L. Buchanan
L. Meramangye
L. Ifould
L. Maurice
L. Macleod

Shark Bay
Dirk Hartog I.
Houtman Abrolhos
Rottnest I.
Geographe B.
C. Leeuwin
Pt. D'Entrecasteaux
West Cape Howe
Archipelago of the Recherche
Eastern Group
Pt. Culver
Pt. Dover
Red Rocks Pt.
Head of Bight
Wilson Bluff
Bremer Bay
Cheyne B.
C. Riche
C. Vancouver
Bald Hd.
5632

Projection: Bonne
East from Greenwich
1 2 3 4 5
E F G

ft m
3000 1000
1200 400
600 200
0 0
200 600
2000 6000
4000 12 000
m ft

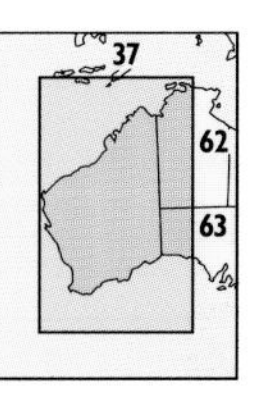

EASTERN AUSTRALIA 1:8 000 000

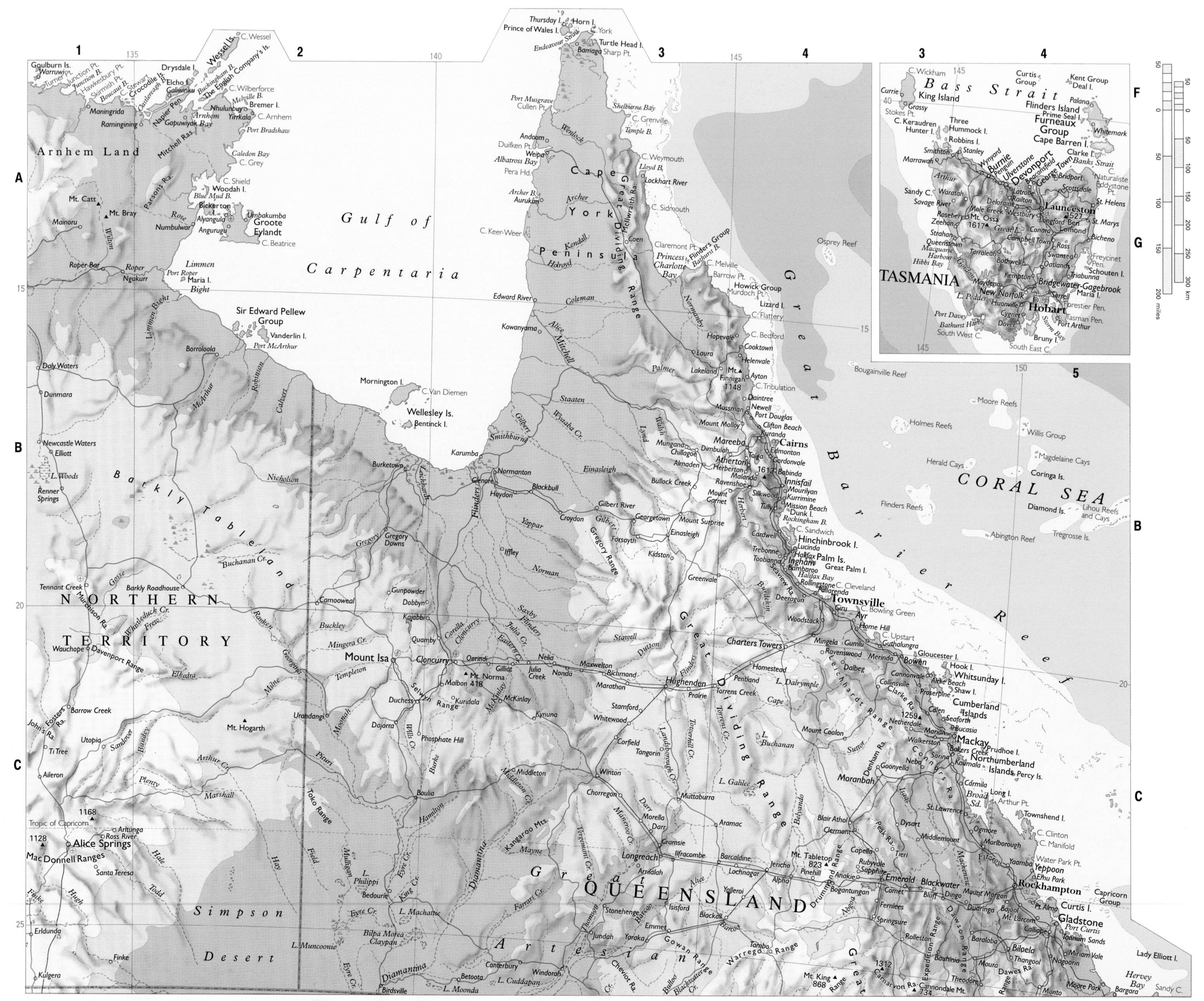

SOUTH AUSTRALIA
NEW SOUTH WALES
VICTORIA
AUSTRALIAN CAPITAL TERR.
TASMAN SEA
SOUTHERN OCEAN
Bass Strait
Spencer Gulf
Gulf St. Vincent
Kangaroo I.
Eyre Peninsula
Yorke Pen.
Lake Eyre (North)
Lake Eyre (South)
Lake Torrens
Lake Frome
Lake Gairdner
Flinders Ranges
Grey Range
Darling Downs
Darling
Murray
BRISBANE
Gold Coast
Tweed Heads
SYDNEY
CANBERRA
MELBOURNE
ADELAIDE
Newcastle
Wollongong
Geelong
Ballarat
Bendigo
Wagga Wagga
Albury-Wodonga
Broken Hill
Mildura
Dubbo
Tamworth
Armidale
Toowoomba
Port Augusta
Whyalla
Port Pirie
Port Lincoln
Mount Gambier
Warrnambool
King Island
Flinders Island
Furneaux Group
Cape Barren I.
Projection: Bonne
East from Greenwich
COPYRIGHT, GEORGE PHILIP LTD.
ft 4500 3000 1200 600 0 200 2000 4000
m 1500 1000 400 200 0 600 6000 12 000

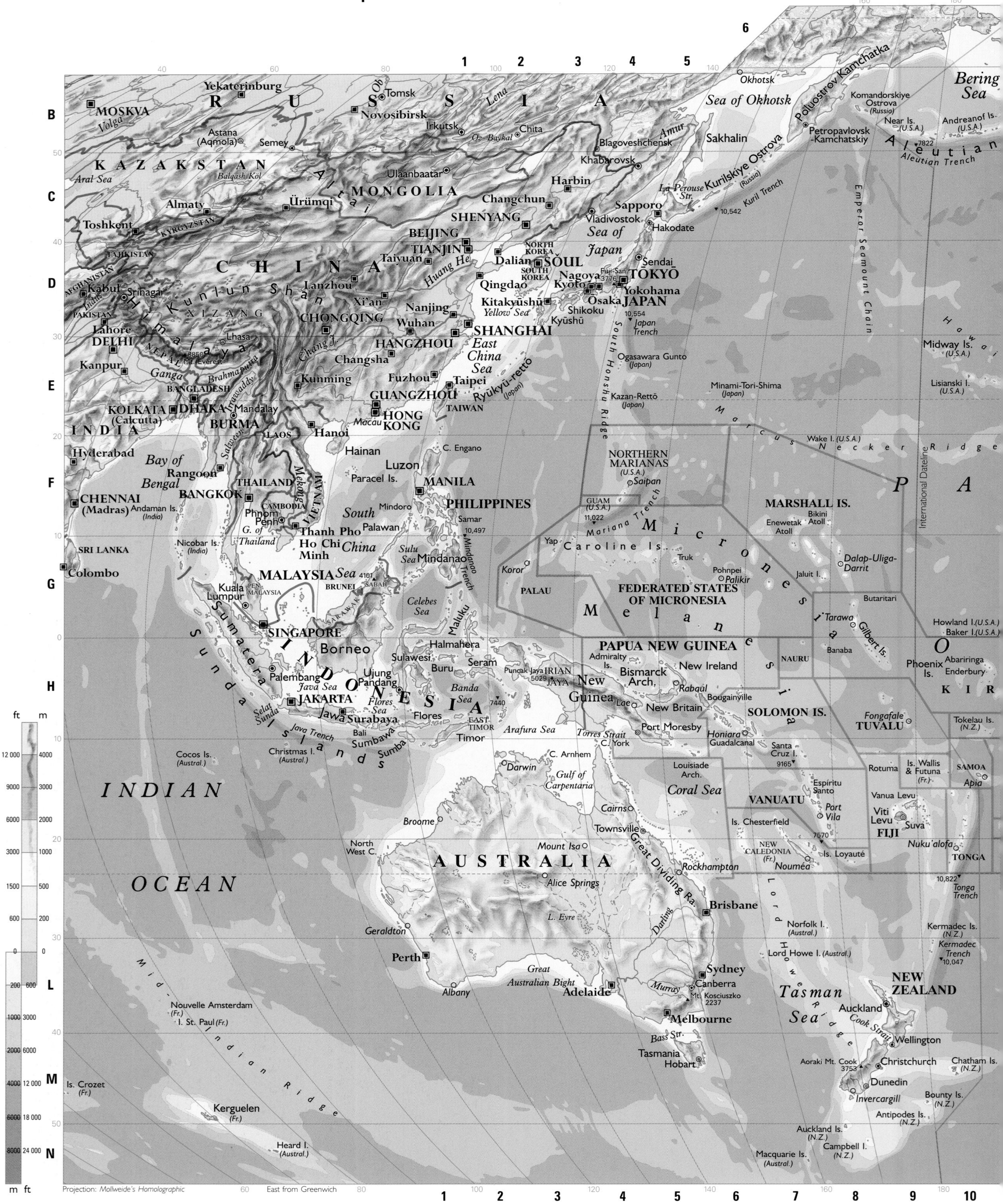

PACIFIC OCEAN Equatorial Scale 1:54 000 000

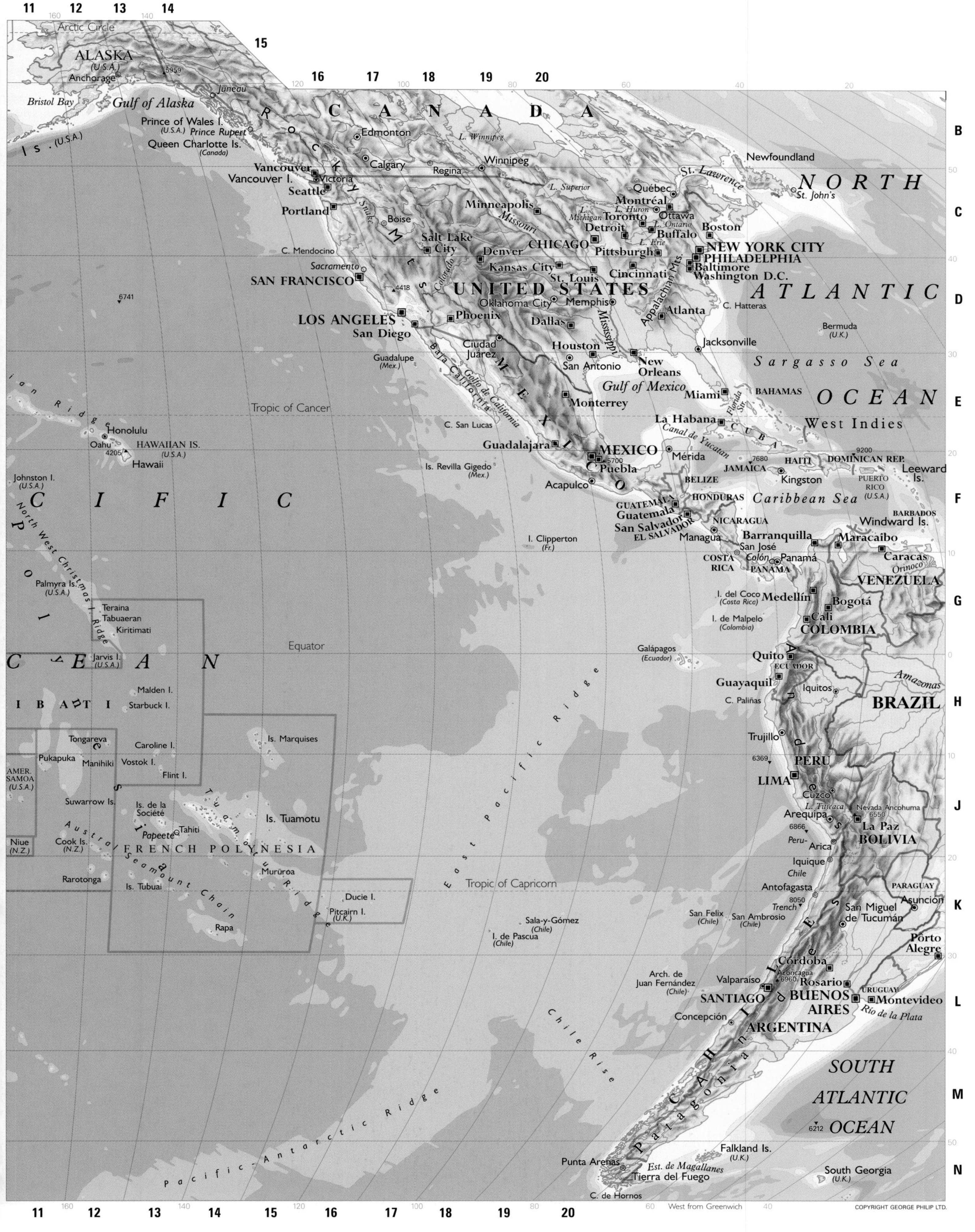
Arctic Circle
ALASKA
(U.S.A.)
Anchorage
Bristol Bay
Gulf of Alaska
Juneau
Prince of Wales I.
(U.S.A.)
Prince Rupert
Queen Charlotte Is.
(Canada)
C A N A D A
Edmonton
Calgary
Regina
Winnipeg
L. Winnipeg
Vancouver
Vancouver I.
Victoria
Seattle
Portland
Boise
Salt Lake City
Minneapolis
Missouri
Denver
CHICAGO
Kansas City
St. Louis
UNITED STATES
Oklahoma City
Memphis
Dallas
Houston
San Antonio
New Orleans
Atlanta
Jacksonville
Miami
C. Mendocino
Sacramento
SAN FRANCISCO
LOS ANGELES
San Diego
Phoenix
Ciudad Juárez
Newfoundland
St. Lawrence
Québec
Montréal
Ottawa
Toronto
L. Superior
L. Huron
L. Michigan
L. Ontario
L. Erie
Detroit
Buffalo
Boston
Pittsburgh
Cincinnati
NEW YORK CITY
PHILADELPHIA
Baltimore
Washington D.C.
Appalachian Mts.
Mississippi
C. Hatteras
St. John's
NORTH
ATLANTIC
OCEAN
Bermuda
(U.K.)
Sargasso Sea
BAHAMAS
West Indies
Gulf of Mexico
Monterrey
Guadalupe
(Mex.)
Baja California
Golfo de California
C. San Lucas
Guadalajara
MEXICO
Puebla
Acapulco
Mérida
La Habana
CUBA
Canal de Yucatan
Florida Str.
Is. Revilla Gigedo
(Mex.)
Tropic of Cancer
Honolulu
Oahu
HAWAIIAN IS.
(U.S.A.)
Hawaii
Johnston I.
(U.S.A.)
JAMAICA
Kingston
HAITI
DOMINICAN REP.
PUERTO RICO
(U.S.A.)
Leeward Is.
BELIZE
HONDURAS
Caribbean Sea
GUATEMALA
Guatemala
San Salvador
EL SALVADOR
NICARAGUA
Managua
COSTA RICA
San José
Colón
Panamá
PANAMA
BARBADOS
Windward Is.
Barranquilla
Maracaibo
Caracas
Orinoco
VENEZUELA
I. Clipperton
(Fr.)
PACIFIC
OCEAN
North West Christmas Ridge
Palmyra Is.
(U.S.A.)
Teraina
Tabuaeran
Kiritimati
Jarvis I.
(U.S.A.)
Malden I.
Starbuck I.
KIRIBATI
Equator
I. del Coco
(Costa Rica)
Medellín
Bogotá
Cali
I. de Malpelo
(Colombia)
COLOMBIA
Galápagos
(Ecuador)
Quito
ECUADOR
Guayaquil
C. Paliñas
Iquitos
Amazonas
BRAZIL
Tongareva
Pukapuka
Manihiki
Caroline I.
Vostok I.
Flint I.
AMER. SAMOA
(U.S.A.)
Suwarrow Is.
Is. de la Société
Papeete
Tahiti
Is. Marquises
Is. Tuamotu
Tuamotu Ridge
Niue
(N.Z.)
Cook Is.
(N.Z.)
FRENCH POLYNESIA
Austral Seamount Chain
Rarotonga
Is. Tubuai
Mururoa
Rapa
Ducie I.
Pitcairn I.
(U.K.)
East Pacific Ridge
Tropic of Capricorn
Sala-y-Gómez
(Chile)
I. de Pascua
(Chile)
Trujillo
PERU
LIMA
Andes
Cuzco
L. Titicaca
Arequipa
Nevada Ancohuma
La Paz
BOLIVIA
Peru-Chile Trench
Arica
Iquique
Antofagasta
PARAGUAY
Asunción
San Felix
(Chile)
San Ambrosio
(Chile)
San Miguel de Tucumán
Porto Alegre
Arch. de Juan Fernández
(Chile)
Córdoba
Aconcagua
Valparaíso
Rosario
SANTIAGO
BUENOS AIRES
URUGUAY
Montevideo
Río de la Plata
Concepción
ARGENTINA
Chile Rise
SOUTH
ATLANTIC
OCEAN
Patagonia
Falkland Is.
(U.K.)
Punta Arenas
Est. de Magallanes
Tierra del Fuego
C. de Hornos
South Georgia
(U.K.)
Pacific-Antarctic Ridge
West from Greenwich
COPYRIGHT GEORGE PHILIP LTD.

NORTH AMERICA : Physical 1:35 000 000

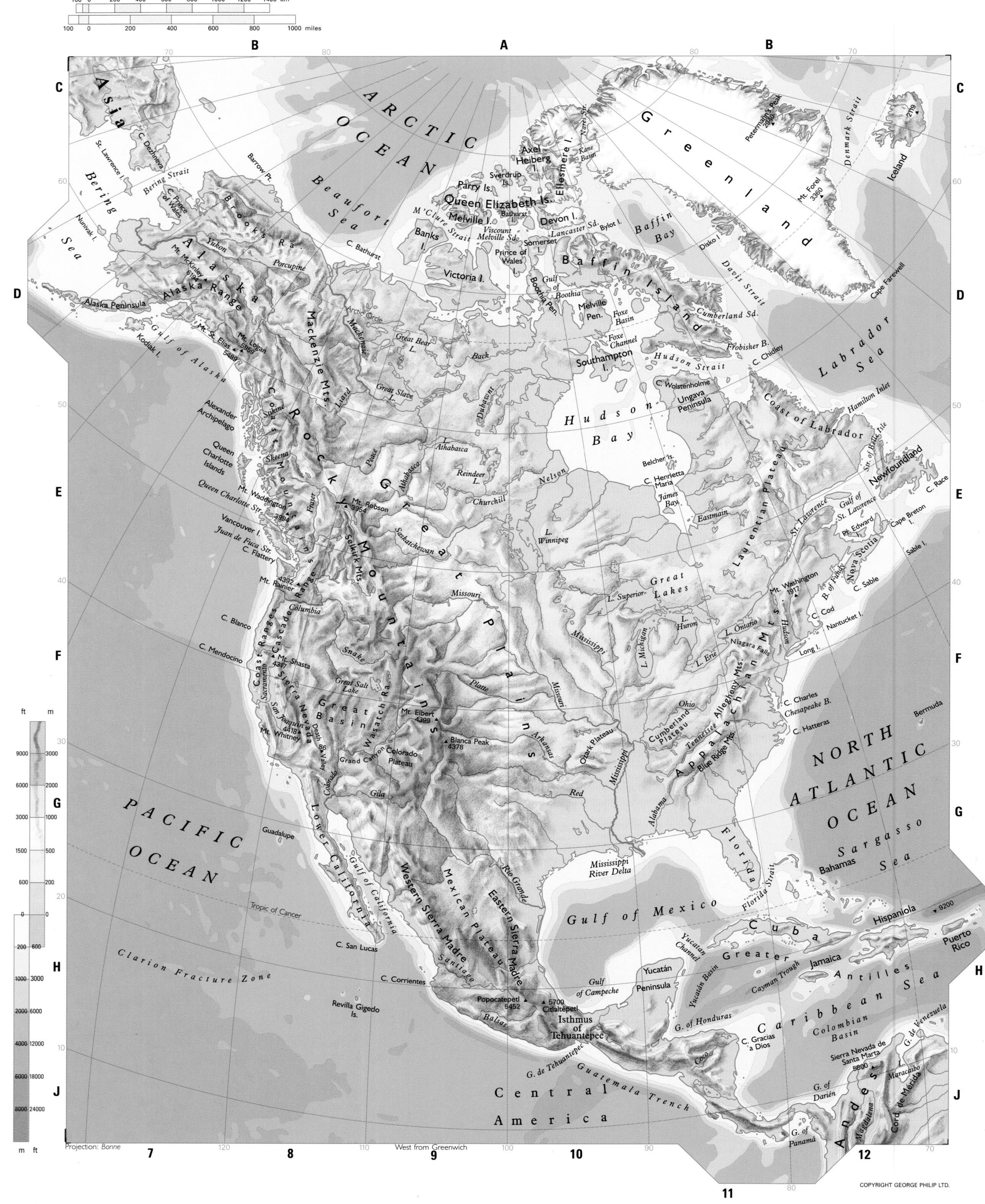

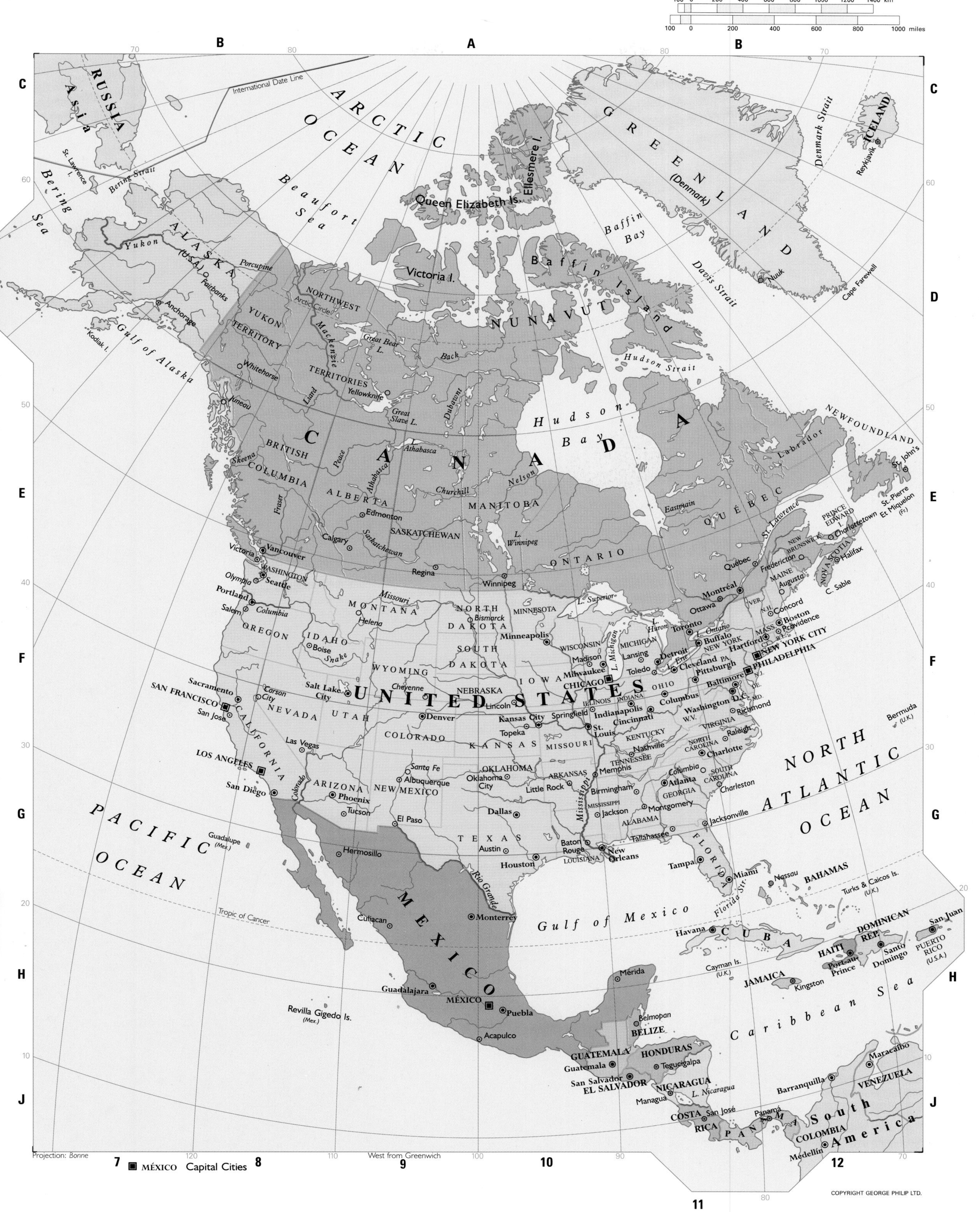
100 0 200 400 600 800 1000 1200 1400 km
100 0 200 400 600 800 1000 miles
RUSSIA
Asia
International Date Line
ARCTIC OCEAN
Beaufort Sea
Queen Elizabeth Is.
Ellesmere I.
GREENLAND (Denmark)
Denmark Strait
ICELAND
Reykjavík
Baffin Bay
Davis Strait
Nuuk
Cape Farewell
St. Lawrence I.
Bering Strait
Bering Sea
Yukon
ALASKA (U.S.A.)
Porcupine
Fairbanks
Anchorage
Kodiak I.
Gulf of Alaska
Victoria I.
Baffin Island
NUNAVUT
NORTHWEST TERRITORIES
Arctic Circle
YUKON TERRITORY
Mackenzie
Great Bear L.
Back
Whitehorse
Yellowknife
Liard
Great Slave L.
Dubawnt
Juneau
Hudson Strait
Hudson Bay
CANADA
NEWFOUNDLAND
Labrador
St. John's
BRITISH COLUMBIA
Skeena
Peace
Athabasca
Fraser
ALBERTA
Churchill
Nelson
MANITOBA
Edmonton
SASKATCHEWAN
Saskatchewan
Calgary
L. Winnipeg
Eastmain
QUÉBEC
St. Lawrence
PRINCE EDWARD I.
Charlottetown
St.-Pierre Et Miquelon (Fr.)
NEW BRUNSWICK
NOVA SCOTIA
Halifax
Fredericton
C. Sable
Victoria
Vancouver
WASHINGTON
Olympia
Seattle
Regina
Winnipeg
ONTARIO
Québec
MAINE
Augusta
Montréal
Ottawa
Portland
Salem
Columbia
OREGON
MONTANA
Missouri
Helena
NORTH DAKOTA
Bismarck
MINNESOTA
L. Superior
L. Huron
Toronto
L. Ontario
N.H.
Concord
Boston
Providence
MASS.
IDAHO
Boise
Snake
SOUTH DAKOTA
Minneapolis
WISCONSIN
Madison
L. Michigan
MICHIGAN
Lansing
Buffalo
NEW YORK
Hartford
NEW YORK CITY
PHILADELPHIA
WYOMING
Cheyenne
Milwaukee
Detroit
L. Erie
Toledo
Cleveland
PA.
Pittsburgh
N.J.
Sacramento
SAN FRANCISCO
San Jose
Carson City
NEVADA
Salt Lake City
UNITED STATES
NEBRASKA
IOWA
CHICAGO
ILLINOIS
INDIANA
OHIO
Columbus
Baltimore
DE.
MD.
Washington D.C.
Richmond
Bermuda (U.K.)
UTAH
Denver
Lincoln
Kansas City
Springfield
Indianapolis
Cincinnati
W.V.
VIRGINIA
CALIFORNIA
COLORADO
Topeka
KANSAS
MISSOURI
St. Louis
KENTUCKY
Raleigh
NORTH CAROLINA
Las Vegas
Nashville
TENNESSEE
Charlotte
LOS ANGELES
Santa Fe
OKLAHOMA
ARKANSAS
Memphis
SOUTH CAROLINA
NORTH ATLANTIC OCEAN
Columbia
Oklahoma City
Albuquerque
Little Rock
Birmingham
Atlanta
Charleston
San Diego
Colorado
ARIZONA
NEW MEXICO
Phoenix
Mississippi
MISSISSIPPI
GEORGIA
Jackson
Montgomery
ALABAMA
Jacksonville
PACIFIC OCEAN
Tucson
El Paso
Dallas
Tallahassee
Guadalupe (Mex.)
TEXAS
Austin
Baton Rouge
New Orleans
LOUISIANA
FLORIDA
Hermosillo
Houston
Tampa
Miami
Nassau
BAHAMAS
Rio Grande
Florida Str.
Turks & Caicos Is. (U.K.)
Tropic of Cancer
Culiacan
MEXICO
Monterrey
Gulf of Mexico
Havana
CUBA
DOMINICAN REP.
San Juan
HAITI
Port-au-Prince
Santo Domingo
PUERTO RICO (U.S.A.)
Cayman Is. (U.K.)
JAMAICA
Kingston
Mérida
Guadalajara
MÉXICO
Puebla
Revilla Gigedo Is. (Mex.)
Caribbean Sea
Belmopan
BELIZE
Acapulco
GUATEMALA
Guatemala
HONDURAS
Tegucigalpa
Maracaibo
San Salvador
EL SALVADOR
NICARAGUA
L. Nicaragua
Managua
Barranquilla
VENEZUELA
COSTA RICA
San José
Panamá
PANAMA
COLOMBIA
Medellín
South America
Projection: Bonne
West from Greenwich
MÉXICO Capital Cities
COPYRIGHT GEORGE PHILIP LTD.

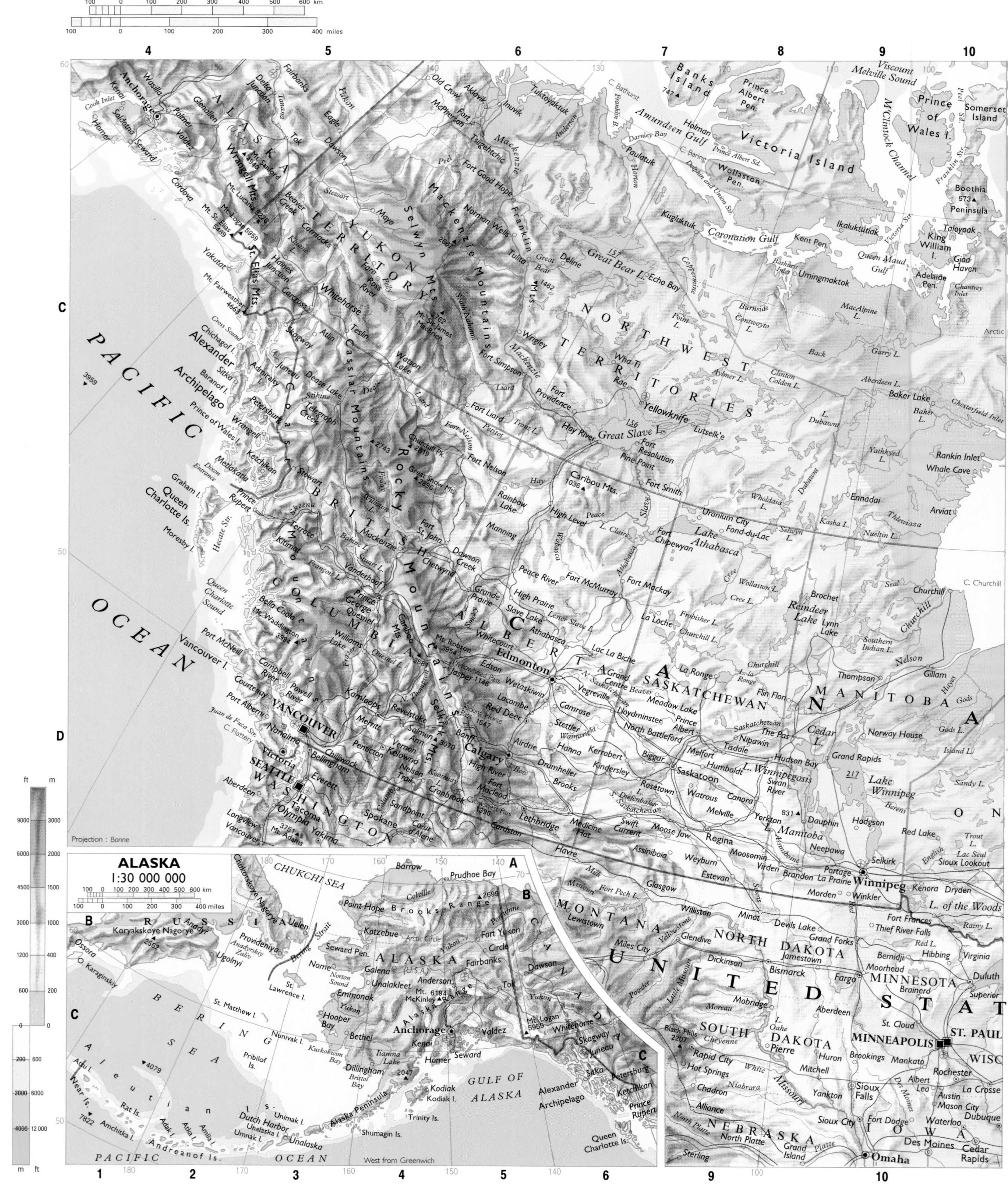

100 0 100 200 300 400 500 600 km
100 0 100 200 300 400 miles
4
5
6
7
8
9
10
C
D
PACIFIC OCEAN
ALASKA
YUKON TERRITORY
NORTHWEST TERRITORIES
BRITISH COLUMBIA
ALBERTA
SASKATCHEWAN
MANITOBA
WASHINGTON
MONTANA
NORTH DAKOTA
SOUTH DAKOTA
MINNESOTA
NEBRASKA
IOWA
UNITED STATES
Anchorage
Fairbanks
Dawson
Whitehorse
Inuvik
Tuktoyaktuk
Yellowknife
Great Bear L.
Great Slave L.
Lake Athabasca
Victoria Island
Banks Island
Prince of Wales I.
Somerset Island
Boothia Peninsula
King William I.
Coronation Gulf
Amundsen Gulf
Queen Maud Gulf
M'Clintock Channel
Mackenzie Mountains
Selwyn Mts.
Cassiar Mountains
Rocky Mountains
Coast Mountains
Wrangell Mts.
St. Elias Mts.
Mt. Logan 5959
Mt. Lucania 5226
Mt. St. Elias 5489
Mt. Fairweather 4663
Mt. Waddington 3994
Mt. Robson 3954
Alexander Archipelago
Queen Charlotte Is.
Vancouver I.
Prince Rupert
Prince George
Fort St. John
Dawson Creek
Grande Prairie
Edmonton
Calgary
Red Deer
Lethbridge
Medicine Hat
VANCOUVER
Victoria
SEATTLE
Tacoma
Olympia
Spokane
Kamloops
Kelowna
Saskatoon
Regina
Moose Jaw
Prince Albert
Lloydminster
North Battleford
Swift Current
Flin Flon
The Pas
Lake Winnipeg
L. Winnipegosis
L. Manitoba
Winnipeg
Brandon
Portage La Prairie
Thompson
Churchill
Reindeer Lake
Baker Lake
Rankin Inlet
Arviat
Fort McMurray
Fort Smith
Hay River
Fort Simpson
Fort Nelson
Fort Liard
Norman Wells
Kugluktuk
Umingmaktok
Ikaluktutiak
Gjoa Haven
Taloyoak
Minot
Bismarck
Fargo
Grand Forks
Duluth
MINNEAPOLIS
ST. PAUL
Pierre
Rapid City
Sioux Falls
Omaha
Des Moines
Projection : Bonne
ALASKA
1:30 000 000
100 0 100 200 300 400 500 600 km
100 0 100 200 300 400 miles
CHUKCHI SEA
BERING SEA
GULF OF ALASKA
Brooks Range
Alaska Range
Mt. McKinley 6194
Aleutian Is.
Alaska Peninsula
Kodiak I.
St. Lawrence I.
Nunivak I.
Pribilof Is.
RUSSIA
Barrow
Prudhoe Bay
Nome
Kotzebue
Point Hope
Fort Yukon
Juneau
Sitka
Ketchikan
Valdez
Seward
Homer
Dutch Harbor
Unalaska
West from Greenwich
PACIFIC OCEAN
ft
m
9000
6000
4500
3000
1200
600
0
200
2000
4000
3000
2000
1500
1000
400
200
0
600
6000
12 000
1
2
3
4
5
6
9
10

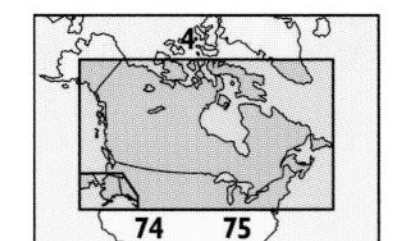

11 12 13 14 15 16

B
C
D
E

Devon I.
Lancaster Sound
Bylot I.
1890
Arctic Bay
Nanisivik
Borden Pen.
Eclipse Sd.
Pond Inlet
Brodeur Peninsula
Gulf of Boothia
Fury and Hecla Str.
Igloolik
Simpson Pen.
Pelly Bay
Committee B.
Melville Peninsula
Sanirajak
Foxe Basin
Prince Charles I.
Air Force I.
Rae Isthmus
Repulse Bay
Circle
NUNAVUT
Wager B.
Roes Welcome Sd.
Southampton I.
Salliq
Bell Pen.
C. Dorchester
Foxe Channel
Foxe Pen.
Cape Dorset
Amadjuak L.
Nettilling L.
Salisbury I.
Nottingham I.
Igluligaarjuk
Coats I.
Mansel I.
Baffin Island
Baffin Bay
2136
C. Adair
Clyde River
C. Raper
Home B.
Qikiqtarjuaq
C. Dyer
2591
Cumberland Peninsula
Pangnirtung
Hoare B.
Mercy C.
Cumberland Sd.
Meta Incognita Peninsula
Iqaluit
Hall Peninsula
Kimmirut
Frobisher Bay
Resolution I.
Hudson Strait
C. Chidley
Akpatok I.
Davis Strait
Nunavik
Uummannaq
Qeqertarsuaq
Qeqertarsuup Tunua
Ilulissat
Qasigiannguit
Kangerlussuaq
Sisimiut
Maniitsoq
Nuuk
GREENLAND (KALAALLIT NUNAAT) (Denmark)
2850
Kong Frederik VI's Kyst
Tasiilak
Qeqertarsuatsiaat
Paamiut
Arsuk
Qaqortoq
Nanortalik
Alluitsup Paa
Uummannarsuaq
ATLANTIC OCEAN
Labrador Sea
3809
Ivujivik
Salluit
Kangiqsujuaq
Quaqtaq
Péninsule d'Ungava
Kangirsuk
Ungava Bay
Arnaud
L. Payne
Puvirnituq
Feuilles
Koksoak
Kuujjuaq
1652
Kangiqsualujjuaq
Hebron
George
Baleine
Nain
Hudson Bay
257
Ottawa Is.
Inukjuak
L. Minto
Mélèzes
Caniapiscau
NEWFOUNDLAND
Hopedale
C. Harrison
Rigolet
Cartwright
Port Hope Simpson
Belle Isle
C. Bauld
St. Anthony
Sleeper Is.
King George Is.
Baker's Dozen Is.
Sanikiluaq
Belcher Is.
C. Tatnam
L. à l'Eau Claire
Grande Baleine
L. Bienville
Schefferville
Smallwood Res.
Labrador
North West River
Happy Valley-Goose Bay
Petitsikapau L.
Esker
Churchill Falls
Churchill
Kuujjuarapik
C. Henrietta Maria
Pte. Louis XIV
Kanaaupscow
La Grande
Rés. de Caniapiscau
Labrador City
Fermont
L. Ashuanipi
Natashquan
St-Augustin
Str. of Belle Isle
Notre Dame B.
Lewisporte
Gander
Bonavista
Trinity B.
Carbonear
St. John's
Baie Verte
Deer Lake
Grand Falls
Corner Brook
814
Stephenville
Newfoundland
Marystown
Placentia B.
Placentia
C. Race
Channel-Port aux Basques
ST.-PIERRE et MIQUELON (Fr.)
Peawanuck
Winisk
Severn
Big Trout L.
James Bay
Chisasibi
1135
Gagnon
Romaine
Moisie
Havre-St-Pierre
Î. d'Anticosti
Akimiski I.
Wemindji
Eastmain
QUÉBEC
Rés. Manicouagan
Attawapiskat
Fort Albany
Charlton I.
Waskaganish
Rupert
L. Mistassini
L. Albanel
Péribonca
Manicouagan
Sept-Îles
Port-Cartier
Gulf of St. Lawrence
Cabot Str.
C. Ray
North C.
ONTARIO
Albany
Moosonee
Harricana
Nottaway
Missinaibi
L. St. Joseph
Nakina
Kenogami
Matagami
L. Matagami
Chibougamau
Baie Comeau
St. Lawrence
Matane
Gaspé
Pén. de Gaspé
Îs. de la Madeleine
Cape Breton I.
Glace Bay
Sydney
Port Hawkesbury
L. Nipigon
Nipigon
Geraldton
Hearst
Cochrane
Abitibi L.
Rés. Gouin
Dolbeau
L. St-Jean
Roberval
Jonquière
Chicoutimi
Rimouski
Rivière-du-Loup
Campbellton
Bathurst
Edmundston
Miramichi
PR. EDWARD I.
Summerside
Charlottetown
Northumberland Str.
Antigonish
New Glasgow
Marathon
Kapuskasing
Oba
Amos
Timmins
Kirkland Lake
Rouyn-Noranda
Val-d'Or
1190
La Tuque
Québec
Lévis
Thetford Mines
Grand Falls
NEW BRUNSWICK
Woodstock
Moncton
Fredericton
Saint John
Amherst
Truro
Kentville
Dartmouth
Halifax
NOVA SCOTIA
Sable I. (Nova Scotia)
Thunder Bay
Chapleau
New Liskeard
Wawa
Lake Superior
Mont-Laurier
Rés. Cabonga
Shawinigan
Trois-Rivières
Joliette
St-Hyacinthe
Sherbrooke
MAINE
Digby
B. of Fundy
Bridgewater
Liverpool
Yarmouth
C. Sable
6309
Houghton
183
Sault Ste. Marie
Elliot Lake
Sudbury
Ottawa
L. Nipissing
North Bay
MONTRÉAL
Hull
Granby
L. Champlain
Bangor
Augusta
Lewiston
Portland
Ironwood
Marquette
MICHIGAN
Sault Ste. Marie
Manitoulin I.
Parry Sound
Georgian Bay
Pembroke
Ottawa
Cornwall
Montpelier
Burlington
VERMONT
NEW HAMPSHIRE
Concord
Manchester
Rhinelander
Manistique
Escanaba
Menominee
Petoskey
Traverse City
Lake Huron
Huntsville
Barrie
Peterborough
Kingston
Belleville
Wausau
Green Bay
Cadillac
Owen Sound
Oshawa
TORONTO
L. Ontario
Syracuse
MASS.
BOSTON
C. Cod
WISCONSIN
Appleton
Sheboygan
L. Michigan
Saginaw
Kitchener
Hamilton
Rochester
Albany
Springfield
Providence
MILWAUKEE
Grand Rapids
Flint
London
Niagara Falls
BUFFALO
NEW YORK
HARTFORD
CONN.
R.I.
Madison
Racine
Kenosha
Lansing
Sarnia
174
Elmira
Binghamton
New Haven
Rockford
CHICAGO
DETROIT
Windsor
L. Erie
Erie
Jamestown
Scranton
Bridgeport
NEW YORK
ILLINOIS
Gary
South Bend
INDIANA
Toledo
OHIO
CLEVELAND
PENNSYLVANIA
Newark
N.J.
Allentown
Trenton

90 80 70 60 50 40 30
60 50 40

West from Greenwich

11 12 13 14

EASTERN CANADA 1:7 000 000

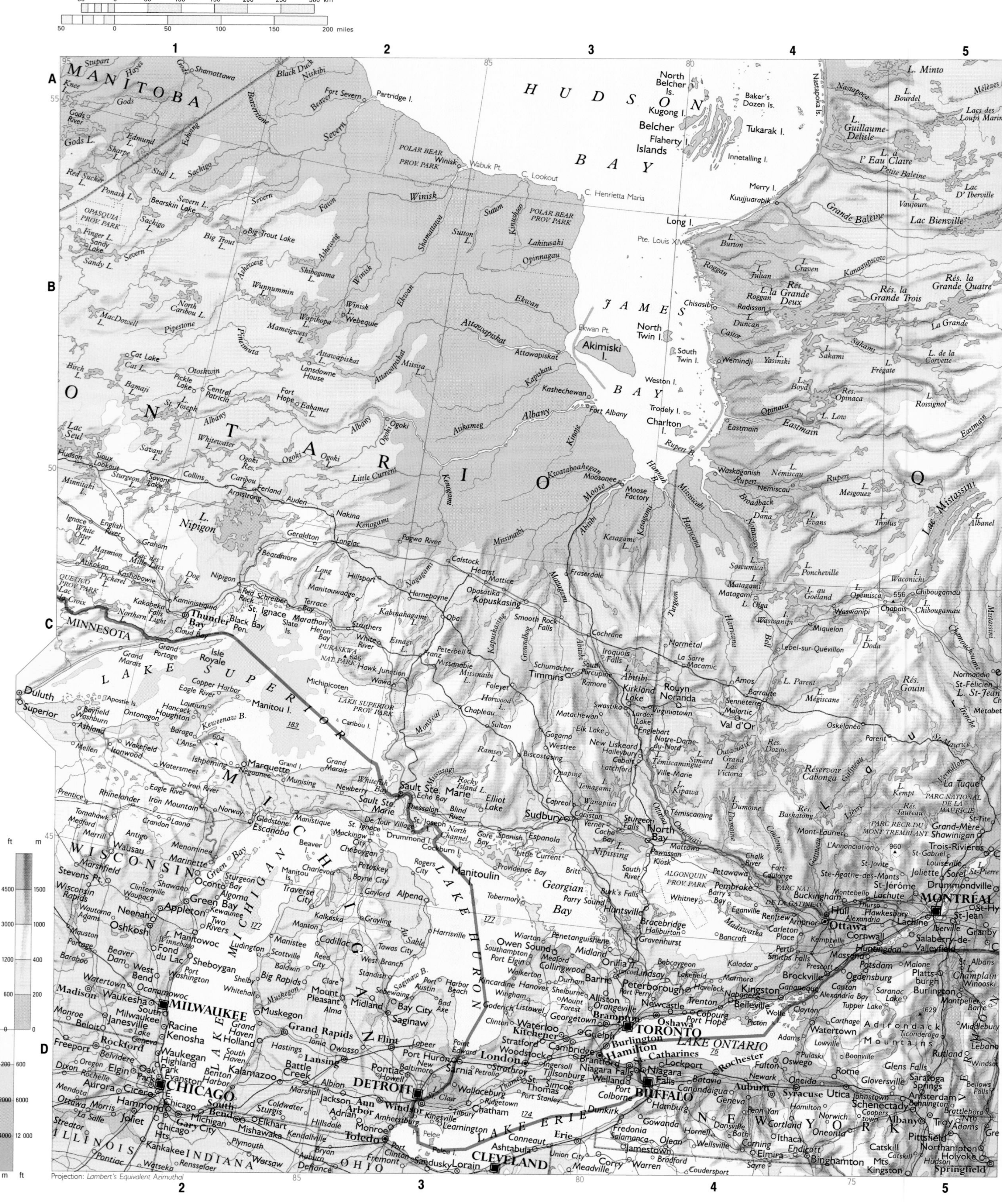

69
73
80
76

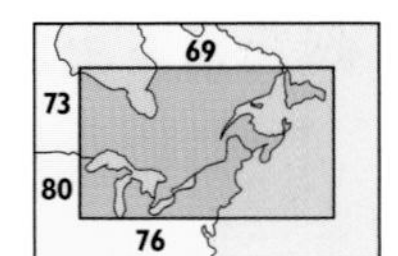

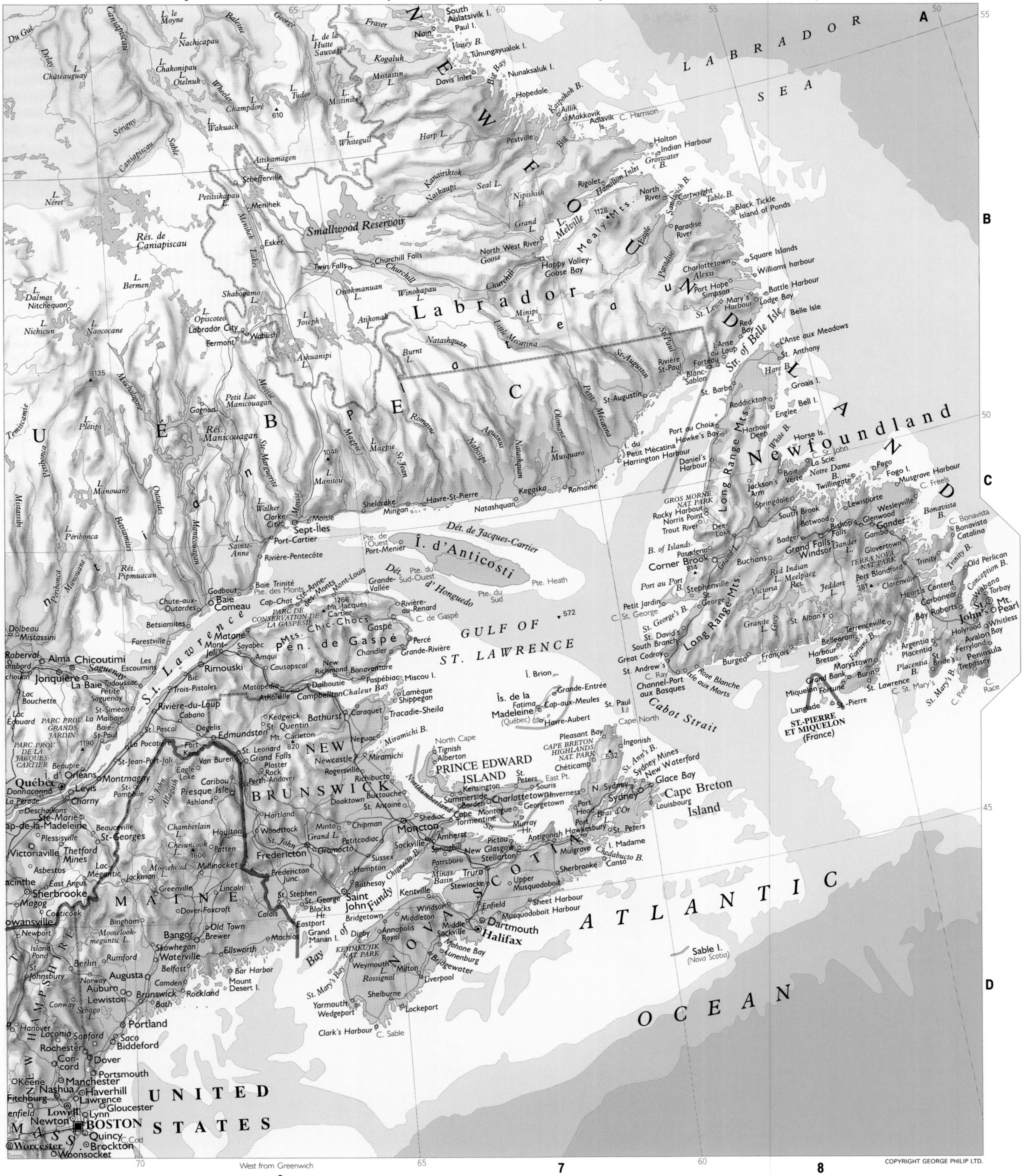

6
7
8
9
A
B
C
D
LABRADOR SEA
NEWFOUNDLAND
Labrador
QUÉBEC
Newfoundland
GULF OF ST. LAWRENCE
ATLANTIC OCEAN
UNITED STATES
MAINE
NEW BRUNSWICK
NOVA SCOTIA
PRINCE EDWARD ISLAND
Cape Breton Island
Smallwood Reservoir
Rés. de Caniapiscau
Rés. Manicouagan
Mealy Mts.
Long Range Mts.
Î. d'Anticosti
Pén. de Gaspé
St. Lawrence
Cabot Strait
Str. of Belle Isle
Bay of Fundy
Chaleur Bay
Northumberland Str.
Dét. de Jacques-Cartier
Dét. d'Honguedo
Îs. de la Madeleine (Québec)
Sable I. (Nova Scotia)
ST-PIERRE ET MIQUELON (France)
GROS MORNE NAT. PARK
TERRA NOVA NAT. PARK
CAPE BRETON HIGHLANDS NAT. PARK
KEJIMKUJIK NAT. PARK
Nain
Davis Inlet
Hopedale
Makkovik
Postville
Cartwright
Rigolet
North West River
Happy Valley-Goose Bay
Churchill Falls
Schefferville
Labrador City
Wabush
Fermont
Sept-Îles
Port-Cartier
Baie Comeau
Havre-St-Pierre
Natashquan
Blanc-Sablon
St. Anthony
Corner Brook
Stephenville
Deer Lake
Grand Falls-Windsor
Gander
Botwood
Lewisporte
Clarenville
Carbonear
St. John's
Mt. Pearl
Placentia
Marystown
Burin
Channel-Port aux Basques
Gaspé
Percé
Matane
Rimouski
Rivière-du-Loup
Chicoutimi
Jonquière
Alma
Québec
Lévis
Sherbrooke
Edmundston
Campbellton
Bathurst
Miramichi
Moncton
Fredericton
Saint John
Charlottetown
Summerside
Amherst
Truro
New Glasgow
Halifax
Dartmouth
Sydney
Glace Bay
Yarmouth
Lunenburg
Bridgewater
Liverpool
Bangor
Augusta
Lewiston
Auburn
Portland
Biddeford
Portsmouth
Manchester
Nashua
Lowell
Lawrence
Haverhill
BOSTON
Quincy
Brockton
Worcester
C. Sable
C. Race
C. Bonavista
C. North
C. Ray
C. de Gaspé
West from Greenwich
70
65
60
55
50
45
COPYRIGHT GEORGE PHILIP LTD.

WESTERN CANADA 1:7 000 000

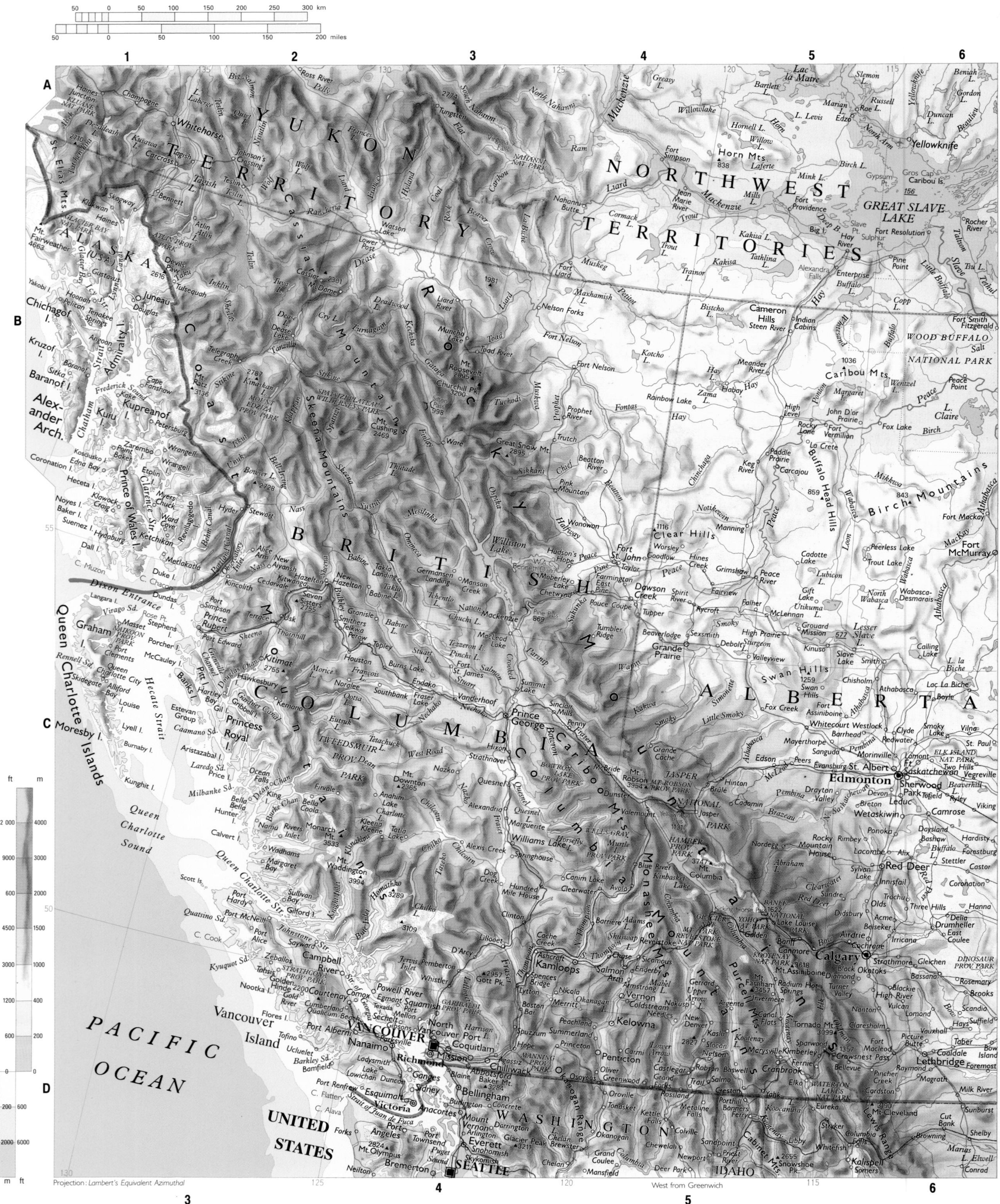

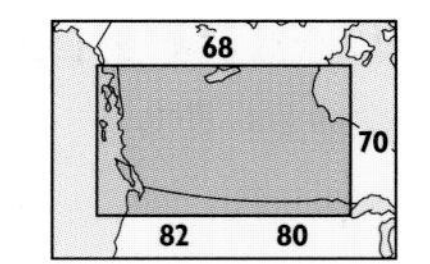

7 8 9 10 11

A B C D

110 105 100 95 90

60 55 50

NUNAVUT

HUDSON BAY

MANITOBA

SASKATCHEWAN

ONTARIO

NORTH DAKOTA

MINNESOTA

MONTANA

LAKE WINNIPEG

Lake Athabasca

Lake Winnipegosis

Lake Manitoba

Cedar Lake

Reindeer Lake

Wollaston L.

Southern Indian L.

Lac La Ronge

Lake of the Woods

Dubawnt L.

Yathkyed L.

Nueltin L.

Kasba L.

Wholdaia L.

Dawson Inlet

Arviat

Churchill

C. Churchill

C. Tatnam

Nelson

Churchill

Hayes

Thompson

Flin Flon

The Pas

Gillam

Saskatchewan

Prince Albert

North Battleford

Lloydminster

Saskatoon

Regina

Moose Jaw

Swift Current

Medicine Hat

Yorkton

Brandon

Winnipeg

Portage la Prairie

Dauphin

Kenora

Dryden

Fort Frances

Estevan

Weyburn

Minot

Williston

Grand Forks

Devils Lake

Bemidji

Duluth

Superior

Havre

Cypress Hills

Lac la Croix

7 8 9 10

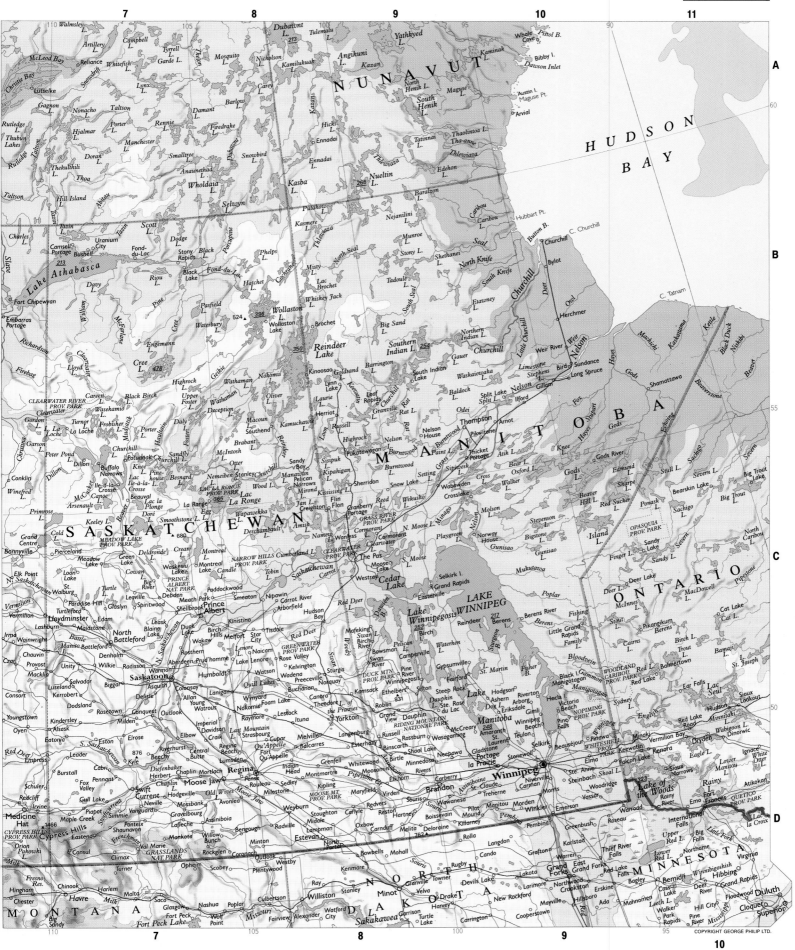

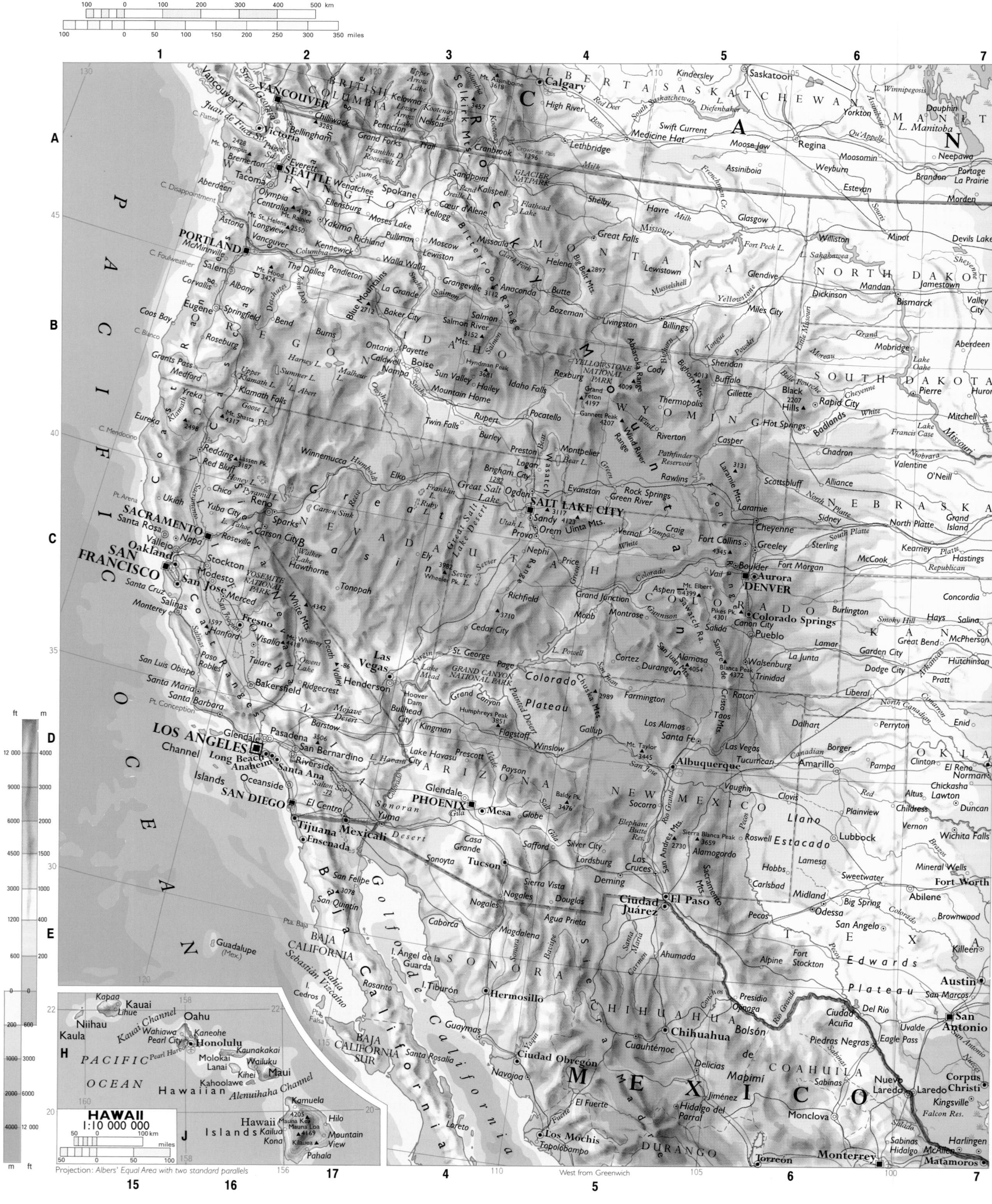

Projection: Albers' Equal Area with two standard parallels
West from Greenwich
HAWAII
1:10 000 000
PACIFIC OCEAN
MEXICO

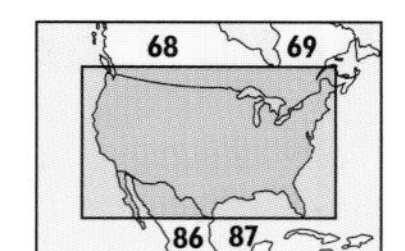
68
69
86
87

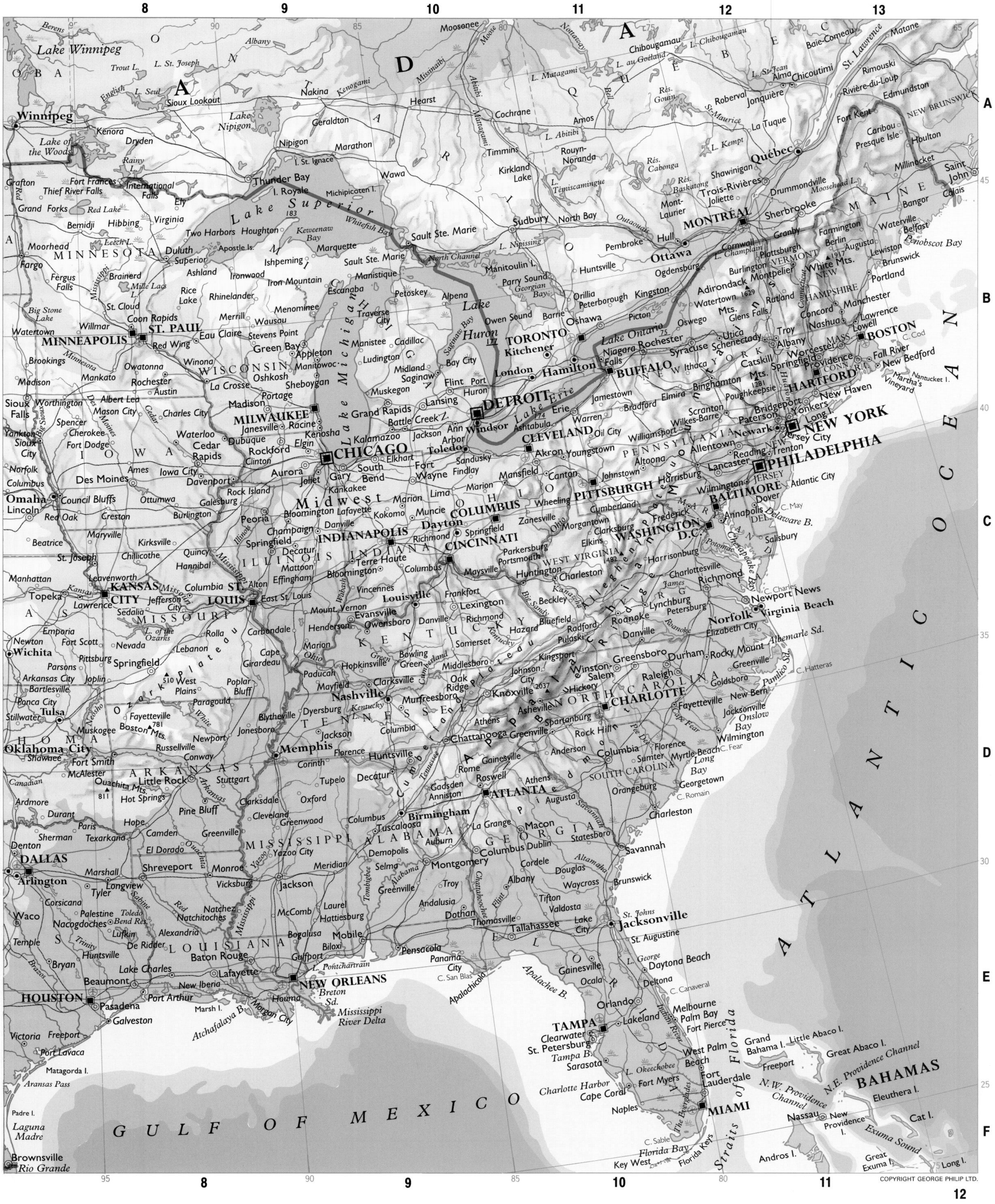

EASTERN UNITED STATES 1:6 000 000

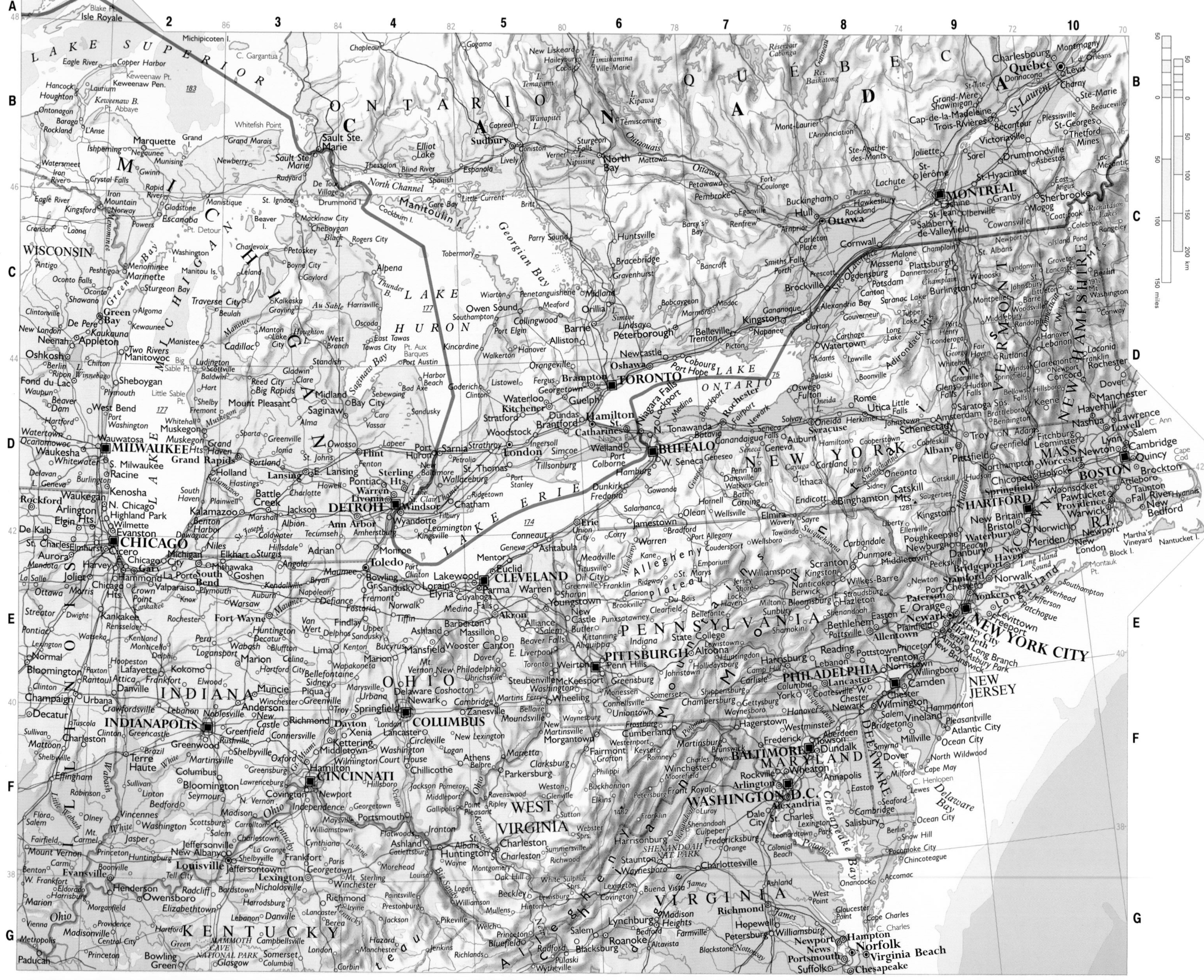

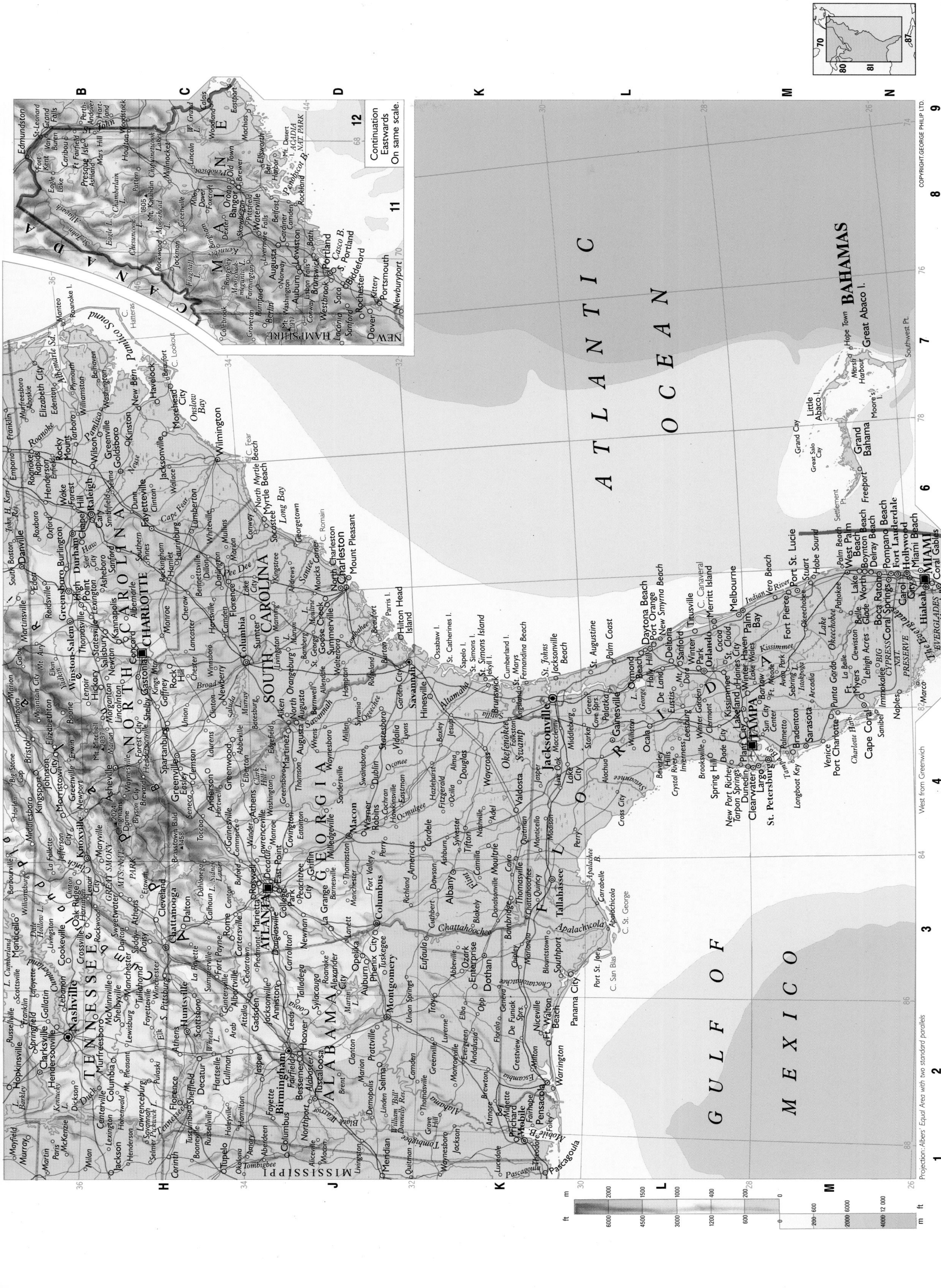
ATLANTIC
OCEAN
GULF OF
MEXICO
BAHAMAS
TENNESSEE
NORTH CAROLINA
SOUTH CAROLINA
GEORGIA
ALABAMA
MISSISSIPPI
FLORIDA
CANADA
MAINE
NEW HAMPSHIRE
Nashville
Knoxville
Chattanooga
Atlanta
Birmingham
Montgomery
Charlotte
Raleigh
Columbia
Charleston
Savannah
Jacksonville
Tallahassee
Tampa
Orlando
Miami
Mobile
Pensacola
Great Abaco I.
Grand Bahama
Continuation Eastwards On same scale.
Projection: Albers' Equal Area with two standard parallels
West from Greenwich
COPYRIGHT GEORGE PHILIP LTD.

NORTH-EASTERN UNITED STATES 1:2 500 000

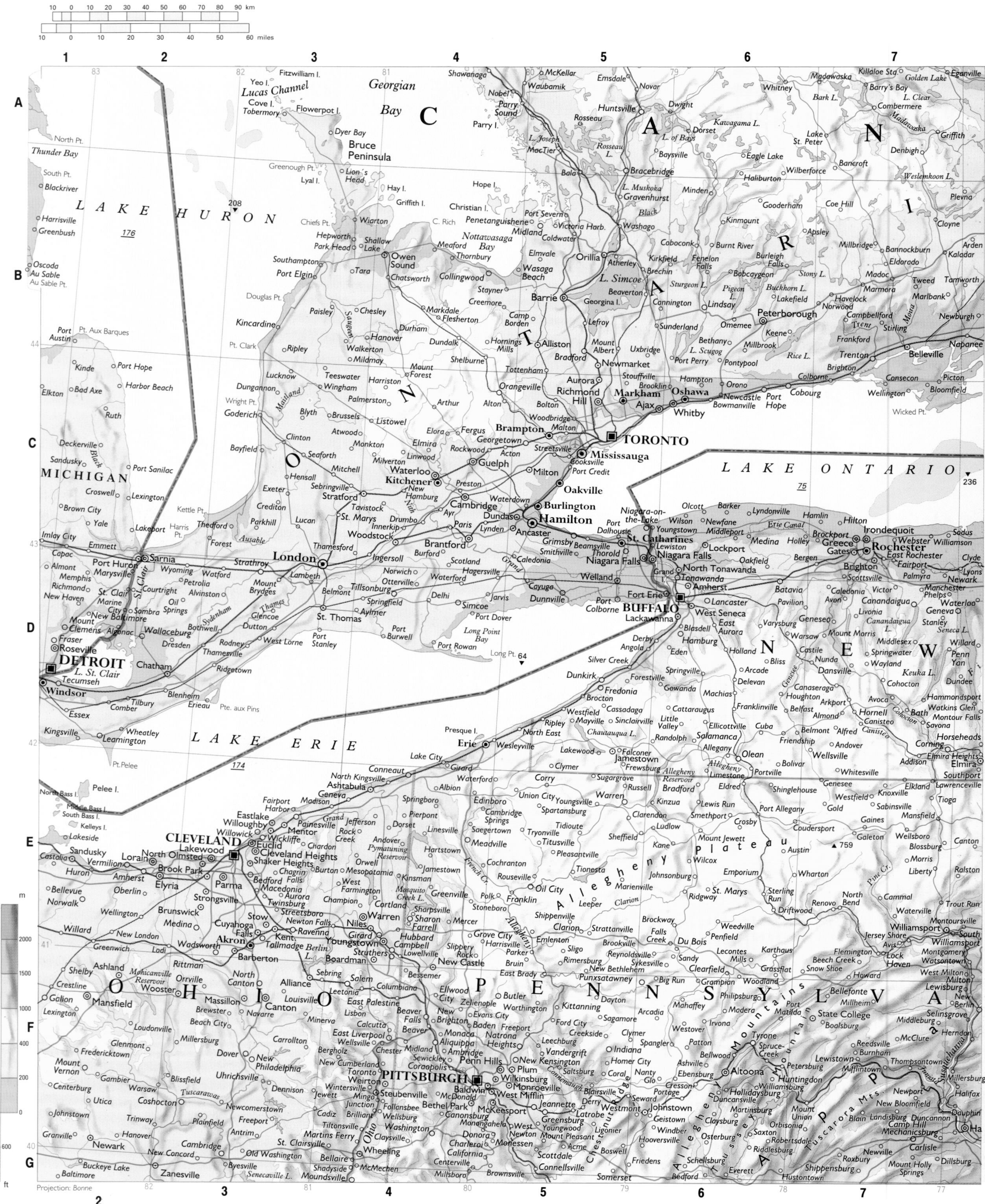

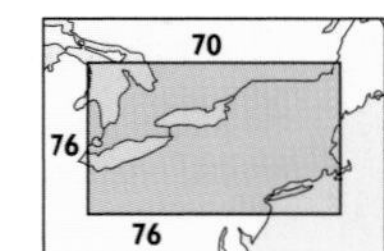

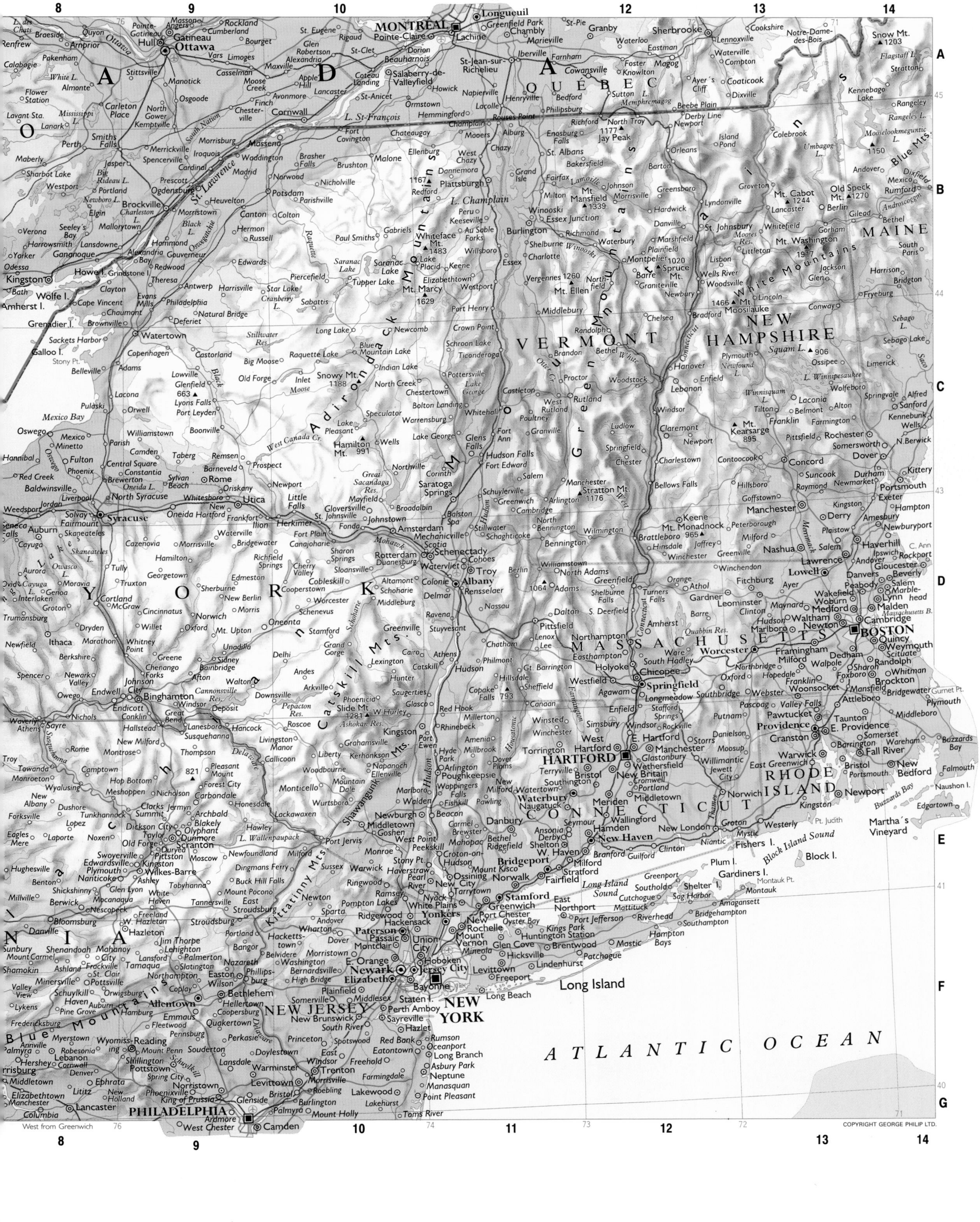

8 9 10 11 12 13 14

A

L. des Chats, Braeside, Quyon, Arnprior, Renfrew, Pointe-Gatineau, Masson, Angers, Rockland, Cumberland, Gatineau, Hull, Ottawa, Bourget, Ottawa, St. Eugène, Rigaud, MONTREAL, Pointe-Claire, Longueuil, Lachine, Greenfield Park, Chambly, St-Pie, Granby, Sherbrooke, Lennoxville, Cookshire, Notre-Dame-des-Bois, Snow Mt. 1203, Calabogie, Pakenham, Vars, Limoges, Glen Robertson, Alexandria, St-Clet, Dorion, Beauharnois, Marieville, Iberville, Farnham, Waterloo, Eastman, Waterville, Compton, Flagstaff L., Stratton, White L., Almonte, Stittsville, Manotick, Casselman, Maxville, Coteau Landing, Salaberry-de-Valleyfield, St-Jean-sur-Richelieu, Cowansville, Foster, Magog, Knowlton, Ayer's Cliff, Coaticook, Dixville, Kennebago Lake, Rangeley, Flower Station, Carleton Place, Osgoode, Moose Creek, Apple Hill, Lancaster, St-Anicet, Howick, Napierville, Henryville, Bedford, Sutton, L. Memphremagog, Beebe Plain, Rangeley L., Lavant Sta., Mississippi L., North Gower, Kemptville, Chesterville, Finch, Avonmore, Cornwall, L. St-François, Ormstown, Hemmingford, Lacolle, Philipsburg, Derby Line, Newport, Lanark, Smiths Falls, Perth, Massena, Fort Covington, Chateaugay, Champlain, Rouses Point, Mooers, Alburg, Richford, North Troy, Jay Peak 1177, Enosburg Falls, Island Pond, Colebrook, Mooselookmeguntic L., Umbagog L., 1150, Blue Mts.

A D A · Q U É B E C · O

B

Maberly, Sharbot Lake, Westport, Merrickville, Spencerville, Iroquois, Morrisburg, South Nation, Waddington, Cardinal, Jasper, Big Rideau L., Portland, Newboro L., Prescott, Ogdensburg, Madrid, Brasher Falls, Brushton, Malone, Ellenburg, West Chazy, Chazy, St. Albans, Bakersfield, Orleans, Barton, Andover, Dixfield, Norwood, Nicholville, Dannemora, Plattsburgh, Grand Isle, Fairfax, Lamoille, Johnson, Greensboro, Groveton, Mt. Cabot 1244, Old Speck Mt. 1270, Mexico, Rumford, Brockville, Elgin, Charleston L., Morristown, Heuvelton, Potsdam, Parishville, 1167, Redford, L. Champlain, Milton, Mt. Mansfield 1339, Morrisville, Lyndonville, Lancaster, Berlin, Androscoggin, Verona, Seeley's Bay, Mallorytown, Black L., Canton, Colton, Raquette, Peru, Keeseville, Au Sable Forks, Winooski, Essex Junction, Burlington, Hardwick, Danville, St. Johnsbury, Whitefield, Gorham, Gilead, Bethel, MAINE, Harrowsmith, Lansdowne, Ganonoque, Hammond, Gouverneur, Oswegatchie, Hermon, Russell, Paul Smiths, Gabriels, Whiteface Mt. 1483, Shelburne, Richmond, Waterbury, Marshfield, Plainfield, Moores Res., Littleton, Mt. Washington 1917, South Paris, Yorker, Odessa, Kingston, Howe I., Grindstone I., Alexandria Bay, Redwood, Edwards, Saranac Lake, Lake Placid, Keene, Willsboro, Charlotte, Winooski, Montpelier, Spruce Mt. 1020, Barre, Lisbon, Wells River, Woodsville, White Mountains, Jackson, Glen, Harrison, Bridgton, Bath, Wolfe I., Theresa, Clayton, Antwerp, Harrisville, Piercefield, Tupper Lake, Elizabethtown, Westport, Essex, Vergennes 1260, Mt. Ellen, Northfield, Graniteville, Newbury, 1466 Mt. Moosilauke, Lincoln, Fryeburg, Amherst I., Cape Vincent, Evans Mills, Philadelphia, Star Lake, Cranberry L., Sabattis, Mt. Marcy 1629, Port Henry, Middlebury, Conway, Sebago L., Chaumont, Natural Bridge, Brownville, Deferiet, Grenadier I.

C

Sackets Harbor, Galloo I., Stony Pt., Watertown, Stillwater Res., Long Lake, Newcomb, Crown Point, Chelsea, Bradford, Randolph, NEW HAMPSHIRE, Sebago Lake, Copenhagen, Castorland, Big Moose, Raquette Lake, Blue Mountain Lake, Schroon Lake, Ticonderoga, V E R M O N T, Bethel, Squam L., 906, Plymouth, Newfound L., Limerick, Saco, Belleville, Adams, Lowville, Glenfield, Black, Old Forge, Inlet, Moose, Snowy Mt. 1188, Indian Lake, North Creek, Pottersville, Lake George, Brandon, Otter Cr., White, Hanover, Enfield, Ossipee, L. Winnipesaukee, Wolfeboro, Alfred, Sanford, Lyons Falls 663, Port Leyden, Chestertown, Bolton Landing, Castleton, Proctor, Rutland, Woodstock, Lebanon, Winnisquam L., Laconia, Belmont, Alton, Springvale, Kennebunk, Wells, Pulaski, Lacona, Orwell, Speculator, Warrensburg, Whitehall, West Rutland, Poultney, Windsor, Tilton, Franklin, Farmington, Mexico Bay, Oswego, Mexico, Minetto, Williamstown, Boonville, West Canada Cr., Lake Pleasant, Hamilton Mt. 991, Wells, Lake George, Glens Falls, Fort Ann, Granville, Ludlow, Claremont, Newport, Mt. Kearsarge 895, Pittsfield, Rochester, Somersworth, N. Berwick, Hannibal, Fulton, Phoenix, Parish, Camden, Taberg, Remsen, Prospect, Northville, Corinth, Hudson Falls, Fort Edward, Springfield, Chester, Charlestown, Contoocook, Concord, Dover, Kittery, Red Creek, Baldwinsville, Central Square, Constantia, Brewerton, Oneida L., Sylvan Beach, Barneveld, Rome, Great Sacandaga Res., Saratoga Springs, Salem, Manchester, Stratton Mt. 1176, Bellows Falls, Hillsboro, Suncook, Durham, Raymond, Newmarket, Portsmouth, Liverpool, North Syracuse, Oriskany, Whitesboro, Newport, Mayfield, Schuylerville, Greenwich, Arlington, West, Goffstown, Manchester, Exeter, Hampton

D

Weedsport, Jordan, Solvay, Fairmount, Syracuse, Oneida, Hartford, New Frankfort, Utica, Little Falls, Gloversville, Broadalbin, Ballston Spa, Cambridge, North Bennington, Keene, Mt. Monadnock 965, Peterborough, Kingston, Derry, Amesbury, Newburyport, Seneca Falls, Auburn, Skaneateles, Ilion, Herkimer, St. Johnsville, Johnstown, Amsterdam, Stillwater, Schaghticoke, Bennington, Wilmington, Brattleboro, Jaffrey, Milford, Plaistow, Haverhill, C. Ann, Cayuga, Skaneateles L., Cazenovia, Morrisville, Waterville, Bridgewater, Fort Plain, Canajoharie, Mohawk, Mechanicville, Scotia, Schenectady, Cohoes, Hinsdale, Winchester, Greenville, Nashua, Salem, Andover, Ipswich, Rockport, Owasco L., Aurora, Hamilton, Richfield Springs, Sharon Springs, Rotterdam, Duanesburg, Watervliet, Troy, Berlin, Williamstown, North Adams, Winchendon, Lawrence, Gloucester, Beverly, Tully, Georgetown, Edmeston, Cherry Valley, Sloansville, Cobleskill, Altamont, Colonie, Albany, Rensselaer, 1064, Adams, Greenfield, Orange, Athol, Fitchburg, Lowell, Danvers, Peabody, Salem, Marblehead, Ovid, Cayuga L., Genoa, Moravia, Truxton, Sherburne, New Berlin, Cooperstown, Schoharie, Delmar, Shelburne Falls, Turners Falls, Gardner, Leominster, Ayer, Wakefield, Woburn, Lynn, Interlaken, Groton, Cortland, McGraw, Cincinnatus, Norwich, Morris, Worcester, Schenevus, Middleburg, Ravena, Nassau, Dalton, S. Deerfield, Barre, Clinton, Maynard, Medford, Malden, Massachusetts B., Trumansburg, Dryden, Willet, Oxford, Mt. Upton, Oneonta, Stamford, Greenville, Stuyvesant, Pittsfield, Northampton, Amherst, Quabbin Res., Hudson, Marlboro, Waltham, Newton, Cambridge, BOSTON, Quincy, Weymouth, Newfield, Ithaca, Marathon, Whitney Point, Unadilla, Sidney, Delhi, Grand Gorge, Catskill Mts., Cairo, Athens, Chatham, Lenox, Lee, Easthampton, Worcester, Ware, Framingham, Milford, Dedham, Scituate, Berkshire, Greene, Chenango Forks, Bainbridge, Afton, Andes, Lexington, Catskill, Hudson, Philmont, Gt. Barrington, Holyoke, South Hadley, Northbridge, Hopedale, Walpole, Sharon, Randolph, Whitman, Spencer, Newark Valley, Johnson City, Owego, Endwell, Binghamton, Cannonsville Res., Walton, Downsville, Hunter, Arkville, Saugerties, Hillsdale, Sheffield, Westfield, Chicopee, Springfield, Oxford, Franklin, Foxboro, Brockton

E

Endicott, Conklin, Windsor, Deposit, Pepacton Res., Phoenicia, Slide Mt. 1281, W. Hurley, Glasco, Copake Falls, 793, Agawam, Longmeadow, Southbridge, Webster, Woonsocket, Mansfield, Bridgewater, Gurnet Pt., Plymouth, Nichols, Waverly, Athens, Sayre, Great Bend, Hallstead, Lanesboro, Hancock, Roscoe, Ashokan Res., Kingston, Red Hook, Rhinebeck, Millerton, Canaan, Enfield, Stafford Springs, Rockville, Putnam, Pascoag, Valley Falls, Attleboro, Taunton, Middleboro, Susquehanna, Rome, New Milford, Montrose, Thompson, Delaware, Livingston Manor, Callicoon, Grahamsville, Port Ewen, Amenia, Millbrook, Winsted, Winchester, Simsbury, Windsor, E. Hartford, Manchester, Storrs, Danielson, Pawtucket, Providence, E. Providence, Somerset, Buzzards Bay, Troy, Towanda, Monroeton, Camptown, 821, Pleasant Mount, Liberty, Kerhonkson, Napanoch, Ellenville, Hyde Park, Arlington, Poughkeepsie, Dover Plains, Torrington, West Hartford, HARTFORD, Glastonbury, Wethersfield, Moosup, Willimantic, Cranston, Warwick, East Greenwich, Barrington, Fall River, Wareham, New Bedford, Falmouth, Hop Bottom, Forest City, Carbondale, Woodbourne, Mountain Dale, Monticello, Wappingers Falls, Marlboro, Pawling, New Milford, Terryville, Bristol, Southington, New Britain, Cromwell, Portland, Jewett City, Bristol, Portsmouth, R H O D E I S L A N D, Newport, Buzzards Bay, Naushon I., Wyalusing, Meshoppen, Nicholson, Honesdale, Wurtsboro, Walden, Fishkill, Watertown, Waterbury, Naugatuck, Meriden, Middletown, Norwich, Kingston, Edgartown, New Albany, Dushore, Clarks Summit, Jermyn, Archbald, Lackawaxen, Newburgh, Beacon, Danbury, C O N N E C T I C U T, Wallingford, Thames, Groton, Westerly, Pt. Judith, Martha's Vineyard, Forksville, Lopez, Tunkhannock, Blakely, Olyphant, Dickson City, Hawley, Middletown, Goshen, Carmel, Brewster, Bethel, Ridgefield, Seymour, Ansonia, Derby, Hamden, New Haven, New London, Mystic, Eagles Mere, Laporte, Noxen, Taylor, Dunmore, Scranton, L. Wallenpaupack, Port Jervis, West Point, Peekskill, Mahopac, Shelton, Branford, Guilford, Clinton, Niantic, Fishers I., Block Island Sound, Block I.

F

Old Forge, Pittston, Duryea, Newfoundland, Milford, Monroe, Stony Pt., Croton-on-Hudson, W. Haven, Milford, Plum I., Gardiners I., Sweyersville, Edwardsville, Plymouth, Kingston, Wilkes-Barre, Moscow, Dingmans Ferry, Sussex, Warwick, Haverstraw, Ossining, Mount Kisco, Bridgeport, Stratford, Greenport, Southold, Shelter I., Montauk Pt., Hughesville, Nanticoke, Ashley, Tobyhanna, Buck Hill Falls, Ringwood, Pearl River, New City, Norwalk, Fairfield, Long Island Sound, Cutchogue, Mattituck, Sag Harbor, Montauk, Benton, Shickshinny, Glen Lyon, White Haven, Mount Pocono, Kittatinny Mts., Ramsey, Nyack, Tarrytown, Stamford, Greenwich, East Northport, Amagansett, Millville, Berwick, Mocanaqua, Nescopeck, Tannersville, East Stroudsburg, Newton, Sparta, Pompton Lakes, White Plains, Port Chester, Port Jefferson, Riverhead, Bridgehampton, Danville, Bloomsburg, Freeland, W. Hazleton, Stroudsburg, Andover, Ridgewood, Hackensack, Yonkers, New Rochelle, Oyster Bay, Kings Park, Southampton, Hazleton, Portland, Wharton, Paterson, Passaic, Mount Vernon, Huntington Station, Hampton Bays, N I A, Jim Thorpe, Lehighton, Bangor, Hackettstown, Dover, Montclair, Union City, Glen Cove, Brentwood, Mastic, Sunbury, Shenandoah, Mahanoy City, Palmerton, Belvidere, Morristown, E. Orange, Mineola, Hicksville, Patchogue, Mount Carmel, Lansford, Slatington, Nazareth, Washington, Hoboken, Lindenhurst, Shamokin, Ashland, Frackville, Tamaqua, Northampton, Phillipsburg, Easton, Bernardsville, Newark, Jersey City, Levittown, Freeport, Minersville, St. Clair, Pottsville, Wilson, High Bridge, Elizabeth, Bayonne, Long Beach, Long Island, Valley View, Schuylkill Haven, Orwigsburg, Coplay, Bethlehem, Plainfield, Middlesex, Staten I., Lykens, Auburn, Pine Grove, Blue Mountains, Allentown, Hellertown, Somerville, Perth Amboy, NEW YORK, Hamburg, Emmaus, Coopersburg, NEW JERSEY, Sayreville, Fredericksburg, Fleetwood, Quakertown, New Brunswick, South River, Hazlet, Myerstown, Pennsburg, Perkasie, Princeton, Red Bank, Rumson, Oceanport, Annville, Palmyra, Robesonia, Wyomissing, Reading, Mount Penn, Souderton, Doylestown, Spotswood, Eatontown, Long Branch

G

Hershey, Lebanon, Cornwall, Shillington, Schuylkill, Lansdale, Warminster, East Windsor, Freehold, Asbury Park, A T L A N T I C   O C E A N, Harrisburg, Denver, Pottstown, Spring City, Trenton, Morrisville, Farmingdale, Neptune, Middletown, Ephrata, Norristown, Levittown, Roebling, Manasquan, Elizabethtown, Lititz, New Holland, Phoenixville, King of Prussia, Bristol, Burlington, Lakewood, Point Pleasant, Manchester, Lancaster, Glenside, Palmyra, Lakehurst, Columbia, PHILADELPHIA, Ardmore, Mount Holly, Toms River, West Chester, Camden

45 44 43 42 41 40
76 75 74 73 72 71

West from Greenwich

8 9 10 11 12 13 14

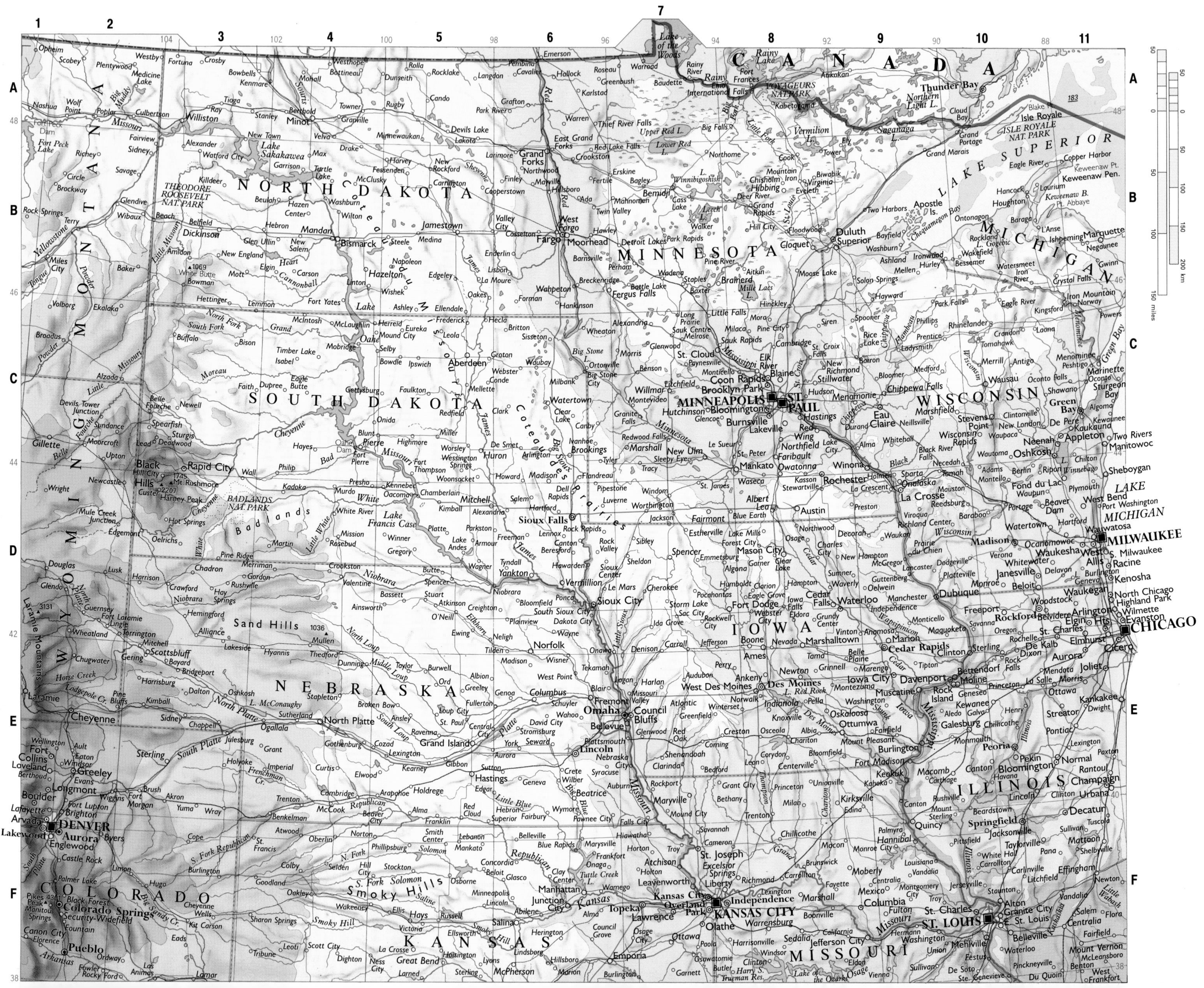
50 0 50 100 150 200 km
50 0 50 100 150 miles
C A N A D A
LAKE SUPERIOR
LAKE MICHIGAN
MICHIGAN
WISCONSIN
MINNESOTA
NORTH DAKOTA
SOUTH DAKOTA
IOWA
ILLINOIS
MISSOURI
NEBRASKA
KANSAS
WYOMING
MONTANA
COLORADO
MILWAUKEE
CHICAGO
MINNEAPOLIS
ST PAUL
Des Moines
KANSAS CITY
ST. LOUIS
DENVER
Lake of the Woods
Sand Hills
Smoky Hills
Laramie Mountains
Badlands
Coteau des Prairies
Mississippi
Missouri
THEODORE ROOSEVELT NAT. PARK
BADLANDS NAT. PARK
VOYAGEURS NAT. PARK
ISLE ROYALE NAT. PARK

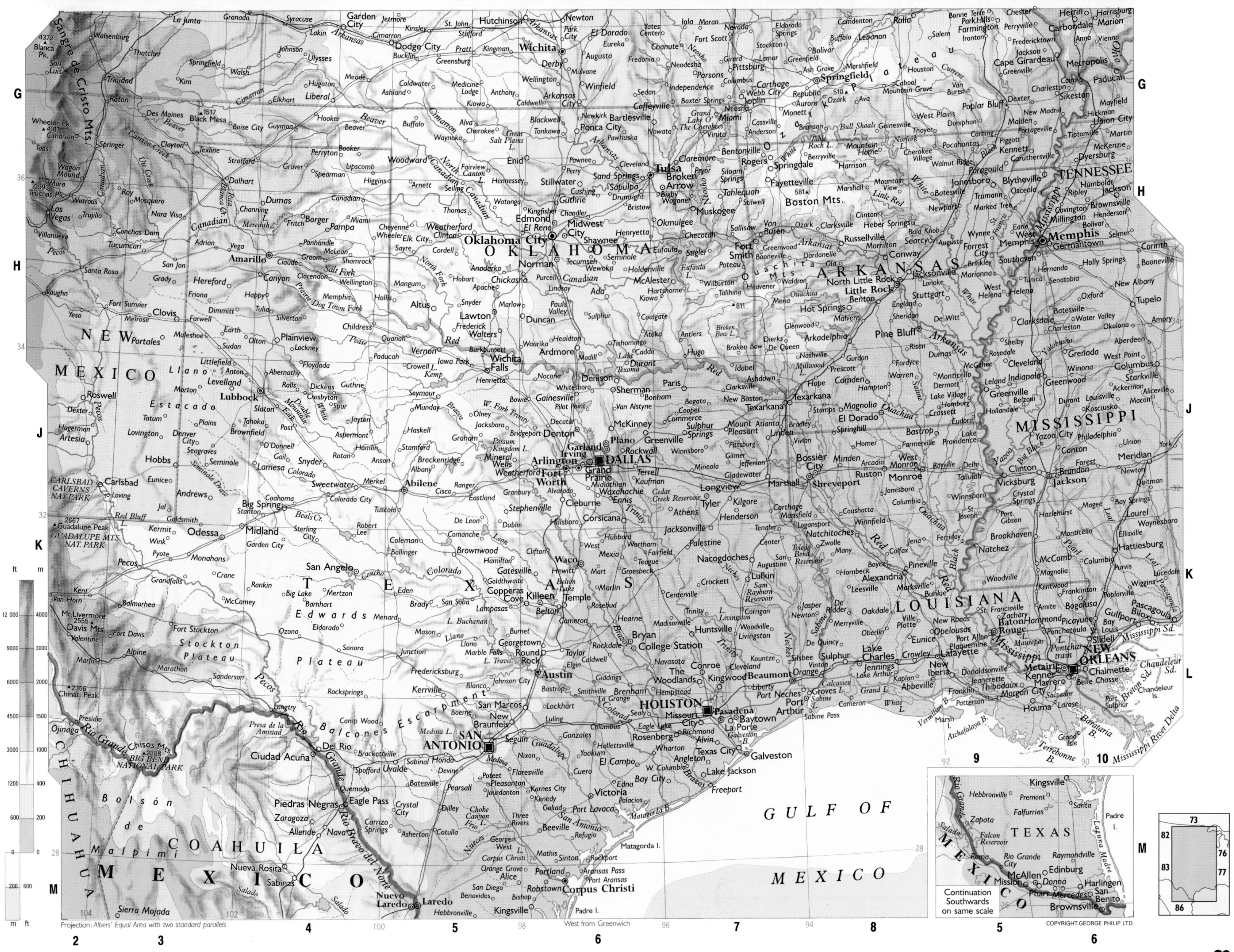

NEW MEXICO

OKLAHOMA

ARKANSAS

TENNESSEE

MISSISSIPPI

LOUISIANA

TEXAS

CHIHUAHUA

COAHUILA

MEXICO

GULF OF MEXICO

Sangre de Cristo Mts.

Llano Estacado

Edwards Plateau

Stockton Plateau

Balcones Escarpment

Ouachita Mts.

Ozark Plateau

Boston Mts.

Bolsón de Mapimí

Rio Grande

Rio Bravo del Norte

Pecos

Red

Arkansas

Canadian

Brazos

Colorado

Mississippi

Ohio

Mississippi River Delta

CARLSBAD CAVERNS NAT. PARK

GUADALUPE MTS. NAT. PARK

BIG BEND NATIONAL PARK

Dallas · Fort Worth · Houston · San Antonio · Austin · Oklahoma City · Tulsa · Wichita · Amarillo · Lubbock · Midland · Odessa · El Paso · Abilene · Waco · Corpus Christi · Laredo · Brownsville · Shreveport · Little Rock · Memphis · Jackson · Baton Rouge · New Orleans · Springfield · Fort Smith · Galveston · Beaumont · Lake Charles · Lafayette · Alexandria · Monroe · Texarkana · Pine Bluff · Hot Springs · Vicksburg · Natchez · Hattiesburg · Gulfport · Biloxi · Pascagoula · Tupelo · Columbus · Meridian · Roswell · Carlsbad · Hobbs · Clovis · Tucumcari · Raton · Trinidad · La Junta · Dodge City · Garden City · Liberal · Hutchinson · Joplin · Fayetteville · Nuevo Laredo · Piedras Negras · Ciudad Acuña · Del Rio · Eagle Pass

Inset: TEXAS · MEXICO · Kingsville · Harlingen · McAllen · Edinburg · Brownsville · Laguna Madre · Padre I. · Falcon Reservoir · Rio Grande City · Zapata · Hebbronville

Continuation Southwards on same scale

Key to adjoining maps: 73 · 76 · 77 · 82 · 83 · 86

Elevation scale:

m	ft
4000	12 000
3000	9000
2000	6000
1500	4500
1000	3000
400	1200
200	600
0	0
200	600

Grid letters: G H J K L M

Grid numbers: 2 3 4 5 6 7 8 9 10

Longitudes: 104 102 100 98 96 94 92 90 · West from Greenwich

Latitudes: 36 34 32 28

Projection: Albers' Equal Area with two standard parallels

50 0 50 100 150 200 km

50 0 50 100 150 miles

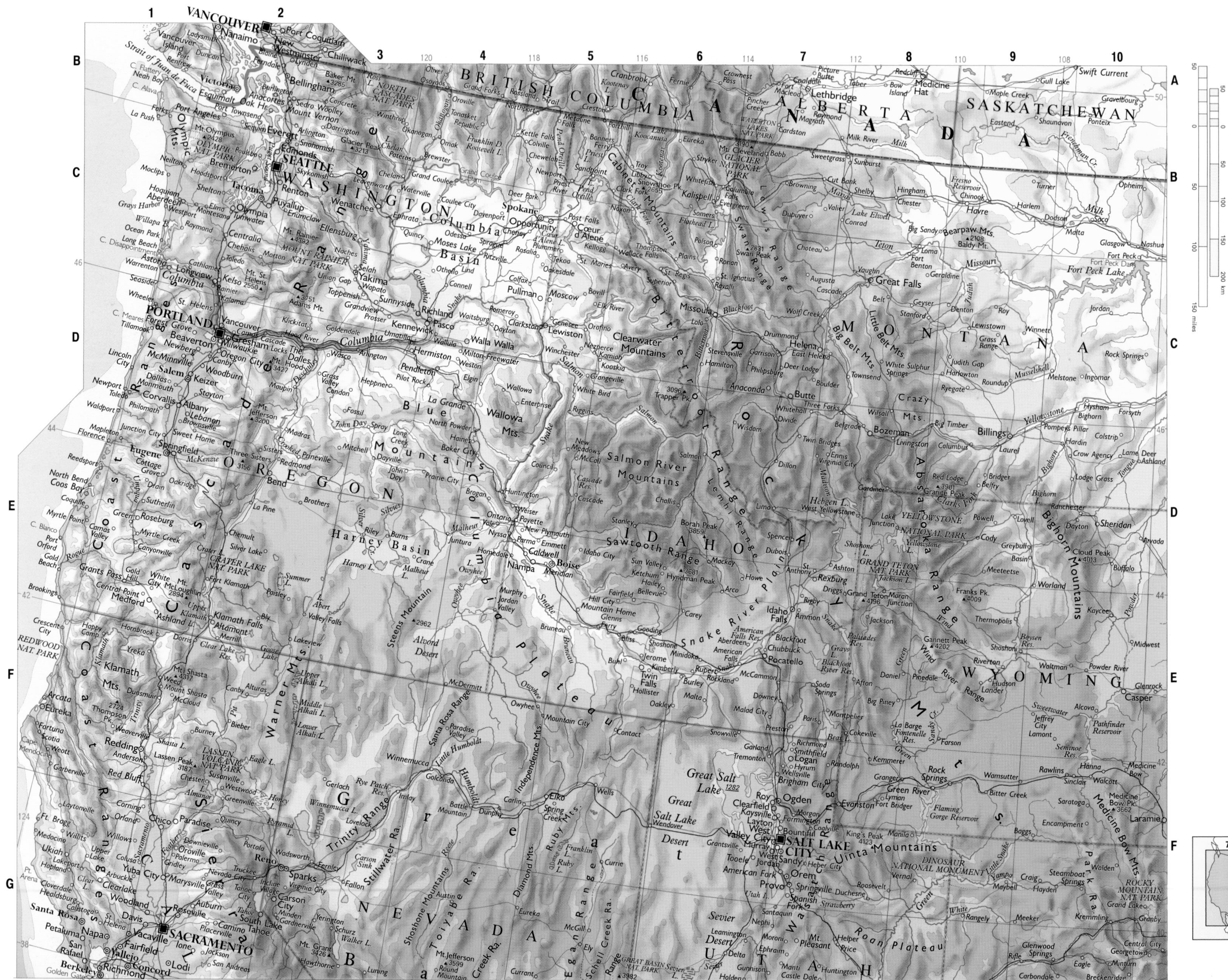

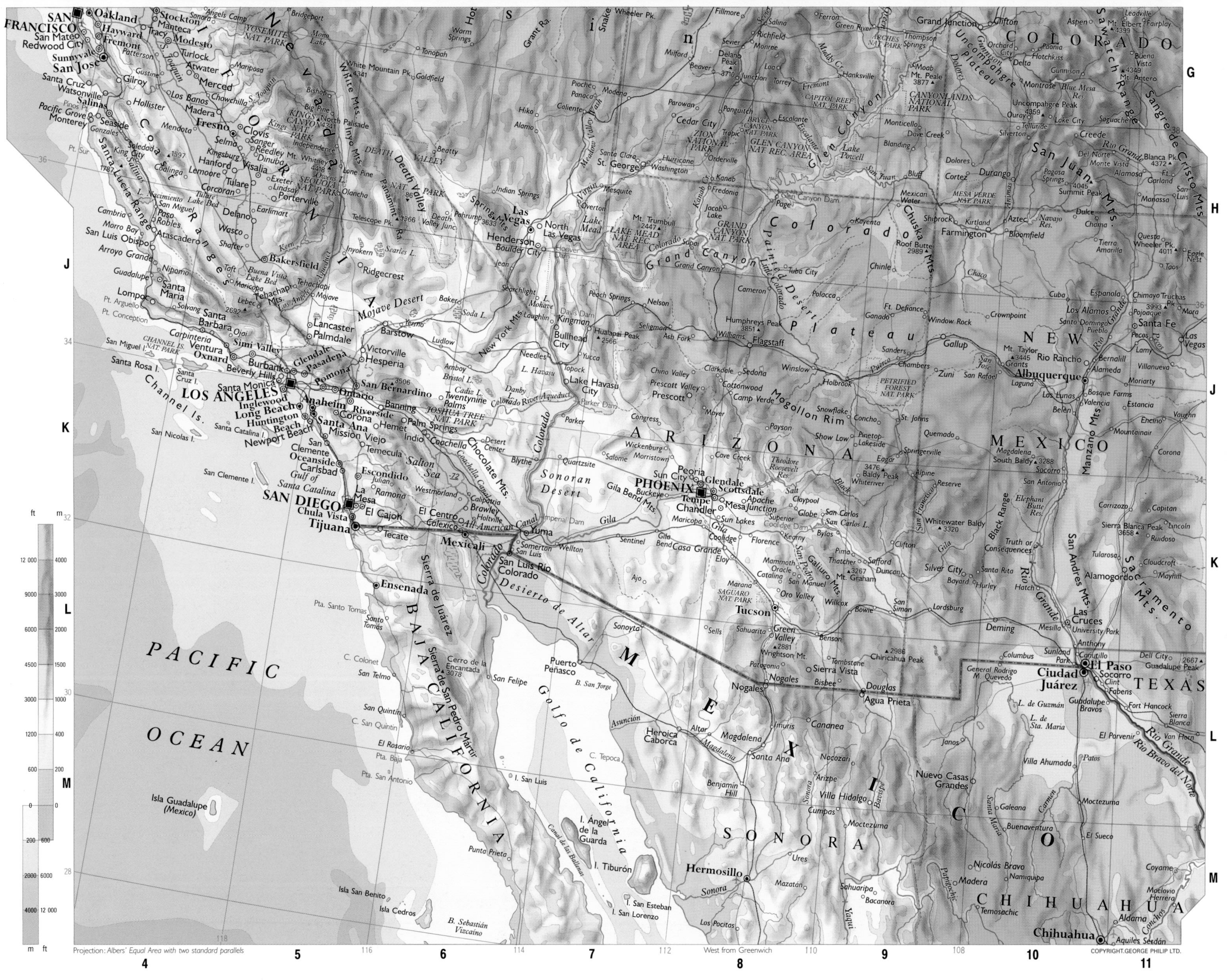

C O L O R A D O
N E V A D A
C A L I F O R N I A
U T A H
A R I Z O N A
N E W   M E X I C O
T E X A S
S O N O R A
C H I H U A H U A
B A J A   C A L I F O R N I A
M E X I C O
PACIFIC
OCEAN
Golfo de California
Colorado Plateau
Painted Desert
Grand Canyon
Mojave Desert
Sonoran Desert
Desierto de Altar
Death Valley
Coast Ranges
Sawatch Range
Sangre de Cristo Mts.
San Juan Mts.
Uncompahgre Plateau
Sacramento Mts.
San Andres Mts.
Manzano Mts.
Mogollon Rim
Chuska Mts.
Chocolate Mts.
Santa Lucia Range
Sierra de Juárez
Sierra de San Pedro Mártir
Channel Is.
Rio Grande
SAN FRANCISCO
LOS ANGELES
SAN DIEGO
PHOENIX
Las Vegas
Tucson
Albuquerque
Santa Fe
El Paso
Ciudad Juárez
Chihuahua
Hermosillo
Tijuana
Mexicali
Ensenada
Isla Guadalupe (Mexico)
West from Greenwich
Projection: Albers' Equal Area with two standard parallels
COPYRIGHT.GEORGE PHILIP LTD.

CENTRAL AND SOUTHERN CALIFORNIA AND WESTERN WASHINGTON 1:2 500 000

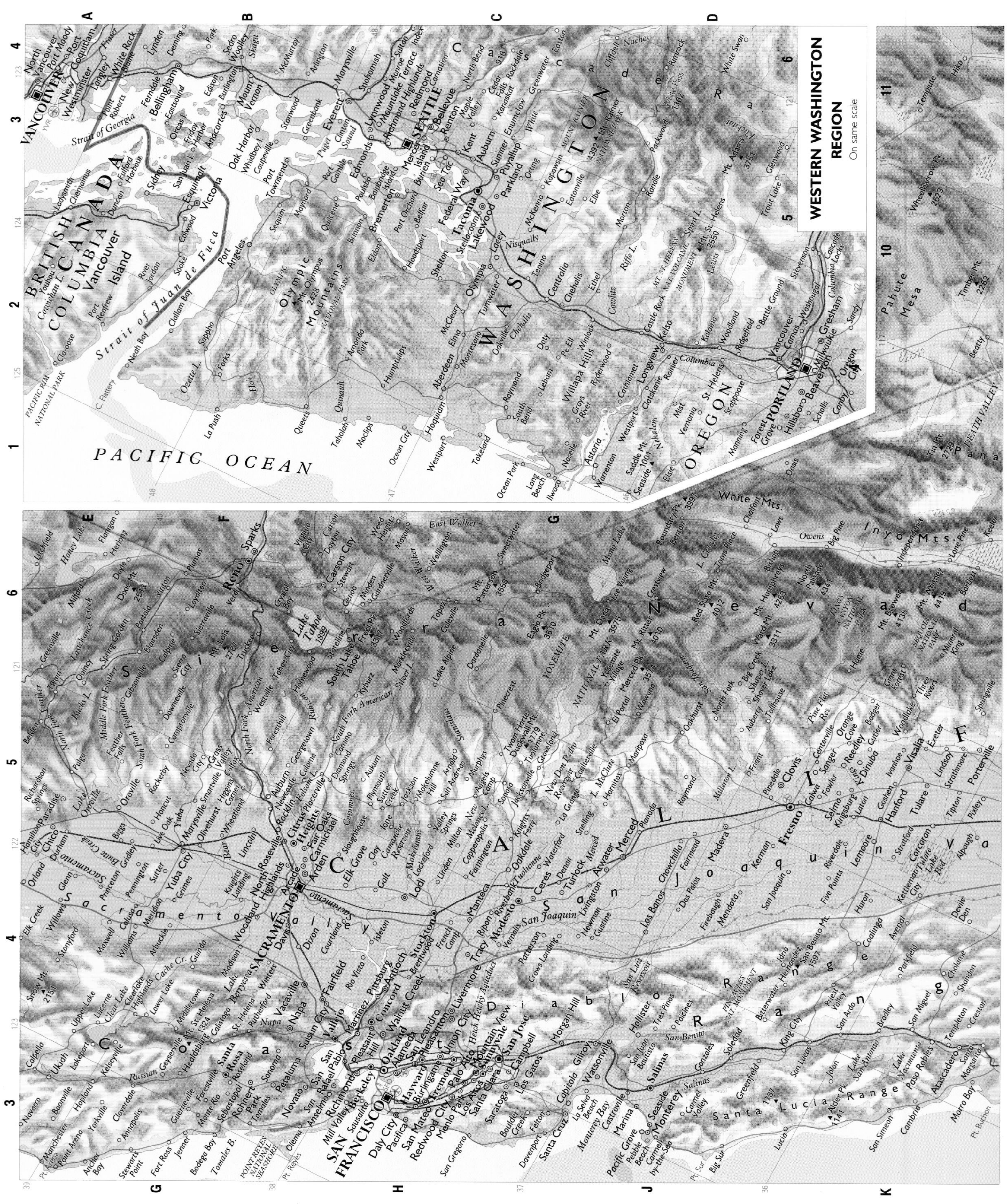

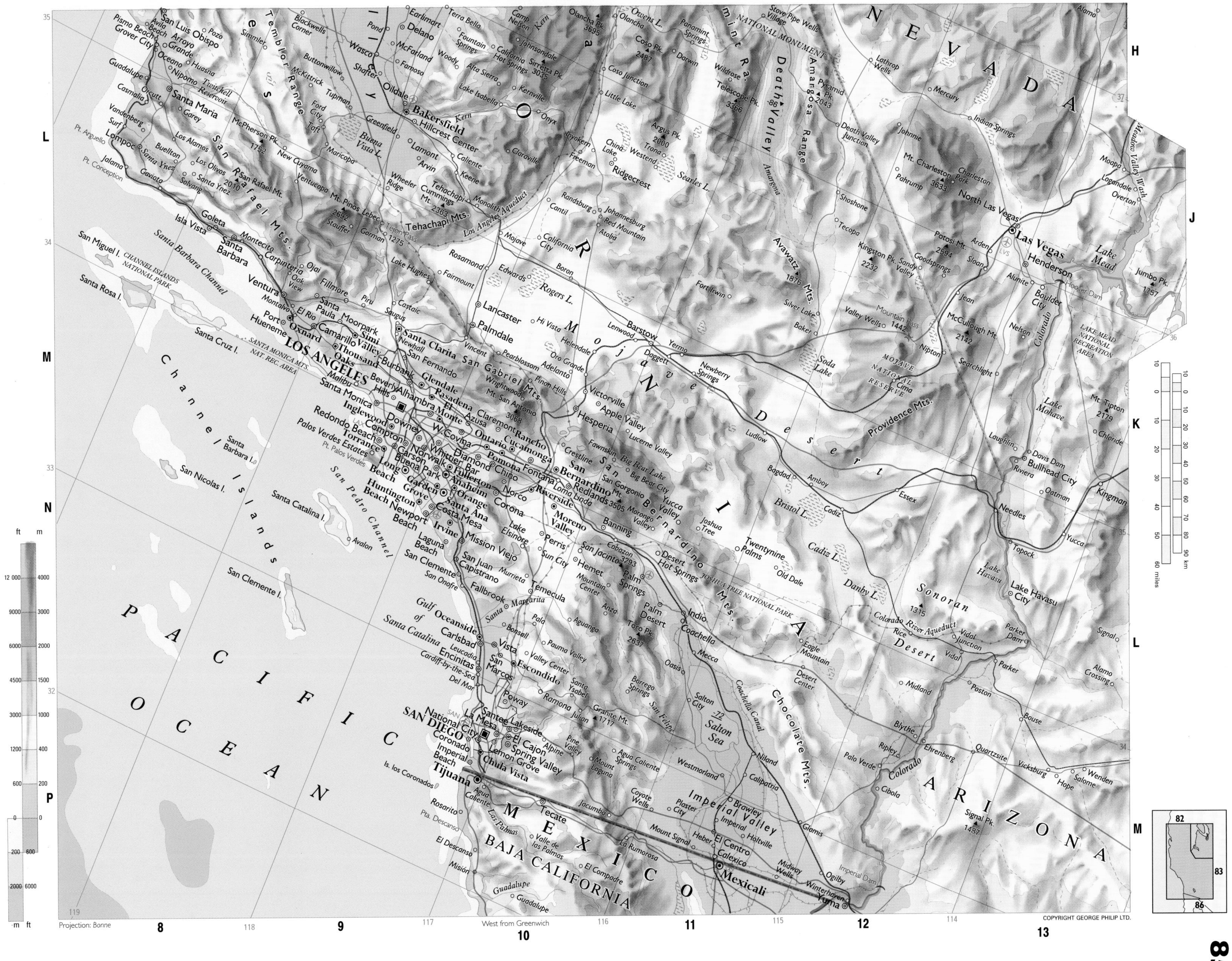

NEVADA
ARIZONA
MEXICO
BAJA CALIFORNIA
PACIFIC
OCEAN
Mojave Desert
Sonoran Desert
Death Valley
Amargosa Range
Chocolate Mts.
San Bernardino Mts.
San Gabriel Mts.
Tehachapi Mts.
San Rafael Mts.
Temblor Range
Providence Mts.
Channel Islands
Lake Mead
Lake Mojave
Salton Sea
Imperial Valley
Las Vegas
Henderson
North Las Vegas
Boulder City
Kingman
Bullhead City
Needles
Lake Havasu City
Parker
Blythe
Yuma
Mexicali
El Centro
Calexico
Indio
Palm Springs
Barstow
Victorville
Hesperia
Lancaster
Palmdale
Bakersfield
San Bernardino
Riverside
LOS ANGELES
Long Beach
Santa Ana
Anaheim
Oceanside
Escondido
SAN DIEGO
Chula Vista
Tijuana
Tecate
Santa Barbara
Ventura
Oxnard
Santa Maria
San Luis Obispo
Lompoc
Santa Catalina I.
San Clemente I.
San Nicolas I.
Santa Cruz I.
Santa Rosa I.
San Miguel I.
Santa Barbara Channel
San Pedro Channel
Gulf of Santa Catalina
Pt. Conception
COPYRIGHT GEORGE PHILIP LTD.
Projection: Bonne
West from Greenwich
km
miles

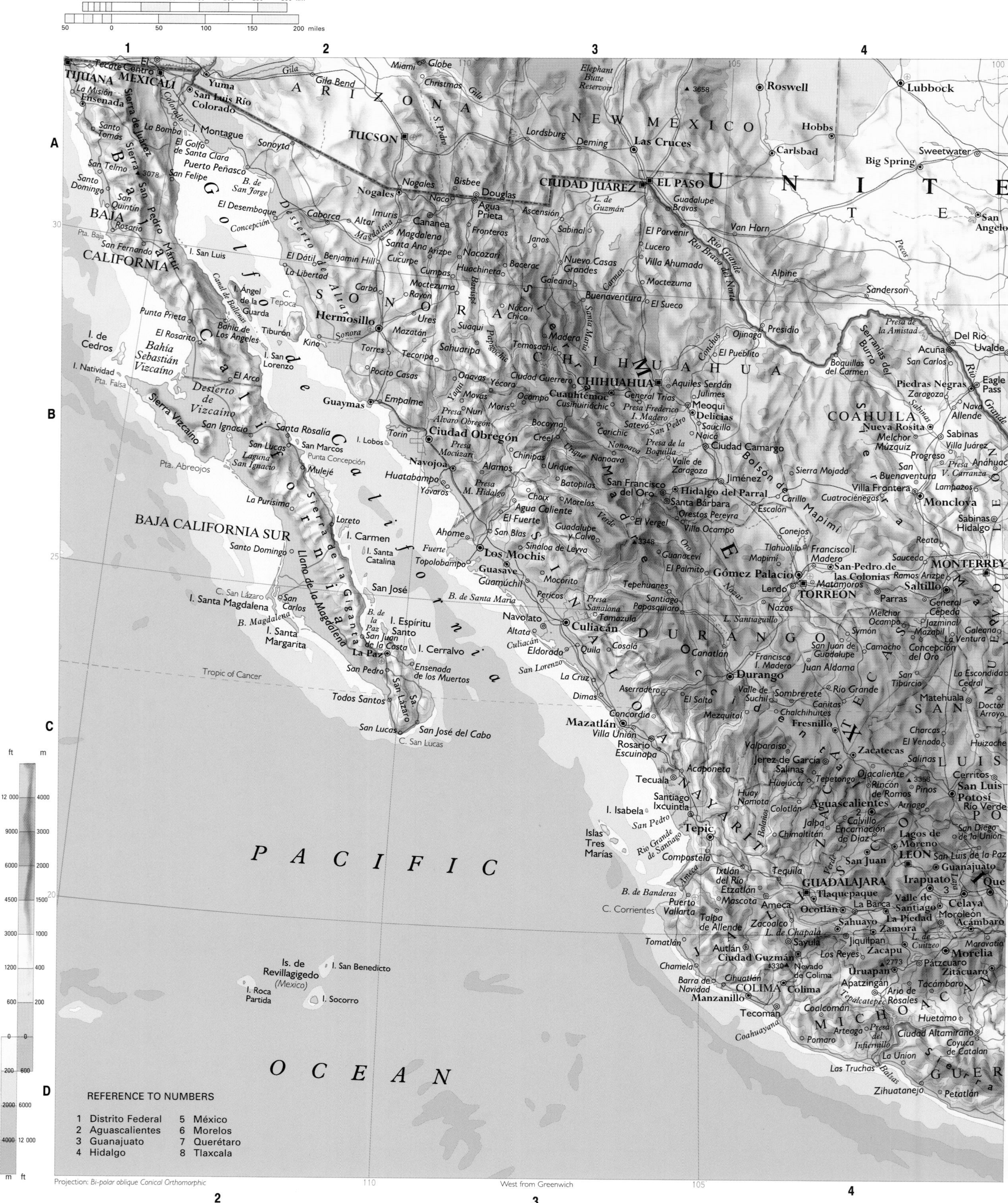
50 0 50 100 150 200 250 300 km
50 0 50 100 150 200 miles
1 2 3 4
A B C D
ft m
12 000 4000
9000 3000
6000 2000
4500 1500
3000 1000
1200 400
600 200
0 0
200 600
2000 6000
4000 12 000
m ft
REFERENCE TO NUMBERS
1 Distrito Federal
2 Aguascalientes
3 Guanajuato
4 Hidalgo
5 México
6 Morelos
7 Querétaro
8 Tlaxcala
Projection: Bi-polar oblique Conical Orthomorphic
West from Greenwich
110
105
100
30
25
20
Tropic of Cancer
PACIFIC OCEAN
Golfo de California
A R I Z O N A
N E W M E X I C O
U N I T E
T E
TIJUANA
MEXICALI
Tecate
El Centro
Yuma
San Luis Río Colorado
Ensenada
La Misión
Santo Tomás
Sierra de Juárez
La Bomba
I. Montague
Sonoyta
El Golfo de Santa Clara
Puerto Peñasco
San Felipe
B. de San Jorge
San Telmo
Santo Domingo
San Quintín
BAJA CALIFORNIA
Sierra San Pedro Mártir
3078
Rosario
Pta. Baja
San Fernando
I. San Luis
El Desemboque
Concepción
Desierto de Altar
Caborca
Altar
Canal de Ballenas
Ángel de la Guarda
Punta Prieta
El Rosarito
Bahía de Los Ángeles
I. Tiburón
C. Tepoca
Bahía Sebastián Vizcaíno
I. de Cedros
I. Natividad
Pta. Falsa
El Arco
Desierto de Vizcaíno
Sierra Vizcaíno
San Ignacio
Laguna San Ignacio
Pta. Abreojos
Santa Rosalía
San Marcos
Punta Concepción
Mulejé
San Lucas
La Purísima
Loreto
I. Carmen
BAJA CALIFORNIA SUR
Santo Domingo
Llano de la Magdalena
Sierra de la Giganta
I. Santa Catalina
San José
C. San Lázaro
San Carlos
I. Santa Magdalena
B. Magdalena
I. Santa Margarita
B. de la Paz
I. Espíritu Santo
San Juan de la Costa
La Paz
I. Cerralvo
San Pedro
Ensenada de los Muertos
Todos Santos
Sa. San Lázaro
San Lucas
San José del Cabo
C. San Lucas
Is. de Revillagigedo (Mexico)
I. San Benedicto
I. Roca Partida
I. Socorro
TUCSON
Miami
Globe
Gila
Gila Bend
Christmas
S. Pedro
Nogales
Bisbee
Naco
Douglas
Agua Prieta
Imuris
Magdalena
Cananea
Santa Ana
Arizpe
Fronteras
Nacozari
El Dátil
Benjamin Hill
Cucurpe
La Libertad
Cumpas
Huachinera
Carbó
Moctezuma
Rayón
Ures
Bavispe
S O N O R A
Hermosillo
Kino
Sonora
Mazatán
Torres
Tecoripa
Suaqui
Sahuaripa
Pocito Casas
Guaymas
Empalme
Onavas
Yécora
Movas
Nuri
Presa Alvaro Obregón
Torin
I. Lobos
Ciudad Obregón
Presa Mocúzari
Navojoa
Huatabampo
Yavaros
Alamos
Presa M. Hidalgo
Ahome
Fuerte
Topolobampo
Los Mochis
El Fuerte
San Blas
Sinaloa de Leyva
Guasave
Guamúchil
Mocorito
B. de Santa María
Pericos
Navolato
Culiacán
Altata
Eldorado
Quila
Cosalá
San Lorenzo
La Cruz
Dimas
Mazatlán
Villa Unión
Concordia
Rosario
Escuinapa
Tecuala
Acaponeta
Santiago Ixcuintla
I. Isabela
San Pedro
Islas Tres Marías
Río Grande de Santiago
Tepic
Compostela
B. de Banderas
Puerto Vallarta
C. Corrientes
Tomatlán
Chamela
Barra de Navidad
Manzanillo
Tecomán
COLIMA
Colima
Coahuayana
Elephant Butte Reservoir
3658
Roswell
Lubbock
Lordsburg
Deming
Las Cruces
Hobbs
Carlsbad
Sweetwater
Big Spring
CIUDAD JUÁREZ
EL PASO
L. de Guzmán
Guadalupe Bravos
Ascensión
Janos
Sabinal
El Porvenir
Van Horn
San Angelo
Pecos
Lucero
Villa Ahumada
Río Bravo del Norte
Río Grande
Nuevo Casas Grandes
Bacerac
Galeana
Moctezuma
Buenaventura
El Sueco
Alpine
Sanderson
Nácori Chico
Temósachic
Madera
Santa María
Papigochic
Presidio
Ojinaga
Conchos
El Pueblito
Presa de la Amistad
Del Rio
Uvalde
Acuña
San Carlos
Boquillas del Carmen
Serranías del Burro
C H I H U A H U A
CHIHUAHUA
Aquiles Serdán
Julimes
Ciudad Guerrero
Cuauhtémoc
Cusihuiriáchic
General Trías
Presa Frederico I. Madero
Meoqui
Delicias
Satevó
San Pedro
Saucillo
Naica
Ocampo
Moris
Bocoyna
Creel
Carichic
Nonoava
Presa de la Boquilla
Ciudad Camargo
Valle de Zaragoza
Chínipas
Urique
Uruachic
Batopilas
Choix
Agua Caliente
Morelos
Guadalupe y Calvo
Sierra Madre Occidental
San Francisco del Oro
Hidalgo del Parral
Santa Bárbara
Orestes Pereyra
El Vergel
Villa Ocampo
3348
Guanaceví
El Palmito
Jiménez
Bolsón de Mapimí
Sierra Mojada
Carillo
Escalón
Conejos
Tlahualilo
Mapimí
Francisco I. Madero
Gómez Palacio
Lerdo
TORREÓN
Matamoros
San Pedro de las Colonias
Tepehuanes
Santiago Papasquiaro
Presa Sanalona
Tamazula
Nazas
L. Santiaguillo
D U R A N G O
Canatlán
Francisco I. Madero
Durango
Juan Aldama
Valle de Suchil
Sombrerete
Río Grande
Cañitas
Chalchihuites
El Salto
Mezquital
Fresnillo
Aserradero
Z A C A T E C A S
Zacatecas
Valparaíso
Jerez de García Salinas
Huejúcar
Tepetongo
Ojocaliente
Rincón de Romos
Aguascalientes
Calvillo
Encarnación de Díaz
Huay Namota
Colotlán
Jalpa
Chimaltitán
Bolaños
N A Y A R I T
Tequila
Ixtlán del Río
Etzatlán
Ameca
Mascota
GUADALAJARA
Tlaquepaque
Ocotlán
Talpa de Allende
Zacoalco
L. de Chapala
Sayula
Autlán
Ciudad Guzmán
4330
Nevado de Colima
Cihuatlán
J A L I S C O
Verde
COAHUILA
Piedras Negras
Eagle Pass
Zaragoza
Sabinas
Nava
Allende
Nueva Rosita
Melchor Múzquiz
Sabinas
Villa Juárez
Progreso
Presa V. Carranza
Anáhuac
San Buenaventura
Villa Frontera
Cuatrociénegas
Lampazos
Monclova
Sabinas Hidalgo
Reata
Sauceda
MONTERREY
Ramos Arizpe
Saltillo
Parras
General Cepeda
Jazminal
Mazapil
Melchor Ocampo
Symón
Camacho
Galeana
La Ventura
San Juan de Guadalupe
Concepción del Oro
San Tiburcio
La Escondida
Cedral
Matehuala
Doctor Arroyo
Charcas
El Venado
Huizache
Salinas
S A N L U I S P O T O S Í
Cerritos
3356
Pinos
San Luis Potosí
Río Verde
Arriaga
Lagos de Moreno
San Diego de la Unión
San Luis de la Paz
LEÓN
San Juan
Guanajuato
Irapuato
Querétaro
Valle de Santiago
Celaya
La Barca
La Piedad
Moroleón
Sahuayo
Zamora
Acámbaro
Jiquilpan
Zacapu
L. de Cuitzeo
Maravatío
Los Reyes
2773
Pátzcuaro
Morelia
Uruapan
Zitácuaro
Apatzingán
Tacámbaro
Ario de Rosales
Tepalcatepec
Coalcomán
M I C H O A C Á N
Huetamo
Arteaga
Presa del Infiernillo
Ciudad Altamirano
Pomaro
Coyuca de Catalán
La Unión
Las Truchas
Balsas
Zihuatanejo
Petatlán
G U E R R E R O
Sierra Madre del Sur
Sierra Madre Oriental
NUEVO LEÓN

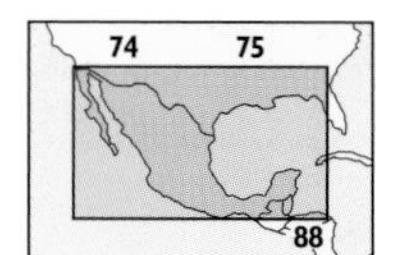

5 6 7 8

A B C D E

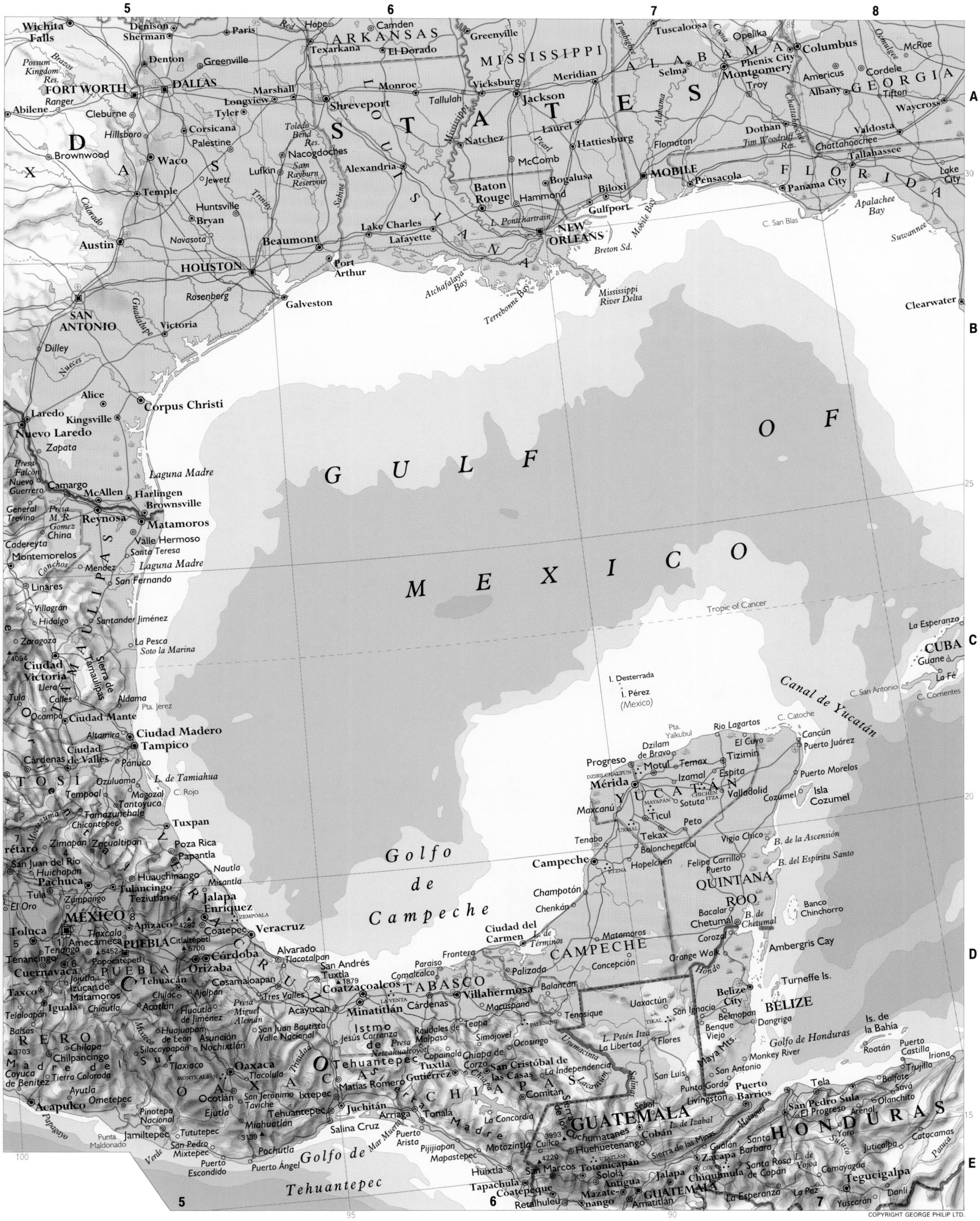

UNITED STATES
TEXAS
ARKANSAS
LOUISIANA
MISSISSIPPI
ALABAMA
GEORGIA
FLORIDA

Wichita Falls
Denison
Sherman
Paris
Hope
Camden
Texarkana
El Dorado
Greenville
Tuscaloosa
Opelika
Phenix City
Columbus
McRae
Denton
Greenville
Possum Kingdom Res.
FORT WORTH
DALLAS
Marshall
Monroe
Vicksburg
Meridian
Selma
Montgomery
Troy
Americus
Cordele
Albany
Tifton
Waycross
Abilene
Ranger
Cleburne
Longview
Tyler
Shreveport
Tallulah
Jackson
Laurel
Hattiesburg
Dothan
Jim Woodruff Res.
Valdosta
Chattahoochee
Tallahassee
Hillsboro
Corsicana
Palestine
Toledo Bend Res.
Nacogdoches
Natchez
McComb
Flomaton
Brownwood
Waco
Lufkin
Sam Rayburn Reservoir
Alexandria
Bogalusa
MOBILE
Pensacola
Panama City
Lake City
Jewett
Temple
Huntsville
Bryan
Baton Rouge
Hammond
Biloxi
Gulfport
Apalachee Bay
Navasota
Lake Charles
Lafayette
L. Pontchartrain
NEW ORLEANS
Mobile Bay
C. San Blas
Austin
Beaumont
Port Arthur
Breton Sd.
Suwannee
HOUSTON
Atchafalaya Bay
Terrebonne Bay
Mississippi River Delta
Rosenberg
Galveston
SAN ANTONIO
Victoria
Clearwater
Dilley
Alice
Corpus Christi
Laredo
Kingsville
Nuevo Laredo
Zapata
Presa Falcón
Laguna Madre
Nuevo Guerrero
Camargo
McAllen
Harlingen
Brownsville
General Treviño
Presa M. R. Gómez
Reynosa
Matamoros
China
Cadereyta
Valle Hermoso
Montemorelos
Santa Teresa
Laguna Madre
Linares
Mendez
San Fernando
Villagrán
Hidalgo
Santander Jiménez
Zaragoza
La Pesca
Soto la Marina
Ciudad Victoria
Sierra de Tamaulipas
TAMAULIPAS
Llera
Tula
Calles
Aldama
Pta. Jerez
Ocampo
Ciudad Mante
Altamira
Ciudad Madero
Tampico
Ciudad de Valles
Cárdenas
Pánuco
Ozuluama
L. de Tamiahua
Tempoal
Mapozal
Tantoyuca
C. Rojo
Tamazunchale
Chicontepec
Tuxpan
Zimapán
Zacualtipán
Poza Rica
Papantla
San Juan del Río
Huichapan
Nautla
Pachuca
Huauchinango
Misantla
Tulancingo
Tula
Zumpango
Teziutlán
El Oro
Jalapa Enríquez
MÉXICO
Apizaco
Toluca
Amecameca
Tlaxcala
PUEBLA
Citlaltépetl 5700
Coatepec
Veracruz
Tenango
Popocatépetl 5452
Córdoba
Orizaba
Alvarado
Tlacotalpan
Tenancingo
Cuernavaca
Tehuacán
Cosamaloapan
San Andrés Tuxtla 1879
Jojutla
Izúcar de Matamoros
Chilac
Ajalpan
Tres Valles
Coatzacoalcos
Minatitlán
Taxco
Iguala
Chiautla
Acatlán
Huautla de Jiménez
Presa Miguel Alemán
Acayucan
Teloloapan
Huajuapan de León
Asunción Nochixtlán
San Juan Bautista Valle Nacional
Istmo de Tehuantepec
Jesús Carranza
Balsas
Chilapa
Silacayoapan
Chilpancingo
Tlaxiaco
Oaxaca
Tlacolula
Tehuantepec
Matías Romero
Coyuca de Benítez
Tierra Colorada
Ayutla
Ometepec
Ocotlán
San Jerónimo Taviche
Ixtepec
Juchitán
Acapulco
Ejutla
Tehuantepec
Pinotepa Nacional
Miahuatlán
Salina Cruz
Punta Maldonado
Jamiltepec
Tututepec
San Pedro Mixtepec
Pochutla
Puerto Escondido
Puerto Ángel
Golfo de Tehuantepec
GUERRERO
OAXACA
VERACRUZ
Madre del Sur
MONTE ALBÁN
ZEMPOALA
Papagayo
Verde
Mixteca
Trinidad

GULF OF MEXICO
Tropic of Cancer
Golfo de Campeche

I. Desterrada
I. Pérez (Mexico)
Canal de Yucatán
C. San Antonio
La Esperanza
CUBA
Guane
La Fe
C. Corrientes
C. Catoche
Pta. Yalkubul
Río Lagartos
El Cuyo
Cancún
Puerto Juárez
Dzilam de Bravo
Progreso
Motul
Temax
Tizimín
DZIBILCHALTÚN
Izamal
Espita
Puerto Morelos
Mérida
YUCATÁN
CHICHÉN ITZÁ
Valladolid
Cozumel
Isla Cozumel
Maxcanú
MAYAPÁN
Sotuta
Ticul
UXMAL
Tekax
Peto
Tenabo
Vigía Chico
B. de la Ascensión
Bolonchenticul
Campeche
Hopelchén
Felipe Carrillo Puerto
B. del Espíritu Santo
EDZNÁ
QUINTANA ROO
Champotón
Chenkán
Bacalar
Chetumal
B. de Chetumal
Banco Chinchorro
Ciudad del Carmen
L. de Términos
Matamoros
CAMPECHE
Corozal
Ambergris Cay
Frontera
Paraíso
Comalcalco
TABASCO
Villahermosa
Palizada
Concepción
Orange Walk
Hondo
Turneffe Is.
LA VENTA
Cárdenas
Macuspana
Balancán
Tenosique
Uaxactún
San Ignacio
Belize City
Belmopan
BELIZE
Teapa
Raudales de Malpaso
Presa Netzahualcóyotl
Simojovel
PALENQUE
TIKAL
Benque Viejo
Dangriga
Golfo de Honduras
Is. de la Bahía
Ocosingo
Usumacinta
L. Petén Itzá
La Libertad
Flores
Maya Mts.
Roatán
Puerto Castilla
Iriona
Copainalá
Chiapa de Corzo
San Cristóbal de las Casas
La Independencia
Monkey River
Trujillo
Tuxtla Gutiérrez
CHIAPAS
Lacantún
Salinas
San Luis
San Antonio
Punta Gorda
Puerto Barrios
Tela
Balfate
Savá
Olanchito
Comitán
Sierra de los Cuchumatanes
Sebol
Livingston
San Pedro Sula
El Progreso
Arenal
Arriaga
Tonalá
Sierra Madre
La Concordia
GUATEMALA
L. de Izabal
Motagua
HONDURAS
Cobán
Yoro
Puerto Arista
Mar Muerto
Pijijiapan
Mapastepec
Motozintla
Cuilco 3993
Huehuetenango
Sierra de las Minas
Gualán
Zacapa
Santa Bárbara
Juticalpa
Catacamas
Santa Rosa de Copán
L. de Yojoa
Comayagua
Patuca
Sulaco
UTATLÁN
COPÁN
Huixtla
4220
San Marcos
Totonicapán
Sololá
Jalapa
Chiquimula
Tapachula
Coatepeque
Antigua
Mazatenango
GUATEMALA
Amatitlán
Retalhuleu
La Esperanza
La Paz
Tegucigalpa
Yuscarán
Danlí

4054
3703
3139
4282

100
95
90
85
30
25
20
15

1:8 000 000

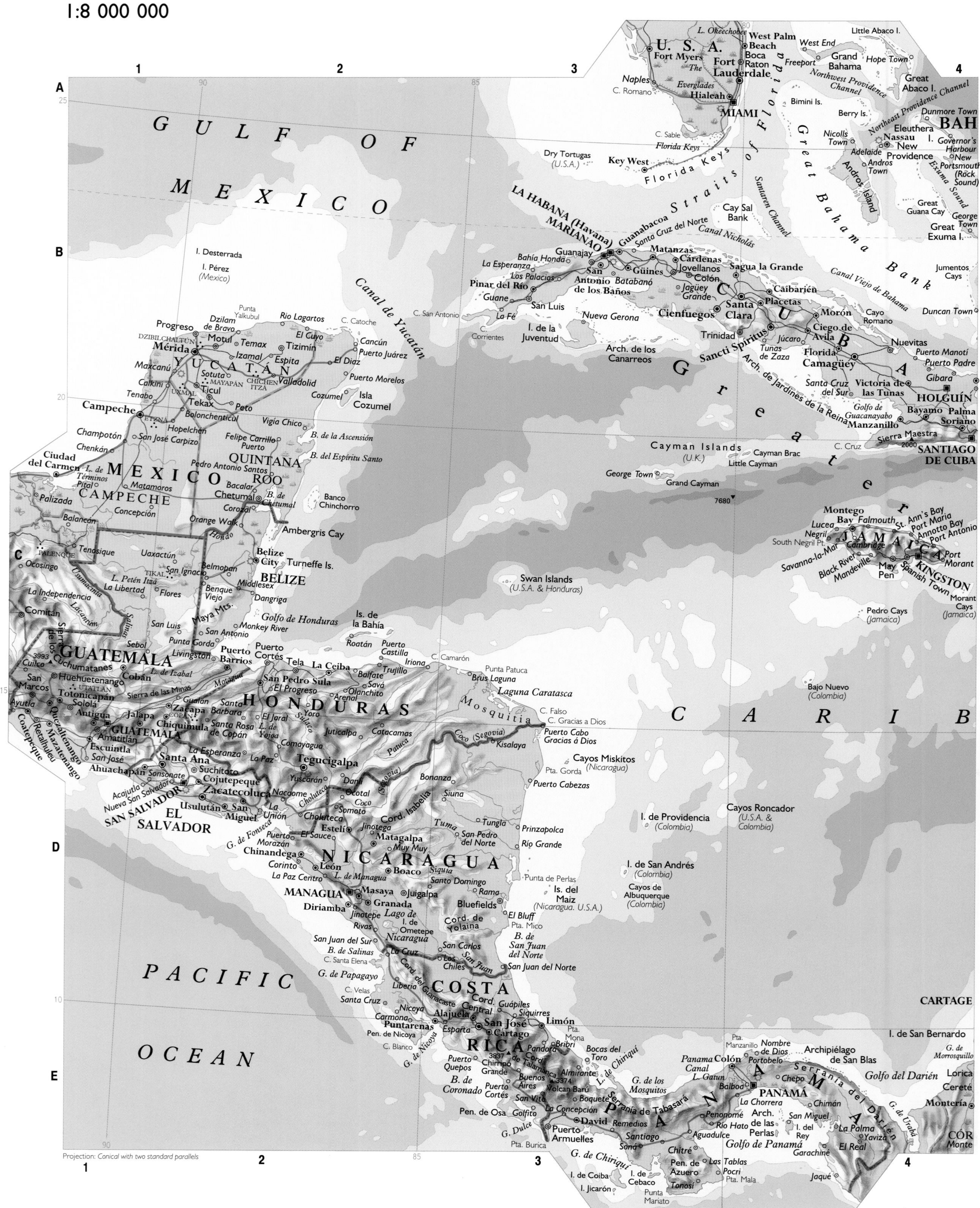
GULF OF MEXICO
Caribbean Sea
PACIFIC OCEAN
U. S. A.
MEXICO
YUCATÁN
CAMPECHE
QUINTANA ROO
BELIZE
GUATEMALA
HONDURAS
EL SALVADOR
NICARAGUA
COSTA RICA
PANAMÁ
CUBA
JAMAICA
Greater Antilles
Great Bahama Bank
Straits of Florida
Florida Keys
Canal de Yucatán
Golfo de Honduras
Mosquitia
Cayman Islands (U.K.)
Swan Islands (U.S.A. & Honduras)
Miami
Hialeah
Fort Lauderdale
West Palm Beach
Boca Raton
Fort Myers
Naples
Key West
Dry Tortugas (U.S.A.)
Freeport
Grand Bahama
Nassau
Andros Island
Eleuthera
La Habana (Havana)
Marianao
Matanzas
Cárdenas
Pinar del Río
Cienfuegos
Santa Clara
Sancti Spíritus
Trinidad
Camagüey
Holguín
Santiago de Cuba
Manzanillo
Sierra Maestra
I. de la Juventud
Nueva Gerona
George Town
Grand Cayman
Cayman Brac
Little Cayman
Montego Bay
Kingston
Spanish Town
Mandeville
Port Antonio
Pedro Cays (Jamaica)
Morant Cays (Jamaica)
Mérida
Progreso
Campeche
Ciudad del Carmen
Champotón
Chetumal
Cancún
Isla Cozumel
Valladolid
Belmopan
Belize City
Ambergris Cay
Turneffe Is.
Dangriga
Flores
Guatemala
Cobán
Quetzaltenango
Huehuetenango
Antigua
Puerto Barrios
Livingston
San Salvador
Santa Ana
San Miguel
Tegucigalpa
San Pedro Sula
La Ceiba
Choluteca
Managua
León
Granada
Masaya
Chinandega
Matagalpa
Bluefields
Puerto Cabezas
Lago de Nicaragua
San José
Cartago
Alajuela
Puntarenas
Limón
Liberia
Panamá
Colón
David
Golfo de Panamá
Golfo del Darién
Archipiélago de San Blas
Cayos Miskitos (Nicaragua)
I. de Providencia (Colombia)
I. de San Andrés (Colombia)
Cayos Roncador (U.S.A. & Colombia)
Bajo Nuevo (Colombia)
Banco Chinchorro
Is. de la Bahía
Roatán
C. Gracias a Dios
G. de Fonseca
G. de Nicoya
G. de Papagayo
G. de Chiriquí
Pen. de Azuero
Pen. de Nicoya
Pen. de Osa
I. de Coiba
CARTAGE
Lorica
Montería
7680
3993
3837
2000

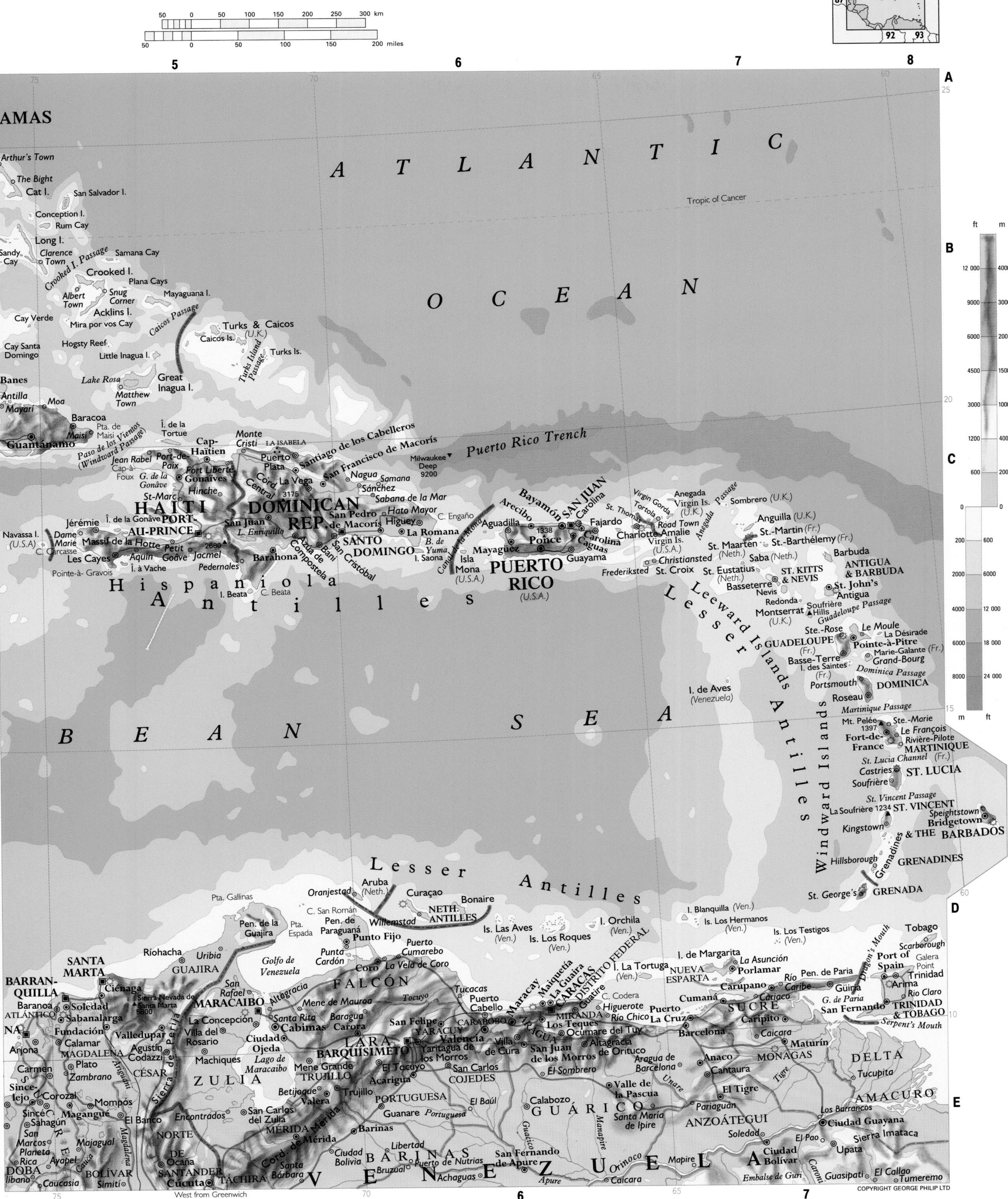

SOUTH AMERICA : Physical 1:35 000 000

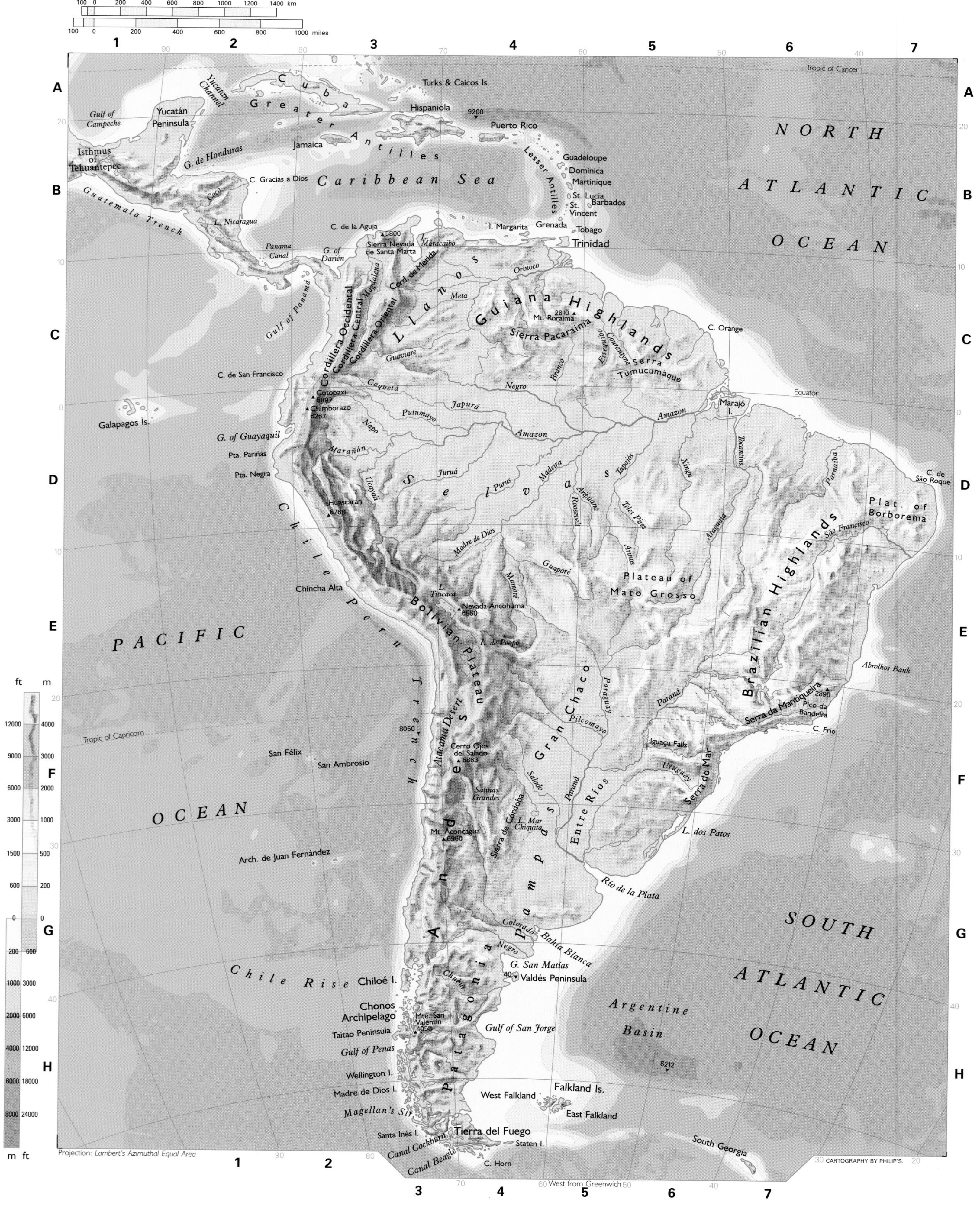

NORTH ATLANTIC OCEAN
Caribbean Sea
PACIFIC OCEAN
SOUTH ATLANTIC OCEAN
MEXICO
BELIZE
GUATEMALA
HONDURAS
NICARAGUA
EL SALVADOR
COSTA RICA
PANAMA
CUBA
BAHAMAS
JAMAICA
HAITI
DOMINICAN REP.
PUERTO RICO (U.S.A.)
Turks & Caicos Is. (U.K.)
Virgin Is. (U.K.)
ANTIGUA & BARBUDA
ST. KITTS & NEVIS
GUADELOUPE (Fr.)
DOMINICA
MARTINIQUE (Fr.)
ST. LUCIA
ST. VINCENT
BARBADOS
GRENADA
TRINIDAD & TOBAGO
VENEZUELA
COLOMBIA
GUYANA
SURINAM
FRENCH GUIANA
ECUADOR
PERU
BRAZIL
BOLIVIA
PARAGUAY
CHILE
ARGENTINA
URUGUAY
FALKLAND IS. (U.K.)
Galapagos Is. (Ecuador)
San Félix (Chile)
San Ambrosio (Chile)
Arch. de Juan Fernández (Chile)
South Georgia (U.K.)
Tropic of Cancer
Equator
Tropic of Capricorn
Projection: Lambert's Azimuthal Equal Area
CARTOGRAPHY BY PHILIP'S.
West from Greenwich
LIMA Capital Cities

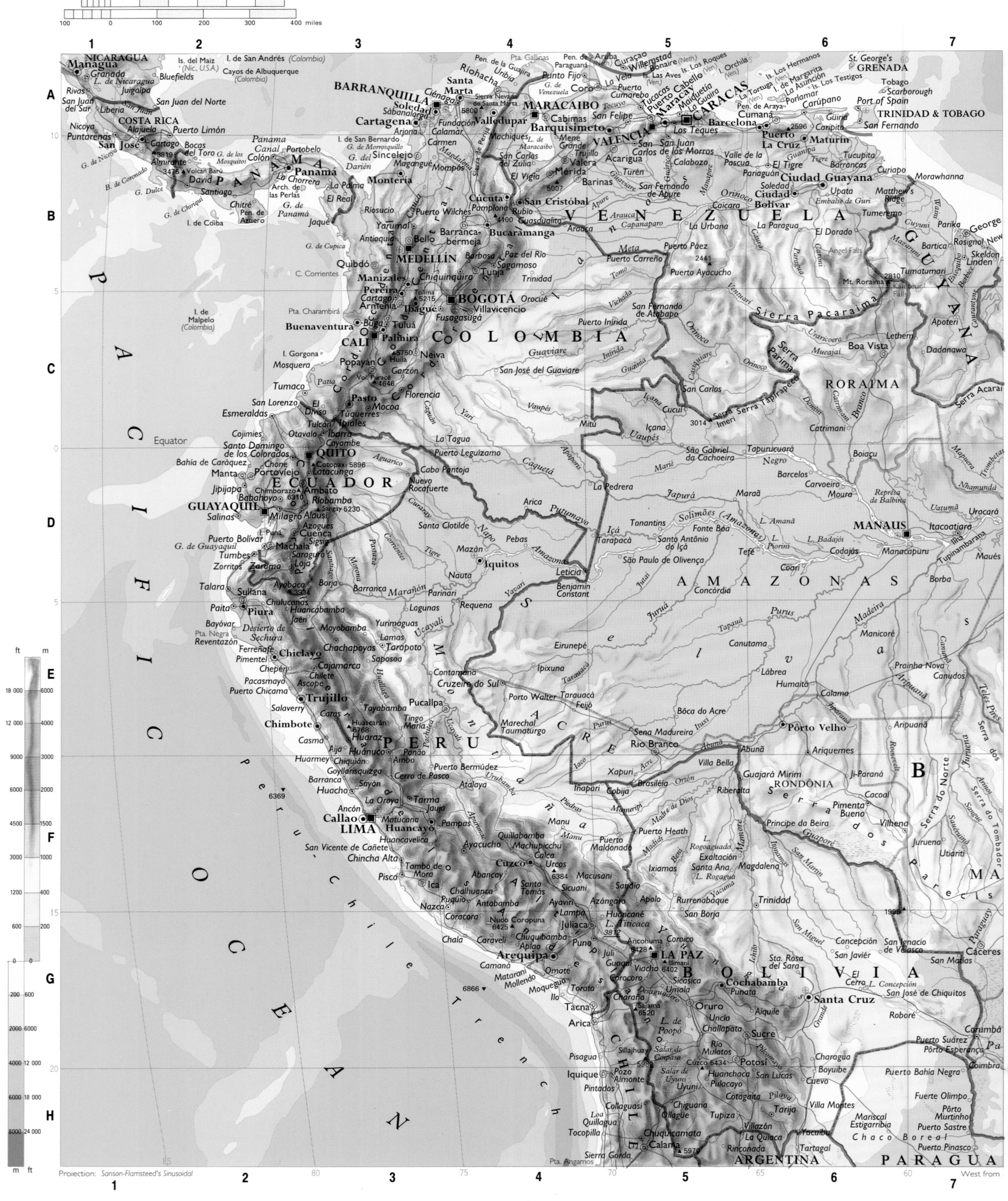

100 0 100 200 300 400 500 km
100 0 100 200 300 400 miles
1 2 3 4 5 6 7
A B C D E F G H
NICARAGUA
Managua
Granada
L. de Nicaragua
Juigalpa
Bluefields
Is. del Maiz (Nic., U.S.A.)
I. de San Andrés (Colombia)
Cayos de Albuquerque (Colombia)
Rivas
San Juan del Sur
Liberia
San Juan del Norte
COSTA RICA
Nicoya
Puntarenas
Alajuela
Puerto Limón
San José
Cartago
Bocas del Toro
3819 Almirante
3475 Volcán Barú
David
G. de los Mosquitos
Panama Canal
Portobelo
Colón
Panamá
La Chorrera
P A N A M A
Santiago
Chitré
Pen. de Azuero
I. de Coiba
G. de Chiriquí
G. Dulce
B. de Coronado
G. de Nicoya
Arch. de las Perlas
G. de Panamá
Jaqué
La Palma
El Real
G. del Darién
BARRANQUILLA
Cartagena
Soledad
Sabanalarga
Ciénaga
Santa Marta
Sierra Nevada de Santa Marta
5800
Fundación
Calamar
Arjona
Valledupar
Riohacha
Uribia
Pen. de la Guajira
Pta. Gallinas
I. de San Bernardo
G. de Morrosquillo
Sincelejo
Magangué
Mompós
Montería
Carmen
Magdalena
Machiques
MARACAIBO
L. de Maracaibo
Cabimas
Mene Grande
San Carlos del Zulia
El Vigía
Mérida
5007
Trujillo
Valera
Barquisimeto
VALENCIA
Maracay
CARACAS
La Guaira
Maiquetía
Los Teques
Puerto Cabello
Tucacas
San Felipe
Coro
Punto Fijo
Pen. de Paraguaná
G. de Venezuela
La Vela
Puerto Cumarebo
Curaçao
Willemstad
Aruba
Bonaire (Neth.)
Is. Las Aves
Is. Los Roques
I. Orchila
Is. Los Hermanos
I. de Margarita
La Asunción
Porlamar
Is. Los Testigos
La Tortuga
Barcelona
Cumaná
Pen. de Araya
Carúpano
Güiria
Caripito
Maturín
Puerto La Cruz
2596
Acarigua
San Carlos
San Juan de los Morros
Calabozo
Valle de la Pascua
El Tigre
Barrancas
Tucupita
Pariaguán
Ciudad Guayana
Ciudad Bolívar
Soledad
Upata
Caicara
Embalse de Guri
Curiapo
St. George's GRENADA
Tobago
Scarborough
Port of Spain
TRINIDAD & TOBAGO
San Fernando
Morawhanna
Matthew's Ridge
Tumeremo
Barinas
Guanare
Turén
San Fernando de Apure
San Cristóbal
Rubio
Guasdualito
Cúcuta
Pamplona
4100
Bucaramanga
Barrancabermeja
Puerto Wilches
Riosucio
Yarumal
Antioquia
Bello
MEDELLÍN
Quibdó
G. de Cupica
C. Corrientes
Manizales
Pereira
Cartago
Armenia
Ibagué
Tolima 5215
Chiquinquirá
Tunja
Sogamoso
Barbosa
Paz del Rio
BOGOTÁ
Fusagasugá
Villavicencio
Orocué
Trinidad
Pta. Charambirá
I. de Malpelo (Colombia)
Buenaventura
Buga
Tuluá
Palmira
CALI
I. Gorgona
Mosquera
Popayán
Huila 5750
Neiva
Garzón
Volc. Puracé 4646
Tumaco
San Lorenzo
Esmeraldas
Pasto
Mocoa
Florencia
Túquerres
Ipiales
Tulcán
El Diviso
C O L O M B I A
V E N E Z U E L A
Arauca
Capanaparo
La Urbana
La Paragua
El Dorado
Puerto Páez
Puerto Carreño
Meta
2441
Puerto Ayacucho
Angel Falls
Mt. Roraima 2810
Sierra Pacaraima
Puerto Inírida
San Fernando de Atabapo
Guaviare
San José del Guaviare
Serra Parima
Uraricoera
Mucajaí
Boa Vista
Lethem
Apoteri
Dadanawa
Bartica
Georgetown
Rosignol
New Amsterdam
Skeldon
Linden
Tumatumari
G U Y A N A
RORAIMA
San Carlos
Cucuí
3014
Serra Imeri
Serra Tapirapecó
Catrimani
Mitú
Vaupés
Içana
Uaupés
La Tagua
Puerto Leguízamo
Caquetá
São Gabriel da Cachoeira
Tapurucuará
Negro
Barcelos
Carvoeiro
Moura
Represa de Balbina
Boiaçu
Uatumã
Uracará
Itacoatiara
MANAUS
Manacapuru
Codajás
Coari
Tefé
Maués
Ilha Tupinambarana
Japurá
Maraã
L. Amanã
L. Badajós
Solimões (Amazonas)
Fonte Boa
Tonantins
Içá
Tarapacá
Santo Antônio do Içá
São Paulo de Olivença
Leticia
Benjamin Constant
Arica
Putumayo
La Pedrera
Otavalo
Ibarra
Cayambe
Cojimíes
Equator
Santo Domingo de los Colorados
QUITO
Cotopaxi 5896
Latacunga
Bahía de Caráquez
Chone
Portoviejo
Manta
Jipijapa
E C U A D O R
Chimborazo 6310
Ambato
Riobamba
Sangay 5230
Babahoyo
GUAYAQUIL
Salinas
Milagro
Alausí
Azogues
Cuenca
Sígsig
I. Puná
Puerto Bolívar
G. de Guayaquil
Machala
Tumbes
Zorritos
Zaruma
Saraguro
Loja
Cabo Pantoja
Nuevo Rocafuerte
Aguarico
Curaray
Santa Clotilde
Napo
Pebas
Mazán
Iquitos
Nauta
Amazonas
Tigre
Pastaza
Morona
Santiago
Corrientes
Talara
Sullana
Ayabaca
3934
Borja
Barranca
Marañón
Parinari
Requena
Paita
Piura
Chulucanas
Huancabamba
Jaén
Bayóvar
Pta. Negra
Desierto de Sechura
Reventazón
Lagunas
Yurimaguas
Moyobamba
Lamas
Tarapoto
Saposoa
Chachapoyas
Ferreñafe
Chiclayo
Pimentel
Chepén
Cajamarca
Chilete
Pacasmayo
Puerto Chicama
Ascope
Trujillo
Salaverry
Chimbote
Huascarán 6768
Huaraz
Casma
Huarmey
Caraz
Tayabamba
Tingo María
Pucallpa
Contamana
Cruzeiro do Sul
Ucayali
Huallaga
Huánuco
Panao
Ambo
Chiquián
Goyllarisquizga
Cerro de Pasco
Puerto Bermúdez
Barranca
Huacho
Sayán
La Oroya
Tarma
Jauja
Atalaya
Urubamba
6369
Ancón
Callao
LIMA
Matucana
Huancayo
Pampas
Huancavelica
San Vicente de Cañete
Chincha Alta
Pisco
Tambo de Mora
Ica
Nazca
Puquio
Chalhuanca
Coracora
Antabamba
Nudo Coropuna 6425
Chala
Caravelí
Chuquibamba
Aplao
Arequipa
Camaná
Mollendo
Matarani
Moquegua
Ilo
Omate
Puno
Juliaca
L. Titicaca
3812
Ayacucho
Quillabamba
Machupicchu
Calca
Cuzco
Urcos
6384
Abancay
Santo Tomás
Sicuani
Macusani
Ayaviri
Lampa
Azángaro
Sandia
P E R U
Peru-Chile Trench
6866
P A C I F I C   O C E A N
Eirunepé
Ipixuna
Tarauacá
Feijó
Porto Walter
Marechal Taumaturgo
A C R E
Purus
Sena Madureira
Rio Branco
Bôca do Acre
Juruá
Tapauá
Canutama
Lábrea
Humaitá
Calama
Pôrto Velho
Ariquemes
Ji-Paraná
Cacoal
Pimenta Bueno
Vilhena
Rondônia
RONDÔNIA
Guajará Mirim
Villa Bella
Abunã
Xapuri
Brasiléia
Cobija
Iñapari
Riberalta
Manu
Puerto Maldonado
Puerto Heath
Madre de Dios
Ixiamas
Exaltación
Santa Ana
L. Rogaguado
L. Rogagua
Magdalena
Principe da Beira
Guaporé
Mamoré
Beni
Rurrenabaque
San Borja
Trinidad
Apolo
Concepción
San Ignacio de Velasco
San Javier
Sta. Rosa del Sara
Cáceres
San Matías
San José de Chiquitos
El Cerro
L. Concepción
Roboré
Santa Cruz
Cochabamba
Punata
Aiquile
LA PAZ
Ancohuma 6428
Illimani 6402
Viacha
Guaqui
Juli
Coroico
Corocoro
Sicasica
Umala
Desaguadero
Charaña
Sajama 6520
Tacna
Tarata
Arica
Oruro
Uncia
Challapata
L. de Poopó
Sucre
Río Mulatos
Potosí
Cuzco 5434
Pisagua
Sillajhuay 5995
Salar de Coipasa
Salar de Uyuni
Uyuni
Iquique
Pozo Almonte
Pintados
Huanchaca
Pulacayo
Cotagaita
Tupiza
Tarija
Chiguana
Ollagüe
Collaguasi
Loa
Quillagua
Tocopilla
Chuquicamata
Calama
5979
Sierra Gorda
Pta. Angamos
Villazón
La Quiaca
Yacuiba
Rinconada
Tartagal
ARGENTINA
Villa Montes
Boyuibe
Charagua
Cuevo
Camiri
Puerto Suárez
Pôrto Esperança
Corumbá
Coimbra
Puerto Bahía Negra
Fuerte Olimpo
Pôrto Murtinho
Mariscal Estigarribia
Puerto Sastre
Puerto Pinasco
Chaco Boreal
PARAGUAY
B O L I V I A
A M A Z O N A S
Manicoré
Madeira
Prainha Nova
Canudos
Aripuanã
Borba
Jurena
Utiariti
Serra dos Parecis
Serra do Norte
1995
ft m
18 000 6000
12 000 4000
9000 3000
6000 2000
4500 1500
3000 1000
1200 400
600 200
0 0
200 600
2000 6000
4000 12 000
6000 18 000
8000 24 000
m ft
Projection: Sanson-Flamsteed's Sinusoidal
West from Greenwich

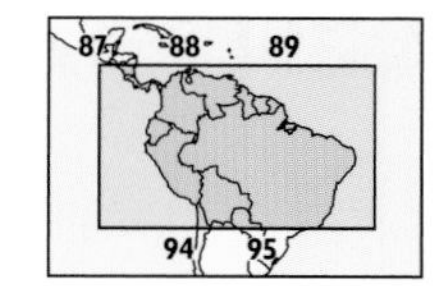

8 9 10 11 12 13

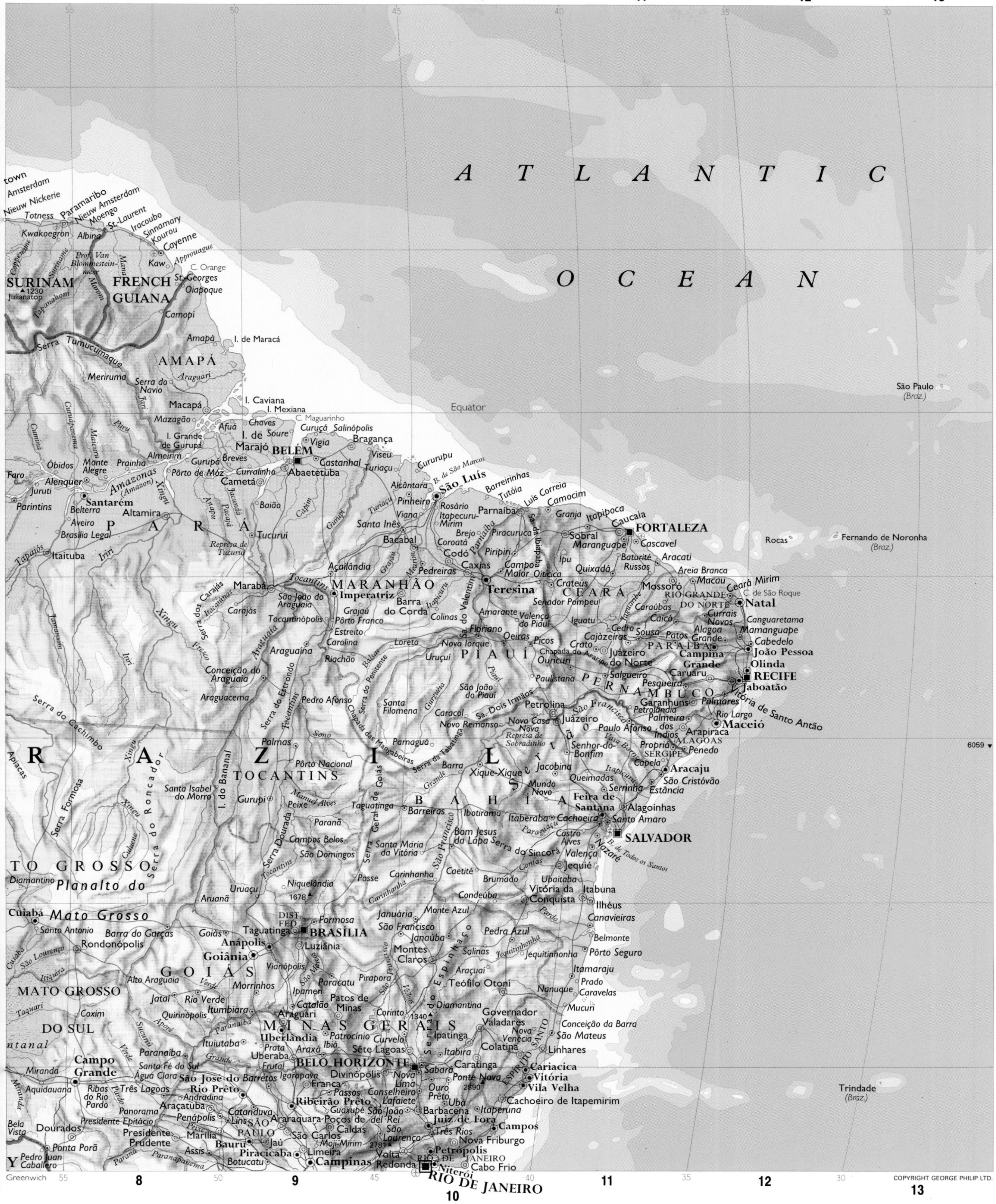

ATLANTIC OCEAN

CENTRAL SOUTH AMERICA 1:8 000 000

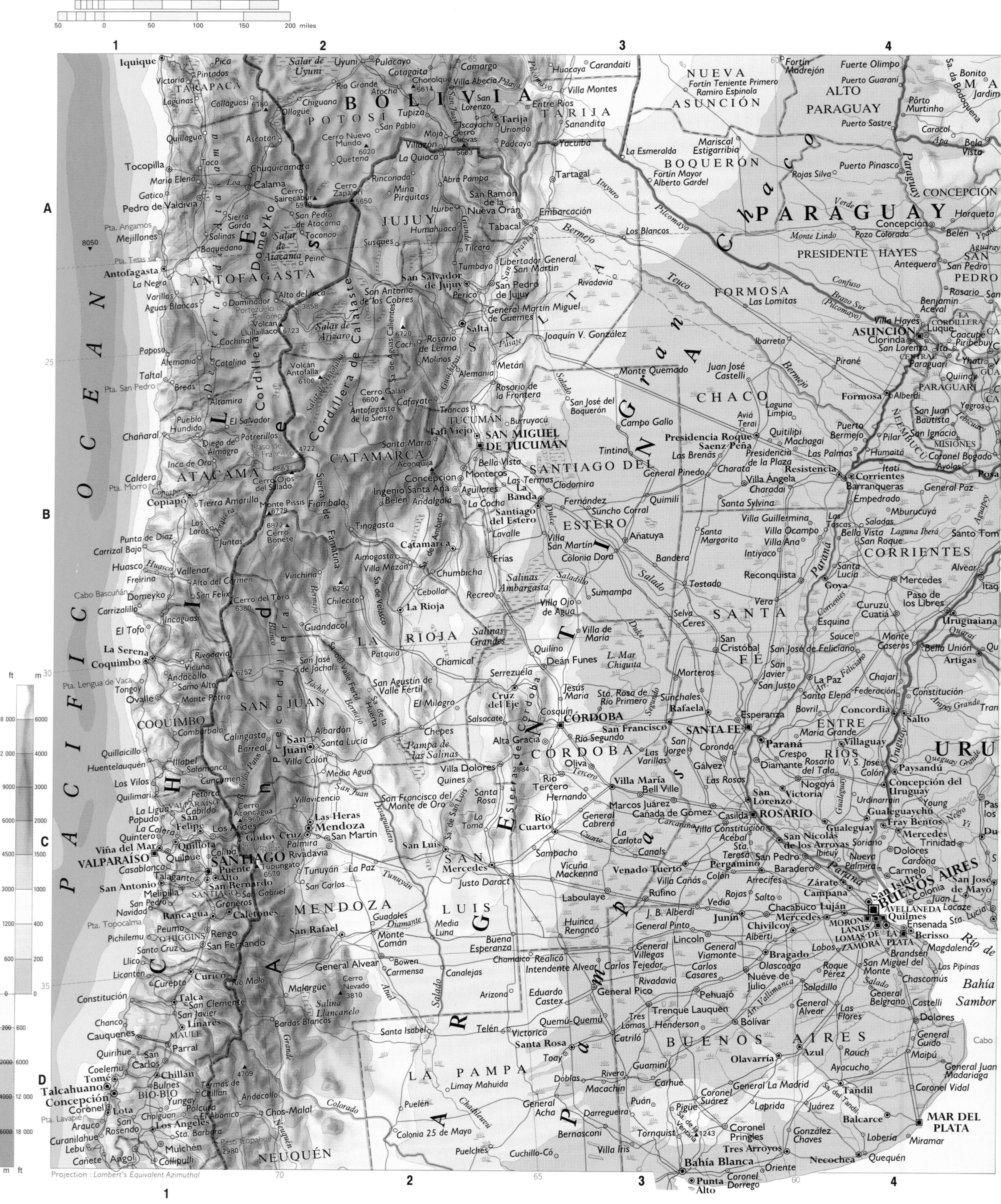

ATLANTIC
OCEAN
BRAZIL
SÃO PAULO
PARANÁ
SANTA CATARINA
RIO GRANDE DO SUL
MATO GROSSO DO SUL
RIO DE JANEIRO
URUGUAY
MISIONES
ITAPUÁ
ALTO PARANÁ
BELO HORIZONTE
Nova Lima
Itabirito
Vitória
Vila Velha
Guarapari
Campos
Cabo de São Tomé
Macaé
Cabo Frio
La. de Araruama
NITERÓI
RIO DE JANEIRO
DUQUE DE CAXIAS
SÃO GONÇALO
NOVA IGUAÇU
Petrópolis
Nova Friburgo
Volta Redonda
Barra Mansa
Angra dos Reis
Ilha Grande
Baía da Ilha Grande
Tropic of Capricorn
Juiz de Fora
Barbacena
Cataguases
Conselheiro Lafaiete
Congonhas
Ouro Prêto
Ponte Nova
São João del Rei
Três Corações
Santos Dumont
Leopoldina
Ubá
Muriaé
Carangola
Cachoeiro de Itapemirim
Pico da Bandeira 2890
Poços de Caldas
Pouso Alegre
Itajubá
Guaratinguetá
Taubaté
São José dos Campos
Jacareí
Mogi das Cruzes
SANTO ANDRÉ
SÃO PAULO
São Bernardo do Campo
SANTOS
São Vicente
Guarujá
Ilha de São Sebastião
Itanhaém
Jundiaí
CAMPINAS
Sorocaba
Piracicaba
Limeira
Americana
Rio Claro
São Carlos
Araraquara
Ribeirão Prêto
Franca
Bebedouro
São José do Rio Prêto
Catanduva
Araçatuba
Birigui
Bauru
Marília
Presidente Prudente
Assis
Ourinhos
Botucatu
Avaré
Itapetininga
Três Lagoas
Andradina
Londrina
Maringá
Apucarana
Arapongas
Umuarama
Cascavel
Foz do Iguaçu
Ciudad del Este
Guarapuava
Ponta Grossa
CURITIBA
Paranaguá
Joinville
São Francisco do Sul
Blumenau
Itajaí
Brusque
Florianópolis
Ilha de Santa Catarina
Lajes
Tubarão
Laguna
Criciúma
Cabo Santa Marta Grande
Araranguá
Torres
Caxias do Sul
Bento Gonçalves
Nôvo Hamburgo
São Leopoldo
Canoas
PÔRTO ALEGRE
Viamão
Lagoa dos Patos
Pelotas
Rio Grande
São José do Norte
Lagoa Mirim
Lagoa Mangueira
Santa Vitória do Palmar
Chuy
Passo Fundo
Santa Maria
Santa Cruz do Sul
Cachoeira do Sul
Bagé
Santana do Livramento
Rivera
Alegrete
Uruguaiana
Santo Ângelo
Tacuarembó
Melo
Treinta y Tres
Rocha
Minas
Maldonado
San Carlos
MONTEVIDEO
Río de la Plata
Encarnación
Posadas
Pedro Juan Caballero
Ponta Porã
Dourados
Campo Grande
Ilha Comprida
Ilha do Cardoso
5304
West from Greenwich
55
50
45
40
25
30
35
5
6
7
A
B
C
D
92
93
96
COPYRIGHT GEORGE PHILIP LTD

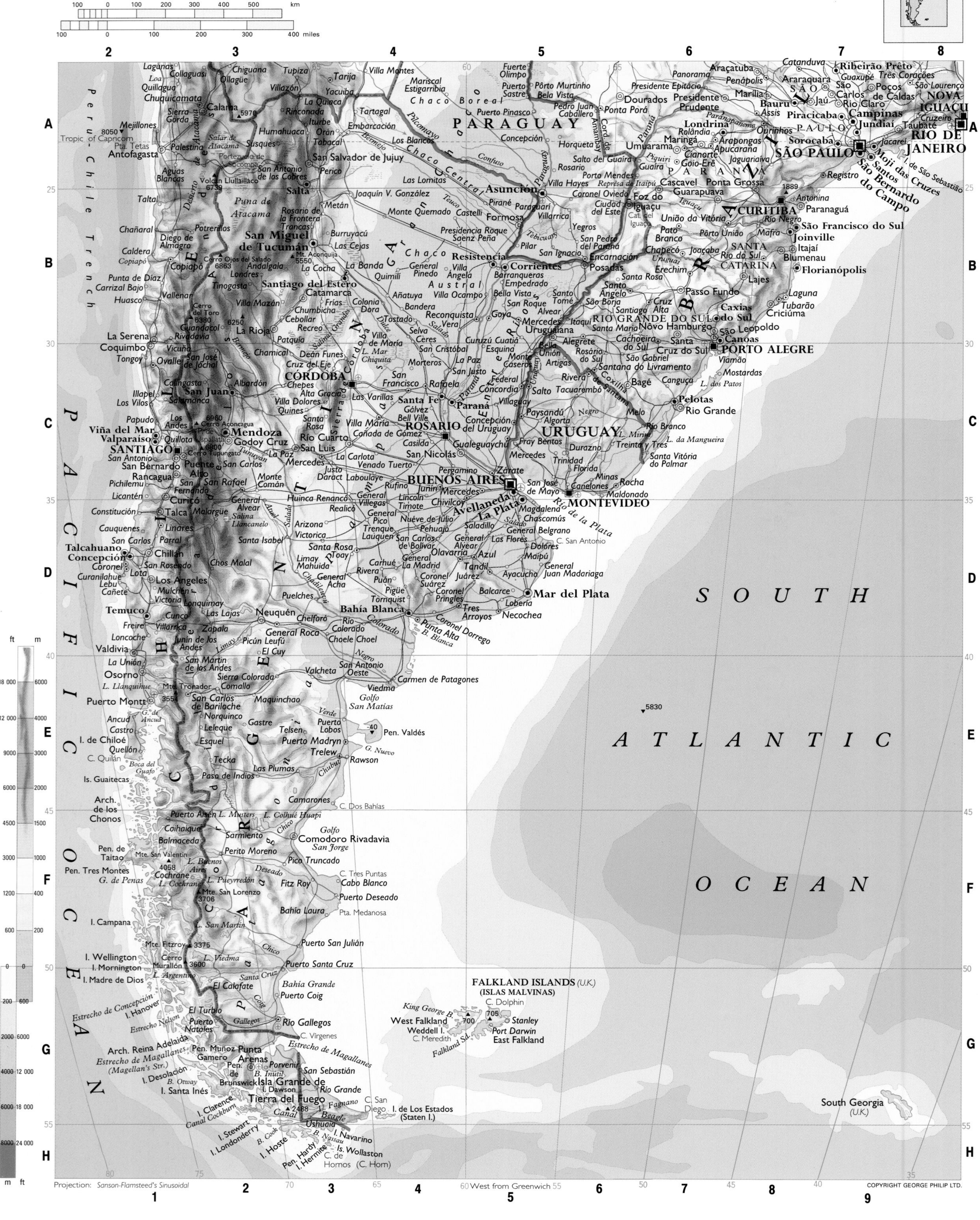
PARAGUAY
URUGUAY
SOUTH ATLANTIC OCEAN
PACIFIC OCEAN
FALKLAND ISLANDS (U.K.)
(ISLAS MALVINAS)
South Georgia (U.K.)
BUENOS AIRES
MONTEVIDEO
SANTIAGO
Asunción
SÃO PAULO
RIO DE JANEIRO
PORTO ALEGRE
CURITIBA
CÓRDOBA
ROSARIO
Mendoza
Mar del Plata
Bahía Blanca
Comodoro Rivadavia
Tierra del Fuego
Projection: Sanson-Flamsteed's Sinusoidal
West from Greenwich
COPYRIGHT GEORGE PHILIP LTD.

INDEX

The index contains the names of all the principal places and features shown on the World Maps. Each name is followed by an additional entry in italics giving the country or region within which it is located. The alphabetical order of names composed of two or more words is governed primarily by the first word and then by the second. This is an example of the rule:

Mīr Kūh, *Iran*	**45 E8**	26 22N	58 55 E
Mīr Shahdād, *Iran*	**45 E8**	26 15N	58 29 E
Mira, *Italy*	**20 B5**	45 26N	12 8 E
Mira por vos Cay, *Bahamas*	**89 B5**	22 9N	74 30 W
Miraj, *India*	**40 L9**	16 50N	74 45 E

Physical features composed of a proper name (Erie) and a description (Lake) are positioned alphabetically by the proper name. The description is positioned after the proper name and is usually abbreviated:

Erie, L., *N. Amer.* .... **78 D4** 42 15N 81 0 W

Where a description forms part of a settlement or administrative name however, it is always written in full and put in its true alphabetic position:

Mount Morris, *U.S.A.* ..... **78 D7** 42 44N 77 52 W

Names beginning with M' and Mc are indexed as if they were spelled Mac. Names beginning St. are alphabetised under Saint, but Sankt, Sint, Sant', Santa and San are all spelt in full and are alphabetised accordingly. If the same place name occurs two or more times in the index and all are in the same country, each is followed by the name of the administrative subdivision in which it is located. The names are placed in the alphabetical order of the subdivisions. For example:

Jackson, *Ky., U.S.A.*	**76 G4**	37 33N	83 23 W
Jackson, *Mich., U.S.A.*	**76 D3**	42 15N	84 24 W
Jackson, *Minn., U.S.A.*	**80 D7**	43 37N	95 1 W

The number in bold type which follows each name in the index refers to the number of the map page where that feature or place will be found. This is usually the largest scale at which the place or feature appears.

The letter and figure which are in bold type immediately after the page number give the grid square on the map page, within which the feature is situated. The letter represents the latitude and the figure the longitude.

In some cases the feature itself may fall within the specified square, while the name is outside. This is usually the case only with features which are larger than a grid square.

For a more precise location the geographical coordinates which follow the letter/figure references give the latitude and the longitude of each place. The first set of figures represent the latitude which is the distance north or south of the Equator measured as an angle at the centre of the earth. The Equator is latitude 0°, the North Pole is 90°N, and the South Pole 90°S.

The second set of figures represent the longitude, which is the distance East or West of the prime meridian, which runs through Greenwich, England. Longitude is also measured as an angle at the centre of the earth and is given East or West of the prime meridian, from 0° to 180° in either direction.

The unit of measurement for latitude and longitude is the degree, which is subdivided into 60 minutes. Each index entry states the position of a place in degrees and minutes, a space being left between the degrees and the minutes.

The latitude is followed by N(orth) or S(outh) and the longitude by E(ast) or W(est).

Rivers are indexed to their mouths or confluences, and carry the symbol → after their names. A solid square ■ follows the name of a country, while an open square □ refers to a first order administrative area.

Abbreviations used in the index

A.C.T. – Australian Capital Territory
Afghan. – Afghanistan
Ala. – Alabama
Alta. – Alberta
Amer. – America(n)
Arch. – Archipelago
Ariz. – Arizona
Ark. – Arkansas
Atl. Oc. – Atlantic Ocean
B. – Baie, Bahía, Bay, Bucht, Bugt
B.C. – British Columbia
Bangla. – Bangladesh
Barr. – Barrage
Bos.-H. – Bosnia-Herzegovina
C. – Cabo, Cap, Cape, Coast
C.A.R. – Central African Republic
C. Prov. – Cape Province
Calif. – California
Cent. – Central
Chan. – Channel
Colo. – Colorado
Conn. – Connecticut
Cord. – Cordillera
Cr. – Creek
Czech. – Czech Republic
D.C. – District of Columbia
Del. – Delaware
Dep. – Dependency
Des. – Desert
Dist. – District
Dj. – Djebel
Domin. – Dominica
Dom. Rep. – Dominican Republic
E. – East
E. Salv. – El Salvador
Eq. Guin. – Equatorial Guinea
Fla. – Florida
Falk. Is. – Falkland Is.
G. – Golfe, Golfo, Gulf, Guba, Gebel
Ga. – Georgia
Gt. – Great, Greater
Guinea-Biss. – Guinea-Bissau
H.K. – Hong Kong
H.P. – Himachal Pradesh
Hants. – Hampshire
Harb. – Harbor, Harbour
Hd. – Head
Hts. – Heights
I.(s). – Île, Ilha, Insel, Isla, Island, Isle
Ill. – Illinois
Ind. – Indiana
Ind. Oc. – Indian Ocean
Ivory C. – Ivory Coast
J. – Jabal, Jebel, Jazira
Junc. – Junction
K. – Kap, Kapp
Kans. – Kansas
Kep. – Kepulauan
Ky. – Kentucky
L. – Lac, Lacul, Lago, Lagoa, Lake, Limni, Loch, Lough
La. – Louisiana
Liech. – Liechtenstein
Lux. – Luxembourg
Mad. P. – Madhya Pradesh
Madag. – Madagascar
Man. – Manitoba
Mass. – Massachusetts
Md. – Maryland
Me. – Maine
Medit. S. – Mediterranean Sea
Mich. – Michigan
Minn. – Minnesota
Miss. – Mississippi
Mo. – Missouri
Mont. – Montana
Mozam. – Mozambique
Mt.(e) – Mont, Monte, Monti, Montaña, Mountain
N. – Nord, Norte, North, Northern, Nouveau
N.B. – New Brunswick
N.C. – North Carolina
N. Cal. – New Caledonia
N. Dak. – North Dakota
N.H. – New Hampshire
N.I. – North Island
N.J. – New Jersey
N. Mex. – New Mexico
N.S. – Nova Scotia
N.S.W. – New South Wales
N.W.T. – North West Territory
N.Y. – New York
N.Z. – New Zealand
Nebr. – Nebraska
Neths. – Netherlands
Nev. – Nevada
Nfld. – Newfoundland
Nic. – Nicaragua
O. – Oued, Ouadi
Occ. – Occidentale
Okla. – Oklahoma
Ont. – Ontario
Or. – Orientale
Oreg. – Oregon
Os. – Ostrov
Oz. – Ozero
P. – Pass, Passo, Pasul, Pulau
P.E.I. – Prince Edward Island
Pa. – Pennsylvania
Pac. Oc. – Pacific Ocean
Papua N.G. – Papua New Guinea
Pass. – Passage
Pen. – Peninsula, Péninsule
Phil. – Philippines
Pk. – Park, Peak
Plat. – Plateau
Prov. – Province, Provincial
Pt. – Point
Pta. – Ponta, Punta
Pte. – Pointe
Qué. – Québec
Queens. – Queensland
R. – Rio, River
R.I. – Rhode Island
Ra.(s). – Range(s)
Raj. – Rajasthan
Reg. – Region
Rep. – Republic
Res. – Reserve, Reservoir
S. – San, South, Sea
Si. Arabia – Saudi Arabia
S.C. – South Carolina
S. Dak. – South Dakota
S.I. – South Island
S. Leone – Sierra Leone
Sa. – Serra, Sierra
Sask. – Saskatchewan
Scot. – Scotland
Sd. – Sound
Sev. – Severnaya
Sib. – Siberia
Sprs. – Springs
St. – Saint
Sta. – Santa, Station
Ste. – Sainte
Sto. – Santo
Str. – Strait, Stretto
Switz. – Switzerland
Tas. – Tasmania
Tenn. – Tennessee
Tex. – Texas
Tg. – Tanjung
Trin. & Tob. – Trinidad & Tobago
U.A.E. – United Arab Emirates
U.K. – United Kingdom
U.S.A. – United States of America
Ut. P. – Uttar Pradesh
Va. – Virginia
Vdkhr. – Vodokhranilishche
Vf. – Vîrful
Vic. – Victoria
Vol. – Volcano
Vt. – Vermont
W. – Wadi, West
W. Va. – West Virginia
Wash. – Washington
Wis. – Wisconsin
Wlkp. – Wielkopolski
Wyo. – Wyoming
Yorks. – Yorkshire
Yug. – Yugoslavia

A

A Coruña, *Spain* **19 A1** 43 20N 8 25W
A Estrada, *Spain* **19 A1** 42 43N 8 27W
A Fonsagrada, *Spain* **19 A2** 43 8N 7 4W
Aachen, *Germany* **16 C4** 50 45N 6 6 E
Aalborg = Ålborg, *Denmark* **9 H13** 57 2N 9 54 E
Aalen, *Germany* **16 D6** 48 51N 10 6 E
Aalst, *Belgium* **15 D4** 50 56N 4 2 E
Aalten, *Neths.* **15 C6** 51 56N 6 35 E
Aalter, *Belgium* **15 C3** 51 5N 3 28 E
Äänekoski, *Finland* **9 E21** 62 36N 25 44 E
Aarau, *Switz.* **18 C8** 47 23N 8 4 E
Aare →, *Switz.* **18 C8** 47 33N 8 14 E
Aarhus = Århus, *Denmark* **9 H14** 56 8N 10 11 E
Aarschot, *Belgium* **15 D4** 50 59N 4 49 E
Aba, *Dem. Rep. of the Congo* **54 B3** 3 58N 30 17 E
Aba, *Nigeria* **50 G7** 5 10N 7 19 E
Ābādān, *Iran* **45 D6** 30 22N 48 20 E
Ābādeh, *Iran* **45 D7** 31 8N 52 40 E
Abadla, *Algeria* **50 B5** 31 2N 2 45W
Abaetetuba, *Brazil* **93 D9** 1 40S 48 50W
Abagnar Qi, *China* **34 C9** 43 52N 116 2 E
Abai, *Paraguay* **95 B4** 25 58S 55 54W
Abakan, *Russia* **27 D10** 53 40N 91 10 E
Abancay, *Peru* **92 F4** 13 35S 72 55W
Abariringa, *Kiribati* **64 H10** 2 50S 171 40W
Abarqū, *Iran* **45 D7** 31 10N 53 20 E
Abashiri, *Japan* **30 B12** 44 0N 144 15 E
Abashiri-Wan, *Japan* **30 C12** 44 0N 144 30 E
Ābay = Nîl el Azraq →, *Sudan* **51 E12** 15 38N 32 31 E
Abay, *Kazakstan* **26 E8** 49 38N 72 53 E
Abaya, L., *Ethiopia* **46 F2** 6 30N 37 50 E
Abaza, *Russia* **26 D9** 52 39N 90 6 E
'Abbāsābād, *Iran* **45 C8** 33 34N 58 23 E
Abbay = Nîl el Azraq →, *Sudan* **51 E12** 15 38N 32 31 E
Abbaye, Pt., *U.S.A.* **76 B1** 46 58N 88 8W
Abbé, L., *Ethiopia* **46 E3** 11 8N 41 47 E
Abbeville, *France* **18 A4** 50 6N 1 49 E
Abbeville, *Ala., U.S.A.* **77 K3** 31 34N 85 15W
Abbeville, *La., U.S.A.* **81 L8** 29 58N 92 8W
Abbeville, *S.C., U.S.A.* **77 H4** 34 11N 82 23W
Abbot Ice Shelf, *Antarctica* **5 D16** 73 0S 92 0W
Abbottabad, *Pakistan* **42 B5** 34 10N 73 15 E
Abd al Kūrī, *Yemen* **46 E5** 12 5N 52 20 E
Ābdar, *Iran* **45 D7** 30 16N 55 19 E
'Abdolābād, *Iran* **45 C8** 34 12N 56 30 E
Abdulpur, *Bangla.* **43 G13** 24 15N 88 59 E
Abéché, *Chad* **51 F10** 13 50N 20 35 E
Abengourou, *Ivory C.* **50 G5** 6 42N 3 27W
Åbenrå, *Denmark* **9 J13** 55 3N 9 25 E
Abeokuta, *Nigeria* **50 G6** 7 3N 3 19 E
Aber, *Uganda* **54 B3** 2 12N 32 25 E
Aberaeron, *U.K.* **11 E3** 52 15N 4 15W
Aberayron = Aberaeron, *U.K.* **11 E3** 52 15N 4 15W
Aberchirder, *U.K.* **12 D6** 57 34N 2 37W
Abercorn = Mbala, *Zambia* **55 D3** 8 46S 31 24 E
Abercorn, *Australia* **63 D5** 25 12S 151 5 E
Aberdare, *U.K.* **11 F4** 51 43N 3 27W
Aberdare Ra., *Kenya* **54 C4** 0 15S 36 50 E
Aberdeen, *Australia* **63 E5** 32 9S 150 56 E
Aberdeen, *Canada* **73 C7** 52 20N 106 8W
Aberdeen, *S. Africa* **56 E3** 32 28S 24 2 E
Aberdeen, *U.K.* **12 D6** 57 9N 2 5W
Aberdeen, *Ala., U.S.A.* **77 J1** 33 49N 88 33W
Aberdeen, *Idaho, U.S.A.* **82 E7** 42 57N 112 50W
Aberdeen, *Md., U.S.A.* **76 F7** 39 31N 76 10W
Aberdeen, *S. Dak., U.S.A.* **80 C5** 45 28N 98 29W
Aberdeen, *Wash., U.S.A.* **84 D3** 46 59N 123 50W
Aberdeen, City of □, *U.K.* **12 D6** 57 10N 2 10W
Aberdeenshire □, *U.K.* **12 D6** 57 17N 2 36W
Aberdovey = Aberdyfi, *U.K.* **11 E3** 52 33N 4 3W
Aberdyfi, *U.K.* **11 E3** 52 33N 4 3W
Aberfeldy, *U.K.* **12 E5** 56 37N 3 51W
Abergavenny, *U.K.* **11 F4** 51 49N 3 1W
Abergele, *U.K.* **10 D4** 53 17N 3 35W
Abernathy, *U.S.A.* **81 J4** 33 50N 101 51W
Abert, L., *U.S.A.* **82 E3** 42 38N 120 14W
Aberystwyth, *U.K.* **11 E3** 52 25N 4 5W
Abhā, *Si. Arabia* **46 D3** 18 0N 42 34 E
Abhar, *Iran* **45 B6** 36 9N 49 13 E
Abhayapuri, *India* **43 F14** 26 24N 90 38 E
Abidjan, *Ivory C.* **50 G5** 5 26N 3 58W
Abilene, *Kans., U.S.A.* **80 F6** 38 55N 97 13W
Abilene, *Tex., U.S.A.* **81 J5** 32 28N 99 43W
Abingdon, *U.K.* **11 F6** 51 40N 1 17W
Abingdon, *U.S.A.* **77 G5** 36 43N 81 59W
Abington Reef, *Australia* **62 B4** 18 0S 149 35 E
Abitau →, *Canada* **73 B7** 59 53N 109 3W
Abitibi →, *Canada* **70 B3** 51 3N 80 55W
Abitibi, L., *Canada* **70 C4** 48 40N 79 40W
Abkhaz Republic = Abkhazia □, *Georgia* **25 F7** 43 12N 41 5 E
Abkhazia □, *Georgia* **25 F7** 43 12N 41 5 E
Abminga, *Australia* **63 D1** 26 8S 134 51 E
Åbo = Turku, *Finland* **9 F20** 60 30N 22 19 E
Abohar, *India* **42 D6** 30 10N 74 10 E
Abomey, *Benin* **50 G6** 7 10N 2 5 E
Abong-Mbang, *Cameroon* **52 D2** 4 0N 13 8 E
Abou-Deïa, *Chad* **51 F9** 11 20N 19 20 E
Aboyne, *U.K.* **12 D6** 57 4N 2 47W
Abra Pampa, *Argentina* **94 A2** 22 43S 65 42W
Abraham L., *Canada* **72 C5** 52 15N 116 35W
Abreojos, Pta., *Mexico* **86 B2** 26 50N 113 40W
Abrud, *Romania* **17 E12** 46 19N 23 5 E
Absaroka Range, *U.S.A.* **82 D9** 44 45N 109 50W
Abu, *India* **42 G5** 24 41N 72 50 E
Abū al Abyad, *U.A.E.* **45 E7** 24 11N 53 50 E
Abū al Khaṣīb, *Iraq* **45 D6** 30 25N 48 0 E
Abū 'Alī, *Si. Arabia* **45 E6** 27 20N 49 27 E
Abū 'Alī →, *Lebanon* **47 A4** 34 25N 35 50 E
Abu Dhabi = Abū Ẓāby, *U.A.E.* **46 C5** 24 28N 54 22 E
Abū Du'ān, *Syria* **44 B3** 36 25N 38 15 E
Abu el Gairi, W. →, *Egypt* **47 F2** 29 35N 33 30 E
Abu Ga'da, W. →, *Egypt* **47 F1** 29 15N 32 53 E
Abū Ḥadrīyah, *Si. Arabia* **45 E6** 27 20N 48 58 E
Abu Hamed, *Sudan* **51 E12** 19 32N 33 13 E
Abū Kamāl, *Syria* **44 C4** 34 30N 41 0 E
Abū Madd, Ra's, *Si. Arabia* **44 E3** 24 50N 37 7 E
Abū Mūsā, *U.A.E.* **45 E7** 25 52N 55 3 E
Abū Qaṣr, *Si. Arabia* **44 D3** 30 21N 38 34 E
Abu Ṣafāt, W. →, *Jordan* **47 E5** 30 24N 36 7 E
Abu Simbel, *Egypt* **51 D12** 22 18N 31 40 E
Abū Şukhayr, *Iraq* **44 D5** 31 54N 44 30 E
Abu Zabad, *Sudan* **51 F11** 12 25N 29 10 E
Abū Ẓāby, *U.A.E.* **46 C5** 24 28N 54 22 E
Abū Zeydābād, *Iran* **45 C6** 33 54N 51 45 E
Abuja, *Nigeria* **50 G7** 9 5N 7 32 E
Abukuma-Gawa →, *Japan* **30 E10** 38 6N 140 52 E
Abukuma-Sammyaku, *Japan* **30 F10** 37 30N 140 45 E
Abunã, *Brazil* **92 E5** 9 40S 65 20W
Abunã →, *Brazil* **92 E5** 9 41S 65 20W
Aburo, *Dem. Rep. of the Congo* **54 B3** 2 4N 30 53 E
Abut Hd., *N.Z.* **59 K3** 43 7S 170 15 E
Acadia Nat. Park, *U.S.A.* **77 C11** 44 20N 68 13W
Açailândia, *Brazil* **93 D9** 4 57S 47 0W
Acajutla, *El Salv.* **88 D2** 13 36N 89 50W
Acámbaro, *Mexico* **86 D4** 20 0N 100 40W
Acaponeta, *Mexico* **86 C3** 22 30N 105 20W
Acapulco, *Mexico* **87 D5** 16 51N 99 56W
Acarai, Serra, *Brazil* **92 C7** 1 50N 57 50W
Acarigua, *Venezuela* **92 B5** 9 33N 69 12W
Acatlán, *Mexico* **87 D5** 18 10N 98 3W
Acayucan, *Mexico* **87 D6** 17 59N 94 58W
Accomac, *U.S.A.* **76 G8** 37 43N 75 40W
Accra, *Ghana* **50 G5** 5 35N 0 6W
Accrington, *U.K.* **10 D5** 53 45N 2 22W
Acebal, *Argentina* **94 C3** 33 20S 60 50W
Aceh □, *Indonesia* **36 D1** 4 15N 97 30 E
Achalpur, *India* **40 J10** 21 22N 77 32 E
Acheng, *China* **35 B14** 45 30N 126 58 E
Acher, *India* **42 H5** 23 10N 72 32 E
Achill Hd., *Ireland* **13 C1** 53 58N 10 15W
Achill I., *Ireland* **13 C1** 53 58N 10 1W
Achinsk, *Russia* **27 D10** 56 20N 90 20 E
Acireale, *Italy* **20 F6** 37 37N 15 10 E
Ackerman, *U.S.A.* **81 J10** 33 19N 89 11W
Acklins I., *Bahamas* **89 B5** 22 30N 74 0W
Acme, *Canada* **72 C6** 51 33N 113 30W
Acme, *U.S.A.* **78 F5** 40 8N 79 26W
Aconcagua, Cerro, *Argentina* **94 C2** 32 39S 70 0W
Aconquija, Mt., *Argentina* **94 B2** 27 0S 66 0W
Açores, Is. dos, *Atl. Oc.* **50 A1** 38 0N 27 0W
Acornhoek, *S. Africa* **57 C5** 24 37S 31 2 E
Acraman, L., *Australia* **63 E2** 32 2S 135 23 E
Acre = 'Akko, *Israel* **47 C4** 32 55N 35 4 E
Acre □, *Brazil* **92 E4** 9 1S 71 0W
Acre →, *Brazil* **92 E5** 8 45S 67 22W
Acton, *Canada* **78 C4** 43 38N 80 3W
Acuña, *Mexico* **86 B4** 29 18N 100 55W
Ad Dammām, *Si. Arabia* **45 E6** 26 20N 50 5 E
Ad Dāmūr, *Lebanon* **47 B4** 33 44N 35 27 E
Ad Dawādimī, *Si. Arabia* **44 E5** 24 35N 44 15 E
Ad Dawḥah, *Qatar* **46 B5** 25 15N 51 35 E
Ad Dawr, *Iraq* **44 C4** 34 27N 43 47 E
Ad Dir'īyah, *Si. Arabia* **44 E5** 24 44N 46 35 E
Ad Dīwānīyah, *Iraq* **44 D5** 32 0N 45 0 E
Ad Dujayl, *Iraq* **44 C5** 33 51N 44 14 E
Ad Duwayd, *Si. Arabia* **44 D4** 30 15N 42 17 E
Ada, *Minn., U.S.A.* **80 B6** 47 18N 96 31W
Ada, *Okla., U.S.A.* **81 H6** 34 46N 96 41W
Adabiya, *Egypt* **47 F1** 29 53N 32 28 E
Adair, C., *Canada* **69 A12** 71 31N 71 24W
Adaja →, *Spain* **19 B3** 41 32N 4 52W
Adak I., *U.S.A.* **68 C2** 51 45N 176 45W
Adamaoua, Massif de l', *Cameroon* **51 G7** 7 20N 12 20 E
Adamawa Highlands = Adamaoua, Massif de l', *Cameroon* **51 G7** 7 20N 12 20 E
Adamello, Mte., *Italy* **18 C9** 46 9N 10 30 E
Adaminaby, *Australia* **63 F4** 36 0S 148 45 E
Adams, *Mass., U.S.A.* **79 D11** 42 38N 73 7W
Adams, *N.Y., U.S.A.* **79 C8** 43 49N 76 1W
Adams, *Wis., U.S.A.* **80 D10** 43 57N 89 49W
Adam's Bridge, *Sri Lanka* **40 Q11** 9 15N 79 40 E
Adams L., *Canada* **72 C5** 51 10N 119 40W
Adams Mt., *U.S.A.* **84 D5** 46 12N 121 30W
Adam's Peak, *Sri Lanka* **40 R12** 6 48N 80 30 E
Adana, *Turkey* **25 G6** 37 0N 35 16 E
Adapazarı = Sakarya, *Turkey* **25 F5** 40 48N 30 25 E
Adarama, *Sudan* **51 E12** 17 10N 34 52 E
Adare, C., *Antarctica* **5 D11** 71 0S 171 0 E
Adaut, *Indonesia* **37 F8** 8 8S 131 7 E
Adavale, *Australia* **63 D3** 25 52S 144 32 E
Adda →, *Italy* **18 D8** 45 8N 9 53 E
Addis Ababa = Addis Abeba, *Ethiopia* **46 F2** 9 2N 38 42 E
Addis Abeba, *Ethiopia* **46 F2** 9 2N 38 42 E
Addison, *U.S.A.* **78 D7** 42 1N 77 14W
Addo, *S. Africa* **56 E4** 33 32S 25 45 E
Ādeh, *Iran* **44 B5** 37 42N 45 11 E
Adel, *U.S.A.* **77 K4** 31 8N 83 25W
Adelaide, *Australia* **63 E2** 34 52S 138 30 E
Adelaide, *Bahamas* **88 A4** 25 4N 77 31W
Adelaide, *S. Africa* **56 E4** 32 42S 26 20 E
Adelaide I., *Antarctica* **5 C17** 67 15S 68 30W
Adelaide Pen., *Canada* **68 B10** 68 15N 97 30W
Adelaide River, *Australia* **60 B5** 13 15S 131 7 E
Adelanto, *U.S.A.* **85 L9** 34 35N 117 22W
Adele I., *Australia* **60 C3** 15 32S 123 9 E
Adélie, Terre, *Antarctica* **5 C10** 68 0S 140 0 E
Adélie Land = Adélie, Terre, *Antarctica* **5 C10** 68 0S 140 0 E
Aden = Al 'Adan, *Yemen* **46 E4** 12 45N 45 0 E
Aden, G. of, *Asia* **46 E4** 12 30N 47 30 E
Adendorp, *S. Africa* **56 E3** 32 15S 24 30 E
Adh Dhayd, *U.A.E.* **45 E7** 25 17N 55 53 E
Adhoi, *India* **42 H4** 23 26N 70 32 E
Adi, *Indonesia* **37 E8** 4 15S 133 30 E
Adieu, C., *Australia* **61 F5** 32 0S 132 10 E
Adieu Pt., *Australia* **60 C3** 15 14S 124 35 E
Adige →, *Italy* **20 B5** 45 9N 12 20 E
Adigrat, *Ethiopia* **46 E2** 14 20N 39 26 E
Adilabad, *India* **40 K11** 19 33N 78 20 E
Adirondack Mts., *U.S.A.* **79 C10** 44 0N 74 0W
Adjumani, *Uganda* **54 B3** 3 20N 31 50 E
Adlavik Is., *Canada* **71 B8** 55 0N 58 40W
Admiralty G., *Australia* **60 B4** 14 20S 125 55 E
Admiralty I., *U.S.A.* **72 B2** 57 30N 134 30W
Admiralty Is., *Papua N. G.* **64 H6** 2 0S 147 0 E
Adonara, *Indonesia* **37 F6** 8 15S 123 5 E
Adoni, *India* **40 M10** 15 33N 77 18 E
Adour →, *France* **18 E3** 43 32N 1 32W
Adra, *India* **43 H12** 23 30N 86 42 E
Adra, *Spain* **19 D4** 36 43N 3 3W
Adrano, *Italy* **20 F6** 37 40N 14 50 E
Adrar, *Mauritania* **50 D3** 20 30N 7 30 E
Adrar des Iforas, *Algeria* **50 C5** 27 51N 0 11 E
Adrian, *Mich., U.S.A.* **76 E3** 41 54N 84 2W
Adrian, *Tex., U.S.A.* **81 H3** 35 16N 102 40W
Adriatic Sea, *Medit. S.* **20 C6** 43 0N 16 0 E
Adua, *Indonesia* **37 E7** 1 45S 129 50 E
Adwa, *Ethiopia* **46 E2** 14 15N 38 52 E
Adygea □, *Russia* **25 F7** 45 0N 40 0 E
Adzhar Republic = Ajaria □, *Georgia* **25 F7** 41 30N 42 0 E
Adzopé, *Ivory C.* **50 G5** 6 7N 3 49W
Ægean Sea, *Medit. S.* **21 E11** 38 30N 25 0 E
Aerhtai Shan, *Mongolia* **32 B4** 46 40N 92 45 E
'Afak, *Iraq* **44 C5** 32 4N 45 15 E
Afándou, *Greece* **23 C10** 36 18N 28 12 E
Afghanistan ■, *Asia* **40 C4** 33 0N 65 0 E
Aflou, *Algeria* **50 B6** 34 7N 2 3 E
Africa **48 E6** 10 0N 20 0 E
'Afrīn, *Syria* **44 B3** 36 32N 36 50 E
Afton, *N.Y., U.S.A.* **79 D9** 42 14N 75 32W
Afton, *Wyo., U.S.A.* **82 E8** 42 44N 110 56W
Afuá, *Brazil* **93 D8** 0 15S 50 20W
'Afula, *Israel* **47 C4** 32 37N 35 17 E
Afyon, *Turkey* **25 G5** 38 45N 30 33 E
Afyonkarahisar = Afyon, *Turkey* **25 G5** 38 45N 30 33 E
Agadès = Agadez, *Niger* **50 E7** 16 58N 7 59 E
Agadez, *Niger* **50 E7** 16 58N 7 59 E
Agadir, *Morocco* **50 B4** 30 28N 9 55W
Agaete, *Canary Is.* **22 F4** 28 6N 15 43W
Agar, *India* **42 H7** 23 40N 76 2 E
Agartala, *India* **41 H17** 23 50N 91 23 E
Agassiz, *Canada* **72 D4** 49 14N 121 46W
Agats, *Indonesia* **37 F9** 5 33S 138 0 E
Agawam, *U.S.A.* **79 D12** 42 5N 72 37W
Agboville, *Ivory C.* **50 G5** 5 55N 4 15W
Ağdam, *Azerbaijan* **44 B5** 40 0N 46 58 E
Agde, *France* **18 E5** 43 19N 3 28 E
Agen, *France* **18 D4** 44 12N 0 38 E
Āgh Kand, *Iran* **45 B6** 37 15N 48 4 E
Aginskoye, *Russia* **27 D12** 51 6N 114 32 E
Agnew, *Australia* **61 E3** 28 1S 120 31 E
Agori, *India* **43 G10** 24 33N 82 57 E
Agra, *India* **42 F7** 27 17N 77 58 E
Ağri, *Turkey* **25 G7** 39 44N 43 3 E
Agri →, *Italy* **20 D7** 40 13N 16 44 E
Ağrı Dağı, *Turkey* **25 G7** 39 50N 44 15 E
Ağri Karakose = Ağri, *Turkey* **25 G7** 39 44N 43 3 E
Agrigento, *Italy* **20 F5** 37 19N 13 34 E
Agrínion, *Greece* **21 E9** 38 37N 21 27 E
Agua Caliente, *Baja Calif., Mexico* **85 N10** 32 29N 116 59W
Agua Caliente, *Sinaloa, Mexico* **86 B3** 26 30N 108 20W
Agua Caliente Springs, *U.S.A.* **85 N10** 32 56N 116 19W
Água Clara, *Brazil* **93 H8** 20 25S 52 45W
Agua Hechicero, *Mexico* **85 N10** 32 26N 116 14W
Agua Prieta, *Mexico* **86 A3** 31 20N 109 32W
Aguadilla, *Puerto Rico* **89 C6** 18 26N 67 10W
Aguadulce, *Panama* **88 E3** 8 15N 80 32W
Aguanga, *U.S.A.* **85 M10** 33 27N 116 51W
Aguanish, *Canada* **71 B7** 50 14N 62 2W
Aguanus →, *Canada* **71 B7** 50 13N 62 5W
Aguapey →, *Argentina* **94 B4** 29 7S 56 36W
Aguaray Guazú →, *Paraguay* **94 A4** 24 47S 57 19W
Aguarico →, *Ecuador* **92 D3** 0 59S 75 11W
Aguas Blancas, *Chile* **94 A2** 24 15S 69 55W
Aguas Calientes, Sierra de, *Argentina* **94 B2** 25 26S 66 40W
Aguascalientes, *Mexico* **86 C4** 21 53N 102 12W
Aguascalientes □, *Mexico* **86 C4** 22 0N 102 20W
Aguilares, *Argentina* **94 B2** 27 26S 65 35W
Aguilas, *Spain* **19 D5** 37 23N 1 35W
Agüimes, *Canary Is.* **22 G4** 27 58N 15 27W
Aguja, C. de la, *Colombia* **90 B3** 11 18N 74 12W
Agulhas, C., *S. Africa* **56 E3** 34 52S 20 0 E
Agulo, *Canary Is.* **22 F2** 28 11N 17 12W
Agung, Gunung, *Indonesia* **36 F5** 8 20S 115 28 E
Agur, *Uganda* **54 B3** 2 28N 32 55 E
Agusan →, *Phil.* **37 C7** 9 0N 125 30 E
Aha Mts., *Botswana* **56 B3** 19 45S 21 0 E
Ahaggar, *Algeria* **50 D7** 23 0N 6 30 E
Ahar, *Iran* **44 B5** 38 35N 47 0 E
Ahipara B., *N.Z.* **59 F4** 35 5S 173 5 E
Ahiri, *India* **40 K12** 19 30N 80 0 E
Ahmad Wal, *Pakistan* **42 E1** 29 18N 65 58 E
Ahmadabad, *India* **42 H5** 23 0N 72 40 E
Aḥmadābād, *Khorāsān, Iran* **45 C9** 35 3N 60 50 E
Aḥmadābād, *Khorāsān, Iran* **45 C8** 35 49N 59 42 E
Aḥmadī, *Iran* **45 E8** 27 56N 56 42 E
Ahmadnagar, *India* **40 K9** 19 7N 74 46 E
Ahmadpur, *Pakistan* **42 E4** 29 12N 71 10 E
Ahmadpur Lamma, *Pakistan* **42 E4** 28 19N 70 3 E
Ahmedabad = Ahmadabad, *India* **42 H5** 23 0N 72 40 E
Ahmednagar = Ahmadnagar, *India* **40 K9** 19 7N 74 46 E
Ahome, *Mexico* **86 B3** 25 55N 109 11W
Ahoskie, *U.S.A.* **77 G7** 36 17N 76 59W
Ahram, *Iran* **45 D6** 28 52N 51 16 E
Ahrax Pt., *Malta* **23 D1** 36 0N 14 22 E
Āhū, *Iran* **45 C6** 34 33N 50 2 E
Ahuachapán, *El Salv.* **88 D2** 13 54N 89 52W
Ahvāz, *Iran* **45 D6** 31 20N 48 40 E
Ahvenanmaa = Åland, *Finland* **9 F19** 60 15N 20 0 E
Aḥwar, *Yemen* **46 E4** 13 30N 46 40 E
Ai →, *India* **43 F14** 26 26N 90 44 E
Ai-Ais, *Namibia* **56 D2** 27 54S 17 59 E
Aichi □, *Japan* **31 G8** 35 0N 137 15 E
Aigua, *Uruguay* **95 C5** 34 13S 54 46W
Aigues-Mortes, *France* **18 E6** 43 35N 4 12 E
Aihui, *China* **33 A7** 50 10N 127 30 E
Aija, *Peru* **92 E3** 9 50S 77 45W
Aikawa, *Japan* **30 E9** 38 2N 138 15 E
Aiken, *U.S.A.* **77 J5** 33 34N 81 43W
Aileron, *Australia* **62 C1** 22 39S 133 20 E
Aillik, *Canada* **71 A8** 55 11N 59 18W
Ailsa Craig, *U.K.* **12 F3** 55 15N 5 6W
'Ailūn, *Jordan* **47 C4** 32 18N 35 47 E
Aim, *Russia* **27 D14** 59 0N 133 55 E
Aimere, *Indonesia* **37 F6** 8 45S 121 3 E
Aimogasta, *Argentina* **94 B2** 28 33S 66 50W
Aïn Ben Tili, *Mauritania* **50 C4** 25 59N 9 27W
Aïn Sefra, *Algeria* **50 B5** 32 47N 0 37W
Ain Sudr, *Egypt* **47 F2** 29 50N 33 6 E
Ainaži, *Latvia* **9 H21** 57 50N 24 24 E
Ainsworth, *U.S.A.* **80 D5** 42 33N 99 52W
Aiquile, *Bolivia* **92 G5** 18 10S 65 10W
Aïr, *Niger* **50 E7** 18 30N 8 0 E
Air Force I., *Canada* **69 B12** 67 58N 74 5W
Air Hitam, *Malaysia* **39 M4** 1 55N 103 11 E
Airdrie, *Canada* **72 C6** 51 18N 114 2W
Airdrie, *U.K.* **12 F5** 55 52N 3 57W
Aire →, *U.K.* **10 D7** 53 43N 0 55W
Aire, I. de l', *Spain* **22 B11** 39 48N 4 16 E
Airlie Beach, *Australia* **62 C4** 20 16S 148 43 E
Aisne →, *France* **18 B5** 49 26N 2 50 E
Ait, *India* **43 G8** 25 54N 79 14 E
Aitkin, *U.S.A.* **80 B8** 46 32N 93 42W
Aiud, *Romania* **17 E12** 46 19N 23 44 E
Aix-en-Provence, *France* **18 E6** 43 32N 5 27 E
Aix-la-Chapelle = Aachen, *Germany* **16 C4** 50 45N 6 6 E
Aix-les-Bains, *France* **18 D6** 45 41N 5 53 E
Aiyion, *Greece* **21 E10** 38 15N 22 5 E
Aizawl, *India* **41 H18** 23 40N 92 44 E
Aizkraukle, *Latvia* **9 H21** 56 36N 25 11 E
Aizpute, *Latvia* **9 H19** 56 43N 21 40 E
Aizuwakamatsu, *Japan* **30 F9** 37 30N 139 56 E
Ajaccio, *France* **18 F8** 41 55N 8 40 E
Ajaigarh, *India* **43 G9** 24 52N 80 16 E
Ajalpan, *Mexico* **87 D5** 18 22N 97 15W
Ajanta Ra., *India* **40 J9** 20 28N 75 50 E
Ajari Rep. = Ajaria □, *Georgia* **25 F7** 41 30N 42 0 E
Ajaria □, *Georgia* **25 F7** 41 30N 42 0 E
Ajax, *Canada* **78 C5** 43 50N 79 1W
Ajdābiyā, *Libya* **51 B10** 30 54N 20 4 E
Ajka, *Hungary* **17 E9** 47 4N 17 31 E
'Ajmān, *U.A.E.* **45 E7** 25 25N 55 30 E
Ajmer, *India* **42 F6** 26 28N 74 37 E
Ajnala, *India* **42 D6** 31 50N 74 48 E
Ajo, *U.S.A.* **83 K7** 32 22N 112 52W
Ajo, C. de, *Spain* **19 A4** 43 31N 3 35W
Akabira, *Japan* **30 C11** 43 33N 142 5 E
Akamas, *Cyprus* **23 D11** 35 3N 32 18 E
Akanthou, *Cyprus* **23 D12** 35 22N 33 45 E
Akaroa, *N.Z.* **59 K4** 43 49S 172 59 E
Akashi, *Japan* **31 G7** 34 45N 134 58 E
Akbarpur, *Bihar, India* **43 G10** 24 39N 83 58 E
Akbarpur, *Ut. P., India* **43 F10** 26 25N 82 32 E
Akelamo, *Indonesia* **37 D7** 1 35N 129 40 E
Aketi, *Dem. Rep. of the Congo* **52 D4** 2 38N 23 47 E
Akharnaí, *Greece* **21 E10** 38 5N 23 44 E
Akhelóös →, *Greece* **21 E9** 38 19N 21 7 E
Akhisar, *Turkey* **21 E12** 38 56N 27 48 E
Akhnur, *India* **43 C6** 32 52N 74 45 E
Akhtyrka = Okhtyrka, *Ukraine* **25 D5** 50 25N 35 0 E
Aki, *Japan* **31 H6** 33 30N 133 54 E
Akimiski I., *Canada* **70 B3** 52 50N 81 30W
Akita, *Japan* **30 E10** 39 45N 140 7 E
Akita □, *Japan* **30 E10** 39 40N 140 30 E
Akjoujt, *Mauritania* **50 E3** 19 45N 14 15W
Akkeshi, *Japan* **30 C12** 43 2N 144 51 E
'Akko, *Israel* **47 C4** 32 55N 35 4 E
Aklavik, *Canada* **68 B6** 68 12N 135 0W
Aklera, *India* **42 G7** 24 26N 76 32 E
Akmolinsk = Astana, *Kazakstan* **26 D8** 51 10N 71 30 E
Akō, *Japan* **31 G7** 34 45N 134 24 E
Akola, *India* **40 J10** 20 42N 77 2 E
Akordat, *Eritrea* **46 D2** 15 30N 37 40 E
Akpatok I., *Canada* **69 B13** 60 25N 68 8W
Åkrahamn, *Norway* **9 G11** 59 15N 5 10 E
Akranes, *Iceland* **8 D2** 64 19N 22 5W
Akron, *Colo., U.S.A.* **80 E3** 40 10N 103 13W
Akron, *Ohio, U.S.A.* **78 E3** 41 5N 81 31W
Akrotiri, *Cyprus* **23 E11** 34 36N 32 57 E
Akrotiri Bay, *Cyprus* **23 E12** 34 35N 33 10 E
Aksai Chin, *China* **43 B8** 35 15N 79 55 E
Aksaray, *Turkey* **25 G5** 38 25N 34 2 E
Aksay, *Kazakstan* **25 D9** 51 11N 53 0 E
Akşehir, *Turkey* **44 B1** 38 18N 31 30 E
Akşehir Gölü, *Turkey* **25 G5** 38 30N 31 25 E
Aksu, *China* **32 B3** 41 5N 80 10 E
Aksum, *Ethiopia* **46 E2** 14 5N 38 40 E
Aktogay, *Kazakstan* **26 E8** 46 57N 79 40 E
Aktsyabrski, *Belarus* **17 B15** 52 38N 28 53 E
Aktyubinsk = Aqtöbe, *Kazakstan* **25 D10** 50 17N 57 10 E
Akure, *Nigeria* **50 G7** 7 15N 5 5 E
Akureyri, *Iceland* **8 D4** 65 40N 18 6W
Akuseki-Shima, *Japan* **31 K4** 29 27N 129 37 E
Akyab = Sittwe, *Burma* **41 J18** 20 18N 92 45 E
Al 'Adan, *Yemen* **46 E4** 12 45N 45 0 E
Al Aḥsā = Hasa □, *Si. Arabia* **45 E6** 25 50N 49 0 E
Al Ajfar, *Si. Arabia* **44 E4** 27 26N 43 0 E
Al Amādīyah, *Iraq* **44 B4** 37 5N 43 30 E
Al 'Amārah, *Iraq* **44 D5** 31 55N 47 15 E
Al 'Aqabah, *Jordan* **47 F4** 29 31N 35 0 E
Al Arak, *Syria* **44 C3** 34 38N 38 35 E
Al 'Aramah, *Si. Arabia* **44 E5** 25 30N 46 0 E
Al Arṭāwīyah, *Si. Arabia* **44 E5** 26 31N 45 20 E
Al 'Āṣimah = 'Ammān □, *Jordan* **47 D5** 31 40N 36 30 E
Al 'Assāfīyah, *Si. Arabia* **44 D3** 28 17N 38 59 E
Al 'Ayn, *Oman* **45 E7** 24 15N 55 45 E
Al 'Ayn, *Si. Arabia* **44 E3** 25 4N 38 6 E
Al 'Aẓamīyah, *Iraq* **44 C5** 33 22N 44 22 E
Al 'Azīzīyah, *Iraq* **44 C5** 32 54N 45 4 E
Al Bāb, *Syria* **44 B3** 36 23N 37 29 E
Al Bad', *Si. Arabia* **44 D2** 28 28N 35 1 E
Al Bādī, *Iraq* **44 C4** 35 56N 41 32 E
Al Baḥrah, *Kuwait* **44 D5** 29 40N 47 52 E
Al Baḥral Mayyit = Dead Sea, *Asia* **47 D4** 31 30N 35 30 E
Al Balqā' □, *Jordan* **47 C4** 32 5N 35 45 E
Al Bārūk, J., *Lebanon* **47 B4** 33 39N 35 40 E
Al Baṣrah, *Iraq* **44 D5** 30 30N 47 50 E
Al Baṭḥā, *Iraq* **44 D5** 31 6N 45 53 E
Al Batrūn, *Lebanon* **47 A4** 34 15N 35 40 E
Al Bayḍā, *Libya* **51 B10** 32 50N 21 44 E
Al Biqā, *Lebanon* **47 A5** 34 10N 36 10 E
Al Bi'r, *Si. Arabia* **44 D3** 28 51N 36 16 E
Al Burayj, *Syria* **47 A5** 34 15N 36 46 E
Al Faḍilī, *Si. Arabia* **45 E6** 26 58N 49 10 E
Al Fallūjah, *Iraq* **44 C4** 33 20N 43 55 E
Al Fāw, *Iraq* **45 D6** 30 0N 48 30 E
Al Fujayrah, *U.A.E.* **45 E8** 25 7N 56 18 E
Al Ghadaf, W. →, *Jordan* **47 D5** 31 26N 36 43 E
Al Ghammās, *Iraq* **44 D5** 31 45N 44 37 E

Al Ghazālah, *Si. Arabia* **44 E4** 26 48N 41 19 E
Al Ḥadīthah, *Iraq* **44 C4** 34 0N 41 13 E
Al Ḥadīthah, *Si. Arabia* **47 D6** 31 28N 37 8 E
Al Ḥaḍr, *Iraq* **44 C4** 35 35N 42 44 E
Al Hājānah, *Syria* **47 B5** 33 20N 36 33 E
Al Ḥajar al Gharbī, *Oman* **45 E8** 24 10N 56 15 E
Al Hāmad, *Si. Arabia* **44 D3** 31 30N 39 30 E
Al Hamdānīyah, *Syria* **44 C3** 35 25N 36 50 E
Al Ḥamīdīyah, *Syria* **47 A4** 34 42N 35 57 E
Al Ḥammār, *Iraq* **44 D5** 30 57N 46 51 E
Al Ḥamrā', *Si. Arabia* **44 E3** 24 2N 38 55 E
Al Ḥanākīyah, *Si. Arabia* **44 E4** 24 51N 40 31 E
Al Harīr, W. →, *Syria* **47 C4** 32 44N 35 59 E
Al Ḥasā, W. →, *Jordan* **47 D4** 31 4N 35 29 E
Al Ḥasakah, *Syria* **44 B4** 36 35N 40 45 E
Al Haydān, W. →, *Jordan* **47 D4** 31 29N 35 34 E
Al Ḥayy, *Iraq* **44 C5** 32 5N 46 5 E
Al Ḥijarah, *Asia* **44 D4** 30 0N 44 0 E
Al Ḥillah, *Iraq* **44 C5** 32 30N 44 25 E
Al Ḥillah, *Si. Arabia* **46 B4** 23 35N 46 50 E
Al Hindīyah, *Iraq* **44 C5** 32 30N 44 10 E
Al Hirmil, *Lebanon* **47 A5** 34 26N 36 24 E
Al Hoceïma, *Morocco* **50 A5** 35 8N 3 58W
Al Ḥudaydah, *Yemen* **46 E3** 14 50N 43 0 E
Al Hufūf, *Si. Arabia* **46 B4** 25 25N 49 45 E
Al Ḥumayḍah, *Si. Arabia* **44 D2** 29 14N 34 56 E
Al Ḥunayy, *Si. Arabia* **45 E6** 25 58N 48 45 E
Al Īsāwīyah, *Si. Arabia* **44 D3** 30 43N 37 59 E
Al Jafr, *Jordan* **47 E5** 30 18N 36 14 E
Al Jāfūrah, *Si. Arabia* **45 E7** 25 0N 50 15 E
Al Jaghbūb, *Libya* **51 C10** 29 42N 24 38 E
Al Jahrah, *Kuwait* **44 D5** 29 25N 47 40 E
Al Jalāmīd, *Si. Arabia* **44 D3** 31 20N 40 6 E
Al Jamalīyah, *Qatar* **45 E6** 25 37N 51 5 E
Al Janūb □, *Lebanon* **47 B4** 33 20N 35 20 E
Al Jawf, *Libya* **51 D10** 24 10N 23 24 E
Al Jawf, *Si. Arabia* **44 D3** 29 55N 39 40 E
Al Jazirah, *Iraq* **44 C5** 33 30N 44 0 E
Al Jithāmīyah, *Si. Arabia* **44 E4** 27 41N 41 43 E
Al Jubayl, *Si. Arabia* **45 E6** 27 0N 49 50 E
Al Jubaylah, *Si. Arabia* **44 E5** 24 55N 46 25 E
Al Jubb, *Si. Arabia* **44 E4** 27 11N 42 17 E
Al Junaynah, *Sudan* **51 F10** 13 27N 22 45 E
Al Kaba'ish, *Iraq* **44 D5** 30 58N 47 0 E
Al Karak, *Jordan* **47 D4** 31 11N 35 42 E
Al Karak □, *Jordan* **47 E5** 31 0N 36 0 E
Al Kāzim Tyah, *Iraq* **44 C5** 33 22N 44 12 E
Al Khābūra, *Oman* **45 F8** 23 57N 57 5 E
Al Khafji, *Si. Arabia* **45 E6** 28 24N 48 29 E
Al Khalīl, *West Bank* **47 D4** 31 32N 35 6 E
Al Khāliṣ, *Iraq* **44 C5** 33 49N 44 32 E
Al Kharsānīyah, *Si. Arabia* **45 E6** 27 13N 49 18 E
Al Khaṣab, *Oman* **45 E8** 26 14N 56 15 E
Al Khawr, *Qatar* **45 E6** 25 41N 51 30 E
Al Khiḍr, *Iraq* **44 D5** 31 12N 45 33 E
Al Khiyām, *Lebanon* **47 B4** 33 20N 35 36 E
Al Kiswah, *Syria* **47 B5** 33 23N 36 14 E
Al Kūfah, *Iraq* **44 C5** 32 2N 44 24 E
Al Kufrah, *Libya* **51 D10** 24 17N 23 15 E
Al Kuhayfiyah, *Si. Arabia* **44 E4** 27 12N 43 3 E
Al Kūt, *Iraq* **44 C5** 32 30N 46 0 E
Al Kuwayt, *Kuwait* **46 B4** 29 30N 48 0 E
Al Labwah, *Lebanon* **47 A5** 34 11N 36 20 E
Al Lādhiqīyah, *Syria* **44 C2** 35 30N 35 45 E
Al Lith, *Si. Arabia* **46 C3** 20 9N 40 15 E
Al Liwā', *Oman* **45 E8** 24 31N 56 36 E
Al Luḥayyah, *Yemen* **46 D3** 15 45N 42 40 E
Al Madīnah, *Iraq* **44 D5** 30 57N 47 16 E
Al Madīnah, *Si. Arabia* **46 C2** 24 35N 39 52 E
Al Mafraq, *Jordan* **47 C5** 32 17N 36 14 E
Al Maḥmūdīyah, *Iraq* **44 C5** 33 3N 44 21 E
Al Majma'ah, *Si. Arabia* **44 E5** 25 57N 45 22 E
Al Makhruq, W. →, *Jordan* **47 D6** 31 28N 37 0 E
Al Makḥūl, *Si. Arabia* **44 E4** 26 37N 42 39 E
Al Manāmah, *Bahrain* **46 B5** 26 10N 50 30 E
Al Maqwa', *Kuwait* **44 D5** 29 10N 47 59 E
Al Marj, *Libya* **51 B10** 32 25N 20 30 E
Al Maṭlā, *Kuwait* **44 D5** 29 24N 47 40 E
Al Mawjib, W. →, *Jordan* **47 D4** 31 28N 35 36 E
Al Mawṣil, *Iraq* **44 B4** 36 15N 43 5 E
Al Mayādin, *Syria* **44 C4** 35 1N 40 27 E
Al Mazār, *Jordan* **47 D4** 31 4N 35 41 E
Al Midhnab, *Si. Arabia* **44 E5** 25 50N 44 18 E
Al Minā', *Lebanon* **47 A4** 34 24N 35 49 E
Al Miqdādīyah, *Iraq* **44 C5** 34 0N 45 0 E
Al Mubarraz, *Si. Arabia* **45 E6** 25 30N 49 40 E
Al Mudawwarah, *Jordan* **47 F5** 29 19N 36 0 E
Al Mughayrā', *U.A.E.* **45 E7** 24 5N 53 32 E
Al Muḥarraq, *Bahrain* **45 E6** 26 15N 50 40 E
Al Mukallā, *Yemen* **46 E4** 14 33N 49 2 E
Al Mukhā, *Yemen* **46 E3** 13 18N 43 15 E
Al Musayjīd, *Si. Arabia* **44 E3** 24 5N 39 5 E
Al Musayyib, *Iraq* **44 C5** 32 49N 44 20 E
Al Muwayliḥ, *Si. Arabia* **44 E2** 27 40N 35 30 E
Al Qā'im, *Iraq* **44 C4** 34 21N 41 7 E
Al Qalībah, *Si. Arabia* **44 D3** 28 24N 37 42 E
Al Qāmishlī, *Syria* **44 B4** 37 2N 41 14 E
Al Qaryatayn, *Syria* **47 A6** 34 12N 37 13 E
Al Qaṣīm, *Si. Arabia* **44 E4** 26 0N 43 0 E
Al Qaṭ'ā, *Syria* **44 C4** 34 40N 40 48 E
Al Qaṭīf, *Si. Arabia* **45 E6** 26 35N 50 0 E
Al Qaṭrānah, *Jordan* **47 D5** 31 12N 36 6 E
Al Qaṭrūn, *Libya* **51 D9** 24 56N 15 3 E
Al Qayṣūmah, *Si. Arabia* **44 D5** 28 20N 46 7 E
Al Quds = Jerusalem, *Israel* **47 D4** 31 47N 35 10 E
Al Qunayṭirah, *Syria* **47 C4** 32 55N 35 45 E
Al Qurnah, *Iraq* **44 D5** 31 1N 47 25 E
Al Quṣayr, *Iraq* **44 D5** 30 39N 45 50 E
Al Quṣayr, *Syria* **47 A5** 34 31N 36 34 E
Al Quṭayfah, *Syria* **47 B5** 33 44N 36 36 E
Al 'Ubaylah, *Si. Arabia* **46 C5** 21 59N 50 57 E
Al 'Uḍaylīyah, *Si. Arabia* **45 E6** 25 8N 49 18 E
Al 'Ulā, *Si. Arabia* **44 E3** 26 35N 38 0 E
Al 'Uqayr, *Si. Arabia* **45 E6** 25 40N 50 15 E
Al 'Uwaynid, *Si. Arabia* **44 E5** 24 50N 46 0 E
Al 'Uwayqīlah, *Si. Arabia* **44 D4** 30 30N 42 10 E
Al 'Uyūn, *Ḥijāz, Si. Arabia* **44 E3** 24 33N 39 35 E
Al 'Uyūn, *Najd, Si. Arabia* **44 E4** 26 30N 43 50 E
Al 'Uzayr, *Iraq* **44 D5** 31 19N 47 25 E
Al Wajh, *Si. Arabia* **44 E3** 26 10N 36 30 E
Al Wakrah, *Qatar* **45 E6** 25 10N 51 40 E
Al Waqbah, *Si. Arabia* **44 D5** 28 48N 45 33 E
Al Wari'āh, *Si. Arabia* **44 E5** 27 51N 47 25 E
Ala Dağ, *Turkey* **44 B2** 37 44N 35 9 E
Ala Tau Shankou = Dzungarian Gates, *Asia* **32 B3** 45 0N 82 0 E
Alabama □, *U.S.A.* **77 J2** 33 0N 87 0W
Alabama →, *U.S.A.* **77 K2** 31 8N 87 57W
Alabaster, *U.S.A.* **77 J2** 33 15N 86 49W
Alaçam Dağları, *Turkey* **21 E13** 39 18N 28 49 E
Alachua, *U.S.A.* **77 L4** 29 47N 82 30W
Alaérma, *Greece* **23 C9** 36 9N 27 57 E
Alagoa Grande, *Brazil* **93 E11** 7 3S 35 35W
Alagoas □, *Brazil* **93 E11** 9 0S 36 0W
Alagoinhas, *Brazil* **93 F11** 12 7S 38 20W
Alaior, *Spain* **22 B11** 39 57N 4 8 E
Alajero, *Canary Is.* **22 F2** 28 3N 17 13W
Alajuela, *Costa Rica* **88 D3** 10 2N 84 8W
Alakamisy, *Madag.* **57 C8** 21 19S 47 14 E
Alaknanda →, *India* **43 D8** 30 8N 78 36 E
Alakurtti, *Russia* **24 A5** 67 0N 30 30 E
Alamarvdasht, *Iran* **45 E7** 27 37N 52 59 E
Alameda, *Calif., U.S.A.* **84 H4** 37 46N 122 15W
Alameda, *N. Mex., U.S.A.* **83 J10** 35 11N 106 37W
Alamo, *U.S.A.* **85 J11** 37 22N 115 10W
Alamo Crossing, *U.S.A.* **85 L13** 34 16N 113 33W
Alamogordo, *U.S.A.* **83 K11** 32 54N 105 57W
Alamos, *Mexico* **86 B3** 27 0N 109 0W
Alamosa, *U.S.A.* **83 H11** 37 28N 105 52W
Åland, *Finland* **9 F19** 60 15N 20 0 E
Ålands hav, *Sweden* **9 F18** 60 0N 19 30 E
Alania = North Ossetia □, *Russia* **25 F7** 43 30N 44 30 E
Alanya, *Turkey* **25 G5** 36 38N 32 0 E
Alaotra, Farihin', *Madag.* **57 B8** 17 30S 48 30 E
Alapayevsk, *Russia* **26 D7** 57 52N 61 42 E
Alappuzha = Alleppey, *India* **40 Q10** 9 30N 76 28 E
Alarobia-Vohiposa, *Madag.* **57 C8** 20 59S 47 9 E
Alaşehir, *Turkey* **21 E13** 38 23N 28 30 E
Alaska □, *U.S.A.* **68 B5** 64 0N 154 0W
Alaska, G. of, *Pac. Oc.* **68 C5** 58 0N 145 0W
Alaska Peninsula, *U.S.A.* **68 C4** 56 0N 159 0W
Alaska Range, *U.S.A.* **68 B4** 62 50N 151 0W
Älät, *Azerbaijan* **25 G8** 39 58N 49 25 E
Alatyr, *Russia* **24 D8** 54 55N 46 35 E
Alausi, *Ecuador* **92 D3** 2 0S 78 50W
Alava, C., *U.S.A.* **82 B1** 48 10N 124 44W
Alavus, *Finland* **9 E20** 62 35N 23 36 E
Alawoona, *Australia* **63 E3** 34 45S 140 30 E
'Alayh, *Lebanon* **47 B4** 33 46N 35 33 E
Alba, *Italy* **18 D8** 44 42N 8 2 E
Alba-Iulia, *Romania* **17 E12** 46 8N 23 39 E
Albacete, *Spain* **19 C5** 39 0N 1 50W
Albacutya, L., *Australia* **63 F3** 35 45S 141 58 E
Albanel, L., *Canada* **70 B5** 50 55N 73 12W
Albania ■, *Europe* **21 D9** 41 0N 20 0 E
Albany, *Australia* **61 G2** 35 1S 117 58 E
Albany, *Ga., U.S.A.* **77 K3** 31 35N 84 10W
Albany, *N.Y., U.S.A.* **79 D11** 42 39N 73 45W
Albany, *Oreg., U.S.A.* **82 D2** 44 38N 123 6W
Albany, *Tex., U.S.A.* **81 J5** 32 44N 99 18W
Albany →, *Canada* **70 B3** 52 17N 81 31W
Albardón, *Argentina* **94 C2** 31 20S 68 30W
Albatross B., *Australia* **62 A3** 12 45S 141 30 E
Albemarle, *U.S.A.* **77 H5** 35 21N 80 11W
Albemarle Sd., *U.S.A.* **77 H7** 36 5N 76 0W
Alberche →, *Spain* **19 C3** 39 58N 4 46W
Alberdi, *Paraguay* **94 B4** 26 14S 58 20W
Albert, L., *Africa* **54 B3** 1 30N 31 0 E
Albert, L., *Australia* **63 F2** 35 30S 139 10 E
Albert Edward Ra., *Australia* **60 C4** 18 17S 127 57 E
Albert Lea, *U.S.A.* **80 D8** 43 39N 93 22W
Albert Nile →, *Uganda* **54 B3** 3 36N 32 2 E
Albert Town, *Bahamas* **89 B5** 22 37N 74 33W
Alberta □, *Canada* **72 C6** 54 40N 115 0W
Alberti, *Argentina* **94 D3** 35 1S 60 16W
Albertinia, *S. Africa* **56 E3** 34 11S 21 34 E
Alberton, *Canada* **71 C7** 46 50N 64 0W
Albertville = Kalemie, *Dem. Rep. of the Congo* **54 D2** 5 55S 29 9 E
Albertville, *France* **18 D7** 45 40N 6 22 E
Albertville, *U.S.A.* **77 H2** 34 16N 86 13W
Albi, *France* **18 E5** 43 56N 2 9 E
Albia, *U.S.A.* **80 E8** 41 2N 92 48W
Albina, *Surinam* **93 B8** 5 37N 54 15W
Albina, Ponta, *Angola* **56 B1** 15 52S 11 44 E
Albion, *Mich., U.S.A.* **76 D3** 42 15N 84 45W
Albion, *Nebr., U.S.A.* **80 E6** 41 42N 98 0W
Albion, *Pa., U.S.A.* **78 E4** 41 53N 80 22W
Alborán, *Medit. S.* **19 E4** 35 57N 3 0W
Ålborg, *Denmark* **9 H13** 57 2N 9 54 E
Alborz, Reshteh-ye Kūhhā-ye, *Iran* **45 C7** 36 0N 52 0 E
Albuquerque, *U.S.A.* **83 J10** 35 5N 106 39W
Albuquerque, Cayos de, *Caribbean* **88 D3** 12 10N 81 50W
Alburg, *U.S.A.* **79 B11** 44 59N 73 18W
Albury = Albury-Wodonga, *Australia* **63 F4** 36 3S 146 56 E
Albury-Wodonga, *Australia* **63 F4** 36 3S 146 56 E
Alcalá de Henares, *Spain* **19 B4** 40 28N 3 22W
Alcalá la Real, *Spain* **19 D4** 37 27N 3 57W
Álcamo, *Italy* **20 F5** 37 59N 12 55 E
Alcaníz, *Spain* **19 B5** 41 2N 0 8W
Alcântara, *Brazil* **93 D10** 2 20S 44 30W
Alcántara, Embalse de, *Spain* **19 C2** 39 44N 6 50W
Alcantarilla, *Spain* **19 D5** 37 59N 1 12W
Alcaraz, Sierra de, *Spain* **19 C4** 38 40N 2 20W
Alcaudete, *Spain* **19 D3** 37 35N 4 5W
Alcázar de San Juan, *Spain* **19 C4** 39 24N 3 12W
Alchevsk, *Ukraine* **25 E6** 48 30N 38 45 E
Alcira = Alzira, *Spain* **19 C5** 39 9N 0 30W
Alcova, *U.S.A.* **82 E10** 42 34N 106 43W
Alcoy, *Spain* **19 C5** 38 43N 0 30W
Alcúdia, *Spain* **22 B10** 39 51N 3 7 E
Alcúdia, B. d', *Spain* **22 B10** 39 47N 3 15 E
Aldabra Is., *Seychelles* **49 G8** 9 22S 46 28 E
Aldama, *Mexico* **87 C5** 23 0N 98 4W
Aldan, *Russia* **27 D13** 58 40N 125 30 E
Aldan →, *Russia* **27 C13** 63 28N 129 35 E
Aldea, Pta. de la, *Canary Is.* **22 G4** 28 0N 15 50W
Aldeburgh, *U.K.* **11 E9** 52 10N 1 37 E
Alder Pk., *U.S.A.* **84 K5** 35 53N 121 22W
Alderney, *U.K.* **11 H5** 49 42N 2 11W
Aldershot, *U.K.* **11 F7** 51 15N 0 44W
Aledo, *U.S.A.* **80 E9** 41 12N 90 45W
Aleg, *Mauritania* **50 E3** 17 3N 13 55W
Alegranza, *Canary Is.* **22 E6** 29 23N 13 32W
Alegranza, I., *Canary Is.* **22 E6** 29 23N 13 32W
Alegre, *Brazil* **95 A7** 20 50S 41 30W
Alegrete, *Brazil* **95 B4** 29 40S 56 0W
Aleisk, *Russia* **26 D9** 52 40N 83 0 E
Aleksandriya = Oleksandriya, *Ukraine* **17 C14** 50 37N 26 19 E
Aleksandrov Gay, *Russia* **25 D8** 50 9N 48 34 E
Aleksandrovsk-Sakhalinskiy, *Russia* **27 D15** 50 50N 142 20 E
Além Paraíba, *Brazil* **95 A7** 21 52S 42 41W
Alemania, *Argentina* **94 B2** 25 40S 65 30W
Alemania, *Chile* **94 B2** 25 10S 69 55W
Alençon, *France* **18 B4** 48 27N 0 4 E
Alenquer, *Brazil* **93 D8** 1 56S 54 46W
Alenuihaha Channel, *U.S.A.* **74 H17** 20 30N 156 0W
Aleppo = Ḥalab, *Syria* **44 B3** 36 10N 37 15 E
Alès, *France* **18 D6** 44 9N 4 5 E
Alessándria, *Italy* **18 D8** 44 54N 8 37 E
Ålesund, *Norway* **9 E12** 62 28N 6 12 E
Aleutian Is., *Pac. Oc.* **68 C2** 52 0N 175 0W
Aleutian Trench, *Pac. Oc.* **64 C10** 48 0N 180 0 E
Alexander, *U.S.A.* **80 B3** 47 51N 103 39W
Alexander, Mt., *Australia* **61 E3** 28 58S 120 16 E
Alexander Arch., *U.S.A.* **68 C6** 56 0N 136 0W
Alexander Bay, *S. Africa* **56 D2** 28 40S 16 30 E
Alexander City, *U.S.A.* **77 J3** 32 56N 85 58W
Alexander I., *Antarctica* **5 C17** 69 0S 70 0W
Alexandra, *Australia* **63 F4** 37 8S 145 40 E
Alexandra, *N.Z.* **59 L2** 45 14S 169 25 E
Alexandra Falls, *Canada* **72 A5** 60 29N 116 18W
Alexandria = El Iskandarîya, *Egypt* **51 B11** 31 13N 29 58 E
Alexandria, *B.C., Canada* **72 C4** 52 35N 122 27W
Alexandria, *Ont., Canada* **79 A10** 45 19N 74 38W
Alexandria, *Romania* **17 G13** 43 57N 25 24 E
Alexandria, *S. Africa* **56 E4** 33 38S 26 28 E
Alexandria, *U.K.* **12 F4** 55 59N 4 35W
Alexandria, *La., U.S.A.* **81 K8** 31 18N 92 27W
Alexandria, *Minn., U.S.A.* **80 C7** 45 53N 95 22W
Alexandria, *S. Dak., U.S.A.* **80 D6** 43 39N 97 47W
Alexandria, *Va., U.S.A.* **76 F7** 38 48N 77 3W
Alexandria Bay, *U.S.A.* **79 B9** 44 20N 75 55W
Alexandrina, L., *Australia* **63 F2** 35 25S 139 10 E
Alexandroúpolis, *Greece* **21 D11** 40 50N 25 54 E
Alexis →, *Canada* **71 B8** 52 33N 56 8W
Alexis Creek, *Canada* **72 C4** 52 10N 123 20W
Alfabia, *Spain* **22 B9** 39 44N 2 44 E
Alfenas, *Brazil* **95 A6** 21 20S 46 10W
Alford, *Aberds., U.K.* **12 D6** 57 14N 2 41W
Alford, *Lincs., U.K.* **10 D8** 53 15N 0 10 E
Alfred, *Maine, U.S.A.* **79 C14** 43 29N 70 43W
Alfred, *N.Y., U.S.A.* **78 D7** 42 16N 77 48W
Alfreton, *U.K.* **10 D6** 53 6N 1 24W
Alga, *Kazakstan* **25 E10** 49 53N 57 20 E
Algaida, *Spain* **22 B9** 39 33N 2 53 E
Ålgård, *Norway* **9 G11** 58 46N 5 53 E
Algarve, *Portugal* **19 D1** 36 58N 8 20W
Algeciras, *Spain* **19 D3** 36 9N 5 28W
Algemesí, *Spain* **19 C5** 39 11N 0 27W
Alger, *Algeria* **50 A6** 36 42N 3 8 E
Algeria ■, *Africa* **50 C6** 28 30N 2 0 E
Alghero, *Italy* **20 D3** 40 33N 8 19 E
Algiers = Alger, *Algeria* **50 A6** 36 42N 3 8 E
Algoa B., *S. Africa* **56 E4** 33 50S 25 45 E
Algoma, *U.S.A.* **76 C2** 44 36N 87 26W
Algona, *U.S.A.* **80 D7** 43 4N 94 14W
Algonac, *U.S.A.* **78 D2** 42 37N 82 32W
Algonquin Prov. Park, *Canada* **70 C4** 45 50N 78 30W
Algorta, *Uruguay* **96 C5** 32 25S 57 23W
Alhambra, *U.S.A.* **85 L8** 34 8N 118 6W
Alhucemas = Al Hoceïma, *Morocco* **50 A5** 35 8N 3 58W
'Alī al Gharbī, *Iraq* **44 C5** 32 30N 46 45 E
'Alī ash Sharqī, *Iraq* **44 C5** 32 7N 46 44 E
'Alī Khēl, *Afghan.* **42 C3** 33 57N 69 43 E
Alī Shāh, *Iran* **44 B5** 38 9N 45 50 E
'Alīābād, *Khorāsān, Iran* **45 C8** 32 30N 57 30 E
'Alīābād, *Kordestān, Iran* **44 C5** 35 4N 46 58 E
'Alīābād, *Yazd, Iran* **45 D7** 31 41N 53 49 E
Aliağa, *Turkey* **21 E12** 38 47N 26 59 E
Aliákmon →, *Greece* **21 D10** 40 30N 22 36 E
Alicante, *Spain* **19 C5** 38 23N 0 30W
Alice, *S. Africa* **56 E4** 32 48S 26 55 E
Alice, *U.S.A.* **81 M5** 27 45N 98 5W
Alice →, *Queens., Australia* **62 C3** 24 2S 144 50 E
Alice →, *Queens., Australia* **62 B3** 15 35S 142 20 E
Alice Arm, *Canada* **72 B3** 55 29N 129 31W
Alice Springs, *Australia* **62 C1** 23 40S 133 50 E
Alicedale, *S. Africa* **56 E4** 33 15S 26 4 E
Aliceville, *U.S.A.* **77 J1** 33 8N 88 9W
Aliganj, *India* **43 F8** 27 30N 79 10 E
Aligarh, *Raj., India* **42 G7** 25 55N 76 15 E
Aligarh, *Ut. P., India* **42 F8** 27 55N 78 10 E
Alīgūdarz, *Iran* **45 C6** 33 25N 49 45 E
Alimnía, *Greece* **23 C9** 36 16N 27 43 E
Alingsås, *Sweden* **9 H15** 57 56N 12 31 E
Alipur, *Pakistan* **42 E4** 29 25N 70 55 E
Alipur Duar, *India* **41 F16** 26 30N 89 35 E
Aliquippa, *U.S.A.* **78 F4** 40 37N 80 15W
Alitus = Alytus, *Lithuania* **9 J21** 54 24N 24 3 E
Aliwal North, *S. Africa* **56 E4** 30 45S 26 45 E
Alix, *Canada* **72 C6** 52 24N 113 11W
Aljustrel, *Portugal* **19 D1** 37 55N 8 10W
Alkmaar, *Neths.* **15 B4** 52 37N 4 45 E
All American Canal, *U.S.A.* **83 K6** 32 45N 115 15W
Allagash →, *U.S.A.* **77 B11** 47 5N 69 3W
Allah Dad, *Pakistan* **42 G2** 25 38N 67 34 E
Allahabad, *India* **43 G9** 25 25N 81 58 E
Allan, *Canada* **73 C7** 51 53N 106 4W
Allanridge, *S. Africa* **56 D4** 27 45S 26 40 E
Allegany, *U.S.A.* **78 D6** 42 6N 78 30W
Allegheny →, *U.S.A.* **78 F5** 40 27N 80 1W
Allegheny Mts., *U.S.A.* **76 G6** 38 15N 80 10W
Allegheny Reservoir, *U.S.A.* **78 E6** 41 50N 79 0W
Allen, Bog of, *Ireland* **13 C5** 53 15N 7 0W
Allen, L., *Ireland* **13 B3** 54 8N 8 4W
Allendale, *U.S.A.* **77 J5** 33 1N 81 18W
Allende, *Mexico* **86 B4** 28 20N 100 50W
Allentown, *U.S.A.* **79 F9** 40 37N 75 29W
Alleppey, *India* **40 Q10** 9 30N 76 28 E
Aller →, *Germany* **16 B5** 52 56N 9 12 E
Alliance, *Nebr., U.S.A.* **80 D3** 42 6N 102 52W
Alliance, *Ohio, U.S.A.* **78 F3** 40 55N 81 6W
Allier →, *France* **18 C5** 46 57N 3 4 E
Alliford Bay, *Canada* **72 C2** 53 12N 131 58W
Alliston, *Canada* **78 B5** 44 9N 79 52W
Alloa, *U.K.* **12 E5** 56 7N 3 47W
Allora, *Australia* **63 D5** 28 2S 152 0 E
Alluitsup Paa, *Greenland* **4 C5** 60 30N 45 35W
Alma, *Canada* **71 C5** 48 35N 71 40W
Alma, *Ga., U.S.A.* **77 K4** 31 33N 82 28W
Alma, *Kans., U.S.A.* **80 F6** 39 1N 96 17W
Alma, *Mich., U.S.A.* **76 D3** 43 23N 84 39W
Alma, *Nebr., U.S.A.* **80 E5** 40 6N 99 22W
Alma Ata = Almaty, *Kazakstan* **26 E8** 43 15N 76 57 E
Almada, *Portugal* **19 C1** 38 40N 9 9W
Almaden, *Australia* **62 B3** 17 22S 144 40 E
Almadén, *Spain* **19 C3** 38 49N 4 52W
Almanor, L., *U.S.A.* **82 F3** 40 14N 121 9W
Almansa, *Spain* **19 C5** 38 51N 1 5W
Almanzor, Pico, *Spain* **19 B3** 40 15N 5 18W
Almanzora →, *Spain* **19 D5** 37 14N 1 46W
Almaty, *Kazakstan* **26 E8** 43 15N 76 57 E
Almazán, *Spain* **19 B4** 41 30N 2 30W
Almeirim, *Brazil* **93 D8** 1 30S 52 34W
Almelo, *Neths.* **15 B6** 52 22N 6 42 E
Almendralejo, *Spain* **19 C2** 38 41N 6 26W
Almere-Stad, *Neths.* **15 B5** 52 20N 5 15 E
Almería, *Spain* **19 D4** 36 52N 2 27W
Almirante, *Panama* **88 E3** 9 10N 82 30W
Almiroú, Kólpos, *Greece* **23 D6** 35 23N 24 20 E
Almond, *U.S.A.* **78 D7** 42 19N 77 44W
Almont, *U.S.A.* **78 D1** 42 55N 83 3W
Almonte, *Canada* **79 A8** 45 14N 76 12W
Almora, *India* **43 E8** 29 38N 79 40 E
Alness, *U.K.* **12 D4** 57 41N 4 16W
Alnmouth, *U.K.* **10 B6** 55 24N 1 37W
Alnwick, *U.K.* **10 B6** 55 24N 1 42W
Aloi, *Uganda* **54 B3** 2 16N 33 10 E
Alon, *Burma* **41 H19** 22 12N 95 5 E
Alor, *Indonesia* **37 F6** 8 15S 124 30 E
Alor Setar, *Malaysia* **39 J3** 6 7N 100 22 E
Alot, *India* **42 H6** 23 56N 75 40 E
Aloysius, Mt., *Australia* **61 E4** 26 0S 128 38 E
Alpaugh, *U.S.A.* **84 K7** 35 53N 119 29W
Alpena, *U.S.A.* **76 C4** 45 4N 83 27W
Alpha, *Australia* **62 C4** 23 39S 146 37 E
Alphen aan den Rijn, *Neths.* **15 B4** 52 7N 4 40 E
Alpine, *Ariz., U.S.A.* **83 K9** 33 51N 109 9W
Alpine, *Calif., U.S.A.* **85 N10** 32 50N 116 46W
Alpine, *Tex., U.S.A.* **81 K3** 30 22N 103 40W
Alps, *Europe* **18 C8** 46 30N 9 30 E
Alsace, *France* **18 B7** 48 15N 7 25 E
Alsask, *Canada* **73 C7** 51 21N 109 59W
Alsasua, *Spain* **19 A4** 42 54N 2 10W
Alsek →, *U.S.A.* **72 B1** 59 10N 138 12W
Alsten, *Norway* **8 D15** 65 58N 12 40 E
Alston, *U.K.* **10 C5** 54 49N 2 25W
Alta, *Norway* **8 B20** 69 57N 23 10 E
Alta Gracia, *Argentina* **94 C3** 31 40S 64 30W
Alta Sierra, *U.S.A.* **85 K8** 35 42N 118 33W
Altaelva →, *Norway* **8 B20** 69 54N 23 17 E
Altafjorden, *Norway* **8 A20** 70 5N 23 5 E
Altai = Aerhtai Shan, *Mongolia* **32 B4** 46 40N 92 45 E
Altamaha →, *U.S.A.* **77 K5** 31 20N 81 20W
Altamira, *Brazil* **93 D8** 3 12S 52 10W
Altamira, *Chile* **94 B2** 25 47S 69 51W
Altamira, *Mexico* **87 C5** 22 24N 97 55W
Altamont, *U.S.A.* **79 D10** 42 43N 74 3W
Altamura, *Italy* **20 D7** 40 49N 16 33 E
Altanbulag, *Mongolia* **32 A5** 50 16N 106 30 E
Altar, *Mexico* **86 A2** 30 40N 111 50W
Altar, Desierto de, *Mexico* **86 B2** 30 10N 112 0W
Altata, *Mexico* **86 C3** 24 30N 108 0W
Altavista, *U.S.A.* **76 G6** 37 6N 79 17W
Altay, *China* **32 B3** 47 48N 88 10 E
Altea, *Spain* **19 C5** 38 38N 0 2W
Altiplano = Bolivian Plateau, *S. Amer.* **90 E4** 20 0S 67 30W
Alto Araguaia, *Brazil* **93 G8** 17 15S 53 20W
Alto Cuchumatanes = Cuchumatanes, Sierra de los, *Guatemala* **88 C1** 15 35N 91 25W
Alto del Carmen, *Chile* **94 B1** 28 46S 70 30W
Alto del Inca, *Chile* **94 A2** 24 10S 68 10W
Alto Ligonha, *Mozam.* **55 F4** 15 30S 38 11 E
Alto Molocue, *Mozam.* **55 F4** 15 50S 37 35 E
Alto Paraguay □, *Paraguay* **94 A4** 21 0S 58 30W
Alto Paraná □, *Paraguay* **95 B5** 25 30S 54 50W
Alton, *Canada* **78 C4** 43 54N 80 5W
Alton, *U.K.* **11 F7** 51 9N 0 59W
Alton, *Ill., U.S.A.* **80 F9** 38 53N 90 11W
Alton, *N.H., U.S.A.* **79 C13** 43 27N 71 13W
Altoona, *U.S.A.* **78 F6** 40 31N 78 24W
Altūn Kūprī, *Iraq* **44 C5** 35 45N 44 9 E
Altun Shan, *China* **32 C3** 38 30N 88 0 E
Alturas, *U.S.A.* **82 F3** 41 29N 120 32W
Altus, *U.S.A.* **81 H5** 34 38N 99 20W
Alucra, *Turkey* **25 F6** 40 22N 38 47 E
Alūksne, *Latvia* **9 H22** 57 24N 27 3 E
Alunite, *U.S.A.* **85 K12** 35 59N 114 55W
Alusi, *Indonesia* **37 F8** 7 35S 131 40 E
Alva, *U.S.A.* **81 G5** 36 48N 98 40W
Alvarado, *Mexico* **87 D5** 18 40N 95 50W
Alvarado, *U.S.A.* **81 J6** 32 24N 97 13W
Alvaro Obregón, Presa, *Mexico* **86 B3** 27 55N 109 52W
Alvear, *Argentina* **94 B4** 29 5S 56 30W
Alvesta, *Sweden* **9 H16** 56 54N 14 35 E
Alvin, *U.S.A.* **81 L7** 29 26N 95 15W
Alvinston, *Canada* **78 D3** 42 49N 81 52W
Älvkarleby, *Sweden* **9 F17** 60 34N 17 26 E
Alvord Desert, *U.S.A.* **82 E4** 42 30N 118 25W
Älvsbyn, *Sweden* **8 D19** 65 40N 21 0 E
Alwar, *India* **42 F7** 27 38N 76 34 E
Alxa Zuoqi, *China* **34 E3** 38 50N 105 40 E
Alyangula, *Australia* **62 A2** 13 55S 136 30 E
Alyata = Älät, *Azerbaijan* **25 G8** 39 58N 49 25 E
Alyth, *U.K.* **12 E5** 56 38N 3 13W
Alytus, *Lithuania* **9 J21** 54 24N 24 3 E
Alzada, *U.S.A.* **80 C2** 45 2N 104 25W
Alzira, *Spain* **19 C5** 39 9N 0 30W
Am Timan, *Chad* **51 F10** 11 0N 20 10 E
Amadeus, L., *Australia* **61 D5** 24 54S 131 0 E
Amadi, *Dem. Rep. of the Congo* **54 B2** 3 40N 26 40 E
Amâdi, *Sudan* **51 G12** 5 29N 30 25 E
Amadjuak L., *Canada* **69 B12** 65 0N 71 8W
Amagansett, *U.S.A.* **79 F12** 40 59N 72 9W
Amagasaki, *Japan* **31 G7** 34 42N 135 20 E
Amahai, *Indonesia* **37 E7** 3 20S 128 55 E
Amakusa-Shotō, *Japan* **31 H5** 32 15N 130 10 E

Åmål, *Sweden* **9 G15** 59 3N 12 42 E
Amaliás, *Greece* **21 F9** 37 47N 21 22 E
Amalner, *India* **40 J9** 21 5N 75 5 E
Amamapare, *Indonesia* **37 E9** 4 53S 136 38 E
Amambai, *Brazil* **95 A4** 23 5S 55 13W
Amambai →, *Brazil* **95 A5** 23 22S 53 56W
Amambay □, *Paraguay* **95 A4** 23 0S 56 0W
Amambay, Cordillera de, *S. Amer.* **95 A4** 23 0S 55 45W
Amami-Guntō, *Japan* **31 L4** 27 16N 129 21 E
Amami-Ō-Shima, *Japan* **31 L4** 28 0N 129 0 E
Amanã, L., *Brazil* **92 D6** 2 35S 64 40W
Amanat →, *India* **43 G11** 24 7N 84 4 E
Amanda Park, *U.S.A.* **84 C3** 47 28N 123 55W
Amangeldy, *Kazakstan* **26 D7** 50 10N 65 10 E
Amapá, *Brazil* **93 C8** 2 5N 50 50W
Amapá □, *Brazil* **93 C8** 1 40N 52 0W
Amarante, *Brazil* **93 E10** 6 14S 42 50W
Amaranth, *Canada* **73 C9** 50 36N 98 43W
Amargosa →, *U.S.A.* **85 J10** 36 14N 116 51W
Amargosa Range, *U.S.A.* **85 J10** 36 20N 116 45W
Amári, *Greece* **23 D6** 35 13N 24 40 E
Amarillo, *U.S.A.* **81 H4** 35 13N 101 50W
Amarkantak, *India* **43 H9** 22 40N 81 45 E
Amaro, Mte., *Italy* **20 C6** 42 5N 14 5 E
Amarpur, *India* **43 G12** 25 5N 87 0 E
Amarwara, *India* **43 H8** 22 18N 79 10 E
Amasya □, *Turkey* **25 F6** 40 40N 35 50 E
Amata, *Australia* **61 E5** 26 9S 131 9 E
Amatikulu, *S. Africa* **57 D5** 29 3S 31 33 E
Amatitlán, *Guatemala* **88 D1** 14 29N 90 38W
Amay, *Belgium* **15 D5** 50 33N 5 19 E
Amazon = Amazonas →, *S. Amer.* **93 D9** 0 5S 50 0W
Amazonas □, *Brazil* **92 E6** 5 0S 65 0W
Amazonas →, *S. Amer.* **93 D9** 0 5S 50 0W
Ambah, *India* **42 F8** 26 43N 78 13 E
Ambahakily, *Madag.* **57 C7** 21 36S 43 41 E
Ambahita, *Madag.* **57 C8** 24 1S 45 16 E
Ambala, *India* **42 D7** 30 23N 76 56 E
Ambalavao, *Madag.* **57 C8** 21 50S 46 56 E
Ambanja, *Madag.* **57 A8** 13 40S 48 27 E
Ambararata, *Madag.* **57 B8** 15 3S 48 33 E
Ambarchik, *Russia* **27 C17** 69 40N 162 20 E
Ambarijeby, *Madag.* **57 A8** 14 56S 47 41 E
Ambaro, Helodranon', *Madag.* **57 A8** 13 23S 48 38 E
Ambato, *Ecuador* **92 D3** 1 5S 78 42W
Ambato, *Madag.* **57 A8** 13 24S 48 29 E
Ambato, Sierra de, *Argentina* **94 B2** 28 25S 66 10W
Ambato Boeny, *Madag.* **57 B8** 16 28S 46 43 E
Ambatofinandrahana, *Madag.* **57 C8** 20 33S 46 48 E
Ambatolampy, *Madag.* **57 B8** 19 20S 47 35 E
Ambatomainty, *Madag.* **57 B8** 17 41S 45 40 E
Ambatomanoina, *Madag.* **57 B8** 18 18S 47 37 E
Ambatondrazaka, *Madag.* **57 B8** 17 55S 48 28 E
Ambatosoratra, *Madag.* **57 B8** 17 37S 48 31 E
Ambenja, *Madag.* **57 B8** 15 17S 46 58 E
Amberg, *Germany* **16 D6** 49 26N 11 52 E
Ambergris Cay, *Belize* **87 D7** 18 0N 88 0W
Amberley, *N.Z.* **59 K4** 43 9S 172 44 E
Ambikapur, *India* **43 H10** 23 15N 83 15 E
Ambilobé, *Madag.* **57 A8** 13 10S 49 3 E
Ambinanindrano, *Madag.* **57 C8** 20 5S 48 23 E
Ambinanitelo, *Madag.* **57 B8** 15 21S 49 35 E
Ambinda, *Madag.* **57 B8** 16 25S 45 52 E
Amble, *U.K.* **10 B6** 55 20N 1 36W
Ambleside, *U.K.* **10 C5** 54 26N 2 58W
Ambo, *Peru* **92 F3** 10 5S 76 10W
Amboahangy, *Madag.* **57 C8** 24 15S 46 22 E
Ambodifototra, *Madag.* **57 B8** 16 59S 49 52 E
Ambodilazana, *Madag.* **57 B8** 18 6S 49 10 E
Ambodiriana, *Madag.* **57 B8** 17 55S 49 18 E
Ambohidratrimo, *Madag.* **57 B8** 18 50S 47 26 E
Ambohidray, *Madag.* **57 B8** 18 36S 48 18 E
Ambohimahamasina, *Madag.* **57 C8** 21 56S 47 11 E
Ambohimahasoa, *Madag.* **57 C8** 21 7S 47 13 E
Ambohimanga, *Madag.* **57 C8** 20 52S 47 36 E
Ambohimitombo, *Madag.* **57 C8** 20 43S 47 26 E
Ambohitra, *Madag.* **57 A8** 12 30S 49 10 E
Amboise, *France* **18 C4** 47 24N 1 2 E
Ambon, *Indonesia* **37 E7** 3 43S 128 12 E
Ambondro, *Madag.* **57 D8** 25 13S 45 44 E
Amboseli, L., *Kenya* **54 C4** 2 40S 37 10 E
Ambositra, *Madag.* **57 C8** 20 31S 47 25 E
Ambovombe, *Madag.* **57 D8** 25 11S 46 5 E
Amboy, *U.S.A.* **85 L11** 34 33N 115 45W
Amboyna Cay, *S. China Sea* **36 C4** 7 50N 112 50 E
Ambridge, *U.S.A.* **78 F4** 40 36N 80 14W
Ambriz, *Angola* **52 F2** 7 48S 13 8 E
Amchitka I., *U.S.A.* **68 C1** 51 32N 179 0 E
Amderma, *Russia* **26 C7** 69 45N 61 30 E
Amdhi, *India* **43 H9** 23 51N 81 27 E
Ameca, *Mexico* **86 C4** 20 30N 104 0W
Ameca →, *Mexico* **86 C3** 20 40N 105 15W
Amecameca, *Mexico* **87 D5** 19 7N 98 46W
Ameland, *Neths.* **15 A5** 53 27N 5 45 E
Amenia, *U.S.A.* **79 E11** 41 51N 73 33W
American Falls, *U.S.A.* **82 E7** 42 47N 112 51W
American Falls Reservoir, *U.S.A.* **82 E7** 42 47N 112 52W
American Fork, *U.S.A.* **82 F8** 40 23N 111 48W
American Highland, *Antarctica* **5 D6** 73 0S 75 0 E
American Samoa ■, *Pac. Oc.* **59 B13** 14 20S 170 40W
Americana, *Brazil* **95 A6** 22 45S 47 20W
Americus, *U.S.A.* **77 K3** 32 4N 84 14W
Amersfoort, *Neths.* **15 B5** 52 9N 5 23 E
Amersfoort, *S. Africa* **57 D4** 26 59S 29 53 E
Amery Ice Shelf, *Antarctica* **5 C6** 69 30S 72 0 E
Ames, *U.S.A.* **80 E8** 42 2N 93 37W
Amesbury, *U.S.A.* **79 D14** 42 51N 70 56W
Amet, *India* **42 G5** 25 18N 73 56 E
Amga, *Russia* **27 C14** 60 50N 132 0 E
Amga →, *Russia* **27 C14** 62 38N 134 32 E
Amgu, *Russia* **27 E14** 45 45N 137 15 E
Amgun →, *Russia* **27 D14** 52 56N 139 38 E
Amherst, *Canada* **71 C7** 45 48N 64 8W
Amherst, *Mass., U.S.A.* **79 D12** 42 23N 72 31W
Amherst, *N.Y., U.S.A.* **78 D6** 42 59N 78 48W
Amherst, *Ohio, U.S.A.* **78 E2** 41 24N 82 14W
Amherst I., *Canada* **79 B8** 44 8N 76 43W
Amherstburg, *Canada* **70 D3** 42 6N 83 6W
Amiata, Mte., *Italy* **20 C4** 42 53N 11 37 E
Amidon, *U.S.A.* **80 B3** 46 29N 103 19W
Amiens, *France* **18 B5** 49 54N 2 16 E
Aminuis, *Namibia* **56 C2** 23 43S 19 21 E
Amīrābād, *Iran* **44 C5** 33 20N 46 16 E
Amirante Is., *Seychelles* **28 K9** 6 0S 53 0 E
Amisk L., *Canada* **73 C8** 54 35N 102 15W
Amistad, Presa de la, *Mexico* **86 B4** 29 24N 101 0W
Amite, *U.S.A.* **81 K9** 30 44N 90 30W
Amla, *India* **42 J8** 21 56N 78 7 E
Amlia I., *U.S.A.* **68 C2** 52 4N 173 30W
Amlwch, *U.K.* **10 D3** 53 24N 4 20W
'Ammān, *Jordan* **47 D4** 31 57N 35 52 E
'Ammān □, *Jordan* **47 D5** 31 40N 36 30 E
Ammanford, *U.K.* **11 F4** 51 48N 3 59W
Ammassalik = Tasiilaq, *Greenland* **4 C6** 65 40N 37 20W
Ammochostos = Famagusta, *Cyprus* **23 D12** 35 8N 33 55 E
Ammon, *U.S.A.* **82 E8** 43 28N 111 58W
Amnat Charoen, *Thailand* **38 E5** 15 51N 104 38 E
Amnura, *Bangla.* **43 G13** 24 37N 88 25 E
Āmol, *Iran* **45 B7** 36 23N 52 20 E
Amorgós, *Greece* **21 F11** 36 50N 25 57 E
Amory, *U.S.A.* **77 J1** 33 59N 88 29W
Amos, *Canada* **70 C4** 48 35N 78 5W
Åmot, *Norway* **9 G13** 59 57N 9 54 E
Amoy = Xiamen, *China* **33 D6** 24 25N 118 4 E
Ampanavoana, *Madag.* **57 B9** 15 41S 50 22 E
Ampang, *Malaysia* **39 L3** 3 8N 101 45 E
Ampangalana, Lakandranon', *Madag.* **57 C8** 22 48S 47 50 E
Ampanihy, *Madag.* **57 C7** 24 40S 44 45 E
Amparafaravola, *Madag.* **57 B8** 17 35S 48 13 E
Ampasinambo, *Madag.* **57 C8** 20 31S 48 0 E
Ampasindava, Helodranon', *Madag.* **57 A8** 13 40S 48 15 E
Ampasindava, Saikanosy, *Madag.* **57 A8** 13 42S 47 55 E
Ampenan, *Indonesia* **36 F5** 8 34S 116 4 E
Amper →, *Germany* **16 D6** 48 29N 11 55 E
Ampitsikinana, *Réunion* **57 A8** 12 57S 49 49 E
Ampombiantambo, *Madag.* **57 A8** 12 42S 48 57 E
Ampotaka, *Madag.* **57 D7** 25 3S 44 41 E
Ampoza, *Madag.* **57 C7** 22 20S 44 44 E
Amqui, *Canada* **71 C6** 48 28N 67 27W
Amravati, *India* **40 J10** 20 55N 77 45 E
Amreli, *India* **42 J4** 21 35N 71 17 E
Amritsar, *India* **42 D6** 31 35N 74 57 E
Amroha, *India* **43 E8** 28 53N 78 30 E
Amsterdam, *Neths.* **15 B4** 52 23N 4 54 E
Amsterdam, *U.S.A.* **79 D10** 42 56N 74 11W
Amsterdam, I. = Nouvelle-Amsterdam, I., *Ind. Oc.* **3 F13** 38 30S 77 30 E
Amstetten, *Austria* **16 D8** 48 7N 14 51 E
Amudarya →, *Uzbekistan* **26 E6** 43 58N 59 34 E
Amundsen Gulf, *Canada* **68 A7** 71 0N 124 0W
Amundsen Sea, *Antarctica* **5 D15** 72 0S 115 0W
Amuntai, *Indonesia* **36 E5** 2 28S 115 25 E
Amur →, *Russia* **27 D15** 52 56N 141 10 E
Amurang, *Indonesia* **37 D6** 1 5N 124 40 E
Amursk, *Russia* **27 D14** 50 14N 136 54 E
Amyderya = Amudarya →, *Uzbekistan* **26 E6** 43 58N 59 34 E
An Bien, *Vietnam* **39 H5** 9 45N 105 0 E
An Hoa, *Vietnam* **38 E7** 15 40N 108 5 E
An Nabatīyah at Tahta, *Lebanon* **47 B4** 33 23N 35 27 E
An Nabk, *Si. Arabia* **44 D3** 31 20N 37 20 E
An Nabk, *Syria* **47 A5** 34 2N 36 44 E
An Nafūd, *Si. Arabia* **44 D4** 28 15N 41 0 E
An Najaf, *Iraq* **44 C5** 32 3N 44 15 E
An Nāşirīyah, *Iraq* **44 D5** 31 0N 46 15 E
An Nhon, *Vietnam* **38 F7** 13 55N 109 7 E
An Nu'ayrīyah, *Si. Arabia* **45 E6** 27 30N 48 30 E
An Nuwayb'ī, W. →, *Si. Arabia* **47 F3** 29 18N 34 57 E
An Thoi, Dao, *Vietnam* **39 H4** 9 58N 104 0 E
An Uaimh, *Ireland* **13 C5** 53 39N 6 41W
Anabar →, *Russia* **27 B12** 73 8N 113 36 E
'Anabtā, *West Bank* **47 C4** 32 19N 35 7 E
Anaconda, *U.S.A.* **82 C7** 46 8N 112 57W
Anacortes, *U.S.A.* **84 B4** 48 30N 122 37W
Anadarko, *U.S.A.* **81 H5** 35 4N 98 15W
Anadolu, *Turkey* **25 G5** 39 0N 30 0 E
Anadyr, *Russia* **27 C18** 64 35N 177 20 E
Anadyr →, *Russia* **27 C18** 64 55N 176 5 E
Anadyrskiy Zaliv, *Russia* **27 C19** 64 0N 180 0 E
Anaga, Pta. de, *Canary Is.* **22 F3** 28 34N 16 9W
'Ānah, *Iraq* **44 C4** 34 25N 42 0 E
Anaheim, *U.S.A.* **85 M9** 33 50N 117 55W
Anahim Lake, *Canada* **72 C3** 52 28N 125 18W
Anáhuac, *Mexico* **86 B4** 27 14N 100 9W
Anakapalle, *India* **41 L13** 17 42N 83 6 E
Anakie, *Australia* **62 C4** 23 32S 147 45 E
Analalava, *Madag.* **57 A8** 14 35S 48 0 E
Analavoka, *Madag.* **57 C8** 22 23S 46 30 E
Análipsis, *Greece* **23 A3** 39 36N 19 55 E
Anambar →, *Pakistan* **42 D3** 30 15N 68 50 E
Anambas, Kepulauan, *Indonesia* **39 L6** 3 20N 106 30 E
Anambas Is. = Anambas, Kepulauan, *Indonesia* **39 L6** 3 20N 106 30 E
Anamosa, *U.S.A.* **80 D9** 42 7N 91 17W
Anamur, *Turkey* **25 G5** 36 8N 32 58 E
Anan, *Japan* **31 H7** 33 54N 134 40 E
Anand, *India* **42 H5** 22 32N 72 59 E
Anantnag, *India* **43 C6** 33 45N 75 10 E
Ananyiv, *Ukraine* **17 E15** 47 44N 29 58 E
Anapodháris →, *Greece* **23 E7** 34 59N 25 20 E
Anápolis, *Brazil* **93 G9** 16 15S 48 50W
Anapu →, *Brazil* **93 D8** 1 53S 50 53W
Anār, *Iran* **45 D7** 30 55N 55 13 E
Anārak, *Iran* **45 C7** 33 25N 53 40 E
Anas →, *India* **42 H5** 23 26N 74 0 E
Anatolia = Anadolu, *Turkey* **25 G5** 39 0N 30 0 E
Anatsogno, *Madag.* **57 C7** 23 33S 43 46 E
Añatuya, *Argentina* **94 B3** 28 20S 62 50W
Anaunethad L., *Canada* **73 A8** 60 55N 104 25W
Anbyŏn, *N. Korea* **35 E14** 39 1N 127 35 E
Ancaster, *Canada* **78 C5** 43 13N 79 59W
Anchor Bay, *U.S.A.* **84 G3** 38 48N 123 34W
Anchorage, *U.S.A.* **68 B5** 61 13N 149 54W
Anci, *China* **34 E9** 39 20N 116 40 E
Ancohuma, Nevada, *Bolivia* **92 G5** 16 0S 68 50W
Ancón, *Peru* **92 F3** 11 50S 77 10W
Ancona, *Italy* **20 C5** 43 38N 13 30 E
Ancud, *Chile* **96 E2** 42 0S 73 50W
Ancud, G. de, *Chile* **96 E2** 42 0S 73 0W
Anda, *China* **33 B7** 46 24N 125 19 E
Andacollo, *Argentina* **94 D1** 37 10S 70 42W
Andacollo, *Chile* **94 C1** 30 14S 71 6W
Andaingo, *Madag.* **57 B8** 18 12S 48 17 E
Andalgalá, *Argentina* **94 B2** 27 40S 66 30W
Åndalsnes, *Norway* **9 E12** 62 35N 7 43 E
Andalucía □, *Spain* **19 D3** 37 35N 5 0W
Andalusia = Andalucía □, *Spain* **19 D3** 37 35N 5 0W
Andalusia, *U.S.A.* **77 K2** 31 18N 86 29W
Andaman Is., *Ind. Oc.* **29 H13** 12 30N 92 45 E
Andaman Sea, *Ind. Oc.* **36 B1** 13 0N 96 0 E
Andamooka Opal Fields, *Australia* **63 E2** 30 27S 137 9 E
Andapa, *Madag.* **57 A8** 14 39S 49 39 E
Andara, *Namibia* **56 B3** 18 2S 21 9 E
Andenes, *Norway* **8 B17** 69 19N 16 18 E
Andenne, *Belgium* **15 D5** 50 28N 5 5 E
Anderson, *Alaska, U.S.A.* **68 B5** 64 25N 149 15W
Anderson, *Calif., U.S.A.* **82 F2** 40 27N 122 18W
Anderson, *Ind., U.S.A.* **76 E3** 40 10N 85 41W
Anderson, *Mo., U.S.A.* **81 G7** 36 39N 94 27W
Anderson, *S.C., U.S.A.* **77 H4** 34 31N 82 39W
Anderson →, *Canada* **68 B7** 69 42N 129 0W
Andes, *U.S.A.* **79 D10** 42 12N 74 47W
Andes, Cord. de los, *S. Amer.* **92 H5** 20 0S 68 0W
Andfjorden, *Norway* **8 B17** 69 10N 16 20 E
Andhra Pradesh □, *India* **40 L11** 18 0N 79 0 E
Andijon, *Uzbekistan* **26 E8** 41 10N 72 15 E
Andikíthira, *Greece* **21 G10** 35 52N 23 15 E
Andilamena, *Madag.* **57 B8** 17 1S 48 35 E
Andīmeshk, *Iran* **45 C6** 32 27N 48 21 E
Andizhan = Andijon, *Uzbekistan* **26 E8** 41 10N 72 15 E
Andoany, *Madag.* **57 A8** 13 25S 48 16 E
Andong, *S. Korea* **35 F15** 36 40N 128 43 E
Andongwei, *China* **35 G10** 35 6N 119 20 E
Andoom, *Australia* **62 A3** 12 25S 141 53 E
Andorra ■, *Europe* **18 E4** 42 30N 1 30 E
Andorra La Vella, *Andorra* **18 E4** 42 31N 1 32 E
Andover, *U.K.* **11 F6** 51 12N 1 29W
Andover, *Maine, U.S.A.* **79 B14** 44 38N 70 45W
Andover, *Mass., U.S.A.* **79 D13** 42 40N 71 8W
Andover, *N.J., U.S.A.* **79 F10** 40 59N 74 45W
Andover, *N.Y., U.S.A.* **78 D7** 42 10N 77 48W
Andover, *Ohio, U.S.A.* **78 E4** 41 36N 80 34W
Andøya, *Norway* **8 B16** 69 10N 15 50 E
Andradina, *Brazil* **93 H8** 20 54S 51 23W
Andrahary, Mt., *Madag.* **57 A8** 13 37S 49 17 E
Andramasina, *Madag.* **57 B8** 19 11S 47 35 E
Andranopasy, *Madag.* **57 C7** 21 17S 43 44 E
Andranovory, *Madag.* **57 C7** 23 8S 44 10 E
Andratx, *Spain* **22 B9** 39 39N 2 25 E
Andreanof Is., *U.S.A.* **68 C2** 51 30N 176 0W
Andrews, *S.C., U.S.A.* **77 J6** 33 27N 79 34W
Andrews, *Tex., U.S.A.* **81 J3** 32 19N 102 33W
Ándria, *Italy* **20 D7** 41 13N 16 17 E
Andriamena, *Madag.* **57 B8** 17 26S 47 30 E
Andriandampy, *Madag.* **57 C8** 22 45S 45 41 E
Andriba, *Madag.* **57 B8** 17 30S 46 58 E
Androka, *Madag.* **57 C7** 24 58S 44 2 E
Andropov = Rybinsk, *Russia* **24 C6** 58 5N 38 50 E
Ándros, *Greece* **21 F11** 37 50N 24 57 E
Andros I., *Bahamas* **88 B4** 24 30N 78 0W
Andros Town, *Bahamas* **88 B4** 24 43N 77 47W
Androscoggin →, *U.S.A.* **79 C14** 43 58N 70 0W
Andselv, *Norway* **8 B18** 69 4N 18 34 E
Andújar, *Spain* **19 C3** 38 3N 4 5W
Andulo, *Angola* **52 G3** 11 25S 16 45 E
Anegada I., *Br. Virgin Is.* **89 C7** 18 45N 64 20W
Anegada Passage, *W. Indies* **89 C7** 18 15N 63 45W
Aneto, Pico de, *Spain* **19 A6** 42 37N 0 40 E
Ang Thong, *Thailand* **38 E3** 14 35N 100 31 E
Angamos, Punta, *Chile* **94 A1** 23 1S 70 32W
Angara →, *Russia* **27 D10** 58 5N 94 20 E
Angarsk, *Russia* **27 D11** 52 30N 104 0 E
Angas Hills, *Australia* **60 D4** 23 0S 127 50 E
Angaston, *Australia* **63 E2** 34 30S 139 8 E
Ånge, *Sweden* **9 E16** 62 31N 15 35 E
Ángel, Salto = Angel Falls, *Venezuela* **92 B6** 5 57N 62 30W
Ángel de la Guarda, I., *Mexico* **86 B2** 29 30N 113 30W
Angel Falls, *Venezuela* **92 B6** 5 57N 62 30W
Angeles, *Phil.* **37 A6** 15 9N 120 33 E
Ängelholm, *Sweden* **9 H15** 56 15N 12 58 E
Angels Camp, *U.S.A.* **84 G6** 38 4N 120 32W
Ångermanälven →, *Sweden* **8 E17** 62 40N 18 0 E
Ångermanland, *Sweden* **8 E18** 63 36N 17 45 E
Angers, *Canada* **79 A9** 45 31N 75 29W
Angers, *France* **18 C3** 47 30N 0 35W
Ängesån →, *Sweden* **8 C20** 66 16N 22 47 E
Angikuni L., *Canada* **73 A9** 62 0N 100 0W
Angkor, *Cambodia* **38 F4** 13 22N 103 50 E
Anglesey, Isle of □, *U.K.* **10 D3** 53 16N 4 18W
Angleton, *U.S.A.* **81 L7** 29 10N 95 26W
Anglisidhes, *Cyprus* **23 E12** 34 51N 33 27 E
Angmagssalik = Tasiilaq, *Greenland* **4 C6** 65 40N 37 20W
Ango, *Dem. Rep. of the Congo* **54 B2** 4 10N 26 5 E
Angoche, *Mozam.* **55 F4** 16 8S 39 55 E
Angoche, I., *Mozam.* **55 F4** 16 20S 39 50 E
Angol, *Chile* **94 D1** 37 56S 72 45W
Angola, *Ind., U.S.A.* **76 E3** 41 38N 85 0W
Angola, *N.Y., U.S.A.* **78 D5** 42 38N 79 2W
Angola ■, *Africa* **53 G3** 12 0S 18 0 E
Angoulême, *France* **18 D4** 45 39N 0 10 E
Angoumois, *France* **18 D3** 45 50N 0 25 E
Angra dos Reis, *Brazil* **95 A7** 23 0S 44 10W
Angren, *Uzbekistan* **26 E8** 41 1N 70 12 E
Angtassom, *Cambodia* **39 G5** 11 1N 104 41 E
Angu, *Dem. Rep. of the Congo* **54 B1** 3 23N 24 30 E
Anguang, *China* **35 B12** 45 15N 123 45 E
Anguilla ■, *W. Indies* **89 C7** 18 14N 63 5W
Anguo, *China* **34 E8** 38 28N 115 15 E
Angurugu, *Australia* **62 A2** 14 0S 136 25 E
Angus □, *U.K.* **12 E6** 56 46N 2 56W
Angwa →, *Zimbabwe* **57 B5** 16 0S 30 23 E
Anhanduí →, *Brazil* **95 A5** 21 46S 52 9W
Anholt, *Denmark* **9 H14** 56 42N 11 33 E
Anhui □, *China* **33 C6** 32 0N 117 0 E
Anhwei = Anhui □, *China* **33 C6** 32 0N 117 0 E
Anichab, *Namibia* **56 C1** 21 0S 14 46 E
Animas →, *U.S.A.* **83 H9** 36 43N 108 13W
Anivorano, *Madag.* **57 B8** 18 44S 48 58 E
Anjalankoski, *Finland* **9 F22** 60 45N 26 51 E
Anjar, *India* **42 H4** 23 6N 70 10 E
Anjou, *France* **18 C3** 47 20N 0 15W
Anjozorobe, *Madag.* **57 B8** 18 22S 47 52 E
Anju, *N. Korea* **35 E13** 39 36N 125 40 E
Ankaboa, Tanjona, *Madag.* **57 C7** 21 58S 43 20 E
Ankang, *China* **34 H5** 32 40N 109 1 E
Ankara, *Turkey* **25 G5** 39 57N 32 54 E
Ankaramena, *Madag.* **57 C8** 21 57S 46 39 E
Ankaratra, *Madag.* **53 H9** 19 25S 47 12 E
Ankasakasa, *Madag.* **57 B7** 16 21S 44 52 E
Ankavandra, *Madag.* **57 B8** 18 46S 45 18 E
Ankazoabo, *Madag.* **57 C7** 22 18S 44 31 E
Ankazobe, *Madag.* **57 B8** 18 20S 47 10 E
Ankeny, *U.S.A.* **80 E8** 41 44N 93 36W
Ankilimalinika, *Madag.* **57 C7** 22 58S 43 45 E
Ankilizato, *Madag.* **57 C8** 20 25S 45 1 E
Ankisabe, *Madag.* **57 B8** 19 17S 46 29 E
Ankoro, *Dem. Rep. of the Congo* **54 D2** 6 45S 26 55 E
Ankororoka, *Madag.* **57 D8** 25 30S 45 11 E
Anmyŏn-do, *S. Korea* **35 F14** 36 25N 126 25 E
Ann, C., *U.S.A.* **79 D14** 42 38N 70 35W
Ann Arbor, *U.S.A.* **76 D4** 42 17N 83 45W
Anna, *U.S.A.* **81 G10** 37 28N 89 15W
Annaba, *Algeria* **50 A7** 36 50N 7 46 E
Annalee →, *Ireland* **13 B4** 54 2N 7 24W
Annam, *Vietnam* **38 E7** 16 0N 108 0 E
Annamitique, Chaîne, *Asia* **38 D6** 17 0N 106 0 E
Annan, *U.K.* **12 G5** 54 59N 3 16W
Annan →, *U.K.* **12 G5** 54 58N 3 16W
Annapolis, *U.S.A.* **76 F7** 38 59N 76 30W
Annapolis Royal, *Canada* **71 D6** 44 44N 65 32W
Annapurna, *Nepal* **43 E10** 28 34N 83 50 E
Annean, L., *Australia* **61 E2** 26 54S 118 14 E
Annecy, *France* **18 D7** 45 55N 6 8 E
Anning, *China* **32 D5** 24 55N 102 26 E
Anniston, *U.S.A.* **77 J3** 33 39N 85 50W
Annobón, *Atl. Oc.* **49 G4** 1 25S 5 36 E
Annotto Bay, *Jamaica* **88 C4** 18 17N 76 45W
Annville, *U.S.A.* **79 F8** 40 20N 76 31W
Áno Viánnos, *Greece* **23 D7** 35 2N 25 21 E
Anorotsangana, *Madag.* **57 A8** 13 56S 47 55 E
Anosibe, *Madag.* **57 B8** 19 26S 48 13 E
Anóyia, *Greece* **23 D6** 35 16N 24 52 E
Anping, *Hebei, China* **34 E8** 38 15N 115 30 E
Anping, *Liaoning, China* **35 D12** 41 5N 123 30 E
Anqing, *China* **33 C6** 30 30N 117 3 E
Anqiu, *China* **35 F10** 36 25N 119 10 E
Ansai, *China* **34 F5** 36 50N 109 20 E
Ansbach, *Germany* **16 D6** 49 28N 10 34 E
Anshan, *China* **35 D12** 41 5N 122 58 E
Anshun, *China* **32 D5** 26 18N 105 57 E
Ansley, *U.S.A.* **80 E5** 41 18N 99 23W
Anson, *U.S.A.* **81 J5** 32 45N 99 54W
Anson B., *Australia* **60 B5** 13 20S 130 6 E
Ansongo, *Mali* **50 E6** 15 25N 0 35 E
Ansonia, *U.S.A.* **79 E11** 41 21N 73 5W
Anstruther, *U.K.* **12 E6** 56 14N 2 41W
Ansudu, *Indonesia* **37 E9** 2 11S 139 22 E
Antabamba, *Peru* **92 F4** 14 40S 73 0W
Antakya, *Turkey* **25 G6** 36 14N 36 10 E
Antalaha, *Madag.* **57 A9** 14 57S 50 20 E
Antalya, *Turkey* **25 G5** 36 52N 30 45 E
Antalya Körfezi, *Turkey* **25 G5** 36 15N 31 30 E
Antambohobe, *Madag.* **57 C8** 22 20S 46 47 E
Antanambao-Manampotsy, *Madag.* **57 B8** 19 29S 48 34 E
Antanambe, *Madag.* **57 B8** 16 26S 49 52 E
Antananarivo, *Madag.* **57 B8** 18 55S 47 31 E
Antananarivo □, *Madag.* **57 B8** 19 0S 47 0 E
Antanifotsy, *Madag.* **57 B8** 19 39S 47 19 E
Antanimbaribe, *Madag.* **57 C7** 21 30S 44 48 E
Antanimora, *Madag.* **57 C8** 24 49S 45 40 E
Antarctic Pen., *Antarctica* **5 C18** 67 0S 60 0W
Antarctica **5 E3** 90 0S 0 0W
Antelope, *Zimbabwe* **55 G2** 21 2S 28 31 E
Antequera, *Paraguay* **94 A4** 24 8S 57 7W
Antequera, *Spain* **19 D3** 37 5N 4 33W
Antero, Mt., *U.S.A.* **83 G10** 38 41N 106 15W
Antevamena, *Madag.* **57 C7** 21 2S 44 8 E
Anthony, *Kans., U.S.A.* **81 G5** 37 9N 98 2W
Anthony, *N. Mex., U.S.A.* **83 K10** 32 0N 106 36W
Anti Atlas, *Morocco* **50 C4** 30 0N 8 30W
Anti-Lebanon = Ash Sharqi, Al Jabal, *Lebanon* **47 B5** 33 40N 36 10 E
Antibes, *France* **18 E7** 43 34N 7 6 E
Anticosti, Î. d', *Canada* **71 C7** 49 30N 63 0W
Antigo, *U.S.A.* **80 C10** 45 9N 89 9W
Antigonish, *Canada* **71 C7** 45 38N 61 58W
Antigua, *Canary Is.* **22 F5** 28 24N 14 1W
Antigua, *Guatemala* **88 D1** 14 34N 90 41W
Antigua, *W. Indies* **89 C7** 17 0N 61 50W
Antigua & Barbuda ■, *W. Indies* **89 C7** 17 20N 61 48W
Antilla, *Cuba* **88 B4** 20 40N 75 50W
Antilles = West Indies, *Cent. Amer.* **89 D7** 15 0N 65 0W
Antioch, *U.S.A.* **84 G5** 38 1N 121 48W
Antioquia, *Colombia* **92 B3** 6 40N 75 55W
Antipodes Is., *Pac. Oc.* **64 M9** 49 45S 178 40 E
Antlers, *U.S.A.* **81 H7** 34 14N 95 37W
Antoetra, *Madag.* **57 C8** 20 46S 47 20 E
Antofagasta, *Chile* **94 A1** 23 50S 70 30W
Antofagasta □, *Chile* **94 A2** 24 0S 69 0W
Antofagasta de la Sierra, *Argentina* **94 B2** 26 5S 67 20W
Antofalla, *Argentina* **94 B2** 25 30S 68 5W
Antofalla, Salar de, *Argentina* **94 B2** 25 40S 67 45W
Anton, *U.S.A.* **81 J3** 33 49N 102 10W
Antongila, Helodrano, *Madag.* **57 B8** 15 30S 49 50 E
Antonibé, *Madag.* **57 B8** 15 7S 47 24 E
Antonibé, Presqu'île d', *Madag.* **57 A8** 14 55S 47 20 E
Antonina, *Brazil* **95 B6** 25 26S 48 42W
Antrim, *U.K.* **13 B5** 54 43N 6 14W
Antrim, *U.S.A.* **78 F3** 40 7N 81 21W
Antrim □, *U.K.* **13 B5** 54 56N 6 25W
Antrim, Mts. of, *U.K.* **13 A5** 55 3N 6 14W
Antrim Plateau, *Australia* **60 C4** 18 8S 128 20 E
Antsakabary, *Madag.* **57 B8** 15 3S 48 56 E
Antsalova, *Madag.* **57 B7** 18 40S 44 37 E

Antsenavolo, Madag. 57 C8 21 24S 48 3 E
Antsiafabositra, Madag. 57 B8 17 18S 46 57 E
Antsirabe, Antananarivo, Madag. 57 B8 19 55S 47 2 E
Antsirabe, Antsiranana, Madag. 57 A8 14 0S 49 59 E
Antsirabe, Mahajanga, Madag. 57 B8 15 57S 48 58 E
Antsiranana, Madag. 57 A8 12 25S 49 20 E
Antsiranana □, Madag. 57 A8 12 16S 49 17 E
Antsohihy, Madag. 57 A8 14 50S 47 59 E
Antsohimbondrona Seranana, Madag. 57 A8 13 7S 48 48 E
Antu, China 35 C15 42 30N 128 20 E
Antwerp = Antwerpen, Belgium 15 C4 51 13N 4 25 E
Antwerp, U.S.A. 79 B9 44 12N 75 37W
Antwerpen, Belgium 15 C4 51 13N 4 25 E
Antwerpen □, Belgium 15 C4 51 15N 4 40 E
Anupgarh, India 42 E5 29 10N 73 10 E
Anuppur, India 43 H9 23 6N 81 41 E
Anuradhapura, Sri Lanka 40 Q12 8 22N 80 28 E
Anveh, Iran 45 E7 27 23N 54 11 E
Anvers = Antwerpen, Belgium 15 C4 51 13N 4 25 E
Anvers I., Antarctica 5 C17 64 30S 63 40W
Anxi, China 32 B4 40 30N 95 43 E
Anxious B., Australia 63 E1 33 24S 134 45 E
Anyang, China 34 F8 36 5N 114 21 E
Anyer-Kidul, Indonesia 37 G11 6 4S 105 53 E
Anyi, China 34 G6 35 2N 111 2 E
Anza, U.S.A. 85 M10 33 35N 116 39W
Anze, China 34 F7 36 10N 112 12 E
Anzhero-Sudzhensk, Russia 26 D9 56 10N 86 0 E
Ánzio, Italy 20 D5 41 27N 12 37 E
Aoga-Shima, Japan 31 H9 32 28N 139 46 E
Aomen = Macau, China 33 D6 22 12N 113 33 E
Aomori, Japan 30 D10 40 45N 140 45 E
Aomori □, Japan 30 D10 40 45N 140 40 E
Aonla, India 43 E8 28 16N 79 11 E
Aoraki Mount Cook, N.Z. 59 K3 43 36S 170 9 E
Aosta, Italy 18 D7 45 45N 7 20 E
Aoukâr, Mauritania 50 E4 17 40N 10 0W
Apa →, S. Amer. 94 A4 22 6S 58 2W
Apache, U.S.A. 81 H5 34 54N 98 22W
Apache Junction, U.S.A. 83 K8 33 25N 111 33W
Apalachee B., U.S.A. 77 L4 30 0N 84 0W
Apalachicola, U.S.A. 77 L3 29 43N 84 59W
Apalachicola →, U.S.A. 77 L3 29 43N 84 58W
Apaporis →, Colombia 92 D5 1 23S 69 25W
Aparri, Phil. 37 A6 18 22N 121 38 E
Apatity, Russia 24 A5 67 34N 33 22 E
Apatzingán, Mexico 86 D4 19 0N 102 20W
Apeldoorn, Neths. 15 B5 52 13N 5 57 E
Apennines = Appennini, Italy 20 B4 44 0N 10 0 E
Apia, Samoa 59 A13 13 50S 171 50W
Apiacás, Serra dos, Brazil 92 E7 9 50S 57 0W
Apies →, S. Africa 57 D4 25 15S 28 8 E
Apizaco, Mexico 87 D5 19 26N 98 9W
Aplao, Peru 92 G4 16 0S 72 40W
Apo, Mt., Phil. 37 C7 6 53N 125 14 E
Apolakkiá, Greece 23 C9 36 5N 27 48 E
Apolakkiá, Órmos, Greece 23 C9 36 5N 27 45 E
Apolo, Bolivia 92 F5 14 30S 68 30W
Aporé →, Brazil 93 G8 19 27S 50 57W
Apostle Is., U.S.A. 80 B9 47 0N 90 40W
Apóstoles, Argentina 95 B4 28 0S 56 0W
Apostolos Andreas, C., Cyprus 23 D13 35 42N 34 35 E
Apoteri, Guyana 92 C7 4 2N 58 32W
Appalachian Mts., U.S.A. 76 G6 38 0N 80 0W
Appennini, Italy 20 B4 44 0N 10 0 E
Apple Hill, Canada 79 A10 45 13N 74 46W
Apple Valley, U.S.A. 85 L9 34 32N 117 14W
Appleby-in-Westmorland, U.K. 10 C5 54 35N 2 29W
Appleton, U.S.A. 76 C1 44 16N 88 25W
Approuague →, Fr. Guiana 93 C8 4 30N 51 57W
Aprilia, Italy 20 D5 41 36N 12 39 E
Apsley, Canada 78 B6 44 45N 78 6W
Apucarana, Brazil 95 A5 23 55S 51 33W
Apure →, Venezuela 92 B5 7 37N 66 25W
Apurimac →, Peru 92 F4 12 17S 73 56W
Āqā Jari, Iran 45 D6 30 42N 49 50 E
Aqaba = Al 'Aqabah, Jordan 47 F4 29 31N 35 0 E
Aqaba, G. of, Red Sea 44 D2 28 15N 33 20 E
'Aqabah, Khalīj al = Aqaba, G. of, Red Sea 44 D2 28 15N 33 20 E
'Aqdā, Iran 45 C7 32 26N 53 37 E
Aqmola = Astana, Kazakstan 26 D8 51 10N 71 30 E
'Aqrah, Iraq 44 B4 36 46N 43 45 E
Aqtaū, Kazakstan 26 E6 43 39N 51 12 E
Aqtöbe, Kazakstan 25 D10 50 17N 57 10 E
Aquidauana, Brazil 93 H7 20 30S 55 50W
Aquiles Serdán, Mexico 86 B3 28 37N 105 54W
Aquin, Haiti 89 C5 18 16N 73 24W
Aquitain, Bassin, France 18 D3 44 0N 0 30W
Aqviligjuaq = Pelly Bay, Canada 69 B11 68 38N 89 50W
Ar Rachidiya = Er Rachidia, Morocco 50 B5 31 58N 4 20W
Ar Rafīd, Syria 47 C4 32 57N 35 52 E
Ar Raḥḥālīyah, Iraq 44 C4 32 44N 43 23 E
Ar Ramādī, Iraq 44 C4 33 25N 43 20 E
Ar Ramthā, Jordan 47 C5 32 34N 36 0 E
Ar Raqqah, Syria 44 C3 35 59N 39 8 E
Ar Rass, Si. Arabia 44 E4 25 50N 43 40 E
Ar Rifā'ī, Iraq 44 D5 31 50N 46 10 E
Ar Riyāḍ, Si. Arabia 46 C4 24 41N 46 42 E
Ar Ru'ays, Qatar 45 E6 26 8N 51 12 E
Ar Rukhaymīyah, Iraq 44 D5 29 22N 45 38 E
Ar Ruṣāfah, Syria 44 C3 35 45N 38 49 E
Ar Ruṭbah, Iraq 44 C4 33 0N 40 15 E
Ara, India 43 G11 25 35N 84 32 E
Arab, U.S.A. 77 H2 34 19N 86 30W
'Arab, Bahr el →, Sudan 51 G11 9 0N 29 30 E
Arab, Shatt al →, Asia 45 D6 30 0N 48 31 E
'Arabābād, Iran 45 C8 33 2N 57 41 E
Arabia, Asia 28 G8 25 0N 45 0 E
Arabian Desert = Es Sahrâ' Esh Sharqîya, Egypt 51 C12 27 30N 32 30 E
Arabian Gulf = Gulf, The, Asia 45 E6 27 0N 50 0 E
Arabian Sea, Ind. Oc. 29 H10 16 0N 65 0 E
Aracaju, Brazil 93 F11 10 55S 37 4W
Aracati, Brazil 93 D11 4 30S 37 44W
Araçatuba, Brazil 95 A5 21 10S 50 30W
Aracena, Spain 19 D2 37 53N 6 38W
Araçuaí, Brazil 93 G10 16 52S 42 4W
'Arad, Israel 47 D4 31 15N 35 12 E
Arad, Romania 17 E11 46 10N 21 20 E
Arādān, Iran 45 C7 35 21N 52 30 E
Aradhippou, Cyprus 23 E12 34 57N 33 36 E
Arafura Sea, E. Indies 28 K17 9 0S 135 0 E
Aragón □, Spain 19 B5 41 25N 0 40W
Aragón →, Spain 19 A5 42 13N 1 44W
Araguacema, Brazil 93 E9 8 50S 49 20W
Araguaia →, Brazil 93 E9 5 21S 48 41W
Araguaína, Brazil 93 E9 7 12S 48 12W
Araguari, Brazil 93 G9 18 38S 48 11W
Araguari →, Brazil 93 C9 1 15N 49 55W
Arain, India 42 F6 26 27N 75 2 E
Arak, Algeria 50 C6 25 20N 3 45 E
Arāk, Iran 45 C6 34 0N 49 40 E
Arakan Coast, Burma 41 K19 19 0N 94 0 E
Arakan Yoma, Burma 41 K19 20 0N 94 40 E
Araks = Aras, Rūd-e →, Asia 44 B5 40 5N 48 29 E
Aral, Kazakstan 26 E7 46 41N 61 45 E
Aral Sea, Asia 26 E7 44 30N 60 0 E
Aral Tengizi = Aral Sea, Asia 26 E7 44 30N 60 0 E
Aralsk = Aral, Kazakstan 26 E7 46 41N 61 45 E
Aralskoye More = Aral Sea, Asia 26 E7 44 30N 60 0 E
Aramac, Australia 62 C4 22 58S 145 14 E
Aran I., Ireland 13 A3 55 0N 8 30W
Aran Is., Ireland 13 C2 53 6N 9 38W
Aranda de Duero, Spain 19 B4 41 39N 3 42W
Arandān, Iran 44 C5 35 23N 46 55 E
Aranjuez, Spain 19 B4 40 1N 3 40W
Aranos, Namibia 56 C2 24 9S 19 7 E
Aransas Pass, U.S.A. 81 M6 27 55N 97 9W
Aranyaprathet, Thailand 38 F4 13 41N 102 30 E
Arapahoe, U.S.A. 80 E5 40 18N 99 54W
Arapey Grande →, Uruguay 94 C4 30 55S 57 49W
Arapgir, Turkey 44 B3 39 5N 38 30 E
Arapiraca, Brazil 93 E11 9 45S 36 39W
Arapongas, Brazil 95 A5 23 29S 51 28W
Ar'ar, Si. Arabia 44 D4 30 59N 41 2 E
Araranguá, Brazil 95 B6 29 0S 49 30W
Araraquara, Brazil 93 H9 21 50S 48 0W
Ararás, Serra das, Brazil 95 B5 25 0S 53 10W
Ararat, Australia 63 F3 37 16S 143 0 E
Ararat, Mt. = Ağrı Dağı, Turkey 25 G7 39 50N 44 15 E
Araria, India 43 F12 26 9N 87 33 E
Araripe, Chapada do, Brazil 93 E11 7 20S 40 0W
Araruama, L. de, Brazil 95 A7 22 53S 42 12W
Aras, Rūd-e →, Asia 44 B5 40 5N 48 29 E
Arauca, Colombia 92 B4 7 0N 70 40W
Arauca →, Venezuela 92 B5 7 24N 66 35W
Arauco, Chile 94 D1 37 16S 73 25W
Araxá, Brazil 93 G9 19 35S 46 55W
Araya, Pen. de, Venezuela 92 A6 10 40N 64 0W
Arba Minch, Ethiopia 46 F2 6 0N 37 30 E
Arbat, Iraq 44 C5 35 25N 45 35 E
Árbatax, Italy 20 E3 39 56N 9 42 E
Arbīl, Iraq 44 B5 36 15N 44 5 E
Arborfield, Canada 73 C8 53 6N 103 39W
Arborg, Canada 73 C9 50 54N 97 13W
Arbroath, U.K. 12 E6 56 34N 2 35W
Arbuckle, U.S.A. 84 F4 39 1N 122 3W
Arcachon, France 18 D3 44 40N 1 10W
Arcade, Calif., U.S.A. 85 L8 34 2N 118 15W
Arcade, N.Y., U.S.A. 78 D6 42 32N 78 25W
Arcadia, Fla., U.S.A. 77 M5 27 13N 81 52W
Arcadia, La., U.S.A. 81 J8 32 33N 92 55W
Arcadia, Pa., U.S.A. 78 F6 40 47N 78 51W
Arcata, U.S.A. 82 F1 40 52N 124 5W
Archangel = Arkhangelsk, Russia 24 B7 64 38N 40 36 E
Archbald, U.S.A. 79 E9 41 30N 75 32W
Archer →, Australia 62 A3 13 28S 141 41 E
Archer B., Australia 62 A3 13 20S 141 30 E
Archers Post, Kenya 54 B4 0 35N 37 35 E
Arches Nat. Park, U.S.A. 83 G9 38 45N 109 25W
Arckaringa Cr. →, Australia 63 D2 28 10S 135 22 E
Arco, U.S.A. 82 E7 43 38N 113 18W
Arcos de la Frontera, Spain 19 D3 36 45N 5 49W
Arcot, India 40 N11 12 53N 79 20 E
Arctic Bay, Canada 69 A11 73 1N 85 7W
Arctic Ocean, Arctic 4 B18 78 0N 160 0W
Arctic Red River = Tsiigehtchic, Canada 68 B6 67 15N 134 0W
Arda →, Bulgaria 21 D12 41 40N 26 30 E
Ardabīl, Iran 45 B6 38 15N 48 18 E
Ardakān = Sepīdān, Iran 45 D7 30 20N 52 5 E
Ardakān, Iran 45 C7 32 19N 53 59 E
Ardee, Ireland 13 C5 53 52N 6 33W
Arden, Canada 78 B8 44 43N 76 56W
Arden, Calif., U.S.A. 84 G5 38 36N 121 33W
Arden, Nev., U.S.A. 85 J11 36 1N 115 14W
Ardenne, Belgium 16 D3 49 50N 5 5 E
Ardennes = Ardenne, Belgium 16 D3 49 50N 5 5 E
Arderin, Ireland 13 C4 53 2N 7 39W
Ardestān, Iran 45 C7 33 20N 52 25 E
Ardivachar Pt., U.K. 12 D1 57 23N 7 26W
Ardlethan, Australia 63 E4 34 22S 146 53 E
Ardmore, Okla., U.S.A. 81 H6 34 10N 97 8W
Ardmore, Pa., U.S.A. 79 G9 39 58N 75 18W
Ardnamurchan, Pt. of, U.K. 12 E2 56 43N 6 14W
Ardnave Pt., U.K. 12 F2 55 53N 6 20W
Ardrossan, Australia 63 E2 34 26S 137 53 E
Ardrossan, U.K. 12 F4 55 39N 4 49W
Ards Pen., U.K. 13 B6 54 33N 5 34W
Arecibo, Puerto Rico 89 C6 18 29N 66 43W
Areia Branca, Brazil 93 E11 5 0S 37 0W
Arena, Pt., U.S.A. 84 G3 38 57N 123 44W
Arenal, Honduras 88 C2 15 21N 86 50W
Arendal, Norway 9 G13 58 28N 8 46 E
Arequipa, Peru 92 G4 16 20S 71 30W
Arévalo, Spain 19 B3 41 3N 4 43W
Arezzo, Italy 20 C4 43 25N 11 53 E
Arga, Turkey 44 B3 38 21N 37 59 E
Arganda, Spain 19 B4 40 19N 3 26W
Argenta, Canada 72 C5 50 11N 116 56W
Argentan, France 18 B3 48 45N 0 1W
Argentário, Mte., Italy 20 C4 42 24N 11 9 E
Argentia, Canada 71 C9 47 18N 53 58W
Argentina ■, S. Amer. 96 D3 35 0S 66 0W
Argentino Is., Antarctica 5 C17 66 0S 64 0W
Argentino, L., Argentina 96 G2 50 10S 73 0W
Argeş →, Romania 17 F14 44 5N 26 38 E
Arghandab →, Afghan. 42 D1 31 30N 64 15 E
Argolikós Kólpos, Greece 21 F10 37 20N 22 52 E
Árgos, Greece 21 F10 37 40N 22 43 E
Argostólion, Greece 21 E9 38 11N 20 29 E
Arguello, Pt., U.S.A. 85 L6 34 35N 120 39W
Arguineguín, Canary Is. 22 G4 27 46N 15 41W
Argun →, Russia 27 D13 53 20N 121 28 E
Argus Pk., U.S.A. 85 K9 35 52N 117 26W
Argyle, L., Australia 60 C4 16 20S 128 40 E
Argyll & Bute □, U.K. 12 E3 56 13N 5 28W
Århus, Denmark 9 H14 56 8N 10 11 E
Ariadnoye, Russia 30 B7 45 8N 134 25 E
Ariamsvlei, Namibia 56 D2 28 9S 19 51 E
Arica, Chile 92 G4 18 32S 70 20W
Arica, Colombia 92 D4 2 0S 71 50W
Arico, Canary Is. 22 F3 28 9N 16 29W
Arid, C., Australia 61 F3 34 1S 123 10 E
Arida, Japan 31 G7 34 5N 135 8 E
Arílla, Ákra, Greece 23 A3 39 43N 19 39 E
Arima, Trin. & Tob. 89 D7 10 38N 61 17W
Arinos →, Brazil 92 F7 10 25S 58 20W
Ario de Rosales, Mexico 86 D4 19 12N 102 0W
Aripuanã, Brazil 92 E6 9 25S 60 30W
Aripuanã →, Brazil 92 E6 5 7S 60 25W
Ariquemes, Brazil 92 E6 9 55S 63 6W
Arisaig, U.K. 12 E3 56 55N 5 51W
Aristazabal I., Canada 72 C3 52 40N 129 10W
Arivonimamo, Madag. 57 B8 19 1S 47 11 E
Arizaro, Salar de, Argentina 94 A2 24 40S 67 50W
Arizona, Argentina 94 D2 35 45S 65 25W
Arizona □, U.S.A. 83 J8 34 0N 112 0W
Arizpe, Mexico 86 A2 30 20N 110 11W
Arjeplog, Sweden 8 D18 66 3N 18 2 E
Arjona, Colombia 92 A3 10 14N 75 22W
Arjuna, Indonesia 37 G15 7 49S 112 34 E
Arka, Russia 27 C15 60 15N 142 0 E
Arkadelphia, U.S.A. 81 H8 34 7N 93 4W
Arkaig, L., U.K. 12 E3 56 59N 5 10W
Arkalyk = Arqalyk, Kazakstan 26 D7 50 13N 66 50 E
Arkansas □, U.S.A. 81 H8 35 0N 92 30W
Arkansas →, U.S.A. 81 J9 33 47N 91 4W
Arkansas City, U.S.A. 81 G6 37 4N 97 2W
Arkaroola, Australia 63 E2 30 20S 139 22 E
Arkhángelos, Greece 23 C10 36 13N 28 7 E
Arkhangelsk, Russia 24 B7 64 38N 40 36 E
Arki, India 42 D7 31 9N 76 58 E
Arklow, Ireland 13 D5 52 48N 6 10W
Arkport, U.S.A. 78 D7 42 24N 77 42W
Arkticheskiy, Mys, Russia 27 A10 81 10N 95 0 E
Arkville, U.S.A. 79 D10 42 9N 74 37W
Arlanzón →, Spain 19 A3 42 3N 4 17W
Arlbergpass, Austria 16 E6 47 9N 10 12 E
Arles, France 18 E6 43 41N 4 40 E
Arlington, S. Africa 57 D4 28 1S 27 53 E
Arlington, N.Y., U.S.A. 79 E11 41 42N 73 54W
Arlington, Oreg., U.S.A. 82 D3 45 43N 120 12W
Arlington, S. Dak., U.S.A. 80 C6 44 22N 97 8W
Arlington, Tex., U.S.A. 81 J6 32 44N 97 7W
Arlington, Va., U.S.A. 76 F7 38 53N 77 7W
Arlington, Vt., U.S.A. 79 C11 43 5N 73 9W
Arlington, Wash., U.S.A. 84 B4 48 12N 122 8W
Arlington Heights, U.S.A. 76 D2 42 5N 87 59W
Arlit, Niger 50 E7 19 0N 7 38 E
Arlon, Belgium 15 E5 49 42N 5 49 E
Arltunga, Australia 62 C1 23 26S 134 41 E
Armagh, U.K. 13 B5 54 21N 6 39W
Armagh □, U.K. 13 B5 54 18N 6 37W
Armavir, Russia 25 E7 45 2N 41 7 E
Armenia, Colombia 92 C3 4 35N 75 45W
Armenia ■, Asia 25 F7 40 20N 45 0 E
Armenistís, Ákra, Greece 23 C9 36 8N 27 42 E
Armidale, Australia 63 E5 30 30S 151 40 E
Armour, U.S.A. 80 D5 43 19N 98 21W
Armstrong, B.C., Canada 72 C5 50 25N 119 10W
Armstrong, Ont., Canada 70 B2 50 18N 89 4W
Arnarfjörður, Iceland 8 D2 65 48N 23 40W
Arnaud →, Canada 69 B12 60 0N 70 0W
Arnauti, C., Cyprus 23 D11 35 6N 32 17 E
Arnett, U.S.A. 81 G5 36 8N 99 46W
Arnhem, Neths. 15 C5 51 58N 5 55 E
Arnhem, C., Australia 62 A2 12 20S 137 30 E
Arnhem B., Australia 62 A2 12 20S 136 10 E
Arnhem Land, Australia 62 A1 13 10S 134 30 E
Arno →, Italy 20 C4 43 41N 10 17 E
Arno Bay, Australia 63 E2 33 54S 136 34 E
Arnold, U.K. 10 D6 53 1N 1 7W
Arnold, U.S.A. 84 G6 38 15N 120 20W
Arnot, Canada 73 B9 55 56N 96 41W
Arnøy, Norway 8 A19 70 9N 20 40 E
Arnprior, Canada 79 A8 45 26N 76 21W
Arnsberg, Germany 16 C5 51 24N 8 5 E
Aroab, Namibia 56 D2 26 41S 19 39 E
Aron, India 42 G6 25 57N 77 56 E
Arqalyk, Kazakstan 26 D7 50 13N 66 50 E
Arrah = Ara, India 43 G11 25 35N 84 32 E
Arran, U.K. 12 F3 55 34N 5 12W
Arras, France 18 A5 50 17N 2 46 E
Arrecife, Canary Is. 22 F6 28 57N 13 37W
Arrecifes, Argentina 94 C3 34 6S 60 9W
Arrée, Mts. d', France 18 B2 48 26N 3 55W
Arriaga, Chiapas, Mexico 87 D6 16 15N 93 52W
Arriaga, San Luis Potosí, Mexico 86 C4 21 55N 101 23W
Arrilalah, Australia 62 C3 23 43S 143 54 E
Arrino, Australia 61 E2 29 30S 115 40 E
Arrow, L., Ireland 13 B3 54 3N 8 19W
Arrowhead, L., U.S.A. 85 L9 34 16N 117 10W
Arrowtown, N.Z. 59 L2 44 57S 168 50 E
Arroyo Grande, U.S.A. 85 K6 35 7N 120 35W
Ars, Iran 44 B5 37 9N 47 46 E
Arsenault L., Canada 73 B7 55 6N 108 32W
Arsenev, Russia 30 B6 44 10N 133 15 E
Árta, Greece 21 E9 39 8N 21 2 E
Artà, Spain 22 B10 39 41N 3 21 E
Arteaga, Mexico 86 D4 18 50N 102 20W
Artem, Russia 30 C6 43 22N 132 13 E
Artemovsk, Russia 27 D10 54 45N 93 35 E
Artemovsk, Ukraine 25 E6 48 35N 38 0 E
Artesia = Mosomane, Botswana 56 C4 24 2S 26 19 E
Artesia, U.S.A. 81 J2 32 51N 104 24W
Arthur, Canada 78 C4 43 50N 80 32W
Arthur →, Australia 62 G3 41 2S 144 40 E
Arthur Cr. →, Australia 62 C2 22 30S 136 25 E
Arthur Pt., Australia 62 C5 22 7S 150 3 E
Arthur River, Australia 61 F2 33 20S 117 2 E
Arthur's Pass, N.Z. 59 K3 42 54S 171 35 E
Arthur's Town, Bahamas 89 B4 24 38N 75 42W
Artigas, Uruguay 94 C4 30 20S 56 30W
Artillery L., Canada 73 A7 63 9N 107 52W
Artois, France 18 A5 50 20N 2 30 E
Artrutx, C. de, Spain 22 B10 39 55N 3 49 E
Artsyz, Ukraine 17 E15 46 4N 29 26 E
Artvin, Turkey 25 F7 41 14N 41 44 E
Aru, Kepulauan, Indonesia 37 F8 6 0S 134 30 E
Aru Is. = Aru, Kepulauan, Indonesia 37 F8 6 0S 134 30 E
Arua, Uganda 54 B3 3 1N 30 58 E
Aruanã, Brazil 93 F8 14 54S 51 10W
Aruba ■, W. Indies 89 D6 12 30N 70 0W
Arucas, Canary Is. 22 F4 28 7N 15 32W
Arun →, Nepal 43 F12 26 55N 87 10 E
Arun →, U.K. 11 G7 50 49N 0 33W
Arunachal Pradesh □, India 41 F19 28 0N 95 0 E
Arusha, Tanzania 54 C4 3 20S 36 40 E
Arusha □, Tanzania 54 C4 4 0S 36 30 E
Arusha Chini, Tanzania 54 C4 3 32S 37 20 E
Aruwimi →, Dem. Rep. of the Congo 54 B1 1 13N 23 36 E
Arvada, Colo., U.S.A. 80 F2 39 48N 105 5W
Arvada, Wyo., U.S.A. 82 D10 44 39N 106 8W
Árvi, Greece 23 E7 34 59N 25 28 E
Arviat, Canada 73 A10 61 6N 93 59W
Arvidsjaur, Sweden 8 D18 65 35N 19 10 E
Arvika, Sweden 9 G15 59 40N 12 36 E
Arvin, U.S.A. 85 K8 35 12N 118 50W
Arwal, India 43 G11 25 15N 84 41 E
Arxan, China 33 B6 47 11N 119 57 E
Aryirádhes, Greece 23 B3 39 27N 19 58 E
Aryiroúpolis, Greece 23 D6 35 17N 24 20 E
Arys, Kazakstan 26 E7 42 26N 68 48 E
Arzamas, Russia 24 C7 55 27N 43 55 E
Aş Şafā, Syria 47 B6 33 10N 37 0 E
As Saffānīyah, Si. Arabia 45 E6 27 55N 48 50 E
As Safīrah, Syria 44 B3 36 5N 37 21 E
Aş Şahm, Oman 45 E8 24 10N 56 53 E
As Sājir, Si. Arabia 44 E5 25 11N 44 36 E
As Salamīyah, Syria 44 C3 35 1N 37 2 E
As Salmān, Iraq 44 D5 30 30N 44 32 E
As Salṭ, Jordan 47 C4 32 2N 35 43 E
As Sal'w'a, Qatar 45 E6 24 23N 50 50 E
As Samāwah, Iraq 44 D5 31 15N 45 15 E
As Sanamayn, Syria 47 B5 33 3N 36 10 E
As Sohar = Şuḥār, Oman 46 C6 24 20N 56 40 E
As Sukhnah, Syria 44 C3 34 52N 38 52 E
As Sulaymānīyah, Iraq 44 C5 35 35N 45 29 E
As Sulaymī, Si. Arabia 44 E4 26 17N 41 21 E
As Sulayyil, Si. Arabia 46 C4 20 27N 45 34 E
As Summān, Si. Arabia 44 E5 25 0N 47 0 E
As Suwaydā', Syria 47 C5 32 40N 36 30 E
As Suwaydā' □, Syria 47 C5 32 45N 36 45 E
As Suwayq, Oman 45 F8 23 51N 57 26 E
Aş Şuwayrah, Iraq 44 C5 32 55N 45 0 E
Asab, Namibia 56 D2 25 30S 18 0 E
Asad, Buḥayrat al, Syria 44 C3 36 0N 38 15 E
Asahi-Gawa →, Japan 31 G6 34 36N 133 58 E
Asahigawa, Japan 30 C11 43 46N 142 22 E
Asamankese, Ghana 50 G5 5 50N 0 40W
Asan →, India 43 F8 26 37N 78 24 E
Asansol, India 43 H12 23 40N 87 1 E
Asbesberge, S. Africa 56 D3 29 0S 23 0 E
Asbestos, Canada 71 C5 45 47N 71 58W
Asbury Park, U.S.A. 79 F10 40 13N 74 1W
Ascensión, Mexico 86 A3 31 6N 107 59W
Ascensión, B. de la, Mexico 87 D7 19 50N 87 20W
Ascension I., Atl. Oc. 49 G2 7 57S 14 23W
Aschaffenburg, Germany 16 D5 49 58N 9 6 E
Aschersleben, Germany 16 C6 51 45N 11 29 E
Áscoli Piceno, Italy 20 C5 42 51N 13 34 E
Ascope, Peru 92 E3 7 46S 79 8W
Ascotán, Chile 94 A2 21 45S 68 17W
Aseb, Eritrea 46 E3 13 0N 42 40 E
Asela, Ethiopia 46 F2 8 0N 39 0 E
Asenovgrad, Bulgaria 21 C11 42 1N 24 51 E
Aserradero, Mexico 86 C3 23 40N 105 43W
Asgata, Cyprus 23 E12 34 46N 33 15 E
Ash Fork, U.S.A. 83 J7 35 13N 112 29W
Ash Grove, U.S.A. 81 G8 37 19N 93 35W
Ash Shabakah, Iraq 44 D4 30 49N 43 39 E
Ash Shamāl □, Lebanon 47 A5 34 25N 36 0 E
Ash Shāmīyah, Iraq 44 D5 31 55N 44 35 E
Ash Shāriqah, U.A.E. 46 B6 25 23N 55 26 E
Ash Sharmah, Si. Arabia 44 D2 28 1N 35 16 E
Ash Sharqāt, Iraq 44 C4 35 27N 43 16 E
Ash Sharqi, Al Jabal, Lebanon 47 B5 33 40N 36 10 E
Ash Shaṭrah, Iraq 44 D5 31 30N 46 10 E
Ash Shawbak, Jordan 44 D2 30 32N 35 34 E
Ash Shawmari, J., Jordan 47 E5 30 35N 36 35 E
Ash Shināfīyah, Iraq 44 D5 31 35N 44 39 E
Ash Shu'bah, Si. Arabia 44 D5 28 54N 44 44 E
Ash Shumlūl, Si. Arabia 44 E5 26 31N 47 20 E
Ash Shūr'a, Iraq 44 C4 35 58N 43 13 E
Ash Shurayf, Si. Arabia 44 E3 25 43N 39 14 E
Ash Shuwayfāt, Lebanon 47 B4 33 45N 35 30 E
Asha, Russia 24 D10 55 0N 57 16 E
Ashau, Vietnam 38 D6 16 6N 107 22 E
Ashbourne, U.K. 10 D6 53 2N 1 43W
Ashburn, U.S.A. 77 K4 31 43N 83 39W
Ashburton, N.Z. 59 K3 43 53S 171 48 E
Ashburton →, Australia 60 D1 21 40S 114 56 E
Ashcroft, Canada 72 C4 50 40N 121 20W
Ashdod, Israel 47 D3 31 49N 34 35 E
Ashdown, U.S.A. 81 J7 33 40N 94 8W
Asheboro, U.S.A. 77 H6 35 43N 79 49W
Ashern, Canada 73 C9 51 11N 98 21W
Asherton, U.S.A. 81 L5 28 27N 99 46W
Asheville, U.S.A. 77 H4 35 36N 82 33W
Ashewat, Pakistan 42 D3 31 22N 68 32 E
Asheweig →, Canada 70 B2 54 17N 87 12W
Ashford, Australia 63 D5 29 15S 151 3 E
Ashford, U.K. 11 F8 51 8N 0 53 E
Ashgabat, Turkmenistan 26 F6 38 0N 57 50 E
Ashibetsu, Japan 30 C11 43 31N 142 11 E
Ashikaga, Japan 31 F9 36 28N 139 29 E
Ashington, U.K. 10 B6 55 11N 1 33W
Ashizuri-Zaki, Japan 31 H6 32 44N 133 0 E
Ashkarkot, Afghan. 42 C2 33 3N 67 58 E
Ashkhabad = Ashgabat, Turkmenistan 26 F6 38 0N 57 50 E

Āshkhāneh, Iran 45 B8 37 26N 56 55 E
Ashland, Kans., U.S.A. 81 G5 37 11N 99 46W
Ashland, Ky., U.S.A. 76 F4 38 28N 82 38W
Ashland, Mont., U.S.A. 82 D10 45 36N 106 16W
Ashland, Ohio, U.S.A. 78 F2 40 52N 82 19W
Ashland, Oreg., U.S.A. 82 E2 42 12N 122 43W
Ashland, Pa., U.S.A. 79 F8 40 45N 76 22W
Ashland, Va., U.S.A. 76 G7 37 46N 77 29W
Ashland, Wis., U.S.A. 80 B9 46 35N 90 53W
Ashley, N. Dak., U.S.A. 80 B5 46 2N 99 22W
Ashley, Pa., U.S.A. 79 E9 41 12N 75 55W
Ashmore Reef, Australia 60 B3 12 14S 123 5 E
Ashmyany, Belarus 9 J21 54 26N 25 52 E
Ashokan Reservoir, U.S.A. 79 E10 41 56N 74 13W
Ashqelon, Israel 47 D3 31 42N 34 35 E
Ashta, India 42 H7 23 1N 76 43 E
Ashtabula, U.S.A. 78 E4 41 52N 80 47W
Ashton, S. Africa 56 E3 33 50S 20 5 E
Ashton, U.S.A. 82 D8 44 4N 111 27W
Ashuanipi, L., Canada 71 B6 52 45N 66 15W
Ashville, U.S.A. 78 F6 40 34N 78 33W
Asia 28 E11 45 0N 75 0 E
Asia, Kepulauan, Indonesia 37 D8 1 0N 131 13 E
Āsīā Bak, Iran 45 C6 35 19N 50 30 E
Asifabad, India 40 K11 19 20N 79 24 E
Asinara, Italy 20 D3 41 4N 8 16 E
Asinara, G. dell', Italy 20 D3 41 0N 8 30 E
Asino, Russia 26 D9 57 0N 86 0 E
Asipovichy, Belarus 17 B15 53 19N 28 33 E
'Asīr □, Si. Arabia 46 D3 18 40N 42 30 E
Asir, Ras, Somali Rep. 46 E5 11 55N 51 10 E
Askersund, Sweden 9 G16 58 53N 14 55 E
Askham, S. Africa 56 D3 26 59S 20 47 E
Askim, Norway 9 G14 59 35N 11 10 E
Askja, Iceland 8 D5 65 3N 16 48W
Askøy, Norway 9 F11 60 29N 5 10 E
Asmara = Asmera, Eritrea 46 D2 15 19N 38 55 E
Asmera, Eritrea 46 D2 15 19N 38 55 E
Åsnen, Sweden 9 H16 56 37N 14 45 E
Aspen, U.S.A. 83 G10 39 11N 106 49W
Aspermont, U.S.A. 81 J4 33 8N 100 14W
Aspiring, Mt., N.Z. 59 L2 44 23S 168 46 E
Asprókavos, Ákra, Greece 23 B4 39 21N 20 6 E
Aspur, India 42 H6 23 58N 74 7 E
Asquith, Canada 73 C7 52 8N 107 13W
Assab = Aseb, Eritrea 46 E3 13 0N 42 40 E
Assam □, India 41 G18 26 0N 93 0 E
Asse, Belgium 15 D4 50 24N 4 10 E
Assen, Neths. 15 A6 53 0N 6 35 E
Assiniboia, Canada 73 D7 49 40N 105 59W
Assiniboine ➔, Canada 73 D9 49 53N 97 8W
Assiniboine, Mt., Canada 72 C5 50 52N 115 39W
Assis, Brazil 95 A5 22 40S 50 20W
Assisi, Italy 20 C5 43 4N 12 37 E
Assynt, L., U.K. 12 C3 58 10N 5 3W
Astana, Kazakstan 26 D8 51 10N 71 30 E
Āstāneh, Iran 45 B6 37 17N 49 59 E
Astara, Azerbaijan 25 G8 38 30N 48 50 E
Asteroúsia, Greece 23 E7 34 59N 25 3 E
Asti, Italy 18 D8 44 54N 8 12 E
Astipálaia, Greece 21 F12 36 32N 26 22 E
Astorga, Spain 19 A2 42 29N 6 8W
Astoria, U.S.A. 84 D3 46 11N 123 50W
Astrakhan, Russia 25 E8 46 25N 48 5 E
Asturias □, Spain 19 A3 43 15N 6 0W
Asunción, Paraguay 94 B4 25 10S 57 30W
Asunción Nochixtlán, Mexico 87 D5 17 28N 97 14W
Aswa ➔, Uganda 54 B3 3 43N 31 55 E
Aswân, Egypt 51 D12 24 4N 32 57 E
Aswân High Dam = Sadd el Aali, Egypt 51 D12 23 54N 32 54 E
Asyût, Egypt 51 C12 27 11N 31 4 E
At Ṭafīlah, Jordan 47 E4 30 45N 35 30 E
Aṭ Ṭā'if, Si. Arabia 46 C3 21 5N 40 27 E
Aţ Ţirāq, Si. Arabia 44 E5 27 19N 44 33 E
Aţ Tubayq, Si. Arabia 44 D3 29 30N 37 0 E
Atacama □, Chile 94 B2 27 30S 70 0W
Atacama, Desierto de, Chile 94 A2 24 0S 69 20W
Atacama, Salar de, Chile 94 A2 23 30S 68 20W
Atalaya, Peru 92 F4 10 45S 73 50W
Atalaya de Femes, Canary Is. 22 F6 28 56N 13 47W
Atami, Japan 31 G9 35 5N 139 4 E
Atapupu, E. Timor 37 F6 9 0S 124 51 E
Atâr, Mauritania 50 D3 20 30N 13 5W
Atari, Pakistan 42 D6 30 56N 74 2 E
Atascadero, U.S.A. 84 K6 35 29N 120 40W
Atasu, Kazakstan 26 E8 48 30N 71 0 E
Atatürk Barajı, Turkey 25 G6 37 28N 38 30 E
Atauro, E. Timor 37 F7 8 10S 125 30 E
'Atbara, Sudan 51 E12 17 42N 33 59 E
'Atbara, Nahr ➔, Sudan 51 E12 17 40N 33 56 E
Atbasar, Kazakstan 26 D7 51 48N 68 20 E
Atchafalaya B., U.S.A. 81 L9 29 25N 91 25W
Atchison, U.S.A. 80 F7 39 34N 95 7W
Āteshān, Iran 45 C7 35 35N 52 37 E
Ath, Belgium 15 D3 50 38N 3 47 E
Athabasca, Canada 72 C6 54 45N 113 20W
Athabasca ➔, Canada 73 B6 58 40N 110 50W
Athabasca, L., Canada 73 B7 59 15N 109 15W
Athboy, Ireland 13 C5 53 37N 6 56W
Athenry, Ireland 13 C3 53 18N 8 44W
Athens = Athínai, Greece 21 F10 37 58N 23 46 E
Athens, Ala., U.S.A. 77 H2 34 48N 86 58W
Athens, Ga., U.S.A. 77 J4 33 57N 83 23W
Athens, N.Y., U.S.A. 79 D11 42 16N 73 49W
Athens, Ohio, U.S.A. 76 F4 39 20N 82 6W
Athens, Pa., U.S.A. 79 E8 41 57N 76 31W
Athens, Tenn., U.S.A. 77 H3 35 27N 84 36W
Athens, Tex., U.S.A. 81 J7 32 12N 95 51W
Atherley, Canada 78 B5 44 37N 79 20W
Atherton, Australia 62 B4 17 17S 145 30 E
Athienou, Cyprus 23 D12 35 3N 33 32 E
Athínai, Greece 21 F10 37 58N 23 46 E
Athlone, Ireland 13 C4 53 25N 7 56W
Athna, Cyprus 23 D12 35 3N 33 47 E
Athol, U.S.A. 79 D12 42 36N 72 14W
Atholl, Forest of, U.K. 12 E5 56 51N 3 50W
Atholville, Canada 71 C6 47 59N 66 43W
Áthos, Greece 21 D11 40 9N 24 22 E
Athy, Ireland 13 C5 53 0N 7 0W
Ati, Chad 51 F9 13 13N 18 20 E
Atiak, Uganda 54 B3 3 12N 32 2 E
Atik L., Canada 73 B9 55 15N 96 0W
Atikameg ➔, Canada 70 B3 52 30N 82 46W
Atikokan, Canada 70 C1 48 45N 91 37W
Atikonak L., Canada 71 B7 52 40N 64 32W
Atka, Russia 27 C16 60 50N 151 48 E
Atka I., U.S.A. 68 C2 52 7N 174 30W
Atkinson, U.S.A. 80 D5 42 32N 98 59W
Atlanta, Ga., U.S.A. 77 J3 33 45N 84 23W
Atlanta, Tex., U.S.A. 81 J7 33 7N 94 10W
Atlantic, U.S.A. 80 E7 41 24N 95 1W
Atlantic City, U.S.A. 76 F8 39 21N 74 27W
Atlantic Ocean 2 E9 0 0 20 0W
Atlas Mts. = Haut Atlas, Morocco 50 B4 32 30N 5 0W
Atlin, Canada 72 B2 59 31N 133 41W
Atlin, L., Canada 72 B2 59 26N 133 45W
Atlin Prov. Park, Canada 72 B2 59 10N 134 30W
Atmore, U.S.A. 77 K2 31 2N 87 29W
Atoka, U.S.A. 81 H6 34 23N 96 8W
Atolia, U.S.A. 85 K9 35 19N 117 37W
Atrai ➔, Bangla. 43 G13 24 7N 89 22 E
Atrak = Atrek ➔, Turkmenistan 45 B8 37 35N 53 58 E
Atrauli, India 42 E8 28 2N 78 20 E
Atrek ➔, Turkmenistan 45 B8 37 35N 53 58 E
Atsuta, Japan 30 C10 43 24N 141 26 E
Attalla, U.S.A. 77 H2 34 1N 86 6W
Attapu, Laos 38 E6 14 48N 106 50 E
Attáviros, Greece 23 C9 36 12N 27 50 E
Attawapiskat, Canada 70 B3 52 56N 82 24W
Attawapiskat ➔, Canada 70 B3 52 57N 82 18W
Attawapiskat L., Canada 70 B2 52 18N 87 54W
Attica, Ind., U.S.A. 76 E2 40 18N 87 15W
Attica, Ohio, U.S.A. 78 E2 41 4N 82 53W
Attikamagen L., Canada 71 B6 55 0N 66 30W
Attleboro, U.S.A. 79 E13 41 57N 71 17W
Attock, Pakistan 42 C5 33 52N 72 20 E
Attopeu = Attapu, Laos 38 E6 14 48N 106 50 E
Attu I., U.S.A. 68 C1 52 55N 172 55 E
Attur, India 40 P11 11 35N 78 30 E
Atuel ➔, Argentina 94 D2 36 17S 66 50W
Åtvidaberg, Sweden 9 G17 58 12N 16 0 E
Atwater, U.S.A. 84 H6 37 21N 120 37W
Atwood, Canada 78 C3 43 40N 81 1W
Atwood, U.S.A. 80 F4 39 48N 101 3W
Atyraū, Kazakstan 25 E9 47 5N 52 0 E
Au Sable, U.S.A. 78 B1 44 25N 83 20W
Au Sable ➔, U.S.A. 76 C4 44 25N 83 20W
Au Sable Forks, U.S.A. 79 B11 44 27N 73 41W
Au Sable Pt., U.S.A. 78 B1 44 20N 83 20W
Aubagne, France 18 E6 43 17N 5 37 E
Aubarca, C. d', Spain 22 B7 39 4N 1 22 E
Aube ➔, France 18 B5 48 34N 3 43 E
Auberry, U.S.A. 84 H7 37 7N 119 29W
Auburn, Ala., U.S.A. 77 J3 32 36N 85 29W
Auburn, Calif., U.S.A. 84 G5 38 54N 121 4W
Auburn, Ind., U.S.A. 76 E3 41 22N 85 4W
Auburn, Maine, U.S.A. 77 C10 44 6N 70 14W
Auburn, N.Y., U.S.A. 79 D8 42 56N 76 34W
Auburn, Nebr., U.S.A. 80 E7 40 23N 95 51W
Auburn, Pa., U.S.A. 79 F8 40 36N 76 6W
Auburn, Wash., U.S.A. 84 C4 47 18N 122 14W
Auburn Ra., Australia 63 D5 25 15S 150 30 E
Auburndale, U.S.A. 77 L5 28 4N 81 48W
Aubusson, France 18 D5 45 57N 2 11 E
Auch, France 18 E4 43 39N 0 36 E
Auckland, N.Z. 59 G5 36 52S 174 46 E
Auckland Is., Pac. Oc. 64 N8 50 40S 166 5 E
Aude ➔, France 18 E5 43 13N 3 14 E
Auden, Canada 70 B2 50 14N 87 53W
Audubon, U.S.A. 80 E7 41 43N 94 56W
Augathella, Australia 63 D4 25 48S 146 35 E
Aughnacloy, U.K. 13 B5 54 25N 6 59W
Augrabies Falls, S. Africa 56 D3 28 35S 20 20 E
Augsburg, Germany 16 D6 48 25N 10 52 E
Augusta, Australia 61 F2 34 19S 115 9 E
Augusta, Italy 20 F6 37 13N 15 13 E
Augusta, Ark., U.S.A. 81 H9 35 17N 91 22W
Augusta, Ga., U.S.A. 77 J5 33 28N 81 58W
Augusta, Kans., U.S.A. 81 G6 37 41N 96 59W
Augusta, Maine, U.S.A. 69 D13 44 19N 69 47W
Augusta, Mont., U.S.A. 82 C7 47 30N 112 24W
Augustów, Poland 17 B12 53 51N 23 0 E
Augustus, Mt., Australia 61 D2 24 20S 116 50 E
Augustus I., Australia 60 C3 15 20S 124 30 E
Aukum, U.S.A. 84 G6 38 34N 120 43W
Auld, L., Australia 60 D3 22 25S 123 50 E
Ault, U.S.A. 80 E2 40 35N 104 44W
Aunis, France 18 C3 46 5N 0 50W
Auponhia, Indonesia 37 E7 1 58S 125 27 E
Aur, Pulau, Malaysia 39 L5 2 35N 104 10 E
Auraiya, India 43 F8 26 28N 79 33 E
Aurangabad, Bihar, India 43 G11 24 45N 84 18 E
Aurangabad, Maharashtra, India 40 K9 19 50N 75 23 E
Aurich, Germany 16 B4 53 28N 7 28 E
Aurillac, France 18 D5 44 55N 2 26 E
Aurora, Canada 78 C5 44 0N 79 28W
Aurora, S. Africa 56 E2 32 40S 18 29 E
Aurora, Colo., U.S.A. 80 F2 39 44N 104 52W
Aurora, Ill., U.S.A. 76 E1 41 45N 88 19W
Aurora, Mo., U.S.A. 81 G8 36 58N 93 43W
Aurora, N.Y., U.S.A. 79 D8 42 45N 76 42W
Aurora, Nebr., U.S.A. 80 E6 40 52N 98 0W
Aurora, Ohio, U.S.A. 78 E3 41 21N 81 20W
Aurukun, Australia 62 A3 13 20S 141 45 E
Aus, Namibia 56 D2 26 35S 16 12 E
Ausable ➔, Canada 78 C3 43 19N 81 46W
Auschwitz = Oświęcim, Poland 17 C10 50 2N 19 11 E
Austin, Minn., U.S.A. 80 D8 43 40N 92 58W
Austin, Nev., U.S.A. 82 G5 39 30N 117 4W
Austin, Pa., U.S.A. 78 E6 41 38N 78 6W
Austin, Tex., U.S.A. 81 K6 30 17N 97 45W
Austin, L., Australia 61 E2 27 40S 118 0 E
Austin I., Canada 73 A10 61 10N 94 0W
Austra, Norway 8 D14 65 8N 11 55 E
Austral Is. = Tubuai Is., Pac. Oc. 65 K13 25 0S 150 0W
Austral Seamount Chain, Pac. Oc. 65 K13 24 0S 150 0W
Australia ■, Oceania 64 K5 23 0S 135 0 E
Australian Capital Territory □, Australia 63 F4 35 30S 149 0 E
Australind, Australia 61 F2 33 17S 115 42 E
Austria ■, Europe 16 E8 47 0N 14 0 E
Austvågøy, Norway 8 B16 68 20N 14 40 E
Autlán, Mexico 86 D4 19 40N 104 30W
Autun, France 18 C6 46 58N 4 17 E
Auvergne, France 18 D5 45 20N 3 15 E
Auvergne, Mts. d', France 18 D5 45 20N 2 55 E
Auxerre, France 18 C5 47 48N 3 32 E
Ava, U.S.A. 81 G8 36 57N 92 40W
Avallon, France 18 C5 47 30N 3 53 E
Avalon, U.S.A. 85 M8 33 21N 118 20W
Avalon Pen., Canada 71 C9 47 30N 53 20W
Avanos, Turkey 44 B2 38 43N 34 51 E
Avaré, Brazil 95 A6 23 4S 48 58W
Avawatz Mts., U.S.A. 85 K10 35 40N 116 30W
Aveiro, Brazil 93 D7 3 10S 55 5W
Aveiro, Portugal 19 B1 40 37N 8 38W
Āvej, Iran 45 C6 35 40N 49 15 E
Avellaneda, Argentina 94 C4 34 50S 58 10W
Avellino, Italy 20 D6 40 54N 14 47 E
Avenal, U.S.A. 84 K6 36 0N 120 8W
Aversa, Italy 20 D6 40 58N 14 12 E
Avery, U.S.A. 82 C6 47 15N 115 49W
Aves, Is. las, Venezuela 89 D6 12 0N 67 30W
Avesta, Sweden 9 F17 60 9N 16 10 E
Avezzano, Italy 20 C5 42 2N 13 25 E
Aviá Terai, Argentina 94 B3 26 45S 60 50W
Aviemore, U.K. 12 D5 57 12N 3 50W
Avignon, France 18 E6 43 57N 4 50 E
Ávila, Spain 19 B3 40 39N 4 43W
Avila Beach, U.S.A. 85 K6 35 11N 120 44W
Avilés, Spain 19 A3 43 35N 5 57W
Avis, U.S.A. 78 E7 41 11N 77 19W
Avoca, U.S.A. 78 D7 42 25N 77 25W
Avoca ➔, Australia 63 F3 35 40S 143 43 E
Avoca ➔, Ireland 13 D5 52 48N 6 10W
Avola, Canada 72 C5 51 45N 119 19W
Avola, Italy 20 F6 36 56N 15 7 E
Avon, U.S.A. 78 D7 42 55N 77 45W
Avon ➔, Australia 61 F2 31 40S 116 7 E
Avon ➔, Bristol, U.K. 11 F5 51 29N 2 41W
Avon ➔, Dorset, U.K. 11 G6 50 44N 1 46W
Avon ➔, Warks., U.K. 11 E5 52 0N 2 8W
Avon Park, U.S.A. 77 M5 27 36N 81 31W
Avondale, Zimbabwe 55 F3 17 43S 30 58 E
Avonlea, Canada 73 D8 50 0N 105 0W
Avonmore, Canada 79 A10 45 10N 74 58W
Avranches, France 18 B3 48 40N 1 20W
A'waj ➔, Syria 47 B5 33 23N 36 20 E
Awaji-Shima, Japan 31 G7 34 30N 134 50 E
'Awālī, Bahrain 45 E6 26 0N 50 30 E
Awantipur, India 43 C6 33 55N 75 3 E
Awasa, Ethiopia 46 F2 7 2N 38 28 E
Awash, Ethiopia 46 F3 9 1N 40 10 E
Awatere ➔, N.Z. 59 J5 41 37S 174 10 E
Awbārī, Libya 51 C8 26 46N 12 57 E
Awe, L., U.K. 12 E3 56 17N 5 16W
Awjilah, Libya 51 C10 29 8N 21 7 E
Axe ➔, U.K. 11 F5 50 42N 3 4W
Axel Heiberg I., Canada 4 B3 80 0N 90 0W
Axim, Ghana 50 H5 4 51N 2 15W
Axiós ➔, Greece 21 D10 40 57N 22 35 E
Axminster, U.K. 11 G4 50 46N 3 0W
Ayabaca, Peru 92 D3 4 40S 79 53W
Ayabe, Japan 31 G7 35 20N 135 20 E
Ayacucho, Argentina 94 D4 37 5S 58 20W
Ayacucho, Peru 92 F4 13 0S 74 0W
Ayaguz, Kazakstan 26 E9 48 10N 80 10 E
Ayamonte, Spain 19 D2 37 12N 7 24W
Ayan, Russia 27 D14 56 30N 138 16 E
Ayaviri, Peru 92 F4 14 50S 70 35W
Aydın, Turkey 21 F12 37 51N 27 51 E
Aydin □, Turkey 25 G4 37 50N 28 0 E
Ayer, U.S.A. 79 D13 42 34N 71 35W
Ayer's Cliff, Canada 79 A12 45 10N 72 3W
Ayers Rock, Australia 61 E5 25 23S 131 5 E
Ayia Aikateríni, Ákra, Greece 23 A3 39 50N 19 50 E
Ayia Dhéka, Greece 23 D6 35 3N 24 58 E
Ayia Gálini, Greece 23 D6 35 6N 24 41 E
Áyia Napa, Cyprus 23 E13 34 59N 34 0 E
Áyia Phyla, Cyprus 23 E12 34 43N 33 1 E
Áyia Varvára, Greece 23 D7 35 8N 25 1 E
Áyios Amvrósios, Cyprus 23 D12 35 20N 33 35 E
Áyios Evstrátios, Greece 21 E11 39 34N 24 58 E
Áyios Ioánnis, Ákra, Greece 23 D7 35 20N 25 40 E
Áyios Isidhoros, Greece 23 C9 36 9N 27 51 E
Áyios Matthaíos, Greece 23 B3 39 30N 19 47 E
Áyios Nikólaos, Greece 23 D7 35 11N 25 41 E
Áyios Seryios, Cyprus 23 D12 35 12N 33 53 E
Áyios Theodhoros, Cyprus 23 D13 35 22N 34 1 E
Aykino, Russia 24 B8 62 15N 49 56 E
Aylesbury, U.K. 11 F7 51 49N 0 49W
Aylmer, Canada 78 D4 42 46N 80 59W
Aylmer, L., Canada 68 B8 64 0N 110 8W
'Ayn, Wādī al, Oman 45 F7 22 15N 55 28 E
Ayn Dār, Si. Arabia 45 E7 25 55N 49 10 E
Ayn Zālah, Iraq 44 B4 36 45N 42 35 E
Ayolas, Paraguay 94 B4 27 10S 56 59W
Ayon, Ostrov, Russia 27 C17 69 50N 169 0 E
'Ayoûn el 'Atroûs, Mauritania 50 E4 16 38N 9 37W
Ayr, Australia 62 B4 19 35S 147 25 E
Ayr, Canada 78 C4 43 17N 80 27W
Ayr, U.K. 12 F4 55 28N 4 38W
Ayr ➔, U.K. 12 F4 55 28N 4 38W
Ayre, Pt. of, U.K. 10 C3 54 25N 4 21W
Ayton, Australia 62 B4 15 56S 145 22 E
Aytos, Bulgaria 21 C12 42 42N 27 16 E
Ayu, Kepulauan, Indonesia 37 D8 0 35N 131 5 E
Ayutla, Guatemala 88 D1 14 40N 92 10W
Ayutla, Mexico 87 D5 16 58N 99 17W
Ayvacık, Turkey 21 E12 39 36N 26 24 E
Ayvalık, Turkey 21 E12 39 20N 26 46 E
Az Zabadānī, Syria 47 B5 33 43N 36 5 E
Aẓ Ẓāhirīyah, West Bank 47 D3 31 25N 34 58 E
Aẓ Ẓahrān, Si. Arabia 45 E6 26 10N 50 7 E
Az Zarqā, Jordan 47 C5 32 5N 36 4 E
Az Zarqā', U.A.E. 45 E7 24 53N 53 4 E
Az Zībār, Iraq 44 B5 36 52N 44 4 E
Az Zilfī, Si. Arabia 44 E5 26 12N 44 52 E
Az Zubayr, Iraq 44 D5 30 26N 47 40 E
Azamgarh, India 43 F10 26 5N 83 13 E
Azangaro, Peru 92 F4 14 55S 70 13W
Āzār Shahr, Iran 44 B5 37 45N 45 59 E
Azarān, Iran 44 B5 37 25N 47 16 E
Azärbayjan = Azerbaijan ■, Asia 25 F8 40 20N 48 0 E
Āzarbāyjān-e Gharbī □, Iran 44 B5 37 0N 44 30 E
Āzarbāyjān-e Sharqī □, Iran 44 B5 37 20N 47 0 E
Azare, Nigeria 50 F8 11 55N 10 10 E
A'zāz, Syria 44 B3 36 36N 37 4 E
Azbine = Aïr, Niger 50 E7 18 30N 8 0 E
Azerbaijan ■, Asia 25 F8 40 20N 48 0 E
Azerbaijchan = Azerbaijan ■, Asia 25 F8 40 20N 48 0 E
Azimganj, India 43 G13 24 14N 88 16 E
Azogues, Ecuador 92 D3 2 35S 78 0W
Azores = Açores, Is. dos, Atl. Oc. 50 A1 38 0N 27 0W
Azov, Russia 25 E6 47 3N 39 25 E
Azov, Sea of, Europe 25 E6 46 0N 36 30 E
Azovskoye More = Azov, Sea of, Europe 25 E6 46 0N 36 30 E
Azraq ash Shīshān, Jordan 47 D5 31 50N 36 49 E
Aztec, U.S.A. 83 H10 36 49N 107 59W
Azúa de Compostela, Dom. Rep. 89 C5 18 25N 70 44W
Azuaga, Spain 19 C3 38 16N 5 39W
Azuero, Pen. de, Panama 88 E3 7 30N 80 30W
Azul, Argentina 94 D4 36 42S 59 43W
Azusa, U.S.A. 85 L9 34 8N 117 52W

B

Ba Don, Vietnam 38 D6 17 45N 106 26 E
Ba Dong, Vietnam 39 H6 9 40N 106 33 E
Ba Ngoi = Cam Lam, Vietnam 39 G7 11 54N 109 10 E
Ba Tri, Vietnam 39 G6 10 2N 106 36 E
Ba Xian = Bazhou, China 34 E9 39 8N 116 22 E
Baa, Indonesia 37 F6 10 50S 123 0 E
Baardeere = Bardera, Somali Rep. 46 G3 2 20N 42 27 E
Baarle-Nassau, Belgium 15 C4 51 27N 4 56 E
Bab el Mandeb, Red Sea 46 E3 12 35N 43 25 E
Bābā, Koh-i-, Afghan. 40 B5 34 30N 67 0 E
Baba Burnu, Turkey 21 E12 39 29N 26 2 E
Bābā Kalū, Iran 45 D6 30 7N 50 49 E
Babadag, Romania 17 F15 44 53N 28 44 E
Babadayhan, Turkmenistan 26 F7 37 42N 60 23 E
Babaeski, Turkey 21 D12 41 26N 27 6 E
Babahoyo, Ecuador 92 D3 1 40S 79 30W
Babai = Sarju ➔, India 43 F9 27 21N 81 23 E
Babar, Indonesia 37 F7 8 0S 129 30 E
Babar, Pakistan 42 D3 31 7N 69 32 E
Babarkach, Pakistan 42 E3 29 45N 68 0 E
Babb, U.S.A. 82 B7 48 51N 113 27W
Baberu, India 43 G9 25 33N 80 43 E
Babi Besar, Pulau, Malaysia 39 L4 2 25N 103 59 E
Babinda, Australia 62 B4 17 20S 145 56 E
Babine, Canada 72 B3 55 22N 126 37W
Babine ➔, Canada 72 B3 55 45N 127 44W
Babine L., Canada 72 C3 54 48N 126 0W
Babo, Indonesia 37 E8 2 30S 133 30 E
Bābol, Iran 45 B7 36 40N 52 50 E
Bābol Sar, Iran 45 B7 36 45N 52 45 E
Babruysk, Belarus 17 B15 53 10N 29 15 E
Babuhri, India 42 F3 26 49N 69 43 E
Babusar Pass, Pakistan 43 B5 35 12N 73 59 E
Babuyan Chan., Phil. 37 A6 18 40N 121 30 E
Babylon, Iraq 44 C5 32 34N 44 22 E
Bac Can, Vietnam 38 A5 22 8N 105 49 E
Bac Giang, Vietnam 38 B6 21 16N 106 11 E
Bac Lieu, Vietnam 39 H5 9 17N 105 43 E
Bac Ninh, Vietnam 38 B6 21 13N 106 4 E
Bac Phan, Vietnam 38 B5 22 0N 105 0 E
Bac Quang, Vietnam 38 A5 22 30N 104 48 E
Bacabal, Brazil 93 D10 4 15S 44 45W
Bacalar, Mexico 87 D7 18 50N 87 27W
Bacan, Kepulauan, Indonesia 37 E7 0 35S 127 30 E
Bacarra, Phil. 37 A6 18 15N 120 37 E
Bacău, Romania 17 E14 46 35N 26 55 E
Bacerac, Mexico 86 A3 30 18N 108 50W
Bach Long Vi, Dao, Vietnam 38 B6 20 10N 107 40 E
Bachelina, Russia 26 D7 57 45N 67 20 E
Bachhwara, India 43 G11 25 35N 85 54 E
Back ➔, Canada 68 B9 65 10N 104 0W
Bacolod, Phil. 37 B6 10 40N 122 57 E
Bacuk, Malaysia 39 J4 6 4N 102 25 E
Bād, Iran 45 C7 33 41N 52 1 E
Bad ➔, U.S.A. 80 C4 44 21N 100 22W
Bad Axe, U.S.A. 78 C2 43 48N 83 0W
Bad Ischl, Austria 16 E7 47 44N 13 38 E
Bad Kissingen, Germany 16 C6 50 11N 10 4 E
Bad Lands, U.S.A. 80 D3 43 40N 102 10W
Bada Barabil, India 43 H11 22 7N 85 24 E
Badagara, India 40 P9 11 35N 75 40 E
Badajós, L., Brazil 92 D6 3 15S 62 50W
Badajoz, Spain 19 C2 38 50N 6 59W
Badakhshān □, Afghan. 40 A7 36 30N 71 0 E
Badalona, Spain 19 B7 41 26N 2 15 E
Badalzai, Afghan. 42 E1 29 50N 65 35 E
Badampahar, India 41 H15 22 10N 86 10 E
Badanah, Si. Arabia 44 D4 30 58N 41 30 E
Badarinath, India 43 D8 30 45N 79 30 E
Badas, Kepulauan, Indonesia 36 D3 0 45N 107 5 E
Baddo ➔, Pakistan 40 F4 28 0N 64 20 E
Bade, Indonesia 37 F9 7 10S 139 35 E
Baden, Austria 16 D9 48 1N 16 13 E
Baden, U.S.A. 78 F4 40 38N 80 14W
Baden-Baden, Germany 16 D5 48 44N 8 13 E
Baden-Württemberg □, Germany 16 D5 48 20N 8 40 E
Badgastein, Austria 16 E7 47 7N 13 9 E
Badger, Canada 71 C8 49 0N 56 4W
Badger, U.S.A. 84 J7 36 38N 119 1W
Bādghīs □, Afghan. 40 B3 35 0N 63 0 E
Badgom, India 43 B6 34 1N 74 45 E
Badin, Pakistan 42 G3 24 38N 68 54 E
Badlands Nat. Park, U.S.A. 80 D3 43 38N 102 56W
Badrah, Iraq 44 C5 33 6N 45 58 E
Badrinath, India 43 D8 30 44N 79 29 E
Badulla, Sri Lanka 40 R12 7 1N 81 7 E
Baena, Spain 19 D3 37 37N 4 20W
Baeza, Spain 19 D4 37 57N 3 25W
Baffin B., Canada 69 A13 72 0N 64 0W
Baffin I., Canada 69 B12 68 0N 75 0W
Bafing ➔, Mali 50 F3 13 49N 10 50W
Bafliyūn, Syria 44 B3 36 37N 36 59 E
Bafoulabé, Mali 50 F3 13 50N 10 55W
Bāfq, Iran 45 D7 31 40N 55 25 E
Bafra, Turkey 25 F6 41 34N 35 54 E
Bāft, Iran 45 D8 29 15N 56 38 E
Bafwasende, Dem. Rep. of the Congo 54 B2 1 3N 27 5 E

Bagamoyo, Tanzania 54 D4 6 28S 38 55 E
Bagan Datoh, Malaysia 39 L3 3 59N 100 47 E
Bagan Serai, Malaysia 39 K3 5 1N 100 32 E
Baganga, Phil. 37 C7 7 34N 126 33 E
Bagani, Namibia 56 B3 18 7S 21 41 E
Bagansiapiapi, Indonesia 36 D2 2 12N 100 50 E
Bagasra, India 42 J4 21 30N 71 0 E
Bagaud, India 42 H6 22 19N 75 53 E
Bagdad, U.S.A. 85 L11 34 35N 115 53W
Bagdarin, Russia 27 D12 54 26N 113 36 E
Bagé, Brazil 95 C5 31 20S 54 15W
Bagenalstown = Muine Bheag, Ireland 13 D5 52 42N 6 58W
Baggs, U.S.A. 82 F10 41 2N 107 39W
Bagh, Pakistan 43 C5 33 59N 73 45 E
Baghain →, India 43 G9 25 32N 81 1 E
Baghdād, Iraq 44 C5 33 20N 44 30 E
Bagheria, Italy 20 E5 38 5N 13 30 E
Baghlān, Afghan. 40 A6 32 12N 68 46 E
Baghlān □, Afghan. 40 B6 36 0N 68 30 E
Bagley, U.S.A. 80 B7 47 32N 95 24W
Bago = Pegu, Burma 41 L20 17 20N 96 29 E
Bagodar, India 43 G11 24 5N 85 52 E
Bagrationovsk, Russia 9 J19 54 23N 20 39 E
Baguio, Phil. 37 A6 16 26N 120 34 E
Bah, India 43 F8 26 53N 78 36 E
Bahadurganj, India 43 F12 26 16N 87 49 E
Bahadurgarh, India 42 E7 28 40N 76 57 E
Bahama, Canal Viejo de, W. Indies 88 B4 22 10N 77 30W
Bahamas ■, N. Amer. 89 B5 24 0N 75 0W
Baharampur, India 43 G13 24 2N 88 27 E
Bahawalnagar, Pakistan 42 E5 30 0N 73 15 E
Bahawalpur, Pakistan 42 E4 29 24N 71 40 E
Baheri, India 43 E8 28 45N 79 34 E
Bahgul →, India 43 F8 27 45N 79 36 E
Bahi, Tanzania 54 D4 5 58S 35 21 E
Bahi Swamp, Tanzania 54 D4 6 10S 35 0 E
Bahía = Salvador, Brazil 93 F11 13 0S 38 30W
Bahía □, Brazil 93 F10 12 0S 42 0W
Bahía, Is. de la, Honduras 88 C2 16 45N 86 15W
Bahía Blanca, Argentina 94 D3 38 35S 62 13W
Bahía de Caráquez, Ecuador 92 D2 0 40S 80 27W
Bahía Honda, Cuba 88 B3 22 54N 83 10W
Bahía Laura, Argentina 96 F3 48 10S 66 30W
Bahía Negra, Paraguay 92 H7 20 5S 58 5W
Bahir Dar, Ethiopia 46 E2 11 37N 37 10 E
Bahmanzād, Iran 45 D6 31 15N 51 47 E
Bahr el Ghazâl □, Sudan 51 G11 7 0N 28 0 E
Bahraich, India 43 F9 27 38N 81 37 E
Bahrain ■, Asia 46 B5 26 0N 50 35 E
Bahror, India 42 F7 27 51N 76 20 E
Bāhū Kalāt, Iran 45 E9 25 43N 61 25 E
Bai Bung, Mui = Ca Mau, Mui, Vietnam 39 H5 8 38N 104 44 E
Bai Duc, Vietnam 38 C5 18 3N 105 49 E
Bai Thuong, Vietnam 38 C5 19 54N 105 23 E
Baia Mare, Romania 17 E12 47 40N 23 35 E
Baião, Brazil 93 D9 2 40S 49 40W
Baïbokoum, Chad 51 G9 7 46N 15 43 E
Baicheng, China 35 B12 45 38N 122 42 E
Baidoa, Somali Rep. 46 G3 3 8N 43 30 E
Baie Comeau, Canada 71 C6 49 12N 68 10W
Baie-St-Paul, Canada 71 C5 47 28N 70 32W
Baie Trinité, Canada 71 C6 49 25N 67 20W
Baie Verte, Canada 71 C8 49 55N 56 12W
Baihar, India 43 H9 22 6N 80 33 E
Baihe, China 34 H6 32 50N 110 5 E
Ba'ījī, Iraq 44 C4 35 0N 43 30 E
Baijnath, India 43 E8 29 55N 79 37 E
Baikal, L. = Baykal, Oz., Russia 27 D11 53 0N 108 0 E
Baikunthpur, India 43 H10 23 15N 82 33 E
Baile Atha Cliath = Dublin, Ireland 13 C5 53 21N 6 15W
Băileşti, Romania 17 F12 44 1N 23 20 E
Bainbridge, Ga., U.S.A. 77 K3 30 55N 84 35W
Bainbridge, N.Y., U.S.A. 79 D9 42 18N 75 29W
Baing, Indonesia 37 F6 10 14S 120 34 E
Bainiu, China 34 H7 32 50N 112 15 E
Bā'ir, Jordan 47 E5 30 45N 36 55 E
Bairin Youqi, China 35 C10 43 30N 118 35 E
Bairin Zuoqi, China 35 C10 43 58N 119 15 E
Bairnsdale, Australia 63 F4 37 48S 147 36 E
Baisha, China 34 G7 34 20N 112 32 E
Baitadi, Nepal 43 E9 29 35N 80 25 E
Baiyin, China 34 F3 36 45N 104 14 E
Baiyu Shan, China 34 F4 37 15N 107 30 E
Baj Baj, India 43 H13 22 30N 88 5 E
Baja, Hungary 17 E10 46 12N 18 59 E
Baja, Pta., Mexico 86 B1 29 50N 116 0W
Baja California, Mexico 86 A1 31 10N 115 12W
Baja California □, Mexico 86 B2 30 0N 115 0W
Baja California Sur □, Mexico 86 B2 25 50N 111 50W
Bajag, India 43 H9 22 40N 81 21 E
Bajamar, Canary Is. 22 F3 28 33N 16 20W
Bajana, India 42 H4 23 7N 71 49 E
Bājgīrān, Iran 45 B8 37 36N 58 24 E
Bajimba, Mt., Australia 63 D5 29 17S 152 6 E
Bajo Nuevo, Caribbean 88 C4 15 40N 78 50W
Bajoga, Nigeria 51 F8 10 57N 11 20 E
Bajool, Australia 62 C5 23 40S 150 35 E
Bakel, Senegal 50 F3 14 56N 12 20W
Baker, Calif., U.S.A. 85 K10 35 16N 116 4W
Baker, Mont., U.S.A. 80 B2 46 22N 104 17W
Baker, L., Canada 68 B10 64 0N 96 0W
Baker City, U.S.A. 82 D5 44 47N 117 50W
Baker I., Pac. Oc. 64 G10 0 10N 176 35W
Baker I., U.S.A. 72 B2 55 20N 133 40W
Baker L., Australia 61 E4 26 54S 126 5 E
Baker Lake, Canada 68 B10 64 20N 96 3W
Baker Mt., U.S.A. 82 B3 48 50N 121 49W
Bakers Creek, Australia 62 C4 21 13S 149 7 E
Baker's Dozen Is., Canada 70 A4 56 45N 78 45W
Bakersfield, Calif., U.S.A. 85 K8 35 23N 119 1W
Bakersfield, Vt., U.S.A. 79 B12 44 45N 72 48W
Bākhtarān, Iran 44 C5 34 23N 47 0 E
Bākhtarān □, Iran 44 C5 34 0N 46 30 E
Bakı, Azerbaijan 25 F8 40 29N 49 56 E
Bakkafjörður, Iceland 8 C6 66 2N 14 48W
Bakony, Hungary 17 E9 47 10N 17 30 E
Bakony Forest = Bakony, Hungary 17 E9 47 10N 17 30 E
Bakouma, C.A.R. 52 C4 5 40N 22 56 E
Bakswaho, India 43 G8 24 15N 79 18 E
Baku = Bakı, Azerbaijan 25 F8 40 29N 49 56 E
Bakutis Coast, Antarctica 5 D15 74 0S 120 0W
Baky = Bakı, Azerbaijan 25 F8 40 29N 49 56 E
Bala, Canada 78 A5 45 1N 79 37W
Bala, U.K. 10 E4 52 54N 3 36W
Bala, L., U.K. 10 E4 52 53N 3 37W
Balabac I., Phil. 36 C5 8 0N 117 0 E
Balabac Str., E. Indies 36 C5 7 53N 117 5 E
Balabagh, Afghan. 42 B4 34 25N 70 12 E
Ba'labakk, Lebanon 47 B5 34 0N 36 10 E
Balabalangan, Kepulauan, Indonesia 36 E5 2 20S 117 30 E
Balad, Iraq 44 C5 34 1N 44 9 E
Balad Rūz, Iraq 44 C5 33 42N 45 5 E
Bālādeh, Fārs, Iran 45 D6 29 17N 51 56 E
Bālādeh, Māzandaran, Iran 45 B6 36 12N 51 48 E
Balaghat, India 40 J12 21 49N 80 12 E
Balaghat Ra., India 40 K10 18 50N 76 30 E
Balaguer, Spain 19 B6 41 50N 0 50 E
Balaklava, Ukraine 25 F5 44 30N 33 30 E
Balakovo, Russia 24 D8 52 4N 47 55 E
Balamau, India 43 F9 27 10N 80 21 E
Balancán, Mexico 87 D6 17 48N 91 32W
Balashov, Russia 25 D7 51 30N 43 10 E
Balasinor, India 42 H5 22 57N 73 23 E
Balasore = Baleshwar, India 41 J15 21 35N 87 3 E
Balaton, Hungary 17 E9 46 50N 17 40 E
Balbina, Represa de, Brazil 92 D7 2 0S 59 30W
Balboa, Panama 88 E4 8 57N 79 34W
Balbriggan, Ireland 13 C5 53 37N 6 11W
Balcarce, Argentina 94 D4 38 0S 58 10W
Balcarres, Canada 73 C8 50 50N 103 35W
Balchik, Bulgaria 21 C13 43 28N 28 11 E
Balclutha, N.Z. 59 M2 46 15S 169 45 E
Balcones Escarpment, U.S.A. 81 L5 29 30N 99 15W
Bald Hd., Australia 61 G2 35 6S 118 1 E
Bald I., Australia 61 F2 34 57S 118 27 E
Bald Knob, U.S.A. 81 H9 35 19N 91 34W
Baldock L., Canada 73 B9 56 33N 97 57W
Baldwin, Mich., U.S.A. 76 D3 43 54N 85 51W
Baldwin, Pa., U.S.A. 78 F5 40 23N 79 59W
Baldwinsville, U.S.A. 79 C8 43 10N 76 20W
Baldy Mt., U.S.A. 82 B9 48 9N 109 39W
Baldy Peak, U.S.A. 83 K9 33 54N 109 34W
Baleares, Is., Spain 22 B10 39 30N 3 0 E
Balearic Is. = Baleares, Is., Spain 22 B10 39 30N 3 0 E
Baleine = Whale →, Canada 71 A6 58 15N 67 40W
Baler, Phil. 37 A6 15 46N 121 34 E
Baleshare, U.K. 12 D1 57 31N 7 22W
Baleshwar, India 41 J15 21 35N 87 3 E
Balfate, Honduras 88 C2 15 48N 86 25W
Bali, Greece 23 D6 35 25N 24 47 E
Bali, India 42 G5 25 11N 73 17 E
Bali, Indonesia 36 F4 8 20S 115 0 E
Bali □, Indonesia 36 F5 8 20S 115 0 E
Bali, Selat, Indonesia 37 H16 8 18S 114 25 E
Baliapal, India 43 J12 21 40N 87 17 E
Balikeşir, Turkey 21 E12 39 39N 27 53 E
Balikpapan, Indonesia 36 E5 1 10S 116 55 E
Balimbing, Phil. 37 C5 5 5N 119 58 E
Baling, Malaysia 39 K3 5 41N 100 55 E
Balipara, India 41 F18 26 50N 92 45 E
Balkan Mts. = Stara Planina, Bulgaria 21 C10 43 15N 23 0 E
Balkhash = Balqash, Kazakstan 26 E8 46 50N 74 50 E
Balkhash, Ozero = Balqash Köl, Kazakstan 26 E8 46 0N 74 50 E
Balla, Bangla. 41 G17 24 10N 91 35 E
Ballachulish, U.K. 12 E3 56 41N 5 8W
Balladonia, Australia 61 F3 32 27S 123 51 E
Ballaghaderreen, Ireland 13 C3 53 55N 8 34W
Ballarat, Australia 63 F3 37 33S 143 50 E
Ballard, L., Australia 61 E3 29 20S 120 40 E
Ballater, U.K. 12 D5 57 3N 3 3W
Ballenas, Canal de, Mexico 86 B2 29 10N 113 45W
Balleny Is., Antarctica 5 C11 66 30S 163 0 E
Ballia, India 43 G11 25 46N 84 12 E
Ballina, Australia 63 D5 28 50S 153 31 E
Ballina, Ireland 13 B2 54 7N 9 9W
Ballinasloe, Ireland 13 C3 53 20N 8 13W
Ballinger, U.S.A. 81 K5 31 45N 99 57W
Ballinrobe, Ireland 13 C2 53 38N 9 13W
Ballinskelligs B., Ireland 13 E1 51 48N 10 13W
Ballston Spa, U.S.A. 79 D11 43 0N 73 51W
Ballycastle, U.K. 13 A5 55 12N 6 15W
Ballyclare, U.K. 13 B5 54 46N 6 0W
Ballyhaunis, Ireland 13 C3 53 46N 8 46W
Ballymena, U.K. 13 B5 54 52N 6 17W
Ballymoney, U.K. 13 A5 55 5N 6 31W
Ballymote, Ireland 13 B3 54 5N 8 31W
Ballynahinch, U.K. 13 B6 54 24N 5 54W
Ballyquintin Pt., U.K. 13 B6 54 20N 5 30W
Ballyshannon, Ireland 13 B3 54 30N 8 11W
Balmaceda, Chile 96 F2 46 0S 71 50W
Balmertown, Canada 73 C10 51 4N 93 41W
Balmoral, Australia 63 F3 37 15S 141 48 E
Balmorhea, U.S.A. 81 K3 30 59N 103 45W
Balochistan = Baluchistan □, Pakistan 40 F4 27 30N 65 0 E
Balonne →, Australia 63 D4 28 47S 147 56 E
Balotra, India 42 G5 25 50N 72 14 E
Balqash, Kazakstan 26 E8 46 50N 74 50 E
Balqash Köl, Kazakstan 26 E8 46 0N 74 50 E
Balrampur, India 43 F10 27 30N 82 20 E
Balranald, Australia 63 E3 34 38S 143 33 E
Balsas, Mexico 87 D5 18 0N 99 40W
Balsas →, Brazil 93 E9 7 15S 44 35W
Balsas →, Mexico 86 D4 17 55N 102 10W
Balston Spa, U.S.A. 79 D11 43 0N 73 52W
Balta, Ukraine 17 D15 48 2N 29 45 E
Bălţi, Moldova 17 E14 47 48N 27 58 E
Baltic Sea, Europe 9 H18 57 0N 19 0 E
Baltimore, Ireland 13 E2 51 29N 9 22W
Baltimore, Md., U.S.A. 76 F7 39 17N 76 37W
Baltimore, Ohio, U.S.A. 78 G2 39 51N 82 36W
Baltit, Pakistan 43 A6 36 15N 74 40 E
Baltiysk, Russia 9 J18 54 41N 19 58 E
Baluchistan □, Pakistan 40 F4 27 30N 65 0 E
Balurghat, India 43 G13 25 15N 88 44 E
Balvi, Latvia 9 H22 57 8N 27 15 E
Balya, Turkey 21 E12 39 44N 27 35 E
Bam, Iran 45 D8 29 7N 58 14 E
Bama, Nigeria 51 F8 11 33N 13 41 E
Bamaga, Australia 62 A3 10 50S 142 25 E
Bamaji L., Canada 70 B1 51 9N 91 25W
Bamako, Mali 50 F4 12 34N 7 55W
Bambari, C.A.R. 52 C4 5 40N 20 35 E
Bambaroo, Australia 62 B4 18 50S 146 10 E
Bamberg, Germany 16 D6 49 54N 10 54 E
Bamberg, U.S.A. 77 J5 33 18N 81 2W
Bambili, Dem. Rep. of the Congo 54 B2 3 40N 26 0 E
Bamfield, Canada 72 D3 48 45N 125 10W
Bāmīān □, Afghan. 40 B5 35 0N 67 0 E
Bamiancheng, China 35 C13 43 15N 124 2 E
Bampūr, Iran 45 E9 27 15N 60 21 E
Ban Ban, Laos 38 C4 19 31N 103 30 E
Ban Bang Hin, Thailand 39 H2 9 32N 98 35 E
Ban Chiang Klang, Thailand 38 C3 19 25N 100 55 E
Ban Chik, Laos 38 D4 17 15N 102 22 E
Ban Choho, Thailand 38 E4 15 2N 102 9 E
Ban Dan Lan Hoi, Thailand 38 D2 17 0N 99 35 E
Ban Don = Surat Thani, Thailand 39 H2 9 6N 99 20 E
Ban Don, Vietnam 38 F6 12 53N 107 48 E
Ban Don, Ao →, Thailand 39 H2 9 20N 99 25 E
Ban Dong, Thailand 38 C3 19 30N 100 59 E
Ban Hong, Thailand 38 C2 18 18N 98 50 E
Ban Kaeng, Thailand 38 D3 17 29N 100 7 E
Ban Kantang, Thailand 39 J2 7 25N 99 31 E
Ban Keun, Laos 38 C4 18 22N 102 35 E
Ban Khai, Thailand 38 F3 12 46N 101 18 E
Ban Kheun, Laos 38 B3 20 13N 101 7 E
Ban Khlong Kua, Thailand 39 J3 6 57N 100 8 E
Ban Khuan Mao, Thailand 39 J2 7 50N 99 37 E
Ban Ko Yai Chim, Thailand 39 G2 11 17N 99 26 E
Ban Kok, Thailand 38 D4 16 40N 103 40 E
Ban Laem, Thailand 38 F2 13 13N 99 59 E
Ban Lao Ngam, Laos 38 E6 15 28N 106 10 E
Ban Le Kathe, Thailand 38 E2 15 49N 98 53 E
Ban Mae Chedi, Thailand 38 C2 19 11N 99 31 E
Ban Mae Laeng, Thailand 38 B2 20 1N 99 17 E
Ban Mae Sariang, Thailand 38 C1 18 10N 97 56 E
Ban Mê Thuôt = Buon Ma Thuot, Vietnam 38 F7 12 40N 108 3 E
Ban Mi, Thailand 38 E3 15 3N 100 32 E
Ban Muong Mo, Laos 38 C4 19 4N 103 58 E
Ban Na Mo, Laos 38 D5 17 7N 105 40 E
Ban Na San, Thailand 39 H2 8 53N 99 52 E
Ban Na Tong, Laos 38 B3 20 56N 101 47 E
Ban Nam Bac, Laos 38 B4 20 38N 102 20 E
Ban Nam Ma, Laos 38 A3 22 2N 101 37 E
Ban Ngang, Laos 38 E6 15 59N 106 11 E
Ban Nong Bok, Laos 38 D5 17 5N 104 48 E
Ban Nong Boua, Laos 38 E6 15 40N 106 33 E
Ban Nong Pling, Thailand 38 E3 15 40N 100 10 E
Ban Pak Chan, Thailand 39 G2 10 32N 98 51 E
Ban Phai, Thailand 38 D4 16 4N 102 44 E
Ban Pong, Thailand 38 F2 13 50N 99 55 E
Ban Ron Phibun, Thailand 39 H2 8 9N 99 51 E
Ban Sanam Chai, Thailand 39 J3 7 33N 100 25 E
Ban Sangkha, Thailand 38 E4 14 37N 103 52 E
Ban Tak, Thailand 38 D2 17 2N 99 4 E
Ban Tako, Thailand 38 E4 14 5N 102 40 E
Ban Tha Dua, Thailand 38 D2 17 59N 98 39 E
Ban Tha Li, Thailand 38 D3 17 37N 101 25 E
Ban Tha Nun, Thailand 39 H2 8 12N 98 18 E
Ban Thahine, Laos 38 E5 14 12N 105 33 E
Ban Xien Kok, Laos 38 B3 20 54N 100 39 E
Ban Yen Nhan, Vietnam 38 B6 20 57N 106 2 E
Banaba, Kiribati 64 H8 0 45S 169 50 E
Banalia, Dem. Rep. of the Congo 54 B2 1 32N 25 5 E
Banam, Cambodia 39 G5 11 20N 105 17 E
Bananal, I. do, Brazil 93 F8 11 30S 50 30W
Banaras = Varanasi, India 43 G10 25 22N 83 0 E
Banas →, Gujarat, India 42 H4 23 45N 71 25 E
Banas →, Mad. P., India 43 G9 24 15N 81 30 E
Bânâs, Ras, Egypt 51 D13 23 57N 35 59 E
Banbridge, U.K. 13 B5 54 22N 6 16W
Banbury, U.K. 11 E6 52 4N 1 20W
Banchory, U.K. 12 D6 57 3N 2 29W
Bancroft, Canada 78 A7 45 3N 77 51W
Band Bonī, Iran 45 E8 25 30N 59 33 E
Band Qīr, Iran 45 D6 31 39N 48 53 E
Banda, Mad. P., India 43 G8 24 3N 78 57 E
Banda, Ut. P., India 43 G9 25 30N 80 26 E
Banda, Kepulauan, Indonesia 37 E7 4 37S 129 50 E
Banda Aceh, Indonesia 36 C1 5 35N 95 20 E
Banda Banda, Mt., Australia 63 E5 31 10S 152 28 E
Banda Elat, Indonesia 37 F8 5 40S 133 5 E
Banda Is. = Banda, Kepulauan, Indonesia 37 E7 4 37S 129 50 E
Banda Sea, Indonesia 37 F7 6 0S 130 0 E
Bandai-San, Japan 30 F10 37 36N 140 4 E
Bandān, Iran 45 D9 31 23N 60 44 E
Bandanaira, Indonesia 37 E7 4 32S 129 54 E
Bandanwara, India 42 F6 26 9N 74 38 E
Bandar = Machilipatnam, India 41 L12 16 12N 81 8 E
Bandār 'Abbās, Iran 45 E8 27 15N 56 15 E
Bandar-e Anzalī, Iran 45 B6 37 30N 49 30 E
Bandar-e Bushehr = Būshehr, Iran 45 D6 28 55N 50 55 E
Bandar-e Chārak, Iran 45 E7 26 45N 54 20 E
Bandar-e Deylam, Iran 45 D6 30 5N 50 10 E
Bandar-e Khomeynı, Iran 45 D6 30 30N 49 5 E
Bandar-e Lengeh, Iran 45 E7 26 35N 54 58 E
Bandar-e Maqām, Iran 45 E7 26 56N 53 29 E
Bandar-e Ma'shur, Iran 45 D6 30 35N 49 10 E
Bandar-e Rīg, Iran 45 D6 29 29N 50 38 E
Bandar-e Torkeman, Iran 45 B7 37 0N 54 10 E
Bandar Maharani = Muar, Malaysia 39 L4 2 3N 102 34 E
Bandar Penggaram = Batu Pahat, Malaysia 39 M4 1 50N 102 56 E
Bandar Seri Begawan, Brunei 36 C4 4 52N 115 0 E
Bandar Sri Aman, Malaysia 36 D4 1 15N 111 32 E
Bandawe, Malawi 55 E3 11 58S 34 5 E
Bandeira, Pico da, Brazil 95 A7 20 26S 41 47W
Bandera, Argentina 94 B3 28 55S 62 20W
Banderas, B. de, Mexico 86 C3 20 40N 105 30W
Bandhogarh, India 43 H9 23 40N 81 2 E
Bandi →, India 42 F6 26 12N 75 47 E
Bandikui, India 42 F7 27 3N 76 34 E
Bandırma, Turkey 21 D13 40 20N 28 0 E
Bandon, Ireland 13 E3 51 44N 8 44W
Bandon →, Ireland 13 E3 51 43N 8 37W
Bandula, Mozam. 55 F3 19 0S 33 7 E
Bandundu, Dem. Rep. of the Congo 52 E3 3 15S 17 22 E
Bandung, Indonesia 36 F3 6 54S 107 36 E
Bāneh, Iran 44 C5 35 59N 45 53 E
Banes, Cuba 89 B4 21 0N 75 42W
Banff, Canada 72 C5 51 10N 115 34W
Banff, U.K. 12 D6 57 40N 2 33W
Banff Nat. Park, Canada 72 C5 51 30N 116 15W
Bang Fai →, Laos 38 D5 16 57N 104 45 E
Bang Hieng →, Laos 38 D5 16 10N 105 10 E
Bang Krathum, Thailand 38 D3 16 34N 100 18 E
Bang Lamung, Thailand 38 F3 13 3N 100 56 E
Bang Mun Nak, Thailand 38 D3 16 2N 100 23 E
Bang Pa In, Thailand 38 E3 14 14N 100 35 E
Bang Rakam, Thailand 38 D3 16 45N 100 7 E
Bang Saphan, Thailand 39 G2 11 14N 99 28 E
Bangaduni I., India 43 J13 21 34N 88 52 E
Bangala Dam, Zimbabwe 55 G3 21 7S 31 25 E
Bangalore, India 40 N10 12 59N 77 40 E
Banganga →, India 42 F6 27 6N 77 25 E
Bangaon, India 43 H13 23 0N 88 47 E
Bangassou, C.A.R. 52 D4 4 55N 23 7 E
Banggai, Indonesia 37 E6 1 34S 123 30 E
Banggai, Kepulauan, Indonesia 37 E6 1 40S 123 30 E
Banggai Arch. = Banggai, Kepulauan, Indonesia 37 E6 1 40S 123 30 E
Banggi, Malaysia 36 C5 7 17N 117 12 E
Banghāzī, Libya 51 B10 32 11N 20 3 E
Bangka, Sulawesi, Indonesia 37 D7 1 50N 125 5 E
Bangka, Sumatera, Indonesia 36 E3 2 0S 105 50 E
Bangka, Selat, Indonesia 36 E3 2 30S 105 30 E
Bangkalan, Indonesia 37 G15 7 2S 112 46 E
Bangkinang, Indonesia 36 D2 0 18N 101 5 E
Bangko, Indonesia 36 E2 2 5S 102 9 E
Bangkok, Thailand 38 F3 13 45N 100 35 E
Bangladesh ■, Asia 41 H17 24 0N 90 0 E
Bangong Co, India 43 B8 35 50N 79 20 E
Bangor, Down, U.K. 13 B6 54 40N 5 40W
Bangor, Gwynedd, U.K. 10 D3 53 14N 4 8W
Bangor, Maine, U.S.A. 69 D13 44 48N 68 46W
Bangor, Pa., U.S.A. 79 F9 40 52N 75 13W
Bangued, Phil. 37 A6 17 40N 120 37 E
Bangui, C.A.R. 52 D3 4 23N 18 35 E
Banguru, Dem. Rep. of the Congo 54 B2 0 30N 27 10 E
Bangweulu, L., Zambia 55 E3 11 0S 30 0 E
Bangweulu Swamp, Zambia 55 E3 11 20S 30 15 E
Bani, Dom. Rep. 89 C5 18 16N 70 22W
Banī Sa'd, Iraq 44 C5 33 34N 44 32 E
Banihal Pass, India 43 C6 33 30N 75 12 E
Bāniyās, Syria 44 C3 35 10N 36 0 E
Banja Luka, Bos.-H. 20 B7 44 49N 17 11 E
Banjar, India 42 D7 31 38N 77 21 E
Banjar →, India 43 H9 22 36N 80 22 E
Banjarmasin, Indonesia 36 E4 3 20S 114 35 E
Banjul, Gambia 50 F2 13 28N 16 40W
Banka, India 43 G12 24 53N 86 55 E
Banket, Zimbabwe 55 F3 17 27S 30 19 E
Bankipore, India 41 G14 25 35N 85 10 E
Banks I., B.C., Canada 72 C3 53 20N 130 0W
Banks I., N.W.T., Canada 68 A7 73 15N 121 30W
Banks Pen., N.Z. 59 K4 43 45S 173 15 E
Banks Str., Australia 62 G4 40 40S 148 10 E
Bankura, India 43 H12 23 11N 87 18 E
Banmankhi, India 43 G12 25 53N 87 11 E
Bann →, Arm., U.K. 13 B5 54 30N 6 31W
Bann →, L'derry., U.K. 13 A5 55 8N 6 41W
Bannang Sata, Thailand 39 J3 6 16N 101 16 E
Banning, U.S.A. 85 M10 33 56N 116 53W
Banningville = Bandundu, Dem. Rep. of the Congo 52 E3 3 15S 17 22 E
Bannockburn, Canada 78 B7 44 39N 77 33W
Bannockburn, U.K. 12 E5 56 5N 3 55W
Bannockburn, Zimbabwe 55 G2 20 17S 29 48 E
Bannu, Pakistan 40 C7 33 0N 70 18 E
Bano, India 43 H11 22 40N 84 55 E
Bansgaon, India 43 F10 26 33N 83 21 E
Banská Bystrica, Slovak Rep. 17 D10 48 46N 19 14 E
Banswara, India 42 H6 23 32N 74 24 E
Bantaeng, Indonesia 37 F5 5 32S 119 56 E
Bantry, Ireland 13 E2 51 41N 9 27W
Bantry B., Ireland 13 E2 51 37N 9 44W
Bantul, Indonesia 37 G14 7 55S 110 19 E
Bantva, India 42 J4 21 29N 70 12 E
Banyak, Kepulauan, Indonesia 36 D1 2 10N 97 10 E
Banyalbufar, Spain 22 B9 39 42N 2 31 E
Banyo, Cameroon 52 C2 6 52N 11 45 E
Banyumas, Indonesia 37 G13 7 32S 109 18 E
Banyuwangi, Indonesia 37 H16 8 13S 114 21 E
Banzare Coast, Antarctica 5 C9 68 0S 125 0 E
Bao Ha, Vietnam 38 A5 22 11N 104 21 E
Bao Lac, Vietnam 38 A5 22 57N 105 40 E
Bao Loc, Vietnam 39 G6 11 32N 107 48 E
Baocheng, China 34 H4 33 12N 106 56 E
Baode, China 34 E6 39 1N 111 5 E
Baodi, China 35 E9 39 38N 117 20 E
Baoding, China 34 E8 38 50N 115 28 E
Baoji, China 34 G4 34 20N 107 5 E
Baoshan, China 32 D4 25 10N 99 5 E
Baotou, China 34 D6 40 32N 110 2 E
Baoying, China 35 H10 33 17N 119 20 E
Bap, India 42 F5 27 23N 72 18 E
Bapatla, India 41 M12 15 55N 80 30 E
Bāqerābād, Iran 45 C6 33 2N 51 58 E
Ba'qūbah, Iraq 44 C5 33 45N 44 50 E
Baquedano, Chile 94 A2 23 20S 69 52W
Bar, Montenegro, Yug. 21 C8 42 8N 19 6 E
Bar, Ukraine 17 D14 49 4N 27 40 E
Bar Bigha, India 43 G11 25 21N 85 47 E
Bar Harbor, U.S.A. 77 C11 44 23N 68 13W
Bar-le-Duc, France 18 B6 48 47N 5 10 E
Bara, India 43 G9 25 16N 81 43 E
Bara Banki, India 43 F9 26 55N 81 12 E
Barabai, Indonesia 36 E5 2 32S 115 34 E
Baraboo, U.S.A. 80 D10 43 28N 89 45W
Baracoa, Cuba 89 B5 20 20N 74 30W
Baradā →, Syria 47 B5 33 33N 36 34 E
Baradero, Argentina 94 C4 33 52S 59 29W
Baraga, U.S.A. 80 B10 46 47N 88 30W
Barah →, India 42 F6 27 42N 77 5 E
Barahona, Dom. Rep. 89 C5 18 13N 71 7W
Barail Range, India 41 G18 25 15N 93 20 E
Barakaldo, Spain 19 A4 43 18N 2 59W
Barakar →, India 43 G12 24 7N 86 14 E
Barakhola, India 41 G18 25 0N 92 45 E
Barakot, India 43 J11 21 33N 84 59 E

Barakpur, India 43 H13 22 44N 88 30 E
Baralaba, Australia 62 C4 24 13S 149 50 E
Baralzon L., Canada 73 B9 60 0N 98 3W
Baramula, India 43 B6 34 15N 74 20 E
Baran, India 42 G7 25 9N 76 40 E
Baran →, Pakistan 42 G3 25 13N 68 17 E
Baranavichy, Belarus 17 B14 53 10N 26 0 E
Baranof, U.S.A. 72 B2 57 5N 134 50W
Baranof I., U.S.A. 68 C6 57 0N 135 0W
Barapasi, Indonesia 37 E9 2 15S 137 5 E
Barasat, India 43 H13 22 46N 88 31 E
Barat Daya, Kepulauan, Indonesia 37 F7 7 30S 128 0 E
Barataria B., U.S.A. 81 L10 29 20N 89 55W
Barauda, India 42 H6 23 33N 75 15 E
Baraut, India 42 E7 29 13N 77 7 E
Barbacena, Brazil 95 A7 21 15S 43 56W
Barbados ■, W. Indies 89 D8 13 10N 59 30W
Barbària, C. de, Spain 22 C7 38 39N 1 24 E
Barbastro, Spain 19 A6 42 2N 0 5 E
Barberton, S. Africa 57 D5 25 42S 31 2 E
Barberton, U.S.A. 78 E3 41 0N 81 39W
Barbosa, Colombia 92 B4 5 57N 73 37W
Barbourville, U.S.A. 77 G4 36 52N 83 53W
Barbuda, W. Indies 89 C7 17 30N 61 40W
Barcaldine, Australia 62 C4 23 43S 145 6 E
Barcellona Pozzo di Gotto, Italy 20 E6 38 9N 15 13 E
Barcelona, Spain 19 B7 41 21N 2 10 E
Barcelona, Venezuela 92 A6 10 10N 64 40W
Barcelos, Brazil 92 D6 1 0S 63 0W
Barcoo →, Australia 62 D3 25 30S 142 50 E
Barda", Chad 51 D9 21 25N 17 0 E
Bardas Blancas, Argentina 94 D2 35 49S 69 45W
Bardawîl, Sabkhet el, Egypt 47 D2 31 10N 33 15 E
Barddhaman, India 43 H12 23 14N 87 39 E
Bardejov, Slovak Rep. 17 D11 49 18N 21 15 E
Bardera, Somali Rep. 46 G3 2 20N 42 27 E
Bardīyah, Libya 51 B10 31 45N 25 5 E
Bardsey I., U.K. 10 E3 52 45N 4 47W
Bardstown, U.S.A. 76 G3 37 49N 85 28W
Bareilly, India 43 E8 28 22N 79 27 E
Barela, India 43 H9 23 6N 80 3 E
Barents Sea, Arctic 4 B9 73 0N 39 0 E
Barfleur, Pte. de, France 18 B3 49 42N 1 16W
Bargara, Australia 62 C5 24 50S 152 25 E
Barguzin, Russia 27 D11 53 37N 109 37 E
Barh, India 43 G11 25 29N 85 46 E
Barhaj, India 43 F10 26 18N 83 44 E
Barharwa, India 43 G12 24 52N 87 47 E
Barhi, India 43 G11 24 15N 85 25 E
Bari, India 42 F7 26 39N 77 39 E
Bari, Italy 20 D7 41 8N 16 51 E
Bari Doab, Pakistan 42 D5 30 20N 73 0 E
Bari Sadri, India 42 G6 24 28N 74 30 E
Barīdī, Ra's, Si. Arabia 44 E3 24 17N 37 31 E
Barim, Yemen 48 E8 12 39N 43 25 E
Barinas, Venezuela 92 B4 8 36N 70 15W
Baring, C., Canada 68 B8 70 0N 117 30W
Baringo, Kenya 54 B4 0 47N 36 16 E
Baringo, L., Kenya 54 B4 0 47N 36 16 E
Barisal, Bangla. 41 H17 22 45N 90 20 E
Barisan, Bukit, Indonesia 36 E2 3 30S 102 15 E
Barito →, Indonesia 36 E4 4 0S 114 50 E
Bark L., Canada 78 A7 45 27N 77 51W
Barkakana, India 43 H11 23 37N 85 29 E
Barker, U.S.A. 78 C6 43 20N 78 33W
Barkley, L., U.S.A. 77 G2 37 1N 88 14W
Barkley Sound, Canada 72 D3 48 50N 125 10W
Barkly East, S. Africa 56 E4 30 58S 27 33 E
Barkly Roadhouse, Australia 62 B2 19 52S 135 50 E
Barkly Tableland, Australia 62 B2 17 50S 136 40 E
Barkly West, S. Africa 56 D3 28 5S 24 31 E
Barkol Kazak Zizhixian, China 32 B4 43 37N 93 2 E
Bârlad, Romania 17 E14 46 15N 27 38 E
Bârlad →, Romania 17 F14 45 38N 27 32 E
Barlee, L., Australia 61 E2 29 15S 119 30 E
Barlee, Mt., Australia 61 D4 24 38S 128 13 E
Barletta, Italy 20 D7 41 19N 16 17 E
Barlovento, Canary Is. 22 F2 28 48N 17 48W
Barlow L., Canada 73 A8 62 0N 103 0W
Barmedman, Australia 63 E4 34 9S 147 21 E
Barmer, India 42 G4 25 45N 71 20 E
Barmera, Australia 63 E3 34 15S 140 28 E
Barmouth, U.K. 10 E3 52 44N 4 4W
Barna →, India 43 G10 25 21N 83 3 E
Barnagar, India 42 H6 23 7N 75 19 E
Barnala, India 42 D6 30 23N 75 33 E
Barnard Castle, U.K. 10 C6 54 33N 1 55W
Barnaul, Russia 26 D9 53 20N 83 40 E
Barnesville, U.S.A. 77 J3 33 3N 84 9W
Barnet □, U.K. 11 F7 51 38N 0 9W
Barneveld, Neths. 15 B5 52 7N 5 36 E
Barneveld, U.S.A. 79 C9 43 16N 75 14W
Barnhart, U.S.A. 81 K4 31 8N 101 10W
Barnsley, U.K. 10 D6 53 34N 1 27W
Barnstaple, U.K. 11 F3 51 5N 4 4W
Barnstaple Bay = Bideford Bay, U.K. 11 F3 51 5N 4 20W
Barnsville, U.S.A. 80 B6 46 43N 96 28W
Barnwell, U.S.A. 77 J5 33 15N 81 23W
Baro, Nigeria 50 G7 8 35N 6 18 E
Baroda = Vadodara, India 42 H5 22 20N 73 10 E
Baroda, India 42 G7 25 29N 76 35 E
Baroe, S. Africa 56 E3 33 13S 24 33 E
Baron Ra., Australia 60 D4 23 30S 127 45 E
Barotseland, Zambia 53 H4 15 0S 24 0 E
Barpeta, India 41 F17 26 20N 91 10 E
Barques, Pt. Aux, U.S.A. 78 B2 44 4N 82 58W
Barquisimeto, Venezuela 92 A5 10 4N 69 19W
Barr Smith Range, Australia 61 E3 27 4S 120 20 E
Barra, Brazil 93 F10 11 5S 43 10W
Barra, U.K. 12 E1 57 0N 7 29W
Barra, Sd. of, U.K. 12 D1 57 4N 7 25W
Barra de Navidad, Mexico 86 D4 19 12N 104 41W
Barra do Corda, Brazil 93 E9 5 30S 45 10W
Barra do Piraí, Brazil 95 A7 22 30S 43 50W
Barra Falsa, Pta. da, Mozam. 57 C6 22 58S 35 37 E
Barra Hd., U.K. 12 E1 56 47N 7 40W
Barra Mansa, Brazil 95 A7 22 35S 44 12W
Barraba, Australia 63 E5 30 21S 150 35 E
Barrackpur = Barakpur, India 43 H13 22 44N 88 30 E
Barradale Roadhouse, Australia 60 D1 22 42S 114 58 E
Barraigh = Barra, U.K. 12 E1 57 0N 7 29W
Barranca, Lima, Peru 92 F3 10 45S 77 50W
Barranca, Loreto, Peru 92 D3 4 50S 76 50W
Barrancabermeja, Colombia 92 B4 7 0N 73 50W
Barrancas, Venezuela 92 B6 8 55N 62 5W
Barrancos, Portugal 19 C2 38 10N 6 58W
Barranqueras, Argentina 94 B4 27 30S 59 0W
Barranquilla, Colombia 92 A4 11 0N 74 50W
Barraute, Canada 70 C4 48 26N 77 38W
Barre, Mass., U.S.A. 79 D12 42 25N 72 6W
Barre, Vt., U.S.A. 79 B12 44 12N 72 30W
Barreal, Argentina 94 C2 31 33S 69 28W
Barreiras, Brazil 93 F10 12 8S 45 0W
Barreirinhas, Brazil 93 D10 2 30S 42 50W
Barreiro, Portugal 19 C1 38 40N 9 6W
Barren, Nosy, Madag. 57 B7 18 25S 43 40 E
Barretos, Brazil 93 H9 20 30S 48 35W
Barrhead, Canada 72 C6 54 10N 114 24W
Barrie, Canada 78 B5 44 24N 79 40W
Barrier Ra., Australia 63 E3 31 0S 141 30 E
Barrière, Canada 72 C4 51 12N 120 7W
Barrington, U.S.A. 79 E13 41 44N 71 18W
Barrington L., Canada 73 B8 56 55N 100 15W
Barrington Tops, Australia 63 E5 32 6S 151 28 E
Barringun, Australia 63 D4 29 1S 145 41 E
Barro do Garças, Brazil 93 G8 15 54S 52 16W
Barron, U.S.A. 80 C9 45 24N 91 51W
Barrow, U.S.A. 68 A4 71 18N 156 47W
Barrow →, Ireland 13 D5 52 25N 6 58W
Barrow Creek, Australia 62 C1 21 30S 133 55 E
Barrow I., Australia 60 D2 20 45S 115 20 E
Barrow-in-Furness, U.K. 10 C4 54 7N 3 14W
Barrow Pt., Australia 62 A3 14 20S 144 40 E
Barrow Pt., U.S.A. 66 B4 71 10N 156 20W
Barrow Ra., Australia 61 E4 26 0S 127 40 E
Barrow Str., Canada 4 B3 74 20N 95 0W
Barry, U.K. 11 F4 51 24N 3 16W
Barry's Bay, Canada 78 A7 45 29N 77 41W
Barsat, Pakistan 43 A5 36 10N 72 45 E
Barsham, Syria 44 C4 35 21N 40 33 E
Barsi, India 40 K9 18 10N 75 50 E
Barsoi, India 41 G15 25 48N 87 57 E
Barstow, U.S.A. 85 L9 34 54N 117 1W
Barthélemy, Col, Vietnam 38 C5 19 26N 104 6 E
Bartica, Guyana 92 B7 6 25N 58 40W
Bartlesville, U.S.A. 81 G7 36 45N 95 59W
Bartlett, U.S.A. 84 J8 36 29N 118 2W
Bartlett, L., Canada 72 A5 63 5N 118 20W
Bartolomeu Dias, Mozam. 55 G4 21 10S 35 8 E
Barton, U.S.A. 79 B12 44 45N 72 11W
Barton upon Humber, U.K. 10 D7 53 41N 0 25W
Bartow, U.S.A. 77 M5 27 54N 81 50W
Barú, Volcan, Panama 88 E3 8 55N 82 35W
Barumba, Dem. Rep. of the Congo 54 B1 1 3N 23 37 E
Baruunsuu, Mongolia 34 C3 43 43N 105 35 E
Barwani, India 42 H6 22 2N 74 57 E
Barysaw, Belarus 17 A15 54 17N 28 28 E
Barzān, Iraq 44 B5 36 55N 44 3 E
Bāsa'idū, Iran 45 E7 26 35N 55 20 E
Basal, Pakistan 42 C5 33 33N 72 13 E
Basankusa, Dem. Rep. of the Congo 52 D3 1 5N 19 50 E
Basarabeasca, Moldova 17 E15 46 21N 28 58 E
Basarabia = Bessarabiya, Moldova 17 E15 47 0N 28 10 E
Basawa, Afghan. 42 B4 34 15N 70 50 E
Bascuñán, C., Chile 94 B1 28 52S 71 35W
Basel, Switz. 18 C7 47 35N 7 35 E
Bashākerd, Kūhhā-ye, Iran 45 E8 26 42N 58 35 E
Bashaw, Canada 72 C6 52 35N 112 58W
Bāshī, Iran 45 D6 28 41N 51 4 E
Bashkir Republic = Bashkortostan □, Russia 24 D10 54 0N 57 0 E
Bashkortostan □, Russia 24 D10 54 0N 57 0 E
Basibasy, Madag. 57 C7 22 10S 43 40 E
Basilan I., Phil. 37 C6 6 35N 122 0 E
Basilan Str., Phil. 37 C6 6 50N 122 0 E
Basildon, U.K. 11 F8 51 34N 0 28 E
Basim = Washim, India 40 J10 20 3N 77 0 E
Basin, U.S.A. 82 D9 44 23N 108 2W
Basingstoke, U.K. 11 F6 51 15N 1 5W
Baskatong, Rés., Canada 70 C4 46 46N 75 50W
Basle = Basel, Switz. 18 C7 47 35N 7 35 E
Basoda, India 42 H7 23 52N 77 54 E
Basoko, Dem. Rep. of the Congo 54 B1 1 16N 23 40 E
Basque Provinces = País Vasco □, Spain 19 A4 42 50N 2 45W
Basra = Al Başrah, Iraq 44 D5 30 30N 47 50 E
Bass Str., Australia 62 F4 39 15S 146 30 E
Bassano, Canada 72 C6 50 48N 112 20W
Bassano del Grappa, Italy 20 B4 45 46N 11 44 E
Bassas da India, Ind. Oc. 53 J7 22 0S 39 0 E
Basse-Terre, Guadeloupe 89 C7 16 0N 61 44W
Bassein, Burma 41 L19 16 45N 94 30 E
Basseterre, St. Kitts & Nevis 89 C7 17 17N 62 43W
Bassett, U.S.A. 80 D5 42 35N 99 32W
Bassi, India 42 D7 30 44N 76 21 E
Bastak, Iran 45 E7 27 15N 54 25 E
Baştām, Iran 45 B7 36 29N 55 4 E
Bastar, India 41 K12 19 15N 81 40 E
Basti, India 43 F10 26 52N 82 55 E
Bastia, France 18 E8 42 40N 9 30 E
Bastogne, Belgium 15 D5 50 1N 5 43 E
Bastrop, La., U.S.A. 81 J9 32 47N 91 55W
Bastrop, Tex., U.S.A. 81 K6 30 7N 97 19W
Bat Yam, Israel 47 C3 32 2N 34 44 E
Bata, Eq. Guin. 52 D1 1 57N 9 50 E
Bataan □, Phil. 37 B6 14 40N 120 25 E
Batabanó, Cuba 88 B3 22 40N 82 20W
Batabanó, G. de, Cuba 88 B3 22 30N 82 30W
Batac, Phil. 37 A6 18 3N 120 34 E
Batagai, Russia 27 C14 67 38N 134 38 E
Batala, India 42 D6 31 48N 75 12 E
Batama, Dem. Rep. of the Congo 54 B2 0 58N 26 33 E
Batamay, Russia 27 C13 63 30N 129 15 E
Batang, Indonesia 37 G13 6 55S 109 45 E
Batangas, Phil. 37 B6 13 35N 121 10 E
Batanta, Indonesia 37 E8 0 55S 130 40 E
Batatais, Brazil 95 A6 20 54S 47 37W
Batavia, U.S.A. 78 D6 43 0N 78 11W
Batchelor, Australia 60 B5 13 4S 131 1 E
Batdambang, Cambodia 38 F4 13 7N 103 12 E
Batemans B., Australia 63 F5 35 40S 150 12 E
Batemans Bay, Australia 63 F5 35 44S 150 11 E
Bates Ra., Australia 61 E3 27 27S 121 5 E
Batesburg-Leesville, U.S.A. 77 J5 33 54N 81 33W
Batesville, Ark., U.S.A. 81 H9 35 46N 91 39W
Batesville, Miss., U.S.A. 81 H10 34 19N 89 57W
Batesville, Tex., U.S.A. 81 L5 28 58N 99 37W
Bath, Canada 79 B8 44 11N 76 47W
Bath, U.K. 11 F5 51 23N 2 22W
Bath, Maine, U.S.A. 77 D11 43 55N 69 49W
Bath, N.Y., U.S.A. 78 D7 42 20N 77 19W
Bath & North East Somerset □, U.K. 11 F5 51 21N 2 27W
Batheay, Cambodia 39 G5 11 59N 104 57 E
Bathurst = Banjul, Gambia 50 F2 13 28N 16 40W
Bathurst, Australia 63 E4 33 25S 149 31 E
Bathurst, Canada 71 C6 47 37N 65 43W
Bathurst, S. Africa 56 E4 33 30S 26 50 E
Bathurst, C., Canada 68 A7 70 34N 128 0W
Bathurst B., Australia 62 A3 14 16S 144 25 E
Bathurst Harb., Australia 62 G4 43 15S 146 10 E
Bathurst I., Australia 60 B5 11 30S 130 10 E
Bathurst I., Canada 4 B2 76 0N 100 30W
Bathurst Inlet, Canada 68 B9 66 50N 108 1W
Batlow, Australia 63 F4 35 31S 148 9 E
Batman, Turkey 25 G7 37 55N 41 5 E
Baṭn al Ghūl, Jordan 47 F4 29 36N 35 56 E
Batna, Algeria 50 A7 35 34N 6 15 E
Batoka, Zambia 55 F2 16 45S 27 15 E
Baton Rouge, U.S.A. 81 K9 30 27N 91 11W
Batong, Ko, Thailand 39 J2 6 32N 99 12 E
Batopilas, Mexico 86 B3 27 0N 107 45W
Batouri, Cameroon 52 D2 4 30N 14 25 E
Båtsfjord, Norway 8 A23 70 38N 29 39 E
Battambang = Batdambang, Cambodia 38 F4 13 7N 103 12 E
Batticaloa, Sri Lanka 40 R12 7 43N 81 45 E
Battipáglia, Italy 20 D6 40 37N 14 58 E
Battle, U.K. 11 G8 50 55N 0 30 E
Battle →, Canada 73 C7 52 43N 108 15W
Battle Creek, U.S.A. 76 D3 42 19N 85 11W
Battle Ground, U.S.A. 84 E4 45 47N 122 32W
Battle Harbour, Canada 71 B8 52 16N 55 35W
Battle Lake, U.S.A. 80 B7 46 17N 95 43W
Battle Mountain, U.S.A. 82 F5 40 38N 116 56W
Battlefields, Zimbabwe 55 F2 18 37S 29 47 E
Battleford, Canada 73 C7 52 45N 108 15W
Batu, Ethiopia 46 F2 6 55N 39 45 E
Batu, Kepulauan, Indonesia 36 E1 0 30S 98 25 E
Batu Caves, Malaysia 39 L3 3 15N 101 40 E
Batu Gajah, Malaysia 39 K3 4 28N 101 3 E
Batu Is. = Batu, Kepulauan, Indonesia 36 E1 0 30S 98 25 E
Batu Pahat, Malaysia 39 M4 1 50N 102 56 E
Batuata, Indonesia 37 F6 6 12S 122 42 E
Batumi, Georgia 25 F7 41 39N 41 44 E
Baturaja, Indonesia 36 E2 4 11S 104 15 E
Baturité, Brazil 93 D11 4 28S 38 45W
Bau, Malaysia 36 D4 1 25N 110 9 E
Baubau, Indonesia 37 F6 5 25S 122 38 E
Baucau, E. Timor 37 F7 8 27S 126 27 E
Bauchi, Nigeria 50 F7 10 22N 9 48 E
Baudette, U.S.A. 80 A7 48 43N 94 36W
Bauer, C., Australia 63 E1 32 44S 134 4 E
Bauhinia, Australia 62 C4 24 35S 149 18 E
Baukau = Baucau, E. Timor 37 F7 8 27S 126 27 E
Bauld, C., Canada 69 C14 51 38N 55 26W
Bauru, Brazil 95 A6 22 10S 49 0W
Bausi, India 43 G12 24 48N 87 1 E
Bauska, Latvia 9 H21 56 24N 24 15 E
Bautzen, Germany 16 C8 51 10N 14 26 E
Bavānāt, Iran 45 D7 30 28N 53 27 E
Bavaria = Bayern □, Germany 16 D6 48 50N 12 0 E
Bavispe →, Mexico 86 B3 29 30N 109 11W
Bawdwin, Burma 41 H20 23 5N 97 20 E
Bawean, Indonesia 36 F4 5 46S 112 35 E
Bawku, Ghana 50 F5 11 3N 0 19W
Bawlake, Burma 41 K20 19 11N 97 21 E
Baxley, U.S.A. 77 K4 31 47N 82 21W
Baxter, U.S.A. 80 B7 46 21N 94 17W
Baxter Springs, U.S.A. 81 G7 37 2N 94 44W
Bay City, Mich., U.S.A. 76 D4 43 36N 83 54W
Bay City, Tex., U.S.A. 81 L7 28 59N 95 58W
Bay Minette, U.S.A. 77 K2 30 53N 87 46W
Bay Roberts, Canada 71 C9 47 36N 53 16W
Bay St. Louis, U.S.A. 81 K10 30 19N 89 20W
Bay Springs, U.S.A. 81 K10 31 59N 89 17W
Bay View, N.Z. 59 H6 39 25S 176 50 E
Baya, Dem. Rep. of the Congo 55 E2 11 53S 27 25 E
Bayamo, Cuba 88 B4 20 20N 76 40W
Bayamón, Puerto Rico 89 C6 18 24N 66 10W
Bayan Har Shan, China 32 C4 34 0N 98 0 E
Bayan Hot = Alxa Zuoqi, China 34 E3 38 50N 105 40 E
Bayan Obo, China 34 D5 41 52N 109 59 E
Bayan-Ovoo = Erdenetsogt, Mongolia 34 C4 42 55N 106 5 E
Bayana, India 42 F7 26 55N 77 18 E
Bayanaūyl, Kazakstan 26 D8 50 45N 75 45 E
Bayandalay, Mongolia 34 C2 43 30N 103 29 E
Bayanhongor, Mongolia 32 B5 46 8N 102 43 E
Bayard, N. Mex., U.S.A. 83 K9 32 46N 108 8W
Bayard, Nebr., U.S.A. 80 E3 41 45N 103 20W
Baybay, Phil. 37 B6 10 40N 124 55 E
Baydhabo = Baidoa, Somali Rep. 46 G3 3 8N 43 30 E
Bayern □, Germany 16 D6 48 50N 12 0 E
Bayeux, France 18 B3 49 17N 0 42W
Bayfield, Canada 78 C3 43 34N 81 42W
Bayfield, U.S.A. 80 B9 46 49N 90 49W
Bayındır, Turkey 21 E12 38 13N 27 39 E
Baykal, Oz., Russia 27 D11 53 0N 108 0 E
Baykan, Turkey 44 B4 38 7N 41 44 E
Baykonur = Bayqongyr, Kazakstan 26 E7 47 48N 65 50 E
Baymak, Russia 24 D10 52 36N 58 19 E
Baynes Mts., Namibia 56 B1 17 15S 13 0 E
Bayombong, Phil. 37 A6 16 30N 121 10 E
Bayonne, France 18 E3 43 30N 1 28W
Bayonne, U.S.A. 79 F10 40 40N 74 7W
Bayovar, Peru 92 E2 5 50S 81 0W
Bayqongyr, Kazakstan 26 E7 47 48N 65 50 E
Bayram-Ali = Bayramaly, Turkmenistan 26 F7 37 37N 62 10 E
Bayramaly, Turkmenistan 26 F7 37 37N 62 10 E
Bayramiç, Turkey 21 E12 39 48N 26 36 E
Bayreuth, Germany 16 D6 49 56N 11 35 E
Bayrūt, Lebanon 47 B4 33 53N 35 31 E
Bays, L. of, Canada 78 A5 45 15N 79 4W
Baysville, Canada 78 A5 45 9N 79 7W
Bayt Lahm, West Bank 47 D4 31 43N 35 12 E
Baytown, U.S.A. 81 L7 29 43N 94 59W
Baza, Spain 19 D4 37 30N 2 47W
Bazaruto, I. do, Mozam. 57 C6 21 40S 35 28 E
Bazhou, China 34 E9 39 8N 116 22 E
Bazmān, Kūh-e, Iran 45 D9 28 4N 60 1 E
Beach, U.S.A. 80 B3 46 58N 104 0W
Beach City, U.S.A. 78 F3 40 39N 81 35W
Beachport, Australia 63 F3 37 29S 140 0 E
Beachy Hd., U.K. 11 G8 50 44N 0 15 E
Beacon, Australia 61 F2 30 26S 117 52 E
Beacon, U.S.A. 79 E11 41 30N 73 58W
Beaconsfield, Australia 62 G4 41 11S 146 48 E
Beagle, Canal, S. Amer. 96 H3 55 0S 68 30W
Beagle Bay, Australia 60 C3 16 58S 122 40 E
Bealanana, Madag. 57 A8 14 33S 48 44 E
Beals Cr. →, U.S.A. 81 J4 32 10N 100 51W
Beamsville, Canada 78 C5 43 12N 79 28W
Bear →, Calif., U.S.A. 84 G5 38 56N 121 36W
Bear →, Utah, U.S.A. 74 B4 41 30N 112 8W
Bear I., Ireland 13 E2 51 38N 9 50W
Bear L., Canada 73 B9 55 8N 96 0W
Bear L., U.S.A. 82 F8 41 59N 111 21W
Beardmore, Canada 70 C2 49 36N 87 57W
Beardmore Glacier, Antarctica 5 E11 84 30S 170 0 E
Beardstown, U.S.A. 80 F9 40 1N 90 26W
Bearma →, India 43 G8 24 20N 79 51 E
Béarn, France 18 E3 43 20N 0 30W
Bearpaw Mts., U.S.A. 82 B9 48 12N 109 30W
Bearskin Lake, Canada 70 B1 53 58N 91 2W
Beas →, India 42 D6 31 10N 74 59 E
Beata, C., Dom. Rep. 89 C5 17 40N 71 30W
Beata, I., Dom. Rep. 89 C5 17 34N 71 31W
Beatrice, U.S.A. 80 E6 40 16N 96 45W
Beatrice, Zimbabwe 55 F3 18 15S 30 55 E
Beatrice, C., Australia 62 A2 14 20S 136 55 E
Beatton →, Canada 72 B4 56 15N 120 45W
Beatton River, Canada 72 B4 57 26N 121 20W
Beatty, U.S.A. 84 J10 36 54N 116 46W
Beauce, Plaine de la, France 18 B4 48 10N 1 45 E
Beauceville, Canada 71 C5 46 13N 70 46W
Beaudesert, Australia 63 D5 27 59S 153 0 E
Beaufort, Malaysia 36 C5 5 30N 115 40 E
Beaufort, N.C., U.S.A. 77 H7 34 43N 76 40W
Beaufort, S.C., U.S.A. 77 J5 32 26N 80 40W
Beaufort Sea, Arctic 4 B1 72 0N 140 0W
Beaufort West, S. Africa 56 E3 32 18S 22 36 E
Beauharnois, Canada 79 A11 45 20N 73 52W
Beaulieu →, Canada 72 A6 62 3N 113 11W
Beauly, U.K. 12 D4 57 30N 4 28W
Beauly →, U.K. 12 D4 57 29N 4 27W
Beaumaris, U.K. 10 D3 53 16N 4 6W
Beaumont, Belgium 15 D4 50 15N 4 14 E
Beaumont, U.S.A. 81 K7 30 5N 94 6W
Beaune, France 18 C6 47 2N 4 50 E
Beaupré, Canada 71 C5 47 3N 70 54W
Beauraing, Belgium 15 D4 50 7N 4 57 E
Beauséjour, Canada 73 C9 50 5N 96 35W
Beauvais, France 18 B5 49 25N 2 8 E
Beauval, Canada 73 B7 55 9N 107 37W
Beaver, Okla., U.S.A. 81 G4 36 49N 100 31W
Beaver, Pa., U.S.A. 78 F4 40 42N 80 19W
Beaver, Utah, U.S.A. 83 G7 38 17N 112 38W
Beaver →, B.C., Canada 72 B4 59 52N 124 20W
Beaver →, Ont., Canada 70 A2 55 55N 87 48W
Beaver →, Sask., Canada 73 B7 55 26N 107 45W
Beaver →, U.S.A. 81 G5 36 35N 99 30W
Beaver City, U.S.A. 80 E5 40 8N 99 50W
Beaver Creek, Canada 68 B5 63 0N 141 0W
Beaver Dam, U.S.A. 80 D10 43 28N 88 50W
Beaver Falls, U.S.A. 78 F4 40 46N 80 20W
Beaver Hill L., Canada 73 C10 54 5N 94 50W
Beaver I., U.S.A. 76 C3 45 40N 85 33W
Beaverhill L., Canada 72 C6 53 27N 112 32W
Beaverlodge, Canada 72 B5 55 11N 119 29W
Beaverstone →, Canada 70 B2 54 59N 89 25W
Beaverton, Canada 78 B5 44 26N 79 9W
Beaverton, U.S.A. 84 E4 45 29N 122 48W
Beawar, India 42 F6 26 3N 74 18 E
Bebedouro, Brazil 95 A6 21 0S 48 25W
Beboa, Madag. 57 B7 17 22S 44 33 E
Beccles, U.K. 11 E9 52 27N 1 35 E
Bečej, Serbia, Yug. 21 B9 45 36N 20 3 E
Béchar, Algeria 50 B5 31 38N 2 18W
Beckley, U.S.A. 76 G5 37 47N 81 11W
Beddouza, Ras, Morocco 50 B4 32 33N 9 9W
Bedford, Canada 79 A12 45 7N 72 59W
Bedford, S. Africa 56 E4 32 40S 26 10 E
Bedford, U.K. 11 E7 52 8N 0 28W
Bedford, Ind., U.S.A. 76 F2 38 52N 86 29W
Bedford, Iowa, U.S.A. 80 E7 40 40N 94 44W
Bedford, Ohio, U.S.A. 78 E3 41 23N 81 32W
Bedford, Pa., U.S.A. 78 F6 40 1N 78 30W
Bedford, Va., U.S.A. 76 G6 37 20N 79 31W
Bedford, C., Australia 62 B4 15 14S 145 21 E
Bedfordshire □, U.K. 11 E7 52 4N 0 28W
Bedourie, Australia 62 C2 24 30S 139 30 E
Bedum, Neths. 15 A6 53 18N 6 36 E
Beebe Plain, Canada 79 A12 45 1N 72 9W
Beech Creek, U.S.A. 78 E7 41 5N 77 36W
Beenleigh, Australia 63 D5 27 43S 153 10 E
Be'er Menuḥa, Israel 44 D2 30 19N 35 8 E
Be'er Sheva, Israel 47 D3 31 15N 34 48 E
Beersheba = Be'er Sheva, Israel 47 D3 31 15N 34 48 E
Beestekraal, S. Africa 57 D4 25 23S 27 38 E
Beeston, U.K. 10 E6 52 56N 1 14W
Beeville, U.S.A. 81 L6 28 24N 97 45W
Befale, Dem. Rep. of the Congo 52 D4 0 25N 20 45 E
Befandriana, Mahajanga, Madag. 57 B8 15 16S 48 32 E
Befandriana, Toliara, Madag. 57 C7 21 55S 44 0 E
Befasy, Madag. 57 C7 20 33S 44 23 E
Befotaka, Antsiranana, Madag. 57 A8 13 15S 48 16 E
Befotaka, Fianarantsoa, Madag. 57 C8 23 49S 47 0 E
Bega, Australia 63 F4 36 41S 149 51 E
Begusarai, India 43 G12 25 24N 86 9 E
Behābād, Iran 45 C8 32 24N 59 47 E

Behala, India 43 H13 22 30N 88 20 E
Behara, Madag. 57 C8 24 55S 46 20 E
Behbehān, Iran 45 D6 30 30N 50 15 E
Behm Canal, U.S.A. 72 B2 55 10N 131 0W
Behshahr, Iran 45 B7 36 45N 53 35 E
Bei Jiang →, China 33 D6 23 2N 112 58 E
Bei'an, China 33 B7 48 10N 126 20 E
Beihai, China 33 D5 21 28N 109 6 E
Beijing, China 34 E9 39 55N 116 20 E
Beijing □, China 34 E9 39 55N 116 20 E
Beilen, Neths. 15 B6 52 52N 6 27 E
Beilpajah, Australia 63 E3 32 54S 143 52 E
Beinn na Faoghla = Benbecula, U.K. 12 D1 57 26N 7 21W
Beipiao, China 35 D11 41 52N 120 32 E
Beira, Mozam. 55 F3 19 50S 34 52 E
Beirut = Bayrūt, Lebanon 47 B4 33 53N 35 31 E
Beiseker, Canada 72 C6 51 23N 113 32W
Beitaolaizhao, China 35 B13 44 58N 125 58 E
Beitbridge, Zimbabwe 55 G3 22 12S 30 0 E
Beizhen = Binzhou, China 35 F10 37 20N 118 2 E
Beizhen, China 35 D11 41 38N 121 54 E
Beizhengzhen, China 35 B12 44 31N 123 30 E
Beja, Portugal 19 C2 38 2N 7 53W
Béja, Tunisia 51 A7 36 43N 9 12 E
Bejaïa, Algeria 50 A7 36 42N 5 2 E
Béjar, Spain 19 B3 40 23N 5 46W
Bejestān, Iran 45 C8 34 30N 58 5 E
Békéscsaba, Hungary 17 E11 46 40N 21 5 E
Bekily, Madag. 57 C8 24 13S 45 19 E
Bekisopa, Madag. 57 C8 21 40S 45 54 E
Bekitro, Madag. 57 C8 24 33S 45 18 E
Bekodoka, Madag. 57 B8 16 58S 45 7 E
Bekok, Malaysia 39 L4 2 20N 103 7 E
Bekopaka, Madag. 57 B7 19 9S 44 48 E
Bela, India 43 G10 25 50N 82 0 E
Bela, Pakistan 42 F2 26 12N 66 20 E
Bela Crkva, Serbia, Yug. 21 B9 44 55N 21 27 E
Bela Vista, Brazil 94 A4 22 12S 56 20W
Bela Vista, Mozam. 57 D5 26 10S 32 44 E
Belan →, India 43 G9 24 2N 81 45 E
Belarus ■, Europe 17 B14 53 30N 27 0 E
Belau = Palau ■, Pac. Oc. 28 J17 7 30N 134 30 E
Belavenona, Madag. 57 C8 24 50S 47 4 E
Belawan, Indonesia 36 D1 3 33N 98 32 E
Belaya →, Russia 24 C9 54 40N 56 0 E
Belaya Tserkov = Bila Tserkva, Ukraine 17 D16 49 45N 30 10 E
Belcher Is., Canada 70 A3 56 15N 78 45W
Belden, U.S.A. 84 E5 40 2N 121 17W
Belebey, Russia 24 D9 54 7N 54 7 E
Beled Weyne = Belet Uen, Somali Rep. 46 G4 4 30N 45 5 E
Belém, Brazil 93 D9 1 20S 48 30W
Belén, Argentina 94 B2 27 40S 67 5W
Belén, Paraguay 94 A4 23 30S 57 6W
Belen, U.S.A. 83 J10 34 40N 106 46W
Belet Uen, Somali Rep. 46 G4 4 30N 45 5 E
Belev, Russia 24 D6 53 50N 36 5 E
Belfair, U.S.A. 84 C4 47 27N 122 50W
Belfast, S. Africa 57 D5 25 42S 30 2 E
Belfast, U.K. 13 B6 54 37N 5 56W
Belfast, Maine, U.S.A. 77 C11 44 26N 69 1W
Belfast, N.Y., U.S.A. 78 D6 42 21N 78 7W
Belfast L., U.K. 13 B6 54 40N 5 50W
Belfield, U.S.A. 80 B3 46 53N 103 12W
Belfort, France 18 C7 47 38N 6 50 E
Belfry, U.S.A. 82 D9 45 9N 109 1W
Belgaum, India 40 M9 15 55N 74 35 E
Belgium ■, Europe 15 D4 50 30N 5 0 E
Belgorod, Russia 25 D6 50 35N 36 35 E
Belgorod-Dnestrovskiy = Bilhorod-Dnistrovskyy, Ukraine 25 E5 46 11N 30 23 E
Belgrade = Beograd, Serbia, Yug. 21 B9 44 50N 20 37 E
Belgrade, U.S.A. 82 D8 45 47N 111 11W
Belhaven, U.S.A. 77 H7 35 33N 76 37W
Beli Drim →, Europe 21 C9 42 6N 20 25 E
Belinyu, Indonesia 36 E3 1 35S 105 50 E
Beliton Is. = Belitung, Indonesia 36 E3 3 10S 107 50 E
Belitung, Indonesia 36 E3 3 10S 107 50 E
Belize ■, Cent. Amer. 87 D7 17 0N 88 30W
Belize City, Belize 87 D7 17 25N 88 0W
Belkovskiy, Ostrov, Russia 27 B14 75 32N 135 44 E
Bell →, Canada 70 C4 49 48N 77 38W
Bell I., Canada 71 B8 50 46N 55 35W
Bell-Irving →, Canada 72 B3 56 12N 129 5W
Bell Peninsula, Canada 69 B11 63 50N 82 0W
Bell Ville, Argentina 94 C3 32 40S 62 40W
Bella Bella, Canada 72 C3 52 10N 128 10W
Bella Coola, Canada 72 C3 52 25N 126 40W
Bella Unión, Uruguay 94 C4 30 15S 57 40W
Bella Vista, Corrientes, Argentina 94 B4 28 33S 59 0W
Bella Vista, Tucuman, Argentina 94 B2 27 10S 65 25W
Bellaire, U.S.A. 78 F4 40 1N 80 45W
Bellary, India 40 M10 15 10N 76 56 E
Bellata, Australia 63 D4 29 53S 149 46 E
Belle-Chasse, U.S.A. 81 L10 29 51N 89 59W
Belle Fourche, U.S.A. 80 C3 44 40N 103 51W
Belle Fourche →, U.S.A. 80 C3 44 26N 102 18W
Belle Glade, U.S.A. 77 M5 26 41N 80 40W
Belle-Île, France 18 C2 47 20N 3 10W
Belle Isle, Canada 71 B8 51 57N 55 25W
Belle Isle, Str. of, Canada 71 B8 51 30N 56 30W
Belle Plaine, U.S.A. 80 E8 41 54N 92 17W
Bellefontaine, U.S.A. 76 E4 40 22N 83 46W
Bellefonte, U.S.A. 78 F7 40 55N 77 47W
Belleoram, Canada 71 C8 47 31N 55 25W
Belleville, Canada 78 B7 44 10N 77 23W
Belleville, Ill., U.S.A. 80 F10 38 31N 89 59W
Belleville, Kans., U.S.A. 80 F6 39 50N 97 38W
Belleville, N.Y., U.S.A. 79 C8 43 46N 76 10W
Bellevue, Canada 72 D6 49 35N 114 22W
Bellevue, Idaho, U.S.A. 82 E6 43 28N 114 16W
Bellevue, Nebr., U.S.A. 80 E7 41 8N 95 53W
Bellevue, Ohio, U.S.A. 78 E2 41 17N 82 51W
Bellevue, Wash., U.S.A. 84 C4 47 37N 122 12W
Bellin = Kangirsuk, Canada 69 B13 60 0N 70 0W
Bellingen, Australia 63 E5 30 25S 152 50 E
Bellingham, U.S.A. 68 D7 48 46N 122 29W
Bellingshausen Sea, Antarctica 5 C17 66 0S 80 0W
Bellinzona, Switz. 18 C8 46 11N 9 1 E
Bello, Colombia 92 B3 6 20N 75 33W
Bellows Falls, U.S.A. 79 C12 43 8N 72 27W
Bellpat, Pakistan 42 E3 29 0N 68 5 E
Belluno, Italy 20 A5 46 9N 12 13 E
Bellwood, U.S.A. 78 F6 40 36N 78 20W
Belmont, Canada 78 D3 42 53N 81 5W
Belmont, S. Africa 56 D3 29 28S 24 22 E
Belmont, U.S.A. 78 D6 42 14N 78 2W
Belmonte, Brazil 93 G11 16 0S 39 0W
Belmopan, Belize 87 D7 17 18N 88 30W
Belmullet, Ireland 13 B2 54 14N 9 58W
Belo Horizonte, Brazil 93 G10 19 55S 43 56W
Belo-sur-Mer, Madag. 57 C7 20 42S 44 0 E
Belo-Tsiribihina, Madag. 57 B7 19 40S 44 30 E
Belogorsk, Russia 27 D13 51 0N 128 20 E
Beloha, Madag. 57 D8 25 10S 45 3 E
Beloit, Kans., U.S.A. 80 F5 39 28N 98 6W
Beloit, Wis., U.S.A. 80 D10 42 31N 89 2W
Belokorovichi, Ukraine 17 C15 51 7N 28 2 E
Belomorsk, Russia 24 B5 64 35N 34 54 E
Belonia, India 41 H17 23 15N 91 30 E
Beloretsk, Russia 24 D10 53 58N 58 24 E
Belorussia = Belarus ■, Europe 17 B14 53 30N 27 0 E
Belovo, Russia 26 D9 54 30N 86 0 E
Beloye, Ozero, Russia 24 B6 60 10N 37 35 E
Beloye More, Russia 24 A6 66 30N 38 0 E
Belozersk, Russia 24 B6 60 1N 37 45 E
Belpre, U.S.A. 76 F5 39 17N 81 34W
Belrain, India 43 E9 28 23N 80 55 E
Belt, U.S.A. 82 C8 47 23N 110 55W
Beltana, Australia 63 E2 30 48S 138 25 E
Belterra, Brazil 93 D8 2 45S 55 0W
Belton, U.S.A. 81 K6 31 3N 97 28W
Belton L., U.S.A. 81 K6 31 8N 97 32W
Beltsy = Bălţi, Moldova 17 E14 47 48N 27 58 E
Belturbet, Ireland 13 B4 54 6N 7 26W
Belukha, Russia 26 E9 49 50N 86 50 E
Beluran, Malaysia 36 C5 5 48N 117 35 E
Belvidere, Ill., U.S.A. 80 D10 42 15N 88 50W
Belvidere, N.J., U.S.A. 79 F9 40 50N 75 5W
Belyando →, Australia 62 C4 21 38S 146 50 E
Belyy, Ostrov, Russia 26 B8 73 30N 71 0 E
Belyy Yar, Russia 26 D9 58 26N 84 39 E
Belzoni, U.S.A. 81 J9 33 11N 90 29W
Bemaraha, Lembalemban' i, Madag. 57 B7 18 40S 44 45 E
Bemarivo, Madag. 57 C7 21 45S 44 45 E
Bemarivo →, Antsiranana, Madag. 57 A9 14 9S 50 9 E
Bemarivo →, Mahajanga, Madag. 57 B8 15 27S 47 40 E
Bemavo, Madag. 57 C8 21 33S 45 25 E
Bembéréke, Benin 50 F6 10 11N 2 43 E
Bembesi, Zimbabwe 55 G2 20 0S 28 58 E
Bembesi →, Zimbabwe 55 F2 18 57S 27 47 E
Bemetara, India 43 J9 21 42N 81 32 E
Bemidji, U.S.A. 80 B7 47 28N 94 53W
Bemolanga, Madag. 57 B8 17 44S 45 6 E
Ben, Iran 45 C6 32 32N 50 45 E
Ben Cruachan, U.K. 12 E3 56 26N 5 8W
Ben Dearg, U.K. 12 D4 57 47N 4 56W
Ben Hope, U.K. 12 C4 58 25N 4 36W
Ben Lawers, U.K. 12 E4 56 32N 4 14W
Ben Lomond, N.S.W., Australia 63 E5 30 1S 151 43 E
Ben Lomond, Tas., Australia 62 G4 41 38S 147 42 E
Ben Lomond, U.K. 12 E4 56 11N 4 38W
Ben Luc, Vietnam 39 G6 10 39N 106 29 E
Ben Macdhui, U.K. 12 D5 57 4N 3 40W
Ben Mhor, U.K. 12 D1 57 15N 7 18W
Ben More, Arg. & Bute, U.K. 12 E2 56 26N 6 1W
Ben More, Stirl., U.K. 12 E4 56 23N 4 32W
Ben More Assynt, U.K. 12 C4 58 8N 4 52W
Ben Nevis, U.K. 12 E3 56 48N 5 1W
Ben Quang, Vietnam 38 D6 17 3N 106 55 E
Ben Vorlich, U.K. 12 E4 56 21N 4 14W
Ben Wyvis, U.K. 12 D4 57 40N 4 35W
Bena, Nigeria 50 F7 11 20N 5 50 E
Benalla, Australia 63 F4 36 30S 146 0 E
Benares = Varanasi, India 43 G10 25 22N 83 0 E
Benavente, Spain 19 A3 42 2N 5 43W
Benavides, U.S.A. 81 M5 27 36N 98 25W
Benbecula, U.K. 12 D1 57 26N 7 21W
Benbonyathe, Australia 63 E2 30 25S 139 11 E
Bend, U.S.A. 82 D3 44 4N 121 19W
Bender Beila, Somali Rep. 46 F5 9 30N 50 48 E
Bendery = Tighina, Moldova 17 E15 46 50N 29 30 E
Bendigo, Australia 63 F3 36 40S 144 15 E
Benē Beraq, Israel 47 C3 32 6N 34 51 E
Benenitra, Madag. 57 C8 23 27S 45 5 E
Benevento, Italy 20 D6 41 8N 14 45 E
Benga, Mozam. 55 F3 16 11S 33 40 E
Bengal, Bay of, Ind. Oc. 41 M17 15 0N 90 0 E
Bengbu, China 35 H9 32 58N 117 20 E
Benghazi = Banghāzī, Libya 51 B10 32 11N 20 3 E
Bengkalis, Indonesia 36 D2 1 30N 102 10 E
Bengkulu, Indonesia 36 E2 3 50S 102 12 E
Bengkulu □, Indonesia 36 E2 3 48S 102 16 E
Bengough, Canada 73 D7 49 25N 105 10W
Benguela, Angola 53 G2 12 37S 13 25 E
Benguérua, I., Mozam. 57 C6 21 58S 35 28 E
Beni, Dem. Rep. of the Congo 54 B2 0 30N 29 27 E
Beni →, Bolivia 92 F5 10 23S 65 24W
Beni Mellal, Morocco 50 B4 32 21N 6 21W
Beni Suef, Egypt 51 C12 29 5N 31 6 E
Beniah L., Canada 72 A6 63 23N 112 17W
Benicia, U.S.A. 84 G4 38 3N 122 9W
Benidorm, Spain 19 C5 38 33N 0 9W
Benin ■, Africa 50 G6 10 0N 2 0 E
Benin, Bight of, W. Afr. 50 H6 5 0N 3 0 E
Benin City, Nigeria 50 G7 6 20N 5 31 E
Benitses, Greece 23 A3 39 32N 19 55 E
Benjamin Aceval, Paraguay 94 A4 24 58S 57 34W
Benjamin Constant, Brazil 92 D4 4 40S 70 15W
Benjamin Hill, Mexico 86 A2 30 10N 111 10W
Benkelman, U.S.A. 80 E4 40 3N 101 32W
Bennett, Canada 72 B2 59 56N 134 53W
Bennett, L., Australia 60 D5 22 50S 131 2 E
Bennetta, Ostrov, Russia 27 B15 76 21N 148 56 E
Bennettsville, U.S.A. 77 H6 34 37N 79 41W
Bennington, N.H., U.S.A. 79 D11 43 0N 71 55W
Bennington, Vt., U.S.A. 79 D11 42 53N 73 12W
Benoni, S. Africa 57 D4 26 11S 28 18 E
Benque Viejo, Belize 87 D7 17 5N 89 8W
Benson, Ariz., U.S.A. 83 L8 31 58N 110 18W
Benson, Minn., U.S.A. 80 C7 45 19N 95 36W
Bent, Iran 45 E8 26 20N 59 31 E
Benteng, Indonesia 37 F6 6 10S 120 30 E
Bentinck I., Australia 62 B2 17 3S 139 35 E
Bento Gonçalves, Brazil 95 B5 29 10S 51 31W
Benton, Ark., U.S.A. 81 H8 34 34N 92 35W
Benton, Calif., U.S.A. 84 H8 37 48N 118 32W
Benton, Ill., U.S.A. 80 G10 38 0N 88 55W
Benton, Pa., U.S.A. 79 E8 41 12N 76 23W
Benton Harbor, U.S.A. 76 D2 42 6N 86 27W
Bentonville, U.S.A. 81 G7 36 22N 94 13W
Bentung, Malaysia 39 L3 3 31N 101 55 E
Benue →, Nigeria 50 G7 7 48N 6 46 E
Benxi, China 35 D12 41 20N 123 48 E
Beo, Indonesia 37 D7 4 25N 126 50 E
Beograd, Serbia, Yug. 21 B9 44 50N 20 37 E
Beppu, Japan 31 H5 33 15N 131 30 E
Beqaa Valley = Al Biqā, Lebanon 47 A5 34 10N 36 10 E
Ber Mota, India 42 H3 23 27N 68 34 E
Berach →, India 42 G6 25 15N 75 2 E
Beraketa, Madag. 57 C7 23 7S 44 25 E
Berat, Albania 21 D8 40 43N 19 59 E
Berau, Teluk, Indonesia 37 E8 2 30S 132 30 E
Beravina, Madag. 57 B8 18 10S 45 14 E
Berber, Sudan 51 E12 18 0N 34 0 E
Berbera, Somali Rep. 46 E4 10 30N 45 2 E
Berbérati, C.A.R. 52 D3 4 15N 15 40 E
Berbice →, Guyana 92 B7 6 20N 57 32W
Berdichev = Berdychiv, Ukraine 17 D15 49 57N 28 30 E
Berdsk, Russia 26 D9 54 47N 83 2 E
Berdyansk, Ukraine 25 E6 46 45N 36 50 E
Berdychiv, Ukraine 17 D15 49 57N 28 30 E
Berea, U.S.A. 76 G3 37 34N 84 17W
Berebere, Indonesia 37 D7 2 25N 128 45 E
Bereda, Somali Rep. 46 E5 11 45N 51 0 E
Berehove, Ukraine 17 D12 48 15N 22 35 E
Berekum, Ghana 50 G5 7 29N 2 34W
Berens →, Canada 73 C9 52 25N 97 2W
Berens I., Canada 73 C9 52 18N 97 18W
Berens River, Canada 73 C9 52 25N 97 0W
Beresford, U.S.A. 80 D6 43 5N 96 47W
Berestechko, Ukraine 17 C13 50 22N 25 5 E
Berevo, Mahajanga, Madag. 57 B7 17 14S 44 17 E
Berevo, Toliara, Madag. 57 B7 19 44S 44 58 E
Bereza = Byaroza, Belarus 17 B13 52 31N 24 51 E
Berezhany, Ukraine 17 D13 49 26N 24 58 E
Berezina = Byarezina →, Belarus 17 B16 52 33N 30 14 E
Bereznik, Russia 24 B7 62 51N 42 40 E
Berezniki, Russia 24 C10 59 24N 56 46 E
Berezovo, Russia 26 C7 64 0N 65 0 E
Berga, Spain 19 A6 42 6N 1 48 E
Bergama, Turkey 21 E12 39 8N 27 11 E
Bérgamo, Italy 18 D8 45 41N 9 43 E
Bergen, Neths. 15 B4 52 40N 4 43 E
Bergen, Norway 9 F11 60 20N 5 20 E
Bergen, U.S.A. 78 C7 43 5N 77 57W
Bergen op Zoom, Neths. 15 C4 51 28N 4 18 E
Bergerac, France 18 D4 44 51N 0 30 E
Bergholz, U.S.A. 78 F4 40 31N 80 53W
Bergisch Gladbach, Germany 15 D7 50 59N 7 8 E
Bergville, S. Africa 57 D4 28 52S 29 18 E
Berhala, Selat, Indonesia 36 E2 1 0S 104 15 E
Berhampore = Baharampur, India 43 G13 24 2N 88 27 E
Berhampur = Brahmapur, India 41 K14 19 15N 84 54 E
Bering Sea, Pac. Oc. 68 C1 58 0N 171 0 E
Bering Strait, Pac. Oc. 68 B3 65 30N 169 0W
Beringovskiy, Russia 27 C18 63 3N 179 19 E
Berisso, Argentina 94 C4 34 56S 57 50W
Berja, Spain 19 D4 36 50N 2 56W
Berkeley, U.S.A. 84 H4 37 52N 122 16W
Berkner I., Antarctica 5 D18 79 30S 50 0W
Berkshire, U.S.A. 79 D8 42 19N 76 11W
Berkshire Downs, U.K. 11 F6 51 33N 1 29W
Berlin, Germany 16 B7 52 30N 13 25 E
Berlin, Md., U.S.A. 76 F8 38 20N 75 13W
Berlin, N.H., U.S.A. 79 B13 44 28N 71 11W
Berlin, N.Y., U.S.A. 79 D11 42 42N 73 23W
Berlin, Wis., U.S.A. 76 D1 43 58N 88 57W
Berlin L., U.S.A. 78 E4 41 3N 81 0W
Bermejo →, Formosa, Argentina 94 B4 26 51S 58 23W
Bermejo →, San Juan, Argentina 94 C2 32 30S 67 30W
Bermen, L., Canada 71 B6 53 35N 68 55W
Bermuda ■, Atl. Oc. 66 F13 32 45N 65 0W
Bern, Switz. 18 C7 46 57N 7 28 E
Bernalillo, U.S.A. 83 J10 35 18N 106 33W
Bernardo de Irigoyen, Argentina 95 B5 26 15S 53 40W
Bernardo O'Higgins □, Chile 94 C1 34 15S 70 45W
Bernardsville, U.S.A. 79 F10 40 43N 74 34W
Bernasconi, Argentina 94 D3 37 55S 63 44W
Bernburg, Germany 16 C6 51 47N 11 44 E
Berne = Bern, Switz. 18 C7 46 57N 7 28 E
Berneray, U.K. 12 D1 57 43N 7 11W
Bernier I., Australia 61 D1 24 50S 113 12 E
Bernina, Piz, Switz. 18 C8 46 20N 9 54 E
Beroroha, Madag. 57 C8 21 40S 45 10 E
Beroun, Czech Rep. 16 D8 49 57N 14 5 E
Berri, Australia 63 E3 34 14S 140 35 E
Berriane, Algeria 50 B6 32 50N 3 46 E
Berry, Australia 63 E5 34 46S 150 43 E
Berry, France 18 C5 46 50N 2 0 E
Berry Is., Bahamas 88 A4 25 40N 77 50W
Berryessa L., U.S.A. 84 G4 38 31N 122 6W
Berryville, U.S.A. 81 G8 36 22N 93 34W
Berseba, Namibia 56 D2 26 0S 17 46 E
Bershad, Ukraine 17 D15 48 22N 29 31 E
Berthold, U.S.A. 80 A4 48 19N 101 44W
Berthoud, U.S.A. 80 E2 40 19N 105 5W
Bertoua, Cameroon 52 D2 4 30N 13 45 E
Bertraghboy B., Ireland 13 C2 53 22N 9 54W
Berwick, U.S.A. 79 E8 41 3N 76 14W
Berwick-upon-Tweed, U.K. 10 B6 55 46N 2 0W
Berwyn Mts., U.K. 10 E4 52 54N 3 26W
Besal, Pakistan 43 B5 35 4N 73 56 E
Besalampy, Madag. 57 B7 16 43S 44 29 E
Besançon, France 18 C7 47 15N 6 2 E
Besar, Indonesia 36 E5 2 40S 116 0 E
Besnard L., Canada 73 B7 55 25N 106 0W
Besni, Turkey 44 B3 37 41N 37 52 E
Besor, N. →, Egypt 47 D3 31 28N 34 22 E
Bessarabiya, Moldova 17 E15 47 0N 28 10 E
Bessarabka = Basarabeasca, Moldova 17 E15 46 21N 28 58 E
Bessemer, Ala., U.S.A. 77 J2 33 24N 86 58W
Bessemer, Mich., U.S.A. 80 B9 46 29N 90 3W
Bessemer, Pa., U.S.A. 78 F4 40 59N 80 30W
Beswick, Australia 60 B5 14 34S 132 53 E
Bet She'an, Israel 47 C4 32 30N 35 30 E
Bet Shemesh, Israel 47 D4 31 44N 35 0 E
Betafo, Madag. 57 B8 19 50S 46 51 E
Betancuria, Canary Is. 22 F5 28 25N 14 3W
Betanzos, Spain 19 A1 43 15N 8 12W
Bétaré Oya, Cameroon 52 C2 5 40N 14 5 E
Betatao, Madag. 57 B8 18 11S 47 52 E
Bethal, S. Africa 57 D4 26 27S 29 28 E
Bethanien, Namibia 56 D2 26 31S 17 8 E
Bethany, Canada 78 B6 44 11N 78 34W
Bethany, U.S.A. 80 E7 40 16N 94 2W
Bethel, Alaska, U.S.A. 68 B3 60 48N 161 45W
Bethel, Conn., U.S.A. 79 E11 41 22N 73 25W
Bethel, Maine, U.S.A. 79 B14 44 25N 70 47W
Bethel, Vt., U.S.A. 79 C12 43 50N 72 38W
Bethel Park, U.S.A. 78 F4 40 20N 80 1W
Bethlehem = Bayt Lahm, West Bank 47 D4 31 43N 35 12 E
Bethlehem, S. Africa 57 D4 28 14S 28 18 E
Bethlehem, U.S.A. 79 F9 40 37N 75 23W
Bethulie, S. Africa 56 E4 30 30S 25 59 E
Béthune, France 18 A5 50 30N 2 38 E
Betioky, Madag. 57 C7 23 48S 44 20 E
Betong, Thailand 39 K3 5 45N 101 5 E
Betoota, Australia 62 D3 25 45S 140 42 E
Betroka, Madag. 57 C8 23 16S 46 0 E
Betsiamites, Canada 71 C6 48 56N 68 40W
Betsiamites →, Canada 71 C6 48 56N 68 38W
Betsiboka →, Madag. 57 B8 16 3S 46 36 E
Bettendorf, U.S.A. 80 E9 41 32N 90 30W
Bettiah, India 43 F11 26 48N 84 33 E
Betul, India 40 J10 21 58N 77 59 E
Betung, Malaysia 36 D4 1 24N 111 31 E
Betws-y-Coed, U.K. 10 D4 53 5N 3 48W
Beulah, Mich., U.S.A. 76 C2 44 38N 86 6W
Beulah, N. Dak., U.S.A. 80 B4 47 16N 101 47W
Beveren, Belgium 15 C4 51 12N 4 16 E
Beverley, Australia 61 F2 32 9S 116 56 E
Beverley, U.K. 10 D7 53 51N 0 26W
Beverley Hills, U.S.A. 77 L4 28 56N 82 28W
Beverly, U.S.A. 79 D14 42 33N 70 53W
Beverly Hills, U.S.A. 85 L8 34 4N 118 25W
Bevoalavo, Madag. 57 D7 25 13S 45 26 E
Bewas →, India 43 H8 23 59N 79 21 E
Bexhill, U.K. 11 G8 50 51N 0 29 E
Beyānlū, Iran 44 C5 36 0N 47 51 E
Beyneu, Kazakstan 25 E10 45 18N 55 9 E
Beypazarı, Turkey 25 F5 40 10N 31 56 E
Beyşehir Gölü, Turkey 25 G5 37 41N 31 33 E
Béziers, France 18 E5 43 20N 3 12 E
Bezwada = Vijayawada, India 41 L12 16 31N 80 39 E
Bhabua, India 43 G10 25 3N 83 37 E
Bhachau, India 40 H7 23 20N 70 16 E
Bhadar →, Gujarat, India 42 H5 22 17N 72 20 E
Bhadar →, Gujarat, India 42 J3 21 27N 69 47 E
Bhadarwah, India 43 C6 32 58N 75 46 E
Bhadohi, India 43 G10 25 25N 82 34 E
Bhadra, India 42 E6 29 8N 75 14 E
Bhadrakh, India 41 J15 21 10N 86 30 E
Bhadran, India 42 H5 22 19N 72 6 E
Bhadravati, India 40 N9 13 49N 75 40 E
Bhag, Pakistan 42 E2 29 2N 67 49 E
Bhagalpur, India 43 G12 25 10N 87 0 E
Bhagirathi →, Uttaranchal, India 43 D8 30 8N 78 35 E
Bhagirathi →, W. Bengal, India 43 H13 23 25N 88 23 E
Bhakkar, Pakistan 42 D4 31 40N 71 5 E
Bhakra Dam, India 42 D7 31 30N 76 45 E
Bhaktapur, Nepal 43 F11 27 38N 85 24 E
Bhamo, Burma 41 G20 24 15N 97 15 E
Bhandara, India 40 J11 21 5N 79 42 E
Bhanpura, India 42 G6 24 31N 75 44 E
Bhanrer Ra., India 43 H8 23 40N 79 45 E
Bhaptiahi, India 43 F12 26 19N 86 44 E
Bharat = India ■, Asia 40 K11 20 0N 78 0 E
Bharatpur, Chhattisgarh, India 43 H9 23 44N 81 46 E
Bharatpur, Raj., India 42 F7 27 15N 77 30 E
Bharno, India 43 H11 23 14N 84 53 E
Bhatinda, India 42 D6 30 15N 74 57 E
Bhatpara, India 43 H13 22 50N 88 25 E
Bhattu, India 42 E6 29 36N 75 19 E
Bhaun, Pakistan 42 C5 32 55N 72 40 E
Bhaunagar = Bhavnagar, India 40 J8 21 45N 72 10 E
Bhavnagar, India 40 J8 21 45N 72 10 E
Bhawari, India 42 G5 25 42N 73 4 E
Bhayavadar, India 42 J4 21 51N 70 15 E
Bhera, Pakistan 42 C5 32 29N 72 57 E
Bhikangaon, India 42 J6 21 52N 75 57 E
Bhilsa = Vidisha, India 42 H7 23 28N 77 53 E
Bhilwara, India 42 G6 25 25N 74 38 E
Bhima →, India 40 L10 16 25N 77 17 E
Bhimbar, Pakistan 43 C6 32 59N 74 3 E
Bhind, India 43 F8 26 30N 78 46 E
Bhinga, India 43 F9 27 43N 81 56 E
Bhinmal, India 42 G5 25 0N 72 15 E
Bhiwandi, India 40 K8 19 20N 73 0 E
Bhiwani, India 42 E7 28 50N 76 9 E
Bhogava →, India 42 H5 22 26N 72 20 E
Bhola, Bangla. 41 H17 22 45N 90 35 E
Bholari, Pakistan 42 G3 25 19N 68 13 E
Bhopal, India 42 H7 23 20N 77 30 E
Bhubaneshwar, India 41 J14 20 15N 85 50 E
Bhuj, India 42 H3 23 15N 69 49 E
Bhusaval, India 40 J9 21 3N 75 46 E
Bhutan ■, Asia 41 F17 27 25N 90 30 E
Biafra, B. of = Bonny, Bight of, Africa 52 D1 3 30N 9 20 E
Biak, Indonesia 37 E9 1 10S 136 6 E
Biała Podlaska, Poland 17 B12 52 4N 23 6 E
Białogard, Poland 16 A8 54 2N 15 58 E
Białystok, Poland 17 B12 53 10N 23 10 E
Biaora, India 42 H7 23 56N 76 56 E

Bīārjmand, Iran 45 B7 36 6N 55 53 E
Biaro, Indonesia 37 D7 2 5N 125 26 E
Biarritz, France 18 E3 43 29N 1 33W
Bibai, Japan 30 C10 43 19N 141 52 E
Bibby I., Canada 73 A10 61 55N 93 0W
Biberach, Germany 16 D5 48 5N 9 47 E
Bibungwa, Dem. Rep. of the Congo 54 C2 2 40S 28 15 E
Bic, Canada 71 C6 48 20N 68 41W
Bicester, U.K. 11 F6 51 54N 1 9W
Bicheno, Australia 62 G4 41 52S 148 18 E
Bichia, India 43 H9 22 27N 80 42 E
Bickerton I., Australia 62 A2 13 45S 136 10 E
Bida, Nigeria 50 G7 9 3N 5 58 E
Bidar, India 40 L10 17 55N 77 35 E
Biddeford, U.S.A. 77 D10 43 30N 70 28W
Bideford, U.K. 11 F3 51 1N 4 13W
Bideford Bay, U.K. 11 F3 51 5N 4 20W
Bidhuna, India 43 F8 26 49N 79 31 E
Bidor, Malaysia 39 K3 4 6N 101 15 E
Bié, Planalto de, Angola 53 G3 12 0S 16 0 E
Bieber, U.S.A. 82 F3 41 7N 121 8W
Biel, Switz. 18 C7 47 8N 7 14 E
Bielefeld, Germany 16 B5 52 1N 8 33 E
Biella, Italy 18 D8 45 34N 8 3 E
Bielsk Podlaski, Poland 17 B12 52 47N 23 12 E
Bielsko-Biała, Poland 17 D10 49 50N 19 2 E
Bien Hoa, Vietnam 39 G6 10 57N 106 49 E
Bienne = Biel, Switz. 18 C7 47 8N 7 14 E
Bienville, L., Canada 70 A5 55 5N 72 40W
Biesiesfontein, S. Africa 56 E2 30 57S 17 58 E
Big →, Canada 71 B8 54 50N 58 55W
Big B., Canada 71 A7 55 43N 60 35W
Big Bear City, U.S.A. 85 L10 34 16N 116 51W
Big Bear Lake, U.S.A. 85 L10 34 15N 116 56W
Big Belt Mts., U.S.A. 82 C8 46 30N 111 25W
Big Bend, Swaziland 57 D5 26 50S 31 58 E
Big Bend Nat. Park, U.S.A. 81 L3 29 20N 103 5W
Big Black →, U.S.A. 81 K9 32 3N 91 4W
Big Blue →, U.S.A. 80 F6 39 35N 96 34W
Big Creek, U.S.A. 84 H7 37 11N 119 14W
Big Cypress Nat. Preserve, U.S.A. 77 M5 26 0N 81 10W
Big Cypress Swamp, U.S.A. 77 M5 26 15N 81 30W
Big Falls, U.S.A. 80 A8 48 12N 93 48W
Big Fork →, U.S.A. 80 A8 48 31N 93 43W
Big Horn Mts. = Bighorn Mts., U.S.A. 82 D10 44 30N 107 30W
Big I., Canada 72 A5 61 7N 116 45W
Big Lake, U.S.A. 81 K4 31 12N 101 28W
Big Moose, U.S.A. 79 C10 43 49N 74 58W
Big Muddy Cr. →, U.S.A. 80 A2 48 8N 104 36W
Big Pine, U.S.A. 84 H8 37 10N 118 17W
Big Piney, U.S.A. 82 E8 42 32N 110 7W
Big Rapids, U.S.A. 76 D3 43 42N 85 29W
Big Rideau L., Canada 79 B8 44 40N 76 15W
Big River, Canada 73 C7 53 50N 107 0W
Big Run, U.S.A. 78 F6 40 57N 78 55W
Big Sable Pt., U.S.A. 76 C2 44 3N 86 1W
Big Salmon →, Canada 72 A2 61 52N 134 55W
Big Sand L., Canada 73 B9 57 45N 99 45W
Big Sandy, U.S.A. 82 B8 48 11N 110 7W
Big Sandy →, U.S.A. 76 F4 38 25N 82 36W
Big Sandy Cr. →, U.S.A. 80 F3 38 7N 102 29W
Big Sioux →, U.S.A. 80 D6 42 29N 96 27W
Big Spring, U.S.A. 81 J4 32 15N 101 28W
Big Stone City, U.S.A. 80 C6 45 18N 96 28W
Big Stone Gap, U.S.A. 77 G4 36 52N 82 47W
Big Stone L., U.S.A. 80 C6 45 30N 96 35W
Big Sur, U.S.A. 84 J5 36 15N 121 48W
Big Timber, U.S.A. 82 D9 45 50N 109 57W
Big Trout L., Canada 70 B2 53 40N 90 0W
Big Trout Lake, Canada 70 B2 53 45N 90 0W
Biğa, Turkey 21 D12 40 13N 27 14 E
Bigadiç, Turkey 21 E13 39 22N 28 7 E
Biggar, Canada 73 C7 52 4N 108 0W
Biggar, U.K. 12 F5 55 38N 3 32W
Bigge I., Australia 60 B4 14 35S 125 10 E
Biggenden, Australia 63 D5 25 31S 152 4 E
Biggleswade, U.K. 11 E7 52 5N 0 14W
Biggs, U.S.A. 84 F5 39 25N 121 43W
Bighorn, U.S.A. 82 C10 46 10N 107 27W
Bighorn →, U.S.A. 82 C10 46 10N 107 28W
Bighorn L., U.S.A. 82 D9 44 55N 108 15W
Bighorn Mts., U.S.A. 82 D10 44 30N 107 30W
Bigstone L., Canada 73 C9 53 42N 95 44W
Bigwa, Tanzania 54 D4 7 10S 39 10 E
Bihać, Bos.-H. 16 F8 44 49N 15 57 E
Bihar, India 43 G11 25 5N 85 40 E
Bihar □, India 43 G12 25 0N 86 0 E
Biharamulo, Tanzania 54 C3 2 25S 31 25 E
Bihariganj, India 43 G12 25 44N 86 59 E
Bihor, Munţii, Romania 17 E12 46 29N 22 47 E
Bijagós, Arquipélago dos, Guinea-Biss. 50 F2 11 15N 16 10W
Bijaipur, India 42 F7 26 2N 77 20 E
Bijapur, Chhattisgarh, India 41 K12 18 50N 80 50 E
Bijapur, Karnataka, India 40 L9 16 50N 75 55 E
Bījār, Iran 44 C5 35 52N 47 35 E
Bijawar, India 43 G8 24 38N 79 30 E
Bijeljina, Bos.-H. 21 B8 44 46N 19 14 E
Bijnor, India 42 E8 29 27N 78 11 E
Bikaner, India 42 E5 28 2N 73 18 E
Bikapur, India 43 F10 26 30N 82 7 E
Bikeqi, China 34 D6 40 43N 111 20 E
Bikfayyā, Lebanon 47 B4 33 55N 35 41 E
Bikin, Russia 27 E14 46 50N 134 20 E
Bikin →, Russia 30 A7 46 51N 134 2 E
Bikini Atoll, Marshall Is. 64 F8 12 0N 167 30 E
Bikita, Zimbabwe 57 C5 20 6S 31 41 E
Bila Tserkva, Ukraine 17 D16 49 45N 30 10 E
Bilara, India 42 F5 26 14N 73 53 E
Bilaspur, Chhattisgarh, India 43 H10 22 2N 82 15 E
Bilaspur, Punjab, India 42 D7 31 19N 76 50 E
Bilauk Taungdan, Thailand 38 F2 13 0N 99 0 E
Bilbao, Spain 19 A4 43 16N 2 56W
Bilbo = Bilbao, Spain 19 A4 43 16N 2 56W
Bíldudalur, Iceland 8 D2 65 41N 23 36W
Bílé Karpaty, Europe 17 D9 49 5N 18 0 E
Bilecik, Turkey 25 F5 40 5N 30 5 E
Bilgram, India 43 F9 27 11N 80 2 E
Bilhaur, India 43 F9 26 51N 80 5 E
Bilhorod-Dnistrovskyy, Ukraine 25 E5 46 11N 30 23 E
Bilibino, Russia 27 C17 68 3N 166 20 E
Bilibiza, Mozam. 55 E5 12 30S 40 20 E
Billabalong Roadhouse, Australia 61 E2 27 25S 115 49 E
Billiluna, Australia 60 C4 19 37S 127 41 E
Billings, U.S.A. 82 D9 45 47N 108 30W
Billiton Is. = Belitung, Indonesia 36 E3 3 10S 107 50 E
Bilma, Niger 51 E8 18 50N 13 30 E
Biloela, Australia 62 C5 24 24S 150 31 E
Biloxi, U.S.A. 81 K10 30 24N 88 53W
Bilpa Morea Claypan, Australia 62 D3 25 0S 140 0 E
Biltine, Chad 51 F10 14 40N 20 50 E
Bima, Indonesia 37 F5 8 22S 118 49 E
Bimini Is., Bahamas 88 A4 25 42N 79 25W
Bin Xian, Heilongjiang, China 35 B14 45 42N 127 32 E
Bin Xian, Shaanxi, China 34 G5 35 2N 108 4 E
Bina-Etawah, India 42 G8 24 13N 78 14 E
Bināb, Iran 45 B6 36 35N 48 41 E
Binalbagan, Phil. 37 B6 10 12N 122 50 E
Binalong, Australia 63 E4 34 40S 148 39 E
Bīnālūd, Kūh-e, Iran 45 B8 36 30N 58 30 E
Binatang = Bintangor, Malaysia 36 D4 2 10N 111 40 E
Binche, Belgium 15 D4 50 26N 4 10 E
Bindki, India 43 F9 26 2N 80 36 E
Bindura, Zimbabwe 55 F3 17 18S 31 18 E
Bingara, Australia 63 D5 29 52S 150 36 E
Bingham, U.S.A. 77 C11 45 3N 69 53W
Binghamton, U.S.A. 79 D9 42 6N 75 55W
Bingöl, Turkey 44 B4 38 53N 40 29 E
Binh Dinh = An Nhon, Vietnam 38 F7 13 55N 109 7 E
Binh Khe, Vietnam 38 F7 13 57N 108 51 E
Binh Son, Vietnam 38 E7 15 20N 108 40 E
Binhai, China 35 G10 34 2N 119 49 E
Binisatua, Spain 22 B11 39 50N 4 11 E
Binjai, Indonesia 36 D3 3 20N 98 30 E
Binnaway, Australia 63 E4 31 28S 149 24 E
Binongko, Indonesia 37 F6 5 57S 124 2 E
Binscarth, Canada 73 C8 50 37N 101 17W
Bintan, Indonesia 36 D2 1 0N 104 0 E
Bintangor, Malaysia 36 D4 2 10N 111 40 E
Bintulu, Malaysia 36 D4 3 10N 113 0 E
Bintuni, Indonesia 37 E8 2 7S 133 32 E
Binzert = Bizerte, Tunisia 51 A7 37 15N 9 50 E
Binzhou, China 35 F10 37 20N 118 2 E
Bío Bío □, Chile 94 D1 37 35S 72 0W
Bioko, Eq. Guin. 52 D1 3 30N 8 40 E
Bir, India 40 K9 19 4N 75 46 E
Bi'r Abu Muḩammad, Egypt 47 F3 29 44N 34 14 E
Bi'r ad Dabbāghāt, Jordan 47 E4 30 26N 35 32 E
Bi'r al Butayyihāt, Jordan 47 F4 29 47N 35 20 E
Bi'r al Mārī, Jordan 47 E4 30 4N 35 33 E
Bi'r al Qattār, Jordan 47 F4 29 47N 35 32 E
Bir Atrun, Sudan 51 E11 18 15N 26 40 E
Bîr Beiḍa, Egypt 47 E3 30 25N 34 29 E
Bi'r el 'Abd, Egypt 47 D2 31 2N 33 0 E
Bîr el Biarât, Egypt 47 F3 29 30N 34 43 E
Bîr el Duweidar, Egypt 47 E1 30 56N 32 32 E
Bîr el Garârât, Egypt 47 D2 31 3N 33 34 E
Bîr el Heisi, Egypt 47 F3 29 22N 34 36 E
Bîr el Jafir, Egypt 47 E1 30 50N 32 41 E
Bîr el Mâlḩi, Egypt 47 E2 30 38N 33 19 E
Bîr el Thamâda, Egypt 47 E2 30 12N 33 27 E
Bîr Gebeil Ḩişn, Egypt 47 E2 30 2N 33 18 E
Bi'r Ghadīr, Syria 47 A6 34 6N 37 3 E
Bîr Ḩasana, Egypt 47 E2 30 29N 33 46 E
Bîr Kaseiba, Egypt 47 E2 31 0N 33 17 E
Bîr Lahfân, Egypt 47 E2 31 0N 33 51 E
Bîr Madkûr, Egypt 47 E1 30 44N 32 33 E
Bîr Mogreïn, Mauritania 50 C3 25 10N 11 25W
Bi'r Muţribah, Kuwait 44 D5 29 54N 47 17 E
Bîr Qaţia, Egypt 47 E1 30 58N 32 45 E
Bîr Shalatein, Egypt 51 D13 23 5N 35 25 E
Biratnagar, Nepal 43 F12 26 27N 87 17 E
Birawa, Dem. Rep. of the Congo 54 C2 2 20S 28 48 E
Birch →, Canada 72 B6 58 28N 112 17W
Birch Hills, Canada 73 C7 52 59N 105 25W
Birch I., Canada 73 C9 52 26N 99 54W
Birch L., N.W.T., Canada 72 A5 62 4N 116 33W
Birch L., Ont., Canada 70 B1 51 23N 92 18W
Birch Mts., Canada 72 B6 57 30N 113 10W
Birch River, Canada 73 C8 52 24N 101 6W
Birchip, Australia 63 F3 35 56S 142 55 E
Bird, Canada 73 B10 56 30N 94 13W
Bird I. = Las Aves, Is., W. Indies 89 C7 15 45N 63 55W
Birdsville, Australia 62 D2 25 51S 139 20 E
Birdum Cr. →, Australia 60 C5 15 14S 133 0 E
Birecik, Turkey 44 B3 37 2N 38 0 E
Birein, Israel 47 E3 30 50N 34 28 E
Bireuen, Indonesia 36 C1 5 14N 96 39 E
Birigui, Brazil 95 A5 21 18S 50 16W
Birjand, Iran 45 C8 32 53N 59 13 E
Birkenhead, U.K. 10 D4 53 23N 3 2W
Bîrlad = Bârlad, Romania 17 E14 46 15N 27 38 E
Birmingham, U.K. 11 E6 52 29N 1 52W
Birmingham, U.S.A. 77 J2 33 31N 86 48W
Birmitrapur, India 41 H14 22 24N 84 46 E
Birni Nkonni, Niger 50 F7 13 55N 5 15 E
Birnin Kebbi, Nigeria 50 F6 12 32N 4 12 E
Birobidzhan, Russia 27 E14 48 50N 132 50 E
Birr, Ireland 13 C4 53 6N 7 54W
Birrie →, Australia 63 D4 29 43S 146 37 E
Birsilpur, India 42 E5 28 11N 72 15 E
Birsk, Russia 24 C10 55 25N 55 30 E
Birtle, Canada 73 C8 50 30N 101 5W
Birur, India 40 N9 13 30N 75 55 E
Biržai, Lithuania 9 H21 56 11N 24 45 E
Birzebbugga, Malta 23 D2 35 50N 14 32 E
Bisa, Indonesia 37 E7 1 15S 127 28 E
Bisalpur, India 43 E8 28 14N 79 48 E
Bisbee, U.S.A. 83 L9 31 27N 109 55W
Biscay, B. of, Atl. Oc. 18 D1 45 0N 2 0W
Biscayne B., U.S.A. 77 N5 25 40N 80 12W
Biscoe Bay, Antarctica 5 D13 77 0S 152 0W
Biscoe Is., Antarctica 5 C17 66 0S 67 0W
Biscostasing, Canada 70 C3 47 18N 82 9W
Bishkek, Kyrgyzstan 26 E8 42 54N 74 46 E
Bishnupur, India 43 H12 23 8N 87 20 E
Bisho, S. Africa 57 E4 32 50S 27 23 E
Bishop, Calif., U.S.A. 84 H8 37 22N 118 24W
Bishop, Tex., U.S.A. 81 M6 27 35N 97 48W
Bishop Auckland, U.K. 10 C6 54 39N 1 40W
Bishop's Falls, Canada 71 C8 49 2N 55 30W
Bishop's Stortford, U.K. 11 F8 51 52N 0 10 E
Bisina, L., Uganda 54 B3 1 38N 33 56 E
Biskra, Algeria 50 B7 34 50N 5 44 E
Bismarck, U.S.A. 80 B4 46 48N 100 47W
Bismarck Arch., Papua N. G. 64 H7 2 30S 150 0 E
Biso, Uganda 54 B3 1 44N 31 26 E
Bison, U.S.A. 80 C3 45 31N 102 28W
Bīsotūn, Iran 44 C5 34 23N 47 26 E
Bissagos = Bijagós, Arquipélago dos, Guinea-Biss. 50 F2 11 15N 16 10W
Bissau, Guinea-Biss. 50 F2 11 45N 15 45W
Bistcho L., Canada 72 B5 59 45N 118 50W
Bistriţa, Romania 17 E13 47 9N 24 35 E
Bistriţa →, Romania 17 E14 46 30N 26 57 E
Biswan, India 43 F9 27 29N 81 2 E
Bitlis, Turkey 44 B4 38 20N 42 3 E
Bitola, Macedonia 21 D9 41 1N 21 20 E
Bitolj = Bitola, Macedonia 21 D9 41 1N 21 20 E
Bitter Creek, U.S.A. 82 F9 41 33N 108 33W
Bitterfontein, S. Africa 56 E2 31 1S 18 32 E
Bitterroot →, U.S.A. 82 C6 46 52N 114 7W
Bitterroot Range, U.S.A. 82 D6 46 0N 114 20W
Bitterwater, U.S.A. 84 J6 36 23N 121 0W
Biu, Nigeria 51 F8 10 40N 12 3 E
Biwa-Ko, Japan 31 G8 35 15N 136 10 E
Biwabik, U.S.A. 80 B8 47 32N 92 21W
Bixby, U.S.A. 81 H7 35 57N 95 53W
Biyang, China 34 H7 32 38N 113 21 E
Biysk, Russia 26 D9 52 40N 85 0 E
Bizana, S. Africa 57 E4 30 50S 29 52 E
Bizen, Japan 31 G7 34 43N 134 8 E
Bizerte, Tunisia 51 A7 37 15N 9 50 E
Bjargtangar, Iceland 8 D1 65 30N 24 30W
Bjelovar, Croatia 20 B7 45 56N 16 49 E
Bjørnevatn, Norway 8 B23 69 40N 30 0 E
Bjørnøya, Arctic 4 B8 74 30N 19 0 E
Black = Da →, Vietnam 38 B5 21 15N 105 20 E
Black →, Canada 78 B5 44 42N 79 19W
Black →, Ariz., U.S.A. 83 K8 33 44N 110 13W
Black →, Ark., U.S.A. 81 H9 35 38N 91 20W
Black →, Mich., U.S.A. 78 D2 42 59N 82 27W
Black →, N.Y., U.S.A. 79 C8 43 59N 76 4W
Black →, Wis., U.S.A. 80 D9 43 57N 91 22W
Black Bay Pen., Canada 70 C2 48 38N 88 21W
Black Birch L., Canada 73 B7 56 53N 107 45W
Black Diamond, Canada 72 C6 50 45N 114 14W
Black Duck →, Canada 70 A2 56 51N 89 2W
Black Forest = Schwarzwald, Germany 16 D5 48 30N 8 20 E
Black Forest, U.S.A. 80 F2 39 0N 104 43W
Black Hd., Ireland 13 C2 53 9N 9 16W
Black Hills, U.S.A. 80 D3 44 0N 103 45W
Black I., Canada 73 C9 51 12N 96 30W
Black L., Canada 73 B7 59 12N 105 15W
Black L., Mich., U.S.A. 76 C3 45 28N 84 16W
Black L., N.Y., U.S.A. 79 B9 44 31N 75 36W
Black Lake, Canada 73 B7 59 11N 105 20W
Black Mesa, U.S.A. 81 G3 36 58N 102 58W
Black Mt. = Mynydd Du, U.K. 11 F4 51 52N 3 50W
Black Mts., U.K. 11 F4 51 55N 3 7W
Black Range, U.S.A. 83 K10 33 15N 107 50W
Black River, Jamaica 88 C4 18 0N 77 50W
Black River Falls, U.S.A. 80 C9 44 18N 90 51W
Black Sea, Eurasia 25 F6 43 30N 35 0 E
Black Tickle, Canada 71 B8 53 28N 55 45W
Black Volta →, Africa 50 G5 8 41N 1 33W
Black Warrior →, U.S.A. 77 J2 32 32N 87 51W
Blackall, Australia 62 C4 24 25S 145 45 E
Blackball, N.Z. 59 K3 42 22S 171 26 E
Blackbull, Australia 62 B3 17 55S 141 45 E
Blackburn, U.K. 10 D5 53 45N 2 29W
Blackburn with Darwen □, U.K. 10 D5 53 45N 2 29W
Blackfoot, U.S.A. 82 E7 43 11N 112 21W
Blackfoot →, U.S.A. 82 C7 46 52N 113 53W
Blackfoot River Reservoir, U.S.A. 82 E8 43 0N 111 43W
Blackpool, U.K. 10 D4 53 49N 3 3W
Blackpool □, U.K. 10 D4 53 49N 3 3W
Blackriver, U.S.A. 78 B1 44 46N 83 17W
Blacks Harbour, Canada 71 C6 45 3N 66 49W
Blacksburg, U.S.A. 76 G5 37 14N 80 25W
Blacksod B., Ireland 13 B1 54 6N 10 0W
Blackstone, U.S.A. 76 G7 37 4N 78 0W
Blackstone Ra., Australia 61 E4 26 0S 128 30 E
Blackwater, Australia 62 C4 23 35S 148 53 E
Blackwater →, Meath, Ireland 13 C4 53 39N 6 41W
Blackwater →, Waterford, Ireland 13 D4 52 4N 7 52W
Blackwater →, U.K. 13 B5 54 31N 6 35W
Blackwell, U.S.A. 81 G6 36 48N 97 17W
Blackwells Corner, U.S.A. 85 K7 35 37N 119 47W
Blaenau Ffestiniog, U.K. 10 E4 53 0N 3 56W
Blaenau Gwent □, U.K. 11 F4 51 48N 3 12W
Blagodarnoye = Blagodarnyy, Russia 25 E7 45 7N 43 37 E
Blagodarnyy, Russia 25 E7 45 7N 43 37 E
Blagoevgrad, Bulgaria 21 C10 42 2N 23 5 E
Blagoveshchensk, Russia 27 D13 50 20N 127 30 E
Blain, U.S.A. 78 F7 40 20N 77 31W
Blaine, Minn., U.S.A. 80 C8 45 10N 93 13W
Blaine, Wash., U.S.A. 84 B4 48 59N 122 45W
Blaine Lake, Canada 73 C7 52 51N 106 52W
Blair, U.S.A. 80 E6 41 33N 96 8W
Blair Athol, Australia 62 C4 22 42S 147 31 E
Blair Atholl, U.K. 12 E5 56 46N 3 50W
Blairgowrie, U.K. 12 E5 56 35N 3 21W
Blairsden, U.S.A. 84 F6 39 47N 120 37W
Blairsville, U.S.A. 78 F5 40 26N 79 16W
Blake Pt., U.S.A. 80 A10 48 11N 88 25W
Blakely, Ga., U.S.A. 77 K3 31 23N 84 56W
Blakely, Pa., U.S.A. 79 E9 41 28N 75 37W
Blanc, C., Spain 22 B9 39 21N 2 51 E
Blanc, Mont, Alps 18 D7 45 48N 6 50 E
Blanc-Sablon, Canada 71 B8 51 24N 57 12W
Blanca, B., Argentina 96 D4 39 10S 61 30W
Blanca Peak, U.S.A. 83 H11 37 35N 105 29W
Blanche, C., Australia 63 E1 33 1S 134 9 E
Blanche, L., S. Austral., Australia 63 D2 29 15S 139 40 E
Blanche, L., W. Austral., Australia 60 D3 22 25S 123 17 E
Blanco, S. Africa 56 E3 33 55S 22 23 E
Blanco, U.S.A. 81 K5 30 6N 98 25W
Blanco →, Argentina 94 C2 30 20S 68 42W
Blanco, C., Costa Rica 88 E2 9 34N 85 8W
Blanco, C., U.S.A. 82 E1 42 51N 124 34W
Blanda →, Iceland 8 D3 65 37N 20 9W
Blandford Forum, U.K. 11 G5 50 51N 2 9W
Blanding, U.S.A. 83 H9 37 37N 109 29W
Blanes, Spain 19 B7 41 40N 2 48 E
Blankenberge, Belgium 15 C3 51 20N 3 9 E
Blanquilla, I., Venezuela 89 D7 11 51N 64 37W
Blanquillo, Uruguay 95 C4 32 53S 55 37W
Blantyre, Malawi 55 F4 15 45S 35 0 E
Blarney, Ireland 13 E3 51 56N 8 33W
Blasdell, U.S.A. 78 D6 42 48N 78 50W
Blåvands Huk, Denmark 9 J13 55 33N 8 4 E
Blaydon, U.K. 10 C6 54 58N 1 42W
Blayney, Australia 63 E4 33 32S 149 14 E
Blaze, Pt., Australia 60 B5 12 56S 130 11 E
Blekinge, Sweden 9 H16 56 25N 15 20 E
Blenheim, Canada 78 D3 42 20N 82 0W
Blenheim, N.Z. 59 J4 41 38S 173 57 E
Bletchley, U.K. 11 F7 51 59N 0 44W
Blida, Algeria 50 A6 36 30N 2 49 E
Bligh Sound, N.Z. 59 L1 44 47S 167 32 E
Blind River, Canada 70 C3 46 10N 82 58W
Bliss, Idaho, U.S.A. 82 E6 42 56N 114 57W
Bliss, N.Y., U.S.A. 78 D6 42 34N 78 15W
Blissfield, U.S.A. 78 F3 40 24N 81 58W
Blitar, Indonesia 37 H15 8 5S 112 11 E
Block I., U.S.A. 79 E13 41 11N 71 35W
Block Island Sd., U.S.A. 79 E13 41 15N 71 40W
Bloemfontein, S. Africa 56 D4 29 6S 26 7 E
Bloemhof, S. Africa 56 D4 27 38S 25 32 E
Blois, France 18 C4 47 35N 1 20 E
Blönduós, Iceland 8 D3 65 40N 20 12W
Bloodvein →, Canada 73 C9 51 47N 96 43W
Bloody Foreland, Ireland 13 A3 55 10N 8 17W
Bloomer, U.S.A. 80 C9 45 6N 91 29W
Bloomfield, Canada 78 C7 43 59N 77 14W
Bloomfield, Iowa, U.S.A. 80 E8 40 45N 92 25W
Bloomfield, N. Mex., U.S.A. 83 H10 36 43N 107 59W
Bloomfield, Nebr., U.S.A. 80 D6 42 36N 97 39W
Bloomington, Ill., U.S.A. 80 E10 40 28N 89 0W
Bloomington, Ind., U.S.A. 76 F2 39 10N 86 32W
Bloomington, Minn., U.S.A. 80 C8 44 50N 93 17W
Bloomsburg, U.S.A. 79 F8 41 0N 76 27W
Blora, Indonesia 37 G14 6 57S 111 25 E
Blossburg, U.S.A. 78 E7 41 41N 77 4W
Blouberg, S. Africa 57 C4 23 8S 28 59 E
Blountstown, U.S.A. 77 K3 30 27N 85 3W
Blue Earth, U.S.A. 80 D8 43 38N 94 6W
Blue Mesa Reservoir, U.S.A. 83 G10 38 28N 107 20W
Blue Mountain Lake, U.S.A. 79 C10 43 52N 74 30W
Blue Mts., Maine, U.S.A. 79 B14 44 50N 70 35W
Blue Mts., Oreg., U.S.A. 82 D4 45 15N 119 0W
Blue Mts., Pa., U.S.A. 79 F8 40 30N 76 30W
Blue Mud B., Australia 62 A2 13 30S 136 0 E
Blue Nile = Nîl el Azraq →, Sudan 51 E12 15 38N 32 31 E
Blue Rapids, U.S.A. 80 F6 39 41N 96 39W
Blue Ridge Mts., U.S.A. 77 G5 36 30N 80 15W
Blue River, Canada 72 C5 52 6N 119 18W
Bluefield, U.S.A. 76 G5 37 15N 81 17W
Bluefields, Nic. 88 D3 12 20N 83 50W
Bluff, Australia 62 C4 23 35S 149 4 E
Bluff, N.Z. 59 M2 46 37S 168 20 E
Bluff, U.S.A. 83 H9 37 17N 109 33W
Bluff Knoll, Australia 61 F2 34 24S 118 15 E
Bluff Pt., Australia 61 E1 27 50S 114 5 E
Bluffton, U.S.A. 76 E3 40 44N 85 11W
Blumenau, Brazil 95 B6 27 0S 49 0W
Blunt, U.S.A. 80 C5 44 31N 99 59W
Bly, U.S.A. 82 E3 42 24N 121 3W
Blyth, Canada 78 C3 43 44N 81 26W
Blyth, U.K. 10 B6 55 8N 1 31W
Blythe, U.S.A. 85 M12 33 37N 114 36W
Blytheville, U.S.A. 81 H10 35 56N 89 55W
Bo, S. Leone 50 G3 7 55N 11 50W
Bo Duc, Vietnam 39 G6 11 58N 106 50 E
Bo Hai, China 35 E10 39 0N 119 0 E
Bo Xian = Bozhou, China 34 H8 33 55N 115 41 E
Boa Vista, Brazil 92 C6 2 48N 60 30W
Boaco, Nic. 88 D2 12 29N 85 35W
Bo'ai, China 34 G7 35 10N 113 3 E
Boalsburg, U.S.A. 78 F7 40 46N 77 47W
Boane, Mozam. 57 D5 26 6S 32 19 E
Boardman, U.S.A. 78 E4 41 2N 80 40W
Bobadah, Australia 63 E4 32 19S 146 41 E
Bobbili, India 41 K13 18 35N 83 30 E
Bobcaygeon, Canada 78 B6 44 33N 78 33W
Bobo-Dioulasso, Burkina Faso 50 F5 11 8N 4 13W
Bóbr →, Poland 16 B8 52 4N 15 4 E
Bobraomby, Tanjon' i, Madag. 57 A8 12 40S 49 10 E
Bobruysk = Babruysk, Belarus 17 B15 53 10N 29 15 E
Boby, Pic, Madag. 53 J9 22 12S 46 55 E
Bôca do Acre, Brazil 92 E5 8 50S 67 27W
Boca Raton, U.S.A. 77 M5 26 21N 80 5W
Bocas del Toro, Panama 88 E3 9 15N 82 20W
Bochnia, Poland 17 D11 49 58N 20 27 E
Bochum, Germany 16 C4 51 28N 7 13 E
Bocoyna, Mexico 86 B3 27 52N 107 35W
Bodaybo, Russia 27 D12 57 50N 114 0 E
Boddam, U.K. 12 B7 59 56N 1 17W
Boddington, Australia 61 F2 32 50S 116 30 E
Bodega Bay, U.S.A. 84 G3 38 20N 123 3W
Boden, Sweden 8 D19 65 50N 21 42 E
Bodensee, Europe 18 C8 47 35N 9 25 E
Bodhan, India 40 K10 18 40N 77 44 E
Bodmin, U.K. 11 G3 50 28N 4 43W
Bodmin Moor, U.K. 11 G3 50 33N 4 36W
Bodø, Norway 8 C16 67 17N 14 24 E
Bodrog →, Hungary 17 D11 48 11N 21 22 E
Bodrum, Turkey 21 F12 37 3N 27 30 E
Boende, Dem. Rep. of the Congo 52 E4 0 24S 21 12 E
Boerne, U.S.A. 81 L5 29 47N 98 44W
Boesmans →, S. Africa 56 E4 33 42S 26 39 E
Bogalusa, U.S.A. 81 K10 30 47N 89 52W
Bogan →, Australia 63 D4 29 59S 146 17 E
Bogan Gate, Australia 63 E4 33 7S 147 49 E
Bogantungan, Australia 62 C4 23 41S 147 17 E
Bogata, U.S.A. 81 J7 33 28N 95 13W
Boggabilla, Australia 63 D5 28 36S 150 24 E

Boggabri, *Australia* **63 E5** 30 45S 150 5 E
Boggeragh Mts., *Ireland* **13 D3** 52 2N 8 55W
Boglan = Solhan, *Turkey* **44 B4** 38 57N 41 3 E
Bognor Regis, *U.K.* **11 G7** 50 47N 0 40W
Bogo, *Phil.* **37 B6** 11 3N 124 0 E
Bogong, Mt., *Australia* **63 F4** 36 47S 147 17 E
Bogor, *Indonesia* **36 F3** 6 36S 106 48 E
Bogotá, *Colombia* **92 C4** 4 34N 74 0W
Bogotol, *Russia* **26 D9** 56 15N 89 50 E
Bogra, *Bangla.* **41 G16** 24 51N 89 22 E
Boguchany, *Russia* **27 D10** 58 40N 97 30 E
Bohemian Forest = Böhmerwald, *Germany* **16 D7** 49 8N 13 14 E
Böhmerwald, *Germany* **16 D7** 49 8N 13 14 E
Bohol □, *Phil.* **37 C6** 9 50N 124 10 E
Bohol Sea, *Phil.* **37 C6** 9 0N 124 0 E
Bohuslän, *Sweden* **9 G14** 58 25N 12 0 E
Boi, Pta. de, *Brazil* **95 A6** 23 55S 45 15W
Boiaçu, *Brazil* **92 D6** 0 27S 61 46W
Boileau, C., *Australia* **60 C3** 17 40S 122 7 E
Boise, *U.S.A.* **82 E5** 43 37N 116 13W
Boise City, *U.S.A.* **81 G3** 36 44N 102 31W
Boissevain, *Canada* **73 D8** 49 15N 100 5W
Bojador, C., *W. Sahara* **50 C3** 26 0N 14 30W
Bojana →, *Albania* **21 D8** 41 52N 19 22 E
Bojnūrd, *Iran* **45 B8** 37 30N 57 20 E
Bojonegoro, *Indonesia* **37 G14** 7 11S 111 54 E
Bokaro, *India* **43 H11** 23 46N 85 55 E
Bokhara →, *Australia* **63 D4** 29 55S 146 42 E
Boknafjorden, *Norway* **9 G11** 59 14N 5 40 E
Bokoro, *Chad* **51 F9** 12 25N 17 14 E
Bokpyin, *Burma* **39 G2** 11 18N 98 42 E
Bolan →, *Pakistan* **42 E2** 28 38N 67 42 E
Bolan Pass, *Pakistan* **40 E5** 29 50N 67 20 E
Bolaños →, *Mexico* **86 C4** 21 14N 104 8W
Bolbec, *France* **18 B4** 49 30N 0 30 E
Boldājī, *Iran* **45 D6** 31 56N 51 3 E
Bole, *China* **32 B3** 45 11N 81 37 E
Bolekhiv, *Ukraine* **17 D12** 49 0N 23 57 E
Bolesławiec, *Poland* **16 C8** 51 17N 15 37 E
Bolgrad = Bolhrad, *Ukraine* **17 F15** 45 40N 28 32 E
Bolhrad, *Ukraine* **17 F15** 45 40N 28 32 E
Bolívar, *Argentina* **94 D3** 36 15S 60 53W
Bolivar, *Mo., U.S.A.* **81 G8** 37 37N 93 25W
Bolivar, *N.Y., U.S.A.* **78 D6** 42 4N 78 10W
Bolivar, *Tenn., U.S.A.* **81 H10** 35 12N 89 0W
Bolivia ■, *S. Amer.* **92 G6** 17 6S 64 0W
Bolivian Plateau, *S. Amer.* **90 E4** 20 0S 67 30W
Bollnäs, *Sweden* **9 F17** 61 21N 16 24 E
Bollon, *Australia* **63 D4** 28 2S 147 29 E
Bolmen, *Sweden* **9 H15** 56 55N 13 40 E
Bolobo, *Dem. Rep. of the Congo* **52 E3** 2 6S 16 20 E
Bologna, *Italy* **20 B4** 44 29N 11 20 E
Bologoye, *Russia* **24 C5** 57 55N 34 5 E
Bolonchenticul, *Mexico* **87 D7** 20 0N 89 49W
Boloven, Cao Nguyen, *Laos* **38 E6** 15 10N 106 30 E
Bolpur, *India* **43 H12** 23 40N 87 45 E
Bolsena, L. di, *Italy* **20 C4** 42 36N 11 56 E
Bolshevik, Ostrov, *Russia* **27 B11** 78 30N 102 0 E
Bolshoi Kavkas = Caucasus Mountains, *Eurasia* **25 F7** 42 50N 44 0 E
Bolshoy Anyuy →, *Russia* **27 C17** 68 30N 160 49 E
Bolshoy Begichev, Ostrov, *Russia* **27 B12** 74 20N 112 30 E
Bolshoy Lyakhovskiy, Ostrov, *Russia* **27 B15** 73 35N 142 0 E
Bolshoy Tyuters, Ostrov, *Russia* **9 G22** 59 51N 27 13 E
Bolsward, *Neths.* **15 A5** 53 3N 5 32 E
Bolt Head, *U.K.* **11 G4** 50 12N 3 48W
Bolton, *Canada* **78 C5** 43 54N 79 45W
Bolton, *U.K.* **10 D5** 53 35N 2 26W
Bolton Landing, *U.S.A.* **79 C11** 43 32N 73 35W
Bolu, *Turkey* **25 F5** 40 45N 31 35 E
Bolungavík, *Iceland* **8 C2** 66 9N 23 15W
Bolvadin, *Turkey* **25 G5** 38 45N 31 4 E
Bolzano, *Italy* **20 A4** 46 31N 11 22 E
Bom Jesus da Lapa, *Brazil* **93 F10** 13 15S 43 25W
Boma, *Dem. Rep. of the Congo* **52 F2** 5 50S 13 4 E
Bombala, *Australia* **63 F4** 36 56S 149 15 E
Bombay = Mumbai, *India* **40 K8** 18 55N 72 50 E
Bomboma, *Dem. Rep. of the Congo* **52 D3** 2 25N 18 55 E
Bombombwa, *Dem. Rep. of the Congo* **54 B2** 1 40N 25 40 E
Bomili, *Dem. Rep. of the Congo* **54 B2** 1 45N 27 5 E
Bømlo, *Norway* **9 G11** 59 37N 5 13 E
Bomokandi →, *Dem. Rep. of the Congo* **54 B2** 3 39N 26 8 E
Bomu →, *C.A.R.* **52 D4** 4 40N 22 30 E
Bon, C., *Tunisia* **48 C5** 37 1N 11 2 E
Bon Sar Pa, *Vietnam* **38 F6** 12 24N 107 35 E
Bonaigarh, *India* **43 J11** 21 50N 84 57 E
Bonaire, *Neth. Ant.* **89 D6** 12 10N 68 15W
Bonang, *Australia* **63 F4** 37 11S 148 41 E
Bonanza, *Nic.* **88 D3** 13 54N 84 35W
Bonaparte Arch., *Australia* **60 B3** 14 0S 124 30 E
Bonaventure, *Canada* **71 C6** 48 5N 65 32W
Bonavista, *Canada* **71 C9** 48 40N 53 5W
Bonavista, C., *Canada* **71 C9** 48 42N 53 5W
Bonavista B., *Canada* **71 C9** 48 45N 53 25W
Bondo, *Dem. Rep. of the Congo* **54 B1** 3 55N 23 53 E
Bondoukou, *Ivory C.* **50 G5** 8 2N 2 47W
Bondowoso, *Indonesia* **37 G15** 7 55S 113 49 E
Bone, Teluk, *Indonesia* **37 E6** 4 10S 120 50 E
Bonerate, *Indonesia* **37 F6** 7 25S 121 5 E
Bonerate, Kepulauan, *Indonesia* **37 F6** 6 30S 121 10 E
Bo'ness, *U.K.* **12 E5** 56 1N 3 37W
Bonete, Cerro, *Argentina* **94 B2** 27 55S 68 40W
Bong Son = Hoai Nhon, *Vietnam* **38 E7** 14 28N 109 1 E
Bongor, *Chad* **51 F9** 10 35N 15 20 E
Bonham, *U.S.A.* **81 J6** 33 35N 96 11W
Bonifacio, *France* **18 F8** 41 24N 9 10 E
Bonifacio, Bouches de, *Medit. S.* **20 D3** 41 12N 9 15 E
Bonin Is. = Ogasawara Gunto, *Pac. Oc.* **28 G18** 27 0N 142 0 E
Bonn, *Germany* **16 C4** 50 46N 7 6 E
Bonne Terre, *U.S.A.* **81 G9** 37 55N 90 33W
Bonners Ferry, *U.S.A.* **82 B5** 48 42N 116 19W
Bonney, L., *Australia* **63 F3** 37 50S 140 20 E
Bonnie Rock, *Australia* **61 F2** 30 29S 118 22 E
Bonny, Bight of, *Africa* **52 D1** 3 30N 9 20 E
Bonnyrigg, *U.K.* **12 F5** 55 53N 3 6W
Bonnyville, *Canada* **73 C6** 54 20N 110 45W
Bonoi, *Indonesia* **37 E9** 1 45S 137 41 E
Bonsall, *U.S.A.* **85 M9** 33 16N 117 14W
Bontang, *Indonesia* **36 D5** 0 10N 117 30 E
Bonthe, *S. Leone* **50 G3** 7 30N 12 33W
Bontoc, *Phil.* **37 A6** 17 7N 120 58 E
Bonython Ra., *Australia* **60 D4** 23 40S 128 45 E
Bookabie, *Australia* **61 F5** 31 50S 132 41 E
Booker, *U.S.A.* **81 G4** 36 27N 100 32W
Boolaboolka L., *Australia* **63 E3** 32 38S 143 10 E
Booligal, *Australia* **63 E3** 33 58S 144 53 E
Boonah, *Australia* **63 D5** 27 58S 152 41 E
Boone, *Iowa, U.S.A.* **80 D8** 42 4N 93 53W
Boone, *N.C., U.S.A.* **77 G5** 36 13N 81 41W
Booneville, *Ark., U.S.A.* **81 H8** 35 8N 93 55W
Booneville, *Miss., U.S.A.* **77 H1** 34 39N 88 34W
Boonville, *Calif., U.S.A.* **84 F3** 39 1N 123 22W
Boonville, *Ind., U.S.A.* **76 F2** 38 3N 87 16W
Boonville, *Mo., U.S.A.* **80 F8** 38 58N 92 44W
Boonville, *N.Y., U.S.A.* **79 C9** 43 29N 75 20W
Boorindal, *Australia* **63 E4** 30 22S 146 11 E
Boorowa, *Australia* **63 E4** 34 28S 148 44 E
Boosaaso = Bosaso, *Somali Rep.* **46 E4** 11 12N 49 18 E
Boothia, Gulf of, *Canada* **69 A11** 71 0N 90 0W
Boothia Pen., *Canada* **68 A10** 71 0N 94 0W
Bootle, *U.K.* **10 D4** 53 28N 3 1W
Booué, *Gabon* **52 E2** 0 5S 11 55 E
Boquete, *Panama* **88 E3** 8 46N 82 27W
Boquilla, Presa de la, *Mexico* **86 B3** 27 40N 105 30W
Boquillas del Carmen, *Mexico* **86 B4** 29 17N 102 53W
Bor, *Serbia, Yug.* **21 B10** 44 5N 22 7 E
Bôr, *Sudan* **51 G12** 6 10N 31 40 E
Bor Mashash, *Israel* **47 D3** 31 7N 34 50 E
Borah Peak, *U.S.A.* **82 D7** 44 8N 113 47W
Borås, *Sweden* **9 H15** 57 43N 12 56 E
Borāzjān, *Iran* **45 D6** 29 22N 51 10 E
Borba, *Brazil* **92 D7** 4 12S 59 34W
Borborema, Planalto da, *Brazil* **90 D7** 7 0S 37 0W
Bord Khūn-e Now, *Iran* **45 D6** 28 3N 51 28 E
Borda, C., *Australia* **63 F2** 35 45S 136 34 E
Bordeaux, *France* **18 D3** 44 50N 0 36W
Borden, *Australia* **61 F2** 34 3S 118 12 E
Borden, *Canada* **71 C7** 46 18N 63 47W
Borden I., *Canada* **4 B2** 78 30N 111 30W
Borden Pen., *Canada* **69 A11** 73 0N 83 0W
Borders = Scottish Borders □, *U.K.* **12 F6** 55 35N 2 50W
Bordertown, *Australia* **63 F3** 36 19S 140 45 E
Borðeyri, *Iceland* **8 D3** 65 12N 21 6W
Bordj Fly Ste. Marie, *Algeria* **50 C5** 27 19N 2 32W
Bordj-in-Eker, *Algeria* **50 D7** 24 9N 5 3 E
Bordj Omar Driss, *Algeria* **50 C7** 28 10N 6 40 E
Borehamwood, *U.K.* **11 F7** 51 40N 0 15W
Borgå = Porvoo, *Finland* **9 F21** 60 24N 25 40 E
Borgarfjörður, *Iceland* **8 D7** 65 31N 13 49W
Borgarnes, *Iceland* **8 D3** 64 32N 21 55W
Børgefjellet, *Norway* **8 D15** 65 20N 13 45 E
Borger, *Neths.* **15 B6** 52 54N 6 44 E
Borger, *U.S.A.* **81 H4** 35 39N 101 24W
Borgholm, *Sweden* **9 H17** 56 52N 16 39 E
Borhoyn Tal, *Mongolia* **34 C6** 43 50N 111 58 E
Borikhane, *Laos* **38 C4** 18 33N 103 43 E
Borisoglebsk, *Russia* **25 D7** 51 27N 42 5 E
Borisov = Barysaw, *Belarus* **17 A15** 54 17N 28 28 E
Borja, *Peru* **92 D3** 4 20S 77 40W
Borkou, *Chad* **51 E9** 18 15N 18 50 E
Borkum, *Germany* **16 B4** 53 34N 6 40 E
Borlänge, *Sweden* **9 F16** 60 29N 15 26 E
Borley, C., *Antarctica* **5 C5** 66 15S 52 30 E
Borneo, *E. Indies* **36 D5** 1 0N 115 0 E
Bornholm, *Denmark* **9 J16** 55 10N 15 0 E
Borogontsy, *Russia* **27 C14** 62 42N 131 8 E
Boron, *U.S.A.* **85 L9** 35 0N 117 39W
Borongan, *Phil.* **37 B7** 11 37N 125 26 E
Borovichi, *Russia* **24 C5** 58 25N 33 55 E
Borrego Springs, *U.S.A.* **85 M10** 33 15N 116 23W
Borroloola, *Australia* **62 B2** 16 4S 136 17 E
Borşa, *Romania* **17 E13** 47 41N 24 50 E
Borsad, *India* **42 H5** 22 25N 72 54 E
Borth, *U.K.* **11 E3** 52 29N 4 2W
Borūjerd, *Iran* **45 C6** 33 55N 48 50 E
Boryslav, *Ukraine* **17 D12** 49 18N 23 28 E
Borzya, *Russia* **27 D12** 50 24N 116 31 E
Bosa, *Italy* **20 D3** 40 18N 8 30 E
Bosanska Gradiška, *Bos.-H.* **20 B7** 45 10N 17 15 E
Bosaso, *Somali Rep.* **46 E4** 11 12N 49 18 E
Boscastle, *U.K.* **11 G3** 50 41N 4 42W
Boshan, *China* **35 F9** 36 28N 117 49 E
Boshof, *S. Africa* **56 D4** 28 31S 25 13 E
Boshrūyeh, *Iran* **45 C8** 33 50N 57 30 E
Bosna →, *Bos.-H.* **21 B8** 45 4N 18 29 E
Bosna i Hercegovina = Bosnia-Herzegovina ■, *Europe* **20 B7** 44 0N 18 0 E
Bosnia-Herzegovina ■, *Europe* **20 B7** 44 0N 18 0 E
Bosnik, *Indonesia* **37 E9** 1 5S 136 10 E
Bosobolo, *Dem. Rep. of the Congo* **52 D3** 4 15N 19 50 E
Bosporus = İstanbul Boğazı, *Turkey* **21 D13** 41 10N 29 10 E
Bosque Farms, *U.S.A.* **83 J10** 34 53N 106 40W
Bossangoa, *C.A.R.* **52 C3** 6 35N 17 30 E
Bossier City, *U.S.A.* **81 J8** 32 31N 93 44W
Bosso, *Niger* **51 F8** 13 43N 13 19 E
Bostan, *Pakistan* **42 D2** 30 26N 67 2 E
Bostānābād, *Iran* **44 B5** 37 50N 46 50 E
Bosten Hu, *China* **32 B3** 41 55N 87 40 E
Boston, *U.K.* **10 E7** 52 59N 0 2W
Boston, *U.S.A.* **79 D13** 42 22N 71 4W
Boston Bar, *Canada* **72 D4** 49 52N 121 30W
Boston Mts., *U.S.A.* **81 H8** 35 42N 93 15W
Boswell, *Canada* **72 D5** 49 28N 116 45W
Boswell, *U.S.A.* **78 F5** 40 10N 79 2W
Botad, *India* **42 H4** 22 15N 71 40 E
Botene, *Laos* **38 D3** 17 35N 101 12 E
Bothaville, *S. Africa* **56 D4** 27 23S 26 34 E
Bothnia, G. of, *Europe* **8 E19** 63 0N 20 15 E
Bothwell, *Australia* **62 G4** 42 20S 147 1 E
Bothwell, *Canada* **78 D3** 42 38N 81 52W
Botletle →, *Botswana* **56 C3** 20 10S 23 15 E
Botoşani, *Romania* **17 E14** 47 42N 26 41 E
Botou, *Burkina Faso* **50 F6** 12 42N 1 59 E
Botswana ■, *Africa* **56 C3** 22 0S 24 0 E
Bottineau, *U.S.A.* **80 A4** 48 50N 100 27W
Bottrop, *Germany* **15 C6** 51 31N 6 58 E
Botucatu, *Brazil* **95 A6** 22 55S 48 30W
Botwood, *Canada* **71 C8** 49 6N 55 23W
Bouaflé, *Ivory C.* **50 G4** 7 1N 5 47W
Bouaké, *Ivory C.* **50 G4** 7 40N 5 2W
Bouar, *C.A.R.* **52 C3** 6 0N 15 40 E
Bouârfa, *Morocco* **50 B5** 32 32N 1 58W
Boucaut B., *Australia* **62 A1** 12 0S 134 25 E
Bougainville, C., *Australia* **60 B4** 13 57S 126 4 E
Bougainville I., *Papua N. G.* **64 H7** 6 0S 155 0 E
Bougainville Reef, *Australia* **62 B4** 15 30S 147 5 E
Bougie = Bejaïa, *Algeria* **50 A7** 36 42N 5 2 E
Bougouni, *Mali* **50 F4** 11 30N 7 20W
Bouillon, *Belgium* **15 E5** 49 44N 5 3 E
Boulder, *Colo., U.S.A.* **80 E2** 40 1N 105 17W
Boulder, *Mont., U.S.A.* **82 C7** 46 14N 112 7W
Boulder City, *U.S.A.* **85 K12** 35 59N 114 50W
Boulder Creek, *U.S.A.* **84 H4** 37 7N 122 7W
Boulder Dam = Hoover Dam, *U.S.A.* **85 K12** 36 1N 114 44W
Boulia, *Australia* **62 C2** 22 52S 139 51 E
Boulogne-sur-Mer, *France* **18 A4** 50 42N 1 36 E
Boultoum, *Niger* **51 F8** 14 45N 10 25 E
Boun Neua, *Laos* **38 B3** 21 38N 101 54 E
Boun Tai, *Laos* **38 B3** 21 23N 101 58 E
Bouna, *Ivory C.* **50 G5** 9 10N 3 0W
Boundary Peak, *U.S.A.* **84 H8** 37 51N 118 21W
Boundiali, *Ivory C.* **50 G4** 9 30N 6 20W
Bountiful, *U.S.A.* **82 F8** 40 53N 111 53W
Bounty Is., *Pac. Oc.* **64 M9** 48 0S 178 30 E
Bourbonnais, *France* **18 C5** 46 28N 3 0 E
Bourdel L., *Canada* **70 A5** 56 43N 74 10W
Bourem, *Mali* **50 E5** 17 0N 0 24W
Bourg-en-Bresse, *France* **18 C6** 46 13N 5 12 E
Bourg-St-Maurice, *France* **18 D7** 45 35N 6 46 E
Bourges, *France* **18 C5** 47 9N 2 25 E
Bourget, *Canada* **79 A9** 45 26N 75 9W
Bourgogne, *France* **18 C6** 47 0N 4 50 E
Bourke, *Australia* **63 E4** 30 8S 145 55 E
Bourne, *U.K.* **10 E7** 52 47N 0 22W
Bournemouth, *U.K.* **11 G6** 50 43N 1 52W
Bournemouth □, *U.K.* **11 G6** 50 43N 1 52W
Bouse, *U.S.A.* **85 M13** 33 56N 114 0W
Bouvet I. = Bouvetøya, *Antarctica* **3 G10** 54 26S 3 24 E
Bouvetøya, *Antarctica* **3 G10** 54 26S 3 24 E
Bovill, *U.S.A.* **82 C5** 46 51N 116 24W
Bovril, *Argentina* **94 C4** 31 21S 59 26W
Bow →, *Canada* **72 C6** 49 57N 111 41W
Bow Island, *Canada* **72 D6** 49 50N 111 23W
Bowbells, *U.S.A.* **80 A3** 48 48N 102 15W
Bowdle, *U.S.A.* **80 C5** 45 27N 99 39W
Bowelling, *Australia* **61 F2** 33 25S 116 30 E
Bowen, *Argentina* **94 D2** 35 0S 67 31W
Bowen, *Australia* **62 C4** 20 0S 148 16 E
Bowen Mts., *Australia* **63 F4** 37 0S 147 50 E
Bowie, *Ariz., U.S.A.* **83 K9** 32 19N 109 29W
Bowie, *Tex., U.S.A.* **81 J6** 33 34N 97 51W
Bowkān, *Iran* **44 B5** 36 31N 46 12 E
Bowland, Forest of, *U.K.* **10 D5** 54 0N 2 30W
Bowling Green, *Ky., U.S.A.* **76 G2** 36 59N 86 27W
Bowling Green, *Ohio, U.S.A.* **76 E4** 41 23N 83 39W
Bowling Green, C., *Australia* **62 B4** 19 19S 147 25 E
Bowman, *U.S.A.* **80 B3** 46 11N 103 24W
Bowman I., *Antarctica* **5 C8** 65 0S 104 0 E
Bowmanville, *Canada* **78 C6** 43 55N 78 41W
Bowmore, *U.K.* **12 F2** 55 45N 6 17W
Bowral, *Australia* **63 E5** 34 26S 150 27 E
Bowraville, *Australia* **63 E5** 30 37S 152 52 E
Bowron →, *Canada* **72 C4** 54 3N 121 50W
Bowron Lake Prov. Park, *Canada* **72 C4** 53 10N 121 5W
Bowser L., *Canada* **72 B3** 56 30N 129 30W
Bowsman, *Canada* **73 C8** 52 14N 101 12W
Bowwood, *Zambia* **55 F2** 17 5S 26 20 E
Box Cr. →, *Australia* **63 E3** 34 10S 143 50 E
Boxmeer, *Neths.* **15 C5** 51 38N 5 56 E
Boxtel, *Neths.* **15 C5** 51 36N 5 20 E
Boyce, *U.S.A.* **81 K8** 31 23N 92 40W
Boyd L., *Canada* **70 B4** 52 46N 76 42W
Boyle, *Canada* **72 C6** 54 35N 112 49W
Boyle, *Ireland* **13 C3** 53 59N 8 18W
Boyne →, *Ireland* **13 C5** 53 43N 6 15W
Boyne City, *U.S.A.* **76 C3** 45 13N 85 1W
Boynton Beach, *U.S.A.* **77 M5** 26 32N 80 4W
Boyolali, *Indonesia* **37 G14** 7 32S 110 35 E
Boyoma, Chutes, *Dem. Rep. of the Congo* **54 B2** 0 35N 25 23 E
Boysen Reservoir, *U.S.A.* **82 E9** 43 25N 108 11W
Boyuibe, *Bolivia* **92 G6** 20 25S 63 17W
Boyup Brook, *Australia* **61 F2** 33 50S 116 23 E
Boz Dağları, *Turkey* **21 E13** 38 20N 28 0 E
Bozburun, *Turkey* **21 F13** 36 43N 28 4 E
Bozcaada, *Turkey* **21 E12** 39 49N 26 3 E
Bozdoğan, *Turkey* **21 F13** 37 40N 28 17 E
Bozeman, *U.S.A.* **82 D8** 45 41N 111 2W
Bozen = Bolzano, *Italy* **20 A4** 46 31N 11 22 E
Bozhou, *China* **34 H8** 33 55N 115 41 E
Bozoum, *C.A.R.* **52 C3** 6 25N 16 35 E
Bra, *Italy* **18 D7** 44 42N 7 51 E
Brabant □, *Belgium* **15 D4** 50 46N 4 30 E
Brabant L., *Canada* **73 B8** 55 58N 103 43W
Brač, *Croatia* **20 C7** 43 20N 16 40 E
Bracadale, L., *U.K.* **12 D2** 57 20N 6 30W
Bracciano, L. di, *Italy* **20 C5** 42 7N 12 14 E
Bracebridge, *Canada* **78 A5** 45 2N 79 19W
Brach, *Libya* **51 C8** 27 31N 14 20 E
Bräcke, *Sweden* **9 E16** 62 45N 15 26 E
Brackettville, *U.S.A.* **81 L4** 29 19N 100 25W
Bracknell, *U.K.* **11 F7** 51 25N 0 43W
Bracknell Forest □, *U.K.* **11 F7** 51 25N 0 44W
Brad, *Romania* **17 E12** 46 10N 22 50 E
Bradenton, *U.S.A.* **77 M4** 27 30N 82 34W
Bradford, *Canada* **78 B5** 44 7N 79 34W
Bradford, *U.K.* **10 D6** 53 47N 1 45W
Bradford, *Pa., U.S.A.* **78 E6** 41 58N 78 38W
Bradford, *Vt., U.S.A.* **79 C12** 43 59N 72 9W
Bradley, *Ark., U.S.A.* **81 J8** 33 6N 93 39W
Bradley, *Calif., U.S.A.* **84 K6** 35 52N 120 48W
Bradley Institute, *Zimbabwe* **55 F3** 17 7S 31 25 E
Brady, *U.S.A.* **81 K5** 31 9N 99 20W
Braeside, *Canada* **79 A8** 45 28N 76 24W
Braga, *Portugal* **19 B1** 41 35N 8 25W
Bragado, *Argentina* **94 D3** 35 2S 60 27W
Bragança, *Brazil* **93 D9** 1 0S 47 2W
Bragança, *Portugal* **19 B2** 41 48N 6 50W
Bragança Paulista, *Brazil* **95 A6** 22 55S 46 32W
Brahmanbaria, *Bangla.* **41 H17** 23 58N 91 15 E
Brahmani →, *India* **41 J15** 20 39N 86 46 E
Brahmapur, *India* **41 K14** 19 15N 84 54 E
Brahmaputra →, *India* **41 F19** 27 48N 95 30 E
Braich-y-pwll, *U.K.* **10 E3** 52 47N 4 46W
Braidwood, *Australia* **63 F4** 35 27S 149 49 E
Brăila, *Romania* **17 F14** 45 19N 27 59 E
Brainerd, *U.S.A.* **80 B7** 46 22N 94 12W
Braintree, *U.K.* **11 F8** 51 53N 0 34 E
Braintree, *U.S.A.* **79 D14** 42 13N 71 0W
Brak →, *S. Africa* **56 D3** 29 35S 22 55 E
Brakwater, *Namibia* **56 C2** 22 28S 17 3 E
Brampton, *Canada* **78 C5** 43 45N 79 45W
Brampton, *U.K.* **10 C5** 54 57N 2 44W
Branco →, *Brazil* **92 D6** 1 20S 61 50W
Brandberg, *Namibia* **56 B2** 21 10S 14 33 E
Brandenburg = Neubrandenburg, *Germany* **16 B7** 53 33N 13 15 E
Brandenburg, *Germany* **16 B7** 52 25N 12 33 E
Brandenburg □, *Germany* **16 B6** 52 50N 13 0 E
Brandfort, *S. Africa* **56 D4** 28 40S 26 30 E
Brandon, *Canada* **73 D9** 49 50N 99 57W
Brandon, *U.S.A.* **79 C11** 43 48N 73 4W
Brandon B., *Ireland* **13 D1** 52 17N 10 8W
Brandon Mt., *Ireland* **13 D1** 52 15N 10 15W
Brandsen, *Argentina* **94 D4** 35 10S 58 15W
Brandvlei, *S. Africa* **56 E3** 30 25S 20 30 E
Branford, *U.S.A.* **79 E12** 41 17N 72 49W
Braniewo, *Poland* **17 A10** 54 25N 19 50 E
Bransfield Str., *Antarctica* **5 C18** 63 0S 59 0W
Branson, *U.S.A.* **81 G8** 36 39N 93 13W
Brantford, *Canada* **78 C4** 43 10N 80 15W
Bras d'Or L., *Canada* **71 C7** 45 50N 60 50W
Brasher Falls, *U.S.A.* **79 B10** 44 49N 74 47W
Brasil, Planalto, *Brazil* **90 E6** 18 0S 46 30W
Brasiléia, *Brazil* **92 F5** 11 0S 68 45W
Brasília, *Brazil* **93 G9** 15 47S 47 55W
Brasília Legal, *Brazil* **93 D7** 3 49S 55 36W
Braslaw, *Belarus* **9 J22** 55 38N 27 0 E
Braşov, *Romania* **17 F13** 45 38N 25 35 E
Brasschaat, *Belgium* **15 C4** 51 19N 4 27 E
Brassey, Banjaran, *Malaysia* **36 D5** 5 0N 117 15 E
Brassey Ra., *Australia* **61 E3** 25 8S 122 15 E
Brasstown Bald, *U.S.A.* **77 H4** 34 53N 83 49W
Brastad, *Sweden* **9 G14** 58 23N 11 30 E
Bratislava, *Slovak Rep.* **17 D9** 48 10N 17 7 E
Bratsk, *Russia* **27 D11** 56 10N 101 30 E
Brattleboro, *U.S.A.* **79 D12** 42 51N 72 34W
Braunau, *Austria* **16 D7** 48 15N 13 3 E
Braunschweig, *Germany* **16 B6** 52 15N 10 31 E
Braunton, *U.K.* **11 F3** 51 7N 4 10W
Bravo del Norte, Rio = Grande, Rio →, *U.S.A.* **81 N6** 25 58N 97 9W
Brawley, *U.S.A.* **85 N11** 32 59N 115 31W
Bray, *Ireland* **13 C5** 53 13N 6 7W
Bray, Mt., *Australia* **62 A1** 14 0S 134 30 E
Bray, Pays de, *France* **18 B4** 49 46N 1 26 E
Brazeau →, *Canada* **72 C5** 52 55N 115 14W
Brazil, *U.S.A.* **76 F2** 39 32N 87 8W
Brazil ■, *S. Amer.* **93 F9** 12 0S 50 0W
Brazilian Highlands = Brasil, Planalto, *Brazil* **90 E6** 18 0S 46 30W
Brazo Sur →, *S. Amer.* **94 B4** 25 21S 57 42W
Brazos →, *U.S.A.* **81 L7** 28 53N 95 23W
Brazzaville, *Congo* **52 E3** 4 9S 15 12 E
Brčko, *Bos.-H.* **21 B8** 44 54N 18 46 E
Breaden, L., *Australia* **61 E4** 25 51S 125 28 E
Breaksea Sd., *N.Z.* **59 L1** 45 35S 166 35 E
Bream B., *N.Z.* **59 F5** 35 56S 174 28 E
Bream Hd., *N.Z.* **59 F5** 35 51S 174 36 E
Breas, *Chile* **94 B1** 25 29S 70 24W
Brebes, *Indonesia* **37 G13** 6 52S 109 3 E
Brechin, *Canada* **78 B5** 44 32N 79 10W
Brechin, *U.K.* **12 E6** 56 44N 2 39W
Brecht, *Belgium* **15 C4** 51 21N 4 38 E
Breckenridge, *Colo., U.S.A.* **82 G10** 39 29N 106 3W
Breckenridge, *Minn., U.S.A.* **80 B6** 46 16N 96 35W
Breckenridge, *Tex., U.S.A.* **81 J5** 32 45N 98 54W
Breckland, *U.K.* **11 E8** 52 30N 0 40 E
Brecon, *U.K.* **11 F4** 51 57N 3 23W
Brecon Beacons, *U.K.* **11 F4** 51 53N 3 26W
Breda, *Neths.* **15 C4** 51 35N 4 45 E
Bredasdorp, *S. Africa* **56 E3** 34 33S 20 2 E
Bree, *Belgium* **15 C5** 51 8N 5 35 E
Bregenz, *Austria* **16 E5** 47 30N 9 45 E
Breiðafjörður, *Iceland* **8 D2** 65 15N 23 15W
Brejo, *Brazil* **93 D10** 3 41S 42 47W
Bremen, *Germany* **16 B5** 53 4N 8 47 E
Bremer Bay, *Australia* **61 F2** 34 21S 119 20 E
Bremer I., *Australia* **62 A2** 12 5S 136 45 E
Bremerhaven, *Germany* **16 B5** 53 33N 8 36 E
Bremerton, *U.S.A.* **84 C4** 47 34N 122 38W
Brenham, *U.S.A.* **81 K6** 30 10N 96 24W
Brennerpass, *Austria* **16 E6** 47 2N 11 30 E
Brent, *U.S.A.* **77 J2** 32 56N 87 10W
Brentwood, *U.K.* **11 F8** 51 37N 0 19 E
Brentwood, *Calif., U.S.A.* **84 H5** 37 56N 121 42W
Brentwood, *N.Y., U.S.A.* **79 F11** 40 47N 73 15W
Bréscia, *Italy* **18 D9** 45 33N 10 15 E
Breskens, *Neths.* **15 C3** 51 23N 3 33 E
Breslau = Wrocław, *Poland* **17 C9** 51 5N 17 5 E
Bressanone, *Italy* **20 A4** 46 43N 11 39 E
Bressay, *U.K.* **12 A7** 60 9N 1 6W
Brest, *Belarus* **17 B12** 52 10N 23 40 E
Brest, *France* **18 B1** 48 24N 4 31W
Brest-Litovsk = Brest, *Belarus* **17 B12** 52 10N 23 40 E
Bretagne, *France* **18 B2** 48 10N 3 0W
Breton, *Canada* **72 C6** 53 7N 114 28W
Breton Sd., *U.S.A.* **81 L10** 29 35N 89 15W
Brett, C., *N.Z.* **59 F5** 35 10S 174 20 E
Brevard, *U.S.A.* **77 H4** 35 14N 82 44W
Breves, *Brazil* **93 D8** 1 40S 50 29W
Brewarrina, *Australia* **63 E4** 30 0S 146 51 E
Brewer, *U.S.A.* **77 C11** 44 48N 68 46W
Brewer, Mt., *U.S.A.* **84 J8** 36 44N 118 28W
Brewster, *N.Y., U.S.A.* **79 E11** 41 23N 73 37W

Brewster, Ohio, U.S.A. 78 F3 40 43N 81 36W
Brewster, Wash., U.S.A. 82 B4 48 6N 119 47W
Brewster, Kap = Kangikajik, Greenland 4 B6 70 7N 22 0W
Brewton, U.S.A. 77 K2 31 7N 87 4W
Breyten, S. Africa 57 D5 26 16S 30 0 E
Brezhnev = Naberezhnyye Chelny, Russia 24 C9 55 42N 52 19 E
Briançon, France 18 D7 44 54N 6 39 E
Bribie I., Australia 63 D5 27 0S 153 10 E
Bribri, Costa Rica 88 E3 9 38N 82 50W
Bridgehampton, U.S.A. 79 F12 40 56N 72 19W
Bridgend, U.K. 11 F4 51 30N 3 34W
Bridgend □, U.K. 11 F4 51 36N 3 36W
Bridgeport, Calif., U.S.A. 84 G7 38 15N 119 14W
Bridgeport, Conn., U.S.A. 79 E11 41 11N 73 12W
Bridgeport, Nebr., U.S.A. 80 E3 41 40N 103 6W
Bridgeport, Tex., U.S.A. 81 J6 33 13N 97 45W
Bridger, U.S.A. 82 D9 45 18N 108 55W
Bridgeton, U.S.A. 76 F8 39 26N 75 14W
Bridgetown, Australia 61 F2 33 58S 116 7 E
Bridgetown, Barbados 89 D8 13 5N 59 30W
Bridgetown, Canada 71 D6 44 55N 65 18W
Bridgewater, Canada 71 D7 44 25N 64 31W
Bridgewater, Mass., U.S.A. 79 E14 41 59N 70 58W
Bridgewater, N.Y., U.S.A. 79 D9 42 53N 75 15W
Bridgewater, C., Australia 63 F3 38 23S 141 23 E
Bridgewater-Gagebrook, Australia 62 G4 42 44S 147 14 E
Bridgnorth, U.K. 11 E5 52 32N 2 25W
Bridgton, U.S.A. 79 B14 44 3N 70 42W
Bridgwater, U.K. 11 F5 51 8N 2 59W
Bridgwater B., U.K. 11 F4 51 15N 3 15W
Bridlington, U.K. 10 C7 54 5N 0 12W
Bridlington B., U.K. 10 C7 54 4N 0 10W
Bridport, Australia 62 G4 40 59S 147 23 E
Bridport, U.K. 11 G5 50 44N 2 45W
Brig, Switz. 18 C7 46 18N 7 59 E
Brigg, U.K. 10 D7 53 34N 0 28W
Brigham City, U.S.A. 82 F7 41 31N 112 1W
Bright, Australia 63 F4 36 42S 146 56 E
Brighton, Australia 63 F2 35 5S 138 30 E
Brighton, Canada 78 B7 44 2N 77 44W
Brighton, U.K. 11 G7 50 49N 0 7W
Brighton, Colo., U.S.A. 80 F2 39 59N 104 49W
Brighton, N.Y., U.S.A. 78 C7 43 8N 77 34W
Brilliant, U.S.A. 78 F4 40 15N 80 39W
Brindisi, Italy 21 D7 40 39N 17 55 E
Brinkley, U.S.A. 81 H9 34 53N 91 12W
Brinnon, U.S.A. 84 C4 47 41N 122 54W
Brion, I., Canada 71 C7 47 46N 61 26W
Brisbane, Australia 63 D5 27 25S 153 2 E
Brisbane →, Australia 63 D5 27 24S 153 9 E
Bristol, U.K. 11 F5 51 26N 2 35W
Bristol, Conn., U.S.A. 79 E12 41 40N 72 57W
Bristol, Pa., U.S.A. 79 F10 40 6N 74 51W
Bristol, R.I., U.S.A. 79 E13 41 40N 71 16W
Bristol, Tenn., U.S.A. 77 G4 36 36N 82 11W
Bristol, City of □, U.K. 11 F5 51 27N 2 36W
Bristol B., U.S.A. 68 C4 58 0N 160 0W
Bristol Channel, U.K. 11 F3 51 18N 4 30W
Bristol I., Antarctica 5 B1 58 45S 28 0W
Bristol L., U.S.A. 83 J5 34 23N 116 50W
Bristow, U.S.A. 81 H6 35 50N 96 23W
Britain = Great Britain, Europe 6 E5 54 0N 2 15W
British Columbia □, Canada 72 C3 55 0N 125 15W
British Indian Ocean Terr. = Chagos Arch., Ind. Oc. 29 K11 6 0S 72 0 E
British Isles, Europe 6 E5 54 0N 4 0W
Brits, S. Africa 57 D4 25 37S 27 48 E
Britstown, S. Africa 56 E3 30 37S 23 30 E
Britt, Canada 70 C3 45 46N 80 34W
Brittany = Bretagne, France 18 B2 48 10N 3 0W
Britton, U.S.A. 80 C6 45 48N 97 45W
Brive-la-Gaillarde, France 18 D4 45 10N 1 32 E
Brixen = Bressanone, Italy 20 A4 46 43N 11 39 E
Brixham, U.K. 11 G4 50 23N 3 31W
Brno, Czech Rep. 17 D9 49 10N 16 35 E
Broad →, U.S.A. 77 J5 34 1N 81 4W
Broad Arrow, Australia 61 F3 30 23S 121 15 E
Broad B., U.K. 12 C2 58 14N 6 18W
Broad Haven, Ireland 13 B2 54 20N 9 55W
Broad Law, U.K. 12 F5 55 30N 3 21W
Broad Sd., Australia 62 C4 22 0S 149 45 E
Broadalbin, U.S.A. 79 C10 43 4N 74 12W
Broadback →, Canada 70 B4 51 21N 78 52W
Broadhurst Ra., Australia 60 D3 22 30S 122 30 E
Broads, The, U.K. 10 E9 52 45N 1 30 E
Broadus, U.S.A. 80 C2 45 27N 105 25W
Brochet, Canada 73 B8 57 53N 101 40W
Brochet, L., Canada 73 B8 58 36N 101 35W
Brocken, Germany 16 C6 51 47N 10 37 E
Brockport, U.S.A. 78 C7 43 13N 77 56W
Brockton, U.S.A. 79 D13 42 5N 71 1W
Brockville, Canada 79 B9 44 35N 75 41W
Brockway, Mont., U.S.A. 80 B2 47 18N 105 45W
Brockway, Pa., U.S.A. 78 E6 41 15N 78 47W
Brocton, U.S.A. 78 D5 42 23N 79 26W
Brodeur Pen., Canada 69 A11 72 30N 88 10W
Brodhead, Mt., U.S.A. 78 E7 41 39N 77 47W
Brodick, U.K. 12 F3 55 35N 5 9W
Brodnica, Poland 17 B10 53 15N 19 25 E
Brody, Ukraine 17 C13 50 5N 25 10 E
Brogan, U.S.A. 82 D5 44 15N 117 31W
Broken Arrow, U.S.A. 81 G7 36 3N 95 48W
Broken Bow, Nebr., U.S.A. 80 E5 41 24N 99 38W
Broken Bow, Okla., U.S.A. 81 H7 34 2N 94 44W
Broken Bow Lake, U.S.A. 81 H7 34 9N 94 40W
Broken Hill = Kabwe, Zambia 55 E2 14 30S 28 29 E
Broken Hill, Australia 63 E3 31 58S 141 29 E
Bromley □, U.K. 11 F8 51 24N 0 2 E
Bromsgrove, U.K. 11 E5 52 21N 2 2W
Brønderslev, Denmark 9 H13 57 16N 9 57 E
Bronkhorstspruit, S. Africa 57 D4 25 46S 28 45 E
Brønnøysund, Norway 8 D15 65 28N 12 14 E
Brook Park, U.S.A. 78 E4 41 24N 81 51W
Brookhaven, U.S.A. 81 K9 31 35N 90 26W
Brookings, Oreg., U.S.A. 82 E1 42 3N 124 17W
Brookings, S. Dak., U.S.A. 80 C6 44 19N 96 48W
Brooklin, Canada 78 C6 43 55N 78 55W
Brooklyn Park, U.S.A. 80 C8 45 6N 93 23W
Brooks, Canada 72 C6 50 35N 111 55W
Brooks Range, U.S.A. 68 B5 68 0N 152 0W
Brooksville, U.S.A. 77 L4 28 33N 82 23W
Brookton, Australia 61 F2 32 22S 117 0 E
Brookville, U.S.A. 78 E5 41 10N 79 5W
Broom, L., U.K. 12 D3 57 55N 5 15W
Broome, Australia 60 C3 18 0S 122 15 E
Brora, U.K. 12 C5 58 0N 3 52W
Brora →, U.K. 12 C5 58 0N 3 51W
Brosna →, Ireland 13 C4 53 14N 7 58W
Brothers, U.S.A. 82 E3 43 49N 120 36W
Brough, U.K. 10 C5 54 32N 2 18W
Brough Hd., U.K. 12 B5 59 8N 3 20W
Broughton Island = Qikiqtarjuaq, Canada 69 B13 67 33N 63 0W
Brown, L., Australia 61 F2 31 5S 118 15 E
Brown, Pt., Australia 63 E1 32 32S 133 50 E
Brown City, U.S.A. 78 C2 43 13N 82 59W
Brown Willy, U.K. 11 G3 50 35N 4 37W
Brownfield, U.S.A. 81 J3 33 11N 102 17W
Browning, U.S.A. 82 B7 48 34N 113 1W
Brownsville, Oreg., U.S.A. 82 D2 44 24N 122 59W
Brownsville, Pa., U.S.A. 78 F5 40 1N 79 53W
Brownsville, Tenn., U.S.A. 81 H10 35 36N 89 16W
Brownsville, Tex., U.S.A. 81 N6 25 54N 97 30W
Brownville, U.S.A. 79 C9 44 0N 75 59W
Brownwood, U.S.A. 81 K5 31 43N 98 59W
Browse I., Australia 60 B3 14 7S 123 33 E
Bruas, Malaysia 39 K3 4 30N 100 47 E
Bruay-la-Buissière, France 18 A5 50 29N 2 33 E
Bruce, Mt., Australia 60 D2 22 37S 118 8 E
Bruce Pen., Canada 78 B3 45 0N 81 30W
Bruce Rock, Australia 61 F2 31 52S 118 8 E
Bruck an der Leitha, Austria 17 D9 48 1N 16 47 E
Bruck an der Mur, Austria 16 E8 47 24N 15 16 E
Brue →, U.K. 11 F5 51 13N 2 59W
Bruges = Brugge, Belgium 15 C3 51 13N 3 13 E
Brugge, Belgium 15 C3 51 13N 3 13 E
Bruin, U.S.A. 78 E5 41 3N 79 43W
Brûlé, Canada 72 C5 53 15N 117 58W
Brumado, Brazil 93 F10 14 14S 41 40W
Brumunddal, Norway 9 F14 60 53N 10 56 E
Bruneau, U.S.A. 82 E6 42 53N 115 48W
Bruneau →, U.S.A. 82 E6 42 56N 115 57W
Brunei = Bandar Seri Begawan, Brunei 36 C4 4 52N 115 0 E
Brunei ■, Asia 36 D4 4 50N 115 0 E
Brunner, L., N.Z. 59 K3 42 37S 171 27 E
Brunssum, Neths. 15 D5 50 57N 5 59 E
Brunswick = Braunschweig, Germany 16 B6 52 15N 10 31 E
Brunswick, Ga., U.S.A. 77 K5 31 10N 81 30W
Brunswick, Maine, U.S.A. 77 D11 43 55N 69 58W
Brunswick, Md., U.S.A. 76 F7 39 19N 77 38W
Brunswick, Mo., U.S.A. 80 F8 39 26N 93 8W
Brunswick, Ohio, U.S.A. 78 E3 41 14N 81 51W
Brunswick, Pen. de, Chile 96 G2 53 30S 71 30W
Brunswick B., Australia 60 C3 15 15S 124 50 E
Brunswick Junction, Australia 61 F2 33 15S 115 50 E
Bruny I., Australia 62 G4 43 20S 147 15 E
Brus Laguna, Honduras 88 C3 15 47N 84 35W
Brush, U.S.A. 80 E3 40 15N 103 37W
Brushton, U.S.A. 79 B10 44 50N 74 31W
Brusque, Brazil 95 B6 27 5S 49 0W
Brussel, Belgium 15 D4 50 51N 4 21 E
Brussels = Brussel, Belgium 15 D4 50 51N 4 21 E
Brussels, Canada 78 C3 43 44N 81 15W
Bruthen, Australia 63 F4 37 42S 147 50 E
Bruxelles = Brussel, Belgium 15 D4 50 51N 4 21 E
Bryan, Ohio, U.S.A. 76 E3 41 28N 84 33W
Bryan, Tex., U.S.A. 81 K6 30 40N 96 22W
Bryan, Mt., Australia 63 E2 33 30S 139 0 E
Bryansk, Russia 24 D4 53 13N 34 25 E
Bryce Canyon Nat. Park, U.S.A. 83 H7 37 30N 112 10W
Bryne, Norway 9 G11 58 44N 5 38 E
Bryson City, U.S.A. 77 H4 35 26N 83 27W
Bsharri, Lebanon 47 A5 34 15N 36 0 E
Bū Baqarah, U.A.E. 45 E8 25 35N 56 25 E
Bu Craa, W. Sahara 50 C3 26 45N 12 50W
Bū Ḩasā, U.A.E. 45 F7 23 30N 53 20 E
Bua Yai, Thailand 38 E4 15 33N 102 26 E
Buapinang, Indonesia 37 E6 4 40S 121 30 E
Bubanza, Burundi 54 C2 3 6S 29 23 E
Būbiyān, Kuwait 46 B4 29 45N 48 15 E
Bucaramanga, Colombia 92 B4 7 0N 73 0W
Bucasia, Australia 62 C4 21 2S 149 10 E
Buccaneer Arch., Australia 60 C3 16 7S 123 20 E
Buchach, Ukraine 17 D13 49 5N 25 25 E
Buchan, U.K. 12 D6 57 32N 2 21W
Buchan Ness, U.K. 12 D7 57 29N 1 46W
Buchanan, Canada 73 C8 51 40N 102 45W
Buchanan, Liberia 50 G3 5 57N 10 2W
Buchanan, L., Queens., Australia 62 C4 21 35S 145 52 E
Buchanan, L., W. Austral., Australia 61 E3 25 33S 123 2 E
Buchanan, L., U.S.A. 81 K5 30 45N 98 25W
Buchanan Cr. →, Australia 62 B2 19 13S 136 33 E
Buchans, Canada 71 C8 48 50N 56 52W
Bucharest = Bucureşti, Romania 17 F14 44 27N 26 10 E
Buchon, Pt., U.S.A. 84 K6 35 15N 120 54W
Buck Hill Falls, U.S.A. 79 E9 41 11N 75 16W
Buckeye, U.S.A. 83 K7 33 22N 112 35W
Buckeye Lake, U.S.A. 78 G2 39 55N 82 29W
Buckhannon, U.S.A. 76 F5 39 0N 80 8W
Buckhaven, U.K. 12 E5 56 11N 3 3W
Buckhorn L., Canada 78 B6 44 29N 78 23W
Buckie, U.K. 12 D6 57 41N 2 58W
Buckingham, Canada 70 C4 45 37N 75 24W
Buckingham, U.K. 11 F7 51 59N 0 57W
Buckingham B., Australia 62 A2 12 10S 135 40 E
Buckinghamshire □, U.K. 11 F7 51 53N 0 55W
Buckle Hd., Australia 60 B4 14 26S 127 52 E
Buckleboo, Australia 63 E2 32 54S 136 12 E
Buckley, U.K. 10 D4 53 10N 3 5W
Buckley →, Australia 62 C2 20 10S 138 49 E
Bucklin, U.S.A. 81 G5 37 33N 99 38W
Bucks L., U.S.A. 84 F5 39 54N 121 12W
Buctouche, Canada 71 C7 46 30N 64 45W
Bucureşti, Romania 17 F14 44 27N 26 10 E
Bucyrus, U.S.A. 76 E4 40 48N 82 59W
Budalin, Burma 41 H19 22 20N 95 10 E
Budapest, Hungary 17 E10 47 29N 19 5 E
Budaun, India 43 E8 28 5N 79 10 E
Budd Coast, Antarctica 5 C8 68 0S 112 0 E
Bude, U.K. 11 G3 50 49N 4 34W
Budennovsk, Russia 25 F7 44 50N 44 10 E
Budge Budge = Baj Baj, India 43 H13 22 30N 88 5 E
Budgewoi, Australia 63 E5 33 13S 151 34 E
Budjala, Dem. Rep. of the Congo 52 D3 2 50N 19 40 E
Buellton, U.S.A. 85 L6 34 37N 120 12W
Buena Esperanza, Argentina 94 C2 34 45S 65 15W
Buena Park, U.S.A. 85 M9 33 52N 117 59W
Buena Vista, Colo., U.S.A. 83 G10 38 51N 106 8W
Buena Vista, Va., U.S.A. 76 G6 37 44N 79 21W
Buena Vista Lake Bed, U.S.A. 85 K7 35 12N 119 18W
Buenaventura, Colombia 92 C3 3 53N 77 4W
Buenaventura, Mexico 86 B3 29 50N 107 30W
Buenos Aires, Argentina 94 C4 34 30S 58 20W
Buenos Aires, Costa Rica 88 E3 9 10N 83 20W
Buenos Aires □, Argentina 94 D4 36 30S 60 0W
Buenos Aires, L., Chile 96 F2 46 35S 72 30W
Buffalo, Mo., U.S.A. 81 G8 37 39N 93 6W
Buffalo, N.Y., U.S.A. 78 D6 42 53N 78 53W
Buffalo, Okla., U.S.A. 81 G5 36 50N 99 38W
Buffalo, S. Dak., U.S.A. 80 C3 45 35N 103 33W
Buffalo, Wyo., U.S.A. 82 D10 44 21N 106 42W
Buffalo →, Canada 72 A5 60 5N 115 5W
Buffalo →, S. Africa 57 D5 28 43S 30 37 E
Buffalo Head Hills, Canada 72 B5 57 25N 115 55W
Buffalo L., Alta., Canada 72 C6 52 27N 112 54W
Buffalo L., N.W.T., Canada 72 A5 60 12N 115 25W
Buffalo Narrows, Canada 73 B7 55 51N 108 29W
Buffels →, S. Africa 56 D2 29 36S 17 3 E
Buford, U.S.A. 77 H4 34 10N 84 0W
Bug = Buh →, Ukraine 25 E5 46 59N 31 58 E
Bug →, Poland 17 B11 52 31N 21 5 E
Buga, Colombia 92 C3 4 0N 76 15W
Bugala I., Uganda 54 C3 0 40S 32 20 E
Buganda, Uganda 54 C3 0 0 31 30 E
Buganga, Uganda 54 C3 0 3S 32 0 E
Bugel, Tanjung, Indonesia 37 G14 6 26S 111 3 E
Bugibba, Malta 23 D1 35 57N 14 25 E
Bugsuk, Phil. 36 C5 8 15N 117 15 E
Bugulma, Russia 24 D9 54 33N 52 48 E
Bugun Shara, Mongolia 32 B5 49 0N 104 0 E
Buguruslan, Russia 24 D9 53 39N 52 26 E
Buh →, Ukraine 25 E5 46 59N 31 58 E
Buhera, Zimbabwe 57 B5 19 18S 31 29 E
Buhl, U.S.A. 82 E6 42 36N 114 46W
Builth Wells, U.K. 11 E4 52 9N 3 25W
Buir Nur, Mongolia 33 B6 47 50N 117 42 E
Bujumbura, Burundi 54 C2 3 16S 29 18 E
Bukachacha, Russia 27 D12 52 55N 116 50 E
Bukama, Dem. Rep. of the Congo 55 D2 9 10S 25 50 E
Bukavu, Dem. Rep. of the Congo 54 C2 2 20S 28 52 E
Bukene, Tanzania 54 C3 4 15S 32 48 E
Bukhara = Bukhoro, Uzbekistan 26 F7 39 48N 64 25 E
Bukhoro, Uzbekistan 26 F7 39 48N 64 25 E
Bukima, Tanzania 54 C3 1 50S 33 25 E
Bukit Mertajam, Malaysia 39 K3 5 22N 100 28 E
Bukittinggi, Indonesia 36 E2 0 20S 100 20 E
Bukoba, Tanzania 54 C3 1 20S 31 49 E
Bukuya, Uganda 54 B3 0 40N 31 52 E
Būl, Kuh-e, Iran 45 D7 30 48N 52 45 E
Bula, Indonesia 37 E8 3 6S 130 30 E
Bulahdelah, Australia 63 E5 32 23S 152 13 E
Bulan, Phil. 37 B6 12 40N 123 52 E
Bulandshahr, India 42 E7 28 28N 77 51 E
Bulawayo, Zimbabwe 55 G2 20 7S 28 32 E
Buldan, Turkey 21 E13 38 2N 28 50 E
Bulgar, Russia 24 D8 54 57N 49 4 E
Bulgaria ■, Europe 21 C11 42 35N 25 30 E
Buli, Teluk, Indonesia 37 D7 0 48N 128 25 E
Buliluyan, C., Phil. 36 C5 8 20N 117 15 E
Bulkley →, Canada 72 B3 55 15N 127 40W
Bull Shoals L., U.S.A. 81 G8 36 22N 92 35W
Bullhead City, U.S.A. 85 K12 35 8N 114 32W
Büllingen, Belgium 15 D6 50 25N 6 16 E
Bullock Creek, Australia 62 B3 17 43S 144 31 E
Bulloo →, Australia 63 D3 28 43S 142 30 E
Bulloo L., Australia 63 D3 28 43S 142 25 E
Bulls, N.Z. 59 J5 40 10S 175 24 E
Bulnes, Chile 94 D1 36 42S 72 19W
Bulsar = Valsad, India 40 J8 20 40N 72 58 E
Bultfontein, S. Africa 56 D4 28 18S 26 10 E
Bulukumba, Indonesia 37 F6 5 33S 120 11 E
Bulun, Russia 27 B13 70 37N 127 30 E
Bumba, Dem. Rep. of the Congo 52 D4 2 13N 22 30 E
Bumbiri I., Tanzania 54 C3 1 40S 31 55 E
Bumhpa Bum, Burma 41 F20 26 51N 97 14 E
Bumi →, Zimbabwe 55 F2 17 0S 28 20 E
Buna, Kenya 54 B4 2 58N 39 30 E
Bunazi, Tanzania 54 C3 1 3S 31 23 E
Bunbury, Australia 61 F2 33 20S 115 35 E
Bunclody, Ireland 13 D5 52 39N 6 40W
Buncrana, Ireland 13 A4 55 8N 7 27W
Bundaberg, Australia 63 C5 24 54S 152 22 E
Bundey →, Australia 62 C2 21 46S 135 37 E
Bundi, India 42 G6 25 30N 75 35 E
Bundoran, Ireland 13 B3 54 28N 8 16W
Bung Kan, Thailand 38 C4 18 23N 103 37 E
Bungay, U.K. 11 E9 52 27N 1 28 E
Bungil Cr. →, Australia 63 D4 27 5S 149 5 E
Bungo-Suidō, Japan 31 H6 33 0N 132 15 E
Bungoma, Kenya 54 B3 0 34N 34 34 E
Bungotakada, Japan 31 H5 33 35N 131 25 E
Bungu, Tanzania 54 D4 7 35S 39 0 E
Bunia, Dem. Rep. of the Congo 54 B3 1 35N 30 20 E
Bunji, Pakistan 43 B6 35 45N 74 40 E
Bunkie, U.S.A. 81 K8 30 57N 92 11W
Bunnell, U.S.A. 77 L5 29 28N 81 16W
Buntok, Indonesia 36 E4 1 40S 114 58 E
Bunyu, Indonesia 36 D5 3 35N 117 50 E
Buol, Indonesia 37 D6 1 15N 121 32 E
Buon Brieng, Vietnam 38 F7 13 9N 108 12 E
Buon Ma Thuot, Vietnam 38 F7 12 40N 108 3 E
Buong Long, Cambodia 38 F6 13 44N 106 59 E
Buorkhaya, Mys, Russia 27 B14 71 50N 132 40 E
Buqayq, Si. Arabia 45 E6 26 0N 49 45 E
Bur Acaba, Somali Rep. 46 G3 3 12N 44 20 E
Bûr Safâga, Egypt 44 E2 26 43N 33 57 E
Bûr Sa'îd, Egypt 51 B12 31 16N 32 18 E
Bûr Sûdân, Sudan 51 E13 19 32N 37 9 E
Bura, Kenya 54 C4 1 4S 39 58 E
Burakin, Australia 61 F2 30 31S 117 10 E
Burao, Somali Rep. 46 F4 9 32N 45 32 E
Burāq, Syria 47 B5 33 11N 36 29 E
Buraydah, Si. Arabia 44 E4 26 20N 43 59 E
Burbank, U.S.A. 85 L8 34 11N 118 19W
Burda, India 42 G6 25 50N 77 35 E
Burdekin →, Australia 62 B4 19 38S 147 25 E
Burdur, Turkey 25 G5 37 45N 30 17 E
Burdwan = Barddhaman, India 43 H12 23 14N 87 39 E
Bure, Ethiopia 46 E2 10 40N 37 4 E
Bure →, U.K. 10 E9 52 38N 1 43 E
Bureya →, Russia 27 E13 49 27N 129 30 E
Burford, Canada 78 C4 43 7N 80 27W
Burgas, Bulgaria 21 C12 42 33N 27 29 E
Burgeo, Canada 71 C8 47 37N 57 38W
Burgersdorp, S. Africa 56 E4 31 0S 26 20 E
Burges, Mt., Australia 61 F3 30 50S 121 5 E
Burgos, Spain 19 A4 42 21N 3 41W
Burgsvik, Sweden 9 H18 57 3N 18 19 E
Burgundy = Bourgogne, France 18 C6 47 0N 4 50 E
Burhaniye, Turkey 21 E12 39 30N 26 58 E
Burhanpur, India 40 J10 21 18N 76 14 E
Burhi Gandak →, India 43 G12 25 20N 86 37 E
Burhner →, India 43 H9 22 43N 80 31 E
Burias I., Phil. 37 B6 12 55N 123 5 E
Burica, Pta., Costa Rica 88 E3 8 3N 82 51W
Burien, U.S.A. 84 C4 47 28N 122 21W
Burigi, L., Tanzania 54 C3 2 2S 31 22 E
Burin, Canada 71 C8 47 1N 55 14W
Buriram, Thailand 38 E4 15 0N 103 0 E
Burj Sāfitā, Syria 44 C3 34 48N 36 7 E
Burkburnett, U.S.A. 81 H5 34 6N 98 34W
Burke →, Australia 62 C2 23 12S 139 33 E
Burke Chan., Canada 72 C3 52 10N 127 30W
Burketown, Australia 62 B2 17 45S 139 33 E
Burkina Faso ■, Africa 50 F5 12 0N 1 0W
Burk's Falls, Canada 70 C4 45 37N 79 24W
Burleigh Falls, Canada 78 B6 44 33N 78 12W
Burley, U.S.A. 82 E7 42 32N 113 48W
Burlingame, U.S.A. 84 H4 37 35N 122 21W
Burlington, Canada 78 C5 43 18N 79 45W
Burlington, Colo., U.S.A. 80 F3 39 18N 102 16W
Burlington, Iowa, U.S.A. 80 E9 40 49N 91 14W
Burlington, Kans., U.S.A. 80 F7 38 12N 95 45W
Burlington, N.C., U.S.A. 77 G6 36 6N 79 26W
Burlington, N.J., U.S.A. 79 F10 40 4N 74 51W
Burlington, Vt., U.S.A. 79 B11 44 29N 73 12W
Burlington, Wash., U.S.A. 84 B4 48 28N 122 20W
Burlington, Wis., U.S.A. 76 D1 42 41N 88 17W
Burlyu-Tyube, Kazakstan 26 E8 46 30N 79 10 E
Burma ■, Asia 41 J20 21 0N 96 30 E
Burnaby I., Canada 72 C2 52 25N 131 19W
Burnet, U.S.A. 81 K5 30 45N 98 14W
Burney, U.S.A. 82 F3 40 53N 121 40W
Burnham, U.S.A. 78 F7 40 38N 77 34W
Burnham-on-Sea, U.K. 11 F5 51 14N 3 0W
Burnie, Australia 62 G4 41 4S 145 56 E
Burnley, U.K. 10 D5 53 47N 2 14W
Burns, U.S.A. 82 E4 43 35N 119 3W
Burns Lake, Canada 72 C3 54 20N 125 45W
Burnside →, Canada 68 B9 66 51N 108 4W
Burnside, L., Australia 61 E3 25 22S 123 0 E
Burnsville, U.S.A. 80 C8 44 47N 93 17W
Burnt L., Canada 71 B7 53 35N 64 4W
Burnt River, Canada 78 B6 44 41N 78 42W
Burntwood →, Canada 73 B9 56 8N 96 34W
Burntwood L., Canada 73 B8 55 22N 100 26W
Burqān, Kuwait 44 D5 29 0N 47 57 E
Burra, Australia 63 E2 33 40S 138 55 E
Burray, U.K. 12 C6 58 51N 2 54W
Burren Junction, Australia 63 E4 30 7S 148 59 E
Burrinjuck Res., Australia 63 F4 35 0S 148 36 E
Burro, Serranías del, Mexico 86 B4 29 0N 102 0W
Burrow Hd., U.K. 12 G4 54 41N 4 24W
Burruyacú, Argentina 94 B3 26 30S 64 40W
Burry Port, U.K. 11 F3 51 41N 4 15W
Bursa, Turkey 21 D13 40 15N 29 5 E
Burstall, Canada 73 C7 50 39N 109 54W
Burton, Ohio, U.S.A. 78 E3 41 28N 81 8W
Burton, S.C., U.S.A. 77 J5 32 25N 80 45W
Burton, L., Canada 70 B4 54 45N 78 20W
Burton upon Trent, U.K. 10 E6 52 48N 1 38W
Buru, Indonesia 37 E7 3 30S 126 30 E
Burûn, Râs, Egypt 47 D2 31 14N 33 7 E
Burundi ■, Africa 54 C3 3 15S 30 0 E
Bururi, Burundi 54 C2 3 57S 29 37 E
Burutu, Nigeria 50 G7 5 20N 5 29 E
Burwell, U.S.A. 80 E5 41 47N 99 8W
Burwick, U.K. 12 C5 58 45N 2 58W
Bury, U.K. 10 D5 53 35N 2 17W
Bury St. Edmunds, U.K. 11 E8 52 15N 0 43 E
Buryatia □, Russia 27 D11 53 0N 110 0 E
Busan = Pusan, S. Korea 35 G15 35 5N 129 0 E
Busango Swamp, Zambia 55 E2 14 15S 25 45 E
Buşayrah, Syria 44 C4 35 9N 40 26 E
Būshehr, Iran 45 D6 28 55N 50 55 E
Būshehr □, Iran 45 D6 28 20N 51 45 E
Bushell, Canada 73 B7 59 31N 108 45W
Bushenyi, Uganda 54 C3 0 35S 30 10 E
Bushire = Būshehr, Iran 45 D6 28 55N 50 55 E
Businga, Dem. Rep. of the Congo 52 D4 3 16N 20 59 E
Buşra ash Shām, Syria 47 C5 32 30N 36 25 E
Busselton, Australia 61 F2 33 42S 115 15 E
Bussum, Neths. 15 B5 52 16N 5 10 E
Busto Arsizio, Italy 18 D8 45 37N 8 51 E
Busu Djanoa, Dem. Rep. of the Congo 52 D4 1 43N 21 23 E
Busuanga I., Phil. 37 B5 12 10N 120 0 E
Buta, Dem. Rep. of the Congo 54 B1 2 50N 24 53 E
Butare, Rwanda 54 C2 2 31S 29 52 E
Butaritari, Kiribati 64 G9 3 30N 174 0 E
Bute, U.K. 12 F3 55 48N 5 2W
Bute Inlet, Canada 72 C4 50 40N 124 53W
Butemba, Uganda 54 B3 1 9N 31 37 E
Butembo, Dem. Rep. of the Congo 54 B2 0 9N 29 18 E
Butha Qi, China 33 B7 48 0N 122 32 E
Butiaba, Uganda 54 B3 1 50N 31 20 E
Butler, Mo., U.S.A. 80 F7 38 16N 94 20W
Butler, Pa., U.S.A. 78 F5 40 52N 79 54W
Buton, Indonesia 37 E6 5 0S 122 45 E
Butte, Mont., U.S.A. 82 C7 46 0N 112 32W
Butte, Nebr., U.S.A. 80 D5 42 58N 98 51W

Butte Creek →, *U.S.A.* **84 F5** 39 12N 121 56W
Butterworth = Gcuwa, *S. Africa* **57 E4** 32 20S 28 11 E
Butterworth, *Malaysia* **39 K3** 5 24N 100 23 E
Buttevant, *Ireland* **13 D3** 52 14N 8 40W
Buttfield, Mt., *Australia* **61 D4** 24 45S 128 9 E
Button B., *Canada* **73 B10** 58 45N 94 23W
Buttonwillow, *U.S.A.* **85 K7** 35 24N 119 28W
Butty Hd., *Australia* **61 F3** 33 54S 121 39 E
Butuan, *Phil.* **37 C7** 8 57N 125 33 E
Butung = Buton, *Indonesia* **37 E6** 5 0S 122 45 E
Buturlinovka, *Russia* **25 D7** 50 50N 40 35 E
Buur Hakaba = Bur Acaba, *Somali Rep.* **46 G3** 3 12N 44 20 E
Buxa Duar, *India* **43 F13** 27 45N 89 35 E
Buxar, *India* **43 G10** 25 34N 83 58 E
Buxtehude, *Germany* **16 B5** 53 28N 9 39 E
Buxton, *U.K.* **10 D6** 53 16N 1 54W
Buy, *Russia* **24 C7** 58 28N 41 28 E
Büyük Menderes →, *Turkey* **21 F12** 37 28N 27 11 E
Büyükçekmece, *Turkey* **21 D13** 41 2N 28 35 E
Buzău, *Romania* **17 F14** 45 10N 26 50 E
Buzău →, *Romania* **17 F14** 45 26N 27 44 E
Buzen, *Japan* **31 H5** 33 35N 131 5 E
Buzi →, *Mozam.* **55 F3** 19 50S 34 43 E
Buzuluk, *Russia* **24 D9** 52 48N 52 12 E
Buzzards B., *U.S.A.* **79 E14** 41 45N 70 37W
Buzzards Bay, *U.S.A.* **79 E14** 41 44N 70 37W
Bwana Mkubwe, *Dem. Rep. of the Congo* **55 E2** 13 8S 28 38 E
Byarezina →, *Belarus* **17 B16** 52 33N 30 14 E
Byaroza, *Belarus* **17 B13** 52 31N 24 51 E
Bydgoszcz, *Poland* **17 B9** 53 10N 18 0 E
Byelarus = Belarus ■, *Europe* **17 B14** 53 30N 27 0 E
Byelorussia = Belarus ■, *Europe* **17 B14** 53 30N 27 0 E
Byers, *U.S.A.* **80 F2** 39 43N 104 14W
Byesville, *U.S.A.* **78 G3** 39 58N 81 32W
Byford, *Australia* **61 F2** 32 15S 116 0 E
Bykhaw, *Belarus* **17 B16** 53 31N 30 14 E
Bykhov = Bykhaw, *Belarus* **17 B16** 53 31N 30 14 E
Bylas, *U.S.A.* **83 K8** 33 8N 110 7W
Bylot, *Canada* **73 B10** 58 25N 94 8W
Bylot I., *Canada* **69 A12** 73 13N 78 34W
Byrd, C., *Antarctica* **5 C17** 69 38S 76 7W
Byrock, *Australia* **63 E4** 30 40S 146 27 E
Byron Bay, *Australia* **63 D5** 28 43S 153 37 E
Byrranga, Gory, *Russia* **27 B11** 75 0N 100 0 E
Byrranga Mts. = Byrranga, Gory, *Russia* **27 B11** 75 0N 100 0 E
Byske, *Sweden* **8 D19** 64 57N 21 11 E
Byske älv →, *Sweden* **8 D19** 64 57N 21 13 E
Bytom, *Poland* **17 C10** 50 25N 18 54 E
Bytów, *Poland* **17 A9** 54 10N 17 30 E
Byumba, *Rwanda* **54 C3** 1 35S 30 4 E

C

Ca →, *Vietnam* **38 C5** 18 45N 105 45 E
Ca Mau, *Vietnam* **39 H5** 9 7N 105 8 E
Ca Mau, Mui, *Vietnam* **39 H5** 8 38N 104 44 E
Ca Na, *Vietnam* **39 G7** 11 20N 108 54 E
Caacupé, *Paraguay* **94 B4** 25 23S 57 5W
Caála, *Angola* **53 G3** 12 46S 15 30 E
Caamano Sd., *Canada* **72 C3** 52 55N 129 25W
Caazapá, *Paraguay* **94 B4** 26 8S 56 19W
Caazapá □, *Paraguay* **95 B4** 26 10S 56 0W
Caballeria, C. de, *Spain* **22 A11** 40 5N 4 5 E
Cabanatuan, *Phil.* **37 A6** 15 30N 120 58 E
Cabano, *Canada* **71 C6** 47 40N 68 56W
Cabazon, *U.S.A.* **85 M10** 33 55N 116 47W
Cabedelo, *Brazil* **93 E12** 7 0S 34 50W
Cabildo, *Chile* **94 C1** 32 30S 71 5W
Cabimas, *Venezuela* **92 A4** 10 23N 71 25W
Cabinda, *Angola* **52 F2** 5 33S 12 11 E
Cabinda □, *Angola* **52 F2** 5 0S 12 30 E
Cabinet Mts., *U.S.A.* **82 C6** 48 0N 115 30W
Cabo Blanco, *Argentina* **96 F3** 47 15S 65 47W
Cabo Frio, *Brazil* **95 A7** 22 51S 42 3W
Cabo Pantoja, *Peru* **92 D3** 1 0S 75 10W
Cabonga, Réservoir, *Canada* **70 C4** 47 20N 76 40W
Cabool, *U.S.A.* **81 G8** 37 7N 92 6W
Caboolture, *Australia* **63 D5** 27 5S 152 58 E
Cabora Bassa Dam = Cahora Bassa, Représa de, *Mozam.* **55 F3** 15 20S 32 50 E
Caborca, *Mexico* **86 A2** 30 40N 112 10W
Cabot, Mt., *U.S.A.* **79 B13** 44 30N 71 25W
Cabot Hd., *Canada* **78 A3** 45 14N 81 17W
Cabot Str., *Canada* **71 C8** 47 15N 59 40W
Cabra, *Spain* **19 D3** 37 30N 4 28W
Cabrera, *Spain* **22 B9** 39 8N 2 57 E
Cabri, *Canada* **73 C7** 50 35N 108 25W
Cabriel →, *Spain* **19 C5** 39 14N 1 3W
Caçador, *Brazil* **95 B5** 26 47S 51 0W
Čačak, *Serbia, Yug.* **21 C9** 43 54N 20 20 E
Caçapava do Sul, *Brazil* **95 C5** 30 30S 53 30W
Cáceres, *Brazil* **92 G7** 16 5S 57 40W
Cáceres, *Spain* **19 C2** 39 26N 6 23W
Cache Bay, *Canada* **70 C4** 46 22N 80 0W
Cache Cr. →, *U.S.A.* **84 G5** 38 42N 121 42W
Cache Creek, *Canada* **72 C4** 50 48N 121 19W
Cachi, *Argentina* **94 B2** 25 5S 66 10W
Cachimbo, Serra do, *Brazil* **93 E7** 9 30S 55 30W
Cachinal de la Sierra, *Chile* **94 A2** 24 58S 69 32W
Cachoeira, *Brazil* **93 F11** 12 30S 39 0W
Cachoeira do Sul, *Brazil* **95 C5** 30 3S 52 53W
Cachoeiro de Itapemirim, *Brazil* **95 A7** 20 51S 41 7W
Cacoal, *Brazil* **92 F6** 11 32S 61 18W
Cacólo, *Angola* **52 G3** 10 9S 19 21 E
Caconda, *Angola* **53 G3** 13 48S 15 8 E
Caddo, *U.S.A.* **81 H6** 34 7N 96 16W
Cader Idris, *U.K.* **11 E4** 52 42N 3 53W
Cadereyta, *Mexico* **86 B5** 25 36N 100 0W
Cadibarrawirracanna, L., *Australia* **63 D2** 28 52S 135 27 E
Cadillac, *U.S.A.* **76 C3** 44 15N 85 24W
Cadiz, *Phil.* **37 B6** 10 57N 123 15 E
Cádiz, *Spain* **19 D2** 36 30N 6 20W
Cadiz, *Calif., U.S.A.* **85 L11** 34 30N 115 28W
Cadiz, *Ohio, U.S.A.* **78 F4** 40 22N 81 0W
Cádiz, G. de, *Spain* **19 D2** 36 40N 7 0W
Cadiz L., *U.S.A.* **83 J6** 34 18N 115 24W
Cadney Park, *Australia* **63 D1** 27 55S 134 3 E
Cadomin, *Canada* **72 C5** 53 2N 117 20W
Cadotte Lake, *Canada* **72 B5** 56 26N 116 23W
Cadoux, *Australia* **61 F2** 30 46S 117 7 E
Caen, *France* **18 B3** 49 10N 0 22W
Caernarfon, *U.K.* **10 D3** 53 8N 4 16W
Caernarfon B., *U.K.* **10 D3** 53 4N 4 40W
Caernarvon = Caernarfon, *U.K.* **10 D3** 53 8N 4 16W
Caerphilly, *U.K.* **11 F4** 51 35N 3 13W
Caerphilly □, *U.K.* **11 F4** 51 37N 3 12W
Caesarea, *Israel* **47 C3** 32 30N 34 53 E
Caetité, *Brazil* **93 F10** 13 50S 42 32W
Cafayate, *Argentina* **94 B2** 26 2S 66 0W
Cafu, *Angola* **56 B2** 16 30S 15 8 E
Cagayan de Oro, *Phil.* **37 C6** 8 30N 124 40 E
Cagayan Is., *Phil.* **37 C5** 9 40N 121 16 E
Cágliari, *Italy* **20 E3** 39 13N 9 7 E
Cágliari, G. di, *Italy* **20 E3** 39 8N 9 11 E
Caguán →, *Colombia* **92 D4** 0 8S 74 18W
Caguas, *Puerto Rico* **89 C6** 18 14N 66 2W
Caha Mts., *Ireland* **13 E2** 51 45N 9 40W
Cahama, *Angola* **56 B1** 16 17S 14 19 E
Caher, *Ireland* **13 D4** 52 22N 7 56W
Cahersiveen, *Ireland* **13 E1** 51 56N 10 14W
Cahora Bassa, L. de, *Mozam.* **55 F3** 15 35S 32 0 E
Cahora Bassa, Représa de, *Mozam.* **55 F3** 15 20S 32 50 E
Cahore Pt., *Ireland* **13 D5** 52 33N 6 12W
Cahors, *France* **18 D4** 44 27N 1 27 E
Cahul, *Moldova* **17 F15** 45 50N 28 15 E
Cai Bau, Dao, *Vietnam* **38 B6** 21 10N 107 27 E
Cai Nuoc, *Vietnam* **39 H5** 8 56N 105 1 E
Caia, *Mozam.* **55 F4** 17 51S 35 24 E
Caianda, *Angola* **55 E1** 11 2S 23 31 E
Caibarién, *Cuba* **88 B4** 22 30N 79 30W
Caicara, *Venezuela* **92 B5** 7 38N 66 10W
Caicó, *Brazil* **93 E11** 6 20S 37 0W
Caicos Is., *Turks & Caicos* **89 B5** 21 40N 71 40W
Caicos Passage, *W. Indies* **89 B5** 22 45N 72 45W
Caird Coast, *Antarctica* **5 D1** 75 0S 25 0W
Cairn Gorm, *U.K.* **12 D5** 57 7N 3 39W
Cairngorm Mts., *U.K.* **12 D5** 57 6N 3 42W
Cairnryan, *U.K.* **12 G3** 54 59N 5 1W
Cairns, *Australia* **62 B4** 16 57S 145 45 E
Cairns L., *Canada* **73 C10** 51 42N 94 30W
Cairo = El Qâhira, *Egypt* **51 B12** 30 1N 31 14 E
Cairo, *Ga., U.S.A.* **77 K3** 30 52N 84 13W
Cairo, *Ill., U.S.A.* **81 G10** 37 0N 89 11W
Cairo, *N.Y., U.S.A.* **79 D11** 42 18N 74 0W
Caithness, Ord of, *U.K.* **12 C5** 58 8N 3 36W
Cajamarca, *Peru* **92 E3** 7 5S 78 28W
Cajàzeiras, *Brazil* **93 E11** 6 52S 38 30W
Cala d'Or, *Spain* **22 B10** 39 23N 3 14 E
Cala en Porter, *Spain* **22 B11** 39 52N 4 8 E
Cala Figuera, C. de, *Spain* **22 B9** 39 27N 2 31 E
Cala Forcat, *Spain* **22 B10** 40 0N 3 47 E
Cala Major, *Spain* **22 B9** 39 33N 2 37 E
Cala Mezquida = Sa Mesquida, *Spain* **22 B11** 39 55N 4 16 E
Cala Millor, *Spain* **22 B10** 39 35N 3 22 E
Cala Ratjada, *Spain* **22 B10** 39 43N 3 27 E
Cala Santa Galdana, *Spain* **22 B10** 39 56N 3 58 E
Calabar, *Nigeria* **50 H7** 4 57N 8 20 E
Calabogie, *Canada* **79 A8** 45 18N 76 43W
Calabozo, *Venezuela* **92 B5** 9 0N 67 28W
Calábria □, *Italy* **20 E7** 39 0N 16 30 E
Calafate, *Argentina* **96 G2** 50 19S 72 15W
Calahorra, *Spain* **19 A5** 42 18N 1 59W
Calais, *France* **18 A4** 50 57N 1 56 E
Calais, *U.S.A.* **77 C12** 45 11N 67 17W
Calalaste, Cord. de, *Argentina* **94 B2** 25 0S 67 0W
Calama, *Brazil* **92 E6** 8 0S 62 50W
Calama, *Chile* **94 A2** 22 30S 68 55W
Calamar, *Colombia* **92 A4** 10 15N 74 55W
Calamian Group, *Phil.* **37 B5** 11 50N 119 55 E
Calamocha, *Spain* **19 B5** 40 50N 1 17W
Calang, *Indonesia* **36 D1** 4 37N 95 37 E
Calapan, *Phil.* **37 B6** 13 25N 121 7 E
Călăraşi, *Romania* **17 F14** 44 12N 27 20 E
Calatayud, *Spain* **19 B5** 41 20N 1 40W
Calauag, *Phil.* **37 B6** 13 55N 122 15 E
Calavite, C., *Phil.* **37 B6** 13 26N 120 20 E
Calbayog, *Phil.* **37 B6** 12 4N 124 38 E
Calca, *Peru* **92 F4** 13 22S 72 0W
Calcasieu L., *U.S.A.* **81 L8** 29 55N 93 18W
Calcutta = Kolkata, *India* **43 H13** 22 36N 88 24 E
Calcutta, *U.S.A.* **78 F4** 40 40N 80 34W
Caldas da Rainha, *Portugal* **19 C1** 39 24N 9 8W
Calder →, *U.K.* **10 D6** 53 44N 1 22W
Caldera, *Chile* **94 B1** 27 5S 70 55W
Caldwell, *Idaho, U.S.A.* **82 E5** 43 40N 116 41W
Caldwell, *Kans., U.S.A.* **81 G6** 37 2N 97 37W
Caldwell, *Tex., U.S.A.* **81 K6** 30 32N 96 42W
Caledon, *S. Africa* **56 E2** 34 14S 19 26 E
Caledon →, *S. Africa* **56 E4** 30 31S 26 5 E
Caledon B., *Australia* **62 A2** 12 45S 137 0 E
Caledonia, *Canada* **78 C5** 43 7N 79 58W
Caledonia, *U.S.A.* **78 D7** 42 58N 77 51W
Calemba, *Angola* **56 B2** 16 0S 15 44 E
Calen, *Australia* **62 C4** 20 56S 148 48 E
Caletones, *Chile* **94 C1** 34 6S 70 27W
Calexico, *U.S.A.* **85 N11** 32 40N 115 30W
Calf of Man, *U.K.* **10 C3** 54 3N 4 48W
Calgary, *Canada* **72 C6** 51 0N 114 10W
Calheta, *Madeira* **22 D2** 32 44N 17 11W
Calhoun, *U.S.A.* **77 H3** 34 30N 84 57W
Cali, *Colombia* **92 C3** 3 25N 76 35W
Calicut, *India* **40 P9** 11 15N 75 43 E
Caliente, *U.S.A.* **83 H6** 37 37N 114 31W
California, *Mo., U.S.A.* **80 F8** 38 38N 92 34W
California, *Pa., U.S.A.* **78 F5** 40 4N 79 54W
California □, *U.S.A.* **84 H7** 37 30N 119 30W
California, Baja, *Mexico* **86 A1** 32 10N 115 12W
California, Baja, T.N. = Baja California □, *Mexico* **86 B2** 30 0N 115 0W
California, Baja, T.S. = Baja California Sur □, *Mexico* **86 B2** 25 50N 111 50W
California, G. de, *Mexico* **86 B2** 27 0N 111 0W
California City, *U.S.A.* **85 K9** 35 10N 117 55W
California Hot Springs, *U.S.A.* **85 K8** 35 51N 118 41W
Calingasta, *Argentina* **94 C2** 31 15S 69 30W
Calipatria, *U.S.A.* **85 M11** 33 8N 115 31W
Calistoga, *U.S.A.* **84 G4** 38 35N 122 35W
Calitzdorp, *S. Africa* **56 E3** 33 33S 21 42 E
Callabonna, L., *Australia* **63 D3** 29 40S 140 5 E
Callan, *Ireland* **13 D4** 52 32N 7 24W
Callander, *U.K.* **12 E4** 56 15N 4 13W
Callao, *Peru* **92 F3** 12 0S 77 0W
Calles, *Mexico* **87 C5** 23 2N 98 42W
Callicoon, *U.S.A.* **79 E9** 41 46N 75 3W
Calling Lake, *Canada* **72 B6** 55 15N 113 12W
Calliope, *Australia* **62 C5** 24 0S 151 16 E
Calne, *U.K.* **11 F6** 51 26N 2 0W
Calola, *Angola* **56 B2** 16 25S 17 48 E
Caloundra, *Australia* **63 D5** 26 45S 153 10 E
Calpella, *U.S.A.* **84 F3** 39 14N 123 12W
Calpine, *U.S.A.* **84 F6** 39 40N 120 27W
Calstock, *Canada* **70 C3** 49 47N 84 9W
Caltagirone, *Italy* **20 F6** 37 14N 14 31 E
Caltanissetta, *Italy* **20 F6** 37 29N 14 4 E
Calulo, *Angola* **52 G2** 10 1S 14 56 E
Calvert →, *Australia* **62 B2** 16 17S 137 44 E
Calvert I., *Canada* **72 C3** 51 30N 128 0W
Calvert Ra., *Australia* **60 D3** 24 0S 122 30 E
Calvi, *France* **18 E8** 42 34N 8 45 E
Calvià, *Spain* **19 C7** 39 34N 2 31 E
Calvillo, *Mexico* **86 C4** 21 51N 102 43W
Calvinia, *S. Africa* **56 E2** 31 28S 19 45 E
Calwa, *U.S.A.* **84 J7** 36 42N 119 46W
Cam →, *U.K.* **11 E8** 52 21N 0 16 E
Cam Lam, *Vietnam* **39 G7** 11 54N 109 10 E
Cam Pha, *Vietnam* **38 B6** 21 7N 107 18 E
Cam Ranh, *Vietnam* **39 G7** 11 54N 109 12 E
Cam Xuyen, *Vietnam* **38 C6** 18 15N 106 0 E
Camabatela, *Angola* **52 F3** 8 20S 15 26 E
Camacha, *Madeira* **22 D3** 32 41N 16 49W
Camacho, *Mexico* **86 C4** 24 25N 102 18W
Camacupa, *Angola* **53 G3** 11 58S 17 22 E
Camagüey, *Cuba* **88 B4** 21 20N 78 0W
Camaná, *Peru* **92 G4** 16 30S 72 50W
Camanche Reservoir, *U.S.A.* **84 G6** 38 14N 121 1W
Camaquã, *Brazil* **95 C5** 30 51S 51 49W
Camaquã →, *Brazil* **95 C5** 31 17S 51 47W
Câmara de Lobos, *Madeira* **22 D3** 32 39N 16 59W
Camargo, *Mexico* **87 B5** 26 19N 98 50W
Camargue, *France* **18 E6** 43 34N 4 34 E
Camarillo, *U.S.A.* **85 L7** 34 13N 119 2W
Camarón, C., *Honduras* **88 C2** 16 0N 85 5W
Camarones, *Argentina* **96 E3** 44 50S 65 40W
Camas, *U.S.A.* **84 E4** 45 35N 122 24W
Camas Valley, *U.S.A.* **82 E2** 43 2N 123 40W
Camballin, *Australia* **60 C3** 17 59S 124 12 E
Cambará, *Brazil* **95 A5** 23 2S 50 5W
Cambay = Khambhat, *India* **42 H5** 22 23N 72 33 E
Cambay, G. of = Khambhat, G. of, *India* **40 J8** 20 45N 72 30 E
Cambodia ■, *Asia* **38 F5** 12 15N 105 0 E
Camborne, *U.K.* **11 G2** 50 12N 5 19W
Cambrai, *France* **18 A5** 50 11N 3 14 E
Cambria, *U.S.A.* **84 K5** 35 34N 121 5W
Cambrian Mts., *U.K.* **11 E4** 52 3N 3 57W
Cambridge, *Canada* **78 C4** 43 23N 80 15W
Cambridge, *Jamaica* **88 C4** 18 18N 77 54W
Cambridge, *N.Z.* **59 G5** 37 54S 175 29 E
Cambridge, *U.K.* **11 E8** 52 12N 0 8 E
Cambridge, *Mass., U.S.A.* **79 D13** 42 22N 71 6W
Cambridge, *Minn., U.S.A.* **80 C8** 45 34N 93 13W
Cambridge, *N.Y., U.S.A.* **79 C11** 43 2N 73 22W
Cambridge, *Nebr., U.S.A.* **80 E4** 40 17N 100 10W
Cambridge, *Ohio, U.S.A.* **78 F3** 40 2N 81 35W
Cambridge Bay = Ikaluktutiak, *Canada* **68 B9** 69 10N 105 0W
Cambridge G., *Australia* **60 B4** 14 55S 128 15 E
Cambridge Springs, *U.S.A.* **78 E4** 41 48N 80 4W
Cambridgeshire □, *U.K.* **11 E7** 52 25N 0 7W
Cambuci, *Brazil* **95 A7** 21 35S 41 55W
Cambundi-Catembo, *Angola* **52 G3** 10 10S 17 35 E
Camden, *Ala., U.S.A.* **77 K2** 31 59N 87 17W
Camden, *Ark., U.S.A.* **81 J8** 33 35N 92 50W
Camden, *Maine, U.S.A.* **77 C11** 44 13N 69 4W
Camden, *N.J., U.S.A.* **79 G9** 39 56N 75 7W
Camden, *N.Y., U.S.A.* **79 C9** 43 20N 75 45W
Camden, *S.C., U.S.A.* **77 H5** 34 16N 80 36W
Camden Sd., *Australia* **60 C3** 15 27S 124 25 E
Camdenton, *U.S.A.* **81 F8** 38 1N 92 45W
Cameron, *Ariz., U.S.A.* **83 J8** 35 53N 111 25W
Cameron, *La., U.S.A.* **81 L8** 29 48N 93 20W
Cameron, *Mo., U.S.A.* **80 F7** 39 44N 94 14W
Cameron, *Tex., U.S.A.* **81 K6** 30 51N 96 59W
Cameron Highlands, *Malaysia* **39 K3** 4 27N 101 22 E
Cameron Hills, *Canada* **72 B5** 59 48N 118 0W
Cameroon ■, *Africa* **52 C2** 6 0N 12 30 E
Cameroun, Mt., *Cameroon* **52 D1** 4 13N 9 10 E
Cametá, *Brazil* **93 D9** 2 12S 49 30W
Camiguin I., *Phil.* **37 C6** 18 56N 121 55 E
Camilla, *U.S.A.* **77 K3** 31 14N 84 12W
Caminha, *Portugal* **19 B1** 41 50N 8 50W
Camino, *U.S.A.* **84 G6** 38 44N 120 41W
Camira Creek, *Australia* **63 D5** 29 15S 152 58 E
Cammal, *U.S.A.* **78 E7** 41 24N 77 28W
Camocim, *Brazil* **93 D10** 2 55S 40 50W
Camooweal, *Australia* **62 B2** 19 56S 138 7 E
Camopi, *Fr. Guiana* **93 C8** 3 12N 52 17W
Camp Borden, *Canada* **78 B5** 44 18N 79 56W
Camp Hill, *U.S.A.* **78 F8** 40 14N 76 55W
Camp Nelson, *U.S.A.* **85 J8** 36 8N 118 39W
Camp Pendleton, *U.S.A.* **85 M9** 33 16N 117 23W
Camp Verde, *U.S.A.* **83 J8** 34 34N 111 51W
Camp Wood, *U.S.A.* **81 L5** 29 40N 100 1W
Campana, *Argentina* **94 C4** 34 10S 58 55W
Campana, I., *Chile* **96 F1** 48 20S 75 20W
Campanário, *Madeira* **22 D2** 32 39N 17 2W
Campánia □, *Italy* **20 D6** 41 0N 14 30 E
Campbell, *S. Africa* **56 D3** 28 48S 23 44 E
Campbell, *Calif., U.S.A.* **84 H5** 37 17N 121 57W
Campbell, *Ohio, U.S.A.* **78 E4** 41 5N 80 37W
Campbell I., *Pac. Oc.* **64 N8** 52 30S 169 0 E
Campbell L., *Canada* **73 A7** 63 14N 106 55W
Campbell River, *Canada* **72 C3** 50 5N 125 20W
Campbell Town, *Australia* **62 G4** 41 52S 147 30 E
Campbellford, *Canada* **78 B7** 44 18N 77 48W
Campbellpur, *Pakistan* **42 C5** 33 46N 72 26 E
Campbellsville, *U.S.A.* **76 G3** 37 21N 85 20W
Campbellton, *Canada* **71 C6** 47 57N 66 43W
Campbelltown, *Australia* **63 E5** 34 4S 150 49 E
Campbeltown, *U.K.* **12 F3** 55 26N 5 36W
Campeche, *Mexico* **87 D6** 19 50N 90 32W
Campeche □, *Mexico* **87 D6** 19 50N 90 32W
Campeche, Golfo de, *Mexico* **87 D6** 19 30N 93 0W
Camperdown, *Australia* **63 F3** 38 14S 143 9 E
Camperville, *Canada* **73 C8** 51 59N 100 9W
Câmpina, *Romania* **17 F13** 45 10N 25 45 E
Campina Grande, *Brazil* **93 E11** 7 20S 35 47W
Campinas, *Brazil* **95 A6** 22 50S 47 0W
Campo Grande, *Brazil* **93 H8** 20 25S 54 40W
Campo Maíor, *Brazil* **93 D10** 4 50S 42 12W
Campo Mourão, *Brazil* **95 A5** 24 3S 52 22W
Campobasso, *Italy* **20 D6** 41 34N 14 39 E
Campos, *Brazil* **95 A7** 21 50S 41 20W
Campos Belos, *Brazil* **93 F9** 13 10S 47 3W
Campos del Port, *Spain* **22 B10** 39 26N 3 1 E
Campos Novos, *Brazil* **95 B5** 27 21S 51 50W
Camptonville, *U.S.A.* **84 F5** 39 27N 121 3W
Camptown, *U.S.A.* **79 E8** 41 44N 76 14W
Câmpulung, *Romania* **17 F13** 45 17N 25 3 E
Camrose, *Canada* **72 C6** 53 0N 112 50W
Camsell Portage, *Canada* **73 B7** 59 37N 109 15W
Çan, *Turkey* **21 D12** 40 2N 27 3 E
Can Clavo, *Spain* **22 C7** 38 57N 1 27 E
Can Creu, *Spain* **22 C7** 38 58N 1 28 E
Can Gio, *Vietnam* **39 G6** 10 25N 106 58 E
Can Tho, *Vietnam* **39 G5** 10 2N 105 46 E
Canaan, *U.S.A.* **79 D11** 42 2N 73 20W
Canada ■, *N. Amer.* **68 C10** 60 0N 100 0W
Cañada de Gómez, *Argentina* **94 C3** 32 40S 61 30W
Canadian, *U.S.A.* **81 H4** 35 55N 100 23W
Canadian →, *U.S.A.* **81 H7** 35 28N 95 3W
Canajoharie, *U.S.A.* **79 D10** 42 54N 74 35W
Çanakkale, *Turkey* **21 D12** 40 8N 26 24 E
Çanakkale Boğazı, *Turkey* **21 D12** 40 17N 26 32 E
Canal Flats, *Canada* **72 C5** 50 10N 115 48W
Canalejas, *Argentina* **94 D2** 35 15S 66 34W
Canals, *Argentina* **94 C3** 33 35S 62 53W
Canandaigua, *U.S.A.* **78 D7** 42 54N 77 17W
Canandaigua L., *U.S.A.* **78 D7** 42 47N 77 19W
Cananea, *Mexico* **86 A2** 31 0N 110 20W
Canarias, Is., *Atl. Oc.* **22 F4** 28 30N 16 0W
Canarreos, Arch. de los, *Cuba* **88 B3** 21 35N 81 40W
Canary Is. = Canarias, Is., *Atl. Oc.* **22 F4** 28 30N 16 0W
Canaseraga, *U.S.A.* **78 D7** 42 27N 77 45W
Canatlán, *Mexico* **86 C4** 24 31N 104 47W
Canaveral, C., *U.S.A.* **77 L5** 28 27N 80 32W
Canavieiras, *Brazil* **93 G11** 15 39S 39 0W
Canberra, *Australia* **63 F4** 35 15S 149 8 E
Canby, *Calif., U.S.A.* **82 F3** 41 27N 120 52W
Canby, *Minn., U.S.A.* **80 C6** 44 43N 96 16W
Canby, *Oreg., U.S.A.* **84 E4** 45 16N 122 42W
Cancún, *Mexico* **87 C7** 21 8N 86 44W
Candelaria, *Argentina* **95 B4** 27 29S 55 44W
Candelaria, *Canary Is.* **22 F3** 28 22N 16 22W
Candelo, *Australia* **63 F4** 36 47S 149 43 E
Candia = Iráklion, *Greece* **23 D7** 35 20N 25 12 E
Candle L., *Canada* **73 C7** 53 50N 105 18W
Candlemas I., *Antarctica* **5 B1** 57 3S 26 40W
Cando, *U.S.A.* **80 A5** 48 32N 99 12W
Canea = Khaniá, *Greece* **23 D6** 35 30N 24 4 E
Canelones, *Uruguay* **95 C4** 34 32S 56 17W
Cañete, *Chile* **94 D1** 37 50S 73 30W
Cañete, *Peru* **92 F3** 13 8S 76 30W
Cangas de Narcea, *Spain* **19 A2** 43 10N 6 32W
Canguaretama, *Brazil* **93 E11** 6 20S 35 5W
Canguçu, *Brazil* **95 C5** 31 22S 52 43W
Canguçu, Serra do, *Brazil* **95 C5** 31 20S 52 40W
Cangzhou, *China* **34 E9** 38 19N 116 52 E
Caniapiscau →, *Canada* **71 A6** 56 40N 69 30W
Caniapiscau, Rés. de, *Canada* **71 B6** 54 10N 69 55W
Canicattì, *Italy* **20 F5** 37 21N 13 51 E
Canim Lake, *Canada* **72 C4** 51 47N 120 54W
Canindeyu □, *Paraguay* **95 A5** 24 10S 55 0W
Canisteo, *U.S.A.* **78 D7** 42 16N 77 36W
Canisteo →, *U.S.A.* **78 D7** 42 7N 77 8W
Cañitas, *Mexico* **86 C4** 23 36N 102 43W
Çankırı, *Turkey* **25 F5** 40 40N 33 37 E
Cankuzo, *Burundi* **54 C3** 3 10S 30 31 E
Canmore, *Canada* **72 C5** 51 7N 115 18W
Cann River, *Australia* **63 F4** 37 35S 149 7 E
Canna, *U.K.* **12 D2** 57 3N 6 33W
Cannanore, *India* **40 P9** 11 53N 75 27 E
Cannes, *France* **18 E7** 43 32N 7 1 E
Canning Town = Port Canning, *India* **43 H13** 22 23N 88 40 E
Cannington, *Canada* **78 B5** 44 20N 79 2W
Cannock, *U.K.* **11 E5** 52 41N 2 1W
Cannon Ball →, *U.S.A.* **80 B4** 46 20N 100 38W
Cannondale Mt., *Australia* **62 D4** 25 13S 148 57 E
Cannonsville Reservoir, *U.S.A.* **79 D9** 42 4N 75 22W
Cannonvale, *Australia* **62 C4** 20 17S 148 43 E
Canoas, *Brazil* **95 B5** 29 56S 51 11W
Canoe L., *Canada* **73 B7** 55 10N 108 15W
Canon City, *U.S.A.* **80 F2** 38 27N 105 14W
Canora, *Canada* **73 C8** 51 40N 102 30W
Canowindra, *Australia* **63 E4** 33 35S 148 38 E
Canso, *Canada* **71 C7** 45 20N 61 0W
Cantabria □, *Spain* **19 A4** 43 10N 4 0W
Cantabrian Mts. = Cantábrica, Cordillera, *Spain* **19 A3** 43 0N 5 10W
Cantábrica, Cordillera, *Spain* **19 A3** 43 0N 5 10W
Cantal, Plomb du, *France* **18 D5** 45 3N 2 45 E
Canterbury, *Australia* **62 D3** 25 23S 141 53 E
Canterbury, *U.K.* **11 F9** 51 16N 1 6 E
Canterbury Bight, *N.Z.* **59 L3** 44 16S 171 55 E
Canterbury Plains, *N.Z.* **59 K3** 43 55S 171 22 E
Cantil, *U.S.A.* **85 K9** 35 18N 117 58W
Canton = Guangzhou, *China* **33 D6** 23 5N 113 10 E
Canton, *Ga., U.S.A.* **77 H3** 34 14N 84 29W
Canton, *Ill., U.S.A.* **80 E9** 40 33N 90 2W
Canton, *Miss., U.S.A.* **81 J9** 32 37N 90 2W
Canton, *Mo., U.S.A.* **80 E9** 40 8N 91 32W
Canton, *N.Y., U.S.A.* **79 B9** 44 36N 75 10W
Canton, *Ohio, U.S.A.* **78 F3** 40 48N 81 23W
Canton, *Pa., U.S.A.* **78 E8** 41 39N 76 51W
Canton, *S. Dak., U.S.A.* **80 D6** 43 18N 96 35W
Canton L., *U.S.A.* **81 G5** 36 6N 98 35W
Canudos, *Brazil* **92 E7** 7 13S 58 5W
Canumã →, *Brazil* **92 D7** 3 55S 59 10W
Canutama, *Brazil* **92 E6** 6 30S 64 20W
Canutillo, *U.S.A.* **83 L10** 31 55N 106 36W
Canvey, *U.K.* **11 F8** 51 31N 0 37 E
Canyon, *U.S.A.* **81 H4** 34 59N 101 55W
Canyonlands Nat. Park, *U.S.A.* **83 G9** 38 15N 110 0W
Canyonville, *U.S.A.* **82 E2** 42 56N 123 17W

Cao Bang, Vietnam 38 A6 22 40N 106 15 E
Cao He →, China 35 D13 40 10N 124 32 E
Cao Lanh, Vietnam 39 G5 10 27N 105 38 E
Cao Xian, China 34 G8 34 50N 115 35 E
Cap-aux-Meules, Canada 71 C7 47 23N 61 52W
Cap-Chat, Canada 71 C6 49 6N 66 40W
Cap-de-la-Madeleine, Canada 70 C5 46 22N 72 31W
Cap-Haïtien, Haiti 89 C5 19 40N 72 20W
Capac, U.S.A. 78 C2 43 1N 82 56W
Capanaparo →, Venezuela 92 B5 7 1N 67 7W
Cape →, Australia 62 C4 20 59S 146 51 E
Cape Barren I., Australia 62 G4 40 25S 148 15 E
Cape Breton Highlands Nat. Park, Canada 71 C7 46 50N 60 40W
Cape Breton I., Canada 71 C7 46 0N 60 30W
Cape Charles, U.S.A. 76 G8 37 16N 76 1W
Cape Coast, Ghana 50 G5 5 5N 1 15W
Cape Coral, U.S.A. 77 M5 26 33N 81 57W
Cape Dorset, Canada 69 B12 64 14N 76 32W
Cape Fear →, U.S.A. 77 H6 33 53N 78 1W
Cape Girardeau, U.S.A. 81 G10 37 19N 89 32W
Cape May, U.S.A. 76 F8 38 56N 74 56W
Cape May Point, U.S.A. 76 F8 38 56N 74 58W
Cape Province, S. Africa 53 L3 32 0S 23 0 E
Cape Tormentine, Canada 71 C7 46 8N 63 47W
Cape Town, S. Africa 56 E2 33 55S 18 22 E
Cape Verde Is. ■, Atl. Oc. 49 E1 16 0N 24 0W
Cape Vincent, U.S.A. 79 B8 44 8N 76 20W
Cape York Peninsula, Australia 62 A3 12 0S 142 30 E
Capela, Brazil 93 F11 10 30S 37 0W
Capella, Australia 62 C4 23 2S 148 1 E
Capim →, Brazil 93 D9 1 40S 47 47W
Capitan, U.S.A. 83 K11 33 35N 105 35W
Capitol Reef Nat. Park, U.S.A. 83 G8 38 15N 111 10W
Capitola, U.S.A. 84 J5 36 59N 121 57W
Capoche →, Mozam. 55 F3 15 35S 33 0 E
Capraia, Italy 18 E8 43 2N 9 50 E
Capreol, Canada 70 C3 46 43N 80 56W
Capri, Italy 20 D6 40 33N 14 14 E
Capricorn Group, Australia 62 C5 23 30S 151 55 E
Capricorn Ra., Australia 60 D2 23 20S 116 50 E
Caprivi Strip, Namibia 56 B3 18 0S 23 0 E
Captain's Flat, Australia 63 F4 35 35S 149 27 E
Caquetá →, Colombia 92 D5 1 15S 69 15W
Caracal, Romania 17 F13 44 8N 24 22 E
Caracas, Venezuela 92 A5 10 30N 66 55W
Caracol, Mato Grosso do Sul, Brazil 94 A4 22 18S 57 1W
Caracol, Piauí, Brazil 93 E10 9 15S 43 22W
Carajas, Brazil 93 E8 6 5S 50 23W
Carajás, Serra dos, Brazil 93 E8 6 0S 51 30W
Carangola, Brazil 95 A7 20 44S 42 5W
Caransebeş, Romania 17 F12 45 28N 22 18 E
Caraquet, Canada 71 C6 47 48N 64 57W
Caras, Peru 92 E3 9 3S 77 47W
Caratasca, L., Honduras 88 C3 15 20N 83 40W
Caratinga, Brazil 93 G10 19 50S 42 10W
Caraúbas, Brazil 93 E11 5 43S 37 33W
Caravaca = Caravaca de la Cruz, Spain 19 C5 38 8N 1 52W
Caravaca de la Cruz, Spain 19 C5 38 8N 1 52W
Caravelas, Brazil 93 G11 17 45S 39 15W
Caraveli, Peru 92 G4 15 45S 73 25W
Caràzinho, Brazil 95 B5 28 16S 52 46W
Carballo, Spain 19 A1 43 13N 8 41W
Carberry, Canada 73 D9 49 50N 99 25W
Carbó, Mexico 86 B2 29 42N 110 58W
Carbonara, C., Italy 20 E3 39 6N 9 31 E
Carbondale, Colo., U.S.A. 82 G10 39 24N 107 13W
Carbondale, Ill., U.S.A. 81 G10 37 44N 89 13W
Carbondale, Pa., U.S.A. 79 E9 41 35N 75 30W
Carbonear, Canada 71 C9 47 42N 53 13W
Carbónia, Italy 20 E3 39 10N 8 30 E
Carcajou, Canada 72 B5 57 47N 117 6W
Carcarana →, Argentina 94 C3 32 27S 60 48W
Carcasse, C., Haiti 89 C5 18 30N 74 28W
Carcassonne, France 18 E5 43 13N 2 20 E
Carcross, Canada 72 A2 60 13N 134 45W
Cardamon Hills, India 40 Q10 9 30N 77 15 E
Cárdenas, Cuba 88 B3 23 0N 81 30W
Cárdenas, San Luis Potosí, Mexico 87 C5 22 0N 99 41W
Cárdenas, Tabasco, Mexico 87 D6 17 59N 93 21W
Cardiff, U.K. 11 F4 51 29N 3 10W
Cardiff □, U.K. 11 F4 51 31N 3 12W
Cardiff-by-the-Sea, U.S.A. 85 M9 33 1N 117 17W
Cardigan, U.K. 11 E3 52 5N 4 40W
Cardigan B., U.K. 11 E3 52 30N 4 30W
Cardinal, Canada 79 B9 44 47N 75 23W
Cardona, Uruguay 94 C4 33 53S 57 18W
Cardoso, Ilha do, Brazil 95 B5 25 8S 47 58W
Cardston, Canada 72 D6 49 15N 113 20W
Cardwell, Australia 62 B4 18 14S 146 2 E
Careen L., Canada 73 B7 57 0N 108 11W
Carei, Romania 17 E12 47 40N 22 29 E
Careme = Ciremai, Indonesia 37 G13 6 55S 108 27 E
Carey, U.S.A. 82 E7 43 19N 113 57W
Carey, L., Australia 61 E3 29 0S 122 15 E
Carey L., Canada 73 A8 62 12N 102 55W
Carhué, Argentina 94 D3 37 10S 62 50W
Caria, Turkey 21 F13 37 20N 28 10 E
Cariacica, Brazil 93 H10 20 16S 40 25W
Caribbean Sea, W. Indies 89 D5 15 0N 75 0W
Cariboo Mts., Canada 72 C4 53 0N 121 0W
Caribou, U.S.A. 77 B12 46 52N 68 1W
Caribou →, Man., Canada 73 B10 59 20N 94 44W
Caribou →, N.W.T., Canada 72 A3 61 27N 125 45W
Caribou I., Canada 70 C2 47 22N 85 49W
Caribou Is., Canada 72 A6 61 55N 113 15W
Caribou L., Man., Canada 73 B9 59 21N 96 10W
Caribou L., Ont., Canada 70 B2 50 25N 89 5W
Caribou Mts., Canada 72 B5 59 12N 115 40W
Carichic, Mexico 86 B3 27 56N 107 3W
Carillo, Mexico 86 B4 26 50N 103 55W
Carinda, Australia 63 E4 30 28S 147 41 E
Carinhanha, Brazil 93 F10 14 15S 44 46W
Carinhanha →, Brazil 93 F10 14 20S 43 47W
Carinthia = Kärnten □, Austria 16 E8 46 52N 13 30 E
Caripito, Venezuela 92 A6 10 8N 63 6W
Carleton, Mt., Canada 71 C6 47 23N 66 53W
Carleton Place, Canada 79 A8 45 8N 76 9W
Carletonville, S. Africa 56 D4 26 23S 27 22 E
Carlin, U.S.A. 82 F5 40 43N 116 7W
Carlingford L., U.K. 13 B5 54 3N 6 9W
Carlinville, U.S.A. 80 F10 39 17N 89 53W
Carlisle, U.K. 10 C5 54 54N 2 56W
Carlisle, U.S.A. 78 F7 40 12N 77 12W
Carlos Casares, Argentina 94 D3 35 32S 61 20W
Carlos Tejedor, Argentina 94 D3 35 25S 62 25W
Carlow, Ireland 13 D5 52 50N 6 56W
Carlow □, Ireland 13 D5 52 43N 6 50W
Carlsbad, Calif., U.S.A. 85 M9 33 10N 117 21W
Carlsbad, N. Mex., U.S.A. 81 J2 32 25N 104 14W
Carlsbad Caverns Nat. Park, U.S.A. 81 J2 32 10N 104 35W
Carluke, U.K. 12 F5 55 45N 3 50W
Carlyle, Canada 73 D8 49 40N 102 20W
Carmacks, Canada 68 B6 62 5N 136 16W
Carman, Canada 73 D9 49 30N 98 0W
Carmarthen, U.K. 11 F3 51 52N 4 19W
Carmarthen B., U.K. 11 F3 51 40N 4 30W
Carmarthenshire □, U.K. 11 F3 51 55N 4 13W
Carmaux, France 18 D5 44 3N 2 10 E
Carmel, U.S.A. 79 E11 41 26N 73 41W
Carmel-by-the-Sea, U.S.A. 84 J5 36 33N 121 55W
Carmel Valley, U.S.A. 84 J5 36 29N 121 43W
Carmelo, Uruguay 94 C4 34 0S 58 20W
Carmen, Colombia 92 B3 9 43N 75 8W
Carmen, Paraguay 95 B4 27 13S 56 12W
Carmen →, Mexico 86 A3 30 42N 106 29W
Carmen, I., Mexico 86 B2 26 0N 111 20W
Carmen de Patagones, Argentina 96 E4 40 50S 63 0W
Carmensa, Argentina 94 D2 35 15S 67 40W
Carmi, Canada 72 D5 49 36N 119 8W
Carmi, U.S.A. 76 F1 38 5N 88 10W
Carmichael, U.S.A. 84 G5 38 38N 121 19W
Carmila, Australia 62 C4 21 55S 149 24 E
Carmona, Costa Rica 88 E2 10 0N 85 15W
Carmona, Spain 19 D3 37 28N 5 42W
Carn Ban, U.K. 12 D4 57 7N 4 15W
Carn Eige, U.K. 12 D3 57 17N 5 8W
Carnac, France 18 C2 47 35N 3 6W
Carnamah, Australia 61 E2 29 41S 115 53 E
Carnarvon, Australia 61 D1 24 51S 113 42 E
Carnarvon, S. Africa 56 E3 30 56S 22 8 E
Carnarvon Ra., Queens., Australia 62 D4 25 15S 148 30 E
Carnarvon Ra., W. Austral., Australia 61 E3 25 20S 120 45 E
Carnation, U.S.A. 84 C5 47 39N 121 55W
Carndonagh, Ireland 13 A4 55 16N 7 15W
Carnduff, Canada 73 D8 49 10N 101 50W
Carnegie, U.S.A. 78 F4 40 24N 80 5W
Carnegie, L., Australia 61 E3 26 5S 122 30 E
Carnic Alps = Karnische Alpen, Europe 16 E7 46 36N 13 0 E
Carniche Alpi = Karnische Alpen, Europe 16 E7 46 36N 13 0 E
Carnot, C.A.R. 52 D3 4 59N 15 56 E
Carnot, C., Australia 63 E2 34 57S 135 38 E
Carnot B., Australia 60 C3 17 20S 122 15 E
Carnoustie, U.K. 12 E6 56 30N 2 42W
Carnsore Pt., Ireland 13 D5 52 10N 6 22W
Caro, U.S.A. 76 D4 43 29N 83 24W
Carol City, U.S.A. 77 N5 25 56N 80 16W
Carolina, Brazil 93 E9 7 10S 47 30W
Carolina, Puerto Rico 89 C6 18 23N 65 58W
Carolina, S. Africa 57 D5 26 5S 30 6 E
Caroline I., Kiribati 65 H12 9 58S 150 13W
Caroline Is., Micronesia 28 J17 8 0N 150 0 E
Caroni →, Venezuela 92 B6 8 21N 62 43W
Caronie = Nébrodi, Monti, Italy 20 F6 37 54N 14 35 E
Caroona, Australia 63 E5 31 24S 150 26 E
Carpathians, Europe 17 D11 49 30N 21 0 E
Carpaţii Meridionali, Romania 17 F13 45 30N 25 0 E
Carpentaria, G. of, Australia 62 A2 14 0S 139 0 E
Carpentras, France 18 D6 44 3N 5 2 E
Carpi, Italy 20 B4 44 47N 10 53 E
Carpinteria, U.S.A. 85 L7 34 24N 119 31W
Carr Boyd Ra., Australia 60 C4 16 15S 128 35 E
Carrabelle, U.S.A. 77 L3 29 51N 84 40W
Carranza, Presa V., Mexico 86 B4 27 20N 100 50W
Carrara, Italy 18 D9 44 5N 10 6 E
Carrauntoohill, Ireland 13 D2 52 0N 9 45W
Carrick-on-Shannon, Ireland 13 C3 53 57N 8 5W
Carrick-on-Suir, Ireland 13 D4 52 21N 7 24W
Carrickfergus, U.K. 13 B6 54 43N 5 49W
Carrickmacross, Ireland 13 C5 53 59N 6 43W
Carrieton, Australia 63 E2 32 25S 138 31 E
Carrington, U.S.A. 80 B5 47 27N 99 8W
Carrizal Bajo, Chile 94 B1 28 5S 71 20W
Carrizalillo, Chile 94 B1 29 5S 71 30W
Carrizo Cr. →, U.S.A. 81 G3 36 55N 103 55W
Carrizo Springs, U.S.A. 81 L5 28 31N 99 52W
Carrizozo, U.S.A. 83 K11 33 38N 105 53W
Carroll, U.S.A. 80 D7 42 4N 94 52W
Carrollton, Ga., U.S.A. 77 J3 33 35N 85 5W
Carrollton, Ill., U.S.A. 80 F9 39 18N 90 24W
Carrollton, Ky., U.S.A. 76 F3 38 41N 85 11W
Carrollton, Mo., U.S.A. 80 F8 39 22N 93 30W
Carrollton, Ohio, U.S.A. 78 F3 40 34N 81 5W
Carron →, U.K. 12 D4 57 53N 4 22W
Carron, L., U.K. 12 D3 57 22N 5 35W
Carrot →, Canada 73 C8 53 50N 101 17W
Carrot River, Canada 73 C8 53 17N 103 35W
Carruthers, Canada 73 C7 52 52N 109 16W
Carson, Calif., U.S.A. 85 M8 33 48N 118 17W
Carson, N. Dak., U.S.A. 80 B4 46 25N 101 34W
Carson →, U.S.A. 84 F8 39 45N 118 40W
Carson City, U.S.A. 84 F7 39 10N 119 46W
Carson Sink, U.S.A. 82 G4 39 50N 118 25W
Cartagena, Colombia 92 A3 10 25N 75 33W
Cartagena, Spain 19 D5 37 38N 0 59W
Cartago, Colombia 92 C3 4 45N 75 55W
Cartago, Costa Rica 88 E3 9 50N 83 55W
Cartersville, U.S.A. 77 H3 34 10N 84 48W
Carterton, N.Z. 59 J5 41 2S 175 31 E
Carthage, Tunisia 51 A8 36 50N 10 21 E
Carthage, Ill., U.S.A. 80 E9 40 25N 91 8W
Carthage, Mo., U.S.A. 81 G7 37 11N 94 19W
Carthage, N.Y., U.S.A. 76 D8 43 59N 75 37W
Carthage, Tex., U.S.A. 81 J7 32 9N 94 20W
Cartier I., Australia 60 B3 12 31S 123 29 E
Cartwright, Canada 71 B8 53 41N 56 58W
Caruaru, Brazil 93 E11 8 15S 35 55W
Carúpano, Venezuela 92 A6 10 39N 63 15W
Caruthersville, U.S.A. 81 G10 36 11N 89 39W
Carvoeiro, Brazil 92 D6 1 30S 61 59W
Carvoeiro, C., Portugal 19 C1 39 21N 9 24W
Cary, U.S.A. 77 H6 35 47N 78 46W
Casa Grande, U.S.A. 83 K8 32 53N 111 45W
Casablanca, Chile 94 C1 33 20S 71 25W
Casablanca, Morocco 50 B4 33 36N 7 36W
Cascade, Idaho, U.S.A. 82 D5 44 31N 116 2W
Cascade, Mont., U.S.A. 82 C8 47 16N 111 42W
Cascade Locks, U.S.A. 84 E5 45 40N 121 54W
Cascade Ra., U.S.A. 84 D5 47 0N 121 30W
Cascade Reservoir, U.S.A. 82 D5 44 32N 116 3W
Cascais, Portugal 19 C1 38 41N 9 25W
Cascavel, Brazil 95 A5 24 57S 53 28W
Cáscina, Italy 20 C4 43 41N 10 33 E
Casco B., U.S.A. 77 D10 43 45N 70 0W
Caserta, Italy 20 D6 41 4N 14 20 E
Caseyr, Raas = Asir, Ras, Somali Rep. 46 E5 11 55N 51 10 E
Cashel, Ireland 13 D4 52 30N 7 53W
Casiguran, Phil. 37 A6 16 22N 122 7 E
Casilda, Argentina 94 C3 33 10S 61 10W
Casino, Australia 63 D5 28 52S 153 3 E
Casiquiare →, Venezuela 92 C5 2 1N 67 7W
Casma, Peru 92 E3 9 30S 78 20W
Casmalia, U.S.A. 85 L6 34 50N 120 32W
Caspe, Spain 19 B5 41 14N 0 1W
Casper, U.S.A. 82 E10 42 51N 106 19W
Caspian Depression, Eurasia 25 E8 47 0N 48 0 E
Caspian Sea, Eurasia 25 F9 43 0N 50 0 E
Cass Lake, U.S.A. 80 B7 47 23N 94 37W
Cassadaga, U.S.A. 78 D5 42 20N 79 19W
Casselman, Canada 79 A9 45 19N 75 5W
Casselton, U.S.A. 80 B6 46 54N 97 13W
Cassiar, Canada 72 B3 59 16N 129 40W
Cassiar Mts., Canada 72 B2 59 30N 130 30W
Cassino, Italy 20 D5 41 30N 13 49 E
Cassville, U.S.A. 81 G8 36 41N 93 52W
Castaic, U.S.A. 85 L8 34 30N 118 38W
Castalia, U.S.A. 78 E2 41 24N 82 49W
Castanhal, Brazil 93 D9 1 18S 47 55W
Castellammare di Stábia, Italy 20 D6 40 42N 14 29 E
Castelli, Argentina 94 D4 36 7S 57 47W
Castelló de la Plana, Spain 19 C5 39 58N 0 3W
Castelo, Brazil 95 A7 20 33S 41 14W
Castelo Branco, Portugal 19 C2 39 50N 7 31W
Castelsarrasin, France 18 E4 44 2N 1 7 E
Castelvetrano, Italy 20 F5 37 41N 12 47 E
Casterton, Australia 63 F3 37 30S 141 30 E
Castile, U.S.A. 78 D6 42 38N 78 3W
Castilla-La Mancha □, Spain 19 C4 39 30N 3 30W
Castilla y Leon □, Spain 19 B3 42 0N 5 0W
Castillos, Uruguay 95 C5 34 12S 53 52W
Castle Dale, U.S.A. 82 G8 39 13N 111 1W
Castle Douglas, U.K. 12 G5 54 56N 3 56W
Castle Rock, Colo., U.S.A. 80 F2 39 22N 104 51W
Castle Rock, Wash., U.S.A. 84 D4 46 17N 122 54W
Castlebar, Ireland 13 C2 53 52N 9 18W
Castleblaney, Ireland 13 B5 54 7N 6 44W
Castlederg, U.K. 13 B4 54 42N 7 35W
Castleford, U.K. 10 D6 53 43N 1 21W
Castlegar, Canada 72 D5 49 20N 117 40W
Castlemaine, Australia 63 F3 37 2S 144 12 E
Castlepollard, Ireland 13 C4 53 41N 7 19W
Castlerea, Ireland 13 C3 53 46N 8 29W
Castlereagh →, Australia 63 E4 30 12S 147 32 E
Castlereagh B., Australia 62 A2 12 10S 135 10 E
Castleton, U.S.A. 79 C11 43 37N 73 11W
Castletown, U.K. 10 C3 54 5N 4 38W
Castletown Bearhaven, Ireland 13 E2 51 39N 9 55W
Castor, Canada 72 C6 52 15N 111 50W
Castor →, Canada 70 B4 53 24N 78 58W
Castorland, U.S.A. 79 C9 43 53N 75 31W
Castres, France 18 E5 43 37N 2 13 E
Castricum, Neths. 15 B4 52 33N 4 40 E
Castries, St. Lucia 89 D7 14 2N 60 58W
Castro, Brazil 95 A6 24 45S 50 0W
Castro, Chile 96 E2 42 30S 73 50W
Castro Alves, Brazil 93 F11 12 46S 39 33W
Castroville, U.S.A. 84 J5 36 46N 121 45W
Castuera, Spain 19 C3 38 43N 5 37W
Cat Ba, Dao, Vietnam 38 B6 20 50N 107 0 E
Cat I., Bahamas 89 B4 24 30N 75 30W
Cat L., Canada 70 B1 51 40N 91 50W
Cat Lake, Canada 70 B1 51 40N 91 50W
Catacamas, Honduras 88 D2 14 54N 85 56W
Cataguases, Brazil 95 A7 21 23S 42 39W
Catalão, Brazil 93 G9 18 10S 47 57W
Çatalca, Turkey 21 D13 41 8N 28 27 E
Catalina, Canada 71 C9 48 31N 53 4W
Catalina, Chile 94 B2 25 13S 69 43W
Catalina, U.S.A. 83 K8 32 30N 110 50W
Catalonia = Cataluña □, Spain 19 B6 41 40N 1 15 E
Cataluña □, Spain 19 B6 41 40N 1 15 E
Catamarca, Argentina 94 B2 28 30S 65 50W
Catamarca □, Argentina 94 B2 27 0S 65 50W
Catanduanes □, Phil. 37 B6 13 50N 124 20 E
Catanduva, Brazil 95 A6 21 5S 48 58W
Catánia, Italy 20 F6 37 30N 15 6 E
Catanzaro, Italy 20 E7 38 54N 16 35 E
Catarman, Phil. 37 B6 12 28N 124 35 E
Cateel, Phil. 37 C7 7 47N 126 24 E
Catembe, Mozam. 57 D5 26 0S 32 33 E
Caterham, U.K. 11 F7 51 15N 0 4W
Cathcart, S. Africa 56 E4 32 18S 27 10 E
Cathlamet, U.S.A. 84 D3 46 12N 123 23W
Catlettsburg, U.S.A. 76 F4 38 25N 82 36W
Catoche, C., Mexico 87 C7 21 40N 87 8W
Catriló, Argentina 94 D3 36 26S 63 24W
Catrimani, Brazil 92 C6 0 27N 61 41W
Catrimani →, Brazil 92 C6 0 28N 61 44W
Catskill, U.S.A. 79 D11 42 14N 73 52W
Catskill Mts., U.S.A. 79 D10 42 10N 74 25W
Catt, Mt., Australia 62 A1 13 49S 134 23 E
Cattaraugus, U.S.A. 78 D6 42 22N 78 52W
Catuala, Angola 56 B2 16 25S 19 2 E
Catuane, Mozam. 57 D5 26 48S 32 18 E
Catur, Mozam. 55 E4 13 45S 35 30 E
Catwick Is., Vietnam 39 G7 10 0N 109 0 E
Cauca →, Colombia 92 B4 8 54N 74 28W
Caucaia, Brazil 93 D11 3 40S 38 35W
Caucasus Mountains, Eurasia 25 F7 42 50N 44 0 E
Caungula, Angola 52 F3 8 26S 18 38 E
Cauquenes, Chile 94 D1 36 0S 72 22W
Caura →, Venezuela 92 B6 7 38N 64 53W
Cauresi →, Mozam. 55 F3 17 8S 33 0 E
Causapscal, Canada 71 C6 48 19N 67 12W
Cauvery →, India 40 P11 11 9N 78 52 E
Caux, Pays de, France 18 B4 49 38N 0 35 E
Cavalier, U.S.A. 80 A6 48 48N 97 37W
Cavan, Ireland 13 B4 54 0N 7 22W
Cavan □, Ireland 13 C4 54 1N 7 16W
Cave Creek, U.S.A. 83 K7 33 50N 111 57W
Cavenagh Ra., Australia 61 E4 26 12S 127 55 E
Cavendish, Australia 63 F3 37 31S 142 2 E
Caviana, I., Brazil 93 C8 0 10N 50 10W
Cavite, Phil. 37 B6 14 29N 120 55 E
Cawndilla L., Australia 63 E3 32 30S 142 15 E
Cawnpore = Kanpur, India 43 F9 26 28N 80 20 E
Caxias, Brazil 93 D10 4 55S 43 20W
Caxias do Sul, Brazil 95 B5 29 10S 51 10W
Cay Sal Bank, Bahamas 88 B4 23 45N 80 0W
Cayambe, Ecuador 92 C3 0 3N 78 8W
Cayenne, Fr. Guiana 93 B8 5 5N 52 18W
Cayman Brac, Cayman Is. 88 C4 19 43N 79 49W
Cayman Is. ■, W. Indies 88 C3 19 40N 80 30W
Cayo Romano, Cuba 88 B4 22 0N 78 0W
Cayuga, Canada 78 D5 42 59N 79 50W
Cayuga, U.S.A. 79 D8 42 54N 76 44W
Cayuga L., U.S.A. 79 D8 42 41N 76 41W
Cazenovia, U.S.A. 79 D9 42 56N 75 51W
Cazombo, Angola 53 G4 11 54S 22 56 E
Ceanannus Mor, Ireland 13 C5 53 44N 6 53W
Ceará = Fortaleza, Brazil 93 D11 3 45S 38 35W
Ceará □, Brazil 93 E11 5 0S 40 0W
Ceará Mirim, Brazil 93 E11 5 38S 35 25W
Cebaco, I. de, Panama 88 E3 7 33N 81 9W
Cebollar, Argentina 94 B2 29 10S 66 35W
Cebu, Phil. 37 B6 10 18N 123 54 E
Cecil Plains, Australia 63 D5 27 30S 151 11 E
Cedar →, U.S.A. 80 E9 41 17N 91 21W
Cedar City, U.S.A. 83 H7 37 41N 113 4W
Cedar Creek Reservoir, U.S.A. 81 J6 32 11N 96 4W
Cedar Falls, Iowa, U.S.A. 80 D8 42 32N 92 27W
Cedar Falls, Wash., U.S.A. 84 C5 47 25N 121 45W
Cedar Key, U.S.A. 77 L4 29 8N 83 2W
Cedar L., Canada 73 C9 53 10N 100 0W
Cedar Rapids, U.S.A. 80 E9 41 59N 91 40W
Cedartown, U.S.A. 77 H3 34 1N 85 15W
Cedarvale, Canada 72 B3 55 1N 128 22W
Cedarville, S. Africa 57 E4 30 23S 29 3 E
Cedral, Mexico 86 C4 23 50N 100 42W
Cedro, Brazil 93 E11 6 34S 39 3W
Cedros, I. de, Mexico 86 B1 28 10N 115 20W
Ceduna, Australia 63 E1 32 7S 133 46 E
Ceerigaabo = Erigavo, Somali Rep. 46 E4 10 35N 47 20 E
Cefalù, Italy 20 E6 38 2N 14 1 E
Cegléd, Hungary 17 E10 47 11N 19 47 E
Celaya, Mexico 86 C4 20 31N 100 37W
Celebes Sea, Indonesia 37 D6 3 0N 123 0 E
Celina, U.S.A. 76 E3 40 33N 84 35W
Celje, Slovenia 16 E8 46 16N 15 18 E
Celle, Germany 16 B6 52 37N 10 4 E
Cenderwasih, Teluk, Indonesia 37 E9 3 0S 135 20 E
Center, N. Dak., U.S.A. 80 B4 47 7N 101 18W
Center, Tex., U.S.A. 81 K7 31 48N 94 11W
Centerburg, U.S.A. 78 F2 40 18N 82 42W
Centerville, Calif., U.S.A. 84 J7 36 44N 119 30W
Centerville, Iowa, U.S.A. 80 E8 40 44N 92 52W
Centerville, Pa., U.S.A. 78 F5 40 3N 79 59W
Centerville, Tenn., U.S.A. 77 H2 35 47N 87 28W
Centerville, Tex., U.S.A. 81 K7 31 16N 95 59W
Central □, Kenya 54 C4 0 30S 37 30 E
Central □, Malawi 55 E3 13 30S 33 30 E
Central □, Zambia 55 E2 14 25S 28 50 E
Central, Cordillera, Colombia 92 C4 5 0N 75 0W
Central, Cordillera, Costa Rica 88 D3 10 10N 84 5W
Central, Cordillera, Dom. Rep. 89 C5 19 15N 71 0W
Central African Rep. ■, Africa 52 C4 7 0N 20 0 E
Central America, America 66 H11 12 0N 85 0W
Central Butte, Canada 73 C7 50 48N 106 31W
Central City, Colo., U.S.A. 82 G11 39 48N 105 31W
Central City, Ky., U.S.A. 76 G2 37 18N 87 7W
Central City, Nebr., U.S.A. 80 E6 41 7N 98 0W
Central I., Kenya 54 B4 3 30N 36 0 E
Central Makran Range, Pakistan 40 F4 26 30N 64 15 E
Central Patricia, Canada 70 B1 51 30N 90 9W
Central Point, U.S.A. 82 E2 42 23N 122 55W
Central Russian Uplands, Europe 6 E13 54 0N 36 0 E
Central Siberian Plateau, Russia 28 C14 65 0N 105 0 E
Central Square, U.S.A. 79 C8 43 17N 76 9W
Centralia, Ill., U.S.A. 80 F10 38 32N 89 8W
Centralia, Mo., U.S.A. 80 F8 39 13N 92 8W
Centralia, Wash., U.S.A. 84 D4 46 43N 122 58W
Cephalonia = Kefallinía, Greece 21 E9 38 15N 20 30 E
Cepu, Indonesia 37 G14 7 9S 111 35 E
Ceram = Seram, Indonesia 37 E7 3 10S 129 0 E
Ceram Sea = Seram Sea, Indonesia 37 E7 2 30S 128 30 E
Ceredigion □, U.K. 11 E3 52 16N 4 15W
Ceres, Argentina 94 B3 29 55S 61 55W
Ceres, S. Africa 56 E2 33 21S 19 18 E
Ceres, U.S.A. 84 H6 37 35N 120 57W
Cerignola, Italy 20 D6 41 17N 15 53 E
Cerigo = Kíthira, Greece 21 F10 36 8N 23 0 E
Çerkezköy, Turkey 21 D12 41 17N 28 0 E
Cerralvo, I., Mexico 86 C3 24 20N 109 45W
Cerritos, Mexico 86 C4 22 27N 100 20W
Cerro Chato, Uruguay 95 C4 33 6S 55 8W
Cerventes, Australia 61 F2 30 31S 115 3 E
Cervera, Spain 19 B6 41 40N 1 16 E
Cesena, Italy 20 B5 44 8N 12 15 E
Cēsis, Latvia 9 H21 57 18N 25 15 E
České Budějovice, Czech Rep. 16 D8 48 55N 14 25 E
Českomoravská Vrchovina, Czech Rep. 16 D8 49 30N 15 40 E
Çeşme, Turkey 21 E12 38 20N 26 23 E
Cessnock, Australia 63 E5 32 50S 151 21 E
Cetinje, Montenegro, Yug. 21 C8 42 23N 18 59 E
Cetraro, Italy 20 E6 39 31N 15 55 E
Ceuta, N. Afr. 19 E3 35 52N 5 18W
Cévennes, France 18 D5 44 10N 3 50 E
Ceyhan, Turkey 44 B2 37 4N 35 47 E
Ceylon = Sri Lanka ■, Asia 40 R12 7 30N 80 50 E

Cha-am, *Thailand* **38 F2** 12 48N 99 58 E
Cha Pa, *Vietnam* **38 A4** 22 20N 103 47 E
Chacabuco, *Argentina* **94 C3** 34 40S 60 27W
Chachapoyas, *Peru* **92 E3** 6 15S 77 50W
Chachoengsao, *Thailand* **38 F3** 13 42N 101 5 E
Chachran, *Pakistan* **40 E7** 28 55N 70 30 E
Chachro, *Pakistan* **42 G4** 25 5N 70 15 E
Chaco □, *Argentina* **94 B3** 26 30S 61 0W
Chaco □, *Paraguay* **94 B4** 26 0S 60 0W
Chaco →, *U.S.A.* **83 H9** 36 46N 108 39W
Chaco Austral, *S. Amer.* **96 B4** 27 0S 61 30W
Chaco Boreal, *S. Amer.* **92 H6** 22 0S 60 0W
Chaco Central, *S. Amer.* **96 A4** 24 0S 61 0W
Chacon, C., *U.S.A.* **72 C2** 54 42N 132 0W
Chad ■, *Africa* **51 F8** 15 0N 17 15 E
Chad, L. = Tchad, L., *Chad* **51 F8** 13 30N 14 30 E
Chadan, *Russia* **27 D10** 51 17N 91 35 E
Chadileuvú →, *Argentina* **94 D2** 37 46S 66 0W
Chadiza, *Zambia* **55 E3** 14 45S 32 27 E
Chadron, *U.S.A.* **80 D3** 42 50N 103 0W
Chadyr-Lunga = Ciadâr-Lunga, *Moldova* **17 E15** 46 3N 28 51 E
Chae Hom, *Thailand* **38 C2** 18 43N 99 35 E
Chaem →, *Thailand* **38 C2** 18 11N 98 38 E
Chaeryŏng, *N. Korea* **35 E13** 38 24N 125 36 E
Chagai Hills = Chāh Gay Hills, *Afghan.* **40 E3** 29 30N 64 0 E
Chagda, *Russia* **27 D14** 58 45N 130 38 E
Chaghcharān, *Afghan.* **40 B4** 34 31N 65 15 E
Chagos Arch., *Ind. Oc.* **29 K11** 6 0S 72 0 E
Chagrin Falls, *U.S.A.* **78 E3** 41 26N 81 24W
Chāh Ākhvor, *Iran* **45 C8** 32 41N 59 40 E
Chāh Bahar, *Iran* **45 E9** 25 20N 60 40 E
Chāh-e Kavīr, *Iran* **45 C8** 34 29N 56 52 E
Chāh Gay Hills, *Afghan.* **40 E3** 29 30N 64 0 E
Chahar Burjak, *Afghan.* **40 D3** 30 15N 62 0 E
Chahār Mahāll va Bakhtīarī □, *Iran* **45 C6** 32 0N 49 0 E
Chaibasa, *India* **41 H14** 22 42N 85 49 E
Chainat, *Thailand* **38 E3** 15 11N 100 8 E
Chaiya, *Thailand* **39 H2** 9 23N 99 14 E
Chaj Doab, *Pakistan* **42 C5** 32 15N 73 0 E
Chajari, *Argentina* **94 C4** 30 42S 58 0W
Chak Amru, *Pakistan* **42 C6** 32 22N 75 11 E
Chakar →, *Pakistan* **42 E3** 29 29N 68 2 E
Chakari, *Zimbabwe* **57 B4** 18 5S 29 51 E
Chake Chake, *Tanzania* **54 D4** 5 15S 39 45 E
Chakhānsūr, *Afghan.* **40 D3** 31 10N 62 0 E
Chakonipau, L., *Canada* **71 A6** 56 18N 68 30W
Chakradharpur, *India* **43 H11** 22 45N 85 40 E
Chakrata, *India* **42 D7** 30 42N 77 51 E
Chakwal, *Pakistan* **42 C5** 32 56N 72 53 E
Chala, *Peru* **92 G4** 15 48S 74 20W
Chalchihuites, *Mexico* **86 C4** 23 29N 103 53W
Chalcis = Khalkís, *Greece* **21 E10** 38 27N 23 42 E
Chaleur B., *Canada* **71 C6** 47 55N 65 30W
Chalfant, *U.S.A.* **84 H8** 37 32N 118 21W
Chalhuanca, *Peru* **92 F4** 14 15S 73 15W
Chalisgaon, *India* **40 J9** 20 30N 75 10 E
Chalk River, *Canada* **70 C4** 46 1N 77 27W
Chalky Inlet, *N.Z.* **59 M1** 46 3S 166 31 E
Challapata, *Bolivia* **92 G5** 18 53S 66 50W
Challis, *U.S.A.* **82 D6** 44 30N 114 14W
Chalmette, *U.S.A.* **81 L10** 29 56N 89 58W
Chalon-sur-Saône, *France* **18 C6** 46 48N 4 50 E
Châlons-en-Champagne, *France* **18 B6** 48 58N 4 20 E
Chalyaphum, *Thailand* **38 E4** 15 48N 102 2 E
Cham, Cu Lao, *Vietnam* **38 E7** 15 57N 108 30 E
Chama, *U.S.A.* **83 H10** 36 54N 106 35W
Chamaicó, *Argentina* **94 D3** 35 3S 64 58W
Chaman, *Pakistan* **40 D5** 30 58N 66 25 E
Chamba, *India* **42 C7** 32 35N 76 10 E
Chamba, *Tanzania* **55 E4** 11 37S 37 0 E
Chambal →, *India* **43 F8** 26 29N 79 15 E
Chamberlain, *U.S.A.* **80 D5** 43 49N 99 20W
Chamberlain →, *Australia* **60 C4** 15 30S 127 54 E
Chamberlain L., *U.S.A.* **77 B11** 46 14N 69 19W
Chambers, *U.S.A.* **83 J9** 35 11N 109 26W
Chambersburg, *U.S.A.* **76 F7** 39 56N 77 40W
Chambéry, *France* **18 D6** 45 34N 5 55 E
Chambeshi →, *Zambia* **52 G6** 11 53S 29 48 E
Chambly, *Canada* **79 A11** 45 27N 73 17W
Chambord, *Canada* **71 C5** 48 25N 72 6W
Chamchamal, *Iraq* **44 C5** 35 32N 44 50 E
Chamela, *Mexico* **86 D3** 19 32N 105 5W
Chamical, *Argentina* **94 C2** 30 22S 66 27W
Chamkar Luong, *Cambodia* **39 G4** 11 0N 103 45 E
Chamoli, *India* **43 D8** 30 24N 79 21 E
Chamonix-Mont Blanc, *France* **18 D7** 45 55N 6 51 E
Chamouchouane →, *Canada* **70 C5** 48 37N 72 20W
Champa, *India* **43 H10** 22 2N 82 43 E
Champagne, *Canada* **72 A1** 60 49N 136 30W
Champagne, *France* **18 B6** 48 40N 4 20 E
Champaign, *U.S.A.* **76 E1** 40 7N 88 15W
Champassak, *Laos* **38 E5** 14 53N 105 52 E
Champawat, *India* **43 E9** 29 20N 80 6 E
Champdoré, L., *Canada* **71 A6** 55 55N 65 49W
Champion, *U.S.A.* **78 E4** 41 19N 80 51W
Champlain, *U.S.A.* **79 B11** 44 59N 73 27W
Champlain, L., *U.S.A.* **79 B11** 44 40N 73 20W
Champotón, *Mexico* **87 D6** 19 20N 90 50W
Champua, *India* **43 H11** 22 5N 85 40 E
Chana, *Thailand* **39 J3** 6 55N 100 44 E
Chañaral, *Chile* **94 B1** 26 23S 70 40W
Chanārān, *Iran* **45 B8** 36 39N 59 6 E
Chanasma, *India* **42 H5** 23 44N 72 5 E
Chanco, *Chile* **94 D1** 35 44S 72 32W
Chand, *India* **43 J8** 21 57N 79 7 E
Chandan, *India* **43 G12** 24 38N 86 40 E
Chandan Chauki, *India* **43 E9** 28 33N 80 47 E
Chandannagar, *India* **43 H13** 22 52N 88 24 E
Chandausi, *India* **43 E8** 28 27N 78 49 E
Chandeleur Is., *U.S.A.* **81 L10** 29 55N 88 57W
Chandeleur Sd., *U.S.A.* **81 L10** 29 55N 89 0W
Chandigarh, *India* **42 D7** 30 43N 76 47 E
Chandil, *India* **43 H12** 22 58N 86 3 E
Chandler, *Australia* **63 D1** 27 0S 133 19 E
Chandler, *Canada* **71 C7** 48 18N 64 46W
Chandler, *Ariz., U.S.A.* **83 K8** 33 18N 111 50W
Chandler, *Okla., U.S.A.* **81 H6** 35 42N 96 53W
Chandod, *India* **42 J5** 21 59N 73 28 E
Chandpur, *Bangla.* **41 H17** 23 8N 90 45 E
Chandrapur, *India* **40 K11** 19 57N 79 25 E
Chānf, *Iran* **45 E9** 26 38N 60 29 E
Chang, *Pakistan* **42 F3** 26 59N 68 30 E
Chang, Ko, *Thailand* **39 F4** 12 0N 102 23 E
Ch'ang Chiang = Chang Jiang →, *China* **33 C7** 31 48N 121 10 E
Chang Jiang →, *China* **33 C7** 31 48N 121 10 E
Changa, *India* **43 C7** 33 53N 77 35 E
Changanacheri, *India* **40 Q10** 9 25N 76 31 E
Changane →, *Mozam.* **57 C5** 24 30S 33 30 E
Changbai, *China* **35 D15** 41 25N 128 5 E
Changbai Shan, *China* **35 C15** 42 20N 129 0 E
Changchiak'ou = Zhangjiakou, *China* **34 D8** 40 48N 114 55 E
Ch'angchou = Changzhou, *China* **33 C6** 31 47N 119 58 E
Changchun, *China* **35 C13** 43 57N 125 17 E
Changchunling, *China* **35 B13** 45 18N 125 27 E
Changde, *China* **33 D6** 29 4N 111 35 E
Changdo-ri, *N. Korea* **35 E14** 38 30N 127 40 E
Changhai = Shanghai, *China* **33 C7** 31 15N 121 26 E
Changhua, *Taiwan* **33 D7** 24 2N 120 30 E
Changhŭng, *S. Korea* **35 G14** 34 41N 126 52 E
Changhŭngni, *N. Korea* **35 D15** 40 24N 128 19 E
Changjiang, *China* **38 C7** 19 20N 108 55 E
Changjin, *N. Korea* **35 D14** 40 23N 127 15 E
Changjin-chŏsuji, *N. Korea* **35 D14** 40 30N 127 15 E
Changli, *China* **35 E10** 39 40N 119 13 E
Changling, *China* **35 B12** 44 20N 123 58 E
Changlun, *Malaysia* **39 J3** 6 25N 100 26 E
Changping, *China* **34 D9** 40 14N 116 12 E
Changsha, *China* **33 D6** 28 12N 113 0 E
Changwu, *China* **34 G4** 35 10N 107 45 E
Changyi, *China* **35 F10** 36 40N 119 30 E
Changyŏn, *N. Korea* **35 E13** 38 15N 125 6 E
Changyuan, *China* **34 G8** 35 15N 114 42 E
Changzhi, *China* **34 F7** 36 10N 113 6 E
Changzhou, *China* **33 C6** 31 47N 119 58 E
Chanhanga, *Angola* **56 B1** 16 0S 14 8 E
Channapatna, *India* **40 N10** 12 40N 77 15 E
Channel Is., *U.K.* **11 H5** 49 19N 2 24W
Channel Is., *U.S.A.* **85 M7** 33 40N 119 15W
Channel Islands Nat. Park, *U.S.A.* **85 M8** 33 30N 119 0W
Channel-Port aux Basques, *Canada* **71 C8** 47 30N 59 9W
Channel Tunnel, *Europe* **11 F9** 51 0N 1 30 E
Channing, *U.S.A.* **81 H3** 35 41N 102 20W
Chantada, *Spain* **19 A2** 42 36N 7 46W
Chanthaburi, *Thailand* **38 F4** 12 38N 102 12 E
Chantrey Inlet, *Canada* **68 B10** 67 48N 96 20W
Chanute, *U.S.A.* **81 G7** 37 41N 95 27W
Chao Phraya →, *Thailand* **38 F3** 13 32N 100 36 E
Chao Phraya Lowlands, *Thailand* **38 E3** 15 30N 100 0 E
Chaocheng, *China* **34 F8** 36 4N 115 37 E
Chaoyang, *China* **35 D11** 41 35N 120 22 E
Chaozhou, *China* **33 D6** 23 42N 116 32 E
Chapais, *Canada* **70 C5** 49 47N 74 51W
Chapala, *Mozam.* **55 F4** 15 50S 37 35 E
Chapala, L. de, *Mexico* **86 C4** 20 10N 103 20W
Chapayev, *Kazakstan* **25 D9** 50 25N 51 10 E
Chapayevsk, *Russia* **24 D8** 53 0N 49 40 E
Chapecó, *Brazil* **95 B5** 27 14S 52 41W
Chapel Hill, *U.S.A.* **77 H6** 35 55N 79 4W
Chapleau, *Canada* **70 C3** 47 50N 83 24W
Chaplin, *Canada* **73 C7** 50 28N 106 40W
Chaplin L., *Canada* **73 C7** 50 22N 106 36W
Chappell, *U.S.A.* **80 E3** 41 6N 102 28W
Chapra = Chhapra, *India* **43 G11** 25 48N 84 44 E
Chara, *Russia* **27 D12** 56 54N 118 20 E
Charadai, *Argentina* **94 B4** 27 35S 59 55W
Charagua, *Bolivia* **92 G6** 19 45S 63 10W
Charambirá, Punta, *Colombia* **92 C3** 4 16N 77 32W
Charaña, *Bolivia* **92 G5** 17 30S 69 25W
Charanwala, *India* **42 F5** 27 51N 72 10 E
Charata, *Argentina* **94 B3** 27 13S 61 14W
Charcas, *Mexico* **86 C4** 23 10N 101 20W
Chard, *U.K.* **11 G5** 50 52N 2 58W
Chardon, *U.S.A.* **78 E3** 41 35N 81 12W
Chardzhou = Chärjew, *Turkmenistan* **26 F7** 39 6N 63 34 E
Charente →, *France* **18 D3** 45 57N 1 5W
Chari →, *Chad* **51 F8** 12 58N 14 31 E
Chārīkār, *Afghan.* **40 B6** 35 0N 69 10 E
Chariton →, *U.S.A.* **80 F8** 39 19N 92 58W
Chärjew, *Turkmenistan* **26 F7** 39 6N 63 34 E
Charkhari, *India* **43 G8** 25 24N 79 45 E
Charkhi Dadri, *India* **42 E7** 28 37N 76 17 E
Charleroi, *Belgium* **15 D4** 50 24N 4 27 E
Charleroi, *U.S.A.* **78 F5** 40 9N 79 57W
Charles, C., *U.S.A.* **76 G8** 37 7N 75 58W
Charles City, *U.S.A.* **80 D8** 43 4N 92 41W
Charles L., *Canada* **73 B6** 59 50N 110 33W
Charles Town, *U.S.A.* **76 F7** 39 17N 77 52W
Charleston, *Ill., U.S.A.* **76 F1** 39 30N 88 10W
Charleston, *Miss., U.S.A.* **81 H9** 34 1N 90 4W
Charleston, *Mo., U.S.A.* **81 G10** 36 55N 89 21W
Charleston, *S.C., U.S.A.* **77 J6** 32 46N 79 56W
Charleston, *W. Va., U.S.A.* **76 F5** 38 21N 81 38W
Charleston L., *Canada* **79 B9** 44 32N 76 0W
Charleston Peak, *U.S.A.* **85 J11** 36 16N 115 42W
Charlestown, *Ireland* **13 C3** 53 58N 8 48W
Charlestown, *S. Africa* **57 D4** 27 26S 29 53 E
Charlestown, *Ind., U.S.A.* **76 F3** 38 27N 85 40W
Charlestown, *N.H., U.S.A.* **79 C12** 43 14N 72 25W
Charleville = Rath Luirc, *Ireland* **13 D3** 52 21N 8 40W
Charleville, *Australia* **63 D4** 26 24S 146 15 E
Charleville-Mézières, *France* **18 B6** 49 44N 4 40 E
Charlevoix, *U.S.A.* **76 C3** 45 19N 85 16W
Charlotte, *Mich., U.S.A.* **76 D3** 42 34N 84 50W
Charlotte, *N.C., U.S.A.* **77 H5** 35 13N 80 51W
Charlotte, *Vt., U.S.A.* **79 B11** 44 19N 73 14W
Charlotte Amalie, *U.S. Virgin Is.* **89 C7** 18 21N 64 56W
Charlotte Harbor, *U.S.A.* **77 M4** 26 50N 82 10W
Charlotte L., *Canada* **72 C3** 52 12N 125 19W
Charlottesville, *U.S.A.* **76 F6** 38 2N 78 30W
Charlottetown, *Nfld., Canada* **71 B8** 52 46N 56 7W
Charlottetown, *P.E.I., Canada* **71 C7** 46 14N 63 8W
Charlton, *Australia* **63 F3** 36 16S 143 24 E
Charlton, *U.S.A.* **80 E8** 40 59N 93 20W
Charlton I., *Canada* **70 B4** 52 0N 79 20W
Charny, *Canada* **71 C5** 46 43N 71 15W
Charolles, *France* **18 C6** 46 27N 4 16 E
Charre, *Mozam.* **55 F4** 17 13S 35 10 E
Charsadda, *Pakistan* **42 B4** 34 7N 71 45 E
Charters Towers, *Australia* **62 C4** 20 5S 146 13 E
Chartres, *France* **18 B4** 48 29N 1 30 E
Chascomús, *Argentina* **94 D4** 35 30S 58 0W
Chasefu, *Zambia* **55 E3** 11 55S 33 8 E
Chashma Barrage, *Pakistan* **42 C4** 32 27N 71 20 E
Chāt, *Iran* **45 B7** 37 59N 55 16 E
Châteaubriant, *France* **18 C3** 47 43N 1 23W
Chateaugay, *U.S.A.* **79 B10** 44 56N 74 5W
Châteauguay, L., *Canada* **71 A5** 56 26N 70 3W
Châteaulin, *France* **18 B1** 48 11N 4 8W
Châteauroux, *France* **18 C4** 46 50N 1 40 E
Châtellerault, *France* **18 C4** 46 50N 0 30 E
Chatham = Miramichi, *Canada* **71 C6** 47 2N 65 28W
Chatham, *Canada* **78 D2** 42 24N 82 11W
Chatham, *U.K.* **11 F8** 51 22N 0 32 E
Chatham, *U.S.A.* **79 D11** 42 21N 73 36W
Chatham Is., *Pac. Oc.* **64 M10** 44 0S 176 40W
Chatmohar, *Bangla.* **43 G13** 24 15N 89 15 E
Chatra, *India* **43 G11** 24 12N 84 56 E
Chatrapur, *India* **41 K14** 19 22N 85 2 E
Chats, L. des, *Canada* **79 A8** 45 30N 76 20W
Chatsu, *India* **42 F6** 26 36N 75 57 E
Chatsworth, *Canada* **78 B4** 44 27N 80 54W
Chatsworth, *Zimbabwe* **55 F3** 19 38S 31 13 E
Chattahoochee, *U.S.A.* **77 K3** 30 42N 84 51W
Chattahoochee →, *U.S.A.* **77 K3** 30 54N 84 57W
Chattanooga, *U.S.A.* **77 H3** 35 3N 85 19W
Chatteris, *U.K.* **11 E8** 52 28N 0 2 E
Chaturat, *Thailand* **38 E3** 15 40N 101 51 E
Chau Doc, *Vietnam* **39 G5** 10 42N 105 7 E
Chaukan Pass, *Burma* **41 F20** 27 0N 97 15 E
Chaumont, *France* **18 B6** 48 7N 5 8 E
Chaumont, *U.S.A.* **79 B8** 44 4N 76 8W
Chautauqua L., *U.S.A.* **78 D5** 42 10N 79 24W
Chauvin, *Canada* **73 C6** 52 45N 110 10W
Chaves, *Brazil* **93 D9** 0 15S 49 55W
Chaves, *Portugal* **19 B2** 41 45N 7 32W
Chawang, *Thailand* **39 H2** 8 25N 99 30 E
Chaykovskiy, *Russia* **24 C9** 56 47N 54 9 E
Chazy, *U.S.A.* **79 B11** 44 53N 73 26W
Cheb, *Czech Rep.* **16 C7** 50 9N 12 28 E
Cheboksary, *Russia* **24 C8** 56 8N 47 12 E
Cheboygan, *U.S.A.* **76 C3** 45 39N 84 29W
Chech, Erg, *Africa* **50 D5** 25 0N 2 15W
Chechenia □, *Russia* **25 F8** 43 30N 45 29 E
Checheno-Ingush Republic = Chechenia □, *Russia* **25 F8** 43 30N 45 29 E
Chechnya = Chechenia □, *Russia* **25 F8** 43 30N 45 29 E
Chech'ŏn, *S. Korea* **35 F15** 37 8N 128 12 E
Checotah, *U.S.A.* **81 H7** 35 28N 95 31W
Chedabucto B., *Canada* **71 C7** 45 25N 61 8W
Cheduba I., *Burma* **41 K18** 18 45N 93 40 E
Cheepie, *Australia* **63 D4** 26 33S 145 1 E
Chegdomyn, *Russia* **27 D14** 51 7N 133 1 E
Chegga, *Mauritania* **50 C4** 25 27N 5 40W
Chegutu, *Zimbabwe* **55 F3** 18 10S 30 14 E
Chehalis, *U.S.A.* **84 D4** 46 40N 122 58W
Chehalis →, *U.S.A.* **84 D3** 46 57N 123 50W
Cheju do, *S. Korea* **35 H14** 33 29N 126 34 E
Chekiang = Zhejiang □, *China* **33 D7** 29 0N 120 0 E
Chela, Sa. da, *Angola* **56 B1** 16 20S 13 20 E
Chelan, *U.S.A.* **82 C4** 47 51N 120 1W
Chelan, L., *U.S.A.* **82 B3** 48 11N 120 30W
Cheleken, *Turkmenistan* **25 G9** 39 34N 53 16 E
Cheleken Yarymadasy, *Turkmenistan* **45 B7** 39 30N 53 15 E
Chelforó, *Argentina* **96 D3** 39 0S 66 33W
Chelkar = Shalqar, *Kazakstan* **26 E6** 47 48N 59 39 E
Chelkar Tengiz, Solonchak, *Kazakstan* **26 E7** 48 5N 63 7 E
Chełm, *Poland* **17 C12** 51 8N 23 30 E
Chełmno, *Poland* **17 B10** 53 20N 18 30 E
Chelmsford, *U.K.* **11 F8** 51 44N 0 29 E
Chelsea, *U.S.A.* **79 C12** 43 59N 72 27W
Cheltenham, *U.K.* **11 F5** 51 54N 2 4W
Chelyabinsk, *Russia* **26 D7** 55 10N 61 24 E
Chelyuskin, C., *Russia* **28 B14** 77 30N 103 0 E
Chemainus, *Canada* **84 B3** 48 55N 123 42W
Chemba, *Mozam.* **53 H6** 17 9S 34 53 E
Chemnitz, *Germany* **16 C7** 50 51N 12 54 E
Chemult, *U.S.A.* **82 E3** 43 14N 121 47W
Chen, Gora, *Russia* **27 C15** 65 16N 141 50 E
Chenab →, *Pakistan* **42 D4** 30 23N 71 2 E
Chenango Forks, *U.S.A.* **79 D9** 42 15N 75 51W
Cheney, *U.S.A.* **82 C5** 47 30N 117 35W
Cheng Xian, *China* **34 H3** 33 43N 105 42 E
Chengcheng, *China* **34 G5** 35 8N 109 56 E
Chengchou = Zhengzhou, *China* **34 G7** 34 45N 113 34 E
Chengde, *China* **35 D9** 40 59N 117 58 E
Chengdu, *China* **32 C5** 30 38N 104 2 E
Chenggu, *China* **34 H4** 33 10N 107 21 E
Chengjiang, *China* **32 D5** 24 39N 103 0 E
Ch'engmai, *China* **38 C7** 19 50N 109 58 E
Ch'engtu = Chengdu, *China* **32 C5** 30 38N 104 2 E
Chengwu, *China* **34 G8** 34 58N 115 50 E
Chengyang, *China* **35 F11** 36 18N 120 21 E
Chenjiagang, *China* **35 G10** 34 23N 119 47 E
Chenkán, *Mexico* **87 D6** 19 8N 90 58W
Chennai, *India* **40 N12** 13 8N 80 19 E
Cheo Reo, *Vietnam* **36 B3** 13 25N 108 28 E
Cheom Ksan, *Cambodia* **38 E5** 14 13N 104 56 E
Chepén, *Peru* **92 E3** 7 15S 79 23W
Chepes, *Argentina* **94 C2** 31 20S 66 35W
Chepo, *Panama* **88 E4** 9 10N 79 6W
Chepstow, *U.K.* **11 F5** 51 38N 2 41W
Cheptulil, Mt., *Kenya* **54 B4** 1 25N 35 35 E
Chequamegon B., *U.S.A.* **80 B9** 46 40N 90 30W
Cher →, *France* **18 C4** 47 21N 0 29 E
Cheraw, *U.S.A.* **77 H6** 34 42N 79 53W
Cherbourg, *France* **18 B3** 49 39N 1 40W
Cherdyn, *Russia* **24 B10** 60 24N 56 29 E
Cheremkhovo, *Russia* **27 D11** 53 8N 103 1 E
Cherepanovo, *Russia* **26 D9** 54 15N 83 30 E
Cherepovets, *Russia* **24 C6** 59 5N 37 55 E
Chergui, Chott ech, *Algeria* **50 B6** 34 21N 0 25 E
Cherikov = Cherykaw, *Belarus* **17 B16** 53 32N 31 20 E
Cherkasy, *Ukraine* **25 E5** 49 27N 32 4 E
Cherkessk, *Russia* **25 F7** 44 15N 42 5 E
Cherlak, *Russia* **26 D8** 54 15N 74 55 E
Chernaya, *Russia* **27 B9** 70 30N 89 10 E
Chernigov = Chernihiv, *Ukraine* **24 D5** 51 28N 31 20 E
Chernihiv, *Ukraine* **24 D5** 51 28N 31 20 E
Chernivtsi, *Ukraine* **17 D13** 48 15N 25 52 E
Chernobyl = Chornobyl, *Ukraine* **17 C16** 51 20N 30 15 E
Chernogorsk, *Russia* **27 D10** 53 49N 91 18 E
Chernovtsy = Chernivtsi, *Ukraine* **17 D13** 48 15N 25 52 E
Chernyakhovsk, *Russia* **9 J19** 54 36N 21 48 E
Chernysheyskiy, *Russia* **27 C12** 63 0N 112 30 E
Cherokee, *Iowa, U.S.A.* **80 D7** 42 45N 95 33W
Cherokee, *Okla., U.S.A.* **81 G5** 36 45N 98 21W
Cherokee Village, *U.S.A.* **81 G9** 36 17N 91 30W
Cherokees, Grand Lake O' The, *U.S.A.* **81 G7** 36 28N 95 2W
Cherrapunji, *India* **41 G17** 25 17N 91 47 E
Cherry Valley, *Calif., U.S.A.* **85 M10** 33 59N 116 57W
Cherry Valley, *N.Y., U.S.A.* **79 D10** 42 48N 74 45W
Cherskiy, *Russia* **27 C17** 68 45N 161 18 E
Cherskogo Khrebet, *Russia* **27 C15** 65 0N 143 0 E
Cherven, *Belarus* **17 B15** 53 45N 28 28 E
Chervonohrad, *Ukraine* **17 C13** 50 25N 24 10 E
Cherwell →, *U.K.* **11 F6** 51 44N 1 14W
Cherykaw, *Belarus* **17 B16** 53 32N 31 20 E
Chesapeake, *U.S.A.* **76 G7** 36 50N 76 17W
Chesapeake B., *U.S.A.* **76 G7** 38 0N 76 10W
Cheshire □, *U.K.* **10 D5** 53 14N 2 30W
Cheshskaya Guba, *Russia* **24 A8** 67 20N 47 0 E
Cheshunt, *U.K.* **11 F7** 51 43N 0 1W
Chesil Beach, *U.K.* **11 G5** 50 37N 2 33W
Chesley, *Canada* **78 B3** 44 17N 81 5W
Chester, *U.K.* **10 D5** 53 12N 2 53W
Chester, *Calif., U.S.A.* **82 F3** 40 19N 121 14W
Chester, *Ill., U.S.A.* **81 G10** 37 55N 89 49W
Chester, *Mont., U.S.A.* **82 B8** 48 31N 110 58W
Chester, *Pa., U.S.A.* **76 F8** 39 51N 75 22W
Chester, *S.C., U.S.A.* **77 H5** 34 43N 81 12W
Chester, *Vt., U.S.A.* **79 C12** 43 16N 72 36W
Chester, *W. Va., U.S.A.* **78 F4** 40 37N 80 34W
Chester-le-Street, *U.K.* **10 C6** 54 51N 1 34W
Chesterfield, *U.K.* **10 D6** 53 15N 1 25W
Chesterfield, Is., *N. Cal.* **64 J7** 19 52S 158 15 E
Chesterfield Inlet, *Canada* **68 B10** 63 30N 90 45W
Chesterton Ra., *Australia* **63 D4** 25 30S 147 27 E
Chestertown, *U.S.A.* **79 C11** 43 40N 73 48W
Chesterville, *Canada* **79 A9** 45 6N 75 14W
Chestnut Ridge, *U.S.A.* **78 F5** 40 20N 79 10W
Chesuncook L., *U.S.A.* **77 C11** 46 0N 69 21W
Chéticamp, *Canada* **71 C7** 46 37N 60 59W
Chetumal, *Mexico* **87 D7** 18 30N 88 20W
Chetumal, B. de, *Mexico* **87 D7** 18 40N 88 10W
Chetwynd, *Canada* **72 B4** 55 45N 121 36W
Cheviot, The, *U.K.* **10 B5** 55 29N 2 9W
Cheviot Hills, *U.K.* **10 B5** 55 20N 2 30W
Cheviot Ra., *Australia* **62 D3** 25 20S 143 45 E
Chew Bahir, *Ethiopia* **46 G2** 4 40N 36 50 E
Chewelah, *U.S.A.* **82 B5** 48 17N 117 43W
Cheyenne, *Okla., U.S.A.* **81 H5** 35 37N 99 40W
Cheyenne, *Wyo., U.S.A.* **80 E2** 41 8N 104 49W
Cheyenne →, *U.S.A.* **80 C4** 44 41N 101 18W
Cheyenne Wells, *U.S.A.* **80 F3** 38 49N 102 21W
Cheyne B., *Australia* **61 F2** 34 35S 118 50 E
Chhabra, *India* **42 G7** 24 40N 76 54 E
Chhaktala, *India* **42 H6** 22 6N 74 11 E
Chhapra, *India* **43 G11** 25 48N 84 44 E
Chhata, *India* **42 F7** 27 42N 77 30 E
Chhatarpur, *Jharkhand, India* **43 G11** 24 23N 84 11 E
Chhatarpur, *Mad. P., India* **43 G8** 24 55N 79 35 E
Chhattisgarh □, *India* **43 J10** 22 0N 82 0 E
Chhep, *Cambodia* **38 F5** 13 45N 105 24 E
Chhindwara, *Mad. P., India* **43 H8** 23 3N 79 29 E
Chhindwara, *Mad. P., India* **43 H8** 22 2N 78 59 E
Chhlong, *Cambodia* **39 F5** 12 15N 105 58 E
Chhota Tawa →, *India* **42 H7** 22 14N 76 36 E
Chhoti Kali Sindh →, *India* **42 G6** 24 2N 75 31 E
Chhuikhadan, *India* **43 J9** 21 32N 80 59 E
Chhuk, *Cambodia* **39 G5** 10 46N 104 28 E
Chi →, *Thailand* **38 E5** 15 11N 104 43 E
Chiai, *Taiwan* **33 D7** 23 29N 120 25 E
Chiamboni, *Somali Rep.* **52 E8** 1 39S 41 35 E
Chiamussu = Jiamusi, *China* **33 B8** 46 40N 130 26 E
Chiang Dao, *Thailand* **38 C2** 19 22N 98 58 E
Chiang Kham, *Thailand* **38 C3** 19 32N 100 18 E
Chiang Khan, *Thailand* **38 D3** 17 52N 101 36 E
Chiang Khong, *Thailand* **38 B3** 20 17N 100 24 E
Chiang Mai, *Thailand* **38 C2** 18 47N 98 59 E
Chiang Rai, *Thailand* **38 C2** 19 52N 99 50 E
Chiang Saen, *Thailand* **38 B3** 20 16N 100 5 E
Chiapa →, *Mexico* **87 D6** 16 42N 93 0W
Chiapa de Corzo, *Mexico* **87 D6** 16 42N 93 0W
Chiapas □, *Mexico* **87 D6** 17 0N 92 45W
Chiautla, *Mexico* **87 D5** 18 18N 98 34W
Chiávari, *Italy* **18 D8** 44 19N 9 19 E
Chiavenna, *Italy* **18 C8** 46 19N 9 24 E
Chiba, *Japan* **31 G10** 35 30N 140 7 E
Chiba □, *Japan* **31 G10** 35 30N 140 20 E
Chibabava, *Mozam.* **57 C5** 20 17S 33 35 E
Chibemba, *Cunene, Angola* **53 H2** 15 48S 14 8 E
Chibemba, *Huila, Angola* **56 B2** 16 20S 15 20 E
Chibi, *Zimbabwe* **57 C5** 20 18S 30 25 E
Chibia, *Angola* **53 H2** 15 10S 13 42 E
Chibougamau, *Canada* **70 C5** 49 56N 74 24W
Chibougamau, L., *Canada* **70 C5** 49 50N 74 20W
Chibuto, *Mozam.* **57 C5** 24 40S 33 33 E
Chic-Chocs, Mts., *Canada* **71 C6** 48 55N 66 0W
Chicacole = Srikakulam, *India* **41 K13** 18 14N 83 58 E
Chicago, *U.S.A.* **76 E2** 41 53N 87 38W
Chicago Heights, *U.S.A.* **76 E2** 41 30N 87 38W
Chichagof I., *U.S.A.* **68 C6** 57 30N 135 30W
Chichén-Itzá, *Mexico* **87 C7** 20 40N 88 36W
Chicheng, *China* **34 D8** 40 55N 115 55 E
Chichester, *U.K.* **11 G7** 50 50N 0 47W
Chichester Ra., *Australia* **60 D2** 22 12S 119 15 E
Chichibu, *Japan* **31 F9** 35 59N 139 10 E
Ch'ich'ihaerh = Qiqihar, *China* **27 E13** 47 26N 124 0 E
Chicholi, *India* **42 H8** 22 1N 77 40 E
Chickasha, *U.S.A.* **81 H6** 35 3N 97 58W
Chiclana de la Frontera, *Spain* **19 D2** 36 26N 6 9W
Chiclayo, *Peru* **92 E3** 6 42S 79 50W
Chico, *U.S.A.* **84 F5** 39 44N 121 50W
Chico →, *Chubut, Argentina* **96 E3** 44 0S 67 0W
Chico →, *Santa Cruz, Argentina* **96 G3** 50 0S 68 30W
Chicomo, *Mozam.* **57 C5** 24 31S 34 6 E
Chicontepec, *Mexico* **87 C5** 20 58N 98 10W
Chicopee, *U.S.A.* **79 D12** 42 9N 72 37W

Chicoutimi, *Canada* **71 C5** 48 28N 71 5W
Chicualacuala, *Mozam.* **57 C5** 22 6S 31 42 E
Chidambaram, *India* **40 P11** 11 20N 79 45 E
Chidenguele, *Mozam.* **57 C5** 24 55S 34 11 E
Chidley, C., *Canada* **69 B13** 60 23N 64 26W
Chiducuane, *Mozam.* **57 C5** 24 35S 34 25 E
Chiede, *Angola* **56 B2** 17 15S 16 22 E
Chiefs Pt., *Canada* **78 B3** 44 41N 81 18W
Chiem Hoa, *Vietnam* **38 A5** 22 12N 105 17 E
Chiemsee, *Germany* **16 E7** 47 53N 12 28 E
Chiengi, *Zambia* **55 D2** 8 45S 29 10 E
Chiengmai = Chiang Mai, *Thailand* **38 C2** 18 47N 98 59 E
Chiese →, *Italy* **18 D9** 45 8N 10 25 E
Chieti, *Italy* **20 C6** 42 21N 14 10 E
Chifeng, *China* **35 C10** 42 18N 118 58 E
Chignecto B., *Canada* **71 C7** 45 30N 64 40W
Chiguana, *Bolivia* **94 A2** 21 0S 67 58W
Chigwell, *U.K.* **11 F8** 51 37N 0 5 E
Chiha-ri, *N. Korea* **35 E14** 38 40N 126 30 E
Chihli, G. of = Bo Hai, *China* **35 E10** 39 0N 119 0 E
Chihuahua, *Mexico* **86 B3** 28 40N 106 3W
Chihuahua □, *Mexico* **86 B3** 28 40N 106 3W
Chiili = Shīeli, *Kazakstan* **26 E7** 44 20N 66 15 E
Chik Bollapur, *India* **40 N10** 13 25N 77 45 E
Chikmagalur, *India* **40 N9** 13 15N 75 45 E
Chikwawa, *Malawi* **55 F3** 16 2S 34 50 E
Chilac, *Mexico* **87 D5** 18 20N 97 24W
Chilam Chavki, *Pakistan* **43 B6** 35 5N 75 5 E
Chilanga, *Zambia* **55 F2** 15 33S 28 16 E
Chilapa, *Mexico* **87 D5** 17 40N 99 11W
Chilas, *Pakistan* **43 B6** 35 25N 74 5 E
Chilaw, *Sri Lanka* **40 R11** 7 30N 79 50 E
Chilcotin →, *Canada* **72 C4** 51 44N 122 23W
Childers, *Australia* **63 D5** 25 15S 152 17 E
Childress, *U.S.A.* **81 H4** 34 25N 100 13W
Chile ■, *S. Amer.* **96 D2** 35 0S 72 0W
Chile Rise, *Pac. Oc.* **65 L18** 38 0S 92 0W
Chilecito, *Argentina* **94 B2** 29 10S 67 30W
Chilete, *Peru* **92 E3** 7 10S 78 50W
Chililabombwe, *Zambia* **55 E2** 12 18S 27 43 E
Chilin = Jilin, *China* **35 C14** 43 44N 126 30 E
Chilka L., *India* **41 K14** 19 40N 85 25 E
Chilko →, *Canada* **72 C4** 52 0N 123 40W
Chilko L., *Canada* **72 C4** 51 20N 124 10W
Chillagoe, *Australia* **62 B3** 17 7S 144 33 E
Chillán, *Chile* **94 D1** 36 40S 72 10W
Chillicothe, *Ill., U.S.A.* **80 E10** 40 55N 89 29W
Chillicothe, *Mo., U.S.A.* **80 F8** 39 48N 93 33W
Chillicothe, *Ohio, U.S.A.* **76 F4** 39 20N 82 59W
Chilliwack, *Canada* **72 D4** 49 10N 121 54W
Chilo, *India* **42 F5** 27 25N 73 32 E
Chiloane, I., *Mozam.* **57 C5** 20 40S 34 55 E
Chiloé, I. de, *Chile* **96 E2** 42 30S 73 50W
Chilpancingo, *Mexico* **87 D5** 17 30N 99 30W
Chiltern Hills, *U.K.* **11 F7** 51 40N 0 53W
Chilton, *U.S.A.* **76 C1** 44 2N 88 10W
Chilubi, *Zambia* **55 E2** 11 5S 29 58 E
Chilubula, *Zambia* **55 E3** 10 14S 30 51 E
Chilumba, *Malawi* **55 E3** 10 28S 34 12 E
Chilung, *Taiwan* **33 D7** 25 3N 121 45 E
Chilwa, L., *Malawi* **55 F4** 15 15S 35 40 E
Chimaltitán, *Mexico* **86 C4** 21 46N 103 50W
Chimán, *Panama* **88 E4** 8 45N 78 40W
Chimanimani, *Zimbabwe* **57 B5** 19 48S 32 52 E
Chimay, *Belgium* **15 D4** 50 3N 4 20 E
Chimayo, *U.S.A.* **83 H11** 36 0N 105 56W
Chimbay, *Uzbekistan* **26 E6** 42 57N 59 47 E
Chimborazo, *Ecuador* **92 D3** 1 29S 78 55W
Chimbote, *Peru* **92 E3** 9 0S 78 35W
Chimkent = Shymkent, *Kazakstan* **26 E7** 42 18N 69 36 E
Chimoio, *Mozam.* **55 F3** 19 4S 33 30 E
Chimpembe, *Zambia* **55 D2** 9 31S 29 33 E
Chin □, *Burma* **41 J18** 22 0N 93 0 E
Chin Ling Shan = Qinling Shandi, *China* **34 H5** 33 50N 108 10 E
China, *Mexico* **87 B5** 25 40N 99 20W
China ■, *Asia* **33 C6** 30 0N 110 0 E
China Lake, *U.S.A.* **85 K9** 35 44N 117 37W
Chinan = Jinan, *China* **34 F9** 36 38N 117 1 E
Chinandega, *Nic.* **88 D2** 12 35N 87 12W
Chinati Peak, *U.S.A.* **81 L2** 29 57N 104 29W
Chincha Alta, *Peru* **92 F3** 13 25S 76 7W
Chinchaga →, *Canada* **72 B5** 58 53N 118 20W
Chinchilla, *Australia* **63 D5** 26 45S 150 38 E
Chinchorro, Banco, *Mexico* **87 D7** 18 35N 87 20W
Chinchou = Jinzhou, *China* **35 D11** 41 5N 121 3 E
Chincoteague, *U.S.A.* **76 G8** 37 56N 75 23W
Chinde, *Mozam.* **55 F4** 18 35S 36 30 E
Chindo, *S. Korea* **35 G14** 34 28N 126 15 E
Chindwin →, *Burma* **41 J19** 21 26N 95 15 E
Chineni, *India* **43 C6** 33 2N 75 15 E
Chinga, *Mozam.* **55 F4** 15 13S 38 35 E
Chingola, *Zambia* **55 E2** 12 31S 27 53 E
Chingole, *Malawi* **55 E3** 13 4S 34 17 E
Ch'ingtao = Qingdao, *China* **35 F11** 36 5N 120 20 E
Chinguetti, *Mauritania* **50 D3** 20 25N 12 24W
Chingune, *Mozam.* **57 C5** 20 33S 34 58 E
Chinhae, *S. Korea* **35 G15** 35 9N 128 47 E
Chinhanguanine, *Mozam.* **57 D5** 25 21S 32 30 E
Chinhoyi, *Zimbabwe* **55 F3** 17 20S 30 8 E
Chini, *India* **42 D8** 31 32N 78 15 E
Chiniot, *Pakistan* **42 D5** 31 45N 73 0 E
Chínipas, *Mexico* **86 B3** 27 22N 108 32W
Chinji, *Pakistan* **42 C5** 32 42N 72 22 E
Chinju, *S. Korea* **35 G15** 35 12N 128 2 E
Chinle, *U.S.A.* **83 H9** 36 9N 109 33W
Chinnampo = Namp'o, *N. Korea* **35 E13** 38 52N 125 10 E
Chino, *Japan* **31 G9** 35 59N 138 9 E
Chino, *U.S.A.* **85 L9** 34 1N 117 41W
Chino Valley, *U.S.A.* **83 J7** 34 45N 112 27W
Chinon, *France* **18 C4** 47 10N 0 15 E
Chinook, *U.S.A.* **82 B9** 48 35N 109 14W
Chinsali, *Zambia* **55 E3** 10 30S 32 2 E
Chióggia, *Italy* **20 B5** 45 13N 12 17 E
Chíos = Khíos, *Greece* **21 E12** 38 27N 26 9 E
Chipata, *Zambia* **55 E3** 13 38S 32 28 E
Chipinge, *Zimbabwe* **55 G3** 20 13S 32 28 E
Chipley, *U.S.A.* **77 K3** 30 47N 85 32W
Chipman, *Canada* **71 C6** 46 6N 65 53W
Chipoka, *Malawi* **55 E3** 13 57S 34 28 E
Chippenham, *U.K.* **11 F5** 51 27N 2 6W
Chippewa →, *U.S.A.* **80 C8** 44 25N 92 5W
Chippewa Falls, *U.S.A.* **80 C9** 44 56N 91 24W
Chipping Norton, *U.K.* **11 F6** 51 56N 1 32W
Chiputneticook Lakes, *U.S.A.* **77 C11** 45 35N 67 35W
Chiquián, *Peru* **92 F3** 10 10S 77 0W
Chiquimula, *Guatemala* **88 D2** 14 51N 89 37W
Chiquinquira, *Colombia* **92 B4** 5 37N 73 50W
Chirala, *India* **40 M12** 15 50N 80 26 E
Chiramba, *Mozam.* **55 F3** 16 55S 34 39 E
Chirawa, *India* **42 E6** 28 14N 75 42 E
Chirchiq, *Uzbekistan* **26 E7** 41 29N 69 35 E
Chiredzi, *Zimbabwe* **57 C5** 21 0S 31 38 E
Chiricahua Peak, *U.S.A.* **83 L9** 31 51N 109 18W
Chiriquí, G. de, *Panama* **88 E3** 8 0N 82 10W
Chiriquí, L. de, *Panama* **88 E3** 9 10N 82 0W
Chirivira Falls, *Zimbabwe* **55 G3** 21 10S 32 12 E
Chirmiri, *India* **41 H13** 23 15N 82 20 E
Chirripó Grande, Cerro, *Costa Rica* **88 E3** 9 29N 83 29W
Chirundu, *Zimbabwe* **57 B4** 16 3S 28 50 E
Chisamba, *Zambia* **55 E2** 14 55S 28 20 E
Chisapani Garhi, *Nepal* **41 F14** 27 30N 84 2 E
Chisasibi, *Canada* **70 B4** 53 50N 79 0W
Chisholm, *Canada* **72 C6** 54 55N 114 10W
Chisholm, *U.S.A.* **80 B8** 47 29N 92 53W
Chishtian Mandi, *Pakistan* **42 E5** 29 50N 72 55 E
Chisimaio, *Somali Rep.* **49 G8** 0 22S 42 32 E
Chisimba Falls, *Zambia* **55 E3** 10 12S 30 56 E
Chişinău, *Moldova* **17 E15** 47 2N 28 50 E
Chisos Mts., *U.S.A.* **81 L3** 29 5N 103 15W
Chistopol, *Russia* **24 C9** 55 25N 50 38 E
Chita, *Russia* **27 D12** 52 0N 113 35 E
Chitipa, *Malawi* **55 D3** 9 41S 33 19 E
Chitose, *Japan* **30 C10** 42 49N 141 39 E
Chitral, *Pakistan* **40 B7** 35 50N 71 56 E
Chitré, *Panama* **88 E3** 7 59N 80 27W
Chittagong, *Bangla.* **41 H17** 22 19N 91 48 E
Chittagong □, *Bangla.* **41 G17** 24 5N 91 0 E
Chittaurgarh, *India* **42 G6** 24 52N 74 38 E
Chittoor, *India* **40 N11** 13 15N 79 5 E
Chitungwiza, *Zimbabwe* **55 F3** 18 0S 31 6 E
Chiusi, *Italy* **20 C4** 43 1N 11 57 E
Chivasso, *Italy* **18 D7** 45 11N 7 53 E
Chivhu, *Zimbabwe* **55 F3** 19 2S 30 52 E
Chivilcoy, *Argentina* **94 C4** 34 55S 60 0W
Chiwanda, *Tanzania* **55 E3** 11 23S 34 55 E
Chizarira, *Zimbabwe* **55 F2** 17 36S 27 45 E
Chizera, *Zambia* **55 E2** 13 10S 25 0 E
Chkalov = Orenburg, *Russia* **24 D10** 51 45N 55 6 E
Chloride, *U.S.A.* **85 K12** 35 25N 114 12W
Cho Bo, *Vietnam* **38 B5** 20 46N 105 10 E
Cho-do, *N. Korea* **35 E13** 38 30N 124 40 E
Cho Phuoc Hai, *Vietnam* **39 G6** 10 26N 107 18 E
Choba, *Kenya* **54 B4** 2 30N 38 5 E
Choch'iwŏn, *S. Korea* **35 F14** 36 37N 127 18 E
Chocolate Mts., *U.S.A.* **85 M11** 33 15N 115 15W
Choctawhatchee →, *U.S.A.* **77 K3** 30 25N 86 8W
Choele Choel, *Argentina* **96 D3** 39 11S 65 40W
Choix, *Mexico* **86 B3** 26 40N 108 23W
Chojnice, *Poland* **17 B9** 53 42N 17 32 E
Chōkai-San, *Japan* **30 E10** 39 6N 140 3 E
Choke Canyon L., *U.S.A.* **81 L5** 28 30N 98 20W
Chokurdakh, *Russia* **27 B15** 70 38N 147 55 E
Cholame, *U.S.A.* **84 K6** 35 44N 120 18W
Cholet, *France* **18 C3** 47 4N 0 52W
Cholguan, *Chile* **94 D1** 37 10S 72 3W
Choluteca, *Honduras* **88 D2** 13 20N 87 14W
Choluteca →, *Honduras* **88 D2** 13 0N 87 20W
Chom Bung, *Thailand* **38 F2** 13 37N 99 36 E
Chom Thong, *Thailand* **38 C2** 18 25N 98 41 E
Choma, *Zambia* **55 F2** 16 48S 26 59 E
Chomun, *India* **42 F6** 27 15N 75 40 E
Chomutov, *Czech Rep.* **16 C7** 50 28N 13 23 E
Chon Buri, *Thailand* **38 F3** 13 21N 101 1 E
Chon Thanh, *Vietnam* **39 G6** 11 24N 106 36 E
Ch'onan, *S. Korea* **35 F14** 36 48N 127 9 E
Chone, *Ecuador* **92 D3** 0 40S 80 0W
Chong Kai, *Cambodia* **38 F4** 13 57N 103 35 E
Chong Mek, *Thailand* **38 E5** 15 10N 105 27 E
Chŏngdo, *S. Korea* **35 G15** 35 38N 128 42 E
Chŏngha, *S. Korea* **35 F15** 36 12N 129 21 E
Chŏngjin, *N. Korea* **35 D15** 41 47N 129 50 E
Chŏngjiu, *S. Korea* **35 F14** 36 39N 127 27 E
Chŏngju, *N. Korea* **35 E13** 39 40N 125 5 E
Chongli, *China* **34 D8** 40 58N 115 15 E
Chongqing, *China* **32 D5** 29 35N 106 25 E
Chongqing Shi □, *China* **32 C5** 30 0N 108 0 E
Chonguene, *Mozam.* **57 C5** 25 3S 33 49 E
Chŏngŭp, *S. Korea* **35 G14** 35 35N 126 50 E
Chŏnju, *S. Korea* **35 G14** 35 50N 127 4 E
Chonos, Arch. de los, *Chile* **96 F2** 45 0S 75 0W
Chop, *Ukraine* **17 D12** 48 26N 22 12 E
Chopim →, *Brazil* **95 B5** 25 35S 53 5W
Chor, *Pakistan* **42 G3** 25 31N 69 46 E
Chorbat La, *India* **43 B7** 34 42N 76 37 E
Chorley, *U.K.* **10 D5** 53 39N 2 38W
Chornobyl, *Ukraine* **17 C16** 51 20N 30 15 E
Chorolque, Cerro, *Bolivia* **94 A2** 20 59S 66 5W
Chorregon, *Australia* **62 C3** 22 40S 143 32 E
Chortkiv, *Ukraine* **17 D13** 49 2N 25 46 E
Ch'ŏrwon, *S. Korea* **35 E14** 38 15N 127 10 E
Chorzów, *Poland* **17 C10** 50 18N 18 57 E
Chos-Malal, *Argentina* **94 D1** 37 20S 70 15W
Ch'osan, *N. Korea* **35 D13** 40 50N 125 47 E
Choszczno, *Poland* **16 B8** 53 7N 15 25 E
Choteau, *U.S.A.* **82 C7** 47 49N 112 11W
Chotila, *India* **42 H4** 22 23N 71 15 E
Chotta Udepur, *India* **42 H6** 22 19N 74 1 E
Chowchilla, *U.S.A.* **84 H6** 37 7N 120 16W
Choybalsan, *Mongolia* **33 B6** 48 4N 114 30 E
Christchurch, *N.Z.* **59 K4** 43 33S 172 47 E
Christchurch, *U.K.* **11 G6** 50 44N 1 47W
Christian I., *Canada* **78 B4** 44 50N 80 12W
Christiana, *S. Africa* **56 D4** 27 52S 25 8 E
Christiansted, *U.S. Virgin Is.* **89 C7** 17 45N 64 42W
Christie B., *Canada* **73 A6** 62 32N 111 10W
Christina →, *Canada* **73 B6** 56 40N 111 3W
Christmas Cr. →, *Australia* **60 C4** 18 29S 125 23 E
Christmas I. = Kiritimati, *Kiribati* **65 G12** 1 58N 157 27W
Christmas I., *Ind. Oc.* **64 J2** 10 30S 105 40 E
Christopher L., *Australia* **61 D4** 24 49S 127 42 E
Chtimba, *Malawi* **55 E3** 10 35S 34 13 E
Chu = Shū, *Kazakstan* **26 E8** 43 36N 73 42 E
Chu →, *Vietnam* **38 C5** 19 53N 105 45 E
Chu Lai, *Vietnam* **38 E7** 15 28N 108 45 E
Ch'uanchou = Quanzhou, *China* **33 D6** 24 55N 118 34 E
Chuankou, *China* **34 G6** 34 20N 110 59 E
Chubbuck, *U.S.A.* **82 E7** 42 55N 112 28W
Chūbu □, *Japan* **31 F8** 36 45N 137 30 E
Chubut →, *Argentina* **96 E3** 43 20S 65 5W
Chuchi L., *Canada* **72 B4** 55 12N 124 30W
Chuda, *India* **42 H4** 22 29N 71 41 E
Chudskoye, Ozero, *Russia* **9 G22** 58 13N 27 30 E
Chūgoku □, *Japan* **31 G6** 35 0N 133 0 E
Chūgoku-Sanchi, *Japan* **31 G6** 35 0N 133 0 E
Chugwater, *U.S.A.* **80 E2** 41 46N 104 50W
Chukchi Sea, *Russia* **27 C19** 68 0N 175 0W
Chukotskoye Nagorye, *Russia* **27 C18** 68 0N 175 0 E
Chula Vista, *U.S.A.* **85 N9** 32 39N 117 5W
Chulucanas, *Peru* **92 E2** 5 8S 80 10W
Chulym →, *Russia* **26 D9** 57 43N 83 51 E
Chum Phae, *Thailand* **38 D4** 16 40N 102 6 E
Chum Saeng, *Thailand* **38 E3** 15 55N 100 15 E
Chumar, *India* **43 C8** 32 40N 78 35 E
Chumbicha, *Argentina* **94 B2** 29 0S 66 10W
Chumikan, *Russia* **27 D14** 54 40N 135 10 E
Chumphon, *Thailand* **39 G2** 10 35N 99 14 E
Chumuare, *Mozam.* **55 E3** 14 31S 31 50 E
Chumunjin, *S. Korea* **35 F15** 37 55N 128 54 E
Chuna →, *Russia* **27 D10** 57 47N 94 37 E
Ch'unch'ŏn, *S. Korea* **35 F14** 37 58N 127 44 E
Chunchura, *India* **43 H13** 22 53N 88 27 E
Chunga, *Zambia* **55 F2** 15 0S 26 2 E
Chunggang-ŭp, *N. Korea* **35 D14** 41 48N 126 48 E
Chunghwa, *N. Korea* **35 E13** 38 52N 125 47 E
Ch'ungju, *S. Korea* **35 F14** 36 58N 127 58 E
Chungking = Chongqing, *China* **32 D5** 29 35N 106 25 E
Ch'ungmu, *S. Korea* **35 G15** 34 50N 128 20 E
Chungt'iaoshan = Zhongtiao Shan, *China* **34 G6** 35 0N 111 10 E
Chunian, *Pakistan* **42 D6** 30 57N 74 0 E
Chunya, *Tanzania* **55 D3** 8 30S 33 27 E
Chunyang, *China* **35 C15** 43 38N 129 23 E
Chuquibamba, *Peru* **92 G4** 15 47S 72 44W
Chuquicamata, *Chile* **94 A2** 22 15S 69 0W
Chur, *Switz.* **18 C8** 46 52N 9 32 E
Churachandpur, *India* **41 G18** 24 20N 93 40 E
Churchill, *Canada* **73 B10** 58 47N 94 11W
Churchill →, *Man., Canada* **73 B10** 58 47N 94 12W
Churchill →, *Nfld., Canada* **71 B7** 53 19N 60 10W
Churchill, C., *Canada* **73 B10** 58 46N 93 12W
Churchill Falls, *Canada* **71 B7** 53 36N 64 19W
Churchill L., *Canada* **73 B7** 55 55N 108 20W
Churchill Pk., *Canada* **72 B3** 58 10N 125 10W
Churki, *India* **43 H10** 23 50N 83 12 E
Churu, *India* **42 E6** 28 20N 74 50 E
Churún Merú = Angel Falls, *Venezuela* **92 B6** 5 57N 62 30W
Chushal, *India* **43 C8** 33 40N 78 40 E
Chuska Mts., *U.S.A.* **83 H9** 36 15N 108 50W
Chusovoy, *Russia* **24 C10** 58 22N 57 50 E
Chute-aux-Outardes, *Canada* **71 C6** 49 7N 68 24W
Chuuronjang, *N. Korea* **35 D15** 41 35N 129 40 E
Chuvash Republic = Chuvashia □, *Russia* **24 C8** 55 30N 47 0 E
Chuvashia □, *Russia* **24 C8** 55 30N 47 0 E
Chuwārtah, *Iraq* **44 C5** 35 43N 45 34 E
Chūy = Shū →, *Kazakstan* **28 E10** 45 0N 67 44 E
Chuy, *Uruguay* **95 C5** 33 41S 53 27W
Ci Xian, *China* **34 F8** 36 20N 114 25 E
Ciadâr-Lunga, *Moldova* **17 E15** 46 3N 28 51 E
Ciamis, *Indonesia* **37 G13** 7 20S 108 21 E
Cianjur, *Indonesia* **37 G12** 6 49S 107 8 E
Cianorte, *Brazil* **95 A5** 23 37S 52 37W
Cibola, *U.S.A.* **85 M12** 33 17N 114 42W
Cicero, *U.S.A.* **76 E2** 41 51N 87 45W
Ciechanów, *Poland* **17 B11** 52 52N 20 38 E
Ciego de Avila, *Cuba* **88 B4** 21 50N 78 50W
Ciénaga, *Colombia* **92 A4** 11 1N 74 15W
Cienfuegos, *Cuba* **88 B3** 22 10N 80 30W
Cieszyn, *Poland* **17 D10** 49 45N 18 35 E
Cieza, *Spain* **19 C5** 38 17N 1 23W
Cihuatlán, *Mexico* **86 D4** 19 14N 104 35W
Cijara, Embalse de, *Spain* **19 C3** 39 18N 4 52W
Cijulang, *Indonesia* **37 G13** 7 42S 108 27 E
Cilacap, *Indonesia* **37 G13** 7 43S 109 0 E
Cill Chainnigh = Kilkenny, *Ireland* **13 D4** 52 39N 7 15W
Cilo Dağı, *Turkey* **25 G7** 37 28N 43 55 E
Cima, *U.S.A.* **85 K11** 35 14N 115 30W
Cimarron, *Kans., U.S.A.* **81 G4** 37 48N 100 21W
Cimarron, *N. Mex., U.S.A.* **81 G2** 36 31N 104 55W
Cimarron →, *U.S.A.* **81 G6** 36 10N 96 17W
Cimişlia, *Moldova* **17 E15** 46 34N 28 44 E
Cimone, Mte., *Italy* **20 B4** 44 12N 10 42 E
Cinca →, *Spain* **19 B6** 41 26N 0 21 E
Cincar, *Bos.-H.* **20 C7** 43 55N 17 5 E
Cincinnati, *U.S.A.* **76 F3** 39 6N 84 31W
Cincinnatus, *U.S.A.* **79 D9** 42 33N 75 54W
Çine, *Turkey* **21 F13** 37 37N 28 2 E
Ciney, *Belgium* **15 D5** 50 18N 5 5 E
Cinto, Mte., *France* **18 E8** 42 24N 8 54 E
Circle, *Alaska, U.S.A.* **68 B5** 65 50N 144 4W
Circle, *Mont., U.S.A.* **80 B2** 47 25N 105 35W
Circleville, *U.S.A.* **76 F4** 39 36N 82 57W
Cirebon, *Indonesia* **36 F3** 6 45S 108 32 E
Ciremai, *Indonesia* **37 G13** 6 55S 108 27 E
Cirencester, *U.K.* **11 F6** 51 43N 1 57W
Cirium, *Cyprus* **23 E11** 34 40N 32 53 E
Cisco, *U.S.A.* **81 J5** 32 23N 98 59W
Citlaltépetl, *Mexico* **87 D5** 19 0N 97 20W
Citrus Heights, *U.S.A.* **84 G5** 38 42N 121 17W
Citrusdal, *S. Africa* **56 E2** 32 35S 19 0 E
Città di Castello, *Italy* **20 C5** 43 27N 12 14 E
Ciudad Altamirano, *Mexico* **86 D4** 18 20N 100 40W
Ciudad Bolívar, *Venezuela* **92 B6** 8 5N 63 36W
Ciudad Camargo, *Mexico* **86 B3** 27 41N 105 10W
Ciudad de Valles, *Mexico* **87 C5** 22 0N 99 0W
Ciudad del Carmen, *Mexico* **87 D6** 18 38N 91 50W
Ciudad del Este, *Paraguay* **95 B5** 25 30S 54 50W
Ciudad Delicias = Delicias, *Mexico* **86 B3** 28 10N 105 30W
Ciudad Guayana, *Venezuela* **92 B6** 8 0N 62 30W
Ciudad Guerrero, *Mexico* **86 B3** 28 33N 107 28W
Ciudad Guzmán, *Mexico* **86 D4** 19 40N 103 30W
Ciudad Juárez, *Mexico* **86 A3** 31 40N 106 28W
Ciudad Madero, *Mexico* **87 C5** 22 19N 97 50W
Ciudad Mante, *Mexico* **87 C5** 22 50N 99 0W
Ciudad Obregón, *Mexico* **86 B3** 27 28N 109 59W
Ciudad Real, *Spain* **19 C4** 38 59N 3 55W
Ciudad Rodrigo, *Spain* **19 B2** 40 35N 6 32W
Ciudad Trujillo = Santo Domingo, *Dom. Rep.* **89 C6** 18 30N 69 59W
Ciudad Victoria, *Mexico* **87 C5** 23 41N 99 9W
Ciudadela, *Spain* **22 B10** 40 0N 3 50 E
Civitanova Marche, *Italy* **20 C5** 43 18N 13 44 E
Civitavécchia, *Italy* **20 C4** 42 6N 11 48 E
Cizre, *Turkey* **25 G7** 37 19N 42 10 E
Clackmannanshire □, *U.K.* **12 E5** 56 10N 3 43W
Clacton-on-Sea, *U.K.* **11 F9** 51 47N 1 11 E
Claire, L., *Canada* **72 B6** 58 35N 112 5W
Clairton, *U.S.A.* **78 F5** 40 18N 79 53W
Clallam Bay, *U.S.A.* **84 B2** 48 15N 124 16W
Clanton, *U.S.A.* **77 J2** 32 51N 86 38W
Clanwilliam, *S. Africa* **56 E2** 32 11S 18 52 E
Clara, *Ireland* **13 C4** 53 21N 7 37W
Claraville, *U.S.A.* **85 K8** 35 24N 118 20W
Clare, *Australia* **63 E2** 33 50S 138 37 E
Clare, *U.S.A.* **76 D3** 43 49N 84 46W
Clare □, *Ireland* **13 D3** 52 45N 9 0W
Clare →, *Ireland* **13 C2** 53 20N 9 2W
Clare I., *Ireland* **13 C1** 53 49N 10 0W
Claremont, *Calif., U.S.A.* **85 L9** 34 6N 117 43W
Claremont, *N.H., U.S.A.* **79 C12** 43 23N 72 20W
Claremont Pt., *Australia* **62 A3** 14 1S 143 41 E
Claremore, *U.S.A.* **81 G7** 36 19N 95 36W
Claremorris, *Ireland* **13 C3** 53 45N 9 0W
Clarence →, *Australia* **63 D5** 29 25S 153 22 E
Clarence →, *N.Z.* **59 K4** 42 10S 173 56 E
Clarence, I., *Chile* **96 G2** 54 0S 72 0W
Clarence I., *Antarctica* **5 C18** 61 10S 54 0W
Clarence Str., *Australia* **60 B5** 12 0S 131 0 E
Clarence Town, *Bahamas* **89 B5** 23 6N 74 59W
Clarendon, *Pa., U.S.A.* **78 E5** 41 47N 79 6W
Clarendon, *Tex., U.S.A.* **81 H4** 34 56N 100 53W
Clarenville, *Canada* **71 C9** 48 10N 54 1W
Claresholm, *Canada* **72 D6** 50 0N 113 33W
Clarie Coast, *Antarctica* **5 C9** 68 0S 135 0 E
Clarinda, *U.S.A.* **80 E7** 40 44N 95 2W
Clarion, *Iowa, U.S.A.* **80 D8** 42 44N 93 44W
Clarion, *Pa., U.S.A.* **78 E5** 41 13N 79 23W
Clarion →, *U.S.A.* **78 E5** 41 7N 79 41W
Clark, *U.S.A.* **80 C6** 44 53N 97 44W
Clark, Pt., *Canada* **78 B3** 44 4N 81 45W
Clark Fork, *U.S.A.* **82 B5** 48 9N 116 11W
Clark Fork →, *U.S.A.* **82 B5** 48 9N 116 15W
Clarkdale, *U.S.A.* **83 J7** 34 46N 112 3W
Clarke City, *Canada* **71 B6** 50 12N 66 38W
Clarke I., *Australia* **62 G4** 40 32S 148 10 E
Clarke Ra., *Australia* **62 C4** 20 40S 148 30 E
Clark's Fork →, *U.S.A.* **82 D9** 45 39N 108 43W
Clark's Harbour, *Canada* **71 D6** 43 25N 65 38W
Clarks Hill L., *U.S.A.* **77 J4** 33 40N 82 12W
Clarks Summit, *U.S.A.* **79 E9** 41 30N 75 42W
Clarksburg, *U.S.A.* **76 F5** 39 17N 80 30W
Clarksdale, *U.S.A.* **81 H9** 34 12N 90 35W
Clarksville, *Ark., U.S.A.* **81 H8** 35 28N 93 28W
Clarksville, *Tenn., U.S.A.* **77 G2** 36 32N 87 21W
Clarksville, *Tex., U.S.A.* **81 J7** 33 37N 95 3W
Clatskanie, *U.S.A.* **84 D3** 46 6N 123 12W
Claude, *U.S.A.* **81 H4** 35 7N 101 22W
Claveria, *Phil.* **37 A6** 18 37N 121 4 E
Clay, *U.S.A.* **84 G5** 38 17N 121 10W
Clay Center, *U.S.A.* **80 F6** 39 23N 97 8W
Claypool, *U.S.A.* **83 K8** 33 25N 110 51W
Claysburg, *U.S.A.* **78 F6** 40 17N 78 27W
Claysville, *U.S.A.* **78 F4** 40 7N 80 25W
Clayton, *N. Mex., U.S.A.* **81 G3** 36 27N 103 11W
Clayton, *N.Y., U.S.A.* **79 B8** 44 14N 76 5W
Clear, C., *Ireland* **13 E2** 51 25N 9 32W
Clear, L., *Canada* **78 A7** 45 26N 77 12W
Clear Hills, *Canada* **72 B5** 56 40N 119 30W
Clear I., *Ireland* **13 E2** 51 26N 9 30W
Clear L., *U.S.A.* **84 F4** 39 2N 122 47W
Clear Lake, *Iowa, U.S.A.* **80 D8** 43 8N 93 23W
Clear Lake, *S. Dak., U.S.A.* **80 C6** 44 45N 96 41W
Clear Lake Reservoir, *U.S.A.* **82 F3** 41 56N 121 5W
Clearfield, *Pa., U.S.A.* **78 E6** 41 2N 78 27W
Clearfield, *Utah, U.S.A.* **82 F8** 41 7N 112 2W
Clearlake, *U.S.A.* **82 G2** 38 57N 122 38W
Clearlake Highlands, *U.S.A.* **84 G4** 38 57N 122 38W
Clearwater, *Canada* **72 C4** 51 38N 120 2W
Clearwater, *U.S.A.* **77 M4** 27 58N 82 48W
Clearwater →, *Alta., Canada* **72 C6** 52 22N 114 57W
Clearwater →, *Alta., Canada* **73 B6** 56 44N 111 23W
Clearwater L., *Canada* **73 C9** 53 34N 99 49W
Clearwater Mts., *U.S.A.* **82 C6** 46 5N 115 20W
Clearwater Prov. Park, *Canada* **73 C8** 54 0N 101 0W
Clearwater River Prov. Park, *Canada* **73 B7** 56 55N 109 10W
Cleburne, *U.S.A.* **81 J6** 32 21N 97 23W
Clee Hills, *U.K.* **11 E5** 52 26N 2 35W
Cleethorpes, *U.K.* **10 D7** 53 33N 0 3W
Cleeve Cloud, *U.K.* **11 F6** 51 56N 2 0W
Clemson, *U.S.A.* **77 H4** 34 41N 82 50W
Clerke Reef, *Australia* **60 C2** 17 22S 119 20 E
Clermont, *Australia* **62 C4** 22 49S 147 39 E
Clermont, *U.S.A.* **77 L5** 28 33N 81 46W
Clermont-Ferrand, *France* **18 D5** 45 46N 3 4 E
Clervaux, *Lux.* **15 D6** 50 4N 6 2 E
Clevedon, *U.K.* **11 F5** 51 26N 2 52W
Cleveland, *Miss., U.S.A.* **81 J9** 33 45N 90 43W
Cleveland, *Ohio, U.S.A.* **78 E3** 41 30N 81 42W
Cleveland, *Okla., U.S.A.* **81 G6** 36 19N 96 28W
Cleveland, *Tenn., U.S.A.* **77 H3** 35 10N 84 53W
Cleveland, *Tex., U.S.A.* **81 K7** 30 21N 95 5W
Cleveland, C., *Australia* **62 B4** 19 11S 147 1 E
Cleveland, Mt., *U.S.A.* **82 B7** 48 56N 113 51W
Cleveland Heights, *U.S.A.* **78 E3** 41 30N 81 34W
Clevelândia, *Brazil* **95 B5** 26 24S 52 23W
Clew B., *Ireland* **13 C2** 53 50N 9 49W
Clewiston, *U.S.A.* **77 M5** 26 45N 80 56W
Clifden, *Ireland* **13 C1** 53 29N 10 1W
Clifden, *N.Z.* **59 M1** 46 1S 167 42 E
Cliffdell, *U.S.A.* **84 D5** 46 56N 121 5W
Cliffy Hd., *Australia* **61 G2** 35 1S 116 29 E
Clifton, *Australia* **63 D5** 27 59S 151 53 E
Clifton, *Ariz., U.S.A.* **83 K9** 33 3N 109 18W
Clifton, *Colo., U.S.A.* **83 G9** 39 7N 108 25W
Clifton, *Tex., U.S.A.* **81 K6** 31 47N 97 35W
Clifton Beach, *Australia* **62 B4** 16 46S 145 39 E
Climax, *Canada* **73 D7** 49 10N 108 20W

Clinch →, U.S.A. 77 H3 35 53N 84 29W
Clingmans Dome, U.S.A. 77 H4 35 34N 83 30W
Clint, U.S.A. 83 L10 31 35N 106 14W
Clinton, B.C., Canada 72 C4 51 6N 121 35W
Clinton, Ont., Canada 78 C3 43 37N 81 32W
Clinton, N.Z. 59 M2 46 12S 169 23 E
Clinton, Ark., U.S.A. 81 H8 35 36N 92 28W
Clinton, Conn., U.S.A. 79 E12 41 17N 72 32W
Clinton, Ill., U.S.A. 80 E10 40 9N 88 57W
Clinton, Ind., U.S.A. 76 F2 39 40N 87 24W
Clinton, Iowa, U.S.A. 80 E9 41 51N 90 12W
Clinton, Mass., U.S.A. 79 D13 42 25N 71 41W
Clinton, Miss., U.S.A. 81 J9 32 20N 90 20W
Clinton, Mo., U.S.A. 80 F8 38 22N 93 46W
Clinton, N.C., U.S.A. 77 H6 35 0N 78 22W
Clinton, Okla., U.S.A. 81 H5 35 31N 98 58W
Clinton, S.C., U.S.A. 77 H5 34 29N 81 53W
Clinton, Tenn., U.S.A. 77 G3 36 6N 84 8W
Clinton, Wash., U.S.A. 84 C4 47 59N 122 21W
Clinton C., Australia 62 C5 22 30S 150 45 E
Clinton Colden L., Canada 68 B9 63 58N 107 27W
Clintonville, U.S.A. 80 C10 44 37N 88 46W
Clipperton, I., Pac. Oc. 65 F17 10 18N 109 13W
Clisham, U.K. 12 D2 57 57N 6 49W
Clitheroe, U.K. 10 D5 53 53N 2 22W
Clo-oose, Canada 84 B2 48 39N 124 49W
Cloates, Pt., Australia 60 D1 22 43S 113 40 E
Clocolan, S. Africa 57 D4 28 55S 27 34 E
Clodomira, Argentina 94 B3 27 35S 64 14W
Clogher Hd., Ireland 13 C5 53 48N 6 14W
Clonakilty, Ireland 13 E3 51 37N 8 53W
Clonakilty B., Ireland 13 E3 51 35N 8 51W
Cloncurry, Australia 62 C3 20 40S 140 28 E
Cloncurry →, Australia 62 B3 18 37S 140 40 E
Clondalkin, Ireland 13 C5 53 19N 6 25W
Clones, Ireland 13 B4 54 11N 7 15W
Clonmel, Ireland 13 D4 52 21N 7 42W
Cloquet, U.S.A. 80 B8 46 43N 92 28W
Clorinda, Argentina 94 B4 25 16S 57 45W
Cloud Bay, Canada 70 C2 48 5N 89 26W
Cloud Peak, U.S.A. 82 D10 44 23N 107 11W
Cloudcroft, U.S.A. 83 K11 32 58N 105 45W
Cloverdale, U.S.A. 84 G4 38 48N 123 1W
Clovis, Calif., U.S.A. 84 J7 36 49N 119 42W
Clovis, N. Mex., U.S.A. 81 H3 34 24N 103 12W
Cloyne, Canada 78 B7 44 49N 77 11W
Cluj-Napoca, Romania 17 E12 46 47N 23 38 E
Clunes, Australia 63 F3 37 20S 143 45 E
Clutha →, N.Z. 59 M2 46 20S 169 49 E
Clwyd →, U.K. 10 D4 53 19N 3 31W
Clyde, Canada 72 C6 54 9N 113 39W
Clyde, N.Z. 59 L2 45 12S 169 20 E
Clyde, U.S.A. 78 C8 43 5N 76 52W
Clyde →, U.K. 12 F4 55 55N 4 30W
Clyde, Firth of, U.K. 12 F3 55 22N 5 1W
Clyde River, Canada 69 A13 70 30N 68 30W
Clydebank, U.K. 12 F4 55 54N 4 23W
Clymer, N.Y., U.S.A. 78 D5 42 1N 79 37W
Clymer, Pa., U.S.A. 78 D5 40 40N 79 1W
Coachella, U.S.A. 85 M10 33 41N 116 10W
Coachella Canal, U.S.A. 85 N12 32 43N 114 57W
Coahoma, U.S.A. 81 J4 32 18N 101 18W
Coahuayana →, Mexico 86 D4 18 41N 103 45W
Coahuila □, Mexico 86 B4 27 0N 103 0W
Coal →, Canada 72 B3 59 39N 126 57W
Coalane, Mozam. 55 F4 17 48S 37 2 E
Coalcomán, Mexico 86 D4 18 40N 103 10W
Coaldale, Canada 72 D6 49 45N 112 35W
Coalgate, U.S.A. 81 H6 34 32N 96 13W
Coalinga, U.S.A. 84 J6 36 9N 120 21W
Coalisland, U.K. 13 B5 54 33N 6 42W
Coalville, U.K. 10 E6 52 44N 1 23W
Coalville, U.S.A. 82 F8 40 55N 111 24W
Coari, Brazil 92 D6 4 8S 63 7W
Coast □, Kenya 54 C4 2 40S 39 45 E
Coast Mts., Canada 72 C3 55 0N 129 20W
Coast Ranges, U.S.A. 84 G4 39 0N 123 0W
Coatbridge, U.K. 12 F4 55 52N 4 6W
Coatepec, Mexico 87 D5 19 27N 96 58W
Coatepeque, Guatemala 88 D1 14 46N 91 55W
Coatesville, U.S.A. 76 F8 39 59N 75 50W
Coaticook, Canada 79 A13 45 10N 71 46W
Coats I., Canada 69 B11 62 30N 83 0W
Coats Land, Antarctica 5 D1 77 0S 25 0W
Coatzacoalcos, Mexico 87 D6 18 7N 94 25W
Cobalt, Canada 70 C4 47 25N 79 42W
Cobán, Guatemala 88 C1 15 30N 90 21W
Cobar, Australia 63 E4 31 27S 145 48 E
Cóbh, Ireland 13 E3 51 51N 8 17W
Cobija, Bolivia 92 F5 11 0S 68 50W
Cobleskill, U.S.A. 79 D10 42 41N 74 29W
Coboconk, Canada 78 B6 44 39N 78 48W
Cobourg, Canada 78 C6 43 58N 78 10W
Cobourg Pen., Australia 60 B5 11 20S 132 15 E
Cobram, Australia 63 F4 35 54S 145 40 E
Cóbuè, Mozam. 55 E3 12 0S 34 58 E
Coburg, Germany 16 C6 50 15N 10 58 E
Cocanada = Kakinada, India 41 L13 16 57N 82 11 E
Cochabamba, Bolivia 92 G5 17 26S 66 10W
Cochemane, Mozam. 55 F3 17 0S 32 54 E
Cochin, India 40 Q10 9 58N 76 20 E
Cochin China = Nam-Phan, Vietnam 39 G6 10 30N 106 0 E
Cochran, U.S.A. 77 J4 32 23N 83 21W
Cochrane, Alta., Canada 72 C6 51 11N 114 30W
Cochrane, Ont., Canada 70 C3 49 0N 81 0W
Cochrane, Chile 96 F2 47 15S 72 33W
Cochrane →, Canada 73 B8 59 0N 103 40W
Cochrane, L., Chile 96 F2 47 10S 72 0W
Cochranton, U.S.A. 78 E4 41 31N 80 3W
Cockburn, Australia 63 E3 32 5S 141 0 E
Cockburn, Canal, Chile 96 G2 54 30S 72 0W
Cockburn I., Canada 70 C3 45 55N 83 22W
Cockburn Ra., Australia 60 C4 15 46S 128 0 E
Cockermouth, U.K. 10 C4 54 40N 3 22W
Cocklebiddy, Australia 61 F4 32 0S 126 3 E
Coco →, Cent. Amer. 88 D3 15 0N 83 8W
Coco, I. del, Pac. Oc. 65 G19 5 25N 87 55W
Cocoa, U.S.A. 77 L5 28 21N 80 44W
Cocobeach, Gabon 52 D1 0 59N 9 34 E
Cocos Is., Ind. Oc. 64 J1 12 10S 96 55 E
Cod, C., U.S.A. 76 D10 42 5N 70 10W
Codajás, Brazil 92 D6 3 55S 62 0W
Codó, Brazil 93 D10 4 30S 43 55W
Cody, U.S.A. 82 D9 44 32N 109 3W
Coe Hill, Canada 78 B7 44 52N 77 50W
Coelemu, Chile 94 D1 36 30S 72 48W
Coen, Australia 62 A3 13 52S 143 12 E
Cœur d'Alene, U.S.A. 82 C5 47 45N 116 51W
Cœur d'Alene L., U.S.A. 82 C5 47 32N 116 48W
Coevorden, Neths. 15 B6 52 40N 6 44 E
Cofete, Canary Is. 22 F5 28 6N 14 23W
Coffeyville, U.S.A. 81 G7 37 2N 95 37W
Coffin B., Australia 63 E2 34 38S 135 28 E
Coffin Bay, Australia 63 E2 34 37S 135 29 E
Coffin Bay Peninsula, Australia 63 E2 34 32S 135 15 E
Coffs Harbour, Australia 63 E5 30 16S 153 5 E
Cognac, France 18 D3 45 41N 0 20W
Cohocton, U.S.A. 78 D7 42 30N 77 30W
Cohocton →, U.S.A. 78 D7 42 9N 77 6W
Cohoes, U.S.A. 79 D11 42 46N 73 42W
Cohuna, Australia 63 F3 35 45S 144 15 E
Coiba, I., Panama 88 E3 7 30N 81 40W
Coig →, Argentina 96 G3 51 0S 69 10W
Coigeach, Rubha, U.K. 12 C3 58 6N 5 26W
Coihaique, Chile 96 F2 45 30S 71 45W
Coimbatore, India 40 P10 11 2N 76 59 E
Coimbra, Brazil 92 G7 19 55S 57 48W
Coimbra, Portugal 19 B1 40 15N 8 27W
Coín, Spain 19 D3 36 40N 4 48W
Coipasa, Salar de, Bolivia 92 G5 19 26S 68 9W
Cojimies, Ecuador 92 C3 0 20N 80 0W
Cojutepequé, El Salv. 88 D2 13 41N 88 54W
Cokeville, U.S.A. 82 E8 42 5N 110 57W
Colac, Australia 63 F3 38 21S 143 35 E
Colatina, Brazil 93 G10 19 32S 40 37W
Colbeck, C., Antarctica 5 D13 77 6S 157 48W
Colborne, Canada 78 C7 44 0N 77 53W
Colby, U.S.A. 80 F4 39 24N 101 3W
Colchester, U.K. 11 F8 51 54N 0 55 E
Cold L., Canada 73 C7 54 33N 110 5W
Coldstream, Canada 72 C5 50 13N 119 11W
Coldstream, U.K. 12 F6 55 39N 2 15W
Coldwater, Canada 78 B5 44 42N 79 40W
Coldwater, Kans., U.S.A. 81 G5 37 16N 99 20W
Coldwater, Mich., U.S.A. 76 E3 41 57N 85 0W
Colebrook, U.S.A. 79 B13 44 54N 71 30W
Coleman, U.S.A. 81 K5 31 50N 99 26W
Coleman →, Australia 62 B3 15 6S 141 38 E
Colenso, S. Africa 57 D4 28 44S 29 50 E
Coleraine, Australia 63 F3 37 36S 141 40 E
Coleraine, U.K. 13 A5 55 8N 6 41W
Coleridge, L., N.Z. 59 K3 43 17S 171 30 E
Colesberg, S. Africa 56 E4 30 45S 25 5 E
Coleville, U.S.A. 84 G7 38 34N 119 30W
Colfax, Calif., U.S.A. 84 F6 39 6N 120 57W
Colfax, La., U.S.A. 81 K8 31 31N 92 42W
Colfax, Wash., U.S.A. 82 C5 46 53N 117 22W
Colhué Huapi, L., Argentina 96 F3 45 30S 69 0W
Coligny, S. Africa 57 D4 26 17S 26 15 E
Colima, Mexico 86 D4 19 14N 103 43W
Colima □, Mexico 86 D4 19 10N 103 40W
Colima, Nevado de, Mexico 86 D4 19 35N 103 45W
Colina, Chile 94 C1 33 13S 70 45W
Colinas, Brazil 93 E10 6 0S 44 10W
Coll, U.K. 12 E2 56 39N 6 34W
Collaguasi, Chile 94 A2 21 5S 68 45W
Collarenebri, Australia 63 D4 29 33S 148 34 E
Colleen Bawn, Zimbabwe 55 G2 21 0S 29 12 E
College Park, U.S.A. 77 J3 33 40N 84 27W
College Station, U.S.A. 81 K6 30 37N 96 21W
Collie, Australia 61 F2 33 22S 116 8 E
Collier B., Australia 60 C3 16 10S 124 15 E
Collier Ra., Australia 61 D2 24 45S 119 10 E
Collina, Passo di, Italy 20 B4 44 2N 10 56 E
Collingwood, Canada 78 B4 44 29N 80 13W
Collingwood, N.Z. 59 J4 40 41S 172 40 E
Collins, Canada 70 B2 50 17N 89 27W
Collinsville, Australia 62 C4 20 30S 147 56 E
Collipulli, Chile 94 D1 37 55S 72 30W
Collooney, Ireland 13 B3 54 11N 8 29W
Colmar, France 18 B7 48 5N 7 20 E
Colo →, Australia 63 E5 33 25S 150 52 E
Cologne = Köln, Germany 16 C4 50 56N 6 57 E
Colom, I. d'en, Spain 22 B11 39 58N 4 16 E
Coloma, U.S.A. 84 G6 38 48N 120 53W
Colomb-Béchar = Béchar, Algeria 50 B5 31 38N 2 18W
Colombia ■, S. Amer. 92 C4 3 45N 73 0W
Colombian Basin, S. Amer. 66 H12 14 0N 76 0W
Colombo, Sri Lanka 40 R11 6 56N 79 58 E
Colón, Buenos Aires, Argentina 94 C3 33 53S 61 7W
Colón, Entre Ríos, Argentina 94 C4 32 12S 58 10W
Colón, Cuba 88 B3 22 42N 80 54W
Colón, Panama 88 E4 9 20N 79 54W
Colònia de Sant Jordi, Spain 22 B9 39 19N 2 59 E
Colonia del Sacramento, Uruguay 94 C4 34 25S 57 50W
Colonia Dora, Argentina 94 B3 28 34S 62 59W
Colonial Beach, U.S.A. 76 F7 38 15N 76 58W
Colonie, U.S.A. 79 D11 42 43N 73 50W
Colonsay, Canada 73 C7 51 59N 105 52W
Colonsay, U.K. 12 E2 56 5N 6 12W
Colorado □, U.S.A. 83 G10 39 30N 105 30W
Colorado →, Argentina 96 D4 39 50S 62 8W
Colorado →, N. Amer. 83 L6 31 45N 114 40W
Colorado →, U.S.A. 81 L7 28 36N 95 59W
Colorado City, U.S.A. 81 J4 32 24N 100 52W
Colorado Plateau, U.S.A. 83 H8 37 0N 111 0W
Colorado River Aqueduct, U.S.A. 85 L12 34 17N 114 10W
Colorado Springs, U.S.A. 80 F2 38 50N 104 49W
Colotlán, Mexico 86 C4 22 6N 103 16W
Colstrip, U.S.A. 82 D10 45 53N 106 38W
Colton, U.S.A. 79 B10 44 33N 74 56W
Columbia, Ky., U.S.A. 76 G3 37 6N 85 18W
Columbia, La., U.S.A. 81 J8 32 6N 92 5W
Columbia, Miss., U.S.A. 81 K10 31 15N 89 50W
Columbia, Mo., U.S.A. 80 F8 38 57N 92 20W
Columbia, Pa., U.S.A. 79 F8 40 2N 76 30W
Columbia, S.C., U.S.A. 77 J5 34 0N 81 2W
Columbia, Tenn., U.S.A. 77 H2 35 37N 87 2W
Columbia →, N. Amer. 84 D2 46 15N 124 5W
Columbia, C., Canada 4 A4 83 0N 70 0W
Columbia, District of □, U.S.A. 76 F7 38 55N 77 0W
Columbia, Mt., Canada 72 C5 52 8N 117 20W
Columbia Basin, U.S.A. 82 C4 46 45N 119 5W
Columbia Falls, U.S.A. 82 B6 48 23N 114 11W
Columbia Mts., Canada 72 C5 52 0N 119 0W
Columbia Plateau, U.S.A. 82 D5 44 0N 117 30W
Columbiana, U.S.A. 78 F4 40 53N 80 42W
Columbretes, Is., Spain 19 C6 39 50N 0 50 E
Columbus, Ga., U.S.A. 77 J3 32 28N 84 59W
Columbus, Ind., U.S.A. 76 F3 39 13N 85 55W
Columbus, Kans., U.S.A. 81 G7 37 10N 94 50W
Columbus, Miss., U.S.A. 77 J1 33 30N 88 25W
Columbus, Mont., U.S.A. 82 D9 45 38N 109 15W
Columbus, N. Mex., U.S.A. 83 L10 31 50N 107 38W
Columbus, Nebr., U.S.A. 80 E6 41 26N 97 22W
Columbus, Ohio, U.S.A. 76 F4 39 58N 83 0W
Columbus, Tex., U.S.A. 81 L6 29 42N 96 33W
Colusa, U.S.A. 84 F4 39 13N 122 1W
Colville, U.S.A. 82 B5 48 33N 117 54W
Colville →, U.S.A. 68 A4 70 25N 150 30W
Colville, C., N.Z. 59 G5 36 29S 175 21 E
Colwood, Canada 84 B3 48 26N 123 29W
Colwyn Bay, U.K. 10 D4 53 18N 3 44W
Comácchio, Italy 20 B5 44 42N 12 11 E
Comalcalco, Mexico 87 D6 18 16N 93 13W
Comallo, Argentina 96 E2 41 0S 70 5W
Comanche, U.S.A. 81 K5 31 54N 98 36W
Comayagua, Honduras 88 D2 14 25N 87 37W
Combahee →, U.S.A. 77 J5 32 30N 80 31W
Combarbalá, Chile 94 C1 31 11S 71 2W
Comber, Canada 78 D2 42 14N 82 33W
Comber, U.K. 13 B6 54 33N 5 45W
Combermere, Canada 78 A7 45 22N 77 37W
Comblain-au-Pont, Belgium 15 D5 50 29N 5 35 E
Comeragh Mts., Ireland 13 D4 52 18N 7 34W
Comet, Australia 62 C4 23 36S 148 38 E
Comilla, Bangla. 41 H17 23 28N 91 10 E
Comino, Malta 23 C1 36 1N 14 20 E
Comino, C., Italy 20 D3 40 32N 9 49 E
Comitán, Mexico 87 D6 16 18N 92 9W
Commerce, Ga., U.S.A. 77 H4 34 12N 83 28W
Commerce, Tex., U.S.A. 81 J7 33 15N 95 54W
Committee B., Canada 69 B11 68 30N 86 30W
Commonwealth B., Antarctica 5 C10 67 0S 144 0 E
Commoron Cr. →, Australia 63 D5 28 22S 150 8 E
Communism Pk. = Kommunizma, Pik, Tajikistan 26 F8 39 0N 72 2 E
Como, Italy 18 D8 45 47N 9 5 E
Como, Lago di, Italy 18 D8 46 0N 9 11 E
Comodoro Rivadavia, Argentina 96 F3 45 50S 67 40W
Comorin, C., India 40 Q10 8 3N 77 40 E
Comoro Is. = Comoros ■, Ind. Oc. 49 H8 12 10S 44 15 E
Comoros ■, Ind. Oc. 49 H8 12 10S 44 15 E
Comox, Canada 72 D4 49 42N 124 55W
Compiègne, France 18 B5 49 24N 2 50 E
Compostela, Mexico 86 C4 21 15N 104 53W
Comprida, I., Brazil 95 A6 24 50S 47 42W
Compton, Canada 79 A13 45 14N 71 49W
Compton, U.S.A. 85 M8 33 54N 118 13W
Comrat, Moldova 17 E15 46 18N 28 40 E
Con Cuong, Vietnam 38 C5 19 2N 104 54 E
Con Son, Vietnam 39 H6 8 41N 106 37 E
Conakry, Guinea 50 G3 9 29N 13 49W
Conara, Australia 62 G4 41 50S 147 26 E
Concarneau, France 18 C2 47 52N 3 56W
Conceição, Mozam. 55 F4 18 47S 36 7 E
Conceição da Barra, Brazil 93 G11 18 35S 39 45W
Conceição do Araguaia, Brazil 93 E9 8 0S 49 2W
Concepción, Argentina 94 B2 27 20S 65 35W
Concepción, Bolivia 92 G6 16 15S 62 8W
Concepción, Chile 94 D1 36 50S 73 0W
Concepción, Mexico 87 D6 18 15N 90 5W
Concepción, Paraguay 94 A4 23 22S 57 26W
Concepción □, Chile 94 D1 37 0S 72 30W
Concepción →, Mexico 86 A2 30 32N 113 2W
Concepción, Est. de, Chile 96 G2 50 30S 74 55W
Concepción, L., Bolivia 92 G6 17 20S 61 20W
Concepción, Punta, Mexico 86 B2 26 55N 111 59W
Concepción del Oro, Mexico 86 C4 24 40N 101 30W
Concepción del Uruguay, Argentina 94 C4 32 35S 58 20W
Conception, Pt., U.S.A. 85 L6 34 27N 120 28W
Conception B., Canada 71 C9 47 45N 53 0W
Conception B., Namibia 56 C1 23 55S 14 22 E
Conception I., Bahamas 89 B4 23 52N 75 9W
Concession, Zimbabwe 55 F3 17 27S 30 56 E
Conchas Dam, U.S.A. 81 H2 35 22N 104 11W
Concho, U.S.A. 83 J9 34 28N 109 36W
Concho →, U.S.A. 81 K5 31 34N 99 43W
Conchos →, Chihuahua, Mexico 86 B4 29 32N 105 0W
Conchos →, Tamaulipas, Mexico 87 B5 25 9N 98 35W
Concord, Calif., U.S.A. 84 H4 37 59N 122 2W
Concord, N.C., U.S.A. 77 H5 35 25N 80 35W
Concord, N.H., U.S.A. 79 C13 43 12N 71 32W
Concordia, Argentina 94 C4 31 20S 58 2W
Concórdia, Brazil 92 D5 4 36S 66 36W
Concordia, Mexico 86 C3 23 18N 106 2W
Concordia, U.S.A. 80 F6 39 34N 97 40W
Concrete, U.S.A. 82 B3 48 32N 121 45W
Condamine, Australia 63 D5 26 56S 150 9 E
Conde, U.S.A. 80 C5 45 9N 98 6W
Condeúba, Brazil 93 F10 14 52S 42 0W
Condobolin, Australia 63 E4 33 4S 147 6 E
Condon, U.S.A. 82 D3 45 14N 120 11W
Conegliano, Italy 20 B5 45 53N 12 18 E
Conejera, I. = Conills, I. des, Spain 22 B9 39 11N 2 58 E
Conejos, Mexico 86 B4 26 14N 103 53W
Confuso →, Paraguay 94 B4 25 9S 57 34W
Congleton, U.K. 10 D5 53 10N 2 13W
Congo (Kinshasa) = Congo, Dem. Rep. of the ■, Africa 52 E4 3 0S 23 0 E
Congo ■, Africa 52 E3 1 0S 16 0 E
Congo →, Africa 52 F2 6 4S 12 24 E
Congo, Dem. Rep. of the ■, Africa 52 E4 3 0S 23 0 E
Congo Basin, Africa 52 E4 0 10S 24 30 E
Congonhas, Brazil 95 A7 20 30S 43 52W
Congress, U.S.A. 83 J7 34 9N 112 51W
Conills, I. des, Spain 22 B9 39 11N 2 58 E
Coniston, Canada 70 C3 46 29N 80 51W
Conjeeveram = Kanchipuram, India 40 N11 12 52N 79 45 E
Conklin, Canada 73 B6 55 38N 111 5W
Conklin, U.S.A. 79 D9 42 2N 75 49W
Conn, L., Ireland 13 B2 54 3N 9 15W
Connacht □, Ireland 13 C2 53 43N 9 12W
Conneaut, U.S.A. 78 E4 41 57N 80 34W
Connecticut □, U.S.A. 79 E12 41 30N 72 45W
Connecticut →, U.S.A. 79 E12 41 16N 72 20W
Connell, U.S.A. 82 C4 46 40N 118 52W
Connellsville, U.S.A. 78 F5 40 1N 79 35W
Connemara, Ireland 13 C2 53 29N 9 45W
Connemaugh →, U.S.A. 78 F5 40 28N 79 19W
Connersville, U.S.A. 76 F3 39 39N 85 8W
Connors Ra., Australia 62 C4 21 40S 149 10 E
Conquest, Canada 73 C7 51 32N 107 14W
Conrad, U.S.A. 82 B8 48 10N 111 57W
Conran, C., Australia 63 F4 37 49S 148 44 E
Conroe, U.S.A. 81 K7 30 19N 95 27W
Consecon, Canada 78 C7 44 0N 77 31W
Conselheiro Lafaiete, Brazil 95 A7 20 40S 43 48W
Consett, U.K. 10 C6 54 51N 1 50W
Consort, Canada 73 C6 52 1N 110 46W
Constance = Konstanz, Germany 16 E5 47 40N 9 10 E
Constance, L. = Bodensee, Europe 18 C8 47 35N 9 25 E
Constanța, Romania 17 F15 44 14N 28 38 E
Constantia, U.S.A. 79 C8 43 15N 76 1W
Constantine, Algeria 50 A7 36 25N 6 42 E
Constitución, Chile 94 D1 35 20S 72 30W
Constitución, Uruguay 94 C4 31 0S 57 50W
Consul, Canada 73 D7 49 20N 109 30W
Contact, U.S.A. 82 F6 41 46N 114 45W
Contai, India 43 J12 21 54N 87 46 E
Contamana, Peru 92 E4 7 19S 74 55W
Contas →, Brazil 93 F11 14 17S 39 1W
Contoocook, U.S.A. 79 C13 43 13N 71 45W
Contra Costa, Mozam. 57 D5 25 9S 33 30 E
Contwoyto L., Canada 68 B8 65 42N 110 50W
Conway = Conwy, U.K. 10 D4 53 17N 3 50W
Conway = Conwy →, U.K. 10 D4 53 17N 3 50W
Conway, Ark., U.S.A. 81 H8 35 5N 92 26W
Conway, N.H., U.S.A. 79 C13 43 59N 71 7W
Conway, S.C., U.S.A. 77 J6 33 51N 79 3W
Conway, L., Australia 63 D2 28 17S 135 35 E
Conwy, U.K. 10 D4 53 17N 3 50W
Conwy □, U.K. 10 D4 53 10N 3 44W
Conwy →, U.K. 10 D4 53 17N 3 50W
Coober Pedy, Australia 63 D1 29 1S 134 43 E
Cooch Behar = Koch Bihar, India 41 F16 26 22N 89 29 E
Cooinda, Australia 60 B5 13 15S 130 5 E
Cook, Australia 61 F5 30 37S 130 25 E
Cook, U.S.A. 80 B8 47 49N 92 39W
Cook, B., Chile 96 H3 55 10S 70 0W
Cook, C., Canada 72 C3 50 8N 127 55W
Cook, Mt. = Aoraki Mount Cook, N.Z. 59 K3 43 36S 170 9 E
Cook Inlet, U.S.A. 68 C4 60 0N 152 0W
Cook Is., Pac. Oc. 65 J12 17 0S 160 0W
Cook Strait, N.Z. 59 J5 41 15S 174 29 E
Cookeville, U.S.A. 77 G3 36 10N 85 30W
Cookhouse, S. Africa 56 E4 32 44S 25 47 E
Cookshire, Canada 79 A13 45 25N 71 38W
Cookstown, U.K. 13 B5 54 39N 6 45W
Cooksville, Canada 78 C5 43 36N 79 35W
Cooktown, Australia 62 B4 15 30S 145 16 E
Coolabah, Australia 63 E4 31 1S 146 43 E
Cooladdi, Australia 63 D4 26 37S 145 23 E
Coolah, Australia 63 E4 31 48S 149 41 E
Coolamon, Australia 63 E4 34 46S 147 8 E
Coolgardie, Australia 61 F3 30 55S 121 8 E
Coolidge, U.S.A. 83 K8 32 59N 111 31W
Coolidge Dam, U.S.A. 83 K8 33 0N 110 20W
Cooma, Australia 63 F4 36 12S 149 8 E
Coon Rapids, U.S.A. 80 C8 45 9N 93 19W
Coonabarabran, Australia 63 E4 31 14S 149 18 E
Coonamble, Australia 63 E4 30 56S 148 27 E
Coonana, Australia 61 F3 31 0S 123 0 E
Coondapoor, India 40 N9 13 42N 74 40 E
Cooninie, L., Australia 63 D2 26 4S 139 59 E
Cooper, U.S.A. 81 J7 33 23N 95 42W
Cooper Cr. →, Australia 63 D2 28 29S 137 46 E
Cooperstown, N. Dak., U.S.A. 80 B5 47 27N 98 8W
Cooperstown, N.Y., U.S.A. 79 D10 42 42N 74 56W
Coorabie, Australia 61 F5 31 54S 132 18 E
Coorong, The, Australia 63 F2 35 50S 139 20 E
Coorow, Australia 61 E2 29 53S 116 2 E
Cooroy, Australia 63 D5 26 22S 152 54 E
Coos Bay, U.S.A. 82 E1 43 22N 124 13W
Coosa →, U.S.A. 77 J2 32 30N 86 16W
Cootamundra, Australia 63 E4 34 36S 148 1 E
Cootehill, Ireland 13 B4 54 4N 7 5W
Copahue Paso, Argentina 94 D1 37 49S 71 8W
Copainalá, Mexico 87 D6 17 8N 93 11W
Copake Falls, U.S.A. 79 D11 42 7N 73 31W
Copán, Honduras 88 D2 14 50N 89 9W
Cope, U.S.A. 80 F3 39 40N 102 51W
Copenhagen = København, Denmark 9 J15 55 41N 12 34 E
Copenhagen, U.S.A. 79 C9 43 54N 75 41W
Copiapó, Chile 94 B1 27 30S 70 20W
Copiapó →, Chile 94 B1 27 19S 70 56W
Coplay, U.S.A. 79 F9 40 44N 75 29W
Copp L., Canada 72 A6 60 14N 114 40W
Coppename →, Surinam 93 B7 5 48N 55 55W
Copper Harbor, U.S.A. 76 B2 47 28N 87 53W
Copper Queen, Zimbabwe 55 F2 17 29S 29 18 E
Copperas Cove, U.S.A. 81 K6 31 8N 97 54W
Copperbelt □, Zambia 55 E2 13 15S 27 30 E
Coppermine = Kugluktuk, Canada 68 B8 67 50N 115 5W
Coppermine →, Canada 68 B8 67 49N 116 4W
Copperopolis, U.S.A. 84 H6 37 58N 120 38W
Coquet →, U.K. 10 B6 55 20N 1 32W
Coquille, U.S.A. 82 E1 43 11N 124 11W
Coquimbo, Chile 94 C1 30 0S 71 20W
Coquimbo □, Chile 94 C1 31 0S 71 0W
Corabia, Romania 17 G13 43 48N 24 30 E
Coracora, Peru 92 G4 15 5S 73 45W
Coraki, Australia 63 D5 28 59S 153 17 E
Coral, U.S.A. 78 F5 40 29N 79 10W
Coral Gables, U.S.A. 77 N5 25 45N 80 16W
Coral Harbour = Salliq, Canada 69 B11 64 8N 83 10W
Coral Sea, Pac. Oc. 64 J7 15 0S 150 0 E

Coral Springs, U.S.A. **77 M5** 26 16N 80 13W
Coraopolis, U.S.A. **78 F4** 40 31N 80 10W
Corato, Italy **20 D7** 41 9N 16 25 E
Corbin, U.S.A. **76 G3** 36 57N 84 6W
Corby, U.K. **11 E7** 52 30N 0 41W
Corcaigh = Cork, Ireland **13 E3** 51 54N 8 29W
Corcoran, U.S.A. **84 J7** 36 6N 119 33W
Corcubión, Spain **19 A1** 42 56N 9 12W
Cordele, U.S.A. **77 K4** 31 58N 83 47W
Cordell, U.S.A. **81 H5** 35 17N 98 59W
Córdoba, Argentina **94 C3** 31 20S 64 10W
Córdoba, Mexico **87 D5** 18 50N 97 0W
Córdoba, Spain **19 D3** 37 50N 4 50W
Córdoba □, Argentina **94 C3** 31 22S 64 15W
Córdoba, Sierra de, Argentina **94 C3** 31 10S 64 25W
Cordova, U.S.A. **68 B5** 60 33N 145 45W
Corella →, Australia **62 B3** 19 34S 140 47 E
Corfield, Australia **62 C3** 21 40S 143 21 E
Corfu = Kérkira, Greece **23 A3** 39 38N 19 50 E
Corfu, Str. of, Greece **23 A4** 39 34N 20 0 E
Coria, Spain **19 C2** 39 58N 6 33W
Corigliano Cálabro, Italy **20 E7** 39 36N 16 31 E
Coringa Is., Australia **62 B4** 16 58S 149 58 E
Corinth = Kórinthos, Greece **21 F10** 37 56N 22 55 E
Corinth, Miss., U.S.A. **77 H1** 34 56N 88 31W
Corinth, N.Y., U.S.A. **79 C11** 43 15N 73 49W
Corinth, G. of = Korinthiakós Kólpos, Greece **21 E10** 38 16N 22 30 E
Corinto, Brazil **93 G10** 18 20S 44 30W
Corinto, Nic. **88 D2** 12 30N 87 10W
Cork, Ireland **13 E3** 51 54N 8 29W
Cork □, Ireland **13 E3** 51 57N 8 40W
Cork Harbour, Ireland **13 E3** 51 47N 8 16W
Çorlu, Turkey **21 D12** 41 11N 27 49 E
Cormack L., Canada **72 A4** 60 56N 121 37W
Cormorant, Canada **73 C8** 54 14N 100 35W
Cormorant L., Canada **73 C8** 54 15N 100 50W
Corn Is. = Maiz, Is. del, Nic. **88 D3** 12 15N 83 4W
Cornélio Procópio, Brazil **95 A5** 23 7S 50 40W
Corner Brook, Canada **71 C8** 48 57N 57 58W
Corneşti, Moldova **17 E15** 47 21N 28 1 E
Corning, Ark., U.S.A. **81 G9** 36 25N 90 35W
Corning, Calif., U.S.A. **82 G2** 39 56N 122 11W
Corning, Iowa, U.S.A. **80 E7** 40 59N 94 44W
Corning, N.Y., U.S.A. **78 D7** 42 9N 77 3W
Cornwall, Canada **79 A10** 45 2N 74 44W
Cornwall, U.S.A. **79 F8** 40 17N 76 25W
Cornwall □, U.K. **11 G3** 50 26N 4 40W
Corny Pt., Australia **63 E2** 34 55S 137 0 E
Coro, Venezuela **92 A5** 11 25N 69 41W
Coroatá, Brazil **93 D10** 4 8S 44 0W
Corocoro, Bolivia **92 G5** 17 15S 68 28W
Coroico, Bolivia **92 G5** 16 0S 67 50W
Coromandel, N.Z. **59 G5** 36 45S 175 31 E
Coromandel Coast, India **40 N12** 12 30N 81 0 E
Corona, Calif., U.S.A. **85 M9** 33 53N 117 34W
Corona, N. Mex., U.S.A. **83 J11** 34 15N 105 36W
Coronach, Canada **73 D7** 49 7N 105 31W
Coronado, U.S.A. **85 N9** 32 41N 117 11W
Coronado, B. de, Costa Rica **88 E3** 9 0N 83 40W
Coronados, Is. los, U.S.A. **85 N9** 32 25N 117 15W
Coronation, Canada **72 C6** 52 5N 111 27W
Coronation Gulf, Canada **68 B8** 68 25N 110 0W
Coronation I., Antarctica **5 C18** 60 45S 46 0W
Coronation Is., Australia **60 B3** 14 57S 124 55 E
Coronda, Argentina **94 C3** 31 58S 60 56W
Coronel, Chile **94 D1** 37 0S 73 10W
Coronel Bogado, Paraguay **94 B4** 27 11S 56 18W
Coronel Dorrego, Argentina **94 D3** 38 40S 61 10W
Coronel Oviedo, Paraguay **94 B4** 25 24S 56 30W
Coronel Pringles, Argentina **94 D3** 38 0S 61 30W
Coronel Suárez, Argentina **94 D3** 37 30S 61 52W
Coronel Vidal, Argentina **94 D4** 37 28S 57 45W
Coropuna, Nevado, Peru **92 G4** 15 30S 72 41W
Corowa, Australia **63 F4** 35 58S 146 21 E
Corozal, Belize **87 D7** 18 23N 88 23W
Corpus, Argentina **95 B4** 27 10S 55 30W
Corpus Christi, U.S.A. **81 M6** 27 47N 97 24W
Corpus Christi, L., U.S.A. **81 L6** 28 2N 97 52W
Corralejo, Canary Is. **22 F6** 28 43N 13 53W
Corraun Pen., Ireland **13 C2** 53 54N 9 54W
Correntes, C. das, Mozam. **57 C6** 24 6S 35 34 E
Corrib, L., Ireland **13 C2** 53 27N 9 16W
Corrientes, Argentina **94 B4** 27 30S 58 45W
Corrientes □, Argentina **94 B4** 28 0S 57 0W
Corrientes →, Argentina **94 C4** 30 42S 59 38W
Corrientes →, Peru **92 D4** 3 43S 74 35W
Corrientes, C., Colombia **92 B3** 5 30N 77 34W
Corrientes, C., Cuba **88 B3** 21 43N 84 30W
Corrientes, C., Mexico **86 C3** 20 25N 105 42W
Corrigan, U.S.A. **81 K7** 31 0N 94 52W
Corrigin, Australia **61 F2** 32 20S 117 53 E
Corry, U.S.A. **78 E5** 41 55N 79 39W
Corse, France **18 F8** 42 0N 9 0 E
Corse, C., France **18 E8** 43 1N 9 25 E
Corsica = Corse, France **18 F8** 42 0N 9 0 E
Corsicana, U.S.A. **81 J6** 32 6N 96 28W
Corte, France **18 E8** 42 19N 9 11 E
Cortez, U.S.A. **83 H9** 37 21N 108 35W
Cortland, N.Y., U.S.A. **79 D8** 42 36N 76 11W
Cortland, Ohio, U.S.A. **78 E4** 41 20N 80 44W
Çorum, Turkey **25 F5** 40 30N 34 57 E
Corumbá, Brazil **92 G7** 19 0S 57 30W
Corunna = A Coruña, Spain **19 A1** 43 20N 8 25W
Corvallis, U.S.A. **82 D2** 44 34N 123 16W
Corvette, L. de la, Canada **70 B5** 53 25N 74 3W
Corydon, U.S.A. **80 E8** 40 46N 93 19W
Cosalá, Mexico **86 C3** 24 28N 106 40W
Cosamaloapan, Mexico **87 D5** 18 23N 95 50W
Cosenza, Italy **20 E7** 39 18N 16 15 E
Coshocton, U.S.A. **78 F3** 40 16N 81 51W
Cosmo Newberry, Australia **61 E3** 28 0S 122 54 E
Coso Junction, U.S.A. **85 J9** 36 3N 117 57W
Coso Pk., U.S.A. **85 J9** 36 13N 117 44W
Cosquín, Argentina **94 C3** 31 15S 64 30W
Costa Blanca, Spain **19 C5** 38 25N 0 10W
Costa Brava, Spain **19 B7** 41 30N 3 0 E
Costa del Sol, Spain **19 D3** 36 30N 4 30W
Costa Dorada, Spain **19 B6** 41 12N 1 15 E
Costa Mesa, U.S.A. **85 M9** 33 38N 117 55W
Costa Rica ■, Cent. Amer. **88 E3** 10 0N 84 0W
Cosumnes →, U.S.A. **84 G5** 38 16N 121 26W
Cotabato, Phil. **37 C6** 7 14N 124 15 E
Cotagaita, Bolivia **94 A2** 20 45S 65 40W
Côte d'Azur, France **18 E7** 43 25N 7 10 E
Côte-d'Ivoire = Ivory Coast ■, Africa **50 G4** 7 30N 5 0W
Coteau des Prairies, U.S.A. **80 C6** 45 20N 97 50W
Coteau du Missouri, U.S.A. **80 B4** 47 0N 100 0W
Coteau Landing, Canada **79 A10** 45 15N 74 13W
Cotentin, France **18 B3** 49 15N 1 30W
Cotillo, Canary Is. **22 F5** 28 41N 14 1W
Cotonou, Benin **50 G6** 6 20N 2 25 E
Cotopaxi, Ecuador **92 D3** 0 40S 78 30W
Cotswold Hills, U.K. **11 F5** 51 42N 2 10W
Cottage Grove, U.S.A. **82 E2** 43 48N 123 3W
Cottbus, Germany **16 C8** 51 45N 14 20 E
Cottonwood, U.S.A. **83 J7** 34 45N 112 1W
Cotulla, U.S.A. **81 L5** 28 26N 99 14W
Coudersport, U.S.A. **78 E6** 41 46N 78 1W
Couedic, C. du, Australia **63 F2** 36 5S 136 40 E
Coulee City, U.S.A. **82 C4** 47 37N 119 17W
Coulman I., Antarctica **5 D11** 73 35S 170 0 E
Coulonge →, Canada **70 C4** 45 52N 76 46W
Coulterville, U.S.A. **84 H6** 37 43N 120 12W
Council, U.S.A. **82 D5** 44 44N 116 26W
Council Bluffs, U.S.A. **80 E7** 41 16N 95 52W
Council Grove, U.S.A. **80 F6** 38 40N 96 29W
Coupeville, U.S.A. **84 B4** 48 13N 122 41W
Courantyne →, S. Amer. **92 B7** 5 55N 57 5W
Courcelles, Belgium **15 D4** 50 28N 4 22 E
Courtenay, Canada **72 D4** 49 45N 125 0W
Courtland, U.S.A. **84 G5** 38 20N 121 34W
Courtrai = Kortrijk, Belgium **15 D3** 50 50N 3 17 E
Courtright, Canada **78 D2** 42 49N 82 28W
Coushatta, U.S.A. **81 J8** 32 1N 93 21W
Coutts Crossing, Australia **63 D5** 29 49S 152 55 E
Couvin, Belgium **15 D4** 50 3N 4 29 E
Cove I., Canada **78 A3** 45 17N 81 44W
Coventry, U.K. **11 E6** 52 25N 1 28W
Covilhã, Portugal **19 B2** 40 17N 7 31W
Covington, Ga., U.S.A. **77 J4** 33 36N 83 51W
Covington, Ky., U.S.A. **76 F3** 39 5N 84 31W
Covington, Okla., U.S.A. **81 G6** 36 18N 97 35W
Covington, Tenn., U.S.A. **81 H10** 35 34N 89 39W
Covington, Va., U.S.A. **76 G5** 37 47N 79 59W
Cowal, L., Australia **63 E4** 33 40S 147 25 E
Cowan, L., Australia **61 F3** 31 45S 121 45 E
Cowan L., Canada **73 C7** 54 0N 107 15W
Cowangie, Australia **63 F3** 35 12S 141 26 E
Cowansville, Canada **79 A12** 45 14N 72 46W
Coward Springs, Australia **63 D2** 29 24S 136 49 E
Cowcowing Lakes, Australia **61 F2** 30 55S 117 20 E
Cowdenbeath, U.K. **12 E5** 56 7N 3 21W
Cowell, Australia **63 E2** 33 39S 136 56 E
Cowes, U.K. **11 G6** 50 45N 1 18W
Cowichan L., Canada **84 B2** 48 53N 124 17W
Cowlitz →, U.S.A. **84 D4** 46 6N 122 55W
Cowra, Australia **63 E4** 33 49S 148 42 E
Coxilha Grande, Brazil **95 B5** 28 18S 51 30W
Coxim, Brazil **93 G8** 18 30S 54 55W
Cox's Bazar, Bangla. **41 J17** 21 26N 91 59 E
Coyote Wells, U.S.A. **85 N11** 32 44N 115 58W
Coyuca de Benítez, Mexico **87 D4** 17 1N 100 8W
Coyuca de Catalan, Mexico **86 D4** 18 18N 100 41W
Cozad, U.S.A. **80 E5** 40 52N 99 59W
Cozumel, Mexico **87 C7** 20 31N 86 55W
Cozumel, Isla, Mexico **87 C7** 20 30N 86 40W
Cracow = Kraków, Poland **17 C10** 50 4N 19 57 E
Cracow, Australia **63 D5** 25 17S 150 17 E
Cradock, Australia **63 E2** 32 6S 138 31 E
Cradock, S. Africa **56 E4** 32 8S 25 36 E
Craig, U.S.A. **82 F10** 40 31N 107 33W
Craigavon, U.K. **13 B5** 54 27N 6 23W
Craigmore, Zimbabwe **55 G3** 20 28S 32 50 E
Craik, Canada **73 C7** 51 3N 105 49W
Crailsheim, Germany **16 D6** 49 8N 10 5 E
Craiova, Romania **17 F12** 44 21N 23 48 E
Cramsie, Australia **62 C3** 23 20S 144 15 E
Cranberry L., U.S.A. **79 B10** 44 11N 74 50W
Cranberry Portage, Canada **73 C8** 54 35N 101 23W
Cranbrook, Australia **61 F2** 34 18S 117 33 E
Cranbrook, Canada **72 D5** 49 30N 115 46W
Crandon, U.S.A. **80 C10** 45 34N 88 54W
Crane, Oreg., U.S.A. **82 E4** 43 25N 118 35W
Crane, Tex., U.S.A. **81 K3** 31 24N 102 21W
Cranston, U.S.A. **79 E13** 41 47N 71 26W
Crater L., U.S.A. **82 E2** 42 56N 122 6W
Crater Lake Nat. Park, U.S.A. **82 E2** 42 55N 122 10W
Crateús, Brazil **93 E10** 5 10S 40 39W
Crato, Brazil **93 E11** 7 10S 39 25W
Craven, L., Canada **70 B4** 54 20N 76 56W
Crawford, U.S.A. **80 D3** 42 41N 103 25W
Crawfordsville, U.S.A. **76 E2** 40 2N 86 54W
Crawley, U.K. **11 F7** 51 7N 0 11W
Crazy Mts., U.S.A. **82 C8** 46 12N 110 20W
Crean L., Canada **73 C7** 54 5N 106 9W
Crediton, Canada **78 C3** 43 17N 81 33W
Cree →, Canada **73 B7** 58 57N 105 47W
Cree →, U.K. **12 G4** 54 55N 4 25W
Cree L., Canada **73 B7** 57 30N 106 30W
Creede, U.S.A. **83 H10** 37 51N 106 56W
Creekside, U.S.A. **78 F5** 40 40N 79 11W
Creel, Mexico **86 B3** 27 45N 107 38W
Creemore, Canada **78 B4** 44 19N 80 6W
Creighton, Canada **73 C8** 54 45N 101 54W
Creighton, U.S.A. **80 D6** 42 28N 97 54W
Crema, Italy **18 D8** 45 22N 9 41 E
Cremona, Italy **18 D9** 45 7N 10 2 E
Cres, Croatia **16 F8** 44 58N 14 25 E
Crescent City, U.S.A. **82 F1** 41 45N 124 12W
Crespo, Argentina **94 C3** 32 2S 60 19W
Cresson, U.S.A. **78 F6** 40 28N 78 36W
Crestline, Calif., U.S.A. **85 L9** 34 14N 117 18W
Crestline, Ohio, U.S.A. **78 F2** 40 47N 82 44W
Creston, Canada **72 D5** 49 10N 116 31W
Creston, Calif., U.S.A. **84 K6** 35 32N 120 33W
Creston, Iowa, U.S.A. **80 E7** 41 4N 94 22W
Crestview, Calif., U.S.A. **84 H8** 37 46N 118 58W
Crestview, Fla., U.S.A. **77 K2** 30 46N 86 34W
Crete = Kríti, Greece **23 D7** 35 15N 25 0 E
Crete, U.S.A. **80 E6** 40 38N 96 58W
Créteil, France **18 B5** 48 47N 2 28 E
Creus, C. de, Spain **19 A7** 42 20N 3 19 E
Creuse →, France **18 C4** 47 0N 0 34 E
Crewe, U.K. **10 D5** 53 6N 2 26W
Crewkerne, U.K. **11 G5** 50 53N 2 48W
Criciúma, Brazil **95 B6** 28 40S 49 23W
Crieff, U.K. **12 E5** 56 22N 3 50W
Crimea □, Ukraine **25 E5** 45 30N 33 10 E
Crimean Pen. = Krymskyy Pivostriv, Ukraine **25 F5** 45 0N 34 0 E
Crişul Alb →, Romania **17 E11** 46 42N 21 17 E
Crişul Negru →, Romania **17 E11** 46 42N 21 16 E
Crna →, Macedonia **21 D9** 41 33N 21 59 E
Crna Gora = Montenegro □, Yugoslavia **21 C8** 42 40N 19 20 E
Crna Gora, Macedonia **21 C9** 42 10N 21 30 E
Crna Reka = Crna →, Macedonia **21 D9** 41 33N 21 59 E
Croagh Patrick, Ireland **13 C2** 53 46N 9 40W
Croatia ■, Europe **16 F9** 45 20N 16 0 E
Crocker, Banjaran, Malaysia **36 C5** 5 40N 116 30 E
Crockett, U.S.A. **81 K7** 31 19N 95 27W
Crocodile = Krokodil →, Mozam. **57 D5** 25 14S 32 18 E
Crocodile Is., Australia **62 A1** 12 3S 134 58 E
Crohy Hd., Ireland **13 B3** 54 55N 8 26W
Croix, L. La, Canada **70 C1** 48 20N 92 15W
Croker, C., Australia **60 B5** 10 58S 132 35 E
Croker, C., Canada **78 B4** 44 58N 80 59W
Croker I., Australia **60 B5** 11 12S 132 32 E
Cromarty, U.K. **12 D4** 57 40N 4 2W
Cromer, U.K. **10 E9** 52 56N 1 17 E
Cromwell, N.Z. **59 L2** 45 3S 169 14 E
Cromwell, U.S.A. **79 E12** 41 36N 72 39W
Crook, U.K. **10 C6** 54 43N 1 45W
Crooked →, Canada **72 C4** 54 50N 122 54W
Crooked →, U.S.A. **82 D3** 44 32N 121 16W
Crooked I., Bahamas **89 B5** 22 50N 74 10W
Crooked Island Passage, Bahamas **89 B5** 23 0N 74 30W
Crookston, Minn., U.S.A. **80 B6** 47 47N 96 37W
Crookston, Nebr., U.S.A. **80 D4** 42 56N 100 45W
Crookwell, Australia **63 E4** 34 28S 149 24 E
Crosby, U.K. **10 D4** 53 30N 3 3W
Crosby, N. Dak., U.S.A. **80 A3** 48 55N 103 18W
Crosby, Pa., U.S.A. **78 E6** 41 45N 78 23W
Crosbyton, U.S.A. **81 J4** 33 40N 101 14W
Cross City, U.S.A. **77 L4** 29 38N 83 7W
Cross Fell, U.K. **10 C5** 54 43N 2 28W
Cross L., Canada **73 C9** 54 45N 97 30W
Cross Lake, Canada **73 C9** 54 37N 97 47W
Cross Sound, U.S.A. **68 C6** 58 0N 135 0W
Crossett, U.S.A. **81 J9** 33 8N 91 58W
Crosshaven, Ireland **13 E3** 51 47N 8 17W
Crossville, U.S.A. **77 G3** 35 57N 85 2W
Croswell, U.S.A. **78 C2** 43 16N 82 37W
Croton-on-Hudson, U.S.A. **79 E11** 41 12N 73 55W
Crotone, Italy **20 E7** 39 5N 17 8 E
Crow →, Canada **72 B4** 59 41N 124 20W
Crow Agency, U.S.A. **82 D10** 45 36N 107 28W
Crow Hd., Ireland **13 E1** 51 35N 10 9W
Crowell, U.S.A. **81 J5** 33 59N 99 43W
Crowley, U.S.A. **81 K8** 30 13N 92 22W
Crowley, L., U.S.A. **84 H8** 37 35N 118 42W
Crown Point, Ind., U.S.A. **76 E2** 41 25N 87 22W
Crown Point, N.Y., U.S.A. **79 C11** 43 57N 73 26W
Crownpoint, U.S.A. **83 J9** 35 41N 108 9W
Crows Landing, U.S.A. **84 H5** 37 23N 121 6W
Crows Nest, Australia **63 D5** 27 16S 152 4 E
Crowsnest Pass, Canada **72 D6** 49 40N 114 40W
Croydon, Australia **62 B3** 18 13S 142 14 E
Croydon □, U.K. **11 F7** 51 22N 0 5W
Crozet, Is., Ind. Oc. **3 G12** 46 27S 52 0 E
Cruz, C., Cuba **88 C4** 19 50N 77 50W
Cruz Alta, Brazil **95 B5** 28 45S 53 40W
Cruz del Eje, Argentina **94 C3** 30 45S 64 50W
Cruzeiro, Brazil **95 A7** 22 33S 45 0W
Cruzeiro do Oeste, Brazil **95 A5** 23 46S 53 4W
Cruzeiro do Sul, Brazil **92 E4** 7 35S 72 35W
Cry L., Canada **72 B3** 58 45N 129 0W
Crystal Bay, U.S.A. **84 F7** 39 15N 120 0W
Crystal Brook, Australia **63 E2** 33 21S 138 12 E
Crystal City, U.S.A. **81 L5** 28 41N 99 50W
Crystal Falls, U.S.A. **76 B1** 46 5N 88 20W
Crystal River, U.S.A. **77 L4** 28 54N 82 35W
Crystal Springs, U.S.A. **81 K9** 31 59N 90 21W
Csongrád, Hungary **17 E11** 46 43N 20 12 E
Cu Lao Hon, Vietnam **39 G7** 10 54N 108 18 E
Cua Rao, Vietnam **38 C5** 19 16N 104 27 E
Cuácua →, Mozam. **55 F4** 17 54S 37 0 E
Cuamato, Angola **56 B2** 17 2S 15 7 E
Cuamba, Mozam. **55 E4** 14 45S 36 22 E
Cuando →, Angola **53 H4** 17 30S 23 15 E
Cuando Cubango □, Angola **56 B3** 16 25S 20 0 E
Cuangar, Angola **56 B2** 17 36S 18 39 E
Cuango = Kwango →, Dem. Rep. of the Congo **52 E3** 3 14S 17 22 E
Cuanza →, Angola **52 F2** 9 21S 13 9 E
Cuarto →, Argentina **94 C3** 33 25S 63 2W
Cuatrociénegas, Mexico **86 B4** 26 59N 102 5W
Cuauhtémoc, Mexico **86 B3** 28 25N 106 52W
Cuba, N. Mex., U.S.A. **83 J10** 36 1N 107 4W
Cuba, N.Y., U.S.A. **78 D6** 42 13N 78 17W
Cuba ■, W. Indies **88 B4** 22 0N 79 0W
Cubango →, Africa **56 B3** 18 50S 22 25 E
Cuchumatanes, Sierra de los, Guatemala **88 C1** 15 35N 91 25W
Cuckfield, U.K. **11 F7** 51 1N 0 8W
Cucuí, Brazil **92 C5** 1 12N 66 50W
Cucurpe, Mexico **86 A2** 30 20N 110 43W
Cúcuta, Colombia **92 B4** 7 54N 72 31W
Cuddalore, India **40 P11** 11 46N 79 45 E
Cuddapah, India **40 M11** 14 30N 78 47 E
Cuddapan, L., Australia **62 D3** 25 45S 141 26 E
Cue, Australia **61 E2** 27 25S 117 54 E
Cuenca, Ecuador **92 D3** 2 50S 79 9W
Cuenca, Spain **19 B4** 40 5N 2 10W
Cuenca, Serranía de, Spain **19 C5** 39 55N 1 50W
Cuernavaca, Mexico **87 D5** 18 55N 99 15W
Cuero, U.S.A. **81 L6** 29 6N 97 17W
Cuevas del Almanzora, Spain **19 D5** 37 18N 1 58W
Cuevo, Bolivia **92 H6** 20 15S 63 30W
Cuiabá, Brazil **93 G7** 15 30S 56 0W
Cuiabá →, Brazil **93 G7** 17 5S 56 36W
Cuijk, Neths. **15 C5** 51 44N 5 50 E
Cuilco, Guatemala **88 C1** 15 24N 91 58W
Cuillin Hills, U.K. **12 D2** 57 13N 6 15W
Cuillin Sd., U.K. **12 D2** 57 4N 6 20W
Cuito →, Angola **56 B3** 18 1S 20 48 E
Cuitzeo, L. de, Mexico **86 D4** 19 55N 101 5W
Cukai, Malaysia **39 K4** 4 13N 103 25 E
Culbertson, U.S.A. **80 A2** 48 9N 104 31W
Culcairn, Australia **63 F4** 35 41S 147 3 E
Culgoa →, Australia **63 D4** 29 56S 146 20 E
Culiacán, Mexico **86 C3** 24 50N 107 23W
Culiacán →, Mexico **86 C3** 24 30N 107 42W
Culion, Phil. **37 B6** 11 54N 119 58 E
Cullarin Ra., Australia **63 E4** 34 30S 149 30 E
Cullen, U.K. **12 D6** 57 42N 2 49W
Cullen Pt., Australia **62 A3** 11 57S 141 54 E
Cullera, Spain **19 C5** 39 9N 0 17W
Cullman, U.S.A. **77 H2** 34 11N 86 51W
Culpeper, U.S.A. **76 F7** 38 30N 78 0W
Culuene →, Brazil **93 F8** 12 56S 52 51W
Culver, Pt., Australia **61 F3** 32 54S 124 43 E
Culverden, N.Z. **59 K4** 42 47S 172 49 E
Cumaná, Venezuela **92 A6** 10 30N 64 5W
Cumberland, B.C., Canada **72 D4** 49 40N 125 0W
Cumberland, Ont., Canada **79 A9** 45 29N 75 24W
Cumberland, U.S.A. **76 F6** 39 39N 78 46W
Cumberland →, U.S.A. **77 G2** 36 15N 87 0W
Cumberland, L., U.S.A. **77 G3** 36 57N 84 55W
Cumberland I., U.S.A. **77 K5** 30 50N 81 25W
Cumberland Is., Australia **62 C4** 20 35S 149 10 E
Cumberland L., Canada **73 C8** 54 3N 102 18W
Cumberland Pen., Canada **69 B13** 67 0N 64 0W
Cumberland Plateau, U.S.A. **77 H3** 36 0N 85 0W
Cumberland Sd., Canada **69 B13** 65 30N 66 0W
Cumbernauld, U.K. **12 F5** 55 57N 3 58W
Cumborah, Australia **63 D4** 29 40S 147 45 E
Cumbria □, U.K. **10 C5** 54 42N 2 52W
Cumbrian Mts., U.K. **10 C5** 54 30N 3 0W
Cumbum, India **40 M11** 15 40N 79 10 E
Cuminá →, Brazil **93 D7** 1 30S 56 0W
Cummings Mt., U.S.A. **85 K8** 35 2N 118 34W
Cummins, Australia **63 E2** 34 16S 135 43 E
Cumnock, Australia **63 E4** 32 59S 148 46 E
Cumnock, U.K. **12 F4** 55 28N 4 17W
Cumpas, Mexico **86 B3** 30 0N 109 48W
Cumplida, Pta., Canary Is. **22 F2** 28 50N 17 48W
Cunco, Chile **96 D2** 38 55S 72 2W
Cuncumén, Chile **94 C1** 31 53S 70 38W
Cunderdin, Australia **61 F2** 31 37S 117 12 E
Cunene →, Angola **56 B1** 17 20S 11 50 E
Cúneo, Italy **18 D7** 44 23N 7 32 E
Çüngüş, Turkey **44 B3** 38 13N 39 17 E
Cunillera, I. = Sa Conillera, Spain **22 C7** 38 59N 1 13 E
Cunnamulla, Australia **63 D4** 28 2S 145 38 E
Cupar, Canada **73 C8** 50 57N 104 10W
Cupar, U.K. **12 E5** 56 19N 3 1W
Cupica, G. de, Colombia **92 B3** 6 25N 77 30W
Curaçao, Neth. Ant. **89 D6** 12 10N 69 0W
Curanilahue, Chile **94 D1** 37 29S 73 28W
Curaray →, Peru **92 D4** 2 20S 74 5W
Curepto, Chile **94 D1** 35 8S 72 1W
Curiapo, Venezuela **92 B6** 8 33N 61 5W
Curicó, Chile **94 C1** 34 55S 71 20W
Curitiba, Brazil **95 B6** 25 20S 49 10W
Curitibanos, Brazil **95 B5** 27 18S 50 36W
Currabubula, Australia **63 E5** 31 16S 150 44 E
Currais Novos, Brazil **93 E11** 6 13S 36 30W
Curralinho, Brazil **93 D9** 1 45S 49 46W
Currant, U.S.A. **82 G6** 38 51N 115 32W
Current →, U.S.A. **81 G9** 36 15N 90 55W
Currie, Australia **62 F3** 39 56S 143 53 E
Currie, U.S.A. **82 F6** 40 16N 114 45W
Curtea de Argeş, Romania **17 F13** 45 12N 24 42 E
Curtis, U.S.A. **80 E4** 40 38N 100 31W
Curtis Group, Australia **62 F4** 39 30S 146 37 E
Curtis I., Australia **62 C5** 23 35S 151 10 E
Curuápanema →, Brazil **93 D7** 2 25S 55 2W
Curuçá, Brazil **93 D9** 0 43S 47 50W
Curuguaty, Paraguay **95 A4** 24 31S 55 42W
Curup, Indonesia **36 E2** 4 26S 102 13 E
Cururupu, Brazil **93 D10** 1 50S 44 50W
Curuzú Cuatiá, Argentina **94 B4** 29 50S 58 5W
Curvelo, Brazil **93 G10** 18 45S 44 27W
Cushing, U.S.A. **81 H6** 35 59N 96 46W
Cushing, Mt., Canada **72 B3** 57 35N 126 57W
Cusihuiriáchic, Mexico **86 B3** 28 10N 106 50W
Custer, U.S.A. **80 D3** 43 46N 103 36W
Cut Bank, U.S.A. **82 B7** 48 38N 112 20W
Cutchogue, U.S.A. **79 E12** 41 1N 72 30W
Cuthbert, U.S.A. **77 K3** 31 46N 84 48W
Cutler, U.S.A. **84 J7** 36 31N 119 17W
Cuttaburra →, Australia **63 D3** 29 43S 144 22 E
Cuttack, India **41 J14** 20 25N 85 57 E
Cuvier, C., Australia **61 D1** 23 14S 113 22 E
Cuvier I., N.Z. **59 G5** 36 27S 175 50 E
Cuxhaven, Germany **16 B5** 53 51N 8 41 E
Cuyahoga Falls, U.S.A. **78 E3** 41 8N 81 29W
Cuyo, Phil. **37 B6** 10 50N 121 5 E
Cuyuni →, Guyana **92 B7** 6 23N 58 41W
Cuzco, Bolivia **92 H5** 20 0S 66 50W
Cuzco, Peru **92 F4** 13 32S 72 0W
Cwmbran, U.K. **11 F4** 51 39N 3 2W
Cyangugu, Rwanda **54 C2** 2 29S 28 54 E
Cyclades = Kikládhes, Greece **21 F11** 37 0N 24 30 E
Cygnet, Australia **62 G4** 43 8S 147 1 E
Cynthiana, U.S.A. **76 F3** 38 23N 84 18W
Cypress Hills, Canada **73 D7** 49 40N 109 30W
Cypress Hills Prov. Park, Canada **73 D7** 49 40N 109 30W
Cyprus ■, Asia **23 E12** 35 0N 33 0 E
Cyrenaica, Libya **51 C10** 27 0N 23 0 E
Czar, Canada **73 C6** 52 27N 110 50W
Czech Rep. ■, Europe **16 D8** 50 0N 15 0 E
Częstochowa, Poland **17 C10** 50 49N 19 7 E

D

Da →, Vietnam **38 B5** 21 15N 105 20 E
Da Hinggan Ling, China **33 B7** 48 0N 121 0 E
Da Lat, Vietnam **39 G7** 11 56N 108 25 E
Da Nang, Vietnam **38 D7** 16 4N 108 13 E
Da Qaidam, China **32 C4** 37 50N 95 15 E
Da Yunhe →, China **35 G11** 34 25N 120 5 E
Da'an, China **35 B13** 45 30N 124 7 E
Daba Shan, China **33 C5** 32 0N 109 0 E
Dabbagh, Jabal, Si. Arabia **44 E2** 27 52N 35 45 E
Dabhoi, India **42 H5** 22 10N 73 20 E
Dabo = Pasirkuning, Indonesia **36 E2** 0 30S 104 33 E
Dabola, Guinea **50 F3** 10 50N 11 5W
Dabung, Malaysia **39 K4** 5 23N 102 1 E

Dacca = Dhaka, *Bangla.* **43 H14** 23 43N 90 26 E
Dacca = Dhaka □, *Bangla.* **43 G14** 24 25N 90 25 E
Dachau, *Germany* **16 D6** 48 15N 11 26 E
Dadanawa, *Guyana* **92 C7** 2 50N 59 30W
Dade City, *U.S.A.* **77 L4** 28 22N 82 11W
Dadhar, *Pakistan* **42 E2** 29 28N 67 39 E
Dadra & Nagar Haveli □, *India* **40 J8** 20 5N 73 0 E
Dadri = Charkhi Dadri, *India* **42 E7** 28 37N 76 17 E
Dadu, *Pakistan* **42 F2** 26 45N 67 45 E
Daet, *Phil.* **37 B6** 14 2N 122 55 E
Dagana, *Senegal* **50 E2** 16 30N 15 35W
Dagestan □, *Russia* **25 F8** 42 30N 47 0 E
Daggett, *U.S.A.* **85 L10** 34 52N 116 52W
Daghestan Republic = Dagestan □, *Russia* **25 F8** 42 30N 47 0 E
Dağlıq Qarabağ = Nagorno-Karabakh, *Azerbaijan* **25 F8** 39 55N 46 45 E
Dagö = Hiiumaa, *Estonia* **9 G20** 58 50N 22 45 E
Dagu, *China* **35 E9** 38 59N 117 40 E
Dagupan, *Phil.* **37 A6** 16 3N 120 20 E
Daguragu, *Australia* **60 C5** 17 33S 130 30 E
Dahlak Kebir, *Eritrea* **46 D3** 15 50N 40 10 E
Dahlonega, *U.S.A.* **77 H4** 34 32N 83 59W
Dahod, *India* **42 H6** 22 50N 74 15 E
Dahomey = Benin ■, *Africa* **50 G6** 10 0N 2 0 E
Dahūk, *Iraq* **44 B3** 36 50N 43 1 E
Dai Hao, *Vietnam* **38 C6** 18 1N 106 25 E
Dai-Sen, *Japan* **31 G6** 35 22N 133 32 E
Dai Xian, *China* **34 E7** 39 4N 112 58 E
Daicheng, *China* **34 E9** 38 42N 116 38 E
Daingean, *Ireland* **13 C4** 53 18N 7 17W
Daintree, *Australia* **62 B4** 16 20S 145 20 E
Daiō-Misaki, *Japan* **31 G8** 34 15N 136 45 E
Daisetsu-Zan, *Japan* **30 C11** 43 30N 142 57 E
Dajarra, *Australia* **62 C2** 21 42S 139 30 E
Dak Dam, *Cambodia* **38 F6** 12 20N 107 21 E
Dak Nhe, *Vietnam* **38 E6** 15 28N 107 48 E
Dak Pek, *Vietnam* **38 E6** 15 4N 107 44 E
Dak Song, *Vietnam* **39 F6** 12 19N 107 35 E
Dak Sui, *Vietnam* **38 E6** 14 55N 107 43 E
Dakar, *Senegal* **50 F2** 14 34N 17 29W
Dakhla, *W. Sahara* **50 D2** 23 50N 15 53W
Dakhla, El Wâhât el-, *Egypt* **51 C11** 25 30N 28 50 E
Dakor, *India* **42 H5** 22 45N 73 11 E
Dakota City, *U.S.A.* **80 D6** 42 25N 96 25W
Đakovica, *Kosovo, Yug.* **21 C9** 42 22N 20 26 E
Dalachi, *China* **34 F3** 36 48N 105 0 E
Dalai Nur, *China* **34 C9** 43 20N 116 45 E
Dālaki, *Iran* **45 D6** 29 26N 51 17 E
Dalälven →, *Sweden* **9 F17** 60 12N 16 43 E
Dalaman →, *Turkey* **21 F13** 36 41N 28 43 E
Dalandzadgad, *Mongolia* **34 C3** 43 27N 104 30 E
Dalap-Uliga-Darrit, *Marshall Is.* **64 G9** 7 7N 171 24 E
Dalarna, *Sweden* **9 F16** 61 0N 14 0 E
Dālbandīn, *Pakistan* **40 E4** 29 0N 64 23 E
Dalbeattie, *U.K.* **12 G5** 54 56N 3 50W
Dalbeg, *Australia* **62 C4** 20 16S 147 18 E
Dalby, *Australia* **63 D5** 27 10S 151 17 E
Dale City, *U.S.A.* **76 F7** 38 38N 77 18W
Dale Hollow L., *U.S.A.* **77 G3** 36 32N 85 27W
Dalgān, *Iran* **45 E8** 27 31N 59 19 E
Dalhart, *U.S.A.* **81 G3** 36 4N 102 31W
Dalhousie, *Canada* **71 C6** 48 5N 66 26W
Dalhousie, *India* **42 C6** 32 38N 75 58 E
Dali, *Shaanxi, China* **34 G5** 34 48N 109 58 E
Dali, *Yunnan, China* **32 D5** 25 40N 100 10 E
Dalian, *China* **35 E11** 38 50N 121 40 E
Daliang Shan, *China* **32 D5** 28 0N 102 45 E
Daling He →, *China* **35 D11** 40 55N 121 40 E
Dāliyat el Karmel, *Israel* **47 C4** 32 43N 35 2 E
Dalkeith, *U.K.* **12 F5** 55 54N 3 4W
Dallas, *Oreg., U.S.A.* **82 D2** 44 55N 123 19W
Dallas, *Tex., U.S.A.* **81 J6** 32 47N 96 49W
Dalmā, *U.A.E.* **45 E7** 24 30N 52 20 E
Dalmacija, *Croatia* **20 C7** 43 20N 17 0 E
Dalmas, L., *Canada* **71 B5** 53 30N 71 50W
Dalmatia = Dalmacija, *Croatia* **20 C7** 43 20N 17 0 E
Dalmau, *India* **43 F9** 26 4N 81 2 E
Dalmellington, *U.K.* **12 F4** 55 19N 4 23W
Dalnegorsk, *Russia* **27 E14** 44 32N 135 33 E
Dalnerechensk, *Russia* **27 E14** 45 50N 133 40 E
Daloa, *Ivory C.* **50 G4** 7 0N 6 30W
Dalry, *U.K.* **12 F4** 55 42N 4 43W
Dalrymple, L., *Australia* **62 C4** 20 40S 147 0 E
Dalsland, *Sweden* **9 G14** 58 50N 12 15 E
Daltenganj, *India* **43 H11** 24 0N 84 4 E
Dalton, *Ga., U.S.A.* **77 H3** 34 46N 84 58W
Dalton, *Mass., U.S.A.* **79 D11** 42 28N 73 11W
Dalton, *Nebr., U.S.A.* **80 E3** 41 25N 102 58W
Dalton-in-Furness, *U.K.* **10 C4** 54 10N 3 11W
Dalvík, *Iceland* **8 D4** 65 58N 18 32W
Dalwallinu, *Australia* **61 F2** 30 17S 116 40 E
Daly →, *Australia* **60 B5** 13 35S 130 19 E
Daly City, *U.S.A.* **84 H4** 37 42N 122 28W
Daly L., *Canada* **73 B7** 56 32N 105 39W
Daly River, *Australia* **60 B5** 13 46S 130 42 E
Daly Waters, *Australia* **62 B1** 16 15S 133 24 E
Dam Doi, *Vietnam* **39 H5** 8 50N 105 12 E
Dam Ha, *Vietnam* **38 B6** 21 21N 107 36 E
Daman, *India* **40 J8** 20 25N 72 57 E
Dāmaneh, *Iran* **45 C6** 33 1N 50 29 E
Damanhûr, *Egypt* **51 B12** 31 0N 30 30 E
Damant L., *Canada* **73 A7** 61 45N 105 5W
Damanzhuang, *China* **34 E9** 38 5N 116 35 E
Damar, *Indonesia* **37 F7** 7 7S 128 40 E
Damaraland, *Namibia* **56 C2** 20 0S 15 0 E
Damascus = Dimashq, *Syria* **47 B5** 33 30N 36 18 E
Damāvand, *Iran* **45 C7** 35 47N 52 0 E
Damāvand, Qolleh-ye, *Iran* **45 C7** 35 56N 52 10 E
Damba, *Angola* **52 F3** 6 44S 15 20 E
Dâmboviţa →, *Romania* **17 F14** 44 12N 26 26 E
Dame Marie, *Haiti* **89 C5** 18 36N 74 26W
Dāmghān, *Iran* **45 B7** 36 10N 54 17 E
Damiel, *Spain* **19 C4** 39 4N 3 37W
Damietta = Dumyât, *Egypt* **51 B12** 31 24N 31 48 E
Daming, *China* **34 F8** 36 15N 115 6 E
Damīr Qābū, *Syria* **44 B4** 36 58N 41 51 E
Dammam = Ad Dammām, *Si. Arabia* **45 E6** 26 20N 50 5 E
Damodar →, *India* **43 H12** 23 17N 87 35 E
Damoh, *India* **43 H8** 23 50N 79 28 E
Dampier, *Australia* **60 D2** 20 41S 116 42 E
Dampier, Selat, *Indonesia* **37 E8** 0 40S 131 0 E
Dampier Arch., *Australia* **60 D2** 20 38S 116 32 E
Damrei, Chuor Phnum, *Cambodia* **39 G4** 11 30N 103 0 E
Dan Xian, *China* **38 C7** 19 31N 109 33 E
Dana, *Indonesia* **37 F6** 11 0S 122 52 E
Dana, L., *Canada* **70 B4** 50 53N 77 20W
Dana, Mt., *U.S.A.* **84 H7** 37 54N 119 12W
Danakil Desert, *Ethiopia* **46 E3** 12 45N 41 0 E
Danané, *Ivory C.* **50 G4** 7 16N 8 9W
Danau Poso, *Indonesia* **37 E6** 1 52S 120 35 E
Danbury, *U.S.A.* **79 E11** 41 24N 73 28W
Danby L., *U.S.A.* **83 J6** 34 13N 115 5W
Dand, *Afghan.* **42 D1** 31 28N 65 32 E
Dandeldhura, *Nepal* **43 E9** 29 20N 80 35 E
Dandeli, *India* **40 M9** 15 5N 74 30 E
Dandenong, *Australia* **63 F4** 38 0S 145 15 E
Dandong, *China* **35 D13** 40 10N 124 20 E
Danfeng, *China* **34 H6** 33 45N 110 25 E
Danger Is. = Pukapuka, *Cook Is.* **65 J11** 10 53S 165 49W
Danger Pt., *S. Africa* **56 E2** 34 40S 19 17 E
Dangla Shan = Tanggula Shan, *China* **32 C4** 32 40N 92 10 E
Dangrek, Phnom, *Thailand* **38 E5** 14 15N 105 0 E
Dangriga, *Belize* **87 D7** 17 0N 88 13W
Dangshan, *China* **34 G9** 34 27N 116 22 E
Daniel, *U.S.A.* **82 E8** 42 52N 110 4W
Daniel's Harbour, *Canada* **71 B8** 50 13N 57 35W
Danielskuil, *S. Africa* **56 D3** 28 11S 23 33 E
Danielson, *U.S.A.* **79 E13** 41 48N 71 53W
Danilov, *Russia* **24 C7** 58 16N 40 13 E
Daning, *China* **34 F6** 36 28N 110 45 E
Danissa, *Kenya* **54 B5** 3 15N 40 58 E
Dank, *Oman* **45 F8** 23 33N 56 16 E
Dankhar Gompa, *India* **40 C11** 32 10N 78 10 E
Danlí, *Honduras* **88 D2** 14 4N 86 35W
Dannemora, *U.S.A.* **79 B11** 44 43N 73 44W
Dannevirke, *N.Z.* **59 J6** 40 12S 176 8 E
Dannhauser, *S. Africa* **57 D5** 28 0S 30 3 E
Dansville, *U.S.A.* **78 D7** 42 34N 77 42W
Danta, *India* **42 G5** 24 11N 72 46 E
Dantan, *India* **43 J12** 21 57N 87 20 E
Danube = Dunărea →, *Europe* **17 F15** 45 20N 29 40 E
Danvers, *U.S.A.* **79 D14** 42 34N 70 56W
Danville, *Ill., U.S.A.* **76 E2** 40 8N 87 37W
Danville, *Ky., U.S.A.* **76 G3** 37 39N 84 46W
Danville, *Pa., U.S.A.* **78 F8** 40 58N 76 37W
Danville, *Va., U.S.A.* **77 G6** 36 36N 79 23W
Danville, *Vt., U.S.A.* **79 B12** 44 25N 72 9W
Danzig = Gdańsk, *Poland* **17 A10** 54 22N 18 40 E
Dapaong, *Togo* **50 F6** 10 55N 0 16 E
Daqing Shan, *China* **34 D6** 40 40N 111 0 E
Dar Banda, *Africa* **48 F6** 8 0N 23 0 E
Dar el Beida = Casablanca, *Morocco* **50 B4** 33 36N 7 36W
Dar es Salaam, *Tanzania* **54 D4** 6 50S 39 12 E
Dar Mazār, *Iran* **45 D8** 29 14N 57 20 E
Dar'ā, *Syria* **47 C5** 32 36N 36 7 E
Dar'ā □, *Syria* **47 C5** 32 55N 36 10 E
Dārāb, *Iran* **45 D7** 28 50N 54 30 E
Daraban, *Pakistan* **42 D4** 31 44N 70 20 E
Daraina, *Madag.* **57 A8** 13 12S 49 40 E
Daraj, *Libya* **51 B8** 30 10N 10 28 E
Dārān, *Iran* **45 C6** 32 59N 50 24 E
Dārayyā, *Syria* **47 B5** 33 28N 36 15 E
Darband, *Pakistan* **42 B5** 34 20N 72 50 E
Darband, Kūh-e, *Iran* **45 D8** 31 34N 57 8 E
Darbhanga, *India* **43 F11** 26 15N 85 55 E
D'Arcy, *Canada* **72 C4** 50 27N 122 35W
Dardanelle, *Ark., U.S.A.* **81 H8** 35 13N 93 9W
Dardanelle, *Calif., U.S.A.* **84 G7** 38 20N 119 50W
Dardanelles = Çanakkale Boğazı, *Turkey* **21 D12** 40 17N 26 32 E
Dārestān, *Iran* **45 D8** 29 9N 58 42 E
Dārfûr, *Sudan* **51 F10** 13 40N 24 0 E
Dargai, *Pakistan* **42 B4** 34 25N 71 55 E
Dargan Ata, *Turkmenistan* **26 E7** 40 29N 62 10 E
Dargaville, *N.Z.* **59 F4** 35 57S 173 52 E
Darhan Muminggan Lianheqi, *China* **34 D6** 41 40N 110 28 E
Darhan, *Mongolia* **32 B5** 49 37N 106 21 E
Darıca, *Turkey* **21 D13** 40 45N 29 23 E
Darién, G. del, *Colombia* **92 B3** 9 0N 77 0W
Dariganga = Ovoot, *Mongolia* **34 B7** 45 21N 113 45 E
Darjeeling = Darjiling, *India* **43 F13** 27 3N 88 18 E
Darjiling, *India* **43 F13** 27 3N 88 18 E
Darkan, *Australia* **61 F2** 33 20S 116 43 E
Darkhana, *Pakistan* **42 D5** 30 39N 72 11 E
Darkhazineh, *Iran* **45 D6** 31 54N 48 39 E
Darkot Pass, *Pakistan* **43 A5** 36 45N 73 26 E
Darling →, *Australia* **63 E3** 34 4S 141 54 E
Darling Downs, *Australia* **63 D5** 27 30S 150 30 E
Darling Ra., *Australia* **61 F2** 32 30S 116 0 E
Darlington, *U.K.* **10 C6** 54 32N 1 33W
Darlington, *U.S.A.* **77 H6** 34 18N 79 52W
Darlington □, *U.K.* **10 C6** 54 32N 1 33W
Darlington, L., *S. Africa* **56 E4** 33 10S 25 9 E
Darlot, L., *Australia* **61 E3** 27 48S 121 35 E
Darłowo, *Poland* **16 A9** 54 25N 16 25 E
Darmstadt, *Germany* **16 D5** 49 51N 8 39 E
Darnah, *Libya* **51 B10** 32 45N 22 45 E
Darnall, *S. Africa* **57 D5** 29 23S 31 18 E
Darnley, C., *Antarctica* **5 C6** 68 0S 69 0 E
Darnley B., *Canada* **68 B7** 69 30N 123 30W
Darr →, *Australia* **62 C3** 23 39S 143 50 E
Darra Pezu, *Pakistan* **42 C4** 32 19N 70 44 E
Darrequeira, *Argentina* **94 D3** 37 42S 63 10W
Darrington, *U.S.A.* **82 B3** 48 15N 121 36W
Dart →, *U.K.* **11 G4** 50 24N 3 39W
Dart, C., *Antarctica* **5 D14** 73 6S 126 20W
Dartford, *U.K.* **11 F8** 51 26N 0 13 E
Dartmoor, *U.K.* **11 G4** 50 38N 3 57W
Dartmouth, *Canada* **71 D7** 44 40N 63 30W
Dartmouth, *U.K.* **11 G4** 50 21N 3 36W
Dartmouth, L., *Australia* **63 D4** 26 4S 145 18 E
Dartuch, C. = Artrutx, C. de, *Spain* **22 B10** 39 55N 3 49 E
Darvaza, *Turkmenistan* **26 E6** 40 11N 58 24 E
Darvel, Teluk = Lahad Datu, Teluk, *Malaysia* **37 D5** 4 50N 118 20 E
Darwen, *U.K.* **10 D5** 53 42N 2 29W
Darwendale, *Zimbabwe* **57 B5** 17 41S 30 33 E
Darwha, *India* **40 J10** 20 15N 77 45 E
Darwin, *Australia* **60 B5** 12 25S 130 51 E
Darwin, *U.S.A.* **85 J9** 36 15N 117 35W
Darya Khan, *Pakistan* **42 D4** 31 48N 71 6 E
Daryoi Amu = Amudarya →, *Uzbekistan* **26 E6** 43 58N 59 34 E
Dās, *U.A.E.* **45 E7** 25 20N 53 30 E
Dashen, Ras, *Ethiopia* **46 E2** 13 8N 38 26 E
Dashetai, *China* **34 D5** 41 0N 109 5 E
Dashhowuz, *Turkmenistan* **26 E6** 41 49N 59 58 E
Dashköpri, *Turkmenistan* **45 B9** 36 16N 62 8 E
Dasht, *Iran* **45 B8** 37 17N 56 7 E
Dasht →, *Pakistan* **40 G2** 25 10N 61 40 E
Daska, *Pakistan* **42 C6** 32 20N 74 20 E
Dasuya, *India* **42 D6** 31 49N 75 38 E
Datça, *Turkey* **21 F12** 36 46N 27 40 E
Datia, *India* **43 G8** 25 39N 78 27 E
Datong, *China* **34 D7** 40 6N 113 18 E
Dattakhel, *Pakistan* **42 C3** 32 54N 69 46 E
Datu, Tanjung, *Indonesia* **36 D3** 2 5N 109 39 E
Datu Piang, *Phil.* **37 C6** 7 2N 124 30 E
Datuk, Tanjong = Datu, Tanjung, *Indonesia* **36 D3** 2 5N 109 39 E
Daud Khel, *Pakistan* **42 C4** 32 53N 71 34 E
Daudnagar, *India* **43 G11** 25 2N 84 24 E
Daugava →, *Latvia* **9 H21** 57 4N 24 3 E
Daugavpils, *Latvia* **9 J22** 55 53N 26 32 E
Daulpur, *India* **42 F7** 26 45N 77 59 E
Dauphin, *Canada* **73 C8** 51 9N 100 5W
Dauphin, *U.S.A.* **78 F8** 40 22N 76 56W
Dauphin L., *Canada* **73 C9** 51 20N 99 45W
Dauphiné, *France* **18 D6** 45 15N 5 25 E
Dausa, *India* **42 F7** 26 52N 76 20 E
Davangere, *India* **40 M9** 14 25N 75 55 E
Davao, *Phil.* **37 C7** 7 0N 125 40 E
Davao G., *Phil.* **37 C7** 6 30N 125 48 E
Dāvar Panāh, *Iran* **45 E9** 27 25N 62 15 E
Davenport, *Calif., U.S.A.* **84 H4** 37 1N 122 12W
Davenport, *Iowa, U.S.A.* **80 E9** 41 32N 90 35W
Davenport, *Wash., U.S.A.* **82 C4** 47 39N 118 9W
Davenport Ra., *Australia* **62 C1** 20 28S 134 0 E
Daventry, *U.K.* **11 E6** 52 16N 1 10W
David, *Panama* **88 E3** 8 30N 82 30W
David City, *U.S.A.* **80 E6** 41 15N 97 8W
David Gorodok = Davyd Haradok, *Belarus* **17 B14** 52 4N 27 8 E
Davidson, *Canada* **73 C7** 51 16N 105 59W
Davis, *U.S.A.* **84 G5** 38 33N 121 44W
Davis Dam, *U.S.A.* **85 K12** 35 11N 114 34W
Davis Inlet, *Canada* **71 A7** 55 50N 60 59W
Davis Mts., *U.S.A.* **81 K2** 30 50N 103 55W
Davis Sea, *Antarctica* **5 C7** 66 0S 92 0 E
Davis Str., *N. Amer.* **69 B14** 65 0N 58 0W
Davos, *Switz.* **18 C8** 46 48N 9 49 E
Davy L., *Canada* **73 B7** 58 53N 108 18W
Davyd Haradok, *Belarus* **17 B14** 52 4N 27 8 E
Dawei, *Burma* **38 E2** 14 2N 98 12 E
Dawes Ra., *Australia* **62 C5** 24 40S 150 40 E
Dawlish, *U.K.* **11 G4** 50 35N 3 28W
Dawna Ra., *Burma* **38 D2** 16 30N 98 30 E
Dawros Hd., *Ireland* **13 B3** 54 50N 8 33W
Dawson, *Canada* **68 B6** 64 10N 139 30W
Dawson, *U.S.A.* **77 K3** 31 46N 84 27W
Dawson, I., *Chile* **96 G2** 53 50S 70 50W
Dawson B., *Canada* **73 C8** 52 53N 100 49W
Dawson Creek, *Canada* **72 B4** 55 45N 120 15W
Dawson Inlet, *Canada* **73 A10** 61 50N 93 25W
Dawson Ra., *Australia* **62 C4** 24 30S 149 48 E
Dax, *France* **18 E3** 43 44N 1 3W
Daxian, *China* **32 C5** 31 15N 107 23 E
Daxindian, *China* **35 F11** 37 30N 120 50 E
Daxinggou, *China* **35 C15** 43 25N 129 40 E
Daxue Shan, *China* **32 C5** 30 30N 101 30 E
Daylesford, *Australia* **63 F3** 37 21S 144 9 E
Dayr az Zawr, *Syria* **44 C4** 35 20N 40 5 E
Daysland, *Canada* **72 C6** 52 50N 112 20W
Dayton, *Nev., U.S.A.* **84 F7** 39 14N 119 36W
Dayton, *Ohio, U.S.A.* **76 F3** 39 45N 84 12W
Dayton, *Pa., U.S.A.* **78 F5** 40 53N 79 15W
Dayton, *Tenn., U.S.A.* **77 H3** 35 30N 85 1W
Dayton, *Wash., U.S.A.* **82 C4** 46 19N 117 59W
Dayton, *Wyo., U.S.A.* **82 D10** 44 53N 107 16W
Daytona Beach, *U.S.A.* **77 L5** 29 13N 81 1W
Dayville, *U.S.A.* **82 D4** 44 28N 119 32W
De Aar, *S. Africa* **56 E3** 30 39S 24 0 E
De Funiak Springs, *U.S.A.* **77 K2** 30 43N 86 7W
De Grey →, *Australia* **60 D2** 20 12S 119 13 E
De Haan, *Belgium* **15 C3** 51 16N 3 2 E
De Kalb, *U.S.A.* **80 E10** 41 56N 88 46W
De Land, *U.S.A.* **77 L5** 29 2N 81 18W
De Leon, *U.S.A.* **81 J5** 32 7N 98 32W
De Panne, *Belgium* **15 C2** 51 6N 2 34 E
De Pere, *U.S.A.* **76 C1** 44 27N 88 4W
De Queen, *U.S.A.* **81 H7** 34 2N 94 21W
De Quincy, *U.S.A.* **81 K8** 30 27N 93 26W
De Ridder, *U.S.A.* **81 K8** 30 51N 93 17W
De Smet, *U.S.A.* **80 C6** 44 23N 97 33W
De Soto, *U.S.A.* **80 F9** 38 8N 90 34W
De Tour Village, *U.S.A.* **76 C4** 46 0N 83 56W
De Witt, *U.S.A.* **81 H9** 34 18N 91 20W
Dead Sea, *Asia* **47 D4** 31 30N 35 30 E
Deadwood, *U.S.A.* **80 C3** 44 23N 103 44W
Deadwood L., *Canada* **72 B3** 59 10N 128 30W
Deal, *U.K.* **11 F9** 51 13N 1 25 E
Deal I., *Australia* **62 F4** 39 30S 147 20 E
Dealesville, *S. Africa* **56 D4** 28 41S 25 44 E
Dean →, *Canada* **72 C3** 52 49N 126 58W
Dean, Forest of, *U.K.* **11 F5** 51 45N 2 33W
Dean Chan., *Canada* **72 C3** 52 30N 127 15W
Deán Funes, *Argentina* **94 C3** 30 20S 64 20W
Dease →, *Canada* **72 B3** 59 56N 128 32W
Dease L., *Canada* **72 B2** 58 40N 130 5W
Dease Lake, *Canada* **72 B2** 58 25N 130 6W
Death Valley, *U.S.A.* **85 J10** 36 15N 116 50W
Death Valley Junction, *U.S.A.* **85 J10** 36 20N 116 25W
Death Valley Nat. Park, *U.S.A.* **85 J10** 36 45N 117 15W
Debar, *Macedonia* **21 D9** 41 31N 20 30 E
Debden, *Canada* **73 C7** 53 30N 106 50W
Dębica, *Poland* **17 C11** 50 2N 21 25 E
Debolt, *Canada* **72 B5** 55 12N 118 1W
Deborah East, L., *Australia* **61 F2** 30 45S 119 0 E
Deborah West, L., *Australia* **61 F2** 30 45S 118 50 E
Debre Markos, *Ethiopia* **46 E2** 10 20N 37 40 E
Debre Tabor, *Ethiopia* **46 E2** 11 50N 38 26 E
Debre Zeyit, *Ethiopia* **46 F2** 11 48N 38 30 E
Debrecen, *Hungary* **17 E11** 47 33N 21 42 E
Decatur, *Ala., U.S.A.* **77 H2** 34 36N 86 59W
Decatur, *Ga., U.S.A.* **77 J3** 33 47N 84 18W
Decatur, *Ill., U.S.A.* **80 F10** 39 51N 88 57W
Decatur, *Ind., U.S.A.* **76 E3** 40 50N 84 56W
Decatur, *Tex., U.S.A.* **81 J6** 33 14N 97 35W
Deccan, *India* **40 L11** 18 0N 79 0 E
Deception Bay, *Australia* **63 D5** 27 10S 153 5 E
Deception L., *Canada* **73 B8** 56 33N 104 13W
Dechhu, *India* **42 F5** 26 46N 72 20 E
Děčín, *Czech Rep.* **16 C8** 50 47N 14 12 E
Deckerville, *U.S.A.* **78 C2** 43 32N 82 44W
Decorah, *U.S.A.* **80 D9** 43 18N 91 48W
Dedéagach = Alexandroúpolis, *Greece* **21 D11** 40 50N 25 54 E
Dedham, *U.S.A.* **79 D13** 42 15N 71 10W
Dedza, *Malawi* **55 E3** 14 20S 34 20 E
Dee →, *Aberds., U.K.* **12 D6** 57 9N 2 5W
Dee →, *Dumf. & Gall., U.K.* **12 G4** 54 51N 4 3W
Dee →, *Wales, U.K.* **10 D4** 53 22N 3 17W
Deep B., *Canada* **72 A5** 61 15N 116 35W
Deepwater, *Australia* **63 D5** 29 25S 151 51 E
Deer →, *Canada* **73 B10** 58 23N 94 13W
Deer L., *Canada* **73 C10** 52 40N 94 20W
Deer Lake, *Nfld., Canada* **71 C8** 49 11N 57 27W
Deer Lake, *Ont., Canada* **73 C10** 52 36N 94 20W
Deer Lodge, *U.S.A.* **82 C7** 46 24N 112 44W
Deer Park, *U.S.A.* **82 C5** 47 57N 117 28W
Deer River, *U.S.A.* **80 B8** 47 20N 93 48W
Deeragun, *Australia* **62 B4** 19 16S 146 33 E
Deerdepoort, *S. Africa* **56 C4** 24 37S 26 27 E
Deferiet, *U.S.A.* **79 B9** 44 2N 75 41W
Defiance, *U.S.A.* **76 E3** 41 17N 84 22W
Degana, *India* **42 F6** 26 50N 74 20 E
Dégelis, *Canada* **71 C6** 47 30N 68 35W
Deggendorf, *Germany* **16 D7** 48 50N 12 57 E
Degh →, *Pakistan* **42 D5** 31 3N 73 21 E
Deh Bīd, *Iran* **45 D7** 30 39N 53 11 E
Deh-e Shīr, *Iran* **45 D7** 31 29N 53 45 E
Dehaj, *Iran* **45 D7** 30 42N 54 53 E
Dehak, *Iran* **45 E9** 27 11N 62 37 E
Dehdez, *Iran* **45 D6** 31 43N 50 17 E
Dehej, *India* **42 J5** 21 44N 72 40 E
Dehestān, *Iran* **45 D7** 28 30N 55 35 E
Dehgolān, *Iran* **44 C5** 35 17N 47 25 E
Dehibat, *Tunisia* **51 B8** 32 0N 10 47 E
Dehlorān, *Iran* **44 C5** 32 41N 47 16 E
Dehnow-e Kūhestān, *Iran* **45 E8** 27 58N 58 32 E
Dehra Dun, *India* **42 D8** 30 20N 78 4 E
Dehri, *India* **43 G11** 24 50N 84 15 E
Dehui, *China* **35 B13** 44 30N 125 40 E
Deinze, *Belgium* **15 D3** 50 59N 3 32 E
Dej, *Romania* **17 E12** 47 10N 23 52 E
Deka →, *Zimbabwe* **56 B4** 18 4S 26 42 E
Dekese, *Dem. Rep. of the Congo* **52 E4** 3 24S 21 24 E
Del Mar, *U.S.A.* **85 N9** 32 58N 117 16W
Del Norte, *U.S.A.* **83 H10** 37 41N 106 21W
Del Rio, *U.S.A.* **81 L4** 29 22N 100 54W
Delambre I., *Australia* **60 D2** 20 26S 117 5 E
Delano, *U.S.A.* **85 K7** 35 46N 119 15W
Delano Peak, *U.S.A.* **83 G7** 38 22N 112 22W
Delareyville, *S. Africa* **56 D4** 26 41S 25 26 E
Delaronde L., *Canada* **73 C7** 54 3N 107 3W
Delavan, *U.S.A.* **80 D10** 42 38N 88 39W
Delaware, *U.S.A.* **76 E4** 40 18N 83 4W
Delaware □, *U.S.A.* **76 F8** 39 0N 75 20W
Delaware →, *U.S.A.* **79 G9** 39 15N 75 20W
Delaware B., *U.S.A.* **76 F8** 39 0N 75 10W
Delay →, *Canada* **71 A5** 56 56N 71 28W
Delegate, *Australia* **63 F4** 37 4S 148 56 E
Delevan, *U.S.A.* **78 D6** 42 29N 78 29W
Delft, *Neths.* **15 B4** 52 1N 4 22 E
Delfzijl, *Neths.* **15 A6** 53 20N 6 55 E
Delgado, C., *Mozam.* **55 E5** 10 45S 40 40 E
Delgerhet, *Mongolia* **34 B6** 45 50N 110 30 E
Delgo, *Sudan* **51 D12** 20 6N 30 40 E
Delhi, *Canada* **78 D4** 42 51N 80 30W
Delhi, *India* **42 E7** 28 38N 77 17 E
Delhi, *La., U.S.A.* **81 J9** 32 28N 91 30W
Delhi, *N.Y., U.S.A.* **79 D10** 42 17N 74 55W
Delia, *Canada* **72 C6** 51 38N 112 23W
Delice, *Turkey* **25 G5** 39 54N 34 2 E
Delicias, *Mexico* **86 B3** 28 10N 105 30W
Delījān, *Iran* **45 C6** 33 59N 50 40 E
Déline, *Canada* **68 B7** 65 10N 123 30W
Delisle, *Canada* **73 C7** 51 55N 107 8W
Dell City, *U.S.A.* **83 L11** 31 56N 105 12W
Dell Rapids, *U.S.A.* **80 D6** 43 50N 96 43W
Delmar, *U.S.A.* **79 D11** 42 37N 73 47W
Delmenhorst, *Germany* **16 B5** 53 3N 8 37 E
Delonga, Ostrova, *Russia* **27 B15** 76 40N 149 20 E
Deloraine, *Australia* **62 G4** 41 30S 146 40 E
Deloraine, *Canada* **73 D8** 49 15N 100 29W
Delphi, *U.S.A.* **76 E2** 40 36N 86 41W
Delphos, *U.S.A.* **76 E3** 40 51N 84 21W
Delportshoop, *S. Africa* **56 D3** 28 22S 24 20 E
Delray Beach, *U.S.A.* **77 M5** 26 28N 80 4W
Delta, *Colo., U.S.A.* **83 G9** 38 44N 108 4W
Delta, *Utah, U.S.A.* **82 G7** 39 21N 112 35W
Delta Junction, *U.S.A.* **68 B5** 64 2N 145 44W
Deltona, *U.S.A.* **77 L5** 28 54N 81 16W
Delungra, *Australia* **63 D5** 29 39S 150 51 E
Delvada, *India* **42 J4** 20 46N 71 2 E
Delvinë, *Albania* **21 E9** 39 59N 20 6 E
Demak, *Indonesia* **37 G14** 6 53S 110 38 E
Demanda, Sierra de la, *Spain* **19 A4** 42 15N 3 0W
Demavand = Damāvand, *Iran* **45 C7** 35 47N 52 0 E
Dembia, *Dem. Rep. of the Congo* **54 B2** 3 33N 25 48 E
Dembidolo, *Ethiopia* **46 F1** 8 34N 34 50 E
Demchok, *India* **43 C8** 32 42N 79 29 E
Demer →, *Belgium* **15 D4** 50 57N 4 42 E
Deming, *N. Mex., U.S.A.* **83 K10** 32 16N 107 46W
Deming, *Wash., U.S.A.* **84 B4** 48 50N 122 13W
Demini →, *Brazil* **92 D6** 0 46S 62 56W
Demirci, *Turkey* **21 E13** 39 2N 28 38 E
Demirköy, *Turkey* **21 D12** 41 49N 27 45 E
Demopolis, *U.S.A.* **77 J2** 32 31N 87 50W
Dempo, *Indonesia* **36 E2** 4 2S 103 15 E
Den Burg, *Neths.* **15 A4** 53 3N 4 47 E
Den Chai, *Thailand* **38 D3** 17 59N 100 4 E
Den Haag = 's-Gravenhage, *Neths.* **15 B4** 52 7N 4 17 E
Den Helder, *Neths.* **15 B4** 52 57N 4 45 E
Den Oever, *Neths.* **15 B5** 52 56N 5 2 E
Denair, *U.S.A.* **84 H6** 37 32N 120 48W
Denau, *Uzbekistan* **26 F7** 38 16N 67 54 E

Denbigh, Canada 78 A7 45 8N 77 15W
Denbigh, U.K. 10 D4 53 12N 3 25W
Denbighshire □, U.K. 10 D4 53 8N 3 22W
Dendang, Indonesia 36 E3 3 7S 107 56 E
Dendermonde, Belgium 15 C4 51 2N 4 5 E
Dengfeng, China 34 G7 34 25N 113 2 E
Dengkou, China 34 D4 40 18N 106 55 E
Denham, Australia 61 E1 25 56S 113 31 E
Denham Ra., Australia 62 C4 21 55S 147 46 E
Denham Sd., Australia 61 E1 25 45S 113 15 E
Denholm, Canada 73 C7 52 39N 108 1W
Denia, Spain 19 C6 38 49N 0 8 E
Denial B., Australia 63 E1 32 14S 133 32 E
Deniliquin, Australia 63 F3 35 30S 144 58 E
Denison, Iowa, U.S.A. 80 E7 42 1N 95 21W
Denison, Tex., U.S.A. 81 J6 33 45N 96 33W
Denison Plains, Australia 60 C4 18 35S 128 0 E
Denizli, Turkey 25 G4 37 42N 29 2 E
Denman Glacier, Antarctica 5 C7 66 45S 99 25 E
Denmark, Australia 61 F2 34 59S 117 25 E
Denmark ■, Europe 9 J13 55 45N 10 0 E
Denmark Str., Atl. Oc. 4 C6 66 0N 30 0W
Dennison, U.S.A. 78 F3 40 24N 81 19W
Denny, U.K. 12 E5 56 1N 3 55W
Denpasar, Indonesia 36 F5 8 39S 115 13 E
Denton, Mont., U.S.A. 82 C9 47 19N 109 57W
Denton, Tex., U.S.A. 81 J6 33 13N 97 8W
D'Entrecasteaux, Pt., Australia 61 F2 34 50S 115 57 E
Denver, Colo., U.S.A. 80 F2 39 44N 104 59W
Denver, Pa., U.S.A. 79 F8 40 14N 76 8W
Denver City, U.S.A. 81 J3 32 58N 102 50W
Deoband, India 42 E7 29 42N 77 43 E
Deogarh, India 42 G5 25 32N 73 54 E
Deoghar, India 43 G12 24 30N 86 42 E
Deolali, India 40 K8 19 58N 73 50 E
Deoli = Devli, India 42 G6 25 50N 75 20 E
Deora, India 42 F4 26 22N 70 55 E
Deori, India 43 H8 23 24N 79 1 E
Deoria, India 43 F10 26 31N 83 48 E
Deosai Mts., Pakistan 43 B6 35 40N 75 0 E
Deosri, India 43 F14 26 46N 90 29 E
Depalpur, India 42 H6 22 51N 75 33 E
Deping, China 35 F9 37 25N 116 58 E
Deposit, U.S.A. 79 D9 42 4N 75 25W
Depuch I., Australia 60 D2 20 37S 117 44 E
Deputatskiy, Russia 27 C14 69 18N 139 54 E
Dera Ghazi Khan, Pakistan 42 D4 30 5N 70 43 E
Dera Ismail Khan, Pakistan 42 D4 31 50N 70 50 E
Derabugti, Pakistan 42 E3 29 2N 69 9 E
Derawar Fort, Pakistan 42 E4 28 46N 71 20 E
Derbent, Russia 25 F8 42 5N 48 15 E
Derby, Australia 60 C3 17 18S 123 38 E
Derby, U.K. 10 E6 52 56N 1 28W
Derby, Conn., U.S.A. 79 E11 41 19N 73 5W
Derby, Kans., U.S.A. 81 G6 37 33N 97 16W
Derby, N.Y., U.S.A. 78 D6 42 41N 78 58W
Derby City □, U.K. 10 E6 52 56N 1 28W
Derby Line, U.S.A. 79 B12 45 0N 72 6W
Derbyshire □, U.K. 10 D6 53 11N 1 38W
Derg →, U.K. 13 B4 54 44N 7 26W
Derg, L., Ireland 13 D3 53 0N 8 20W
Dergaon, India 41 F19 26 45N 94 0 E
Dermott, U.S.A. 81 J9 33 32N 91 26W
Derry = Londonderry, U.K. 13 B4 55 0N 7 20W
Derry = Londonderry □, U.K. 13 B4 55 0N 7 20W
Derry, N.H., U.S.A. 79 D13 42 53N 71 19W
Derry, Pa., U.S.A. 78 F5 40 20N 79 18W
Derryveagh Mts., Ireland 13 B3 54 56N 8 11W
Derwent →, Cumb., U.K. 10 C4 54 39N 3 33W
Derwent →, Derby, U.K. 10 E6 52 57N 1 28W
Derwent →, N. Yorks., U.K. 10 D7 53 45N 0 58W
Derwent Water, U.K. 10 C4 54 35N 3 9W
Des Moines, Iowa, U.S.A. 80 E8 41 35N 93 37W
Des Moines, N. Mex., U.S.A. 81 G3 36 46N 103 50W
Des Moines →, U.S.A. 80 E9 40 23N 91 25W
Desaguadero →, Argentina 94 C2 34 30S 66 46W
Desaguadero →, Bolivia 92 G5 16 35S 69 5W
Descanso, Pta., Mexico 85 N9 32 21N 117 3W
Deschaillons, Canada 71 C5 46 32N 72 7W
Deschambault L., Canada 73 C8 54 50N 103 30W
Deschutes →, U.S.A. 82 D3 45 38N 120 55W
Dese, Ethiopia 46 E2 11 5N 39 40 E
Deseado →, Argentina 96 F3 47 45S 65 54W
Desert Center, U.S.A. 85 M11 33 43N 115 24W
Desert Hot Springs, U.S.A. 85 M10 33 58N 116 30W
Deshnok, India 42 F5 27 48N 73 21 E
Desna →, Ukraine 17 C16 50 33N 30 32 E
Desolación, I., Chile 96 G2 53 0S 74 0W
Despeñaperros, Paso, Spain 19 C4 38 24N 3 30W
Dessau, Germany 16 C7 51 51N 12 14 E
Dessye = Dese, Ethiopia 46 E2 11 5N 39 40 E
D'Estrees B., Australia 63 F2 35 55S 137 45 E
Desuri, India 42 G5 25 18N 73 35 E
Det Udom, Thailand 38 E5 14 54N 105 5 E
Dete, Zimbabwe 56 B4 18 38S 26 50 E
Detmold, Germany 16 C5 51 56N 8 52 E
Detour, Pt., U.S.A. 76 C2 45 40N 86 40W
Detroit, U.S.A. 78 D1 42 20N 83 3W
Detroit Lakes, U.S.A. 80 B7 46 49N 95 51W
Deurne, Neths. 15 C5 51 27N 5 49 E
Deutsche Bucht, Germany 16 A5 54 15N 8 0 E
Deva, Romania 17 F12 45 53N 22 55 E
Devakottai, India 40 Q11 9 55N 78 45 E
Devaprayag, India 43 D8 30 13N 78 35 E
Deventer, Neths. 15 B6 52 15N 6 10 E
Deveron →, U.K. 12 D6 57 41N 2 32W
Devgadh Bariya, India 42 H5 22 40N 73 55 E
Devikot, India 42 F4 26 42N 71 12 E
Devils Den, U.S.A. 84 K7 35 46N 119 58W
Devils Lake, U.S.A. 80 A5 48 7N 98 52W
Devils Paw, Canada 72 B2 58 47N 134 0W
Devils Tower Junction, U.S.A. 80 C2 44 31N 104 57W
Devine, U.S.A. 81 L5 29 8N 98 54W
Devizes, U.K. 11 F6 51 22N 1 58W
Devli, India 42 G6 25 50N 75 20 E
Devon, Canada 72 C6 53 24N 113 44W
Devon □, U.K. 11 G4 50 50N 3 40W
Devon I., Canada 4 B3 75 10N 85 0W
Devonport, Australia 62 G4 41 10S 146 22 E
Devonport, N.Z. 59 G5 36 49S 174 49 E
Dewas, India 42 H7 22 59N 76 3 E
Dewetsdorp, S. Africa 56 D4 29 33S 26 39 E
Dexter, Maine, U.S.A. 77 C11 45 1N 69 18W
Dexter, Mo., U.S.A. 81 G10 36 48N 89 57W
Dexter, N. Mex., U.S.A. 81 J2 33 12N 104 22W
Dey-Dey, L., Australia 61 E5 29 12S 131 4 E
Deyhūk, Iran 45 C8 33 15N 57 30 E
Deyyer, Iran 45 E6 27 55N 51 55 E
Dezadeash L., Canada 72 A1 60 28N 136 58W
Dezfūl, Iran 45 C6 32 20N 48 30 E
Dezhneva, Mys, Russia 27 C19 66 5N 169 40W
Dezhou, China 34 F9 37 26N 116 18 E
Dhadhar →, India 43 G11 24 56N 85 24 E
Dháfni, Greece 23 D7 35 13N 25 3 E
Dhahiriya = Az̧ Z̧āhirīyah, West Bank 47 D3 31 25N 34 58 E
Dhahran = Az̧ Z̧ahrān, Si. Arabia 45 E6 26 10N 50 7 E
Dhak, Pakistan 42 C5 32 25N 72 33 E
Dhaka, Bangla. 43 H14 23 43N 90 26 E
Dhaka □, Bangla. 43 G14 24 25N 90 25 E
Dhali, Cyprus 23 D12 35 1N 33 25 E
Dhampur, India 43 E8 29 19N 78 33 E
Dhamtari, India 41 J12 20 42N 81 35 E
Dhanbad, India 43 H12 23 50N 86 30 E
Dhangarhi, Nepal 41 E12 28 55N 80 40 E
Dhankuta, Nepal 43 F12 26 55N 87 40 E
Dhar, India 42 H6 22 35N 75 26 E
Dharampur, India 42 H6 22 13N 75 18 E
Dharamsala = Dharmsala, India 42 C7 32 16N 76 23 E
Dhariwal, India 42 D6 31 57N 75 19 E
Dharla →, Bangla. 43 G13 25 46N 89 42 E
Dharmapuri, India 40 N11 12 10N 78 10 E
Dharmjaygarh, India 43 H10 22 28N 83 13 E
Dharmsala, India 42 C7 32 16N 76 23 E
Dharni, India 42 J7 21 33N 76 53 E
Dharwad, India 40 M9 15 30N 75 4 E
Dhasan →, India 43 G8 25 48N 79 24 E
Dhaulagiri, Nepal 43 E10 28 39N 83 28 E
Dhebar, L., India 42 G6 24 10N 74 0 E
Dheftera, Cyprus 23 D12 35 5N 33 16 E
Dhenkanal, India 41 J14 20 45N 85 35 E
Dherinia, Cyprus 23 D12 35 3N 33 57 E
Dhiarrizos →, Cyprus 23 E11 34 41N 32 34 E
Dhībān, Jordan 47 D4 31 30N 35 46 E
Dhíkti Óros, Greece 23 D7 35 8N 25 30 E
Dhilwan, India 42 D6 31 31N 75 21 E
Dhimarkhera, India 43 H9 23 28N 80 22 E
Dhírfis Óros, Greece 21 E10 38 40N 23 54 E
Dhodhekánisos, Greece 21 F12 36 35N 27 0 E
Dholka, India 42 H5 22 44N 72 29 E
Dhoraji, India 42 J4 21 45N 70 37 E
Dhráhstis, Ákra, Greece 23 A3 39 48N 19 40 E
Dhrangadhra, India 42 H4 22 59N 71 31 E
Dhrápanon, Ákra, Greece 23 D6 35 28N 24 14 E
Dhrol, India 42 H4 22 33N 70 25 E
Dhuburi, India 41 F16 26 2N 89 59 E
Dhule, India 40 J9 20 58N 74 50 E
Di Linh, Vietnam 39 G7 11 35N 108 4 E
Di Linh, Cao Nguyen, Vietnam 39 G7 11 30N 108 0 E
Dia, Greece 23 D7 35 28N 25 14 E
Diablo, Mt., U.S.A. 84 H5 37 53N 121 56W
Diablo Range, U.S.A. 84 J5 37 20N 121 25W
Diafarabé, Mali 50 F5 14 9N 4 57W
Diamante, Argentina 94 C3 32 5S 60 40W
Diamante →, Argentina 94 C2 34 30S 66 46W
Diamantina, Brazil 93 G10 18 17S 43 40W
Diamantina →, Australia 63 D2 26 45S 139 10 E
Diamantino, Brazil 93 F7 14 30S 56 30W
Diamond Bar, U.S.A. 85 L9 34 1N 117 48W
Diamond Harbour, India 43 H13 22 11N 88 14 E
Diamond Is., Australia 62 B5 17 25S 151 5 E
Diamond Mts., U.S.A. 82 G6 39 50N 115 30W
Diamond Springs, U.S.A. 84 G6 38 42N 120 49W
Dibā, Oman 45 E8 25 45N 56 16 E
Dibai, India 42 E8 28 13N 78 15 E
Dibaya-Lubue, Dem. Rep. of the Congo 52 E3 4 12S 19 54 E
Dibete, Botswana 56 C4 23 45S 26 32 E
Dibrugarh, India 41 F19 27 29N 94 55 E
Dickens, U.S.A. 81 J4 33 37N 100 50W
Dickinson, U.S.A. 80 B3 46 53N 102 47W
Dickson = Dikson, Russia 26 B9 73 40N 80 5 E
Dickson, U.S.A. 77 G2 36 5N 87 23W
Dickson City, U.S.A. 79 E9 41 29N 75 40W
Didiéni, Mali 50 F4 13 53N 8 6W
Didsbury, Canada 72 C6 51 35N 114 10W
Didwana, India 42 F6 27 23N 74 36 E
Diefenbaker, L., Canada 73 C7 51 0N 106 55W
Diego de Almagro, Chile 94 B1 26 22S 70 3W
Diego Garcia, Ind. Oc. 3 E13 7 50S 72 50 E
Diekirch, Lux. 15 E6 49 52N 6 10 E
Dien Ban, Vietnam 38 E7 15 53N 108 16 E
Dien Bien, Vietnam 38 B4 21 20N 103 0 E
Dien Khanh, Vietnam 39 F7 12 15N 109 6 E
Dieppe, France 18 B4 49 54N 1 4 E
Dierks, U.S.A. 81 H8 34 7N 94 1W
Diest, Belgium 15 D5 50 58N 5 4 E
Dif, Somali Rep. 46 G3 0 59N 0 56 E
Differdange, Lux. 15 E5 49 31N 5 54 E
Dig, India 42 F7 27 28N 77 20 E
Digba, Dem. Rep. of the Congo 54 B2 4 25N 25 48 E
Digby, Canada 71 D6 44 38N 65 50W
Diggi, India 42 F6 26 22N 75 26 E
Dighinala, Bangla. 41 H18 23 15N 92 5 E
Dighton, U.S.A. 80 F4 38 29N 100 28W
Digne-les-Bains, France 18 D7 44 5N 6 12 E
Digos, Phil. 37 C7 6 45N 125 20 E
Digranes, Iceland 8 C6 66 4N 14 44W
Digul →, Indonesia 37 F9 7 7S 138 42 E
Dihang = Brahmaputra →, India 41 F19 27 48N 95 30 E
Dijlah, Nahr →, Asia 44 D5 31 0N 47 25 E
Dijon, France 18 C6 47 20N 5 3 E
Dikhil, Djibouti 46 E3 11 8N 42 20 E
Dikkil = Dikhil, Djibouti 46 E3 11 8N 42 20 E
Diksmuide, Belgium 15 C2 51 2N 2 52 E
Dikson, Russia 26 B9 73 40N 80 5 E
Dila, Ethiopia 46 F2 6 21N 38 22 E
Dili, E. Timor 37 F7 8 39S 125 34 E
Dilley, U.S.A. 81 L5 28 40N 99 10W
Dillingham, U.S.A. 68 C4 59 3N 158 28W
Dillon, Canada 73 B7 55 56N 108 35W
Dillon, Mont., U.S.A. 82 D7 45 13N 112 38W
Dillon, S.C., U.S.A. 77 H6 34 25N 79 22W
Dillon →, Canada 73 B7 55 56N 108 56W
Dillsburg, U.S.A. 78 F7 40 7N 77 2W
Dilolo, Dem. Rep. of the Congo 52 G4 10 28S 22 18 E
Dimas, Mexico 86 C3 23 43N 106 47W
Dimashq, Syria 47 B5 33 30N 36 18 E
Dimashq □, Syria 47 B5 33 30N 36 30 E
Dimbaza, S. Africa 57 E4 32 50S 27 14 E
Dimboola, Australia 63 F3 36 28S 142 7 E
Dîmboviţa = Dâmboviţa →, Romania 17 F14 44 12N 26 26 E
Dimbulah, Australia 62 B4 17 8S 145 4 E
Dimitrovgrad, Bulgaria 21 C11 42 5N 25 35 E
Dimitrovgrad, Russia 24 D8 54 14N 49 39 E
Dimitrovo = Pernik, Bulgaria 21 C10 42 35N 23 2 E
Dimmitt, U.S.A. 81 H3 34 33N 102 19W
Dimona, Israel 47 D4 31 2N 35 1 E
Dinagat, Phil. 37 B7 10 10N 125 40 E
Dinajpur, Bangla. 41 G16 25 33N 88 43 E
Dinan, France 18 B2 48 28N 2 2W
Dīnān Āb, Iran 45 C8 32 4N 56 49 E
Dinant, Belgium 15 D4 50 16N 4 55 E
Dinapur, India 43 G11 25 38N 85 5 E
Dīnār, Kūh-e, Iran 45 D6 30 42N 51 46 E
Dinara Planina, Croatia 20 C7 44 0N 16 30 E
Dinard, France 18 B2 48 38N 2 6W
Dinaric Alps = Dinara Planina, Croatia 20 C7 44 0N 16 30 E
Dindigul, India 40 P11 10 25N 78 0 E
Dindori, India 43 H9 22 57N 81 5 E
Ding Xian = Dingzhou, China 34 E8 38 30N 114 59 E
Dinga, Pakistan 42 G2 25 26N 67 10 E
Dingbian, China 34 F4 37 35N 107 32 E
Dingle, Ireland 13 D1 52 9N 10 17W
Dingle B., Ireland 13 D1 52 3N 10 20W
Dingmans Ferry, U.S.A. 79 E10 41 13N 74 55W
Dingo, Australia 62 C4 23 38S 149 19 E
Dingtao, China 34 G8 35 5N 115 35 E
Dingwall, U.K. 12 D4 57 36N 4 26W
Dingxi, China 34 G3 35 30N 104 33 E
Dingxiang, China 34 E7 38 30N 112 58 E
Dingzhou, China 34 E8 38 30N 114 59 E
Dinh, Mui, Vietnam 39 G7 11 22N 109 1 E
Dinh Lap, Vietnam 38 B6 21 33N 107 6 E
Dinokwe, Botswana 56 C4 23 29S 26 37 E
Dinorwic, Canada 73 D10 49 41N 92 30W
Dinosaur Nat. Monument, U.S.A. 82 F9 40 30N 108 45W
Dinosaur Prov. Park, Canada 72 C6 50 47N 111 30W
Dinuba, U.S.A. 84 J7 36 32N 119 23W
Dipalpur, Pakistan 42 D5 30 40N 73 39 E
Diplo, Pakistan 42 G3 24 35N 69 35 E
Dipolog, Phil. 37 C6 8 36N 123 20 E
Dir, Pakistan 40 B7 35 8N 71 59 E
Dire Dawa, Ethiopia 46 F3 9 35N 41 45 E
Diriamba, Nic. 88 D2 11 51N 86 19W
Dirk Hartog I., Australia 61 E1 25 50S 113 5 E
Dirranbandi, Australia 63 D4 28 33S 148 17 E
Disa, India 42 G5 24 18N 72 10 E
Disappointment, C., U.S.A. 82 C2 46 18N 124 5W
Disappointment, L., Australia 60 D3 23 20S 122 40 E
Disaster B., Australia 63 F4 37 15S 149 58 E
Discovery B., Australia 63 F3 38 10S 140 40 E
Disko = Qeqertarsuaq, Greenland 69 B5 69 45N 53 30W
Disko Bugt, Greenland 4 C5 69 10N 52 0W
Diss, U.K. 11 E9 52 23N 1 7 E
Disteghil Sar, Pakistan 43 A6 36 20N 75 12 E
Distrito Federal □, Brazil 93 G9 15 45S 47 45W
Distrito Federal □, Mexico 87 D5 19 15N 99 10W
Diu, India 42 J4 20 45N 70 58 E
Divāndarreh, Iran 44 C5 35 55N 47 2 E
Divide, U.S.A. 82 D7 45 45N 112 45W
Dividing Ra., Australia 61 E2 27 45S 116 0 E
Divinópolis, Brazil 93 H10 20 10S 44 54W
Divnoye, Russia 25 E7 45 55N 43 21 E
Divo, Ivory C. 50 G4 5 48N 5 15W
Dīwāl Kol, Afghan. 42 B2 34 23N 67 52 E
Dixie Mt., U.S.A. 84 F6 39 55N 120 16W
Dixon, Calif., U.S.A. 84 G5 38 27N 121 49W
Dixon, Ill., U.S.A. 80 E10 41 50N 89 29W
Dixon Entrance, U.S.A. 68 C6 54 30N 132 0W
Dixville, Canada 79 A13 45 4N 71 46W
Diyālā →, Iraq 44 C5 33 14N 44 31 E
Diyarbakır, Turkey 25 G7 37 55N 40 18 E
Diyodar, India 42 G4 24 8N 71 50 E
Djakarta = Jakarta, Indonesia 36 F3 6 9S 106 49 E
Djamba, Angola 56 B1 16 45S 13 58 E
Djambala, Congo 52 E2 2 32S 14 30 E
Djanet, Algeria 50 D7 24 35N 9 32 E
Djawa = Jawa, Indonesia 36 F3 7 0S 110 0 E
Djelfa, Algeria 50 B6 34 40N 3 15 E
Djema, C.A.R. 54 A2 6 3N 25 15 E
Djerba, I. de, Tunisia 51 B8 33 50N 10 48 E
Djerid, Chott, Tunisia 50 B7 33 42N 8 30 E
Djibouti, Djibouti 46 E3 11 30N 43 5 E
Djibouti ■, Africa 46 E3 12 0N 43 0 E
Djolu, Dem. Rep. of the Congo 52 D4 0 35N 22 5 E
Djoum, Cameroon 52 D2 2 41N 12 35 E
Djourab, Erg du, Chad 51 E9 16 40N 18 50 E
Djugu, Dem. Rep. of the Congo 54 B3 1 55N 30 35 E
Djúpivogur, Iceland 8 D6 64 39N 14 17W
Dmitriya Lapteva, Proliv, Russia 27 B15 73 0N 140 0 E
Dnepr → = Dnipro →, Ukraine 25 E5 46 30N 32 18 E
Dneprodzerzhinsk = Dniprodzerzhynsk, Ukraine 25 E5 48 32N 34 37 E
Dnepropetrovsk = Dnipropetrovsk, Ukraine 25 E6 48 30N 35 0 E
Dnestr → = Dnister →, Europe 17 E16 46 18N 30 17 E
Dnestrovski = Belgorod, Russia 25 D6 50 35N 36 35 E
Dnieper = Dnipro →, Ukraine 25 E5 46 30N 32 18 E
Dniester = Dnister →, Europe 17 E16 46 18N 30 17 E
Dnipro →, Ukraine 25 E5 46 30N 32 18 E
Dniprodzerzhynsk, Ukraine 25 E5 48 32N 34 37 E
Dnipropetrovsk, Ukraine 25 E6 48 30N 35 0 E
Dnister →, Europe 17 E16 46 18N 30 17 E
Dnistrovskyy Lyman, Ukraine 17 E16 46 15N 30 17 E
Dno, Russia 24 C4 57 50N 29 58 E
Dnyapro = Dnipro →, Ukraine 25 E5 46 30N 32 18 E
Doaktown, Canada 71 C6 46 33N 66 8W
Doan Hung, Vietnam 38 B5 21 30N 105 10 E
Doany, Madag. 57 A8 14 21S 49 30 E
Doba, Chad 51 G9 8 40N 16 50 E
Dobandi, Pakistan 42 D2 31 13N 66 50 E
Dobbyn, Australia 62 B3 19 44S 140 2 E
Dobele, Latvia 9 H20 56 37N 23 16 E
Doberai, Jazirah, Indonesia 37 E8 1 25S 133 0 E
Doblas, Argentina 94 D3 37 5S 64 0W
Dobo, Indonesia 37 F8 5 45S 134 15 E
Doboj, Bos.-H. 21 B8 44 46N 18 4 E
Dobrich, Bulgaria 21 C12 43 37N 27 49 E
Dobruja, Europe 17 F15 44 30N 28 15 E
Dobrush, Belarus 17 B16 52 25N 31 22 E
Doc, Mui, Vietnam 38 D6 17 58N 106 30 E
Docker River, Australia 61 D4 24 52S 129 5 E
Doctor Arroyo, Mexico 86 C4 23 40N 100 11W
Doda, India 43 C6 33 10N 75 34 E
Doda, L., Canada 70 C4 49 25N 75 13W
Dodecanese = Dhodhekánisos, Greece 21 F12 36 35N 27 0 E
Dodge City, U.S.A. 81 G5 37 45N 100 1W
Dodge L., Canada 73 B7 59 50N 105 36W
Dodgeville, U.S.A. 80 D9 42 58N 90 8W
Dodoma, Tanzania 54 D4 6 8S 35 45 E
Dodoma □, Tanzania 54 D4 6 0S 36 0 E
Dodsland, Canada 73 C7 51 50N 108 45W
Dodson, U.S.A. 82 B9 48 24N 108 15W
Doesburg, Neths. 15 B6 52 1N 6 9 E
Doetinchem, Neths. 15 C6 51 59N 6 18 E
Dog Creek, Canada 72 C4 51 35N 122 14W
Dog L., Man., Canada 73 C9 51 2N 98 31W
Dog L., Ont., Canada 70 C2 48 48N 89 30W
Dogran, Pakistan 42 D5 31 48N 73 35 E
Doğubayazıt, Turkey 44 B5 39 31N 44 5 E
Doha = Ad Dawḩah, Qatar 46 B5 25 15N 51 35 E
Dohazari, Bangla. 41 H18 22 10N 92 5 E
Dohrighat, India 43 F10 26 16N 83 31 E
Doi, Indonesia 37 D7 2 14N 127 49 E
Doi Luang, Thailand 38 C3 18 30N 101 0 E
Doi Saket, Thailand 38 C2 18 52N 99 9 E
Dois Irmãos, Sa., Brazil 93 E10 9 0S 42 30W
Dokkum, Neths. 15 A5 53 20N 5 59 E
Dokri, Pakistan 42 F3 27 25N 68 7 E
Dolak, Pulau, Indonesia 37 F9 8 0S 138 30 E
Dolbeau, Canada 71 C5 48 53N 72 18W
Dole, France 18 C6 47 7N 5 31 E
Dolgellau, U.K. 10 E4 52 45N 3 53W
Dolgelley = Dolgellau, U.K. 10 E4 52 45N 3 53W
Dollard, Neths. 15 A7 53 20N 7 10 E
Dolo, Ethiopia 46 G3 4 11N 42 3 E
Dolomites = Dolomiti, Italy 20 A4 46 23N 11 51 E
Dolomiti, Italy 20 A4 46 23N 11 51 E
Dolores, Argentina 94 D4 36 20S 57 40W
Dolores, Uruguay 94 C4 33 34S 58 15W
Dolores, U.S.A. 83 H9 37 28N 108 30W
Dolores →, U.S.A. 83 G9 38 49N 109 17W
Dolphin, C., Falk. Is. 96 G5 51 10S 59 0W
Dolphin and Union Str., Canada 68 B8 69 5N 114 45W
Dom Pedrito, Brazil 95 C5 31 0S 54 40W
Domariaganj →, India 43 F10 26 17N 83 44 E
Domasi, Malawi 55 F4 15 15S 35 22 E
Dombarovskiy, Russia 26 D6 50 46N 59 32 E
Dombås, Norway 9 E13 62 4N 9 8 E
Domel I. = Letsôk-aw Kyun, Burma 39 G2 11 30N 98 25 E
Domeyko, Chile 94 B1 29 0S 71 0W
Domeyko, Cordillera, Chile 94 A2 24 30S 69 0W
Dominador, Chile 94 A2 24 21S 69 20W
Dominica ■, W. Indies 89 C7 15 20N 61 20W
Dominica Passage, W. Indies 89 C7 15 10N 61 20W
Dominican Rep. ■, W. Indies 89 C5 19 0N 70 30W
Domodóssola, Italy 18 C8 46 7N 8 17 E
Domville, Mt., Australia 63 D5 28 1S 151 15 E
Don →, Russia 25 E6 47 4N 39 18 E
Don →, Aberds., U.K. 12 D6 57 11N 2 5W
Don →, S. Yorks., U.K. 10 D7 53 41N 0 52W
Don, C., Australia 60 B5 11 18S 131 46 E
Don Benito, Spain 19 C3 38 53N 5 51W
Dona Ana = Nhamaabué, Mozam. 55 F4 17 25S 35 5 E
Donaghadee, U.K. 13 B6 54 39N 5 33W
Donald, Australia 63 F3 36 23S 143 0 E
Donaldsonville, U.S.A. 81 K9 30 6N 90 59W
Donalsonville, U.S.A. 77 K3 31 3N 84 53W
Donau = Dunărea →, Europe 17 F15 45 20N 29 40 E
Donau →, Austria 15 D3 48 10N 17 0 E
Donauwörth, Germany 16 D6 48 43N 10 47 E
Doncaster, U.K. 10 D6 53 32N 1 6W
Dondo, Mozam. 55 F3 19 33S 34 46 E
Dondo, Teluk, Indonesia 37 D6 0 50N 120 30 E
Dondra Head, Sri Lanka 40 S12 5 55N 80 40 E
Donegal, Ireland 13 B3 54 39N 8 5W
Donegal □, Ireland 13 B4 54 53N 8 0W
Donegal B., Ireland 13 B3 54 31N 8 49W
Donets →, Russia 25 E7 47 33N 40 55 E
Donetsk, Ukraine 25 E6 48 0N 37 45 E
Dong Ba Thin, Vietnam 39 F7 12 8N 109 13 E
Dong Dang, Vietnam 38 B6 21 54N 106 42 E
Dong Giam, Vietnam 38 C5 19 25N 105 31 E
Dong Ha, Vietnam 38 D6 16 55N 107 8 E
Dong Hene, Laos 38 D5 16 40N 105 18 E
Dong Hoi, Vietnam 38 D6 17 29N 106 36 E
Dong Khe, Vietnam 38 A6 22 26N 106 27 E
Dong Ujimqin Qi, China 34 B9 45 32N 116 55 E
Dong Van, Vietnam 38 A5 23 16N 105 22 E
Dong Xoai, Vietnam 39 G6 11 32N 106 55 E
Dongara, Australia 61 E1 29 14S 114 57 E
Dongbei, China 35 D13 45 0N 125 0 E
Dongchuan, China 32 D5 26 8N 103 1 E
Dongfang, China 38 C7 18 50N 108 33 E
Dongfeng, China 35 C13 42 40N 125 34 E
Donggala, Indonesia 37 E5 0 30S 119 40 E
Donggou, China 35 E13 39 52N 124 10 E
Dongguang, China 34 F9 37 50N 116 30 E
Dongjingcheng, China 35 B15 44 5N 129 10 E
Dongning, China 35 B16 44 2N 131 5 E
Dongola, Sudan 51 E12 19 9N 30 22 E
Dongping, China 34 G9 35 55N 116 20 E
Dongsheng, China 34 E6 39 50N 110 0 E
Dongtai, China 35 H11 32 51N 120 21 E
Dongting Hu, China 33 D6 29 18N 112 45 E
Donington, C., Australia 63 E2 34 45S 136 0 E
Doniphan, U.S.A. 81 G9 36 37N 90 50W
Dønna, Norway 8 C15 66 6N 12 30 E
Donna, U.S.A. 81 M5 26 9N 98 4W
Donnaconna, Canada 71 C5 46 41N 71 41W
Donnelly's Crossing, N.Z. 59 F4 35 42S 173 38 E

Donnybrook, *Australia* **61 F2** 33 34S 115 48 E
Donnybrook, *S. Africa* **57 D4** 29 59S 29 48 E
Donora, *U.S.A.* **78 F5** 40 11N 79 52W
Donostia = Donostia-San Sebastián, *Spain* **19 A5** 43 17N 1 58W
Donostia-San Sebastián, *Spain* **19 A5** 43 17N 1 58W
Doon →, *U.K.* **12 F4** 55 27N 4 39W
Dora, L., *Australia* **60 D3** 22 0S 123 0 E
Dora Báltea →, *Italy* **18 D8** 45 11N 8 3 E
Doran L., *Canada* **73 A7** 61 13N 108 6W
Dorchester, *U.K.* **11 G5** 50 42N 2 27W
Dorchester, C., *Canada* **69 B12** 65 27N 77 27W
Dordabis, *Namibia* **56 C2** 22 52S 17 38 E
Dordogne →, *France* **18 D3** 45 2N 0 36W
Dordrecht, *Neths.* **15 C4** 51 48N 4 39 E
Dordrecht, *S. Africa* **56 E4** 31 20S 27 3 E
Doré L., *Canada* **73 C7** 54 46N 107 17W
Doré Lake, *Canada* **73 C7** 54 38N 107 36W
Dori, *Burkina Faso* **50 F5** 14 3N 0 2W
Doring →, *S. Africa* **56 E2** 31 54S 18 39 E
Doringbos, *S. Africa* **56 E2** 31 59S 19 16 E
Dorion, *Canada* **79 A10** 45 23N 74 3W
Dornbirn, *Austria* **16 E5** 47 25N 9 45 E
Dornie, *U.K.* **12 D3** 57 17N 5 31W
Dornoch, *U.K.* **12 D4** 57 53N 4 2W
Dornoch Firth, *U.K.* **12 D4** 57 51N 4 4W
Dornogovĭ □, *Mongolia* **34 C6** 44 0N 110 0 E
Dorohoi, *Romania* **17 E14** 47 56N 26 23 E
Döröö Nuur, *Mongolia* **32 B4** 48 0N 93 0 E
Dorr, *Iran* **45 C6** 33 17N 50 38 E
Dorre I., *Australia* **61 E1** 25 13S 113 12 E
Dorrigo, *Australia* **63 E5** 30 20S 152 44 E
Dorris, *U.S.A.* **82 F3** 41 58N 121 55W
Dorset, *Canada* **78 A6** 45 14N 78 54W
Dorset, *U.S.A.* **78 E4** 41 40N 80 40W
Dorset □, *U.K.* **11 G5** 50 45N 2 26W
Dortmund, *Germany* **16 C4** 51 30N 7 28 E
Doruma, *Dem. Rep. of the Congo* **54 B2** 4 42N 27 33 E
Dorūneh, *Iran* **45 C8** 35 10N 57 18 E
Dos Bahías, C., *Argentina* **96 E3** 44 58S 65 32W
Dos Hermanas, *Spain* **19 D3** 37 16N 5 55W
Dos Palos, *U.S.A.* **84 J6** 36 59N 120 37W
Dosso, *Niger* **50 F6** 13 0N 3 13 E
Dothan, *U.S.A.* **77 K3** 31 13N 85 24W
Doty, *U.S.A.* **84 D3** 46 38N 123 17W
Douai, *France* **18 A5** 50 21N 3 4 E
Douala, *Cameroon* **52 D1** 4 0N 9 45 E
Douarnenez, *France* **18 B1** 48 6N 4 21W
Double Island Pt., *Australia* **63 D5** 25 56S 153 11 E
Double Mountain Fork →, *U.S.A.* **81 J4** 33 16N 100 0W
Doubs →, *France* **18 C6** 46 53N 5 1 E
Doubtful Sd., *N.Z.* **59 L1** 45 20S 166 49 E
Doubtless B., *N.Z.* **59 F4** 34 55S 173 26 E
Douglas, *S. Africa* **56 D3** 29 4S 23 46 E
Douglas, *U.K.* **10 C3** 54 10N 4 28W
Douglas, *Ariz., U.S.A.* **83 L9** 31 21N 109 33W
Douglas, *Ga., U.S.A.* **77 K4** 31 31N 82 51W
Douglas, *Wyo., U.S.A.* **80 D2** 42 45N 105 24W
Douglas Chan., *Canada* **72 C3** 53 40N 129 20W
Douglas Pt., *Canada* **78 B3** 44 19N 81 37W
Douglasville, *U.S.A.* **77 J3** 33 45N 84 45W
Dounreay, *U.K.* **12 C5** 58 35N 3 44W
Dourada, Serra, *Brazil* **93 F9** 13 10S 48 45W
Dourados, *Brazil* **95 A5** 22 9S 54 50W
Dourados →, *Brazil* **95 A5** 21 58S 54 18W
Dourados, Serra dos, *Brazil* **95 A5** 23 30S 53 30W
Douro →, *Europe* **19 B1** 41 8N 8 40W
Dove →, *U.K.* **10 E6** 52 51N 1 36W
Dove Creek, *U.S.A.* **83 H9** 37 46N 108 54W
Dover, *Australia* **62 G4** 43 18S 147 2 E
Dover, *U.K.* **11 F9** 51 7N 1 19 E
Dover, *Del., U.S.A.* **76 F8** 39 10N 75 32W
Dover, *N.H., U.S.A.* **79 C14** 43 12N 70 56W
Dover, *N.J., U.S.A.* **79 F10** 40 53N 74 34W
Dover, *Ohio, U.S.A.* **78 F3** 40 32N 81 29W
Dover, Pt., *Australia* **61 F4** 32 32S 125 32 E
Dover, Str. of, *Europe* **11 G9** 51 0N 1 30 E
Dover-Foxcroft, *U.S.A.* **77 C11** 45 11N 69 13W
Dover Plains, *U.S.A.* **79 E11** 41 43N 73 35W
Dovey = Dyfi →, *U.K.* **11 E3** 52 32N 4 3W
Dovrefjell, *Norway* **9 E13** 62 15N 9 33 E
Dow Rūd, *Iran* **45 C6** 33 28N 49 4 E
Dowa, *Malawi* **55 E3** 13 38S 33 58 E
Dowagiac, *U.S.A.* **76 E2** 41 59N 86 6W
Dowerin, *Australia* **61 F2** 31 12S 117 2 E
Dowgha'i, *Iran* **45 B8** 36 54N 58 32 E
Dowlatābād, *Iran* **45 D8** 28 20N 56 40 E
Down □, *U.K.* **13 B5** 54 23N 6 2W
Downey, *Calif., U.S.A.* **85 M8** 33 56N 118 7W
Downey, *Idaho, U.S.A.* **82 E7** 42 26N 112 7W
Downham Market, *U.K.* **11 E8** 52 37N 0 23 E
Downieville, *U.S.A.* **84 F6** 39 34N 120 50W
Downpatrick, *U.K.* **13 B6** 54 20N 5 43W
Downpatrick Hd., *Ireland* **13 B2** 54 20N 9 21W
Downsville, *U.S.A.* **79 D10** 42 5N 74 50W
Downton, Mt., *Canada* **72 C4** 52 42N 124 52W
Dowsārī, *Iran* **45 D8** 28 25N 57 59 E
Doyle, *U.S.A.* **84 E6** 40 2N 120 6W
Doylestown, *U.S.A.* **79 F9** 40 21N 75 10W
Dozois, Rés., *Canada* **70 C4** 47 30N 77 5W
Dra Khel, *Pakistan* **42 F2** 27 58N 66 45 E
Drachten, *Neths.* **15 A6** 53 7N 6 5 E
Drăgăşani, *Romania* **17 F13** 44 39N 24 17 E
Dragichyn, *Belarus* **17 B13** 52 15N 25 8 E
Dragoman, Prokhod, *Bulgaria* **21 C10** 42 58N 22 53 E
Draguignan, *France* **18 E7** 43 32N 6 27 E
Drain, *U.S.A.* **82 E2** 43 40N 123 19W
Drake, *U.S.A.* **80 B4** 47 55N 100 23W
Drake Passage, *S. Ocean* **5 B17** 58 0S 68 0W
Drakensberg, *S. Africa* **57 D4** 31 0S 28 0 E
Dráma, *Greece* **21 D11** 41 9N 24 10 E
Drammen, *Norway* **9 G14** 59 42N 10 12 E
Drangajökull, *Iceland* **8 C2** 66 9N 22 15W
Dras, *India* **43 B6** 34 25N 75 48 E
Drau = Drava →, *Croatia* **21 B8** 45 33N 18 55 E
Drava →, *Croatia* **21 B8** 45 33N 18 55 E
Drayton Valley, *Canada* **72 C6** 53 12N 114 58W
Drenthe □, *Neths.* **15 B6** 52 52N 6 40 E
Drepanum, C., *Cyprus* **23 E11** 34 54N 32 19 E
Dresden, *Canada* **78 D2** 42 35N 82 11W
Dresden, *Germany* **16 C7** 51 3N 13 44 E
Dreux, *France* **18 B4** 48 44N 1 23 E
Driffield, *U.K.* **10 C7** 54 0N 0 26W
Driftwood, *U.S.A.* **78 E6** 41 20N 78 8W
Driggs, *U.S.A.* **82 E8** 43 44N 111 6W
Drin →, *Albania* **21 C8** 42 1N 19 38 E
Drina →, *Bos.-H.* **21 B8** 44 53N 19 21 E
Drøbak, *Norway* **9 G14** 59 39N 10 39 E
Drobeta-Turnu Severin, *Romania* **17 F12** 44 39N 22 41 E
Drochia, *Moldova* **17 D14** 48 2N 27 48 E
Drogheda, *Ireland* **13 C5** 53 43N 6 22W
Drogichin = Dragichyn, *Belarus* **17 B13** 52 15N 25 8 E
Drogobych = Drohobych, *Ukraine* **17 D12** 49 20N 23 30 E
Drohobych, *Ukraine* **17 D12** 49 20N 23 30 E
Droichead Atha = Drogheda, *Ireland* **13 C5** 53 43N 6 22W
Droichead Nua, *Ireland* **13 C5** 53 11N 6 48W
Droitwich, *U.K.* **11 E5** 52 16N 2 8W
Dromedary, C., *Australia* **63 F5** 36 17S 150 10 E
Dromore, *U.K.* **13 B4** 54 31N 7 28W
Dromore West, *Ireland* **13 B3** 54 15N 8 52W
Dronfield, *U.K.* **10 D6** 53 19N 1 27W
Dronten, *Neths.* **15 B5** 52 32N 5 43 E
Drumbo, *Canada* **78 C4** 43 16N 80 35W
Drumheller, *Canada* **72 C6** 51 25N 112 40W
Drummond, *U.S.A.* **82 C7** 46 40N 113 9W
Drummond I., *U.S.A.* **76 C4** 46 1N 83 39W
Drummond Pt., *Australia* **63 E2** 34 9S 135 16 E
Drummond Ra., *Australia* **62 C4** 23 45S 147 10 E
Drummondville, *Canada* **70 C5** 45 55N 72 25W
Drumright, *U.S.A.* **81 H6** 35 59N 96 36W
Druskininkai, *Lithuania* **9 J20** 54 3N 23 58 E
Drut →, *Belarus* **17 B16** 53 8N 30 5 E
Druzhina, *Russia* **27 C15** 68 14N 145 18 E
Dry Tortugas, *U.S.A.* **88 B3** 24 38N 82 55W
Dryden, *Canada* **73 D10** 49 47N 92 50W
Dryden, *U.S.A.* **79 D8** 42 30N 76 18W
Drygalski I., *Antarctica* **5 C7** 66 0S 92 0 E
Drysdale →, *Australia* **60 B4** 13 59S 126 51 E
Drysdale I., *Australia* **62 A2** 11 41S 136 0 E
Du Bois, *U.S.A.* **78 E6** 41 8N 78 46W
Du Gué →, *Canada* **70 A5** 57 21N 70 45W
Du Quoin, *U.S.A.* **80 G10** 38 1N 89 14W
Duanesburg, *U.S.A.* **79 D10** 42 45N 74 11W
Duaringa, *Australia* **62 C4** 23 42S 149 42 E
Dubā, *Si. Arabia* **44 E2** 27 10N 35 40 E
Dubai = Dubayy, *U.A.E.* **46 B6** 25 18N 55 20 E
Dubăsari, *Moldova* **17 E15** 47 15N 29 10 E
Dubăsari Vdkhr., *Moldova* **17 E15** 47 30N 29 0 E
Dubawnt →, *Canada* **73 A8** 64 33N 100 6W
Dubawnt, L., *Canada* **73 A8** 63 4N 101 42W
Dubayy, *U.A.E.* **46 B6** 25 18N 55 20 E
Dubbo, *Australia* **63 E4** 32 11S 148 35 E
Dubele, *Dem. Rep. of the Congo* **54 B2** 2 56N 29 35 E
Dublin, *Ireland* **13 C5** 53 21N 6 15W
Dublin, *Ga., U.S.A.* **77 J4** 32 32N 82 54W
Dublin, *Tex., U.S.A.* **81 J5** 32 5N 98 21W
Dublin □, *Ireland* **13 C5** 53 24N 6 20W
Dubno, *Ukraine* **17 C13** 50 25N 25 45 E
Dubois, *U.S.A.* **82 D7** 44 10N 112 14W
Dubossary = Dubăsari, *Moldova* **17 E15** 47 15N 29 10 E
Dubossary Vdkhr. = Dubăsari Vdkhr., *Moldova* **17 E15** 47 30N 29 0 E
Dubovka, *Russia* **25 E7** 49 5N 44 50 E
Dubrajpur, *India* **43 H12** 23 48N 87 25 E
Dubréka, *Guinea* **50 G3** 9 46N 13 31W
Dubrovitsa = Dubrovytsya, *Ukraine* **17 C14** 51 31N 26 35 E
Dubrovnik, *Croatia* **21 C8** 42 39N 18 6 E
Dubrovytsya, *Ukraine* **17 C14** 51 31N 26 35 E
Dubuque, *U.S.A.* **80 D9** 42 30N 90 41W
Duchesne, *U.S.A.* **82 F8** 40 10N 110 24W
Duchess, *Australia* **62 C2** 21 20S 139 50 E
Ducie I., *Pac. Oc.* **65 K15** 24 40S 124 48W
Duck →, *U.S.A.* **77 G2** 36 2N 87 52W
Duck Cr. →, *Australia* **60 D2** 22 37S 116 53 E
Duck Lake, *Canada* **73 C7** 52 50N 106 16W
Duck Mountain Prov. Park, *Canada* **73 C8** 51 45N 101 0W
Duckwall, Mt., *U.S.A.* **84 H6** 37 58N 120 7W
Dudhi, *India* **41 G13** 24 15N 83 10 E
Dudinka, *Russia* **27 C9** 69 30N 86 13 E
Dudley, *U.K.* **11 E5** 52 31N 2 5W
Dudwa, *India* **43 E9** 28 30N 80 41 E
Duero = Douro →, *Europe* **19 B1** 41 8N 8 40W
Dufftown, *U.K.* **12 D5** 57 27N 3 8W
Dūghī Kalā, *Afghan.* **40 C3** 32 20N 62 50 E
Dugi Otok, *Croatia* **16 G8** 44 0N 15 3 E
Duifken Pt., *Australia* **62 A3** 12 33S 141 38 E
Duisburg, *Germany* **16 C4** 51 26N 6 45 E
Duiwelskloof, *S. Africa* **57 C5** 23 42S 30 10 E
Dūkdamīn, *Iran* **45 C8** 35 59N 57 43 E
Dukelský Průsmyk, *Slovak Rep.* **17 D11** 49 25N 21 42 E
Dukhān, *Qatar* **45 E6** 25 25N 50 50 E
Duki, *Pakistan* **40 D6** 30 14N 68 25 E
Duku, *Nigeria* **51 F8** 10 43N 10 43 E
Dulce, *U.S.A.* **83 H10** 36 56N 107 0W
Dulce →, *Argentina* **94 C3** 30 32S 62 33W
Dulce, G., *Costa Rica* **88 E3** 8 40N 83 20W
Dulf, *Iraq* **44 C5** 35 7N 45 51 E
Dulit, Banjaran, *Malaysia* **36 D4** 3 15N 114 30 E
Duliu, *China* **34 E9** 39 2N 116 55 E
Dullewala, *Pakistan* **42 D4** 31 50N 71 25 E
Dullstroom, *S. Africa* **57 D5** 25 27S 30 7 E
Dulq Maghār, *Syria* **44 B3** 36 22N 38 39 E
Duluth, *U.S.A.* **80 B8** 46 47N 92 6W
Dum Dum, *India* **43 H13** 22 39N 88 33 E
Dum Duma, *India* **41 F19** 27 40N 95 40 E
Dūmā, *Syria* **47 B5** 33 34N 36 24 E
Dumaguete, *Phil.* **37 C6** 9 17N 123 15 E
Dumai, *Indonesia* **36 D2** 1 35N 101 28 E
Dumaran, *Phil.* **37 B5** 10 33N 119 50 E
Dumas, *Ark., U.S.A.* **81 J9** 33 53N 91 29W
Dumas, *Tex., U.S.A.* **81 H4** 35 52N 101 58W
Dumayr, *Syria* **47 B5** 33 39N 36 42 E
Dumbarton, *U.K.* **12 F4** 55 57N 4 33W
Dumbleyung, *Australia* **61 F2** 33 17S 117 42 E
Dumfries, *U.K.* **12 F5** 55 4N 3 37W
Dumfries & Galloway □, *U.K.* **12 F5** 55 9N 3 58W
Dumka, *India* **43 G12** 24 12N 87 15 E
Dumoine →, *Canada* **70 C4** 46 13N 77 51W
Dumoine, L., *Canada* **70 C4** 46 55N 77 55W
Dumraon, *India* **43 G11** 25 33N 84 8 E
Dumyât, *Egypt* **51 B12** 31 24N 31 48 E
Dún Dealgan = Dundalk, *Ireland* **13 B5** 54 1N 6 24W
Dun Laoghaire, *Ireland* **13 C5** 53 17N 6 8W
Duna = Dunărea →, *Europe* **17 F15** 45 20N 29 40 E
Dunagiri, *India* **43 D8** 30 31N 79 52 E
Dunaj = Dunărea →, *Europe* **17 F15** 45 20N 29 40 E
Dunakeszi, *Hungary* **17 E10** 47 37N 19 8 E
Dunărea →, *Europe* **17 F15** 45 20N 29 40 E
Dunaújváros, *Hungary* **17 E10** 46 58N 18 57 E
Dunav = Dunărea →, *Europe* **17 F15** 45 20N 29 40 E
Dunay, *Russia* **30 C6** 42 52N 132 22 E
Dunback, *N.Z.* **59 L3** 45 23S 170 36 E
Dunbar, *U.K.* **12 E6** 56 0N 2 31W
Dunblane, *U.K.* **12 E5** 56 11N 3 58W
Duncan, *Canada* **72 D4** 48 45N 123 40W
Duncan, *Ariz., U.S.A.* **83 K9** 32 43N 109 6W
Duncan, *Okla., U.S.A.* **81 H6** 34 30N 97 57W
Duncan, L., *Canada* **70 B4** 53 29N 77 58W
Duncan L., *Canada* **72 A6** 62 51N 113 58W
Duncan Town, *Bahamas* **88 B4** 22 15N 75 45W
Duncannon, *U.S.A.* **78 F7** 40 23N 77 2W
Duncansby Head, *U.K.* **12 C5** 58 38N 3 1W
Duncansville, *U.S.A.* **78 F6** 40 25N 78 26W
Dundalk, *Canada* **78 B4** 44 10N 80 24W
Dundalk, *Ireland* **13 B5** 54 1N 6 24W
Dundalk, *U.S.A.* **76 F7** 39 16N 76 32W
Dundalk Bay, *Ireland* **13 C5** 53 55N 6 15W
Dundas, *Canada* **78 C5** 43 17N 79 59W
Dundas, L., *Australia* **61 F3** 32 35S 121 50 E
Dundas I., *Canada* **72 C2** 54 30N 130 50W
Dundas Str., *Australia* **60 B5** 11 15S 131 35 E
Dundee, *S. Africa* **57 D5** 28 11S 30 15 E
Dundee, *U.K.* **12 E6** 56 28N 2 59W
Dundee, *U.S.A.* **78 D8** 42 32N 76 59W
Dundee City □, *U.K.* **12 E6** 56 30N 2 58W
Dundgovĭ □, *Mongolia* **34 B4** 45 10N 106 0 E
Dundrum, *U.K.* **13 B6** 54 16N 5 52W
Dundrum B., *U.K.* **13 B6** 54 13N 5 47W
Dunedin, *N.Z.* **59 L3** 45 50S 170 33 E
Dunedin, *U.S.A.* **77 L4** 28 1N 82 47W
Dunfermline, *U.K.* **12 E5** 56 5N 3 27W
Dungannon, *Canada* **78 C3** 43 51N 81 36W
Dungannon, *U.K.* **13 B5** 54 31N 6 46W
Dungarpur, *India* **42 H5** 23 52N 73 45 E
Dungarvan, *Ireland* **13 D4** 52 5N 7 37W
Dungarvan Harbour, *Ireland* **13 D4** 52 4N 7 35W
Dungeness, *U.K.* **11 G8** 50 54N 0 59 E
Dungo, L. do, *Angola* **56 B2** 17 15S 19 0 E
Dungog, *Australia* **63 E5** 32 22S 151 46 E
Dungu, *Dem. Rep. of the Congo* **54 B2** 3 40N 28 32 E
Dungun, *Malaysia* **39 K4** 4 45N 103 25 E
Dunhua, *China* **35 C15** 43 20N 128 14 E
Dunhuang, *China* **32 B4** 40 8N 94 36 E
Dunk I., *Australia* **62 B4** 17 59S 146 29 E
Dunkeld, *Australia* **63 E4** 33 25S 149 29 E
Dunkeld, *U.K.* **12 E5** 56 34N 3 35W
Dunkerque, *France* **18 A5** 51 2N 2 20 E
Dunkery Beacon, *U.K.* **11 F4** 51 9N 3 36W
Dunkirk = Dunkerque, *France* **18 A5** 51 2N 2 20 E
Dunkirk, *U.S.A.* **78 D5** 42 29N 79 20W
Dúnleary = Dun Laoghaire, *Ireland* **13 C5** 53 17N 6 8W
Dunleer, *Ireland* **13 C5** 53 50N 6 24W
Dunmanus B., *Ireland* **13 E2** 51 31N 9 50W
Dunmanway, *Ireland* **13 E2** 51 43N 9 6W
Dunmara, *Australia* **62 B1** 16 42S 133 25 E
Dunmore, *U.S.A.* **79 E9** 41 25N 75 38W
Dunmore Hd., *Ireland* **13 D1** 52 10N 10 35W
Dunmore Town, *Bahamas* **88 A4** 25 30N 76 39W
Dunn, *U.S.A.* **77 H6** 35 19N 78 37W
Dunnellon, *U.S.A.* **77 L4** 29 3N 82 28W
Dunnet Hd., *U.K.* **12 C5** 58 40N 3 21W
Dunning, *U.S.A.* **80 E4** 41 50N 100 6W
Dunnville, *Canada* **78 D5** 42 54N 79 36W
Dunolly, *Australia* **63 F3** 36 51S 143 44 E
Dunoon, *U.K.* **12 F4** 55 57N 4 56W
Dunphy, *U.S.A.* **82 F5** 40 42N 116 31W
Duns, *U.K.* **12 F6** 55 47N 2 20W
Dunseith, *U.S.A.* **80 A4** 48 50N 100 3W
Dunsmuir, *U.S.A.* **82 F2** 41 13N 122 16W
Dunstable, *U.K.* **11 F7** 51 53N 0 32W
Dunstan Mts., *N.Z.* **59 L2** 44 53S 169 35 E
Dunster, *Canada* **72 C5** 53 8N 119 50W
Dunvegan L., *Canada* **73 A7** 60 8N 107 10W
Duolun, *China* **34 C9** 42 12N 116 28 E
Duong Dong, *Vietnam* **39 G4** 10 13N 103 58 E
Dupree, *U.S.A.* **80 C4** 45 4N 101 35W
Dupuyer, *U.S.A.* **82 B7** 48 13N 112 30W
Duque de Caxias, *Brazil* **95 A7** 22 45S 43 19W
Durack →, *Australia* **60 C4** 15 33S 127 52 E
Durack Ra., *Australia* **60 C4** 16 50S 127 40 E
Durance →, *France* **18 E6** 43 55N 4 45 E
Durand, *U.S.A.* **80 C9** 44 38N 91 58W
Durango, *Mexico* **86 C4** 24 3N 104 39W
Durango, *U.S.A.* **83 H10** 37 16N 107 53W
Durango □, *Mexico* **86 C4** 25 0N 105 0W
Durant, *Miss., U.S.A.* **81 J10** 33 4N 89 51W
Durant, *Okla., U.S.A.* **81 J6** 33 59N 96 25W
Durazno, *Uruguay* **94 C4** 33 25S 56 31W
Durazzo = Durrës, *Albania* **21 D8** 41 19N 19 28 E
Durban, *S. Africa* **57 D5** 29 49S 31 1 E
Durbuy, *Belgium* **15 D5** 50 21N 5 28 E
Düren, *Germany* **16 C4** 50 48N 6 29 E
Durg, *India* **41 J12** 21 15N 81 22 E
Durgapur, *India* **43 H12** 23 30N 87 20 E
Durham, *Canada* **78 B4** 44 10N 80 49W
Durham, *U.K.* **10 C6** 54 47N 1 34W
Durham, *Calif., U.S.A.* **84 F5** 39 39N 121 48W
Durham, *N.C., U.S.A.* **77 H6** 35 59N 78 54W
Durham, *N.H., U.S.A.* **79 C14** 43 8N 70 56W
Durham □, *U.K.* **10 C6** 54 42N 1 45W
Durmā, *Si. Arabia* **44 E5** 24 37N 46 8 E
Durmitor, *Montenegro, Yug.* **21 C8** 43 10N 19 0 E
Durness, *U.K.* **12 C4** 58 34N 4 45W
Durrës, *Albania* **21 D8** 41 19N 19 28 E
Durrow, *Ireland* **13 D4** 52 51N 7 24W
Dursey I., *Ireland* **13 E1** 51 36N 10 12W
Dursunbey, *Turkey* **21 E13** 39 35N 28 37 E
Duru, *Dem. Rep. of the Congo* **54 B2** 4 14N 28 50 E
Durūz, Jabal ad, *Jordan* **47 C5** 32 35N 36 40 E
D'Urville, Tanjung, *Indonesia* **37 E9** 1 28S 137 54 E
D'Urville I., *N.Z.* **59 J4** 40 50S 173 55 E
Duryea, *U.S.A.* **79 E9** 41 20N 75 45W
Dushak, *Turkmenistan* **26 F7** 37 13N 60 1 E
Dushanbe, *Tajikistan* **26 F7** 38 33N 68 48 E
Dushore, *U.S.A.* **79 E8** 41 31N 76 24W
Dusky Sd., *N.Z.* **59 L1** 45 47S 166 30 E
Dussejour, C., *Australia* **60 B4** 14 45S 128 13 E
Düsseldorf, *Germany* **16 C4** 51 14N 6 47 E
Dutch Harbor, *U.S.A.* **68 C3** 53 53N 166 32W
Dutlwe, *Botswana* **56 C3** 23 58S 23 46 E
Dutton, *Canada* **78 D3** 42 39N 81 30W
Dutton →, *Australia* **62 C3** 20 44S 143 10 E
Duwayhin, Khawr, *U.A.E.* **45 E6** 24 20N 51 25 E
Duyun, *China* **32 D5** 26 18N 107 29 E
Duzdab = Zāhedān, *Iran* **45 D9** 29 30N 60 50 E
Dvina, Severnaya →, *Russia* **24 B7** 64 32N 40 30 E
Dvinsk = Daugavpils, *Latvia* **9 J22** 55 53N 26 32 E
Dvinskaya Guba, *Russia* **24 B6** 65 0N 39 0 E
Dwarka, *India* **42 H3** 22 18N 69 8 E
Dwellingup, *Australia* **61 F2** 32 43S 116 4 E
Dwight, *Canada* **78 A5** 45 20N 79 1W
Dwight, *U.S.A.* **76 E1** 41 5N 88 26W
Dyatlovo = Dzyatlava, *Belarus* **17 B13** 53 28N 25 28 E
Dyce, *U.K.* **12 D6** 57 13N 2 12W
Dyer, C., *Canada* **69 B13** 66 40N 61 0W
Dyer Bay, *Canada* **78 A3** 45 10N 81 20W
Dyer Plateau, *Antarctica* **5 D17** 70 45S 65 30W
Dyersburg, *U.S.A.* **81 G10** 36 3N 89 23W
Dyfi →, *U.K.* **11 E3** 52 32N 4 3W
Dymer, *Ukraine* **17 C16** 50 47N 30 18 E
Dysart, *Australia* **62 C4** 22 32S 148 23 E
Dzamin Üüd = Borhoyn Tal, *Mongolia* **34 C6** 43 50N 111 58 E
Dzerzhinsk, *Russia* **24 C7** 56 14N 43 30 E
Dzhalinda, *Russia* **27 D13** 53 26N 124 0 E
Dzhambul = Taraz, *Kazakstan* **26 E8** 42 54N 71 22 E
Dzhankoy, *Ukraine* **25 E5** 45 40N 34 20 E
Dzhezkazgan = Zhezqazghan, *Kazakstan* **26 E7** 47 44N 67 40 E
Dzhizak = Jizzakh, *Uzbekistan* **26 E7** 40 6N 67 50 E
Dzhugdzur, Khrebet, *Russia* **27 D14** 57 30N 138 0 E
Dzhungarskiye Vorota = Dzungarian Gates, *Asia* **32 B3** 45 0N 82 0 E
Działdowo, *Poland* **17 B11** 53 15N 20 15 E
Dzibilchaltun, *Mexico* **87 C7** 21 5N 89 36W
Dzierżoniów, *Poland* **17 C9** 50 45N 16 39 E
Dzilam de Bravo, *Mexico* **87 C7** 21 24N 88 53W
Dzungaria = Junggar Pendi, *China* **32 B3** 44 30N 86 0 E
Dzungarian Gates, *Asia* **32 B3** 45 0N 82 0 E
Dzuumod, *Mongolia* **32 B5** 47 45N 106 58 E
Dzyarzhynsk, *Belarus* **17 B14** 53 40N 27 1 E
Dzyatlava, *Belarus* **17 B13** 53 28N 25 28 E

E

Eabamet L., *Canada* **70 B2** 51 30N 87 46W
Eads, *U.S.A.* **80 F3** 38 29N 102 47W
Eagar, *U.S.A.* **83 J9** 34 6N 109 17W
Eagle, *Alaska, U.S.A.* **68 B5** 64 47N 141 12W
Eagle, *Colo., U.S.A.* **82 G10** 39 39N 106 50W
Eagle →, *Canada* **71 B8** 53 36N 57 26W
Eagle Butte, *U.S.A.* **80 C4** 45 0N 101 10W
Eagle Grove, *U.S.A.* **80 D8** 42 40N 93 54W
Eagle L., *Canada* **73 D10** 49 42N 93 13W
Eagle L., *Calif., U.S.A.* **82 F3** 40 39N 120 45W
Eagle L., *Maine, U.S.A.* **77 B11** 46 20N 69 22W
Eagle Lake, *Canada* **78 A6** 45 8N 78 29W
Eagle Lake, *Maine, U.S.A.* **77 B11** 47 3N 68 36W
Eagle Lake, *Tex., U.S.A.* **81 L6** 29 35N 96 20W
Eagle Mountain, *U.S.A.* **85 M11** 33 49N 115 27W
Eagle Nest, *U.S.A.* **83 H11** 36 33N 105 16W
Eagle Pass, *U.S.A.* **81 L4** 28 43N 100 30W
Eagle Pk., *U.S.A.* **84 G7** 38 10N 119 25W
Eagle Pt., *Australia* **60 C3** 16 11S 124 23 E
Eagle River, *Mich., U.S.A.* **76 B1** 47 24N 88 18W
Eagle River, *Wis., U.S.A.* **80 C10** 45 55N 89 15W
Eaglehawk, *Australia* **63 F3** 36 44S 144 15 E
Eagles Mere, *U.S.A.* **79 E8** 41 25N 76 33W
Ealing □, *U.K.* **11 F7** 51 31N 0 20W
Ear Falls, *Canada* **73 C10** 50 38N 93 13W
Earle, *U.S.A.* **81 H9** 35 16N 90 28W
Earlimart, *U.S.A.* **85 K7** 35 53N 119 16W
Earn →, *U.K.* **12 E5** 56 21N 3 18W
Earn, L., *U.K.* **12 E4** 56 23N 4 13W
Earnslaw, Mt., *N.Z.* **59 L2** 44 32S 168 27 E
Earth, *U.S.A.* **81 H3** 34 14N 102 24W
Easley, *U.S.A.* **77 H4** 34 50N 82 36W
East Anglia, *U.K.* **10 E9** 52 30N 1 0 E
East Angus, *Canada* **71 C5** 45 30N 71 40W
East Aurora, *U.S.A.* **78 D6** 42 46N 78 37W
East Ayrshire □, *U.K.* **12 F4** 55 26N 4 11W
East Bengal, *Bangla.* **41 H17** 24 0N 90 0 E
East Beskids = Vychodné Beskydy, *Europe* **17 D11** 49 20N 22 0 E
East Brady, *U.S.A.* **78 F5** 40 59N 79 36W
East C., *N.Z.* **59 G7** 37 42S 178 35 E
East Chicago, *U.S.A.* **76 E2** 41 38N 87 27W
East China Sea, *Asia* **33 D7** 30 0N 126 0 E
East Coulee, *Canada* **72 C6** 51 23N 112 27W
East Dereham, *U.K.* **11 E8** 52 41N 0 57 E
East Dunbartonshire □, *U.K.* **12 F4** 55 57N 4 13W
East Falkland, *Falk. Is.* **96 G5** 51 30S 58 30W
East Grand Forks, *U.S.A.* **80 B6** 47 56N 97 1W
East Greenwich, *U.S.A.* **79 E13** 41 40N 71 27W
East Grinstead, *U.K.* **11 F8** 51 7N 0 0W
East Hartford, *U.S.A.* **79 E12** 41 46N 72 39W
East Helena, *U.S.A.* **82 C8** 46 35N 111 56W
East Indies, *Asia* **28 K15** 0 0 120 0 E
East Kilbride, *U.K.* **12 F4** 55 47N 4 11W
East Lansing, *U.S.A.* **76 D3** 42 44N 84 29W
East Liverpool, *U.S.A.* **78 F4** 40 37N 80 35W
East London, *S. Africa* **57 E4** 33 0S 27 55 E
East Lothian □, *U.K.* **12 F6** 55 58N 2 44W
East Main = Eastmain, *Canada* **70 B4** 52 10N 78 30W
East Northport, *U.S.A.* **79 F11** 40 53N 73 20W
East Orange, *U.S.A.* **79 F10** 40 46N 74 13W
East Pacific Ridge, *Pac. Oc.* **65 J17** 15 0S 110 0W
East Palestine, *U.S.A.* **78 F4** 40 50N 80 33W
East Pine, *Canada* **72 B4** 55 48N 120 12W
East Point, *U.S.A.* **77 J3** 33 41N 84 27W
East Providence, *U.S.A.* **79 E13** 41 49N 71 23W

East Pt., Canada 71 C7 46 27N 61 58W
East Renfrewshire □, U.K. 12 F4 55 46N 4 21W
East Retford = Retford, U.K. 10 D7 53 19N 0 56W
East Riding of Yorkshire □, U.K. 10 D7 53 55N 0 30W
East Rochester, U.S.A. 78 C7 43 7N 77 29W
East St. Louis, U.S.A. 80 F9 38 37N 90 9W
East Schelde = Oosterschelde →, Neths. 15 C4 51 33N 4 0 E
East Sea = Japan, Sea of, Asia 30 E7 40 0N 135 0 E
East Siberian Sea, Russia 27 B17 73 0N 160 0 E
East Stroudsburg, U.S.A. 79 E9 41 1N 75 11W
East Sussex □, U.K. 11 G8 50 56N 0 19 E
East Tawas, U.S.A. 76 C4 44 17N 83 29W
East Timor ■, Asia 37 F7 8 50S 126 0 E
East Toorale, Australia 63 E4 30 27S 145 28 E
East Walker →, U.S.A. 84 G7 38 52N 119 10W
East Windsor, U.S.A. 79 F10 40 17N 74 34W
Eastbourne, N.Z. 59 J5 41 19S 174 55 E
Eastbourne, U.K. 11 G8 50 46N 0 18 E
Eastend, Canada 73 D7 49 32N 108 50W
Easter I. = Pascua, I. de, Chile 65 K17 27 7S 109 23W
Eastern □, Kenya 54 C4 0 0 38 30 E
Eastern Cape □, S. Africa 56 E4 32 0S 26 0 E
Eastern Cr. →, Australia 62 C3 20 40S 141 35 E
Eastern Ghats, India 40 N11 14 0N 78 50 E
Eastern Group = Lau Group, Fiji 59 C9 17 0S 178 30W
Eastern Group, Australia 61 F3 33 30S 124 30 E
Eastern Transvaal = Mpumalanga □, S. Africa 57 B5 26 0S 30 0 E
Easterville, Canada 73 C9 53 8N 99 49W
Easthampton, U.S.A. 79 D12 42 16N 72 40W
Eastlake, U.S.A. 78 E3 41 40N 81 26W
Eastland, U.S.A. 81 J5 32 24N 98 49W
Eastleigh, U.K. 11 G6 50 58N 1 21W
Eastmain, Canada 70 B4 52 10N 78 30W
Eastmain →, Canada 70 B4 52 27N 78 26W
Eastman, Canada 79 A12 45 18N 72 19W
Eastman, U.S.A. 77 J4 32 12N 83 11W
Easton, Md., U.S.A. 76 F7 38 47N 76 5W
Easton, Pa., U.S.A. 79 F9 40 41N 75 13W
Easton, Wash., U.S.A. 84 C5 47 14N 121 11W
Eastpointe, U.S.A. 78 D2 42 27N 82 56W
Eastport, U.S.A. 77 C12 44 56N 67 0W
Eastsound, U.S.A. 84 B4 48 42N 122 55W
Eaton, U.S.A. 80 E2 40 32N 104 42W
Eatonia, Canada 73 C7 51 13N 109 25W
Eatonton, U.S.A. 77 J4 33 20N 83 23W
Eatontown, U.S.A. 79 F10 40 19N 74 4W
Eatonville, U.S.A. 84 D4 46 52N 122 16W
Eau Claire, U.S.A. 80 C9 44 49N 91 30W
Eau Claire, L. à l', Canada 70 A5 56 10N 74 25W
Ebbw Vale, U.K. 11 F4 51 46N 3 12W
Ebeltoft, Denmark 9 H14 56 12N 10 41 E
Ebensburg, U.S.A. 78 F6 40 29N 78 44W
Eberswalde-Finow, Germany 16 B7 52 50N 13 49 E
Ebetsu, Japan 30 C10 43 7N 141 34 E
Ebolowa, Cameroon 52 D2 2 55N 11 10 E
Ebro →, Spain 19 B6 40 43N 0 54 E
Eceabat, Turkey 21 D12 40 11N 26 21 E
Ech Chéliff, Algeria 50 A6 36 10N 1 20 E
Echigo-Sammyaku, Japan 31 F9 36 50N 139 50 E
Echizen-Misaki, Japan 31 G7 35 59N 135 57 E
Echo Bay, N.W.T., Canada 68 B8 66 5N 117 55W
Echo Bay, Ont., Canada 70 C3 46 29N 84 4W
Echoing →, Canada 70 B1 55 51N 92 5W
Echternach, Lux. 15 E6 49 49N 6 25 E
Echuca, Australia 63 F3 36 10S 144 45 E
Ecija, Spain 19 D3 37 30N 5 10W
Eclipse Is., Australia 60 B4 13 54S 126 19 E
Eclipse Sd., Canada 69 A11 72 38N 79 0W
Ecuador ■, S. Amer. 92 D3 2 0S 78 0W
Ed Damazin, Sudan 51 F12 11 46N 34 21 E
Ed Debba, Sudan 51 E12 18 0N 30 51 E
Ed Dueim, Sudan 51 F12 14 0N 32 10 E
Edam, Canada 73 C7 53 11N 108 46W
Edam, Neths. 15 B5 52 31N 5 3 E
Eday, U.K. 12 B6 59 11N 2 47W
Eddrachillis B., U.K. 12 C3 58 17N 5 14W
Eddystone Pt., Australia 62 G4 40 59S 148 20 E
Ede, Neths. 15 B5 52 4N 5 40 E
Edehon L., Canada 73 A9 60 25N 97 15W
Eden, Australia 63 F4 37 3S 149 55 E
Eden, N.C., U.S.A. 77 G6 36 29N 79 53W
Eden, N.Y., U.S.A. 78 D6 42 39N 78 55W
Eden, Tex., U.S.A. 81 K5 31 13N 99 51W
Eden →, U.K. 10 C4 54 57N 3 1W
Edenburg, S. Africa 56 D4 29 43S 25 58 E
Edendale, S. Africa 57 D5 29 39S 30 18 E
Edenderry, Ireland 13 C4 53 21N 7 4W
Edenton, U.S.A. 77 G7 36 4N 76 39W
Edenville, S. Africa 57 D4 27 37S 27 34 E
Eder →, Germany 16 C5 51 12N 9 28 E
Edgar, U.S.A. 80 E6 40 22N 97 58W
Edgartown, U.S.A. 79 E14 41 23N 70 31W
Edge Hill, U.K. 11 E6 52 8N 1 26W
Edgefield, U.S.A. 77 J5 33 47N 81 56W
Edgeley, U.S.A. 80 B5 46 22N 98 43W
Edgemont, U.S.A. 80 D3 43 18N 103 50W
Edgeøya, Svalbard 4 B9 77 45N 22 30 E
Édhessa, Greece 21 D10 40 48N 22 5 E
Edievale, N.Z. 59 L2 45 49S 169 22 E
Edina, U.S.A. 80 E8 40 10N 92 11W
Edinboro, U.S.A. 78 E4 41 52N 80 8W
Edinburg, U.S.A. 81 M5 26 18N 98 10W
Edinburgh, U.K. 12 F5 55 57N 3 13W
Edinburgh, City of □, U.K. 12 F5 55 57N 3 17W
Edineţ, Moldova 17 D14 48 9N 27 18 E
Edirne, Turkey 21 D12 41 40N 26 34 E
Edison, U.S.A. 84 B4 48 33N 122 27W
Edithburgh, Australia 63 F2 35 5S 137 43 E
Edmeston, U.S.A. 79 D9 42 42N 75 15W
Edmond, U.S.A. 81 H6 35 39N 97 29W
Edmonds, U.S.A. 84 C4 47 49N 122 23W
Edmonton, Australia 62 B4 17 2S 145 46 E
Edmonton, Canada 72 C6 53 30N 113 30W
Edmund L., Canada 70 B1 54 45N 93 17W
Edmundston, Canada 71 C6 47 23N 68 20W
Edna, U.S.A. 81 L6 28 59N 96 39W
Edremit, Turkey 21 E12 39 34N 27 0 E
Edremit Körfezi, Turkey 21 E12 39 30N 26 45 E
Edson, Canada 72 C5 53 35N 116 28W
Eduardo Castex, Argentina 94 D3 35 50S 64 18W
Edward →, Australia 63 F3 35 5S 143 30 E
Edward, L., Africa 54 C2 0 25S 29 40 E
Edward River, Australia 62 A3 14 59S 141 26 E
Edward VII Land, Antarctica 5 E13 80 0S 150 0W
Edwards, Calif., U.S.A. 85 L9 34 55N 117 51W
Edwards, N.Y., U.S.A. 79 B9 44 20N 75 15W
Edwards Air Force Base, U.S.A. 85 L9 34 50N 117 40W
Edwards Plateau, U.S.A. 81 K4 30 45N 101 20W
Edwardsville, U.S.A. 79 E9 41 15N 75 56W
Edzo, Canada 72 A5 62 49N 116 4W
Eeklo, Belgium 15 C3 51 11N 3 33 E
Effingham, U.S.A. 76 F1 39 7N 88 33W
Égadi, Ísole, Italy 20 F5 37 55N 12 16 E
Egan Range, U.S.A. 82 G6 39 35N 114 55W
Eganville, Canada 78 A7 45 32N 77 5W
Eger = Cheb, Czech Rep. 16 C7 50 9N 12 28 E
Eger, Hungary 17 E11 47 53N 20 27 E
Egersund, Norway 9 G12 58 26N 6 1 E
Egg L., Canada 73 B7 55 5N 105 30W
Éghezée, Belgium 15 D4 50 35N 4 55 E
Egmont, Canada 72 D4 49 45N 123 56W
Egmont, C., N.Z. 59 H4 39 16S 173 45 E
Egmont, Mt. = Taranaki, Mt., N.Z. 59 H5 39 17S 174 5 E
Egra, India 43 J12 21 54N 87 32 E
Eğridir, Turkey 25 G5 37 52N 30 51 E
Eğridir Gölü, Turkey 25 G5 37 53N 30 50 E
Egvekinot, Russia 27 C19 66 19N 179 50W
Egypt ■, Africa 51 C12 28 0N 31 0 E
Ehime □, Japan 31 H6 33 30N 132 40 E
Ehrenberg, U.S.A. 85 M12 33 36N 114 31W
Eibar, Spain 19 A4 43 11N 2 28W
Eidsvold, Australia 63 D5 25 25S 151 12 E
Eidsvoll, Norway 9 F14 60 19N 11 14 E
Eifel, Germany 16 C4 50 15N 6 50 E
Eiffel Flats, Zimbabwe 55 F3 18 20S 30 0 E
Eigg, U.K. 12 E2 56 54N 6 10W
Eighty Mile Beach, Australia 60 C3 19 30S 120 40 E
Eil, Somali Rep. 46 F4 8 0N 49 50 E
Eil, L., U.K. 12 E3 56 51N 5 16W
Eildon, L., Australia 63 F4 37 10S 146 0 E
Einasleigh, Australia 62 B3 18 32S 144 5 E
Einasleigh →, Australia 62 B3 17 30S 142 17 E
Eindhoven, Neths. 15 C5 51 26N 5 28 E
Eire = Ireland ■, Europe 13 C4 53 50N 7 52W
Eiríksjökull, Iceland 8 D3 64 46N 20 24W
Eirunepé, Brazil 92 E5 6 35S 69 53W
Eiseb →, Namibia 56 C2 20 33S 20 59 E
Eisenach, Germany 16 C6 50 58N 10 19 E
Eisenerz, Austria 16 E8 47 32N 14 54 E
Eivissa, Spain 22 C7 38 54N 1 26 E
Ejeda, Madag. 57 C7 24 20S 44 31 E
Ejutla, Mexico 87 D5 16 34N 96 44W
Ekalaka, U.S.A. 80 C2 45 53N 104 33W
Eketahuna, N.Z. 59 J5 40 38S 175 43 E
Ekibastuz, Kazakstan 26 D8 51 50N 75 10 E
Ekoli, Dem. Rep. of the Congo 54 C1 0 23S 24 13 E
Eksjö, Sweden 9 H16 57 40N 14 58 E
Ekuma →, Namibia 56 B2 18 40S 16 2 E
Ekwan →, Canada 70 B3 53 12N 82 15W
Ekwan Pt., Canada 70 B3 53 16N 82 7W
El Aaiún, W. Sahara 50 C3 27 9N 13 12W
El Abanico, Chile 94 D1 37 20S 71 31W
El 'Agrûd, Egypt 47 E3 30 14N 34 24 E
El Alamein, Egypt 51 B11 30 48N 28 58 E
El 'Aqaba, W. →, Egypt 47 E2 30 7N 33 54 E
El Arīḥā, West Bank 47 D4 31 52N 35 27 E
El 'Arîsh, Egypt 47 D2 31 8N 33 50 E
El 'Arîsh, W. →, Egypt 47 D2 31 8N 33 47 E
El Asnam = Ech Chéliff, Algeria 50 A6 36 10N 1 20 E
El Bayadh, Algeria 50 B6 33 40N 1 1 E
El Bluff, Nic. 88 D3 11 59N 83 40W
El Brûk, W. →, Egypt 47 E2 30 15N 33 50 E
El Cajon, U.S.A. 85 N10 32 48N 116 58W
El Campo, U.S.A. 81 L6 29 12N 96 16W
El Centro, U.S.A. 85 N11 32 48N 115 34W
El Cerro, Bolivia 92 G6 17 30S 61 40W
El Compadre, Mexico 85 N10 32 20N 116 14W
El Cuy, Argentina 96 D3 39 55S 68 25W
El Cuyo, Mexico 87 C7 21 30N 87 40W
El Daheir, Egypt 47 D3 31 13N 34 10 E
El Dátil, Mexico 86 B2 30 7N 112 15W
El Dere, Somali Rep. 46 G4 3 50N 47 8 E
El Descanso, Mexico 85 N10 32 12N 116 58W
El Desemboque, Mexico 86 A2 30 30N 112 57W
El Diviso, Colombia 92 C3 1 22N 78 14W
El Djouf, Mauritania 50 D4 20 0N 9 0W
El Dorado, Ark., U.S.A. 81 J8 33 12N 92 40W
El Dorado, Kans., U.S.A. 81 G6 37 49N 96 52W
El Dorado, Venezuela 92 B6 6 55N 61 37W
El Escorial, Spain 19 B3 40 35N 4 7W
El Faiyûm, Egypt 51 C12 29 19N 30 50 E
El Fâsher, Sudan 51 F11 13 33N 25 26 E
El Ferrol = Ferrol, Spain 19 A1 43 29N 8 15W
El Fuerte, Mexico 86 B3 26 30N 108 40W
El Gal, Somali Rep. 46 E5 10 58N 50 20 E
El Geneina = Al Junaynah, Sudan 51 F10 13 27N 22 45 E
El Gîza, Egypt 51 C12 30 0N 31 10 E
El Goléa, Algeria 50 B6 30 30N 2 50 E
El Iskandarîya, Egypt 51 B11 31 13N 29 58 E
El Istiwa'iya, Sudan 51 G11 5 0N 28 0 E
El Jadida, Morocco 50 B4 33 11N 8 17W
El Jardal, Honduras 88 D2 14 54N 88 50W
El Kabrît, G., Egypt 47 F2 29 42N 33 16 E
El Khârga, Egypt 51 C12 25 30N 30 33 E
El Khartûm, Sudan 51 E12 15 31N 32 35 E
El Kuntilla, Egypt 47 E3 30 1N 34 45 E
El Maestrazgo, Spain 19 B5 40 30N 0 25W
El Mahalla el Kubra, Egypt 51 B12 31 0N 31 0 E
El Mansûra, Egypt 51 B12 31 0N 31 19 E
El Medano, Canary Is. 22 F3 28 3N 16 32W
El Milagro, Argentina 94 C2 30 59S 65 59W
El Minyâ, Egypt 51 C12 28 7N 30 33 E
El Monte, U.S.A. 85 L8 34 4N 118 1W
El Obeid, Sudan 51 F12 13 8N 30 10 E
El Odaiya, Sudan 51 F11 12 8N 28 12 E
El Oro, Mexico 87 D4 19 48N 100 8W
El Oued, Algeria 50 B7 33 20N 6 58 E
El Palmito, Presa, Mexico 86 B3 25 40N 105 30W
El Paso, U.S.A. 83 L10 31 45N 106 29W
El Paso Robles, U.S.A. 84 K6 35 38N 120 41W
El Portal, U.S.A. 84 H7 37 41N 119 47W
El Porvenir, Mexico 86 A3 31 15N 105 51W
El Prat de Llobregat, Spain 19 B7 41 18N 2 3 E
El Progreso, Honduras 88 C2 15 26N 87 51W
El Pueblito, Mexico 86 B3 29 3N 105 4W
El Pueblo, Canary Is. 22 F2 28 36N 17 47W
El Puerto de Santa María, Spain 19 D2 36 36N 6 13W
El Qâhira, Egypt 51 B12 30 1N 31 14 E
El Qantara, Egypt 47 E1 30 51N 32 20 E
El Quseima, Egypt 47 E3 30 40N 34 15 E
El Real, Panama 92 B3 8 0N 77 40W
El Reno, U.S.A. 81 H6 35 32N 97 57W
El Rio, U.S.A. 85 L7 34 14N 119 10W
El Roque, Pta., Canary Is. 22 F4 28 10N 15 25W
El Rosarito, Mexico 86 B2 28 38N 114 4W
El Saheira, W. →, Egypt 47 E2 30 5N 33 25 E
El Salto, Mexico 86 C3 23 47N 105 22W
El Salvador ■, Cent. Amer. 88 D2 13 50N 89 0W
El Sauce, Nic. 88 D2 13 0N 86 40W
El Sueco, Mexico 86 B3 29 54N 106 24W
El Suweis, Egypt 51 C12 29 58N 32 31 E
El Tamarâni, W. →, Egypt 47 E3 30 7N 34 43 E
El Thamad, Egypt 47 F3 29 40N 34 28 E
El Tigre, Venezuela 92 B6 8 44N 64 15W
El Tîh, Gebal, Egypt 47 F2 29 40N 33 50 E
El Tîna, Khalîg, Egypt 47 D1 31 10N 32 40 E
El Tofo, Chile 94 B1 29 22S 71 18W
El Tránsito, Chile 94 B1 28 52S 70 17W
El Tûr, Egypt 44 D2 28 14N 33 36 E
El Turbio, Argentina 96 G2 51 45S 72 5W
El Uqsur, Egypt 51 C12 25 41N 32 38 E
El Venado, Mexico 86 C4 22 56N 101 10W
El Vergel, Mexico 86 B3 26 28N 106 22W
El Vigía, Venezuela 92 B4 8 38N 71 39W
El Wabeira, Egypt 47 F2 29 34N 33 6 E
El Wak, Kenya 54 B5 2 49N 40 56 E
El Wuz, Sudan 51 E12 15 5N 30 7 E
Elat, Israel 47 F3 29 30N 34 56 E
Elâzığ, Turkey 25 G6 38 37N 39 14 E
Elba, Italy 20 C4 42 46N 10 17 E
Elba, U.S.A. 77 K2 31 25N 86 4W
Elbasan, Albania 21 D9 41 9N 20 9 E
Elbe, U.S.A. 84 D4 46 45N 122 10W
Elbe →, Europe 16 B5 53 50N 9 0 E
Elbert, Mt., U.S.A. 83 G10 39 7N 106 27W
Elberton, U.S.A. 77 H4 34 7N 82 52W
Elbeuf, France 18 B4 49 17N 1 2 E
Elbidtan, Turkey 44 B3 38 13N 37 12 E
Elbing = Elbląg, Poland 17 A10 54 10N 19 25 E
Elbląg, Poland 17 A10 54 10N 19 25 E
Elbow, Canada 73 C7 51 7N 106 35W
Elbrus, Asia 25 F7 43 21N 42 30 E
Elburz Mts. = Alborz, Reshteh-ye Kūhhā-ye, Iran 45 C7 36 0N 52 0 E
Elche, Spain 19 C5 38 15N 0 42W
Elcho I., Australia 62 A2 11 55S 135 45 E
Elda, Spain 19 C5 38 29N 0 47W
Elde →, Germany 16 B6 53 7N 11 15 E
Eldon, Mo., U.S.A. 80 F8 38 21N 92 35W
Eldon, Wash., U.S.A. 84 C3 47 33N 123 3W
Eldora, U.S.A. 80 D8 42 22N 93 5W
Eldorado, Argentina 95 B5 26 28S 54 43W
Eldorado, Canada 78 B7 44 35N 77 31W
Eldorado, Mexico 86 C3 24 20N 107 22W
Eldorado, Ill., U.S.A. 76 G1 37 49N 88 26W
Eldorado, Tex., U.S.A. 81 K4 30 52N 100 36W
Eldorado Springs, U.S.A. 81 G8 37 52N 94 1W
Eldoret, Kenya 54 B4 0 30N 35 17 E
Eldred, U.S.A. 78 E6 41 58N 78 23W
Elea, C., Cyprus 23 D13 35 19N 34 4 E
Eleanora, Pk., Australia 61 F3 32 57S 121 9 E
Elefantes →, Mozam. 57 C5 24 10S 32 40 E
Elektrostal, Russia 24 C6 55 41N 38 32 E
Elephant Butte Reservoir, U.S.A. 83 K10 33 9N 107 11W
Elephant I., Antarctica 5 C18 61 0S 55 0W
Eleuthera, Bahamas 88 B4 25 0N 76 20W
Elgin, Canada 79 B8 44 36N 76 13W
Elgin, U.K. 12 D5 57 39N 3 19W
Elgin, Ill., U.S.A. 76 D1 42 2N 88 17W
Elgin, N. Dak., U.S.A. 80 B4 46 24N 101 51W
Elgin, Oreg., U.S.A. 82 D5 45 34N 117 55W
Elgin, Tex., U.S.A. 81 K6 30 21N 97 22W
Elgon, Mt., Africa 54 B3 1 10N 34 30 E
Eliase, Indonesia 37 F8 8 21S 130 48 E
Elim, Namibia 56 B2 17 48S 15 31 E
Elim, S. Africa 56 E2 34 35S 19 45 E
Elista, Russia 25 E7 46 16N 44 14 E
Elizabeth, Australia 63 E2 34 42S 138 41 E
Elizabeth, N.J., U.S.A. 79 F10 40 39N 74 13W
Elizabeth, N.J., U.S.A. 79 F10 40 40N 74 13W
Elizabeth City, U.S.A. 77 G7 36 18N 76 14W
Elizabethton, U.S.A. 77 G4 36 21N 82 13W
Elizabethtown, Ky., U.S.A. 76 G3 37 42N 85 52W
Elizabethtown, N.Y., U.S.A. 79 B11 44 13N 73 36W
Elizabethtown, Pa., U.S.A. 79 F8 40 9N 76 36W
Ełk, Poland 17 B12 53 50N 22 21 E
Elk →, Canada 72 C5 49 11N 115 14W
Elk →, U.S.A. 77 H2 34 46N 87 16W
Elk City, U.S.A. 81 H5 35 25N 99 25W
Elk Creek, U.S.A. 84 F4 39 36N 122 32W
Elk Grove, U.S.A. 84 G5 38 25N 121 22W
Elk Island Nat. Park, Canada 72 C6 53 35N 112 59W
Elk Lake, Canada 70 C3 47 40N 80 25W
Elk Point, Canada 73 C6 53 54N 110 55W
Elk River, Idaho, U.S.A. 82 C5 46 47N 116 11W
Elk River, Minn., U.S.A. 80 C8 45 18N 93 35W
Elkedra →, Australia 62 C2 21 8S 136 22 E
Elkhart, Ind., U.S.A. 76 E3 41 41N 85 58W
Elkhart, Kans., U.S.A. 81 G4 37 0N 101 54W
Elkhorn, Canada 73 D8 49 59N 101 14W
Elkhorn →, U.S.A. 80 E6 41 8N 96 19W
Elkhovo, Bulgaria 21 C12 42 10N 26 35 E
Elkin, U.S.A. 77 G5 36 15N 80 51W
Elkins, U.S.A. 76 F6 38 55N 79 51W
Elkland, U.S.A. 78 E7 41 59N 77 19W
Elko, Canada 72 D5 49 20N 115 10W
Elko, U.S.A. 82 F6 40 50N 115 46W
Elkton, U.S.A. 78 C1 43 49N 83 11W
Ell, L., Australia 61 E4 29 13S 127 46 E
Ellef Ringnes I., Canada 4 B2 78 30N 102 2W
Ellen, Mt., U.S.A. 79 B12 44 9N 72 56W
Ellenburg, U.S.A. 79 B11 44 54N 73 48W
Ellendale, U.S.A. 80 B5 46 0N 98 32W
Ellensburg, U.S.A. 82 C3 46 59N 120 34W
Ellenville, U.S.A. 79 E10 41 43N 74 24W
Ellery, Mt., Australia 63 F4 37 28S 148 47 E
Ellesmere, L., N.Z. 59 M4 43 47S 172 28 E
Ellesmere I., Canada 4 B4 79 30N 80 0W
Ellesmere Port, U.K. 10 D5 53 17N 2 54W
Ellice Is. = Tuvalu ■, Pac. Oc. 64 H9 8 0S 178 0 E
Ellicottville, U.S.A. 78 D6 42 17N 78 40W
Elliot, Australia 62 B1 17 33S 133 32 E
Elliot, S. Africa 57 E4 31 22S 27 48 E
Elliot Lake, Canada 70 C3 46 25N 82 35W
Elliotdale = Xhora, S. Africa 57 E4 31 55S 28 38 E
Ellis, U.S.A. 80 F5 38 56N 99 34W
Elliston, Australia 63 E1 33 39S 134 53 E
Ellisville, U.S.A. 81 K10 31 36N 89 12W
Ellon, U.K. 12 D6 57 22N 2 4W
Ellore = Eluru, India 41 L12 16 48N 81 8 E
Ellsworth, Kans., U.S.A. 80 F5 38 44N 98 14W
Ellsworth, Maine, U.S.A. 77 C11 44 33N 68 25W
Ellsworth Land, Antarctica 5 D16 76 0S 89 0W
Ellsworth Mts., Antarctica 5 D16 78 30S 85 0W
Ellwood City, U.S.A. 78 F4 40 52N 80 17W
Elma, Canada 73 D9 49 52N 95 55W
Elma, U.S.A. 84 D3 47 0N 123 25W
Elmalı, Turkey 25 G4 36 44N 29 56 E
Elmhurst, U.S.A. 76 E2 41 53N 87 56W
Elmira, Canada 78 C4 43 36N 80 33W
Elmira, U.S.A. 78 D8 42 6N 76 48W
Elmira Heights, U.S.A. 78 D8 42 8N 76 50W
Elmore, Australia 63 F3 36 30S 144 37 E
Elmore, U.S.A. 85 M11 33 7N 115 49W
Elmshorn, Germany 16 B5 53 43N 9 40 E
Elmvale, Canada 78 B5 44 35N 79 52W
Elora, Canada 78 C4 43 41N 80 26W
Eloúnda, Greece 23 D7 35 16N 25 42 E
Eloy, U.S.A. 83 K8 32 45N 111 33W
Elrose, Canada 73 C7 51 12N 108 0W
Elsie, U.S.A. 84 E3 45 52N 123 36W
Elsinore = Helsingør, Denmark 9 H15 56 2N 12 35 E
Eltham, N.Z. 59 H5 39 26S 174 19 E
Eluru, India 41 L12 16 48N 81 8 E
Elvas, Portugal 19 C2 38 50N 7 10W
Elverum, Norway 9 F14 60 53N 11 34 E
Elvire →, Australia 60 C4 17 51S 128 11 E
Elvire, Mt., Australia 61 E2 29 22S 119 36 E
Elwell, L., U.S.A. 82 B8 48 22N 111 17W
Elwood, Ind., U.S.A. 76 E3 40 17N 85 50W
Elwood, Nebr., U.S.A. 80 E5 40 36N 99 52W
Elx = Elche, Spain 19 C5 38 15N 0 42W
Ely, U.K. 11 E8 52 24N 0 16 E
Ely, Minn., U.S.A. 80 B9 47 55N 91 51W
Ely, Nev., U.S.A. 82 G6 39 15N 114 54W
Elyria, U.S.A. 78 E2 41 22N 82 7W
Emāmrūd, Iran 45 B7 36 30N 55 0 E
Emba, Kazakstan 26 E6 48 50N 58 8 E
Emba →, Kazakstan 25 E9 46 55N 53 28 E
Embarcación, Argentina 94 A3 23 10S 64 0W
Embarras Portage, Canada 73 B6 58 27N 111 28W
Embetsu, Japan 30 B10 44 44N 141 47 E
Embi = Emba, Kazakstan 26 E6 48 50N 58 8 E
Embi = Emba →, Kazakstan 25 E9 46 55N 53 28 E
Embóna, Greece 23 C9 36 13N 27 51 E
Embrun, France 18 D7 44 34N 6 30 E
Embu, Kenya 54 C4 0 32S 37 38 E
Emden, Germany 16 B4 53 21N 7 12 E
Emerald, Australia 62 C4 23 32S 148 10 E
Emerson, Canada 73 D9 49 0N 97 10W
Emet, Turkey 21 E13 39 20N 29 15 E
Emi Koussi, Chad 51 E9 19 45N 18 55 E
Eminabad, Pakistan 42 C6 32 2N 74 8 E
Emine, Nos, Bulgaria 21 C12 42 40N 27 56 E
Emissi, Tarso, Chad 51 D9 21 27N 18 36 E
Emlenton, U.S.A. 78 E5 41 11N 79 43W
Emmaus, S. Africa 56 D4 29 2S 25 15 E
Emmaus, U.S.A. 79 F9 40 32N 75 30W
Emmeloord, Neths. 15 B5 52 44N 5 46 E
Emmen, Neths. 15 B6 52 48N 6 57 E
Emmet, Australia 62 C3 24 45S 144 30 E
Emmetsburg, U.S.A. 80 D7 43 7N 94 41W
Emmett, Idaho, U.S.A. 82 E5 43 52N 116 30W
Emmett, Mich., U.S.A. 78 D2 42 59N 82 46W
Emmonak, U.S.A. 68 B3 62 46N 164 30W
Emo, Canada 73 D10 48 38N 93 50W
Empalme, Mexico 86 B2 28 1N 110 49W
Empangeni, S. Africa 57 D5 28 50S 31 52 E
Empedrado, Argentina 94 B4 28 0S 58 46W
Emperor Seamount Chain, Pac. Oc. 64 D9 40 0N 170 0 E
Emporia, Kans., U.S.A. 80 F6 38 25N 96 11W
Emporia, Va., U.S.A. 77 G7 36 42N 77 32W
Emporium, U.S.A. 78 E6 41 31N 78 14W
Empress, Canada 73 C7 50 57N 110 0W
Empty Quarter = Rub' al Khālī, Si. Arabia 46 D4 19 0N 48 0 E
Ems →, Germany 16 B4 53 20N 7 12 E
Emsdale, Canada 78 A5 45 32N 79 19W
Emu, China 35 C15 43 40N 128 6 E
Emu Park, Australia 62 C5 23 13S 150 50 E
'En 'Avrona, Israel 47 F4 29 43N 35 0 E
En Nahud, Sudan 51 F11 12 45N 28 25 E
Ena, Japan 31 G8 35 25N 137 25 E
Enana, Namibia 56 B2 17 30S 16 23 E
Enard B., U.K. 12 C3 58 5N 5 20W
Enare = Inarijärvi, Finland 8 B22 69 0N 28 0 E
Enarotali, Indonesia 37 E9 3 55S 136 21 E
Encampment, U.S.A. 82 F10 41 12N 106 47W
Encantadas, Serra, Brazil 95 C5 30 40S 53 0W
Encarnación, Paraguay 95 B4 27 15S 55 50W
Encarnación de Diaz, Mexico 86 C4 21 30N 102 13W
Encinitas, U.S.A. 85 M9 33 3N 117 17W
Encino, U.S.A. 83 J11 34 39N 105 28W
Encounter B., Australia 63 F2 35 45S 138 45 E
Endako, Canada 72 C3 54 6N 125 2W
Ende, Indonesia 37 F6 8 45S 121 40 E
Endeavour Str., Australia 62 A3 10 45S 142 0 E
Enderbury I., Kiribati 64 H10 3 8S 171 5W
Enderby, Canada 72 C5 50 35N 119 10W
Enderby I., Australia 60 D2 20 35S 116 30 E
Enderby Land, Antarctica 5 C5 66 0S 53 0 E
Enderlin, U.S.A. 80 B6 46 38N 97 36W
Endicott, U.S.A. 79 D8 42 6N 76 4W
Endwell, U.S.A. 79 D8 42 6N 76 2W
Endyalgout I., Australia 60 B5 11 40S 132 35 E
Eneabba, Australia 61 E2 29 49S 115 16 E
Enewetak Atoll, Marshall Is. 64 F8 11 30N 162 15 E
Enez, Turkey 21 D12 40 45N 26 5 E

Enfield, *Canada* 71 D7 44 56N 63 32W
Enfield, *Conn., U.S.A.* 79 E12 41 58N 72 36W
Enfield, *N.H., U.S.A.* 79 C12 43 39N 72 9W
Engadin, *Switz.* 18 C9 46 45N 10 10 E
Engaño, C., *Dom. Rep.* 89 C6 18 30N 68 20W
Engaño, C., *Phil.* 37 A6 18 35N 122 23 E
Engaru, *Japan* 30 B11 44 3N 143 31 E
Engcobo, *S. Africa* 57 E4 31 37S 28 0 E
Engels, *Russia* 25 D8 51 28N 46 6 E
Engemann L., *Canada* 73 B7 58 0N 106 55W
Enggano, *Indonesia* 36 F2 5 20S 102 40 E
England, *U.S.A.* 81 H9 34 33N 91 58W
England □, *U.K.* 10 D7 53 0N 2 0W
Englee, *Canada* 71 B8 50 45N 56 5W
Englehart, *Canada* 70 C4 47 49N 79 52W
Englewood, *U.S.A.* 80 F2 39 39N 104 59W
English →, *Canada* 73 C10 50 35N 93 30W
English Bazar = Ingraj Bazar, *India* 43 G13 24 58N 88 10 E
English Channel, *Europe* 11 G6 50 0N 2 0W
English River, *Canada* 70 C1 49 14N 91 0W
Enid, *U.S.A.* 81 G6 36 24N 97 53W
Enkhuizen, *Neths.* 15 B5 52 42N 5 17 E
Enna, *Italy* 20 F6 37 34N 14 16 E
Ennadai, *Canada* 73 A8 61 8N 100 53W
Ennadai L., *Canada* 73 A8 61 0N 101 0W
Ennedi, *Chad* 51 E10 17 15N 22 0 E
Enngonia, *Australia* 63 D4 29 21S 145 50 E
Ennis, *Ireland* 13 D3 52 51N 8 59W
Ennis, *Mont., U.S.A.* 82 D8 45 21N 111 44W
Ennis, *Tex., U.S.A.* 81 J6 32 20N 96 38W
Enniscorthy, *Ireland* 13 D5 52 30N 6 34W
Enniskillen, *U.K.* 13 B4 54 21N 7 39W
Ennistimon, *Ireland* 13 D2 52 57N 9 17W
Enns →, *Austria* 16 D8 48 14N 14 32 E
Enontekiö, *Finland* 8 B20 68 23N 23 37 E
Enosburg Falls, *U.S.A.* 79 B12 44 55N 72 48W
Enriquillo, L., *Dom. Rep.* 89 C5 18 20N 72 5W
Enschede, *Neths.* 15 B6 52 13N 6 53 E
Ensenada, *Argentina* 94 C4 34 55S 57 55W
Ensenada, *Mexico* 86 A1 31 50N 116 50W
Ensenada de los Muertos, *Mexico* 86 C2 23 59N 109 50W
Ensiola, Pta. de n', *Spain* 22 B9 39 7N 2 55 E
Entebbe, *Uganda* 54 B3 0 4N 32 28 E
Enterprise, *Canada* 72 A5 60 47N 115 45W
Enterprise, *Ala., U.S.A.* 77 K3 31 19N 85 51W
Enterprise, *Oreg., U.S.A.* 82 D5 45 25N 117 17W
Entre Ríos, *Bolivia* 94 A3 21 30S 64 25W
Entre Ríos □, *Argentina* 94 C4 30 30S 58 30W
Entroncamento, *Portugal* 19 C1 39 28N 8 28W
Enugu, *Nigeria* 50 G7 6 30N 7 30 E
Enumclaw, *U.S.A.* 84 C5 47 12N 121 59W
Eólie, Ís., *Italy* 20 E6 38 30N 14 57 E
Epe, *Neths.* 15 B5 52 21N 5 59 E
Épernay, *France* 18 B5 49 3N 3 56 E
Ephesus, *Turkey* 21 F12 37 55N 27 22 E
Ephraim, *U.S.A.* 82 G8 39 22N 111 35W
Ephrata, *Pa., U.S.A.* 79 F8 40 11N 76 11W
Ephrata, *Wash., U.S.A.* 82 C4 47 19N 119 33W
Épinal, *France* 18 B7 48 10N 6 27 E
Episkopi, *Cyprus* 23 E11 34 40N 32 54 E
Episkopí, *Greece* 23 D6 35 20N 24 20 E
Episkopi Bay, *Cyprus* 23 E11 34 35N 32 50 E
Epsom, *U.K.* 11 F7 51 19N 0 16W
Epukiro, *Namibia* 56 C2 21 40S 19 9 E
Equatorial Guinea ■, *Africa* 52 D1 2 0N 8 0 E
Er Rachidia, *Morocco* 50 B5 31 58N 4 20W
Er Rahad, *Sudan* 51 F12 12 45N 30 32 E
Er Rif, *Morocco* 50 A5 35 1N 4 1W
Erāwadī Myit = Irrawaddy →, *Burma* 41 M19 15 50N 95 6 E
Erāwadī Myitwanya = Irrawaddy, Mouths of the, *Burma* 41 M19 15 30N 95 0 E
Erbil = Arbīl, *Iraq* 44 B5 36 15N 44 5 E
Erçek, *Turkey* 44 B4 38 39N 43 36 E
Erciyaş Dağı, *Turkey* 25 G6 38 30N 35 30 E
Érd, *Hungary* 17 E10 47 22N 18 56 E
Erdao Jiang →, *China* 35 C14 43 0N 127 0 E
Erdek, *Turkey* 21 D12 40 23N 27 47 E
Erdene = Ulaan-Uul, *Mongolia* 34 B6 44 13N 111 10 E
Erdenetsogt, *Mongolia* 34 C4 42 55N 106 5 E
Erebus, Mt., *Antarctica* 5 D11 77 35S 167 0 E
Erechim, *Brazil* 95 B5 27 35S 52 15W
Ereğli, *Konya, Turkey* 25 G5 37 31N 34 4 E
Ereğli, *Zonguldak, Turkey* 25 F5 41 15N 31 24 E
Erenhot, *China* 34 C7 43 48N 112 2 E
Eresma →, *Spain* 19 B3 41 26N 4 45W
Erfenisdam, *S. Africa* 56 D4 28 30S 26 50 E
Erfurt, *Germany* 16 C6 50 58N 11 2 E
Erg Iguidi, *Africa* 50 C4 27 0N 7 0 E
Ergani, *Turkey* 44 B3 38 17N 39 49 E
Ergel, *Mongolia* 34 C5 43 8N 109 5 E
Ergeni Vozvyshennost, *Russia* 25 E7 47 0N 44 0 E
Ērgli, *Latvia* 9 H21 56 54N 25 38 E
Eriboll, L., *U.K.* 12 C4 58 30N 4 42W
Érice, *Italy* 20 E5 38 2N 12 35 E
Erie, *U.S.A.* 78 D4 42 8N 80 5W
Erie, L., *N. Amer.* 78 D4 42 15N 81 0W
Erie Canal, *U.S.A.* 78 C7 43 5N 78 43W
Erieau, *Canada* 78 D3 42 16N 81 57W
Erigavo, *Somali Rep.* 46 E4 10 35N 47 20 E
Erikoúsa, *Greece* 23 A3 39 53N 19 34 E
Eriksdale, *Canada* 73 C9 50 52N 98 7W
Erimanthos, *Greece* 21 F9 37 57N 21 50 E
Erimo-misaki, *Japan* 30 D11 41 50N 143 15 E
Erinpura, *India* 42 G5 25 9N 73 3 E
Eriskay, *U.K.* 12 D1 57 4N 7 18W
Eritrea ■, *Africa* 46 D2 14 0N 38 30 E
Erlangen, *Germany* 16 D6 49 36N 11 0 E
Erldunda, *Australia* 62 D1 25 14S 133 12 E
Ermelo, *Neths.* 15 B5 52 18N 5 35 E
Ermelo, *S. Africa* 57 D4 26 31S 29 59 E
Ermenek, *Turkey* 44 B2 36 38N 33 0 E
Ermones, *Greece* 23 A3 39 37N 19 46 E
Ermoúpolis = Síros, *Greece* 21 F11 37 28N 24 57 E
Erne →, *Ireland* 13 B3 54 30N 8 16W
Erne, Lower L., *U.K.* 13 B4 54 28N 7 47W
Erne, Upper L., *U.K.* 13 B4 54 14N 7 32W
Ernest Giles Ra., *Australia* 61 E3 27 0S 123 45 E
Erode, *India* 40 P10 11 24N 77 45 E
Eromanga, *Australia* 63 D3 26 40S 143 11 E
Erongo, *Namibia* 56 C2 21 39S 15 58 E
Erramala Hills, *India* 40 M11 15 30N 78 15 E
Errigal, *Ireland* 13 A3 55 2N 8 6W
Erris Hd., *Ireland* 13 B1 54 19N 10 0W
Erskine, *U.S.A.* 80 B7 47 40N 96 0W
Ertis = Irtysh →, *Russia* 26 C7 61 4N 68 52 E
Erwin, *U.S.A.* 77 G4 36 9N 82 25W
Erzgebirge, *Germany* 16 C7 50 27N 12 55 E
Erzin, *Russia* 27 D10 50 15N 95 10 E
Erzincan, *Turkey* 25 G6 39 46N 39 30 E
Erzurum, *Turkey* 25 G7 39 57N 41 15 E
Es Caló, *Spain* 22 C8 38 40N 1 30 E
Es Canar, *Spain* 22 B8 39 2N 1 36 E
Es Mercadal, *Spain* 22 B11 39 59N 4 5 E
Es Migjorn Gran, *Spain* 22 B11 39 57N 4 3 E
Es Sahrā' Esh Sharqîya, *Egypt* 51 C12 27 30N 32 30 E
Es Sînâ', *Egypt* 47 F3 29 0N 34 0 E
Es Vedrà, *Spain* 22 C7 38 52N 1 12 E
Esambo, *Dem. Rep. of the Congo* 54 C1 3 48S 23 30 E
Esan-Misaki, *Japan* 30 D10 41 40N 141 10 E
Esashi, *Hokkaidō, Japan* 30 B11 44 56N 142 35 E
Esashi, *Hokkaidō, Japan* 30 D10 41 52N 140 7 E
Esbjerg, *Denmark* 9 J13 55 29N 8 29 E
Escalante, *U.S.A.* 83 H8 37 47N 111 36W
Escalante →, *U.S.A.* 83 H8 37 24N 110 57W
Escalón, *Mexico* 86 B4 26 46N 104 20W
Escambia →, *U.S.A.* 77 K2 30 32N 87 11W
Escanaba, *U.S.A.* 76 C2 45 45N 87 4W
Esch-sur-Alzette, *Lux.* 18 B6 49 32N 6 0 E
Escondido, *U.S.A.* 85 M9 33 7N 117 5W
Escuinapa, *Mexico* 86 C3 22 50N 105 50W
Escuintla, *Guatemala* 88 D1 14 20N 90 48W
Esenguly, *Turkmenistan* 26 F6 37 37N 53 59 E
Eşfahān, *Iran* 45 C6 32 39N 51 43 E
Eşfahān □, *Iran* 45 C6 32 50N 51 50 E
Esfarāyen, *Iran* 45 B8 37 4N 57 30 E
Esfīdeh, *Iran* 45 C8 33 39N 59 46 E
Esh Sham = Dimashq, *Syria* 47 B5 33 30N 36 18 E
Esha Ness, *U.K.* 12 A7 60 29N 1 38W
Esher, *U.K.* 11 F7 51 21N 0 20W
Eshowe, *S. Africa* 57 D5 28 50S 31 30 E
Esigodini, *Zimbabwe* 57 C4 20 18S 28 56 E
Esil = Ishim →, *Russia* 26 D8 57 45N 71 10 E
Esira, *Madag.* 57 C8 24 20S 46 42 E
Esk →, *Cumb., U.K.* 12 G5 54 58N 3 2W
Esk →, *N. Yorks., U.K.* 10 C7 54 30N 0 37W
Eskān, *Iran* 45 E9 26 48N 63 9 E
Esker, *Canada* 71 B6 53 53N 66 25W
Eskifjörður, *Iceland* 8 D7 65 3N 13 55W
Eskilstuna, *Sweden* 9 G17 59 22N 16 32 E
Eskimo Pt., *Canada* 68 B10 61 10N 94 15W
Eskişehir, *Turkey* 25 G5 39 50N 30 30 E
Esla →, *Spain* 19 B2 41 29N 6 3W
Eslāmābād-e Gharb, *Iran* 44 C5 34 10N 46 30 E
Eslāmshahr, *Iran* 45 C6 35 40N 51 10 E
Eşme, *Turkey* 21 E13 38 23N 28 58 E
Esmeraldas, *Ecuador* 92 C3 1 0N 79 40W
Esnagi L., *Canada* 70 C3 48 36N 84 33W
Espanola, *Canada* 70 C3 46 15N 81 46W
Espanola, *U.S.A.* 83 H10 35 59N 106 5W
Esparta, *Costa Rica* 88 E3 9 59N 84 40W
Esperance, *Australia* 61 F3 33 45S 121 55 E
Esperance B., *Australia* 61 F3 33 48S 121 55 E
Esperanza, *Argentina* 94 C3 31 29S 61 3W
Espichel, C., *Portugal* 19 C1 38 22N 9 16W
Espigão, Serra do, *Brazil* 95 B5 26 35S 50 30W
Espinazo, Sierra del = Espinhaço, Serra do, *Brazil* 93 G10 17 30S 43 30W
Espinhaço, Serra do, *Brazil* 93 G10 17 30S 43 30W
Espinilho, Serra do, *Brazil* 95 B5 28 30S 55 0W
Espírito Santo □, *Brazil* 93 H10 20 0S 40 45W
Espíritu Santo, *Vanuatu* 64 J8 15 15S 166 50 E
Espíritu Santo, B. del, *Mexico* 87 D7 19 15N 87 0W
Espíritu Santo, I., *Mexico* 86 C2 24 30N 110 23W
Espita, *Mexico* 87 C7 21 1N 88 19W
Espoo, *Finland* 9 F21 60 12N 24 40 E
Espungabera, *Mozam.* 57 C5 20 29S 32 45 E
Esquel, *Argentina* 96 E2 42 55S 71 20W
Esquimalt, *Canada* 72 D4 48 26N 123 25W
Esquina, *Argentina* 94 C4 30 0S 59 30W
Essaouira, *Morocco* 50 B4 31 32N 9 42W
Essebie, *Dem. Rep. of the Congo* 54 B3 2 58N 30 40 E
Essen, *Belgium* 15 C4 51 28N 4 28 E
Essen, *Germany* 16 C4 51 28N 7 2 E
Essendon, Mt., *Australia* 61 E3 25 0S 120 29 E
Essequibo →, *Guyana* 92 B7 6 50N 58 30W
Essex, *Canada* 78 D2 42 10N 82 49W
Essex, *Calif., U.S.A.* 85 L11 34 44N 115 15W
Essex, *N.Y., U.S.A.* 79 B11 44 19N 73 21W
Essex □, *U.K.* 11 F8 51 54N 0 27 E
Essex Junction, *U.S.A.* 79 B11 44 29N 73 7W
Esslingen, *Germany* 16 D5 48 44N 9 18 E
Estados, I. de Los, *Argentina* 96 G4 54 40S 64 30W
Eşţahbānāt, *Iran* 45 D7 29 8N 54 4 E
Estância, *Brazil* 93 F11 11 16S 37 26W
Estancia, *U.S.A.* 83 J10 34 46N 106 4W
Estārm, *Iran* 45 D8 28 21N 58 21 E
Estcourt, *S. Africa* 57 D4 29 0S 29 53 E
Esteli, *Nic.* 88 D2 13 9N 86 22W
Estellencs, *Spain* 22 B9 39 39N 2 29 E
Esterhazy, *Canada* 73 C8 50 37N 102 5W
Estevan, *Canada* 73 D8 49 10N 102 59W
Estevan Group, *Canada* 72 C3 53 3N 129 38W
Estherville, *U.S.A.* 80 D7 43 24N 94 50W
Eston, *Canada* 73 C7 51 8N 108 40W
Estonia ■, *Europe* 9 G21 58 30N 25 30 E
Estreito, *Brazil* 93 E9 6 32S 47 25W
Estrela, Serra da, *Portugal* 19 B2 40 10N 7 45W
Estremoz, *Portugal* 19 C2 38 51N 7 39W
Estrondo, Serra do, *Brazil* 93 E9 7 20S 48 0W
Esztergom, *Hungary* 17 E10 47 47N 18 44 E
Etah, *India* 43 F8 27 35N 78 40 E
Étampes, *France* 18 B5 48 26N 2 10 E
Etanga, *Namibia* 56 B1 17 55S 13 0 E
Etawah, *India* 43 F8 26 48N 79 6 E
Etawney L., *Canada* 73 B9 57 50N 96 50W
Ethel, *U.S.A.* 84 D4 46 32N 122 46W
Ethelbert, *Canada* 73 C8 51 32N 100 25W
Ethiopia ■, *Africa* 46 F3 8 0N 40 0 E
Ethiopian Highlands, *Ethiopia* 28 J7 10 0N 37 0 E
Etive, L., *U.K.* 12 E3 56 29N 5 10W
Etna, *Italy* 20 F6 37 50N 14 55 E
Etoile, *Dem. Rep. of the Congo* 55 E2 11 33S 27 30 E
Etosha Pan, *Namibia* 56 B2 18 40S 16 30 E
Etowah, *U.S.A.* 77 H3 35 20N 84 32W
Ettelbruck, *Lux.* 15 E6 49 51N 6 5 E
Ettrick Water →, *U.K.* 12 F6 55 31N 2 55W
Etuku, *Dem. Rep. of the Congo* 54 C2 3 42S 25 45 E
Etzatlán, *Mexico* 86 C4 20 48N 104 5W
Etzná, *Mexico* 87 D6 19 35N 90 15W
Euboea = Évvoia, *Greece* 21 E11 38 30N 24 0 E
Eucla, *Australia* 61 F4 31 41S 128 52 E
Euclid, *U.S.A.* 78 E3 41 34N 81 32W
Eucumbene, L., *Australia* 63 F4 36 2S 148 40 E
Eudora, *U.S.A.* 81 J9 33 7N 91 16W
Eufaula, *Ala., U.S.A.* 77 K3 31 54N 85 9W
Eufaula, *Okla., U.S.A.* 81 H7 35 17N 95 35W
Eufaula L., *U.S.A.* 81 H7 35 18N 95 21W
Eugene, *U.S.A.* 82 E2 44 5N 123 4W
Eugowra, *Australia* 63 E4 33 22S 148 24 E
Eulo, *Australia* 63 D4 28 10S 145 3 E
Eunice, *La., U.S.A.* 81 K8 30 30N 92 25W
Eunice, *N. Mex., U.S.A.* 81 J3 32 26N 103 10W
Eupen, *Belgium* 15 D6 50 37N 6 3 E
Euphrates = Furāt, Nahr al →, *Asia* 44 D5 31 0N 47 25 E
Eureka, *Canada* 4 B3 80 0N 85 56W
Eureka, *Calif., U.S.A.* 82 F1 40 47N 124 9W
Eureka, *Kans., U.S.A.* 81 G6 37 49N 96 17W
Eureka, *Mont., U.S.A.* 82 B6 48 53N 115 3W
Eureka, *Nev., U.S.A.* 82 G5 39 31N 115 58W
Eureka, *S. Dak., U.S.A.* 80 C5 45 46N 99 38W
Eureka, Mt., *Australia* 61 E3 26 35S 121 35 E
Euroa, *Australia* 63 F4 36 44S 145 35 E
Europa, Île, *Ind. Oc.* 53 J8 22 20S 40 22 E
Europa, Picos de, *Spain* 19 A3 43 10N 4 49W
Europa, Pta. de, *Gib.* 19 D3 36 3N 5 21W
Europe 6 E10 50 0N 20 0 E
Europoort, *Neths.* 15 C4 51 57N 4 10 E
Eustis, *U.S.A.* 77 L5 28 51N 81 41W
Eutsuk L., *Canada* 72 C3 53 20N 126 45W
Evale, *Angola* 56 B2 16 33S 15 44 E
Evans, *U.S.A.* 80 E2 40 23N 104 41W
Evans, L., *Canada* 70 B4 50 50N 77 0W
Evans City, *U.S.A.* 78 F4 40 46N 80 4W
Evans Head, *Australia* 63 D5 29 7S 153 27 E
Evans Mills, *U.S.A.* 79 B9 44 6N 75 48W
Evansburg, *Canada* 72 C5 53 36N 114 59W
Evanston, *Ill., U.S.A.* 76 E2 42 3N 87 41W
Evanston, *Wyo., U.S.A.* 82 F8 41 16N 110 58W
Evansville, *U.S.A.* 76 G2 37 58N 87 35W
Evaz, *Iran* 45 E7 27 46N 53 59 E
Eveleth, *U.S.A.* 80 B8 47 28N 92 32W
Evensk, *Russia* 27 C16 62 12N 159 30 E
Everard, L., *Australia* 63 E2 31 30S 135 0 E
Everard Ranges, *Australia* 61 E5 27 5S 132 28 E
Everest, Mt., *Nepal* 43 E12 28 5N 86 58 E
Everett, *Pa., U.S.A.* 78 F6 40 1N 78 23W
Everett, *Wash., U.S.A.* 84 C4 47 59N 122 12W
Everglades, The, *U.S.A.* 77 N5 25 50N 81 0W
Everglades City, *U.S.A.* 77 N5 25 52N 81 23W
Everglades Nat. Park, *U.S.A.* 77 N5 25 30N 81 0W
Evergreen, *Ala., U.S.A.* 77 K2 31 26N 86 57W
Evergreen, *Mont., U.S.A.* 82 B6 48 9N 114 13W
Evesham, *U.K.* 11 E6 52 6N 1 56W
Evje, *Norway* 9 G12 58 36N 7 51 E
Évora, *Portugal* 19 C2 38 33N 7 57W
Evowghlī, *Iran* 44 B5 38 43N 45 13 E
Évreux, *France* 18 B4 49 3N 1 8 E
Évros →, *Greece* 21 D12 41 40N 26 34 E
Évry, *France* 18 B5 48 38N 2 27 E
Évvoia, *Greece* 21 E11 38 30N 24 0 E
Ewe, L., *U.K.* 12 D3 57 49N 5 38W
Ewing, *U.S.A.* 80 D5 42 16N 98 21W
Ewo, *Congo* 52 E2 0 48S 14 45 E
Exaltación, *Bolivia* 92 F5 13 10S 65 20W
Excelsior Springs, *U.S.A.* 80 F7 39 20N 94 13W
Exe →, *U.K.* 11 G4 50 41N 3 29W
Exeter, *Canada* 78 C3 43 21N 81 29W
Exeter, *U.K.* 11 G4 50 43N 3 31W
Exeter, *Calif., U.S.A.* 84 J7 36 18N 119 9W
Exeter, *N.H., U.S.A.* 79 D14 42 59N 70 57W
Exmoor, *U.K.* 11 F4 51 12N 3 45W
Exmouth, *Australia* 60 D1 21 54S 114 10 E
Exmouth, *U.K.* 11 G4 50 37N 3 25W
Exmouth G., *Australia* 60 D1 22 15S 114 15 E
Expedition Ra., *Australia* 62 C4 24 30S 149 12 E
Extremadura □, *Spain* 19 C2 39 30N 6 5W
Exuma Sound, *Bahamas* 88 B4 24 30N 76 20W
Eyasi, L., *Tanzania* 54 C4 3 30S 35 0 E
Eye Pen., *U.K.* 12 C2 58 13N 6 10W
Eyemouth, *U.K.* 12 F6 55 52N 2 5W
Eyjafjörður, *Iceland* 8 C4 66 15N 18 30W
Eyre (North), L., *Australia* 63 D2 28 30S 137 20 E
Eyre (South), L., *Australia* 63 D2 29 18S 137 25 E
Eyre Mts., *N.Z.* 59 L2 45 25S 168 25 E
Eyre Pen., *Australia* 63 E2 33 30S 136 17 E
Eysturoy, *Færoe Is.* 8 E9 62 13N 6 54W
Eyvānkī, *Iran* 45 C6 35 24N 51 56 E
Ezine, *Turkey* 21 E12 39 48N 26 20 E
Ezouza →, *Cyprus* 23 E11 34 44N 32 27 E

F

F.Y.R.O.M. = Macedonia ■, *Europe* 21 D9 41 53N 21 40 E
Fabala, *Guinea* 50 G4 9 44N 9 5W
Fabens, *U.S.A.* 83 L10 31 30N 106 10W
Fabriano, *Italy* 20 C5 43 20N 12 54 E
Fachi, *Niger* 51 E8 18 6N 11 34 E
Fada, *Chad* 51 E10 17 13N 21 34 E
Fada-n-Gourma, *Burkina Faso* 50 F6 12 10N 0 30 E
Faddeyevskiy, Ostrov, *Russia* 27 B15 76 0N 144 0 E
Fadghāmī, *Syria* 44 C4 35 53N 40 52 E
Faenza, *Italy* 20 B4 44 17N 11 53 E
Færoe Is. = Føroyar, *Atl. Oc.* 8 F9 62 0N 7 0W
Făgăras, *Romania* 17 F13 45 48N 24 58 E
Fagersta, *Sweden* 9 F16 60 1N 15 46 E
Fagnano, L., *Argentina* 96 G3 54 30S 68 0W
Fahliān, *Iran* 45 D6 30 11N 51 28 E
Fahraj, *Kermān, Iran* 45 D8 29 0N 59 0 E
Fahraj, *Yazd, Iran* 45 D7 31 46N 54 36 E
Faial, *Madeira* 22 D3 32 47N 16 53W
Fair Haven, *U.S.A.* 76 D9 43 36N 73 16W
Fair Hd., *U.K.* 13 A5 55 14N 6 9W
Fair Oaks, *U.S.A.* 84 G5 38 39N 121 16W
Fairbanks, *U.S.A.* 68 B5 64 51N 147 43W
Fairbury, *U.S.A.* 80 E6 40 8N 97 11W
Fairfax, *U.S.A.* 79 B11 44 40N 73 1W
Fairfield, *Ala., U.S.A.* 77 J2 33 29N 86 55W
Fairfield, *Calif., U.S.A.* 84 G4 38 15N 122 3W
Fairfield, *Conn., U.S.A.* 79 E11 41 9N 73 16W
Fairfield, *Idaho, U.S.A.* 82 E6 43 21N 114 44W
Fairfield, *Ill., U.S.A.* 76 F1 38 23N 88 22W
Fairfield, *Iowa, U.S.A.* 80 E9 40 56N 91 57W
Fairfield, *Tex., U.S.A.* 81 K7 31 44N 96 10W
Fairford, *Canada* 73 C9 51 37N 98 38W
Fairhope, *U.S.A.* 77 K2 30 31N 87 54W
Fairlie, *N.Z.* 59 L3 44 5S 170 49 E
Fairmead, *U.S.A.* 84 H6 37 5N 120 10W
Fairmont, *Minn., U.S.A.* 80 D7 43 39N 94 28W
Fairmont, *W. Va., U.S.A.* 76 F5 39 29N 80 9W
Fairmount, *Calif., U.S.A.* 85 L8 34 45N 118 26W
Fairmount, *N.Y., U.S.A.* 79 C8 43 5N 76 12W
Fairplay, *U.S.A.* 83 G11 39 15N 106 2W
Fairport, *U.S.A.* 78 C7 43 6N 77 27W
Fairport Harbor, *U.S.A.* 78 E3 41 45N 81 17W
Fairview, *Canada* 72 B5 56 5N 118 25W
Fairview, *Mont., U.S.A.* 80 B2 47 51N 104 3W
Fairview, *Okla., U.S.A.* 81 G5 36 16N 98 29W
Fairweather, Mt., *U.S.A.* 72 B1 58 55N 137 32W
Faisalabad, *Pakistan* 42 D5 31 30N 73 5 E
Faith, *U.S.A.* 80 C3 45 2N 102 2W
Faizabad, *India* 43 F10 26 45N 82 10 E
Fajardo, *Puerto Rico* 89 C6 18 20N 65 39W
Fajr, W. →, *Si. Arabia* 44 D3 29 10N 38 10 E
Fakenham, *U.K.* 10 E8 52 51N 0 51 E
Fakfak, *Indonesia* 37 E8 2 55S 132 18 E
Faku, *China* 35 C12 42 32N 123 21 E
Falaise, *France* 18 B3 48 54N 0 12W
Falaise, Mui, *Vietnam* 38 C5 19 6N 105 45 E
Falam, *Burma* 41 H18 23 0N 93 45 E
Falcó, C. des, *Spain* 22 C7 38 50N 1 23 E
Falcón, Presa, *Mexico* 87 B5 26 35N 99 10W
Falcon Lake, *Canada* 73 D9 49 42N 95 15W
Falcon Reservoir, *U.S.A.* 81 M5 26 34N 99 10W
Falconara Marittima, *Italy* 20 C5 43 37N 13 24 E
Falcone, C. del, *Italy* 20 D3 40 58N 8 12 E
Falconer, *U.S.A.* 78 D5 42 7N 79 13W
Faleshty = Făleşti, *Moldova* 17 E14 47 32N 27 44 E
Făleşti, *Moldova* 17 E14 47 32N 27 44 E
Falfurrias, *U.S.A.* 81 M5 27 14N 98 9W
Falher, *Canada* 72 B5 55 44N 117 15W
Faliraki, *Greece* 23 C10 36 22N 28 12 E
Falkenberg, *Sweden* 9 H15 56 54N 12 30 E
Falkirk, *U.K.* 12 F5 56 0N 3 47W
Falkirk □, *U.K.* 12 F5 55 58N 3 49W
Falkland, *U.K.* 12 E5 56 16N 3 12W
Falkland Is. □, *Atl. Oc.* 96 G5 51 30S 59 0W
Falkland Sd., *Falk. Is.* 96 G5 52 0S 60 0W
Falköping, *Sweden* 9 G15 58 12N 13 33 E
Fall River, *U.S.A.* 79 E13 41 43N 71 10W
Fallbrook, *U.S.A.* 85 M9 33 23N 117 15W
Fallon, *U.S.A.* 82 G4 39 28N 118 47W
Falls City, *U.S.A.* 80 E7 40 3N 95 36W
Falls Creek, *U.S.A.* 78 E6 41 9N 78 48W
Falmouth, *Jamaica* 88 C4 18 30N 77 40W
Falmouth, *U.K.* 11 G2 50 9N 5 5W
Falmouth, *U.S.A.* 79 E14 41 33N 70 37W
Falsa, Pta., *Mexico* 86 B1 27 51N 115 3W
False B., *S. Africa* 56 E2 34 15S 18 40 E
Falso, C., *Honduras* 88 C3 15 12N 83 21W
Falster, *Denmark* 9 J14 54 45N 11 55 E
Falsterbo, *Sweden* 9 J15 55 23N 12 50 E
Fălticeni, *Romania* 17 E14 47 21N 26 20 E
Falun, *Sweden* 9 F16 60 37N 15 37 E
Famagusta, *Cyprus* 23 D12 35 8N 33 55 E
Famagusta Bay, *Cyprus* 23 D13 35 15N 34 0 E
Famalé, *Niger* 50 F6 14 33N 1 5 E
Famatina, Sierra de, *Argentina* 94 B2 27 30S 68 0W
Family L., *Canada* 73 C9 51 54N 95 27W
Famoso, *U.S.A.* 85 K7 35 37N 119 12W
Fan Xian, *China* 34 G8 35 55N 115 38 E
Fanad Hd., *Ireland* 13 A4 55 17N 7 38W
Fandriana, *Madag.* 57 C8 20 14S 47 21 E
Fang, *Thailand* 38 C2 19 55N 99 13 E
Fangcheng, *China* 34 H7 33 18N 112 59 E
Fangshan, *China* 34 E6 38 3N 111 25 E
Fangzi, *China* 35 F10 36 33N 119 10 E
Fanjakana, *Madag.* 57 C8 21 10S 46 53 E
Fanjiatun, *China* 35 C13 43 40N 125 15 E
Fannich, L., *U.K.* 12 D4 57 38N 4 59W
Fannūj, *Iran* 45 E8 26 35N 59 38 E
Fanø, *Denmark* 9 J13 55 25N 8 25 E
Fano, *Italy* 20 C5 43 50N 13 1 E
Fanshi, *China* 34 E7 39 12N 113 20 E
Fao = Al Fāw, *Iraq* 45 D6 30 0N 48 30 E
Faqirwali, *Pakistan* 42 E5 29 27N 73 0 E
Faradje, *Dem. Rep. of the Congo* 54 B2 3 50N 29 45 E
Farafangana, *Madag.* 57 C8 22 49S 47 50 E
Farāh, *Afghan.* 40 C3 32 20N 62 7 E
Farāh □, *Afghan.* 40 C3 32 25N 62 10 E
Farahalana, *Madag.* 57 A9 14 26S 50 10 E
Faranah, *Guinea* 50 F3 10 3N 10 45W
Farasān, Jazā'ir, *Si. Arabia* 46 D3 16 45N 41 55 E
Farasan Is. = Farasān, Jazā'ir, *Si. Arabia* 46 D3 16 45N 41 55 E
Faratsiho, *Madag.* 57 B8 19 24S 46 57 E
Fareham, *U.K.* 11 G6 50 51N 1 11W
Farewell, C., *N.Z.* 59 J4 40 29S 172 43 E
Farewell C. = Nunap Isua, *Greenland* 69 C15 59 48N 43 55W
Farghona, *Uzbekistan* 26 E8 40 23N 71 19 E
Fargo, *U.S.A.* 80 B6 46 53N 96 48W
Fār'iah, W. al →, *West Bank* 47 C4 32 12N 35 27 E
Faribault, *U.S.A.* 80 C8 44 18N 93 16W
Faridabad, *India* 42 E6 28 26N 77 19 E
Faridkot, *India* 42 D6 30 44N 74 45 E
Faridpur, *Bangla.* 43 H13 23 15N 89 55 E
Faridpur, *India* 43 E8 28 13N 79 33 E
Farīmān, *Iran* 45 C8 35 40N 59 49 E
Farina, *Australia* 63 E2 30 3S 138 15 E
Fariones, Pta., *Canary Is.* 22 E6 29 13N 13 28W
Farmerville, *U.S.A.* 81 J8 32 47N 92 24W
Farmingdale, *U.S.A.* 79 F10 40 12N 74 10W
Farmington, *Canada* 72 B4 55 54N 120 30W
Farmington, *Calif., U.S.A.* 84 H6 37 55N 120 59W
Farmington, *Maine, U.S.A.* 77 C10 44 40N 70 9W

Farmington, Mo., U.S.A. **81 G9** 37 47N 90 25W
Farmington, N.H., U.S.A. **79 C13** 43 24N 71 4W
Farmington, N. Mex., U.S.A. **83 H9** 36 44N 108 12W
Farmington, Utah, U.S.A. **82 F8** 41 0N 111 12W
Farmington →, U.S.A. **79 E12** 41 51N 72 38W
Farmville, U.S.A. **76 G6** 37 18N 78 24W
Farne Is., U.K. **10 B6** 55 38N 1 37W
Farnham, Canada **79 A12** 45 17N 72 59W
Farnham, Mt., Canada **72 C5** 50 29N 116 30W
Faro, Brazil **93 D7** 2 10S 56 39W
Faro, Canada **68 B6** 62 11N 133 22W
Faro, Portugal **19 D2** 37 2N 7 55W
Fårö, Sweden **9 H18** 57 55N 19 5 E
Farquhar, C., Australia **61 D1** 23 50S 113 36 E
Farrars Cr. →, Australia **62 D3** 25 35S 140 43 E
Farrāshband, Iran **45 D7** 28 57N 52 5 E
Farrell, U.S.A. **78 E4** 41 13N 80 30W
Farrokhī, Iran **45 C8** 33 50N 59 31 E
Farruch, C. = Ferrutx, C., Spain **22 B10** 39 47N 3 21 E
Fārs □, Iran **45 D7** 29 30N 55 0 E
Fársala, Greece **21 E10** 39 17N 22 23 E
Farson, U.S.A. **82 E9** 42 6N 109 27W
Farsund, Norway **9 G12** 58 5N 6 55 E
Fartak, Râs, Si. Arabia **44 D2** 28 5N 34 34 E
Fartak, Ra's, Yemen **46 D5** 15 38N 52 15 E
Fartura, Serra da, Brazil **95 B5** 26 21S 52 52W
Fārūj, Iran **45 B8** 37 14N 58 14 E
Farvel, Kap = Nunap Isua, Greenland **69 C15** 59 48N 43 55W
Farwell, U.S.A. **81 H3** 34 23N 103 2W
Fāryāb □, Afghan. **40 B4** 36 0N 65 0 E
Fasā, Iran **45 D7** 29 0N 53 39 E
Fasano, Italy **20 D7** 40 50N 17 22 E
Fastiv, Ukraine **17 C15** 50 7N 29 57 E
Fastov = Fastiv, Ukraine **17 C15** 50 7N 29 57 E
Fatagar, Tanjung, Indonesia **37 E8** 2 46S 131 57 E
Fatehabad, Haryana, India **42 E6** 29 31N 75 27 E
Fatehabad, Ut. P., India **42 F8** 27 1N 78 19 E
Fatehgarh, India **43 F8** 27 25N 79 35 E
Fatehpur, Bihar, India **43 G11** 24 38N 85 14 E
Fatehpur, Raj., India **42 F6** 28 0N 74 40 E
Fatehpur, Ut. P., India **43 G9** 25 56N 81 13 E
Fatehpur, Ut. P., India **43 F9** 27 10N 81 13 E
Fatehpur Sikri, India **42 F6** 27 6N 77 40 E
Fatima, Canada **71 C7** 47 24N 61 53W
Faulkton, U.S.A. **80 C5** 45 2N 99 8W
Faure I., Australia **61 E1** 25 52S 113 50 E
Fauresmith, S. Africa **56 D4** 29 44S 25 17 E
Fauske, Norway **8 C16** 67 17N 15 25 E
Favara, Italy **20 F5** 37 19N 13 39 E
Faváritx, C. de, Spain **22 B11** 40 0N 4 15 E
Favignana, Italy **20 F5** 37 56N 12 20 E
Fawcett, Pt., Australia **60 B5** 11 46S 130 2 E
Fawn →, Canada **70 A2** 55 20N 87 35W
Fawnskin, U.S.A. **85 L10** 34 16N 116 56W
Faxaflói, Iceland **8 D2** 64 29N 23 0W
Faya-Largeau, Chad **51 E9** 17 58N 19 6 E
Fayd, Si. Arabia **44 E4** 27 1N 42 52 E
Fayette, Ala., U.S.A. **77 J2** 33 41N 87 50W
Fayette, Mo., U.S.A. **80 F8** 39 9N 92 41W
Fayetteville, Ark., U.S.A. **81 G7** 36 4N 94 10W
Fayetteville, N.C., U.S.A. **77 H6** 35 3N 78 53W
Fayetteville, Tenn., U.S.A. **77 H2** 35 9N 86 34W
Fazilka, India **42 D6** 30 27N 74 2 E
Fazilpur, Pakistan **42 E4** 29 18N 70 29 E
Fdérik, Mauritania **50 D3** 22 40N 12 45W
Feale →, Ireland **13 D2** 52 27N 9 37W
Fear, C., U.S.A. **77 J7** 33 50N 77 58W
Feather →, U.S.A. **82 G3** 38 47N 121 36W
Feather Falls, U.S.A. **84 F5** 39 36N 121 16W
Featherston, N.Z. **59 J5** 41 6S 175 20 E
Featherstone, Zimbabwe **55 F3** 18 42S 30 55 E
Fécamp, France **18 B4** 49 45N 0 22 E
Fedala = Mohammedia, Morocco **50 B4** 33 44N 7 21W
Federación, Argentina **94 C4** 31 0S 57 55W
Féderal, Argentina **96 C5** 30 57S 58 48W
Federal Way, U.S.A. **84 C4** 47 18N 122 19W
Fedeshkūh, Iran **45 D7** 28 49N 53 50 E
Fehmarn, Germany **16 A6** 54 27N 11 7 E
Fehmarn Bælt, Europe **9 J14** 54 35N 11 20 E
Fehmarn Belt = Fehmarn Bælt, Europe **9 J14** 54 35N 11 20 E
Fei Xian, China **35 G9** 35 18N 117 59 E
Feijó, Brazil **92 E4** 8 9S 70 21W
Feilding, N.Z. **59 J5** 40 13S 175 35 E
Feira de Santana, Brazil **93 F11** 12 15S 38 57W
Feixiang, China **34 F8** 36 30N 114 45 E
Felanitx, Spain **22 B10** 39 28N 3 9 E
Feldkirch, Austria **16 E5** 47 15N 9 37 E
Felipe Carrillo Puerto, Mexico **87 D7** 19 38N 88 3W
Felixburg, Zimbabwe **57 B5** 19 29S 30 51 E
Felixstowe, U.K. **11 F9** 51 58N 1 23 E
Felton, U.S.A. **84 H4** 37 3N 122 4W
Femer Bælt = Fehmarn Bælt, Europe **9 J14** 54 35N 11 20 E
Femunden, Norway **9 E14** 62 10N 11 53 E
Fen He →, China **34 G6** 35 36N 110 42 E
Fenelon Falls, Canada **78 B6** 44 32N 78 45W
Feng Xian, Jiangsu, China **34 G9** 34 43N 116 35 E
Feng Xian, Shaanxi, China **34 H4** 33 54N 106 40 E
Fengcheng, China **35 D13** 40 28N 124 5 E
Fengfeng, China **34 F8** 36 28N 114 8 E
Fengning, China **34 D9** 41 10N 116 33 E
Fengqiu, China **34 G8** 35 2N 114 25 E
Fengrun, China **35 E10** 39 48N 118 8 E
Fengtai, China **34 E9** 39 50N 116 18 E
Fengxiang, China **34 G4** 34 29N 107 25 E
Fengyang, China **35 H9** 32 51N 117 29 E
Fengzhen, China **34 D7** 40 25N 113 2 E
Fenoarivo, Fianarantsoa, Madag. **57 C8** 21 43S 46 24 E
Fenoarivo, Fianarantsoa, Madag. **57 C8** 20 52S 46 53 E
Fenoarivo Afovoany, Madag. **57 B8** 18 26S 46 34 E
Fenoarivo Atsinanana, Madag. **57 B8** 17 22S 49 25 E
Fens, The, U.K. **10 E7** 52 38N 0 2W
Fenton, U.S.A. **76 D4** 42 48N 83 42W
Fenxi, China **34 F6** 36 40N 111 31 E
Fenyang, China **34 F6** 37 18N 111 48 E
Feodosiya, Ukraine **25 E6** 45 2N 35 16 E
Ferdows, Iran **45 C8** 33 58N 58 2 E
Ferfer, Somali Rep. **46 F4** 5 4N 45 9 E
Fergana = Farghona, Uzbekistan **26 E8** 40 23N 71 19 E
Fergus, Canada **78 C4** 43 43N 80 24W
Fergus Falls, U.S.A. **80 B6** 46 17N 96 4W
Ferkéssédougou, Ivory C. **50 G4** 9 35N 5 6W
Ferland, Canada **70 B2** 50 19N 88 27W
Fermanagh □, U.K. **13 B4** 54 21N 7 40W
Fermo, Italy **20 C5** 43 9N 13 43 E
Fermont, Canada **71 B6** 52 47N 67 5W
Fermoy, Ireland **13 D3** 52 9N 8 16W
Fernández, Argentina **94 B3** 27 55S 63 50W
Fernandina Beach, U.S.A. **77 K5** 30 40N 81 27W
Fernando de Noronha, Brazil **93 D12** 4 0S 33 10W
Fernando Póo = Bioko, Eq. Guin. **52 D1** 3 30N 8 40 E
Ferndale, U.S.A. **84 B4** 48 51N 122 36W
Fernie, Canada **72 D5** 49 30N 115 5W
Fernlees, Australia **62 C4** 23 51S 148 7 E
Fernley, U.S.A. **82 G4** 39 36N 119 15W
Ferozepore = Firozpur, India **42 D6** 30 55N 74 40 E
Ferrara, Italy **20 B4** 44 50N 11 35 E
Ferreñafe, Peru **92 E3** 6 42S 79 50W
Ferrerías, Spain **22 B11** 39 59N 4 1 E
Ferret, C., France **18 D3** 44 38N 1 15W
Ferriday, U.S.A. **81 K9** 31 38N 91 33W
Ferrol, Spain **19 A1** 43 29N 8 15W
Ferron, U.S.A. **83 G8** 39 5N 111 8W
Ferrutx, C., Spain **22 B10** 39 47N 3 21 E
Ferryland, Canada **71 C9** 47 2N 52 53W
Fertile, U.S.A. **80 B6** 47 32N 96 17W
Fès, Morocco **50 B5** 34 0N 5 0W
Fessenden, U.S.A. **80 B5** 47 39N 99 38W
Festus, U.S.A. **80 F9** 38 13N 90 24W
Feteşti, Romania **17 F14** 44 22N 27 51 E
Fethiye, Turkey **25 G4** 36 36N 29 6 E
Fetlar, U.K. **12 A8** 60 36N 0 52W
Feuilles →, Canada **69 C12** 58 47N 70 4W
Fez = Fès, Morocco **50 B5** 34 0N 5 0W
Fezzan, Libya **51 C8** 27 0N 13 0 E
Fiambalá, Argentina **94 B2** 27 45S 67 37W
Fianarantsoa, Madag. **57 C8** 21 26S 47 5 E
Fianarantsoa □, Madag. **57 B8** 19 30S 47 0 E
Ficksburg, S. Africa **57 D4** 28 51S 27 53 E
Field →, Australia **62 C2** 23 48S 138 0 E
Field I., Australia **60 B5** 12 5S 132 23 E
Fier, Albania **21 D8** 40 43N 19 33 E
Fife □, U.K. **12 E5** 56 16N 3 1W
Fife Ness, U.K. **12 E6** 56 17N 2 35W
Fifth Cataract, Sudan **51 E12** 18 22N 33 50 E
Figeac, France **18 D5** 44 37N 2 2 E
Figtree, Zimbabwe **55 G2** 20 22S 28 20 E
Figueira da Foz, Portugal **19 B1** 40 7N 8 54W
Figueres, Spain **19 A7** 42 18N 2 58 E
Figuig, Morocco **50 B5** 32 5N 1 11W
Fihaonana, Madag. **57 B8** 18 36S 47 12 E
Fiherenana, Madag. **57 B8** 18 29S 48 24 E
Fiherenana →, Madag. **57 C7** 23 19S 43 37 E
Fiji ■, Pac. Oc. **59 C8** 17 20S 179 0 E
Filabusi, Zimbabwe **57 C4** 20 34S 29 20 E
Filey, U.K. **10 C7** 54 12N 0 18W
Filey B., U.K. **10 C7** 54 12N 0 15W
Filfla, Malta **23 D1** 35 47N 14 24 E
Filiatrá, Greece **21 F9** 37 9N 21 35 E
Filingué, Niger **50 F6** 14 21N 3 22 E
Filipstad, Sweden **9 G16** 59 43N 14 9 E
Fillmore, Calif., U.S.A. **85 L8** 34 24N 118 55W
Fillmore, Utah, U.S.A. **83 G7** 38 58N 112 20W
Finch, Canada **79 A9** 45 11N 75 7W
Findhorn →, U.K. **12 D5** 57 38N 3 38W
Findlay, U.S.A. **76 E4** 41 2N 83 39W
Finger L., Canada **70 B1** 53 33N 93 30W
Finger Lakes, U.S.A. **79 D8** 42 40N 76 30W
Fingoè, Mozam. **55 E3** 14 55S 31 50 E
Finisterre, C. = Fisterra, C., Spain **19 A1** 42 50N 9 19W
Finke, Australia **62 D1** 25 34S 134 35 E
Finland ■, Europe **8 E22** 63 0N 27 0 E
Finland, G. of, Europe **9 G21** 60 0N 26 0 E
Finlay →, Canada **72 B3** 57 0N 125 10W
Finley, Australia **63 F4** 35 38S 145 35 E
Finley, U.S.A. **80 B6** 47 31N 97 50W
Finn →, Ireland **13 B4** 54 51N 7 28W
Finnigan, Mt., Australia **62 B4** 15 49S 145 17 E
Finniss, C., Australia **63 E1** 33 8S 134 51 E
Finnmark, Norway **8 B20** 69 37N 23 57 E
Finnsnes, Norway **8 B18** 69 14N 18 0 E
Finspång, Sweden **9 G16** 58 43N 15 47 E
Fiora →, Italy **20 C4** 42 20N 11 34 E
Fiq, Syria **47 C4** 32 46N 35 41 E
Firat = Furāt, Nahr al →, Asia **44 D5** 31 0N 47 25 E
Firebag →, Canada **73 B6** 57 45N 111 21W
Firebaugh, U.S.A. **84 J6** 36 52N 120 27W
Firedrake L., Canada **73 A8** 61 25N 104 30W
Firenze, Italy **20 C4** 43 46N 11 15 E
Firk →, Iraq **44 D5** 30 59N 44 34 E
Firozabad, India **43 F8** 27 10N 78 25 E
Firozpur, India **42 D6** 30 55N 74 40 E
Firozpur-Jhirka, India **42 F7** 27 48N 76 57 E
Fīrūzābād, Iran **45 D7** 28 52N 52 35 E
Fīrūzkūh, Iran **45 C7** 35 50N 52 50 E
Firvale, Canada **72 C3** 52 27N 126 13W
Fish →, Namibia **56 D2** 28 7S 17 10 E
Fish →, S. Africa **56 E3** 31 30S 20 16 E
Fish River Canyon, Namibia **56 D2** 27 40S 17 35 E
Fisher, Australia **61 F5** 30 30S 131 0 E
Fisher B., Canada **73 C9** 51 35N 97 13W
Fishers I., U.S.A. **79 E13** 41 15N 72 0W
Fishguard, U.K. **11 E3** 52 0N 4 58W
Fishing L., Canada **73 C9** 52 10N 95 24W
Fishkill, U.S.A. **79 E11** 41 32N 73 53W
Fisterra, C., Spain **19 A1** 42 50N 9 19W
Fitchburg, U.S.A. **79 D13** 42 35N 71 48W
Fitz Roy, Argentina **96 F3** 47 0S 67 0W
Fitzgerald, Canada **72 B6** 59 51N 111 36W
Fitzgerald, U.S.A. **77 K4** 31 43N 83 15W
Fitzmaurice →, Australia **60 B5** 14 45S 130 5 E
Fitzroy →, Queens., Australia **62 C5** 23 32S 150 52 E
Fitzroy →, W. Austral., Australia **60 C3** 17 31S 123 35 E
Fitzroy, Mte., Argentina **96 F2** 49 17S 73 5W
Fitzroy Crossing, Australia **60 C4** 18 9S 125 38 E
Fitzwilliam I., Canada **78 A3** 45 30N 81 45W
Fiume = Rijeka, Croatia **16 F8** 45 20N 14 21 E
Five Points, U.S.A. **84 J6** 36 26N 120 6W
Fizi, Dem. Rep. of the Congo **54 C2** 4 17S 28 55 E
Flagstaff, U.S.A. **83 J8** 35 12N 111 39W
Flagstaff L., U.S.A. **77 C10** 45 12N 70 18W
Flaherty I., Canada **70 A4** 56 15N 79 15W
Flåm, Norway **9 F12** 60 50N 7 7 E
Flambeau →, U.S.A. **80 C9** 45 18N 91 14W
Flamborough Hd., U.K. **10 C7** 54 7N 0 5W
Flaming Gorge Reservoir, U.S.A. **82 F9** 41 10N 109 25W
Flamingo, Teluk, Indonesia **37 F9** 5 30S 138 0 E
Flanders = Flandre, Europe **18 A5** 50 50N 2 30 E
Flandre, Europe **18 A5** 50 50N 2 30 E
Flandre Occidentale = West-Vlaanderen □, Belgium **15 D2** 51 0N 3 0 E
Flandre Orientale = Oost-Vlaanderen □, Belgium **15 C3** 51 5N 3 50 E
Flandreau, U.S.A. **80 C6** 44 3N 96 36W
Flanigan, U.S.A. **84 E7** 40 10N 119 53W
Flannan Is., U.K. **12 C1** 58 9N 7 52W
Flåsjön, Sweden **8 D16** 64 5N 15 40 E
Flat →, Canada **72 A3** 61 33N 125 18W
Flathead L., U.S.A. **82 C7** 47 51N 114 8W
Flattery, C., Australia **62 A4** 14 58S 145 21 E
Flattery, C., U.S.A. **84 B2** 48 23N 124 29W
Flatwoods, U.S.A. **76 F4** 38 31N 82 43W
Fleetwood, U.K. **10 D4** 53 55N 3 1W
Fleetwood, U.S.A. **79 F9** 40 27N 75 49W
Flekkefjord, Norway **9 G12** 58 18N 6 39 E
Flemington, U.S.A. **78 E7** 41 7N 77 28W
Flensburg, Germany **16 A5** 54 47N 9 27 E
Flers, France **18 B3** 48 47N 0 33W
Flesherton, Canada **78 B4** 44 16N 80 33W
Flesko, Tanjung, Indonesia **37 D6** 0 29N 124 30 E
Fleurieu Pen., Australia **63 F2** 35 40S 138 5 E
Flevoland □, Neths. **15 B5** 52 30N 5 30 E
Flin Flon, Canada **73 C8** 54 46N 101 53W
Flinders →, Australia **62 B3** 17 36S 140 36 E
Flinders B., Australia **61 F2** 34 19S 115 19 E
Flinders Group, Australia **62 A3** 14 11S 144 15 E
Flinders I., S. Austral., Australia **63 E1** 33 44S 134 41 E
Flinders I., Tas., Australia **62 G4** 40 0S 148 0 E
Flinders Ranges, Australia **63 E2** 31 30S 138 30 E
Flinders Reefs, Australia **62 B4** 17 37S 148 31 E
Flint, U.K. **10 D4** 53 15N 3 8W
Flint, U.S.A. **76 D4** 43 1N 83 41W
Flint →, U.S.A. **77 K3** 30 57N 84 34W
Flint I., Kiribati **65 J12** 11 26S 151 48W
Flintshire □, U.K. **10 D4** 53 17N 3 17W
Flodden, U.K. **10 B5** 55 37N 2 8W
Floodwood, U.S.A. **80 B8** 46 55N 92 55W
Flora, U.S.A. **76 F1** 38 40N 88 29W
Florala, U.S.A. **77 K2** 31 0N 86 20W
Florence = Firenze, Italy **20 C4** 43 46N 11 15 E
Florence, Ala., U.S.A. **77 H2** 34 48N 87 41W
Florence, Ariz., U.S.A. **83 K8** 33 2N 111 23W
Florence, Colo., U.S.A. **80 F2** 38 23N 105 8W
Florence, Oreg., U.S.A. **82 E1** 43 58N 124 7W
Florence, S.C., U.S.A. **77 H6** 34 12N 79 46W
Florence, L., Australia **63 D2** 28 53S 138 9 E
Florencia, Colombia **92 C3** 1 36N 75 36W
Florennes, Belgium **15 D4** 50 15N 4 35 E
Florenville, Belgium **15 E5** 49 40N 5 19 E
Flores, Guatemala **88 C2** 16 59N 89 50W
Flores, Indonesia **37 F6** 8 35S 121 0 E
Flores I., Canada **72 D3** 49 20N 126 10W
Flores Sea, Indonesia **37 F6** 6 30S 120 0 E
Floreşti, Moldova **17 E15** 47 53N 28 17 E
Floresville, U.S.A. **81 L5** 29 8N 98 10W
Floriano, Brazil **93 E10** 6 50S 43 0W
Florianópolis, Brazil **95 B6** 27 30S 48 30W
Florida, Cuba **88 B4** 21 32N 78 14W
Florida, Uruguay **95 C4** 34 7S 56 10W
Florida □, U.S.A. **77 L5** 28 0N 82 0W
Florida, Straits of, U.S.A. **88 B4** 25 0N 80 0W
Florida B., U.S.A. **88 B3** 25 0N 80 45W
Florida Keys, U.S.A. **77 N5** 24 40N 81 0W
Flórina, Greece **21 D9** 40 48N 21 26 E
Florø, Norway **9 F11** 61 35N 5 1 E
Flower Station, Canada **79 A8** 45 10N 76 41W
Flowerpot I., Canada **78 A3** 45 18N 81 38W
Floydada, U.S.A. **81 J4** 33 59N 101 20W
Fluk, Indonesia **37 E7** 1 42S 127 44 E
Flushing = Vlissingen, Neths. **15 C3** 51 26N 3 34 E
Flying Fish, C., Antarctica **5 D15** 72 6S 102 29W
Foam Lake, Canada **73 C8** 51 40N 103 32W
Foça, Turkey **21 E12** 38 39N 26 46 E
Focşani, Romania **17 F14** 45 41N 27 15 E
Fóggia, Italy **20 D6** 41 27N 15 34 E
Fogo, Canada **71 C9** 49 43N 54 17W
Fogo I., Canada **71 C9** 49 40N 54 5W
Föhr, Germany **16 A5** 54 43N 8 30 E
Foix, France **18 E4** 42 58N 1 38 E
Folda, Nord-Trøndelag, Norway **8 D14** 64 32N 10 30 E
Folda, Nordland, Norway **8 C16** 67 38N 14 50 E
Foley, Botswana **56 C4** 21 34S 27 21 E
Foley, U.S.A. **77 K2** 30 24N 87 41W
Foleyet, Canada **70 C3** 48 15N 82 25W
Folgefonni, Norway **9 F12** 60 3N 6 23 E
Foligno, Italy **20 C5** 42 57N 12 42 E
Folkestone, U.K. **11 F9** 51 5N 1 12 E
Folkston, U.S.A. **77 K5** 30 50N 82 0W
Follansbee, U.S.A. **78 F4** 40 19N 80 35W
Folsom L., U.S.A. **84 G5** 38 42N 121 9W
Fond-du-Lac, Canada **73 B7** 59 19N 107 12W
Fond du Lac, U.S.A. **80 D10** 43 47N 88 27W
Fond-du-Lac →, Canada **73 B7** 59 17N 106 0W
Fonda, U.S.A. **79 D10** 42 57N 74 22W
Fondi, Italy **20 D5** 41 21N 13 25 E
Fongafale, Tuvalu **64 H9** 8 31S 179 13 E
Fonsagrada = A Fonsagrada, Spain **19 A2** 43 8N 7 4W
Fonseca, G. de, Cent. Amer. **88 D2** 13 10N 87 40W
Fontainebleau, France **18 B5** 48 24N 2 40 E
Fontana, U.S.A. **85 L9** 34 6N 117 26W
Fontas →, Canada **72 B4** 58 14N 121 48W
Fonte Boa, Brazil **92 D5** 2 33S 66 0W
Fontenay-le-Comte, France **18 C3** 46 28N 0 48W
Fontenelle Reservoir, U.S.A. **82 E8** 42 1N 110 3W
Fontur, Iceland **8 C6** 66 23N 14 32W
Foochow = Fuzhou, China **33 D6** 26 5N 119 16 E
Foping, China **34 H5** 33 41N 108 0 E
Forbes, Australia **63 E4** 33 22S 148 5 E
Forbesganj, India **43 F12** 26 17N 87 18 E
Ford City, Calif., U.S.A. **85 K7** 35 9N 119 27W
Ford City, Pa., U.S.A. **78 F5** 40 46N 79 32W
Førde, Norway **9 F11** 61 27N 5 53 E
Ford's Bridge, Australia **63 D4** 29 41S 145 29 E
Fordyce, U.S.A. **81 J8** 33 49N 92 25W
Forel, Mt., Greenland **4 C6** 66 52N 36 55W
Foremost, Canada **72 D6** 49 26N 111 34W
Forest, Canada **78 C3** 43 6N 82 0W
Forest, U.S.A. **81 J10** 32 22N 89 29W
Forest City, Iowa, U.S.A. **80 D8** 43 16N 93 39W
Forest City, N.C., U.S.A. **77 H5** 35 20N 81 52W
Forest City, Pa., U.S.A. **79 E9** 41 39N 75 28W
Forest Grove, U.S.A. **84 E3** 45 31N 123 7W
Forestburg, Canada **72 C6** 52 35N 112 1W
Foresthill, U.S.A. **84 F6** 39 1N 120 49W
Forestier Pen., Australia **62 G4** 43 0S 148 0 E
Forestville, Canada **71 C6** 48 48N 69 2W
Forestville, Calif., U.S.A. **84 G4** 38 28N 122 54W
Forestville, N.Y., U.S.A. **78 D5** 42 28N 79 10W
Forfar, U.K. **12 E6** 56 39N 2 53W
Forks, U.S.A. **84 C2** 47 57N 124 23W
Forksville, U.S.A. **79 E8** 41 29N 76 35W
Forlì, Italy **20 B5** 44 13N 12 3 E
Forman, U.S.A. **80 B6** 46 7N 97 38W
Formby Pt., U.K. **10 D4** 53 33N 3 6W
Formentera, Spain **22 C7** 38 43N 1 27 E
Formentor, C. de, Spain **22 B10** 39 58N 3 13 E
Former Yugoslav Republic of Macedonia = Macedonia ■, Europe **21 D9** 41 53N 21 40 E
Fórmia, Italy **20 D5** 41 15N 13 37 E
Formosa = Taiwan ■, Asia **33 D7** 23 30N 121 0 E
Formosa, Argentina **94 B4** 26 15S 58 10W
Formosa, Brazil **93 G9** 15 32S 47 20W
Formosa □, Argentina **94 B4** 25 0S 60 0W
Formosa, Serra, Brazil **93 F8** 12 0S 55 0W
Formosa Bay, Kenya **54 C5** 2 40S 40 20 E
Fornells, Spain **22 A11** 40 3N 4 7 E
Føroyar, Atl. Oc. **8 F9** 62 0N 7 0W
Forres, U.K. **12 D5** 57 37N 3 37W
Forrest, Australia **61 F4** 30 51S 128 6 E
Forrest, Mt., Australia **61 D4** 24 48S 127 45 E
Forrest City, U.S.A. **81 H9** 35 1N 90 47W
Forsayth, Australia **62 B3** 18 33S 143 34 E
Forssa, Finland **9 F20** 60 49N 23 38 E
Forst, Germany **16 C8** 51 45N 14 37 E
Forsyth, U.S.A. **82 C10** 46 16N 106 41W
Fort Abbas, Pakistan **42 E5** 29 12N 72 52 E
Fort Albany, Canada **70 B3** 52 15N 81 35W
Fort Ann, U.S.A. **79 C11** 43 25N 73 30W
Fort Assiniboine, Canada **72 C6** 54 20N 114 45W
Fort Augustus, U.K. **12 D4** 57 9N 4 42W
Fort Beaufort, S. Africa **56 E4** 32 46S 26 40 E
Fort Benton, U.S.A. **82 C8** 47 49N 110 40W
Fort Bragg, U.S.A. **82 G2** 39 26N 123 48W
Fort Bridger, U.S.A. **82 F8** 41 19N 110 23W
Fort Chipewyan, Canada **73 B6** 58 42N 111 8W
Fort Collins, U.S.A. **80 E2** 40 35N 105 5W
Fort-Coulonge, Canada **70 C4** 45 50N 76 45W
Fort Covington, U.S.A. **79 B10** 44 59N 74 29W
Fort Davis, U.S.A. **81 K3** 30 35N 103 54W
Fort-de-France, Martinique **89 D7** 14 36N 61 2W
Fort Defiance, U.S.A. **83 J9** 35 45N 109 5W
Fort Dodge, U.S.A. **80 D7** 42 30N 94 11W
Fort Edward, U.S.A. **79 C11** 43 16N 73 35W
Fort Erie, Canada **78 D6** 42 54N 78 56W
Fort Fairfield, U.S.A. **77 B12** 46 46N 67 50W
Fort Frances, Canada **73 D10** 48 36N 93 24W
Fort Garland, U.S.A. **83 H11** 37 26N 105 26W
Fort George = Chisasibi, Canada **70 B4** 53 50N 79 0W
Fort Good-Hope, Canada **68 B7** 66 14N 128 40W
Fort Hancock, U.S.A. **83 L11** 31 18N 105 51W
Fort Hertz = Putao, Burma **41 F20** 27 28N 97 30 E
Fort Hope, Canada **70 B2** 51 30N 88 0W
Fort Irwin, U.S.A. **85 K10** 35 16N 116 34W
Fort Kent, U.S.A. **77 B11** 47 15N 68 36W
Fort Klamath, U.S.A. **82 E3** 42 42N 122 0W
Fort Laramie, U.S.A. **80 D2** 42 13N 104 31W
Fort Lauderdale, U.S.A. **77 M5** 26 7N 80 8W
Fort Liard, Canada **72 A4** 60 14N 123 30W
Fort Liberté, Haiti **89 C5** 19 42N 71 51W
Fort Lupton, U.S.A. **80 E2** 40 5N 104 49W
Fort Mackay, Canada **72 B6** 57 12N 111 41W
Fort Macleod, Canada **72 D6** 49 45N 113 30W
Fort McMurray, Canada **72 B6** 56 44N 111 7W
Fort McPherson, Canada **68 B6** 67 30N 134 55W
Fort Madison, U.S.A. **80 E9** 40 38N 91 27W
Fort Meade, U.S.A. **77 M5** 27 45N 81 48W
Fort Morgan, U.S.A. **80 E3** 40 15N 103 48W
Fort Myers, U.S.A. **77 M5** 26 39N 81 52W
Fort Nelson, Canada **72 B4** 58 50N 122 44W
Fort Nelson →, Canada **72 B4** 59 32N 124 0W
Fort Norman = Tulita, Canada **68 B7** 64 57N 125 30W
Fort Payne, U.S.A. **77 H3** 34 26N 85 43W
Fort Peck, U.S.A. **82 B10** 48 1N 106 27W
Fort Peck Dam, U.S.A. **82 C10** 48 0N 106 26W
Fort Peck L., U.S.A. **82 C10** 48 0N 106 26W
Fort Pierce, U.S.A. **77 M5** 27 27N 80 20W
Fort Pierre, U.S.A. **80 C4** 44 21N 100 22W
Fort Plain, U.S.A. **79 D10** 42 56N 74 37W
Fort Portal, Uganda **54 B3** 0 40N 30 20 E
Fort Providence, Canada **72 A5** 61 3N 117 40W
Fort Qu'Appelle, Canada **73 C8** 50 45N 103 50W
Fort Resolution, Canada **72 A6** 61 10N 113 40W
Fort Rixon, Zimbabwe **55 G2** 20 2S 29 17 E
Fort Ross, U.S.A. **84 G3** 38 32N 123 13W
Fort Rupert = Waskaganish, Canada **70 B4** 51 30N 78 40W
Fort St. James, Canada **72 C4** 54 30N 124 10W
Fort St. John, Canada **72 B4** 56 15N 120 50W
Fort Saskatchewan, Canada **72 C6** 53 40N 113 15W
Fort Scott, U.S.A. **81 G7** 37 50N 94 42W
Fort Severn, Canada **70 A2** 56 0N 87 40W
Fort Shevchenko, Kazakstan **25 F9** 44 35N 50 23 E
Fort Simpson, Canada **72 A4** 61 45N 121 15W
Fort Smith, Canada **72 B6** 60 0N 111 51W
Fort Smith, U.S.A. **81 H7** 35 23N 94 25W
Fort Stockton, U.S.A. **81 K3** 30 53N 102 53W
Fort Sumner, U.S.A. **81 H2** 34 28N 104 15W
Fort Thompson, U.S.A. **80 C5** 44 3N 99 26W
Fort Valley, U.S.A. **77 J4** 32 33N 83 53W
Fort Vermilion, Canada **72 B5** 58 24N 116 0W
Fort Walton Beach, U.S.A. **77 K2** 30 25N 86 36W
Fort Wayne, U.S.A. **76 E3** 41 4N 85 9W
Fort William, U.K. **12 E3** 56 49N 5 7W
Fort Worth, U.S.A. **81 J6** 32 45N 97 18W
Fort Yates, U.S.A. **80 B4** 46 5N 100 38W

Fort Yukon, U.S.A. 68 B5 66 34N 145 16W
Fortaleza, Brazil 93 D11 3 45S 38 35W
Forteau, Canada 71 B8 51 28N 56 58W
Fortescue →, Australia 60 D2 21 0S 116 4 E
Forth →, U.K. 12 E5 56 9N 3 50W
Forth, Firth of, U.K. 12 E6 56 5N 2 55W
Fortrose, U.K. 12 D4 57 35N 4 9W
Fortuna, Calif., U.S.A. 82 F1 40 36N 124 9W
Fortuna, N. Dak., U.S.A. 80 A3 48 55N 103 47W
Fortune, Canada 71 C8 47 4N 55 50W
Fortune B., Canada 71 C8 47 30N 55 22W
Forūr, Iran 45 E7 26 17N 54 32 E
Foshan, China 33 D6 23 4N 113 5 E
Fosna, Norway 8 E14 63 50N 10 20 E
Fosnavåg, Norway 9 E11 62 22N 5 38 E
Fossano, Italy 18 D7 44 33N 7 43 E
Fossil, U.S.A. 82 D3 45 0N 120 9W
Foster, Canada 79 A12 45 17N 72 30W
Foster →, Canada 73 B7 55 47N 105 49W
Fosters Ra., Australia 62 C1 21 35S 133 48 E
Fostoria, U.S.A. 76 E4 41 10N 83 25W
Fotadrevo, Madag. 57 C8 24 3S 45 1 E
Fougères, France 18 B3 48 21N 1 14W
Foul Pt., Sri Lanka 40 Q12 8 35N 81 18 E
Foula, U.K. 12 A6 60 10N 2 5W
Foulness I., U.K. 11 F8 51 36N 0 55 E
Foulpointe, Madag. 57 B8 17 41S 49 31 E
Foulweather, C., U.S.A. 74 B2 44 50N 124 5W
Foumban, Cameroon 52 C2 5 45N 10 50 E
Fountain, U.S.A. 80 F2 38 41N 104 42W
Fountain Springs, U.S.A. 85 K8 35 54N 118 51W
Fouriesburg, S. Africa 56 D4 28 38S 28 14 E
Foúrnoi, Greece 21 F12 37 36N 26 32 E
Fourth Cataract, Sudan 51 E12 18 47N 32 3 E
Fouta Djalon, Guinea 50 F3 11 20N 12 10W
Foux, Cap-à-, Haiti 89 C5 19 43N 73 27W
Foveaux Str., N.Z. 59 M2 46 42S 168 10 E
Fowey, U.K. 11 G3 50 20N 4 39W
Fowler, Calif., U.S.A. 84 J7 36 38N 119 41W
Fowler, Colo., U.S.A. 80 F3 38 8N 104 2W
Fowlers B., Australia 61 F5 31 59S 132 34 E
Fowman, Iran 45 B6 37 13N 49 19 E
Fox →, Canada 73 B10 56 3N 93 18W
Fox Creek, Canada 72 C5 54 24N 116 48W
Fox Lake, Canada 72 B6 58 28N 114 31W
Fox Valley, Canada 73 C7 50 30N 109 25W
Foxboro, U.S.A. 79 D13 42 4N 71 16W
Foxe Basin, Canada 69 B12 66 0N 77 0W
Foxe Chan., Canada 69 B11 65 0N 80 0W
Foxe Pen., Canada 69 B12 65 0N 76 0W
Foxton, N.Z. 59 J5 40 29S 175 18 E
Foyle, Lough, U.K. 13 A4 55 7N 7 4W
Foynes, Ireland 13 D2 52 37N 9 7W
Foz do Cunene, Angola 56 B1 17 15S 11 48 E
Foz do Iguaçu, Brazil 95 B5 25 30S 54 30W
Frackville, U.S.A. 79 F8 40 47N 76 14W
Fraile Muerto, Uruguay 95 C5 32 31S 54 32W
Framingham, U.S.A. 79 D13 42 17N 71 25W
Franca, Brazil 93 H9 20 33S 47 30W
Francavilla Fontana, Italy 21 D7 40 32N 17 35 E
France ■, Europe 18 C5 47 0N 3 0 E
Frances, Australia 63 F3 36 41S 140 55 E
Frances →, Canada 72 A3 60 16N 129 10W
Frances L., Canada 72 A3 61 23N 129 30W
Franceville, Gabon 52 E2 1 40S 13 32 E
Franche-Comté, France 18 C6 46 50N 5 55 E
Francis Case, L., U.S.A. 80 D5 43 4N 98 34W
Francisco Beltrão, Brazil 95 B5 26 5S 53 4W
Francisco I. Madero, Coahuila, Mexico 86 B4 25 48N 103 18W
Francisco I. Madero, Durango, Mexico 86 C4 24 32N 104 22W
Francistown, Botswana 57 C4 21 7S 27 33 E
François, Canada 71 C8 47 35N 56 45W
François L., Canada 72 C3 54 0N 125 30W
Franeker, Neths. 15 A5 53 12N 5 33 E
Frankford, Canada 78 B7 44 12N 77 36W
Frankfort, S. Africa 57 D4 27 17S 28 30 E
Frankfort, Ind., U.S.A. 76 E2 40 17N 86 31W
Frankfort, Kans., U.S.A. 80 F6 39 42N 96 25W
Frankfort, Ky., U.S.A. 76 F3 38 12N 84 52W
Frankfort, N.Y., U.S.A. 79 C9 43 2N 75 4W
Frankfurt, Brandenburg, Germany 16 B8 52 20N 14 32 E
Frankfurt, Hessen, Germany 16 C5 50 7N 8 41 E
Fränkische Alb, Germany 16 D6 49 10N 11 23 E
Frankland →, Australia 61 G2 35 0S 116 48 E
Franklin, Ky., U.S.A. 77 G2 36 43N 86 35W
Franklin, La., U.S.A. 81 L9 29 48N 91 30W
Franklin, Mass., U.S.A. 79 D13 42 5N 71 24W
Franklin, N.H., U.S.A. 79 C13 43 27N 71 39W
Franklin, Nebr., U.S.A. 80 E5 40 6N 98 57W
Franklin, Pa., U.S.A. 78 E5 41 24N 79 50W
Franklin, Va., U.S.A. 77 G7 36 41N 76 56W
Franklin, W. Va., U.S.A. 76 F6 38 39N 79 20W
Franklin B., Canada 68 B7 69 45N 126 0W
Franklin D. Roosevelt L., U.S.A. 82 B4 48 18N 118 9W
Franklin I., Antarctica 5 D11 76 10S 168 30 E
Franklin L., U.S.A. 82 F6 40 25N 115 22W
Franklin Mts., Canada 68 B7 65 0N 125 0W
Franklin Str., Canada 68 A10 72 0N 96 0W
Franklinton, U.S.A. 81 K9 30 51N 90 9W
Franklinville, U.S.A. 78 D6 42 20N 78 27W
Franks Pk., U.S.A. 82 E9 43 58N 109 18W
Frankston, Australia 63 F4 38 8S 145 8 E
Fransfontein, Namibia 56 C2 20 12S 15 1 E
Frantsa Iosifa, Zemlya, Russia 26 A6 82 0N 55 0 E
Franz, Canada 70 C3 48 25N 84 30W
Franz Josef Land = Frantsa Iosifa, Zemlya, Russia 26 A6 82 0N 55 0 E
Fraser, U.S.A. 78 D2 42 32N 82 57W
Fraser →, B.C., Canada 72 D4 49 7N 123 11W
Fraser →, Nfld., Canada 71 A7 56 39N 62 10W
Fraser, Mt., Australia 61 E2 25 35S 118 20 E
Fraser I., Australia 63 D5 25 15S 153 10 E
Fraser Lake, Canada 72 C4 54 0N 124 50W
Fraserburg, S. Africa 56 E3 31 55S 21 30 E
Fraserburgh, U.K. 12 D6 57 42N 2 1W
Fraserdale, Canada 70 C3 49 55N 81 37W
Fray Bentos, Uruguay 94 C4 33 10S 58 15W
Fredericia, Denmark 9 J13 55 34N 9 45 E
Frederick, Md., U.S.A. 76 F7 39 25N 77 25W
Frederick, Okla., U.S.A. 81 H5 34 23N 99 1W
Frederick, S. Dak., U.S.A. 80 C5 45 50N 98 31W
Fredericksburg, Pa., U.S.A. 79 F8 40 27N 76 26W
Fredericksburg, Tex., U.S.A. 81 K5 30 16N 98 52W
Fredericksburg, Va., U.S.A. 76 F7 38 18N 77 28W
Fredericktown, Mo., U.S.A. 81 G9 37 34N 90 18W
Fredericktown, Ohio, U.S.A. 78 F2 40 29N 82 33W
Frederico I. Madero, Presa, Mexico 86 B3 28 7N 105 40W
Frederico Westphalen, Brazil 95 B5 27 22S 53 24W
Fredericton, Canada 71 C6 45 57N 66 40W
Fredericton Junction, Canada 71 C6 45 41N 66 40W
Frederikshåb = Paamiut, Greenland 4 C5 62 0N 49 43W
Frederikshavn, Denmark 9 H14 57 28N 10 31 E
Frederiksted, U.S. Virgin Is. 89 C7 17 43N 64 53W
Fredonia, Ariz., U.S.A. 83 H7 36 57N 112 32W
Fredonia, Kans., U.S.A. 81 G7 37 32N 95 49W
Fredonia, N.Y., U.S.A. 78 D5 42 26N 79 20W
Fredrikstad, Norway 9 G14 59 13N 10 57 E
Free State □, S. Africa 56 D4 28 30S 27 0 E
Freehold, U.S.A. 79 F10 40 16N 74 17W
Freel Peak, U.S.A. 84 G7 38 52N 119 54W
Freeland, U.S.A. 79 E9 41 1N 75 54W
Freels, C., Canada 71 C9 49 15N 53 30W
Freeman, Calif., U.S.A. 85 K9 35 35N 117 53W
Freeman, S. Dak., U.S.A. 80 D6 43 21N 97 26W
Freeport, Bahamas 88 A4 26 30N 78 47W
Freeport, Ill., U.S.A. 80 D10 42 17N 89 36W
Freeport, N.Y., U.S.A. 79 F11 40 39N 73 35W
Freeport, Ohio, U.S.A. 78 F3 40 12N 81 15W
Freeport, Pa., U.S.A. 78 F5 40 41N 79 41W
Freeport, Tex., U.S.A. 81 L7 28 57N 95 21W
Freetown, S. Leone 50 G3 8 30N 13 17W
Frégate, L., Canada 70 B5 53 15N 74 45W
Fregenal de la Sierra, Spain 19 C2 38 10N 6 39W
Freibourg = Fribourg, Switz. 18 C7 46 49N 7 9 E
Freiburg, Germany 16 E4 47 59N 7 51 E
Freire, Chile 96 D2 38 54S 72 38W
Freirina, Chile 94 B1 28 30S 71 10W
Freising, Germany 16 D6 48 24N 11 45 E
Freistadt, Austria 16 D8 48 30N 14 30 E
Fréjus, France 18 E7 43 25N 6 44 E
Fremantle, Australia 61 F2 32 7S 115 47 E
Fremont, Calif., U.S.A. 84 H4 37 32N 121 57W
Fremont, Mich., U.S.A. 76 D3 43 28N 85 57W
Fremont, Nebr., U.S.A. 80 E6 41 26N 96 30W
Fremont, Ohio, U.S.A. 76 E4 41 21N 83 7W
Fremont →, U.S.A. 83 G8 38 24N 110 42W
French Camp, U.S.A. 84 H5 37 53N 121 16W
French Creek →, U.S.A. 78 E5 41 24N 79 50W
French Guiana ■, S. Amer. 93 C8 4 0N 53 0W
French Polynesia ■, Pac. Oc. 65 K13 20 0S 145 0W
Frenchman Cr. →, N. Amer. 82 B10 48 31N 107 10W
Frenchman Cr. →, U.S.A. 80 E4 40 14N 100 50W
Fresco →, Brazil 93 E8 7 15S 51 30W
Freshfield, C., Antarctica 5 C10 68 25S 151 10 E
Fresnillo, Mexico 86 C4 23 10N 103 0W
Fresno, U.S.A. 84 J7 36 44N 119 47W
Fresno Reservoir, U.S.A. 82 B9 48 36N 109 57W
Frew →, Australia 62 C2 20 0S 135 38 E
Frewsburg, U.S.A. 78 D5 42 3N 79 10W
Freycinet Pen., Australia 62 G4 42 10S 148 25 E
Fria, C., Namibia 56 B1 18 0S 12 0 E
Friant, U.S.A. 84 J7 36 59N 119 43W
Frías, Argentina 94 B2 28 40S 65 5W
Fribourg, Switz. 18 C7 46 49N 7 9 E
Friday Harbor, U.S.A. 84 B3 48 32N 123 1W
Friedens, U.S.A. 78 F6 40 3N 78 59W
Friedrichshafen, Germany 16 E5 47 39N 9 30 E
Friendly Is. = Tonga ■, Pac. Oc. 59 D11 19 50S 174 30W
Friendship, U.S.A. 78 D6 42 12N 78 8W
Friesland □, Neths. 15 A5 53 5N 5 50 E
Frio →, U.S.A. 81 L5 28 26N 98 11W
Frio, C., Brazil 90 F6 22 50S 41 50W
Friona, U.S.A. 81 H3 34 38N 102 43W
Fritch, U.S.A. 81 H4 35 38N 101 36W
Frobisher B., Canada 69 B13 62 30N 66 0W
Frobisher Bay = Iqaluit, Canada 69 B13 63 44N 68 31W
Frobisher L., Canada 73 B7 56 20N 108 15W
Frohavet, Norway 8 E13 64 0N 9 30 E
Frome, U.K. 11 F5 51 14N 2 19W
Frome →, U.K. 11 G5 50 41N 2 6W
Frome, L., Australia 63 E2 30 45S 139 45 E
Front Range, U.S.A. 74 C5 40 25N 105 45W
Front Royal, U.S.A. 76 F6 38 55N 78 12W
Frontera, Canary Is. 22 G2 27 47N 17 59W
Frontera, Mexico 87 D6 18 30N 92 40W
Fronteras, Mexico 86 A3 30 56N 109 31W
Frosinone, Italy 20 D5 41 38N 13 19 E
Frostburg, U.S.A. 76 F6 39 39N 78 56W
Frostisen, Norway 8 B17 68 14N 17 10 E
Frøya, Norway 8 E13 63 43N 8 40 E
Frunze = Bishkek, Kyrgyzstan 26 E8 42 54N 74 46 E
Frutal, Brazil 93 H9 20 0S 49 0W
Frýdek-Místek, Czech Rep. 17 D10 49 40N 18 20 E
Fryeburg, U.S.A. 79 B14 44 1N 70 59W
Fu Xian = Wafangdian, China 35 E11 39 38N 121 58 E
Fu Xian, China 34 G5 36 0N 109 20 E
Fucheng, China 34 F9 37 50N 116 10 E
Fuchou = Fuzhou, China 33 D6 26 5N 119 16 E
Fuchū, Japan 31 G6 34 34N 133 14 E
Fuencaliente, Canary Is. 22 F2 28 28N 17 50W
Fuencaliente, Pta., Canary Is. 22 F2 28 27N 17 51W
Fuengirola, Spain 19 D3 36 32N 4 41W
Fuentes de Oñoro, Spain 19 B2 40 33N 6 52W
Fuerte →, Mexico 86 B3 25 50N 109 25W
Fuerte Olimpo, Paraguay 94 A4 21 0S 57 51W
Fuerteventura, Canary Is. 22 F6 28 30N 14 0W
Fufeng, China 34 G5 34 22N 108 0 E
Fugou, China 34 G8 34 3N 114 25 E
Fugu, China 34 E6 39 2N 111 3 E
Fuhai, China 32 B3 47 2N 87 25 E
Fuḩaymī, Iraq 44 C4 34 16N 42 10 E
Fuji, Japan 31 G9 35 9N 138 39 E
Fuji-San, Japan 31 G9 35 22N 138 44 E
Fuji-Yoshida, Japan 31 G9 35 30N 138 46 E
Fujian □, China 33 D6 26 0N 118 0 E
Fujinomiya, Japan 31 G9 35 10N 138 40 E
Fujisawa, Japan 31 G9 35 22N 139 29 E
Fujiyama, Mt. = Fuji-San, Japan 31 G9 35 22N 138 44 E
Fukien = Fujian □, China 33 D6 26 0N 118 0 E
Fukuchiyama, Japan 31 G7 35 19N 135 9 E
Fukue-Shima, Japan 31 H4 32 40N 128 45 E
Fukui, Japan 31 F8 36 5N 136 10 E
Fukui □, Japan 31 G8 36 0N 136 12 E
Fukuoka, Japan 31 H5 33 39N 130 21 E
Fukuoka □, Japan 31 H5 33 30N 131 0 E
Fukushima, Japan 30 F10 37 44N 140 28 E
Fukushima □, Japan 30 F10 37 30N 140 15 E
Fukuyama, Japan 31 G6 34 35N 133 20 E
Fulda, Germany 16 C5 50 32N 9 40 E
Fulda →, Germany 16 C5 51 25N 9 39 E
Fulford Harbour, Canada 84 B3 48 47N 123 27W
Fullerton, Calif., U.S.A. 85 M9 33 53N 117 56W
Fullerton, Nebr., U.S.A. 80 E6 41 22N 97 58W
Fulongquan, China 35 B13 44 20N 124 42 E
Fulton, Mo., U.S.A. 80 F9 38 52N 91 57W
Fulton, N.Y., U.S.A. 79 C8 43 19N 76 25W
Funabashi, Japan 31 G10 35 45N 140 0 E
Funafuti = Fongafale, Tuvalu 64 H9 8 31S 179 13 E
Funchal, Madeira 22 D3 32 38N 16 54W
Fundación, Colombia 92 A4 10 31N 74 11W
Fundão, Portugal 19 B2 40 8N 7 30W
Fundy, B. of, Canada 71 D6 45 0N 66 0W
Funhalouro, Mozam. 57 C5 23 3S 34 25 E
Funing, Hebei, China 35 E10 39 53N 119 12 E
Funing, Jiangsu, China 35 H10 33 45N 119 50 E
Funiu Shan, China 34 H7 33 30N 112 20 E
Funtua, Nigeria 50 F7 11 30N 7 18 E
Fuping, Hebei, China 34 E8 38 48N 114 12 E
Fuping, Shaanxi, China 34 G5 34 42N 109 10 E
Furano, Japan 30 C11 43 21N 142 23 E
Furāt, Nahr al →, Asia 44 D5 31 0N 47 25 E
Fürg, Iran 45 D7 28 18N 55 13 E
Furnás, Spain 22 B8 39 3N 1 32 E
Furnas, Represa de, Brazil 95 A6 20 50S 45 30W
Furneaux Group, Australia 62 G4 40 10S 147 50 E
Furqlus, Syria 47 A6 34 36N 37 8 E
Fürstenwalde, Germany 16 B8 52 22N 14 3 E
Fürth, Germany 16 D6 49 28N 10 59 E
Furukawa, Japan 30 E10 38 34N 140 58 E
Fury and Hecla Str., Canada 69 B11 69 56N 84 0W
Fusagasuga, Colombia 92 C4 4 21N 74 22W
Fushan, Shandong, China 35 F11 37 30N 121 15 E
Fushan, Shanxi, China 34 G6 35 58N 111 51 E
Fushun, China 35 D12 41 50N 123 56 E
Fusong, China 35 C14 42 20N 127 15 E
Futuna, Wall. & F. Is. 59 B8 14 25S 178 20W
Fuxin, China 35 C11 42 5N 121 48 E
Fuyang, China 34 H8 33 0N 115 48 E
Fuyang He →, China 34 E9 38 12N 117 0 E
Fuyu, China 35 B13 45 12N 124 43 E
Fuzhou, China 33 D6 26 5N 119 16 E
Fylde, U.K. 10 D5 53 50N 2 58W
Fyn, Denmark 9 J14 55 20N 10 30 E
Fyne, L., U.K. 12 F3 55 59N 5 23W

G

Gabela, Angola 52 G2 11 0S 14 24 E
Gabès, Tunisia 51 B8 33 53N 10 2 E
Gabès, G. de, Tunisia 51 B8 34 0N 10 30 E
Gabon ■, Africa 52 E2 0 10S 10 0 E
Gaborone, Botswana 56 C4 24 45S 25 57 E
Gabriels, U.S.A. 79 B10 44 26N 74 12W
Gābrīk, Iran 45 E8 25 44N 58 28 E
Gabrovo, Bulgaria 21 C11 42 52N 25 19 E
Gāch Sār, Iran 45 B6 36 7N 51 19 E
Gachsārān, Iran 45 D6 30 15N 50 45 E
Gadag, India 40 M9 15 30N 75 45 E
Gadap, Pakistan 42 G2 25 5N 67 28 E
Gadarwara, India 43 H8 22 50N 78 50 E
Gadhada, India 42 J4 22 0N 71 35 E
Gadra, Pakistan 42 G4 25 40N 70 38 E
Gadsden, U.S.A. 77 H3 34 1N 86 1W
Gadwal, India 40 L10 16 10N 77 50 E
Gaffney, U.S.A. 77 H5 35 5N 81 39W
Gafsa, Tunisia 50 B7 34 24N 8 43 E
Gagaria, India 42 G4 25 43N 70 46 E
Gagnoa, Ivory C. 50 G4 6 56N 5 16W
Gagnon, Canada 71 B6 51 50N 68 5W
Gagnon, L., Canada 73 A6 62 3N 110 27W
Gahini, Rwanda 54 C3 1 50S 30 30 E
Gahmar, India 43 G10 25 27N 83 49 E
Gai Xian = Gaizhou, China 35 D12 40 22N 122 20 E
Gaïdhouronísi, Greece 23 E7 34 53N 25 41 E
Gail, U.S.A. 81 J4 32 46N 101 27W
Gaillimh = Galway, Ireland 13 C2 53 17N 9 3W
Gaines, U.S.A. 78 E7 41 46N 77 35W
Gainesville, Fla., U.S.A. 77 L4 29 40N 82 20W
Gainesville, Ga., U.S.A. 77 H4 34 18N 83 50W
Gainesville, Mo., U.S.A. 81 G8 36 36N 92 26W
Gainesville, Tex., U.S.A. 81 J6 33 38N 97 8W
Gainsborough, U.K. 10 D7 53 24N 0 46W
Gairdner, L., Australia 63 E2 31 30S 136 0 E
Gairloch, L., U.K. 12 D3 57 43N 5 45W
Gaizhou, China 35 D12 40 22N 122 20 E
Gaj →, Pakistan 42 F2 26 26N 67 21 E
Gakuch, Pakistan 43 A5 36 7N 73 45 E
Galán, Cerro, Argentina 94 B2 25 55S 66 52W
Galana →, Kenya 54 C5 3 9S 40 8 E
Galápagos, Pac. Oc. 90 D1 0 0 91 0W
Galashiels, U.K. 12 F6 55 37N 2 49W
Galaţi, Romania 17 F15 45 27N 28 2 E
Galatina, Italy 21 D8 40 10N 18 10 E
Galax, U.S.A. 77 G5 36 40N 80 56W
Galcaio, Somali Rep. 46 F4 6 30N 47 30 E
Galdhøpiggen, Norway 9 F12 61 38N 8 18 E
Galeana, Chihuahua, Mexico 86 A3 30 7N 107 38W
Galeana, Nuevo León, Mexico 86 A3 24 50N 100 4W
Galela, Indonesia 37 D7 1 50N 127 49 E
Galena, U.S.A. 68 B4 64 44N 156 56W
Galera Pt., Trin. & Tob. 89 D7 10 49N 60 54W
Galesburg, U.S.A. 80 E9 40 57N 90 22W
Galeton, U.S.A. 78 E7 41 44N 77 39W
Galich, Russia 24 C7 58 22N 42 24 E
Galicia □, Spain 19 A2 42 43N 7 45W
Galilee = Hagalil, Israel 47 C4 32 53N 35 18 E
Galilee, L., Australia 62 C4 22 20S 145 50 E
Galilee, Sea of = Yam Kinneret, Israel 47 C4 32 45N 35 35 E
Galinoporni, Cyprus 23 D13 35 31N 34 18 E
Galion, U.S.A. 78 F2 40 44N 82 47W
Galiuro Mts., U.S.A. 83 K8 32 30N 110 20W
Galiwinku, Australia 62 A2 12 2S 135 34 E
Gallan Hd., U.K. 12 C1 58 15N 7 2W
Gallatin, U.S.A. 77 G2 36 24N 86 27W
Galle, Sri Lanka 40 R12 6 5N 80 10 E
Gállego →, Spain 19 B5 41 39N 0 51W
Gallegos →, Argentina 96 G3 51 35S 69 0W
Galley Hd., Ireland 13 E3 51 32N 8 55W
Gallinas, Pta., Colombia 92 A4 12 28N 71 40W
Gallipoli = Gelibolu, Turkey 21 D12 40 28N 26 43 E
Gallípoli, Italy 21 D8 40 3N 17 58 E
Gallipolis, U.S.A. 76 F4 38 49N 82 12W
Gällivare, Sweden 8 C19 67 9N 20 40 E
Galloo I., U.S.A. 79 C8 43 55N 76 25W
Galloway, U.K. 12 F4 55 1N 4 29W
Galloway, Mull of, U.K. 12 G4 54 39N 4 52W
Gallup, U.S.A. 83 J9 35 32N 108 45W
Galoya, Sri Lanka 40 Q12 8 10N 80 55 E
Galt, U.S.A. 84 G5 38 15N 121 18W
Galty Mts., Ireland 13 D3 52 22N 8 10W
Galtymore, Ireland 13 D3 52 21N 8 11W
Galva, U.S.A. 80 E9 41 10N 90 3W
Galveston, U.S.A. 81 L7 29 18N 94 48W
Galveston B., U.S.A. 81 L7 29 36N 94 50W
Gálvez, Argentina 94 C3 32 0S 61 14W
Galway, Ireland 13 C2 53 17N 9 3W
Galway □, Ireland 13 C2 53 22N 9 1W
Galway B., Ireland 13 C2 53 13N 9 10W
Gam →, Vietnam 38 B5 21 55N 105 12 E
Gamagōri, Japan 31 G8 34 50N 137 14 E
Gambat, Pakistan 42 F3 27 17N 68 26 E
Gambhir →, India 42 F6 26 58N 77 27 E
Gambia ■, W. Afr. 50 F2 13 25N 16 0W
Gambia →, W. Afr. 50 F2 13 28N 16 34W
Gambier, U.S.A. 78 F2 40 22N 82 23W
Gambier, C., Australia 60 B5 11 56S 130 57 E
Gambier Is., Australia 63 F2 35 3S 136 30 E
Gambo, Canada 71 C9 48 47N 54 13W
Gamboli, Pakistan 42 E3 29 53N 68 24 E
Gamboma, Congo 52 E3 1 55S 15 52 E
Gamka →, S. Africa 56 E3 33 18S 21 39 E
Gamkab →, Namibia 56 D2 28 4S 17 54 E
Gamlakarleby = Kokkola, Finland 8 E20 63 50N 23 8 E
Gammon →, Canada 73 C9 51 24N 95 44W
Gamtoos →, S. Africa 56 E4 33 58S 25 1 E
Gan Jiang →, China 33 D6 29 15N 116 0 E
Ganado, U.S.A. 83 J9 35 43N 109 33W
Gananoque, Canada 79 B8 44 20N 76 10W
Ganāveh, Iran 45 D6 29 35N 50 35 E
Gäncä, Azerbaijan 25 F8 40 45N 46 20 E
Gancheng, China 38 C7 18 51N 108 37 E
Gand = Gent, Belgium 15 C3 51 2N 3 42 E
Ganda, Angola 53 G2 13 3S 14 35 E
Gandajika, Dem. Rep. of the Congo 52 F4 6 45S 23 57 E
Gandak →, India 43 G11 25 39N 85 13 E
Gandava, Pakistan 42 E2 28 32N 67 32 E
Gander, Canada 71 C9 48 58N 54 35W
Gander L., Canada 71 C9 48 58N 54 35W
Ganderowe Falls, Zimbabwe 55 F2 17 20S 29 10 E
Gandhi Sagar, India 42 G6 24 40N 75 40 E
Gandhinagar, India 42 H5 23 15N 72 45 E
Gandía, Spain 19 C5 38 58N 0 9W
Gando, Pta., Canary Is. 22 G4 27 55N 15 22W
Ganedidalem = Gani, Indonesia 37 E7 0 48S 128 14 E
Ganga →, India 43 H14 23 20N 90 30 E
Ganga Sagar, India 43 J13 21 38N 88 5 E
Gangan →, India 43 E8 28 38N 78 58 E
Ganganagar, India 42 E5 29 56N 73 56 E
Gangapur, India 42 F7 26 32N 76 49 E
Gangaw, Burma 41 H19 22 5N 94 5 E
Gangdisê Shan, China 41 D12 31 20N 81 0 E
Ganges = Ganga →, India 43 H14 23 20N 90 30 E
Ganges, Canada 72 D4 48 51N 123 31W
Ganges, Mouths of the, India 43 J14 21 30N 90 0 E
Gangoh, India 42 E7 29 46N 77 18 E
Gangroti, India 43 D8 30 50N 79 10 E
Gangtok, India 41 F16 27 20N 88 37 E
Gangu, China 34 G3 34 40N 105 15 E
Gangyao, China 35 B14 44 12N 126 37 E
Gani, Indonesia 37 E7 0 48S 128 14 E
Ganj, India 43 F8 27 45N 78 57 E
Gannett Peak, U.S.A. 82 E9 43 11N 109 39W
Ganquan, China 34 F5 36 20N 109 20 E
Gansu □, China 34 G3 36 0N 104 0 E
Ganta, Liberia 50 G4 7 15N 8 59W
Gantheaume, C., Australia 63 F2 36 4S 137 32 E
Gantheaume B., Australia 61 E1 27 40S 114 10 E
Gantsevichi = Hantsavichy, Belarus 17 B14 52 49N 26 30 E
Ganyem = Genyem, Indonesia 37 E10 2 46S 140 12 E
Ganyu, China 35 G10 34 50N 119 8 E
Ganzhou, China 33 D6 25 51N 114 56 E
Gao, Mali 50 E5 16 15N 0 5W
Gaomi, China 35 F10 36 20N 119 42 E
Gaoping, China 34 G7 35 45N 112 55 E
Gaotang, China 34 F9 36 50N 116 15 E
Gaoua, Burkina Faso 50 F5 10 20N 3 8W
Gaoual, Guinea 50 F3 11 45N 13 25W
Gaoxiong = Kaohsiung, Taiwan 33 D7 22 35N 120 16 E
Gaoyang, China 34 E8 38 40N 115 45 E
Gaoyou Hu, China 35 H10 32 45N 119 20 E
Gaoyuan, China 35 F9 37 8N 117 58 E
Gap, France 18 D7 44 33N 6 5 E
Gapat →, India 43 G10 24 30N 82 28 E
Gapuwiyak, Australia 62 A2 12 25S 135 43 E
Gar, China 32 C2 32 10N 79 58 E
Garabogazköl Aylagy, Turkmenistan 25 F9 41 0N 53 30 E
Garachico, Canary Is. 22 F3 28 22N 16 46W
Garachiné, Panama 88 E4 8 0N 78 12W
Garafia, Canary Is. 22 F2 28 48N 17 57W
Garah, Australia 63 D4 29 5S 149 38 E
Garajonay, Canary Is. 22 F2 28 7N 17 14W
Garanhuns, Brazil 93 E11 8 50S 36 30W
Garautha, India 43 G8 25 34N 79 18 E
Garba Tula, Kenya 54 B4 0 30N 38 32 E
Garberville, U.S.A. 82 F2 40 6N 123 48W
Garbiyang, India 43 D9 30 8N 80 54 E
Garda, L. di, Italy 20 B4 45 40N 10 41 E
Garde L., Canada 73 A7 62 50N 106 13W
Garden City, Ga., U.S.A. 77 J5 32 6N 81 9W
Garden City, Kans., U.S.A. 81 G4 37 58N 100 53W
Garden City, Tex., U.S.A. 81 K4 31 52N 101 29W

Garden Grove, *U.S.A.* **85 M9** 33 47N 117 55W
Gardēz, *Afghan.* **42 C3** 33 37N 69 9 E
Gardiner, *Maine, U.S.A.* **77 C11** 44 14N 69 47W
Gardiner, *Mont., U.S.A.* **82 D8** 45 2N 110 22W
Gardiners I., *U.S.A.* **79 E12** 41 6N 72 6W
Gardner, *U.S.A.* **79 D13** 42 34N 71 59W
Gardner Canal, *Canada* **72 C3** 53 27N 128 8W
Gardnerville, *U.S.A.* **84 G7** 38 56N 119 45W
Gardo, *Somali Rep.* **46 F4** 9 30N 49 6 E
Garey, *U.S.A.* **85 L6** 34 53N 120 19W
Garfield, *U.S.A.* **82 C5** 47 1N 117 9W
Garforth, *U.K.* **10 D6** 53 47N 1 24W
Gargano, Mte., *Italy* **20 D6** 41 43N 15 43 E
Garibaldi Prov. Park, *Canada* **72 D4** 49 50N 122 40W
Gariep, L., *S. Africa* **56 E4** 30 40S 25 40 E
Garies, *S. Africa* **56 E2** 30 32S 17 59 E
Garigliano →, *Italy* **20 D5** 41 13N 13 45 E
Garissa, *Kenya* **54 C4** 0 25S 39 40 E
Garland, *Tex., U.S.A.* **81 J6** 32 55N 96 38W
Garland, *Utah, U.S.A.* **82 F7** 41 47N 112 10W
Garm, *Tajikistan* **26 F8** 39 0N 70 20 E
Garmāb, *Iran* **45 C8** 35 25N 56 45 E
Garmisch-Partenkirchen, *Germany* **16 E6** 47 30N 11 6 E
Garmo, Qullai = Kommunizma, Pik, *Tajikistan* **26 F8** 39 0N 72 2 E
Garmsār, *Iran* **45 C7** 35 20N 52 25 E
Garner, *U.S.A.* **80 D8** 43 6N 93 36W
Garnett, *U.S.A.* **80 F7** 38 17N 95 14W
Garo Hills, *India* **43 G14** 25 30N 90 30 E
Garoe, *Somali Rep.* **46 F4** 8 25N 48 33 E
Garonne →, *France* **18 D3** 45 2N 0 36W
Garoowe = Garoe, *Somali Rep.* **46 F4** 8 25N 48 33 E
Garot, *India* **42 G6** 24 19N 75 41 E
Garoua, *Cameroon* **51 G8** 9 19N 13 21 E
Garrauli, *India* **43 G8** 25 5N 79 22 E
Garrison, *Mont., U.S.A.* **82 C7** 46 31N 112 49W
Garrison, *N. Dak., U.S.A.* **80 B4** 47 40N 101 25W
Garrison Res. = Sakakawea, L., *U.S.A.* **80 B4** 47 30N 101 25W
Garron Pt., *U.K.* **13 A6** 55 3N 5 59W
Garry →, *U.K.* **12 E5** 56 44N 3 47W
Garry, L., *Canada* **68 B9** 65 58N 100 18W
Garsen, *Kenya* **54 C5** 2 20S 40 5 E
Garson L., *Canada* **73 B6** 56 19N 110 2W
Garu, *India* **43 H11** 23 40N 84 14 E
Garub, *Namibia* **56 D2** 26 37S 16 0 E
Garut, *Indonesia* **37 G12** 7 14S 107 53 E
Garvie Mts., *N.Z.* **59 L2** 45 30S 168 50 E
Garwa = Garoua, *Cameroon* **51 G8** 9 19N 13 21 E
Garwa, *India* **43 G10** 24 11N 83 47 E
Gary, *U.S.A.* **76 E2** 41 36N 87 20W
Garzê, *China* **32 C5** 31 38N 100 1 E
Garzón, *Colombia* **92 C3** 2 10N 75 40W
Gas-San, *Japan* **30 E10** 38 32N 140 1 E
Gasan Kuli = Esenguly, *Turkmenistan* **26 F6** 37 37N 53 59 E
Gascogne, *France* **18 E4** 43 45N 0 20 E
Gascogne, G. de, *Europe* **18 D2** 44 0N 2 0W
Gascony = Gascogne, *France* **18 E4** 43 45N 0 20 E
Gascoyne →, *Australia* **61 D1** 24 52S 113 37 E
Gascoyne Junction, *Australia* **61 E2** 25 2S 115 17 E
Gashaka, *Nigeria* **51 G8** 7 20N 11 29 E
Gasherbrum, *Pakistan* **43 B7** 35 40N 76 40 E
Gashua, *Nigeria* **51 F8** 12 54N 11 0 E
Gaspé, *Canada* **71 C7** 48 52N 64 30W
Gaspé, C. de, *Canada* **71 C7** 48 48N 64 7W
Gaspé, Pén. de, *Canada* **71 C6** 48 45N 65 40W
Gaspésie, Parc de Conservation de la, *Canada* **71 C6** 48 55N 65 50W
Gasteiz = Vitoria-Gasteiz, *Spain* **19 A4** 42 50N 2 41W
Gastonia, *U.S.A.* **77 H5** 35 16N 81 11W
Gastre, *Argentina* **96 E3** 42 20S 69 15W
Gata, C., *Cyprus* **23 E12** 34 34N 33 2 E
Gata, C. de, *Spain* **19 D4** 36 41N 2 13W
Gata, Sierra de, *Spain* **19 B2** 40 20N 6 45W
Gataga →, *Canada* **72 B3** 58 35N 126 59W
Gatehouse of Fleet, *U.K.* **12 G4** 54 53N 4 12W
Gates, *U.S.A.* **78 C7** 43 9N 77 42W
Gateshead, *U.K.* **10 C6** 54 57N 1 35W
Gatesville, *U.S.A.* **81 K6** 31 26N 97 45W
Gaths, *Zimbabwe* **55 G3** 20 2S 30 32 E
Gatico, *Chile* **94 A1** 22 29S 70 20W
Gatineau, *Canada* **79 A9** 45 29N 75 38W
Gatineau →, *Canada* **70 C4** 45 27N 75 42W
Gatineau, Parc Nat. de la, *Canada* **70 C4** 45 40N 76 0W
Gatton, *Australia* **63 D5** 27 32S 152 17 E
Gatun, L., *Panama* **88 E4** 9 7N 79 56W
Gatyana, *S. Africa* **57 E4** 32 16S 28 31 E
Gau, *Fiji* **59 D8** 18 2S 179 18 E
Gauer L., *Canada* **73 B9** 57 0N 97 50W
Gauhati = Guwahati, *India* **41 F17** 26 10N 91 45 E
Gauja →, *Latvia* **9 H21** 57 10N 24 16 E
Gaula →, *Norway* **8 E14** 63 21N 10 14 E
Gauri Phanta, *India* **43 E9** 28 41N 80 36 E
Gausta, *Norway* **9 G13** 59 48N 8 40 E
Gauteng □, *S. Africa* **57 D4** 26 0S 28 0 E
Gāv Koshī, *Iran* **45 D8** 28 38N 57 12 E
Gāvakān, *Iran* **45 D7** 29 37N 53 10 E
Gavāter, *Iran* **45 E9** 25 10N 61 31 E
Gāvbandī, *Iran* **45 E7** 27 12N 53 4 E
Gavdhopoúla, *Greece* **23 E6** 34 56N 24 0 E
Gávdhos, *Greece* **23 E6** 34 50N 24 5 E
Gaviota, *U.S.A.* **85 L6** 34 29N 120 13W
Gāvkhūnī, Bāṭlāq-e, *Iran* **45 C7** 32 6N 52 52 E
Gävle, *Sweden* **9 F17** 60 40N 17 9 E
Gawachab, *Namibia* **56 D2** 27 4S 17 55 E
Gawilgarh Hills, *India* **40 J10** 21 15N 76 45 E
Gawler, *Australia* **63 E2** 34 30S 138 42 E
Gaxun Nur, *China* **32 B5** 42 22N 100 30 E
Gay, *Russia* **24 D10** 51 27N 58 27 E
Gaya, *India* **43 G11** 24 47N 85 4 E
Gaya, *Niger* **50 F6** 11 52N 3 28 E
Gaylord, *U.S.A.* **76 C3** 45 2N 84 41W
Gayndah, *Australia* **63 D5** 25 35S 151 32 E
Gaysin = Haysyn, *Ukraine* **17 D15** 48 57N 29 25 E
Gayvoron = Hayvoron, *Ukraine* **17 D15** 48 22N 29 52 E
Gaza, *Gaza Strip* **47 D3** 31 30N 34 28 E
Gaza □, *Mozam.* **57 C5** 23 10S 32 45 E
Gaza Strip □, *Asia* **47 D3** 31 29N 34 25 E
Gazanjyk, *Turkmenistan* **45 B7** 39 16N 55 32 E
Gāzbor, *Iran* **45 D8** 28 5N 58 51 E
Gazi, *Dem. Rep. of the Congo* **54 B1** 1 3N 24 30 E
Gaziantep, *Turkey* **25 G6** 37 6N 37 23 E
Gcoverega, *Botswana* **56 B3** 19 8S 24 18 E
Gcuwa, *S. Africa* **57 E4** 32 20S 28 11 E
Gdańsk, *Poland* **17 A10** 54 22N 18 40 E
Gdańska, Zatoka, *Poland* **17 A10** 54 30N 19 20 E
Gdov, *Russia* **9 G22** 58 48N 27 55 E
Gdynia, *Poland* **17 A10** 54 35N 18 33 E
Gebe, *Indonesia* **37 D7** 0 5N 129 25 E
Gebze, *Turkey* **21 D13** 40 47N 29 25 E
Gedaref, *Sudan* **51 F13** 14 2N 35 28 E
Gediz →, *Turkey* **21 E12** 38 35N 26 48 E
Gedser, *Denmark* **9 J14** 54 35N 11 55 E
Geegully Cr. →, *Australia* **60 C3** 18 32S 123 41 E
Geel, *Belgium* **15 C4** 51 10N 4 59 E
Geelong, *Australia* **63 F3** 38 10S 144 22 E
Geelvink B. = Cenderwasih, Teluk, *Indonesia* **37 E9** 3 0S 135 20 E
Geelvink Chan., *Australia* **61 E1** 28 30S 114 0 E
Geesthacht, *Germany* **16 B6** 53 26N 10 22 E
Geidam, *Nigeria* **51 F8** 12 57N 11 57 E
Geikie →, *Canada* **73 B8** 57 45N 103 52W
Geistown, *U.S.A.* **78 F6** 40 18N 78 52W
Geita, *Tanzania* **54 C3** 2 48S 32 12 E
Gejiu, *China* **32 D5** 23 20N 103 10 E
Gel, Meydān-e, *Iran* **45 D7** 29 4N 54 50 E
Gela, *Italy* **20 F6** 37 4N 14 15 E
Gelderland □, *Neths.* **15 B6** 52 5N 6 10 E
Geldrop, *Neths.* **15 C5** 51 25N 5 32 E
Geleen, *Neths.* **15 D5** 50 57N 5 49 E
Gelibolu, *Turkey* **21 D12** 40 28N 26 43 E
Gelsenkirchen, *Germany* **16 C4** 51 32N 7 6 E
Gemas, *Malaysia* **39 L4** 2 37N 102 36 E
Gembloux, *Belgium* **15 D4** 50 34N 4 43 E
Gemena, *Dem. Rep. of the Congo* **52 D3** 3 13N 19 48 E
Gemerek, *Turkey* **44 B3** 39 15N 36 10 E
Gemlik, *Turkey* **21 D13** 40 26N 29 9 E
Genale →, *Ethiopia* **46 F2** 6 2N 39 1 E
General Acha, *Argentina* **94 D3** 37 20S 64 38W
General Alvear, *Buenos Aires, Argentina* **94 D4** 36 0S 60 0W
General Alvear, *Mendoza, Argentina* **94 D2** 35 0S 67 40W
General Artigas, *Paraguay* **94 B4** 26 52S 56 16W
General Belgrano, *Argentina* **94 D4** 36 35S 58 47W
General Cabrera, *Argentina* **94 C3** 32 53S 63 52W
General Cepeda, *Mexico* **86 B4** 25 23N 101 27W
General Guido, *Argentina* **94 D4** 36 40S 57 50W
General Juan Madariaga, *Argentina* **94 D4** 37 0S 57 0W
General La Madrid, *Argentina* **94 D3** 37 17S 61 20W
General MacArthur, *Phil.* **37 B7** 11 18N 125 28 E
General Martin Miguel de Güemes, *Argentina* **94 A3** 24 50S 65 0W
General Paz, *Argentina* **94 B4** 27 45S 57 36W
General Pico, *Argentina* **94 D3** 35 45S 63 50W
General Pinedo, *Argentina* **94 B3** 27 15S 61 20W
General Pinto, *Argentina* **94 C3** 34 45S 61 50W
General Roca, *Argentina* **96 D3** 39 2S 67 35W
General Santos, *Phil.* **37 C7** 6 5N 125 14 E
General Trevino, *Mexico* **87 B5** 26 14N 99 29W
General Trías, *Mexico* **86 B3** 28 21N 106 22W
General Viamonte, *Argentina* **94 D3** 35 1S 61 3W
General Villegas, *Argentina* **94 D3** 35 5S 63 0W
Genesee, *Idaho, U.S.A.* **82 C5** 46 33N 116 56W
Genesee, *Pa., U.S.A.* **78 E7** 41 59N 77 54W
Genesee →, *U.S.A.* **78 C7** 43 16N 77 36W
Geneseo, *Ill., U.S.A.* **80 E9** 41 27N 90 9W
Geneseo, *N.Y., U.S.A.* **78 D7** 42 48N 77 49W
Geneva = Genève, *Switz.* **18 C7** 46 12N 6 9 E
Geneva, *Ala., U.S.A.* **77 K3** 31 2N 85 52W
Geneva, *N.Y., U.S.A.* **78 D8** 42 52N 76 59W
Geneva, *Nebr., U.S.A.* **80 E6** 40 32N 97 36W
Geneva, *Ohio, U.S.A.* **78 E4** 41 48N 80 57W
Geneva, L. = Léman, L., *Europe* **18 C7** 46 26N 6 30 E
Geneva, L., *U.S.A.* **76 D1** 42 38N 88 30W
Genève, *Switz.* **18 C7** 46 12N 6 9 E
Genil →, *Spain* **19 D3** 37 42N 5 19W
Genk, *Belgium* **15 D5** 50 58N 5 32 E
Gennargentu, Mti. del, *Italy* **20 D3** 40 1N 9 19 E
Genoa = Génova, *Italy* **18 D8** 44 25N 8 57 E
Genoa, *Australia* **63 F4** 37 29S 149 35 E
Genoa, *N.Y., U.S.A.* **79 D8** 42 40N 76 32W
Genoa, *Nebr., U.S.A.* **80 E6** 41 27N 97 44W
Genoa, *Nev., U.S.A.* **84 F7** 39 2N 119 50W
Génova, *Italy* **18 D8** 44 25N 8 57 E
Génova, G. di, *Italy* **20 C3** 44 0N 9 0 E
Genriyetty, Ostrov, *Russia* **27 B16** 77 6N 156 30 E
Gent, *Belgium* **15 C3** 51 2N 3 42 E
Genteng, *Indonesia* **37 G12** 7 22S 106 24 E
Genyem, *Indonesia* **37 E10** 2 46S 140 12 E
Geographe B., *Australia* **61 F2** 33 30S 115 15 E
Geographe Chan., *Australia* **61 D1** 24 30S 113 0 E
Georga, Zemlya, *Russia* **26 A5** 80 30N 49 0 E
George, *S. Africa* **56 E3** 33 58S 22 29 E
George →, *Canada* **71 A6** 58 49N 66 10W
George, L., *N.S.W., Australia* **63 F4** 35 10S 149 25 E
George, L., *S. Austral., Australia* **63 F3** 37 25S 140 0 E
George, L., *W. Austral., Australia* **60 D3** 22 45S 123 40 E
George, L., *Uganda* **54 B3** 0 5N 30 10 E
George, L., *Fla., U.S.A.* **77 L5** 29 17N 81 36W
George, L., *N.Y., U.S.A.* **79 C11** 43 37N 73 33W
George Gill Ra., *Australia* **60 D5** 24 22S 131 45 E
George River = Kangiqsualujjuaq, *Canada* **69 C13** 58 30N 65 59W
George Sound, *N.Z.* **59 L1** 44 52S 167 25 E
George Town, *Australia* **62 G4** 41 6S 146 49 E
George Town, *Bahamas* **88 B4** 23 33N 75 47W
George Town, *Cayman Is.* **88 C3** 19 20N 81 24W
George Town, *Malaysia* **39 K3** 5 25N 100 20 E
George V Land, *Antarctica* **5 C10** 69 0S 148 0 E
George VI Sound, *Antarctica* **5 D17** 71 0S 68 0W
George West, *U.S.A.* **81 L5** 28 20N 98 7W
Georgetown, *Australia* **62 B3** 18 17S 143 33 E
Georgetown, *Ont., Canada* **78 C5** 43 40N 79 56W
Georgetown, *P.E.I., Canada* **71 C7** 46 13N 62 24W
Georgetown, *Gambia* **50 F3** 13 30N 14 47W
Georgetown, *Guyana* **92 B7** 6 50N 58 12W
Georgetown, *Calif., U.S.A.* **84 G6** 38 54N 120 50W
Georgetown, *Colo., U.S.A.* **82 G11** 39 42N 105 42W
Georgetown, *Ky., U.S.A.* **76 F3** 38 13N 84 33W
Georgetown, *N.Y., U.S.A.* **79 D9** 42 46N 75 44W
Georgetown, *Ohio, U.S.A.* **76 F4** 38 52N 83 54W
Georgetown, *S.C., U.S.A.* **77 J6** 33 23N 79 17W
Georgetown, *Tex., U.S.A.* **81 K6** 30 38N 97 41W
Georgia □, *U.S.A.* **77 K5** 32 50N 83 15W
Georgia ■, *Asia* **25 F7** 42 0N 43 0 E
Georgia, Str. of, *Canada* **72 D4** 49 25N 124 0W
Georgian B., *Canada* **78 A4** 45 15N 81 0W
Georgina →, *Australia* **62 C2** 23 30S 139 47 E
Georgina I., *Canada* **78 B5** 44 22N 79 17W
Georgiu-Dezh = Liski, *Russia* **25 D6** 51 3N 39 30 E
Georgiyevsk, *Russia* **25 F7** 44 12N 43 28 E
Gera, *Germany* **16 C7** 50 53N 12 4 E
Geraardsbergen, *Belgium* **15 D3** 50 45N 3 53 E
Geral, Serra, *Brazil* **95 B6** 26 25S 50 0W
Geral de Goiás, Serra, *Brazil* **93 F9** 12 0S 46 0W
Geraldine, *U.S.A.* **82 C8** 47 36N 110 16W
Geraldton, *Australia* **61 E1** 28 48S 114 32 E
Geraldton, *Canada* **70 C2** 49 44N 86 59W
Gereshk, *Afghan.* **40 D4** 31 47N 64 35 E
Gerik, *Malaysia* **39 K3** 5 50N 101 15 E
Gering, *U.S.A.* **80 E3** 41 50N 103 40W
Gerlach, *U.S.A.* **82 F4** 40 39N 119 21W
Germansen Landing, *Canada* **72 B4** 55 43N 124 40W
Germantown, *U.S.A.* **81 M10** 35 5N 89 49W
Germany ■, *Europe* **16 C6** 51 0N 10 0 E
Germī, *Iran* **45 B6** 39 1N 48 3 E
Germiston, *S. Africa* **57 D4** 26 15S 28 10 E
Gernika-Lumo, *Spain* **19 A4** 43 19N 2 40W
Gero, *Japan* **31 G8** 35 48N 137 14 E
Gerona = Girona, *Spain* **19 B7** 41 58N 2 46 E
Gerrard, *Canada* **72 C5** 50 30N 117 17W
Geser, *Indonesia* **37 E8** 3 50S 130 54 E
Getafe, *Spain* **19 B4** 40 18N 3 44W
Gettysburg, *Pa., U.S.A.* **76 F7** 39 50N 77 14W
Gettysburg, *S. Dak., U.S.A.* **80 C5** 45 1N 99 57W
Getxo, *Spain* **19 A4** 43 21N 2 59W
Getz Ice Shelf, *Antarctica* **5 D14** 75 0S 130 0W
Geyser, *U.S.A.* **82 C8** 47 16N 110 30W
Geyserville, *U.S.A.* **84 G4** 38 42N 122 54W
Ghaggar →, *India* **42 E6** 29 30N 74 53 E
Ghaghara →, *India* **43 G11** 25 45N 84 40 E
Ghaghat →, *Bangla.* **43 G13** 25 19N 89 38 E
Ghagra, *India* **43 H11** 23 17N 84 33 E
Ghagra →, *India* **43 F9** 27 29N 81 9 E
Ghana ■, *W. Afr.* **50 G5** 8 0N 1 0W
Ghansor, *India* **43 H9** 22 39N 80 1 E
Ghanzi, *Botswana* **56 C3** 21 50S 21 34 E
Ghardaïa, *Algeria* **50 B6** 32 20N 3 37 E
Gharyān, *Libya* **51 B8** 32 10N 13 0 E
Ghat, *Libya* **51 D8** 24 59N 10 11 E
Ghatal, *India* **43 H12** 22 40N 87 46 E
Ghatampur, *India* **43 F9** 26 8N 80 13 E
Ghatsila, *India* **43 H12** 22 36N 86 29 E
Ghaṭṭī, *Si. Arabia* **44 D3** 31 16N 37 31 E
Ghawdex = Gozo, *Malta* **23 C1** 36 3N 14 15 E
Ghazal, Bahr el →, *Chad* **51 F9** 13 0N 15 47 E
Ghazâl, Bahr el →, *Sudan* **51 G12** 9 31N 30 25 E
Ghaziabad, *India* **42 E7** 28 42N 77 26 E
Ghazipur, *India* **43 G10** 25 38N 83 35 E
Ghaznī, *Afghan.* **42 C3** 33 30N 68 28 E
Ghaznī □, *Afghan.* **40 C6** 32 10N 68 20 E
Ghent = Gent, *Belgium* **15 C3** 51 2N 3 42 E
Gheorghe Gheorghiu-Dej = Oneşti, *Romania* **17 E14** 46 17N 26 47 E
Ghīnah, Wādī al →, *Si. Arabia* **44 D3** 30 27N 38 14 E
Ghizao, *Afghan.* **42 C1** 33 20N 65 44 E
Ghizar →, *Pakistan* **43 A5** 36 15N 73 43 E
Ghotaru, *India* **42 F4** 27 20N 70 1 E
Ghotki, *Pakistan* **42 E3** 28 5N 69 21 E
Ghowr □, *Afghan.* **40 C4** 34 0N 64 20 E
Ghudaf, W. al →, *Iraq* **44 C4** 32 56N 43 30 E
Ghudāmis, *Libya* **49 C4** 30 11N 9 29 E
Ghughri, *India* **43 H9** 22 39N 80 41 E
Ghugus, *India* **40 K11** 19 58N 79 12 E
Ghulam Mohammad Barrage, *Pakistan* **42 G3** 25 30N 68 20 E
Ghūrīān, *Afghan.* **40 B2** 34 17N 61 25 E
Gia Dinh, *Vietnam* **39 G6** 10 49N 106 42 E
Gia Lai = Plei Ku, *Vietnam* **38 F7** 13 57N 108 0 E
Gia Nghia, *Vietnam* **39 G6** 11 58N 107 42 E
Gia Ngoc, *Vietnam* **38 E7** 14 50N 108 58 E
Gia Vuc, *Vietnam* **38 E7** 14 42N 108 34 E
Giant Forest, *U.S.A.* **84 J8** 36 36N 118 43W
Giants Causeway, *U.K.* **13 A5** 55 16N 6 29W
Giarabub = Al Jaghbūb, *Libya* **51 C10** 29 42N 24 38 E
Giarre, *Italy* **20 F6** 37 43N 15 11 E
Gibara, *Cuba* **88 B4** 21 9N 76 11W
Gibb River, *Australia* **60 C4** 16 26S 126 26 E
Gibbon, *U.S.A.* **80 E5** 40 45N 98 51W
Gibeon, *Namibia* **56 D2** 25 9S 17 43 E
Gibraltar ■, *Europe* **19 D3** 36 7N 5 22W
Gibraltar, Str. of, *Medit. S.* **19 E3** 35 55N 5 40W
Gibson Desert, *Australia* **60 D4** 24 0S 126 0 E
Gibsons, *Canada* **72 D4** 49 24N 123 32W
Gibsonville, *U.S.A.* **84 F6** 39 46N 120 54W
Giddings, *U.S.A.* **81 K6** 30 11N 96 56W
Giebnegáisi = Kebnekaise, *Sweden* **8 C18** 67 53N 18 33 E
Giessen, *Germany* **16 C5** 50 34N 8 41 E
Gīfān, *Iran* **45 B8** 37 54N 57 28 E
Gift Lake, *Canada* **72 B5** 55 53N 115 49W
Gifu, *Japan* **31 G8** 35 30N 136 45 E
Gifu □, *Japan* **31 G8** 35 40N 137 0 E
Giganta, Sa. de la, *Mexico* **86 B2** 25 30N 111 30W
Gigha, *U.K.* **12 F3** 55 42N 5 44W
Giglio, *Italy* **20 C4** 42 20N 10 52 E
Gijón, *Spain* **19 A3** 43 32N 5 42W
Gil I., *Canada* **72 C3** 53 12N 129 15W
Gila →, *U.S.A.* **83 K6** 32 43N 114 33W
Gila Bend, *U.S.A.* **83 K7** 32 57N 112 43W
Gila Bend Mts., *U.S.A.* **83 K7** 33 10N 113 0W
Gīlān □, *Iran* **45 B6** 37 0N 50 0 E
Gilbert →, *Australia* **62 B3** 16 35S 141 15 E
Gilbert Is., *Kiribati* **64 G9** 1 0N 172 0 E
Gilbert River, *Australia* **62 B3** 18 9S 142 52 E
Gilead, *U.S.A.* **79 B14** 44 24N 70 59W
Gilford I., *Canada* **72 C3** 50 40N 126 30W
Gilgandra, *Australia* **63 E4** 31 43S 148 39 E
Gilgil, *Kenya* **54 C4** 0 30S 36 20 E
Gilgit, *India* **43 B6** 35 50N 74 15 E
Gilgit →, *Pakistan* **43 B6** 35 44N 74 37 E
Gillam, *Canada* **73 B10** 56 20N 94 40W
Gillen, L., *Australia* **61 E3** 26 11S 124 38 E
Gilles, L., *Australia* **63 E2** 32 50S 136 45 E
Gillette, *U.S.A.* **80 C2** 44 18N 105 30W
Gilliat, *Australia* **62 C3** 20 40S 141 28 E
Gillingham, *U.K.* **11 F8** 51 23N 0 33 E
Gilmer, *U.S.A.* **81 J7** 32 44N 94 57W
Gilmore, L., *Australia* **61 F3** 32 29S 121 37 E
Gilroy, *U.S.A.* **84 H5** 37 1N 121 34W
Gimli, *Canada* **73 C9** 50 40N 97 0W
Gin Gin, *Australia* **63 D5** 25 0S 151 58 E
Gingin, *Australia* **61 F2** 31 22S 115 54 E
Gingindlovu, *S. Africa* **57 D5** 29 2S 31 30 E
Ginir, *Ethiopia* **46 F3** 7 6N 40 40 E
Gióna, Óros, *Greece* **21 E10** 38 38N 22 14 E
Gir Hills, *India* **42 J4** 21 0N 71 0 E
Girab, *India* **42 F4** 26 2N 70 38 E
Girâfi, W. →, *Egypt* **47 F3** 29 58N 34 39 E
Girard, *Kans., U.S.A.* **81 G7** 37 31N 94 51W
Girard, *Ohio, U.S.A.* **78 E4** 41 9N 80 42W
Girard, *Pa., U.S.A.* **78 E4** 42 0N 80 19W
Girdle Ness, *U.K.* **12 D6** 57 9N 2 3W
Giresun, *Turkey* **25 F6** 40 55N 38 30 E
Girga, *Egypt* **51 C12** 26 17N 31 55 E
Giri →, *India* **42 D7** 30 28N 77 41 E
Giridih, *India* **43 G12** 24 10N 86 21 E
Girne = Kyrenia, *Cyprus* **23 D12** 35 20N 33 20 E
Girona, *Spain* **19 B7** 41 58N 2 46 E
Gironde →, *France* **18 D3** 45 32N 1 7W
Giru, *Australia* **62 B4** 19 30S 147 5 E
Girvan, *U.K.* **12 F4** 55 14N 4 51W
Gisborne, *N.Z.* **59 H7** 38 39S 178 5 E
Gisenyi, *Rwanda* **54 C2** 1 41S 29 15 E
Gislaved, *Sweden* **9 H15** 57 19N 13 32 E
Gitega, *Burundi* **54 C2** 3 26S 29 56 E
Giuba →, *Somali Rep.* **46 G3** 1 30N 42 35 E
Giurgiu, *Romania* **17 G13** 43 52N 25 57 E
Giza = El Gîza, *Egypt* **51 C12** 30 0N 31 10 E
Gizhiga, *Russia* **27 C17** 62 3N 160 30 E
Gizhiginskaya Guba, *Russia* **27 C16** 61 0N 158 0 E
Giżycko, *Poland* **17 A11** 54 2N 21 48 E
Gjirokastër, *Albania* **21 D9** 40 7N 20 10 E
Gjoa Haven, *Canada* **68 B10** 68 20N 96 8W
Gjøvik, *Norway* **9 F14** 60 47N 10 43 E
Glace Bay, *Canada* **71 C8** 46 11N 59 58W
Glacier Bay Nat. Park and Preserve, *U.S.A.* **72 B1** 58 45N 136 30W
Glacier Nat. Park, *Canada* **72 C5** 51 15N 117 30W
Glacier Nat. Park, *U.S.A.* **82 B7** 48 30N 113 18W
Glacier Peak, *U.S.A.* **82 B3** 48 7N 121 7W
Gladewater, *U.S.A.* **81 J7** 32 33N 94 56W
Gladstone, *Queens., Australia* **62 C5** 23 52S 151 16 E
Gladstone, *S. Austral., Australia* **63 E2** 33 15S 138 22 E
Gladstone, *Canada* **73 C9** 50 13N 98 57W
Gladstone, *U.S.A.* **76 C2** 45 51N 87 1W
Gladwin, *U.S.A.* **76 D3** 43 59N 84 29W
Glåma = Glomma →, *Norway* **9 G14** 59 12N 10 57 E
Gláma, *Iceland* **8 D2** 65 48N 23 0W
Glamis, *U.S.A.* **85 N11** 32 55N 115 5W
Glasco, *Kans., U.S.A.* **80 F6** 39 22N 97 50W
Glasco, *N.Y., U.S.A.* **79 D11** 42 3N 73 57W
Glasgow, *U.K.* **12 F4** 55 51N 4 15W
Glasgow, *Ky., U.S.A.* **76 G3** 37 0N 85 55W
Glasgow, *Mont., U.S.A.* **82 B10** 48 12N 106 38W
Glasgow, City of □, *U.K.* **12 F4** 55 51N 4 12W
Glaslyn, *Canada* **73 C7** 53 22N 108 21W
Glastonbury, *U.K.* **11 F5** 51 9N 2 43W
Glastonbury, *U.S.A.* **79 E12** 41 43N 72 37W
Glazov, *Russia* **24 C9** 58 9N 52 40 E
Gleichen, *Canada* **72 C6** 50 52N 113 3W
Gleiwitz = Gliwice, *Poland* **17 C10** 50 22N 18 41 E
Glen, *U.S.A.* **79 B13** 44 7N 71 11W
Glen Affric, *U.K.* **12 D3** 57 17N 5 1W
Glen Canyon, *U.S.A.* **83 H8** 37 30N 110 40W
Glen Canyon Dam, *U.S.A.* **83 H8** 36 57N 111 29W
Glen Canyon Nat. Recr. Area, *U.S.A.* **83 H8** 37 15N 111 0W
Glen Coe, *U.K.* **12 E3** 56 40N 5 0W
Glen Cove, *U.S.A.* **79 F11** 40 52N 73 38W
Glen Garry, *U.K.* **12 D3** 57 3N 5 7W
Glen Innes, *Australia* **63 D5** 29 44S 151 44 E
Glen Lyon, *U.S.A.* **79 E8** 41 10N 76 5W
Glen Mor, *U.K.* **12 D4** 57 9N 4 37W
Glen Moriston, *U.K.* **12 D4** 57 11N 4 52W
Glen Robertson, *Canada* **79 A10** 45 22N 74 30W
Glen Spean, *U.K.* **12 E4** 56 53N 4 40W
Glen Ullin, *U.S.A.* **80 B4** 46 49N 101 50W
Glencoe, *Canada* **78 D3** 42 45N 81 43W
Glencoe, *S. Africa* **57 D5** 28 11S 30 11 E
Glencoe, *U.S.A.* **80 C7** 44 46N 94 9W
Glendale, *Ariz., U.S.A.* **83 K7** 33 32N 112 11W
Glendale, *Calif., U.S.A.* **85 L8** 34 9N 118 15W
Glendale, *Zimbabwe* **55 F3** 17 22S 31 5 E
Glendive, *U.S.A.* **80 B2** 47 7N 104 43W
Glendo, *U.S.A.* **80 D2** 42 30N 105 2W
Glenelg →, *Australia* **63 F3** 38 4S 140 59 E
Glenfield, *U.S.A.* **79 C9** 43 43N 75 24W
Glengarriff, *Ireland* **13 E2** 51 45N 9 34W
Glenmont, *U.S.A.* **78 F2** 40 31N 82 6W
Glenmorgan, *Australia* **63 D4** 27 14S 149 42 E
Glenn, *U.S.A.* **84 F4** 39 31N 122 1W
Glennallen, *U.S.A.* **68 B5** 62 7N 145 33W
Glennamaddy, *Ireland* **13 C3** 53 37N 8 33W
Glenns Ferry, *U.S.A.* **82 E6** 42 57N 115 18W
Glenore, *Australia* **62 B3** 17 50S 141 12 E
Glenreagh, *Australia* **63 E5** 30 2S 153 1 E
Glenrock, *U.S.A.* **82 E11** 42 52N 105 52W
Glenrothes, *U.K.* **12 E5** 56 12N 3 10W
Glens Falls, *U.S.A.* **79 C11** 43 19N 73 39W
Glenside, *U.S.A.* **79 F9** 40 6N 75 9W
Glenties, *Ireland* **13 B3** 54 49N 8 16W
Glenville, *U.S.A.* **76 F5** 38 56N 80 50W
Glenwood, *Canada* **71 C9** 49 0N 54 58W
Glenwood, *Ark., U.S.A.* **81 H8** 34 20N 93 33W
Glenwood, *Iowa, U.S.A.* **80 E7** 41 3N 95 45W
Glenwood, *Minn., U.S.A.* **80 C7** 45 39N 95 23W
Glenwood, *Wash., U.S.A.* **84 D5** 46 1N 121 17W
Glenwood Springs, *U.S.A.* **82 G10** 39 33N 107 19W
Glettinganes, *Iceland* **8 D7** 65 30N 13 37W
Gliwice, *Poland* **17 C10** 50 22N 18 41 E
Globe, *U.S.A.* **83 K8** 33 24N 110 47W
Głogów, *Poland* **16 C9** 51 37N 16 5 E
Glomma →, *Norway* **9 G14** 59 12N 10 57 E
Glorieuses, Is., *Ind. Oc.* **57 A8** 11 30S 47 20 E
Glossop, *U.K.* **10 D6** 53 27N 1 56W

Gloucester, Australia 63 E5 32 0S 151 59 E
Gloucester, U.K. 11 F5 51 53N 2 15W
Gloucester, U.S.A. 79 D14 42 37N 70 40W
Gloucester I., Australia 62 C4 20 0S 148 30 E
Gloucester Point, U.S.A. 76 G7 37 15N 76 29W
Gloucestershire □, U.K. 11 F5 51 46N 2 15W
Gloversville, U.S.A. 79 C10 43 3N 74 21W
Glovertown, Canada 71 C9 48 40N 54 3W
Glusk, Belarus 17 B15 52 53N 28 41 E
Gmünd, Austria 16 D8 48 45N 15 0 E
Gmunden, Austria 16 E7 47 55N 13 48 E
Gniezno, Poland 17 B9 52 30N 17 35 E
Gnowangerup, Australia 61 F2 33 58S 117 59 E
Go Cong, Vietnam 39 G6 10 22N 106 40 E
Gō-no-ura, Japan 31 H4 33 44N 129 40 E
Goa, India 40 M8 15 33N 73 59 E
Goa □, India 40 M8 15 33N 73 59 E
Goalen Hd., Australia 63 F5 36 33S 150 4 E
Goalpara, India 41 F17 26 10N 90 40 E
Goaltor, India 43 H12 22 43N 87 10 E
Goalundo Ghat, Bangla. 43 H13 23 50N 89 47 E
Goat Fell, U.K. 12 F3 55 38N 5 11W
Goba, Ethiopia 46 F2 7 1N 39 59 E
Goba, Mozam. 57 D5 26 15S 32 13 E
Gobabis, Namibia 56 C2 22 30S 19 0 E
Gobi, Asia 34 C6 44 0N 110 0 E
Gobō, Japan 31 H7 33 53N 135 10 E
Gochas, Namibia 56 C2 24 59S 18 55 E
Godavari →, India 41 L13 16 25N 82 18 E
Godavari Pt., India 41 L13 17 0N 82 20 E
Godbout, Canada 71 C6 49 20N 67 38W
Godda, India 43 G12 24 50N 87 13 E
Goderich, Canada 78 C3 43 45N 81 41W
Godfrey Ra., Australia 61 D2 24 0S 117 0 E
Godhavn = Qeqertarsuaq, Greenland 4 C5 69 15N 53 38W
Godhra, India 42 H5 22 49N 73 40 E
Godoy Cruz, Argentina 94 C2 32 56S 68 52W
Gods →, Canada 70 A1 56 22N 92 51W
Gods L., Canada 70 B1 54 40N 94 15W
Gods River, Canada 73 C10 54 50N 94 5W
Godthåb = Nuuk, Greenland 69 B14 64 10N 51 35W
Godwin Austen = K2, Pakistan 43 B7 35 58N 76 32 E
Goeie Hoop, Kaap die = Good Hope, C. of, S. Africa 56 E2 34 24S 18 30 E
Goéland, L. au, Canada 70 C4 49 50N 76 48W
Goeree, Neths. 15 C3 51 50N 4 0 E
Goes, Neths. 15 C3 51 30N 3 55 E
Goffstown, U.S.A. 79 C13 43 1N 71 36W
Gogama, Canada 70 C3 47 35N 81 43W
Gogebic, L., U.S.A. 80 B10 46 30N 89 35W
Gogra = Ghaghara →, India 43 G11 25 45N 84 40 E
Gogriâl, Sudan 51 G11 8 30N 28 8 E
Gohana, India 42 E7 29 8N 76 42 E
Goharganj, India 42 H7 23 1N 77 41 E
Goi →, India 42 H6 22 4N 74 46 E
Goiânia, Brazil 93 G9 16 43S 49 20W
Goiás, Brazil 93 G8 15 55S 50 10W
Goiás □, Brazil 93 F9 12 10S 48 0W
Goio-Erê, Brazil 95 A5 24 12S 53 1W
Gojō, Japan 31 G7 34 21N 135 42 E
Gojra, Pakistan 42 D5 31 10N 72 40 E
Gökçeada, Turkey 21 D11 40 10N 25 50 E
Gökova Körfezi, Turkey 21 F12 36 55N 27 50 E
Gokteik, Burma 41 H20 22 26N 97 0 E
Gokurt, Pakistan 42 E2 29 40N 67 26 E
Gokwe, Zimbabwe 57 B4 18 7S 28 58 E
Gola, India 43 E9 28 3N 80 32 E
Golakganj, India 43 F13 26 8N 89 52 E
Golan Heights = Hagolan, Syria 47 C4 33 0N 35 45 E
Golāshkerd, Iran 45 E8 27 59N 57 16 E
Golchikha, Russia 4 B12 71 45N 83 30 E
Golconda, U.S.A. 82 F5 40 58N 117 30W
Gold, U.S.A. 78 E7 41 52N 77 50W
Gold Beach, U.S.A. 82 E1 42 25N 124 25W
Gold Coast, W. Afr. 50 H5 4 0N 1 40W
Gold Hill, U.S.A. 82 E2 42 26N 123 3W
Gold River, Canada 72 D3 49 46N 126 3W
Golden, Canada 72 C5 51 20N 116 59W
Golden B., N.Z. 59 J4 40 40S 172 50 E
Golden Gate, U.S.A. 82 H2 37 54N 122 30W
Golden Hinde, Canada 72 D3 49 40N 125 44W
Golden Lake, Canada 78 A7 45 34N 77 21W
Golden Vale, Ireland 13 D3 52 33N 8 17W
Goldendale, U.S.A. 82 D3 45 49N 120 50W
Goldfield, U.S.A. 83 H5 37 42N 117 14W
Goldsand L., Canada 73 B8 57 2N 101 8W
Goldsboro, U.S.A. 77 H7 35 23N 77 59W
Goldsmith, U.S.A. 81 K3 31 59N 102 37W
Goldsworthy, Australia 60 D2 20 21S 119 30 E
Goldthwaite, U.S.A. 81 K5 31 27N 98 34W
Goleniów, Poland 16 B8 53 35N 14 50 E
Golestānak, Iran 45 D7 30 36N 54 14 E
Goleta, U.S.A. 85 L7 34 27N 119 50W
Golfito, Costa Rica 88 E3 8 41N 83 5W
Golfo Aranci, Italy 20 D3 40 59N 9 38 E
Goliad, U.S.A. 81 L6 28 40N 97 23W
Golpāyegān, Iran 45 C6 33 27N 50 18 E
Golra, Pakistan 42 C5 33 37N 72 56 E
Golspie, U.K. 12 D5 57 58N 3 59W
Goma, Dem. Rep. of the Congo 54 C2 1 37S 29 10 E
Gomal Pass, Pakistan 42 D3 31 56N 69 20 E
Gomati →, India 43 G10 25 32N 83 11 E
Gombari, Dem. Rep. of the Congo 54 B2 2 45N 29 3 E
Gombe, Nigeria 51 F8 10 19N 11 2 E
Gombe →, Tanzania 54 C3 4 38S 31 40 E
Gomel = Homyel, Belarus 17 B16 52 28N 31 0 E
Gomera, Canary Is. 22 F2 28 7N 17 14W
Gómez Palacio, Mexico 86 B4 25 40N 104 0W
Gomishān, Iran 45 B7 37 4N 54 6 E
Gomogomo, Indonesia 37 F8 6 39S 134 43 E
Gomoh, India 41 H15 23 52N 86 10 E
Gompa = Ganta, Liberia 50 G4 7 15N 8 59W
Gonābād, Iran 45 C8 34 15N 58 45 E
Gonaïves, Haiti 89 C5 19 20N 72 42W
Gonâve, G. de la, Haiti 89 C5 19 29N 72 42W
Gonâve, I. de la, Haiti 89 C5 18 45N 73 0W
Gonbad-e Kāvūs, Iran 45 B7 37 20N 55 25 E
Gonda, India 43 F9 27 9N 81 58 E
Gondal, India 42 J4 21 58N 70 52 E
Gonder, Ethiopia 46 E2 12 39N 37 30 E
Gondia, India 40 J12 21 23N 80 10 E
Gondola, Mozam. 55 F3 19 10S 33 37 E
Gönen, Turkey 21 D12 40 6N 27 39 E
Gonghe, China 32 C5 36 18N 100 32 E
Gongolgon, Australia 63 E4 30 21S 146 54 E
Gongzhuling, China 35 C13 43 30N 124 40 E
Gonzales, Calif., U.S.A. 84 J5 36 30N 121 26W
Gonzales, Tex., U.S.A. 81 L6 29 30N 97 27W
González Chaves, Argentina 94 D3 38 2S 60 5W
Good Hope, C. of, S. Africa 56 E2 34 24S 18 30 E
Gooderham, Canada 78 B6 44 54N 78 21W
Goodhouse, S. Africa 56 D2 28 57S 18 13 E
Gooding, U.S.A. 82 E6 42 56N 114 43W
Goodland, U.S.A. 80 F4 39 21N 101 43W
Goodlow, Canada 72 B4 56 20N 120 8W
Goodooga, Australia 63 D4 29 3S 147 28 E
Goodsprings, U.S.A. 85 K11 35 49N 115 27W
Goole, U.K. 10 D7 53 42N 0 53W
Goolgowi, Australia 63 E4 33 58S 145 41 E
Goomalling, Australia 61 F2 31 15S 116 49 E
Goomeri, Australia 63 D5 26 12S 152 6 E
Goonda, Mozam. 55 F3 19 48S 33 57 E
Goondiwindi, Australia 63 D5 28 30S 150 21 E
Goongarrie, L., Australia 61 F3 30 3S 121 9 E
Goonyella, Australia 62 C4 21 47S 147 58 E
Goose →, Canada 71 B7 53 20N 60 35W
Goose Creek, U.S.A. 77 J5 32 59N 80 2W
Goose L., U.S.A. 82 F3 41 56N 120 26W
Gop, India 40 H6 22 5N 69 50 E
Gopalganj, India 43 F11 26 28N 84 30 E
Göppingen, Germany 16 D5 48 42N 9 39 E
Gorakhpur, India 43 F10 26 47N 83 23 E
Goražde, Bos.-H. 21 C8 43 38N 18 58 E
Gorda, U.S.A. 84 K5 35 53N 121 26W
Gorda, Pta., Canary Is. 22 F2 28 45N 18 0W
Gorda, Pta., Nic. 88 D3 14 20N 83 10W
Gordan B., Australia 60 B5 11 35S 130 10 E
Gordon, U.S.A. 80 D3 42 48N 102 12W
Gordon →, Australia 62 G4 42 27S 145 30 E
Gordon L., Alta., Canada 73 B6 56 30N 110 25W
Gordon L., N.W.T., Canada 72 A6 63 5N 113 11W
Gordonvale, Australia 62 B4 17 5S 145 50 E
Gore, Ethiopia 46 F2 8 12N 35 32 E
Gore, N.Z. 59 M2 46 5S 168 58 E
Gore Bay, Canada 70 C3 45 57N 82 28W
Gorey, Ireland 13 D5 52 41N 6 18W
Gorg, Iran 45 D8 29 29N 59 43 E
Gorgān, Iran 45 B7 36 50N 54 29 E
Gorgona, I., Colombia 92 C3 3 0N 78 10W
Gorham, U.S.A. 79 B13 44 23N 71 10W
Goriganga →, India 43 E9 29 45N 80 23 E
Gorinchem, Neths. 15 C4 51 50N 4 59 E
Goris, Armenia 25 G8 39 31N 46 22 E
Gorízia, Italy 20 B5 45 56N 13 37 E
Gorki = Nizhniy Novgorod, Russia 24 C7 56 20N 44 0 E
Gorkiy = Nizhniy Novgorod, Russia 24 C7 56 20N 44 0 E
Gorkovskoye Vdkhr., Russia 24 C7 57 2N 43 4 E
Görlitz, Germany 16 C8 51 9N 14 58 E
Gorlovka = Horlivka, Ukraine 25 E6 48 19N 38 5 E
Gorman, U.S.A. 85 L8 34 47N 118 51W
Gorna Dzhumayo = Blagoevgrad, Bulgaria 21 C10 42 2N 23 5 E
Gorna Oryakhovitsa, Bulgaria 21 C11 43 7N 25 40 E
Gorno-Altay □, Russia 26 D9 51 0N 86 0 E
Gorno-Altaysk, Russia 26 D9 51 50N 86 5 E
Gornyatski, Russia 24 A11 67 32N 64 3 E
Gornyy, Russia 30 B6 44 57N 133 59 E
Gorodenka = Horodenka, Ukraine 17 D13 48 41N 25 29 E
Gorodok = Horodok, Ukraine 17 D12 49 46N 23 32 E
Gorokhov = Horokhiv, Ukraine 17 C13 50 30N 24 45 E
Goromonzi, Zimbabwe 55 F3 17 52S 31 22 E
Gorong, Kepulauan, Indonesia 37 E8 3 59S 131 25 E
Gorongose →, Mozam. 57 C5 20 30S 34 40 E
Gorongoza, Mozam. 55 F3 18 44S 34 2 E
Gorongoza, Sa. da, Mozam. 55 F3 18 27S 34 2 E
Gorontalo, Indonesia 37 D6 0 35N 123 5 E
Gort, Ireland 13 C3 53 3N 8 49W
Gortis, Greece 23 D6 35 4N 24 58 E
Gorzów Wielkopolski, Poland 16 B8 52 43N 15 15 E
Gosford, Australia 63 E5 33 23S 151 18 E
Goshen, Calif., U.S.A. 84 J7 36 21N 119 25W
Goshen, Ind., U.S.A. 76 E3 41 35N 85 50W
Goshen, N.Y., U.S.A. 79 E10 41 24N 74 20W
Goshogawara, Japan 30 D10 40 48N 140 27 E
Goslar, Germany 16 C6 51 54N 10 25 E
Gospič, Croatia 16 F8 44 35N 15 23 E
Gosport, U.K. 11 G6 50 48N 1 9W
Gosse →, Australia 62 B1 19 32S 134 37 E
Göta älv →, Sweden 9 H14 57 42N 11 54 E
Göta kanal, Sweden 9 G16 58 30N 15 58 E
Götaland, Sweden 9 G15 57 30N 14 30 E
Göteborg, Sweden 9 H14 57 43N 11 59 E
Gotha, Germany 16 C6 50 56N 10 42 E
Gothenburg = Göteborg, Sweden 9 H14 57 43N 11 59 E
Gothenburg, U.S.A. 80 E4 40 56N 100 10W
Gotland, Sweden 9 H18 57 30N 18 33 E
Gotō-Rettō, Japan 31 H4 32 55N 129 5 E
Gotska Sandön, Sweden 9 G18 58 24N 19 15 E
Gōtsu, Japan 31 G6 35 0N 132 14 E
Gott Pk., Canada 72 C4 50 18N 122 16W
Göttingen, Germany 16 C5 51 31N 9 55 E
Gottwaldov = Zlín, Czech Rep. 17 D9 49 14N 17 40 E
Goubangzi, China 35 D11 41 20N 121 52 E
Gouda, Neths. 15 B4 52 1N 4 42 E
Goúdhoura, Ákra, Greece 23 E8 34 59N 26 6 E
Gough I., Atl. Oc. 2 G9 40 10S 9 45W
Gouin, Rés., Canada 70 C5 48 35N 74 40W
Goulburn, Australia 63 E4 34 44S 149 44 E
Goulburn Is., Australia 62 A1 11 40S 133 20 E
Goulimine, Morocco 50 C3 28 56N 10 0W
Gourits →, S. Africa 56 E3 34 21S 21 52 E
Goúrnais, Greece 23 D7 35 19N 25 16 E
Gouverneur, U.S.A. 79 B9 44 20N 75 28W
Gouviá, Greece 23 A3 39 39N 19 50 E
Governador Valadares, Brazil 93 G10 18 15S 41 57W
Governor's Harbour, Bahamas 88 A4 25 10N 76 14W
Govindgarh, India 43 G9 24 23N 81 18 E
Gowan Ra., Australia 62 D4 25 0S 145 0 E
Gowanda, U.S.A. 78 D6 42 28N 78 56W
Gower, U.K. 11 F3 51 35N 4 10W
Gowna, L., Ireland 13 C4 53 51N 7 34W
Goya, Argentina 94 B4 29 10S 59 10W
Goyder Lagoon, Australia 63 D2 27 3S 138 58 E
Goyllarisquisga, Peru 92 F3 10 31S 76 24W
Goz Beïda, Chad 51 F10 12 10N 21 20 E
Gozo, Malta 23 C1 36 3N 14 15 E
Graaff-Reinet, S. Africa 56 E3 32 13S 24 32 E
Gračac, Croatia 16 F8 44 18N 15 57 E
Gracias a Dios, C., Honduras 88 D3 15 0N 83 10W
Graciosa, I., Canary Is. 22 E6 29 15N 13 32W
Grado, Spain 19 A2 43 23N 6 4W
Grady, U.S.A. 81 H3 34 49N 103 19W
Grafham Water, U.K. 11 E7 52 19N 0 18W
Grafton, Australia 63 D5 29 38S 152 58 E
Grafton, N. Dak., U.S.A. 80 A6 48 25N 97 25W
Grafton, W. Va., U.S.A. 76 F5 39 21N 80 2W
Graham, Canada 70 C1 49 20N 90 30W
Graham, U.S.A. 81 J5 33 6N 98 35W
Graham, Mt., U.S.A. 83 K9 32 42N 109 52W
Graham Bell, Ostrov = Greem-Bell, Ostrov, Russia 26 A7 81 0N 62 0 E
Graham I., Canada 72 C2 53 40N 132 30W
Graham Land, Antarctica 5 C17 65 0S 64 0W
Grahamstown, S. Africa 56 E4 33 19S 26 31 E
Grahamsville, U.S.A. 79 E10 41 51N 74 33W
Grain Coast, W. Afr. 50 H3 4 20N 10 0W
Grajaú, Brazil 93 E9 5 50S 46 4W
Grajaú →, Brazil 93 D10 3 41S 44 48W
Grampian, U.S.A. 78 F6 40 58N 78 37W
Grampian Highlands = Grampian Mts., U.K. 12 E5 56 50N 4 0W
Grampian Mts., U.K. 12 E5 56 50N 4 0W
Grampians, The, Australia 63 F3 37 0S 142 20 E
Gran Canaria, Canary Is. 22 G4 27 55N 15 35W
Gran Chaco, S. Amer. 94 B3 25 0S 61 0W
Gran Paradiso, Italy 18 D7 45 33N 7 17 E
Gran Sasso d'Itália, Italy 20 C5 42 27N 13 42 E
Granada, Nic. 88 D2 11 58N 86 0W
Granada, Spain 19 D4 37 10N 3 35W
Granada, U.S.A. 81 F3 38 4N 102 19W
Granadilla de Abona, Canary Is. 22 F3 28 7N 16 33W
Granard, Ireland 13 C4 53 47N 7 30W
Granbury, U.S.A. 81 J6 32 27N 97 47W
Granby, Canada 79 A12 45 25N 72 45W
Granby, U.S.A. 82 F11 40 5N 105 56W
Grand →, Canada 78 D5 42 51N 79 34W
Grand →, Mo., U.S.A. 80 F8 39 23N 93 7W
Grand →, S. Dak., U.S.A. 80 C4 45 40N 100 45W
Grand Bahama, Bahamas 88 A4 26 40N 78 30W
Grand Bank, Canada 71 C8 47 6N 55 48W
Grand Bassam, Ivory C. 50 G5 5 10N 3 49W
Grand-Bourg, Guadeloupe 89 C7 15 53N 61 19W
Grand Canal = Yun Ho →, China 35 E9 39 10N 117 10 E
Grand Canyon, U.S.A. 83 H7 36 3N 112 9W
Grand Canyon Nat. Park, U.S.A. 83 H7 36 15N 112 30W
Grand Cayman, Cayman Is. 88 C3 19 20N 81 20W
Grand Centre, Canada 73 C6 54 25N 110 13W
Grand Coulee, U.S.A. 82 C4 47 57N 119 0W
Grand Coulee Dam, U.S.A. 82 C4 47 57N 118 59W
Grand Falls, Canada 71 C6 47 3N 67 44W
Grand Falls-Windsor, Canada 71 C8 48 56N 55 40W
Grand Forks, Canada 72 D5 49 0N 118 30W
Grand Forks, U.S.A. 80 B6 47 55N 97 3W
Grand Gorge, U.S.A. 79 D10 42 21N 74 29W
Grand Haven, U.S.A. 76 D2 43 4N 86 13W
Grand I., Mich., U.S.A. 76 B2 46 31N 86 40W
Grand I., N.Y., U.S.A. 78 D6 43 0N 78 58W
Grand Island, U.S.A. 80 E5 40 55N 98 21W
Grand Isle, La., U.S.A. 81 L9 29 14N 90 0W
Grand Isle, Vt., U.S.A. 79 B11 44 43N 73 18W
Grand Junction, U.S.A. 83 G9 39 4N 108 33W
Grand L., N.B., Canada 71 C6 45 57N 66 7W
Grand L., Nfld., Canada 71 C8 49 0N 57 30W
Grand L., Nfld., Canada 71 B7 53 40N 60 30W
Grand L., U.S.A. 81 L8 29 55N 92 47W
Grand Lake, U.S.A. 82 F11 40 15N 105 49W
Grand Manan I., Canada 71 D6 44 45N 66 52W
Grand Marais, Canada 80 B9 47 45N 90 25W
Grand Marais, U.S.A. 76 B3 46 40N 85 59W
Grand-Mère, Canada 70 C5 46 36N 72 40W
Grand Portage, U.S.A. 80 B10 47 58N 89 41W
Grand Prairie, U.S.A. 81 J6 32 47N 97 0W
Grand Rapids, Canada 73 C9 53 12N 99 19W
Grand Rapids, Mich., U.S.A. 76 D2 42 58N 85 40W
Grand Rapids, Minn., U.S.A. 80 B8 47 14N 93 31W
Grand St-Bernard, Col du, Europe 18 D7 45 50N 7 10 E
Grand Teton, U.S.A. 82 E8 43 54N 111 50W
Grand Teton Nat. Park, U.S.A. 82 D8 43 50N 110 50W
Grand Union Canal, U.K. 11 E7 52 7N 0 53W
Grand View, Canada 73 C8 51 10N 100 42W
Grande →, Jujuy, Argentina 94 A2 24 20S 65 2W
Grande →, Mendoza, Argentina 94 D2 36 52S 69 45W
Grande →, Bolivia 92 G6 15 51S 64 39W
Grande →, Bahia, Brazil 93 F10 11 30S 44 30W
Grande →, Minas Gerais, Brazil 93 H8 20 6S 51 4W
Grande, B., Argentina 96 G3 50 30S 68 20W
Grande, Rio →, U.S.A. 81 N6 25 58N 97 9W
Grande Baleine, R. de la →, Canada 70 A4 55 16N 77 47W
Grande Cache, Canada 72 C5 53 53N 119 8W
Grande-Entrée, Canada 71 C7 47 30N 61 40W
Grande Prairie, Canada 72 B5 55 10N 118 50W
Grande-Rivière, Canada 71 C7 48 26N 64 30W
Grande-Vallée, Canada 71 C6 49 14N 65 8W
Grandfalls, U.S.A. 81 K3 31 20N 102 51W
Grandview, U.S.A. 82 C4 46 15N 119 54W
Graneros, Chile 94 C1 34 5S 70 45W
Grangemouth, U.K. 12 E5 56 1N 3 42W
Granger, U.S.A. 82 F9 41 35N 109 58W
Grangeville, U.S.A. 82 D5 45 56N 116 7W
Granisle, Canada 72 C3 54 53N 126 13W
Granite City, U.S.A. 80 F9 38 42N 90 9W
Granite Falls, U.S.A. 80 C7 44 49N 95 33W
Granite L., Canada 71 C8 48 8N 57 5W
Granite Mt., U.S.A. 85 M10 33 5N 116 28W
Granite Pk., U.S.A. 82 D9 45 10N 109 48W
Graniteville, U.S.A. 79 B12 44 8N 72 29W
Granity, N.Z. 59 J3 41 39S 171 51 E
Granja, Brazil 93 D10 3 7S 40 50W
Granollers, Spain 19 B7 41 39N 2 18 E
Grant, U.S.A. 80 E4 40 53N 101 42W
Grant, Mt., U.S.A. 82 G4 38 34N 118 48W
Grant City, U.S.A. 80 E7 40 29N 94 25W
Grant I., Australia 60 B5 11 10S 132 52 E
Grant Range, U.S.A. 83 G6 38 30N 115 25W
Grantham, U.K. 10 E7 52 55N 0 38W
Grantown-on-Spey, U.K. 12 D5 57 20N 3 36W
Grants, U.S.A. 83 J10 35 9N 107 52W
Grants Pass, U.S.A. 82 E2 42 26N 123 19W
Grantsville, U.S.A. 82 F7 40 36N 112 28W
Granville, France 18 B3 48 50N 1 35W
Granville, N. Dak., U.S.A. 80 A4 48 16N 100 47W
Granville, N.Y., U.S.A. 79 C11 43 24N 73 16W
Granville, Ohio, U.S.A. 78 F2 40 4N 82 31W
Granville L., Canada 73 B8 56 18N 100 30W
Graskop, S. Africa 57 C5 24 56S 30 49 E
Grass →, Canada 73 B9 56 3N 96 33W
Grass Range, U.S.A. 82 C9 47 0N 109 0W
Grass River Prov. Park, Canada 73 C8 54 40N 100 50W
Grass Valley, Calif., U.S.A. 84 F6 39 13N 121 4W
Grass Valley, Oreg., U.S.A. 82 D3 45 22N 120 47W
Grasse, France 18 E7 43 38N 6 56 E
Grassflat, U.S.A. 78 F6 41 0N 78 6W
Grasslands Nat. Park, Canada 73 D7 49 11N 107 38W
Grassy, Australia 62 G3 40 3S 144 5 E
Graulhet, France 18 E4 43 45N 1 59 E
Gravelbourg, Canada 73 D7 49 50N 106 35W
's-Gravenhage, Neths. 15 B4 52 7N 4 17 E
Gravenhurst, Canada 78 B5 44 52N 79 20W
Gravesend, Australia 63 D5 29 35S 150 20 E
Gravesend, U.K. 11 F8 51 26N 0 22 E
Gravois, Pointe-à-, Haiti 89 C5 18 15N 73 56W
Grayling, U.S.A. 76 C3 44 40N 84 43W
Grays Harbor, U.S.A. 82 C1 46 59N 124 1W
Grays L., U.S.A. 82 E8 43 4N 111 26W
Grays River, U.S.A. 84 D3 46 21N 123 37W
Graz, Austria 16 E8 47 4N 15 27 E
Greasy L., Canada 72 A4 62 55N 122 12W
Great Abaco I., Bahamas 88 A4 26 25N 77 10W
Great Artesian Basin, Australia 62 C3 23 0S 144 0 E
Great Australian Bight, Australia 61 F5 33 30S 130 0 E
Great Bahama Bank, Bahamas 88 B4 23 15N 78 0W
Great Barrier I., N.Z. 59 G5 36 11S 175 25 E
Great Barrier Reef, Australia 62 B4 18 0S 146 50 E
Great Barrington, U.S.A. 79 D11 42 12N 73 22W
Great Basin, U.S.A. 82 G5 40 0N 117 0W
Great Basin Nat. Park, U.S.A. 82 G6 38 55N 114 14W
Great Bear →, Canada 68 B7 65 0N 124 0W
Great Bear L., Canada 68 B7 65 30N 120 0W
Great Belt = Store Bælt, Denmark 9 J14 55 20N 11 0 E
Great Bend, Kans., U.S.A. 80 F5 38 22N 98 46W
Great Bend, Pa., U.S.A. 79 E9 41 58N 75 45W
Great Blasket I., Ireland 13 D1 52 6N 10 32W
Great Britain, Europe 6 E5 54 0N 2 15W
Great Codroy, Canada 71 C8 47 51N 59 16W
Great Dividing Ra., Australia 62 C4 23 0S 146 0 E
Great Driffield = Driffield, U.K. 10 C7 54 0N 0 26W
Great Exuma I., Bahamas 88 B4 23 30N 75 50W
Great Falls, U.S.A. 82 C8 47 30N 111 17W
Great Fish = Groot Vis →, S. Africa 56 E4 33 28S 27 5 E
Great Guana Cay, Bahamas 88 B4 24 0N 76 20W
Great Inagua I., Bahamas 89 B5 21 0N 73 20W
Great Indian Desert = Thar Desert, India 42 F5 28 0N 72 0 E
Great Karoo, S. Africa 56 E3 31 55S 21 0 E
Great Lake, Australia 62 G4 41 50S 146 40 E
Great Lakes, N. Amer. 66 E11 46 0N 84 0W
Great Malvern, U.K. 11 E5 52 7N 2 18W
Great Miami →, U.S.A. 76 F3 39 20N 84 40W
Great Ormes Head, U.K. 10 D4 53 20N 3 52W
Great Ouse →, U.K. 10 E8 52 48N 0 21 E
Great Palm I., Australia 62 B4 18 45S 146 40 E
Great Plains, N. Amer. 74 A6 47 0N 105 0W
Great Ruaha →, Tanzania 54 D4 7 56S 37 52 E
Great Sacandaga Res., U.S.A. 79 C10 43 6N 74 16W
Great Saint Bernard Pass = Grand St-Bernard, Col du, Europe 18 D7 45 50N 7 10 E
Great Salt L., U.S.A. 82 F7 41 15N 112 40W
Great Salt Lake Desert, U.S.A. 82 F7 40 50N 113 30W
Great Salt Plains L., U.S.A. 81 G5 36 45N 98 8W
Great Sandy Desert, Australia 60 D3 21 0S 124 0 E
Great Sangi = Sangihe, Pulau, Indonesia 37 D7 3 35N 125 30 E
Great Skellig, Ireland 13 E1 51 47N 10 33W
Great Slave L., Canada 72 A5 61 23N 115 38W
Great Smoky Mts. Nat. Park, U.S.A. 77 H4 35 40N 83 40W
Great Snow Mt., Canada 72 B4 57 26N 124 0W
Great Stour = Stour →, U.K. 11 F9 51 18N 1 22 E
Great Victoria Desert, Australia 61 E4 29 30S 126 30 E
Great Wall, China 34 E5 38 30N 109 30 E
Great Whernside, U.K. 10 C6 54 10N 1 58W
Great Yarmouth, U.K. 11 E9 52 37N 1 44 E
Greater Antilles, W. Indies 89 C5 17 40N 74 0W
Greater London □, U.K. 11 F7 51 31N 0 6W
Greater Manchester □, U.K. 10 D5 53 30N 2 15W
Greater Sunda Is., Indonesia 36 F4 7 0S 112 0 E
Greco, C., Cyprus 23 E13 34 57N 34 5 E
Gredos, Sierra de, Spain 19 B3 40 20N 5 0W
Greece, U.S.A. 78 C7 43 13N 77 41W
Greece ■, Europe 21 E9 40 0N 23 0 E
Greeley, Colo., U.S.A. 80 E2 40 25N 104 42W
Greeley, Nebr., U.S.A. 80 E5 41 33N 98 32W
Greem-Bell, Ostrov, Russia 26 A7 81 0N 62 0 E
Green, U.S.A. 82 E2 43 9N 123 22W
Green →, Ky., U.S.A. 76 G2 37 54N 87 30W
Green →, Utah, U.S.A. 83 G9 38 11N 109 53W
Green B., U.S.A. 76 C2 45 0N 87 30W
Green Bay, U.S.A. 76 C2 44 31N 88 0W
Green C., Australia 63 F5 37 13S 150 1 E
Green Cove Springs, U.S.A. 77 L5 29 59N 81 42W
Green Lake, Canada 73 C7 54 17N 107 47W
Green Mts., U.S.A. 79 C12 43 45N 72 45W
Green River, Utah, U.S.A. 83 G8 38 59N 110 10W
Green River, Wyo., U.S.A. 82 F9 41 32N 109 28W

Green Valley, U.S.A. 83 L8 31 52N 110 56W
Greenbank, U.S.A. 84 B4 48 6N 122 34W
Greenbush, Mich., U.S.A. 78 B1 44 35N 83 19W
Greenbush, Minn., U.S.A. 80 A6 48 42N 96 11W
Greencastle, U.S.A. 76 F2 39 38N 86 52W
Greene, U.S.A. 79 D9 42 20N 75 46W
Greenfield, Calif., U.S.A. 84 J5 36 19N 121 15W
Greenfield, Calif., U.S.A. 85 K8 35 15N 119 0W
Greenfield, Ind., U.S.A. 76 F3 39 47N 85 46W
Greenfield, Iowa, U.S.A. 80 E7 41 18N 94 28W
Greenfield, Mass., U.S.A. 79 D12 42 35N 72 36W
Greenfield, Mo., U.S.A. 81 G8 37 25N 93 51W
Greenfield Park, Canada 79 A11 45 29N 73 29W
Greenland ■, N. Amer. 4 C5 66 0N 45 0W
Greenland Sea, Arctic 4 B7 73 0N 10 0W
Greenock, U.K. 12 F4 55 57N 4 46W
Greenore, Ireland 13 B5 54 2N 6 8W
Greenore Pt., Ireland 13 D5 52 14N 6 19W
Greenough, Australia 61 E1 28 58S 114 43 E
Greenough →, Australia 61 E1 28 51S 114 38 E
Greenough Pt., Canada 78 B3 44 58N 81 26W
Greenport, U.S.A. 79 E12 41 6N 72 22W
Greensboro, Ga., U.S.A. 77 J4 33 35N 83 11W
Greensboro, N.C., U.S.A. 77 G6 36 4N 79 48W
Greensboro, Vt., U.S.A. 79 B12 44 36N 72 18W
Greensburg, Ind., U.S.A. 76 F3 39 20N 85 29W
Greensburg, Kans., U.S.A. 81 G5 37 36N 99 18W
Greensburg, Pa., U.S.A. 78 F5 40 18N 79 33W
Greenstone Pt., U.K. 12 D3 57 55N 5 37W
Greenvale, Australia 62 B4 18 59S 145 7 E
Greenville, Ala., U.S.A. 77 K2 31 50N 86 38W
Greenville, Calif., U.S.A. 84 E6 40 8N 120 57W
Greenville, Maine, U.S.A. 77 C11 45 28N 69 35W
Greenville, Mich., U.S.A. 76 D3 43 11N 85 15W
Greenville, Miss., U.S.A. 81 J9 33 24N 91 4W
Greenville, Mo., U.S.A. 81 G9 37 8N 90 27W
Greenville, N.C., U.S.A. 77 H7 35 37N 77 23W
Greenville, N.H., U.S.A. 79 D13 42 46N 71 49W
Greenville, N.Y., U.S.A. 79 D10 42 25N 74 1W
Greenville, Ohio, U.S.A. 76 E3 40 6N 84 38W
Greenville, Pa., U.S.A. 78 E4 41 24N 80 23W
Greenville, S.C., U.S.A. 77 H4 34 51N 82 24W
Greenville, Tenn., U.S.A. 77 G4 36 13N 82 51W
Greenville, Tex., U.S.A. 81 J6 33 8N 96 7W
Greenwater Lake Prov. Park, Canada 73 C8 52 32N 103 30W
Greenwich, Conn., U.S.A. 79 E11 41 2N 73 38W
Greenwich, N.Y., U.S.A. 79 C11 43 5N 73 30W
Greenwich, Ohio, U.S.A. 78 E2 41 2N 82 31W
Greenwich □, U.K. 11 F8 51 29N 0 1 E
Greenwood, Canada 72 D5 49 10N 118 40W
Greenwood, Ark., U.S.A. 81 H7 35 13N 94 16W
Greenwood, Ind., U.S.A. 76 F2 39 37N 86 7W
Greenwood, Miss., U.S.A. 81 J9 33 31N 90 11W
Greenwood, S.C., U.S.A. 77 H4 34 12N 82 10W
Greenwood, Mt., Australia 60 B5 13 48S 130 4 E
Gregory, U.S.A. 80 D5 43 14N 99 20W
Gregory →, Australia 62 B2 17 53S 139 17 E
Gregory, L., S. Austral., Australia 63 D2 28 55S 139 0 E
Gregory, L., W. Austral., Australia 61 E2 25 38S 119 58 E
Gregory Downs, Australia 62 B2 18 35S 138 45 E
Gregory L., Australia 60 D4 20 0S 127 40 E
Gregory Ra., Queens., Australia 62 B3 19 30S 143 40 E
Gregory Ra., W. Austral., Australia 60 D3 21 20S 121 12 E
Greifswald, Germany 16 A7 54 5N 13 23 E
Greiz, Germany 16 C7 50 39N 12 10 E
Gremikha, Russia 24 A6 67 59N 39 47 E
Grenå, Denmark 9 H14 56 25N 10 53 E
Grenada, U.S.A. 81 J10 33 47N 89 49W
Grenada ■, W. Indies 89 D7 12 10N 61 40W
Grenadier I., U.S.A. 79 B8 44 3N 76 22W
Grenadines, St. Vincent 89 D7 12 40N 61 20W
Grenen, Denmark 9 H14 57 44N 10 40 E
Grenfell, Australia 63 E4 33 52S 148 8 E
Grenfell, Canada 73 C8 50 30N 102 56W
Grenoble, France 18 D6 45 12N 5 42 E
Grenville, C., Australia 62 A3 12 0S 143 13 E
Grenville Chan., Canada 72 C3 53 40N 129 46W
Gresham, U.S.A. 84 E4 45 30N 122 26W
Gresik, Indonesia 37 G15 7 13S 112 38 E
Gretna, U.K. 12 F5 55 0N 3 3W
Grevenmacher, Lux. 15 E6 49 41N 6 26 E
Grey →, Canada 71 C8 47 34N 57 6W
Grey →, N.Z. 59 K3 42 27S 171 12 E
Grey, C., Australia 62 A2 13 0S 136 35 E
Grey Ra., Australia 63 D3 27 0S 143 30 E
Greybull, U.S.A. 82 D9 44 30N 108 3W
Greymouth, N.Z. 59 K3 42 29S 171 13 E
Greystones, Ireland 13 C5 53 9N 6 5W
Greytown, N.Z. 59 J5 41 5S 175 29 E
Greytown, S. Africa 57 D5 29 1S 30 36 E
Gribbell I., Canada 72 C3 53 23N 129 0W
Gridley, U.S.A. 84 F5 39 22N 121 42W
Griekwastad, S. Africa 56 D3 28 49S 23 15 E
Griffin, U.S.A. 77 J3 33 15N 84 16W
Griffith, Australia 63 E4 34 18S 146 2 E
Griffith, Canada 78 A7 45 15N 77 10W
Griffith I., Canada 78 B4 44 50N 80 55W
Grimaylov = Hrymayliv, Ukraine 17 D14 49 20N 26 5 E
Grimes, U.S.A. 84 F5 39 4N 121 54W
Grimsay, U.K. 12 D1 57 29N 7 14W
Grimsby, Canada 78 C5 43 12N 79 34W
Grimsby, U.K. 10 D7 53 34N 0 5W
Grímsey, Iceland 8 C5 66 33N 17 58W
Grimshaw, Canada 72 B5 56 10N 117 40W
Grimstad, Norway 9 G13 58 20N 8 35 E
Grindstone I., Canada 79 B8 44 43N 76 14W
Grinnell, U.S.A. 80 E8 41 45N 92 43W
Gris-Nez, C., France 18 A4 50 52N 1 35 E
Groais I., Canada 71 B8 50 55N 55 35W
Groblersdal, S. Africa 57 D4 25 15S 29 25 E
Grodno = Hrodna, Belarus 17 B12 53 42N 23 52 E
Grodzyanka = Hrodzyanka, Belarus 17 B15 53 31N 28 42 E
Groesbeck, U.S.A. 81 K6 31 31N 96 31W
Grójec, Poland 17 C11 51 50N 20 58 E
Grong, Norway 8 D15 64 25N 12 8 E
Groningen, Neths. 15 A6 53 15N 6 35 E
Groningen □, Neths. 15 A6 53 16N 6 40 E
Groom, U.S.A. 81 H4 35 12N 101 6W
Groot →, S. Africa 56 E3 33 45S 24 36 E
Groot Berg →, S. Africa 56 E2 32 47S 18 8 E
Groot-Brakrivier, S. Africa 56 E3 34 2S 22 18 E
Groot Karasberge, Namibia 56 D2 27 20S 18 40 E
Groot-Kei →, S. Africa 57 E4 32 41S 28 22 E
Groot Vis →, S. Africa 56 E4 33 28S 27 5 E
Grootdrink, S. Africa 56 D3 28 33S 21 42 E
Groote Eylandt, Australia 62 A2 14 0S 136 40 E
Grootfontein, Namibia 56 B2 19 31S 18 6 E
Grootlaagte →, Africa 56 C3 20 55S 21 27 E
Grootvloer →, S. Africa 56 E3 30 0S 20 40 E
Gros C., Canada 72 A6 61 59N 113 32W
Gros Morne Nat. Park, Canada 71 C8 49 40N 57 50W
Grossa, Pta., Spain 22 B8 39 6N 1 36 E
Grosser Arber, Germany 16 D7 49 6N 13 8 E
Grosseto, Italy 20 C4 42 46N 11 8 E
Grossglockner, Austria 16 E7 47 5N 12 40 E
Groswater B., Canada 71 B8 54 20N 57 40W
Groton, Conn., U.S.A. 79 E12 41 21N 72 5W
Groton, N.Y., U.S.A. 79 D8 42 36N 76 22W
Groton, S. Dak., U.S.A. 80 C5 45 27N 98 6W
Grouard Mission, Canada 72 B5 55 33N 116 9W
Groundhog →, Canada 70 C3 48 45N 82 58W
Grouw, Neths. 15 A5 53 5N 5 51 E
Grove City, U.S.A. 78 E4 41 10N 80 5W
Grove Hill, U.S.A. 77 K2 31 42N 87 47W
Groveland, U.S.A. 84 H6 37 50N 120 14W
Grover City, U.S.A. 85 K6 35 7N 120 37W
Groves, U.S.A. 81 L8 29 57N 93 54W
Groveton, U.S.A. 79 B13 44 36N 71 31W
Groznyy, Russia 25 F8 43 20N 45 45 E
Grudziądz, Poland 17 B10 53 30N 18 47 E
Gruinard B., U.K. 12 D3 57 56N 5 35W
Grundy Center, U.S.A. 80 D8 42 22N 92 47W
Gruver, U.S.A. 81 G4 36 16N 101 24W
Gryazi, Russia 24 D6 52 30N 39 58 E
Gryazovets, Russia 24 C7 58 50N 40 10 E
Gua, India 41 H14 22 18N 85 20 E
Gua Musang, Malaysia 39 K3 4 53N 101 58 E
Guacanayabo, G. de, Cuba 88 B4 20 40N 77 20W
Guachípas →, Argentina 94 B2 25 40S 65 30W
Guadalajara, Mexico 86 C4 20 40N 103 20W
Guadalajara, Spain 19 B4 40 37N 3 12W
Guadalcanal, Solomon Is. 64 H8 9 32S 160 12 E
Guadales, Argentina 94 C2 34 30S 67 55W
Guadalete →, Spain 19 D2 36 35N 6 13W
Guadalquivir →, Spain 19 D2 36 47N 6 22W
Guadalupe = Guadeloupe ■, W. Indies 89 C7 16 20N 61 40W
Guadalupe, Mexico 85 N10 32 4N 116 32W
Guadalupe, U.S.A. 85 L6 34 59N 120 33W
Guadalupe →, Mexico 85 N10 32 6N 116 51W
Guadalupe →, U.S.A. 81 L6 28 27N 96 47W
Guadalupe, Sierra de, Spain 19 C3 39 28N 5 30W
Guadalupe Bravos, Mexico 86 A3 31 20N 106 10W
Guadalupe I., Pac. Oc. 66 G8 29 0N 118 50W
Guadalupe Mts. Nat. Park, U.S.A. 81 K2 32 0N 104 30W
Guadalupe Peak, U.S.A. 81 K2 31 50N 104 52W
Guadalupe y Calvo, Mexico 86 B3 26 6N 106 58W
Guadarrama, Sierra de, Spain 19 B4 41 0N 4 0W
Guadeloupe ■, W. Indies 89 C7 16 20N 61 40W
Guadeloupe Passage, W. Indies 89 C7 16 50N 62 15W
Guadiana →, Portugal 19 D2 37 14N 7 22W
Guadix, Spain 19 D4 37 18N 3 11W
Guafo, Boca del, Chile 96 E2 43 35S 74 0W
Guainía →, Colombia 92 C5 2 1N 67 7W
Guaíra, Brazil 95 A5 24 5S 54 10W
Guaira □, Paraguay 94 B4 25 45S 56 30W
Guaitecas, Is., Chile 96 E2 44 0S 74 30W
Guajará-Mirim, Brazil 92 F5 10 50S 65 20W
Guajira, Pen. de la, Colombia 92 A4 12 0N 72 0W
Gualán, Guatemala 88 C2 15 8N 89 22W
Gualeguay, Argentina 94 C4 33 10S 59 14W
Gualeguaychú, Argentina 94 C4 33 3S 59 31W
Gualequay →, Argentina 94 C4 33 19S 59 39W
Guam ■, Pac. Oc. 64 F6 13 27N 144 45 E
Guaminí, Argentina 94 D3 37 1S 62 28W
Guamúchil, Mexico 86 B3 25 25N 108 3W
Guanabacoa, Cuba 88 B3 23 8N 82 18W
Guanacaste, Cordillera del, Costa Rica 88 D2 10 40N 85 4W
Guanaceví, Mexico 86 B3 25 40N 106 0W
Guanahani = San Salvador I., Bahamas 89 B5 24 0N 74 40W
Guanajay, Cuba 88 B3 22 56N 82 42W
Guanajuato, Mexico 86 C4 21 0N 101 20W
Guanajuato □, Mexico 86 C4 20 40N 101 20W
Guandacol, Argentina 94 B2 29 30S 68 40W
Guane, Cuba 88 B3 22 10N 84 7W
Guangdong □, China 33 D6 23 0N 113 0 E
Guangling, China 34 E8 39 47N 114 22 E
Guangrao, China 35 F10 37 5N 118 25 E
Guangwu, China 34 F3 37 48N 105 57 E
Guangxi Zhuangzu Zizhiqu □, China 33 D5 24 0N 109 0 E
Guangzhou, China 33 D6 23 5N 113 10 E
Guanipa →, Venezuela 92 B6 9 56N 62 26W
Guannan, China 35 G10 34 8N 119 21 E
Guantánamo, Cuba 89 B4 20 10N 75 14W
Guantao, China 34 F8 36 42N 115 25 E
Guanyun, China 35 G10 34 20N 119 18 E
Guápiles, Costa Rica 88 D3 10 10N 83 46W
Guaporé, Brazil 95 B5 28 51S 51 54W
Guaporé →, Brazil 92 F5 11 55S 65 4W
Guaqui, Bolivia 92 G5 16 41S 68 54W
Guarapari, Brazil 95 A7 20 40S 40 30W
Guarapuava, Brazil 95 B5 25 20S 51 30W
Guaratinguetá, Brazil 95 A6 22 49S 45 9W
Guaratuba, Brazil 95 B6 25 53S 48 38W
Guarda, Portugal 19 B2 40 32N 7 20W
Guardafui, C. = Asir, Ras, Somali Rep. 46 E5 11 55N 51 10 E
Guárico □, Venezuela 92 B5 8 40N 66 35W
Guarujá, Brazil 95 A6 24 2S 46 25W
Guarus, Brazil 95 A7 21 44S 41 20W
Guasave, Mexico 86 B3 25 34N 108 27W
Guasdualito, Venezuela 92 B4 7 15N 70 44W
Guatemala, Guatemala 88 D1 14 40N 90 22W
Guatemala ■, Cent. Amer. 88 C1 15 40N 90 30W
Guaviare →, Colombia 92 C5 4 3N 67 44W
Guaxupé, Brazil 95 A6 21 10S 47 5W
Guayama, Puerto Rico 89 C6 17 59N 66 7W
Guayaquil, Ecuador 92 D3 2 15S 79 52W
Guayaquil, G. de, Ecuador 92 D2 3 10S 81 0W
Guaymas, Mexico 86 B2 27 59N 110 54W
Guba, Dem. Rep. of the Congo 55 E2 10 38S 26 27 E
Gubkin, Russia 25 D6 51 17N 37 32 E
Gudbrandsdalen, Norway 9 F14 61 33N 10 10 E
Guddu Barrage, Pakistan 40 E6 28 30N 69 50 E
Gudur, India 40 M11 14 12N 79 55 E
Guecho = Getxo, Spain 19 A4 43 21N 2 59W
Guelmine = Goulimine, Morocco 50 C3 28 56N 10 0W
Guelph, Canada 78 C4 43 35N 80 20W
Guéret, France 18 C4 46 11N 1 51 E
Guerneville, U.S.A. 84 G4 38 30N 123 0W
Guernica = Gernika-Lumo, Spain 19 A4 43 19N 2 40W
Guernsey, U.K. 11 H5 49 26N 2 35W
Guernsey, U.S.A. 80 D2 42 19N 104 45W
Guerrero □, Mexico 87 D5 17 30N 100 0W
Gügher, Iran 45 D8 29 28N 56 27 E
Guhakolak, Tanjung, Indonesia 37 G11 6 50S 105 14 E
Guia, Canary Is. 22 F4 28 8N 15 38W
Guia de Isora, Canary Is. 22 F3 28 12N 16 46W
Guia Lopes da Laguna, Brazil 95 A4 21 26S 56 7W
Guiana, S. Amer. 90 C4 5 10N 60 40W
Guidónia-Montecélio, Italy 20 C5 42 1N 12 45 E
Guijá, Mozam. 57 C5 24 27S 33 0 E
Guildford, U.K. 11 F7 51 14N 0 34W
Guilford, U.S.A. 79 E12 41 17N 72 41W
Guilin, China 33 D6 25 18N 110 15 E
Guillaume-Delisle L., Canada 70 A4 56 15N 76 17W
Güimar, Canary Is. 22 F3 28 18N 16 24W
Guimarães, Portugal 19 B1 41 28N 8 24W
Guimaras □, Phil. 37 B6 10 35N 122 37 E
Guinda, U.S.A. 84 G4 38 50N 122 12W
Guinea, Africa 48 F4 8 0N 8 0 E
Guinea ■, W. Afr. 50 F3 10 20N 11 30W
Guinea, Gulf of, Atl. Oc. 49 F4 3 0N 2 30 E
Guinea-Bissau ■, Africa 50 F3 12 0N 15 0W
Güines, Cuba 88 B3 22 50N 82 0W
Guingamp, France 18 B2 48 34N 3 10W
Güiria, Venezuela 92 A6 10 32N 62 18W
Guiuan, Phil. 37 B7 11 5N 125 55 E
Guiyang, China 32 D5 26 32N 106 40 E
Guizhou □, China 32 D5 27 0N 107 0 E
Gujar Khan, Pakistan 42 C5 33 16N 73 19 E
Gujarat □, India 42 H4 23 20N 71 0 E
Gujranwala, Pakistan 42 C6 32 10N 74 12 E
Gujrat, Pakistan 42 C6 32 40N 74 2 E
Gulbarga, India 40 L10 17 20N 76 50 E
Gulbene, Latvia 9 H22 57 8N 26 52 E
Gulf, The, Asia 45 E6 27 0N 50 0 E
Gulfport, U.S.A. 81 K10 30 22N 89 6W
Gulgong, Australia 63 E4 32 20S 149 49 E
Gulistan, Pakistan 42 D2 30 30N 66 35 E
Gull Lake, Canada 73 C7 50 10N 108 29W
Güllük, Turkey 21 F12 37 14N 27 35 E
Gulmarg, India 43 B6 34 3N 74 25 E
Gulshad, Kazakstan 26 E8 46 45N 74 25 E
Gulu, Uganda 54 B3 2 48N 32 17 E
Gulwe, Tanzania 54 D4 6 30S 36 25 E
Gumal →, Pakistan 42 D4 31 40N 71 50 E
Gumbaz, Pakistan 42 D3 30 2N 69 0 E
Gumel, Nigeria 50 F7 12 39N 9 22 E
Gumla, India 43 H11 23 3N 84 33 E
Gumlu, Australia 62 B4 19 53S 147 41 E
Gumma □, Japan 31 F9 36 30N 138 20 E
Gumzai, Indonesia 37 F8 5 28S 134 42 E
Guna, India 42 G7 24 40N 77 19 E
Gunisao →, Canada 73 C9 53 56N 97 53W
Gunisao L., Canada 73 C9 53 33N 96 15W
Gunjyal, Pakistan 42 C4 32 20N 71 55 E
Gunnbjørn Fjeld, Greenland 4 C6 68 55N 29 47W
Gunnedah, Australia 63 E5 30 59S 150 15 E
Gunnewin, Australia 63 D4 25 59S 148 33 E
Gunningbar Cr. →, Australia 63 E4 31 14S 147 6 E
Gunnison, Colo., U.S.A. 83 G10 38 33N 106 56W
Gunnison, Utah, U.S.A. 82 G8 39 9N 111 49W
Gunnison →, U.S.A. 83 G9 39 4N 108 35W
Gunpowder, Australia 62 B2 19 42S 139 22 E
Guntakal, India 40 M10 15 11N 77 27 E
Guntersville, U.S.A. 77 H2 34 21N 86 18W
Guntong, Malaysia 39 K3 4 36N 101 3 E
Guntur, India 41 L12 16 23N 80 30 E
Gunungapi, Indonesia 37 F7 6 45S 126 30 E
Gunungsitoli, Indonesia 36 D1 1 15N 97 30 E
Gunza, Angola 52 G2 10 50S 13 50 E
Guo He →, China 35 H9 32 59N 117 10 E
Guoyang, China 34 H9 33 32N 116 12 E
Gupis, Pakistan 43 A5 36 15N 73 20 E
Gurdaspur, India 42 C6 32 5N 75 31 E
Gurdon, U.S.A. 81 J8 33 55N 93 9W
Gurgaon, India 42 E7 28 27N 77 1 E
Gurgueia →, Brazil 93 E10 6 50S 43 24W
Gurha, India 42 G4 25 12N 71 39 E
Guri, Embalse de, Venezuela 92 B6 7 50N 62 52W
Gurkha, Nepal 43 E11 28 5N 84 40 E
Gurley, Australia 63 D4 29 45S 149 48 E
Gurnet Point, U.S.A. 79 D14 42 1N 70 34W
Guro, Mozam. 55 F3 17 26S 32 30 E
Gurué, Mozam. 55 F4 15 25S 36 58 E
Gurun, Malaysia 39 K3 5 49N 100 27 E
Gürün, Turkey 25 G6 38 43N 37 15 E
Gurupá, Brazil 93 D8 1 25S 51 35W
Gurupá, I. Grande de, Brazil 93 D8 1 25S 51 45W
Gurupi, Brazil 93 F9 11 43S 49 4W
Gurupi →, Brazil 93 D9 1 13S 46 6W
Guruwe, Zimbabwe 57 B5 16 40S 30 42 E
Guryev = Atyraū, Kazakstan 25 E9 47 5N 52 0 E
Gusau, Nigeria 50 F7 12 12N 6 40 E
Gusev, Russia 9 J20 54 35N 22 10 E
Gushan, China 35 E12 39 50N 123 35 E
Gushgy, Turkmenistan 26 F7 35 20N 62 18 E
Gusinoozersk, Russia 27 D11 51 16N 106 27 E
Gustavus, U.S.A. 72 B1 58 25N 135 44W
Gustine, U.S.A. 84 H6 37 16N 121 0W
Güstrow, Germany 16 B7 53 47N 12 10 E
Gütersloh, Germany 16 C5 51 54N 8 24 E
Gutha, Australia 61 E2 28 58S 115 55 E
Guthalungra, Australia 62 B4 19 52S 147 50 E
Guthrie, Okla., U.S.A. 81 H6 35 53N 97 25W
Guthrie, Tex., U.S.A. 81 J4 33 37N 100 19W
Guttenberg, U.S.A. 80 D9 42 47N 91 6W
Gutu, Zimbabwe 57 B5 19 41S 31 9 E
Guwahati, India 41 F17 26 10N 91 45 E
Guyana ■, S. Amer. 92 C7 5 0N 59 0W
Guyane française = French Guiana ■, S. Amer. 93 C8 4 0N 53 0W
Guyang, China 34 D6 41 0N 110 5 E
Guyenne, France 18 D4 44 30N 0 40 E
Guymon, U.S.A. 81 G4 36 41N 101 29W
Guyra, Australia 63 E5 30 15S 151 40 E
Guyuan, Hebei, China 34 D8 41 37N 115 40 E
Guyuan, Ningxia Huizu, China 34 G4 36 0N 106 20 E
Guzhen, China 35 H9 33 22N 117 18 E
Guzmán, L. de, Mexico 86 A3 31 25N 107 25W
Gvardeysk, Russia 9 J19 54 39N 21 5 E
Gwa, Burma 41 L19 17 36N 94 34 E
Gwaai, Zimbabwe 55 F2 19 15S 27 45 E
Gwaai →, Zimbabwe 55 F2 17 59S 26 52 E
Gwabegar, Australia 63 E4 30 31S 149 0 E
Gwādar, Pakistan 40 G3 25 10N 62 18 E
Gwalior, India 42 F8 26 12N 78 10 E
Gwanda, Zimbabwe 55 G2 20 55S 29 0 E
Gwane, Dem. Rep. of the Congo 54 B2 4 45N 25 48 E
Gweebarra B., Ireland 13 B3 54 51N 8 23W
Gweedore, Ireland 13 A3 55 3N 8 13W
Gweru, Zimbabwe 55 F2 19 28S 29 45 E
Gwinn, U.S.A. 76 B2 46 19N 87 27W
Gwydir →, Australia 63 D4 29 27S 149 48 E
Gwynedd □, U.K. 10 E3 52 52N 4 10W
Gyandzha = Gäncä, Azerbaijan 25 F8 40 45N 46 20 E
Gyaring Hu, China 32 C4 34 50N 97 40 E
Gydanskiy Poluostrov, Russia 26 C8 70 0N 78 0 E
Gympie, Australia 63 D5 26 11S 152 38 E
Gyöngyös, Hungary 17 E10 47 48N 19 56 E
Győr, Hungary 17 E9 47 41N 17 40 E
Gypsum Pt., Canada 72 A6 61 53N 114 35W
Gypsumville, Canada 73 C9 51 45N 98 40W
Gyula, Hungary 17 E11 46 38N 21 17 E
Gyumri, Armenia 25 F7 40 47N 43 50 E
Gyzylarbat, Turkmenistan 26 F6 39 4N 56 23 E
Gyzyletrek, Turkmenistan 45 B7 37 36N 54 46 E

H

Ha 'Arava →, Israel 47 E4 30 50N 35 20 E
Ha Coi, Vietnam 38 B6 21 26N 107 46 E
Ha Dong, Vietnam 38 B5 20 58N 105 46 E
Ha Giang, Vietnam 38 A5 22 50N 104 59 E
Ha Tien, Vietnam 39 G5 10 23N 104 29 E
Ha Tinh, Vietnam 38 C5 18 20N 105 54 E
Ha Trung, Vietnam 38 C5 19 58N 105 50 E
Haaksbergen, Neths. 15 B6 52 9N 6 45 E
Haapsalu, Estonia 9 G20 58 56N 23 30 E
Haarlem, Neths. 15 B4 52 23N 4 39 E
Haast →, N.Z. 59 K2 43 50S 169 2 E
Haast Bluff, Australia 60 D5 23 22S 132 0 E
Hab →, Pakistan 42 G3 24 53N 66 41 E
Hab Nadi Chauki, Pakistan 42 G2 25 0N 66 50 E
Habaswein, Kenya 54 B4 1 2N 39 30 E
Habay, Canada 72 B5 58 50N 118 44W
Ḩabbānīyah, Iraq 44 C4 33 17N 43 29 E
Haboro, Japan 30 B10 44 22N 141 42 E
Ḩabshān, U.A.E. 45 F7 23 50N 53 37 E
Hachijō-Jima, Japan 31 H9 33 5N 139 45 E
Hachinohe, Japan 30 D10 40 30N 141 29 E
Hachiōji, Japan 31 G9 35 40N 139 20 E
Hachŏn, N. Korea 35 D15 41 29N 129 2 E
Hackensack, U.S.A. 79 F10 40 53N 74 3W
Hackettstown, U.S.A. 79 F10 40 51N 74 50W
Hadali, Pakistan 42 C5 32 16N 72 11 E
Hadarba, Ras, Sudan 51 D13 22 4N 36 51 E
Hadarom □, Israel 47 E4 31 0N 35 0 E
Ḩadd, Ra's al, Oman 46 C6 22 35N 59 50 E
Hadejia, Nigeria 50 F7 12 30N 10 5 E
Hadera, Israel 47 C3 32 27N 34 55 E
Hadera, N. →, Israel 47 C3 32 28N 34 52 E
Haderslev, Denmark 9 J13 55 15N 9 30 E
Hadhramaut = Ḩaḑramawt, Yemen 46 D4 15 30N 49 30 E
Hadiboh, Yemen 46 E5 12 39N 54 2 E
Hadong, S. Korea 35 G14 35 5N 127 44 E
Ḩaḑramawt, Yemen 46 D4 15 30N 49 30 E
Ḩadrānīyah, Iraq 44 C4 35 38N 43 14 E
Hadrian's Wall, U.K. 10 B5 55 0N 2 30W
Haeju, N. Korea 35 E13 38 3N 125 45 E
Haenam, S. Korea 35 G14 34 34N 126 35 E
Haenertsburg, S. Africa 57 C4 24 0S 29 50 E
Haerhpin = Harbin, China 35 B14 45 48N 126 40 E
Hafar al Bāţin, Si. Arabia 44 D5 28 32N 45 52 E
Ḩafīrat al 'Aydā, Si. Arabia 44 E3 26 26N 39 12 E
Ḩafit, Oman 45 F7 23 59N 55 49 E
Hafizabad, Pakistan 42 C5 32 5N 73 40 E
Haflong, India 41 G18 25 10N 93 5 E
Hafnarfjörður, Iceland 8 D3 64 4N 21 57W
Haft Gel, Iran 45 D6 31 30N 49 32 E
Hafun, Ras, Somali Rep. 46 E5 10 29N 51 30 E
Hagalil, Israel 47 C4 32 53N 35 18 E
Hagen, Germany 16 C4 51 21N 7 27 E
Hagerman, U.S.A. 81 J2 33 7N 104 20W
Hagerstown, U.S.A. 76 F7 39 39N 77 43W
Hagersville, Canada 78 D4 42 58N 80 3W
Hagfors, Sweden 9 F15 60 3N 13 45 E
Hagi, Japan 31 G5 34 30N 131 22 E
Hagolan, Syria 47 C4 33 0N 35 45 E
Hagondange, France 18 B7 49 16N 6 11 E
Hags Hd., Ireland 13 D2 52 57N 9 28W
Hague, C. de la, France 18 B3 49 44N 1 56W
Hague, The = 's-Gravenhage, Neths. 15 B4 52 7N 4 17 E
Haguenau, France 18 B7 48 49N 7 47 E
Hai Duong, Vietnam 38 B6 20 56N 106 19 E
Haicheng, China 35 D12 40 50N 122 45 E
Haidar Khel, Afghan. 42 C3 33 58N 68 38 E
Haidargarh, India 43 F9 26 37N 81 22 E
Haifa = Ḩefa, Israel 47 C4 32 46N 35 0 E
Haikou, China 33 D6 20 1N 110 16 E
Ḩā'il, Si. Arabia 44 E4 27 28N 41 45 E
Hailar, China 33 B6 49 10N 119 38 E
Hailey, U.S.A. 82 E6 43 31N 114 19W
Haileybury, Canada 70 C4 47 30N 79 38W
Hailin, China 35 B15 44 37N 129 30 E
Hailong, China 35 C13 42 32N 125 40 E

Hailuoto, *Finland* **8 D21** 65 3N 24 45 E
Hainan □, *China* **33 E5** 19 0N 109 30 E
Hainaut □, *Belgium* **15 D4** 50 30N 4 0 E
Haines, *Alaska, U.S.A.* **72 B1** 59 14N 135 26W
Haines, *Oreg., U.S.A.* **82 D5** 44 55N 117 56W
Haines City, *U.S.A.* **77 L5** 28 7N 81 38W
Haines Junction, *Canada* **72 A1** 60 45N 137 30W
Haiphong, *Vietnam* **32 D5** 20 47N 106 41 E
Haiti ■, *W. Indies* **89 C5** 19 0N 72 30W
Haiya, *Sudan* **51 E13** 18 20N 36 21 E
Haiyang, *China* **35 F11** 36 47N 121 9 E
Haiyuan, *China* **34 F3** 36 35N 105 52 E
Haizhou, *China* **35 G10** 34 37N 119 7 E
Haizhou Wan, *China* **35 G10** 34 50N 119 20 E
Hajdúböszörmény, *Hungary* **17 E11** 47 40N 21 30 E
Hajipur, *India* **43 G11** 25 45N 85 13 E
Ḩājjī Muḩsin, *Iraq* **44 C5** 32 35N 45 29 E
Ḩājjīābād, *Iran* **45 D7** 28 19N 55 55 E
Ḩājjīābād-e Zarrīn, *Iran* **45 C7** 33 9N 54 51 E
Hajnówka, *Poland* **17 B12** 52 47N 23 35 E
Hakansson, Mts., *Dem. Rep. of the Congo* **55 D2** 8 40S 25 45 E
Hakkâri, *Turkey* **44 B4** 37 34N 43 44 E
Hakken-Zan, *Japan* **31 G7** 34 10N 135 54 E
Hakodate, *Japan* **30 D10** 41 45N 140 44 E
Hakos, *Namibia* **56 C2** 23 13S 16 21 E
Haku-San, *Japan* **31 F8** 36 9N 136 46 E
Hakui, *Japan* **31 F8** 36 53N 136 47 E
Hala, *Pakistan* **40 G6** 25 43N 68 20 E
Ḩalab, *Syria* **44 B3** 36 10N 37 15 E
Ḩalabjah, *Iraq* **44 C5** 35 10N 45 58 E
Halaib, *Sudan* **51 D13** 22 12N 36 30 E
Hālat 'Ammār, *Si. Arabia* **44 D3** 29 10N 36 4 E
Halbā, *Lebanon* **47 A5** 34 34N 36 6 E
Halberstadt, *Germany* **16 C6** 51 54N 11 3 E
Halcombe, *N.Z.* **59 J5** 40 8S 175 30 E
Halcon, *Phil.* **37 B6** 13 0N 121 30 E
Halden, *Norway* **9 G14** 59 9N 11 23 E
Haldia, *India* **41 H16** 22 5N 88 3 E
Haldwani, *India* **43 E8** 29 31N 79 30 E
Hale →, *Australia* **62 C2** 24 56S 135 53 E
Halesowen, *U.K.* **11 E5** 52 27N 2 3W
Haleyville, *U.S.A.* **77 H2** 34 14N 87 37W
Halfmoon Bay, *N.Z.* **59 M2** 46 50S 168 5 E
Halfway →, *Canada* **72 B4** 56 12N 121 32W
Halia, *India* **43 G10** 24 50N 82 19 E
Haliburton, *Canada* **78 A6** 45 3N 78 30W
Halifax, *Australia* **62 B4** 18 32S 146 22 E
Halifax, *Canada* **71 D7** 44 38N 63 35W
Halifax, *U.K.* **10 D6** 53 43N 1 52W
Halifax, *U.S.A.* **78 F8** 40 25N 76 55W
Halifax B., *Australia* **62 B4** 18 50S 147 0 E
Halifax I., *Namibia* **56 D2** 26 38S 15 4 E
Halīl →, *Iran* **45 E8** 27 40N 58 30 E
Halkirk, *U.K.* **12 C5** 58 30N 3 29W
Hall Beach = Sanirajak, *Canada* **69 B11** 68 46N 81 12W
Hall Pen., *Canada* **69 B13** 63 30N 66 0W
Hall Pt., *Australia* **60 C3** 15 40S 124 23 E
Halland, *Sweden* **9 H15** 57 8N 12 47 E
Halle, *Belgium* **15 D4** 50 44N 4 13 E
Halle, *Germany* **16 C6** 51 30N 11 56 E
Hällefors, *Sweden* **9 G16** 59 47N 14 31 E
Hallett, *Australia* **63 E2** 33 25S 138 55 E
Hallettsville, *U.S.A.* **81 L6** 29 27N 96 57W
Hallim, *S. Korea* **35 H14** 33 24N 126 15 E
Hallingdalselvi →, *Norway* **9 F13** 60 23N 9 35 E
Hallock, *U.S.A.* **80 A6** 48 47N 96 57W
Halls Creek, *Australia* **60 C4** 18 16S 127 38 E
Hallsberg, *Sweden* **9 G16** 59 5N 15 7 E
Hallstead, *U.S.A.* **79 E9** 41 58N 75 45W
Halmahera, *Indonesia* **37 D7** 0 40N 128 0 E
Halmstad, *Sweden* **9 H15** 56 41N 12 52 E
Hälsingborg = Helsingborg, *Sweden* **9 H15** 56 3N 12 42 E
Hälsingland, *Sweden* **9 F16** 61 40N 16 5 E
Halstead, *U.K.* **11 F8** 51 57N 0 40 E
Halti, *Finland* **8 B19** 69 17N 21 18 E
Halton □, *U.K.* **10 D5** 53 22N 2 45W
Haltwhistle, *U.K.* **10 C5** 54 58N 2 26W
Ḩālūl, *Qatar* **45 E7** 25 40N 52 40 E
Halvad, *India* **42 H4** 23 1N 71 11 E
Ḩalvān, *Iran* **45 C8** 33 57N 56 15 E
Ham Tan, *Vietnam* **39 G6** 10 40N 107 45 E
Ham Yen, *Vietnam* **38 A5** 22 4N 105 3 E
Hamab, *Namibia* **56 D2** 28 7S 19 16 E
Hamada, *Japan* **31 G6** 34 56N 132 4 E
Hamadān, *Iran* **45 C6** 34 52N 48 32 E
Hamadān □, *Iran* **45 C6** 35 0N 49 0 E
Ḩamāh, *Syria* **44 C3** 35 5N 36 40 E
Hamamatsu, *Japan* **31 G8** 34 45N 137 45 E
Hamar, *Norway* **9 F14** 60 48N 11 7 E
Hamâta, Gebel, *Egypt* **44 E2** 24 17N 35 0 E
Hambantota, *Sri Lanka* **40 R12** 6 10N 81 10 E
Hamber Prov. Park, *Canada* **72 C5** 52 20N 118 0W
Hamburg, *Germany* **16 B5** 53 33N 9 59 E
Hamburg, *Ark., U.S.A.* **81 J9** 33 14N 91 48W
Hamburg, *N.Y., U.S.A.* **78 D6** 42 43N 78 50W
Hamburg, *Pa., U.S.A.* **79 F9** 40 33N 75 59W
Ḩamḑ, W. al →, *Si. Arabia* **44 E3** 24 55N 36 20 E
Hamden, *U.S.A.* **79 E12** 41 23N 72 54W
Häme, *Finland* **9 F20** 61 38N 25 10 E
Hämeenlinna, *Finland* **9 F21** 61 0N 24 28 E
Hamelin Pool, *Australia* **61 E1** 26 22S 114 20 E
Hameln, *Germany* **16 B5** 52 6N 9 21 E
Hamerkaz □, *Israel* **47 C3** 32 15N 34 55 E
Hamersley Ra., *Australia* **60 D2** 22 0S 117 45 E
Hamhung, *N. Korea* **35 E14** 39 54N 127 30 E
Hami, *China* **32 B4** 42 55N 93 25 E
Hamilton, *Australia* **63 F3** 37 45S 142 2 E
Hamilton, *Canada* **78 C5** 43 15N 79 50W
Hamilton, *N.Z.* **59 G5** 37 47S 175 19 E
Hamilton, *U.K.* **12 F4** 55 46N 4 2W
Hamilton, *Ala., U.S.A.* **77 H1** 34 9N 87 59W
Hamilton, *Mont., U.S.A.* **82 C6** 46 15N 114 10W
Hamilton, *N.Y., U.S.A.* **79 D9** 42 50N 75 33W
Hamilton, *Ohio, U.S.A.* **76 F3** 39 24N 84 34W
Hamilton, *Tex., U.S.A.* **81 K5** 31 42N 98 7W
Hamilton →, *Australia* **62 C2** 23 30S 139 47 E
Hamilton City, *U.S.A.* **84 F4** 39 45N 122 1W
Hamilton Inlet, *Canada* **71 B8** 54 0N 57 30W
Hamilton Mt., *U.S.A.* **79 C10** 43 25N 74 22W
Hamina, *Finland* **9 F22** 60 34N 27 12 E
Hamirpur, *H.P., India* **42 D7** 31 41N 76 31 E
Hamirpur, *Ut. P., India* **43 G9** 25 57N 80 9 E
Hamlet, *U.S.A.* **77 H6** 34 53N 79 42W
Hamley Bridge, *Australia* **63 E2** 34 17S 138 35 E
Hamlin = Hameln, *Germany* **16 B5** 52 6N 9 21 E
Hamlin, *N.Y., U.S.A.* **78 C7** 43 17N 77 55W
Hamlin, *Tex., U.S.A.* **81 J4** 32 53N 100 8W
Hamm, *Germany* **16 C4** 51 40N 7 50 E
Ḩammār, Hawr al, *Iraq* **44 D5** 30 50N 47 10 E
Hammerfest, *Norway* **8 A20** 70 39N 23 41 E
Hammond, *Ind., U.S.A.* **76 E2** 41 38N 87 30W
Hammond, *La., U.S.A.* **81 K9** 30 30N 90 28W
Hammond, *N.Y., U.S.A.* **79 B9** 44 27N 75 42W
Hammondsport, *U.S.A.* **78 D7** 42 25N 77 13W
Hammonton, *U.S.A.* **76 F8** 39 39N 74 48W
Hampden, *N.Z.* **59 L3** 45 18S 170 50 E
Hampshire □, *U.K.* **11 F6** 51 7N 1 23W
Hampshire Downs, *U.K.* **11 F6** 51 15N 1 10W
Hampton, *N.B., Canada* **71 C6** 45 32N 65 51W
Hampton, *Ont., Canada* **78 C6** 43 58N 78 45W
Hampton, *Ark., U.S.A.* **81 J8** 33 32N 92 28W
Hampton, *Iowa, U.S.A.* **80 D8** 42 45N 93 13W
Hampton, *N.H., U.S.A.* **79 D14** 42 57N 70 50W
Hampton, *S.C., U.S.A.* **77 J5** 32 52N 81 7W
Hampton, *Va., U.S.A.* **76 G7** 37 2N 76 21W
Hampton Bays, *U.S.A.* **79 F12** 40 53N 72 30W
Hampton Tableland, *Australia* **61 F4** 32 0S 127 0 E
Hamyang, *S. Korea* **35 G14** 35 32N 127 42 E
Han Pijesak, *Bos.-H.* **21 B8** 44 5N 18 57 E
Hanak, *Si. Arabia* **44 E3** 25 32N 37 0 E
Hanamaki, *Japan* **30 E10** 39 23N 141 7 E
Hanang, *Tanzania* **54 C4** 4 30S 35 25 E
Hanau, *Germany* **16 C5** 50 7N 8 56 E
Hanbogd = Ihbulag, *Mongolia* **34 C4** 43 11N 107 10 E
Hancheng, *China* **34 G6** 35 31N 110 25 E
Hancock, *Mich., U.S.A.* **80 B10** 47 8N 88 35W
Hancock, *N.Y., U.S.A.* **79 E9** 41 57N 75 17W
Handa, *Japan* **31 G8** 34 53N 136 55 E
Handan, *China* **34 F8** 36 35N 114 28 E
Handeni, *Tanzania* **54 D4** 5 25S 38 2 E
Handwara, *India* **43 B6** 34 21N 74 20 E
Hanegev, *Israel* **47 E4** 30 50N 35 0 E
Hanford, *U.S.A.* **84 J7** 36 20N 119 39W
Hang Chat, *Thailand* **38 C2** 18 20N 99 21 E
Hang Dong, *Thailand* **38 C2** 18 41N 98 55 E
Hangang →, *S. Korea* **35 F14** 37 50N 126 30 E
Hangayn Nuruu, *Mongolia* **32 B4** 47 30N 99 0 E
Hangchou = Hangzhou, *China* **33 C7** 30 18N 120 11 E
Hanggin Houqi, *China* **34 D4** 40 58N 107 4 E
Hanggin Qi, *China* **34 E5** 39 52N 108 50 E
Hangu, *China* **35 E9** 39 18N 117 53 E
Hangzhou, *China* **33 C7** 30 18N 120 11 E
Hangzhou Wan, *China* **33 C7** 30 15N 120 45 E
Hanhongor, *Mongolia* **34 C3** 43 55N 104 28 E
Ḩanīdh, *Si. Arabia* **45 E6** 26 35N 48 38 E
Ḩanīsh, *Yemen* **46 E3** 13 45N 42 46 E
Hankinson, *U.S.A.* **80 B6** 46 4N 96 54W
Hanko, *Finland* **9 G20** 59 50N 22 57 E
Hanksville, *U.S.A.* **83 G8** 38 22N 110 43W
Hanle, *India* **43 C8** 32 42N 79 4 E
Hanmer Springs, *N.Z.* **59 K4** 42 32S 172 50 E
Hann →, *Australia* **60 C4** 17 26S 126 17 E
Hann, Mt., *Australia* **60 C4** 15 45S 126 0 E
Hanna, *Canada* **72 C6** 51 40N 111 54W
Hanna, *U.S.A.* **82 F10** 41 52N 106 34W
Hannah B., *Canada* **70 B4** 51 40N 80 0W
Hannibal, *Mo., U.S.A.* **80 F9** 39 42N 91 22W
Hannibal, *N.Y., U.S.A.* **79 C8** 43 19N 76 35W
Hannover, *Germany* **16 B5** 52 22N 9 46 E
Hanoi, *Vietnam* **32 D5** 21 5N 105 55 E
Hanover = Hannover, *Germany* **16 B5** 52 22N 9 46 E
Hanover, *Canada* **78 B3** 44 9N 81 2W
Hanover, *S. Africa* **56 E3** 31 4S 24 29 E
Hanover, *N.H., U.S.A.* **79 C12** 43 42N 72 17W
Hanover, *Ohio, U.S.A.* **78 F2** 40 4N 82 16W
Hanover, *Pa., U.S.A.* **76 F7** 39 48N 76 59W
Hanover, I., *Chile* **96 G2** 51 0S 74 50W
Hansdiha, *India* **43 G12** 24 36N 87 5 E
Hansi, *India* **42 E6** 29 10N 75 57 E
Hanson, L., *Australia* **63 E2** 31 0S 136 15 E
Hantsavichy, *Belarus* **17 B14** 52 49N 26 30 E
Hanumangarh, *India* **42 E6** 29 35N 74 19 E
Hanzhong, *China* **34 H4** 33 10N 107 1 E
Hanzhuang, *China* **35 G9** 34 33N 117 23 E
Haora, *India* **43 H13** 22 37N 88 20 E
Haparanda, *Sweden* **8 D21** 65 52N 24 8 E
Happy, *U.S.A.* **81 H4** 34 45N 101 52W
Happy Camp, *U.S.A.* **82 F2** 41 48N 123 23W
Happy Valley-Goose Bay, *Canada* **71 B7** 53 15N 60 20W
Hapsu, *N. Korea* **35 D15** 41 13N 128 51 E
Hapur, *India* **42 E7** 28 45N 77 45 E
Ḩaql, *Si. Arabia* **47 F3** 29 10N 34 58 E
Har, *Indonesia* **37 F8** 5 16S 133 14 E
Har-Ayrag, *Mongolia* **34 B5** 45 47N 109 16 E
Har Hu, *China* **32 C4** 38 20N 97 38 E
Har Us Nuur, *Mongolia* **32 B4** 48 0N 92 0 E
Har Yehuda, *Israel* **47 D3** 31 35N 34 57 E
Ḩaraḑ, *Si. Arabia* **46 C4** 24 22N 49 0 E
Haranomachi, *Japan* **30 F10** 37 38N 140 58 E
Harare, *Zimbabwe* **55 F3** 17 43S 31 2 E
Harbin, *China* **35 B14** 45 48N 126 40 E
Harbor Beach, *U.S.A.* **78 C2** 43 51N 82 39W
Harbour Breton, *Canada* **71 C8** 47 29N 55 50W
Harbour Deep, *Canada* **71 B8** 50 25N 56 32W
Harda, *India* **42 H7** 22 27N 77 5 E
Hardangerfjorden, *Norway* **9 F12** 60 5N 6 0 E
Hardangervidda, *Norway* **9 F12** 60 7N 7 20 E
Hardap Dam, *Namibia* **56 C2** 24 32S 17 50 E
Hardenberg, *Neths.* **15 B6** 52 34N 6 37 E
Harderwijk, *Neths.* **15 B5** 52 21N 5 38 E
Hardey →, *Australia* **60 D2** 22 45S 116 8 E
Hardin, *U.S.A.* **82 D10** 45 44N 107 37W
Harding, *S. Africa* **57 E4** 30 35S 29 55 E
Harding Ra., *Australia* **60 C3** 16 17S 124 55 E
Hardisty, *Canada* **72 C6** 52 40N 111 18W
Hardoi, *India* **43 F9** 27 26N 80 6 E
Hardwar = Haridwar, *India* **42 E8** 29 58N 78 9 E
Hardwick, *U.S.A.* **79 B12** 44 30N 72 22W
Hardy, Pen., *Chile* **96 H3** 55 30S 68 20W
Hare B., *Canada* **71 B8** 51 15N 55 45W
Hareid, *Norway* **9 E12** 62 22N 6 1 E
Harer, *Ethiopia* **46 F3** 9 20N 42 8 E
Hargeisa, *Somali Rep.* **46 F3** 9 30N 44 2 E
Hari →, *Indonesia* **36 E2** 1 16S 104 5 E
Haria, *Canary Is.* **22 E6** 29 8N 13 32W
Haridwar, *India* **42 E8** 29 58N 78 9 E
Harim, Jabal al, *Oman* **45 E8** 25 58N 56 14 E
Haringhata →, *Bangla.* **41 J16** 22 0N 89 58 E
Harīrūd →, *Asia* **40 A2** 37 24N 60 38 E
Härjedalen, *Sweden* **9 E15** 62 22N 13 5 E
Harlan, *Iowa, U.S.A.* **80 E7** 41 39N 95 19W
Harlan, *Ky., U.S.A.* **77 G4** 36 51N 83 19W
Harlech, *U.K.* **10 E3** 52 52N 4 6W
Harlem, *U.S.A.* **82 B9** 48 32N 108 47W
Harlingen, *Neths.* **15 A5** 53 11N 5 25 E
Harlingen, *U.S.A.* **81 M6** 26 12N 97 42W
Harlow, *U.K.* **11 F8** 51 46N 0 8 E
Harlowton, *U.S.A.* **82 C9** 46 26N 109 50W
Harnai, *Pakistan* **42 D2** 30 6N 67 56 E
Harney Basin, *U.S.A.* **82 E4** 43 30N 119 0W
Harney L., *U.S.A.* **82 E4** 43 14N 119 8W
Harney Peak, *U.S.A.* **80 D3** 43 52N 103 32W
Härnösand, *Sweden* **9 E17** 62 38N 17 55 E
Haroldswick, *U.K.* **12 A8** 60 48N 0 50W
Harp L., *Canada* **71 A7** 55 5N 61 50W
Harper, *Liberia* **50 H4** 4 25N 7 43W
Harrai, *India* **43 H8** 22 37N 79 13 E
Harrand, *Pakistan* **42 E4** 29 28N 70 3 E
Harricana →, *Canada* **70 B4** 50 56N 79 32W
Harriman, *U.S.A.* **77 H3** 35 56N 84 33W
Harrington Harbour, *Canada* **71 B8** 50 31N 59 30W
Harris, *U.K.* **12 D2** 57 50N 6 55W
Harris, Sd. of, *U.K.* **12 D1** 57 44N 7 6W
Harris L., *Australia* **63 E2** 31 10S 135 10 E
Harris Pt., *Canada* **78 C2** 43 6N 82 9W
Harrisburg, *Ill., U.S.A.* **81 G10** 37 44N 88 32W
Harrisburg, *Nebr., U.S.A.* **80 E3** 41 33N 103 44W
Harrisburg, *Pa., U.S.A.* **78 F8** 40 16N 76 53W
Harrismith, *S. Africa* **57 D4** 28 15S 29 8 E
Harrison, *Ark., U.S.A.* **81 G8** 36 14N 93 7W
Harrison, *Maine, U.S.A.* **79 B14** 44 7N 70 39W
Harrison, *Nebr., U.S.A.* **80 D3** 42 41N 103 53W
Harrison, C., *Canada* **71 B8** 54 55N 57 55W
Harrison L., *Canada* **72 D4** 49 33N 121 50W
Harrisonburg, *U.S.A.* **76 F6** 38 27N 78 52W
Harrisonville, *U.S.A.* **80 F7** 38 39N 94 21W
Harriston, *Canada* **78 C4** 43 57N 80 53W
Harrisville, *Mich., U.S.A.* **78 B1** 44 39N 83 17W
Harrisville, *N.Y., U.S.A.* **79 B9** 44 9N 75 19W
Harrisville, *Pa., U.S.A.* **78 E5** 41 8N 80 0W
Harrodsburg, *U.S.A.* **76 G3** 37 46N 84 51W
Harrogate, *U.K.* **10 C6** 54 0N 1 33W
Harrow □, *U.K.* **11 F7** 51 35N 0 21W
Harrowsmith, *Canada* **79 B8** 44 24N 76 40W
Harry S. Truman Reservoir, *U.S.A.* **80 F7** 38 16N 93 24W
Harsin, *Iran* **44 C5** 34 18N 47 33 E
Harstad, *Norway* **8 B17** 68 48N 16 30 E
Harsud, *India* **42 H7** 22 6N 76 44 E
Hart, *U.S.A.* **76 D2** 43 42N 86 22W
Hart, L., *Australia* **63 E2** 31 10S 136 25 E
Hartbees →, *S. Africa* **56 D3** 28 45S 20 32 E
Hartford, *Conn., U.S.A.* **79 E12** 41 46N 72 41W
Hartford, *Ky., U.S.A.* **76 G2** 37 27N 86 55W
Hartford, *S. Dak., U.S.A.* **80 D6** 43 38N 96 57W
Hartford, *Wis., U.S.A.* **80 D10** 43 19N 88 22W
Hartford City, *U.S.A.* **76 E3** 40 27N 85 22W
Hartland, *Canada* **71 C6** 46 20N 67 32W
Hartland Pt., *U.K.* **11 F3** 51 1N 4 32W
Hartlepool, *U.K.* **10 C6** 54 42N 1 13W
Hartlepool □, *U.K.* **10 C6** 54 42N 1 17W
Hartley Bay, *Canada* **72 C3** 53 25N 129 15W
Hartmannberge, *Namibia* **56 B1** 17 0S 13 0 E
Hartney, *Canada* **73 D8** 49 30N 100 35W
Harts →, *S. Africa* **56 D3** 28 24S 24 17 E
Hartselle, *U.S.A.* **77 H2** 34 27N 86 56W
Hartshorne, *U.S.A.* **81 H7** 34 51N 95 34W
Hartstown, *U.S.A.* **78 E4** 41 33N 80 23W
Hartsville, *U.S.A.* **77 H5** 34 23N 80 4W
Hartswater, *S. Africa* **56 D3** 27 34S 24 43 E
Hartwell, *U.S.A.* **77 H4** 34 21N 82 56W
Harunabad, *Pakistan* **42 E5** 29 35N 73 8 E
Harvand, *Iran* **45 D7** 28 25N 55 43 E
Harvey, *Australia* **61 F2** 33 5S 115 54 E
Harvey, *Ill., U.S.A.* **76 E2** 41 36N 87 50W
Harvey, *N. Dak., U.S.A.* **80 B5** 47 47N 99 56W
Harwich, *U.K.* **11 F9** 51 56N 1 17 E
Haryana □, *India* **42 E7** 29 0N 76 10 E
Haryn →, *Belarus* **17 B14** 52 7N 27 17 E
Harz, *Germany* **16 C6** 51 38N 10 44 E
Hasa □, *Si. Arabia* **45 E6** 25 50N 49 0 E
Ḩasanābād, *Iran* **45 C7** 32 8N 52 44 E
Hasdo →, *India* **43 J10** 21 44N 82 44 E
Hashimoto, *Japan* **31 G7** 34 19N 135 37 E
Hashtjerd, *Iran* **45 C6** 35 52N 50 40 E
Haskell, *U.S.A.* **81 J5** 33 10N 99 44W
Haslemere, *U.K.* **11 F7** 51 5N 0 43W
Hasselt, *Belgium* **15 D5** 50 56N 5 21 E
Hassi Messaoud, *Algeria* **50 B7** 31 51N 6 1 E
Hässleholm, *Sweden* **9 H15** 56 10N 13 46 E
Hastings, *N.Z.* **59 H6** 39 39S 176 52 E
Hastings, *U.K.* **11 G8** 50 51N 0 35 E
Hastings, *Mich., U.S.A.* **76 D3** 42 39N 85 17W
Hastings, *Minn., U.S.A.* **80 C8** 44 44N 92 51W
Hastings, *Nebr., U.S.A.* **80 E5** 40 35N 98 23W
Hastings Ra., *Australia* **63 E5** 31 15S 152 14 E
Hat Yai, *Thailand* **39 J3** 7 1N 100 27 E
Hatanbulag = Ergel, *Mongolia* **34 C5** 43 8N 109 5 E
Hatay = Antalya, *Turkey* **25 G5** 36 52N 30 45 E
Hatch, *U.S.A.* **83 K10** 32 40N 107 9W
Hatchet L., *Canada* **73 B8** 58 36N 103 40W
Hateruma-Shima, *Japan* **31 M1** 24 3N 123 47 E
Hatfield P.O., *Australia* **63 E3** 33 54S 143 49 E
Hatgal, *Mongolia* **32 A5** 50 26N 100 9 E
Hathras, *India* **42 F8** 27 36N 78 6 E
Hatia, *Bangla.* **41 H17** 22 30N 91 5 E
Hato Mayor, *Dom. Rep.* **89 C6** 18 46N 69 15W
Hatta, *India* **43 G8** 24 7N 79 36 E
Hattah, *Australia* **63 E3** 34 48S 142 17 E
Hatteras, C., *U.S.A.* **77 H8** 35 14N 75 32W
Hattiesburg, *U.S.A.* **81 K10** 31 20N 89 17W
Hatvan, *Hungary* **17 E10** 47 40N 19 45 E
Hau Bon = Cheo Reo, *Vietnam* **36 B3** 13 25N 108 28 E
Hau Duc, *Vietnam* **38 E7** 15 20N 108 13 E
Haugesund, *Norway* **9 G11** 59 23N 5 13 E
Haukipudas, *Finland* **8 D21** 65 12N 25 20 E
Haultain →, *Canada* **73 B7** 55 51N 106 46W
Hauraki G., *N.Z.* **59 G5** 36 35S 175 5 E
Haut Atlas, *Morocco* **50 B4** 32 30N 5 0W
Haut-Zaïre = Orientale □, *Dem. Rep. of the Congo* **54 B2** 2 20N 26 0 E
Hautes Fagnes = Hohe Venn, *Belgium* **15 D6** 50 30N 6 5 E
Hauts Plateaux, *Algeria* **48 C4** 35 0N 1 0 E
Havana = La Habana, *Cuba* **88 B3** 23 8N 82 22W
Havana, *U.S.A.* **80 E9** 40 18N 90 4W
Havant, *U.K.* **11 G7** 50 51N 0 58W
Havasu, L., *U.S.A.* **85 L12** 34 18N 114 28W
Havel →, *Germany* **16 B7** 52 50N 12 3 E
Havelian, *Pakistan* **42 B5** 34 2N 73 10 E
Havelock, *Canada* **78 B7** 44 26N 77 53W
Havelock, *N.Z.* **59 J4** 41 17S 173 48 E
Havelock, *U.S.A.* **77 H7** 34 53N 76 54W
Haverfordwest, *U.K.* **11 F3** 51 48N 4 58W
Haverhill, *U.S.A.* **79 D13** 42 47N 71 5W
Haverstraw, *U.S.A.* **79 E11** 41 12N 73 58W
Havirga, *Mongolia* **34 B7** 45 41N 113 5 E
Havířov, *Czech Rep.* **17 D10** 49 46N 18 20 E
Havlíčkův Brod, *Czech Rep.* **16 D8** 49 36N 15 33 E
Havre, *U.S.A.* **82 B9** 48 33N 109 41W
Havre-Aubert, *Canada* **71 C7** 47 12N 61 56W
Havre-St.-Pierre, *Canada* **71 B7** 50 18N 63 33W
Haw →, *U.S.A.* **77 H6** 35 36N 79 3W
Hawaii □, *U.S.A.* **74 H16** 19 30N 156 30W
Hawaii I., *Pac. Oc.* **74 J17** 20 0N 155 0W
Hawaiian Is., *Pac. Oc.* **74 H17** 20 30N 156 0W
Hawaiian Ridge, *Pac. Oc.* **65 E11** 24 0N 165 0W
Hawarden, *U.S.A.* **80 D6** 43 0N 96 29W
Hawea, L., *N.Z.* **59 L2** 44 28S 169 19 E
Hawera, *N.Z.* **59 H5** 39 35S 174 19 E
Hawick, *U.K.* **12 F6** 55 26N 2 47W
Hawk Junction, *Canada* **70 C3** 48 5N 84 38W
Hawke B., *N.Z.* **59 H6** 39 25S 177 20 E
Hawker, *Australia* **63 E2** 31 59S 138 22 E
Hawkesbury, *Canada* **70 C5** 45 37N 74 37W
Hawkesbury I., *Canada* **72 C3** 53 37N 129 3W
Hawkesbury Pt., *Australia* **62 A1** 11 55S 134 5 E
Hawkinsville, *U.S.A.* **77 J4** 32 17N 83 28W
Hawley, *Minn., U.S.A.* **80 B6** 46 53N 96 19W
Hawley, *Pa., U.S.A.* **79 E9** 41 28N 75 11W
Ḩawrān, W. →, *Iraq* **44 C4** 33 58N 42 34 E
Hawsh Mūssá, *Lebanon* **47 B4** 33 45N 35 55 E
Hawthorne, *U.S.A.* **82 G4** 38 32N 118 38W
Hay, *Australia* **63 E3** 34 30S 144 51 E
Hay →, *Australia* **62 C2** 24 50S 138 0 E
Hay →, *Canada* **72 A5** 60 50N 116 26W
Hay, C., *Australia* **60 B4** 14 5S 129 29 E
Hay I., *Canada* **78 B4** 44 53N 80 58W
Hay L., *Canada* **72 B5** 58 50N 118 50W
Hay-on-Wye, *U.K.* **11 E4** 52 5N 3 8W
Hay River, *Canada* **72 A5** 60 51N 115 44W
Hay Springs, *U.S.A.* **80 D3** 42 41N 102 41W
Haya = Tehoru, *Indonesia* **37 E7** 3 23S 129 30 E
Hayachine-San, *Japan* **30 E10** 39 34N 141 29 E
Hayden, *U.S.A.* **82 F10** 40 30N 107 16W
Haydon, *Australia* **62 B3** 18 0S 141 30 E
Hayes, *U.S.A.* **80 C4** 44 23N 101 1W
Hayes →, *Canada* **70 A1** 57 3N 92 12W
Hayes Creek, *Australia* **60 B5** 13 43S 131 22 E
Hayle, *U.K.* **11 G2** 50 11N 5 26W
Hayling I., *U.K.* **11 G7** 50 48N 0 59W
Hayrabolu, *Turkey* **21 D12** 41 12N 27 5 E
Hays, *Canada* **72 C6** 50 6N 111 48W
Hays, *U.S.A.* **80 F5** 38 53N 99 20W
Haysyn, *Ukraine* **17 D15** 48 57N 29 25 E
Hayvoron, *Ukraine* **17 D15** 48 22N 29 52 E
Hayward, *Calif., U.S.A.* **84 H4** 37 40N 122 5W
Hayward, *Wis., U.S.A.* **80 B9** 46 1N 91 29W
Haywards Heath, *U.K.* **11 G7** 51 0N 0 5W
Hazafon □, *Israel* **47 C4** 32 40N 35 20 E
Hazārān, Kūh-e, *Iran* **45 D8** 29 35N 57 20 E
Hazard, *U.S.A.* **76 G4** 37 15N 83 12W
Hazaribag, *India* **43 H11** 23 58N 85 26 E
Hazaribag Road, *India* **43 G11** 24 12N 85 57 E
Hazelton, *Canada* **72 B3** 55 20N 127 42W
Hazelton, *U.S.A.* **80 B4** 46 29N 100 17W
Hazen, *U.S.A.* **80 B4** 47 18N 101 38W
Hazlehurst, *Ga., U.S.A.* **77 K4** 31 52N 82 36W
Hazlehurst, *Miss., U.S.A.* **81 K9** 31 52N 90 24W
Hazlet, *U.S.A.* **79 F10** 40 25N 74 12W
Hazleton, *U.S.A.* **79 F9** 40 57N 75 59W
Hazlett, L., *Australia* **60 D4** 21 30S 128 48 E
Hazro, *Turkey* **44 B4** 38 15N 40 47 E
Head of Bight, *Australia* **61 F5** 31 30S 131 25 E
Headlands, *Zimbabwe* **55 F3** 18 15S 32 2 E
Healdsburg, *U.S.A.* **84 G4** 38 37N 122 52W
Healdton, *U.S.A.* **81 H6** 34 14N 97 29W
Healesville, *Australia* **63 F4** 37 35S 145 30 E
Heany Junction, *Zimbabwe* **57 C4** 20 6S 28 54 E
Heard I., *Ind. Oc.* **3 G13** 53 0S 74 0 E
Hearne, *U.S.A.* **81 K6** 30 53N 96 36W
Hearst, *Canada* **70 C3** 49 40N 83 41W
Heart →, *U.S.A.* **80 B4** 46 46N 100 50W
Heart's Content, *Canada* **71 C9** 47 54N 53 27W
Heath Pt., *Canada* **71 C7** 49 8N 61 40W
Heavener, *U.S.A.* **81 H7** 34 53N 94 36W
Hebbronville, *U.S.A.* **81 M5** 27 18N 98 41W
Hebei □, *China* **34 E9** 39 0N 116 0 E
Hebel, *Australia* **63 D4** 28 58S 147 47 E
Heber, *U.S.A.* **85 N11** 32 44N 115 32W
Heber City, *U.S.A.* **82 F8** 40 31N 111 25W
Heber Springs, *U.S.A.* **81 H9** 35 30N 92 2W
Hebert, *Canada* **73 C7** 50 30N 107 10W
Hebgen L., *U.S.A.* **82 D8** 44 52N 111 20W
Hebi, *China* **34 G8** 35 57N 114 7 E
Hebrides, *U.K.* **6 D4** 57 30N 7 0W
Hebrides, Sea of the, *U.K.* **12 D2** 57 5N 7 0W
Hebron = Al Khalīl, *West Bank* **47 D4** 31 32N 35 6 E
Hebron, *Canada* **69 C13** 58 5N 62 30W
Hebron, *N. Dak., U.S.A.* **80 B3** 46 54N 102 3W
Hebron, *Nebr., U.S.A.* **80 E6** 40 10N 97 35W
Hecate Str., *Canada* **72 C2** 53 10N 130 30W
Heceta I., *U.S.A.* **72 B2** 55 46N 133 40W
Hechi, *China* **32 D5** 24 40N 108 2 E
Hechuan, *China* **32 C5** 30 2N 106 12 E
Hecla, *U.S.A.* **80 C5** 45 53N 98 9W
Hecla I., *Canada* **73 C9** 51 10N 96 43W
Hede, *Sweden* **9 E15** 62 23N 13 30 E
Hedemora, *Sweden* **9 F16** 60 18N 15 58 E
Heerde, *Neths.* **15 B6** 52 24N 6 2 E
Heerenveen, *Neths.* **15 B5** 52 57N 5 55 E
Heerhugowaard, *Neths.* **15 B4** 52 40N 4 51 E
Heerlen, *Neths.* **18 A6** 50 55N 5 58 E
Ḩefa, *Israel* **47 C4** 32 46N 35 0 E
Ḩefa □, *Israel* **47 C4** 32 40N 35 0 E
Hefei, *China* **33 C6** 31 52N 117 18 E

Hegang, *China* 33 B8 47 20N 130 19 E
Heichengzhen, *China* 34 F4 36 24N 106 3 E
Heidelberg, *Germany* 16 D5 49 24N 8 42 E
Heidelberg, *S. Africa* 56 E3 34 6S 20 59 E
Heilbron, *S. Africa* 57 D4 27 16S 27 59 E
Heilbronn, *Germany* 16 D5 49 9N 9 13 E
Heilongjiang □, *China* 33 B7 48 0N 126 0 E
Heilunkiang = Heilongjiang □, *China* 33 B7 48 0N 126 0 E
Heimaey, *Iceland* 8 E3 63 26N 20 17W
Heinola, *Finland* 9 F22 61 13N 26 2 E
Heinze Kyun, *Burma* 38 E1 14 25N 97 45 E
Heishan, *China* 35 D12 41 40N 122 5 E
Heishui, *China* 35 C10 42 8N 119 30 E
Hejaz = Ḥijāz □, *Si. Arabia* 46 C2 24 0N 40 0 E
Hejian, *China* 34 E9 38 25N 116 5 E
Hejin, *China* 34 G6 35 35N 110 42 E
Hekımhan, *Turkey* 44 B3 38 50N 37 55 E
Hekla, *Iceland* 8 E4 63 56N 19 35W
Hekou, *China* 32 D5 22 30N 103 59 E
Helan Shan, *China* 34 E3 38 30N 105 55 E
Helen Atoll, *Pac. Oc.* 37 D8 2 40N 132 0 E
Helena, *Ark., U.S.A.* 81 H9 34 32N 90 36W
Helena, *Mont., U.S.A.* 82 C7 46 36N 112 2W
Helendale, *U.S.A.* 85 L9 34 44N 117 19W
Helensburgh, *U.K.* 12 E4 56 1N 4 43W
Helensville, *N.Z.* 59 G5 36 41S 174 29 E
Helenvale, *Australia* 62 B4 15 43S 145 14 E
Helgeland, *Norway* 8 C15 66 7N 13 29 E
Helgoland, *Germany* 16 A4 54 10N 7 53 E
Heligoland = Helgoland, *Germany* 16 A4 54 10N 7 53 E
Heligoland B. = Deutsche Bucht, *Germany* 16 A5 54 15N 8 0 E
Hella, *Iceland* 8 E3 63 50N 20 24W
Hellertown, *U.S.A.* 79 F9 40 35N 75 21W
Hellespont = Çanakkale Boğazı, *Turkey* 21 D12 40 17N 26 32 E
Hellevoetsluis, *Neths.* 15 C4 51 50N 4 8 E
Hellín, *Spain* 19 C5 38 31N 1 40W
Helmand □, *Afghan.* 40 D4 31 20N 64 0 E
Helmand →, *Afghan.* 40 D2 31 12N 61 34 E
Helmeringhausen, *Namibia* 56 D2 25 54S 16 57 E
Helmond, *Neths.* 15 C5 51 29N 5 41 E
Helmsdale, *U.K.* 12 C5 58 7N 3 39W
Helmsdale →, *U.K.* 12 C5 58 7N 3 40W
Helong, *China* 35 C15 42 40N 129 0 E
Helper, *U.S.A.* 82 G8 39 41N 110 51W
Helsingborg, *Sweden* 9 H15 56 3N 12 42 E
Helsingfors = Helsinki, *Finland* 9 F21 60 15N 25 3 E
Helsingør, *Denmark* 9 H15 56 2N 12 35 E
Helsinki, *Finland* 9 F21 60 15N 25 3 E
Helston, *U.K.* 11 G2 50 6N 5 17W
Helvellyn, *U.K.* 10 C4 54 32N 3 1W
Helwân, *Egypt* 51 C12 29 50N 31 20 E
Hemel Hempstead, *U.K.* 11 F7 51 44N 0 28W
Hemet, *U.S.A.* 85 M10 33 45N 116 58W
Hemingford, *U.S.A.* 80 D3 42 19N 103 4W
Hemmingford, *Canada* 79 A11 45 3N 73 35W
Hempstead, *U.S.A.* 81 K6 30 6N 96 5W
Hemse, *Sweden* 9 H18 57 15N 18 22 E
Henan □, *China* 34 H8 34 0N 114 0 E
Henares →, *Spain* 19 B4 40 24N 3 30W
Henashi-Misaki, *Japan* 30 D9 40 37N 139 51 E
Henderson, *Argentina* 94 D3 36 18S 61 43W
Henderson, *Ky., U.S.A.* 76 G2 37 50N 87 35W
Henderson, *N.C., U.S.A.* 77 G6 36 20N 78 25W
Henderson, *Nev., U.S.A.* 85 J12 36 2N 114 59W
Henderson, *Tenn., U.S.A.* 77 H1 35 26N 88 38W
Henderson, *Tex., U.S.A.* 81 J7 32 9N 94 48W
Hendersonville, *N.C., U.S.A.* 77 H4 35 19N 82 28W
Hendersonville, *Tenn., U.S.A.* 77 G2 36 18N 86 37W
Hendījān, *Iran* 45 D6 30 14N 49 43 E
Hendorābī, *Iran* 45 E7 26 40N 53 37 E
Hengcheng, *China* 34 E4 38 18N 106 28 E
Hengdaohezi, *China* 35 B15 44 52N 129 0 E
Hengelo, *Neths.* 15 B6 52 16N 6 48 E
Hengshan, *China* 34 F5 37 58N 109 5 E
Hengshui, *China* 34 F8 37 41N 115 40 E
Hengyang, *China* 33 D6 26 59N 112 22 E
Henlopen, C., *U.S.A.* 76 F8 38 48N 75 6W
Hennenman, *S. Africa* 56 D4 27 59S 27 1 E
Hennessey, *U.S.A.* 81 G6 36 6N 97 54W
Henrietta, *U.S.A.* 81 J5 33 49N 98 12W
Henrietta, Ostrov = Genriyetty, Ostrov, *Russia* 27 B16 77 6N 156 30 E
Henrietta Maria, C., *Canada* 70 A3 55 9N 82 20W
Henry, *U.S.A.* 80 E10 41 7N 89 22W
Henryetta, *U.S.A.* 81 H7 35 27N 95 59W
Henryville, *Canada* 79 A11 45 8N 73 11W
Hensall, *Canada* 78 C3 43 26N 81 30W
Hentiesbaai, *Namibia* 56 C1 22 8S 14 18 E
Hentiyn Nuruu, *Mongolia* 33 B5 48 30N 108 30 E
Henty, *Australia* 63 F4 35 30S 147 0 E
Henzada, *Burma* 41 L19 17 38N 95 26 E
Heppner, *U.S.A.* 82 D4 45 21N 119 33W
Hepworth, *Canada* 78 B3 44 37N 81 9W
Hequ, *China* 34 E6 39 20N 111 15 E
Héraðsflói, *Iceland* 8 D6 65 42N 14 12W
Héraðsvötn →, *Iceland* 8 D4 65 45N 19 25W
Herald Cays, *Australia* 62 B4 16 58S 149 9 E
Herāt, *Afghan.* 40 B3 34 20N 62 7 E
Herāt □, *Afghan.* 40 B3 35 0N 62 0 E
Herbert →, *Australia* 62 B4 18 31S 146 17 E
Herberton, *Australia* 62 B4 17 20S 145 25 E
Herbertsdale, *S. Africa* 56 E3 34 1S 21 46 E
Herceg-Novi, *Montenegro, Yug.* 21 C8 42 30N 18 33 E
Herchmer, *Canada* 73 B10 57 22N 94 10W
Herðubreið, *Iceland* 8 D5 65 11N 16 21W
Hereford, *U.K.* 11 E5 52 4N 2 43W
Hereford, *U.S.A.* 81 H3 34 49N 102 24W
Herefordshire □, *U.K.* 11 E5 52 8N 2 40W
Herentals, *Belgium* 15 C4 51 12N 4 51 E
Herford, *Germany* 16 B5 52 7N 8 39 E
Herington, *U.S.A.* 80 F6 38 40N 96 57W
Herkimer, *U.S.A.* 79 D10 43 0N 74 59W
Herlong, *U.S.A.* 84 E6 40 8N 120 8W
Herm, *U.K.* 11 H5 49 30N 2 28W
Hermann, *U.S.A.* 80 F9 38 42N 91 27W
Hermannsburg, *Australia* 60 D5 23 57S 132 45 E
Hermanus, *S. Africa* 56 E2 34 27S 19 12 E
Hermidale, *Australia* 63 E4 31 30S 146 42 E
Hermiston, *U.S.A.* 82 D4 45 51N 119 17W
Hermite, I., *Chile* 96 H3 55 50S 68 0W
Hermon, *U.S.A.* 79 B9 44 28N 75 14W
Hermon, Mt. = Shaykh, J. ash, *Lebanon* 47 B4 33 25N 35 50 E
Hermosillo, *Mexico* 86 B2 29 10N 111 0W
Hernád →, *Hungary* 17 D11 47 56N 21 8 E
Hernandarias, *Paraguay* 95 B5 25 20S 54 40W
Hernandez, *U.S.A.* 84 J6 36 24N 120 46W
Hernando, *Argentina* 94 C3 32 28S 63 40W
Hernando, *U.S.A.* 81 H10 34 50N 90 0W
Herndon, *U.S.A.* 78 F8 40 43N 76 51W
Herne, *Germany* 15 C7 51 32N 7 14 E
Herne Bay, *U.K.* 11 F9 51 21N 1 8 E
Herning, *Denmark* 9 H13 56 8N 8 58 E
Heroica = Caborca, *Mexico* 86 A2 30 40N 112 10W
Heroica Nogales = Nogales, *Mexico* 86 A2 31 20N 110 56W
Heron Bay, *Canada* 70 C2 48 40N 86 25W
Herradura, Pta. de la, *Canary Is.* 22 F5 28 26N 14 8W
Herreid, *U.S.A.* 80 C4 45 50N 100 4W
Herrin, *U.S.A.* 81 G10 37 48N 89 2W
Herriot, *Canada* 73 B8 56 22N 101 16W
Hershey, *U.S.A.* 79 F8 40 17N 76 39W
Hersonissos, *Greece* 23 D7 35 18N 25 22 E
Herstal, *Belgium* 15 D5 50 40N 5 38 E
Hertford, *U.K.* 11 F7 51 48N 0 4W
Hertfordshire □, *U.K.* 11 F7 51 51N 0 5W
's-Hertogenbosch, *Neths.* 15 C5 51 42N 5 17 E
Hertzogville, *S. Africa* 56 D4 28 9S 25 30 E
Hervey B., *Australia* 62 C5 25 0S 152 52 E
Herzliyya, *Israel* 47 C3 32 10N 34 50 E
Ḥeṣār, *Fārs, Iran* 45 D6 29 52N 50 16 E
Ḥeṣār, *Markazī, Iran* 45 C6 35 50N 49 12 E
Heshui, *China* 34 G5 35 48N 108 0 E
Heshun, *China* 34 F7 37 22N 113 32 E
Hesperia, *U.S.A.* 85 L9 34 25N 117 18W
Hesse = Hessen □, *Germany* 16 C5 50 30N 9 0 E
Hessen □, *Germany* 16 C5 50 30N 9 0 E
Hetch Hetchy Aqueduct, *U.S.A.* 84 H5 37 29N 122 19W
Hettinger, *U.S.A.* 80 C3 46 0N 102 42W
Heuvelton, *U.S.A.* 79 B9 44 37N 75 25W
Hewitt, *U.S.A.* 81 K6 31 27N 97 11W
Hexham, *U.K.* 10 C5 54 58N 2 4W
Hexigten Qi, *China* 35 C9 43 18N 117 30 E
Ḥeydarābād, *Iran* 45 D7 30 33N 55 38 E
Heysham, *U.K.* 10 C5 54 3N 2 53W
Heywood, *Australia* 63 F3 38 8S 141 37 E
Heze, *China* 34 G8 35 14N 115 20 E
Hi Vista, *U.S.A.* 85 L9 34 45N 117 46W
Hialeah, *U.S.A.* 77 N5 25 50N 80 17W
Hiawatha, *U.S.A.* 80 F7 39 51N 95 32W
Hibbing, *U.S.A.* 80 B8 47 25N 92 56W
Hibbs B., *Australia* 62 G4 42 35S 145 15 E
Hibernia Reef, *Australia* 60 B3 12 0S 123 23 E
Hickman, *U.S.A.* 81 G10 36 34N 89 11W
Hickory, *U.S.A.* 77 H5 35 44N 81 21W
Hicks, Pt., *Australia* 63 F4 37 49S 149 17 E
Hicks L., *Canada* 73 A9 61 25N 100 0W
Hicksville, *U.S.A.* 79 F11 40 46N 73 32W
Hida-Gawa →, *Japan* 31 G8 35 26N 137 3 E
Hida-Sammyaku, *Japan* 31 F8 36 30N 137 40 E
Hidaka-Sammyaku, *Japan* 30 C11 42 35N 142 45 E
Hidalgo, *Mexico* 87 C5 24 15N 99 26W
Hidalgo □, *Mexico* 87 C5 20 30N 99 10W
Hidalgo, Presa M., *Mexico* 86 B3 26 30N 108 35W
Hidalgo del Parral, *Mexico* 86 B3 26 58N 105 40W
Hierro, *Canary Is.* 22 G1 27 44N 18 0W
Higashiajima-San, *Japan* 30 F10 37 40N 140 10 E
Higashiōsaka, *Japan* 31 G7 34 40N 135 37 E
Higgins, *U.S.A.* 81 G4 36 7N 100 2W
Higgins Corner, *U.S.A.* 84 F5 39 2N 121 5W
High Atlas = Haut Atlas, *Morocco* 50 B4 32 30N 5 0W
High Bridge, *U.S.A.* 79 F10 40 40N 74 54W
High Level, *Canada* 72 B5 58 31N 117 8W
High Point, *U.S.A.* 77 H6 35 57N 80 0W
High Prairie, *Canada* 72 B5 55 30N 116 30W
High River, *Canada* 72 C6 50 30N 113 50W
High Tatra = Tatry, *Slovak Rep.* 17 D11 49 20N 20 0 E
High Veld, *Africa* 48 J6 27 0S 27 0 E
High Wycombe, *U.K.* 11 F7 51 37N 0 45W
Highland □, *U.K.* 12 D4 57 17N 4 21W
Highland Park, *U.S.A.* 76 D2 42 11N 87 48W
Highmore, *U.S.A.* 80 C5 44 31N 99 27W
Highrock L., *Man., Canada* 73 B8 55 45N 100 30W
Highrock L., *Sask., Canada* 73 B7 57 5N 105 32W
Higüey, *Dom. Rep.* 89 C6 18 37N 68 42W
Hiiumaa, *Estonia* 9 G20 58 50N 22 45 E
Ḥijāz □, *Si. Arabia* 46 C2 24 0N 40 0 E
Hijo = Tagum, *Phil.* 37 C7 7 33N 125 53 E
Hikari, *Japan* 31 H5 33 58N 131 58 E
Hiko, *U.S.A.* 84 H11 37 32N 115 14W
Hikone, *Japan* 31 G8 35 15N 136 10 E
Hikurangi, *Gisborne, N.Z.* 59 H6 37 55S 178 4 E
Hikurangi, *Northland, N.Z.* 59 F5 35 36S 174 17 E
Hildesheim, *Germany* 16 B5 52 9N 9 56 E
Hill →, *Australia* 61 F2 30 23S 115 3 E
Hill City, *Idaho, U.S.A.* 82 E6 43 18N 115 3W
Hill City, *Kans., U.S.A.* 80 F5 39 22N 99 51W
Hill City, *S. Dak., U.S.A.* 80 D3 43 56N 103 35W
Hill Island L., *Canada* 73 A7 60 30N 109 50W
Hillcrest Center, *U.S.A.* 85 K8 35 23N 118 57W
Hillegom, *Neths.* 15 B4 52 18N 4 35 E
Hillerød, *Denmark* 9 J15 55 56N 12 19 E
Hillsboro, *Kans., U.S.A.* 80 F6 38 21N 97 12W
Hillsboro, *N. Dak., U.S.A.* 80 B6 47 26N 97 3W
Hillsboro, *N.H., U.S.A.* 79 C13 43 7N 71 54W
Hillsboro, *Ohio, U.S.A.* 76 F4 39 12N 83 37W
Hillsboro, *Oreg., U.S.A.* 84 E4 45 31N 122 59W
Hillsboro, *Tex., U.S.A.* 81 J6 32 1N 97 8W
Hillsborough, *Grenada* 89 D7 12 28N 61 28W
Hillsdale, *Mich., U.S.A.* 76 E3 41 56N 84 38W
Hillsdale, *N.Y., U.S.A.* 79 D11 42 11N 73 30W
Hillsport, *Canada* 70 C2 49 27N 85 34W
Hillston, *Australia* 63 E4 33 30S 145 31 E
Hilo, *U.S.A.* 74 J17 19 44N 155 5W
Hilton, *U.S.A.* 78 C7 43 17N 77 48W
Hilton Head Island, *U.S.A.* 77 J5 32 13N 80 45W
Hilversum, *Neths.* 15 B5 52 14N 5 10 E
Himachal Pradesh □, *India* 42 D7 31 30N 77 0 E
Himalaya, *Asia* 43 E11 29 0N 84 0 E
Himatnagar, *India* 40 H8 23 37N 72 57 E
Himeji, *Japan* 31 G7 34 50N 134 40 E
Himi, *Japan* 31 F8 36 50N 136 55 E
Ḥimş, *Syria* 47 A5 34 40N 36 45 E
Ḥimş □, *Syria* 47 A6 34 30N 37 0 E
Hinche, *Haiti* 89 C5 19 9N 72 1W
Hinchinbrook I., *Australia* 62 B4 18 20S 146 15 E
Hinckley, *U.K.* 11 E6 52 33N 1 22W
Hinckley, *U.S.A.* 80 B8 46 1N 92 56W
Hindaun, *India* 42 F7 26 44N 77 5 E
Hindmarsh, L., *Australia* 63 F3 36 5S 141 55 E
Hindu Bagh, *Pakistan* 42 D2 30 56N 67 50 E
Hindu Kush, *Asia* 40 B7 36 0N 71 0 E
Hindubagh, *Pakistan* 40 D5 30 56N 67 57 E
Hindupur, *India* 40 N10 13 49N 77 32 E
Hines Creek, *Canada* 72 B5 56 20N 118 40W
Hinesville, *U.S.A.* 77 K5 31 51N 81 36W
Hinganghat, *India* 40 J11 20 30N 78 52 E
Hingham, *U.S.A.* 82 B8 48 33N 110 25W
Hingir, *India* 43 J10 21 57N 83 41 E
Hingoli, *India* 40 K10 19 41N 77 15 E
Hinna = Imi, *Ethiopia* 46 F3 6 28N 42 10 E
Hinnøya, *Norway* 8 B16 68 35N 15 50 E
Hinojosa del Duque, *Spain* 19 C3 38 30N 5 9W
Hinsdale, *U.S.A.* 79 D12 42 47N 72 29W
Hinton, *Canada* 72 C5 53 26N 117 34W
Hinton, *U.S.A.* 76 G5 37 40N 80 54W
Hirado, *Japan* 31 H4 33 22N 129 33 E
Hirakud Dam, *India* 41 J13 21 32N 83 45 E
Hiran →, *India* 43 H8 23 6N 79 21 E
Hirapur, *India* 43 G8 24 22N 79 13 E
Hiratsuka, *Japan* 31 G9 35 19N 139 21 E
Hiroo, *Japan* 30 C11 42 17N 143 19 E
Hirosaki, *Japan* 30 D10 40 34N 140 28 E
Hiroshima, *Japan* 31 G6 34 24N 132 30 E
Hiroshima □, *Japan* 31 G6 34 50N 133 0 E
Hisar, *India* 42 E6 29 12N 75 45 E
Hisb →, *Iraq* 44 D5 31 45N 44 17 E
Ḥismá, *Si. Arabia* 44 D3 28 30N 36 0 E
Hispaniola, *W. Indies* 89 C5 19 0N 71 0W
Hīt, *Iraq* 44 C4 33 38N 42 49 E
Hita, *Japan* 31 H5 33 20N 130 58 E
Hitachi, *Japan* 31 F10 36 36N 140 39 E
Hitchin, *U.K.* 11 F7 51 58N 0 16W
Hitoyoshi, *Japan* 31 H5 32 13N 130 45 E
Hitra, *Norway* 8 E13 63 30N 8 45 E
Hixon, *Canada* 72 C4 53 25N 122 35W
Ḥiyyon, N. →, *Israel* 47 E4 30 25N 35 10 E
Hjalmar L., *Canada* 73 A7 61 33N 109 25W
Hjälmaren, *Sweden* 9 G16 59 18N 15 40 E
Hjørring, *Denmark* 9 H13 57 29N 9 59 E
Hkakabo Razi, *Burma* 41 E20 28 25N 97 23 E
Hlobane, *S. Africa* 57 D5 27 42S 31 0 E
Hluhluwe, *S. Africa* 57 D5 28 1S 32 15 E
Hlyboka, *Ukraine* 17 D13 48 5N 25 56 E
Ho Chi Minh City = Thanh Pho Ho Chi Minh, *Vietnam* 39 G6 10 58N 106 40 E
Ho Thuong, *Vietnam* 38 C5 19 32N 105 48 E
Hoa Binh, *Vietnam* 38 B5 20 50N 105 20 E
Hoa Da, *Vietnam* 39 G7 11 16N 108 40 E
Hoa Hiep, *Vietnam* 39 G5 11 34N 105 51 E
Hoai Nhon, *Vietnam* 38 E7 14 28N 109 1 E
Hoang Lien Son, *Vietnam* 38 A4 22 0N 104 0 E
Hoanib →, *Namibia* 56 B2 19 27S 12 46 E
Hoare B., *Canada* 69 B13 65 17N 62 30W
Hoarusib →, *Namibia* 56 B2 19 3S 12 36 E
Hobart, *Australia* 62 G4 42 50S 147 21 E
Hobart, *U.S.A.* 81 H5 35 1N 99 6W
Hobbs, *U.S.A.* 81 J3 32 42N 103 8W
Hobbs Coast, *Antarctica* 5 D14 74 50S 131 0W
Hobe Sound, *U.S.A.* 77 M5 27 4N 80 8W
Hoboken, *U.S.A.* 79 F10 40 45N 74 4W
Hobro, *Denmark* 9 H13 56 39N 9 46 E
Hoburgen, *Sweden* 9 H18 56 55N 18 7 E
Hochfeld, *Namibia* 56 C2 21 28S 17 58 E
Hodaka-Dake, *Japan* 31 F8 36 17N 137 39 E
Hodeida = Al Ḥudaydah, *Yemen* 46 E3 14 50N 43 0 E
Hodgeville, *Canada* 73 C7 50 7N 106 58W
Hodgson, *Canada* 73 C9 51 13N 97 36W
Hódmezővásárhely, *Hungary* 17 E11 46 28N 20 22 E
Hodna, Chott el, *Algeria* 50 A6 35 26N 4 43 E
Hodonín, *Czech Rep.* 17 D9 48 50N 17 10 E
Hoeamdong, *N. Korea* 35 C16 42 30N 130 16 E
Hoek van Holland, *Neths.* 15 C4 52 0N 4 7 E
Hoengsŏng, *S. Korea* 35 F14 37 29N 127 59 E
Hoeryong, *N. Korea* 35 C15 42 30N 129 45 E
Hoeyang, *N. Korea* 35 E14 38 43N 127 36 E
Hof, *Germany* 16 C6 50 19N 11 55 E
Hofmeyr, *S. Africa* 56 E4 31 39S 25 50 E
Höfn, *Iceland* 8 D6 64 15N 15 13W
Hofors, *Sweden* 9 F17 60 31N 16 15 E
Hofsjökull, *Iceland* 8 D4 64 49N 18 48W
Hōfu, *Japan* 31 G5 34 3N 131 34 E
Hogan Group, *Australia* 63 F4 39 13S 147 1 E
Hogarth, Mt., *Australia* 62 C2 21 48S 136 58 E
Hoggar = Ahaggar, *Algeria* 50 D7 23 0N 6 30 E
Hogsty Reef, *Bahamas* 89 B5 21 41N 73 48W
Hoh →, *U.S.A.* 84 C2 47 45N 124 29W
Hohe Venn, *Belgium* 15 D6 50 30N 6 5 E
Hohenwald, *U.S.A.* 77 H2 35 33N 87 33W
Hoher Rhön = Rhön, *Germany* 16 C5 50 24N 9 58 E
Hohhot, *China* 34 D6 40 52N 111 40 E
Hóhlakas, *Greece* 23 D9 35 57N 27 53 E
Hoi An, *Vietnam* 38 E7 15 30N 108 19 E
Hoi Xuan, *Vietnam* 38 B5 20 25N 105 9 E
Hoisington, *U.S.A.* 80 F5 38 31N 98 47W
Hōjō, *Japan* 31 H6 33 58N 132 46 E
Hokianga Harbour, *N.Z.* 59 F4 35 31S 173 22 E
Hokitika, *N.Z.* 59 K3 42 42S 171 0 E
Hokkaidō □, *Japan* 30 C11 43 30N 143 0 E
Holbrook, *Australia* 63 F4 35 42S 147 18 E
Holbrook, *U.S.A.* 83 J8 34 54N 110 10W
Holden, *U.S.A.* 82 G7 39 6N 112 16W
Holdenville, *U.S.A.* 81 H6 35 5N 96 24W
Holdrege, *U.S.A.* 80 E5 40 26N 99 23W
Holguín, *Cuba* 88 B4 20 50N 76 20W
Hollams Bird I., *Namibia* 56 C1 24 40S 14 30 E
Holland, *Mich., U.S.A.* 76 D2 42 47N 86 7W
Holland, *N.Y., U.S.A.* 78 D6 42 38N 78 32W
Hollandale, *U.S.A.* 81 J9 33 10N 90 51W
Hollandia = Jayapura, *Indonesia* 37 E10 2 28S 140 38 E
Holley, *U.S.A.* 78 C6 43 14N 78 2W
Hollidaysburg, *U.S.A.* 78 F6 40 26N 78 24W
Hollis, *U.S.A.* 81 H5 34 41N 99 55W
Hollister, *Calif., U.S.A.* 84 J5 36 51N 121 24W
Hollister, *Idaho, U.S.A.* 82 E6 42 21N 114 35W
Holly Hill, *U.S.A.* 77 L5 29 16N 81 3W
Holly Springs, *U.S.A.* 81 H10 34 46N 89 27W
Hollywood, *U.S.A.* 77 N5 26 1N 80 9W
Holman, *Canada* 68 A8 70 44N 117 44W
Hólmavík, *Iceland* 8 D3 65 42N 21 40W
Holmen, *U.S.A.* 80 D9 43 58N 91 15W
Holmes Reefs, *Australia* 62 B4 16 27S 148 0 E
Holmsund, *Sweden* 8 E19 63 41N 20 20 E
Holroyd →, *Australia* 62 A3 14 10S 141 36 E
Holstebro, *Denmark* 9 H13 56 22N 8 37 E
Holsworthy, *U.K.* 11 G3 50 48N 4 22W
Holton, *Canada* 71 B8 54 31N 57 12W
Holton, *U.S.A.* 80 F7 39 28N 95 44W
Holtville, *U.S.A.* 85 N11 32 49N 115 23W
Holwerd, *Neths.* 15 A5 53 22N 5 54 E
Holy I., *Angl., U.K.* 10 D3 53 17N 4 37W
Holy I., *Northumb., U.K.* 10 B6 55 40N 1 47W
Holyhead, *U.K.* 10 D3 53 18N 4 38W
Holyoke, *Colo., U.S.A.* 80 E3 40 35N 102 18W
Holyoke, *Mass., U.S.A.* 79 D12 42 12N 72 37W
Holyrood, *Canada* 71 C9 47 27N 53 8W
Homa Bay, *Kenya* 54 C3 0 36S 34 30 E
Homalin, *Burma* 41 G19 24 55N 95 0 E
Homand, *Iran* 45 C8 32 28N 59 37 E
Homathko →, *Canada* 72 C4 51 0N 124 56W
Hombori, *Mali* 50 E5 15 20N 1 38W
Home B., *Canada* 69 B13 68 40N 67 10W
Home Hill, *Australia* 62 B4 19 43S 147 25 E
Homedale, *U.S.A.* 82 E5 43 37N 116 56W
Homer, *Alaska, U.S.A.* 68 C4 59 39N 151 33W
Homer, *La., U.S.A.* 81 J8 32 48N 93 4W
Homer City, *U.S.A.* 78 F5 40 32N 79 10W
Homestead, *Australia* 62 C4 20 20S 145 40 E
Homestead, *U.S.A.* 77 N5 25 28N 80 29W
Homewood, *U.S.A.* 84 F6 39 4N 120 8W
Homoine, *Mozam.* 57 C6 23 55S 35 8 E
Homs = Ḥimş, *Syria* 47 A5 34 40N 36 45 E
Homyel, *Belarus* 17 B16 52 28N 31 0 E
Hon Chong, *Vietnam* 39 G5 10 25N 104 30 E
Hon Me, *Vietnam* 38 C5 19 23N 105 56 E
Honan = Henan □, *China* 34 H8 34 0N 114 0 E
Honbetsu, *Japan* 30 C11 43 7N 143 37 E
Honcut, *U.S.A.* 84 F5 39 20N 121 32W
Hondeklipbaai, *S. Africa* 56 E2 30 19S 17 17 E
Hondo, *Japan* 31 H5 32 27N 130 12 E
Hondo, *U.S.A.* 81 L5 29 21N 99 9W
Hondo →, *Belize* 87 D7 18 25N 88 21W
Honduras ■, *Cent. Amer.* 88 D2 14 40N 86 30W
Honduras, G. de, *Caribbean* 88 C2 16 50N 87 0W
Hønefoss, *Norway* 9 F14 60 10N 10 18 E
Honesdale, *U.S.A.* 79 E9 41 34N 75 16W
Honey L., *U.S.A.* 84 E6 40 15N 120 19W
Honfleur, *France* 18 B4 49 25N 0 13 E
Hong →, *Vietnam* 32 D5 22 0N 104 0 E
Hong Gai, *Vietnam* 38 B6 20 57N 107 5 E
Hong He →, *China* 34 H8 32 25N 115 35 E
Hong Kong □, *China* 33 D6 22 11N 114 14 E
Hongch'ŏn, *S. Korea* 35 F14 37 44N 127 53 E
Hongjiang, *China* 33 D5 27 7N 109 59 E
Hongliu He →, *China* 34 F5 38 0N 109 50 E
Hongor, *Mongolia* 34 B7 45 45N 112 50 E
Hongsa, *Laos* 38 C3 19 43N 101 20 E
Hongshui He →, *China* 33 D5 23 48N 109 30 E
Hongsŏng, *S. Korea* 35 F14 36 37N 126 38 E
Hongtong, *China* 34 F6 36 16N 111 40 E
Honguedo, Détroit d', *Canada* 71 C7 49 15N 64 0W
Hongwon, *N. Korea* 35 E14 40 0N 127 56 E
Hongze Hu, *China* 35 H10 33 15N 118 35 E
Honiara, *Solomon Is.* 64 H7 9 27S 159 57 E
Honiton, *U.K.* 11 G4 50 47N 3 11W
Honjō, *Japan* 30 E10 39 23N 140 3 E
Honningsvåg, *Norway* 8 A21 70 59N 25 59 E
Honolulu, *U.S.A.* 74 H16 21 19N 157 52W
Honshū, *Japan* 33 C8 36 0N 138 0 E
Hood, Mt., *U.S.A.* 82 D3 45 23N 121 42W
Hood, Pt., *Australia* 61 F2 34 23S 119 34 E
Hood River, *U.S.A.* 82 D3 45 43N 121 31W
Hoodsport, *U.S.A.* 84 C3 47 24N 123 9W
Hoogeveen, *Neths.* 15 B6 52 44N 6 28 E
Hoogezand-Sappemeer, *Neths.* 15 A6 53 9N 6 45 E
Hooghly →, *India* 43 J13 21 56N 88 4 E
Hooghly-Chinsura = Chunchura, *India* 43 H13 22 53N 88 27 E
Hook Hd., *Ireland* 13 D5 52 7N 6 56W
Hook I., *Australia* 62 C4 20 4S 149 0 E
Hook of Holland = Hoek van Holland, *Neths.* 15 C4 52 0N 4 7 E
Hooker, *U.S.A.* 81 G4 36 52N 101 13W
Hooker Creek, *Australia* 60 C5 18 23S 130 38 E
Hoonah, *U.S.A.* 72 B1 58 7N 135 27W
Hooper Bay, *U.S.A.* 68 B3 61 32N 166 6W
Hoopeston, *U.S.A.* 76 E2 40 28N 87 40W
Hoopstad, *S. Africa* 56 D4 27 50S 25 55 E
Hoorn, *Neths.* 15 B5 52 38N 5 4 E
Hoover, *U.S.A.* 77 J2 33 20N 86 11W
Hoover Dam, *U.S.A.* 85 K12 36 1N 114 44W
Hooversville, *U.S.A.* 78 F6 40 9N 78 55W
Hop Bottom, *U.S.A.* 79 E9 41 42N 75 46W
Hope, *Canada* 72 D4 49 25N 121 25W
Hope, *Ariz., U.S.A.* 85 M13 33 43N 113 42W
Hope, *Ark., U.S.A.* 81 J8 33 40N 93 36W
Hope, L., *S. Austral., Australia* 63 D2 28 24S 139 18 E
Hope, L., *W. Austral., Australia* 61 F3 32 35S 120 15 E
Hope I., *Canada* 78 B4 44 55N 80 11W
Hope Town, *Bahamas* 88 A4 26 35N 76 57W
Hopedale, *Canada* 71 A7 55 28N 60 13W
Hopedale, *U.S.A.* 79 D13 42 8N 71 33W
Hopefield, *S. Africa* 56 E2 33 3S 18 22 E
Hopei = Hebei □, *China* 34 E9 39 0N 116 0 E
Hopelchén, *Mexico* 87 D7 19 46N 89 50W
Hopetoun, *Vic., Australia* 63 F3 35 42S 142 22 E
Hopetoun, *W. Austral., Australia* 61 F3 33 57S 120 7 E
Hopetown, *S. Africa* 56 D3 29 34S 24 3 E
Hopevale, *Australia* 62 B4 15 16S 145 20 E
Hopewell, *U.S.A.* 76 G7 37 18N 77 17W
Hopkins, L., *Australia* 60 D4 24 15S 128 35 E
Hopkinsville, *U.S.A.* 77 G2 36 52N 87 29W
Hopland, *U.S.A.* 84 G3 38 58N 123 7W
Hoquiam, *U.S.A.* 84 D3 46 59N 123 53W
Horden Hills, *Australia* 60 D5 20 15S 130 0 E

Horinger, *China* 34 D6 40 28N 111 48 E
Horlick Mts., *Antarctica* 5 E15 84 0S 102 0W
Horlivka, *Ukraine* 25 E6 48 19N 38 5 E
Hormak, *Iran* 45 D9 29 58N 60 51 E
Hormoz, *Iran* 45 E7 27 35N 55 0 E
Hormoz, Jaz.-ye, *Iran* 45 E8 27 8N 56 28 E
Hormozgān □, *Iran* 45 E8 27 30N 56 0 E
Hormuz, Kūh-e, *Iran* 45 E7 27 27N 55 10 E
Hormuz, Str. of, *The Gulf* 45 E8 26 30N 56 30 E
Horn, *Austria* 16 D8 48 39N 15 40 E
Horn, *Iceland* 8 C2 66 28N 22 28W
Horn →, *Canada* 72 A5 61 30N 118 1W
Horn, Cape = Hornos, C. de, *Chile* 96 H3 55 50S 67 30W
Horn Head, *Ireland* 13 A3 55 14N 8 0W
Horn I., *Australia* 62 A3 10 37S 142 17 E
Horn Mts., *Canada* 72 A5 62 15N 119 15W
Hornavan, *Sweden* 8 C17 66 15N 17 30 E
Hornbeck, *U.S.A.* 81 K8 31 20N 93 24W
Hornbrook, *U.S.A.* 82 F2 41 55N 122 33W
Horncastle, *U.K.* 10 D7 53 13N 0 7W
Hornell, *U.S.A.* 78 D7 42 20N 77 40W
Hornell L., *Canada* 72 A5 62 20N 119 25W
Hornepayne, *Canada* 70 C3 49 14N 84 48W
Hornings Mills, *Canada* 78 B4 44 9N 80 12W
Hornitos, *U.S.A.* 84 H6 37 30N 120 14W
Hornos, C. de, *Chile* 96 H3 55 50S 67 30W
Hornsea, *U.K.* 10 D7 53 55N 0 11W
Horobetsu, *Japan* 30 C10 42 24N 141 6 E
Horodenka, *Ukraine* 17 D13 48 41N 25 29 E
Horodok, *Khmelnytskyy, Ukraine* 17 D14 49 10N 26 34 E
Horodok, *Lviv, Ukraine* 17 D12 49 46N 23 32 E
Horokhiv, *Ukraine* 17 C13 50 30N 24 45 E
Horqin Youyi Qianqi, *China* 35 A12 46 5N 122 3 E
Horqueta, *Paraguay* 94 A4 23 15S 56 55W
Horse Creek, *U.S.A.* 80 E3 41 57N 105 10W
Horse Is., *Canada* 71 B8 50 15N 55 50W
Horsefly L., *Canada* 72 C4 52 25N 121 0W
Horseheads, *U.S.A.* 78 D8 42 10N 76 49W
Horsens, *Denmark* 9 J13 55 52N 9 51 E
Horsham, *Australia* 63 F3 36 44S 142 13 E
Horsham, *U.K.* 11 F7 51 4N 0 20W
Horten, *Norway* 9 G14 59 25N 10 32 E
Horton, *U.S.A.* 80 F7 39 40N 95 32W
Horton →, *Canada* 68 B7 69 56N 126 52W
Horwood L., *Canada* 70 C3 48 5N 82 20W
Hose, Gunung-Gunung, *Malaysia* 36 D4 2 5N 114 6 E
Hoseynābād, *Khuzestān, Iran* 45 C6 32 45N 48 20 E
Hoseynābād, *Kordestān, Iran* 44 C5 35 33N 47 8 E
Hoshangabad, *India* 42 H7 22 45N 77 45 E
Hoshiarpur, *India* 42 D6 31 30N 75 58 E
Hospet, *India* 40 M10 15 15N 76 20 E
Hoste, I., *Chile* 96 H3 55 0S 69 0W
Hot, *Thailand* 38 C2 18 8N 98 29 E
Hot Creek Range, *U.S.A.* 82 G6 38 40N 116 20W
Hot Springs, *Ark., U.S.A.* 81 H8 34 31N 93 3W
Hot Springs, *S. Dak., U.S.A.* 80 D3 43 26N 103 29W
Hotagen, *Sweden* 8 E16 63 50N 14 30 E
Hotan, *China* 32 C2 37 25N 79 55 E
Hotazel, *S. Africa* 56 D3 27 17S 22 58 E
Hotchkiss, *U.S.A.* 83 G10 38 48N 107 43W
Hotham, C., *Australia* 60 B5 12 2S 131 18 E
Hoting, *Sweden* 8 D17 64 8N 16 15 E
Hotte, Massif de la, *Haiti* 89 C5 18 30N 73 45W
Hottentotsbaai, *Namibia* 56 D1 26 8S 14 59 E
Houei Sai, *Laos* 38 B3 20 18N 100 26 E
Houffalize, *Belgium* 15 D5 50 8N 5 48 E
Houghton, *Mich., U.S.A.* 80 B10 47 7N 88 34W
Houghton, *N.Y., U.S.A.* 78 D6 42 25N 78 10W
Houghton L., *U.S.A.* 76 C3 44 21N 84 44W
Houhora Heads, *N.Z.* 59 F4 34 49S 173 9 E
Houlton, *U.S.A.* 77 B12 46 8N 67 51W
Houma, *U.S.A.* 81 L9 29 36N 90 43W
Housatonic →, *U.S.A.* 79 E11 41 10N 73 7W
Houston, *Canada* 72 C3 54 25N 126 39W
Houston, *Mo., U.S.A.* 81 G9 37 22N 91 58W
Houston, *Tex., U.S.A.* 81 L7 29 46N 95 22W
Hout →, *S. Africa* 57 C4 23 4S 29 36 E
Houtkraal, *S. Africa* 56 E3 30 23S 24 5 E
Houtman Abrolhos, *Australia* 61 E1 28 43S 113 48 E
Hovd, *Mongolia* 32 B4 48 2N 91 37 E
Hove, *U.K.* 11 G7 50 50N 0 10W
Hoveyzeh, *Iran* 45 D6 31 27N 48 4 E
Hövsgöl, *Mongolia* 34 C5 43 37N 109 39 E
Hövsgöl Nuur, *Mongolia* 32 A5 51 0N 100 30 E
Howard, *Australia* 63 D5 25 16S 152 32 E
Howard, *Pa., U.S.A.* 78 F7 41 1N 77 40W
Howard, *S. Dak., U.S.A.* 80 C6 44 1N 97 32W
Howe, *U.S.A.* 82 E7 43 48N 113 0W
Howe, C., *Australia* 63 F5 37 30S 150 0 E
Howe I., *Canada* 79 B8 44 16N 76 17W
Howell, *U.S.A.* 76 D4 42 36N 83 56W
Howick, *Canada* 79 A11 45 11N 73 51W
Howick, *S. Africa* 57 D5 29 28S 30 14 E
Howick Group, *Australia* 62 A4 14 20S 145 30 E
Howitt, L., *Australia* 63 D2 27 40S 138 40 E
Howland I., *Pac. Oc.* 64 G10 0 48N 176 38W
Howrah = Haora, *India* 43 H13 22 37N 88 20 E
Howth Hd., *Ireland* 13 C5 53 22N 6 3W
Höxter, *Germany* 16 C5 51 46N 9 22 E
Hoy, *U.K.* 12 C5 58 50N 3 15W
Høyanger, *Norway* 9 F12 61 13N 6 4 E
Hoyerswerda, *Germany* 16 C8 51 26N 14 14 E
Hoylake, *U.K.* 10 D4 53 24N 3 10W
Hpa-an = Pa-an, *Burma* 41 L20 16 51N 97 40 E
Hpungan Pass, *Burma* 41 F20 27 30N 96 55 E
Hradec Králové, *Czech Rep.* 16 C8 50 15N 15 50 E
Hrodna, *Belarus* 17 B12 53 42N 23 52 E
Hrodzyanka, *Belarus* 17 B15 53 31N 28 42 E
Hron →, *Slovak Rep.* 17 E10 47 49N 18 45 E
Hrvatska = Croatia ■, *Europe* 16 F9 45 20N 16 0 E
Hrymayliv, *Ukraine* 17 D14 49 20N 26 5 E
Hsenwi, *Burma* 41 H20 23 22N 97 55 E
Hsiamen = Xiamen, *China* 33 D6 24 25N 118 4 E
Hsian = Xi'an, *China* 34 G5 34 15N 109 0 E
Hsinchu, *Taiwan* 33 D7 24 48N 120 58 E
Hsinhailien = Lianyungang, *China* 35 G10 34 40N 119 11 E
Hsüchou = Xuzhou, *China* 35 G9 34 18N 117 10 E
Hu Xian, *China* 34 G5 34 8N 108 42 E
Hua Hin, *Thailand* 38 F2 12 34N 99 58 E
Hua Xian, *Henan, China* 34 G8 35 30N 114 30 E
Hua Xian, *Shaanxi, China* 34 G5 34 30N 109 48 E
Huab →, *Namibia* 56 B2 20 52S 13 25 E
Huachinera, *Mexico* 86 A3 30 9N 108 55W
Huacho, *Peru* 92 F3 11 10S 77 35W
Huade, *China* 34 D7 41 55N 113 59 E
Huadian, *China* 35 C14 43 0N 126 40 E
Huai He →, *China* 33 C6 33 0N 118 30 E
Huai Yot, *Thailand* 39 J2 7 45N 99 37 E
Huai'an, *Hebei, China* 34 D8 40 30N 114 20 E
Huai'an, *Jiangsu, China* 35 H10 33 30N 119 10 E
Huaibei, *China* 34 G9 34 0N 116 48 E
Huaide = Gongzhuling, *China* 35 C13 43 30N 124 40 E
Huaidezhen, *China* 35 C13 43 48N 124 50 E
Huainan, *China* 33 C6 32 38N 116 58 E
Huairen, *China* 34 E7 39 48N 113 20 E
Huairou, *China* 34 D9 40 20N 116 35 E
Huaiyang, *China* 34 H8 33 40N 114 52 E
Huaiyin, *China* 35 H10 33 30N 119 2 E
Huaiyuan, *China* 35 H9 32 55N 117 10 E
Huajianzi, *China* 35 D13 41 23N 125 20 E
Huajuapan de Leon, *Mexico* 87 D5 17 50N 97 48W
Hualapai Peak, *U.S.A.* 83 J7 35 5N 113 54W
Huallaga →, *Peru* 92 E3 5 15S 75 30W
Huambo, *Angola* 53 G3 12 42S 15 54 E
Huan Jiang →, *China* 34 G5 34 28N 109 0 E
Huan Xian, *China* 34 F4 36 33N 107 7 E
Huancabamba, *Peru* 92 E3 5 10S 79 15W
Huancane, *Peru* 92 G5 15 10S 69 44W
Huancavelica, *Peru* 92 F3 12 50S 75 5W
Huancayo, *Peru* 92 F3 12 5S 75 12W
Huanchaca, *Bolivia* 92 H5 20 15S 66 40W
Huang Hai = Yellow Sea, *China* 35 G12 35 0N 123 0 E
Huang He →, *China* 35 F10 37 55N 118 50 E
Huang Xian, *China* 35 F11 37 38N 120 30 E
Huangling, *China* 34 G5 35 34N 109 15 E
Huanglong, *China* 34 G5 35 30N 109 59 E
Huangshan, *China* 33 D6 29 42N 118 25 E
Huangshi, *China* 33 C6 30 10N 115 3 E
Huangsongdian, *China* 35 C14 43 45N 127 25 E
Huantai, *China* 35 F9 36 58N 117 56 E
Huánuco, *Peru* 92 E3 9 55S 76 15W
Huaraz, *Peru* 92 E3 9 30S 77 32W
Huarmey, *Peru* 92 F3 10 5S 78 5W
Huascarán, *Peru* 92 E3 9 8S 77 36W
Huasco, *Chile* 94 B1 28 30S 71 15W
Huasco →, *Chile* 94 B1 28 27S 71 13W
Huasna, *U.S.A.* 85 K6 35 6N 120 24W
Huatabampo, *Mexico* 86 B3 26 50N 109 50W
Huauchinango, *Mexico* 87 C5 20 11N 98 3W
Huautla de Jiménez, *Mexico* 87 D5 18 8N 96 51W
Huay Namota, *Mexico* 86 C4 21 56N 104 30W
Huayin, *China* 34 G6 34 35N 110 5 E
Hubbard, *Ohio, U.S.A.* 78 E4 41 9N 80 34W
Hubbard, *Tex., U.S.A.* 81 K6 31 51N 96 48W
Hubbart Pt., *Canada* 73 B10 59 21N 94 41W
Hubei □, *China* 33 C6 31 0N 112 0 E
Huch'ang, *N. Korea* 35 D14 41 25N 127 2 E
Hucknall, *U.K.* 10 D6 53 3N 1 13W
Huddersfield, *U.K.* 10 D6 53 39N 1 47W
Hudiksvall, *Sweden* 9 F17 61 43N 17 10 E
Hudson, *Canada* 70 B1 50 6N 92 9W
Hudson, *Mass., U.S.A.* 79 D13 42 23N 71 34W
Hudson, *N.Y., U.S.A.* 79 D11 42 15N 73 46W
Hudson, *Wis., U.S.A.* 80 C8 44 58N 92 45W
Hudson, *Wyo., U.S.A.* 82 E9 42 54N 108 35W
Hudson →, *U.S.A.* 79 F10 40 42N 74 2W
Hudson Bay, *Nunavut, Canada* 69 C11 60 0N 86 0W
Hudson Bay, *Sask., Canada* 73 C8 52 51N 102 23W
Hudson Falls, *U.S.A.* 79 C11 43 18N 73 35W
Hudson Mts., *Antarctica* 5 D16 74 32S 99 20W
Hudson Str., *Canada* 69 B13 62 0N 70 0W
Hudson's Hope, *Canada* 72 B4 56 0N 121 54W
Hue, *Vietnam* 38 D6 16 30N 107 35 E
Huehuetenango, *Guatemala* 88 C1 15 20N 91 28W
Huejúcar, *Mexico* 86 C4 22 21N 103 13W
Huelva, *Spain* 19 D2 37 18N 6 57W
Huentelauquén, *Chile* 94 C1 31 38S 71 33W
Huerta, Sa. de la, *Argentina* 94 C2 31 10S 67 30W
Huesca, *Spain* 19 A5 42 8N 0 25W
Huetamo, *Mexico* 86 D4 18 36N 100 54W
Hugh →, *Australia* 62 D1 25 1S 134 1 E
Hughenden, *Australia* 62 C3 20 52S 144 10 E
Hughes, *Australia* 61 F4 30 42S 129 31 E
Hughesville, *U.S.A.* 79 E8 41 14N 76 44W
Hugli →, *India* 43 J13 21 56N 88 4 E
Hugo, *Colo., U.S.A.* 80 F3 39 8N 103 28W
Hugo, *Okla., U.S.A.* 81 H7 34 1N 95 31W
Hugoton, *U.S.A.* 81 G4 37 11N 101 21W
Hui Xian = Huixian, *China* 34 G7 35 27N 113 12 E
Hui Xian, *China* 34 H4 33 50N 106 4 E
Hui'anbu, *China* 34 F4 37 28N 106 38 E
Huichapán, *Mexico* 87 C5 20 24N 99 40W
Huifa He →, *China* 35 C14 43 0N 127 50 E
Huila, Nevado del, *Colombia* 92 C3 3 0N 76 0W
Huimin, *China* 35 F9 37 27N 117 28 E
Huinan, *China* 35 C14 42 40N 126 2 E
Huinca Renancó, *Argentina* 94 C3 34 51S 64 22W
Huining, *China* 34 G3 35 38N 105 0 E
Huinong, *China* 34 E4 39 5N 106 35 E
Huisache, *Mexico* 86 C4 22 55N 100 25W
Huiting, *China* 34 G9 34 5N 116 5 E
Huixian, *China* 34 G7 35 27N 113 12 E
Huixtla, *Mexico* 87 D6 15 9N 92 28W
Huize, *China* 32 D5 26 24N 103 15 E
Hukawng Valley, *Burma* 41 F20 26 30N 96 30 E
Hŭksan-chedo, *S. Korea* 35 G13 34 40N 125 30 E
Hukuntsi, *Botswana* 56 C3 23 58S 21 45 E
Ḩulayfā', *Si. Arabia* 44 E4 25 58N 40 45 E
Huld = Ulaanjirem, *Mongolia* 34 B3 45 5N 105 30 E
Hulin He →, *China* 35 B12 45 0N 122 10 E
Hull = Kingston upon Hull, *U.K.* 10 D7 53 45N 0 21W
Hull, *Canada* 79 A9 45 25N 75 44W
Hull →, *U.K.* 10 D7 53 44N 0 20W
Hulst, *Neths.* 15 C4 51 17N 4 2 E
Hulun Nur, *China* 33 B6 49 0N 117 30 E
Humahuaca, *Argentina* 94 A2 23 10S 65 25W
Humaitá, *Brazil* 92 E6 7 35S 63 1W
Humaitá, *Paraguay* 94 B4 27 2S 58 31W
Humansdorp, *S. Africa* 56 E3 34 2S 24 46 E
Humbe, *Angola* 56 B1 16 40S 14 55 E
Humber →, *U.K.* 10 D7 53 42N 0 27W
Humboldt, *Canada* 73 C7 52 15N 105 9W
Humboldt, *Iowa, U.S.A.* 80 D7 42 44N 94 13W
Humboldt, *Tenn., U.S.A.* 81 H10 35 50N 88 55W
Humboldt →, *U.S.A.* 82 F4 39 59N 118 36W
Humboldt Gletscher, *Greenland* 4 B4 79 30N 62 0W
Hume, *U.S.A.* 84 J8 36 48N 118 54W
Hume, L., *Australia* 63 F4 36 0S 147 5 E
Humenné, *Slovak Rep.* 17 D11 48 55N 21 50 E
Humphreys, Mt., *U.S.A.* 84 H8 37 17N 118 40W
Humphreys Peak, *U.S.A.* 83 J8 35 21N 111 41W
Humptulips, *U.S.A.* 84 C3 47 14N 123 57W
Hūn, *Libya* 51 C9 29 2N 16 0 E
Hun Jiang →, *China* 35 D13 40 50N 125 38 E
Húnaflói, *Iceland* 8 D3 65 50N 20 50W
Hunan □, *China* 33 D6 27 30N 112 0 E
Hunchun, *China* 35 C16 42 52N 130 28 E
Hundewali, *Pakistan* 42 D5 31 55N 72 38 E
Hundred Mile House, *Canada* 72 C4 51 38N 121 18W
Hunedoara, *Romania* 17 F12 45 40N 22 50 E
Hung Yen, *Vietnam* 38 B6 20 39N 106 4 E
Hungary ■, *Europe* 17 E10 47 20N 19 20 E
Hungary, Plain of, *Europe* 6 F10 47 0N 20 0 E
Hungerford, *Australia* 63 D3 28 58S 144 24 E
Hŭngnam, *N. Korea* 35 E14 39 49N 127 45 E
Hunsberge, *Namibia* 56 D2 27 45S 17 12 E
Hunsrück, *Germany* 16 D4 49 56N 7 27 E
Hunstanton, *U.K.* 10 E8 52 56N 0 29 E
Hunter, *U.S.A.* 79 D10 42 13N 74 13W
Hunter I., *Australia* 62 G3 40 30S 144 45 E
Hunter I., *Canada* 72 C3 51 55N 128 0W
Hunter Ra., *Australia* 63 E5 32 45S 150 15 E
Hunters Road, *Zimbabwe* 55 F2 19 9S 29 49 E
Hunterville, *N.Z.* 59 H5 39 56S 175 35 E
Huntingburg, *U.S.A.* 76 F2 38 18N 86 57W
Huntingdon, *Canada* 70 C5 45 6N 74 10W
Huntingdon, *U.K.* 11 E7 52 20N 0 11W
Huntingdon, *U.S.A.* 78 F6 40 30N 78 1W
Huntington, *Ind., U.S.A.* 76 E3 40 53N 85 30W
Huntington, *Oreg., U.S.A.* 82 D5 44 21N 117 16W
Huntington, *Utah, U.S.A.* 82 G8 39 20N 110 58W
Huntington, *W. Va., U.S.A.* 76 F4 38 25N 82 27W
Huntington Beach, *U.S.A.* 85 M9 33 40N 118 5W
Huntington Station, *U.S.A.* 79 F11 40 52N 73 26W
Huntly, *N.Z.* 59 G5 37 34S 175 11 E
Huntly, *U.K.* 12 D6 57 27N 2 47W
Huntsville, *Canada* 78 A5 45 20N 79 14W
Huntsville, *Ala., U.S.A.* 77 H2 34 44N 86 35W
Huntsville, *Tex., U.S.A.* 81 K7 30 43N 95 33W
Hunyani →, *Zimbabwe* 55 F3 15 57S 30 39 E
Hunyuan, *China* 34 E7 39 42N 113 42 E
Hunza →, *India* 43 B6 35 54N 74 20 E
Huo Xian = Huozhou, *China* 34 F6 36 36N 111 42 E
Huong Hoa, *Vietnam* 38 D6 16 37N 106 45 E
Huong Khe, *Vietnam* 38 C5 18 13N 105 41 E
Huonville, *Australia* 62 G4 43 0S 147 5 E
Huozhou, *China* 34 F6 36 36N 111 42 E
Hupeh = Hubei □, *China* 33 C6 31 0N 112 0 E
Ḩūr, *Iran* 45 D8 30 50N 57 7 E
Hurd, C., *Canada* 78 A3 45 13N 81 44W
Hure Qi, *China* 35 C11 42 45N 121 45 E
Hurghada, *Egypt* 51 C12 27 15N 33 50 E
Hurley, *N. Mex., U.S.A.* 83 K9 32 42N 108 8W
Hurley, *Wis., U.S.A.* 80 B9 46 27N 90 11W
Huron, *Calif., U.S.A.* 84 J6 36 12N 120 6W
Huron, *Ohio, U.S.A.* 78 E2 41 24N 82 33W
Huron, *S. Dak., U.S.A.* 80 C5 44 22N 98 13W
Huron, L., *U.S.A.* 78 B2 44 30N 82 40W
Hurricane, *U.S.A.* 83 H7 37 11N 113 17W
Hurunui →, *N.Z.* 59 K4 42 54S 173 18 E
Húsavík, *Iceland* 8 C5 66 3N 17 21W
Huşi, *Romania* 17 E15 46 41N 28 7 E
Huskvarna, *Sweden* 9 H16 57 47N 14 15 E
Hustadvika, *Norway* 8 E12 63 0N 7 0 E
Hustontown, *U.S.A.* 78 F6 40 3N 78 2W
Hutchinson, *Kans., U.S.A.* 81 F6 38 5N 97 56W
Hutchinson, *Minn., U.S.A.* 80 C7 44 54N 94 22W
Hutte Sauvage, L. de la, *Canada* 71 A7 56 15N 64 45W
Hutton, Mt., *Australia* 63 D4 25 51S 148 20 E
Huy, *Belgium* 15 D5 50 31N 5 15 E
Huzhou, *China* 33 C7 30 51N 120 8 E
Hvammstangi, *Iceland* 8 D3 65 24N 20 57W
Hvar, *Croatia* 20 C7 43 11N 16 28 E
Hvítá →, *Iceland* 8 D3 64 30N 21 58W
Hwachŏn-chŏsuji, *S. Korea* 35 E14 38 5N 127 50 E
Hwang Ho = Huang He →, *China* 35 F10 37 55N 118 50 E
Hwange, *Zimbabwe* 55 F2 18 18S 26 30 E
Hwange Nat. Park, *Zimbabwe* 56 B4 19 0S 26 30 E
Hyannis, *Mass., U.S.A.* 76 E10 41 39N 70 17W
Hyannis, *Nebr., U.S.A.* 80 E4 42 0N 101 46W
Hyargas Nuur, *Mongolia* 32 B4 49 0N 93 0 E
Hydaburg, *U.S.A.* 72 B2 55 15N 132 50W
Hyde Park, *U.S.A.* 79 E11 41 47N 73 56W
Hyden, *Australia* 61 F2 32 24S 118 53 E
Hyder, *U.S.A.* 72 B2 55 55N 130 5W
Hyderabad, *India* 40 L11 17 22N 78 29 E
Hyderabad, *Pakistan* 42 G3 25 23N 68 24 E
Hyères, *France* 18 E7 43 8N 6 9 E
Hyères, Îs. d', *France* 18 E7 43 0N 6 20 E
Hyesan, *N. Korea* 35 D15 41 20N 128 10 E
Hyland →, *Canada* 72 B3 59 52N 128 12W
Hymia, *India* 43 C8 33 40N 78 2 E
Hyndman Peak, *U.S.A.* 82 E6 43 45N 114 8W
Hyōgo □, *Japan* 31 G7 35 15N 134 50 E
Hyrum, *U.S.A.* 82 F8 41 38N 111 51W
Hysham, *U.S.A.* 82 C10 46 18N 107 14W
Hythe, *U.K.* 11 F9 51 4N 1 5 E
Hyūga, *Japan* 31 H5 32 25N 131 35 E
Hyvinge = Hyvinkää, *Finland* 9 F21 60 38N 24 50 E
Hyvinkää, *Finland* 9 F21 60 38N 24 50 E

I

I-n-Gall, *Niger* 50 E7 16 51N 7 1 E
Iaco →, *Brazil* 92 E5 9 3S 68 34W
Iakora, *Madag.* 57 C8 23 6S 46 40 E
Ialomiţa →, *Romania* 17 F14 44 42N 27 51 E
Iaşi, *Romania* 17 E14 47 10N 27 40 E
Ib →, *India* 43 J10 21 34N 83 48 E
Iba, *Phil.* 37 A6 15 22N 120 0 E
Ibadan, *Nigeria* 50 G6 7 22N 3 58 E
Ibagué, *Colombia* 92 C3 4 20N 75 20W
Ibar →, *Serbia, Yug.* 21 C9 43 43N 20 45 E
Ibaraki □, *Japan* 31 F10 36 10N 140 10 E
Ibarra, *Ecuador* 92 C3 0 21N 78 7W
Ibembo, *Dem. Rep. of the Congo* 54 B1 2 35N 23 35 E
Ibera, L., *Argentina* 94 B4 28 30S 57 9W
Iberian Peninsula, *Europe* 6 H5 40 0N 5 0W
Iberville, *Canada* 79 A11 45 19N 73 17W
Iberville, Lac d', *Canada* 70 A5 55 55N 73 15W
Ibiá, *Brazil* 93 G9 19 30S 46 30W
Ibiapaba, Sa. da, *Brazil* 93 D10 4 0S 41 30W
Ibicuí →, *Brazil* 95 B4 29 25S 56 47W
Ibicuy, *Argentina* 94 C4 33 55S 59 10W
Ibiza = Eivissa, *Spain* 22 C7 38 54N 1 26 E
Ibo, *Mozam.* 55 E5 12 22S 40 40 E
Ibonma, *Indonesia* 37 E8 3 29S 133 31 E
Ibotirama, *Brazil* 93 F10 12 13S 43 12W
Ibrāhīm →, *Lebanon* 47 A4 34 4N 35 38 E
'Ibrī, *Oman* 45 F8 23 14N 56 30 E
Ibu, *Indonesia* 37 D7 1 35N 127 33 E
Ibusuki, *Japan* 31 J5 31 12N 130 40 E
Ica, *Peru* 92 F3 14 0S 75 48W
Iça →, *Brazil* 92 D5 2 55S 67 58W
Içana, *Brazil* 92 C5 0 21N 67 19W
Içana →, *Brazil* 92 C5 0 26N 67 19W
İçel = Mersin, *Turkey* 25 G5 36 51N 34 36 E
Iceland ■, *Europe* 8 D4 64 45N 19 0W
Ich'ang = Yichang, *China* 33 C6 30 40N 111 20 E
Ichchapuram, *India* 41 K14 19 10N 84 40 E
Ichhawar, *India* 42 H7 23 1N 77 1 E
Ichihara, *Japan* 31 G10 35 28N 140 5 E
Ichikawa, *Japan* 31 G9 35 44N 139 55 E
Ichilo →, *Bolivia* 92 G6 15 57S 64 50W
Ichinohe, *Japan* 30 D10 40 13N 141 17 E
Ichinomiya, *Japan* 31 G8 35 18N 136 48 E
Ichinoseki, *Japan* 30 E10 38 55N 141 8 E
Icod, *Canary Is.* 22 F3 28 22N 16 43W
Ida Grove, *U.S.A.* 80 D7 42 21N 95 28W
Idabel, *U.S.A.* 81 J7 33 54N 94 50W
Idaho □, *U.S.A.* 82 D7 45 0N 115 0W
Idaho City, *U.S.A.* 82 E6 43 50N 115 50W
Idaho Falls, *U.S.A.* 82 E7 43 30N 112 2W
Idar-Oberstein, *Germany* 16 D4 49 43N 7 16 E
Idfû, *Egypt* 51 D12 24 55N 32 49 E
Ídhi Óros, *Greece* 23 D6 35 15N 24 45 E
Ídhra, *Greece* 21 F10 37 20N 23 28 E
Idi, *Indonesia* 36 C1 5 2N 97 37 E
Idiofa, *Dem. Rep. of the Congo* 52 E3 4 55S 19 42 E
Idlib, *Syria* 44 C3 35 55N 36 36 E
Idria, *U.S.A.* 84 J6 36 25N 120 41W
Idutywa, *S. Africa* 57 E4 32 8S 28 18 E
Ieper, *Belgium* 15 D2 50 51N 2 53 E
Ierápetra, *Greece* 23 E7 35 1N 25 44 E
Iesi, *Italy* 20 C5 43 31N 13 14 E
Ifakara, *Tanzania* 52 F7 8 8S 36 41 E
'Ifāl, W. al →, *Si. Arabia* 44 D2 28 7N 35 3 E
Ifanadiana, *Madag.* 57 C8 21 19S 47 39 E
Ife, *Nigeria* 50 G6 7 30N 4 31 E
Iffley, *Australia* 62 B3 18 53S 141 12 E
Iforas, Adrar des, *Africa* 50 E6 19 40N 1 40 E
Ifould, L., *Australia* 61 F5 30 52S 132 6 E
Iganga, *Uganda* 54 B3 0 37N 33 28 E
Igarapava, *Brazil* 93 H9 20 3S 47 47W
Igarka, *Russia* 26 C9 67 30N 86 33 E
Igatimi, *Paraguay* 95 A4 24 5S 55 40W
Iggesund, *Sweden* 9 F17 61 39N 17 10 E
Iglésias, *Italy* 20 E3 39 19N 8 32 E
Igloolik, *Canada* 69 B11 69 20N 81 49W
Igluligaarjuk, *Canada* 69 B10 63 21N 90 42W
Iglulik = Igloolik, *Canada* 69 B11 69 20N 81 49W
Ignace, *Canada* 70 C1 49 30N 91 40W
İğneada Burnu, *Turkey* 21 D13 41 53N 28 2 E
Igoumenitsa, *Greece* 21 E9 39 32N 20 18 E
Iguaçu →, *Brazil* 95 B5 25 36S 54 36W
Iguaçu, Cat. del, *Brazil* 95 B5 25 41S 54 26W
Iguaçu Falls = Iguaçu, Cat. del, *Brazil* 95 B5 25 41S 54 26W
Iguala, *Mexico* 87 D5 18 20N 99 40W
Igualada, *Spain* 19 B6 41 37N 1 37 E
Iguassu = Iguaçu →, *Brazil* 95 B5 25 36S 54 36W
Iguatu, *Brazil* 93 E11 6 20S 39 18W
Iharana, *Madag.* 57 A9 13 25S 50 0 E
Ihbulag, *Mongolia* 34 C4 43 11N 107 10 E
Iheya-Shima, *Japan* 31 L3 27 4N 127 58 E
Ihosy, *Madag.* 57 C8 22 24S 46 8 E
Ihotry, Farihy, *Madag.* 57 C7 21 56S 43 41 E
Ii, *Finland* 8 D21 65 19N 25 22 E
Ii-Shima, *Japan* 31 L3 26 43N 127 47 E
Iida, *Japan* 31 G8 35 35N 137 50 E
Iijoki →, *Finland* 8 D21 65 20N 25 20 E
Iisalmi, *Finland* 8 E22 63 32N 27 10 E
Iiyama, *Japan* 31 F9 36 51N 138 22 E
Iizuka, *Japan* 31 H5 33 38N 130 42 E
Ijebu-Ode, *Nigeria* 50 G6 6 47N 3 58 E
IJmuiden, *Neths.* 15 B4 52 28N 4 35 E
IJssel →, *Neths.* 15 B5 52 35N 5 50 E
IJsselmeer, *Neths.* 15 B5 52 45N 5 20 E
Ijuí, *Brazil* 95 B5 28 23S 53 55W
Ijuí →, *Brazil* 95 B4 27 58S 55 20W
Ikalamavony, *Madag.* 57 C8 21 9S 46 35 E
Ikaluktutiak, *Canada* 68 B9 69 10N 105 0W
Ikare, *Nigeria* 50 G7 7 32N 5 40 E
Ikaría, *Greece* 21 F12 37 35N 26 10 E
Ikeda, *Japan* 31 G6 34 1N 133 48 E
Ikela, *Dem. Rep. of the Congo* 52 E4 1 6S 23 6 E
Iki, *Japan* 31 H4 33 45N 129 42 E
Ikimba L., *Tanzania* 54 C3 1 30S 31 20 E
Ikongo, *Madag.* 57 C8 21 52S 47 27 E
Ikopa →, *Madag.* 57 B8 16 45S 46 40 E
Ikungu, *Tanzania* 54 C3 1 33S 33 42 E
Ilagan, *Phil.* 37 A6 17 7N 121 53 E
Ilaka, *Madag.* 57 B8 19 33S 48 52 E
Īlām, *Iran* 44 C5 33 36N 46 36 E
Ilam, *Nepal* 43 F12 26 58N 87 58 E
Īlām □, *Iran* 44 C5 33 0N 47 0 E
Ilanskiy, *Russia* 27 D10 56 14N 96 3 E
Iława, *Poland* 17 B10 53 36N 19 34 E
Ile →, *Kazakstan* 26 E8 45 53N 77 10 E
Ile-à-la-Crosse, *Canada* 73 B7 55 27N 107 53W
Ile-à-la-Crosse, Lac, *Canada* 73 B7 55 40N 107 45W
Île-de-France □, *France* 18 B5 49 0N 2 20 E
Ilebo, *Dem. Rep. of the Congo* 52 E4 4 17S 20 55 E
Ilek, *Russia* 26 D6 51 32N 53 21 E
Ilek →, *Russia* 24 D9 51 30N 53 22 E
Ilesha, *Nigeria* 50 G6 7 37N 4 40 E
Ilford, *Canada* 73 B9 56 4N 95 35W
Ilfracombe, *Australia* 62 C3 23 30S 144 30 E

Ilfracombe, *U.K.* **11 F3** 51 12N 4 8W
Ilhéus, *Brazil* **93 F11** 14 49S 39 2W
Ili = Ile →, *Kazakstan* **26 E8** 45 53N 77 10 E
Iliamna L., *U.S.A.* **68 C4** 59 30N 155 0W
Iligan, *Phil.* **37 C6** 8 12N 124 13 E
Ilion, *U.S.A.* **79 D9** 43 1N 75 2W
Ilkeston, *U.K.* **10 E6** 52 58N 1 19W
Ilkley, *U.K.* **10 D6** 53 56N 1 48W
Illampu = Ancohuma, Nevada, *Bolivia* **92 G5** 16 0S 68 50W
Illana B., *Phil.* **37 C6** 7 35N 123 45 E
Illapel, *Chile* **94 C1** 32 0S 71 10W
Iller →, *Germany* **16 D6** 48 23N 9 58 E
Illetas, *Spain* **22 B9** 39 32N 2 35 E
Illimani, Nevado, *Bolivia* **92 G5** 16 30S 67 50W
Illinois □, *U.S.A.* **80 E10** 40 15N 89 30W
Illinois →, *U.S.A.* **80 F9** 38 58N 90 28W
Illium = Troy, *Turkey* **21 E12** 39 57N 26 12 E
Illizi, *Algeria* **50 C7** 26 31N 8 32 E
Ilmajoki, *Finland* **9 E20** 62 44N 22 34 E
Ilmen, Ozero, *Russia* **24 C5** 58 15N 31 10 E
Ilo, *Peru* **92 G4** 17 40S 71 20W
Iloilo, *Phil.* **37 B6** 10 45N 122 33 E
Ilorin, *Nigeria* **50 G6** 8 30N 4 35 E
Ilwaco, *U.S.A.* **84 D2** 46 19N 124 3W
Ilwaki, *Indonesia* **37 F7** 7 55S 126 30 E
Imabari, *Japan* **31 G6** 34 4N 133 0 E
Imaloto →, *Madag.* **57 C8** 23 27S 45 13 E
Imandra, Ozero, *Russia* **24 A5** 67 30N 33 0 E
Imanombo, *Madag.* **57 C8** 24 26S 45 49 E
Imari, *Japan* **31 H4** 33 15N 129 52 E
Imatra, *Finland* **24 B4** 61 12N 28 48 E
Imbil, *Australia* **63 D5** 26 22S 152 32 E
imeni 26 Bakinskikh Komissarov = Neftçala, *Azerbaijan* **25 G8** 39 19N 49 12 E
imeni 26 Bakinskikh Komissarov, *Turkmenistan* **45 B7** 39 22N 54 10 E
Imeri, Serra, *Brazil* **92 C5** 0 50N 65 25W
Imerimandroso, *Madag.* **57 B8** 17 26S 48 35 E
Imi, *Ethiopia* **46 F3** 6 28N 42 10 E
Imlay, *U.S.A.* **82 F4** 40 40N 118 9W
Imlay City, *U.S.A.* **78 D1** 43 2N 83 5W
Immingham, *U.K.* **10 D7** 53 37N 0 13W
Immokalee, *U.S.A.* **77 M5** 26 25N 81 25W
Ímola, *Italy* **20 B4** 44 20N 11 42 E
Imperatriz, *Brazil* **93 E9** 5 30S 47 29W
Impéria, *Italy* **18 E8** 43 53N 8 3 E
Imperial, *Canada* **73 C7** 51 21N 105 28W
Imperial, *Calif., U.S.A.* **85 N11** 32 51N 115 34W
Imperial, *Nebr., U.S.A.* **80 E4** 40 31N 101 39W
Imperial Beach, *U.S.A.* **85 N9** 32 35N 117 8W
Imperial Dam, *U.S.A.* **85 N12** 32 55N 114 25W
Imperial Reservoir, *U.S.A.* **85 N12** 32 53N 114 28W
Imperial Valley, *U.S.A.* **85 N11** 33 0N 115 30W
Imperieuse Reef, *Australia* **60 C2** 17 36S 118 50 E
Impfondo, *Congo* **52 D3** 1 40N 18 0 E
Imphal, *India* **41 G18** 24 48N 93 56 E
İmroz = Gökçeada, *Turkey* **21 D11** 40 10N 25 50 E
Imuris, *Mexico* **86 A2** 30 47N 110 52W
Imuruan B., *Phil.* **37 B5** 10 40N 119 10 E
In Salah, *Algeria* **50 C6** 27 10N 2 32 E
Ina, *Japan* **31 G8** 35 50N 137 55 E
Inangahua, *N.Z.* **59 J3** 41 52S 171 59 E
Inanwatan, *Indonesia* **37 E8** 2 8S 132 10 E
Iñapari, *Peru* **92 F5** 11 0S 69 40W
Inari, *Finland* **8 B22** 68 54N 27 5 E
Inarijärvi, *Finland* **8 B22** 69 0N 28 0 E
Inawashiro-Ko, *Japan* **30 F10** 37 29N 140 6 E
Inca, *Spain* **22 B9** 39 43N 2 54 E
Inca de Oro, *Chile* **94 B2** 26 45S 69 54W
Incaguasi, *Chile* **94 B1** 29 12S 71 5W
İnce Burun, *Turkey* **25 F5** 42 7N 34 56 E
İncesu, *Turkey* **44 B2** 38 38N 35 11 E
Inch'ŏn, *S. Korea* **35 F14** 37 27N 126 40 E
İncirliova, *Turkey* **21 F12** 37 50N 27 41 E
Incline Village, *U.S.A.* **82 G4** 39 10N 119 58W
Incomáti →, *Mozam.* **57 D5** 25 46S 32 43 E
Indalsälven →, *Sweden* **9 E17** 62 36N 17 30 E
Indaw, *Burma* **41 G20** 24 15N 96 5 E
Independence, *Calif., U.S.A.* **84 J8** 36 48N 118 12W
Independence, *Iowa, U.S.A.* **80 D9** 42 28N 91 54W
Independence, *Kans., U.S.A.* **81 G7** 37 14N 95 42W
Independence, *Ky., U.S.A.* **76 F3** 38 57N 84 33W
Independence, *Mo., U.S.A.* **80 F7** 39 6N 94 25W
Independence Fjord, *Greenland* **4 A6** 82 10N 29 0W
Independence Mts., *U.S.A.* **82 F5** 41 20N 116 0W
Index, *U.S.A.* **84 C5** 47 50N 121 33W
India ■, *Asia* **40 K11** 20 0N 78 0 E
Indian →, *U.S.A.* **77 M5** 27 59N 80 34W
Indian Cabins, *Canada* **72 B5** 59 52N 117 40W
Indian Harbour, *Canada* **71 B8** 54 27N 57 13W
Indian Head, *Canada* **73 C8** 50 30N 103 41W
Indian Lake, *U.S.A.* **79 C10** 43 47N 74 16W
Indian Ocean **28 K11** 5 0S 75 0 E
Indian Springs, *U.S.A.* **85 J11** 36 35N 115 40W
Indiana, *U.S.A.* **78 F5** 40 37N 79 9W
Indiana □, *U.S.A.* **76 F3** 40 0N 86 0W
Indianapolis, *U.S.A.* **76 F2** 39 46N 86 9W
Indianola, *Iowa, U.S.A.* **80 E8** 41 22N 93 34W
Indianola, *Miss., U.S.A.* **81 J9** 33 27N 90 39W
Indiga, *Russia* **24 A8** 67 38N 49 9 E
Indigirka →, *Russia* **27 B15** 70 48N 148 54 E
Indio, *U.S.A.* **85 M10** 33 43N 116 13W
Indo-China, *Asia* **28 H14** 15 0N 102 0 E
Indonesia ■, *Asia* **36 F5** 5 0S 115 0 E
Indore, *India* **42 H6** 22 42N 75 53 E
Indramayu, *Indonesia* **37 G13** 6 20S 108 19 E
Indravati →, *India* **41 K12** 19 20N 80 20 E
Indre →, *France* **18 C4** 47 16N 0 11 E
Indulkana, *Australia* **63 D1** 26 58S 133 5 E
Indus →, *Pakistan* **42 G2** 24 20N 67 47 E
Indus, Mouths of the, *Pakistan* **42 H3** 24 0N 68 0 E
İnebolu, *Turkey* **25 F5** 41 55N 33 40 E
Infiernillo, Presa del, *Mexico* **86 D4** 18 9N 102 0W
Ingenio, *Canary Is.* **22 G4** 27 55N 15 26W
Ingenio Santa Ana, *Argentina* **94 B2** 27 25S 65 40W
Ingersoll, *Canada* **78 C4** 43 4N 80 55W
Ingham, *Australia* **62 B4** 18 43S 146 10 E
Ingleborough, *U.K.* **10 C5** 54 10N 2 22W
Inglewood, *Queens., Australia* **63 D5** 28 25S 151 2 E
Inglewood, *Vic., Australia* **63 F3** 36 29S 143 53 E
Inglewood, *N.Z.* **59 H5** 39 9S 174 14 E
Inglewood, *U.S.A.* **85 M8** 33 58N 118 21W
Ingólfshöfði, *Iceland* **8 E5** 63 48N 16 39W
Ingolstadt, *Germany* **16 D6** 48 46N 11 26 E
Ingomar, *U.S.A.* **82 C10** 46 35N 107 23W
Ingonish, *Canada* **71 C7** 46 42N 60 18W
Ingraj Bazar, *India* **43 G13** 24 58N 88 10 E
Ingrid Christensen Coast, *Antarctica* **5 C6** 69 30S 76 0 E
Ingulec = Inhulec, *Ukraine* **25 E5** 47 42N 33 14 E
Ingushetia □, *Russia* **25 F8** 43 20N 44 50 E
Ingwavuma, *S. Africa* **57 D5** 27 9S 31 59 E
Inhaca, *Mozam.* **57 D5** 26 1S 32 57 E
Inhafenga, *Mozam.* **57 C5** 20 36S 33 53 E
Inhambane, *Mozam.* **57 C6** 23 54S 35 30 E
Inhambane □, *Mozam.* **57 C5** 22 30S 34 20 E
Inhaminga, *Mozam.* **55 F4** 18 26S 35 0 E
Inharrime, *Mozam.* **57 C6** 24 30S 35 0 E
Inharrime →, *Mozam.* **57 C6** 24 30S 35 0 E
Inhulec, *Ukraine* **25 E5** 47 42N 33 14 E
Ining = Yining, *China* **26 E9** 43 58N 81 10 E
Inírida →, *Colombia* **92 C5** 3 55N 67 52W
Inishbofin, *Ireland* **13 C1** 53 37N 10 13W
Inisheer, *Ireland* **13 C2** 53 3N 9 32W
Inishfree B., *Ireland* **13 A3** 55 4N 8 23W
Inishkea North, *Ireland* **13 B1** 54 9N 10 11W
Inishkea South, *Ireland* **13 B1** 54 7N 10 12W
Inishmaan, *Ireland* **13 C2** 53 5N 9 35W
Inishmore, *Ireland* **13 C2** 53 8N 9 45W
Inishowen Pen., *Ireland* **13 A4** 55 14N 7 15W
Inishshark, *Ireland* **13 C1** 53 37N 10 16W
Inishturk, *Ireland* **13 C1** 53 42N 10 7W
Inishvickillane, *Ireland* **13 D1** 52 3N 10 37W
Injune, *Australia* **63 D4** 25 53S 148 32 E
Inklin →, *Canada* **72 B2** 58 50N 133 10W
Inland Sea = Setonaikai, *Japan* **31 G6** 34 20N 133 30 E
Inle L., *Burma* **41 J20** 20 30N 96 58 E
Inlet, *U.S.A.* **79 C10** 43 45N 74 48W
Inn →, *Austria* **16 D7** 48 35N 13 28 E
Innamincka, *Australia* **63 D3** 27 44S 140 46 E
Inner Hebrides, *U.K.* **12 E2** 57 0N 6 30W
Inner Mongolia = Nei Monggol Zizhiqu □, *China* **34 D7** 42 0N 112 0 E
Inner Sound, *U.K.* **12 D3** 57 30N 5 55W
Innerkip, *Canada* **78 C4** 43 13N 80 42W
Innetalling I., *Canada* **70 A4** 56 0N 79 0W
Innisfail, *Australia* **62 B4** 17 33S 146 5 E
Innisfail, *Canada* **72 C6** 52 0N 113 57W
In'noshima, *Japan* **31 G6** 34 19N 133 10 E
Innsbruck, *Austria* **16 E6** 47 16N 11 23 E
Inny →, *Ireland* **13 C4** 53 30N 7 50W
Inongo, *Dem. Rep. of the Congo* **52 E3** 1 55S 18 30 E
Inoucdjouac = Inukjuak, *Canada* **69 C12** 58 25N 78 15W
Inowrocław, *Poland* **17 B10** 52 50N 18 12 E
Inpundong, *N. Korea* **35 D14** 41 25N 126 34 E
Inscription, C., *Australia* **61 E1** 25 29S 112 59 E
Insein, *Burma* **41 L20** 16 50N 96 5 E
Inta, *Russia* **24 A11** 66 5N 60 8 E
Intendente Alvear, *Argentina* **94 D3** 35 12S 63 32W
Interlaken, *Switz.* **18 C7** 46 41N 7 50 E
Interlaken, *U.S.A.* **79 D8** 42 37N 76 44W
International Falls, *U.S.A.* **80 A8** 48 36N 93 25W
Intiyaco, *Argentina* **94 B3** 28 43S 60 5W
Inukjuak, *Canada* **69 C12** 58 25N 78 15W
Inútil, B., *Chile* **96 G2** 53 30S 70 15W
Inuvik, *Canada* **68 B6** 68 16N 133 40W
Inveraray, *U.K.* **12 E3** 56 14N 5 5W
Inverbervie, *U.K.* **12 E6** 56 51N 2 17W
Invercargill, *N.Z.* **59 M2** 46 24S 168 24 E
Inverclyde □, *U.K.* **12 F4** 55 55N 4 49W
Inverell, *Australia* **63 D5** 29 45S 151 8 E
Invergordon, *U.K.* **12 D4** 57 41N 4 10W
Inverloch, *Australia* **63 F4** 38 38S 145 45 E
Invermere, *Canada* **72 C5** 50 30N 116 2W
Inverness, *Canada* **71 C7** 46 15N 61 19W
Inverness, *U.K.* **12 D4** 57 29N 4 13W
Inverness, *U.S.A.* **77 L4** 28 50N 82 20W
Inverurie, *U.K.* **12 D6** 57 17N 2 23W
Investigator Group, *Australia* **63 E1** 34 45S 134 20 E
Investigator Str., *Australia* **63 F2** 35 30S 137 0 E
Inya, *Russia* **26 D9** 50 28N 86 37 E
Inyanga, *Zimbabwe* **55 F3** 18 12S 32 40 E
Inyangani, *Zimbabwe* **55 F3** 18 5S 32 50 E
Inyantue, *Zimbabwe* **56 B4** 18 33S 26 39 E
Inyo Mts., *U.S.A.* **84 J9** 36 40N 118 0W
Inyokern, *U.S.A.* **85 K9** 35 39N 117 49W
Inza, *Russia* **24 D8** 53 55N 46 25 E
Iō-Jima, *Japan* **31 J5** 30 48N 130 18 E
Ioánnina, *Greece* **21 E9** 39 42N 20 47 E
Iola, *U.S.A.* **81 G7** 37 55N 95 24W
Iona, *U.K.* **12 E2** 56 20N 6 25W
Ione, *U.S.A.* **84 G6** 38 21N 120 56W
Ionia, *U.S.A.* **76 D3** 42 59N 85 4W
Ionian Is. = Iónioi Nísoi, *Greece* **21 E9** 38 40N 20 0 E
Ionian Sea, *Medit. S.* **21 E7** 37 30N 17 30 E
Iónioi Nísoi, *Greece* **21 E9** 38 40N 20 0 E
Íos, *Greece* **21 F11** 36 41N 25 20 E
Iowa □, *U.S.A.* **80 D8** 42 18N 93 30W
Iowa →, *U.S.A.* **80 E9** 41 10N 91 1W
Iowa City, *U.S.A.* **80 E9** 41 40N 91 32W
Iowa Falls, *U.S.A.* **80 D8** 42 31N 93 16W
Iowa Park, *U.S.A.* **81 J5** 33 57N 98 40W
Ipala, *Tanzania* **54 C3** 4 30S 32 52 E
Ipameri, *Brazil* **93 G9** 17 44S 48 9W
Ipatinga, *Brazil* **93 G10** 19 32S 42 30W
Ipiales, *Colombia* **92 C3** 0 50N 77 37W
Ipin = Yibin, *China* **32 D5** 28 45N 104 32 E
Ipixuna, *Brazil* **92 E4** 7 0S 71 40W
Ipoh, *Malaysia* **39 K3** 4 35N 101 5 E
Ippy, *C.A.R.* **52 C4** 6 5N 21 7 E
İpsala, *Turkey* **21 D12** 40 55N 26 23 E
Ipswich, *Australia* **63 D5** 27 35S 152 40 E
Ipswich, *U.K.* **11 E9** 52 4N 1 10 E
Ipswich, *Mass., U.S.A.* **79 D14** 42 41N 70 50W
Ipswich, *S. Dak., U.S.A.* **80 C5** 45 27N 99 2W
Ipu, *Brazil* **93 D10** 4 23S 40 44W
Iqaluit, *Canada* **69 B13** 63 44N 68 31W
Iquique, *Chile* **92 H4** 20 19S 70 5W
Iquitos, *Peru* **92 D4** 3 45S 73 10W
Irabu-Jima, *Japan* **31 M2** 24 50N 125 10 E
Iracoubo, *Fr. Guiana* **93 B8** 5 30N 53 10W
Īrafshān, *Iran* **45 E9** 26 42N 61 56 E
Iráklion, *Greece* **23 D7** 35 20N 25 12 E
Iráklion □, *Greece* **23 D7** 35 10N 25 10 E
Irala, *Paraguay* **95 B5** 25 55S 54 35W
Iran ■, *Asia* **45 C7** 33 0N 53 0 E
Iran, Gunung-Gunung, *Malaysia* **36 D4** 2 20N 114 50 E
Iran, Plateau of, *Asia* **28 F9** 32 0N 55 0 E
Iran Ra. = Iran, Gunung-Gunung, *Malaysia* **36 D4** 2 20N 114 50 E
Īrānshahr, *Iran* **45 E9** 27 15N 60 40 E
Irapuato, *Mexico* **86 C4** 20 40N 101 30W
Iraq ■, *Asia* **44 C5** 33 0N 44 0 E
Irati, *Brazil* **95 B5** 25 25S 50 38W
Irbid, *Jordan* **47 C4** 32 35N 35 48 E
Irbid □, *Jordan* **47 C5** 32 15N 36 35 E
Ireland ■, *Europe* **13 C4** 53 50N 7 52W
Irhyangdong, *N. Korea* **35 D15** 41 15N 129 30 E
Iri, *S. Korea* **35 G14** 35 59N 127 0 E
Irian Jaya □, *Indonesia* **37 E9** 4 0S 137 0 E
Iringa, *Tanzania* **54 D4** 7 48S 35 43 E
Iringa □, *Tanzania* **54 D4** 7 48S 35 43 E
Iriomote-Jima, *Japan* **31 M1** 24 19N 123 48 E
Iriona, *Honduras* **88 C2** 15 57N 85 11W
Iriri →, *Brazil* **93 D8** 3 52S 52 37W
Irish Republic ■, *Europe* **13 C3** 53 0N 8 0W
Irish Sea, *U.K.* **10 D3** 53 38N 4 48W
Irkutsk, *Russia* **27 D11** 52 18N 104 20 E
Irma, *Canada* **73 C6** 52 55N 111 14W
Irō-Zaki, *Japan* **31 G9** 34 36N 138 51 E
Iron Baron, *Australia* **63 E2** 32 58S 137 11 E
Iron Gate = Portile de Fier, *Europe* **17 F12** 44 44N 22 30 E
Iron Knob, *Australia* **63 E2** 32 46S 137 8 E
Iron Mountain, *U.S.A.* **76 C1** 45 49N 88 4W
Iron River, *U.S.A.* **80 B10** 46 6N 88 39W
Irondequoit, *U.S.A.* **78 C7** 43 13N 77 35W
Ironton, *Mo., U.S.A.* **81 G9** 37 36N 90 38W
Ironton, *Ohio, U.S.A.* **76 F4** 38 32N 82 41W
Ironwood, *U.S.A.* **80 B9** 46 27N 90 9W
Iroquois, *Canada* **79 B9** 44 51N 75 19W
Iroquois Falls, *Canada* **70 C3** 48 46N 80 41W
Irpin, *Ukraine* **17 C16** 50 30N 30 15 E
Irrara Cr. →, *Australia* **63 D4** 29 35S 145 31 E
Irrawaddy □, *Burma* **41 L19** 17 0N 95 0 E
Irrawaddy →, *Burma* **41 M19** 15 50N 95 6 E
Irrawaddy, Mouths of the, *Burma* **41 M19** 15 30N 95 0 E
Irricana, *Canada* **72 C6** 51 19N 113 37W
Irtysh →, *Russia* **26 C7** 61 4N 68 52 E
Irumu, *Dem. Rep. of the Congo* **54 B2** 1 32N 29 53 E
Irún, *Spain* **19 A5** 43 20N 1 52W
Irunea = Pamplona, *Spain* **19 A5** 42 48N 1 38W
Irvine, *U.K.* **12 F4** 55 37N 4 41W
Irvine, *Calif., U.S.A.* **85 M9** 33 41N 117 46W
Irvine, *Ky., U.S.A.* **76 G4** 37 42N 83 58W
Irvinestown, *U.K.* **13 B4** 54 28N 7 39W
Irving, *U.S.A.* **81 J6** 32 49N 96 56W
Irvona, *U.S.A.* **78 F6** 40 46N 78 33W
Irwin →, *Australia* **61 E1** 29 15S 114 54 E
Irymple, *Australia* **63 E3** 34 14S 142 8 E
Isa Khel, *Pakistan* **42 C4** 32 41N 71 17 E
Isaac →, *Australia* **62 C4** 22 55S 149 20 E
Isabel, *U.S.A.* **80 C4** 45 24N 101 26W
Isabela, *Phil.* **37 C6** 6 40N 121 59 E
Isabela, I., *Mexico* **86 C3** 21 51N 105 55W
Isabelia, Cord., *Nic.* **88 D2** 13 30N 85 25W
Isabella Ra., *Australia* **60 D3** 21 0S 121 4 E
Ísafjarðardjúp, *Iceland* **8 C2** 66 10N 23 0W
Ísafjörður, *Iceland* **8 C2** 66 5N 23 9W
Isagarh, *India* **42 G7** 24 48N 77 51 E
Isahaya, *Japan* **31 H5** 32 52N 130 2 E
Isaka, *Tanzania* **54 C3** 3 56S 32 59 E
Isan →, *India* **43 F9** 26 51N 80 7 E
Isana = Içana →, *Brazil* **92 C5** 0 26N 67 19W
Isar →, *Germany* **16 D7** 48 48N 12 57 E
Íschia, *Italy* **20 D5** 40 44N 13 57 E
Isdell →, *Australia* **60 C3** 16 27S 124 51 E
Ise, *Japan* **31 G8** 34 25N 136 45 E
Ise-Wan, *Japan* **31 G8** 34 43N 136 43 E
Iseramagazi, *Tanzania* **54 C3** 4 37S 32 10 E
Isère →, *France* **18 D6** 44 59N 4 51 E
Isérnia, *Italy* **20 D6** 41 36N 14 14 E
Isfahan = Eşfahān, *Iran* **45 C6** 32 39N 51 43 E
Ishigaki-Shima, *Japan* **31 M2** 24 20N 124 10 E
Ishikari-Gawa →, *Japan* **30 C10** 43 15N 141 23 E
Ishikari-Sammyaku, *Japan* **30 C11** 43 30N 143 0 E
Ishikari-Wan, *Japan* **30 C10** 43 25N 141 1 E
Ishikawa □, *Japan* **31 F8** 36 30N 136 30 E
Ishim, *Russia* **26 D7** 56 10N 69 30 E
Ishim →, *Russia* **26 D8** 57 45N 71 10 E
Ishinomaki, *Japan* **30 E10** 38 32N 141 20 E
Ishioka, *Japan* **31 F10** 36 11N 140 16 E
Ishkuman, *Pakistan* **43 A5** 36 30N 73 50 E
Ishpeming, *U.S.A.* **76 B2** 46 29N 87 40W
Isil Kul, *Russia* **26 D8** 54 55N 71 16 E
Isiolo, *Kenya* **54 B4** 0 24N 37 33 E
Isiro, *Dem. Rep. of the Congo* **54 B2** 2 53N 27 40 E
Isisford, *Australia* **62 C3** 24 15S 144 21 E
İskenderun, *Turkey* **25 G6** 36 32N 36 10 E
İskenderun Körfezi, *Turkey* **25 G6** 36 40N 35 50 E
Iskŭr →, *Bulgaria* **21 C11** 43 45N 24 25 E
Iskut →, *Canada* **72 B2** 56 45N 131 49W
Isla →, *U.K.* **12 E5** 56 32N 3 20W
Isla Vista, *U.S.A.* **85 L7** 34 25N 119 53W
Islam Headworks, *Pakistan* **42 E5** 29 49N 72 33 E
Islamabad, *Pakistan* **42 C5** 33 40N 73 10 E
Islamgarh, *Pakistan* **42 F4** 27 51N 70 48 E
Islamkot, *Pakistan* **42 G4** 24 42N 70 13 E
Islampur, *India* **43 G11** 25 9N 85 12 E
Island L., *Canada* **73 C10** 53 47N 94 25W
Island Lagoon, *Australia* **63 E2** 31 30S 136 40 E
Island Pond, *U.S.A.* **79 B13** 44 49N 71 53W
Islands, B. of, *Canada* **71 C8** 49 11N 58 15W
Islands, B. of, *N.Z.* **59 F5** 35 15S 174 6 E
Islay, *U.K.* **12 F2** 55 46N 6 10W
Isle →, *France* **18 D3** 44 55N 0 15W
Isle aux Morts, *Canada* **71 C8** 47 35N 59 0W
Isle of Wight □, *U.K.* **11 G6** 50 41N 1 17W
Isle Royale Nat. Park, *U.S.A.* **80 B10** 48 0N 88 55W
Isleton, *U.S.A.* **84 G5** 38 10N 121 37W
Ismail = Izmayil, *Ukraine* **17 F15** 45 22N 28 46 E
Ismâ'ilîya, *Egypt* **51 B12** 30 37N 32 18 E
Isoanala, *Madag.* **57 C8** 23 50S 45 44 E
Isogstalo, *India* **43 B8** 34 15N 78 46 E
İsparta, *Turkey* **25 G5** 37 47N 30 30 E
Íspica, *Italy* **20 F6** 36 47N 14 55 E
Israel ■, *Asia* **47 D3** 32 0N 34 50 E
Issoire, *France* **18 D5** 45 32N 3 15 E
Issyk-Kul, Ozero = Ysyk-Köl, *Kyrgyzstan* **26 E8** 42 25N 77 15 E
İstanbul, *Turkey* **21 D13** 41 0N 29 0 E
İstanbul Boğazı, *Turkey* **21 D13** 41 10N 29 10 E
Istiaía, *Greece* **21 E10** 38 57N 23 9 E
Istokpoga, L., *U.S.A.* **77 M5** 27 23N 81 17W
Istra, *Croatia* **16 F7** 45 10N 14 0 E
Istres, *France* **18 E6** 43 31N 4 59 E
Istria = Istra, *Croatia* **16 F7** 45 10N 14 0 E
Itá, *Paraguay* **94 B4** 25 29S 57 21W
Itaberaba, *Brazil* **93 F10** 12 32S 40 18W
Itabira, *Brazil* **93 G10** 19 37S 43 13W
Itabirito, *Brazil* **95 A7** 20 15S 43 48W
Itabuna, *Brazil* **93 F11** 14 48S 39 16W
Itacaunas →, *Brazil* **93 E9** 5 21S 49 8W
Itacoatiara, *Brazil* **92 D7** 3 8S 58 25W
Itaipú, Repêsa de, *Brazil* **95 B5** 25 30S 54 30W
Itaituba, *Brazil* **93 D7** 4 10S 55 50W
Itajaí, *Brazil* **95 B6** 27 50S 48 39W
Itajubá, *Brazil* **95 A6** 22 24S 45 30W
Itaka, *Tanzania* **55 D3** 8 50S 32 49 E
Italy ■, *Europe* **20 C5** 42 0N 13 0 E
Itamaraju, *Brazil* **93 G11** 17 5S 39 31W
Itampolo, *Madag.* **57 C7** 24 41S 43 57 E
Itandrano, *Madag.* **57 C8** 21 47S 45 17 E
Itapecuru-Mirim, *Brazil* **93 D10** 3 24S 44 20W
Itaperuna, *Brazil* **95 A7** 21 10S 41 54W
Itapetininga, *Brazil* **95 A6** 23 36S 48 7W
Itapeva, *Brazil* **95 A6** 23 59S 48 59W
Itapicuru →, *Bahia, Brazil* **93 F11** 11 47S 37 32W
Itapicuru →, *Maranhão, Brazil* **93 D10** 2 52S 44 12W
Itapipoca, *Brazil* **93 D11** 3 30S 39 35W
Itapuá □, *Paraguay* **95 B4** 26 40S 55 40W
Itaquari, *Brazil* **95 A7** 20 20S 40 25W
Itaquí, *Brazil* **94 B4** 29 8S 56 30W
Itararé, *Brazil* **95 A6** 24 6S 49 23W
Itarsi, *India* **42 H7** 22 36N 77 51 E
Itatí, *Argentina* **94 B4** 27 16S 58 15W
Itchen →, *U.K.* **11 G6** 50 55N 1 22W
Itezhi Tezhi, L., *Zambia* **55 F2** 15 30S 25 30 E
Ithaca = Itháki, *Greece* **21 E9** 38 25N 20 40 E
Ithaca, *U.S.A.* **79 D8** 42 27N 76 30W
Itháki, *Greece* **21 E9** 38 25N 20 40 E
Itiquira →, *Brazil* **93 G7** 17 18S 56 44W
Itō, *Japan* **31 G9** 34 58N 139 5 E
Itoigawa, *Japan* **31 F8** 37 2N 137 51 E
Itonamas →, *Bolivia* **92 F6** 12 28S 64 24W
Ittoqqortoormiit, *Greenland* **4 B6** 70 20N 23 0W
Itu, *Brazil* **95 A6** 23 17S 47 15W
Itu Aba I., *S. China Sea* **36 B4** 10 23N 114 21 E
Ituiutaba, *Brazil* **93 G9** 19 0S 49 25W
Itumbiara, *Brazil* **93 G9** 18 20S 49 10W
Ituna, *Canada* **73 C8** 51 10N 103 24W
Itunge Port, *Tanzania* **55 D3** 9 40S 33 55 E
Iturbe, *Argentina* **94 A2** 23 0S 65 25W
Ituri →, *Dem. Rep. of the Congo* **54 B2** 1 40N 27 1 E
Iturup, Ostrov, *Russia* **27 E15** 45 0N 148 0 E
Ituxi →, *Brazil* **92 E6** 7 18S 64 51W
Ituyuro →, *Argentina* **94 A3** 22 40S 63 50W
Itzehoe, *Germany* **16 B5** 53 55N 9 31 E
Ivahona, *Madag.* **57 C8** 23 27S 46 10 E
Ivaí →, *Brazil* **95 A5** 23 18S 53 42W
Ivalo, *Finland* **8 B22** 68 38N 27 35 E
Ivalojoki →, *Finland* **8 B22** 68 40N 27 40 E
Ivanava, *Belarus* **17 B13** 52 7N 25 29 E
Ivanhoe, *Australia* **63 E3** 32 56S 144 20 E
Ivanhoe, *Calif., U.S.A.* **84 J7** 36 23N 119 13W
Ivanhoe, *Minn., U.S.A.* **80 C6** 44 28N 96 15W
Ivano-Frankivsk, *Ukraine* **17 D13** 48 40N 24 40 E
Ivano-Frankovsk = Ivano-Frankivsk, *Ukraine* **17 D13** 48 40N 24 40 E
Ivanovo = Ivanava, *Belarus* **17 B13** 52 7N 25 29 E
Ivanovo, *Russia* **24 C7** 57 5N 41 0 E
Ivato, *Madag.* **57 C8** 20 37S 47 10 E
Ivatsevichy, *Belarus* **17 B13** 52 43N 25 21 E
Ivdel, *Russia* **24 B11** 60 42N 60 24 E
Ivinheima →, *Brazil* **95 A5** 23 14S 53 42W
Ivinhema, *Brazil* **95 A5** 22 10S 53 37W
Ivohibe, *Madag.* **57 C8** 22 31S 46 57 E
Ivory Coast, *W. Afr.* **50 H4** 4 20N 5 0W
Ivory Coast ■, *Africa* **50 G4** 7 30N 5 0W
Ivrea, *Italy* **18 D7** 45 28N 7 52 E
Ivujivik, *Canada* **69 B12** 62 24N 77 55W
Ivybridge, *U.K.* **11 G4** 50 23N 3 56W
Iwaizumi, *Japan* **30 E10** 39 50N 141 45 E
Iwaki, *Japan* **31 F10** 37 3N 140 55 E
Iwakuni, *Japan* **31 G6** 34 15N 132 8 E
Iwamizawa, *Japan* **30 C10** 43 12N 141 46 E
Iwanai, *Japan* **30 C10** 42 58N 140 30 E
Iwata, *Japan* **31 G8** 34 42N 137 51 E
Iwate □, *Japan* **30 E10** 39 30N 141 30 E
Iwate-San, *Japan* **30 E10** 39 51N 141 0 E
Iwo, *Nigeria* **50 G6** 7 39N 4 9 E
Ixiamas, *Bolivia* **92 F5** 13 50S 68 5W
Ixopo, *S. Africa* **57 E5** 30 11S 30 5 E
Ixtepec, *Mexico* **87 D5** 16 32N 95 10W
Ixtlán del Río, *Mexico* **86 C4** 21 5N 104 21W
Iyo, *Japan* **31 H6** 33 45N 132 45 E
Izabal, L. de, *Guatemala* **88 C2** 15 30N 89 10W
Izamal, *Mexico* **87 C7** 20 56N 89 1W
Izena-Shima, *Japan* **31 L3** 26 56N 127 56 E
Izhevsk, *Russia* **24 C9** 56 51N 53 14 E
Izhma →, *Russia* **24 A9** 65 19N 52 54 E
Izmayil, *Ukraine* **17 F15** 45 22N 28 46 E
İzmir, *Turkey* **21 E12** 38 25N 27 8 E
İzmit = Kocaeli, *Turkey* **25 F4** 40 45N 29 50 E
İznik Gölü, *Turkey* **21 D13** 40 27N 29 30 E
Izra, *Syria* **47 C5** 32 51N 36 15 E
Izu-Shotō, *Japan* **31 G10** 34 30N 140 0 E
Izúcar de Matamoros, *Mexico* **87 D5** 18 36N 98 28W
Izumi-Sano, *Japan* **31 G7** 34 23N 135 18 E
Izumo, *Japan* **31 G6** 35 20N 132 46 E
Izyaslav, *Ukraine* **17 C14** 50 5N 26 50 E

J

Jabalpur, *India* **43 H8** 23 9N 79 58 E
Jabbūl, *Syria* **44 B3** 36 4N 37 30 E
Jabiru, *Australia* **60 B5** 12 40S 132 53 E
Jablah, *Syria* **44 C3** 35 20N 36 0 E
Jablonec nad Nisou, *Czech Rep.* **16 C8** 50 43N 15 10 E

Jaboatão, *Brazil* 93 E11 8 7S 35 1W
Jaboticabal, *Brazil* 95 A6 21 15S 48 17W
Jaca, *Spain* 19 A5 42 35N 0 33W
Jacareí, *Brazil* 95 A6 23 20S 46 0W
Jacarèzinho, *Brazil* 95 A6 23 5S 49 58W
Jackman, *U.S.A.* 77 C10 45 35N 70 17W
Jacksboro, *U.S.A.* 81 J5 33 14N 98 15W
Jackson, *Ala., U.S.A.* 77 K2 31 31N 87 53W
Jackson, *Calif., U.S.A.* 84 G6 38 21N 120 46W
Jackson, *Ky., U.S.A.* 76 G4 37 33N 83 23W
Jackson, *Mich., U.S.A.* 76 D3 42 15N 84 24W
Jackson, *Minn., U.S.A.* 80 D7 43 37N 95 1W
Jackson, *Miss., U.S.A.* 81 J9 32 18N 90 12W
Jackson, *Mo., U.S.A.* 81 G10 37 23N 89 40W
Jackson, *N.H., U.S.A.* 79 B13 44 10N 71 11W
Jackson, *Ohio, U.S.A.* 76 F4 39 3N 82 39W
Jackson, *Tenn., U.S.A.* 77 H1 35 37N 88 49W
Jackson, *Wyo., U.S.A.* 82 E8 43 29N 110 46W
Jackson B., *N.Z.* 59 K2 43 58S 168 42 E
Jackson L., *U.S.A.* 82 E8 43 52N 110 36W
Jacksons, *N.Z.* 59 K3 42 46S 171 32 E
Jackson's Arm, *Canada* 71 C8 49 52N 56 47W
Jacksonville, *Ala., U.S.A.* 77 J3 33 49N 85 46W
Jacksonville, *Ark., U.S.A.* 81 H8 34 52N 92 7W
Jacksonville, *Calif., U.S.A.* 84 H6 37 52N 120 24W
Jacksonville, *Fla., U.S.A.* 77 K5 30 20N 81 39W
Jacksonville, *Ill., U.S.A.* 80 F9 39 44N 90 14W
Jacksonville, *N.C., U.S.A.* 77 H7 34 45N 77 26W
Jacksonville, *Tex., U.S.A.* 81 K7 31 58N 95 17W
Jacksonville Beach, *U.S.A.* 77 K5 30 17N 81 24W
Jacmel, *Haiti* 89 C5 18 14N 72 32W
Jacob Lake, *U.S.A.* 83 H7 36 43N 112 13W
Jacobabad, *Pakistan* 42 E3 28 20N 68 29 E
Jacobina, *Brazil* 93 F10 11 11S 40 30W
Jacques Cartier, Dét. de, *Canada* 71 C7 50 0N 63 30W
Jacques Cartier, Mt., *Canada* 71 C6 48 57N 66 0W
Jacques Cartier, Parc Prov., *Canada* 71 C5 47 15N 71 33W
Jacuí →, *Brazil* 95 C5 30 2S 51 15W
Jacumba, *U.S.A.* 85 N10 32 37N 116 11W
Jacundá →, *Brazil* 93 D8 1 57S 50 26W
Jadotville = Likasi, *Dem. Rep. of the Congo* 55 E2 10 55S 26 48 E
Jaén, *Peru* 92 E3 5 25S 78 40W
Jaén, *Spain* 19 D4 37 44N 3 43W
Jafarabad, *India* 42 J4 20 52N 71 22 E
Jaffa = Tel Aviv-Yafo, *Israel* 47 C3 32 4N 34 48 E
Jaffa, C., *Australia* 63 F2 36 58S 139 40 E
Jaffna, *Sri Lanka* 40 Q12 9 45N 80 2 E
Jaffrey, *U.S.A.* 79 D12 42 49N 72 2W
Jagadhri, *India* 42 D7 30 10N 77 20 E
Jagadishpur, *India* 43 G11 25 30N 84 21 E
Jagdalpur, *India* 41 K13 19 3N 82 0 E
Jagersfontein, *S. Africa* 56 D4 29 44S 25 27 E
Jaghīn →, *Iran* 45 E8 27 17N 57 13 E
Jagodina, *Serbia, Yug.* 21 C9 44 5N 21 15 E
Jagraon, *India* 40 D9 30 50N 75 25 E
Jagtial, *India* 40 K11 18 50N 79 0 E
Jaguariaíva, *Brazil* 95 A6 24 10S 49 50W
Jaguaribe →, *Brazil* 93 D11 4 25S 37 45W
Jagüey Grande, *Cuba* 88 B3 22 35N 81 7W
Jahanabad, *India* 43 G11 25 13N 84 59 E
Jahazpur, *India* 42 G6 25 37N 75 17 E
Jahrom, *Iran* 45 D7 28 30N 53 31 E
Jaijon, *India* 42 D7 31 21N 76 9 E
Jailolo, *Indonesia* 37 D7 1 5N 127 30 E
Jailolo, Selat, *Indonesia* 37 D7 0 5N 129 5 E
Jaipur, *India* 42 F6 27 0N 75 50 E
Jais, *India* 43 F9 26 15N 81 32 E
Jaisalmer, *India* 42 F4 26 55N 70 54 E
Jaisinghnagar, *India* 43 H8 23 38N 78 34 E
Jaitaran, *India* 42 F5 26 12N 73 56 E
Jaithari, *India* 43 H8 23 14N 78 37 E
Jājarm, *Iran* 45 B8 36 58N 56 27 E
Jakam →, *India* 42 H6 23 54N 74 13 E
Jakarta, *Indonesia* 36 F3 6 9S 106 49 E
Jakhal, *India* 42 E6 29 48N 75 50 E
Jakhau, *India* 42 H3 23 13N 68 43 E
Jakobstad = Pietarsaari, *Finland* 8 E20 63 40N 22 43 E
Jal, *U.S.A.* 81 J3 32 7N 103 12W
Jalālābād, *Afghan.* 42 B4 34 30N 70 29 E
Jalalabad, *India* 43 F8 27 41N 79 42 E
Jalalpur Jattan, *Pakistan* 42 C6 32 38N 74 11 E
Jalama, *U.S.A.* 85 L6 34 29N 120 29W
Jalapa, *Guatemala* 88 D2 14 39N 89 59W
Jalapa Enríquez, *Mexico* 87 D5 19 32N 96 55W
Jalasjärvi, *Finland* 9 E20 62 29N 22 47 E
Jalaun, *India* 43 F8 26 8N 79 25 E
Jaldhaka →, *Bangla.* 43 F13 26 16N 89 16 E
Jalesar, *India* 42 F8 27 29N 78 19 E
Jaleswar, *Nepal* 43 F11 26 38N 85 48 E
Jalgaon, *India* 40 J9 21 0N 75 42 E
Jalībah, *Iraq* 44 D5 30 35N 46 32 E
Jalisco □, *Mexico* 86 D4 20 0N 104 0W
Jalkot, *Pakistan* 43 B5 35 14N 73 24 E
Jalna, *India* 40 K9 19 48N 75 38 E
Jalón →, *Spain* 19 B5 41 47N 1 4W
Jalor, *India* 42 G5 25 21N 72 37 E
Jalpa, *Mexico* 86 C4 21 38N 102 58W
Jalpaiguri, *India* 41 F16 26 32N 88 46 E
Jaluit I., *Marshall Is.* 64 G8 6 0N 169 30 E
Jalūlā, *Iraq* 44 C5 34 16N 45 10 E
Jamaica ■, *W. Indies* 88 C4 18 10N 77 30W
Jamalpur, *Bangla.* 41 G16 24 52N 89 56 E
Jamalpur, *India* 43 G12 25 18N 86 28 E
Jamalpurganj, *India* 43 H13 23 2N 87 59 E
Jamanxim →, *Brazil* 93 D7 4 43S 56 18W
Jambi, *Indonesia* 36 E2 1 38S 103 30 E
Jambi □, *Indonesia* 36 E2 1 30S 102 30 E
Jambusar, *India* 42 H5 22 3N 72 51 E
James →, *S. Dak., U.S.A.* 80 D6 42 52N 97 18W
James →, *Va., U.S.A.* 76 G7 36 56N 76 27W
James B., *Canada* 70 B3 54 0N 80 0W
James Ranges, *Australia* 60 D5 24 10S 132 30 E
James Ross I., *Antarctica* 5 C18 63 58S 57 50W
Jamesabad, *Pakistan* 42 G3 25 17N 69 15 E
Jamestown, *Australia* 63 E2 33 10S 138 32 E
Jamestown, *S. Africa* 56 E4 31 6S 26 45 E
Jamestown, *N. Dak., U.S.A.* 80 B5 46 54N 98 42W
Jamestown, *N.Y., U.S.A.* 78 D5 42 6N 79 14W
Jamestown, *Pa., U.S.A.* 78 E4 41 29N 80 27W
Jamīlābād, *Iran* 45 C6 34 24N 48 28 E
Jamiltepec, *Mexico* 87 D5 16 17N 97 49W
Jamira →, *India* 43 J13 21 35N 88 28 E
Jamkhandi, *India* 40 L9 16 30N 75 15 E
Jammu, *India* 42 C6 32 43N 74 54 E
Jammu & Kashmir □, *India* 43 B7 34 25N 77 0 E
Jamnagar, *India* 42 H4 22 30N 70 6 E
Jamni →, *India* 43 G8 25 13N 78 35 E
Jampur, *Pakistan* 42 E4 29 39N 70 40 E
Jamrud, *Pakistan* 42 C4 33 59N 71 24 E
Jämsä, *Finland* 9 F21 61 53N 25 10 E
Jamshedpur, *India* 43 H12 22 44N 86 12 E
Jamtara, *India* 43 H12 23 59N 86 49 E
Jämtland, *Sweden* 8 E15 63 31N 14 0 E
Jan L., *Canada* 73 C8 54 56N 102 55W
Jan Mayen, *Arctic* 4 B7 71 0N 9 0W
Janakkala, *Finland* 9 F21 60 54N 24 36 E
Janaúba, *Brazil* 93 G10 15 48S 43 19W
Jand, *Pakistan* 42 C5 33 30N 72 6 E
Jandaq, *Iran* 45 C7 34 3N 54 22 E
Jandia, *Canary Is.* 22 F5 28 6N 14 21W
Jandia, Pta. de, *Canary Is.* 22 F5 28 3N 14 31W
Jandola, *Pakistan* 42 C4 32 20N 70 9 E
Jandowae, *Australia* 63 D5 26 45S 151 7 E
Janesville, *U.S.A.* 80 D10 42 41N 89 1W
Jangamo, *Mozam.* 57 C6 24 6S 35 21 E
Janghai, *India* 43 G10 25 33N 82 19 E
Janīn, *West Bank* 47 C4 32 28N 35 18 E
Janjgir, *India* 43 J10 22 1N 82 34 E
Janjina, *Madag.* 57 C8 20 30S 45 50 E
Janos, *Mexico* 86 A3 30 45N 108 10W
Januária, *Brazil* 93 G10 15 25S 44 25W
Janubio, *Canary Is.* 22 F6 28 56N 13 50W
Jaora, *India* 42 H6 23 40N 75 10 E
Japan ■, *Asia* 31 G8 36 0N 136 0 E
Japan, Sea of, *Asia* 30 E7 40 0N 135 0 E
Japan Trench, *Pac. Oc.* 28 F18 32 0N 142 0 E
Japen = Yapen, *Indonesia* 37 E9 1 50S 136 0 E
Japla, *India* 43 G11 24 33N 84 1 E
Japurá →, *Brazil* 92 D5 3 8S 65 46W
Jaquarão, *Brazil* 95 C5 32 34S 53 23W
Jaqué, *Panama* 88 E4 7 27N 78 8W
Jarābulus, *Syria* 44 B3 36 49N 38 1 E
Jarama →, *Spain* 19 B4 40 24N 3 32W
Jaranwala, *Pakistan* 42 D5 31 15N 73 26 E
Jarash, *Jordan* 47 C4 32 17N 35 54 E
Jardim, *Brazil* 94 A4 21 28S 56 2W
Jardines de la Reina, Arch. de los, *Cuba* 88 B4 20 50N 78 50W
Jargalang, *China* 35 C12 43 5N 122 55 E
Jargalant = Hovd, *Mongolia* 32 B4 48 2N 91 37 E
Jari →, *Brazil* 93 D8 1 9S 51 54W
Jarīr, W. al →, *Si. Arabia* 44 E4 25 38N 42 30 E
Jarosław, *Poland* 17 C12 50 2N 22 42 E
Jarrahdale, *Australia* 61 F2 32 24S 116 5 E
Jarrahi →, *Iran* 45 D6 30 49N 48 48 E
Jarres, Plaine des, *Laos* 38 C4 19 27N 103 10 E
Jartai, *China* 34 E3 39 45N 105 48 E
Jarud Qi, *China* 35 B11 44 28N 120 50 E
Järvenpää, *Finland* 9 F21 60 29N 25 5 E
Jarvis, *Canada* 78 D4 42 53N 80 6W
Jarvis I., *Pac. Oc.* 65 H12 0 15S 160 5W
Jarwa, *India* 43 F10 27 38N 82 30 E
Jasdan, *India* 42 H4 22 2N 71 12 E
Jashpurnagar, *India* 43 H11 22 54N 84 9 E
Jasidih, *India* 43 G12 24 31N 86 39 E
Jāsimīyah, *Iraq* 44 C5 33 45N 44 41 E
Jasin, *Malaysia* 39 L4 2 20N 102 26 E
Jāsk, *Iran* 45 E8 25 38N 57 45 E
Jasło, *Poland* 17 D11 49 45N 21 30 E
Jaso, *India* 43 G9 24 30N 80 29 E
Jasper, *Alta., Canada* 72 C5 52 55N 118 5W
Jasper, *Ont., Canada* 79 B9 44 52N 75 57W
Jasper, *Ala., U.S.A.* 77 J2 33 50N 87 17W
Jasper, *Fla., U.S.A.* 77 K4 30 31N 82 57W
Jasper, *Ind., U.S.A.* 76 F2 38 24N 86 56W
Jasper, *Tex., U.S.A.* 81 K8 30 56N 94 1W
Jasper Nat. Park, *Canada* 72 C5 52 50N 118 8W
Jasrasar, *India* 42 F5 27 43N 73 49 E
Jászberény, *Hungary* 17 E10 47 30N 19 55 E
Jataí, *Brazil* 93 G8 17 58S 51 48W
Jati, *Pakistan* 42 G3 24 20N 68 19 E
Jatibarang, *Indonesia* 37 G13 6 28S 108 18 E
Jatinegara, *Indonesia* 37 G12 6 13S 106 52 E
Játiva = Xátiva, *Spain* 19 C5 38 59N 0 32W
Jaú, *Brazil* 95 A6 22 10S 48 30W
Jauja, *Peru* 92 F3 11 45S 75 15W
Jaunpur, *India* 43 G10 25 46N 82 44 E
Java = Jawa, *Indonesia* 36 F3 7 0S 110 0 E
Java Barat □, *Indonesia* 37 G12 7 0S 107 0 E
Java Sea, *Indonesia* 36 E3 4 35S 107 15 E
Java Tengah □, *Indonesia* 37 G14 7 0S 110 0 E
Java Timur □, *Indonesia* 37 G15 8 0S 113 0 E
Java Trench, *Ind. Oc.* 36 F3 9 0S 105 0 E
Javhlant = Ulyasutay, *Mongolia* 32 B4 47 56N 97 28 E
Jawa, *Indonesia* 36 F3 7 0S 110 0 E
Jawad, *India* 42 G6 24 36N 74 51 E
Jay Peak, *U.S.A.* 79 B12 44 55N 72 32W
Jaya, Puncak, *Indonesia* 37 E9 3 57S 137 17 E
Jayanti, *India* 41 F16 26 45N 89 40 E
Jayapura, *Indonesia* 37 E10 2 28S 140 38 E
Jayawijaya, Pegunungan, *Indonesia* 37 E9 5 0S 139 0 E
Jaynagar, *India* 41 F15 26 43N 86 9 E
Jayrūd, *Syria* 44 C3 33 49N 36 44 E
Jayton, *U.S.A.* 81 J4 33 15N 100 34W
Jāz Mūrīān, Hāmūn-e, *Iran* 45 E8 27 20N 58 55 E
Jazīreh-ye Shīf, *Iran* 45 D6 29 4N 50 54 E
Jazminal, *Mexico* 86 C4 24 56N 101 25W
Jazzīn, *Lebanon* 47 B4 33 31N 35 35 E
Jean, *U.S.A.* 85 K11 35 47N 115 20W
Jean Marie River, *Canada* 72 A4 61 32N 120 38W
Jean Rabel, *Haiti* 89 C5 19 50N 73 5W
Jeanerette, *U.S.A.* 81 L9 29 55N 91 40W
Jeanette, Ostrov = Zhannetty, Ostrov, *Russia* 27 B16 76 43N 158 0 E
Jeannette, *U.S.A.* 78 F5 40 20N 79 36W
Jebāl Bārez, Kūh-e, *Iran* 45 D8 28 30N 58 20 E
Jebel, Bahr el →, *Sudan* 51 G12 9 30N 30 25 E
Jedburgh, *U.K.* 12 F6 55 29N 2 33W
Jedda = Jiddah, *Si. Arabia* 46 C2 21 29N 39 10 E
Jeddore L., *Canada* 71 C8 48 3N 55 55W
Jędrzejów, *Poland* 17 C11 50 35N 20 15 E
Jefferson, *Iowa, U.S.A.* 80 D7 42 1N 94 23W
Jefferson, *Ohio, U.S.A.* 78 E4 41 44N 80 46W
Jefferson, *Tex., U.S.A.* 81 J7 32 46N 94 21W
Jefferson, Mt., *Nev., U.S.A.* 82 G5 38 51N 117 0W
Jefferson, Mt., *Oreg., U.S.A.* 82 D3 44 41N 121 48W
Jefferson City, *Mo., U.S.A.* 80 F8 38 34N 92 10W
Jefferson City, *Tenn., U.S.A.* 77 G4 36 7N 83 30W
Jeffersontown, *U.S.A.* 76 F3 38 12N 85 35W
Jeffersonville, *U.S.A.* 76 F3 38 17N 85 44W
Jeffrey City, *U.S.A.* 82 E10 42 30N 107 49W
Jega, *Nigeria* 50 F6 12 15N 4 23 E
Jēkabpils, *Latvia* 9 H21 56 29N 25 57 E
Jekyll I., *U.S.A.* 77 K5 31 4N 81 25W
Jelenia Góra, *Poland* 16 C8 50 50N 15 45 E
Jelgava, *Latvia* 9 H20 56 41N 23 49 E
Jemaja, *Indonesia* 39 L5 3 5N 105 45 E
Jemaluang, *Malaysia* 39 L4 2 16N 103 52 E
Jember, *Indonesia* 37 H15 8 11S 113 41 E
Jembongan, *Malaysia* 36 C5 6 45N 117 20 E
Jena, *Germany* 16 C6 50 54N 11 35 E
Jena, *U.S.A.* 81 K8 31 41N 92 8W
Jenkins, *U.S.A.* 76 G4 37 10N 82 38W
Jenner, *U.S.A.* 84 G3 38 27N 123 7W
Jennings, *U.S.A.* 81 K8 30 13N 92 40W
Jepara, *Indonesia* 37 G14 7 40S 109 14 E
Jeparit, *Australia* 63 F3 36 8S 142 1 E
Jequié, *Brazil* 93 F10 13 51S 40 5W
Jequitinhonha, *Brazil* 93 G10 16 30S 41 0W
Jequitinhonha →, *Brazil* 93 G11 15 51S 38 53W
Jerantut, *Malaysia* 39 L4 3 56N 102 22 E
Jérémie, *Haiti* 89 C5 18 40N 74 10W
Jerez, Punta, *Mexico* 87 C5 22 58N 97 40W
Jerez de García Salinas, *Mexico* 86 C4 22 39N 103 0W
Jerez de la Frontera, *Spain* 19 D2 36 41N 6 7W
Jerez de los Caballeros, *Spain* 19 C2 38 20N 6 45W
Jericho = El Arīḥā, *West Bank* 47 D4 31 52N 35 27 E
Jericho, *Australia* 62 C4 23 38S 146 6 E
Jerid, Chott el = Djerid, Chott, *Tunisia* 50 B7 33 42N 8 30 E
Jerilderie, *Australia* 63 F4 35 20S 145 41 E
Jermyn, *U.S.A.* 79 E9 41 31N 75 31W
Jerome, *U.S.A.* 82 E6 42 44N 114 31W
Jerramungup, *Australia* 61 F2 33 55S 118 55 E
Jersey, *U.K.* 11 H5 49 11N 2 7W
Jersey City, *U.S.A.* 79 F10 40 44N 74 4W
Jersey Shore, *U.S.A.* 78 E7 41 12N 77 15W
Jerseyville, *U.S.A.* 80 F9 39 7N 90 20W
Jerusalem, *Israel* 47 D4 31 47N 35 10 E
Jervis B., *Australia* 63 F5 35 8S 150 46 E
Jervis Inlet, *Canada* 72 C4 50 0N 123 57W
Jesi = Iesi, *Italy* 20 C5 43 31N 13 14 E
Jesselton = Kota Kinabalu, *Malaysia* 36 C5 6 0N 116 4 E
Jessore, *Bangla.* 41 H16 23 10N 89 10 E
Jesup, *U.S.A.* 77 K5 31 36N 81 53W
Jesús Carranza, *Mexico* 87 D5 17 28N 95 1W
Jesús María, *Argentina* 94 C3 30 59S 64 5W
Jetmore, *U.S.A.* 81 F5 38 4N 99 54W
Jetpur, *India* 42 J4 21 45N 70 10 E
Jevnaker, *Norway* 9 F14 60 15N 10 26 E
Jewett, *U.S.A.* 78 F3 40 22N 81 2W
Jewett City, *U.S.A.* 79 E13 41 36N 72 0W
Jeyḥūnābād, *Iran* 45 C6 34 58N 48 59 E
Jeypore, *India* 41 K13 18 50N 82 38 E
Jha Jha, *India* 43 G12 24 46N 86 22 E
Jhaarkand = Jharkhand □, *India* 43 H11 24 0N 85 50 E
Jhabua, *India* 42 H6 22 46N 74 36 E
Jhajjar, *India* 42 E7 28 37N 76 42 E
Jhal, *Pakistan* 42 E2 28 17N 67 27 E
Jhal Jhao, *Pakistan* 40 F4 26 20N 65 35 E
Jhalawar, *India* 42 G7 24 40N 76 10 E
Jhalida, *India* 43 H11 23 22N 85 58 E
Jhalrapatan, *India* 42 G7 24 33N 76 10 E
Jhang Maghiana, *Pakistan* 42 D5 31 15N 72 22 E
Jhansi, *India* 43 G8 25 30N 78 36 E
Jhargram, *India* 43 H12 22 27N 86 59 E
Jharia, *India* 43 H12 23 45N 86 26 E
Jharkhand □, *India* 43 H11 24 0N 85 50 E
Jharsuguda, *India* 41 J14 21 56N 84 5 E
Jhelum, *Pakistan* 42 C5 33 0N 73 45 E
Jhelum →, *Pakistan* 42 D5 31 20N 72 10 E
Jhilmilli, *India* 43 H10 23 24N 82 51 E
Jhudo, *Pakistan* 42 G3 24 58N 69 18 E
Jhunjhunu, *India* 42 E6 28 10N 75 30 E
Ji-Paraná, *Brazil* 92 F6 10 52S 62 57W
Ji Xian, *Hebei, China* 34 F8 37 35N 115 30 E
Ji Xian, *Henan, China* 34 G8 35 22N 114 5 E
Ji Xian, *Shanxi, China* 34 F6 36 7N 110 40 E
Jia Xian, *Henan, China* 34 H7 33 59N 113 12 E
Jia Xian, *Shaanxi, China* 34 E6 38 12N 110 28 E
Jiamusi, *China* 33 B8 46 40N 130 26 E
Ji'an, *Jiangxi, China* 33 D6 27 6N 114 59 E
Ji'an, *Jilin, China* 35 D14 41 5N 126 10 E
Jianchang, *China* 35 D11 40 55N 120 35 E
Jianchangying, *China* 35 D10 40 10N 118 50 E
Jiangcheng, *China* 32 D5 22 36N 101 52 E
Jiangmen, *China* 33 D6 22 32N 113 0 E
Jiangsu □, *China* 35 H11 33 0N 120 0 E
Jiangxi □, *China* 33 D6 27 30N 116 0 E
Jiao Xian = Jiaozhou, *China* 35 F11 36 18N 120 1 E
Jiaohe, *Hebei, China* 34 E9 38 2N 116 20 E
Jiaohe, *Jilin, China* 35 C14 43 40N 127 22 E
Jiaozhou, *China* 35 F11 36 18N 120 1 E
Jiaozhou Wan, *China* 35 F11 36 5N 120 10 E
Jiaozuo, *China* 34 G7 35 16N 113 12 E
Jiawang, *China* 35 G9 34 28N 117 26 E
Jiaxiang, *China* 34 G9 35 25N 116 20 E
Jiaxing, *China* 33 C7 30 49N 120 45 E
Jiayi = Chiai, *Taiwan* 33 D7 23 29N 120 25 E
Jibuti = Djibouti ■, *Africa* 46 E3 12 0N 43 0 E
Jicarón, I., *Panama* 88 E3 7 10N 81 50W
Jiddah, *Si. Arabia* 46 C2 21 29N 39 10 E
Jido, *India* 41 E19 29 2N 94 58 E
Jieshou, *China* 34 H8 33 18N 115 22 E
Jiexiu, *China* 34 F6 37 2N 111 55 E
Jiggalong, *Australia* 60 D3 23 21S 120 47 E
Jigni, *India* 43 G8 25 45N 79 25 E
Jihlava, *Czech Rep.* 16 D8 49 28N 15 35 E
Jihlava →, *Czech Rep.* 17 D9 48 55N 16 36 E
Jijiga, *Ethiopia* 46 F3 9 20N 42 50 E
Jilin, *China* 35 C14 43 44N 126 30 E
Jilin □, *China* 35 C14 44 0N 127 0 E
Jilong = Chilung, *Taiwan* 33 D7 25 3N 121 45 E
Jim Thorpe, *U.S.A.* 79 F9 40 52N 75 44W
Jima, *Ethiopia* 46 F2 7 40N 36 47 E
Jiménez, *Mexico* 86 B4 27 10N 104 54W
Jimo, *China* 35 F11 36 23N 120 30 E
Jin Xian = Jinzhou, *China* 34 E8 38 2N 115 2 E
Jin Xian, *China* 35 E11 38 55N 121 42 E
Jinan, *China* 34 F9 36 38N 117 1 E
Jinchang, *China* 32 C5 38 30N 102 10 E
Jincheng, *China* 34 G7 35 29N 112 50 E
Jind, *India* 42 E7 29 19N 76 22 E
Jindabyne, *Australia* 63 F4 36 25S 148 35 E
Jindřichův Hradec, *Czech Rep.* 16 D8 49 10N 15 2 E
Jing He →, *China* 34 G5 34 27N 109 4 E
Jingbian, *China* 34 F5 37 20N 108 30 E
Jingchuan, *China* 34 G4 35 20N 107 20 E
Jingdezhen, *China* 33 D6 29 20N 117 11 E
Jinggu, *China* 32 D5 23 35N 100 41 E
Jinghai, *China* 34 E9 38 55N 116 55 E
Jingle, *China* 34 E6 38 20N 111 55 E
Jingning, *China* 34 G3 35 30N 105 43 E
Jingpo Hu, *China* 35 C15 43 55N 128 55 E
Jingtai, *China* 34 F3 37 10N 104 6 E
Jingxing, *China* 34 E8 38 2N 114 8 E
Jingyang, *China* 34 G5 34 30N 108 50 E
Jingyu, *China* 35 C14 42 25N 126 45 E
Jingyuan, *China* 34 F3 36 30N 104 40 E
Jingziguan, *China* 34 H6 33 15N 111 0 E
Jinhua, *China* 33 D6 29 8N 119 38 E
Jining, *Nei Monggol Zizhiqu, China* 34 D7 41 5N 113 0 E
Jining, *Shandong, China* 34 G9 35 22N 116 34 E
Jinja, *Uganda* 54 B3 0 25N 33 12 E
Jinjang, *Malaysia* 39 L3 3 13N 101 39 E
Jinji, *China* 34 F4 37 58N 106 8 E
Jinnah Barrage, *Pakistan* 40 C7 32 58N 71 33 E
Jinotega, *Nic.* 88 D2 13 6N 85 59W
Jinotepe, *Nic.* 88 D2 11 50N 86 10W
Jinsha Jiang →, *China* 32 D5 28 50N 104 36 E
Jinxi, *China* 35 D11 40 52N 120 50 E
Jinxiang, *China* 34 G9 35 5N 116 22 E
Jinzhou, *Hebei, China* 34 E8 38 2N 115 2 E
Jinzhou, *Liaoning, China* 35 D11 41 5N 121 3 E
Jiparaná →, *Brazil* 92 E6 8 3S 62 52W
Jipijapa, *Ecuador* 92 D2 1 0S 80 40W
Jiquilpan, *Mexico* 86 D4 19 57N 102 42W
Jishan, *China* 34 G6 35 34N 110 58 E
Jisr ash Shughūr, *Syria* 44 C3 35 49N 36 18 E
Jitarning, *Australia* 61 F2 32 48S 117 57 E
Jitra, *Malaysia* 39 J3 6 16N 100 25 E
Jiu →, *Romania* 17 F12 43 47N 23 48 E
Jiudengkou, *China* 34 E4 39 56N 106 40 E
Jiujiang, *China* 33 D6 29 42N 115 58 E
Jiutai, *China* 35 B13 44 10N 125 50 E
Jiuxincheng, *China* 34 E8 39 17N 115 59 E
Jixi, *China* 35 B16 45 20N 130 50 E
Jiyang, *China* 35 F9 37 0N 117 12 E
Jiyuan, *China* 34 G7 35 7N 112 57 E
Jīzān, *Si. Arabia* 46 D3 17 0N 42 20 E
Jize, *China* 34 F8 36 54N 114 56 E
Jizl, Wādī al, *Si. Arabia* 44 E3 25 39N 38 25 E
Jizō-Zaki, *Japan* 31 G6 35 34N 133 20 E
Jizzakh, *Uzbekistan* 26 E7 40 6N 67 50 E
Joaçaba, *Brazil* 95 B5 27 5S 51 31W
João Pessoa, *Brazil* 93 E12 7 10S 34 52W
Joaquín V. González, *Argentina* 94 B3 25 10S 64 0W
Jobat, *India* 42 H6 22 25N 74 34 E
Jodhpur, *India* 42 F5 26 23N 73 8 E
Jodiya, *India* 42 H4 22 42N 70 18 E
Joensuu, *Finland* 24 B4 62 37N 29 49 E
Jōetsu, *Japan* 31 F9 37 12N 138 10 E
Jofane, *Mozam.* 57 C5 21 15S 34 18 E
Jogbani, *India* 43 F12 26 25N 87 15 E
Jõgeva, *Estonia* 9 G22 58 45N 26 24 E
Jogjakarta = Yogyakarta, *Indonesia* 36 F4 7 49S 110 22 E
Johannesburg, *S. Africa* 57 D4 26 10S 28 2 E
Johannesburg, *U.S.A.* 85 K9 35 22N 117 38W
Johilla →, *India* 43 H9 23 37N 81 14 E
John Day, *U.S.A.* 82 D4 44 25N 118 57W
John Day →, *U.S.A.* 82 D3 45 44N 120 39W
John D'Or Prairie, *Canada* 72 B5 58 30N 115 8W
John H. Kerr Reservoir, *U.S.A.* 77 G6 36 36N 78 18W
John o' Groats, *U.K.* 12 C5 58 38N 3 4W
Johnnie, *U.S.A.* 85 J10 36 25N 116 5W
John's Ra., *Australia* 62 C1 21 55S 133 23 E
Johnson, *Kans., U.S.A.* 81 G4 37 34N 101 45W
Johnson, *Vt., U.S.A.* 79 B12 44 38N 72 41W
Johnson City, *N.Y., U.S.A.* 79 D9 42 7N 75 58W
Johnson City, *Tenn., U.S.A.* 77 G4 36 19N 82 21W
Johnson City, *Tex., U.S.A.* 81 K5 30 17N 98 25W
Johnsonburg, *U.S.A.* 78 E6 41 29N 78 41W
Johnsondale, *U.S.A.* 85 K8 35 58N 118 32W
Johnson's Crossing, *Canada* 72 A2 60 29N 133 18W
Johnston, L., *Australia* 61 F3 32 25S 120 30 E
Johnston Falls = Mambilima Falls, *Zambia* 55 E2 10 31S 28 45 E
Johnston I., *Pac. Oc.* 65 F11 17 10N 169 8W
Johnstone Str., *Canada* 72 C3 50 28N 126 0W
Johnstown, *N.Y., U.S.A.* 79 C10 43 0N 74 22W
Johnstown, *Ohio, U.S.A.* 78 F2 40 9N 82 41W
Johnstown, *Pa., U.S.A.* 78 F6 40 20N 78 55W
Johor Baharu, *Malaysia* 39 M4 1 28N 103 46 E
Jõhvi, *Estonia* 9 G22 59 22N 27 27 E
Joinville, *Brazil* 95 B6 26 15S 48 55W
Joinville I., *Antarctica* 5 C18 65 0S 55 30W
Jojutla, *Mexico* 87 D5 18 37N 99 11W
Jokkmokk, *Sweden* 8 C18 66 35N 19 50 E
Jökulsá á Bru →, *Iceland* 8 D6 65 40N 14 16W
Jökulsá á Fjöllum →, *Iceland* 8 C5 66 10N 16 30W
Jolfā, *Āzarbājān-e Sharqī, Iran* 44 B5 38 57N 45 38 E
Jolfā, *Eşfahan, Iran* 45 C6 32 58N 51 37 E
Joliet, *U.S.A.* 76 E1 41 32N 88 5W
Joliette, *Canada* 70 C5 46 3N 73 24W
Jolo, *Phil.* 37 C6 6 0N 121 0 E
Jolon, *U.S.A.* 84 K5 35 58N 121 9W
Jombang, *Indonesia* 37 G15 7 33S 112 14 E
Jonava, *Lithuania* 9 J21 55 8N 24 12 E
Jones Sound, *Canada* 4 B3 76 0N 85 0W
Jonesboro, *Ark., U.S.A.* 81 H9 35 50N 90 42W
Jonesboro, *La., U.S.A.* 81 J8 32 15N 92 43W
Joniškis, *Lithuania* 9 H20 56 13N 23 35 E
Jönköping, *Sweden* 9 H16 57 45N 14 8 E
Jonquière, *Canada* 71 C5 48 27N 71 14W
Joplin, *U.S.A.* 81 G7 37 6N 94 31W

Jora, India 42 F6 26 20N 77 49 E
Jordan, Mont., U.S.A. 82 C10 47 19N 106 55W
Jordan, N.Y., U.S.A. 79 C8 43 4N 76 29W
Jordan ■, Asia 47 E5 31 0N 36 0 E
Jordan →, Asia 47 D4 31 48N 35 32 E
Jordan Valley, U.S.A. 82 E5 42 59N 117 3W
Jorhat, India 41 F19 26 45N 94 12 E
Jörn, Sweden 8 D19 65 4N 20 1 E
Jorong, Indonesia 36 E4 3 58S 114 56 E
Jørpeland, Norway 9 G11 59 3N 6 1 E
Jorquera →, Chile 94 B2 28 3S 69 58W
Jos, Nigeria 50 G7 9 53N 8 51 E
José Batlle y Ordóñez, Uruguay 95 C4 33 20S 55 10W
Joseph, L., Nfld., Canada 71 B6 52 45N 65 18W
Joseph, L., Ont., Canada 78 A5 45 10N 79 44W
Joseph Bonaparte G., Australia 60 B4 14 35S 128 50 E
Joshinath, India 43 D8 30 34N 79 34 E
Joshua Tree, U.S.A. 85 L10 34 8N 116 19W
Joshua Tree Nat. Park, U.S.A. 85 M10 33 55N 116 0W
Jostedalsbreen, Norway 9 F12 61 40N 6 59 E
Jotunheimen, Norway 9 F13 61 35N 8 25 E
Joubertberge, Namibia 56 B1 18 30S 14 0 E
Jourdanton, U.S.A. 81 L5 28 55N 98 33W
Jovellanos, Cuba 88 B3 22 40N 81 10W
Ju Xian, China 35 F10 36 35N 118 20 E
Juan Aldama, Mexico 86 C4 24 20N 103 23W
Juan Bautista Alberdi, Argentina 94 C3 34 26S 61 48W
Juan de Fuca Str., Canada 84 B3 48 15N 124 0W
Juan de Nova, Ind. Oc. 57 B7 17 3S 43 45 E
Juan Fernández, Arch. de, Pac. Oc. 90 G2 33 50S 80 0W
Juan José Castelli, Argentina 94 B3 25 27S 60 57W
Juan L. Lacaze, Uruguay 94 C4 34 26S 57 25W
Juankoski, Finland 8 E23 63 3N 28 19 E
Juárez, Argentina 94 D4 37 40S 59 43W
Juárez, Mexico 85 N11 32 20N 115 57W
Juárez, Sierra de, Mexico 86 A1 32 0N 116 0W
Juàzeiro, Brazil 93 E10 9 30S 40 30W
Juàzeiro do Norte, Brazil 93 E11 7 10S 39 18W
Juba = Giuba →, Somali Rep. 46 G3 1 30N 42 35 E
Juba, Sudan 51 H12 4 50N 31 35 E
Jubayl, Lebanon 47 A4 34 5N 35 39 E
Jubbah, Si. Arabia 44 D4 28 2N 40 56 E
Jubbal, India 42 D7 31 5N 77 40 E
Jubbulpore = Jabalpur, India 43 H8 23 9N 79 58 E
Jubilee L., Australia 61 E4 29 0S 126 50 E
Juby, C., Morocco 50 C3 28 0N 12 59W
Júcar = Xúquer →, Spain 19 C5 39 5N 0 10W
Júcaro, Cuba 88 B4 21 37N 78 51W
Juchitán, Mexico 87 D5 16 27N 95 5W
Judaea = Har Yehuda, Israel 47 D3 31 35N 34 57 E
Judith →, U.S.A. 82 C9 47 44N 109 39W
Judith, Pt., U.S.A. 79 E13 41 22N 71 29W
Judith Gap, U.S.A. 82 C9 46 41N 109 45W
Jugoslavia = Yugoslavia ■, Europe 21 B9 43 20N 20 0 E
Juigalpa, Nic. 88 D2 12 6N 85 26W
Juiz de Fora, Brazil 95 A7 21 43S 43 19W
Jujuy □, Argentina 94 A2 23 20S 65 40W
Julesburg, U.S.A. 80 E3 40 59N 102 16W
Juli, Peru 92 G5 16 10S 69 25W
Julia Cr. →, Australia 62 C3 20 0S 141 11 E
Julia Creek, Australia 62 C3 20 39S 141 44 E
Juliaca, Peru 92 G4 15 25S 70 10W
Julian, U.S.A. 85 M10 33 4N 116 38W
Julian L., Canada 70 B4 54 25N 77 57W
Julianatop, Surinam 93 C7 3 40N 56 30W
Julianehåb = Qaqortoq, Greenland 69 B6 60 43N 46 0W
Julimes, Mexico 86 B3 28 25N 105 27W
Jullundur, India 42 D6 31 20N 75 40 E
Julu, China 34 F8 37 15N 115 2 E
Jumbo, Zimbabwe 55 F3 17 30S 30 58 E
Jumbo Pk., U.S.A. 85 J12 36 12N 114 11W
Jumentos Cays, Bahamas 88 B4 23 0N 75 40W
Jumilla, Spain 19 C5 38 28N 1 19W
Jumla, Nepal 43 E10 29 15N 82 13 E
Jumna = Yamuna →, India 43 G9 25 30N 81 53 E
Junagadh, India 42 J4 21 30N 70 30 E
Junction, Tex., U.S.A. 81 K5 30 29N 99 46W
Junction, Utah, U.S.A. 83 G7 38 14N 112 13W
Junction B., Australia 62 A1 11 52S 133 55 E
Junction City, Kans., U.S.A. 80 F6 39 2N 96 50W
Junction City, Oreg., U.S.A. 82 D2 44 13N 123 12W
Junction Pt., Australia 62 A1 11 45S 133 50 E
Jundah, Australia 62 C3 24 46S 143 2 E
Jundiaí, Brazil 95 A6 24 30S 47 0W
Juneau, U.S.A. 72 B2 58 18N 134 25W
Junee, Australia 63 E4 34 53S 147 35 E
Jungfrau, Switz. 18 C7 46 32N 7 58 E
Junggar Pendi, China 32 B3 44 30N 86 0 E
Jungshahi, Pakistan 42 G2 24 52N 67 44 E
Juniata →, U.S.A. 78 F7 40 30N 77 40W
Junín, Argentina 94 C3 34 33S 60 57W
Junín de los Andes, Argentina 96 D2 39 45S 71 0W
Jūniyah, Lebanon 47 B4 33 59N 35 38 E
Juntas, Chile 94 B2 28 24S 69 58W
Juntura, U.S.A. 82 E4 43 45N 118 5W
Jur, Nahr el →, Sudan 51 G11 8 45N 29 15 E
Jura = Jura, Mts. du, Europe 18 C7 46 40N 6 5 E
Jura = Schwäbische Alb, Germany 16 D5 48 20N 9 30 E
Jura, U.K. 12 F3 56 0N 5 50W
Jura, Mts. du, Europe 18 C7 46 40N 6 5 E
Jura, Sd. of, U.K. 12 F3 55 57N 5 45W
Jurbarkas, Lithuania 9 J20 55 4N 22 46 E
Jurien, Australia 61 F2 30 18S 115 2 E
Jūrmala, Latvia 9 H20 56 58N 23 34 E
Juruá →, Brazil 92 D5 2 37S 65 44W
Juruena, Brazil 92 F7 13 0S 58 10W
Juruena →, Brazil 92 E7 7 20S 58 3W
Juruti, Brazil 93 D7 2 9S 56 4W
Justo Daract, Argentina 94 C2 33 52S 65 12W
Jutaí →, Brazil 92 D5 2 43S 66 57W
Juticalpa, Honduras 88 D2 14 40N 86 12W
Jutland = Jylland, Denmark 9 H13 56 25N 9 30 E
Juventud, I. de la, Cuba 88 B3 21 40N 82 40W
Jūy Zar, Iran 44 C5 33 50N 46 18 E
Juye, China 34 G9 35 22N 116 5 E
Jwaneng, Botswana 53 J4 24 45S 24 50 E
Jylland, Denmark 9 H13 56 25N 9 30 E
Jyväskylä, Finland 9 E21 62 14N 25 50 E

K

K2, Pakistan 43 B7 35 58N 76 32 E
Kaap Plateau, S. Africa 56 D3 28 30S 24 0 E
Kaapkruis, Namibia 56 C1 21 55S 13 57 E
Kaapstad = Cape Town, S. Africa 56 E2 33 55S 18 22 E
Kabaena, Indonesia 37 F6 5 15S 122 0 E
Kabala, S. Leone 50 G3 9 38N 11 37W
Kabale, Uganda 54 C3 1 15S 30 0 E
Kabalo, Dem. Rep. of the Congo 54 D2 6 0S 27 0 E
Kabambare, Dem. Rep. of the Congo 54 C2 4 41S 27 39 E
Kabango, Dem. Rep. of the Congo 55 D2 8 35S 28 30 E
Kabanjahe, Indonesia 36 D1 3 6N 98 30 E
Kabardino-Balkar Republic = Kabardino-Balkaria □, Russia 25 F7 43 30N 43 30 E
Kabardino-Balkaria □, Russia 25 F7 43 30N 43 30 E
Kabarega Falls = Murchison Falls, Uganda 54 B3 2 15N 31 30 E
Kabasalan, Phil. 37 C6 7 47N 122 44 E
Kabetogama, U.S.A. 80 A8 48 28N 92 59W
Kabin Buri, Thailand 38 F3 13 57N 101 43 E
Kabinakagami L., Canada 70 C3 48 54N 84 25W
Kabinda, Dem. Rep. of the Congo 52 F4 6 19S 24 20 E
Kabompo, Zambia 55 E1 13 36S 24 14 E
Kabompo →, Zambia 53 G4 14 10S 23 11 E
Kabondo, Dem. Rep. of the Congo 55 D2 8 58S 25 40 E
Kabongo, Dem. Rep. of the Congo 54 D2 7 22S 25 33 E
Kabūd Gonbad, Iran 45 B8 37 5N 59 45 E
Kābul, Afghan. 42 B3 34 28N 69 11 E
Kābul □, Afghan. 40 B6 34 30N 69 0 E
Kābul →, Pakistan 42 C5 33 55N 72 14 E
Kabunga, Dem. Rep. of the Congo 54 C2 1 38S 28 3 E
Kaburuang, Indonesia 37 D7 3 50N 126 30 E
Kabwe, Zambia 55 E2 14 30S 28 29 E
Kachchh, Gulf of, India 42 H3 22 50N 69 15 E
Kachchh, Rann of, India 42 H4 24 0N 70 0 E
Kachchhidhana, India 43 J8 21 44N 78 46 E
Kachebera, Zambia 55 E3 13 50S 32 50 E
Kachikau, Botswana 56 B3 18 8S 24 26 E
Kachin □, Burma 41 G20 26 0N 97 30 E
Kachira, L., Uganda 54 C3 0 40S 31 7 E
Kachiry, Kazakstan 26 D8 53 10N 75 50 E
Kachnara, India 42 H6 23 50N 75 6 E
Kachot, Cambodia 39 G4 11 30N 103 3 E
Kaçkar, Turkey 25 F7 40 45N 41 10 E
Kadan Kyun, Burma 38 F2 12 30N 98 20 E
Kadanai →, Afghan. 42 D1 31 22N 65 45 E
Kadavu, Fiji 59 D8 19 0S 178 15 E
Kadi, India 42 H5 23 18N 72 23 E
Kadina, Australia 63 E2 33 55S 137 43 E
Kadipur, India 43 F10 26 10N 82 23 E
Kadirli, Turkey 44 B3 37 23N 36 5 E
Kadiyevka = Stakhanov, Ukraine 25 E6 48 35N 38 40 E
Kadoka, U.S.A. 80 D4 43 50N 101 31W
Kadoma, Zimbabwe 55 F2 18 20S 29 52 E
Kâdugli, Sudan 51 F11 11 0N 29 45 E
Kaduna, Nigeria 50 F7 10 30N 7 21 E
Kaédi, Mauritania 50 E3 16 9N 13 28W
Kaeng Khoï, Thailand 38 E3 14 35N 101 0 E
Kaesŏng, N. Korea 35 F14 37 58N 126 35 E
Kāf, Si. Arabia 44 D3 31 25N 37 29 E
Kafan = Kapan, Armenia 25 G8 39 18N 46 27 E
Kafanchan, Nigeria 50 G7 9 40N 8 20 E
Kafinda, Zambia 55 E3 12 32S 30 20 E
Kafirévs, Ákra, Greece 21 E11 38 9N 24 38 E
Kafue, Zambia 55 F2 15 46S 28 9 E
Kafue →, Zambia 53 H5 15 30S 29 0 E
Kafue Flats, Zambia 55 F2 15 40S 27 25 E
Kafulwe, Zambia 55 D2 9 0S 29 1 E
Kaga, Afghan. 42 B4 34 14N 70 10 E
Kaga Bandoro, C.A.R. 52 C3 7 0N 19 10 E
Kagan, Uzbekistan 26 F7 39 43N 64 33 E
Kagawa □, Japan 31 G7 34 15N 134 0 E
Kagera = Ziwa Maghariba □, Tanzania 54 C3 2 0S 31 30 E
Kagera →, Uganda 54 C3 0 57S 31 47 E
Kağizman, Turkey 44 B4 40 5N 43 10 E
Kagoshima, Japan 31 J5 31 35N 130 33 E
Kagoshima □, Japan 31 J5 31 30N 130 30 E
Kagul = Cahul, Moldova 17 F15 45 50N 28 15 E
Kahak, Iran 45 B6 36 6N 49 46 E
Kahama, Tanzania 54 C3 4 8S 32 30 E
Kahan, Pakistan 42 E3 29 18N 68 54 E
Kahang, Malaysia 39 L4 2 12N 103 32 E
Kahayan →, Indonesia 36 E4 3 40S 114 0 E
Kahe, Tanzania 54 C4 3 30S 37 25 E
Kahnūj, Iran 45 E8 27 55N 57 40 E
Kahoka, U.S.A. 80 E9 40 25N 91 44W
Kahoolawe, U.S.A. 74 H16 20 33N 156 37W
Kahramanmaraş, Turkey 25 G6 37 37N 36 53 E
Kahuta, Pakistan 42 C5 33 35N 73 24 E
Kai, Kepulauan, Indonesia 37 F8 5 55S 132 45 E
Kai Besar, Indonesia 37 F8 5 35S 133 0 E
Kai Is. = Kai, Kepulauan, Indonesia 37 F8 5 55S 132 45 E
Kai Kecil, Indonesia 37 F8 5 45S 132 40 E
Kaiapoi, N.Z. 59 K4 43 24S 172 40 E
Kaieteur Falls, Guyana 92 B7 5 1N 59 10W
Kaifeng, China 34 G8 34 48N 114 21 E
Kaikohe, N.Z. 59 F4 35 25S 173 49 E
Kaikoura, N.Z. 59 K4 42 25S 173 43 E
Kaikoura Ra., N.Z. 59 J4 41 59S 173 41 E
Kailu, China 35 C11 43 38N 121 18 E
Kailua Kona, U.S.A. 74 J17 19 39N 155 59W
Kaimana, Indonesia 37 E8 3 39S 133 45 E
Kaimanawa Mts., N.Z. 59 H5 39 15S 175 56 E
Kaimganj, India 43 F8 27 33N 79 24 E
Kaimur Hills, India 43 G10 24 30N 82 0 E
Kainab →, Namibia 56 D2 28 32S 19 34 E
Kainji Res., Nigeria 50 F6 10 1N 4 40 E
Kainuu, Finland 8 D23 64 30N 29 7 E
Kaipara Harbour, N.Z. 59 G5 36 25S 174 14 E
Kaipokok B., Canada 71 B8 54 54N 59 47W
Kaira, India 42 H5 22 45N 72 50 E
Kairana, India 42 E7 29 24N 77 15 E
Kaironi, Indonesia 37 E8 0 47S 133 40 E
Kairouan, Tunisia 51 A8 35 45N 10 5 E
Kaiserslautern, Germany 16 D4 49 26N 7 45 E
Kaitaia, N.Z. 59 F4 35 8S 173 17 E
Kaitangata, N.Z. 59 M2 46 17S 169 51 E
Kaithal, India 42 E7 29 48N 76 26 E
Kaitu →, Pakistan 42 C4 33 10N 70 30 E
Kaiyuan, China 35 C13 42 28N 124 1 E
Kajaani, Finland 8 D22 64 17N 27 46 E
Kajabbi, Australia 62 C3 20 0S 140 1 E
Kajana = Kajaani, Finland 8 D22 64 17N 27 46 E
Kajang, Malaysia 39 L3 2 59N 101 48 E
Kajiado, Kenya 54 C4 1 53S 36 48 E
Kajo Kaji, Sudan 51 H12 3 58N 31 40 E
Kakabeka Falls, Canada 70 C2 48 24N 89 37W
Kakamas, S. Africa 56 D3 28 45S 20 33 E
Kakamega, Kenya 54 B3 0 20N 34 46 E
Kakanui Mts., N.Z. 59 L3 45 10S 170 30 E
Kakdwip, India 43 J13 21 53N 88 11 E
Kake, Japan 31 G6 34 36N 132 19 E
Kake, U.S.A. 72 B2 56 59N 133 57W
Kakegawa, Japan 31 G9 34 45N 138 1 E
Kakeroma-Jima, Japan 31 K4 28 8N 129 14 E
Kakhovka, Ukraine 25 E5 46 45N 33 30 E
Kakhovske Vdskh., Ukraine 25 E5 47 5N 34 0 E
Kakinada, India 41 L13 16 57N 82 11 E
Kakisa →, Canada 72 A5 61 3N 118 10W
Kakisa L., Canada 72 A5 60 56N 117 43W
Kakogawa, Japan 31 G7 34 46N 134 51 E
Kakwa →, Canada 72 C5 54 37N 118 28W
Kāl Gūsheh, Iran 45 D8 30 59N 58 12 E
Kal Safīd, Iran 44 C5 34 52N 47 23 E
Kalaallit Nunaat = Greenland ■, N. Amer. 4 C5 66 0N 45 0W
Kalabagh, Pakistan 42 C4 33 0N 71 28 E
Kalabahi, Indonesia 37 F6 8 13S 124 31 E
Kalach, Russia 25 D7 50 22N 41 0 E
Kaladan →, Burma 41 J18 20 20N 93 5 E
Kaladar, Canada 78 B7 44 37N 77 5W
Kalahari, Africa 56 C3 24 0S 21 30 E
Kalajoki, Finland 8 D20 64 12N 24 10 E
Kālak, Iran 45 E8 25 29N 59 22 E
Kalakamati, Botswana 57 C4 20 40S 27 25 E
Kalakan, Russia 27 D12 55 15N 116 45 E
K'alak'unlun Shank'ou = Karakoram Pass, Asia 43 B7 35 33N 77 50 E
Kalam, Pakistan 43 B5 35 34N 72 30 E
Kalama, Dem. Rep. of the Congo 54 C2 2 52S 28 35 E
Kalama, U.S.A. 84 E4 46 1N 122 51W
Kalámai, Greece 21 F10 37 3N 22 10 E
Kalamata = Kalámai, Greece 21 F10 37 3N 22 10 E
Kalamazoo, U.S.A. 76 D3 42 17N 85 35W
Kalamazoo →, U.S.A. 76 D2 42 40N 86 10W
Kalambo Falls, Tanzania 55 D3 8 37S 31 35 E
Kalan, Turkey 44 B3 39 7N 39 32 E
Kalannie, Australia 61 F2 30 22S 117 5 E
Kalāntarī, Iran 45 C7 32 10N 54 8 E
Kalao, Indonesia 37 F6 7 21S 121 0 E
Kalaotoa, Indonesia 37 F6 7 20S 121 50 E
Kalasin, Thailand 38 D4 16 26N 103 30 E
Kalat, Pakistan 40 E5 29 8N 66 31 E
Kalāteh, Iran 45 B7 36 33N 55 41 E
Kalāteh-ye Ganj, Iran 45 E8 27 31N 57 55 E
Kalbarri, Australia 61 E1 27 40S 114 10 E
Kalce, Slovenia 16 F8 45 54N 14 13 E
Kale, Turkey 21 F13 37 27N 28 49 E
Kalegauk Kyun, Burma 41 M20 15 33N 97 35 E
Kalehe, Dem. Rep. of the Congo 54 C2 2 6S 28 50 E
Kalema, Tanzania 54 C3 1 12S 31 55 E
Kalemie, Dem. Rep. of the Congo 54 D2 5 55S 29 9 E
Kalewa, Burma 41 H19 23 10N 94 15 E
Kaleybar, Iran 44 B5 38 47N 47 2 E
Kalgan = Zhangjiakou, China 34 D8 40 48N 114 55 E
Kalgoorlie-Boulder, Australia 61 F3 30 40S 121 22 E
Kali →, India 43 F8 27 6N 79 55 E
Kali Sindh →, India 42 G6 25 32N 76 17 E
Kaliakra, Nos, Bulgaria 21 C13 43 21N 28 30 E
Kalianda, Indonesia 36 F3 5 50S 105 45 E
Kalibo, Phil. 37 B6 11 43N 122 22 E
Kalima, Dem. Rep. of the Congo 54 C2 2 33S 26 32 E
Kalimantan □, Indonesia 36 E4 0 0 114 0 E
Kalimantan Barat □, Indonesia 36 E4 0 0 110 30 E
Kalimantan Selatan □, Indonesia 36 E5 2 30S 115 30 E
Kalimantan Tengah □, Indonesia 36 E4 2 0S 113 30 E
Kalimantan Timur □, Indonesia 36 D5 1 30N 116 30 E
Kálimnos, Greece 21 F12 37 0N 27 0 E
Kalimpong, India 43 F13 27 4N 88 35 E
Kalinin = Tver, Russia 24 C6 56 55N 35 55 E
Kaliningrad, Russia 9 J19 54 42N 20 32 E
Kalinkavichy, Belarus 17 B15 52 12N 29 20 E
Kalinkovichi = Kalinkavichy, Belarus 17 B15 52 12N 29 20 E
Kaliro, Uganda 54 B3 0 56N 33 30 E
Kalispell, U.S.A. 82 B6 48 12N 114 19W
Kalisz, Poland 17 C10 51 45N 18 8 E
Kaliua, Tanzania 54 D3 5 5S 31 48 E
Kalix, Sweden 8 D20 65 53N 23 12 E
Kalix →, Sweden 8 D20 65 50N 23 11 E
Kalka, India 42 D7 30 46N 76 57 E
Kalkarindji, Australia 60 C5 17 30S 130 47 E
Kalkaska, U.S.A. 76 C3 44 44N 85 11W
Kalkfeld, Namibia 56 C2 20 57S 16 14 E
Kalkfontein, Botswana 56 C3 22 4S 20 57 E
Kalkrand, Namibia 56 C2 24 1S 17 35 E
Kallavesi, Finland 8 E22 62 58N 27 30 E
Kallsjön, Sweden 8 E15 63 38N 13 0 E
Kalmar, Sweden 9 H17 56 40N 16 20 E
Kalmyk Republic = Kalmykia □, Russia 25 E8 46 5N 46 1 E
Kalmykia □, Russia 25 E8 46 5N 46 1 E
Kalmykovo, Kazakstan 25 E9 49 0N 51 47 E
Kalna, India 43 H13 23 13N 88 25 E
Kalnai, India 43 H10 22 46N 83 30 E
Kalocsa, Hungary 17 E10 46 32N 19 0 E
Kalokhorio, Cyprus 23 E12 34 51N 33 2 E
Kaloko, Dem. Rep. of the Congo 54 D2 6 47S 25 48 E
Kalol, Gujarat, India 42 H5 22 37N 73 31 E
Kalol, Gujarat, India 42 H5 23 15N 72 33 E
Kalomo, Zambia 55 F2 17 0S 26 30 E
Kalpi, India 43 F8 26 8N 79 47 E
Kalu, Pakistan 42 G2 25 5N 67 39 E
Kaluga, Russia 24 D6 54 35N 36 10 E
Kalulushi, Zambia 55 E2 12 50S 28 3 E
Kalundborg, Denmark 9 J14 55 41N 11 5 E
Kalush, Ukraine 17 D13 49 3N 24 23 E
Kalutara, Sri Lanka 40 R12 6 35N 80 0 E
Kalya, Russia 24 B10 60 15N 59 59 E
Kama, Dem. Rep. of the Congo 54 C2 3 30S 27 5 E
Kama →, Russia 24 C9 55 45N 52 0 E
Kamachumu, Tanzania 54 C3 1 37S 31 37 E
Kamaishi, Japan 30 E10 39 16N 141 53 E
Kamalia, Pakistan 42 D5 30 44N 72 42 E
Kaman, India 42 F6 27 39N 77 16 E
Kamanjab, Namibia 56 B2 19 35S 14 51 E
Kamapanda, Zambia 55 E1 12 5S 24 0 E
Kamarān, Yemen 46 D3 15 21N 42 35 E
Kamativi, Zimbabwe 56 B4 18 20S 27 6 E
Kambalda, Australia 61 F3 31 10S 121 37 E
Kambar, Pakistan 42 F3 27 37N 68 1 E
Kambarka, Russia 24 C9 56 15N 54 11 E
Kambolé, Zambia 55 D3 8 47S 30 48 E
Kambos, Cyprus 23 D11 35 2N 32 44 E
Kambove, Dem. Rep. of the Congo 55 E2 10 51S 26 33 E
Kamchatka, Poluostrov, Russia 27 D16 57 0N 160 0 E
Kamchatka Pen. = Kamchatka, Poluostrov, Russia 27 D16 57 0N 160 0 E
Kamchiya →, Bulgaria 21 C12 43 4N 27 44 E
Kamen, Russia 26 D9 53 50N 81 30 E
Kamen-Rybolov, Russia 30 B6 44 46N 132 2 E
Kamenjak, Rt, Croatia 16 F7 44 47N 13 55 E
Kamenka, Russia 24 A7 65 58N 44 0 E
Kamenka Bugskaya = Kamyanka-Buzka, Ukraine 17 C13 50 8N 24 16 E
Kamensk Uralskiy, Russia 26 D7 56 25N 62 2 E
Kamenskoye, Russia 27 C17 62 45N 165 30 E
Kameoka, Japan 31 G7 35 0N 135 35 E
Kamiah, U.S.A. 82 C5 46 14N 116 2W
Kamieskroon, S. Africa 56 E2 30 9S 17 56 E
Kamilukuak, L., Canada 73 A8 62 22N 101 40W
Kamin-Kashyrskyy, Ukraine 17 C13 51 39N 24 56 E
Kamina, Dem. Rep. of the Congo 55 D2 8 45S 25 0 E
Kaminak L., Canada 73 A10 62 10N 95 0W
Kaministiquia, Canada 70 C1 48 32N 89 35W
Kaminoyama, Japan 30 E10 38 9N 140 17 E
Kamiros, Greece 23 C9 36 20N 27 56 E
Kamituga, Dem. Rep. of the Congo 54 C2 3 2S 28 10 E
Kamla →, India 43 G12 25 35N 86 36 E
Kamloops, Canada 72 C4 50 40N 120 20W
Kamo, Japan 30 F9 37 39N 139 3 E
Kamoke, Pakistan 42 C6 32 4N 74 4 E
Kampala, Uganda 54 B3 0 20N 32 30 E
Kampang Chhnang, Cambodia 39 F5 12 20N 104 35 E
Kampar, Malaysia 39 K3 4 18N 101 9 E
Kampar →, Indonesia 36 D2 0 30N 103 8 E
Kampen, Neths. 15 B5 52 33N 5 53 E
Kampene, Dem. Rep. of the Congo 52 E5 3 36S 26 40 E
Kamphaeng Phet, Thailand 38 D2 16 28N 99 30 E
Kampolombo, L., Zambia 55 E2 11 37S 29 42 E
Kampong Saom, Cambodia 39 G4 10 38N 103 30 E
Kampong Saom, Chaak, Cambodia 39 G4 10 50N 103 32 E
Kampong To, Thailand 39 J3 6 3N 101 13 E
Kampot, Cambodia 39 G5 10 36N 104 10 E
Kampuchea = Cambodia ■, Asia 38 F5 12 15N 105 0 E
Kampung Air Putih, Malaysia 39 K4 4 15N 103 10 E
Kampung Jerangau, Malaysia 39 K4 4 50N 103 10 E
Kampung Raja, Malaysia 39 K4 5 45N 102 35 E
Kampungbaru = Tolitoli, Indonesia 37 D6 1 5N 120 50 E
Kamrau, Teluk, Indonesia 37 E8 3 30S 133 36 E
Kamsack, Canada 73 C8 51 34N 101 54W
Kamskoye Vdkhr., Russia 24 C10 58 41N 56 7 E
Kamuchawie L., Canada 73 B8 56 18N 101 59W
Kamui-Misaki, Japan 30 C10 43 20N 140 21 E
Kamyanets-Podilskyy, Ukraine 17 D14 48 45N 26 40 E
Kamyanka-Buzka, Ukraine 17 C13 50 8N 24 16 E
Kāmyārān, Iran 44 C5 34 47N 46 56 E
Kamyshin, Russia 25 D8 50 10N 45 24 E
Kanaaupscow, Canada 70 B4 54 2N 76 30W
Kanaaupscow →, Canada 69 C12 53 39N 77 9W
Kanab, U.S.A. 83 H7 37 3N 112 32W
Kanab →, U.S.A. 83 H7 36 24N 112 38W
Kanagi, Japan 30 D10 40 54N 140 27 E
Kanairiktok →, Canada 71 A7 55 2N 60 18W
Kananga, Dem. Rep. of the Congo 52 F4 5 55S 22 18 E
Kanash, Russia 24 C8 55 30N 47 32 E
Kanaskat, U.S.A. 84 C5 47 19N 121 54W
Kanastraíon, Ákra = Paliouríon, Ákra, Greece 21 E10 39 57N 23 45 E
Kanawha →, U.S.A. 76 F4 38 50N 82 9W
Kanazawa, Japan 31 F8 36 30N 136 38 E
Kanchanaburi, Thailand 38 E2 14 2N 99 31 E
Kanchenjunga, Nepal 43 F13 27 50N 88 10 E
Kanchipuram, India 40 N11 12 52N 79 45 E
Kandaghat, India 42 D7 30 59N 77 7 E
Kandahar = Qandahār, Afghan. 40 D4 31 32N 65 43 E
Kandalaksha, Russia 24 A5 67 9N 32 30 E
Kandalakshskiy Zaliv, Russia 24 A6 66 0N 35 0 E
Kandangan, Indonesia 36 E5 2 50S 115 20 E
Kandanghaur, Indonesia 37 G13 6 21S 108 6 E
Kandanos, Greece 23 D5 35 19N 23 44 E
Kandavu = Kadavu, Fiji 59 D8 19 0S 178 15 E
Kandhkot, Pakistan 42 E3 28 16N 69 8 E
Kandhla, India 42 E7 29 18N 77 19 E
Kandi, Benin 50 F6 11 7N 2 55 E
Kandi, India 43 H13 23 58N 88 5 E
Kandiaro, Pakistan 42 F3 27 4N 68 13 E
Kandla, India 42 H4 23 0N 70 10 E
Kandos, Australia 63 E4 32 45S 149 58 E
Kandreho, Madag. 57 B8 17 29S 46 6 E

Kandy, *Sri Lanka* 40 R12 7 18N 80 43 E
Kane, *U.S.A.* 78 E6 41 40N 78 49W
Kane Basin, *Greenland* 4 B4 79 1N 70 0W
Kaneohe, *U.S.A.* 74 H16 21 25N 157 48W
Kang, *Botswana* 56 C3 23 41S 22 50 E
Kangān, *Fārs, Iran* 45 E7 27 50N 52 3 E
Kangān, *Hormozgān, Iran* 45 E8 25 48N 57 28 E
Kangar, *Malaysia* 39 J3 6 27N 100 12 E
Kangaroo I., *Australia* 63 F2 35 45S 137 0 E
Kangaroo Mts., *Australia* 62 C3 23 29S 141 51 E
Kangasala, *Finland* 9 F21 61 28N 24 4 E
Kangāvar, *Iran* 45 C6 34 40N 48 0 E
Kangdong, *N. Korea* 35 E14 39 9N 126 5 E
Kangean, Kepulauan, *Indonesia* 36 F5 6 55S 115 23 E
Kangean Is. = Kangean, Kepulauan, *Indonesia* 36 F5 6 55S 115 23 E
Kanggye, *N. Korea* 35 D14 41 0N 126 35 E
Kanggyŏng, *S. Korea* 35 F14 36 10N 127 0 E
Kanghwa, *S. Korea* 35 F14 37 45N 126 30 E
Kangikajik, *Greenland* 4 B6 70 7N 22 0W
Kangiqsliniq = Rankin Inlet, *Canada* 68 B10 62 30N 93 0W
Kangiqsualujjuaq, *Canada* 69 C13 58 30N 65 59W
Kangiqsujuaq, *Canada* 69 B12 61 30N 72 0W
Kangiqtugaapik = Clyde River, *Canada* 69 A13 70 30N 68 30W
Kangirsuk, *Canada* 69 B13 60 0N 70 0W
Kangnŭng, *S. Korea* 35 F15 37 45N 128 54 E
Kangping, *China* 35 C12 42 43N 123 18 E
Kangra, *India* 42 C7 32 6N 76 16 E
Kangto, *India* 41 F18 27 50N 92 35 E
Kanhar →, *India* 43 G10 24 28N 83 8 E
Kaniama, *Dem. Rep. of the Congo* 54 D1 7 30S 24 12 E
Kaniapiskau = Caniapiscau →, *Canada* 71 A6 56 40N 69 30W
Kaniapiskau, Res. = Caniapiscau, Rés. de, *Canada* 71 B6 54 10N 69 55W
Kanin, Poluostrov, *Russia* 24 A8 68 0N 45 0 E
Kanin Nos, Mys, *Russia* 24 A7 68 39N 43 32 E
Kanin Pen. = Kanin, Poluostrov, *Russia* 24 A8 68 0N 45 0 E
Kaniva, *Australia* 63 F3 36 22S 141 18 E
Kanjut Sar, *Pakistan* 43 A6 36 7N 75 25 E
Kankaanpää, *Finland* 9 F20 61 44N 22 50 E
Kankakee, *U.S.A.* 76 E2 41 7N 87 52W
Kankakee →, *U.S.A.* 76 E1 41 23N 88 15W
Kankan, *Guinea* 50 F4 10 23N 9 15W
Kankendy = Xankändi, *Azerbaijan* 25 G8 39 52N 46 49 E
Kanker, *India* 41 J12 20 10N 81 40 E
Kankroli, *India* 42 G5 25 4N 73 53 E
Kannapolis, *U.S.A.* 77 H5 35 30N 80 37W
Kannauj, *India* 43 F8 27 3N 79 56 E
Kannod, *India* 40 H10 22 45N 76 40 E
Kano, *Nigeria* 50 F7 12 2N 8 30 E
Kan'onji, *Japan* 31 G6 34 7N 133 39 E
Kanowit, *Malaysia* 36 D4 2 14N 112 20 E
Kanoya, *Japan* 31 J5 31 25N 130 50 E
Kanpetlet, *Burma* 41 J18 21 10N 93 59 E
Kanpur, *India* 43 F9 26 28N 80 20 E
Kansas □, *U.S.A.* 80 F6 38 30N 99 0W
Kansas →, *U.S.A.* 80 F7 39 7N 94 37W
Kansas City, *Kans., U.S.A.* 80 F7 39 7N 94 38W
Kansas City, *Mo., U.S.A.* 80 F7 39 6N 94 35W
Kansenia, *Dem. Rep. of the Congo* 55 E2 10 20S 26 0 E
Kansk, *Russia* 27 D10 56 20N 95 37 E
Kansŏng, *S. Korea* 35 E15 38 24N 128 30 E
Kansu = Gansu □, *China* 34 G3 36 0N 104 0 E
Kantaphor, *India* 42 H7 22 35N 76 34 E
Kantharalak, *Thailand* 38 E5 14 39N 104 39 E
Kantli →, *India* 42 E6 28 20N 75 30 E
Kantō □, *Japan* 31 F9 36 15N 139 30 E
Kantō-Sanchi, *Japan* 31 G9 35 59N 138 50 E
Kanturk, *Ireland* 13 D3 52 11N 8 54W
Kanuma, *Japan* 31 F9 36 34N 139 42 E
Kanus, *Namibia* 56 D2 27 50S 18 39 E
Kanye, *Botswana* 56 C4 24 55S 25 28 E
Kanzenze, *Dem. Rep. of the Congo* 55 E2 10 30S 25 12 E
Kanzi, Ras, *Tanzania* 54 D4 7 1S 39 33 E
Kaohsiung, *Taiwan* 33 D7 22 35N 120 16 E
Kaokoveld, *Namibia* 56 B1 19 15S 14 30 E
Kaolack, *Senegal* 50 F2 14 5N 16 8W
Kaoshan, *China* 35 B13 44 38N 124 50 E
Kapaa, *U.S.A.* 74 G15 22 5N 159 19W
Kapadvanj, *India* 42 H5 23 5N 73 0 E
Kapan, *Armenia* 25 G8 39 18N 46 27 E
Kapanga, *Dem. Rep. of the Congo* 52 F4 8 30S 22 40 E
Kapchagai = Qapshaghay, *Kazakstan* 26 E8 43 51N 77 14 E
Kapela = Velika Kapela, *Croatia* 16 F8 45 10N 15 5 E
Kapema, *Dem. Rep. of the Congo* 55 E2 10 45S 28 22 E
Kapfenberg, *Austria* 16 E8 47 26N 15 18 E
Kapiri Mposhi, *Zambia* 55 E2 13 59S 28 43 E
Kāpīsā □, *Afghan.* 40 B6 35 0N 69 20 E
Kapiskau →, *Canada* 70 B3 52 47N 81 55W
Kapit, *Malaysia* 36 D4 2 0N 112 55 E
Kapiti I., *N.Z.* 59 J5 40 50S 174 56 E
Kaplan, *U.S.A.* 81 K8 30 0N 92 17W
Kapoe, *Thailand* 39 H2 9 34N 98 32 E
Kapoeta, *Sudan* 51 H12 4 50N 33 35 E
Kaposvár, *Hungary* 17 E9 46 25N 17 47 E
Kapowsin, *U.S.A.* 84 D4 46 59N 122 13W
Kapps, *Namibia* 56 C2 22 32S 17 18 E
Kapsan, *N. Korea* 35 D15 41 4N 128 19 E
Kapsukas = Marijampolė, *Lithuania* 9 J20 54 33N 23 19 E
Kapuas →, *Indonesia* 36 E3 0 25S 109 20 E
Kapuas Hulu, Pegunungan, *Malaysia* 36 D4 1 30N 113 30 E
Kapuas Hulu Ra. = Kapuas Hulu, Pegunungan, *Malaysia* 36 D4 1 30N 113 30 E
Kapulo, *Dem. Rep. of the Congo* 55 D2 8 18S 29 15 E
Kapunda, *Australia* 63 E2 34 20S 138 56 E
Kapuni, *N.Z.* 59 H5 39 29S 174 8 E
Kapurthala, *India* 42 D6 31 23N 75 25 E
Kapuskasing, *Canada* 70 C3 49 25N 82 30W
Kapuskasing →, *Canada* 70 C3 49 49N 82 0W
Kaputar, *Australia* 63 E5 30 15S 150 10 E
Kaputir, *Kenya* 54 B4 2 5N 35 28 E
Kara, *Russia* 26 C7 69 10N 65 0 E
Kara Bogaz Gol, Zaliv = Garabogazköl Aylagy, *Turkmenistan* 25 F9 41 0N 53 30 E
Kara Kalpak Republic = Qoraqalpoghistan □, *Uzbekistan* 26 E6 43 0N 58 0 E
Kara Kum, *Turkmenistan* 26 F6 39 30N 60 0 E
Kara Sea, *Russia* 26 B7 75 0N 70 0 E
Karabiğa, *Turkey* 21 D12 40 23N 27 17 E
Karabük, *Turkey* 25 F5 41 12N 32 37 E
Karaburun, *Turkey* 21 E12 38 41N 26 28 E
Karabutak = Qarabutaq, *Kazakstan* 26 E7 49 59N 60 14 E
Karacabey, *Turkey* 21 D13 40 12N 28 21 E
Karacasu, *Turkey* 21 F13 37 43N 28 35 E
Karachey-Cherkessia □, *Russia* 25 F7 43 40N 41 30 E
Karachi, *Pakistan* 42 G2 24 53N 67 0 E
Karad, *India* 40 L9 17 15N 74 10 E
Karaganda = Qaraghandy, *Kazakstan* 26 E8 49 50N 73 10 E
Karagayly, *Kazakstan* 26 E8 49 26N 76 0 E
Karaginskiy, Ostrov, *Russia* 27 D17 58 45N 164 0 E
Karagiye, Vpadina, *Kazakstan* 25 F9 43 27N 51 45 E
Karagiye Depression = Karagiye, Vpadina, *Kazakstan* 25 F9 43 27N 51 45 E
Karagola Road, *India* 43 G12 25 29N 87 23 E
Karaikal, *India* 40 P11 10 59N 79 50 E
Karaikkudi, *India* 40 P11 10 5N 78 45 E
Karaj, *Iran* 45 C6 35 48N 51 0 E
Karak, *Malaysia* 39 L4 3 25N 102 2 E
Karakalpakstan = Qoraqalpoghistan □, *Uzbekistan* 26 E6 43 0N 58 0 E
Karakelong, *Indonesia* 37 D7 4 35N 126 50 E
Karakitang, *Indonesia* 37 D7 3 14N 125 28 E
Karaklis = Vanadzor, *Armenia* 25 F7 40 48N 44 30 E
Karakol, *Kyrgyzstan* 26 E8 42 30N 78 20 E
Karakoram Pass, *Asia* 43 B7 35 33N 77 50 E
Karakoram Ra., *Pakistan* 43 B7 35 30N 77 0 E
Karakuwisa, *Namibia* 56 B2 18 56S 19 40 E
Karalon, *Russia* 27 D12 57 5N 115 50 E
Karama, *Jordan* 47 D4 31 57N 35 35 E
Karaman, *Turkey* 25 G5 37 14N 33 13 E
Karamay, *China* 32 B3 45 30N 84 58 E
Karambu, *Indonesia* 36 E5 3 53S 116 6 E
Karamea Bight, *N.Z.* 59 J3 41 22S 171 40 E
Karamnasa →, *India* 43 G10 25 31N 83 52 E
Karand, *Iran* 44 C5 34 16N 46 15 E
Karanganyar, *Indonesia* 37 G13 7 38S 109 37 E
Karanjia, *India* 43 J11 21 47N 85 58 E
Karasburg, *Namibia* 56 D2 28 0S 18 44 E
Karasino, *Russia* 26 C9 66 50N 86 50 E
Karasjok, *Norway* 8 B21 69 27N 25 30 E
Karasuk, *Russia* 26 D8 53 44N 78 2 E
Karasuyama, *Japan* 31 F10 36 39N 140 9 E
Karatau, Khrebet = Qarataū, *Kazakstan* 26 E7 43 30N 69 30 E
Karatsu, *Japan* 31 H4 33 26N 129 58 E
Karaul, *Russia* 26 B9 70 6N 82 15 E
Karauli, *India* 42 F7 26 30N 77 4 E
Karavostasi, *Cyprus* 23 D11 35 8N 32 50 E
Karawang, *Indonesia* 37 G12 6 30S 107 15 E
Karawanken, *Europe* 16 E8 46 30N 14 40 E
Karayazı, *Turkey* 25 G7 39 41N 42 9 E
Karazhal, *Kazakstan* 26 E8 48 2N 70 49 E
Karbalā', *Iraq* 44 C5 32 36N 44 3 E
Karcag, *Hungary* 17 E11 47 19N 20 57 E
Karcha →, *Pakistan* 43 B7 34 45N 76 10 E
Karchana, *India* 43 G9 25 17N 81 56 E
Kardhítsa, *Greece* 21 E9 39 23N 21 54 E
Kärdla, *Estonia* 9 G20 58 50N 22 40 E
Kareeberge, *S. Africa* 56 E3 30 59S 21 50 E
Kareha →, *India* 43 G12 25 44N 86 21 E
Kareima, *Sudan* 51 E12 18 30N 31 49 E
Karelia □, *Russia* 24 A5 65 30N 32 30 E
Karelian Republic = Karelia □, *Russia* 24 A5 65 30N 32 30 E
Karera, *India* 42 G8 25 32N 78 9 E
Kārevāndar, *Iran* 45 E9 27 53N 60 44 E
Kargasok, *Russia* 26 D9 59 3N 80 53 E
Kargat, *Russia* 26 D9 55 10N 80 15 E
Kargil, *India* 43 B7 34 32N 76 12 E
Kargopol, *Russia* 24 B6 61 30N 38 58 E
Karhal, *India* 43 F8 27 1N 78 57 E
Karīān, *Iran* 45 E8 26 57N 57 14 E
Karianga, *Madag.* 57 C8 22 25S 47 22 E
Kariba, *Zimbabwe* 55 F2 16 28S 28 50 E
Kariba, L., *Zimbabwe* 55 F2 16 40S 28 25 E
Kariba Dam, *Zimbabwe* 55 F2 16 30S 28 35 E
Kariba Gorge, *Zambia* 55 F2 16 30S 28 50 E
Karibib, *Namibia* 56 C2 22 0S 15 56 E
Karimata, Kepulauan, *Indonesia* 36 E3 1 25S 109 0 E
Karimata, Selat, *Indonesia* 36 E3 2 0S 108 40 E
Karimata Is. = Karimata, Kepulauan, *Indonesia* 36 E3 1 25S 109 0 E
Karimnagar, *India* 40 K11 18 26N 79 10 E
Karimunjawa, Kepulauan, *Indonesia* 36 F4 5 50S 110 30 E
Karin, *Somali Rep.* 46 E4 10 50N 45 52 E
Karīt, *Iran* 45 C8 33 29N 56 55 E
Kariya, *Japan* 31 G8 34 58N 137 1 E
Kariyangwe, *Zimbabwe* 57 B4 18 0S 27 38 E
Karkaralinsk = Qarqaraly, *Kazakstan* 26 E8 49 26N 75 30 E
Karkheh →, *Iran* 44 D5 31 2N 47 29 E
Karkinitska Zatoka, *Ukraine* 25 E5 45 56N 33 0 E
Karkinitskiy Zaliv = Karkinitska Zatoka, *Ukraine* 25 E5 45 56N 33 0 E
Karl-Marx-Stadt = Chemnitz, *Germany* 16 C7 50 51N 12 54 E
Karlovac, *Croatia* 16 F8 45 31N 15 36 E
Karlovo, *Bulgaria* 21 C11 42 38N 24 47 E
Karlovy Vary, *Czech Rep.* 16 C7 50 13N 12 51 E
Karlsbad = Karlovy Vary, *Czech Rep.* 16 C7 50 13N 12 51 E
Karlsborg, *Sweden* 9 G16 58 33N 14 33 E
Karlshamn, *Sweden* 9 H16 56 10N 14 51 E
Karlskoga, *Sweden* 9 G16 59 28N 14 33 E
Karlskrona, *Sweden* 9 H16 56 10N 15 35 E
Karlsruhe, *Germany* 16 D5 49 0N 8 23 E
Karlstad, *Sweden* 9 G15 59 23N 13 30 E
Karlstad, *U.S.A.* 80 A6 48 35N 96 31W
Karmi'el, *Israel* 47 C4 32 55N 35 18 E
Karnak, *Egypt* 51 C12 25 43N 32 39 E
Karnal, *India* 42 E7 29 42N 77 2 E
Karnali →, *Nepal* 43 E9 28 45N 81 16 E
Karnaphuli Res., *Bangla.* 41 H18 22 40N 92 20 E
Karnaprayag, *India* 43 D8 30 16N 79 15 E
Karnataka □, *India* 40 N10 13 15N 77 0 E
Karnes City, *U.S.A.* 81 L6 28 53N 97 54W
Karnische Alpen, *Europe* 16 E7 46 36N 13 0 E
Kärnten □, *Austria* 16 E8 46 52N 13 30 E
Karoi, *Zimbabwe* 55 F2 16 48S 29 45 E
Karonga, *Malawi* 55 D3 9 57S 33 55 E
Karoonda, *Australia* 63 F2 35 1S 139 59 E
Karor, *Pakistan* 42 D4 31 15N 70 59 E
Karora, *Sudan* 51 E13 17 44N 38 15 E
Karpasia, *Cyprus* 23 D13 35 32N 34 15 E
Kárpathos, *Greece* 21 G12 35 37N 27 10 E
Karpinsk, *Russia* 24 C11 59 45N 60 1 E
Karpogory, *Russia* 24 B7 64 0N 44 27 E
Karpuz Burnu = Apostolos Andreas, C., *Cyprus* 23 D13 35 42N 34 35 E
Karratha, *Australia* 60 D2 20 53S 116 40 E
Kars, *Turkey* 25 F7 40 40N 43 5 E
Karsakpay, *Kazakstan* 26 E7 47 55N 66 40 E
Karshi = Qarshi, *Uzbekistan* 26 F7 38 53N 65 48 E
Karsiyang, *India* 43 F13 26 56N 88 18 E
Karsog, *India* 42 D7 31 23N 77 12 E
Kartaly, *Russia* 26 D7 53 3N 60 40 E
Kartapur, *India* 42 D6 31 27N 75 32 E
Karthaus, *U.S.A.* 78 E6 41 8N 78 9W
Karufa, *Indonesia* 37 E8 3 50S 133 20 E
Karumba, *Australia* 62 B3 17 31S 140 50 E
Karumo, *Tanzania* 54 C3 2 25S 32 50 E
Karumwa, *Tanzania* 54 C3 3 12S 32 38 E
Kārūn →, *Iran* 45 D6 30 26N 48 10 E
Karungu, *Kenya* 54 C3 0 50S 34 10 E
Karviná, *Czech Rep.* 17 D10 49 53N 18 31 E
Karwan →, *India* 42 F8 27 26N 78 4 E
Karwar, *India* 40 M9 14 55N 74 13 E
Karwi, *India* 43 G9 25 12N 80 57 E
Kasache, *Malawi* 55 E3 13 25S 34 20 E
Kasai →, *Dem. Rep. of the Congo* 52 E3 3 30S 16 10 E
Kasai-Oriental □, *Dem. Rep. of the Congo* 54 D1 5 0S 24 30 E
Kasaji, *Dem. Rep. of the Congo* 55 E1 10 25S 23 27 E
Kasama, *Zambia* 55 E3 10 16S 31 9 E
Kasan-dong, *N. Korea* 35 D14 41 18N 126 55 E
Kasane, *Namibia* 56 B3 17 34S 24 50 E
Kasanga, *Tanzania* 55 D3 8 30S 31 10 E
Kasaragod, *India* 40 N9 12 30N 74 58 E
Kasba L., *Canada* 73 A8 60 20N 102 10W
Kāseh Garān, *Iran* 44 C5 34 5N 46 2 E
Kasempa, *Zambia* 55 E2 13 30S 25 44 E
Kasenga, *Dem. Rep. of the Congo* 55 E2 10 20S 28 45 E
Kasese, *Uganda* 54 B3 0 13N 30 3 E
Kasewa, *Zambia* 55 E2 14 28S 28 53 E
Kasganj, *India* 43 F8 27 48N 78 42 E
Kashabowie, *Canada* 70 C1 48 40N 90 26W
Kashaf, *Iran* 45 C9 35 58N 61 7 E
Kāshān, *Iran* 45 C6 34 5N 51 30 E
Kashechewan, *Canada* 70 B3 52 18N 81 37W
Kashgar = Kashi, *China* 32 C2 39 30N 76 2 E
Kashi, *China* 32 C2 39 30N 76 2 E
Kashimbo, *Dem. Rep. of the Congo* 55 E2 11 12S 26 19 E
Kashipur, *India* 43 E8 29 15N 79 0 E
Kashiwazaki, *Japan* 31 F9 37 22N 138 33 E
Kashk-e Kohneh, *Afghan.* 40 B3 34 55N 62 30 E
Kashkū'iyeh, *Iran* 45 D7 30 31N 55 40 E
Kāshmar, *Iran* 45 C8 35 16N 58 26 E
Kashmir, *Asia* 43 C7 34 0N 76 0 E
Kashmor, *Pakistan* 42 E3 28 28N 69 32 E
Kashun Noerh = Gaxun Nur, *China* 32 B5 42 22N 100 30 E
Kasiari, *India* 43 H12 22 8N 87 14 E
Kasimov, *Russia* 24 D7 54 55N 41 20 E
Kasinge, *Dem. Rep. of the Congo* 54 D2 6 15S 26 58 E
Kasiruta, *Indonesia* 37 E7 0 25S 127 12 E
Kaskaskia →, *U.S.A.* 80 G10 37 58N 89 57W
Kaskattama →, *Canada* 73 B10 57 3N 90 4W
Kaskinen, *Finland* 9 E19 62 22N 21 15 E
Kaslo, *Canada* 72 D5 49 55N 116 55W
Kasmere L., *Canada* 73 B8 59 34N 101 10W
Kasongo, *Dem. Rep. of the Congo* 54 C2 4 30S 26 33 E
Kasongo Lunda, *Dem. Rep. of the Congo* 52 F3 6 35S 16 49 E
Kásos, *Greece* 21 G12 35 20N 26 55 E
Kassalâ, *Sudan* 51 E13 15 30N 36 0 E
Kassel, *Germany* 16 C5 51 18N 9 26 E
Kassiópi, *Greece* 23 A3 39 48N 19 53 E
Kasson, *U.S.A.* 80 C8 44 2N 92 45W
Kastamonu, *Turkey* 25 F5 41 25N 33 43 E
Kastélli, *Greece* 23 D5 35 29N 23 38 E
Kastéllion, *Greece* 23 D7 35 12N 25 20 E
Kasterlee, *Belgium* 15 C4 51 15N 4 59 E
Kastoría, *Greece* 21 D9 40 30N 21 19 E
Kasulu, *Tanzania* 54 C3 4 37S 30 5 E
Kasumi, *Japan* 31 G7 35 38N 134 38 E
Kasungu, *Malawi* 55 E3 13 0S 33 29 E
Kasur, *Pakistan* 42 D6 31 5N 74 25 E
Kataba, *Zambia* 55 F2 16 5S 25 10 E
Katahdin, Mt., *U.S.A.* 77 C11 45 54N 68 56W
Kataka Kombe, *Dem. Rep. of the Congo* 54 C1 3 25S 24 20 E
Katale, *Tanzania* 54 C3 4 52S 31 7 E
Katanda, Katanga, *Dem. Rep. of the Congo* 54 D1 7 52S 24 13 E
Katanda, Nord-Kivu, *Dem. Rep. of the Congo* 54 C2 0 55S 29 21 E
Katanga □, *Dem. Rep. of the Congo* 54 D2 8 0S 25 0 E
Katangi, *India* 40 J11 21 56N 79 50 E
Katanning, *Australia* 61 F2 33 40S 117 33 E
Katavi Swamp, *Tanzania* 54 D3 6 50S 31 10 E
Kateríni, *Greece* 21 D10 40 18N 22 37 E
Katghora, *India* 43 H10 22 30N 82 33 E
Katha, *Burma* 41 G20 24 10N 96 30 E
Katherîna, Gebel, *Egypt* 44 D2 28 30N 33 57 E
Katherine, *Australia* 60 B5 14 27S 132 20 E
Katherine Gorge, *Australia* 60 B5 14 18S 132 28 E
Kathi, *India* 42 J6 21 47N 74 3 E
Kathiawar, *India* 42 H4 22 20N 71 0 E
Kathikas, *Cyprus* 23 E11 34 55N 32 25 E
Kathmandu = Katmandu, *Nepal* 43 F11 27 45N 85 20 E
Kathua, *India* 42 C6 32 23N 75 34 E
Katihar, *India* 43 G12 25 34N 87 36 E
Katima Mulilo, *Zambia* 56 B3 17 28S 24 13 E
Katimbira, *Malawi* 55 E3 12 40S 34 0 E
Katingan = Mendawai →, *Indonesia* 36 E4 3 30S 113 0 E
Katiola, *Ivory C.* 50 G4 8 10N 5 10W
Katmandu, *Nepal* 43 F11 27 45N 85 20 E
Katni, *India* 43 H9 23 51N 80 24 E
Káto Arkhánai, *Greece* 23 D7 35 15N 25 10 E
Káto Khorió, *Greece* 23 D7 35 3N 25 47 E
Káto Pyrgos, *Cyprus* 23 D11 35 11N 32 41 E
Katompe, *Dem. Rep. of the Congo* 54 D2 6 2S 26 23 E
Katonga →, *Uganda* 54 B3 0 34N 31 50 E
Katoomba, *Australia* 63 E5 33 41S 150 19 E
Katowice, *Poland* 17 C10 50 17N 19 5 E
Katrine, L., *U.K.* 12 E4 56 15N 4 30W
Katrineholm, *Sweden* 9 G17 59 9N 16 12 E
Katsepe, *Madag.* 57 B8 15 45S 46 15 E
Katsina, *Nigeria* 50 F7 13 0N 7 32 E
Katsumoto, *Japan* 31 H4 33 51N 129 42 E
Katsuura, *Japan* 31 G10 35 10N 140 20 E
Katsuyama, *Japan* 31 F8 36 3N 136 30 E
Kattaviá, *Greece* 23 D9 35 57N 27 46 E
Kattegat, *Denmark* 9 H14 56 40N 11 20 E
Katumba, *Dem. Rep. of the Congo* 54 D2 7 40S 25 17 E
Katungu, *Kenya* 54 C5 2 55S 40 3 E
Katwa, *India* 43 H13 23 30N 88 5 E
Katwijk, *Neths.* 15 B4 52 12N 4 24 E
Kauai, *U.S.A.* 74 H15 22 3N 159 30W
Kauai Channel, *U.S.A.* 74 H15 21 45N 158 50W
Kaufman, *U.S.A.* 81 J6 32 35N 96 19W
Kauhajoki, *Finland* 9 E20 62 25N 22 10 E
Kaukauna, *U.S.A.* 76 C1 44 17N 88 17W
Kaukauveld, *Namibia* 56 C3 20 0S 20 15 E
Kaunakakai, *U.S.A.* 74 H16 21 6N 157 1W
Kaunas, *Lithuania* 9 J20 54 54N 23 54 E
Kaunia, *Bangla.* 43 G13 25 46N 89 26 E
Kautokeino, *Norway* 8 B20 69 0N 23 4 E
Kauwapur, *India* 43 F10 27 31N 82 18 E
Kavacha, *Russia* 27 C17 60 16N 169 51 E
Kavalerovo, *Russia* 30 B7 44 15N 135 4 E
Kavali, *India* 40 M12 14 55N 80 1 E
Kavála, *Greece* 21 D11 40 57N 24 28 E
Kavār, *Iran* 45 D7 29 11N 52 44 E
Kavi, *India* 42 H5 22 12N 72 38 E
Kavimba, *Botswana* 56 B3 18 2S 24 38 E
Kavīr, Dasht-e, *Iran* 45 C7 34 30N 55 0 E
Kavos, *Greece* 23 B4 39 23N 20 3 E
Kaw, *Fr. Guiana* 93 C8 4 30N 52 15W
Kawagama L., *Canada* 78 A6 45 18N 78 45W
Kawagoe, *Japan* 31 G9 35 55N 139 29 E
Kawaguchi, *Japan* 31 G9 35 52N 139 45 E
Kawambwa, *Zambia* 55 D2 9 48S 29 3 E
Kawanoe, *Japan* 31 G6 34 1N 133 34 E
Kawardha, *India* 43 J9 22 0N 81 17 E
Kawasaki, *Japan* 31 G9 35 35N 139 42 E
Kawasi, *Indonesia* 37 E7 1 38S 127 28 E
Kawerau, *N.Z.* 59 H6 38 7S 176 42 E
Kawhia Harbour, *N.Z.* 59 H5 38 5S 174 51 E
Kawio, Kepulauan, *Indonesia* 37 D7 4 30N 125 30 E
Kawnro, *Burma* 41 H21 22 48N 99 8 E
Kawthaung, *Burma* 39 H2 10 5N 98 36 E
Kawthoolei = Kayin □, *Burma* 41 L20 18 0N 97 30 E
Kawthule = Kayin □, *Burma* 41 L20 18 0N 97 30 E
Kaya, *Burkina Faso* 50 F5 13 4N 1 10W
Kayah □, *Burma* 41 K20 19 15N 97 15 E
Kayan →, *Indonesia* 36 D5 2 55N 117 35 E
Kaycee, *U.S.A.* 82 E10 43 43N 106 38W
Kayeli, *Indonesia* 37 E7 3 20S 127 10 E
Kayenta, *U.S.A.* 83 H8 36 44N 110 15W
Kayes, *Mali* 50 F3 14 25N 11 30W
Kayin □, *Burma* 41 L20 18 0N 97 30 E
Kayoa, *Indonesia* 37 D7 0 1N 127 28 E
Kayomba, *Zambia* 55 E1 13 11S 24 2 E
Kayseri, *Turkey* 25 G6 38 45N 35 30 E
Kaysville, *U.S.A.* 82 F8 41 2N 111 56W
Kazachye, *Russia* 27 B14 70 52N 135 58 E
Kazakstan ■, *Asia* 26 E7 50 0N 70 0 E
Kazan, *Russia* 24 C8 55 50N 49 10 E
Kazan →, *Canada* 73 A9 64 3N 95 35W
Kazan-Rettō, *Pac. Oc.* 64 E6 25 0N 141 0 E
Kazanlŭk, *Bulgaria* 21 C11 42 38N 25 20 E
Kazatin = Kozyatyn, *Ukraine* 17 D15 49 45N 28 50 E
Kāzerūn, *Iran* 45 D6 29 38N 51 40 E
Kazi Magomed = Qazimämmäd, *Azerbaijan* 45 A6 40 3N 49 0 E
Kazuno, *Japan* 30 D10 40 10N 140 45 E
Kazym →, *Russia* 26 C7 63 54N 65 50 E
Kéa, *Greece* 21 F11 37 35N 24 22 E
Keady, *U.K.* 13 B5 54 15N 6 42W
Kearney, *U.S.A.* 80 E5 40 42N 99 5W
Kearny, *U.S.A.* 83 K8 33 3N 110 55W
Kearsarge, Mt., *U.S.A.* 79 C13 43 22N 71 50W
Keban, *Turkey* 25 G6 38 50N 38 50 E
Keban Barajı, *Turkey* 25 G6 38 41N 38 33 E
Kebnekaise, *Sweden* 8 C18 67 53N 18 33 E
Kebri Dehar, *Ethiopia* 46 F3 6 45N 44 17 E
Kebumen, *Indonesia* 37 G13 7 42S 109 40 E
Kechika →, *Canada* 72 B3 59 41N 127 12W
Kecskemét, *Hungary* 17 E10 46 57N 19 42 E
Kėdainiai, *Lithuania* 9 J21 55 15N 24 2 E
Kedarnath, *India* 43 D8 30 44N 79 4 E
Kedgwick, *Canada* 71 C6 47 40N 67 20W
Kédhros Óros, *Greece* 23 D6 35 11N 24 37 E
Kediri, *Indonesia* 36 F4 7 51S 112 1 E
Keeler, *U.S.A.* 84 J9 36 29N 117 52W
Keeley L., *Canada* 73 C7 54 54N 108 8W
Keeling Is. = Cocos Is., *Ind. Oc.* 64 J1 12 10S 96 55 E
Keelung = Chilung, *Taiwan* 33 D7 25 3N 121 45 E
Keene, *Canada* 78 B6 44 15N 78 10W
Keene, *Calif., U.S.A.* 85 K8 35 13N 118 33W
Keene, *N.H., U.S.A.* 79 D12 42 56N 72 17W

Keene, N.Y., U.S.A. 79 B11 44 16N 73 46W
Keeper Hill, Ireland 13 D3 52 45N 8 16W
Keer-Weer, C., Australia 62 A3 14 0S 141 32 E
Keeseville, U.S.A. 79 B11 44 29N 73 30W
Keetmanshoop, Namibia 56 D2 26 35S 18 8 E
Keewatin, Canada 73 D10 49 46N 94 34W
Keewatin →, Canada 73 B8 56 29N 100 46W
Kefallinia, Greece 21 E9 38 15N 20 30 E
Kefamenanu, Indonesia 37 F6 9 28S 124 29 E
Kefar Sava, Israel 47 C3 32 11N 34 54 E
Keffi, Nigeria 50 G7 8 55N 7 43 E
Keflavík, Iceland 8 D2 64 2N 22 35W
Keg River, Canada 72 B5 57 54N 117 55W
Kegaska, Canada 71 B7 50 9N 61 18W
Keighley, U.K. 10 D6 53 52N 1 54W
Keila, Estonia 9 G21 59 18N 24 25 E
Keimoes, S. Africa 56 D3 28 41S 20 59 E
Keitele, Finland 8 E22 63 10N 26 20 E
Keith, Australia 63 F3 36 6S 140 20 E
Keith, U.K. 12 D6 57 32N 2 57W
Keizer, U.S.A. 82 D2 44 57N 123 1W
Kejimkujik Nat. Park, Canada 71 D6 44 25N 65 25W
Kejserr Franz Joseph Fd., Greenland 4 B6 73 30N 24 30W
Kekri, India 42 G6 26 0N 75 10 E
Kelan, China 34 E6 38 43N 111 31 E
Kelang, Malaysia 39 L3 3 2N 101 26 E
Kelantan →, Malaysia 39 J4 6 13N 102 14 E
Kelkit →, Turkey 25 F6 40 45N 36 32 E
Kellerberrin, Australia 61 F2 31 36S 117 38 E
Kellett, C., Canada 4 B1 72 0N 126 0W
Kelleys I., U.S.A. 78 E2 41 36N 82 42W
Kellogg, U.S.A. 82 C5 47 32N 116 7W
Kells = Ceanannus Mor, Ireland 13 C5 53 44N 6 53W
Kelokedhara, Cyprus 23 E11 34 48N 32 39 E
Kelowna, Canada 72 D5 49 50N 119 25W
Kelseyville, U.S.A. 84 G4 38 59N 122 50W
Kelso, N.Z. 59 L2 45 54S 169 15 E
Kelso, U.K. 12 F6 55 36N 2 26W
Kelso, U.S.A. 84 D4 46 9N 122 54W
Keluang, Malaysia 39 L4 2 3N 103 18 E
Kelvington, Canada 73 C8 52 10N 103 30W
Kem, Russia 24 B5 65 0N 34 38 E
Kem →, Russia 24 B5 64 57N 34 41 E
Kema, Indonesia 37 D7 1 22N 125 8 E
Kemah, Turkey 44 B3 39 32N 39 5 E
Kemaman, Malaysia 36 D2 4 12N 103 18 E
Kemano, Canada 72 C3 53 35N 128 0W
Kemasik, Malaysia 39 K4 4 25N 103 27 E
Kemerovo, Russia 26 D9 55 20N 86 5 E
Kemi, Finland 8 D21 65 44N 24 34 E
Kemi älv = Kemijoki →, Finland 8 D21 65 47N 24 32 E
Kemijärvi, Finland 8 C22 66 43N 27 22 E
Kemijoki →, Finland 8 D21 65 47N 24 32 E
Kemmerer, U.S.A. 82 F8 41 48N 110 32W
Kemmuna = Comino, Malta 23 C1 36 1N 14 20 E
Kemp, L., U.S.A. 81 J5 33 46N 99 9W
Kemp Land, Antarctica 5 C5 69 0S 55 0 E
Kempsey, Australia 63 E5 31 1S 152 50 E
Kempt, L., Canada 70 C5 47 25N 74 22W
Kempten, Germany 16 E6 47 45N 10 17 E
Kempton, Australia 62 G4 42 31S 147 12 E
Kemptville, Canada 79 B9 45 0N 75 38W
Ken →, India 43 G9 25 13N 80 27 E
Kenai, U.S.A. 68 B4 60 33N 151 16W
Kendai, India 43 H10 22 45N 82 37 E
Kendal, Indonesia 37 G14 6 56S 110 14 E
Kendal, U.K. 10 C5 54 20N 2 44W
Kendall, Australia 63 E5 31 35S 152 44 E
Kendall, U.S.A. 77 N5 25 41N 80 19W
Kendall →, Australia 62 A3 14 4S 141 35 E
Kendallville, U.S.A. 76 E3 41 27N 85 16W
Kendari, Indonesia 37 E6 3 50S 122 30 E
Kendawangan, Indonesia 36 E4 2 32S 110 17 E
Kendrapara, India 41 J15 20 35N 86 30 E
Kendrew, S. Africa 56 E3 32 32S 24 30 E
Kene Thao, Laos 38 D3 17 44N 101 10 E
Kenedy, U.S.A. 81 L6 28 49N 97 51W
Kenema, S. Leone 50 G3 7 50N 11 14W
Keng Kok, Laos 38 D5 16 26N 105 12 E
Keng Tawng, Burma 41 J21 20 45N 98 18 E
Keng Tung, Burma 41 J21 21 0N 99 30 E
Kengeja, Tanzania 54 D4 5 26S 39 45 E
Kenhardt, S. Africa 56 D3 29 19S 21 12 E
Kenitra, Morocco 50 B4 34 15N 6 40W
Kenli, China 35 F10 37 30N 118 20 E
Kenmare, Ireland 13 E2 51 53N 9 36W
Kenmare, U.S.A. 80 A3 48 41N 102 5W
Kenmare River, Ireland 13 E2 51 48N 9 51W
Kennebago Lake, U.S.A. 79 A14 45 4N 70 40W
Kennebec, U.S.A. 80 D5 43 54N 99 52W
Kennebec →, U.S.A. 77 D11 43 45N 69 46W
Kennebunk, U.S.A. 79 C14 43 23N 70 33W
Kennedy, Zimbabwe 56 B4 18 52S 27 10 E
Kennedy Ra., Australia 61 D2 24 45S 115 10 E
Kennedy Taungdeik, Burma 41 H18 23 15N 93 45 E
Kenner, U.S.A. 81 L9 29 59N 90 15W
Kennet →, U.K. 11 F7 51 27N 0 57W
Kenneth Ra., Australia 61 D2 23 50S 117 8 E
Kennett, U.S.A. 81 G9 36 14N 90 3W
Kennewick, U.S.A. 82 C4 46 12N 119 7W
Kenogami →, Canada 70 B3 51 6N 84 28W
Kenora, Canada 73 D10 49 47N 94 29W
Kenosha, U.S.A. 76 D2 42 35N 87 49W
Kensington, Canada 71 C7 46 28N 63 34W
Kent, Ohio, U.S.A. 78 E3 41 9N 81 22W
Kent, Tex., U.S.A. 81 K2 31 4N 104 13W
Kent, Wash., U.S.A. 84 C4 47 23N 122 14W
Kent □, U.K. 11 F8 51 12N 0 40 E
Kent Group, Australia 62 F4 39 30S 147 20 E
Kent Pen., Canada 68 B9 68 30N 107 0W
Kentaū, Kazakstan 26 E7 43 32N 68 36 E
Kentland, U.S.A. 76 E2 40 46N 87 27W
Kenton, U.S.A. 76 E4 40 39N 83 37W
Kentucky □, U.S.A. 76 G3 37 0N 84 0W
Kentucky →, U.S.A. 76 F3 38 41N 85 11W
Kentucky L., U.S.A. 77 G2 37 1N 88 16W
Kentville, Canada 71 C7 45 6N 64 29W
Kentwood, U.S.A. 81 K9 30 56N 90 31W
Kenya ■, Africa 54 B4 1 0N 38 0 E
Kenya, Mt., Kenya 54 C4 0 10S 37 18 E
Keo Neua, Deo, Vietnam 38 C5 18 23N 105 10 E
Keokuk, U.S.A. 80 E9 40 24N 91 24W
Keonjhargarh, India 43 J11 21 28N 85 35 E
Kep, Cambodia 39 G5 10 29N 104 19 E
Kep, Vietnam 38 B6 21 24N 106 16 E
Kepi, Indonesia 37 F9 6 32S 139 19 E
Kerala □, India 40 P10 11 0N 76 15 E
Kerama-Rettō, Japan 31 L3 26 5N 127 15 E
Keran, Pakistan 43 B5 34 35N 73 59 E
Kerang, Australia 63 F3 35 40S 143 55 E
Keraudren, C., Australia 60 C2 19 58S 119 45 E
Kerava, Finland 9 F21 60 25N 25 5 E
Kerch, Ukraine 25 E6 45 20N 36 20 E
Kerguelen, Ind. Oc. 3 G13 49 15S 69 10 E
Kericho, Kenya 54 C4 0 22S 35 15 E
Kerinci, Indonesia 36 E2 1 40S 101 15 E
Kerki, Turkmenistan 26 F7 37 50N 65 12 E
Kérkira, Greece 23 A3 39 38N 19 50 E
Kerkrade, Neths. 15 D6 50 53N 6 4 E
Kermadec Is., Pac. Oc. 64 L10 30 0S 178 15W
Kermadec Trench, Pac. Oc. 64 L10 30 30S 176 0W
Kermān, Iran 45 D8 30 15N 57 1 E
Kerman, U.S.A. 84 J6 36 43N 120 4W
Kermān □, Iran 45 D8 30 0N 57 0 E
Kermān, Bīābān-e, Iran 45 D8 28 45N 59 45 E
Kermānshāh = Bākhtarān, Iran 44 C5 34 23N 47 0 E
Kermit, U.S.A. 81 K3 31 52N 103 6W
Kern →, U.S.A. 85 K7 35 16N 119 18W
Kernow = Cornwall □, U.K. 11 G3 50 26N 4 40W
Kernville, U.S.A. 85 K8 35 45N 118 26W
Keroh, Malaysia 39 K3 5 43N 101 1 E
Kerrera, U.K. 12 E3 56 24N 5 33W
Kerrobert, Canada 73 C7 51 56N 109 8W
Kerrville, U.S.A. 81 K5 30 3N 99 8W
Kerry □, Ireland 13 D2 52 7N 9 35W
Kerry Hd., Ireland 13 D2 52 25N 9 56W
Kerulen →, Asia 33 B6 48 48N 117 0 E
Kerzaz, Algeria 50 C5 29 29N 1 37W
Kesagami →, Canada 70 B4 51 40N 79 45W
Kesagami L., Canada 70 B3 50 23N 80 15W
Keşan, Turkey 21 D12 40 49N 26 38 E
Kesennuma, Japan 30 E10 38 54N 141 35 E
Keshit, Iran 45 D8 29 43N 58 17 E
Kestell, S. Africa 57 D4 28 17S 28 42 E
Kestenga, Russia 24 A5 65 50N 31 45 E
Keswick, U.K. 10 C4 54 36N 3 8W
Ket →, Russia 26 D9 58 55N 81 32 E
Ketapang, Indonesia 36 E4 1 55S 110 0 E
Ketchikan, U.S.A. 72 B2 55 21N 131 39W
Ketchum, U.S.A. 82 E6 43 41N 114 22W
Ketef, Khalîg Umm el, Egypt 44 F2 23 40N 35 35 E
Keti Bandar, Pakistan 42 G2 24 8N 67 27 E
Ketri, India 42 E6 28 1N 75 50 E
Kętrzyn, Poland 17 A11 54 7N 21 22 E
Kettering, U.K. 11 E7 52 24N 0 43W
Kettering, U.S.A. 76 F3 39 41N 84 10W
Kettle →, Canada 73 B11 56 40N 89 34W
Kettle Falls, U.S.A. 82 B4 48 37N 118 3W
Kettle Pt., Canada 78 C2 43 13N 82 1W
Kettleman City, U.S.A. 84 J7 36 1N 119 58W
Keuka L., U.S.A. 78 D7 42 30N 77 9W
Keuruu, Finland 9 E21 62 16N 24 41 E
Kewanee, U.S.A. 80 E10 41 14N 89 56W
Kewaunee, U.S.A. 76 C2 44 27N 87 31W
Keweenaw B., U.S.A. 76 B1 47 0N 88 15W
Keweenaw Pen., U.S.A. 76 B2 47 30N 88 0W
Keweenaw Pt., U.S.A. 76 B2 47 25N 87 43W
Key Largo, U.S.A. 77 N5 25 5N 80 27W
Key West, U.S.A. 75 F10 24 33N 81 48W
Keynsham, U.K. 11 F5 51 24N 2 29W
Keyser, U.S.A. 76 F6 39 26N 78 59W
Kezhma, Russia 27 D11 58 59N 101 9 E
Kezi, Zimbabwe 57 C4 20 58S 28 32 E
Khabarovsk, Russia 27 E14 48 30N 135 5 E
Khabr, Iran 45 D8 28 51N 56 22 E
Khābūr →, Syria 44 C4 35 17N 40 35 E
Khachmas = Xaçmaz, Azerbaijan 25 F8 41 31N 48 42 E
Khachrod, India 42 H6 23 25N 75 20 E
Khadro, Pakistan 42 F3 26 11N 68 50 E
Khadzhilyangar, China 43 B8 35 45N 79 20 E
Khaga, India 43 G9 25 47N 81 7 E
Khagaria, India 43 G12 25 30N 86 32 E
Khaipur, Pakistan 42 E5 29 34N 72 17 E
Khair, India 42 F7 27 57N 77 46 E
Khairabad, India 43 F9 27 33N 80 47 E
Khairagarh, India 43 J9 21 27N 81 2 E
Khairpur, Pakistan 42 F3 27 32N 68 49 E
Khairpur Nathan Shah, Pakistan 42 F2 27 6N 67 44 E
Khairwara, India 42 H5 23 58N 73 38 E
Khaisor →, Pakistan 42 D3 31 17N 68 59 E
Khajuri Kach, Pakistan 42 C3 32 4N 69 51 E
Khakassia □, Russia 26 D9 53 0N 90 0 E
Khakhea, Botswana 56 C3 24 48S 23 22 E
Khalafābād, Iran 45 D6 30 54N 49 24 E
Khalilabad, India 43 F10 26 48N 83 5 E
Khalīlī, Iran 45 E7 27 38N 53 17 E
Khalkhāl, Iran 45 B6 37 37N 48 32 E
Khalkís, Greece 21 E10 38 27N 23 42 E
Khalmer-Sede = Tazovskiy, Russia 26 C8 67 30N 78 44 E
Khalmer Yu, Russia 26 C7 67 58N 65 1 E
Khalturin, Russia 24 C8 58 40N 48 50 E
Khalūf, Oman 46 C6 20 30N 58 13 E
Kham Keut, Laos 38 C5 18 15N 104 43 E
Khamaria, India 43 H9 23 5N 80 48 E
Khambhaliya, India 42 H3 22 14N 69 41 E
Khambhat, India 42 H5 22 23N 72 33 E
Khambhat, G. of, India 40 J8 20 45N 72 30 E
Khamir, Iran 45 E7 26 57N 55 36 E
Khamir, Yemen 46 D3 16 2N 44 0 E
Khamsa, Egypt 47 E1 30 27N 32 23 E
Khan →, Namibia 56 C2 22 37S 14 56 E
Khān Abū Shāmat, Syria 47 B5 33 39N 36 53 E
Khān Azād, Iraq 44 C5 33 7N 44 22 E
Khān Mujiddah, Iraq 44 C4 32 21N 43 48 E
Khān Shaykhūn, Syria 44 C3 35 26N 36 38 E
Khān Yūnis, Gaza Strip 47 D3 31 21N 34 18 E
Khanai, Pakistan 42 D2 30 30N 67 8 E
Khānaqīn, Iraq 44 C5 34 23N 45 25 E
Khānbāghī, Iran 45 B7 36 10N 55 25 E
Khandwa, India 40 J10 21 49N 76 22 E
Khandyga, Russia 27 C14 62 42N 135 35 E
Khāneh, Iran 44 B5 36 41N 45 8 E
Khanewal, Pakistan 42 D4 30 20N 71 55 E
Khangah Dogran, Pakistan 42 D5 31 50N 73 37 E
Khanh Duong, Vietnam 38 F7 12 44N 108 44 E
Khaniá, Greece 23 D6 35 30N 24 4 E
Khaniá □, Greece 23 D6 35 30N 24 0 E
Khaniadhana, India 42 G8 25 1N 78 8 E
Khanion, Kólpos, Greece 23 D5 35 33N 23 55 E
Khanka, L., Asia 27 E14 45 0N 132 24 E
Khankendy = Xankändi, Azerbaijan 25 G8 39 52N 46 49 E
Khanna, India 42 D7 30 42N 76 16 E
Khanozai, Pakistan 42 D2 30 37N 67 19 E
Khanpur, Pakistan 42 E4 28 42N 70 35 E
Khanty-Mansiysk, Russia 26 C7 61 0N 69 0 E
Khapalu, Pakistan 43 B7 35 10N 76 20 E
Khapcheranga, Russia 27 E12 49 42N 112 24 E
Kharaghoda, India 42 H4 23 11N 71 46 E
Kharagpur, India 43 H12 22 20N 87 25 E
Khárakas, Greece 23 D7 35 1N 25 7 E
Kharan Kalat, Pakistan 40 E4 28 34N 65 21 E
Kharānaq, Iran 45 C7 32 20N 54 45 E
Kharda, India 40 K9 18 40N 75 34 E
Khardung La, India 43 B7 34 20N 77 43 E
Khârga, El Wâhât-el, Egypt 51 C12 25 10N 30 35 E
Khargon, India 40 J9 21 45N 75 40 E
Khari →, India 42 G6 25 54N 74 31 E
Kharian, Pakistan 42 C5 32 49N 73 52 E
Khārk, Jazīreh-ye, Iran 45 D6 29 15N 50 28 E
Kharkiv, Ukraine 25 E6 49 58N 36 20 E
Kharkov = Kharkiv, Ukraine 25 E6 49 58N 36 20 E
Kharovsk, Russia 24 C7 59 56N 40 13 E
Kharsawangarh, India 43 H11 22 48N 85 50 E
Kharta, Turkey 21 D13 40 55N 29 7 E
Khartoum = El Khartûm, Sudan 51 E12 15 31N 32 35 E
Khasan, Russia 30 C5 42 25N 130 40 E
Khāsh, Iran 40 E2 28 15N 61 15 E
Khashm el Girba, Sudan 51 F13 14 59N 35 58 E
Khaskovo, Bulgaria 21 D11 41 56N 25 30 E
Khatanga, Russia 27 B11 72 0N 102 20 E
Khatanga →, Russia 27 B11 72 55N 106 0 E
Khatauli, India 42 E7 29 17N 77 43 E
Khatra, India 43 H12 22 59N 86 51 E
Khātūnābād, Iran 45 D7 30 1N 55 25 E
Khatyrka, Russia 27 C18 62 3N 175 15 E
Khavda, India 42 H3 23 51N 69 43 E
Khaybar, Ḩarrat, Si. Arabia 44 E4 25 45N 40 0 E
Khayelitsha, S. Africa 53 L3 34 5S 18 42 E
Khāzimiyah, Iraq 44 C4 34 46N 43 37 E
Khe Bo, Vietnam 38 C5 19 8N 104 41 E
Khe Long, Vietnam 38 B5 21 29N 104 46 E
Khed Brahma, India 40 G8 24 7N 73 5 E
Khekra, India 42 E7 28 52N 77 20 E
Khemarak Phouminville, Cambodia 39 G4 11 37N 102 59 E
Khemisset, Morocco 50 B4 33 50N 6 1W
Khemmarat, Thailand 38 D5 16 10N 105 15 E
Khenāmān, Iran 45 D8 30 27N 56 29 E
Khenchela, Algeria 50 A7 35 28N 7 11 E
Khersān →, Iran 45 D6 31 33N 50 22 E
Kherson, Ukraine 25 E5 46 35N 32 35 E
Khersónisos Akrotíri, Greece 23 D6 35 30N 24 10 E
Kheta →, Russia 27 B11 71 54N 102 6 E
Khewari, Pakistan 42 F3 26 36N 68 52 E
Khilchipur, India 42 G7 24 2N 76 34 E
Khilok, Russia 27 D12 51 30N 110 45 E
Khíos, Greece 21 E12 38 27N 26 9 E
Khirsadoh, India 43 H8 22 11N 78 47 E
Khiuma = Hiiumaa, Estonia 9 G20 58 50N 22 45 E
Khiva, Uzbekistan 26 E7 41 30N 60 18 E
Khīyāv, Iran 44 B5 38 30N 47 45 E
Khlong Khlung, Thailand 38 D2 16 12N 99 43 E
Khmelnik, Ukraine 17 D14 49 33N 27 58 E
Khmelnitskiy = Khmelnytskyy, Ukraine 17 D14 49 23N 27 0 E
Khmelnytskyy, Ukraine 17 D14 49 23N 27 0 E
Khmer Rep. = Cambodia ■, Asia 38 F5 12 15N 105 0 E
Khoai, Hon, Vietnam 39 H5 8 26N 104 50 E
Khodoriv, Ukraine 17 D13 49 24N 24 19 E
Khodzent = Khŭjand, Tajikistan 26 E7 40 17N 69 37 E
Khojak Pass, Afghan. 42 D2 30 51N 66 34 E
Khok Kloi, Thailand 39 H2 8 17N 98 19 E
Khok Pho, Thailand 39 J3 6 43N 101 6 E
Kholm, Russia 24 C5 57 10N 31 15 E
Kholmsk, Russia 27 E15 47 40N 142 5 E
Khomas Hochland, Namibia 56 C2 22 40S 16 0 E
Khomeyn, Iran 45 C6 33 40N 50 7 E
Khomeynī Shahr, Iran 45 C6 32 41N 51 31 E
Khomodino, Botswana 56 C3 22 46S 23 52 E
Khon Kaen, Thailand 38 D4 16 30N 102 47 E
Khong →, Cambodia 38 F5 13 32N 105 58 E
Khong Sedone, Laos 38 E5 15 34N 105 49 E
Khonuu, Russia 27 C15 66 30N 143 12 E
Khoper →, Russia 25 D6 49 30N 42 20 E
Khóra Sfakion, Greece 23 D6 35 15N 24 9 E
Khorāsān □, Iran 45 C8 34 0N 58 0 E
Khorat = Nakhon Ratchasima, Thailand 38 E4 14 59N 102 12 E
Khorat, Cao Nguyen, Thailand 38 E4 15 30N 102 50 E
Khorixas, Namibia 56 C1 20 16S 14 59 E
Khorramābād, Khorāsān, Iran 45 C8 35 6N 57 57 E
Khorramābād, Lorestān, Iran 45 C6 33 30N 48 25 E
Khorrāmshahr, Iran 45 D6 30 29N 48 15 E
Khorugh, Tajikistan 26 F8 37 30N 71 36 E
Khosravī, Iran 45 D6 30 48N 51 28 E
Khosrowābād, Khuzestān, Iran 45 D6 30 10N 48 25 E
Khosrowābād, Kordestān, Iran 44 C5 35 31N 47 38 E
Khost, Pakistan 42 D2 30 13N 67 35 E
Khosūyeh, Iran 45 D7 28 32N 54 26 E
Khotyn, Ukraine 17 D14 48 31N 26 27 E
Khouribga, Morocco 50 B4 32 58N 6 57W
Khowst, Afghan. 42 C3 33 22N 69 58 E
Khowst □, Afghan. 40 C6 33 20N 70 0 E
Khoyniki, Belarus 17 C15 51 54N 29 55 E
Khrysokhou B., Cyprus 23 D11 35 6N 32 25 E
Khu Khan, Thailand 38 E5 14 42N 104 12 E
Khudzhand = Khŭjand, Tajikistan 26 E7 40 17N 69 37 E
Khuff, Si. Arabia 44 E5 24 55N 44 53 E
Khūgīānī, Afghan. 42 D2 31 37N 65 4 E
Khuis, Botswana 56 D3 26 40S 21 49 E
Khuiyala, India 42 F4 27 9N 70 25 E
Khŭjand, Tajikistan 26 E7 40 17N 69 37 E
Khujner, India 42 H7 23 47N 76 36 E
Khulna, Bangla. 41 H16 22 45N 89 34 E
Khulna □, Bangla. 41 H16 22 25N 89 35 E
Khumago, Botswana 56 C3 20 26S 24 32 E
Khūnsorkh, Iran 45 E8 27 9N 56 7 E
Khunti, India 43 H11 23 5N 85 17 E
Khūr, Iran 45 C8 32 55N 58 18 E
Khurai, India 42 G8 24 3N 78 23 E
Khurayş, Si. Arabia 45 E6 25 6N 48 2 E
Khuriyā Muriyā, Jazā'ir, Oman 46 D6 17 30N 55 58 E
Khurja, India 42 E7 28 15N 77 58 E
Khūrmāl, Iraq 44 C5 35 18N 46 2 E
Khurr, Wādī al, Iraq 44 C4 32 3N 43 52 E
Khūsf, Iran 45 C8 32 46N 58 53 E
Khush, Afghan. 40 C3 32 55N 62 10 E
Khushab, Pakistan 42 C5 32 20N 72 20 E
Khust, Ukraine 17 D12 48 10N 23 18 E
Khuzdar, Pakistan 42 F2 27 52N 66 30 E
Khūzestān □, Iran 45 D6 31 0N 49 0 E
Khvāf, Iran 45 C9 34 33N 60 8 E
Khvājeh, Iran 44 B5 38 9N 46 35 E
Khvānsār, Iran 45 D7 29 56N 54 8 E
Khvor, Iran 45 C7 33 45N 55 0 E
Khvorgū, Iran 45 E8 27 34N 56 27 E
Khvormūj, Iran 45 D6 28 40N 51 30 E
Khvoy, Iran 44 B5 38 35N 45 0 E
Khyber Pass, Afghan. 42 B4 34 10N 71 8 E
Kiabukwa, Dem. Rep. of the Congo 55 D1 8 40S 24 48 E
Kiama, Australia 63 E5 34 40S 150 50 E
Kiamba, Phil. 37 C6 6 2N 124 46 E
Kiambi, Dem. Rep. of the Congo 54 D2 7 15S 28 0 E
Kiambu, Kenya 54 C4 1 8S 36 50 E
Kiangara, Madag. 57 B8 17 58S 47 2 E
Kiangsi = Jiangxi □, China 33 D6 27 30N 116 0 E
Kiangsu = Jiangsu □, China 35 H11 33 0N 120 0 E
Kibanga Port, Uganda 54 B3 0 10N 32 58 E
Kibara, Tanzania 54 C3 2 8S 33 30 E
Kibare, Mts., Dem. Rep. of the Congo 54 D2 8 25S 27 10 E
Kibombo, Dem. Rep. of the Congo 54 C2 3 57S 25 53 E
Kibondo, Tanzania 54 C3 3 35S 30 45 E
Kibre Mengist, Ethiopia 46 F2 5 54N 38 59 E
Kibumbu, Burundi 54 C2 3 32S 29 45 E
Kibungo, Rwanda 54 C3 2 10S 30 32 E
Kibuye, Burundi 54 C2 3 39S 29 59 E
Kibuye, Rwanda 54 C2 2 3S 29 21 E
Kibwesa, Tanzania 54 D2 6 30S 29 58 E
Kibwezi, Kenya 54 C4 2 27S 37 57 E
Kichha, India 43 E8 28 53N 79 30 E
Kichha →, India 43 E8 28 41N 79 18 E
Kichmengskiy Gorodok, Russia 24 B8 59 59N 45 48 E
Kicking Horse Pass, Canada 72 C5 51 28N 116 16W
Kidal, Mali 50 E6 18 26N 1 22 E
Kidderminster, U.K. 11 E5 52 24N 2 15W
Kidete, Tanzania 54 D4 6 25S 37 17 E
Kidnappers, C., N.Z. 59 H6 39 38S 177 5 E
Kidsgrove, U.K. 10 D5 53 5N 2 14W
Kidston, Australia 62 B3 18 52S 144 8 E
Kidugallo, Tanzania 54 D4 6 49S 38 15 E
Kiel, Germany 16 A6 54 19N 10 8 E
Kiel Canal = Nord-Ostsee-Kanal, Germany 16 A5 54 12N 9 32 E
Kielce, Poland 17 C11 50 52N 20 42 E
Kielder Water, U.K. 10 B5 55 11N 2 31W
Kieler Bucht, Germany 16 A6 54 35N 10 25 E
Kien Binh, Vietnam 39 H5 9 55N 105 19 E
Kien Tan, Vietnam 39 G5 10 7N 105 17 E
Kienge, Dem. Rep. of the Congo 55 E2 10 30S 27 30 E
Kiev = Kyyiv, Ukraine 17 C16 50 30N 30 28 E
Kiffa, Mauritania 50 E3 16 37N 11 24W
Kifrī, Iraq 44 C5 34 45N 45 0 E
Kigali, Rwanda 54 C3 1 59S 30 4 E
Kigarama, Tanzania 54 C3 1 1S 31 50 E
Kigoma □, Tanzania 54 D3 5 0S 30 0 E
Kigoma-Ujiji, Tanzania 54 C2 4 55S 29 36 E
Kigomasha, Ras, Tanzania 54 C4 4 58S 38 58 E
Kığzı, Turkey 44 B4 38 18N 43 25 E
Kihei, U.S.A. 74 H16 20 47N 156 28W
Kihnu, Estonia 9 G21 58 9N 24 1 E
Kii-Sanchi, Japan 31 G8 34 20N 136 0 E
Kii-Suidō, Japan 31 H7 33 40N 134 45 E
Kikaiga-Shima, Japan 31 K4 28 19N 129 59 E
Kikinda, Serbia, Yug. 21 B9 45 50N 20 30 E
Kikládhes, Greece 21 F11 37 0N 24 30 E
Kikwit, Dem. Rep. of the Congo 52 E3 5 0S 18 45 E
Kilar, India 42 C7 33 6N 76 25 E
Kilauea Crater, U.S.A. 74 J17 19 25N 155 17W
Kilbrannan Sd., U.K. 12 F3 55 37N 5 26W
Kilchu, N. Korea 35 D15 40 57N 129 25 E
Kilcoy, Australia 63 D5 26 59S 152 30 E
Kildare, Ireland 13 C5 53 9N 6 55W
Kildare □, Ireland 13 C5 53 10N 6 50W
Kilfinnane, Ireland 13 D3 52 21N 8 28W
Kilgore, U.S.A. 81 J7 32 23N 94 53W
Kilifi, Kenya 54 C4 3 40S 39 48 E
Kilimanjaro, Tanzania 54 C4 3 7S 37 20 E
Kilimanjaro □, Tanzania 54 C4 4 0S 38 0 E
Kilindini, Kenya 54 C4 4 4S 39 40 E
Kilis, Turkey 44 B3 36 42N 37 6 E
Kiliya, Ukraine 17 F15 45 28N 29 16 E
Kilkee, Ireland 13 D2 52 41N 9 39W
Kilkeel, U.K. 13 B5 54 4N 6 0W
Kilkenny, Ireland 13 D4 52 39N 7 15W
Kilkenny □, Ireland 13 D4 52 35N 7 15W
Kilkieran B., Ireland 13 C2 53 20N 9 41W
Kilkís, Greece 21 D10 40 58N 22 57 E
Killala, Ireland 13 B2 54 13N 9 12W
Killala B., Ireland 13 B2 54 16N 9 8W
Killaloe, Ireland 13 D3 52 48N 8 28W
Killaloe Station, Canada 78 A7 45 33N 77 25W
Killarney, Australia 63 D5 28 20S 152 18 E
Killarney, Canada 73 D9 49 10N 99 40W
Killarney, Ireland 13 D2 52 4N 9 30W
Killary Harbour, Ireland 13 C2 53 38N 9 52W
Killdeer, U.S.A. 80 B3 47 26N 102 48W
Killeen, U.S.A. 81 K6 31 7N 97 44W
Killin, U.K. 12 E4 56 28N 4 19W
Killíni, Greece 21 F10 37 54N 22 25 E
Killorglin, Ireland 13 D2 52 6N 9 47W
Killybegs, Ireland 13 B3 54 38N 8 26W
Kilmarnock, U.K. 12 F4 55 37N 4 29W
Kilmore, Australia 63 F3 37 25S 144 53 E

Kilondo, *Tanzania* **55 D3** 9 45S 34 20 E
Kilosa, *Tanzania* **54 D4** 6 48S 37 0 E
Kilrush, *Ireland* **13 D2** 52 38N 9 29W
Kilwa Kisiwani, *Tanzania* **55 D4** 8 58S 39 32 E
Kilwa Kivinje, *Tanzania* **55 D4** 8 45S 39 25 E
Kilwa Masoko, *Tanzania* **55 D4** 8 55S 39 30 E
Kilwinning, *U.K.* **12 F4** 55 39N 4 43W
Kim, *U.S.A.* **81 G3** 37 15N 103 21W
Kimaam, *Indonesia* **37 F9** 7 58S 138 53 E
Kimamba, *Tanzania* **54 D4** 6 45S 37 10 E
Kimba, *Australia* **63 E2** 33 8S 136 23 E
Kimball, *Nebr., U.S.A.* **80 E3** 41 14N 103 40W
Kimball, *S. Dak., U.S.A.* **80 D5** 43 45N 98 57W
Kimberley, *Australia* **60 C4** 16 20S 127 0 E
Kimberley, *Canada* **72 D5** 49 40N 115 59W
Kimberley, *S. Africa* **56 D3** 28 43S 24 46 E
Kimberly, *U.S.A.* **82 E6** 42 32N 114 22W
Kimch'aek, *N. Korea* **35 D15** 40 40N 129 10 E
Kimch'ŏn, *S. Korea* **35 F15** 36 11N 128 4 E
Kimje, *S. Korea* **35 G14** 35 48N 126 45 E
Kimmirut, *Canada* **69 B13** 62 50N 69 50W
Kimpese, *Dem. Rep. of the Congo* **52 F2** 5 35S 14 26 E
Kimry, *Russia* **24 C6** 56 55N 37 15 E
Kinabalu, Gunong, *Malaysia* **36 C5** 6 3N 116 14 E
Kinaskan L., *Canada* **72 B2** 57 38N 130 8W
Kinbasket L., *Canada* **72 C5** 52 0N 118 10W
Kincardine, *Canada* **78 B3** 44 10N 81 40W
Kincolith, *Canada* **72 B3** 55 0N 129 57W
Kinda, *Dem. Rep. of the Congo* **55 D2** 9 18S 25 4 E
Kinde, *U.S.A.* **78 C2** 43 56N 83 0W
Kinder Scout, *U.K.* **10 D6** 53 24N 1 52W
Kindersley, *Canada* **73 C7** 51 30N 109 10W
Kindia, *Guinea* **50 F3** 10 0N 12 52W
Kindu, *Dem. Rep. of the Congo* **54 C2** 2 55S 25 50 E
Kineshma, *Russia* **24 C7** 57 30N 42 5 E
Kinesi, *Tanzania* **54 C3** 1 25S 33 50 E
King, L., *Australia* **61 F2** 33 10S 119 35 E
King, Mt., *Australia* **62 D4** 25 10S 147 30 E
King City, *U.S.A.* **84 J5** 36 13N 121 8W
King Cr. →, *Australia* **62 C2** 24 35S 139 30 E
King Edward →, *Australia* **60 B4** 14 14S 126 35 E
King Frederick VI Land = Kong Frederik VI Kyst, *Greenland* **4 C5** 63 0N 43 0W
King George B., *Falk. Is.* **96 G4** 51 30S 60 30W
King George I., *Antarctica* **5 C18** 60 0S 60 0W
King George Is., *Canada* **69 C11** 57 20N 80 30W
King I. = Kadan Kyun, *Burma* **38 F2** 12 30N 98 20 E
King I., *Australia* **62 F3** 39 50S 144 0 E
King I., *Canada* **72 C3** 52 10N 127 40W
King Leopold Ranges, *Australia* **60 C4** 17 30S 125 45 E
King of Prussia, *U.S.A.* **79 F9** 40 5N 75 23W
King Sd., *Australia* **60 C3** 16 50S 123 20 E
King William I., *Canada* **68 B10** 69 10N 97 25W
King William's Town, *S. Africa* **56 E4** 32 51S 27 22 E
Kingaok = Bathurst Inlet, *Canada* **68 B9** 66 50N 108 1W
Kingaroy, *Australia* **63 D5** 26 32S 151 51 E
Kingfisher, *U.S.A.* **81 H6** 35 52N 97 56W
Kingirbān, *Iraq* **44 C5** 34 40N 44 54 E
Kingisepp = Kuressaare, *Estonia* **9 G20** 58 15N 22 30 E
Kingman, *Ariz., U.S.A.* **85 K12** 35 12N 114 4W
Kingman, *Kans., U.S.A.* **81 G5** 37 39N 98 7W
Kingoonya, *Australia* **63 E2** 30 55S 135 19 E
Kingri, *Pakistan* **42 D3** 30 27N 69 49 E
Kings →, *U.S.A.* **84 J7** 36 3N 119 50W
Kings Canyon Nat. Park, *U.S.A.* **84 J8** 36 50N 118 40W
King's Lynn, *U.K.* **10 E8** 52 45N 0 24 E
Kings Mountain, *U.S.A.* **77 H5** 35 15N 81 20W
Kings Park, *U.S.A.* **79 F11** 40 53N 73 16W
King's Peak, *U.S.A.* **82 F8** 40 46N 110 27W
Kingsbridge, *U.K.* **11 G4** 50 17N 3 47W
Kingsburg, *U.S.A.* **84 J7** 36 31N 119 33W
Kingscote, *Australia* **63 F2** 35 40S 137 38 E
Kingscourt, *Ireland* **13 C5** 53 55N 6 48W
Kingsford, *U.S.A.* **76 C1** 45 48N 88 4W
Kingsland, *U.S.A.* **77 K5** 30 48N 81 41W
Kingsley, *U.S.A.* **80 D7** 42 35N 95 58W
Kingsport, *U.S.A.* **77 G4** 36 33N 82 33W
Kingston, *Canada* **79 B8** 44 14N 76 30W
Kingston, *Jamaica* **88 C4** 18 0N 76 50W
Kingston, *N.Z.* **59 L2** 45 20S 168 43 E
Kingston, *N.H., U.S.A.* **79 D13** 42 56N 71 3W
Kingston, *N.Y., U.S.A.* **79 E11** 41 56N 73 59W
Kingston, *Pa., U.S.A.* **79 E9** 41 16N 75 54W
Kingston, *R.I., U.S.A.* **79 E13** 41 29N 71 30W
Kingston Pk., *U.S.A.* **85 K11** 35 45N 115 54W
Kingston South East, *Australia* **63 F2** 36 51S 139 55 E
Kingston upon Hull, *U.K.* **10 D7** 53 45N 0 21W
Kingston upon Hull □, *U.K.* **10 D7** 53 45N 0 21W
Kingston-upon-Thames □, *U.K.* **11 F7** 51 24N 0 17W
Kingstown, *St. Vincent* **89 D7** 13 10N 61 10W
Kingstree, *U.S.A.* **77 J6** 33 40N 79 50W
Kingsville, *Canada* **78 D2** 42 2N 82 45W
Kingsville, *U.S.A.* **81 M6** 27 31N 97 52W
Kingussie, *U.K.* **12 D4** 57 6N 4 2W
Kingwood, *U.S.A.* **81 K7** 29 54N 95 18W
Kınık, *Turkey* **21 E12** 39 6N 27 24 E
Kinistino, *Canada* **73 C7** 52 57N 105 2W
Kinkala, *Congo* **52 E2** 4 18S 14 49 E
Kinki □, *Japan* **31 H8** 33 45N 136 0 E
Kinleith, *N.Z.* **59 H5** 38 20S 175 56 E
Kinmount, *Canada* **78 B6** 44 48N 78 45W
Kinna, *Sweden* **9 H15** 57 32N 12 42 E
Kinnairds Hd., *U.K.* **12 D6** 57 43N 2 1W
Kinnarodden, *Norway* **6 A11** 71 8N 27 40 E
Kinngait = Cape Dorset, *Canada* **69 B12** 64 14N 76 32W
Kino, *Mexico* **86 B2** 28 45N 111 59W
Kinoje →, *Canada* **70 B3** 52 8N 81 25W
Kinomoto, *Japan* **31 G8** 35 30N 136 13 E
Kinoni, *Uganda* **54 C3** 0 41S 30 28 E
Kinoosao, *Canada* **73 B8** 57 5N 102 1W
Kinross, *U.K.* **12 E5** 56 13N 3 25W
Kinsale, *Ireland* **13 E3** 51 42N 8 31W
Kinsale, Old Hd. of, *Ireland* **13 E3** 51 37N 8 33W
Kinsha = Chang Jiang →, *China* **33 C7** 31 48N 121 10 E
Kinshasa, *Dem. Rep. of the Congo* **52 E3** 4 20S 15 15 E
Kinsley, *U.S.A.* **81 G5** 37 55N 99 25W
Kinsman, *U.S.A.* **78 E4** 41 26N 80 35W
Kinston, *U.S.A.* **77 H7** 35 16N 77 35W
Kintore Ra., *Australia* **60 D4** 23 15S 128 47 E
Kintyre, *U.K.* **12 F3** 55 30N 5 35W
Kintyre, Mull of, *U.K.* **12 F3** 55 17N 5 47W
Kinushseo →, *Canada* **70 A3** 55 15N 83 45W
Kinuso, *Canada* **72 B5** 55 20N 115 25W
Kinyangiri, *Tanzania* **54 C3** 4 25S 34 37 E
Kinzua, *U.S.A.* **78 E6** 41 52N 78 58W
Kinzua Dam, *U.S.A.* **78 E6** 41 53N 79 0W
Kiosk, *Canada* **70 C4** 46 6N 78 53W
Kiowa, *Kans., U.S.A.* **81 G5** 37 1N 98 29W
Kiowa, *Okla., U.S.A.* **81 H7** 34 43N 95 54W
Kipahigan L., *Canada* **73 B8** 55 20N 101 55W
Kipanga, *Tanzania* **54 D4** 6 15S 35 20 E
Kiparissia, *Greece* **21 F9** 37 15N 21 40 E
Kiparissiakós Kólpos, *Greece* **21 F9** 37 25N 21 25 E
Kipawa, L., *Canada* **70 C4** 46 50N 79 0W
Kipembawe, *Tanzania* **54 D3** 7 38S 33 27 E
Kipengere Ra., *Tanzania* **55 D3** 9 12S 34 15 E
Kipili, *Tanzania* **54 D3** 7 28S 30 32 E
Kipini, *Kenya* **54 C5** 2 30S 40 32 E
Kipling, *Canada* **73 C8** 50 6N 102 38W
Kippure, *Ireland* **13 C5** 53 11N 6 21W
Kipushi, *Dem. Rep. of the Congo* **55 E2** 11 48S 27 12 E
Kiranomena, *Madag.* **57 B8** 18 17S 46 2 E
Kirensk, *Russia* **27 D11** 57 50N 107 55 E
Kirghizia = Kyrgyzstan ■, *Asia* **26 E8** 42 0N 75 0 E
Kirghizstan = Kyrgyzstan ■, *Asia* **26 E8** 42 0N 75 0 E
Kirgiziya Steppe, *Eurasia* **25 E10** 50 0N 55 0 E
Kiribati ■, *Pac. Oc.* **64 H10** 5 0S 180 0 E
Kırıkkale, *Turkey* **25 G5** 39 51N 33 32 E
Kirillov, *Russia* **24 C6** 59 49N 38 24 E
Kirin = Jilin, *China* **35 C14** 43 44N 126 30 E
Kirinyaga = Kenya, Mt., *Kenya* **54 C4** 0 10S 37 18 E
Kiritimati, *Kiribati* **65 G12** 1 58N 157 27W
Kirkby, *U.K.* **10 D5** 53 30N 2 54W
Kirkby Lonsdale, *U.K.* **10 C5** 54 12N 2 36W
Kirkcaldy, *U.K.* **12 E5** 56 7N 3 9W
Kirkcudbright, *U.K.* **12 G4** 54 50N 4 2W
Kirkee, *India* **40 K8** 18 34N 73 56 E
Kirkenes, *Norway* **8 B23** 69 40N 30 5 E
Kirkfield, *Canada* **78 B6** 44 34N 78 59W
Kirkjubæjarklaustur, *Iceland* **8 E4** 63 47N 18 4W
Kirkkonummi, *Finland* **9 F21** 60 8N 24 26 E
Kirkland Lake, *Canada* **70 C3** 48 9N 80 2W
Kırklareli, *Turkey* **21 D12** 41 44N 27 15 E
Kirksville, *U.S.A.* **80 E8** 40 12N 92 35W
Kirkūk, *Iraq* **44 C5** 35 30N 44 21 E
Kirkwall, *U.K.* **12 C6** 58 59N 2 58W
Kirkwood, *S. Africa* **56 E4** 33 22S 25 15 E
Kirov, *Russia* **24 C8** 58 35N 49 40 E
Kirovabad = Gäncä, *Azerbaijan* **25 F8** 40 45N 46 20 E
Kirovakan = Vanadzor, *Armenia* **25 F7** 40 48N 44 30 E
Kirovograd = Kirovohrad, *Ukraine* **25 E5** 48 35N 32 20 E
Kirovohrad, *Ukraine* **25 E5** 48 35N 32 20 E
Kirovsk = Babadayhan, *Turkmenistan* **26 F7** 37 42N 60 23 E
Kirovsk, *Russia* **24 A5** 67 32N 33 41 E
Kirovskiy, *Kamchatka, Russia* **27 D16** 54 27N 155 42 E
Kirovskiy, *Primorsk, Russia* **30 B6** 45 7N 133 30 E
Kirriemuir, *U.K.* **12 E5** 56 41N 3 1W
Kirsanov, *Russia* **24 D7** 52 35N 42 40 E
Kırşehir, *Turkey* **25 G5** 39 14N 34 5 E
Kirthar Range, *Pakistan* **42 F2** 27 0N 67 0 E
Kirtland, *U.S.A.* **83 H9** 36 44N 108 21W
Kiruna, *Sweden* **8 C19** 67 52N 20 15 E
Kirundu, *Dem. Rep. of the Congo* **54 C2** 0 50S 25 35 E
Kiryū, *Japan* **31 F9** 36 24N 139 20 E
Kisaga, *Tanzania* **54 C3** 4 30S 34 23 E
Kisalaya, *Nic.* **88 D3** 14 40N 84 3W
Kisámou, Kólpos, *Greece* **23 D5** 35 30N 23 38 E
Kisanga, *Dem. Rep. of the Congo* **54 B2** 2 30N 26 35 E
Kisangani, *Dem. Rep. of the Congo* **54 B2** 0 35N 25 15 E
Kisar, *Indonesia* **37 F7** 8 5S 127 10 E
Kisarawe, *Tanzania* **54 D4** 6 53S 39 0 E
Kisarazu, *Japan* **31 G9** 35 23N 139 55 E
Kishanganga →, *Pakistan* **43 B5** 34 18N 73 28 E
Kishanganj, *India* **43 F13** 26 3N 88 14 E
Kishangarh, *Raj., India* **42 F6** 26 34N 74 52 E
Kishangarh, *Raj., India* **42 F4** 27 50N 70 30 E
Kishinev = Chişinău, *Moldova* **17 E15** 47 2N 28 50 E
Kishiwada, *Japan* **31 G7** 34 28N 135 22 E
Kishtwar, *India* **43 C6** 33 20N 75 48 E
Kisii, *Kenya* **54 C3** 0 40S 34 45 E
Kisiju, *Tanzania* **54 D4** 7 23S 39 19 E
Kisizi, *Uganda* **54 C2** 1 0S 29 58 E
Kiskőrös, *Hungary* **17 E10** 46 37N 19 20 E
Kiskunfélegyháza, *Hungary* **17 E10** 46 42N 19 53 E
Kiskunhalas, *Hungary* **17 E10** 46 28N 19 37 E
Kislovodsk, *Russia* **25 F7** 43 50N 42 45 E
Kismayu = Chisimaio, *Somali Rep.* **49 G8** 0 22S 42 32 E
Kiso-Gawa →, *Japan* **31 G8** 35 20N 136 45 E
Kiso-Sammyaku, *Japan* **31 G8** 35 45N 137 45 E
Kisofukushima, *Japan* **31 G8** 35 52N 137 43 E
Kisoro, *Uganda* **54 C2** 1 17S 29 48 E
Kissidougou, *Guinea* **50 G3** 9 5N 10 5W
Kissimmee, *U.S.A.* **77 L5** 28 18N 81 24W
Kissimmee →, *U.S.A.* **77 M5** 27 9N 80 52W
Kississing L., *Canada* **73 B8** 55 10N 101 20W
Kissónerga, *Cyprus* **23 E11** 34 49N 32 24 E
Kisumu, *Kenya* **54 C3** 0 3S 34 45 E
Kiswani, *Tanzania* **54 C4** 4 5S 37 57 E
Kiswere, *Tanzania* **55 D4** 9 27S 39 30 E
Kit Carson, *U.S.A.* **80 F3** 38 46N 102 48W
Kita, *Mali* **50 F4** 13 5N 9 25W
Kitaibaraki, *Japan* **31 F10** 36 50N 140 45 E
Kitakami, *Japan* **30 E10** 39 20N 141 10 E
Kitakami-Gawa →, *Japan* **30 E10** 38 25N 141 19 E
Kitakami-Sammyaku, *Japan* **30 E10** 39 30N 141 30 E
Kitakata, *Japan* **30 F9** 37 39N 139 52 E
Kitakyūshū, *Japan* **31 H5** 33 50N 130 50 E
Kitale, *Kenya* **54 B4** 1 0N 35 0 E
Kitami, *Japan* **30 C11** 43 48N 143 54 E
Kitami-Sammyaku, *Japan* **30 B11** 44 22N 142 43 E
Kitangiri, L., *Tanzania* **54 C3** 4 5S 34 20 E
Kitaya, *Tanzania* **55 E5** 10 38S 40 8 E
Kitchener, *Canada* **78 C4** 43 27N 80 29W
Kitega = Gitega, *Burundi* **54 C2** 3 26S 29 56 E
Kitengo, *Dem. Rep. of the Congo* **54 D1** 7 26S 24 8 E
Kitgum, *Uganda* **54 B3** 3 17N 32 52 E
Kíthira, *Greece* **21 F10** 36 8N 23 0 E
Kíthnos, *Greece* **21 F11** 37 26N 24 27 E
Kiti, *Cyprus* **23 E12** 34 50N 33 34 E
Kiti, C., *Cyprus* **23 E12** 34 48N 33 36 E
Kitimat, *Canada* **72 C3** 54 3N 128 38W
Kitinen →, *Finland* **8 C22** 67 14N 27 27 E
Kitsuki, *Japan* **31 H5** 33 25N 131 37 E
Kittakittaooloo, L., *Australia* **63 D2** 28 3S 138 14 E
Kittanning, *U.S.A.* **78 F5** 40 49N 79 31W
Kittatinny Mts., *U.S.A.* **79 F10** 41 0N 75 0W
Kittery, *U.S.A.* **77 D10** 43 5N 70 45W
Kittilä, *Finland* **8 C21** 67 40N 24 51 E
Kitui, *Kenya* **54 C4** 1 17S 38 0 E
Kitwanga, *Canada* **72 B3** 55 6N 128 4W
Kitwe, *Zambia* **55 E2** 12 54S 28 13 E
Kivarli, *India* **42 G5** 24 33N 72 46 E
Kivertsi, *Ukraine* **17 C13** 50 50N 25 28 E
Kividhes, *Cyprus* **23 E11** 34 46N 32 51 E
Kivu, L., *Dem. Rep. of the Congo* **54 C2** 1 48S 29 0 E
Kiyev = Kyyiv, *Ukraine* **17 C16** 50 30N 30 28 E
Kiyevskoye Vdkhr. = Kyyivske Vdskh., *Ukraine* **17 C16** 51 0N 30 25 E
Kizel, *Russia* **24 C10** 59 3N 57 40 E
Kiziguru, *Rwanda* **54 C3** 1 46S 30 23 E
Kızıl Irmak →, *Turkey* **25 F6** 41 44N 35 58 E
Kizil Jilga, *China* **43 B8** 35 26N 78 50 E
Kızıltepe, *Turkey* **44 B4** 37 12N 40 35 E
Kizimkazi, *Tanzania* **54 D4** 6 28S 39 30 E
Kizlyar, *Russia* **25 F8** 43 51N 46 40 E
Kizyl-Arvat = Gyzylarbat, *Turkmenistan* **26 F6** 39 4N 56 23 E
Kjölur, *Iceland* **8 D4** 64 50N 19 25W
Kladno, *Czech Rep.* **16 C8** 50 10N 14 7 E
Klaeng, *Thailand* **38 F3** 12 47N 101 39 E
Klagenfurt, *Austria* **16 E8** 46 38N 14 20 E
Klaipėda, *Lithuania* **9 J19** 55 43N 21 10 E
Klaksvík, *Færoe Is.* **8 E9** 62 14N 6 35W
Klamath →, *U.S.A.* **82 F1** 41 33N 124 5W
Klamath Falls, *U.S.A.* **82 E3** 42 13N 121 46W
Klamath Mts., *U.S.A.* **82 F2** 41 20N 123 0W
Klamono, *Indonesia* **37 E8** 1 8S 131 30 E
Klappan →, *Canada* **72 B3** 58 0N 129 43W
Klarälven →, *Sweden* **9 G15** 59 23N 13 32 E
Klatovy, *Czech Rep.* **16 D7** 49 23N 13 18 E
Klawer, *S. Africa* **56 E2** 31 44S 18 36 E
Klazienaveen, *Neths.* **15 B6** 52 44N 7 0 E
Kleena Kleene, *Canada* **72 C4** 52 0N 124 59W
Klein-Karas, *Namibia* **56 D2** 27 33S 18 7 E
Klerksdorp, *S. Africa* **56 D4** 26 53S 26 38 E
Kletsk = Klyetsk, *Belarus* **17 B14** 53 5N 26 45 E
Kletskiy, *Russia* **25 E7** 49 16N 43 11 E
Klickitat, *U.S.A.* **82 D3** 45 49N 121 9W
Klickitat →, *U.S.A.* **84 E5** 45 42N 121 17W
Klidhes, *Cyprus* **23 D13** 35 42N 34 36 E
Klinaklini →, *Canada* **72 C3** 51 21N 125 40W
Klip →, *S. Africa* **57 D4** 27 3S 29 3 E
Klipdale, *S. Africa* **56 E2** 34 19S 19 57 E
Klipplaat, *S. Africa* **56 E3** 33 1S 24 22 E
Kłodzko, *Poland* **17 C9** 50 28N 16 38 E
Klouto, *Togo* **50 G6** 6 57N 0 44 E
Kluane L., *Canada* **68 B6** 61 15N 138 40W
Kluane Nat. Park, *Canada* **72 A1** 60 45N 139 30W
Kluczbork, *Poland* **17 C10** 50 58N 18 12 E
Klukwan, *U.S.A.* **72 B1** 59 24N 135 54W
Klyetsk, *Belarus* **17 B14** 53 5N 26 45 E
Klyuchevskaya, Gora, *Russia* **27 D17** 55 50N 160 30 E
Knaresborough, *U.K.* **10 C6** 54 1N 1 28W
Knee L., *Man., Canada* **70 A1** 55 3N 94 45W
Knee L., *Sask., Canada* **73 B7** 55 51N 107 0W
Knight Inlet, *Canada* **72 C3** 50 45N 125 40W
Knighton, *U.K.* **11 E4** 52 21N 3 3W
Knights Ferry, *U.S.A.* **84 H6** 37 50N 120 40W
Knights Landing, *U.S.A.* **84 G5** 38 48N 121 43W
Knob, C., *Australia* **61 F2** 34 32S 119 16 E
Knock, *Ireland* **13 C3** 53 48N 8 55W
Knockmealdown Mts., *Ireland* **13 D4** 52 14N 7 56W
Knokke-Heist, *Belgium* **15 C3** 51 21N 3 17 E
Knossós, *Greece* **23 D7** 35 16N 25 10 E
Knowlton, *Canada* **79 A12** 45 13N 72 31W
Knox, *U.S.A.* **76 E2** 41 18N 86 37W
Knox Coast, *Antarctica* **5 C8** 66 30S 108 0 E
Knoxville, *Iowa, U.S.A.* **80 E8** 41 19N 93 6W
Knoxville, *Pa., U.S.A.* **78 E7** 41 57N 77 27W
Knoxville, *Tenn., U.S.A.* **77 H4** 35 58N 83 55W
Knysna, *S. Africa* **56 E3** 34 2S 23 2 E
Ko Kha, *Thailand* **38 C2** 18 11N 99 24 E
Koartac = Quaqtaq, *Canada* **69 B13** 60 55N 69 40W
Koba, *Indonesia* **37 F8** 6 37S 134 37 E
Kobarid, *Slovenia* **16 E7** 46 15N 13 30 E
Kobayashi, *Japan* **31 J5** 31 56N 130 59 E
Kobdo = Hovd, *Mongolia* **32 B4** 48 2N 91 37 E
Kōbe, *Japan* **31 G7** 34 45N 135 10 E
København, *Denmark* **9 J15** 55 41N 12 34 E
Kōbi-Sho, *Japan* **31 M1** 25 56N 123 41 E
Koblenz, *Germany* **16 C4** 50 21N 7 36 E
Kobryn, *Belarus* **17 B13** 52 15N 24 22 E
Kocaeli, *Turkey* **25 F4** 40 45N 29 50 E
Kočani, *Macedonia* **21 D10** 41 55N 22 25 E
Koch Bihar, *India* **41 F16** 26 22N 89 29 E
Kochang, *S. Korea* **35 G14** 35 41N 127 55 E
Kochas, *India* **43 G10** 25 15N 83 56 E
Kochi = Cochin, *India* **40 Q10** 9 58N 76 20 E
Kōchi, *Japan* **31 H6** 33 30N 133 35 E
Kōchi □, *Japan* **31 H6** 33 40N 133 30 E
Kochiu = Gejiu, *China* **32 D5** 23 20N 103 10 E
Kodarma, *India* **43 G11** 24 28N 85 36 E
Kodiak, *U.S.A.* **68 C4** 57 47N 152 24W
Kodiak I., *U.S.A.* **68 C4** 57 30N 152 45W
Kodinar, *India* **42 J4** 20 46N 70 46 E
Koedoesberge, *S. Africa* **56 E3** 32 40S 20 11 E
Koes, *Namibia* **56 D2** 26 0S 19 15 E
Koffiefontein, *S. Africa* **56 D4** 29 30S 25 0 E
Kofiau, *Indonesia* **37 E7** 1 11S 129 50 E
Koforidua, *Ghana* **50 G5** 6 3N 0 17W
Kōfu, *Japan* **31 G9** 35 40N 138 30 E
Koga, *Japan* **31 F9** 36 11N 139 43 E
Kogaluk →, *Canada* **71 A7** 56 12N 61 44W
Køge, *Denmark* **9 J15** 55 27N 12 11 E
Koh-i-Khurd, *Afghan.* **42 C1** 33 30N 65 59 E
Koh-i-Maran, *Pakistan* **42 E2** 29 18N 66 50 E
Kohat, *Pakistan* **42 C4** 33 40N 71 29 E
Kohima, *India* **41 G19** 25 35N 94 10 E
Kohkīlūyeh va Būyer Aḥmadi □, *Iran* **45 D6** 31 30N 50 30 E
Kohler Ra., *Antarctica* **5 D15** 77 0S 110 0W
Kohlu, *Pakistan* **42 E3** 29 54N 69 15 E
Kohtla-Järve, *Estonia* **9 G22** 59 20N 27 20 E
Koillismaa, *Finland* **8 D23** 65 44N 28 36 E
Koin-dong, *N. Korea* **35 D14** 40 28N 126 18 E
Kojŏ, *N. Korea* **35 E14** 38 58N 127 58 E
Kojonup, *Australia* **61 F2** 33 48S 117 10 E
Kojūr, *Iran* **45 B6** 36 23N 51 43 E
Kokand = Qŭqon, *Uzbekistan* **26 E8** 40 30N 70 57 E
Kokas, *Indonesia* **37 E8** 2 42S 132 26 E
Kokchetav = Kökshetaū, *Kazakstan* **26 D7** 53 20N 69 25 E
Kokemäenjoki →, *Finland* **9 F19** 61 32N 21 44 E
Kokkola, *Finland* **8 E20** 63 50N 23 8 E
Koko Kyunzu, *Burma* **41 M18** 14 10N 93 25 E
Kokomo, *U.S.A.* **76 E2** 40 29N 86 8W
Koksan, *N. Korea* **35 E14** 38 46N 126 40 E
Kökshetaū, *Kazakstan* **26 D7** 53 20N 69 25 E
Koksoak →, *Canada* **69 C13** 58 30N 68 10W
Kokstad, *S. Africa* **57 E4** 30 32S 29 29 E
Kokubu, *Japan* **31 J5** 31 44N 130 46 E
Kola, *Indonesia* **37 F8** 5 35S 134 30 E
Kola, *Russia* **24 A5** 68 45N 33 8 E
Kola Pen. = Kolskiy Poluostrov, *Russia* **24 A6** 67 30N 38 0 E
Kolachi →, *Pakistan* **42 F2** 27 8N 67 2 E
Kolahoi, *India* **43 B6** 34 12N 75 22 E
Kolaka, *Indonesia* **37 E6** 4 3S 121 46 E
Kolar, *India* **40 N11** 13 12N 78 15 E
Kolar Gold Fields, *India* **40 N11** 12 58N 78 16 E
Kolaras, *India* **42 G6** 25 14N 77 36 E
Kolari, *Finland* **8 C20** 67 20N 23 48 E
Kolayat, *India* **40 F8** 27 50N 72 50 E
Kolchugino = Leninsk-Kuznetskiy, *Russia* **26 D9** 54 44N 86 10 E
Kolding, *Denmark* **9 J13** 55 30N 9 29 E
Kolepom = Dolak, Pulau, *Indonesia* **37 F9** 8 0S 138 30 E
Kolguyev, Ostrov, *Russia* **24 A8** 69 20N 48 30 E
Kolhapur, *India* **40 L9** 16 43N 74 15 E
Kolín, *Czech Rep.* **16 C8** 50 2N 15 9 E
Kolkas rags, *Latvia* **9 H20** 57 46N 22 37 E
Kolkata, *India* **43 H13** 22 36N 88 24 E
Kollam = Quilon, *India* **40 Q10** 8 50N 76 38 E
Kollum, *Neths.* **15 A6** 53 17N 6 10 E
Kolmanskop, *Namibia* **56 D2** 26 45S 15 14 E
Köln, *Germany* **16 C4** 50 56N 6 57 E
Koło, *Poland* **17 B10** 52 14N 18 40 E
Kołobrzeg, *Poland* **16 A8** 54 10N 15 35 E
Kolomna, *Russia* **24 C6** 55 8N 38 45 E
Kolomyya, *Ukraine* **17 D13** 48 31N 25 2 E
Kolonodale, *Indonesia* **37 E6** 2 0S 121 19 E
Kolosib, *India* **41 G18** 24 15N 92 45 E
Kolpashevo, *Russia* **26 D9** 58 20N 83 5 E
Kolpino, *Russia* **24 C5** 59 44N 30 39 E
Kolskiy Poluostrov, *Russia* **24 A6** 67 30N 38 0 E
Kolskiy Zaliv, *Russia* **24 A5** 69 23N 34 0 E
Kolwezi, *Dem. Rep. of the Congo* **55 E2** 10 40S 25 25 E
Kolyma →, *Russia* **27 C17** 69 30N 161 0 E
Kolymskoye Nagorye, *Russia* **27 C16** 63 0N 157 0 E
Kôm Ombo, *Egypt* **51 D12** 24 25N 32 52 E
Komandorskiye Is. = Komandorskiye Ostrova, *Russia* **27 D17** 55 0N 167 0 E
Komandorskiye Ostrova, *Russia* **27 D17** 55 0N 167 0 E
Komárno, *Slovak Rep.* **17 E10** 47 49N 18 5 E
Komatipoort, *S. Africa* **57 D5** 25 25S 31 55 E
Komatou Yialou, *Cyprus* **23 D13** 35 25N 34 8 E
Komatsu, *Japan* **31 F8** 36 25N 136 30 E
Komatsushima, *Japan* **31 H7** 34 0N 134 35 E
Komi □, *Russia* **24 B10** 64 0N 55 0 E
Kommunarsk = Alchevsk, *Ukraine* **25 E6** 48 30N 38 45 E
Kommunizma, Pik, *Tajikistan* **26 F8** 39 0N 72 2 E
Komodo, *Indonesia* **37 F5** 8 37S 119 20 E
Komoran, Pulau, *Indonesia* **37 F9** 8 18S 138 45 E
Komoro, *Japan* **31 F9** 36 19N 138 26 E
Komotini, *Greece* **21 D11** 41 9N 25 26 E
Kompasberg, *S. Africa* **56 E3** 31 45S 24 32 E
Kompong Bang, *Cambodia* **39 F5** 12 24N 104 40 E
Kompong Cham, *Cambodia* **39 F5** 12 0N 105 30 E
Kompong Chhnang = Kampang Chhnang, *Cambodia* **39 F5** 12 20N 104 35 E
Kompong Chikreng, *Cambodia* **38 F5** 13 5N 104 18 E
Kompong Kleang, *Cambodia* **38 F5** 13 6N 104 8 E
Kompong Luong, *Cambodia* **39 G5** 11 49N 104 48 E
Kompong Pranak, *Cambodia* **38 F5** 13 35N 104 55 E
Kompong Som = Kampong Saom, *Cambodia* **39 G4** 10 38N 103 30 E
Kompong Som, Chhung = Kampong Saom, Chaak, *Cambodia* **39 G4** 10 50N 103 32 E
Kompong Speu, *Cambodia* **39 G5** 11 26N 104 32 E
Kompong Sralao, *Cambodia* **38 E5** 14 5N 105 46 E
Kompong Thom, *Cambodia* **38 F5** 12 35N 104 51 E
Kompong Trabeck, *Cambodia* **38 F5** 13 6N 105 14 E
Kompong Trabeck, *Cambodia* **39 G5** 11 9N 105 28 E
Kompong Trach, *Cambodia* **39 G5** 11 25N 105 48 E
Kompong Tralach, *Cambodia* **39 G5** 11 54N 104 47 E
Komrat = Comrat, *Moldova* **17 E15** 46 18N 28 40 E
Komsberg, *S. Africa* **56 E3** 32 40S 20 45 E
Komsomolets, Ostrov, *Russia* **27 A10** 80 30N 95 0 E
Komsomolsk, *Russia* **27 D14** 50 30N 137 0 E
Kon Tum, *Vietnam* **38 E7** 14 24N 108 0 E
Kon Tum, Plateau du, *Vietnam* **38 E7** 14 30N 108 30 E
Konarhā □, *Afghan.* **40 B7** 34 30N 71 3 E
Konārī, *Iran* **45 D6** 28 13N 51 36 E
Konch, *India* **43 G8** 26 0N 79 10 E
Konde, *Tanzania* **54 C4** 4 57S 39 45 E
Kondinin, *Australia* **61 F2** 32 34S 118 8 E
Kondoa, *Tanzania* **54 C4** 4 55S 35 50 E
Kondókali, *Greece* **23 A3** 39 38N 19 51 E
Kondopaga, *Russia* **24 B5** 62 12N 34 17 E
Kondratyevo, *Russia* **27 D10** 57 22N 98 15 E

Köneürgench, Turkmenistan 26 E6 42 19N 59 10 E
Konevo, Russia 24 B6 62 8N 39 20 E
Kong = Khong →, Cambodia 38 F5 13 32N 105 58 E
Kong, Ivory C. 50 G5 8 54N 4 36W
Kong, Koh, Cambodia 39 G4 11 20N 103 0 E
Kong Christian IX Land, Greenland 4 C6 68 0N 36 0W
Kong Christian X Land, Greenland 4 B6 74 0N 29 0W
Kong Frederik IX Land, Greenland 4 C5 67 0N 52 0W
Kong Frederik VI Kyst, Greenland 4 C5 63 0N 43 0W
Kong Frederik VIII Land, Greenland 4 B6 78 30N 26 0W
Kong Oscar Fjord, Greenland 4 B6 72 20N 24 0W
Kongju, S. Korea 35 F14 36 30N 127 0 E
Konglu, Burma 41 F20 27 13N 97 57 E
Kongola, Namibia 56 B3 17 45S 23 20 E
Kongolo, Kasai-Or., Dem. Rep. of the Congo 54 D1 5 26S 24 49 E
Kongolo, Katanga, Dem. Rep. of the Congo 54 D2 5 22S 27 0 E
Kongsberg, Norway 9 G13 59 39N 9 39 E
Kongsvinger, Norway 9 F15 60 12N 12 2 E
Kongwa, Tanzania 54 D4 6 11S 36 26 E
Koni, Dem. Rep. of the Congo 55 E2 10 40S 27 11 E
Koni, Mts., Dem. Rep. of the Congo 55 E2 10 36S 27 10 E
Königsberg = Kaliningrad, Russia 9 J19 54 42N 20 32 E
Konin, Poland 17 B10 52 12N 18 15 E
Konjic, Bos.-H. 21 C7 43 42N 17 58 E
Konkiep, Namibia 56 D2 26 49S 17 15 E
Konosha, Russia 24 B7 61 0N 40 5 E
Kōnosu, Japan 31 F9 36 3N 139 31 E
Konotop, Ukraine 25 D5 51 12N 33 7 E
Końskie, Poland 17 C11 51 15N 20 23 E
Konstanz, Germany 16 E5 47 40N 9 10 E
Kont, Iran 45 E9 26 55N 61 50 E
Kontagora, Nigeria 50 F7 10 23N 5 27 E
Konya, Turkey 25 G5 37 52N 32 35 E
Konza, Kenya 54 C4 1 45S 37 7 E
Koocanusa, L., Canada 82 B6 49 20N 115 15W
Kookynie, Australia 61 E3 29 17S 121 22 E
Koolyanobbing, Australia 61 F2 30 48S 119 36 E
Koonibba, Australia 63 E1 31 54S 133 25 E
Koorawatha, Australia 63 E4 34 2S 148 33 E
Koorda, Australia 61 F2 30 48S 117 35 E
Kooskia, U.S.A. 82 C6 46 9N 115 59W
Kootenay →, U.S.A. 72 D5 49 19N 117 39W
Kootenay L., Canada 72 D5 49 45N 116 50W
Kootenay Nat. Park, Canada 72 C5 51 0N 116 0W
Kootjieskolk, S. Africa 56 E3 31 15S 20 21 E
Kopaonik, Yugoslavia 21 C9 43 10N 20 50 E
Kópavogur, Iceland 8 D3 64 6N 21 55W
Koper, Slovenia 16 F7 45 31N 13 44 E
Kopervik, Norway 9 G11 59 17N 5 17 E
Kopet Dagh, Asia 45 B8 38 0N 58 0 E
Kopi, Australia 63 E2 33 24S 135 40 E
Köping, Sweden 9 G17 59 31N 16 3 E
Koppeh Dāgh = Kopet Dagh, Asia 45 B8 38 0N 58 0 E
Koppies, S. Africa 57 D4 27 20S 27 30 E
Koprivnica, Croatia 20 A7 46 12N 16 45 E
Kopychyntsi, Ukraine 17 D13 49 7N 25 58 E
Korab, Macedonia 21 D9 41 44N 20 40 E
Korakiána, Greece 23 A3 39 42N 19 45 E
Koral, India 42 J5 21 50N 73 12 E
Korba, India 43 H10 22 20N 82 45 E
Korbu, G., Malaysia 39 K3 4 41N 101 18 E
Korce = Korçë, Albania 21 D9 40 37N 20 50 E
Korçë, Albania 21 D9 40 37N 20 50 E
Korčula, Croatia 20 C7 42 56N 16 57 E
Kord Kūy, Iran 45 B7 36 48N 54 7 E
Kord Sheykh, Iran 45 D7 28 31N 52 53 E
Kordestān □, Iran 44 C5 36 0N 47 0 E
Kordofân, Sudan 51 F11 13 0N 29 0 E
Korea, North ■, Asia 35 E14 40 0N 127 0 E
Korea, South ■, Asia 35 G15 36 0N 128 0 E
Korea Bay, Korea 35 E13 39 0N 124 0 E
Korea Strait, Asia 35 H15 34 0N 129 30 E
Korets, Ukraine 17 C14 50 40N 27 5 E
Korhogo, Ivory C. 50 G4 9 29N 5 28W
Korinthiakós Kólpos, Greece 21 E10 38 16N 22 30 E
Kórinthos, Greece 21 F10 37 56N 22 55 E
Korissa, Límni, Greece 23 B3 39 27N 19 53 E
Kōriyama, Japan 30 F10 37 24N 140 23 E
Korla, China 32 B3 41 45N 86 4 E
Kormakiti, C., Cyprus 23 D11 35 23N 32 56 E
Korneshty = Corneşti, Moldova 17 E15 47 21N 28 1 E
Koro, Fiji 59 C8 17 19S 179 23 E
Koro, Ivory C. 50 G4 8 32N 7 30W
Koro Sea, Fiji 59 C9 17 30S 179 45W
Korogwe, Tanzania 54 D4 5 5S 38 25 E
Koronadal, Phil. 37 C6 6 12N 125 1 E
Koror, Palau 64 G5 7 20N 134 28 E
Körös →, Hungary 17 E11 46 43N 20 12 E
Korosten, Ukraine 17 C15 50 54N 28 36 E
Korostyshev, Ukraine 17 C15 50 19N 29 4 E
Korraraika, Helodranon' i, Madag. 57 B7 17 45S 43 57 E
Korsakov, Russia 27 E15 46 36N 142 42 E
Korshunovo, Russia 27 D12 58 37N 110 10 E
Korsør, Denmark 9 J14 55 20N 11 9 E
Kortrijk, Belgium 15 D3 50 50N 3 17 E
Korwai, India 42 G8 24 7N 78 5 E
Koryakskoye Nagorye, Russia 27 C18 61 0N 171 0 E
Koryŏng, S. Korea 35 G15 35 44N 128 15 E
Kos, Greece 21 F12 36 50N 27 15 E
Koschagyl, Kazakstan 25 E9 46 40N 54 0 E
Kościan, Poland 17 B9 52 5N 16 40 E
Kosciusko, U.S.A. 81 J10 33 4N 89 35W
Kosciuszko, Mt., Australia 63 F4 36 27S 148 16 E
Kosha, Sudan 51 D12 20 50N 30 30 E
K'oshih = Kashi, China 32 C2 39 30N 76 2 E
Koshiki-Rettō, Japan 31 J4 31 45N 129 49 E
Kosi, India 42 F7 27 48N 77 29 E
Kosi →, India 43 E8 28 41N 78 57 E
Košice, Slovak Rep. 17 D11 48 42N 21 15 E
Koskhinoú, Greece 23 C10 36 23N 28 13 E
Koslan, Russia 24 B8 63 34N 49 14 E
Kosŏng, N. Korea 35 E15 38 40N 128 22 E
Kosovo □, Yugoslavia 21 C9 42 30N 21 0 E
Kosovska Mitrovica, Kosovo, Yug. 21 C9 42 54N 20 52 E
Kossou, L. de, Ivory C. 50 G4 6 59N 5 31W
Koster, S. Africa 56 D4 25 52S 26 54 E
Kôstî, Sudan 51 F12 13 8N 32 43 E
Kostopil, Ukraine 17 C14 50 51N 26 22 E
Kostroma, Russia 24 C7 57 50N 40 58 E
Kostrzyn, Poland 16 B8 52 35N 14 39 E
Koszalin, Poland 16 A9 54 11N 16 8 E
Kot Addu, Pakistan 42 D4 30 30N 71 0 E
Kot Kapura, India 42 D6 30 35N 74 50 E
Kot Moman, Pakistan 42 C5 32 13N 73 0 E
Kot Sultan, Pakistan 42 D4 30 46N 70 56 E
Kota, India 42 G6 25 14N 75 49 E
Kota Baharu, Malaysia 39 J4 6 7N 102 14 E
Kota Barrage, India 42 G6 25 6N 75 51 E
Kota Belud, Malaysia 36 C5 6 21N 116 26 E
Kota Kinabalu, Malaysia 36 C5 6 0N 116 4 E
Kota Kubu Baharu, Malaysia 39 L3 3 34N 101 39 E
Kota Tinggi, Malaysia 39 M4 1 44N 103 53 E
Kotaagung, Indonesia 36 F2 5 38S 104 29 E
Kotabaru, Indonesia 36 E5 3 20S 116 20 E
Kotabumi, Indonesia 36 E2 4 49S 104 54 E
Kotamobagu, Indonesia 37 D6 0 57N 124 31 E
Kotcho L., Canada 72 B4 59 7N 121 12W
Kotdwara, India 43 E8 29 45N 78 32 E
Kotelnich, Russia 24 C8 58 22N 48 24 E
Kotelnikovo, Russia 25 E7 47 38N 43 8 E
Kotelnyy, Ostrov, Russia 27 B14 75 10N 139 0 E
Kothari →, India 42 G6 25 20N 75 4 E
Kothi, Chhattisgarh, India 43 H10 23 21N 82 3 E
Kothi, Mad. P., India 43 G9 24 45N 80 40 E
Kotiro, Pakistan 42 F2 26 17N 67 13 E
Kotka, Finland 9 F22 60 28N 26 58 E
Kotlas, Russia 24 B8 61 17N 46 43 E
Kotli, Pakistan 42 C5 33 30N 73 55 E
Kotma, India 43 H9 23 12N 81 58 E
Kotmul, Pakistan 43 B6 35 32N 75 10 E
Kotor, Montenegro, Yug. 21 C8 42 25N 18 47 E
Kotovsk, Ukraine 17 E15 47 45N 29 35 E
Kotputli, India 42 F7 27 43N 76 12 E
Kotri, Pakistan 42 G3 25 22N 68 22 E
Kotturu, India 40 M10 14 45N 76 10 E
Kotuy →, Russia 27 B11 71 54N 102 6 E
Kotzebue, U.S.A. 68 B3 66 53N 162 39W
Koudougou, Burkina Faso 50 F5 12 10N 2 20W
Koufonisi, Greece 23 E8 34 56N 26 8 E
Kougaberge, S. Africa 56 E3 33 48S 23 50 E
Kouilou →, Congo 52 E2 4 10S 12 5 E
Koula Moutou, Gabon 52 E2 1 15S 12 25 E
Koulen = Kulen, Cambodia 38 F5 13 50N 104 40 E
Kouloúra, Greece 23 A3 39 42N 19 54 E
Koúm-bournoú, Ákra, Greece 23 C10 36 15N 28 11 E
Koumala, Australia 62 C4 21 38S 149 15 E
Koumra, Chad 51 G9 8 50N 17 35 E
Kounradskiy, Kazakstan 26 E8 46 59N 75 0 E
Kountze, U.S.A. 81 K7 30 22N 94 19W
Kouris →, Cyprus 23 E11 34 38N 32 54 E
Kourou, Fr. Guiana 93 B8 5 9N 52 39W
Kousseri, Cameroon 51 F8 12 0N 14 55 E
Kouvola, Finland 9 F22 60 52N 26 43 E
Kovdor, Russia 24 A5 67 34N 30 24 E
Kovel, Ukraine 17 C13 51 11N 24 38 E
Kovrov, Russia 24 C7 56 25N 41 25 E
Kowanyama, Australia 62 B3 15 29S 141 44 E
Kowŏn, N. Korea 35 E14 39 26N 127 14 E
Köyceğiz, Turkey 21 F13 36 57N 28 40 E
Koza, Japan 31 L3 26 19N 127 46 E
Kozan, Turkey 44 B2 37 26N 35 50 E
Kozáni, Greece 21 D9 40 19N 21 47 E
Kozhikode = Calicut, India 40 P9 11 15N 75 43 E
Kozhva, Russia 24 A10 65 10N 57 0 E
Kozyatyn, Ukraine 17 D15 49 45N 28 50 E
Kra, Isthmus of = Kra, Kho Khot, Thailand 39 G2 10 15N 99 30 E
Kra, Kho Khot, Thailand 39 G2 10 15N 99 30 E
Kra Buri, Thailand 39 G2 10 22N 98 46 E
Kraai →, S. Africa 56 E4 30 40S 26 45 E
Krabi, Thailand 39 H2 8 4N 98 55 E
Kracheh, Cambodia 38 F6 12 32N 106 10 E
Kragan, Indonesia 37 G14 6 43S 111 38 E
Kragerø, Norway 9 G13 58 52N 9 25 E
Kragujevac, Serbia, Yug. 21 B9 44 2N 20 56 E
Krajina, Bos.-H. 20 B7 44 45N 16 35 E
Krakatau = Rakata, Pulau, Indonesia 36 F3 6 10S 105 20 E
Krakatoa = Rakata, Pulau, Indonesia 36 F3 6 10S 105 20 E
Krakor, Cambodia 38 F5 12 32N 104 12 E
Kraków, Poland 17 C10 50 4N 19 57 E
Kralanh, Cambodia 38 F4 13 35N 103 25 E
Kraljevo, Serbia, Yug. 21 C9 43 44N 20 41 E
Kramatorsk, Ukraine 25 E6 48 50N 37 30 E
Kramfors, Sweden 9 E17 62 55N 17 48 E
Kranj, Slovenia 16 E8 46 16N 14 22 E
Krankskop, S. Africa 57 D5 28 0S 30 47 E
Krasavino, Russia 24 B8 60 58N 46 29 E
Kraskino, Russia 27 E14 42 44N 130 48 E
Kraśnik, Poland 17 C12 50 55N 22 15 E
Krasnoarmeysk, Russia 26 D5 51 0N 45 42 E
Krasnodar, Russia 25 E6 45 5N 39 0 E
Krasnokamsk, Russia 24 C10 58 4N 55 48 E
Krasnoperekopsk, Ukraine 25 E5 46 0N 33 54 E
Krasnorechenskiy, Russia 30 B7 44 41N 135 14 E
Krasnoselkup, Russia 26 C9 65 20N 82 10 E
Krasnoturinsk, Russia 24 C11 59 46N 60 12 E
Krasnoufimsk, Russia 24 C10 56 36N 57 38 E
Krasnouralsk, Russia 24 C11 58 21N 60 3 E
Krasnovishersk, Russia 24 B10 60 23N 57 3 E
Krasnovodsk = Türkmenbashi, Turkmenistan 25 G9 40 5N 53 5 E
Krasnoyarsk, Russia 27 D10 56 8N 93 0 E
Krasnyy Kut, Russia 25 D8 50 50N 47 0 E
Krasnyy Luch, Ukraine 25 E6 48 13N 39 0 E
Krasnyy Yar, Russia 25 E8 46 43N 48 23 E
Kratie = Kracheh, Cambodia 38 F6 12 32N 106 10 E
Krau, Indonesia 37 E10 3 19S 140 5 E
Kravanh, Chuor Phnum, Cambodia 39 G4 12 0N 103 32 E
Krefeld, Germany 16 C4 51 20N 6 33 E
Kremen, Croatia 16 F8 44 28N 15 53 E
Kremenchuk, Ukraine 25 E5 49 5N 33 25 E
Kremenchuksk Vdskh., Ukraine 25 E5 49 20N 32 30 E
Kremenets, Ukraine 17 C13 50 8N 25 43 E
Kremmling, U.S.A. 82 F10 40 4N 106 24W
Krems, Austria 16 D8 48 25N 15 36 E
Kretinga, Lithuania 9 J19 55 53N 21 15 E
Kribi, Cameroon 52 D1 2 57N 9 56 E
Krichev = Krychaw, Belarus 17 B16 53 40N 31 41 E
Kriós, Ákra, Greece 23 D5 35 13N 23 34 E
Krishna →, India 41 M12 15 57N 80 59 E
Krishnanagar, India 43 H13 23 24N 88 33 E
Kristiansand, Norway 9 G13 58 8N 8 1 E
Kristianstad, Sweden 9 H16 56 2N 14 9 E
Kristiansund, Norway 8 E12 63 7N 7 45 E
Kristiinankaupunki, Finland 9 E19 62 16N 21 21 E
Kristinehamn, Sweden 9 G16 59 18N 14 7 E
Kristinestad = Kristiinankaupunki, Finland 9 E19 62 16N 21 21 E
Kríti, Greece 23 D7 35 15N 25 0 E
Kritsá, Greece 23 D7 35 10N 25 41 E
Krivoy Rog = Kryvyy Rih, Ukraine 25 E5 47 51N 33 20 E
Krk, Croatia 16 F8 45 8N 14 40 E
Krokodil →, Mozam. 57 D5 25 14S 32 18 E
Krong Kaoh Kong, Cambodia 36 B2 11 35N 103 0 E
Kronprins Olav Kyst, Antarctica 5 C5 69 0S 42 0 E
Kronshtadt, Russia 24 B4 59 57N 29 51 E
Kroonstad, S. Africa 56 D4 27 43S 27 19 E
Kropotkin, Russia 25 E7 45 28N 40 28 E
Krosno, Poland 17 D11 49 42N 21 46 E
Krotoszyn, Poland 17 C9 51 42N 17 23 E
Kroussón, Greece 23 D6 35 13N 24 59 E
Krugersdorp, S. Africa 57 D4 26 5S 27 46 E
Kruisfontein, S. Africa 56 E3 33 59S 24 43 E
Krung Thep = Bangkok, Thailand 38 F3 13 45N 100 35 E
Krupki, Belarus 17 A15 54 19N 29 8 E
Kruševac, Serbia, Yug. 21 C9 43 35N 21 28 E
Krychaw, Belarus 17 B16 53 40N 31 41 E
Krymskiy Poluostrov = Krymskyy Pivostriv, Ukraine 25 F5 45 0N 34 0 E
Krymskyy Pivostriv, Ukraine 25 F5 45 0N 34 0 E
Kryvyy Rih, Ukraine 25 E5 47 51N 33 20 E
Ksar el Kebir, Morocco 50 B4 35 0N 6 0W
Ksar es Souk = Er Rachidia, Morocco 50 B5 31 58N 4 20W
Kuala Belait, Malaysia 36 D4 4 35N 114 11 E
Kuala Berang, Malaysia 39 K4 5 5N 103 1 E
Kuala Dungun = Dungun, Malaysia 39 K4 4 45N 103 25 E
Kuala Kangsar, Malaysia 39 K3 4 46N 100 56 E
Kuala Kelawang, Malaysia 39 L4 2 56N 102 5 E
Kuala Kerai, Malaysia 39 K4 5 30N 102 12 E
Kuala Lipis, Malaysia 39 K4 4 10N 102 3 E
Kuala Lumpur, Malaysia 39 L3 3 9N 101 41 E
Kuala Nerang, Malaysia 39 J3 6 16N 100 37 E
Kuala Pilah, Malaysia 39 L4 2 45N 102 15 E
Kuala Rompin, Malaysia 39 L4 2 49N 103 29 E
Kuala Selangor, Malaysia 39 L3 3 20N 101 15 E
Kuala Sepetang, Malaysia 39 K3 4 49N 100 28 E
Kuala Terengganu, Malaysia 39 K4 5 20N 103 8 E
Kualajelai, Indonesia 36 E4 2 58S 110 46 E
Kualakapuas, Indonesia 36 E4 2 55S 114 20 E
Kualakurun, Indonesia 36 E4 1 10S 113 50 E
Kualapembuang, Indonesia 36 E4 3 14S 112 38 E
Kualasimpang, Indonesia 36 D1 4 17N 98 3 E
Kuancheng, China 35 D10 40 37N 118 30 E
Kuandang, Indonesia 37 D6 0 56N 123 1 E
Kuandian, China 35 D13 40 45N 124 45 E
Kuangchou = Guangzhou, China 33 D6 23 5N 113 10 E
Kuantan, Malaysia 39 L4 3 49N 103 20 E
Kuba = Quba, Azerbaijan 25 F8 41 21N 48 32 E
Kuban →, Russia 25 E6 45 20N 37 30 E
Kubokawa, Japan 31 H6 33 12N 133 8 E
Kucha Gompa, India 43 B7 34 25N 76 56 E
Kuchaman, India 42 F6 27 13N 74 47 E
Kuchinda, India 43 J11 21 44N 84 21 E
Kuching, Malaysia 36 D4 1 33N 110 25 E
Kuchino-eruba-Jima, Japan 31 J5 30 28N 130 12 E
Kuchino-Shima, Japan 31 K4 29 57N 129 55 E
Kuchinotsu, Japan 31 H5 32 36N 130 11 E
Kucing = Kuching, Malaysia 36 D4 1 33N 110 25 E
Kud →, Pakistan 42 F2 26 5N 66 20 E
Kuda, India 40 H7 23 10N 71 15 E
Kudat, Malaysia 36 C5 6 55N 116 55 E
Kudus, Indonesia 37 G14 6 48S 110 51 E
Kudymkar, Russia 24 C9 59 1N 54 39 E
Kueiyang = Guiyang, China 32 D5 26 32N 106 40 E
Kufra Oasis = Al Kufrah, Libya 51 D10 24 17N 23 15 E
Kufstein, Austria 16 E7 47 35N 12 11 E
Kugluktuk, Canada 68 B8 67 50N 115 5W
Kugong I., Canada 70 A4 56 18N 79 50W
Kūhak, Iran 40 F3 27 12N 63 10 E
Kuhan, Pakistan 42 E2 28 19N 67 14 E
Kūhbonān, Iran 45 D8 31 23N 56 19 E
Kūhestak, Iran 45 E8 26 47N 57 2 E
Kuhin, Iran 45 B6 36 22N 49 40 E
Kūhīrī, Iran 45 E9 26 55N 61 2 E
Kūhpāyeh, Eşfahan, Iran 45 C7 32 44N 52 20 E
Kūhpāyeh, Kermān, Iran 45 D8 30 35N 57 15 E
Kūhrān, Kūh-e, Iran 45 E8 26 46N 58 12 E
Kui Buri, Thailand 39 F2 12 3N 99 52 E
Kuiseb →, Namibia 56 B2 22 59S 14 31 E
Kuito, Angola 53 G3 12 22S 16 55 E
Kuiu I., U.S.A. 72 B2 57 45N 134 10W
Kujang, N. Korea 35 E14 39 57N 126 1 E
Kuji, Japan 30 D10 40 11N 141 46 E
Kujū-San, Japan 31 H5 33 5N 131 15 E
Kukës, Albania 21 C9 42 5N 20 27 E
Kukup, Malaysia 39 M4 1 20N 103 27 E
Kula, Turkey 21 E13 38 32N 28 40 E
Kulachi, Pakistan 42 D4 31 56N 70 27 E
Kulai, Malaysia 39 M4 1 44N 103 35 E
Kulal, Mt., Kenya 54 B4 2 42N 36 57 E
Kulasekarappattinam, India 40 Q11 8 20N 78 5 E
Kuldīga, Latvia 9 H19 56 58N 21 59 E
Kuldja = Yining, China 26 E9 43 58N 81 10 E
Kulen, Cambodia 38 F5 13 50N 104 40 E
Kulgam, India 43 C6 33 36N 75 2 E
Kulgera, Australia 62 D1 25 50S 133 18 E
Kulim, Malaysia 39 K3 5 22N 100 34 E
Kulin, Australia 61 F2 32 40S 118 2 E
Kŭlob, Tajikistan 26 F7 37 55N 69 50 E
Kulsary, Kazakstan 25 E9 46 59N 54 1 E
Kulti, India 43 H12 23 43N 86 50 E
Kulu, India 42 D7 31 58N 77 6 E
Kulumbura, Australia 60 B4 13 55S 126 35 E
Kulunda, Russia 26 D8 52 35N 78 57 E
Kulungar, Afghan. 42 C3 34 0N 69 2 E
Kūlvand, Iran 45 D7 31 21N 54 35 E
Kulwin, Australia 63 F3 35 0S 142 42 E
Kulyab = Kŭlob, Tajikistan 26 F7 37 55N 69 50 E
Kuma →, Russia 25 F8 44 55N 47 0 E
Kumagaya, Japan 31 F9 36 9N 139 22 E
Kumai, Indonesia 36 E4 2 44S 111 43 E
Kumamba, Kepulauan, Indonesia 37 E9 1 36S 138 45 E
Kumamoto, Japan 31 H5 32 45N 130 45 E
Kumamoto □, Japan 31 H5 32 55N 130 55 E
Kumanovo, Macedonia 21 C9 42 9N 21 42 E
Kumara, N.Z. 59 K3 42 37S 171 12 E
Kumarina, Australia 61 D2 24 41S 119 32 E
Kumasi, Ghana 50 G5 6 41N 1 38W
Kumayri = Gyumri, Armenia 25 F7 40 47N 43 50 E
Kumba, Cameroon 52 D1 4 36N 9 24 E
Kumbakonam, India 40 P11 10 58N 79 25 E
Kumbarilla, Australia 63 D5 27 15S 150 55 E
Kumbhraj, India 42 G7 24 22N 77 3 E
Kumbia, Australia 63 D5 26 41S 151 39 E
Kŭmch'ŏn, N. Korea 35 E14 38 10N 126 29 E
Kumdok, India 43 C8 33 32N 78 10 E
Kume-Shima, Japan 31 L3 26 20N 126 47 E
Kumertau, Russia 24 D10 52 45N 55 57 E
Kumharsain, India 42 D7 31 19N 77 27 E
Kŭmhwa, S. Korea 35 E14 38 17N 127 28 E
Kumi, Uganda 54 B3 1 30N 33 58 E
Kumla, Sweden 9 G16 59 8N 15 10 E
Kumo, Nigeria 51 F8 10 1N 11 12 E
Kumon Bum, Burma 41 F20 26 30N 97 15 E
Kunashir, Ostrov, Russia 27 E15 44 0N 146 0 E
Kunda, Estonia 9 G22 59 30N 26 34 E
Kunda, India 43 G9 25 43N 81 31 E
Kundar →, Pakistan 42 D3 31 56N 69 19 E
Kundian, Pakistan 42 C4 32 27N 71 28 E
Kundla, India 42 J4 21 21N 71 25 E
Kunga →, Bangla. 43 J13 21 46N 89 30 E
Kunghit I., Canada 72 C2 52 6N 131 3W
Kungrad = Qŭnghirot, Uzbekistan 26 E6 43 6N 58 54 E
Kungsbacka, Sweden 9 H15 57 30N 12 5 E
Kungur, Russia 24 C10 57 25N 56 57 E
Kunhar →, Pakistan 43 B5 34 20N 73 30 E
Kuningan, Indonesia 37 G13 6 59S 108 29 E
Kunlong, Burma 41 H21 23 20N 98 50 E
Kunlun Shan, Asia 32 C3 36 0N 86 30 E
Kunming, China 32 D5 25 1N 102 41 E
Kunsan, S. Korea 35 G14 35 59N 126 45 E
Kununurra, Australia 60 C4 15 40S 128 50 E
Kunwari →, India 43 F8 26 26N 79 11 E
Kunya-Urgench = Köneürgench, Turkmenistan 26 E6 42 19N 59 10 E
Kuopio, Finland 8 E22 62 53N 27 35 E
Kupa →, Croatia 16 F9 45 28N 16 24 E
Kupang, Indonesia 37 F6 10 19S 123 39 E
Kupreanof I., U.S.A. 72 B2 56 50N 133 30W
Kupyansk-Uzlovoi, Ukraine 25 E6 49 40N 37 43 E
Kuqa, China 32 B3 41 35N 82 30 E
Kür →, Azerbaijan 25 G8 39 29N 49 15 E
Kür Dili, Azerbaijan 45 B6 39 3N 49 13 E
Kura = Kür →, Azerbaijan 25 G8 39 29N 49 15 E
Kuranda, Australia 62 B4 16 48S 145 35 E
Kuranga, India 42 H3 22 4N 69 10 E
Kurashiki, Japan 31 G6 34 40N 133 50 E
Kurayoshi, Japan 31 G6 35 26N 133 50 E
Kŭrdzhali, Bulgaria 21 D11 41 38N 25 21 E
Kure, Japan 31 G6 34 14N 132 32 E
Kuressaare, Estonia 9 G20 58 15N 22 30 E
Kurgan, Russia 26 D7 55 26N 65 18 E
Kuri, India 42 F4 26 37N 70 43 E
Kuria Maria Is. = Khurīyā Murīyā, Jazā'ir, Oman 46 D6 17 30N 55 58 E
Kuridala, Australia 62 C3 21 16S 140 29 E
Kurigram, Bangla. 41 G16 25 49N 89 39 E
Kurikka, Finland 9 E20 62 36N 22 24 E
Kuril Is. = Kurilskiye Ostrova, Russia 27 E15 45 0N 150 0 E
Kuril Trench, Pac. Oc. 28 E19 44 0N 153 0 E
Kurilsk, Russia 27 E15 45 14N 147 53 E
Kurilskiye Ostrova, Russia 27 E15 45 0N 150 0 E
Kurino, Japan 31 J5 31 57N 130 43 E
Kurinskaya Kosa = Kür Dili, Azerbaijan 45 B6 39 3N 49 13 E
Kurnool, India 40 M11 15 45N 78 0 E
Kuro-Shima, Kagoshima, Japan 31 J4 30 50N 129 57 E
Kuro-Shima, Okinawa, Japan 31 M2 24 14N 124 1 E
Kurow, N.Z. 59 L3 44 44S 170 29 E
Kurram →, Pakistan 42 C4 32 36N 71 20 E
Kurri Kurri, Australia 63 E5 32 50S 151 28 E
Kurrimine, Australia 62 B4 17 47S 146 6 E
Kurshskiy Zaliv, Russia 9 J19 55 9N 21 6 E
Kursk, Russia 24 D6 51 42N 36 11 E
Kuruçay, Turkey 44 B3 39 39N 38 29 E
Kuruktag, China 32 B3 41 0N 89 0 E
Kuruman, S. Africa 56 D3 27 28S 23 28 E
Kuruman →, S. Africa 56 D3 26 56S 20 39 E
Kurume, Japan 31 H5 33 15N 130 30 E
Kurunegala, Sri Lanka 40 R12 7 30N 80 23 E
Kurya, Russia 24 B10 61 42N 57 9 E
Kuş Gölü, Turkey 21 D12 40 10N 27 55 E
Kuşadası, Turkey 21 F12 37 52N 27 15 E
Kusatsu, Japan 31 F9 36 37N 138 36 E
Kusawa L., Canada 72 A1 60 20N 136 13W
Kushalgarh, India 42 H6 23 10N 74 27 E
Kushikino, Japan 31 J5 31 44N 130 16 E
Kushima, Japan 31 J5 31 29N 131 14 E
Kushimoto, Japan 31 H7 33 28N 135 47 E
Kushiro, Japan 30 C12 43 0N 144 25 E
Kushiro-Gawa →, Japan 30 C12 42 59N 144 23 E
Kūshk, Iran 45 D8 28 46N 56 51 E
Kushka = Gushgy, Turkmenistan 26 F7 35 20N 62 18 E
Kūshkī, Iran 44 C5 33 31N 47 13 E
Kushol, India 43 C7 33 40N 76 36 E
Kushtia, Bangla. 41 H16 23 55N 89 5 E
Kushva, Russia 24 C10 58 18N 59 45 E
Kuskokwim B., U.S.A. 68 C3 59 45N 162 25W
Kusmi, India 43 H10 23 17N 83 55 E
Kussharo-Ko, Japan 30 C12 43 38N 144 21 E
Kustanay = Qostanay, Kazakstan 26 D7 53 10N 63 35 E

Kut, Ko, *Thailand* .... **39 G4** 11 40N 102 35 E
Kütahya, *Turkey* .... **25 G5** 39 30N 30 2 E
Kutaisi, *Georgia* .... **25 F7** 42 19N 42 40 E
Kutaraja = Banda Aceh, *Indonesia* .... **36 C1** 5 35N 95 20 E
Kutch, Gulf of = Kachchh, Gulf of, *India* .... **42 H3** 22 50N 69 15 E
Kutch, Rann of = Kachchh, Rann of, *India* .... **42 H4** 24 0N 70 0 E
Kutiyana, *India* .... **42 J4** 21 36N 70 2 E
Kutno, *Poland* .... **17 B10** 52 15N 19 23 E
Kutse, *Botswana* .... **56 C3** 21 7S 22 16 E
Kutu, *Dem. Rep. of the Congo* **52 E3** 2 40S 18 11 E
Kutum, *Sudan* .... **51 F10** 14 10N 24 40 E
Kuujjuaq, *Canada* **69 C13** 58 6N 68 15W
Kuujjuarapik, *Canada* **70 A4** 55 20N 77 35W
Kuŭp-tong, *N. Korea* .... **35 D14** 40 45N 126 1 E
Kuusamo, *Finland* .... **8 D23** 65 57N 29 8 E
Kuusankoski, *Finland* .... **9 F22** 60 55N 26 38 E
Kuwait = Al Kuwayt, *Kuwait* . **46 B4** 29 30N 48 0 E
Kuwait ■, *Asia* .... **46 B4** 29 30N 47 30 E
Kuwana, *Japan* .... **31 G8** 35 5N 136 43 E
Kuwana →, *India* .... **43 F10** 26 25N 83 15 E
Kuybyshev = Samara, *Russia* **24 D9** 53 8N 50 6 E
Kuybyshev, *Russia* .... **26 D8** 55 27N 78 19 E
Kuybyshevskoye Vdkhr., *Russia* .... **24 C8** 55 2N 49 30 E
Kuye He →, *China* .... **34 E6** 38 23N 110 46 E
Kūyeh, *Iran* .... **44 B5** 38 45N 47 57 E
Kūysanjaq, *Iraq* .... **44 B5** 36 5N 44 38 E
Kuyto, Ozero, *Russia* .... **24 B5** 65 6N 31 20 E
Kuyumba, *Russia* .... **27 C10** 60 58N 96 59 E
Kuzey Anadolu Dağları, *Turkey* .... **25 F6** 41 30N 35 0 E
Kuznetsk, *Russia* .... **24 D8** 53 12N 46 40 E
Kuzomen, *Russia* .... **24 A6** 66 22N 36 50 E
Kvænangen, *Norway* .... **8 A19** 70 5N 21 15 E
Kvaløy, *Norway* .... **8 B18** 69 40N 18 30 E
Kvarner, *Croatia* .... **16 F8** 44 50N 14 10 E
Kvarnerič, *Croatia* .... **16 F8** 44 43N 14 37 E
Kwa-Nobuhle, *S. Africa* .... **53 L5** 33 50S 25 22 E
Kwabhaca, *S. Africa* .... **57 E4** 30 51S 29 0 E
Kwakhanai, *Botswana* .... **56 C3** 21 39S 21 16 E
Kwakoegron, *Surinam* **93 B7** 5 12N 55 25W
Kwale, *Kenya* .... **54 C4** 4 15S 39 31 E
KwaMashu, *S. Africa* .... **57 D5** 29 45S 30 58 E
Kwando →, *Africa* .... **56 B3** 18 27S 23 32 E
Kwangdaeri, *N. Korea* .... **35 D14** 40 31N 127 32 E
Kwangju, *S. Korea* .... **35 G14** 35 9N 126 54 E
Kwango →, *Dem. Rep. of the Congo* .... **52 E3** 3 14S 17 22 E
Kwangsi-Chuang = Guangxi Zhuangzu Zizhiqu □, *China* **33 D5** 24 0N 109 0 E
Kwangtung = Guangdong □, *China* .... **33 D6** 23 0N 113 0 E
Kwataboahegan →, *Canada* **70 B3** 51 9N 80 50W
Kwatisore, *Indonesia* .... **37 E8** 3 18S 134 50 E
KwaZulu Natal □, *S. Africa* . **57 D5** 29 0S 30 0 E
Kweichow = Guizhou □, *China* .... **32 D5** 27 0N 107 0 E
Kwekwe, *Zimbabwe* .... **55 F2** 18 58S 29 48 E
Kwidzyn, *Poland* .... **17 B10** 53 44N 18 55 E
Kwinana New Town, *Australia* .... **61 F2** 32 15S 115 47 E
Kwoka, *Indonesia* .... **37 E8** 0 31S 132 27 E
Kyabra Cr. →, *Australia* .... **63 D3** 25 36S 142 55 E
Kyabram, *Australia* .... **63 F4** 36 19S 145 4 E
Kyaikto, *Burma* .... **38 D1** 17 20N 97 3 E
Kyakhta, *Russia* .... **27 D11** 50 30N 106 25 E
Kyancutta, *Australia* .... **63 E2** 33 8S 135 33 E
Kyaukpadaung, *Burma* .... **41 J19** 20 52N 95 8 E
Kyaukpyu, *Burma* .... **41 K18** 19 28N 93 30 E
Kyaukse, *Burma* .... **41 J20** 21 36N 96 10 E
Kyburz, *U.S.A.* **84 G6** 38 47N 120 18W
Kyelang, *India* .... **42 C7** 32 35N 77 2 E
Kyenjojo, *Uganda* .... **54 B3** 0 40N 30 37 E
Kyle, *Canada* **73 C7** 50 50N 108 2W
Kyle Dam, *Zimbabwe* .... **55 G3** 20 15S 31 0 E
Kyle of Lochalsh, *U.K.* **12 D3** 57 17N 5 44W
Kymijoki →, *Finland* .... **9 F22** 60 30N 26 55 E
Kyneton, *Australia* .... **63 F3** 37 10S 144 29 E
Kynuna, *Australia* .... **62 C3** 21 37S 141 55 E
Kyō-ga-Saki, *Japan* .... **31 G7** 35 45N 135 15 E
Kyoga, L., *Uganda* .... **54 B3** 1 35N 33 0 E
Kyogle, *Australia* .... **63 D5** 28 40S 153 0 E
Kyongju, *S. Korea* .... **35 G15** 35 51N 129 14 E
Kyongpyaw, *Burma* .... **41 L19** 17 12N 95 10 E
Kyŏngsŏng, *N. Korea* .... **35 D15** 41 35N 129 36 E
Kyōto, *Japan* .... **31 G7** 35 0N 135 45 E
Kyōto □, *Japan* .... **31 G7** 35 15N 135 45 E
Kyparissovouno, *Cyprus* .... **23 D12** 35 19N 33 10 E
Kyperounda, *Cyprus* .... **23 E11** 34 56N 32 58 E
Kyrenia, *Cyprus* .... **23 D12** 35 20N 33 20 E
Kyrgyzstan ■, *Asia* .... **26 E8** 42 0N 75 0 E
Kyrönjoki →, *Finland* .... **8 E19** 63 14N 21 45 E
Kystatyam, *Russia* .... **27 C13** 67 20N 123 10 E
Kythréa, *Cyprus* .... **23 D12** 35 15N 33 29 E
Kyunhla, *Burma* .... **41 H19** 23 25N 95 15 E
Kyuquot Sound, *Canada* **72 D3** 50 2N 127 22W
Kyūshū, *Japan* .... **31 H5** 33 0N 131 0 E
Kyūshū □, *Japan* .... **31 H5** 33 0N 131 0 E
Kyūshū-Sanchi, *Japan* .... **31 H5** 32 35N 131 17 E
Kyustendil, *Bulgaria* .... **21 C10** 42 16N 22 41 E
Kyusyur, *Russia* .... **27 B13** 70 19N 127 30 E
Kyyiv, *Ukraine* .... **17 C16** 50 30N 30 28 E
Kyyivske Vdskh., *Ukraine* .... **17 C16** 51 0N 30 25 E
Kyzyl, *Russia* .... **27 D10** 51 50N 94 30 E
Kyzyl Kum, *Uzbekistan* .... **26 E7** 42 30N 65 0 E
Kyzyl-Kyya, *Kyrgyzstan* .... **26 E8** 40 16N 72 8 E
Kzyl-Orda = Qyzylorda, *Kazakstan* .... **26 E7** 44 48N 65 28 E

L

La Alcarria, *Spain* **19 B4** 40 31N 2 45W
La Asunción, *Venezuela* **92 A6** 11 2N 63 53W
La Baie, *Canada* **71 C5** 48 19N 70 53W
La Banda, *Argentina* **94 B3** 27 45S 64 10W
La Barca, *Mexico* **86 C4** 20 20N 102 40W
La Barge, *U.S.A.* **82 E8** 42 16N 110 12W
La Belle, *U.S.A.* **77 M5** 26 46N 81 26W
La Biche →, *Canada* **72 B4** 59 57N 123 50W
La Biche, L., *Canada* **72 C6** 54 50N 112 5W
La Bomba, *Mexico* **86 A1** 31 53N 115 2W
La Calera, *Chile* **94 C1** 32 50S 71 10W
La Canal = Sa Canal, *Spain* . **22 C7** 38 51N 1 23 E
La Carlota, *Argentina* **94 C3** 33 30S 63 20W
La Ceiba, *Honduras* **88 C2** 15 40N 86 50W
La Chaux-de-Fonds, *Switz.* .. **18 C7** 47 7N 6 50 E
La Chorrera, *Panama* **88 E4** 8 53N 79 47W
La Cocha, *Argentina* **94 B2** 27 50S 65 40W
La Concepción, *Panama* **88 E3** 8 31N 82 37W
La Concordia, *Mexico* **87 D6** 16 8N 92 38W
La Coruña = A Coruña, *Spain* **19 A1** 43 20N 8 25W
La Crescent, *U.S.A.* **80 D9** 43 50N 91 18W
La Crete, *Canada* **72 B5** 58 11N 116 24W
La Crosse, *Kans., U.S.A.* **80 F5** 38 32N 99 18W
La Crosse, *Wis., U.S.A.* **80 D9** 43 48N 91 15W
La Cruz, *Costa Rica* **88 D2** 11 4N 85 39W
La Cruz, *Mexico* **86 C3** 23 55N 106 54W
La Désirade, *Guadeloupe* **89 C7** 16 18N 61 3W
La Escondida, *Mexico* **86 C5** 24 6N 99 55W
La Esmeralda, *Paraguay* **94 A3** 22 16S 62 33W
La Esperanza, *Cuba* **88 B3** 22 46N 83 44W
La Esperanza, *Honduras* **88 D2** 14 15N 88 10W
La Estrada = A Estrada, *Spain* **19 A1** 42 43N 8 27W
La Fayette, *U.S.A.* **77 H3** 34 42N 85 17W
La Fé, *Cuba* **88 B3** 22 2N 84 15W
La Follette, *U.S.A.* **77 G3** 36 23N 84 7W
La Grande, *U.S.A.* **82 D4** 45 20N 118 5W
La Grande →, *Canada* **70 B5** 53 50N 79 0W
La Grande Deux, Rés., *Canada* **70 B4** 53 40N 76 55W
La Grande Quatre, Rés., *Canada* **70 B5** 54 0N 73 15W
La Grande Trois, Rés., *Canada* **70 B4** 53 40N 75 10W
La Grange, *Calif., U.S.A.* **84 H6** 37 42N 120 27W
La Grange, *Ga., U.S.A.* **77 J3** 33 2N 85 2W
La Grange, *Ky., U.S.A.* **76 F3** 38 25N 85 23W
La Grange, *Tex., U.S.A.* **81 L6** 29 54N 96 52W
La Guaira, *Venezuela* **92 A5** 10 36N 66 56W
La Habana, *Cuba* **88 B3** 23 8N 82 22W
La Independencia, *Mexico* .. **87 D6** 16 31N 91 47W
La Isabela, *Dom. Rep.* **89 C5** 19 58N 71 2W
La Junta, *U.S.A.* **81 F3** 37 59N 103 33W
La Laguna, *Canary Is.* **22 F3** 28 28N 16 18W
La Libertad, *Guatemala* **88 C1** 16 47N 90 7W
La Libertad, *Mexico* **86 B2** 29 55N 112 41W
La Ligua, *Chile* **94 C1** 32 30S 71 16W
La Línea de la Concepción, *Spain* **19 D3** 36 15N 5 23W
La Loche, *Canada* **73 B7** 56 29N 109 26W
La Louvière, *Belgium* .... **15 D4** 50 27N 4 10 E
La Malbaie, *Canada* **71 C5** 47 40N 70 10W
La Mancha, *Spain* **19 C4** 39 10N 2 54W
La Martre, L., *Canada* **72 A5** 63 15N 117 55W
La Mesa, *U.S.A.* **85 N9** 32 46N 117 3W
La Misión, *Mexico* **86 A1** 32 5N 116 50W
La Moure, *U.S.A.* **80 B5** 46 21N 98 18W
La Negra, *Chile* **94 A1** 23 46S 70 18W
La Oliva, *Canary Is.* **22 F6** 28 36N 13 57W
La Orotava, *Canary Is.* **22 F3** 28 22N 16 31W
La Oroya, *Peru* **92 F3** 11 32S 75 54W
La Palma, *Canary Is.* **22 F2** 28 40N 17 50W
La Palma, *Panama* **88 E4** 8 15N 78 0W
La Palma del Condado, *Spain* **19 D2** 37 21N 6 38W
La Paloma, *Chile* **94 C1** 30 35S 71 0W
La Pampa □, *Argentina* **94 D2** 36 50S 66 0W
La Paragua, *Venezuela* **92 B6** 6 50N 63 20W
La Paz, *Entre Ríos, Argentina* **94 C4** 30 50S 59 45W
La Paz, *San Luis, Argentina* . **94 C2** 33 30S 67 20W
La Paz, *Bolivia* **92 G5** 16 20S 68 10W
La Paz, *Honduras* **88 D2** 14 20N 87 47W
La Paz, *Mexico* **86 C2** 24 10N 110 20W
La Paz Centro, *Nic.* **88 D2** 12 20N 86 41W
La Pedrera, *Colombia* **92 D5** 1 18S 69 43W
La Pérade, *Canada* **71 C5** 46 35N 72 12W
La Perouse Str., *Asia* .... **30 B11** 45 40N 142 0 E
La Pesca, *Mexico* **87 C5** 23 46N 97 47W
La Piedad, *Mexico* **86 C4** 20 20N 102 1W
La Pine, *U.S.A.* **82 E3** 43 40N 121 30W
La Plata, *Argentina* **94 D4** 35 0S 57 55W
La Pocatière, *Canada* **71 C5** 47 22N 70 2W
La Porte, *Ind., U.S.A.* **76 E2** 41 36N 86 43W
La Porte, *Tex., U.S.A.* **81 L7** 29 39N 95 1W
La Purísima, *Mexico* **86 B2** 26 10N 112 4W
La Push, *U.S.A.* **84 C2** 47 55N 124 38W
La Quiaca, *Argentina* **94 A2** 22 5S 65 35W
La Restinga, *Canary Is.* **22 G2** 27 38N 17 59W
La Rioja, *Argentina* **94 B2** 29 20S 67 0W
La Rioja □, *Argentina* **94 B2** 29 30S 67 0W
La Rioja □, *Spain* **19 A4** 42 20N 2 20W
La Robla, *Spain* **19 A3** 42 50N 5 41W
La Roche-en-Ardenne, *Belgium* .... **15 D5** 50 11N 5 35 E
La Roche-sur-Yon, *France* .. **18 C3** 46 40N 1 25W
La Rochelle, *France* **18 C3** 46 10N 1 9W
La Roda, *Spain* **19 C4** 39 13N 2 15W
La Romana, *Dom. Rep.* **89 C6** 18 27N 68 57W
La Ronge, *Canada* **73 B7** 55 5N 105 20W
La Rumorosa, *Mexico* **85 N10** 32 33N 116 4W
La Sabina = Sa Savina, *Spain* **22 C7** 38 44N 1 25 E
La Salle, *U.S.A.* **80 E10** 41 20N 89 6W
La Santa, *Canary Is.* **22 E6** 29 5N 13 40W
La Sarre, *Canada* **70 C4** 48 45N 79 15W
La Scie, *Canada* **71 C8** 49 57N 55 36W
La Selva Beach, *U.S.A.* **84 J5** 36 56N 121 51W
La Serena, *Chile* **94 B1** 29 55S 71 10W
La Seu d'Urgell, *Spain* .... **19 A6** 42 22N 1 23 E
La Seyne-sur-Mer, *France* .. **18 E6** 43 7N 5 52 E
La Soufrière, *St. Vincent* **89 D7** 13 20N 61 11W
La Spézia, *Italy* .... **18 D8** 44 7N 9 50 E
La Tagua, *Colombia* **92 C4** 0 3N 74 40W
La Tortuga, *Venezuela* **89 D6** 11 0N 65 22W
La Tuque, *Canada* **70 C5** 47 30N 72 50W
La Unión, *Chile* **96 E2** 40 10S 73 0W
La Unión, *El Salv.* **88 D2** 13 20N 87 50W
La Unión, *Mexico* **86 D4** 17 58N 101 49W
La Urbana, *Venezuela* **92 B5** 7 8N 66 56W
La Vall d'Uixó, *Spain* **19 C5** 39 49N 0 15W
La Vega, *Dom. Rep.* **89 C5** 19 20N 70 30W
La Vela de Coro, *Venezuela* . **92 A5** 11 27N 69 34W
La Venta, *Mexico* **87 D6** 18 8N 94 3W
La Ventura, *Mexico* **86 C4** 24 38N 100 54W
Laas Caanood = Las Anod, *Somali Rep.* .... **46 F4** 8 26N 47 19 E
Labasa, *Fiji* .... **59 C8** 16 30S 179 27 E
Labe = Elbe →, *Europe* .... **16 B5** 53 50N 9 0 E
Labé, *Guinea* **50 F3** 11 24N 12 16W
Laberge, L., *Canada* **72 A1** 61 11N 135 12W
Labinsk, *Russia* .... **25 F7** 44 40N 40 48 E
Labis, *Malaysia* .... **39 L4** 2 22N 103 2 E
Laboulaye, *Argentina* **94 C3** 34 10S 63 30W
Labrador, *Canada* **71 B7** 53 20N 61 0W
Labrador City, *Canada* **71 B6** 52 57N 66 55W
Labrador Sea, *Atl. Oc.* **69 C14** 57 0N 54 0W
Lábrea, *Brazil* **92 E6** 7 15S 64 51W
Labuan, *Malaysia* .... **36 C5** 5 20N 115 14 E
Labuan, Pulau, *Malaysia* ... **36 C5** 5 21N 115 13 E
Labuha, *Indonesia* .... **37 E7** 0 30S 127 30 E
Labuhan, *Indonesia* .... **37 G11** 6 22S 105 50 E
Labuhanbajo, *Indonesia* .... **37 F6** 8 28S 119 54 E
Labuk, Telok, *Malaysia* .... **36 C5** 6 10N 117 50 E
Labyrinth, L., *Australia* .... **63 E2** 30 40S 135 11 E
Labytnangi, *Russia* .... **26 C7** 66 39N 66 21 E
Lac Bouchette, *Canada* **71 C5** 48 16N 72 11W
Lac Édouard, *Canada* **70 C5** 47 40N 72 16W
Lac La Biche, *Canada* **72 C6** 54 45N 111 58W
Lac la Martre = Wha Ti, *Canada* **68 B8** 63 8N 117 16W
Lac La Ronge Prov. Park, *Canada* **73 B7** 55 9N 104 41W
Lac-Mégantic, *Canada* **71 C5** 45 35N 70 53W
Lac Thien, *Vietnam* .... **38 F7** 12 25N 108 11 E
Lacanau, *France* **18 D3** 44 58N 1 5W
Lacantúm →, *Mexico* **87 D6** 16 36N 90 40W
Laccadive Is. = Lakshadweep Is., *India* .... **29 H11** 10 0N 72 30 E
Lacepede B., *Australia* .... **63 F2** 36 40S 139 40 E
Lacepede Is., *Australia* .... **60 C3** 16 55S 122 0 E
Lacerdónia, *Mozam.* .... **55 F4** 18 3S 35 35 E
Lacey, *U.S.A.* **84 C4** 47 7N 122 49W
Lachhmangarh, *India* .... **42 F6** 27 50N 75 4 E
Lachi, *Pakistan* .... **42 C4** 33 25N 71 20 E
Lachine, *Canada* **79 A11** 45 30N 73 40W
Lachlan →, *Australia* .... **63 E3** 34 22S 143 55 E
Lachute, *Canada* **70 C5** 45 39N 74 21W
Lackawanna, *U.S.A.* **78 D6** 42 50N 78 50W
Lackawaxen, *U.S.A.* **79 E10** 41 29N 74 59W
Lacolle, *Canada* **79 A11** 45 5N 73 22W
Lacombe, *Canada* **72 C6** 52 30N 113 44W
Lacona, *U.S.A.* **79 C8** 43 39N 76 10W
Laconia, *U.S.A.* **79 C13** 43 32N 71 28W
Ladakh Ra., *India* .... **43 C8** 34 0N 78 0 E
Ladismith, *S. Africa* .... **56 E3** 33 28S 21 15 E
Lādīz, *Iran* .... **45 D9** 28 55N 61 15 E
Ladnun, *India* .... **42 F6** 27 38N 74 25 E
Ladoga, L. = Ladozhskoye Ozero, *Russia* .... **24 B5** 61 15N 30 30 E
Ladozhskoye Ozero, *Russia* . **24 B5** 61 15N 30 30 E
Lady Elliott I., *Australia* .... **62 C5** 24 7S 152 42 E
Lady Grey, *S. Africa* .... **56 E4** 30 43S 27 13 E
Ladybrand, *S. Africa* .... **56 D4** 29 9S 27 29 E
Ladysmith, *Canada* **72 D4** 49 0N 123 49W
Ladysmith, *S. Africa* .... **57 D4** 28 32S 29 46 E
Ladysmith, *U.S.A.* **80 C9** 45 28N 91 12W
Lae, *Papua N. G.* .... **64 H6** 6 40S 147 2 E
Laem Ngop, *Thailand* .... **39 F4** 12 10N 102 26 E
Laem Pho, *Thailand* .... **39 J3** 6 55N 101 19 E
Læsø, *Denmark* .... **9 H14** 57 15N 11 5 E
Lafayette, *Colo., U.S.A.* **80 F2** 39 58N 105 12W
Lafayette, *Ind., U.S.A.* **76 E2** 40 25N 86 54W
Lafayette, *La., U.S.A.* **81 K9** 30 14N 92 1W
Lafayette, *Tenn., U.S.A.* **77 G2** 36 31N 86 2W
Laferte →, *Canada* **72 A5** 61 53N 117 44W
Lafia, *Nigeria* .... **50 G7** 8 30N 8 34 E
Lafleche, *Canada* **73 D7** 49 45N 106 40W
Lagan →, *U.K.* **13 B6** 54 36N 5 55W
Lagarfljót →, *Iceland* **8 D6** 65 40N 14 18W
Lågen →, *Oppland, Norway* . **9 F14** 61 8N 10 25 E
Lågen →, *Vestfold, Norway* . **9 G14** 59 3N 10 3 E
Laghouat, *Algeria* .... **50 B6** 33 50N 2 59 E
Lagoa Vermelha, *Brazil* **95 B5** 28 13S 51 32W
Lagonoy G., *Phil.* .... **37 B6** 13 35N 123 50 E
Lagos, *Nigeria* .... **50 G6** 6 25N 3 27 E
Lagos, *Portugal* **19 D1** 37 5N 8 41W
Lagos de Moreno, *Mexico* **86 C4** 21 21N 101 55W
Lagrange, *Australia* .... **60 C3** 18 45S 121 43 E
Lagrange B., *Australia* .... **60 C3** 18 38S 121 42 E
Laguna, *Brazil* **95 B6** 28 30S 48 50W
Laguna, *U.S.A.* **83 J10** 35 2N 107 25W
Laguna Beach, *U.S.A.* **85 M9** 33 33N 117 47W
Laguna Limpia, *Argentina* .. **94 B4** 26 32S 59 45W
Lagunas, *Chile* **94 A2** 21 0S 69 45W
Lagunas, *Peru* **92 E3** 5 10S 75 35W
Lahad Datu, *Malaysia* .... **37 C5** 5 0N 118 20 E
Lahad Datu, Teluk, *Malaysia* **37 D5** 4 50N 118 20 E
Lahan Sai, *Thailand* .... **38 E4** 14 25N 102 52 E
Lahanam, *Laos* .... **38 D5** 16 16N 105 16 E
Lahar, *India* .... **43 F8** 26 12N 78 57 E
Laharpur, *India* .... **43 F9** 27 43N 80 56 E
Lahat, *Indonesia* .... **36 E2** 3 45S 103 30 E
Lahewa, *Indonesia* .... **36 D1** 1 22N 97 12 E
Lāhījān, *Iran* .... **45 B6** 37 10N 50 6 E
Lahn →, *Germany* .... **16 C4** 50 19N 7 37 E
Laholm, *Sweden* .... **9 H15** 56 30N 13 2 E
Lahore, *Pakistan* .... **42 D6** 31 32N 74 22 E
Lahri, *Pakistan* .... **42 E3** 29 11N 68 13 E
Lahti, *Finland* .... **9 F21** 60 58N 25 40 E
Lahtis = Lahti, *Finland* .... **9 F21** 60 58N 25 40 E
Laï, *Chad* .... **51 G9** 9 25N 16 18 E
Lai Chau, *Vietnam* .... **38 A4** 22 5N 103 3 E
Laila = Layla, *Si. Arabia* .... **46 C4** 22 10N 46 40 E
Laingsburg, *S. Africa* .... **56 E3** 33 9S 20 52 E
Lainio älv →, *Sweden* .... **8 C20** 67 35N 22 40 E
Lairg, *U.K.* **12 C4** 58 2N 4 24W
Laishui, *China* .... **34 E8** 39 23N 115 45 E
Laiwu, *China* .... **35 F9** 36 15N 117 40 E
Laixi, *China* .... **35 F11** 36 50N 120 31 E
Laiyang, *China* .... **35 F11** 36 59N 120 45 E
Laiyuan, *China* .... **34 E8** 39 20N 114 40 E
Laizhou, *China* .... **35 F10** 37 8N 119 57 E
Laizhou Wan, *China* .... **35 F10** 37 30N 119 30 E
Laja →, *Mexico* **86 C4** 20 55N 100 46W
Lajes, *Brazil* **95 B5** 27 48S 50 20W
Lak Sao, *Laos* .... **38 C5** 18 11N 104 59 E
Lakaband, *Pakistan* .... **42 D3** 31 2N 69 15 E
Lake Alpine, *U.S.A.* **84 G7** 38 29N 120 0W
Lake Andes, *U.S.A.* **80 D5** 43 9N 98 32W
Lake Arthur, *U.S.A.* **81 K8** 30 5N 92 41W
Lake Cargelligo, *Australia* .. **63 E4** 33 15S 146 22 E
Lake Charles, *U.S.A.* **81 K8** 30 14N 93 13W
Lake City, *Colo., U.S.A.* **83 G10** 38 2N 107 19W
Lake City, *Fla., U.S.A.* **77 K4** 30 11N 82 38W
Lake City, *Mich., U.S.A.* **76 C3** 44 20N 85 13W
Lake City, *Minn., U.S.A.* **80 C8** 44 27N 92 16W
Lake City, *Pa., U.S.A.* **78 D4** 42 1N 80 21W
Lake City, *S.C., U.S.A.* **77 J6** 33 52N 79 45W
Lake Cowichan, *Canada* **72 D4** 48 49N 124 3W
Lake District, *U.K.* .... **10 C4** 54 35N 3 20 E
Lake Elsinore, *U.S.A.* **85 M9** 33 38N 117 20W
Lake George, *U.S.A.* **79 C11** 43 26N 73 43W
Lake Grace, *Australia* .... **61 F2** 33 7S 118 28 E
Lake Harbour = Kimmirut, *Canada* **69 B13** 62 50N 69 50W
Lake Havasu City, *U.S.A.* **85 L12** 34 27N 114 22W
Lake Hughes, *U.S.A.* **85 L8** 34 41N 118 26W
Lake Isabella, *U.S.A.* **85 K8** 35 38N 118 28W
Lake Jackson, *U.S.A.* **81 L7** 29 3N 95 27W
Lake Junction, *U.S.A.* **82 D8** 44 35N 110 28W
Lake King, *Australia* .... **61 F2** 33 5S 119 45 E
Lake Lenore, *Canada* **73 C8** 52 24N 104 59W
Lake Louise, *Canada* **72 C5** 51 30N 116 10W
Lake Mead Nat. Recr. Area, *U.S.A.* **85 K12** 36 15N 114 30W
Lake Mills, *U.S.A.* **80 D8** 43 25N 93 32W
Lake Placid, *U.S.A.* **79 B11** 44 17N 73 59W
Lake Pleasant, *U.S.A.* **79 C10** 43 28N 74 25W
Lake Providence, *U.S.A.* **81 J9** 32 48N 91 10W
Lake St. Peter, *Canada* **78 A6** 45 18N 78 2W
Lake Superior Prov. Park, *Canada* **70 C3** 47 45N 84 45W
Lake Village, *U.S.A.* **81 J9** 33 20N 91 17W
Lake Wales, *U.S.A.* **77 M5** 27 54N 81 35W
Lake Worth, *U.S.A.* **77 M5** 26 37N 80 3W
Lakeba, *Fiji* **59 D9** 18 13S 178 47W
Lakefield, *Canada* **78 B6** 44 25N 78 16W
Lakehurst, *U.S.A.* **79 F10** 40 1N 74 19W
Lakeland, *Australia* .... **62 B3** 15 49S 144 57 E
Lakeland, *U.S.A.* **77 M5** 28 3N 81 57W
Lakemba = Lakeba, *Fiji* **59 D9** 18 13S 178 47W
Lakeport, *Calif., U.S.A.* **84 F4** 39 3N 122 55W
Lakeport, *Mich., U.S.A.* **78 C2** 43 7N 82 30W
Lakes Entrance, *Australia* .. **63 F4** 37 50S 148 0 E
Lakeside, *Ariz., U.S.A.* **83 J9** 34 9N 109 58W
Lakeside, *Calif., U.S.A.* **85 N10** 32 52N 116 55W
Lakeside, *Nebr., U.S.A.* **80 D3** 42 3N 102 26W
Lakeside, *Ohio, U.S.A.* **78 E2** 41 32N 82 46W
Lakeview, *U.S.A.* **82 E3** 42 11N 120 21W
Lakeville, *U.S.A.* **80 C8** 44 39N 93 14W
Lakewood, *Colo., U.S.A.* **80 F2** 39 44N 105 5W
Lakewood, *N.J., U.S.A.* **79 F10** 40 6N 74 13W
Lakewood, *N.Y., U.S.A.* **78 D5** 42 6N 79 19W
Lakewood, *Ohio, U.S.A.* **78 E3** 41 29N 81 48W
Lakewood, *Wash., U.S.A.* **84 C4** 47 11N 122 32W
Lakha, *India* .... **42 F4** 26 9N 70 54 E
Lakhaniá, *Greece* .... **23 D9** 35 58N 27 54 E
Lakhimpur, *India* .... **43 F9** 27 57N 80 46 E
Lakhnadon, *India* .... **43 H8** 22 36N 79 36 E
Lakhonpheng, *Laos* .... **38 E5** 15 54N 105 34 E
Lakhpat, *India* .... **42 H3** 23 48N 68 47 E
Lakin, *U.S.A.* **81 G4** 37 57N 101 15W
Lakitusaki →, *Canada* **70 B3** 54 21N 82 25W
Lakki, *Pakistan* .... **42 C4** 32 36N 70 55 E
Lákkoi, *Greece* .... **23 D5** 35 24N 23 57 E
Lakonikós Kólpos, *Greece* .. **21 F10** 36 40N 22 40 E
Lakor, *Indonesia* .... **37 F7** 8 15S 128 17 E
Lakota, *Ivory C.* **50 G4** 5 50N 5 30W
Lakota, *U.S.A.* **80 A5** 48 2N 98 21W
Laksar, *India* .... **42 E8** 29 46N 78 3 E
Laksefjorden, *Norway* .... **8 A22** 70 45N 26 50 E
Lakselv, *Norway* .... **8 A21** 70 2N 25 0 E
Lakshadweep Is., *India* .... **29 H11** 10 0N 72 30 E
Lakshmanpur, *India* .... **43 H10** 22 58N 83 3 E
Lakshmikantapur, *India* .... **43 H13** 22 5N 88 20 E
Lala Ghat, *India* .... **41 G18** 24 30N 92 40 E
Lala Musa, *Pakistan* .... **42 C5** 32 40N 73 57 E
Lalago, *Tanzania* .... **54 C3** 3 28S 33 58 E
Lalapanzi, *Zimbabwe* .... **55 F3** 19 20S 30 15 E
L'Albufera, *Spain* **19 C5** 39 20N 0 27W
Lalganj, *India* .... **43 G11** 25 52N 85 13 E
Lalgola, *India* .... **43 G13** 24 25N 88 15 E
Lālī, *Iran* .... **45 C6** 32 21N 49 6 E
Lalibela, *Ethiopia* .... **46 E2** 12 3N 39 0 E
Lalin, *China* .... **35 B14** 45 12N 127 0 E
Lalín, *Spain* **19 A1** 42 40N 8 5W
Lalin He →, *China* .... **35 B13** 45 32N 125 40 E
Lalitapur, *Nepal* .... **43 F11** 27 40N 85 20 E
Lalitpur, *India* .... **43 G8** 24 42N 78 28 E
Lalkua, *India* .... **43 E8** 29 5N 79 31 E
Lalsot, *India* .... **42 F7** 26 34N 76 20 E
Lam, *Vietnam* .... **38 B6** 21 21N 106 31 E
Lam Pao Res., *Thailand* .... **38 D4** 16 50N 103 15 E
Lamaing, *Burma* .... **41 M20** 15 25N 97 53 E
Lamar, *Colo., U.S.A.* **80 F3** 38 5N 102 37W
Lamar, *Mo., U.S.A.* **81 G7** 37 30N 94 16W
Lamas, *Peru* **92 E3** 6 28S 76 31W
Lambaréné, *Gabon* .... **52 E2** 0 41S 10 12 E
Lambasa = Labasa, *Fiji* .... **59 C8** 16 30S 179 27 E
Lambay I., *Ireland* **13 C5** 53 29N 6 1W
Lambert Glacier, *Antarctica* . **5 D6** 71 0S 70 0 E
Lambert's Bay, *S. Africa* .... **56 E2** 32 5S 18 17 E
Lambeth, *Canada* **78 D3** 42 54N 81 18W
Lambomakondro, *Madag.* .... **57 C7** 22 41S 44 44 E
Lame Deer, *U.S.A.* **82 D10** 45 37N 106 40W
Lamego, *Portugal* **19 B2** 41 5N 7 52W
Lamèque, *Canada* **71 C7** 47 45N 64 38W
Lameroo, *Australia* .... **63 F3** 35 19S 140 33 E
Lamesa, *U.S.A.* **81 J4** 32 44N 101 58W
Lamía, *Greece* .... **21 E10** 38 55N 22 26 E
Lammermuir Hills, *U.K.* **12 F6** 55 50N 2 40W
Lamoille →, *U.S.A.* **79 B11** 44 38N 73 13W
Lamon B., *Phil.* .... **37 B6** 14 30N 122 20 E
Lamont, *Canada* **72 C6** 53 46N 112 50W
Lamont, *Calif., U.S.A.* **85 K8** 35 15N 118 55W
Lamont, *Wyo., U.S.A.* **82 E10** 42 13N 107 29W
Lampa, *Peru* **92 G4** 15 22S 70 22W
Lampang, *Thailand* .... **38 C2** 18 16N 99 32 E
Lampasas, *U.S.A.* **81 K5** 31 4N 98 11W
Lampazos de Naranjo, *Mexico* **86 B4** 27 2N 100 32W
Lampedusa, *Medit. S.* .... **20 G5** 35 36N 12 40 E
Lampeter, *U.K.* **11 E3** 52 7N 4 4W
Lampione, *Medit. S.* .... **20 G5** 35 33N 12 20 E
Lampman, *Canada* **73 D8** 49 25N 102 50W
Lampung □, *Indonesia* .... **36 F2** 5 30S 104 30 E
Lamta, *India* .... **43 H9** 22 8N 80 7 E
Lamu, *Kenya* .... **54 C5** 2 16S 40 55 E
Lamy, *U.S.A.* **83 J11** 35 29N 105 53W
Lan Xian, *China* .... **34 E6** 38 15N 111 35 E
Lanak La, *China* .... **43 B8** 34 27N 79 32 E

Lanak'o Shank'ou = Lanak La, *China* **43 B8** 34 27N 79 32 E
Lanark, *Canada* **79 A8** 45 1N 76 22W
Lanark, *U.K.* **12 F5** 55 40N 3 47W
Lanbi Kyun, *Burma* **39 G2** 10 50N 98 20 E
Lancang Jiang →, *China* **32 D5** 21 40N 101 10 E
Lancashire □, *U.K.* **10 D5** 53 50N 2 48W
Lancaster, *Canada* **79 A10** 45 10N 74 30W
Lancaster, *U.K.* **10 C5** 54 3N 2 48W
Lancaster, *Calif., U.S.A.* **85 L8** 34 42N 118 8W
Lancaster, *Ky., U.S.A.* **76 G3** 37 37N 84 35W
Lancaster, *N.H., U.S.A.* **79 B13** 44 29N 71 34W
Lancaster, *N.Y., U.S.A.* **78 D6** 42 54N 78 40W
Lancaster, *Ohio, U.S.A.* **76 F4** 39 43N 82 36W
Lancaster, *Pa., U.S.A.* **79 F8** 40 2N 76 19W
Lancaster, *S.C., U.S.A.* **77 H5** 34 43N 80 46W
Lancaster, *Wis., U.S.A.* **80 D9** 42 51N 90 43W
Lancaster Sd., *Canada* **69 A11** 74 13N 84 0W
Lancelin, *Australia* **61 F2** 31 0S 115 18 E
Lanchow = Lanzhou, *China* **34 F2** 36 1N 103 52 E
Lanciano, *Italy* **20 C6** 42 14N 14 23 E
Lancun, *China* **35 F11** 36 25N 120 10 E
Landeck, *Austria* **16 E6** 47 9N 10 34 E
Lander, *U.S.A.* **82 E9** 42 50N 108 44W
Lander →, *Australia* **60 D5** 22 0S 132 0 E
Landes, *France* **18 D3** 44 0N 1 0W
Landi Kotal, *Pakistan* **42 B4** 34 7N 71 6 E
Landisburg, *U.S.A.* **78 F7** 40 21N 77 19W
Land's End, *U.K.* **11 G2** 50 4N 5 44W
Landsborough Cr. →, *Australia* **62 C3** 22 28S 144 35 E
Landshut, *Germany* **16 D7** 48 34N 12 8 E
Landskrona, *Sweden* **9 J15** 55 53N 12 50 E
Lanesboro, *U.S.A.* **79 E9** 41 57N 75 34W
Lanett, *U.S.A.* **77 J3** 32 52N 85 12W
Lang Qua, *Vietnam* **38 A5** 22 16N 104 27 E
Lang Shan, *China* **34 D4** 41 0N 106 30 E
Lang Son, *Vietnam* **38 B6** 21 52N 106 42 E
Lang Suan, *Thailand* **39 H2** 9 57N 99 4 E
La'nga Co, *China* **41 D12** 30 45N 81 15 E
Langar, *Iran* **45 C9** 35 23N 60 25 E
Langara I., *Canada* **72 C2** 54 14N 133 1W
Langdon, *U.S.A.* **80 A5** 48 45N 98 22W
Langeberg, *S. Africa* **56 E3** 33 55S 21 0 E
Langeberge, *S. Africa* **56 D3** 28 15S 22 33 E
Langeland, *Denmark* **9 J14** 54 56N 10 48 E
Langenburg, *Canada* **73 C8** 50 51N 101 43W
Langholm, *U.K.* **12 F5** 55 9N 3 0W
Langjökull, *Iceland* **8 D3** 64 39N 20 12W
Langkawi, Pulau, *Malaysia* **39 J2** 6 25N 99 45 E
Langklip, *S. Africa* **56 D3** 28 12S 20 20 E
Langkon, *Malaysia* **36 C5** 6 30N 116 40 E
Langlade, *St- P. & M.* **71 C8** 46 50N 56 20W
Langley, *Canada* **84 A4** 49 7N 122 39W
Langøya, *Norway* **8 B16** 68 45N 14 50 E
Langreo, *Spain* **19 A3** 43 18N 5 40W
Langres, *France* **18 C6** 47 52N 5 20 E
Langres, Plateau de, *France* **18 C6** 47 45N 5 3 E
Langsa, *Indonesia* **36 D1** 4 30N 97 57 E
Langtry, *U.S.A.* **81 L4** 29 49N 101 34W
Langu, *Thailand* **39 J2** 6 53N 99 47 E
Languedoc, *France* **18 E5** 43 58N 3 55 E
Langxiangzhen, *China* **34 E9** 39 43N 116 8 E
Lanigan, *Canada* **73 C7** 51 51N 105 2W
Lankao, *China* **34 G8** 34 48N 114 50 E
Länkäran, *Azerbaijan* **25 G8** 38 48N 48 52 E
Lannion, *France* **18 B2** 48 46N 3 29W
L'Annonciation, *Canada* **70 C5** 46 25N 74 55W
Lansdale, *U.S.A.* **79 F9** 40 14N 75 17W
Lansdowne, *Australia* **63 E5** 31 48S 152 30 E
Lansdowne, *Canada* **79 B8** 44 24N 76 1W
Lansdowne, *India* **43 E8** 29 50N 78 41 E
Lansdowne House, *Canada* **70 B2** 52 14N 87 53W
L'Anse, *U.S.A.* **76 B1** 46 45N 88 27W
L'Anse au Loup, *Canada* **71 B8** 51 32N 56 50W
L'Anse aux Meadows, *Canada* **71 B8** 51 36N 55 32W
Lansford, *U.S.A.* **79 F9** 40 50N 75 53W
Lansing, *U.S.A.* **76 D3** 42 44N 84 33W
Lanta Yai, Ko, *Thailand* **39 J2** 7 35N 99 3 E
Lantian, *China* **34 G5** 34 11N 109 20 E
Lanus, *Argentina* **94 C4** 34 44S 58 27W
Lanusei, *Italy* **20 E3** 39 52N 9 34 E
Lanzarote, *Canary Is.* **22 F6** 29 0N 13 40W
Lanzhou, *China* **34 F2** 36 1N 103 52 E
Lao Bao, *Laos* **38 D6** 16 35N 106 30 E
Lao Cai, *Vietnam* **38 A4** 22 30N 103 57 E
Laoag, *Phil.* **37 A6** 18 7N 120 34 E
Laoang, *Phil.* **37 B7** 12 32N 125 8 E
Laoha He →, *China* **35 C11** 43 25N 120 35 E
Laois □, *Ireland* **13 D4** 52 57N 7 36W
Laon, *France* **18 B5** 49 33N 3 35 E
Laona, *U.S.A.* **76 C1** 45 34N 88 40W
Laos ■, *Asia* **38 D5** 17 45N 105 0 E
Lapa, *Brazil* **95 B6** 25 46S 49 44W
Lapeer, *U.S.A.* **76 D4** 43 3N 83 19W
Lapithos, *Cyprus* **23 D12** 35 21N 33 11 E
Lapland = Lappland, *Europe* **8 B21** 68 7N 24 0 E
Laporte, *U.S.A.* **79 E8** 41 25N 76 30W
Lappeenranta, *Finland* **9 F23** 61 3N 28 12 E
Lappland, *Europe* **8 B21** 68 7N 24 0 E
Laprida, *Argentina* **94 D3** 37 34S 60 45W
Lapseki, *Turkey* **21 D12** 40 20N 26 41 E
Laptev Sea, *Russia* **27 B13** 76 0N 125 0 E
Lapua, *Finland* **8 E20** 62 58N 23 0 E
L'Áquila, *Italy* **20 C5** 42 22N 13 22 E
Lār, *Āzarbājān-e Sharqī, Iran* **44 B5** 38 30N 47 52 E
Lār, *Fārs, Iran* **45 E7** 27 40N 54 14 E
Laramie, *U.S.A.* **80 E2** 41 19N 105 35W
Laramie →, *U.S.A.* **82 F11** 42 13N 104 33W
Laramie Mts., *U.S.A.* **80 E2** 42 0N 105 30W
Laranjeiras do Sul, *Brazil* **95 B5** 25 23S 52 23W
Larantuka, *Indonesia* **37 F6** 8 21S 122 55 E
Larat, *Indonesia* **37 F8** 7 0S 132 0 E
Larde, *Mozam.* **55 F4** 16 28S 39 43 E
Larder Lake, *Canada* **70 C4** 48 5N 79 40W
Lardhos, Ákra = Líndhos, Ákra, *Greece* **23 C10** 36 4N 28 10 E
Lardhos, Órmos, *Greece* **23 C10** 36 4N 28 2 E
Laredo, *U.S.A.* **81 M5** 27 30N 99 30W
Laredo Sd., *Canada* **72 C3** 52 30N 128 53W
Largo, *U.S.A.* **77 M4** 27 55N 82 47W
Largs, *U.K.* **12 F4** 55 47N 4 52W
Lariang, *Indonesia* **37 E5** 1 26S 119 17 E
Larimore, *U.S.A.* **80 B6** 47 54N 97 38W
Lārīn, *Iran* **45 C7** 35 55N 52 19 E
Lárisa, *Greece* **21 E10** 39 36N 22 27 E
Larkana, *Pakistan* **42 F3** 27 32N 68 18 E
Larnaca, *Cyprus* **23 E12** 34 55N 33 38 E
Larnaca Bay, *Cyprus* **23 E12** 34 53N 33 45 E
Larne, *U.K.* **13 B6** 54 51N 5 51W
Larned, *U.S.A.* **80 F5** 38 11N 99 6W
Larose, *U.S.A.* **81 L9** 29 34N 90 23W
Larrimah, *Australia* **60 C5** 15 35S 133 12 E
Larsen Ice Shelf, *Antarctica* **5 C17** 67 0S 62 0W
Larvik, *Norway* **9 G14** 59 4N 10 2 E
Las Animas, *U.S.A.* **80 F3** 38 4N 103 13W
Las Anod, *Somali Rep.* **46 F4** 8 26N 47 19 E
Las Aves, Is., *W. Indies* **89 C7** 15 45N 63 55W
Las Brenãs, *Argentina* **94 B3** 27 5S 61 7W
Las Cejas, *Argentina* **96 B4** 26 53S 64 44W
Las Chimeneas, *Mexico* **85 N10** 32 8N 116 5W
Las Cruces, *U.S.A.* **83 K10** 32 19N 106 47W
Las Flores, *Argentina* **94 D4** 36 10S 59 7W
Las Heras, *Argentina* **94 C2** 32 51S 68 49W
Las Lajas, *Argentina* **96 D2** 38 30S 70 25W
Las Lomitas, *Argentina* **94 A3** 24 43S 60 35W
Las Palmas, *Argentina* **94 B4** 27 8S 58 45W
Las Palmas, *Canary Is.* **22 F4** 28 7N 15 26W
Las Palmas →, *Mexico* **85 N10** 32 26N 116 54W
Las Piedras, *Uruguay* **95 C4** 34 44S 56 14W
Las Pipinas, *Argentina* **94 D4** 35 30S 57 19W
Las Plumas, *Argentina* **96 E3** 43 40S 67 15W
Las Rosas, *Argentina* **94 C3** 32 30S 61 35W
Las Tablas, *Panama* **88 E3** 7 49N 80 14W
Las Termas, *Argentina* **94 B3** 27 29S 64 52W
Las Toscas, *Argentina* **94 B4** 28 21S 59 18W
Las Truchas, *Mexico* **86 D4** 17 57N 102 13W
Las Varillas, *Argentina* **94 C3** 31 50S 62 50W
Las Vegas, *N. Mex., U.S.A.* **83 J11** 35 36N 105 13W
Las Vegas, *Nev., U.S.A.* **85 J11** 36 10N 115 9W
Lascano, *Uruguay* **95 C5** 33 35S 54 12W
Lash-e Joveyn, *Afghan.* **40 D2** 31 45N 61 30 E
Lashburn, *Canada* **73 C7** 53 10N 109 40W
Lashio, *Burma* **41 H20** 22 56N 97 45 E
Lashkar, *India* **42 F8** 26 10N 78 10 E
Lasíthi, *Greece* **23 D7** 35 11N 25 31 E
Lasíthi □, *Greece* **23 D7** 35 5N 25 50 E
Lāsjerd, *Iran* **45 C7** 35 24N 53 4 E
Lassen Pk., *U.S.A.* **82 F3** 40 29N 121 31W
Lassen Volcanic Nat. Park, *U.S.A.* **82 F3** 40 30N 121 20W
Last Mountain L., *Canada* **73 C7** 51 5N 105 14W
Lastchance Cr. →, *U.S.A.* **84 E5** 40 2N 121 15W
Lastoursville, *Gabon* **52 E2** 0 55S 12 38 E
Lastovo, *Croatia* **20 C7** 42 46N 16 55 E
Lat Yao, *Thailand* **38 E2** 15 45N 99 48 E
Latacunga, *Ecuador* **92 D3** 0 50S 78 35W
Latakia = Al Lādhiqīyah, *Syria* **44 C2** 35 30N 35 45 E
Latchford, *Canada* **70 C4** 47 20N 79 50W
Latehar, *India* **43 H11** 23 45N 84 30 E
Latham, *Australia* **61 E2** 29 44S 116 20 E
Lathi, *India* **42 F4** 27 43N 71 23 E
Lathrop Wells, *U.S.A.* **85 J10** 36 39N 116 24W
Latina, *Italy* **20 D5** 41 28N 12 52 E
Latium = Lazio □, *Italy* **20 C5** 42 10N 12 30 E
Laton, *U.S.A.* **84 J7** 36 26N 119 41W
Latouche Treville, C., *Australia* **60 C3** 18 27S 121 49 E
Latrobe, *Australia* **62 G4** 41 14S 146 30 E
Latrobe, *U.S.A.* **78 F5** 40 19N 79 23W
Latvia ■, *Europe* **9 H20** 56 50N 24 0 E
Lau Group, *Fiji* **59 C9** 17 0S 178 30W
Lauchhammer, *Germany* **16 C7** 51 29N 13 47 E
Laughlin, *U.S.A.* **83 J6** 35 8N 114 35W
Laukaa, *Finland* **9 E21** 62 24N 25 56 E
Launceston, *Australia* **62 G4** 41 24S 147 8 E
Launceston, *U.K.* **11 G3** 50 38N 4 22W
Laune →, *Ireland* **13 D2** 52 7N 9 47W
Launglon Bok, *Burma* **38 F1** 13 50N 97 54 E
Laura, *Australia* **62 B3** 15 32S 144 32 E
Laurel, *Miss., U.S.A.* **81 K10** 31 41N 89 8W
Laurel, *Mont., U.S.A.* **82 D9** 45 40N 108 46W
Laurencekirk, *U.K.* **12 E6** 56 50N 2 28W
Laurens, *U.S.A.* **77 H4** 34 30N 82 1W
Laurentian Plateau, *Canada* **71 B6** 52 0N 70 0W
Lauria, *Italy* **20 E6** 40 2N 15 50 E
Laurie L., *Canada* **73 B8** 56 35N 101 57W
Laurinburg, *U.S.A.* **77 H6** 34 47N 79 28W
Laurium, *U.S.A.* **76 B1** 47 14N 88 27W
Lausanne, *Switz.* **18 C7** 46 32N 6 38 E
Laut, *Indonesia* **39 K6** 4 45N 108 0 E
Laut, Pulau, *Indonesia* **36 E5** 3 40S 116 10 E
Laut Kecil, Kepulauan, *Indonesia* **36 E5** 4 45S 115 40 E
Lautoka, *Fiji* **59 C7** 17 37S 177 27 E
Lavagh More, *Ireland* **13 B3** 54 46N 8 6W
Laval, *France* **18 B3** 48 4N 0 48W
Lavalle, *Argentina* **94 B2** 28 15S 65 15W
Lavant Station, *Canada* **79 A8** 45 3N 76 42W
Lāvar Meydān, *Iran* **45 D7** 30 20N 54 30 E
Laverton, *Australia* **61 E3** 28 44S 122 29 E
Lavras, *Brazil* **95 A7** 21 20S 45 0W
Lávrion, *Greece* **21 F11** 37 40N 24 4 E
Lávris, *Greece* **23 D6** 35 25N 24 40 E
Lavumisa, *Swaziland* **57 D5** 27 20S 31 55 E
Lawas, *Malaysia* **36 D5** 4 55N 115 25 E
Lawele, *Indonesia* **37 F6** 5 13S 122 57 E
Lawng Pit, *Burma* **41 G20** 25 30N 97 25 E
Lawqah, *Si. Arabia* **44 D4** 29 49N 42 45 E
Lawrence, *N.Z.* **59 L2** 45 55S 169 41 E
Lawrence, *Kans., U.S.A.* **80 F7** 38 58N 95 14W
Lawrence, *Mass., U.S.A.* **79 D13** 42 43N 71 10W
Lawrenceburg, *Ind., U.S.A.* **76 F3** 39 6N 84 52W
Lawrenceburg, *Tenn., U.S.A.* **77 H2** 35 14N 87 20W
Lawrenceville, *Ga., U.S.A.* **77 J4** 33 57N 83 59W
Lawrenceville, *Pa., U.S.A.* **78 E7** 41 59N 77 8W
Laws, *U.S.A.* **84 H8** 37 24N 118 20W
Lawton, *U.S.A.* **81 H5** 34 37N 98 25W
Lawu, *Indonesia* **37 G14** 7 40S 111 13 E
Laxford, L., *U.K.* **12 C3** 58 24N 5 6W
Layla, *Si. Arabia* **46 C4** 22 10N 46 40 E
Laylān, *Iraq* **44 C5** 35 18N 44 31 E
Layton, *U.S.A.* **82 F7** 41 4N 111 58W
Laytonville, *U.S.A.* **82 G2** 39 41N 123 29W
Lazarivo, *Madag.* **57 C8** 23 54S 44 59 E
Lazio □, *Italy* **20 C5** 42 10N 12 30 E
Lazo, *Russia* **30 C6** 43 25N 133 55 E
Le Creusot, *France* **18 C6** 46 48N 4 24 E
Le François, *Martinique* **89 D7** 14 38N 60 57W
Le Havre, *France* **18 B4** 49 30N 0 5 E
Le Mans, *France* **18 C4** 48 0N 0 10 E
Le Mars, *U.S.A.* **80 D6** 42 47N 96 10W
Le Mont-St-Michel, *France* **18 B3** 48 40N 1 30W
Le Moule, *Guadeloupe* **89 C7** 16 20N 61 22W
Le Puy-en-Velay, *France* **18 D5** 45 3N 3 52 E
Le Sueur, *U.S.A.* **80 C8** 44 28N 93 55W
Le Thuy, *Vietnam* **38 D6** 17 14N 106 49 E
Le Touquet-Paris-Plage, *France* **18 A4** 50 30N 1 36 E
Le Tréport, *France* **18 A4** 50 3N 1 20 E
Le Verdon-sur-Mer, *France* **18 D3** 45 33N 1 4W
Lea →, *U.K.* **11 F8** 51 31N 0 1 E
Leach, *Cambodia* **39 F4** 12 21N 103 46 E
Lead, *U.S.A.* **80 C3** 44 21N 103 46W
Leader, *Canada* **73 C7** 50 50N 109 30W
Leadville, *U.S.A.* **83 G10** 39 15N 106 18W
Leaf →, *U.S.A.* **81 K10** 30 59N 88 44W
Leaf Rapids, *Canada* **73 B9** 56 30N 99 59W
Leamington, *Canada* **78 D2** 42 3N 82 36W
Leamington, *U.S.A.* **82 G7** 39 32N 112 17W
Leamington Spa = Royal Leamington Spa, *U.K.* **11 E6** 52 18N 1 31W
Leandro Norte Alem, *Argentina* **95 B4** 27 34S 55 15W
Leane, L., *Ireland* **13 D2** 52 2N 9 32W
Learmonth, *Australia* **60 D1** 22 13S 114 10 E
Leask, *Canada* **73 C7** 53 5N 106 45W
Leatherhead, *U.K.* **11 F7** 51 18N 0 20W
Leavenworth, *Kans., U.S.A.* **80 F7** 39 19N 94 55W
Leavenworth, *Wash., U.S.A.* **82 C3** 47 36N 120 40W
Lebak, *Phil.* **37 C6** 6 32N 124 5 E
Lebam, *U.S.A.* **84 D3** 46 34N 123 33W
Lebanon, *Ind., U.S.A.* **76 E2** 40 3N 86 28W
Lebanon, *Kans., U.S.A.* **80 F5** 39 49N 98 33W
Lebanon, *Ky., U.S.A.* **76 G3** 37 34N 85 15W
Lebanon, *Mo., U.S.A.* **81 G8** 37 41N 92 40W
Lebanon, *N.H., U.S.A.* **79 C12** 43 39N 72 15W
Lebanon, *Oreg., U.S.A.* **82 D2** 44 32N 122 55W
Lebanon, *Pa., U.S.A.* **79 F8** 40 20N 76 26W
Lebanon, *Tenn., U.S.A.* **77 G2** 36 12N 86 18W
Lebanon ■, *Asia* **47 B5** 34 0N 36 0 E
Lebec, *U.S.A.* **85 L8** 34 50N 118 52W
Lebel-sur-Quévillon, *Canada* **70 C4** 49 3N 76 59W
Lebomboberge, *S. Africa* **57 C5** 24 30S 32 0 E
Lębork, *Poland* **17 A9** 54 33N 17 46 E
Lebrija, *Spain* **19 D2** 36 53N 6 5W
Lebu, *Chile* **94 D1** 37 40S 73 47W
Lecce, *Italy* **21 D8** 40 23N 18 11 E
Lecco, *Italy* **18 D8** 45 51N 9 23 E
Lech →, *Germany* **16 D6** 48 43N 10 56 E
Lecontes Mills, *U.S.A.* **78 E6** 41 5N 78 17W
Łęczyca, *Poland* **17 B10** 52 5N 19 15 E
Ledong, *China* **38 C7** 18 41N 109 5 E
Leduc, *Canada* **72 C6** 53 15N 113 30W
Lee, *U.S.A.* **79 D11** 42 19N 73 15W
Lee →, *Ireland* **13 E3** 51 53N 8 56W
Lee Vining, *U.S.A.* **84 H7** 37 58N 119 7W
Leech L., *U.S.A.* **80 B7** 47 10N 94 24W
Leechburg, *U.S.A.* **78 F5** 40 37N 79 36W
Leeds, *U.K.* **10 D6** 53 48N 1 33W
Leeds, *U.S.A.* **77 J2** 33 33N 86 33W
Leek, *Neths.* **15 A6** 53 10N 6 24 E
Leek, *U.K.* **10 D5** 53 7N 2 1W
Leeman, *Australia* **61 E1** 29 57S 114 58 E
Leeper, *U.S.A.* **78 E5** 41 22N 79 18W
Leer, *Germany* **16 B4** 53 13N 7 26 E
Leesburg, *U.S.A.* **77 L5** 28 49N 81 53W
Leesville, *U.S.A.* **81 K8** 31 9N 93 16W
Leeton, *Australia* **63 E4** 34 33S 146 23 E
Leetonia, *U.S.A.* **78 F4** 40 53N 80 45W
Leeu Gamka, *S. Africa* **56 E3** 32 47S 21 59 E
Leeuwarden, *Neths.* **15 A5** 53 15N 5 48 E
Leeuwin, C., *Australia* **61 F2** 34 20S 115 9 E
Leeward Is., *Atl. Oc.* **89 C7** 16 30N 63 30W
Lefka, *Cyprus* **23 D11** 35 6N 32 51 E
Lefkoniko, *Cyprus* **23 D12** 35 18N 33 44 E
Lefroy, *Canada* **78 B5** 44 16N 79 34W
Lefroy, L., *Australia* **61 F3** 31 21S 121 40 E
Leganés, *Spain* **19 B4** 40 19N 3 45W
Legazpi, *Phil.* **37 B6** 13 10N 123 45 E
Legendre I., *Australia* **60 D2** 20 22S 116 55 E
Leghorn = Livorno, *Italy* **20 C4** 43 33N 10 19 E
Legionowo, *Poland* **17 B11** 52 25N 20 50 E
Legnago, *Italy* **20 B4** 45 11N 11 18 E
Legnica, *Poland* **16 C9** 51 12N 16 10 E
Leh, *India* **43 B7** 34 9N 77 35 E
Lehigh Acres, *U.S.A.* **77 M5** 26 36N 81 39W
Lehighton, *U.S.A.* **79 F9** 40 50N 75 43W
Lehututu, *Botswana* **56 C3** 23 54S 21 55 E
Leiah, *Pakistan* **42 D4** 30 58N 70 58 E
Leicester, *U.K.* **11 E6** 52 38N 1 8W
Leicester City □, *U.K.* **11 E6** 52 38N 1 8W
Leicestershire □, *U.K.* **11 E6** 52 41N 1 17W
Leichhardt →, *Australia* **62 B2** 17 35S 139 48 E
Leichhardt Ra., *Australia* **62 C4** 20 46S 147 40 E
Leiden, *Neths.* **15 B4** 52 9N 4 30 E
Leie →, *Belgium* **15 C3** 51 2N 3 45 E
Leine →, *Germany* **16 B5** 52 43N 9 36 E
Leinster, *Australia* **61 E3** 27 51S 120 36 E
Leinster □, *Ireland* **13 C4** 53 3N 7 8W
Leinster, Mt., *Ireland* **13 D5** 52 37N 6 46W
Leipzig, *Germany* **16 C7** 51 18N 12 22 E
Leiria, *Portugal* **19 C1** 39 46N 8 53W
Leirvik, *Norway* **9 G11** 59 47N 5 28 E
Leisler, Mt., *Australia* **60 D4** 23 23S 129 20 E
Leith, *U.K.* **12 F5** 55 59N 3 11W
Leith Hill, *U.K.* **11 F7** 51 11N 0 22W
Leitrim, *Ireland* **13 B3** 54 0N 8 5W
Leitrim □, *Ireland* **13 B4** 54 8N 8 0W
Leizhou Bandao, *China* **33 D6** 21 0N 110 0 E
Lek →, *Neths.* **15 C4** 51 54N 4 35 E
Leka, *Norway* **8 D14** 65 5N 11 35 E
Lékva Óros, *Greece* **23 D6** 35 18N 24 3 E
Leland, *Mich., U.S.A.* **76 C3** 45 1N 85 45W
Leland, *Miss., U.S.A.* **81 J9** 33 24N 90 54W
Leleque, *Argentina* **96 E2** 42 28S 71 0W
Lelystad, *Neths.* **15 B5** 52 30N 5 25 E
Léman, L., *Europe* **18 C7** 46 26N 6 30 E
Lemera, *Dem. Rep. of the Congo* **54 C2** 3 0S 28 55 E
Lemhi Ra., *U.S.A.* **82 D7** 44 30N 113 30W
Lemmer, *Neths.* **15 B5** 52 51N 5 43 E
Lemmon, *U.S.A.* **80 C3** 45 57N 102 10W
Lemon Grove, *U.S.A.* **85 N9** 32 45N 117 2W
Lemoore, *U.S.A.* **84 J7** 36 18N 119 46W
Lemvig, *Denmark* **9 H13** 56 33N 8 20 E
Lena →, *Russia* **27 B13** 72 52N 126 40 E
Léndas, *Greece* **23 E6** 34 56N 24 56 E
Lendeh, *Iran* **45 D6** 30 58N 50 25 E
Lenggong, *Malaysia* **39 K3** 5 6N 100 58 E
Lengua de Vaca, Pta., *Chile* **94 C1** 30 14S 71 38W
Leninabad = Khŭjand, *Tajikistan* **26 E7** 40 17N 69 37 E
Leninakan = Gyumri, *Armenia* **25 F7** 40 47N 43 50 E
Leningrad = Sankt-Peterburg, *Russia* **24 C5** 59 55N 30 20 E
Leninogorsk, *Kazakstan* **26 D9** 50 20N 83 30 E
Leninsk, *Russia* **25 E8** 48 40N 45 15 E
Leninsk-Kuznetskiy, *Russia* **26 D9** 54 44N 86 10 E
Lenkoran = Länkäran, *Azerbaijan* **25 G8** 38 48N 48 52 E
Lenmalu, *Indonesia* **37 E8** 1 45S 130 15 E
Lennox, *U.S.A.* **80 D6** 43 21N 96 53W
Lennoxville, *Canada* **79 A13** 45 22N 71 51W
Lenoir, *U.S.A.* **77 H5** 35 55N 81 32W
Lenoir City, *U.S.A.* **77 H3** 35 48N 84 16W
Lenore L., *Canada* **73 C8** 52 30N 104 59W
Lenox, *U.S.A.* **79 D11** 42 22N 73 17W
Lens, *France* **18 A5** 50 26N 2 50 E
Lensk, *Russia* **27 C12** 60 48N 114 55 E
Lentini, *Italy* **20 F6** 37 17N 15 0 E
Lenwood, *U.S.A.* **85 L9** 34 53N 117 7W
Lenya, *Burma* **36 B1** 11 33N 98 57 E
Leoben, *Austria* **16 E8** 47 22N 15 5 E
Leodhas = Lewis, *U.K.* **12 C2** 58 9N 6 40W
Leola, *U.S.A.* **80 C5** 45 43N 98 56W
Leominster, *U.K.* **11 E5** 52 14N 2 43W
Leominster, *U.S.A.* **79 D13** 42 32N 71 46W
León, *Mexico* **86 C4** 21 7N 101 40W
León, *Nic.* **88 D2** 12 20N 86 51W
León, *Spain* **19 A3** 42 38N 5 34W
Leon, *U.S.A.* **80 E8** 40 44N 93 45W
Leon →, *U.S.A.* **81 K6** 31 14N 97 28W
León, Montes de, *Spain* **19 A2** 42 30N 6 18W
Leonardtown, *U.S.A.* **76 F7** 38 17N 76 38W
Leonardville, *Namibia* **56 C2** 23 29S 18 49 E
Leongatha, *Australia* **63 F4** 38 30S 145 58 E
Leonora, *Australia* **61 E3** 28 49S 121 19 E
Leopoldina, *Brazil* **95 A7** 21 28S 42 40W
Leopoldsburg, *Belgium* **15 C5** 51 7N 5 13 E
Leoti, *U.S.A.* **80 F4** 38 29N 101 21W
Leova, *Moldova* **17 E15** 46 28N 28 15 E
Leoville, *Canada* **73 C7** 53 39N 107 33W
Lepel = Lyepyel, *Belarus* **24 D4** 54 50N 28 40 E
Lépo, L. do, *Angola* **56 B2** 17 0S 19 0 E
Leppävirta, *Finland* **9 E22** 62 29N 27 46 E
Lerdo, *Mexico* **86 B4** 25 32N 103 32W
Leribe, *Lesotho* **57 D4** 28 51S 28 3 E
Lérida = Lleida, *Spain* **19 B6** 41 37N 0 39 E
Lerwick, *U.K.* **12 A7** 60 9N 1 9W
Les Cayes, *Haiti* **89 C5** 18 15N 73 46W
Les Sables-d'Olonne, *France* **18 C3** 46 30N 1 45W
Lesbos = Lésvos, *Greece* **21 E12** 39 10N 26 20 E
Leshan, *China* **32 D5** 29 33N 103 41 E
Leshukonskoye, *Russia* **24 B8** 64 54N 45 46 E
Leskov I., *Antarctica* **5 B1** 56 0S 28 0W
Leskovac, *Serbia, Yug.* **21 C9** 43 0N 21 58 E
Lesopilnoye, *Russia* **30 A7** 46 44N 134 20 E
Lesotho ■, *Africa* **57 D4** 29 40S 28 0 E
Lesozavodsk, *Russia* **27 E14** 45 30N 133 29 E
Lesse →, *Belgium* **15 D4** 50 15N 4 54 E
Lesser Antilles, *W. Indies* **89 D7** 15 0N 61 0W
Lesser Slave L., *Canada* **72 B5** 55 30N 115 25W
Lesser Sunda Is., *Indonesia* **37 F6** 8 0S 120 0 E
Lessines, *Belgium* **15 D3** 50 42N 3 50 E
Lester, *U.S.A.* **84 C5** 47 12N 121 29W
Lestock, *Canada* **73 C8** 51 19N 103 59W
Lesuer I., *Australia* **60 B4** 13 50S 127 17 E
Lésvos, *Greece* **21 E12** 39 10N 26 20 E
Leszno, *Poland* **17 C9** 51 50N 16 30 E
Letaba, *S. Africa* **57 C5** 23 59S 31 50 E
Letchworth, *U.K.* **11 F7** 51 59N 0 13W
Lethbridge, *Canada* **72 D6** 49 45N 112 45W
Lethem, *Guyana* **92 C7** 3 20N 59 50W
Leti, Kepulauan, *Indonesia* **37 F7** 8 10S 128 0 E
Leti Is. = Leti, Kepulauan, *Indonesia* **37 F7** 8 10S 128 0 E
Letiahau →, *Botswana* **56 C3** 21 16S 24 0 E
Leticia, *Colombia* **92 D5** 4 9S 70 0W
Leting, *China* **35 E10** 39 23N 118 55 E
Letjiesbos, *S. Africa* **56 E3** 32 34S 22 16 E
Letlhakane, *Botswana* **56 C4** 21 27S 25 30 E
Letlhakeng, *Botswana* **56 C3** 24 0S 24 59 E
Letong, *Indonesia* **36 D3** 2 58N 105 42 E
Letpadan, *Burma* **41 L19** 17 45N 95 45 E
Letpan, *Burma* **41 K19** 19 28N 94 10 E
Letsôk-aw Kyun, *Burma* **39 G2** 11 30N 98 25 E
Letterkenny, *Ireland* **13 B4** 54 57N 7 45W
Leucadia, *U.S.A.* **85 M9** 33 4N 117 18W
Leuser, G., *Indonesia* **36 D1** 3 46N 97 12 E
Leuven, *Belgium* **15 D4** 50 52N 4 42 E
Leuze-en-Hainaut, *Belgium* **15 D3** 50 36N 3 37 E
Levádhia, *Greece* **21 E10** 38 27N 22 54 E
Levanger, *Norway* **8 E14** 63 45N 11 19 E
Levelland, *U.S.A.* **81 J3** 33 35N 102 23W
Leven, *U.K.* **12 E6** 56 12N 3 0W
Leven, L., *U.K.* **12 E5** 56 12N 3 22W
Leven, Toraka, *Madag.* **57 A8** 12 30S 47 45 E
Leveque C., *Australia* **60 C3** 16 20S 123 0 E
Levice, *Slovak Rep.* **17 D10** 48 13N 18 35 E
Levin, *N.Z.* **59 J5** 40 37S 175 18 E
Lévis, *Canada* **71 C5** 46 48N 71 9W
Levis, L., *Canada* **72 A5** 62 37N 117 58W
Levittown, *N.Y., U.S.A.* **79 F11** 40 44N 73 31W
Levittown, *Pa., U.S.A.* **79 F10** 40 9N 74 51W
Levkás, *Greece* **21 E9** 38 40N 20 43 E
Levkímmi, *Greece* **23 B4** 39 25N 20 3 E
Levkímmi, Ákra, *Greece* **23 B4** 39 29N 20 4 E
Levkôsia = Nicosia, *Cyprus* **23 D12** 35 10N 33 25 E
Levskigrad = Karlovo, *Bulgaria* **21 C11** 42 38N 24 47 E
Lewes, *U.K.* **11 G8** 50 52N 0 1 E
Lewes, *U.S.A.* **76 F8** 38 46N 75 9W
Lewis, *U.K.* **12 C2** 58 9N 6 40W
Lewis →, *U.S.A.* **84 E4** 45 51N 122 48W
Lewis, Butt of, *U.K.* **12 C2** 58 31N 6 16W
Lewis Ra., *Australia* **60 D4** 20 3S 128 50 E
Lewis Range, *U.S.A.* **82 C7** 48 5N 113 5W
Lewis Run, *U.S.A.* **78 E6** 41 52N 78 40W
Lewisburg, *Pa., U.S.A.* **78 F8** 40 58N 76 54W
Lewisburg, *Tenn., U.S.A.* **77 H2** 35 27N 86 48W
Lewisburg, *W. Va., U.S.A.* **76 G5** 37 48N 80 27W
Lewisporte, *Canada* **71 C8** 49 15N 55 3W
Lewiston, *Idaho, U.S.A.* **82 C5** 46 25N 117 1W

Lewiston, Maine, U.S.A. 77 C11 44 6N 70 13W
Lewiston, N.Y., U.S.A. 78 C5 43 11N 79 3W
Lewistown, Mont., U.S.A. 82 C9 47 4N 109 26W
Lewistown, Pa., U.S.A. 78 F7 40 36N 77 34W
Lexington, Ill., U.S.A. 80 E10 40 39N 88 47W
Lexington, Ky., U.S.A. 76 F3 38 3N 84 30W
Lexington, Mich., U.S.A. 78 C2 43 16N 82 32W
Lexington, Mo., U.S.A. 80 F8 39 11N 93 52W
Lexington, N.C., U.S.A. 77 H5 35 49N 80 15W
Lexington, N.Y., U.S.A. 79 D10 42 15N 74 22W
Lexington, Nebr., U.S.A. 80 E5 40 47N 99 45W
Lexington, Ohio, U.S.A. 78 F2 40 41N 82 35W
Lexington, Tenn., U.S.A. 77 H1 35 39N 88 24W
Lexington, Va., U.S.A. 76 G6 37 47N 79 27W
Lexington Park, U.S.A. 76 F7 38 16N 76 27W
Leyburn, U.K. 10 C6 54 19N 1 48W
Leyland, U.K. 10 D5 53 42N 2 43W
Leyte □, Phil. 37 B6 11 0N 125 0 E
Lezhë, Albania 21 D8 41 47N 19 39 E
Lhasa, China 32 D4 29 25N 90 58 E
Lhazê, China 32 D3 29 5N 87 38 E
Lhokkruet, Indonesia 36 D1 4 55N 95 24 E
Lhokseumawe, Indonesia 36 C1 5 10N 97 10 E
L'Hospitalet de Llobregat, Spain 19 B7 41 21N 2 6 E
Li, Thailand 38 D2 17 48N 98 57 E
Li Xian, Gansu, China 34 G3 34 10N 105 5 E
Li Xian, Hebei, China 34 E8 38 30N 115 35 E
Lianga, Phil. 37 C7 8 38N 126 6 E
Liangcheng, Nei Monggol Zizhiqu, China 34 D7 40 28N 112 25 E
Liangcheng, Shandong, China 35 G10 35 32N 119 37 E
Liangdang, China 34 H4 33 56N 106 18 E
Liangpran, Indonesia 36 D4 1 4N 114 23 E
Lianshanguan, China 35 D12 40 53N 123 43 E
Lianshui, China 35 H10 33 42N 119 20 E
Lianyungang, China 35 G10 34 40N 119 11 E
Liao He →, China 35 D11 41 0N 121 50 E
Liaocheng, China 34 F8 36 28N 115 58 E
Liaodong Bandao, China 35 E12 40 0N 122 30 E
Liaodong Wan, China 35 D11 40 20N 121 10 E
Liaoning □, China 35 D12 41 40N 122 30 E
Liaoyang, China 35 D12 41 15N 122 58 E
Liaoyuan, China 35 C13 42 58N 125 2 E
Liaozhong, China 35 D12 41 23N 122 50 E
Liard →, Canada 72 A4 61 51N 121 18W
Liard River, Canada 72 B3 59 25N 126 5W
Liari, Pakistan 42 G2 25 37N 66 30 E
Libau = Liepāja, Latvia 9 H19 56 30N 21 0 E
Libby, U.S.A. 82 B6 48 23N 115 33W
Libenge, Dem. Rep. of the Congo 52 D3 3 40N 18 55 E
Liberal, U.S.A. 81 G4 37 3N 100 55W
Liberec, Czech Rep. 16 C8 50 47N 15 7 E
Liberia, Costa Rica 88 D2 10 40N 85 30W
Liberia ■, W. Afr. 50 G4 6 30N 9 30W
Liberty, Mo., U.S.A. 80 F7 39 15N 94 25W
Liberty, N.Y., U.S.A. 79 E10 41 48N 74 45W
Liberty, Pa., U.S.A. 78 E7 41 34N 77 6W
Liberty, Tex., U.S.A. 81 K7 30 3N 94 48W
Lîbîya, Sahrâ', Africa 51 C10 25 0N 25 0 E
Libobo, Tanjung, Indonesia 37 E7 0 54S 128 28 E
Libode, S. Africa 57 E4 31 33S 29 2 E
Libourne, France 18 D3 44 55N 0 14W
Libramont, Belgium 15 E5 49 55N 5 23 E
Libreville, Gabon 52 D1 0 25N 9 26 E
Libya ■, N. Afr. 51 C9 27 0N 17 0 E
Libyan Desert = Lîbîya, Sahrâ', Africa 51 C10 25 0N 25 0 E
Licantén, Chile 94 D1 35 55S 72 0W
Licata, Italy 20 F5 37 6N 13 56 E
Licheng, China 34 F7 36 28N 113 20 E
Lichfield, U.K. 11 E6 52 41N 1 49W
Lichinga, Mozam. 55 E4 13 13S 35 11 E
Lichtenburg, S. Africa 56 D4 26 8S 26 8 E
Licking →, U.S.A. 76 F3 39 6N 84 30W
Licungo →, Mozam. 55 F4 17 40S 37 15 E
Lida, Belarus 9 K21 53 53N 25 15 E
Lidköping, Sweden 9 G15 58 31N 13 7 E
Liebig, Mt., Australia 60 D5 23 18S 131 22 E
Liechtenstein ■, Europe 18 C8 47 8N 9 35 E
Liège, Belgium 15 D5 50 38N 5 35 E
Liège □, Belgium 15 D5 50 32N 5 35 E
Liegnitz = Legnica, Poland 16 C9 51 12N 16 10 E
Lienart, Dem. Rep. of the Congo 54 B2 3 3N 25 31 E
Lienyünchiangshih = Lianyungang, China 35 G10 34 40N 119 11 E
Lienz, Austria 16 E7 46 50N 12 46 E
Liepāja, Latvia 9 H19 56 30N 21 0 E
Lier, Belgium 15 C4 51 7N 4 34 E
Lièvre →, Canada 70 C4 45 31N 75 26W
Liffey →, Ireland 13 C5 53 21N 6 13W
Lifford, Ireland 13 B4 54 51N 7 29W
Lifudzin, Russia 30 B7 44 21N 134 58 E
Lightning Ridge, Australia 63 D4 29 22S 148 0 E
Ligonha →, Mozam. 55 F4 16 54S 39 9 E
Ligonier, U.S.A. 78 F5 40 15N 79 14W
Liguria □, Italy 18 D8 44 30N 8 50 E
Ligurian Sea, Medit. S. 20 C3 43 20N 9 0 E
Lihou Reefs and Cays, Australia 62 B5 17 25S 151 40 E
Lihue, U.S.A. 74 H15 21 59N 159 23W
Lijiang, China 32 D5 26 55N 100 20 E
Likasi, Dem. Rep. of the Congo 55 E2 10 55S 26 48 E
Likoma I., Malawi 55 E3 12 3S 34 45 E
Likumburu, Tanzania 55 D4 9 43S 35 8 E
Lille, France 18 A5 50 38N 3 3 E
Lille Bælt, Denmark 9 J13 55 20N 9 45 E
Lillehammer, Norway 9 F14 61 8N 10 30 E
Lillesand, Norway 9 G13 58 15N 8 23 E
Lillian Pt., Australia 61 E4 27 40S 126 6 E
Lillooet, Canada 72 C4 50 44N 121 57W
Lillooet →, Canada 72 D4 49 15N 121 57W
Lilongwe, Malawi 55 E3 14 0S 33 48 E
Liloy, Phil. 37 C6 8 4N 122 39 E
Lim →, Bos.-H. 21 C8 43 45N 19 15 E
Lima, Indonesia 37 E7 3 39S 127 58 E
Lima, Peru 92 F3 12 0S 77 0W
Lima, Mont., U.S.A. 82 D7 44 38N 112 36W
Lima, Ohio, U.S.A. 76 E3 40 44N 84 6W
Lima →, Portugal 19 B1 41 41N 8 50W
Liman, Indonesia 37 G14 7 48S 111 45 E
Limassol, Cyprus 23 E12 34 42N 33 1 E
Limavady, U.K. 13 A5 55 3N 6 56W
Limay →, Argentina 96 D3 39 0S 68 0W
Limay Mahuida, Argentina 94 D2 37 10S 66 45W
Limbang, Brunei 36 D5 4 42N 115 6 E
Limbaži, Latvia 9 H21 57 31N 24 42 E
Limbdi, India 42 H4 22 34N 71 51 E
Limbe, Cameroon 52 D1 4 1N 9 10 E
Limburg, Germany 16 C5 50 22N 8 4 E
Limburg □, Belgium 15 C5 51 2N 5 25 E
Limburg □, Neths. 15 C5 51 20N 5 55 E
Limeira, Brazil 95 A6 22 35S 47 28W
Limerick, Ireland 13 D3 52 40N 8 37W
Limerick, U.S.A. 79 C14 43 41N 70 48W
Limerick □, Ireland 13 D3 52 30N 8 50W
Limestone, U.S.A. 78 D6 42 2N 78 38W
Limestone →, Canada 73 B10 56 31N 94 7W
Limfjorden, Denmark 9 H13 56 55N 9 0 E
Limia = Lima →, Portugal 19 B1 41 41N 8 50W
Limingen, Norway 8 D15 64 48N 13 35 E
Limmen Bight, Australia 62 A2 14 40S 135 35 E
Limmen Bight →, Australia 62 B2 15 7S 135 44 E
Límnos, Greece 21 E11 39 50N 25 5 E
Limoges, Canada 79 A9 45 20N 75 16W
Limoges, France 18 D4 45 50N 1 15 E
Limón, Costa Rica 88 E3 10 0N 83 2W
Limon, U.S.A. 80 F3 39 16N 103 41W
Limousin, France 18 D4 45 30N 1 30 E
Limoux, France 18 E5 43 4N 2 12 E
Limpopo →, Africa 57 D5 25 5S 33 30 E
Limuru, Kenya 54 C4 1 2S 36 35 E
Lin Xian, China 34 F6 37 57N 110 58 E
Linares, Chile 94 D1 35 50S 71 40W
Linares, Mexico 87 C5 24 50N 99 40W
Linares, Spain 19 C4 38 10N 3 40W
Lincheng, China 34 F8 37 25N 114 30 E
Lincoln, Argentina 94 C3 34 55S 61 30W
Lincoln, N.Z. 59 K4 43 38S 172 30 E
Lincoln, U.K. 10 D7 53 14N 0 32W
Lincoln, Calif., U.S.A. 84 G5 38 54N 121 17W
Lincoln, Ill., U.S.A. 80 E10 40 9N 89 22W
Lincoln, Kans., U.S.A. 80 F5 39 3N 98 9W
Lincoln, Maine, U.S.A. 77 C11 45 22N 68 30W
Lincoln, N.H., U.S.A. 79 B13 44 3N 71 40W
Lincoln, N. Mex., U.S.A. 83 K11 33 30N 105 23W
Lincoln, Nebr., U.S.A. 80 E6 40 49N 96 41W
Lincoln City, U.S.A. 82 D1 44 57N 124 1W
Lincoln Hav = Lincoln Sea, Arctic 4 A5 84 0N 55 0W
Lincoln Sea, Arctic 4 A5 84 0N 55 0W
Lincolnshire □, U.K. 10 D7 53 14N 0 32W
Lincolnshire Wolds, U.K. 10 D7 53 26N 0 13W
Lincolnton, U.S.A. 77 H5 35 29N 81 16W
Lind, U.S.A. 82 C4 46 58N 118 37W
Linda, U.S.A. 84 F5 39 8N 121 34W
Linden, Guyana 92 B7 6 0N 58 10W
Linden, Ala., U.S.A. 77 J2 32 18N 87 48W
Linden, Calif., U.S.A. 84 G5 38 1N 121 5W
Linden, Tex., U.S.A. 81 J7 33 1N 94 22W
Lindenhurst, U.S.A. 79 F11 40 41N 73 23W
Lindesnes, Norway 9 H12 57 58N 7 3 E
Líndhos, Greece 23 C10 36 6N 28 4 E
Líndhos, Ákra, Greece 23 C10 36 4N 28 10 E
Lindi, Tanzania 55 D4 9 58S 39 38 E
Lindi □, Tanzania 55 D4 9 40S 38 30 E
Lindi →, Dem. Rep. of the Congo 54 B2 0 33N 25 5 E
Lindsay, Canada 78 B6 44 22N 78 43W
Lindsay, Calif., U.S.A. 84 J7 36 12N 119 5W
Lindsay, Okla., U.S.A. 81 H6 34 50N 97 38W
Lindsborg, U.S.A. 80 F6 38 35N 97 40W
Linesville, U.S.A. 78 E4 41 39N 80 26W
Linfen, China 34 F6 36 3N 111 30 E
Ling Xian, China 34 F9 37 22N 116 30 E
Lingao, China 38 C7 19 56N 109 42 E
Lingayen, Phil. 37 A6 16 1N 120 14 E
Lingayen G., Phil. 37 A6 16 10N 120 15 E
Lingbi, China 35 H9 33 33N 117 33 E
Lingchuan, China 34 G7 35 45N 113 12 E
Lingen, Germany 16 B4 52 31N 7 19 E
Lingga, Indonesia 36 E2 0 12S 104 37 E
Lingga, Kepulauan, Indonesia 36 E2 0 10S 104 30 E
Lingga Arch. = Lingga, Kepulauan, Indonesia 36 E2 0 10S 104 30 E
Lingle, U.S.A. 80 D2 42 8N 104 21W
Lingqiu, China 34 E8 39 28N 114 22 E
Lingshi, China 34 F6 36 48N 111 48 E
Lingshou, China 34 E8 38 20N 114 20 E
Lingshui, China 38 C8 18 27N 110 0 E
Lingtai, China 34 G4 35 0N 107 40 E
Linguère, Senegal 50 E2 15 25N 15 5W
Lingwu, China 34 E4 38 6N 106 20 E
Lingyuan, China 35 D10 41 10N 119 15 E
Linhai, China 33 D7 28 50N 121 8 E
Linhares, Brazil 93 G10 19 25S 40 4W
Linhe, China 34 D4 40 48N 107 20 E
Linjiang, China 35 D14 41 50N 127 0 E
Linköping, Sweden 9 G16 58 28N 15 36 E
Linkou, China 35 B16 45 15N 130 18 E
Linnhe, L., U.K. 12 E3 56 36N 5 25W
Linosa, Medit. S. 20 G5 35 51N 12 50 E
Linqi, China 34 G7 35 45N 113 52 E
Linqing, China 34 F8 36 50N 115 42 E
Linqu, China 35 F10 36 25N 118 30 E
Linru, China 34 G7 34 11N 112 52 E
Lins, Brazil 95 A6 21 40S 49 44W
Linta →, Madag. 57 D7 25 2S 44 5 E
Linton, Ind., U.S.A. 76 F2 39 2N 87 10W
Linton, N. Dak., U.S.A. 80 B4 46 16N 100 14W
Lintong, China 34 G5 34 20N 109 10 E
Linwood, Canada 78 C4 43 35N 80 43W
Linxi, China 35 C10 43 36N 118 2 E
Linxia, China 32 C5 35 36N 103 10 E
Linyanti →, Africa 56 B4 17 50S 25 5 E
Linyi, China 35 G10 35 5N 118 21 E
Linz, Austria 16 D8 48 18N 14 18 E
Linzhenzhen, China 34 F5 36 30N 109 59 E
Linzi, China 35 F10 36 50N 118 20 E
Lion, G. du, France 18 E6 43 10N 4 0 E
Lionárisso, Cyprus 23 D13 35 28N 34 8 E
Lions, G. of = Lion, G. du, France 18 E6 43 10N 4 0 E
Lion's Den, Zimbabwe 55 F3 17 15S 30 5 E
Lion's Head, Canada 78 B3 44 58N 81 15W
Lipa, Phil. 37 B6 13 57N 121 10 E
Lipali, Mozam. 55 F4 15 50S 35 50 E
Lípari, Italy 20 E6 38 26N 14 58 E
Lípari, Is. = Eólie, Ís., Italy 20 E6 38 30N 14 57 E
Lipcani, Moldova 17 D14 48 14N 26 48 E
Lipetsk, Russia 24 D6 52 37N 39 35 E
Lipkany = Lipcani, Moldova 17 D14 48 14N 26 48 E
Lipovcy Manzovka, Russia 30 B6 44 12N 132 26 E
Lipovets, Ukraine 17 D15 49 12N 29 1 E
Lippe →, Germany 16 C4 51 39N 6 36 E
Lipscomb, U.S.A. 81 G4 36 14N 100 16W
Liptrap C., Australia 63 F4 38 50S 145 55 E
Lira, Uganda 54 B3 2 17N 32 57 E
Liria = Lliria, Spain 19 C5 39 37N 0 35W
Lisala, Dem. Rep. of the Congo 52 D4 2 12N 21 38 E
Lisboa, Portugal 19 C1 38 42N 9 10W
Lisbon = Lisboa, Portugal 19 C1 38 42N 9 10W
Lisbon, N. Dak., U.S.A. 80 B6 46 27N 97 41W
Lisbon, N.H., U.S.A. 79 B13 44 13N 71 55W
Lisbon, Ohio, U.S.A. 78 F4 40 46N 80 46W
Lisbon Falls, U.S.A. 77 D10 44 0N 70 4W
Lisburn, U.K. 13 B5 54 31N 6 3W
Liscannor B., Ireland 13 D2 52 55N 9 24W
Lishi, China 34 F6 37 31N 111 8 E
Lishu, China 35 C13 43 20N 124 18 E
Lisianski I., Pac. Oc. 64 E10 26 2N 174 0W
Lisichansk = Lysychansk, Ukraine 25 E6 48 55N 38 30 E
Lisieux, France 18 B4 49 10N 0 12 E
Liski, Russia 25 D6 51 3N 39 30 E
Lismore, Australia 63 D5 28 44S 153 21 E
Lismore, Ireland 13 D4 52 8N 7 55W
Lista, Norway 9 G12 58 7N 6 39 E
Lister, Mt., Antarctica 5 D11 78 0S 162 0 E
Liston, Australia 63 D5 28 39S 152 6 E
Listowel, Canada 78 C4 43 44N 80 58W
Listowel, Ireland 13 D2 52 27N 9 29W
Litani →, Lebanon 47 B4 33 20N 35 15 E
Litchfield, Calif., U.S.A. 84 E6 40 24N 120 23W
Litchfield, Conn., U.S.A. 79 E11 41 45N 73 11W
Litchfield, Ill., U.S.A. 80 F10 39 11N 89 39W
Litchfield, Minn., U.S.A. 80 C7 45 8N 94 32W
Lithgow, Australia 63 E5 33 25S 150 8 E
Líthinon, Ákra, Greece 23 E6 34 55N 24 44 E
Lithuania ■, Europe 9 J20 55 30N 24 0 E
Lititz, U.S.A. 79 F8 40 9N 76 18W
Litoměřice, Czech Rep. 16 C8 50 33N 14 10 E
Little Abaco I., Bahamas 88 A4 26 50N 77 30W
Little Barrier I., N.Z. 59 G5 36 12S 175 8 E
Little Belt Mts., U.S.A. 82 C8 46 40N 110 45W
Little Blue →, U.S.A. 80 F6 39 42N 96 41W
Little Buffalo →, Canada 72 A6 61 0N 113 46W
Little Cayman, Cayman Is. 88 C3 19 41N 80 3W
Little Churchill →, Canada 73 B9 57 30N 95 22W
Little Colorado →, U.S.A. 83 H8 36 12N 111 48W
Little Current, Canada 70 C3 45 55N 82 0W
Little Current →, Canada 70 B3 50 57N 84 36W
Little Falls, Minn., U.S.A. 80 C7 45 59N 94 22W
Little Falls, N.Y., U.S.A. 79 C10 43 3N 74 51W
Little Fork →, U.S.A. 80 A8 48 31N 93 35W
Little Grand Rapids, Canada 73 C9 52 0N 95 29W
Little Humboldt →, U.S.A. 82 F5 41 1N 117 43W
Little Inagua I., Bahamas 89 B5 21 40N 73 50W
Little Karoo, S. Africa 56 E3 33 45S 21 0 E
Little Lake, U.S.A. 85 K9 35 56N 117 55W
Little Laut Is. = Laut Kecil, Kepulauan, Indonesia 36 E5 4 45S 115 40 E
Little Mecatina = Petit-Mécatina →, Canada 71 B8 50 40N 59 30W
Little Minch, U.K. 12 D2 57 35N 6 45W
Little Missouri →, U.S.A. 80 B3 47 36N 102 25W
Little Ouse →, U.K. 11 E9 52 22N 1 12 E
Little Rann, India 42 H4 23 25N 71 25 E
Little Red →, U.S.A. 81 H9 35 11N 91 27W
Little River, N.Z. 59 K4 43 45S 172 49 E
Little Rock, U.S.A. 81 H8 34 45N 92 17W
Little Ruaha →, Tanzania 54 D4 7 57S 37 53 E
Little Sable Pt., U.S.A. 76 D2 43 38N 86 33W
Little Sioux →, U.S.A. 80 E6 41 48N 96 4W
Little Smoky →, Canada 72 C5 54 44N 117 11W
Little Snake →, U.S.A. 82 F9 40 27N 108 26W
Little Valley, U.S.A. 78 D6 42 15N 78 48W
Little Wabash →, U.S.A. 76 G1 37 55N 88 5W
Little White →, U.S.A. 80 D4 43 40N 100 40W
Littlefield, U.S.A. 81 J3 33 55N 102 20W
Littlehampton, U.K. 11 G7 50 49N 0 32W
Littleton, U.S.A. 79 B13 44 18N 71 46W
Liu He →, China 35 D11 40 55N 121 35 E
Liuba, China 34 H4 33 38N 106 55 E
Liugou, China 35 D10 40 57N 118 15 E
Liuhe, China 35 C13 42 17N 125 43 E
Liukang Tenggaja = Sabalana, Kepulauan, Indonesia 37 F5 6 45S 118 50 E
Liuli, Tanzania 55 E3 11 3S 34 38 E
Liuwa Plain, Zambia 53 G4 14 20S 22 30 E
Liuzhou, China 33 D5 24 22N 109 22 E
Liuzhuang, China 35 H11 33 12N 120 18 E
Livadhia, Cyprus 23 E12 34 57N 33 38 E
Live Oak, Calif., U.S.A. 84 F5 39 17N 121 40W
Live Oak, Fla., U.S.A. 77 K4 30 18N 82 59W
Liveras, Cyprus 23 D11 35 23N 32 57 E
Livermore, U.S.A. 84 H5 37 41N 121 47W
Livermore, Mt., U.S.A. 81 K2 30 38N 104 11W
Livermore Falls, U.S.A. 77 C11 44 29N 70 11W
Liverpool, Canada 71 D7 44 5N 64 41W
Liverpool, U.K. 10 D4 53 25N 3 0W
Liverpool, U.S.A. 79 C8 43 6N 76 13W
Liverpool Bay, U.K. 10 D4 53 30N 3 20W
Liverpool Plains, Australia 63 E5 31 15S 150 15 E
Liverpool Ra., Australia 63 E5 31 50S 150 30 E
Livingston, Guatemala 88 C2 15 50N 88 50W
Livingston, U.K. 12 F5 55 54N 3 30W
Livingston, Ala., U.S.A. 77 J1 32 35N 88 11W
Livingston, Calif., U.S.A. 84 H6 37 23N 120 43W
Livingston, Mont., U.S.A. 82 D8 45 40N 110 34W
Livingston, S.C., U.S.A. 77 J5 33 32N 80 53W
Livingston, Tenn., U.S.A. 77 G3 36 23N 85 19W
Livingston, Tex., U.S.A. 81 K7 30 43N 94 56W
Livingston, L., U.S.A. 81 K7 30 50N 95 10W
Livingston Manor, U.S.A. 79 E10 41 54N 74 50W
Livingstone, Zambia 55 F2 17 46S 25 52 E
Livingstone Mts., Tanzania 55 D3 9 40S 34 20 E
Livingstonia, Malawi 55 E3 10 38S 34 5 E
Livny, Russia 24 D6 52 30N 37 30 E
Livonia, Mich., U.S.A. 76 D4 42 23N 83 23W
Livonia, N.Y., U.S.A. 78 D7 42 49N 77 40W
Livorno, Italy 20 C4 43 33N 10 19 E
Livramento, Brazil 95 C4 30 55S 55 30W
Liwale, Tanzania 55 D4 9 48S 37 58 E
Lizard I., Australia 62 A4 14 42S 145 30 E
Lizard Pt., U.K. 11 H2 49 57N 5 13W
Ljubljana, Slovenia 16 E8 46 4N 14 33 E
Ljungan →, Sweden 9 E17 62 18N 17 23 E
Ljungby, Sweden 9 H15 56 49N 13 55 E
Ljusdal, Sweden 9 F17 61 46N 16 3 E
Ljusnan →, Sweden 9 F17 61 12N 17 8 E
Ljusne, Sweden 9 F17 61 13N 17 7 E
Llancanelo, Salina, Argentina 94 D2 35 40S 69 8W
Llandeilo, U.K. 11 F4 51 53N 3 59W
Llandovery, U.K. 11 F4 51 59N 3 48W
Llandrindod Wells, U.K. 11 E4 52 14N 3 22W
Llandudno, U.K. 10 D4 53 19N 3 50W
Llanelli, U.K. 11 F3 51 41N 4 10W
Llanes, Spain 19 A3 43 25N 4 50W
Llangollen, U.K. 10 E4 52 58N 3 11W
Llanidloes, U.K. 11 E4 52 27N 3 31W
Llano, U.S.A. 81 K5 30 45N 98 41W
Llano →, U.S.A. 81 K5 30 39N 98 26W
Llano Estacado, U.S.A. 81 J3 33 30N 103 0W
Llanos, S. Amer. 92 C4 5 0N 71 35W
Llanquihue, L., Chile 96 E1 41 10S 72 50W
Llanwrtyd Wells, U.K. 11 E4 52 7N 3 38W
Llebeig, C. des, Spain 22 B9 39 33N 2 18 E
Lleida, Spain 19 B6 41 37N 0 39 E
Llentrisca, C., Spain 22 C7 38 52N 1 15 E
Llera, Mexico 87 C5 23 19N 99 1W
Lleyn Peninsula, U.K. 10 E3 52 51N 4 36W
Llico, Chile 94 C1 34 46S 72 5W
Lliria, Spain 19 C5 39 37N 0 35W
Llobregat →, Spain 19 B7 41 19N 2 9 E
Lloret de Mar, Spain 19 B7 41 41N 2 53 E
Lloyd B., Australia 62 A3 12 45S 143 27 E
Lloyd L., Canada 73 B7 57 22N 108 57W
Lloydminster, Canada 73 C7 53 17N 110 0W
Llucmajor, Spain 22 B9 39 29N 2 53 E
Llullaillaco, Volcán, S. Amer. 94 A2 24 43S 68 30W
Lo →, Vietnam 38 B5 21 18N 105 25 E
Loa, U.S.A. 83 G8 38 24N 111 39W
Loa →, Chile 94 A1 21 26S 70 41W
Loaita I., S. China Sea 36 B4 10 41N 114 25 E
Loange →, Dem. Rep. of the Congo 52 E4 4 17S 20 2 E
Lobatse, Botswana 56 D4 25 12S 25 40 E
Lobería, Argentina 94 D4 38 10S 58 40W
Lobito, Angola 53 G2 12 18S 13 35 E
Lobos, Argentina 94 D4 35 10S 59 0W
Lobos, I., Mexico 86 B2 27 15N 110 30W
Lobos, I. de, Canary Is. 22 F6 28 45N 13 50W
Loc Binh, Vietnam 38 B6 21 46N 106 54 E
Loc Ninh, Vietnam 39 G6 11 50N 106 34 E
Locarno, Switz. 18 C8 46 10N 8 47 E
Loch Baghasdail = Lochboisdale, U.K. 12 D1 57 9N 7 20W
Loch Garman = Wexford, Ireland 13 D5 52 20N 6 28W
Loch Nam Madadh = Lochmaddy, U.K. 12 D1 57 36N 7 10W
Lochaber, U.K. 12 E3 56 59N 5 1W
Locharbriggs, U.K. 12 F5 55 7N 3 35W
Lochboisdale, U.K. 12 D1 57 9N 7 20W
Loche, L. La, Canada 73 B7 56 30N 109 30W
Lochem, Neths. 15 B6 52 9N 6 26 E
Loches, France 18 C4 47 7N 1 0 E
Lochgilphead, U.K. 12 E3 56 2N 5 26W
Lochinver, U.K. 12 C3 58 9N 5 14W
Lochmaddy, U.K. 12 D1 57 36N 7 10W
Lochnagar, Australia 62 C4 23 33S 145 38 E
Lochnagar, U.K. 12 E5 56 57N 3 15W
Lochy, L., U.K. 12 E4 57 0N 4 53W
Lock, Australia 63 E2 33 34S 135 46 E
Lock Haven, U.S.A. 78 E7 41 8N 77 28W
Lockeford, U.S.A. 84 G5 38 10N 121 9W
Lockeport, Canada 71 D6 43 47N 65 4W
Lockerbie, U.K. 12 F5 55 7N 3 21W
Lockhart, U.S.A. 81 L6 29 53N 97 40W
Lockhart, L., Australia 61 F2 33 15S 119 3 E
Lockhart River, Australia 62 A3 12 58S 143 30 E
Lockney, U.S.A. 81 H4 34 7N 101 27W
Lockport, U.S.A. 78 C6 43 10N 78 42W
Lod, Israel 47 D3 31 57N 34 54 E
Lodeinoye Pole, Russia 24 B5 60 44N 33 33 E
Lodge Bay, Canada 71 B8 52 14N 55 51W
Lodge Grass, U.S.A. 82 D10 45 19N 107 22W
Lodgepole Cr. →, U.S.A. 80 E2 41 20N 104 30W
Lodhran, Pakistan 42 E4 29 32N 71 30 E
Lodi, Italy 18 D8 45 19N 9 30 E
Lodi, Calif., U.S.A. 84 G5 38 8N 121 16W
Lodi, Ohio, U.S.A. 78 E3 41 2N 82 0W
Lodja, Dem. Rep. of the Congo 54 C1 3 30S 23 23 E
Lodwar, Kenya 54 B4 3 10N 35 40 E
Łódź, Poland 17 C10 51 45N 19 27 E
Loei, Thailand 38 D3 17 29N 101 35 E
Loengo, Dem. Rep. of the Congo 54 C2 4 48S 26 30 E
Loeriesfontein, S. Africa 56 E2 31 0S 19 26 E
Lofoten, Norway 8 B15 68 30N 14 0 E
Logan, Iowa, U.S.A. 80 E7 41 39N 95 47W
Logan, Ohio, U.S.A. 76 F4 39 32N 82 25W
Logan, Utah, U.S.A. 82 F8 41 44N 111 50W
Logan, W. Va., U.S.A. 76 G5 37 51N 81 59W
Logan, Mt., Canada 68 B5 60 31N 140 22W
Logandale, U.S.A. 85 J12 36 36N 114 29W
Logansport, Ind., U.S.A. 76 E2 40 45N 86 22W
Logansport, La., U.S.A. 81 K8 31 58N 94 0W
Logone →, Chad 51 F9 12 6N 15 2 E
Logroño, Spain 19 A4 42 28N 2 27W
Lohardaga, India 43 H11 23 27N 84 45 E
Loharia, India 42 H6 23 45N 74 14 E
Loharu, India 42 E6 28 27N 75 49 E
Lohja, Finland 9 F21 60 12N 24 5 E
Lohri Wah →, Pakistan 42 F2 27 27N 67 37 E
Loi-kaw, Burma 41 K20 19 40N 97 17 E
Loimaa, Finland 9 F20 60 50N 23 5 E
Loir →, France 18 C3 47 33N 0 32W
Loire →, France 18 C3 47 16N 2 10W
Loja, Ecuador 92 D3 3 59S 79 16W
Loja, Spain 19 D3 37 10N 4 10W
Loji = Kawasi, Indonesia 37 E7 1 38S 127 28 E
Lokandu, Dem. Rep. of the Congo 54 C2 2 30S 25 45 E
Lokeren, Belgium 15 C3 51 6N 3 59 E
Lokgwabe, Botswana 56 C3 24 10S 21 50 E
Lokichokio, Kenya 54 B3 4 19N 35 48 E
Lokitaung, Kenya 54 B4 4 12N 35 48 E

Lokkan tekojärvi, Finland 8 C22 67 55N 27 35 E
Lokoja, Nigeria 50 G7 7 47N 6 45 E
Lola, Mt., U.S.A. 84 F6 39 26N 120 22W
Loliondo, Tanzania 54 C4 2 2S 35 39 E
Lolland, Denmark 9 J14 54 45N 11 30 E
Lolo, U.S.A. 82 C6 46 45N 114 5W
Lom, Bulgaria 21 C10 43 48N 23 12 E
Lom Kao, Thailand 38 D3 16 53N 101 14 E
Lom Sak, Thailand 38 D3 16 47N 101 15 E
Loma, U.S.A. 82 C8 47 56N 110 30W
Loma Linda, U.S.A. 85 L9 34 3N 117 16W
Lomami →, Dem. Rep. of the Congo 54 B1 0 46N 24 16 E
Lomas de Zamóra, Argentina 94 C4 34 45S 58 25W
Lombadina, Australia 60 C3 16 31S 122 54 E
Lombárdia □, Italy 18 D8 45 40N 9 30 E
Lombardy = Lombárdia □, Italy 18 D8 45 40N 9 30 E
Lomblen, Indonesia 37 F6 8 30S 123 32 E
Lombok, Indonesia 36 F5 8 45S 116 30 E
Lomé, Togo 50 G6 6 9N 1 20 E
Lomela, Dem. Rep. of the Congo 52 E4 2 19S 23 15 E
Lomela →, Dem. Rep. of the Congo 52 E4 0 15S 20 40 E
Lommel, Belgium 15 C5 51 14N 5 19 E
Lomond, Canada 72 C6 50 24N 112 36W
Lomond, L., U.K. 12 E4 56 8N 4 38W
Lomphat, Cambodia 38 F6 13 30N 106 59 E
Lompobatang, Indonesia 37 F5 5 24S 119 56 E
Lompoc, U.S.A. 85 L6 34 38N 120 28W
Łomża, Poland 17 B12 53 10N 22 2 E
Loncoche, Chile 96 D2 39 20S 72 50W
Londa, India 40 M9 15 30N 74 30 E
Londiani, Kenya 54 C4 0 10S 35 33 E
London, Canada 78 D3 42 59N 81 15W
London, U.K. 11 F7 51 30N 0 3W
London, Ky., U.S.A. 76 G3 37 8N 84 5W
London, Ohio, U.S.A. 76 F4 39 53N 83 27W
London, Greater □, U.K. 11 F7 51 36N 0 5W
Londonderry, U.K. 13 B4 55 0N 7 20W
Londonderry □, U.K. 13 B4 55 0N 7 20W
Londonderry, C., Australia 60 B4 13 45S 126 55 E
Londonderry, I., Chile 96 H2 55 0S 71 0W
Londres, Argentina 96 B3 27 43S 67 7W
Londrina, Brazil 95 A5 23 18S 51 10W
Lone Pine, U.S.A. 84 J8 36 36N 118 4W
Lonely Mine, Zimbabwe 57 B4 19 30S 28 49 E
Long B., U.S.A. 77 J6 33 35N 78 45W
Long Beach, Calif., U.S.A. 85 M8 33 47N 118 11W
Long Beach, N.Y., U.S.A. 79 F11 40 35N 73 39W
Long Beach, Wash., U.S.A. 84 D2 46 21N 124 3W
Long Branch, U.S.A. 79 F11 40 18N 74 0W
Long Creek, U.S.A. 82 D4 44 43N 119 6W
Long Eaton, U.K. 10 E6 52 53N 1 15W
Long I., Australia 62 C4 20 22S 148 51 E
Long I., Bahamas 89 B4 23 20N 75 10W
Long I., Canada 70 B4 54 50N 79 20W
Long I., Ireland 13 E2 51 30N 9 34W
Long I., U.S.A. 79 F11 40 45N 73 30W
Long Island Sd., U.S.A. 79 E12 41 10N 73 0W
Long L., Canada 70 C2 49 30N 86 50W
Long Lake, U.S.A. 79 C10 43 58N 74 25W
Long Point B., Canada 78 D4 42 40N 80 10W
Long Prairie →, U.S.A. 80 C7 46 20N 94 36W
Long Pt., Canada 78 D4 42 35N 80 2W
Long Range Mts., Canada 71 C8 49 30N 57 30W
Long Reef, Australia 60 B4 14 1S 125 48 E
Long Spruce, Canada 73 B10 56 24N 94 21W
Long Str. = Longa, Proliv, Russia 4 C16 70 0N 175 0 E
Long Thanh, Vietnam 39 G6 10 47N 106 57 E
Long Xian, China 34 G4 34 55N 106 55 E
Long Xuyen, Vietnam 39 G5 10 19N 105 28 E
Longa, Proliv, Russia 4 C16 70 0N 175 0 E
Longbenton, U.K. 10 B6 55 1N 1 31W
Longboat Key, U.S.A. 77 M4 27 23N 82 39W
Longde, China 34 G4 35 30N 106 20 E
Longford, Australia 62 G4 41 32S 147 3 E
Longford, Ireland 13 C4 53 43N 7 49W
Longford □, Ireland 13 C4 53 42N 7 45W
Longhua, China 35 D9 41 18N 117 45 E
Longido, Tanzania 54 C4 2 43S 36 42 E
Longiram, Indonesia 36 E5 0 5S 115 45 E
Longkou, China 35 F11 37 40N 120 18 E
Longlac, Canada 70 C2 49 45N 86 25W
Longmeadow, U.S.A. 79 D12 42 3N 72 34W
Longmont, U.S.A. 80 E2 40 10N 105 6W
Longnawan, Indonesia 36 D4 1 51N 114 55 E
Longreach, Australia 62 C3 23 28S 144 14 E
Longueuil, Canada 79 A11 45 32N 73 28W
Longview, Tex., U.S.A. 81 J7 32 30N 94 44W
Longview, Wash., U.S.A. 84 D4 46 8N 122 57W
Longxi, China 34 G3 34 53N 104 40 E
Lonoke, U.S.A. 81 H9 34 47N 91 54W
Lonquimay, Chile 96 D2 38 26S 71 14W
Lons-le-Saunier, France 18 C6 46 40N 5 31 E
Looe, U.K. 11 G3 50 22N 4 28W
Lookout, C., Canada 70 A3 55 18N 83 56W
Lookout, C., U.S.A. 77 H7 34 35N 76 32W
Loolmalasin, Tanzania 54 C4 3 0S 35 53 E
Loon →, Alta., Canada 72 B5 57 8N 115 3W
Loon →, Man., Canada 73 B8 55 53N 101 59W
Loon Lake, Canada 73 C7 54 2N 109 10W
Loongana, Australia 61 F4 30 52S 127 5 E
Loop Hd., Ireland 13 D2 52 34N 9 56W
Lop Buri, Thailand 38 E3 14 48N 100 37 E
Lop Nor = Lop Nur, China 32 B4 40 20N 90 10 E
Lop Nur, China 32 B4 40 20N 90 10 E
Lopatina, Gora, Russia 27 D15 50 47N 143 10 E
Lopez, U.S.A. 79 E8 41 27N 76 20W
Lopez, C., Gabon 52 E1 0 47S 8 40 E
Lopphavet, Norway 8 A19 70 27N 21 15 E
Lora →, Afghan. 40 D4 31 35N 66 32 E
Lora, Hāmūn-i-, Pakistan 40 E4 29 38N 64 58 E
Lora Cr. →, Australia 63 D2 28 10S 135 22 E
Lora del Río, Spain 19 D3 37 39N 5 33W
Lorain, U.S.A. 78 E2 41 28N 82 11W
Loralai, Pakistan 42 D3 30 20N 68 41 E
Lorca, Spain 19 D5 37 41N 1 42W
Lord Howe I., Pac. Oc. 64 L7 31 33S 159 6 E
Lord Howe Ridge, Pac. Oc. 64 L8 30 0S 162 30 E
Lordsburg, U.S.A. 83 K9 32 21N 108 43W
Lorestan □, Iran 45 C6 33 30N 48 40 E
Loreto, Brazil 93 E9 7 5S 45 10W
Loreto, Mexico 86 B2 26 1N 111 21W
Lorient, France 18 C2 47 45N 3 23W
Lormi, India 43 H9 22 17N 81 41 E
Lorn, U.K. 12 E3 56 26N 5 10W
Lorn, Firth of, U.K. 12 E3 56 20N 5 40W
Lorne, Australia 63 F3 38 33S 143 59 E
Lorovouno, Cyprus 23 D11 35 8N 32 36 E
Lorraine □, France 18 B7 48 53N 6 0 E
Los Alamos, Calif., U.S.A. 85 L6 34 44N 120 17W
Los Alamos, N. Mex., U.S.A. 83 J10 35 53N 106 19W
Los Altos, U.S.A. 84 H4 37 23N 122 7W
Los Andes, Chile 94 C1 32 50S 70 40W
Los Angeles, Chile 94 D1 37 28S 72 23W
Los Angeles, U.S.A. 85 M8 34 4N 118 15W
Los Angeles, Bahia de, Mexico 86 B2 28 56N 113 34W
Los Angeles Aqueduct, U.S.A. 85 K9 35 22N 118 5W
Los Banos, U.S.A. 84 H6 37 4N 120 51W
Los Blancos, Argentina 94 A3 23 40S 62 30W
Los Chiles, Costa Rica 88 D3 11 2N 84 43W
Los Cristianos, Canary Is. 22 F3 28 3N 16 42W
Los Gatos, U.S.A. 84 H5 37 14N 121 59W
Los Hermanos Is., Venezuela 89 D7 11 45N 64 25W
Los Islotes, Canary Is. 22 E6 29 4N 13 44W
Los Llanos de Aridane, Canary Is. 22 F2 28 38N 17 54W
Los Loros, Chile 94 B1 27 50S 70 6W
Los Lunas, U.S.A. 83 J10 34 48N 106 44W
Los Mochis, Mexico 86 B3 25 45N 108 57W
Los Olivos, U.S.A. 85 L6 34 40N 120 7W
Los Palacios, Cuba 88 B3 22 35N 83 15W
Los Reyes, Mexico 86 D4 19 34N 102 30W
Los Roques Is., Venezuela 89 D6 11 50N 66 45W
Los Teques, Venezuela 92 A5 10 21N 67 2W
Los Testigos, Is., Venezuela 92 A6 11 23N 63 6W
Los Vilos, Chile 94 C1 32 10S 71 30W
Lošinj, Croatia 16 F8 44 30N 14 30 E
Loskop Dam, S. Africa 57 D4 25 23S 29 20 E
Lossiemouth, U.K. 12 D5 57 42N 3 17W
Lostwithiel, U.K. 11 G3 50 24N 4 41W
Lot →, France 18 D4 44 18N 0 20 E
Lota, Chile 94 D1 37 5S 73 10W
Loṭfābād, Iran 45 B8 37 32N 59 20 E
Lothair, S. Africa 57 D5 26 22S 30 27 E
Loubomo, Congo 52 E2 4 9S 12 47 E
Loudonville, U.S.A. 78 F2 40 38N 82 14W
Louga, Senegal 50 E2 15 45N 16 5W
Loughborough, U.K. 10 E6 52 47N 1 11W
Loughrea, Ireland 13 C3 53 12N 8 33W
Loughros More B., Ireland 13 B3 54 48N 8 32W
Louis Trichardt, S. Africa 57 C4 23 1S 29 43 E
Louis XIV, Pte., Canada 70 B4 54 37N 79 45W
Louisa, U.S.A. 76 F4 38 7N 82 36W
Louisbourg, Canada 71 C8 45 55N 60 0W
Louise I., Canada 72 C2 52 55N 131 50W
Louiseville, Canada 70 C5 46 20N 72 56W
Louisiade Arch., Papua N. G. 64 J7 11 10S 153 0 E
Louisiana, U.S.A. 80 F9 39 27N 91 3W
Louisiana □, U.S.A. 81 K9 30 50N 92 0W
Louisville, Ky., U.S.A. 76 F3 38 15N 85 46W
Louisville, Miss., U.S.A. 81 J10 33 7N 89 3W
Louisville, Ohio, U.S.A. 78 F3 40 50N 81 16W
Loulé, Portugal 19 D1 37 9N 8 0W
Loup City, U.S.A. 80 E5 41 17N 98 58W
Loups Marins, Lacs des, Canada 70 A5 56 30N 73 45W
Lourdes, France 18 E3 43 6N 0 3W
Louth, Australia 63 E4 30 30S 145 8 E
Louth, Ireland 13 C5 53 58N 6 32W
Louth, U.K. 10 D7 53 22N 0 1W
Louth □, Ireland 13 C5 53 56N 6 34W
Louvain = Leuven, Belgium 15 D4 50 52N 4 42 E
Louwsburg, S. Africa 57 D5 27 37S 31 7 E
Lovech, Bulgaria 21 C11 43 8N 24 42 E
Loveland, U.S.A. 80 E2 40 24N 105 5W
Lovell, U.S.A. 82 D9 44 50N 108 24W
Lovelock, U.S.A. 82 F4 40 11N 118 28W
Loviisa, Finland 9 F22 60 28N 26 12 E
Loving, U.S.A. 81 J2 32 17N 104 6W
Lovington, U.S.A. 81 J3 32 57N 103 21W
Lovisa = Loviisa, Finland 9 F22 60 28N 26 12 E
Low, L., Canada 70 B4 52 29N 76 17W
Low Pt., Australia 61 F4 32 25S 127 25 E
Low Tatra = Nízké Tatry, Slovak Rep. 17 D10 48 55N 19 30 E
Lowa, Dem. Rep. of the Congo 54 C2 1 25S 25 47 E
Lowa →, Dem. Rep. of the Congo 54 C2 1 24S 25 51 E
Lowell, U.S.A. 79 D13 42 38N 71 19W
Lowellville, U.S.A. 78 E4 41 2N 80 32W
Löwen →, Namibia 56 D2 26 51S 18 17 E
Lower Alkali L., U.S.A. 82 F3 41 16N 120 2W
Lower Arrow L., Canada 72 D5 49 40N 118 5W
Lower California = Baja California, Mexico 86 A1 31 10N 115 12W
Lower Hutt, N.Z. 59 J5 41 10S 174 55 E
Lower Lake, U.S.A. 84 G4 38 55N 122 37W
Lower Manitou L., Canada 73 D10 49 15N 93 0W
Lower Post, Canada 72 B3 59 58N 128 30W
Lower Red L., U.S.A. 80 B7 47 58N 95 0W
Lower Saxony = Niedersachsen □, Germany 16 B5 52 50N 9 0 E
Lower Tunguska = Tunguska, Nizhnyaya →, Russia 27 C9 65 48N 88 4 E
Lowestoft, U.K. 11 E9 52 29N 1 45 E
Lowgar □, Afghan. 40 B6 34 0N 69 0 E
Łowicz, Poland 17 B10 52 6N 19 55 E
Lowville, U.S.A. 79 C9 43 47N 75 29W
Loxton, Australia 63 E3 34 28S 140 31 E
Loxton, S. Africa 56 E3 31 30S 22 22 E
Loyalton, U.S.A. 84 F6 39 41N 120 14W
Loyalty Is. = Loyauté, Îs., N. Cal. 64 K8 20 50S 166 30 E
Loyang = Luoyang, China 34 G7 34 40N 112 26 E
Loyauté, Îs., N. Cal. 64 K8 20 50S 166 30 E
Loyev = Loyew, Belarus 17 C16 51 56N 30 46 E
Loyew, Belarus 17 C16 51 56N 30 46 E
Loyoro, Uganda 54 B3 3 22N 34 14 E
Luachimo, Angola 52 F4 7 23S 20 48 E
Luajan →, India 43 G11 24 44N 85 1 E
Lualaba →, Dem. Rep. of the Congo 54 B2 0 26N 25 20 E
Luampa, Zambia 55 F1 15 4S 24 20 E
Luan Chau, Vietnam 38 B4 21 38N 103 24 E
Luan He →, China 35 E10 39 20N 119 5 E
Luan Xian, China 35 E10 39 40N 118 40 E
Luancheng, China 34 F8 37 53N 114 40 E
Luanda, Angola 52 F2 8 50S 13 15 E
Luang, Thale, Thailand 39 J3 7 30N 100 15 E
Luang Prabang, Laos 38 C4 19 52N 102 10 E
Luangwa, Zambia 55 F3 15 35S 30 16 E
Luangwa →, Zambia 55 E3 14 25S 30 25 E
Luangwa Valley, Zambia 55 E3 13 30S 31 30 E
Luanne, China 35 D9 40 55N 117 40 E
Luanping, China 35 D9 40 53N 117 23 E
Luanshya, Zambia 55 E2 13 3S 28 28 E
Luapula □, Zambia 55 E2 11 0S 29 0 E
Luapula →, Africa 55 D2 9 26S 28 33 E
Luarca, Spain 19 A2 43 32N 6 32W
Luashi, Dem. Rep. of the Congo 55 E1 10 50S 23 36 E
Luau, Angola 52 G4 10 40S 22 10 E
Lubana, Ozero = Lubānas Ezers, Latvia 9 H22 56 45N 27 0 E
Lubānas Ezers, Latvia 9 H22 56 45N 27 0 E
Lubang Is., Phil. 37 B6 13 50N 120 12 E
Lubao, Dem. Rep. of the Congo 54 D2 5 17S 25 42 E
Lubbock, U.S.A. 81 J4 33 35N 101 51W
Lübeck, Germany 16 B6 53 52N 10 40 E
Lubefu, Dem. Rep. of the Congo 54 C1 4 47S 24 27 E
Lubefu →, Dem. Rep. of the Congo 54 C1 4 10S 23 0 E
Lubero = Luofu, Dem. Rep. of the Congo 54 C2 0 10S 29 15 E
Lubicon L., Canada 72 B5 56 23N 115 56W
Lubilash →, Dem. Rep. of the Congo 52 F4 6 2S 23 45 E
Lubin, Poland 16 C9 51 24N 16 11 E
Lublin, Poland 17 C12 51 12N 22 38 E
Lubnān, Jabal, Lebanon 47 B4 33 45N 35 40 E
Lubny, Ukraine 26 D4 50 3N 32 58 E
Lubongola, Dem. Rep. of the Congo 54 C2 2 35S 27 50 E
Lubudi, Dem. Rep. of the Congo 52 F5 9 57S 25 58 E
Lubudi →, Dem. Rep. of the Congo 55 D2 9 0S 25 35 E
Lubuklinggau, Indonesia 36 E2 3 15S 102 55 E
Lubuksikaping, Indonesia 36 D2 0 10N 100 15 E
Lubumbashi, Dem. Rep. of the Congo 55 E2 11 40S 27 28 E
Lubunda, Dem. Rep. of the Congo 54 D2 5 12S 26 41 E
Lubungu, Zambia 55 E2 14 35S 26 24 E
Lubutu, Dem. Rep. of the Congo 54 C2 0 45S 26 30 E
Luc An Chau, Vietnam 38 A5 22 6N 104 43 E
Lucan, Canada 78 C3 43 11N 81 24W
Lucania, Mt., Canada 68 B5 61 1N 140 29W
Lucas Channel, Canada 78 A3 45 21N 81 45W
Lucca, Italy 20 C4 43 50N 10 29 E
Luce Bay, U.K. 12 G4 54 45N 4 48W
Lucea, Jamaica 88 C4 18 25N 78 10W
Lucedale, U.S.A. 77 K1 30 56N 88 35W
Lucena, Phil. 37 B6 13 56N 121 37 E
Lucena, Spain 19 D3 37 27N 4 31W
Lučenec, Slovak Rep. 17 D10 48 18N 19 42 E
Lucerne = Luzern, Switz. 18 C8 47 3N 8 18 E
Lucerne, U.S.A. 84 F4 39 6N 122 48W
Lucerne Valley, U.S.A. 85 L10 34 27N 116 57W
Lucero, Mexico 86 A3 30 49N 106 30W
Lucheng, China 34 F7 36 20N 113 11 E
Lucheringo →, Mozam. 55 E4 11 43S 36 17 E
Lucia, U.S.A. 84 J5 36 2N 121 33W
Lucinda, Australia 62 B4 18 32S 146 20 E
Luckenwalde, Germany 16 B7 52 5N 13 10 E
Luckhoff, S. Africa 56 D3 29 44S 24 43 E
Lucknow, Canada 78 C3 43 57N 81 31W
Lucknow, India 43 F9 26 50N 81 0 E
Lüda = Dalian, China 35 E11 38 50N 121 40 E
Lüderitz, Namibia 56 D2 26 41S 15 8 E
Lüderitzbaai, Namibia 56 D2 26 36S 15 8 E
Ludhiana, India 42 D6 30 57N 75 56 E
Ludington, U.S.A. 76 D2 43 57N 86 27W
Ludlow, U.K. 11 E5 52 22N 2 42W
Ludlow, Calif., U.S.A. 85 L10 34 43N 116 10W
Ludlow, Pa., U.S.A. 78 E6 41 43N 78 56W
Ludlow, Vt., U.S.A. 79 C12 43 24N 72 42W
Ludvika, Sweden 9 F16 60 8N 15 14 E
Ludwigsburg, Germany 16 D5 48 53N 9 11 E
Ludwigshafen, Germany 16 D5 49 29N 8 26 E
Lueki, Dem. Rep. of the Congo 54 C2 3 20S 25 48 E
Luena, Dem. Rep. of the Congo 55 D2 9 28S 25 43 E
Luena, Zambia 55 E3 10 40S 30 25 E
Lüeyang, China 34 H4 33 22N 106 10 E
Lufira →, Dem. Rep. of the Congo 55 D2 9 30S 27 0 E
Lufkin, U.S.A. 81 K7 31 21N 94 44W
Lufupa, Dem. Rep. of the Congo 55 E1 10 37S 24 56 E
Luga, Russia 24 C4 58 40N 29 55 E
Lugano, Switz. 18 C8 46 1N 8 57 E
Lugansk = Luhansk, Ukraine 25 E6 48 38N 39 15 E
Lugard's Falls, Kenya 54 C4 3 6S 38 41 E
Lugela, Mozam. 55 F4 16 25S 36 43 E
Lugenda →, Mozam. 55 E4 11 25S 38 33 E
Lugh Ganana, Somali Rep. 46 G3 3 48N 42 34 E
Lugnaquilla, Ireland 13 D5 52 58N 6 28W
Lugo, Italy 20 B4 44 25N 11 54 E
Lugo, Spain 19 A2 43 2N 7 35W
Lugoj, Romania 17 F11 45 42N 21 57 E
Lugovoy = Qulan, Kazakstan 26 E8 42 55N 72 43 E
Luhansk, Ukraine 25 E6 48 38N 39 15 E
Luiana, Angola 56 B3 17 25S 22 59 E
Luimneach = Limerick, Ireland 13 D3 52 40N 8 37W
Luing, U.K. 12 E3 56 14N 5 39W
Luis Correia, Brazil 93 D10 3 0S 41 35W
Luitpold Coast, Antarctica 5 D1 78 30S 32 0W
Luiza, Dem. Rep. of the Congo 52 F4 7 40S 22 30 E
Luizi, Dem. Rep. of the Congo 54 D2 6 0S 27 25 E
Luján, Argentina 94 C4 34 45S 59 5W
Lukanga Swamp, Zambia 55 E2 14 30S 27 40 E
Lukenie →, Dem. Rep. of the Congo 52 E3 3 0S 18 50 E
Lukhisaral, India 43 G12 25 11N 86 5 E
Lukolela, Dem. Rep. of the Congo 54 D1 5 23S 24 32 E
Lukosi, Zimbabwe 55 F2 18 30S 26 30 E
Łuków, Poland 17 C12 51 55N 22 23 E
Lule älv →, Sweden 8 D19 65 35N 22 10 E
Luleå, Sweden 8 D20 65 35N 22 10 E
Lüleburgaz, Turkey 21 D12 41 23N 27 22 E
Luling, U.S.A. 81 L6 29 41N 97 39W
Lulong, China 35 E10 39 53N 118 51 E
Lulonga →, Dem. Rep. of the Congo 52 D3 1 0N 18 10 E
Lulua →, Dem. Rep. of the Congo 52 E4 4 30S 20 30 E
Lumajang, Indonesia 37 H15 8 8S 113 13 E
Lumbala N'guimbo, Angola 53 G4 14 18S 21 18 E
Lumberton, U.S.A. 77 H6 34 37N 79 0W
Lumbwa, Kenya 54 C4 0 12S 35 28 E
Lumsden, Canada 73 C8 50 39N 104 52W
Lumsden, N.Z. 59 L2 45 44S 168 27 E
Lumut, Malaysia 39 K3 4 13N 100 37 E
Lumut, Tanjung, Indonesia 36 E3 3 50S 105 58 E
Luna, India 42 H3 23 43N 69 16 E
Lunavada, India 42 H5 23 8N 73 37 E
Lund, Sweden 9 J15 55 44N 13 12 E
Lundazi, Zambia 55 E3 12 20S 33 7 E
Lundi →, Zimbabwe 55 G3 21 43S 32 34 E
Lundu, Malaysia 36 D3 1 40N 109 50 E
Lundy, U.K. 11 F3 51 10N 4 41W
Lune →, U.K. 10 C5 54 0N 2 51W
Lüneburg, Germany 16 B6 53 15N 10 24 E
Lüneburg Heath = Lüneburger Heide, Germany 16 B6 53 10N 10 12 E
Lüneburger Heide, Germany 16 B6 53 10N 10 12 E
Lunenburg, Canada 71 D7 44 22N 64 18W
Lunéville, France 18 B7 48 36N 6 30 E
Lunga →, Zambia 55 E2 14 34S 26 25 E
Lunglei, India 41 H18 22 55N 92 45 E
Luni, India 42 G5 26 0N 73 6 E
Luni →, India 42 G4 24 41N 71 14 E
Luninets = Luninyets, Belarus 17 B14 52 15N 26 50 E
Luning, U.S.A. 82 G4 38 30N 118 11W
Luninyets, Belarus 17 B14 52 15N 26 50 E
Lunkaransar, India 42 E5 28 29N 73 44 E
Lunsemfwa →, Zambia 55 E3 14 54S 30 12 E
Lunsemfwa Falls, Zambia 55 E2 14 30S 29 6 E
Luo He →, China 34 G6 34 35N 110 20 E
Luochuan, China 34 G5 35 45N 109 26 E
Luofu, Dem. Rep. of the Congo 54 C2 0 10S 29 15 E
Luohe, China 34 H8 33 32N 114 2 E
Luonan, China 34 G6 34 5N 110 10 E
Luoning, China 34 G6 34 35N 111 40 E
Luoyang, China 34 G7 34 40N 112 26 E
Luozigou, China 35 C16 43 42N 130 18 E
Lupanshui, China 32 D5 26 38N 104 48 E
Lupilichi, Mozam. 55 E4 11 47S 35 13 E
Luque, Paraguay 94 B4 25 19S 57 25W
Luray, U.S.A. 76 F6 38 40N 78 28W
Lurgan, U.K. 13 B5 54 28N 6 19W
Lusaka, Zambia 55 F2 15 28S 28 16 E
Lusambo, Dem. Rep. of the Congo 54 C1 4 58S 23 28 E
Lusangaye, Dem. Rep. of the Congo 54 C2 4 54S 26 0 E
Luseland, Canada 73 C7 52 5N 109 24W
Lushan, China 34 H7 33 45N 112 55 E
Lushi, China 34 G6 34 3N 111 3 E
Lushnjë, Albania 21 D8 40 55N 19 41 E
Lushoto, Tanzania 54 C4 4 47S 38 20 E
Lüshun, China 35 E11 38 45N 121 15 E
Lusk, U.S.A. 80 D2 42 46N 104 27W
Lūt, Dasht-e, Iran 45 D8 31 30N 58 0 E
Luta = Dalian, China 35 E11 38 50N 121 40 E
Lutherstadt Wittenberg, Germany 16 C7 51 53N 12 39 E
Luton, U.K. 11 F7 51 53N 0 24W
Luton □, U.K. 11 F7 51 53N 0 24W
Lutselke, Canada 73 A6 62 24N 110 44W
Lutsk, Ukraine 17 C13 50 50N 25 15 E
Lützow Holmbukta, Antarctica 5 C4 69 10S 37 30 E
Lutzputs, S. Africa 56 D3 28 3S 20 40 E
Luuq = Lugh Ganana, Somali Rep. 46 G3 3 48N 42 34 E
Luverne, Ala., U.S.A. 77 K2 31 43N 86 16W
Luverne, Minn., U.S.A. 80 D6 43 39N 96 13W
Luvua, Dem. Rep. of the Congo 55 D2 8 48S 25 17 E
Luvua →, Dem. Rep. of the Congo 54 D2 6 50S 27 30 E
Luvuvhu →, S. Africa 57 C5 22 25S 31 18 E
Luwegu →, Tanzania 55 D4 8 31S 37 23 E
Luwuk, Indonesia 37 E6 0 56S 122 47 E
Luxembourg, Lux. 18 B7 49 37N 6 9 E
Luxembourg □, Belgium 15 E5 49 58N 5 30 E
Luxembourg ■, Europe 18 B7 49 45N 6 0 E
Luxi, China 32 D4 24 27N 98 36 E
Luxor = El Uqsur, Egypt 51 C12 25 41N 32 38 E
Luyi, China 34 H8 33 50N 115 35 E
Luza, Russia 24 B8 60 39N 47 10 E
Luzern, Switz. 18 C8 47 3N 8 18 E
Luzern □, Switz. 18 C8 47 2N 7 55 E
Luzhou, China 32 D5 28 52N 105 20 E
Luziânia, Brazil 93 G9 16 20S 48 0W
Luzon, Phil. 37 A6 16 0N 121 0 E
Lviv, Ukraine 17 D13 49 50N 24 0 E
Lvov = Lviv, Ukraine 17 D13 49 50N 24 0 E
Lyakhavichy, Belarus 17 B14 53 2N 26 32 E
Lyakhovskiye, Ostrova, Russia 27 B15 73 40N 141 0 E
Lyal I., Canada 78 B3 44 57N 81 24W
Lyallpur = Faisalabad, Pakistan 42 D5 31 30N 73 5 E
Lybster, U.K. 12 C5 58 18N 3 15W
Lycksele, Sweden 8 D18 64 38N 18 40 E
Lydda = Lod, Israel 47 D3 31 57N 34 54 E
Lydenburg, S. Africa 57 D5 25 10S 30 29 E
Lydia, Turkey 21 E13 38 48N 28 19 E
Lyell, N.Z. 59 J4 41 48S 172 4 E
Lyell I., Canada 72 C2 52 40N 131 35W
Lyepyel, Belarus 24 D4 54 50N 28 40 E
Lykens, U.S.A. 79 F8 40 34N 76 42W
Lyman, U.S.A. 82 F8 41 20N 110 18W
Lyme B., U.K. 11 G4 50 42N 2 53W
Lyme Regis, U.K. 11 G5 50 43N 2 57W
Lymington, U.K. 11 G6 50 45N 1 32W
Łyna →, Poland 9 J19 54 37N 21 14 E
Lynchburg, U.S.A. 76 G6 37 25N 79 9W
Lynd →, Australia 62 B3 16 28S 143 18 E
Lynd Ra., Australia 63 D4 25 30S 149 20 E
Lynden, Canada 78 C4 43 14N 80 9W

Lynden, U.S.A. 84 B4 48 57N 122 27W
Lyndhurst, Australia 63 E2 30 15S 138 18 E
Lyndon →, Australia 61 D1 23 29S 114 6 E
Lyndonville, N.Y., U.S.A. 78 C6 43 20N 78 23W
Lyndonville, Vt., U.S.A. 79 B12 44 31N 72 1W
Lyngen, Norway 8 B19 69 45N 20 30 E
Lynher Reef, Australia 60 C3 15 27S 121 55 E
Lynn, U.S.A. 79 D14 42 28N 70 57W
Lynn Lake, Canada 73 B8 56 51N 101 3W
Lynnwood, U.S.A. 84 C4 47 49N 122 19W
Lynton, U.K. 11 F4 51 13N 3 50W
Lyntupy, Belarus 9 J22 55 4N 26 23 E
Lynx L., Canada 73 A7 62 25N 106 15W
Lyon, France 18 D6 45 46N 4 50 E
Lyonnais, France 18 D6 45 45N 4 15 E
Lyons = Lyon, France 18 D6 45 46N 4 50 E
Lyons, Ga., U.S.A. 77 J4 32 12N 82 19W
Lyons, Kans., U.S.A. 80 F5 38 21N 98 12W
Lyons, N.Y., U.S.A. 78 C8 43 5N 77 0W
Lyons →, Australia 61 E2 25 2S 115 9 E
Lyons Falls, U.S.A. 79 C9 43 37N 75 22W
Lys = Leie →, Belgium 15 C3 51 2N 3 45 E
Lysva, Russia 24 C10 58 7N 57 49 E
Lysychansk, Ukraine 25 E6 48 55N 38 30 E
Lytham St. Anne's, U.K. 10 D4 53 45N 3 0W
Lyttelton, N.Z. 59 K4 43 35S 172 44 E
Lytton, Canada 72 C4 50 13N 121 31W
Lyubertsy, Russia 24 C6 55 39N 37 50 E
Lyuboml, Ukraine 17 C13 51 11N 24 4 E

M

M.R. Gomez, Presa, Mexico 87 B5 26 10N 99 0W
Ma →, Vietnam 38 C5 19 47N 105 56 E
Ma'adaba, Jordan 47 E4 30 43N 35 47 E
Maamba, Zambia 56 B4 17 17S 26 28 E
Ma'ān, Jordan 47 E4 30 12N 35 44 E
Ma'ān □, Jordan 47 F5 30 0N 36 0 E
Maanselkä, Finland 8 C23 63 52N 28 32 E
Ma'anshan, China 33 C6 31 44N 118 29 E
Maarianhamina, Finland 9 F18 60 5N 19 55 E
Ma'arrat an Nu'mān, Syria 44 C3 35 43N 36 43 E
Maas →, Neths. 15 C4 51 45N 4 32 E
Maaseik, Belgium 15 C5 51 6N 5 45 E
Maasin, Phil. 37 B6 10 8N 124 50 E
Maastricht, Neths. 18 A6 50 50N 5 40 E
Maave, Mozam. 57 C5 21 4S 34 47 E
Mababe Depression, Botswana 56 B3 18 50S 24 15 E
Mabalane, Mozam. 57 C5 23 37S 32 31 E
Mabel L., Canada 72 C5 50 35N 118 43W
Mabenge, Dem. Rep. of the Congo 54 B1 4 15N 24 12 E
Maberly, Canada 79 B8 44 50N 76 32W
Mablethorpe, U.K. 10 D8 53 20N 0 15 E
Maboma, Dem. Rep. of the Congo 54 B2 2 30N 28 10 E
Mac Bac, Vietnam 39 H6 9 46N 106 7 E
Macachín, Argentina 94 D3 37 10S 63 43W
Macaé, Brazil 95 A7 22 20S 41 43W
McAlester, U.S.A. 81 H7 34 56N 95 46W
McAllen, U.S.A. 81 M5 26 12N 98 14W
MacAlpine L., Canada 68 B9 66 40N 102 50W
Macamic, Canada 70 C4 48 45N 79 0W
Macao = Macau, China 33 D6 22 12N 113 33 E
Macapá, Brazil 93 C8 0 5N 51 4W
McArthur →, Australia 62 B2 15 54S 136 40 E
McArthur, Port, Australia 62 B2 16 4S 136 23 E
Macau, Brazil 93 E11 5 15S 36 40W
Macau, China 33 D6 22 12N 113 33 E
McBride, Canada 72 C4 53 20N 120 19W
McCall, U.S.A. 82 D5 44 55N 116 6W
McCamey, U.S.A. 81 K3 31 8N 102 14W
McCammon, U.S.A. 82 E7 42 39N 112 12W
McCauley I., Canada 72 C2 53 40N 130 15W
McCleary, U.S.A. 84 C3 47 3N 123 16W
Macclenny, U.S.A. 77 K4 30 17N 82 7W
Macclesfield, U.K. 10 D5 53 15N 2 8W
M'Clintock Chan., Canada 68 A9 72 0N 102 0W
McClintock Ra., Australia 60 C4 18 44S 127 38 E
McCloud, U.S.A. 82 F2 41 15N 122 8W
McCluer I., Australia 60 B5 11 5S 133 0 E
McClure, U.S.A. 78 F7 40 42N 77 19W
McClure, L., U.S.A. 84 H6 37 35N 120 16W
M'Clure Str., Canada 4 B2 75 0N 119 0W
McClusky, U.S.A. 80 B4 47 29N 100 27W
McComb, U.S.A. 81 K9 31 15N 90 27W
McConaughy, L., U.S.A. 80 E4 41 14N 101 40W
McCook, U.S.A. 80 E4 40 12N 100 38W
McCreary, Canada 73 C9 50 47N 99 29W
McCullough Mt., U.S.A. 85 K11 35 35N 115 13W
McCusker →, Canada 73 B7 55 32N 108 39W
McDame, Canada 72 B3 59 44N 128 59W
McDermitt, U.S.A. 82 F5 41 59N 117 43W
McDonald, U.S.A. 78 F4 40 22N 80 14W
Macdonald, L., Australia 60 D4 23 30S 129 0 E
McDonald Is., Ind. Oc. 3 G13 53 0S 73 0 E
MacDonnell Ranges, Australia 60 D5 23 40S 133 0 E
MacDowell L., Canada 70 B1 52 15N 92 45W
Macduff, U.K. 12 D6 57 40N 2 31W
Macedonia = Makedhonía □, Greece 21 D10 40 39N 22 0 E
Macedonia, U.S.A. 78 E3 41 19N 81 31W
Macedonia ■, Europe 21 D9 41 53N 21 40 E
Maceió, Brazil 93 E11 9 40S 35 41W
Macerata, Italy 20 C5 43 18N 13 27 E
McFarland, U.S.A. 85 K7 35 41N 119 14W
McFarlane →, Canada 73 B7 59 12N 107 58W
Macfarlane, L., Australia 63 E2 32 0S 136 40 E
McGehee, U.S.A. 81 J9 33 38N 91 24W
McGill, U.S.A. 82 G6 39 23N 114 47W
Macgillycuddy's Reeks, Ireland 13 E2 51 58N 9 45W
McGraw, U.S.A. 79 D8 42 36N 76 8W
McGregor, U.S.A. 80 D9 43 1N 91 11W
McGregor Ra., Australia 63 D3 27 0S 142 45 E
Mach, Pakistan 40 E5 29 50N 67 20 E
Māch Kowr, Iran 45 E9 25 48N 61 28 E
Machado = Jiparaná →, Brazil 92 E6 8 3S 62 52W
Machagai, Argentina 94 B3 26 56S 60 2W
Machakos, Kenya 54 C4 1 30S 37 15 E
Machala, Ecuador 92 D3 3 20S 79 57W
Machanga, Mozam. 57 C6 20 59S 35 0 E
Machattie, L., Australia 62 C2 24 50S 139 48 E
Machava, Mozam. 57 D5 25 54S 32 28 E
Machece, Mozam. 55 F4 19 15S 35 32 E
Macheke, Zimbabwe 57 B5 18 5S 31 51 E
Machhu →, India 42 H4 23 6N 70 46 E
Machias, Maine, U.S.A. 77 C12 44 43N 67 28W
Machias, N.Y., U.S.A. 78 D6 42 25N 78 30W
Machichi →, Canada 73 B10 57 3N 92 6W
Machico, Madeira 22 D3 32 43N 16 44W
Machilipatnam, India 41 L12 16 12N 81 8 E
Machiques, Venezuela 92 A4 10 4N 72 34W
Machupicchu, Peru 92 F4 13 8S 72 30W
Machynlleth, U.K. 11 E4 52 35N 3 50W
Macia, Mozam. 57 D5 25 2S 33 8 E
McIlwraith Ra., Australia 62 A3 13 50S 143 20 E
McInnes L., Canada 73 C10 52 13N 93 45W
McIntosh, U.S.A. 80 C4 45 55N 101 21W
McIntosh L., Canada 73 B8 55 45N 105 0W
Macintosh Ra., Australia 61 E4 27 39S 125 32 E
Macintyre →, Australia 63 D5 28 37S 150 47 E
Mackay, Australia 62 C4 21 8S 149 11 E
Mackay, U.S.A. 82 E7 43 55N 113 37W
MacKay →, Canada 72 B6 57 10N 111 38W
Mackay, L., Australia 60 D4 22 30S 129 0 E
McKay Ra., Australia 60 D3 23 0S 122 30 E
McKeesport, U.S.A. 78 F5 40 21N 79 52W
McKellar, Canada 78 A5 45 30N 79 55W
McKenna, U.S.A. 84 D4 46 56N 122 33W
Mackenzie, Canada 72 B4 55 20N 123 5W
McKenzie, U.S.A. 77 G1 36 8N 88 31W
Mackenzie →, Australia 62 C4 23 38S 149 46 E
Mackenzie →, Canada 68 B6 69 10N 134 20W
McKenzie →, U.S.A. 82 D2 44 7N 123 6W
Mackenzie Bay, Canada 4 B1 69 0N 137 30W
Mackenzie City = Linden, Guyana 92 B7 6 0N 58 10W
Mackenzie Mts., Canada 68 B6 64 0N 130 0W
Mackinaw City, U.S.A. 76 C3 45 47N 84 44W
McKinlay, Australia 62 C3 21 16S 141 18 E
McKinlay →, Australia 62 C3 20 50S 141 28 E
McKinley, Mt., U.S.A. 68 B4 63 4N 151 0W
McKinley Sea, Arctic 4 A7 82 0N 0 0W
McKinney, U.S.A. 81 J6 33 12N 96 37W
Mackinnon Road, Kenya 54 C4 3 40S 39 1 E
McKittrick, U.S.A. 85 K7 35 18N 119 37W
Macklin, Canada 73 C7 52 20N 109 56W
Macksville, Australia 63 E5 30 40S 152 56 E
McLaughlin, U.S.A. 80 C4 45 49N 100 49W
Maclean, Australia 63 D5 29 26S 153 16 E
McLean, U.S.A. 81 H4 35 14N 100 36W
McLeansboro, U.S.A. 80 F10 38 6N 88 32W
Maclear, S. Africa 57 E4 31 2S 28 23 E
Macleay →, Australia 63 E5 30 56S 153 0 E
McLennan, Canada 72 B5 55 42N 116 50W
McLeod →, Canada 72 C5 54 9N 115 44W
MacLeod, B., Canada 73 A7 62 53N 110 0W
McLeod, L., Australia 61 D1 24 9S 113 47 E
MacLeod Lake, Canada 72 C4 54 58N 123 0W
McLoughlin, Mt., U.S.A. 82 E2 42 27N 122 19W
McMechen, U.S.A. 78 G4 39 57N 80 44W
McMinnville, Oreg., U.S.A. 82 D2 45 13N 123 12W
McMinnville, Tenn., U.S.A. 77 H3 35 41N 85 46W
McMurdo Sd., Antarctica 5 D11 77 0S 170 0 E
McMurray = Fort McMurray, Canada 72 B6 56 44N 111 7W
McMurray, U.S.A. 84 B4 48 19N 122 14W
Macodoene, Mozam. 57 C6 23 32S 35 5 E
Macomb, U.S.A. 80 E9 40 27N 90 40W
Mâcon, France 18 C6 46 19N 4 50 E
Macon, Ga., U.S.A. 77 J4 32 51N 83 38W
Macon, Miss., U.S.A. 77 J1 33 7N 88 34W
Macon, Mo., U.S.A. 80 F8 39 44N 92 28W
Macossa, Mozam. 55 F3 17 55S 33 56 E
Macoun L., Canada 73 B8 56 32N 103 40W
Macovane, Mozam. 57 C6 21 30S 35 2 E
McPherson, U.S.A. 80 F6 38 22N 97 40W
McPherson Pk., U.S.A. 85 L7 34 53N 119 53W
McPherson Ra., Australia 63 D5 28 15S 153 15 E
Macquarie →, Australia 63 E4 30 5S 147 30 E
Macquarie Harbour, Australia 62 G4 42 15S 145 23 E
Macquarie Is., Pac. Oc. 64 N7 54 36S 158 55 E
MacRobertson Land, Antarctica 5 D6 71 0S 64 0 E
Macroom, Ireland 13 E3 51 54N 8 57W
MacTier, Canada 78 A5 45 9N 79 46W
Macubela, Mozam. 55 F4 16 53S 37 49 E
Macuiza, Mozam. 55 F3 18 7S 34 29 E
Macusani, Peru 92 F4 14 4S 70 29W
Macuse, Mozam. 55 F4 17 45S 37 10 E
Macuspana, Mexico 87 D6 17 46N 92 36W
Macusse, Angola 56 B3 17 48S 20 23 E
Madadeni, S. Africa 57 D5 27 43S 30 3 E
Madagascar ■, Africa 57 C8 20 0S 47 0 E
Madā'in Sālih, Si. Arabia 44 E3 26 46N 37 57 E
Madama, Niger 51 D8 22 0N 13 40 E
Madame I., Canada 71 C7 45 30N 60 58W
Madaripur, Bangla. 41 H17 23 19N 90 15 E
Madauk, Burma 41 L20 17 56N 96 52 E
Madawaska, Canada 78 A7 45 30N 78 0W
Madawaska →, Canada 78 A8 45 27N 76 21W
Madaya, Burma 41 H20 22 12N 96 10 E
Maddalena, Italy 20 D3 41 16N 9 23 E
Madeira, Atl. Oc. 22 D3 32 50N 17 0W
Madeira →, Brazil 92 D7 3 22S 58 45W
Madeleine, Îs. de la, Canada 71 C7 47 30N 61 40W
Madera, Mexico 86 B3 29 12N 108 7W
Madera, Calif., U.S.A. 84 J6 36 57N 120 3W
Madera, Pa., U.S.A. 78 F6 40 49N 78 26W
Madha, India 40 L9 18 0N 75 30 E
Madhavpur, India 42 J3 21 15N 69 58 E
Madhepura, India 43 F12 26 11N 86 23 E
Madhubani, India 43 F12 26 21N 86 7 E
Madhupur, India 43 G12 24 16N 86 39 E
Madhya Pradesh □, India 42 J8 22 50N 78 0 E
Madidi →, Bolivia 92 F5 12 32S 66 52W
Madikeri, India 40 N9 12 30N 75 45 E
Madill, U.S.A. 81 H6 34 6N 96 46W
Madimba, Dem. Rep. of the Congo 52 E3 4 58S 15 5 E
Ma'din, Syria 44 C3 35 45N 39 36 E
Madingou, Congo 52 E2 4 10S 13 33 E
Madirovalo, Madag. 57 B8 16 26S 46 32 E
Madison, Calif., U.S.A. 84 G5 38 41N 121 59W
Madison, Fla., U.S.A. 77 K4 30 28N 83 25W
Madison, Ind., U.S.A. 76 F3 38 44N 85 23W
Madison, Nebr., U.S.A. 80 E6 41 50N 97 27W
Madison, Ohio, U.S.A. 78 E3 41 46N 81 3W
Madison, S. Dak., U.S.A. 80 D6 44 0N 97 7W
Madison, Wis., U.S.A. 80 D10 43 4N 89 24W
Madison →, U.S.A. 82 D8 45 56N 111 31W
Madison Heights, U.S.A. 76 G6 37 25N 79 8W
Madisonville, Ky., U.S.A. 76 G2 37 20N 87 30W
Madisonville, Tex., U.S.A. 81 K7 30 57N 95 55W
Madista, Botswana 56 C4 21 15S 25 6 E
Madiun, Indonesia 36 F4 7 38S 111 32 E
Madoc, Canada 78 B7 44 30N 77 28W
Madona, Latvia 9 H22 56 53N 26 5 E
Madrakah, Ra's al, Oman 46 D6 19 0N 57 50 E
Madras = Chennai, India 40 N12 13 8N 80 19 E
Madras = Tamil Nadu □, India 40 P10 11 0N 77 0 E
Madras, U.S.A. 82 D3 44 38N 121 8W
Madre, Laguna, U.S.A. 81 M6 27 0N 97 30W
Madre, Sierra, Phil. 37 A6 17 0N 122 0 E
Madre de Dios →, Bolivia 92 F5 10 59S 66 8W
Madre de Dios, I., Chile 96 G1 50 20S 75 10W
Madre del Sur, Sierra, Mexico 87 D5 17 30N 100 0W
Madre Occidental, Sierra, Mexico 86 B3 27 0N 107 0W
Madre Oriental, Sierra, Mexico 86 C5 25 0N 100 0W
Madri, India 42 G5 24 16N 73 32 E
Madrid, Spain 19 B4 40 25N 3 45W
Madrid, U.S.A. 79 B9 44 45N 75 8W
Madura, Australia 61 F4 31 55S 127 0 E
Madura, Indonesia 37 G15 7 30S 114 0 E
Madura, Selat, Indonesia 37 G15 7 30S 113 20 E
Madurai, India 40 Q11 9 55N 78 10 E
Madurantakam, India 40 N11 12 30N 79 50 E
Mae Chan, Thailand 38 B2 20 9N 99 52 E
Mae Hong Son, Thailand 38 C2 19 16N 97 56 E
Mae Khlong →, Thailand 38 F3 13 24N 100 0 E
Mae Phrik, Thailand 38 D2 17 27N 99 7 E
Mae Ramat, Thailand 38 D2 16 58N 98 31 E
Mae Rim, Thailand 38 C2 18 54N 98 57 E
Mae Sot, Thailand 38 D2 16 43N 98 34 E
Mae Suai, Thailand 38 C2 19 39N 99 33 E
Mae Tha, Thailand 38 C2 18 28N 99 8 E
Maebashi, Japan 31 F9 36 24N 139 4 E
Maesteg, U.K. 11 F4 51 36N 3 40W
Maestra, Sierra, Cuba 88 B4 20 15N 77 0W
Maevatanana, Madag. 57 B8 16 56S 46 49 E
Mafeking = Mafikeng, S. Africa 56 D4 25 50S 25 38 E
Mafeking, Canada 73 C8 52 40N 101 10W
Mafeteng, Lesotho 56 D4 29 51S 27 15 E
Maffra, Australia 63 F4 37 53S 146 58 E
Mafia I., Tanzania 54 D4 7 45S 39 50 E
Mafikeng, S. Africa 56 D4 25 50S 25 38 E
Mafra, Brazil 95 B6 26 10S 49 55W
Mafra, Portugal 19 C1 38 55N 9 20W
Mafungabusi Plateau, Zimbabwe 55 F2 18 30S 29 8 E
Magadan, Russia 27 D16 59 38N 150 50 E
Magadi, Kenya 54 C4 1 54S 36 19 E
Magadi, L., Kenya 54 C4 1 54S 36 19 E
Magaliesburg, S. Africa 57 D4 26 0S 27 32 E
Magallanes, Estrecho de, Chile 96 G2 52 30S 75 0W
Magangué, Colombia 92 B4 9 14N 74 45W
Magdalen Is. = Madeleine, Îs. de la, Canada 71 C7 47 30N 61 40W
Magdalena, Argentina 94 D4 35 5S 57 30W
Magdalena, Bolivia 92 F6 13 13S 63 57W
Magdalena, Mexico 86 A2 30 50N 112 0W
Magdalena, U.S.A. 83 J10 34 7N 107 15W
Magdalena →, Colombia 92 A4 11 6N 74 51W
Magdalena →, Mexico 86 A2 30 40N 112 25W
Magdalena, B., Mexico 86 C2 24 30N 112 10W
Magdalena, Llano de la, Mexico 86 C2 25 0N 111 30W
Magdeburg, Germany 16 B6 52 7N 11 38 E
Magdelaine Cays, Australia 62 B5 16 33S 150 18 E
Magee, U.S.A. 81 K10 31 52N 89 44W
Magelang, Indonesia 37 G14 7 29S 110 13 E
Magellan's Str. = Magallanes, Estrecho de, Chile 96 G2 52 30S 75 0W
Magenta, L., Australia 61 F2 33 30S 119 2 E
Magerøya, Norway 8 A21 71 3N 25 40 E
Maggiore, Lago, Italy 18 D8 45 57N 8 39 E
Maghâgha, Egypt 51 C12 28 38N 30 50 E
Magherafelt, U.K. 13 B5 54 45N 6 37W
Maghreb, N. Afr. 50 B5 32 0N 4 0W
Magistralnyy, Russia 27 D11 56 16N 107 36 E
Magnetic Pole (North) = North Magnetic Pole, Canada 4 B2 77 58N 102 8W
Magnetic Pole (South) = South Magnetic Pole, Antarctica 5 C9 64 8S 138 8 E
Magnitogorsk, Russia 24 D10 53 27N 59 4 E
Magnolia, Ark., U.S.A. 81 J8 33 16N 93 14W
Magnolia, Miss., U.S.A. 81 K9 31 9N 90 28W
Magog, Canada 79 A12 45 18N 72 9W
Magoro, Uganda 54 B3 1 45N 34 12 E
Magosa = Famagusta, Cyprus 23 D12 35 8N 33 55 E
Magouládhes, Greece 23 A3 39 45N 19 42 E
Magoye, Zambia 55 F2 16 1S 27 30 E
Magozal, Mexico 87 C5 21 34N 97 59W
Magpie, L., Canada 71 B7 51 0N 64 41W
Magrath, Canada 72 D6 49 25N 112 50W
Maguarinho, C., Brazil 93 D9 0 15S 48 30W
Mague, Mozam. 57 D5 25 2S 32 40 E
Mağusa = Famagusta, Cyprus 23 D12 35 8N 33 55 E
Maguse L., Canada 73 A9 61 40N 95 10W
Maguse Pt., Canada 73 A10 61 20N 93 50W
Magvana, India 42 H3 23 13N 69 22 E
Magwe, Burma 41 J19 20 10N 95 0 E
Maha Sarakham, Thailand 38 D4 16 12N 103 16 E
Mahābād, Iran 44 B5 36 50N 45 45 E
Mahabharat Lekh, Nepal 43 E10 28 30N 82 0 E
Mahabo, Madag. 57 C7 20 23S 44 40 E
Mahadeo Hills, India 43 H8 22 20N 78 30 E
Mahaffey, U.S.A. 78 F6 40 53N 78 44W
Mahagi, Dem. Rep. of the Congo 54 B3 2 20N 31 0 E
Mahajamba →, Madag. 57 B8 15 33S 47 8 E
Mahajamba, Helodranon' i, Madag. 57 B8 15 24S 47 5 E
Mahajan, India 42 E5 28 48N 73 56 E
Mahajanga, Madag. 57 B8 15 40S 46 25 E
Mahajanga □, Madag. 57 B8 17 0S 47 0 E
Mahajilo →, Madag. 57 B8 19 42S 45 22 E
Mahakam →, Indonesia 36 E5 0 35S 117 17 E
Mahalapye, Botswana 56 C4 23 1S 26 51 E
Maḩallāt, Iran 45 C6 33 55N 50 30 E
Māhān, Iran 45 D8 30 5N 57 18 E
Mahan →, India 43 H10 23 30N 82 50 E
Mahanadi →, India 41 J15 20 20N 86 25 E
Mahananda →, India 43 G12 25 12N 87 52 E
Mahanoro, Madag. 57 B8 19 54S 48 48 E
Mahanoy City, U.S.A. 79 F8 40 49N 76 9W
Maharashtra □, India 40 J9 20 30N 75 30 E
Mahari Mts., Tanzania 54 D3 6 20S 30 0 E
Mahasham, W. →, Egypt 47 E3 30 15N 34 10 E
Mahasoa, Madag. 57 C8 22 12S 46 6 E
Mahasolo, Madag. 57 B8 19 7S 46 22 E
Mahattat ash Shīdīyah, Jordan 47 F4 29 55N 35 55 E
Mahattat 'Unayzah, Jordan 47 E4 30 30N 35 47 E
Mahavavy →, Madag. 57 B8 15 57S 45 54 E
Mahaxay, Laos 38 D5 17 22N 105 12 E
Mahbubnagar, India 40 L10 16 45N 77 59 E
Maḩḑah, Oman 45 E7 24 24N 55 59 E
Mahdia, Tunisia 51 A8 35 28N 11 0 E
Mahe, India 43 C8 33 10N 78 32 E
Mahendragarh, India 42 E7 28 17N 76 14 E
Mahenge, Tanzania 55 D4 8 45S 36 41 E
Maheno, N.Z. 59 L3 45 10S 170 50 E
Mahesana, India 42 H5 23 39N 72 26 E
Maheshwar, India 42 H6 22 11N 75 35 E
Mahgawan, India 43 F8 26 29N 78 37 E
Mahi →, India 42 H5 22 15N 72 55 E
Mahia Pen., N.Z. 59 H6 39 9S 177 55 E
Mahilyow, Belarus 17 B16 53 55N 30 18 E
Mahmud Kot, Pakistan 42 D4 30 16N 71 0 E
Mahnomen, U.S.A. 80 B7 47 19N 95 58W
Mahoba, India 43 G8 25 15N 79 55 E
Mahón = Maó, Spain 22 B11 39 53N 4 16 E
Mahone Bay, Canada 71 D7 44 30N 64 20W
Mahopac, U.S.A. 79 E11 41 22N 73 45W
Mahuva, India 42 J4 21 5N 71 48 E
Mai-Ndombe, L., Dem. Rep. of the Congo 52 E3 2 0S 18 20 E
Mai-Sai, Thailand 38 B2 20 20N 99 55 E
Maicurú →, Brazil 93 D8 2 14S 54 17W
Maidan Khula, Afghan. 42 C3 33 36N 69 50 E
Maidenhead, U.K. 11 F7 51 31N 0 42W
Maidstone, Canada 73 C7 53 5N 109 20W
Maidstone, U.K. 11 F8 51 16N 0 32 E
Maiduguri, Nigeria 51 F8 12 0N 13 20 E
Maihar, India 43 G9 24 16N 80 45 E
Maijdi, Bangla. 41 H17 22 48N 91 10 E
Maikala Ra., India 41 J12 22 0N 81 0 E
Mailani, India 43 E9 28 17N 80 21 E
Mailsi, Pakistan 42 E5 29 48N 72 15 E
Main →, Germany 16 C5 50 0N 8 18 E
Main →, U.K. 13 B5 54 48N 6 18W
Maine, France 18 C3 48 20N 0 15W
Maine □, U.S.A. 77 C11 45 20N 69 0W
Maine →, Ireland 13 D2 52 9N 9 45W
Maingkwan, Burma 41 F20 26 15N 96 37 E
Mainit, L., Phil. 37 C7 9 31N 125 30 E
Mainland, Orkney, U.K. 12 C5 58 59N 3 8W
Mainland, Shet., U.K. 12 A7 60 15N 1 22W
Mainoru, Australia 62 A1 14 0S 134 6 E
Mainpuri, India 43 F8 27 18N 79 4 E
Maintirano, Madag. 57 B7 18 3S 44 1 E
Mainz, Germany 16 C5 50 1N 8 14 E
Maipú, Argentina 94 D4 36 52S 57 50W
Maiquetía, Venezuela 92 A5 10 36N 66 57W
Mairabari, India 41 F18 26 30N 92 22 E
Maisi, Cuba 89 B5 20 17N 74 9W
Maisí, Pta. de, Cuba 89 B5 20 10N 74 10W
Maitland, N.S.W., Australia 63 E5 32 33S 151 36 E
Maitland, S. Austral., Australia 63 E2 34 23S 137 40 E
Maitland →, Canada 78 C3 43 45N 81 43W
Maiz, Is. del, Nic. 88 D3 12 15N 83 4W
Maizuru, Japan 31 G7 35 25N 135 22 E
Majalengka, Indonesia 37 G13 6 50S 108 13 E
Majene, Indonesia 37 E5 3 38S 118 57 E
Majorca = Mallorca, Spain 22 B10 39 30N 3 0 E
Makaha, Zimbabwe 57 B5 17 20S 32 39 E
Makalamabedi, Botswana 56 C3 20 19S 23 51 E
Makale, Indonesia 37 E5 3 6S 119 51 E
Makamba, Burundi 54 C2 4 8S 29 49 E
Makarikari = Makgadikgadi Salt Pans, Botswana 56 C4 20 40S 25 45 E
Makarovo, Russia 27 D11 57 40N 107 45 E
Makasar = Ujung Pandang, Indonesia 37 F5 5 10S 119 20 E
Makasar, Selat, Indonesia 37 E5 1 0S 118 20 E
Makasar, Str. of = Makasar, Selat, Indonesia 37 E5 1 0S 118 20 E
Makat, Kazakstan 25 E9 47 39N 53 19 E
Makedhonía □, Greece 21 D10 40 39N 22 0 E
Makedonija = Macedonia ■, Europe 21 D9 41 53N 21 40 E
Makeyevka = Makiyivka, Ukraine 25 E6 48 0N 38 0 E
Makgadikgadi Salt Pans, Botswana 56 C4 20 40S 25 45 E
Makhachkala, Russia 25 F8 43 0N 47 30 E
Makhmūr, Iraq 44 C4 35 46N 43 35 E
Makian, Indonesia 37 D7 0 20N 127 20 E
Makindu, Kenya 54 C4 2 18S 37 50 E
Makinsk, Kazakstan 26 D8 52 37N 70 26 E
Makiyivka, Ukraine 25 E6 48 0N 38 0 E
Makkah, Si. Arabia 46 C2 21 30N 39 54 E
Makkovik, Canada 71 A8 55 10N 59 10W
Makó, Hungary 17 E11 46 14N 20 33 E
Makokou, Gabon 52 D2 0 40N 12 50 E
Makongo, Dem. Rep. of the Congo 54 B2 3 25N 26 17 E
Makoro, Dem. Rep. of the Congo 54 B2 3 10N 29 59 E
Makrai, India 40 H10 22 2N 77 0 E
Makran Coast Range, Pakistan 40 G4 25 40N 64 0 E
Makrana, India 42 F6 27 2N 74 46 E
Makriyialos, Greece 23 D7 35 2N 25 59 E
Mākū, Iran 44 B5 39 15N 44 31 E
Makunda, Botswana 56 C3 22 30S 20 7 E
Makurazaki, Japan 31 J5 31 15N 130 20 E
Makurdi, Nigeria 50 G7 7 43N 8 35 E
Makūyeh, Iran 45 D7 28 7N 53 9 E
Makwassie, S. Africa 56 D4 27 17S 26 0 E
Makwiro, Zimbabwe 57 B5 17 58S 30 25 E

Mal B., *Ireland* **13 D2** 52 50N 9 30W
Mala, Pta., *Panama* **88 E3** 7 28N 80 2W
Malabar Coast, *India* .... **40 P9** 11 0N 75 0 E
Malabo = Rey Malabo, *Eq. Guin.* .... **52 D1** 3 45N 8 50 E
Malacca, Str. of, *Indonesia* .. **39 L3** 3 0N 101 0 E
Malad City, *U.S.A.* **82 E7** 42 12N 112 15W
Maladzyechna, *Belarus* ..... **17 A14** 54 20N 26 50 E
Málaga, *Spain* **19 D3** 36 43N 4 23W
Malagarasi, *Tanzania* ...... **54 D3** 5 5S 30 50 E
Malagarasi →, *Tanzania* .... **54 D2** 5 12S 29 47 E
Malagasy Rep. = Madagascar ■, *Africa* .... **57 C8** 20 0S 47 0 E
Malahide, *Ireland* **13 C5** 53 26N 6 9W
Malaimbandy, *Madag.* ...... **57 C8** 20 20S 45 36 E
Malakâl, *Sudan* .... **51 G12** 9 33N 31 40 E
Malakand, *Pakistan* .... **42 B4** 34 40N 71 55 E
Malakwal, *Pakistan* .... **42 C5** 32 34N 73 13 E
Malamala, *Indonesia* .... **37 E6** 3 21S 120 55 E
Malanda, *Australia* .... **62 B4** 17 22S 145 35 E
Malang, *Indonesia* .... **36 F4** 7 59S 112 45 E
Malangen, *Norway* .... **8 B18** 69 24N 18 37 E
Malanje, *Angola* .... **52 F3** 9 36S 16 17 E
Mälaren, *Sweden* .... **9 G17** 59 30N 17 10 E
Malargüe, *Argentina* **94 D2** 35 32S 69 30W
Malartic, *Canada* **70 C4** 48 9N 78 9W
Malaryta, *Belarus* .... **17 C13** 51 50N 24 3 E
Malatya, *Turkey* .... **25 G6** 38 25N 38 20 E
Malawi ■, *Africa* .... **55 E3** 11 55S 34 0 E
Malawi, L. = Nyasa, L., *Africa* **55 E3** 12 30S 34 30 E
Malay Pen., *Asia* .... **39 J3** 7 25N 100 0 E
Malaya Vishera, *Russia* ..... **24 C5** 58 55N 32 25 E
Malaybalay, *Phil.* .... **37 C7** 8 5N 125 7 E
Malāyer, *Iran* .... **45 C6** 34 19N 48 51 E
Malaysia ■, *Asia* .... **39 K4** 5 0N 110 0 E
Malazgirt, *Turkey* .... **25 G7** 39 10N 42 33 E
Malbon, *Australia* .... **62 C3** 21 5S 140 17 E
Malbooma, *Australia* .... **63 E1** 30 41S 134 11 E
Malbork, *Poland* .... **17 B10** 54 3N 19 1 E
Malcolm, *Australia* .... **61 E3** 28 51S 121 25 E
Malcolm, Pt., *Australia* ..... **61 F3** 33 48S 123 45 E
Maldah, *India* .... **43 G13** 25 2N 88 9 E
Maldegem, *Belgium* .... **15 C3** 51 14N 3 26 E
Malden, *Mass., U.S.A.* **79 D13** 42 26N 71 4W
Malden, *Mo., U.S.A.* **81 G10** 36 34N 89 57W
Malden I., *Kiribati* **65 H12** 4 3S 155 1W
Maldives ■, *Ind. Oc.* .... **29 J11** 5 0N 73 0 E
Maldonado, *Uruguay* **95 C5** 34 59S 55 0W
Maldonado, Punta, *Mexico* . **87 D5** 16 19N 98 35W
Malé, *Maldives* .... **29 J11** 4 0N 73 28 E
Malé Karpaty, *Slovak Rep.* .. **17 D9** 48 30N 17 20 E
Maléa, Ákra, *Greece* .... **21 F10** 36 28N 23 7 E
Malegaon, *India* .... **40 J9** 20 30N 74 38 E
Malei, *Mozam.* .... **55 F4** 17 12S 36 58 E
Malek Kandī, *Iran* .... **44 B5** 37 9N 46 6 E
Malela, *Dem. Rep. of the Congo* .... **54 C2** 4 22S 26 8 E
Malema, *Mozam.* .... **55 E4** 14 57S 37 20 E
Máleme, *Greece* .... **23 D5** 35 31N 23 49 E
Maleny, *Australia* .... **63 D5** 26 45S 152 52 E
Malerkotla, *India* .... **42 D6** 30 32N 75 58 E
Máles, *Greece* .... **23 D7** 35 6N 25 35 E
Malgomaj, *Sweden* .... **8 D17** 64 40N 16 30 E
Malha, *Sudan* .... **51 E11** 15 8N 25 10 E
Malhargarh, *India* .... **42 G6** 24 17N 74 59 E
Malheur →, *U.S.A.* **82 D5** 44 4N 116 59W
Malheur L., *U.S.A.* **82 E4** 43 20N 118 48W
Mali ■, *Africa* **50 E5** 17 0N 3 0W
Mali →, *Burma* .... **41 G20** 25 40N 97 40 E
Mali Kyun, *Burma* .... **38 F2** 13 0N 98 20 E
Malibu, *U.S.A.* **85 L8** 34 2N 118 41W
Maliku, *Indonesia* .... **37 E6** 0 39S 123 16 E
Malili, *Indonesia* .... **37 E6** 2 42S 121 6 E
Malimba, Mts., *Dem. Rep. of the Congo* .... **54 D2** 7 30S 29 30 E
Malin Hd., *Ireland* **13 A4** 55 23N 7 23W
Malin Pen., *Ireland* **13 A4** 55 20N 7 17W
Malindi, *Kenya* .... **54 C5** 3 12S 40 5 E
Malines = Mechelen, *Belgium* **15 C4** 51 2N 4 29 E
Malino, *Indonesia* .... **37 D6** 1 0N 121 0 E
Malinyi, *Tanzania* .... **55 D4** 8 56S 36 0 E
Malita, *Phil.* .... **37 C7** 6 19N 125 39 E
Maliwun, *Burma* .... **36 B1** 10 17N 98 40 E
Maliya, *India* .... **42 H4** 23 5N 70 46 E
Malkara, *Turkey* .... **21 D12** 40 53N 26 53 E
Mallacoota Inlet, *Australia* .. **63 F4** 37 34S 149 40 E
Mallaig, *U.K.* **12 D3** 57 0N 5 50W
Mallawan, *India* .... **43 F9** 27 4N 80 12 E
Mallawi, *Egypt* .... **51 C12** 27 44N 30 44 E
Mállia, *Greece* .... **23 D7** 35 17N 25 32 E
Mallión, Kólpos, *Greece* .... **23 D7** 35 19N 25 27 E
Mallorca, *Spain* .... **22 B10** 39 30N 3 0 E
Mallorytown, *Canada* **79 B9** 44 29N 75 53W
Mallow, *Ireland* **13 D3** 52 8N 8 39W
Malmberget, *Sweden* ...... **8 C19** 67 11N 20 40 E
Malmédy, *Belgium* .... **15 D6** 50 25N 6 2 E
Malmesbury, *S. Africa* ..... **56 E2** 33 28S 18 41 E
Malmö, *Sweden* .... **9 J15** 55 36N 12 59 E
Malolos, *Phil.* .... **37 B6** 14 50N 120 49 E
Malombe L., *Malawi* .... **55 E4** 14 40S 35 15 E
Malone, *U.S.A.* **79 B10** 44 51N 74 18W
Måløy, *Norway* .... **9 F11** 61 57N 5 6 E
Malpaso, *Canary Is.* **22 G1** 27 43N 18 3W
Malpelo, I. de, *Colombia* ... **92 C2** 4 3N 81 35W
Malpur, *India* .... **42 H5** 23 21N 73 27 E
Malpura, *India* .... **42 F6** 26 17N 75 23 E
Malta, *Idaho, U.S.A.* **82 E7** 42 18N 113 22W
Malta, *Mont., U.S.A.* **82 B10** 48 21N 107 52W
Malta ■, *Europe* .... **23 D2** 35 55N 14 26 E
Maltahöhe, *Namibia* .... **56 C2** 24 55S 17 0 E
Malton, *Canada* **78 C5** 43 42N 79 38W
Malton, *U.K.* **10 C7** 54 8N 0 49W
Maluku, *Indonesia* .... **37 E7** 1 0S 127 0 E
Maluku □, *Indonesia* .... **37 E7** 3 0S 128 0 E
Maluku Sea = Molucca Sea, *Indonesia* .... **37 E6** 0 0 125 0 E
Malvan, *India* .... **40 L8** 16 2N 73 30 E
Malvern, *U.S.A.* **81 H8** 34 22N 92 49W
Malvern Hills, *U.K.* **11 E5** 52 0N 2 19W
Malvinas, Is. = Falkland Is. □, *Atl. Oc.* **96 G5** 51 30S 59 0W
Malya, *Tanzania* .... **54 C3** 3 5S 33 38 E
Malyn, *Ukraine* .... **17 C15** 50 46N 29 3 E
Malyy Lyakhovskiy, Ostrov, *Russia* .... **27 B15** 74 7N 140 36 E
Mama, *Russia* .... **27 D12** 58 18N 112 54 E
Mamanguape, *Brazil* **93 E11** 6 50S 35 4W
Mamarr Mitlā, *Egypt* .... **47 E1** 30 2N 32 54 E
Mamasa, *Indonesia* .... **37 E5** 2 55S 119 20 E
Mambasa, *Dem. Rep. of the Congo* .... **54 B2** 1 22N 29 3 E
Mamberamo →, *Indonesia* . **37 E9** 2 0S 137 50 E
Mambilima Falls, *Zambia* ... **55 E2** 10 31S 28 45 E
Mambirima, *Dem. Rep. of the Congo* .... **55 E2** 11 25S 27 33 E
Mambo, *Tanzania* .... **54 C4** 4 52S 38 22 E
Mambrui, *Kenya* .... **54 C5** 3 5S 40 5 E
Mamburao, *Phil.* .... **37 B6** 13 13N 120 39 E
Mameigwess L., *Canada* ... **70 B2** 52 35N 87 50W
Mammoth, *U.S.A.* **83 K8** 32 43N 110 39W
Mammoth Cave Nat. Park, *U.S.A.* **76 G3** 37 8N 86 13W
Mamoré →, *Bolivia* **92 F5** 10 23S 65 53W
Mamou, *Guinea* **50 F3** 10 15N 12 0W
Mamoudzou, *Mayotte* ..... **49 H8** 12 48S 45 14 E
Mampikony, *Madag.* .... **57 B8** 16 6S 47 38 E
Mamuju, *Indonesia* .... **37 E5** 2 41S 118 50 E
Mamuno, *Botswana* .... **56 C3** 22 16S 20 1 E
Man, *Ivory C.* **50 G4** 7 30N 7 40W
Man, I. of, *U.K.* **10 C3** 54 15N 4 30W
Man-Bazar, *India* .... **43 H12** 23 4N 86 39 E
Man Na, *Burma* .... **41 H20** 23 27N 97 19 E
Mana →, *Fr. Guiana* **93 B8** 5 45N 53 55W
Manaar, G. of = Mannar, G. of, *Asia* .... **40 Q11** 8 30N 79 0 E
Manacapuru, *Brazil* **92 D6** 3 16S 60 37W
Manacor, *Spain* .... **22 B10** 39 34N 3 13 E
Manado, *Indonesia* .... **37 D6** 1 29N 124 51 E
Managua, *Nic.* **88 D2** 12 6N 86 20W
Managua, L. de, *Nic.* **88 D2** 12 20N 86 30W
Manakara, *Madag.* .... **57 C8** 22 8S 48 1 E
Manali, *India* .... **42 C7** 32 16N 77 10 E
Manama = Al Manāmah, *Bahrain* .... **46 B5** 26 10N 50 30 E
Manambao →, *Madag.* ..... **57 B7** 17 35S 44 0 E
Manambato, *Madag.* .... **57 A8** 13 43S 49 7 E
Manambolo →, *Madag.* .... **57 B7** 19 18S 44 22 E
Manambolosy, *Madag.* ..... **57 B8** 16 2S 49 40 E
Mananara, *Madag.* .... **57 B8** 16 10S 49 46 E
Mananara →, *Madag.* ...... **57 C8** 23 21S 47 42 E
Mananjary, *Madag.* .... **57 C8** 21 13S 48 20 E
Manantenina, *Madag.* ...... **57 C8** 24 17S 47 19 E
Manaos = Manaus, *Brazil* ... **92 D7** 3 0S 60 0W
Manapire →, *Venezuela* **92 B5** 7 42N 66 7W
Manapouri, *N.Z.* .... **59 L1** 45 34S 167 39 E
Manapouri, L., *N.Z.* .... **59 L1** 45 32S 167 32 E
Manār, Jabal, *Yemen* ...... **46 E3** 14 2N 44 17 E
Manaravolo, *Madag.* .... **57 C8** 23 59S 45 39 E
Manas, *China* .... **32 B3** 44 17N 85 56 E
Manas →, *India* .... **41 F17** 26 12N 90 40 E
Manaslu, *Nepal* .... **43 E11** 28 33N 84 33 E
Manasquan, *U.S.A.* **79 F10** 40 8N 74 3W
Manassa, *U.S.A.* **83 H11** 37 11N 105 56W
Manaung, *Burma* .... **41 K18** 18 45N 93 40 E
Manaus, *Brazil* **92 D7** 3 0S 60 0W
Manawan L., *Canada* **73 B8** 55 24N 103 14W
Manbij, *Syria* .... **44 B3** 36 31N 37 57 E
Manchegorsk, *Russia* ...... **26 C4** 67 54N 32 58 E
Manchester, *U.K.* **10 D5** 53 29N 2 12W
Manchester, *Calif., U.S.A.* .. **84 G3** 38 58N 123 41W
Manchester, *Conn., U.S.A.* .. **79 E12** 41 47N 72 31W
Manchester, *Ga., U.S.A.* **77 J3** 32 51N 84 37W
Manchester, *Iowa, U.S.A.* ... **80 D9** 42 29N 91 27W
Manchester, *Ky., U.S.A.* **76 G4** 37 9N 83 46W
Manchester, *N.H., U.S.A.* ... **79 D13** 42 59N 71 28W
Manchester, *N.Y., U.S.A.* ... **78 D7** 42 56N 77 16W
Manchester, *Pa., U.S.A.* **79 F8** 40 4N 76 43W
Manchester, *Tenn., U.S.A.* .. **77 H2** 35 29N 86 5W
Manchester, *Vt., U.S.A.* **79 C11** 43 10N 73 5W
Manchester L., *Canada* **73 A7** 61 28N 107 29W
Manchhar L., *Pakistan* ..... **42 F2** 26 25N 67 39 E
Manchuria = Dongbei, *China* **35 D13** 45 0N 125 0 E
Manchurian Plain, *China* ... **28 E16** 47 0N 124 0 E
Mand →, *India* .... **43 J10** 21 42N 83 15 E
Mand →, *Iran* .... **45 D7** 28 20N 52 30 E
Manda, *Ludewe, Tanzania* .. **55 E3** 10 30S 34 40 E
Manda, *Mbeya, Tanzania* ... **54 D3** 7 58S 32 29 E
Manda, *Mbeya, Tanzania* ... **55 D3** 8 30S 32 49 E
Mandabé, *Madag.* .... **57 C7** 21 0S 44 55 E
Mandaguari, *Brazil* **95 A5** 23 32S 51 42W
Mandah = Töhöm, *Mongolia* **34 B5** 44 27N 108 2 E
Mandal, *Norway* .... **9 G12** 58 2N 7 25 E
Mandala, Puncak, *Indonesia* **37 E10** 4 44S 140 20 E
Mandalay, *Burma* .... **41 J20** 22 0N 96 4 E
Mandale = Mandalay, *Burma* **41 J20** 22 0N 96 4 E
Mandalgarh, *India* .... **42 G6** 25 12N 75 6 E
Mandalgovi, *Mongolia* ..... **34 B4** 45 45N 106 10 E
Mandalī, *Iraq* .... **44 C5** 33 43N 45 28 E
Mandan, *U.S.A.* **80 B4** 46 50N 100 54W
Mandar, Teluk, *Indonesia* .. **37 E5** 3 35S 119 15 E
Mandaue, *Phil.* .... **37 B6** 10 20N 123 56 E
Mandera, *Kenya* .... **54 B5** 3 55N 41 53 E
Mandi, *India* .... **42 D7** 31 39N 76 58 E
Mandi Dabwali, *India* ...... **42 E6** 29 58N 74 42 E
Mandimba, *Mozam.* .... **55 E4** 14 20S 35 40 E
Mandioli, *Indonesia* .... **37 E7** 0 40S 127 20 E
Mandla, *India* .... **43 H9** 22 39N 80 30 E
Mandorah, *Australia* ...... **60 B5** 12 32S 130 42 E
Mandoto, *Madag.* .... **57 B8** 19 34S 46 17 E
Mandra, *Pakistan* .... **42 C5** 33 23N 73 12 E
Mandrare →, *Madag.* ...... **57 D8** 25 10S 46 30 E
Mandritsara, *Madag.* ...... **57 B8** 15 50S 48 49 E
Mandronarivo, *Madag.* ..... **57 C8** 21 7S 45 38 E
Mandsaur, *India* .... **42 G6** 24 3N 75 8 E
Mandurah, *Australia* ...... **61 F2** 32 36S 115 48 E
Mandvi, *India* .... **42 H3** 22 51N 69 22 E
Mandya, *India* .... **40 N10** 12 30N 77 0 E
Mandzai, *Pakistan* .... **42 D2** 30 55N 67 6 E
Maneh, *Iran* .... **45 B8** 37 39N 57 7 E
Manera, *Madag.* .... **57 C7** 22 55S 44 20 E
Maneroo Cr. →, *Australia* .. **62 C3** 23 21S 143 53 E
Manfalût, *Egypt* .... **51 C12** 27 20N 30 52 E
Manfredónia, *Italy* .... **20 D6** 41 38N 15 55 E
Mangabeiras, Chapada das, *Brazil* **93 F9** 10 0S 46 30W
Mangalia, *Romania* .... **17 G15** 43 50N 28 35 E
Mangalore, *India* .... **40 N9** 12 55N 74 47 E
Mangan, *India* .... **43 F13** 27 31N 88 32 E
Mangaung, *S. Africa* .... **53 K5** 29 10S 26 25 E
Mangawan, *India* .... **43 G9** 24 41N 81 33 E
Mangaweka, *N.Z.* .... **59 H5** 39 48S 175 47 E
Manggar, *Indonesia* .... **36 E3** 2 50S 108 10 E
Manggawitu, *Indonesia* .... **37 E8** 4 8S 133 32 E
Mangindrano, *Madag.* ..... **57 A8** 14 17S 48 58 E
Mangkalihat, Tanjung, *Indonesia* .... **37 D5** 1 2N 118 59 E
Mangla, *Pakistan* .... **42 C5** 33 7N 73 39 E
Mangla Dam, *Pakistan* ..... **43 C5** 33 9N 73 44 E
Manglaur, *India* .... **42 E7** 29 44N 77 49 E
Mangnai, *China* .... **32 C4** 37 52N 91 43 E
Mango, *Togo* .... **50 F6** 10 20N 0 30 E
Mangoche, *Malawi* .... **55 E4** 14 25S 35 16 E
Mangoky →, *Madag.* .... **57 C7** 21 29S 43 41 E
Mangole, *Indonesia* .... **37 E6** 1 50S 125 55 E
Mangombe, *Dem. Rep. of the Congo* .... **54 C2** 1 20S 26 48 E
Mangonui, *N.Z.* .... **59 F4** 35 1S 173 32 E
Mangoro →, *Madag.* .... **57 B8** 20 0S 48 45 E
Mangrol, *Mad. P., India* .... **42 J4** 21 7N 70 7 E
Mangrol, *Raj., India* .... **42 G6** 25 20N 76 31 E
Mangueira, L. da, *Brazil* ... **95 C5** 33 0S 52 50W
Mangum, *U.S.A.* **81 H5** 34 53N 99 30W
Mangyshlak Poluostrov, *Kazakstan* .... **26 E6** 44 30N 52 30 E
Manhattan, *U.S.A.* **80 F6** 39 11N 96 35W
Manhiça, *Mozam.* .... **57 D5** 25 23S 32 49 E
Mania →, *Madag.* .... **57 B8** 19 42S 45 22 E
Manica, *Mozam.* .... **57 B5** 18 58S 32 59 E
Manica □, *Mozam.* .... **57 B5** 19 10S 33 45 E
Manicaland □, *Zimbabwe* .. **55 F3** 19 0S 32 30 E
Manicoré, *Brazil* **92 E6** 5 48S 61 16W
Manicouagan →, *Canada* ... **71 C6** 49 30N 68 30W
Manicouagan, Rés., *Canada* . **71 B6** 51 5N 68 40W
Maniema □, *Dem. Rep. of the Congo* .... **54 C2** 3 0S 26 0 E
Manifah, *Si. Arabia* .... **45 E6** 27 44N 49 0 E
Manifold, C., *Australia* .... **62 C5** 22 41S 150 50 E
Manigotagan, *Canada* **73 C9** 51 6N 96 18W
Manigotagan →, *Canada* ... **73 C9** 51 7N 96 20W
Manihari, *India* .... **43 G12** 25 21N 87 38 E
Manihiki, *Cook Is.* **65 J11** 10 24S 161 1W
Manika, Plateau de la, *Dem. Rep. of the Congo* .. **55 E2** 10 0S 25 5 E
Manikpur, *India* .... **43 G9** 25 4N 81 7 E
Manila, *Phil.* .... **37 B6** 14 40N 121 3 E
Manila, *U.S.A.* **82 F9** 40 59N 109 43W
Manila B., *Phil.* .... **37 B6** 14 40N 120 35 E
Manilla, *Australia* .... **63 E5** 30 45S 150 43 E
Maningrida, *Australia* ..... **62 A1** 12 3S 134 13 E
Manipur □, *India* .... **41 G19** 25 0N 94 0 E
Manipur →, *Burma* .... **41 H19** 23 45N 94 20 E
Manisa, *Turkey* .... **21 E12** 38 38N 27 30 E
Manistee, *U.S.A.* **76 C2** 44 15N 86 19W
Manistee →, *U.S.A.* **76 C2** 44 15N 86 21W
Manistique, *U.S.A.* **76 C2** 45 57N 86 15W
Manito L., *Canada* **73 C7** 52 43N 109 43W
Manitoba □, *Canada* **73 B9** 55 30N 97 0W
Manitoba, L., *Canada* **73 C9** 51 0N 98 45W
Manitou, *Canada* **73 D9** 49 15N 98 32W
Manitou, L., *Canada* **71 B6** 50 55N 65 17W
Manitou Is., *U.S.A.* **76 C3** 45 8N 86 0W
Manitou Springs, *U.S.A.* ... **80 F2** 38 52N 104 55W
Manitoulin I., *Canada* **70 C3** 45 40N 82 30W
Manitouwadge, *Canada* **70 C2** 49 8N 85 48W
Manitowoc, *U.S.A.* **76 C2** 44 5N 87 40W
Manizales, *Colombia* **92 B3** 5 5N 75 32W
Manja, *Madag.* .... **57 C7** 21 26S 44 20 E
Manjacaze, *Mozam.* .... **57 C5** 24 45S 34 0 E
Manjakandriana, *Madag.* ... **57 B8** 18 55S 47 47 E
Manjhand, *Pakistan* .... **42 G3** 25 50N 68 10 E
Manjil, *Iran* .... **45 B6** 36 46N 49 30 E
Manjimup, *Australia* ...... **61 F2** 34 15S 116 6 E
Manjra →, *India* .... **40 K10** 18 49N 77 52 E
Mankato, *Kans., U.S.A.* **80 F5** 39 47N 98 13W
Mankato, *Minn., U.S.A.* **80 C8** 44 10N 94 0W
Mankayane, *Swaziland* .... **57 D5** 26 40S 31 4 E
Mankera, *Pakistan* .... **42 D4** 31 23N 71 26 E
Mankota, *Canada* **73 D7** 49 25N 107 5W
Manlay = Üydzin, *Mongolia* . **34 B4** 44 9N 107 0 E
Manmad, *India* .... **40 J9** 20 18N 74 28 E
Mann Ranges, *Australia* .... **61 E5** 26 6S 130 5 E
Manna, *Indonesia* .... **36 E2** 4 25S 102 55 E
Mannahill, *Australia* ...... **63 E3** 32 25S 140 0 E
Mannar, *Sri Lanka* .... **40 Q11** 9 1N 79 54 E
Mannar, G. of, *Asia* .... **40 Q11** 8 30N 79 0 E
Mannar I., *Sri Lanka* ...... **40 Q11** 9 5N 79 45 E
Mannheim, *Germany* ...... **16 D5** 49 29N 8 29 E
Manning, *Canada* **72 B5** 56 53N 117 39W
Manning, *Oreg., U.S.A.* **84 E3** 45 45N 123 13W
Manning, *S.C., U.S.A.* **77 J5** 33 42N 80 13W
Manning Prov. Park, *Canada* **72 D4** 49 5N 120 45W
Mannum, *Australia* .... **63 E2** 34 50S 139 20 E
Manoharpur, *India* .... **43 H11** 22 23N 85 12 E
Manokwari, *Indonesia* ..... **37 E8** 0 54S 134 0 E
Manombo, *Madag.* .... **57 C7** 22 57S 43 28 E
Manono, *Dem. Rep. of the Congo* .... **54 D2** 7 15S 27 25 E
Manosque, *France* .... **18 E6** 43 49N 5 47 E
Manotick, *Canada* **79 A9** 45 13N 75 41W
Manouane →, *Canada* **71 C5** 49 30N 71 10W
Manouane, L., *Canada* **71 B5** 50 45N 70 45W
Manp'o, *N. Korea* .... **35 D14** 41 6N 126 24 E
Manpojin = Manp'o, *N. Korea* **35 D14** 41 6N 126 24 E
Manpur, *Chhattisgarh, India* **43 H10** 23 17N 83 35 E
Manpur, *Mad. P., India* .... **42 H6** 22 26N 75 37 E
Manresa, *Spain* .... **19 B6** 41 48N 1 50 E
Mansa, *Gujarat, India* ..... **42 H5** 23 27N 72 45 E
Mansa, *Punjab, India* ...... **42 E6** 30 0N 75 27 E
Mansa, *Zambia* .... **55 E2** 11 13S 28 55 E
Mansehra, *Pakistan* .... **42 B5** 34 20N 73 15 E
Mansel I., *Canada* **69 B11** 62 0N 80 0W
Mansfield, *Australia* .... **63 F4** 37 4S 146 6 E
Mansfield, *U.K.* **10 D6** 53 9N 1 11W
Mansfield, *La., U.S.A.* **81 J8** 32 2N 93 43W
Mansfield, *Mass., U.S.A.* ... **79 D13** 42 2N 71 13W
Mansfield, *Ohio, U.S.A.* **78 F2** 40 45N 82 31W
Mansfield, *Pa., U.S.A.* **78 E7** 41 48N 77 5W
Mansfield, Mt., *U.S.A.* **79 B12** 44 33N 72 49W
Manson Creek, *Canada* **72 B4** 55 37N 124 32W
Manta, *Ecuador* **92 D2** 1 0S 80 40W
Mantalingajan, Mt., *Phil.* ... **36 C5** 8 55N 117 45 E
Mantare, *Tanzania* .... **54 C3** 2 42S 33 13 E
Manteca, *U.S.A.* **84 H5** 37 48N 121 13W
Manteo, *U.S.A.* **77 H8** 35 55N 75 40W
Mantes-la-Jolie, *France* .... **18 B4** 48 58N 1 41 E
Manthani, *India* .... **40 K11** 18 40N 79 35 E
Manti, *U.S.A.* **82 G8** 39 16N 111 38W
Mantiqueira, Serra da, *Brazil* **95 A7** 22 0S 44 0W
Manton, *U.S.A.* **76 C3** 44 25N 85 24W
Mántova, *Italy* .... **20 B4** 45 9N 10 48 E
Mänttä, *Finland* .... **9 E21** 62 0N 24 40 E
Mantua = Mántova, *Italy* ... **20 B4** 45 9N 10 48 E
Manu, *Peru* **92 F4** 12 10S 70 51W
Manu →, *Peru* **92 F4** 12 16S 70 55W
Manu'a Is., *Amer. Samoa* ... **59 B14** 14 13S 169 35W
Manuel Alves →, *Brazil* **93 F9** 11 19S 48 28W
Manui, *Indonesia* .... **37 E6** 3 35S 123 5 E
Manukau, *N.Z.* .... **59 G5** 40 43S 175 13 E
Manuripi →, *Bolivia* **92 F5** 11 6S 67 36W
Many, *U.S.A.* **81 K8** 31 34N 93 29W
Manyara, L., *Tanzania* ..... **54 C4** 3 40S 35 50 E
Manych-Gudilo, Ozero, *Russia* .... **25 E7** 46 24N 42 38 E
Manyonga →, *Tanzania* .... **54 C3** 4 10S 34 15 E
Manyoni, *Tanzania* .... **54 D3** 5 45S 34 55 E
Manzai, *Pakistan* .... **42 C4** 32 12N 70 15 E
Manzanares, *Spain* **19 C4** 39 2N 3 22W
Manzanillo, *Cuba* **88 B4** 20 20N 77 31W
Manzanillo, *Mexico* **86 D4** 19 0N 104 20W
Manzanillo, Pta., *Panama* ... **88 E4** 9 30N 79 40W
Manzano Mts., *U.S.A.* **83 J10** 34 40N 106 20W
Manzarīyeh, *Iran* .... **45 C6** 34 53N 50 50 E
Manzhouli, *China* .... **33 B6** 49 35N 117 25 E
Manzini, *Swaziland* .... **57 D5** 26 30S 31 25 E
Mao, *Chad* .... **51 F9** 14 4N 15 19 E
Maó, *Spain* .... **22 B11** 39 53N 4 16 E
Maoke, Pegunungan, *Indonesia* .... **37 E9** 3 40S 137 30 E
Maolin, *China* .... **35 C12** 43 58N 123 30 E
Maoming, *China* .... **33 D6** 21 50N 110 54 E
Maoxing, *China* .... **35 B13** 45 28N 124 40 E
Mapam Yumco, *China* ..... **32 C3** 30 45N 81 28 E
Mapastepec, *Mexico* **87 D6** 15 26N 92 54W
Mapia, Kepulauan, *Indonesia* **37 D8** 0 50N 134 20 E
Mapimí, *Mexico* **86 B4** 25 50N 103 50W
Mapimí, Bolsón de, *Mexico* . **86 B4** 27 30N 104 15W
Mapinga, *Tanzania* .... **54 D4** 6 40S 39 12 E
Mapinhane, *Mozam.* .... **57 C6** 22 20S 35 0 E
Maple Creek, *Canada* **73 D7** 49 55N 109 29W
Maple Valley, *U.S.A.* **84 C4** 47 25N 122 3W
Mapleton, *U.S.A.* **82 D2** 44 2N 123 52W
Mapuera →, *Brazil* **92 D7** 1 5S 57 2W
Mapulanguene, *Mozam.* .... **57 C5** 24 29S 32 6 E
Maputo, *Mozam.* .... **57 D5** 25 58S 32 32 E
Maputo □, *Mozam.* .... **57 D5** 26 0S 32 25 E
Maputo, B. de, *Mozam.* .... **57 D5** 25 50S 32 45 E
Maqiaohe, *China* .... **35 B16** 44 40N 130 30 E
Maqnā, *Si. Arabia* .... **44 D2** 28 25N 34 50 E
Maquela do Zombo, *Angola* **52 F3** 6 0S 15 15 E
Maquinchao, *Argentina* **96 E3** 41 15S 68 50W
Maquoketa, *U.S.A.* **80 D9** 42 4N 90 40W
Mar, Serra do, *Brazil* **95 B6** 25 30S 49 0W
Mar Chiquita, L., *Argentina* . **94 C3** 30 40S 62 50W
Mar del Plata, *Argentina* ... **94 D4** 38 0S 57 30W
Mar Menor, *Spain* **19 D5** 37 40N 0 45W
Mara, *Tanzania* .... **54 C3** 1 30S 34 32 E
Mara □, *Tanzania* .... **54 C3** 1 45S 34 20 E
Maraã, *Brazil* **92 D5** 1 52S 65 25W
Marabá, *Brazil* **93 E9** 5 20S 49 5W
Maracá, I. de, *Brazil* **93 C8** 2 10N 50 30W
Maracaibo, *Venezuela* **92 A4** 10 40N 71 37W
Maracaibo, L. de, *Venezuela* **92 B4** 9 40N 71 30W
Maracaju, *Brazil* **95 A4** 21 38S 55 9W
Maracay, *Venezuela* **92 A5** 10 15N 67 28W
Maradi, *Niger* .... **50 F7** 13 29N 7 20 E
Marāgheh, *Iran* .... **44 B5** 37 30N 46 12 E
Marāh, *Si. Arabia* .... **44 E5** 25 0N 45 35 E
Marajó, I. de, *Brazil* **93 D9** 1 0S 49 30W
Marākand, *Iran* .... **44 B5** 38 51N 45 16 E
Maralal, *Kenya* .... **54 B4** 1 0N 36 38 E
Maralinga, *Australia* ...... **61 F5** 30 13S 131 32 E
Maran, *Malaysia* .... **39 L4** 3 35N 102 45 E
Marana, *U.S.A.* **83 K8** 32 27N 111 13W
Maranboy, *Australia* ...... **60 B5** 14 40S 132 39 E
Marand, *Iran* .... **44 B5** 38 30N 45 45 E
Marang, *Malaysia* .... **39 K4** 5 12N 103 13 E
Maranguape, *Brazil* **93 D11** 3 55S 38 50W
Maranhão = São Luís, *Brazil* **93 D10** 2 39S 44 15W
Maranhão □, *Brazil* **93 E9** 5 0S 46 0W
Maranoa →, *Australia* ..... **63 D4** 27 50S 148 37 E
Marañón →, *Peru* **92 D4** 4 30S 73 35W
Marão, *Mozam.* .... **57 C5** 24 18S 34 2 E
Maraş = Kahramanmaraş, *Turkey* .... **25 G6** 37 37N 36 53 E
Marathasa, *Cyprus* .... **23 E11** 34 59N 32 51 E
Marathon, *Australia* ...... **62 C3** 20 51S 143 32 E
Marathon, *Canada* **70 C2** 48 44N 86 23W
Marathon, *N.Y., U.S.A.* **79 D8** 42 27N 76 2W
Marathon, *Tex., U.S.A.* **81 K3** 30 12N 103 15W
Marathóvouno, *Cyprus* ..... **23 D12** 35 13N 33 37 E
Maratua, *Indonesia* .... **37 D5** 2 10N 118 35 E
Maravatío, *Mexico* **86 D4** 19 51N 100 25W
Marāwih, *U.A.E.* .... **45 E7** 24 18N 53 18 E
Marbella, *Spain* **19 D3** 36 30N 4 57W
Marble Bar, *Australia* ..... **60 D2** 21 9S 119 44 E
Marble Falls, *U.S.A.* **81 K5** 30 35N 98 16W
Marblehead, *U.S.A.* **79 D14** 42 30N 70 51W
Marburg, *Germany* .... **16 C5** 50 47N 8 46 E
March, *U.K.* .... **11 E8** 52 33N 0 5 E
Marche, *France* .... **18 C4** 46 5N 1 20 E
Marche-en-Famenne, *Belgium* .... **15 D5** 50 14N 5 19 E
Marchena, *Spain* **19 D3** 37 18N 5 23W
Marco, *U.S.A.* **77 N5** 25 58N 81 44W
Marcos Juárez, *Argentina* .. **94 C3** 32 42S 62 5W
Marcus I. = Minami-Tori-Shima, *Pac. Oc.* .... **64 E7** 24 20N 153 58 E
Marcus Necker Ridge, *Pac. Oc.* .... **64 F9** 20 0N 175 0 E
Marcy, Mt., *U.S.A.* **79 B11** 44 7N 73 56W
Mardan, *Pakistan* .... **42 B5** 34 20N 72 0 E
Mardin, *Turkey* .... **25 G7** 37 20N 40 43 E
Maree, L., *U.K.* **12 D3** 57 40N 5 26W
Mareeba, *Australia* .... **62 B4** 16 59S 145 28 E
Mareetsane, *S. Africa* ..... **56 D4** 26 9S 25 25 E
Marek = Stanke Dimitrov, *Bulgaria* .... **21 C10** 42 17N 23 9 E
Marengo, *U.S.A.* **80 E8** 41 48N 92 4W
Marenyi, *Kenya* .... **54 C4** 4 22S 39 8 E
Marerano, *Madag.* .... **57 C7** 21 23S 44 52 E
Marfa, *U.S.A.* **81 K2** 30 19N 104 1W
Marfa Pt., *Malta* .... **23 D1** 35 59N 14 19 E
Margaret →, *Australia* ..... **60 C4** 18 9S 125 41 E
Margaret Bay, *Canada* **72 C3** 51 20N 127 35W

Margaret L., *Canada* **72 B5** 58 56N 115 25W
Margaret River, *Australia* **61 F2** 33 57S 115 4 E
Margarita, I. de, *Venezuela* **92 A6** 11 0N 64 0W
Margaritovo, *Russia* **30 C7** 43 25N 134 45 E
Margate, *S. Africa* **57 E5** 30 50S 30 20 E
Margate, *U.K.* **11 F9** 51 23N 1 23 E
Mārgow, Dasht-e, *Afghan.* **40 D3** 30 40N 62 30 E
Marguerite, *Canada* **72 C4** 52 30N 122 25W
Mari El □, *Russia* **24 C8** 56 30N 48 0 E
Mari Indus, *Pakistan* **42 C4** 32 57N 71 34 E
Mari Republic = Mari El □, *Russia* **24 C8** 56 30N 48 0 E
María Elena, *Chile* **94 A2** 22 18S 69 40W
María Grande, *Argentina* **94 C4** 31 45S 59 55W
Maria I., *N. Terr., Australia* **62 A2** 14 52S 135 45 E
Maria I., *Tas., Australia* **62 G4** 42 35S 148 0 E
Maria van Diemen, C., *N.Z.* **59 F4** 34 29S 172 40 E
Mariakani, *Kenya* **54 C4** 3 50S 39 27 E
Marian, *Australia* **62 C4** 21 9S 148 57 E
Marian L., *Canada* **72 A5** 63 0N 116 15W
Mariana Trench, *Pac. Oc.* **28 H18** 13 0N 145 0 E
Marianao, *Cuba* **88 B3** 23 8N 82 24W
Marianna, *Ark., U.S.A.* **81 H9** 34 46N 90 46W
Marianna, *Fla., U.S.A.* **77 K3** 30 46N 85 14W
Marias →, *U.S.A.* **82 C8** 47 56N 110 30W
Mariato, Punta, *Panama* **88 E3** 7 12N 80 52W
Maribor, *Slovenia* **16 E8** 46 36N 15 40 E
Marico →, *Africa* **56 C4** 23 35S 26 57 E
Maricopa, *Ariz., U.S.A.* **83 K7** 33 4N 112 3W
Maricopa, *Calif., U.S.A.* **85 K7** 35 4N 119 24W
Marié →, *Brazil* **92 D5** 0 27S 66 26W
Marie Byrd Land, *Antarctica* **5 D14** 79 30S 125 0W
Marie-Galante, *Guadeloupe* **89 C7** 15 56N 61 16W
Mariecourt = Kangiqsujuaq, *Canada* **69 B12** 61 30N 72 0W
Mariembourg, *Belgium* **15 D4** 50 6N 4 31 E
Mariental, *Namibia* **56 C2** 24 36S 18 0 E
Marienville, *U.S.A.* **78 E5** 41 28N 79 8W
Mariestad, *Sweden* **9 G15** 58 43N 13 50 E
Marietta, *Ga., U.S.A.* **77 J3** 33 57N 84 33W
Marietta, *Ohio, U.S.A.* **76 F5** 39 25N 81 27W
Marieville, *Canada* **79 A11** 45 26N 73 10W
Mariinsk, *Russia* **26 D9** 56 10N 87 20 E
Marijampolė, *Lithuania* **9 J20** 54 33N 23 19 E
Marília, *Brazil* **95 A6** 22 13S 50 0W
Marín, *Spain* **19 A1** 42 23N 8 42W
Marina, *U.S.A.* **84 J5** 36 41N 121 48W
Marinduque, *Phil.* **37 B6** 13 25N 122 0 E
Marine City, *U.S.A.* **78 D2** 42 43N 82 30W
Marinette, *U.S.A.* **76 C2** 45 6N 87 38W
Maringá, *Brazil* **95 A5** 23 26S 52 2W
Marion, *Ala., U.S.A.* **77 J2** 32 38N 87 19W
Marion, *Ill., U.S.A.* **81 G10** 37 44N 88 56W
Marion, *Ind., U.S.A.* **76 E3** 40 32N 85 40W
Marion, *Iowa, U.S.A.* **80 D9** 42 2N 91 36W
Marion, *Kans., U.S.A.* **80 F6** 38 21N 97 1W
Marion, *N.C., U.S.A.* **77 H5** 35 41N 82 1W
Marion, *Ohio, U.S.A.* **76 E4** 40 35N 83 8W
Marion, *S.C., U.S.A.* **77 H6** 34 11N 79 24W
Marion, *Va., U.S.A.* **77 G5** 36 50N 81 31W
Marion, L., *U.S.A.* **77 J5** 33 28N 80 10W
Mariposa, *U.S.A.* **84 H7** 37 29N 119 58W
Mariscal Estigarribia, *Paraguay* **94 A3** 22 3S 60 40W
Maritime Alps = Maritimes, Alpes, *Europe* **18 D7** 44 10N 7 10 E
Maritimes, Alpes, *Europe* **18 D7** 44 10N 7 10 E
Maritsa = Évros →, *Greece* **21 D12** 41 40N 26 34 E
Maritsá, *Greece* **23 C10** 36 22N 28 8 E
Mariupol, *Ukraine* **25 E6** 47 5N 37 31 E
Marīvān, *Iran* **44 C5** 35 30N 46 25 E
Marj 'Uyūn, *Lebanon* **47 B4** 33 20N 35 35 E
Marka = Merca, *Somali Rep.* **46 G3** 1 48N 44 50 E
Markazī □, *Iran* **45 C6** 35 0N 49 30 E
Markdale, *Canada* **78 B4** 44 19N 80 39W
Marked Tree, *U.S.A.* **81 H9** 35 32N 90 25W
Market Drayton, *U.K.* **10 E5** 52 54N 2 29W
Market Harborough, *U.K.* **11 E7** 52 29N 0 55W
Market Rasen, *U.K.* **10 D7** 53 24N 0 20W
Markham, *Canada* **78 C5** 43 52N 79 16W
Markham, Mt., *Antarctica* **5 E11** 83 0S 164 0 E
Markleeville, *U.S.A.* **84 G7** 38 42N 119 47W
Markovo, *Russia* **27 C17** 64 40N 170 24 E
Marks, *Russia* **24 D8** 51 45N 46 50 E
Marksville, *U.S.A.* **81 K8** 31 8N 92 4W
Marla, *Australia* **63 D1** 27 19S 133 33 E
Marlbank, *Canada* **78 B7** 44 26N 77 6W
Marlboro, *Mass., U.S.A.* **79 D13** 42 19N 71 33W
Marlboro, *N.Y., U.S.A.* **79 E11** 41 36N 73 59W
Marlborough, *Australia* **62 C4** 22 46S 149 52 E
Marlborough, *U.K.* **11 F6** 51 25N 1 43W
Marlborough Downs, *U.K.* **11 F6** 51 27N 1 53W
Marlin, *U.S.A.* **81 K6** 31 18N 96 54W
Marlow, *U.S.A.* **81 H6** 34 39N 97 58W
Marmagao, *India* **40 M8** 15 25N 73 56 E
Marmara, *Turkey* **21 D12** 40 35N 27 34 E
Marmara, Sea of = Marmara Denizi, *Turkey* **21 D13** 40 45N 28 15 E
Marmara Denizi, *Turkey* **21 D13** 40 45N 28 15 E
Marmaris, *Turkey* **21 F13** 36 50N 28 14 E
Marmion, Mt., *Australia* **61 E2** 29 16S 119 50 E
Marmion L., *Canada* **70 C1** 48 55N 91 20W
Marmolada, Mte., *Italy* **20 A4** 46 26N 11 51 E
Marmora, *Canada* **78 B7** 44 28N 77 41W
Marne →, *France* **18 B5** 48 48N 2 24 E
Maroala, *Madag.* **57 B8** 15 23S 47 59 E
Maroantsetra, *Madag.* **57 B8** 15 26S 49 44 E
Maroelaboom, *Namibia* **56 B2** 19 15S 18 53 E
Marofandilia, *Madag.* **57 C7** 20 7S 44 34 E
Marolambo, *Madag.* **57 C8** 20 2S 48 7 E
Maromandia, *Madag.* **57 A8** 14 13S 48 5 E
Marondera, *Zimbabwe* **55 F3** 18 5S 31 42 E
Maroni →, *Fr. Guiana* **93 B8** 5 30N 54 0W
Maroochydore, *Australia* **63 D5** 26 29S 153 5 E
Maroona, *Australia* **63 F3** 37 27S 142 54 E
Marosakoa, *Madag.* **57 B8** 15 26S 46 38 E
Maroseranana, *Madag.* **57 B8** 18 32S 48 51 E
Marotandrano, *Madag.* **57 B8** 16 10S 48 50 E
Marotaolano, *Madag.* **57 A8** 12 47S 49 15 E
Maroua, *Cameroon* **51 F8** 10 40N 14 20 E
Marovato, *Madag.* **57 B8** 15 48S 48 5 E
Marovoay, *Madag.* **57 B8** 16 6S 46 39 E
Marquard, *S. Africa* **56 D4** 28 40S 27 28 E
Marquesas Is. = Marquises, Is., *Pac. Oc.* **65 H14** 9 30S 140 0W
Marquette, *U.S.A.* **76 B2** 46 33N 87 24W
Marquises, Is., *Pac. Oc.* **65 H14** 9 30S 140 0W
Marra, Djebel, *Sudan* **51 F10** 13 10N 24 22 E
Marracuene, *Mozam.* **57 D5** 25 45S 32 35 E
Marrakech, *Morocco* **50 B4** 31 9N 8 0W
Marrawah, *Australia* **62 G3** 40 55S 144 42 E
Marree, *Australia* **63 D2** 29 39S 138 1 E
Marrero, *U.S.A.* **81 L9** 29 54N 90 6W
Marrimane, *Mozam.* **57 C5** 22 58S 33 34 E
Marromeu, *Mozam.* **57 B6** 18 15S 36 25 E
Marrowie Cr. →, *Australia* **63 E4** 33 23S 145 40 E
Marrubane, *Mozam.* **55 F4** 18 0S 37 0 E
Marrupa, *Mozam.* **55 E4** 13 8S 37 30 E
Mars Hill, *U.S.A.* **77 B12** 46 31N 67 52W
Marsá Matrûh, *Egypt* **51 B11** 31 19N 27 9 E
Marsabit, *Kenya* **54 B4** 2 18N 38 0 E
Marsala, *Italy* **20 F5** 37 48N 12 26 E
Marsalforn, *Malta* **23 C1** 36 4N 14 16 E
Marsden, *Australia* **63 E4** 33 47S 147 32 E
Marseille, *France* **18 E6** 43 18N 5 23 E
Marseilles = Marseille, *France* **18 E6** 43 18N 5 23 E
Marsh I., *U.S.A.* **81 L9** 29 34N 91 53W
Marshall, *Ark., U.S.A.* **81 H8** 35 55N 92 38W
Marshall, *Mich., U.S.A.* **76 D3** 42 16N 84 58W
Marshall, *Minn., U.S.A.* **80 C7** 44 25N 95 45W
Marshall, *Mo., U.S.A.* **80 F8** 39 7N 93 12W
Marshall, *Tex., U.S.A.* **81 J7** 32 33N 94 23W
Marshall →, *Australia* **62 C2** 22 59S 136 59 E
Marshall Is. ■, *Pac. Oc.* **64 G9** 9 0N 171 0 E
Marshalltown, *U.S.A.* **80 D8** 42 3N 92 55W
Marshbrook, *Zimbabwe* **57 B5** 18 33S 31 9 E
Marshfield, *Mo., U.S.A.* **81 G8** 37 15N 92 54W
Marshfield, *Vt., U.S.A.* **79 B12** 44 20N 72 20W
Marshfield, *Wis., U.S.A.* **80 C9** 44 40N 90 10W
Marshūn, *Iran* **45 B6** 36 19N 49 23 E
Märsta, *Sweden* **9 G17** 59 37N 17 52 E
Mart, *U.S.A.* **81 K6** 31 33N 96 50W
Martaban, *Burma* **41 L20** 16 30N 97 35 E
Martaban, G. of, *Burma* **41 L20** 16 5N 96 30 E
Martapura, *Kalimantan, Indonesia* **36 E4** 3 22S 114 47 E
Martapura, *Sumatera, Indonesia* **36 E2** 4 19S 104 22 E
Martelange, *Belgium* **15 E5** 49 49N 5 43 E
Martha's Vineyard, *U.S.A.* **79 E14** 41 25N 70 38W
Martigny, *Switz.* **18 C7** 46 6N 7 3 E
Martigues, *France* **18 E6** 43 24N 5 4 E
Martin, *Slovak Rep.* **17 D10** 49 6N 18 58 E
Martin, *S. Dak., U.S.A.* **80 D4** 43 11N 101 44W
Martin, *Tenn., U.S.A.* **81 G10** 36 21N 88 51W
Martin, L., *U.S.A.* **77 J3** 32 41N 85 55W
Martina Franca, *Italy* **20 D7** 40 42N 17 20 E
Martinborough, *N.Z.* **59 J5** 41 14S 175 29 E
Martinez, *Calif., U.S.A.* **84 G4** 38 1N 122 8W
Martinez, *Ga., U.S.A.* **77 J4** 33 31N 82 4W
Martinique ■, *W. Indies* **89 D7** 14 40N 61 0W
Martinique Passage, *W. Indies* **89 C7** 15 15N 61 0W
Martinópolis, *Brazil* **95 A5** 22 11S 51 12W
Martins Ferry, *U.S.A.* **78 F4** 40 6N 80 44W
Martinsburg, *Pa., U.S.A.* **78 F6** 40 19N 78 20W
Martinsburg, *W. Va., U.S.A.* **76 F7** 39 27N 77 58W
Martinsville, *Ind., U.S.A.* **76 F2** 39 26N 86 25W
Martinsville, *Va., U.S.A.* **77 G6** 36 41N 79 52W
Marton, *N.Z.* **59 J5** 40 4S 175 23 E
Martos, *Spain* **19 D4** 37 44N 3 58W
Marudi, *Malaysia* **36 D4** 4 11N 114 19 E
Maruf, *Afghan.* **40 D5** 31 30N 67 6 E
Marugame, *Japan* **31 G6** 34 15N 133 40 E
Marunga, *Angola* **56 B3** 17 28S 20 2 E
Marungu, Mts., *Dem. Rep. of the Congo* **54 D3** 7 30S 30 0 E
Marv Dasht, *Iran* **45 D7** 29 50N 52 40 E
Marvast, *Iran* **45 D7** 30 30N 54 15 E
Marvel Loch, *Australia* **61 F2** 31 28S 119 29 E
Marwar, *India* **42 G5** 25 43N 73 45 E
Mary, *Turkmenistan* **26 F7** 37 40N 61 50 E
Maryborough = Port Laoise, *Ireland* **13 C4** 53 2N 7 18W
Maryborough, *Queens., Australia* **63 D5** 25 31S 152 37 E
Maryborough, *Vic., Australia* **63 F3** 37 0S 143 44 E
Maryfield, *Canada* **73 D8** 49 50N 101 35W
Maryland □, *U.S.A.* **76 F7** 39 0N 76 30W
Maryland Junction, *Zimbabwe* **55 F3** 17 45S 30 31 E
Maryport, *U.K.* **10 C4** 54 44N 3 28W
Mary's Harbour, *Canada* **71 B8** 52 18N 55 51W
Marystown, *Canada* **71 C8** 47 10N 55 10W
Marysville, *Canada* **72 D5** 49 35N 116 0W
Marysville, *Calif., U.S.A.* **84 F5** 39 9N 121 35W
Marysville, *Kans., U.S.A.* **80 F6** 39 51N 96 39W
Marysville, *Mich., U.S.A.* **78 D2** 42 54N 82 29W
Marysville, *Ohio, U.S.A.* **76 E4** 40 14N 83 22W
Marysville, *Wash., U.S.A.* **84 B4** 48 3N 122 11W
Maryville, *Mo., U.S.A.* **80 E7** 40 21N 94 52W
Maryville, *Tenn., U.S.A.* **77 H4** 35 46N 83 58W
Marzūq, *Libya* **51 C8** 25 53N 13 57 E
Masahunga, *Tanzania* **54 C3** 2 6S 33 18 E
Masai Steppe, *Tanzania* **54 C4** 4 30S 36 30 E
Masaka, *Uganda* **54 C3** 0 21S 31 45 E
Masalembo, Kepulauan, *Indonesia* **36 F4** 5 35S 114 30 E
Masalima, Kepulauan, *Indonesia* **36 F5** 5 4S 117 5 E
Masamba, *Indonesia* **37 E6** 2 30S 120 15 E
Masan, *S. Korea* **35 G15** 35 11N 128 32 E
Masandam, Ra's, *Oman* **46 B6** 26 30N 56 30 E
Masasi, *Tanzania* **55 E4** 10 45S 38 52 E
Masaya, *Nic.* **88 D2** 12 0N 86 7W
Masbate, *Phil.* **37 B6** 12 21N 123 36 E
Mascara, *Algeria* **50 A6** 35 26N 0 6 E
Mascota, *Mexico* **86 C4** 20 30N 104 50W
Masela, *Indonesia* **37 F7** 8 9S 129 51 E
Maseru, *Lesotho* **56 D4** 29 18S 27 30 E
Mashaba, *Zimbabwe* **55 G3** 20 2S 30 29 E
Mashābih, *Si. Arabia* **44 E3** 25 35N 36 30 E
Masherbrum, *Pakistan* **43 B7** 35 38N 76 18 E
Mashhad, *Iran* **45 B8** 36 20N 59 35 E
Mashīz, *Iran* **45 D8** 29 56N 56 37 E
Māshkel, Hāmūn-i-, *Pakistan* **40 E3** 28 20N 62 56 E
Mashki Chāh, *Pakistan* **40 E3** 29 5N 62 30 E
Mashonaland, *Zimbabwe* **53 H6** 16 30S 31 0 E
Mashonaland Central □, *Zimbabwe* **57 B5** 17 30S 31 0 E
Mashonaland East □, *Zimbabwe* **57 B5** 18 0S 32 0 E
Mashonaland West □, *Zimbabwe* **57 B4** 17 30S 29 30 E
Mashrakh, *India* **43 F11** 26 7N 84 48 E
Masindi, *Uganda* **54 B3** 1 40N 31 43 E
Masindi Port, *Uganda* **54 B3** 1 43N 32 2 E
Maşīrah, *Oman* **46 C6** 21 0N 58 50 E
Maşīrah, Khalīj, *Oman* **46 C6** 20 10N 58 10 E
Masisi, *Dem. Rep. of the Congo* **54 C2** 1 23S 28 49 E
Masjed Soleyman, *Iran* **45 D6** 31 55N 49 18 E
Mask, L., *Ireland* **13 C2** 53 36N 9 22W
Maskin, *Oman* **45 F8** 23 30N 56 50 E
Masoala, Tanjon' i, *Madag.* **57 B9** 15 59S 50 13 E
Masoarivo, *Madag.* **57 B7** 19 3S 44 19 E
Masohi = Amahai, *Indonesia* **37 E7** 3 20S 128 55 E
Masomeloka, *Madag.* **57 C8** 20 17S 48 37 E
Mason, *Nev., U.S.A.* **84 G7** 38 56N 119 8W
Mason, *Tex., U.S.A.* **81 K5** 30 45N 99 14W
Mason City, *U.S.A.* **80 D8** 43 9N 93 12W
Maspalomas, *Canary Is.* **22 G4** 27 46N 15 35W
Maspalomas, Pta., *Canary Is.* **22 G4** 27 43N 15 36W
Masqat, *Oman* **46 C6** 23 37N 58 36 E
Massa, *Italy* **18 D9** 44 1N 10 9 E
Massachusetts □, *U.S.A.* **79 D13** 42 30N 72 0W
Massachusetts B., *U.S.A.* **79 D14** 42 20N 70 50W
Massakory, *Chad* **51 F9** 13 0N 15 49 E
Massanella, *Spain* **22 B9** 39 48N 2 51 E
Massangena, *Mozam.* **57 C5** 21 34S 33 0 E
Massango, *Angola* **52 F3** 8 2S 16 21 E
Massawa = Mitsiwa, *Eritrea* **46 D2** 15 35N 39 25 E
Massena, *U.S.A.* **79 B10** 44 56N 74 54W
Massénya, *Chad* **51 F9** 11 21N 16 9 E
Masset, *Canada* **72 C2** 54 2N 132 10W
Massif Central, *France* **18 D5** 44 55N 3 0 E
Massillon, *U.S.A.* **78 F3** 40 48N 81 32W
Massinga, *Mozam.* **57 C6** 23 15S 35 22 E
Massingir, *Mozam.* **57 C5** 23 51S 32 4 E
Masson, *Canada* **79 A9** 45 32N 75 25W
Masson I., *Antarctica* **5 C7** 66 10S 93 20 E
Mastanli = Momchilgrad, *Bulgaria* **21 D11** 41 33N 25 23 E
Masterton, *N.Z.* **59 J5** 40 56S 175 39 E
Mastic, *U.S.A.* **79 F12** 40 47N 72 54W
Mastuj, *Pakistan* **43 A5** 36 20N 72 36 E
Mastung, *Pakistan* **40 E5** 29 50N 66 56 E
Masty, *Belarus* **17 B13** 53 27N 24 38 E
Masuda, *Japan* **31 G5** 34 40N 131 51 E
Masvingo, *Zimbabwe* **55 G3** 20 8S 30 49 E
Masvingo □, *Zimbabwe* **55 G3** 21 0S 31 30 E
Maşyāf, *Syria* **44 C3** 35 4N 36 20 E
Matabeleland, *Zimbabwe* **53 H5** 18 0S 27 0 E
Matabeleland North □, *Zimbabwe* **55 F2** 19 0S 28 0 E
Matabeleland South □, *Zimbabwe* **55 G2** 21 0S 29 0 E
Matachewan, *Canada* **70 C3** 47 56N 80 39W
Matadi, *Dem. Rep. of the Congo* **52 F2** 5 52S 13 31 E
Matagalpa, *Nic.* **88 D2** 13 0N 85 58W
Matagami, *Canada* **70 C4** 49 45N 77 34W
Matagami, L., *Canada* **70 C4** 49 50N 77 40W
Matagorda B., *U.S.A.* **81 L6** 28 40N 96 0W
Matagorda I., *U.S.A.* **81 L6** 28 15N 96 30W
Matak, *Indonesia* **39 L6** 3 18N 106 16 E
Mátala, *Greece* **23 E6** 34 59N 24 45 E
Matam, *Senegal* **50 E3** 15 34N 13 17W
Matamoros, *Campeche, Mexico* **87 D6** 18 50N 90 50W
Matamoros, *Coahuila, Mexico* **86 B4** 25 33N 103 15W
Matamoros, *Tamaulipas, Mexico* **87 B5** 25 50N 97 30W
Ma'ţan as Sarra, *Libya* **51 D10** 21 45N 22 0 E
Matandu →, *Tanzania* **55 D3** 8 45S 34 19 E
Matane, *Canada* **71 C6** 48 50N 67 33W
Matanomadh, *India* **42 H3** 23 33N 68 57 E
Matanzas, *Cuba* **88 B3** 23 0N 81 40W
Matapa, *Botswana* **56 C3** 23 11S 24 39 E
Matapan, C. = Taínaron, Ákra, *Greece* **21 F10** 36 22N 22 27 E
Matapédia, *Canada* **71 C6** 48 0N 66 59W
Matara, *Sri Lanka* **40 S12** 5 58N 80 30 E
Mataram, *Indonesia* **36 F5** 8 35S 116 7 E
Matarani, *Peru* **92 G4** 17 0S 72 10W
Mataranka, *Australia* **60 B5** 14 55S 133 4 E
Matarma, Râs, *Egypt* **47 E1** 30 27N 32 44 E
Mataró, *Spain* **19 B7** 41 32N 2 29 E
Matatiele, *S. Africa* **57 E4** 30 20S 28 49 E
Mataura, *N.Z.* **59 M2** 46 11S 168 51 E
Matehuala, *Mexico* **86 C4** 23 40N 100 40W
Mateke Hills, *Zimbabwe* **55 G3** 21 48S 31 0 E
Matera, *Italy* **20 D7** 40 40N 16 36 E
Matetsi, *Zimbabwe* **55 F2** 18 12S 26 0 E
Mathis, *U.S.A.* **81 L6** 28 6N 97 50W
Mathráki, *Greece* **23 A3** 39 48N 19 31 E
Mathura, *India* **42 F7** 27 30N 77 40 E
Mati, *Phil.* **37 C7** 6 55N 126 15 E
Matiali, *India* **43 F13** 26 56N 88 49 E
Matías Romero, *Mexico* **87 D5** 16 53N 95 2W
Matibane, *Mozam.* **55 E5** 14 49S 40 45 E
Matima, *Botswana* **56 C3** 20 15S 24 26 E
Matiri Ra., *N.Z.* **59 J4** 41 38S 172 20 E
Matjiesfontein, *S. Africa* **56 E3** 33 14S 20 35 E
Matla →, *India* **43 J13** 21 40N 88 40 E
Matlamanyane, *Botswana* **56 B4** 19 33S 25 57 E
Matli, *Pakistan* **42 G3** 25 2N 68 39 E
Matlock, *U.K.* **10 D6** 53 9N 1 33W
Mato Grosso □, *Brazil* **93 F8** 14 0S 55 0W
Mato Grosso, Planalto do, *Brazil* **93 G8** 15 0S 55 0W
Mato Grosso do Sul □, *Brazil* **93 G8** 18 0S 55 0W
Matochkin Shar, *Russia* **26 B6** 73 10N 56 40 E
Matopo Hills, *Zimbabwe* **55 G2** 20 36S 28 20 E
Matopos, *Zimbabwe* **55 G2** 20 20S 28 29 E
Matosinhos, *Portugal* **19 B1** 41 11N 8 42W
Matroosberg, *S. Africa* **56 E2** 33 23S 19 40 E
Maţruḩ, *Oman* **46 C6** 23 37N 58 30 E
Matsue, *Japan* **31 G6** 35 25N 133 10 E
Matsumae, *Japan* **30 D10** 41 26N 140 7 E
Matsumoto, *Japan* **31 F9** 36 15N 138 0 E
Matsusaka, *Japan* **31 G8** 34 34N 136 32 E
Matsuura, *Japan* **31 H4** 33 20N 129 49 E
Matsuyama, *Japan* **31 H6** 33 45N 132 45 E
Mattagami →, *Canada* **70 B3** 50 43N 81 29W
Mattancheri, *India* **40 Q10** 9 50N 76 15 E
Mattawa, *Canada* **70 C4** 46 20N 78 45W
Matterhorn, *Switz.* **18 D7** 45 58N 7 39 E
Matthew Town, *Bahamas* **89 B5** 20 57N 73 40W
Matthew's Ridge, *Guyana* **92 B6** 7 37N 60 10W
Mattice, *Canada* **70 C3** 49 40N 83 20W
Mattituck, *U.S.A.* **79 F12** 40 59N 72 32W
Mattō, *Japan* **31 F8** 36 31N 136 34 E
Mattoon, *U.S.A.* **76 F1** 39 29N 88 23W
Matuba, *Mozam.* **57 C5** 24 28S 32 49 E
Matucana, *Peru* **92 F3** 11 55S 76 25W
Matūn = Khowst, *Afghan.* **42 C3** 33 22N 69 58 E
Maturín, *Venezuela* **92 B6** 9 45N 63 11W
Mau, *Mad. P., India* **43 F8** 26 17N 78 41 E
Mau, *Ut. P., India* **43 G10** 25 56N 83 33 E
Mau, *Ut. P., India* **43 G9** 25 17N 81 23 E
Mau Escarpment, *Kenya* **54 C4** 0 40S 36 0 E
Mau Ranipur, *India* **43 G8** 25 16N 79 8 E
Maubeuge, *France* **18 A6** 50 17N 3 57 E
Maud, Pt., *Australia* **60 D1** 23 6S 113 45 E
Maude, *Australia* **63 E3** 34 29S 144 18 E
Maudin Sun, *Burma* **41 M19** 16 0N 94 30 E
Maués, *Brazil* **92 D7** 3 20S 57 45W
Mauganj, *India* **41 G12** 24 50N 81 55 E
Maughold Hd., *U.K.* **10 C3** 54 18N 4 18W
Maui, *U.S.A.* **74 H16** 20 48N 156 20W
Maulamyaing = Moulmein, *Burma* **41 L20** 16 30N 97 40 E
Maule □, *Chile* **94 D1** 36 5S 72 30W
Maumee, *U.S.A.* **76 E4** 41 34N 83 39W
Maumee →, *U.S.A.* **76 E4** 41 42N 83 28W
Maumere, *Indonesia* **37 F6** 8 38S 122 13 E
Maun, *Botswana* **56 C3** 20 0S 23 26 E
Mauna Kea, *U.S.A.* **74 J17** 19 50N 155 28W
Mauna Loa, *U.S.A.* **74 J17** 19 30N 155 35W
Maungmagan Kyunzu, *Burma* **38 E1** 14 0N 97 48 E
Maupin, *U.S.A.* **82 D3** 45 11N 121 5W
Maurepas, L., *U.S.A.* **81 K9** 30 15N 90 30W
Maurice, L., *Australia* **61 E5** 29 30S 131 0 E
Mauricie, Parc Nat. de la, *Canada* **70 C5** 46 45N 73 0W
Mauritania ■, *Africa* **50 E3** 20 50N 10 0W
Mauritius ■, *Ind. Oc.* **49 J9** 20 0S 57 0 E
Mauston, *U.S.A.* **80 D9** 43 48N 90 5W
Mavli, *India* **42 G5** 24 45N 73 55 E
Mavuradonha Mts., *Zimbabwe* **55 F3** 16 30S 31 30 E
Mawa, *Dem. Rep. of the Congo* **54 B2** 2 45N 26 40 E
Mawai, *India* **43 H9** 22 30N 81 4 E
Mawana, *India* **42 E7** 29 6N 77 58 E
Mawand, *Pakistan* **42 E3** 29 33N 68 38 E
Mawk Mai, *Burma* **41 J20** 20 14N 97 37 E
Mawlaik, *Burma* **41 H19** 23 40N 94 26 E
Mawlamyine = Moulmein, *Burma* **41 L20** 16 30N 97 40 E
Mawqaq, *Si. Arabia* **44 E4** 27 25N 41 8 E
Mawson Coast, *Antarctica* **5 C6** 68 30S 63 0 E
Max, *U.S.A.* **80 B4** 47 49N 101 18W
Maxcanú, *Mexico* **87 C6** 20 40N 92 0W
Maxesibeni, *S. Africa* **57 E4** 30 49S 29 23 E
Maxhamish L., *Canada* **72 B4** 59 50N 123 17W
Maxixe, *Mozam.* **57 C6** 23 54S 35 17 E
Maxville, *Canada* **79 A10** 45 17N 74 51W
Maxwell, *U.S.A.* **84 F4** 39 17N 122 11W
Maxwelton, *Australia* **62 C3** 20 43S 142 41 E
May, C., *U.S.A.* **76 F8** 38 56N 74 58W
May Pen, *Jamaica* **88 C4** 17 58N 77 15W
Maya →, *Russia* **27 D14** 60 28N 134 28 E
Maya Mts., *Belize* **87 D7** 16 30N 89 0W
Mayaguana, *Bahamas* **89 B5** 22 30N 72 44W
Mayagüez, *Puerto Rico* **89 C6** 18 12N 67 9W
Mayāmey, *Iran* **45 B7** 36 24N 55 42 E
Mayanup, *Australia* **61 F2** 33 57S 116 27 E
Mayapan, *Mexico* **87 C7** 20 30N 89 25W
Mayarí, *Cuba* **89 B4** 20 40N 75 41W
Maybell, *U.S.A.* **82 F9** 40 31N 108 5W
Maybole, *U.K.* **12 F4** 55 21N 4 42W
Maydān, *Iraq* **44 C5** 34 55N 45 37 E
Maydena, *Australia* **62 G4** 42 45S 146 30 E
Mayenne →, *France* **18 C3** 47 30N 0 32W
Mayer, *U.S.A.* **83 J7** 34 24N 112 14W
Mayerthorpe, *Canada* **72 C5** 53 57N 115 8W
Mayfield, *Ky., U.S.A.* **77 G1** 36 44N 88 38W
Mayfield, *N.Y., U.S.A.* **79 C10** 43 6N 74 16W
Mayhill, *U.S.A.* **83 K11** 32 53N 105 29W
Maykop, *Russia* **25 F7** 44 35N 40 10 E
Maymyo, *Burma* **38 A1** 22 2N 96 28 E
Maynard, *Mass., U.S.A.* **79 D13** 42 26N 71 27W
Maynard, *Wash., U.S.A.* **84 C4** 47 59N 122 55W
Maynard Hills, *Australia* **61 E2** 28 28S 119 49 E
Mayne →, *Australia* **62 C3** 23 40S 141 55 E
Maynooth, *Ireland* **13 C5** 53 23N 6 34W
Mayo, *Canada* **68 B6** 63 38N 135 57W
Mayo □, *Ireland* **13 C2** 53 53N 9 3W
Mayon Volcano, *Phil.* **37 B6** 13 15N 123 41 E
Mayor I., *N.Z.* **59 G6** 37 16S 176 17 E
Mayotte, *Ind. Oc.* **53 G9** 12 50S 45 10 E
Maysville, *U.S.A.* **76 F4** 38 39N 83 46W
Mayu, *Indonesia* **37 D7** 1 30N 126 30 E
Mayville, *N. Dak., U.S.A.* **80 B6** 47 30N 97 20W
Mayville, *N.Y., U.S.A.* **78 D5** 42 15N 79 30W
Mayya, *Russia* **27 C14** 61 44N 130 18 E
Mazabuka, *Zambia* **55 F2** 15 52S 27 44 E
Mazagán = El Jadida, *Morocco* **50 B4** 33 11N 8 17W
Mazagão, *Brazil* **93 D8** 0 7S 51 16W
Mazán, *Peru* **92 D4** 3 30S 73 0W
Māzandarān □, *Iran* **45 B7** 36 30N 52 0 E
Mazapil, *Mexico* **86 C4** 24 38N 101 34W
Mazara del Vallo, *Italy* **20 F5** 37 39N 12 35 E
Mazarrón, *Spain* **19 D5** 37 38N 1 19W
Mazaruni →, *Guyana* **92 B7** 6 25N 58 35W
Mazatán, *Mexico* **86 B2** 29 0N 110 8W
Mazatenango, *Guatemala* **88 D1** 14 35N 91 30W
Mazatlán, *Mexico* **86 C3** 23 13N 106 25W
Mažeikiai, *Lithuania* **9 H20** 56 20N 22 20 E
Māzhān, *Iran* **45 C8** 32 30N 59 0 E
Mazīnān, *Iran* **45 B8** 36 19N 56 56 E
Mazoe, *Mozam.* **55 F3** 16 42S 33 7 E
Mazoe →, *Mozam.* **55 F3** 16 20S 33 30 E
Mazowe, *Zimbabwe* **55 F3** 17 28S 30 58 E
Mazurian Lakes = Mazurski, Pojezierze, *Poland* **17 B11** 53 50N 21 0 E
Mazurski, Pojezierze, *Poland* **17 B11** 53 50N 21 0 E
Mazyr, *Belarus* **17 B15** 51 59N 29 15 E
Mbabane, *Swaziland* **57 D5** 26 18S 31 6 E
Mbaïki, *C.A.R.* **52 D3** 3 53N 18 1 E
Mbala, *Zambia* **55 D3** 8 46S 31 24 E

Mbalabala, Zimbabwe 57 C4 20 27S 29 3 E
Mbale, Uganda 54 B3 1 8N 34 12 E
Mbalmayo, Cameroon 52 D2 3 33N 11 33 E
Mbamba Bay, Tanzania 55 E3 11 13S 34 49 E
Mbandaka, Dem. Rep. of the Congo 52 D3 0 1N 18 18 E
Mbanza Congo, Angola 52 F2 6 18S 14 16 E
Mbanza Ngungu, Dem. Rep. of the Congo 52 F2 5 12S 14 53 E
Mbarangandu, Tanzania 55 D4 10 11S 36 48 E
Mbarara, Uganda 54 C3 0 35S 30 40 E
Mbashe →, S. Africa 57 E4 32 15S 28 54 E
Mbenkuru →, Tanzania 55 D4 9 25S 39 50 E
Mberengwa, Zimbabwe 55 G2 20 29S 29 57 E
Mberengwa, Mt., Zimbabwe 55 G2 20 37S 29 55 E
Mbesuma, Zambia 55 E3 10 0S 32 2 E
Mbeya, Tanzania 55 D3 8 54S 33 29 E
Mbeya □, Tanzania 54 D3 8 15S 33 30 E
Mbinga, Tanzania 55 E4 10 50S 35 0 E
Mbini = Río Muni □, Eq. Guin. 52 D2 1 30N 10 0 E
Mbour, Senegal 50 F2 14 22N 16 54W
Mbuji-Mayi, Dem. Rep. of the Congo 54 D1 6 9S 23 40 E
Mbulu, Tanzania 54 C4 3 45S 35 30 E
Mburucuyá, Argentina 94 B4 28 1S 58 14W
Mchinja, Tanzania 55 D4 9 44S 39 45 E
Mchinji, Malawi 55 E3 13 47S 32 58 E
Mdantsane, S. Africa 53 L5 32 56S 27 46 E
Mead, L., U.S.A. 85 J12 36 1N 114 44W
Meade, U.S.A. 81 G4 37 17N 100 20W
Meadow Lake, Canada 73 C7 54 10N 108 26W
Meadow Lake Prov. Park, Canada 73 C7 54 27N 109 0W
Meadow Valley Wash →, U.S.A. 85 J12 36 40N 114 34W
Meadville, U.S.A. 78 E4 41 39N 80 9W
Meaford, Canada 78 B4 44 36N 80 35W
Mealy Mts., Canada 71 B8 53 10N 58 0W
Meander River, Canada 72 B5 59 2N 117 42W
Meares, C., U.S.A. 82 D2 45 37N 124 0W
Mearim →, Brazil 93 D10 3 4S 44 35W
Meath □, Ireland 13 C5 53 40N 6 57W
Meath Park, Canada 73 C7 53 27N 105 22W
Meaux, France 18 B5 48 58N 2 50 E
Mebechi-Gawa →, Japan 30 D10 40 31N 141 31 E
Mecanhelas, Mozam. 55 F4 15 12S 35 54 E
Mecca = Makkah, Si. Arabia 46 C2 21 30N 39 54 E
Mecca, U.S.A. 85 M10 33 34N 116 5W
Mechanicsburg, U.S.A. 78 F8 40 13N 77 1W
Mechanicville, U.S.A. 79 D11 42 54N 73 41W
Mechelen, Belgium 15 C4 51 2N 4 29 E
Mecheria, Algeria 50 B5 33 35N 0 18W
Mecklenburg, Germany 16 B6 53 33N 11 40 E
Mecklenburger Bucht, Germany 16 A6 54 20N 11 40 E
Meconta, Mozam. 55 E4 14 59S 39 50 E
Medan, Indonesia 36 D1 3 40N 98 38 E
Medanosa, Pta., Argentina 96 F3 48 8S 66 0W
Médéa, Algeria 50 A6 36 12N 2 50 E
Medellín, Colombia 92 B3 6 15N 75 35W
Medelpad, Sweden 9 E17 62 33N 16 30 E
Medemblik, Neths. 15 B5 52 46N 5 8 E
Medford, Mass., U.S.A. 79 D13 42 25N 71 7W
Medford, Oreg., U.S.A. 82 E2 42 19N 122 52W
Medford, Wis., U.S.A. 80 C9 45 9N 90 20W
Medgidia, Romania 17 F15 44 15N 28 19 E
Media Agua, Argentina 94 C2 31 58S 68 25W
Media Luna, Argentina 94 C2 34 45S 66 44W
Medianeira, Brazil 95 B5 25 17S 54 5W
Mediaş, Romania 17 E13 46 9N 24 22 E
Medicine Bow, U.S.A. 82 F10 41 54N 106 12W
Medicine Bow Pk., U.S.A. 82 F10 41 21N 106 19W
Medicine Bow Ra., U.S.A. 82 F10 41 10N 106 25W
Medicine Hat, Canada 73 D6 50 0N 110 45W
Medicine Lake, U.S.A. 80 A2 48 30N 104 30W
Medicine Lodge, U.S.A. 81 G5 37 17N 98 35W
Medina = Al Madīnah, Si. Arabia 46 C2 24 35N 39 52 E
Medina, N. Dak., U.S.A. 80 B5 46 54N 99 18W
Medina, N.Y., U.S.A. 78 C6 43 13N 78 23W
Medina, Ohio, U.S.A. 78 E3 41 8N 81 52W
Medina →, U.S.A. 81 L5 29 16N 98 29W
Medina del Campo, Spain 19 B3 41 18N 4 55W
Medina L., U.S.A. 81 L5 29 32N 98 56W
Medina Sidonia, Spain 19 D3 36 28N 5 57W
Medinipur, India 43 H12 22 25N 87 21 E
Mediterranean Sea, Europe 49 C5 35 0N 15 0 E
Médoc, France 18 D3 45 10N 0 50W
Medveditsa →, Russia 25 E7 49 35N 42 41 E
Medvezhi, Ostrava, Russia 27 B17 71 0N 161 0 E
Medvezhyegorsk, Russia 24 B5 63 0N 34 25 E
Medway □, U.K. 11 F8 51 25N 0 32 E
Medway →, U.K. 11 F8 51 27N 0 46 E
Meekatharra, Australia 61 E2 26 32S 118 29 E
Meeker, U.S.A. 82 F10 40 2N 107 55W
Meelpaeg Res., Canada 71 C8 48 15N 56 33W
Meerut, India 42 E7 29 1N 77 42 E
Meeteetse, U.S.A. 82 D9 44 9N 108 52W
Mega, Ethiopia 46 G2 3 57N 38 19 E
Mégara, Greece 21 F10 37 58N 23 22 E
Megasini, India 43 J12 21 38N 86 21 E
Meghalaya □, India 41 G17 25 50N 91 0 E
Mégiscane, L., Canada 70 C4 48 35N 75 55W
Meharry, Mt., Australia 60 D2 22 59S 118 35 E
Mehlville, U.S.A. 80 F9 38 30N 90 19W
Mehndawal, India 43 F10 26 58N 83 5 E
Mehr Jān, Iran 45 C7 33 50N 55 6 E
Mehrābād, Iran 44 B5 36 53N 47 55 E
Mehrān, Iran 44 C5 33 7N 46 10 E
Mehrīz, Iran 45 D7 31 35N 54 28 E
Mei Xian, China 34 G4 34 18N 107 55 E
Meiktila, Burma 41 J19 20 53N 95 54 E
Meissen, Germany 16 C7 51 9N 13 29 E
Meizhou, China 33 D6 24 16N 116 6 E
Meja, India 43 G10 25 9N 82 7 E
Mejillones, Chile 94 A1 23 10S 70 30W
Mekele, Ethiopia 46 E2 13 33N 39 30 E
Mekhtar, Pakistan 40 D6 30 30N 69 15 E
Meknès, Morocco 50 B4 33 57N 5 33W
Mekong →, Asia 39 H6 9 30N 106 15 E
Mekongga, Indonesia 37 E6 3 39S 121 15 E
Mekvari = Kür →, Azerbaijan 25 G8 39 29N 49 15 E
Melagiri Hills, India 40 N10 12 20N 77 30 E
Melaka, Malaysia 39 L4 2 15N 102 15 E
Melalap, Malaysia 36 C5 5 10N 116 5 E
Mélambes, Greece 23 D6 35 8N 24 40 E
Melanesia, Pac. Oc. 64 H7 4 0S 155 0 E
Melbourne, Australia 63 F4 37 50S 145 0 E
Melbourne, U.S.A. 77 L5 28 5N 80 37W
Melchor Múzquiz, Mexico 86 B4 27 50N 101 30W
Melchor Ocampo, Mexico 86 C4 24 52N 101 40W
Mélèzes →, Canada 70 A5 57 40N 69 29W
Melfort, Canada 73 C8 52 50N 104 37W
Melfort, Zimbabwe 55 F3 18 0S 31 25 E
Melhus, Norway 8 E14 63 17N 10 18 E
Melilla, N. Afr. 19 E4 35 21N 2 57W
Melipilla, Chile 94 C1 33 42S 71 15W
Mélissa, Ákra, Greece 23 D6 35 6N 24 33 E
Melita, Canada 73 D8 49 15N 101 0W
Melitopol, Ukraine 25 E6 46 50N 35 22 E
Melk, Austria 16 D8 48 13N 15 20 E
Mellansel, Sweden 8 E18 63 25N 18 17 E
Mellen, U.S.A. 80 B9 46 20N 90 40W
Mellerud, Sweden 9 G15 58 41N 12 28 E
Mellette, U.S.A. 80 C5 45 9N 98 30W
Mellieha, Malta 23 D1 35 57N 14 22 E
Melo, Uruguay 95 C5 32 20S 54 10W
Melolo, Indonesia 37 F6 9 53S 120 40 E
Melouprey, Cambodia 38 F5 13 48N 105 16 E
Melrose, Australia 63 E4 32 42S 146 57 E
Melrose, U.K. 12 F6 55 36N 2 43W
Melrose, Minn., U.S.A. 80 C7 45 40N 94 49W
Melrose, N. Mex., U.S.A. 81 H3 34 26N 103 38W
Melstone, U.S.A. 82 C10 46 36N 107 52W
Melton Mowbray, U.K. 10 E7 52 47N 0 54W
Melun, France 18 B5 48 32N 2 39 E
Melville, Canada 73 C8 50 55N 102 50W
Melville, C., Australia 62 A3 14 11S 144 30 E
Melville, L., Canada 71 B8 53 30N 60 0W
Melville B., Australia 62 A2 12 0S 136 45 E
Melville I., Australia 60 B5 11 30S 131 0 E
Melville I., Canada 4 B2 75 30N 112 0W
Melville Pen., Canada 69 B11 68 0N 84 0W
Memba, Mozam. 55 E5 14 11S 40 30 E
Memboro, Indonesia 37 F5 9 30S 119 30 E
Memel = Klaipėda, Lithuania 9 J19 55 43N 21 10 E
Memel, S. Africa 57 D4 27 38S 29 36 E
Memmingen, Germany 16 E6 47 58N 10 10 E
Mempawah, Indonesia 36 D3 0 30N 109 5 E
Memphis, Mich., U.S.A. 78 D2 42 54N 82 46W
Memphis, Tenn., U.S.A. 81 H10 35 8N 90 3W
Memphis, Tex., U.S.A. 81 H4 34 44N 100 33W
Memphremagog, L., U.S.A. 79 B12 45 0N 72 12W
Mena, U.S.A. 81 H7 34 35N 94 15W
Menai Strait, U.K. 10 D3 53 11N 4 13W
Ménaka, Mali 50 E6 15 59N 2 18 E
Menan = Chao Phraya →, Thailand 38 F3 13 32N 100 36 E
Menarandra →, Madag. 57 D7 25 17S 44 30 E
Menard, U.S.A. 81 K5 30 55N 99 47W
Mendawai →, Indonesia 36 E4 3 30S 113 0 E
Mende, France 18 D5 44 31N 3 30 E
Mendez, Mexico 87 B5 25 7N 98 34W
Mendhar, India 43 C6 33 35N 74 10 E
Mendip Hills, U.K. 11 F5 51 17N 2 40W
Mendocino, U.S.A. 82 G2 39 19N 123 48W
Mendocino, C., U.S.A. 82 F1 40 26N 124 25W
Mendota, Calif., U.S.A. 84 J6 36 45N 120 23W
Mendota, Ill., U.S.A. 80 E10 41 33N 89 7W
Mendoza, Argentina 94 C2 32 50S 68 52W
Mendoza □, Argentina 94 C2 33 0S 69 0W
Mene Grande, Venezuela 92 B4 9 49N 70 56W
Menemen, Turkey 21 E12 38 34N 27 3 E
Menen, Belgium 15 D3 50 47N 3 7 E
Menggala, Indonesia 36 E3 4 30S 105 15 E
Mengjin, China 34 G7 34 55N 112 45 E
Mengyin, China 35 G9 35 40N 117 58 E
Mengzi, China 32 D5 23 20N 103 22 E
Menihek, Canada 71 B6 54 28N 56 36W
Menihek L., Canada 71 B6 54 0N 67 0W
Menin = Menen, Belgium 15 D3 50 47N 3 7 E
Menindee, Australia 63 E3 32 20S 142 25 E
Menindee L., Australia 63 E3 32 20S 142 25 E
Meningie, Australia 63 F2 35 50S 139 18 E
Menlo Park, U.S.A. 84 H4 37 27N 122 12W
Menominee, U.S.A. 76 C2 45 6N 87 37W
Menominee →, U.S.A. 76 C2 45 6N 87 36W
Menomonie, U.S.A. 80 C9 44 53N 91 55W
Menongue, Angola 53 G3 14 48S 17 52 E
Menorca, Spain 22 B11 40 0N 4 0 E
Mentakab, Malaysia 39 L4 3 29N 102 21 E
Mentawai, Kepulauan, Indonesia 36 E1 2 0S 99 0 E
Menton, France 18 E7 43 50N 7 29 E
Mentor, U.S.A. 78 E3 41 40N 81 21W
Menzelinsk, Russia 24 C9 55 47N 53 11 E
Menzies, Australia 61 E3 29 40S 121 2 E
Meob B., Namibia 56 B2 24 25S 14 34 E
Me'ona, Israel 47 B4 33 1N 35 15 E
Meoqui, Mexico 86 B3 28 17N 105 29W
Mepaco, Mozam. 55 F3 15 57S 30 48 E
Meppel, Neths. 15 B6 52 42N 6 12 E
Merabéllou, Kólpos, Greece 23 D7 35 10N 25 50 E
Merak, Indonesia 37 F12 6 10N 106 26 E
Meramangye, L., Australia 61 E5 28 25S 132 13 E
Meran = Merano, Italy 20 A4 46 40N 11 9 E
Merano, Italy 20 A4 46 40N 11 9 E
Merauke, Indonesia 37 F10 8 29S 140 24 E
Merbein, Australia 63 E3 34 10S 142 2 E
Merca, Somali Rep. 46 G3 1 48N 44 50 E
Merced, U.S.A. 84 H6 37 18N 120 29W
Merced →, U.S.A. 84 H6 37 21N 120 59W
Merced Pk., U.S.A. 84 H7 37 36N 119 24W
Mercedes, Buenos Aires, Argentina 94 C4 34 40S 59 30W
Mercedes, Corrientes, Argentina 94 B4 29 10S 58 5W
Mercedes, San Luis, Argentina 94 C2 33 40S 65 21W
Mercedes, Uruguay 94 C4 33 12S 58 0W
Mercedes, U.S.A. 81 M6 26 9N 97 55W
Merceditas, Chile 94 B1 28 20S 70 35W
Mercer, N.Z. 59 G5 37 16S 175 5 E
Mercer, U.S.A. 78 E4 41 14N 80 15W
Mercer Island, U.S.A. 84 C4 47 35N 122 15W
Mercury, U.S.A. 85 J11 36 40N 115 58W
Mercy C., Canada 69 B13 65 0N 63 30W
Mere, U.K. 11 F5 51 6N 2 16W
Meredith, C., Falk. Is. 96 G4 52 15S 60 40W
Meredith, L., U.S.A. 81 H4 35 43N 101 33W
Mergui, Burma 38 F2 12 26N 98 34 E
Mergui Arch. = Myeik Kyunzu, Burma 39 G1 11 30N 97 30 E
Mérida, Mexico 87 C7 20 58N 89 37W
Mérida, Spain 19 C2 38 55N 6 25W
Mérida, Venezuela 92 B4 8 24N 71 8W
Mérida, Cord. de, Venezuela 92 B4 9 0N 71 0W
Meriden, U.K. 11 E6 52 26N 1 38W
Meriden, U.S.A. 79 E12 41 32N 72 48W
Meridian, Calif., U.S.A. 84 F5 39 9N 121 55W
Meridian, Idaho, U.S.A. 82 E5 43 37N 116 24W
Meridian, Miss., U.S.A. 77 J1 32 22N 88 42W
Merinda, Australia 62 C4 20 2S 148 11 E
Merir, Pac. Oc. 37 D8 4 10N 132 30 E
Merirumã, Brazil 93 C8 1 15N 54 50W
Merkel, U.S.A. 81 J5 32 28N 100 1W
Mermaid Reef, Australia 60 C2 17 6S 119 36 E
Merredin, Australia 61 F2 31 28S 118 18 E
Merrick, U.K. 12 F4 55 8N 4 28W
Merrickville, Canada 79 B9 44 55N 75 50W
Merrill, Oreg., U.S.A. 82 E3 42 1N 121 36W
Merrill, Wis., U.S.A. 80 C10 45 11N 89 41W
Merrimack →, U.S.A. 79 D14 42 49N 70 49W
Merriman, U.S.A. 80 D4 42 55N 101 42W
Merritt, Canada 72 C4 50 10N 120 45W
Merritt Island, U.S.A. 77 L5 28 21N 80 42W
Merriwa, Australia 63 E5 32 6S 150 22 E
Merry I., Canada 70 A4 55 29N 77 31W
Merryville, U.S.A. 81 K8 30 45N 93 33W
Mersch, Lux. 15 E6 49 44N 6 7 E
Mersea I., U.K. 11 F8 51 47N 0 58 E
Merseburg, Germany 16 C6 51 22N 11 59 E
Mersey →, U.K. 10 D4 53 25N 3 1W
Merseyside □, U.K. 10 D4 53 31N 3 2W
Mersin, Turkey 25 G5 36 51N 34 36 E
Mersing, Malaysia 39 L4 2 25N 103 50 E
Merta, India 42 F6 26 39N 74 4 E
Merta Road, India 42 F5 26 43N 73 55 E
Merthyr Tydfil, U.K. 11 F4 51 45N 3 22W
Merthyr Tydfil □, U.K. 11 F4 51 46N 3 21W
Mértola, Portugal 19 D2 37 40N 7 40W
Mertzon, U.S.A. 81 K4 31 16N 100 49W
Meru, Kenya 54 B4 0 3N 37 40 E
Meru, Tanzania 54 C4 3 15S 36 46 E
Mesa, U.S.A. 83 K8 33 25N 111 50W
Mesa Verde Nat. Park, U.S.A. 83 H9 37 11N 108 29W
Mesanagrós, Greece 23 C9 36 1N 27 49 E
Mesaoría, Cyprus 23 D12 35 12N 33 14 E
Mesarás, Kólpos, Greece 23 D6 35 6N 24 47 E
Mesgouez, L., Canada 70 B5 51 20N 75 0W
Meshed = Mashhad, Iran 45 B8 36 20N 59 35 E
Meshoppen, U.S.A. 79 E8 41 36N 76 3W
Meshilinka →, Canada 72 B4 56 6N 124 30W
Mesilla, U.S.A. 83 K10 32 16N 106 48W
Mesolóngion, Greece 21 E9 38 21N 21 28 E
Mesopotamia = Al Jazirah, Iraq 44 C5 33 30N 44 0 E
Mesopotamia, U.S.A. 78 E4 41 27N 80 57W
Mesquite, U.S.A. 83 H6 36 47N 114 6W
Messaad, Algeria 50 B6 34 8N 3 30 E
Messalo →, Mozam. 55 E4 12 25S 39 15 E
Messina, Italy 20 E6 38 11N 15 34 E
Messina, S. Africa 57 C5 22 20S 30 5 E
Messina, Str. di, Italy 20 F6 38 15N 15 35 E
Messíni, Greece 21 F10 37 4N 22 1 E
Messiniakós Kólpos, Greece 21 F10 36 45N 22 5 E
Messonghi, Greece 23 B3 39 29N 19 56 E
Mesta →, Bulgaria 21 D11 40 54N 24 49 E
Meta →, S. Amer. 92 B5 6 12N 67 28W
Meta Incognita Peninsula, Canada 69 B13 62 40N 68 0W
Metabetchouan, Canada 71 C5 48 26N 71 52W
Metairie, U.S.A. 81 L9 29 58N 90 10W
Metaline Falls, U.S.A. 82 B5 48 52N 117 22W
Metán, Argentina 94 B3 25 30S 65 0W
Metangula, Mozam. 55 E3 12 40S 34 50 E
Metengobalame, Mozam. 55 E3 14 49S 34 30 E
Methven, N.Z. 59 K3 43 38S 171 40 E
Metil, Mozam. 55 F4 16 24S 39 0 E
Metlakatla, U.S.A. 68 C6 55 8N 131 35W
Metropolis, U.S.A. 81 G10 37 9N 88 44W
Metu, Ethiopia 46 F2 8 18N 35 35 E
Metz, France 18 B7 49 8N 6 10 E
Meulaboh, Indonesia 36 D1 4 11N 96 3 E
Meureudu, Indonesia 36 C1 5 19N 96 10 E
Meuse →, Europe 18 A6 50 45N 5 41 E
Mexia, U.S.A. 81 K6 31 41N 96 29W
Mexiana, I., Brazil 93 D9 0 0 49 30W
Mexicali, Mexico 85 N11 32 40N 115 30W
Mexican Plateau, Mexico 66 G9 25 0N 104 0W
Mexican Water, U.S.A. 83 H9 36 57N 109 32W
México, Mexico 87 D5 19 20N 99 10W
Mexico, Maine, U.S.A. 79 B14 44 34N 70 33W
Mexico, Mo., U.S.A. 80 F9 39 10N 91 53W
Mexico, N.Y., U.S.A. 79 C8 43 28N 76 18W
México □, Mexico 87 D5 19 20N 99 10W
Mexico ■, Cent. Amer. 86 C4 25 0N 105 0W
Mexico, G. of, Cent. Amer. 87 C7 25 0N 90 0W
Mexico B., U.S.A. 79 C8 43 35N 76 20W
Meydān-e Naftūn, Iran 45 D6 31 56N 49 18 E
Meydani, Ra's-e, Iran 45 E8 25 24N 59 6 E
Meymaneh, Afghan. 40 B4 35 53N 64 38 E
Mezen, Russia 24 A7 65 50N 44 20 E
Mezen →, Russia 24 A7 65 44N 44 22 E
Mézenc, Mt., France 18 D6 44 54N 4 11 E
Mezhdurechenskiy, Russia 26 D7 59 36N 65 56 E
Mezőkövesd, Hungary 17 E11 47 49N 20 35 E
Mezőtúr, Hungary 17 E11 47 1N 20 41 E
Mezquital, Mexico 86 C4 23 29N 104 23W
Mfolozi →, S. Africa 57 D5 28 25S 32 26 E
Mgeta, Tanzania 55 D4 8 22S 36 6 E
Mhlaba Hills, Zimbabwe 55 F3 18 30S 30 30 E
Mhow, India 42 H6 22 33N 75 50 E
Miahuatlán, Mexico 87 D5 16 21N 96 36W
Miami, Fla., U.S.A. 77 N5 25 47N 80 11W
Miami, Okla., U.S.A. 81 G7 36 53N 94 53W
Miami, Tex., U.S.A. 81 H4 35 42N 100 38W
Miami Beach, U.S.A. 77 N5 25 47N 80 8W
Mian Xian, China 34 H4 33 10N 106 32 E
Mianchi, China 34 G6 34 48N 111 48 E
Miāndarreh, Iran 45 C7 35 37N 53 39 E
Miāndowāb, Iran 44 B5 37 0N 46 5 E
Miandrivazo, Madag. 57 B8 19 31S 45 29 E
Mīāneh, Iran 44 B5 37 30N 47 40 E
Mianwali, Pakistan 42 C4 32 38N 71 28 E
Miarinarivo, Antananarivo, Madag. 57 B8 18 57S 46 55 E
Miarinarivo, Toamasina, Madag. 57 B8 16 38S 48 15 E
Miariravaratra, Madag. 57 C8 20 13S 47 31 E
Miass, Russia 24 D11 54 59N 60 6 E
Mica, S. Africa 57 C5 24 10S 30 48 E
Michalovce, Slovak Rep. 17 D11 48 47N 21 58 E
Michigan □, U.S.A. 76 C3 44 0N 85 0W
Michigan, L., U.S.A. 76 D2 44 0N 87 0W
Michigan City, U.S.A. 76 E2 41 43N 86 54W
Michipicoten I., Canada 70 C2 47 40N 85 40W
Michoacan □, Mexico 86 D4 19 0N 102 0W
Michurin, Bulgaria 21 C12 42 9N 27 51 E
Michurinsk, Russia 24 D7 52 58N 40 27 E
Mico, Pta., Nic. 88 D3 12 0N 83 30W
Micronesia, Pac. Oc. 64 G7 11 0N 160 0 E
Micronesia, Federated States of ■, Pac. Oc. 64 G7 9 0N 150 0 E
Midai, Indonesia 39 L6 3 0N 107 47 E
Midale, Canada 73 D8 49 25N 103 20W
Middelburg, Neths. 15 C3 51 30N 3 36 E
Middelburg, Eastern Cape, S. Africa 56 E4 31 30S 25 0 E
Middelburg, Mpumalanga, S. Africa 57 D4 25 49S 29 28 E
Middelpos, S. Africa 56 E3 31 55S 20 13 E
Middelwit, S. Africa 56 C4 24 51S 27 3 E
Middle Alkali L., U.S.A. 82 F3 41 27N 120 5W
Middle Bass I., U.S.A. 78 E2 41 41N 82 49W
Middle East, Asia 28 F7 38 0N 40 0 E
Middle Fork Feather →, U.S.A. 84 F5 38 33N 121 30W
Middle I., Australia 61 F3 34 6S 123 11 E
Middle Loup →, U.S.A. 80 E5 41 17N 98 24W
Middle Sackville, Canada 71 D7 44 47N 63 42W
Middleboro, U.S.A. 79 E14 41 54N 70 55W
Middleburg, Fla., U.S.A. 77 K5 30 4N 81 52W
Middleburg, N.Y., U.S.A. 79 D10 42 36N 74 20W
Middleburg, Pa., U.S.A. 78 F7 40 47N 77 3W
Middlebury, U.S.A. 79 B11 44 1N 73 10W
Middlemount, Australia 62 C4 22 50S 148 40 E
Middleport, N.Y., U.S.A. 78 C6 43 13N 78 29W
Middleport, Ohio, U.S.A. 76 F4 39 0N 82 3W
Middlesboro, U.S.A. 77 G4 36 36N 83 43W
Middlesbrough, U.K. 10 C6 54 35N 1 13W
Middlesbrough □, U.K. 10 C6 54 28N 1 13W
Middlesex, Belize 88 C2 17 2N 88 31W
Middlesex, N.J., U.S.A. 79 F10 40 36N 74 30W
Middlesex, N.Y., U.S.A. 78 D7 42 42N 77 16W
Middleton, Australia 62 C3 22 22S 141 32 E
Middleton, Canada 71 D6 44 57N 65 4W
Middleton Cr. →, Australia 62 C3 22 35S 141 51 E
Middletown, U.K. 13 B5 54 17N 6 51W
Middletown, Calif., U.S.A. 84 G4 38 45N 122 37W
Middletown, Conn., U.S.A. 79 E12 41 34N 72 39W
Middletown, N.Y., U.S.A. 79 E10 41 27N 74 25W
Middletown, Ohio, U.S.A. 76 F3 39 31N 84 24W
Middletown, Pa., U.S.A. 79 F8 40 12N 76 44W
Midhurst, U.K. 11 G7 50 59N 0 44W
Midi, Canal du →, France 18 E4 43 45N 1 21 E
Midland, Canada 78 B5 44 45N 79 50W
Midland, Calif., U.S.A. 85 M12 33 52N 114 48W
Midland, Mich., U.S.A. 76 D3 43 37N 84 14W
Midland, Pa., U.S.A. 78 F4 40 39N 80 27W
Midland, Tex., U.S.A. 81 K3 32 0N 102 3W
Midlands □, Zimbabwe 55 F2 19 40S 29 0 E
Midleton, Ireland 13 E3 51 55N 8 10W
Midlothian, U.S.A. 81 J6 32 30N 97 0W
Midlothian □, U.K. 12 F5 55 51N 3 5W
Midongy, Tangorombohitr' i, Madag. 57 C8 23 30S 47 0 E
Midongy Atsimo, Madag. 57 C8 23 35S 47 1 E
Midway Is., Pac. Oc. 64 E10 28 13N 177 22W
Midway Wells, U.S.A. 85 N11 32 41N 115 7W
Midwest, U.S.A. 82 E10 43 25N 106 16W
Midwest City, U.S.A. 81 H6 35 27N 97 24W
Midyat, Turkey 44 B4 37 25N 41 23 E
Midzŏr, Bulgaria 21 C10 43 24N 22 40 E
Mie □, Japan 31 G8 34 30N 136 10 E
Międzychód, Poland 16 B8 52 35N 15 53 E
Międzyrzec Podlaski, Poland 17 C12 51 58N 22 45 E
Mielec, Poland 17 C11 50 15N 21 25 E
Mienga, Angola 56 B2 17 12S 19 48 E
Miercurea-Ciuc, Romania 17 E13 46 21N 25 48 E
Mieres, Spain 19 A3 43 18N 5 48W
Mifflintown, U.S.A. 78 F7 40 34N 77 24W
Mifraz Hefa, Israel 47 C4 32 52N 35 0 E
Miguel Alemán, Presa, Mexico 87 D5 18 15N 96 40W
Mihara, Japan 31 G6 34 24N 133 5 E
Mikese, Tanzania 54 D4 6 48S 37 55 E
Mikhaylovgrad = Montana, Bulgaria 21 C10 43 27N 23 16 E
Mikhaylovka, Russia 25 D7 50 3N 43 5 E
Mikkeli, Finland 9 F22 61 43N 27 15 E
Mikkwa →, Canada 72 B6 58 25N 114 46W
Míkonos, Greece 21 F11 37 30N 25 25 E
Mikumi, Tanzania 54 D4 7 26S 37 0 E
Mikun, Russia 24 B9 62 20N 50 0 E
Milaca, U.S.A. 80 C8 45 45N 93 39W
Milagro, Ecuador 92 D3 2 11S 79 36W
Milan = Milano, Italy 18 D8 45 28N 9 12 E
Milan, Mo., U.S.A. 80 E8 40 12N 93 7W
Milan, Tenn., U.S.A. 77 H1 35 55N 88 46W
Milange, Mozam. 55 F4 16 3S 35 45 E
Milano, Italy 18 D8 45 28N 9 12 E
Milanoa, Madag. 57 A8 13 35S 49 47 E
Milâs, Turkey 21 F12 37 20N 27 50 E
Mílatos, Greece 23 D7 35 18N 25 34 E
Milazzo, Italy 20 E6 38 13N 15 15 E
Milbank, U.S.A. 80 C6 45 13N 96 38W
Milbanke Sd., Canada 72 C3 52 15N 128 35W
Milden, Canada 73 C7 51 29N 107 32W
Mildenhall, U.K. 11 E8 52 21N 0 32 E
Mildmay, Canada 78 B3 44 3N 81 7W
Mildura, Australia 63 E3 34 13S 142 9 E
Miles, Australia 63 D5 26 40S 150 9 E
Miles City, U.S.A. 80 B2 46 25N 105 51W
Milestone, Canada 73 D8 49 59N 104 31W
Miletus, Turkey 21 F12 37 30N 27 18 E
Milford, Calif., U.S.A. 84 E6 40 10N 120 22W
Milford, Conn., U.S.A. 79 E11 41 14N 73 3W
Milford, Del., U.S.A. 76 F8 38 55N 75 26W
Milford, Mass., U.S.A. 79 D13 42 8N 71 31W
Milford, N.H., U.S.A. 79 D13 42 50N 71 39W
Milford, Pa., U.S.A. 79 E10 41 19N 74 48W
Milford, Utah, U.S.A. 83 G7 38 24N 113 1W

Milford Haven, *U.K.* **11 F2** 51 42N 5 7W
Milford Sd., *N.Z.* .... **59 L1** 44 41S 167 47 E
Milḩ, Baḩr al, *Iraq* .... **44 C4** 32 40N 43 35 E
Milikapiti, *Australia* .... **60 B5** 11 26S 130 40 E
Miling, *Australia* .... **61 F2** 30 30S 116 17 E
Milk →, *U.S.A.* **82 B10** 48 4N 106 19W
Milk River, *Canada* **72 D6** 49 10N 112 5W
Mill I., *Antarctica* .... **5 C8** 66 0S 101 30 E
Mill Valley, *U.S.A.* **84 H4** 37 54N 122 32W
Millau, *France* .... **18 D5** 44 8N 3 4 E
Millbridge, *Canada* **78 B7** 44 41N 77 36W
Millbrook, *Canada* **78 B6** 44 10N 78 29W
Millbrook, *U.S.A.* **79 E11** 41 47N 73 42W
Mille Lacs, L. des, *Canada* .. **70 C1** 48 45N 90 35W
Mille Lacs L., *U.S.A.* **80 B8** 46 15N 93 39W
Milledgeville, *U.S.A.* **77 J4** 33 5N 83 14W
Millen, *U.S.A.* **77 J5** 32 48N 81 57W
Millennium I. = Caroline I., *Kiribati* **65 H12** 9 58S 150 13W
Miller, *U.S.A.* **80 C5** 44 31N 98 59W
Millersburg, *Ohio, U.S.A.* **78 F3** 40 33N 81 55W
Millersburg, *Pa., U.S.A.* **78 F8** 40 32N 76 58W
Millerton, *U.S.A.* **79 E11** 41 57N 73 31W
Millerton L., *U.S.A.* **84 J7** 37 1N 119 41W
Millheim, *U.S.A.* **78 F7** 40 54N 77 29W
Millicent, *Australia* .... **63 F3** 37 34S 140 21 E
Millington, *U.S.A.* **81 H10** 35 20N 89 53W
Millinocket, *U.S.A.* **77 C11** 45 39N 68 43W
Millmerran, *Australia* ...... **63 D5** 27 53S 151 16 E
Millom, *U.K.* **10 C4** 54 13N 3 16W
Mills L., *Canada* **72 A5** 61 30N 118 20W
Millsboro, *U.S.A.* **78 G5** 40 0N 80 0W
Milltown Malbay, *Ireland* **13 D2** 52 52N 9 24W
Millville, *N.J., U.S.A.* **76 F8** 39 24N 75 2W
Millville, *Pa., U.S.A.* **79 E8** 41 7N 76 32W
Millwood L., *U.S.A.* **81 J8** 33 42N 93 58W
Milne →, *Australia* .... **62 C2** 21 10S 137 33 E
Milo, *U.S.A.* **77 C11** 45 15N 68 59W
Milos, *Greece* .... **21 F11** 36 44N 24 25 E
Milparinka, *Australia* .... **63 D3** 29 46S 141 57 E
Milton, *N.S., Canada* **71 D7** 44 4N 64 45W
Milton, *Ont., Canada* **78 C5** 43 31N 79 53W
Milton, *N.Z.* .... **59 M2** 46 7S 169 59 E
Milton, *Calif., U.S.A.* **84 G6** 38 3N 120 51W
Milton, *Fla., U.S.A.* **77 K2** 30 38N 87 3W
Milton, *Pa., U.S.A.* **78 F8** 41 1N 76 51W
Milton, *Vt., U.S.A.* **79 B11** 44 38N 73 7W
Milton-Freewater, *U.S.A.* ... **82 D4** 45 56N 118 23W
Milton Keynes, *U.K.* **11 E7** 52 1N 0 44W
Milton Keynes □, *U.K.* **11 E7** 52 1N 0 44W
Milverton, *Canada* **78 C4** 43 34N 80 55W
Milwaukee, *U.S.A.* **76 D2** 43 2N 87 55W
Milwaukee Deep, *Atl. Oc.* ... **89 C6** 19 50N 68 0W
Milwaukie, *U.S.A.* **84 E4** 45 27N 122 38W
Min Jiang →, *Fujian, China* . **33 D6** 26 0N 119 35 E
Min Jiang →, *Sichuan, China* **32 D5** 28 45N 104 40 E
Min Xian, *China* .... **34 G3** 34 25N 104 5 E
Mina Pirquitas, *Argentina* ... **94 A2** 22 40S 66 30W
Mīnā Su'ud, *Si. Arabia* ..... **45 D6** 28 45N 48 28 E
Mīnā'al Aḩmadī, *Kuwait* .... **45 D6** 29 5N 48 10 E
Minago →, *Canada* **73 C9** 54 33N 98 59W
Minaki, *Canada* **73 D10** 49 59N 94 40W
Minamata, *Japan* .... **31 H5** 32 10N 130 30 E
Minami-Tori-Shima, *Pac. Oc.* **64 E7** 24 20N 153 58 E
Minas, *Uruguay* **95 C4** 34 20S 55 10W
Minas, Sierra de las, *Guatemala* **88 C2** 15 9N 89 31W
Minas Basin, *Canada* **71 C7** 45 20N 64 12W
Minas Gerais □, *Brazil* **93 G9** 18 50S 46 0W
Minatitlán, *Mexico* **87 D6** 17 59N 94 31W
Minbu, *Burma* .... **41 J19** 20 10N 94 52 E
Minchinabad, *Pakistan* ..... **42 D5** 30 10N 73 34 E
Mindanao, *Phil.* .... **37 C6** 8 0N 125 0 E
Mindanao Sea = Bohol Sea, *Phil.* .... **37 C6** 9 0N 124 0 E
Mindanao Trench, *Pac. Oc.* . **37 B7** 12 0N 126 6 E
Minden, *Canada* **78 B6** 44 55N 78 43W
Minden, *Germany* .... **16 B5** 52 17N 8 55 E
Minden, *La., U.S.A.* **81 J8** 32 37N 93 17W
Minden, *Nev., U.S.A.* **84 G7** 38 57N 119 46W
Mindiptana, *Indonesia* ...... **37 F10** 5 55S 140 22 E
Mindoro, *Phil.* .... **37 B6** 13 0N 121 0 E
Mindoro Str., *Phil.* .... **37 B6** 12 30N 120 30 E
Mine, *Japan* .... **31 G5** 34 12N 131 7 E
Minehead, *U.K.* **11 F4** 51 12N 3 29W
Mineola, *N.Y., U.S.A.* **79 F11** 40 45N 73 39W
Mineola, *Tex., U.S.A.* **81 J7** 32 40N 95 29W
Mineral King, *U.S.A.* **84 J8** 36 27N 118 36W
Mineral Wells, *U.S.A.* **81 J5** 32 48N 98 7W
Minersville, *U.S.A.* **79 F8** 40 41N 76 16W
Minerva, *U.S.A.* **78 F3** 40 44N 81 6W
Minetto, *U.S.A.* **79 C8** 43 24N 76 28W
Mingäçevir Su Anbarı, *Azerbaijan* .... **25 F8** 40 57N 46 50 E
Mingan, *Canada* **71 B7** 50 20N 64 0W
Mingechaurskoye Vdkhr. = Mingäçevir Su Anbarı, *Azerbaijan* .... **25 F8** 40 57N 46 50 E
Mingela, *Australia* .... **62 B4** 19 52S 146 38 E
Mingenew, *Australia* .... **61 E2** 29 12S 115 21 E
Mingera Cr. →, *Australia* ... **62 C2** 20 38S 137 45 E
Mingin, *Burma* .... **41 H19** 22 50N 94 30 E
Mingo Junction, *U.S.A.* **78 F4** 40 19N 80 37W
Mingteke Daban = Mintaka Pass, *Pakistan* .... **43 A6** 37 0N 74 58 E
Mingyuegue, *China* .... **35 C15** 43 2N 128 50 E
Minho = Miño →, *Spain* **19 A2** 41 52N 8 40W
Minho, *Portugal* **19 B1** 41 25N 8 20W
Minidoka, *U.S.A.* **82 E7** 42 45N 113 29W
Minigwal, L., *Australia* ..... **61 E3** 29 31S 123 14 E
Minilya →, *Australia* .... **61 D1** 23 45S 114 0 E
Minilya Roadhouse, *Australia* **61 D1** 23 55S 114 0 E
Minipi L., *Canada* **71 B7** 52 25N 60 45W
Mink L., *Canada* **72 A5** 61 54N 117 40W
Minna, *Nigeria* .... **50 G7** 9 37N 6 30 E
Minneapolis, *Kans., U.S.A.* .. **80 F6** 39 8N 97 42W
Minneapolis, *Minn., U.S.A.* .. **80 C8** 44 59N 93 16W
Minnedosa, *Canada* **73 C9** 50 14N 99 50W
Minnesota □, *U.S.A.* **80 B8** 46 0N 94 15W
Minnesota →, *U.S.A.* **80 C8** 44 54N 93 9W
Minnewaukan, *U.S.A.* **80 A5** 48 4N 99 15W
Minnipa, *Australia* .... **63 E2** 32 51S 135 9 E
Minnitaki L., *Canada* **70 C1** 49 57N 92 10W
Mino, *Japan* .... **31 G8** 35 32N 136 55 E
Miño →, *Spain* **19 A2** 41 52N 8 40W
Minorca = Menorca, *Spain* .. **22 B11** 40 0N 4 0 E
Minot, *U.S.A.* **80 A4** 48 14N 101 18W
Minqin, *China* .... **34 E2** 38 38N 103 20 E
Minsk, *Belarus* .... **17 B14** 53 52N 27 30 E
Mińsk Mazowiecki, *Poland* .. **17 B11** 52 10N 21 33 E
Mintabie, *Australia* .... **63 D1** 27 15S 133 7 E
Mintaka Pass, *Pakistan* ..... **43 A6** 37 0N 74 58 E
Minto, *Canada* **71 C6** 46 5N 66 5W
Minto, L., *Canada* **70 A5** 57 13N 75 0W
Minton, *Canada* **73 D8** 49 10N 104 35W
Minturn, *U.S.A.* **82 G10** 39 35N 106 26W
Minusinsk, *Russia* .... **27 D10** 53 43N 91 20 E
Minutang, *India* .... **41 E20** 28 15N 96 30 E
Miquelon, *Canada* **70 C4** 49 25N 76 27W
Miquelon, *St- P. & M.* **71 C8** 47 8N 56 22W
Mīr Kūh, *Iran* .... **45 E8** 26 22N 58 55 E
Mīr Shahdād, *Iran* .... **45 E8** 26 15N 58 29 E
Mira, *Italy* .... **20 B5** 45 26N 12 8 E
Mira por vos Cay, *Bahamas* . **89 B5** 22 9N 74 30W
Miraj, *India* .... **40 L9** 16 50N 74 45 E
Miram Shah, *Pakistan* ...... **42 C4** 33 0N 70 2 E
Miramar, *Argentina* **94 D4** 38 15S 57 50W
Miramar, *Mozam.* .... **57 C6** 23 50S 35 35 E
Miramichi, *Canada* **71 C6** 47 2N 65 28W
Miramichi B., *Canada* **71 C7** 47 15N 65 0W
Miranda, *Brazil* **93 H7** 20 10S 56 15W
Miranda →, *Brazil* **92 G7** 19 25S 57 20W
Miranda de Ebro, *Spain* **19 A4** 42 41N 2 57W
Miranda do Douro, *Portugal* **19 B2** 41 30N 6 16W
Mirandópolis, *Brazil* **95 A5** 21 9S 51 6W
Mirango, *Malawi* .... **55 E3** 13 32S 34 58 E
Mirassol, *Brazil* **95 A6** 20 46S 49 28W
Mirbāţ, *Oman* .... **46 D5** 17 0N 54 45 E
Miri, *Malaysia* .... **36 D4** 4 23N 113 59 E
Miriam Vale, *Australia* ..... **62 C5** 24 20S 151 33 E
Mirim, L., *S. Amer.* **95 C5** 32 45S 52 50W
Mirnyy, *Russia* .... **27 C12** 62 33N 113 53 E
Mirokhan, *Pakistan* .... **42 F3** 27 46N 68 6 E
Mirond L., *Canada* **73 B8** 55 6N 102 47W
Mirpur, *Pakistan* .... **43 C5** 33 32N 73 56 E
Mirpur Batoro, *Pakistan* .... **42 G3** 24 44N 68 16 E
Mirpur Bibiwari, *Pakistan* ... **42 E2** 28 33N 67 44 E
Mirpur Khas, *Pakistan* ..... **42 G3** 25 30N 69 0 E
Mirpur Sakro, *Pakistan* ..... **42 G2** 24 33N 67 41 E
Mirtağ, *Turkey* .... **44 B4** 38 23N 41 56 E
Miryang, *S. Korea* .... **35 G15** 35 31N 128 44 E
Mirzapur, *India* .... **43 G10** 25 10N 82 34 E
Mirzapur-cum-Vindhyachal = Mirzapur, *India* .... **43 G10** 25 10N 82 34 E
Misantla, *Mexico* **87 D5** 19 56N 96 50W
Misawa, *Japan* .... **30 D10** 40 41N 141 24 E
Miscou I., *Canada* **71 C7** 47 57N 64 31W
Mish'āb, Ra's al, *Si. Arabia* . **45 D6** 28 15N 48 43 E
Mishan, *China* .... **33 B8** 45 37N 131 48 E
Mishawaka, *U.S.A.* **76 E2** 41 40N 86 11W
Mishima, *Japan* .... **31 G9** 35 10N 138 52 E
Misión, *Mexico* **85 N10** 32 6N 116 53W
Misiones □, *Argentina* **95 B5** 27 0S 55 0W
Misiones □, *Paraguay* **94 B4** 27 0S 56 0W
Miskah, *Si. Arabia* .... **44 E4** 24 49N 42 56 E
Miskitos, Cayos, *Nic.* **88 D3** 14 26N 82 50W
Miskolc, *Hungary* .... **17 D11** 48 7N 20 50 E
Misoke, *Dem. Rep. of the Congo* .... **54 C2** 0 42S 28 2 E
Misool, *Indonesia* .... **37 E8** 1 52S 130 10 E
Mişrātah, *Libya* .... **51 B9** 32 24N 15 3 E
Missanabie, *Canada* **70 C3** 48 20N 84 6W
Missinaibi →, *Canada* **70 B3** 50 43N 81 29W
Missinaibi L., *Canada* **70 C3** 48 23N 83 40W
Mission, *Canada* **72 D4** 49 10N 122 15W
Mission, *S. Dak., U.S.A.* **80 D4** 43 18N 100 39W
Mission, *Tex., U.S.A.* **81 M5** 26 13N 98 20W
Mission Beach, *Australia* ... **62 B4** 17 53S 146 6 E
Mission Viejo, *U.S.A.* **85 M9** 33 36N 117 40W
Missisa L., *Canada* **70 B2** 52 20N 85 7W
Missisicabi →, *Canada* **70 B4** 51 14N 79 31W
Missisagi →, *Canada* **70 C3** 46 15N 83 9W
Mississauga, *Canada* **78 C5** 43 32N 79 35W
Mississippi □, *U.S.A.* **81 J10** 33 0N 90 0W
Mississippi →, *U.S.A.* **81 L10** 29 9N 89 15W
Mississippi L., *Canada* **79 A8** 45 5N 76 10W
Mississippi River Delta, *U.S.A.* **81 L9** 29 10N 89 15W
Mississippi Sd., *U.S.A.* **81 K10** 30 20N 89 0W
Missoula, *U.S.A.* **82 C7** 46 52N 114 1W
Missouri □, *U.S.A.* **80 F8** 38 25N 92 30W
Missouri →, *U.S.A.* **80 F9** 38 49N 90 7W
Missouri City, *U.S.A.* **81 L7** 29 37N 95 32W
Missouri Valley, *U.S.A.* **80 E7** 41 34N 95 53W
Mist, *U.S.A.* **84 E3** 45 59N 123 15W
Mistassibi →, *Canada* **71 B5** 48 53N 72 13W
Mistassini, *Canada* **71 C5** 48 53N 72 12W
Mistassini →, *Canada* **71 C5** 48 42N 72 20W
Mistassini, L., *Canada* **70 B5** 51 0N 73 30W
Mistastin L., *Canada* **71 A7** 55 57N 63 20W
Mistinibi, L., *Canada* **71 A7** 55 56N 64 17W
Misty L., *Canada* **73 B8** 58 53N 101 40W
Misurata = Mişrātah, *Libya* .. **51 B9** 32 24N 15 3 E
Mitchell, *Australia* .... **63 D4** 26 29S 147 58 E
Mitchell, *Canada* **78 C3** 43 28N 81 12W
Mitchell, *Nebr., U.S.A.* **80 E3** 41 57N 103 49W
Mitchell, *Oreg., U.S.A.* **82 D3** 44 34N 120 9W
Mitchell, *S. Dak., U.S.A.* **80 D6** 43 43N 98 2W
Mitchell →, *Australia* ..... **62 B3** 15 12S 141 35 E
Mitchell, Mt., *U.S.A.* **77 H4** 35 46N 82 16W
Mitchell Ranges, *Australia* .. **62 A2** 12 49S 135 36 E
Mitchelstown, *Ireland* **13 D3** 52 15N 8 16W
Mitha Tiwana, *Pakistan* ..... **42 C5** 32 13N 72 6 E
Mithi, *Pakistan* .... **42 G3** 24 44N 69 48 E
Mithrao, *Pakistan* .... **42 F3** 27 28N 69 40 E
Mitilíni, *Greece* .... **21 E12** 39 6N 26 35 E
Mito, *Japan* .... **31 F10** 36 20N 140 30 E
Mitrovica = Kosovska Mitrovica, *Kosovo, Yug.* .. **21 C9** 42 54N 20 52 E
Mitsinjo, *Madag.* .... **57 B8** 16 1S 45 52 E
Mitsiwa, *Eritrea* .... **46 D2** 15 35N 39 25 E
Mitsukaidō, *Japan* .... **31 F9** 36 1N 139 59 E
Mittagong, *Australia* .... **63 E5** 34 28S 150 29 E
Mittimatalik = Pond Inlet, *Canada* **69 A12** 72 40N 77 0W
Mitú, *Colombia* **92 C4** 1 15N 70 13W
Mitumba, *Tanzania* .... **54 D3** 7 8S 31 2 E
Mitumba, Mts., *Dem. Rep. of the Congo* .... **54 D2** 7 0S 27 30 E
Mitwaba, *Dem. Rep. of the Congo* .... **55 D2** 8 2S 27 17 E
Mityana, *Uganda* .... **54 B3** 0 23N 32 2 E
Mixteco →, *Mexico* **87 D5** 18 11N 98 30W
Miyagi □, *Japan* .... **30 E10** 38 15N 140 45 E
Miyāh, W. el →, *Syria* ...... **44 C3** 34 44N 39 57 E
Miyake-Jima, *Japan* .... **31 G9** 34 5N 139 30 E
Miyako, *Japan* .... **30 E10** 39 40N 141 59 E
Miyako-Jima, *Japan* .... **31 M2** 24 45N 125 20 E
Miyako-Rettō, *Japan* .... **31 M2** 24 24N 125 0 E
Miyakonojō, *Japan* .... **31 J5** 31 40N 131 5 E
Miyani, *India* .... **42 J3** 21 50N 69 26 E
Miyanoura-Dake, *Japan* .... **31 J5** 30 20N 130 31 E
Miyazaki, *Japan* .... **31 J5** 31 56N 131 30 E
Miyazaki □, *Japan* .... **31 H5** 32 30N 131 30 E
Miyazu, *Japan* .... **31 G7** 35 35N 135 10 E
Miyet, Bahr el = Dead Sea, *Asia* .... **47 D4** 31 30N 35 30 E
Miyoshi, *Japan* .... **31 G6** 34 48N 132 51 E
Miyun, *China* .... **34 D9** 40 28N 116 50 E
Miyun Shuiku, *China* ...... **35 D9** 40 30N 117 0 E
Mizdah, *Libya* .... **51 B8** 31 30N 13 0 E
Mizen Hd., *Cork, Ireland* **13 E2** 51 27N 9 50W
Mizen Hd., *Wick., Ireland* ... **13 D5** 52 51N 6 4W
Mizhi, *China* .... **34 F6** 37 47N 110 12 E
Mizoram □, *India* .... **41 H18** 23 30N 92 40 E
Mizpe Ramon, *Israel* .... **47 E3** 30 34N 34 49 E
Mizusawa, *Japan* .... **30 E10** 39 8N 141 8 E
Mjölby, *Sweden* .... **9 G16** 58 20N 15 10 E
Mjøsa, *Norway* .... **9 F14** 60 40N 11 0 E
Mkata, *Tanzania* .... **54 D4** 5 45S 38 20 E
Mkokotoni, *Tanzania* .... **54 D4** 5 55S 39 15 E
Mkomazi, *Tanzania* .... **54 C4** 4 40S 38 7 E
Mkomazi →, *S. Africa* ...... **57 E5** 30 12S 30 50 E
Mkulwe, *Tanzania* .... **55 D3** 8 37S 32 20 E
Mkumbi, Ras, *Tanzania* .... **54 D4** 7 38S 39 55 E
Mkushi, *Zambia* .... **55 E2** 14 25S 29 15 E
Mkushi River, *Zambia* ...... **55 E2** 13 32S 29 45 E
Mkuze, *S. Africa* .... **57 D5** 27 10S 32 0 E
Mladá Boleslav, *Czech Rep.* . **16 C8** 50 27N 14 53 E
Mlala Hills, *Tanzania* ...... **54 D3** 6 50S 31 40 E
Mlange = Mulanje, *Malawi* .. **55 F4** 16 2S 35 33 E
Mlanje, Pic, *Malawi* .... **53 H7** 15 57S 35 38 E
Mława, *Poland* .... **17 B11** 53 9N 20 25 E
Mljet, *Croatia* .... **20 C7** 42 43N 17 30 E
Mmabatho, *S. Africa* .... **56 D4** 25 49S 25 30 E
Mo i Rana, *Norway* .... **8 C16** 66 20N 14 7 E
Moa, *Cuba* **89 B4** 20 40N 74 56W
Moa, *Indonesia* .... **37 F7** 8 0S 128 0 E
Moab, *U.S.A.* **83 G9** 38 35N 109 33W
Moala, *Fiji* .... **59 D8** 18 36S 179 53 E
Moama, *Australia* .... **63 F3** 36 7S 144 46 E
Moamba, *Mozam.* .... **57 D5** 25 36S 32 15 E
Moapa, *U.S.A.* **85 J12** 36 40N 114 37W
Moate, *Ireland* **13 C4** 53 24N 7 44W
Moba, *Dem. Rep. of the Congo* .... **54 D2** 7 0S 29 48 E
Mobārakābād, *Iran* .... **45 D7** 28 24N 53 20 E
Mobaye, *C.A.R.* .... **52 D4** 4 25N 21 5 E
Mobayi, *Dem. Rep. of the Congo* .... **52 D4** 4 15N 21 8 E
Moberley Lake, *Canada* **72 B4** 55 50N 121 44W
Moberly, *U.S.A.* **80 F8** 39 25N 92 26W
Mobile, *U.S.A.* **77 K1** 30 41N 88 3W
Mobile B., *U.S.A.* **77 K2** 30 30N 88 0W
Mobridge, *U.S.A.* **80 C4** 45 32N 100 26W
Mobutu Sese Seko, L. = Albert, L., *Africa* .... **54 B3** 1 30N 31 0 E
Moc Chau, *Vietnam* .... **38 B5** 20 50N 104 38 E
Moc Hoa, *Vietnam* .... **39 G5** 10 46N 105 56 E
Mocabe Kasari, *Dem. Rep. of the Congo* .... **55 D2** 9 58S 26 12 E
Moçambique, *Mozam.* ...... **55 F5** 15 3S 40 42 E
Moçâmedes = Namibe, *Angola* .... **53 H2** 15 7S 12 11 E
Mocanaqua, *U.S.A.* **79 E8** 41 9N 76 8W
Mochudi, *Botswana* .... **56 C4** 24 27S 26 7 E
Mocimboa da Praia, *Mozam.* . **55 E5** 11 25S 40 20 E
Moclips, *U.S.A.* **84 C2** 47 14N 124 13W
Mocoa, *Colombia* **92 C3** 1 7N 76 35W
Mococa, *Brazil* **95 A6** 21 28S 47 0W
Mocorito, *Mexico* **86 B3** 25 30N 107 53W
Moctezuma, *Mexico* **86 B3** 29 50N 109 0W
Moctezuma →, *Mexico* **87 C5** 21 59N 98 34W
Mocuba, *Mozam.* .... **55 F4** 16 54S 36 57 E
Mocúzari, Presa, *Mexico* **86 B3** 27 10N 109 10W
Modane, *France* .... **18 D7** 45 12N 6 40 E
Modasa, *India* .... **42 H5** 23 30N 73 21 E
Modder →, *S. Africa* .... **56 D3** 29 2S 24 37 E
Modderrivier, *S. Africa* ..... **56 D3** 29 2S 24 38 E
Módena, *Italy* .... **20 B4** 44 40N 10 55 E
Modena, *U.S.A.* **83 H7** 37 48N 113 56W
Modesto, *U.S.A.* **84 H6** 37 39N 121 0W
Módica, *Italy* .... **20 F6** 36 52N 14 46 E
Moe, *Australia* .... **63 F4** 38 12S 146 19 E
Moebase, *Mozam.* .... **55 F4** 17 3S 38 41 E
Moengo, *Surinam* **93 B8** 5 45N 54 20W
Moffat, *U.K.* **12 F5** 55 21N 3 27W
Moga, *India* .... **42 D6** 30 48N 75 8 E
Mogadishu = Muqdisho, *Somali Rep.* .... **46 G4** 2 2N 45 25 E
Mogador = Essaouira, *Morocco* **50 B4** 31 32N 9 42W
Mogalakwena →, *S. Africa* .. **57 C4** 22 38S 28 40 E
Mogami-Gawa →, *Japan* .... **30 E10** 38 45N 140 0 E
Mogán, *Canary Is.* **22 G4** 27 53N 15 43W
Mogaung, *Burma* .... **41 G20** 25 20N 97 0 E
Mogi das Cruzes, *Brazil* **95 A6** 23 31S 46 11W
Mogi-Guaçu →, *Brazil* **95 A6** 20 53S 48 10W
Mogi-Mirim, *Brazil* **95 A6** 22 29S 47 0W
Mogilev = Mahilyow, *Belarus* **17 B16** 53 55N 30 18 E
Mogilev-Podolskiy = Mohyliv-Podilskyy, *Ukraine* ...... **17 D14** 48 26N 27 48 E
Mogincual, *Mozam.* .... **55 F5** 15 35S 40 25 E
Mogocha, *Russia* .... **27 D12** 53 40N 119 50 E
Mogok, *Burma* .... **41 H20** 23 0N 96 40 E
Mogollon Rim, *U.S.A.* **83 J8** 34 10N 110 50W
Mogumber, *Australia* .... **61 F2** 31 2S 116 3 E
Mohács, *Hungary* .... **17 F10** 45 58N 18 41 E
Mohales Hoek, *Lesotho* ..... **56 E4** 30 7S 27 26 E
Mohall, *U.S.A.* **80 A4** 48 46N 101 31W
Moḩammadābād, *Iran* ...... **45 B8** 37 52N 59 5 E
Mohammedia, *Morocco* **50 B4** 33 44N 7 21W
Mohana →, *India* .... **43 G11** 24 43N 85 0 E
Mohanlalganj, *India* .... **43 F9** 26 41N 80 58 E
Mohave, L., *U.S.A.* **85 K12** 35 12N 114 34W
Mohawk →, *U.S.A.* **79 D11** 42 47N 73 41W
Mohenjodaro, *Pakistan* ..... **42 F3** 27 19N 68 7 E
Mohicanville Reservoir, *U.S.A.* **78 F3** 40 45N 82 0W
Mohoro, *Tanzania* .... **54 D4** 8 6S 39 8 E
Mohyliv-Podilskyy, *Ukraine* . **17 D14** 48 26N 27 48 E
Moidart, L., *U.K.* **12 E3** 56 47N 5 52W
Moira →, *Canada* **78 B7** 44 21N 77 24W
Moíres, *Greece* .... **23 D6** 35 4N 24 56 E
Moisaküla, *Estonia* .... **9 G21** 58 3N 25 12 E
Moisie, *Canada* **71 B6** 50 12N 66 1W
Moisie →, *Canada* **71 B6** 50 14N 66 5W
Mojave, *U.S.A.* **85 K8** 35 3N 118 10W
Mojave Desert, *U.S.A.* **85 L10** 35 0N 116 30W
Mojo, *Bolivia* **94 A2** 21 48S 65 33W
Mojokerto, *Indonesia* ...... **37 G15** 7 28S 112 26 E
Mokai, *N.Z.* .... **59 H5** 38 32S 175 56 E
Mokambo, *Dem. Rep. of the Congo* .... **55 E2** 12 25S 28 20 E
Mokameh, *India* .... **43 G11** 25 24N 85 55 E
Mokau, *N.Z.* .... **59 H5** 38 42S 174 39 E
Mokelumne →, *U.S.A.* **84 G5** 38 13N 121 28W
Mokelumne Hill, *U.S.A.* **84 G6** 38 18N 120 43W
Mokhós, *Greece* .... **23 D7** 35 16N 25 27 E
Mokhotlong, *Lesotho* ...... **57 D4** 29 22S 29 2 E
Mokokchung, *India* .... **41 F19** 26 15N 94 30 E
Mokolo →, *S. Africa* ...... **57 C4** 23 14S 27 43 E
Mokp'o, *S. Korea* .... **35 G14** 34 50N 126 25 E
Mokra Gora, *Yugoslavia* .... **21 C9** 42 50N 20 30 E
Mol, *Belgium* .... **15 C5** 51 11N 5 5 E
Molchanovo, *Russia* .... **26 D9** 57 40N 83 50 E
Mold, *U.K.* **10 D4** 53 9N 3 8W
Moldavia = Moldova ■, *Europe* .... **17 E15** 47 0N 28 0 E
Molde, *Norway* .... **8 E12** 62 45N 7 9 E
Moldova ■, *Europe* .... **17 E15** 47 0N 28 0 E
Moldoveanu, Vf., *Romania* .. **17 F13** 45 36N 24 45 E
Mole →, *U.K.* **11 F7** 51 24N 0 21W
Mole Creek, *Australia* ...... **62 G4** 41 34S 146 24 E
Molepolole, *Botswana* ..... **56 C4** 24 28S 25 28 E
Molfetta, *Italy* .... **20 D7** 41 12N 16 36 E
Moline, *U.S.A.* **80 E9** 41 30N 90 31W
Molinos, *Argentina* **94 B2** 25 28S 66 15W
Moliro, *Dem. Rep. of the Congo* .... **54 D3** 8 12S 30 30 E
Mollendo, *Peru* **92 G4** 17 0S 72 0W
Mollerin, L., *Australia* ...... **61 F2** 30 30S 117 35 E
Molodechno = Maladzyechna, *Belarus* .... **17 A14** 54 20N 26 50 E
Molokai, *U.S.A.* **74 H16** 21 8N 157 0W
Molong, *Australia* .... **63 E4** 33 5S 148 54 E
Molopo →, *Africa* .... **56 D3** 27 30S 20 13 E
Molotov = Perm, *Russia* .... **24 C10** 58 0N 56 10 E
Molson L., *Canada* **73 C9** 54 22N 96 40W
Molteno, *S. Africa* .... **56 E4** 31 22S 26 22 E
Molu, *Indonesia* .... **37 F8** 6 45S 131 40 E
Molucca Sea, *Indonesia* .... **37 E6** 0 0 125 0 E
Moluccas = Maluku, *Indonesia* .... **37 E7** 1 0S 127 0 E
Moma, *Dem. Rep. of the Congo* .... **54 C1** 1 35S 23 52 E
Moma, *Mozam.* .... **55 F4** 16 47S 39 4 E
Mombasa, *Kenya* .... **54 C4** 4 2S 39 43 E
Mombetsu, *Japan* .... **30 B11** 44 21N 143 22 E
Momchilgrad, *Bulgaria* ..... **21 D11** 41 33N 25 23 E
Momi, *Dem. Rep. of the Congo* .... **54 C2** 1 42S 27 0 E
Mompós, *Colombia* **92 B4** 9 14N 74 26W
Møn, *Denmark* .... **9 J15** 54 57N 12 20 E
Mon □, *Burma* .... **41 L20** 16 0N 97 30 E
Mona, Canal de la, *W. Indies* **89 C6** 18 30N 67 45W
Mona, Isla, *Puerto Rico* **89 C6** 18 5N 67 54W
Mona, Pta., *Costa Rica* **88 E3** 9 37N 82 36W
Monaca, *U.S.A.* **78 F4** 40 41N 80 17W
Monaco ■, *Europe* .... **18 E7** 43 46N 7 23 E
Monadhliath Mts., *U.K.* **12 D4** 57 10N 4 4W
Monadnock, Mt., *U.S.A.* **79 D12** 42 52N 72 7W
Monaghan, *Ireland* **13 B5** 54 15N 6 57W
Monaghan □, *Ireland* **13 B5** 54 11N 6 56W
Monahans, *U.S.A.* **81 K3** 31 36N 102 54W
Monapo, *Mozam.* .... **55 E5** 14 56S 40 19 E
Monar, L., *U.K.* **12 D3** 57 26N 5 8W
Monarch Mt., *Canada* **72 C3** 51 55N 125 57W
Monashee Mts., *Canada* **72 C5** 51 0N 118 43W
Monasterevin, *Ireland* **13 C4** 53 8N 7 4W
Monastir = Bitola, *Macedonia* **21 D9** 41 1N 21 20 E
Moncayo, Sierra del, *Spain* . **19 B5** 41 48N 1 50W
Monchegorsk, *Russia* ...... **24 A5** 67 54N 32 58 E
Mönchengladbach, *Germany* **16 C4** 51 11N 6 27 E
Monchique, *Portugal* **19 D1** 37 19N 8 38W
Moncks Corner, *U.S.A.* **77 J5** 33 12N 80 1W
Monclova, *Mexico* **86 B4** 26 50N 101 30W
Moncton, *Canada* **71 C7** 46 7N 64 51W
Mondego →, *Portugal* **19 B1** 40 9N 8 52W
Mondeodo, *Indonesia* ...... **37 E6** 3 34S 122 9 E
Mondovì, *Italy* .... **18 D7** 44 23N 7 49 E
Mondrain I., *Australia* ...... **61 F3** 34 9S 122 14 E
Monessen, *U.S.A.* **78 F5** 40 9N 79 54W
Monett, *U.S.A.* **81 G8** 36 55N 93 55W
Moneymore, *U.K.* **13 B5** 54 41N 6 40W
Monforte de Lemos, *Spain* .. **19 A2** 42 31N 7 33W
Mông Hsu, *Burma* .... **41 J21** 21 54N 98 30 E
Mong Kung, *Burma* .... **41 J20** 21 35N 97 35 E
Mong Nai, *Burma* .... **41 J20** 20 32N 97 46 E
Mong Pawk, *Burma* .... **41 H21** 22 4N 99 16 E
Mong Ton, *Burma* .... **41 J21** 20 17N 98 45 E
Mong Wa, *Burma* .... **41 J22** 21 26N 100 27 E
Mong Yai, *Burma* .... **41 H21** 22 21N 98 3 E
Mongalla, *Sudan* .... **51 G12** 5 8N 31 42 E
Mongers, L., *Australia* ...... **61 E2** 29 25S 117 5 E
Monghyr = Munger, *India* ... **43 G12** 25 23N 86 30 E
Mongibello = Etna, *Italy* ..... **20 F6** 37 50N 14 55 E
Mongo, *Chad* .... **51 F9** 12 14N 18 43 E
Mongolia ■, *Asia* .... **27 E10** 47 0N 103 0 E
Mongu, *Zambia* .... **53 H4** 15 16S 23 12 E
Môngua, *Angola* .... **56 B2** 16 43S 15 20 E
Monifieth, *U.K.* **12 E6** 56 30N 2 48W
Monkey Bay, *Malawi* .... **55 E4** 14 7S 35 1 E
Monkey Mia, *Australia* ..... **61 E1** 25 48S 113 43 E
Monkey River, *Belize* **87 D7** 16 22N 88 29W
Monkoto, *Dem. Rep. of the Congo* .... **52 E4** 1 38S 20 35 E
Monkton, *Canada* **78 C3** 43 35N 81 5W
Monmouth, *U.K.* **11 F5** 51 48N 2 42W
Monmouth, *Ill., U.S.A.* **80 E9** 40 55N 90 39W
Monmouth, *Oreg., U.S.A.* ... **82 D2** 44 51N 123 14W
Monmouthshire □, *U.K.* **11 F5** 51 48N 2 54W
Mono L., *U.S.A.* **84 H7** 38 1N 119 1W

Monolith, U.S.A. **85 K8** 35 7N 118 22W
Monólithos, Greece **23 C9** 36 7N 27 45 E
Monongahela, U.S.A. **78 F5** 40 12N 79 56W
Monópoli, Italy **20 D7** 40 57N 17 18 E
Monroe, Ga., U.S.A. **77 J4** 33 47N 83 43W
Monroe, La., U.S.A. **81 J8** 32 30N 92 7W
Monroe, Mich., U.S.A. **76 E4** 41 55N 83 24W
Monroe, N.C., U.S.A. **77 H5** 34 59N 80 33W
Monroe, N.Y., U.S.A. **79 E10** 41 20N 74 11W
Monroe, Utah, U.S.A. **83 G7** 38 38N 112 7W
Monroe, Wash., U.S.A. **84 C5** 47 51N 121 58W
Monroe, Wis., U.S.A. **80 D10** 42 36N 89 38W
Monroe City, U.S.A. **80 F9** 39 39N 91 44W
Monroeton, U.S.A. **79 E8** 41 43N 76 29W
Monroeville, Ala., U.S.A. **77 K2** 31 31N 87 20W
Monroeville, Pa., U.S.A. **78 F5** 40 26N 79 45W
Monrovia, Liberia **50 G3** 6 18N 10 47W
Mons, Belgium **15 D3** 50 27N 3 58 E
Monse, Indonesia **37 E6** 4 7S 123 15 E
Mont-de-Marsan, France **18 E3** 43 54N 0 31W
Mont-Joli, Canada **71 C6** 48 37N 68 10W
Mont-Laurier, Canada **70 C4** 46 35N 75 30W
Mont-Louis, Canada **71 C6** 49 15N 65 44W
Mont-St-Michel, Le = Le Mont-St-Michel, France **18 B3** 48 40N 1 30W
Mont Tremblant, Parc Recr. du, Canada **70 C5** 46 30N 74 30W
Montagu, S. Africa **56 E3** 33 45S 20 8 E
Montagu I., Antarctica **5 B1** 58 25S 26 20W
Montague, Canada **71 C7** 46 10N 62 39W
Montague, I., Mexico **86 A2** 31 40N 114 56W
Montague Ra., Australia **61 E2** 27 15S 119 30 E
Montague Sd., Australia **60 B4** 14 28S 125 20 E
Montalbán, Spain **19 B5** 40 50N 0 45W
Montalvo, U.S.A. **85 L7** 34 15N 119 12W
Montana, Bulgaria **21 C10** 43 27N 23 16 E
Montaña, Peru **92 E4** 6 0S 73 0W
Montana □, U.S.A. **82 C9** 47 0N 110 0W
Montaña Clara, I., Canary Is. **22 E6** 29 17N 13 33W
Montargis, France **18 C5** 47 59N 2 43 E
Montauban, France **18 D4** 44 2N 1 21 E
Montauk, U.S.A. **79 E13** 41 3N 71 57W
Montauk Pt., U.S.A. **79 E13** 41 4N 71 52W
Montbéliard, France **18 C7** 47 31N 6 48 E
Montceau-les-Mines, France **18 C6** 46 40N 4 23 E
Montclair, U.S.A. **79 F10** 40 49N 74 13W
Monte Albán, Mexico **87 D5** 17 2N 96 45W
Monte Alegre, Brazil **93 D8** 2 0S 54 0W
Monte Azul, Brazil **93 G10** 15 9S 42 53W
Monte Bello Is., Australia **60 D2** 20 30S 115 45 E
Monte-Carlo, Monaco **18 E7** 43 46N 7 23 E
Monte Caseros, Argentina **94 C4** 30 10S 57 50W
Monte Comán, Argentina **94 C2** 34 40S 67 53W
Monte Cristi, Dom. Rep. **89 C5** 19 52N 71 39W
Monte Lindo →, Paraguay **94 A4** 23 56S 57 12W
Monte Patria, Chile **94 C1** 30 42S 70 58W
Monte Quemado, Argentina **94 B3** 25 53S 62 41W
Monte Rio, U.S.A. **84 G4** 38 28N 123 0W
Monte Santu, C. di, Italy **20 D3** 40 5N 9 44 E
Monte Vista, U.S.A. **83 H10** 37 35N 106 9W
Monteagudo, Argentina **95 B5** 27 14S 54 8W
Montebello, Canada **70 C5** 45 40N 74 55W
Montecito, U.S.A. **85 L7** 34 26N 119 40W
Montecristo, Italy **20 C4** 42 20N 10 19 E
Montego Bay, Jamaica **88 C4** 18 30N 78 0W
Montélimar, France **18 D6** 44 33N 4 45 E
Montello, U.S.A. **80 D10** 43 48N 89 20W
Montemorelos, Mexico **87 B5** 25 11N 99 42W
Montenegro, Brazil **95 B5** 29 39S 51 29W
Montenegro □, Yugoslavia **21 C8** 42 40N 19 20 E
Montepuez, Mozam. **55 E4** 13 8S 38 59 E
Montepuez →, Mozam. **55 E5** 12 32S 40 27 E
Monterey, U.S.A. **84 J5** 36 37N 121 55W
Monterey B., U.S.A. **84 J5** 36 45N 122 0W
Montería, Colombia **92 B3** 8 46N 75 53W
Monteros, Argentina **94 B2** 27 11S 65 30W
Monterrey, Mexico **86 B4** 25 40N 100 30W
Montes Claros, Brazil **93 G10** 16 30S 43 50W
Montesano, U.S.A. **84 D3** 46 59N 123 36W
Montesilvano, Italy **20 C6** 42 29N 14 8 E
Montevideo, Uruguay **95 C4** 34 50S 56 11W
Montevideo, U.S.A. **80 C7** 44 57N 95 43W
Montezuma, U.S.A. **80 E8** 41 35N 92 32W
Montgomery = Sahiwal, Pakistan **42 D5** 30 45N 73 8 E
Montgomery, U.K. **11 E4** 52 34N 3 8W
Montgomery, Ala., U.S.A. **77 J2** 32 23N 86 19W
Montgomery, Pa., U.S.A. **78 E8** 41 10N 76 53W
Montgomery, W. Va., U.S.A. **76 F5** 38 11N 81 19W
Montgomery City, U.S.A. **80 F9** 38 59N 91 30W
Monticello, Ark., U.S.A. **81 J9** 33 38N 91 47W
Monticello, Fla., U.S.A. **77 K4** 30 33N 83 52W
Monticello, Ind., U.S.A. **76 E2** 40 45N 86 46W
Monticello, Iowa, U.S.A. **80 D9** 42 15N 91 12W
Monticello, Ky., U.S.A. **77 G3** 36 50N 84 51W
Monticello, Minn., U.S.A. **80 C8** 45 18N 93 48W
Monticello, Miss., U.S.A. **81 K9** 31 33N 90 7W
Monticello, N.Y., U.S.A. **79 E10** 41 39N 74 42W
Monticello, Utah, U.S.A. **83 H9** 37 52N 109 21W
Montijo, Portugal **19 C1** 38 41N 8 54W
Montilla, Spain **19 D3** 37 36N 4 40W
Montluçon, France **18 C5** 46 22N 2 36 E
Montmagny, Canada **71 C5** 46 58N 70 34W
Montmartre, Canada **73 C8** 50 14N 103 27W
Montmorillon, France **18 C4** 46 26N 0 50 E
Monto, Australia **62 C5** 24 52S 151 6 E
Montoro, Spain **19 C3** 38 1N 4 27W
Montour Falls, U.S.A. **78 D8** 42 21N 76 51W
Montoursville, U.S.A. **78 E8** 41 15N 76 55W
Montpelier, Idaho, U.S.A. **82 E8** 42 19N 111 18W
Montpelier, Vt., U.S.A. **79 B12** 44 16N 72 35W
Montpellier, France **18 E5** 43 37N 3 52 E
Montréal, Canada **79 A11** 45 31N 73 34W
Montreal →, Canada **70 C3** 47 14N 84 39W
Montreal L., Canada **73 C7** 54 20N 105 45W
Montreal Lake, Canada **73 C7** 54 3N 105 46W
Montreux, Switz. **18 C7** 46 26N 6 55 E
Montrose, U.K. **12 E6** 56 44N 2 27W
Montrose, Colo., U.S.A. **83 G10** 38 29N 107 53W
Montrose, Pa., U.S.A. **79 E9** 41 50N 75 53W
Monts, Pte. des, Canada **71 C6** 49 20N 67 12W
Montserrat ■, W. Indies **89 C7** 16 40N 62 10W
Montuiri, Spain **22 B9** 39 34N 2 59 E
Monywa, Burma **41 H19** 22 7N 95 11 E
Monza, Italy **18 D8** 45 35N 9 16 E
Monze, Zambia **55 F2** 16 17S 27 29 E
Monze, C., Pakistan **42 G2** 24 47N 66 37 E
Monzón, Spain **19 B6** 41 52N 0 10 E
Mooers, U.S.A. **79 B11** 44 58N 73 35W
Mooi →, S. Africa **57 D5** 28 45S 30 34 E
Mooi River, S. Africa **57 D4** 29 13S 29 50 E
Moonah →, Australia **62 C2** 22 3S 138 33 E
Moonda, L., Australia **62 D3** 25 52S 140 25 E
Moonie, Australia **63 D5** 27 46S 150 20 E
Moonie →, Australia **63 D4** 29 19S 148 43 E
Moonta, Australia **63 E2** 34 6S 137 32 E
Moora, Australia **61 F2** 30 37S 115 58 E
Moorcroft, U.S.A. **80 C2** 44 16N 104 57W
Moore →, Australia **61 F2** 31 22S 115 30 E
Moore, L., Australia **61 E2** 29 50S 117 35 E
Moore Park, Australia **62 C5** 24 43S 152 17 E
Moore Reefs, Australia **62 B4** 16 0S 149 5 E
Moorefield, U.S.A. **76 F6** 39 5N 78 59W
Moores Res., U.S.A. **79 B13** 44 45N 71 50W
Moorfoot Hills, U.K. **12 F5** 55 44N 3 8W
Moorhead, U.S.A. **80 B6** 46 53N 96 45W
Moorpark, U.S.A. **85 L8** 34 17N 118 53W
Moorreesburg, S. Africa **56 E2** 33 6S 18 38 E
Moose →, Canada **70 B3** 51 20N 80 25W
Moose →, U.S.A. **79 C9** 43 38N 75 24W
Moose Creek, Canada **79 A10** 45 15N 74 58W
Moose Factory, Canada **70 B3** 51 16N 80 32W
Moose Jaw, Canada **73 C7** 50 24N 105 30W
Moose Jaw →, Canada **73 C7** 50 34N 105 18W
Moose Lake, Canada **73 C8** 53 43N 100 20W
Moose Lake, U.S.A. **80 B8** 46 27N 92 46W
Moose Mountain Prov. Park, Canada **73 D8** 49 48N 102 25W
Moosehead L., U.S.A. **77 C11** 45 38N 69 40W
Mooselookmeguntic L., U.S.A. **77 C10** 44 55N 70 49W
Moosilauke, Mt., U.S.A. **79 B13** 44 3N 71 40W
Moosomin, Canada **73 C8** 50 9N 101 40W
Moosonee, Canada **70 B3** 51 17N 80 39W
Moosup, U.S.A. **79 E13** 41 43N 71 53W
Mopane, S. Africa **57 C4** 22 37S 29 52 E
Mopeia Velha, Mozam. **55 F4** 17 30S 35 40 E
Mopipi, Botswana **56 C3** 21 6S 24 55 E
Mopoi, C.A.R. **54 A2** 5 6N 26 54 E
Mopti, Mali **50 F5** 14 30N 4 0W
Moqor, Afghan. **42 C2** 32 50N 67 42 E
Moquegua, Peru **92 G4** 17 15S 70 46W
Mora, Sweden **9 F16** 61 2N 14 38 E
Mora, Minn., U.S.A. **80 C8** 45 53N 93 18W
Mora, N. Mex., U.S.A. **83 J11** 35 58N 105 20W
Mora →, U.S.A. **81 H2** 35 35N 104 25W
Moradabad, India **43 E8** 28 50N 78 50 E
Morafenobe, Madag. **57 B7** 17 50S 44 53 E
Moramanga, Madag. **57 B8** 18 56S 48 12 E
Moran, Kans., U.S.A. **81 G7** 37 55N 95 10W
Moran, Wyo., U.S.A. **82 E8** 43 53N 110 37W
Moranbah, Australia **62 C4** 22 1S 148 6 E
Morant Cays, Jamaica **88 C4** 17 22N 76 0W
Morant Pt., Jamaica **88 C4** 17 55N 76 12W
Morar, India **42 F8** 26 14N 78 14 E
Morar, L., U.K. **12 E3** 56 57N 5 40W
Moratuwa, Sri Lanka **40 R11** 6 45N 79 55 E
Morava →, Serbia, Yug. **21 B9** 44 36N 21 4 E
Morava →, Slovak Rep. **17 D9** 48 10N 16 59 E
Moravia, U.S.A. **79 D8** 42 43N 76 25W
Moravian Hts. = Českomoravská Vrchovina, Czech Rep. **16 D8** 49 30N 15 40 E
Morawa, Australia **61 E2** 29 13S 116 0 E
Morawhanna, Guyana **92 B7** 8 30N 59 40W
Moray □, U.K. **12 D5** 57 31N 3 18W
Moray Firth, U.K. **12 D5** 57 40N 3 52W
Morbi, India **42 H4** 22 50N 70 42 E
Morden, Canada **73 D9** 49 15N 98 10W
Mordovian Republic = Mordvinia □, Russia **24 D7** 54 20N 44 30 E
Mordvinia □, Russia **24 D7** 54 20N 44 30 E
Morea, Greece **6 H10** 37 45N 22 10 E
Moreau →, U.S.A. **80 C4** 45 18N 100 43W
Morecambe, U.K. **10 C5** 54 5N 2 52W
Morecambe B., U.K. **10 C5** 54 7N 3 0W
Moree, Australia **63 D4** 29 28S 149 54 E
Morehead, U.S.A. **76 F4** 38 11N 83 26W
Morehead City, U.S.A. **77 H7** 34 43N 76 43W
Morel →, India **42 F7** 26 13N 76 36 E
Morelia, Mexico **86 D4** 19 42N 101 7W
Morella, Australia **62 C3** 23 0S 143 52 E
Morella, Spain **19 B5** 40 35N 0 5W
Morelos, Mexico **86 B3** 26 42N 107 40W
Morelos □, Mexico **87 D5** 18 40N 99 10W
Morena, India **42 F8** 26 30N 78 4 E
Morena, Sierra, Spain **19 C3** 38 20N 4 0W
Moreno Valley, U.S.A. **85 M10** 33 56N 117 15W
Moresby I., Canada **72 C2** 52 30N 131 40W
Moreton I., Australia **63 D5** 27 10S 153 25 E
Morey, Spain **22 B10** 39 44N 3 20 E
Morgan, Australia **63 E2** 34 2S 139 35 E
Morgan, U.S.A. **82 F8** 41 2N 111 41W
Morgan City, U.S.A. **81 L9** 29 42N 91 12W
Morgan Hill, U.S.A. **84 H5** 37 8N 121 39W
Morganfield, U.S.A. **76 G2** 37 41N 87 55W
Morganton, U.S.A. **77 H5** 35 45N 81 41W
Morgantown, U.S.A. **76 F6** 39 38N 79 57W
Morgenzon, S. Africa **57 D4** 26 45S 29 36 E
Morghak, Iran **45 D8** 29 7N 57 54 E
Morhar →, India **43 G11** 25 29N 85 11 E
Moriarty, U.S.A. **83 J10** 34 59N 106 3W
Morice L., Canada **72 C3** 53 50N 127 40W
Morinville, Canada **72 C6** 53 49N 113 41W
Morioka, Japan **30 E10** 39 45N 141 8 E
Moris, Mexico **86 B3** 28 8N 108 32W
Morlaix, France **18 B2** 48 36N 3 52W
Mornington, Australia **63 F4** 38 15S 145 5 E
Mornington, I., Chile **96 F1** 49 50S 75 30W
Mornington I., Australia **62 B2** 16 30S 139 30 E
Moro, Pakistan **42 F2** 26 40N 68 0 E
Moro →, Pakistan **42 E2** 29 42N 67 22 E
Moro G., Phil. **37 C6** 6 30N 123 0 E
Morocco ■, N. Afr. **50 B4** 32 0N 5 50W
Morogoro, Tanzania **54 D4** 6 50S 37 40 E
Morogoro □, Tanzania **54 D4** 8 0S 37 0 E
Moroleón, Mexico **86 C4** 20 8N 101 32W
Morombe, Madag. **57 C7** 21 45S 43 22 E
Moron, Argentina **94 C4** 34 39S 58 37W
Morón, Cuba **88 B4** 22 8N 78 39W
Morón de la Frontera, Spain **19 D3** 37 6N 5 28W
Morona →, Peru **92 D3** 4 40S 77 10W
Morondava, Madag. **57 C7** 20 17S 44 17 E
Morongo Valley, U.S.A. **85 L10** 34 3N 116 37W
Moroni, Comoros Is. **49 H8** 11 40S 43 16 E
Moroni, U.S.A. **82 G8** 39 32N 111 35W
Morotai, Indonesia **37 D7** 2 10N 128 30 E
Moroto, Uganda **54 B3** 2 28N 34 42 E
Moroto Summit, Kenya **54 B3** 2 30N 34 43 E
Morpeth, U.K. **10 B6** 55 10N 1 41W
Morphou, Cyprus **23 D11** 35 12N 32 59 E
Morphou Bay, Cyprus **23 D11** 35 15N 32 50 E
Morrilton, U.S.A. **81 H8** 35 9N 92 44W
Morrinhos, Brazil **93 G9** 17 45S 49 10W
Morrinsville, N.Z. **59 G5** 37 40S 175 32 E
Morris, Canada **73 D9** 49 25N 97 22W
Morris, Ill., U.S.A. **76 E1** 41 22N 88 26W
Morris, Minn., U.S.A. **80 C7** 45 35N 95 55W
Morris, N.Y., U.S.A. **79 D9** 42 33N 75 15W
Morris, Pa., U.S.A. **78 E7** 41 35N 77 17W
Morris, Mt., Australia **61 E5** 26 9S 131 4 E
Morrisburg, Canada **79 B9** 44 55N 75 7W
Morristown, Ariz., U.S.A. **83 K7** 33 51N 112 37W
Morristown, N.J., U.S.A. **79 F10** 40 48N 74 29W
Morristown, N.Y., U.S.A. **79 B9** 44 35N 75 39W
Morristown, Tenn., U.S.A. **77 G4** 36 13N 83 18W
Morrisville, N.Y., U.S.A. **79 D9** 42 53N 75 35W
Morrisville, Pa., U.S.A. **79 F10** 40 13N 74 47W
Morrisville, Vt., U.S.A. **79 B12** 44 34N 72 36W
Morro, Pta., Chile **94 B1** 27 6S 71 0W
Morro Bay, U.S.A. **84 K6** 35 22N 120 51W
Morro del Jable, Canary Is. **22 F5** 28 3N 14 23W
Morro Jable, Pta. de, Canary Is. **22 F5** 28 2N 14 20W
Morrosquillo, G. de, Colombia **88 E4** 9 35N 75 40W
Morrumbene, Mozam. **57 C6** 23 31S 35 16 E
Morshansk, Russia **24 D7** 53 28N 41 50 E
Morteros, Argentina **94 C3** 30 50S 62 0W
Mortlach, Canada **73 C7** 50 27N 106 4W
Mortlake, Australia **63 F3** 38 5S 142 50 E
Morton, Tex., U.S.A. **81 J3** 33 44N 102 46W
Morton, Wash., U.S.A. **84 D4** 46 34N 122 17W
Morundah, Australia **63 E4** 34 57S 146 19 E
Moruya, Australia **63 F5** 35 58S 150 3 E
Morvan, France **18 C6** 47 5N 4 3 E
Morven, Australia **63 D4** 26 22S 147 5 E
Morvern, U.K. **12 E3** 56 38N 5 44W
Morwell, Australia **63 F4** 38 10S 146 22 E
Morzhovets, Ostrov, Russia **24 A7** 66 44N 42 35 E
Moscos Is., Burma **38 E1** 14 0N 97 30 E
Moscow = Moskva, Russia **24 C6** 55 45N 37 35 E
Moscow, Idaho, U.S.A. **82 C5** 46 44N 117 0W
Moscow, Pa., U.S.A. **79 E9** 41 20N 75 31W
Mosel →, Europe **18 A7** 50 22N 7 36 E
Moselle = Mosel →, Europe **18 A7** 50 22N 7 36 E
Moses Lake, U.S.A. **82 C4** 47 8N 119 17W
Mosgiel, N.Z. **59 L3** 45 53S 170 21 E
Moshaweng →, S. Africa **56 D3** 26 35S 22 50 E
Moshi, Tanzania **54 C4** 3 22S 37 18 E
Moshupa, Botswana **56 C4** 24 46S 25 29 E
Mosjøen, Norway **8 D15** 65 51N 13 12 E
Moskenesøya, Norway **8 C15** 67 58N 13 0 E
Moskenstraumen, Norway **8 C15** 67 47N 12 45 E
Moskva, Russia **24 C6** 55 45N 37 35 E
Mosomane, Botswana **56 C4** 24 2S 26 19 E
Mosonmagyaróvár, Hungary **17 E9** 47 52N 17 18 E
Mosquera, Colombia **92 C3** 2 35N 78 24W
Mosquero, U.S.A. **81 H3** 35 47N 103 58W
Mosquitia, Honduras **88 C3** 15 20N 84 10W
Mosquito Coast = Mosquitia, Honduras **88 C3** 15 20N 84 10W
Mosquito Creek L., U.S.A. **78 E4** 41 18N 80 46W
Mosquito L., Canada **73 A8** 62 35N 103 20W
Mosquitos, G. de los, Panama **88 E3** 9 15N 81 10W
Moss, Norway **9 G14** 59 27N 10 40 E
Moss Vale, Australia **63 E5** 34 32S 150 25 E
Mossbank, Canada **73 D7** 49 56N 105 56W
Mossburn, N.Z. **59 L2** 45 41S 168 15 E
Mosselbaai, S. Africa **56 E3** 34 11S 22 8 E
Mossendjo, Congo **52 E2** 2 55S 12 42 E
Mossgiel, Australia **63 E3** 33 15S 144 5 E
Mossman, Australia **62 B4** 16 21S 145 15 E
Mossoró, Brazil **93 E11** 5 10S 37 15W
Mossuril, Mozam. **55 E5** 14 58S 40 42 E
Most, Czech Rep. **16 C7** 50 31N 13 38 E
Mosta, Malta **23 D1** 35 55N 14 26 E
Mostaganem, Algeria **50 A6** 35 54N 0 5 E
Mostar, Bos.-H. **21 C7** 43 22N 17 50 E
Mostardas, Brazil **95 C5** 31 2S 50 51W
Mostiska = Mostyska, Ukraine **17 D12** 49 48N 23 4 E
Mosty = Masty, Belarus **17 B13** 53 27N 24 38 E
Mostyska, Ukraine **17 D12** 49 48N 23 4 E
Mosul = Al Mawşil, Iraq **44 B4** 36 15N 43 5 E
Mosŭlpo, S. Korea **35 H14** 33 20N 126 17 E
Motagua →, Guatemala **88 C2** 15 44N 88 14W
Motala, Sweden **9 G16** 58 32N 15 1 E
Motaze, Mozam. **57 C5** 24 48S 32 52 E
Moth, India **43 G8** 25 43N 78 57 E
Motherwell, U.K. **12 F5** 55 47N 3 58W
Motihari, India **43 F11** 26 30N 84 55 E
Motozintla de Mendoza, Mexico **87 D6** 15 21N 92 14W
Motril, Spain **19 D4** 36 31N 3 37W
Mott, U.S.A. **80 B3** 46 23N 102 20W
Motueka, N.Z. **59 J4** 41 7S 173 1 E
Motueka →, N.Z. **59 J4** 41 5S 173 1 E
Motul, Mexico **87 C7** 21 0N 89 20W
Mouchalagane →, Canada **71 B6** 50 56N 68 41W
Moúdhros, Greece **21 E11** 39 50N 25 18 E
Mouila, Gabon **52 E2** 1 50S 11 0 E
Moulamein, Australia **63 F3** 35 3S 144 1 E
Moulianá, Greece **23 D7** 35 10N 25 59 E
Moulins, France **18 C5** 46 35N 3 19 E
Moulmein, Burma **41 L20** 16 30N 97 40 E
Moulouya, O. →, Morocco **50 B5** 35 5N 2 25W
Moultrie, U.S.A. **77 K4** 31 11N 83 47W
Moultrie, L., U.S.A. **77 J5** 33 20N 80 5W
Mound City, Mo., U.S.A. **80 E7** 40 7N 95 14W
Mound City, S. Dak., U.S.A. **80 C4** 45 44N 100 4W
Moundou, Chad **51 G9** 8 40N 16 10 E
Moundsville, U.S.A. **78 G4** 39 55N 80 44W
Moung, Cambodia **38 F4** 12 46N 103 27 E
Mount Airy, U.S.A. **77 G5** 36 31N 80 37W
Mount Albert, Canada **78 B5** 44 8N 79 19W
Mount Barker, S. Austral., Australia **63 F2** 35 5S 138 52 E
Mount Barker, W. Austral., Australia **61 F2** 34 38S 117 40 E
Mount Brydges, Canada **78 D3** 42 54N 81 29W
Mount Burr, Australia **63 F3** 37 34S 140 26 E
Mount Carmel, Ill., U.S.A. **76 F2** 38 25N 87 46W
Mount Carmel, Pa., U.S.A. **79 F8** 40 47N 76 24W
Mount Charleston, U.S.A. **85 J11** 36 16N 115 37W
Mount Clemens, U.S.A. **78 D2** 42 35N 82 53W
Mount Coolon, Australia **62 C4** 21 25S 147 25 E
Mount Darwin, Zimbabwe **55 F3** 16 47S 31 38 E
Mount Desert I., U.S.A. **77 C11** 44 21N 68 20W
Mount Dora, U.S.A. **77 L5** 28 48N 81 38W
Mount Edziza Prov. Park, Canada **72 B2** 57 30N 130 45W
Mount Fletcher, S. Africa **57 E4** 30 40S 28 30 E
Mount Forest, Canada **78 C4** 43 59N 80 43W
Mount Gambier, Australia **63 F3** 37 50S 140 46 E
Mount Garnet, Australia **62 B4** 17 37S 145 6 E
Mount Holly, U.S.A. **79 G10** 39 59N 74 47W
Mount Holly Springs, U.S.A. **78 F7** 40 7N 77 12W
Mount Hope, N.S.W., Australia **63 E4** 32 51S 145 51 E
Mount Hope, S. Austral., Australia **63 E2** 34 7S 135 23 E
Mount Isa, Australia **62 C2** 20 42S 139 26 E
Mount Jewett, U.S.A. **78 E6** 41 44N 78 39W
Mount Kisco, U.S.A. **79 E11** 41 12N 73 44W
Mount Laguna, U.S.A. **85 N10** 32 52N 116 25W
Mount Larcom, Australia **62 C5** 23 48S 150 59 E
Mount Lofty Ra., Australia **63 E2** 34 35S 139 5 E
Mount Magnet, Australia **61 E2** 28 2S 117 47 E
Mount Maunganui, N.Z. **59 G6** 37 40S 176 14 E
Mount Molloy, Australia **62 B4** 16 42S 145 20 E
Mount Morgan, Australia **62 C5** 23 40S 150 25 E
Mount Morris, U.S.A. **78 D7** 42 44N 77 52W
Mount Pearl, Canada **71 C9** 47 31N 52 47W
Mount Penn, U.S.A. **79 F9** 40 20N 75 54W
Mount Perry, Australia **63 D5** 25 13S 151 42 E
Mount Pleasant, Iowa, U.S.A. **80 E9** 40 58N 91 33W
Mount Pleasant, Mich., U.S.A. **76 D3** 43 36N 84 46W
Mount Pleasant, Pa., U.S.A. **78 F5** 40 9N 79 33W
Mount Pleasant, S.C., U.S.A. **77 J6** 32 47N 79 52W
Mount Pleasant, Tenn., U.S.A. **77 H2** 35 32N 87 12W
Mount Pleasant, Tex., U.S.A. **81 J7** 33 9N 94 58W
Mount Pleasant, Utah, U.S.A. **82 G8** 39 33N 111 27W
Mount Pocono, U.S.A. **79 E9** 41 7N 75 22W
Mount Rainier Nat. Park, U.S.A. **84 D5** 46 55N 121 50W
Mount Revelstoke Nat. Park, Canada **72 C5** 51 5N 118 30W
Mount Robson Prov. Park, Canada **72 C5** 53 0N 119 0W
Mount Selinda, Zimbabwe **57 C5** 20 24S 32 43 E
Mount Shasta, U.S.A. **82 F2** 41 19N 122 19W
Mount Signal, U.S.A. **85 N11** 32 39N 115 37W
Mount Sterling, Ill., U.S.A. **80 F9** 39 59N 90 45W
Mount Sterling, Ky., U.S.A. **76 F4** 38 4N 83 56W
Mount Surprise, Australia **62 B3** 18 10S 144 17 E
Mount Union, U.S.A. **78 F7** 40 23N 77 53W
Mount Upton, U.S.A. **79 D9** 42 26N 75 23W
Mount Vernon, Ill., U.S.A. **76 F1** 38 19N 88 55W
Mount Vernon, Ind., U.S.A. **80 F10** 38 17N 88 57W
Mount Vernon, N.Y., U.S.A. **79 F11** 40 55N 73 50W
Mount Vernon, Ohio, U.S.A. **78 F2** 40 23N 82 29W
Mount Vernon, Wash., U.S.A. **84 B4** 48 25N 122 20W
Mountain Ash, U.K. **11 F4** 51 40N 3 23W
Mountain Center, U.S.A. **85 M10** 33 42N 116 44W
Mountain City, Nev., U.S.A. **82 F6** 41 50N 115 58W
Mountain City, Tenn., U.S.A. **77 G5** 36 29N 81 48W
Mountain Dale, U.S.A. **79 E10** 41 41N 74 32W
Mountain Grove, U.S.A. **81 G8** 37 8N 92 16W
Mountain Home, Ark., U.S.A. **81 G8** 36 20N 92 23W
Mountain Home, Idaho, U.S.A. **82 E6** 43 8N 115 41W
Mountain Iron, U.S.A. **80 B8** 47 32N 92 37W
Mountain Pass, U.S.A. **85 K11** 35 29N 115 35W
Mountain View, Ark., U.S.A. **81 H8** 35 52N 92 7W
Mountain View, Calif., U.S.A. **84 H4** 37 23N 122 5W
Mountain View, Hawaii, U.S.A. **74 J17** 19 33N 155 7W
Mountainair, U.S.A. **83 J10** 34 31N 106 15W
Mountlake Terrace, U.S.A. **84 C4** 47 47N 122 19W
Mountmellick, Ireland **13 C4** 53 7N 7 20W
Mountrath, Ireland **13 D4** 53 0N 7 28W
Moura, Australia **62 C4** 24 35S 149 58 E
Moura, Brazil **92 D6** 1 32S 61 38W
Moura, Portugal **19 C2** 38 7N 7 30W
Mourdi, Dépression du, Chad **51 E10** 18 10N 23 0 E
Mourilyan, Australia **62 B4** 17 35S 146 3 E
Mourne →, U.K. **13 B4** 54 52N 7 26W
Mourne Mts., U.K. **13 B5** 54 10N 6 0W
Mourniaí, Greece **23 D6** 35 29N 24 1 E
Mournies = Mourniaí, Greece **23 D6** 35 29N 24 1 E
Mouscron, Belgium **15 D3** 50 45N 3 12 E
Moussoro, Chad **51 F9** 13 41N 16 35 E
Moutong, Indonesia **37 D6** 0 28N 121 13 E
Movas, Mexico **86 B3** 28 10N 109 25W
Moville, Ireland **13 A4** 55 11N 7 3W
Mowandjum, Australia **60 C3** 17 22S 123 40 E
Moy →, Ireland **13 B2** 54 8N 9 8W
Moyale, Kenya **54 B4** 3 30N 39 0 E
Moyen Atlas, Morocco **50 B4** 33 0N 5 0W
Moyne, L. le, Canada **71 A6** 56 45N 68 47W
Moyo, Indonesia **36 F5** 8 10S 117 40 E
Moyobamba, Peru **92 E3** 6 0S 77 0W
Moyyero →, Russia **27 C11** 68 44N 103 42 E
Moyynty, Kazakstan **26 E8** 47 10N 73 18 E
Mozambique = Moçambique, Mozam. **55 F5** 15 3S 40 42 E
Mozambique ■, Africa **55 F4** 19 0S 35 0 E
Mozambique Chan., Africa **57 B7** 17 30S 42 30 E
Mozdok, Russia **25 F7** 43 45N 44 48 E
Mozdūrān, Iran **45 B9** 36 9N 60 35 E
Mozhnābād, Iran **45 C9** 34 7N 60 6 E
Mozyr = Mazyr, Belarus **17 B15** 51 59N 29 15 E
Mpanda, Tanzania **54 D3** 6 23S 31 1 E
Mphoengs, Zimbabwe **57 C4** 21 10S 27 51 E
Mpika, Zambia **55 E3** 11 51S 31 25 E
Mpulungu, Zambia **55 D3** 8 51S 31 5 E
Mpumalanga, S. Africa **57 D5** 29 50S 30 33 E
Mpumalanga □, S. Africa **57 B5** 26 0S 30 0 E
Mpwapwa, Tanzania **54 D4** 6 23S 36 30 E
Mqanduli, S. Africa **57 E4** 31 49S 28 45 E
Msambansovu, Zimbabwe **55 F3** 15 50S 30 3 E
M'sila →, Algeria **50 A6** 35 30N 4 29 E
Msoro, Zambia **55 E3** 13 35S 31 50 E
Mstislavl = Mstsislaw, Belarus **17 A16** 54 0N 31 50 E
Mstsislaw, Belarus **17 A16** 54 0N 31 50 E

Mtama, *Tanzania* **55 E4** 10 17S 39 21 E
Mtamvuna →, *S. Africa* **57 E5** 31 6S 30 12 E
Mtilikwe →, *Zimbabwe* **55 G3** 21 9S 31 30 E
Mtubatuba, *S. Africa* **57 D5** 28 30S 32 8 E
Mtwalume, *S. Africa* **57 E5** 30 30S 30 38 E
Mtwara-Mikindani, *Tanzania* **55 E5** 10 20S 40 20 E
Mu Gia, Deo, *Vietnam* **38 D5** 17 40N 105 47 E
Mu Us Shamo, *China* **34 E5** 39 0N 109 0 E
Muang Chiang Rai = Chiang Rai, *Thailand* **38 C2** 19 52N 99 50 E
Muang Khong, *Laos* **38 E5** 14 7N 105 51 E
Muang Lamphun, *Thailand* **38 C2** 18 40N 99 2 E
Muang Pak Beng, *Laos* **38 C3** 19 54N 101 8 E
Muar, *Malaysia* **39 L4** 2 3N 102 34 E
Muarabungo, *Indonesia* **36 E2** 1 28S 102 52 E
Muaraenim, *Indonesia* **36 E2** 3 40S 103 50 E
Muarajuloi, *Indonesia* **36 E4** 0 12S 114 3 E
Muarakaman, *Indonesia* **36 E5** 0 2S 116 45 E
Muaratebo, *Indonesia* **36 E2** 1 30S 102 26 E
Muaratembesi, *Indonesia* **36 E2** 1 42S 103 8 E
Muaratewe, *Indonesia* **36 E4** 0 58S 114 52 E
Mubarakpur, *India* **43 F10** 26 6N 83 18 E
Mubarraz = Al Mubarraz, *Si. Arabia* **45 E6** 25 30N 49 40 E
Mubende, *Uganda* **54 B3** 0 33N 31 22 E
Mubi, *Nigeria* **51 F8** 10 18N 13 16 E
Mubur, Pulau, *Indonesia* **39 L6** 3 20N 106 12 E
Mucajaí →, *Brazil* **92 C6** 2 25N 60 52W
Muchachos, Roque de los, *Canary Is.* **22 F2** 28 44N 17 52W
Muchinga Mts., *Zambia* **55 E3** 11 30S 31 30 E
Muck, *U.K.* **12 E2** 56 50N 6 15W
Muckadilla, *Australia* **63 D4** 26 35S 148 23 E
Mucuri, *Brazil* **93 G11** 18 0S 39 36W
Mucusso, *Angola* **56 B3** 18 1S 21 25 E
Muda, *Canary Is.* **22 F6** 28 34N 13 57W
Mudanjiang, *China* **35 B15** 44 38N 129 30 E
Mudanya, *Turkey* **21 D13** 40 25N 28 50 E
Muddy Cr. →, *U.S.A.* **83 H8** 38 24N 110 42W
Mudgee, *Australia* **63 E4** 32 32S 149 31 E
Mudjatik →, *Canada* **73 B7** 56 1N 107 36W
Muecate, *Mozam.* **55 E4** 14 55S 39 40 E
Mueda, *Mozam.* **55 E4** 11 36S 39 28 E
Mueller Ra., *Australia* **60 C4** 18 18S 126 46 E
Muende, *Mozam.* **55 E3** 14 28S 33 0 E
Muerto, Mar, *Mexico* **87 D6** 16 10N 94 10W
Mufulira, *Zambia* **55 E2** 12 32S 28 15 E
Mufumbiro Range, *Africa* **54 C2** 1 25S 29 30 E
Mughal Sarai, *India* **43 G10** 25 18N 83 7 E
Mughayrā', *Si. Arabia* **44 D3** 29 17N 37 41 E
Mugi, *Japan* **31 H7** 33 40N 134 25 E
Mugila, Mts., *Dem. Rep. of the Congo* **54 D2** 7 0S 28 50 E
Muğla, *Turkey* **21 F13** 37 15N 28 22 E
Mugu, *Nepal* **43 E10** 29 45N 82 30 E
Muhammad, Râs, *Egypt* **44 E2** 27 44N 34 16 E
Muhammad Qol, *Sudan* **51 D13** 20 53N 37 9 E
Muhammadabad, *India* **43 F10** 26 4N 83 25 E
Muhesi →, *Tanzania* **54 D4** 7 0S 35 20 E
Mühlhausen, *Germany* **16 C6** 51 12N 10 27 E
Mühlig Hofmann fjell, *Antarctica* **5 D3** 72 30S 5 0 E
Muhos, *Finland* **8 D22** 64 47N 25 59 E
Muhu, *Estonia* **9 G20** 58 36N 23 11 E
Muhutwe, *Tanzania* **54 C3** 1 35S 31 45 E
Muine Bheag, *Ireland* **13 D5** 52 42N 6 58W
Muir, L., *Australia* **61 F2** 34 30S 116 40 E
Mujnak = Muynak, *Uzbekistan* **26 E6** 43 44N 59 10 E
Mukacheve, *Ukraine* **17 D12** 48 27N 22 45 E
Mukachevo = Mukacheve, *Ukraine* **17 D12** 48 27N 22 45 E
Mukah, *Malaysia* **36 D4** 2 55N 112 5 E
Mukandwara, *India* **42 G6** 24 49N 75 59 E
Mukdahan, *Thailand* **38 D5** 16 32N 104 43 E
Mukden = Shenyang, *China* **35 D12** 41 48N 123 27 E
Mukerian, *India* **42 D6** 31 57N 75 37 E
Mukhtuya = Lensk, *Russia* **27 C12** 60 48N 114 55 E
Mukinbudin, *Australia* **61 F2** 30 55S 118 5 E
Mukishi, *Dem. Rep. of the Congo* **55 D1** 8 30S 24 44 E
Mukomuko, *Indonesia* **36 E2** 2 30S 101 10 E
Mukomwenze, *Dem. Rep. of the Congo* **54 D2** 6 49S 27 15 E
Muktsar, *India* **42 D6** 30 30N 74 30 E
Mukur = Moqor, *Afghan.* **42 C2** 32 50N 67 42 E
Mukutawa →, *Canada* **73 C9** 53 10N 97 24W
Mukwela, *Zambia* **55 F2** 17 0S 26 40 E
Mula, *Spain* **19 C5** 38 3N 1 33W
Mula →, *Pakistan* **42 F2** 27 57N 67 36 E
Mulange, *Dem. Rep. of the Congo* **54 C2** 3 40S 27 10 E
Mulanje, *Malawi* **55 F4** 16 2S 35 33 E
Mulchén, *Chile* **94 D1** 37 45S 72 20W
Mulde →, *Germany* **16 C7** 51 53N 12 15 E
Mule Creek Junction, *U.S.A.* **80 D2** 43 19N 104 8W
Muleba, *Tanzania* **54 C3** 1 50S 31 37 E
Mulejé, *Mexico* **86 B2** 26 53N 112 1W
Muleshoe, *U.S.A.* **81 H3** 34 13N 102 43W
Mulgrave, *Canada* **71 C7** 45 38N 61 31W
Mulhacén, *Spain* **19 D4** 37 4N 3 20W
Mülheim, *Germany* **33 C6** 51 25N 6 54 E
Mulhouse, *France* **18 C7** 47 40N 7 20 E
Muling, *China* **35 B16** 44 35N 130 10 E
Mull, *U.K.* **12 E3** 56 25N 5 56W
Mull, Sound of, *U.K.* **12 E3** 56 30N 5 50W
Mullaittivu, *Sri Lanka* **40 Q12** 9 15N 80 49 E
Mullen, *U.S.A.* **80 D4** 42 3N 101 1W
Mullens, *U.S.A.* **76 G5** 37 35N 81 23W
Muller, Pegunungan, *Indonesia* **36 D4** 0 30N 113 30 E
Mullet Pen., *Ireland* **13 B1** 54 13N 10 2W
Mullewa, *Australia* **61 E2** 28 29S 115 30 E
Mulligan →, *Australia* **62 D2** 25 0S 139 0 E
Mullingar, *Ireland* **13 C4** 53 31N 7 21W
Mullins, *U.S.A.* **77 H6** 34 12N 79 15W
Mullumbimby, *Australia* **63 D5** 28 30S 153 30 E
Mulobezi, *Zambia* **55 F2** 16 45S 25 7 E
Mulroy B., *Ireland* **13 A4** 55 15N 7 46W
Multan, *Pakistan* **42 D4** 30 15N 71 36 E
Mulumbe, Mts., *Dem. Rep. of the Congo* **55 D2** 8 40S 27 30 E
Mulungushi Dam, *Zambia* **55 E2** 14 48S 28 48 E
Mulvane, *U.S.A.* **81 G6** 37 29N 97 15W
Mumbai, *India* **40 K8** 18 55N 72 50 E
Mumbwa, *Zambia* **55 F2** 15 0S 27 0 E
Mun →, *Thailand* **38 E5** 15 19N 105 30 E
Muna, *Indonesia* **37 F6** 5 0S 122 30 E
Munabao, *India* **42 G4** 25 45N 70 17 E
Munamagi, *Estonia* **9 H22** 57 43N 27 4 E
München, *Germany* **16 D6** 48 8N 11 34 E
Munchen-Gladbach = Mönchengladbach, *Germany* **16 C4** 51 11N 6 27 E
Muncho Lake, *Canada* **72 B3** 59 0N 125 50W
Munch'ŏn, *N. Korea* **35 E14** 39 14N 127 19 E
Muncie, *U.S.A.* **76 E3** 40 12N 85 23W
Muncoonie, L., *Australia* **62 D2** 25 12S 138 40 E
Mundabbera, *Australia* **63 D5** 25 36S 151 18 E
Munday, *U.S.A.* **81 J5** 33 27N 99 38W
Münden, *Germany* **16 C5** 51 25N 9 38 E
Mundiwindi, *Australia* **60 D3** 23 47S 120 9 E
Mundo Novo, *Brazil* **93 F10** 11 50S 40 29W
Mundra, *India* **42 H3** 22 54N 69 48 E
Mundrabilla, *Australia* **61 F4** 31 52S 127 51 E
Mungallala, *Australia* **63 D4** 26 28S 147 34 E
Mungallala Cr. →, *Australia* **63 D4** 28 53S 147 5 E
Mungana, *Australia* **62 B3** 17 8S 144 27 E
Mungaoli, *India* **42 G8** 24 24N 78 7 E
Mungari, *Mozam.* **55 F3** 17 12S 33 30 E
Mungbere, *Dem. Rep. of the Congo* **54 B2** 2 36N 28 28 E
Mungeli, *India* **43 H9** 22 4N 81 41 E
Munger, *India* **43 G12** 25 23N 86 30 E
Munich = München, *Germany* **16 D6** 48 8N 11 34 E
Munising, *U.S.A.* **76 B2** 46 25N 86 40W
Munku-Sardyk, *Russia* **27 D11** 51 45N 100 20 E
Muñoz Gamero, Pen., *Chile* **96 G2** 52 30S 73 5W
Munroe L., *Canada* **73 B9** 59 13N 98 35W
Munsan, *S. Korea* **35 F14** 37 51N 126 48 E
Münster, *Germany* **16 C4** 51 58N 7 37 E
Munster □, *Ireland* **13 D3** 52 18N 8 44W
Muntadgin, *Australia* **61 F2** 31 45S 118 33 E
Muntok, *Indonesia* **36 E3** 2 5S 105 10 E
Munyama, *Zambia* **55 F2** 16 5S 28 31 E
Muong Beng, *Laos* **38 B3** 20 23N 101 46 E
Muong Boum, *Vietnam* **38 A4** 22 24N 102 49 E
Muong Et, *Laos* **38 B5** 20 49N 104 1 E
Muong Hai, *Laos* **38 B3** 21 3N 101 49 E
Muong Hiem, *Laos* **38 B4** 20 5N 103 22 E
Muong Houn, *Laos* **38 B3** 20 8N 101 23 E
Muong Hung, *Vietnam* **38 B4** 20 56N 103 53 E
Muong Kau, *Laos* **38 E5** 15 6N 105 47 E
Muong Khao, *Laos* **38 C4** 19 38N 103 32 E
Muong Khoua, *Laos* **38 B4** 21 5N 102 31 E
Muong Liep, *Laos* **38 C3** 18 29N 101 40 E
Muong May, *Laos* **38 E6** 14 49N 106 56 E
Muong Ngeun, *Laos* **38 B3** 20 36N 101 3 E
Muong Ngoi, *Laos* **38 B4** 20 43N 102 41 E
Muong Nhie, *Vietnam* **38 A4** 22 12N 102 28 E
Muong Nong, *Laos* **38 D6** 16 22N 106 30 E
Muong Ou Tay, *Laos* **38 A3** 22 7N 101 48 E
Muong Oua, *Laos* **38 C3** 18 18N 101 20 E
Muong Peun, *Laos* **38 B4** 20 13N 103 52 E
Muong Phalane, *Laos* **38 D5** 16 39N 105 34 E
Muong Phieng, *Laos* **38 C3** 19 6N 101 32 E
Muong Phine, *Laos* **38 D6** 16 32N 106 2 E
Muong Sai, *Laos* **38 B3** 20 42N 101 59 E
Muong Saiapoun, *Laos* **38 C3** 18 24N 101 31 E
Muong Sen, *Vietnam* **38 C5** 19 24N 104 8 E
Muong Sing, *Laos* **38 B3** 21 11N 101 9 E
Muong Son, *Laos* **38 B4** 20 27N 103 19 E
Muong Soui, *Laos* **38 C4** 19 33N 102 52 E
Muong Va, *Laos* **38 B4** 21 53N 102 19 E
Muong Xia, *Vietnam* **38 B5** 20 19N 104 50 E
Muonio, *Finland* **8 C20** 67 57N 23 40 E
Muonionjoki →, *Finland* **8 C20** 67 11N 23 34 E
Muping, *China* **35 F11** 37 22N 121 36 E
Muqdisho, *Somali Rep.* **46 G4** 2 2N 45 25 E
Mur →, *Austria* **17 E9** 46 18N 16 52 E
Murakami, *Japan* **30 E9** 38 14N 139 29 E
Murallón, Cerro, *Chile* **96 F2** 49 48S 73 30W
Muranda, *Rwanda* **54 C2** 1 52S 29 20 E
Murang'a, *Kenya* **54 C4** 0 45S 37 9 E
Murashi, *Russia* **24 C8** 59 30N 49 0 E
Murat →, *Turkey* **25 G7** 38 46N 40 0 E
Muratlı, *Turkey* **21 D12** 41 10N 27 29 E
Murayama, *Japan* **30 E10** 38 30N 140 25 E
Murchison →, *Australia* **61 E1** 27 45S 114 0 E
Murchison, Mt., *Antarctica* **5 D11** 73 0S 168 0 E
Murchison Falls, *Uganda* **54 B3** 2 15N 31 30 E
Murchison Ra., *Australia* **62 C1** 20 0S 134 10 E
Murchison Rapids, *Malawi* **55 F3** 15 55S 34 35 E
Murcia, *Spain* **19 D5** 38 5N 1 10W
Murcia □, *Spain* **19 D5** 37 50N 1 30W
Murdo, *U.S.A.* **80 D4** 43 53N 100 43W
Murdoch Pt., *Australia* **62 A3** 14 37S 144 55 E
Mureș →, *Romania* **17 E11** 46 15N 20 13 E
Mureșul = Mureș →, *Romania* **17 E11** 46 15N 20 13 E
Murewa, *Zimbabwe* **57 B5** 17 39S 31 47 E
Murfreesboro, *N.C., U.S.A.* **77 G7** 36 27N 77 6W
Murfreesboro, *Tenn., U.S.A.* **77 H2** 35 51N 86 24W
Murgab = Murghob, *Tajikistan* **26 F8** 38 10N 74 2 E
Murgab →, *Turkmenistan* **45 B9** 38 18N 61 12 E
Murgenella, *Australia* **60 B5** 11 34S 132 56 E
Murgha Kibzai, *Pakistan* **42 D3** 30 44N 69 25 E
Murghob, *Tajikistan* **26 F8** 38 10N 74 2 E
Murgon, *Australia* **63 D5** 26 15S 151 54 E
Muri, *India* **43 H11** 23 22N 85 52 E
Muria, *Indonesia* **37 G14** 6 36S 110 53 E
Muriaé, *Brazil* **95 A7** 21 8S 42 23W
Muriel Mine, *Zimbabwe* **55 F3** 17 14S 30 40 E
Müritz, *Germany* **16 B7** 53 25N 12 42 E
Murka, *Kenya* **54 C4** 3 27S 38 0 E
Murliganj, *India* **43 G12** 25 54N 86 59 E
Murmansk, *Russia* **24 A5** 68 57N 33 10 E
Muro, *Spain* **22 B10** 39 44N 3 3 E
Murom, *Russia* **24 C7** 55 35N 42 3 E
Muroran, *Japan* **30 C10** 42 25N 141 0 E
Muroto, *Japan* **31 H7** 33 18N 134 9 E
Muroto-Misaki, *Japan* **31 H7** 33 15N 134 10 E
Murphy, *U.S.A.* **82 E5** 43 13N 116 33W
Murphys, *U.S.A.* **84 G6** 38 8N 120 28W
Murray, *Ky., U.S.A.* **77 G1** 36 37N 88 19W
Murray, *Utah, U.S.A.* **82 F8** 40 40N 111 53W
Murray →, *Australia* **63 F2** 35 20S 139 22 E
Murray, L., *U.S.A.* **77 H5** 34 3N 81 13W
Murray Bridge, *Australia* **63 F2** 35 6S 139 14 E
Murray Harbour, *Canada* **71 C7** 46 0N 62 28W
Murraysburg, *S. Africa* **56 E3** 31 58S 23 47 E
Murree, *Pakistan* **42 C5** 33 56N 73 28 E
Murrieta, *U.S.A.* **85 M9** 33 33N 117 13W
Murrumbidgee →, *Australia* **63 E3** 34 43S 143 12 E
Murrumburrah, *Australia* **63 E4** 34 32S 148 22 E
Murrurundi, *Australia* **63 E5** 31 42S 150 51 E
Murshidabad, *India* **43 G13** 24 11N 88 19 E
Murtle L., *Canada* **72 C5** 52 8N 119 38W
Murtoa, *Australia* **63 F3** 36 35S 142 28 E
Murungu, *Tanzania* **54 C3** 4 12S 31 10 E
Mururoa, *Pac. Oc.* **65 K14** 21 52S 138 55W
Murwara, *India* **43 H9** 23 46N 80 28 E
Murwillumbah, *Australia* **63 D5** 28 18S 153 27 E
Mürzzuschlag, *Austria* **16 E8** 47 36N 15 41 E
Muş, *Turkey* **25 G7** 38 45N 41 30 E
Mûsa, Gebel, *Egypt* **44 D2** 28 33N 33 59 E
Musa Khel, *Pakistan* **42 D3** 30 59N 69 52 E
Mūsa Qal'eh, *Afghan.* **40 C4** 32 20N 64 50 E
Musafirkhana, *India* **43 F9** 26 22N 81 48 E
Musala, *Bulgaria* **21 C10** 42 13N 23 37 E
Musala, *Indonesia* **36 D1** 1 41N 98 28 E
Musan, *N. Korea* **35 C15** 42 12N 129 12 E
Musangu, *Dem. Rep. of the Congo* **55 E1** 10 28S 23 55 E
Musasa, *Tanzania* **54 C3** 3 25S 31 30 E
Musay'īd, *Qatar* **45 E6** 25 0N 51 33 E
Muscat = Masqat, *Oman* **46 C6** 23 37N 58 36 E
Muscat & Oman = Oman ■, *Asia* **46 C6** 23 0N 58 0 E
Muscatine, *U.S.A.* **80 E9** 41 25N 91 3W
Musgrave Harbour, *Canada* **71 C9** 49 27N 53 58W
Musgrave Ranges, *Australia* **61 E5** 26 0S 132 0 E
Mushie, *Dem. Rep. of the Congo* **52 E3** 2 56S 16 55 E
Musi →, *Indonesia* **36 E2** 2 20S 104 56 E
Muskeg →, *Canada* **72 A4** 60 20N 123 20W
Muskegon, *U.S.A.* **76 D2** 43 14N 86 16W
Muskegon →, *U.S.A.* **76 D2** 43 14N 86 21W
Muskegon Heights, *U.S.A.* **76 D2** 43 12N 86 16W
Muskogee, *U.S.A.* **81 H7** 35 45N 95 22W
Muskoka, L., *Canada* **78 B5** 45 0N 79 25W
Muskwa →, *Canada* **72 B4** 58 47N 122 48W
Muslimiyah, *Syria* **44 B3** 36 19N 37 12 E
Musofu, *Zambia* **55 E2** 13 30S 29 0 E
Musoma, *Tanzania* **54 C3** 1 30S 33 48 E
Musquaro, L., *Canada* **71 B7** 50 38N 61 5W
Musquodoboit Harbour, *Canada* **71 D7** 44 50N 63 9W
Musselburgh, *U.K.* **12 F5** 55 57N 3 2W
Musselshell →, *U.S.A.* **82 C10** 47 21N 107 57W
Mussoorie, *India* **42 D8** 30 27N 78 6 E
Mussuco, *Angola* **56 B2** 17 2S 19 3 E
Mustafakemalpaşa, *Turkey* **21 D13** 40 2N 28 24 E
Mustang, *Nepal* **43 E10** 29 10N 83 55 E
Musters, L., *Argentina* **96 F3** 45 20S 69 25W
Musudan, *N. Korea* **35 D15** 40 50N 129 43 E
Muswellbrook, *Australia* **63 E5** 32 16S 150 56 E
Mût, *Egypt* **51 C11** 25 28N 28 58 E
Mut, *Turkey* **44 B2** 36 40N 33 28 E
Mutanda, *Mozam.* **57 C5** 21 0S 33 34 E
Mutanda, *Zambia* **55 E2** 12 24S 26 13 E
Mutare, *Zimbabwe* **55 F3** 18 58S 32 38 E
Muting, *Indonesia* **37 F10** 7 23S 140 20 E
Mutoko, *Zimbabwe* **57 B5** 17 24S 32 13 E
Mutoray, *Russia* **27 C11** 60 56N 101 0 E
Mutshatsha, *Dem. Rep. of the Congo* **55 E1** 10 35S 24 20 E
Mutsu, *Japan* **30 D10** 41 5N 140 55 E
Mutsu-Wan, *Japan* **30 D10** 41 5N 140 55 E
Muttaburra, *Australia* **62 C3** 22 38S 144 29 E
Mutton I., *Ireland* **13 D2** 52 49N 9 32W
Mutuáli, *Mozam.* **55 E4** 14 55S 37 0 E
Muweilih, *Egypt* **47 E3** 30 42N 34 19 E
Muy Muy, *Nic.* **88 D2** 12 39N 85 36W
Muyinga, *Burundi* **54 C3** 3 14S 30 33 E
Muynak, *Uzbekistan* **26 E6** 43 44N 59 10 E
Muzaffarabad, *Pakistan* **43 B5** 34 25N 73 30 E
Muzaffargarh, *Pakistan* **42 D4** 30 5N 71 14 E
Muzaffarnagar, *India* **42 E7** 29 26N 77 40 E
Muzaffarpur, *India* **43 F11** 26 7N 85 23 E
Muzafirpur, *Pakistan* **42 D3** 30 58N 69 9 E
Muzhi, *Russia* **24 A11** 65 25N 64 40 E
Mvuma, *Zimbabwe* **55 F3** 19 16S 30 30 E
Mvurwi, *Zimbabwe* **55 F3** 17 0S 30 57 E
Mwadui, *Tanzania* **54 C3** 3 26S 33 32 E
Mwambo, *Tanzania* **55 E5** 10 30S 40 22 E
Mwandi, *Zambia* **55 F1** 17 30S 24 51 E
Mwanza, *Dem. Rep. of the Congo* **54 D2** 7 55S 26 43 E
Mwanza, *Tanzania* **54 C3** 2 30S 32 58 E
Mwanza, *Zambia* **55 F1** 16 58S 24 28 E
Mwanza □, *Tanzania* **54 C3** 2 0S 33 0 E
Mwaya, *Tanzania* **55 D3** 9 32S 33 55 E
Mweelrea, *Ireland* **13 C2** 53 39N 9 49W
Mweka, *Dem. Rep. of the Congo* **52 E4** 4 50S 21 34 E
Mwenezi, *Zimbabwe* **55 G3** 21 15S 30 48 E
Mwenezi →, *Mozam.* **55 G3** 22 40S 31 50 E
Mwenga, *Dem. Rep. of the Congo* **54 C2** 3 1S 28 28 E
Mweru, L., *Zambia* **55 D2** 9 0S 28 40 E
Mweza Range, *Zimbabwe* **55 G3** 21 0S 30 0 E
Mwilambwe, *Dem. Rep. of the Congo* **54 D2** 8 7S 25 5 E
Mwimbi, *Tanzania* **55 D3** 8 38S 31 39 E
Mwinilunga, *Zambia* **55 E1** 11 43S 24 25 E
My Tho, *Vietnam* **39 G6** 10 29N 106 23 E
Myajlar, *India* **42 F4** 26 15N 70 20 E
Myanaung, *Burma* **41 K19** 18 18N 95 22 E
Myanmar = Burma ■, *Asia* **41 J20** 21 0N 96 30 E
Myaungmya, *Burma* **41 L19** 16 30N 94 40 E
Mycenæ, *Greece* **21 F10** 37 39N 22 52 E
Myeik Kyunzu, *Burma* **39 G1** 11 30N 97 30 E
Myers Chuck, *U.S.A.* **72 B2** 55 44N 132 11W
Myerstown, *U.S.A.* **79 F8** 40 22N 76 19W
Myingyan, *Burma* **41 J19** 21 30N 95 20 E
Myitkyina, *Burma* **41 G20** 25 24N 97 26 E
Mykines, *Færoe Is.* **8 E9** 62 7N 7 35W
Mykolayiv, *Ukraine* **25 E5** 46 58N 32 0 E
Mymensingh, *Bangla.* **41 G17** 24 45N 90 24 E
Mynydd Du, *U.K.* **11 F4** 51 52N 3 50W
Mýrdalsjökull, *Iceland* **8 E4** 63 40N 19 6W
Myrtle Beach, *U.S.A.* **77 J6** 33 42N 78 53W
Myrtle Creek, *U.S.A.* **82 E2** 43 1N 123 17W
Myrtle Point, *U.S.A.* **82 E1** 43 4N 124 8W
Myrtou, *Cyprus* **23 D12** 35 18N 33 4 E
Mysia, *Turkey* **21 E12** 39 50N 27 0 E
Mysore = Karnataka □, *India* **40 N10** 13 15N 77 0 E
Mysore, *India* **40 N10** 12 17N 76 41 E
Mystic, *U.S.A.* **79 E13** 41 21N 71 58W
Myszków, *Poland* **17 C10** 50 45N 19 22 E
Mytishchi, *Russia* **24 C6** 55 50N 37 50 E
Mývatn, *Iceland* **8 D5** 65 36N 17 0W
Mzimba, *Malawi* **55 E3** 11 55S 33 39 E
Mzimkulu →, *S. Africa* **57 E5** 30 44S 30 28 E
Mzimvubu →, *S. Africa* **57 E4** 31 38S 29 33 E
Mzuzu, *Malawi* **55 E3** 11 30S 33 55 E

N

Na Hearadh = Harris, *U.K.* **12 D2** 57 50N 6 55W
Na Noi, *Thailand* **38 C3** 18 19N 100 43 E
Na Phao, *Laos* **38 D5** 17 35N 105 44 E
Na Sam, *Vietnam* **38 A6** 22 3N 106 37 E
Na San, *Vietnam* **38 B5** 21 12N 104 2 E
Naab →, *Germany* **16 D6** 49 1N 12 2 E
Naantali, *Finland* **9 F19** 60 29N 22 2 E
Naas, *Ireland* **13 C5** 53 12N 6 40W
Nababeep, *S. Africa* **56 D2** 29 36S 17 46 E
Nabadwip = Navadwip, *India* **43 H13** 23 34N 88 20 E
Nabari, *Japan* **31 G8** 34 37N 136 5 E
Nabawa, *Australia* **61 E1** 28 30S 114 48 E
Nabberu, L., *Australia* **61 E3** 25 50S 120 30 E
Naberezhnyye Chelny, *Russia* **24 C9** 55 42N 52 19 E
Nabeul, *Tunisia* **51 A8** 36 30N 10 44 E
Nabha, *India* **42 D7** 30 26N 76 14 E
Nabīd, *Iran* **45 D8** 29 40N 57 38 E
Nabire, *Indonesia* **37 E9** 3 15S 135 26 E
Nabisar, *Pakistan* **42 G3** 25 8N 69 40 E
Nabisipi →, *Canada* **71 B7** 50 14N 62 13W
Nabiswera, *Uganda* **54 B3** 1 27N 32 15 E
Nablus = Nābulus, *West Bank* **47 C4** 32 14N 35 15 E
Naboomspruit, *S. Africa* **57 C4** 24 32S 28 40 E
Nābulus, *West Bank* **47 C4** 32 14N 35 15 E
Nacala, *Mozam.* **55 E5** 14 31S 40 34 E
Nacala-Velha, *Mozam.* **55 E5** 14 32S 40 34 E
Nacaome, *Honduras* **88 D2** 13 31N 87 30W
Nacaroa, *Mozam.* **55 E4** 14 22S 39 56 E
Naches, *U.S.A.* **82 C3** 46 44N 120 42W
Naches →, *U.S.A.* **84 D6** 46 38N 120 31W
Nachicapau, L., *Canada* **71 A6** 56 40N 68 5W
Nachingwea, *Tanzania* **55 E4** 10 23S 38 49 E
Nachna, *India* **42 F4** 27 34N 71 41 E
Nacimiento L., *U.S.A.* **84 K6** 35 46N 120 53W
Naco, *Mexico* **86 A3** 31 20N 109 56W
Nacogdoches, *U.S.A.* **81 K7** 31 36N 94 39W
Nácori Chico, *Mexico* **86 B3** 29 39N 109 1W
Nacozari, *Mexico* **86 A3** 30 24N 109 39W
Nadi, *Fiji* **59 C7** 17 42S 177 20 E
Nadiad, *India* **42 H5** 22 41N 72 56 E
Nador, *Morocco* **50 B5** 35 14N 2 58W
Nadur, *Malta* **23 C1** 36 2N 14 18 E
Nadūshan, *Iran* **45 C7** 32 2N 53 35 E
Nadvirna, *Ukraine* **17 D13** 48 37N 24 30 E
Nadvoitsy, *Russia* **24 B5** 63 52N 34 14 E
Nadvornaya = Nadvirna, *Ukraine* **17 D13** 48 37N 24 30 E
Nadym, *Russia* **26 C8** 65 35N 72 42 E
Nadym →, *Russia* **26 C8** 66 12N 72 0 E
Nærbø, *Norway* **9 G11** 58 40N 5 39 E
Næstved, *Denmark* **9 J14** 55 13N 11 44 E
Naft-e Safīd, *Iran* **45 D6** 31 40N 49 17 E
Naftshahr, *Iran* **44 C5** 34 0N 45 30 E
Nafud Desert = An Nafūd, *Si. Arabia* **44 D4** 28 15N 41 0 E
Naga, *Phil.* **37 B6** 13 38N 123 15 E
Nagahama, *Japan* **31 G8** 35 23N 136 16 E
Nagai, *Japan* **30 E10** 38 6N 140 2 E
Nagaland □, *India* **41 G19** 26 0N 94 30 E
Nagano, *Japan* **31 F9** 36 40N 138 10 E
Nagano □, *Japan* **31 F9** 36 15N 138 0 E
Nagaoka, *Japan* **31 F9** 37 27N 138 51 E
Nagappattinam, *India* **40 P11** 10 46N 79 51 E
Nagar →, *Bangla.* **43 G13** 24 27N 89 12 E
Nagar Parkar, *Pakistan* **42 G4** 24 28N 70 46 E
Nagasaki, *Japan* **31 H4** 32 47N 129 50 E
Nagasaki □, *Japan* **31 H4** 32 50N 129 40 E
Nagato, *Japan* **31 G5** 34 19N 131 5 E
Nagaur, *India* **42 F5** 27 15N 73 45 E
Nagda, *India* **42 H6** 23 27N 75 25 E
Nagercoil, *India* **40 Q10** 8 12N 77 26 E
Nagina, *India* **43 E8** 29 30N 78 30 E
Nagineh, *Iran* **45 C8** 34 20N 57 15 E
Nagir, *Pakistan* **43 A6** 36 12N 74 42 E
Nagod, *India* **43 G9** 24 34N 80 36 E
Nagoorin, *Australia* **62 C5** 24 17S 151 15 E
Nagorno-Karabakh, *Azerbaijan* **25 F8** 39 55N 46 45 E
Nagornyy, *Russia* **27 D13** 55 58N 124 57 E
Nagoya, *Japan* **31 G8** 35 10N 136 50 E
Nagpur, *India* **40 J11** 21 8N 79 10 E
Nagua, *Dom. Rep.* **89 C6** 19 23N 69 50W
Nagykanizsa, *Hungary* **17 E9** 46 28N 17 0 E
Nagykőrös, *Hungary* **17 E10** 47 5N 19 48 E
Naha, *Japan* **31 L3** 26 13N 127 42 E
Nahan, *India* **42 D7** 30 33N 77 18 E
Nahanni Butte, *Canada* **72 A4** 61 2N 123 31W
Nahanni Nat. Park, *Canada* **72 A4** 61 15N 125 0W
Nahargarh, *Mad. P., India* **42 G6** 24 10N 75 14 E
Nahargarh, *Raj., India* **42 G7** 24 55N 76 50 E
Nahariyya, *Israel* **44 C2** 33 1N 35 5 E
Nahāvand, *Iran* **45 C6** 34 10N 48 22 E
Naicá, *Mexico* **86 B3** 27 53N 105 31W
Naicam, *Canada* **73 C8** 52 30N 104 30W
Naikoon Prov. Park, *Canada* **72 C2** 53 55N 131 55W
Naimisharanya, *India* **43 F9** 27 21N 80 30 E
Nain, *Canada* **71 A7** 56 34N 61 40W
Nā'īn, *Iran* **45 C7** 32 54N 53 0 E
Naini Tal, *India* **43 E8** 29 30N 79 30 E
Nainpur, *India* **40 H12** 22 30N 80 10 E
Nainwa, *India* **42 G6** 25 46N 75 51 E
Nairn, *U.K.* **12 D5** 57 35N 3 53W
Nairobi, *Kenya* **54 C4** 1 17S 36 48 E
Naissaar, *Estonia* **9 G21** 59 34N 24 29 E
Naivasha, *Kenya* **54 C4** 0 40S 36 30 E
Naivasha, L., *Kenya* **54 C4** 0 48S 36 20 E
Najafābād, *Iran* **45 C6** 32 40N 51 15 E
Najd, *Si. Arabia* **46 B3** 26 30N 42 0 E
Najibabad, *India* **42 E8** 29 40N 78 20 E
Najin, *N. Korea* **35 C16** 42 12N 130 15 E
Najmah, *Si. Arabia* **45 E6** 26 42N 50 6 E

Naju, *S. Korea* . . . . **35 G14** 35 3N 126 43 E
Nakadōri-Shima, *Japan* . . . . **31 H4** 32 57N 129 4 E
Nakalagba, *Dem. Rep. of the Congo* . . . . **54 B2** 2 50N 27 58 E
Nakaminato, *Japan* . . . . **31 F10** 36 21N 140 36 E
Nakamura, *Japan* . . . . **31 H6** 32 59N 132 56 E
Nakano, *Japan* . . . . **31 F9** 36 45N 138 22 E
Nakano-Shima, *Japan* . . . . . **31 K4** 29 51N 129 52 E
Nakashibetsu, *Japan* . . . . . . **30 C12** 43 33N 144 59 E
Nakfa, *Eritrea* . . . . **46 D2** 16 40N 38 32 E
Nakhfar al Buşayyah, *Iraq* . . **44 D5** 30 0N 46 10 E
Nakhichevan = Naxçıvan, *Azerbaijan* . . . . **25 G8** 39 12N 45 15 E
Nakhichevan Republic = Naxçıvan □, *Azerbaijan* . . **25 G8** 39 25N 45 26 E
Nakhl, *Egypt* . . . . **47 F2** 29 55N 33 43 E
Nakhl-e Taqī, *Iran* . . . . **45 E7** 27 28N 52 36 E
Nakhodka, *Russia* . . . . **27 E14** 42 53N 132 54 E
Nakhon Nayok, *Thailand* . . . **38 E3** 14 12N 101 13 E
Nakhon Pathom, *Thailand* . . **38 F3** 13 49N 100 3 E
Nakhon Phanom, *Thailand* . . **38 D5** 17 23N 104 43 E
Nakhon Ratchasima, *Thailand* **38 E4** 14 59N 102 12 E
Nakhon Sawan, *Thailand* . . . **38 E3** 15 35N 100 10 E
Nakhon Si Thammarat, *Thailand* . . . . **39 H3** 8 29N 100 0 E
Nakhon Thai, *Thailand* . . . . . **38 D3** 17 5N 100 44 E
Nakhtarana, *India* . . . . **42 H3** 23 20N 69 15 E
Nakina, *Canada* **70 B2** 50 10N 86 40W
Nakodar, *India* . . . . **42 D6** 31 8N 75 31 E
Nakskov, *Denmark* . . . . **9 J14** 54 50N 11 8 E
Naktong →, *S. Korea* . . . . . . **35 G15** 35 7N 128 57 E
Nakuru, *Kenya* . . . . **54 C4** 0 15S 36 4 E
Nakuru, L., *Kenya* . . . . **54 C4** 0 23S 36 5 E
Nakusp, *Canada* **72 C5** 50 20N 117 45W
Nal, *Pakistan* . . . . **42 F2** 27 40N 66 12 E
Nal →, *Pakistan* . . . . **42 G1** 25 20N 65 30 E
Nalázi, *Mozam.* . . . . **57 C5** 24 3S 33 20 E
Nalchik, *Russia* . . . . **25 F7** 43 30N 43 33 E
Nalgonda, *India* . . . . **40 L11** 17 6N 79 15 E
Nalhati, *India* . . . . **43 G12** 24 17N 87 52 E
Naliya, *India* . . . . **42 H3** 23 16N 68 50 E
Nallamalai Hills, *India* . . . . . **40 M11** 15 30N 78 50 E
Nam Can, *Vietnam* . . . . **39 H5** 8 46N 104 59 E
Nam-ch'on, *N. Korea* . . . . . . **35 E14** 38 15N 126 26 E
Nam Co, *China* . . . . **32 C4** 30 30N 90 45 E
Nam Dinh, *Vietnam* . . . . **38 B6** 20 25N 106 5 E
Nam Du, Hon, *Vietnam* . . . . . **39 H5** 9 41N 104 21 E
Nam Ngum Dam, *Laos* . . . . . **38 C4** 18 35N 102 34 E
Nam-Phan, *Vietnam* . . . . **39 G6** 10 30N 106 0 E
Nam Phong, *Thailand* . . . . . . **38 D4** 16 42N 102 52 E
Nam Tha, *Laos* . . . . **38 B3** 20 58N 101 30 E
Nam Tok, *Thailand* . . . . **38 E2** 14 21N 99 4 E
Namacunde, *Angola* . . . . **56 B2** 17 18S 15 50 E
Namacurra, *Mozam.* . . . . **57 B6** 17 30S 36 50 E
Namak, Daryācheh-ye, *Iran* . **45 C7** 34 30N 52 0 E
Namak, Kavir-e, *Iran* . . . . . . **45 C8** 34 30N 57 30 E
Namakzār, Daryācheh-ye, *Iran* **45 C9** 34 0N 60 30 E
Namaland, *Namibia* . . . . **56 C2** 26 0S 17 0 E
Namangan, *Uzbekistan* . . . . **26 E8** 41 0N 71 40 E
Namapa, *Mozam.* . . . . **55 E4** 13 43S 39 50 E
Namaqualand, *S. Africa* . . . . **56 E2** 30 0S 17 25 E
Namasagali, *Uganda* . . . . . . **54 B3** 1 2N 33 0 E
Namber, *Indonesia* . . . . **37 E8** 1 2S 134 49 E
Nambour, *Australia* . . . . **63 D5** 26 32S 152 58 E
Nambucca Heads, *Australia* . **63 E5** 30 37S 153 0 E
Namcha Barwa, *China* . . . . . **32 D4** 29 40N 95 10 E
Namche Bazar, *Nepal* . . . . . . **43 F12** 27 51N 86 47 E
Namchonjŏm = Nam-ch'on, *N. Korea* . . . . **35 E14** 38 15N 126 26 E
Namecunda, *Mozam.* . . . . **55 E4** 14 54S 37 37 E
Nameponda, *Mozam.* . . . . **55 F4** 15 50S 39 50 E
Nametil, *Mozam.* . . . . **55 F4** 15 40S 39 21 E
Namew L., *Canada* **73 C8** 54 14N 101 56W
Namgia, *India* . . . . **43 D8** 31 48N 78 40 E
Namib Desert, *Namibia* . . . . **56 C2** 22 30S 15 0 E
Namibe, *Angola* . . . . **53 H2** 15 7S 12 11 E
Namibe □, *Angola* . . . . **56 B1** 16 35S 12 30 E
Namibia ■, *Africa* . . . . **56 C2** 22 0S 18 9 E
Namibwoestyn = Namib Desert, *Namibia* . . . . **56 C2** 22 30S 15 0 E
Namlea, *Indonesia* . . . . **37 E7** 3 18S 127 5 E
Namoi →, *Australia* . . . . **63 E4** 30 12S 149 30 E
Nampa, *U.S.A.* **82 E5** 43 34N 116 34W
Namp'o, *N. Korea* . . . . **35 E13** 38 52N 125 10 E
Nampō-Shotō, *Japan* . . . . . . **31 J10** 32 0N 140 0 E
Nampula, *Mozam.* . . . . **55 F4** 15 6S 39 15 E
Namrole, *Indonesia* . . . . **37 E7** 3 46S 126 46 E
Namse Shankou, *China* . . . . **41 E13** 30 0N 82 25 E
Namsen →, *Norway* . . . . **8 D14** 64 28N 11 37 E
Namsos, *Norway* . . . . **8 D14** 64 29N 11 30 E
Namtsy, *Russia* . . . . **27 C13** 62 43N 129 37 E
Namtu, *Burma* . . . . **41 H20** 23 5N 97 28 E
Namtumbo, *Tanzania* . . . . . . **55 E4** 10 30S 36 4 E
Namu, *Canada* **72 C3** 51 52N 127 50W
Namur, *Belgium* . . . . **15 D4** 50 27N 4 52 E
Namur □, *Belgium* . . . . **15 D4** 50 17N 5 0 E
Namutoni, *Namibia* . . . . **56 B2** 18 49S 16 55 E
Namwala, *Zambia* . . . . **55 F2** 15 44S 26 30 E
Namwŏn, *S. Korea* . . . . **35 G14** 35 23N 127 23 E
Nan, *Thailand* . . . . **38 C3** 18 48N 100 46 E
Nan →, *Thailand* . . . . **38 E3** 15 42N 100 9 E
Nan-ch'ang = Nanchang, *China* . . . . **33 D6** 28 42N 115 55 E
Nanaimo, *Canada* **72 D4** 49 10N 124 0W
Nanam, *N. Korea* . . . . **35 D15** 41 44N 129 40 E
Nanango, *Australia* . . . . **63 D5** 26 40S 152 0 E
Nanao, *Japan* . . . . **31 F8** 37 0N 137 0 E
Nanchang, *China* . . . . **33 D6** 28 42N 115 55 E
Nanching = Nanjing, *China* . . **33 C6** 32 2N 118 47 E
Nanchong, *China* . . . . **32 C5** 30 43N 106 2 E
Nancy, *France* . . . . **18 B7** 48 42N 6 12 E
Nanda Devi, *India* . . . . **43 D8** 30 23N 79 59 E
Nanda Kot, *India* . . . . **43 D9** 30 17N 80 5 E
Nandan, *Japan* . . . . **31 G7** 34 10N 134 42 E
Nanded, *India* . . . . **40 K10** 19 10N 77 20 E
Nandewar Ra., *Australia* . . . . **63 E5** 30 15S 150 35 E
Nandi = Nadi, *Fiji* . . . . **59 C7** 17 42S 177 20 E
Nandigram, *India* . . . . **43 H12** 22 1N 87 58 E
Nandurbar, *India* . . . . **40 J9** 21 20N 74 15 E
Nandyal, *India* . . . . **40 M11** 15 30N 78 30 E
Nanga-Eboko, *Cameroon* . . . **52 D2** 4 41N 12 22 E
Nanga Parbat, *Pakistan* . . . . **43 B6** 35 10N 74 35 E
Nangade, *Mozam.* . . . . **55 E4** 11 5S 39 36 E
Nangapinoh, *Indonesia* . . . . . **36 E4** 0 20S 111 44 E
Nangarhār □, *Afghan.* . . . . . **40 B7** 34 20N 70 0 E
Nangatayap, *Indonesia* . . . . . **36 E4** 1 32S 110 34 E
Nangeya Mts., *Uganda* . . . . . **54 B3** 3 30N 33 30 E
Nangong, *China* . . . . **34 F8** 37 23N 115 22 E
Nanhuang, *China* . . . . **35 F11** 36 58N 121 48 E
Nanjeko, *Zambia* . . . . **55 F1** 15 31S 23 30 E
Nanjing, *China* . . . . **33 C6** 32 2N 118 47 E
Nanjirinji, *Tanzania* . . . . **55 D4** 9 41S 39 5 E
Nankana Sahib, *Pakistan* . . . **42 D5** 31 27N 73 38 E
Nanking = Nanjing, *China* . . **33 C6** 32 2N 118 47 E
Nankoku, *Japan* . . . . **31 H6** 33 39N 133 44 E
Nanning, *China* . . . . **32 D5** 22 48N 108 20 E
Nannup, *Australia* . . . . **61 F2** 33 59S 115 48 E
Nanpara, *India* . . . . **43 F9** 27 52N 81 33 E
Nanpi, *China* . . . . **34 E9** 38 2N 116 45 E
Nanping, *China* . . . . **33 D6** 26 38N 118 10 E
Nanripe, *Mozam.* . . . . **55 E4** 13 52S 38 52 E
Nansei-Shotō = Ryūkyū-rettō, *Japan* . . . . **31 M3** 26 0N 126 0 E
Nansen Sd., *Canada* **4 A3** 81 0N 91 0W
Nanshan I., *S. China Sea* . . . **36 B5** 10 45N 115 49 E
Nansio, *Tanzania* . . . . **54 C3** 2 3S 33 4 E
Nantes, *France* **18 C3** 47 12N 1 33W
Nanticoke, *U.S.A.* **79 E8** 41 12N 76 0W
Nanton, *Canada* **72 C6** 50 21N 113 46W
Nantong, *China* . . . . **33 C7** 32 1N 120 52 E
Nantucket I., *U.S.A.* **76 E10** 41 16N 70 5W
Nantwich, *U.K.* **10 D5** 53 4N 2 31W
Nanty Glo, *U.S.A.* **78 F6** 40 28N 78 50W
Nanuque, *Brazil* **93 G10** 17 50S 40 21W
Nanusa, Kepulauan, *Indonesia* . . . . **37 D7** 4 45N 127 1 E
Nanutarra Roadhouse, *Australia* . . . . **60 D2** 22 32S 115 30 E
Nanyang, *China* . . . . **34 H7** 33 11N 112 30 E
Nanyuki, *Kenya* . . . . **54 B4** 0 2N 37 4 E
Nao, C. de la, *Spain* . . . . **19 C6** 38 44N 0 14 E
Naococane, L., *Canada* **71 B5** 52 50N 70 45W
Napa, *U.S.A.* **84 G4** 38 18N 122 17W
Napa →, *U.S.A.* **84 G4** 38 10N 122 19W
Napanee, *Canada* **78 B8** 44 15N 77 0W
Napanoch, *U.S.A.* **79 E10** 41 44N 74 22W
Nape, *Laos* . . . . **38 C5** 18 18N 105 6 E
Nape Pass = Keo Neua, Deo, *Vietnam* . . . . **38 C5** 18 23N 105 10 E
Napier, *N.Z.* . . . . **59 H6** 39 30S 176 56 E
Napier Broome B., *Australia* **60 B4** 14 2S 126 37 E
Napier Pen., *Australia* . . . . . . **62 A2** 12 4S 135 43 E
Napierville, *Canada* **79 A11** 45 11N 73 25W
Naples = Nápoli, *Italy* . . . . . . **20 D6** 40 50N 14 15 E
Naples, *U.S.A.* **77 M5** 26 8N 81 48W
Napo →, *Peru* **92 D4** 3 20S 72 40W
Napoleon, *N. Dak., U.S.A.* . . . **80 B5** 46 30N 99 46W
Napoleon, *Ohio, U.S.A.* **76 E3** 41 23N 84 8W
Nápoli, *Italy* . . . . **20 D6** 40 50N 14 15 E
Napopo, *Dem. Rep. of the Congo* . . . . **54 B2** 4 15N 28 0 E
Naqb, Ra's an, *Jordan* . . . . . **47 F4** 30 0N 35 29 E
Naqqāsh, *Iran* . . . . **45 C6** 35 40N 49 6 E
Nara, *Japan* . . . . **31 G7** 34 40N 135 49 E
Nara, *Mali* **50 E4** 15 10N 7 20W
Nara □, *Japan* . . . . **31 G8** 34 30N 136 0 E
Nara Canal, *Pakistan* . . . . **42 G3** 24 30N 69 20 E
Nara Visa, *U.S.A.* **81 H3** 35 37N 103 6W
Naracoorte, *Australia* . . . . **63 F3** 36 58S 140 45 E
Naradhan, *Australia* . . . . **63 E4** 33 34S 146 17 E
Naraini, *India* . . . . **43 G9** 25 11N 80 29 E
Narasapur, *India* . . . . **41 L12** 16 26N 81 40 E
Narathiwat, *Thailand* . . . . **39 J3** 6 30N 101 48 E
Narayanganj, *Bangla.* . . . . . . **41 H17** 23 40N 90 33 E
Narayanpet, *India* . . . . **40 L10** 16 45N 77 30 E
Narbonne, *France* . . . . **18 E5** 43 11N 3 0 E
Nardīn, *Iran* . . . . **45 B7** 37 3N 55 59 E
Nardò, *Italy* . . . . **21 D8** 40 11N 18 2 E
Narembeen, *Australia* . . . . . . **61 F2** 32 7S 118 24 E
Narendranagar, *India* . . . . . . **42 D8** 30 10N 78 18 E
Nares Str., *Arctic* **66 A13** 80 0N 70 0W
Naretha, *Australia* . . . . **61 F3** 31 0S 124 45 E
Narew →, *Poland* . . . . **17 B11** 52 26N 20 41 E
Nari →, *Pakistan* . . . . **42 F2** 28 0N 67 40 E
Narin, *Afghan.* . . . . **40 A6** 36 5N 69 0 E
Narindra, Helodranon' i, *Madag.* . . . . **57 A8** 14 55S 47 30 E
Narita, *Japan* . . . . **31 G10** 35 47N 140 19 E
Narmada →, *India* . . . . **42 J5** 21 38N 72 36 E
Narmland, *Sweden* . . . . **9 F15** 60 0N 13 30 E
Narnaul, *India* . . . . **42 E7** 28 5N 76 11 E
Narodnaya, *Russia* . . . . **24 A10** 65 5N 59 58 E
Narok, *Kenya* . . . . **54 C4** 1 55S 35 52 E
Narooma, *Australia* . . . . **63 F5** 36 14S 150 4 E
Narowal, *Pakistan* . . . . **42 C6** 32 6N 74 52 E
Narrabri, *Australia* . . . . **63 E4** 30 19S 149 46 E
Narran →, *Australia* . . . . **63 D4** 28 37S 148 12 E
Narrandera, *Australia* . . . . . . **63 E4** 34 42S 146 31 E
Narrogin, *Australia* . . . . **61 F2** 32 58S 117 14 E
Narromine, *Australia* . . . . **63 E4** 32 12S 148 12 E
Narrow Hills Prov. Park, *Canada* **73 C8** 54 0N 104 37W
Narsimhapur, *India* . . . . **43 H8** 22 54N 79 14 E
Narsinghgarh, *India* . . . . **42 H7** 23 45N 76 40 E
Naruto, *Japan* . . . . **31 G7** 34 11N 134 37 E
Narva, *Estonia* . . . . **24 C4** 59 23N 28 12 E
Narva →, *Russia* . . . . **9 G22** 59 27N 28 2 E
Narva Bay, *Estonia* . . . . **9 G19** 59 35N 27 35 E
Narvik, *Norway* . . . . **8 B17** 68 28N 17 26 E
Narwana, *India* . . . . **42 E7** 29 39N 76 6 E
Naryan-Mar, *Russia* . . . . **24 A9** 67 42N 53 12 E
Narym, *Russia* . . . . **26 D9** 59 0N 81 30 E
Naryn, *Kyrgyzstan* . . . . **26 E8** 41 26N 75 58 E
Nasa, *Norway* . . . . **8 C16** 66 29N 15 23 E
Naseby, *N.Z.* . . . . **59 L3** 45 1S 170 10 E
Naselle, *U.S.A.* **84 D3** 46 22N 123 49W
Naser, Buheirat en, *Egypt* . . **51 D12** 23 0N 32 30 E
Nashua, *Mont., U.S.A.* **82 B10** 48 8N 106 22W
Nashua, *N.H., U.S.A.* **79 D13** 42 45N 71 28W
Nashville, *Ark., U.S.A.* **81 J8** 33 57N 93 51W
Nashville, *Ga., U.S.A.* **77 K4** 31 12N 83 15W
Nashville, *Tenn., U.S.A.* **77 G2** 36 10N 86 47W
Nasik, *India* . . . . **40 K8** 19 58N 73 50 E
Nasirabad, *India* . . . . **42 F6** 26 15N 74 45 E
Nasirabad, *Pakistan* . . . . **42 E3** 28 23N 68 24 E
Naskaupi →, *Canada* **71 B7** 53 47N 60 51W
Naşrābād, *Iran* . . . . **45 C6** 34 8N 51 26 E
Naşriān-e Pā'īn, *Iran* . . . . **44 C5** 32 52N 46 52 E
Nass →, *Canada* **72 C3** 55 0N 129 40W
Nassau, *Bahamas* **88 A4** 25 5N 77 20W
Nassau, *U.S.A.* **79 D11** 42 31N 73 37W
Nassau, B., *Chile* **96 H3** 55 20S 68 0W
Nasser, L. = Naser, Buheirat en, *Egypt* . . . . **51 D12** 23 0N 32 30 E
Nasser City = Kôm Ombo, *Egypt* . . . . **51 D12** 24 25N 32 52 E
Nässjö, *Sweden* . . . . **9 H16** 57 39N 14 42 E
Nastapoka →, *Canada* **70 A4** 56 55N 76 33W
Nastapoka, Is., *Canada* **70 A4** 56 55N 76 50W
Nata, *Botswana* . . . . **56 C4** 20 12S 26 12 E
Nata →, *Botswana* . . . . **56 C4** 20 14S 26 10 E
Natal, *Brazil* **93 E11** 5 47S 35 13W
Natal, *Indonesia* . . . . **36 D1** 0 35N 99 7 E
Natal, *S. Africa* . . . . **53 K6** 28 30S 30 30 E
Naţanz, *Iran* . . . . **45 C6** 33 30N 51 55 E
Natashquan, *Canada* **71 B7** 50 14N 61 46W
Natashquan →, *Canada* **71 B7** 50 7N 61 50W
Natchez, *U.S.A.* **81 K9** 31 34N 91 24W
Natchitoches, *U.S.A.* **81 K8** 31 46N 93 5W
Nathalia, *Australia* . . . . **63 F4** 36 1S 145 13 E
Nathdwara, *India* . . . . **42 G5** 24 55N 73 50 E
Nati, Pta., *Spain* . . . . **22 A10** 40 3N 3 50 E
Natimuk, *Australia* . . . . **63 F3** 36 42S 142 0 E
Nation →, *Canada* **72 B4** 55 30N 123 32W
National City, *U.S.A.* **85 N9** 32 41N 117 6W
Natitingou, *Benin* . . . . **50 F6** 10 20N 1 26 E
Natividad, I., *Mexico* **86 B1** 27 50N 115 10W
Natkyizin, *Burma* . . . . **38 E1** 14 57N 97 59 E
Natron, L., *Tanzania* . . . . **54 C4** 2 20S 36 0 E
Natrona Heights, *U.S.A.* **78 F5** 40 37N 79 44W
Natukanaoka Pan, *Namibia* . . **56 B2** 18 40S 15 45 E
Natuna Besar, Kepulauan, *Indonesia* . . . . **39 L7** 4 0N 108 15 E
Natuna Is. = Natuna Besar, Kepulauan, *Indonesia* . . . . **39 L7** 4 0N 108 15 E
Natuna Selatan, Kepulauan, *Indonesia* . . . . **39 L7** 2 45N 109 0 E
Natural Bridge, *U.S.A.* **79 B9** 44 5N 75 30W
Naturaliste, C., *Australia* . . . . **62 G4** 40 50S 148 15 E
Nau Qala, *Afghan.* . . . . **42 B3** 34 5N 68 5 E
Naugatuck, *U.S.A.* **79 E11** 41 30N 73 3W
Naujaat = Repulse Bay, *Canada* **69 B11** 66 30N 86 30W
Naumburg, *Germany* . . . . **16 C6** 51 9N 11 47 E
Nā'ūr at Tunayb, *Jordan* . . . . **47 D4** 31 48N 35 57 E
Nauru ■, *Pac. Oc.* . . . . **64 H8** 1 0S 166 0 E
Naushahra = Nowshera, *Pakistan* . . . . **40 C8** 34 0N 72 0 E
Naushahro, *Pakistan* . . . . **42 F3** 26 50N 68 7 E
Naushon I., *U.S.A.* **79 E14** 41 29N 70 45W
Nauta, *Peru* **92 D4** 4 31S 73 35W
Nautanwa, *India* . . . . **41 F13** 27 20N 83 25 E
Nautla, *Mexico* **87 C5** 20 20N 96 50W
Nava, *Mexico* **86 B4** 28 25N 100 46W
Navadwip, *India* . . . . **43 H13** 23 34N 88 20 E
Navahrudak, *Belarus* . . . . **17 B13** 53 40N 25 50 E
Navajo Reservoir, *U.S.A.* **83 H10** 36 48N 107 36W
Navalmoral de la Mata, *Spain* **19 C3** 39 52N 5 33W
Navan = An Uaimh, *Ireland* . . **13 C5** 53 39N 6 41W
Navarino, I., *Chile* **96 H3** 55 0S 67 40W
Navarra □, *Spain* **19 A5** 42 40N 1 40W
Navarre, *U.S.A.* **78 F3** 40 43N 81 31W
Navarro →, *U.S.A.* **84 F3** 39 11N 123 45W
Navasota, *U.S.A.* **81 K6** 30 23N 96 5W
Navassa I., *W. Indies* **89 C5** 18 30N 75 0W
Naver →, *U.K.* **12 C4** 58 32N 4 14W
Navibandar, *India* . . . . **42 J3** 21 26N 69 48 E
Navidad, *Chile* **94 C1** 33 57S 71 50W
Navirai, *Brazil* **95 A5** 23 8S 54 13W
Navlakhi, *India* . . . . **42 H4** 22 58N 70 28 E
Năvodari, *Romania* . . . . **17 F15** 44 19N 28 36 E
Navoi = Nawoiy, *Uzbekistan* . **26 E7** 40 9N 65 22 E
Navojoa, *Mexico* **86 B3** 27 0N 109 30W
Navolato, *Mexico* **86 C3** 24 47N 107 42W
Návpaktos, *Greece* . . . . **21 E9** 38 24N 21 50 E
Návplion, *Greece* . . . . **21 F10** 37 33N 22 50 E
Navsari, *India* . . . . **40 J8** 20 57N 72 59 E
Nawa Kot, *Pakistan* . . . . **42 E4** 28 21N 71 24 E
Nawab Khan, *Pakistan* . . . . . . **42 D3** 30 17N 69 12 E
Nawabganj, *Ut. P., India* . . . . **43 F9** 26 56N 81 14 E
Nawabganj, *Ut. P., India* . . . . **43 E8** 28 32N 79 40 E
Nawabshah, *Pakistan* . . . . **42 F3** 26 15N 68 25 E
Nawada, *India* . . . . **43 G11** 24 50N 85 33 E
Nawakot, *Nepal* . . . . **43 F11** 27 55N 85 10 E
Nawalgarh, *India* . . . . **42 F6** 27 50N 75 15 E
Nawanshahr, *India* . . . . **43 C6** 32 33N 74 48 E
Nawar, Dasht-i-, *Afghan.* . . . . **42 C3** 33 52N 68 0 E
Nawoiy, *Uzbekistan* . . . . **26 E7** 40 9N 65 22 E
Naxçıvan, *Azerbaijan* . . . . **25 G8** 39 12N 45 15 E
Naxçıvan □, *Azerbaijan* . . . . . **25 G8** 39 25N 45 26 E
Náxos, *Greece* . . . . **21 F11** 37 8N 25 25 E
Nay, Mui, *Vietnam* . . . . **36 B3** 12 55N 109 23 E
Nāy Band, *Būshehr, Iran* . . . . **45 E7** 27 20N 52 40 E
Nāy Band, *Khorāsān, Iran* . . . **45 C8** 32 20N 57 34 E
Nayakhan, *Russia* . . . . **27 C16** 61 56N 159 0 E
Nayarit □, *Mexico* **86 C4** 22 0N 105 0W
Nayoro, *Japan* . . . . **30 B11** 44 21N 142 28 E
Nayyāl, W. →, *Si. Arabia* . . . **44 D3** 28 35N 39 4 E
Nazaré, *Brazil* **93 F11** 13 2S 39 0W
Nazareth = Nazerat, *Israel* . . **47 C4** 32 42N 35 17 E
Nazareth, *U.S.A.* **79 F9** 40 44N 75 19W
Nazas, *Mexico* **86 B4** 25 10N 104 6W
Nazas →, *Mexico* **86 B4** 25 35N 103 25W
Nazca, *Peru* **92 F4** 14 50S 74 57W
Naze, The, *U.K.* . . . . **11 F9** 51 53N 1 18 E
Nazerat, *Israel* . . . . **47 C4** 32 42N 35 17 E
Nāzīk, *Iran* . . . . **44 B5** 39 1N 45 4 E
Nazilli, *Turkey* . . . . **21 F13** 37 55N 28 15 E
Nazko, *Canada* **72 C4** 53 1N 123 37W
Nazko →, *Canada* **72 C4** 53 7N 123 34W
Nazret, *Ethiopia* . . . . **46 F2** 8 32N 39 22 E
Nazwa, *Oman* . . . . **46 C6** 22 56N 57 32 E
Nchanga, *Zambia* . . . . **55 E2** 12 30S 27 49 E
Ncheu, *Malawi* . . . . **55 E3** 14 50S 34 47 E
Ndala, *Tanzania* . . . . **54 C3** 4 45S 33 15 E
Ndalatando, *Angola* . . . . **52 F2** 9 12S 14 48 E
Ndareda, *Tanzania* . . . . **54 C4** 4 12S 35 30 E
Ndélé, *C.A.R.* . . . . **52 C4** 8 25N 20 36 E
Ndjamena, *Chad* . . . . **51 F8** 12 10N 14 59 E
Ndola, *Zambia* . . . . **55 E2** 13 0S 28 34 E
Ndoto Mts., *Kenya* . . . . **54 B4** 2 0N 37 0 E
Nduguti, *Tanzania* . . . . **54 C3** 4 18S 34 41 E
Neagh, Lough, *U.K.* **13 B5** 54 37N 6 25W
Neah Bay, *U.S.A.* **84 B2** 48 22N 124 37W
Neale, L., *Australia* . . . . **60 D5** 24 15S 130 0 E
Neápolis, *Greece* . . . . **23 D7** 35 15N 25 37 E
Near Is., *U.S.A.* . . . . **68 C1** 52 30N 174 0 E
Neath, *U.K.* **11 F4** 51 39N 3 48W
Neath Port Talbot □, *U.K.* . . . **11 F4** 51 42N 3 45W
Nebine Cr. →, *Australia* . . . . **63 D4** 29 27S 146 56 E
Nebitdag, *Turkmenistan* . . . . . **25 G9** 39 30N 54 22 E
Nebo, *Australia* . . . . **62 C4** 21 42S 148 42 E
Nebraska □, *U.S.A.* **80 E5** 41 30N 99 30W
Nebraska City, *U.S.A.* **80 E7** 40 41N 95 52W
Nébrodi, Monti, *Italy* . . . . **20 F6** 37 54N 14 35 E
Necedah, *U.S.A.* **80 C9** 44 2N 90 4W
Nechako →, *Canada* **72 C4** 53 30N 122 44W
Neches →, *U.S.A.* **81 L8** 29 58N 93 51W
Neckar →, *Germany* . . . . **16 D5** 49 27N 8 29 E
Necochea, *Argentina* **94 D4** 38 30S 58 50W
Needles, *Canada* **72 D5** 49 53N 118 7W
Needles, *U.S.A.* **85 L12** 34 51N 114 37W
Needles, The, *U.K.* **11 G6** 50 39N 1 35W
Ñeembucú □, *Paraguay* **94 B4** 27 0S 58 0W
Neemuch = Nimach, *India* . . . **42 G6** 24 30N 74 56 E
Neenah, *U.S.A.* **76 C1** 44 11N 88 28W
Neepawa, *Canada* **73 C9** 50 15N 99 30W
Neftçala, *Azerbaijan* . . . . **25 G8** 39 19N 49 12 E
Neftekumsk, *Russia* . . . . **25 F7** 44 46N 44 50 E
Nefyn, *U.K.* **10 E3** 52 56N 4 31W
Negapatam = Nagappattinam, *India* . . . . **40 P11** 10 46N 79 51 E
Negaunee, *U.S.A.* **76 B2** 46 30N 87 36W
Negele, *Ethiopia* . . . . **46 F2** 5 20N 39 36 E
Negev Desert = Hanegev, *Israel* . . . . **47 E4** 30 50N 35 0 E
Negombo, *Sri Lanka* . . . . **40 R11** 7 12N 79 50 E
Negotin, *Serbia, Yug.* . . . . **21 B10** 44 16N 22 37 E
Negra, Pta., *Peru* **92 E2** 6 6S 81 10W
Negrais, C. = Maudin Sun, *Burma* . . . . **41 M19** 16 0N 94 30 E
Negril, *Jamaica* **88 C4** 18 22N 78 20W
Negro →, *Argentina* **96 E4** 41 2S 62 47W
Negro →, *Brazil* **92 D7** 3 0S 60 0W
Negro →, *Uruguay* **95 C4** 33 24S 58 22W
Negros, *Phil.* . . . . **37 C6** 9 30N 122 40 E
Neguac, *Canada* **71 C6** 47 15N 65 5W
Nehalem →, *U.S.A.* **84 E3** 45 40N 123 56W
Nehāvand, *Iran* . . . . **45 C6** 35 56N 49 31 E
Nehbandān, *Iran* . . . . **45 D9** 31 35N 60 5 E
Nei Monggol Zizhiqu □, *China* . . . . **34 D7** 42 0N 112 0 E
Neijiang, *China* . . . . **32 D5** 29 35N 104 55 E
Neillsville, *U.S.A.* **80 C9** 44 34N 90 36W
Neilton, *U.S.A.* **82 C2** 47 25N 123 53W
Neiqiu, *China* . . . . **34 F8** 37 15N 114 30 E
Neiva, *Colombia* **92 C3** 2 56N 75 18W
Neixiang, *China* . . . . **34 H6** 33 10N 111 52 E
Nejanilini L., *Canada* **73 B9** 59 33N 97 48W
Nejd = Najd, *Si. Arabia* . . . . . **46 B3** 26 30N 42 0 E
Nekā, *Iran* . . . . **45 B7** 36 39N 53 19 E
Nekemte, *Ethiopia* . . . . **46 F2** 9 4N 36 30 E
Neksø, *Denmark* . . . . **9 J16** 55 4N 15 8 E
Nelia, *Australia* . . . . **62 C3** 20 39S 142 12 E
Neligh, *U.S.A.* **80 D5** 42 8N 98 2W
Nelkan, *Russia* . . . . **27 D14** 57 40N 136 4 E
Nellore, *India* . . . . **40 M11** 14 27N 79 59 E
Nelson, *Canada* **72 D5** 49 30N 117 20W
Nelson, *N.Z.* . . . . **59 J4** 41 18S 173 16 E
Nelson, *U.K.* **10 D5** 53 50N 2 13W
Nelson, *Ariz., U.S.A.* **83 J7** 35 31N 113 19W
Nelson, *Nev., U.S.A.* **85 K12** 35 42N 114 50W
Nelson →, *Canada* **73 C9** 54 33N 98 2W
Nelson, C., *Australia* . . . . **63 F3** 38 26S 141 32 E
Nelson, Estrecho, *Chile* **96 G2** 51 30S 75 0W
Nelson Forks, *Canada* **72 B4** 59 30N 124 0W
Nelson House, *Canada* **73 B9** 55 47N 98 51W
Nelson L., *Canada* **73 B8** 55 48N 100 7W
Nelspoort, *S. Africa* . . . . **56 E3** 32 7S 23 0 E
Nelspruit, *S. Africa* . . . . **57 D5** 25 29S 30 59 E
Néma, *Mauritania* **50 E4** 16 40N 7 15W
Neman, *Russia* . . . . **9 J20** 55 2N 22 2 E
Neman →, *Lithuania* . . . . **9 J19** 55 25N 21 10 E
Nemeiben L., *Canada* **73 B7** 55 20N 105 20W
Némiscau, *Canada* **70 B4** 51 18N 76 54W
Némiscau, L., *Canada* **70 B4** 51 25N 76 40W
Nemunas = Neman →, *Lithuania* . . . . **9 J19** 55 25N 21 10 E
Nemuro, *Japan* . . . . **30 C12** 43 20N 145 35 E
Nemuro-Kaikyō, *Japan* . . . . . . **30 C12** 43 30N 145 30 E
Nen Jiang →, *China* . . . . **35 B13** 45 28N 124 30 E
Nenagh, *Ireland* **13 D3** 52 52N 8 11W
Nenasi, *Malaysia* . . . . **39 L4** 3 9N 103 23 E
Nene →, *U.K.* . . . . **11 E8** 52 49N 0 11 E
Nenjiang, *China* . . . . **33 B7** 49 10N 125 10 E
Neno, *Malawi* . . . . **55 F3** 15 25S 34 40 E
Neodesha, *U.S.A.* **81 G7** 37 25N 95 41W
Neosho, *U.S.A.* **81 G7** 36 52N 94 22W
Neosho →, *U.S.A.* **81 H7** 36 48N 95 18W
Nepal ■, *Asia* . . . . **43 F11** 28 0N 84 30 E
Nepalganj, *Nepal* . . . . **43 E9** 28 5N 81 40 E
Nepalganj Road, *India* . . . . **43 E9** 28 1N 81 41 E
Nephi, *U.S.A.* **82 G8** 39 43N 111 50W
Nephin, *Ireland* **13 B2** 54 1N 9 22W
Neptune, *U.S.A.* **79 F10** 40 13N 74 2W
Nerang, *Australia* . . . . **63 D5** 27 58S 153 20 E
Nerchinsk, *Russia* . . . . **27 D12** 52 0N 116 39 E
Néret, L., *Canada* **71 B5** 54 45N 70 44W
Neretva →, *Croatia* . . . . **21 C7** 43 1N 17 27 E
Neringa, *Lithuania* . . . . **9 J19** 55 20N 21 5 E
Neryungri, *Russia* . . . . **27 D13** 57 38N 124 28 E
Nescopeck, *U.S.A.* **79 E8** 41 3N 76 12W
Ness, L., *U.K.* **12 D4** 57 15N 4 32W
Ness City, *U.S.A.* **80 F5** 38 27N 99 54W
Nesterov, *Poland* . . . . **17 C12** 50 4N 23 58 E
Nesvizh = Nyasvizh, *Belarus* . **17 B14** 53 14N 26 38 E
Netanya, *Israel* . . . . **47 C3** 32 20N 34 51 E
Netarhat, *India* . . . . **43 H11** 23 29N 84 16 E
Nete →, *Belgium* . . . . **15 C4** 51 7N 4 14 E
Netherdale, *Australia* . . . . **62 C4** 21 10S 148 33 E
Netherlands ■, *Europe* . . . . . . **15 C5** 52 0N 5 30 E
Netherlands Antilles ■, *W. Indies* **92 A5** 12 15N 69 0W
Netrang, *India* . . . . **42 J5** 21 39N 73 21 E
Nettilling L., *Canada* **69 B12** 66 30N 71 0W
Netzahualcoyotl, Presa, *Mexico* **87 D6** 17 10N 93 30W
Neubrandenburg, *Germany* . . **16 B7** 53 33N 13 15 E
Neuchâtel, *Switz.* . . . . **18 C7** 47 0N 6 55 E
Neuchâtel, Lac de, *Switz.* . . . . **18 C7** 46 53N 6 50 E
Neufchâteau, *Belgium* . . . . **15 E5** 49 50N 5 25 E
Neumünster, *Germany* . . . . **16 A5** 54 4N 9 58 E
Neunkirchen, *Germany* . . . . . . **16 D4** 49 20N 7 9 E
Neuquén, *Argentina* **96 D3** 38 55S 68 0W

Neuquén □, *Argentina* **94 D2** 38 0S 69 50W
Neuruppin, *Germany* **16 B7** 52 55N 12 48 E
Neuse →, *U.S.A.* **77 H7** 35 6N 76 29W
Neusiedler See, *Austria* **17 E9** 47 50N 16 47 E
Neustrelitz, *Germany* **16 B7** 53 21N 13 4 E
Neva →, *Russia* **24 C5** 59 50N 30 30 E
Nevada, *Iowa, U.S.A.* **80 D8** 42 1N 93 27W
Nevada, *Mo., U.S.A.* **81 G7** 37 51N 94 22W
Nevada □, *U.S.A.* **82 G5** 39 0N 117 0W
Nevada City, *U.S.A.* **84 F6** 39 16N 121 1W
Nevado, Cerro, *Argentina* **94 D2** 35 30S 68 32W
Nevel, *Russia* **24 C4** 56 0N 29 55 E
Nevers, *France* **18 C5** 47 0N 3 9 E
Nevertire, *Australia* **63 E4** 31 50S 147 44 E
Neville, *Canada* **73 D7** 49 58N 107 39W
Nevinnomyssk, *Russia* **25 F7** 44 40N 42 0 E
Nevis, *St. Kitts & Nevis* **89 C7** 17 0N 62 30W
Nevşehir, *Turkey* **44 B2** 38 33N 34 40 E
Nevyansk, *Russia* **24 C11** 57 30N 60 13 E
New →, *U.S.A.* **76 F5** 38 10N 81 12W
New Aiyansh, *Canada* **72 B3** 55 12N 129 4W
New Albany, *Ind., U.S.A.* **76 F3** 38 18N 85 49W
New Albany, *Miss., U.S.A.* **81 H10** 34 29N 89 0W
New Albany, *Pa., U.S.A.* **79 E8** 41 36N 76 27W
New Amsterdam, *Guyana* **92 B7** 6 15N 57 36W
New Angledool, *Australia* **63 D4** 29 5S 147 55 E
New Baltimore, *U.S.A.* **78 D2** 42 41N 82 44W
New Bedford, *U.S.A.* **79 E14** 41 38N 70 56W
New Berlin, *N.Y., U.S.A.* **79 D9** 42 37N 75 20W
New Berlin, *Pa., U.S.A.* **78 F8** 40 50N 76 57W
New Bern, *U.S.A.* **77 H7** 35 7N 77 3W
New Bethlehem, *U.S.A.* **78 F5** 41 0N 79 20W
New Bloomfield, *U.S.A.* **78 F7** 40 25N 77 11W
New Boston, *U.S.A.* **81 J7** 33 28N 94 25W
New Braunfels, *U.S.A.* **81 L5** 29 42N 98 8W
New Brighton, *N.Z.* **59 K4** 43 29S 172 43 E
New Brighton, *U.S.A.* **78 F4** 40 42N 80 19W
New Britain, *Papua N. G.* **64 H7** 5 50S 150 20 E
New Britain, *U.S.A.* **79 E12** 41 40N 72 47W
New Brunswick, *U.S.A.* **79 F10** 40 30N 74 27W
New Brunswick □, *Canada* **71 C6** 46 50N 66 30W
New Caledonia ■, *Pac. Oc.* **64 K8** 21 0S 165 0 E
New Castile = Castilla-La Mancha □, *Spain* **19 C4** 39 30N 3 30W
New Castle, *Ind., U.S.A.* **76 F3** 39 55N 85 22W
New Castle, *Pa., U.S.A.* **78 F4** 41 0N 80 21W
New City, *U.S.A.* **79 E11** 41 9N 73 59W
New Concord, *U.S.A.* **78 G3** 39 59N 81 54W
New Cumberland, *U.S.A.* **78 F4** 40 30N 80 36W
New Cuyama, *U.S.A.* **85 L7** 34 57N 119 38W
New Delhi, *India* **42 E7** 28 37N 77 13 E
New Denver, *Canada* **72 D5** 50 0N 117 25W
New Don Pedro Reservoir, *U.S.A.* **84 H6** 37 43N 120 24W
New England, *U.S.A.* **80 B3** 46 32N 102 52W
New England Ra., *Australia* **63 E5** 30 20S 151 45 E
New Forest, *U.K.* **11 G6** 50 53N 1 34W
New Galloway, *U.K.* **12 F4** 55 5N 4 9W
New Glasgow, *Canada* **71 C7** 45 35N 62 36W
New Guinea, *Oceania* **28 K17** 4 0S 136 0 E
New Hamburg, *Canada* **78 C4** 43 23N 80 42W
New Hampshire □, *U.S.A.* **79 C13** 44 0N 71 30W
New Hampton, *U.S.A.* **80 D8** 43 3N 92 19W
New Hanover, *S. Africa* **57 D5** 29 22S 30 31 E
New Hartford, *U.S.A.* **79 C9** 43 4N 75 18W
New Haven, *Conn., U.S.A.* **79 E12** 41 18N 72 55W
New Haven, *Mich., U.S.A.* **78 D2** 42 44N 82 48W
New Hazelton, *Canada* **72 B3** 55 20N 127 30W
New Hebrides = Vanuatu ■, *Pac. Oc.* **64 J8** 15 0S 168 0 E
New Holland, *U.S.A.* **79 F8** 40 6N 76 5W
New Iberia, *U.S.A.* **81 K9** 30 1N 91 49W
New Ireland, *Papua N. G.* **64 H7** 3 20S 151 50 E
New Jersey □, *U.S.A.* **76 E8** 40 0N 74 30W
New Kensington, *U.S.A.* **78 F5** 40 34N 79 46W
New Lexington, *U.S.A.* **76 F4** 39 43N 82 13W
New Liskeard, *Canada* **70 C4** 47 31N 79 41W
New London, *Conn., U.S.A.* **79 E12** 41 22N 72 6W
New London, *Ohio, U.S.A.* **78 E2** 41 5N 82 24W
New London, *Wis., U.S.A.* **80 C10** 44 23N 88 45W
New Madrid, *U.S.A.* **81 G10** 36 36N 89 32W
New Martinsville, *U.S.A.* **76 F5** 39 39N 80 52W
New Meadows, *U.S.A.* **82 D5** 44 58N 116 18W
New Melones L., *U.S.A.* **84 H6** 37 57N 120 31W
New Mexico □, *U.S.A.* **83 J10** 34 30N 106 0W
New Milford, *Conn., U.S.A.* **79 E11** 41 35N 73 25W
New Milford, *Pa., U.S.A.* **79 E9** 41 52N 75 44W
New Norcia, *Australia* **61 F2** 30 57S 116 13 E
New Norfolk, *Australia* **62 G4** 42 46S 147 2 E
New Orleans, *U.S.A.* **81 L9** 29 58N 90 4W
New Philadelphia, *U.S.A.* **78 F3** 40 30N 81 27W
New Plymouth, *N.Z.* **59 H5** 39 4S 174 5 E
New Plymouth, *U.S.A.* **82 E5** 43 58N 116 49W
New Port Richey, *U.S.A.* **77 L4** 28 16N 82 43W
New Providence, *Bahamas* **88 A4** 25 25N 78 35W
New Quay, *U.K.* **11 E3** 52 13N 4 21W
New Radnor, *U.K.* **11 E4** 52 15N 3 9W
New Richmond, *Canada* **71 C6** 48 15N 65 45W
New Richmond, *U.S.A.* **80 C8** 45 7N 92 32W
New Roads, *U.S.A.* **81 K9** 30 42N 91 26W
New Rochelle, *U.S.A.* **79 F11** 40 55N 73 47W
New Rockford, *U.S.A.* **80 B5** 47 41N 99 8W
New Romney, *U.K.* **11 G8** 50 59N 0 57 E
New Ross, *Ireland* **13 D5** 52 23N 6 57W
New Salem, *U.S.A.* **80 B4** 46 51N 101 25W
New Scone, *U.K.* **12 E5** 56 25N 3 24W
New Siberian I. = Novaya Sibir, Ostrov, *Russia* **27 B16** 75 10N 150 0 E
New Siberian Is. = Novosibirskiye Ostrova, *Russia* **27 B15** 75 0N 142 0 E
New Smyrna Beach, *U.S.A.* **77 L5** 29 1N 80 56W
New South Wales □, *Australia* **63 E4** 33 0S 146 0 E
New Town, *U.S.A.* **80 B3** 47 59N 102 30W
New Tredegar, *U.K.* **11 F4** 51 44N 3 16W
New Ulm, *U.S.A.* **80 C7** 44 19N 94 28W
New Waterford, *Canada* **71 C7** 46 13N 60 4W
New Westminster, *Canada* **84 A4** 49 13N 122 55W
New York, *U.S.A.* **79 F11** 40 45N 74 0W
New York □, *U.S.A.* **79 D9** 43 0N 75 0W
New York Mts., *U.S.A.* **83 J6** 35 0N 115 20W
New Zealand ■, *Oceania* **59 J6** 40 0S 176 0 E
Newaj →, *India* **42 G7** 24 24N 76 49 E
Newala, *Tanzania* **55 E4** 10 58S 39 18 E
Newark, *Del., U.S.A.* **76 F8** 39 41N 75 46W
Newark, *N.J., U.S.A.* **79 F10** 40 44N 74 10W
Newark, *N.Y., U.S.A.* **78 C7** 43 3N 77 6W
Newark, *Ohio, U.S.A.* **78 F2** 40 3N 82 24W
Newark-on-Trent, *U.K.* **10 D7** 53 5N 0 48W
Newark Valley, *U.S.A.* **79 D8** 42 14N 76 11W
Newberg, *U.S.A.* **82 D2** 45 18N 122 58W
Newberry, *Mich., U.S.A.* **76 B3** 46 21N 85 30W
Newberry, *S.C., U.S.A.* **77 H5** 34 17N 81 37W
Newberry Springs, *U.S.A.* **85 L10** 34 50N 116 41W
Newboro L., *Canada* **79 B8** 44 38N 76 20W
Newbridge = Droichead Nua, *Ireland* **13 C5** 53 11N 6 48W
Newburgh, *Canada* **78 B8** 44 19N 76 52W
Newburgh, *U.S.A.* **79 E10** 41 30N 74 1W
Newbury, *U.K.* **11 F6** 51 24N 1 20W
Newbury, *N.H., U.S.A.* **79 B12** 43 19N 72 3W
Newbury, *Vt., U.S.A.* **79 B12** 44 5N 72 4W
Newburyport, *U.S.A.* **77 D10** 42 49N 70 53W
Newcastle, *Australia* **63 E5** 33 0S 151 46 E
Newcastle, *N.B., Canada* **71 C6** 47 1N 65 38W
Newcastle, *Ont., Canada* **70 D4** 43 55N 78 35W
Newcastle, *S. Africa* **57 D4** 27 45S 29 58 E
Newcastle, *U.K.* **13 B6** 54 13N 5 54W
Newcastle, *Calif., U.S.A.* **84 G5** 38 53N 121 8W
Newcastle, *Wyo., U.S.A.* **80 D2** 43 50N 104 11W
Newcastle Emlyn, *U.K.* **11 E3** 52 2N 4 28W
Newcastle Ra., *Australia* **60 C5** 15 45S 130 15 E
Newcastle-under-Lyme, *U.K.* **10 D5** 53 1N 2 14W
Newcastle-upon-Tyne, *U.K.* **10 C6** 54 58N 1 36W
Newcastle Waters, *Australia* **62 B1** 17 30S 133 28 E
Newcastle West, *Ireland* **13 D2** 52 27N 9 3W
Newcomb, *U.S.A.* **79 C10** 43 58N 74 10W
Newcomerstown, *U.S.A.* **78 F3** 40 16N 81 36W
Newdegate, *Australia* **61 F2** 33 6S 119 0 E
Newell, *Australia* **62 B4** 16 20S 145 16 E
Newell, *U.S.A.* **80 C3** 44 43N 103 25W
Newfane, *U.S.A.* **78 C6** 43 17N 78 43W
Newfield, *U.S.A.* **79 D8** 42 18N 76 33W
Newfound L., *U.S.A.* **79 C13** 43 40N 71 47W
Newfoundland, *Canada* **66 E14** 49 0N 55 0W
Newfoundland, *U.S.A.* **79 E9** 41 18N 75 19W
Newfoundland □, *Canada* **71 B8** 53 0N 58 0W
Newhall, *U.S.A.* **85 L8** 34 23N 118 32W
Newhaven, *U.K.* **11 G8** 50 47N 0 3 E
Newkirk, *U.S.A.* **81 G6** 36 53N 97 3W
Newlyn, *U.K.* **11 G2** 50 6N 5 34W
Newman, *Australia* **60 D2** 23 18S 119 45 E
Newman, *U.S.A.* **84 H5** 37 19N 121 1W
Newmarket, *Canada* **78 B5** 44 3N 79 28W
Newmarket, *Ireland* **13 D2** 52 13N 9 0W
Newmarket, *U.K.* **11 E8** 52 15N 0 25 E
Newmarket, *U.S.A.* **79 C14** 43 4N 70 56W
Newnan, *U.S.A.* **77 J3** 33 23N 84 48W
Newport, *Ireland* **13 C2** 53 53N 9 33W
Newport, *I. of W., U.K.* **11 G6** 50 42N 1 17W
Newport, *Newp., U.K.* **11 F5** 51 35N 3 0W
Newport, *Ark., U.S.A.* **81 H9** 35 37N 91 16W
Newport, *Ky., U.S.A.* **76 F3** 39 5N 84 30W
Newport, *N.H., U.S.A.* **79 C12** 43 22N 72 10W
Newport, *N.Y., U.S.A.* **79 C9** 43 11N 75 1W
Newport, *Oreg., U.S.A.* **82 D1** 44 39N 124 3W
Newport, *Pa., U.S.A.* **78 F7** 40 29N 77 8W
Newport, *R.I., U.S.A.* **79 E13** 41 29N 71 19W
Newport, *Tenn., U.S.A.* **77 H4** 35 58N 83 11W
Newport, *Vt., U.S.A.* **79 B12** 44 56N 72 13W
Newport, *Wash., U.S.A.* **82 B5** 48 11N 117 3W
Newport □, *U.K.* **11 F4** 51 33N 3 1W
Newport Beach, *U.S.A.* **85 M9** 33 37N 117 56W
Newport News, *U.S.A.* **76 G7** 36 59N 76 25W
Newport Pagnell, *U.K.* **11 E7** 52 5N 0 43W
Newquay, *U.K.* **11 G2** 50 25N 5 6W
Newry, *U.K.* **13 B5** 54 11N 6 21W
Newton, *Ill., U.S.A.* **80 F10** 38 59N 88 10W
Newton, *Iowa, U.S.A.* **80 E8** 41 42N 93 3W
Newton, *Kans., U.S.A.* **81 F6** 38 3N 97 21W
Newton, *Mass., U.S.A.* **79 D13** 42 21N 71 12W
Newton, *Miss., U.S.A.* **81 J10** 32 19N 89 10W
Newton, *N.C., U.S.A.* **77 H5** 35 40N 81 13W
Newton, *N.J., U.S.A.* **79 E10** 41 3N 74 45W
Newton, *Tex., U.S.A.* **81 K8** 30 51N 93 46W
Newton Abbot, *U.K.* **11 G4** 50 32N 3 37W
Newton Aycliffe, *U.K.* **10 C6** 54 37N 1 34W
Newton Falls, *U.S.A.* **78 E4** 41 11N 80 59W
Newton Stewart, *U.K.* **12 G4** 54 57N 4 30W
Newtonmore, *U.K.* **12 D4** 57 4N 4 8W
Newtown, *U.K.* **11 E4** 52 31N 3 19W
Newtownabbey, *U.K.* **13 B6** 54 40N 5 56W
Newtownards, *U.K.* **13 B6** 54 36N 5 42W
Newtownbarry = Bunclody, *Ireland* **13 D5** 52 39N 6 40W
Newtownstewart, *U.K.* **13 B4** 54 43N 7 23W
Newville, *U.S.A.* **78 F7** 40 10N 77 24W
Neya, *Russia* **24 C7** 58 21N 43 49 E
Neyrīz, *Iran* **45 D7** 29 15N 54 19 E
Neyshābūr, *Iran* **45 B8** 36 10N 58 50 E
Nezhin = Nizhyn, *Ukraine* **25 D5** 51 5N 31 55 E
Nezperce, *U.S.A.* **82 C5** 46 14N 116 14W
Ngabang, *Indonesia* **36 D3** 0 23N 109 55 E
Ngabordamlu, Tanjung, *Indonesia* **37 F8** 6 56S 134 11 E
N'Gage, *Angola* **52 F3** 7 46S 15 16 E
Ngami Depression, *Botswana* **56 C3** 20 30S 22 46 E
Ngamo, *Zimbabwe* **55 F2** 19 3S 27 32 E
Nganglong Kangri, *China* **41 C12** 33 0N 81 0 E
Ngao, *Thailand* **38 C2** 18 46N 99 59 E
Ngaoundéré, *Cameroon* **52 C2** 7 15N 13 35 E
Ngapara, *N.Z.* **59 L3** 44 57S 170 46 E
Ngara, *Tanzania* **54 C3** 2 29S 30 40 E
Ngawi, *Indonesia* **37 G14** 7 24S 111 26 E
Nghia Lo, *Vietnam* **38 B5** 21 33N 104 28 E
Ngoma, *Malawi* **55 E3** 13 8S 33 45 E
Ngomahura, *Zimbabwe* **55 G3** 20 26S 30 43 E
Ngomba, *Tanzania* **55 D3** 8 20S 32 53 E
Ngoring Hu, *China* **32 C4** 34 55N 97 5 E
Ngorongoro, *Tanzania* **54 C4** 3 11S 35 32 E
Ngozi, *Burundi* **54 C2** 2 54S 29 50 E
Ngudu, *Tanzania* **54 C3** 2 58S 33 25 E
Nguigmi, *Niger* **51 F8** 14 20N 13 20 E
Nguiu, *Australia* **60 B5** 11 46S 130 38 E
Ngukurr, *Australia* **62 A1** 14 44S 134 44 E
Ngunga, *Tanzania* **54 C3** 3 37S 33 37 E
Nguru, *Nigeria* **51 F8** 12 56N 10 29 E
Nguru Mts., *Tanzania* **54 D4** 6 0S 37 30 E
Ngusi, *Malawi* **55 E3** 14 0S 34 50 E
Nguyen Binh, *Vietnam* **38 A5** 22 39N 105 56 E
Nha Trang, *Vietnam* **39 F7** 12 16N 109 10 E
Nhacoongo, *Mozam.* **57 C6** 24 18S 35 14 E
Nhamaabué, *Mozam.* **55 F4** 17 25S 35 5 E
Nhamundá →, *Brazil* **93 D7** 2 12S 56 41W
Nhangulaze, L., *Mozam.* **57 C5** 24 0S 34 30 E
Nhill, *Australia* **63 F3** 36 18S 141 40 E
Nho Quan, *Vietnam* **38 B5** 20 18N 105 45 E
Nhulunbuy, *Australia* **62 A2** 12 10S 137 20 E
Nia-nia, *Dem. Rep. of the Congo* **54 B2** 1 30N 27 40 E
Niagara Falls, *Canada* **78 C5** 43 7N 79 5W
Niagara Falls, *U.S.A.* **78 C6** 43 5N 79 4W
Niagara-on-the-Lake, *Canada* **78 C5** 43 15N 79 4W
Niah, *Malaysia* **36 D4** 3 58N 113 46 E
Niamey, *Niger* **50 F6** 13 27N 2 6 E
Niangara, *Dem. Rep. of the Congo* **54 B2** 3 42N 27 50 E
Niantic, *U.S.A.* **79 E12** 41 20N 72 11W
Nias, *Indonesia* **36 D1** 1 0N 97 30 E
Niassa □, *Mozam.* **55 E4** 13 30S 36 0 E
Nibāk, *Si. Arabia* **45 E7** 24 25N 50 50 E
Nicaragua ■, *Cent. Amer.* **88 D2** 11 40N 85 30W
Nicaragua, L. de, *Nic.* **88 D2** 12 0N 85 30W
Nicastro, *Italy* **20 E7** 38 59N 16 19 E
Nice, *France* **18 E7** 43 42N 7 14 E
Niceville, *U.S.A.* **77 K2** 30 31N 86 30W
Nichicun, L., *Canada* **71 B5** 53 5N 71 0W
Nichinan, *Japan* **31 J5** 31 38N 131 23 E
Nicholás, Canal, *W. Indies* **88 B3** 23 30N 80 5W
Nicholasville, *U.S.A.* **76 G3** 37 53N 84 34W
Nichols, *U.S.A.* **79 D8** 42 1N 76 22W
Nicholson, *Australia* **60 C4** 18 2S 128 54 E
Nicholson, *U.S.A.* **79 E9** 41 37N 75 47W
Nicholson →, *Australia* **62 B2** 17 31S 139 36 E
Nicholson L., *Canada* **73 A8** 62 40N 102 40W
Nicholson Ra., *Australia* **61 E2** 27 15S 116 45 E
Nicholville, *U.S.A.* **79 B10** 44 41N 74 39W
Nicobar Is., *Ind. Oc.* **29 J13** 8 0N 93 30 E
Nicola, *Canada* **72 C4** 50 12N 120 40W
Nicolls Town, *Bahamas* **88 A4** 25 8N 78 0W
Nicosia, *Cyprus* **23 D12** 35 10N 33 25 E
Nicoya, *Costa Rica* **88 D2** 10 9N 85 27W
Nicoya, G. de, *Costa Rica* **88 E3** 10 0N 85 0W
Nicoya, Pen. de, *Costa Rica* **88 E2** 9 45N 85 40W
Nidd →, *U.K.* **10 D6** 53 59N 1 23W
Niedersachsen □, *Germany* **16 B5** 52 50N 9 0 E
Niekerkshoop, *S. Africa* **56 D3** 29 19S 22 51 E
Niemba, *Dem. Rep. of the Congo* **54 D2** 5 58S 28 24 E
Niemen = Neman →, *Lithuania* **9 J19** 55 25N 21 10 E
Nienburg, *Germany* **16 B5** 52 39N 9 13 E
Nieu Bethesda, *S. Africa* **56 E3** 31 51S 24 34 E
Nieuw Amsterdam, *Surinam* **93 B7** 5 53N 55 5W
Nieuw Nickerie, *Surinam* **93 B7** 6 0N 56 59W
Nieuwoudtville, *S. Africa* **56 E2** 31 23S 19 7 E
Nieuwpoort, *Belgium* **15 C2** 51 8N 2 45 E
Nieves, Pico de las, *Canary Is.* **22 G4** 27 57N 15 35W
Niğde, *Turkey* **25 G5** 37 58N 34 40 E
Nigel, *S. Africa* **57 D4** 26 27S 28 25 E
Niger ■, *W. Afr.* **50 E7** 17 30N 10 0 E
Niger →, *W. Afr.* **50 G7** 5 33N 6 33 E
Nigeria ■, *W. Afr.* **50 G7** 8 30N 8 0 E
Nighasin, *India* **43 E9** 28 14N 80 52 E
Nightcaps, *N.Z.* **59 L2** 45 57S 168 2 E
Nii-Jima, *Japan* **31 G9** 34 20N 139 15 E
Niigata, *Japan* **30 F9** 37 58N 139 0 E
Niigata □, *Japan* **31 F9** 37 15N 138 45 E
Niihama, *Japan* **31 H6** 33 55N 133 16 E
Niihau, *U.S.A.* **74 H14** 21 54N 160 9W
Niimi, *Japan* **31 G6** 34 59N 133 28 E
Niitsu, *Japan* **30 F9** 37 48N 139 7 E
Nijil, *Jordan* **47 E4** 30 32N 35 33 E
Nijkerk, *Neths.* **15 B5** 52 13N 5 30 E
Nijmegen, *Neths.* **15 C5** 51 50N 5 52 E
Nijverdal, *Neths.* **15 B6** 52 22N 6 28 E
Nīk Pey, *Iran* **45 B6** 36 50N 48 10 E
Nikiniki, *Indonesia* **37 F6** 9 49S 124 30 E
Nikkō, *Japan* **31 F9** 36 45N 139 35 E
Nikolayev = Mykolayiv, *Ukraine* **25 E5** 46 58N 32 0 E
Nikolayevsk, *Russia* **25 E8** 50 0N 45 35 E
Nikolayevsk-na-Amur, *Russia* **27 D15** 53 8N 140 44 E
Nikolskoye, *Russia* **27 D17** 55 12N 166 0 E
Nikopol, *Ukraine* **25 E5** 47 35N 34 25 E
Nīkshahr, *Iran* **45 E9** 26 15N 60 10 E
Nikšić, *Montenegro, Yug.* **21 C8** 42 50N 18 57 E
Nîl, Nahr en →, *Africa* **51 B12** 30 10N 31 6 E
Nîl el Abyad →, *Sudan* **51 E12** 15 38N 32 31 E
Nîl el Azraq →, *Sudan* **51 E12** 15 38N 32 31 E
Nila, *Indonesia* **37 F7** 6 44S 129 31 E
Niland, *U.S.A.* **85 M11** 33 14N 115 31W
Nile = Nîl, Nahr en →, *Africa* **51 B12** 30 10N 31 6 E
Niles, *Mich., U.S.A.* **76 E2** 41 50N 86 15W
Niles, *Ohio, U.S.A.* **78 E4** 41 11N 80 46W
Nim Ka Thana, *India* **42 F6** 27 44N 75 48 E
Nimach, *India* **42 G6** 24 30N 74 56 E
Nimbahera, *India* **42 G6** 24 37N 74 45 E
Nîmes, *France* **18 E6** 43 50N 4 23 E
Nimfaíon, Ákra = Pínnes, Ákra, *Greece* **21 D11** 40 5N 24 20 E
Nimmitabel, *Australia* **63 F4** 36 29S 149 15 E
Nīnawá, *Iraq* **44 B4** 36 25N 43 10 E
Nindigully, *Australia* **63 D4** 28 21S 148 50 E
Nineveh = Nīnawá, *Iraq* **44 B4** 36 25N 43 10 E
Ning Xian, *China* **34 G4** 35 30N 107 58 E
Ning'an, *China* **35 B15** 44 22N 129 20 E
Ningbo, *China* **33 D7** 29 51N 121 28 E
Ningcheng, *China* **35 D10** 41 32N 119 53 E
Ningjin, *China* **34 F8** 37 35N 114 57 E
Ningjing Shan, *China* **32 D4** 30 0N 98 20 E
Ningling, *China* **34 G8** 34 25N 115 22 E
Ningpo = Ningbo, *China* **33 D7** 29 51N 121 28 E
Ningqiang, *China* **34 H4** 32 47N 106 15 E
Ningshan, *China* **34 H5** 33 21N 108 21 E
Ningsia Hui A.R. = Ningxia Huizu Zizhiqu □, *China* **34 F4** 38 0N 106 0 E
Ningwu, *China* **34 E7** 39 0N 112 18 E
Ningxia Huizu Zizhiqu □, *China* **34 F4** 38 0N 106 0 E
Ningyang, *China* **34 G9** 35 47N 116 45 E
Ninh Binh, *Vietnam* **38 B5** 20 15N 105 55 E
Ninh Giang, *Vietnam* **38 B6** 20 44N 106 24 E
Ninh Hoa, *Vietnam* **38 F7** 12 30N 109 7 E
Ninh Ma, *Vietnam* **38 F7** 12 48N 109 21 E
Ninove, *Belgium* **15 D4** 50 51N 4 2 E
Nioaque, *Brazil* **95 A4** 21 5S 55 50W
Niobrara, *U.S.A.* **80 D6** 42 45N 98 2W
Niobrara →, *U.S.A.* **80 D6** 42 46N 98 3W
Nioro du Sahel, *Mali* **50 E4** 15 15N 9 30W
Niort, *France* **18 C3** 46 19N 0 29W
Nipawin, *Canada* **73 C8** 53 20N 104 0W
Nipigon, *Canada* **70 C2** 49 0N 88 17W
Nipigon, L., *Canada* **70 C2** 49 50N 88 30W
Nipishish L., *Canada* **71 B7** 54 12N 60 45W
Nipissing, L., *Canada* **70 C4** 46 20N 80 0W
Nipomo, *U.S.A.* **85 K6** 35 3N 120 29W
Nipton, *U.S.A.* **85 K11** 35 28N 115 16W
Niquelândia, *Brazil* **93 F9** 14 33S 48 23W
Nīr, *Iran* **44 B5** 38 2N 47 59 E
Nirasaki, *Japan* **31 G9** 35 42N 138 27 E
Nirmal, *India* **40 K11** 19 3N 78 20 E
Nirmali, *India* **43 F12** 26 20N 86 35 E
Niš, *Serbia, Yug.* **21 C9** 43 19N 21 58 E
Nişāb, *Si. Arabia* **44 D5** 29 11N 44 43 E
Nişāb, *Yemen* **46 E4** 14 25N 46 29 E
Nishinomiya, *Japan* **31 G7** 34 45N 135 20 E
Nishin'omote, *Japan* **31 J5** 30 43N 130 59 E
Nishiwaki, *Japan* **31 G7** 34 59N 134 58 E
Niskibi →, *Canada* **70 A2** 56 29N 88 9W
Nisqually →, *U.S.A.* **84 C4** 47 6N 122 42W
Nissáki, *Greece* **23 A3** 39 43N 19 52 E
Nissum Bredning, *Denmark* **9 H13** 56 40N 8 20 E
Nistru = Dnister →, *Europe* **17 E16** 46 18N 30 17 E
Nisutlin →, *Canada* **72 A2** 60 14N 132 34W
Nitchequon, *Canada* **71 B5** 53 10N 70 58W
Niterói, *Brazil* **95 A7** 22 52S 43 0W
Nith →, *Canada* **78 C4** 43 12N 80 23W
Nith →, *U.K.* **12 F5** 55 14N 3 33W
Nitra, *Slovak Rep.* **17 D10** 48 19N 18 4 E
Nitra →, *Slovak Rep.* **17 E10** 47 46N 18 10 E
Niuafo'ou, *Tonga* **59 B11** 15 30S 175 58W
Niue, *Cook Is.* **65 J11** 19 2S 169 54W
Niut, *Indonesia* **36 D4** 0 55N 110 6 E
Niuzhuang, *China* **35 D12** 40 58N 122 28 E
Nivala, *Finland* **8 E21** 63 56N 24 57 E
Nivelles, *Belgium* **15 D4** 50 35N 4 20 E
Nivernais, *France* **18 C5** 47 15N 3 30 E
Niwas, *India* **43 H9** 23 3N 80 26 E
Nixon, *U.S.A.* **81 L6** 29 16N 97 46W
Nizamabad, *India* **40 K11** 18 45N 78 7 E
Nizamghat, *India* **41 E19** 28 20N 95 45 E
Nizhne Kolymsk, *Russia* **27 C17** 68 34N 160 55 E
Nizhnekamsk, *Russia* **24 C9** 55 38N 51 49 E
Nizhneudinsk, *Russia* **27 D10** 54 54N 99 3 E
Nizhnevartovsk, *Russia* **26 C8** 60 56N 76 38 E
Nizhniy Novgorod, *Russia* **24 C7** 56 20N 44 0 E
Nizhniy Tagil, *Russia* **24 C10** 57 55N 59 57 E
Nizhyn, *Ukraine* **25 D5** 51 5N 31 55 E
Nizip, *Turkey* **44 B3** 37 5N 37 50 E
Nízké Tatry, *Slovak Rep.* **17 D10** 48 55N 19 30 E
Njakwa, *Malawi* **55 E3** 11 1S 33 56 E
Njanji, *Zambia* **55 E3** 14 25S 31 46 E
Njinjo, *Tanzania* **55 D4** 8 48S 38 54 E
Njombe, *Tanzania* **55 D3** 9 20S 34 50 E
Njombe →, *Tanzania* **54 D4** 6 56S 35 6 E
Nkana, *Zambia* **55 E2** 12 50S 28 8 E
Nkandla, *S. Africa* **57 D5** 28 37S 31 5 E
Nkayi, *Zimbabwe* **55 F2** 19 41S 29 20 E
Nkhotakota, *Malawi* **55 E3** 12 56S 34 15 E
Nkongsamba, *Cameroon* **52 D1** 4 55N 9 55 E
Nkurenkuru, *Namibia* **56 B2** 17 42S 18 32 E
Nmai →, *Burma* **41 G20** 25 30N 97 25 E
Noakhali = Maijdi, *Bangla.* **41 H17** 22 48N 91 10 E
Nobel, *Canada* **78 A4** 45 25N 80 6W
Nobeoka, *Japan* **31 H5** 32 36N 131 41 E
Noblesville, *U.S.A.* **76 E3** 40 3N 86 1W
Nocera Inferiore, *Italy* **20 D6** 40 44N 14 38 E
Nocona, *U.S.A.* **81 J6** 33 47N 97 44W
Noda, *Japan* **31 G9** 35 56N 139 52 E
Nogales, *Mexico* **86 A2** 31 20N 110 56W
Nogales, *U.S.A.* **83 L8** 31 20N 110 56W
Nōgata, *Japan* **31 H5** 33 48N 130 44 E
Noggerup, *Australia* **61 F2** 33 32S 116 5 E
Noginsk, *Russia* **27 C10** 64 30N 90 50 E
Nogoa →, *Australia* **62 C4** 23 40S 147 55 E
Nogoyá, *Argentina* **94 C4** 32 24S 59 48W
Nohar, *India* **42 E6** 29 11N 74 49 E
Nohta, *India* **43 H8** 23 40N 79 34 E
Noires, Mts., *France* **18 B2** 48 11N 3 40W
Noirmoutier, Î. de, *France* **18 C2** 46 58N 2 10W
Nojane, *Botswana* **56 C3** 23 15S 20 14 E
Nojima-Zaki, *Japan* **31 G9** 34 54N 139 53 E
Nok Kundi, *Pakistan* **40 E3** 28 50N 62 45 E
Nokaneng, *Botswana* **56 B3** 19 40S 22 17 E
Nokia, *Finland* **9 F20** 61 30N 23 30 E
Nokomis, *Canada* **73 C8** 51 35N 105 0W
Nokomis L., *Canada* **73 B8** 57 0N 103 0W
Nola, *C.A.R.* **52 D3** 3 35N 16 4 E
Noma Omuramba →, *Namibia* **56 B3** 18 52S 20 53 E
Nombre de Dios, *Panama* **88 E4** 9 34N 79 28W
Nome, *U.S.A.* **68 B3** 64 30N 165 25W
Nomo-Zaki, *Japan* **31 H4** 32 35N 129 44 E
Nonacho L., *Canada* **73 A7** 61 42N 109 40W
Nonda, *Australia* **62 C3** 20 40S 142 28 E
Nong Chang, *Thailand* **38 E2** 15 23N 99 51 E
Nong Het, *Laos* **38 C4** 19 29N 103 59 E
Nong Khai, *Thailand* **38 D4** 17 50N 102 46 E
Nong'an, *China* **35 B13** 44 25N 125 5 E
Nongoma, *S. Africa* **57 D5** 27 58S 31 35 E
Nonoava, *Mexico* **86 B3** 27 28N 106 44W
Nonoava →, *Mexico* **86 B3** 27 29N 106 45W
Nonthaburi, *Thailand* **38 F3** 13 51N 100 34 E
Noonamah, *Australia* **60 B5** 12 40S 131 4 E
Noord Brabant □, *Neths.* **15 C5** 51 40N 5 0 E
Noord Holland □, *Neths.* **15 B4** 52 30N 4 45 E
Noordbeveland, *Neths.* **15 C3** 51 35N 3 50 E
Noordoostpolder, *Neths.* **15 B5** 52 45N 5 45 E
Noordwijk, *Neths.* **15 B4** 52 14N 4 26 E
Nootka I., *Canada* **72 D3** 49 32N 126 42W
Nopiming Prov. Park, *Canada* **73 C9** 50 30N 95 37W
Noralee, *Canada* **72 C3** 53 59N 126 26W
Noranda = Rouyn-Noranda, *Canada* **70 C4** 48 20N 79 0W
Norco, *U.S.A.* **85 M9** 33 56N 117 33W
Nord-Kivu □, *Dem. Rep. of the Congo* **54 C2** 1 0S 29 0 E
Nord-Ostsee-Kanal, *Germany* **16 A5** 54 12N 9 32 E
Nordaustlandet, *Svalbard* **4 B9** 79 14N 23 0 E
Nordegg, *Canada* **72 C5** 52 29N 116 5W
Norderney, *Germany* **16 B4** 53 42N 7 9 E
Norderstedt, *Germany* **16 B5** 53 42N 10 1 E

Nordfjord, *Norway* 9 F11 61 55N 5 30 E
Nordfriesische Inseln, *Germany* 16 A5 54 40N 8 20 E
Nordhausen, *Germany* 16 C6 51 30N 10 47 E
Norðoyar, *Færoe Is.* 8 E9 62 17N 6 35W
Nordkapp, *Norway* 8 A21 71 10N 25 50 E
Nordkapp, *Svalbard* 4 A9 80 31N 20 0 E
Nordkinn = Kinnarodden, *Norway* 6 A11 71 8N 27 40 E
Nordkinn-halvøya, *Norway* 8 A22 70 55N 27 40 E
Nordrhein-Westfalen □, *Germany* 16 C4 51 45N 7 30 E
Nordvik, *Russia* 27 B12 74 2N 111 32 E
Nore ↝, *Ireland* 13 D4 52 25N 6 58W
Norfolk, *Nebr., U.S.A.* 80 D6 42 2N 97 25W
Norfolk, *Va., U.S.A.* 76 G7 36 51N 76 17W
Norfolk □, *U.K.* 11 E8 52 39N 0 54 E
Norfolk I., *Pac. Oc.* 64 K8 28 58S 168 3 E
Norfork L., *U.S.A.* 81 G8 36 15N 92 14W
Norilsk, *Russia* 27 C9 69 20N 88 6 E
Norma, Mt., *Australia* 62 C3 20 55S 140 42 E
Normal, *U.S.A.* 80 E10 40 31N 88 59W
Norman, *U.S.A.* 81 H6 35 13N 97 26W
Norman ↝, *Australia* 62 B3 19 18S 141 51 E
Norman Wells, *Canada* 68 B7 65 17N 126 51W
Normanby ↝, *Australia* 62 A3 14 23S 144 10 E
Normandie, *France* 18 B4 48 45N 0 10 E
Normandin, *Canada* 70 C5 48 49N 72 31W
Normandy = Normandie, *France* 18 B4 48 45N 0 10 E
Normanhurst, Mt., *Australia* 61 E3 25 4S 122 30 E
Normanton, *Australia* 62 B3 17 40S 141 10 E
Normétal, *Canada* 70 C4 49 0N 79 22W
Norquay, *Canada* 73 C8 51 53N 102 5W
Norquinco, *Argentina* 96 E2 41 51S 70 55W
Norrbotten □, *Sweden* 8 C19 66 30N 22 30 E
Norris Point, *Canada* 71 C8 49 31N 57 53W
Norristown, *U.S.A.* 79 F9 40 7N 75 21W
Norrköping, *Sweden* 9 G17 58 37N 16 11 E
Norrland, *Sweden* 9 E16 62 15N 15 45 E
Norrtälje, *Sweden* 9 G18 59 46N 18 42 E
Norseman, *Australia* 61 F3 32 8S 121 43 E
Norsk, *Russia* 27 D14 52 30N 130 5 E
Norte, Pta. del, *Canary Is.* 22 G2 27 51N 17 57W
Norte, Serra do, *Brazil* 92 F7 11 20S 59 0W
North, C., *Canada* 71 C7 47 2N 60 20W
North Adams, *U.S.A.* 79 D11 42 42N 73 7W
North Arm, *Canada* 72 A5 62 0N 114 30W
North Augusta, *U.S.A.* 77 J5 33 30N 81 59W
North Ayrshire □, *U.K.* 12 F4 55 45N 4 44W
North Bass I., *U.S.A.* 78 E2 41 44N 82 53W
North Battleford, *Canada* 73 C7 52 50N 108 17W
North Bay, *Canada* 70 C4 46 20N 79 30W
North Belcher Is., *Canada* 70 A4 56 50N 79 50W
North Bend, *Oreg., U.S.A.* 82 E1 43 24N 124 14W
North Bend, *Pa., U.S.A.* 78 E7 41 20N 77 42W
North Bend, *Wash., U.S.A.* 84 C5 47 30N 121 47W
North Bennington, *U.S.A.* 79 D11 42 56N 73 15W
North Berwick, *U.K.* 12 E6 56 4N 2 42W
North Berwick, *U.S.A.* 79 C14 43 18N 70 44W
North C., *Canada* 71 C7 47 5N 64 0W
North C., *N.Z.* 59 F4 34 23S 173 4 E
North Canadian ↝, *U.S.A.* 81 H7 35 16N 95 31W
North Canton, *U.S.A.* 78 F3 40 53N 81 24W
North Cape = Nordkapp, *Norway* 8 A21 71 10N 25 50 E
North Cape = Nordkapp, *Svalbard* 4 A9 80 31N 20 0 E
North Caribou L., *Canada* 70 B1 52 50N 90 40W
North Carolina □, *U.S.A.* 77 H6 35 30N 80 0W
North Cascades Nat. Park, *U.S.A.* 82 B3 48 45N 121 10W
North Channel, *Canada* 70 C3 46 0N 83 0W
North Channel, *U.K.* 12 F3 55 13N 5 52W
North Charleston, *U.S.A.* 77 J6 32 53N 79 58W
North Chicago, *U.S.A.* 76 D2 42 19N 87 51W
North Creek, *U.S.A.* 79 C11 43 41N 73 59W
North Dakota □, *U.S.A.* 80 B5 47 30N 100 15W
North Downs, *U.K.* 11 F8 51 19N 0 21 E
North East, *U.S.A.* 78 D5 42 13N 79 50W
North East Frontier Agency = Arunachal Pradesh □, *India* 41 F19 28 0N 95 0 E
North East Lincolnshire □, *U.K.* 10 D7 53 34N 0 2W
North Eastern □, *Kenya* 54 B5 1 30N 40 0 E
North Esk ↝, *U.K.* 12 E6 56 46N 2 24W
North European Plain, *Europe* 6 E10 55 0N 25 0 E
North Foreland, *U.K.* 11 F9 51 22N 1 28 E
North Fork, *U.S.A.* 84 H7 37 14N 119 21W
North Fork American ↝, *U.S.A.* 84 G5 38 57N 120 59W
North Fork Feather ↝, *U.S.A.* 84 F5 38 33N 121 30W
North Fork Grand ↝, *U.S.A.* 80 C3 45 47N 102 16W
North Fork Red ↝, *U.S.A.* 81 H5 34 24N 99 14W
North Frisian Is. = Nordfriesische Inseln, *Germany* 16 A5 54 40N 8 20 E
North Gower, *Canada* 79 A9 45 8N 75 43W
North Hd., *Australia* 61 F1 30 14S 114 59 E
North Henik L., *Canada* 73 A9 61 45N 97 40W
North Highlands, *U.S.A.* 84 G5 38 40N 121 23W
North Horr, *Kenya* 54 B4 3 20N 37 8 E
North I., *Kenya* 54 B4 4 5N 36 5 E
North I., *N.Z.* 59 H5 38 0S 175 0 E
North Kingsville, *U.S.A.* 78 E4 41 54N 80 42W
North Knife ↝, *Canada* 73 B10 58 53N 94 45W
North Koel ↝, *India* 43 G10 24 45N 83 50 E
North Korea ■, *Asia* 35 E14 40 0N 127 0 E
North Lakhimpur, *India* 41 F19 27 14N 94 7 E
North Lanarkshire □, *U.K.* 12 F5 55 52N 3 56W
North Las Vegas, *U.S.A.* 85 J11 36 12N 115 7W
North Lincolnshire □, *U.K.* 10 D7 53 36N 0 30W
North Little Rock, *U.S.A.* 81 H8 34 45N 92 16W
North Loup ↝, *U.S.A.* 80 E5 41 17N 98 24W
North Magnetic Pole, *Canada* 4 B2 77 58N 102 8W
North Minch, *U.K.* 12 C3 58 5N 5 55W
North Moose L., *Canada* 73 C8 54 11N 100 6W
North Myrtle Beach, *U.S.A.* 77 J6 33 48N 78 42W
North Nahanni ↝, *Canada* 72 A4 62 15N 123 20W
North Olmsted, *U.S.A.* 78 E3 41 25N 81 56W
North Ossetia □, *Russia* 25 F7 43 30N 44 30 E
North Pagai, I. = Pagai Utara, Pulau, *Indonesia* 36 E2 2 35S 100 0 E
North Palisade, *U.S.A.* 84 H8 37 6N 118 31W
North Platte, *U.S.A.* 80 E4 41 8N 100 46W
North Platte ↝, *U.S.A.* 80 E4 41 7N 100 42W
North Pole, *Arctic* 4 A 90 0N 0 0W
North Portal, *Canada* 73 D8 49 0N 102 33W
North Powder, *U.S.A.* 82 D5 45 2N 117 55W
North Pt., *U.S.A.* 78 A1 45 2N 83 16W
North Rhine Westphalia = Nordrhein-Westfalen □, *Germany* 16 C4 51 45N 7 30 E
North River, *Canada* 71 B8 53 49N 57 6W
North Ronaldsay, *U.K.* 12 B6 59 22N 2 26W
North Saskatchewan ↝, *Canada* 73 C7 53 15N 105 5W
North Sea, *Europe* 6 D6 56 0N 4 0 E
North Seal ↝, *Canada* 73 B9 58 50N 98 7W
North Somerset □, *U.K.* 11 F5 51 24N 2 45W
North Sporades = Vóriai Sporádhes, *Greece* 21 E10 39 15N 23 30 E
North Sydney, *Canada* 71 C7 46 12N 60 15W
North Syracuse, *U.S.A.* 79 C8 43 8N 76 7W
North Taranaki Bight, *N.Z.* 59 H5 38 50S 174 15 E
North Thompson ↝, *Canada* 72 C4 50 40N 120 20W
North Tonawanda, *U.S.A.* 78 C6 43 2N 78 53W
North Troy, *U.S.A.* 79 B12 45 0N 72 24W
North Truchas Pk., *U.S.A.* 83 J11 36 0N 105 30W
North Twin I., *Canada* 70 B4 53 20N 80 0W
North Tyne ↝, *U.K.* 10 B5 55 0N 2 8W
North Uist, *U.K.* 12 D1 57 40N 7 15W
North Vancouver, *Canada* 72 D4 49 19N 123 4W
North Vernon, *U.S.A.* 76 F3 39 0N 85 38W
North Wabasca L., *Canada* 72 B6 56 0N 113 55W
North Walsham, *U.K.* 10 E9 52 50N 1 22 E
North-West □, *S. Africa* 56 D4 27 0S 25 0 E
North West C., *Australia* 60 D1 21 45S 114 9 E
North West Christmas I. Ridge, *Pac. Oc.* 65 G11 6 30N 165 0W
North West Frontier □, *Pakistan* 42 C4 34 0N 72 0 E
North West Highlands, *U.K.* 12 D4 57 33N 4 58W
North West River, *Canada* 71 B7 53 30N 60 10W
North Western □, *Zambia* 55 E2 13 30S 25 30 E
North Wildwood, *U.S.A.* 76 F8 39 0N 74 48W
North York Moors, *U.K.* 10 C7 54 23N 0 53W
North Yorkshire □, *U.K.* 10 C6 54 15N 1 25W
Northallerton, *U.K.* 10 C6 54 20N 1 26W
Northam, *Australia* 61 F2 31 35S 116 42 E
Northam, *S. Africa* 56 C4 24 56S 27 18 E
Northampton, *Australia* 61 E1 28 27S 114 33 E
Northampton, *U.K.* 11 E7 52 15N 0 53W
Northampton, *Mass., U.S.A.* 79 D12 42 19N 72 38W
Northampton, *Pa., U.S.A.* 79 F9 40 41N 75 30W
Northamptonshire □, *U.K.* 11 E7 52 16N 0 55W
Northbridge, *U.S.A.* 79 D13 42 9N 71 39W
Northcliffe, *Australia* 61 F2 34 39S 116 7 E
Northeast Providence Chan., *W. Indies* 88 A4 26 0N 76 0W
Northern □, *Malawi* 55 E3 11 0S 34 0 E
Northern □, *Zambia* 55 E3 10 30S 31 0 E
Northern Areas □, *Pakistan* 43 A5 36 30N 73 0 E
Northern Cape □, *S. Africa* 56 D3 30 0S 20 0 E
Northern Circars, *India* 41 L13 17 30N 82 30 E
Northern Indian L., *Canada* 73 B9 57 20N 97 20W
Northern Ireland □, *U.K.* 13 B5 54 45N 7 0W
Northern Light L., *Canada* 70 C1 48 15N 90 39W
Northern Marianas ■, *Pac. Oc.* 64 F6 17 0N 145 0 E
Northern Province □, *S. Africa* 57 C4 24 0S 29 0 E
Northern Territory □, *Australia* 60 D5 20 0S 133 0 E
Northfield, *Minn., U.S.A.* 80 C8 44 27N 93 9W
Northfield, *Vt., U.S.A.* 79 B12 44 9N 72 40W
Northland □, *N.Z.* 59 F4 35 30S 173 30 E
Northome, *U.S.A.* 80 B7 47 52N 94 17W
Northport, *Ala., U.S.A.* 77 J2 33 14N 87 35W
Northport, *Wash., U.S.A.* 82 B5 48 55N 117 48W
Northumberland □, *U.K.* 10 B6 55 12N 2 0W
Northumberland, C., *Australia* 63 F3 38 5S 140 40 E
Northumberland Is., *Australia* 62 C4 21 30S 149 50 E
Northumberland Str., *Canada* 71 C7 46 20N 64 0W
Northville, *U.S.A.* 79 C10 43 13N 74 11W
Northwest Providence Channel, *W. Indies* 88 A4 26 0N 78 0W
Northwest Territories □, *Canada* 68 B9 63 0N 118 0W
Northwood, *Iowa, U.S.A.* 80 D8 43 27N 93 13W
Northwood, *N. Dak., U.S.A.* 80 B6 47 44N 97 34W
Norton, *U.S.A.* 80 F5 39 50N 99 53W
Norton, *Zimbabwe* 55 F3 17 52S 30 40 E
Norton Sd., *U.S.A.* 68 B3 63 50N 164 0W
Norwalk, *Calif., U.S.A.* 85 M8 33 54N 118 5W
Norwalk, *Conn., U.S.A.* 79 E11 41 7N 73 22W
Norwalk, *Iowa, U.S.A.* 80 E8 41 29N 93 41W
Norwalk, *Ohio, U.S.A.* 78 E2 41 15N 82 37W
Norway, *Maine, U.S.A.* 77 C10 44 13N 70 32W
Norway, *Mich., U.S.A.* 76 C2 45 47N 87 55W
Norway ■, *Europe* 8 E14 63 0N 11 0 E
Norway House, *Canada* 73 C9 53 59N 97 50W
Norwegian Sea, *Atl. Oc.* 4 C8 66 0N 1 0 E
Norwich, *Canada* 78 D4 42 59N 80 36W
Norwich, *U.K.* 11 E9 52 38N 1 18 E
Norwich, *Conn., U.S.A.* 79 E12 41 31N 72 5W
Norwich, *N.Y., U.S.A.* 79 D9 42 32N 75 32W
Norwood, *Canada* 78 B7 44 23N 77 59W
Norwood, *U.S.A.* 79 B10 44 45N 75 0W
Noshiro, *Japan* 30 D10 40 12N 140 0 E
Nosratābād, *Iran* 45 D8 29 55N 60 0 E
Noss Hd., *U.K.* 12 C5 58 28N 3 3W
Nossob ↝, *S. Africa* 56 D3 26 55S 20 45 E
Nosy Barren, *Madag.* 53 H8 18 25S 43 40 E
Nosy Be, *Madag.* 53 G9 13 25S 48 15 E
Nosy Boraha, *Madag.* 57 B8 16 50S 49 55 E
Nosy Lava, *Madag.* 57 A8 14 33S 47 36 E
Nosy Varika, *Madag.* 57 C8 20 35S 48 32 E
Noteć ↝, *Poland* 16 B8 52 44N 15 26 E
Notikewin ↝, *Canada* 72 B5 57 2N 117 38W
Notodden, *Norway* 9 G13 59 35N 9 17 E
Notre Dame B., *Canada* 71 C8 49 45N 55 30W
Notre Dame de Koartac = Quaqtaq, *Canada* 69 B13 60 55N 69 40W
Notre-Dame-des-Bois, *Canada* 79 A13 45 24N 71 4W
Notre Dame d'Ivugivic = Ivujivik, *Canada* 69 B12 62 24N 77 55W
Notre-Dame-du-Nord, *Canada* 70 C4 47 36N 79 30W
Nottawasaga B., *Canada* 78 B4 44 35N 80 15W
Nottaway ↝, *Canada* 70 B4 51 22N 78 55W
Nottingham, *U.K.* 10 E6 52 58N 1 10W
Nottingham, City of □, *U.K.* 10 E6 52 58N 1 10W
Nottingham I., *Canada* 69 B12 63 20N 77 55W
Nottinghamshire □, *U.K.* 10 D6 53 10N 1 3W
Nottoway ↝, *U.S.A.* 76 G7 36 33N 76 55W
Notwane ↝, *Botswana* 56 C4 23 35S 26 58 E
Nouâdhibou, *Mauritania* 50 D2 20 54N 17 0W
Nouâdhibou, Ras, *Mauritania* 50 D2 20 50N 17 0W
Nouakchott, *Mauritania* 50 E2 18 9N 15 58W
Nouméa, *N. Cal.* 64 K8 22 17S 166 30 E
Noupoort, *S. Africa* 56 E3 31 10S 24 57 E
Nouveau Comptoir = Wemindji, *Canada* 70 B4 53 0N 78 49W
Nouvelle-Amsterdam, I., *Ind. Oc.* 3 F13 38 30S 77 30 E
Nouvelle-Calédonie = New Caledonia ■, *Pac. Oc.* 64 K8 21 0S 165 0 E
Nova Casa Nova, *Brazil* 93 E10 9 25S 41 5W
Nova Esperança, *Brazil* 95 A5 23 8S 52 24W
Nova Friburgo, *Brazil* 95 A7 22 16S 42 30W
Nova Gaia = Cambundi-Catembo, *Angola* 52 G3 10 10S 17 35 E
Nova Iguaçu, *Brazil* 95 A7 22 45S 43 28W
Nova Iorque, *Brazil* 93 E10 7 0S 44 5W
Nova Lima, *Brazil* 95 A7 19 59S 43 51W
Nova Lisboa = Huambo, *Angola* 53 G3 12 42S 15 54 E
Nova Lusitânia, *Mozam.* 55 F3 19 50S 34 34 E
Nova Mambone, *Mozam.* 57 C6 21 0S 35 3 E
Nova Scotia □, *Canada* 71 C7 45 10N 63 0W
Nova Sofala, *Mozam.* 57 C5 20 7S 34 42 E
Nova Venécia, *Brazil* 93 G10 18 45S 40 24W
Nova Zagora, *Bulgaria* 21 C11 42 32N 26 1 E
Novar, *Canada* 78 A5 45 27N 79 15W
Novara, *Italy* 18 D8 45 28N 8 38 E
Novato, *U.S.A.* 84 G4 38 6N 122 35W
Novaya Ladoga, *Russia* 24 B5 60 7N 32 16 E
Novaya Lyalya, *Russia* 24 C11 59 4N 60 45 E
Novaya Sibir, Ostrov, *Russia* 27 B16 75 10N 150 0 E
Novaya Zemlya, *Russia* 26 B6 75 0N 56 0 E
Nové Zámky, *Slovak Rep.* 17 D10 48 2N 18 8 E
Novgorod, *Russia* 24 C5 58 30N 31 25 E
Novgorod-Severskiy = Novhorod-Siverskyy, *Ukraine* 24 D5 52 2N 33 10 E
Novhorod-Siverskyy, *Ukraine* 24 D5 52 2N 33 10 E
Novi Lígure, *Italy* 18 D8 44 46N 8 47 E
Novi Pazar, *Serbia, Yug.* 21 C9 43 12N 20 28 E
Novi Sad, *Serbia, Yug.* 21 B8 45 18N 19 52 E
Novo Hamburgo, *Brazil* 95 B5 29 37S 51 7W
Novo Mesto, *Slovenia* 20 B6 45 47N 15 12 E
Novo Remanso, *Brazil* 93 E10 9 41S 42 4W
Novoataysk, *Russia* 26 D9 53 30N 84 0 E
Novocherkassk, *Russia* 25 E7 47 27N 40 15 E
Novogrudok = Navahrudak, *Belarus* 17 B13 53 40N 25 50 E
Novohrad-Volynskyy, *Ukraine* 17 C14 50 34N 27 35 E
Novokachalinsk, *Russia* 30 B6 45 5N 132 0 E
Novokazalinsk = Zhangaqazaly, *Kazakstan* 26 E7 45 48N 62 6 E
Novokuybyshevsk, *Russia* 24 D8 53 7N 49 58 E
Novokuznetsk, *Russia* 26 D9 53 45N 87 10 E
Novomoskovsk, *Russia* 24 D6 54 5N 38 15 E
Novorossiysk, *Russia* 25 F6 44 43N 37 46 E
Novorybnoye, *Russia* 27 B11 72 50N 105 50 E
Novoselytsya, *Ukraine* 17 D14 48 14N 26 15 E
Novoshakhtinsk, *Russia* 25 E6 47 46N 39 58 E
Novosibirsk, *Russia* 26 D9 55 0N 83 5 E
Novosibirskiye Ostrova, *Russia* 27 B15 75 0N 142 0 E
Novotroitsk, *Russia* 24 D10 51 10N 58 15 E
Novouzensk, *Russia* 25 D8 50 32N 48 17 E
Novovolynsk, *Ukraine* 17 C13 50 45N 24 4 E
Novska, *Croatia* 20 B7 45 19N 17 0 E
Novvy Urengoy, *Russia* 26 C8 65 48N 76 52 E
Novyy Bor, *Russia* 24 A9 66 43N 52 19 E
Novyy Port, *Russia* 26 C8 67 40N 72 30 E
Now Shahr, *Iran* 45 B6 36 40N 51 30 E
Nowa Sól, *Poland* 16 C8 51 48N 15 44 E
Nowata, *U.S.A.* 81 G7 36 42N 95 38W
Nowbarān, *Iran* 45 C6 35 8N 49 42 E
Nowghāb, *Iran* 45 C8 33 53N 59 4 E
Nowgong, *Assam, India* 41 F18 26 20N 92 50 E
Nowgong, *Mad. P., India* 43 G8 25 4N 79 27 E
Nowra, *Australia* 63 E5 34 53S 150 35 E
Nowshera, *Pakistan* 40 C8 34 0N 72 0 E
Nowy Sącz, *Poland* 17 D11 49 40N 20 41 E
Nowy Targ, *Poland* 17 D11 49 29N 20 2 E
Nowy Tomyśl, *Poland* 16 B9 52 19N 16 10 E
Noxen, *U.S.A.* 79 E8 41 25N 76 4W
Noxon, *U.S.A.* 82 C6 48 0N 115 43W
Noyabr'sk, *Russia* 26 C8 64 34N 76 21 E
Noyon, *France* 18 B5 49 34N 2 59 E
Noyon, *Mongolia* 34 C2 43 2N 102 4 E
Nqutu, *S. Africa* 57 D5 28 13S 30 32 E
Nsanje, *Malawi* 55 F4 16 55S 35 12 E
Nsomba, *Zambia* 55 E2 10 45S 29 51 E
Nu Jiang ↝, *China* 32 D4 29 58N 97 25 E
Nu Shan, *China* 32 D4 26 0N 99 20 E
Nubia, *Africa* 48 D7 21 0N 32 0 E
Nubian Desert = Nûbîya, Es Sahrâ en, *Sudan* 51 D12 21 30N 33 30 E
Nûbîya, Es Sahrâ en, *Sudan* 51 D12 21 30N 33 30 E
Nuboai, *Indonesia* 37 E9 2 10S 136 30 E
Nubra ↝, *India* 43 B7 34 35N 77 35 E
Nueces ↝, *U.S.A.* 81 M6 27 51N 97 30W
Nueltin L., *Canada* 73 A9 60 30N 99 30W
Nueva Asunción □, *Paraguay* 94 A3 21 0S 61 0W
Nueva Gerona, *Cuba* 88 B3 21 53N 82 49W
Nueva Palmira, *Uruguay* 94 C4 33 52S 58 20W
Nueva Rosita, *Mexico* 86 B4 28 0N 101 11W
Nueva San Salvador, *El Salv.* 88 D2 13 40N 89 18W
Nuéve de Julio, *Argentina* 94 D3 35 30S 61 0W
Nuevitas, *Cuba* 88 B4 21 30N 77 20W
Nuevo, G., *Argentina* 96 E4 43 0S 64 30W
Nuevo Casas Grandes, *Mexico* 86 A3 30 22N 108 0W
Nuevo Guerrero, *Mexico* 87 B5 26 34N 99 15W
Nuevo Laredo, *Mexico* 87 B5 27 30N 99 30W
Nuevo León □, *Mexico* 86 C5 25 0N 100 0W
Nuevo Rocafuerte, *Ecuador* 92 D3 0 55S 75 27W
Nugget Pt., *N.Z.* 59 M2 46 27S 169 50 E
Nuhaka, *N.Z.* 59 H6 39 3S 177 45 E
Nukey Bluff, *Australia* 63 E2 32 26S 135 29 E
Nukhuyb, *Iraq* 44 C4 32 4N 42 3 E
Nuku'alofa, *Tonga* 59 E12 21 10S 174 0W
Nukus, *Uzbekistan* 26 E6 42 27N 59 41 E
Nullagine, *Australia* 60 D3 21 53S 120 7 E
Nullagine ↝, *Australia* 60 D3 21 20S 120 20 E
Nullarbor, *Australia* 61 F5 31 28S 130 55 E
Nullarbor Plain, *Australia* 61 F4 31 10S 129 0 E
Numalla, L., *Australia* 63 D3 28 43S 144 20 E
Numan, *Nigeria* 51 G8 9 29N 12 3 E
Numata, *Japan* 31 F9 36 45N 139 4 E
Numazu, *Japan* 31 G9 35 7N 138 51 E
Numbulwar, *Australia* 62 A2 14 15S 135 45 E
Numfoor, *Indonesia* 37 E8 1 0S 134 50 E
Numurkah, *Australia* 63 F4 36 5S 145 26 E
Nunaksaluk I., *Canada* 71 A7 55 49N 60 20W
Nunap Isua, *Greenland* 69 C15 59 48N 43 55W
Nunavut □, *Canada* 69 B11 66 0N 85 0W
Nunda, *U.S.A.* 78 D7 42 35N 77 56W
Nungarin, *Australia* 61 F2 31 12S 118 6 E
Nungo, *Mozam.* 55 E4 13 23S 37 43 E
Nungwe, *Tanzania* 54 C3 2 48S 32 2 E
Nunivak I., *U.S.A.* 68 B3 60 10N 166 30W
Nunkun, *India* 43 C7 33 57N 76 2 E
Nùoro, *Italy* 20 D3 40 20N 9 20 E
Nūrābād, *Iran* 45 E8 27 47N 57 12 E
Nuremberg = Nürnberg, *Germany* 16 D6 49 27N 11 3 E
Nuri, *Mexico* 86 B3 28 2N 109 22W
Nuriootpa, *Australia* 63 E2 34 27S 139 0 E
Nuristān □, *Afghan.* 40 B7 35 20N 71 0 E
Nurmes, *Finland* 8 E23 63 33N 29 10 E
Nürnberg, *Germany* 16 D6 49 27N 11 3 E
Nurpur, *Pakistan* 42 D4 31 53N 71 54 E
Nurran, L. = Terewah, L., *Australia* 63 D4 29 52S 147 35 E
Nurrari Lakes, *Australia* 61 E5 29 1S 130 5 E
Nusa Barung, *Indonesia* 37 H15 8 30S 113 30 E
Nusa Kambangan, *Indonesia* 37 G13 7 40S 108 10 E
Nusa Tenggara Barat □, *Indonesia* 36 F5 8 50S 117 30 E
Nusa Tenggara Timur □, *Indonesia* 37 F6 9 30S 122 0 E
Nusaybin, *Turkey* 25 G7 37 3N 41 10 E
Nushki, *Pakistan* 42 E2 29 35N 66 0 E
Nuuk, *Greenland* 69 B14 64 10N 51 35W
Nuwakot, *Nepal* 43 E10 28 10N 83 55 E
Nuweiba', *Egypt* 44 D2 28 59N 34 39 E
Nuwerus, *S. Africa* 56 E2 31 8S 18 24 E
Nuweveldberge, *S. Africa* 56 E3 32 10S 21 45 E
Nuyts, C., *Australia* 61 F5 32 2S 132 21 E
Nuyts, Pt., *Australia* 61 G2 35 4S 116 38 E
Nuyts Arch., *Australia* 63 E1 32 35S 133 20 E
Nxau-Nxau, *Botswana* 56 B3 18 57S 21 4 E
Nyabing, *Australia* 61 F2 33 33S 118 9 E
Nyack, *U.S.A.* 79 E11 41 5N 73 55W
Nyagan, *Russia* 26 C7 62 30N 65 38 E
Nyahanga, *Tanzania* 54 C3 2 20S 33 37 E
Nyahua, *Tanzania* 54 D3 5 25S 33 23 E
Nyahururu, *Kenya* 54 B4 0 2N 36 27 E
Nyainqentanglha Shan, *China* 32 D4 30 0N 90 0 E
Nyakanazi, *Tanzania* 54 C3 3 2S 31 10 E
Nyâlâ, *Sudan* 51 F10 12 2N 24 58 E
Nyamandhlovu, *Zimbabwe* 55 F2 19 55S 28 16 E
Nyambiti, *Tanzania* 54 C3 2 48S 33 27 E
Nyamwaga, *Tanzania* 54 C3 1 27S 34 33 E
Nyandekwa, *Tanzania* 54 C3 3 57S 32 32 E
Nyandoma, *Russia* 24 B7 61 40N 40 12 E
Nyangana, *Namibia* 56 B3 18 0S 20 40 E
Nyanguge, *Tanzania* 54 C3 2 30S 33 12 E
Nyanza, *Rwanda* 54 C2 2 20S 29 42 E
Nyanza □, *Kenya* 54 C3 0 10S 34 15 E
Nyanza-Lac, *Burundi* 54 C2 4 21S 29 36 E
Nyasa, L., *Africa* 55 E3 12 30S 34 30 E
Nyasvizh, *Belarus* 17 B14 53 14N 26 38 E
Nyazepetrovsk, *Russia* 24 C10 56 3N 59 36 E
Nyazura, *Zimbabwe* 55 F3 18 40S 32 16 E
Nyazwidzi ↝, *Zimbabwe* 55 G3 20 0S 31 17 E
Nybro, *Sweden* 9 H16 56 44N 15 55 E
Nyda, *Russia* 26 C8 66 40N 72 58 E
Nyeri, *Kenya* 54 C4 0 23S 36 56 E
Nyíregyháza, *Hungary* 17 E11 47 58N 21 47 E
Nykøbing, *Storstrøm, Denmark* 9 J14 54 56N 11 52 E
Nykøbing, *Vestsjælland, Denmark* 9 J14 55 55N 11 40 E
Nykøbing, *Viborg, Denmark* 9 H13 56 48N 8 51 E
Nyköping, *Sweden* 9 G17 58 45N 17 1 E
Nylstroom, *S. Africa* 57 C4 24 42S 28 22 E
Nymagee, *Australia* 63 E4 32 7S 146 20 E
Nynäshamn, *Sweden* 9 G17 58 54N 17 57 E
Nyngan, *Australia* 63 E4 31 30S 147 8 E
Nyoma Rap, *India* 43 C8 33 10N 78 40 E
Nyoman = Neman ↝, *Lithuania* 9 J19 55 25N 21 10 E
Nysa, *Poland* 17 C9 50 30N 17 22 E
Nysa ↝, *Europe* 16 B8 52 4N 14 46 E
Nyssa, *U.S.A.* 82 E5 43 53N 117 0W
Nyunzu, *Dem. Rep. of the Congo* 54 D2 5 57S 27 58 E
Nyurba, *Russia* 27 C12 63 17N 118 28 E
Nzega, *Tanzania* 54 C3 4 10S 33 12 E
Nzérékoré, *Guinea* 50 G4 7 49N 8 48W
Nzeto, *Angola* 52 F2 7 10S 12 52 E
Nzilo, Chutes de, *Dem. Rep. of the Congo* 55 E2 10 18S 25 27 E
Nzubuka, *Tanzania* 54 C3 4 45S 32 50 E

O

Ō-Shima, *Japan* 31 G9 34 44N 139 24 E
Oa, Mull of, *U.K.* 12 F2 55 35N 6 20W
Oacoma, *U.S.A.* 80 D5 43 48N 99 24W
Oahe, L., *U.S.A.* 80 C4 44 27N 100 24W
Oahe Dam, *U.S.A.* 80 C4 44 27N 100 24W
Oahu, *U.S.A.* 74 H16 21 28N 157 58W
Oak Harbor, *U.S.A.* 84 B4 48 18N 122 39W
Oak Hill, *U.S.A.* 76 G5 37 59N 81 9W
Oak Ridge, *U.S.A.* 77 G3 36 1N 84 16W
Oak View, *U.S.A.* 85 L7 34 24N 119 18W
Oakan-Dake, *Japan* 30 C12 43 27N 144 10 E
Oakdale, *Calif., U.S.A.* 84 H6 37 46N 120 51W
Oakdale, *La., U.S.A.* 81 K8 30 49N 92 40W
Oakes, *U.S.A.* 80 B5 46 8N 98 6W
Oakesdale, *U.S.A.* 82 C5 47 8N 117 15W
Oakey, *Australia* 63 D5 27 25S 151 43 E
Oakfield, *U.S.A.* 78 C6 43 4N 78 16W
Oakham, *U.K.* 11 E7 52 40N 0 43W

Oakhurst, U.S.A. 84 H7 37 19N 119 40W
Oakland, U.S.A. 84 H4 37 49N 122 16W
Oakley, Idaho, U.S.A. 82 E7 42 15N 113 53W
Oakley, Kans., U.S.A. 80 F4 39 8N 100 51W
Oakover →, Australia 60 D3 21 0S 120 40 E
Oakridge, U.S.A. 82 E2 43 45N 122 28W
Oakville, Canada 78 C5 43 27N 79 41W
Oakville, U.S.A. 84 D3 46 51N 123 14W
Oamaru, N.Z. 59 L3 45 5S 170 59 E
Oasis, Calif., U.S.A. 85 M10 33 28N 116 6W
Oasis, Nev., U.S.A. 84 H9 37 29N 117 55W
Oates Land, Antarctica 5 C11 69 0S 160 0 E
Oatlands, Australia 62 G4 42 17S 147 21 E
Oatman, U.S.A. 85 K12 35 1N 114 19W
Oaxaca, Mexico 87 D5 17 2N 96 40W
Oaxaca □, Mexico 87 D5 17 0N 97 0W
Ob →, Russia 26 C7 66 45N 69 30 E
Oba, Canada 70 C3 49 4N 84 7W
Obama, Japan 31 G7 35 30N 135 45 E
Oban, U.K. 12 E3 56 25N 5 29W
Obbia, Somali Rep. 46 F4 5 25N 48 30 E
Obera, Argentina 95 B4 27 21S 55 2W
Oberhausen, Germany 16 C4 51 28N 6 51 E
Oberlin, Kans., U.S.A. 80 F4 39 49N 100 32W
Oberlin, La., U.S.A. 81 K8 30 37N 92 46W
Oberlin, Ohio, U.S.A. 78 E2 41 18N 82 13W
Oberon, Australia 63 E4 33 45S 149 52 E
Obi, Indonesia 37 E7 1 23S 127 45 E
Óbidos, Brazil 93 D7 1 50S 55 30W
Obihiro, Japan 30 C11 42 56N 143 12 E
Obilatu, Indonesia 37 E7 1 25S 127 20 E
Obluchye, Russia 27 E14 49 1N 131 4 E
Obo, C.A.R. 54 A2 5 20N 26 32 E
Oboa, Mt., Uganda 54 B3 1 45N 34 45 E
Oboyan, Russia 26 D4 51 15N 36 21 E
Obozerskaya = Obozerskiy, Russia 24 B7 63 34N 40 21 E
Obozerskiy, Russia 24 B7 63 34N 40 21 E
Observatory Inlet, Canada 72 B3 55 10N 129 54W
Obshchi Syrt, Russia 6 E16 52 0N 53 0 E
Obskaya Guba, Russia 26 C8 69 0N 73 0 E
Obuasi, Ghana 50 G5 6 17N 1 40W
Ocala, U.S.A. 77 L4 29 11N 82 8W
Ocampo, Chihuahua, Mexico 86 B3 28 9N 108 24W
Ocampo, Tamaulipas, Mexico 87 C5 22 50N 99 20W
Ocaña, Spain 19 C4 39 55N 3 30W
Ocanomowoc, U.S.A. 80 D10 43 7N 88 30W
Occidental, Cordillera, Colombia 92 C3 5 0N 76 0W
Occidental, Grand Erg, Algeria 50 B6 30 20N 1 0 E
Ocean City, Md., U.S.A. 76 F8 38 20N 75 5W
Ocean City, N.J., U.S.A. 76 F8 39 17N 74 35W
Ocean City, Wash., U.S.A. 84 C2 47 4N 124 10W
Ocean Falls, Canada 72 C3 52 18N 127 48W
Ocean I. = Banaba, Kiribati 64 H8 0 45S 169 50 E
Ocean Park, U.S.A. 84 D2 46 30N 124 3W
Oceano, U.S.A. 85 K6 35 6N 120 37W
Oceanport, U.S.A. 79 F10 40 19N 74 3W
Oceanside, U.S.A. 85 M9 33 12N 117 23W
Ochil Hills, U.K. 12 E5 56 14N 3 40W
Ocilla, U.S.A. 77 K4 31 36N 83 15W
Ocmulgee →, U.S.A. 77 K4 31 58N 82 33W
Ocniţa, Moldova 17 D14 48 25N 27 30 E
Oconee →, U.S.A. 77 K4 31 58N 82 33W
Oconto, U.S.A. 76 C2 44 53N 87 52W
Oconto Falls, U.S.A. 76 C1 44 52N 88 9W
Ocosingo, Mexico 87 D6 17 10N 92 15W
Ocotal, Nic. 88 D2 13 41N 86 31W
Ocotlán, Mexico 86 C4 20 21N 102 42W
Ocotlán de Morelos, Mexico 87 D5 16 48N 96 40W
Ōda, Japan 31 G6 35 11N 132 30 E
Ódáðahraun, Iceland 8 D5 65 5N 17 0W
Odate, Japan 30 D10 40 16N 140 34 E
Odawara, Japan 31 G9 35 20N 139 6 E
Odda, Norway 9 F12 60 3N 6 35 E
Odei →, Canada 73 B9 56 6N 96 54W
Ödemiş, Turkey 21 E13 38 15N 28 0 E
Odendaalsrus, S. Africa 56 D4 27 48S 26 45 E
Odense, Denmark 9 J14 55 22N 10 23 E
Oder →, Europe 16 B8 53 33N 14 38 E
Odesa, Ukraine 25 E5 46 30N 30 45 E
Odessa = Odesa, Ukraine 25 E5 46 30N 30 45 E
Odessa, Canada 79 B8 44 17N 76 43W
Odessa, Tex., U.S.A. 81 K3 31 52N 102 23W
Odessa, Wash., U.S.A. 82 C4 47 20N 118 41W
Odiakwe, Botswana 56 C4 20 12S 25 17 E
Odienné, Ivory C. 50 G4 9 30N 7 34W
Odintsovo, Russia 24 C6 55 39N 37 15 E
O'Donnell, U.S.A. 81 J4 32 58N 101 50W
Odorheiu Secuiesc, Romania 17 E13 46 21N 25 21 E
Odra = Oder →, Europe 16 B8 53 33N 14 38 E
Odzi, Zimbabwe 57 B5 19 0S 32 20 E
Odzi →, Zimbabwe 57 B5 19 45S 32 23 E
Oeiras, Brazil 93 E10 7 0S 42 8W
Oelrichs, U.S.A. 80 D3 43 11N 103 14W
Oelwein, U.S.A. 80 D9 42 41N 91 55W
Oenpelli, Australia 60 B5 12 20S 133 4 E
Ofanto →, Italy 20 D7 41 22N 16 13 E
Offa, Nigeria 50 G6 8 13N 4 42 E
Offaly □, Ireland 13 C4 53 15N 7 30W
Offenbach, Germany 16 C5 50 6N 8 44 E
Offenburg, Germany 16 D4 48 28N 7 56 E
Ofotfjorden, Norway 8 B17 68 27N 17 0 E
Ōfunato, Japan 30 E10 39 4N 141 43 E
Oga, Japan 30 E9 39 55N 139 50 E
Oga-Hantō, Japan 30 E9 39 58N 139 47 E
Ogaden, Ethiopia 46 F3 7 30N 45 30 E
Ōgaki, Japan 31 G8 35 21N 136 37 E
Ogallala, U.S.A. 80 E4 41 8N 101 43W
Ogasawara Gunto, Pac. Oc. 28 G18 27 0N 142 0 E
Ogbomosho, Nigeria 50 G6 8 1N 4 11 E
Ogden, U.S.A. 82 F7 41 13N 111 58W
Ogdensburg, U.S.A. 79 B9 44 42N 75 30W
Ogeechee →, U.S.A. 77 K5 31 50N 81 3W
Ogilby, U.S.A. 85 N12 32 49N 114 50W
Oglio →, Italy 20 B4 45 2N 10 39 E
Ogmore, Australia 62 C4 22 37S 149 35 E
Ogoki, Canada 70 B2 51 38N 85 58W
Ogoki →, Canada 70 B2 51 38N 85 57W
Ogoki L., Canada 70 B2 50 50N 87 10W
Ogoki Res., Canada 70 B2 50 45N 88 15W
Ogooué →, Gabon 52 E1 1 0S 9 0 E
Ogowe = Ogooué →, Gabon 52 E1 1 0S 9 0 E
Ogre, Latvia 9 H21 56 49N 24 36 E
Ogurchinskiy, Ostrov, Turkmenistan 45 B7 38 55N 53 2 E
Ohai, N.Z. 59 L2 45 55S 168 0 E
Ohakune, N.Z. 59 H5 39 24S 175 24 E
Ohata, Japan 30 D10 41 24N 141 10 E
Ohau, L., N.Z. 59 L2 44 15S 169 53 E
Ohio □, U.S.A. 78 F2 40 15N 82 45W
Ohio →, U.S.A. 76 G1 36 59N 89 8W
Ohře →, Czech Rep. 16 C8 50 30N 14 10 E
Ohrid, Macedonia 21 D9 41 8N 20 52 E
Ohridsko Jezero, Macedonia 21 D9 41 8N 20 52 E
Ohrigstad, S. Africa 57 C5 24 39S 30 36 E
Oiapoque, Brazil 93 3 50N 51 50W
Oikou, China 35 E9 38 35N 117 42 E
Oil City, U.S.A. 78 E5 41 26N 79 42W
Oil Springs, Canada 78 D2 42 47N 82 7W
Oildale, U.S.A. 85 K7 35 25N 119 1W
Oise →, France 18 B5 49 0N 2 4 E
Ōita, Japan 31 H5 33 14N 131 36 E
Ōita □, Japan 31 H5 33 15N 131 30 E
Oiticica, Brazil 93 E10 5 3S 41 5W
Ojacaliente, Mexico 86 C4 22 34N 102 15W
Ojai, U.S.A. 85 L7 34 27N 119 15W
Ojinaga, Mexico 86 B4 29 34N 104 25W
Ojiya, Japan 31 F9 37 18N 138 48 E
Ojos del Salado, Cerro, Argentina 94 B2 27 0S 68 40W
Oka →, Russia 24 C7 56 20N 43 59 E
Okaba, Indonesia 37 F9 8 6S 139 42 E
Okahandja, Namibia 56 C2 22 0S 16 59 E
Okanagan L., Canada 72 D5 50 0N 119 30W
Okanogan, U.S.A. 82 B4 48 22N 119 35W
Okanogan →, U.S.A. 82 B4 48 6N 119 44W
Okaputa, Namibia 56 C2 20 5S 17 0 E
Okara, Pakistan 42 D5 30 50N 73 31 E
Okaukuejo, Namibia 56 B2 19 10S 16 0 E
Okavango Delta, Botswana 56 B3 18 45S 22 45 E
Okavango Swamp = Okavango Delta, Botswana 56 B3 18 45S 22 45 E
Okaya, Japan 31 F9 36 5N 138 10 E
Okayama, Japan 31 G6 34 40N 133 54 E
Okayama □, Japan 31 G6 35 0N 133 50 E
Okazaki, Japan 31 G8 34 57N 137 10 E
Okeechobee, U.S.A. 77 M5 27 15N 80 50W
Okeechobee, L., U.S.A. 77 M5 27 0N 80 50W
Okefenokee Swamp, U.S.A. 77 K4 30 40N 82 20W
Okehampton, U.K. 11 G4 50 44N 4 0W
Okha, India 42 H3 22 27N 69 4 E
Okha, Russia 27 D15 53 40N 143 0 E
Okhotsk, Russia 27 D15 59 20N 143 10 E
Okhotsk, Sea of, Asia 27 D15 55 0N 145 0 E
Okhotskiy Perevoz, Russia 27 C14 61 52N 135 35 E
Okhtyrka, Ukraine 25 D5 50 25N 35 0 E
Oki-Shotō, Japan 31 F6 36 5N 133 15 E
Okiep, S. Africa 56 D2 29 39S 17 53 E
Okinawa □, Japan 31 L4 26 40N 128 0 E
Okinawa-Guntō, Japan 31 L4 26 40N 128 0 E
Okinawa-Jima, Japan 31 L4 26 32N 128 0 E
Okino-erabu-Shima, Japan 31 L4 27 21N 128 33 E
Oklahoma □, U.S.A. 81 H6 35 20N 97 30W
Oklahoma City, U.S.A. 81 H6 35 30N 97 30W
Okmulgee, U.S.A. 81 H7 35 37N 95 58W
Oknitsa = Ocniţa, Moldova 17 D14 48 25N 27 30 E
Okolo, Uganda 54 B3 2 37N 31 8 E
Okolona, U.S.A. 81 J10 34 0N 88 45W
Okombahe, Namibia 56 C2 21 23S 15 22 E
Okotoks, Canada 72 C6 50 43N 113 58W
Oksibil, Indonesia 37 E10 4 59S 140 35 E
Oksovskiy, Russia 24 B6 62 33N 39 57 E
Oktabrsk = Oktyabrsk, Kazakstan 25 E10 49 28N 57 25 E
Oktyabrsk, Kazakstan 25 E10 49 28N 57 25 E
Oktyabrskiy = Aktsyabrski, Belarus 17 B15 52 38N 28 53 E
Oktyabrskiy, Russia 24 D9 54 28N 53 28 E
Oktyabrskoy Revolyutsii, Ostrov, Russia 27 B10 79 30N 97 0 E
Okuru, N.Z. 59 K2 43 55S 168 55 E
Okushiri-Tō, Japan 30 C9 42 15N 139 30 E
Okwa →, Botswana 56 C3 22 30S 23 0 E
Ola, U.S.A. 81 H8 35 2N 93 13W
Ólafsfjörður, Iceland 8 C4 66 4N 18 39W
Ólafsvík, Iceland 8 D2 64 53N 23 43W
Olancha, U.S.A. 85 J8 36 17N 118 1W
Olancha Pk., U.S.A. 85 J8 36 15N 118 7W
Olanchito, Honduras 88 C2 15 30N 86 30W
Öland, Sweden 9 H17 56 45N 16 38 E
Olary, Australia 63 E3 32 18S 140 19 E
Olascoaga, Argentina 94 D3 35 15S 60 39W
Olathe, U.S.A. 80 F7 38 53N 94 49W
Olavarría, Argentina 94 D3 36 55S 60 20W
Oława, Poland 17 C9 50 57N 17 20 E
Ólbia, Italy 20 D3 40 55N 9 31 E
Olcott, U.S.A. 78 C6 43 20N 78 42W
Old Bahama Chan. = Bahama, Canal Viejo de, W. Indies 88 B4 22 10N 77 30W
Old Baldy Pk. = San Antonio, Mt., U.S.A. 85 L9 34 17N 117 38W
Old Castile = Castilla y Leon □, Spain 19 B3 42 0N 5 0W
Old Crow, Canada 68 B6 67 30N 139 55W
Old Dale, U.S.A. 85 L11 34 8N 115 47W
Old Forge, N.Y., U.S.A. 79 C10 43 43N 74 58W
Old Forge, Pa., U.S.A. 79 E9 41 22N 75 45W
Old Perlican, Canada 71 C9 48 5N 53 1W
Old Shinyanga, Tanzania 54 C3 3 33S 33 27 E
Old Speck Mt., U.S.A. 79 B14 44 34N 70 57W
Old Town, U.S.A. 77 C11 44 56N 68 39W
Old Washington, U.S.A. 78 F3 40 2N 81 27W
Old Wives L., Canada 73 C7 50 5N 106 0W
Oldbury, U.K. 11 F5 51 38N 2 33W
Oldcastle, Ireland 13 C4 53 46N 7 10W
Oldeani, Tanzania 54 C4 3 22S 35 35 E
Oldenburg, Germany 16 B5 53 9N 8 13 E
Oldenzaal, Neths. 15 B6 52 19N 6 53 E
Oldham, U.K. 10 D5 53 33N 2 7W
Oldman →, Canada 72 D6 49 57N 111 42W
Oldmeldrum, U.K. 12 D6 57 20N 2 19W
Olds, Canada 72 C6 51 50N 114 10W
Oldziyt, Mongolia 34 B5 44 40N 109 1 E
Olean, U.S.A. 78 D6 42 5N 78 26W
Olekma →, Russia 27 C13 60 22N 120 42 E
Olekminsk, Russia 27 C13 60 25N 120 30 E
Oleksandriya, Ukraine 17 C14 50 37N 26 19 E
Olema, U.S.A. 84 G4 38 3N 122 47W
Olenegorsk, Russia 24 A5 68 9N 33 18 E
Olenek, Russia 27 C12 68 28N 112 18 E
Olenek →, Russia 27 B13 73 0N 120 10 E
Oléron, Î. d', France 18 D3 45 55N 1 15W
Oleśnica, Poland 17 C9 51 13N 17 22 E
Olevsk, Ukraine 17 C14 51 12N 27 39 E
Olga, Russia 27 E14 43 50N 135 14 E
Olga, L., Canada 70 C4 49 47N 77 15W
Olga, Mt., Australia 61 E5 25 20S 130 50 E
Olhão, Portugal 19 D2 37 3N 7 48W
Olifants →, Africa 57 C5 23 57S 31 58 E
Olifants →, Namibia 56 C2 25 30S 19 30 E
Olifantshoek, S. Africa 56 D3 27 57S 22 42 E
Ólimbos, Óros, Greece 21 D10 40 6N 22 23 E
Olímpia, Brazil 95 A6 20 44S 48 54W
Olinda, Brazil 93 E12 8 1S 34 51W
Oliva, Argentina 94 C3 32 0S 63 38W
Olivehurst, U.S.A. 84 F5 39 6N 121 34W
Olivenza, Spain 19 C2 38 41N 7 9W
Oliver, Canada 72 D5 49 13N 119 37W
Oliver L., Canada 73 B8 56 56N 103 22W
Ollagüe, Chile 94 A2 21 15S 68 10W
Olney, Ill., U.S.A. 76 F1 38 44N 88 5W
Olney, Tex., U.S.A. 81 J5 33 22N 98 45W
Olomane →, Canada 71 B7 50 14N 60 37W
Olomouc, Czech Rep. 17 D9 49 38N 17 12 E
Olonets, Russia 24 B5 61 0N 32 54 E
Olongapo, Phil. 37 B6 14 50N 120 18 E
Olot, Spain 19 A7 42 11N 2 30 E
Olovyannaya, Russia 27 D12 50 58N 115 35 E
Oloy →, Russia 27 C16 66 29N 159 29 E
Olsztyn, Poland 17 B11 53 48N 20 29 E
Olt →, Romania 17 G13 43 43N 24 51 E
Olteniţa, Romania 17 F14 44 7N 26 42 E
Olton, U.S.A. 81 H3 34 11N 102 8W
Olymbos, Cyprus 23 D12 35 21N 33 45 E
Olympia, Greece 21 F9 37 39N 21 39 E
Olympia, U.S.A. 84 D4 47 3N 122 53W
Olympic Dam, Australia 63 E2 30 30S 136 55 E
Olympic Mts., U.S.A. 84 C3 47 55N 123 45W
Olympic Nat. Park, U.S.A. 84 C3 47 48N 123 30W
Olympus, Cyprus 23 E11 34 56N 32 52 E
Olympus, Mt. = Ólimbos, Óros, Greece 21 D10 40 6N 22 23 E
Olympus, Mt. = Uludağ, Turkey 21 D13 40 4N 29 13 E
Olympus, Mt., U.S.A. 84 C3 47 48N 123 43W
Olyphant, U.S.A. 79 E9 41 27N 75 36W
Om →, Russia 26 D8 54 59N 73 22 E
Om Koi, Thailand 38 D2 17 48N 98 22 E
Ōma, Japan 30 D10 41 45N 141 5 E
Ōmachi, Japan 31 F8 36 30N 137 50 E
Omae-Zaki, Japan 31 G9 34 36N 138 14 E
Ōmagari, Japan 30 E10 39 27N 140 29 E
Omagh, U.K. 13 B4 54 36N 7 19W
Omagh □, U.K. 13 B4 54 35N 7 15W
Omaha, U.S.A. 80 E7 41 17N 95 58W
Omak, U.S.A. 82 B4 48 25N 119 31W
Omalos, Greece 23 D5 35 19N 23 55 E
Oman ■, Asia 46 C6 23 0N 58 0 E
Oman, G. of, Asia 45 E8 24 30N 58 30 E
Omaruru, Namibia 56 C2 21 26S 16 0 E
Omaruru →, Namibia 56 C1 22 7S 14 15 E
Omate, Peru 92 G4 16 45S 71 0W
Ombai, Selat, Indonesia 37 F6 8 30S 124 50 E
Omboué, Gabon 52 E1 1 35S 9 15 E
Ombrone →, Italy 20 C4 42 42N 11 5 E
Omdurmân, Sudan 51 E12 15 40N 32 28 E
Omemee, Canada 78 B6 44 18N 78 33W
Omeonga, Dem. Rep. of the Congo 54 C1 3 40S 24 22 E
Ometepe, I. de, Nic. 88 D2 11 32N 85 35W
Ometepec, Mexico 87 D5 16 39N 98 23W
Ominato, Japan 30 D10 41 17N 141 10 E
Omineca →, Canada 72 B4 56 3N 124 16W
Omitara, Namibia 56 C2 22 16S 18 2 E
Ōmiya, Japan 31 G9 35 54N 139 38 E
Ommen, Neths. 15 B6 52 31N 6 26 E
Ömnögovĭ □, Mongolia 34 C3 43 15N 104 0 E
Omo →, Ethiopia 46 F2 6 25N 36 10 E
Omodhos, Cyprus 23 E11 34 51N 32 48 E
Omolon →, Russia 27 C16 68 42N 158 36 E
Omono-Gawa →, Japan 30 E10 39 46N 140 3 E
Omsk, Russia 26 D8 55 0N 73 12 E
Omsukchan, Russia 27 C16 62 32N 155 48 E
Ōmu, Japan 30 B11 44 34N 142 58 E
Omul, Vf., Romania 17 F13 45 27N 25 29 E
Ōmura, Japan 31 H4 32 56N 129 57 E
Omuramba Omatako →, Namibia 56 B2 17 45S 20 25 E
Omuramba Ovambo →, Namibia 56 B2 18 45S 16 59 E
Ōmuta, Japan 31 H5 33 5N 130 26 E
Onaga, U.S.A. 80 F6 39 29N 96 10W
Onalaska, U.S.A. 80 D9 43 53N 91 14W
Onancock, U.S.A. 76 G8 37 43N 75 45W
Onang, Indonesia 37 E5 3 2S 118 49 E
Onaping L., Canada 70 C3 47 3N 81 30W
Onavas, Mexico 86 B3 28 28N 109 30W
Onawa, U.S.A. 80 D6 42 2N 96 6W
Oncócua, Angola 56 B1 16 30S 13 25 E
Onda, Spain 19 C5 39 55N 0 17W
Ondaejin, N. Korea 35 D15 41 34N 129 40 E
Ondangwa, Namibia 56 B2 17 57S 16 4 E
Ondjiva, Angola 56 B2 16 48S 15 50 E
Öndörshil, Mongolia 34 B5 45 13N 108 5 E
Öndverðarnes, Iceland 8 D1 64 52N 24 0W
One Tree, Australia 63 E3 34 11S 144 43 E
Onega, Russia 24 B6 64 0N 38 10 E
Onega →, Russia 24 B6 63 58N 38 2 E
Onega, G. of = Onezhskaya Guba, Russia 24 B6 64 24N 36 38 E
Onega, L. = Onezhskoye Ozero, Russia 24 B6 61 44N 35 22 E
Oneida, U.S.A. 79 C9 43 6N 75 39W
Oneida L., U.S.A. 79 C9 43 12N 75 54W
O'Neill, U.S.A. 80 D5 42 27N 98 39W
Onekotan, Ostrov, Russia 27 E16 49 25N 154 45 E
Onema, Dem. Rep. of the Congo 54 C1 4 35S 24 30 E
Oneonta, U.S.A. 79 D9 42 27N 75 4W
Oneşti, Romania 17 E14 46 17N 26 47 E
Onezhskaya Guba, Russia 24 B6 64 24N 36 38 E
Onezhskoye Ozero, Russia 24 B6 61 44N 35 22 E
Ongarue, N.Z. 59 H5 38 42S 175 19 E
Ongers →, S. Africa 56 E3 31 4S 23 13 E
Ongerup, Australia 61 F2 33 58S 118 28 E
Ongjin, N. Korea 35 F13 37 56N 125 21 E
Ongkharak, Thailand 38 E3 14 8N 101 1 E
Ongniud Qi, China 35 C10 43 0N 118 38 E
Ongoka, Dem. Rep. of the Congo 54 C2 1 20S 26 0 E
Ongole, India 40 M12 15 33N 80 2 E
Ongon = Havirga, Mongolia 34 B7 45 41N 113 5 E
Onida, U.S.A. 80 C4 44 42N 100 4W
Onilahy →, Madag. 57 C7 23 34S 43 45 E
Onitsha, Nigeria 50 G7 6 6N 6 42 E
Onoda, Japan 31 G5 33 59N 131 11 E
Onpyŏng-ni, S. Korea 35 H14 33 25N 126 55 E
Onslow, Australia 60 D2 21 40S 115 12 E
Onslow B., U.S.A. 77 H7 34 20N 77 15W
Ontake-San, Japan 31 G8 35 53N 137 29 E
Ontario, Calif., U.S.A. 85 L9 34 4N 117 39W
Ontario, Oreg., U.S.A. 82 D5 44 2N 116 58W
Ontario □, Canada 70 B2 48 0N 83 0W
Ontario, L., N. Amer. 78 C7 43 20N 78 0W
Ontonagon, U.S.A. 80 B10 46 52N 89 19W
Onyx, U.S.A. 85 K8 35 41N 118 14W
Oodnadatta, Australia 63 D2 27 33S 135 30 E
Ooldea, Australia 61 F5 30 27S 131 50 E
Oombulgurri, Australia 60 C4 15 15S 127 45 E
Oorindi, Australia 62 C3 20 40S 141 1 E
Oost-Vlaanderen □, Belgium 15 C3 51 5N 3 50 E
Oostende, Belgium 15 C2 51 15N 2 54 E
Oosterhout, Neths. 15 C4 51 39N 4 47 E
Oosterschelde →, Neths. 15 C4 51 33N 4 0 E
Oosterwolde, Neths. 15 B6 53 0N 6 17 E
Ootacamund = Udagamandalam, India 40 P10 11 30N 76 44 E
Ootsa L., Canada 72 C3 53 50N 126 2W
Opala, Dem. Rep. of the Congo 54 C1 0 40S 24 20 E
Opanake, Sri Lanka 40 R12 6 35N 80 40 E
Opasatika, Canada 70 C3 49 30N 82 50W
Opasquia Prov. Park, Canada 70 B1 53 33N 93 5W
Opava, Czech Rep. 17 D9 49 57N 17 58 E
Opelika, U.S.A. 77 J3 32 39N 85 23W
Opelousas, U.S.A. 81 K8 30 32N 92 5W
Opémisca, L., Canada 70 C5 49 56N 74 52W
Opheim, U.S.A. 82 B10 48 51N 106 24W
Ophthalmia Ra., Australia 60 D2 23 15S 119 30 E
Opinaca →, Canada 70 B4 52 15N 78 2W
Opinaca, Rés., Canada 70 B4 52 39N 76 20W
Opinnagau →, Canada 70 B3 54 12N 82 25W
Opiscoteo, L., Canada 71 B6 53 10N 68 10W
Opole, Poland 17 C9 50 42N 17 58 E
Oponono L., Namibia 56 B2 18 8S 15 45 E
Oporto = Porto, Portugal 19 B1 41 8N 8 40W
Opotiki, N.Z. 59 H6 38 1S 177 19 E
Opp, U.S.A. 77 K2 31 17N 86 16W
Oppdal, Norway 9 E13 62 35N 9 41 E
Opportunity, U.S.A. 82 C5 47 39N 117 15W
Opua, N.Z. 59 F5 35 19S 174 9 E
Opunake, N.Z. 59 H4 39 26S 173 52 E
Opuwo, Namibia 56 B1 18 3S 13 45 E
Ora, Cyprus 23 E12 34 51N 33 12 E
Oracle, U.S.A. 83 K8 32 37N 110 46W
Oradea, Romania 17 E11 47 2N 21 58 E
Öræfajökull, Iceland 8 D5 64 2N 16 39W
Orai, India 43 G8 25 58N 79 30 E
Oral = Zhayyq →, Kazakstan 25 E9 47 0N 51 48 E
Oral, Kazakstan 25 D9 51 20N 51 20 E
Oran, Algeria 50 A5 35 45N 0 39W
Orange, Australia 63 E4 33 15S 149 7 E
Orange, France 18 D6 44 8N 4 47 E
Orange, Calif., U.S.A. 85 M9 33 47N 117 51W
Orange, Mass., U.S.A. 79 D12 42 35N 72 19W
Orange, Tex., U.S.A. 81 K8 30 6N 93 44W
Orange, Va., U.S.A. 76 F6 38 15N 78 7W
Orange →, S. Africa 56 D2 28 41S 16 28 E
Orange, C., Brazil 93 C8 4 20N 51 30W
Orange Cove, U.S.A. 84 J7 36 38N 119 19W
Orange Free State = Free State □, S. Africa 56 D4 28 30S 27 0 E
Orange Grove, U.S.A. 81 M6 27 58N 97 56W
Orange Walk, Belize 87 D7 18 6N 88 33W
Orangeburg, U.S.A. 77 J5 33 30N 80 52W
Orangeville, Canada 78 C4 43 55N 80 5W
Oranienburg, Germany 16 B7 52 45N 13 14 E
Oranje = Orange →, S. Africa 56 D2 28 41S 16 28 E
Oranje Vrystaat = Free State □, S. Africa 56 D4 28 30S 27 0 E
Oranjemund, Namibia 56 D2 28 38S 16 29 E
Oranjerivier, S. Africa 56 D3 29 40S 24 12 E
Oranjestad, Aruba 89 D5 12 32N 70 2W
Orapa, Botswana 53 J5 21 15S 25 30 E
Oras, Phil. 37 B7 12 9N 125 28 E
Oraşul Stalin = Braşov, Romania 17 F13 45 38N 25 35 E
Orbetello, Italy 20 C4 42 27N 11 13 E
Orbisonia, U.S.A. 78 F7 40 15N 77 54W
Orbost, Australia 63 F4 37 40S 148 29 E
Orcas I., U.S.A. 84 B4 48 42N 122 56W
Orchard City, U.S.A. 83 G10 38 50N 107 58W
Orchila, I., Venezuela 89 D6 11 48N 66 10W
Orcutt, U.S.A. 85 L6 34 52N 120 27W
Ord, U.S.A. 80 E5 41 36N 98 56W
Ord →, Australia 60 C4 15 33S 128 15 E
Ord, Mt., Australia 60 C4 17 20S 125 34 E
Orderville, U.S.A. 83 H7 37 17N 112 38W
Ordos = Mu Us Shamo, China 34 E5 39 0N 109 0 E
Ordu, Turkey 25 F6 40 55N 37 53 E
Ordway, U.S.A. 80 F3 38 13N 103 46W
Ordzhonikidze = Vladikavkaz, Russia 25 F7 43 0N 44 35 E
Ore, Dem. Rep. of the Congo 54 B2 3 17N 29 30 E
Ore Mts. = Erzgebirge, Germany 16 C7 50 27N 12 55 E
Örebro, Sweden 9 G16 59 20N 15 18 E
Oregon, U.S.A. 80 D10 42 1N 89 20W
Oregon □, U.S.A. 82 E3 44 0N 121 0W
Oregon City, U.S.A. 84 E4 45 21N 122 36W
Orekhovo-Zuyevo, Russia 24 C6 55 50N 38 55 E
Orel, Russia 24 D6 52 57N 36 3 E
Orem, U.S.A. 82 F8 40 19N 111 42W
Ören, Turkey 21 F12 37 3N 27 57 E
Orenburg, Russia 24 D10 51 45N 55 6 E
Orense = Ourense, Spain 19 A2 42 19N 7 55W
Orepuki, N.Z. 59 M1 46 19S 167 46 E
Orestiás, Greece 21 D12 41 30N 26 33 E
Orestos Pereyra, Mexico 86 B3 26 31N 105 40W
Orford Ness, U.K. 11 E9 52 5N 1 35 E

Organos, Pta. de los, Canary Is. 22 F2 28 12N 17 17W
Orgaz, Spain 19 C4 39 39N 3 53W
Orgeyev = Orhei, Moldova 17 E15 47 24N 28 50 E
Orhaneli, Turkey 21 E13 39 54N 28 59 E
Orhangazi, Turkey 21 D13 40 29N 29 18 E
Orhei, Moldova 17 E15 47 24N 28 50 E
Orhon Gol →, Mongolia 32 A5 50 21N 106 0 E
Oriental, Cordillera, Colombia 92 B4 6 0N 73 0W
Oriental, Grand Erg, Algeria 50 B7 30 0N 6 30 E
Orientale □, Dem. Rep. of the Congo 54 B2 2 20N 26 0 E
Oriente, Argentina 94 D3 38 44S 60 37W
Orihuela, Spain 19 C5 38 7N 0 55W
Orillia, Canada 78 B5 44 40N 79 24W
Orinoco →, Venezuela 92 B6 9 15N 61 30W
Orion, Canada 73 D6 49 27N 110 49W
Oriskany, U.S.A. 79 C9 43 10N 75 20W
Orissa □, India 41 K14 20 0N 84 0 E
Orissaare, Estonia 9 G20 58 34N 23 5 E
Oristano, Italy 20 E3 39 54N 8 36 E
Oristano, G. di, Italy 20 E3 39 50N 8 29 E
Orizaba, Mexico 87 D5 18 51N 97 6W
Orkanger, Norway 8 E13 63 18N 9 52 E
Orkla →, Norway 8 E13 63 18N 9 51 E
Orkney, S. Africa 56 D4 26 58S 26 40 E
Orkney □, U.K. 12 B5 59 2N 3 13W
Orkney Is., U.K. 12 B6 59 0N 3 0W
Orland, U.S.A. 84 F4 39 45N 122 12W
Orlando, U.S.A. 77 L5 28 33N 81 23W
Orléanais, France 18 C5 48 0N 2 0 E
Orléans, France 18 C4 47 54N 1 52 E
Orleans, U.S.A. 79 B12 44 49N 72 12W
Orléans, I. d', Canada 71 C5 46 54N 70 58W
Ormara, Pakistan 40 G4 25 16N 64 33 E
Ormoc, Phil. 37 B6 11 0N 124 37 E
Ormond, N.Z. 59 H6 38 33S 177 56 E
Ormond Beach, U.S.A. 77 L5 29 17N 81 3W
Ormskirk, U.K. 10 D5 53 35N 2 54W
Ormstown, Canada 79 A11 45 8N 74 0W
Örnsköldsvik, Sweden 8 E18 63 17N 18 40 E
Oro, N. Korea 35 D14 40 1N 127 27 E
Oro →, Mexico 86 B3 25 35N 105 2W
Oro Grande, U.S.A. 85 L9 34 36N 117 20W
Oro Valley, U.S.A. 83 K8 32 26N 110 58W
Orocué, Colombia 92 C4 4 48N 71 20W
Orofino, U.S.A. 82 C5 46 29N 116 15W
Orol Dengizi = Aral Sea, Asia 26 E7 44 30N 60 0 E
Oromocto, Canada 71 C6 45 54N 66 29W
Orono, Canada 78 C6 43 59N 78 37W
Orono, U.S.A. 77 C11 44 53N 68 40W
Oronsay, U.K. 12 E2 56 1N 6 15W
Oroqen Zizhiqi, China 33 A7 50 34N 123 43 E
Oroquieta, Phil. 37 C6 8 32N 123 44 E
Orosháza, Hungary 17 E11 46 32N 20 42 E
Orotukan, Russia 27 C16 62 16N 151 42 E
Oroville, Calif., U.S.A. 84 F5 39 31N 121 33W
Oroville, Wash., U.S.A. 82 B4 48 56N 119 26W
Oroville, L., U.S.A. 84 F5 39 33N 121 29W
Orroroo, Australia 63 E2 32 43S 138 38 E
Orrville, U.S.A. 78 F3 40 50N 81 46W
Orsha, Belarus 24 D5 54 30N 30 25 E
Orsk, Russia 26 D6 51 12N 58 34 E
Orşova, Romania 17 F12 44 41N 22 25 E
Ortaca, Turkey 21 F13 36 49N 28 45 E
Ortegal, C., Spain 19 A2 43 43N 7 52W
Orthez, France 18 E3 43 29N 0 48W
Ortigueira, Spain 19 A2 43 40N 7 50W
Orting, U.S.A. 84 C4 47 6N 122 12W
Ortles, Italy 18 C9 46 31N 10 33 E
Ortón →, Bolivia 92 F5 10 50S 67 0W
Ortonville, U.S.A. 80 C6 45 19N 96 27W
Orūmīyeh, Iran 44 B5 37 40N 45 0 E
Orūmīyeh, Daryācheh-ye, Iran 44 B5 37 50N 45 30 E
Oruro, Bolivia 92 G5 18 0S 67 9W
Orust, Sweden 9 G14 58 10N 11 40 E
Oruzgān □, Afghan. 40 C5 33 30N 66 0 E
Orvieto, Italy 20 C5 42 43N 12 7 E
Orwell, N.Y., U.S.A. 79 C9 43 35N 75 50W
Orwell, Ohio, U.S.A. 78 E4 41 32N 80 52W
Orwell →, U.K. 11 F9 51 59N 1 18 E
Orwigsburg, U.S.A. 79 F8 40 38N 76 6W
Oryakhovo, Bulgaria 21 C10 43 40N 23 57 E
Osa, Russia 24 C10 57 17N 55 26 E
Osa, Pen. de, Costa Rica 88 E3 8 0N 84 0W
Osage, U.S.A. 80 D8 43 17N 92 49W
Osage →, U.S.A. 80 F9 38 35N 91 57W
Osage City, U.S.A. 80 F7 38 38N 95 50W
Ōsaka, Japan 31 G7 34 40N 135 30 E
Osan, S. Korea 35 F14 37 11N 127 4 E
Osawatomie, U.S.A. 80 F7 38 31N 94 57W
Osborne, U.S.A. 80 F5 39 26N 98 42W
Osceola, Ark., U.S.A. 81 H10 35 42N 89 58W
Osceola, Iowa, U.S.A. 80 E8 41 2N 93 46W
Oscoda, U.S.A. 78 B1 44 26N 83 20W
Ösel = Saaremaa, Estonia 9 G20 58 30N 22 30 E
Osgoode, Canada 79 A9 45 8N 75 36W
Osh, Kyrgyzstan 26 E8 40 37N 72 49 E
Oshakati, Namibia 53 H3 17 45S 15 40 E
Oshawa, Canada 78 C6 43 50N 78 50W
Oshigambo, Namibia 56 B2 17 45S 16 5 E
Oshkosh, Nebr., U.S.A. 80 E3 41 24N 102 21W
Oshkosh, Wis., U.S.A. 80 C10 44 1N 88 33W
Oshmyany = Ashmyany, Belarus 9 J21 54 26N 25 52 E
Oshnovīyeh, Iran 44 B5 37 2N 45 6 E
Oshogbo, Nigeria 50 G6 7 48N 4 37 E
Oshtorīnān, Iran 45 C6 34 1N 48 38 E
Oshwe, Dem. Rep. of the Congo 52 E3 3 25S 19 28 E
Osijek, Croatia 21 B8 45 34N 18 41 E
Osipenko = Berdyansk, Ukraine 25 E6 46 45N 36 50 E
Osipovichi = Asipovichy, Belarus 17 B15 53 19N 28 33 E
Osiyan, India 42 F5 26 43N 72 55 E
Osizweni, S. Africa 57 D5 27 49S 30 7 E
Oskaloosa, U.S.A. 80 E8 41 18N 92 39W
Oskarshamn, Sweden 9 H17 57 15N 16 27 E
Oskélanéo, Canada 70 C4 48 5N 75 15W
Öskemen, Kazakstan 26 E9 50 0N 82 36 E
Oslo, Norway 9 G14 59 55N 10 45 E
Oslofjorden, Norway 9 G14 59 20N 10 35 E
Osmanabad, India 40 K10 18 5N 76 10 E
Osmaniye, Turkey 25 G6 37 5N 36 10 E
Osnabrück, Germany 16 B5 52 17N 8 3 E
Osorio, Brazil 95 B5 29 53S 50 17W
Osorno, Chile 96 E2 40 25S 73 0W
Osoyoos, Canada 72 D5 49 0N 119 30W
Osøyro, Norway 9 F11 60 9N 5 30 E
Ospika →, Canada 72 B4 56 20N 124 0W
Osprey Reef, Australia 62 A4 13 52S 146 36 E
Oss, Neths. 15 C5 51 46N 5 32 E
Ossa, Mt., Australia 62 G4 41 52S 146 3 E
Óssa, Óros, Greece 21 E10 39 47N 22 42 E
Ossabaw I., U.S.A. 77 K5 31 50N 81 5W
Ossining, U.S.A. 79 E11 41 10N 73 55W
Ossipee, U.S.A. 79 C13 43 41N 71 7W
Ossokmanuan L., Canada 71 B7 53 25N 65 0W
Ossora, Russia 27 D17 59 20N 163 13 E
Ostend = Oostende, Belgium 15 C2 51 15N 2 54 E
Oster, Ukraine 17 C16 50 57N 30 53 E
Osterburg, U.S.A. 78 F6 40 16N 78 31W
Österdalälven, Sweden 9 F16 61 30N 13 45 E
Østerdalen, Norway 9 F14 61 40N 10 50 E
Östersund, Sweden 8 E16 63 10N 14 38 E
Ostfriesische Inseln, Germany 16 B4 53 42N 7 0 E
Ostrava, Czech Rep. 17 D10 49 51N 18 18 E
Ostróda, Poland 17 B10 53 42N 19 58 E
Ostroh, Ukraine 17 C14 50 20N 26 30 E
Ostrołęka, Poland 17 B11 53 4N 21 32 E
Ostrów Mazowiecka, Poland 17 B11 52 50N 21 51 E
Ostrów Wielkopolski, Poland 17 C9 51 36N 17 44 E
Ostrowiec-Świętokrzyski, Poland 17 C11 50 55N 21 22 E
Ostuni, Italy 21 D7 40 44N 17 35 E
Ōsumi-Kaikyō, Japan 31 J5 30 55N 131 0 E
Ōsumi-Shotō, Japan 31 J5 30 30N 130 0 E
Osuna, Spain 19 D3 37 14N 5 8W
Oswegatchie →, U.S.A. 79 B9 44 42N 75 30W
Oswego, U.S.A. 79 C8 43 27N 76 31W
Oswego →, U.S.A. 79 C8 43 27N 76 30W
Oswestry, U.K. 10 E4 52 52N 3 3W
Oświęcim, Poland 17 C10 50 2N 19 11 E
Otago □, N.Z. 59 L2 45 15S 170 0 E
Otago Harbour, N.Z. 59 L3 45 47S 170 42 E
Ōtake, Japan 31 G6 34 12N 132 13 E
Otaki, N.Z. 59 J5 40 45S 175 10 E
Otaru, Japan 30 C10 43 10N 141 0 E
Otaru-Wan = Ishikari-Wan, Japan 30 C10 43 25N 141 1 E
Otavalo, Ecuador 92 C3 0 13N 78 20W
Otavi, Namibia 56 B2 19 40S 17 24 E
Otchinjau, Angola 56 B1 16 30S 13 56 E
Otelnuk L., Canada 71 A6 56 9N 68 12W
Othello, U.S.A. 82 C4 46 50N 119 10W
Otjiwarongo, Namibia 56 C2 20 30S 16 33 E
Otoineppu, Japan 30 B11 44 44N 142 16 E
Otorohanga, N.Z. 59 H5 38 12S 175 14 E
Otoskwin →, Canada 70 B2 52 13N 88 6W
Otra →, Norway 9 G13 58 9N 8 1 E
Otranto, Italy 21 D8 40 9N 18 28 E
Otranto, C. d', Italy 21 D8 40 7N 18 30 E
Otranto, Str. of, Italy 21 D8 40 15N 18 40 E
Otse, S. Africa 56 D4 25 2S 25 45 E
Ōtsu, Japan 31 G7 35 0N 135 50 E
Ōtsuki, Japan 31 G9 35 36N 138 57 E
Ottawa = Outaouais →, Canada 70 C5 45 27N 74 8W
Ottawa, Canada 79 A9 45 27N 75 42W
Ottawa, Ill., U.S.A. 80 E10 41 21N 88 51W
Ottawa, Kans., U.S.A. 80 F7 38 37N 95 16W
Ottawa Is., Canada 69 C11 59 35N 80 10W
Otter Cr. →, U.S.A. 79 B11 44 13N 73 17W
Otter L., Canada 73 B8 55 35N 104 39W
Otterville, Canada 78 D4 42 55N 80 36W
Ottery St. Mary, U.K. 11 G4 50 44N 3 17W
Otto Beit Bridge, Zimbabwe 55 F2 15 59S 28 56 E
Ottosdal, S. Africa 56 D4 26 46S 25 59 E
Ottumwa, U.S.A. 80 E8 41 1N 92 25W
Oturkpo, Nigeria 50 G7 7 16N 8 8 E
Otway, B., Chile 96 G2 53 30S 74 0W
Otway, C., Australia 63 F3 38 52S 143 30 E
Otwock, Poland 17 B11 52 5N 21 20 E
Ou →, Laos 38 B4 20 4N 102 13 E
Ou Neua, Laos 38 A3 22 18N 101 48 E
Ou-Sammyaku, Japan 30 E10 39 20N 140 35 E
Ouachita →, U.S.A. 81 K9 31 38N 91 49W
Ouachita, L., U.S.A. 81 H8 34 34N 93 12W
Ouachita Mts., U.S.A. 81 H7 34 40N 94 25W
Ouagadougou, Burkina Faso 50 F5 12 25N 1 30W
Ouahran = Oran, Algeria 50 A5 35 45N 0 39W
Ouallene, Algeria 50 D6 24 41N 1 11 E
Ouargla, Algeria 50 B7 31 59N 5 16 E
Ouarzazate, Morocco 50 B4 30 55N 6 50W
Oubangi →, Dem. Rep. of the Congo 52 E3 0 30S 17 50 E
Ouddorp, Neths. 15 C3 51 50N 3 57 E
Oude Rijn →, Neths. 15 B4 52 12N 4 24 E
Oudenaarde, Belgium 15 D3 50 50N 3 37 E
Oudtshoorn, S. Africa 56 E3 33 35S 22 14 E
Ouessant, Î. d', France 18 B1 48 28N 5 6W
Ouesso, Congo 52 D3 1 37N 16 5 E
Ouest, Pte. de l', Canada 71 C7 49 52N 64 40W
Ouezzane, Morocco 50 B4 34 51N 5 35W
Oughterard, Ireland 13 C2 53 26N 9 18W
Oujda, Morocco 50 B5 34 41N 1 55W
Oulainen, Finland 8 D21 64 17N 24 47 E
Oulu, Finland 8 D21 65 1N 25 29 E
Oulujärvi, Finland 8 D22 64 25N 27 15 E
Oulujoki →, Finland 8 D21 65 1N 25 30 E
Oum Chalouba, Chad 51 E10 15 48N 20 46 E
Oum Hadjer, Chad 51 F9 13 18N 19 41 E
Ounasjoki →, Finland 8 C21 66 31N 25 40 E
Ounguati, Namibia 56 C2 22 0S 15 46 E
Ounianga Sérir, Chad 51 E10 18 54N 20 51 E
Our →, Lux. 15 E6 49 55N 6 5 E
Ouray, U.S.A. 83 G10 38 1N 107 40W
Ourense, Spain 19 A2 42 19N 7 55W
Ouricuri, Brazil 93 E10 7 53S 40 5W
Ourinhos, Brazil 95 A6 23 0S 49 54W
Ouro Fino, Brazil 95 A6 22 16S 46 25W
Ouro Prêto, Brazil 95 A7 20 20S 43 30W
Ourthe →, Belgium 15 D5 50 29N 5 35 E
Ouse →, E. Susx., U.K. 11 G8 50 47N 0 4 E
Ouse →, N. Yorks., U.K. 10 D7 53 44N 0 55W
Outaouais →, Canada 70 C5 45 27N 74 8W
Outardes →, Canada 71 C6 49 24N 69 30W
Outer Hebrides, U.K. 12 D1 57 30N 7 40W
Outjo, Namibia 56 C2 20 5S 16 7 E
Outlook, Canada 73 C7 51 30N 107 0W
Outokumpu, Finland 8 E23 62 43N 29 1 E
Ouyen, Australia 63 F3 35 1S 142 22 E
Ovalau, Fiji 59 C8 17 40S 178 48 E
Ovalle, Chile 94 C1 30 33S 71 18W
Ovamboland, Namibia 56 B2 18 30S 16 0 E
Overflakkee, Neths. 15 C4 51 44N 4 10 E
Overijssel □, Neths. 15 B6 52 25N 6 35 E
Overland Park, U.S.A. 80 F7 38 55N 94 50W
Overton, U.S.A. 85 J12 36 33N 114 27W
Övertorneå, Sweden 8 C20 66 23N 23 38 E
Ovid, U.S.A. 79 D8 42 41N 76 49W
Oviedo, Spain 19 A3 43 25N 5 50W
Oviši, Latvia 9 H19 57 33N 21 44 E
Ovoot, Mongolia 34 B7 45 21N 113 45 E
Övör Hangay □, Mongolia 34 B2 45 0N 102 30 E
Øvre Årdal, Norway 9 F12 61 19N 7 48 E
Ovruch, Ukraine 17 C15 51 25N 28 45 E
Owaka, N.Z. 59 M2 46 27S 169 40 E
Owambo = Ovamboland, Namibia 56 B2 18 30S 16 0 E
Owasco L., U.S.A. 79 D8 42 50N 76 31W
Owase, Japan 31 G8 34 7N 136 12 E
Owatonna, U.S.A. 80 C8 44 5N 93 14W
Owbeh, Afghan. 40 B3 34 28N 63 10 E
Owego, U.S.A. 79 D8 42 6N 76 16W
Owen Falls Dam, Uganda 54 B3 0 30N 33 5 E
Owen Sound, Canada 78 B4 44 35N 80 55W
Owens →, U.S.A. 84 J9 36 32N 117 59W
Owens L., U.S.A. 85 J9 36 26N 117 57W
Owensboro, U.S.A. 76 G2 37 46N 87 7W
Owl →, Canada 73 B10 57 51N 92 44W
Owo, Nigeria 50 G7 7 10N 5 39 E
Owosso, U.S.A. 76 D3 43 0N 84 10W
Owyhee, U.S.A. 82 F5 41 57N 116 6W
Owyhee →, U.S.A. 82 E5 43 49N 117 2W
Owyhee, L., U.S.A. 82 E5 43 38N 117 14W
Ox Mts. = Slieve Gamph, Ireland 13 B3 54 6N 9 0W
Öxarfjörður, Iceland 8 C5 66 15N 16 45W
Oxbow, Canada 73 D8 49 14N 102 10W
Oxelösund, Sweden 9 G17 58 43N 17 5 E
Oxford, N.Z. 59 K4 43 18S 172 11 E
Oxford, U.K. 11 F6 51 46N 1 15W
Oxford, Mass., U.S.A. 79 D13 42 7N 71 52W
Oxford, Miss., U.S.A. 81 H10 34 22N 89 31W
Oxford, N.C., U.S.A. 77 G6 36 19N 78 35W
Oxford, N.Y., U.S.A. 79 D9 42 27N 75 36W
Oxford, Ohio, U.S.A. 76 F3 39 31N 84 45W
Oxford L., Canada 73 C9 54 51N 95 37W
Oxfordshire □, U.K. 11 F6 51 48N 1 16W
Oxnard, U.S.A. 85 L7 34 12N 119 11W
Oxus = Amudarya →, Uzbekistan 26 E6 43 58N 59 34 E
Oya, Malaysia 36 D4 2 55N 111 55 E
Oyama, Japan 31 F9 36 18N 139 48 E
Oyem, Gabon 52 D2 1 34N 11 31 E
Oyen, Canada 73 C6 51 22N 110 28W
Oykel →, U.K. 12 D4 57 56N 4 26W
Oymyakon, Russia 27 C15 63 25N 142 44 E
Oyo, Nigeria 50 G6 7 46N 3 56 E
Oyster Bay, U.S.A. 79 F11 40 52N 73 32W
Ōyūbari, Japan 30 C11 43 1N 142 5 E
Ozamiz, Phil. 37 C6 8 15N 123 50 E
Ozark, Ala., U.S.A. 77 K3 31 28N 85 39W
Ozark, Ark., U.S.A. 81 H8 35 29N 93 50W
Ozark, Mo., U.S.A. 81 G8 37 1N 93 12W
Ozark Plateau, U.S.A. 81 G9 37 20N 91 40W
Ozarks, L. of the, U.S.A. 80 F8 38 12N 92 38W
Ózd, Hungary 17 D11 48 14N 20 15 E
Ozette L., U.S.A. 84 B2 48 6N 124 38W
Ozona, U.S.A. 81 K4 30 43N 101 12W
Ozuluama, Mexico 87 C5 21 40N 97 50W

P

Pa-an, Burma 41 L20 16 51N 97 40 E
Pa Mong Dam, Thailand 38 D4 18 0N 102 22 E
Pa Sak →, Thailand 36 B2 15 30N 101 0 E
Paamiut, Greenland 4 C5 62 0N 49 43W
Paarl, S. Africa 56 E2 33 45S 18 56 E
Pab Hills, Pakistan 42 F2 26 30N 66 45 E
Pabbay, U.K. 12 D1 57 46N 7 14W
Pabianice, Poland 17 C10 51 40N 19 20 E
Pabna, Bangla. 41 G16 24 1N 89 18 E
Pabo, Uganda 54 B3 3 1N 32 10 E
Pacaja →, Brazil 93 D8 1 56S 50 50W
Pacaraima, Sa., S. Amer. 92 C6 4 0N 62 30W
Pacasmayo, Peru 92 E3 7 20S 79 35W
Pachhar, India 42 G7 24 40N 77 42 E
Pachitea →, Peru 92 E4 8 46S 74 33W
Pachmarhi, India 43 H8 22 28N 78 26 E
Pachpadra, India 40 G8 25 58N 72 10 E
Pachuca, Mexico 87 C5 20 10N 98 40W
Pacific, Canada 72 C3 54 48N 128 28W
Pacific-Antarctic Ridge, Pac. Oc. 65 M16 43 0S 115 0W
Pacific Grove, U.S.A. 84 J5 36 38N 121 56W
Pacific Ocean, Pac. Oc. 65 G14 10 0N 140 0W
Pacific Rim Nat. Park, Canada 84 B2 48 40N 124 45W
Pacifica, U.S.A. 84 H4 37 36N 122 30W
Pacitan, Indonesia 37 H14 8 12S 111 7 E
Packwood, U.S.A. 84 D5 46 36N 121 40W
Padaido, Kepulauan, Indonesia 37 E9 1 15S 136 30 E
Padang, Indonesia 36 E2 1 0S 100 20 E
Padang Endau, Malaysia 39 L4 2 40N 103 38 E
Padangpanjang, Indonesia 36 E2 0 40S 100 20 E
Padangsidempuan, Indonesia 36 D1 1 30N 99 15 E
Paddle Prairie, Canada 72 B5 57 57N 117 29W
Paddockwood, Canada 73 C7 53 30N 105 30W
Paderborn, Germany 16 C5 51 42N 8 45 E
Padma, India 43 G11 24 12N 85 22 E
Pádova, Italy 20 B4 45 25N 11 53 E
Padra, India 42 H5 22 15N 73 7 E
Padrauna, India 43 F10 26 54N 83 59 E
Padre I., U.S.A. 81 M6 27 10N 97 25W
Padstow, U.K. 11 G3 50 33N 4 58W
Padua = Pádova, Italy 20 B4 45 25N 11 53 E
Paducah, Ky., U.S.A. 76 G1 37 5N 88 37W
Paducah, Tex., U.S.A. 81 H4 34 1N 100 18W
Paengnyŏng-do, S. Korea 35 F13 37 57N 124 40 E
Paeroa, N.Z. 59 G5 37 23S 175 41 E
Pafúri, Mozam. 57 C5 22 28S 31 17 E
Pag, Croatia 16 F8 44 25N 15 3 E
Pagadian, Phil. 37 C6 7 55N 123 30 E
Pagai Selatan, Pulau, Indonesia 36 E2 3 0S 100 15 E
Pagai Utara, Pulau, Indonesia 36 E2 2 35S 100 0 E
Pagalu = Annobón, Atl. Oc. 49 G4 1 25S 5 36 E
Pagara, India 43 G9 24 22N 80 1 E
Pagastikós Kólpos, Greece 21 E10 39 15N 23 0 E
Pagatan, Indonesia 36 E5 3 33S 115 59 E
Page, U.S.A. 83 H8 36 57N 111 27W
Pago Pago, Amer. Samoa 59 B13 14 16S 170 43W
Pagosa Springs, U.S.A. 83 H10 37 16N 107 1W
Pagwa River, Canada 70 B2 50 2N 85 14W
Pahala, U.S.A. 74 J17 19 12N 155 29W
Pahang →, Malaysia 39 L4 3 30N 103 9 E
Pahiatua, N.Z. 59 J5 40 27S 175 50 E
Pahokee, U.S.A. 77 M5 26 50N 80 40W
Pahrump, U.S.A. 85 J11 36 12N 115 59W
Pahute Mesa, U.S.A. 84 H10 37 20N 116 45W
Pai, Thailand 38 C2 19 19N 98 27 E
Paicines, U.S.A. 84 J5 36 44N 121 17W
Paide, Estonia 9 G21 58 57N 25 31 E
Paignton, U.K. 11 G4 50 26N 3 35W
Päijänne, Finland 9 F21 61 30N 25 30 E
Pailani, India 43 G9 25 45N 80 26 E
Pailin, Cambodia 38 F4 12 46N 102 36 E
Painan, Indonesia 36 E2 1 21S 100 34 E
Painesville, U.S.A. 78 E3 41 43N 81 15W
Paint Hills = Wemindji, Canada 70 B4 53 0N 78 49W
Paint L., Canada 73 B9 55 28N 97 57W
Painted Desert, U.S.A. 83 J8 36 0N 111 0W
Paintsville, U.S.A. 76 G4 37 49N 82 48W
País Vasco □, Spain 19 A4 42 50N 2 45W
Paisley, Canada 78 B3 44 18N 81 16W
Paisley, U.K. 12 F4 55 50N 4 25W
Paisley, U.S.A. 82 E3 42 42N 120 32W
Paita, Peru 92 E2 5 11S 81 9W
Pajares, Puerto de, Spain 19 A3 42 58N 5 46W
Pak Lay, Laos 38 C3 18 15N 101 27 E
Pak Phanang, Thailand 39 H3 8 21N 100 12 E
Pak Sane, Laos 38 C4 18 22N 103 39 E
Pak Song, Laos 38 E6 15 11N 106 14 E
Pak Suong, Laos 38 C4 19 58N 102 15 E
Pakaur, India 43 G12 24 38N 87 51 E
Pakenham, Canada 79 A8 45 18N 76 18W
Pákhnes, Greece 23 D6 35 16N 24 4 E
Pakhuis, S. Africa 56 E2 32 9S 19 5 E
Pakistan ■, Asia 42 E4 30 0N 70 0 E
Pakkading, Laos 38 C4 18 19N 103 59 E
Pakokku, Burma 41 J19 21 20N 95 0 E
Pakowki L., Canada 73 D6 49 20N 111 0W
Pakpattan, Pakistan 42 D5 30 25N 73 27 E
Paktīā □, Afghan. 40 C6 33 30N 69 15 E
Paktīkā □, Afghan. 40 C6 32 30N 69 0 E
Pakwach, Uganda 54 B3 2 28N 31 27 E
Pakxe, Laos 38 E5 15 5N 105 52 E
Pal Lahara, India 43 J11 21 27N 85 11 E
Pala, Chad 51 G9 9 25N 15 5 E
Pala, Dem. Rep. of the Congo 54 D2 6 45S 29 30 E
Pala, U.S.A. 85 M9 33 22N 117 5W
Palabek, Uganda 54 B3 3 22N 32 33 E
Palacios, U.S.A. 81 L6 28 42N 96 13W
Palagruža, Croatia 20 C7 42 24N 16 15 E
Palaiókastron, Greece 23 D8 35 12N 26 15 E
Palaiokhóra, Greece 23 D5 35 16N 23 39 E
Palam, India 40 K10 19 0N 77 0 E
Palampur, India 42 C7 32 10N 76 30 E
Palana, Australia 62 F4 39 45S 147 55 E
Palana, Russia 27 D16 59 10N 159 59 E
Palanan, Phil. 37 A6 17 8N 122 29 E
Palanan Pt., Phil. 37 A6 17 17N 122 30 E
Palandri, Pakistan 43 C5 33 42N 73 40 E
Palanga, Lithuania 9 J19 55 58N 21 3 E
Palangkaraya, Indonesia 36 E4 2 16S 113 56 E
Palani Hills, India 40 P10 10 14N 77 33 E
Palanpur, India 42 G5 24 10N 72 25 E
Palapye, Botswana 56 C4 22 30S 27 7 E
Palas, Pakistan 43 B5 35 4N 73 14 E
Palashi, India 43 H13 23 47N 88 15 E
Palasponga, India 43 J11 21 47N 85 34 E
Palatka, Russia 27 C16 60 6N 150 54 E
Palatka, U.S.A. 77 L5 29 39N 81 38W
Palau ■, Pac. Oc. 28 J17 7 30N 134 30 E
Palauk, Burma 38 F2 13 10N 98 40 E
Palawan, Phil. 36 C5 9 30N 118 30 E
Palayankottai, India 40 Q10 8 45N 77 45 E
Paldiski, Estonia 9 G21 59 23N 24 9 E
Paleleh, Indonesia 37 D6 1 10N 121 50 E
Palembang, Indonesia 36 E2 3 0S 104 50 E
Palencia, Spain 19 A3 42 1N 4 34W
Palenque, Mexico 87 D6 17 31N 91 58W
Paleokastrítsa, Greece 23 A3 39 40N 19 41 E
Paleometokho, Cyprus 23 D12 35 7N 33 11 E
Palermo, Italy 20 E5 38 7N 13 22 E
Palermo, U.S.A. 82 G3 39 26N 121 33W
Palestina, Chile 96 A3 23 50S 69 47W
Palestine, Asia 47 D4 32 0N 35 0 E
Palestine, U.S.A. 81 K7 31 46N 95 38W
Paletwa, Burma 41 J18 21 10N 92 50 E
Palghat, India 40 P10 10 46N 76 42 E
Palgrave, Mt., Australia 60 D2 23 22S 115 58 E
Pali, India 42 G5 25 50N 73 20 E
Palikir, Micronesia 64 G7 6 55N 158 9 E
Palioúrion, Ákra, Greece 21 E10 39 57N 23 45 E
Palisades Reservoir, U.S.A. 82 E8 43 20N 111 12W
Paliseul, Belgium 15 E5 49 54N 5 8 E
Palitana, India 42 J4 21 32N 71 49 E
Palizada, Mexico 87 D6 18 18N 92 8W
Palk Bay, Asia 40 Q11 9 30N 79 15 E
Palk Strait, Asia 40 Q11 10 0N 79 45 E
Palkānah, Iraq 44 C5 35 49N 44 26 E
Palkot, India 43 H11 22 53N 84 39 E
Palla Road = Dinokwe, Botswana 56 C4 23 29S 26 37 E
Pallanza = Verbánia, Italy 18 D8 45 56N 8 33 E
Pallarenda, Australia 62 B4 19 12S 146 46 E
Pallinup →, Australia 61 F2 34 27S 118 50 E
Pallisa, Uganda 54 B3 1 12N 33 43 E
Pallu, India 42 E6 28 59N 74 14 E
Palm Bay, U.S.A. 77 L5 28 2N 80 35W
Palm Beach, U.S.A. 77 M6 26 43N 80 2W
Palm Coast, U.S.A. 77 L5 29 32N 81 10W
Palm Desert, U.S.A. 85 M10 33 43N 116 22W
Palm Is., Australia 62 B4 18 40S 146 35 E
Palm Springs, U.S.A. 85 M10 33 50N 116 33W
Palma, Mozam. 55 E5 10 46S 40 29 E
Palma, B. de, Spain 22 B9 39 30N 2 39 E

Palma de Mallorca, *Spain* .. **22 B9** 39 35N 2 39 E
Palma Soriano, *Cuba* **88 B4** 20 15N 76 0W
Palmares, *Brazil* **93 E11** 8 41S 35 28W
Palmas, *Brazil* **95 B5** 26 29S 52 0W
Palmas, C., *Liberia* **50 H4** 4 27N 7 46W
Pálmas, G. di, *Italy* .... **20 E3** 39 0N 8 30 E
Palmdale, *U.S.A.* **85 L8** 34 35N 118 7W
Palmeira das Missões, *Brazil* **95 B5** 27 55S 53 17W
Palmeira dos Índios, *Brazil* .. **93 E11** 9 25S 36 37W
Palmer, *U.S.A.* **68 B5** 61 36N 149 7W
Palmer →, *Australia* .... **62 B3** 16 0S 142 26 E
Palmer Arch., *Antarctica* **5 C17** 64 15S 65 0W
Palmer Lake, *U.S.A.* **80 F2** 39 7N 104 55W
Palmer Land, *Antarctica* **5 D18** 73 0S 63 0W
Palmerston, *Canada* **78 C4** 43 50N 80 51W
Palmerston, *N.Z.* .... **59 L3** 45 29S 170 43 E
Palmerston North, *N.Z.* ..... **59 J5** 40 21S 175 39 E
Palmerton, *U.S.A.* **79 F9** 40 48N 75 37W
Palmetto, *U.S.A.* **77 M4** 27 31N 82 34W
Palmi, *Italy* .... **20 E6** 38 21N 15 51 E
Palmira, *Argentina* **94 C2** 32 59S 68 34W
Palmira, *Colombia* **92 C3** 3 32N 76 16W
Palmyra = Tudmur, *Syria* .... **44 C3** 34 36N 38 15 E
Palmyra, *Mo., U.S.A.* **80 F9** 39 48N 91 32W
Palmyra, *N.J., U.S.A.* **79 F9** 40 1N 75 1W
Palmyra, *N.Y., U.S.A.* **78 C7** 43 5N 77 18W
Palmyra, *Pa., U.S.A.* **79 F8** 40 18N 76 36W
Palmyra Is., *Pac. Oc.* **65 G11** 5 52N 162 5W
Palo Alto, *U.S.A.* **84 H4** 37 27N 122 10W
Palo Verde, *U.S.A.* **85 M12** 33 26N 114 44W
Palopo, *Indonesia* .... **37 E6** 3 0S 120 16 E
Palos, C. de, *Spain* **19 D5** 37 38N 0 40W
Palos Verdes, *U.S.A.* **85 M8** 33 48N 118 23W
Palos Verdes, Pt., *U.S.A.* **85 M8** 33 43N 118 26W
Palu, *Indonesia* .... **37 E5** 1 0S 119 52 E
Palu, *Turkey* .... **25 G7** 38 45N 40 0 E
Palwal, *India* .... **42 E7** 28 8N 77 19 E
Pamanukan, *Indonesia* ..... **37 G12** 6 16S 107 49 E
Pamiers, *France* .... **18 E4** 43 7N 1 39 E
Pamir, *Tajikistan* .... **26 F8** 37 40N 73 0 E
Pamlico →, *U.S.A.* **77 H7** 35 20N 76 28W
Pamlico Sd., *U.S.A.* **77 H8** 35 20N 76 0W
Pampa, *U.S.A.* **81 H4** 35 32N 100 58W
Pampa de las Salinas, *Argentina* **94 C2** 32 1S 66 58W
Pampanua, *Indonesia* ...... **37 E6** 4 16S 120 8 E
Pampas, *Argentina* **94 D3** 35 0S 63 0W
Pampas, *Peru* **92 F4** 12 20S 74 50W
Pamplona, *Colombia* **92 B4** 7 23N 72 39W
Pamplona, *Spain* **19 A5** 42 48N 1 38W
Pampoenpoort, *S. Africa* ... **56 E3** 31 3S 22 40 E
Pana, *U.S.A.* **80 F10** 39 23N 89 5W
Panaca, *U.S.A.* **83 H6** 37 47N 114 23W
Panaitan, *Indonesia* .... **37 G11** 6 36S 105 12 E
Panaji, *India* .... **40 M8** 15 25N 73 50 E
Panamá, *Panama* **88 E4** 9 0N 79 25W
Panama ■, *Cent. Amer.* **88 E4** 8 48N 79 55W
Panamá, G. de, *Panama* **88 E4** 8 4N 79 20W
Panama Canal, *Panama* **88 E4** 9 10N 79 37W
Panama City, *U.S.A.* **77 K3** 30 10N 85 40W
Panamint Range, *U.S.A.* **85 J9** 36 20N 117 20W
Panamint Springs, *U.S.A.* ... **85 J9** 36 20N 117 28W
Panão, *Peru* **92 E3** 9 55S 75 55W
Panare, *Thailand* .... **39 J3** 6 51N 101 30 E
Panay, *Phil.* .... **37 B6** 11 10N 122 30 E
Panay, G., *Phil.* .... **37 B6** 11 0N 122 30 E
Pančevo, *Serbia, Yug.* ...... **21 B9** 44 52N 20 41 E
Panda, *Mozam.* .... **57 C5** 24 2S 34 45 E
Pandan, *Phil.* .... **37 B6** 11 45N 122 10 E
Pandegelang, *Indonesia* .... **37 G12** 6 25S 106 5 E
Pandhana, *India* .... **42 J7** 21 42N 76 13 E
Pandharpur, *India* .... **40 L9** 17 41N 75 20 E
Pando, *Uruguay* **95 C4** 34 44S 56 0W
Pando, L. = Hope, L., *Australia* **63 D2** 28 24S 139 18 E
Pandokrátor, *Greece* .... **23 A3** 39 45N 19 50 E
Pandora, *Costa Rica* **88 E3** 9 43N 83 3W
Panevėžys, *Lithuania* ...... **9 J21** 55 42N 24 25 E
Panfilov, *Kazakstan* .... **26 E8** 44 10N 80 0 E
Pang-Long, *Burma* .... **41 H21** 23 11N 98 45 E
Pang-Yang, *Burma* .... **41 H21** 22 7N 98 48 E
Panga, *Dem. Rep. of the Congo* .... **54 B2** 1 52N 26 18 E
Pangalanes, Canal des = Ampangalana, Lakandranon', *Madag.* ... **57 C8** 22 48S 47 50 E
Pangani, *Tanzania* .... **54 D4** 5 25S 38 58 E
Pangani →, *Tanzania* ...... **54 D4** 5 26S 38 58 E
Pangfou = Bengbu, *China* ... **35 H9** 32 58N 117 20 E
Pangil, *Dem. Rep. of the Congo* .... **54 C2** 3 10S 26 35 E
Pangkah, Tanjung, *Indonesia* **37 G15** 6 51S 112 33 E
Pangkajene, *Indonesia* ..... **37 E5** 4 46S 119 34 E
Pangkalanbrandan, *Indonesia* **36 D1** 4 1N 98 20 E
Pangkalanbuun, *Indonesia* .. **36 E4** 2 41S 111 37 E
Pangkalpinang, *Indonesia* .. **36 E3** 2 0S 106 0 E
Pangnirtung, *Canada* **69 B13** 66 8N 65 54W
Pangong Tso, *India* .... **42 B8** 34 40N 78 40 E
Panguitch, *U.S.A.* **83 H7** 37 50N 112 26W
Pangutaran Group, *Phil.* .... **37 C6** 6 18N 120 34 E
Panhandle, *U.S.A.* **81 H4** 35 21N 101 23W
Pani Mines, *India* .... **42 H5** 22 29N 73 50 E
Pania-Mutombo, *Dem. Rep. of the Congo* .... **54 D1** 5 11S 23 51 E
Panikota I., *India* .... **42 J4** 20 46N 71 21 E
Panipat, *India* .... **42 E7** 29 25N 77 2 E
Panjal Range = Pir Panjal Range, *India* .... **42 C7** 32 30N 76 50 E
Panjang, Hon, *Vietnam* ..... **39 H4** 9 20N 103 28 E
Panjgur, *Pakistan* .... **40 F4** 27 0N 64 5 E
Panjim = Panaji, *India* ...... **40 M8** 15 25N 73 50 E
Panjin, *China* .... **35 D12** 41 3N 122 2 E
Panjinad Barrage, *Pakistan* . **40 E7** 29 22N 71 15 E
Panjnad →, *Pakistan* ...... **42 E4** 28 57N 70 30 E
Panjwai, *Afghan.* .... **42 D1** 31 26N 65 27 E
Panmunjŏm, *N. Korea* ..... **35 F14** 37 59N 126 38 E
Panna, *India* .... **43 G9** 24 40N 80 15 E
Panna Hills, *India* .... **43 G9** 24 40N 81 15 E
Pannawonica, *Australia* .... **60 D2** 21 39S 116 19 E
Pannirtuuq = Pangnirtung, *Canada* **69 B13** 66 8N 65 54W
Pano Akil, *Pakistan* .... **42 F3** 27 51N 69 7 E
Pano Lefkara, *Cyprus* ...... **23 E12** 34 53N 33 20 E
Pano Panayia, *Cyprus* ...... **23 E11** 34 55N 32 38 E
Panorama, *Brazil* **95 A5** 21 21S 51 51W
Pánormon, *Greece* .... **23 D6** 35 25N 24 41 E
Pansemal, *India* .... **42 J6** 21 39N 74 42 E
Panshan = Panjin, *China* .... **35 D12** 41 3N 122 2 E
Panshi, *China* .... **35 C14** 42 58N 126 5 E
Pantanal, *Brazil* **92 H7** 17 30S 57 40W
Pantar, *Indonesia* .... **37 F6** 8 28S 124 10 E
Pante Macassar, *E. Timor* ... **37 F6** 9 30S 123 58 E
Pante Makasar = Pante Macassar, *E. Timor* ...... **37 F6** 9 30S 123 58 E
Pantelleria, *Italy* .... **20 F4** 36 50N 11 57 E
Pánuco, *Mexico* **87 C5** 22 0N 98 15W
Paola, *Malta* .... **23 D2** 35 52N 14 30 E
Paola, *U.S.A.* **80 F7** 38 35N 94 53W
Paonia, *U.S.A.* **83 G10** 38 52N 107 36W
Paoting = Baoding, *China* ... **34 E8** 38 50N 115 28 E
Paot'ou = Baotou, *China* .... **34 D6** 40 32N 110 2 E
Paoua, *C.A.R.* .... **52 C3** 7 9N 16 20 E
Pápa, *Hungary* .... **17 E9** 47 22N 17 30 E
Papa Stour, *U.K.* **12 A7** 60 20N 1 42W
Papa Westray, *U.K.* **12 B6** 59 20N 2 55W
Papagayo →, *Mexico* **87 D5** 16 36N 99 43W
Papagayo, G. de, *Costa Rica* **88 D2** 10 30N 85 50W
Papakura, *N.Z.* .... **59 G5** 37 4S 174 59 E
Papantla, *Mexico* **87 C5** 20 30N 97 30W
Papar, *Malaysia* .... **36 C5** 5 45N 116 0 E
Papeete, *Tahiti* **65 J13** 17 32S 149 34W
Paphos, *Cyprus* .... **23 E11** 34 46N 32 25 E
Papien Chiang = Da →, *Vietnam* .... **38 B5** 21 15N 105 20 E
Papigochic →, *Mexico* **86 B3** 29 9N 109 40W
Paposo, *Chile* **94 B1** 25 0S 70 30W
Papoutsa, *Cyprus* .... **23 E12** 34 54N 33 4 E
Papua New Guinea ■, *Oceania* .... **64 H6** 8 0S 145 0 E
Papudo, *Chile* **94 C1** 32 29S 71 27W
Papun, *Burma* .... **41 K20** 18 2N 97 30 E
Papunya, *Australia* .... **60 D5** 23 15S 131 54 E
Pará = Belém, *Brazil* **93 D9** 1 20S 48 30W
Pará □, *Brazil* **93 D8** 3 20S 52 0W
Paraburdoo, *Australia* ...... **60 D2** 23 14S 117 32 E
Paracatu, *Brazil* **93 G9** 17 10S 46 50W
Paracel Is., *S. China Sea* .... **36 A4** 15 50N 112 0 E
Parachilna, *Australia* .... **63 E2** 31 10S 138 21 E
Parachinar, *Pakistan* .... **42 C4** 33 55N 70 5 E
Paradhísi, *Greece* .... **23 C10** 36 18N 28 7 E
Paradip, *India* .... **41 J15** 20 15N 86 35 E
Paradise, *Calif., U.S.A.* **84 F5** 39 46N 121 37W
Paradise, *Nev., U.S.A.* **85 J11** 36 9N 115 10W
Paradise →, *Canada* **71 B8** 53 27N 57 19W
Paradise Hill, *Canada* **73 C7** 53 32N 109 28W
Paradise River, *Canada* **71 B8** 53 27N 57 17W
Paradise Valley, *U.S.A.* **82 F5** 41 30N 117 32W
Parado, *Indonesia* .... **37 F5** 8 42S 118 30 E
Paragould, *U.S.A.* **81 G9** 36 3N 90 29W
Paragua →, *Venezuela* **92 B6** 6 55N 62 55W
Paraguaçu →, *Brazil* **93 F11** 12 45S 38 54W
Paraguaçu Paulista, *Brazil* .. **95 A5** 22 22S 50 35W
Paraguaná, Pen. de, *Venezuela* **92 A5** 12 0N 70 0W
Paraguarí, *Paraguay* **94 B4** 25 36S 57 0W
Paraguarí □, *Paraguay* **94 B4** 26 0S 57 10W
Paraguay ■, *S. Amer.* **94 A4** 23 0S 57 0W
Paraguay →, *Paraguay* **94 B4** 27 18S 58 38W
Paraíba = João Pessoa, *Brazil* **93 E12** 7 10S 34 52W
Paraíba □, *Brazil* **93 E11** 7 0S 36 0W
Paraíba do Sul →, *Brazil* ... **95 A7** 21 37S 41 3W
Parainen, *Finland* .... **9 F20** 60 18N 22 18 E
Paraiso, *Mexico* **87 D6** 18 24N 93 14W
Parak, *Iran* .... **45 E7** 27 38N 52 25 E
Parakou, *Benin* .... **50 G6** 9 25N 2 40 E
Paralimni, *Cyprus* .... **23 D12** 35 2N 33 58 E
Paramaribo, *Surinam* **93 B7** 5 50N 55 10W
Paramushir, Ostrov, *Russia* . **27 D16** 50 24N 156 0 E
Paran →, *Israel* .... **47 E4** 30 20N 35 10 E
Paraná, *Argentina* **94 C3** 31 45S 60 30W
Paranã, *Brazil* **93 F9** 12 30S 47 48W
Paraná □, *Brazil* **95 A5** 24 30S 51 0W
Paraná →, *Argentina* **94 C4** 33 43S 59 15W
Paranaguá, *Brazil* **95 B6** 25 30S 48 30W
Paranaíba, *Brazil* **93 G8** 19 40S 51 11W
Paranaíba →, *Brazil* **93 H8** 20 6S 51 4W
Paranapanema →, *Brazil* ... **95 A5** 22 40S 53 9W
Paranapiacaba, Serra do, *Brazil* **95 A6** 24 31S 48 35W
Paranavai, *Brazil* **95 A5** 23 4S 52 56W
Parang, *Maguindanao, Phil.* . **37 C6** 7 23N 124 16 E
Parang, *Sulu, Phil.* .... **37 C6** 5 55N 120 54 E
Parângul Mare, Vf., *Romania* **17 F12** 45 20N 23 37 E
Paraparaumu, *N.Z.* .... **59 J5** 40 57S 175 3 E
Parbati →, *Mad. P., India* ... **42 G7** 25 50N 76 30 E
Parbati →, *Raj., India* ...... **42 F7** 26 54N 77 53 E
Parbhani, *India* .... **40 K10** 19 8N 76 52 E
Parchim, *Germany* .... **16 B6** 53 26N 11 52 E
Pardes Hanna-Karkur, *Israel* . **47 C3** 32 28N 34 57 E
Pardo →, *Bahia, Brazil* **93 G11** 15 40S 39 0W
Pardo →, *Mato Grosso, Brazil* **95 A5** 21 46S 52 9W
Pardubice, *Czech Rep.* ...... **16 C8** 50 3N 15 45 E
Pare, *Indonesia* .... **37 G15** 7 43S 112 12 E
Pare Mts., *Tanzania* .... **54 C4** 4 0S 37 45 E
Parecis, Serra dos, *Brazil* ... **92 F7** 13 0S 60 0W
Paren, *Russia* .... **27 C17** 62 30N 163 15 E
Parent, *Canada* **70 C5** 47 55N 74 35W
Parent, L., *Canada* **70 C4** 48 31N 77 1W
Parepare, *Indonesia* .... **37 E5** 4 0S 119 40 E
Párga, *Greece* .... **21 E9** 39 15N 20 29 E
Pargo, Pta. do, *Madeira* **22 D2** 32 49N 17 17W
Pariaguán, *Venezuela* **92 B6** 8 51N 64 34W
Paricutín, Cerro, *Mexico* **86 D4** 19 28N 102 15W
Parigi, *Indonesia* .... **37 E6** 0 50S 120 5 E
Parika, *Guyana* **92 B7** 6 50N 58 20W
Parima, Serra, *Brazil* **92 C6** 2 30N 64 0W
Parinari, *Peru* **92 D4** 4 35S 74 25W
Pariñas, Pta., *S. Amer.* **90 D2** 4 30S 82 0W
Parintins, *Brazil* **93 D7** 2 40S 56 50W
Pariparit Kyun, *Burma* ..... **41 M18** 14 55N 93 45 E
Paris, *Canada* **78 C4** 43 12N 80 25W
Paris, *France* .... **18 B5** 48 50N 2 20 E
Paris, *Idaho, U.S.A.* **82 E8** 42 14N 111 24W
Paris, *Ky., U.S.A.* **76 F3** 38 13N 84 15W
Paris, *Tenn., U.S.A.* **77 G1** 36 18N 88 19W
Paris, *Tex., U.S.A.* **81 J7** 33 40N 95 33W
Parish, *U.S.A.* **79 C8** 43 25N 76 8W
Parishville, *U.S.A.* **79 B10** 44 38N 74 49W
Park, *U.S.A.* **84 B4** 48 45N 122 18W
Park City, *U.S.A.* **82 F8** 40 39N 111 30W
Park Falls, *U.S.A.* **80 C9** 45 56N 90 27W
Park Head, *Canada* **78 B3** 44 36N 81 9W
Park Hills, *U.S.A.* **81 G9** 37 53N 90 28W
Park Range, *U.S.A.* **82 G10** 40 0N 106 30W
Park Rapids, *U.S.A.* **80 B7** 46 55N 95 4W
Park River, *U.S.A.* **80 A6** 48 24N 97 45W
Park Rynie, *S. Africa* .... **57 E5** 30 25S 30 45 E
Parkā Bandar, *Iran* .... **45 E8** 25 55N 59 35 E
Parkano, *Finland* .... **9 E20** 62 1N 23 0 E
Parker, *Ariz., U.S.A.* **85 L12** 34 9N 114 17W
Parker, *Pa., U.S.A.* **78 E5** 41 5N 79 41W
Parker Dam, *U.S.A.* **85 L12** 34 18N 114 8W
Parkersburg, *U.S.A.* **76 F5** 39 16N 81 34W
Parkes, *Australia* .... **63 E4** 33 9S 148 11 E
Parkfield, *U.S.A.* **84 K6** 35 54N 120 26W
Parkhill, *Canada* **78 C3** 43 15N 81 38W
Parkland, *U.S.A.* **84 C4** 47 9N 122 26W
Parkston, *U.S.A.* **80 D6** 43 24N 97 59W
Parksville, *Canada* **72 D4** 49 20N 124 21W
Parla, *Spain* **19 B4** 40 14N 3 46W
Parma, *Italy* .... **18 D9** 44 48N 10 20 E
Parma, *Idaho, U.S.A.* **82 E5** 43 47N 116 57W
Parma, *Ohio, U.S.A.* **78 E3** 41 23N 81 43W
Parnaguá, *Brazil* **93 F10** 10 10S 44 38W
Parnaíba, *Brazil* **93 D10** 2 54S 41 47W
Parnaíba →, *Brazil* **93 D10** 3 0S 41 50W
Parnassós, *Greece* .... **21 E10** 38 35N 22 30 E
Pärnu, *Estonia* .... **9 G21** 58 28N 24 33 E
Paroo →, *Australia* .... **63 E3** 31 28S 143 32 E
Páros, *Greece* .... **21 F11** 37 5N 25 12 E
Parowan, *U.S.A.* **83 H7** 37 51N 112 50W
Parral, *Chile* **94 D1** 36 10S 71 52W
Parras, *Mexico* **86 B4** 25 30N 102 20W
Parrett →, *U.K.* **11 F4** 51 12N 3 1W
Parris I., *U.S.A.* **77 J5** 32 20N 80 41W
Parrsboro, *Canada* **71 C7** 45 30N 64 25W
Parry I., *Canada* **78 A4** 45 18N 80 10W
Parry Is., *Canada* **4 B2** 77 0N 110 0W
Parry Sound, *Canada* **78 A5** 45 20N 80 0W
Parsnip →, *Canada* **72 B4** 55 10N 123 2W
Parsons, *U.S.A.* **81 G7** 37 20N 95 16W
Parsons Ra., *Australia* ..... **62 A2** 13 30S 135 15 E
Partinico, *Italy* .... **20 E5** 38 3N 13 7 E
Partridge I., *Canada* **70 A2** 55 59N 87 37W
Paru →, *Brazil* **93 D8** 1 33S 52 38W
Parvān □, *Afghan.* .... **40 B6** 35 0N 69 0 E
Parvatipuram, *India* .... **41 K13** 18 50N 83 25 E
Parvatsar, *India* .... **42 F6** 26 52N 74 49 E
Parys, *S. Africa* .... **56 D4** 26 52S 27 29 E
Pas, Pta. des, *Spain* .... **22 C7** 38 46N 1 26 E
Pasadena, *Canada* **71 C8** 49 1N 57 36W
Pasadena, *Calif., U.S.A.* **85 L8** 34 9N 118 9W
Pasadena, *Tex., U.S.A.* **81 L7** 29 43N 95 13W
Pasaje →, *Argentina* **94 B3** 25 39S 63 56W
Pascagoula, *U.S.A.* **81 K10** 30 21N 88 33W
Pascagoula →, *U.S.A.* **81 K10** 30 23N 88 37W
Paşcani, *Romania* .... **17 E14** 47 14N 26 45 E
Pasco, *U.S.A.* **82 C4** 46 14N 119 6W
Pasco, Cerro de, *Peru* **92 F3** 10 45S 76 10W
Pasco I., *Australia* .... **60 D2** 20 57S 115 20 E
Pascoag, *U.S.A.* **79 E13** 41 57N 71 42W
Pascua, I. de, *Chile* **65 K17** 27 7S 109 23W
Pasfield L., *Canada* **73 B7** 58 24N 105 20W
Pashmakli = Smolyan, *Bulgaria* .... **21 D11** 41 36N 24 38 E
Pasir Mas, *Malaysia* .... **39 J4** 6 2N 102 8 E
Pasir Putih, *Malaysia* .... **39 K4** 5 50N 102 24 E
Pasirian, *Indonesia* .... **37 H15** 8 13S 113 8 E
Pasirkuning, *Indonesia* ..... **36 E2** 0 30S 104 33 E
Paskūh, *Iran* .... **45 E9** 27 34N 61 39 E
Pasley, C., *Australia* .... **61 F3** 33 52S 123 35 E
Pašman, *Croatia* .... **16 G8** 43 58N 15 20 E
Pasni, *Pakistan* .... **40 G3** 25 15N 63 27 E
Paso Cantinela, *Mexico* **85 N11** 32 33N 115 47W
Paso de Indios, *Argentina* .. **96 E3** 43 55S 69 0W
Paso de los Libres, *Argentina* **94 B4** 29 44S 57 10W
Paso de los Toros, *Uruguay* . **94 C4** 32 45S 56 30W
Paso Robles, *U.S.A.* **83 J3** 35 38N 120 41W
Paspébiac, *Canada* **71 C6** 48 3N 65 17W
Pasrur, *Pakistan* .... **42 C6** 32 16N 74 43 E
Passage West, *Ireland* **13 E3** 51 52N 8 21W
Passaic, *U.S.A.* **79 F10** 40 51N 74 7W
Passau, *Germany* .... **16 D7** 48 34N 13 28 E
Passero, C., *Italy* .... **20 F6** 36 41N 15 10 E
Passo Fundo, *Brazil* **95 B5** 28 10S 52 20W
Passos, *Brazil* **93 H9** 20 45S 46 37W
Pastavy, *Belarus* .... **9 J22** 55 4N 26 50 E
Pastaza →, *Peru* **92 D3** 4 50S 76 52W
Pasto, *Colombia* **92 C3** 1 13N 77 17W
Pasuruan, *Indonesia* ...... **37 G15** 7 40S 112 44 E
Patagonia, *Argentina* **96 F3** 45 0S 69 0W
Patagonia, *U.S.A.* **83 L8** 31 33N 110 45W
Patambar, *Iran* .... **45 D9** 29 45N 60 17 E
Patan = Lalitapur, *Nepal* ... **43 F11** 27 40N 85 20 E
Patan, *Gujarat, India* .... **40 H8** 23 54N 72 14 E
Patan, *Maharashtra, India* ... **42 H5** 23 54N 72 14 E
Patani, *Indonesia* .... **37 D7** 0 20N 128 50 E
Pataudi, *India* .... **42 E7** 28 18N 76 48 E
Patchewollock, *Australia* ... **63 F3** 35 22S 142 12 E
Patchogue, *U.S.A.* **79 F11** 40 46N 73 1W
Patea, *N.Z.* .... **59 H5** 39 45S 174 30 E
Patensie, *S. Africa* .... **56 E3** 33 46S 24 49 E
Paternò, *Italy* .... **20 F6** 37 34N 14 54 E
Pateros, *U.S.A.* **82 B4** 48 3N 119 54W
Paterson, *U.S.A.* **79 F10** 40 55N 74 11W
Paterson Ra., *Australia* ..... **60 D3** 21 45S 122 10 E
Pathankot, *India* .... **42 C6** 32 18N 75 45 E
Pathein = Bassein, *Burma* .. **41 L19** 16 45N 94 30 E
Pathfinder Reservoir, *U.S.A.* **82 E10** 42 28N 106 51W
Pathiu, *Thailand* .... **39 G2** 10 42N 99 19 E
Pathum Thani, *Thailand* .... **38 E3** 14 1N 100 32 E
Pati, *Indonesia* .... **37 G14** 6 45S 111 1 E
Patía →, *Colombia* **92 C3** 2 13N 78 40W
Patiala, *Punjab, India* ...... **42 D7** 30 23N 76 26 E
Patiala, *Ut. P., India* .... **43 F8** 27 43N 79 1 E
Patkai Bum, *India* .... **41 F19** 27 0N 95 30 E
Pátmos, *Greece* .... **21 F12** 37 21N 26 36 E
Patna, *India* .... **43 G11** 25 35N 85 12 E
Pato Branco, *Brazil* **95 B5** 26 13S 52 40W
Patonga, *Uganda* .... **54 B3** 2 45N 33 15 E
Patos, *Brazil* **93 E11** 6 55S 37 16W
Patos, L. dos, *Brazil* **95 C5** 31 20S 51 0W
Patos, Río de los →, *Argentina* **94 C2** 31 18S 69 25W
Patos de Minas, *Brazil* **93 G9** 18 35S 46 32W
Patquía, *Argentina* **94 C2** 30 2S 66 55W
Pátrai, *Greece* .... **21 E9** 38 14N 21 47 E
Pátraikós Kólpos, *Greece* ... **21 E9** 38 17N 21 30 E
Patras = Pátrai, *Greece* .... **21 E9** 38 14N 21 47 E
Patrocínio, *Brazil* **93 G9** 18 57S 47 0W
Patta, *Kenya* .... **54 C5** 2 10S 41 0 E
Pattani, *Thailand* .... **39 J3** 6 48N 101 15 E
Pattaya, *Thailand* .... **36 B2** 12 52N 100 55 E
Patten, *U.S.A.* **77 C11** 46 0N 68 38W
Patterson, *Calif., U.S.A.* **84 H5** 37 28N 121 8W
Patterson, *La., U.S.A.* **81 L9** 29 42N 91 18W
Patterson, Mt., *U.S.A.* **84 G7** 38 29N 119 20W
Patti, *Punjab, India* .... **42 D6** 31 17N 74 54 E
Patti, *Ut. P., India* .... **43 G10** 25 55N 82 12 E
Pattoki, *Pakistan* .... **42 D5** 31 5N 73 52 E
Patton, *U.S.A.* **78 F6** 40 38N 78 39W
Patuakhali, *Bangla.* .... **41 H17** 22 20N 90 25 E
Patuanak, *Canada* **73 B7** 55 55N 107 43W
Patuca →, *Honduras* **88 C3** 15 50N 84 18W
Patuca, Punta, *Honduras* ... **88 C3** 15 49N 84 14W
Pátzcuaro, *Mexico* **86 D4** 19 30N 101 40W
Pau, *France* **18 E3** 43 19N 0 25W
Pauk, *Burma* .... **41 J19** 21 27N 94 30 E
Paul I., *Canada* **71 A7** 56 30N 61 20W
Paul Smiths, *U.S.A.* **79 B10** 44 26N 74 15W
Paulatuk, *Canada* **68 B7** 69 25N 124 0W
Paulis = Isiro, *Dem. Rep. of the Congo* .... **54 B2** 2 53N 27 40 E
Paulistana, *Brazil* **93 E10** 8 9S 41 9W
Paulo Afonso, *Brazil* **93 E11** 9 21S 38 15W
Paulpietersburg, *S. Africa* .. **57 D5** 27 23S 30 50 E
Pauls Valley, *U.S.A.* **81 H6** 34 44N 97 13W
Pauma Valley, *U.S.A.* **85 M10** 33 16N 116 58W
Pauri, *India* .... **43 D8** 30 9N 78 47 E
Pāveh, *Iran* .... **44 C5** 35 3N 46 22 E
Pavia, *Italy* .... **18 D8** 45 7N 9 8 E
Pavilion, *U.S.A.* **78 D6** 42 52N 78 1W
Pāvilosta, *Latvia* .... **9 H19** 56 53N 21 14 E
Pavlodar, *Kazakstan* .... **26 D8** 52 33N 77 0 E
Pavlograd = Pavlohrad, *Ukraine* .... **25 E6** 48 30N 35 52 E
Pavlohrad, *Ukraine* .... **25 E6** 48 30N 35 52 E
Pavlovo, *Russia* .... **24 C7** 55 58N 43 5 E
Pavlovsk, *Russia* .... **25 D7** 50 26N 40 5 E
Pavlovskaya, *Russia* .... **25 E6** 46 17N 39 47 E
Pawayan, *India* .... **43 E9** 28 4N 80 6 E
Pawhuska, *U.S.A.* **81 G6** 36 40N 96 20W
Pawling, *U.S.A.* **79 E11** 41 34N 73 36W
Pawnee, *U.S.A.* **81 G6** 36 20N 96 48W
Pawnee City, *U.S.A.* **80 E6** 40 7N 96 9W
Pawtucket, *U.S.A.* **79 E13** 41 53N 71 23W
Paximádhia, *Greece* .... **23 E6** 35 0N 24 35 E
Paxoí, *Greece* .... **21 E9** 39 14N 20 12 E
Paxton, *Ill., U.S.A.* **76 E1** 40 27N 88 6W
Paxton, *Nebr., U.S.A.* **80 E4** 41 7N 101 21W
Payakumbuh, *Indonesia* .... **36 E2** 0 20S 100 35 E
Payette, *U.S.A.* **82 D5** 44 5N 116 56W
Payne Bay = Kangirsuk, *Canada* **69 B13** 60 0N 70 0W
Payne L., *Canada* **69 C12** 59 30N 74 30W
Paynes Find, *Australia* ..... **61 E2** 29 15S 117 42 E
Paynesville, *U.S.A.* **80 C7** 45 23N 94 43W
Paysandú, *Uruguay* **94 C4** 32 19S 58 8W
Payson, *U.S.A.* **83 J8** 34 14N 111 20W
Paz →, *Guatemala* **88 D1** 13 44N 90 10W
Paz, B. de la, *Mexico* **86 C2** 24 15N 110 25W
Pāzanān, *Iran* .... **45 D6** 30 35N 49 59 E
Pazardzhik, *Bulgaria* ...... **21 C11** 42 12N 24 20 E
Pe Ell, *U.S.A.* **84 D3** 46 34N 123 18W
Peabody, *U.S.A.* **79 D14** 42 31N 70 56W
Peace →, *Canada* **72 B6** 59 0N 111 25W
Peace Point, *Canada* **72 B6** 59 7N 112 27W
Peace River, *Canada* **72 B5** 56 15N 117 18W
Peach Springs, *U.S.A.* **83 J7** 35 32N 113 25W
Peachland, *Canada* **72 D5** 49 47N 119 45W
Peachtree City, *U.S.A.* **77 J3** 33 25N 84 35W
Peak, The = Kinder Scout, *U.K.* **10 D6** 53 24N 1 52W
Peak District, *U.K.* **10 D6** 53 10N 1 50W
Peak Hill, *N.S.W., Australia* . **63 E4** 32 47S 148 11 E
Peak Hill, *W. Austral., Australia* .... **61 E2** 25 35S 118 43 E
Peak Ra., *Australia* .... **62 C4** 22 50S 148 20 E
Peake Cr. →, *Australia* .... **63 D2** 28 2S 136 7 E
Peale, Mt., *U.S.A.* **83 G9** 38 26N 109 14W
Pearblossom, *U.S.A.* **85 L9** 34 30N 117 55W
Pearl →, *U.S.A.* **81 K10** 30 11N 89 32W
Pearl City, *U.S.A.* **74 H16** 21 24N 157 59W
Pearl Harbor, *U.S.A.* **74 H16** 21 21N 157 57W
Pearl River, *U.S.A.* **79 E10** 41 4N 74 2W
Pearsall, *U.S.A.* **81 L5** 28 54N 99 6W
Peary Land, *Greenland* **4 A6** 82 40N 33 0W
Pease →, *U.S.A.* **81 H5** 34 12N 99 2W
Peawanuck, *Canada* **69 C11** 55 15N 85 12W
Pebane, *Mozam.* .... **55 F4** 17 10S 38 8 E
Pebas, *Peru* **92 D4** 3 10S 71 46W
Pebble Beach, *U.S.A.* **84 J5** 36 34N 121 57W
Peć, *Kosovo, Yug.* .... **21 C9** 42 40N 20 17 E
Pechenga, *Russia* .... **24 A5** 69 29N 31 4 E
Pechenizhyn, *Ukraine* ..... **17 D13** 48 30N 24 48 E
Pechiguera, Pta., *Canary Is.* . **22 F6** 28 51N 13 53W
Pechora, *Russia* .... **24 A10** 65 10N 57 11 E
Pechora →, *Russia* .... **24 A9** 68 13N 54 15 E
Pechorskaya Guba, *Russia* . **24 A9** 68 40N 54 0 E
Pečory, *Russia* .... **9 H22** 57 48N 27 40 E
Pecos, *U.S.A.* **81 K3** 31 26N 103 30W
Pecos →, *U.S.A.* **81 L3** 29 42N 101 22W
Pécs, *Hungary* .... **17 E10** 46 5N 18 15 E
Pedder, L., *Australia* ...... **62 G4** 42 55S 146 10 E
Peddie, *S. Africa* .... **57 E4** 33 14S 27 7 E
Pedernales, *Dom. Rep.* **89 C5** 18 2N 71 44W
Pedieos →, *Cyprus* .... **23 D12** 35 10N 33 54 E
Pedirka, *Australia* .... **63 D2** 26 40S 135 14 E
Pedra Azul, *Brazil* **93 G10** 16 2S 41 17W
Pedreiras, *Brazil* **93 D10** 4 32S 44 40W
Pedro Afonso, *Brazil* **93 E9** 9 0S 48 10W
Pedro Cays, *Jamaica* **88 C4** 17 5N 77 48W
Pedro de Valdivia, *Chile* **94 A2** 22 55S 69 38W
Pedro Juan Caballero, *Paraguay* **95 A4** 22 30S 55 40W
Pee Dee →, *U.S.A.* **77 J6** 33 22N 79 16W
Peebinga, *Australia* .... **63 E3** 34 52S 140 57 E
Peebles, *U.K.* **12 F5** 55 40N 3 11W
Peekskill, *U.S.A.* **79 E11** 41 17N 73 55W
Peel, *U.K.* **10 C3** 54 13N 4 40W
Peel →, *Australia* .... **63 E5** 30 50S 150 29 E
Peel →, *Canada* **68 B6** 67 0N 135 0W
Peel Sound, *Canada* **68 A10** 73 0N 96 0W
Peera Peera Poolanna L., *Australia* .... **63 D2** 26 30S 138 0 E

Peerless Lake, Canada 72 B6 56 37N 114 40W
Peers, Canada 72 C5 53 40N 116 0W
Pegasus Bay, N.Z. 59 K4 43 20S 173 10 E
Pegu, Burma 41 L20 17 20N 96 29 E
Pegu Yoma, Burma 41 K20 19 0N 96 0 E
Pehuajó, Argentina 94 D3 35 45S 62 0W
Pei Xian = Pizhou, China 34 G9 34 44N 116 55 E
Peine, Chile 94 A2 23 45S 68 8W
Peine, Germany 16 B6 52 19N 10 14 E
Peip'ing = Beijing, China 34 E9 39 55N 116 20 E
Peipus, L. = Chudskoye, Ozero, Russia 9 G22 58 13N 27 30 E
Peixe, Brazil 93 F9 12 0S 48 40W
Peixe →, Brazil 93 H8 21 31S 51 58W
Pekalongan, Indonesia 36 F3 6 53S 109 40 E
Pekan, Malaysia 39 L4 3 30N 103 25 E
Pekanbaru, Indonesia 36 D2 0 30N 101 15 E
Pekin, U.S.A. 80 E10 40 35N 89 40W
Peking = Beijing, China 34 E9 39 55N 116 20 E
Pelabuhan Kelang, Malaysia 39 L3 3 0N 101 23 E
Pelabuhan Ratu, Teluk, Indonesia 37 G12 7 5S 106 30 E
Pelabuhanratu, Indonesia 37 G12 7 0S 106 32 E
Pelagie, Is., Italy 20 G5 35 39N 12 33 E
Pelaihari, Indonesia 36 E4 3 55S 114 45 E
Peleaga, Vf., Romania 17 F12 45 22N 22 55 E
Pelée, Mt., Martinique 89 D7 14 48N 61 10W
Pelee, Pt., Canada 70 D3 41 54N 82 31W
Pelee I., Canada 78 E2 41 47N 82 40W
Pelekech, Kenya 54 B4 3 52N 35 8 E
Peleng, Indonesia 37 E6 1 20S 123 30 E
Pelican, U.S.A. 72 B1 57 58N 136 14W
Pelican L., Canada 73 C8 52 28N 100 20W
Pelican Narrows, Canada 73 B8 55 10N 102 56W
Pelješac, Croatia 20 C7 42 55N 17 25 E
Pelkosenniemi, Finland 8 C22 67 6N 27 28 E
Pella, S. Africa 56 D2 29 1S 19 6 E
Pella, U.S.A. 80 E8 41 25N 92 55W
Pello, Finland 8 C21 66 47N 23 59 E
Pelly →, Canada 68 B6 62 47N 137 19W
Pelly Bay, Canada 69 B11 68 38N 89 50W
Peloponnese = Pelopónnisos □, Greece 21 F10 37 10N 22 0 E
Pelopónnisos □, Greece 21 F10 37 10N 22 0 E
Pelorus Sd., N.Z. 59 J4 40 59S 173 59 E
Pelotas, Brazil 95 C5 31 42S 52 23W
Pelotas →, Brazil 95 B5 27 28S 51 55W
Pelvoux, Massif du, France 18 D7 44 52N 6 20 E
Pemalang, Indonesia 37 G13 6 53S 109 23 E
Pemanggil, Pulau, Malaysia 39 L5 2 37N 104 21 E
Pematangsiantar, Indonesia 36 D1 2 57N 99 5 E
Pemba, Mozam. 55 E5 12 58S 40 30 E
Pemba, Zambia 55 F2 16 30S 27 28 E
Pemba Channel, Tanzania 54 D4 5 0S 39 37 E
Pemba I., Tanzania 54 D4 5 0S 39 45 E
Pemberton, Australia 61 F2 34 30S 116 0 E
Pemberton, Canada 72 C4 50 25N 122 50W
Pembina, U.S.A. 80 A6 48 58N 97 15W
Pembroke, Canada 70 C4 45 50N 77 7W
Pembroke, U.K. 11 F3 51 41N 4 55W
Pembrokeshire □, U.K. 11 F3 51 52N 4 56W
Pen-y-Ghent, U.K. 10 C5 54 10N 2 14W
Penang = Pinang, Malaysia 39 K3 5 25N 100 15 E
Penápolis, Brazil 95 A6 21 30S 50 0W
Peñarroya-Pueblonuevo, Spain 19 C3 38 19N 5 16W
Penarth, U.K. 11 F4 51 26N 3 11W
Peñas, C. de, Spain 19 A3 43 42N 5 52W
Penas, G. de, Chile 96 F2 47 0S 75 0W
Peñas del Chache, Canary Is. 22 E6 29 6N 13 33W
Pench'i = Benxi, China 35 D12 41 20N 123 48 E
Pend Oreille →, U.S.A. 82 B5 49 4N 117 37W
Pend Oreille, L., U.S.A. 82 C5 48 10N 116 21W
Pendembu, S. Leone 50 G3 9 7N 11 14W
Pender B., Australia 60 C3 16 45S 122 42 E
Pendleton, U.S.A. 82 D4 45 40N 118 47W
Pendra, India 43 H9 22 46N 81 57 E
Penedo, Brazil 93 F11 10 15S 36 36W
Penetanguishene, Canada 78 B5 44 50N 79 55W
Penfield, U.S.A. 78 E6 41 13N 78 35W
Pengalengan, Indonesia 37 G12 7 9S 107 30 E
Penge, Kasai-Or., Dem. Rep. of the Congo 54 D1 5 30S 24 33 E
Penge, Sud-Kivu, Dem. Rep. of the Congo 54 C2 4 27S 28 25 E
Penglai, China 35 F11 37 48N 120 42 E
Penguin, Australia 62 G4 41 8S 146 6 E
Penhalonga, Zimbabwe 55 F3 18 52S 32 40 E
Peniche, Portugal 19 C1 39 19N 9 22W
Penicuik, U.K. 12 F5 55 50N 3 13W
Penida, Nusa, Indonesia 36 F5 8 45S 115 30 E
Peninsular Malaysia □, Malaysia 39 L4 4 0N 102 0 E
Penitente, Serra do, Brazil 93 E9 8 45S 46 20W
Penkridge, U.K. 10 E5 52 44N 2 6W
Penmarch, Pte. de, France 18 C1 47 48N 4 22W
Penn Hills, U.S.A. 78 F5 40 28N 79 52W
Penn Yan, U.S.A. 78 D7 42 40N 77 3W
Pennant, Canada 73 C7 50 32N 108 14W
Penner →, India 40 M12 14 35N 80 10 E
Pennines, U.K. 10 C5 54 45N 2 27W
Pennington, U.S.A. 84 F5 39 15N 121 47W
Pennsburg, U.S.A. 79 F9 40 23N 75 29W
Pennsylvania □, U.S.A. 76 E7 40 45N 77 30W
Penny, Canada 72 C4 53 51N 121 20W
Penobscot →, U.S.A. 77 C11 44 30N 68 48W
Penobscot B., U.S.A. 77 C11 44 35N 68 50W
Penola, Australia 63 F3 37 25S 140 48 E
Penong, Australia 61 F5 31 56S 133 1 E
Penonomé, Panama 88 E3 8 31N 80 21W
Penrith, Australia 63 E5 33 43S 150 38 E
Penrith, U.K. 10 C5 54 40N 2 45W
Penryn, U.K. 11 G2 50 9N 5 7W
Pensacola, U.S.A. 77 K2 30 25N 87 13W
Pensacola Mts., Antarctica 5 E1 84 0S 40 0W
Pense, Canada 73 C8 50 25N 104 59W
Penshurst, Australia 63 F3 37 49S 142 20 E
Penticton, Canada 72 D5 49 30N 119 38W
Pentland, Australia 62 C4 20 32S 145 25 E
Pentland Firth, U.K. 12 C5 58 43N 3 10W
Pentland Hills, U.K. 12 F5 55 48N 3 25W
Penza, Russia 24 D8 53 15N 45 5 E
Penzance, U.K. 11 G2 50 7N 5 33W
Penzhino, Russia 27 C17 63 30N 167 55 E
Penzhinskaya Guba, Russia 27 C17 61 30N 163 0 E
Peoria, Ariz., U.S.A. 83 K7 33 35N 112 14W
Peoria, Ill., U.S.A. 80 E10 40 42N 89 36W
Pepacton Reservoir, U.S.A. 79 D10 42 5N 74 58W
Pepani →, S. Africa 56 D3 25 49S 22 47 E
Pera Hd., Australia 62 A3 12 55S 141 37 E
Perabumulih, Indonesia 36 E2 3 27S 104 15 E
Perak →, Malaysia 39 K3 4 0N 100 50 E
Pérama, Kérkira, Greece 23 A3 39 34N 19 54 E
Pérama, Kríti, Greece 23 D6 35 20N 24 40 E
Peräpohjola, Finland 8 C22 66 16N 26 10 E
Percé, Canada 71 C7 48 31N 64 13W
Perche, Collines du, France 18 B4 48 30N 0 40 E
Percival Lakes, Australia 60 D4 21 25S 125 0 E
Percy Is., Australia 62 C5 21 39S 150 16 E
Perdido, Mte., Spain 19 A6 42 40N 0 5 E
Perdu, Mt. = Perdido, Mte., Spain 19 A6 42 40N 0 5 E
Pereira, Colombia 92 C3 4 49N 75 43W
Perenjori, Australia 61 E2 29 26S 116 16 E
Pereyaslav-Khmelnytskyy, Ukraine 25 D5 50 3N 31 28 E
Pérez, I., Mexico 87 C7 22 24N 89 42W
Pergamino, Argentina 94 C3 33 52S 60 30W
Pergau →, Malaysia 39 K3 5 23N 102 2 E
Perham, U.S.A. 80 B7 46 36N 95 34W
Perhentian, Kepulauan, Malaysia 36 C2 5 54N 102 42 E
Péribonca →, Canada 71 C5 48 45N 72 5W
Péribonca, L., Canada 71 B5 50 1N 71 10W
Perico, Argentina 94 A2 24 20S 65 5W
Pericos, Mexico 86 B3 25 3N 107 42W
Périgueux, France 18 D4 45 10N 0 42 E
Perijá, Sierra de, Colombia 92 B4 9 30N 73 3W
Peristerona →, Cyprus 23 D12 35 8N 33 5 E
Perito Moreno, Argentina 96 F2 46 36S 70 56W
Perkasie, U.S.A. 79 F9 40 22N 75 18W
Perlas, Arch. de las, Panama 88 E4 8 41N 79 7W
Perlas, Punta de, Nic. 88 D3 12 30N 83 30W
Perm, Russia 24 C10 58 0N 56 10 E
Pernambuco = Recife, Brazil 93 E12 8 0S 35 0W
Pernambuco □, Brazil 93 E11 8 0S 37 0W
Pernatty Lagoon, Australia 63 E2 31 30S 137 12 E
Pernik, Bulgaria 21 C10 42 35N 23 2 E
Peron Is., Australia 60 B5 13 9S 130 4 E
Peron Pen., Australia 61 E1 26 0S 113 10 E
Perow, Canada 72 C3 54 35N 126 10W
Perpendicular Pt., Australia 63 E5 31 37S 152 52 E
Perpignan, France 18 E5 42 42N 2 53 E
Perris, U.S.A. 85 M9 33 47N 117 14W
Perry, Fla., U.S.A. 77 K4 30 7N 83 35W
Perry, Ga., U.S.A. 77 J4 32 28N 83 44W
Perry, Iowa, U.S.A. 80 E7 41 51N 94 6W
Perry, Okla., U.S.A. 81 G6 36 17N 97 14W
Perryton, U.S.A. 81 G4 36 24N 100 48W
Perryville, U.S.A. 81 G10 37 43N 89 52W
Persepolis, Iran 45 D7 29 55N 52 50 E
Pershotravensk, Ukraine 17 C14 50 13N 27 40 E
Persia = Iran ■, Asia 45 C7 33 0N 53 0 E
Persian Gulf = Gulf, The, Asia 45 E6 27 0N 50 0 E
Perth, Australia 61 F2 31 57S 115 52 E
Perth, Canada 79 B8 44 55N 76 15W
Perth, U.K. 12 E5 56 24N 3 26W
Perth & Kinross □, U.K. 12 E5 56 45N 3 55W
Perth Amboy, U.S.A. 79 F10 40 31N 74 16W
Perth-Andover, Canada 71 C6 46 44N 67 42W
Peru, Ind., U.S.A. 76 E2 40 45N 86 4W
Peru, N.Y., U.S.A. 79 B11 44 35N 73 32W
Peru ■, S. Amer. 92 D4 4 0S 75 0W
Peru Basin, Pac. Oc. 65 J18 20 0S 95 0W
Peru-Chile Trench, Pac. Oc. 92 G3 20 0S 72 0W
Perúgia, Italy 20 C5 43 7N 12 23 E
Pervomaysk, Ukraine 25 E5 48 10N 30 46 E
Pervouralsk, Russia 24 C10 56 59N 59 59 E
Pésaro, Italy 20 C5 43 54N 12 55 E
Pescara, Italy 20 C6 42 28N 14 13 E
Peshawar, Pakistan 42 B4 34 2N 71 37 E
Peshkopi, Albania 21 D9 41 41N 20 25 E
Peshtigo, U.S.A. 76 C2 45 4N 87 46W
Pesqueira, Brazil 93 E11 8 20S 36 42W
Petah Tiqwa, Israel 47 C3 32 6N 34 53 E
Petaling Jaya, Malaysia 39 L3 3 4N 101 42 E
Petaloudhes, Greece 23 C10 36 18N 28 5 E
Petaluma, U.S.A. 84 G4 38 14N 122 39W
Pétange, Lux. 15 E5 49 33N 5 55 E
Petaro, Pakistan 42 G3 25 31N 68 18 E
Petatlán, Mexico 86 D4 17 31N 101 16W
Petauke, Zambia 55 E3 14 14S 31 20 E
Petawawa, Canada 70 C4 45 54N 77 17W
Petén Itzá, L., Guatemala 88 C2 16 58N 89 50W
Peter I.s Øy, Antarctica 5 C16 69 0S 91 0W
Peter Pond L., Canada 73 B7 55 55N 108 44W
Peterbell, Canada 70 C3 48 36N 83 21W
Peterborough, Australia 63 E2 32 58S 138 51 E
Peterborough, Canada 78 B6 44 20N 78 20W
Peterborough, U.K. 11 E7 52 35N 0 15W
Peterborough, U.S.A. 79 D13 42 53N 71 57W
Peterborough □, U.K. 11 E7 52 35N 0 15W
Peterculter, U.K. 12 D6 57 6N 2 16W
Peterhead, U.K. 12 D7 57 31N 1 48W
Peterlee, U.K. 10 C6 54 47N 1 20W
Petermann Bjerg, Greenland 66 B17 73 7N 28 25W
Petermann Ranges, Australia 60 E5 26 0S 130 30 E
Petersburg, Alaska, U.S.A. 68 C6 56 48N 132 58W
Petersburg, Pa., U.S.A. 78 F6 40 34N 78 3W
Petersburg, Va., U.S.A. 76 G7 37 14N 77 24W
Petersburg, W. Va., U.S.A. 76 F6 39 1N 79 5W
Petersfield, U.K. 11 F7 51 1N 0 56W
Petit Goâve, Haiti 89 C5 18 27N 72 51W
Petit Jardin, Canada 71 C8 48 28N 59 14W
Petit Lac Manicouagan, Canada 71 B6 51 25N 67 40W
Petit-Mécatina →, Canada 71 B8 50 40N 59 30W
Petit-Mécatina, I. du, Canada 71 B8 50 30N 59 25W
Petitcodiac, Canada 71 C6 45 57N 65 11W
Petite Baleine →, Canada 70 A4 56 0N 76 45W
Petite Saguenay, Canada 71 C5 48 15N 70 4W
Petitot →, Canada 72 A4 60 14N 123 29W
Petitsikapau L., Canada 71 B6 54 37N 66 25W
Petlad, India 42 H5 22 30N 72 45 E
Peto, Mexico 87 C7 20 10N 88 53W
Petone, N.Z. 59 J5 41 13S 174 53 E
Petorca, Chile 94 C1 32 15S 70 56W
Petoskey, U.S.A. 76 C3 45 22N 84 57W
Petra, Jordan 47 E4 30 20N 35 22 E
Petra, Spain 22 B10 39 37N 3 6 E
Petra, Ostrova, Russia 4 B13 76 15N 118 30 E
Petra Velikogo, Zaliv, Russia 30 C6 42 40N 132 0 E
Petrich, Bulgaria 21 D10 41 24N 23 13 E
Petrified Forest Nat. Park, U.S.A. 83 J9 35 0N 109 30W
Petrikov = Pyetrikaw, Belarus 17 B15 52 11N 28 29 E
Petrograd = Sankt-Peterburg, Russia 24 C5 59 55N 30 20 E
Petrolândia, Brazil 93 E11 9 5S 38 20W
Petrolia, Canada 78 D2 42 54N 82 9W
Petrolina, Brazil 93 E10 9 24S 40 30W
Petropavl, Kazakstan 26 D7 54 53N 69 13 E
Petropavlovsk = Petropavl, Kazakstan 26 D7 54 53N 69 13 E
Petropavlovsk-Kamchatskiy, Russia 27 D16 53 3N 158 43 E
Petrópolis, Brazil 95 A7 22 33S 43 9W
Petroşani, Romania 17 F12 45 28N 23 20 E
Petrovaradin, Serbia, Yug. 21 B8 45 16N 19 55 E
Petrovsk, Russia 24 D8 52 22N 45 19 E
Petrovsk-Zabaykalskiy, Russia 27 D11 51 20N 108 55 E
Petrozavodsk, Russia 24 B5 61 41N 34 20 E
Petrus Steyn, S. Africa 57 D4 27 38S 28 8 E
Petrusburg, S. Africa 56 D4 29 4S 25 26 E
Peumo, Chile 94 C1 34 21S 71 12W
Peureulak, Indonesia 36 D1 4 48N 97 45 E
Pevek, Russia 27 C18 69 41N 171 19 E
Pforzheim, Germany 16 D5 48 52N 8 41 E
Phagwara, India 40 D9 31 10N 75 40 E
Phaistós, Greece 23 D6 35 2N 24 50 E
Phala, Botswana 56 C4 23 45S 26 50 E
Phalera = Phulera, India 42 F6 26 52N 75 16 E
Phalodi, India 42 F5 27 12N 72 24 E
Phan, Thailand 38 C2 19 28N 99 43 E
Phan Rang, Vietnam 39 G7 11 34N 109 0 E
Phan Ri = Hoa Da, Vietnam 39 G7 11 16N 108 40 E
Phan Thiet, Vietnam 39 G7 11 1N 108 9 E
Phanat Nikhom, Thailand 38 F3 13 27N 101 11 E
Phangan, Ko, Thailand 39 H3 9 45N 100 0 E
Phangnga, Thailand 39 H2 8 28N 98 30 E
Phanom Sarakham, Thailand 38 F3 13 45N 101 21 E
Phaphund, India 43 F8 26 36N 79 28 E
Pharenda, India 43 F10 27 5N 83 17 E
Pharr, U.S.A. 81 M5 26 12N 98 11W
Phatthalung, Thailand 39 J3 7 39N 100 6 E
Phayao, Thailand 38 C2 19 11N 99 55 E
Phelps, U.S.A. 78 D7 42 58N 77 3W
Phelps L., Canada 73 B8 59 15N 103 15W
Phenix City, U.S.A. 77 J3 32 28N 85 0W
Phet Buri, Thailand 38 F2 13 1N 99 55 E
Phetchabun, Thailand 38 D3 16 25N 101 8 E
Phetchabun, Thiu Khao, Thailand 38 E3 16 0N 101 20 E
Phetchaburi = Phet Buri, Thailand 38 F2 13 1N 99 55 E
Phi Phi, Ko, Thailand 39 J2 7 45N 98 46 E
Phiafay, Laos 38 E6 14 48N 106 0 E
Phibun Mangsahan, Thailand 38 E5 15 14N 105 14 E
Phichai, Thailand 38 D3 17 22N 100 10 E
Phichit, Thailand 38 D3 16 26N 100 22 E
Philadelphia, Miss., U.S.A. 81 J10 32 46N 89 7W
Philadelphia, N.Y., U.S.A. 79 B9 44 9N 75 43W
Philadelphia, Pa., U.S.A. 79 G9 39 57N 75 10W
Philip, U.S.A. 80 C4 44 2N 101 40W
Philippeville, Belgium 15 D4 50 12N 4 33 E
Philippi, U.S.A. 76 F5 39 9N 80 3W
Philippi L., Australia 62 C2 24 20S 138 55 E
Philippines ■, Asia 37 B6 12 0N 123 0 E
Philippolis, S. Africa 56 E4 30 15S 25 16 E
Philippopolis = Plovdiv, Bulgaria 21 C11 42 8N 24 44 E
Philipsburg, Canada 79 A11 45 2N 73 5W
Philipsburg, Mont., U.S.A. 82 C7 46 20N 113 18W
Philipsburg, Pa., U.S.A. 78 F6 40 54N 78 13W
Philipstown = Daingean, Ireland 13 C4 53 18N 7 17W
Philipstown, S. Africa 56 E3 30 28S 24 30 E
Phillip I., Australia 63 F4 38 30S 145 12 E
Phillips, U.S.A. 80 C9 45 42N 90 24W
Phillipsburg, Kans., U.S.A. 80 F5 39 45N 99 19W
Phillipsburg, N.J., U.S.A. 79 F9 40 42N 75 12W
Philmont, U.S.A. 79 D11 42 15N 73 39W
Philomath, U.S.A. 82 D2 44 32N 123 22W
Phimai, Thailand 38 E4 15 13N 102 30 E
Phitsanulok, Thailand 38 D3 16 50N 100 12 E
Phnom Dangrek, Thailand 36 B2 14 20N 104 0 E
Phnom Penh, Cambodia 39 G5 11 33N 104 55 E
Phnum Penh = Phnom Penh, Cambodia 39 G5 11 33N 104 55 E
Phoenicia, U.S.A. 79 D10 42 5N 74 14W
Phoenix, Ariz., U.S.A. 83 K7 33 27N 112 4W
Phoenix, N.Y., U.S.A. 79 C8 43 14N 76 18W
Phoenix Is., Kiribati 64 H10 3 30S 172 0W
Phoenixville, U.S.A. 79 F9 40 8N 75 31W
Phon, Thailand 38 E4 15 49N 102 36 E
Phon Tiou, Laos 38 D5 17 53N 104 37 E
Phong →, Thailand 38 D4 16 23N 102 56 E
Phong Saly, Laos 38 B4 21 42N 102 9 E
Phong Tho, Vietnam 38 A4 22 32N 103 21 E
Phonhong, Laos 38 C4 18 30N 102 25 E
Phonum, Thailand 39 H2 8 49N 98 48 E
Phosphate Hill, Australia 62 C2 21 53S 139 58 E
Photharam, Thailand 38 F2 13 41N 99 51 E
Phra Nakhon Si Ayutthaya, Thailand 38 E3 14 25N 100 30 E
Phra Thong, Ko, Thailand 39 H2 9 5N 98 17 E
Phrae, Thailand 38 C3 18 7N 100 9 E
Phrom Phiram, Thailand 38 D3 17 2N 100 12 E
Phu Dien, Vietnam 38 C5 18 58N 105 31 E
Phu Loi, Laos 38 B4 20 14N 103 14 E
Phu Ly, Vietnam 38 B5 20 35N 105 50 E
Phu Quoc, Dao, Vietnam 39 G4 10 20N 104 0 E
Phu Tho, Vietnam 38 B5 21 24N 105 13 E
Phuc Yen, Vietnam 38 B5 21 16N 105 45 E
Phuket, Thailand 39 J2 7 53N 98 24 E
Phuket, Ko, Thailand 39 J2 8 0N 98 22 E
Phul, India 42 D6 30 19N 75 14 E
Phulad, India 42 G5 25 38N 73 49 E
Phulchari, Bangla. 43 G13 25 11N 89 37 E
Phulera, India 42 F6 26 52N 75 16 E
Phulpur, India 43 G10 25 31N 82 49 E
Phun Phin, Thailand 39 H2 9 7N 99 12 E
Piacenza, Italy 18 D8 45 1N 9 40 E
Pian Cr. →, Australia 63 E4 30 2S 148 12 E
Pianosa, Italy 20 C4 42 35N 10 5 E
Piapot, Canada 73 D7 49 59N 109 8W
Piatra Neamţ, Romania 17 E14 46 56N 26 21 E
Piauí □, Brazil 93 E10 7 0S 43 0W
Piauí →, Brazil 93 E10 6 38S 42 42W
Piave →, Italy 20 B5 45 32N 12 44 E
Pibor Post, Sudan 51 G12 6 47N 33 3 E
Picardie, France 18 B5 49 50N 3 0 E
Picardy = Picardie, France 18 B5 49 50N 3 0 E
Picayune, U.S.A. 81 K10 30 32N 89 41W
Pichhor, India 43 G8 25 58N 78 20 E
Pichilemu, Chile 94 C1 34 22S 72 0W
Pichor, India 42 G8 25 11N 78 11 E
Pickerel L., Canada 70 C1 48 40N 91 25W
Pickering, U.K. 10 C7 54 15N 0 46W
Pickering, Vale of, U.K. 10 C7 54 14N 0 45W
Pickle Lake, Canada 70 B1 51 30N 90 12W
Pickwick L., U.S.A. 77 H1 35 4N 88 15W
Pico Truncado, Argentina 96 F3 46 40S 68 0W
Picos, Brazil 93 E10 7 5S 41 28W
Picton, Australia 63 E5 34 12S 150 34 E
Picton, Canada 78 B7 44 1N 77 9W
Picton, N.Z. 59 J5 41 18S 174 3 E
Pictou, Canada 71 C7 45 41N 62 42W
Picture Butte, Canada 72 D6 49 55N 112 45W
Picún Leufú, Argentina 96 D3 39 30S 69 5W
Pidurutalagala, Sri Lanka 40 R12 7 10N 80 50 E
Piedmont = Piemonte □, Italy 18 D7 45 0N 8 0 E
Piedmont, Ala., U.S.A. 77 J3 33 55N 85 37W
Piedmont, S.C., U.S.A. 75 D10 34 0N 81 30W
Piedras Negras, Mexico 86 B4 28 42N 100 31W
Pieksämäki, Finland 9 E22 62 18N 27 10 E
Piemonte □, Italy 18 D7 45 0N 8 0 E
Pienaarsrivier, S. Africa 57 D4 25 15S 28 18 E
Piercefield, U.S.A. 79 B10 44 13N 74 35W
Pierceland, Canada 73 C7 54 20N 109 46W
Pierpont, U.S.A. 78 E4 41 45N 80 34W
Pierre, U.S.A. 80 C4 44 22N 100 21W
Pierre E. Trudeau, Mt. = Logan, Mt., Canada 68 B5 60 31N 140 22W
Piet Retief, S. Africa 57 D5 27 1S 30 50 E
Pietarsaari, Finland 8 E20 63 40N 22 43 E
Pietermaritzburg, S. Africa 57 D5 29 35S 30 25 E
Pietersburg, S. Africa 57 C4 23 54S 29 25 E
Pietrosul, Vf., Maramureş, Romania 17 E13 47 35N 24 43 E
Pietrosul, Vf., Suceava, Romania 17 E13 47 12N 25 18 E
Pigeon L., Canada 78 B6 44 27N 78 30W
Piggott, U.S.A. 81 G9 36 23N 90 11W
Pigüe, Argentina 94 D3 37 36S 62 25W
Pihani, India 43 F9 27 36N 80 15 E
Pihlajavesi, Finland 9 F23 61 45N 28 45 E
Pijijiapan, Mexico 87 D6 15 42N 93 14W
Pikangikum Berens, Canada 73 C10 51 49N 94 0W
Pikes Peak, U.S.A. 80 F2 38 50N 105 3W
Piketberg, S. Africa 56 E2 32 55S 18 40 E
Pikeville, U.S.A. 76 G4 37 29N 82 31W
Pikou, China 35 E12 39 18N 122 22 E
Pikwitonei, Canada 73 B9 55 35N 97 9W
Piła, Poland 17 B9 53 10N 16 48 E
Pilani, India 42 E6 28 22N 75 33 E
Pilar, Paraguay 94 B4 26 50S 58 20W
Pilaya →, Bolivia 92 H6 20 55S 64 4W
Pilbara, Australia 60 D2 23 35S 117 25 E
Pilcomayo →, Paraguay 94 B4 25 21S 57 42W
Pilgrim's Rest, S. Africa 57 C5 24 55S 30 44 E
Pilibhit, India 43 E8 28 40N 79 50 E
Pilica →, Poland 17 C11 51 52N 21 17 E
Pilkhawa, India 42 E7 28 43N 77 42 E
Pilliga, Australia 63 E4 30 21S 148 54 E
Pílos, Greece 21 F9 36 55N 21 42 E
Pilot Mound, Canada 73 D9 49 15N 98 54W
Pilot Point, U.S.A. 81 J6 33 24N 96 58W
Pilot Rock, U.S.A. 82 D4 45 29N 118 50W
Pilsen = Plzeň, Czech Rep. 16 D7 49 45N 13 22 E
Pima, U.S.A. 83 K9 32 54N 109 50W
Pimba, Australia 63 E2 31 18S 136 46 E
Pimenta Bueno, Brazil 92 F6 11 35S 61 10W
Pimentel, Peru 92 E3 6 45S 79 55W
Pinang, Malaysia 39 K3 5 25N 100 15 E
Pinar, C. des, Spain 22 B10 39 53N 3 12 E
Pinar del Río, Cuba 88 B3 22 26N 83 40W
Pınarhisar, Turkey 21 D12 41 37N 27 30 E
Pinatubo, Mt., Phil. 37 A6 15 8N 120 21 E
Pincher Creek, Canada 72 D6 49 30N 113 57W
Pinchi L., Canada 72 C4 54 38N 124 30W
Pinckneyville, U.S.A. 80 F10 38 5N 89 23W
Pińczów, Poland 17 C11 50 32N 20 32 E
Pindar, Australia 61 E2 28 30S 115 47 E
Pindi Gheb, Pakistan 42 C5 33 14N 72 21 E
Pindos Óros, Greece 21 E9 40 0N 21 0 E
Pindus Mts. = Pindos Óros, Greece 21 E9 40 0N 21 0 E
Pine →, B.C., Canada 72 B4 56 8N 120 43W
Pine →, Sask., Canada 73 B7 58 50N 105 38W
Pine, C., Canada 71 C9 46 37N 53 32W
Pine Bluff, U.S.A. 81 H9 34 13N 92 1W
Pine Bluffs, U.S.A. 80 E2 41 11N 104 4W
Pine City, U.S.A. 80 C8 45 50N 92 59W
Pine Cr. →, U.S.A. 78 E7 41 10N 77 16W
Pine Creek, Australia 60 B5 13 50S 131 50 E
Pine Falls, Canada 73 C9 50 34N 96 11W
Pine Flat Res., U.S.A. 84 J7 36 50N 119 20W
Pine Grove, U.S.A. 79 F8 40 33N 76 23W
Pine Pass, Canada 72 B4 55 25N 122 42W
Pine Point, Canada 72 A6 60 50N 114 28W
Pine Ridge, U.S.A. 80 D3 43 2N 102 33W
Pine River, Canada 73 C8 51 45N 100 30W
Pine River, U.S.A. 80 B7 46 43N 94 24W
Pine Valley, U.S.A. 85 N10 32 50N 116 32W
Pinecrest, U.S.A. 84 G6 38 12N 120 1W
Pinedale, Calif., U.S.A. 84 J7 36 50N 119 48W
Pinedale, Wyo., U.S.A. 82 E9 42 52N 109 52W
Pinega →, Russia 24 B8 64 30N 44 19 E
Pinehill, Australia 62 C4 23 38S 146 57 E
Pinehouse L., Canada 73 B7 55 32N 106 35W
Pineimuta →, Canada 70 B1 52 8N 88 33W
Pinerolo, Italy 18 D7 44 47N 7 21 E
Pinetop, U.S.A. 83 J9 34 8N 109 56W
Pinetown, S. Africa 57 D5 29 48S 30 54 E
Pineville, U.S.A. 81 K8 31 19N 92 26W
Ping →, Thailand 38 E3 15 42N 100 9 E
Pingaring, Australia 61 F2 32 40S 118 32 E
Pingding, China 34 F7 37 47N 113 38 E
Pingdingshan, China 34 H7 33 43N 113 27 E
Pingdong, Taiwan 33 D7 22 39N 120 30 E
Pingdu, China 35 F10 36 42N 119 59 E
Pingelly, Australia 61 F2 32 32S 117 5 E
Pingliang, China 34 G4 35 35N 106 31 E

Pinglu, China 34 E7 39 31N 112 30 E
Pingluo, China 34 E4 38 52N 106 30 E
Pingquan, China 35 D10 41 1N 118 37 E
Pingrup, Australia 61 F2 33 32S 118 29 E
P'ingtung, Taiwan 33 D7 22 38N 120 30 E
Pingwu, China 34 H3 32 25N 104 30 E
Pingxiang, China 32 D5 22 6N 106 46 E
Pingyao, China 34 F7 37 12N 112 10 E
Pingyi, China 35 G9 35 30N 117 35 E
Pingyin, China 34 F9 36 20N 116 25 E
Pingyuan, China 34 F9 37 10N 116 22 E
Pinhal, Brazil 95 A6 22 10S 46 46W
Pinheiro, Brazil 93 D9 2 31S 45 5W
Pinheiro Machado, Brazil 95 C5 31 34S 53 23W
Pinhel, Portugal 19 B2 40 50N 7 1W
Pini, Indonesia 36 D1 0 10N 98 40 E
Piniós →, Greece 21 E10 39 55N 22 41 E
Pinjarra, Australia 61 F2 32 37S 115 52 E
Pink Mountain, Canada 72 B4 57 3N 122 52W
Pinnacles, U.S.A. 84 J5 36 33N 121 19W
Pinnaroo, Australia 63 F3 35 17S 140 53 E
Pinnes, Ákra, Greece 21 D11 40 5N 24 20 E
Pinon Hills, U.S.A. 85 L9 34 26N 117 39W
Pinos, Mexico 86 C4 22 20N 101 40W
Pinos, Mt., U.S.A. 85 L7 34 49N 119 8W
Pinos Pt., U.S.A. 83 H3 36 38N 121 57W
Pinotepa Nacional, Mexico 87 D5 16 19N 98 3W
Pinrang, Indonesia 37 E5 3 46S 119 41 E
Pins, Pte. aux, Canada 78 D3 42 15N 81 51W
Pinsk, Belarus 17 B14 52 10N 26 1 E
Pintados, Chile 92 H5 20 35S 69 40W
Pinyug, Russia 24 B8 60 5N 48 0 E
Pioche, U.S.A. 83 H6 37 56N 114 27W
Piombino, Italy 20 C4 42 55N 10 32 E
Pioner, Ostrov, Russia 27 B10 79 50N 92 0 E
Piorini, L., Brazil 92 D6 3 15S 62 35W
Piotrków Trybunalski, Poland 17 C10 51 23N 19 43 E
Pip, Iran 45 E9 26 45N 60 10 E
Pipar, India 42 F5 26 25N 73 31 E
Pipar Road, India 42 F5 26 27N 73 27 E
Piparia, Mad. P., India 42 H8 22 45N 78 23 E
Piparia, Mad. P., India 42 J7 21 49N 77 37 E
Pipestone, U.S.A. 80 D6 44 0N 96 19W
Pipestone →, Canada 70 B2 52 53N 89 23W
Pipestone Cr. →, Canada 73 D8 49 38N 100 15W
Piplan, Pakistan 42 C4 32 17N 71 21 E
Piploda, India 42 H6 23 37N 74 56 E
Pipmuacan, Rés., Canada 71 C5 49 45N 70 30W
Pippingarra, Australia 60 D2 20 27S 118 42 E
Piqua, U.S.A. 76 E3 40 9N 84 15W
Piquiri →, Brazil 95 A5 24 3S 54 14W
Pir Panjal Range, India 42 C7 32 30N 76 50 E
Pīr Sohrāb, Iran 45 E9 25 44N 60 54 E
Piracicaba, Brazil 95 A6 22 45S 47 40W
Piracuruca, Brazil 93 D10 3 50S 41 50W
Piræus = Piraiévs, Greece 21 F10 37 57N 23 42 E
Piraiévs, Greece 21 F10 37 57N 23 42 E
Pirajuí, Brazil 95 A6 21 59S 49 29W
Piram I., India 42 J5 21 36N 72 21 E
Pirané, Argentina 94 B4 25 42S 59 6W
Pirapora, Brazil 93 G10 17 20S 44 56W
Pirawa, India 42 G7 24 10N 76 2 E
Pírgos, Greece 21 F9 37 40N 21 27 E
Piribebuy, Paraguay 94 B4 25 26S 57 2W
Pirimapun, Indonesia 37 F9 6 20S 138 24 E
Pirin Planina, Bulgaria 21 D10 41 40N 23 30 E
Pirineos = Pyrénées, Europe 18 E4 42 45N 0 18 E
Piripiri, Brazil 93 D10 4 15S 41 46W
Pirmasens, Germany 16 D4 49 12N 7 36 E
Pirot, Serbia, Yug. 21 C10 43 9N 22 33 E
Piru, Indonesia 37 E7 3 4S 128 12 E
Piru, U.S.A. 85 L8 34 25N 118 48W
Pisa, Italy 20 C4 43 43N 10 23 E
Pisagua, Chile 92 G4 19 40S 70 15W
Pisco, Peru 92 F3 13 50S 76 12W
Písek, Czech Rep. 16 D8 49 19N 14 10 E
Pishan, China 32 C2 37 30N 78 33 E
Pishīn, Iran 45 E9 26 6N 61 47 E
Pishin, Pakistan 42 D2 30 35N 67 0 E
Pishin Lora →, Pakistan 42 E1 29 9N 64 5 E
Pising, Indonesia 37 F6 5 8S 121 53 E
Pismo Beach, U.S.A. 85 K6 35 9N 120 38W
Pissis, Cerro, Argentina 94 B2 27 45S 68 48W
Pissouri, Cyprus 23 E11 34 40N 32 42 E
Pistóia, Italy 20 C4 43 55N 10 54 E
Pistol B., Canada 73 A10 62 25N 92 37W
Pisuerga →, Spain 19 B3 41 33N 4 52W
Pit →, U.S.A. 82 F2 40 47N 122 6W
Pitarpunga, L., Australia 63 E3 34 24S 143 30 E
Pitcairn I., Pac. Oc. 65 K14 25 5S 130 5W
Pite älv →, Sweden 8 D19 65 20N 21 25 E
Piteå, Sweden 8 D19 65 20N 21 25 E
Piteşti, Romania 17 F13 44 52N 24 54 E
Pithapuram, India 41 L13 17 10N 82 15 E
Pithara, Australia 61 F2 30 20S 116 35 E
Pithoragarh, India 43 E9 29 35N 80 13 E
Pithoro, Pakistan 42 G3 25 31N 69 23 E
Pitlochry, U.K. 12 E5 56 42N 3 44W
Pitsilia, Cyprus 23 E12 34 55N 33 0 E
Pitt I., Canada 72 C3 53 30N 129 50W
Pittsburg, Calif., U.S.A. 84 G5 38 2N 121 53W
Pittsburg, Kans., U.S.A. 81 G7 37 25N 94 42W
Pittsburg, Tex., U.S.A. 81 J7 33 0N 94 59W
Pittsburgh, U.S.A. 78 F5 40 26N 80 1W
Pittsfield, Ill., U.S.A. 80 F9 39 36N 90 49W
Pittsfield, Maine, U.S.A. 77 C11 44 47N 69 23W
Pittsfield, Mass., U.S.A. 79 D11 42 27N 73 15W
Pittsfield, N.H., U.S.A. 79 C13 43 18N 71 20W
Pittston, U.S.A. 79 E9 41 19N 75 47W
Pittsworth, Australia 63 D5 27 41S 151 37 E
Pituri →, Australia 62 C2 22 35S 138 30 E
Piura, Peru 92 E2 5 15S 80 38W
Pixley, U.S.A. 84 K7 35 58N 119 18W
Pizhou, China 34 G9 34 44N 116 55 E
Placentia, Canada 71 C9 47 20N 54 0W
Placentia B., Canada 71 C9 47 0N 54 40W
Placerville, U.S.A. 84 G6 38 44N 120 48W
Placetas, Cuba 88 B4 22 15N 79 44W
Plainfield, N.J., U.S.A. 79 F10 40 37N 74 25W
Plainfield, Ohio, U.S.A. 78 F3 40 13N 81 43W
Plainfield, Vt., U.S.A. 79 B12 44 17N 72 26W
Plains, Mont., U.S.A. 82 C6 47 28N 114 53W
Plains, Tex., U.S.A. 81 J3 33 11N 102 50W
Plainview, Nebr., U.S.A. 80 D6 42 21N 97 47W
Plainview, Tex., U.S.A. 81 H4 34 11N 101 43W
Plainwell, U.S.A. 76 D3 42 27N 85 38W
Plaistow, U.S.A. 79 D13 42 50N 71 6W
Pláka, Ákra, Greece 23 D8 35 11N 26 19 E
Plana Cays, Bahamas 89 B5 22 38N 73 30W
Planada, U.S.A. 84 H6 37 16N 120 19W
Plano, U.S.A. 81 J6 33 1N 96 42W
Plant City, U.S.A. 77 M4 28 1N 82 7W
Plaquemine, U.S.A. 81 K9 30 17N 91 14W
Plasencia, Spain 19 B2 40 3N 6 8W
Plaster City, U.S.A. 85 N11 32 47N 115 51W
Plaster Rock, Canada 71 C6 46 53N 67 22W
Plastun, Russia 30 B8 44 45N 136 19 E
Plata, Río de la, S. Amer. 94 C4 34 45S 57 30W
Plátani →, Italy 20 F5 37 23N 13 16 E
Plátanos, Greece 23 D5 35 28N 23 33 E
Platte, U.S.A. 80 D5 43 23N 98 51W
Platte →, Mo., U.S.A. 80 F7 39 16N 94 50W
Platte →, Nebr., U.S.A. 80 E7 41 4N 95 53W
Platteville, U.S.A. 80 D9 42 44N 90 29W
Plattsburgh, U.S.A. 79 B11 44 42N 73 28W
Plattsmouth, U.S.A. 80 E7 41 1N 95 53W
Plauen, Germany 16 C7 50 30N 12 8 E
Plavinas, Latvia 9 H21 56 35N 25 46 E
Playa Blanca, Canary Is. 22 F6 28 55N 13 37W
Playa Blanca Sur, Canary Is. 22 F6 28 51N 13 50W
Playa de las Americas, Canary Is. 22 F3 28 5N 16 43W
Playa de Mogán, Canary Is. 22 G4 27 48N 15 47W
Playa del Inglés, Canary Is. 22 G4 27 45N 15 33W
Playa Esmerelda, Canary Is. 22 F5 28 8N 14 16W
Playgreen L., Canada 73 C9 54 0N 98 15W
Pleasant Bay, Canada 71 C7 46 51N 60 48W
Pleasant Hill, U.S.A. 84 H4 37 57N 122 4W
Pleasant Mount, U.S.A. 79 E9 41 44N 75 26W
Pleasanton, Calif., U.S.A. 84 H5 37 39N 121 52W
Pleasanton, Tex., U.S.A. 81 L5 28 58N 98 29W
Pleasantville, N.J., U.S.A. 76 F8 39 24N 74 32W
Pleasantville, Pa., U.S.A. 78 E5 41 35N 79 34W
Plei Ku, Vietnam 38 F7 13 57N 108 0 E
Plenty →, Australia 62 C2 23 25S 136 31 E
Plenty, B. of, N.Z. 59 G6 37 45S 177 0 E
Plentywood, U.S.A. 80 A2 48 47N 104 34W
Plesetsk, Russia 24 B7 62 43N 40 20 E
Plessisville, Canada 71 C5 46 14N 71 47W
Plétipi, L., Canada 71 B5 51 44N 70 6W
Pleven, Bulgaria 21 C11 43 26N 24 37 E
Plevlja, Montenegro, Yug. 21 C8 43 21N 19 21 E
Plevna, Canada 78 B8 44 58N 76 59W
Płock, Poland 17 B10 52 32N 19 40 E
Plöckenstein, Germany 16 D7 48 46N 13 51 E
Ploieşti, Romania 17 F14 44 57N 26 5 E
Plonge, Lac la, Canada 73 B7 55 8N 107 20W
Plovdiv, Bulgaria 21 C11 42 8N 24 44 E
Plum, U.S.A. 78 F5 40 29N 79 47W
Plum I., U.S.A. 79 E12 41 11N 72 12W
Plumas, U.S.A. 84 F7 39 45N 120 4W
Plummer, U.S.A. 82 C5 47 20N 116 53W
Plumtree, Zimbabwe 55 G2 20 27S 27 55 E
Plungė, Lithuania 9 J19 55 53N 21 59 E
Plymouth, U.K. 11 G3 50 22N 4 10W
Plymouth, Calif., U.S.A. 84 G6 38 29N 120 51W
Plymouth, Ind., U.S.A. 76 E2 41 21N 86 19W
Plymouth, Mass., U.S.A. 79 E14 41 57N 70 40W
Plymouth, N.C., U.S.A. 77 H7 35 52N 76 43W
Plymouth, N.H., U.S.A. 79 C13 43 46N 71 41W
Plymouth, Pa., U.S.A. 79 E9 41 14N 75 57W
Plymouth, Wis., U.S.A. 76 D2 43 45N 87 59W
Plynlimon = Pumlumon Fawr, U.K. 11 E4 52 28N 3 46W
Plzeň, Czech Rep. 16 D7 49 45N 13 22 E
Po →, Italy 20 B5 44 57N 12 4 E
Po Hai = Bo Hai, China 35 E10 39 0N 119 0 E
Pobeda, Russia 27 C15 65 12N 146 12 E
Pobedy, Pik, Kyrgyzstan 26 E8 42 0N 79 58 E
Pocahontas, Ark., U.S.A. 81 G9 36 16N 90 58W
Pocahontas, Iowa, U.S.A. 80 D7 42 44N 94 40W
Pocatello, U.S.A. 82 E7 42 52N 112 27W
Pochutla, Mexico 87 D5 15 50N 96 31W
Pocito Casas, Mexico 86 B2 28 32N 111 6W
Pocomoke City, U.S.A. 76 F8 38 5N 75 34W
Poços de Caldas, Brazil 95 A6 21 50S 46 33W
Podgorica, Montenegro, Yug. 21 C8 42 30N 19 19 E
Podilska Vysochyna, Ukraine 17 D14 49 0N 28 0 E
Podolsk, Russia 24 C6 55 25N 37 30 E
Podporozhye, Russia 24 B5 60 55N 34 2 E
Pofadder, S. Africa 56 D2 29 10S 19 22 E
Pogranitšnyi, Russia 30 B5 44 25N 131 24 E
Poh, Indonesia 37 E6 0 46S 122 51 E
P'ohang, S. Korea 35 F15 36 1N 129 23 E
Pohjanmaa, Finland 8 E20 62 58N 22 50 E
Pohnpei, Micronesia 64 G7 6 55N 158 10 E
Pohri, India 42 G6 25 32N 77 22 E
Poinsett, C., Antarctica 5 C8 65 42S 113 18 E
Point Arena, U.S.A. 84 G3 38 55N 123 41W
Point Baker, U.S.A. 72 B2 56 21N 133 37W
Point Edward, Canada 70 D3 43 0N 82 30W
Point Hope, U.S.A. 68 B3 68 21N 166 47W
Point L., Canada 68 B8 65 15N 113 4W
Point Pedro, Sri Lanka 40 Q12 9 50N 80 15 E
Point Pleasant, N.J., U.S.A. 79 F10 40 5N 74 4W
Point Pleasant, W. Va., U.S.A. 76 F4 38 51N 82 8W
Pointe-à-Pitre, Guadeloupe 89 C7 16 10N 61 32W
Pointe-Claire, Canada 79 A11 45 26N 73 50W
Pointe-Gatineau, Canada 79 A9 45 28N 75 42W
Pointe-Noire, Congo 52 E2 4 48S 11 53 E
Poisonbush Ra., Australia 60 D3 22 30S 121 30 E
Poissonnier Pt., Australia 60 C2 19 57S 119 10 E
Poitiers, France 18 C4 46 35N 0 20 E
Poitou, France 18 C3 46 40N 0 10W
Pojoaque, U.S.A. 83 J11 35 54N 106 1W
Pokaran, India 40 F7 27 0N 71 50 E
Pokataroo, Australia 63 D4 29 30S 148 36 E
Pokhara, Nepal 43 E10 28 14N 83 58 E
Poko, Dem. Rep. of the Congo 54 B2 3 7N 26 52 E
Pokrovsk = Engels, Russia 25 D8 51 28N 46 6 E
Pokrovsk, Russia 27 C13 61 29N 129 0 E
Pola = Pula, Croatia 16 F7 44 54N 13 57 E
Polacca, U.S.A. 83 J8 35 50N 110 23W
Polan, Iran 45 E9 25 30N 61 10 E
Poland ■, Europe 17 C10 52 0N 20 0 E
Polar Bear Prov. Park, Canada 70 A2 55 0N 83 45W
Polatsk, Belarus 24 C4 55 30N 28 50 E
Polcura, Chile 94 D1 37 17S 71 43W
Polessk, Russia 9 J19 54 50N 21 8 E
Polesye = Pripet Marshes, Europe 17 B15 52 10N 28 10 E
Polevskoy, Russia 24 C11 56 26N 60 11 E
Pŏlgyo-ri, S. Korea 35 G14 34 51N 127 21 E
Police, Poland 16 B8 53 33N 14 33 E
Polillo Is., Phil. 37 B6 14 56N 122 0 E
Polis, Cyprus 23 D11 35 2N 32 26 E
Políyiros, Greece 21 D10 40 23N 23 25 E
Polk, U.S.A. 78 E5 41 22N 79 56W
Pollachi, India 40 P10 10 35N 77 0 E
Pollença, Spain 22 B10 39 54N 3 1 E
Pollença, B. de, Spain 22 B10 39 53N 3 8 E
Polnovat, Russia 26 C7 63 50N 65 54 E
Polonne, Ukraine 17 C14 50 6N 27 30 E
Polonnoye = Polonne, Ukraine 17 C14 50 6N 27 30 E
Polson, U.S.A. 82 C6 47 41N 114 9W
Poltava, Ukraine 25 E5 49 35N 34 35 E
Põltsamaa, Estonia 9 G21 58 41N 25 58 E
Polunochnoye, Russia 26 C7 60 52N 60 25 E
Põlva, Estonia 9 G22 58 3N 27 3 E
Polyarny, Russia 24 A5 69 8N 33 20 E
Polynesia, Pac. Oc. 65 J11 10 0S 162 0W
Polynésie française = French Polynesia ■, Pac. Oc. 65 K13 20 0S 145 0W
Pomaro, Mexico 86 D4 18 20N 103 18W
Pombal, Portugal 19 C1 39 55N 8 40W
Pómbia, Greece 23 E6 35 0N 24 51 E
Pomene, Mozam. 57 C6 22 53S 35 33 E
Pomeroy, Ohio, U.S.A. 76 F4 39 2N 82 2W
Pomeroy, Wash., U.S.A. 82 C5 46 28N 117 36W
Pomézia, Italy 20 D5 41 40N 12 30 E
Pomona, Australia 63 D5 26 22S 152 52 E
Pomona, U.S.A. 85 L9 34 4N 117 45W
Pomorskie, Pojezierze, Poland 17 B9 53 40N 16 37 E
Pomos, Cyprus 23 D11 35 9N 32 33 E
Pomos, C., Cyprus 23 D11 35 10N 32 33 E
Pompano Beach, U.S.A. 77 M5 26 14N 80 8W
Pompeys Pillar, U.S.A. 82 D10 45 59N 107 57W
Pompton Lakes, U.S.A. 79 F10 41 0N 74 17W
Ponape = Pohnpei, Micronesia 64 G7 6 55N 158 10 E
Ponask L., Canada 70 B1 54 0N 92 41W
Ponca, U.S.A. 80 D6 42 34N 96 43W
Ponca City, U.S.A. 81 G6 36 42N 97 5W
Ponce, Puerto Rico 89 C6 18 1N 66 37W
Ponchatoula, U.S.A. 81 K9 30 26N 90 26W
Poncheville, L., Canada 70 B4 50 10N 76 55W
Pond, U.S.A. 85 K7 35 43N 119 20W
Pond Inlet, Canada 69 A12 72 40N 77 0W
Pondicherry, India 40 P11 11 59N 79 50 E
Ponds, I. of, Canada 71 B8 53 27N 55 52W
Ponferrada, Spain 19 A2 42 32N 6 35W
Ponnani, India 40 P9 10 45N 75 59 E
Ponoka, Canada 72 C6 52 42N 113 40W
Ponorogo, Indonesia 37 G14 7 52S 111 27 E
Ponoy, Russia 24 A7 67 0N 41 13 E
Ponoy →, Russia 24 A7 66 59N 41 17 E
Ponta do Sol, Madeira 22 D2 32 42N 17 7W
Ponta Grossa, Brazil 95 B5 25 7S 50 10W
Ponta Pora, Brazil 95 A4 22 20S 55 35W
Pontarlier, France 18 C7 46 54N 6 20 E
Pontchartrain L., U.S.A. 81 K10 30 5N 90 5W
Ponte do Pungué, Mozam. 55 F3 19 30S 34 33 E
Ponte Nova, Brazil 95 A7 20 25S 42 54W
Ponteix, Canada 73 D7 49 46N 107 29W
Pontevedra, Spain 19 A1 42 26N 8 40W
Pontiac, Ill., U.S.A. 80 E10 40 53N 88 38W
Pontiac, Mich., U.S.A. 76 D4 42 38N 83 18W
Pontian Kecil, Malaysia 39 M4 1 29N 103 23 E
Pontianak, Indonesia 36 E3 0 3S 109 15 E
Pontine Is. = Ponziane, Ísole, Italy 20 D5 40 55N 12 57 E
Pontine Mts. = Kuzey Anadolu Dağları, Turkey 25 F6 41 30N 35 0 E
Pontivy, France 18 B2 48 5N 2 58W
Pontoise, France 18 B5 49 3N 2 5 E
Ponton →, Canada 72 B5 58 27N 116 11W
Pontypool, Canada 78 B6 44 6N 78 38W
Pontypool, U.K. 11 F4 51 42N 3 2W
Ponziane, Ísole, Italy 20 D5 40 55N 12 57 E
Poochera, Australia 63 E1 32 43S 134 51 E
Poole, U.K. 11 G6 50 43N 1 59W
Poole □, U.K. 11 G6 50 43N 1 59W
Poona = Pune, India 40 K8 18 29N 73 57 E
Pooncarie, Australia 63 E3 33 22S 142 31 E
Poopelloe L., Australia 63 E3 31 40S 144 0 E
Poopó, L. de, Bolivia 92 G5 18 30S 67 35W
Popayán, Colombia 92 C3 2 27N 76 36W
Poperinge, Belgium 15 D2 50 51N 2 42 E
Popilta L., Australia 63 E3 33 10S 141 42 E
Popio L., Australia 63 E3 33 10S 141 52 E
Poplar, U.S.A. 80 A2 48 7N 105 12W
Poplar →, Canada 73 C9 53 0N 97 19W
Poplar Bluff, U.S.A. 81 G9 36 46N 90 24W
Poplarville, U.S.A. 81 K10 30 51N 89 32W
Popocatépetl, Volcán, Mexico 87 D5 19 2N 98 38W
Popokabaka, Dem. Rep. of the Congo 52 F3 5 41S 16 40 E
Poprad, Slovak Rep. 17 D11 49 3N 20 18 E
Porali →, Pakistan 42 G2 25 58N 66 26 E
Porbandar, India 42 J3 21 44N 69 43 E
Porcher I., Canada 72 C2 53 50N 130 30W
Porcupine →, Canada 73 B8 59 11N 104 46W
Porcupine →, U.S.A. 68 B5 66 34N 145 19W
Pordenone, Italy 20 B5 45 57N 12 39 E
Pori, Finland 9 F19 61 29N 21 48 E
Porlamar, Venezuela 92 A6 10 57N 63 51W
Poronaysk, Russia 27 E15 49 13N 143 0 E
Poroshiri-Dake, Japan 30 C11 42 41N 142 52 E
Poroto Mts., Tanzania 55 D3 9 0S 33 30 E
Porpoise B., Antarctica 5 C9 66 0S 127 0 E
Porreres, Spain 22 B10 39 31N 3 2 E
Porsangen, Norway 8 A21 70 40N 25 40 E
Porsgrunn, Norway 9 G13 59 10N 9 40 E
Port Alberni, Canada 72 D4 49 14N 124 50W
Port Alfred, S. Africa 56 E4 33 36S 26 55 E
Port Alice, Canada 72 C3 50 20N 127 25W
Port Allegany, U.S.A. 78 E6 41 48N 78 17W
Port Allen, U.S.A. 81 K9 30 27N 91 12W
Port Alma, Australia 62 C5 23 38S 150 53 E
Port Angeles, U.S.A. 84 B3 48 7N 123 27W
Port Antonio, Jamaica 88 C4 18 10N 76 30W
Port Aransas, U.S.A. 81 M6 27 50N 97 4W
Port Arthur = Lüshun, China 35 E11 38 45N 121 15 E
Port Arthur, Australia 62 G4 43 7S 147 50 E
Port Arthur, U.S.A. 81 L8 29 54N 93 56W
Port au Choix, Canada 71 B8 50 43N 57 22W
Port au Port B., Canada 71 C8 48 40N 58 50W
Port-au-Prince, Haiti 89 C5 18 40N 72 20W
Port Augusta, Australia 63 E2 32 30S 137 50 E
Port Austin, U.S.A. 78 B2 44 3N 83 1W
Port Bell, Uganda 54 B3 0 18N 32 35 E
Port Bergé Vaovao, Madag. 57 B8 15 33S 47 40 E
Port Blandford, Canada 71 C9 48 20N 54 10W
Port Bradshaw, Australia 62 A2 12 30S 137 20 E
Port Broughton, Australia 63 E2 33 37S 137 56 E
Port Burwell, Canada 78 D4 42 40N 80 48W
Port Canning, India 43 H13 22 23N 88 40 E
Port-Cartier, Canada 71 B6 50 2N 66 50W
Port Chalmers, N.Z. 59 L3 45 49S 170 30 E
Port Charlotte, U.S.A. 77 M4 26 59N 82 6W
Port Chester, U.S.A. 79 F11 41 0N 73 40W
Port Clements, Canada 72 C2 53 40N 132 10W
Port Clinton, U.S.A. 76 E4 41 31N 82 56W
Port Colborne, Canada 78 D5 42 50N 79 10W
Port Coquitlam, Canada 72 D4 49 15N 122 45W
Port Credit, Canada 78 C5 43 33N 79 35W
Port Curtis, Australia 62 C5 23 57S 151 20 E
Port d'Alcúdia, Spain 22 B10 39 50N 3 7 E
Port Dalhousie, Canada 78 C5 43 13N 79 16W
Port d'Andratx, Spain 22 B9 39 32N 2 23 E
Port Darwin, Australia 60 B5 12 24S 130 45 E
Port Darwin, Falk. Is. 96 G5 51 50S 59 0W
Port Davey, Australia 62 G4 43 16S 145 55 E
Port-de-Paix, Haiti 89 C5 19 50N 72 50W
Port de Pollença, Spain 22 B10 39 54N 3 4 E
Port de Sóller, Spain 22 B9 39 48N 2 42 E
Port Dickson, Malaysia 39 L3 2 30N 101 49 E
Port Douglas, Australia 62 B4 16 30S 145 30 E
Port Dover, Canada 78 D4 42 47N 80 12W
Port Edward, Canada 72 C2 54 12N 130 10W
Port Elgin, Canada 78 B3 44 25N 81 25W
Port Elizabeth, S. Africa 56 E4 33 58S 25 40 E
Port Ellen, U.K. 12 F2 55 38N 6 11W
Port Erin, U.K. 10 C3 54 5N 4 45W
Port Essington, Australia 60 B5 11 15S 132 10 E
Port Etienne = Nouâdhibou, Mauritania 50 D2 20 54N 17 0W
Port Ewen, U.S.A. 79 E11 41 54N 73 59W
Port Fairy, Australia 63 F3 38 22S 142 12 E
Port Gamble, U.S.A. 84 C4 47 51N 122 35W
Port-Gentil, Gabon 52 E1 0 40S 8 50 E
Port Germein, Australia 63 E2 33 1S 138 1 E
Port Gibson, U.S.A. 81 K9 31 58N 90 59W
Port Glasgow, U.K. 12 F4 55 56N 4 41W
Port Harcourt, Nigeria 50 H7 4 40N 7 10 E
Port Hardy, Canada 72 C3 50 41N 127 30W
Port Harrison = Inukjuak, Canada 69 C12 58 25N 78 15W
Port Hawkesbury, Canada 71 C7 45 36N 61 22W
Port Hedland, Australia 60 D2 20 25S 118 35 E
Port Henry, U.S.A. 79 B11 44 3N 73 28W
Port Hood, Canada 71 C7 46 0N 61 32W
Port Hope, Canada 78 C6 43 56N 78 20W
Port Hope, U.S.A. 78 C2 43 57N 82 43W
Port Hope Simpson, Canada 71 B8 52 33N 56 18W
Port Hueneme, U.S.A. 85 L7 34 7N 119 12W
Port Huron, U.S.A. 78 D2 42 58N 82 26W
Port Jefferson, U.S.A. 79 F11 40 57N 73 3W
Port Jervis, U.S.A. 79 E10 41 22N 74 41W
Port Kelang = Pelabuhan Kelang, Malaysia 39 L3 3 0N 101 23 E
Port Kenny, Australia 63 E1 33 10S 134 41 E
Port Lairge = Waterford, Ireland 13 D4 52 15N 7 8W
Port Laoise, Ireland 13 C4 53 2N 7 18W
Port Lavaca, U.S.A. 81 L6 28 37N 96 38W
Port Leyden, U.S.A. 79 C9 43 35N 75 21W
Port Lincoln, Australia 63 E2 34 42S 135 52 E
Port Loko, S. Leone 50 G3 8 48N 12 46W
Port Louis, Mauritius 49 H9 20 10S 57 30 E
Port MacDonnell, Australia 63 F3 38 5S 140 48 E
Port McNeill, Canada 72 C3 50 35N 127 6W
Port Macquarie, Australia 63 E5 31 25S 152 25 E
Port Maria, Jamaica 88 C4 18 25N 76 55W
Port Matilda, U.S.A. 78 F6 40 48N 78 3W
Port Mellon, Canada 72 D4 49 32N 123 31W
Port-Menier, Canada 71 C7 49 51N 64 15W
Port Moody, Canada 84 A4 49 17N 122 51W
Port Morant, Jamaica 88 C4 17 54N 76 19W
Port Moresby, Papua N. G. 64 H6 9 24S 147 8 E
Port Musgrave, Australia 62 A3 11 55S 141 50 E
Port Neches, U.S.A. 81 L8 30 0N 93 59W
Port Nolloth, S. Africa 56 D2 29 17S 16 52 E
Port Nouveau-Québec = Kangiqsualujjuaq, Canada 69 C13 58 30N 65 59W
Port of Spain, Trin. & Tob. 89 D7 10 40N 61 31W
Port Orange, U.S.A. 77 L5 29 9N 80 59W
Port Orchard, U.S.A. 84 C4 47 32N 122 38W
Port Orford, U.S.A. 82 E1 42 45N 124 30W
Port Pegasus, N.Z. 59 M1 47 12S 167 41 E
Port Perry, Canada 78 B6 44 6N 78 56W
Port Phillip B., Australia 63 F3 38 10S 144 50 E
Port Pirie, Australia 63 E2 33 10S 138 1 E
Port Radium = Echo Bay, Canada 68 B8 66 5N 117 55W
Port Renfrew, Canada 72 D4 48 30N 124 20W
Port Roper, Australia 62 A2 14 45S 135 25 E
Port Rowan, Canada 78 D4 42 40N 80 30W
Port Safaga = Bûr Safâga, Egypt 44 E2 26 43N 33 57 E
Port Said = Bûr Sa'îd, Egypt 51 B12 31 16N 32 18 E
Port St. Joe, U.S.A. 77 L3 29 49N 85 18W
Port St. Johns = Umzimvubu, S. Africa 57 E4 31 38S 29 33 E
Port St. Lucie, U.S.A. 77 M5 27 20N 80 20W
Port Sanilac, U.S.A. 78 C2 43 26N 82 33W
Port Severn, Canada 78 B5 44 48N 79 43W
Port Shepstone, S. Africa 57 E5 30 44S 30 28 E
Port Simpson, Canada 72 C2 54 30N 130 20W
Port Stanley = Stanley, Falk. Is. 96 G5 51 40S 59 51W
Port Stanley, Canada 78 D3 42 40N 81 10W
Port Sudan = Bûr Sûdân, Sudan 51 E13 19 32N 37 9 E
Port Sulphur, U.S.A. 81 L10 29 29N 89 42W
Port Talbot, U.K. 11 F4 51 35N 3 47W
Port Townsend, U.S.A. 84 B4 48 7N 122 45W
Port-Vendres, France 18 E5 42 32N 3 8 E
Port Vila, Vanuatu 64 J8 17 45S 168 18 E
Port Vladimir, Russia 24 A5 69 25N 33 6 E
Port Wakefield, Australia 63 E2 34 12S 138 10 E
Port Washington, U.S.A. 76 D2 43 23N 87 53W

Port Weld = Kuala Sepetang, Malaysia 39 K3 4 49N 100 28 E
Porta Orientalis, Romania 17 F12 45 6N 22 18 E
Portadown, U.K. 13 B5 54 25N 6 27W
Portaferry, U.K. 13 B6 54 23N 5 33W
Portage, Pa., U.S.A. 78 F6 40 23N 78 41W
Portage, Wis., U.S.A. 80 D10 43 33N 89 28W
Portage La Prairie, Canada 73 D9 49 58N 98 18W
Portageville, U.S.A. 81 G10 36 26N 89 42W
Portalegre, Portugal 19 C2 39 19N 7 25W
Portales, U.S.A. 81 H3 34 11N 103 20W
Portarlington, Ireland 13 C4 53 9N 7 14W
Portbou, Spain 19 A7 42 25N 3 9 E
Porter L., N.W.T., Canada 73 A7 61 41N 108 5W
Porter L., Sask., Canada 73 B7 56 20N 107 20W
Porterville, S. Africa 56 E2 33 0S 19 0 E
Porterville, U.S.A. 84 J8 36 4N 119 1W
Porthcawl, U.K. 11 F4 51 29N 3 42W
Porthill, U.S.A. 82 B5 48 59N 116 30W
Porthmadog, U.K. 10 E3 52 55N 4 8W
Portile de Fier, Europe 17 F12 44 44N 22 30 E
Portimão, Portugal 19 D1 37 8N 8 32W
Portishead, U.K. 11 F5 51 29N 2 46W
Portknockie, U.K. 12 D6 57 42N 2 51W
Portland, N.S.W., Australia 63 E5 33 20S 150 0 E
Portland, Vic., Australia 63 F3 38 20S 141 35 E
Portland, Canada 79 B8 44 42N 76 12W
Portland, Conn., U.S.A. 79 E12 41 34N 72 38W
Portland, Maine, U.S.A. 69 D12 43 39N 70 16W
Portland, Mich., U.S.A. 76 D3 42 52N 84 54W
Portland, Oreg., U.S.A. 84 E4 45 32N 122 37W
Portland, Pa., U.S.A. 79 F9 40 55N 75 6W
Portland, Tex., U.S.A. 81 M6 27 53N 97 20W
Portland, I. of, U.K. 11 G5 50 33N 2 26W
Portland B., Australia 63 F3 38 15S 141 45 E
Portland Bill, U.K. 11 G5 50 31N 2 28W
Portland Canal, U.S.A. 72 B2 55 56N 130 0W
Portmadoc = Porthmadog, U.K. 10 E3 52 55N 4 8W
Porto, Portugal 19 B1 41 8N 8 40W
Pôrto Alegre, Brazil 95 C5 30 5S 51 10W
Porto Amboim = Gunza, Angola 52 G2 10 50S 13 50 E
Porto Cristo, Spain 22 B10 39 33N 3 20 E
Pôrto de Móz, Brazil 93 D8 1 41S 52 13W
Porto Empédocle, Italy 20 F5 37 17N 13 32 E
Pôrto Esperança, Brazil 92 G7 19 37S 57 29W
Pôrto Franco, Brazil 93 E9 6 20S 47 24W
Pôrto Mendes, Brazil 95 A5 24 30S 54 15W
Porto Moniz, Madeira 22 D2 32 52N 17 11W
Pôrto Murtinho, Brazil 92 H7 21 45S 57 55W
Pôrto Nacional, Brazil 93 F9 10 40S 48 30W
Porto-Novo, Benin 50 G6 6 23N 2 42 E
Porto Petro, Spain 22 B10 39 22N 3 13 E
Porto Santo, I. de, Madeira 50 B2 33 45N 16 25W
Pôrto São José, Brazil 95 A5 22 43S 53 10W
Pôrto Seguro, Brazil 93 G11 16 26S 39 5W
Porto Tórres, Italy 20 D3 40 50N 8 24 E
Pôrto União, Brazil 95 B5 26 10S 51 10W
Pôrto Válter, Brazil 92 E4 8 15S 72 40W
Porto-Vecchio, France 18 F8 41 35N 9 16 E
Pôrto Velho, Brazil 92 E6 8 46S 63 54W
Portobelo, Panama 88 E4 9 35N 79 42W
Portoferráio, Italy 20 C4 42 48N 10 20 E
Portola, U.S.A. 84 F6 39 49N 120 28W
Portoscuso, Italy 20 E3 39 12N 8 24 E
Portoviejo, Ecuador 92 D2 1 7S 80 28W
Portpatrick, U.K. 12 G3 54 51N 5 7W
Portree, U.K. 12 D2 57 25N 6 12W
Portrush, U.K. 13 A5 55 12N 6 40W
Portsmouth, Domin. 89 C7 15 34N 61 27W
Portsmouth, U.K. 11 G6 50 48N 1 6W
Portsmouth, N.H., U.S.A. 77 D10 43 5N 70 45W
Portsmouth, Ohio, U.S.A. 76 F4 38 44N 82 57W
Portsmouth, R.I., U.S.A. 79 E13 41 36N 71 15W
Portsmouth, Va., U.S.A. 76 G7 36 50N 76 18W
Portsmouth □, U.K. 11 G6 50 48N 1 6W
Portsoy, U.K. 12 D6 57 41N 2 41W
Portstewart, U.K. 13 A5 55 11N 6 43W
Porttipahtan tekojärvi, Finland 8 B22 68 5N 26 40 E
Portugal ■, Europe 19 C1 40 0N 8 0W
Portumna, Ireland 13 C3 53 6N 8 14W
Portville, U.S.A. 78 D6 42 3N 78 20W
Porvenir, Chile 96 G2 53 10S 70 16W
Porvoo, Finland 9 F21 60 24N 25 40 E
Posadas, Argentina 95 B4 27 30S 55 50W
Poshan = Boshan, China 35 F9 36 28N 117 49 E
Posht-e-Badam, Iran 45 C7 33 2N 55 23 E
Poso, Indonesia 37 E6 1 20S 120 55 E
Posong, S. Korea 35 G14 34 46N 127 5 E
Posse, Brazil 93 F9 14 4S 46 18W
Possession I., Antarctica 5 D11 72 4S 172 0 E
Possum Kingdom L., U.S.A. 81 J5 32 52N 98 26W
Post, U.S.A. 81 J4 33 12N 101 23W
Post Falls, U.S.A. 82 C5 47 43N 116 57W
Postavy = Pastavy, Belarus 9 J22 55 4N 26 50 E
Poste-de-la-Baleine = Kuujjuarapik, Canada 70 A4 55 20N 77 35W
Postmasburg, S. Africa 56 D3 28 18S 23 5 E
Postojna, Slovenia 16 F8 45 46N 14 12 E
Poston, U.S.A. 85 M12 34 0N 114 24W
Postville, Canada 71 B8 54 54N 59 47W
Potchefstroom, S. Africa 56 D4 26 41S 27 7 E
Poteau, U.S.A. 81 H7 35 3N 94 37W
Poteet, U.S.A. 81 L5 29 2N 98 35W
Potenza, Italy 20 D6 40 38N 15 48 E
Poteriteri, L., N.Z. 59 M1 46 5S 167 10 E
Potgietersrus, S. Africa 57 C4 24 10S 28 55 E
Poti, Georgia 25 F7 42 10N 41 38 E
Potiskum, Nigeria 51 F8 11 39N 11 2 E
Potomac →, U.S.A. 76 G7 38 0N 76 23W
Potosí, Bolivia 92 G5 19 38S 65 50W
Potosi Mt., U.S.A. 85 K11 35 57N 115 29W
Pototan, Phil. 37 B6 10 54N 122 38 E
Potrerillos, Chile 94 B2 26 30S 69 30W
Potsdam, Germany 16 B7 52 25N 13 4 E
Potsdam, U.S.A. 79 B10 44 40N 74 59W
Pottersville, U.S.A. 79 C11 43 43N 73 50W
Pottstown, U.S.A. 79 F9 40 15N 75 39W
Pottsville, U.S.A. 79 F8 40 41N 76 12W
Pottuvil, Sri Lanka 40 R12 6 55N 81 50 E
Pouce Coupé, Canada 72 B4 55 40N 120 10W
Poughkeepsie, U.S.A. 79 E11 41 42N 73 56W
Poulaphouca Res., Ireland 13 C5 53 8N 6 30W
Poulsbo, U.S.A. 84 C4 47 44N 122 39W
Poultney, U.S.A. 79 C11 43 31N 73 14W
Poulton-le-Fylde, U.K. 10 D5 53 51N 2 58W
Pouso Alegre, Brazil 95 A6 22 14S 45 57W
Pouthisat, Cambodia 38 F4 12 34N 103 50 E
Považská Bystrica, Slovak Rep. 17 D10 49 8N 18 27 E
Povenets, Russia 24 B5 62 50N 34 50 E
Poverty B., N.Z. 59 H7 38 43S 178 2 E
Póvoa de Varzim, Portugal 19 B1 41 25N 8 46W
Povungnituk = Puvirnituq, Canada 69 B12 60 2N 77 10W
Powassan, Canada 70 C4 46 5N 79 25W
Poway, U.S.A. 85 N9 32 58N 117 2W
Powder →, U.S.A. 80 B2 46 45N 105 26W
Powder River, U.S.A. 82 E10 43 2N 106 59W
Powell, U.S.A. 82 D9 44 45N 108 46W
Powell, L., U.S.A. 83 H8 36 57N 111 29W
Powell River, Canada 72 D4 49 50N 124 35W
Powers, U.S.A. 76 C2 45 41N 87 32W
Powys □, U.K. 11 E4 52 20N 3 20W
Poyang Hu, China 33 D6 29 5N 116 20 E
Poyarkovo, Russia 27 E13 49 36N 128 41 E
Poza Rica, Mexico 87 C5 20 33N 97 27W
Požarevac, Serbia, Yug. 21 B9 44 35N 21 18 E
Poznań, Poland 17 B9 52 25N 16 55 E
Pozo, U.S.A. 85 K6 35 20N 120 24W
Pozo Almonte, Chile 92 H5 20 10S 69 50W
Pozo Colorado, Paraguay 94 A4 23 30S 58 45W
Pozoblanco, Spain 19 C3 38 23N 4 51W
Pozzuoli, Italy 20 D6 40 49N 14 7 E
Prachin Buri, Thailand 38 E3 14 0N 101 25 E
Prachuap Khiri Khan, Thailand 39 G2 11 49N 99 48 E
Prado, Brazil 93 G11 17 20S 39 13W
Prague = Praha, Czech Rep. 16 C8 50 5N 14 22 E
Praha, Czech Rep. 16 C8 50 5N 14 22 E
Praia, C. Verde Is. 49 E1 15 2N 23 34W
Prainha, Amazonas, Brazil 92 E6 7 10S 60 30W
Prainha, Pará, Brazil 93 D8 1 45S 53 30W
Prairie, Australia 62 C3 20 50S 144 35 E
Prairie City, U.S.A. 82 D4 44 28N 118 43W
Prairie Dog Town Fork →, U.S.A. 81 H5 34 30N 99 23W
Prairie du Chien, U.S.A. 80 D9 43 3N 91 9W
Prairies, L. of the, Canada 73 C8 51 16N 101 32W
Pran Buri, Thailand 38 F2 12 23N 99 55 E
Prapat, Indonesia 36 D1 2 41N 98 58 E
Prasonísi, Ákra, Greece 23 D9 35 42N 27 46 E
Prata, Brazil 93 G9 19 25S 48 54W
Pratabpur, India 43 H10 23 28N 83 15 E
Pratapgarh, Raj., India 42 G6 24 2N 74 40 E
Pratapgarh, Ut. P., India 43 G9 25 56N 81 59 E
Prato, Italy 20 C4 43 53N 11 6 E
Pratt, U.S.A. 81 G5 37 39N 98 44W
Prattville, U.S.A. 77 J2 32 28N 86 29W
Pravia, Spain 19 A2 43 30N 6 12W
Praya, Indonesia 36 F5 8 39S 116 17 E
Precordillera, Argentina 94 C2 30 0S 69 1W
Preeceville, Canada 73 C8 51 57N 102 40W
Preiļi, Latvia 9 H22 56 18N 26 43 E
Premont, U.S.A. 81 M5 27 22N 98 7W
Prentice, U.S.A. 80 C9 45 33N 90 17W
Preobrazheniye, Russia 30 C6 42 54N 133 54 E
Preparis North Channel, Ind. Oc. 41 M18 15 12N 93 40 E
Preparis South Channel, Ind. Oc. 41 M18 14 36N 93 40 E
Přerov, Czech Rep. 17 D9 49 28N 17 27 E
Prescott, Canada 79 B9 44 45N 75 30W
Prescott, Ariz., U.S.A. 83 J7 34 33N 112 28W
Prescott, Ark., U.S.A. 81 J8 33 48N 93 23W
Prescott Valley, U.S.A. 83 J7 34 40N 112 18W
Preservation Inlet, N.Z. 59 M1 46 8S 166 35 E
Presho, U.S.A. 80 D4 43 54N 100 3W
Presidencia de la Plaza, Argentina 94 B4 27 0S 59 50W
Presidencia Roque Saenz Peña, Argentina 94 B3 26 45S 60 30W
Presidente Epitácio, Brazil 93 H8 21 56S 52 6W
Presidente Hayes □, Paraguay 94 A4 24 0S 59 0W
Presidente Prudente, Brazil 95 A5 22 5S 51 25W
Presidio, Mexico 86 B4 29 29N 104 23W
Presidio, U.S.A. 81 L2 29 34N 104 22W
Prešov, Slovak Rep. 17 D11 49 0N 21 15 E
Prespa, L. = Prespansko Jezero, Macedonia 21 D9 40 55N 21 0 E
Prespansko Jezero, Macedonia 21 D9 40 55N 21 0 E
Presque I., U.S.A. 78 D4 42 9N 80 6W
Presque Isle, U.S.A. 77 B12 46 41N 68 1W
Prestatyn, U.K. 10 D4 53 20N 3 24W
Presteigne, U.K. 11 E5 52 17N 3 0W
Preston, Canada 78 C4 43 23N 80 21W
Preston, U.K. 10 D5 53 46N 2 42W
Preston, Idaho, U.S.A. 82 E8 42 6N 111 53W
Preston, Minn., U.S.A. 80 D8 43 40N 92 5W
Preston, C., Australia 60 D2 20 51S 116 12 E
Prestonburg, U.S.A. 76 G4 37 39N 82 46W
Prestwick, U.K. 12 F4 55 29N 4 37W
Pretoria, S. Africa 57 D4 25 44S 28 12 E
Préveza, Greece 21 E9 38 57N 20 45 E
Prey Veng, Cambodia 39 G5 11 35N 105 29 E
Pribilof Is., U.S.A. 68 C2 57 0N 170 0W
Příbram, Czech Rep. 16 D8 49 41N 14 2 E
Price, U.S.A. 82 G8 39 36N 110 49W
Price I., Canada 72 C3 52 23N 128 41W
Prichard, U.S.A. 77 K1 30 44N 88 5W
Priekule, Latvia 9 H19 56 26N 21 35 E
Prienai, Lithuania 9 J20 54 38N 23 57 E
Prieska, S. Africa 56 D3 29 40S 22 42 E
Priest L., U.S.A. 82 B5 48 35N 116 52W
Priest River, U.S.A. 82 B5 48 10N 116 54W
Priest Valley, U.S.A. 84 J6 36 10N 120 39W
Prievidza, Slovak Rep. 17 D10 48 46N 18 36 E
Prikaspiyskaya Nizmennost = Caspian Depression, Eurasia 25 E8 47 0N 48 0 E
Prilep, Macedonia 21 D9 41 21N 21 32 E
Priluki = Pryluky, Ukraine 25 D5 50 30N 32 24 E
Prime Seal I., Australia 62 G4 40 3S 147 43 E
Primrose L., Canada 73 C7 54 55N 109 45W
Prince Albert, Canada 73 C7 53 15N 105 50W
Prince Albert, S. Africa 56 E3 33 12S 22 2 E
Prince Albert Mts., Antarctica 5 D11 76 0S 161 30 E
Prince Albert Nat. Park, Canada 73 C7 54 0N 106 25W
Prince Albert Pen., Canada 68 A8 72 30N 116 0W
Prince Albert Sd., Canada 68 A8 70 25N 115 0W
Prince Alfred, C., Canada 4 B1 74 20N 124 40W
Prince Charles I., Canada 69 B12 67 47N 76 12W
Prince Charles Mts., Antarctica 5 D6 72 0S 67 0 E
Prince Edward I. □, Canada 71 C7 46 20N 63 20W
Prince Edward Is., Ind. Oc. 3 G11 46 35S 38 0 E
Prince Edward Pt., Canada 78 C8 43 56N 76 52W
Prince George, Canada 72 C4 53 55N 122 50W
Prince of Wales, C., U.S.A. 66 C3 65 36N 168 5W
Prince of Wales I., Australia 62 A3 10 40S 142 10 E
Prince of Wales I., Canada 68 A10 73 0N 99 0W
Prince of Wales I., U.S.A. 68 C6 55 47N 132 50W
Prince Patrick I., Canada 4 B2 77 0N 120 0W
Prince Regent Inlet, Canada 4 B3 73 0N 90 0W
Prince Rupert, Canada 72 C2 54 20N 130 20W
Princess Charlotte B., Australia 62 A3 14 25S 144 0 E
Princess May Ranges, Australia 60 C4 15 30S 125 30 E
Princess Royal I., Canada 72 C3 53 0N 128 40W
Princeton, Canada 72 D4 49 27N 120 30W
Princeton, Calif., U.S.A. 84 F4 39 24N 122 1W
Princeton, Ill., U.S.A. 80 E10 41 23N 89 28W
Princeton, Ind., U.S.A. 76 F2 38 21N 87 34W
Princeton, Ky., U.S.A. 76 G2 37 7N 87 53W
Princeton, Mo., U.S.A. 80 E8 40 24N 93 35W
Princeton, N.J., U.S.A. 79 F10 40 21N 74 39W
Princeton, W. Va., U.S.A. 76 G5 37 22N 81 6W
Principe, I. de, Atl. Oc. 48 F4 1 37N 7 27 E
Principe da Beira, Brazil 92 F6 12 20S 64 30W
Prineville, U.S.A. 82 D3 44 18N 120 51W
Prins Harald Kyst, Antarctica 5 D4 70 0S 35 1 E
Prinsesse Astrid Kyst, Antarctica 5 D3 70 45S 12 30 E
Prinsesse Ragnhild Kyst, Antarctica 5 D4 70 15S 27 30 E
Prinzapolca, Nic. 88 D3 13 20N 83 35W
Priozersk, Russia 24 B5 61 2N 30 7 E
Pripet = Prypyat →, Europe 17 C16 51 20N 30 15 E
Pripet Marshes, Europe 17 B15 52 10N 28 10 E
Pripyat Marshes = Pripet Marshes, Europe 17 B15 52 10N 28 10 E
Pripyats = Prypyat →, Europe 17 C16 51 20N 30 15 E
Priština, Kosovo, Yug. 21 C9 42 40N 21 13 E
Privas, France 18 D6 44 45N 4 37 E
Privolzhskaya Vozvyshennost, Russia 25 D8 51 0N 46 0 E
Prizren, Kosovo, Yug. 21 C9 42 13N 20 45 E
Probolinggo, Indonesia 37 G15 7 46S 113 13 E
Proctor, U.S.A. 79 C11 43 40N 73 2W
Proddatur, India 40 M11 14 45N 78 30 E
Prodhromos, Cyprus 23 E11 34 57N 32 50 E
Profitis Ilías, Greece 23 C9 36 17N 27 56 E
Profondeville, Belgium 15 D4 50 23N 4 52 E
Progreso, Coahuila, Mexico 86 B4 27 28N 101 4W
Progreso, Yucatán, Mexico 87 C7 21 20N 89 40W
Prokopyevsk, Russia 26 D9 54 0N 86 45 E
Prokuplje, Serbia, Yug. 21 C9 43 16N 21 36 E
Prome, Burma 41 K19 18 49N 95 13 E
Prophet →, Canada 72 B4 58 48N 122 40W
Prophet River, Canada 72 B4 58 6N 122 43W
Propriá, Brazil 93 F11 10 13S 36 51W
Proserpine, Australia 62 C4 20 21S 148 36 E
Prosna →, Poland 17 B9 52 6N 17 44 E
Prospect, U.S.A. 79 C9 43 18N 75 9W
Prosser, U.S.A. 82 C4 46 12N 119 46W
Prostějov, Czech Rep. 17 D9 49 30N 17 9 E
Proston, Australia 63 D5 26 8S 151 32 E
Provence, France 18 E6 43 40N 5 46 E
Providence, Ky., U.S.A. 76 G2 37 24N 87 46W
Providence, R.I., U.S.A. 79 E13 41 49N 71 24W
Providence Bay, Canada 70 C3 45 41N 82 15W
Providence Mts., U.S.A. 85 K11 35 10N 115 15W
Providencia, I. de, Colombia 88 D3 13 25N 81 26W
Provideniya, Russia 27 C19 64 23N 173 18W
Provins, France 18 B5 48 33N 3 15 E
Provo, U.S.A. 82 F8 40 14N 111 39W
Provost, Canada 73 C6 52 25N 110 20W
Prudhoe Bay, U.S.A. 68 A5 70 18N 148 22W
Prudhoe I., Australia 62 C4 21 19S 149 41 E
Prud'homme, Canada 73 C7 52 20N 105 54W
Pruszków, Poland 17 B11 52 9N 20 49 E
Prut →, Romania 17 F15 45 28N 28 10 E
Pruzhany, Belarus 17 B13 52 33N 24 28 E
Prydz B., Antarctica 5 C6 69 0S 74 0 E
Pryluky, Ukraine 25 D5 50 30N 32 24 E
Pryor, U.S.A. 81 G7 36 19N 95 19W
Prypyat →, Europe 17 C16 51 20N 30 15 E
Przemyśl, Poland 17 D12 49 50N 22 45 E
Przhevalsk = Karakol, Kyrgyzstan 26 E8 42 30N 78 20 E
Psará, Greece 21 E11 38 37N 25 38 E
Psíra, Greece 23 D7 35 12N 25 52 E
Pskov, Russia 24 C4 57 50N 28 25 E
Ptich = Ptsich →, Belarus 17 B15 52 9N 28 52 E
Ptolemaís, Greece 21 D9 40 30N 21 43 E
Ptsich →, Belarus 17 B15 52 9N 28 52 E
Pu Xian, China 34 F6 36 24N 111 6 E
Pua, Thailand 38 C3 19 11N 100 55 E
Puán, Argentina 94 D3 37 30S 62 45W
Puan, S. Korea 35 G14 35 44N 126 44 E
Pucallpa, Peru 92 E4 8 25S 74 30W
Pudasjärvi, Finland 8 D22 65 23N 26 53 E
Pudozh, Russia 24 B6 61 48N 36 32 E
Puduchcheri = Pondicherry, India 40 P11 11 59N 79 50 E
Pudukkottai, India 40 P11 10 28N 78 47 E
Puebla, Mexico 87 D5 19 3N 98 12W
Puebla □, Mexico 87 D5 18 30N 98 0W
Pueblo, U.S.A. 80 F2 38 16N 104 37W
Pueblo Hundido, Chile 94 B1 26 20S 70 5W
Puelches, Argentina 94 D2 38 5S 65 51W
Puelén, Argentina 94 D2 37 32S 67 38W
Puente Alto, Chile 94 C1 33 32S 70 35W
Puente-Genil, Spain 19 D3 37 22N 4 47W
Puerco →, U.S.A. 83 J10 34 22N 107 50W
Puerto, Canary Is. 22 F2 28 5N 17 20W
Puerto Aisén, Chile 96 F2 45 27S 73 0W
Puerto Ángel, Mexico 87 D5 15 40N 96 29W
Puerto Arista, Mexico 87 D6 15 56N 93 48W
Puerto Armuelles, Panama 88 E3 8 20N 82 51W
Puerto Ayacucho, Venezuela 92 B5 5 40N 67 35W
Puerto Barrios, Guatemala 88 C2 15 40N 88 32W
Puerto Bermejo, Argentina 94 B4 26 55S 58 34W
Puerto Bermúdez, Peru 92 F4 10 20S 74 58W
Puerto Bolívar, Ecuador 92 D3 3 19S 79 55W
Puerto Cabello, Venezuela 92 A5 10 28N 68 1W
Puerto Cabezas, Nic. 88 D3 14 0N 83 30W
Puerto Cabo Gracias á Dios, Nic. 88 D3 15 0N 83 10W
Puerto Carreño, Colombia 92 B5 6 12N 67 22W
Puerto Castilla, Honduras 88 C2 16 0N 86 0W
Puerto Chicama, Peru 92 E3 7 45S 79 20W
Puerto Coig, Argentina 96 G3 50 54S 69 15W
Puerto Cortés, Costa Rica 88 E3 8 55N 84 0W
Puerto Cortés, Honduras 88 C2 15 51N 88 0W
Puerto Cumarebo, Venezuela 92 A5 11 29N 69 30W
Puerto de Alcudia = Port d'Alcúdia, Spain 22 B10 39 50N 3 7 E
Puerto de Cabrera, Spain 22 B9 39 8N 2 56 E
Puerto de Gran Tarajal, Canary Is. 22 F5 28 13N 14 1W
Puerto de la Cruz, Canary Is. 22 F3 28 24N 16 32W
Puerto de Pozo Negro, Canary Is. 22 F6 28 19N 13 55W
Puerto de Sóller = Port de Sóller, Spain 22 B9 39 48N 2 42 E
Puerto del Carmen, Canary Is. 22 F6 28 55N 13 38W
Puerto del Rosario, Canary Is. 22 F6 28 30N 13 52W
Puerto Deseado, Argentina 96 F3 47 55S 66 0W
Puerto Escondido, Mexico 87 D5 15 50N 97 3W
Puerto Heath, Bolivia 92 F5 12 34S 68 39W
Puerto Inírida, Colombia 92 C5 3 53N 67 52W
Puerto Juárez, Mexico 87 C7 21 11N 86 49W
Puerto La Cruz, Venezuela 92 A6 10 13N 64 38W
Puerto Leguízamo, Colombia 92 D4 0 12S 74 46W
Puerto Limón, Colombia 92 C4 3 23N 73 30W
Puerto Lobos, Argentina 96 E3 42 0S 65 3W
Puerto Madryn, Argentina 96 E3 42 48S 65 4W
Puerto Maldonado, Peru 92 F5 12 30S 69 10W
Puerto Manotí, Cuba 88 B4 21 22N 76 50W
Puerto Montt, Chile 96 E2 41 28S 73 0W
Puerto Morazán, Nic. 88 D2 12 51N 87 11W
Puerto Morelos, Mexico 87 C7 20 49N 86 52W
Puerto Natales, Chile 96 G2 51 45S 72 15W
Puerto Padre, Cuba 88 B4 21 13N 76 35W
Puerto Páez, Venezuela 92 B5 6 13N 67 28W
Puerto Peñasco, Mexico 86 A2 31 20N 113 33W
Puerto Pinasco, Paraguay 94 A4 22 36S 57 50W
Puerto Plata, Dom. Rep. 89 C5 19 48N 70 45W
Puerto Pollensa = Port de Pollença, Spain 22 B10 39 54N 3 4 E
Puerto Princesa, Phil. 37 C5 9 46N 118 45 E
Puerto Quepos, Costa Rica 88 E3 9 29N 84 6W
Puerto Rico, Canary Is. 22 G4 27 47N 15 42W
Puerto Rico ■, W. Indies 89 C6 18 15N 66 45W
Puerto Rico Trench, Atl. Oc. 89 C6 19 50N 66 0W
Puerto San Julián, Argentina 96 F3 49 18S 67 43W
Puerto Sastre, Paraguay 94 A4 22 2S 57 55W
Puerto Suárez, Bolivia 92 G7 18 58S 57 52W
Puerto Vallarta, Mexico 86 C3 20 36N 105 15W
Puerto Wilches, Colombia 92 B4 7 21N 73 54W
Puertollano, Spain 19 C3 38 43N 4 7W
Pueyrredón, L., Argentina 96 F2 47 20S 72 0W
Puffin I., Ireland 13 E1 51 50N 10 24W
Pugachev, Russia 24 D8 52 0N 48 49 E
Pugal, India 42 E5 28 30N 72 48 E
Puge, Tanzania 54 C3 4 45S 33 11 E
Puget Sound, U.S.A. 82 C2 47 50N 122 30W
Pugŏdong, N. Korea 35 C16 42 5N 130 0 E
Pugu, Tanzania 54 D4 6 55S 39 4 E
Pūgūnzī, Iran 45 E8 25 49N 59 10 E
Puig Major, Spain 22 B9 39 48N 2 47 E
Puigcerdà, Spain 19 A6 42 24N 1 50 E
Puigpunyent, Spain 22 B9 39 38N 2 32 E
Pujon-chŏsuji, N. Korea 35 D14 40 35N 127 35 E
Pukaki, L., N.Z. 59 L3 44 4S 170 1 E
Pukapuka, Cook Is. 65 J11 10 53S 165 49W
Pukaskwa Nat. Park, Canada 70 C2 48 20N 86 0W
Pukatawagan, Canada 73 B8 55 45N 101 20W
Pukchin, N. Korea 35 D13 40 12N 125 45 E
Pukch'ŏng, N. Korea 35 D15 40 14N 128 10 E
Pukekohe, N.Z. 59 G5 37 12S 174 55 E
Pukhrayan, India 43 F8 26 14N 79 51 E
Pula, Croatia 16 F7 44 54N 13 57 E
Pulacayo, Bolivia 92 H5 20 25S 66 41W
Pulandian, China 35 E11 39 25N 121 58 E
Pularumpi, Australia 60 B5 11 24S 130 26 E
Pulaski, N.Y., U.S.A. 79 C8 43 34N 76 8W
Pulaski, Tenn., U.S.A. 77 H2 35 12N 87 2W
Pulaski, Va., U.S.A. 76 G5 37 3N 80 47W
Pulau →, Indonesia 37 F9 5 50S 138 15 E
Puławy, Poland 17 C11 51 23N 21 59 E
Pulga, U.S.A. 84 F5 39 48N 121 29W
Pulicat L., India 40 N12 13 40N 80 15 E
Pullman, U.S.A. 82 C5 46 44N 117 10W
Pulog, Mt., Phil. 37 A6 16 40N 120 50 E
Pułtusk, Poland 17 B11 52 43N 21 6 E
Pumlumon Fawr, U.K. 11 E4 52 28N 3 46W
Puná, I., Ecuador 92 D2 2 55S 80 5W
Punakha, Bhutan 41 F16 27 42N 89 52 E
Punasar, India 42 F5 27 6N 73 6 E
Punata, Bolivia 92 G5 17 32S 65 50W
Punch, India 43 C6 33 48N 74 4 E
Punch →, Pakistan 42 C5 33 12N 73 40 E
Punda Maria, S. Africa 57 C5 22 40S 31 5 E
Pune, India 40 K8 18 29N 73 57 E
P'ungsan, N. Korea 35 D15 40 50N 128 9 E
Pungue, Ponte de, Mozam. 55 F3 19 0S 34 0 E
Punjab □, India 42 D7 31 0N 76 0 E
Punjab □, Pakistan 42 E6 32 0N 72 30 E
Puno, Peru 92 G4 15 55S 70 3W
Punpun →, India 43 G11 25 31N 85 18 E
Punta Alta, Argentina 96 D4 38 53S 62 4W
Punta Arenas, Chile 96 G2 53 10S 71 0W
Punta de Díaz, Chile 94 B1 28 0S 70 45W
Punta del Hidalgo, Canary Is. 22 F3 28 33N 16 19W
Punta Gorda, Belize 87 D7 16 10N 88 45W
Punta Gorda, U.S.A. 77 M5 26 56N 82 3W
Punta Prieta, Mexico 86 B2 28 58N 114 17W
Punta Prima, Spain 22 B11 39 48N 4 16 E
Puntarenas, Costa Rica 88 E3 10 0N 84 50W
Punto Fijo, Venezuela 92 A4 11 50N 70 13W
Punxsatawney, U.S.A. 78 F6 40 57N 78 59W
Puquio, Peru 92 F4 14 45S 74 10W
Pur →, Russia 26 C8 67 31N 77 55 E
Purace, Vol., Colombia 92 C3 2 21N 76 23W
Puralia = Puruliya, India 43 H12 23 17N 86 24 E
Puranpur, India 43 E9 28 31N 80 9 E
Purbeck, Isle of, U.K. 11 G6 50 39N 1 59W

Purcell, *U.S.A.* **81 H6** 35 1N 97 22W
Purcell Mts., *Canada* **72 D5** 49 55N 116 15W
Puri, *India* **41 K14** 19 50N 85 58 E
Purmerend, *Neths.* **15 B4** 52 32N 4 58 E
Purnia, *India* **43 G12** 25 45N 87 31 E
Pursat = Pouthisat, *Cambodia* **38 F4** 12 34N 103 50 E
Purukcahu, *Indonesia* **36 E4** 0 35S 114 35 E
Puruliya, *India* **43 H12** 23 17N 86 24 E
Purus →, *Brazil* **92 D6** 3 42S 61 28W
Purvis, *U.S.A.* **81 K10** 31 9N 89 25W
Purwa, *India* **43 F9** 26 28N 80 47 E
Purwakarta, *Indonesia* **37 G12** 6 35S 107 29 E
Purwodadi, *Indonesia* **37 G14** 7 7S 110 55 E
Purwokerto, *Indonesia* **37 G13** 7 25S 109 14 E
Puryŏng, *N. Korea* **35 C15** 42 5N 129 43 E
Pusa, *India* **43 G11** 25 59N 85 41 E
Pusan, *S. Korea* **35 G15** 35 5N 129 0 E
Pushkino, *Russia* **25 D8** 51 16N 47 0 E
Putahow L., *Canada* **73 B8** 59 54N 100 40W
Putao, *Burma* **41 F20** 27 28N 97 30 E
Putaruru, *N.Z.* **59 H5** 38 2S 175 50 E
Putignano, *Italy* **20 D7** 40 51N 17 7 E
Puting, Tanjung, *Indonesia* **36 E4** 3 31S 111 46 E
Putnam, *U.S.A.* **79 E13** 41 55N 71 55W
Putorana, Gory, *Russia* **27 C10** 69 0N 95 0 E
Puttalam, *Sri Lanka* **40 Q11** 8 1N 79 55 E
Puttgarden, *Germany* **16 A6** 54 30N 11 10 E
Putumayo →, *S. Amer.* **92 D5** 3 7S 67 58W
Putussibau, *Indonesia* **36 D4** 0 50N 112 56 E
Puvirnituq, *Canada* **69 B12** 60 2N 77 10W
Puy-de-Dôme, *France* **18 D5** 45 46N 2 57 E
Puyallup, *U.S.A.* **84 C4** 47 12N 122 18W
Puyang, *China* **34 G8** 35 40N 115 1 E
Pūzeh Rīg, *Iran* **45 E8** 27 20N 58 40 E
Pwani □, *Tanzania* **54 D4** 7 0S 39 0 E
Pweto, *Dem. Rep. of the Congo* **55 D2** 8 25S 28 51 E
Pwllheli, *U.K.* **10 E3** 52 53N 4 25W
Pya-ozero, *Russia* **24 A5** 66 5N 30 58 E
Pyapon, *Burma* **41 L19** 16 20N 95 40 E
Pyasina →, *Russia* **27 B9** 73 30N 87 0 E
Pyatigorsk, *Russia* **25 F7** 44 2N 43 6 E
Pyè = Prome, *Burma* **41 K19** 18 49N 95 13 E
Pyetrikaw, *Belarus* **17 B15** 52 11N 28 29 E
Pyhäjoki, *Finland* **8 D21** 64 28N 24 14 E
Pyinmana, *Burma* **41 K20** 19 45N 96 12 E
Pyla, C., *Cyprus* **23 E12** 34 56N 33 51 E
Pymatuning Reservoir, *U.S.A.* **78 E4** 41 30N 80 28W
Pyŏktong, *N. Korea* **35 D13** 40 50N 125 50 E
Pyŏnggang, *N. Korea* **35 E14** 38 24N 127 17 E
P'yŏngt'aek, *S. Korea* **35 F14** 37 1N 127 4 E
P'yŏngyang, *N. Korea* **35 E13** 39 0N 125 30 E
Pyote, *U.S.A.* **81 K3** 31 32N 103 8W
Pyramid L., *U.S.A.* **82 G4** 40 1N 119 35W
Pyramid Pk., *U.S.A.* **85 J10** 36 25N 116 37W
Pyrénées, *Europe* **18 E4** 42 45N 0 18 E
Pyu, *Burma* **41 K20** 18 30N 96 28 E

Q

Qaanaaq, *Greenland* **4 B4** 77 40N 69 0W
Qachasnek, *S. Africa* **57 E4** 30 6S 28 42 E
Qa'el Jafr, *Jordan* **47 E5** 30 20N 36 25 E
Qa'emābād, *Iran* **45 D9** 31 44N 60 2 E
Qā'emshahr, *Iran* **45 B7** 36 30N 52 53 E
Qagan Nur, *China* **34 C8** 43 30N 114 55 E
Qahar Youyi Zhongqi, *China* **34 D7** 41 12N 112 40 E
Qahremānshahr = Bākhtarān, *Iran* **44 C5** 34 23N 47 0 E
Qaidam Pendi, *China* **32 C4** 37 0N 95 0 E
Qajarīyeh, *Iran* **45 D6** 31 1N 48 22 E
Qala, Ras il, *Malta* **23 C1** 36 2N 14 20 E
Qala-i-Jadid = Spīn Būldak, *Afghan.* **42 D2** 31 1N 66 25 E
Qala Point = Qala, Ras il, *Malta* **23 C1** 36 2N 14 20 E
Qala Viala, *Pakistan* **42 D2** 30 49N 67 17 E
Qala Yangi, *Afghan.* **42 B2** 34 20N 66 30 E
Qal'at al Akhḑar, *Si. Arabia* **44 E3** 28 0N 37 10 E
Qal'at Dīzah, *Iraq* **44 B5** 36 11N 45 7 E
Qal'at Şāliḩ, *Iraq* **44 D5** 31 31N 47 16 E
Qal'at Sukkar, *Iraq* **44 D5** 31 51N 46 5 E
Qamani'tuaq = Baker Lake, *Canada* **68 B10** 64 20N 96 3W
Qamdo, *China* **32 C4** 31 15N 97 6 E
Qamruddin Karez, *Pakistan* **42 D3** 31 45N 68 20 E
Qandahār, *Afghan.* **40 D4** 31 32N 65 43 E
Qandahār □, *Afghan.* **40 D4** 31 0N 65 0 E
Qapān, *Iran* **45 B7** 37 40N 55 47 E
Qapshaghay, *Kazakstan* **26 E8** 43 51N 77 14 E
Qaqortoq, *Greenland* **69 B6** 60 43N 46 0W
Qara Qash →, *China* **43 B8** 35 0N 78 30 E
Qarabutaq, *Kazakstan* **26 E7** 49 59N 60 14 E
Qaraghandy, *Kazakstan* **26 E8** 49 50N 73 10 E
Qārah, *Si. Arabia* **44 D4** 29 55N 40 3 E
Qarataū, *Kazakstan* **26 E8** 43 10N 70 28 E
Qarataū, *Kazakstan* **26 E7** 43 30N 69 30 E
Qardho = Gardo, *Somali Rep.* **46 F4** 9 30N 49 6 E
Qareh →, *Iran* **44 B5** 39 25N 47 22 E
Qareh Tekān, *Iran* **45 B6** 36 38N 49 29 E
Qarqan He →, *China* **32 C3** 39 30N 88 30 E
Qarqaraly, *Kazakstan* **26 E8** 49 26N 75 30 E
Qarshi, *Uzbekistan* **26 F7** 38 53N 65 48 E
Qartabā, *Lebanon* **47 A4** 34 4N 35 50 E
Qaryat al Gharab, *Iraq* **44 D5** 31 27N 44 48 E
Qaryat al 'Ulyā, *Si. Arabia* **44 E5** 27 33N 47 42 E
Qasr 'Amra, *Jordan* **44 D3** 31 48N 36 35 E
Qaşr-e Qand, *Iran* **45 E9** 26 15N 60 45 E
Qasr Farâfra, *Egypt* **51 C11** 27 0N 28 1 E
Qatanā, *Syria* **47 B5** 33 26N 36 4 E
Qatar ■, *Asia* **46 B5** 25 30N 51 15 E
Qatlīsh, *Iran* **45 B8** 37 50N 57 19 E
Qattâra, Munkhafed el, *Egypt* **51 C11** 29 30N 27 30 E
Qattâra Depression = Qattâra, Munkhafed el, *Egypt* **51 C11** 29 30N 27 30 E
Qawām al Ḩamzah, *Iraq* **44 D5** 31 43N 44 58 E
Qāyen, *Iran* **45 C8** 33 40N 59 10 E
Qazaqstan = Kazakstan ■, *Asia* **26 E7** 50 0N 70 0 E
Qazimämmäd, *Azerbaijan* **45 A6** 40 3N 49 0 E
Qazvin, *Iran* **45 B6** 36 15N 50 0 E
Qena, *Egypt* **51 C12** 26 10N 32 43 E
Qeqertarsuaq, *Greenland* **4 C5** 69 15N 53 38W
Qeqertarsuaq, *Greenland* **69 B5** 69 45N 53 30W
Qeshlāq, *Iran* **44 C5** 34 55N 46 28 E
Qeshm, *Iran* **45 E8** 26 55N 56 10 E
Qeys, *Iran* **45 E7** 26 32N 53 58 E
Qezel Owzen →, *Iran* **45 B6** 36 45N 49 22 E
Qezi'ot, *Israel* **47 E3** 30 52N 34 26 E
Qi Xian, *China* **34 G8** 34 40N 114 48 E
Qian Gorlos, *China* **35 B13** 45 5N 124 42 E
Qian Xian, *China* **34 G5** 34 31N 108 15 E
Qianyang, *China* **34 G4** 34 40N 107 8 E
Qikiqtarjuaq, *Canada* **69 B13** 67 33N 63 0W
Qila Safed, *Pakistan* **40 E2** 29 0N 61 30 E
Qila Saifullāh, *Pakistan* **42 D3** 30 45N 68 17 E
Qilian Shan, *China* **32 C4** 38 30N 96 0 E
Qin He →, *China* **34 G7** 35 1N 113 22 E
Qin Ling = Qinling Shandi, *China* **34 H5** 33 50N 108 10 E
Qin'an, *China* **34 G3** 34 48N 105 40 E
Qing Xian, *China* **34 E9** 38 35N 116 45 E
Qingcheng, *China* **35 F9** 37 15N 117 40 E
Qingdao, *China* **35 F11** 36 5N 120 20 E
Qingfeng, *China* **34 G8** 35 52N 115 8 E
Qinghai □, *China* **32 C4** 36 0N 98 0 E
Qinghai Hu, *China* **32 C5** 36 40N 100 10 E
Qinghecheng, *China* **35 D13** 41 28N 124 15 E
Qinghemen, *China* **35 D11** 41 48N 121 25 E
Qingjian, *China* **34 F6** 37 8N 110 8 E
Qingjiang = Huaiyin, *China* **35 H10** 33 30N 119 2 E
Qingshui, *China* **34 G4** 34 48N 106 8 E
Qingshuihe, *China* **34 E6** 39 55N 111 35 E
Qingtongxia Shuiku, *China* **34 F3** 37 50N 105 58 E
Qingxu, *China* **34 F7** 37 34N 112 22 E
Qingyang, *China* **34 F4** 36 2N 107 55 E
Qingyuan, *China* **35 C13** 42 10N 124 55 E
Qingyun, *China* **35 F9** 37 45N 117 20 E
Qinhuangdao, *China* **35 E10** 39 56N 119 30 E
Qinling Shandi, *China* **34 H5** 33 50N 108 10 E
Qinshui, *China* **34 G7** 35 40N 112 8 E
Qinyang = Jiyuan, *China* **34 G7** 35 7N 112 57 E
Qinyuan, *China* **34 F7** 36 29N 112 20 E
Qinzhou, *China* **32 D5** 21 58N 108 38 E
Qionghai, *China* **38 C8** 19 15N 110 26 E
Qiongzhou Haixia, *China* **38 B8** 20 10N 110 15 E
Qiqihar, *China* **27 E13** 47 26N 124 0 E
Qiraīya, W. →, *Egypt* **47 E3** 30 27N 34 0 E
Qiryat Ata, *Israel* **47 C4** 32 47N 35 6 E
Qiryat Gat, *Israel* **47 D3** 31 32N 34 46 E
Qiryat Mal'akhi, *Israel* **47 D3** 31 44N 34 44 E
Qiryat Shemona, *Israel* **47 B4** 33 13N 35 35 E
Qiryat Yam, *Israel* **47 C4** 32 51N 35 4 E
Qishan, *China* **34 G4** 34 25N 107 38 E
Qitai, *China* **32 B3** 44 2N 89 35 E
Qixia, *China* **35 F11** 37 17N 120 52 E
Qızılağac Körfäzi, *Azerbaijan* **45 B6** 39 9N 49 0 E
Qojūr, *Iran* **44 B5** 36 12N 47 55 E
Qom, *Iran* **45 C6** 34 40N 51 0 E
Qomolangma Feng = Everest, Mt., *Nepal* **43 E12** 28 5N 86 58 E
Qomsheh, *Iran* **45 D6** 32 0N 51 55 E
Qoraqalpoghistan □, *Uzbekistan* **26 E6** 43 0N 58 0 E
Qostanay, *Kazakstan* **26 D7** 53 10N 63 35 E
Quabbin Reservoir, *U.S.A.* **79 D12** 42 20N 72 20W
Quairading, *Australia* **61 F2** 32 0S 117 21 E
Quakertown, *U.S.A.* **79 F9** 40 26N 75 21W
Qualicum Beach, *Canada* **72 D4** 49 22N 124 26W
Quambatook, *Australia* **63 F3** 35 49S 143 34 E
Quambone, *Australia* **63 E4** 30 57S 147 53 E
Quamby, *Australia* **62 C3** 20 22S 140 17 E
Quan Long = Ca Mau, *Vietnam* **39 H5** 9 7N 105 8 E
Quanah, *U.S.A.* **81 H5** 34 18N 99 44W
Quang Ngai, *Vietnam* **38 E7** 15 13N 108 58 E
Quang Tri, *Vietnam* **38 D6** 16 45N 107 13 E
Quang Yen, *Vietnam* **38 B6** 20 56N 106 52 E
Quantock Hills, *U.K.* **11 F4** 51 8N 3 10W
Quanzhou, *China* **33 D6** 24 55N 118 34 E
Qu'Appelle, *Canada* **73 C8** 50 33N 103 53W
Quaqtaq, *Canada* **69 B13** 60 55N 69 40W
Quaraí, *Brazil* **94 C4** 30 15S 56 20W
Quartu Sant'Élena, *Italy* **20 E3** 39 15N 9 10 E
Quartzsite, *U.S.A.* **85 M12** 33 40N 114 13W
Quatsino Sd., *Canada* **72 C3** 50 25N 127 58W
Quba, *Azerbaijan* **25 F8** 41 21N 48 32 E
Qūchān, *Iran* **45 B8** 37 10N 58 27 E
Queanbeyan, *Australia* **63 F4** 35 17S 149 14 E
Québec, *Canada* **71 C5** 46 52N 71 13W
Québec □, *Canada* **71 C6** 48 0N 74 0W
Queen Alexandra Ra., *Antarctica* **5 E11** 85 0S 170 0 E
Queen Charlotte City, *Canada* **72 C2** 53 15N 132 2W
Queen Charlotte Is., *Canada* **72 C2** 53 20N 132 10W
Queen Charlotte Sd., *Canada* **72 C3** 51 0N 128 0W
Queen Charlotte Strait, *Canada* **72 C3** 50 45N 127 10W
Queen Elizabeth Is., *Canada* **66 B10** 76 0N 95 0W
Queen Mary Land, *Antarctica* **5 D7** 70 0S 95 0 E
Queen Maud G., *Canada* **68 B9** 68 15N 102 30W
Queen Maud Land, *Antarctica* **5 D3** 72 30S 12 0 E
Queen Maud Mts., *Antarctica* **5 E13** 86 0S 160 0W
Queens Chan., *Australia* **60 C4** 15 0S 129 30 E
Queenscliff, *Australia* **63 F3** 38 16S 144 39 E
Queensland □, *Australia* **62 C3** 22 0S 142 0 E
Queenstown, *Australia* **62 G4** 42 4S 145 35 E
Queenstown, *N.Z.* **59 L2** 45 1S 168 40 E
Queenstown, *S. Africa* **56 E4** 31 52S 26 52 E
Queets, *U.S.A.* **84 C2** 47 32N 124 20W
Queguay Grande →, *Uruguay* **94 C4** 32 9S 58 9W
Queimadas, *Brazil* **93 F11** 11 0S 39 38W
Quelimane, *Mozam.* **55 F4** 17 53S 36 58 E
Quellón, *Chile* **96 E2** 43 7S 73 37W
Quelpart = Cheju do, *S. Korea* **35 H14** 33 29N 126 34 E
Quemado, *N. Mex., U.S.A.* **83 J9** 34 20N 108 30W
Quemado, *Tex., U.S.A.* **81 L4** 28 58N 100 35W
Quemú-Quemú, *Argentina* **94 D3** 36 3S 63 36W
Quequén, *Argentina* **94 D4** 38 30S 58 30W
Querétaro, *Mexico* **86 C4** 20 36N 100 23W
Querétaro □, *Mexico* **86 C5** 20 30N 100 0W
Queshan, *China* **34 H8** 32 55N 114 2 E
Quesnel, *Canada* **72 C4** 53 0N 122 30W
Quesnel →, *Canada* **72 C4** 52 58N 122 29W
Quesnel L., *Canada* **72 C4** 52 30N 121 20W
Questa, *U.S.A.* **83 H11** 36 42N 105 36W
Quetico Prov. Park, *Canada* **70 C1** 48 30N 91 45W
Quetta, *Pakistan* **42 D2** 30 15N 66 55 E
Quezaltenango, *Guatemala* **88 D1** 14 50N 91 30W
Quezon City, *Phil.* **37 B6** 14 38N 121 0 E
Qufār, *Si. Arabia* **44 E4** 27 26N 41 37 E
Qui Nhon, *Vietnam* **38 F7** 13 40N 109 13 E
Quibaxe, *Angola* **52 F2** 8 24S 14 27 E
Quibdo, *Colombia* **92 B3** 5 42N 76 40W
Quiberon, *France* **18 C2** 47 29N 3 9W
Quiet L., *Canada* **72 A2** 61 5N 133 5W
Quiindy, *Paraguay* **94 B4** 25 58S 57 14W
Quila, *Mexico* **86 C3** 24 23N 107 13W
Quilán, C., *Chile* **96 E2** 43 15S 74 30W
Quilcene, *U.S.A.* **84 C4** 47 49N 122 53W
Quilimarí, *Chile* **94 C1** 32 5S 71 30W
Quilino, *Argentina* **94 C3** 30 14S 64 29W
Quill Lakes, *Canada* **73 C8** 51 55N 104 13W
Quillabamba, *Peru* **92 F4** 12 50S 72 50W
Quillagua, *Chile* **94 A2** 21 40S 69 40W
Quillaicillo, *Chile* **94 C1** 31 17S 71 40W
Quillota, *Chile* **94 C1** 32 54S 71 16W
Quilmes, *Argentina* **94 C4** 34 43S 58 15W
Quilon, *India* **40 Q10** 8 50N 76 38 E
Quilpie, *Australia* **63 D3** 26 35S 144 11 E
Quilpué, *Chile* **94 C1** 33 5S 71 33W
Quilua, *Mozam.* **55 F4** 16 17S 39 54 E
Quimilí, *Argentina* **94 B3** 27 40S 62 30W
Quimper, *France* **18 B1** 48 0N 4 9W
Quimperlé, *France* **18 C2** 47 53N 3 33W
Quinault →, *U.S.A.* **84 C2** 47 21N 124 18W
Quincy, *Calif., U.S.A.* **84 F6** 39 56N 120 57W
Quincy, *Fla., U.S.A.* **77 K3** 30 35N 84 34W
Quincy, *Ill., U.S.A.* **80 F9** 39 56N 91 23W
Quincy, *Mass., U.S.A.* **79 D14** 42 15N 71 0W
Quincy, *Wash., U.S.A.* **82 C4** 47 22N 119 56W
Quines, *Argentina* **94 C2** 32 13S 65 48W
Quinga, *Mozam.* **55 F5** 15 49S 40 15 E
Quinns Rocks, *Australia* **61 F2** 31 40S 115 42 E
Quintana Roo □, *Mexico* **87 D7** 19 0N 88 0W
Quintanar de la Orden, *Spain* **19 C4** 39 36N 3 5W
Quintero, *Chile* **94 C1** 32 45S 71 30W
Quirihue, *Chile* **94 D1** 36 15S 72 35W
Quirindi, *Australia* **63 E5** 31 28S 150 40 E
Quirinópolis, *Brazil* **93 G8** 18 32S 50 30W
Quissanga, *Mozam.* **55 E5** 12 24S 40 28 E
Quissico, *Mozam.* **57 C5** 24 42S 34 44 E
Quitilipi, *Argentina* **94 B3** 26 50S 60 13W
Quitman, *U.S.A.* **77 K4** 30 47N 83 34W
Quito, *Ecuador* **92 D3** 0 15S 78 35W
Quixadá, *Brazil* **93 D11** 4 55S 39 0W
Quixaxe, *Mozam.* **55 F5** 15 17S 40 4 E
Qulan, *Kazakstan* **26 E8** 42 55N 72 43 E
Qul'ân, Jazâ'ir, *Egypt* **44 E2** 24 22N 35 31 E
Qumbu, *S. Africa* **57 E4** 31 10S 28 48 E
Quneitra, *Syria* **47 B4** 33 7N 35 48 E
Qŭnghirot, *Uzbekistan* **26 E6** 43 6N 58 54 E
Quoin I., *Australia* **60 B4** 14 54S 129 32 E
Quoin Pt., *S. Africa* **56 E2** 34 46S 19 37 E
Quorn, *Australia* **63 E2** 32 25S 138 5 E
Qŭqon, *Uzbekistan* **26 E8** 40 30N 70 57 E
Qurnat as Sawdā', *Lebanon* **47 A5** 34 18N 36 6 E
Quşaybā', *Si. Arabia* **44 E4** 26 53N 43 35 E
Qusaybah, *Iraq* **44 C4** 34 24N 40 59 E
Quseir, *Egypt* **44 E2** 26 7N 34 16 E
Qūshchī, *Iran* **44 B5** 37 59N 45 3 E
Quthing, *Lesotho* **57 E4** 30 25S 27 36 E
Qūţīābād, *Iran* **45 C6** 35 47N 48 30 E
Quwo, *China* **34 G6** 35 38N 111 25 E
Quyang, *China* **34 E8** 38 35N 114 40 E
Quynh Nhai, *Vietnam* **38 B4** 21 49N 103 33 E
Quyon, *Canada* **79 A8** 45 31N 76 14W
Quzhou, *China* **33 D6** 28 57N 118 54 E
Quzi, *China* **34 F4** 36 20N 107 20 E
Qyzylorda, *Kazakstan* **26 E7** 44 48N 65 28 E

R

Ra, Ko, *Thailand* **39 H2** 9 13N 98 16 E
Raahe, *Finland* **8 D21** 64 40N 24 28 E
Raalte, *Neths.* **15 B6** 52 23N 6 16 E
Raasay, *U.K.* **12 D2** 57 25N 6 4W
Raasay, Sd. of, *U.K.* **12 D2** 57 30N 6 8W
Raba, *Indonesia* **37 F5** 8 36S 118 55 E
Rába →, *Hungary* **17 E9** 47 38N 17 38 E
Rabai, *Kenya* **54 C4** 3 50S 39 31 E
Rabat = Victoria, *Malta* **23 C1** 36 3N 14 14 E
Rabat, *Malta* **23 D1** 35 53N 14 24 E
Rabat, *Morocco* **50 B4** 34 2N 6 48W
Rabaul, *Papua N. G.* **64 H7** 4 24S 152 18 E
Rābigh, *Si. Arabia* **46 C2** 22 50N 39 5 E
Râbniţa, *Moldova* **17 E15** 47 45N 29 0 E
Rābor, *Iran* **45 D8** 29 17N 56 55 E
Race, C., *Canada* **71 C9** 46 40N 53 5W
Rach Gia, *Vietnam* **39 G5** 10 5N 105 5 E
Rachid, *Mauritania* **50 E3** 18 45N 11 35W
Racibórz, *Poland* **17 C10** 50 7N 18 18 E
Racine, *U.S.A.* **76 D2** 42 41N 87 51W
Rackerby, *U.S.A.* **84 F5** 39 26N 121 22W
Radama, Nosy, *Madag.* **57 A8** 14 0S 47 47 E
Radama, Saikanosy, *Madag.* **57 A8** 14 16S 47 53 E
Rădăuţi, *Romania* **17 E13** 47 50N 25 59 E
Radcliff, *U.S.A.* **76 G3** 37 51N 85 57W
Radekhiv, *Ukraine* **17 C13** 50 25N 24 32 E
Radekhov = Radekhiv, *Ukraine* **17 C13** 50 25N 24 32 E
Radford, *U.S.A.* **76 G5** 37 8N 80 34W
Radhanpur, *India* **42 H4** 23 50N 71 38 E
Radhwa, Jabal, *Si. Arabia* **44 E3** 24 34N 38 18 E
Radisson, *Qué., Canada* **70 B4** 53 47N 77 37W
Radisson, *Sask., Canada* **73 C7** 52 30N 107 20W
Radium Hot Springs, *Canada* **72 C5** 50 35N 116 2W
Radnor Forest, *U.K.* **11 E4** 52 17N 3 10W
Radom, *Poland* **17 C11** 51 23N 21 12 E
Radomsko, *Poland* **17 C10** 51 5N 19 28 E
Radomyshl, *Ukraine* **17 C15** 50 30N 29 12 E
Radstock, C., *Australia* **63 E1** 33 12S 134 20 E
Radviliškis, *Lithuania* **9 J20** 55 49N 23 33 E
Radville, *Canada* **73 D8** 49 30N 104 15W
Rae, *Canada* **72 A5** 62 50N 116 3W
Rae Bareli, *India* **43 F9** 26 18N 81 20 E
Rae Isthmus, *Canada* **69 B11** 66 40N 87 30W
Raeren, *Belgium* **15 D6** 50 41N 6 7 E
Raeside, L., *Australia* **61 E3** 29 20S 122 0 E
Raetihi, *N.Z.* **59 H5** 39 25S 175 17 E
Rafaela, *Argentina* **94 C3** 31 10S 61 30W
Rafah, *Gaza Strip* **47 D3** 31 18N 34 14 E
Rafai, *C.A.R.* **54 B1** 4 59N 23 58 E
Rafḩā, *Si. Arabia* **44 D4** 29 35N 43 35 E
Rafsanjān, *Iran* **45 D8** 30 30N 56 5 E
Raft Pt., *Australia* **60 C3** 16 4S 124 26 E
Râgâ, *Sudan* **51 G11** 8 28N 25 41 E
Ragachow, *Belarus* **17 B16** 53 8N 30 5 E
Ragama, *Sri Lanka* **40 R11** 7 0N 79 50 E
Ragged, Mt., *Australia* **61 F3** 33 27S 123 25 E
Raghunathpalli, *India* **43 H11** 22 14N 84 48 E
Raghunathpur, *India* **43 H12** 23 33N 86 40 E
Raglan, *N.Z.* **59 G5** 37 55S 174 55 E
Ragusa, *Italy* **20 F6** 36 55N 14 44 E
Raha, *Indonesia* **37 E6** 4 55S 123 0 E
Rahaeng = Tak, *Thailand* **38 D2** 16 52N 99 8 E
Rahatgarh, *India* **43 H8** 23 47N 78 22 E
Rahimyar Khan, *Pakistan* **42 E4** 28 30N 70 25 E
Rāhjerd, *Iran* **45 C6** 34 22N 50 22 E
Rahon, *India* **42 D7** 31 3N 76 7 E
Raichur, *India* **40 L10** 16 10N 77 20 E
Raiganj, *India* **43 G13** 25 37N 88 10 E
Raigarh, *India* **41 J13** 21 56N 83 25 E
Raijua, *Indonesia* **37 F6** 10 37S 121 36 E
Raikot, *India* **42 D6** 30 41N 75 42 E
Railton, *Australia* **62 G4** 41 25S 146 28 E
Rainbow Lake, *Canada* **72 B5** 58 30N 119 23W
Rainier, *U.S.A.* **84 D4** 46 53N 122 41W
Rainier, Mt., *U.S.A.* **84 D5** 46 52N 121 46W
Rainy L., *Canada* **73 D10** 48 42N 93 10W
Rainy River, *Canada* **73 D10** 48 43N 94 29W
Raippaluoto, *Finland* **8 E19** 63 13N 21 14 E
Raipur, *India* **41 J12** 21 17N 81 45 E
Raisen, *India* **42 H8** 23 20N 77 48 E
Raisio, *Finland* **9 F20** 60 28N 22 11 E
Raj Nandgaon, *India* **41 J12** 21 5N 81 5 E
Raj Nilgiri, *India* **43 J12** 21 28N 86 46 E
Raja, Ujung, *Indonesia* **36 D1** 3 40N 96 25 E
Raja Ampat, Kepulauan, *Indonesia* **37 E7** 0 30S 130 0 E
Rajahmundry, *India* **41 L12** 17 1N 81 48 E
Rajang →, *Malaysia* **36 D4** 2 30N 112 0 E
Rajanpur, *Pakistan* **42 E4** 29 6N 70 19 E
Rajapalaiyam, *India* **40 Q10** 9 25N 77 35 E
Rajasthan □, *India* **42 F5** 26 45N 73 30 E
Rajasthan Canal, *India* **42 F5** 28 0N 72 0 E
Rajauri, *India* **43 C6** 33 25N 74 21 E
Rajgarh, *Mad. P., India* **42 G7** 24 2N 76 45 E
Rajgarh, *Raj., India* **42 F7** 27 14N 76 38 E
Rajgarh, *Raj., India* **42 E6** 28 40N 75 25 E
Rajgir, *India* **43 G11** 25 2N 85 25 E
Rajkot, *India* **42 H4** 22 15N 70 56 E
Rajmahal Hills, *India* **43 G12** 24 30N 87 30 E
Rajpipla, *India* **40 J8** 21 50N 73 30 E
Rajpur, *India* **42 H6** 22 18N 74 21 E
Rajpura, *India* **42 D7** 30 25N 76 32 E
Rajshahi, *Bangla.* **41 G16** 24 22N 88 39 E
Rajshahi □, *Bangla.* **43 G13** 25 0N 89 0 E
Rajula, *India* **42 J4** 21 3N 71 26 E
Rakaia, *N.Z.* **59 K4** 43 45S 172 1 E
Rakaia →, *N.Z.* **59 K4** 43 36S 172 15 E
Rakan, Ra's, *Qatar* **45 E6** 26 10N 51 20 E
Rakaposhi, *Pakistan* **43 A6** 36 10N 74 25 E
Rakata, Pulau, *Indonesia* **36 F3** 6 10S 105 20 E
Rakhiv, *Ukraine* **17 D13** 48 3N 24 12 E
Rakhni, *Pakistan* **42 D3** 30 4N 69 56 E
Rakhni →, *Pakistan* **42 E3** 29 31N 69 36 E
Rakitnoye, *Russia* **30 B7** 45 36N 134 17 E
Rakops, *Botswana* **56 C3** 21 1S 24 28 E
Rakvere, *Estonia* **9 G22** 59 20N 26 25 E
Raleigh, *U.S.A.* **77 H6** 35 47N 78 39W
Ralls, *U.S.A.* **81 J4** 33 41N 101 24W
Ralston, *U.S.A.* **78 E8** 41 30N 76 57W
Ram →, *Canada* **72 A4** 62 1N 123 41W
Rām Allāh, *West Bank* **47 D4** 31 55N 35 10 E
Rama, *Nic.* **88 D3** 12 9N 84 15W
Ramakona, *India* **43 J8** 21 43N 78 50 E
Raman, *Thailand* **39 J3** 6 29N 101 18 E
Ramanathapuram, *India* **40 Q11** 9 25N 78 55 E
Ramanetaka, B. de, *Madag.* **57 A8** 14 13S 47 52 E
Ramanujganj, *India* **43 H10** 23 48N 83 42 E
Ramat Gan, *Israel* **47 C3** 32 4N 34 48 E
Ramatlhabama, *S. Africa* **56 D4** 25 37S 25 33 E
Ramban, *India* **43 C6** 33 14N 75 12 E
Rambipuji, *Indonesia* **37 H15** 8 12S 113 37 E
Rame Hd., *Australia* **63 F4** 37 47S 149 30 E
Ramechhap, *Nepal* **43 F12** 27 25N 86 10 E
Ramganga →, *India* **43 F8** 27 5N 79 58 E
Ramgarh, *Jharkhand, India* **43 H11** 23 40N 85 35 E
Ramgarh, *Raj., India* **42 F6** 27 16N 75 14 E
Ramgarh, *Raj., India* **42 F4** 27 30N 70 36 E
Rāmhormoz, *Iran* **45 D6** 31 15N 49 35 E
Ramīān, *Iran* **45 B7** 37 3N 55 16 E
Ramingining, *Australia* **62 A2** 12 19S 135 3 E
Ramla, *Israel* **47 D3** 31 55N 34 52 E
Ramnad = Ramanathapuram, *India* **40 Q11** 9 25N 78 55 E
Ramnagar, *Jammu & Kashmir, India* **43 C6** 32 47N 75 18 E
Ramnagar, *Uttaranchal, India* **43 E8** 29 24N 79 7 E
Râmnicu Sărat, *Romania* **17 F14** 45 26N 27 3 E
Râmnicu Vâlcea, *Romania* **17 F13** 45 9N 24 21 E
Ramona, *U.S.A.* **85 M10** 33 2N 116 52W
Ramore, *Canada* **70 C3** 48 30N 80 25W
Ramotswa, *Botswana* **56 C4** 24 50S 25 52 E
Rampur, *H.P., India* **42 D7** 31 26N 77 43 E
Rampur, *Mad. P., India* **42 H5** 23 25N 73 53 E
Rampur, *Ut. P., India* **43 E8** 28 50N 79 5 E
Rampur Hat, *India* **43 G12** 24 10N 87 50 E
Rampura, *India* **42 G6** 24 30N 75 27 E
Ramrama Tola, *India* **43 J8** 21 52N 79 55 E
Ramree I., *Burma* **41 K19** 19 0N 93 40 E
Rāmsar, *Iran* **45 B6** 36 53N 50 41 E
Ramsey, *U.K.* **10 C3** 54 20N 4 22W
Ramsey, *U.S.A.* **79 E10** 41 4N 74 9W
Ramsey L., *Canada* **70 C3** 47 13N 82 15W
Ramsgate, *U.K.* **11 F9** 51 20N 1 25 E
Ramtek, *India* **40 J11** 21 20N 79 15 E
Rana Pratap Sagar Dam, *India* **42 G6** 24 58N 75 38 E
Ranaghat, *India* **43 H13** 23 15N 88 35 E
Ranahu, *Pakistan* **42 G3** 25 55N 69 45 E
Ranau, *Malaysia* **36 C5** 6 2N 116 40 E
Rancagua, *Chile* **94 C1** 34 10S 70 50W
Rancheria →, *Canada* **72 A3** 60 13N 129 7W
Ranchester, *U.S.A.* **82 D10** 44 54N 107 10W
Ranchi, *India* **43 H11** 23 19N 85 27 E
Rancho Cucamonga, *U.S.A.* **85 L9** 34 10N 117 30W
Randalstown, *U.K.* **13 B5** 54 45N 6 19W

Randers, Denmark 9 H14 56 29N 10 1 E
Randfontein, S. Africa 57 D4 26 8S 27 45 E
Randle, U.S.A. 84 D5 46 32N 121 57W
Randolph, Mass., U.S.A. 79 D13 42 10N 71 2W
Randolph, N.Y., U.S.A. 78 D6 42 10N 78 59W
Randolph, Utah, U.S.A. 82 F8 41 40N 111 11W
Randolph, Vt., U.S.A. 79 C12 43 55N 72 40W
Randsburg, U.S.A. 85 K9 35 22N 117 39W
Råne älv →, Sweden 8 D20 65 50N 22 20 E
Rangae, Thailand 39 J3 6 19N 101 44 E
Rangaunu B., N.Z. 59 F4 34 51S 173 15 E
Rangeley, U.S.A. 79 B14 44 58N 70 39W
Rangeley L., U.S.A. 79 B14 44 55N 70 43W
Rangely, U.S.A. 82 F9 40 5N 108 48W
Ranger, U.S.A. 81 J5 32 28N 98 41W
Rangia, India 41 F17 26 28N 91 38 E
Rangiora, N.Z. 59 K4 43 19S 172 36 E
Rangitaiki →, N.Z. 59 G6 37 54S 176 49 E
Rangitata →, N.Z. 59 K3 43 45S 171 15 E
Rangkasbitung, Indonesia 37 G12 6 21S 106 15 E
Rangon →, Burma 41 L20 16 28N 96 40 E
Rangoon, Burma 41 L20 16 45N 96 20 E
Rangpur, Bangla. 41 G16 25 42N 89 22 E
Rangsit, Thailand 38 F3 13 59N 100 37 E
Ranibennur, India 40 M9 14 35N 75 30 E
Raniganj, Ut. P., India 43 F9 27 3N 82 13 E
Raniganj, W. Bengal, India 41 H15 23 40N 87 5 E
Ranikhet, India 43 E8 29 39N 79 25 E
Raniwara, India 40 G8 24 50N 72 10 E
Rāniyah, Iraq 44 B5 36 15N 44 53 E
Ranka, India 43 H10 23 59N 83 47 E
Ranken →, Australia 62 C2 20 31S 137 36 E
Rankin, U.S.A. 81 K4 31 13N 101 56W
Rankin Inlet, Canada 68 B10 62 30N 93 0W
Rankins Springs, Australia 63 E4 33 49S 146 14 E
Rannoch, L., U.K. 12 E4 56 41N 4 20W
Rannoch Moor, U.K. 12 E4 56 38N 4 48W
Ranobe, Helodranon' i, Madag. 57 C7 23 3S 43 33 E
Ranohira, Madag. 57 C8 22 29S 45 24 E
Ranomafana, Toamasina, Madag. 57 B8 18 57S 48 50 E
Ranomafana, Toliara, Madag. 57 C8 24 34S 47 0 E
Ranomena, Madag. 57 C8 23 25S 47 17 E
Ranong, Thailand 39 H2 9 56N 98 40 E
Ranotsara Nord, Madag. 57 C8 22 48S 46 36 E
Rānsa, Iran 45 C6 33 39N 48 18 E
Ransiki, Indonesia 37 E8 1 30S 134 10 E
Rantabe, Madag. 57 B8 15 42S 49 39 E
Rantauprapat, Indonesia 36 D1 2 15N 99 50 E
Rantemario, Indonesia 37 E5 3 15S 119 57 E
Rantoul, U.S.A. 76 E1 40 19N 88 9W
Raoyang, China 34 E8 38 15N 115 45 E
Rapa, Pac. Oc. 65 K13 27 35S 144 20W
Rapa Nui = Pascua, I. de, Chile 65 K17 27 7S 109 23W
Rapallo, Italy 18 D8 44 21N 9 14 E
Rapar, India 42 H4 23 34N 70 38 E
Rāpch, Iran 45 E8 25 40N 59 15 E
Raper, C., Canada 69 B13 69 44N 67 6W
Rapid City, U.S.A. 80 D3 44 5N 103 14W
Rapid River, U.S.A. 76 C2 45 55N 86 58W
Rapla, Estonia 9 G21 59 1N 24 52 E
Rapti →, India 43 F10 26 18N 83 41 E
Raquette →, U.S.A. 79 B10 45 0N 74 42W
Raquette Lake, U.S.A. 79 C10 43 49N 74 40W
Rarotonga, Cook Is. 65 K12 21 30S 160 0W
Ra's al 'Ayn, Syria 44 B4 36 45N 40 12 E
Ra's al Khaymah, U.A.E. 46 B6 25 50N 55 59 E
Rasca, Pta. de la, Canary Is. 22 G3 27 59N 16 41W
Raseiniai, Lithuania 9 J20 55 25N 23 5 E
Rashmi, India 42 G6 25 4N 74 22 E
Rasht, Iran 45 B6 37 20N 49 40 E
Rasi Salai, Thailand 38 E5 15 20N 104 9 E
Rason L., Australia 61 E3 28 45S 124 25 E
Rasra, India 43 G10 25 50N 83 50 E
Rasul, Pakistan 42 C5 32 42N 73 34 E
Rat Buri, Thailand 38 F2 13 30N 99 54 E
Rat Islands, U.S.A. 68 C1 52 0N 178 0 E
Rat L., Canada 73 B9 56 10N 99 40W
Ratangarh, India 42 E6 28 5N 74 35 E
Raṭāwī, Iraq 44 D5 30 38N 47 13 E
Rath, India 43 G8 25 36N 79 37 E
Rath Luirc, Ireland 13 D3 52 21N 8 40W
Rathdrum, Ireland 13 D5 52 56N 6 14W
Rathenow, Germany 16 B7 52 37N 12 19 E
Rathkeale, Ireland 13 D3 52 32N 8 56W
Rathlin I., U.K. 13 A5 55 18N 6 14W
Rathmelton, Ireland 13 A4 55 2N 7 38W
Ratibor = Racibórz, Poland 17 C10 50 7N 18 18 E
Ratlam, India 42 H6 23 20N 75 0 E
Ratnagiri, India 40 L8 16 57N 73 18 E
Ratodero, Pakistan 42 F3 27 48N 68 18 E
Raton, U.S.A. 81 G2 36 54N 104 24W
Rattaphum, Thailand 39 J3 7 8N 100 16 E
Rattray Hd., U.K. 12 D7 57 38N 1 50W
Ratz, Mt., Canada 72 B2 57 23N 132 12W
Raub, Malaysia 39 L3 3 47N 101 52 E
Rauch, Argentina 94 D4 36 45S 59 5W
Raudales de Malpaso, Mexico 87 D6 17 30N 23 30W
Raufarhöfn, Iceland 8 C6 66 27N 15 57W
Raufoss, Norway 9 F14 60 44N 10 37 E
Raukumara Ra., N.Z. 59 H6 38 5S 177 55 E
Rauma, Finland 9 F19 61 10N 21 30 E
Raurkela, India 43 H11 22 14N 84 50 E
Rausu-Dake, Japan 30 B12 44 4N 145 7 E
Rava-Ruska, Poland 17 C12 50 15N 23 42 E
Rava Russkaya = Rava-Ruska, Poland 17 C12 50 15N 23 42 E
Ravalli, U.S.A. 82 C6 47 17N 114 11W
Ravānsar, Iran 44 C5 34 43N 46 40 E
Rāvar, Iran 45 D8 31 20N 56 51 E
Ravena, U.S.A. 79 D11 42 28N 73 49W
Ravenna, Italy 20 B5 44 25N 12 12 E
Ravenna, Nebr., U.S.A. 80 E5 41 1N 98 55W
Ravenna, Ohio, U.S.A. 78 E3 41 9N 81 15W
Ravensburg, Germany 16 E5 47 46N 9 36 E
Ravenshoe, Australia 62 B4 17 37S 145 29 E
Ravensthorpe, Australia 61 F3 33 35S 120 2 E
Ravenswood, Australia 62 C4 20 6S 146 54 E
Ravenswood, U.S.A. 76 F5 38 57N 81 46W
Ravi →, Pakistan 42 D4 30 35N 71 49 E
Rawalpindi, Pakistan 42 C5 33 38N 73 8 E
Rawāndūz, Iraq 44 B5 36 40N 44 30 E
Rawang, Malaysia 39 L3 3 20N 101 35 E
Rawene, N.Z. 59 F4 35 25S 173 32 E
Rawlinna, Australia 61 F4 30 58S 125 28 E
Rawlins, U.S.A. 82 F10 41 47N 107 14W
Rawlinson Ra., Australia 61 D4 24 40S 128 30 E
Rawson, Argentina 96 E3 43 15S 65 5W
Raxaul, India 43 F11 26 59N 84 51 E
Ray, U.S.A. 80 A3 48 21N 103 10W
Ray, C., Canada 71 C8 47 33N 59 15W
Rayadurg, India 40 M10 14 40N 76 50 E
Rayagada, India 41 K13 19 15N 83 20 E
Raychikhinsk, Russia 27 E13 49 46N 129 25 E
Rāyen, Iran 45 D8 29 34N 57 26 E
Rayleigh, U.K. 11 F8 51 36N 0 37 E
Raymond, Canada 72 D6 49 30N 112 35W
Raymond, Calif., U.S.A. 84 H7 37 13N 119 54W
Raymond, N.H., U.S.A. 79 C13 43 2N 71 11W
Raymond, Wash., U.S.A. 84 D3 46 41N 123 44W
Raymondville, U.S.A. 81 M6 26 29N 97 47W
Raymore, Canada 73 C8 51 25N 104 31W
Rayón, Mexico 86 B2 29 43N 110 35W
Rayong, Thailand 38 F3 12 40N 101 20 E
Rayville, U.S.A. 81 J9 32 29N 91 46W
Raz, Pte. du, France 18 C1 48 2N 4 47W
Razan, Iran 45 C6 35 23N 49 2 E
Razdel'naya = Rozdilna, Ukraine 17 E16 46 50N 30 2 E
Razdolnoye, Russia 30 C5 43 30N 131 52 E
Razeh, Iran 45 C6 32 47N 48 9 E
Razgrad, Bulgaria 21 C12 43 33N 26 34 E
Razim, Lacul, Romania 17 F15 44 50N 29 0 E
Razmak, Pakistan 42 C3 32 45N 69 50 E
Ré, Î. de, France 18 C3 46 12N 1 30W
Reading, U.K. 11 F7 51 27N 0 58W
Reading, U.S.A. 79 F9 40 20N 75 56W
Reading □, U.K. 11 F7 51 27N 0 58W
Realicó, Argentina 94 D3 35 0S 64 15W
Ream, Cambodia 39 G4 10 34N 103 39 E
Reata, Mexico 86 B4 26 8N 101 5W
Reay Forest, U.K. 12 C4 58 22N 4 55W
Rebi, Indonesia 37 F8 6 23S 134 7 E
Rebiana, Libya 51 D10 24 12N 22 10 E
Rebun-Tō, Japan 30 B10 45 23N 141 2 E
Recherche, Arch. of the, Australia 61 F3 34 15S 122 50 E
Rechna Doab, Pakistan 42 D5 31 35N 73 30 E
Rechytsa, Belarus 17 B16 52 21N 30 24 E
Recife, Brazil 93 E12 8 0S 35 0W
Recklinghausen, Germany 15 C7 51 37N 7 12 E
Reconquista, Argentina 94 B4 29 10S 59 45W
Recreo, Argentina 94 B2 29 25S 65 10W
Red →, La., U.S.A. 81 K9 31 1N 91 45W
Red →, N. Dak., U.S.A. 68 C10 49 0N 97 15W
Red Bank, U.S.A. 79 F10 40 21N 74 5W
Red Bay, Canada 71 B8 51 44N 56 25W
Red Bluff, U.S.A. 82 F2 40 11N 122 15W
Red Bluff L., U.S.A. 81 K3 31 54N 103 55W
Red Cliffs, Australia 63 E3 34 19S 142 11 E
Red Cloud, U.S.A. 80 E5 40 5N 98 32W
Red Creek, U.S.A. 79 C8 43 14N 76 45W
Red Deer, Canada 72 C6 52 20N 113 50W
Red Deer →, Alta., Canada 73 C7 50 58N 110 0W
Red Deer →, Man., Canada 73 C8 52 53N 101 1W
Red Deer L., Canada 73 C8 52 55N 101 20W
Red Hook, U.S.A. 79 E11 41 55N 73 53W
Red Indian L., Canada 71 C8 48 35N 57 0W
Red L., Canada 73 C10 51 3N 93 49W
Red Lake, Canada 73 C10 51 3N 93 49W
Red Lake Falls, U.S.A. 80 B6 47 53N 96 16W
Red Lake Road, Canada 73 C10 49 59N 93 25W
Red Lodge, U.S.A. 82 D9 45 11N 109 15W
Red Mountain, U.S.A. 85 K9 35 37N 117 38W
Red Oak, U.S.A. 80 E7 41 1N 95 14W
Red Rock, Canada 70 C2 48 55N 88 15W
Red Rock, L., U.S.A. 80 E8 41 22N 92 59W
Red Rocks Pt., Australia 61 F4 32 13S 127 32 E
Red Sea, Asia 46 C2 25 0N 36 0 E
Red Slate Mt., U.S.A. 84 H8 37 31N 118 52W
Red Sucker L., Canada 70 B1 54 9N 93 40W
Red Tower Pass = Turnu Roşu, P., Romania 17 F13 45 33N 24 17 E
Red Wing, U.S.A. 80 C8 44 34N 92 31W
Redang, Malaysia 36 C2 5 49N 103 2 E
Redange, Lux. 15 E5 49 46N 5 52 E
Redcar, U.K. 10 C6 54 37N 1 4W
Redcar & Cleveland □, U.K. 10 C7 54 29N 1 0W
Redcliff, Canada 73 C6 50 10N 110 50W
Redcliffe, Australia 63 D5 27 12S 153 0 E
Redcliffe, Mt., Australia 61 E3 28 30S 121 30 E
Reddersburg, S. Africa 56 D4 29 41S 26 10 E
Redding, U.S.A. 82 F2 40 35N 122 24W
Redditch, U.K. 11 E6 52 18N 1 55W
Redfield, U.S.A. 80 C5 44 53N 98 31W
Redford, U.S.A. 79 B11 44 38N 73 48W
Redlands, U.S.A. 85 M9 34 4N 117 11W
Redmond, Oreg., U.S.A. 82 D3 44 17N 121 11W
Redmond, Wash., U.S.A. 84 C4 47 41N 122 7W
Redon, France 18 C2 47 40N 2 6W
Redonda, Antigua 89 C7 16 58N 62 19W
Redondela, Spain 19 A1 42 15N 8 38W
Redondo Beach, U.S.A. 85 M8 33 50N 118 23W
Redruth, U.K. 11 G2 50 14N 5 14W
Redvers, Canada 73 D8 49 35N 101 40W
Redwater, Canada 72 C6 53 55N 113 6W
Redwood, U.S.A. 79 B9 44 18N 75 48W
Redwood City, U.S.A. 84 H4 37 30N 122 15W
Redwood Falls, U.S.A. 80 C7 44 32N 95 7W
Redwood Nat. Park, U.S.A. 82 F1 41 40N 124 5W
Ree, L., Ireland 13 C3 53 35N 8 0W
Reed, L., Canada 73 C8 54 38N 100 30W
Reed City, U.S.A. 76 D3 43 53N 85 31W
Reedley, U.S.A. 84 J7 36 36N 119 27W
Reedsburg, U.S.A. 80 D9 43 32N 90 0W
Reedsport, U.S.A. 82 E1 43 42N 124 6W
Reedsville, U.S.A. 78 F7 40 39N 77 35W
Reefton, N.Z. 59 K3 42 6S 171 51 E
Reese →, U.S.A. 82 F5 40 48N 117 4W
Refugio, U.S.A. 81 L6 28 18N 97 17W
Regensburg, Germany 16 D7 49 1N 12 6 E
Reggâne = Zaouiet Reggâne, Algeria 50 C6 26 32N 0 3 E
Réggio di Calábria, Italy 20 E6 38 6N 15 39 E
Réggio nell'Emilia, Italy 20 B4 44 43N 10 36 E
Reghin, Romania 17 E13 46 46N 24 42 E
Regina, Canada 73 C8 50 27N 104 35W
Regina Beach, Canada 73 C8 50 47N 105 0W
Registro, Brazil 95 A6 24 29S 47 49W
Rehar →, India 43 H10 23 55N 82 40 E
Rehli, India 43 H8 23 38N 79 5 E
Rehoboth, Namibia 56 C2 23 15S 17 4 E
Rehovot, Israel 47 D3 31 54N 34 48 E
Reichenbach, Germany 16 C7 50 37N 12 17 E
Reid, Australia 61 F4 30 49S 128 26 E
Reidsville, U.S.A. 77 G6 36 21N 79 40W
Reigate, U.K. 11 F7 51 14N 0 12W
Reims, France 18 B6 49 15N 4 1 E
Reina Adelaida, Arch., Chile 96 G2 52 20S 74 0W
Reindeer →, Canada 73 B8 55 36N 103 11W
Reindeer I., Canada 73 C9 52 30N 98 0W
Reindeer L., Canada 73 B8 57 15N 102 15W
Reinga, C., N.Z. 59 F4 34 25S 172 43 E
Reinosa, Spain 19 A3 43 2N 4 15W
Reitz, S. Africa 57 D4 27 48S 28 29 E
Reivilo, S. Africa 56 D3 27 36S 24 8 E
Reliance, Canada 73 A7 63 0N 109 20W
Remarkable, Mt., Australia 63 E2 32 48S 138 10 E
Rembang, Indonesia 37 G14 6 42S 111 21 E
Remedios, Panama 88 E3 8 15N 81 50W
Remeshk, Iran 45 E8 26 55N 58 50 E
Remich, Lux. 15 E6 49 32N 6 22 E
Remscheid, Germany 15 C7 51 11N 7 12 E
Ren Xian, China 34 F8 37 8N 114 40 E
Rendsburg, Germany 16 A5 54 17N 9 39 E
Renfrew, Canada 79 A8 45 30N 76 40W
Renfrewshire □, U.K. 12 F4 55 49N 4 38W
Rengat, Indonesia 36 E2 0 30S 102 45 E
Rengo, Chile 94 C1 34 24S 70 50W
Reni, Ukraine 17 F15 45 28N 28 15 E
Renmark, Australia 63 E3 34 11S 140 43 E
Rennell Sd., Canada 72 C2 53 23N 132 35W
Renner Springs, Australia 62 B1 18 20S 133 47 E
Rennes, France 18 B3 48 7N 1 41W
Rennie L., Canada 73 A7 61 32N 105 35W
Reno, U.S.A. 84 F7 39 31N 119 48W
Reno →, Italy 20 B5 44 38N 12 16 E
Renovo, U.S.A. 78 E7 41 20N 77 45W
Renqiu, China 34 E9 38 43N 116 5 E
Rensselaer, Ind., U.S.A. 76 E2 40 57N 87 9W
Rensselaer, N.Y., U.S.A. 79 D11 42 38N 73 45W
Rentería, Spain 19 A5 43 19N 1 54W
Renton, U.S.A. 84 C4 47 29N 122 12W
Reotipur, India 43 G10 25 33N 83 45 E
Republic, Mo., U.S.A. 81 G8 37 7N 93 29W
Republic, Wash., U.S.A. 82 B4 48 39N 118 44W
Republican →, U.S.A. 80 F6 39 4N 96 48W
Repulse Bay, Canada 69 B11 66 30N 86 30W
Requena, Peru 92 E4 5 5S 73 52W
Requena, Spain 19 C5 39 30N 1 4W
Reşadiye = Datça, Turkey 21 F12 36 46N 27 40 E
Reserve, U.S.A. 83 K9 33 43N 108 45W
Resht = Rasht, Iran 45 B6 37 20N 49 40 E
Resistencia, Argentina 94 B4 27 30S 59 0W
Reşiţa, Romania 17 F11 45 18N 21 53 E
Resolution I., Canada 69 B13 61 30N 65 0W
Resolution I., N.Z. 59 L1 45 40S 166 40 E
Ressano Garcia, Mozam. 57 D5 25 25S 32 0 E
Reston, Canada 73 D8 49 33N 101 6W
Retalhuleu, Guatemala 88 D1 14 33N 91 46W
Retenue, L. de, Dem. Rep. of the Congo 55 E2 11 0S 27 0 E
Retford, U.K. 10 D7 53 19N 0 56W
Réthimnon, Greece 23 D6 35 18N 24 30 E
Réthimnon □, Greece 23 D6 35 23N 24 28 E
Reti, Pakistan 42 E3 28 5N 69 48 E
Réunion ■, Ind. Oc. 49 J9 21 0S 56 0 E
Reus, Spain 19 B6 41 10N 1 5 E
Reutlingen, Germany 16 D5 48 29N 9 12 E
Reval = Tallinn, Estonia 9 G21 59 22N 24 48 E
Revda, Russia 24 C10 56 48N 59 57 E
Revelganj, India 43 G11 25 50N 84 40 E
Revelstoke, Canada 72 C5 51 0N 118 10W
Reventazón, Peru 92 E2 6 10S 80 58W
Revillagigedo, Is. de, Pac. Oc. 86 D2 18 40N 112 0W
Revuè →, Mozam. 55 F3 19 50S 34 0 E
Rewa, India 43 G9 24 33N 81 25 E
Rewari, India 42 E7 28 15N 76 40 E
Rexburg, U.S.A. 82 E8 43 49N 111 47W
Rey, Iran 45 C6 35 35N 51 25 E
Rey, I. del, Panama 88 E4 8 20N 78 30W
Rey Malabo, Eq. Guin. 52 D1 3 45N 8 50 E
Reyðarfjörður, Iceland 8 D6 65 2N 14 13W
Reyes, Pt., U.S.A. 84 H3 38 0N 123 0W
Reykjahlið, Iceland 8 D5 65 40N 16 55W
Reykjanes, Iceland 8 E2 63 48N 22 40W
Reykjavík, Iceland 8 D3 64 10N 21 57W
Reynolds Ra., Australia 60 D5 22 30S 133 0 E
Reynoldsville, U.S.A. 78 E6 41 5N 78 58W
Reynosa, Mexico 87 B5 26 5N 98 18W
Rēzekne, Latvia 9 H22 56 30N 27 17 E
Rezvān, Iran 45 E8 27 34N 56 6 E
Rhayader, U.K. 11 E4 52 18N 3 29W
Rhein →, Europe 15 C6 51 52N 6 2 E
Rhein-Main-Donau-Kanal, Germany 16 D6 49 1N 11 27 E
Rheine, Germany 16 B4 52 17N 7 26 E
Rheinland-Pfalz □, Germany 16 C4 50 0N 7 0 E
Rhin = Rhein →, Europe 15 C6 51 52N 6 2 E
Rhine = Rhein →, Europe 15 C6 51 52N 6 2 E
Rhinebeck, U.S.A. 79 E11 41 56N 73 55W
Rhineland-Palatinate = Rheinland-Pfalz □, Germany 16 C4 50 0N 7 0 E
Rhinelander, U.S.A. 80 C10 45 38N 89 25W
Rhinns Pt., U.K. 12 F2 55 40N 6 29W
Rhino Camp, Uganda 54 B3 3 0N 31 22 E
Rhir, Cap, Morocco 50 B4 30 38N 9 54W
Rhode Island □, U.S.A. 79 E13 41 40N 71 30W
Rhodes = Ródhos, Greece 23 C10 36 15N 28 10 E
Rhodesia = Zimbabwe ■, Africa 55 F3 19 0S 30 0 E
Rhodope Mts. = Rhodopi Planina, Bulgaria 21 D11 41 40N 24 20 E
Rhodopi Planina, Bulgaria 21 D11 41 40N 24 20 E
Rhön, Germany 16 C5 50 24N 9 58 E
Rhondda, U.K. 11 F4 51 39N 3 31W
Rhondda Cynon Taff □, U.K. 11 F4 51 42N 3 27W
Rhône →, France 18 E6 43 28N 4 42 E
Rhum, U.K. 12 E2 57 0N 6 20W
Rhyl, U.K. 10 D4 53 20N 3 29W
Riachão, Brazil 93 E9 7 20S 46 37W
Riasi, India 43 C6 33 10N 74 50 E
Riau □, Indonesia 36 D2 0 0 102 35 E
Riau, Kepulauan, Indonesia 36 D2 0 30N 104 20 E
Riau Arch. = Riau, Kepulauan, Indonesia 36 D2 0 30N 104 20 E
Ribadeo, Spain 19 A2 43 35N 7 5W
Ribas do Rio Pardo, Brazil 93 H8 20 27S 53 46W
Ribauè, Mozam. 55 E4 14 57S 38 17 E
Ribble →, U.K. 10 D5 53 52N 2 25W
Ribe, Denmark 9 J13 55 19N 8 44 E
Ribeira Brava, Madeira 22 D2 32 41N 17 4W
Ribeirão Prêto, Brazil 95 A6 21 10S 47 50W
Riberalta, Bolivia 92 F5 11 0S 66 0W
Riccarton, N.Z. 59 K4 43 32S 172 37 E
Rice, U.S.A. 85 L12 34 5N 114 51W
Rice L., Canada 78 B6 44 12N 78 10W
Rice Lake, U.S.A. 80 C9 45 30N 91 44W
Rich, C., Canada 78 B4 44 43N 80 38W
Richards Bay, S. Africa 57 D5 28 48S 32 6 E
Richardson →, Canada 73 B6 58 25N 111 14W
Richardson Lakes, U.S.A. 76 C10 44 46N 70 58W
Richardson Springs, U.S.A. 84 F5 39 51N 121 46W
Riche, C., Australia 61 F2 34 36S 118 47 E
Richey, U.S.A. 80 B2 47 39N 105 4W
Richfield, U.S.A. 83 G8 38 46N 112 5W
Richfield Springs, U.S.A. 79 D10 42 51N 74 59W
Richford, U.S.A. 79 B12 45 0N 72 40W
Richibucto, Canada 71 C7 46 42N 64 54W
Richland, Ga., U.S.A. 77 J3 32 5N 84 40W
Richland, Wash., U.S.A. 82 C4 46 17N 119 18W
Richland Center, U.S.A. 80 D9 43 21N 90 23W
Richlands, U.S.A. 76 G5 37 6N 81 48W
Richmond, Australia 62 C3 20 43S 143 8 E
Richmond, N.Z. 59 J4 41 20S 173 12 E
Richmond, U.K. 10 C6 54 25N 1 43W
Richmond, Calif., U.S.A. 84 H4 37 56N 122 21W
Richmond, Ind., U.S.A. 76 F3 39 50N 84 53W
Richmond, Ky., U.S.A. 76 G3 37 45N 84 18W
Richmond, Mich., U.S.A. 78 D2 42 49N 82 45W
Richmond, Mo., U.S.A. 80 F8 39 17N 93 58W
Richmond, Tex., U.S.A. 81 L7 29 35N 95 46W
Richmond, Utah, U.S.A. 82 F8 41 56N 111 48W
Richmond, Va., U.S.A. 76 G7 37 33N 77 27W
Richmond, Vt., U.S.A. 79 B12 44 24N 72 59W
Richmond Hill, Canada 78 C5 43 52N 79 27W
Richmond Ra., Australia 63 D5 29 0S 152 45 E
Richwood, U.S.A. 76 F5 38 14N 80 32W
Ridder = Leninogorsk, Kazakstan 26 D9 50 20N 83 30 E
Riddlesburg, U.S.A. 78 F6 40 9N 78 15W
Ridgecrest, U.S.A. 85 K9 35 38N 117 40W
Ridgefield, Conn., U.S.A. 79 E11 41 17N 73 30W
Ridgefield, Wash., U.S.A. 84 E4 45 49N 122 45W
Ridgeland, U.S.A. 77 J5 32 29N 80 59W
Ridgetown, Canada 78 D3 42 26N 81 52W
Ridgewood, U.S.A. 79 F10 40 59N 74 7W
Ridgway, U.S.A. 78 E6 41 25N 78 44W
Riding Mountain Nat. Park, Canada 73 C9 50 50N 100 0W
Ridley, Mt., Australia 61 F3 33 12S 122 7 E
Riebeek-Oos, S. Africa 56 E4 33 10S 26 10 E
Ried, Austria 16 D7 48 14N 13 30 E
Riesa, Germany 16 C7 51 17N 13 17 E
Riet →, S. Africa 56 D3 29 0S 23 54 E
Rietbron, S. Africa 56 E3 32 54S 23 10 E
Rietfontein, Namibia 56 C3 21 58S 20 58 E
Rieti, Italy 20 C5 42 24N 12 51 E
Rif, Er = Er Rif, Morocco 50 A5 35 1N 4 1W
Riffe L., U.S.A. 84 D4 46 32N 122 26W
Rifle, U.S.A. 82 G10 39 32N 107 47W
Rift Valley □, Kenya 54 B4 0 20N 36 0 E
Rīga, Latvia 9 H21 56 53N 24 8 E
Riga, G. of, Latvia 9 H20 57 40N 23 45 E
Rīgān, Iran 45 D8 28 37N 58 58 E
Rīgas Jūras Līcis = Riga, G. of, Latvia 9 H20 57 40N 23 45 E
Rigaud, Canada 79 A10 45 29N 74 18W
Rigby, U.S.A. 82 E8 43 40N 111 55W
Rīgestān, Afghan. 40 D4 30 15N 65 0 E
Riggins, U.S.A. 82 D5 45 25N 116 19W
Rigolet, Canada 71 B8 54 10N 58 23W
Rihand Dam, India 43 G10 24 9N 83 2 E
Riihimäki, Finland 9 F21 60 45N 24 48 E
Riiser-Larsen-halvøya, Antarctica 5 C4 68 0S 35 0 E
Rijeka, Croatia 16 F8 45 20N 14 21 E
Rijssen, Neths. 15 B6 52 19N 6 31 E
Rikuzentakada, Japan 30 E10 39 0N 141 40 E
Riley, U.S.A. 82 E4 43 32N 119 28W
Rimah, Wadi ar →, Si. Arabia 44 E4 26 5N 41 30 E
Rimbey, Canada 72 C6 52 35N 114 15W
Rimersburg, U.S.A. 78 E5 41 3N 79 30W
Rimini, Italy 20 B5 44 3N 12 33 E
Rimouski, Canada 71 C6 48 27N 68 30W
Rimrock, U.S.A. 84 D5 46 38N 121 10W
Rinca, Indonesia 37 F5 8 45S 119 35 E
Rincón de Romos, Mexico 86 C4 22 14N 102 18W
Rinconada, Argentina 94 A2 22 26S 66 10W
Rind →, India 43 G9 25 53N 80 33 E
Ringas, India 42 F6 27 21N 75 34 E
Ringkøbing, Denmark 9 H13 56 5N 8 15 E
Ringvassøy, Norway 8 B18 69 56N 19 15 E
Ringwood, U.S.A. 79 E10 41 7N 74 15W
Rinjani, Indonesia 36 F5 8 24S 116 28 E
Rio Branco, Brazil 92 E5 9 58S 67 49W
Río Branco, Uruguay 95 C5 32 40S 53 40W
Río Bravo del Norte →, Mexico 87 B5 25 57N 97 9W
Rio Brilhante, Brazil 95 A5 21 48S 54 33W
Rio Claro, Brazil 95 A6 22 19S 47 35W
Rio Claro, Trin. & Tob. 89 D7 10 20N 61 25W
Río Colorado, Argentina 96 D4 39 0S 64 0W
Río Cuarto, Argentina 94 C3 33 10S 64 25W
Rio das Pedras, Mozam. 57 C6 23 8S 35 28 E
Rio de Janeiro, Brazil 95 A7 23 0S 43 12W
Rio de Janeiro □, Brazil 95 A7 22 50S 43 0W
Rio do Sul, Brazil 95 B6 27 13S 49 37W
Río Gallegos, Argentina 96 G3 51 35S 69 15W
Rio Grande = Grande, Rio →, U.S.A. 81 N6 25 58N 97 9W
Río Grande, Argentina 96 G3 53 50S 67 45W
Rio Grande, Brazil 95 C5 32 0S 52 20W
Río Grande, Mexico 86 C4 23 50N 103 2W
Río Grande, Nic. 88 D3 12 54N 83 33W
Rio Grande City, U.S.A. 81 M5 26 23N 98 49W
Río Grande de Santiago →, Mexico 86 C3 21 36N 105 26W
Rio Grande do Norte □, Brazil 93 E11 5 40S 36 0W
Rio Grande do Sul □, Brazil 95 C5 30 0S 53 0W

Río Hato, *Panama* **88 E3** 8 22N 80 10W
Río Lagartos, *Mexico* **87 C7** 21 36N 88 10W
Rio Largo, *Brazil* **93 E11** 9 28S 35 50W
Río Mulatos, *Bolivia* **92 G5** 19 40S 66 50W
Río Muni □, *Eq. Guin.* **52 D2** 1 30N 10 0 E
Rio Negro, *Brazil* **95 B6** 26 0S 49 55W
Rio Pardo, *Brazil* **95 C5** 30 0S 52 30W
Rio Rancho, *U.S.A.* **83 J10** 35 14N 106 38W
Río Segundo, *Argentina* **94 C3** 31 40S 63 59W
Río Tercero, *Argentina* **94 C3** 32 15S 64 8W
Rio Verde, *Brazil* **93 G8** 17 50S 51 0W
Río Verde, *Mexico* **87 C5** 21 56N 99 59W
Rio Vista, *U.S.A.* **84 G5** 38 10N 121 42W
Riobamba, *Ecuador* **92 D3** 1 50S 78 45W
Ríohacha, *Colombia* **92 A4** 11 33N 72 55W
Ríosucio, *Colombia* **92 B3** 7 27N 77 7W
Riou L., *Canada* **73 B7** 59 7N 106 25W
Ripley, *Canada* **78 B3** 44 4N 81 35W
Ripley, *Calif., U.S.A.* **85 M12** 33 32N 114 39W
Ripley, *N.Y., U.S.A.* **78 D5** 42 16N 79 43W
Ripley, *Tenn., U.S.A.* **81 H10** 35 45N 89 32W
Ripley, *W. Va., U.S.A.* **76 F5** 38 49N 81 43W
Ripon, *U.K.* **10 C6** 54 9N 1 31W
Ripon, *Calif., U.S.A.* **84 H5** 37 44N 121 7W
Ripon, *Wis., U.S.A.* **76 D1** 43 51N 88 50W
Rishā', W. ar →, *Si. Arabia* **44 E5** 25 33N 44 5 E
Rishiri-Tō, *Japan* **30 B10** 45 11N 141 15 E
Rishon le Ẕiyyon, *Israel* **47 D3** 31 58N 34 48 E
Rison, *U.S.A.* **81 J8** 33 58N 92 11W
Risør, *Norway* **9 G13** 58 43N 9 13 E
Rita Blanca Cr. →, *U.S.A.* **81 H3** 35 40N 102 29W
Ritter, Mt., *U.S.A.* **84 H7** 37 41N 119 12W
Rittman, *U.S.A.* **78 F3** 40 58N 81 47W
Ritzville, *U.S.A.* **82 C4** 47 8N 118 23W
Riva del Garda, *Italy* **20 B4** 45 53N 10 50 E
Rivadavia, *Buenos Aires,*
Argentina **94 D3** 35 29S 62 59W
Rivadavia, *Mendoza,*
Argentina **94 C2** 33 13S 68 30W
Rivadavia, *Salta, Argentina* **94 A3** 24 5S 62 54W
Rivadavia, *Chile* **94 B1** 29 57S 70 35W
Rivas, *Nic.* **88 D2** 11 30N 85 50W
River Cess, *Liberia* **50 G4** 5 30N 9 32W
River Jordan, *Canada* **84 B2** 48 26N 124 3W
Rivera, *Argentina* **94 D3** 37 12S 63 14W
Rivera, *Uruguay* **95 C4** 31 0S 55 50W
Riverbank, *U.S.A.* **84 H6** 37 44N 120 56W
Riverdale, *U.S.A.* **84 J7** 36 26N 119 52W
Riverhead, *U.S.A.* **79 F12** 40 55N 72 40W
Riverhurst, *Canada* **73 C7** 50 55N 106 50W
Rivers, *Canada* **73 C8** 50 2N 100 14W
Rivers Inlet, *Canada* **72 C3** 51 42N 127 15W
Riversdale, *S. Africa* **56 E3** 34 7S 21 15 E
Riverside, *U.S.A.* **85 M9** 33 59N 117 22W
Riverton, *Australia* **63 E2** 34 10S 138 46 E
Riverton, *Canada* **73 C9** 51 1N 97 0W
Riverton, *N.Z.* **59 M2** 46 21S 168 0 E
Riverton, *U.S.A.* **82 E9** 43 2N 108 23W
Riverton Heights, *U.S.A.* **84 C4** 47 28N 122 17W
Riviera, *U.S.A.* **85 K12** 35 4N 114 35W
Riviera di Levante, *Italy* **18 D8** 44 15N 9 30 E
Riviera di Ponente, *Italy* **18 D8** 44 10N 8 20 E
Rivière-au-Renard, *Canada* **71 C7** 48 59N 64 23W
Rivière-du-Loup, *Canada* **71 C6** 47 50N 69 30W
Rivière-Pentecôte, *Canada* **71 C6** 49 57N 67 1W
Rivière-Pilote, *Martinique* **89 D7** 14 26N 60 53W
Rivière St. Paul, *Canada* **71 B8** 51 28N 57 45W
Rivne, *Ukraine* **17 C14** 50 40N 26 10 E
Rívoli, *Italy* **18 D7** 45 3N 7 31 E
Rivoli B., *Australia* **63 F3** 37 32S 140 3 E
Riyadh = Ar Riyāḍ, *Si. Arabia* **46 C4** 24 41N 46 42 E
Rize, *Turkey* **25 F7** 41 0N 40 30 E
Rizhao, *China* **35 G10** 35 25N 119 30 E
Rizokarpaso, *Cyprus* **23 D13** 35 36N 34 23 E
Rizzuto, C., *Italy* **20 E7** 38 53N 17 5 E
Rjukan, *Norway* **9 G13** 59 54N 8 33 E
Road Town, *Br. Virgin Is.* **89 C7** 18 27N 64 37W
Roan Plateau, *U.S.A.* **82 G9** 39 20N 109 20W
Roanne, *France* **18 C6** 46 3N 4 4 E
Roanoke, *Ala., U.S.A.* **77 J3** 33 9N 85 22W
Roanoke, *Va., U.S.A.* **76 G6** 37 16N 79 56W
Roanoke →, *U.S.A.* **77 H7** 35 57N 76 42W
Roanoke I., *U.S.A.* **77 H8** 35 55N 75 40W
Roanoke Rapids, *U.S.A.* **77 G7** 36 28N 77 40W
Roatán, *Honduras* **88 C2** 16 18N 86 35W
Robāt Sang, *Iran* **45 C8** 35 35N 59 10 E
Robbins I., *Australia* **62 G4** 40 42S 145 0 E
Robe →, *Australia* **60 D2** 21 42S 116 15 E
Robert Lee, *U.S.A.* **81 K4** 31 54N 100 29W
Robertsdale, *U.S.A.* **78 F6** 40 11N 78 6W
Robertsganj, *India* **43 G10** 24 44N 83 4 E
Robertson, *S. Africa* **56 E2** 33 46S 19 50 E
Robertson I., *Antarctica* **5 C18** 65 15S 59 30W
Robertson Ra., *Australia* **60 D3** 23 15S 121 0 E
Robertstown, *Australia* **63 E2** 33 58S 139 5 E
Roberval, *Canada* **71 C5** 48 32N 72 15W
Robeson Chan., *Greenland* **4 A4** 82 0N 61 30W
Robesonia, *U.S.A.* **79 F8** 40 21N 76 8W
Robinson, *U.S.A.* **76 F2** 39 0N 87 44W
Robinson →, *Australia* **62 B2** 16 3S 137 16 E
Robinson Ra., *Australia* **61 E2** 25 40S 119 0 E
Robinvale, *Australia* **63 E3** 34 40S 142 45 E
Roblin, *Canada* **73 C8** 51 14N 101 21W
Roboré, *Bolivia* **92 G7** 18 10S 59 45W
Robson, *Canada* **72 D5** 49 20N 117 41W
Robson, Mt., *Canada* **72 C5** 53 10N 119 10W
Robstown, *U.S.A.* **81 M6** 27 47N 97 40W
Roca, C. da, *Portugal* **19 C1** 38 40N 9 31W
Roca Partida, I., *Mexico* **86 D2** 19 1N 112 2W
Rocas, I., *Brazil* **93 D12** 4 0S 34 1W
Rocha, *Uruguay* **95 C5** 34 30S 54 25W
Rochdale, *U.K.* **10 D5** 53 38N 2 9W
Rochefort, *Belgium* **15 D5** 50 9N 5 12 E
Rochefort, *France* **18 D3** 45 56N 0 57W
Rochelle, *U.S.A.* **80 E10** 41 56N 89 4W
Rocher River, *Canada* **72 A6** 61 23N 112 44W
Rochester, *U.K.* **11 F8** 51 23N 0 31 E
Rochester, *Ind., U.S.A.* **76 E2** 41 4N 86 13W
Rochester, *Minn., U.S.A.* **80 C8** 44 1N 92 28W
Rochester, *N.H., U.S.A.* **79 C14** 43 18N 70 59W
Rochester, *N.Y., U.S.A.* **78 C7** 43 10N 77 37W
Rock →, *Canada* **72 A3** 60 7N 127 7W
Rock Creek, *U.S.A.* **78 E4** 41 40N 80 52W
Rock Falls, *U.S.A.* **80 E10** 41 47N 89 41W
Rock Hill, *U.S.A.* **77 H5** 34 56N 81 1W
Rock Island, *U.S.A.* **80 E9** 41 30N 90 34W
Rock Rapids, *U.S.A.* **80 D6** 43 26N 96 10W
Rock Sound, *Bahamas* **88 B4** 24 54N 76 12W
Rock Springs, *Mont., U.S.A.* **82 C10** 46 49N 106 15W
Rock Springs, *Wyo., U.S.A.* **82 F9** 41 35N 109 14W
Rock Valley, *U.S.A.* **80 D6** 43 12N 96 18W
Rockall, *Atl. Oc.* **6 D3** 57 37N 13 42W
Rockdale, *Tex., U.S.A.* **81 K6** 30 39N 97 0W
Rockdale, *Wash., U.S.A.* **84 C5** 47 22N 121 28W
Rockefeller Plateau,
Antarctica **5 E14** 80 0S 140 0W
Rockford, *U.S.A.* **80 D10** 42 16N 89 6W
Rockglen, *Canada* **73 D7** 49 11N 105 57W
Rockhampton, *Australia* **62 C5** 23 22S 150 32 E
Rockingham, *Australia* **61 F2** 32 15S 115 38 E
Rockingham, *U.S.A.* **77 H6** 34 57N 79 46W
Rockingham B., *Australia* **62 B4** 18 5S 146 10 E
Rocklake, *U.S.A.* **80 A5** 48 47N 99 15W
Rockland, *Canada* **79 A9** 45 33N 75 17W
Rockland, *Idaho, U.S.A.* **82 E7** 42 34N 112 53W
Rockland, *Maine, U.S.A.* **77 C11** 44 6N 69 7W
Rockland, *Mich., U.S.A.* **80 B10** 46 44N 89 11W
Rocklin, *U.S.A.* **84 G5** 38 48N 121 14W
Rockmart, *U.S.A.* **77 H3** 34 0N 85 3W
Rockport, *Mass., U.S.A.* **79 D14** 42 39N 70 37W
Rockport, *Mo., U.S.A.* **80 E7** 40 25N 95 31W
Rockport, *Tex., U.S.A.* **81 L6** 28 2N 97 3W
Rocksprings, *U.S.A.* **81 K4** 30 1N 100 13W
Rockville, *Conn., U.S.A.* **79 E12** 41 52N 72 28W
Rockville, *Md., U.S.A.* **76 F7** 39 5N 77 9W
Rockwall, *U.S.A.* **81 J6** 32 56N 96 28W
Rockwell City, *U.S.A.* **80 D7** 42 24N 94 38W
Rockwood, *Canada* **78 C4** 43 37N 80 8W
Rockwood, *Maine, U.S.A.* **77 C11** 45 41N 69 45W
Rockwood, *Tenn., U.S.A.* **77 H3** 35 52N 84 41W
Rocky Ford, *U.S.A.* **80 F3** 38 3N 103 43W
Rocky Gully, *Australia* **61 F2** 34 30S 116 57 E
Rocky Harbour, *Canada* **71 C8** 49 36N 57 55W
Rocky Island L., *Canada* **70 C3** 46 55N 83 0W
Rocky Lane, *Canada* **72 B5** 58 31N 116 22W
Rocky Mount, *U.S.A.* **77 H7** 35 57N 77 48W
Rocky Mountain House,
Canada **72 C6** 52 22N 114 55W
Rocky Mountain Nat. Park,
U.S.A. **82 F11** 40 25N 105 45W
Rocky Mts., *N. Amer.* **82 G10** 49 0N 115 0W
Rocky Point, *Namibia* **56 B2** 19 3S 12 30 E
Rod, *Pakistan* **40 E3** 28 10N 63 5 E
Rødbyhavn, *Denmark* **9 J14** 54 39N 11 22 E
Roddickton, *Canada* **71 B8** 50 51N 56 8W
Rodez, *France* **18 D5** 44 21N 2 33 E
Rodhopoú, *Greece* **23 D5** 35 34N 23 45 E
Ródhos, *Greece* **23 C10** 36 15N 28 10 E
Rodney, *Canada* **78 D3** 42 34N 81 41W
Rodney, C., *N.Z.* **59 G5** 36 17S 174 50 E
Rodriguez, *Ind. Oc.* **3 E13** 19 45S 63 20 E
Roe →, *U.K.* **13 A5** 55 6N 6 59W
Roebling, *U.S.A.* **79 F10** 40 7N 74 47W
Roebourne, *Australia* **60 D2** 20 44S 117 9 E
Roebuck B., *Australia* **60 C3** 18 5S 122 20 E
Roermond, *Neths.* **15 C6** 51 12N 6 0 E
Roes Welcome Sd., *Canada* **69 B11** 65 0N 87 0W
Roeselare, *Belgium* **15 D3** 50 57N 3 7 E
Rogachev = Ragachow,
Belarus **17 B16** 53 8N 30 5 E
Rogagua, L., *Bolivia* **92 F5** 13 43S 66 50W
Rogatyn, *Ukraine* **17 D13** 49 24N 24 36 E
Rogdhia, *Greece* **23 D7** 35 22N 25 1 E
Rogers, *U.S.A.* **81 G7** 36 20N 94 7W
Rogers City, *U.S.A.* **76 C4** 45 25N 83 49W
Rogersville, *Canada* **71 C6** 46 44N 65 26W
Roggan →, *Canada* **70 B4** 54 24N 79 25W
Roggan L., *Canada* **70 B4** 54 8N 77 50W
Roggeveldberge, *S. Africa* **56 E3** 32 10S 20 10 E
Rogoaguado, L., *Bolivia* **92 F5** 13 0S 65 30W
Rogue →, *U.S.A.* **82 E1** 42 26N 124 26W
Róhda, *Greece* **23 A3** 39 48N 19 46 E
Rohnert Park, *U.S.A.* **84 G4** 38 16N 122 40W
Rohri, *Pakistan* **42 F3** 27 45N 68 51 E
Rohri Canal, *Pakistan* **42 F3** 26 15N 68 27 E
Rohtak, *India* **42 E7** 28 55N 76 43 E
Roi Et, *Thailand* **38 D4** 16 4N 103 40 E
Roja, *Latvia* **9 H20** 57 29N 22 43 E
Rojas, *Argentina* **94 C3** 34 10S 60 45W
Rojo, C., *Mexico* **87 C5** 21 33N 97 20W
Rokan →, *Indonesia* **36 D2** 2 0N 100 50 E
Rokiškis, *Lithuania* **9 J21** 55 55N 25 35 E
Rolândia, *Brazil* **95 A5** 23 18S 51 23W
Rolla, *U.S.A.* **81 G9** 37 57N 91 46W
Rolleston, *Australia* **62 C4** 24 28S 148 35 E
Rollingstone, *Australia* **62 B4** 19 2S 146 24 E
Roma, *Australia* **63 D4** 26 32S 148 49 E
Roma, *Italy* **20 D5** 41 54N 12 29 E
Roma, *Sweden* **9 H18** 57 32N 18 26 E
Roma, *U.S.A.* **81 M5** 26 25N 99 1W
Romain C., *U.S.A.* **77 J6** 33 0N 79 22W
Romaine, *Canada* **71 B7** 50 13N 60 40W
Romaine →, *Canada* **71 B7** 50 18N 63 47W
Roman, *Romania* **17 E14** 46 57N 26 55 E
Romang, *Indonesia* **37 F7** 7 30S 127 20 E
Români, *Egypt* **47 E1** 30 59N 32 38 E
Romania ■, *Europe* **17 F12** 46 0N 25 0 E
Romano, Cayo, *Cuba* **88 B4** 22 0N 77 30W
Romanovka = Basarabeasca,
Moldova **17 E15** 46 21N 28 58 E
Romans-sur-Isère, *France* **18 D6** 45 3N 5 3 E
Romblon, *Phil.* **37 B6** 12 33N 122 17 E
Rome = Roma, *Italy* **20 D5** 41 54N 12 29 E
Rome, *Ga., U.S.A.* **77 H3** 34 15N 85 10W
Rome, *N.Y., U.S.A.* **79 C9** 43 13N 75 27W
Rome, *Pa., U.S.A.* **79 E8** 41 51N 76 21W
Romney, *U.S.A.* **76 F6** 39 21N 78 45W
Romney Marsh, *U.K.* **11 F8** 51 2N 0 54 E
Rømø, *Denmark* **9 J13** 55 10N 8 30 E
Romorantin-Lanthenay,
France **18 C4** 47 21N 1 45 E
Romsdalen, *Norway* **9 E12** 62 25N 7 52 E
Romsey, *U.K.* **11 G6** 51 0N 1 29W
Ron, *Vietnam* **38 D6** 17 53N 106 27 E
Rona, *U.K.* **12 D3** 57 34N 5 59W
Ronan, *U.S.A.* **82 C6** 47 32N 114 6W
Roncador, Cayos, *Colombia* **88 D3** 13 32N 80 4W
Roncador, Serra do, *Brazil* **93 F8** 12 30S 52 30W
Ronda, *Spain* **19 D3** 36 46N 5 12W
Rondane, *Norway* **9 F13** 61 57N 9 50 E
Rondônia □, *Brazil* **92 F6** 11 0S 63 0W
Rondonópolis, *Brazil* **93 G8** 16 28S 54 38W
Rong, Koh, *Cambodia* **39 G4** 10 45N 103 15 E
Ronge, L. la, *Canada* **73 B7** 55 6N 105 17W
Rønne, *Denmark* **9 J16** 55 6N 14 43 E
Ronne Ice Shelf, *Antarctica* **5 D18** 78 0S 60 0W
Ronsard, C., *Australia* **61 D1** 24 46S 113 10 E
Ronse, *Belgium* **15 D3** 50 45N 3 35 E
Roodepoort, *S. Africa* **57 D4** 26 11S 27 54 E
Roof Butte, *U.S.A.* **83 H9** 36 28N 109 5W
Rooiboklaagte →, *Namibia* **56 C3** 20 50S 21 0 E
Roorkee, *India* **42 E7** 29 52N 77 59 E
Roosendaal, *Neths.* **15 C4** 51 32N 4 29 E
Roosevelt, *U.S.A.* **82 F8** 40 18N 109 59W
Roosevelt →, *Brazil* **92 E6** 7 35S 60 20W
Roosevelt, Mt., *Canada* **72 B3** 58 26N 125 20W
Roosevelt I., *Antarctica* **5 D12** 79 30S 162 0W
Roper →, *Australia* **62 A2** 14 43S 135 27 E
Roper Bar, *Australia* **62 A1** 14 44S 134 44 E
Roque Pérez, *Argentina* **94 D4** 35 25S 59 24W
Roquetas de Mar, *Spain* **19 D4** 36 46N 2 36W
Roraima □, *Brazil* **92 C6** 2 0N 61 30W
Roraima, Mt., *Venezuela* **92 B6** 5 10N 60 40W
Røros, *Norway* **9 E14** 62 35N 11 23 E
Rosa, *Zambia* **55 D3** 9 33S 31 15 E
Rosa, L., *Bahamas* **89 B5** 21 0N 73 30W
Rosa, Monte, *Europe* **18 D7** 45 57N 7 53 E
Rosalia, *U.S.A.* **82 C5** 47 14N 117 22W
Rosamond, *U.S.A.* **85 L8** 34 52N 118 10W
Rosario, *Argentina* **94 C3** 33 0S 60 40W
Rosário, *Brazil* **93 D10** 3 0S 44 15W
Rosario, *Baja Calif., Mexico* **86 B1** 30 0N 115 50W
Rosario, *Sinaloa, Mexico* **86 C3** 23 0N 105 52W
Rosario, *Paraguay* **94 A4** 24 30S 57 35W
Rosario de la Frontera,
Argentina **94 B3** 25 50S 65 0W
Rosario de Lerma, *Argentina* **94 A2** 24 59S 65 35W
Rosario del Tala, *Argentina* **94 C4** 32 20S 59 10W
Rosário do Sul, *Brazil* **95 C5** 30 15S 54 55W
Rosarito, *Mexico* **85 N9** 32 18N 117 4W
Roscoe, *U.S.A.* **79 E10** 41 56N 74 55W
Roscommon, *Ireland* **13 C3** 53 38N 8 11W
Roscommon □, *Ireland* **13 C3** 53 49N 8 23W
Roscrea, *Ireland* **13 D4** 52 57N 7 49W
Rose →, *Australia* **62 A2** 14 16S 135 45 E
Rose Blanche, *Canada* **71 C8** 47 38N 58 45W
Rose Pt., *Canada* **72 C2** 54 11N 131 39W
Rose Valley, *Canada* **73 C8** 52 19N 103 49W
Roseau, *Domin.* **89 C7** 15 20N 61 24W
Roseau, *U.S.A.* **80 A7** 48 51N 95 46W
Rosebery, *Australia* **62 G4** 41 46S 145 33 E
Rosebud, *S. Dak., U.S.A.* **80 D4** 43 14N 100 51W
Rosebud, *Tex., U.S.A.* **81 K6** 31 4N 96 59W
Roseburg, *U.S.A.* **82 E2** 43 13N 123 20W
Rosedale, *U.S.A.* **81 J9** 33 51N 91 2W
Roseland, *U.S.A.* **84 G4** 38 25N 122 43W
Rosemary, *Canada* **72 C6** 50 46N 112 5W
Rosenberg, *U.S.A.* **81 L7** 29 34N 95 49W
Rosenheim, *Germany* **16 E7** 47 51N 12 7 E
Roses, G. de, *Spain* **19 A7** 42 10N 3 15 E
Rosetown, *Canada* **73 C7** 51 35N 107 59W
Roseville, *Calif., U.S.A.* **84 G5** 38 45N 121 17W
Roseville, *Mich., U.S.A.* **78 D2** 42 30N 82 56W
Rosewood, *Australia* **63 D5** 27 38S 152 36 E
Roshkhvār, *Iran* **45 C8** 34 58N 59 37 E
Rosignano Marittimo, *Italy* **20 C4** 43 24N 10 28 E
Rosignol, *Guyana* **92 B7** 6 15N 57 30W
Roşiori de Vede, *Romania* **17 F13** 44 9N 25 0 E
Roskilde, *Denmark* **9 J15** 55 38N 12 3 E
Roslavl, *Russia* **24 D5** 53 57N 32 55 E
Rosmead, *S. Africa* **56 E4** 31 29S 25 8 E
Ross, *Australia* **62 G4** 42 2S 147 30 E
Ross, *N.Z.* **59 K3** 42 53S 170 49 E
Ross I., *Antarctica* **5 D11** 77 30S 168 0 E
Ross Ice Shelf, *Antarctica* **5 E12** 80 0S 180 0 E
Ross L., *U.S.A.* **82 B3** 48 44N 121 4W
Ross-on-Wye, *U.K.* **11 F5** 51 54N 2 34W
Ross River, *Australia* **62 C1** 23 44S 134 30 E
Ross River, *Canada* **72 A2** 62 30N 131 30W
Ross Sea, *Antarctica* **5 D11** 74 0S 178 0 E
Rossall Pt., *U.K.* **10 D4** 53 55N 3 3W
Rossan Pt., *Ireland* **13 B3** 54 42N 8 47W
Rossano, *Italy* **20 E7** 39 36N 16 39 E
Rossburn, *Canada* **73 C8** 50 40N 100 49W
Rosseau, *Canada* **78 A5** 45 16N 79 39W
Rosseau L., *Canada* **78 A5** 45 10N 79 35W
Rosses, The, *Ireland* **13 A3** 55 2N 8 20W
Rossignol, L., *Canada* **70 B5** 52 43N 73 40W
Rossignol Res., *Canada* **71 D6** 44 12N 65 10W
Rossland, *Canada* **72 D5** 49 6N 117 50W
Rosslare, *Ireland* **13 D5** 52 17N 6 24W
Rosso, *Mauritania* **50 E2** 16 40N 15 45W
Rossosh, *Russia* **25 D6** 50 15N 39 28 E
Røssvatnet, *Norway* **8 D16** 65 45N 14 5 E
Røst, *Norway* **8 C15** 67 32N 12 0 E
Rosthern, *Canada* **73 C7** 52 40N 106 20W
Rostock, *Germany* **16 A7** 54 5N 12 8 E
Rostov, *Don, Russia* **25 E6** 47 15N 39 45 E
Rostov, *Yaroslavl, Russia* **24 C6** 57 14N 39 25 E
Roswell, *Ga., U.S.A.* **77 H3** 34 2N 84 22W
Roswell, *N. Mex., U.S.A.* **81 J2** 33 24N 104 32W
Rotan, *U.S.A.* **81 J4** 32 51N 100 28W
Rother →, *U.K.* **11 G8** 50 59N 0 45 E
Rotherham, *U.K.* **10 D6** 53 26N 1 20W
Rothes, *U.K.* **12 D5** 57 32N 3 13W
Rothesay, *Canada* **71 C6** 45 23N 66 0W
Rothesay, *U.K.* **12 F3** 55 50N 5 3W
Roti, *Indonesia* **37 F6** 10 50S 123 0 E
Roto, *Australia* **63 E4** 33 0S 145 30 E
Rotondo, Mte., *France* **18 E8** 42 14N 9 8 E
Rotoroa, L., *N.Z.* **59 J4** 41 55S 172 39 E
Rotorua, *N.Z.* **59 H6** 38 9S 176 16 E
Rotorua, L., *N.Z.* **59 H6** 38 5S 176 18 E
Rotterdam, *Neths.* **15 C4** 51 55N 4 30 E
Rotterdam, *U.S.A.* **79 D10** 42 48N 74 1W
Rottnest I., *Australia* **61 F2** 32 0S 115 27 E
Rottumeroog, *Neths.* **15 A6** 53 33N 6 34 E
Rottweil, *Germany* **16 D5** 48 9N 8 37 E
Rotuma, *Fiji* **64 J9** 12 25S 177 5 E
Roubaix, *France* **18 A5** 50 40N 3 10 E
Rouen, *France* **18 B4** 49 27N 1 4 E
Rouleau, *Canada* **73 C8** 50 10N 104 56W
Round Mountain, *U.S.A.* **82 G5** 38 43N 117 4W
Round Mt., *Australia* **63 E5** 30 26S 152 16 E
Round Rock, *U.S.A.* **81 K6** 30 31N 97 41W
Roundup, *U.S.A.* **82 C9** 46 27N 108 33W
Rousay, *U.K.* **12 B5** 59 10N 3 2W
Rouses Point, *U.S.A.* **79 B11** 44 59N 73 22W
Rouseville, *U.S.A.* **78 E5** 41 28N 79 42W
Roussillon, *France* **18 E5** 42 30N 2 35 E
Rouxville, *S. Africa* **56 E4** 30 25S 26 50 E
Rouyn-Noranda, *Canada* **70 C4** 48 20N 79 0W
Rovaniemi, *Finland* **8 C21** 66 29N 25 41 E
Rovereto, *Italy* **20 B4** 45 53N 11 3 E
Rovigo, *Italy* **20 B4** 45 4N 11 47 E
Rovinj, *Croatia* **16 F7** 45 5N 13 40 E
Rovno = Rivne, *Ukraine* **17 C14** 50 40N 26 10 E
Rovuma = Ruvuma →,
Tanzania **55 E5** 10 29S 40 28 E
Row'ān, *Iran* **45 C6** 35 8N 48 51 E
Rowena, *Australia* **63 D4** 29 48S 148 55 E
Rowley Shoals, *Australia* **60 C2** 17 30S 119 0 E
Roxas, *Phil.* **37 B6** 11 36N 122 49 E
Roxboro, *U.S.A.* **77 G6** 36 24N 78 59W
Roxburgh, *N.Z.* **59 L2** 45 33S 169 19 E
Roxbury, *U.S.A.* **78 F7** 40 6N 77 39W
Roy, *Mont., U.S.A.* **82 C9** 47 20N 108 58W
Roy, *N. Mex., U.S.A.* **81 H2** 35 57N 104 12W
Roy, *Utah, U.S.A.* **82 F7** 41 10N 112 2W
Royal Canal, *Ireland* **13 C4** 53 30N 7 13W
Royal Leamington Spa, *U.K.* **11 E6** 52 18N 1 31W
Royal Tunbridge Wells, *U.K.* **11 F8** 51 7N 0 16 E
Royale, Isle, *U.S.A.* **80 B10** 48 0N 88 54W
Royan, *France* **18 D3** 45 37N 1 2W
Royston, *U.K.* **11 E7** 52 3N 0 0W
Rozdilna, *Ukraine* **17 E16** 46 50N 30 2 E
Rozhyshche, *Ukraine* **17 C13** 50 54N 25 15 E
Rtishchevo, *Russia* **24 C7** 52 18N 43 46 E
Ruacaná, *Namibia* **56 B1** 17 27S 14 21 E
Ruahine Ra., *N.Z.* **59 H6** 39 55S 176 2 E
Ruapehu, *N.Z.* **59 H5** 39 17S 175 35 E
Ruapuke I., *N.Z.* **59 M2** 46 46S 168 31 E
Ruâq, W. →, *Egypt* **47 F2** 30 0N 33 49 E
Rub' al Khālī, *Si. Arabia* **46 D4** 19 0N 48 0 E
Rubeho Mts., *Tanzania* **54 D4** 6 50S 36 25 E
Rubh a' Mhail, *U.K.* **12 F2** 55 56N 6 8W
Rubha Hunish, *U.K.* **12 D2** 57 42N 6 20W
Rubha Robhanais = Lewis,
Butt of, *U.K.* **12 C2** 58 31N 6 16W
Rubicon →, *U.S.A.* **84 G5** 38 53N 121 4W
Rubio, *Venezuela* **92 B4** 7 43N 72 22W
Rubtsovsk, *Russia* **26 D9** 51 30N 81 10 E
Ruby L., *U.S.A.* **82 F6** 40 10N 115 28W
Ruby Mts., *U.S.A.* **82 F6** 40 30N 115 20W
Rubyvale, *Australia* **62 C4** 23 25S 147 42 E
Rūd Sar, *Iran* **45 B6** 37 8N 50 18 E
Rudall, *Australia* **63 E2** 33 43S 136 17 E
Rudall →, *Australia* **60 D3** 22 34S 122 13 E
Rudewa, *Tanzania* **55 E3** 10 7S 34 40 E
Rudnyy, *Kazakstan* **26 D7** 52 57N 63 7 E
Rudolfa, Ostrov, *Russia* **26 A6** 81 45N 58 30 E
Rudyard, *U.S.A.* **76 B3** 46 14N 84 36W
Ruenya →, *Africa* **55 F3** 16 24S 33 48 E
Rufiji →, *Tanzania* **54 D4** 7 50S 39 15 E
Rufino, *Argentina* **94 C3** 34 20S 62 50W
Rufunsa, *Zambia* **55 F2** 15 4S 29 34 E
Rugby, *U.K.* **11 E6** 52 23N 1 16W
Rugby, *U.S.A.* **80 A5** 48 22N 100 0W
Rügen, *Germany* **16 A7** 54 22N 13 24 E
Ruhengeri, *Rwanda* **54 C2** 1 30S 29 36 E
Ruhnu, *Estonia* **9 H20** 57 48N 23 15 E
Ruhr →, *Germany* **16 C4** 51 27N 6 43 E
Ruhuhu →, *Tanzania* **55 E3** 10 31S 34 34 E
Ruidoso, *U.S.A.* **83 K11** 33 20N 105 41W
Ruivo, Pico, *Madeira* **22 D3** 32 45N 16 56W
Rujm Tal'at al Jamā'ah,
Jordan **47 E4** 30 24N 35 30 E
Ruk, *Pakistan* **42 F3** 27 50N 68 42 E
Rukhla, *Pakistan* **42 C4** 32 27N 71 57 E
Ruki →, *Dem. Rep. of*
the Congo **52 E3** 0 5N 18 17 E
Rukwa □, *Tanzania* **54 D3** 7 0S 31 30 E
Rukwa, L., *Tanzania* **54 D3** 8 0S 32 20 E
Rulhieres, C., *Australia* **60 B4** 13 56S 127 22 E
Rum = Rhum, *U.K.* **12 E2** 57 0N 6 20W
Rum Cay, *Bahamas* **89 B5** 23 40N 74 58W
Rum Jungle, *Australia* **60 B5** 13 0S 130 59 E
Rumāḥ, *Si. Arabia* **44 E5** 25 29N 47 10 E
Rumania = Romania ■,
Europe **17 F12** 46 0N 25 0 E
Rumaylah, *Iraq* **44 D5** 30 47N 47 37 E
Rumbêk, *Sudan* **51 G11** 6 54N 29 37 E
Rumford, *U.S.A.* **77 C10** 44 33N 70 33W
Rumia, *Poland* **17 A10** 54 37N 18 25 E
Rumoi, *Japan* **30 C10** 43 56N 141 39 E
Rumonge, *Burundi* **54 C2** 3 59S 29 26 E
Rumson, *U.S.A.* **79 F11** 40 23N 74 0W
Rumuruti, *Kenya* **54 B4** 0 17N 36 32 E
Runan, *China* **34 H8** 33 0N 114 30 E
Runanga, *N.Z.* **59 K3** 42 25S 171 15 E
Runaway, C., *N.Z.* **59 G6** 37 32S 177 59 E
Runcorn, *U.K.* **10 D5** 53 21N 2 44W
Rundu, *Namibia* **56 B2** 17 52S 19 43 E
Rungwa, *Tanzania* **54 D3** 6 55S 33 32 E
Rungwa →, *Tanzania* **54 D3** 7 36S 31 50 E
Rungwe, *Tanzania* **55 D3** 9 11S 33 32 E
Rungwe, Mt., *Tanzania* **52 F6** 9 8S 33 40 E
Runton Ra., *Australia* **60 D3** 23 31S 123 6 E
Ruoqiang, *China* **32 C3** 38 55N 88 10 E
Rupa, *India* **41 F18** 27 15N 92 21 E
Rupar, *India* **42 D7** 31 2N 76 38 E
Rupat, *Indonesia* **36 D2** 1 45N 101 40 E
Rupen →, *India* **42 H4** 23 28N 71 31 E
Rupert, *U.S.A.* **82 E7** 42 37N 113 41W
Rupert →, *Canada* **70 B4** 51 29N 78 45W
Rupert B., *Canada* **70 B4** 51 35N 79 0W
Rupert House = Waskaganish,
Canada **70 B4** 51 30N 78 40W
Rupsa, *India* **43 J12** 21 37N 87 1 E
Rurrenabaque, *Bolivia* **92 F5** 14 30S 67 32W
Rusambo, *Zimbabwe* **55 F3** 16 30S 32 4 E
Rusape, *Zimbabwe* **55 F3** 18 35S 32 8 E
Ruschuk = Ruse, *Bulgaria* **21 C12** 43 48N 25 59 E
Ruse, *Bulgaria* **21 C12** 43 48N 25 59 E
Rush, *Ireland* **13 C5** 53 31N 6 6W
Rushan, *China* **35 F11** 36 56N 121 30 E
Rushden, *U.K.* **11 E7** 52 18N 0 35W
Rushmore, Mt., *U.S.A.* **80 D3** 43 53N 103 28W
Rushville, *Ill., U.S.A.* **80 E9** 40 7N 90 34W
Rushville, *Ind., U.S.A.* **76 F3** 39 37N 85 27W
Rushville, *Nebr., U.S.A.* **80 D3** 42 43N 102 28W
Russas, *Brazil* **93 D11** 4 55S 37 50W
Russell, *Canada* **73 C8** 50 50N 101 20W
Russell, *Kans., U.S.A.* **80 F5** 38 54N 98 52W

Russell, N.Y., U.S.A. 79 B9 44 27N 75 9W
Russell, Pa., U.S.A. 78 E5 41 56N 79 8W
Russell L., Man., Canada 73 B8 56 15N 101 30W
Russell L., N.W.T., Canada 72 A5 63 5N 115 44W
Russellkonda, India 41 K14 19 57N 84 42 E
Russellville, Ala., U.S.A. 77 H2 34 30N 87 44W
Russellville, Ark., U.S.A. 81 H8 35 17N 93 8W
Russellville, Ky., U.S.A. 77 G2 36 51N 86 53W
Russia ■, Eurasia 27 C11 62 0N 105 0 E
Russian →, U.S.A. 84 G3 38 27N 123 8W
Russkoye Ustie, Russia 4 B15 71 0N 149 0 E
Rustam, Pakistan 42 B5 34 25N 72 13 E
Rustam Shahr, Pakistan 42 F2 26 58N 66 6 E
Rustavi, Georgia 25 F8 41 30N 45 0 E
Rustenburg, S. Africa 56 D4 25 41S 27 14 E
Ruston, U.S.A. 81 J8 32 32N 92 38W
Rutana, Burundi 54 C3 3 55S 30 0 E
Ruteng, Indonesia 37 F6 8 35S 120 30 E
Ruth, U.S.A. 78 C2 43 42N 82 45W
Rutherford, U.S.A. 84 G4 38 26N 122 24W
Rutland, U.S.A. 79 C12 43 37N 72 58W
Rutland □, U.K. 11 E7 52 38N 0 40W
Rutland Water, U.K. 11 E7 52 39N 0 38W
Rutledge →, Canada 73 A6 61 4N 112 0W
Rutledge L., Canada 73 A6 61 33N 110 47W
Rutshuru, Dem. Rep. of the Congo 54 C2 1 13S 29 25 E
Ruvu, Tanzania 54 D4 6 49S 38 43 E
Ruvu →, Tanzania 54 D4 6 23S 38 52 E
Ruvuma □, Tanzania 55 E4 10 20S 36 0 E
Ruvuma →, Tanzania 55 E5 10 29S 40 28 E
Ruwais, U.A.E. 45 E7 24 5N 52 50 E
Ruwenzori, Africa 54 B2 0 30N 29 55 E
Ruya →, Zimbabwe 57 B5 16 27S 32 5 E
Ruyigi, Burundi 54 C3 3 29S 30 15 E
Ružomberok, Slovak Rep. 17 D10 49 3N 19 17 E
Rwanda ■, Africa 54 C3 2 0S 30 0 E
Ryan, L., U.K. 12 G3 55 0N 5 2W
Ryazan, Russia 24 D6 54 40N 39 40 E
Ryazhsk, Russia 24 D7 53 45N 40 3 E
Rybache = Rybachye, Kazakstan 26 E9 46 40N 81 20 E
Rybachiy Poluostrov, Russia 24 A5 69 43N 32 0 E
Rybachye, Kazakstan 26 E9 46 40N 81 20 E
Rybinsk, Russia 24 C6 58 5N 38 50 E
Rybinskoye Vdkhr., Russia 24 C6 58 30N 38 25 E
Rybnitsa = Râbniţa, Moldova 17 E15 47 45N 29 0 E
Rycroft, Canada 72 B5 55 45N 118 40W
Ryde, U.K. 11 G6 50 43N 1 9W
Ryderwood, U.S.A. 84 D3 46 23N 123 3W
Rye, U.K. 11 G8 50 57N 0 45 E
Rye →, U.K. 10 C7 54 11N 0 44W
Rye Bay, U.K. 11 G8 50 52N 0 49 E
Rye Patch Reservoir, U.S.A. 82 F4 40 28N 118 19W
Ryegate, U.S.A. 82 C9 46 18N 109 15W
Ryley, Canada 72 C6 53 17N 112 26W
Rylstone, Australia 63 E4 32 46S 149 58 E
Ryōtsu, Japan 30 E9 38 5N 138 26 E
Rypin, Poland 17 B10 53 3N 19 25 E
Ryūgasaki, Japan 31 G10 35 54N 140 11 E
Ryūkyū Is. = Ryūkyū-rettō, Japan 31 M3 26 0N 126 0 E
Ryūkyū-rettō, Japan 31 M3 26 0N 126 0 E
Rzeszów, Poland 17 C11 50 5N 21 58 E
Rzhev, Russia 24 C5 56 20N 34 20 E

S

Sa, Thailand 38 C3 18 34N 100 45 E
Sa Canal, Spain 22 C7 38 51N 1 23 E
Sa Conillera, Spain 22 C7 38 59N 1 13 E
Sa Dec, Vietnam 39 G5 10 20N 105 46 E
Sa Dragonera, Spain 22 B9 39 35N 2 19 E
Sa Mesquida, Spain 22 B11 39 55N 4 16 E
Sa Savina, Spain 22 C7 38 44N 1 25 E
Sa'ādatābād, Fārs, Iran 45 D7 30 10N 53 5 E
Sa'ādatābād, Hormozgān, Iran 45 D7 28 3N 55 53 E
Sa'ādatābād, Kermān, Iran 45 D7 29 40N 55 51 E
Saale →, Germany 16 C6 51 56N 11 54 E
Saalfeld, Germany 16 C6 50 38N 11 21 E
Saar →, Europe 18 B7 49 41N 6 32 E
Saarbrücken, Germany 16 D4 49 14N 6 59 E
Saaremaa, Estonia 9 G20 58 30N 22 30 E
Saarijärvi, Finland 9 E21 62 43N 25 16 E
Saariselkä, Finland 8 B23 68 16N 28 15 E
Sab 'Ābar, Syria 44 C3 33 46N 37 41 E
Saba, W. Indies 89 C7 17 42N 63 26W
Šabac, Serbia, Yug. 21 B8 44 48N 19 42 E
Sabadell, Spain 19 B7 41 28N 2 7 E
Sabah □, Malaysia 36 C5 6 0N 117 0 E
Sabak Bernam, Malaysia 39 L3 3 46N 100 58 E
Sabalān, Kūhhā-ye, Iran 44 B5 38 15N 47 45 E
Sabalana, Kepulauan, Indonesia 37 F5 6 45S 118 50 E
Sábana de la Mar, Dom. Rep. 89 C6 19 7N 69 24W
Sábanalarga, Colombia 92 A4 10 38N 74 55W
Sabang, Indonesia 36 C1 5 50N 95 15 E
Sabará, Brazil 93 G10 19 55S 43 46W
Sabarmati →, India 42 H5 22 18N 72 22 E
Sabattis, U.S.A. 79 B10 44 6N 74 40W
Saberania, Indonesia 37 E9 2 5S 138 18 E
Sabhah, Libya 51 C8 27 9N 14 29 E
Sabi →, India 42 E7 28 29N 76 44 E
Sabie, S. Africa 57 D5 25 10S 30 48 E
Sabinal, Mexico 86 A3 30 58N 107 25W
Sabinal, U.S.A. 81 L5 29 19N 99 28W
Sabinas, Mexico 86 B4 27 50N 101 10W
Sabinas →, Mexico 86 B4 27 37N 100 42W
Sabinas Hidalgo, Mexico 86 B4 26 33N 100 10W
Sabine →, U.S.A. 81 L8 29 59N 93 47W
Sabine L., U.S.A. 81 L8 29 53N 93 51W
Sabine Pass, U.S.A. 81 L8 29 44N 93 54W
Sabinsville, U.S.A. 78 E7 41 52N 77 31W
Sablayan, Phil. 37 B6 12 50N 120 50 E
Sable, Canada 71 A6 55 30N 68 21W
Sable, C., Canada 71 D6 43 29N 65 38W
Sable, C., U.S.A. 75 E10 25 9N 81 8W
Sable I., Canada 71 D8 44 0N 60 0W
Sabrina Coast, Antarctica 5 C9 68 0S 120 0 E
Sabulubbek, Indonesia 36 E1 1 36S 98 40 E
Sabzevār, Iran 45 B8 36 15N 57 40 E
Sabzvārān, Iran 45 D8 28 45N 57 50 E
Sac City, U.S.A. 80 D7 42 25N 95 0W
Săcele, Romania 17 F13 45 37N 25 41 E
Sachigo →, Canada 70 A2 55 6N 88 58W
Sachigo, L., Canada 70 B1 53 50N 92 12W
Sachsen □, Germany 16 C7 50 55N 13 10 E
Sachsen-Anhalt □, Germany 16 C7 52 0N 12 0 E
Sackets Harbor, U.S.A. 79 C8 43 57N 76 7W
Sackville, Canada 71 C7 45 54N 64 22W
Saco, Maine, U.S.A. 77 D10 43 30N 70 27W
Saco, Mont., U.S.A. 82 B10 48 28N 107 21W
Sacramento, U.S.A. 84 G5 38 35N 121 29W
Sacramento →, U.S.A. 84 G5 38 3N 121 56W
Sacramento Mts., U.S.A. 83 K11 32 30N 105 30W
Sacramento Valley, U.S.A. 84 G5 39 30N 122 0W
Sada-Misaki, Japan 31 H6 33 20N 132 1 E
Sadabad, India 42 F8 27 27N 78 3 E
Sadani, Tanzania 54 D4 5 58S 38 35 E
Sadao, Thailand 39 J3 6 38N 100 26 E
Sadd el Aali, Egypt 51 D12 23 54N 32 54 E
Saddle Mt., U.S.A. 84 E3 45 58N 123 41W
Sadimi, Dem. Rep. of the Congo 55 D1 9 25S 23 32 E
Sado, Japan 30 F9 38 0N 138 25 E
Sadon, Burma 41 G20 25 28N 97 55 E
Sadra, India 42 H5 23 21N 72 43 E
Sadri, India 42 G5 25 11N 73 26 E
Sæby, Denmark 9 H14 57 21N 10 30 E
Saegertown, U.S.A. 78 E4 41 43N 80 9W
Şafājah, Si. Arabia 44 E3 26 25N 39 0 E
Säffle, Sweden 9 G15 59 8N 12 55 E
Safford, U.S.A. 83 K9 32 50N 109 43W
Saffron Walden, U.K. 11 E8 52 1N 0 16 E
Safi, Morocco 50 B4 32 18N 9 20W
Şafīābād, Iran 45 B8 36 45N 57 58 E
Safīd Dasht, Iran 45 C6 33 27N 48 11 E
Safīd Kūh, Afghan. 40 B3 34 45N 63 0 E
Safīd Rūd →, Iran 45 B6 37 23N 50 11 E
Safipur, India 43 F9 26 44N 80 21 E
Safwān, Iraq 44 D5 30 7N 47 43 E
Sag Harbor, U.S.A. 79 F12 41 0N 72 18W
Saga, Japan 31 H5 33 15N 130 16 E
Saga □, Japan 31 H5 33 15N 130 20 E
Sagae, Japan 30 E10 38 22N 140 17 E
Sagamore, U.S.A. 78 F5 40 46N 79 14W
Sagar, Karnataka, India 40 M9 14 14N 75 6 E
Sagar, Mad. P., India 43 H8 23 50N 78 44 E
Sagara, L., Tanzania 54 D3 5 20S 31 0 E
Saginaw, U.S.A. 76 D4 43 26N 83 56W
Saginaw →, U.S.A. 76 D4 43 39N 83 51W
Saginaw B., U.S.A. 76 D4 43 50N 83 40W
Saglouc = Salluit, Canada 69 B12 62 14N 75 38W
Sagŏ-ri, S. Korea 35 G14 35 25N 126 49 E
Sagua la Grande, Cuba 88 B3 22 50N 80 10W
Saguache, U.S.A. 83 G10 38 5N 106 8W
Saguaro Nat. Park, U.S.A. 83 K8 32 12N 110 38W
Saguenay →, Canada 71 C5 48 22N 71 0W
Sagunt, Spain 19 C5 39 42N 0 18W
Sagunto = Sagunt, Spain 19 C5 39 42N 0 18W
Sagwara, India 42 H6 23 41N 74 1 E
Sahagún, Spain 19 A3 42 18N 5 2W
Saḩam al Jawlān, Syria 47 C4 32 45N 35 55 E
Sahamandrevo, Madag. 57 C8 23 15S 45 35 E
Sahand, Kūh-e, Iran 44 B5 37 44N 46 27 E
Sahara, Africa 50 D6 23 0N 5 0 E
Saharan Atlas = Saharien, Atlas, Algeria 50 B6 33 30N 1 0 E
Saharanpur, India 42 E7 29 58N 77 33 E
Saharien, Atlas, Algeria 50 B6 33 30N 1 0 E
Saharsa, India 43 G12 25 53N 86 36 E
Sahasinaka, Madag. 57 C8 21 49S 47 49 E
Sahaswan, India 43 E8 28 5N 78 45 E
Sahel, Africa 50 E5 16 0N 5 0 E
Sahibganj, India 43 G12 25 12N 87 40 E
Sāḩilīyah, Iraq 44 C4 33 43N 42 42 E
Sahiwal, Pakistan 42 D5 30 45N 73 8 E
Şaḩneh, Iran 44 C5 34 29N 47 41 E
Sahuaripa, Mexico 86 B3 29 0N 109 13W
Sahuarita, U.S.A. 83 L8 31 57N 110 58W
Sahuayo, Mexico 86 C4 20 4N 102 43W
Sai →, India 43 G10 25 39N 82 47 E
Sai Buri, Thailand 39 J3 6 43N 101 45 E
Sa'id Bundas, Sudan 51 G10 8 24N 24 48 E
Sa'īdābād, Kermān, Iran 45 D7 29 30N 55 45 E
Sa'īdābād, Semnān, Iran 45 B7 36 8N 54 11 E
Sa'īdīyeh, Iran 45 B6 36 20N 48 55 E
Saidpur, Bangla. 41 G16 25 48N 89 0 E
Saidpur, India 43 G10 25 33N 83 11 E
Saidu, Pakistan 43 B5 34 43N 72 24 E
Saigon = Thanh Pho Ho Chi Minh, Vietnam 39 G6 10 58N 106 40 E
Saijō, Japan 31 H6 33 55N 133 11 E
Saikanosy Masoala, Madag. 57 B9 15 45S 50 10 E
Saikhoa Ghat, India 41 F19 27 50N 95 40 E
Saiki, Japan 31 H5 32 58N 131 51 E
Sailana, India 42 H6 23 28N 74 55 E
Sailolof, Indonesia 37 E8 1 15S 130 46 E
Saimaa, Finland 9 F23 61 15N 28 15 E
Şa'in Dezh, Iran 44 B5 36 40N 46 25 E
St. Abb's Head, U.K. 12 F6 55 55N 2 8W
St. Alban's, Canada 71 C8 47 51N 55 50W
St. Albans, U.K. 11 F7 51 45N 0 19W
St. Albans, Vt., U.S.A. 79 B11 44 49N 73 5W
St. Albans, W. Va., U.S.A. 76 F5 38 23N 81 50W
St. Alban's Head, U.K. 11 G5 50 34N 2 4W
St. Albert, Canada 72 C6 53 37N 113 32W
St. Andrew's, Canada 71 C8 47 45N 59 15W
St. Andrews, U.K. 12 E6 56 20N 2 47W
St-Anicet, Canada 79 A10 45 8N 74 22W
St. Ann B., Canada 71 C7 46 22N 60 25W
St. Ann's Bay, Jamaica 88 C4 18 26N 77 15W
St. Anthony, Canada 71 B8 51 22N 55 35W
St. Anthony, U.S.A. 82 E8 43 58N 111 41W
St. Antoine, Canada 71 C7 46 22N 64 45W
St. Arnaud, Australia 63 F3 36 40S 143 16 E
St-Augustin →, Canada 71 B8 51 16N 58 40W
St-Augustin-Saguenay, Canada 71 B8 51 13N 58 38W
St. Augustine, U.S.A. 77 L5 29 54N 81 19W
St. Austell, U.K. 11 G3 50 20N 4 47W
St. Barbe, Canada 71 B8 51 12N 56 46W
St-Barthélemy, W. Indies 89 C7 17 50N 62 50W
St. Bees Hd., U.K. 10 C4 54 31N 3 38W
St. Bride's, Canada 71 C9 46 56N 54 10W
St. Brides B., U.K. 11 F2 51 49N 5 9W
St-Brieuc, France 18 B2 48 30N 2 46W
St. Catharines, Canada 78 C5 43 10N 79 15W
St. Catherines I., U.S.A. 77 K5 31 40N 81 10W
St. Catherine's Pt., U.K. 11 G6 50 34N 1 18W
St-Chamond, France 18 D6 45 28N 4 31 E
St. Charles, Ill., U.S.A. 76 E1 41 54N 88 19W
St. Charles, Mo., U.S.A. 80 F9 38 47N 90 29W
St. Charles, Va., U.S.A. 76 F7 36 48N 83 4W
St. Christopher-Nevis = St. Kitts & Nevis ■, W. Indies 89 C7 17 20N 62 40W
St. Clair, Mich., U.S.A. 78 D2 42 50N 82 30W
St. Clair, Pa., U.S.A. 79 F8 40 43N 76 12W
St. Clair →, U.S.A. 78 D2 42 38N 82 31W
St. Clair, L., Canada 70 D3 42 30N 82 45W
St. Clair, L., U.S.A. 78 D2 42 27N 82 39W
St. Clairsville, U.S.A. 78 F4 40 5N 80 54W
St. Claude, Canada 73 D9 49 40N 98 20W
St-Clet, Canada 79 A10 45 21N 74 13W
St. Cloud, Fla., U.S.A. 77 L5 28 15N 81 17W
St. Cloud, Minn., U.S.A. 80 C7 45 34N 94 10W
St. Cricq, C., Australia 61 E1 25 17S 113 6 E
St. Croix, U.S. Virgin Is. 89 C7 17 45N 64 45W
St. Croix →, U.S.A. 80 C8 44 45N 92 48W
St. Croix Falls, U.S.A. 80 C8 45 24N 92 38W
St. David's, Canada 71 C8 48 12N 58 52W
St. David's, U.K. 11 F2 51 53N 5 16W
St. David's Head, U.K. 11 F2 51 54N 5 19W
St-Denis, France 18 B5 48 56N 2 22 E
St-Dizier, France 18 B6 48 38N 4 56 E
St. Elias, Mt., U.S.A. 68 B5 60 18N 140 56W
St. Elias Mts., Canada 72 A1 60 33N 139 28W
St. Elias Mts., U.S.A. 68 C6 60 0N 138 0W
St-Étienne, France 18 D6 45 27N 4 22 E
St. Eugène, Canada 79 A10 45 30N 74 28W
St. Eustatius, W. Indies 89 C7 17 20N 63 0W
St-Félicien, Canada 70 C5 48 40N 72 25W
St-Flour, France 18 D5 45 2N 3 6 E
St. Francis, U.S.A. 80 F4 39 47N 101 48W
St. Francis →, U.S.A. 81 H9 34 38N 90 36W
St. Francis, C., S. Africa 56 E3 34 14S 24 49 E
St. Francisville, U.S.A. 81 K9 30 47N 91 23W
St-François, L., Canada 79 A10 45 10N 74 22W
St-Gabriel, Canada 70 C5 46 17N 73 24W
St. Gallen = Sankt Gallen, Switz. 18 C8 47 26N 9 22 E
St-Gaudens, France 18 E4 43 6N 0 44 E
St. George, Australia 63 D4 28 1S 148 30 E
St. George, Canada 71 C6 45 11N 66 50W
St. George, S.C., U.S.A. 77 J5 33 11N 80 35W
St. George, Utah, U.S.A. 83 H7 37 6N 113 35W
St. George, C., Canada 71 C8 48 30N 59 16W
St. George, C., U.S.A. 77 L3 29 40N 85 5W
St. George Ra., Australia 60 C4 18 40S 125 0 E
St. George's, Canada 71 C8 48 26N 58 31W
St-Georges, Canada 71 C5 46 8N 70 40W
St. George's, Grenada 89 D7 12 5N 61 43W
St. George's B., Canada 71 C8 48 24N 58 53W
St. Georges Basin, N.S.W., Australia 63 F5 35 7S 150 36 E
St. Georges Basin, W. Austral., Australia 60 C4 15 23S 125 2 E
St. George's Channel, Europe 13 E6 52 0N 6 0W
St. Georges Hd., Australia 63 F5 35 12S 150 42 E
St. Gotthard P. = San Gottardo, P. del, Switz. 18 C8 46 33N 8 33 E
St. Helena, Atl. Oc. 48 H3 15 58S 5 42W
St. Helena, U.S.A. 82 G2 38 30N 122 28W
St. Helena, Mt., U.S.A. 84 G4 38 40N 122 36W
St. Helena B., S. Africa 56 E2 32 40S 18 10 E
St. Helens, Australia 62 G4 41 20S 148 15 E
St. Helens, U.K. 10 D5 53 27N 2 44W
St. Helens, U.S.A. 84 E4 45 52N 122 48W
St. Helens, Mt., U.S.A. 84 D4 46 12N 122 12W
St. Helier, U.K. 11 H5 49 10N 2 7W
St-Hubert, Belgium 15 D5 50 2N 5 23 E
St-Hyacinthe, Canada 70 C5 45 40N 72 58W
St. Ignace, U.S.A. 76 C3 45 52N 84 44W
St. Ignace I., Canada 70 C2 48 45N 88 0W
St. Ignatius, U.S.A. 82 C6 47 19N 114 6W
St. Ives, U.K. 11 G2 50 12N 5 30W
St. James, U.S.A. 80 D7 43 59N 94 38W
St-Jean →, Canada 71 B7 50 17N 64 20W
St-Jean, L., Canada 71 C5 48 40N 72 0W
St-Jean-Port-Joli, Canada 71 C5 47 15N 70 13W
St-Jean-sur-Richelieu, Canada 79 A11 45 20N 73 20W
St-Jérôme, Canada 70 C5 45 47N 74 0W
St. John, Canada 71 C6 45 20N 66 8W
St. John, U.S.A. 81 G5 38 0N 98 46W
St. John →, U.S.A. 77 C12 45 12N 66 5W
St. John, C., Canada 71 C8 50 0N 55 32W
St. John's, Antigua 89 C7 17 6N 61 51W
St. John's, Canada 71 C9 47 35N 52 40W
St. Johns, Ariz., U.S.A. 83 J9 34 30N 109 22W
St. Johns, Mich., U.S.A. 76 D3 43 0N 84 33W
St. Johns →, U.S.A. 77 K5 30 24N 81 24W
St. John's Pt., Ireland 13 B3 54 34N 8 27W
St. Johnsbury, U.S.A. 79 B12 44 25N 72 1W
St. Johnsville, U.S.A. 79 D10 43 0N 74 43W
St. Joseph, La., U.S.A. 81 K9 31 55N 91 14W
St. Joseph, Mo., U.S.A. 80 F7 39 46N 94 50W
St. Joseph →, U.S.A. 76 D2 42 7N 86 29W
St. Joseph, I., Canada 70 C3 46 12N 83 58W
St. Joseph, L., Canada 70 B1 51 10N 90 35W
St-Jovite, Canada 70 C5 46 8N 74 38W
St. Kitts & Nevis ■, W. Indies 89 C7 17 20N 62 40W
St. Laurent, Canada 73 C9 50 25N 97 58W
St. Lawrence, Australia 62 C4 22 16S 149 31 E
St. Lawrence, Canada 71 C8 46 54N 55 23W
St. Lawrence →, Canada 71 C6 49 30N 66 0W
St. Lawrence, Gulf of, Canada 71 C7 48 25N 62 0W
St. Lawrence I., U.S.A. 68 B3 63 30N 170 30W
St. Leonard, Canada 71 C6 47 12N 67 58W
St. Lewis →, Canada 71 B8 52 26N 56 11W
St-Lô, France 18 B3 49 7N 1 5W
St. Louis, Senegal 50 E2 16 8N 16 27W
St. Louis, U.S.A. 80 F9 38 37N 90 12W
St. Louis →, U.S.A. 80 B8 47 15N 92 45W
St. Lucia ■, W. Indies 89 D7 14 0N 60 50W
St. Lucia, L., S. Africa 57 D5 28 5S 32 30 E
St. Lucia Channel, W. Indies 89 D7 14 15N 61 0W
St. Maarten, W. Indies 89 C7 18 0N 63 5W
St. Magnus B., U.K. 12 A7 60 25N 1 35W
St-Malo, France 18 B2 48 39N 2 1W
St-Marc, Haiti 89 C5 19 10N 72 41W
St. Maries, U.S.A. 82 C5 47 19N 116 35W
St-Martin, W. Indies 89 C7 18 0N 63 0W
St. Martin, L., Canada 73 C9 51 40N 98 30W
St. Mary Pk., Australia 63 E2 31 32S 138 34 E
St. Marys, Australia 62 G4 41 35S 148 11 E
St. Marys, Canada 78 C3 43 20N 81 10W
St. Mary's, Corn., U.K. 11 H1 49 55N 6 18W
St. Mary's, Orkney, U.K. 12 C6 58 54N 2 54W
St. Marys, Ga., U.S.A. 77 K5 30 44N 81 33W
St. Marys, Pa., U.S.A. 78 E6 41 26N 78 34W
St. Mary's, C., Canada 71 C9 46 50N 54 12W
St. Mary's B., Canada 71 C9 46 50N 53 50W
St. Marys Bay, Canada 71 D6 44 25N 66 10W
St-Mathieu, Pte., France 18 B1 48 20N 4 45W
St. Matthew I., U.S.A. 68 B2 60 24N 172 42W
St. Matthews, I. = Zadetkyi Kyun, Burma 39 G1 10 0N 98 25 E
St-Maurice →, Canada 70 C5 46 21N 72 31W
St-Nazaire, France 18 C2 47 17N 2 12W
St. Neots, U.K. 11 E7 52 14N 0 15W
St-Niklaas, Belgium 15 C4 51 10N 4 8 E
St-Omer, France 18 A5 50 45N 2 15 E
St-Pamphile, Canada 71 C6 46 58N 69 48W
St. Pascal, Canada 71 C6 47 32N 69 48W
St. Paul, Canada 72 C6 54 0N 111 17W
St. Paul, Minn., U.S.A. 80 C8 44 57N 93 6W
St. Paul, Nebr., U.S.A. 80 E5 41 13N 98 27W
St-Paul →, Canada 71 B8 51 27N 57 42W
St. Paul, I., Ind. Oc. 3 F13 38 55S 77 34 E
St. Paul I., Canada 71 C7 47 12N 60 9W
St. Peter, U.S.A. 80 C8 44 20N 93 57W
St. Peter Port, U.K. 11 H5 49 26N 2 33W
St. Peters, N.S., Canada 71 C7 45 40N 60 53W
St. Peters, P.E.I., Canada 71 C7 46 25N 62 35W
St. Petersburg = Sankt-Peterburg, Russia 24 C5 59 55N 30 20 E
St. Petersburg, U.S.A. 77 M4 27 46N 82 39W
St-Pie, Canada 79 A12 45 30N 72 54W
St-Pierre, St- P. & M. 71 C8 46 46N 56 12W
St-Pierre, L., Canada 70 C5 46 12N 72 52W
St-Pierre et Miquelon □, St- P. & M. 71 C8 46 55N 56 10W
St. Quentin, Canada 71 C6 47 30N 67 23W
St-Quentin, France 18 B5 49 50N 3 16 E
St. Regis, U.S.A. 82 C6 47 18N 115 6W
St. Sebastien, Tanjon' i, Madag. 57 A8 12 26S 48 44 E
St-Siméon, Canada 71 C6 47 51N 69 54W
St. Simons I., U.S.A. 77 K5 31 12N 81 15W
St. Simons Island, U.S.A. 77 K5 31 9N 81 22W
St. Stephen, Canada 71 C6 45 16N 67 17W
St. Thomas, Canada 78 D3 42 45N 81 10W
St. Thomas I., U.S. Virgin Is. 89 C7 18 20N 64 55W
St-Tite, Canada 70 C5 46 45N 72 34W
St-Tropez, France 18 E7 43 17N 6 38 E
St. Troud = St. Truiden, Belgium 15 D5 50 48N 5 10 E
St. Truiden, Belgium 15 D5 50 48N 5 10 E
St. Vincent, G., Australia 63 F2 35 0S 138 0 E
St. Vincent & the Grenadines ■, W. Indies 89 D7 13 0N 61 10W
St. Vincent Passage, W. Indies 89 D7 13 30N 61 0W
St-Vith, Belgium 15 D6 50 17N 6 9 E
St. Walburg, Canada 73 C7 53 39N 109 12W
Ste-Agathe-des-Monts, Canada 70 C5 46 3N 74 17W
Ste-Anne, L., Canada 71 B6 50 0N 67 42W
Ste-Anne-des-Monts, Canada 71 C6 49 8N 66 30W
Ste. Genevieve, U.S.A. 80 G9 37 59N 90 2W
Ste-Marguerite →, Canada 71 B6 50 9N 66 36W
Ste-Marie, Martinique 89 D7 14 48N 61 1W
Ste-Marie de la Madeleine, Canada 71 C5 46 26N 71 0W
Ste-Rose, Guadeloupe 89 C7 16 20N 61 45W
Ste. Rose du Lac, Canada 73 C9 51 4N 99 30W
Saintes, France 18 D3 45 45N 0 37W
Saintes, I. des, Guadeloupe 89 C7 15 50N 61 35W
Saintfield, U.K. 13 B6 54 28N 5 49W
Saintonge, France 18 D3 45 40N 0 50W
Saipan, Pac. Oc. 64 F6 15 12N 145 45 E
Sairang, India 41 H18 23 50N 92 45 E
Sairecábur, Cerro, Bolivia 94 A2 22 43S 67 54W
Saitama □, Japan 31 F9 36 25N 139 30 E
Saiyid, Pakistan 42 C5 33 7N 73 2 E
Sajama, Bolivia 92 G5 18 7S 69 0W
Sajószentpéter, Hungary 17 D11 48 12N 20 44 E
Sajum, India 43 C8 33 20N 79 0 E
Sak →, S. Africa 56 E3 30 52S 20 25 E
Sakai, Japan 31 G7 34 30N 135 30 E
Sakaide, Japan 31 G6 34 19N 133 50 E
Sakaiminato, Japan 31 G6 35 38N 133 11 E
Sakākah, Si. Arabia 44 D4 30 0N 40 8 E
Sakakawea, L., U.S.A. 80 B4 47 30N 101 25W
Sakami →, Canada 70 B4 53 40N 76 40W
Sakami, L., Canada 70 B4 53 15N 77 0W
Sakania, Dem. Rep. of the Congo 55 E2 12 43S 28 30 E
Sakarara, Madag. 57 C7 22 55S 44 32 E
Sakarya, Turkey 25 F5 40 48N 30 25 E
Sakashima-Guntō, Japan 31 M2 24 46N 124 0 E
Sakata, Japan 30 E9 38 55N 139 50 E
Sakchu, N. Korea 35 D13 40 23N 125 2 E
Sakeny →, Madag. 57 C8 20 0S 45 25 E
Sakha □, Russia 27 C13 66 0N 130 0 E
Sakhalin, Russia 27 D15 51 0N 143 0 E
Sakhalinskiy Zaliv, Russia 27 D15 54 0N 141 0 E
Šakiai, Lithuania 9 J20 54 59N 23 2 E
Sakon Nakhon, Thailand 38 D5 17 10N 104 9 E
Sakrand, Pakistan 42 F3 26 10N 68 15 E
Sakri, India 43 F12 26 13N 86 5 E
Sakrivier, S. Africa 56 E3 30 54S 20 28 E
Sakti, India 43 H10 22 2N 82 58 E
Sakuma, Japan 31 G8 35 3N 137 49 E
Sakurai, Japan 31 G7 34 30N 135 51 E
Sala, Sweden 9 G17 59 58N 16 35 E
Sala Consilina, Italy 20 D6 40 23N 15 36 E
Sala-y-Gómez, Pac. Oc. 65 K17 26 28S 105 28W
Salaberry-de-Valleyfield, Canada 79 A10 45 15N 74 8W
Saladas, Argentina 94 B4 28 15S 58 40W
Saladillo, Argentina 94 D4 35 40S 59 55W
Salado →, Buenos Aires, Argentina 94 D4 35 44S 57 22W
Salado →, La Pampa, Argentina 96 D3 37 30S 67 0W
Salado →, Santa Fe, Argentina 94 C3 31 40S 60 41W
Salado →, Mexico 81 M5 26 52N 99 19W
Salaga, Ghana 50 G5 8 31N 0 31W
Sālah, Syria 47 C5 32 40N 36 45 E

Sálakhos, Greece 23 C9 36 17N 27 57 E
Salālah, Oman 46 D5 16 56N 53 59 E
Salamanca, Chile 94 C1 31 46S 70 59W
Salamanca, Spain 19 B3 40 58N 5 39W
Salamanca, U.S.A. 78 D6 42 10N 78 43W
Salāmatābād, Iran 44 C5 35 39N 47 50 E
Salamis, Cyprus 23 D12 35 11N 33 54 E
Salamís, Greece 21 F10 37 56N 23 30 E
Salar de Atacama, Chile 94 A2 23 30S 68 25W
Salar de Uyuni, Bolivia 92 H5 20 30S 67 45W
Salatiga, Indonesia 37 G14 7 19S 110 30 E
Salavat, Russia 24 D10 53 21N 55 55 E
Salaverry, Peru 92 E3 8 15S 79 0W
Salawati, Indonesia 37 E8 1 7S 130 52 E
Salaya, India 42 H3 22 19N 69 35 E
Salayar, Indonesia 37 F6 6 7S 120 30 E
Salcombe, U.K. 11 G4 50 14N 3 47W
Saldanha, S. Africa 56 E2 33 0S 17 58 E
Saldanha B., S. Africa 56 E2 33 6S 18 0 E
Saldus, Latvia 9 H20 56 38N 22 30 E
Sale, Australia 63 F4 38 6S 147 6 E
Salé, Morocco 50 B4 34 3N 6 48W
Sale, U.K. 10 D5 53 26N 2 19W
Salekhard, Russia 26 C7 66 30N 66 35 E
Salem, India 40 P11 11 40N 78 11 E
Salem, Ill., U.S.A. 76 F1 38 38N 88 57W
Salem, Ind., U.S.A. 76 F2 38 36N 86 6W
Salem, Mass., U.S.A. 79 D14 42 31N 70 53W
Salem, Mo., U.S.A. 81 G9 37 39N 91 32W
Salem, N.H., U.S.A. 79 D13 42 45N 71 12W
Salem, N.J., U.S.A. 76 F8 39 34N 75 28W
Salem, N.Y., U.S.A. 79 C11 43 10N 73 20W
Salem, Ohio, U.S.A. 78 F4 40 54N 80 52W
Salem, Oreg., U.S.A. 82 D2 44 56N 123 2W
Salem, S. Dak., U.S.A. 80 D6 43 44N 97 23W
Salem, Va., U.S.A. 76 G5 37 18N 80 3W
Salerno, Italy 20 D6 40 41N 14 47 E
Salford, U.K. 10 D5 53 30N 2 18W
Salgótarján, Hungary 17 D10 48 5N 19 47 E
Salgueiro, Brazil 93 E11 8 4S 39 6W
Salibabu, Indonesia 37 D7 3 51N 126 40 E
Salida, U.S.A. 74 C5 38 32N 106 0W
Salihli, Turkey 21 E13 38 28N 28 8 E
Salihorsk, Belarus 17 B14 52 51N 27 27 E
Salima, Malawi 53 G6 13 47S 34 28 E
Salina, Italy 20 E6 38 34N 14 50 E
Salina, Kans., U.S.A. 80 F6 38 50N 97 37W
Salina, Utah, U.S.A. 83 G8 38 58N 111 51W
Salina Cruz, Mexico 87 D5 16 10N 95 10W
Salinas, Brazil 93 G10 16 10S 42 10W
Salinas, Chile 94 A2 23 31S 69 29W
Salinas, Ecuador 92 D2 2 10S 80 58W
Salinas, U.S.A. 84 J5 36 40N 121 39W
Salinas →, Guatemala 87 D6 16 28N 90 31W
Salinas →, U.S.A. 84 J5 36 45N 121 48W
Salinas, B. de, Nic. 88 D2 11 4N 85 45W
Salinas, Pampa de las, Argentina 94 C2 31 58S 66 42W
Salinas Ambargasta, Argentina 94 B3 29 0S 65 0W
Salinas de Hidalgo, Mexico 86 C4 22 30N 101 40W
Salinas Grandes, Argentina 94 C3 30 0S 65 0W
Saline →, Ark., U.S.A. 81 J8 33 10N 92 8W
Saline →, Kans., U.S.A. 80 F6 38 52N 97 30W
Salines, C. de ses, Spain 22 B10 39 16N 3 4 E
Salinópolis, Brazil 93 D9 0 40S 47 20W
Salisbury = Harare, Zimbabwe 55 F3 17 43S 31 2 E
Salisbury, U.K. 11 F6 51 4N 1 47W
Salisbury, Md., U.S.A. 76 F8 38 22N 75 36W
Salisbury, N.C., U.S.A. 77 H5 35 40N 80 29W
Salisbury I., Canada 69 B12 63 30N 77 0W
Salisbury Plain, U.K. 11 F6 51 14N 1 55W
Şalkhad, Syria 47 C5 32 29N 36 43 E
Salla, Finland 8 C23 66 50N 28 49 E
Salliq, Canada 69 B11 64 8N 83 10W
Sallisaw, U.S.A. 81 H7 35 28N 94 47W
Salluit, Canada 69 B12 62 14N 75 38W
Salmās, Iran 44 B5 38 11N 44 47 E
Salmo, Canada 72 D5 49 10N 117 20W
Salmon, U.S.A. 82 D7 45 11N 113 54W
Salmon →, Canada 72 C4 54 3N 122 40W
Salmon →, U.S.A. 82 D5 45 51N 116 47W
Salmon Arm, Canada 72 C5 50 40N 119 15W
Salmon Gums, Australia 61 F3 32 59S 121 38 E
Salmon River Mts., U.S.A. 82 D6 45 0N 114 30W
Salo, Finland 9 F20 60 22N 23 10 E
Salome, U.S.A. 85 M13 33 47N 113 37W
Salon, India 43 F9 26 2N 81 27 E
Salon-de-Provence, France 18 E6 43 39N 5 6 E
Salonica = Thessaloníki, Greece 21 D10 40 38N 22 58 E
Salonta, Romania 17 E11 46 49N 21 42 E
Salpausselkä, Finland 9 F22 61 0N 27 0 E
Salsacate, Argentina 94 C2 31 20S 65 5W
Salsk, Russia 25 E7 46 28N 41 30 E
Salso →, Italy 20 F5 37 6N 13 57 E
Salt →, Canada 72 B6 60 0N 112 25W
Salt →, U.S.A. 83 K7 33 23N 112 19W
Salt Lake City, U.S.A. 82 F8 40 45N 111 53W
Salt Range, Pakistan 42 C5 32 30N 72 25 E
Salta, Argentina 94 A2 24 57S 65 25W
Salta □, Argentina 94 A2 24 48S 65 30W
Saltash, U.K. 11 G3 50 24N 4 14W
Saltburn by the Sea, U.K. 10 C7 54 35N 0 58W
Saltcoats, U.K. 12 F4 55 38N 4 47W
Saltee Is., Ireland 13 D5 52 7N 6 37W
Saltfjellet, Norway 8 C16 66 40N 15 15 E
Saltfjorden, Norway 8 C16 67 15N 14 10 E
Saltillo, Mexico 86 B4 25 25N 101 0W
Salto, Argentina 94 C3 34 20S 60 15W
Salto, Uruguay 94 C4 31 27S 57 50W
Salto →, Italy 20 C5 42 26N 12 25 E
Salto del Guaíra, Paraguay 95 A5 24 3S 54 17W
Salton City, U.S.A. 85 M11 33 29N 115 51W
Salton Sea, U.S.A. 85 M11 33 15N 115 45W
Saltsburg, U.S.A. 78 F5 40 29N 79 27W
Saluda →, U.S.A. 77 J5 34 1N 81 4W
Salûm, Egypt 51 B11 31 31N 25 7 E
Salur, India 41 K13 18 27N 83 18 E
Salvador, Brazil 93 F11 13 0S 38 30W
Salvador, Canada 73 C7 52 10N 109 32W
Salvador, L., U.S.A. 81 L9 29 43N 90 15W
Salween →, Burma 41 L20 16 31N 97 37 E
Salyan, Azerbaijan 25 G8 39 33N 48 59 E
Salzach →, Austria 16 D7 48 12N 12 56 E
Salzburg, Austria 16 E7 47 48N 13 2 E
Salzgitter, Germany 16 B6 52 9N 10 19 E
Salzwedel, Germany 16 B6 52 52N 11 10 E
Sam, India 42 F4 26 50N 70 31 E
Sam Neua, Laos 38 B5 20 29N 104 5 E
Sam Ngao, Thailand 38 D2 17 18N 99 0 E
Sam Rayburn Reservoir, U.S.A. 81 K7 31 4N 94 5W
Sam Son, Vietnam 38 C5 19 44N 105 54 E
Sam Teu, Laos 38 C5 19 59N 104 38 E
Sama de Langreo = Langreo, Spain 19 A3 43 18N 5 40W
Samagaltay, Russia 27 D10 50 36N 95 3 E
Samales Group, Phil. 37 C6 6 0N 122 0 E
Samana, India 42 D7 30 10N 76 13 E
Samana Cay, Bahamas 89 B5 23 3N 73 45W
Samanga, Tanzania 55 D4 8 20S 39 13 E
Samangān □, Afghan. 40 B5 36 15N 68 3 E
Samangwa, Dem. Rep. of the Congo 54 C1 4 23S 24 10 E
Samani, Japan 30 C11 42 7N 142 56 E
Samar, Phil. 37 B7 12 0N 125 0 E
Samara, Russia 24 D9 53 8N 50 6 E
Samaria = Shōmrōn, West Bank 47 C4 32 15N 35 13 E
Samariá, Greece 23 D5 35 17N 23 58 E
Samarinda, Indonesia 36 E5 0 30S 117 9 E
Samarkand = Samarqand, Uzbekistan 26 F7 39 40N 66 55 E
Samarqand, Uzbekistan 26 F7 39 40N 66 55 E
Sāmarrā, Iraq 44 C4 34 12N 43 52 E
Samastipur, India 43 G11 25 50N 85 50 E
Samba, Dem. Rep. of the Congo 54 C2 4 38S 26 22 E
Samba, India 43 C6 32 32N 75 10 E
Sambalpur, India 41 J14 21 28N 84 4 E
Sambar, Tanjung, Indonesia 36 E4 2 59S 110 19 E
Sambas, Indonesia 36 D3 1 20N 109 20 E
Sambava, Madag. 57 A9 14 16S 50 10 E
Sambawizi, Zimbabwe 55 F2 18 24S 26 13 E
Sambhal, India 43 E8 28 35N 78 37 E
Sambhar, India 42 F6 26 52N 75 6 E
Sambhar L., India 42 F6 26 55N 75 12 E
Sambiase, Italy 20 E7 38 58N 16 17 E
Sambir, Ukraine 17 D12 49 30N 23 10 E
Sambor, Cambodia 38 F6 12 46N 106 0 E
Samborombón, B., Argentina 94 D4 36 5S 57 20W
Samch'ŏk, S. Korea 35 F15 37 30N 129 10 E
Samch'onp'o, S. Korea 35 G15 35 0N 128 6 E
Same, Tanzania 54 C4 4 2S 37 38 E
Samfya, Zambia 55 E2 11 22S 29 31 E
Samnah, Si. Arabia 44 E3 25 10N 37 15 E
Samo Alto, Chile 94 C1 30 22S 71 0W
Samoa ■, Pac. Oc. 59 B13 14 0S 172 0W
Samokov, Bulgaria 21 C10 42 18N 23 35 E
Sámos, Greece 21 F12 37 45N 26 50 E
Samothráki = Mathráki, Greece 23 A3 39 48N 19 31 E
Samothráki, Greece 21 D11 40 28N 25 28 E
Sampacho, Argentina 94 C3 33 20S 64 50W
Sampang, Indonesia 37 G15 7 11S 113 13 E
Sampit, Indonesia 36 E4 2 34S 113 0 E
Sampit, Teluk, Indonesia 36 E4 3 5S 113 3 E
Samrong, Cambodia 38 E4 14 15N 103 30 E
Samrong, Thailand 38 E3 15 10N 100 40 E
Samsø, Denmark 9 J14 55 50N 10 35 E
Samsun, Turkey 25 F6 41 15N 36 22 E
Samui, Ko, Thailand 39 H3 9 30N 100 0 E
Samusole, Dem. Rep. of the Congo 55 E1 10 2S 24 0 E
Samut Prakan, Thailand 38 F3 13 32N 100 40 E
Samut Songkhram →, Thailand 36 B1 13 24N 100 1 E
Samwari, Pakistan 42 E2 28 30N 66 46 E
San, Mali 50 F5 13 15N 4 57W
San →, Cambodia 38 F5 13 32N 105 57 E
San →, Poland 17 C11 50 45N 21 51 E
San Agustin, C., Phil. 37 C7 6 20N 126 13 E
San Agustín de Valle Fértil, Argentina 94 C2 30 35S 67 30W
San Ambrosio, Pac. Oc. 90 F3 26 28S 79 53W
San Andreas, U.S.A. 84 G6 38 12N 120 41W
San Andrés, I. de, Caribbean 88 D3 12 42N 81 46W
San Andres Mts., U.S.A. 83 K10 33 0N 106 30W
San Andrés Tuxtla, Mexico 87 D5 18 30N 95 20W
San Angelo, U.S.A. 81 K4 31 28N 100 26W
San Anselmo, U.S.A. 84 H4 37 59N 122 34W
San Antonio, Belize 87 D7 16 15N 89 2W
San Antonio, Chile 94 C1 33 40S 71 40W
San Antonio, N. Mex., U.S.A. 83 K10 33 55N 106 52W
San Antonio, Tex., U.S.A. 81 L5 29 25N 98 30W
San Antonio →, U.S.A. 81 L6 28 30N 96 54W
San Antonio, C., Argentina 94 D4 36 15S 56 40W
San Antonio, C., Cuba 88 B3 21 50N 84 57W
San Antonio, Mt., U.S.A. 85 L9 34 17N 117 38W
San Antonio de los Baños, Cuba 88 B3 22 54N 82 31W
San Antonio de los Cobres, Argentina 94 A2 24 10S 66 17W
San Antonio Oeste, Argentina 96 E4 40 40S 65 0W
San Ardo, U.S.A. 84 J6 36 1N 120 54W
San Augustín, Canary Is. 22 G4 27 47N 15 32W
San Augustine, U.S.A. 81 K7 31 30N 94 7W
San Bartolomé, Canary Is. 22 F6 28 59N 13 37W
San Bartolomé de Tirajana, Canary Is. 22 G4 27 54N 15 34W
San Benedetto del Tronto, Italy 20 C5 42 57N 13 53 E
San Benedicto, I., Mexico 86 D2 19 18N 110 49W
San Benito, U.S.A. 81 M6 26 8N 97 38W
San Benito →, U.S.A. 84 J5 36 53N 121 34W
San Benito Mt., U.S.A. 84 J6 36 22N 120 37W
San Bernardino, U.S.A. 85 L9 34 7N 117 19W
San Bernardino Mts., U.S.A. 85 L10 34 10N 116 45W
San Bernardino Str., Phil. 37 B6 13 0N 125 0 E
San Bernardo, Chile 94 C1 33 40S 70 50W
San Bernardo, I. de, Colombia 92 B3 9 45N 75 50W
San Blas, Mexico 86 B3 26 4N 108 46W
San Blas, Arch. de, Panama 88 E4 9 50N 78 31W
San Blas, C., U.S.A. 77 L3 29 40N 85 21W
San Borja, Bolivia 92 F5 14 50S 66 52W
San Buenaventura, Mexico 86 B4 27 5N 101 32W
San Carlos = Sant Carles, Spain 22 B8 39 3N 1 34 E
San Carlos, Argentina 94 C2 33 50S 69 0W
San Carlos, Chile 94 D1 36 10S 72 0W
San Carlos, Baja Calif. S., Mexico 86 C2 24 47N 112 6W
San Carlos, Coahuila, Mexico 86 B4 29 0N 100 54W
San Carlos, Nic. 88 D3 11 12N 84 50W
San Carlos, Phil. 37 B6 10 29N 123 25 E
San Carlos, Uruguay 95 C5 34 46S 54 58W
San Carlos, U.S.A. 83 K8 33 21N 110 27W
San Carlos, Venezuela 92 B5 9 40N 68 36W
San Carlos de Bariloche, Argentina 96 E2 41 10S 71 25W
San Carlos de Bolívar, Argentina 96 D4 36 15S 61 6W
San Carlos del Zulia, Venezuela 92 B4 9 1N 71 55W
San Carlos L., U.S.A. 83 K8 33 11N 110 32W
San Clemente, Chile 94 D1 35 30S 71 29W
San Clemente, U.S.A. 85 M9 33 26N 117 37W
San Clemente I., U.S.A. 85 N8 32 53N 118 29W
San Cristóbal = Es Migjorn Gran, Spain 22 B11 39 57N 4 3 E
San Cristóbal, Argentina 94 C3 30 20S 61 10W
San Cristóbal, Dom. Rep. 89 C5 18 25N 70 6W
San Cristóbal, Venezuela 92 B4 7 46N 72 14W
San Cristóbal de la Casas, Mexico 87 D6 16 50N 92 33W
San Diego, Calif., U.S.A. 85 N9 32 43N 117 9W
San Diego, Tex., U.S.A. 81 M5 27 46N 98 14W
San Diego, C., Argentina 96 G3 54 40S 65 10W
San Diego de la Unión, Mexico 86 C4 21 28N 100 52W
San Dimitri, Ras, Malta 23 C1 36 4N 14 11 E
San Dimitri Point = San Dimitri, Ras, Malta 23 C1 36 4N 14 11 E
San Estanislao, Paraguay 94 A4 24 39S 56 26W
San Felipe, Chile 94 C1 32 43S 70 42W
San Felipe, Mexico 86 A2 31 0N 114 52W
San Felipe, Venezuela 92 A5 10 20N 68 44W
San Felipe →, U.S.A. 85 M11 33 12N 115 49W
San Félix, Chile 94 B1 28 56S 70 28W
San Félix, Pac. Oc. 90 F2 26 23S 80 0W
San Fernando = Sant Ferran, Spain 22 C7 38 42N 1 28 E
San Fernando, Chile 94 C1 34 30S 71 0W
San Fernando, Baja Calif., Mexico 86 B1 29 55N 115 10W
San Fernando, Tamaulipas, Mexico 87 C5 24 51N 98 10W
San Fernando, La Union, Phil. 37 A6 16 40N 120 23 E
San Fernando, Pampanga, Phil. 37 A6 15 5N 120 37 E
San Fernando, Spain 19 D2 36 28N 6 17W
San Fernando, Trin. & Tob. 89 D7 10 20N 61 30W
San Fernando, U.S.A. 85 L8 34 17N 118 26W
San Fernando de Apure, Venezuela 92 B5 7 54N 67 15W
San Fernando de Atabapo, Venezuela 92 C5 4 3N 67 42W
San Francisco, Argentina 94 C3 31 30S 62 5W
San Francisco, U.S.A. 84 H4 37 47N 122 25W
San Francisco →, U.S.A. 83 K9 32 59N 109 22W
San Francisco, Paso de, S. Amer. 94 B2 27 0S 68 0W
San Francisco de Macorís, Dom. Rep. 89 C5 19 19N 70 15W
San Francisco del Monte de Oro, Argentina 94 C2 32 36S 66 8W
San Francisco del Oro, Mexico 86 B3 26 52N 105 50W
San Francisco Javier = Sant Francesc de Formentera, Spain 22 C7 38 42N 1 26 E
San Francisco Solano, Pta., Colombia 90 C3 6 18N 77 29W
San Gabriel, Chile 94 C1 33 47S 70 15W
San Gabriel Mts., U.S.A. 85 L9 34 20N 118 0W
San Gorgonio Mt., U.S.A. 85 L10 34 7N 116 51W
San Gottardo, P. del, Switz. 18 C8 46 33N 8 33 E
San Gregorio, Uruguay 95 C4 32 37S 55 40W
San Gregorio, U.S.A. 84 H4 37 20N 122 23W
San Ignacio, Belize 87 D7 17 10N 89 0W
San Ignacio, Bolivia 92 G6 16 20S 60 55W
San Ignacio, Mexico 86 B2 27 27N 113 0W
San Ignacio, Paraguay 88 C2 26 52S 57 3W
San Ignacio, L., Mexico 86 B2 26 50N 113 11W
San Ildefonso, C., Phil. 37 A6 16 0N 122 1 E
San Isidro, Argentina 94 C4 34 29S 58 31W
San Jacinto, U.S.A. 85 M10 33 47N 116 57W
San Jaime = Sant Jaume, Spain 22 B11 39 54N 4 4 E
San Javier, Misiones, Argentina 95 B4 27 55S 55 5W
San Javier, Santa Fe, Argentina 94 C4 30 40S 59 55W
San Javier, Bolivia 92 G6 16 18S 62 30W
San Javier, Chile 94 D1 35 40S 71 45W
San Jeronimo Taviche, Mexico 87 D5 16 38N 96 32W
San Joaquin, U.S.A. 84 J6 36 36N 120 11W
San Joaquin →, U.S.A. 84 G5 38 4N 121 51W
San Joaquin Valley, U.S.A. 84 J6 37 20N 121 0W
San Jon, U.S.A. 81 H3 35 6N 103 20W
San Jordi = Sant Jordi, Spain 22 B9 39 33N 2 46 E
San Jorge, Argentina 94 C3 31 54S 61 50W
San Jorge, B. de, Mexico 86 A2 31 20N 113 20W
San Jorge, G., Argentina 96 F3 46 0S 66 0W
San José = San Josep, Spain 22 C7 38 55N 1 18 E
San José, Costa Rica 88 E3 9 55N 84 2W
San José, Guatemala 88 D1 14 0N 90 50W
San José, Mexico 86 C2 25 0N 110 50W
San Jose, Mind. Occ., Phil. 37 B6 12 27N 121 4 E
San Jose, Nueva Ecija, Phil. 37 A6 15 45N 120 55 E
San Jose, U.S.A. 84 H5 37 20N 121 53W
San Jose →, U.S.A. 83 J10 34 25N 106 45W
San Jose de Buenavista, Phil. 37 B6 10 45N 121 56 E
San José de Chiquitos, Bolivia 92 G6 17 53S 60 50W
San José de Feliciano, Argentina 94 C4 30 26S 58 46W
San José de Jáchal, Argentina 94 C2 30 15S 68 46W
San José de Mayo, Uruguay 94 C4 34 27S 56 40W
San José del Cabo, Mexico 86 C3 23 0N 109 40W
San José del Guaviare, Colombia 92 C4 2 35N 72 38W
San Josep, Spain 22 C7 38 55N 1 18 E
San Juan, Argentina 94 C2 31 30S 68 30W
San Juan, Mexico 86 C4 21 20N 102 50W
San Juan, Puerto Rico 89 C6 18 28N 66 7W
San Juan □, Argentina 94 C2 31 9S 69 0W
San Juan →, Argentina 94 C2 32 20S 67 25W
San Juan →, Nic. 88 D3 10 56N 83 42W
San Juan →, U.S.A. 83 H8 37 16N 110 26W
San Juan Bautista = Sant Joan Baptista, Spain 22 B8 39 5N 1 31 E
San Juan Bautista, Paraguay 94 B4 26 37S 57 6W
San Juan Bautista, U.S.A. 84 J5 36 51N 121 32W
San Juan Bautista Valle Nacional, Mexico 87 D5 17 47N 96 19W
San Juan Capistrano, U.S.A. 85 M9 33 30N 117 40W
San Juan Cr. →, U.S.A. 84 J5 35 40N 120 22W
San Juan de Guadalupe, Mexico 86 C4 24 38N 102 44W
San Juan de la Costa, Mexico 86 C2 24 23N 110 45W
San Juan de los Morros, Venezuela 92 B5 9 55N 67 21W
San Juan del Norte, Nic. 88 D3 10 58N 83 40W
San Juan del Norte, B. de, Nic. 88 D3 11 0N 83 40W
San Juan del Río, Mexico 87 C5 20 25N 100 0W
San Juan del Sur, Nic. 88 D2 11 20N 85 51W
San Juan I., U.S.A. 84 B3 48 32N 123 5W
San Juan Mts., U.S.A. 83 H10 37 30N 107 0W
San Justo, Argentina 94 C3 30 47S 60 30W
San Kamphaeng, Thailand 38 C2 18 45N 99 8 E
San Lázaro, C., Mexico 86 C2 24 50N 112 18W
San Lázaro, Sa., Mexico 86 C3 23 25N 110 0W
San Leandro, U.S.A. 84 H4 37 44N 122 9W
San Lorenzo = Sant Llorenç des Cardassar, Spain 22 B10 39 37N 3 17 E
San Lorenzo, Argentina 94 C3 32 45S 60 45W
San Lorenzo, Ecuador 92 C3 1 15N 78 50W
San Lorenzo, Paraguay 94 B4 25 20S 57 32W
San Lorenzo →, Mexico 86 C3 24 15N 107 24W
San Lorenzo, I., Mexico 86 B2 28 35N 112 50W
San Lorenzo, Mte., Argentina 96 F2 47 40S 72 20W
San Lucas, Bolivia 92 H5 20 5S 65 7W
San Lucas, Baja Calif. S., Mexico 86 C3 22 53N 109 54W
San Lucas, Baja Calif. S., Mexico 86 B2 27 10N 112 14W
San Lucas, U.S.A. 84 J5 36 8N 121 1W
San Lucas, C., Mexico 86 C3 22 50N 110 0W
San Luis, Argentina 94 C2 33 20S 66 20W
San Luis, Cuba 88 B3 22 17N 83 46W
San Luis, Guatemala 88 C2 16 14N 89 27W
San Luis, Ariz., U.S.A. 83 K6 32 29N 114 47W
San Luis, Colo., U.S.A. 83 H11 37 12N 105 25W
San Luis □, Argentina 94 C2 34 0S 66 0W
San Luis, I., Mexico 86 B2 29 58N 114 26W
San Luis, Sierra de, Argentina 94 C2 32 30S 66 10W
San Luis de la Paz, Mexico 86 C4 21 19N 100 32W
San Luis Obispo, U.S.A. 85 K6 35 17N 120 40W
San Luis Potosí, Mexico 86 C4 22 9N 100 59W
San Luis Potosí □, Mexico 86 C4 22 10N 101 0W
San Luis Reservoir, U.S.A. 84 H5 37 4N 121 5W
San Luis Río Colorado, Mexico 86 A2 32 29N 114 58W
San Manuel, U.S.A. 83 K8 32 36N 110 38W
San Marcos, Guatemala 88 D1 14 59N 91 52W
San Marcos, Mexico 86 B2 27 13N 112 6W
San Marcos, Calif., U.S.A. 85 M9 33 9N 117 10W
San Marcos, Tex., U.S.A. 81 L6 29 53N 97 56W
San Marino, San Marino 16 G7 43 55N 12 30 E
San Marino ■, Europe 20 C5 43 56N 12 25 E
San Martín, Argentina 94 C2 33 5S 68 28W
San Martín →, Bolivia 92 F6 13 8S 63 43W
San Martín, L., Argentina 96 F2 48 50S 72 50W
San Martín de los Andes, Argentina 96 E2 40 10S 71 20W
San Mateo = Sant Mateu, Spain 22 B7 39 3N 1 23 E
San Mateo, U.S.A. 84 H4 37 34N 122 19W
San Matías, Bolivia 92 G7 16 25S 58 20W
San Matías, G., Argentina 96 E4 41 30S 64 0W
San Miguel = Sant Miguel, Spain 22 B7 39 3N 1 26 E
San Miguel, El Salv. 88 D2 13 30N 88 12W
San Miguel, Panama 88 E4 8 27N 78 55W
San Miguel, U.S.A. 84 K6 35 45N 120 42W
San Miguel →, Bolivia 92 F6 13 52S 63 56W
San Miguel de Tucumán, Argentina 94 B2 26 50S 65 20W
San Miguel del Monte, Argentina 94 D4 35 23S 58 50W
San Miguel I., U.S.A. 85 L6 34 2N 120 23W
San Nicolás, Canary Is. 22 G4 27 58N 15 47W
San Nicolás de los Arroyas, Argentina 94 C3 33 25S 60 10W
San Nicolas I., U.S.A. 85 M7 33 15N 119 30W
San Onofre, U.S.A. 85 M9 33 22N 117 34W
San Pablo, Bolivia 94 A2 21 43S 66 38W
San Pablo, U.S.A. 84 H4 37 58N 122 21W
San Pedro, Buenos Aires, Argentina 94 C4 33 40S 59 40W
San Pedro, Misiones, Argentina 95 B5 26 30S 54 10W
San Pedro, Chile 94 C1 33 54S 71 28W
San Pédro, Ivory C. 50 H4 4 50N 6 33W
San Pedro, Mexico 86 C2 23 55N 110 17W
San Pedro □, Paraguay 94 A4 24 0S 57 0W
San Pedro →, Chihuahua, Mexico 86 B3 28 20N 106 10W
San Pedro →, Nayarit, Mexico 86 C3 21 45N 105 30W
San Pedro →, U.S.A. 83 K8 32 59N 110 47W
San Pedro, Pta., Chile 94 B1 25 30S 70 38W
San Pedro Channel, U.S.A. 85 M8 33 30N 118 25W
San Pedro de Atacama, Chile 94 A2 22 55S 68 15W
San Pedro de Jujuy, Argentina 94 A3 24 12S 64 55W
San Pedro de las Colonias, Mexico 86 B4 25 50N 102 59W
San Pedro de Macorís, Dom. Rep. 89 C6 18 30N 69 18W
San Pedro del Norte, Nic. 88 D3 13 4N 84 33W
San Pedro del Paraná, Paraguay 94 B4 26 43S 56 13W
San Pedro Mártir, Sierra, Mexico 86 A1 31 0N 115 30W
San Pedro Mixtepec, Mexico 87 D5 16 2N 97 7W
San Pedro Ocampo = Melchor Ocampo, Mexico 86 C4 24 52N 101 40W

San Pedro Sula, Honduras **88 C2** 15 30N 88 0W
San Pietro, Italy **20 E3** 39 8N 8 17 E
San Quintín, Mexico **86 A1** 30 29N 115 57W
San Rafael, Argentina **94 C2** 34 40S 68 21W
San Rafael, Calif., U.S.A. **84 H4** 37 58N 122 32W
San Rafael, N. Mex., U.S.A. **83 J10** 35 7N 107 53W
San Rafael Mt., U.S.A. **85 L7** 34 41N 119 52W
San Rafael Mts., U.S.A. **85 L7** 34 40N 119 50W
San Ramón de la Nueva Orán, Argentina **94 A3** 23 10S 64 20W
San Remo, Italy **18 E7** 43 49N 7 46 E
San Roque, Argentina **94 B4** 28 25S 58 45W
San Roque, Spain **19 D3** 36 17N 5 21W
San Rosendo, Chile **94 D1** 37 16S 72 43W
San Saba, U.S.A. **81 K5** 31 12N 98 43W
San Salvador, El Salv. **88 D2** 13 40N 89 10W
San Salvador, Spain **22 B10** 39 27N 3 11 E
San Salvador de Jujuy, Argentina **94 A3** 24 10S 64 48W
San Salvador I., Bahamas **89 B5** 24 0N 74 40W
San Sebastián = Donostia-San Sebastián, Spain **19 A5** 43 17N 1 58W
San Sebastián, Argentina **96 G3** 53 10S 68 30W
San Sebastián de la Gomera, Canary Is. **22 F2** 28 5N 17 7W
San Serra = Son Serra, Spain **22 B10** 39 43N 3 13 E
San Severo, Italy **20 D6** 41 41N 15 23 E
San Simeon, U.S.A. **84 K5** 35 39N 121 11W
San Simon, U.S.A. **83 K9** 32 16N 109 14W
San Telmo = Sant Telm, Spain **22 B9** 39 35N 2 21 E
San Telmo, Mexico **86 A1** 30 58N 116 6W
San Tiburcio, Mexico **86 C4** 24 8N 101 32W
San Valentin, Mte., Chile **96 F2** 46 30S 73 30W
San Vicente de la Barquera, Spain **19 A3** 43 23N 4 29W
San Vito, Costa Rica **88 E3** 8 50N 82 58W
Sana', Yemen **46 D3** 15 27N 44 12 E
Sana →, Bos.-H. **16 F9** 45 3N 16 23 E
Sanaga →, Cameroon **52 D1** 3 35N 9 38 E
Sanaloa, Presa, Mexico **86 C3** 24 50N 107 20W
Sanana, Indonesia **37 E7** 2 4S 125 58 E
Sanand, India **42 H5** 22 59N 72 25 E
Sanandaj, Iran **44 C5** 35 18N 47 1 E
Sanandita, Bolivia **94 A3** 21 40S 63 45W
Sanawad, India **42 H7** 22 11N 76 5 E
Sancellas = Sencelles, Spain **22 B9** 39 39N 2 54 E
Sanchahe, China **35 B14** 44 50N 126 2 E
Sánchez, Dom. Rep. **89 C6** 19 15N 69 36W
Sanchor, India **42 G4** 24 45N 71 55 E
Sancti Spíritus, Cuba **88 B4** 21 52N 79 33W
Sancy, Puy de, France **18 D5** 45 32N 2 50 E
Sand →, S. Africa **57 C5** 22 25S 30 5 E
Sand Hills, U.S.A. **80 D4** 42 10N 101 30W
Sand Springs, U.S.A. **81 G6** 36 9N 96 7W
Sanda, Japan **31 G7** 34 53N 135 14 E
Sandakan, Malaysia **36 C5** 5 53N 118 4 E
Sandan = Sambor, Cambodia **38 F6** 12 46N 106 0 E
Sandanski, Bulgaria **21 D10** 41 35N 23 16 E
Sanday, U.K. **12 B6** 59 16N 2 31W
Sandefjord, Norway **9 G14** 59 10N 10 15 E
Sanders, U.S.A. **83 J9** 35 13N 109 20W
Sanderson, U.S.A. **81 K3** 30 9N 102 24W
Sandersville, U.S.A. **77 J4** 32 59N 82 48W
Sandfire Roadhouse, Australia **60 C3** 19 45S 121 15 E
Sandfly L., Canada **73 B7** 55 43N 106 6W
Sandfontein, Namibia **56 C2** 23 48S 29 1 E
Sandia, Peru **92 F5** 14 10S 69 30W
Sandila, India **43 F9** 27 5N 80 31 E
Sandnes, Norway **9 G11** 58 50N 5 45 E
Sandnessjøen, Norway **8 C15** 66 2N 12 38 E
Sandoa, Dem. Rep. of the Congo **52 F4** 9 41S 23 0 E
Sandomierz, Poland **17 C11** 50 40N 21 43 E
Sandover →, Australia **62 C2** 21 43S 136 32 E
Sandoway, Burma **41 K19** 18 20N 94 30 E
Sandoy, Færoe Is. **8 F9** 61 52N 6 46W
Sandpoint, U.S.A. **82 B5** 48 17N 116 33W
Sandray, U.K. **12 E1** 56 53N 7 31W
Sandringham, U.K. **10 E8** 52 51N 0 31 E
Sandstone, Australia **61 E2** 27 59S 119 16 E
Sandusky, Mich., U.S.A. **78 C2** 43 25N 82 50W
Sandusky, Ohio, U.S.A. **78 E2** 41 27N 82 42W
Sandviken, Sweden **9 F17** 60 38N 16 46 E
Sandwich, C., Australia **62 B4** 18 14S 146 18 E
Sandwich B., Canada **71 B8** 53 40N 57 15W
Sandwich B., Namibia **56 C1** 23 25S 14 20 E
Sandy, Oreg., U.S.A. **84 E4** 45 24N 122 16W
Sandy, Pa., U.S.A. **78 E6** 41 6N 78 46W
Sandy, Utah, U.S.A. **82 F8** 40 35N 111 50W
Sandy Bay, Canada **73 B8** 55 31N 102 19W
Sandy Bight, Australia **61 F3** 33 50S 123 20 E
Sandy C., Queens., Australia **62 C5** 24 42S 153 15 E
Sandy C., Tas., Australia **62 G3** 41 25S 144 45 E
Sandy Cay, Bahamas **89 B4** 23 13N 75 18W
Sandy Cr. →, U.S.A. **82 F9** 41 51N 109 47W
Sandy L., Canada **70 B1** 53 2N 93 0W
Sandy Lake, Canada **70 B1** 53 0N 93 15W
Sandy Valley, U.S.A. **85 K11** 35 49N 115 36W
Sanford, Fla., U.S.A. **77 L5** 28 48N 81 16W
Sanford, Maine, U.S.A. **77 D10** 43 27N 70 47W
Sanford, N.C., U.S.A. **77 H6** 35 29N 79 10W
Sanford →, Australia **61 E2** 27 22S 115 53 E
Sanford, Mt., U.S.A. **68 B5** 62 13N 144 8W
Sang-i-Masha, Afghan. **42 C2** 33 8N 67 27 E
Sanga, Mozam. **55 E4** 12 22S 35 21 E
Sanga →, Congo **52 E3** 1 5S 17 0 E
Sangamner, India **40 K9** 19 37N 74 15 E
Sangar, Afghan. **42 C1** 32 56N 65 30 E
Sangar, Russia **27 C13** 64 2N 127 31 E
Sangar Sarai, Afghan. **42 B4** 34 27N 70 35 E
Sangarh →, Pakistan **42 D4** 30 43N 70 44 E
Sangay, Ecuador **92 D3** 2 0S 78 20W
Sange, Dem. Rep. of the Congo **54 D2** 6 58S 28 21 E
Sangeang, Indonesia **37 F5** 8 12S 119 6 E
Sanger, U.S.A. **84 J7** 36 42N 119 33W
Sangerhausen, Germany **16 C6** 51 28N 11 18 E
Sanggan He →, China **34 E9** 38 12N 117 15 E
Sanggau, Indonesia **36 D4** 0 5N 110 30 E
Sanghar, Pakistan **42 F3** 26 2N 68 57 E
Sangihe, Kepulauan, Indonesia **37 D7** 3 0N 125 30 E
Sangihe, Pulau, Indonesia **37 D7** 3 35N 125 30 E
Sangju, S. Korea **35 F15** 36 25N 128 10 E
Sangkapura, Indonesia **36 F4** 5 52S 112 40 E
Sangkhla, Thailand **38 E2** 14 57N 98 28 E
Sangkulirang, Indonesia **36 D5** 0 59N 117 58 E
Sangla, Pakistan **42 D5** 31 43N 73 23 E
Sangli, India **40 L9** 16 55N 74 33 E
Sangmélima, Cameroon **52 D2** 2 57N 12 1 E
Sangod, India **42 G7** 24 55N 76 17 E
Sangre de Cristo Mts., U.S.A. **81 G2** 37 30N 105 20W
Sangrur, India **42 D6** 30 14N 75 50 E
Sangudo, Canada **72 C6** 53 50N 114 54W
Sangue →, Brazil **92 F7** 11 1S 58 39W
Sanibel, U.S.A. **77 M4** 26 26N 82 1W
Sanirajak, Canada **69 B11** 68 46N 81 12W
Sanjawi, Pakistan **42 D3** 30 17N 68 21 E
Sanje, Uganda **54 C3** 0 49S 31 30 E
Sanjo, Japan **30 F9** 37 37N 138 57 E
Sankh →, India **43 H11** 22 15N 84 48 E
Sankt Gallen, Switz. **18 C8** 47 26N 9 22 E
Sankt Moritz, Switz. **18 C8** 46 30N 9 50 E
Sankt-Peterburg, Russia **24 C5** 59 55N 30 20 E
Sankt Pölten, Austria **16 D8** 48 12N 15 38 E
Sankuru →, Dem. Rep. of the Congo **52 E4** 4 17S 20 25 E
Sanliurfa, Turkey **25 G6** 37 12N 38 50 E
Sanlúcar de Barrameda, Spain **19 D2** 36 46N 6 21W
Sanmenxia, China **34 G6** 34 47N 111 12 E
Sanming, China **33 D6** 26 15N 117 40 E
Sannaspos, S. Africa **56 D4** 29 6S 26 34 E
Sannicandro Gargánico, Italy **20 D6** 41 50N 15 34 E
Sânnicolau Mare, Romania **17 E11** 46 5N 20 39 E
Sannieshof, S. Africa **56 D4** 26 30S 25 47 E
Sannin, J., Lebanon **47 B4** 33 57N 35 52 E
Sanniquellie, Liberia **50 G4** 7 19N 8 38W
Sanok, Poland **17 D12** 49 35N 22 10 E
Sanquhar, U.K. **12 F5** 55 22N 3 54W
Sant Antoni Abat, Spain **22 C7** 38 59N 1 19 E
Sant Carles, Spain **22 B8** 39 3N 1 34 E
Sant Feliu de Guíxols, Spain **19 B7** 41 45N 3 1 E
Sant Ferran, Spain **22 C7** 38 42N 1 28 E
Sant Francesc de Formentera, Spain **22 C7** 38 42N 1 26 E
Sant Jaume, Spain **22 B11** 39 54N 4 4 E
Sant Joan Baptista, Spain **22 B8** 39 5N 1 31 E
Sant Jordi, Ibiza, Spain **22 C7** 38 53N 1 24 E
Sant Jordi, Mallorca, Spain **22 B9** 39 33N 2 46 E
Sant Jordi, G. de, Spain **19 B6** 40 53N 1 2 E
Sant Llorenç des Cardassar, Spain **22 B10** 39 37N 3 17 E
Sant Mateu, Spain **22 B7** 39 3N 1 23 E
Sant Miquel, Spain **22 B7** 39 3N 1 26 E
Sant Telm, Spain **22 B9** 39 35N 2 21 E
Santa Agnés, Spain **22 B7** 39 3N 1 21 E
Santa Ana, Bolivia **92 F5** 13 50S 65 40W
Santa Ana, El Salv. **88 D2** 14 0N 89 31W
Santa Ana, Mexico **86 A2** 30 31N 111 8W
Santa Ana, U.S.A. **85 M9** 33 46N 117 52W
Sant' Antioco, Italy **20 E3** 39 4N 8 27 E
Santa Bárbara, Chile **94 D1** 37 40S 72 1W
Santa Bárbara, Honduras **88 D2** 14 53N 88 14W
Santa Bárbara, Mexico **86 B3** 26 48N 105 50W
Santa Barbara, U.S.A. **85 L7** 34 25N 119 42W
Santa Barbara Channel, U.S.A. **85 L7** 34 15N 120 0W
Santa Barbara I., U.S.A. **85 M7** 33 29N 119 2W
Santa Catalina, Gulf of, U.S.A. **85 N9** 33 10N 117 50W
Santa Catalina, I., Mexico **86 B2** 25 40N 110 50W
Santa Catalina I., U.S.A. **85 M8** 33 23N 118 25W
Santa Catarina □, Brazil **95 B6** 27 25S 48 30W
Santa Catarina, I. de, Brazil **95 B6** 27 30S 48 40W
Santa Cecília, Brazil **95 B5** 26 56S 50 18W
Santa Clara, Cuba **88 B4** 22 20N 80 0W
Santa Clara, Calif., U.S.A. **84 H5** 37 21N 121 57W
Santa Clara, Utah, U.S.A. **83 H7** 37 8N 113 39W
Santa Clara, El Golfo de, Mexico **86 A2** 31 42N 114 30W
Santa Clara de Olimar, Uruguay **95 C5** 32 50S 54 54W
Santa Clarita, U.S.A. **85 L8** 34 24N 118 30W
Santa Clotilde, Peru **92 D4** 2 33S 73 45W
Santa Coloma de Gramenet, Spain **19 B7** 41 27N 2 13 E
Santa Cruz, Argentina **96 G3** 50 0S 68 32W
Santa Cruz, Bolivia **92 G6** 17 43S 63 10W
Santa Cruz, Chile **94 C1** 34 38S 71 27W
Santa Cruz, Costa Rica **88 D2** 10 15N 85 35W
Santa Cruz, Madeira **22 D3** 32 42N 16 46W
Santa Cruz, Phil. **37 B6** 14 20N 121 24 E
Santa Cruz, U.S.A. **84 J4** 36 58N 122 1W
Santa Cruz →, Argentina **96 G3** 50 10S 68 20W
Santa Cruz de la Palma, Canary Is. **22 F2** 28 41N 17 46W
Santa Cruz de Tenerife, Canary Is. **22 F3** 28 28N 16 15W
Santa Cruz del Norte, Cuba **88 B3** 23 9N 81 55W
Santa Cruz del Sur, Cuba **88 B4** 20 44N 78 0W
Santa Cruz do Rio Pardo, Brazil **95 A6** 22 54S 49 37W
Santa Cruz do Sul, Brazil **95 B5** 29 42S 52 25W
Santa Cruz I., U.S.A. **85 M7** 34 1N 119 43W
Santa Cruz Is., Solomon Is. **64 J8** 10 30S 166 0 E
Santa Domingo, Cay, Bahamas **88 B4** 21 25N 75 15W
Santa Elena, Argentina **94 C4** 30 58S 59 47W
Santa Elena, C., Costa Rica **88 D2** 10 54N 85 56W
Santa Eulàlia des Riu, Spain **22 C8** 38 59N 1 32 E
Santa Fe, Argentina **94 C3** 31 35S 60 41W
Santa Fe, U.S.A. **83 J11** 35 41N 105 57W
Santa Fé □, Argentina **94 C3** 31 50S 60 55W
Santa Fé do Sul, Brazil **93 H8** 20 13S 50 56W
Santa Filomena, Brazil **93 E9** 9 6S 45 50W
Santa Gertrudis, Spain **22 C7** 39 0N 1 26 E
Santa Inês, Brazil **93 F11** 13 17S 39 48W
Santa Inés, I., Chile **96 G2** 54 0S 73 0W
Santa Isabel = Rey Malabo, Eq. Guin. **52 D1** 3 45N 8 50 E
Santa Isabel, Argentina **94 D2** 36 10S 66 54W
Santa Isabel do Morro, Brazil **93 F8** 11 34S 50 40W
Santa Lucía, Corrientes, Argentina **94 B4** 28 58S 59 5W
Santa Lucía, San Juan, Argentina **94 C2** 31 30S 68 30W
Santa Lucia, Uruguay **94 C4** 34 27S 56 24W
Santa Lucia Range, U.S.A. **84 K5** 36 0N 121 20W
Santa Magdalena, I., Mexico **86 C2** 24 40N 112 15W
Santa Margarita, Argentina **94 D3** 38 28S 61 35W
Santa Margarita, Spain **22 B10** 39 42N 3 6 E
Santa Margarita, U.S.A. **84 K6** 35 23N 120 37W
Santa Margarita →, U.S.A. **85 M9** 33 13N 117 23W
Santa Margarita, I., Mexico **86 C2** 24 30N 111 50W
Santa María, Argentina **94 B2** 26 40S 66 0W
Santa Maria, Brazil **95 B5** 29 40S 53 48W
Santa Maria, U.S.A. **85 L6** 34 57N 120 26W
Santa María →, Mexico **86 A3** 31 0N 107 14W
Santa María, B. de, Mexico **86 B3** 25 10N 108 40W
Santa Maria da Vitória, Brazil **93 F10** 13 24S 44 12W
Santa Maria del Camí, Spain **22 B9** 39 38N 2 47 E
Santa Maria di Léuca, C., Italy **21 E8** 39 47N 18 22 E
Santa Marta, Colombia **92 A4** 11 15N 74 13W
Santa Marta, Sierra Nevada de, Colombia **92 A4** 10 55N 73 50W
Santa Marta Grande, C., Brazil **95 B6** 28 43S 48 50W
Santa Maura = Levkás, Greece **21 E9** 38 40N 20 43 E
Santa Monica, U.S.A. **85 M8** 34 1N 118 29W
Santa Paula, U.S.A. **85 L7** 34 21N 119 4W
Santa Ponça, Spain **22 B9** 39 30N 2 28 E
Santa Rita, U.S.A. **83 K10** 32 48N 108 4W
Santa Rosa, La Pampa, Argentina **94 D3** 36 40S 64 17W
Santa Rosa, San Luis, Argentina **94 C2** 32 21S 65 10W
Santa Rosa, Brazil **95 B5** 27 52S 54 29W
Santa Rosa, Calif., U.S.A. **84 G4** 38 26N 122 43W
Santa Rosa, N. Mex., U.S.A. **81 H2** 34 57N 104 41W
Santa Rosa de Copán, Honduras **88 D2** 14 47N 88 46W
Santa Rosa de Río Primero, Argentina **94 C3** 31 8S 63 20W
Santa Rosa del Sara, Bolivia **92 G6** 17 7S 63 35W
Santa Rosa I., Calif., U.S.A. **85 M6** 33 58N 120 6W
Santa Rosa I., Fla., U.S.A. **77 K2** 30 20N 86 50W
Santa Rosa Range, U.S.A. **82 F5** 41 45N 117 40W
Santa Rosalía, Mexico **86 B2** 27 20N 112 20W
Santa Sylvina, Argentina **94 B3** 27 50S 61 10W
Santa Tecla = Nueva San Salvador, El Salv. **88 D2** 13 40N 89 18W
Santa Teresa, Argentina **94 C3** 33 25S 60 47W
Santa Teresa, Australia **62 C1** 24 8S 134 22 E
Santa Teresa, Mexico **87 B5** 25 17N 97 51W
Santa Vitória do Palmar, Brazil **95 C5** 33 32S 53 25W
Santa Ynez →, U.S.A. **85 L6** 35 41N 120 36W
Santa Ynez Mts., U.S.A. **85 L6** 34 30N 120 0W
Santa Ysabel, U.S.A. **85 M10** 33 7N 116 40W
Santai, China **32 C5** 31 5N 104 58 E
Santana, Madeira **22 D3** 32 48N 16 52W
Santana, Coxilha de, Brazil **95 C4** 30 50S 55 35W
Santana do Livramento, Brazil **95 C4** 30 55S 55 30W
Santander, Spain **19 A4** 43 27N 3 51W
Santander Jiménez, Mexico **87 C5** 24 11N 98 29W
Santanilla, Is., Honduras **88 C3** 17 22N 83 57W
Santanyí, Spain **22 B10** 39 20N 3 5 E
Santaquin, U.S.A. **82 G8** 39 59N 111 47W
Santarém, Brazil **93 D8** 2 25S 54 42W
Santarém, Portugal **19 C1** 39 12N 8 42W
Santaren Channel, W. Indies **88 B4** 24 0N 79 30W
Santee, U.S.A. **85 N10** 32 50N 116 58W
Santee →, U.S.A. **77 J6** 33 7N 79 17W
Santiago, Brazil **95 B5** 29 11S 54 52W
Santiago, Chile **94 C1** 33 24S 70 40W
Santiago, Panama **88 E3** 8 0N 81 0W
Santiago □, Chile **94 C1** 33 30S 70 50W
Santiago →, Mexico **66 G9** 25 11N 105 26W
Santiago →, Peru **92 D3** 4 27S 77 38W
Santiago de Compostela, Spain **19 A1** 42 52N 8 37W
Santiago de Cuba, Cuba **88 C4** 20 0N 75 49W
Santiago de los Cabelleros, Dom. Rep. **89 C5** 19 30N 70 40W
Santiago del Estero, Argentina **94 B3** 27 50S 64 15W
Santiago del Estero □, Argentina **94 B3** 27 40S 63 15W
Santiago del Teide, Canary Is. **22 F3** 28 17N 16 48W
Santiago Ixcuintla, Mexico **86 C3** 21 50N 105 11W
Santiago Papasquiaro, Mexico **86 C3** 25 0N 105 20W
Santiaguillo, L. de, Mexico **86 C4** 24 50N 104 50W
Santo Amaro, Brazil **93 F11** 12 30S 38 43W
Santo Anastácio, Brazil **95 A5** 21 58S 51 39W
Santo André, Brazil **95 A6** 23 39S 46 29W
Santo Ângelo, Brazil **95 B5** 28 15S 54 15W
Santo Antônio do Içá, Brazil **92 D5** 3 5S 67 57W
Santo Antônio do Leverger, Brazil **93 G7** 15 52S 56 5W
Santo Domingo, Dom. Rep. **89 C6** 18 30N 69 59W
Santo Domingo, Baja Calif., Mexico **86 A1** 30 43N 116 2W
Santo Domingo, Baja Calif. S., Mexico **86 B2** 25 32N 112 2W
Santo Domingo, Nic. **88 D3** 12 14N 84 59W
Santo Domingo de los Colorados, Ecuador **92 D3** 0 15S 79 9W
Santo Domingo Pueblo, U.S.A. **83 J10** 35 31N 106 22W
Santo Tomás, Mexico **86 A1** 31 33N 116 24W
Santo Tomás, Peru **92 F4** 14 26S 72 8W
Santo Tomé, Argentina **95 B4** 28 40S 56 5W
Santo Tomé de Guayana = Ciudad Guayana, Venezuela **92 B6** 8 0N 62 30W
Santoña, Spain **19 A4** 43 29N 3 27W
Santorini = Thira, Greece **21 F11** 36 23N 25 27 E
Santos, Brazil **95 A6** 24 0S 46 20W
Santos Dumont, Brazil **95 A7** 22 55S 43 10W
Sanwer, India **42 H6** 22 59N 75 50 E
Sanyuan, China **34 G5** 34 35N 108 58 E
São Bernardo do Campo, Brazil **95 A6** 23 45S 46 34W
São Borja, Brazil **95 B4** 28 39S 56 0W
São Carlos, Brazil **95 A6** 22 0S 47 50W
São Cristóvão, Brazil **93 F11** 11 1S 37 15W
São Domingos, Brazil **93 F9** 13 25S 46 19W
São Francisco, Brazil **93 G10** 16 0S 44 50W
São Francisco →, Brazil **93 F11** 10 30S 36 24W
São Francisco do Sul, Brazil **95 B6** 26 15S 48 36W
São Gabriel, Brazil **95 C5** 30 20S 54 20W
São Gonçalo, Brazil **95 A7** 22 48S 43 5W
Sao Hill, Tanzania **55 D4** 8 20S 35 12 E
São João da Boa Vista, Brazil **95 A6** 22 0S 46 52W
São João da Madeira, Portugal **19 B1** 40 54N 8 30W
São João del Rei, Brazil **95 A7** 21 8S 44 15W
São João do Araguaia, Brazil **93 E9** 5 23S 48 46W
São João do Piauí, Brazil **93 E10** 8 21S 42 15W
São Joaquim, Brazil **95 B6** 28 18S 49 56W
São Jorge, Pta. de, Madeira **22 D3** 32 50N 16 53W
São José, Brazil **95 B5** 27 38S 48 39W
São José do Norte, Brazil **95 C5** 32 1S 52 3W
São José do Rio Prêto, Brazil **95 A6** 20 50S 49 20W
São José dos Campos, Brazil **95 A6** 23 7S 45 52W
São Leopoldo, Brazil **95 B5** 29 50S 51 10W
São Lourenço, Brazil **95 A6** 22 7S 45 3W
São Lourenço →, Brazil **93 G7** 17 53S 57 27W
São Lourenço, Pta. de, Madeira **22 D3** 32 44N 16 39W
São Lourenço do Sul, Brazil **95 C5** 31 22S 51 58W
São Luís, Brazil **93 D10** 2 39S 44 15W
São Luís Gonzaga, Brazil **95 B5** 28 25S 55 0W
São Marcos →, Brazil **93 G9** 18 15S 47 37W
São Marcos, B. de, Brazil **93 D10** 2 0S 44 0W
São Mateus, Brazil **93 G11** 18 44S 39 50W
São Mateus do Sul, Brazil **95 B5** 25 52S 50 23W
São Miguel do Oeste, Brazil **95 B5** 26 45S 53 34W
São Paulo, Brazil **95 A6** 23 32S 46 37W
São Paulo □, Brazil **95 A6** 22 0S 49 0W
São Paulo, I., Atl. Oc. **2 D8** 0 50N 31 40W
São Paulo de Olivença, Brazil **92 D5** 3 27S 68 48W
São Roque, Madeira **22 D3** 32 46N 16 48W
São Roque, C. de, Brazil **93 E11** 5 30S 35 16W
São Sebastião, I. de, Brazil **95 A6** 23 50S 45 18W
São Sebastião do Paraíso, Brazil **95 A6** 20 54S 46 59W
São Tomé, São Tomé & Principe **48 F4** 0 10N 6 39 E
São Tomé, C. de, Brazil **95 A7** 22 0S 40 59W
São Tomé & Principe ■, Africa **49 F4** 0 12N 6 39 E
São Vicente, Brazil **95 A6** 23 57S 46 23W
São Vicente, Madeira **22 D2** 32 48N 17 3W
São Vicente, C. de, Portugal **19 D1** 37 0N 9 0W
Saona, I., Dom. Rep. **89 C6** 18 10N 68 40W
Saône →, France **18 D6** 45 44N 4 50 E
Saonek, Indonesia **37 E8** 0 22S 130 55 E
Saparua, Indonesia **37 E7** 3 33S 128 40 E
Sapele, Nigeria **50 G7** 5 50N 5 40 E
Sapelo I., U.S.A. **77 K5** 31 25N 81 12W
Saposoa, Peru **92 E3** 6 55S 76 45W
Sapphire, Australia **62 C4** 23 28S 147 43 E
Sappho, U.S.A. **84 B2** 48 4N 124 16W
Sapporo, Japan **30 C10** 43 0N 141 21 E
Sapulpa, U.S.A. **81 H6** 35 59N 96 5W
Saqqez, Iran **44 B5** 36 15N 46 20 E
Sar Dasht, Iran **45 C6** 32 32N 48 52 E
Sar-e Pol □, Afghan. **40 B4** 36 20N 65 50 E
Sar Gachineh = Yāsūj, Iran **45 D6** 30 31N 51 31 E
Sar Planina, Macedonia **21 C9** 42 0N 21 0 E
Sara Buri = Saraburi, Thailand **38 E3** 14 30N 100 55 E
Sarāb, Iran **44 B5** 37 55N 47 40 E
Sarabadi, Iraq **44 C5** 33 1N 44 48 E
Saraburi, Thailand **38 E3** 14 30N 100 55 E
Saradiya, India **42 J4** 21 34N 70 2 E
Saragossa = Zaragoza, Spain **19 B5** 41 39N 0 53W
Saraguro, Ecuador **92 D3** 3 35S 79 16W
Sarai Naurang, Pakistan **42 C4** 32 50N 70 47 E
Saraikela, India **43 H11** 22 42N 85 56 E
Sarajevo, Bos.-H. **21 C8** 43 52N 18 26 E
Sarakhs, Turkmenistan **45 B9** 36 32N 61 13 E
Saran, Gunung, Indonesia **36 E4** 0 30S 111 25 E
Saranac L., U.S.A. **79 B10** 44 20N 74 10W
Saranac Lake, U.S.A. **79 B10** 44 20N 74 8W
Saranda, Tanzania **54 D3** 5 45S 34 59 E
Sarandí del Yi, Uruguay **95 C4** 33 18S 55 38W
Sarandí Grande, Uruguay **94 C4** 33 44S 56 20W
Sarangani B., Phil. **37 C7** 6 0N 125 13 E
Sarangani Is., Phil. **37 C7** 5 25N 125 25 E
Sarangarh, India **41 J13** 21 30N 83 5 E
Saransk, Russia **24 D8** 54 10N 45 10 E
Sarapul, Russia **24 C9** 56 28N 53 48 E
Sarasota, U.S.A. **77 M4** 27 20N 82 32W
Saratoga, Calif., U.S.A. **84 H4** 37 16N 122 2W
Saratoga, Wyo., U.S.A. **82 F10** 41 27N 106 49W
Saratoga Springs, U.S.A. **79 C11** 43 5N 73 47W
Saratok, Malaysia **36 D4** 1 55N 111 17 E
Saratov, Russia **25 D8** 51 30N 46 2 E
Saravane, Laos **38 E6** 15 43N 106 25 E
Sarawak □, Malaysia **36 D4** 2 0N 113 0 E
Saray, Turkey **21 D12** 41 26N 27 55 E
Sarayköy, Turkey **21 F13** 37 55N 28 54 E
Sarbāz, Iran **45 E9** 26 38N 61 19 E
Sarbīsheh, Iran **45 C8** 32 30N 59 40 E
Sarda →, India **41 F12** 27 21N 81 23 E
Sardarshahr, India **42 E6** 28 30N 74 29 E
Sardegna □, Italy **20 D3** 40 0N 9 0 E
Sardhana, India **42 E7** 29 9N 77 39 E
Sardina, Pta., Canary Is. **22 F4** 28 9N 15 44W
Sardinia = Sardegna □, Italy **20 D3** 40 0N 9 0 E
Sardis, Turkey **21 E12** 38 28N 28 2 E
Sārdūīyeh = Dar Mazār, Iran **45 D8** 29 14N 57 20 E
S'Arenal, Spain **22 B9** 39 30N 2 45 E
Sargasso Sea, Atl. Oc. **66 G13** 27 0N 72 0W
Sargodha, Pakistan **42 C5** 32 10N 72 40 E
Sarh, Chad **51 G9** 9 5N 18 23 E
Sārī, Iran **45 B7** 36 30N 53 4 E
Saria, India **43 J10** 21 38N 83 22 E
Sariab, Pakistan **42 D2** 30 6N 66 59 E
Sarıgöl, Turkey **21 E13** 38 14N 28 41 E
Sarikei, Malaysia **36 D4** 2 8N 111 30 E
Sarila, India **43 G8** 25 46N 79 41 E
Sarina, Australia **62 C4** 21 22S 149 13 E
Sarita, U.S.A. **81 M6** 27 13N 97 47W
Sariwŏn, N. Korea **35 E13** 38 31N 125 46 E
Sarju →, India **43 F9** 27 21N 81 23 E
Sark, U.K. **11 H5** 49 25N 2 22W
Sarkari Tala, India **42 F4** 27 39N 70 52 E
Şarköy, Turkey **21 D12** 40 36N 27 6 E
Sarlat-la-Canéda, France **18 D4** 44 54N 1 13 E
Sarmi, Indonesia **37 E9** 1 49S 138 44 E
Sarmiento, Argentina **96 F3** 45 35S 69 5W
Särna, Sweden **9 F15** 61 41N 13 8 E
Sarnia, Canada **78 D2** 42 58N 82 23W
Sarolangun, Indonesia **36 E2** 2 19S 102 42 E
Saronikós Kólpos, Greece **21 F10** 37 45N 23 45 E
Saros Körfezi, Turkey **21 D12** 40 30N 26 15 E
Sarpsborg, Norway **9 G14** 59 16N 11 7 E
Sarre = Saar →, Europe **18 B7** 49 41N 6 32 E
Sarreguemines, France **18 B7** 49 5N 7 4 E
Sarthe →, France **18 C3** 47 33N 0 31W
Saruna →, Pakistan **42 F2** 26 31N 67 7 E

Sarvar, *India* **42 F6** 26 4N 75 0 E
Sarvestān, *Iran* **45 D7** 29 20N 53 10 E
Sary-Tash, *Kyrgyzstan* **26 F8** 39 44N 73 15 E
Saryshagan, *Kazakstan* **26 E8** 46 12N 73 38 E
Sasan Gir, *India* **42 J4** 21 10N 70 36 E
Sasaram, *India* **43 G11** 24 57N 84 5 E
Sasebo, *Japan* **31 H4** 33 10N 129 43 E
Saser, *India* **43 B7** 34 50N 77 50 E
Saskatchewan □, *Canada* **73 C7** 54 40N 106 0W
Saskatchewan →, *Canada* **73 C8** 53 37N 100 40W
Saskatoon, *Canada* **73 C7** 52 10N 106 38W
Saskylakh, *Russia* **27 B12** 71 55N 114 1 E
Sasolburg, *S. Africa* **57 D4** 26 46S 27 49 E
Sasovo, *Russia* **24 D7** 54 25N 41 55 E
Sassandra, *Ivory C.* **50 H4** 4 55N 6 8W
Sassandra →, *Ivory C.* **50 H4** 4 58N 6 5W
Sássari, *Italy* **20 D3** 40 43N 8 34 E
Sassnitz, *Germany* **16 A7** 54 29N 13 39 E
Sassuolo, *Italy* **20 B4** 44 33N 10 47 E
Sasumua Dam, *Kenya* **54 C4** 0 45S 36 40 E
Sasyk, Ozero, *Ukraine* **17 F15** 45 45N 29 20 E
Sata-Misaki, *Japan* **31 J5** 31 0N 130 40 E
Satadougou, *Mali* **50 F3** 12 25N 11 25W
Satakunta, *Finland* **9 F20** 61 45N 23 0 E
Satara, *India* **40 L8** 17 44N 73 58 E
Satara, *S. Africa* **57 C5** 24 29S 31 47 E
Satbarwa, *India* **43 H11** 23 55N 84 16 E
Satevó, *Mexico* **86 B3** 27 57N 106 7W
Satilla →, *U.S.A.* **77 K5** 30 59N 81 29W
Satka, *Russia* **24 C10** 55 3N 59 1 E
Satmala Hills, *India* **40 J9** 20 15N 74 40 E
Satna, *India* **43 G9** 24 35N 80 50 E
Sátoraljaújhely, *Hungary* **17 D11** 48 25N 21 41 E
Satpura Ra., *India* **40 J10** 21 25N 76 10 E
Satsuna-Shotō, *Japan* **31 K5** 30 0N 130 0 E
Sattahip, *Thailand* **38 F3** 12 41N 100 54 E
Satu Mare, *Romania* **17 E12** 47 46N 22 55 E
Satui, *Indonesia* **36 E5** 3 50S 115 27 E
Satun, *Thailand* **39 J3** 6 43N 100 2 E
Saturnina →, *Brazil* **92 F7** 12 15S 58 10W
Sauce, *Argentina* **94 C4** 30 5S 58 46W
Sauceda, *Mexico* **86 B4** 25 55N 101 18W
Saucillo, *Mexico* **86 B3** 28 1N 105 17W
Sauda, *Norway* **9 G12** 59 40N 6 20 E
Sauðarkrókur, *Iceland* **8 D4** 65 45N 19 40W
Saudi Arabia ■, *Asia* **46 B3** 26 0N 44 0 E
Sauerland, *Germany* **16 C4** 51 12N 7 59 E
Saugeen →, *Canada* **78 B3** 44 30N 81 22W
Saugerties, *U.S.A.* **79 D11** 42 5N 73 57W
Saugus, *U.S.A.* **85 L8** 34 25N 118 32W
Sauk Centre, *U.S.A.* **80 C7** 45 44N 94 57W
Sauk Rapids, *U.S.A.* **80 C7** 45 35N 94 10W
Sault Ste. Marie, *Canada* **70 C3** 46 30N 84 20W
Sault Ste. Marie, *U.S.A.* **69 D11** 46 30N 84 21W
Saumlaki, *Indonesia* **37 F8** 7 55S 131 20 E
Saumur, *France* **18 C3** 47 15N 0 5W
Saunders, C., *N.Z.* **59 L3** 45 53S 170 45 E
Saunders I., *Antarctica* **5 B1** 57 48S 26 28W
Saunders Point, *Australia* **61 E4** 27 52S 125 38 E
Saurimo, *Angola* **52 F4** 9 40S 20 12 E
Sausalito, *U.S.A.* **84 H4** 37 51N 122 29W
Savá, *Honduras* **88 C2** 15 32N 86 15W
Sava →, *Serbia, Yug.* **21 B9** 44 50N 20 26 E
Savage, *U.S.A.* **80 B2** 47 27N 104 21W
Savage I. = Niue, *Cook Is.* **65 J11** 19 2S 169 54W
Savage River, *Australia* **62 G4** 41 31S 145 14 E
Savai'i, *Samoa* **59 A12** 13 28S 172 24W
Savalou, *Benin* **50 G6** 7 57N 1 58 E
Savane, *Mozam.* **55 F4** 19 37S 35 8 E
Savanna, *U.S.A.* **80 D9** 42 5N 90 8W
Savanna-la-Mar, *Jamaica* **88 C4** 18 10N 78 10W
Savannah, *Ga., U.S.A.* **77 J5** 32 5N 81 6W
Savannah, *Mo., U.S.A.* **80 F7** 39 56N 94 50W
Savannah, *Tenn., U.S.A.* **77 H1** 35 14N 88 15W
Savannah →, *U.S.A.* **77 J5** 32 2N 80 53W
Savannakhet, *Laos* **38 D5** 16 30N 104 49 E
Savant L., *Canada* **70 B1** 50 16N 90 44W
Savant Lake, *Canada* **70 B1** 50 14N 90 40W
Save →, *Mozam.* **57 C5** 21 16S 34 0 E
Sāveh, *Iran* **45 C6** 35 2N 50 20 E
Savelugu, *Ghana* **50 G5** 9 38N 0 54W
Savo, *Finland* **8 E22** 62 45N 27 30 E
Savoie □, *France* **18 D7** 45 26N 6 25 E
Savona, *Italy* **18 D8** 44 17N 8 30 E
Savona, *U.S.A.* **78 D7** 42 17N 77 13W
Savonlinna, *Finland* **24 B4** 61 52N 28 53 E
Savoy = Savoie □, *France* **18 D7** 45 26N 6 25 E
Savur, *Turkey* **44 B4** 37 34N 40 53 E
Sawahlunto, *Indonesia* **36 E2** 0 40S 100 52 E
Sawai, *Indonesia* **37 E7** 3 0S 129 5 E
Sawai Madhopur, *India* **42 G7** 26 0N 76 25 E
Sawang Daen Din, *Thailand* **38 D4** 17 28N 103 28 E
Sawankhalok, *Thailand* **38 D2** 17 19N 99 50 E
Sawara, *Japan* **31 G10** 35 55N 140 30 E
Sawatch Range, *U.S.A.* **83 G10** 38 30N 106 30W
Sawel Mt., *U.K.* **13 B4** 54 50N 7 2W
Sawi, *Thailand* **39 G2** 10 14N 99 5 E
Sawmills, *Zimbabwe* **55 F2** 19 30S 28 2 E
Sawtooth Range, *U.S.A.* **82 E6** 44 3N 114 58W
Sawu, *Indonesia* **37 F6** 10 35S 121 50 E
Sawu Sea, *Indonesia* **37 F6** 9 30S 121 50 E
Saxby →, *Australia* **62 B3** 18 25S 140 53 E
Saxmundham, *U.K.* **11 E9** 52 13N 1 30 E
Saxony = Sachsen □, *Germany* **16 C7** 50 55N 13 10 E
Saxony, Lower = Niedersachsen □, *Germany* **16 B5** 52 50N 9 0 E
Saxton, *U.S.A.* **78 F6** 40 13N 78 15W
Sayabec, *Canada* **71 C6** 48 35N 67 41W
Sayaboury, *Laos* **38 C3** 19 15N 101 45 E
Sayán, *Peru* **92 F3** 11 8S 77 12W
Sayan, Vostochnyy, *Russia* **27 D10** 54 0N 96 0 E
Sayan, Zapadnyy, *Russia* **27 D10** 52 30N 94 0 E
Saydā, *Lebanon* **47 B4** 33 35N 35 25 E
Sayhandulaan = Oldziyt, *Mongolia* **34 B5** 44 40N 109 1 E
Sayḥūt, *Yemen* **46 D5** 15 12N 51 10 E
Saylac = Zeila, *Somali Rep.* **46 E3** 11 21N 43 30 E
Saynshand, *Mongolia* **33 B6** 44 55N 110 11 E
Sayre, *Okla., U.S.A.* **81 H5** 35 18N 99 38W
Sayre, *Pa., U.S.A.* **79 E8** 41 59N 76 32W
Sayreville, *U.S.A.* **79 F10** 40 28N 74 22W
Sayula, *Mexico* **86 D4** 19 50N 103 40W
Sayward, *Canada* **72 C3** 50 21N 125 55W
Sazanit, *Albania* **21 D8** 40 30N 19 20 E
Sázava →, *Czech Rep.* **16 D8** 49 53N 14 24 E
Sazin, *Pakistan* **43 B5** 35 35N 73 30 E
Scafell Pike, *U.K.* **10 C4** 54 27N 3 14W
Scalloway, *U.K.* **12 A7** 60 9N 1 17W
Scalpay, *U.K.* **12 D3** 57 18N 6 0W
Scandia, *Canada* **72 C6** 50 20N 112 0W
Scandicci, *Italy* **20 C4** 43 45N 11 11 E
Scandinavia, *Europe* **8 E16** 64 0N 12 0 E
Scapa Flow, *U.K.* **12 C5** 58 53N 3 3W
Scappoose, *U.S.A.* **84 E4** 45 45N 122 53W
Scarba, *U.K.* **12 E3** 56 11N 5 43W
Scarborough, *Trin. & Tob.* **89 D7** 11 11N 60 42W
Scarborough, *U.K.* **10 C7** 54 17N 0 24W
Scariff I., *Ireland* **13 E1** 51 44N 10 15W
Scarp, *U.K.* **12 C1** 58 1N 7 8W
Scebeli, Wabi →, *Somali Rep.* **46 G3** 2 0N 44 0 E
Schaffhausen, *Switz.* **18 C8** 47 42N 8 39 E
Schagen, *Neths.* **15 B4** 52 49N 4 48 E
Schaghticoke, *U.S.A.* **79 D11** 42 54N 73 35W
Schefferville, *Canada* **71 B6** 54 48N 66 50W
Schelde →, *Belgium* **15 C4** 51 15N 4 16 E
Schell Creek Ra., *U.S.A.* **82 G6** 39 15N 114 30W
Schellsburg, *U.S.A.* **78 F6** 40 3N 78 39W
Schenectady, *U.S.A.* **79 D11** 42 49N 73 57W
Schenevus, *U.S.A.* **79 D10** 42 33N 74 50W
Schiedam, *Neths.* **15 C4** 51 55N 4 25 E
Schiermonnikoog, *Neths.* **15 A6** 53 30N 6 15 E
Schio, *Italy* **20 B4** 45 43N 11 21 E
Schleswig, *Germany* **16 A5** 54 31N 9 34 E
Schleswig-Holstein □, *Germany* **16 A5** 54 30N 9 30 E
Schoharie, *U.S.A.* **79 D10** 42 40N 74 19W
Schoharie →, *U.S.A.* **79 D10** 42 57N 74 18W
Scholls, *U.S.A.* **84 E4** 45 24N 122 56W
Schouten I., *Australia* **62 G4** 42 20S 148 20 E
Schouten Is. = Supiori, *Indonesia* **37 E9** 1 0S 136 0 E
Schouwen, *Neths.* **15 C3** 51 43N 3 45 E
Schreiber, *Canada* **70 C2** 48 45N 87 20W
Schroffenstein, *Namibia* **56 D2** 27 11S 18 42 E
Schroon Lake, *U.S.A.* **79 C11** 43 50N 73 46W
Schuler, *Canada* **73 C6** 50 20N 110 6W
Schumacher, *Canada* **70 C3** 48 30N 81 16W
Schurz, *U.S.A.* **82 G4** 38 57N 118 49W
Schuyler, *U.S.A.* **80 E6** 41 27N 97 4W
Schuylerville, *U.S.A.* **79 C11** 43 6N 73 35W
Schuylkill →, *U.S.A.* **79 G9** 39 53N 75 12W
Schuylkill Haven, *U.S.A.* **79 F8** 40 37N 76 11W
Schwäbische Alb, *Germany* **16 D5** 48 20N 9 30 E
Schwaner, Pegunungan, *Indonesia* **36 E4** 1 0S 112 30 E
Schwarzrand, *Namibia* **56 D2** 25 37S 16 50 E
Schwarzwald, *Germany* **16 D5** 48 30N 8 20 E
Schwedt, *Germany* **16 B8** 53 3N 14 16 E
Schweinfurt, *Germany* **16 C6** 50 3N 10 14 E
Schweizer-Reneke, *S. Africa* **56 D4** 27 11S 25 18 E
Schwenningen = Villingen-Schwenningen, *Germany* **16 D5** 48 3N 8 26 E
Schwerin, *Germany* **16 B6** 53 36N 11 22 E
Schwyz, *Switz.* **18 C8** 47 2N 8 39 E
Sciacca, *Italy* **20 F5** 37 31N 13 3 E
Scilla, *Italy* **20 E6** 38 15N 15 43 E
Scilly, Isles of, *U.K.* **11 H1** 49 56N 6 22W
Scioto →, *U.S.A.* **76 F4** 38 44N 83 1W
Scituate, *U.S.A.* **79 D14** 42 12N 70 44W
Scobey, *U.S.A.* **80 A2** 48 47N 105 25W
Scone, *Australia* **63 E5** 32 5S 150 52 E
Scoresbysund = Ittoqqortoormiit, *Greenland* **4 B6** 70 20N 23 0W
Scotia, *Calif., U.S.A.* **82 F1** 40 29N 124 6W
Scotia, *N.Y., U.S.A.* **79 D11** 42 50N 73 58W
Scotia Sea, *Antarctica* **5 B18** 56 5S 56 0W
Scotland, *Canada* **78 C4** 43 1N 80 22W
Scotland □, *U.K.* **12 E5** 57 0N 4 0W
Scott, C., *Australia* **60 B4** 13 30S 129 49 E
Scott City, *U.S.A.* **80 F4** 38 29N 100 54W
Scott Glacier, *Antarctica* **5 C8** 66 15S 100 5 E
Scott I., *Antarctica* **5 C11** 67 0S 179 0 E
Scott Is., *Canada* **72 C3** 50 48N 128 40W
Scott L., *Canada* **73 B7** 59 55N 106 18W
Scott Reef, *Australia* **60 B3** 14 0S 121 50 E
Scottburgh, *S. Africa* **57 E5** 30 15S 30 47 E
Scottdale, *U.S.A.* **78 F5** 40 6N 79 35W
Scottish Borders □, *U.K.* **12 F6** 55 35N 2 50W
Scottsbluff, *U.S.A.* **80 E3** 41 52N 103 40W
Scottsboro, *U.S.A.* **77 H3** 34 40N 86 2W
Scottsburg, *U.S.A.* **76 F3** 38 41N 85 47W
Scottsdale, *Australia* **62 G4** 41 9S 147 31 E
Scottsdale, *U.S.A.* **83 K7** 33 29N 111 56W
Scottsville, *Ky., U.S.A.* **77 G2** 36 45N 86 11W
Scottsville, *N.Y., U.S.A.* **78 C7** 43 2N 77 47W
Scottville, *U.S.A.* **76 D2** 43 58N 86 17W
Scranton, *U.S.A.* **79 E9** 41 25N 75 40W
Scugog, L., *Canada* **78 B6** 44 10N 78 55W
Scunthorpe, *U.K.* **10 D7** 53 36N 0 39W
Scutari = Shkodër, *Albania* **21 C8** 42 4N 19 32 E
Seabrook, L., *Australia* **61 F2** 30 55S 119 40 E
Seaford, *U.K.* **11 G8** 50 47N 0 7 E
Seaford, *U.S.A.* **76 F8** 38 39N 75 37W
Seaforth, *Australia* **62 C4** 20 55S 148 57 E
Seaforth, *Canada* **78 C3** 43 35N 81 25W
Seaforth, L., *U.K.* **12 D2** 57 52N 6 36W
Seagraves, *U.S.A.* **81 J3** 32 57N 102 34W
Seaham, *U.K.* **10 C6** 54 50N 1 20W
Seal →, *Canada* **73 B10** 59 4N 94 48W
Seal L., *Canada* **71 B7** 54 20N 61 30W
Sealy, *U.S.A.* **81 L6** 29 47N 96 9W
Searchlight, *U.S.A.* **85 K12** 35 28N 114 55W
Searcy, *U.S.A.* **81 H9** 35 15N 91 44W
Searles L., *U.S.A.* **85 K9** 35 44N 117 21W
Seascale, *U.K.* **10 C4** 54 24N 3 29W
Seaside, *Calif., U.S.A.* **84 J5** 36 37N 121 50W
Seaside, *Oreg., U.S.A.* **84 E3** 46 0N 123 56W
Seaspray, *Australia* **63 F4** 38 25S 147 15 E
Seattle, *U.S.A.* **84 C4** 47 36N 122 20W
Seaview Ra., *Australia* **62 B4** 18 40S 145 45 E
Sebago L., *U.S.A.* **79 C14** 43 52N 70 34W
Sebago Lake, *U.S.A.* **79 C14** 43 51N 70 34W
Sebastián Vizcaíno, B., *Mexico* **86 B2** 28 0N 114 30W
Sebastopol = Sevastopol, *Ukraine* **25 F5** 44 35N 33 30 E
Sebastopol, *U.S.A.* **84 G4** 38 24N 122 49W
Sebewaing, *U.S.A.* **76 D4** 43 44N 83 27W
Sebha = Sabhah, *Libya* **51 C8** 27 9N 14 29 E
Şebinkarahisar, *Turkey* **25 F6** 40 22N 38 28 E
Sebring, *Fla., U.S.A.* **77 M5** 27 30N 81 27W
Sebring, *Ohio, U.S.A.* **78 F3** 40 55N 81 2W
Sebringville, *Canada* **78 C3** 43 24N 81 4W
Sebta = Ceuta, *N. Afr.* **19 E3** 35 52N 5 18W
Sebuku, *Indonesia* **36 E5** 3 30S 116 25 E
Sebuku, Teluk, *Malaysia* **36 D5** 4 0N 118 10 E
Sechelt, *Canada* **72 D4** 49 25N 123 42W
Sechura, Desierto de, *Peru* **92 E2** 6 0S 80 30W
Secretary I., *N.Z.* **59 L1** 45 15S 166 56 E
Secunderabad, *India* **40 L11** 17 28N 78 30 E
Security-Widefield, *U.S.A.* **80 F2** 38 45N 104 45W
Sedalia, *U.S.A.* **80 F8** 38 42N 93 14W
Sedan, *France* **18 B6** 49 43N 4 57 E
Sedan, *U.S.A.* **81 G6** 37 8N 96 11W
Seddon, *N.Z.* **59 J5** 41 40S 174 7 E
Seddonville, *N.Z.* **59 J4** 41 33S 172 1 E
Sedé Boqér, *Israel* **47 E3** 30 52N 34 47 E
Sedeh, *Fārs, Iran* **45 D7** 30 45N 52 11 E
Sedeh, *Khorāsān, Iran* **45 C8** 33 20N 59 14 E
Sederot, *Israel* **47 D3** 31 32N 34 37 E
Sédhiou, *Senegal* **50 F2** 12 44N 15 30W
Sedley, *Canada* **73 C8** 50 10N 104 0W
Sedona, *U.S.A.* **83 J8** 34 52N 111 46W
Sedova, Pik, *Russia* **26 B6** 73 29N 54 58 E
Sedro Woolley, *U.S.A.* **84 B4** 48 30N 122 14W
Seeheim, *Namibia* **56 D2** 26 50S 17 45 E
Seeis, *Namibia* **56 C2** 22 29S 17 39 E
Seekoei →, *S. Africa* **56 E4** 30 18S 25 1 E
Seeley's Bay, *Canada* **79 B8** 44 29N 76 14W
Seferihisar, *Turkey* **21 E12** 38 10N 26 50 E
Seg-ozero, *Russia* **24 B5** 63 20N 33 46 E
Segamat, *Malaysia* **39 L4** 2 30N 102 50 E
Segesta, *Italy* **20 F5** 37 56N 12 50 E
Seget, *Indonesia* **37 E8** 1 24S 130 58 E
Segezha, *Russia* **24 B5** 63 44N 34 19 E
Ségou, *Mali* **50 F4** 13 30N 6 16W
Segovia = Coco →, *Cent. Amer.* **88 D3** 15 0N 83 8W
Segovia, *Spain* **19 B3** 40 57N 4 10W
Segre →, *Spain* **19 B6** 41 40N 0 43 E
Séguéla, *Ivory C.* **50 G4** 7 55N 6 40W
Seguin, *U.S.A.* **81 L6** 29 34N 97 58W
Segundo →, *Argentina* **94 C3** 30 53S 62 44W
Segura →, *Spain* **19 C5** 38 3N 0 44W
Seh Konj, Kūh-e, *Iran* **45 D8** 30 6N 57 30 E
Seh Qal'eh, *Iran* **45 C8** 33 40N 58 24 E
Sehitwa, *Botswana* **56 C3** 20 30S 22 30 E
Sehore, *India* **42 H7** 23 10N 77 5 E
Sehwan, *Pakistan* **42 F2** 26 28N 67 53 E
Seil, *U.K.* **12 E3** 56 18N 5 38W
Seiland, *Norway* **8 A20** 70 25N 23 15 E
Seiling, *U.S.A.* **81 G5** 36 9N 98 56W
Seinäjoki, *Finland* **9 E20** 62 40N 22 51 E
Seine →, *France* **18 B4** 49 26N 0 26 E
Seistan = Sīstān, *Asia* **45 D9** 30 50N 61 0 E
Seistan, Daryācheh-ye = Sīstān, Daryācheh-ye, *Iran* **45 D9** 31 0N 61 0 E
Sekayu, *Indonesia* **36 E2** 2 51S 103 51 E
Seke, *Tanzania* **54 C3** 3 20S 33 31 E
Sekenke, *Tanzania* **54 C3** 4 18S 34 11 E
Sekondi-Takoradi, *Ghana* **50 H5** 4 58N 1 45W
Sekuma, *Botswana* **56 C3** 24 36S 23 50 E
Selah, *U.S.A.* **82 C3** 46 39N 120 32W
Selama, *Malaysia* **39 K3** 5 12N 100 42 E
Selaru, *Indonesia* **37 F8** 8 9S 131 0 E
Selby, *U.K.* **10 D6** 53 47N 1 5W
Selby, *U.S.A.* **80 C4** 45 31N 100 2W
Selçuk, *Turkey* **21 F12** 37 56N 27 22 E
Selden, *U.S.A.* **80 F4** 39 33N 100 34W
Sele →, *Italy* **20 D6** 40 29N 14 56 E
Selebi-Pikwe, *Botswana* **57 C4** 21 58S 27 48 E
Selemdzha →, *Russia* **27 D13** 51 42N 128 53 E
Selenga = Selenge Mörön →, *Asia* **32 A5** 52 16N 106 16 E
Selenge Mörön →, *Asia* **32 A5** 52 16N 106 16 E
Seletan, Tanjung, *Indonesia* **36 E4** 4 10S 114 40 E
Sélibabi, *Mauritania* **50 E3** 15 10N 12 15W
Seligman, *U.S.A.* **83 J7** 35 20N 112 53W
Selîma, El Wâhât el, *Sudan* **51 D11** 21 22N 29 19 E
Selinda Spillway →, *Botswana* **56 B3** 18 35S 23 10 E
Selinsgrove, *U.S.A.* **78 F8** 40 48N 76 52W
Selkirk, *Canada* **73 C9** 50 10N 96 55W
Selkirk, *U.K.* **12 F6** 55 33N 2 50W
Selkirk I., *Canada* **73 C9** 53 20N 99 6W
Selkirk Mts., *Canada* **68 C8** 51 15N 117 40W
Selliá, *Greece* **23 D6** 35 12N 24 23 E
Sells, *U.S.A.* **83 L8** 31 55N 111 53W
Selma, *Ala., U.S.A.* **77 J2** 32 25N 87 1W
Selma, *Calif., U.S.A.* **84 J7** 36 34N 119 37W
Selma, *N.C., U.S.A.* **77 H6** 35 32N 78 17W
Selmer, *U.S.A.* **77 H1** 35 10N 88 36W
Selowandoma Falls, *Zimbabwe* **55 G3** 21 15S 31 50 E
Selpele, *Indonesia* **37 E8** 0 1S 130 5 E
Selsey Bill, *U.K.* **11 G7** 50 43N 0 47W
Seltso, *Russia* **24 D5** 53 22N 34 4 E
Selu, *Indonesia* **37 F8** 7 32S 130 55 E
Selva, *Argentina* **94 B3** 29 50S 62 0W
Selvas, *Brazil* **92 E5** 6 30S 67 0W
Selwyn L., *Canada* **73 B8** 60 0N 104 30W
Selwyn Mts., *Canada* **68 B6** 63 0N 130 0W
Selwyn Ra., *Australia* **62 C3** 21 10S 140 0 E
Seman →, *Albania* **21 D8** 40 47N 19 30 E
Semarang, *Indonesia* **36 F4** 7 0S 110 26 E
Sembabule, *Uganda* **54 C3** 0 4S 31 25 E
Semeru, *Indonesia* **37 H15** 8 4S 112 55 E
Semey, *Kazakstan* **26 D9** 50 30N 80 10 E
Seminoe Reservoir, *U.S.A.* **82 F10** 42 9N 106 55W
Seminole, *Okla., U.S.A.* **81 H6** 35 14N 96 41W
Seminole, *Tex., U.S.A.* **81 J3** 32 43N 102 39W
Seminole Draw →, *U.S.A.* **81 J3** 32 27N 102 20W
Semipalatinsk = Semey, *Kazakstan* **26 D9** 50 30N 80 10 E
Semirara Is., *Phil.* **37 B6** 12 0N 121 20 E
Semitau, *Indonesia* **36 D4** 0 29N 111 57 E
Semiyarka, *Kazakstan* **26 D8** 50 55N 78 23 E
Semiyarskoye = Semiyarka, *Kazakstan* **26 D8** 50 55N 78 23 E
Semmering P., *Austria* **16 E8** 47 41N 15 45 E
Semnān, *Iran* **45 C7** 35 40N 53 23 E
Semnān □, *Iran* **45 C7** 36 0N 54 0 E
Semporna, *Malaysia* **37 D5** 4 30N 118 33 E
Semuda, *Indonesia* **36 E4** 2 51S 112 58 E
Sen →, *Cambodia* **38 B3** 13 45N 105 12 E
Senā, *Iran* **45 D6** 28 27N 51 36 E
Sena, *Mozam.* **55 F4** 17 25S 35 0 E
Sena Madureira, *Brazil* **92 E5** 9 5S 68 45W
Senador Pompeu, *Brazil* **93 E11** 5 40S 39 20W
Senanga, *Zambia* **53 H4** 16 7S 23 16 E
Senatobia, *U.S.A.* **81 H10** 34 37N 89 58W
Sencelles, *Spain* **22 B9** 39 39N 2 54 E
Sendai, *Kagoshima, Japan* **31 J5** 31 50N 130 20 E
Sendai, *Miyagi, Japan* **30 E10** 38 15N 140 53 E
Sendai-Wan, *Japan* **30 E10** 38 15N 141 0 E
Sendhwa, *India* **42 J6** 21 41N 75 6 E
Seneca, *U.S.A.* **77 H4** 34 41N 82 57W
Seneca Falls, *U.S.A.* **79 D8** 42 55N 76 48W
Seneca L., *U.S.A.* **78 D8** 42 40N 76 54W
Senecaville L., *U.S.A.* **78 G3** 39 55N 81 25W
Senegal ■, *W. Afr.* **50 F3** 14 30N 14 30W
Sénégal →, *W. Afr.* **50 E2** 15 48N 16 32W
Senegambia, *Africa* **48 E2** 12 45N 12 0W
Senekal, *S. Africa* **57 D4** 28 20S 27 36 E
Senga Hill, *Zambia* **55 D3** 9 19S 31 11 E
Senge Khambab = Indus →, *Pakistan* **42 G2** 24 20N 67 47 E
Sengua →, *Zimbabwe* **55 F2** 17 7S 28 5 E
Senhor-do-Bonfim, *Brazil* **93 F10** 10 30S 40 10W
Senigállia, *Italy* **20 C5** 43 43N 13 13 E
Senj, *Croatia* **16 F8** 45 0N 14 58 E
Senja, *Norway* **8 B17** 69 25N 17 30 E
Senkaku-Shotō, *Japan* **31 L1** 25 45N 124 0 E
Senlis, *France* **18 B5** 49 13N 2 35 E
Senmonorom, *Cambodia* **38 F6** 12 27N 107 12 E
Senneterre, *Canada* **70 C4** 48 25N 77 15W
Seno, *Laos* **38 D5** 16 35N 104 50 E
Sens, *France* **18 B5** 48 11N 3 15 E
Senta, *Serbia, Yug.* **21 B9** 45 55N 20 3 E
Sentani, *Indonesia* **37 E10** 2 36S 140 37 E
Sentery = Lubao, *Dem. Rep. of the Congo* **54 D2** 5 17S 25 42 E
Sentinel, *U.S.A.* **83 K7** 32 52N 113 13W
Seo de Urgel = La Seu d'Urgell, *Spain* **19 A6** 42 22N 1 23 E
Seohara, *India* **43 E8** 29 15N 78 33 E
Seonath →, *India* **43 J10** 21 44N 82 28 E
Seondha, *India* **43 F8** 26 9N 78 48 E
Seoni, *India* **43 H8** 22 5N 79 30 E
Seoni Malwa, *India* **42 H8** 22 27N 77 28 E
Seoul = Sŏul, *S. Korea* **35 F14** 37 31N 126 58 E
Sepīdān, *Iran* **45 D7** 30 20N 52 5 E
Sepo-ri, *N. Korea* **35 E14** 38 57N 127 25 E
Sepone, *Laos* **38 D6** 16 45N 106 13 E
Sept-Îles, *Canada* **71 B6** 50 13N 66 22W
Sequim, *U.S.A.* **84 B3** 48 5N 123 6W
Sequoia Nat. Park, *U.S.A.* **84 J8** 36 30N 118 30W
Seraing, *Belgium* **15 D5** 50 35N 5 32 E
Seraja, *Indonesia* **39 L7** 2 41N 108 35 E
Serakhis →, *Cyprus* **23 D11** 35 13N 32 55 E
Seram, *Indonesia* **37 E7** 3 10S 129 0 E
Seram Sea, *Indonesia* **37 E7** 2 30S 128 30 E
Seranantsara, *Madag.* **57 B8** 18 30S 49 5 E
Serang, *Indonesia* **37 G12** 6 8S 106 10 E
Serasan, *Indonesia* **39 L7** 2 29N 109 4 E
Serbia □, *Yugoslavia* **21 C9** 43 30N 21 0 E
Serdobsk, *Russia* **24 D7** 52 28N 44 10 E
Seremban, *Malaysia* **39 L3** 2 43N 101 53 E
Serengeti Plain, *Tanzania* **54 C4** 2 40S 35 0 E
Serenje, *Zambia* **55 E3** 13 14S 30 15 E
Sereth = Siret →, *Romania* **17 F14** 45 24N 28 1 E
Sergino, *Russia* **26 C7** 62 25N 65 12 E
Sergipe □, *Brazil* **93 F11** 10 30S 37 30W
Sergiyev Posad, *Russia* **24 C6** 56 20N 38 10 E
Seria, *Brunei* **36 D4** 4 37N 114 23 E
Serian, *Malaysia* **36 D4** 1 10N 110 31 E
Seribu, Kepulauan, *Indonesia* **36 F3** 5 36S 106 33 E
Sérifos, *Greece* **21 F11** 37 9N 24 30 E
Sérigny →, *Canada* **71 A6** 56 47N 66 0W
Seringapatam Reef, *Australia* **60 B3** 13 38S 122 5 E
Sermata, *Indonesia* **37 F7** 8 15S 128 50 E
Serov, *Russia* **24 C11** 59 29N 60 35 E
Serowe, *Botswana* **56 C4** 22 25S 26 43 E
Serpentine Lakes, *Australia* **61 E4** 28 30S 129 10 E
Serpukhov, *Russia* **24 D6** 54 55N 37 28 E
Serra do Navio, *Brazil* **93 C8** 0 59N 52 3W
Sérrai, *Greece* **21 D10** 41 5N 23 31 E
Serrezuela, *Argentina* **94 C2** 30 40S 65 20W
Serrinha, *Brazil* **93 F11** 11 39S 39 0W
Sertanópolis, *Brazil* **95 A5** 23 4S 51 2W
Serua, *Indonesia* **37 F8** 6 18S 130 1 E
Serui, *Indonesia* **37 E9** 1 53S 136 10 E
Serule, *Botswana* **56 C4** 21 57S 27 20 E
Ses Salines, *Spain* **22 B10** 39 21N 3 3 E
Sese Is., *Uganda* **54 C3** 0 20S 32 20 E
Sesepe, *Indonesia* **37 E7** 1 30S 127 59 E
Sesfontein, *Namibia* **56 B1** 19 7S 13 39 E
Sesheke, *Zambia* **56 B3** 17 29S 24 13 E
S'Espalmador, *Spain* **22 C7** 38 47N 1 26 E
S'Espardell, *Spain* **22 C7** 38 48N 1 29 E
S'Estanyol, *Spain* **22 B9** 39 22N 2 54 E
Setana, *Japan* **30 C9** 42 26N 139 51 E
Sète, *France* **18 E5** 43 25N 3 42 E
Sete Lagôas, *Brazil* **93 G10** 19 27S 44 16W
Sétif, *Algeria* **50 A7** 36 9N 5 26 E
Seto, *Japan* **31 G8** 35 14N 137 6 E
Setonaikai, *Japan* **31 G6** 34 20N 133 30 E
Settat, *Morocco* **50 B4** 33 0N 7 40W
Setting L., *Canada* **73 C9** 55 0N 98 38W
Settle, *U.K.* **10 C5** 54 5N 2 16W
Settlement Pt., *Bahamas* **77 M6** 26 40N 79 0W
Settlers, *S. Africa* **57 C4** 25 2S 28 30 E
Setúbal, *Portugal* **19 C1** 38 30N 8 58W
Setúbal, B. de, *Portugal* **19 C1** 38 40N 8 56W
Seul, Lac, *Canada* **70 B1** 50 20N 92 30W
Sevan, Ozero = Sevana Lich, *Armenia* **25 F8** 40 30N 45 20 E
Sevana Lich, *Armenia* **25 F8** 40 30N 45 20 E
Sevastopol, *Ukraine* **25 F5** 44 35N 33 30 E
Seven Sisters, *Canada* **72 C3** 54 56N 128 10W
Severn →, *Canada* **70 A2** 56 2N 87 36W
Severn →, *U.K.* **11 F5** 51 35N 2 40W
Severn L., *Canada* **70 B1** 53 54N 90 48W
Severnaya Zemlya, *Russia* **27 B10** 79 0N 100 0 E
Severnyye Uvaly, *Russia* **24 C8** 60 0N 50 0 E
Severo-Kurilsk, *Russia* **27 D16** 50 40N 156 8 E
Severo-Yeniseyskiy, *Russia* **27 C10** 60 22N 93 1 E
Severodvinsk, *Russia* **24 B6** 64 27N 39 58 E
Severomorsk, *Russia* **24 A5** 69 5N 33 27 E
Severouralsk, *Russia* **24 B10** 60 9N 59 57 E
Sevier, *U.S.A.* **83 G7** 38 39N 112 11W
Sevier →, *U.S.A.* **83 G7** 39 4N 113 6W
Sevier Desert, *U.S.A.* **82 G7** 39 40N 112 45W

Sevier L., *U.S.A.* **82 G7** 38 54N 113 9W
Sevilla, *Spain* **19 D2** 37 23N 5 58W
Seville = Sevilla, *Spain* **19 D2** 37 23N 5 58W
Sevlievo, *Bulgaria* **21 C11** 43 2N 25 6 E
Sewani, *India* **42 E6** 28 58N 75 39 E
Seward, *Alaska, U.S.A.* **68 B5** 60 7N 149 27W
Seward, *Nebr., U.S.A.* **80 E6** 40 55N 97 6W
Seward, *Pa., U.S.A.* **78 F5** 40 25N 79 1W
Seward Peninsula, *U.S.A.* **68 B3** 65 30N 166 0W
Sewell, *Chile* **94 C1** 34 10S 70 23W
Sewer, *Indonesia* **37 F8** 5 53S 134 40 E
Sewickley, *U.S.A.* **78 F4** 40 32N 80 12W
Sexsmith, *Canada* **72 B5** 55 21N 118 47W
Seychelles ■, *Ind. Oc.* **29 K9** 5 0S 56 0 E
Seyðisfjörður, *Iceland* **8 D6** 65 16N 13 57W
Seydişehir, *Turkey* **25 G5** 37 25N 31 51 E
Seydvān, *Iran* **44 B5** 38 34N 45 2 E
Seyhan →, *Turkey* **44 B2** 36 43N 34 53 E
Seym →, *Ukraine* **25 D5** 51 27N 32 34 E
Seymour, *Australia* **63 F4** 37 0S 145 10 E
Seymour, *S. Africa* **57 E4** 32 33S 26 46 E
Seymour, *Conn., U.S.A.* **79 E11** 41 24N 73 4W
Seymour, *Ind., U.S.A.* **76 F3** 38 58N 85 53W
Seymour, *Tex., U.S.A.* **81 J5** 33 35N 99 16W
Sfântu Gheorghe, *Romania* **17 F13** 45 52N 25 48 E
Sfax, *Tunisia* **51 B8** 34 49N 10 48 E
Shaanxi □, *China* **34 G5** 35 0N 109 0 E
Shaba = Katanga □, *Dem. Rep. of the Congo* **54 D2** 8 0S 25 0 E
Shaballe = Scebeli, Wabi →, *Somali Rep.* **46 G3** 2 0N 44 0 E
Shabogamo L., *Canada* **71 B6** 53 15N 66 30W
Shabunda, *Dem. Rep. of the Congo* **54 C2** 2 40S 27 16 E
Shache, *China* **32 C2** 38 20N 77 10 E
Shackleton Ice Shelf, *Antarctica* **5 C8** 66 0S 100 0 E
Shackleton Inlet, *Antarctica* **5 E11** 83 0S 160 0 E
Shādegān, *Iran* **45 D6** 30 40N 48 38 E
Shadi, *India* **43 C7** 33 24N 77 14 E
Shadrinsk, *Russia* **26 D7** 56 5N 63 32 E
Shadyside, *U.S.A.* **78 G4** 39 58N 80 45W
Shafter, *U.S.A.* **85 K7** 35 30N 119 16W
Shaftesbury, *U.K.* **11 F5** 51 0N 2 11W
Shagram, *Pakistan* **43 A5** 36 24N 72 20 E
Shah Alizai, *Pakistan* **42 E2** 29 25N 66 33 E
Shah Bunder, *Pakistan* **42 G2** 24 13N 67 56 E
Shahabad, *Punjab, India* **42 D7** 30 10N 76 55 E
Shahabad, *Raj., India* **42 G7** 25 15N 77 11 E
Shahabad, *Ut. P., India* **43 F8** 27 36N 79 56 E
Shahadpur, *Pakistan* **42 G3** 25 55N 68 35 E
Shahba, *Syria* **47 C5** 32 52N 36 38 E
Shahdād, *Iran* **45 D8** 30 30N 57 40 E
Shahdād, Namakzār-e, *Iran* **45 D8** 30 20N 58 20 E
Shahdadkot, *Pakistan* **42 F2** 27 50N 67 55 E
Shahdol, *India* **43 H9** 23 19N 81 26 E
Shahe, *China* **34 F8** 37 0N 114 32 E
Shahganj, *India* **43 F10** 26 3N 82 44 E
Shahgarh, *India* **40 F6** 27 15N 69 50 E
Shahjahanpur, *India* **43 F8** 27 54N 79 57 E
Shahpur, *India* **42 H7** 22 12N 77 58 E
Shahpur, *Baluchistan, Pakistan* **42 E3** 28 46N 68 27 E
Shahpur, *Punjab, Pakistan* **42 C5** 32 17N 72 26 E
Shahpur Chakar, *Pakistan* **42 F3** 26 9N 68 39 E
Shahpura, *Mad. P., India* **43 H9** 23 10N 80 45 E
Shahpura, *Raj., India* **42 G6** 25 38N 74 56 E
Shahr-e Bābak, *Iran* **45 D7** 30 7N 55 9 E
Shahr-e Kord, *Iran* **45 C6** 32 15N 50 55 E
Shāhrakht, *Iran* **45 C9** 33 38N 60 16 E
Shahrig, *Pakistan* **42 D2** 30 15N 67 40 E
Shahukou, *China* **34 D7** 40 20N 112 18 E
Shaikhabad, *Afghan.* **42 B3** 34 2N 68 45 E
Shajapur, *India* **42 H7** 23 27N 76 21 E
Shakargarh, *Pakistan* **42 C6** 32 17N 75 10 E
Shakawe, *Botswana* **56 B3** 18 28S 21 49 E
Shaker Heights, *U.S.A.* **78 E3** 41 29N 81 32W
Shakhty, *Russia* **25 E7** 47 40N 40 16 E
Shakhunya, *Russia* **24 C8** 57 40N 46 46 E
Shaki, *Nigeria* **50 G6** 8 41N 3 21 E
Shallow Lake, *Canada* **78 B3** 44 36N 81 5W
Shalqar, *Kazakstan* **26 E6** 47 48N 59 39 E
Shaluli Shan, *China* **32 C4** 30 40N 99 55 E
Shām, *Iran* **45 E8** 26 39N 57 21 E
Shām, Bādiyat ash, *Asia* **44 C3** 32 0N 40 0 E
Shamâl Kordofân □, *Sudan* **48 E6** 15 0N 30 0 E
Shamattawa, *Canada* **70 A1** 55 51N 92 5W
Shamattawa →, *Canada* **70 A2** 55 1N 85 23W
Shamīl, *Iran* **45 E8** 27 30N 56 55 E
Shāmkūh, *Iran* **45 C8** 35 47N 57 50 E
Shamli, *India* **42 E7** 29 32N 77 18 E
Shammar, Jabal, *Si. Arabia* **44 E4** 27 40N 41 0 E
Shamo = Gobi, *Asia* **34 C6** 44 0N 110 0 E
Shamo, L., *Ethiopia* **46 F2** 5 45N 37 30 E
Shamokin, *U.S.A.* **79 F8** 40 47N 76 34W
Shamrock, *U.S.A.* **81 H4** 35 13N 100 15W
Shamva, *Zimbabwe* **55 F3** 17 20S 31 32 E
Shan □, *Burma* **41 J21** 21 30N 98 30 E
Shan Xian, *China* **34 G9** 34 50N 116 5 E
Shanchengzhen, *China* **35 C13** 42 20N 125 20 E
Shāndak, *Iran* **45 D9** 28 28N 60 27 E
Shandon, *U.S.A.* **84 K6** 35 39N 120 23W
Shandong □, *China* **35 G10** 36 0N 118 0 E
Shandong Bandao, *China* **35 F11** 37 0N 121 0 E
Shang Xian = Shangzhou, *China* **34 H5** 33 50N 109 58 E
Shanga, *Nigeria* **50 F6** 11 12N 4 33 E
Shangalowe, *Dem. Rep. of the Congo* **55 E2** 10 50S 26 30 E
Shangani, *Zimbabwe* **57 B4** 19 41S 29 20 E
Shangani →, *Zimbabwe* **55 F2** 18 41S 27 10 E
Shangbancheng, *China* **35 D10** 40 50N 118 1 E
Shangdu, *China* **34 D7** 41 30N 113 30 E
Shanghai, *China* **33 C7** 31 15N 121 26 E
Shanghe, *China* **35 F9** 37 20N 117 10 E
Shangnan, *China* **34 H6** 33 32N 110 50 E
Shangqiu, *China* **34 G8** 34 26N 115 36 E
Shangrao, *China* **33 D6** 28 25N 117 59 E
Shangshui, *China* **33 C6** 33 42N 114 35 E
Shangzhi, *China* **35 B14** 45 22N 127 56 E
Shangzhou, *China* **34 H5** 33 50N 109 58 E
Shanhetun, *China* **35 B14** 44 33N 127 15 E
Shannon, *N.Z.* **59 J5** 40 33S 175 25 E
Shannon →, *Ireland* **13 D2** 52 35N 9 30W
Shannon, Mouth of the, *Ireland* **13 D2** 52 30N 9 55W
Shannon Airport, *Ireland* **13 D3** 52 42N 8 57W
Shansi = Shanxi □, *China* **34 F7** 37 0N 112 0 E
Shantar, Ostrov Bolshoy, *Russia* **27 D14** 55 9N 137 40 E
Shantipur, *India* **43 H13** 23 17N 88 25 E
Shantou, *China* **33 D6** 23 18N 116 40 E
Shantung = Shandong □, *China* **35 G10** 36 0N 118 0 E
Shanxi □, *China* **34 F7** 37 0N 112 0 E
Shanyang, *China* **34 H5** 33 31N 109 55 E
Shanyin, *China* **34 E7** 39 25N 112 56 E
Shaoguan, *China* **33 D6** 24 48N 113 35 E
Shaoxing, *China* **33 D7** 30 0N 120 35 E
Shaoyang, *China* **33 D6** 27 14N 111 25 E
Shap, *U.K.* **10 C5** 54 32N 2 40W
Shapinsay, *U.K.* **12 B6** 59 3N 2 51W
Shaqra', *Si. Arabia* **44 E5** 25 15N 45 16 E
Shaqrā', *Yemen* **46 E4** 13 22N 45 44 E
Sharafkhāneh, *Iran* **44 B5** 38 11N 45 29 E
Sharbot Lake, *Canada* **79 B8** 44 46N 76 41W
Shari, *Japan* **30 C12** 43 55N 144 40 E
Sharjah = Ash Shāriqah, *U.A.E.* **46 B6** 25 23N 55 26 E
Shark B., *Australia* **61 E1** 25 30S 113 32 E
Sharon, *Mass., U.S.A.* **79 D13** 42 7N 71 11W
Sharon, *Pa., U.S.A.* **78 E4** 41 14N 80 31W
Sharon Springs, *Kans., U.S.A.* **80 F4** 38 54N 101 45W
Sharon Springs, *N.Y., U.S.A.* **79 D10** 42 48N 74 37W
Sharp Pt., *Australia* **62 A3** 10 58S 142 43 E
Sharpe L., *Canada* **70 B1** 54 24N 93 40W
Sharpsville, *U.S.A.* **78 E4** 41 15N 80 29W
Sharya, *Russia* **24 C8** 58 22N 45 20 E
Shashemene, *Ethiopia* **46 F2** 7 13N 38 33 E
Shashi, *Botswana* **57 C4** 21 15S 27 27 E
Shashi, *China* **33 C6** 30 25N 112 14 E
Shashi →, *Africa* **55 G2** 21 14S 29 20 E
Shasta, Mt., *U.S.A.* **82 F2** 41 25N 122 12W
Shasta L., *U.S.A.* **82 F2** 40 43N 122 25W
Shatt al Arab = Arab, Shatt al →, *Asia* **45 D6** 30 0N 48 31 E
Shaunavon, *Canada* **73 D7** 49 35N 108 25W
Shaver L., *U.S.A.* **84 H7** 37 9N 119 18W
Shaw →, *Australia* **60 D2** 20 21S 119 17 E
Shaw I., *Australia* **62 C4** 20 30S 149 2 E
Shawanaga, *Canada* **78 A4** 45 31N 80 17W
Shawangunk Mts., *U.S.A.* **79 E10** 41 35N 74 30W
Shawano, *U.S.A.* **76 C1** 44 47N 88 36W
Shawinigan, *Canada* **70 C5** 46 35N 72 50W
Shawnee, *U.S.A.* **81 H6** 35 20N 96 55W
Shay Gap, *Australia* **60 D3** 20 30S 120 10 E
Shaybārā, *Si. Arabia* **44 E3** 25 26N 36 47 E
Shaykh, J. ash, *Lebanon* **47 B4** 33 25N 35 50 E
Shaykh Miskīn, *Syria* **47 C5** 32 49N 36 9 E
Shaykh Sa'īd, *Iraq* **44 C5** 32 34N 46 17 E
Shcherbakov = Rybinsk, *Russia* **24 C6** 58 5N 38 50 E
Shchuchinsk, *Kazakstan* **26 D8** 52 56N 70 12 E
She Xian, *China* **34 F7** 36 30N 113 40 E
Shebele = Scebeli, Wabi →, *Somali Rep.* **46 G3** 2 0N 44 0 E
Sheboygan, *U.S.A.* **76 D2** 43 46N 87 45W
Shediac, *Canada* **71 C7** 46 14N 64 32W
Sheelin, L., *Ireland* **13 C4** 53 48N 7 20W
Sheep Haven, *Ireland* **13 A4** 55 11N 7 52W
Sheerness, *U.K.* **11 F8** 51 26N 0 47 E
Sheet Harbour, *Canada* **71 D7** 44 56N 62 31W
Sheffield, *U.K.* **10 D6** 53 23N 1 28W
Sheffield, *Ala., U.S.A.* **77 H2** 34 46N 87 41W
Sheffield, *Mass., U.S.A.* **79 D11** 42 5N 73 21W
Sheffield, *Pa., U.S.A.* **78 E5** 41 42N 79 3W
Sheikhpura, *India* **43 G11** 25 9N 85 53 E
Shekhupura, *Pakistan* **42 D5** 31 42N 73 58 E
Shelburne, *N.S., Canada* **71 D6** 43 47N 65 20W
Shelburne, *Ont., Canada* **78 B4** 44 4N 80 15W
Shelburne, *U.S.A.* **79 B11** 44 23N 73 14W
Shelburne B., *Australia* **62 A3** 11 50S 142 50 E
Shelburne Falls, *U.S.A.* **79 D12** 42 36N 72 45W
Shelby, *Mich., U.S.A.* **76 D2** 43 37N 86 22W
Shelby, *Miss., U.S.A.* **81 J9** 33 57N 90 46W
Shelby, *Mont., U.S.A.* **82 B8** 48 30N 111 51W
Shelby, *N.C., U.S.A.* **77 H5** 35 17N 81 32W
Shelby, *Ohio, U.S.A.* **78 F2** 40 53N 82 40W
Shelbyville, *Ill., U.S.A.* **80 F10** 39 24N 88 48W
Shelbyville, *Ind., U.S.A.* **76 F3** 39 31N 85 47W
Shelbyville, *Ky., U.S.A.* **76 F3** 38 13N 85 14W
Shelbyville, *Tenn., U.S.A.* **77 H2** 35 29N 86 28W
Sheldon, *U.S.A.* **80 D7** 43 11N 95 51W
Sheldrake, *Canada* **71 B7** 50 20N 64 51W
Shelikhova, Zaliv, *Russia* **27 D16** 59 30N 157 0 E
Shell Lakes, *Australia* **61 E4** 29 20S 127 30 E
Shellbrook, *Canada* **73 C7** 53 13N 106 24W
Shellharbour, *Australia* **63 E5** 34 31S 150 51 E
Shelter I, *U.S.A.* **79 E12** 41 5N 72 21W
Shelton, *Conn., U.S.A.* **79 E11** 41 19N 73 5W
Shelton, *Wash., U.S.A.* **84 C3** 47 13N 123 6W
Shen Xian, *China* **34 F8** 36 15N 115 40 E
Shenandoah, *Iowa, U.S.A.* **80 E7** 40 46N 95 22W
Shenandoah, *Pa., U.S.A.* **79 F8** 40 49N 76 12W
Shenandoah, *Va., U.S.A.* **76 F6** 38 29N 78 37W
Shenandoah →, *U.S.A.* **76 F7** 39 19N 77 44W
Shenandoah Nat. Park, *U.S.A.* **76 F6** 38 35N 78 22W
Shenchi, *China* **34 E7** 39 8N 112 10 E
Shendam, *Nigeria* **50 G7** 8 49N 9 30 E
Shendî, *Sudan* **51 E12** 16 46N 33 22 E
Shengfang, *China* **34 E9** 39 3N 116 42 E
Shenjingzi, *China* **35 B13** 44 40N 124 30 E
Shenmu, *China* **34 E6** 38 50N 110 29 E
Shenqiu, *China* **34 H8** 33 25N 115 5 E
Shensi = Shaanxi □, *China* **34 G5** 35 0N 109 0 E
Shenyang, *China* **35 D12** 41 48N 123 27 E
Sheo, *India* **42 F4** 26 11N 71 15 E
Sheopur Kalan, *India* **40 G10** 25 40N 76 40 E
Shepetivka, *Ukraine* **17 C14** 50 10N 27 10 E
Shepetovka = Shepetivka, *Ukraine* **17 C14** 50 10N 27 10 E
Shepparton, *Australia* **63 F4** 36 23S 145 26 E
Sheppey, I. of, *U.K.* **11 F8** 51 25N 0 48 E
Shepton Mallet, *U.K.* **11 F5** 51 11N 2 33W
Sheqi, *China* **34 H7** 33 12N 112 57 E
Sher Qila, *Pakistan* **43 A6** 36 7N 74 2 E
Sherborne, *U.K.* **11 G5** 50 57N 2 31W
Sherbro I., *S. Leone* **50 G3** 7 30N 12 40W
Sherbrooke, *N.S., Canada* **71 C7** 45 8N 61 59W
Sherbrooke, *Qué., Canada* **79 A13** 45 28N 71 57W
Sherburne, *U.S.A.* **79 D9** 42 41N 75 30W
Shergarh, *India* **42 F5** 26 20N 72 18 E
Sherghati, *India* **43 G11** 24 34N 84 47 E
Sheridan, *Ark., U.S.A.* **81 H8** 34 19N 92 24W
Sheridan, *Wyo., U.S.A.* **82 D10** 44 48N 106 58W
Sheringham, *U.K.* **10 E9** 52 56N 1 13 E
Sherkin I., *Ireland* **13 E2** 51 28N 9 26W
Sherkot, *India* **43 E8** 29 22N 78 35 E
Sherman, *U.S.A.* **81 J6** 33 40N 96 35W
Sherpur, *India* **43 G10** 25 34N 83 47 E
Sherridon, *Canada* **73 B8** 55 8N 101 5W
Sherwood Forest, *U.K.* **10 D6** 53 6N 1 7W
Sherwood Park, *Canada* **72 C6** 53 31N 113 19W
Sheslay →, *Canada* **72 B2** 58 48N 132 5W
Shethanei L., *Canada* **73 B9** 58 48N 97 50W
Shetland □, *U.K.* **12 A7** 60 30N 1 30W
Shetland Is., *U.K.* **12 A7** 60 30N 1 30W
Shetrunji →, *India* **42 J5** 21 19N 72 7 E
Sheyenne →, *U.S.A.* **80 B6** 47 2N 96 50W
Shibām, *Yemen* **46 D4** 15 59N 48 36 E
Shibata, *Japan* **30 F9** 37 57N 139 20 E
Shibecha, *Japan* **30 C12** 43 17N 144 36 E
Shibetsu, *Japan* **30 B11** 44 10N 142 23 E
Shibogama L., *Canada* **70 B2** 53 35N 88 15W
Shibushi, *Japan* **31 J5** 31 25N 131 8 E
Shickshinny, *U.S.A.* **79 E8** 41 9N 76 9W
Shickshock Mts. = Chic-Chocs, Mts., *Canada* **71 C6** 48 55N 66 0W
Shidao, *China* **35 F12** 36 50N 122 25 E
Shido, *Japan* **31 G7** 34 19N 134 10 E
Shiel, L., *U.K.* **12 E3** 56 48N 5 34W
Shield, C., *Australia* **62 A2** 13 20S 136 20 E
Shieli, *Kazakstan* **26 E7** 44 20N 66 15 E
Shiga □, *Japan* **31 G8** 35 20N 136 0 E
Shiguaigou, *China* **34 D6** 40 52N 110 15 E
Shihchiachuangi = Shijiazhuang, *China* **34 E8** 38 2N 114 28 E
Shihezi, *China* **32 B3** 44 15N 86 2 E
Shijiazhuang, *China* **34 E8** 38 2N 114 28 E
Shikarpur, *India* **42 E8** 28 17N 78 7 E
Shikarpur, *Pakistan* **42 F3** 27 57N 68 39 E
Shikohabad, *India* **43 F8** 27 6N 78 36 E
Shikoku □, *Japan* **31 H6** 33 30N 133 30 E
Shikoku-Sanchi, *Japan* **31 H6** 33 30N 133 30 E
Shiliguri, *India* **41 F16** 26 45N 88 25 E
Shilka, *Russia* **27 D12** 52 0N 115 55 E
Shilka →, *Russia* **27 D13** 53 20N 121 26 E
Shillelagh, *Ireland* **13 D5** 52 45N 6 32W
Shillington, *U.S.A.* **79 F9** 40 18N 75 58W
Shillong, *India* **41 G17** 25 35N 91 53 E
Shilo, *West Bank* **47 C4** 32 4N 35 18 E
Shilou, *China* **34 F6** 37 0N 110 48 E
Shimabara, *Japan* **31 H5** 32 48N 130 20 E
Shimada, *Japan* **31 G9** 34 49N 138 10 E
Shimane □, *Japan* **31 G6** 35 0N 132 30 E
Shimanovsk, *Russia* **27 D13** 52 15N 127 30 E
Shimizu, *Japan* **31 G9** 35 0N 138 30 E
Shimodate, *Japan* **31 F9** 36 20N 139 55 E
Shimoga, *India* **40 N9** 13 57N 75 32 E
Shimoni, *Kenya* **54 C4** 4 38S 39 20 E
Shimonoseki, *Japan* **31 H5** 33 58N 130 55 E
Shimpuru Rapids, *Namibia* **56 B2** 17 45S 19 55 E
Shin, L., *U.K.* **12 C4** 58 5N 4 30W
Shinano-Gawa →, *Japan* **31 F9** 36 50N 138 30 E
Shināş, *Oman* **45 E8** 24 46N 56 28 E
Shīndand, *Afghan.* **40 C3** 33 12N 62 8 E
Shinglehouse, *U.S.A.* **78 E6** 41 58N 78 12W
Shingū, *Japan* **31 H7** 33 40N 135 55 E
Shingwidzi, *S. Africa* **57 C5** 23 5S 31 25 E
Shinjō, *Japan* **30 E10** 38 46N 140 18 E
Shinshār, *Syria* **47 A5** 34 36N 36 43 E
Shinyanga, *Tanzania* **54 C3** 3 45S 33 27 E
Shinyanga □, *Tanzania* **54 C3** 3 50S 34 0 E
Shio-no-Misaki, *Japan* **31 H7** 33 25N 135 45 E
Shiogama, *Japan* **30 E10** 38 19N 141 1 E
Shiojiri, *Japan* **31 F8** 36 6N 137 58 E
Shipchenski Prokhod, *Bulgaria* **21 C11** 42 45N 25 15 E
Shiping, *China* **32 D5** 23 45N 102 23 E
Shippegan, *Canada* **71 C7** 47 45N 64 45W
Shippensburg, *U.S.A.* **78 F7** 40 3N 77 31W
Shippenville, *U.S.A.* **78 E5** 41 15N 79 28W
Shiprock, *U.S.A.* **83 H9** 36 47N 108 41W
Shiqma, N. →, *Israel* **47 D3** 31 37N 34 30 E
Shiquan, *China* **34 H5** 33 5N 108 15 E
Shiquan He = Indus →, *Pakistan* **42 G2** 24 20N 67 47 E
Shīr Kūh, *Iran* **45 D7** 31 39N 54 3 E
Shiragami-Misaki, *Japan* **30 D10** 41 24N 140 12 E
Shirakawa, *Fukushima, Japan* **31 F10** 37 7N 140 13 E
Shirakawa, *Gifu, Japan* **31 F8** 36 17N 136 56 E
Shirane-San, *Gumma, Japan* **31 F9** 36 48N 139 22 E
Shirane-San, *Yamanashi, Japan* **31 G9** 35 42N 138 9 E
Shiraoi, *Japan* **30 C10** 42 33N 141 21 E
Shīrāz, *Iran* **45 D7** 29 42N 52 30 E
Shire →, *Africa* **55 F4** 17 42S 35 19 E
Shiretoko-Misaki, *Japan* **30 B12** 44 21N 145 20 E
Shirinab →, *Pakistan* **42 D2** 30 15N 66 28 E
Shiriya-Zaki, *Japan* **30 D10** 41 25N 141 30 E
Shiroishi, *Japan* **30 F10** 38 0N 140 37 E
Shīrvān, *Iran* **45 B8** 37 30N 57 50 E
Shirwa, L. = Chilwa, L., *Malawi* **55 F4** 15 15S 35 40 E
Shivpuri, *India* **42 G7** 25 26N 77 42 E
Shixian, *China* **35 C15** 43 5N 129 50 E
Shizuishan, *China* **34 E4** 39 15N 106 50 E
Shizuoka, *Japan* **31 G9** 34 57N 138 24 E
Shizuoka □, *Japan* **31 G9** 35 15N 138 40 E
Shklov = Shklow, *Belarus* **17 A16** 54 16N 30 15 E
Shklow, *Belarus* **17 A16** 54 16N 30 15 E
Shkodër, *Albania* **21 C8** 42 4N 19 32 E
Shkumbini →, *Albania* **21 D8** 41 2N 19 31 E
Shmidta, Ostrov, *Russia* **27 A10** 81 0N 91 0 E
Shō-Gawa →, *Japan* **31 F8** 36 47N 137 4 E
Shoal L., *Canada* **73 D9** 49 33N 95 1W
Shoal Lake, *Canada* **73 C8** 50 30N 100 35W
Shōdo-Shima, *Japan* **31 G7** 34 30N 134 15 E
Sholapur = Solapur, *India* **40 L9** 17 43N 75 56 E
Shologontsy, *Russia* **27 C12** 66 13N 114 0 E
Shōmrōn, *West Bank* **47 C4** 32 15N 35 13 E
Shoreham by Sea, *U.K.* **11 G7** 50 50N 0 16W
Shori →, *Pakistan* **42 E3** 28 29N 69 44 E
Shorkot Road, *Pakistan* **42 D5** 30 47N 72 15 E
Shoshone, *Calif., U.S.A.* **85 K10** 35 58N 116 16W
Shoshone, *Idaho, U.S.A.* **82 E6** 42 56N 114 25W
Shoshone L., *U.S.A.* **82 D8** 44 22N 110 43W
Shoshone Mts., *U.S.A.* **82 G5** 39 20N 117 25W
Shoshong, *Botswana* **56 C4** 22 56S 26 31 E
Shoshoni, *U.S.A.* **82 E9** 43 14N 108 7W
Shouguang, *China* **35 F10** 37 52N 118 45 E
Shouyang, *China* **34 F7** 37 54N 113 8 E
Show Low, *U.S.A.* **83 J9** 34 15N 110 2W
Shreveport, *U.S.A.* **81 J8** 32 31N 93 45W
Shrewsbury, *U.K.* **11 E5** 52 43N 2 45W
Shri Mohangarh, *India* **42 F4** 27 17N 71 18 E
Shrirampur, *India* **43 H13** 22 44N 88 21 E
Shropshire □, *U.K.* **11 E5** 52 36N 2 45W
Shū, *Kazakstan* **26 E8** 43 36N 73 42 E
Shū →, *Kazakstan* **28 E10** 45 0N 67 44 E
Shuangcheng, *China* **35 B14** 45 20N 126 15 E
Shuanggou, *China* **35 G9** 34 2N 117 30 E
Shuangliao, *China* **35 C12** 43 29N 123 30 E
Shuangshanzi, *China* **35 D10** 40 20N 119 8 E
Shuangyang, *China* **35 C13** 43 28N 125 40 E
Shuangyashan, *China* **33 B8** 46 28N 131 5 E
Shuguri Falls, *Tanzania* **55 D4** 8 33S 37 22 E
Shuiye, *China* **34 F8** 36 7N 114 8 E
Shujalpur, *India* **42 H7** 23 18N 76 46 E
Shukpa Kunzang, *India* **43 B8** 34 22N 78 22 E
Shulan, *China* **35 B14** 44 28N 127 0 E
Shule, *China* **32 C2** 39 25N 76 3 E
Shumagin Is., *U.S.A.* **68 C4** 55 7N 160 30W
Shumen, *Bulgaria* **21 C12** 43 18N 26 55 E
Shumikha, *Russia* **26 D7** 55 10N 63 15 E
Shuo Xian = Shuozhou, *China* **34 E7** 39 20N 112 33 E
Shuozhou, *China* **34 E7** 39 20N 112 33 E
Shūr →, *Fārs, Iran* **45 D7** 28 30N 55 0 E
Shūr →, *Kermān, Iran* **45 D8** 30 52N 57 37 E
Shūr →, *Yazd, Iran* **45 D7** 31 45N 55 15 E
Shūr Āb, *Iran* **45 C6** 34 23N 51 11 E
Shūr Gaz, *Iran* **45 D8** 29 10N 59 20 E
Shūrāb, *Iran* **45 C8** 33 43N 56 29 E
Shūrjestān, *Iran* **45 D7** 31 24N 52 25 E
Shurugwi, *Zimbabwe* **55 F3** 19 40S 30 0 E
Shūsf, *Iran* **45 D9** 31 50N 60 5 E
Shūshtar, *Iran* **45 D6** 32 0N 48 50 E
Shuswap L., *Canada* **72 C5** 50 55N 119 3W
Shuyang, *China* **35 G10** 34 10N 118 42 E
Shūzū, *Iran* **45 D7** 29 52N 54 30 E
Shwebo, *Burma* **41 H19** 22 30N 95 45 E
Shwegu, *Burma* **41 G20** 24 15N 96 26 E
Shweli →, *Burma* **41 H20** 23 45N 96 45 E
Shymkent, *Kazakstan* **26 E7** 42 18N 69 36 E
Shyok, *India* **43 B8** 34 13N 78 12 E
Shyok →, *Pakistan* **43 B6** 35 13N 75 53 E
Si Chon, *Thailand* **39 H2** 9 0N 99 54 E
Si Kiang = Xi Jiang →, *China* **33 D6** 22 5N 113 20 E
Si-ngan = Xi'an, *China* **34 G5** 34 15N 109 0 E
Si Prachan, *Thailand* **38 E3** 14 37N 100 9 E
Si Racha, *Thailand* **38 F3** 13 10N 100 48 E
Si Xian, *China* **35 H9** 33 30N 117 50 E
Siachen Glacier, *Asia* **43 B7** 35 20N 77 30 E
Siahaf →, *Pakistan* **42 E3** 29 3N 68 57 E
Siahan Range, *Pakistan* **40 F4** 27 30N 64 40 E
Siaksriindrapura, *Indonesia* **36 D2** 0 51N 102 0 E
Sialkot, *Pakistan* **42 C6** 32 32N 74 30 E
Siam = Thailand ■, *Asia* **38 E4** 16 0N 102 0 E
Sian = Xi'an, *China* **34 G5** 34 15N 109 0 E
Siantan, *Indonesia* **36 D3** 3 10N 106 15 E
Siāreh, *Iran* **45 D9** 28 5N 60 14 E
Siargao I., *Phil.* **37 C7** 9 52N 126 3 E
Siari, *Pakistan* **43 B7** 34 55N 76 40 E
Siasi, *Phil.* **37 C6** 5 34N 120 50 E
Siau, *Indonesia* **37 D7** 2 50N 125 25 E
Šiauliai, *Lithuania* **9 J20** 55 56N 23 15 E
Sibâi, Gebel el, *Egypt* **44 E2** 25 45N 34 10 E
Sibay, *Russia* **24 D10** 52 42N 58 39 E
Sibayi, L., *S. Africa* **57 D5** 27 20S 32 45 E
Šibenik, *Croatia* **20 C6** 43 48N 15 54 E
Siberia, *Russia* **4 D13** 60 0N 100 0 E
Siberut, *Indonesia* **36 E1** 1 30S 99 0 E
Sibi, *Pakistan* **42 E2** 29 30N 67 54 E
Sibil = Oksibil, *Indonesia* **37 E10** 4 59S 140 35 E
Sibiti, *Congo* **52 E2** 3 38S 13 19 E
Sibiu, *Romania* **17 F13** 45 45N 24 9 E
Sibley, *U.S.A.* **80 D7** 43 24N 95 45W
Sibolga, *Indonesia* **36 D1** 1 42N 98 45 E
Sibsagar, *India* **41 F19** 27 0N 94 36 E
Sibu, *Malaysia* **36 D4** 2 18N 111 49 E
Sibuco, *Phil.* **37 C6** 7 20N 122 10 E
Sibuguey B., *Phil.* **37 C6** 7 50N 122 45 E
Sibut, *C.A.R.* **52 C3** 5 46N 19 10 E
Sibutu, *Phil.* **37 D5** 4 45N 119 30 E
Sibutu Passage, *E. Indies* **37 D5** 4 50N 120 0 E
Sibuyan I., *Phil.* **37 B6** 12 25N 122 40 E
Sibuyan Sea, *Phil.* **37 B6** 12 30N 122 20 E
Sicamous, *Canada* **72 C5** 50 49N 119 0W
Siccus →, *Australia* **63 E2** 31 26S 139 30 E
Sichuan □, *China* **32 C5** 30 30N 103 0 E
Sicilia, *Italy* **20 F6** 37 30N 14 30 E
Sicily = Sicilia, *Italy* **20 F6** 37 30N 14 30 E
Sicuani, *Peru* **92 F4** 14 21S 71 10W
Sidári, *Greece* **23 A3** 39 47N 19 41 E
Siddhapur, *India* **42 H5** 23 56N 72 25 E
Siddipet, *India* **40 K11** 18 5N 78 51 E
Sidhauli, *India* **43 F9** 27 17N 80 50 E
Sídheros, Ákra, *Greece* **23 D8** 35 19N 26 19 E
Sidhi, *India* **43 G9** 24 25N 81 53 E
Sidi-bel-Abbès, *Algeria* **50 A5** 35 13N 0 39W
Sidi Ifni, *Morocco* **50 C3** 29 29N 10 12W
Sidlaw Hills, *U.K.* **12 E5** 56 32N 3 2W
Sidley, Mt., *Antarctica* **5 D14** 77 2S 126 2W
Sidmouth, *U.K.* **11 G4** 50 40N 3 15W
Sidmouth, C., *Australia* **62 A3** 13 25S 143 36 E
Sidney, *Canada* **72 D4** 48 39N 123 24W
Sidney, *Mont., U.S.A.* **80 B2** 47 43N 104 9W
Sidney, *N.Y., U.S.A.* **79 D9** 42 19N 75 24W
Sidney, *Nebr., U.S.A.* **80 E3** 41 8N 102 59W
Sidney, *Ohio, U.S.A.* **76 E3** 40 17N 84 9W
Sidney Lanier, L., *U.S.A.* **77 H4** 34 10N 84 4W
Sidoarjo, *Indonesia* **37 G15** 7 27S 112 43 E
Sidon = Saydā, *Lebanon* **47 B4** 33 35N 35 25 E
Sidra, G. of = Surt, Khalīj, *Libya* **51 B9** 31 40N 18 30 E
Siedlce, *Poland* **17 B12** 52 10N 22 20 E
Sieg →, *Germany* **16 C4** 50 46N 7 6 E
Siegen, *Germany* **16 C5** 50 51N 8 0 E
Siem Pang, *Cambodia* **38 E6** 14 7N 106 23 E
Siem Reap = Siemreab, *Cambodia* **38 F4** 13 20N 103 52 E
Siemreab, *Cambodia* **38 F4** 13 20N 103 52 E
Siena, *Italy* **20 C4** 43 19N 11 21 E
Sieradz, *Poland* **17 C10** 51 37N 18 41 E

Sierra Blanca, *U.S.A.* **83 L11** 31 11N 105 22W
Sierra Blanca Peak, *U.S.A.* .. **83 K11** 33 23N 105 49W
Sierra City, *U.S.A.* **84 F6** 39 34N 120 38W
Sierra Colorada, *Argentina* . **96 E3** 40 35S 67 50W
Sierra Gorda, *Chile* **94 A2** 22 50S 69 15W
Sierra Leone ■, *W. Afr.* **50 G3** 9 0N 12 0W
Sierra Madre, *Mexico* **87 D6** 16 0N 93 0W
Sierra Mojada, *Mexico* **86 B4** 27 19N 103 42W
Sierra Nevada, *Spain* **19 D4** 37 3N 3 15W
Sierra Nevada, *U.S.A.* **84 H8** 39 0N 120 30W
Sierra Vista, *U.S.A.* **83 L8** 31 33N 110 18W
Sierraville, *U.S.A.* **84 F6** 39 36N 120 22W
Sífnos, *Greece* .... **21 F11** 37 0N 24 45 E
Sifton, *Canada* **73 C8** 51 21N 100 8W
Sifton Pass, *Canada* **72 B3** 57 52N 126 15W
Sighetu-Marmației, *Romania* **17 E12** 47 57N 23 52 E
Sighişoara, *Romania* ...... **17 E13** 46 12N 24 50 E
Sigli, *Indonesia* .... **36 C1** 5 25N 96 0 E
Siglufjörður, *Iceland* **8 C4** 66 12N 18 55W
Signal, *U.S.A.* **85 L13** 34 30N 113 38W
Signal Pk., *U.S.A.* **85 M12** 33 20N 114 2W
Sigsig, *Ecuador* **92 D3** 3 0S 78 50W
Sigüenza, *Spain* **19 B4** 41 3N 2 40W
Siguiri, *Guinea* **50 F4** 11 31N 9 10W
Sigulda, *Latvia* .... **9 H21** 57 10N 24 55 E
Sihanoukville = Kampong
Saom, *Cambodia* .... **39 G4** 10 38N 103 30 E
Sihora, *India* .... **43 H9** 23 29N 80 6 E
Siikajoki →, *Finland* .... **8 D21** 64 50N 24 43 E
Siilinjärvi, *Finland* .... **8 E22** 63 4N 27 39 E
Sijarira Ra. = Chizarira,
Zimbabwe .... **55 F2** 17 36S 27 45 E
Sika, *India* .... **42 H3** 22 26N 69 47 E
Sikao, *Thailand* .... **39 J2** 7 34N 99 21 E
Sikar, *India* .... **42 F6** 27 33N 75 10 E
Sikasso, *Mali* **50 F4** 11 18N 5 35W
Sikeston, *U.S.A.* **81 G10** 36 53N 89 35W
Sikhote Alin, Khrebet, *Russia* **27 E14** 45 0N 136 0 E
Sikhote Alin Ra. = Sikhote
Alin, Khrebet, *Russia* ..... **27 E14** 45 0N 136 0 E
Síkinos, *Greece* .... **21 F11** 36 40N 25 8 E
Sikkani Chief →, *Canada* ... **72 B4** 57 47N 122 15W
Sikkim □, *India* .... **41 F16** 27 50N 88 30 E
Sikotu-Ko, *Japan* .... **30 C10** 42 45N 141 25 E
Sil →, *Spain* **19 A2** 42 27N 7 43W
Silacayoapan, *Mexico* **87 D5** 17 30N 98 9W
Silawad, *India* .... **42 J6** 21 54N 74 54 E
Silchar, *India* .... **41 G18** 24 49N 92 48 E
Siler City, *U.S.A.* **77 H6** 35 44N 79 28W
Silesia = Śląsk, *Poland* ..... **16 C9** 51 0N 16 30 E
Silgarhi Doti, *Nepal* .... **43 E9** 29 15N 81 0 E
Silghat, *India* .... **41 F18** 26 35N 93 0 E
Silifke, *Turkey* .... **25 G5** 36 22N 33 58 E
Siliguri = Shiliguri, *India* ... **41 F16** 26 45N 88 25 E
Siling Co, *China* .... **32 C3** 31 50N 89 20 E
Silistra, *Bulgaria* .... **21 B12** 44 6N 27 19 E
Silivri, *Turkey* .... **21 D13** 41 4N 28 14 E
Siljan, *Sweden* .... **9 F16** 60 55N 14 45 E
Silkeborg, *Denmark* .... **9 H13** 56 10N 9 32 E
Silkwood, *Australia* .... **62 B4** 17 45S 146 2 E
Sillajhuay, Cordillera, *Chile* . **92 G5** 19 46S 68 40W
Sillamäe, *Estonia* .... **9 G22** 59 24N 27 45 E
Silloth, *U.K.* **10 C4** 54 52N 3 23W
Siloam Springs, *U.S.A.* **81 G7** 36 11N 94 32W
Silsbee, *U.S.A.* **81 K7** 30 21N 94 11W
Šilutė, *Lithuania* .... **9 J19** 55 21N 21 33 E
Silva Porto = Kuito, *Angola* . **53 G3** 12 22S 16 55 E
Silvani, *India* .... **43 H8** 23 18N 78 25 E
Silver City, *U.S.A.* **83 K9** 32 46N 108 17W
Silver Cr. →, *U.S.A.* **82 E4** 43 16N 119 13W
Silver Creek, *U.S.A.* **78 D5** 42 33N 79 10W
Silver L., *U.S.A.* **84 G6** 38 39N 120 6W
Silver Lake, *Calif., U.S.A.* ... **85 K10** 35 21N 116 7W
Silver Lake, *Oreg., U.S.A.* ... **82 E3** 43 8N 121 3W
Silverton, *Colo., U.S.A.* **83 H10** 37 49N 107 40W
Silverton, *Tex., U.S.A.* **81 H4** 34 28N 101 19W
Silvies →, *U.S.A.* **82 E4** 43 34N 119 2W
Simaltala, *India* .... **43 G12** 24 43N 86 33 E
Simanggang = Bandar Sri
Aman, *Malaysia* .... **36 D4** 1 15N 111 32 E
Simard, L., *Canada* **70 C4** 47 40N 78 40W
Simav, *Turkey* .... **21 E13** 39 4N 28 58 E
Simba, *Tanzania* .... **54 C4** 2 10S 37 36 E
Simbirsk, *Russia* .... **24 D8** 54 20N 48 25 E
Simbo, *Tanzania* .... **54 C2** 4 51S 29 41 E
Simcoe, *Canada* **78 D4** 42 50N 80 20W
Simcoe, L., *Canada* **78 B5** 44 25N 79 20W
Simdega, *India* .... **43 H11** 22 37N 84 31 E
Simeria, *Romania* .... **17 F12** 45 51N 23 1 E
Simeulue, *Indonesia* .... **36 D1** 2 45N 95 45 E
Simferopol, *Ukraine* .... **25 F5** 44 55N 34 3 E
Sími, *Greece* .... **21 F12** 36 35N 27 50 E
Simi Valley, *U.S.A.* **85 L8** 34 16N 118 47W
Simikot, *Nepal* .... **43 E9** 30 0N 81 50 E
Simla, *India* .... **42 D7** 31 2N 77 9 E
Simmie, *Canada* **73 D7** 49 56N 108 6W
Simmler, *U.S.A.* **85 K7** 35 21N 119 59W
Simojoki →, *Finland* .... **8 D21** 65 35N 25 1 E
Simojovel, *Mexico* **87 D6** 17 12N 92 38W
Simonette →, *Canada* **72 B5** 55 9N 118 15W
Simonstown, *S. Africa* ...... **56 E2** 34 14S 18 26 E
Simplonpass, *Switz.* .... **18 C8** 46 15N 8 3 E
Simpson Desert, *Australia* .. **62 D2** 25 0S 137 0 E
Simpson Pen., *Canada* **69 B11** 68 34N 88 45W
Simpungdong, *N. Korea* ..... **35 D15** 40 56N 129 29 E
Simrishamn, *Sweden* .... **9 J16** 55 33N 14 22 E
Simsbury, *U.S.A.* **79 E12** 41 53N 72 48W
Simushir, Ostrov, *Russia* ... **27 E16** 46 50N 152 30 E
Sin Cowe I., *S. China Sea* ... **36 C4** 9 53N 114 19 E
Sinabang, *Indonesia* .... **36 D1** 2 30N 96 24 E
Sinadogo, *Somali Rep.* ...... **46 F4** 5 50N 47 0 E
Sinai = Es Sînâ', *Egypt* ..... **47 F3** 29 0N 34 0 E
Sinai, Mt. = Mûsa, Gebel,
Egypt .... **44 D2** 28 33N 33 59 E
Sinai Peninsula, *Egypt* ..... **47 F3** 29 30N 34 0 E
Sinaloa □, *Mexico* **86 C3** 25 0N 107 30W
Sinaloa de Leyva, *Mexico* ... **86 B3** 25 50N 108 20W
Sinarádhes, *Greece* .... **23 A3** 39 34N 19 51 E
Sincelejo, *Colombia* **92 B3** 9 18N 75 24W
Sinch'ang, *N. Korea* .... **35 D15** 40 7N 128 28 E
Sinchang-ni, *N. Korea* ...... **35 E14** 39 24N 126 8 E
Sinclair, *U.S.A.* **82 F10** 41 47N 107 7W
Sinclair Mills, *Canada* **72 C4** 54 5N 121 40W
Sinclair's B., *U.K.* **12 C5** 58 31N 3 5W
Sinclairville, *U.S.A.* **78 D5** 42 16N 79 16W
Sincorá, Serra do, *Brazil* **93 F10** 13 30S 41 0W
Sind, *Pakistan* .... **42 G3** 26 0N 68 30 E
Sind □, *Pakistan* .... **42 G3** 26 0N 69 0 E
Sind →, *Jammu & Kashmir,*
India .... **43 B6** 34 18N 74 45 E
Sind →, *Mad. P., India* ..... **43 F8** 26 26N 79 13 E
Sind Sagar Doab, *Pakistan* .. **42 D4** 32 0N 71 30 E
Sindangan, *Phil.* .... **37 C6** 8 10N 123 5 E
Sindangbarang, *Indonesia* .. **37 G12** 7 27S 107 1 E
Sinde, *Zambia* .... **55 F2** 17 28S 25 51 E
Sindh = Sind □, *Pakistan* ... **42 G3** 26 0N 69 0 E
Sindri, *India* .... **43 H12** 23 45N 86 42 E
Sines, *Portugal* **19 D1** 37 56N 8 51W
Sines, C. de, *Portugal* **19 D1** 37 58N 8 53W
Sineu, *Spain* .... **22 B10** 39 38N 3 1 E
Sing Buri, *Thailand* .... **38 E3** 14 53N 100 25 E
Singa, *Sudan* .... **51 F12** 13 10N 33 57 E
Singapore ■, *Asia* .... **39 M4** 1 17N 103 51 E
Singapore, Straits of, *Asia* .. **39 M5** 1 15N 104 0 E
Singaraja, *Indonesia* .... **36 F5** 8 7S 115 6 E
Singida, *Tanzania* .... **54 C3** 4 49S 34 48 E
Singida □, *Tanzania* .... **54 D3** 6 0S 34 30 E
Singitikós Kólpos, *Greece* .. **21 D11** 40 6N 24 0 E
Singkaling Hkamti, *Burma* .. **41 G19** 26 0N 95 39 E
Singkang, *Indonesia* .... **37 E6** 4 8S 120 1 E
Singkawang, *Indonesia* ..... **36 D3** 1 0N 108 57 E
Singkep, *Indonesia* .... **36 E2** 0 30S 104 25 E
Singleton, *Australia* .... **63 E5** 32 33S 151 0 E
Singleton, Mt., *N. Terr.,*
Australia .... **60 D5** 22 0S 130 46 E
Singleton, Mt., *W. Austral.,*
Australia .... **61 E2** 29 27S 117 15 E
Singoli, *India* .... **42 G6** 25 0N 75 22 E
Singora = Songkhla, *Thailand* **39 J3** 7 13N 100 37 E
Singosan, *N. Korea* .... **35 E14** 38 52N 127 25 E
Sinhung, *N. Korea* .... **35 D14** 40 11N 127 34 E
Sinjai, *Indonesia* .... **37 F6** 5 7S 120 20 E
Sinjār, *Iraq* .... **44 B4** 36 19N 41 52 E
Sinkat, *Sudan* .... **51 E13** 18 55N 36 49 E
Sinkiang Uighur = Xinjiang
Uygur Zizhiqu □, *China* .... **32 C3** 42 0N 86 0 E
Sinmak, *N. Korea* .... **35 E14** 38 25N 126 14 E
Sinnamary, *Fr. Guiana* **93 B8** 5 25N 53 0W
Sinni →, *Italy* .... **20 D7** 40 8N 16 41 E
Sinop, *Turkey* .... **25 F6** 42 1N 35 11 E
Sinor, *India* .... **42 J5** 21 55N 73 20 E
Sinp'o, *N. Korea* .... **35 E15** 40 0N 128 13 E
Sinsk, *Russia* .... **27 C13** 61 8N 126 48 E
Sintang, *Indonesia* .... **36 D4** 0 5N 111 35 E
Sinton, *U.S.A.* **81 L6** 28 2N 97 31W
Sintra, *Portugal* **19 C1** 38 47N 9 25W
Sinŭiju, *N. Korea* .... **35 D13** 40 5N 124 24 E
Siocon, *Phil.* .... **37 C6** 7 40N 122 10 E
Siófok, *Hungary* .... **17 E10** 46 54N 18 3 E
Sion, *Switz.* .... **18 C7** 46 14N 7 20 E
Sion Mills, *U.K.* **13 B4** 54 48N 7 29W
Sioux City, *U.S.A.* **80 D6** 42 30N 96 24W
Sioux Falls, *U.S.A.* **80 D6** 43 33N 96 44W
Sioux Lookout, *Canada* **70 B1** 50 10N 91 50W
Sioux Narrows, *Canada* **73 D10** 49 25N 94 10W
Siping, *China* .... **35 C13** 43 8N 124 21 E
Sipiwesk L., *Canada* **73 B9** 55 5N 97 35W
Sipra →, *India* .... **42 H6** 23 55N 75 28 E
Sipura, *Indonesia* .... **36 E1** 2 18S 99 40 E
Siquia →, *Nic.* **88 D3** 12 10N 84 20W
Siquijor, *Phil.* .... **37 C6** 9 12N 123 35 E
Siquirres, *Costa Rica* **88 D3** 10 6N 83 30W
Şīr Banī Yās, *U.A.E.* .... **45 E7** 24 19N 52 37 E
Sir Edward Pellew Group,
Australia .... **62 B2** 15 40S 137 10 E
Sir Graham Moore Is.,
Australia .... **60 B4** 13 53S 126 34 E
Sir James MacBrien, Mt.,
Canada **68 B7** 62 8N 127 40W
Sira →, *Norway* .... **9 G12** 58 23N 6 34 E
Siracusa, *Italy* .... **20 F6** 37 4N 15 17 E
Sirajganj, *Bangla.* .... **43 G13** 24 25N 89 47 E
Sirathu, *India* .... **43 G9** 25 39N 81 19 E
Sīrdān, *Iran* .... **45 B6** 36 39N 49 12 E
Sirdaryo = Syrdarya →,
Kazakstan .... **26 E7** 46 3N 61 0 E
Siren, *U.S.A.* **80 C8** 45 47N 92 24W
Sirer, *Spain* .... **22 C7** 38 56N 1 22 E
Siret →, *Romania* .... **17 F14** 45 24N 28 1 E
Sirghāyā, *Syria* .... **47 B5** 33 51N 36 8 E
Sirmaur, *India* .... **43 G9** 24 51N 81 23 E
Sirohi, *India* .... **42 G5** 24 52N 72 53 E
Sironj, *India* .... **42 G7** 24 5N 77 39 E
Síros, *Greece* .... **21 F11** 37 28N 24 57 E
Sirretta Pk., *U.S.A.* **85 K8** 35 56N 118 19W
Sīrrī, *Iran* .... **45 E7** 25 55N 54 32 E
Sirsa, *India* .... **42 E6** 29 33N 75 4 E
Sirsa →, *India* .... **43 F8** 26 51N 79 4 E
Sisak, *Croatia* .... **16 F9** 45 30N 16 21 E
Sisaket, *Thailand* .... **38 E5** 15 8N 104 23 E
Sishen, *S. Africa* .... **56 D3** 27 47S 22 59 E
Sishui, *Henan, China* .... **34 G7** 34 48N 113 15 E
Sishui, *Shandong, China* .... **35 G9** 35 42N 117 18 E
Sisipuk L., *Canada* **73 B8** 55 45N 101 50W
Sisophon, *Cambodia* .... **38 F4** 13 38N 102 59 E
Sisseton, *U.S.A.* **80 C6** 45 40N 97 3W
Sīstān, *Asia* .... **45 D9** 30 50N 61 0 E
Sīstān, Daryācheh-ye, *Iran* .. **45 D9** 31 0N 61 0 E
Sīstān va Balūchestān □, *Iran* **45 E9** 27 0N 62 0 E
Sisters, *U.S.A.* **82 D3** 44 18N 121 33W
Siswa Bazar, *India* .... **43 F10** 27 9N 83 46 E
Sitamarhi, *India* .... **43 F11** 26 37N 85 30 E
Sitampiky, *Madag.* .... **57 B8** 16 41S 46 6 E
Sitapur, *India* .... **43 F9** 27 38N 80 45 E
Siteki, *Swaziland* .... **57 D5** 26 32S 31 58 E
Sitges, *Spain* .... **19 B6** 41 17N 1 47 E
Sitía, *Greece* .... **23 D8** 35 13N 26 6 E
Sitka, *U.S.A.* **72 B1** 57 3N 135 20W
Sitoti, *Botswana* .... **56 C3** 23 15S 23 40 E
Sittang Myit →, *Burma* ..... **41 L20** 17 20N 96 45 E
Sittard, *Neths.* .... **15 C5** 51 0N 5 52 E
Sittingbourne, *U.K.* .... **11 F8** 51 21N 0 45 E
Sittoung = Sittang Myit →,
Burma .... **41 L20** 17 20N 96 45 E
Sittwe, *Burma* .... **41 J18** 20 18N 92 45 E
Situbondo, *Indonesia* ...... **37 G16** 7 42S 114 0 E
Siuna, *Nic.* **88 D3** 13 37N 84 45W
Siuri, *India* .... **43 H12** 23 50N 87 34 E
Sīvand, *Iran* .... **45 D7** 30 5N 52 55 E
Sivas, *Turkey* .... **25 G6** 39 43N 36 58 E
Siverek, *Turkey* .... **44 B3** 37 50N 39 19 E
Sivomaskinskiy, *Russia* .... **24 A11** 66 40N 62 35 E
Sivrihisar, *Turkey* .... **25 G5** 39 30N 31 35 E
Sîwa, *Egypt* .... **51 C11** 29 11N 25 31 E
Sîwa, El Wâhât es, *Egypt* ... **48 D6** 29 10N 25 30 E
Siwa Oasis = Sîwa, El Wâhât
es, *Egypt* .... **48 D6** 29 10N 25 30 E
Siwalik Range, *Nepal* ...... **43 F10** 28 0N 83 0 E
Siwan, *India* .... **43 F11** 26 13N 84 21 E
Siwana, *India* .... **42 G5** 25 38N 72 25 E
Sixmilebridge, *Ireland* **13 D3** 52 44N 8 46W
Sixth Cataract, *Sudan* ..... **51 E12** 16 20N 32 42 E
Siziwang Qi, *China* .... **34 D6** 41 25N 111 40 E
Sjælland, *Denmark* .... **9 J14** 55 30N 11 30 E
Sjumen = Shumen, *Bulgaria* **21 C12** 43 18N 26 55 E
Skadarsko Jezero,
Montenegro, Yug. .... **21 C8** 42 10N 19 20 E
Skaftafell, *Iceland* **8 D5** 64 1N 17 0W
Skagafjörður, *Iceland* **8 D4** 65 54N 19 35W
Skagastølstindane, *Norway* . **9 F12** 61 28N 7 52 E
Skagaströnd, *Iceland* **8 D3** 65 50N 20 19W
Skagen, *Denmark* .... **9 H14** 57 43N 10 35 E
Skagerrak, *Denmark* .... **9 H13** 57 30N 9 0 E
Skagit →, *U.S.A.* **84 B4** 48 23N 122 22W
Skagway, *U.S.A.* **68 C6** 59 28N 135 19W
Skala-Podilska, *Ukraine* .... **17 D14** 48 50N 26 15 E
Skala Podolskaya = Skala-
Podilska, *Ukraine* .... **17 D14** 48 50N 26 15 E
Skalat, *Ukraine* .... **17 D13** 49 23N 25 55 E
Skåne, *Sweden* .... **9 J15** 55 59N 13 30 E
Skaneateles, *U.S.A.* **79 D8** 42 57N 76 26W
Skaneateles L., *U.S.A.* **79 D8** 42 51N 76 22W
Skara, *Sweden* .... **9 G15** 58 25N 13 30 E
Skardu, *Pakistan* .... **43 B6** 35 20N 75 44 E
Skarżysko-Kamienna, *Poland* **17 C11** 51 7N 20 52 E
Skeena →, *Canada* **72 C2** 54 9N 130 5W
Skeena Mts., *Canada* **72 B3** 56 40N 128 30W
Skegness, *U.K.* .... **10 D8** 53 9N 0 20 E
Skeldon, *Guyana* **92 B7** 5 55N 57 20W
Skellefte älv →, *Sweden* ... **8 D19** 64 45N 21 10 E
Skellefteå, *Sweden* .... **8 D19** 64 45N 20 50 E
Skelleftehamn, *Sweden* .... **8 D19** 64 40N 21 9 E
Skerries, The, *U.K.* **10 D3** 53 25N 4 36W
Ski, *Norway* .... **9 G14** 59 43N 10 52 E
Skíathos, *Greece* .... **21 E10** 39 12N 23 30 E
Skibbereen, *Ireland* **13 E2** 51 33N 9 16W
Skiddaw, *U.K.* **10 C4** 54 39N 3 9W
Skidegate, *Canada* **72 C2** 53 15N 132 1W
Skien, *Norway* .... **9 G13** 59 12N 9 35 E
Skierniewice, *Poland* ...... **17 C11** 51 58N 20 10 E
Skikda, *Algeria* .... **50 A7** 36 50N 6 58 E
Skilloura, *Cyprus* .... **23 D12** 35 14N 33 10 E
Skipton, *U.K.* **10 D5** 53 58N 2 3W
Skirmish Pt., *Australia* ..... **62 A1** 11 59S 134 17 E
Skíros, *Greece* .... **21 E11** 38 55N 24 34 E
Skive, *Denmark* .... **9 H13** 56 33N 9 2 E
Skjálfandafljót →, *Iceland* .. **8 D5** 65 59N 17 25W
Skjálfandi, *Iceland* **8 C5** 66 5N 17 30W
Skoghall, *Sweden* .... **9 G15** 59 20N 13 30 E
Skole, *Ukraine* .... **17 D12** 49 3N 23 30 E
Skópelos, *Greece* .... **21 E10** 39 9N 23 47 E
Skopí, *Greece* .... **23 D8** 35 11N 26 2 E
Skopje, *Macedonia* .... **21 C9** 42 1N 21 26 E
Skövde, *Sweden* .... **9 G15** 58 24N 13 50 E
Skovorodino, *Russia* .... **27 D13** 54 0N 124 0 E
Skowhegan, *U.S.A.* **77 C11** 44 46N 69 43W
Skull, *Ireland* **13 E2** 51 32N 9 34W
Skunk →, *U.S.A.* **80 E9** 40 42N 91 7W
Skuodas, *Lithuania* .... **9 H19** 56 16N 21 33 E
Skvyra, *Ukraine* .... **17 D15** 49 44N 29 40 E
Skye, *U.K.* **12 D2** 57 15N 6 10W
Skykomish, *U.S.A.* **82 C3** 47 42N 121 22W
Skyros = Skíros, *Greece* .... **21 E11** 38 55N 24 34 E
Slættaratindur, *Færoe Is.* ... **8 E9** 62 18N 7 1W
Slagelse, *Denmark* .... **9 J14** 55 23N 11 19 E
Slamet, *Indonesia* .... **37 G13** 7 16S 109 8 E
Slaney →, *Ireland* **13 D5** 52 26N 6 33W
Slangberge, *S. Africa* ...... **56 E3** 31 32S 20 48 E
Śląsk, *Poland* .... **16 C9** 51 0N 16 30 E
Slate Is., *Canada* **70 C2** 48 40N 87 0W
Slatina, *Romania* .... **17 F13** 44 28N 24 22 E
Slatington, *U.S.A.* **79 F9** 40 45N 75 37W
Slaton, *U.S.A.* **81 J4** 33 26N 101 39W
Slave →, *Canada* **72 A6** 61 18N 113 39W
Slave Coast, *W. Afr.* .... **50 G6** 6 0N 2 30 E
Slave Lake, *Canada* **72 B6** 55 17N 114 43W
Slave Pt., *Canada* **72 A5** 61 11N 115 56W
Slavgorod, *Russia* .... **26 D8** 53 1N 78 37 E
Slavonski Brod, *Croatia* .... **21 B8** 45 11N 18 1 E
Slavuta, *Ukraine* .... **17 C14** 50 15N 27 2 E
Slavyanka, *Russia* .... **30 C5** 42 53N 131 21 E
Slavyansk = Slovyansk,
Ukraine .... **25 E6** 48 55N 37 36 E
Slawharad, *Belarus* .... **17 B16** 53 27N 31 0 E
Sleaford, *U.K.* **10 D7** 53 0N 0 24W
Sleaford B., *Australia* ...... **63 E2** 34 55S 135 45 E
Sleat, Sd. of, *U.K.* **12 D3** 57 5N 5 47W
Sleeper Is., *Canada* **69 C11** 58 30N 81 0W
Sleepy Eye, *U.S.A.* **80 C7** 44 18N 94 43W
Slemon L., *Canada* **72 A5** 63 13N 116 4W
Slide Mt., *U.S.A.* **79 E10** 42 0N 74 25W
Slidell, *U.S.A.* **81 K10** 30 17N 89 47W
Sliema, *Malta* .... **23 D2** 35 55N 14 30 E
Slieve Aughty, *Ireland* **13 C3** 53 4N 8 30W
Slieve Bloom, *Ireland* **13 C4** 53 4N 7 40W
Slieve Donard, *U.K.* **13 B6** 54 11N 5 55W
Slieve Gamph, *Ireland* **13 B3** 54 6N 9 0W
Slieve Gullion, *U.K.* **13 B5** 54 7N 6 26W
Slieve Mish, *Ireland* **13 D2** 52 12N 9 50W
Slievenamon, *Ireland* **13 D4** 52 25N 7 34W
Sligeach = Sligo, *Ireland* ... **13 B3** 54 16N 8 28W
Sligo, *Ireland* **13 B3** 54 16N 8 28W
Sligo, *U.S.A.* **78 E5** 41 6N 79 29W
Sligo □, *Ireland* **13 B3** 54 8N 8 42W
Sligo B., *Ireland* **13 B3** 54 18N 8 40W
Slippery Rock, *U.S.A.* **78 E4** 41 3N 80 3W
Slite, *Sweden* .... **9 H18** 57 42N 18 48 E
Sliven, *Bulgaria* .... **21 C12** 42 42N 26 19 E
Sloan, *U.S.A.* **85 K11** 35 57N 115 13W
Sloansville, *U.S.A.* **79 D10** 42 45N 74 22W
Slobodskoy, *Russia* .... **24 C9** 58 40N 50 6 E
Slobozia, *Romania* .... **17 F14** 44 34N 27 23 E
Slocan, *Canada* **72 D5** 49 48N 117 28W
Slonim, *Belarus* .... **17 B13** 53 4N 25 19 E
Slough, *U.K.* **11 F7** 51 30N 0 36W
Slough □, *U.K.* **11 F7** 51 30N 0 36W
Sloughhouse, *U.S.A.* **84 G5** 38 26N 121 12W
Slovak Rep. ■, *Europe* ..... **17 D10** 48 30N 20 0 E
Slovakia = Slovak Rep. ■,
Europe .... **17 D10** 48 30N 20 0 E
Slovakian Ore Mts. =
Slovenské Rudohorie,
Slovak Rep. .... **17 D10** 48 45N 20 0 E
Slovenia ■, *Europe* .... **16 F8** 45 58N 14 30 E
Slovenija = Slovenia ■,
Europe .... **16 F8** 45 58N 14 30 E
Slovenské Rudohorie,
Slovak Rep. .... **17 D10** 48 45N 20 0 E
Slovyansk, *Ukraine* .... **25 E6** 48 55N 37 36 E
Sluch →, *Ukraine* .... **17 C14** 51 37N 26 38 E
Sluis, *Neths.* .... **15 C3** 51 18N 3 23 E
Słupsk, *Poland* .... **17 A9** 54 30N 17 3 E
Slurry, *S. Africa* .... **56 D4** 25 49S 25 42 E
Slutsk, *Belarus* .... **17 B14** 53 2N 27 31 E
Slyne Hd., *Ireland* **13 C1** 53 25N 10 10W
Slyudyanka, *Russia* .... **27 D11** 51 40N 103 40 E
Småland, *Sweden* .... **9 H16** 57 15N 15 25 E
Smalltree L., *Canada* **73 A8** 61 0N 105 0W
Smallwood Res., *Canada* ... **71 B7** 54 0N 64 0W
Smarhon, *Belarus* .... **17 A14** 54 20N 26 24 E
Smartt Syndicate Dam,
S. Africa .... **56 E3** 30 45S 23 10 E
Smartville, *U.S.A.* **84 F5** 39 13N 121 18W
Smeaton, *Canada* **73 C8** 53 30N 104 49W
Smederevo, *Serbia, Yug.* .... **21 B9** 44 40N 20 57 E
Smerwick Harbour, *Ireland* . **13 D1** 52 12N 10 23W
Smethport, *U.S.A.* **78 E6** 41 49N 78 27W
Smidovich, *Russia* .... **27 E14** 48 36N 133 49 E
Smith, *Canada* **72 B6** 55 10N 114 0W
Smith Center, *U.S.A.* **80 F5** 39 47N 98 47W
Smith Sund, *Greenland* **4 B4** 78 30N 74 0W
Smithburne →, *Australia* ... **62 B3** 17 3S 140 57 E
Smithers, *Canada* **72 C3** 54 45N 127 10W
Smithfield, *S. Africa* .... **57 E4** 30 9S 26 30 E
Smithfield, *N.C., U.S.A.* **77 H6** 35 31N 78 21W
Smithfield, *Utah, U.S.A.* **82 F8** 41 50N 111 50W
Smiths Falls, *Canada* **79 B9** 44 55N 76 0W
Smithton, *Australia* .... **62 G4** 40 53S 145 6 E
Smithville, *Canada* **78 C5** 43 6N 79 33W
Smithville, *U.S.A.* **81 K6** 30 1N 97 10W
Smoky →, *Canada* **72 B5** 56 10N 117 21W
Smoky Bay, *Australia* ...... **63 E1** 32 22S 134 13 E
Smoky Hill →, *U.S.A.* **80 F6** 39 4N 96 48W
Smoky Hills, *U.S.A.* **80 F5** 39 15N 99 30W
Smoky Lake, *Canada* **72 C6** 54 10N 112 30W
Smøla, *Norway* .... **8 E13** 63 23N 8 3 E
Smolensk, *Russia* .... **24 D5** 54 45N 32 5 E
Smolikas, Óros, *Greece* .... **21 D9** 40 9N 20 58 E
Smolyan, *Bulgaria* .... **21 D11** 41 36N 24 38 E
Smooth Rock Falls, *Canada* . **70 C3** 49 17N 81 37W
Smoothstone L., *Canada* ... **73 C7** 54 40N 106 50W
Smorgon = Smarhon, *Belarus* **17 A14** 54 20N 26 24 E
Smyrna = İzmir, *Turkey* ..... **21 E12** 38 25N 27 8 E
Smyrna, *U.S.A.* **76 F8** 39 18N 75 36W
Snæfell, *Iceland* **8 D6** 64 48N 15 34W
Snaefell, *U.K.* **10 C3** 54 16N 4 27W
Snæfellsjökull, *Iceland* **8 D2** 64 49N 23 46W
Snake →, *U.S.A.* **82 C4** 46 12N 119 2W
Snake I., *Australia* .... **63 F4** 38 47S 146 33 E
Snake Range, *U.S.A.* **82 G6** 39 0N 114 20W
Snake River Plain, *U.S.A.* ... **82 E7** 42 50N 114 0W
Snåsavatnet, *Norway* ...... **8 D14** 64 12N 12 0 E
Sneek, *Neths.* .... **15 A5** 53 2N 5 40 E
Sneeuberge, *S. Africa* ...... **56 E3** 31 46S 24 20 E
Snelling, *U.S.A.* **84 H6** 37 31N 120 26W
Sněžka, *Europe* .... **16 C8** 50 41N 15 50 E
Snizort, L., *U.K.* **12 D2** 57 33N 6 28W
Snøhetta, *Norway* .... **9 E13** 62 19N 9 16 E
Snohomish, *U.S.A.* **84 C4** 47 55N 122 6W
Snoul, *Cambodia* .... **39 F6** 12 4N 106 26 E
Snow Hill, *U.S.A.* **76 F8** 38 11N 75 24W
Snow Lake, *Canada* **73 C8** 54 52N 100 3W
Snow Mt., *Calif., U.S.A.* **84 F4** 39 23N 122 45W
Snow Mt., *Maine, U.S.A.* ... **79 A14** 45 18N 70 48W
Snow Shoe, *U.S.A.* **78 E7** 41 2N 77 57W
Snowbird L., *Canada* **73 A8** 60 45N 103 0W
Snowdon, *U.K.* **10 D3** 53 4N 4 5W
Snowdrift →, *Canada* **73 A6** 62 24N 110 44W
Snowflake, *U.S.A.* **83 J8** 34 30N 110 5W
Snowshoe Pk., *U.S.A.* **82 B6** 48 13N 115 41W
Snowtown, *Australia* .... **63 E2** 33 46S 138 14 E
Snowville, *U.S.A.* **82 F7** 41 58N 112 43W
Snowy →, *Australia* .... **63 F4** 37 46S 148 30 E
Snowy Mt., *U.S.A.* **79 C10** 43 42N 74 23W
Snowy Mts., *Australia* ..... **63 F4** 36 30S 148 20 E
Snug Corner, *Bahamas* **89 B5** 22 33N 73 52W
Snyatyn, *Ukraine* .... **17 D13** 48 27N 25 38 E
Snyder, *Okla., U.S.A.* **81 H5** 34 40N 98 57W
Snyder, *Tex., U.S.A.* **81 J4** 32 44N 100 55W
Soahanina, *Madag.* .... **57 B7** 18 42S 44 13 E
Soalala, *Madag.* .... **57 B8** 16 6S 45 20 E
Soaloka, *Madag.* .... **57 B8** 18 32S 45 15 E
Soamanonga, *Madag.* ...... **57 C7** 23 52S 44 47 E
Soan →, *Pakistan* .... **42 C4** 33 1N 71 44 E
Soanierana-Ivongo, *Madag.* . **57 B8** 16 55S 49 35 E
Soanindraniny, *Madag.* ..... **57 B8** 19 54S 47 14 E
Soavina, *Madag.* .... **57 C8** 20 23S 46 56 E
Soavinandriana, *Madag.* ... **57 B8** 19 9S 46 45 E
Sobat, Nahr →, *Sudan* ..... **51 G12** 9 22N 31 33 E
Sobhapur, *India* .... **42 H8** 22 47N 78 17 E
Sobradinho, Reprêsa de,
Brazil .... **93 E10** 9 30S 42 0 E
Sobral, *Brazil* **93 D10** 3 50S 40 20W
Soc Giang, *Vietnam* .... **38 A6** 22 54N 106 1 E
Soc Trang, *Vietnam* .... **39 H5** 9 37N 105 50 E
Socastee, *U.S.A.* **77 J6** 33 41N 79 1W
Soch'e = Shache, *China* .... **32 C2** 38 20N 77 10 E
Sochi, *Russia* .... **25 F6** 43 35N 39 40 E
Société, Is. de la, *Pac. Oc.* ... **65 J12** 17 0S 151 0W
Society Is. = Société, Is. de la,
Pac. Oc. **65 J12** 17 0S 151 0W
Socompa, Portezuelo de,
Chile **94 A2** 24 27S 68 18W
Socorro, *N. Mex., U.S.A.* ... **83 J10** 34 4N 106 54W
Socorro, *Tex., U.S.A.* **83 L10** 31 39N 106 18W
Socorro, I., *Mexico* **86 D2** 18 45N 110 58W
Socotra, *Yemen* .... **46 E5** 12 30N 54 0 E
Soda L., *U.S.A.* **83 J5** 35 10N 116 4W
Soda Plains, *India* .... **43 B8** 35 30N 79 0 E
Soda Springs, *U.S.A.* **82 E8** 42 39N 111 36W
Sodankylä, *Finland* .... **8 C22** 67 29N 26 40 E
Soddy-Daisy, *U.S.A.* **77 H3** 35 17N 85 10W
Söderhamn, *Sweden* .... **9 F17** 61 18N 17 10 E

Söderköping, Sweden 9 G17 58 31N 16 20 E
Södermanland, Sweden 9 G17 58 56N 16 55 E
Södertälje, Sweden 9 G17 59 12N 17 39 E
Sodiri, Sudan 51 F11 14 27N 29 0 E
Sodus, U.S.A. 78 C7 43 14N 77 4W
Soekmekaar, S. Africa 57 C4 23 30S 29 55 E
Soest, Neths. 15 B5 52 9N 5 19 E
Sofala □, Mozam. 57 B5 19 30S 34 30 E
Sofia = Sofiya, Bulgaria 21 C10 42 45N 23 20 E
Sofia →, Madag. 57 B8 15 27S 47 23 E
Sofiya, Bulgaria 21 C10 42 45N 23 20 E
Sōfu-Gan, Japan 31 K10 29 49N 140 21 E
Sogamoso, Colombia 92 B4 5 43N 72 56W
Sogār, Iran 45 E8 25 53N 58 6 E
Sogndalsfjøra, Norway 9 F12 61 14N 7 5 E
Søgne, Norway 9 G12 58 5N 7 48 E
Sognefjorden, Norway 9 F11 61 10N 5 50 E
Sŏgwipo, S. Korea 35 H14 33 13N 126 34 E
Soh, Iran 45 C6 33 26N 51 27 E
Sohâg, Egypt 51 C12 26 33N 31 43 E
Sohagpur, India 42 H8 22 42N 78 12 E
Sŏhori, N. Korea 35 D15 40 7N 128 23 E
Soignies, Belgium 15 D4 50 35N 4 5 E
Soissons, France 18 B5 49 25N 3 19 E
Sōja, Japan 31 G6 34 40N 133 45 E
Sojat, India 42 G5 25 55N 73 45 E
Sokal, Ukraine 17 C13 50 31N 24 15 E
Söke, Turkey 21 F12 37 48N 27 28 E
Sokelo, Dem. Rep. of the Congo 55 D1 9 55S 24 36 E
Sokhumi, Georgia 25 F7 43 0N 41 0 E
Sokodé, Togo 50 G6 9 0N 1 11 E
Sokol, Russia 24 C7 59 30N 40 5 E
Sokółka, Poland 17 B12 53 25N 23 30 E
Sokołów Podlaski, Poland 17 B12 52 25N 22 15 E
Sokoto, Nigeria 50 F7 13 2N 5 16 E
Sol Iletsk, Russia 24 D10 51 10N 55 0 E
Solai, Kenya 54 B4 0 2N 36 12 E
Solan, India 42 D7 30 55N 77 7 E
Solano, Phil. 37 A6 16 31N 121 15 E
Solapur, India 40 L9 17 43N 75 56 E
Soldotna, U.S.A. 68 B4 60 29N 151 3W
Soléa, Cyprus 23 D12 35 5N 33 4 E
Soledad, Colombia 92 A4 10 55N 74 46W
Soledad, U.S.A. 84 J5 36 26N 121 20W
Soledad, Venezuela 92 B6 8 10N 63 34W
Solent, The, U.K. 11 G6 50 45N 1 25W
Solfonn, Norway 9 F12 60 2N 6 57 E
Solhan, Turkey 44 B4 38 57N 41 3 E
Soligalich, Russia 24 C7 59 5N 42 10 E
Soligorsk = Salihorsk, Belarus 17 B14 52 51N 27 27 E
Solihull, U.K. 11 E6 52 26N 1 47W
Solikamsk, Russia 24 C10 59 38N 56 50 E
Solila, Madag. 57 C8 21 25S 46 37 E
Solimões = Amazonas →, S. Amer. 93 D9 0 5S 50 0W
Solingen, Germany 16 C4 51 10N 7 5 E
Sollefteå, Sweden 8 E17 63 12N 17 20 E
Sóller, Spain 22 B9 39 46N 2 43 E
Solo →, Indonesia 37 G15 6 47S 112 22 E
Sologne, France 18 C4 47 40N 1 45 E
Solok, Indonesia 36 E2 0 45S 100 40 E
Sololá, Guatemala 88 D1 14 49N 91 10W
Solomon, N. Fork →, U.S.A. 80 F5 39 29N 98 26W
Solomon, S. Fork →, U.S.A. 80 F5 39 25N 99 12W
Solomon Is. ■, Pac. Oc. 64 H7 6 0S 155 0 E
Solon, China 33 B7 46 32N 121 10 E
Solon Springs, U.S.A. 80 B9 46 22N 91 49W
Solor, Indonesia 37 F6 8 27S 123 0 E
Solothurn, Switz. 18 C7 47 13N 7 32 E
Šolta, Croatia 20 C7 43 24N 16 15 E
Solṭānābād, Khorāsān, Iran 45 C8 34 13N 59 58 E
Solṭānābād, Khorāsān, Iran 45 B8 36 29N 58 5 E
Solunska Glava, Macedonia 21 D9 41 44N 21 31 E
Solvang, U.S.A. 85 L6 34 36N 120 8W
Solvay, U.S.A. 79 C8 43 3N 76 13W
Sölvesborg, Sweden 9 H16 56 5N 14 35 E
Solvychegodsk, Russia 24 B8 61 21N 46 56 E
Solway Firth, U.K. 10 C4 54 49N 3 35W
Solwezi, Zambia 55 E2 12 11S 26 21 E
Sōma, Japan 30 F10 37 40N 140 50 E
Soma, Turkey 21 E12 39 10N 27 35 E
Somabhula, Zimbabwe 57 B4 19 42S 29 40 E
Somali Pen., Africa 48 F8 7 0N 46 0 E
Somali Rep. ■, Africa 46 F4 7 0N 47 0 E
Somalia = Somali Rep. ■, Africa 46 F4 7 0N 47 0 E
Sombor, Serbia, Yug. 21 B8 45 46N 19 9 E
Sombra, Canada 78 D2 42 43N 82 29W
Sombrerete, Mexico 86 C4 23 40N 103 40W
Sombrero, Anguilla 89 C7 18 37N 63 30W
Somdari, India 42 G5 25 47N 72 38 E
Somers, U.S.A. 82 B6 48 5N 114 13W
Somerset, Ky., U.S.A. 76 G3 37 5N 84 36W
Somerset, Mass., U.S.A. 79 E13 41 47N 71 8W
Somerset, Pa., U.S.A. 78 F5 40 1N 79 5W
Somerset □, U.K. 11 F5 51 9N 3 0W
Somerset East, S. Africa 56 E4 32 42S 25 35 E
Somerset I., Canada 68 A10 73 30N 93 0W
Somerset West, S. Africa 56 E2 34 8S 18 50 E
Somersworth, U.S.A. 79 C14 43 16N 70 52W
Somerton, U.S.A. 83 K6 32 36N 114 43W
Somerville, U.S.A. 79 F10 40 35N 74 38W
Someş →, Romania 17 D12 47 49N 22 43 E
Somme →, France 18 A4 50 11N 1 38 E
Somnath, India 42 J4 20 53N 70 22 E
Somosierra, Puerto de, Spain 19 B4 41 4N 3 35W
Somoto, Nic. 88 D2 13 28N 86 37W
Somport, Puerto de, Spain 18 E3 42 48N 0 31W
Son →, India 43 G11 25 42N 84 52 E
Son Ha, Vietnam 38 E7 15 3N 108 34 E
Son Hoa, Vietnam 38 F7 13 2N 108 58 E
Son La, Vietnam 38 B4 21 20N 103 50 E
Son Serra, Spain 22 B10 39 43N 3 13 E
Son Tay, Vietnam 38 B5 21 8N 105 30 E
Soná, Panama 88 E3 8 0N 81 20W
Sonamarg, India 43 B6 34 18N 75 21 E
Sonamukhi, India 43 H12 23 18N 87 27 E
Sonar →, India 43 G8 24 24N 79 56 E
Sŏnch'ŏn, N. Korea 35 E13 39 48N 124 55 E
Sondags →, S. Africa 56 E4 33 44S 25 51 E
Sondar, India 43 C6 33 28N 75 56 E
Sønderborg, Denmark 9 J13 54 55N 9 49 E
Sóndrio, Italy 18 C8 46 10N 9 52 E
Sone, Mozam. 55 F3 17 23S 34 55 E
Sonepur, India 41 J13 20 55N 83 50 E
Song, Thailand 38 C3 18 28N 100 11 E
Song Cau, Vietnam 38 F7 13 27N 109 18 E
Song Xian, China 34 G7 34 12N 112 8 E
Songch'ŏn, N. Korea 35 E14 39 12N 126 15 E
Songea, Tanzania 55 E4 10 40S 35 40 E
Songhua Hu, China 35 C14 43 35N 126 50 E
Songhua Jiang →, China 33 B8 47 45N 132 30 E
Songjin, N. Korea 35 D15 40 40N 129 10 E
Songjŏng-ni, S. Korea 35 G14 35 8N 126 47 E
Songkhla, Thailand 39 J3 7 13N 100 37 E
Songnim, N. Korea 35 E13 38 45N 125 39 E
Songo, Mozam. 53 H6 15 34S 32 38 E
Songo, Sudan 51 G10 9 47N 24 21 E
Songpan, China 32 C5 32 40N 103 30 E
Songwe, Dem. Rep. of the Congo 54 C2 3 20S 26 16 E
Songwe →, Africa 55 D3 9 44S 33 58 E
Sonhat, India 43 H10 23 29N 82 31 E
Sonid Youqi, China 34 C7 42 45N 112 48 E
Sonipat, India 42 E7 29 0N 77 5 E
Sonkach, India 42 H7 22 59N 76 21 E
Sonmiani, Pakistan 42 G2 25 25N 66 40 E
Sonmiani B., Pakistan 42 G2 25 15N 66 30 E
Sono →, Brazil 93 E9 9 58S 48 11W
Sonoma, U.S.A. 84 G4 38 18N 122 28W
Sonora, Calif., U.S.A. 84 H6 37 59N 120 23W
Sonora, Tex., U.S.A. 81 K4 30 34N 100 39W
Sonora □, Mexico 86 B2 29 0N 111 0W
Sonora →, Mexico 86 B2 28 50N 111 33W
Sonoran Desert, U.S.A. 85 L12 33 40N 114 15W
Sonoyta, Mexico 86 A2 31 51N 112 50W
Sŏnsan, S. Korea 35 F15 36 14N 128 17 E
Sonsonate, El Salv. 88 D2 13 43N 89 44W
Soochow = Suzhou, China 33 C7 31 19N 120 38 E
Sooke, Canada 84 B3 48 13N 123 43W
Sop Hao, Laos 38 B5 20 33N 104 27 E
Sop Prap, Thailand 38 D2 17 53N 99 20 E
Sopi, Indonesia 37 D7 2 34N 128 28 E
Sopot, Poland 17 A10 54 27N 18 31 E
Sopron, Hungary 17 E9 47 45N 16 32 E
Sopur, India 43 B6 34 18N 74 27 E
Sør-Rondane, Antarctica 5 D4 72 0S 25 0 E
Sorah, Pakistan 42 F3 27 13N 68 56 E
Soraon, India 43 G9 25 37N 81 51 E
Sorel, Canada 70 C5 46 0N 73 10W
Sórgono, Italy 20 D3 40 1N 9 6 E
Soria, Spain 19 B4 41 43N 2 32W
Soriano, Uruguay 94 C4 33 24S 58 19W
Sorkh, Kuh-e, Iran 45 C8 35 40N 58 30 E
Soroca, Moldova 17 D15 48 8N 28 12 E
Sorocaba, Brazil 95 A6 23 31S 47 27W
Sorochinsk, Russia 24 D9 52 26N 53 10 E
Soroki = Soroca, Moldova 17 D15 48 8N 28 12 E
Sorong, Indonesia 37 E8 0 55S 131 15 E
Soroni, Greece 23 C10 36 21N 28 1 E
Soroti, Uganda 54 B3 1 43N 33 35 E
Sørøya, Norway 8 A20 70 40N 22 30 E
Sørøysundet, Norway 8 A20 70 25N 23 0 E
Sorrell, Australia 62 G4 42 47S 147 34 E
Sorsele, Sweden 8 D17 65 31N 17 30 E
Sorsogon, Phil. 37 B6 13 0N 124 0 E
Sortavala, Russia 24 B5 61 42N 30 41 E
Sortland, Norway 8 B16 68 42N 15 25 E
Sŏsan, S. Korea 35 F14 36 47N 126 27 E
Soscumica, L., Canada 70 B4 50 15N 77 27W
Sosnogorsk, Russia 24 B9 63 37N 53 51 E
Sosnowiec, Poland 17 C10 50 20N 19 10 E
Sossus Vlei, Namibia 56 C2 24 40S 15 23 E
Sŏsura, N. Korea 35 C16 42 16N 130 36 E
Sot →, India 43 F8 27 27N 79 37 E
Sotkamo, Finland 8 D23 64 8N 28 23 E
Soto la Marina →, Mexico 87 C5 23 40N 97 40W
Sotuta, Mexico 87 C7 20 29N 89 43W
Souanké, Congo 52 D2 2 10N 14 3 E
Souderton, U.S.A. 79 F9 40 19N 75 19W
Soúdha, Greece 23 D6 35 29N 24 4 E
Soúdhas, Kólpos, Greece 23 D6 35 25N 24 10 E
Soufrière, St. Lucia 89 D7 13 51N 61 3W
Soukhouma, Laos 38 E5 14 38N 105 48 E
Sŏul, S. Korea 35 F14 37 31N 126 58 E
Sound, The, U.K. 11 G3 50 20N 4 10W
Sources, Mt. aux, Lesotho 57 D4 28 45S 28 50 E
Soure, Brazil 93 D9 0 35S 48 30W
Souris, Man., Canada 73 D8 49 40N 100 20W
Souris, P.E.I., Canada 71 C7 46 21N 62 15W
Souris →, Canada 80 A5 49 40N 99 34W
Sousa, Brazil 93 E11 6 45S 38 10W
Sousse, Tunisia 51 A8 35 50N 10 38 E
Sout →, S. Africa 56 E2 31 35S 18 24 E
South Africa ■, Africa 56 E3 32 0S 23 0 E
South America 90 E5 10 0S 60 0W
South Atlantic Ocean 90 H7 20 0S 10 0W
South Aulatsivik I., Canada 71 A7 56 45N 61 30W
South Australia □, Australia 63 E2 32 0S 139 0 E
South Ayrshire □, U.K. 12 F4 55 18N 4 41W
South Baldy, U.S.A. 83 J10 33 59N 107 11W
South Bass I., U.S.A. 78 E2 41 38N 82 53W
South Bend, Ind., U.S.A. 76 E2 41 41N 86 15W
South Bend, Wash., U.S.A. 84 D3 46 40N 123 48W
South Boston, U.S.A. 77 G6 36 42N 78 54W
South Branch, Canada 71 C8 47 55N 59 2W
South Brook, Canada 71 C8 49 26N 56 5W
South Carolina □, U.S.A. 77 J5 34 0N 81 0W
South Charleston, U.S.A. 76 F5 38 22N 81 44W
South China Sea, Asia 36 C4 10 0N 113 0 E
South Dakota □, U.S.A. 80 C5 44 15N 100 0W
South Deerfield, U.S.A. 79 D12 42 29N 72 37W
South Downs, U.K. 11 G7 50 52N 0 25W
South East C., Australia 62 G4 43 40S 146 50 E
South East Is., Australia 61 F3 34 17S 123 30 E
South Esk →, U.K. 12 E6 56 43N 2 31W
South Foreland, U.K. 11 F9 51 8N 1 24 E
South Fork American →, U.S.A. 84 G5 38 45N 121 5W
South Fork Feather →, U.S.A. 84 F5 39 17N 121 36W
South Fork Grand →, U.S.A. 80 C3 45 43N 102 17W
South Fork Republican →, U.S.A. 80 E4 40 3N 101 31W
South Georgia, Antarctica 96 G9 54 30S 37 0W
South Gloucestershire □, U.K. 11 F5 51 32N 2 28W
South Hadley, U.S.A. 79 D12 42 16N 72 35W
South Haven, U.S.A. 76 D2 42 24N 86 16W
South Henik, L., Canada 73 A9 61 30N 97 30W
South Honshu Ridge, Pac. Oc. 64 E6 23 0N 143 0 E
South Horr, Kenya 54 B4 2 12N 36 56 E
South I., Kenya 54 B4 2 35N 36 35 E
South I., N.Z. 59 L3 44 0S 170 0 E
South Indian Lake, Canada 73 B9 56 47N 98 56W
South Invercargill, N.Z. 59 M2 46 26S 168 23 E
South Knife →, Canada 73 B10 58 55N 94 37W
South Koel →, India 43 H11 22 32N 85 14 E
South Korea ■, Asia 35 G15 36 0N 128 0 E
South Lake Tahoe, U.S.A. 84 G6 38 57N 119 59W
South Lanarkshire □, U.K. 12 F5 55 37N 3 53W
South Loup →, U.S.A. 80 E5 41 4N 98 39W
South Magnetic Pole, Antarctica 5 C9 64 8S 138 8 E
South Milwaukee, U.S.A. 76 D2 42 55N 87 52W
South Molton, U.K. 11 F4 51 1N 3 51W
South Moose L., Canada 73 C8 53 46N 100 8W
South Nahanni →, Canada 72 A4 61 3N 123 21W
South Nation →, Canada 79 A9 45 34N 75 6W
South Natuna Is. = Natuna Selatan, Kepulauan, Indonesia 39 L7 2 45N 109 0 E
South Negril Pt., Jamaica 88 C4 18 14N 78 30W
South Orkney Is., Antarctica 5 C18 63 0S 45 0W
South Ossetia □, Georgia 25 F7 42 21N 44 2 E
South Pagai, I. = Pagai Selatan, Pulau, Indonesia 36 E2 3 0S 100 15 E
South Paris, U.S.A. 79 B14 44 14N 70 31W
South Pittsburg, U.S.A. 77 H3 35 1N 85 42W
South Platte →, U.S.A. 80 E4 41 7N 100 42W
South Pole, Antarctica 5 E 90 0S 0 0W
South Porcupine, Canada 70 C3 48 30N 81 12W
South Portland, U.S.A. 77 D10 43 38N 70 15W
South Pt., U.S.A. 78 B1 44 52N 83 19W
South River, Canada 70 C4 45 52N 79 23W
South River, U.S.A. 79 F10 40 27N 74 23W
South Ronaldsay, U.K. 12 C6 58 48N 2 58W
South Sandwich Is., Antarctica 5 B1 57 0S 27 0W
South Saskatchewan →, Canada 73 C7 53 15N 105 5W
South Seal →, Canada 73 B9 58 48N 98 8W
South Shetland Is., Antarctica 5 C18 62 0S 59 0W
South Shields, U.K. 10 C6 55 0N 1 25W
South Sioux City, U.S.A. 80 D6 42 28N 96 24W
South Taranaki Bight, N.Z. 59 H5 39 40S 174 5 E
South Thompson →, Canada 72 C4 50 40N 120 20W
South Twin I., Canada 70 B4 53 7N 79 52W
South Tyne →, U.K. 10 C5 54 59N 2 8W
South Uist, U.K. 12 D1 57 20N 7 15W
South West Africa = Namibia ■, Africa 56 C2 22 0S 18 9 E
South West C., Australia 62 G4 43 34S 146 3 E
South Williamsport, U.S.A. 78 E8 41 13N 77 0W
South Yorkshire □, U.K. 10 D6 53 27N 1 36W
Southampton, Canada 78 B3 44 30N 81 25W
Southampton, U.K. 11 G6 50 54N 1 23W
Southampton, U.S.A. 79 F12 40 53N 72 23W
Southampton □, U.K. 11 G6 50 54N 1 23W
Southampton I., Canada 69 B11 64 30N 84 0W
Southaven, U.S.A. 81 H9 34 59N 90 2W
Southbank, Canada 72 C3 54 2N 125 46W
Southbridge, N.Z. 59 K4 43 48S 172 16 E
Southbridge, U.S.A. 79 D12 42 5N 72 2W
Southend, Canada 73 B8 56 19N 103 22W
Southend-on-Sea, U.K. 11 F8 51 32N 0 44 E
Southend-on-Sea □, U.K. 11 F8 51 32N 0 44 E
Southern □, Malawi 55 F4 15 0S 35 0 E
Southern □, Zambia 55 F2 16 20S 26 20 E
Southern Alps, N.Z. 59 K3 43 41S 170 11 E
Southern Cross, Australia 61 F2 31 12S 119 15 E
Southern Indian L., Canada 73 B9 57 10N 98 30W
Southern Ocean, Antarctica 5 C6 62 0S 60 0 E
Southern Pines, U.S.A. 77 H6 35 11N 79 24W
Southern Uplands, U.K. 12 F5 55 28N 3 52W
Southington, U.S.A. 79 E12 41 36N 72 53W
Southland □, N.Z. 59 L1 45 30S 168 0 E
Southold, U.S.A. 79 E12 41 4N 72 26W
Southport, Australia 63 D5 27 58S 153 25 E
Southport, U.K. 10 D4 53 39N 3 0W
Southport, Fla., U.S.A. 77 K3 30 17N 85 38W
Southport, N.Y., U.S.A. 78 D8 42 3N 76 49W
Southwest C., N.Z. 59 M1 47 17S 167 28 E
Southwold, U.K. 11 E9 52 20N 1 41 E
Soutpansberg, S. Africa 57 C4 23 0S 29 30 E
Sovetsk, Kaliningd., Russia 9 J19 55 6N 21 50 E
Sovetsk, Kirov, Russia 24 C8 57 38N 48 53 E
Sovetskaya Gavan = Vanino, Russia 27 E15 48 50N 140 5 E
Soweto, S. Africa 57 D4 26 14S 27 54 E
Sōya-Kaikyō = La Perouse Str., Asia 30 B11 45 40N 142 0 E
Sōya-Misaki, Japan 30 B10 45 30N 141 55 E
Sozh →, Belarus 17 B16 51 57N 30 48 E
Spa, Belgium 15 D5 50 29N 5 53 E
Spain ■, Europe 19 B4 39 0N 4 0W
Spalding, Australia 63 E2 33 30S 138 37 E
Spalding, U.K. 10 E7 52 48N 0 9W
Spangler, U.S.A. 78 F6 40 39N 78 48W
Spanish, Canada 70 C3 46 12N 82 20W
Spanish Fork, U.S.A. 82 F8 40 7N 111 39W
Spanish Town, Jamaica 88 C4 18 0N 76 57W
Sparks, U.S.A. 84 F7 39 32N 119 45W
Sparta = Spárti, Greece 21 F10 37 5N 22 25 E
Sparta, Mich., U.S.A. 76 D3 43 10N 85 42W
Sparta, N.J., U.S.A. 79 E10 41 2N 74 38W
Sparta, Wis., U.S.A. 80 D9 43 56N 90 49W
Spartanburg, U.S.A. 77 H5 34 56N 81 57W
Spartansburg, U.S.A. 78 E5 41 49N 79 41W
Spárti, Greece 21 F10 37 5N 22 25 E
Spartivento, C., Calabria, Italy 20 F7 37 55N 16 4 E
Spartivento, C., Sard., Italy 20 E3 38 53N 8 50 E
Sparwood, Canada 72 D6 49 44N 114 53W
Spassk Dalniy, Russia 27 E14 44 40N 132 48 E
Spátha, Ákra, Greece 23 D5 35 42N 23 43 E
Spatsizi →, Canada 72 B3 57 42N 128 7W
Spatsizi Plateau Wilderness Park, Canada 72 B3 57 40N 128 0W
Spean →, U.K. 12 E4 56 55N 4 59W
Spearfish, U.S.A. 80 C3 44 30N 103 52W
Spearman, U.S.A. 81 G4 36 12N 101 12W
Speculator, U.S.A. 79 C10 43 30N 74 25W
Speightstown, Barbados 89 D8 13 15N 59 39W
Speke Gulf, Tanzania 54 C3 2 20S 32 50 E
Spencer, Idaho, U.S.A. 82 D7 44 22N 112 11W
Spencer, Iowa, U.S.A. 80 D7 43 9N 95 9W
Spencer, N.Y., U.S.A. 79 D8 42 13N 76 30W
Spencer, Nebr., U.S.A. 80 D5 42 53N 98 42W
Spencer, C., Australia 63 F2 35 20S 136 53 E
Spencer B., Namibia 56 D1 25 30S 14 47 E
Spencer G., Australia 63 E2 34 0S 137 20 E
Spencerville, Canada 79 B9 44 51N 75 33W
Spences Bridge, Canada 72 C4 50 25N 121 20W
Spennymoor, U.K. 10 C6 54 42N 1 36W
Spenser Mts., N.Z. 59 K4 42 15S 172 45 E
Sperrin Mts., U.K. 13 B5 54 50N 7 0W
Spey →, U.K. 12 D5 57 40N 3 6W
Speyer, Germany 16 D5 49 29N 8 25 E
Spezand, Pakistan 42 E2 29 59N 67 0 E
Spili, Greece 23 D6 35 13N 24 31 E
Spin Büldak, Afghan. 42 D2 31 1N 66 25 E
Spinalónga, Greece 23 D7 35 18N 25 44 E
Spirit Lake, U.S.A. 84 D4 46 15N 122 9W
Spirit River, Canada 72 B5 55 45N 118 50W
Spiritwood, Canada 73 C7 53 24N 107 33W
Spithead, U.K. 11 G6 50 45N 1 10W
Spitzbergen = Svalbard, Arctic 4 B8 78 0N 17 0 E
Spjelkavik, Norway 9 E12 62 28N 6 22 E
Split, Croatia 20 C7 43 31N 16 26 E
Split L., Canada 73 B9 56 8N 96 15W
Split Lake, Canada 73 B9 56 8N 96 15W
Spofford, U.S.A. 81 L4 29 10N 100 25W
Spokane, U.S.A. 82 C5 47 40N 117 24W
Spoleto, Italy 20 C5 42 44N 12 44 E
Spooner, U.S.A. 80 C9 45 50N 91 53W
Sporyy Navolok, Mys, Russia 26 B7 75 50N 68 40 E
Sprague, U.S.A. 82 C5 47 18N 117 59W
Spratly I., S. China Sea 36 C4 8 38N 111 55 E
Spratly Is., S. China Sea 36 C4 8 20N 112 0 E
Spray, U.S.A. 82 D4 44 50N 119 48W
Spree →, Germany 16 B7 52 32N 13 13 E
Sprengisandur, Iceland 8 D5 64 52N 18 7W
Spring City, U.S.A. 79 F9 40 11N 75 33W
Spring Creek, U.S.A. 82 F6 40 45N 115 38W
Spring Garden, U.S.A. 84 F6 39 52N 120 47W
Spring Hill, U.S.A. 77 L4 28 27N 82 41W
Spring Mts., U.S.A. 83 H6 36 0N 115 45W
Spring Valley, U.S.A. 85 N10 32 45N 117 5W
Springbok, S. Africa 56 D2 29 42S 17 54 E
Springboro, U.S.A. 78 E4 41 48N 80 22W
Springdale, Canada 71 C8 49 30N 56 6W
Springdale, U.S.A. 81 G7 36 11N 94 8W
Springer, U.S.A. 81 G2 36 22N 104 36W
Springerville, U.S.A. 83 J9 34 8N 109 17W
Springfield, Canada 78 D4 42 50N 80 56W
Springfield, N.Z. 59 K3 43 19S 171 56 E
Springfield, Colo., U.S.A. 81 G3 37 24N 102 37W
Springfield, Ill., U.S.A. 80 F10 39 48N 89 39W
Springfield, Mass., U.S.A. 79 D12 42 6N 72 35W
Springfield, Mo., U.S.A. 81 G8 37 13N 93 17W
Springfield, Ohio, U.S.A. 76 F4 39 55N 83 49W
Springfield, Oreg., U.S.A. 82 D2 44 3N 123 1W
Springfield, Tenn., U.S.A. 77 G2 36 31N 86 53W
Springfield, Vt., U.S.A. 79 C12 43 18N 72 29W
Springfontein, S. Africa 56 E4 30 15S 25 40 E
Springhill, Canada 71 C7 45 40N 64 4W
Springhill, U.S.A. 81 J8 33 0N 93 28W
Springhouse, Canada 72 C4 51 56N 122 7W
Springs, S. Africa 57 D4 26 13S 28 25 E
Springsure, Australia 62 C4 24 8S 148 6 E
Springvale, U.S.A. 79 C14 43 28N 70 48W
Springville, Calif., U.S.A. 84 J8 36 8N 118 49W
Springville, N.Y., U.S.A. 78 D6 42 31N 78 40W
Springville, Utah, U.S.A. 82 F8 40 10N 111 37W
Springwater, U.S.A. 78 D7 42 38N 77 35W
Spruce-Creek, U.S.A. 78 F6 40 36N 78 9W
Spruce Mt., U.S.A. 79 B12 44 12N 72 19W
Spur, U.S.A. 81 J4 33 28N 100 52W
Spurn Hd., U.K. 10 D8 53 35N 0 8 E
Spuzzum, Canada 72 D4 49 37N 121 23W
Squam L., U.S.A. 79 C13 43 45N 71 32W
Squamish, Canada 72 D4 49 45N 123 10W
Square Islands, Canada 71 B8 52 47N 55 47W
Squires, Mt., Australia 61 E4 26 14S 127 28 E
Srbija = Serbia □, Yugoslavia 21 C9 43 30N 21 0 E
Sre Ambel, Cambodia 39 G4 11 8N 103 46 E
Sre Khtum, Cambodia 39 F6 12 10N 106 52 E
Sre Umbell = Sre Ambel, Cambodia 39 G4 11 8N 103 46 E
Srebrenica, Bos.-H. 21 B8 44 6N 19 18 E
Sredinny Ra. = Sredinnyy Khrebet, Russia 27 D16 57 0N 160 0 E
Sredinnyy Khrebet, Russia 27 D16 57 0N 160 0 E
Srednekolymsk, Russia 27 C16 67 27N 153 40 E
Śrem, Poland 17 B9 52 6N 17 2 E
Sremska Mitrovica, Serbia, Yug. 21 B8 44 59N 19 38 E
Srepok →, Cambodia 38 F6 13 33N 106 16 E
Sretensk, Russia 27 D12 52 10N 117 40 E
Sri Lanka ■, Asia 40 R12 7 30N 80 50 E
Srikakulam, India 41 K13 18 14N 83 58 E
Srinagar, India 43 B6 34 5N 74 50 E
Staaten →, Australia 62 B3 16 24S 141 17 E
Stade, Germany 16 B5 53 35N 9 29 E
Stadskanaal, Neths. 15 A6 53 4N 6 55 E
Staffa, U.K. 12 E2 56 27N 6 21W
Stafford, U.K. 10 E5 52 49N 2 7W
Stafford, U.S.A. 81 G5 37 58N 98 36W
Stafford Springs, U.S.A. 79 E12 41 57N 72 18W
Staffordshire □, U.K. 10 E5 52 53N 2 10W
Staines, U.K. 11 F7 51 26N 0 29W
Stakhanov, Ukraine 25 E6 48 35N 38 40 E
Stalingrad = Volgograd, Russia 25 E7 48 40N 44 25 E
Staliniri = Tskhinvali, Georgia 25 F7 42 14N 44 1 E
Stalino = Donetsk, Ukraine 25 E6 48 0N 37 45 E
Stalinogorsk = Novomoskovsk, Russia 24 D6 54 5N 38 15 E
Stalis, Greece 23 D7 35 17N 25 25 E
Stalowa Wola, Poland 17 C12 50 34N 22 3 E
Stalybridge, U.K. 10 D5 53 28N 2 3W
Stamford, Australia 62 C3 21 15S 143 46 E
Stamford, U.K. 11 E7 52 39N 0 29W
Stamford, Conn., U.S.A. 79 E11 41 3N 73 32W
Stamford, N.Y., U.S.A. 79 D10 42 25N 74 38W
Stamford, Tex., U.S.A. 81 J5 32 57N 99 48W
Stampriet, Namibia 56 C2 24 20S 18 28 E
Stamps, U.S.A. 81 J8 33 22N 93 30W
Standerton, S. Africa 57 D4 26 55S 29 7 E
Standish, U.S.A. 76 D4 43 59N 83 57W
Stanford, S. Africa 56 E2 34 26S 19 29 E
Stanford, U.S.A. 82 C8 47 9N 110 13W
Stanger, S. Africa 57 D5 29 27S 31 14 E
Stanislaus →, U.S.A. 84 H5 37 40N 121 14W

Stanislav = Ivano-Frankivsk, Ukraine 17 D13 48 40N 24 40 E
Stanke Dimitrov, Bulgaria 21 C10 42 17N 23 9 E
Stanley, Australia 62 G4 40 46S 145 19 E
Stanley, Canada 73 B8 55 24N 104 22W
Stanley, Falk. Is. 96 G5 51 40S 59 51W
Stanley, U.K. 10 C6 54 53N 1 41W
Stanley, Idaho, U.S.A. 82 D6 44 13N 114 56W
Stanley, N. Dak., U.S.A. 80 A3 48 19N 102 23W
Stanley, N.Y., U.S.A. 78 D7 42 48N 77 6W
Stanovoy Khrebet, Russia 27 D13 55 0N 130 0 E
Stanovoy Ra. = Stanovoy Khrebet, Russia 27 D13 55 0N 130 0 E
Stansmore Ra., Australia 60 D4 21 23S 128 33 E
Stanthorpe, Australia 63 D5 28 36S 151 59 E
Stanton, U.S.A. 81 J4 32 8N 101 48W
Stanwood, U.S.A. 84 B4 48 15N 122 23W
Staples, U.S.A. 80 B7 46 21N 94 48W
Star City, Canada 73 C8 52 50N 104 20W
Star Lake, U.S.A. 79 B9 44 10N 75 2W
Stara Planina, Bulgaria 21 C10 43 15N 23 0 E
Stara Zagora, Bulgaria 21 C11 42 26N 25 39 E
Starachowice, Poland 17 C11 51 3N 21 2 E
Staraya Russa, Russia 24 C5 57 58N 31 23 E
Starbuck I., Kiribati 65 H12 5 37S 155 55W
Stargard Szczeciński, Poland 16 B8 53 20N 15 0 E
Staritsa, Russia 24 C5 56 33N 34 55 E
Starke, U.S.A. 77 L4 29 57N 82 7W
Starogard Gdański, Poland 17 B10 53 59N 18 30 E
Starokonstantinov = Starokonstyantyniv, Ukraine 17 D14 49 48N 27 10 E
Starokonstyantyniv, Ukraine 17 D14 49 48N 27 10 E
Start Pt., U.K. 11 G4 50 13N 3 39W
Staryy Chartoriysk, Ukraine 17 C13 51 15N 25 54 E
Staryy Oskol, Russia 25 D6 51 19N 37 55 E
State College, U.S.A. 78 F7 40 48N 77 52W
Stateline, U.S.A. 84 G7 38 57N 119 56W
Staten, I. = Estados, I. de Los, Argentina 96 G4 54 40S 64 30W
Staten I., U.S.A. 79 F10 40 35N 74 9W
Statesboro, U.S.A. 77 J5 32 27N 81 47W
Statesville, U.S.A. 77 H5 35 47N 80 53W
Stauffer, U.S.A. 85 L7 34 45N 119 3W
Staunton, Ill., U.S.A. 80 F10 39 1N 89 47W
Staunton, Va., U.S.A. 76 F6 38 9N 79 4W
Stavanger, Norway 9 G11 58 57N 5 40 E
Staveley, N.Z. 59 K3 43 40S 171 32 E
Stavelot, Belgium 15 D5 50 23N 5 55 E
Stavern, Norway 9 G14 59 0N 10 1 E
Stavoren, Neths. 15 B5 52 53N 5 22 E
Stavropol, Russia 25 E7 45 5N 42 0 E
Stavros, Cyprus 23 D11 35 1N 32 38 E
Stavrós, Greece 23 D6 35 12N 24 45 E
Stavrós, Ákra, Greece 23 D6 35 26N 24 58 E
Stawell, Australia 63 F3 37 5S 142 47 E
Stawell →, Australia 62 C3 20 20S 142 55 E
Stayner, Canada 78 B4 44 25N 80 5W
Stayton, U.S.A. 82 D2 44 48N 122 48W
Steamboat Springs, U.S.A. 82 F10 40 29N 106 50W
Steele, U.S.A. 80 B5 46 51N 99 55W
Steelton, U.S.A. 78 F8 40 14N 76 50W
Steen River, Canada 72 B5 59 40N 117 12W
Steenkool = Bintuni, Indonesia 37 E8 2 7S 133 32 E
Steens Mt., U.S.A. 82 E4 42 35N 118 40W
Steenwijk, Neths. 15 B6 52 47N 6 7 E
Steep Pt., Australia 61 E1 26 8S 113 8 E
Steep Rock, Canada 73 C9 51 30N 98 48W
Stefanie L. = Chew Bahir, Ethiopia 46 G2 4 40N 36 50 E
Stefansson Bay, Antarctica 5 C5 67 20S 59 8 E
Steiermark □, Austria 16 E8 47 26N 15 0 E
Steilacoom, U.S.A. 84 C4 47 10N 122 36W
Steilrandberge, Namibia 56 B1 17 45S 13 20 E
Steinbach, Canada 73 D9 49 32N 96 40W
Steinhausen, Namibia 56 C2 21 49S 18 20 E
Steinkjer, Norway 8 D14 64 1N 11 31 E
Steinkopf, S. Africa 56 D2 29 18S 17 43 E
Stellarton, Canada 71 C7 45 32N 62 30W
Stellenbosch, S. Africa 56 E2 33 58S 18 50 E
Stendal, Germany 16 B6 52 36N 11 53 E
Steornabhaigh = Stornoway, U.K. 12 C2 58 13N 6 23W
Stepanakert = Xankändi, Azerbaijan 25 G8 39 52N 46 49 E
Stephens Creek, Australia 63 E3 31 50S 141 30 E
Stephens I., Canada 72 C2 54 10N 130 45W
Stephens L., Canada 73 B9 56 32N 95 0W
Stephenville, Canada 71 C8 48 31N 58 35W
Stephenville, U.S.A. 81 J5 32 13N 98 12W
Stepnoi = Elista, Russia 25 E7 46 16N 44 14 E
Steppe, Asia 28 D9 50 0N 50 0 E
Sterkstroom, S. Africa 56 E4 31 32S 26 32 E
Sterling, Colo., U.S.A. 80 E3 40 37N 103 13W
Sterling, Ill., U.S.A. 80 E10 41 48N 89 42W
Sterling, Kans., U.S.A. 80 F5 38 13N 98 12W
Sterling City, U.S.A. 81 K4 31 51N 101 0W
Sterling Heights, U.S.A. 76 D4 42 35N 83 0W
Sterling Run, U.S.A. 78 E6 41 25N 78 12W
Sterlitamak, Russia 24 D10 53 40N 56 0 E
Stérnes, Greece 23 D6 35 30N 24 9 E
Stettin = Szczecin, Poland 16 B8 53 27N 14 27 E
Stettiner Haff, Germany 16 B8 53 47N 14 15 E
Stettler, Canada 72 C6 52 19N 112 40W
Steubenville, U.S.A. 78 F4 40 22N 80 37W
Stevenage, U.K. 11 F7 51 55N 0 13W
Stevens Point, U.S.A. 80 C10 44 31N 89 34W
Stevenson, U.S.A. 84 E5 45 42N 121 53W
Stevenson L., Canada 73 C9 53 55N 96 0W
Stevensville, U.S.A. 82 C6 46 30N 114 5W
Stewart, Canada 72 B3 55 56N 129 57W
Stewart, U.S.A. 84 F7 39 5N 119 46W
Stewart →, Canada 68 B6 63 19N 139 26W
Stewart, C., Australia 62 A1 11 57S 134 56 E
Stewart, I., Chile 96 G2 54 50S 71 15W
Stewart I., N.Z. 59 M1 46 58S 167 54 E
Stewarts Point, U.S.A. 84 G3 38 39N 123 24W
Stewartville, U.S.A. 80 D8 43 51N 92 29W
Stewiacke, Canada 71 C7 45 9N 63 22W
Steynsburg, S. Africa 56 E4 31 15S 25 49 E
Steyr, Austria 16 D8 48 3N 14 25 E
Steytlerville, S. Africa 56 E3 33 17S 24 19 E
Stigler, U.S.A. 81 H7 35 15N 95 8W
Stikine →, Canada 72 B2 56 40N 132 30W
Stilfontein, S. Africa 56 D4 26 51S 26 50 E
Stillwater, N.Z. 59 K3 42 27S 171 20 E
Stillwater, Minn., U.S.A. 80 C8 45 3N 92 49W
Stillwater, N.Y., U.S.A. 79 D11 42 55N 73 41W
Stillwater, Okla., U.S.A. 81 G6 36 7N 97 4W
Stillwater Range, U.S.A. 82 G4 39 50N 118 5W
Stillwater Reservoir, U.S.A. 79 C9 43 54N 75 3W
Stilwell, U.S.A. 81 H7 35 49N 94 38W
Štip, Macedonia 21 D10 41 42N 22 10 E
Stirling, Canada 78 B7 44 18N 77 33W
Stirling, U.K. 12 E5 56 8N 3 57W
Stirling □, U.K. 12 E4 56 12N 4 18W
Stirling Ra., Australia 61 F2 34 23S 118 0 E
Stittsville, Canada 79 A9 45 15N 75 55W
Stjernøya, Norway 8 A20 70 20N 22 40 E
Stjørdalshalsen, Norway 8 E14 63 29N 10 51 E
Stockerau, Austria 16 D9 48 24N 16 12 E
Stockholm, Sweden 9 G18 59 20N 18 3 E
Stockport, U.K. 10 D5 53 25N 2 9W
Stocksbridge, U.K. 10 D6 53 29N 1 35W
Stockton, Calif., U.S.A. 84 H5 37 58N 121 17W
Stockton, Kans., U.S.A. 80 F5 39 26N 99 16W
Stockton, Mo., U.S.A. 81 G8 37 42N 93 48W
Stockton-on-Tees, U.K. 10 C6 54 35N 1 19W
Stockton-on-Tees □, U.K. 10 C6 54 35N 1 19W
Stockton Plateau, U.S.A. 81 K3 30 30N 102 30W
Stoeng Treng, Cambodia 38 F5 13 31N 105 58 E
Stoer, Pt. of, U.K. 12 C3 58 16N 5 23W
Stoke-on-Trent, U.K. 10 D5 53 1N 2 11W
Stoke-on-Trent □, U.K. 10 D5 53 1N 2 11W
Stokes Pt., Australia 62 G3 40 10S 143 56 E
Stokes Ra., Australia 60 C5 15 50S 130 50 E
Stokksnes, Iceland 8 D6 64 14N 14 58W
Stokmarknes, Norway 8 B16 68 34N 14 54 E
Stolac, Bos.-H. 21 C7 43 5N 17 59 E
Stolbovoy, Ostrov, Russia 27 B14 74 44N 135 14 E
Stolbtsy = Stowbtsy, Belarus 17 B14 53 30N 26 43 E
Stolin, Belarus 17 C14 51 53N 26 50 E
Stomion, Greece 23 D5 35 21N 23 32 E
Stone, U.K. 10 E5 52 55N 2 9W
Stoneboro, U.S.A. 78 E4 41 20N 80 7W
Stonehaven, U.K. 12 E6 56 59N 2 12W
Stonehenge, Australia 62 C3 24 22S 143 17 E
Stonehenge, U.K. 11 F6 51 9N 1 45W
Stonewall, Canada 73 C9 50 10N 97 19W
Stony L., Man., Canada 73 B9 58 51N 98 40W
Stony L., Ont., Canada 78 B6 44 30N 78 5W
Stony Point, U.S.A. 79 E11 41 14N 73 59W
Stony Pt., U.S.A. 79 C8 43 50N 76 18W
Stony Rapids, Canada 73 B7 59 16N 105 50W
Stony Tunguska = Tunguska, Podkamennaya →, Russia 27 C10 61 50N 90 13 E
Stonyford, U.S.A. 84 F4 39 23N 122 33W
Stora Lulevatten, Sweden 8 C18 67 10N 19 30 E
Storavan, Sweden 8 D18 65 45N 18 10 E
Stord, Norway 9 G11 59 52N 5 23 E
Store Bælt, Denmark 9 J14 55 20N 11 0 E
Storm B., Australia 62 G4 43 10S 147 30 E
Storm Lake, U.S.A. 80 D7 42 39N 95 13W
Stormberge, S. Africa 56 E4 31 16S 26 17 E
Stormsrivier, S. Africa 56 E3 33 59S 23 52 E
Stornoway, U.K. 12 C2 58 13N 6 23W
Storozhinets = Storozhynets, Ukraine 17 D13 48 14N 25 45 E
Storozhynets, Ukraine 17 D13 48 14N 25 45 E
Storrs, U.S.A. 79 E12 41 49N 72 15W
Storsjön, Sweden 8 E16 63 9N 14 30 E
Storuman, Sweden 8 D17 65 5N 17 10 E
Storuman, sjö, Sweden 8 D17 65 13N 16 50 E
Stouffville, Canada 78 C5 43 58N 79 15W
Stoughton, Canada 73 D8 49 40N 103 0W
Stour →, Dorset, U.K. 11 G6 50 43N 1 47W
Stour →, Kent, U.K. 11 F9 51 18N 1 22 E
Stour →, Suffolk, U.K. 11 F9 51 57N 1 4 E
Stourbridge, U.K. 11 E5 52 28N 2 8W
Stout L., Canada 73 C10 52 0N 94 40W
Stove Pipe Wells Village, U.S.A. 85 J9 36 35N 117 11W
Stow, U.S.A. 78 E3 41 10N 81 27W
Stowbtsy, Belarus 17 B14 53 30N 26 43 E
Stowmarket, U.K. 11 E9 52 12N 1 0 E
Strabane, U.K. 13 B4 54 50N 7 27W
Strahan, Australia 62 G4 42 9S 145 20 E
Stralsund, Germany 16 A7 54 18N 13 4 E
Strand, S. Africa 56 E2 34 9S 18 48 E
Stranda, Møre og Romsdal, Norway 9 E12 62 19N 6 58 E
Stranda, Nord-Trøndelag, Norway 8 E14 63 33N 10 14 E
Strangford L., U.K. 13 B6 54 30N 5 37W
Stranraer, U.K. 12 G3 54 54N 5 1W
Strasbourg, Canada 73 C8 51 4N 104 55W
Strasbourg, France 18 B7 48 35N 7 42 E
Stratford, Canada 78 C4 43 23N 81 0W
Stratford, N.Z. 59 H5 39 20S 174 19 E
Stratford, Calif., U.S.A. 84 J7 36 11N 119 49W
Stratford, Conn., U.S.A. 79 E11 41 12N 73 8W
Stratford, Tex., U.S.A. 81 G3 36 20N 102 4W
Stratford-upon-Avon, U.K. 11 E6 52 12N 1 42W
Strath Spey, U.K. 12 D5 57 9N 3 49W
Strathalbyn, Australia 63 F2 35 13S 138 53 E
Strathaven, U.K. 12 F4 55 40N 4 5W
Strathcona Prov. Park, Canada 72 D3 49 38N 125 40W
Strathmore, Canada 72 C6 51 5N 113 18W
Strathmore, U.K. 12 E5 56 37N 3 7W
Strathmore, U.S.A. 84 J7 36 9N 119 4W
Strathnaver, Canada 72 C4 53 20N 122 33W
Strathpeffer, U.K. 12 D4 57 35N 4 32W
Strathroy, Canada 78 D3 42 58N 81 38W
Strathy Pt., U.K. 12 C4 58 36N 4 1W
Strattanville, U.S.A. 78 E5 41 12N 79 19W
Stratton, U.S.A. 79 A14 45 8N 70 26W
Stratton Mt., U.S.A. 79 C12 43 4N 72 55W
Straubing, Germany 16 D7 48 52N 12 34 E
Straumnes, Iceland 8 C2 66 26N 23 8W
Strawberry →, U.S.A. 82 F8 40 10N 110 24W
Streaky B., Australia 63 E1 32 48S 134 13 E
Streaky Bay, Australia 63 E1 32 51S 134 18 E
Streator, U.S.A. 80 E10 41 8N 88 50W
Streetsboro, U.S.A. 78 E3 41 14N 81 21W
Streetsville, Canada 78 C5 43 35N 79 42W
Strelka, Russia 27 D10 58 5N 93 3 E
Streng →, Cambodia 38 F4 13 12N 103 37 E
Streymoy, Færoe Is. 8 E9 62 8N 7 5W
Strezhevoy, Russia 26 C8 60 42N 77 34 E
Strimón →, Greece 21 D10 40 46N 23 51 E
Strimonikós Kólpos, Greece 21 D11 40 33N 24 0 E
Stroma, U.K. 12 C5 58 41N 3 7W
Strómboli, Italy 20 E6 38 47N 15 13 E
Stromeferry, U.K. 12 D3 57 21N 5 33W
Stromness, U.K. 12 C5 58 58N 3 17W
Stromsburg, U.S.A. 80 E6 41 7N 97 36W
Strömstad, Sweden 9 G14 58 56N 11 10 E
Strömsund, Sweden 8 E16 63 51N 15 33 E
Strongsville, U.S.A. 78 E3 41 19N 81 50W
Stronsay, U.K. 12 B6 59 7N 2 35W
Stroud, U.K. 11 F5 51 45N 2 13W
Stroud Road, Australia 63 E5 32 18S 151 57 E
Stroudsburg, U.S.A. 79 F9 40 59N 75 12W
Stroumbi, Cyprus 23 E11 34 53N 32 29 E
Struer, Denmark 9 H13 56 30N 8 35 E
Strumica, Macedonia 21 D10 41 28N 22 41 E
Struthers, Canada 70 C2 48 41N 85 51W
Struthers, U.S.A. 78 E4 41 4N 80 39W
Stryker, U.S.A. 82 B6 48 41N 114 46W
Stryy, Ukraine 17 D12 49 16N 23 48 E
Strzelecki Cr. →, Australia 63 D2 29 37S 139 59 E
Stuart, Fla., U.S.A. 77 M5 27 12N 80 15W
Stuart, Nebr., U.S.A. 80 D5 42 36N 99 8W
Stuart →, Canada 72 C4 54 0N 123 35W
Stuart Bluff Ra., Australia 60 D5 22 50S 131 52 E
Stuart L., Canada 72 C4 54 30N 124 30W
Stuart Ra., Australia 63 D1 29 10S 134 56 E
Stull L., Canada 70 B1 54 24N 92 34W
Stung Treng = Stoeng Treng, Cambodia 38 F5 13 31N 105 58 E
Stupart →, Canada 70 A1 56 0N 93 25W
Sturgeon B., Canada 73 C9 52 0N 97 50W
Sturgeon Bay, U.S.A. 76 C2 44 50N 87 23W
Sturgeon Falls, Canada 70 C4 46 25N 79 57W
Sturgeon L., Alta., Canada 72 B5 55 6N 117 32W
Sturgeon L., Ont., Canada 70 C1 50 0N 90 45W
Sturgeon L., Ont., Canada 78 B6 44 28N 78 43W
Sturgis, Canada 73 C8 51 56N 102 36W
Sturgis, Mich., U.S.A. 76 E3 41 48N 85 25W
Sturgis, S. Dak., U.S.A. 80 C3 44 25N 103 31W
Sturt Cr. →, Australia 60 C4 19 8S 127 50 E
Stutterheim, S. Africa 56 E4 32 33S 27 28 E
Stuttgart, Germany 16 D5 48 48N 9 11 E
Stuttgart, U.S.A. 81 H9 34 30N 91 33W
Stuyvesant, U.S.A. 79 D11 42 23N 73 45W
Stykkishólmur, Iceland 8 D2 65 2N 22 40W
Styria = Steiermark □, Austria 16 E8 47 26N 15 0 E
Su Xian = Suzhou, China 34 H9 33 41N 116 59 E
Suakin, Sudan 51 E13 19 8N 37 20 E
Suan, N. Korea 35 E14 38 42N 126 22 E
Suaqui, Mexico 86 B3 29 12N 109 41W
Suar, India 43 E8 29 2N 79 3 E
Subang, Indonesia 37 G12 6 34S 107 45 E
Subansiri →, India 41 F18 26 48N 93 50 E
Subarnarekha →, India 43 H12 22 34N 87 24 E
Subayhah, Si. Arabia 44 D3 30 2N 38 50 E
Subi, Indonesia 39 L7 2 58N 108 50 E
Subotica, Serbia, Yug. 21 A8 46 6N 19 39 E
Suceava, Romania 17 E14 47 38N 26 16 E
Suchan, Russia 30 C6 43 8N 133 9 E
Suchitoto, El Salv. 88 D2 13 56N 89 0W
Suchou = Suzhou, China 33 C7 31 19N 120 38 E
Süchow = Xuzhou, China 35 G9 34 18N 117 10 E
Suck →, Ireland 13 C3 53 17N 8 3W
Sucre, Bolivia 92 G5 19 0S 65 15W
Sucuriú →, Brazil 93 H8 20 47S 51 38W
Sud, Pte. du, Canada 71 C7 49 3N 62 14W
Sud-Kivu □, Dem. Rep. of the Congo 54 C2 3 0S 28 30 E
Sud-Ouest, Pte. du, Canada 71 C7 49 23N 63 36W
Sudan, U.S.A. 81 H3 34 4N 102 32W
Sudan ■, Africa 51 E11 15 0N 30 0 E
Sudbury, Canada 70 C3 46 30N 81 0W
Sudbury, U.K. 11 E8 52 2N 0 45 E
Sûdd, Sudan 51 G12 8 20N 30 0 E
Sudeten Mts. = Sudety, Europe 17 C9 50 20N 16 45 E
Sudety, Europe 17 C9 50 20N 16 45 E
Suðuroy, Færoe Is. 8 F9 61 32N 6 50W
Sudi, Tanzania 55 E4 10 11S 39 57 E
Sudirman, Pegunungan, Indonesia 37 E9 4 30S 137 0 E
Sueca, Spain 19 C5 39 12N 0 21W
Suemez I., U.S.A. 72 B2 55 15N 133 20W
Suez = El Suweis, Egypt 51 C12 29 58N 32 31 E
Suez, G. of = Suweis, Khalîg el, Egypt 51 C12 28 40N 33 0 E
Suez Canal = Suweis, Qanâ es, Egypt 51 B12 31 0N 32 20 E
Suffield, Canada 72 C6 50 12N 111 10W
Suffolk, U.S.A. 76 G7 36 44N 76 35W
Suffolk □, U.K. 11 E9 52 16N 1 0 E
Sugargrove, U.S.A. 78 E5 41 59N 79 21W
Sugarive →, India 43 F12 26 16N 86 24 E
Sugluk = Salluit, Canada 69 B12 62 14N 75 38W
Şuḩār, Oman 46 C6 24 20N 56 40 E
Sühbaatar □, Mongolia 34 B8 45 30N 114 0 E
Suhl, Germany 16 C6 50 36N 10 42 E
Sui, Pakistan 42 E3 28 37N 69 19 E
Sui Xian, China 34 G8 34 25N 115 2 E
Suide, China 34 F6 37 30N 110 12 E
Suifenhe, China 35 B16 44 25N 131 10 E
Suihua, China 33 B7 46 32N 126 55 E
Suining, China 35 H9 33 56N 117 58 E
Suiping, China 34 H7 33 10N 113 59 E
Suir →, Ireland 13 D4 52 16N 7 9W
Suisun City, U.S.A. 84 G4 38 15N 122 2W
Suiyang, China 35 B16 44 30N 130 56 E
Suizhong, China 35 D11 40 21N 120 20 E
Sujangarh, India 42 F6 27 42N 74 31 E
Sukabumi, Indonesia 37 G12 6 56S 106 50 E
Sukadana, Indonesia 36 E3 1 10S 110 0 E
Sukagawa, Japan 31 F10 37 17N 140 23 E
Sukaraja, Indonesia 36 E4 2 28S 110 25 E
Sukarnapura = Jayapura, Indonesia 37 E10 2 28S 140 38 E
Sukch'ŏn, N. Korea 35 E13 39 22N 125 35 E
Sukhona →, Russia 24 C6 61 15N 46 39 E
Sukhothai, Thailand 38 D2 17 1N 99 49 E
Sukhumi = Sokhumi, Georgia 25 F7 43 0N 41 0 E
Sukkur, Pakistan 42 F3 27 42N 68 54 E
Sukkur Barrage, Pakistan 42 F3 27 40N 68 50 E
Sukri →, India 42 G4 25 4N 71 43 E
Sukumo, Japan 31 H6 32 56N 132 44 E
Sukunka →, Canada 72 B4 55 45N 121 15W
Sula, Kepulauan, Indonesia 37 E7 1 45S 125 0 E
Sulaco →, Honduras 88 C2 15 2N 87 44W
Sulaiman Range, Pakistan 42 D3 30 30N 69 50 E
Sūlār, Iran 45 D6 31 53N 51 54 E
Sulawesi Sea = Celebes Sea, Indonesia 37 D6 3 0N 123 0 E
Sulawesi Selatan □, Indonesia 37 E6 2 30S 120 0 E
Sulawesi Utara □, Indonesia 37 D6 1 0N 122 30 E
Sulima, S. Leone 50 G3 6 58N 11 32W
Sulina, Romania 17 F15 45 10N 29 40 E
Sulitjelma, Norway 8 C17 67 9N 16 3 E
Sullana, Peru 92 D2 4 52S 80 39W
Sullivan, Ill., U.S.A. 80 F10 39 36N 88 37W
Sullivan, Ind., U.S.A. 76 F2 39 6N 87 24W
Sullivan, Mo., U.S.A. 80 F9 38 13N 91 10W
Sullivan Bay, Canada 72 C3 50 55N 126 50W
Sullivan I. = Lanbi Kyun, Burma 39 G2 10 50N 98 20 E
Sulphur, La., U.S.A. 81 K8 30 14N 93 23W
Sulphur, Okla., U.S.A. 81 H6 34 31N 96 58W
Sulphur Pt., Canada 72 A6 60 56N 114 48W
Sulphur Springs, U.S.A. 81 J7 33 8N 95 36W
Sultan, Canada 70 C3 47 36N 82 47W
Sultan, U.S.A. 84 C5 47 52N 121 49W
Sultanpur, Mad. P., India 42 H8 23 9N 77 56 E
Sultanpur, Punjab, India 42 D6 31 13N 75 11 E
Sultanpur, Ut. P., India 43 F10 26 18N 82 4 E
Sulu Arch., Phil. 37 C6 6 0N 121 0 E
Sulu Sea, E. Indies 37 C6 8 0N 120 0 E
Suluq, Libya 51 B10 31 44N 20 14 E
Sulzberger Ice Shelf, Antarctica 5 D10 78 0S 150 0 E
Sumalata, Indonesia 37 D6 1 0N 122 31 E
Sumampa, Argentina 94 B3 29 25S 63 29W
Sumatera □, Indonesia 36 D2 0 40N 100 20 E
Sumatera Barat □, Indonesia 36 E2 1 0S 101 0 E
Sumatera Utara □, Indonesia 36 D1 2 30N 98 0 E
Sumatra = Sumatera □, Indonesia 36 D2 0 40N 100 20 E
Sumba, Indonesia 37 F5 9 45S 119 35 E
Sumba, Selat, Indonesia 37 F5 9 0S 118 40 E
Sumbawa, Indonesia 36 F5 8 26S 117 30 E
Sumbawa Besar, Indonesia 36 F5 8 30S 117 26 E
Sumbawanga □, Tanzania 52 F6 8 0S 31 30 E
Sumbe, Angola 52 G2 11 10S 13 48 E
Sumburgh Hd., U.K. 12 B7 59 52N 1 17W
Sumdeo, India 43 D8 31 26N 78 44 E
Sumdo, China 43 B8 35 6N 78 41 E
Sumedang, Indonesia 37 G12 6 52S 107 55 E
Šumen = Shumen, Bulgaria 21 C12 43 18N 26 55 E
Sumenep, Indonesia 37 G15 7 1S 113 52 E
Sumgait = Sumqayıt, Azerbaijan 25 F8 40 34N 49 38 E
Summer L., U.S.A. 82 E3 42 50N 120 45W
Summerland, Canada 72 D5 49 32N 119 41W
Summerside, Canada 71 C7 46 24N 63 47W
Summersville, U.S.A. 76 F5 38 17N 80 51W
Summerville, Ga., U.S.A. 77 H3 34 29N 85 21W
Summerville, S.C., U.S.A. 77 J5 33 1N 80 11W
Summit Lake, Canada 72 C4 54 20N 122 40W
Summit Peak, U.S.A. 83 H10 37 21N 106 42W
Sumner, Iowa, U.S.A. 80 D8 42 51N 92 6W
Sumner, Wash., U.S.A. 84 C4 47 12N 122 14W
Sumoto, Japan 31 G7 34 21N 134 54 E
Šumperk, Czech Rep. 17 D9 49 59N 16 59 E
Sumqayıt, Azerbaijan 25 F8 40 34N 49 38 E
Sumter, U.S.A. 77 J5 33 55N 80 21W
Sumy, Ukraine 25 D5 50 57N 34 50 E
Sun City, S. Africa 56 D4 25 17S 27 3 E
Sun City, Ariz., U.S.A. 83 K7 33 36N 112 17W
Sun City, Calif., U.S.A. 85 M9 33 42N 117 11W
Sun City Center, U.S.A. 77 M4 27 43N 82 18W
Sun Lakes, U.S.A. 83 K8 33 10N 111 52W
Sun Valley, U.S.A. 82 E6 43 42N 114 21W
Sunagawa, Japan 30 C10 43 29N 141 55 E
Sunan, N. Korea 35 E13 39 15N 125 40 E
Sunart, L., U.K. 12 E3 56 42N 5 43W
Sunburst, U.S.A. 82 B8 48 53N 111 55W
Sunbury, Australia 63 F3 37 35S 144 44 E
Sunbury, U.S.A. 79 F8 40 52N 76 48W
Sunchales, Argentina 94 C3 30 58S 61 35W
Suncho Corral, Argentina 94 B3 27 55S 63 27W
Sunch'ŏn, S. Korea 35 G14 34 52N 127 31 E
Suncook, U.S.A. 79 C13 43 8N 71 27W
Sunda, Selat, Indonesia 36 F3 6 20S 105 30 E
Sunda Is., Indonesia 28 K14 5 0S 105 0 E
Sunda Str. = Sunda, Selat, Indonesia 36 F3 6 20S 105 30 E
Sundance, Canada 73 B10 56 32N 94 4W
Sundance, U.S.A. 80 C2 44 24N 104 23W
Sundar Nagar, India 42 D7 31 32N 76 53 E
Sundarbans, Asia 41 J16 22 0N 89 0 E
Sundargarh, India 41 H14 22 4N 84 5 E
Sundays = Sondags →, S. Africa 56 E4 33 44S 25 51 E
Sunderland, Canada 78 B5 44 16N 79 4W
Sunderland, U.K. 10 C6 54 55N 1 23W
Sundre, Canada 72 C6 51 49N 114 38W
Sundsvall, Sweden 9 E17 62 23N 17 17 E
Sung Hei, Vietnam 39 G6 10 20N 106 2 E
Sungai Kolok, Thailand 39 J3 6 2N 101 58 E
Sungai Lembing, Malaysia 39 L4 3 55N 103 3 E
Sungai Petani, Malaysia 39 K3 5 37N 100 30 E
Sungaigerong, Indonesia 36 E2 2 59S 104 52 E
Sungailiat, Indonesia 36 E3 1 51S 106 8 E
Sungaipenuh, Indonesia 36 E2 2 1S 101 20 E
Sungari = Songhua Jiang →, China 33 B8 47 45N 132 30 E
Sunghua Chiang = Songhua Jiang →, China 33 B8 47 45N 132 30 E
Sunland Park, U.S.A. 83 L10 31 50N 106 40W
Sunndalsøra, Norway 9 E13 62 40N 8 33 E
Sunnyside, U.S.A. 82 C3 46 20N 120 0W
Sunnyvale, U.S.A. 84 H4 37 23N 122 2W
Suntar, Russia 27 C12 62 15N 117 30 E
Suomenselkä, Finland 8 E21 62 52N 24 0 E
Suomussalmi, Finland 8 D23 64 54N 29 10 E
Suoyarvi, Russia 24 B5 62 3N 32 20 E
Supai, U.S.A. 83 H7 36 15N 112 41W
Supaul, India 43 F12 26 10N 86 40 E
Superior, Ariz., U.S.A. 83 K8 33 18N 111 6W
Superior, Mont., U.S.A. 82 C6 47 12N 114 53W
Superior, Nebr., U.S.A. 80 E5 40 1N 98 4W
Superior, Wis., U.S.A. 80 B8 46 44N 92 6W
Superior, L., N. Amer. 70 C2 47 0N 87 0W
Suphan Buri, Thailand 38 E3 14 14N 100 10 E

Suphan Dağı, Turkey 44 B4 38 54N 42 48 E
Supiori, Indonesia 37 E9 1 0S 136 0 E
Supung Shuiku, China 35 D13 40 35N 124 50 E
Sūq Suwayq, Si. Arabia 44 E3 24 23N 38 27 E
Suqian, China 35 H10 33 54N 118 8 E
Sūr, Lebanon 47 B4 33 19N 35 16 E
Şūr, Oman 46 C6 22 34N 59 32 E
Sur, Pt., U.S.A. 84 J5 36 18N 121 54W
Sura →, Russia 24 C8 56 6N 46 0 E
Surab, Pakistan 42 E2 28 25N 66 15 E
Surabaja = Surabaya, Indonesia 36 F4 7 17S 112 45 E
Surabaya, Indonesia 36 F4 7 17S 112 45 E
Surakarta, Indonesia 36 F4 7 35S 110 48 E
Surat, Australia 63 D4 27 10S 149 6 E
Surat, India 40 J8 21 12N 72 55 E
Surat Thani, Thailand 39 H2 9 6N 99 20 E
Suratgarh, India 42 E5 29 18N 73 55 E
Surendranagar, India 42 H4 22 45N 71 40 E
Surf, U.S.A. 85 L6 34 41N 120 36W
Surgut, Russia 26 C8 61 14N 73 20 E
Suriapet, India 40 L11 17 10N 79 40 E
Surigao, Phil. 37 C7 9 47N 125 29 E
Surin, Thailand 38 E4 14 50N 103 34 E
Surin Nua, Ko, Thailand 39 H1 9 30N 97 55 E
Surinam ■, S. Amer. 93 C7 4 0N 56 0W
Suriname = Surinam ■, S. Amer. 93 C7 4 0N 56 0W
Suriname →, Surinam 93 B7 5 50N 55 15W
Sūrmaq, Iran 45 D7 31 3N 52 48 E
Surrey □, U.K. 11 F7 51 15N 0 31W
Sursand, India 43 F11 26 39N 85 43 E
Sursar →, India 43 F12 26 14N 87 3 E
Surt, Libya 51 B9 31 11N 16 39 E
Surt, Khalīj, Libya 51 B9 31 40N 18 30 E
Surtanahu, Pakistan 42 F4 26 22N 70 0 E
Surtsey, Iceland 8 E3 63 20N 20 30W
Suruga-Wan, Japan 31 G9 34 45N 138 30 E
Susaki, Japan 31 H6 33 22N 133 17 E
Sūsangerd, Iran 45 D6 31 35N 48 6 E
Susanville, U.S.A. 82 F3 40 25N 120 39W
Susner, India 42 H7 23 57N 76 5 E
Susquehanna, U.S.A. 79 E9 41 57N 75 36W
Susquehanna →, U.S.A. 79 G8 39 33N 76 5W
Susques, Argentina 94 A2 23 35S 66 25W
Sussex, Canada 71 C6 45 45N 65 37W
Sussex, U.S.A. 79 E10 41 13N 74 37W
Sussex, E. □, U.K. 11 G8 51 0N 0 20 E
Sussex, W. □, U.K. 11 G7 51 0N 0 30W
Sustut →, Canada 72 B3 56 20N 127 30W
Susuman, Russia 27 C15 62 47N 148 10 E
Susunu, Indonesia 37 E8 3 7S 133 39 E
Susurluk, Turkey 21 E13 39 54N 28 8 E
Sutherland, S. Africa 56 E3 32 24S 20 40 E
Sutherland, U.S.A. 80 E4 41 10N 101 8W
Sutherland Falls, N.Z. 59 L1 44 48S 167 46 E
Sutherlin, U.S.A. 82 E2 43 23N 123 19W
Suthri, India 42 H3 23 3N 68 55 E
Sutlej →, Pakistan 42 E4 29 23N 71 3 E
Sutter, U.S.A. 84 F5 39 10N 121 45W
Sutter Creek, U.S.A. 84 G6 38 24N 120 48W
Sutton, Canada 79 A12 45 6N 72 37W
Sutton, Nebr., U.S.A. 80 E6 40 36N 97 52W
Sutton, W. Va., U.S.A. 76 F5 38 40N 80 43W
Sutton →, Canada 70 A3 55 15N 83 45W
Sutton Coldfield, U.K. 11 E6 52 35N 1 49W
Sutton in Ashfield, U.K. 10 D6 53 8N 1 16W
Sutton L., Canada 70 B3 54 15N 84 42W
Suttor →, Australia 62 C4 21 36S 147 2 E
Suttsu, Japan 30 C10 42 48N 140 14 E
Suva, Fiji 59 D8 18 6S 178 30 E
Suva Planina, Serbia, Yug. 21 C10 43 10N 22 5 E
Suvorov Is. = Suwarrow Is., Cook Is. 65 J11 15 0S 163 0W
Suwałki, Poland 17 A12 54 8N 22 59 E
Suwannaphum, Thailand 38 E4 15 33N 103 47 E
Suwannee →, U.S.A. 77 L4 29 17N 83 10W
Suwanose-Jima, Japan 31 K4 29 38N 129 43 E
Suwarrow Is., Cook Is. 65 J11 15 0S 163 0W
Suwayq aş Şuqban, Iraq 44 D5 31 32N 46 7 E
Suweis, Khalîg el, Egypt 51 C12 28 40N 33 0 E
Suweis, Qanâ es, Egypt 51 B12 31 0N 32 20 E
Suwŏn, S. Korea 35 F14 37 17N 127 1 E
Suzdal, Russia 24 C7 56 29N 40 26 E
Suzhou, Anhui, China 34 H9 33 41N 116 59 E
Suzhou, Jiangsu, China 33 C7 31 19N 120 38 E
Suzu, Japan 31 F8 37 25N 137 17 E
Suzu-Misaki, Japan 31 F8 37 31N 137 21 E
Suzuka, Japan 31 G8 34 55N 136 36 E
Svalbard, Arctic 4 B8 78 0N 17 0 E
Svappavaara, Sweden 8 C19 67 40N 21 3 E
Svartisen, Norway 8 C15 66 40N 13 50 E
Svay Chek, Cambodia 38 F4 13 48N 102 58 E
Svay Rieng, Cambodia 39 G5 11 9N 105 45 E
Svealand □, Sweden 9 G16 60 20N 15 0 E
Sveg, Sweden 9 E16 62 2N 14 21 E
Svendborg, Denmark 9 J14 55 4N 10 35 E
Sverdlovsk = Yekaterinburg, Russia 26 D7 56 50N 60 30 E
Sverdrup Is., Canada 4 B3 79 0N 97 0W
Svetlaya, Russia 30 A9 46 33N 138 18 E
Svetlogorsk = Svyetlahorsk, Belarus 17 B15 52 38N 29 46 E
Svir →, Russia 24 B5 60 30N 32 48 E
Svishtov, Bulgaria 21 C11 43 36N 25 23 E
Svislach, Belarus 17 B13 53 3N 24 2 E
Svobodnyy, Russia 27 D13 51 20N 128 0 E
Svolvær, Norway 8 B16 68 15N 14 34 E
Svyetlahorsk, Belarus 17 B15 52 38N 29 46 E
Swabian Alps = Schwäbische Alb, Germany 16 D5 48 20N 9 30 E
Swainsboro, U.S.A. 77 J4 32 36N 82 20W
Swakop →, Namibia 56 C2 22 38S 14 36 E
Swakopmund, Namibia 56 C1 22 37S 14 30 E
Swale →, U.K. 10 C6 54 5N 1 20W
Swan →, Australia 61 F2 32 3S 115 45 E
Swan →, Canada 73 C8 52 30N 100 45W
Swan Hill, Australia 63 F3 35 20S 143 33 E
Swan Hills, Canada 72 C5 54 43N 115 24W
Swan Is. = Santanilla, Is., Honduras 88 C3 17 22N 83 57W
Swan L., Canada 73 C8 52 30N 100 40W
Swan Peak, U.S.A. 82 C7 47 43N 113 38W
Swan Ra., U.S.A. 82 C7 48 0N 113 45W
Swan River, Canada 73 C8 52 10N 101 16W
Swanage, U.K. 11 G6 50 36N 1 58W
Swansea, Australia 62 G4 42 8S 148 4 E
Swansea, Canada 78 C5 43 38N 79 28W
Swansea, U.K. 11 F4 51 37N 3 57W
Swansea □, U.K. 11 F3 51 38N 4 3W
Swar →, Pakistan 43 B5 34 40N 72 5 E
Swartberge, S. Africa 56 E3 33 20S 22 0 E
Swartmodder, S. Africa 56 D3 28 1S 20 32 E
Swartnossob →, Namibia 56 C2 23 8S 18 42 E
Swartruggens, S. Africa 56 D4 25 39S 26 42 E
Swastika, Canada 70 C3 48 7N 80 6W
Swatow = Shantou, China 33 D6 23 18N 116 40 E
Swaziland ■, Africa 57 D5 26 30S 31 30 E
Sweden ■, Europe 9 G16 57 0N 15 0 E
Sweet Home, U.S.A. 82 D2 44 24N 122 44W
Sweetgrass, U.S.A. 82 B8 48 59N 111 58W
Sweetwater, Nev., U.S.A. 84 G7 38 27N 119 9W
Sweetwater, Tenn., U.S.A. 77 H3 35 36N 84 28W
Sweetwater, Tex., U.S.A. 81 J4 32 28N 100 25W
Sweetwater →, U.S.A. 82 E10 42 31N 107 2W
Swellendam, S. Africa 56 E3 34 1S 20 26 E
Świdnica, Poland 17 C9 50 50N 16 30 E
Świdnik, Poland 17 C12 51 13N 22 39 E
Świebodzin, Poland 16 B8 52 15N 15 31 E
Świecie, Poland 17 B10 53 25N 18 30 E
Swift Current, Canada 73 C7 50 20N 107 45W
Swiftcurrent →, Canada 73 C7 50 38N 107 44W
Swilly, L., Ireland 13 A4 55 12N 7 33W
Swindon, U.K. 11 F6 51 34N 1 46W
Swindon □, U.K. 11 F6 51 34N 1 46W
Swinemünde = Świnoujście, Poland 16 B8 53 54N 14 16 E
Swinford, Ireland 13 C3 53 57N 8 58W
Świnoujście, Poland 16 B8 53 54N 14 16 E
Switzerland ■, Europe 18 C8 46 30N 8 0 E
Swords, Ireland 13 C5 53 28N 6 13W
Swoyerville, U.S.A. 79 E9 41 18N 75 53W
Sydenham →, Canada 78 D2 42 33N 82 25W
Sydney, Australia 63 E5 33 53S 151 10 E
Sydney, Canada 71 C7 46 7N 60 7W
Sydney L., Canada 73 C10 50 41N 94 25W
Sydney Mines, Canada 71 C7 46 18N 60 15W
Sydprøven = Alluitsup Paa, Greenland 4 C5 60 30N 45 35W
Sydra, G. of = Surt, Khalīj, Libya 51 B9 31 40N 18 30 E
Sykesville, U.S.A. 78 E6 41 3N 78 50W
Syktyvkar, Russia 24 B9 61 45N 50 40 E
Sylacauga, U.S.A. 77 J2 33 10N 86 15W
Sylarna, Sweden 8 E15 63 2N 12 13 E
Sylhet, Bangla. 41 G17 24 54N 91 52 E
Sylhet □, Bangla. 41 G17 24 50N 91 50 E
Sylt, Germany 16 A5 54 54N 8 22 E
Sylvan Beach, U.S.A. 79 C9 43 12N 75 44W
Sylvan Lake, Canada 72 C6 52 20N 114 3W
Sylvania, U.S.A. 77 J5 32 45N 81 38W
Sylvester, U.S.A. 77 K4 31 32N 83 50W
Sym, Russia 26 C9 60 20N 88 18 E
Symón, Mexico 86 C4 24 42N 102 35W
Synnott Ra., Australia 60 C4 16 30S 125 20 E
Syracuse, Kans., U.S.A. 81 G4 37 59N 101 45W
Syracuse, N.Y., U.S.A. 79 C8 43 3N 76 9W
Syracuse, Nebr., U.S.A. 80 E6 40 39N 96 11W
Syrdarya →, Kazakstan 26 E7 46 3N 61 0 E
Syria ■, Asia 44 C3 35 0N 38 0 E
Syrian Desert = Shām, Bādiyat ash, Asia 44 C3 32 0N 40 0 E
Syzran, Russia 24 D8 53 12N 48 30 E
Szczecin, Poland 16 B8 53 27N 14 27 E
Szczecinek, Poland 17 B9 53 43N 16 41 E
Szczeciński, Zalew = Stettiner Haff, Germany 16 B8 53 47N 14 15 E
Szczytno, Poland 17 B11 53 33N 21 0 E
Szechwan = Sichuan □, China 32 C5 30 30N 103 0 E
Szeged, Hungary 17 E11 46 16N 20 10 E
Székesfehérvár, Hungary 17 E10 47 15N 18 25 E
Szekszárd, Hungary 17 E10 46 22N 18 42 E
Szentes, Hungary 17 E11 46 39N 20 21 E
Szolnok, Hungary 17 E11 47 10N 20 15 E
Szombathely, Hungary 17 E9 47 14N 16 38 E

T

Ta Khli Khok, Thailand 38 E3 15 18N 100 20 E
Ta Lai, Vietnam 39 G6 11 24N 107 23 E
Tabacal, Argentina 94 A3 23 15S 64 15W
Tabaco, Phil. 37 B6 13 22N 123 44 E
Ţābah, Si. Arabia 44 E4 26 55N 42 38 E
Ţabas, Khorāsān, Iran 45 C9 32 48N 60 12 E
Ţabas, Khorāsān, Iran 45 C8 33 35N 56 55 E
Tabasará, Serranía de, Panama 88 E3 8 35N 81 40W
Tabasco □, Mexico 87 D6 17 45N 93 30W
Tābāsīn, Iran 45 D8 31 12N 57 54 E
Tabatinga, Serra da, Brazil 93 F10 10 30S 44 0W
Taber, Canada 72 D6 49 47N 112 8W
Taberg, U.S.A. 79 C9 43 18N 75 37W
Tablas I., Phil. 37 B6 12 25N 122 2 E
Table B. = Tafelbaai, S. Africa 56 E2 33 35S 18 25 E
Table B., Canada 71 B8 53 40N 56 25W
Table Mt., S. Africa 56 E2 34 0S 18 22 E
Table Rock L., U.S.A. 81 G8 36 36N 93 19W
Tabletop, Mt., Australia 62 C4 23 24S 147 11 E
Tábor, Czech Rep. 16 D8 49 25N 14 39 E
Tabora, Tanzania 54 D3 5 2S 32 50 E
Tabora □, Tanzania 54 D3 5 0S 33 0 E
Tabou, Ivory C. 50 H4 4 30N 7 20W
Tabrīz, Iran 44 B5 38 7N 46 20 E
Tabuaeran, Kiribati 65 G12 3 51N 159 22W
Tabūk, Si. Arabia 44 D3 28 23N 36 36 E
Tacámbaro de Codallos, Mexico 86 D4 19 14N 101 28W
Tacheng, China 32 B3 46 40N 82 58 E
Tach'ing Shan = Daqing Shan, China 34 D6 40 40N 111 0 E
Tacloban, Phil. 37 B6 11 15N 124 58 E
Tacna, Peru 92 G4 18 0S 70 20W
Tacoma, U.S.A. 84 C4 47 14N 122 26W
Tacuarembó, Uruguay 95 C4 31 45S 56 0W
Tademaït, Plateau du, Algeria 50 C6 28 30N 2 30 E
Tadjoura, Djibouti 46 E3 11 50N 42 55 E
Tadmor, N.Z. 59 J4 41 27S 172 45 E
Tadoule, L., Canada 73 B9 58 36N 98 20W
Tadoussac, Canada 71 C6 48 11N 69 42W
Tadzhikistan = Tajikistan ■, Asia 26 F8 38 30N 70 0 E
Taechŏn-ni, S. Korea 35 F14 36 21N 126 36 E
Taegu, S. Korea 35 G15 35 50N 128 37 E
Taegwan, N. Korea 35 D13 40 13N 125 12 E
Taejŏn, S. Korea 35 F14 36 20N 127 28 E
Tafalla, Spain 19 A5 42 30N 1 41W
Tafelbaai, S. Africa 56 E2 33 35S 18 25 E
Tafermaar, Indonesia 37 F8 6 47S 134 10 E
Tafí Viejo, Argentina 94 B2 26 43S 65 17W
Tafīhān, Iran 45 D7 29 25N 52 39 E
Tafresh, Iran 45 C6 34 45N 49 57 E
Taft, Iran 45 D7 31 45N 54 14 E
Taft, Phil. 37 B7 11 57N 125 30 E
Taft, U.S.A. 85 K7 35 8N 119 28W
Taftān, Kūh-e, Iran 45 D9 28 40N 61 0 E
Taga Dzong, Bhutan 41 F16 27 5N 89 55 E
Taganrog, Russia 25 E6 47 12N 38 50 E
Tagbilaran, Phil. 37 C6 9 39N 123 51 E
Tagish, Canada 72 A2 60 19N 134 16W
Tagish L., Canada 72 A2 60 10N 134 20W
Tagliamento →, Italy 20 B5 45 38N 13 6 E
Tagomago, Spain 22 B8 39 2N 1 39 E
Taguatinga, Brazil 93 F10 12 16S 42 26W
Tagum, Phil. 37 C7 7 33N 125 53 E
Tagus = Tejo →, Europe 19 C1 38 40N 9 24W
Tahakopa, N.Z. 59 M2 46 30S 169 23 E
Tahan, Gunong, Malaysia 39 K4 4 34N 102 17 E
Tahat, Algeria 50 D7 23 18N 5 33 E
Tāherī, Iran 45 E7 27 43N 52 20 E
Tahiti, Pac. Oc. 65 J13 17 37S 149 27W
Tahlequah, U.S.A. 81 H7 35 55N 94 58W
Tahoe, L., U.S.A. 84 G6 39 6N 120 2W
Tahoe City, U.S.A. 84 F6 39 10N 120 9W
Tahoka, U.S.A. 81 J4 33 10N 101 48W
Taholah, U.S.A. 84 C2 47 21N 124 17W
Tahoua, Niger 50 F7 14 57N 5 16 E
Tahrūd, Iran 45 D8 29 26N 57 49 E
Tahsis, Canada 72 D3 49 55N 126 40W
Tahta, Egypt 51 C12 26 44N 31 32 E
Tahulandang, Indonesia 37 D7 2 27N 125 23 E
Tahuna, Indonesia 37 D7 3 38N 125 30 E
Tai Shan, China 35 F9 36 25N 117 20 E
Tai'an, China 35 F9 36 12N 117 8 E
Taibei = T'aipei, Taiwan 33 D7 25 2N 121 30 E
Taibique, Canary Is. 22 G2 27 42N 17 58W
Taibus Qi, China 34 D8 41 54N 115 22 E
T'aichung, Taiwan 33 D7 24 9N 120 37 E
Taieri →, N.Z. 59 M3 46 3S 170 12 E
Taigu, China 34 F7 37 28N 112 30 E
Taihang Shan, China 34 G7 36 0N 113 30 E
Taihape, N.Z. 59 H5 39 41S 175 48 E
Taihe, China 34 H8 33 20N 115 42 E
Taikang, China 34 G8 34 5N 114 50 E
Tailem Bend, Australia 63 F2 35 12S 139 29 E
Taimyr Peninsula = Taymyr, Poluostrov, Russia 27 B11 75 0N 100 0 E
Tain, U.K. 12 D4 57 49N 4 4W
T'ainan, Taiwan 33 D7 23 0N 120 10 E
Tainaron, Ákra, Greece 21 F10 36 22N 22 27 E
T'aipei, Taiwan 33 D7 25 2N 121 30 E
Taiping, Malaysia 39 K3 4 51N 100 44 E
Taipingzhen, China 34 H6 33 35N 111 42 E
Tairbeart = Tarbert, U.K. 12 D2 57 54N 6 49W
Taita Hills, Kenya 54 C4 3 25S 38 15 E
Taitao, Pen. de, Chile 96 F2 46 30S 75 0W
T'aitung, Taiwan 33 D7 22 43N 121 4 E
Taivalkoski, Finland 8 D23 65 33N 28 12 E
Taiwan ■, Asia 33 D7 23 30N 121 0 E
Taïyetos Óros, Greece 21 F10 37 0N 22 23 E
Taiyiba, Israel 47 C4 32 36N 35 27 E
Taiyuan, China 34 F7 37 52N 112 33 E
Taizhong = T'aichung, Taiwan 33 D7 24 9N 120 37 E
Ta'izz, Yemen 46 E3 13 35N 44 2 E
Tājābād, Iran 45 D7 30 2N 54 24 E
Tajikistan ■, Asia 26 F8 38 30N 70 0 E
Tajima, Japan 31 F9 37 12N 139 46 E
Tajo = Tejo →, Europe 19 C1 38 40N 9 24W
Tajrīsh, Iran 45 C6 35 48N 51 25 E
Tak, Thailand 38 D2 16 52N 99 8 E
Takāb, Iran 44 B5 36 24N 47 7 E
Takachiho, Japan 31 H5 32 42N 131 18 E
Takachu, Botswana 56 C3 22 37S 21 58 E
Takada, Japan 31 F9 37 7N 138 15 E
Takahagi, Japan 31 F10 36 43N 140 45 E
Takaka, N.Z. 59 J4 40 51S 172 50 E
Takamatsu, Japan 31 G7 34 20N 134 5 E
Takaoka, Japan 31 F8 36 47N 137 0 E
Takapuna, N.Z. 59 G5 36 47S 174 47 E
Takasaki, Japan 31 F9 36 20N 139 0 E
Takatsuki, Japan 31 G7 34 51N 135 37 E
Takaungu, Kenya 54 C4 3 38S 39 52 E
Takayama, Japan 31 F8 36 18N 137 11 E
Take-Shima, Japan 31 J5 30 49N 130 26 E
Takefu, Japan 31 G8 35 50N 136 10 E
Takengon, Indonesia 36 D1 4 45N 96 50 E
Takeo, Japan 31 H5 33 12N 130 1 E
Tākestān, Iran 45 C6 36 0N 49 40 E
Taketa, Japan 31 H5 32 58N 131 24 E
Takev, Cambodia 39 G5 10 59N 104 47 E
Takh, India 43 C7 33 6N 77 32 E
Takht-Sulaiman, Pakistan 42 D3 31 40N 69 58 E
Takikawa, Japan 30 C10 43 33N 141 54 E
Takla L., Canada 72 B3 55 15N 125 45W
Takla Landing, Canada 72 B3 55 30N 125 50W
Takla Makan = Taklamakan Shamo, China 32 C3 38 0N 83 0 E
Taklamakan Shamo, China 32 C3 38 0N 83 0 E
Taku →, Canada 72 B2 58 30N 133 50W
Tal Halāl, Iran 45 D7 28 54N 55 1 E
Tala, Uruguay 95 C4 34 21S 55 46W
Talagang, Pakistan 42 C5 32 55N 72 25 E
Talagante, Chile 94 C1 33 40S 70 50W
Talamanca, Cordillera de, Cent. Amer. 88 E3 9 20N 83 20W
Talara, Peru 92 D2 4 38S 81 18W
Talas, Kyrgyzstan 26 E8 42 30N 72 13 E
Talâta, Egypt 47 E1 30 36N 32 20 E
Talaud, Kepulauan, Indonesia 37 D7 4 30N 126 50 E
Talaud Is. = Talaud, Kepulauan, Indonesia 37 D7 4 30N 126 50 E
Talavera de la Reina, Spain 19 C3 39 55N 4 46W
Talayan, Phil. 37 C6 6 52N 124 24 E
Talbandh, India 43 H12 22 3N 86 20 E
Talbot, C., Australia 60 B4 13 48S 126 43 E
Talbragar →, Australia 63 E4 32 12S 148 37 E
Talca, Chile 94 D1 35 28S 71 40W
Talcahuano, Chile 94 D1 36 40S 73 10W
Talcher, India 41 J14 21 0N 85 18 E
Taldy Kurgan = Taldyqorghan, Kazakstan 26 E8 45 10N 78 45 E
Taldyqorghan, Kazakstan 26 E8 45 10N 78 45 E
Tālesh, Iran 45 B6 37 58N 48 58 E
Tālesh, Kūhhā-ye, Iran 45 B6 37 42N 48 55 E
Tali Post, Sudan 51 G12 5 55N 30 44 E
Taliabu, Indonesia 37 E6 1 50S 125 0 E
Talibon, Phil. 37 B6 10 9N 124 20 E
Talibong, Ko, Thailand 39 J2 7 15N 99 23 E
Talihina, U.S.A. 81 H7 34 45N 95 3W
Taliwang, Indonesia 36 F5 8 50S 116 55 E
Tall 'Afar, Iraq 44 B4 36 22N 42 27 E
Tall Kalakh, Syria 47 A5 34 41N 36 15 E
Talladega, U.S.A. 77 J2 33 26N 86 6W
Tallahassee, U.S.A. 77 K3 30 27N 84 17W
Tallangatta, Australia 63 F4 36 15S 147 19 E
Tallering Pk., Australia 61 E2 28 6S 115 37 E
Talli, Pakistan 42 E3 29 32N 68 8 E
Tallinn, Estonia 9 G21 59 22N 24 48 E
Tallmadge, U.S.A. 78 E3 41 6N 81 27W
Tallulah, U.S.A. 81 J9 32 25N 91 11W
Taloyoak, Canada 68 B10 69 32N 93 32W
Talpa de Allende, Mexico 86 C4 20 23N 104 51W
Talsi, Latvia 9 H20 57 10N 22 30 E
Taltal, Chile 94 B1 25 23S 70 33W
Taltson →, Canada 72 A6 61 24N 112 46W
Talurqjuak = Taloyoak, Canada 68 B10 69 32N 93 32W
Talwood, Australia 63 D4 28 29S 149 29 E
Talyawalka Cr. →, Australia 63 E3 32 28S 142 22 E
Tam Chau, Vietnam 39 G5 10 48N 105 12 E
Tam Ky, Vietnam 38 E7 15 34N 108 29 E
Tam Quan, Vietnam 38 E7 14 35N 109 3 E
Tama, U.S.A. 80 E8 41 58N 92 35W
Tamale, Ghana 50 G5 9 22N 0 50W
Tamano, Japan 31 G6 34 29N 133 59 E
Tamanrasset, Algeria 50 D7 22 50N 5 30 E
Tamaqua, U.S.A. 79 F9 40 48N 75 58W
Tamar →, U.K. 11 G3 50 27N 4 15W
Tamarinda, Spain 22 B10 39 55N 3 49 E
Tamashima, Japan 31 G6 34 32N 133 40 E
Tamaulipas □, Mexico 87 C5 24 0N 99 0W
Tamaulipas, Sierra de, Mexico 87 C5 23 30N 98 20W
Tamazula, Mexico 86 C3 24 55N 106 58W
Tamazunchale, Mexico 87 C5 21 16N 98 47W
Tambacounda, Senegal 50 F3 13 45N 13 40W
Tambelan, Kepulauan, Indonesia 36 D3 1 0N 107 30 E
Tambellup, Australia 61 F2 34 4S 117 37 E
Tambo, Australia 62 C4 24 54S 146 14 E
Tambo de Mora, Peru 92 F3 13 30S 76 8W
Tambohorano, Madag. 57 B7 17 30S 43 58 E
Tambora, Indonesia 36 F5 8 12S 118 5 E
Tambov, Russia 24 D7 52 45N 41 28 E
Tambuku, Indonesia 37 G15 7 8S 113 40 E
Tâmega →, Portugal 19 B1 41 5N 8 21W
Tamenglong, India 41 G18 25 0N 93 35 E
Tamiahua, L. de, Mexico 87 C5 21 30N 97 30W
Tamil Nadu □, India 40 P10 11 0N 77 0 E
Tamluk, India 43 H12 22 18N 87 58 E
Tammerfors = Tampere, Finland 9 F20 61 30N 23 50 E
Tammisaari, Finland 9 F20 60 0N 23 26 E
Tamo Abu, Pegunungan, Malaysia 36 D5 3 10N 115 5 E
Tampa, U.S.A. 77 M4 27 57N 82 27W
Tampa B., U.S.A. 77 M4 27 50N 82 30W
Tampere, Finland 9 F20 61 30N 23 50 E
Tampico, Mexico 87 C5 22 20N 97 50W
Tampin, Malaysia 39 L4 2 28N 102 13 E
Tamu, Burma 41 G19 24 13N 94 12 E
Tamworth, Australia 63 E5 31 7S 150 58 E
Tamworth, Canada 78 B8 44 29N 77 0W
Tamworth, U.K. 11 E6 52 39N 1 41W
Tamyang, S. Korea 35 G14 35 19N 126 59 E
Tan An, Vietnam 39 G6 10 32N 106 25 E
Tan-Tan, Morocco 50 C3 28 29N 11 1W
Tana →, Kenya 54 C5 2 32S 40 31 E
Tana →, Norway 8 A23 70 30N 28 14 E
Tana, L., Ethiopia 46 E2 13 5N 37 30 E
Tana River, Kenya 54 C4 2 0S 39 30 E
Tanabe, Japan 31 H7 33 44N 135 22 E
Tanafjorden, Norway 8 A23 70 45N 28 25 E
Tanaga, Pta., Canary Is. 22 G1 27 42N 18 10W
Tanahbala, Indonesia 36 E1 0 30S 98 30 E
Tanahgrogot, Indonesia 36 E5 1 55S 116 15 E
Tanahjampea, Indonesia 37 F6 7 10S 120 35 E
Tanahmasa, Indonesia 36 E1 0 12S 98 39 E
Tanahmerah, Indonesia 37 F10 6 5S 140 16 E
Tanakpur, India 43 E9 29 5N 80 7 E
Tanakura, Japan 31 F10 37 10N 140 20 E
Tanami, Australia 60 C4 19 59S 129 43 E
Tanami Desert, Australia 60 C5 18 50S 132 0 E
Tanana →, U.S.A. 68 B4 65 10N 151 58W
Tananarive = Antananarivo, Madag. 57 B8 18 55S 47 31 E
Tânaro →, Italy 18 D8 44 55N 8 40 E
Tancheng, China 35 G10 34 25N 118 20 E
Tanch'ŏn, N. Korea 35 D15 40 27N 128 54 E
Tanda, Ut. P., India 43 F10 26 33N 82 35 E
Tanda, Ut. P., India 43 E8 28 57N 78 56 E
Tandag, Phil. 37 C7 9 4N 126 9 E
Tandaia, Tanzania 55 D3 9 25S 34 15 E
Tandaué, Angola 56 B2 16 58S 18 5 E
Tandil, Argentina 94 D4 37 15S 59 6W
Tandil, Sa. del, Argentina 94 D4 37 30S 59 0W
Tandlianwala, Pakistan 42 D5 31 3N 73 9 E
Tando Adam, Pakistan 42 G3 25 45N 68 40 E
Tando Allahyar, Pakistan 42 G3 25 28N 68 43 E
Tando Bago, Pakistan 42 G3 24 47N 68 58 E
Tando Mohommed Khan, Pakistan 42 G3 25 8N 68 32 E
Tandou L., Australia 63 E3 32 40S 142 5 E
Tandragee, U.K. 13 B5 54 21N 6 24W
Tane-ga-Shima, Japan 31 J5 30 30N 131 0 E
Taneatua, N.Z. 59 H6 38 4S 177 1 E
Tanen Tong Dan = Dawna Ra., Burma 38 D2 16 30N 98 30 E
Tanezrouft, Algeria 50 D6 23 9N 0 11 E
Tang, Koh, Cambodia 39 G4 10 16N 103 7 E
Tang, Ra's-e, Iran 45 E8 25 21N 59 52 E
Tang Krasang, Cambodia 38 F5 12 34N 105 3 E

Tanga, *Tanzania* 54 D4 5 5S 39 2 E
Tanga □, *Tanzania* 54 D4 5 20S 38 0 E
Tanganyika, L., *Africa* 54 D3 6 40S 30 0 E
Tanger, *Morocco* 50 A4 35 50N 5 49W
Tangerang, *Indonesia* 37 G12 6 11S 106 37 E
Tanggu, *China* 35 E9 39 2N 117 40 E
Tanggula Shan, *China* 32 C4 32 40N 92 10 E
Tanghe, *China* 34 H7 32 47N 112 50 E
Tangier = Tanger, *Morocco* 50 A4 35 50N 5 49W
Tangorin, *Australia* 62 C3 21 47S 144 12 E
Tangorombohitr'i Makay, *Madag.* 57 C8 21 0S 45 15 E
Tangshan, *China* 35 E10 39 38N 118 10 E
Tangtou, *China* 35 G10 35 28N 118 30 E
Tanimbar, Kepulauan, *Indonesia* 37 F8 7 30S 131 30 E
Tanimbar Is. = Tanimbar, Kepulauan, *Indonesia* 37 F8 7 30S 131 30 E
Taninthari = Tenasserim □, *Burma* 38 F2 14 0N 98 30 E
Tanjay, *Phil.* 37 C6 9 30N 123 5 E
Tanjong Malim, *Malaysia* 39 L3 3 42N 101 31 E
Tanjore = Thanjavur, *India* 40 P11 10 48N 79 12 E
Tanjung, *Phil.* 36 E5 2 10S 115 25 E
Tanjungbalai, *Indonesia* 36 D1 2 55N 99 44 E
Tanjungbatu, *Indonesia* 36 D5 2 23N 118 3 E
Tanjungkarang Telukbetung, *Indonesia* 36 F3 5 20S 105 10 E
Tanjungpandan, *Indonesia* 36 E3 2 43S 107 38 E
Tanjungpinang, *Indonesia* 36 D2 1 5N 104 30 E
Tanjungredeb, *Indonesia* 36 D5 2 9N 117 29 E
Tanjungselor, *Indonesia* 36 D5 2 55N 117 25 E
Tank, *Pakistan* 42 C4 32 14N 70 25 E
Tankhala, *India* 42 J5 21 58N 73 47 E
Tannersville, *U.S.A.* 79 E9 41 3N 75 18W
Tannu-Ola, *Russia* 27 D10 51 0N 94 0 E
Tannum Sands, *Australia* 62 C5 23 57S 151 22 E
Tanout, *Niger* 50 F7 14 50N 8 55 E
Tanta, *Egypt* 51 B12 30 45N 30 57 E
Tantoyuca, *Mexico* 87 C5 21 21N 98 10W
Tantung = Dandong, *China* 35 D13 40 10N 124 20 E
Tanunda, *Australia* 63 E2 34 30S 139 0 E
Tanzania ■, *Africa* 54 D3 6 0S 34 0 E
Tanzilla →, *Canada* 72 B2 58 8N 130 43W
Tao, Ko, *Thailand* 39 G2 10 5N 99 52 E
Tao'an = Taonan, *China* 35 B12 45 22N 122 40 E
Tao'er He →, *China* 35 B13 45 45N 124 5 E
Taolanaro, *Madag.* 57 D8 25 2S 47 0 E
Taole, *China* 34 E4 38 48N 106 40 E
Taonan, *China* 35 B12 45 22N 122 40 E
Taos, *U.S.A.* 83 H11 36 24N 105 35W
Taoudenni, *Mali* 50 D5 22 40N 3 55W
Tapa, *Estonia* 9 G21 59 15N 25 50 E
Tapa Shan = Daba Shan, *China* 33 C5 32 0N 109 0 E
Tapachula, *Mexico* 87 E6 14 54N 92 17W
Tapah, *Malaysia* 39 K3 4 12N 101 15 E
Tapajós →, *Brazil* 93 D8 2 24S 54 41W
Tapaktuan, *Indonesia* 36 D1 3 15N 97 10 E
Tapanahoni →, *Surinam* 93 C8 4 20N 54 25W
Tapanui, *N.Z.* 59 L2 45 56S 169 18 E
Tapauá →, *Brazil* 92 E6 5 40S 64 21W
Tapes, *Brazil* 95 C5 30 40S 51 23W
Tapeta, *Liberia* 50 G4 6 29N 8 52W
Taphan Hin, *Thailand* 38 D3 16 13N 100 26 E
Tapi →, *India* 40 J8 21 8N 72 41 E
Tapirapecó, Serra, *Venezuela* 92 C6 1 10N 65 0W
Tapuaenuku, *N.Z.* 59 K4 42 0S 173 39 E
Tapul Group, *Phil.* 37 C6 5 35N 120 50 E
Tapurucuará, *Brazil* 92 D5 0 24S 65 2W
Ţaqţaq, *Iraq* 44 C5 35 53N 44 35 E
Taquara, *Brazil* 95 B5 29 36S 50 46W
Taquari →, *Brazil* 92 G7 19 15S 57 17W
Tara, *Australia* 63 D5 27 17S 150 31 E
Tara, *Canada* 78 B3 44 28N 81 9W
Tara, *Russia* 26 D8 56 55N 74 24 E
Tara, *Zambia* 55 F2 16 58S 26 45 E
Tara →, *Montenegro, Yug.* 21 C8 43 21N 18 51 E
Tarabagatay, Khrebet, *Kazakstan* 26 E9 48 0N 83 0 E
Tarâbulus, *Lebanon* 47 A4 34 31N 35 50 E
Tarâbulus, *Libya* 51 B8 32 49N 13 7 E
Taradehi, *India* 43 H8 23 18N 79 21 E
Tarajalejo, *Canary Is.* 22 F5 28 12N 14 7W
Tarakan, *Indonesia* 36 D5 3 20N 117 35 E
Tarakit, Mt., *Kenya* 54 B4 2 2N 35 10 E
Tarama-Jima, *Japan* 31 M2 24 39N 124 42 E
Taran, Mys, *Russia* 9 J18 54 56N 19 59 E
Taranagar, *India* 42 E6 28 43N 74 50 E
Taranaki □, *N.Z.* 59 H5 39 25S 174 30 E
Taranaki, Mt., *N.Z.* 59 H5 39 17S 174 5 E
Tarancón, *Spain* 19 B4 40 1N 3 0W
Taransay, *U.K.* 12 D1 57 54N 7 0W
Táranto, *Italy* 20 D7 40 28N 17 14 E
Táranto, G. di, *Italy* 20 D7 40 8N 17 20 E
Tarapacá, *Colombia* 92 D5 2 56S 69 46W
Tarapacá □, *Chile* 94 A2 20 45S 69 30W
Tarapoto, *Peru* 92 E3 6 30S 76 20W
Tararua Ra., *N.Z.* 59 J5 40 45S 175 25 E
Tarashcha, *Ukraine* 17 D16 49 30N 30 31 E
Tarauacá, *Brazil* 92 E4 8 6S 70 48W
Tarauacá →, *Brazil* 92 E5 6 42S 69 48W
Tarawa, *Kiribati* 64 G9 1 30N 173 0 E
Tarawera, *N.Z.* 59 H6 39 2S 176 36 E
Tarawera, L., *N.Z.* 59 H6 38 13S 176 27 E
Taraz, *Kazakstan* 26 E8 42 54N 71 22 E
Tarazona, *Spain* 19 B5 41 55N 1 43W
Tarbat Ness, *U.K.* 12 D5 57 52N 3 47W
Tarbela Dam, *Pakistan* 42 B5 34 8N 72 52 E
Tarbert, *Arg. & Bute, U.K.* 12 F3 55 52N 5 25W
Tarbert, *W. Isles, U.K.* 12 D2 57 54N 6 49W
Tarbes, *France* 18 E4 43 15N 0 3 E
Tarboro, *U.S.A.* 77 H7 35 54N 77 32W
Tarcoola, *Australia* 63 E1 30 44S 134 36 E
Tarcoon, *Australia* 63 E4 30 15S 146 43 E
Taree, *Australia* 63 E5 31 50S 152 30 E
Tarfaya, *Morocco* 50 C3 27 55N 12 55W
Târgovişte, *Romania* 17 F13 44 55N 25 27 E
Târgu-Jiu, *Romania* 17 F12 45 5N 23 19 E
Târgu Mureş, *Romania* 17 E13 46 31N 24 38 E
Ţarif, *U.A.E.* 45 E7 24 3N 53 46 E
Tarifa, *Spain* 19 D3 36 1N 5 36W
Tarija, *Bolivia* 94 A3 21 30S 64 40W
Tarija □, *Bolivia* 94 A3 21 30S 63 30W
Tariku →, *Indonesia* 37 E9 2 55S 138 26 E
Tarim Basin = Tarim Pendi, *China* 32 B3 40 0N 84 0 E
Tarim He →, *China* 32 C3 39 30N 88 30 E
Tarim Pendi, *China* 32 B3 40 0N 84 0 E
Taritatu →, *Indonesia* 37 E9 2 54S 138 27 E
Tarka →, *S. Africa* 56 E4 32 10S 26 0 E
Tarkastad, *S. Africa* 56 E4 32 0S 26 16 E
Tarkhankut, Mys, *Ukraine* 25 E5 45 25N 32 30 E
Tarko Sale, *Russia* 26 C8 64 55N 77 50 E
Tarkwa, *Ghana* 50 G5 5 20N 2 0W
Tarlac, *Phil.* 37 A6 15 29N 120 35 E
Tarma, *Peru* 92 F3 11 25S 75 45W
Tarn →, *France* 18 E4 44 5N 1 6 E
Târnăveni, *Romania* 17 E13 46 19N 24 13 E
Tarnobrzeg, *Poland* 17 C11 50 35N 21 41 E
Tarnów, *Poland* 17 C11 50 3N 21 0 E
Tarnowskie Góry, *Poland* 17 C10 50 27N 18 54 E
Ţārom, *Iran* 45 D7 28 11N 55 46 E
Taroom, *Australia* 63 D4 25 36S 149 48 E
Taroudannt, *Morocco* 50 B4 30 30N 8 52W
Tarpon Springs, *U.S.A.* 77 L4 28 9N 82 45W
Tarragona, *Spain* 19 B6 41 5N 1 17 E
Tarraleah, *Australia* 62 G4 42 17S 146 26 E
Tarrasa = Terrassa, *Spain* 19 B7 41 34N 2 1 E
Tarrytown, *U.S.A.* 79 E11 41 4N 73 52W
Tarshiha = Me'ona, *Israel* 47 B4 33 1N 35 15 E
Tarsus, *Turkey* 25 G5 36 58N 34 55 E
Tartagal, *Argentina* 94 A3 22 30S 63 50W
Tartu, *Estonia* 9 G22 58 20N 26 44 E
Ţarţūs, *Syria* 44 C2 34 55N 35 55 E
Tarumizu, *Japan* 31 J5 31 29N 130 42 E
Tarutao, Ko, *Thailand* 39 J2 6 33N 99 40 E
Tarutung, *Indonesia* 36 D1 2 0N 98 54 E
Taseko →, *Canada* 72 C4 52 8N 123 45W
Tash-Kömür, *Kyrgyzstan* 26 E8 41 40N 72 10 E
Tash-Kumyr = Tash-Kömür, *Kyrgyzstan* 26 E8 41 40N 72 10 E
Tashauz = Dashhowuz, *Turkmenistan* 26 E6 41 49N 59 58 E
Tashi Chho Dzong = Thimphu, *Bhutan* 41 F16 27 31N 89 45 E
Ţashk, Daryācheh-ye, *Iran* 45 D7 29 45N 53 35 E
Tashkent = Toshkent, *Uzbekistan* 26 E7 41 20N 69 10 E
Tashtagol, *Russia* 26 D9 52 47N 87 53 E
Tasiilaq, *Greenland* 4 C6 65 40N 37 20W
Tasikmalaya, *Indonesia* 37 G13 7 18S 108 12 E
Tåsjön, *Sweden* 8 D16 64 15N 15 40 E
Taskan, *Russia* 27 C16 62 59N 150 20 E
Tasman B., *N.Z.* 59 J4 40 59S 173 25 E
Tasman Mts., *N.Z.* 59 J4 41 3S 172 25 E
Tasman Pen., *Australia* 62 G4 43 10S 148 0 E
Tasman Sea, *Pac. Oc.* 64 L8 36 0S 160 0 E
Tasmania □, *Australia* 62 G4 42 0S 146 30 E
Tassili n'Ajjer, *Algeria* 50 C7 25 47N 8 1 E
Tatabánya, *Hungary* 17 E10 47 32N 18 25 E
Tatahouine, *Tunisia* 51 B8 32 56N 10 27 E
Tatar Republic = Tatarstan □, *Russia* 24 C9 55 30N 51 30 E
Tatarbunary, *Ukraine* 17 F15 45 50N 29 39 E
Tatarsk, *Russia* 26 D8 55 14N 76 0 E
Tatarstan □, *Russia* 24 C9 55 30N 51 30 E
Tateyama, *Japan* 31 G9 35 0N 139 50 E
Tathlina L., *Canada* 72 A5 60 33N 117 39W
Tathra, *Australia* 63 F4 36 44S 149 59 E
Tatinnai L., *Canada* 73 A9 60 55N 97 40W
Tatla L., *Canada* 72 C4 52 0N 124 20W
Tatnam, C., *Canada* 73 B10 57 16N 91 0W
Tatra = Tatry, *Slovak Rep.* 17 D11 49 20N 20 0 E
Tatry, *Slovak Rep.* 17 D11 49 20N 20 0 E
Tatshenshini →, *Canada* 72 B1 59 28N 137 45W
Tatsuno, *Japan* 31 G7 34 52N 134 33 E
Tatta, *Pakistan* 42 G2 24 42N 67 55 E
Tatuí, *Brazil* 95 A6 23 25S 47 53W
Tatum, *U.S.A.* 81 J3 33 16N 103 19W
Tat'ung = Datong, *China* 34 D7 40 6N 113 18 E
Tatvan, *Turkey* 25 G7 38 31N 42 15 E
Taubaté, *Brazil* 95 A6 23 0S 45 36W
Tauern, *Austria* 16 E7 47 15N 12 40 E
Taumarunui, *N.Z.* 59 H5 38 53S 175 15 E
Taumaturgo, *Brazil* 92 E4 8 54S 72 51W
Taung, *S. Africa* 56 D3 27 33S 24 47 E
Taungdwingyi, *Burma* 41 J19 20 1N 95 40 E
Taunggyi, *Burma* 41 J20 20 50N 97 0 E
Taungup, *Burma* 41 K19 18 51N 94 14 E
Taungup Taunggya, *Burma* 41 K18 18 20N 93 40 E
Taunsa, *Pakistan* 42 D4 30 42N 70 39 E
Taunsa Barrage, *Pakistan* 42 D4 30 42N 70 50 E
Taunton, *U.K.* 11 F4 51 1N 3 5W
Taunton, *U.S.A.* 79 E13 41 54N 71 6W
Taunus, *Germany* 16 C5 50 13N 8 34 E
Taupo, *N.Z.* 59 H6 38 41S 176 7 E
Taupo, L., *N.Z.* 59 H5 38 46S 175 55 E
Tauragė, *Lithuania* 9 J20 55 14N 22 16 E
Tauranga, *N.Z.* 59 G6 37 42S 176 11 E
Tauranga Harb., *N.Z.* 59 G6 37 30S 176 5 E
Taureau, Rés., *Canada* 70 C5 46 46N 73 50W
Taurianova, *Italy* 20 E7 38 21N 16 1 E
Taurus Mts. = Toros Dağları, *Turkey* 25 G5 37 0N 32 30 E
Tavda, *Russia* 26 D7 58 7N 65 8 E
Tavda →, *Russia* 26 D7 57 47N 67 18 E
Taveta, *Tanzania* 54 C4 3 23S 37 37 E
Taveuni, *Fiji* 59 C9 16 51S 179 58W
Tavira, *Portugal* 19 D2 37 8N 7 40W
Tavistock, *Canada* 78 C4 43 19N 80 50W
Tavistock, *U.K.* 11 G3 50 33N 4 9W
Tavoy = Dawei, *Burma* 38 E2 14 2N 98 12 E
Taw →, *U.K.* 11 F3 51 4N 4 4W
Tawa →, *India* 42 H8 22 48N 77 48 E
Tawas City, *U.S.A.* 76 C4 44 16N 83 31W
Tawau, *Malaysia* 36 D5 4 20N 117 55 E
Tawitawi, *Phil.* 37 B6 5 10N 120 0 E
Taxco de Alarcón, *Mexico* 87 D5 18 33N 99 36W
Taxila, *Pakistan* 42 C5 33 42N 72 52 E
Tay →, *U.K.* 12 E5 56 37N 3 38W
Tay, Firth of, *U.K.* 12 E5 56 25N 3 8W
Tay, L., *Australia* 61 F3 32 55S 120 48 E
Tay, L., *U.K.* 12 E4 56 32N 4 8W
Tay Ninh, *Vietnam* 39 G6 11 20N 106 5 E
Tayabamba, *Peru* 92 E3 8 15S 77 16W
Taylakova, *Russia* 26 D8 59 13N 74 0 E
Taylakovy = Taylakova, *Russia* 26 D8 59 13N 74 0 E
Taylor, *Canada* 72 B4 56 13N 120 40W
Taylor, *Nebr., U.S.A.* 80 E5 41 46N 99 23W
Taylor, *Pa., U.S.A.* 79 E9 41 23N 75 43W
Taylor, *Tex., U.S.A.* 81 K6 30 34N 97 25W
Taylor, Mt., *U.S.A.* 83 J10 35 14N 107 37W
Taylorville, *U.S.A.* 80 F10 39 33N 89 18W
Taymā, *Si. Arabia* 44 E3 27 35N 38 45 E
Taymyr, Oz., *Russia* 27 B11 74 20N 102 0 E
Taymyr, Poluostrov, *Russia* 27 B11 75 0N 100 0 E
Tayport, *U.K.* 12 E6 56 27N 2 52W
Tayshet, *Russia* 27 D10 55 58N 98 1 E
Taytay, *Phil.* 37 B5 10 45N 119 30 E
Taz →, *Russia* 26 C8 67 32N 78 40 E
Taza, *Morocco* 50 B5 34 16N 4 6W
Tāzah Khurmātū, *Iraq* 44 C5 35 18N 44 20 E
Tazawa-Ko, *Japan* 30 E10 39 43N 140 40 E
Tazin, *Canada* 73 B7 59 48N 109 55W
Tazin L., *Canada* 73 B7 59 44N 108 42W
Tazovskiy, *Russia* 26 C8 67 30N 78 44 E
Tbilisi, *Georgia* 25 F7 41 43N 44 50 E
Tchad = Chad ■, *Africa* 51 F8 15 0N 17 15 E
Tchad, L., *Chad* 51 F8 13 30N 14 30 E
Tch'eng-tou = Chengdu, *China* 32 C5 30 38N 104 2 E
Tchentlo L., *Canada* 72 B4 55 15N 125 0W
Tchibanga, *Gabon* 52 E2 2 45S 11 0 E
Tch'ong-k'ing = Chongqing, *China* 32 D5 29 35N 106 25 E
Tczew, *Poland* 17 A10 54 8N 18 50 E
Te Anau, *N.Z.* 59 L1 45 25S 167 43 E
Te Anau, L., *N.Z.* 59 L1 45 15S 167 45 E
Te Aroha, *N.Z.* 59 G5 37 32S 175 44 E
Te Awamutu, *N.Z.* 59 H5 38 1S 175 20 E
Te Kuiti, *N.Z.* 59 H5 38 20S 175 11 E
Te Puke, *N.Z.* 59 G6 37 46S 176 22 E
Te Waewae B., *N.Z.* 59 M1 46 13S 167 33 E
Teague, *U.S.A.* 81 K6 31 38N 96 17W
Teapa, *Mexico* 87 D6 18 35N 92 56W
Tebakang, *Malaysia* 36 D4 1 6N 110 30 E
Tébessa, *Algeria* 50 A7 35 22N 8 8 E
Tebicuary →, *Paraguay* 94 B4 26 36S 58 16W
Tebingtinggi, *Indonesia* 36 D1 3 20N 99 9 E
Tecate, *Mexico* 85 N10 32 34N 116 38W
Tecka, *Argentina* 96 E2 43 29S 70 48W
Tecomán, *Mexico* 86 D4 18 55N 103 53W
Tecopa, *U.S.A.* 85 K10 35 51N 116 13W
Tecoripa, *Mexico* 86 B3 28 37N 109 57W
Tecuala, *Mexico* 86 C3 22 23N 105 27W
Tecuci, *Romania* 17 F14 45 51N 27 27 E
Tecumseh, *Canada* 78 D2 42 19N 82 54W
Tecumseh, *Mich., U.S.A.* 76 D4 42 0N 83 57W
Tecumseh, *Okla., U.S.A.* 81 H6 35 15N 96 56W
Tedzhen = Tejen, *Turkmenistan* 26 F7 37 23N 60 31 E
Tees →, *U.K.* 10 C6 54 37N 1 10W
Tees B., *U.K.* 10 C6 54 40N 1 9W
Teeswater, *Canada* 78 C3 43 59N 81 17W
Tefé, *Brazil* 92 D6 3 25S 64 50W
Tegal, *Indonesia* 36 F3 6 52S 109 8 E
Tegid, L. = Bala, L., *U.K.* 10 E4 52 53N 3 37W
Tegucigalpa, *Honduras* 88 D2 14 5N 87 14W
Tehachapi, *U.S.A.* 85 K8 35 8N 118 27W
Tehachapi Mts., *U.S.A.* 85 L8 35 0N 118 30W
Tehoru, *Indonesia* 37 E7 3 23S 129 30 E
Tehrān, *Iran* 45 C6 35 44N 51 30 E
Tehri, *India* 43 D8 30 23N 78 29 E
Tehuacán, *Mexico* 87 D5 18 30N 97 30W
Tehuantepec, *Mexico* 87 D5 16 21N 95 13W
Tehuantepec, G. de, *Mexico* 87 D5 15 50N 95 12W
Tehuantepec, Istmo de, *Mexico* 87 D6 17 0N 94 30W
Teide, *Canary Is.* 22 F3 28 15N 16 38W
Teifi →, *U.K.* 11 E3 52 5N 4 41W
Teign →, *U.K.* 11 G4 50 32N 3 32W
Teignmouth, *U.K.* 11 G4 50 33N 3 31W
Tejam, *India* 43 E9 29 57N 80 11 E
Tejen, *Turkmenistan* 26 F7 37 23N 60 31 E
Tejen →, *Turkmenistan* 45 B9 37 24N 60 38 E
Tejo →, *Europe* 19 C1 38 40N 9 24W
Tejon Pass, *U.S.A.* 85 L8 34 49N 118 53W
Tekamah, *U.S.A.* 80 E6 41 47N 96 13W
Tekapo, L., *N.Z.* 59 K3 43 53S 170 33 E
Tekax, *Mexico* 87 C7 20 11N 89 18W
Tekeli, *Kazakstan* 26 E8 44 50N 79 0 E
Tekirdağ, *Turkey* 21 D12 40 58N 27 30 E
Tekkali, *India* 41 K14 18 37N 84 15 E
Tekoa, *U.S.A.* 82 C5 47 14N 117 4W
Tel Aviv-Yafo, *Israel* 47 C3 32 4N 34 48 E
Tel Lakhish, *Israel* 47 D3 31 34N 34 51 E
Tel Megiddo, *Israel* 47 C4 32 35N 35 11 E
Tela, *Honduras* 88 C2 15 40N 87 28W
Telanaipura = Jambi, *Indonesia* 36 E2 1 38S 103 30 E
Telavi, *Georgia* 25 F8 42 0N 45 30 E
Telde, *Canary Is.* 22 G4 27 59N 15 25W
Telegraph Creek, *Canada* 72 B2 58 0N 131 10W
Telekhany = Tsyelyakhany, *Belarus* 17 B13 52 30N 25 46 E
Telemark, *Norway* 9 G12 59 15N 7 40 E
Telén, *Argentina* 94 D2 36 15S 65 31W
Teleng, *Iran* 45 E9 25 47N 61 3 E
Teles Pires →, *Brazil* 92 E7 7 21S 58 3W
Telescope Pk., *U.S.A.* 85 J9 36 10N 117 5W
Telfer Mine, *Australia* 60 C3 21 40S 122 12 E
Telford, *U.K.* 11 E5 52 40N 2 27W
Telford and Wrekin □, *U.K.* 10 E5 52 45N 2 27W
Telkwa, *Canada* 72 C3 54 41N 127 5W
Tell City, *U.S.A.* 76 G2 37 57N 86 46W
Tellicherry, *India* 40 P9 11 45N 75 30 E
Telluride, *U.S.A.* 83 H10 37 56N 107 49W
Teloloapán, *Mexico* 87 D5 18 21N 99 51W
Telpos Iz, *Russia* 24 B10 63 16N 59 13 E
Telsen, *Argentina* 96 E3 42 30S 66 50W
Telšiai, *Lithuania* 9 H20 55 59N 22 14 E
Teluk Anson = Teluk Intan, *Malaysia* 39 K3 4 3N 101 0 E
Teluk Betung = Tanjungkarang Telukbetung, *Indonesia* 36 F3 5 20S 105 10 E
Teluk Intan, *Malaysia* 39 K3 4 3N 101 0 E
Telukbutun, *Indonesia* 39 K7 4 13N 108 12 E
Telukdalem, *Indonesia* 36 D1 0 33N 97 50 E
Tema, *Ghana* 50 G5 5 41N 0 0W
Temax, *Mexico* 87 C7 21 10N 88 50W
Temba, *S. Africa* 57 D4 25 20S 28 17 E
Tembagapura, *Indonesia* 37 E9 4 20S 137 0 E
Tembe, *Dem. Rep. of the Congo* 54 C2 0 16S 28 14 E
Temblor Range, *U.S.A.* 85 K7 35 20N 119 50W
Teme →, *U.K.* 11 E5 52 11N 2 13W
Temecula, *U.S.A.* 85 M9 33 30N 117 9W
Temerloh, *Malaysia* 36 D2 3 27N 102 25 E
Teminabuan, *Indonesia* 37 E8 1 26S 132 1 E
Temir, *Kazakstan* 25 E10 49 1N 57 14 E
Temirtau, *Kazakstan* 26 D8 50 5N 72 56 E
Temirtau, *Russia* 26 D9 53 10N 87 30 E
Temiscamie →, *Canada* 71 B5 50 59N 73 5W
Témiscaming, *Canada* 70 C4 46 44N 79 5W
Témiscamingue, L., *Canada* 70 C4 47 10N 79 25W
Temosachic, *Mexico* 86 B3 28 58N 107 50W
Tempe, *U.S.A.* 83 K8 33 25N 111 56W
Tempiute, *U.S.A.* 84 H11 37 39N 115 38W
Temple, *U.S.A.* 81 K6 31 6N 97 21W
Temple B., *Australia* 62 A3 12 15S 143 3 E
Templemore, *Ireland* 13 D4 52 47N 7 51W
Templeton, *U.S.A.* 84 K6 35 33N 120 42W
Templeton →, *Australia* 62 C2 21 0S 138 40 E
Tempoal, *Mexico* 87 C5 21 31N 98 23W
Temuco, *Chile* 96 D2 38 45S 72 40W
Temuka, *N.Z.* 59 L3 44 14S 171 17 E
Tenabo, *Mexico* 87 C6 20 2N 90 12W
Tenaha, *U.S.A.* 81 K7 31 57N 94 15W
Tenakee Springs, *U.S.A.* 72 B1 57 47N 135 13W
Tenali, *India* 41 L12 16 15N 80 35 E
Tenancingo, *Mexico* 87 D5 19 0N 99 33W
Tenango, *Mexico* 87 D5 19 7N 99 33W
Tenasserim, *Burma* 39 F2 12 6N 99 3 E
Tenasserim □, *Burma* 38 F2 14 0N 98 30 E
Tenby, *U.K.* 11 F3 51 40N 4 42W
Tenda, Colle di, *France* 18 D7 44 7N 7 36 E
Tendaho, *Ethiopia* 46 E3 11 48N 40 54 E
Tendukhera, *India* 43 H8 23 24N 79 33 E
Tenerife, *Canary Is.* 22 F3 28 15N 16 35W
Tenerife, Pico, *Canary Is.* 22 G1 27 43N 18 1W
Teng Xian, *China* 35 G9 35 5N 117 10 E
Tengah □, *Indonesia* 37 E6 1 30S 121 0 E
Tengah, Kepulauan, *Indonesia* 36 F5 7 5S 118 15 E
Tengchong, *China* 32 D4 25 0N 98 28 E
Tengchowfu = Penglai, *China* 35 F11 37 48N 120 42 E
Tenggara □, *Indonesia* 37 E6 3 50S 122 0 E
Tenggarong, *Indonesia* 36 E5 0 24S 116 58 E
Tenggol, Pulau, *Malaysia* 39 K4 4 48N 103 41 E
Tengiz, Ozero, *Kazakstan* 26 D7 50 30N 69 0 E
Tenino, *U.S.A.* 84 D4 46 51N 122 51W
Tenkasi, *India* 40 Q10 8 55N 77 20 E
Tenke, *Katanga, Dem. Rep. of the Congo* 55 E2 11 22S 26 40 E
Tenke, *Katanga, Dem. Rep. of the Congo* 55 E2 10 32S 26 7 E
Tennant Creek, *Australia* 62 B1 19 30S 134 15 E
Tennessee □, *U.S.A.* 77 H2 36 0N 86 30W
Tennessee →, *U.S.A.* 76 G1 37 4N 88 34W
Teno, Pta. de, *Canary Is.* 22 F3 28 21N 16 55W
Tenom, *Malaysia* 36 C5 5 4N 115 57 E
Tenosique, *Mexico* 87 D6 17 30N 91 24W
Tenryū-Gawa →, *Japan* 31 G8 35 39N 137 48 E
Tenterden, *U.K.* 11 F8 51 4N 0 42 E
Tenterfield, *Australia* 63 D5 29 0S 152 0 E
Teófilo Otoni, *Brazil* 93 G10 17 50S 41 30W
Tepa, *Indonesia* 37 F7 7 52S 129 31 E
Tepalcatepec →, *Mexico* 86 D4 18 35N 101 59W
Tepehuanes, *Mexico* 86 B3 25 21N 105 44W
Tepetongo, *Mexico* 86 C4 22 28N 103 9W
Tepic, *Mexico* 86 C4 21 30N 104 54W
Teplice, *Czech Rep.* 16 C7 50 40N 13 48 E
Tepoca, C., *Mexico* 86 A2 30 20N 112 25W
Tequila, *Mexico* 86 C4 20 54N 103 47W
Ter →, *Spain* 19 A7 42 2N 3 12 E
Ter Apel, *Neths.* 15 B7 52 53N 7 5 E
Teraina, *Kiribati* 65 G11 4 43N 160 25W
Téramo, *Italy* 20 C5 42 39N 13 42 E
Terang, *Australia* 63 F3 38 15S 142 55 E
Tercero →, *Argentina* 94 C3 32 58S 61 47W
Terebovlya, *Ukraine* 17 D13 49 18N 25 44 E
Terek →, *Russia* 25 F8 44 0N 47 30 E
Teresina, *Brazil* 93 E10 5 9S 42 45W
Terewah, L., *Australia* 63 D4 29 52S 147 35 E
Teridgerie Cr. →, *Australia* 63 E4 30 25S 148 50 E
Termez = Termiz, *Uzbekistan* 26 F7 37 15N 67 15 E
Términi Imerese, *Italy* 20 F5 37 59N 13 42 E
Términos, L. de, *Mexico* 87 D6 18 35N 91 30W
Termiz, *Uzbekistan* 26 F7 37 15N 67 15 E
Térmoli, *Italy* 20 C6 42 0N 15 0 E
Ternate, *Indonesia* 37 D7 0 45N 127 25 E
Terneuzen, *Neths.* 15 C3 51 20N 3 50 E
Terney, *Russia* 27 E14 45 3N 136 37 E
Terni, *Italy* 20 C5 42 34N 12 37 E
Ternopil, *Ukraine* 17 D13 49 30N 25 40 E
Ternopol = Ternopil, *Ukraine* 17 D13 49 30N 25 40 E
Terowie, *Australia* 63 E2 33 8S 138 55 E
Terra Bella, *U.S.A.* 85 K7 35 58N 119 3W
Terra Nova Nat. Park, *Canada* 71 C9 48 33N 53 55W
Terrace, *Canada* 72 C3 54 30N 128 35W
Terrace Bay, *Canada* 70 C2 48 47N 87 5W
Terracina, *Italy* 20 D5 41 17N 13 15 E
Terralba, *Italy* 20 E3 39 43N 8 39 E
Terranova = Ólbia, *Italy* 20 D3 40 55N 9 31 E
Terrassa, *Spain* 19 B7 41 34N 2 1 E
Terre Haute, *U.S.A.* 76 F2 39 28N 87 25W
Terrebonne B., *U.S.A.* 81 L9 29 5N 90 35W
Terrell, *U.S.A.* 81 J6 32 44N 96 17W
Terrenceville, *Canada* 71 C9 47 40N 54 44W
Terry, *U.S.A.* 80 B2 46 47N 105 19W
Terryville, *U.S.A.* 79 E11 41 41N 73 3W
Terschelling, *Neths.* 15 A5 53 25N 5 20 E
Teruel, *Spain* 19 B5 40 22N 1 8W
Tervola, *Finland* 8 C21 66 6N 24 49 E
Teryaweyna L., *Australia* 63 E3 32 18S 143 22 E
Teshio, *Japan* 30 B10 44 53N 141 44 E
Teshio-Gawa →, *Japan* 30 B10 44 53N 141 45 E
Tesiyn Gol →, *Mongolia* 32 A4 50 40N 93 20 E
Teslin, *Canada* 72 A2 60 10N 132 43W
Teslin →, *Canada* 72 A2 61 34N 134 35W
Teslin L., *Canada* 72 A2 60 15N 132 57W
Tessalit, *Mali* 50 D6 20 12N 1 0 E
Test →, *U.K.* 11 G6 50 56N 1 29W
Testigos, Is. Las, *Venezuela* 89 D7 11 23N 63 7W
Tetachuck L., *Canada* 72 C3 53 18N 125 55W
Tetas, Pta., *Chile* 94 A1 23 31S 70 38W
Tete, *Mozam.* 55 F3 16 13S 33 33 E
Tete □, *Mozam.* 55 F3 15 15S 32 40 E
Teterev →, *Ukraine* 17 C16 51 1N 30 5 E
Teteven, *Bulgaria* 21 C11 42 58N 24 17 E

Tethul →, Canada 72 A6 60 35N 112 12W
Tetiyev, Ukraine 17 D15 49 22N 29 38 E
Teton →, U.S.A. 82 C8 47 56N 110 31W
Tétouan, Morocco 50 A4 35 35N 5 21W
Tetovo, Macedonia 21 C9 42 1N 20 59 E
Teuco →, Argentina 94 B3 25 35S 60 11W
Teulon, Canada 73 C9 50 23N 97 16W
Teun, Indonesia 37 F7 6 59S 129 8 E
Teutoburger Wald, Germany 16 B5 52 5N 8 22 E
Tevere →, Italy 20 D5 41 44N 12 14 E
Teverya, Israel 47 C4 32 47N 35 32 E
Teviot →, U.K. 12 F6 55 29N 2 38W
Tewantin, Australia 63 D5 26 27S 153 3 E
Tewkesbury, U.K. 11 F5 51 59N 2 9W
Texada I., Canada 72 D4 49 40N 124 25W
Texarkana, Ark., U.S.A. 81 J8 33 26N 94 2W
Texarkana, Tex., U.S.A. 81 J7 33 26N 94 3W
Texas, Australia 63 D5 28 49S 151 9 E
Texas □, U.S.A. 81 K5 31 40N 98 30W
Texas City, U.S.A. 81 L7 29 24N 94 54W
Texel, Neths. 15 A4 53 5N 4 50 E
Texline, U.S.A. 81 G3 36 23N 103 2W
Texoma, L., U.S.A. 81 J6 33 50N 96 34W
Tezin, Afghan. 42 B3 34 24N 69 30 E
Teziutlán, Mexico 87 D5 19 50N 97 22W
Tezpur, India 41 F18 26 40N 92 45 E
Tezzeron L., Canada 72 C4 54 43N 124 30W
Tha-anne →, Canada 73 A10 60 31N 94 37W
Tha Deua, Laos 38 D4 17 57N 102 53 E
Tha Deua, Laos 38 C3 19 26N 101 50 E
Tha Pla, Thailand 38 D3 17 48N 100 32 E
Tha Rua, Thailand 38 E3 14 34N 100 44 E
Tha Sala, Thailand 39 H2 8 40N 99 56 E
Tha Song Yang, Thailand 38 D1 17 34N 97 55 E
Thaba Putsoa, Lesotho 57 D4 29 45S 28 0 E
Thabana Ntlenyana, Lesotho 57 D4 29 30S 29 16 E
Thabazimbi, S. Africa 57 C4 24 40S 27 21 E
Thādiq, Si. Arabia 44 E5 25 18N 45 52 E
Thai Binh, Vietnam 38 B6 20 35N 106 1 E
Thai Muang, Thailand 39 H2 8 24N 98 16 E
Thai Nguyen, Vietnam 38 B5 21 35N 105 55 E
Thailand ■, Asia 38 E4 16 0N 102 0 E
Thailand, G. of, Asia 39 G3 11 30N 101 0 E
Thakhek, Laos 38 D5 17 25N 104 45 E
Thal, Pakistan 42 C4 33 28N 70 33 E
Thal Desert, Pakistan 42 D4 31 10N 71 30 E
Thala La = Hkakabo Razi, Burma 41 E20 28 25N 97 23 E
Thalabarivat, Cambodia 38 F5 13 33N 105 57 E
Thallon, Australia 63 D4 28 39S 148 49 E
Thames, N.Z. 59 G5 37 7S 175 34 E
Thames →, Canada 78 D2 42 20N 82 25W
Thames →, U.K. 11 F8 51 29N 0 34 E
Thames →, U.S.A. 79 E12 41 18N 72 5W
Thames Estuary, U.K. 11 F8 51 29N 0 52 E
Thamesford, Canada 78 C4 43 4N 81 0W
Thamesville, Canada 78 D3 42 33N 81 59W
Than, India 42 H4 22 34N 71 11 E
Than Uyen, Vietnam 38 B4 22 0N 103 54 E
Thana Gazi, India 42 F7 27 25N 76 19 E
Thandla, India 42 H6 23 0N 74 34 E
Thane, India 40 K8 19 12N 72 59 E
Thanesar, India 42 D7 30 1N 76 52 E
Thanet, I. of, U.K. 11 F9 51 21N 1 20 E
Thangool, Australia 62 C5 24 38S 150 42 E
Thanh Hoa, Vietnam 38 C5 19 48N 105 46 E
Thanh Hung, Vietnam 39 H5 9 55N 105 43 E
Thanh Pho Ho Chi Minh, Vietnam 39 G6 10 58N 106 40 E
Thanh Thuy, Vietnam 38 A5 22 55N 104 51 E
Thanjavur, India 40 P11 10 48N 79 12 E
Thano Bula Khan, Pakistan 42 G2 25 22N 67 50 E
Thaolinta L., Canada 73 A9 61 30N 96 25W
Thap Sakae, Thailand 39 G2 11 30N 99 37 E
Thap Than, Thailand 38 E2 15 27N 99 54 E
Thar Desert, India 42 F5 28 0N 72 0 E
Tharad, India 42 G4 24 30N 71 44 E
Thargomindah, Australia 63 D3 27 58S 143 46 E
Tharrawaddy, Burma 41 L19 17 38N 95 48 E
Tharthār, Mileh, Iraq 44 C4 34 0N 43 15 E
Tharthār, W. ath →, Iraq 44 C4 33 59N 43 12 E
Thásos, Greece 21 D11 40 40N 24 40 E
That Khe, Vietnam 38 A6 22 16N 106 28 E
Thatcher, Ariz., U.S.A. 83 K9 32 51N 109 46W
Thatcher, Colo., U.S.A. 81 G2 37 33N 104 7W
Thaton, Burma 41 L20 16 55N 97 22 E
Thaungdut, Burma 41 G19 24 30N 94 40 E
Thayer, U.S.A. 81 G9 36 31N 91 33W
Thayetmyo, Burma 41 K19 19 20N 95 10 E
Thazi, Burma 41 J20 21 0N 96 5 E
The Alberga →, Australia 63 D2 27 6S 135 33 E
The Bight, Bahamas 89 B4 24 19N 75 24W
The Dalles, U.S.A. 82 D3 45 36N 121 10W
The English Company's Is., Australia 62 A2 11 50S 136 32 E
The Frome →, Australia 63 D2 29 8S 137 54 E
The Great Divide = Great Dividing Ra., Australia 62 C4 23 0S 146 0 E
The Hague = 's-Gravenhage, Neths. 15 B4 52 7N 4 17 E
The Hamilton →, Australia 63 D2 26 40S 135 19 E
The Macumba →, Australia 63 D2 27 52S 137 12 E
The Neales →, Australia 63 D2 28 8S 136 47 E
The Officer →, Australia 61 E5 27 46S 132 30 E
The Pas, Canada 73 C8 53 45N 101 15W
The Range, Zimbabwe 55 F3 19 2S 31 2 E
The Rock, Australia 63 F4 35 15S 147 2 E
The Salt L., Australia 63 E3 30 6S 142 8 E
The Sandheads, India 43 J13 21 10N 88 20 E
The Stevenson →, Australia 63 D2 27 6S 135 33 E
The Warburton →, Australia 63 D2 28 4S 137 28 E
The Woodlands, U.S.A. 81 K7 30 9N 95 27W
Thebes = Thívai, Greece 21 E10 38 19N 23 19 E
Thebes, Egypt 51 C12 25 40N 32 35 E
Thedford, Canada 78 C3 43 9N 81 51W
Thedford, U.S.A. 80 E4 41 59N 100 35W
Theebine, Australia 63 D5 25 57S 152 34 E
Thekulthili L., Canada 73 A7 61 3N 110 0W
Thelon →, Canada 73 A8 62 35N 104 3W
Theodore, Australia 62 C5 24 55S 150 3 E
Theodore, Canada 73 C8 51 26N 102 55W
Theodore, U.S.A. 77 K1 30 33N 88 10W
Theodore Roosevelt Nat. Memorial Park, U.S.A. 80 B3 47 0N 103 25W
Theodore Roosevelt Res., U.S.A. 83 K8 33 46N 111 0W
Thepha, Thailand 39 J3 6 52N 100 58 E
Theresa, U.S.A. 79 B9 44 13N 75 48W
Thermaïkós Kólpos, Greece 21 D10 40 15N 22 45 E
Thermopolis, U.S.A. 82 E9 43 39N 108 13W
Thermopylae P., Greece 21 E10 38 48N 22 35 E
Thessalon, Canada 70 C3 46 20N 83 30W
Thessaloniki, Greece 21 D10 40 38N 22 58 E
Thessaloniki, Gulf of = Thermaïkós Kólpos, Greece 21 D10 40 15N 22 45 E
Thetford, U.K. 11 E8 52 25N 0 45 E
Thetford Mines, Canada 71 C5 46 8N 71 18W
Theun →, Laos 38 C5 18 19N 104 0 E
Theunissen, S. Africa 56 D4 28 26S 26 43 E
Thevenard, Australia 63 E1 32 9S 133 38 E
Thibodaux, U.S.A. 81 L9 29 48N 90 49W
Thicket Portage, Canada 73 B9 55 19N 97 42W
Thief River Falls, U.S.A. 80 A6 48 7N 96 10W
Thiel Mts., Antarctica 5 E16 85 15S 91 0W
Thiers, France 18 D5 45 52N 3 33 E
Thiès, Senegal 50 F2 14 50N 16 51W
Thika, Kenya 54 C4 1 1S 37 5 E
Thikombia, Fiji 59 B9 15 44S 179 55W
Thimphu, Bhutan 41 F16 27 31N 89 45 E
Þingvallavatn, Iceland 8 D3 64 11N 21 9W
Thionville, France 18 B7 49 20N 6 10 E
Thíra, Greece 21 F11 36 23N 25 27 E
Third Cataract, Sudan 51 E12 19 42N 30 20 E
Thirsk, U.K. 10 C6 54 14N 1 19W
Thiruvananthapuram = Trivandrum, India 40 Q10 8 41N 77 0 E
Thisted, Denmark 9 H13 56 58N 8 40 E
Thistle I., Australia 63 F2 35 0S 136 8 E
Thívai, Greece 21 E10 38 19N 23 19 E
Þjórsá →, Iceland 8 E3 63 47N 20 48W
Thlewiaza →, Man., Canada 73 B8 59 43N 100 5W
Thlewiaza →, N.W.T., Canada 73 A10 60 29N 94 40W
Thmar Puok, Cambodia 38 F4 13 57N 103 4 E
Tho Vinh, Vietnam 38 C5 19 16N 105 42 E
Thoa →, Canada 73 A7 60 31N 109 47W
Thoen, Thailand 38 D2 17 43N 99 12 E
Thoeng, Thailand 38 C3 19 41N 100 12 E
Thohoyandou, S. Africa 53 J6 22 58S 30 29 E
Tholdi, Pakistan 43 B7 35 5N 76 6 E
Thomas, U.S.A. 81 H5 35 45N 98 45W
Thomas, L., Australia 63 D2 26 4S 137 58 E
Thomaston, U.S.A. 77 J3 32 53N 84 20W
Thomasville, Ala., U.S.A. 77 K2 31 55N 87 44W
Thomasville, Ga., U.S.A. 77 K4 30 50N 83 59W
Thomasville, N.C., U.S.A. 77 H5 35 53N 80 5W
Thompson, Canada 73 B9 55 45N 97 52W
Thompson, U.S.A. 79 E9 41 52N 75 31W
Thompson →, Canada 72 C4 50 15N 121 24W
Thompson →, U.S.A. 80 F8 39 46N 93 37W
Thompson Falls, U.S.A. 82 C6 47 36N 115 21W
Thompson Pk., U.S.A. 82 F2 41 0N 123 0W
Thompson Springs, U.S.A. 83 G9 38 58N 109 43W
Thompsontown, U.S.A. 78 F7 40 33N 77 14W
Thomson, U.S.A. 77 J4 33 28N 82 30W
Thomson →, Australia 62 C3 25 11S 142 53 E
Thomson's Falls = Nyahururu, Kenya 54 B4 0 2N 36 27 E
Þórisvatn, Iceland 8 D4 64 20N 18 55W
Thornaby on Tees, U.K. 10 C6 54 33N 1 18W
Thornbury, Canada 78 B4 44 34N 80 26W
Thorne, U.K. 10 D7 53 37N 0 57W
Thornhill, Canada 72 C3 54 31N 128 32W
Thorold, Canada 78 C5 43 7N 79 12W
Þórshöfn, Iceland 8 C6 66 12N 15 20W
Thouin, C., Australia 60 D2 20 20S 118 10 E
Thousand Oaks, U.S.A. 85 L8 34 10N 118 50W
Thrace, Turkey 21 D12 41 0N 27 0 E
Three Forks, U.S.A. 82 D8 45 54N 111 33W
Three Hills, Canada 72 C6 51 43N 113 15W
Three Hummock I., Australia 62 G3 40 25S 144 55 E
Three Points, C., Ghana 50 H5 4 42N 2 6W
Three Rivers, Calif., U.S.A. 84 J8 36 26N 118 54W
Three Rivers, Tex., U.S.A. 81 L5 28 28N 98 11W
Three Sisters, U.S.A. 82 D3 44 4N 121 51W
Three Springs, Australia 61 E2 29 32S 115 45 E
Throssell, L., Australia 61 E3 27 33S 124 10 E
Throssell Ra., Australia 60 D3 22 3S 121 43 E
Thuan Hoa, Vietnam 39 H5 8 58N 105 30 E
Thubun Lakes, Canada 73 A6 61 30N 112 0W
Thuin, Belgium 15 D4 50 20N 4 17 E
Thule = Qaanaaq, Greenland 4 B4 77 40N 69 0W
Thun, Switz. 18 C7 46 45N 7 38 E
Thunder B., U.S.A. 78 B1 45 0N 83 20W
Thunder Bay, Canada 70 C2 48 20N 89 15W
Thung Song, Thailand 39 H2 8 10N 99 40 E
Thunkar, Bhutan 41 F17 27 55N 91 0 E
Thuong Tra, Vietnam 38 D6 16 2N 107 42 E
Thüringer Wald, Germany 16 C6 50 35N 11 0 E
Thurles, Ireland 13 D4 52 41N 7 49W
Thurrock □, U.K. 11 F8 51 31N 0 23 E
Thursday I., Australia 62 A3 10 30S 142 3 E
Thurso, Canada 70 C4 45 36N 75 15W
Thurso, U.K. 12 C5 58 36N 3 32W
Thurso →, U.K. 12 C5 58 36N 3 32W
Thurston I., Antarctica 5 D16 72 0S 100 0W
Thutade L., Canada 72 B3 57 0N 126 55W
Thyolo, Malawi 55 F4 16 7S 35 5 E
Thysville = Mbanza Ngungu, Dem. Rep. of the Congo 52 F2 5 12S 14 53 E
Ti Tree, Australia 62 C1 22 5S 133 22 E
Tian Shan, Asia 32 B3 40 30N 76 0 E
Tianjin, China 35 E9 39 8N 117 10 E
Tianshui, China 34 G3 34 32N 105 40 E
Tianzhen, China 34 D8 40 24N 114 5 E
Tianzhuangtai, China 35 D12 40 43N 122 5 E
Tiaret, Algeria 50 A6 35 20N 1 21 E
Tibagi, Brazil 95 A5 24 30S 50 24W
Tibagi →, Brazil 95 A5 22 47S 51 1W
Tiber = Tevere →, Italy 20 D5 41 44N 12 14 E
Tiberias = Teverya, Israel 47 C4 32 47N 35 32 E
Tiberias, L. = Yam Kinneret, Israel 47 C4 32 45N 35 35 E
Tibesti, Chad 51 D9 21 0N 17 30 E
Tibet = Xizang Zizhiqu □, China 32 C3 32 0N 88 0 E
Tibet, Plateau of, Asia 28 F12 32 0N 86 0 E
Tibnī, Syria 44 C3 35 36N 39 50 E
Tibooburra, Australia 63 D3 29 26S 142 1 E
Tiburón, I., Mexico 86 B2 29 0N 112 30W
Ticino →, Italy 18 D8 45 9N 9 14 E
Ticonderoga, U.S.A. 79 C11 43 51N 73 26W
Ticul, Mexico 87 C7 20 20N 89 31W
Tidaholm, Sweden 9 G15 58 12N 13 58 E
Tiddim, Burma 41 H18 23 28N 93 45 E
Tidioute, U.S.A. 78 E5 41 41N 79 24W
Tidjikja, Mauritania 50 E3 18 29N 11 35W
Tidore, Indonesia 37 D7 0 40N 127 25 E
Tiel, Neths. 15 C5 51 53N 5 26 E
Tieling, China 35 C12 42 20N 123 55 E
Tielt, Belgium 15 C3 51 0N 3 20 E
Tien Shan = Tian Shan, Asia 32 B3 40 30N 76 0 E
Tien-tsin = Tianjin, China 35 E9 39 8N 117 10 E
Tien Yen, Vietnam 38 B6 21 20N 107 24 E
T'ienching = Tianjin, China 35 E9 39 8N 117 10 E
Tienen, Belgium 15 D4 50 48N 4 57 E
Tientsin = Tianjin, China 35 E9 39 8N 117 10 E
Tieri, Australia 62 C4 23 2S 148 21 E
Tierra Amarilla, Chile 94 B1 27 28S 70 18W
Tierra Amarilla, U.S.A. 83 H10 36 42N 106 33W
Tierra Colorada, Mexico 87 D5 17 10N 99 35W
Tierra de Campos, Spain 19 A3 42 10N 4 50W
Tierra del Fuego, I. Gr. de, Argentina 96 G3 54 0S 69 0W
Tiétar →, Spain 19 C3 39 50N 6 1W
Tieté →, Brazil 95 A5 20 40S 51 35W
Tiffin, U.S.A. 76 E4 41 7N 83 11W
Tiflis = Tbilisi, Georgia 25 F7 41 43N 44 50 E
Tifton, U.S.A. 77 K4 31 27N 83 31W
Tifu, Indonesia 37 E7 3 39S 126 24 E
Tighina, Moldova 17 E15 46 50N 29 30 E
Tigil, Russia 27 D16 57 49N 158 40 E
Tignish, Canada 71 C7 46 58N 64 2W
Tigre →, Peru 92 D4 4 30S 74 10W
Tigre →, Venezuela 92 B6 9 20N 62 30W
Tigris = Dijlah, Nahr →, Asia 44 D5 31 0N 47 25 E
Tigyaing, Burma 41 H20 23 45N 96 10 E
Tījara, India 42 F7 27 56N 76 31 E
Tijuana, Mexico 85 N9 32 30N 117 10W
Tikal, Guatemala 88 C2 17 13N 89 24W
Tikamgarh, India 43 G8 24 44N 78 50 E
Tikhoretsk, Russia 25 E7 45 56N 40 5 E
Tikhvin, Russia 24 C5 59 35N 33 30 E
Tikrit, Iraq 44 C4 34 35N 43 37 E
Tiksi, Russia 27 B13 71 40N 128 45 E
Tilamuta, Indonesia 37 D6 0 32N 122 23 E
Tilburg, Neths. 15 C5 51 31N 5 6 E
Tilbury, Canada 78 D2 42 17N 82 23W
Tilbury, U.K. 11 F8 51 27N 0 22 E
Tilcara, Argentina 94 A2 23 36S 65 23W
Tilden, U.S.A. 80 D6 42 3N 97 50W
Tilhar, India 43 F8 28 0N 79 45 E
Tilichiki, Russia 27 C17 60 27N 166 5 E
Tilissos, Greece 23 D7 35 20N 25 1 E
Till →, U.K. 10 B5 55 41N 2 13W
Tillamook, U.S.A. 82 D2 45 27N 123 51W
Tillsonburg, Canada 78 D4 42 53N 80 44W
Tillyeria, Cyprus 23 D11 35 6N 32 40 E
Tílos, Greece 21 F12 36 27N 27 27 E
Tilpa, Australia 63 E3 30 57S 144 24 E
Tilsit = Sovetsk, Russia 9 J19 55 6N 21 50 E
Tilt →, U.K. 12 E5 56 46N 3 51W
Tilton, U.S.A. 79 C13 43 27N 71 36W
Tiltonsville, U.S.A. 78 F4 40 10N 80 41W
Timagami, L., Canada 70 C3 47 0N 80 10W
Timanskiy Kryazh, Russia 24 A9 65 58N 50 5 E
Timaru, N.Z. 59 L3 44 23S 171 14 E
Timau, Kenya 54 B4 0 4N 37 15 E
Timbákion, Greece 23 D6 35 4N 24 45 E
Timber Creek, Australia 60 C5 15 40S 130 29 E
Timber Lake, U.S.A. 80 C4 45 26N 101 5W
Timber Mt., U.S.A. 84 H10 37 6N 116 28W
Timbuktu = Tombouctou, Mali 50 E5 16 50N 3 0W
Timi, Cyprus 23 E11 34 44N 32 31 E
Timimoun, Algeria 50 C6 29 14N 0 16 E
Timirist, Râs, Mauritania 50 E2 19 21N 16 30W
Timişoara, Romania 17 F11 45 43N 21 15 E
Timmins, Canada 70 C3 48 28N 81 25W
Timok →, Serbia, Yug. 21 B10 44 10N 22 40 E
Timor, Indonesia 37 F7 9 0S 125 0 E
Timor Sea, Ind. Oc. 60 B4 12 0S 127 0 E
Timor Timur = East Timor ■, Asia 37 F7 8 50S 126 0 E
Tin Can Bay, Australia 63 D5 25 56S 153 0 E
Tin Mt., U.S.A. 84 J9 36 50N 117 10W
Tina →, S. Africa 57 E4 31 18S 29 13 E
Tinaca Pt., Phil. 37 C7 5 30N 125 25 E
Tinajo, Canary Is. 22 E6 29 4N 13 42W
Tindal, Australia 60 B5 14 31S 132 22 E
Tindouf, Algeria 50 C4 27 42N 8 10W
Tinggi, Pulau, Malaysia 39 L5 2 18N 104 7 E
Tingo Maria, Peru 92 E3 9 10S 75 54W
Tingrela, Ivory C. 50 F4 10 27N 6 25W
Tinh Bien, Vietnam 39 G5 10 36N 104 57 E
Tinnevelly = Tirunelveli, India 40 Q10 8 45N 77 45 E
Tinogasta, Argentina 94 B2 28 5S 67 32W
Tínos, Greece 21 F11 37 33N 25 8 E
Tinpahar, India 43 G12 24 59N 87 44 E
Tintina, Argentina 94 B3 27 2S 62 45W
Tintinara, Australia 63 F3 35 48S 140 2 E
Tioga, N. Dak., U.S.A. 80 A3 48 23N 102 56W
Tioga, Pa., U.S.A. 78 E7 41 55N 77 8W
Tioman, Pulau, Malaysia 39 L5 2 50N 104 10 E
Tionesta, U.S.A. 78 E5 41 30N 79 28W
Tipongpani, India 41 F19 27 20N 95 55 E
Tipperary, Ireland 13 D3 52 28N 8 10W
Tipperary □, Ireland 13 D4 52 37N 7 55W
Tipton, Calif., U.S.A. 84 J7 36 4N 119 19W
Tipton, Iowa, U.S.A. 80 E9 41 46N 91 8W
Tipton Mt., U.S.A. 85 K12 35 32N 114 12W
Tiptonville, U.S.A. 81 G10 36 23N 89 29W
Tīrān, Iran 45 C6 32 45N 51 8 E
Tiranë, Albania 21 D8 41 18N 19 49 E
Tiraspol, Moldova 17 E15 46 55N 29 35 E
Tire, Turkey 21 E12 38 5N 27 45 E
Tirebolu, Turkey 25 F6 40 58N 38 45 E
Tiree, U.K. 12 E2 56 31N 6 55W
Tiree, Passage of, U.K. 12 E2 56 30N 6 30W
Tîrgovişte = Târgovişte, Romania 17 F13 44 55N 25 27 E
Tîrgu-Jiu = Târgu-Jiu, Romania 17 F12 45 5N 23 19 E
Tîrgu Mureş = Târgu Mureş, Romania 17 E13 46 31N 24 38 E
Tirich Mir, Pakistan 40 A7 36 15N 71 55 E
Tírnavos, Greece 21 E10 39 45N 22 18 E
Tirodi, India 40 J11 21 40N 79 44 E
Tirol □, Austria 16 E6 47 3N 10 43 E
Tirso →, Italy 20 E3 39 53N 8 32 E
Tiruchchirappalli, India 40 P11 10 45N 78 45 E
Tirunelveli, India 40 Q10 8 45N 77 45 E
Tirupati, India 40 N11 13 39N 79 25 E
Tiruppur, India 40 P10 11 5N 77 22 E
Tiruvannamalai, India 40 N11 12 15N 79 5 E
Tisa, India 42 C7 32 50N 76 9 E
Tisa →, Serbia, Yug. 21 B9 45 15N 20 17 E
Tisdale, Canada 73 C8 52 50N 104 0W
Tishomingo, U.S.A. 81 H6 34 14N 96 41W
Tisza = Tisa →, Serbia, Yug. 21 B9 45 15N 20 17 E
Tit-Ary, Russia 27 B13 71 55N 127 2 E
Tithwal, Pakistan 43 B5 34 21N 73 50 E
Titicaca, L., S. Amer. 92 G5 15 30S 69 30W
Titograd = Podgorica, Montenegro, Yug. 21 C8 42 30N 19 19 E
Titule, Dem. Rep. of the Congo 54 B2 3 15N 25 31 E
Titusville, Fla., U.S.A. 77 L5 28 37N 80 49W
Titusville, Pa., U.S.A. 78 E5 41 38N 79 41W
Tivaouane, Senegal 50 F2 14 56N 16 45W
Tiverton, U.K. 11 G4 50 54N 3 29W
Tívoli, Italy 20 D5 41 58N 12 45 E
Tizi-Ouzou, Algeria 50 A6 36 42N 4 3 E
Tizimín, Mexico 87 C7 21 0N 88 1W
Tjeggelvas, Sweden 8 C17 66 37N 17 45 E
Tjirebon = Cirebon, Indonesia 36 F3 6 45S 108 32 E
Tjörn, Sweden 9 G14 58 0N 11 35 E
Tlacotalpan, Mexico 87 D5 18 37N 95 40W
Tlahualilo, Mexico 86 B4 26 20N 103 30W
Tlaquepaque, Mexico 86 C4 20 39N 103 19W
Tlaxcala, Mexico 87 D5 19 20N 98 14W
Tlaxcala □, Mexico 87 D5 19 30N 98 20W
Tlaxiaco, Mexico 87 D5 17 18N 97 40W
Tlemcen, Algeria 50 B5 34 52N 1 21W
To Bong, Vietnam 38 F7 12 45N 109 16 E
Toad →, Canada 72 B4 59 25N 124 57W
Toad River, Canada 72 B3 58 51N 125 14W
Toamasina, Madag. 57 B8 18 10S 49 25 E
Toamasina □, Madag. 57 B8 18 0S 49 0 E
Toay, Argentina 94 D3 36 43S 64 38W
Toba, Japan 31 G8 34 30N 136 51 E
Toba, Danau, Indonesia 36 D1 2 30N 97 30 E
Toba Kakar, Pakistan 42 D3 31 30N 69 0 E
Toba Tek Singh, Pakistan 42 D5 30 55N 72 25 E
Tobago, Trin. & Tob. 89 D7 11 10N 60 30W
Tobelo, Indonesia 37 D7 1 45N 127 56 E
Tobermory, Canada 78 A3 45 12N 81 40W
Tobermory, U.K. 12 E2 56 38N 6 5W
Tobi, Pac. Oc. 37 D8 2 40N 131 10 E
Tobin, U.S.A. 84 F5 39 55N 121 19W
Tobin, L., Australia 60 D4 21 45S 125 49 E
Tobin L., Canada 73 C8 53 35N 103 30W
Toboali, Indonesia 36 E3 3 0S 106 25 E
Tobol →, Russia 26 D7 58 10N 68 12 E
Toboli, Indonesia 37 E6 0 38S 120 5 E
Tobolsk, Russia 26 D7 58 15N 68 10 E
Tobruk = Tubruq, Libya 51 B10 32 7N 23 55 E
Tobyhanna, U.S.A. 79 E9 41 11N 75 25W
Tobyl = Tobol →, Russia 26 D7 58 10N 68 12 E
Tocantinópolis, Brazil 93 E9 6 20S 47 25W
Tocantins □, Brazil 93 F9 10 0S 48 0W
Tocantins →, Brazil 93 D9 1 45S 49 10W
Toccoa, U.S.A. 77 H4 34 35N 83 19W
Tochi →, Pakistan 42 C4 32 49N 70 41 E
Tochigi, Japan 31 F9 36 25N 139 45 E
Tochigi □, Japan 31 F9 36 45N 139 45 E
Toconao, Chile 94 A2 23 11S 68 1W
Tocopilla, Chile 94 A1 22 5S 70 10W
Tocumwal, Australia 63 F4 35 51S 145 31 E
Tocuyo →, Venezuela 92 A5 11 3N 68 23W
Todd →, Australia 62 C2 24 52S 135 48 E
Todeli, Indonesia 37 E6 1 40S 124 29 E
Todenyang, Kenya 54 B4 4 35N 35 56 E
Todgarh, India 42 G5 25 42N 73 58 E
Todos os Santos, B. de, Brazil 93 F11 12 48S 38 38W
Todos Santos, Mexico 86 C2 23 27N 110 13W
Toe Hd., U.K. 12 D1 57 50N 7 8W
Tofield, Canada 72 C6 53 25N 112 40W
Tofino, Canada 72 D3 49 11N 125 55W
Tofua, Tonga 59 D11 19 45S 175 5W
Tōgane, Japan 31 G10 35 33N 140 22 E
Togian, Kepulauan, Indonesia 37 E6 0 20S 121 50 E
Togliatti, Russia 24 D8 53 32N 49 24 E
Togo ■, W. Afr. 50 G6 8 30N 1 35 E
Togtoh, China 34 D6 40 15N 111 10 E
Tōhoku □, Japan 30 E10 39 50N 141 45 E
Töhöm, Mongolia 34 B5 44 27N 108 2 E
Toinya, Sudan 51 G11 6 17N 29 46 E
Toiyabe Range, U.S.A. 82 G5 39 30N 117 0W
Tojikiston = Tajikistan ■, Asia 26 F8 38 30N 70 0 E
Tojo, Indonesia 37 E6 1 20S 121 15 E
Tōjō, Japan 31 G6 34 53N 133 16 E
Tok, U.S.A. 68 B5 63 20N 142 59W
Tok-do, Japan 31 F5 37 15N 131 52 E
Tokachi-Dake, Japan 30 C11 43 17N 142 5 E
Tokachi-Gawa →, Japan 30 C11 42 44N 143 42 E
Tokala, Indonesia 37 E6 1 30S 121 40 E
Tōkamachi, Japan 31 F9 37 8N 138 43 E
Tokanui, N.Z. 59 M2 46 34S 168 56 E
Tokara-Rettō, Japan 31 K4 29 37N 129 43 E
Tokarahi, N.Z. 59 L3 44 56S 170 39 E
Tokashiki-Shima, Japan 31 L3 26 11N 127 21 E
Tokat □, Turkey 25 F6 40 15N 36 30 E
Tŏkch'ŏn, N. Korea 35 E14 39 45N 126 18 E
Tokeland, U.S.A. 84 D3 46 42N 123 59W
Tokelau Is., Pac. Oc. 64 H10 9 0S 171 45W
Tokmak, Kyrgyzstan 26 E8 42 49N 75 15 E
Toko Ra., Australia 62 C2 23 5S 138 20 E
Tokoro-Gawa →, Japan 30 B12 44 7N 144 5 E
Tokuno-Shima, Japan 31 L4 27 56N 128 55 E
Tokushima, Japan 31 G7 34 4N 134 34 E
Tokushima □, Japan 31 H7 33 55N 134 0 E
Tokuyama, Japan 31 G5 34 3N 131 50 E
Tōkyō, Japan 31 G9 35 45N 139 45 E
Tolaga Bay, N.Z. 59 H7 38 21S 178 20 E
Tolbukhin = Dobrich, Bulgaria 21 C12 43 37N 27 49 E
Toledo, Brazil 95 A5 24 44S 53 45W
Toledo, Spain 19 C3 39 50N 4 2W
Toledo, Ohio, U.S.A. 76 E4 41 39N 83 33W
Toledo, Oreg., U.S.A. 82 D2 44 37N 123 56W
Toledo, Wash., U.S.A. 82 C2 46 26N 122 51W
Toledo, Montes de, Spain 19 C3 39 33N 4 20W
Toledo Bend Reservoir, U.S.A. 81 K8 31 11N 93 34W
Tolga, Australia 62 B4 17 15S 145 29 E

Toliara, *Madag.* **57 C7** 23 21S 43 40 E
Toliara □, *Madag.* **57 C8** 21 0S 45 0 E
Tolima, *Colombia* **92 C3** 4 40N 75 19W
Tolitoli, *Indonesia* **37 D6** 1 5N 120 50 E
Tollhouse, *U.S.A.* **84 H7** 37 1N 119 24W
Tolo, Teluk, *Indonesia* **37 E6** 2 20S 122 10 E
Toluca, *Mexico* **87 D5** 19 20N 99 40W
Tom Burke, *S. Africa* **57 C4** 23 5S 28 0 E
Tom Price, *Australia* **60 D2** 22 40S 117 48 E
Tomah, *U.S.A.* **80 D9** 43 59N 90 30W
Tomahawk, *U.S.A.* **80 C10** 45 28N 89 44W
Tomakomai, *Japan* **30 C10** 42 38N 141 36 E
Tomales, *U.S.A.* **84 G4** 38 15N 122 53W
Tomales B., *U.S.A.* **84 G3** 38 15N 123 58W
Tomar, *Portugal* **19 C1** 39 36N 8 25W
Tomaszów Mazowiecki, *Poland* **17 C10** 51 30N 20 2 E
Tomatlán, *Mexico* **86 D3** 19 56N 105 15W
Tombador, Serra do, *Brazil* **92 F7** 12 0S 58 0W
Tombigbee →, *U.S.A.* **77 K2** 31 8N 87 57W
Tombouctou, *Mali* **50 E5** 16 50N 3 0W
Tombstone, *U.S.A.* **83 L8** 31 43N 110 4W
Tombua, *Angola* **56 B1** 15 55S 11 55 E
Tomé, *Chile* **94 D1** 36 36S 72 57W
Tomelloso, *Spain* **19 C4** 39 10N 3 2W
Tomini, *Indonesia* **37 D6** 0 30N 120 30 E
Tomini, Teluk, *Indonesia* **37 E6** 0 10S 121 0 E
Tomintoul, *U.K.* **12 D5** 57 15N 3 23W
Tomkinson Ranges, *Australia* **61 E4** 26 11S 129 5 E
Tommot, *Russia* **27 D13** 59 4N 126 20 E
Tomnop Ta Suos, *Cambodia* **39 G5** 11 20N 104 15 E
Tomo →, *Colombia* **92 B5** 5 20N 67 48W
Toms Place, *U.S.A.* **84 H8** 37 34N 118 41W
Toms River, *U.S.A.* **79 G10** 39 58N 74 12W
Tomsk, *Russia* **26 D9** 56 30N 85 5 E
Tonalá, *Mexico* **87 D6** 16 8N 93 41W
Tonantins, *Brazil* **92 D5** 2 45S 67 45W
Tonasket, *U.S.A.* **82 B4** 48 42N 119 26W
Tonawanda, *U.S.A.* **78 D6** 43 1N 78 53W
Tonbridge, *U.K.* **11 F8** 51 11N 0 17 E
Tondano, *Indonesia* **37 D6** 1 35N 124 54 E
Tondoro, *Namibia* **56 B2** 17 45S 18 50 E
Tone →, *Australia* **61 F2** 34 25S 116 25 E
Tone-Gawa →, *Japan* **31 F9** 35 44N 140 51 E
Tonekābon, *Iran* **45 B6** 36 45N 51 12 E
Tong Xian, *China* **34 E9** 39 55N 116 35 E
Tonga ■, *Pac. Oc.* **59 D11** 19 50S 174 30W
Tonga Trench, *Pac. Oc.* **64 J10** 18 0S 173 0W
Tongaat, *S. Africa* **57 D5** 29 33S 31 9 E
Tongareva, *Cook Is.* **65 H12** 9 0S 158 0W
Tongatapu Group, *Tonga* **59 E12** 21 0S 175 0W
Tongchŏn-ni, *N. Korea* **35 E14** 39 50N 127 25 E
Tongchuan, *China* **34 G5** 35 6N 109 3 E
Tongeren, *Belgium* **15 D5** 50 47N 5 28 E
Tongguan, *China* **34 G6** 34 40N 110 25 E
Tonghua, *China* **35 D13** 41 42N 125 58 E
Tongjosŏn Man, *N. Korea* **35 E15** 39 30N 128 0 E
Tongking, G. of = Tonkin, G. of, *Asia* **32 E5** 20 0N 108 0 E
Tongliao, *China* **35 C12** 43 38N 122 18 E
Tongling, *China* **33 C6** 30 55N 117 48 E
Tongnae, *S. Korea* **35 G15** 35 12N 129 5 E
Tongobory, *Madag.* **57 C7** 23 32S 44 20 E
Tongoy, *Chile* **94 C1** 30 16S 71 31W
Tongres = Tongeren, *Belgium* **15 D5** 50 47N 5 28 E
Tongsa Dzong, *Bhutan* **41 F17** 27 31N 90 31 E
Tongue, *U.K.* **12 C4** 58 29N 4 25W
Tongue →, *U.S.A.* **80 B2** 46 25N 105 52W
Tongwei, *China* **34 G3** 35 0N 105 5 E
Tongxin, *China* **34 F3** 36 59N 105 58 E
Tongyang, *N. Korea* **35 E14** 39 9N 126 53 E
Tongyu, *China* **35 B12** 44 45N 123 4 E
Tonj, *Sudan* **51 G11** 7 20N 28 44 E
Tonk, *India* **42 F6** 26 6N 75 54 E
Tonkawa, *U.S.A.* **81 G6** 36 41N 97 18W
Tonkin = Bac Phan, *Vietnam* **38 B5** 22 0N 105 0 E
Tonkin, G. of, *Asia* **32 E5** 20 0N 108 0 E
Tonle Sap, *Cambodia* **38 F4** 13 0N 104 0 E
Tono, *Japan* **30 E10** 39 19N 141 32 E
Tonopah, *U.S.A.* **83 G5** 38 4N 117 14W
Tonosí, *Panama* **88 E3** 7 20N 80 20W
Tons →, *Haryana, India* **42 D7** 30 30N 77 39 E
Tons →, *Ut. P., India* **43 F10** 26 1N 83 33 E
Tønsberg, *Norway* **9 G14** 59 19N 10 25 E
Toobanna, *Australia* **62 B4** 18 42S 146 9 E
Toodyay, *Australia* **61 F2** 31 34S 116 28 E
Tooele, *U.S.A.* **82 F7** 40 32N 112 18W
Toompine, *Australia* **63 D3** 27 15S 144 19 E
Toora, *Australia* **63 F4** 38 39S 146 23 E
Toora-Khem, *Russia* **27 D10** 52 28N 96 17 E
Toowoomba, *Australia* **63 D5** 27 32S 151 56 E
Top-ozero, *Russia* **24 A5** 65 35N 32 0 E
Top Springs, *Australia* **60 C5** 16 37S 131 51 E
Topaz, *U.S.A.* **84 G7** 38 41N 119 30W
Topeka, *U.S.A.* **80 F7** 39 3N 95 40W
Topley, *Canada* **72 C3** 54 49N 126 18W
Topocalma, Pta., *Chile* **94 C1** 34 10S 72 2W
Topock, *U.S.A.* **85 L12** 34 46N 114 29W
Topol'čany, *Slovak Rep.* **17 D10** 48 35N 18 12 E
Topolobampo, *Mexico* **86 B3** 25 40N 109 4W
Toppenish, *U.S.A.* **82 C3** 46 23N 120 19W
Toraka Vestale, *Madag.* **57 B7** 16 20S 43 58 E
Torata, *Peru* **92 G4** 17 23S 70 1W
Torbalı, *Turkey* **21 E12** 38 10N 27 21 E
Torbat-e Heydārīyeh, *Iran* **45 C8** 35 15N 59 12 E
Torbat-e Jām, *Iran* **45 C9** 35 16N 60 35 E
Torbay, *Canada* **71 C9** 47 40N 52 42W
Torbay □, *U.K.* **11 G4** 50 26N 3 31W
Tordesillas, *Spain* **19 B3** 41 30N 5 0W
Torfaen □, *U.K.* **11 F4** 51 43N 3 3W
Torgau, *Germany* **16 C7** 51 34N 13 0 E
Torhout, *Belgium* **15 C3** 51 5N 3 7 E
Tori-Shima, *Japan* **31 J10** 30 29N 140 19 E
Torin, *Mexico* **86 B2** 27 33N 110 15W
Torino, *Italy* **18 D7** 45 3N 7 40 E
Torit, *Sudan* **51 H12** 4 27N 32 31 E
Torkamān, *Iran* **44 B5** 37 35N 47 23 E
Tormes →, *Spain* **19 B2** 41 18N 6 29W
Tornado Mt., *Canada* **72 D6** 49 55N 114 40W
Torne älv →, *Sweden* **8 D21** 65 50N 24 12 E
Torneå = Tornio, *Finland* **8 D21** 65 50N 24 12 E
Torneträsk, *Sweden* **8 B18** 68 24N 19 15 E
Tornio, *Finland* **8 D21** 65 50N 24 12 E
Tornionjoki →, *Finland* **8 D21** 65 50N 24 12 E
Tornquist, *Argentina* **94 D3** 38 8S 62 15W
Toro, *Spain* **22 B11** 39 59N 4 8 E
Toro, Cerro del, *Chile* **94 B2** 29 10S 69 50W
Toro Pk., *U.S.A.* **85 M10** 33 34N 116 24W
Toronios Kólpos, *Greece* **21 D10** 40 5N 23 30 E
Toronto, *Canada* **78 C5** 43 39N 79 20W
Toronto, *U.S.A.* **78 F4** 40 28N 80 36W
Toropets, *Russia* **24 C5** 56 30N 31 40 E
Tororo, *Uganda* **54 B3** 0 45N 34 12 E
Toros Dağları, *Turkey* **25 G5** 37 0N 32 30 E
Torpa, *India* **43 H11** 22 57N 85 6 E
Torquay, *U.K.* **11 G4** 50 27N 3 32W
Torrance, *U.S.A.* **85 M8** 33 50N 118 19W
Torre de Moncorvo, *Portugal* **19 B2** 41 12N 7 8W
Torre del Greco, *Italy* **20 D6** 40 47N 14 22 E
Torrejón de Ardoz, *Spain* **19 B4** 40 27N 3 29W
Torrelavega, *Spain* **19 A3** 43 20N 4 5W
Torremolinos, *Spain* **19 D3** 36 38N 4 30W
Torrens, L., *Australia* **63 E2** 31 0S 137 50 E
Torrens Cr. →, *Australia* **62 C4** 22 23S 145 9 E
Torrens Creek, *Australia* **62 C4** 20 48S 145 3 E
Torrent, *Spain* **19 C5** 39 27N 0 28W
Torreón, *Mexico* **86 B4** 25 33N 103 26W
Torres, *Brazil* **95 B5** 29 21S 49 44W
Torres, *Mexico* **86 B2** 28 46N 110 47W
Torres Strait, *Australia* **64 H6** 9 50S 142 20 E
Torres Vedras, *Portugal* **19 C1** 39 5N 9 15W
Torrevieja, *Spain* **19 D5** 37 59N 0 42W
Torrey, *U.S.A.* **83 G8** 38 18N 111 25W
Torridge →, *U.K.* **11 G3** 51 0N 4 13W
Torridon, L., *U.K.* **12 D3** 57 35N 5 50W
Torrington, *Conn., U.S.A.* **79 E11** 41 48N 73 7W
Torrington, *Wyo., U.S.A.* **80 D2** 42 4N 104 11W
Tórshavn, *Færoe Is.* **8 E9** 62 5N 6 56W
Tortola, *Br. Virgin Is.* **89 C7** 18 19N 64 45W
Tortosa, *Spain* **19 B6** 40 49N 0 31 E
Tortosa, C., *Spain* **19 B6** 40 41N 0 52 E
Tortue, I. de la, *Haiti* **89 B5** 20 5N 72 57W
Torūd, *Iran* **45 C7** 35 25N 55 5 E
Toruń, *Poland* **17 B10** 53 2N 18 39 E
Tory I., *Ireland* **13 A3** 55 16N 8 14W
Tosa, *Japan* **31 H6** 33 24N 133 23 E
Tosa-Shimizu, *Japan* **31 H6** 32 52N 132 58 E
Tosa-Wan, *Japan* **31 H6** 33 15N 133 30 E
Toscana □, *Italy* **20 C4** 43 25N 11 0 E
Toshkent, *Uzbekistan* **26 E7** 41 20N 69 10 E
Tostado, *Argentina* **94 B3** 29 15S 61 50W
Tostón, Pta. de, *Canary Is.* **22 F5** 28 42N 14 2W
Tosu, *Japan* **31 H5** 33 22N 130 31 E
Toteng, *Botswana* **56 C3** 20 22S 22 58 E
Totma, *Russia* **24 C7** 60 0N 42 40 E
Totnes, *U.K.* **11 G4** 50 26N 3 42W
Totness, *Surinam* **93 B7** 5 53N 56 19W
Totonicapán, *Guatemala* **88 D1** 14 58N 91 12W
Totten Glacier, *Antarctica* **5 C8** 66 45S 116 10 E
Tottenham, *Australia* **63 E4** 32 14S 147 21 E
Tottenham, *Canada* **78 B5** 44 1N 79 49W
Tottori, *Japan* **31 G7** 35 30N 134 15 E
Tottori □, *Japan* **31 G7** 35 30N 134 12 E
Toubkal, Djebel, *Morocco* **50 B4** 31 0N 8 0W
Tougan, *Burkina Faso* **50 F5** 13 11N 2 58W
Touggourt, *Algeria* **50 B7** 33 6N 6 4 E
Toul, *France* **18 B6** 48 40N 5 53 E
Toulon, *France* **18 E6** 43 10N 5 55 E
Toulouse, *France* **18 E4** 43 37N 1 27 E
Toummo, *Niger* **51 D8** 22 45N 14 8 E
Toungoo, *Burma* **41 K20** 19 0N 96 30 E
Touraine, *France* **18 C4** 47 20N 0 30 E
Tourane = Da Nang, *Vietnam* **38 D7** 16 4N 108 13 E
Tourcoing, *France* **18 A5** 50 42N 3 10 E
Touriñán, C., *Spain* **19 A1** 43 3N 9 18W
Tournai, *Belgium* **15 D3** 50 35N 3 25 E
Tournon-sur-Rhône, *France* **18 D6** 45 4N 4 50 E
Tours, *France* **18 C4** 47 22N 0 40 E
Toussora, Mt., *C.A.R.* **52 C4** 9 7N 23 14 E
Touws →, *S. Africa* **56 E3** 33 45S 21 11 E
Touwsrivier, *S. Africa* **56 E3** 33 20S 20 2 E
Towada, *Japan* **30 D10** 40 37N 141 13 E
Towada-Ko, *Japan* **30 D10** 40 28N 140 55 E
Towanda, *U.S.A.* **79 E8** 41 46N 76 27W
Towang, *India* **41 F17** 27 37N 91 50 E
Tower, *U.S.A.* **80 B8** 47 48N 92 17W
Towerhill Cr. →, *Australia* **62 C3** 22 28S 144 35 E
Towner, *U.S.A.* **80 A4** 48 21N 100 25W
Townsend, *U.S.A.* **82 C8** 46 19N 111 31W
Townshend I., *Australia* **62 C5** 22 10S 150 31 E
Townsville, *Australia* **62 B4** 19 15S 146 45 E
Towraghondi, *Afghan.* **40 B3** 35 13N 62 16 E
Towson, *U.S.A.* **76 F7** 39 24N 76 36W
Towuti, Danau, *Indonesia* **37 E6** 2 45S 121 32 E
Toya-Ko, *Japan* **30 C10** 42 35N 140 51 E
Toyama, *Japan* **31 F8** 36 40N 137 15 E
Toyama □, *Japan* **31 F8** 36 45N 137 30 E
Toyama-Wan, *Japan* **31 F8** 37 0N 137 30 E
Toyohashi, *Japan* **31 G8** 34 45N 137 25 E
Toyokawa, *Japan* **31 G8** 34 48N 137 27 E
Toyonaka, *Japan* **31 G7** 34 50N 135 28 E
Toyooka, *Japan* **31 G7** 35 35N 134 48 E
Toyota, *Japan* **31 G8** 35 3N 137 7 E
Tozeur, *Tunisia* **50 B7** 33 56N 8 8 E
Trá Li = Tralee, *Ireland* **13 D2** 52 16N 9 42W
Tra On, *Vietnam* **39 H5** 9 58N 105 55 E
Trabzon, *Turkey* **25 F6** 41 0N 39 45 E
Tracadie, *Canada* **71 C7** 47 30N 64 55W
Tracy, *Calif., U.S.A.* **84 H5** 37 44N 121 26W
Tracy, *Minn., U.S.A.* **80 C7** 44 14N 95 37W
Trafalgar, C., *Spain* **19 D2** 36 10N 6 2W
Trail, *Canada* **72 D5** 49 5N 117 40W
Trainor L., *Canada* **72 A4** 60 24N 120 17W
Trákhonas, *Cyprus* **23 D12** 35 12N 33 21 E
Tralee, *Ireland* **13 D2** 52 16N 9 42W
Tralee B., *Ireland* **13 D2** 52 17N 9 55W
Tramore, *Ireland* **13 D4** 52 10N 7 10W
Tramore B., *Ireland* **13 D4** 52 9N 7 10W
Tran Ninh, Cao Nguyen, *Laos* **38 C4** 19 30N 103 10 E
Tranås, *Sweden* **9 G16** 58 3N 14 59 E
Trancas, *Argentina* **94 B2** 26 11S 65 20W
Trang, *Thailand* **39 J2** 7 33N 99 38 E
Trangahy, *Madag.* **57 B7** 19 7S 44 31 E
Trangan, *Indonesia* **37 F8** 6 40S 134 20 E
Trangie, *Australia* **63 E4** 32 4S 148 0 E
Trani, *Italy* **20 D7** 41 17N 16 25 E
Tranoroa, *Madag.* **57 C8** 24 42S 45 4 E
Tranqueras, *Uruguay* **95 C4** 31 13S 55 45W
Transantarctic Mts., *Antarctica* **5 E12** 85 0S 170 0W
Transilvania, *Romania* **17 E12** 46 30N 24 0 E
Transilvanian Alps = Carpaţii Meridionali, *Romania* **17 F13** 45 30N 25 0 E
Transvaal, *S. Africa* **53 K5** 25 0S 29 0 E
Transylvania = Transilvania, *Romania* **17 E12** 46 30N 24 0 E
Trápani, *Italy* **20 E5** 38 1N 12 29 E
Trapper Pk., *U.S.A.* **82 D6** 45 54N 114 18W
Traralgon, *Australia* **63 F4** 38 12S 146 34 E
Trasimeno, L., *Italy* **20 C5** 43 8N 12 6 E
Trat, *Thailand* **39 F4** 12 14N 102 33 E
Tratani →, *Pakistan* **42 E3** 29 19N 68 20 E
Traun, *Austria* **16 D8** 48 14N 14 15 E
Traveller's L., *Australia* **63 E3** 33 20S 142 0 E
Travemünde, *Germany* **16 B6** 53 57N 10 52 E
Travers, Mt., *N.Z.* **59 K4** 42 1S 172 45 E
Traverse City, *U.S.A.* **76 C3** 44 46N 85 38W
Travis, L., *U.S.A.* **81 K5** 30 24N 97 55W
Travnik, *Bos.-H.* **21 B7** 44 17N 17 39 E
Trébbia →, *Italy* **18 D8** 45 4N 9 41 E
Třebíč, *Czech Rep.* **16 D8** 49 14N 15 55 E
Trebinje, *Bos.-H.* **21 C8** 42 44N 18 22 E
Trebonne, *Australia* **62 B4** 18 37S 146 5 E
Tregaron, *U.K.* **11 E4** 52 14N 3 56W
Tregrosse Is., *Australia* **62 B5** 17 41S 150 43 E
Treherne, *Canada* **73 D9** 49 38N 98 42W
Treinta y Tres, *Uruguay* **95 C5** 33 16S 54 17W
Trelawney, *Zimbabwe* **57 B5** 17 30S 30 30 E
Trelew, *Argentina* **96 E3** 43 10S 65 20W
Trelleborg, *Sweden* **9 J15** 55 20N 13 10 E
Tremadog Bay, *U.K.* **10 E3** 52 51N 4 18W
Tremonton, *U.S.A.* **82 F7** 41 43N 112 10W
Tremp, *Spain* **19 A6** 42 10N 0 52 E
Trenche →, *Canada* **70 C5** 47 46N 72 53W
Trenčín, *Slovak Rep.* **17 D10** 48 52N 18 4 E
Trenggalek, *Indonesia* **37 H14** 8 3S 111 43 E
Trenque Lauquen, *Argentina* **94 D3** 36 5S 62 45W
Trent →, *Canada* **78 B7** 44 6N 77 34W
Trent →, *U.K.* **10 D7** 53 41N 0 42W
Trento, *Italy* **20 A4** 46 4N 11 8 E
Trenton, *Canada* **78 B7** 44 10N 77 34W
Trenton, *Mo., U.S.A.* **80 E8** 40 5N 93 37W
Trenton, *N.J., U.S.A.* **79 F10** 40 14N 74 46W
Trenton, *Nebr., U.S.A.* **80 E4** 40 11N 101 1W
Trepassey, *Canada* **71 C9** 46 43N 53 25W
Tres Arroyos, *Argentina* **94 D3** 38 26S 60 20W
Três Corações, *Brazil* **95 A6** 21 44S 45 15W
Três Lagoas, *Brazil* **93 H8** 20 50S 51 43W
Tres Lomas, *Argentina* **94 D3** 36 27S 62 51W
Tres Marías, Islas, *Mexico* **86 C3** 21 25N 106 28W
Tres Montes, C., *Chile* **96 F1** 46 50S 75 30W
Tres Pinos, *U.S.A.* **84 J5** 36 48N 121 19W
Três Pontas, *Brazil* **95 A6** 21 23S 45 29W
Tres Puentes, *Chile* **94 B1** 27 50S 70 15W
Tres Puntas, C., *Argentina* **96 F3** 47 0S 66 0W
Três Rios, *Brazil* **95 A7** 22 6S 43 15W
Tres Valles, *Mexico* **87 D5** 18 15N 96 8W
Tresco, *U.K.* **11 H1** 49 57N 6 20W
Treviso, *Italy* **20 B5** 45 40N 12 15 E
Triabunna, *Australia* **62 G4** 42 30S 147 55 E
Triánda, *Greece* **23 C10** 36 25N 28 10 E
Triangle, *Zimbabwe* **57 C5** 21 2S 31 28 E
Tribal Areas □, *Pakistan* **42 C4** 33 0N 70 0 E
Tribulation, C., *Australia* **62 B4** 16 5S 145 29 E
Tribune, *U.S.A.* **80 F4** 38 28N 101 45W
Trichinopoly = Tiruchchirappalli, *India* **40 P11** 10 45N 78 45 E
Trichur, *India* **40 P10** 10 30N 76 18 E
Trida, *Australia* **63 E4** 33 1S 145 1 E
Trier, *Germany* **16 D4** 49 45N 6 38 E
Trieste, *Italy* **20 B5** 45 40N 13 46 E
Triglav, *Slovenia* **16 E7** 46 21N 13 50 E
Tríkkala, *Greece* **21 E9** 39 34N 21 47 E
Trikomo, *Cyprus* **23 D12** 35 17N 33 52 E
Trikora, Puncak, *Indonesia* **37 E9** 4 15S 138 45 E
Trim, *Ireland* **13 C5** 53 33N 6 48W
Trincomalee, *Sri Lanka* **40 Q12** 8 38N 81 15 E
Trindade, *Brazil* **93 G9** 16 40S 49 30W
Trindade, I., *Atl. Oc.* **2 F8** 20 20S 29 50W
Trinidad, *Bolivia* **92 F6** 14 46S 64 50W
Trinidad, *Cuba* **88 B4** 21 48N 80 0W
Trinidad, *Trin. & Tob.* **89 D7** 10 30N 61 15W
Trinidad, *Uruguay* **94 C4** 33 30S 56 50W
Trinidad, *U.S.A.* **81 G2** 37 10N 104 31W
Trinidad →, *Mexico* **87 D5** 17 49N 95 9W
Trinidad & Tobago ■, *W. Indies* **89 D7** 10 30N 61 20W
Trinity, *Canada* **71 C9** 48 59N 53 55W
Trinity, *U.S.A.* **81 K7** 30 57N 95 22W
Trinity →, *Calif., U.S.A.* **82 F2** 41 11N 123 42W
Trinity →, *Tex., U.S.A.* **81 L7** 29 45N 94 43W
Trinity B., *Canada* **71 C9** 48 20N 53 10W
Trinity Is., *U.S.A.* **68 C4** 56 33N 154 25W
Trinity Range, *U.S.A.* **82 F4** 40 15N 118 45W
Trinkitat, *Sudan* **51 E13** 18 45N 37 51 E
Trinway, *U.S.A.* **78 F2** 40 9N 82 1W
Tripoli = Tarābulus, *Lebanon* **47 A4** 34 31N 35 50 E
Tripoli = Tarābulus, *Libya* **51 B8** 32 49N 13 7 E
Trípolis, *Greece* **21 F10** 37 31N 22 25 E
Tripolitania, *N. Afr.* **51 B8** 31 0N 13 0 E
Tripura □, *India* **41 H18** 24 0N 92 0 E
Tripylos, *Cyprus* **23 E11** 34 59N 32 41 E
Tristan da Cunha, *Atl. Oc.* **49 K2** 37 6S 12 20W
Trisul, *India* **43 D8** 30 19N 79 47 E
Trivandrum, *India* **40 Q10** 8 41N 77 0 E
Trnava, *Slovak Rep.* **17 D9** 48 23N 17 35 E
Trochu, *Canada* **72 C6** 51 50N 113 13W
Trodely I., *Canada* **70 B4** 52 15N 79 26W
Troglav, *Croatia* **20 C7** 43 56N 16 36 E
Troilus, L., *Canada* **70 B5** 50 50N 74 35W
Trois-Pistoles, *Canada* **71 C6** 48 5N 69 10W
Trois-Rivières, *Canada* **70 C5** 46 25N 72 34W
Troitsk, *Russia* **26 D7** 54 10N 61 35 E
Troitsko Pechorsk, *Russia* **24 B10** 62 40N 56 10 E
Trölladyngja, *Iceland* **8 D5** 64 54N 17 16W
Trollhättan, *Sweden* **9 G15** 58 17N 12 20 E
Trollheimen, *Norway* **8 E13** 62 46N 9 1 E
Trombetas →, *Brazil* **93 D7** 1 55S 55 35W
Tromsø, *Norway* **8 B18** 69 40N 18 56 E
Trona, *U.S.A.* **85 K9** 35 46N 117 23W
Tronador, Mte., *Argentina* **96 E2** 41 10S 71 50W
Trøndelag, *Norway* **8 D14** 64 17N 11 50 E
Trondheim, *Norway* **8 E14** 63 36N 10 25 E
Trondheimsfjorden, *Norway* **8 E14** 63 35N 10 30 E
Troodos, *Cyprus* **23 E11** 34 55N 32 52 E
Troon, *U.K.* **12 F4** 55 33N 4 39W
Tropic, *U.S.A.* **83 H7** 37 37N 112 5W
Trostan, *U.K.* **13 A5** 55 3N 6 10W
Trout →, *Canada* **72 A5** 61 19N 119 51W
Trout L., *N.W.T., Canada* **72 A4** 60 40N 121 14W
Trout L., *Ont., Canada* **73 C10** 51 20N 93 15W
Trout Lake, *Canada* **72 B6** 56 30N 114 32W
Trout Lake, *U.S.A.* **84 E5** 46 0N 121 32W
Trout River, *Canada* **71 C8** 49 29N 58 8W
Trout Run, *U.S.A.* **78 E7** 41 23N 77 3W
Trouville-sur-Mer, *France* **18 B4** 49 21N 0 5 E
Trowbridge, *U.K.* **11 F5** 51 18N 2 12W
Troy, *Turkey* **21 E12** 39 57N 26 12 E
Troy, *Ala., U.S.A.* **77 K3** 31 48N 85 58W
Troy, *Kans., U.S.A.* **80 F7** 39 47N 95 5W
Troy, *Mo., U.S.A.* **80 F9** 38 59N 90 59W
Troy, *Mont., U.S.A.* **82 B6** 48 28N 115 53W
Troy, *N.Y., U.S.A.* **79 D11** 42 44N 73 41W
Troy, *Ohio, U.S.A.* **76 E3** 40 2N 84 12W
Troy, *Pa., U.S.A.* **79 E8** 41 47N 76 47W
Troyes, *France* **18 B6** 48 19N 4 3 E
Truchas Peak, *U.S.A.* **81 H2** 35 58N 105 39W
Trucial States = United Arab Emirates ■, *Asia* **46 C5** 23 50N 54 0 E
Truckee, *U.S.A.* **84 F6** 39 20N 120 11W
Trudovoye, *Russia* **30 C6** 43 17N 132 5 E
Trujillo, *Honduras* **88 C2** 16 0N 86 0W
Trujillo, *Peru* **92 E3** 8 6S 79 0W
Trujillo, *Spain* **19 C3** 39 28N 5 55W
Trujillo, *U.S.A.* **81 H2** 35 32N 104 42W
Trujillo, *Venezuela* **92 B4** 9 22N 70 38W
Truk, *Micronesia* **64 G7** 7 25N 151 46 E
Trumann, *U.S.A.* **81 H9** 35 41N 90 31W
Trumansburg, *U.S.A.* **79 D8** 42 33N 76 40W
Trumbull, Mt., *U.S.A.* **83 H7** 36 25N 113 8W
Trundle, *Australia* **63 E4** 32 53S 147 35 E
Trung-Phan = Annam, *Vietnam* **38 E7** 16 0N 108 0 E
Truro, *Canada* **71 C7** 45 21N 63 14W
Truro, *U.K.* **11 G2** 50 16N 5 4W
Truskavets, *Ukraine* **17 D12** 49 17N 23 30 E
Trutch, *Canada* **72 B4** 57 44N 122 57W
Truth or Consequences, *U.S.A.* **83 K10** 33 8N 107 15W
Trutnov, *Czech Rep.* **16 C8** 50 37N 15 54 E
Truxton, *U.S.A.* **79 D8** 42 45N 76 2W
Tryonville, *U.S.A.* **78 E5** 41 42N 79 48W
Tsandi, *Namibia* **56 B1** 17 42S 14 50 E
Tsaratanana, *Madag.* **57 B8** 16 47S 47 39 E
Tsaratanana, Mt. de, *Madag.* **57 A8** 14 0S 49 0 E
Tsarevo = Michurin, *Bulgaria* **21 C12** 42 9N 27 51 E
Tsau, *Botswana* **56 C3** 20 8S 22 22 E
Tselinograd = Astana, *Kazakstan* **26 D8** 51 10N 71 30 E
Tses, *Namibia* **56 D2** 25 58S 18 8 E
Tsetserleg, *Mongolia* **32 B5** 47 36N 101 32 E
Tshabong, *Botswana* **56 D3** 26 2S 22 29 E
Tshane, *Botswana* **56 C3** 24 5S 21 54 E
Tshela, *Dem. Rep. of the Congo* **52 E2** 4 57S 13 4 E
Tshesebe, *Botswana* **57 C4** 21 51S 27 32 E
Tshibeke, *Dem. Rep. of the Congo* **54 C2** 2 40S 28 35 E
Tshibinda, *Dem. Rep. of the Congo* **54 C2** 2 23S 28 43 E
Tshikapa, *Dem. Rep. of the Congo* **52 F4** 6 28S 20 48 E
Tshilenge, *Dem. Rep. of the Congo* **54 D1** 6 17S 23 48 E
Tshinsenda, *Dem. Rep. of the Congo* **55 E2** 12 20S 28 0 E
Tshofa, *Dem. Rep. of the Congo* **54 D2** 5 13S 25 16 E
Tshwane, *Botswana* **56 C3** 22 24S 22 1 E
Tsigara, *Botswana* **56 C4** 20 22S 25 54 E
Tsihombe, *Madag.* **57 D8** 25 10S 45 41 E
Tsiigehtchic, *Canada* **68 B6** 67 15N 134 0W
Tsimlyansk Res. = Tsimlyanskoye Vdkhr., *Russia* **25 E7** 48 0N 43 0 E
Tsimlyanskoye Vdkhr., *Russia* **25 E7** 48 0N 43 0 E
Tsinan = Jinan, *China* **34 F9** 36 38N 117 1 E
Tsineng, *S. Africa* **56 D3** 27 5S 23 5 E
Tsinghai = Qinghai □, *China* **32 C4** 36 0N 98 0 E
Tsingtao = Qingdao, *China* **35 F11** 36 5N 120 20 E
Tsinjoarivo, *Madag.* **57 B8** 19 37S 47 40 E
Tsinjomitondraka, *Madag.* **57 B8** 15 40S 47 8 E
Tsiroanomandidy, *Madag.* **57 B8** 18 46S 46 2 E
Tsitondroina, *Madag.* **57 C8** 21 19S 46 0 E
Tsivory, *Madag.* **57 C8** 24 4S 46 5 E
Tskhinvali, *Georgia* **25 F7** 42 14N 44 1 E
Tsna →, *Russia* **24 D7** 54 55N 41 58 E
Tso Moriri, L., *India* **43 C8** 32 50N 78 20 E
Tsobis, *Namibia* **56 B2** 19 27S 17 30 E
Tsodilo Hill, *Botswana* **56 B3** 18 49S 21 43 E
Tsogttsetsiy = Baruunsuu, *Mongolia* **34 C3** 43 43N 105 35 E
Tsolo, *S. Africa* **57 E4** 31 18S 28 37 E
Tsomo, *S. Africa* **57 E4** 32 0S 27 42 E
Tsu, *Japan* **31 G8** 34 45N 136 25 E
Tsu L., *Canada* **72 A6** 60 40N 111 52W
Tsuchiura, *Japan* **31 F10** 36 5N 140 15 E
Tsugaru-Kaikyō, *Japan* **30 D10** 41 35N 141 0 E
Tsumeb, *Namibia* **56 B2** 19 9S 17 44 E
Tsumis, *Namibia* **56 C2** 23 39S 17 29 E
Tsuruga, *Japan* **31 G8** 35 45N 136 2 E
Tsurugi-San, *Japan* **31 H7** 33 51N 134 6 E
Tsuruoka, *Japan* **30 E9** 38 44N 139 50 E
Tsushima, *Gifu, Japan* **31 G8** 35 10N 136 43 E
Tsushima, *Nagasaki, Japan* **31 G4** 34 20N 129 20 E
Tsuyama, *Japan* **31 G7** 35 3N 134 0 E
Tsyelyakhany, *Belarus* **17 B13** 52 30N 25 46 E
Tual, *Indonesia* **37 F8** 5 38S 132 44 E
Tuam, *Ireland* **13 C3** 53 31N 8 51W
Tuamotu Arch. = Tuamotu Is., *Pac. Oc.* **65 J13** 17 0S 144 0W
Tuamotu Is., *Pac. Oc.* **65 J13** 17 0S 144 0W
Tuamotu Ridge, *Pac. Oc.* **65 K14** 20 0S 138 0W
Tuao, *Phil.* **37 A6** 17 55N 121 22 E
Tuapse, *Russia* **25 F6** 44 5N 39 10 E
Tuatapere, *N.Z.* **59 M1** 46 8S 167 41 E
Tuba City, *U.S.A.* **83 H8** 36 8N 111 14W
Tuban, *Indonesia* **37 G15** 6 54S 112 3 E
Tubani, *Botswana* **56 C3** 24 46S 24 18 E
Tubarão, *Brazil* **95 B6** 28 30S 49 0W
Ṭūbās, *West Bank* **47 C4** 32 20N 35 22 E
Tubas →, *Namibia* **56 C2** 22 54S 14 35 E
Tübingen, *Germany* **16 D5** 48 31N 9 4 E
Tubruq, *Libya* **51 B10** 32 7N 23 55 E

Tubuai Is., *Pac. Oc.* **65 K13** 25 0S 150 0W
Tuc Trung, *Vietnam* **39 G6** 11 1N 107 12 E
Tucacas, *Venezuela* **92 A5** 10 48N 68 19W
Tuchodi →, *Canada* **72 B4** 58 17N 123 42W
Tuckanarra, *Australia* **61 E2** 27 7S 118 5 E
Tucson, *U.S.A.* **83 K8** 32 13N 110 58W
Tucumán □, *Argentina* **94 B2** 26 48S 66 2W
Tucumcari, *U.S.A.* **81 H3** 35 10N 103 44W
Tucupita, *Venezuela* **92 B6** 9 2N 62 3W
Tucuruí, *Brazil* **93 D9** 3 42S 49 44W
Tucuruí, Reprêsa de, *Brazil* **93 D9** 4 0S 49 30W
Tudela, *Spain* **19 A5** 42 4N 1 39W
Tudmur, *Syria* **44 C3** 34 36N 38 15 E
Tudor, L., *Canada* **71 A6** 55 50N 65 25W
Tugela →, *S. Africa* **57 D5** 29 14S 31 30 E
Tuguegarao, *Phil.* **37 A6** 17 35N 121 42 E
Tugur, *Russia* **27 D14** 53 44N 136 45 E
Tui, *Spain* **19 A1** 42 3N 8 39W
Tuineje, *Canary Is.* **22 F5** 28 19N 14 3W
Tukangbesi, Kepulauan, *Indonesia* **37 F6** 6 0S 124 0 E
Tukarak I., *Canada* **70 A4** 56 15N 78 45W
Tukayyid, *Iraq* **44 D5** 29 47N 45 36 E
Tuktoyaktuk, *Canada* **68 B6** 69 27N 133 2W
Tukums, *Latvia* **9 H20** 56 58N 23 10 E
Tukuyu, *Tanzania* **55 D3** 9 17S 33 35 E
Tula, *Hidalgo, Mexico* **87 C5** 20 5N 99 20W
Tula, *Tamaulipas, Mexico* **87 C5** 23 0N 99 40W
Tula, *Russia* **24 D6** 54 13N 37 38 E
Tulancingo, *Mexico* **87 C5** 20 5N 99 22W
Tulare, *U.S.A.* **84 J7** 36 13N 119 21W
Tulare Lake Bed, *U.S.A.* **84 K7** 36 0N 119 48W
Tularosa, *U.S.A.* **83 K10** 33 5N 106 1W
Tulbagh, *S. Africa* **56 E2** 33 16S 19 6 E
Tulcán, *Ecuador* **92 C3** 0 48N 77 43W
Tulcea, *Romania* **17 F15** 45 13N 28 46 E
Tulchyn, *Ukraine* **17 D15** 48 41N 28 49 E
Tūleh, *Iran* **45 C7** 34 35N 52 33 E
Tulemalu L., *Canada* **73 A9** 62 58N 99 25W
Tuli, *Zimbabwe* **55 G2** 21 58S 29 13 E
Tulia, *U.S.A.* **81 H4** 34 32N 101 46W
Tulita, *Canada* **68 B7** 64 57N 125 30W
Ţūlkarm, *West Bank* **47 C4** 32 19N 35 2 E
Tulla, *Ireland* **13 D3** 52 53N 8 46W
Tullahoma, *U.S.A.* **77 H2** 35 22N 86 13W
Tullamore, *Australia* **63 E4** 32 39S 147 36 E
Tullamore, *Ireland* **13 C4** 53 16N 7 31W
Tulle, *France* **18 D4** 45 16N 1 46 E
Tullow, *Ireland* **13 D5** 52 49N 6 45W
Tully, *Australia* **62 B4** 17 56S 145 55 E
Tully, *U.S.A.* **79 D8** 42 48N 76 7W
Tulsa, *U.S.A.* **81 G7** 36 10N 95 55W
Tulsequah, *Canada* **72 B2** 58 39N 133 35W
Tulua, *Colombia* **92 C3** 4 6N 76 11W
Tulun, *Russia* **27 D11** 54 32N 100 35 E
Tulungagung, *Indonesia* **37 H14** 8 5S 111 54 E
Tuma →, *Nic.* **88 D3** 13 6N 84 35W
Tumaco, *Colombia* **92 C3** 1 50N 78 45W
Tumatumari, *Guyana* **92 B7** 5 20N 58 55W
Tumba, *Sweden* **9 G17** 59 12N 17 48 E
Tumba, L., *Dem. Rep. of the Congo* **52 E3** 0 50S 18 0 E
Tumbarumba, *Australia* **63 F4** 35 44S 148 0 E
Tumbaya, *Argentina* **94 A2** 23 50S 65 26W
Tumbes, *Peru* **92 D2** 3 37S 80 27W
Tumbwe, *Dem. Rep. of the Congo* **55 E2** 11 25S 27 15 E
Tumby Bay, *Australia* **63 E2** 34 21S 136 8 E
Tumd Youqi, *China* **34 D6** 40 30N 110 30 E
Tumen, *China* **35 C15** 43 0N 129 50 E
Tumen Jiang →, *China* **35 C16** 42 20N 130 35 E
Tumeremo, *Venezuela* **92 B6** 7 18N 61 30W
Tumkur, *India* **40 N10** 13 18N 77 6 E
Tump, *Pakistan* **40 F3** 26 7N 62 16 E
Tumpat, *Malaysia* **39 J4** 6 11N 102 10 E
Tumu, *Ghana* **50 F5** 10 56N 1 56W
Tumucumaque, Serra, *Brazil* **93 C8** 2 0N 55 0W
Tumut, *Australia* **63 F4** 35 16S 148 13 E
Tumwater, *U.S.A.* **84 C4** 47 1N 122 54W
Tuna, *India* **42 H4** 22 59N 70 5 E
Tunas de Zaza, *Cuba* **88 B4** 21 39N 79 34W
Tunbridge Wells = Royal Tunbridge Wells, *U.K.* **11 F8** 51 7N 0 16 E
Tuncurry, *Australia* **63 E5** 32 17S 152 29 E
Tundla, *India* **42 F8** 27 12N 78 17 E
Tunduru, *Tanzania* **55 E4** 11 8S 37 25 E
Tundzha →, *Bulgaria* **21 C11** 41 40N 26 35 E
Tungabhadra →, *India* **40 M11** 15 57N 78 15 E
Tungla, *Nic.* **88 D3** 13 24N 84 21W
Tungsten, *Canada* **72 A3** 61 57N 128 16W
Tunguska, Nizhnyaya →, *Russia* **27 C9** 65 48N 88 4 E
Tunguska, Podkamennaya →, *Russia* **27 C10** 61 50N 90 13 E
Tunica, *U.S.A.* **81 H9** 34 41N 90 23W
Tunis, *Tunisia* **50 A7** 36 50N 10 11 E
Tunisia ■, *Africa* **50 B6** 33 30N 9 10 E
Tunja, *Colombia* **92 B4** 5 33N 73 25W
Tunkhannock, *U.S.A.* **79 E9** 41 32N 75 57W
Tunliu, *China* **34 F7** 36 13N 112 52 E
Tunnsjøen, *Norway* **8 D15** 64 45N 13 25 E
Tunungayualok I., *Canada* **71 A7** 56 0N 61 0W
Tununirusiq = Arctic Bay, *Canada* **69 A11** 73 1N 85 7W
Tunuyán, *Argentina* **94 C2** 33 35S 69 0W
Tunuyán →, *Argentina* **94 C2** 33 33S 67 30W
Tuolumne, *U.S.A.* **84 H6** 37 58N 120 15W
Tuolumne →, *U.S.A.* **84 H5** 37 36N 121 13W
Tūp Āghāj, *Iran* **44 B5** 36 3N 47 50 E
Tupã, *Brazil* **95 A5** 21 57S 50 28W
Tupelo, *U.S.A.* **77 H1** 34 16N 88 43W
Tupinambaranas, *Brazil* **92 D7** 3 0S 58 0W
Tupiza, *Bolivia* **94 A2** 21 30S 65 40W
Tupman, *U.S.A.* **85 K7** 35 18N 119 21W
Tupper, *Canada* **72 B4** 55 32N 120 1W
Tupper Lake, *U.S.A.* **79 B10** 44 14N 74 28W
Tupungato, Cerro, *S. Amer.* **94 C2** 33 15S 69 50W
Tuquan, *China* **35 B11** 45 18N 121 38 E
Túquerres, *Colombia* **92 C3** 1 5N 77 37W
Tura, *Russia* **27 C11** 64 20N 100 17 E
Turabah, *Si. Arabia* **46 C3** 28 20N 43 15 E
Tūrān, *Iran* **45 C8** 35 39N 56 42 E
Turan, *Russia* **27 D10** 51 55N 95 0 E
Ţurayf, *Si. Arabia* **44 D3** 31 41N 38 39 E
Turda, *Romania* **17 E12** 46 34N 23 47 E
Turek, *Poland* **17 B10** 52 3N 18 30 E
Turen, *Venezuela* **92 B5** 9 17N 69 6W
Turfan = Turpan, *China* **32 B3** 43 58N 89 10 E
Turfan Depression = Turpan Hami, *China* **28 E12** 42 40N 89 25 E
Turgeon →, *Canada* **70 C4** 50 0N 78 56W
Tŭrgovishte, *Bulgaria* **21 C12** 43 17N 26 38 E
Turgutlu, *Turkey* **21 E12** 38 30N 27 43 E
Turgwe →, *Zimbabwe* **57 C5** 21 31S 32 15 E
Turia →, *Spain* **19 C5** 39 27N 0 19W
Turiaçu, *Brazil* **93 D9** 1 40S 45 19W
Turiaçu →, *Brazil* **93 D9** 1 36S 45 19W
Turin = Torino, *Italy* **18 D7** 45 3N 7 40 E
Turkana, L., *Africa* **54 B4** 3 30N 36 5 E
Turkestan = Türkistan, *Kazakstan* **26 E7** 43 17N 68 16 E
Turkey ■, *Eurasia* **25 G6** 39 0N 36 0 E
Turkey Creek, *Australia* **60 C4** 17 2S 128 12 E
Türkistan, *Kazakstan* **26 E7** 43 17N 68 16 E
Türkmenbashi, *Turkmenistan* **25 G9** 40 5N 53 5 E
Turkmenistan ■, *Asia* **26 F6** 39 0N 59 0 E
Turks & Caicos Is. ■, *W. Indies* **89 B5** 21 20N 71 20W
Turks Island Passage, *W. Indies* **89 B5** 21 30N 71 30W
Turku, *Finland* **9 F20** 60 30N 22 19 E
Turkwel →, *Kenya* **54 B4** 3 6N 36 6 E
Turlock, *U.S.A.* **84 H6** 37 30N 120 51W
Turnagain →, *Canada* **72 B3** 59 12N 127 35W
Turnagain, C., *N.Z.* **59 J6** 40 28S 176 38 E
Turneffe Is., *Belize* **87 D7** 17 20N 87 50W
Turner, *U.S.A.* **82 B9** 48 51N 108 24W
Turner Pt., *Australia* **62 A1** 11 47S 133 32 E
Turner Valley, *Canada* **72 C6** 50 40N 114 17W
Turners Falls, *U.S.A.* **79 D12** 42 36N 72 33W
Turnhout, *Belgium* **15 C4** 51 19N 4 57 E
Turnor L., *Canada* **73 B7** 56 35N 108 35W
Tŭrnovo = Veliko Tŭrnovo, *Bulgaria* **21 C11** 43 5N 25 41 E
Turnu Măgurele, *Romania* **17 G13** 43 46N 24 56 E
Turnu Roşu, P., *Romania* **17 F13** 45 33N 24 17 E
Turpan, *China* **32 B3** 43 58N 89 10 E
Turpan Hami, *China* **28 E12** 42 40N 89 25 E
Turriff, *U.K.* **12 D6** 57 32N 2 27W
Tursāq, *Iraq* **44 C5** 33 27N 45 47 E
Turtle Head I., *Australia* **62 A3** 10 56S 142 37 E
Turtle L., *Canada* **73 C7** 53 36N 108 38W
Turtle Lake, *U.S.A.* **80 B4** 47 31N 100 53W
Turtleford, *Canada* **73 C7** 53 23N 108 57W
Turukhansk, *Russia* **27 C9** 65 21N 88 5 E
Tuscaloosa, *U.S.A.* **77 J2** 33 12N 87 34W
Tuscany = Toscana □, *Italy* **20 C4** 43 25N 11 0 E
Tuscarawas →, *U.S.A.* **78 F3** 40 24N 81 25W
Tuscarora Mt., *U.S.A.* **78 F7** 40 55N 77 55W
Tuscola, *Ill., U.S.A.* **76 F1** 39 48N 88 17W
Tuscola, *Tex., U.S.A.* **81 J5** 32 12N 99 48W
Tuscumbia, *U.S.A.* **77 H2** 34 44N 87 42W
Tuskegee, *U.S.A.* **77 J3** 32 25N 85 42W
Tustin, *U.S.A.* **85 M9** 33 44N 117 49W
Tuticorin, *India* **40 Q11** 8 50N 78 12 E
Tutóia, *Brazil* **93 D10** 2 45S 42 20W
Tutong, *Brunei* **36 D4** 4 47N 114 40 E
Tutrakan, *Bulgaria* **21 B12** 44 2N 26 40 E
Tuttle Creek L., *U.S.A.* **80 F6** 39 22N 96 40W
Tuttlingen, *Germany* **16 E5** 47 58N 8 48 E
Tutuala, *E. Timor* **37 F7** 8 25S 127 15 E
Tutuila, *Amer. Samoa* **59 B13** 14 19S 170 50W
Tutume, *Botswana* **53 J5** 20 30S 27 5 E
Tututepec, *Mexico* **87 D5** 16 9N 97 38W
Tuva □, *Russia* **27 D10** 51 30N 95 0 E
Tuvalu ■, *Pac. Oc.* **64 H9** 8 0S 178 0 E
Tuxpan, *Mexico* **87 C5** 20 58N 97 23W
Tuxtla Gutiérrez, *Mexico* **87 D6** 16 50N 93 10W
Tuy = Tui, *Spain* **19 A1** 42 3N 8 39W
Tuy An, *Vietnam* **38 F7** 13 17N 109 16 E
Tuy Duc, *Vietnam* **39 F6** 12 15N 107 27 E
Tuy Hoa, *Vietnam* **38 F7** 13 5N 109 10 E
Tuy Phong, *Vietnam* **39 G7** 11 14N 108 43 E
Tuya L., *Canada* **72 B2** 59 7N 130 35W
Tuyen Hoa, *Vietnam* **38 D6** 17 50N 106 10 E
Tuyen Quang, *Vietnam* **38 B5** 21 50N 105 10 E
Tūysarkān, *Iran* **45 C6** 34 33N 48 27 E
Tuz Gölü, *Turkey* **25 G5** 38 42N 33 18 E
Ţūz Khurmātū, *Iraq* **44 C5** 34 56N 44 38 E
Tuzla, *Bos.-H.* **21 B8** 44 34N 18 41 E
Tver, *Russia* **24 C6** 56 55N 35 55 E
Twain, *U.S.A.* **84 E5** 40 1N 121 3W
Twain Harte, *U.S.A.* **84 G6** 38 2N 120 14W
Tweed, *Canada* **78 B7** 44 29N 77 19W
Tweed →, *U.K.* **12 F6** 55 45N 2 0W
Tweed Heads, *Australia* **63 D5** 28 10S 153 31 E
Tweedsmuir Prov. Park, *Canada* **72 C3** 53 0N 126 20W
Twentynine Palms, *U.S.A.* **85 L10** 34 8N 116 3W
Twillingate, *Canada* **71 C9** 49 42N 54 45W
Twin Bridges, *U.S.A.* **82 D7** 45 33N 112 20W
Twin Falls, *Canada* **71 B7** 53 30N 64 32W
Twin Falls, *U.S.A.* **82 E6** 42 34N 114 28W
Twin Valley, *U.S.A.* **80 B6** 47 16N 96 16W
Twinsburg, *U.S.A.* **78 E3** 41 18N 81 26W
Twitchell Reservoir, *U.S.A.* **85 L6** 34 59N 120 19W
Two Harbors, *U.S.A.* **80 B9** 47 2N 91 40W
Two Hills, *Canada* **72 C6** 53 43N 111 52W
Two Rivers, *U.S.A.* **76 C2** 44 9N 87 34W
Two Rocks, *Australia* **61 F2** 31 30S 115 35 E
Twofold B., *Australia* **63 F4** 37 8S 149 59 E
Tyachiv, *Ukraine* **17 D12** 48 1N 23 35 E
Tychy, *Poland* **17 C10** 50 9N 18 59 E
Tyler, *Minn., U.S.A.* **80 C6** 44 18N 96 8W
Tyler, *Tex., U.S.A.* **81 J7** 32 21N 95 18W
Tynda, *Russia* **27 D13** 55 10N 124 43 E
Tyndall, *U.S.A.* **80 D6** 43 0N 97 50W
Tyne →, *U.K.* **10 C6** 54 59N 1 32W
Tyne & Wear □, *U.K.* **10 B6** 55 6N 1 17W
Tynemouth, *U.K.* **10 B6** 55 1N 1 26W
Tyre = Sūr, *Lebanon* **47 B4** 33 19N 35 16 E
Tyrifjorden, *Norway* **9 F14** 60 2N 10 8 E
Tyrol = Tirol □, *Austria* **16 E6** 47 3N 10 43 E
Tyrone, *U.S.A.* **78 F6** 40 40N 78 14W
Tyrone □, *U.K.* **13 B4** 54 38N 7 11W
Tyrrell →, *Australia* **63 F3** 35 26S 142 51 E
Tyrrell, L., *Australia* **63 F3** 35 20S 142 50 E
Tyrrell L., *Canada* **73 A7** 63 7N 105 27W
Tyrrhenian Sea, *Medit. S.* **20 E5** 40 0N 12 30 E
Tysfjorden, *Norway* **8 B17** 68 7N 16 25 E
Tyulgan, *Russia* **24 D10** 52 22N 56 12 E
Tyumen, *Russia* **26 D7** 57 11N 65 29 E
Tywi →, *U.K.* **11 F3** 51 48N 4 21W
Tywyn, *U.K.* **11 E3** 52 35N 4 5W
Tzaneen, *S. Africa* **57 C5** 23 47S 30 9 E
Tzermiádhes, *Greece* **23 D7** 35 12N 25 29 E
Tzukong = Zigong, *China* **32 D5** 29 15N 104 48 E

U

U Taphao, *Thailand* **38 F3** 12 35N 101 0 E
U.S.A. = United States of America ■, *N. Amer.* **74 C7** 37 0N 96 0W
Uatumã →, *Brazil* **92 D7** 2 26S 57 37W
Uaupés, *Brazil* **92 D5** 0 8S 67 5W
Uaupés →, *Brazil* **92 C5** 0 2N 67 16W
Uaxactún, *Guatemala* **88 C2** 17 25N 89 29W
Ubá, *Brazil* **95 A7** 21 8S 43 0W
Ubaitaba, *Brazil* **93 F11** 14 18S 39 20W
Ubangi = Oubangi →, *Dem. Rep. of the Congo* **52 E3** 0 30S 17 50 E
Ubauro, *Pakistan* **42 E3** 28 15N 69 45 E
Ubayyiḍ, W. al →, *Iraq* **44 C4** 32 34N 43 48 E
Ube, *Japan* **31 H5** 33 56N 131 15 E
Úbeda, *Spain* **19 C4** 38 3N 3 23W
Uberaba, *Brazil* **93 G9** 19 50S 47 55W
Uberlândia, *Brazil* **93 G9** 19 0S 48 20W
Ubolratna Res., *Thailand* **38 D4** 16 45N 102 30 E
Ubombo, *S. Africa* **57 D5** 27 31S 32 4 E
Ubon Ratchathani, *Thailand* **38 E5** 15 15N 104 50 E
Ubondo, *Dem. Rep. of the Congo* **54 C2** 0 55S 25 42 E
Ubort →, *Belarus* **17 B15** 52 6N 28 30 E
Ubundu, *Dem. Rep. of the Congo* **54 C2** 0 22S 25 30 E
Ucayali →, *Peru* **92 D4** 4 30S 73 30W
Uchab, *Namibia* **56 B2** 19 47S 17 42 E
Uchiura-Wan, *Japan* **30 C10** 42 25N 140 40 E
Uchquduq, *Uzbekistan* **26 E7** 41 50N 62 50 E
Uchur →, *Russia* **27 D14** 58 48N 130 35 E
Ucluelet, *Canada* **72 D3** 48 57N 125 32W
Uda →, *Russia* **27 D14** 54 42N 135 14 E
Udagamandalam, *India* **40 P10** 11 30N 76 44 E
Udainagar, *India* **42 H7** 22 33N 76 13 E
Udaipur, *India* **42 G5** 24 36N 73 44 E
Udaipur Garhi, *Nepal* **43 F12** 27 0N 86 35 E
Udala, *India* **43 J12** 21 35N 86 34 E
Uddevalla, *Sweden* **9 G14** 58 21N 11 55 E
Uddjaur, *Sweden* **8 D17** 65 56N 17 49 E
Uden, *Neths.* **15 C5** 51 40N 5 37 E
Udgir, *India* **40 K10** 18 25N 77 5 E
Udhampur, *India* **43 C6** 33 0N 75 5 E
Údine, *Italy* **20 A5** 46 3N 13 14 E
Udmurtia □, *Russia* **24 C9** 57 30N 52 30 E
Udon Thani, *Thailand* **38 D4** 17 29N 102 46 E
Udupi, *India* **40 N9** 13 25N 74 42 E
Udzungwa Range, *Tanzania* **55 D4** 9 30S 35 10 E
Ueda, *Japan* **31 F9** 36 24N 138 16 E
Uedineniya, Os., *Russia* **4 B12** 78 0N 85 0 E
Uele →, *Dem. Rep. of the Congo* **52 D4** 3 45N 24 45 E
Uelen, *Russia* **27 C19** 66 10N 170 0W
Uelzen, *Germany* **16 B6** 52 57N 10 32 E
Ufa, *Russia* **24 D10** 54 45N 55 55 E
Ufa →, *Russia* **24 D10** 54 40N 56 0 E
Ugab →, *Namibia* **56 C1** 20 55S 13 30 E
Ugalla →, *Tanzania* **54 D3** 5 8S 30 42 E
Uganda ■, *Africa* **54 B3** 2 0N 32 0 E
Ugie, *S. Africa* **57 E4** 31 10S 28 13 E
Uglegorsk, *Russia* **27 E15** 49 5N 142 2 E
Ugljan, *Croatia* **16 F8** 44 12N 15 10 E
Uhlenhorst, *Namibia* **56 C2** 23 45S 17 55 E
Uhrichsville, *U.S.A.* **78 F3** 40 24N 81 21W
Uibhist a Deas = South Uist, *U.K.* **12 D1** 57 20N 7 15W
Uibhist a Tuath = North Uist, *U.K.* **12 D1** 57 40N 7 15W
Uig, *U.K.* **12 D2** 57 35N 6 21W
Uíge, *Angola* **52 F2** 7 30S 14 40 E
Uijŏngbu, *S. Korea* **35 F14** 37 48N 127 0 E
Ŭiju, *N. Korea* **35 D13** 40 15N 124 35 E
Uinta Mts., *U.S.A.* **82 F8** 40 45N 110 30W
Uis, *Namibia* **56 B2** 21 8S 14 49 E
Uitenhage, *S. Africa* **56 E4** 33 40S 25 28 E
Uithuizen, *Neths.* **15 A6** 53 24N 6 41 E
Ujh →, *India* **42 C6** 32 10N 75 18 E
Ujhani, *India* **43 F8** 28 0N 79 6 E
Uji-guntō, *Japan* **31 J4** 31 15N 129 25 E
Ujjain, *India* **42 H6** 23 9N 75 43 E
Ujung Pandang, *Indonesia* **37 F5** 5 10S 119 20 E
Uka, *Russia* **27 D17** 57 50N 162 0 E
Ukara I., *Tanzania* **54 C3** 1 50S 33 0 E
Uke-Shima, *Japan* **31 K4** 28 2N 129 14 E
Ukerewe I., *Tanzania* **54 C3** 2 0S 33 0 E
Ukhrul, *India* **41 G19** 25 10N 94 25 E
Ukhta, *Russia* **24 B9** 63 34N 53 41 E
Ukiah, *U.S.A.* **84 F3** 39 9N 123 13W
Ukki Fort, *India* **43 C7** 33 28N 76 54 E
Ukmergė, *Lithuania* **9 J21** 55 15N 24 45 E
Ukraine ■, *Europe* **25 E5** 49 0N 32 0 E
Ukwi, *Botswana* **56 C3** 23 29S 20 30 E
Ulaan-Uul, *Mongolia* **34 B6** 44 13N 111 10 E
Ulaanbaatar, *Mongolia* **27 E11** 47 55N 106 53 E
Ulaangom, *Mongolia* **32 A4** 50 5N 92 10 E
Ulaanjirem, *Mongolia* **34 B3** 45 5N 105 30 E
Ulamba, *Dem. Rep. of the Congo* **55 D1** 9 3S 23 38 E
Ulan Bator = Ulaanbaatar, *Mongolia* **27 E11** 47 55N 106 53 E
Ulan Ude, *Russia* **27 D11** 51 45N 107 40 E
Ulaya, *Morogoro, Tanzania* **54 D4** 7 3S 36 55 E
Ulaya, *Tabora, Tanzania* **54 C3** 4 25S 33 30 E
Ulcinj, *Montenegro, Yug.* **21 D8** 41 58N 19 10 E
Ulco, *S. Africa* **56 D3** 28 21S 24 15 E
Ulefoss, *Norway* **9 G13** 59 17N 9 16 E
Ulhasnagar, *India* **40 K8** 19 15N 73 10 E
Uliastay = Ulyasutay, *Mongolia* **32 B4** 47 56N 97 28 E
Ulladulla, *Australia* **63 F5** 35 21S 150 29 E
Ullapool, *U.K.* **12 D3** 57 54N 5 9W
Ullswater, *U.K.* **10 C5** 54 34N 2 52W
Ullŭng-do, *S. Korea* **31 F5** 37 30N 130 30 E
Ulm, *Germany* **16 D5** 48 23N 9 58 E
Ulmarra, *Australia* **63 D5** 29 37S 153 4 E
Ulongué, *Mozam.* **55 E3** 14 37S 34 19 E
Ulricehamn, *Sweden* **9 H15** 57 46N 13 26 E
Ulsan, *S. Korea* **35 G15** 35 20N 129 15 E
Ulsta, *U.K.* **12 A7** 60 30N 1 9W
Ulster □, *U.K.* **13 B5** 54 35N 6 30W
Ulubat Gölü, *Turkey* **21 D13** 40 9N 28 35 E
Uludağ, *Turkey* **21 D13** 40 4N 29 13 E
Uluguru Mts., *Tanzania* **54 D4** 7 15S 37 40 E
Ulungur He →, *China* **32 B3** 47 1N 87 24 E
Uluru = Ayers Rock, *Australia* **61 E5** 25 23S 131 5 E
Ulutau, *Kazakstan* **26 E7** 48 39N 67 1 E
Ulva, *U.K.* **12 E2** 56 29N 6 13W
Ulverston, *U.K.* **10 C4** 54 13N 3 5W
Ulverstone, *Australia* **62 G4** 41 11S 146 11 E
Ulya, *Russia* **27 D15** 59 10N 142 0 E
Ulyanovsk = Simbirsk, *Russia* **24 D8** 54 20N 48 25 E
Ulyasutay, *Mongolia* **32 B4** 47 56N 97 28 E
Ulysses, *U.S.A.* **81 G4** 37 35N 101 22W
Umala, *Bolivia* **92 G5** 17 25S 68 5W
Uman, *Ukraine* **17 D16** 48 40N 30 12 E
Umaria, *India* **41 H12** 23 35N 80 50 E
Umarkot, *Pakistan* **40 G6** 25 15N 69 40 E
Umarpada, *India* **42 J5** 21 27N 73 30 E
Umatilla, *U.S.A.* **82 D4** 45 55N 119 21W
Umba, *Russia* **24 A5** 66 42N 34 11 E
Umbagog L., *U.S.A.* **79 B13** 44 46N 71 3W
Umbakumba, *Australia* **62 A2** 13 47S 136 50 E
Umbrella Mts., *N.Z.* **59 L2** 45 35S 169 5 E
Ume älv →, *Sweden* **8 E19** 63 45N 20 20 E
Umeå, *Sweden* **8 E19** 63 45N 20 20 E
Umera, *Indonesia* **37 E7** 0 12S 129 37 E
Umfuli →, *Zimbabwe* **55 F2** 17 30S 29 23 E
Umgusa, *Zimbabwe* **55 F2** 19 29S 27 52 E
Umkomaas, *S. Africa* **57 E5** 30 13S 30 48 E
Umlazi, *S. Africa* **53 L6** 29 59S 30 54 E
Umm ad Daraj, J., *Jordan* **47 C4** 32 18N 35 48 E
Umm al Qaywayn, *U.A.E.* **45 E7** 25 30N 55 35 E
Umm al Qittayn, *Jordan* **47 C5** 32 18N 36 40 E
Umm Bāb, *Qatar* **45 E6** 25 12N 50 48 E
Umm el Fahm, *Israel* **47 C4** 32 31N 35 9 E
Umm Keddada, *Sudan* **51 F11** 13 33N 26 35 E
Umm Lajj, *Si. Arabia* **44 E3** 25 0N 37 23 E
Umm Ruwaba, *Sudan* **51 F12** 12 50N 31 20 E
Umnak I., *U.S.A.* **68 C3** 53 15N 168 20W
Umniati →, *Zimbabwe* **55 F2** 16 49S 28 45 E
Umpqua →, *U.S.A.* **82 E1** 43 40N 124 12W
Umreth, *India* **42 H5** 22 41N 73 4 E
Umtata, *S. Africa* **57 E4** 31 36S 28 49 E
Umuarama, *Brazil* **95 A5** 23 45S 53 20W
Umvukwe Ra., *Zimbabwe* **55 F3** 16 45S 30 45 E
Umzimvubu, *S. Africa* **57 E4** 31 38S 29 33 E
Umzingwane →, *Zimbabwe* **55 G2** 22 12S 29 56 E
Umzinto, *S. Africa* **57 E5** 30 15S 30 45 E
Una, *India* **42 J4** 20 46N 71 8 E
Una →, *Bos.-H.* **16 F9** 45 0N 16 20 E
Unadilla, *U.S.A.* **79 D9** 42 20N 75 19W
Unalakleet, *U.S.A.* **68 B3** 63 52N 160 47W
Unalaska, *U.S.A.* **68 C3** 53 53N 166 32W
Unalaska I., *U.S.A.* **68 C3** 53 35N 166 50W
'Unayzah, *Si. Arabia* **44 E4** 26 6N 43 58 E
'Unāzah, J., *Asia* **44 C3** 32 12N 39 18 E
Uncía, *Bolivia* **92 G5** 18 25S 66 40W
Uncompahgre Peak, *U.S.A.* **83 G10** 38 4N 107 28W
Uncompahgre Plateau, *U.S.A.* **83 G9** 38 20N 108 15W
Underbool, *Australia* **63 F3** 35 10S 141 51 E
Ungarie, *Australia* **63 E4** 33 38S 146 56 E
Ungarra, *Australia* **63 E2** 34 12S 136 2 E
Ungava, Pén. d', *Canada* **69 C12** 60 0N 74 0W
Ungava B., *Canada* **69 C13** 59 30N 67 30W
Ungeny = Ungheni, *Moldova* **17 E14** 47 11N 27 51 E
Unggi, *N. Korea* **35 C16** 42 16N 130 28 E
Ungheni, *Moldova* **17 E14** 47 11N 27 51 E
União da Vitória, *Brazil* **95 B5** 26 13S 51 5W
Unimak I., *U.S.A.* **68 C3** 54 45N 164 0W
Union, *Miss., U.S.A.* **81 J10** 32 34N 89 7W
Union, *Mo., U.S.A.* **80 F9** 38 27N 91 0W
Union, *S.C., U.S.A.* **77 H5** 34 43N 81 37W
Union City, *Calif., U.S.A.* **84 H4** 37 36N 122 1W
Union City, *N.J., U.S.A.* **79 F10** 40 45N 74 2W
Union City, *Pa., U.S.A.* **78 E5** 41 54N 79 51W
Union City, *Tenn., U.S.A.* **81 G10** 36 26N 89 3W
Union Gap, *U.S.A.* **82 C3** 46 33N 120 28W
Union Springs, *U.S.A.* **77 J3** 32 9N 85 43W
Uniondale, *S. Africa* **56 E3** 33 39S 23 7 E
Uniontown, *U.S.A.* **76 F6** 39 54N 79 44W
Unionville, *U.S.A.* **80 E8** 40 29N 93 1W
United Arab Emirates ■, *Asia* **46 C5** 23 50N 54 0 E
United Kingdom ■, *Europe* **7 E5** 53 0N 2 0W
United States of America ■, *N. Amer.* **74 C7** 37 0N 96 0W
Unity, *Canada* **73 C7** 52 30N 109 5W
University Park, *U.S.A.* **83 K10** 32 17N 106 45W
Unjha, *India* **42 H5** 23 46N 72 24 E
Unnao, *India* **43 F9** 26 35N 80 30 E
Unsengedsi →, *Zimbabwe* **55 F3** 15 43S 31 14 E
Unst, *U.K.* **12 A8** 60 44N 0 53W
Unuk →, *Canada* **72 B2** 56 5N 131 3W
Uozu, *Japan* **31 F8** 36 48N 137 24 E
Upata, *Venezuela* **92 B6** 8 1N 62 24W
Upemba, L., *Dem. Rep. of the Congo* **55 D2** 8 30S 26 20 E
Upernavik, *Greenland* **4 B5** 72 49N 56 20W
Upington, *S. Africa* **56 D3** 28 25S 21 15 E
Upleta, *India* **42 J4** 21 46N 70 16 E
'Upolu, *Samoa* **59 A13** 13 58S 172 0W
Upper Alkali L., *U.S.A.* **82 F3** 41 47N 120 8W
Upper Arrow L., *Canada* **72 C5** 50 30N 117 50W
Upper Foster L., *Canada* **73 B7** 56 47N 105 20W
Upper Hutt, *N.Z.* **59 J5** 41 8S 175 5 E
Upper Klamath L., *U.S.A.* **82 E3** 42 25N 121 55W
Upper Lake, *U.S.A.* **84 F4** 39 10N 122 54W
Upper Musquodoboit, *Canada* **71 C7** 45 10N 62 58W
Upper Red L., *U.S.A.* **80 A7** 48 8N 94 45W
Upper Sandusky, *U.S.A.* **76 E4** 40 50N 83 17W
Upper Volta = Burkina Faso ■, *Africa* **50 F5** 12 0N 1 0W
Uppland, *Sweden* **9 F17** 59 59N 17 48 E
Uppsala, *Sweden* **9 G17** 59 53N 17 38 E
Upshi, *India* **43 C7** 33 48N 77 52 E
Upstart, C., *Australia* **62 B4** 19 41S 147 45 E
Upton, *U.S.A.* **80 C2** 44 6N 104 38W
Ur, *Iraq* **44 D5** 30 55N 46 25 E
Urad Qianqi, *China* **34 D5** 40 40N 108 30 E
Urakawa, *Japan* **30 C11** 42 9N 142 47 E

Ural = Zhayyq →, *Kazakstan* **25 E9** 47 0N 51 48 E
Ural, *Australia* **63 E4** 33 21S 146 12 E
Ural Mts. = Uralskie Gory, *Eurasia* **24 C10** 60 0N 59 0 E
Uralla, *Australia* **63 E5** 30 37S 151 29 E
Uralsk = Oral, *Kazakstan* **25 D9** 51 20N 51 20 E
Uralskie Gory, *Eurasia* **24 C10** 60 0N 59 0 E
Urambo, *Tanzania* **54 D3** 5 4S 32 0 E
Urandangi, *Australia* **62 C2** 21 32S 138 14 E
Uranium City, *Canada* **73 B7** 59 34N 108 37W
Uraricoera →, *Brazil* **92 C6** 3 2N 60 30W
Urawa, *Japan* **31 G9** 35 50N 139 40 E
Uray, *Russia* **26 C7** 60 5N 65 15 E
'Uray'irah, *Si. Arabia* **45 E6** 25 57N 48 53 E
Urbana, *Ill., U.S.A.* **76 E1** 40 7N 88 12W
Urbana, *Ohio, U.S.A.* **76 E4** 40 7N 83 45W
Urbino, *Italy* **20 C5** 43 43N 12 38 E
Urbión, Picos de, *Spain* **19 A4** 42 1N 2 52W
Urcos, *Peru* **92 F4** 13 40S 71 38W
Urdinarrain, *Argentina* **94 C4** 32 37S 58 52W
Urdzhar, *Kazakstan* **26 E9** 47 5N 81 38 E
Ure →, *U.K.* **10 C6** 54 5N 1 20W
Ures, *Mexico* **86 B2** 29 30N 110 30W
Urfa = Sanliurfa, *Turkey* **25 G6** 37 12N 38 50 E
Urganch, *Uzbekistan* **26 E7** 41 40N 60 41 E
Urgench = Urganch, *Uzbekistan* **26 E7** 41 40N 60 41 E
Ürgüp, *Turkey* **44 B2** 38 38N 34 56 E
Uri, *India* **43 B6** 34 8N 74 2 E
Uribia, *Colombia* **92 A4** 11 43N 72 16W
Uriondo, *Bolivia* **94 A3** 21 41S 64 41W
Urique, *Mexico* **86 B3** 27 13N 107 55W
Urique →, *Mexico* **86 B3** 26 29N 107 58W
Urk, *Neths.* **15 B5** 52 39N 5 36 E
Urla, *Turkey* **21 E12** 38 20N 26 47 E
Urmia = Orūmīyeh, *Iran* **44 B5** 37 40N 45 0 E
Urmia, L. = Orūmīyeh, Daryācheh-ye, *Iran* **44 B5** 37 50N 45 30 E
Uroševac, *Kosovo, Yug.* **21 C9** 42 23N 21 10 E
Uruaçu, *Brazil* **93 F9** 14 30S 49 10W
Uruapan, *Mexico* **86 D4** 19 30N 102 0W
Urubamba →, *Peru* **92 F4** 10 43S 73 48W
Uruçara, *Brazil* **92 D7** 2 32S 57 45W
Uruçui, *Brazil* **93 E10** 7 20S 44 28W
Uruguai →, *Brazil* **95 B5** 26 0S 53 30W
Uruguaiana, *Brazil* **94 B4** 29 50S 57 0W
Uruguay ■, *S. Amer.* **94 C4** 32 30S 56 30W
Uruguay →, *S. Amer.* **94 C4** 34 12S 58 18W
Urumchi = Ürümqi, *China* **26 E9** 43 45N 87 45 E
Ürümqi, *China* **26 E9** 43 45N 87 45 E
Urup, Ostrov, *Russia* **27 E16** 46 0N 151 0 E
Usa →, *Russia* **24 A10** 66 16N 59 49 E
Uşak, *Turkey* **25 G4** 38 43N 29 28 E
Usakos, *Namibia* **56 C2** 21 54S 15 31 E
Usedom, *Germany* **16 B8** 53 55N 14 2 E
Useless Loop, *Australia* **61 E1** 26 8S 113 23 E
Ush-Tobe, *Kazakstan* **26 E8** 45 16N 78 0 E
Ushakova, Ostrov, *Russia* **4 A12** 82 0N 80 0 E
Ushant = Ouessant, Î. d', *France* **18 B1** 48 28N 5 6W
Ushashi, *Tanzania* **54 C3** 1 59S 33 57 E
Ushibuka, *Japan* **31 H5** 32 11N 130 1 E
Ushuaia, *Argentina* **96 G3** 54 50S 68 23W
Ushumun, *Russia* **27 D13** 52 47N 126 32 E
Usk, *Canada* **72 C3** 54 38N 128 26W
Usk →, *U.K.* **11 F5** 51 33N 2 58W
Uska, *India* **43 F10** 27 12N 83 7 E
Usman, *Russia* **24 D6** 52 5N 39 48 E
Usoke, *Tanzania* **54 D3** 5 8S 32 24 E
Usolye Sibirskoye, *Russia* **27 D11** 52 48N 103 40 E
Uspallata, P. de, *Argentina* **94 C2** 32 37S 69 22W
Uspenskiy, *Kazakstan* **26 E8** 48 41N 72 43 E
Ussuri →, *Asia* **30 A7** 48 27N 135 0 E
Ussuriysk, *Russia* **27 E14** 43 48N 131 59 E
Ussurka, *Russia* **30 B6** 45 12N 133 31 E
Ust-Aldan = Batamay, *Russia* **27 C13** 63 30N 129 15 E
Ust-Amginskoye = Khandyga, *Russia* **27 C14** 62 42N 135 35 E
Ust-Bolsheretsk, *Russia* **27 D16** 52 50N 156 15 E
Ust-Chaun, *Russia* **27 C18** 68 47N 170 30 E
Ust-Ilimpeya = Yukta, *Russia* **27 C11** 63 26N 105 42 E
Ust-Ilimsk, *Russia* **27 D11** 58 3N 102 39 E
Ust-Ishim, *Russia* **26 D8** 57 45N 71 10 E
Ust-Kamchatsk, *Russia* **27 D17** 56 10N 162 28 E
Ust-Kamenogorsk = Öskemen, *Kazakstan* **26 E9** 50 0N 82 36 E
Ust-Khayryuzovo, *Russia* **27 D16** 57 15N 156 45 E
Ust-Kut, *Russia* **27 D11** 56 50N 105 42 E
Ust-Kuyga, *Russia* **27 B14** 70 1N 135 43 E
Ust-Maya, *Russia* **27 C14** 60 30N 134 28 E
Ust-Mil, *Russia* **27 D14** 59 40N 133 11 E
Ust-Nera, *Russia* **27 C15** 64 35N 143 15 E
Ust-Nyukzha, *Russia* **27 D13** 56 34N 121 37 E
Ust-Olenek, *Russia* **27 B12** 73 0N 120 5 E
Ust-Omchug, *Russia* **27 C15** 61 9N 149 38 E
Ust-Port, *Russia* **26 C9** 69 40N 84 26 E
Ust-Tsilma, *Russia* **24 A9** 65 28N 52 11 E
Ust Urt = Ustyurt Plateau, *Asia* **26 E6** 44 0N 55 0 E
Ust-Usa, *Russia* **24 A10** 66 2N 56 57 E
Ust-Vorkuta, *Russia* **24 A11** 67 24N 64 0 E
Ústí nad Labem, *Czech Rep.* **16 C8** 50 41N 14 3 E
Ústica, *Italy* **20 E5** 38 42N 13 11 E
Ustinov = Izhevsk, *Russia* **24 C9** 56 51N 53 14 E
Ustyurt Plateau, *Asia* **26 E6** 44 0N 55 0 E
Usu, *China* **32 B3** 44 27N 84 40 E
Usuki, *Japan* **31 H5** 33 8N 131 49 E
Usulután, *El Salv.* **88 D2** 13 25N 88 28W
Usumacinta →, *Mexico* **87 D6** 17 0N 91 0W
Usumbura = Bujumbura, *Burundi* **54 C2** 3 16S 29 18 E
Usure, *Tanzania* **54 C3** 4 40S 34 22 E
Usutuo →, *Mozam.* **57 D5** 26 48S 32 7 E
Uta, *Indonesia* **37 E9** 4 33S 136 0 E
Utah □, *U.S.A.* **82 G8** 39 20N 111 30W
Utah L., *U.S.A.* **82 F8** 40 10N 111 58W
Utarni, *India* **42 F4** 26 5N 71 58 E
Utatlan, *Guatemala* **88 C1** 15 2N 91 11W
Ute Creek →, *U.S.A.* **81 H3** 35 21N 103 50W
Utena, *Lithuania* **9 J21** 55 27N 25 40 E
Utete, *Tanzania* **54 D4** 8 0S 38 45 E
Uthai Thani, *Thailand* **38 E3** 15 22N 100 3 E
Uthal, *Pakistan* **42 G2** 25 44N 66 40 E
Utiariti, *Brazil* **92 F7** 13 0S 58 10W
Utica, *N.Y., U.S.A.* **79 C9** 43 6N 75 14W
Utica, *Ohio, U.S.A.* **78 F2** 40 14N 82 27W
Utikuma L., *Canada* **72 B5** 55 50N 115 30W
Utopia, *Australia* **62 C1** 22 14S 134 33 E
Utraula, *India* **43 F10** 27 19N 82 25 E
Utrecht, *Neths.* **15 B5** 52 5N 5 8 E
Utrecht, *S. Africa* **57 D5** 27 38S 30 20 E
Utrecht □, *Neths.* **15 B5** 52 6N 5 7 E
Utrera, *Spain* **19 D3** 37 12N 5 48W
Utsjoki, *Finland* **8 B22** 69 51N 26 59 E
Utsunomiya, *Japan* **31 F9** 36 30N 139 50 E
Uttar Pradesh □, *India* **43 F9** 27 0N 80 0 E
Uttaradit, *Thailand* **38 D3** 17 36N 100 5 E
Uttaranchal □, *India* **43 D8** 30 0N 79 30 E
Uttoxeter, *U.K.* **10 E6** 52 54N 1 52W
Uummannarsuaq = Nunap Isua, *Greenland* **69 C15** 59 48N 43 55W
Uusikaarlepyy, *Finland* **8 E20** 63 32N 22 31 E
Uusikaupunki, *Finland* **9 F19** 60 47N 21 25 E
Uva, *Russia* **24 C9** 56 59N 52 13 E
Uvalde, *U.S.A.* **81 L5** 29 13N 99 47W
Uvat, *Russia* **26 D7** 59 5N 68 50 E
Uvinza, *Tanzania* **54 D3** 5 5S 30 24 E
Uvira, *Dem. Rep. of the Congo* **54 C2** 3 22S 29 3 E
Uvs Nuur, *Mongolia* **32 A4** 50 20N 92 30 E
'Uwairidh, Ḥarrat al, *Si. Arabia* **44 E3** 26 50N 38 0 E
Uwajima, *Japan* **31 H6** 33 10N 132 35 E
Uweinat, Jebel, *Sudan* **51 D10** 21 54N 24 58 E
Uxbridge, *Canada* **78 B5** 44 6N 79 7W
Uxin Qi, *China* **34 E5** 38 50N 109 5 E
Uxmal, *Mexico* **87 C7** 20 22N 89 46W
Üydzin, *Mongolia* **34 B4** 44 9N 107 0 E
Uyo, *Nigeria* **50 G7** 5 1N 7 53 E
Uyûn Mûsa, *Egypt* **47 F1** 29 53N 32 40 E
Uyuni, *Bolivia* **92 H5** 20 28S 66 47W
Uzbekistan ■, *Asia* **26 E7** 41 30N 65 0 E
Uzen, *Kazakstan* **25 F9** 43 29N 52 54 E
Uzen, Mal →, *Kazakstan* **25 E8** 49 4N 49 44 E
Uzerche, *France* **18 D4** 45 25N 1 34 E
Uzh →, *Ukraine* **17 C16** 51 15N 30 12 E
Uzhgorod = Uzhhorod, *Ukraine* **17 D12** 48 36N 22 18 E
Uzhhorod, *Ukraine* **17 D12** 48 36N 22 18 E
Užice, *Serbia, Yug.* **21 C8** 43 55N 19 50 E
Uzunköprü, *Turkey* **21 D12** 41 16N 26 43 E

V

Vaal →, *S. Africa* **56 D3** 29 4S 23 38 E
Vaal Dam, *S. Africa* **57 D4** 27 0S 28 14 E
Vaalwater, *S. Africa* **57 C4** 24 15S 28 8 E
Vaasa, *Finland* **8 E19** 63 6N 21 38 E
Vác, *Hungary* **17 E10** 47 49N 19 10 E
Vacaria, *Brazil* **95 B5** 28 31S 50 52W
Vacaville, *U.S.A.* **84 G5** 38 21N 121 59W
Vach = Vakh →, *Russia* **26 C8** 60 45N 76 45 E
Vache, Î. à, *Haiti* **89 C5** 18 2N 73 35W
Vadnagar, *India* **42 H5** 23 47N 72 40 E
Vadodara, *India* **42 H5** 22 20N 73 10 E
Vadsø, *Norway* **8 A23** 70 3N 29 50 E
Vaduz, *Liech.* **18 C8** 47 8N 9 31 E
Værøy, *Norway* **8 C15** 67 40N 12 40 E
Vågar, *Færoe Is.* **8 E9** 62 5N 7 15W
Vågsfjorden, *Norway* **8 B17** 68 50N 16 50 E
Váh →, *Slovak Rep.* **17 D9** 47 43N 18 7 E
Vahsel B., *Antarctica* **5 D1** 75 0S 35 0W
Váï, *Greece* **23 D8** 35 15N 26 18 E
Vaigach, *Russia* **26 B6** 70 10N 59 0 E
Vail, *U.S.A.* **74 C5** 39 40N 106 20W
Vaisali →, *India* **43 F8** 26 28N 78 53 E
Vakh →, *Russia* **26 C8** 60 45N 76 45 E
Val-d'Or, *Canada* **70 C4** 48 7N 77 47W
Val Marie, *Canada* **73 D7** 49 15N 107 45W
Valahia, *Romania* **17 F13** 44 35N 25 0 E
Valandovo, *Macedonia* **21 D10** 41 19N 22 34 E
Valcheta, *Argentina* **96 E3** 40 40S 66 8W
Valdayskaya Vozvyshennost, *Russia* **24 C5** 57 0N 33 30 E
Valdepeñas, *Spain* **19 C4** 38 43N 3 25W
Valdés, Pen., *Argentina* **96 E4** 42 30S 63 45W
Valdez, *U.S.A.* **68 B5** 61 7N 146 16W
Valdivia, *Chile* **96 D2** 39 50S 73 14W
Valdosta, *U.S.A.* **77 K4** 30 50N 83 17W
Valdres, *Norway* **9 F13** 61 5N 9 5 E
Vale, *U.S.A.* **82 E5** 43 59N 117 15W
Vale of Glamorgan □, *U.K.* **11 F4** 51 28N 3 25W
Valemount, *Canada* **72 C5** 52 50N 119 15W
Valença, *Brazil* **93 F11** 13 20S 39 5W
Valença do Piaui, *Brazil* **93 E10** 6 20S 41 45W
Valence, *France* **18 D6** 44 57N 4 54 E
Valencia, *Spain* **19 C5** 39 27N 0 23W
Valencia, *U.S.A.* **83 J10** 34 48N 106 43W
Valencia, *Venezuela* **92 A5** 10 11N 68 0W
Valencia □, *Spain* **19 C5** 39 20N 0 40W
Valencia, G. de, *Spain* **19 C6** 39 30N 0 20 E
Valencia de Alcántara, *Spain* **19 C2** 39 25N 7 14W
Valencia I., *Ireland* **13 E1** 51 54N 10 22W
Valenciennes, *France* **18 A5** 50 20N 3 34 E
Valentim, Sa. do, *Brazil* **93 E10** 6 0S 43 30W
Valentin, *Russia* **30 C7** 43 8N 134 17 E
Valentine, *U.S.A.* **81 K2** 30 35N 104 30W
Valera, *Venezuela* **92 B4** 9 19N 70 37W
Valga, *Estonia* **9 H22** 57 47N 26 2 E
Valier, *U.S.A.* **82 B7** 48 18N 112 16W
Valjevo, *Serbia, Yug.* **21 B8** 44 18N 19 53 E
Valka, *Latvia* **9 H21** 57 42N 25 57 E
Valkeakoski, *Finland* **9 F20** 61 16N 24 2 E
Valkenswaard, *Neths.* **15 C5** 51 21N 5 29 E
Vall de Uxó = La Vall d'Uixó, *Spain* **19 C5** 39 49N 0 15W
Valladolid, *Mexico* **87 C7** 20 40N 88 11W
Valladolid, *Spain* **19 B3** 41 38N 4 43W
Valldemossa, *Spain* **22 B9** 39 43N 2 37 E
Valle de la Pascua, *Venezuela* **92 B5** 9 13N 66 0W
Valle de las Palmas, *Mexico* **85 N10** 32 20N 116 43W
Valle de Santiago, *Mexico* **86 C4** 20 25N 101 15W
Valle de Suchil, *Mexico* **86 C4** 23 38N 103 55W
Valle de Zaragoza, *Mexico* **86 B3** 27 28N 105 49W
Valle Fértil, Sierra del, *Argentina* **94 C2** 30 20S 68 0W
Valle Hermoso, *Mexico* **87 B5** 25 35N 97 40W
Valledupar, *Colombia* **92 A4** 10 29N 73 15W
Vallehermoso, *Canary Is.* **22 F2** 28 10N 17 15W
Vallejo, *U.S.A.* **84 G4** 38 7N 122 14W
Vallenar, *Chile* **94 B1** 28 30S 70 50W
Valletta, *Malta* **23 D2** 35 54N 14 31 E
Valley Center, *U.S.A.* **85 M9** 33 13N 117 2W
Valley City, *U.S.A.* **80 B6** 46 55N 98 0W
Valley Falls, *Oreg., U.S.A.* **82 E3** 42 29N 120 17W
Valley Falls, *R.I., U.S.A.* **79 E13** 41 54N 71 24W
Valley Springs, *U.S.A.* **84 G6** 38 12N 120 50W
Valley View, *U.S.A.* **79 F8** 40 39N 76 33W
Valley Wells, *U.S.A.* **85 K11** 35 27N 115 46W
Valleyview, *Canada* **72 B5** 55 5N 117 17W
Vallimanca, Arroyo, *Argentina* **94 D4** 35 40S 59 10W
Valls, *Spain* **19 B6** 41 18N 1 15 E
Valmiera, *Latvia* **9 H21** 57 37N 25 29 E
Valognes, *France* **18 B3** 49 30N 1 28W
Valona = Vlorë, *Albania* **21 D8** 40 32N 19 28 E
Valozhyn, *Belarus* **17 A14** 54 3N 26 30 E
Valparaíso, *Chile* **94 C1** 33 2S 71 40W
Valparaíso, *Mexico* **86 C4** 22 50N 103 32W
Valparaiso, *U.S.A.* **76 E2** 41 28N 87 4W
Valparaíso □, *Chile* **94 C1** 33 2S 71 40W
Vals →, *S. Africa* **56 D4** 27 23S 26 30 E
Vals, Tanjung, *Indonesia* **37 F9** 8 26S 137 25 E
Valsad, *India* **40 J8** 20 40N 72 58 E
Valverde, *Canary Is.* **22 G2** 27 48N 17 55W
Valverde del Camino, *Spain* **19 D2** 37 35N 6 47W
Vammala, *Finland* **9 F20** 61 20N 22 54 E
Vámos, *Greece* **23 D6** 35 24N 24 13 E
Van, *Turkey* **25 G7** 38 30N 43 20 E
Van, L. = Van Gölü, *Turkey* **25 G7** 38 30N 43 0 E
Van Alstyne, *U.S.A.* **81 J6** 33 25N 96 35W
Van Blommestein Meer, *Surinam* **93 C7** 4 45N 55 5W
Van Buren, *Canada* **71 C6** 47 10N 67 55W
Van Buren, *Ark., U.S.A.* **81 H7** 35 26N 94 21W
Van Buren, *Maine, U.S.A.* **77 B11** 47 10N 67 58W
Van Buren, *Mo., U.S.A.* **81 G9** 37 0N 91 1W
Van Canh, *Vietnam* **38 F7** 13 37N 109 0 E
Van Diemen, C., *N. Terr., Australia* **60 B5** 11 9S 130 24 E
Van Diemen, C., *Queens., Australia* **62 B2** 16 30S 139 46 E
Van Diemen G., *Australia* **60 B5** 11 45S 132 0 E
Van Gölü, *Turkey* **25 G7** 38 30N 43 0 E
Van Horn, *U.S.A.* **81 K2** 31 3N 104 50W
Van Ninh, *Vietnam* **38 F7** 12 42N 109 14 E
Van Rees, Pegunungan, *Indonesia* **37 E9** 2 35S 138 15 E
Van Wert, *U.S.A.* **76 E3** 40 52N 84 35W
Van Yen, *Vietnam* **38 B5** 21 4N 104 42 E
Vanadzor, *Armenia* **25 F7** 40 48N 44 30 E
Vanavara, *Russia* **27 C11** 60 22N 102 16 E
Vancouver, *Canada* **72 D4** 49 15N 123 10W
Vancouver, *U.S.A.* **84 E4** 45 38N 122 40W
Vancouver, C., *Australia* **61 G2** 35 2S 118 11 E
Vancouver I., *Canada* **72 D3** 49 50N 126 0W
Vandalia, *Ill., U.S.A.* **80 F10** 38 58N 89 6W
Vandalia, *Mo., U.S.A.* **80 F9** 39 19N 91 29W
Vandenburg, *U.S.A.* **85 L6** 34 35N 120 33W
Vanderbijlpark, *S. Africa* **57 D4** 26 42S 27 54 E
Vandergrift, *U.S.A.* **78 F5** 40 36N 79 34W
Vanderhoof, *Canada* **72 C4** 54 0N 124 0W
Vanderkloof Dam, *S. Africa* **56 E3** 30 4S 24 40 E
Vanderlin I., *Australia* **62 B2** 15 44S 137 2 E
Vänern, *Sweden* **9 G15** 58 47N 13 30 E
Vänersborg, *Sweden* **9 G15** 58 26N 12 19 E
Vang Vieng, *Laos* **38 C4** 18 58N 102 32 E
Vanga, *Kenya* **54 C4** 4 35S 39 12 E
Vangaindrano, *Madag.* **57 C8** 23 21S 47 36 E
Vanguard, *Canada* **73 D7** 49 55N 107 20W
Vanino, *Russia* **27 E15** 48 50N 140 5 E
Vanna, *Norway* **8 A18** 70 6N 19 50 E
Vännäs, *Sweden* **8 E18** 63 58N 19 48 E
Vannes, *France* **18 C2** 47 40N 2 47W
Vanrhynsdorp, *S. Africa* **56 E2** 31 36S 18 44 E
Vansbro, *Sweden* **9 F16** 60 32N 14 15 E
Vansittart B., *Australia* **60 B4** 14 3S 126 17 E
Vantaa, *Finland* **9 F21** 60 18N 24 58 E
Vanua Balavu, *Fiji* **59 C9** 17 40S 178 57W
Vanua Levu, *Fiji* **59 C8** 16 33S 179 15 E
Vanuatu ■, *Pac. Oc.* **64 J8** 15 0S 168 0 E
Vanwyksvlei, *S. Africa* **56 E3** 30 18S 21 49 E
Vanzylsrus, *S. Africa* **56 D3** 26 52S 22 4 E
Vapnyarka, *Ukraine* **17 D15** 48 32N 28 45 E
Varanasi, *India* **43 G10** 25 22N 83 0 E
Varangerfjorden, *Norway* **8 A23** 70 3N 29 25 E
Varangerhalvøya, *Norway* **8 A23** 70 25N 29 30 E
Varaždin, *Croatia* **16 E9** 46 20N 16 20 E
Varberg, *Sweden* **9 H15** 57 6N 12 20 E
Vardak □, *Afghan.* **40 B6** 34 0N 68 0 E
Vardar = Axiós →, *Greece* **21 D10** 40 57N 22 35 E
Varde, *Denmark* **9 J13** 55 38N 8 29 E
Vardø, *Norway* **8 A24** 70 23N 31 5 E
Varella, Mui, *Vietnam* **38 F7** 12 54N 109 26 E
Varėna, *Lithuania* **9 J21** 54 12N 24 30 E
Varese, *Italy* **18 D8** 45 48N 8 50 E
Varginha, *Brazil* **95 A6** 21 33S 45 25W
Varillas, *Chile* **94 A1** 24 0S 70 10W
Varkaus, *Finland* **9 E22** 62 19N 27 50 E
Varna, *Bulgaria* **21 C12** 43 13N 27 56 E
Värnamo, *Sweden* **9 H16** 57 10N 14 3 E
Vars, *Canada* **79 A9** 45 21N 75 21W
Varysburg, *U.S.A.* **78 D6** 42 46N 78 19W
Varzaneh, *Iran* **45 C7** 32 25N 52 40 E
Vasa Barris →, *Brazil* **93 F11** 11 10S 37 10W
Vascongadas = País Vasco □, *Spain* **19 A4** 42 50N 2 45W
Vasht = Khāsh, *Iran* **40 E2** 28 15N 61 15 E
Vasilevichi, *Belarus* **17 B15** 52 15N 29 50 E
Vasilkov = Vasylkiv, *Ukraine* **17 C16** 50 7N 30 15 E
Vaslui, *Romania* **17 E14** 46 38N 27 42 E
Vassar, *Canada* **73 D9** 49 10N 95 55W
Vassar, *U.S.A.* **76 D4** 43 22N 83 35W
Västerås, *Sweden* **9 G17** 59 37N 16 38 E
Västerbotten, *Sweden* **8 D18** 64 36N 20 4 E
Västerdalälven →, *Sweden* **9 F16** 60 30N 14 7 E
Västervik, *Sweden* **9 H17** 57 43N 16 33 E
Västmanland, *Sweden* **9 G16** 59 45N 16 20 E
Vasto, *Italy* **20 C6** 42 8N 14 40 E
Vasylkiv, *Ukraine* **17 C16** 50 7N 30 15 E
Vatersay, *U.K.* **12 E1** 56 55N 7 32W
Vatican City ■, *Europe* **20 D5** 41 54N 12 27 E
Vatili, *Cyprus* **23 D12** 35 6N 33 40 E
Vatnajökull, *Iceland* **8 D5** 64 30N 16 48W
Vatoa, *Fiji* **59 D9** 19 50S 178 13W
Vatólakkos, *Greece* **23 D5** 35 27N 23 53 E
Vatoloha, *Madag.* **57 B8** 17 52S 47 48 E
Vatomandry, *Madag.* **57 B8** 19 20S 48 59 E
Vatra-Dornei, *Romania* **17 E13** 47 22N 25 22 E
Vatrak →, *India* **42 H5** 23 9N 73 2 E
Vättern, *Sweden* **9 G16** 58 25N 14 30 E
Vaughn, *Mont., U.S.A.* **82 C8** 47 33N 111 33W
Vaughn, *N. Mex., U.S.A.* **83 J11** 34 36N 105 13W
Vaujours L., *Canada* **70 A5** 55 27N 74 15W
Vaupés = Uaupés →, *Brazil* **92 C5** 0 2N 67 16W
Vaupes □, *Colombia* **92 C4** 1 0N 71 0W
Vauxhall, *Canada* **72 C6** 50 5N 112 9W
Vav, *India* **42 G4** 24 22N 71 31 E
Vavatenina, *Madag.* **57 B8** 17 28S 49 12 E
Vava'u, *Tonga* **59 D12** 18 36S 174 0W
Vawkavysk, *Belarus* **17 B13** 53 9N 24 30 E
Växjö, *Sweden* **9 H16** 56 52N 14 50 E
Vaygach, Ostrov, *Russia* **26 C6** 70 0N 60 0 E
Váyia, Ákra, *Greece* **23 C10** 36 15N 28 11 E
Vechte →, *Neths.* **15 B6** 52 34N 6 6 E
Vedea →, *Romania* **17 G13** 43 42N 25 41 E
Vedia, *Argentina* **94 C3** 34 30S 61 31W
Veendam, *Neths.* **15 A6** 53 5N 6 52 E
Veenendaal, *Neths.* **15 B5** 52 2N 5 34 E
Vefsna →, *Norway* **8 D15** 65 48N 13 10 E
Vega, *Norway* **8 D14** 65 40N 11 55 E
Vega, *U.S.A.* **81 H3** 35 15N 102 26W
Vegreville, *Canada* **72 C6** 53 30N 112 5W
Vejer de la Frontera, *Spain* **19 D3** 36 15N 5 59W
Vejle, *Denmark* **9 J13** 55 43N 9 30 E
Velas, C., *Costa Rica* **88 D2** 10 21N 85 52W
Velasco, Sierra de, *Argentina* **94 B2** 29 20S 67 10W
Velddrif, *S. Africa* **56 E2** 32 42S 18 11 E
Velebit Planina, *Croatia* **16 F8** 44 50N 15 20 E
Veles, *Macedonia* **21 D9** 41 46N 21 47 E
Vélez-Málaga, *Spain* **19 D3** 36 48N 4 5W
Vélez Rubio, *Spain* **19 D4** 37 41N 2 5W
Velhas →, *Brazil* **93 G10** 17 13S 44 49W
Velika Kapela, *Croatia* **16 F8** 45 10N 15 5 E
Velikaya →, *Russia* **24 C4** 57 48N 28 10 E
Velikaya Kema, *Russia* **30 B8** 45 30N 137 12 E
Veliki Ustyug, *Russia* **24 B8** 60 47N 46 20 E
Velikiye Luki, *Russia* **24 C5** 56 25N 30 32 E
Veliko Tŭrnovo, *Bulgaria* **21 C11** 43 5N 25 41 E
Velikonda Range, *India* **40 M11** 14 45N 79 10 E
Velletri, *Italy* **20 D5** 41 41N 12 47 E
Vellore, *India* **40 N11** 12 57N 79 10 E
Velsk, *Russia* **24 B7** 61 10N 42 5 E
Velva, *U.S.A.* **80 A4** 48 4N 100 56W
Venado Tuerto, *Argentina* **94 C3** 33 50S 62 0W
Vendée □, *France* **18 C3** 46 50N 1 35W
Vendôme, *France* **18 C4** 47 47N 1 3 E
Venézia, *Italy* **20 B5** 45 27N 12 21 E
Venézia, G. di, *Italy* **20 B5** 45 15N 13 0 E
Venezuela ■, *S. Amer.* **92 B5** 8 0N 66 0W
Venezuela, G. de, *Venezuela* **92 A4** 11 30N 71 0W
Vengurla, *India* **40 M8** 15 53N 73 45 E
Venice = Venézia, *Italy* **20 B5** 45 27N 12 21 E
Venice, *U.S.A.* **77 M4** 27 6N 82 27W
Venkatapuram, *India* **41 K12** 18 20N 80 30 E
Venlo, *Neths.* **15 C6** 51 22N 6 11 E
Vennesla, *Norway* **9 G12** 58 15N 7 59 E
Venray, *Neths.* **15 C6** 51 31N 6 0 E
Ventana, Punta de la, *Mexico* **86 C3** 24 4N 109 48W
Ventana, Sa. de la, *Argentina* **94 D3** 38 0S 62 30W
Ventersburg, *S. Africa* **56 D4** 28 7S 27 9 E
Venterstad, *S. Africa* **56 E4** 30 47S 25 48 E
Ventnor, *U.K.* **11 G6** 50 36N 1 12W
Ventotène, *Italy* **20 D5** 40 47N 13 25 E
Ventoux, Mt., *France* **18 D6** 44 10N 5 17 E
Ventspils, *Latvia* **9 H19** 57 25N 21 32 E
Ventuarí →, *Venezuela* **92 C5** 3 58N 67 2W
Ventucopa, *U.S.A.* **85 L7** 34 50N 119 29W
Ventura, *U.S.A.* **85 L7** 34 17N 119 18W
Venus B., *Australia* **63 F4** 38 40S 145 42 E
Vera, *Argentina* **94 B3** 29 30S 60 20W
Vera, *Spain* **19 D5** 37 15N 1 51W
Veracruz, *Mexico* **87 D5** 19 10N 96 10W
Veracruz □, *Mexico* **87 D5** 19 0N 96 15W
Veraval, *India* **42 J4** 20 53N 70 27 E
Verbánia, *Italy* **18 D8** 45 56N 8 33 E
Vercelli, *Italy* **18 D8** 45 19N 8 25 E
Verdalsøra, *Norway* **8 E14** 63 48N 11 30 E
Verde →, *Argentina* **96 E3** 41 56S 65 5W
Verde →, *Goiás, Brazil* **93 G8** 18 1S 50 14W
Verde →, *Mato Grosso do Sul, Brazil* **93 H8** 21 25S 52 20W
Verde →, *Chihuahua, Mexico* **86 B3** 26 29N 107 58W
Verde →, *Oaxaca, Mexico* **87 D5** 15 59N 97 50W
Verde →, *Veracruz, Mexico* **86 C4** 21 10N 102 50W
Verde →, *Paraguay* **94 A4** 23 9S 57 37W
Verde →, *U.S.A.* **74 D4** 33 33N 111 40W
Verde, Cay, *Bahamas* **88 B4** 23 0N 75 5W
Verden, *Germany* **16 B5** 52 55N 9 14 E
Verdi, *U.S.A.* **84 F7** 39 31N 119 59W
Verdun, *France* **18 B6** 49 9N 5 24 E
Vereeniging, *S. Africa* **57 D4** 26 38S 27 57 E
Verga, C., *Guinea* **50 F3** 10 30N 14 10W
Vergara, *Uruguay* **95 C5** 32 56S 53 57W
Vergemont Cr. →, *Australia* **62 C3** 24 16S 143 16 E
Vergennes, *U.S.A.* **79 B11** 44 10N 73 15W
Verín, *Spain* **19 B2** 41 57N 7 27W
Verkhnevilyuysk, *Russia* **27 C13** 63 27N 120 18 E
Verkhniy Baskunchak, *Russia* **25 E8** 48 14N 46 44 E
Verkhoyansk, *Russia* **27 C14** 67 35N 133 25 E
Verkhoyansk Ra. = Verkhoyanskiy Khrebet, *Russia* **27 C13** 66 0N 129 0 E
Verkhoyanskiy Khrebet, *Russia* **27 C13** 66 0N 129 0 E
Vermilion, *Canada* **73 C6** 53 20N 110 50W
Vermilion, *U.S.A.* **78 E2** 41 25N 82 22W
Vermilion →, *Alta., Canada* **73 C6** 53 22N 110 51W
Vermilion →, *Qué., Canada* **70 C5** 47 38N 72 56W
Vermilion, B., *U.S.A.* **81 L9** 29 45N 91 55W
Vermilion Bay, *Canada* **73 D10** 49 51N 93 34W
Vermilion L., *U.S.A.* **80 B8** 47 53N 92 26W
Vermillion, *U.S.A.* **80 D6** 42 47N 96 56W
Vermont □, *U.S.A.* **79 C12** 44 0N 73 0W
Vernal, *U.S.A.* **82 F9** 40 27N 109 32W
Vernalis, *U.S.A.* **84 H5** 37 36N 121 17W
Verner, *Canada* **70 C3** 46 25N 80 8W
Verneukpan, *S. Africa* **56 E3** 30 0S 21 0 E
Vernon, *Canada* **72 C5** 50 20N 119 15W
Vernon, *U.S.A.* **81 H5** 34 9N 99 17W
Vernonia, *U.S.A.* **84 E3** 45 52N 123 11W
Vero Beach, *U.S.A.* **77 M5** 27 38N 80 24W

Véroia, Greece 21 D10 40 34N 22 12 E
Verona, Canada 79 B8 44 29N 76 42W
Verona, Italy 20 B4 45 27N 10 59 E
Verona, U.S.A. 80 D10 42 59N 89 32W
Versailles, France 18 B5 48 48N 2 8 E
Vert, C., Senegal 50 F2 14 45N 17 30W
Verulam, S. Africa 57 D5 29 38S 31 2 E
Verviers, Belgium 15 D5 50 37N 5 52 E
Veselovskoye Vdkhr., Russia 25 E7 46 58N 41 25 E
Vesoul, France 18 C7 47 40N 6 11 E
Vesterålen, Norway 8 B16 68 45N 15 0 E
Vestfjorden, Norway 8 C15 67 55N 14 0 E
Vestmannaeyjar, Iceland 8 E3 63 27N 20 15W
Vestspitsbergen, Svalbard 4 B8 78 40N 17 0 E
Vestvågøy, Norway 8 B15 68 18N 13 50 E
Vesuvio, Italy 20 D6 40 49N 14 26 E
Vesuvius, Mt. = Vesuvio, Italy 20 D6 40 49N 14 26 E
Veszprém, Hungary 17 E9 47 8N 17 57 E
Vetlanda, Sweden 9 H16 57 24N 15 3 E
Vetlugu →, Russia 24 C8 56 36N 46 4 E
Vettore, Mte., Italy 20 C5 42 49N 13 16 E
Veurne, Belgium 15 C2 51 5N 2 40 E
Veys, Iran 45 D6 31 30N 49 0 E
Vezhen, Bulgaria 21 C11 42 50N 24 20 E
Vi Thanh, Vietnam 39 H5 9 42N 105 26 E
Viacha, Bolivia 92 G5 16 39S 68 18W
Viamão, Brazil 95 C5 30 5S 51 0W
Viana, Brazil 93 D10 3 13S 44 55W
Viana do Alentejo, Portugal 19 C2 38 17N 7 59W
Viana do Castelo, Portugal 19 B1 41 42N 8 50W
Vianden, Lux. 15 E6 49 56N 6 12 E
Viangchan = Vientiane, Laos 38 D4 17 58N 102 36 E
Vianópolis, Brazil 93 G9 16 40S 48 35W
Viaréggio, Italy 20 C4 43 52N 10 14 E
Vibo Valéntia, Italy 20 E7 38 40N 16 6 E
Viborg, Denmark 9 H13 56 27N 9 23 E
Vic, Spain 19 B7 41 58N 2 19 E
Vicenza, Italy 20 B4 45 33N 11 33 E
Vich = Vic, Spain 19 B7 41 58N 2 19 E
Vichada →, Colombia 92 C5 4 55N 67 50W
Vichy, France 18 C5 46 9N 3 26 E
Vicksburg, Ariz., U.S.A. 85 M13 33 45N 113 45W
Vicksburg, Miss., U.S.A. 81 J9 32 21N 90 53W
Victor, India 42 J4 21 0N 71 30 E
Victor, U.S.A. 78 D7 42 58N 77 24W
Victor Harbor, Australia 63 F2 35 30S 138 37 E
Victoria = Labuan, Malaysia 36 C5 5 20N 115 14 E
Victoria, Argentina 94 C3 32 40S 60 10W
Victoria, Canada 72 D4 48 30N 123 25W
Victoria, Chile 96 D2 38 13S 72 20W
Victoria, Malta 23 C1 36 3N 14 14 E
Victoria, Kans., U.S.A. 80 F5 38 52N 99 9W
Victoria, Tex., U.S.A. 81 L6 28 48N 97 0W
Victoria □, Australia 63 F3 37 0S 144 0 E
Victoria →, Australia 60 C4 15 10S 129 40 E
Victoria, Grand L., Canada 70 C4 47 31N 77 30W
Victoria, L., Africa 54 C3 1 0S 33 0 E
Victoria, L., Australia 63 E3 33 57S 141 15 E
Victoria, Mt., Burma 41 J18 21 15N 93 55 E
Victoria Beach, Canada 73 C9 50 40N 96 35W
Victoria de Durango = Durango, Mexico 86 C4 24 3N 104 39W
Victoria de las Tunas, Cuba 88 B4 20 58N 76 59W
Victoria Falls, Zimbabwe 55 F2 17 58S 25 52 E
Victoria Harbour, Canada 78 B5 44 45N 79 45W
Victoria I., Canada 68 A8 71 0N 111 0W
Victoria L., Canada 71 C8 48 20N 57 27W
Victoria Ld., Antarctica 5 D11 75 0S 160 0 E
Victoria Nile →, Uganda 54 B3 2 14N 31 26 E
Victoria River, Australia 60 C5 16 25S 131 0 E
Victoria Str., Canada 68 B9 69 30N 100 0W
Victoria West, S. Africa 56 E3 31 25S 23 4 E
Victoriaville, Canada 71 C5 46 4N 71 56W
Victorica, Argentina 94 D2 36 20S 65 30W
Victorville, U.S.A. 85 L9 34 32N 117 18W
Vicuña, Chile 94 C1 30 0S 70 50W
Vicuña Mackenna, Argentina 94 C3 33 53S 64 25W
Vidal, U.S.A. 85 L12 34 7N 114 31W
Vidal Junction, U.S.A. 85 L12 34 11N 114 34W
Vidalia, U.S.A. 77 J4 32 13N 82 25W
Vídho, Greece 23 A3 39 38N 19 55 E
Vidin, Bulgaria 21 C10 43 59N 22 50 E
Vidisha, India 42 H7 23 28N 77 53 E
Vidzy, Belarus 9 J22 55 23N 26 37 E
Viedma, Argentina 96 E4 40 50S 63 0W
Viedma, L., Argentina 96 F2 49 30S 72 30W
Vielsalm, Belgium 15 D5 50 17N 5 54 E
Vieng Pou Kha, Laos 38 B3 20 41N 101 4 E
Vienna = Wien, Austria 16 D9 48 12N 16 22 E
Vienna, Ill., U.S.A. 81 G10 37 25N 88 54W
Vienna, Mo., U.S.A. 80 F9 38 11N 91 57W
Vienne, France 18 D6 45 31N 4 53 E
Vienne →, France 18 C4 47 13N 0 5 E
Vientiane, Laos 38 D4 17 58N 102 36 E
Vientos, Paso de los, Caribbean 89 C5 20 0N 74 0W
Vierzon, France 18 C5 47 13N 2 5 E
Vietnam ■, Asia 38 C6 19 0N 106 0 E
Vigan, Phil. 37 A6 17 35N 120 28 E
Vigévano, Italy 18 D8 45 19N 8 51 E
Vigia, Brazil 93 D9 0 50S 48 5W
Vigía Chico, Mexico 87 D7 19 46N 87 35W
Vígla, Ákra, Greece 23 D9 35 54N 27 51 E
Vigo, Spain 19 A1 42 12N 8 41W
Vihowa, Pakistan 42 D4 31 8N 70 30 E
Vihowa →, Pakistan 42 D4 31 8N 70 41 E
Vijayawada, India 41 L12 16 31N 80 39 E
Vijosë →, Albania 21 D8 40 37N 19 24 E
Vík, Iceland 8 E4 63 25N 19 1W
Vikeke = Viqueque, E. Timor 37 F7 8 52S 126 23 E
Viking, Canada 72 C6 53 7N 111 50W
Vikna, Norway 8 D14 64 55N 10 58 E
Vila da Maganja, Mozam. 55 F4 17 18S 37 30 E
Vila de João Belo = Xai-Xai, Mozam. 57 D5 25 6S 33 31 E
Vila do Bispo, Portugal 19 D1 37 5N 8 53W
Vila Franca de Xira, Portugal 19 C1 38 57N 8 59W
Vila Gamito, Mozam. 55 E3 14 12S 33 0 E
Vila Gomes da Costa, Mozam. 57 C5 24 20S 33 37 E
Vila Machado, Mozam. 55 F3 19 15S 34 14 E
Vila Mouzinho, Mozam. 55 E3 14 48S 34 25 E
Vila Nova de Gaia, Portugal 19 B1 41 8N 8 37W
Vila Real, Portugal 19 B2 41 17N 7 48W
Vila-real de los Infantes, Spain 19 C5 39 55N 0 3W
Vila Real de Santo António, Portugal 19 D2 37 10N 7 28W
Vila Vasco da Gama, Mozam. 55 E3 14 54S 32 14 E
Vila Velha, Brazil 95 A7 20 20S 40 17W
Vilagarcía de Arousa, Spain 19 A1 42 34N 8 46W
Vilaine →, France 18 C2 47 30N 2 27W
Vilanandro, Tanjona, Madag. 57 B7 16 11S 44 27 E
Vilanculos, Mozam. 57 C6 22 1S 35 17 E
Vilanova i la Geltrú, Spain 19 B6 41 13N 1 40 E
Vileyka, Belarus 17 A14 54 30N 26 53 E
Vilhelmina, Sweden 8 D17 64 35N 16 39 E
Vilhena, Brazil 92 F6 12 40S 60 5W
Viliga, Russia 27 C16 61 36N 156 56 E
Viliya →, Lithuania 9 J21 55 8N 24 16 E
Viljandi, Estonia 9 G21 58 28N 25 30 E
Vilkitskogo, Proliv, Russia 27 B11 78 0N 103 0 E
Vilkovo = Vylkove, Ukraine 17 F15 45 28N 29 32 E
Villa Abecia, Bolivia 94 A2 21 0S 68 18W
Villa Ahumada, Mexico 86 A3 30 38N 106 30W
Villa Ana, Argentina 94 B4 28 28S 59 40W
Villa Ángela, Argentina 94 B3 27 34S 60 45W
Villa Bella, Bolivia 92 F5 10 25S 65 22W
Villa Bens = Tarfaya, Morocco 50 C3 27 55N 12 55W
Villa Cañás, Argentina 94 C3 34 0S 61 35W
Villa Cisneros = Dakhla, W. Sahara 50 D2 23 50N 15 53W
Villa Colón, Argentina 94 C2 31 38S 68 20W
Villa Constitución, Argentina 94 C3 33 15S 60 20W
Villa de María, Argentina 94 B3 29 55S 63 43W
Villa Dolores, Argentina 94 C2 31 58S 65 15W
Villa Frontera, Mexico 86 B4 26 56N 101 27W
Villa Guillermina, Argentina 94 B4 28 15S 59 29W
Villa Hayes, Paraguay 94 B4 25 5S 57 20W
Villa Iris, Argentina 94 D3 38 12S 63 12W
Villa Juárez, Mexico 86 B4 27 37N 100 44W
Villa María, Argentina 94 C3 32 20S 63 10W
Villa Mazán, Argentina 94 B2 28 40S 66 30W
Villa Montes, Bolivia 94 A3 21 10S 63 30W
Villa Ocampo, Argentina 94 B4 28 30S 59 20W
Villa Ocampo, Mexico 86 B3 26 29N 105 30W
Villa Ojo de Agua, Argentina 94 B3 29 30S 63 44W
Villa San José, Argentina 94 C4 32 12S 58 15W
Villa San Martín, Argentina 94 B3 28 15S 64 9W
Villa Unión, Mexico 86 C3 23 12N 106 14W
Villacarlos, Spain 22 B11 39 53N 4 17 E
Villacarrillo, Spain 19 C4 38 7N 3 3W
Villach, Austria 16 E7 46 37N 13 51 E
Villafranca de los Caballeros, Spain 22 B10 39 34N 3 25 E
Villagrán, Mexico 87 C5 24 29N 99 29W
Villaguay, Argentina 94 C4 32 0S 59 0W
Villahermosa, Mexico 87 D6 17 59N 92 55W
Villajoyosa, Spain 19 C5 38 30N 0 12W
Villalba, Spain 19 A2 43 26N 7 40W
Villanueva, U.S.A. 81 H2 35 16N 105 22W
Villanueva de la Serena, Spain 19 C3 38 59N 5 50W
Villanueva y Geltrú = Vilanova i la Geltrú, Spain 19 B6 41 13N 1 40 E
Villarreal = Vila-real de los Infantes, Spain 19 C5 39 55N 0 3W
Villarrica, Chile 96 D2 39 15S 72 15W
Villarrica, Paraguay 94 B4 25 40S 56 30W
Villarrobledo, Spain 19 C4 39 18N 2 36W
Villavicencio, Argentina 94 C2 32 28S 69 0W
Villavicencio, Colombia 92 C4 4 9N 73 37W
Villaviciosa, Spain 19 A3 43 32N 5 27W
Villazón, Bolivia 94 A2 22 0S 65 35W
Ville-Marie, Canada 70 C4 47 20N 79 30W
Ville Platte, U.S.A. 81 K8 30 41N 92 17W
Villena, Spain 19 C5 38 39N 0 52W
Villeneuve-d'Ascq, France 18 A5 50 38N 3 9 E
Villeneuve-sur-Lot, France 18 D4 44 24N 0 42 E
Villiers, S. Africa 57 D4 27 2S 28 36 E
Villingen-Schwenningen, Germany 16 D5 48 3N 8 26 E
Vilna, Canada 72 C6 54 7N 111 55W
Vilnius, Lithuania 9 J21 54 38N 25 19 E
Vilvoorde, Belgium 15 D4 50 56N 4 26 E
Vilyuy →, Russia 27 C13 64 24N 126 26 E
Vilyuysk, Russia 27 C13 63 40N 121 35 E
Viña del Mar, Chile 94 C1 33 0S 71 30W
Vinarós, Spain 19 B6 40 30N 0 27 E
Vincennes, U.S.A. 76 F2 38 41N 87 32W
Vincent, U.S.A. 85 L8 34 33N 118 11W
Vinchina, Argentina 94 B2 28 45S 68 15W
Vindelälven →, Sweden 8 E18 63 55N 19 50 E
Vindeln, Sweden 8 D18 64 12N 19 43 E
Vindhya Ra., India 42 H7 22 50N 77 0 E
Vineland, U.S.A. 76 F8 39 29N 75 2W
Vinh, Vietnam 38 C5 18 45N 105 38 E
Vinh Linh, Vietnam 38 D6 17 4N 107 2 E
Vinh Long, Vietnam 39 G5 10 16N 105 57 E
Vinh Yen, Vietnam 38 B5 21 21N 105 35 E
Vinita, U.S.A. 81 G7 36 39N 95 9W
Vinkovci, Croatia 21 B8 45 19N 18 48 E
Vinnitsa = Vinnytsya, Ukraine 17 D15 49 15N 28 30 E
Vinnytsya, Ukraine 17 D15 49 15N 28 30 E
Vinton, Calif., U.S.A. 84 F6 39 48N 120 10W
Vinton, Iowa, U.S.A. 80 D8 42 10N 92 1W
Vinton, La., U.S.A. 81 K8 30 11N 93 35W
Viqueque, E. Timor 37 F7 8 52S 126 23 E
Virac, Phil. 37 B6 13 30N 124 20 E
Virachei, Cambodia 38 F6 13 59N 106 49 E
Virago Sd., Canada 72 C2 54 0N 132 30W
Viramgam, India 42 H5 23 5N 72 0 E
Viranşehir, Turkey 44 B3 37 13N 39 45 E
Virawah, Pakistan 42 G4 24 31N 70 46 E
Virden, Canada 73 D8 49 50N 100 56W
Vire, France 18 B3 48 50N 0 53W
Virgenes, C., Argentina 96 G3 52 19S 68 21W
Virgin →, U.S.A. 83 H6 36 28N 114 21W
Virgin Gorda, Br. Virgin Is. 89 C7 18 30N 64 26W
Virgin Is. (British) ■, W. Indies 89 C7 18 30N 64 30W
Virgin Is. (U.S.) ■, W. Indies 89 C7 18 20N 65 0W
Virginia, S. Africa 56 D4 28 8S 26 55 E
Virginia, U.S.A. 80 B8 47 31N 92 32W
Virginia □, U.S.A. 76 G7 37 30N 78 45W
Virginia Beach, U.S.A. 76 G8 36 51N 75 59W
Virginia City, Mont., U.S.A. 82 D8 45 18N 111 56W
Virginia City, Nev., U.S.A. 84 F7 39 19N 119 39W
Virginia Falls, Canada 72 A3 61 38N 125 42W
Virginiatown, Canada 70 C4 48 9N 79 36W
Viroqua, U.S.A. 80 D9 43 34N 90 53W
Virovitica, Croatia 20 B7 45 51N 17 21 E
Virpur, India 42 J4 21 51N 70 42 E
Virton, Belgium 15 E5 49 35N 5 32 E
Virudunagar, India 40 Q10 9 30N 77 58 E
Vis, Croatia 20 C7 43 4N 16 10 E
Visalia, U.S.A. 84 J7 36 20N 119 18W
Visayan Sea, Phil. 37 B6 11 30N 123 30 E
Visby, Sweden 9 H18 57 37N 18 18 E
Viscount Melville Sd., Canada 4 B2 74 10N 108 0W
Visé, Belgium 15 D5 50 44N 5 41 E
Višegrad, Bos.-H. 21 C8 43 47N 19 17 E
Viseu, Brazil 93 D9 1 10S 46 5W
Viseu, Portugal 19 B2 40 40N 7 55W
Vishakhapatnam, India 41 L13 17 45N 83 20 E
Visnagar, India 42 H5 23 45N 72 32 E
Viso, Mte., Italy 18 D7 44 38N 7 5 E
Visokoi I., Antarctica 5 B1 56 43S 27 15W
Vista, U.S.A. 85 M9 33 12N 117 14W
Vistula = Wisła →, Poland 17 A10 54 22N 18 55 E
Vitebsk = Vitsyebsk, Belarus 24 C5 55 10N 30 15 E
Viterbo, Italy 20 C5 42 25N 12 6 E
Viti Levu, Fiji 59 C7 17 30S 177 30 E
Vitigudino, Spain 19 B2 41 1N 6 26W
Vitim, Russia 27 D12 59 28N 112 35 E
Vitim →, Russia 27 D12 59 26N 112 34 E
Vitória, Brazil 93 H10 20 20S 40 22W
Vitória da Conquista, Brazil 93 F10 14 51S 40 51W
Vitória de São Antão, Brazil 93 E11 8 10S 35 20W
Vitoria-Gasteiz, Spain 19 A4 42 50N 2 41W
Vitsyebsk, Belarus 24 C5 55 10N 30 15 E
Vittória, Italy 20 F6 36 57N 14 32 E
Vittório Véneto, Italy 20 B5 45 59N 12 18 E
Viveiro, Spain 19 A2 43 39N 7 38W
Vivian, U.S.A. 81 J8 32 53N 93 59W
Vizcaíno, Desierto de, Mexico 86 B2 27 40N 113 50W
Vizcaíno, Sierra, Mexico 86 B2 27 30N 114 0W
Vize, Turkey 21 D12 41 34N 27 45 E
Vizianagaram, India 41 K13 18 6N 83 30 E
Vlaardingen, Neths. 15 C4 51 55N 4 21 E
Vladikavkaz, Russia 25 F7 43 0N 44 35 E
Vladimir, Russia 24 C7 56 15N 40 30 E
Vladimir Volynskiy = Volodymyr-Volynskyy, Ukraine 17 C13 50 50N 24 18 E
Vladivostok, Russia 27 E14 43 10N 131 53 E
Vlieland, Neths. 15 A4 53 16N 4 55 E
Vlissingen, Neths. 15 C3 51 26N 3 34 E
Vlorë, Albania 21 D8 40 32N 19 28 E
Vltava →, Czech Rep. 16 D8 50 21N 14 30 E
Vo Dat, Vietnam 39 G6 11 9N 107 31 E
Voe, U.K. 12 A7 60 21N 1 16W
Vogelkop = Doberai, Jazirah, Indonesia 37 E8 1 25S 133 0 E
Vogelsberg, Germany 16 C5 50 31N 9 12 E
Voghera, Italy 18 D8 44 59N 9 1 E
Vohibinany, Madag. 57 B8 18 49S 49 4 E
Vohilava, Madag. 57 C8 21 4S 48 0 E
Vohimarina = Iharana, Madag. 57 A9 13 25S 50 0 E
Vohimena, Tanjon' i, Madag. 57 D8 25 36S 45 8 E
Vohipeno, Madag. 57 C8 22 22S 47 51 E
Voi, Kenya 54 C4 3 25S 38 32 E
Voiron, France 18 D6 45 22N 5 35 E
Voisey B., Canada 71 A7 56 15N 61 50W
Vojmsjön, Sweden 8 D17 64 55N 16 40 E
Vojvodina □, Serbia, Yug. 21 B9 45 20N 20 0 E
Volborg, U.S.A. 80 C2 45 51N 105 41W
Volcano Is. = Kazan-Rettō, Pac. Oc. 64 E6 25 0N 141 0 E
Volda, Norway 9 E12 62 9N 6 5 E
Volga →, Russia 25 E8 46 0N 48 30 E
Volga Hts. = Privolzhskaya Vozvyshennost, Russia 25 D8 51 0N 46 0 E
Volgodonsk, Russia 25 E7 47 33N 42 5 E
Volgograd, Russia 25 E7 48 40N 44 25 E
Volgogradskoye Vdkhr., Russia 25 D8 50 0N 45 20 E
Volkhov →, Russia 24 B5 60 8N 32 20 E
Volkovysk = Vawkavysk, Belarus 17 B13 53 9N 24 30 E
Volksrust, S. Africa 57 D4 27 24S 29 53 E
Volochanka, Russia 27 B10 71 0N 94 28 E
Volodymyr-Volynskyy, Ukraine 17 C13 50 50N 24 18 E
Vologda, Russia 24 C6 59 10N 39 45 E
Vólos, Greece 21 E10 39 24N 22 59 E
Volovets, Ukraine 17 D12 48 43N 23 11 E
Volozhin = Valozhyn, Belarus 17 A14 54 3N 26 30 E
Volsk, Russia 24 D8 52 5N 47 22 E
Volta →, Ghana 48 F4 5 46N 0 41 E
Volta, L., Ghana 50 G6 7 30N 0 0 E
Volta Redonda, Brazil 95 A7 22 31S 44 5W
Voltaire, C., Australia 60 B4 14 16S 125 35 E
Volterra, Italy 20 C4 43 24N 10 51 E
Volturno →, Italy 20 D5 41 1N 13 55 E
Volzhskiy, Russia 25 E7 48 56N 44 46 E
Vondrozo, Madag. 57 C8 22 49S 47 20 E
Vopnafjörður, Iceland 8 D6 65 45N 14 50W
Vóriai Sporádhes, Greece 21 E10 39 15N 23 30 E
Vorkuta, Russia 24 A11 67 48N 64 20 E
Vormsi, Estonia 9 G20 59 1N 23 13 E
Voronezh, Russia 25 D6 51 40N 39 10 E
Voroshilovgrad = Luhansk, Ukraine 25 E6 48 38N 39 15 E
Voroshilovsk = Alchevsk, Ukraine 25 E6 48 30N 38 45 E
Võrts Järv, Estonia 9 G22 58 16N 26 3 E
Võru, Estonia 9 H22 57 48N 26 54 E
Vosges, France 18 B7 48 20N 7 10 E
Voss, Norway 9 F12 60 38N 6 26 E
Vostok I., Kiribati 65 J12 10 5S 152 23W
Votkinsk, Russia 24 C9 57 0N 53 55 E
Votkinskoye Vdkhr., Russia 24 C10 57 22N 55 12 E
Votsuri-Shima, Japan 31 M1 25 45N 123 29 E
Vouga →, Portugal 19 B1 40 41N 8 40W
Voúxa, Ákra, Greece 23 D5 35 37N 23 32 E
Vozhe, Ozero, Russia 24 B6 60 45N 39 0 E
Voznesensk, Ukraine 25 E5 47 35N 31 21 E
Voznesenye, Russia 24 B6 61 0N 35 28 E
Vrangelya, Ostrov, Russia 27 B19 71 0N 180 0 E
Vranje, Serbia, Yug. 21 C9 42 34N 21 54 E
Vratsa, Bulgaria 21 C10 43 15N 23 30 E
Vrbas →, Bos.-H. 20 B7 45 8N 17 29 E
Vrede, S. Africa 57 D4 27 24S 29 6 E
Vredefort, S. Africa 56 D4 27 0S 27 22 E
Vredenburg, S. Africa 56 E2 32 56S 18 0 E
Vredendal, S. Africa 56 E2 31 41S 18 35 E
Vrindavan, India 42 F7 27 37N 77 40 E
Vrises, Greece 23 D6 35 23N 24 13 E
Vršac, Serbia, Yug. 21 B9 45 8N 21 20 E
Vryburg, S. Africa 56 D3 26 55S 24 45 E
Vryheid, S. Africa 57 D5 27 45S 30 47 E
Vu Liet, Vietnam 38 C5 18 43N 105 23 E
Vukovar, Croatia 21 B8 45 21N 18 59 E
Vulcan, Canada 72 C6 50 25N 113 15W
Vulcan, Romania 17 F12 45 23N 23 17 E
Vulcaneşti, Moldova 17 F15 45 41N 28 18 E
Vulcano, Italy 20 E6 38 24N 14 58 E
Vulkaneshty = Vulcaneşti, Moldova 17 F15 45 41N 28 18 E
Vunduzi →, Mozam. 55 F3 18 56S 34 1 E
Vung Tau, Vietnam 39 G6 10 21N 107 4 E
Vyatka = Kirov, Russia 24 C8 58 35N 49 40 E
Vyatka →, Russia 24 C9 55 37N 51 28 E
Vyatskiye Polyany, Russia 24 C9 56 14N 51 5 E
Vyazemskiy, Russia 27 E14 47 32N 134 45 E
Vyazma, Russia 24 C5 55 10N 34 15 E
Vyborg, Russia 24 B4 60 43N 28 47 E
Vychegda →, Russia 24 B8 61 18N 46 36 E
Vychodné Beskydy, Europe 17 D11 49 20N 22 0 E
Vyg-ozero, Russia 24 B5 63 47N 34 29 E
Vylkove, Ukraine 17 F15 45 28N 29 32 E
Vynohradiv, Ukraine 17 D12 48 9N 23 2 E
Vyrnwy, L., U.K. 10 E4 52 48N 3 31W
Vyshniy Volochek, Russia 24 C5 57 30N 34 30 E
Vyshzha = imeni 26 Bakinskikh Komissarov, Turkmenistan 45 B7 39 22N 54 10 E
Vyškov, Czech Rep. 17 D9 49 17N 17 0 E
Vytegra, Russia 24 B6 61 0N 36 27 E

W

W.A.C. Bennett Dam, Canada 72 B4 56 2N 122 6W
Waal →, Neths. 15 C5 51 37N 5 0 E
Waalwijk, Neths. 15 C5 51 42N 5 4 E
Wabana, Canada 71 C9 47 40N 53 0W
Wabasca →, Canada 72 B5 58 22N 115 20W
Wabasca-Desmarais, Canada 72 B6 55 57N 113 56W
Wabash, U.S.A. 76 E3 40 48N 85 49W
Wabash →, U.S.A. 76 G1 37 48N 88 2W
Wabigoon L., Canada 73 D10 49 44N 92 44W
Wabowden, Canada 73 C9 54 55N 98 38W
Wabuk Pt., Canada 70 A2 55 20N 85 5W
Wabush, Canada 71 B6 52 55N 66 52W
Waco, U.S.A. 81 K6 31 33N 97 9W
Waconichi, L., Canada 70 B5 50 8N 74 0W
Wad Hamid, Sudan 51 E12 16 30N 32 45 E
Wad Medanī, Sudan 51 F12 14 28N 33 30 E
Wad Thana, Pakistan 42 F2 27 22N 66 23 E
Wadai, Africa 48 E5 12 0N 19 0 E
Wadayama, Japan 31 G7 35 19N 134 52 E
Waddeneilanden, Neths. 15 A5 53 20N 5 10 E
Waddenzee, Neths. 15 A5 53 6N 5 10 E
Waddington, U.S.A. 79 B9 44 52N 75 12W
Waddington, Mt., Canada 72 C3 51 23N 125 15W
Waddy Pt., Australia 63 C5 24 58S 153 21 E
Wadebridge, U.K. 11 G3 50 31N 4 51W
Wadena, Canada 73 C8 51 57N 103 47W
Wadena, U.S.A. 80 B7 46 26N 95 8W
Wadeye, Australia 60 B4 14 28S 129 52 E
Wadhams, Canada 72 C3 51 30N 127 30W
Wādī as Sir, Jordan 47 D4 31 56N 35 49 E
Wadi Halfa, Sudan 51 D12 21 53N 31 19 E
Wadsworth, Nev., U.S.A. 82 G4 39 38N 119 17W
Wadsworth, Ohio, U.S.A. 78 E3 41 2N 81 44W
Waegwan, S. Korea 35 G15 35 59N 128 23 E
Wafangdian, China 35 E11 39 38N 121 58 E
Wafrah, Si. Arabia 44 D5 28 33N 47 56 E
Wageningen, Neths. 15 C5 51 58N 5 40 E
Wager B., Canada 69 B11 65 26N 88 40W
Wagga Wagga, Australia 63 F4 35 7S 147 24 E
Waghete, Indonesia 37 E9 4 10S 135 50 E
Wagin, Australia 61 F2 33 17S 117 25 E
Wagner, U.S.A. 80 D5 43 5N 98 18W
Wagon Mound, U.S.A. 81 G2 36 1N 104 42W
Wagoner, U.S.A. 81 H7 35 58N 95 22W
Wah, Pakistan 42 C5 33 45N 72 40 E
Wahai, Indonesia 37 E7 2 48S 129 35 E
Wahiawa, U.S.A. 74 H15 21 30N 158 2W
Wâḥid, Egypt 47 E1 30 48N 32 21 E
Wahnai, Afghan. 42 C1 32 40N 65 50 E
Wahoo, U.S.A. 80 E6 41 13N 96 37W
Wahpeton, U.S.A. 80 B6 46 16N 96 36W
Waiau →, N.Z. 59 K4 42 47S 173 22 E
Waibeem, Indonesia 37 E8 0 30S 132 59 E
Waigeo, Indonesia 37 E8 0 20S 130 40 E
Waihi, N.Z. 59 G5 37 23S 175 52 E
Waihou →, N.Z. 59 G5 37 15S 175 40 E
Waika, Dem. Rep. of the Congo 54 C2 2 22S 25 42 E
Waikabubak, Indonesia 37 F5 9 45S 119 25 E
Waikari, N.Z. 59 K4 42 58S 172 41 E
Waikato →, N.Z. 59 G5 37 23S 174 43 E
Waikerie, Australia 63 E3 34 9S 140 0 E
Waikokopu, N.Z. 59 H6 39 3S 177 52 E
Waikouaiti, N.Z. 59 L3 45 36S 170 41 E
Wailuku, U.S.A. 74 H16 20 53N 156 30W
Waimakariri →, N.Z. 59 K4 43 24S 172 42 E
Waimate, N.Z. 59 L3 44 45S 171 3 E
Wainganga →, India 40 K11 18 50N 79 55 E
Waingapu, Indonesia 37 F6 9 35S 120 11 E
Waini →, Guyana 92 B7 8 20N 59 50W
Wainwright, Canada 73 C6 52 50N 110 50W
Waiouru, N.Z. 59 H5 39 28S 175 41 E
Waipara, N.Z. 59 K4 43 3S 172 46 E
Waipawa, N.Z. 59 H6 39 56S 176 38 E
Waipiro, N.Z. 59 H7 38 2S 178 22 E
Waipu, N.Z. 59 F5 35 59S 174 29 E
Waipukurau, N.Z. 59 J6 40 1S 176 33 E
Wairakei, N.Z. 59 H6 38 37S 176 6 E
Wairarapa, L., N.Z. 59 J5 41 14S 175 15 E
Wairoa, N.Z. 59 H6 39 3S 177 25 E
Waitaki →, N.Z. 59 L3 44 56S 171 7 E
Waitara, N.Z. 59 H5 38 59S 174 15 E
Waitsburg, U.S.A. 82 C5 46 16N 118 9W
Waiuku, N.Z. 59 G5 37 15S 174 45 E
Wajima, Japan 31 F8 37 30N 137 0 E

Wajir, Kenya **54 B5** 1 42N 40 5 E
Wakasa, Japan **31 G7** 35 20N 134 24 E
Wakasa-Wan, Japan **31 G7** 35 40N 135 30 E
Wakatipu, L., N.Z. **59 L2** 45 5S 168 33 E
Wakaw, Canada **73 C7** 52 39N 105 44W
Wakayama, Japan **31 G7** 34 15N 135 15 E
Wakayama □, Japan **31 H7** 33 50N 135 30 E
Wake Forest, U.S.A. **77 H6** 35 59N 78 30W
Wake I., Pac. Oc. **64 F8** 19 18N 166 36 E
WaKeeney, U.S.A. **80 F5** 39 1N 99 53W
Wakefield, N.Z. **59 J4** 41 24S 173 5 E
Wakefield, U.K. **10 D6** 53 41N 1 29W
Wakefield, Mass., U.S.A. **79 D13** 42 30N 71 4W
Wakefield, Mich., U.S.A. **80 B10** 46 29N 89 56W
Wakkanai, Japan **30 B10** 45 28N 141 35 E
Wakkerstroom, S. Africa **57 D5** 27 24S 30 10 E
Wakool, Australia **63 F3** 35 28S 144 23 E
Wakool →, Australia **63 F3** 35 5S 143 33 E
Wakre, Indonesia **37 E8** 0 19S 131 5 E
Wakuach, L., Canada **71 A6** 55 34N 67 32W
Walamba, Zambia **55 E2** 13 30S 28 42 E
Wałbrzych, Poland **16 C9** 50 45N 16 18 E
Walbury Hill, U.K. **11 F6** 51 21N 1 28W
Walcha, Australia **63 E5** 30 55S 151 31 E
Walcheren, Neths. **15 C3** 51 30N 3 35 E
Walcott, U.S.A. **82 F10** 41 46N 106 51W
Wałcz, Poland **16 B9** 53 17N 16 27 E
Waldburg Ra., Australia **61 D2** 24 40S 117 35 E
Walden, Colo., U.S.A. **82 F10** 40 44N 106 17W
Walden, N.Y., U.S.A. **79 E10** 41 34N 74 11W
Waldport, U.S.A. **82 D1** 44 26N 124 4W
Waldron, U.S.A. **81 H7** 34 54N 94 5W
Walebing, Australia **61 F2** 30 41S 116 13 E
Wales □, U.K. **11 E3** 52 19N 4 43W
Walgett, Australia **63 E4** 30 0S 148 5 E
Walgreen Coast, Antarctica **5 D15** 75 15S 105 0W
Walker, U.S.A. **80 B7** 47 6N 94 35W
Walker, L., Canada **71 B6** 50 20N 67 11W
Walker L., Canada **73 C9** 54 42N 95 57W
Walker L., U.S.A. **82 G4** 38 42N 118 43W
Walkerston, Australia **62 C4** 21 11S 149 8 E
Walkerton, Canada **78 B3** 44 10N 81 10W
Wall, U.S.A. **80 D3** 44 0N 102 8W
Walla Walla, U.S.A. **82 C4** 46 4N 118 20W
Wallace, Idaho, U.S.A. **82 C6** 47 28N 115 56W
Wallace, N.C., U.S.A. **77 H7** 34 44N 77 59W
Wallaceburg, Canada **78 D2** 42 34N 82 23W
Wallachia = Valahia, Romania **17 F13** 44 35N 25 0 E
Wallal, Australia **63 D4** 26 32S 146 7 E
Wallam Cr. →, Australia **63 D4** 28 40S 147 20 E
Wallambin, L., Australia **61 F2** 30 57S 117 35 E
Wallangarra, Australia **63 D5** 28 56S 151 58 E
Wallaroo, Australia **63 E2** 33 56S 137 39 E
Wallenpaupack, L., U.S.A. **79 E9** 41 25N 75 15W
Wallingford, U.S.A. **79 E12** 41 27N 72 50W
Wallis & Futuna, Is., Pac. Oc. **64 J10** 13 18S 176 10W
Wallowa, U.S.A. **82 D5** 45 34N 117 32W
Wallowa Mts., U.S.A. **82 D5** 45 20N 117 30W
Walls, U.K. **12 A7** 60 14N 1 33W
Wallula, U.S.A. **82 C4** 46 5N 118 54W
Wallumbilla, Australia **63 D4** 26 33S 149 9 E
Walmsley, L., Canada **73 A7** 63 25N 108 36W
Walney, I. of, U.K. **10 C4** 54 6N 3 15W
Walnut Creek, U.S.A. **84 H4** 37 54N 122 4W
Walnut Ridge, U.S.A. **81 G9** 36 4N 90 57W
Walpole, Australia **61 F2** 34 58S 116 44 E
Walpole, U.S.A. **79 D13** 42 9N 71 15W
Walsall, U.K. **11 E6** 52 35N 1 58W
Walsenburg, U.S.A. **81 G2** 37 38N 104 47W
Walsh, U.S.A. **81 G3** 37 23N 102 17W
Walsh →, Australia **62 B3** 16 31S 143 42 E
Walterboro, U.S.A. **77 J5** 32 55N 80 40W
Walters, U.S.A. **81 H5** 34 22N 98 19W
Waltham, U.S.A. **79 D13** 42 23N 71 14W
Waltman, U.S.A. **82 E10** 43 4N 107 12W
Walton, U.S.A. **79 D9** 42 10N 75 8W
Walton-on-the-Naze, U.K. **11 F9** 51 51N 1 17 E
Walvis Bay, Namibia **56 C1** 23 0S 14 28 E
Walvisbaai = Walvis Bay, Namibia **56 C1** 23 0S 14 28 E
Wamba, Dem. Rep. of the Congo **54 B2** 2 10N 27 57 E
Wamba, Kenya **54 B4** 0 58N 37 19 E
Wamego, U.S.A. **80 F6** 39 12N 96 18W
Wamena, Indonesia **37 E9** 4 4S 138 57 E
Wamsutter, U.S.A. **82 F9** 41 40N 107 58W
Wamulan, Indonesia **37 E7** 3 27S 126 7 E
Wan Xian, China **34 E8** 38 47N 115 7 E
Wana, Pakistan **42 C3** 32 20N 69 32 E
Wanaaring, Australia **63 D3** 29 38S 144 9 E
Wanaka, N.Z. **59 L2** 44 42S 169 9 E
Wanaka, L., N.Z. **59 L2** 44 33S 169 7 E
Wanapitei L., Canada **70 C3** 46 45N 80 40W
Wandel Sea = McKinley Sea, Arctic **4 A7** 82 0N 0 0W
Wanderer, Zimbabwe **55 F3** 19 36S 30 1 E
Wandhari, Pakistan **42 F2** 27 42N 66 48 E
Wandoan, Australia **63 D4** 26 5S 149 55 E
Wanfu, China **35 D12** 40 8N 122 38 E
Wang →, Thailand **38 D2** 17 8N 99 2 E
Wang Noi, Thailand **38 E3** 14 13N 100 44 E
Wang Saphung, Thailand **38 D3** 17 18N 101 46 E
Wang Thong, Thailand **38 D3** 16 50N 100 26 E
Wanga, Dem. Rep. of the Congo **54 B2** 2 58N 29 12 E
Wangal, Indonesia **37 F8** 6 8S 134 9 E
Wanganella, Australia **63 F3** 35 6S 144 49 E
Wanganui, N.Z. **59 H5** 39 56S 175 3 E
Wangaratta, Australia **63 F4** 36 21S 146 19 E
Wangary, Australia **63 E2** 34 35S 135 29 E
Wangdu, China **34 E8** 38 40N 115 7 E
Wangerooge, Germany **16 B4** 53 47N 7 54 E
Wangi, Kenya **54 C5** 1 58S 40 58 E
Wangiwangi, Indonesia **37 F6** 5 22S 123 37 E
Wangqing, China **35 C15** 43 12N 129 42 E
Wankaner, India **42 H4** 22 35N 71 0 E
Wanless, Canada **73 C8** 54 11N 101 21W
Wanning, China **38 C8** 18 48N 110 22 E
Wanon Niwat, Thailand **38 D4** 17 38N 103 46 E
Wanquan, China **34 D8** 40 50N 114 40 E
Wanrong, China **34 G6** 35 25N 110 50 E
Wantage, U.K. **11 F6** 51 35N 1 25W
Wapakoneta, U.S.A. **76 E3** 40 34N 84 12W
Wapato, U.S.A. **82 C3** 46 27N 120 25W
Wapawekka L., Canada **73 C8** 54 55N 104 40W
Wapikopa L., Canada **70 B2** 52 56N 87 53W
Wapiti →, Canada **72 B5** 55 5N 118 18W
Wappingers Falls, U.S.A. **79 E11** 41 36N 73 55W
Wapsipinicon →, U.S.A. **80 E9** 41 44N 90 19W
Warangal, India **40 L11** 17 58N 79 35 E
Waraseoni, India **43 J9** 21 45N 80 2 E
Waratah, Australia **62 G4** 41 30S 145 30 E
Waratah B., Australia **63 F4** 38 54S 146 5 E
Warburton, Vic., Australia **63 F4** 37 47S 145 42 E
Warburton, W. Austral., Australia **61 E4** 26 8S 126 35 E
Warburton Ra., Australia **61 E4** 25 55S 126 28 E
Ward, N.Z. **59 J5** 41 49S 174 11 E
Ward →, Australia **63 D4** 26 28S 146 6 E
Ward Mt., U.S.A. **84 H8** 37 12N 118 54W
Warden, S. Africa **57 D4** 27 50S 29 0 E
Wardha, India **40 J11** 20 45N 78 39 E
Wardha →, India **40 K11** 19 57N 79 11 E
Ware, Canada **72 B3** 57 26N 125 41W
Ware, U.S.A. **79 D12** 42 16N 72 14W
Waregem, Belgium **15 D3** 50 53N 3 27 E
Wareham, U.S.A. **79 E14** 41 46N 70 43W
Waremme, Belgium **15 D5** 50 43N 5 15 E
Warialda, Australia **63 D5** 29 29S 150 33 E
Wariap, Indonesia **37 E8** 1 30S 134 5 E
Warin Chamrap, Thailand **38 E5** 15 12N 104 53 E
Warkopi, Indonesia **37 E8** 1 12S 134 9 E
Warm Springs, U.S.A. **83 G5** 38 10N 116 20W
Warman, Canada **73 C7** 52 19N 106 30W
Warmbad, Namibia **56 D2** 28 25S 18 42 E
Warmbad, S. Africa **57 C4** 24 51S 28 19 E
Warminster, U.K. **11 F5** 51 12N 2 10W
Warminster, U.S.A. **79 F9** 40 12N 75 6W
Warner Mts., U.S.A. **82 F3** 41 40N 120 15W
Warner Robins, U.S.A. **77 J4** 32 37N 83 36W
Waroona, Australia **61 F2** 32 50S 115 58 E
Warracknabeal, Australia **63 F3** 36 9S 142 26 E
Warragul, Australia **63 F4** 38 10S 145 58 E
Warrego →, Australia **63 E4** 30 24S 145 21 E
Warrego Ra., Australia **62 C4** 24 58S 146 0 E
Warren, Australia **63 E4** 31 42S 147 51 E
Warren, Ark., U.S.A. **81 J8** 33 37N 92 4W
Warren, Mich., U.S.A. **76 D4** 42 30N 83 0W
Warren, Minn., U.S.A. **80 A6** 48 12N 96 46W
Warren, Ohio, U.S.A. **78 E4** 41 14N 80 49W
Warren, Pa., U.S.A. **78 E5** 41 51N 79 9W
Warrenpoint, U.K. **13 B5** 54 6N 6 15W
Warrensburg, Mo., U.S.A. **80 F8** 38 46N 93 44W
Warrensburg, N.Y., U.S.A. **79 C11** 43 29N 73 46W
Warrenton, S. Africa **56 D3** 28 9S 24 47 E
Warrenton, U.S.A. **84 D3** 46 10N 123 56W
Warri, Nigeria **50 G7** 5 30N 5 41 E
Warrina, Australia **63 D2** 28 12S 135 50 E
Warrington, U.K. **10 D5** 53 24N 2 35W
Warrington, U.S.A. **77 K2** 30 23N 87 17W
Warrington □, U.K. **10 D5** 53 24N 2 35W
Warrnambool, Australia **63 F3** 38 25S 142 30 E
Warroad, U.S.A. **80 A7** 48 54N 95 19W
Warruwi, Australia **62 A1** 11 36S 133 20 E
Warsa, Indonesia **37 E9** 0 47S 135 55 E
Warsak Dam, Pakistan **42 B4** 34 11N 71 19 E
Warsaw = Warszawa, Poland **17 B11** 52 13N 21 0 E
Warsaw, Ind., U.S.A. **76 E3** 41 14N 85 51W
Warsaw, N.Y., U.S.A. **78 D6** 42 45N 78 8W
Warsaw, Ohio, U.S.A. **78 F3** 40 20N 82 0W
Warszawa, Poland **17 B11** 52 13N 21 0 E
Warta →, Poland **16 B8** 52 35N 14 39 E
Warthe = Warta →, Poland **16 B8** 52 35N 14 39 E
Waru, Indonesia **37 E8** 3 30S 130 36 E
Warwick, Australia **63 D5** 28 10S 152 1 E
Warwick, U.K. **11 E6** 52 18N 1 35W
Warwick, N.Y., U.S.A. **79 E10** 41 16N 74 22W
Warwick, R.I., U.S.A. **79 E13** 41 42N 71 28W
Warwickshire □, U.K. **11 E6** 52 14N 1 38W
Wasaga Beach, Canada **78 B4** 44 31N 80 1W
Wasagaming, Canada **73 C9** 50 39N 99 58W
Wasatch Ra., U.S.A. **82 F8** 40 30N 111 15W
Wasbank, S. Africa **57 D5** 28 15S 30 9 E
Wasco, Calif., U.S.A. **85 K7** 35 36N 119 20W
Wasco, Oreg., U.S.A. **82 D3** 45 36N 120 42W
Waseca, U.S.A. **80 C8** 44 5N 93 30W
Wasekamio L., Canada **73 B7** 56 45N 108 45W
Wash, The, U.K. **10 E8** 52 58N 0 20 E
Washago, Canada **78 B5** 44 45N 79 20W
Washburn, N. Dak., U.S.A. **80 B4** 47 17N 101 2W
Washburn, Wis., U.S.A. **80 B9** 46 40N 90 54W
Washim, India **40 J10** 20 3N 77 0 E
Washington, U.K. **10 C6** 54 55N 1 30W
Washington, D.C., U.S.A. **76 F7** 38 54N 77 2W
Washington, Ga., U.S.A. **77 J4** 33 44N 82 44W
Washington, Ind., U.S.A. **76 F2** 38 40N 87 10W
Washington, Iowa, U.S.A. **80 E9** 41 18N 91 42W
Washington, Mo., U.S.A. **80 F9** 38 33N 91 1W
Washington, N.C., U.S.A. **77 H7** 35 33N 77 3W
Washington, N.J., U.S.A. **79 F10** 40 46N 74 59W
Washington, Pa., U.S.A. **78 F4** 40 10N 80 15W
Washington, Utah, U.S.A. **83 H7** 37 8N 113 31W
Washington □, U.S.A. **82 C3** 47 30N 120 30W
Washington, Mt., U.S.A. **79 B13** 44 16N 71 18W
Washington Court House, U.S.A. **76 F4** 39 32N 83 26W
Washington I., U.S.A. **76 C2** 45 23N 86 54W
Washougal, U.S.A. **84 E4** 45 35N 122 21W
Wasian, Indonesia **37 E8** 1 47S 133 19 E
Wasilla, U.S.A. **68 B5** 61 35N 149 26W
Wasior, Indonesia **37 E8** 2 43S 134 30 E
Waskaganish, Canada **70 B4** 51 30N 78 40W
Waskaiowaka, L., Canada **73 B9** 56 33N 96 23W
Waskesiu Lake, Canada **73 C7** 53 55N 106 5W
Wasserkuppe, Germany **16 C5** 50 29N 9 55 E
Waswanipi, Canada **70 C4** 49 40N 76 29W
Waswanipi, L., Canada **70 C4** 49 35N 76 40W
Watampone, Indonesia **37 E6** 4 29S 120 25 E
Water Park Pt., Australia **62 C5** 22 56S 150 47 E
Water Valley, U.S.A. **81 H10** 34 10N 89 38W
Waterberge, S. Africa **57 C4** 24 10S 28 0 E
Waterbury, Conn., U.S.A. **79 E11** 41 33N 73 3W
Waterbury, Vt., U.S.A. **79 B12** 44 20N 72 46W
Waterbury L., Canada **73 B8** 58 10N 104 22W
Waterdown, Canada **78 C5** 43 20N 79 53W
Waterford, Canada **78 D4** 42 56N 80 17W
Waterford, Ireland **13 D4** 52 15N 7 8W
Waterford, Calif., U.S.A. **84 H6** 37 38N 120 46W
Waterford, Pa., U.S.A. **78 E5** 41 57N 79 59W
Waterford □, Ireland **13 D4** 52 10N 7 40W
Waterford Harbour, Ireland **13 D5** 52 8N 6 58W
Waterhen L., Canada **73 C9** 52 10N 99 40W
Waterloo, Belgium **15 D4** 50 43N 4 25 E
Waterloo, Ont., Canada **78 C4** 43 30N 80 32W
Waterloo, Qué., Canada **79 A12** 45 22N 72 32W
Waterloo, Ill., U.S.A. **80 F9** 38 20N 90 9W
Waterloo, Iowa, U.S.A. **80 D8** 42 30N 92 21W
Waterloo, N.Y., U.S.A. **78 D8** 42 54N 76 52W
Watersmeet, U.S.A. **80 B10** 46 16N 89 11W
Waterton Lakes Nat. Park, U.S.A. **82 B7** 48 45N 115 0W
Watertown, Conn., U.S.A. **79 E11** 41 36N 73 7W
Watertown, N.Y., U.S.A. **79 C9** 43 59N 75 55W
Watertown, S. Dak., U.S.A. **80 C6** 44 54N 97 7W
Watertown, Wis., U.S.A. **80 D10** 43 12N 88 43W
Waterval-Boven, S. Africa **57 D5** 25 40S 30 18 E
Waterville, Canada **79 A13** 45 16N 71 54W
Waterville, Maine, U.S.A. **77 C11** 44 33N 69 38W
Waterville, N.Y., U.S.A. **79 D9** 42 56N 75 23W
Waterville, Pa., U.S.A. **78 E7** 41 19N 77 21W
Waterville, Wash., U.S.A. **82 C3** 47 39N 120 4W
Watervliet, U.S.A. **79 D11** 42 44N 73 42W
Wates, Indonesia **37 G14** 7 51S 110 10 E
Watford, Canada **78 D3** 42 57N 81 53W
Watford, U.K. **11 F7** 51 40N 0 24W
Watford City, U.S.A. **80 B3** 47 48N 103 17W
Wathaman →, Canada **73 B8** 57 16N 102 59W
Wathaman L., Canada **73 B8** 56 58N 103 44W
Watheroo, Australia **61 F2** 30 15S 116 0 E
Wating, China **34 G4** 35 40N 106 38 E
Watkins Glen, U.S.A. **78 D8** 42 23N 76 52W
Watling I. = San Salvador I., Bahamas **89 B5** 24 0N 74 40W
Watonga, U.S.A. **81 H5** 35 51N 98 25W
Watrous, Canada **73 C7** 51 40N 105 25W
Watrous, U.S.A. **81 H2** 35 48N 104 59W
Watsa, Dem. Rep. of the Congo **54 B2** 3 4N 29 30 E
Watseka, U.S.A. **76 E2** 40 47N 87 44W
Watson, Australia **61 F5** 30 29S 131 31 E
Watson, Canada **73 C8** 52 10N 104 30W
Watson Lake, Canada **72 A3** 60 6N 128 49W
Watsontown, U.S.A. **78 E8** 41 5N 76 52W
Watsonville, U.S.A. **84 J5** 36 55N 121 45W
Wattiwarriganna Cr. →, Australia **63 D2** 28 57S 136 10 E
Watuata = Batuata, Indonesia **37 F6** 6 12S 122 42 E
Watubela, Kepulauan, Indonesia **37 E8** 4 28S 131 35 E
Watubela Is. = Watubela, Kepulauan, Indonesia **37 E8** 4 28S 131 35 E
Wau = Wâw, Sudan **51 G11** 7 45N 28 1 E
Waubamik, Canada **78 A4** 45 27N 80 1W
Waubay, U.S.A. **80 C6** 45 20N 97 18W
Wauchope, N.S.W., Australia **63 E5** 31 28S 152 45 E
Wauchope, N. Terr., Australia **62 C1** 20 36S 134 15 E
Wauchula, U.S.A. **77 M5** 27 33N 81 49W
Waukarlycarly, L., Australia **60 D3** 21 18S 121 56 E
Waukegan, U.S.A. **76 D2** 42 22N 87 50W
Waukesha, U.S.A. **76 D1** 43 1N 88 14W
Waukon, U.S.A. **80 D9** 43 16N 91 29W
Waupaca, U.S.A. **80 C10** 44 21N 89 5W
Waupun, U.S.A. **80 D10** 43 38N 88 44W
Waurika, U.S.A. **81 H6** 34 10N 98 0W
Wausau, U.S.A. **80 C10** 44 58N 89 38W
Wautoma, U.S.A. **80 C10** 44 4N 89 18W
Wauwatosa, U.S.A. **76 D2** 43 3N 88 0W
Waveney →, U.K. **11 E9** 52 35N 1 39 E
Waverley, N.Z. **59 H5** 39 46S 174 37 E
Waverly, Iowa, U.S.A. **80 D8** 42 44N 92 29W
Waverly, N.Y., U.S.A. **79 E8** 42 1N 76 32W
Wavre, Belgium **15 D4** 50 43N 4 38 E
Wâw, Sudan **51 G11** 7 45N 28 1 E
Wâw al Kabir, Libya **51 C9** 25 20N 16 43 E
Wawa, Canada **70 C3** 47 59N 84 47W
Wawanesa, Canada **73 D9** 49 36N 99 40W
Wawona, U.S.A. **84 H7** 37 32N 119 39W
Waxahachie, U.S.A. **81 J6** 32 24N 96 51W
Way, L., Australia **61 E3** 26 45S 120 16 E
Waycross, U.S.A. **77 K4** 31 13N 82 21W
Wayland, U.S.A. **78 D7** 42 34N 77 35W
Wayne, Nebr., U.S.A. **80 D6** 42 14N 97 1W
Wayne, W. Va., U.S.A. **76 F4** 38 13N 82 27W
Waynesboro, Ga., U.S.A. **77 J4** 33 6N 82 1W
Waynesboro, Miss., U.S.A. **77 K1** 31 40N 88 39W
Waynesboro, Pa., U.S.A. **76 F7** 39 45N 77 35W
Waynesboro, Va., U.S.A. **76 F6** 38 4N 78 53W
Waynesburg, U.S.A. **76 F5** 39 54N 80 11W
Waynesville, U.S.A. **77 H4** 35 28N 82 58W
Waynoka, U.S.A. **81 G5** 36 35N 98 53W
Wazirabad, Pakistan **42 C6** 32 30N 74 8 E
We, Indonesia **36 C1** 5 51N 95 18 E
Weald, The, U.K. **11 F8** 51 4N 0 20 E
Wear →, U.K. **10 C6** 54 55N 1 23W
Weatherford, Okla., U.S.A. **81 H5** 35 32N 98 43W
Weatherford, Tex., U.S.A. **81 J6** 32 46N 97 48W
Weaverville, U.S.A. **82 F2** 40 44N 122 56W
Webb City, U.S.A. **81 G7** 37 9N 94 28W
Webequie, Canada **70 B2** 52 59N 87 21W
Webster, Mass., U.S.A. **79 D13** 42 3N 71 53W
Webster, N.Y., U.S.A. **78 C7** 43 13N 77 26W
Webster, S. Dak., U.S.A. **80 C6** 45 20N 97 31W
Webster City, U.S.A. **80 D8** 42 28N 93 49W
Webster Springs, U.S.A. **76 F5** 38 29N 80 25W
Weda, Indonesia **37 D7** 0 21N 127 50 E
Weda, Teluk, Indonesia **37 D7** 0 20N 128 0 E
Weddell I., Falk. Is. **96 G4** 51 50S 61 0W
Weddell Sea, Antarctica **5 D1** 72 30S 40 0W
Wedderburn, Australia **63 F3** 36 26S 143 33 E
Wedgeport, Canada **71 D6** 43 44N 65 59W
Wedza, Zimbabwe **55 F3** 18 40S 31 33 E
Wee Waa, Australia **63 E4** 30 11S 149 26 E
Weed, U.S.A. **82 F2** 41 25N 122 23W
Weed Heights, U.S.A. **84 G7** 38 59N 119 13W
Weedsport, U.S.A. **79 C8** 43 3N 76 35W
Weedville, U.S.A. **78 E6** 41 17N 78 30W
Weenen, S. Africa **57 D5** 28 48S 30 7 E
Weert, Neths. **15 C5** 51 15N 5 43 E
Wei He →, Hebei, China **34 F8** 36 10N 115 45 E
Wei He →, Shaanxi, China **34 G6** 34 38N 110 15 E
Weichang, China **35 D9** 41 58N 117 49 E
Weichuan, China **34 G7** 34 20N 113 59 E
Weiden, Germany **16 D7** 49 41N 12 10 E
Weifang, China **35 F10** 36 44N 119 7 E
Weihai, China **35 F12** 37 30N 122 6 E
Weimar, Germany **16 C6** 50 58N 11 19 E
Weinan, China **34 G5** 34 31N 109 29 E
Weipa, Australia **62 A3** 12 40S 141 50 E
Weir →, Australia **63 D4** 28 20S 149 50 E
Weir →, Canada **73 B10** 56 54N 93 21W
Weir River, Canada **73 B10** 56 49N 94 6W
Weirton, U.S.A. **78 F4** 40 24N 80 35W
Weiser, U.S.A. **82 D5** 44 10N 117 0W
Weishan, China **35 G9** 34 47N 117 5 E
Weiyuan, China **34 G3** 35 7N 104 10 E
Wejherowo, Poland **17 A10** 54 35N 18 12 E
Wekusko L., Canada **73 C9** 54 40N 99 50W
Welch, U.S.A. **76 G5** 37 26N 81 35W
Welkom, S. Africa **56 D4** 28 0S 26 46 E
Welland, Canada **78 D5** 43 0N 79 15W
Welland →, U.K. **11 E7** 52 51N 0 5W
Wellesley Is., Australia **62 B2** 16 42S 139 30 E
Wellingborough, U.K. **11 E7** 52 19N 0 41W
Wellington, Australia **63 E4** 32 35S 148 59 E
Wellington, Canada **78 C7** 43 57N 77 20W
Wellington, N.Z. **59 J5** 41 19S 174 46 E
Wellington, S. Africa **56 E2** 33 38S 19 1 E
Wellington, Somst., U.K. **11 G4** 50 58N 3 13W
Wellington, Telford & Wrekin, U.K. **11 E5** 52 42N 2 30W
Wellington, Colo., U.S.A. **80 E2** 40 42N 105 0W
Wellington, Kans., U.S.A. **81 G6** 37 16N 97 24W
Wellington, Nev., U.S.A. **84 G7** 38 45N 119 23W
Wellington, Ohio, U.S.A. **78 E2** 41 10N 82 13W
Wellington, Tex., U.S.A. **81 H4** 34 51N 100 13W
Wellington, I., Chile **96 F2** 49 30S 75 0W
Wellington, L., Australia **63 F4** 38 6S 147 20 E
Wells, U.K. **11 F5** 51 13N 2 39W
Wells, Maine, U.S.A. **79 C14** 43 20N 70 35W
Wells, N.Y., U.S.A. **79 C10** 43 24N 74 17W
Wells, Nev., U.S.A. **82 F6** 41 7N 114 58W
Wells, L., Australia **61 E3** 26 44S 123 15 E
Wells, Mt., Australia **60 C4** 17 25S 127 8 E
Wells Gray Prov. Park, Canada **72 C4** 52 30N 120 15W
Wells-next-the-Sea, U.K. **10 E8** 52 57N 0 51 E
Wells River, U.S.A. **79 B12** 44 9N 72 4W
Wellsboro, U.S.A. **78 E7** 41 45N 77 18W
Wellsburg, U.S.A. **78 F4** 40 16N 80 37W
Wellsville, N.Y., U.S.A. **78 D7** 42 7N 77 57W
Wellsville, Ohio, U.S.A. **78 F4** 40 36N 80 39W
Wellsville, Utah, U.S.A. **82 F8** 41 38N 111 56W
Wellton, U.S.A. **83 K6** 32 40N 114 8W
Wels, Austria **16 D8** 48 9N 14 1 E
Welshpool, U.K. **11 E4** 52 39N 3 8W
Welwyn Garden City, U.K. **11 F7** 51 48N 0 12W
Wem, U.K. **10 E5** 52 52N 2 44W
Wembere →, Tanzania **54 C3** 4 10S 34 15 E
Wemindji, Canada **70 B4** 53 0N 78 49W
Wen Xian, China **34 G7** 34 55N 113 5 E
Wenatchee, U.S.A. **82 C3** 47 25N 120 19W
Wenchang, China **38 C8** 19 38N 110 42 E
Wenchi, Ghana **50 G5** 7 46N 2 8W
Wenchow = Wenzhou, China **33 D7** 28 0N 120 38 E
Wenden, U.S.A. **85 M13** 33 49N 113 33W
Wendeng, China **35 F12** 37 15N 122 5 E
Wendesi, Indonesia **37 E8** 2 30S 134 17 E
Wendover, U.S.A. **82 F6** 40 44N 114 2W
Wenlock →, Australia **62 A3** 12 2S 141 55 E
Wenshan, China **32 D5** 23 20N 104 18 E
Wenshang, China **34 G9** 35 45N 116 30 E
Wenshui, China **34 F7** 37 26N 112 1 E
Wensleydale, U.K. **10 C6** 54 17N 2 0W
Wensu, China **32 B3** 41 15N 80 10 E
Wensum →, U.K. **10 E8** 52 40N 1 15 E
Wentworth, Australia **63 E3** 34 2S 141 54 E
Wentzel L., Canada **72 B6** 59 2N 114 28W
Wenut, Indonesia **37 E8** 3 11S 133 19 E
Wenxi, China **34 G6** 35 20N 111 10 E
Wenxian, China **34 H3** 32 43N 104 36 E
Wenzhou, China **33 D7** 28 0N 120 38 E
Weott, U.S.A. **82 F2** 40 20N 123 55W
Wepener, S. Africa **56 D4** 29 42S 27 3 E
Werda, Botswana **56 D3** 25 24S 23 15 E
Weri, Indonesia **37 E8** 3 10S 132 38 E
Werra →, Germany **16 C5** 51 24N 9 39 E
Werrimull, Australia **63 E3** 34 25S 141 38 E
Werris Creek, Australia **63 E5** 31 18S 150 38 E
Weser →, Germany **16 B5** 53 36N 8 28 E
Wesiri, Indonesia **37 F7** 7 30S 126 30 E
Weslemkoon L., Canada **78 A7** 45 2N 77 25W
Wesleyville, Canada **71 C9** 49 8N 53 36W
Wesleyville, U.S.A. **78 D4** 42 9N 80 0W
Wessel, C., Australia **62 A2** 10 59S 136 46 E
Wessel Is., Australia **62 A2** 11 10S 136 45 E
Wessington Springs, U.S.A. **80 C5** 44 5N 98 34W
West, U.S.A. **81 K6** 31 48N 97 6W
West →, U.S.A. **79 D12** 42 52N 72 33W
West Baines →, Australia **60 C4** 15 38S 129 59 E
West Bank □, Asia **47 C4** 32 6N 35 13 E
West Bend, U.S.A. **76 D1** 43 25N 88 11W
West Bengal □, India **43 H13** 23 0N 88 0 E
West Berkshire □, U.K. **11 F6** 51 25N 1 17W
West Beskids = Západné Beskydy, Europe **17 D10** 49 30N 19 0 E
West Branch, U.S.A. **76 C3** 44 17N 84 14W
West Branch Susquehanna →, U.S.A. **79 F8** 40 53N 76 48W
West Bromwich, U.K. **11 E6** 52 32N 1 59W
West Burra, U.K. **12 A7** 60 5N 1 21W
West Canada Cr. →, U.S.A. **79 C10** 43 1N 74 58W
West Cape Howe, Australia **61 G2** 35 8S 117 36 E
West Chazy, U.S.A. **79 B11** 44 49N 73 28W
West Chester, U.S.A. **79 G9** 39 58N 75 36W
West Columbia, U.S.A. **81 L7** 29 9N 95 39W
West Covina, U.S.A. **85 L9** 34 4N 117 54W
West Des Moines, U.S.A. **80 E8** 41 35N 93 43W
West Dunbartonshire □, U.K. **12 F4** 55 59N 4 30W
West End, Bahamas **88 A4** 26 41N 78 58W
West Falkland, Falk. Is. **96 G5** 51 40S 60 0W
West Fargo, U.S.A. **80 B6** 46 52N 96 54W
West Farmington, U.S.A. **78 E4** 41 23N 80 58W
West Fjord = Vestfjorden, Norway **8 C15** 67 55N 14 0 E
West Fork Trinity →, U.S.A. **81 J6** 32 48N 96 54W
West Frankfort, U.S.A. **80 G10** 37 54N 88 55W
West Hartford, U.S.A. **79 E12** 41 45N 72 44W
West Haven, U.S.A. **79 E12** 41 17N 72 57W
West Hazleton, U.S.A. **79 F9** 40 58N 76 0W
West Helena, U.S.A. **81 H9** 34 33N 90 38W

West Hurley, *U.S.A.* **79 E10** 41 59N 74 7W
West Ice Shelf, *Antarctica* **5 C7** 67 0S 85 0 E
West Indies, *Cent. Amer.* **89 D7** 15 0N 65 0W
West Jordan, *U.S.A.* **82 F8** 40 36N 111 56W
West Lorne, *Canada* **78 D3** 42 36N 81 36W
West Lothian □, *U.K.* **12 F5** 55 54N 3 36W
West Lunga →, *Zambia* **55 E1** 13 6S 24 39 E
West Memphis, *U.S.A.* **81 H9** 35 9N 90 11W
West Midlands □, *U.K.* **11 E6** 52 26N 2 0W
West Mifflin, *U.S.A.* **78 F5** 40 22N 79 52W
West Milton, *U.S.A.* **78 E8** 41 1N 76 50W
West Monroe, *U.S.A.* **81 J8** 32 31N 92 9W
West Newton, *U.S.A.* **78 F5** 40 14N 79 46W
West Nicholson, *Zimbabwe* **55 G2** 21 2S 29 20 E
West Palm Beach, *U.S.A.* **77 M5** 26 43N 80 3W
West Plains, *U.S.A.* **81 G9** 36 44N 91 51W
West Point, *N.Y., U.S.A.* **79 E11** 41 24N 73 58W
West Point, *Nebr., U.S.A.* **80 E6** 41 51N 96 43W
West Point, *Va., U.S.A.* **76 G7** 37 32N 76 48W
West Pt. = Ouest, Pte. de l', *Canada* **71 C7** 49 52N 64 40W
West Pt., *Australia* **63 F2** 35 1S 135 56 E
West Road →, *Canada* **72 C4** 53 18N 122 53W
West Rutland, *U.S.A.* **79 C11** 43 38N 73 5W
West Schelde = Westerschelde →, *Neths.* **15 C3** 51 25N 3 25 E
West Seneca, *U.S.A.* **78 D6** 42 51N 78 48W
West Siberian Plain, *Russia* **28 C11** 62 0N 75 0 E
West Sussex □, *U.K.* **11 G7** 50 55N 0 30W
West-Terschelling, *Neths.* **15 A5** 53 22N 5 13 E
West Valley City, *U.S.A.* **82 F8** 40 42N 111 57W
West Virginia □, *U.S.A.* **76 F5** 38 45N 80 30W
West-Vlaanderen □, *Belgium* **15 D2** 51 0N 3 0 E
West Walker →, *U.S.A.* **84 G7** 38 54N 119 9W
West Wyalong, *Australia* **63 E4** 33 56S 147 10 E
West Yellowstone, *U.S.A.* **82 D8** 44 40N 111 6W
West Yorkshire □, *U.K.* **10 D6** 53 45N 1 40W
Westall Pt., *Australia* **63 E1** 32 55S 134 4 E
Westbrook, *U.S.A.* **77 D10** 43 41N 70 22W
Westbury, *Australia* **62 G4** 41 30S 146 51 E
Westby, *U.S.A.* **80 A2** 48 52N 104 3W
Westend, *U.S.A.* **85 K9** 35 42N 117 24W
Westerland, *Germany* **9 J13** 54 54N 8 17 E
Westerly, *U.S.A.* **79 E13** 41 22N 71 50W
Western □, *Kenya* **54 B3** 0 30N 34 30 E
Western □, *Zambia* **55 F1** 15 0S 24 4 E
Western Australia □, *Australia* **61 E2** 25 0S 118 0 E
Western Cape □, *S. Africa* **56 E3** 34 0S 20 0 E
Western Dvina = Daugava →, *Latvia* **9 H21** 57 4N 24 3 E
Western Ghats, *India* **40 N9** 14 0N 75 0 E
Western Isles □, *U.K.* **12 D1** 57 30N 7 10W
Western Sahara ■, *Africa* **50 D3** 25 0N 13 0W
Western Samoa = Samoa ■, *Pac. Oc.* **59 B13** 14 0S 172 0W
Westernport, *U.S.A.* **76 F6** 39 29N 79 3W
Westerschelde →, *Neths.* **15 C3** 51 25N 3 25 E
Westerwald, *Germany* **16 C4** 50 38N 7 56 E
Westfield, *Mass., U.S.A.* **79 D12** 42 7N 72 45W
Westfield, *N.Y., U.S.A.* **78 D5** 42 20N 79 35W
Westfield, *Pa., U.S.A.* **78 E7** 41 55N 77 32W
Westhill, *U.K.* **12 D6** 57 9N 2 19W
Westhope, *U.S.A.* **80 A4** 48 55N 101 1W
Westland Bight, *N.Z.* **59 K3** 42 55S 170 5 E
Westlock, *Canada* **72 C6** 54 9N 113 55W
Westmar, *Australia* **63 D4** 27 55S 149 44 E
Westmeath □, *Ireland* **13 C4** 53 33N 7 34W
Westminster, *U.S.A.* **76 F7** 39 34N 76 59W
Westmont, *U.S.A.* **78 F6** 40 19N 78 58W
Westmorland, *U.S.A.* **85 M11** 33 2N 115 37W
Weston, *Oreg., U.S.A.* **82 D4** 45 49N 118 26W
Weston, *W. Va., U.S.A.* **76 F5** 39 2N 80 28W
Weston I., *Canada* **70 B4** 52 33N 79 36W
Weston-super-Mare, *U.K.* **11 F5** 51 21N 2 58W
Westover, *U.S.A.* **78 F6** 40 45N 78 40W
Westport, *Canada* **79 B8** 44 40N 76 25W
Westport, *Ireland* **13 C2** 53 48N 9 31W
Westport, *N.Z.* **59 J3** 41 46S 171 37 E
Westport, *N.Y., U.S.A.* **79 B11** 44 11N 73 26W
Westport, *Oreg., U.S.A.* **84 D3** 46 8N 123 23W
Westport, *Wash., U.S.A.* **84 D2** 46 53N 124 6W
Westray, *Canada* **73 C8** 53 36N 101 24W
Westray, *U.K.* **12 B5** 59 18N 3 0W
Westree, *Canada* **70 C3** 47 26N 81 34W
Westville, *U.S.A.* **84 F6** 39 8N 120 42W
Westwood, *U.S.A.* **82 F3** 40 18N 121 0W
Wetar, *Indonesia* **37 F7** 7 48S 126 30 E
Wetaskiwin, *Canada* **72 C6** 52 55N 113 24W
Wete, *Tanzania* **52 F7** 5 4S 39 43 E
Wetherby, *U.K.* **10 D6** 53 56N 1 23W
Wethersfield, *U.S.A.* **79 E12** 41 42N 72 40W
Wetteren, *Belgium* **15 D3** 51 0N 3 53 E
Wetzlar, *Germany* **16 C5** 50 32N 8 31 E
Wewoka, *U.S.A.* **81 H6** 35 9N 96 30W
Wexford, *Ireland* **13 D5** 52 20N 6 28W
Wexford □, *Ireland* **13 D5** 52 20N 6 25W
Wexford Harbour, *Ireland* **13 D5** 52 20N 6 25W
Weyburn, *Canada* **73 D8** 49 40N 103 50W
Weymouth, *Canada* **71 D6** 44 30N 66 1W
Weymouth, *U.K.* **11 G5** 50 37N 2 28W
Weymouth, *U.S.A.* **79 D14** 42 13N 70 58W
Weymouth, C., *Australia* **62 A3** 12 37S 143 27 E
Wha Ti, *Canada* **68 B8** 63 8N 117 16W
Whakatane, *N.Z.* **59 G6** 37 57S 177 1 E
Whale →, *Canada* **71 A6** 58 15N 67 40W
Whale Cove, *Canada* **73 A10** 62 11N 92 36W
Whales, B. of, *Antarctica* **5 D12** 78 0S 165 0W
Whalsay, *U.K.* **12 A8** 60 22N 0 59W
Whangamomona, *N.Z.* **59 H5** 39 8S 174 44 E
Whangarei, *N.Z.* **59 F5** 35 43S 174 21 E
Whangarei Harb., *N.Z.* **59 F5** 35 45S 174 28 E
Wharfe →, *U.K.* **10 D6** 53 51N 1 9W
Wharfedale, *U.K.* **10 C5** 54 6N 2 1W
Wharton, *N.J., U.S.A.* **79 F10** 40 54N 74 35W
Wharton, *Pa., U.S.A.* **78 E6** 41 31N 78 1W
Wharton, *Tex., U.S.A.* **81 L6** 29 19N 96 6W
Wheatland, *Calif., U.S.A.* **84 F5** 39 1N 121 25W
Wheatland, *Wyo., U.S.A.* **80 D2** 42 3N 104 58W
Wheatley, *Canada* **78 D2** 42 6N 82 27W
Wheaton, *Md., U.S.A.* **76 F7** 39 3N 77 3W
Wheaton, *Minn., U.S.A.* **80 C6** 45 48N 96 30W
Wheelbarrow Pk., *U.S.A.* **84 H10** 37 26N 116 5W
Wheeler, *Oreg., U.S.A.* **82 D2** 45 41N 123 53W
Wheeler, *Tex., U.S.A.* **81 H4** 35 27N 100 16W
Wheeler →, *Canada* **71 A6** 57 2N 67 13W
Wheeler L., *U.S.A.* **77 H2** 34 48N 87 23W
Wheeler Pk., *N. Mex., U.S.A.* **83 H11** 36 34N 105 25W
Wheeler Pk., *Nev., U.S.A.* **83 G6** 38 57N 114 15W
Wheeler Ridge, *U.S.A.* **85 L8** 35 0N 118 57W
Wheeling, *U.S.A.* **78 F4** 40 4N 80 43W
Whernside, *U.K.* **10 C5** 54 14N 2 24W
Whiskey Jack L., *Canada* **73 B8** 58 23N 101 55W
Whistleduck Cr. →, *Australia* **62 C2** 20 15S 135 18 E
Whistler, *Canada* **72 C4** 50 7N 122 58W
Whitby, *Canada* **78 C6** 43 52N 78 56W
Whitby, *U.K.* **10 C7** 54 29N 0 37W
White →, *Ark., U.S.A.* **81 J9** 33 57N 91 5W
White →, *Ind., U.S.A.* **76 F2** 38 25N 87 45W
White →, *S. Dak., U.S.A.* **80 D5** 43 42N 99 27W
White →, *Tex., U.S.A.* **81 J4** 33 14N 100 56W
White →, *Utah, U.S.A.* **82 F9** 40 4N 109 41W
White →, *Vt., U.S.A.* **79 C12** 43 37N 72 20W
White →, *Wash., U.S.A.* **84 C4** 47 12N 122 15W
White, L., *Australia* **60 D4** 21 9S 128 56 E
White B., *Canada* **71 C8** 50 0N 56 35W
White Bird, *U.S.A.* **82 D5** 45 46N 116 18W
White Butte, *U.S.A.* **80 B3** 46 23N 103 18W
White City, *U.S.A.* **82 E2** 42 26N 122 51W
White Cliffs, *Australia* **63 E3** 30 50S 143 10 E
White Hall, *U.S.A.* **80 F9** 39 26N 90 24W
White Haven, *U.S.A.* **79 E9** 41 4N 75 47W
White Horse, Vale of, *U.K.* **11 F6** 51 37N 1 30W
White I., *N.Z.* **59 G6** 37 30S 177 13 E
White L., *Canada* **79 A8** 45 18N 76 31W
White L., *U.S.A.* **81 L8** 29 44N 92 30W
White Mountain Peak, *U.S.A.* **83 G4** 37 38N 118 15W
White Mts., *Calif., U.S.A.* **84 H8** 37 30N 118 15W
White Mts., *N.H., U.S.A.* **79 B13** 44 15N 71 15W
White Nile = Nîl el Abyad →, *Sudan* **51 E12** 15 38N 32 31 E
White Otter L., *Canada* **70 C1** 49 5N 91 55W
White Pass, *U.S.A.* **84 D5** 46 38N 121 24W
White Plains, *U.S.A.* **79 E11** 41 2N 73 46W
White River, *Canada* **70 C2** 48 35N 85 20W
White River, *S. Africa* **57 D5** 25 20S 31 0 E
White River, *U.S.A.* **80 D4** 43 34N 100 45W
White Rock, *Canada* **84 A4** 49 2N 122 48W
White Russia = Belarus ■, *Europe* **17 B14** 53 30N 27 0 E
White Sea = Beloye More, *Russia* **24 A6** 66 30N 38 0 E
White Sulphur Springs, *Mont., U.S.A.* **82 C8** 46 33N 110 54W
White Sulphur Springs, *W. Va., U.S.A.* **76 G5** 37 48N 80 18W
White Swan, *U.S.A.* **84 D6** 46 23N 120 44W
Whitecliffs, *N.Z.* **59 K3** 43 26S 171 55 E
Whitecourt, *Canada* **72 C5** 54 10N 115 45W
Whiteface Mt., *U.S.A.* **79 B11** 44 22N 73 54W
Whitefield, *U.S.A.* **79 B13** 44 23N 71 37W
Whitefish, *U.S.A.* **82 B6** 48 25N 114 20W
Whitefish L., *Canada* **73 A7** 62 41N 106 48W
Whitefish Point, *U.S.A.* **76 B3** 46 45N 84 59W
Whitegull, L., *Canada* **71 A7** 55 27N 64 17W
Whitehall, *Mich., U.S.A.* **76 D2** 43 24N 86 21W
Whitehall, *Mont., U.S.A.* **82 D7** 45 52N 112 6W
Whitehall, *N.Y., U.S.A.* **79 C11** 43 33N 73 24W
Whitehall, *Wis., U.S.A.* **80 C9** 44 22N 91 19W
Whitehaven, *U.K.* **10 C4** 54 33N 3 35W
Whitehorse, *Canada* **72 A1** 60 43N 135 3W
Whitemark, *Australia* **62 G4** 40 7S 148 3 E
Whiteriver, *U.S.A.* **83 K9** 33 50N 109 58W
Whitesand →, *Canada* **72 A5** 60 9N 115 45W
Whitesands, *S. Africa* **56 E3** 34 23S 20 50 E
Whitesboro, *N.Y., U.S.A.* **79 C9** 43 7N 75 18W
Whitesboro, *Tex., U.S.A.* **81 J6** 33 39N 96 54W
Whiteshell Prov. Park, *Canada* **73 D9** 50 0N 95 40W
Whitesville, *U.S.A.* **78 D7** 42 2N 77 46W
Whiteville, *U.S.A.* **77 H6** 34 20N 78 42W
Whitewater, *U.S.A.* **76 D1** 42 50N 88 44W
Whitewater Baldy, *U.S.A.* **83 K9** 33 20N 108 39W
Whitewater L., *Canada* **70 B2** 50 50N 89 10W
Whitewood, *Australia* **62 C3** 21 28S 143 30 E
Whitewood, *Canada* **73 C8** 50 20N 102 20W
Whithorn, *U.K.* **12 G4** 54 44N 4 26W
Whitianga, *N.Z.* **59 G5** 36 47S 175 41 E
Whitman, *U.S.A.* **79 D14** 42 5N 70 56W
Whitney, *Canada* **78 A6** 45 31N 78 14W
Whitney, Mt., *U.S.A.* **84 J8** 36 35N 118 18W
Whitney Point, *U.S.A.* **79 D9** 42 20N 75 58W
Whitstable, *U.K.* **11 F9** 51 21N 1 3 E
Whitsunday I., *Australia* **62 C4** 20 15S 149 4 E
Whittier, *U.S.A.* **85 M8** 33 58N 118 3W
Whittlesea, *Australia* **63 F4** 37 27S 145 9 E
Wholdaia L., *Canada* **73 A8** 60 43N 104 20W
Whyalla, *Australia* **63 E2** 33 2S 137 30 E
Wiarton, *Canada* **78 B3** 44 40N 81 10W
Wiay, *U.K.* **12 D1** 57 24N 7 13W
Wibaux, *U.S.A.* **80 B2** 46 59N 104 11W
Wichian Buri, *Thailand* **38 E3** 15 39N 101 7 E
Wichita, *U.S.A.* **81 G6** 37 42N 97 20W
Wichita Falls, *U.S.A.* **81 J5** 33 54N 98 30W
Wick, *U.K.* **12 C5** 58 26N 3 5W
Wicked Pt., *Canada* **78 C7** 43 52N 77 15W
Wickenburg, *U.S.A.* **83 K7** 33 58N 112 44W
Wickepin, *Australia* **61 F2** 32 50S 117 30 E
Wickham, *Australia* **60 D2** 20 42S 117 11 E
Wickham, C., *Australia* **62 F3** 39 35S 143 57 E
Wickliffe, *U.S.A.* **78 E3** 41 36N 81 28W
Wicklow, *Ireland* **13 D5** 52 59N 6 3W
Wicklow □, *Ireland* **13 D5** 52 57N 6 25W
Wicklow Hd., *Ireland* **13 D6** 52 58N 6 0W
Wicklow Mts., *Ireland* **13 C5** 52 58N 6 26W
Widgeegoara Cr. →, *Australia* **63 D4** 28 51S 146 34 E
Widgiemooltha, *Australia* **61 F3** 31 30S 121 34 E
Widnes, *U.K.* **10 D5** 53 23N 2 45W
Wieluń, *Poland* **17 C10** 51 15N 18 34 E
Wien, *Austria* **16 D9** 48 12N 16 22 E
Wiener Neustadt, *Austria* **16 E9** 47 49N 16 16 E
Wiesbaden, *Germany* **16 C5** 50 4N 8 14 E
Wigan, *U.K.* **10 D5** 53 33N 2 38W
Wiggins, *Colo., U.S.A.* **80 E2** 40 14N 104 4W
Wiggins, *Miss., U.S.A.* **81 K10** 30 51N 89 8W
Wight, I. of □, *U.K.* **11 G6** 50 40N 1 20W
Wigston, *U.K.* **11 E6** 52 35N 1 6W
Wigton, *U.K.* **10 C4** 54 50N 3 10W
Wigtown, *U.K.* **12 G4** 54 53N 4 27W
Wigtown B., *U.K.* **12 G4** 54 46N 4 15W
Wilber, *U.S.A.* **80 E6** 40 29N 96 58W
Wilberforce, *Canada* **78 A6** 45 2N 78 13W
Wilberforce, C., *Australia* **62 A2** 11 54S 136 35 E
Wilburton, *U.S.A.* **81 H7** 34 55N 95 19W
Wilcannia, *Australia* **63 E3** 31 30S 143 26 E
Wilcox, *U.S.A.* **78 E6** 41 35N 78 41W
Wildrose, *U.S.A.* **85 J9** 36 14N 117 11W
Wildspitze, *Austria* **16 E6** 46 53N 10 53 E
Wilge →, *S. Africa* **57 D4** 27 3S 28 20 E
Wilhelm II Coast, *Antarctica* **5 C7** 68 0S 90 0 E
Wilhelmshaven, *Germany* **16 B5** 53 31N 8 7 E
Wilhelmstal, *Namibia* **56 C2** 21 58S 16 21 E
Wilkes-Barre, *U.S.A.* **79 E9** 41 15N 75 53W
Wilkie, *Canada* **73 C7** 52 27N 108 42W
Wilkinsburg, *U.S.A.* **78 F5** 40 26N 79 53W
Wilkinson Lakes, *Australia* **61 E5** 29 40S 132 39 E
Willandra Creek →, *Australia* **63 E4** 33 22S 145 52 E
Willapa B., *U.S.A.* **82 C2** 46 40N 124 0W
Willapa Hills, *U.S.A.* **84 D3** 46 35N 123 25W
Willard, *N.Y., U.S.A.* **78 D8** 42 40N 76 50W
Willard, *Ohio, U.S.A.* **78 E2** 41 3N 82 44W
Willcox, *U.S.A.* **83 K9** 32 15N 109 50W
Willemstad, *Neth. Ant.* **89 D6** 12 5N 69 0W
Willet, *U.S.A.* **79 D9** 42 28N 75 55W
William →, *Canada* **73 B7** 59 8N 109 19W
William 'Bill' Dannely Res., *U.S.A.* **77 J2** 32 10N 87 10W
William Creek, *Australia* **63 D2** 28 58S 136 22 E
Williams, *Australia* **61 F2** 33 2S 116 52 E
Williams, *Ariz., U.S.A.* **83 J7** 35 15N 112 11W
Williams, *Calif., U.S.A.* **84 F4** 39 9N 122 9W
Williams Harbour, *Canada* **71 B8** 52 33N 55 47W
Williams Lake, *Canada* **72 C4** 52 10N 122 10W
Williamsburg, *Ky., U.S.A.* **77 G3** 36 44N 84 10W
Williamsburg, *Pa., U.S.A.* **78 F6** 40 28N 78 12W
Williamsburg, *Va., U.S.A.* **76 G7** 37 17N 76 44W
Williamson, *N.Y., U.S.A.* **78 C7** 43 14N 77 11W
Williamson, *W. Va., U.S.A.* **76 G4** 37 41N 82 17W
Williamsport, *U.S.A.* **78 E7** 41 15N 77 0W
Williamston, *U.S.A.* **77 H7** 35 51N 77 4W
Williamstown, *Australia* **63 F3** 37 51S 144 52 E
Williamstown, *Ky., U.S.A.* **76 F3** 38 38N 84 34W
Williamstown, *Mass., U.S.A.* **79 D11** 42 41N 73 12W
Williamstown, *N.Y., U.S.A.* **79 C9** 43 26N 75 53W
Willimantic, *U.S.A.* **79 E12** 41 43N 72 13W
Willingboro, *U.S.A.* **76 E8** 40 3N 74 54W
Willis Group, *Australia* **62 B5** 16 18S 150 0 E
Williston, *S. Africa* **56 E3** 31 20S 20 53 E
Williston, *Fla., U.S.A.* **77 L4** 29 23N 82 27W
Williston, *N. Dak., U.S.A.* **80 A3** 48 9N 103 37W
Williston L., *Canada* **72 B4** 56 0N 124 0W
Willits, *U.S.A.* **82 G2** 39 25N 123 21W
Willmar, *U.S.A.* **80 C7** 45 7N 95 3W
Willoughby, *U.S.A.* **78 E3** 41 39N 81 24W
Willow Bunch, *Canada* **73 D7** 49 20N 105 35W
Willow L., *Canada* **72 A5** 62 10N 119 8W
Willow Wall, The, *China* **35 C12** 42 10N 122 0 E
Willowick, *U.S.A.* **78 E3** 41 38N 81 28W
Willowlake →, *Canada* **72 A4** 62 42N 123 8W
Willowmore, *S. Africa* **56 E3** 33 15S 23 30 E
Willows, *U.S.A.* **84 F4** 39 31N 122 12W
Willowvale = Gatyana, *S. Africa* **57 E4** 32 16S 28 31 E
Wills, L., *Australia* **60 D4** 21 25S 128 51 E
Wills Cr. →, *Australia* **62 C3** 22 43S 140 2 E
Willsboro, *U.S.A.* **79 B11** 44 21N 73 24W
Willunga, *Australia* **63 F2** 35 15S 138 30 E
Wilmette, *U.S.A.* **76 D2** 42 5N 87 42W
Wilmington, *Australia* **63 E2** 32 39S 138 7 E
Wilmington, *Del., U.S.A.* **76 F8** 39 45N 75 33W
Wilmington, *N.C., U.S.A.* **77 H7** 34 14N 77 55W
Wilmington, *Ohio, U.S.A.* **76 F4** 39 27N 83 50W
Wilmington, *Vt., U.S.A.* **79 D12** 42 52N 72 52W
Wilmslow, *U.K.* **10 D5** 53 19N 2 13W
Wilpena Cr. →, *Australia* **63 E2** 31 25S 139 29 E
Wilsall, *U.S.A.* **82 D8** 45 59N 110 38W
Wilson, *N.C., U.S.A.* **77 H7** 35 44N 77 55W
Wilson, *N.Y., U.S.A.* **78 C6** 43 19N 78 50W
Wilson, *Pa., U.S.A.* **79 F9** 40 41N 75 15W
Wilson →, *Australia* **60 C4** 16 48S 128 16 E
Wilson Bluff, *Australia* **61 F4** 31 41S 129 0 E
Wilson Inlet, *Australia* **61 G2** 35 0S 117 22 E
Wilsons Promontory, *Australia* **63 F4** 38 55S 146 25 E
Wilton, *U.S.A.* **80 B4** 47 10N 100 47W
Wilton →, *Australia* **62 A1** 14 45S 134 33 E
Wiltshire □, *U.K.* **11 F6** 51 18N 1 53W
Wiltz, *Lux.* **15 E5** 49 57N 5 55 E
Wiluna, *Australia* **61 E3** 26 36S 120 14 E
Wimborne Minster, *U.K.* **11 G6** 50 48N 1 59W
Wimmera →, *Australia* **63 F3** 36 8S 141 56 E
Winam G., *Kenya* **54 C3** 0 20S 34 15 E
Winburg, *S. Africa* **56 D4** 28 30S 27 2 E
Winchendon, *U.S.A.* **79 D12** 42 41N 72 3W
Winchester, *U.K.* **11 F6** 51 4N 1 18W
Winchester, *Conn., U.S.A.* **79 E11** 41 53N 73 9W
Winchester, *Idaho, U.S.A.* **82 C5** 46 14N 116 38W
Winchester, *Ind., U.S.A.* **76 E3** 40 10N 84 59W
Winchester, *Ky., U.S.A.* **76 G3** 38 0N 84 11W
Winchester, *N.H., U.S.A.* **79 D12** 42 46N 72 23W
Winchester, *Nev., U.S.A.* **85 J11** 36 6N 115 10W
Winchester, *Tenn., U.S.A.* **77 H2** 35 11N 86 7W
Winchester, *Va., U.S.A.* **76 F6** 39 11N 78 10W
Wind →, *U.S.A.* **82 E9** 43 12N 108 12W
Wind River Range, *U.S.A.* **82 E9** 43 0N 109 30W
Windau = Ventspils, *Latvia* **9 H19** 57 25N 21 32 E
Windber, *U.S.A.* **78 F6** 40 14N 78 50W
Winder, *U.S.A.* **77 J4** 34 0N 83 45W
Windermere, *U.K.* **10 C5** 54 23N 2 55W
Windhoek, *Namibia* **56 C2** 22 35S 17 4 E
Windom, *U.S.A.* **80 D7** 43 52N 95 7W
Windorah, *Australia* **62 D3** 25 24S 142 36 E
Window Rock, *U.S.A.* **83 J9** 35 41N 109 3W
Windrush →, *U.K.* **11 F6** 51 43N 1 24W
Windsor, *Australia* **63 E5** 33 37S 150 50 E
Windsor, *N.S., Canada* **71 D7** 44 59N 64 5W
Windsor, *Ont., Canada* **78 D2** 42 18N 83 0W
Windsor, *U.K.* **11 F7** 51 29N 0 36W
Windsor, *Colo., U.S.A.* **80 E2** 40 29N 104 54W
Windsor, *Conn., U.S.A.* **79 E12** 41 50N 72 39W
Windsor, *Mo., U.S.A.* **80 F8** 38 32N 93 31W
Windsor, *N.Y., U.S.A.* **79 D9** 42 5N 75 37W
Windsor, *Vt., U.S.A.* **79 C12** 43 29N 72 24W
Windsor & Maidenhead □, *U.K.* **11 F7** 51 29N 0 40W
Windsorton, *S. Africa* **56 D3** 28 16S 24 44 E
Windward Is., *W. Indies* **89 D7** 13 0N 61 0W
Windward Passage = Vientos, Paso de los, *Caribbean* **89 C5** 20 0N 74 0W
Winefred L., *Canada* **73 B6** 55 30N 110 30W
Winfield, *U.S.A.* **81 G6** 37 15N 96 59W
Wingate Mts., *Australia* **60 B5** 14 25S 130 40 E
Wingham, *Australia* **63 E5** 31 48S 152 22 E
Wingham, *Canada* **78 C3** 43 55N 81 20W
Winisk, *Canada* **70 A2** 55 20N 85 15W
Winisk →, *Canada* **70 A2** 55 17N 85 5W
Winisk L., *Canada* **70 B2** 52 55N 87 22W
Wink, *U.S.A.* **81 K3** 31 45N 103 9W
Winkler, *Canada* **73 D9** 49 10N 97 56W
Winlock, *U.S.A.* **84 D4** 46 30N 122 56W
Winnebago, L., *U.S.A.* **76 D1** 44 0N 88 26W
Winnecke Cr. →, *Australia* **60 C5** 18 35S 131 34 E
Winnemucca, *U.S.A.* **82 F5** 40 58N 117 44W
Winnemucca L., *U.S.A.* **82 F4** 40 7N 119 21W
Winnett, *U.S.A.* **82 C9** 47 0N 108 21W
Winnfield, *U.S.A.* **81 K8** 31 56N 92 38W
Winnibigoshish, L., *U.S.A.* **80 B7** 47 27N 94 13W
Winnipeg, *Canada* **73 D9** 49 54N 97 9W
Winnipeg →, *Canada* **73 C9** 50 38N 96 19W
Winnipeg, L., *Canada* **73 C9** 52 0N 97 0W
Winnipeg Beach, *Canada* **73 C9** 50 30N 96 58W
Winnipegosis, *Canada* **73 C9** 51 39N 99 55W
Winnipegosis L., *Canada* **73 C9** 52 30N 100 0W
Winnipesaukee, L., *U.S.A.* **79 C13** 43 38N 71 21W
Winnisquam L., *U.S.A.* **79 C13** 43 33N 71 31W
Winnsboro, *La., U.S.A.* **81 J9** 32 10N 91 43W
Winnsboro, *S.C., U.S.A.* **77 H5** 34 23N 81 5W
Winnsboro, *Tex., U.S.A.* **81 J7** 32 58N 95 17W
Winokapau, L., *Canada* **71 B7** 53 15N 62 50W
Winona, *Minn., U.S.A.* **80 C9** 44 3N 91 39W
Winona, *Miss., U.S.A.* **81 J10** 33 29N 89 44W
Winooski, *U.S.A.* **79 B11** 44 29N 73 11W
Winooski →, *U.S.A.* **79 B11** 44 32N 73 17W
Winschoten, *Neths.* **15 A7** 53 9N 7 3 E
Winsford, *U.K.* **10 D5** 53 12N 2 31W
Winslow, *Ariz., U.S.A.* **83 J8** 35 2N 110 42W
Winslow, *Wash., U.S.A.* **84 C4** 47 38N 122 31W
Winsted, *U.S.A.* **79 E11** 41 55N 73 4W
Winston-Salem, *U.S.A.* **77 G5** 36 6N 80 15W
Winter Garden, *U.S.A.* **77 L5** 28 34N 81 35W
Winter Haven, *U.S.A.* **77 M5** 28 1N 81 44W
Winter Park, *U.S.A.* **77 L5** 28 36N 81 20W
Winterhaven, *U.S.A.* **85 N12** 32 47N 114 39W
Winters, *U.S.A.* **84 G5** 38 32N 121 58W
Wintersville, *U.S.A.* **78 F4** 40 23N 80 42W
Winterswijk, *Neths.* **15 C6** 51 58N 6 43 E
Winterthur, *Switz.* **18 C8** 47 30N 8 44 E
Winthrop, *U.S.A.* **82 B3** 48 28N 120 10W
Winton, *Australia* **62 C3** 22 24S 143 3 E
Winton, *N.Z.* **59 M2** 46 8S 168 20 E
Wirrulla, *Australia* **63 E1** 32 24S 134 31 E
Wisbech, *U.K.* **11 E8** 52 41N 0 9 E
Wisconsin □, *U.S.A.* **80 C10** 44 45N 89 30W
Wisconsin →, *U.S.A.* **80 D9** 43 0N 91 15W
Wisconsin Rapids, *U.S.A.* **80 C10** 44 23N 89 49W
Wisdom, *U.S.A.* **82 D7** 45 37N 113 27W
Wishaw, *U.K.* **12 F5** 55 46N 3 54W
Wishek, *U.S.A.* **80 B5** 46 16N 99 33W
Wisła →, *Poland* **17 A10** 54 22N 18 55 E
Wismar, *Germany* **16 B6** 53 54N 11 29 E
Wisner, *U.S.A.* **80 E6** 41 59N 96 55W
Witbank, *S. Africa* **57 D4** 25 51S 29 14 E
Witdraai, *S. Africa* **56 D3** 26 58S 20 48 E
Witham, *U.K.* **11 F8** 51 48N 0 40 E
Witham →, *U.K.* **10 E7** 52 59N 0 2W
Withernsea, *U.K.* **10 D8** 53 44N 0 1 E
Witney, *U.K.* **11 F6** 51 48N 1 28W
Witnossob →, *Namibia* **56 D3** 23 55S 18 45 E
Wittenberge, *Germany* **16 B6** 53 0N 11 45 E
Wittenoom, *Australia* **60 D2** 22 15S 118 20 E
Witvlei, *Namibia* **56 C2** 22 23S 18 32 E
Wkra →, *Poland* **17 B11** 52 27N 20 44 E
Wlingi, *Indonesia* **37 H15** 8 5S 112 25 E
Włocławek, *Poland* **17 B10** 52 40N 19 3 E
Włodawa, *Poland* **17 C12** 51 33N 23 31 E
Woburn, *U.S.A.* **79 D13** 42 29N 71 9W
Wodian, *China* **34 H7** 32 50N 112 35 E
Wodonga = Albury-Wodonga, *Australia* **63 F4** 36 3S 146 56 E
Wokam, *Indonesia* **37 F8** 5 45S 134 28 E
Woking, *U.K.* **11 F7** 51 19N 0 34W
Wokingham □, *U.K.* **11 F7** 51 25N 0 51W
Wolf →, *Canada* **72 A2** 60 17N 132 33W
Wolf Creek, *U.S.A.* **82 C7** 47 0N 112 4W
Wolf L., *Canada* **72 A2** 60 24N 131 40W
Wolf Point, *U.S.A.* **80 A2** 48 5N 105 39W
Wolfe I., *Canada* **79 B8** 44 7N 76 20W
Wolfeboro, *U.S.A.* **79 C13** 43 35N 71 13W
Wolfsberg, *Austria* **16 E8** 46 50N 14 52 E
Wolfsburg, *Germany* **16 B6** 52 25N 10 48 E
Wolin, *Poland* **16 B8** 53 50N 14 37 E
Wollaston, Is., *Chile* **96 H3** 55 40S 67 30W
Wollaston L., *Canada* **73 B8** 58 7N 103 10W
Wollaston Lake, *Canada* **73 B8** 58 3N 103 33W
Wollaston Pen., *Canada* **68 B8** 69 30N 115 0W
Wollongong, *Australia* **63 E5** 34 25S 150 54 E
Wolmaransstad, *S. Africa* **56 D4** 27 12S 25 59 E
Wolseley, *S. Africa* **56 E2** 33 26S 19 7 E
Wolsey, *U.S.A.* **80 C5** 44 24N 98 28W
Wolstenholme, C., *Canada* **66 C12** 62 35N 77 30W
Wolvega, *Neths.* **15 B6** 52 52N 6 0 E
Wolverhampton, *U.K.* **11 E5** 52 35N 2 7W
Wondai, *Australia* **63 D5** 26 20S 151 49 E
Wongalarroo L., *Australia* **63 E3** 31 32S 144 0 E
Wongan Hills, *Australia* **61 F2** 30 51S 116 37 E
Wŏnju, *S. Korea* **35 F14** 37 22N 127 58 E
Wonosari, *Indonesia* **37 G14** 7 58S 110 36 E
Wonosobo, *Indonesia* **37 G13** 7 22S 109 54 E
Wonowon, *Canada* **72 B4** 56 44N 121 48W
Wŏnsan, *N. Korea* **35 E14** 39 11N 127 27 E
Wonthaggi, *Australia* **63 F4** 38 37S 145 37 E
Wood Buffalo Nat. Park, *Canada* **72 B6** 59 0N 113 41W
Wood Is., *Australia* **60 C3** 16 24S 123 19 E
Wood L., *Canada* **73 B8** 55 17N 103 17W
Woodah I., *Australia* **62 A2** 13 27S 136 10 E
Woodbourne, *U.S.A.* **79 E10** 41 46N 74 36W
Woodbridge, *Canada* **78 C5** 43 47N 79 36W
Woodbridge, *U.K.* **11 E9** 52 6N 1 20 E
Woodburn, *U.S.A.* **82 D2** 45 9N 122 51W
Woodenbong, *Australia* **63 D5** 28 24S 152 39 E

Woodend, *Australia* **63 F3** 37 20S 144 33 E
Woodford, *Australia* **63 D5** 26 58S 152 47 E
Woodfords, *U.S.A.* **84 G7** 38 47N 119 50W
Woodlake, *U.S.A.* **84 J7** 36 25N 119 6W
Woodland, *Calif., U.S.A.* **84 G5** 38 41N 121 46W
Woodland, *Maine, U.S.A.* **77 C12** 45 9N 67 25W
Woodland, *Pa., U.S.A.* **78 F6** 40 59N 78 21W
Woodland, *Wash., U.S.A.* **84 E4** 45 54N 122 45W
Woodland Caribou Prov. Park, *Canada* **73 C10** 51 0N 94 45W
Woodridge, *Canada* **73 D9** 49 20N 96 9W
Woodroffe, Mt., *Australia* **61 E5** 26 20S 131 45 E
Woods, L., *Australia* **62 B1** 17 50S 133 30 E
Woods, L. of the, *Canada* **73 D10** 49 15N 94 45W
Woodstock, *Australia* **62 B4** 19 35S 146 50 E
Woodstock, *N.B., Canada* **71 C6** 46 11N 67 37W
Woodstock, *Ont., Canada* **78 C4** 43 10N 80 45W
Woodstock, *U.K.* **11 F6** 51 51N 1 20W
Woodstock, *Ill., U.S.A.* **80 D10** 42 19N 88 27W
Woodstock, *Vt., U.S.A.* **79 C12** 43 37N 72 31W
Woodsville, *U.S.A.* **79 B13** 44 9N 72 2W
Woodville, *N.Z.* **59 J5** 40 20S 175 53 E
Woodville, *Miss., U.S.A.* **81 K9** 31 6N 91 18W
Woodville, *Tex., U.S.A.* **81 K7** 30 47N 94 25W
Woodward, *U.S.A.* **81 G5** 36 26N 99 24W
Woody, *U.S.A.* **85 K8** 35 42N 118 50W
Woody →, *Canada* **73 C8** 52 31N 100 51W
Woolamai, C., *Australia* **63 F4** 38 30S 145 23 E
Wooler, *U.K.* **10 B5** 55 33N 2 1W
Woolgoolga, *Australia* **63 E5** 30 6S 153 11 E
Woomera, *Australia* **63 E2** 31 5S 136 50 E
Woonsocket, *R.I., U.S.A.* **79 E13** 42 0N 71 31W
Woonsocket, *S. Dak., U.S.A.* **80 C5** 44 3N 98 17W
Wooramel →, *Australia* **61 E1** 25 47S 114 10 E
Wooramel Roadhouse, *Australia* **61 E1** 25 45S 114 17 E
Wooster, *U.S.A.* **78 F3** 40 48N 81 56W
Worcester, *S. Africa* **56 E2** 33 39S 19 27 E
Worcester, *U.K.* **11 E5** 52 11N 2 12W
Worcester, *Mass., U.S.A.* **79 D13** 42 16N 71 48W
Worcester, *N.Y., U.S.A.* **79 D10** 42 36N 74 45W
Worcestershire □, *U.K.* **11 E5** 52 13N 2 10W
Workington, *U.K.* **10 C4** 54 39N 3 33W
Worksop, *U.K.* **10 D6** 53 18N 1 7W
Workum, *Neths.* **15 B5** 52 59N 5 26 E
Worland, *U.S.A.* **82 D10** 44 1N 107 57W
Worms, *Germany* **16 D5** 49 37N 8 21 E
Worsley, *Canada* **72 B5** 56 31N 119 8W
Wortham, *U.S.A.* **81 K6** 31 47N 96 28W
Worthing, *U.K.* **11 G7** 50 49N 0 21W
Worthington, *Minn., U.S.A.* **80 D7** 43 37N 95 36W
Worthington, *Pa., U.S.A.* **78 F5** 40 50N 79 38W
Wosi, *Indonesia* **37 E7** 0 15S 128 0 E
Wou-han = Wuhan, *China* **33 C6** 30 31N 114 18 E
Wousi = Wuxi, *China* **33 C7** 31 33N 120 18 E
Wowoni, *Indonesia* **37 E6** 4 5S 123 5 E
Wrangel I. = Vrangelya, Ostrov, *Russia* **27 B19** 71 0N 180 0 E
Wrangell, *U.S.A.* **72 B2** 56 28N 132 23W
Wrangell Mts., *U.S.A.* **68 B5** 61 30N 142 0W
Wrath, C., *U.K.* **12 C3** 58 38N 5 1W
Wray, *U.S.A.* **80 E3** 40 5N 102 13W
Wrekin, The, *U.K.* **11 E5** 52 41N 2 32W
Wrens, *U.S.A.* **77 J4** 33 12N 82 23W
Wrexham, *U.K.* **10 D4** 53 3N 3 0W
Wrexham □, *U.K.* **10 D5** 53 1N 2 58W
Wright, *U.S.A.* **80 D2** 43 47N 105 30W
Wright Pt., *Canada* **78 C3** 43 48N 81 44W
Wrightson Mt., *U.S.A.* **83 L8** 31 42N 110 51W
Wrightwood, *U.S.A.* **85 L9** 34 21N 117 38W
Wrigley, *Canada* **68 B7** 63 16N 123 37W
Wrocław, *Poland* **17 C9** 51 5N 17 5 E
Września, *Poland* **17 B9** 52 21N 17 36 E
Wu Jiang →, *China* **32 D5** 29 40N 107 20 E
Wu'an, *China* **34 F8** 36 40N 114 15 E
Wubin, *Australia* **61 F2** 30 6S 116 37 E
Wubu, *China* **34 F6** 37 28N 110 42 E
Wuchang, *China* **35 B14** 44 55N 127 5 E
Wucheng, *China* **34 F9** 37 12N 116 20 E
Wuchuan, *China* **34 D6** 41 5N 111 28 E
Wudi, *China* **35 F9** 37 40N 117 35 E
Wuding He →, *China* **34 F6** 37 2N 110 23 E
Wudinna, *Australia* **63 E2** 33 0S 135 22 E
Wudu, *China* **34 H3** 33 22N 104 54 E
Wuhan, *China* **33 C6** 30 31N 114 18 E
Wuhe, *China* **35 H9** 33 10N 117 50 E
Wuhsi = Wuxi, *China* **33 C7** 31 33N 120 18 E
Wuhu, *China* **33 C6** 31 22N 118 21 E
Wukari, *Nigeria* **50 G7** 7 51N 9 42 E
Wulajie, *China* **35 B14** 44 6N 126 33 E
Wulanbulang, *China* **34 D6** 41 5N 110 55 E
Wular L., *India* **43 B6** 34 20N 74 30 E
Wulian, *China* **35 G10** 35 40N 119 12 E
Wuliaru, *Indonesia* **37 F8** 7 27S 131 0 E
Wuluk'omushih Ling, *China* **32 C3** 36 25N 87 25 E
Wulumuchi = Ürümqi, *China* **26 E9** 43 45N 87 45 E
Wundowie, *Australia* **61 F2** 31 47S 116 23 E
Wunnummin L., *Canada* **70 B2** 52 55N 89 10W
Wuntho, *Burma* **41 H19** 23 55N 95 45 E
Wuppertal, *Germany* **16 C4** 51 16N 7 12 E
Wuppertal, *S. Africa* **56 E2** 32 13S 19 12 E
Wuqing, *China* **35 E9** 39 23N 117 4 E
Wurtsboro, *U.S.A.* **79 E10** 41 35N 74 29W
Würzburg, *Germany* **16 D5** 49 46N 9 55 E
Wushan, *China* **34 G3** 34 43N 104 53 E
Wusuli Jiang = Ussuri →, *Asia* **30 A7** 48 27N 135 0 E
Wutai, *China* **34 E7** 38 40N 113 12 E
Wuting = Huimin, *China* **35 F9** 37 27N 117 28 E
Wutonghaolai, *China* **35 C11** 42 50N 120 5 E
Wutongqiao, *China* **32 D5** 29 22N 103 50 E
Wuwei, *China* **32 C5** 37 57N 102 34 E
Wuxi, *China* **33 C7** 31 33N 120 18 E
Wuxiang, *China* **34 F7** 36 49N 112 50 E
Wuyang, *China* **34 H7** 33 25N 113 35 E
Wuyi, *China* **34 F8** 37 46N 115 56 E
Wuyi Shan, *China* **33 D6** 27 0N 117 0 E
Wuyuan, *China* **34 D5** 41 2N 108 20 E
Wuzhai, *China* **34 E6** 38 54N 111 48 E
Wuzhi Shan, *China* **38 C7** 18 45N 109 45 E
Wuzhong, *China* **34 E4** 38 2N 106 12 E
Wuzhou, *China* **33 D6** 23 30N 111 18 E
Wyaaba Cr. →, *Australia* **62 B3** 16 27S 141 35 E
Wyalkatchem, *Australia* **61 F2** 31 8S 117 22 E
Wyalusing, *U.S.A.* **79 E8** 41 40N 76 16W
Wyandotte, *U.S.A.* **76 D4** 42 12N 83 9W
Wyandra, *Australia* **63 D4** 27 12S 145 56 E
Wyangala, L., *Australia* **63 E4** 33 54S 149 0 E
Wyara, L., *Australia* **63 D3** 28 42S 144 14 E
Wycheproof, *Australia* **63 F3** 36 5S 143 17 E
Wye →, *U.K.* **11 F5** 51 38N 2 40W
Wyemandoo, *Australia* **61 E2** 28 28S 118 29 E
Wymondham, *U.K.* **11 E9** 52 35N 1 7 E
Wymore, *U.S.A.* **80 E6** 40 7N 96 40W
Wyndham, *Australia* **60 C4** 15 33S 128 3 E
Wyndham, *N.Z.* **59 M2** 46 20S 168 51 E
Wynne, *U.S.A.* **81 H9** 35 14N 90 47W
Wynyard, *Australia* **62 G4** 41 5S 145 44 E
Wynyard, *Canada* **73 C8** 51 45N 104 10W
Wyola L., *Australia* **61 E5** 29 8S 130 17 E
Wyoming, *Canada* **78 D2** 42 57N 82 7W
Wyoming □, *U.S.A.* **82 E10** 43 0N 107 30W
Wyomissing, *U.S.A.* **79 F9** 40 20N 75 59W
Wyong, *Australia* **63 E5** 33 14S 151 24 E
Wytheville, *U.S.A.* **76 G5** 36 57N 81 5W

X

Xaçmaz, *Azerbaijan* **25 F8** 41 31N 48 42 E
Xai-Xai, *Mozam.* **57 D5** 25 6S 33 31 E
Xainza, *China* **32 C3** 30 58N 88 35 E
Xangongo, *Angola* **56 B2** 16 45S 15 5 E
Xankändi, *Azerbaijan* **25 G8** 39 52N 46 49 E
Xánthi, *Greece* **21 D11** 41 10N 24 58 E
Xanxerê, *Brazil* **95 B5** 26 53S 52 23W
Xapuri, *Brazil* **92 F5** 10 35S 68 35W
Xar Moron He →, *China* **35 C11** 43 25N 120 35 E
Xátiva, *Spain* **19 C5** 38 59N 0 32W
Xau, L., *Botswana* **56 C3** 21 15S 24 44 E
Xavantina, *Brazil* **95 A5** 21 15S 52 48W
Xenia, *U.S.A.* **76 F4** 39 41N 83 56W
Xeropotamos →, *Cyprus* **23 E11** 34 42N 32 33 E
Xhora, *S. Africa* **57 E4** 31 55S 28 38 E
Xhumo, *Botswana* **56 C3** 21 7S 24 35 E
Xi Jiang →, *China* **33 D6** 22 5N 113 20 E
Xi Xian, *China* **34 F6** 36 41N 110 58 E
Xia Xian, *China* **34 G6** 35 8N 111 12 E
Xiachengzi, *China* **35 B16** 44 40N 130 18 E
Xiaguan, *China* **32 D5** 25 32N 100 16 E
Xiajin, *China* **34 F9** 36 56N 116 0 E
Xiamen, *China* **33 D6** 24 25N 118 4 E
Xi'an, *China* **34 G5** 34 15N 109 0 E
Xian Xian, *China* **34 E9** 38 12N 116 6 E
Xiang Jiang →, *China* **33 D6** 28 55N 112 50 E
Xiangcheng, *Henan, China* **34 H8** 33 29N 114 52 E
Xiangcheng, *Henan, China* **34 H7** 33 50N 113 27 E
Xiangfan, *China* **33 C6** 32 2N 112 8 E
Xianggang = Hong Kong □, *China* **33 D6** 22 11N 114 14 E
Xianghuang Qi, *China* **34 C7** 42 2N 113 50 E
Xiangning, *China* **34 G6** 35 58N 110 50 E
Xiangquan, *China* **34 F7** 36 30N 113 1 E
Xiangquan He = Sutlej →, *Pakistan* **42 E4** 29 23N 71 3 E
Xiangshui, *China* **35 G10** 34 12N 119 33 E
Xiangtan, *China* **33 D6** 27 51N 112 54 E
Xianyang, *China* **34 G5** 34 20N 108 40 E
Xiao Hinggan Ling, *China* **33 B7** 49 0N 127 0 E
Xiao Xian, *China* **34 G9** 34 15N 116 55 E
Xiaoyi, *China* **34 F6** 37 8N 111 48 E
Xiawa, *China* **35 C11** 42 35N 120 38 E
Xiayi, *China* **34 G9** 34 15N 116 10 E
Xichang, *China* **32 D5** 27 51N 102 19 E
Xichuan, *China* **34 H6** 33 0N 111 30 E
Xieng Khouang, *Laos* **38 C4** 19 17N 103 25 E
Xifei He →, *China* **34 H9** 32 45N 116 40 E
Xifeng, *Gansu, China* **34 G4** 35 40N 107 40 E
Xifeng, *Liaoning, China* **35 C13** 42 42N 124 45 E
Xifengzhen = Xifeng, *China* **34 G4** 35 40N 107 40 E
Xigazê, *China* **32 D3** 29 5N 88 45 E
Xihe, *China* **34 G3** 34 2N 105 20 E
Xihua, *China* **34 H8** 33 45N 114 30 E
Xiliao He →, *China* **35 C12** 43 32N 123 35 E
Ximana, *Mozam.* **55 F3** 19 24S 33 58 E
Xin Xian = Xinzhou, *China* **34 E7** 38 22N 112 46 E
Xinavane, *Mozam.* **57 D5** 25 2S 32 47 E
Xinbin, *China* **35 D13** 41 40N 125 2 E
Xing Xian, *China* **34 E6** 38 27N 111 7 E
Xing'an, *China* **33 D6** 25 38N 110 40 E
Xingcheng, *China* **35 D11** 40 40N 120 45 E
Xinghe, *China* **34 D7** 40 55N 113 55 E
Xinghua, *China* **35 H10** 32 58N 119 48 E
Xinglong, *China* **35 D9** 40 25N 117 30 E
Xingping, *China* **34 G5** 34 20N 108 28 E
Xingtai, *China* **34 F8** 37 3N 114 32 E
Xingu →, *Brazil* **93 D8** 1 30S 51 53W
Xingyang, *China* **34 G7** 34 45N 112 52 E
Xinhe, *China* **34 F8** 37 30N 115 15 E
Xining, *China* **32 C5** 36 34N 101 40 E
Xinjiang, *China* **34 G6** 35 34N 111 11 E
Xinjiang Uygur Zizhiqu □, *China* **32 C3** 42 0N 86 0 E
Xinjin = Pulandian, *China* **35 E11** 39 25N 121 58 E
Xinkai He →, *China* **35 C12** 43 32N 123 35 E
Xinle, *China* **34 E8** 38 25N 114 40 E
Xinlitun, *China* **35 D12** 42 0N 122 8 E
Xinmin, *China* **35 D12** 41 59N 122 50 E
Xintai, *China* **35 G9** 35 55N 117 45 E
Xinxiang, *China* **34 G7** 35 18N 113 50 E
Xinzhan, *China* **35 C14** 43 50N 127 18 E
Xinzheng, *China* **34 G7** 34 20N 113 45 E
Xinzhou, *China* **34 E7** 38 22N 112 46 E
Xiongyuecheng, *China* **35 D12** 40 12N 122 5 E
Xiping, *Henan, China* **34 H8** 33 22N 114 5 E
Xiping, *Henan, China* **34 H6** 33 25N 111 8 E
Xique-Xique, *Brazil* **93 F10** 10 50S 42 40W
Xisha Qundao = Paracel Is., *S. China Sea* **36 A4** 15 50N 112 0 E
Xiuyan, *China* **35 D12** 40 18N 123 11 E
Xixabangma Feng, *China* **41 E14** 28 20N 85 40 E
Xixia, *China* **34 H6** 33 25N 111 29 E
Xixiang, *China* **34 H4** 33 0N 107 44 E
Xiyang, *China* **34 F7** 37 38N 113 38 E
Xizang Zizhiqu □, *China* **32 C3** 32 0N 88 0 E
Xlendi, *Malta* **23 C1** 36 1N 14 12 E
Xuan Loc, *Vietnam* **39 G6** 10 56N 107 14 E
Xuanhua, *China* **34 D8** 40 40N 115 2 E
Xuchang, *China* **34 G7** 34 2N 113 48 E
Xun Xian, *China* **34 G8** 35 42N 114 33 E
Xunyang, *China* **34 H5** 32 48N 109 22 E
Xunyi, *China* **34 G5** 35 8N 108 20 E
Xúquer →, *Spain* **19 C5** 39 5N 0 10W
Xushui, *China* **34 E8** 39 2N 115 40 E
Xuyen Moc, *Vietnam* **39 G6** 10 34N 107 25 E
Xuzhou, *China* **35 G9** 34 18N 117 10 E
Xylophagou, *Cyprus* **23 E12** 34 54N 33 51 E

Y

Ya Xian, *China* **38 C7** 18 14N 109 29 E
Yaamba, *Australia* **62 C5** 23 8S 150 22 E
Yaapeet, *Australia* **63 F3** 35 45S 142 3 E
Yablonovy Ra. = Yablonovyy Khrebet, *Russia* **27 D12** 53 0N 114 0 E
Yablonovyy Khrebet, *Russia* **27 D12** 53 0N 114 0 E
Yabrai Shan, *China* **34 E2** 39 40N 103 0 E
Yabrūd, *Syria* **47 B5** 33 58N 36 39 E
Yacheng, *China* **33 E5** 18 22N 109 6 E
Yacuiba, *Bolivia* **94 A3** 22 0S 63 43W
Yacuma →, *Bolivia* **92 F5** 13 38S 65 23W
Yadgir, *India* **40 L10** 16 45N 77 5 E
Yadkin →, *U.S.A.* **77 H5** 35 29N 80 9W
Yaeyama-Rettō, *Japan* **31 M1** 24 30N 123 40 E
Yagodnoye, *Russia* **27 C15** 62 33N 149 40 E
Yahila, *Dem. Rep. of the Congo* **54 B1** 0 13N 24 28 E
Yahk, *Canada* **72 D5** 49 6N 116 10W
Yahuma, *Dem. Rep. of the Congo* **52 D4** 1 0N 23 10 E
Yaita, *Japan* **31 F9** 36 48N 139 56 E
Yaiza, *Canary Is.* **22 F6** 28 57N 13 46W
Yakima, *U.S.A.* **82 C3** 46 36N 120 31W
Yakima →, *U.S.A.* **82 C3** 47 0N 120 30W
Yakobi I., *U.S.A.* **72 B1** 58 0N 136 30W
Yakovlevka, *Russia* **30 B6** 44 26N 133 28 E
Yaku-Shima, *Japan* **31 J5** 30 20N 130 30 E
Yakumo, *Japan* **30 C10** 42 15N 140 16 E
Yakutat, *U.S.A.* **68 C6** 59 33N 139 44W
Yakutia = Sakha □, *Russia* **27 C13** 66 0N 130 0 E
Yakutsk, *Russia* **27 C13** 62 5N 129 50 E
Yala, *Thailand* **39 J3** 6 33N 101 18 E
Yale, *U.S.A.* **78 C2** 43 8N 82 48W
Yalgoo, *Australia* **61 E2** 28 16S 116 39 E
Yalinga, *C.A.R.* **52 C4** 6 33N 23 10 E
Yalkubul, Punta, *Mexico* **87 C7** 21 32N 88 37W
Yalleroi, *Australia* **62 C4** 24 3S 145 42 E
Yalobusha →, *U.S.A.* **81 J9** 33 33N 90 10W
Yalong Jiang →, *China* **32 D5** 26 40N 101 55 E
Yalova, *Turkey* **21 D13** 40 41N 29 15 E
Yalta, *Ukraine* **25 F5** 44 30N 34 10 E
Yalu Jiang →, *China* **35 E13** 40 0N 124 22 E
Yam Ha Melaḥ = Dead Sea, *Asia* **47 D4** 31 30N 35 30 E
Yam Kinneret, *Israel* **47 C4** 32 45N 35 35 E
Yamada, *Japan* **31 H5** 33 33N 130 49 E
Yamagata, *Japan* **30 E10** 38 15N 140 15 E
Yamagata □, *Japan* **30 E10** 38 30N 140 0 E
Yamaguchi, *Japan* **31 G5** 34 10N 131 32 E
Yamaguchi □, *Japan* **31 G5** 34 20N 131 40 E
Yamal, Poluostrov, *Russia* **26 B8** 71 0N 70 0 E
Yamal Pen. = Yamal, Poluostrov, *Russia* **26 B8** 71 0N 70 0 E
Yamanashi □, *Japan* **31 G9** 35 40N 138 40 E
Yamantau, Gora, *Russia* **24 D10** 54 15N 58 6 E
Yamba, *Australia* **63 D5** 29 26S 153 23 E
Yambarran Ra., *Australia* **60 C5** 15 10S 130 25 E
Yâmbiô, *Sudan* **51 H11** 4 35N 28 16 E
Yambol, *Bulgaria* **21 C12** 42 30N 26 30 E
Yamdena, *Indonesia* **37 F8** 7 45S 131 20 E
Yame, *Japan* **31 H5** 33 13N 130 35 E
Yamethin, *Burma* **41 J20** 20 29N 96 18 E
Yamma-Yamma, L., *Australia* **63 D3** 26 16S 141 20 E
Yamoussoukro, *Ivory C.* **50 G4** 6 49N 5 17W
Yampa →, *U.S.A.* **82 F9** 40 32N 108 59W
Yampi Sd., *Australia* **60 C3** 16 8S 123 38 E
Yampil, *Moldova* **17 D15** 48 15N 28 15 E
Yampol = Yampil, *Moldova* **17 D15** 48 15N 28 15 E
Yamuna →, *India* **43 G9** 25 30N 81 53 E
Yamunanagar, *India* **42 D7** 30 7N 77 17 E
Yamzho Yumco, *China* **32 D4** 28 48N 90 35 E
Yana →, *Russia* **27 B14** 71 30N 136 0 E
Yanagawa, *Japan* **31 H5** 33 10N 130 24 E
Yanai, *Japan* **31 H6** 33 58N 132 7 E
Yan'an, *China* **34 F5** 36 35N 109 26 E
Yanaul, *Russia* **24 C10** 56 25N 55 0 E
Yanbu 'al Baḥr, *Si. Arabia* **46 C2** 24 0N 38 5 E
Yanchang, *China* **34 F6** 36 43N 110 1 E
Yancheng, *Henan, China* **34 H8** 33 35N 114 0 E
Yancheng, *Jiangsu, China* **35 H11** 33 23N 120 8 E
Yanchep Beach, *Australia* **61 F2** 31 33S 115 37 E
Yanchi, *China* **34 F4** 37 48N 107 20 E
Yanchuan, *China* **34 F6** 36 51N 110 10 E
Yanco Cr. →, *Australia* **63 F4** 35 14S 145 35 E
Yandoon, *Burma* **41 L19** 17 0N 95 40 E
Yang Xian, *China* **34 H4** 33 15N 107 30 E
Yangambi, *Dem. Rep. of the Congo* **54 B1** 0 47N 24 24 E
Yangcheng, *China* **34 G7** 35 28N 112 22 E
Yangch'ü = Taiyuan, *China* **34 F7** 37 52N 112 33 E
Yanggao, *China* **34 D7** 40 21N 113 55 E
Yanggu, *China* **34 F8** 36 8N 115 43 E
Yangliuqing, *China* **35 E9** 39 2N 117 5 E
Yangon = Rangoon, *Burma* **41 L20** 16 45N 96 20 E
Yangpingguan, *China* **34 H4** 32 58N 106 5 E
Yangquan, *China* **34 F7** 37 58N 113 31 E
Yangtse = Chang Jiang →, *China* **33 C7** 31 48N 121 10 E
Yangtze Kiang = Chang Jiang →, *China* **33 C7** 31 48N 121 10 E
Yangyang, *S. Korea* **35 E15** 38 4N 128 38 E
Yangyuan, *China* **34 D8** 40 1N 114 10 E
Yangzhou, *China* **33 C6** 32 21N 119 26 E
Yanji, *China* **35 C15** 42 59N 129 30 E
Yankton, *U.S.A.* **80 D6** 42 53N 97 23W
Yanonge, *Dem. Rep. of the Congo* **54 B1** 0 35N 24 38 E
Yanqi, *China* **32 B3** 42 5N 86 35 E
Yanqing, *China* **34 D8** 40 30N 115 58 E
Yanshan, *China* **35 E9** 38 4N 117 22 E
Yanshou, *China* **35 B15** 45 28N 128 22 E
Yantabulla, *Australia* **63 D4** 29 21S 145 0 E
Yantai, *China* **35 F11** 37 34N 121 22 E
Yanzhou, *China* **34 G9** 35 35N 116 49 E
Yao Xian, *China* **34 G5** 34 55N 108 59 E
Yao Yai, Ko, *Thailand* **39 J2** 8 0N 98 35 E
Yaoundé, *Cameroon* **52 D2** 3 50N 11 35 E
Yaowan, *China* **35 G10** 34 15N 118 3 E
Yap I., *Pac. Oc.* **64 G5** 9 30N 138 10 E
Yapen, *Indonesia* **37 E9** 1 50S 136 0 E
Yapen, Selat, *Indonesia* **37 E9** 1 20S 136 10 E
Yapero, *Indonesia* **37 E9** 4 59S 137 11 E
Yappar →, *Australia* **62 B3** 18 22S 141 16 E
Yaqui →, *Mexico* **86 B2** 27 37N 110 39W
Yar-Sale, *Russia* **26 C8** 66 50N 70 50 E
Yaraka, *Australia* **62 C3** 24 53S 144 3 E
Yaransk, *Russia* **24 C8** 57 22N 47 49 E
Yare →, *U.K.* **11 E9** 52 35N 1 38 E
Yaremcha, *Ukraine* **17 D13** 48 27N 24 33 E
Yarensk, *Russia* **24 B8** 62 11N 49 15 E
Yarí →, *Colombia* **92 D4** 0 20S 72 20W
Yarkand = Shache, *China* **32 C2** 38 20N 77 10 E
Yarker, *Canada* **79 B8** 44 23N 76 46W
Yarkhun →, *Pakistan* **43 A5** 36 17N 72 30 E
Yarmouth, *Canada* **71 D6** 43 50N 66 7W
Yarmūk →, *Syria* **47 C4** 32 42N 35 40 E
Yaroslavl, *Russia* **24 C6** 57 35N 39 55 E
Yarqa, W. →, *Egypt* **47 F2** 30 0N 33 49 E
Yarra Yarra Lakes, *Australia* **61 E2** 29 40S 115 45 E
Yarram, *Australia* **63 F4** 38 29S 146 39 E
Yarraman, *Australia* **63 D5** 26 50S 152 0 E
Yarras, *Australia* **63 E5** 31 25S 152 20 E
Yartsevo, *Russia* **27 C10** 60 20N 90 0 E
Yarumal, *Colombia* **92 B3** 6 58N 75 24W
Yasawa Group, *Fiji* **59 C7** 17 0S 177 23 E
Yaselda, *Belarus* **17 B14** 52 7N 26 28 E
Yasin, *Pakistan* **43 A5** 36 24N 73 23 E
Yasinski, L., *Canada* **70 B4** 53 16N 77 35W
Yasinya, *Ukraine* **17 D13** 48 16N 24 21 E
Yasothon, *Thailand* **38 E5** 15 50N 104 10 E
Yass, *Australia* **63 E4** 34 49S 148 54 E
Yāsūj, *Iran* **45 D6** 30 31N 51 31 E
Yatağan, *Turkey* **21 F13** 37 20N 28 10 E
Yates Center, *U.S.A.* **81 G7** 37 53N 95 44W
Yathkyed L., *Canada* **73 A9** 62 40N 98 0W
Yatsushiro, *Japan* **31 H5** 32 30N 130 40 E
Yatta Plateau, *Kenya* **54 C4** 2 0S 38 0 E
Yavari →, *Peru* **92 D4** 4 21S 70 2W
Yávaros, *Mexico* **86 B3** 26 42N 109 31W
Yavatmal, *India* **40 J11** 20 20N 78 15 E
Yavne, *Israel* **47 D3** 31 52N 34 45 E
Yavoriv, *Ukraine* **17 D12** 49 55N 23 20 E
Yavorov = Yavoriv, *Ukraine* **17 D12** 49 55N 23 20 E
Yawatahama, *Japan* **31 H6** 33 27N 132 24 E
Yazd, *Iran* **45 D7** 31 55N 54 27 E
Yazd □, *Iran* **45 D7** 32 0N 55 0 E
Yazd-e Khvāst, *Iran* **45 D7** 31 31N 52 7 E
Yazman, *Pakistan* **42 E4** 29 8N 71 45 E
Yazoo →, *U.S.A.* **81 J9** 32 22N 90 54W
Yazoo City, *U.S.A.* **81 J9** 32 51N 90 25W
Yding Skovhøj, *Denmark* **9 J13** 55 59N 9 46 E
Ye Xian = Laizhou, *China* **35 F10** 37 8N 119 57 E
Ye Xian, *China* **34 H7** 33 35N 113 25 E
Yebyu, *Burma* **38 E2** 14 15N 98 13 E
Yechŏn, *S. Korea* **35 F15** 36 39N 128 27 E
Yecla, *Spain* **19 C5** 38 35N 1 5W
Yécora, *Mexico* **86 B3** 28 20N 108 58W
Yedintsy = Edineţ, *Moldova* **17 D14** 48 9N 27 18 E
Yegros, *Paraguay* **94 B4** 26 20S 56 25W
Yehuda, Midbar, *Israel* **47 D4** 31 35N 35 15 E
Yei, *Sudan* **51 H12** 4 9N 30 40 E
Yekaterinburg, *Russia* **26 D7** 56 50N 60 30 E
Yekaterinodar = Krasnodar, *Russia* **25 E6** 45 5N 39 0 E
Yelarbon, *Australia* **63 D5** 28 33S 150 38 E
Yelets, *Russia* **24 D6** 52 40N 38 30 E
Yelizavetgrad = Kirovohrad, *Ukraine* **25 E5** 48 35N 32 20 E
Yell, *U.K.* **12 A7** 60 35N 1 5W
Yell Sd., *U.K.* **12 A7** 60 33N 1 15W
Yellow Sea, *China* **35 G12** 35 0N 123 0 E
Yellowhead Pass, *Canada* **72 C5** 52 53N 118 25W
Yellowknife, *Canada* **72 A6** 62 27N 114 29W
Yellowknife →, *Canada* **72 A6** 62 31N 114 19W
Yellowstone →, *U.S.A.* **80 B3** 47 59N 103 59W
Yellowstone L., *U.S.A.* **82 D8** 44 27N 110 22W
Yellowstone Nat. Park, *U.S.A.* **82 D9** 44 40N 110 30W
Yelsk, *Belarus* **17 C15** 51 50N 29 10 E
Yemen ■, *Asia* **46 E3** 15 0N 44 0 E
Yen Bai, *Vietnam* **38 B5** 21 42N 104 52 E
Yenangyaung, *Burma* **41 J19** 20 30N 95 0 E
Yenbo = Yanbu 'al Baḥr, *Si. Arabia* **46 C2** 24 0N 38 5 E
Yenda, *Australia* **63 E4** 34 13S 146 14 E
Yenice, *Turkey* **21 E12** 39 55N 27 17 E
Yenisey →, *Russia* **26 B9** 71 50N 82 40 E
Yeniseysk, *Russia* **27 D10** 58 27N 92 13 E
Yeniseyskiy Zaliv, *Russia* **26 B9** 72 20N 81 0 E
Yennádhi, *Greece* **23 C9** 36 2N 27 56 E
Yenyuka, *Russia* **27 D13** 57 57N 121 15 E
Yeo →, *U.K.* **11 G5** 51 2N 2 49W
Yeo, L., *Australia* **61 E3** 28 0S 124 30 E
Yeo I., *Canada* **78 A3** 45 24N 81 48W
Yeola, *India* **40 J9** 20 2N 74 30 E
Yeoryioúpolis, *Greece* **23 D6** 35 20N 24 15 E
Yeovil, *U.K.* **11 G5** 50 57N 2 38W
Yeppoon, *Australia* **62 C5** 23 5S 150 47 E
Yerbent, *Turkmenistan* **26 F6** 39 30N 58 50 E
Yerbogachen, *Russia* **27 C11** 61 16N 108 0 E
Yerevan, *Armenia* **25 F7** 40 10N 44 31 E
Yerington, *U.S.A.* **82 G4** 38 59N 119 10W
Yermak, *Kazakstan* **26 D8** 52 2N 76 55 E
Yermo, *U.S.A.* **85 L10** 34 54N 116 50W
Yerólakkos, *Cyprus* **23 D12** 35 11N 33 15 E
Yeropol, *Russia* **27 C17** 65 15N 168 40 E
Yeropótamos →, *Greece* **23 D6** 35 3N 24 50 E
Yeroskipos, *Cyprus* **23 E11** 34 46N 32 28 E
Yershov, *Russia* **25 D8** 51 23N 48 27 E
Yerushalayim = Jerusalem, *Israel* **47 D4** 31 47N 35 10 E
Yes Tor, *U.K.* **11 G4** 50 41N 4 0W
Yesan, *S. Korea* **35 F14** 36 41N 126 51 E
Yeso, *U.S.A.* **81 H2** 34 26N 104 37W
Yessey, *Russia* **27 C11** 68 29N 102 10 E
Yetman, *Australia* **63 D5** 28 56S 150 48 E

Yeu, Î. d', *France* **18 C2** 46 42N 2 20W
Yevpatoriya, *Ukraine* **25 E5** 45 15N 33 20 E
Yeysk, *Russia* **25 E6** 46 40N 38 12 E
Yezd = Yazd, *Iran* **45 D7** 31 55N 54 27 E
Yhati, *Paraguay* **94 B4** 25 45S 56 35W
Yhú, *Paraguay* **95 B4** 25 0S 56 0W
Yi →, *Uruguay* **94 C4** 33 7S 57 8W
Yi 'Allaq, G., *Egypt* **47 E2** 30 22N 33 32 E
Yi He →, *China* **35 G10** 34 10N 118 8 E
Yi Xian, *Hebei, China* **34 E8** 39 20N 115 30 E
Yi Xian, *Liaoning, China* **35 D11** 41 30N 121 22 E
Yialiás →, *Cyprus* **23 D12** 35 9N 33 44 E
Yialousa, *Cyprus* **23 D13** 35 32N 34 10 E
Yianisádhes, *Greece* **23 D8** 35 20N 26 10 E
Yiannitsa, *Greece* **21 D10** 40 46N 22 24 E
Yibin, *China* **32 D5** 28 45N 104 32 E
Yichang, *China* **33 C6** 30 40N 111 20 E
Yicheng, *China* **34 G6** 35 42N 111 40 E
Yichuan, *China* **34 F6** 36 2N 110 10 E
Yichun, *China* **33 B7** 47 44N 128 52 E
Yidu, *China* **35 F10** 36 43N 118 28 E
Yijun, *China* **34 G5** 35 28N 109 8 E
Yıldız Dağları, *Turkey* **21 D12** 41 48N 27 36 E
Yilehuli Shan, *China* **33 A7** 51 20N 124 20 E
Yimianpo, *China* **35 B15** 45 7N 128 2 E
Yinchuan, *China* **34 E4** 38 30N 106 15 E
Yindarlgooda, L., *Australia* **61 F3** 30 40S 121 52 E
Ying He →, *China* **34 H9** 32 30N 116 30 E
Ying Xian, *China* **34 E7** 39 32N 113 10 E
Yingkou, *China* **35 D12** 40 37N 122 18 E
Yining, *China* **26 E9** 43 58N 81 10 E
Yinmabin, *Burma* **41 H19** 22 10N 94 55 E
Yiofiros →, *Greece* **23 D7** 35 20N 25 6 E
Yirga Alem, *Ethiopia* **46 F2** 6 48N 38 22 E
Yirrkala, *Australia* **62 A2** 12 14S 136 56 E
Yishan, *China* **32 D5** 24 28N 108 38 E
Yishui, *China* **35 G10** 35 47N 118 30 E
Yíthion, *Greece* **21 F10** 36 46N 22 34 E
Yitong, *China* **35 C13** 43 13N 125 20 E
Yiyang, *Henan, China* **34 G7** 34 27N 112 10 E
Yiyang, *Hunan, China* **33 D6** 28 35N 112 18 E
Yli-Kitka, *Finland* **8 C23** 66 8N 28 30 E
Ylitornio, *Finland* **8 C20** 66 19N 23 39 E
Ylivieska, *Finland* **8 D21** 64 4N 24 28 E
Yoakum, *U.S.A.* **81 L6** 29 17N 97 9W
Yog Pt., *Phil.* **37 B6** 14 6N 124 12 E
Yogyakarta, *Indonesia* **36 F4** 7 49S 110 22 E
Yoho Nat. Park, *Canada* **72 C5** 51 25N 116 30W
Yojoa, L. de, *Honduras* **88 D2** 14 53N 88 0W
Yŏju, *S. Korea* **35 F14** 37 20N 127 35 E
Yokadouma, *Cameroon* **52 D2** 3 26N 14 55 E
Yokkaichi, *Japan* **31 G8** 34 55N 136 38 E
Yoko, *Cameroon* **52 C2** 5 32N 12 20 E
Yokohama, *Japan* **31 G9** 35 27N 139 28 E
Yokosuka, *Japan* **31 G9** 35 20N 139 40 E
Yokote, *Japan* **30 E10** 39 20N 140 30 E
Yola, *Nigeria* **51 G8** 9 10N 12 29 E
Yolaina, Cordillera de, *Nic.* **88 D3** 11 30N 84 0W
Yoloten, *Turkmenistan* **45 B9** 37 18N 62 21 E
Yom →, *Thailand* **36 A2** 15 35N 100 1 E
Yonago, *Japan* **31 G6** 35 25N 133 19 E
Yonaguni-Jima, *Japan* **31 M1** 24 27N 123 0 E
Yŏnan, *N. Korea* **35 F14** 37 55N 126 11 E
Yonezawa, *Japan* **30 F10** 37 57N 140 4 E
Yong Peng, *Malaysia* **39 L4** 2 0N 103 3 E
Yong Sata, *Thailand* **39 J2** 7 8N 99 41 E
Yongamp'o, *N. Korea* **35 E13** 39 56N 124 23 E
Yongcheng, *China* **34 H9** 33 55N 116 20 E
Yŏngch'ŏn, *S. Korea* **35 G15** 35 58N 128 56 E
Yongdeng, *China* **34 F2** 36 38N 103 25 E
Yŏngdŏk, *S. Korea* **35 F15** 36 24N 129 22 E
Yŏngdŭngpo, *S. Korea* **35 F14** 37 31N 126 54 E
Yonghe, *China* **34 F6** 36 46N 110 38 E
Yŏnghŭng, *N. Korea* **35 E14** 39 31N 127 18 E
Yongji, *China* **34 G6** 34 52N 110 28 E
Yŏngju, *S. Korea* **35 F15** 36 50N 128 40 E
Yongnian, *China* **34 F8** 36 47N 114 29 E
Yongning, *China* **34 E4** 38 15N 106 14 E
Yongqing, *China* **34 E9** 39 25N 116 28 E
Yŏngwŏl, *S. Korea* **35 F15** 37 11N 128 28 E
Yonibana, *S. Leone* **50 G3** 8 30N 12 19W
Yonkers, *U.S.A.* **79 F11** 40 56N 73 54W
Yonne →, *France* **18 B5** 48 23N 2 58 E
York, *Australia* **61 F2** 31 52S 116 47 E
York, *U.K.* **10 D6** 53 58N 1 6W
York, *Ala., U.S.A.* **81 J10** 32 29N 88 18W
York, *Nebr., U.S.A.* **80 E6** 40 52N 97 36W
York, *Pa., U.S.A.* **76 F7** 39 58N 76 44W
York, C., *Australia* **62 A3** 10 42S 142 31 E
York, City of □, *U.K.* **10 D6** 53 58N 1 6W
York, Kap, *Greenland* **4 B4** 75 55N 66 25W
York, Vale of, *U.K.* **10 C6** 54 15N 1 25W
York Haven, *U.S.A.* **78 F8** 40 7N 76 46W
York Sd., *Australia* **60 C4** 15 0S 125 5 E
Yorke Pen., *Australia* **63 E2** 34 50S 137 40 E
Yorkshire Wolds, *U.K.* **10 C7** 54 8N 0 31W
Yorkton, *Canada* **73 C8** 51 11N 102 28W
Yorkville, *U.S.A.* **84 G3** 38 52N 123 13W
Yoro, *Honduras* **88 C2** 15 9N 87 7W
Yoron-Jima, *Japan* **31 L4** 27 2N 128 26 E
Yos Sudarso, Pulau = Dolak, Pulau, *Indonesia* **37 F9** 8 0S 138 30 E
Yosemite Nat. Park, *U.S.A.* **84 H7** 37 45N 119 40W
Yosemite Village, *U.S.A.* **84 H7** 37 45N 119 35W
Yoshkar Ola, *Russia* **24 C8** 56 38N 47 55 E
Yŏsu, *S. Korea* **35 G14** 34 47N 127 45 E
Yotvata, *Israel* **47 F4** 29 55N 35 2 E
Youbou, *Canada* **84 B2** 48 53N 124 13W
Youghal, *Ireland* **13 E4** 51 56N 7 52W
Youghal B., *Ireland* **13 E4** 51 55N 7 49W
Young, *Australia* **63 E4** 34 19S 148 18 E
Young, *Canada* **73 C7** 51 47N 105 45W
Young, *Uruguay* **94 C4** 32 44S 57 36W
Younghusband, L., *Australia* **63 E2** 30 50S 136 5 E
Younghusband Pen., *Australia* **63 F2** 36 0S 139 25 E
Youngstown, *Canada* **73 C6** 51 35N 111 10W
Youngstown, *N.Y., U.S.A.* **78 C5** 43 15N 79 3W
Youngstown, *Ohio, U.S.A.* **78 E4** 41 6N 80 39W
Youngsville, *U.S.A.* **78 E5** 41 51N 79 19W
Youngwood, *U.S.A.* **78 F5** 40 14N 79 34W
Youyu, *China* **34 D7** 40 10N 112 20 E
Yozgat, *Turkey* **25 G5** 39 51N 34 47 E
Ypané →, *Paraguay* **94 A4** 23 29S 57 19W
Ypres = Ieper, *Belgium* **15 D2** 50 51N 2 53 E
Yreka, *U.S.A.* **82 F2** 41 44N 122 38W
Ystad, *Sweden* **9 J15** 55 26N 13 50 E
Ysyk-Köl, *Kyrgyzstan* **26 E8** 42 25N 77 15 E
Ythan →, *U.K.* **12 D7** 57 19N 1 59W
Ytyk-Kyuyel, *Russia* **27 C14** 62 30N 133 45 E
Yu Jiang →, *China* **33 D6** 23 22N 110 3 E
Yu Xian = Yuzhou, *China* **34 G7** 34 10N 113 28 E
Yu Xian, *Hebei, China* **34 E8** 39 50N 114 35 E
Yu Xian, *Shanxi, China* **34 E7** 38 5N 113 20 E
Yuan Jiang →, *China* **33 D6** 28 55N 111 50 E
Yuanqu, *China* **34 G6** 35 18N 111 40 E
Yuanyang, *China* **34 G7** 35 3N 113 58 E
Yuba →, *U.S.A.* **84 F5** 39 8N 121 36W
Yuba City, *U.S.A.* **84 F5** 39 8N 121 37W
Yūbari, *Japan* **30 C10** 43 4N 141 59 E
Yūbetsu, *Japan* **30 B11** 44 13N 143 50 E
Yucatán □, *Mexico* **87 C7** 21 30N 86 30W
Yucatán, Canal de, *Caribbean* **88 B2** 22 0N 86 30W
Yucatán, Península de, *Mexico* **66 H11** 19 30N 89 0W
Yucatán Basin, *Cent. Amer.* **66 H11** 19 0N 86 0W
Yucatan Channel = Yucatán, Canal de, *Caribbean* **88 B2** 22 0N 86 30W
Yucca, *U.S.A.* **85 L12** 34 52N 114 9W
Yucca Valley, *U.S.A.* **85 L10** 34 8N 116 27W
Yucheng, *China* **34 F9** 36 55N 116 32 E
Yuci, *China* **34 F7** 37 42N 112 46 E
Yuendumu, *Australia* **60 D5** 22 16S 131 49 E
Yugoslavia ■, *Europe* **21 B9** 43 20N 20 0 E
Yukon →, *U.S.A.* **68 B3** 62 32N 163 54W
Yukon Territory □, *Canada* **68 B6** 63 0N 135 0W
Yukta, *Russia* **27 C11** 63 26N 105 42 E
Yukuhashi, *Japan* **31 H5** 33 44N 130 59 E
Yulara, *Australia* **61 E5** 25 10S 130 55 E
Yule →, *Australia* **60 D2** 20 41S 118 17 E
Yuleba, *Australia* **63 D4** 26 37S 149 24 E
Yülin, *Hainan, China* **39 C7** 18 10N 109 31 E
Yulin, *Shaanxi, China* **34 E5** 38 20N 109 30 E
Yuma, *Ariz., U.S.A.* **85 N12** 32 43N 114 37W
Yuma, *Colo., U.S.A.* **80 E3** 40 8N 102 43W
Yuma, B. de, *Dom. Rep.* **89 C6** 18 20N 68 35W
Yumbe, *Uganda* **54 B3** 3 28N 31 15 E
Yumbi, *Dem. Rep. of the Congo* **54 C2** 1 12S 26 15 E
Yumen, *China* **32 C4** 39 50N 97 30 E
Yun Ho →, *China* **35 E9** 39 10N 117 10 E
Yuna, *Australia* **61 E2** 28 20S 115 0 E
Yuncheng, *Henan, China* **34 G8** 35 36N 115 57 E
Yuncheng, *Shanxi, China* **34 G6** 35 2N 111 0 E
Yungas, *Bolivia* **92 G5** 17 0S 66 0W
Yungay, *Chile* **94 D1** 37 10S 72 5W
Yunnan □, *China* **32 D5** 25 0N 102 0 E
Yunta, *Australia* **63 E2** 32 34S 139 36 E
Yunxi, *China* **34 H6** 33 0N 110 22 E
Yupyongdong, *N. Korea* **35 D15** 41 49N 128 53 E
Yurga, *Russia* **26 D9** 55 42N 84 51 E
Yurimaguas, *Peru* **92 E3** 5 55S 76 7W
Yuscarán, *Honduras* **88 D2** 13 58N 86 45W
Yushe, *China* **34 F7** 37 4N 112 58 E
Yushu, *Jilin, China* **35 B14** 44 43N 126 38 E
Yushu, *Qinghai, China* **32 C4** 33 5N 96 55 E
Yutai, *China* **34 G9** 35 0N 116 45 E
Yutian, *China* **35 E9** 39 53N 117 45 E
Yuxarı Qarabağ = Nagorno-Karabakh, *Azerbaijan* **25 F8** 39 55N 46 45 E
Yuxi, *China* **32 D5** 24 30N 102 35 E
Yuzawa, *Japan* **30 E10** 39 10N 140 30 E
Yuzhno-Sakhalinsk, *Russia* **27 E15** 46 58N 142 45 E
Yuzhou, *China* **34 G7** 34 10N 113 28 E
Yvetot, *France* **18 B4** 49 37N 0 44 E

Z

Zaanstad, *Neths.* **15 B4** 52 27N 4 50 E
Zāb al Kabīr →, *Iraq* **44 C4** 36 1N 43 24 E
Zāb aş Şagīr →, *Iraq* **44 C4** 35 17N 43 29 E
Zabaykalsk, *Russia* **27 E12** 49 40N 117 25 E
Zābol, *Iran* **45 D9** 31 0N 61 32 E
Zābol □, *Afghan.* **40 D5** 32 0N 67 0 E
Zābolī, *Iran* **45 E9** 27 10N 61 35 E
Zabrze, *Poland* **17 C10** 50 18N 18 50 E
Zacapa, *Guatemala* **88 D2** 14 59N 89 31W
Zacapu, *Mexico* **86 D4** 19 50N 101 43W
Zacatecas, *Mexico* **86 C4** 22 49N 102 34W
Zacatecas □, *Mexico* **86 C4** 23 30N 103 0W
Zacatecoluca, *El Salv.* **88 D2** 13 29N 88 51W
Zachary, *U.S.A.* **81 K9** 30 39N 91 9W
Zacoalco, *Mexico* **86 C4** 20 14N 103 33W
Zacualtipán, *Mexico* **87 C5** 20 39N 98 36W
Zadar, *Croatia* **16 F8** 44 8N 15 14 E
Zadetkyi Kyun, *Burma* **39 G1** 10 0N 98 25 E
Zafarqand, *Iran* **45 C7** 33 11N 52 29 E
Zafra, *Spain* **19 C2** 38 26N 6 30W
Żagań, *Poland* **16 C8** 51 39N 15 22 E
Zagaoua, *Chad* **51 E10** 15 30N 22 24 E
Zagazig, *Egypt* **51 B12** 30 40N 31 30 E
Zāgheh, *Iran* **45 C6** 33 30N 48 42 E
Zagorsk = Sergiyev Posad, *Russia* **24 C6** 56 20N 38 10 E
Zagreb, *Croatia* **16 F9** 45 50N 15 58 E
Zāgros, Kūhhā-ye, *Iran* **45 C6** 33 45N 48 5 E
Zagros Mts. = Zāgros, Kūhhā-ye, *Iran* **45 C6** 33 45N 48 5 E
Zāhedān, *Fārs, Iran* **45 D7** 28 46N 53 52 E
Zāhedān, *Sīstān va Balūchestān, Iran* **45 D9** 29 30N 60 50 E
Zahlah, *Lebanon* **47 B4** 33 52N 35 50 E
Zaïre = Congo →, *Africa* **52 F2** 6 4S 12 24 E
Zaječar, *Serbia, Yug.* **21 C10** 43 53N 22 18 E
Zaka, *Zimbabwe* **57 C5** 20 20S 31 29 E
Zakamensk, *Russia* **27 D11** 50 23N 103 17 E
Zakhodnaya Dzvina = Daugava →, *Latvia* **9 H21** 57 4N 24 3 E
Zākhū, *Iraq* **44 B4** 37 10N 42 50 E
Zákinthos, *Greece* **21 F9** 37 47N 20 54 E
Zakopane, *Poland* **17 D10** 49 18N 19 57 E
Zákros, *Greece* **23 D8** 35 6N 26 10 E
Zalaegerszeg, *Hungary* **17 E9** 46 53N 16 47 E
Zalău, *Romania* **17 E12** 47 12N 23 3 E
Zaleshchiki = Zalishchyky, *Ukraine* **17 D13** 48 45N 25 45 E
Zalew Wiślany, *Poland* **17 A10** 54 20N 19 50 E
Zalingei, *Sudan* **51 F10** 12 51N 23 29 E
Zalishchyky, *Ukraine* **17 D13** 48 45N 25 45 E
Zama L., *Canada* **72 B5** 58 45N 119 5W
Zambeke, *Dem. Rep. of the Congo* **54 B2** 2 8N 25 17 E
Zambeze →, *Africa* **55 F4** 18 35S 36 20 E
Zambezi = Zambeze →, *Africa* **55 F4** 18 35S 36 20 E
Zambezi, *Zambia* **53 G4** 13 30S 23 15 E
Zambezia □, *Mozam.* **55 F4** 16 15S 37 30 E
Zambia ■, *Africa* **55 F2** 15 0S 28 0 E
Zamboanga, *Phil.* **37 C6** 6 59N 122 3 E
Zamora, *Mexico* **86 D4** 20 0N 102 21W
Zamora, *Spain* **19 B3** 41 30N 5 45W
Zamość, *Poland* **17 C12** 50 43N 23 15 E
Zandvoort, *Neths.* **15 B4** 52 22N 4 32 E
Zanesville, *U.S.A.* **78 G2** 39 56N 82 1W
Zangābād, *Iran* **44 B5** 38 26N 46 44 E
Zangue →, *Mozam.* **55 F4** 17 50S 35 21 E
Zanjān, *Iran* **45 B6** 36 40N 48 35 E
Zanjān □, *Iran* **45 B6** 37 20N 49 30 E
Zanjān →, *Iran* **45 B6** 37 8N 47 47 E
Zante = Zákinthos, *Greece* **21 F9** 37 47N 20 54 E
Zanthus, *Australia* **61 F3** 31 2S 123 34 E
Zanzibar, *Tanzania* **54 D4** 6 12S 39 12 E
Zaouiet El-Kala = Bordj Omar Driss, *Algeria* **50 C7** 28 10N 6 40 E
Zaouiet Reggâne, *Algeria* **50 C6** 26 32N 0 3 E
Zaozhuang, *China* **35 G9** 34 50N 117 35 E
Zap Suyu = Zāb al Kabīr →, *Iraq* **44 C4** 36 1N 43 24 E
Zapadnaya Dvina = Daugava →, *Latvia* **9 H21** 57 4N 24 3 E
Západné Beskydy, *Europe* **17 D10** 49 30N 19 0 E
Zapala, *Argentina* **96 D2** 39 0S 70 5W
Zapaleri, Cerro, *Bolivia* **94 A2** 22 49S 67 11W
Zapata, *U.S.A.* **81 M5** 26 55N 99 16W
Zapolyarnyy, *Russia* **24 A5** 69 26N 30 51 E
Zaporizhzhya, *Ukraine* **25 E6** 47 50N 35 10 E
Zaporozhye = Zaporizhzhya, *Ukraine* **25 E6** 47 50N 35 10 E
Zara, *Turkey* **44 B3** 39 58N 37 43 E
Zaragoza, *Coahuila, Mexico* **86 B4** 28 30N 101 0W
Zaragoza, *Nuevo León, Mexico* **87 C5** 24 0N 99 46W
Zaragoza, *Spain* **19 B5** 41 39N 0 53W
Zarand, *Kermān, Iran* **45 D8** 30 46N 56 34 E
Zarand, *Markazī, Iran* **45 C6** 35 18N 50 25 E
Zaranj, *Afghan.* **40 D2** 30 55N 61 55 E
Zarasai, *Lithuania* **9 J22** 55 40N 26 20 E
Zárate, *Argentina* **94 C4** 34 7S 59 0W
Zard, Kūh-e, *Iran* **45 C6** 32 22N 50 4 E
Zāreh, *Iran* **45 C6** 35 7N 49 9 E
Zaria, *Nigeria* **50 F7** 11 0N 7 40 E
Zarneh, *Iran* **44 C5** 33 55N 46 10 E
Zarós, *Greece* **23 D6** 35 8N 24 54 E
Zarqā', Nahr az →, *Jordan* **47 C4** 32 10N 35 37 E
Zarrin, *Iran* **45 C7** 32 46N 54 37 E
Zaruma, *Ecuador* **92 D3** 3 40S 79 38W
Żary, *Poland* **16 C8** 51 37N 15 10 E
Zarzis, *Tunisia* **51 B8** 33 31N 11 2 E
Zaskar →, *India* **43 B7** 34 13N 77 20 E
Zaskar Mts., *India* **43 C7** 33 15N 77 30 E
Zastron, *S. Africa* **56 E4** 30 18S 27 7 E
Zavāreh, *Iran* **45 C7** 33 29N 52 28 E
Zave, *Zimbabwe* **57 B5** 17 6S 30 1 E
Zavitinsk, *Russia* **27 D13** 50 10N 129 20 E
Zavodovski, I., *Antarctica* **5 B1** 56 0S 27 45W
Zawiercie, *Poland* **17 C10** 50 30N 19 24 E
Zāwiyat al Bayḍā = Al Bayḍā, *Libya* **51 B10** 32 50N 21 44 E
Zāyā, *Iraq* **44 C5** 33 33N 44 13 E
Zāyandeh →, *Iran* **45 C7** 32 35N 52 0 E
Zaysan, *Kazakstan* **26 E9** 47 28N 84 52 E
Zaysan, Oz., *Kazakstan* **26 E9** 48 0N 83 0 E
Zayü, *China* **32 D4** 28 48N 97 27 E
Zazafotsy, *Madag.* **57 C8** 21 11S 46 21 E
Zbarazh, *Ukraine* **17 D13** 49 43N 25 44 E
Zdolbuniv, *Ukraine* **17 C14** 50 30N 26 15 E
Zduńska Wola, *Poland* **17 C10** 51 37N 18 59 E
Zeballos, *Canada* **72 D3** 49 59N 126 50W
Zebediela, *S. Africa* **57 C4** 24 20S 29 17 E
Zeebrugge, *Belgium* **15 C3** 51 19N 3 12 E
Zeehan, *Australia* **62 G4** 41 52S 145 25 E
Zeeland □, *Neths.* **15 C3** 51 30N 3 50 E
Zeerust, *S. Africa* **56 D4** 25 31S 26 4 E
Ẕefat, *Israel* **47 C4** 32 58N 35 29 E
Zeil, Mt., *Australia* **60 D5** 23 30S 132 23 E
Zeila, *Somali Rep.* **46 E3** 11 21N 43 30 E
Zeist, *Neths.* **15 B5** 52 5N 5 15 E
Zeitz, *Germany* **16 C7** 51 2N 12 7 E
Zelenograd, *Russia* **24 C6** 56 1N 37 12 E
Zelenogradsk, *Russia* **9 J19** 54 53N 20 29 E
Zelienople, *U.S.A.* **78 F4** 40 48N 80 8W
Zémio, *C.A.R.* **54 A2** 5 2N 25 5 E
Zemun, *Serbia, Yug.* **21 B9** 44 51N 20 25 E
Zenica, *Bos.-H.* **21 B7** 44 10N 17 57 E
Žepče, *Bos.-H.* **21 B8** 44 28N 18 2 E
Zevenaar, *Neths.* **15 C6** 51 56N 6 5 E
Zeya, *Russia* **27 D13** 53 48N 127 14 E
Zeya →, *Russia* **27 D13** 51 42N 128 53 E
Zêzere →, *Portugal* **19 C1** 39 28N 8 20W
Zghartā, *Lebanon* **47 A4** 34 21N 35 53 E
Zgorzelec, *Poland* **16 C8** 51 10N 15 0 E
Zhabinka, *Belarus* **17 B13** 52 13N 24 2 E
Zhailma, *Kazakstan* **26 D7** 51 37N 61 33 E
Zhambyl = Taraz, *Kazakstan* **26 E8** 42 54N 71 22 E
Zhangaqazaly, *Kazakstan* **26 E7** 45 48N 62 6 E
Zhangbei, *China* **34 D8** 41 10N 114 45 E
Zhangguangcai Ling, *China* **35 B15** 45 0N 129 0 E
Zhangjiakou, *China* **34 D8** 40 48N 114 55 E
Zhangwu, *China* **35 C12** 42 43N 123 52 E
Zhangye, *China* **32 C5** 38 50N 100 23 E
Zhangzhou, *China* **33 D6** 24 30N 117 35 E
Zhanhua, *China* **35 F10** 37 40N 118 8 E
Zhanjiang, *China* **33 D6** 21 15N 110 20 E
Zhannetty, Ostrov, *Russia* **27 B16** 76 43N 158 0 E
Zhanyi, *China* **32 D5** 25 38N 103 48 E
Zhanyu, *China* **35 B12** 44 30N 122 30 E
Zhao Xian, *China* **34 F8** 37 43N 114 45 E
Zhaocheng, *China* **34 F6** 36 22N 111 38 E
Zhaotong, *China* **32 D5** 27 20N 103 44 E
Zhaoyuan, *Heilongjiang, China* **35 B13** 45 27N 125 0 E
Zhaoyuan, *Shandong, China* **35 F11** 37 20N 120 23 E
Zhashkiv, *Ukraine* **17 D16** 49 15N 30 5 E
Zhashui, *China* **34 H5** 33 40N 109 8 E
Zhayyq →, *Kazakstan* **25 E9** 47 0N 51 48 E
Zhdanov = Mariupol, *Ukraine* **25 E6** 47 5N 37 31 E
Zhecheng, *China* **34 G8** 34 7N 115 20 E
Zhejiang □, *China* **33 D7** 29 0N 120 0 E
Zheleznodorozhnyy, *Russia* **24 B9** 62 35N 50 55 E
Zheleznogorsk-Ilimskiy, *Russia* **27 D11** 56 34N 104 8 E
Zhen'an, *China* **34 H5** 33 27N 109 9 E
Zhengding, *China* **34 E8** 38 8N 114 32 E
Zhengzhou, *China* **34 G7** 34 45N 113 34 E
Zhenlai, *China* **35 B12** 45 50N 123 5 E
Zhenping, *China* **34 H7** 33 10N 112 16 E
Zhenyuan, *China* **34 G4** 35 35N 107 30 E
Zhetiqara, *Kazakstan* **26 D7** 52 11N 61 12 E
Zhezqazghan, *Kazakstan* **26 E7** 47 44N 67 40 E
Zhidan, *China* **34 F5** 36 48N 108 48 E
Zhigansk, *Russia* **27 C13** 66 48N 123 27 E
Zhilinda, *Russia* **27 C12** 70 0N 114 20 E
Zhitomir = Zhytomyr, *Ukraine* **17 C15** 50 20N 28 40 E
Zhlobin, *Belarus* **17 B16** 52 55N 30 0 E
Zhmerinka = Zhmerynka, *Ukraine* **17 D15** 49 2N 28 2 E
Zhmerynka, *Ukraine* **17 D15** 49 2N 28 2 E
Zhob, *Pakistan* **42 D3** 31 20N 69 31 E
Zhob →, *Pakistan* **42 C3** 32 4N 69 50 E
Zhodino = Zhodzina, *Belarus* **17 A15** 54 5N 28 17 E
Zhodzina, *Belarus* **17 A15** 54 5N 28 17 E
Zhokhova, Ostrov, *Russia* **27 B16** 76 4N 152 40 E
Zhongdian, *China* **32 D4** 27 48N 99 42 E
Zhongning, *China* **34 F3** 37 29N 105 40 E
Zhongtiao Shan, *China* **34 G6** 35 0N 111 10 E
Zhongwei, *China* **34 F3** 37 30N 105 12 E
Zhongyang, *China* **34 F6** 37 20N 111 11 E
Zhoucun, *China* **35 F9** 36 47N 117 48 E
Zhouzhi, *China* **34 G5** 34 10N 108 12 E
Zhuanghe, *China* **35 E12** 39 40N 123 0 E
Zhucheng, *China* **35 G10** 36 0N 119 27 E
Zhugqu, *China* **34 H3** 33 40N 104 30 E
Zhumadian, *China* **34 H8** 32 59N 114 2 E
Zhuo Xian = Zhuozhou, *China* **34 E8** 39 28N 115 58 E
Zhuolu, *China* **34 D8** 40 20N 115 12 E
Zhuozhou, *China* **34 E8** 39 28N 115 58 E
Zhuozi, *China* **34 D7** 41 0N 112 25 E
Zhytomyr, *Ukraine* **17 C15** 50 20N 28 40 E
Ziārān, *Iran* **45 B6** 36 7N 50 32 E
Ziarat, *Pakistan* **42 D2** 30 25N 67 49 E
Zibo, *China* **35 F10** 36 47N 118 3 E
Zichang, *China* **34 F5** 37 18N 109 40 E
Zielona Góra, *Poland* **16 C8** 51 57N 15 31 E
Zierikzee, *Neths.* **15 C3** 51 40N 3 55 E
Zigey, *Chad* **51 F9** 14 43N 15 50 E
Zigong, *China* **32 D5** 29 15N 104 48 E
Ziguinchor, *Senegal* **50 F2** 12 35N 16 20W
Zihuatanejo, *Mexico* **86 D4** 17 38N 101 33W
Žilina, *Slovak Rep.* **17 D10** 49 12N 18 42 E
Zillah, *Libya* **51 C9** 28 30N 17 33 E
Zima, *Russia* **27 D11** 54 0N 102 5 E
Zimapán, *Mexico* **87 C5** 20 54N 99 20W
Zimba, *Zambia* **55 F2** 17 20S 26 11 E
Zimbabwe, *Zimbabwe* **55 G3** 20 16S 30 54 E
Zimbabwe ■, *Africa* **55 F3** 19 0S 30 0 E
Zimnicea, *Romania* **17 G13** 43 40N 25 22 E
Zinder, *Niger* **50 F7** 13 48N 9 0 E
Zinga, *Tanzania* **55 D4** 9 16S 38 49 E
Zion Nat. Park, *U.S.A.* **83 H7** 37 15N 113 5W
Ziros, *Greece* **23 D8** 35 5N 26 8 E
Zirreh, Gowd-e, *Afghan.* **40 E3** 29 45N 62 0 E
Zitácuaro, *Mexico* **86 D4** 19 28N 100 21W
Zitundo, *Mozam.* **57 D5** 26 48S 32 47 E
Ziwa Maghariba □, *Tanzania* **54 C3** 2 0S 31 30 E
Ziway, L., *Ethiopia* **46 F2** 8 0N 38 50 E
Ziyang, *China* **34 H5** 32 32N 108 31 E
Zlatograd, *Bulgaria* **21 D11** 41 22N 25 7 E
Zlatoust, *Russia* **24 C10** 55 10N 59 40 E
Zlín, *Czech Rep.* **17 D9** 49 14N 17 40 E
Zmeinogorsk, *Kazakstan* **26 D9** 51 10N 82 13 E
Znojmo, *Czech Rep.* **16 D9** 48 50N 16 2 E
Zobeyrī, *Iran* **44 C5** 34 10N 46 40 E
Zobia, *Dem. Rep. of the Congo* **54 B2** 3 0N 25 59 E
Zoetermeer, *Neths.* **15 B4** 52 3N 4 30 E
Zolochev = Zolochiv, *Ukraine* **17 D13** 49 45N 24 51 E
Zolochiv, *Ukraine* **17 D13** 49 45N 24 51 E
Zomba, *Malawi* **55 F4** 15 22S 35 19 E
Zongo, *Dem. Rep. of the Congo* **52 D3** 4 20N 18 35 E
Zonguldak, *Turkey* **25 F5** 41 28N 31 50 E
Zonqor Pt., *Malta* **23 D2** 35 52N 14 34 E
Zorritos, *Peru* **92 D2** 3 43S 80 40W
Zou Xiang, *China* **34 G9** 35 30N 116 58 E
Zouar, *Chad* **51 D9** 20 30N 16 32 E
Zouérate = Zouîrât, *Mauritania* **50 D3** 22 44N 12 21W
Zouîrât, *Mauritania* **50 D3** 22 44N 12 21W
Zoutkamp, *Neths.* **15 A6** 53 20N 6 18 E
Zrenjanin, *Serbia, Yug.* **21 B9** 45 22N 20 23 E
Zufār, *Oman* **46 D5** 17 40N 54 0 E
Zug, *Switz.* **18 C8** 47 10N 8 31 E
Zugspitze, *Germany* **16 E6** 47 25N 10 59 E
Zuid-Holland □, *Neths.* **15 C4** 52 0N 4 35 E
Zuidbeveland, *Neths.* **15 C3** 51 30N 3 50 E
Zuidhorn, *Neths.* **15 A6** 53 15N 6 23 E
Zula, *Eritrea* **46 D2** 15 17N 39 40 E
Zumbo, *Mozam.* **55 F3** 15 35S 30 26 E
Zumpango, *Mexico* **87 D5** 19 48N 99 6W
Zunhua, *China* **35 D9** 40 18N 117 58 E
Zuni, *U.S.A.* **83 J9** 35 4N 108 51W
Zunyi, *China* **32 D5** 27 42N 106 53 E
Zurbātīyah, *Iraq* **44 C5** 33 9N 46 3 E
Zürich, *Switz.* **18 C8** 47 22N 8 32 E
Zutphen, *Neths.* **15 B6** 52 9N 6 12 E
Zuwārah, *Libya* **51 B8** 32 58N 12 1 E
Zūzan, *Iran* **45 C8** 34 22N 59 53 E
Zverinogolovskoye, *Russia* **26 D7** 54 26N 64 50 E
Zvishavane, *Zimbabwe* **55 G3** 20 17S 30 2 E
Zvolen, *Slovak Rep.* **17 D10** 48 33N 19 10 E
Zwettl, *Austria* **16 D8** 48 35N 15 9 E
Zwickau, *Germany* **16 C7** 50 44N 12 30 E
Zwolle, *Neths.* **15 B6** 52 31N 6 6 E
Zwolle, *U.S.A.* **81 K8** 31 38N 93 39W
Żyrardów, *Poland* **17 B11** 52 3N 20 28 E
Zyryan, *Kazakstan* **26 E9** 49 43N 84 20 E
Zyryanka, *Russia* **27 C16** 65 45N 150 51 E
Zyryanovsk = Zyryan, *Kazakstan* **26 E9** 49 43N 84 20 E
Żywiec, *Poland* **17 D10** 49 42N 19 10 E
Zyyi, *Cyprus* **23 E12** 34 43N 33 20 E